FANTASY LITERATURE FOR CHILDREN AND YOUNG ADULTS

FANTASY LITERATURE FOR CHILDREN AND YOUNG ADULTS

AN ANNOTATED BIBLIOGRAPHY

FOURTH EDITION

RUTH NADELMAN LYNN

R. R. BOWKER

New Providence, New Jersey

Published by R. R. Bowker,
a Reed Reference Publishing Company
Copyright © 1995 by Reed Elsevier Inc.
All rights reserved
Printed and bound in the United States of America

Library of Congress Cataloging-in-Publication Data

Lynn, Ruth Nadelman, 1948–
    Fantasy literature for children and young adults : an annotated
bibliography / Ruth Nadelman Lynn.—4th ed.
        p.   cm.
    Rev. ed. of: Fantasy for children. 3rd ed., 1989.
    Includes indexes.
    ISBN 0-8352-3456-8
    1. Children—Books and reading.
2. Children's literature—Bibliography.
3. Young adult literature—Bibliography.
4. Fantastic literature—Bibliography.
I. Title.
Z1037.L97 1989
[PN1009.A1]
016.80883'8766—dc20
                                                    94-42549
                                                    CIP

3143 4318

Ruth Nadelman Lynn is the supervisor of children's services at
Cary Memorial Library in Lexington, Massachusetts. In addi-
tion to four editions of *Fantasy Literature for Children and
Young Adults: An Annotated Bibliography*, two of her bibli-
ographies have been published in *Booklist* (Chicago: American
Library Association) and *The Children's Book Bag*
(Watertown, Mass.: The Foundation for Children's Books,
Inc.). She lives in Lexington, Massachusetts, with her husband
and two sons.

With love to Bruce, to Joshua, and to Noah, who continue to illuminate my reality with delight and with joy.

CONTENTS

Preface ix
Guide to Use xvii
Abbreviations of Books and Review Journals Cited xix
Introduction xxiii
Outstanding Contemporary Fantasy lv
Award-Winning Fantasy Literature lxv

Part One ANNOTATED BIBLIOGRAPHY
     1. Allegorical Fantasy and Literary Fairy Tales 3
     2. Animal Fantasy 71
     3. Fantasy Collections 133
     4. Ghost Fantasy 176
     5. High Fantasy (Heroic or Secondary World
          Fantasy) 211
          A. Alternate Worlds or Histories 211
          B. Myth Fantasy 275
          C. Travel to Other Worlds 320
     6. Humorous Fantasy 355
     7. Magic Adventure Fantasy 407
     8. Time Travel Fantasy 466
     9. Toy Fantasy 499
    10. Witchcraft and Sorcery Fantasy 512

Part Two RESEARCH GUIDE
    11. Bibliographical and Reference Sources
          on Fantasy Literature 553
    12. Critical and Historical Studies
          of Fantasy Literature 562
    13. Educational Resources on Fantasy Literature . . .591
    14. Fantasy Literature Author Studies 598

Author and Illustrator Index 925
Title Index 997
Subject Index 1043

PREFACE

Fantasy Literature for Children and Young Adults is an annotated bibliography of 4,800 fantasy novels and story collections for children and young adults in grades 3 through 12, as well as a research guide to more than 10,500 articles, books, and Ph.D. dissertations about the authors who write fantasy literature for children and young adults. The book is intended for use by librarians, teachers, parents, and students in children's and young adult literature courses.

Significant improvements have been made in this, the fourth, edition. Nearly 1,500 books have been added to the 3,300 books in the last edition (1989) for a total of more than 4,800 books in Part One, the Annotated Bibliography—a 45 percent increase. Almost 3,150 are numbered main entry titles; the remaining 1,650 titles are sequels or related works by the same author, which are cited in the main entry's annotation. Sixty books that have been out of print for over fifty years have been deleted (see "Books Deleted from the Fourth Edition," below). In Part Two, the Research Guide, nearly 4,000 new books, Ph.D. dissertations, and articles have been added to the more than 6,700 resources listed in the third edition, a 60 percent increase, for a total of more than 10,500 research sources.

The books in Part One, the Annotated Bibliography, are novels and story collections published in English in the United States (including translations) between 1900 and 1994. A few nineteenth-century classics such as Lewis Carroll's *Alice's Adventures in Wonderland* (1865) and Mark Twain's *A Connecticut Yankee in King Arthur's Court* (1889) have also been included. Careful attention has been given to original publication dates and to recommended (by professional review sources discussed later) twentieth-century U.S. editions of these significant works. The same can be said for those works originally published abroad, both in English and in foreign languages that were translated into English. Review citations from professional journals continue to be given in each entry, and only books recommended in two or more sources have been included. Neither science fiction novels nor horror literature has been included, although a number of "science fantasies" with more fantasy elements than science fiction (e.g., McCaffrey's Pern series) and a few short story anthologies containing both fantasy and science fiction or horror will be found.

Part One, Annotated Bibliography

While the genre of children's fantasy is frequently discussed in the professional literature, very little attention has been paid to the burgeoning young adult interest in fantasy. Furthermore, with the exception of a few book lists published in such journals as *Booklist, English Journal,* and *VOYA,* and one recently revised non-selective list of fantasy and horror paperbacks entitled *Supernatural Fiction for Teens,* there has been no other comprehensive list of recommended fantasy titles to help middle school, junior high school, high school, and young adult librarians find books for the young people they serve. Therefore, the scope of this bibliography continues to include young adult fantasy and those so-called adult fantasy novels that have found an eager audience in young adults.

Grade-Level Designation. All books, whether for children or young adults, have been interfiled and arranged in 10 topical chapters, with numerous cross-references. Each entry has been given a specific grade-level designation (for example, Gr. 3–5 or Gr. 8–10).

Reviewing Sources Cited. Five professional reviewing sources and five updated review sources have been added to the 24 books and review journals cited in the previous edition. (see Abbreviations of Books and Review Journals Cited on p. xix). All of the books included in this bibliography have been recommended in at least 2 of these 29 professional reviewing sources.

Out-of-Print Entries. An ever-growing number of recommended but out-of-print works of fantasy continue to appear in this bibliography. These books still deserve inclusion since many are available in library collections. As in the previous edition, all out-of-print entries have a descriptive annotation, and its out-of-print status is noted.

Recommendation Symbols. In this edition, the symbol ✓✓ denotes books of outstanding quality recommended in five or more professional review sources or generally regarded as "classics" by librarians who work with children and young adults; a single ✓ denotes books that have been recommended in four review sources. These symbols, if applicable, will be found directly under the entry number. Note that all of the books included in this bibliography have received at least two professional recommendations.

Chapter Title Changes. For ease of access, the books in chapter 2, Animal Fantasy, have been interfiled into one list, rather than separated into "Beast Tales" and "Talking Animal Fantasy."

Sequels. The titles and publication dates of all sequels continue to be given within the main entry annotation. Books with significant sequels have been given expanded annotations, which also include brief plot summaries. The reference book *Science Fiction and Fantasy Series and Sequels,* edited by Tim Cottrill, Martin H. Greenberg, and Charles G. Waugh (New York: Garland, 1986) was an invaluable resource for identifying sequels of young adult fantasy novels published before 1986.

Title Entries for Anthologies. Since it is now commonly accepted library practice to use title entries for anthologies of stories written by many authors and/or compiled by an editor, such anthologies continue to be listed by title.

Books Deleted from the Fourth Edition. In preparing this fourth edition of *Fantasy Literature for Children and Young Adults,* the reviews of all of the 3,300 books included in the third edition were reexamined. In this edition the recommendation symbols of numerous entries have been revised and 58 books have been deleted. In most cases these deleted titles have been out of print for more than fifty years (since before 1940), and can be found on few library shelves today. However, since the majority of these books were recommended by at least two of the professional review sources of their time, they may be of historical interest to children's literature scholars. Therefore, an unannotated list of the deleted titles has been included here.

Alden, Raymond Macdonald. *The Boy Who Found the King; a Tournament of Stories.* Illus. by W. R. Lohse, Bobbs Merrill, 1922; illus. by Evelyn Copelman, Bobbs Merrill, 1946, entitled: *Once There Was a King; a Tournament of Stories.* (BL 19:127, 43:90; Mahony 2:269)

Baker, Margaret. *Pedlar's Ware.* Illus. by Mary Baker, Duffield, 1925. (BL 21:386)

Barrie, Sir James M. *Peter Pan in Kensington Gardens.* (Orig. British pub. as part of *The Little White Bird; or, Adventures in Kensington Gardens,* 1902; pub. separately, 1906.) Illus. by Arthur Rackham, Scribner, 1906, 1934. (BL 7:173)

Barzini, Luigi. *The Little Match Man.* Illus. by Hattie Longstreet, Penn, 1917, 1923. (BL 14:202; Bookshelf 1923–1924, p. 8)

Baum, L(yman) Frank. *The Sea Fairies.* Illus. by John R. Neill, Reilly, 1911; Contemporary Books, 1969. The sequel is *Sky Island,* 1912, 1970. (LJ 95:1936)

Bianco, Margery (Williams). *The Adventures of Andy.* Illus. by Lech Underwood, Doran, 1927. (HB 3:47; Mahony 2:122; Moore:124)

Bianco, Margery (Williams). *The Apple Tree.* Illus. by Boris Artyzybasheff, Doran, 1926. (BL 22:425)

Bowen, William A. *The Enchanted Forest.* Illus. by Maud Petersham and Miska Petersham, Macmillan, 1920, 1926. (BL 17:220; Bookshelf, 1923–1924, p. 8)

Branch, M(ary) L(ydia) (Bolles). *Guld the Cavern Kind.* French, 1917; Bookshop for Boys and Girls, 1918. (BL 15:189; Mahony 2:274)

Brentano, Clemens Maria. *Fairy Tales from Brentano.* (Orig. German pub. 1846–1847; U.S. 1886.) Trans. by Kate Freiligrath Kroeker, illus. by F. Carruthers Gould, Stokes, 1925. *More Fairy Tales from Brentano* (1888) is a companion volume. (BL 22:425)

Bullett, Gerald W(illiam). *The Happy Mariners.* (Orig. British pub. 1930.) Illus. by C. Walter Hodges, Dodge, 1936, *The Spanish Mariners* (British pub. 1928) is a related book. (HB 12:355; TLS 1930 p. 805)

Burgess, Thornton Waldo. *Tommy and the Wishing-Stone.* Illus. by Harrison Cady, Century, 1915. The sequels are: *Tommy's Change of Heart* (Little, 1921) and *Tommy's Wishes Come True* (Little, 1921). (BL 12:294; Mahony 1:24)

Colum, Padraic. *The Children Who Followed the Piper.* Illus. by Dugald Stewart Walker, Macmillan, 1922, 1935, 1944. (BL 19:91; Mahony 2:134)

Cranch, Christopher P(earse). *The Last of the Huggermuggers, a Giant Story.* (Orig. British pub. 1855; U.S. 1856.) Illus. by J. Watson Davis, Burt, 1901(?). The sequel is: *Kobboltozo* (orig. British pub. 1856; U.S. 1857). (HB 20:172–175)

Crownfield, Gertrude. *The Little Tailor of the Winding Way.* Illus. by Willy Pogany, Macmillan, 1917. (BL 14:230; Mahony 2:163)

Crownfield, Gertrude. *Princess Whiteflame.* Illus. by Anne Merriman Peck, Dutton, 1920. (BL 17:352; Mahony 1:39)

Dunbar, Aldis. *The Sons O'Cormac an' Tales of Other Men's Sons.* (Orig. pub. in England.) Illus. by Myra Luxmoore, Longmans, 1904; illus. by Ferdinand Hussszti-Horvath, Dutton, 1920, 1929. (BL 17:235, 26:77; Mahony 1:40)

Farjeon, Eleanor. *Gypsy and Ginger.* (Orig. pub. in England.) Dutton, 1920. (BL 17:353)

Farjeon, Eleanor. *Kaleidoscope.* (Orig. British pub. 1928; U.S. 1929.) Illus. by Edward Ardizzone. Walck, 1963 (LJ 88:4083)

Farjeon, Eleanor. *The Tale of Tim Tiddler, with Rhymes of London Town.* (Orig. British pub. 1929.) Illus. by Norman Tealby, Stokes, 1930. (BL 27:67)

Franchi, Anna. *The Little Lead Soldier.* Illus. by Hattie Longstreet Price, Penn, 1919. (BL 16:316; Bookshelf 1923–1924, p. 8)

Fyleman, Rose (Amy). *A Princess Came to Our Town.* Illus. by Erick Berry. Doubleday, 1928. (BL 16:316; Mahoney 2:279)

Fyleman, Rose (Amy). *The Strange Adventures of Captain Marwhopple.* (Orig. British pub. 1931.) Illus. by Gertrude Lindsay, Doubleday, 1932. (LJ 57:864; TLS 1931 p. 957)

Gate, Ethel M(ay). *The Broom Fairies, and Other Stories.* Illus. by Maud Petersham and Miska Petersham, Yale, 1917. (BL 14:172; 19:134; Mahony 2:280)

King, Beulah. *Ruffs and Pompoms.* Illus. by Maurice Day, Little 1924. (HB 1:8; Mahony 2:282)

La Motte Fouqué, Baron Friedrich Heinrich Karl de. *Sintram and His Companions, a Northern Romance.* (Written 1814; orig. U.S. pub. 1869.) Lippincott, 1901; illus. by Gordon Browne, Stokes, 1909, 1912. Pub. as part of *Sintramm and His Companions, and Undine.* Illus. by Gordon Browne, Stokes, 189?, 1909, 1912, 1930. (BL 6:420; Mahony 1:31; Mahony 2:669)

Lang, Andrew. *My Own Fairy Book.* (Orig. British and U.S. pub. 1895.) Illus. by Gertrude A. Kay, McKay, 1927. (BL 24:75)

MacDonald, George. *Phantastes: A Faerie Romance for Men and Women.* (Orig. British pub. 1858; U.S. 1871.) McKay 1911; Dutton, 1916, 1923, 1940. (HB 3:17–22)

Mamin-Siberiak (pseud. of Dmitrii Narkisovich Mamin). *Verotchka's Tales.* (Orig pub. in Russia.) Trans. by Ray Davidson, illus. by Boris Artzybasheff, Dutton, 1922. (BL 19:129; Mahony 2:290)

Maria, Consort of Ferdinand, King of Rumania. *The Magic Doll of Rumania; a Wonder Story in Which East and West Do Meet; Written for American Children.* Illus.

by Maud Petersham and Miska Petersham, Stokes, 1929. (Bookshelf, 1925–1926, p. 1; Mahony 3:54)

Maria, Consort of Ferdinand, King of Rumania. *The Story of Naughty Kildeen.* (Orig. British pub. 1921.) Illus. by Job, Harcourt, 1926. (BL 24:169; Bookshelf, 1923–1924, p. 2)

Meyer, Zoe, *The Little Green Door.* Illus. by Clara E. Atwood, Little, 1921. (BL 18:161; Bookshelf, 1923–1924, p. 8)

Molesworth, Mary Louisa (Stewart). *Stories by Mrs. Molesworth.* Comp. by Sidney Baldwin, illus. by Edna Cooke, Duffield, 1922. (BL 19:95; Mahony 2:292)

Musset, Paul Edmé de. *Mr. Wind and Madam Rain.* (Orig. pub. in France; orig. U.S. pub. Harper, 1864.) Trans. by Emily Makepeace, illus. by Charles Bennett, Putnam, 1905; Harper, 1908. (BL 1:23, 5:64; Mahony 1:23)

Petersham, Maud (Fuller) and Petersham, Miska. *Get A-Way and Hary Janos.* Illus. by the authors, Viking, 1933. (BL 30:90; Mahony 3:59)

Phillips, Ethel Calvert. *Pretty Polly Perkins.* Illus. by E. F. Butler, Houghton, 1925. (BL 22:123; HB 2:17; Mahony 2:128)

Pyle, Katherine. *The Counterpane Fairy.* Illus. by the author, Dutton, 1898, 1928. (BL 25:174; Mahony 1:40; 2:136)

Sawyer, Ruth. *This Way to Christmas.* Illus. by Maginel Barney, Harper, 1916, 1952, rev. ed. 1967. (BL 13:185)

Scott, Evelyn. *Witch Perkins; a Story of the Kentucky Hills.* Illus. by Vera Clare, Holt, 1929. (HB 5:30–33; Mahony 3:404; Moore: 93)

Sègur, Comtesse Sophie (Rotopchine) de. *The Wise Little Donkey [Memoirs of a Donkey].* (Orig. French pub. 1860; orig. U.S. pub. 1880, entitled: *The Adventures of a Donkey*; 1901, entitled: *The Story of a Donkey.*) Trans. by Marguerite Fellows Melcher, illus. by Lauren Ford, Macmillan, 1924, entitled: *Memoirs of a Donkey*; trans. by Louis Auguste Loiseaux, illus. by Emma Brock, Whitman, 1931, entitled: *The Wise Little Donkey.* (BL 21:161, 28:313; Mahony 2:114)

Stephens, James. *In the Land of Youth.* Macmillan, 1924. (BL 21:199)

Townsend, Ralph M. *A Journey to the Garden Gate.* Illus. by Milo Winter, Houghton, 1919. (BL 16:208; Mahony 2:298)

Turner, Nancy Byrd. *Zodiac Town; the Rhymes of Amos and Ann.* Illus. by Winifred Bromhall, Little, 1921. (BL 18:93; LJ 47:869)

Wilde, Oscar. *The Birthday of the Infanta.* (Orig. British pub. 1891; U.S. 1905.) Illus. by Pamela Bianco, Macmillan, 1929. (BL 26:170; Mahony 3:486)

Wilkins (Freeman), Mary Eleanor. *The Pot of Gold, and Other Stories.* Lothrop, 1892; Books for Libraries, 1970; Ayer, 1974. (Mahony 1:27, 2:27)

Williams, Ursula Moray. *Adventures of a Little Wooden Horse.* (Orig. British pub. 1938.) Illus. by Joyce Brisley, Lippincott, 1939; illus. by Peggy Fortnum, Penguin, 1959. (LJ 65:37)

Award-Winning Fantasy Literature. A listing of the hundreds of fantasy novels and authors that have won international and national literary awards has been added to this edition, following the Introduction.

Part Two, Research Guide

There are 3,645 new articles, Ph.D. dissertations, and books on fantasy literature and its authors that have been added to the 6,720 resources listed in the third edition, a 60 percent increase.

The following sources were used in compiling this Research Guide:

American Writers for Children (*Dictionary of Literary Biography*, Vols.22, 42, and 52). Detroit: Gale, 1983 (ed. by John Cech), 1985 (ed. by Glen E. Estes), and 1986 (ed. by Glen E. Estes), respectively.

Cannons, H. G. T. *Bibliography of Library Economy . . . 1876 to 1920.* Chicago: American Library Association, 1927.

Children's Literature, Vols. 1–21. Storrs, CT: Journal of the Modern Language Association, 1972–1974; Philadelphia: Temple University Press, 1975–1978; New Haven, CT: Yale University Press, 1980–1993.

Children's Literature Abstracts. Rowys, Wales. Children's Libraries Section of the International Federation of Library Associations, 1973–March 1991; Austin, Texas: International Federation of Library Associations, Children's Library Section and Round Table of Children's Literature Documentation Centers, June 1991– .

Children's Literature Association Quarterly. Annual "Bibliography: The Year's Work in Children's Literature Studies," Battle Creek: MI: Children's Literature Association, 1987– .

Clareson, Thomas D. *Science Fiction Criticism: An Annotated Checklist.* Kent, OH: Kent State University Press, 1972.

Dictionary of American Children's Fiction, 2 vols. Edited by Alethea K. Helbig. Westport, CT: Greenwood, 1985 and 1986.

Education Index. New York: Wilson, 1932– .

Hendrickson, Linnea. *Children's Literature: A Guide to the Criticism.* Boston: G. K. Hall, 1987.

Humanities Index. New York: Wilson, 1974– .

International Index. New York: Wilson, 1907–1965.

Junior Book of Authors, 5 vols. New York: Wilson, 1951–1983.

Leif, Irving P. *Children's Literature: An Historical and Contemporary Bibliography.* Troy, NY: Whitson, 1977.

Library Literature. Chicago: American Library Association, 1921–1934; New York: Wilson, 1935– .

The Oxford Companion to Children's Literature. Edited by Humphrey Carpenter. New York: Oxford University Press, 1984.

Pflieger, Pat, and Helen M. Hill. *A Reference Guide to Modern Fantasy for Children.* Westport, CT: Greenwood, 1984.

Phaedrus: An International Annual of Children's Literature Research. New York: Columbia University School of Library Science, 1973–1988.

Rahn, Suzanne. *Children's Literature: An Annotated Bibliography of the History and Criticism.* New York: Garland, 1981.

Roginski, Jim. *Newbery and Caldecott Medalists and Honor Book Winners: Bibliography and Resource Materials Through 1977.* Littleton, CO: Libraries Unlimited, 1982.

Science Fiction and Fantasy Reference Index, 1878–1985. Edited by H. W. Hall. Detroit: Gale, 1987.

Social Science and Humanities Index. New York: Wilson, 1965–1974.

Supernatural Fiction Writers: Fantasy and Horror, 2 vols. Edited by E. F. Bleiler. New York: Scribner, 1985.

Survey of Modern Fantasy Literature, 5 vols. Edited by Frank N. Magill. Topsfield, MA: Salem, 1983.

Twentieth-Century Children's Writers, 3rd ed. Edited by Tracy Chevalier. Chicago: St. James, 1989.

Twentieth Century Science Fiction Writers, 3rd ed. Edited by Noelle Watson and Paul E. Schellinger. Chicago: St. James, 1991.

Tymn, Marshall B., and Roger C. Schlobin. *The Year's Scholarship in Science Fiction, Fantasy [and Horror Literature],* 1972–1987. (These annual lists were published in the journal *Extrapolation.* Some were also published as monographs by Kent State University Press, Kent, Ohio. For complete publication information see Chapter 11, "Bibliographical and Reference Sources on Fantasy Literature.")

Tymn, Marshall B., Roger C. Schlobin, and L. W. Currey. *A Research Guide to Science Fiction Studies.* New York: Garland, 1977.

Writers for Children. Edited by Jane M. Bingham. New York: Scribner, 1988.

Indexes. The Subject Index has been expanded in this edition. It includes topical headings on fantasy worlds (e.g., Narnia) and headings on imaginary beings (for example, lilliputians, minnipins, and hobbits). The Subject Index also includes historical periods such as the Middle Ages and World War II, and series titles. The titles listed in the Title Index and the Author Index may be titles of main entry listings or titles of sequels and related works that have been noted in the main entry annotation. The numbers in each of the three indexes (Author and Illustrator; Title; and Subject) refer to entry numbers, not page numbers.

Once again, I acknowledge the invaluable help of my husband, Bruce, who not only offered loads of encouragement and child care, but spent months of evenings and weekends typing this book! I would also like to thank Simmons College Graduate School of Library and Information Science, Boston, for allowing me to use its collection for my research.

GUIDE TO USE

Entries in Part One, the Annotated Bibliography, contain, where applicable, the following bibliographic information: author's name or pseudonym (the real names of pseudonymous authors are included in parentheses), title, series title in parentheses, suggested grade level, original country of publication other than the United States, and alternate or British title.

Recommendation symbols have been assigned by considering both the number of favorable reviews cited for each title and the degree of recommendation expressed in those reviews. Most entries include a recommendation symbol. If no recommendation symbol appears it is understood that the book received two recommendations from professional reviewing sources. A ✓ indicates recommended (titles receiving four recommendations), and ✓✓ denotes outstanding quality (titles receiving five or more recommendations or those works generally regarded as "classics" by librarians who work with children and young adults). These symbols will be found directly below the entry number.

Annotations provide a brief description of each title. A list of sequels or related works by the same author, including publisher and date, follows the annotation. If the publisher of a series title or related work is the same as that for the main entry title, only the date of publication is given. Sequels or related works judged to be important and significantly different from the main entry have also been given brief descriptive annotations within the main entry.

Each annotation concludes with a notation of any major awards won and a list of review citations. Reviews cited pertain to all editions listed in the entry, including out-of-print editions. (For a complete list of the review sources used see Abbreviations of Books and Review Journals Cited following this Guide to Use.) Following the annotation, data is provided regarding the illustrator, translator, and adaptor; publisher and date of publication; pagination of the most recent edition; ISBN number(s); or an o.p. (out of print) designation if applicable.

In cases where a book fits into two or more categories (e.g., time travel and ghost fantasy), it is placed in the chapter that best fits it and a cross-reference is entered in the alternate chapter(s). Cross-references are interfiled alphabetically with the main entries and are listed by author's surname, first name, title of book, and chapter or section reference where the main entry is found.

Each main entry must have been recommended by at least two professional reviewing sources to be considered for inclusion. In addition to the 29 review sources cited (see Abbreviations of Books and Review Journals Cited), publication information has been verified in *American Book Publishing Record, Books in Print 1994, Whitaker's Books in Print, Cumulative Book Index,* and *The National Union Catalog, Pre-1956 Imprints.*

Part Two, the Research Guide, is divided into four chapters: Chapter 11, "Bibliographical and Reference Sources on Fantasy Literature"; Chapter 12, "Critical and Historical Studies of Fantasy Literature"; Chapter 13, "Educational Resources on Fantasy Literature"; and Chapter 14, "Fantasy Literature Author Studies." Entries were culled from general periodical indexes, general bibliographies of children's and young adult literature, research lists of adult science fiction and fantasy, and an issue-by-issue search of numerous children's and young adult literature periodicals. A list of the sources used to compile this Research Guide can be found in the Preface. In addition, the specific journals listed in Abbreviations of Books and Review Journals Cited, which follows this Guide to Use, were used.

ABBREVIATIONS OF BOOKS
AND REVIEW JOURNALS CITED

Most journal reviews have been cited by volume and page number. The exceptions are those reviews from *Center for Children's Books, Bulletin* prior to December 1949, *The Horn Book Magazine* prior to 1930, *Library Journal* beginning in 1985, *Times Literary Supplement* for those few years when Roman numerals were used for page numbers, and *VOYA* prior to April 1983. Since these five journals were not given consecutive paging throughout the year, the reviews have been cited by month, year, and page number. For this same reason, all reviews from *Kliatt* and *School Library Journal* have been cited by month, year, and page number.

Five reviewing sources of children's and young adult literature have been used in this edition for the first time and are preceded by an asterisk (*) below. Five other sources have been updated.

*BBC	*Best Books for Children, Preschool Through Grade 6*, Fourth ed. Edited by John T. Gillespie and Corinne J. Naden. New Providence, NJ: Bowker, 1990. (Note that a fifth edition was published in mid-1994.)
*BBJ	*Best Books for Junior High Readers.* Edited by John T. Gillespie. New Providence, NJ: Bowker, 1991.
*BBS	*Best Books for Senior High Readers.* Edited by John T. Gillespie. New Providence, NJ: Bowker, 1991.
BL	*Booklist.* Chicago: American Library Association, 1904– .
Bookshelf	*The Bookshelf for Boys and Girls.* Edited by Clara W. Hunt, and others. New York: R. R. Bowker, 1918–1935.
CC	*Children's Catalog,* 16th ed. Edited by Juliette Yaakov. New York: H. W. Wilson, 1991; supplements, 1992, 1993.
Ch&Bks	Sutherland, Zena, and May Hill Arbuthnot. *Children and Books,* 8th ed. Glenview, IL: Scott, Foresman, 1991.

CCBB *Center for Children's Books, Bulletin.* Chicago: University of Chicago Press, 1948–1992. Urbana: University of Illinois Press, 1992– .

Eakin Eakin, Mary. *Good Books for Children, 1950–1965,* 3rd ed. Chicago: University of Chicago Press, 1966.

HB *The Horn Book Magazine.* Boston: Horn Book, 1924– .

*HBG *The Horn Book Guide to Children's and Young Adult Books.* Boston: Horn Book, 1990– .

JHC *Junior High School Library Catalog,* 6th ed. Edited by Juliette Yaakov. New York: H. W. Wilson, 1990; supplements, 1991, 1992.

Kies Kies, Cosette. *Supernatural Fiction for Teens: More Than 1300 Good Paperbacks to Read for Wonderment, Fear, and Fun,* 2nd ed. Englewood, CO: Libraries Unlimited, 1992.

Kliatt *Kliatt Young Adult Paperback Book Guide.* Newton, MA: Kliatt Paperback Book Guide, 1966– .

KR *Kirkus Reviews.* New York: Kirkus Service, 1932– .

LJ *Library Journal.* New York: R. R. Bowker, 1875– .

Mahony 1 Mahony, Bertha E. *Books for Boys and Girls: A Suggestive Purchase List.* Boston: Woman's Educational and Industrial Union, Bookshop for Boys and Girls, 1914–1922.

Mahony 2 Mahony, Bertha E., and Elinor Whitney. *Realms of Gold in Children's Books.* Garden City, NY: Doubleday, 1929.

Mahony 3 Mahony, Bertha E., and Elinor Whitney. *Five Years of Children's Books: A Supplement to "Realms of Gold."* Garden City, NY: Doubleday, 1936.

Moore Moore, Anne Carroll. *The Three Owls,* Vol. 3. New York: Macmillan, 1931.

SHC *Senior High School Library Catalog,* 14th ed. Edited by Brenda Smith and Juliette Yaakov. New York: H. W. Wilson, 1992.

SLJ *School Library Journal.* New York: R. R. Bowker, 1953– .

Suth Sutherland, Zena. *The Best in Children's Books, 1966–1972.* Chicago: University of Chicago Press, 1973.

Suth 2 Sutherland, Zena. *The Best in Children's Books, 1973–1978.* Chicago: University of Chicago Press, 1980.

Suth 3 Sutherland, Zena. *The Best in Children's Books; The University of Chicago Guide to Children's Literature, 1979–1984.* Chicago: University of Chicago Press, 1986.

*Suth 4 Sutherland, Zena, Betsy Hearne, and Roger Sutton. *The Best in Children's Books: The University of Chicago Guide to Children's Literature, 1985–1990.* Chicago: University of Chicago Press, 1991.

TLS   [London] *Times Literary Supplement.* London, England: Times Newspapers, Ltd., 1938– .

Tymn   Tymn, Marshall B., Kenneth J. Zahorski, and Robert H. Boyer. *Fantasy Literature: A Core Collection and Reference Guide.* New York: R. R. Bowker, 1979.

VOYA   *VOYA: Voice of Youth Advocates.* Metuchen, NJ: Scarecrow Press, 1977– .

INTRODUCTION

True fantasy . . . is not so much created as it is distilled and interpreted—from impressions that go far back into pre-history, impressions that, so far as we can tell from the study of folk tales, are common to us all, no matter what our age or nationality. True fantasy . . . aims to define the universe. Fantasy offers a system of symbols everyone of every age understands; it enriches and simplifies our lives and makes them bearable.[1]

These are the words of author and illustrator Natalie Babbitt, whose book *Tuck Everlasting* has become a modern fantasy classic.

She and the other authors of contemporary fantasy literature for young people, whose work will be discussed here, have created stories that have been called "the most wrenching, depth-provoking kind of fiction available to our children,"[2] in a literary genre that has been described as "the richest and most varied of all the genres."[3] According to critic Elizabeth Nesbit, " . . . it is probable that no other type of book has done more to give genuine distinction to children's literature than has fantasy."[4]

"Fantasy literature" is a broad term used to describe books in which magic causes impossible, and often wondrous, events to occur. Either a quest or a struggle between good and evil is often central to the plot of contemporary fantasy novels, and many of these works are steeped in myth or legend. Fantasy tales can be set in our own everyday world or in a "secondary" world somewhat like our own. The existence of the magic cannot be explained. Tales of fantasy should not be confused with science fiction stories, which involve a future made more or less possible by scientific or technological advances.

Paradoxically, imaginative fantasies, especially those written for young people over the past three decades, often contain the most serious of underlying themes. Such themes as the conflict between good and evil, the struggle to preserve joy and hope in a cruel and frightening world, and the acceptance of the inevitability of death have led some critics to suggest that fantasies may portray a truer version of reality than many or most realistic novels.

What is fantasy literature for children and young adults? How does it differ from fantasy written for adults? What is the appeal of fantasy? How does the development of fantasy fit into the development of children's and young adult literature in general? Why do authors write fantasy? Hundreds of articles and books have attempted to answer these questions. This introduction surveys the important critical literature on these topics and contains an updated historical overview of the outstanding fantasy literature for children and young adults.

Defining Fantasy

The Oxford English Dictionary, Second Edition (1989) states that the two forms of the word *fantasy,* spelled "fantasy" and "phantasy," come from the Latin *phantasia* and the Greek *φavraoia,* the sense of which combines spectral apparitions or phantoms with the faculties of "sensuous perception" and imagination. The predominant modern sense of *fantasy* is described as "caprice, whim, fanciful invention," and that of *phantasy* as "imagination, visionary notion." Fantasy as a genre of literary composition "deals with things that are not and cannot be," [while] science fiction deals with things that can be, that some day may be.[5]

The Random House Dictionary of the English Language, Second Edition, Unabridged, defines fantasy literature as "an imaginative or fanciful work, especially one dealing with supernatural or unnatural events or characters."[6] Literary critics and fantasists have enlarged upon these definitions.

Critical definitions of fantasy vary from the ambiguous, for example, "Fantasy may be almost all things to all men" and "Fantasy . . . is so many different things that attempts to define it seem rather pointless," to the obscure: "[In fantasy] the perspectives enforced by the ground rules of the narrative world must be diametrically contradicted." Between these poles lies a great variety of interpretations.[7]

The two elements of fantastic literature given the greatest weight by critics and fantasists alike are the presence of magic[8] and of the impossible or inexplicable.[9] Critic Jane Mobley has observed that within a fantasy narrative no attempt is made to explain the origin of the magic, it simply exists; and she suggests that the narrative itself is in a sense magical in its ability to enchant readers, drawing them into another world where they demand no explanation as to how they got there.[10]

Many critics have written of fantasy's violation of natural laws,[11] and others give the element of "wonder"[12] prime importance in defining fantasy literature. Still others point to fantasy literature's propensity for pushing past the boundaries of the realities of our own world, the so-called primary world, into secondary otherworlds. Ann Swinfen describes modern fantasy as "a serious form of the modern novel, often characterized by notable literary merit, and concerned both with heightened awareness of the complex nature of primary reality and with the exploration beyond empirical experience into the transcendent reality embodied in imaginative and spiritual otherworlds."[13]

Critic Sheila Egoff and fantasist Eleanor Cameron have pointed out the paradoxes inherent in fantasy. According to Egoff:

> Fantasy is a literature of paradox. It is the discovery of the real within the unreal, the credible within the incredible, the believable within the unbelievable. . . . The

creators of fantasy may use the most fantastic, weird and bizarre images and happenings but their basic concern is with the wholesomeness of the human soul, or to use a more contemporary term, the integrity of the self. . . . The tenet of the fantasist is "there is another kind of real, one that is truer to the human spirit, demanding a pilgrim's progress to find it."[14]

To Cameron, the paradox of fantasy is that all fantasy that works has a sense of reality; that within the everyday world of the novel there exists a pool of magic possessing a strange but powerful and convincing reality of its own.[15]

It should come as no surprise that fantasists should have their own unique visions of the nature of fantasy. To J. R. R. Tolkien, in *Tree and Leaf* (Houghton, 1965), fantasy is the making or glimpsing of otherworlds. For Jane Langton, fantasy novels are "waking dreams. They make up to us for the sense of loss we feel when we wake up and find our dreams shrinking out of memory. A literary fantasy gives us a dream back to keep." Lloyd Alexander also speaks of dreams, as he succinctly calls attention to the psychological depths that fantasy probes and the fact that even so-called realistic novels are an author's invention: "I suppose you might define realism as fantasy pretending to be true; and fantasy as reality pretending to be a dream. "And Mollie Hunter explains that her vision of fantasy comes from her memories of childhood: "As a writer . . . I find that the form of children's literature which best exemplifies both the fascinated terror [of childhood memory] and the yearning [for a sudden glimpse of something strange and wonderful] is what—for lack of a more exact name—we refer to as fantasy."[16]

Fantasy has been variously described as imaginative, fanciful, visionary, strange, otherworldly, supernatural, mysterious, frightening, magical, inexplicable, wondrous, dreamlike, and, paradoxically, realistic. It has been termed an awareness of the inexplicable existence of "magic" in the everyday world, a yearning for a sudden glimpse of something strange and wonderful, and a different and perhaps truer version of reality.

If it is difficult to encapsulate the entire genre of fantasy literature into a single definition, we can, nevertheless, acknowledge the powerful effect that fantasy can have on its readers. As Ursula K. Le Guin asserts:

> [Fantasy] is a different approach to reality, an alternative technique for apprehending and coping with existence. It is not antirational, but pararational; not realistic, but surrealistic, superrealistic; a heightening of reality. . . . Fantasy is nearer to poetry, to mysticism, and to insanity than naturalistic fiction is. . . .
> A fantasy is a journey. It is a journey into the subconscious mind, just as psychoanalysis is. Like psychoanalysis, it can be dangerous; and *it will change you*.[17]

The Purpose of Fantasy

Does fantasy have any function beyond entertainment? Certainly, it can be entertaining. It can also provide the reader with insights into himself or herself through identification with or rejection of a particular character. In these ways it parallels the literature of other genres. But critics and fantasists agree that good fantasy does more. Jane Mobley writes in *Phantasmagoria* (Anchor, 1977) that fantasy's purpose is to evoke wonder and mystery, and Lloyd Alexander tells readers in a *Library Journal* article (December 15, 1966) that its purpose is to refresh the heart through escape or "liberation."

Sheila Egoff and Ursula K. Le Guin have pointed out fantasy's unique way of helping us to better understand our own world. Unlike other genres, which tend to offer either a total escape from or total immersion in reality, fantasy can meet both needs. Egoff puts it this way, "The purpose of fantasy is not to escape reality, but to illuminate it: to transport us to a world different from the real world, yet to demonstrate certain immutable truths that persist even there—and in every possible world."[18]

Critic Swinfen agrees that "the fundamental purpose of serious fantasy is to comment upon the real world and to explore the moral, philosophical and other dilemmas posed by it."[19]

According to Egoff, "What distinguishes fine fantasy from other fine literature is not merely its framework or its view of life, but its inner core. The writer of fantasy goes beyond realism to disclose that we do not live entirely in a world of the perceived senses, that we also inhabit an inner world of the mind and spirit where the creative imagination is permanently struggling to expand vision and perception. . . . It is from the 'worlds within' created by fantasists that the faculty of the imagination can be seen at its most powerful and stimulating."[20]

The Imagery of Fantasy

Some authors assert that they begin their writing with a mental image, rather than specific characters or a completely developed plot. It is interesting, therefore, to compare the variety of images that some fantasists have used to describe fantasy itself. These images range from onions to soap bubbles.

Alan Garner likens the many layers of meaning found in a serious fantasy to an onion:

In order to connect, the book must be written for all levels of experience. This means that any given piece of text must work at simple plot level . . . and it must also work for me, and for every stage between. . . . An onion can be peeled down through its layers, but it is always, at every layer, an onion, whole in itself. I try to write onions.[21]

Jane Louise Curry also uses a spherical image in her analogy between the structure of a "visionary" fantasy and that of a pearl:

The fantasy of the lost "ph" . . . is rarely, if ever, simply a picaresque series of adventures like bright Venetian beads on a string. More often—if it approaches real excellence—it is shaped as a single pearl is shaped: a whole built up around a theme, or person, or place, or relationship.[22]

Susan Cooper compares the ephemeral nature of fantasy to a soap bubble:

[Fantasy is] the most magnificent bubble I have ever seen, iridescent, gleaming . . . and in the sunlight all the colors in the world were swimming over that gleaming sphere—swirling, glowing, achingly beautiful. Like a dancing rainbow the bubble hung there for a long moment; then it was gone.[23]

French literary scholar Paul Hazard describes the nature of fairy tales as a deep pool: "Fairy tales are like beautiful mirrors of water, so deep and crystal clear! In their depth we sense the mysterious experience of a thousand years. Their contents date from the primeval ages of humanity."[24]

A final example of descriptive imagery comes from the *Green and Burning Tree* (Little, Brown, 1969), in which Eleanor Cameron likens fantasists to wizards, whose imaginative virtuosity allows them to toss up ideas like dazzling, brilliantly colored balls; wizards able to juggle past, present, and future with a deftness that almost defies analysis.[25]

Children's and Young Adult Fantasy versus Adult Fantasy

It is obvious that novels for children and young adults can usually be distinguished from novels for adults on the superficial level of format: Children's and young adult novels are often (but not always) shorter and printed in a larger typeface with wider margins. Some children's novels are illustrated. Most, but not all, human protagonists of children's and young adult novels tend to be young people.

Fantasist Natalie Babbitt maintains that although children's literature deals with all of the so-called adult emotions of love, pride, grief, fear of death, violence, and the yearning for success, there is one emotion to be found only in children's books, and that is joy.[26]

Although overt sexuality is usually avoided in books for children, children's and young adult fantasies can be as complex in terms of plot, theme, and writing style as "adult" fantasies. According to Swinfen: "It is quite clear from any prolonged study of what might be termed 'high fantasy,' that to label them as children's books is grossly misleading. They operate on an adult level of meaning and the issue of deciding the dividing line, if such could ever exist, between worthwhile literature for children and for adults seems to be a futile exercise."[27]

Indeed, Sheila Egoff asserts in *Thursday's Child* that "fantasy written for children is far superior to that written for adults." In the not-too-distant past, however, critical agreement seemed to be quite the opposite. "Adult" literary critics tended to lump children's fantasies under the heading "light entertainment." *Peter Pan* was frequently offered as an example of the frivolousness of fantasy literature for children.[28]

Even librarian Donnarae MacCann, a proponent of children's fantasy, concluded that

> The only notable difference in an author's stylistic treatment when he writes for the child audience is the overall tone of gaiety or sympathetic understanding pervading the story. The same writer, perhaps, may allow some bitterness to colour his communications with his peers.[29]

And as recently as 1973, Lin Carter, an author of "adult" fantasy, maintained that "A fantasy is a book or story . . . in which magic really works—not a fairy tale, not a story for children, like *Peter Pan* or *The Wizard of Oz,* but a work of fiction for adults—a story which challenges the mind, which sets it working."[30]

Obviously, Carter was unaware that such powerful "children's" fantasies as William Mayne's *Earthfasts,* Alan Garner's *The Owl Service,* Ursula K. Le Guin's *A Wizard of Earthsea,* and Susan Cooper's *The Dark Is Rising* had already been published. Certainly, none of these "children's" fantasies could be characterized as whimsical, or lighthearted, and it is even more certain that reading any of these novels would "challenge the mind."

What, then, *does* differentiate a "children's" fantasy from an "adult" fantasy, if it is not lightness of tone or the absence of substance? Natalie Babbitt feels that the one tangible difference is that all the children's stories we remember longest and love best have "happy endings."

> Not, please . . . a simple "happily ever after," or . . . the kind of contrived final sugar coating that seems to be tacked on . . . but . . . something which goes much deeper, something which turns a story ultimately toward hope rather than resignation and contains within it a difference not only between the two literatures but also between youth and age.[31]

Youth Response versus Adult Response

Other critics and fantasists have turned the question around, proposing that it is not the books that are different, but the level of response to the story that separates adult readers from child readers. "A fantasy," says Sheila Egoff, "may often be read on two levels. It may be only an adventure story for some children; others will have—at once, or on later reflection—the richer experience of sensing the inner truths behind the exciting and entertaining tale."[32]

Critic Neil Philip proposes that children respond to what they read on an emotional level, whereas adults are more analytical. Adults, according to Philip, think like philosophers, using a logical progression of ideas to produce a solution. Whereas children think like poets, gaining insight from a condensation of images, allowing them to experience emotions they may not be able to explain or to completely understand.[33]

Fantasist Susan Cooper feels that children are more open to accepting the fantastic than are adults:

> [It is not] surprising that we [fantasists] should be read, today, mainly by children . . . children are the natural audience for fantasy. They aren't a different species. They're us, a little while ago. It's just that they are still able to accept mystery. . . . They still know the essence of wonder, which is to live without ever being quite sure what to expect. And therefore, quite often, to encounter delight.[34]

According to Ursula K. Le Guin, "Fantasy is the great age-equalizer, if it's good when you're twelve, it's quite likely to be just as good, or better when you're thirty-six."[35]

In the genre of fantasy as a whole, there are great variations in tone and complexity, both in literature written for children and young adults and that written for adults. It seems clear, however, that as in all literature, it is the level of the reader's understanding and his or her willingness to accept the presence of magic and impossibility that determine an individual's choice of reading material.

The Appeal of Fantasy

Fantasy has appeal for adults as well as for children and young adults. Adults find it "a source of marvel and mystery and wonder and joy that [they] find nowhere else." It brings "a sense of the strange, the numinous, the totally Other, . . . [into their lives, as well as something that] cannot be found in any human relationship . . . queer pricklings of delight, excitement and terror . . . magic."[36]

Young people can find adventure, humor, and nonsense in fantasy, while their emotions are being touched and their imaginations stretched. Susan Cooper explains fantasy's appeal for children:

> Very young children, their conscious minds not yet developed, are all feeling and instinct. Closer to the unconscious than they will ever be again, they respond naturally to the archetypes and the deep echoes of fairy story, ritual, and myth. . . . Some children . . . go on seeking out fantasy all their lives, instinctively aware that far from being babyish, it is probably the most complex form of fiction they will ever find.[37]

For fantasist Jane Langton ("The Weak Place . . ."), fantasy "feeds a hunger we didn't know we had," and for critic Jane Mobley (*Phantasmagoria*), it satisfies "the human craving to be carried or enchanted to worlds beyond the one we know, or to have revealed to us here in this world some glimpse of the other."

Fantasy can also provide a fresh perspective on our own world. C. S. Lewis observed that

> fairyland arouses a longing [in the reader] for he knows not what. It stirs and troubles him (to his lifelong enrichment) with the dim sense of something beyond his reach and, far from dulling or emptying the actual world, gives it a new dimension of depth. He does not despise the real woods because he has read of enchanted woods: the reading makes all real woods a little enchanted. This is a special kind of longing.[38]

The concept of time is one aspect of contemporary fantasy that many readers find particularly intriguing. According to Jane Louise Curry: "There is great force in the recognition that today holds yesterday and tomorrow within it: that 'past,' 'present,' and 'future' are not labels to put on isolated pigeonholes . . . [that] the same moment *does* contain the mundane and the marvellous."[39] And Tolkien emphasizes the profound emotional effect great fantasy can have on its readers: "in a serious tale of faerie . . . when the sudden 'turn' comes, we get a piercing glimpse of joy, and heart's desire, that for a moment passes outside the frame, rends indeed the very web of the story, and lets a gleam come through."[40]

Critics Francis J. Molson and Susan G. Miles have written that:

> YA fantasy flourishes today because it satisfies two genuine needs of the audience it is designed to reach. The first is aesthetic. YA fantasy at its best is very effective storytelling, providing believable characters, stimulating description, original setting, and distinctive writing. . . .The second need is psychological, . . .Youth do need and deserve assistance as they confront the central concerns of adolescence. YA fantasy, like most YA literature, speaks to those in passage from childhood to adulthood. . . .YA fantasy provides imaginative and vicarious opportunities to identify and empathize; to try out different roles or assume new faces; or to pursue different options or to take off in new directions. As an especially effective medium of dramatizing the journey of self-discovery or coming of age, YA fantasy assists in revealing to adolescents that they are not immortal, that evil exists both within and outside, that they are capable of great evil as well as great good, and that they must make choices or render judgments if they are to grow into authentic adulthood.[41]

Young adult fantasist Tamora Pierce has written that the idealism and imagination in fantasy literature is especially appealing to young people, who have the time and emotional energy to devote to social and political causes,

> but they need fuel to spark and refine ideas, the same kind of fuel that fires idealism. That fuel can be found—according to the writings of Jung, Bettelheim, M. Ester Harding, and Joseph Campbell—in the mighty symbols of myth, fairy tales, dreams, legends—and fantasy. . . . [F]antasy, in its flesh and modern (i.e., post-1900) forms, using contemporary sensibilities and characters youngsters identify with, reigns supreme. Here the symbols of meaningful struggle and of truth as an inner constant exist in their most undiluted form outside myth and fairy tale. . . .
> These stories appear to have little to do with reality, but they do provide readers with the impetus to challenge the way things are, something YAs respond to wholeheartedly. Young people are drawn to battles for a discernable higher good: the images of such battles evoke their passion. . . .
> Fantasy, more than any other genre, is a literature of empowerment. In the real world, kids have little say. This is a given; it is the nature of childhood. In fantasy, however short, fat, unbeautiful, weak, dreamy or unlearned individuals may be, they find a realm in which those things are negated by strength. . . . Young readers seem to come away from the characters' mishaps not depressed but energized, as if the protagonist's struggle was something they survived as well.
> Most important of all in fantasy is that great equalizer between the powerful and the powerless: magic, the thing that keeps young children captivated by fairy tales and older one enthralled by wizards. . . . Fantasy creates hope and optimism in readers. It is the pure stuff of wonder, the kind that carries over into everyday life and colors the way readers perceive things around them.[42]

Fantasy's direct relationship to our own lives is conveyed by Lloyd Alexander:

If a work of fantasy delights, refreshes, or gloriously terrifies us, it also encourages us on our own adventures, richer and more exciting than any fiction . . .whether we're children or grownups, fantasy can move us because it suggests a world where all we value as human beings—courage, justice, love—really work.[43]

The Effect of Fantasy on Children and Young Adults

It seems clear that reading fantasy is beneficial as well as enjoyable for young people. According to Kornei Chukovskii, literary critic and preeminent Soviet children's author:

> Fantasy is the most valuable attribute of the human mind and it should be diligently nurtured from earliest childhood, as one nurtures musical sensitivity—and not crushed. . . . Without imaginative fantasy there would be complete stagnation in both physics and chemistry . . . the value of such tales [is] in developing, strengthening, enriching, and directing children's thinking and emotional responses.[44]

Psychologist Bruno Bettelheim and others have explored the therapeutic value of fairy tales in defusing children's anxieties and resolving their emotional conflicts. And fantasist Lloyd Alexander feels that "Fantasy, by its power to move us so deeply, to dramatize, even melodramatize, morality, can be one of the most effective means of establishing a capacity for adult values."[45]

It is logical to presume that an exposure to fairy tales and fantasy as a child will aid the adult in appreciating more sophisticated literature. Indeed, the lack of exposure to imaginative tales as a child may preclude an adult's interest in epic, allegory, and folklore; at the very least it may make a "suspension of belief" difficult to achieve. Fantasist Penelope Lively contends that fantasy helps children learn about human nature and develop a sense of place and time.

> Children need to sense that we live in a permanent world that reaches away and behind and ahead of us, and that the span of a lifetime is something to be wondered at, and thought about, and that—above all—people evolve during their own lives . . . [They] end up a curious irrational blend of experience and memory. . . . Perhaps books can help, just a little.[46]

Eleanor Cameron finds hope for adult perceptions in children's response to fantasy:

> [Fantasy is] a form of literature which . . . [helps] young children to orient themselves in the surrounding world, that enriches their spiritual development, that enables them to regard themselves as fearless participants in imaginary struggles for justice, goodness, and freedom. . . . I feel that in a child's longing for what cannot be expressed, in his love of what cannot be proved, his cherishing of a vision, there lies a kind of hope. If he guards it and has faith in it, there is nothing more powerful. It may even be the beginning of illumination, and this is to me the precious element in any work of art.[47]

In a *Journal of Youth Services in Libraries* article on gender bias in young adult fiction, Linda Forrest cites studies showing that as recently as 1986 "the cultural stereotype of the dependent female, "the perennial damsel in distress,' needing a man's protection, was still being reflected."

She urges librarians to "help counteract gender bias by deliberately selecting and promoting materials that help young people develop positive views of females and an awareness of the obstacles women face in overcoming sexual stereotypes. . . . Fantasy is one area of young adult literature that offers a rich source of gender-fair fiction. It is popular with both male and female adolescents and has traditionally been a genre in which women escape the standard cultural roles. Portrayals of passive females can certainly be found; nevertheless, readers are often offered a chance to experience what females *could be* instead of what they *are*. . . . Well-written fantasy novels . . . shatter the 'dependent damsel' stereotype [with characters who] develop into fully fleshed people who struggle, grow, change in their attempts to conquer evil."[48]

Adverse Criticism of Fantasy Literature

Those critics who feel that fantasy is not an important literary genre often dismiss such works as "escapist." According to Ursula K. Le Guin:

> There is still, in this country, a deep puritanical distrust of fantasy. . . . Fantasy, to
> [its critics] is escapism. . . . They confuse fantasy, which in the psychological sense
> is a universal and essential faculty of the human mind, with infantilism and
> pathological regression. . . . [On the contrary,] fantasy is the natural, the appropriate
> language for the recounting of the spiritual journey and the struggle of good and
> evil in the soul.[49]

Donnarae MacCann points out that

> Some adults distrust fantasies as being somehow "unhealthy." They raise the
> question, "won't these dwarfs and talking beasts encourage unwholesome
> fantasizing on the part of children or make them withdraw from the real world?"
> These fears result from a confusion of terms: confusion of the word fantasy when it
> refers to a *literary form* with fantasy as a *psychological illness.*[50]

Fantasists Alan Garner and Susan Cooper have refuted such suspicions. According to Garner: "Mythology is not an escape, it is not an entertainment. It is an attempt to come to terms with reality, and therefore I would say that fantasy that works is not an escape from life. . . . It is a coming to terms with reality, it is a clarification . . ."; and Cooper contends: "When we depart from our own reality into the reality of the book . . . we're going out of time, out of space, into the unconscious. . . . We aren't escaping out, we're escaping in, without any idea of what we may encounter. Fantasy is the metaphor through which we discover ourselves."[51]

It is interesting to note that two otherwise valuable and scholarly works on children's literature, psychologist Bruno Bettelheim's *The Uses of Enchantment* and French literary critic Isabelle Jan's *On Children's Literature,* disparage contemporary fantasy for young people. Both authors have, it would seem, based their criticisms on an outdated reading of the genre. In 1969 Jan wrote: "Apart from [Kipling and de Ségur] the modern fairy tale has definitely had its day," and proceeds to accuse children's fantasy novels of static settings, a lack of character development, and stereotypical protagonists. She concludes that "Children who are not brought up by nurses in a nursery and for whom [boarding] school lore is something they know only by hearsay or from books, find it difficult to appreciate fantasy. . . . To be successful, children's stories must correspond to real experiences."[52]

That final sentence is most important. "Real experience" always underlies the fantasies written by Alan Garner, William Mayne, Ursula K. Le Guin, Susan Cooper, and Philippa Pearce, to name but a few contemporary children's and young adult fantasists. A reading of even one or two of these authors' novels would demonstrate that such criticisms are unfounded. In spite of their lack of a "nursery upbringing" or a "boarding school education," children and young adults today still read and enjoy fantasy.

A second example of what would appear to be unfounded criticism of modern fantasy is found in Bruno Bettelheim's *The Uses of Enchantment.* Bettelheim devoted only 5 of the 328 pages of his analysis of the effects of fairy tales on children to the thousands of "modern" fantasy novels for children. In these five pages, he makes two questionable judgments. The first is that "Many of these modern tales have sad endings, which fail to provide the escape and consolation which the fearsome events in the fairy tale make necessary, to strengthen the child for meeting the vagaries of his life."[53] Oddly enough, the only "modern" tale Bettelheim mentions by name is *The Blue Bird,* a play written by Maurice Maeterlinck in 1909. A more up-to-date reading of children's fantasy novels would seem warranted. In this light, fantasist Natalie Babbitt's remarks about hope and happy endings are particularly to the point (see notes 30 and 60).

In his second criticism, Bettelheim dismisses "modern" fantasy because "when children are asked to name their favorite fairy tales, hardly any modern tales are among their choices." To back up this statement, he cites a 1958 study in which 264 college students were asked to recall their favorite children's stories. The study found that 59 percent of the women and 30 percent of the men preferred "fairy tales" (including "new tales of magic like *The Wizard of Oz, Brer Rabbit,* and *Little Black Sambo*") to "fiction."[54]

Putting aside the fact that *The Wizard of Oz* is a fantasy novel, not a fairy tale, and that the study's findings do not seem to support Bettelheim's thesis, one obvious question arises: What "modern" tales could students who read children's books before 1950 be expected to mention? A study of adult recollections of books read over 40 years ago could not possibly render relevant information about the reading habits of contemporary children. To dismiss the entire genre of children's fantasy on such a basis is indefensible.

Why Write Fantasy?

Why do writers create fantasy and what makes their work successful? The critical view is expressed by Sheila Egoff, Jane Mobley, and Ann Swinfen. According to Egoff: "Modern fantasists . . . engender a sense of wonder in readers, not so much by making us realize that the fantastic and the real can coexist, as by convincing us that they already do so." Elsewhere she has written: "Fantasists . . . respect the qualities of children—curiosity, a sense of wonder, a love of the fabulous, and an ability to see to the heart of things with courage and honesty. Fantasists recognize that such assets should not be lost with the ending of childhood, but are ones that are necessary for all mature and sensitive human beings."[55] Mobley writes: "The skillful fantasist is the true wizard. Through the magic of naming he makes reality, he calls things into being. As namer, the wonder-storyteller is a poet, and his is the oldest form of poetry: incantation, the making of magic through words."[56] According to Swinfen:

> It is noteworthy that fantasy, which some might expect to be a literature of "withdrawal," since it is so often carelessly dismissed as "escapist," is in reality employed to condemn [the temptation toward violence and withdrawal]. . . . Those views of society which are expressed with such remarkable consistency by so many of the writers of serious modern fantasy arise from a desperate dissatisfaction with contemporary life, a need to break free and realize full human potential. These writers of fantasy are thus amongst the latest voices in the long tradition of liberal humanism in English literature.[57]

Each fantasist has, of course, his or her own answers. According to Andre Norton in *The Book of Andre Norton* (DAW, 1975), "You cannot write fantasy unless you love it, unless you yourself can believe in what you're telling." Helen Cresswell asserts: "I write fantasy . . . because I have always had a very strong sense of the miraculous being about to erupt into the everyday."[58] And Roger W. Drury writes fantasy stories "because they make children creative; because children reared on such stories grow into resourceful adults, who are never bored or cornered. . . . I write such tales because I like them that way. My realism comes naturally with a wide fringe."[59]

In his well-known article "On Three Ways of Writing for Children," C. S. Lewis states that he writes "a children's story because a children's story is the best art-form for something you have to say . . . of course readers who want to hear that will read the story or reread it at any age."[60]

Natalie Babbitt feels that children's fantasists are people who have not settled for compromise in their lives, who have retained their childlike hope that in the end, everything will turn out all right.[61]

Like any artist, a fantasist must draw his or her creations from within, both from his or her conscious experiences and from the unconscious. According to Susan Cooper, "I think those of us who write fantasy are dedicated to making impossible things seem likely, making dreams seem real. . . . Our writing is haunted by those parts of our experience which we do not understand, or even consciously remember."[62] Ursula K. Le Guin carries this one step further. She proposes that writers of fantasy inevitably draw on the "collective unconscious" for their inspiration, whether they intend to or not.

> The artist who goes into himself most deeply—and it is a painful journey—is the artist who touches us most closely, speaks to us most clearly. . . .
> So it would seem that true myth arises only in the process of connecting the conscious and the unconscious realms. . . .

The writer who draws not upon the works and thoughts of others, but upon his own thoughts and his own deep being, will inevitably hit upon common material. The more original his work, the more imperiously *recognizable* it will be. "Yes, of course!" says the reader, recognizing himself, his dreams, his nightmares.[63]

Mollie Hunter concurs: "no such thing as pure fantasy exists. There is only a succession of folk memories filtered through the storyteller's imagination, and since all mankind shares in these memories, they are the common store on which the modern storyteller must draw in his attempts to create fantasy."[64]

Whether or not a fantasist realizes that his or her works are rooted in "the collective unconscious," good fantasy must have all of the elements of good fiction—unique style, memorable plot and characters, and deep meaning. The additional element needed to ensure the creation of lasting works of fantasy is the author's ability to share his or her wholehearted belief that the impossible is possible.

Patricia Wrightson describes her craft: "What it is that writers do . . . they drop stones into pools: finding a visionary stone, handling and weighing it; dropping it into a pool of another mind; watching for the ripples to spread, and perhaps for the stirred water to give something back."[65]

Women as Fantasists

It should not be necessary to point out that there have been great fantasies written by women as well as by men. Yet it has been asserted that women have not been, and could not be, great fantasists. In an article published in *New Society* in 1962, critic Helen Lourie characterizes Hans Christian Andersen, Lewis Carroll, George MacDonald, and J. M. Barrie as writers of genius, and concludes:

> Is it an accident that all these writers, and those in the same group who are writing today are men? No. . . . Women can be excellent storytellers: their powers of invention and fancy are not inferior to that of men. But what they lack is the wholehearted abandonment to their inspiration: the power to enter the other world . . . without keeping some conscious hold on normality.[66]

Aside from the antifeminist bias of Lourie's conclusions, she seems to have overlooked a few authors. E. Nesbit and Selma Lagerlöf were both writing during the early years of children's fantasy. As for writers of Lourie's day, L. M. Boston, Rumer Godden, Carol Kendall, Mary Norton, and Philippa Pearce have produced unquestionable literary masterpieces. And today, Natalie Babbitt, Eleanor Cameron, Susan Cooper, Diana Wynne Jones, Ursula K. Le Guin, Anne McCaffrey, Robin McKinley, Margaret Mahy, Rosemary Sutcliff, and Patricia Wrightson are only a few of the masters of young people's fantasy who are women.

Classifying Fantasy

In an effort to analyze the many works grouped under the heading Fantasy Literature, the genre has often been subdivided. Fantasies have been categorized by subject matter, by setting, by degree of seriousness of treatment, and by the sex of the author. Psychologist Ravenna Helson, writing in *Horn Book Magazine* (April 1970), feels that fantasies written by men differ from those written by women. Her categories for men's novels are "wish fulfillment and humor," "heroism," and "tender feelings"; and for women's novels, "independence and self-expression," "transformation," and "inner mystery and awe."

In his essay, "On Fairy-Stories," J. R. R. Tolkien separated stories that are set in, or involve, a world other than our own from those tales set in the real world. He called the otherworlds "Secondary Worlds," and our world the "Primary World." Tolkien concluded that only those stories involving secondary worlds were "true" fairy stories. In addition, he outlined four essential elements of a good fairy story: "Fantasy, Recovery, Escape, and Consolation." He described Fantasy as the author's "image-making" or "subcreation"; Recovery as insight or renewal; Escape as a liberation from life's evils, rather than an evasion of reality; and Consolation as a happy ending or "eucatastrophe."

Like Tolkien, critics Tymn, Zahorski, and Boyer, in their *Fantasy Literature* (Bowker, 1979), use setting to distinguish various types of fantasy written for adults. They label those stories set in the real world as Low Fantasy and those set in secondary worlds as High Fantasy. The High Fantasy category includes "myth fantasy" (interpreted retellings of myth), "faery tales," "gothic fantasy" (weird tales with no rational explanation), and "science fantasy" (tales offering a scientific explanation for the existence of the secondary world, but that use magic during the remainder of the story).

Fantasist Jane Louise Curry divides fantasy stories into two categories, whimsical and visionary.

> There are excellences and excellences. I would suggest, always with qualifications and reservations in mind, that the two broad types of fantasy differ in focus, tone, technique, and quality of insight in much the same way that fairy tale differs from myth. In one, our attention is focused primarily on the story or action, itself; in the other it is the feeling, the emotional dimension, that holds us.[67]

Although both types of fantasy story can be well written, they appeal to the reader in different ways. For example, Norton's *The Borrowers* and Grahame's *The Wind in the Willows* and *The Reluctant Dragon* "are 'dear' to us," writes Curry, whereas Boston's *Green Knowe* books, Mayne's *Earthfasts,* Lewis's *Chronicles of Narnia,* Tolkien's *Lord of the Rings,* Garner's *Elidor* and *The Owl Service,* and Pearce's *Tom's Midnight Garden*

> are not "dear" to us. It may be nearer the truth to say that they are a power *over* us . . . . Our feeling for them is of quite a different quality. . . . Fantasy offers on one hand entertainment, reassurance, and—yes—escape: on the other, involvement, provocative ideas and insights, consolation, and the intensification of feeling. . . . Whimsical fantasy may give us deep delight, but "visionary" fantasy can give us joy.[68]

The Mythic Element in Contemporary Fantasy

Critics Sheila Egoff and Ralph Lavender have noted that children's novels that relive or reinterpret myth or legend and those that "cast fantasy within the structure of legend" were a notable development of the 1970s.[69] Ursula K. Le Guin, Alan Garner, William Mayne, Susan Cooper, and others have written fantasies of great seriousness and depth. These books, which usually center around a battle of good versus evil, are of two types. Some involve modern-day characters in dangerous encounters with the mythological past—and a magic that breaks into their everyday world. In others, entirely new mythologies are created. Egoff has observed that

> the mythic element in modern fantasy gives a quasi-religious tone to the narrative; we are persuaded that we are concerned with major moral issues, that the very stability and continuity of our world is at stake. This is in contrast to the magical, almost capricious supernatural efforts of older fantasies [such as *Mary Poppins, Peter Pan,* or E. Nesbit's stories of magic].[70]

A Historical Overview of Children's and Young Adult Fantasy

> Most children's classics that have lasted from earlier times are fantasies, mainly because they are a literature least dependent upon the immediacy of time and surroundings.[71]

In *Thursday's Child: Trends and Patterns in Contemporary Children's Literature,* Sheila Egoff has done an impressive job of relating the historical development of children's literature to the evolution of Western society's attitude toward children, and the following is an attempt to relate her theory to the development of European and American children's fantasy as a genre. I have inserted additional information about the history of young adult fantasy.

The Nineteenth Century

Original fantasy stories for children and young adults are a fairly recent phenomenon. Invented tales of wonder and magic began appearing in English only around the middle of the nineteenth century, and fantasies written specifically for young adults did not really proliferate until after the middle of the twentieth century, although a number of earlier books written for adults and containing elements of fantasy were later adopted by young people, including John Bunyan's *The Pilgrim's Progress* (1671) and Jonathan Swift's *Gulliver's Travels* (1726). The first literary fairy tale in the English language is thought to have been "Uncle David's Nonsensical Story of Giants and Fairies," contained in the otherwise realistic novel *Holiday House* by Catherine Sinclair, published in 1839. *The Hope of the Katzekopfs,* written in 1844 by F. E. Paget, is considered to be the first English children's fantasy novel. It was preceded, of course, by a rich tradition of oral folklore, anonymous tales of magical creatures and occurrences, passed from one generation to the next. Before 1850, however, books written specifically for children tended to be didactic, moralistic tales, and the children themselves were regarded as miniature adults who were constantly admonished to be "good." The stories they were given were for the purpose of saving them from damnation. There were no "teenagers" in the nineteenth century; young people in their teens were considered to be adults, and those who could read were given adult books.

Hans Christian Andersen was the first great writer of original fantasy for children. His tales, published in Denmark beginning in 1835, were translated into English in 1846 and are still among the most loved of all children's stories. Critic Margery Fisher describes Andersen's genius:

> There are plenty of writers since Andersen who have animated tin soldiers. . . . But to draw tears and smiles, quite spontaneous and genuine, on account of a lead soldier with one leg and a paper doll—that takes genius. Not cleverness or wit or ingenuity, but the power to compel truth out of yourself that has grown slowly out of childhood impressions. This is how writers of fairy tale work.[72]

The latter half of the nineteenth century has been called the first "golden age" of children's literature and it was during this period, the Victorian era, that Western children were finally deemed worthy of a literature of their own. Children were now seen as basically good, but needing to be guided onto the path of conformity. They were looked at as mischievous but perceptive, and they were finally given books with interesting characters and exciting plots, books written specifically for them, whose authors wanted to amuse them, rather than to subdue them.

Many of the Victorian fantasies are now considered classics. They include John Ruskin's *The King of the Golden River* (written in 1841, published in 1851), Mrs. Fairstar's *Memoirs of a London Doll* (1846 in England; 1852 in the United States), the first talking doll fantasy, William Makepeace Thackeray's *The Rose and the Ring* (1855), Frances Browne's *Granny's Wonderful Chair* (1856 in England; 1892 in the United States), the Comtesse de Sègur's *The Enchanted Forest* (1856 in France; 1869 in the United States), Charles Kingsley's *The Water Babies* (1863), Lewis Carroll's *Alice's Adventures in Wonderland* (1865), Jean Ingelow's *Mopsa the Fairy* (1869), and George MacDonald's *At the Back of the North Wind* (1871, 1875) and *The Princess and the Goblin* (1872).

These books were followed by Mary L. Molesworth's *The Cuckoo Clock* (1877), Carlo Collodi's *The Adventures of Pinocchio* (written in Italy in 1880; published in the United States in 1892), Lucretia P. Hale's *The Peterkin Papers* (1880), Richard Jeffries's *Wood Magic* (1881), which is considered to be the first animal fantasy novel written for children; Louise de la Ramée's *The Nürnberg Stove* (1882 in France; 1901 in the United States), Frank R. Stockton's *The Bee-Man of Orn and Other Fanciful Tales* (1884), Howard Pyle's *Pepper and Salt* (1886) and *The Wonder Clock* (1887), Oscar Wilde's *The Happy Prince and Other Tales* (1888), Andrew Lang's *Prince Prigio* (1889), Rudyard Kipling's *The Jungle Book* (1894), Laurence Housman's *A Doorway in Fairyland* (1894–1904 in England; 1905 in the United States), and Kenneth Grahame's *The Reluctant Dragon* (1898 in England; 1938 in the United States).

"An interesting fact," notes critic Naomi Lewis, "is that the fantasy genre was attracting (if briefly) most of the leading adult novelists. Ruskin, Thackeray, Dickens, Kingsley—MacDonald too—were all basically writers for adults when they turned to this new kind [of novel]; and though they chose themes of magic, they did not temper their manner or approach, so their books interest adults too."[73]

As a matter of fact, some of the "adult" fantasy works of this period are still read today, both by adults and young adults. This list might include Edward Bellamy's *Looking Backward: 2000–1887* (1888), Mark Twain's *A Connecticut Yankee in King Arthur's Court* (1889), Oscar Wilde's *The Picture of Dorian Gray* (1891), and William Morris's *The Well at the World's End* (1896). William Morris has been called the father of modern high fantasy, and his work influenced many others, including Lord Dunsany, J. R. R. Tolkien, and C. S. Lewis.

The Twentieth Century

During the first half of the twentieth century, childhood was still considered an idyllic time, a period to be prolonged and kept separate from adulthood. This attitude was, of course, reflected in the books written for children. In spite of the fact that "most of the major writers of the [Edwardian] period—Nesbit, Potter, Kipling, and Grahame—had far from idyllic childhoods," writes Egoff, "these writers drew a curtain firmly down on the adult world, and therefore on pain and distress."[74]

A decade-by-decade examination of the development of twentieth-century children's fantasy shows the surprising number of "old" books that are still being read.

The early years of the century produced a number of memorable books, beginning with the first truly American children's fantasy, L. Frank Baum's *The Wonderful Wizard of Oz* (1900). According to Sheila Egoff, *The Wonderful Wizard of Oz* was "not only the first other world fantasy in American children's literature; it [was] the first fully created imaginative world in the whole of children's literature."[75] Those that followed include E. Nesbit's *Five Children and It* (1902 in England; 1905 in the United States), *The Story of the Amulet* (1906 in England; 1906 in the United States), which was the first time travel fantasy was written for children, Howard Pyle's *The Story of King Arthur and His Knights* (1903), J. M. Barrie's *Peter Pan* (1904; 1911), W. H. Hudson's *A Little Boy Lost* (1905 in England; 1918 in the United States), Frances Hodgson Burnett's *Racketty-Packetty House* (1906), Rudyard Kipling's *Puck of Pook's Hill* (1906), Kenneth Grahame's *The Wind in the Willows* (1907 in England; 1908 in the United States), Selma Lagerlöf's *The Wonderful Adventures of Nils* (1907 in Sweden; 1908 in the United States), Friedrich de la Motte Fouqué's *Undine* (written in 1811; published in the United States in 1908), Walter de la Mare's *The Three Mulla-Mulgars* (1910 in England; 1919 in the United States), and E. F. Benson's *David Blaize and the Blue Door* (1918 in England; 1919 in the United States).

The 1920s and 1930s

During and following World War I, there was an understandable lull in the writing and publishing of all types of children's books; other needs were more pressing. In contrast, the 1920s, a period of relative prosperity, produced a number of lighthearted fantasies, including talking toy and animal stories and tales of voyages to wondrous lands. Some of the better known books from this period are W. W. Tarn's *Treasure of the Isle of Mist* (1919, 1920), which contained the first real-world villain in children's fantasy literature,

Padraic Colum's *The Boy Apprenticed to an Enchanter* (1920), Hugh Lofting's *The Story of Doctor Dolittle* (1920), Margery Williams Bianco's *The Velveteen Rabbit,* (1922), which was the first toy animal fantasy novel written for children, Carl Sandburg's *Rootabaga Stories* (1922), Stewart Edward White's *The Magic Forest* (1923), A. A. Milne's *Winnie-the-Pooh* (1926), Walter Brooks's Freddy books (1927–1958), John Masefield's *The Midnight Folk* (1927), which, according to Egoff, included "the first feisty girl character in children's literature," Paul Fenimore Cooper's *Tal* (1929), Rachel Field's *Hitty* (1929), and Beatrix Potter's *The Fairy Caravan* (1929). Laurence Housman's gentle tales of fairies and princesses, first published during the 1890s, were reissued in new collections in the 1920s, and Walter De La Mare's memorable short story collections began appearing in 1925.

The years of the Great Depression produced two of the best loved English fantasies—P. L. Travers's *Mary Poppins* (1931) and J. R. R. Tolkien's *The Hobbit* (1937)—as well as Elizabeth Coatsworth's *The Cat Who Went to Heaven* (1930), Anne Parrish's *Floating Island* (1930), Eleanor Farjeon's *The Little Book Room* (1931 in England; 1956 in the United States), Ella Young's *The Unicorn with Silver Shoes* (1932), Kate Seredy's *The White Stag* (1937), Richard Atwater and Florence Atwater's *Mr. Popper's Penguins* (1938), Dr. Seuss's *The 500 Hats of Bartholomew Cubbins* (1938), Robert Lawson's *Ben and Me* (1939), and Alison Uttley's *A Traveller in Time* (1939, 1940).

During the 1920s and 1930s, teenagers were expected to read the classics, and school reading lists of this period often included Tennyson's Arthurian poem, "Idylls of the King," written in 1859. Westerns, mysteries, and adventure stories, rather than fantasies, seem to have been the recreational reading of young people at this time, although we should note that a number of the fantasies written for adults during the 1920s and 1930s are still read today by both adults and young adults.

These include E. R. Eddison's *The Worm Ouroboros* (1922 in England; 1926 in the United States), James Stephens's *Deirdre* (1923), Lord Dunsany's *The King of Elfland's Daughter* (1924), Robert Nathan's *Portrait of Jenny* (1929), James Hilton's *Lost Horizon* (1933), Evangeline Walton's *The Virgin and the Swine* (1936, later retitled *The Island of the Mighty*), Stephen Vincent Benét's *The Devil and Daniel Webster* (1937), J. R. R. Tolkien's *The Hobbit* (1937), and T. H. White's *A Sword in the Stone* (1938, 1939). *The Hobbit,* with its richly detailed other-world and its imaginative tribe of small people called "hobbits" broke new ground in the world of fantasy literature. Tolkien's ability to meld an exciting plot, a memorable setting, and a strong sense of a moral code, with characters who are changed by their experiences had an impact on the genre that is still felt today.

The 1940s and 1950s

Unlike the World War I period, a number of noteworthy children's fantasies were published during World War II. These include B. B.'s (D. J. Watkins-Pitchford) *The Little Grey Men* (1942 in England; 1949 in the United States), Enys Tregarthen's *The Doll Who Came Alive* (1942), Mary Norton's *The Magic Bedknob* (1943 in England; 1957 in the United States), Antoine de Saint-Exupéry's *The Little Prince* (1943), Julia L. Sauer's

Fog Magic (1943), James Thurber's *Many Moons* (1943), Robert Lawson's *Rabbit Hill* (1944), Eric Linklater's *The Wind on the Moon* (1944), Astrid Lindgren's *Pippi Long-stocking* (1945 in Sweden; 1950 in the United States), Carolyn Bailey's *Miss Hickory* (1946), Eleanor Farjeon's *The Glass Slipper* (1946 in England; 1956 in the United States), Elizabeth Goudge's *The Little White Horse* (1946, 1947), T. H. White's *Mistress Masham's Repose* (1946), William Pène Du Bois's *The Twenty-One Balloons* (1947), Rumer Godden's *The Doll's House* (1947), Ruth Stiles Gannett's *My Father's Dragon* (1948), Tove Jansson's *Finn Family Moomintroll* (1949 in Finland; 1958 in the United States), and Rumer Godden's *The Mousewife* (1951).

According to Sheila Egoff, "In general . . . [the fantasies] of the 1940s have a sense of children at play, but with play used as a metaphor for experiencing life. . . . Play is not seen as a trivial, time-filling activity. . . . Chiefly, there is a scenario of mini-war. Tyranny is fought and defeated. Might goes down before courage and cunning, goodness and generosity. The writers of this decade present their ideas quite plainly and endow their young heroes and heroines with a kind of stylized innocence. . . . [These fantasies] are halfway houses to those stories of the 1960s and 1970s where time and distance from real battles resulted in a highly mythic and symbolic approach to the struggle between good and evil."[76]

Following World War II, childhood came to be seen as preparation for adulthood. Adults were peripheral characters in the books of this era, and the children were depicted as resourceful and imaginative. The 1950s were again golden years for children's fantasy. Included among the many outstanding works were, according to critics,[77] three "perfect" fantasies: E. B. White's *Charlotte's Web* (1952), L. M. Boston's *The Children of Green Knowe* (1954, 1955), and Philippa Pearce's *Tom's Midnight Garden* (1958 in England; 1959 in the United States).

In addition to these three books, many of the memorable children's fantasies from the 1950s and early 1960s were magic adventure tales: C. S. Lewis's Chronicles of Narnia (1951–1956), Edward Eager's *Half Magic* (1954), K. M. Briggs's *Hobberdy Dick* (1955 in England; 1977 in the United States), Barbara Sleigh's *Carbonel* (1955, 1956), William Mayne's *A Grass Rope* (1957 in England; 1962 in the United States), Mary Chase's *Loretta Mason Potts* (1958), Elizabeth Marie Pope's *The Sherwood Ring* (1958), Agnes Smith's *An Edge of the Forest* (1959), and Norton Juster's *The Phantom Tollbooth* (1961).

A number of others involved miniature worlds, including Mary Norton's The Borrowers series (1952–1982), Carol Kendall's *The Gammage Cup* (1959), and Pauline Clarke's *The Return of the Twelves* (1962, 1963).

Still others involved humorous exaggeration or were lighthearted talking animal tales: Oliver Butterworth's *The Enormous Egg* (1956), Dodie Smith's *The Hundred and One Dalmatians* (1956, 1957), Eve Titus's Basil of Baker Street series (1958–1982), Margery Sharp's Miss Bianca books (1959–1978), Michael Bond's Paddington series (1960–1982), George Selden's *The Cricket in Times Square* (1960), Mary Stolz's *Belling the Tiger* (1961), Beverly Cleary's Ralph Mouse trilogy (1965–1982), and Maurice Sendak's *Higglety Pigglety Pop!* (1967).

One criticism could be leveled at many of the children's fantasies written during the 1950s: In spite of their fantastic adventures, the children in most of these stories never grew or changed. With the exception of a few books, such as Philippa Pearce's *Tom's Midnight Garden* (1958), L. M. Boston's *The Children of Green Knowe* (1959), and Mary Chase's *Loretta Mason Potts,* children with "problems" did not appear; the children were almost repetitiously pictured as happy and safe.

According to Egoff, "Simplicity combined with depth of feeling is one of the chief hallmarks of the fantasy novels of the 1950s. . . . These are all child-centered books and childhood is seen as a very natural state. . . . The emphasis was on the family and family life. The children's books of the period all have this sense of security and hope. . . . The greatest triumph of these writers lay in their ability to present such concepts [as empathy with others and with the natural world] in a clear, lucid style and with memorable images."[78]

Most of the books popular with teenagers during the two decades following World War II were not fantasies, but were war stories, sports stories, car stories, and romances, beginning with Maureen Daly's *Seventeenth Summer* (1942). The immediate popularity of J. D. Salinger's realistic novel *The Catcher in the Rye* (1951) marked the beginning of a new body of literature written with the teenage reader in mind, although the term "young adult literature" did not come into use for more than 20 years.

In spite of the development of this "new" category of books aimed at teenagers, the fantasy novels written between 1945 and 1965 were still mainly "adult" works that only later gained popularity with young people. These works include George Orwell's *Animal Farm* (1945), Valentine Davies's *The Miracle on 34th Street* (1947), John Myers Myers's *Silverlock* (1949), Jack Vance's *Dying Earth* (1950), J. R. R. Tolkien's Lord of the Rings trilogy (1954–1956), Leonard Wibberley's *The Mouse That Roared* (1955), Mary Renault's *The King Must Die* (1958), T. H. White's *The Once and Future King* (1958), Peter Beagles's *A Fine and Private Place* (1960), Ray Bradbury's *Something Wicked This Way Comes* (1962), Marion Zimmer Bradley's first Darkover novel (*The Sword of Aldones,* 1962), and Andre Norton's *Witch World* (1963).

Contemporary Fantasy, 1965 to the Present

By the mid-1960s, children, particularly in the United States and England, were thought to be more mature than their earlier counterparts, capable of handling many heretofore "adult" problems. As a consequence, children's and young adult novels of all genres written during the last three decades became much more open about the realities of parental conflict, divorce, death, child abuse, love, and sexual identity. The protagonists of contemporary fantasy novels must also deal with these issues. In addition, the magic in these stories is now seen to have serious consequences if misused, and those characters whose lives are touched by magic are themselves changed by the experience.

The 1960s

It was not until the reissue of J. R. R. Tolkien's *The Hobbit* (1966) and Lord of the Rings trilogy (1967) that young adults began to find *fantasy* novels written specifically for them. Indeed, the term "young adult literature" first came into use in the early 1970s, along with the rise of problem novels aimed at young people, the first of which was S. E. Hinton's *The Outsiders* (1967).

Two types of fantasy have gained special prominence during the last three decades: stories in which characters in the real world become involved with forces of myth and legend, which have been called myth fantasy, and stories set in imaginary worlds, variously called epic fantasy, high fantasy, heroic fantasy, other-world fantasy, and alternate world fantasy.

The prime example of the latter type of fantasy written for young people during the 1960s was Ursula K. Le Guin's Earthsea quartet, begun in 1968 with *A Wizard of Earthsea,* which Egoff calls "The most intellectual and quotable of modern fantasies written for the young."[79] Two well-known other-world fantasy series written for adults and read by young adults arrived on the scene during the 1960s: Marion Zimmer Bradley's Darkover series (1962–1994) and Anne McCaffrey's Dragonriders of Pern series (1968–1994).

One variation on the other-world fantasy novel is the alternate-history fantasy, which is a story set in an alternate version of real-world history, such as Joan Aiken's Wolves Chronicles, begun in 1962 with *The Wolves of Willoughby Chase,* and Peter Dickinson's Changes trilogy, begun in 1968 with *The Weathermonger.* A second variation on the other-world theme is the story of real-world protagonists who visit another world, best exemplified during the 1960s by Alan Garner's *Elidor* (1965, 1967).

In the category of contemporary involvement with myth, the three outstanding examples from the 1960s are William Mayne's *Earthfasts* (1966, 1967), Susan Cooper's The Dark Is Rising sequence, which began with *Over Sea, Under Stone* in 1966, and Alan Garner's *The Owl Service* (1967, 1968). Garner's story brought a Welsh myth to life, while Mayne and Cooper utilized Arthurian themes, which have become increasingly important in contemporary fantasy literature.

Other authors began to expand mythical and legendary tales into novel-length, or even saga-length stories during the 1960s, including K. M. Briggs's *Kate Crackernuts* (1963), Lloyd Alexander's Chronicles of Prydain, which began with *The Book of Three* (1964), and Rosemary Harris's Reuben trilogy, which began with *The Moon in the Cloud* (1968).

During the 1960s, adolescent main characters became much more common in fantasy literature. As in the realistic fiction being written for young people after 1960, an important aspect of these "new" fantasies was the coming of age of their protagonists, who deal with serious problems and mature from childhood through adolescence into adulthood.

There were, of course, outstanding fantasies with child protagonists still being written during the 1960s, many of which were magic adventure and time travel stories. These included Penelope Farmer's *The Summer Birds* (1962), John Lawson's *You Better Come Home with Me* (1966), Leon Garfield's *Mister Corbett's Ghost* (1968), Antonia Barber's *The Ghosts* (1969), Helen Cresswell's *A Game of Catch* (1969, 1977), and Penelope Farmer's *Charlotte Sometimes* (1969).

A number of memorable animal fantasies were written during the 1960s, including George Selden's *A Cricket in Times Square* (1960), Beverly Cleary's *The Mouse and the*

Motorcycle (1965), Randall Jarrell's *The Animal Family* (1965, 1985), and Russell Hoban's multi-leveled masterpiece, *The Mouse and His Child* (1967), which describes a father and son's attempts to build a family for themselves, while satirizing American society.

The 1970s

The genre of fantasy literature for children and young adults expanded prodigiously during the 1970s. In addition to the already prominent fantasy authors such as Joan Aiken, Lloyd Alexander, Susan Cooper, Helen Cresswell, Peter Dickinson, Penelope Farmer, Leon Garfield, Alan Garner, Mollie Hunter, Ursula K. Le Guin, and William Mayne, a number of important new fantasy authors appeared, including Richard Adams, Natalie Babbitt, Diana Wynne Jones, Penelope Lively, Robin McKinley, Robert Westall, and Patricia Wrightson.

"High Fantasy" novels, including both stories set in other-worlds and those involving myth and legend, proliferated during this decade. Outstanding examples of alternate world fantasy written during the 1970s include Joy Chant's *Red Moon and Black Mountain* (1970, 1971, 1976), Patricia McKillip's *The Forgotten Beasts of Eld* (1974), Elizabeth Pope's *The Perilous Gard* (1974), Diana Wynne Jones's *Cart and Cwidder* (1975, 1977), Peter Dickinson's *The Blue Hawk* (1976), Anne McCaffrey's Harper Hall trilogy, which began with *Dragonsong* (1976), and Lloyd Alexander's *The First Two Lives of Lukas-Kasha* (1978).

A number of so-called adult other-world fantasy series also began appearing during the 1970s: Katherine Kurtz's The Chronicles of Deryni (1970–1991), Roger Zelazny's Amber series (1970–1991), Gordon R. Dickson's Dragon series (1976–1992), Stephen R. Donaldson's Chronicles of Thomas Covenant, the Unbeliever (1977–1983), Piers Anthony's Magic of Xanth series (1977–1994), and Robert L. Asprin's Myth Adventure series (1978–1987).

Critically acclaimed "myth fantasies" written for young people during the 1970s included Penelope Lively's *The Wild Hunt of the Ghost Hounds* (1971, 1972), Dahlov Ipcar's *The Queen of Spells* (1973), Patricia Wrightson's *The Nargun and the Stars* (1973), and Natalie Babbitt's *Tuck Everlasting* (1975), which Sheila Egoff called "one of the simplest yet most profound fantasies in children's literature. In asking—and answering—questions about morality, it takes its place alongside E. B. White's *Charlotte's Web.*"[80]

Other outstanding myth fantasies of the decade were Susan Cooper's *The Grey King* (1975), Mollie Hunter's *A Stranger Came Ashore* (1975), Robin McKinley's *Beauty* (1978), and Rosemary Sutcliff's The Sword and the Circle trilogy (1979–1982). Cooper used Arthurian themes in her The Dark Is Rising series, and Sutcliff retold the Arthurian legends themselves, while Mary Stewart re-created the King Arthur stories by telling them from Merlin's point of view in her "adult" quartet that began with *The Crystal Cave* (1970).

Memorable animal fantasies written for young people during the 1970s included Robert C. O'Brien's *Mrs. Frisby and the Rats of NIMH* (1971) and Richard Adams's *Watership Down* (1972, 1974). Ghost fantasies included Eleanor Cameron's *The Court of the Stone Children* (1973), Penelope Lively's *The Ghost of Thomas Kempe* (1973), Richard Peck's Blossom Culp trilogy (1975–1986), and Robert Westall's *The Watch House* (1977, 1978). Humorous fantasies included Mary Rogers's *Freaky Friday* (1972), Natalie Babbitt's *The Devil's Storybook* (1974), and Christine Nöstlinger's *Konrad* (1977). Magic adventure and time travel fantasies from this decade included Otfried Preussler's *The Satanic Mill* (1971, 1973), Diana Wynne Jones's *The Ogre Downstairs* (1974, 1990), and Andrew Davies's *Conrad's War* (1978, 1980). Two well-received adult time travel novels were published during this decade: Jack Finney's *Time and Again* (1970) and Richard Matheson's *Bid Time Return* (1975).

Sheila Egoff has one criticism for the authors of contemporary fantasy for young people: "Modern writers who endow their young characters with supernatural powers (that is beyond the use of talismans) deprive us of a chance to deal with our own humanity. The best fantasies remind us of our humanity, not allowing us to fantasize beyond our innate capabilities, but encouraging us to use these capabilities to the utmost."[81]

During the past twenty years, alternate world or epic fantasy seems to have become the fastest-growing category of fantasy literature. There is, however, one problem that has plagued the genre of contemporary young adult fantasy, and is perhaps tied to the growing popularity of fantasy role-playing games such as "Dungeons and Dragons," fantasy video, and computer games: the publication of numerous derivative "adult" fantasy novels and series, often referred to as "sword- and-sorcery fantasy." In a 1990 *New York Times Book Review* front page article, editor David G. Hartwell decries the proliferation of formulaic mass-market fantasy novels written for adults, a literary subgenre that, according to him, accounts for nearly 10 percent of all fiction sales in the United States. He deplores the authors' "slavish imitation of Tolkien," and outlines the criteria for these formula books that were set up by Bantam editor Lester del Rey in the late 1970s:

> The books would be original novels set in invented worlds in which magic works. Each would have a male central character who triumphed over the forces of evil (usually associated with technical knowledge of some variety) by innate virtue, and with the help of a tutor or tutelary spirit. . . . The covers would be rich, detailed illustrations of a colorful scene. . . . Mr. del Rey had codified a children's literature that could be sold as adult. It was nostalgic, conservative, pastoral and optimistic. . . . By the late '70s, the success of the Del Rey formula was so confirmed that many other publishers had begun to publish in imitation. Dragons and unicorns began to appear all over the mass-market racks. . . . In the '80s most mass-market publishers [got into this new market]. Trilogies were the order of the day. Some authors complained that publishers often requested revisions in the endings of their fantasy works so that a single novel, if popular, might be extended by two more volumes. . . . Unquestionably, [mass-market publishers] created an enormous wave of trash writing [for] an audience trained . . . to accept tiny nuances and gestures overlaying mediocrity and repetition as true originality.

Mr. Hartwell concludes his article on an optimistic note by commending a number of distinguished examples of contemporary fantasy literature, which have "rich artistic possibilities when properly executed, especially when in the hands of the finest writers working in fantasy today. . . . These works have individual excellences that are expanding the literary boundaries of stylistic and imaginative achievement in fantasy and in contemporary literature."[82]

The 1980s to the 1990s

Many outstanding fantasies for children and young adults were written and published during the 1980s, and more have appeared in the first quarter of the 1990s. Well-respected fantasy authors such as Ursula K. Le Guin, Diana Wynne Jones, Lloyd Alexander, and Robin McKinley added to their *oeuvre,* while new and talented authors have begun writing fantasy, including Pam Conrad, Virginia Hamilton, Margaret Mahy, Ruth Park, and Cynthia Voigt.

Some of these special books include animal fantasies such as Clare Bell's *Ratha's Creature* (1983), Brian Jacques's Redwall saga (1986–1994), and Ursula K. Le Guin's Catwings books (1988–1994), and ghost fantasies such as Virginia Hamilton's *Sweet Whispers, Brother Rush* (1982), Sylvia Cassedy's *Behind the Attic Wall* (1983), and Nicholas Wilde's *Into the Dark* (1987, 1990). There were also humorous fantasies such as Roald Dahl's *Matilda* (1988), and magic adventure stories such as Jane Langton's *The Fledgling* (1980), Lynne Reid Banks's The Indian in the Cupboard quartet (1980–1993), Bill Brittain's Coven Tree saga, which began with *The Devil's Donkey* (1981), Chris Van Allsburg's *Jumanji* (1981), Margaret Mahy's *The Haunting* (1982), Mary Norton's *The Borrowers Avenged* (1982), Diana Wynne Jones's *Fire and Hemlock* (1984), and Margaret Mahy's *The Changeover* (1984).

The category of time travel fantasy has also continued to be enriched by memorable books for children and young adults, including David Wiseman's *Jeremy Visick* (1981), Ruth Park's *Playing Beatie Bow* (1982), Jane Yolen's *The Devil's Arithmetic* (1988), and Pam Conrad's *Stonewords* (1990). Humor and witchcraft are effectively combined in Kate Gilmore's *Enter Three Witches* (1990) and Patrice Kindl's *Owl in Love* (1993).

There have been numerous well-written alternate world fantasies for young people written during the past decade, including Lloyd Alexander's *Westmark* (1981), Robin McKinley's *The Blue Sword* (1982), Meredith Ann Pierce's *The Darkangel* (1982), Patricia McKillip's *Moon-Flash* (1984), Sid Fleischman's *The Whipping Boy* (1986), Monica Furlong's *Wise Child* (1987), Diana Wynne Jones's *The Lives of Christopher Chant* (1988), Susan Fletcher's *Dragon's Milk* (1989), William Mayne's *Antar and the Eagles* (1989, 1990), Terry Pratchett's Bromeliad trilogy, which began with *Truckers* (1989), Pauline Fisk's *Midnight Blue* (1990), Ursula K. Le Guin's *Tehanu* (1990), Cynthia Voigt's *On Fortune's Wheel* (1990), Patricia C. Wrede's Enchanted Forest Chronicles (1990–1993), Gillian Bradshaw's *The Dragon and the Thief* (1991), Grace

Chetwin's *Child of the Air* (1991), Vivian Vande Velde's *Dragon's Bait* (1992), and Sherryl Jordan's *Winter of Fire* (1993). Vivien Alcock's *Singer to the Sea God* (1992) brings to life the Greek myth of Perseus and Medusa, and Elizabeth E. Wein's *The Winter Prince* (1993) tells the Arthurian story from a new point of view.

Well-written adult fantasies of the 1980s read by young adults include Marion Zimmer Bradley's *The Mists of Avalon* (1982), Nancy Willard's *Things Invisible to See* (1985), and Barbara Hambley's *Dragonsbane* (1986).

One welcome development in the genre of fantasy literature for young people written during the past twenty years has been the growing number of strong female protagonists, including Dido Twite in Aiken's The Wolves Chronicles, Zoe in Conrad's *Stonewords,* Kaeldra in Fletcher's *Dragon's Milk,* Juniper in Furlong's *Wise Child,* Polly in Jones's *Fire and Hemlock,* Tenar in Le Guin's *Tehanu,* Menolly in McCaffrey's *Dragonsong,* Sybel in McKillip's *The Forgotten Beasts of Eld,* Harry Crew in McKinley's *The Blue Sword,* Laura in Mahy's *The Changeover,* Aeriel in Pearce's *The Darkangel,* Kate in Pope's *The Perilous Gard,* Cimorene in Wrede's The Enchanted Forest Chronicles, and Hannah in Yolen's *The Devil's Arithmetic.*

For this edition of *Fantasy Literature for Children and Young Adults,* I have added a listing of national and international "Award-Winning Fantasy Literature," which follows the list of "Outstanding Contemporary Fantasy." I decided to retain and update the "Outstanding" list, which includes many titles discussed above, because so many well-written books never win awards. As Jane Langton put it in a *New York Times* review of the 1992 Newbery award-winning book: "Did *Shiloh* really deserve the prize? Surely there must have been a book more important than this agreeable but slight story. Like the Oscar, the Newbery has sometimes passed over the good and the great. There have been embarrassing omissions. Where were the prizes for Ursula K. Le Guin's *A Wizard of Earthsea* [and] Natalie Babbitt's *Tuck Everlasting . . .* ? Possibly the greatest children's book ever written in the English language, E. B. White's *Charlotte's Web,* ran second to an otherwise forgotten wonder, *Secret of the Andes,* by Ann Nolan Clark. . . . The Newbery judges . . . are all members of the American Library Association, good workers in the vineyard. . . . Can a committee of 15 do anything but compromise?"[83]

Conclusion

Natalie Babbitt has written that one of the special qualities of fantasy literature is that it not only lets us share the hero's hopes and triumphs but that it ends on a note of hope. She feels that fantasy "is not a sop for the terminally optimistic, but an affirmation of one of the things that makes us, as a species, unique: the always present hope that something will happen to change everything, once and for all, for the better."[84]

It is hoped that the authors of fantasy literature will continue to create stories that illuminate reality, delight us, refresh our hearts, provide us with hope for the future, and give us joy.

Notes

1. Natalie Babbitt, "The Purposes of Fantasy." In *Proceedings of the Ninth Annual Conference of the Children's Literature Association* (Ypsilanti, Mich.: Children's Literature Association, 1983), pp. 22, 29. Reprinted with permission. Reprinted in *Innocence & Experience,* ed. by Barbara Harrison and Gregory Maguire (New York: Lothrop, 1987), pp. 174–181.
2. Jane Yolen, "Tough Magic," *Top of the News* 35 (Winter, 1979): 186.
3. Sheila Egoff, *Thursday's Child: Trends and Patterns in Contemporary Children's Literature* (Chicago: American Library Association, 1981), p. 82.
4. Elizabeth Nesbit, *A Critical History of Children's Literature: A Survey of Children's Books in English,* rev. ed. Cornelia Meigs, Anne Thaxter Eaton, Elizabeth Nesbit, and Ruth Hill Viguers (New York: Macmillan, 1969), p. 347.
5. *The Oxford English Dictionary,* Second Edition (Oxford, England: Clarendon Press, 1989), Vol. V, pp. 722–723.
6. *The Random House Dictionary of the English Language* Second Edition, Unabridged (New York: Random House, 1987), p. 698.
7. Everett F. Bleiler, *The Checklist of Fantastic Literature: A Bibliography of Fantasy, Weird and Science Fiction Published in the English Language* (Chicago: Shasta, 1948), p. 3; Perry Nodelman, "Defining Children's Literature," in *Children's Literature* 8 (New Haven, Conn.: Yale University Press, 1980), p. 187; Eric S. Rabkin, *The Fantastic in Literature* (Princeton, N.J.: Princeton University Press, 1976), p. 8; and Tsvetan Todorov, *The Fantastic: A Structural Approach to a Literary Genre* (Cleveland, Ohio: Case Western Reserve University Press, 1973), p. 25. "[Fantasy is] that hesitation experienced by a person . . . confronting an apparently supernatural event." *See also* Pierre Castex, *Le Conte Fantastique en France de Nodier à Maupassant* (Paris: Corti, 1951), quoted in Todorov, *The Fantastic,* p. 26. "[Fantasy is] the brutal intrusion of mystery [into real life.]"; H. P. Lovecraft, quoted in Todorov, *The Fantastic,* p. 34; Peter Penzoldt, *The Supernatural in Fiction* (Atlantic Highlands, N.J.: Humanities Press, 1965), quoted in Todorov, *The Fantastic,* p. 35. "A fantasy is a tale of fear and terror"; and Julius Kagarlitski, "Realism and Fantasy," in *Science Fiction: The Other Side of Realism–Essays in Modern Fantasy and Science Fiction,* ed. by Thomas D. Clareson. (Bowling Green, Ohio: Bowling Green University Popular Press, 1971), p. 29. "[Fantasy is a tale in which] disbelief arises side by side with belief."
8. Lin Carter, *Imaginary Worlds: The Art of Fantasy* (New York: Ballantine, 1973), p. 6. *See also* James E. Higgins, *Beyond Words: Mystical Fancy in Children's Literature* (New York: Columbia University Press, 1970), p. 5; Naomi Lewis, *Fantasy Books for Children,* rev. ed. (London: National Book League, 1977), p. 5; and Patrick Merla, " 'What Is Real?' Asked the Rabbit One Day; Realism vs. Fantasy in Children's and Adult Literature," in *Only Connect,* 2nd ed., ed. by Sheila Egoff, G. T. Stubbs, and L. F. Ashley (New York: Oxford University Press, 1980), p. 348. ". . . the essential element of any true work of fantasy is magic—a force that affects the lives and actions of all the creatures that inhabit the fantastic world. . . . Always it is

a *supernatural* force whose use, *mis*use, or *dis*use irrevocably changes the lives of those it touches. . . . Real magic cannot be explained in material terms, nor manufactured with mechanical devices, nor achieved through ingested substances."

9. Louis Vax, *L'Art et la Litérature Fantastiques* (Paris: Presses Universitaires de France, 1960), quoted in Todorov, *The Fantastic,* p. 26. "The fantastic narrative generally describes men like ourselves, inhabiting the real world, suddenly confronted by the inexplicable." *See also* Roger Caillois, *Au Coeur de Fantastique* (Paris), quoted in Todorov, *The Fantastic,* p. 26. "The fantastic is always a break in the acknowledged order, an irruption of the inadmissible, within the changeless everyday legality."

10. Jane Mobley, ed., *Phantasmagoria: Tales of Fantasy and the Supernatural* (New York: Anchor Press, 1977), pp. 17, 23.

11. Brian Attebery, *The Fantasy Tradition in American Literature from Irving to Le Guin* (Bloomington: Indiana University Press, 1980), p. 2. "Any narrative which includes as a significant part of its make-up some violation of what the author clearly believes to be natural law—that is fantasy." *See also* W. R. Irwin, *The Game of the Impossible: A Rhetoric of Fantasy* (Champaign: University of Illinois Press, 1976), pp. 4, 9. "[The primary feature of fantasy is] an overt violation of what is generally accepted as possibility . . . a narrative is fantasy if it presents the persuasive establishment and development of an impossibility."; Leo P. Kelley, ed., *Fantasy: The Literature of the Marvelous* (New York: McGraw-Hill, 1974), p. v. "[Fantasy] tells us of events which could not occur in a universe whose major physical laws are known and necessarily obeyed"; and Marshall B. Tymn, Kenneth J. Zahorski, and Robert H. Boyer, *Fantasy Literature: A Core Collection and Reference Guide* (New York: Bowker, 1979), pp. 3, 4. "[Fantasies are] works in which events occur, or places or creatures exist that could not exist according to rational standards or scientific explanations. . . . Fantasy . . . has its own vision of reality."

12. Attebery, *Fantasy Tradition,* p. 3. "The most important thing [works of fantasy] share is a sense of wonder . . . invoke[d] . . . by making the impossible seem familiar and the familiar seem new and strange." See also C. N. Manlove, *Modern Fantasy: Five Studies* (New York: Cambridge University Press, 1975), p. 1. "A fantasy is 'A fiction evoking wonder and containing a substantial and irreducible element of the supernatural with which the mortal characters in the story or the readers become on at least partly familiar terms.'"

13. Ann Swinfen, *In Defense of Fantasy: A Study of the Genre in English and American Literature Since 1945* (Boston: Routledge, 1984), p. 234. Reprinted with permission of the publisher.

14. Egoff, *Thursday's Child,* p. 80. Reprinted with permission of the American Library Association, excerpt taken from "Thursday's Child: Trends and Patterns in Contemporary Children's Literature" by Sheila Egoff; copyright © 1981 by ALA.

15. Eleanor Cameron, *The Green and Burning Tree: On the Writing and Enjoyment of Children's Books* (Boston: Little, Brown, 1969), p. 16.

16. Jane Langton, "The Weak Place in the Cloth: A Study of Fantasy for Children," *Horn Book Magazine* 49 (October 1973): 433; Lloyd Alexander, "Wishful Think-

ing—Or Hopeful Dreaming?" *Horn Book Magazine* 44 (August 1968): 386; and Mollie Hunter, "One World," *Horn Book Magazine* 51 (December 1975): 557.

17. Ursula K. Le Guin, "From Elfland to Poughkeepsie," in *The Language of the Night: Essays on Fantasy and Science Fiction,* edited by Susan Wood. (New York: Putnam, 1979), pp. 84, 93. Reprinted with the permission of the editor's Estate, the Author, and their joint agent, Virginia Kidd.

18. Sheila Egoff, *The Republic of Childhood,* 2nd ed. (New York: Oxford University Press, 1975), p. 134.

19. Swinfen, *In Defense of Fantasy,* p. 231. Reprinted with permission of the publisher.

20. Sheila Egoff, *Worlds Within: Children's Fantasy from the Middle Ages to Today.* (Chicago: American Library Association, 1988), p. 19.

21. Alan Garner, "A Bit More Practice," [London] *Times Literary Supplement,* June 6, 1968, p. 577.

22. Jane Louise Curry, "On the Elvish Craft," *Signal* 2 (May 1970): 44.

23. Susan Cooper, "Escaping into Ourselves," in Betsy Hearne and Marilyn Kaye, *Celebrating Children's Books* (New York: Lothrop, 1981), pp. 22–23.

24. Paul Hazard, *Books, Children and Men,* 4th ed. (Boston: Horn Book, 1960), p. 157.

25. Cameron, *Green and Burning Tree,* pp. 15–16.

26. Natalie Babbitt, "Happy Endings? Of Course, and Also Joy," *New York Times Book Review,* November 8, 1970, p. 1.

27. Swinfen, *In Defense of Fantasy,* p. 2. Reprinted with permission of the publisher.

28. See, for example, Carter, *Imaginary Worlds,* p. 1; Louis Macneice, *Varieties of Parable* (New York: Cambridge University Press, 1965), p. 102. "When we reach the twentieth century, children's fantasy is represented, I suppose, typically by *Peter Pan,* a work which is not only frivolous but perverse"; and Isabelle Jan, *On Children's Literature* (New York: Schocken, 1974), pp. 67–68.

29. Donnarae MacCann, "Wells of Fancy, 1865–1965," *Wilson Library Bulletin* 40 (December 1965): 403.

30. Carter, *Imaginary Worlds,* p. 1.

31. Babbitt, "Happy Endings?" p. 50.

32. Egoff, *The Republic of Childhood,* p. 134. *See also* Cameron, *Green and Burning Tree,* pp. 87–88. "A writer, it seems to me, should feel himself no more under necessity to restrict the complexity of his plotting because of differences in child understanding . . . than he feels the necessity of restricting his vocabulary. What is important is not, I think, that a child shall have understood each turn of the author's thinking, but that his excitement be set simmering as vista after vista of mental and spiritual distances, hitherto unguessed at, open before him. [These implications and overtones of meaning] will haunt the child long after he has forgotten the plot. . . . [These stories] are satisfying to [an adult] in ways which the child is not yet aware of . . . but the child can experience a very deep sense of satisfaction without in the least knowing why."

33. Neil Philip, "Fantasy: Double Cream or Instant Whip?" *Signal* 35 (May 1981): 83.

34. Susan Cooper, "Newbery Award Acceptance Address," *Horn Book Magazine* 52 (August 1976): 362.

35. Le Guin, "Dreams Must Explain Themselves," in *Language of the Night,* p. 55. *See also* C. S. Lewis, "On Three Ways of Writing for Children," in *Of Other Worlds: Essays and Stories* (New York: Harcourt, 1967), p. 24. "I am almost inclined to set it up as a canon that a children's story which is enjoyed only by children is a bad children's story. The good ones last."

36. Carter, *Imaginary Worlds,* p. 1; Elizabeth Cook, *The Ordinary and the Fabulous* (New York: Cambridge University Press, 1969), p. 5.

37. Cooper, "Escaping into Ourselves," pp. 15–16.

38. Lewis, "On Three Ways," pp. 29–30.

39. Curry, "On the Elvish Craft," p. 47.

40. J. R. R. Tolkien, *Tree and Leaf* (Boston: Houghton Mifflin, 1965), pp. 46–55.

41. Neil Barron, *Fantasy Literature: A Reader's Guide* (New York: Garland, 1990), pp. 309–310.

42. Tamora Pierce, "Fantasy: Why Kids Read It, Why Kids Need It," *School Library Journal* 39(October 1993): 50–51.

43. Lloyd Alexander, "Substance and Fantasy," *Library Journal* 91 (December 15, 1966): 6159; and Lloyd Alexander, "The Truth about Fantasy, " *Top of the News* 24 (January 1968): 174.

44. Kornei Chukovskii, *From Two to Five* (Berkeley: University of California Press, 1963), pp. 116–117, 124.

45. Alexander, "Wishful Thinking," p. 389.

46. Penelope Lively, "Children and Memory," *Horn Book Magazine* 49 (August 1973): 407.

47. Eleanor Cameron, "The Dearest Freshness Deep Down Things." Reprinted with the permission of Eleanor Cameron, *The Green and Burning Tree: On the Writing and Enjoyment of Children's Books* (Boston: Atlantic-Little, 1969), pp. 272–273; also in *Horn Book Magazine* 40 (October 1964): pp. 471–472.

48. Linda A. Forrest, "Young Adult Fantasy and the Search for Gender-Fair Genres," *Journal of Youth Services in Libraries* 7 (Fall 1993): 37–42.

49. Le Guin, "The Child and the Shadow," in *The Language of the Night,* pp. 68–69. *See also* Swinfen, *In Defense of Fantasy,* p. 229.

50. MacCann, "Wells of Fancy," p. 334.

51. Alan Garner, "Coming to Terms," *Children's Literature in Education* 2 (July 1970): 17; and Cooper, "Escaping into Ourselves," p. 16.

52. Isabelle Jan, *On Children's Literature* (New York: Schocken, 1974, published in France in 1969), pp. 44, 67, 75.

53. Bruno Bettleheim, *The Uses of Enchantment* (New York: Knopf, 1976), p. 144.

54. Mary J. Collier and Eugene L. Gaier, "Adult Reactions to Preferred Childhood Stories," *Child Development* 29 (March 1958): 97–103.

55. Egoff, *Worlds Within,* p.20.

56. Egoff, *Thursday's Child,* p. 87; and Mobley, *Phantasmagoria,* p. 35.

57. Swinfen, *In Defense of Fantasy,* p. 229. Reprinted with permission of the publisher.

58. Helen Cresswell, "If It's Someone from Porlock, Don't Answer the Door," *Children's Literature in Education* 4 (March 1971): 37.

59. Roger W. Drury, "Realism Plus Fantasy Equals Magic," *Horn Book Magazine* 48 (April 1972): 119.
60. Lewis, "On Three Ways," p. 23.
61. Babbitt, "Happy Endings?," p. 50.
62. Cooper, "Escaping into Ourselves," p. 22.
63. Le Guin, "Myth and Archetype in Science Fiction," in *The Language of the Night,* pp. 78–79, edited by Susan Wood. Reprinted with permission of the editor's Estate, the Author, and their joint agent, Virginia Kidd. *See also* Attebery, *Fantasy Traditions,* p. 15. "The materials of fantasy, the things that call forth feelings of wonder . . . are partly individual invention and partly community property."
64. Mollie Hunter, "One World," *Horn Book Magazine* 51 (December 1975): 562 (continued in 52 [January 1976]: 32–38).
65. Patricia Wrightson, "Stones into Pools," *Top of the News* 41 (Spring 1985): 286.
66. Helen Lourie, "Where Is Fancy Bred?" in Egoff, *Only Connect,* p. 110.
67. Curry, "On the Elvish Craft," pp. 42–43.
68. Ibid., pp. 43, 49. Other critics who divide fantasy into two basic categories are Frank Eyre, *British Children's Books in the Twentieth Century* (New York: Dutton, 1971), pp. 116–117. "[The first kind is] a story of ordinary life but with some extra quality added—wishes granted, time travel, talking animals, fairy creatures—the adventures happen in the real world. . . . [The second kind is] either about a different world altogether, or about our own world but in a completely different time in which everything is different"; Göte Klingberg, "The Fantastic and the Mythical as Reading for Modern Children and Young People," in *How Can Children's Literature Meet the Needs of Modern Children* (15th IBBY conference, 1976), p. 32. "I will call here a novel where some strange world is united with an everyday world . . . a fantastic tale, and a novel telling only of a mystical country wholly outside our ordinary world, a mythical tale"; Manlove, *Modern Fantasy,* p. 11. "The two broad classes of fantasy are 'comic' or 'escapist' or 'fanciful' [in which] the point of the work . . . is the reader's pleasure in the invented characters or situations, [and] 'imaginative fantasy' [in which] the object is to enlist [the author's] experience and invention into giving a total version of reality transformed: that is to make their fantastic worlds as real as our own"; and Diana Waggoner, *The Hills of Faraway: A Guide to Fantasy* (New York: Atheneum, 1978). Waggoner uses the term "Magic in Operation" for tales set in our world and "Magic of Situation" for tales that take place in a magical world.
69. Egoff, *Thursday's Child,* p. 82; Ralph Lavender, "Other Worlds: Myth and Fantasy, 1970–1980," *Children's Literature in Education* 12, no. 3 (Autumn 1981): 141–142.
70. Egoff, *Thursday's Child,* p. 92.
71. Egoff, *Thursday's Child,* p. 83.
72. Margery Fisher, *Intent upon Reading* (New York: Watts, 1962), p. 100.
73. Lewis, *Fantasy Books,* p. 5.
74. Egoff, *Worlds Within,* p. 78.
75. Ibid., p. 73.

76. Ibid., p. 150.
77. Frank Eyre, *British Children's Books in the Twentieth Century* (New York: Dutton, 1971), p. 128. "[*Tom's Midnight Garden* and *The Children of Green Knowe* are the two] perfect fantasies of our time." *See also* John Rowe Townsend, *Written for Children* (New York: Lothrop, 1967), pp. 127–128. "*Tom's Midnight Garden* . . . has not a flaw . . . it is as near to being perfect in its construction and its writing as any book I know. . . . If I were asked to name a single masterpiece of English children's literature since the last war . . . it would be this outstandingly beautiful and absorbing book"; and Eudora Welty, "Life in the Barn Was Very Good," *New York Times Book Review,* October 19, 1952, p. 49. "As a piece of work [*Charlotte's Web*] is just about perfect, and just about magical in the way it is done."
78. Egoff, *Worlds Within,* pp. 171–172.
79. Ibid., p. 182.
80. Ibid., p. 248.
81. Ibid., p. 310.
82. David G. Hartwell, "Dollars and Dragons: The Truth About Fantasy," *New York Times Book Review,* April 29, 1990, pp. 1, 40–41.
83. Jane Langton, Review of *Shiloh* by Phyllis Reynolds Naylor (Atheneum, 1991), *New York Times Book Review,* May 10, 1992, p. 21.
84. Babbitt, "The Purposes of Fantasy," p. 28.

OUTSTANDING CONTEMPORARY FANTASY

The following alphabetical lists of books and series published since 1960 are outstanding examples of fantasy literature for children and young adults. These lists are based on personal opinion as well as that expressed in professional review sources. For a list of the professional review sources used see Abbreviations of Books and Review Journals Cited. The first ten headings in this section correspond to Chapters 1 through 10. The final list, Crossover Books for Young Adults, includes those "adult" fantasy works that have become popular with young adults. Occasionally, a title will fit into two or more categories; if this is the case that title will appear on more than one list. To locate complete information on a specific book see the Title Index or the Author and Illustrator Index.

Allegorical Fantasy and Literary Fairy Tales

A number of fine contemporary allegorical stories and literary fairy tales have been written in the tradition of the classic stories by Hans Christian Andersen, Saavedra Miguel de Cervantes, Padraic Colum, Charles Dickens, Rudyard Kipling, Andrew Lang, George MacDonald, Antoine de Saint-Exupéry, Frank R. Stockton, William Makepeace Thackeray, James Thurber, and Oscar Wilde, including:

Adams, Richard. *Watership Down.* 1972, 1974
Alexander, Lloyd. *The Remarkable Journey of Prince Jen.* 1991
Beagle, Peter S. *The Last Unicorn.* 1968, 1988
Brittain, Bill. *Dr. Dredd's Wagon of Wonders.* 1987
Fleischman, Paul. *Coming-and-Going Men.* 1985
Fleischman, Sid. *The Whipping Boy.* 1986
Garfield, Leon. *The Wedding Ghost.* 1985, 1987
Hoban, Russell. *The Mouse and His Child.* 1967
Lawson, John. *You Better Come Home with Me.* 1966
Le Vert, John. *The Flight of the Cassowary.* 1986

Moeri, Louise. *Star Mother's Youngest Child.* 1975
Paterson, Katherine. *The King's Equal.* 1992
Price, Susan. *The Ghost Drum.* 1987
Stockton, Frank R. *The Bee-Man of Orn.* 1964, 1987
Thurber, James. *Many Moons.* 1943, 1990
Wangerin, Walter. *The Book of the Dun Cow.* 1978

Animal Fantasy

Two types of animal fantasy novels are represented on this list: allegorical tales of animals attempting to escape human evils, and more lighthearted talking animal stories. George Orwell's *Animal Farm* (1945) and E. B. White's *Charlotte's Web* (1952) are two classic animal fantasy novels written before 1960 that set the standard for those that have followed.

Adams, Richard. *Watership Down.* 1972, 1974
Bell, Clare. *Ratha's Creature.* 1983
Bond, Michael. Paddington series. 1960–1984
Cleary, Beverly. Ralph S. Mouse series. 1965–1982
Corbett, W. J. *The Song of Pentecost.* 1982, 1983
Erickson, Russell E. Warton and Morton series. 1974–1986
Hoban, Russell. *The Mouse and His Child.* 1967
Howe, James. Bunnicula series. 1979–1993
Jacques, Brian. Redwall saga. 1986–1994
Jarrell, Randall. *The Animal Family.* 1965, 1985
King-Smith, Dick. *Babe: The Gallant Pig* (1983, 1985); *Martin's Mice.* 1988
Le Guin, Ursula K. Catwings books. 1988, 1989, 1994
Lively, Penelope. *The Voyage of QV66.* 1978, 1979
Marshall, James. *Rats on the Roof and Other Stories.* 1991
O'Brien, Robert C. *Mrs. Frisby and the Rats of NIMH.* 1971
Selden, George. The Cricket in Times Square series. 1960–1987
Sendak, Maurice. *Higglety Pigglety Pop! Or, There Must Be More to Life.* 1967
Sharp, Margery. Miss Bianca series. 1959–1978
Steig, William. *Abel's Island.* 1976
Stolz, Mary. *Belling the Tiger.* 1961, 1989

Fantasy Collections

During the so-called golden age of the fantasy short story genre—the latter half of the nineteenth and the early years of the twentieth centuries—classic stories were created by Hans Christian Andersen, Arthur Bowie Chrisman, Padraic Colum, Walter de la Mare, Eleanor Farjeon, Laurence Housman, Rudyard Kipling, E. Nesbit, Barbara Leonie Picard, Howard Pyle, Carl Sandburg, Frank R. Stockton, and Oscar Wilde.

Since the early 1970s there has been a renewed interest in the fantasy short story, leading to the publication of a number of excellent collections. These include:

Aiken, Joan. *Up the Chimney Down and Other Stories.* 1984, 1985
Babbitt, Natalie. *The Devil's Storybook.* 1974
Brooke, William J. *A Telling of the Tales.* 1990
Harris, Rosemary. *Sea Magic and Other Stories of Enchantment.* 1974
Housman, Laurence. *The Rat Catcher's Daughter.* 1974
Jones, Diana Wynne. *Warlock at the Wheel and Other Stories.* 1984, 1985
Kennedy, Richard. *Richard Kennedy: Collected Stories.* 1987
Le Guin, Ursula K. *The Wind's Twelve Quarters.* 1975
Lively, Penelope. *Uninvited Ghosts and Other Stories.* 1984, 1985
McKinley, Robin. *Imaginary Lands.* 1985
Mahy, Margaret. *The Girl with the Green Ear.* 1992
Pearce, Philippa. *Lion at School: And Other Stories.* 1985, 1986
Singer, Isaac Bashevis. *Stories for Children.* 1984
Westall, Robert. *The Haunting of Chas McGill and Other Stories.* 1983
Williams, Jay. *The Practical Princess and Other Liberating Fairy Tales.* 1978
Yolen, Jane. *The Girl Who Cried Flowers and Other Tales.* 1974; *The Faery Flag* 1989

Ghost Fantasy

The most memorable recent books in the category of ghost fantasy include:

Aiken, Joan. *The Shadow Guests.* 1980
Beware! Beware! Chilling Tales. Ed. by Jean Richardson. 1989
Boston, Lucy. *The Children of Green Knowe* 1955, 1967
Burgess, Barbara Hood. *Oren Bell.* 1991
Cameron, Eleanor. *The Court of the Stone Children.* 1973
Cassedy, Sylvia. *Behind the Attic Wall.* 1983
Cresswell, Helen. *A Game of Catch.* 1969, 1977
Fleischman, Sid. *The Midnight Horse.* 1990
Garfield, Leon. *Mister Corbett's Ghost.* 1968; *The Empty Sleeve.* 1988
Hahn, Mary Downing. *Wait Till Helen Comes.* 1986
Hamilton, Virginia. *Sweet Whispers, Brother Rush.* 1982
Lively, Penelope. *The Ghost of Thomas Kempe.* 1973
Lunn, Janet. *Shadow in Hawthorne Bay.* 1986, 1987
McKissack, Patricia C. *The Dark-Thirty.* 1992
Mahy, Margaret. *The Tricksters.* 1986, 1987
Pearce, Philippa. *The Shadow Cage and Other Tales of the Supernatural.* 1977
Peck, Richard. The Blossom Culp trilogy. 1975–1986
Things That Go Bump in the Night. Ed. by Jane Yolen and Martin H. Greenberg. 1989

Westall, Robert. *The Watch House.* 1977, 1978; *The Scarecrows.* 1981
Wilde, Nicholas. *Into the Dark.* 1987, 1990
Wright, Betty Ren. *A Ghost in the House.* 1991

High Fantasy

The late 1960s and the 1970s were marked by the development of a relatively new type of children's and young adult novel—high fantasy, also called heroic fantasy or secondary world fantasy. The numerous books of high fantasy published during the last 25 years have been divided into three subcategories in this bibliography: (1) alternate world fantasy, stories set entirely in a secondary world; (2) myth fantasy, retellings of myth and stories of contemporary involvement in myth; and (3) travel to other worlds, stories in which a character from the "real" or primary world visits a secondary world.

ALTERNATE WORLDS OR HISTORIES. The outstanding alternate world fantasy novels written since Tolkien's *The Hobbit* (1937) include:

Aiken, Joan. The Wolves Chronicles. 1962–1993; *The Whispering Mountain.* 1969
Alexander, Lloyd. Westmark trilogy. 1981–1984
Beagle, Peter S. *The Last Unicorn.* 1968, 1988
Bradshaw, Gillian. The Dragon and the Thief books. 1991, 1992
Chetwin, Grace. Tales of Gom series. 1986–1989; *Child of the Air.* 1991
Christopher, John. Winchester trilogy. 1970–1972
Dickinson, Peter. *The Blue Hawk.* 1976; Changes trilogy. 1968–1970
Downer, Ann. Caitlin and Badger series. 1987–1993
Fleischman, Sid. *The Whipping Boy.* 1986
Fletcher, Susan. *Dragon's Milk.* 1989; *Flight of the Dragon Kyn.* 1993
Gloss, Molly. *Outside the Gates.* 1986
Halam, Ann. *The Daymaker.* 1987
Harris, Geraldine. Seven Citadels quartet. 1982–1984
James, Betsy. *Long Night Dance.* 1989
Jones, Diana Wynne. *Cart and Cwidder.* 1975, 1977; *Howl's Moving Castle.* 1986
Jordan, Sherryl. *Winter of Fire,* 1993
King, Stephen. *The Eyes of the Dragon.* 1987
Kisling, Lee. *Fool's War.* 1992
Lee, Tanith. *Black Unicorn.* 1991
Le Guin, Ursula K. Earthsea quartet. 1968–1990
Levin, Betty. *The Ice Bear.* 1986
Lovett, Margaret. *The Great and Terrible Quest.* 1967
McCaffrey, Anne. Harper Hall trilogy. 1976–1979
McKillip, Patricia. *The Forgotten Beasts of Eld.* 1974; *Moon-Flash.* 1984; Star-Bearer trilogy. 1976–1979; *The Changeling Sea.* 1988
McKinley, Robin. *The Blue Sword.* 1982; *The Hero and the Crown.* 1984
Mark, Jan. *Aquarius.* 1982, 1984

Mayne, William. *Antar and the Eagles.* 1989, 1990
Murphy, Shirley Rousseau. Nightpool trilogy. 1985–1988
Norton, Andre. *The Crystal Gryphon.* 1972
Pierce, Meredith Ann. The Darkangel trilogy. 1982–1990
Pierce, Tamora. Song of the Lioness series. 1983–1988; *Wild Magic: The Immortals.* 1992
Pratchett, Terry. Bromeliad trilogy. 1989–1991
Vande Velde, Vivian. *Dragon's Bait.* 1992
Voigt, Cynthia. *On Fortune's Wheel.* 1990
Wilder, Cherry. Rulers of Hylor trilogy. 1984–1986
Wrede, Patricia C. Enchanted Forest Chronicles. 1990–1993
Yep, Laurence M. Dragon quartet. 1982–1992
Yolen, Jane. Pit Dragons trilogy. 1982–1987
Zettner, Pat. *The Shadow Warrior.* 1990

MYTH FANTASY. T. H. White's *The Sword in the Stone* (1938, 1939) was the forerunner of the retold-myth type of fantasy, represented more recently by:

Alcock, Vivien. *Singer to the Sea God.* 1992
Alexander, Lloyd. Chronicles of Prydain series. 1964–1968
Bradshaw, Gillian. *Hawk of May.* 1980
Briggs, K. M. *Kate Crackernuts.* 1963, 1979, 1980
Coolidge, Olivia. *The King of Men.* 1966
Curry, Jane Louise. *The Sleepers.* 1968
Farjeon, Eleanor. *The Glass Slipper.* 1945, 1956, 1986
Gardner, John C. *Grendel.* 1971
Garfield, Leon, and Blishen, Edward. *The God Beneath the Sea.* 1970, 1971
Hamilton, Virginia. *The Magical Adventures of Pretty Pearl.* 1983
Harris, Rosemary. Reuben trilogy. 1968–1972
Ipcar, Dahlov. *The Queen of Spells.* 1973
Johnston, Norma. *Strangers Dark and Gold.* 1975
McKinley, Robin. *Beauty.* 1978
Seraillier, Ian. *The Challenge of the Green Knight.* 1967
Sutcliff, Rosemary. The Sword and the Circle trilogy. 1979–1982
Wein, Elizabeth E. *The Winter Prince.* 1993
Yolen, Jane. *The Dragon's Boy.* 1990

Outstanding stories of contemporary involvement with myth include:

Alcock, Vivien. *The Stonewalkers.* 1983
Babbitt, Natalie. *Tuck Everlasting.* 1975
Cooper, Susan. The Dark Is Rising sequence. 1966–1977
Curry, Jane Louise. *The Sleepers.* 1968
Dunlop, Eileen. *Clementina.* 1985, 1987
Farmer, Penelope. *A Castle of Bone.* 1972
Garfield, Leon. *The Wedding Ghost.* 1985, 1987

Garner, Alan. *The Owl Service.* 1967, 1968; *The Weirdstone of Brisingamen.* 1960
Harris, Rosemary. *The Seal-Singing.* 1971
Hunter, Mollie. *A Stranger Came Ashore.* 1975
Lawrence, Louise. *Star Lord.* 1978
Lively, Penelope. *The Wild Hunt of the Ghost Hounds.* 1971, 1972
Mayne, William. *Earthfasts.* 1966, 1967
O'Shea, Pat. *The Hounds of the Morrigan.* 1985, 1986
Service, Pamela. *Winter of Magic's Return.* 1985
Wrightson, Patricia. Wirrun trilogy. 1977–1981; *Balyet.* 1989

TRAVEL TO OTHER WORLDS. The best contemporary children's and young adult books in the category of travel to other worlds include:

Alexander, Lloyd. *The First Two Lives of Lukas-Kasha.* 1978
Chant, Joy. *Red Moon and Black Mountain.* 1970, 1971, 1976
Christopher, John. Fireball trilogy. 1981–1986
Cooper, Susan. *Seaward.* 1983
Dalton, Annie. *Out of the Ordinary.* 1988, 1990
Duane, Diane. *So You Want to Be a Wizard.* 1983
Ende, Michael. *The Neverending Story.* 1983
Fisk, Pauline. *Midnight Blue.* 1990
Garner, Alan. *Elidor.* 1965, 1967
Hilgartner, Beth. *Colors of the Dreamweaver's Loom.* 1989
Jones, Diana Wynne. *The Lives of Christopher Chant.* 1988
Le Guin, Ursula K. *The Beginning Place.* 1980
Mahy, Margaret. *Dangerous Spaces.* 1991
Pope, Elizabeth. *The Perilous Gard.* 1974
Westall, Robert. *The Devil on the Road.* 1979
Winthrop, Elizabeth. The Castle in the Attic books. 1985, 1993

Humorous Fantasy

Humorous fantasy continues to be popular, although more humorous stories seem to be written for children than for young adults. The well-loved stories by Dr. Seuss, Richard Atwater and Florence Atwater, William Pène du Bois, and Oliver Butterworth have been followed by:

Babbitt, Natalie. *The Devil's Storybook.* 1974
Cresswell, Helen. *The Piemakers.* 1967, 1980
Dahl, Roald. *Matilda.* 1988
Fleischman, Sid. Numerous tall tales. 1962–1990
King-Smith, Dick. *Harry's Mad.* 1986
Le Vert, John. *The Flight of the Cassowary.* 1986
Mahy, Margaret. *The Great White Man-Eating Shark.* 1989, 1990

Nöstlinger, Christine. *Konrad.* 1977
Peck, Richard. Blossom Culp series. 1975–1986
Pinkwater, Daniel Manus. Numerous offbeat stories. 1976–1986
Raskin, Ellen. *Figgs and Phantoms.* 1974
Rodgers, Mary. Annabel Andrews trilogy. 1972–1983
Scieszka, Jon. *The Stinky Cheese Man and Other Fairly Stupid Tales.* 1992

Magic Adventure Fantasy

The magic adventure tradition of E. Nesbit, P. L. Travers, and C. S. Lewis has been continued in:

Brittain, Bill. *The Wish Giver.* 1983
Cassedy, Sylvia. *Behind the Attic Wall.* 1983
Cresswell, Helen. *The Secret World of Polly Flint.* 1982
Curry, Jane Louise. *Mindy's Mysterious Miniature.* 1970
Farmer, Penelope. *The Summer Birds.* 1962
Jones, Diana Wynne. *The Ogre Downstairs.* 1974, 1990
Konigsburg, E. L. *Up from Jericho Tel.* 1986
Langton, Jane. *The Fledgling.* 1980
McCaughrean, Geraldine. *A Pack of Lies.* 1988, 1989
Mahy, Margaret. *The Haunting.* 1982
Norton, Mary. *The Borrowers Avenged.* 1982
Reid Banks, Lynne. The Indian in the Cupboard quartet. 1980–1993
Selden, George. *The Genie of Sutton Place.* 1973
Snyder, Zilpha Keatley. *Black and Blue Magic.* 1966
Townsend, John Rowe. *The Persuading Stick.* 1986, 1987
Van Allsburg, Chris. *Jumanji.* 1981
Winthrop, Elizabeth. The Castle in the Attic books. 1985, 1993

Time Travel Fantasy

The concept of time travel continues to fascinate readers of all ages, although its complexities can best be understood by young people from about age 10 up. Outstanding books that have followed in the footsteps of E. Nesbit's *The Story of the Amulet,* Alison Uttley's *A Traveller in Time,* and Philippa Pearce's *Tom's Midnight Garden* include:

Barber, Antonia. *The Ghosts.* 1969
Bond, Nancy. *A String in the Harp.* 1976
Buffie, Margaret. *The Haunting of Frances Rain.* 1987, 1989
Cameron, Eleanor. *Beyond Silence.* 1980
Conrad, Pan. *Stonewords.* 1990
Cresswell, Helen. *Moondial.* 1987; *Up the Pier.* 1971
Curry, Jane Louise. *Over the Sea's Edge.* 1971

Davies, Andrew. *Conrad's War.* 1978, 1980
Dexter, Catherine. *Mazemaker.* 1989
Farmer, Penelope. *Charlotte Sometimes.* 1969
Garner, Alan. *The Red Shift.* 1973
James, J. Alison. *Sing for a Gentle Rain.* 1990
Jones, Diana Wynne. *A Charmed Life.* 1977, 1978
Mayne, William. *A Game of Dark.* 1971
Naylor, Phyllis Reynolds. York trilogy. 1980–1981
Park, Ruth. *Playing Beatie Bow.* 1982
Parker, Richard. *The Old Powder Line.* 1971
Paton Walsh, Jill. *A Chance Child.* 1978
Peck, Richard. *Voices After Midnight.* 1989
Reiss, Kathryn. *Time Windows.* 1991; *Dreadful Sorry.* 1993
Stolz, Mary. *Cat in the Mirror.* 1975
Wesley, Mary. *Haphazard House.* 1983, 1993
Westall, Robert. *The Devil on the Road.* 1978, 1980; *The Wind Eye.* 1976, 1977
Wiseman, David. *Jeremy Visick.* 1981
Yolen, Jane. *The Devil's Arithmetic.* 1988

Toy Fantasy

Novels about toys or other inanimate objects that come to life are less common now than they were in the past, although such old favorites as E. T. A. Hoffmann's *The Nutcracker* (1819), Margery Williams Bianco's *The Velveteen Rabbit* (1922), A. A. Milne's *Winnie-the-Pooh* (1926), Rachel FIeld's *Hitty, Her First Hundred Years* (1929), Anne Parrish's *Floating Island* (1930), Carolyn Sherwin Bailey's *Miss Hickory* (1946), and Rumer Godden's doll stories (1947–1964) are still popular and frequently reprinted. The most memorable contemporary toy fantasies include:

Cassedy, Sylvia. *Behind the Attic Wall.* 1983
Gardam, Jane. *Through the Doll's House Door.* 1987
Kennedy, Richard. *Amy's Eyes.* 1985
Nabb, Magdalen. *The Enchanted Horse.* 1992, 1993
O'Connell, Jean. *The Dollhouse Caper.* 1976
Reid Banks, Lynne. The Indian in the Cupboard quartet. 1980–1993
Sleator, William. *Among the Dolls.* 1975, 1985
Wright, Betty Ren. *The Dollhouse Murders.* 1983

Witchcraft and Sorcery Fantasy

The best of the contemporary witchcraft and sorcery novels for young people include:

Bedard, Michael. *A Darker Magic.* 1987
Brittain, Bill. Coven Tree saga. 1981–1990

Duane, Diane. *So You Want to Be a Wizard.* 1983

Furlong, Monica. *Wise Child.* 1987; *Juniper.* 1990, 1991

Gilmore, Kate. *Enter Three Witches.* 1990

Harris, Deborah Turner. *The Burning Stone.* 1987

Hunter, Mollie. *Thomas and the Warlock.* 1967, 1986

Jones, Diana Wynne. *Fire and Hemlock.* 1984; *Howl's Moving Castle.* 1986; *The Lives of Christopher Chant.* 1988

Kindl, Patrice. *Owl in Love.* 1993

Mahy, Margaret. *The Changeover.* 1984; *The Haunting.* 1982

Preussler, Otfried. *The Satanic Mill.* 1971, 1973

Turner, Ann. *Rosemary's Witch.* 1991

Zambreno, Mary Frances. *A Plague of Sorcerers.* 1991

Crossover Fantasy for Young Adults

Many readers who devoured children's and young adult fantasy novels have discovered the fast-growing genre of "adult" fantasy and have claimed these books for themselves. These crossover novels, many of which are part of a series, include:

Anthony, Piers. Magic of Xanth series. 1977–1994

Asimov, Isaac, Charles G. Waugh, and Martin H. Greenberg. *Dragon Tales.* 1982

Asprin, Robert L. Myth Adventure series. 1978–1987

Beagle, Peter S. *The Last Unicorn.* 1968

Bradley, Marion Zimmer. Darkover series. 1962–1994; *Hawkmistress!* 1982; *The Mists of Avalon.* 1982

Butler, Octavia E. *Kindred.* 1979

Card, Orson Scott. *Seventh Son.* 1987

Cherryh, C. J. *Angel with the Sword.* 1985

Dickson, Gordon R. Dragon series. 1976–1992

Donaldson, Stephen R. Chronicles of Thomas Covenant, the Unbeliever. 1977–1983

Egan, Doris. *The Gate of Ivory.* 1989

Feist, Raymond E. *Silverthorn.* 1985

Finney, Jack. *Time and Again.* 1970

Goldstein, Lisa. *The Red Magician.* 1982, 1993

Hambley, Barbara. *Dragonsbane.* 1986

Kurtz, Katherine. The Chronicles of Deryni. 1970–1991

Lackey, Mercedes. Mage Wind trilogy. 1991–1993

MacAvoy, R. A. *The Book of Kells.* 1985

McCaffrey, Anne. Dragonriders of Pern series. 1968–1994

McKinley, Robin. *Deerskin.* 1993

Matheson, Richard. *Bid Time Return.* 1975

Orwell, George. *Animal Farm.* 1945, 1982

The Pendragon Chronicles. Ed. by Mike Ashley. 1989, 1990

Shwartz, Susan. *Moonsinger's Friends.* 1985
Silverberg, Robert. *Lord Valentine's Castle.* 1980
Springer, Nancy. *Chains of Gold.* 1986
Stewart, Mary. Merlin quartet. 1970–1979
Tarr, Judith. The Hounds of God cycle. 1985–1991; *A Fall of Princes.* 1988
Tolkien, J. R. R. Lord of the Rings trilogy. 1954, 1967, 1992
Warner, Sylvia Townsend. *Kingdoms of Elfin.* 1976
Wellman, Manly Wade. Silver John series. 1963–1984
Willard, Nancy. *Things Invisible to See.* 1985
Wolfe, Gene. Book of the New Sun series. 1980–1983
Zelazny, Roger. Amber series. 1970–1991

AWARD-WINNING FANTASY LITERATURE

This list includes international and national literary awards won by children's and young adult fantasy novels, story collections, authors, and illustrators. State and provincial award winners are not listed.

The American Book Award

Awarded between 1980 and 1986 by the Association of American Publishers for the most distinguished books of the preceding year published in the United States, in a number of categories. It replaced the National Book Award (see below), and was renamed the National Book Award in 1987. The Children's Book categories were discontinued in 1984.

- 1980 Science Fiction. *The Book of the Dun Cow*. Walter Wangerin
- 1982 Children's Fiction. *Westmark*. Lloyd Alexander
- 1982 Graphic Design. *Jumanji*. Chris Van Allsburg
- 1983 Pictorial Design. *Alice's Adventures in Wonderland*, illus. by Barry Moser. Lewis Carroll
- 1983 Original Paperback. *The Red Magician*. Lisa Goldstein

Hans Christian Andersen Award

Awarded biennially by the International Board on Books for Young People (I.B.B.Y. Secretariat, Nonnenweg 12, Postfach, CH-4003 Basel, Switzerland) to an author and an illustrator in recognition of his or her entire body of work.

- 1956 Author. Eleanor Farjeon (Great Britain)
- 1958 Author. Astrid Lindgren (Sweden)
- 1960 Author. Erich Kästner (Germany)
- 1964 Author. René Guillot (France)

1966 Author. Tove Jansson (Finland)

1968 Author. José Maria Sanchez-Silva (Spain)

1968 Author. James Krüss (Germany)

1968 Highly Commended Author. Elizabeth Coatsworth (United States)

1970 Highly Commended Author. E. B. White (United States)

1970 Illustrator. Maurice Sendak (United States)

1972 Highly Commended Author. Otfried Preussler (Germany)

1972 Highly Commended Author. Maria Gripe (Sweden)

1974 Author. Maria Gripe (Sweden)

1974 Highly Commended Author. Rosemary Sutcliff (Great Britain)

1976 Highly Commended Author. E. B. White (United States)

1978 Highly Commended Author. Alan Garner (Great Britain)

1984 Author. Christine Nöstlinger (Austria)

1986 Author. Patricia Wrightson (Australia)

1992 Author. Virginia Hamilton (United States)

Australian Children's Book of the Year Award

See Children's Book Council of Australia Book of the Year Award

Mildred L. Batchelder Award

Awarded by the Association for Library Service to Children, American Library Association (50 E. Huron St., Chicago, IL 60611), to a U.S. publisher for the most outstanding English translation of a children's book originally published in a foreign language in a foreign country during the preceding year.

1968 *The Little Man* (Harcourt). Erich Kästner

1978 *Konrad* (Watts). Christine Nöstlinger

1979 *Rabbit Island* (Harcourt). Jörg Steiner

1984 *Ronia, the Robber's Daughter* (Viking). Astrid Lindgren

Boston Globe–Horn Book Award

Co-sponsored by *The Boston Globe* (P.O. Box 2378, Boston, MA 02107) and *The Horn Book Magazine* (14 Beacon St., Boston, MA 02115), for outstanding fiction, nonfiction, and illustration.

1968 Text. *The Spring Rider*. John Lawson

1969 Text. *A Wizard of Earthsea*. Ursula K. Le Guin

1971 Text Honor. *Mrs. Frisby and the Rats of NIMH*. Robert C. O'Brien

1972 Text. *Tristan and Iseult*. Rosemary Sutcliff

1973 Text. *The Dark Is Rising*. Susan Cooper

1973 Illustration. *King Stork,* illus. by Trina Schart Hyman. Howard Pyle

1976 Fiction Honor. *A Stranger Came Ashore*. Mollie Hunter

1976 Fiction Honor. *A String in the Harp*. Nancy Bond

1979 Fiction. *Humug Mountain*. Sid Fleischman

1980 Fiction. *Conrad's War*. Andrew Davies

1980 Illustration. *The Garden of Abdul Gasazi*. Chris Van Allsburg

1981 Illustration Honor. *Jumanji*. Chris Van Allsburg

1982 Fiction. *Playing Beatie Bow*. Ruth Park

1982 Fiction Honor. *The Scarecrows*. Robert Westall

1983 Fiction. *Sweet Whispers, Brother Rush*. Virginia Hamilton

1983 Fiction Honor. *The Road to Camlann*. Rosemary Sutcliff

1984 Fiction. *A Little Fear*. Patricia Wrightson

1984 Fiction Honor. *Archer's Goon*. Diana Wynne Jones

1985 Fiction Honor. *The Changeover*. Margaret Mahy

1986 Fiction Honor. *Howl's Moving Castle*. Diana Wynne Jones

1990 Fiction Honor. *Stonewords*. Pam Conrad

British Fantasy Award

Awarded annually by the British Fantasy Society (c/o Di Wathen, 15 Stanley Rd., Morden SM4 5DE, UK). Not limited to British authors. Named the August Derleth Fantasy Award from 1971 to 1976. From 1977 on, the August Derleth Fantasy Award has been given in the best novel category. Winners in the remaining categories receive the British Fantasy Award.

1976 Best Novel. *The Dragon and the George*. Gordon R. Dickson

1977 Best Novel. *A Spell for Chameleon*. Piers Anthony

1978 Best Novel. *The Chronicles of Thomas Covenant* (trilogy). Stephen Donaldson

1982 Best Novel. *The Sword of the Lictor*. Gene Wolfe

1984 Special Award. Manley Wade Wellman

Randolph Caldecott Medal

Awarded by the Association for Library Service to Children, American Library Association (50 E. Huron St., Chicago, IL 60611), to the artist of the most distinguished American picture book for children published in the United States during the preceding year.

1944 *Many Moons*, illus. by Louis Slobodkin. James Thurber

1950 Honor. *Bartholomew and the Oobleck*. Dr. Seuss

1954 Honor. *The Steadfast Tin Soldier*, illus. by Marcia Brown. Hans Christian Andersen

1980 Honor. *The Garden of Abdul Gazasi*. Chris Van Allsburg

1982 *Jumanji*. Chris Van Allsburg

1993 Honor. *The Stinky Cheese Man and Other Fairly Stupid Tales*, illus. by Lane Smith. Jon Scieszka

Canadian Governor General's Award for Children's Literature

See Governor General's Literary Award for Children's Literature

Canadian Library Association Book of the Year for Children Award

Awarded by the Canadian Library Association (200 Elgin St., Suite 602, Ottawa, ON K2P 1L5, Canada) to an outstanding children's book by a Canadian author.

1973 *Marrow of the World*. Ruth Nichols

1976 *Jacob Two-Two Meets the Hooded Fang*. Mordecai Richler

1980 *Uncle Jacob's Ghost Story*. Don Kushner

1981 *The Violin-Maker's Gift*. Don Kushner

1982 *The Root Cellar*. Janet Lunn

1987 *Shadow in Hawthorn Bay*. Janet Lunn

1988 *A Handful of Time*. Kit Pearson

1989 Runner-Up. *The Third Magic*. Welwyn W. Katz

1991 *Redwork*. Michael Bedard

1994 (illustration) *The Dragon's Pearl*. Julie Lawson; illus. by Paul Morin

Canadian Science Fiction and Fantasy Award

Awarded annually to English- or French-speaking Canadian writers of science fiction and fantasy novels.

1987 *The Wandering Fire*. Guy Gavriel Kay

1988 *Jack the Giant Killer*. Charles de Lint

Carnegie Medal

Awarded by The [British] Library Association (7 Ridgemount St., London WC1E 7AE, UK) to the outstanding book for children written in English and published in the United Kingdom.

1942 *The Little Grey Men*. B. B. [Denys Watkins-Pitchford]

1944 *The Wind on the Moon*. Eric Linklater

1946 *The Little White Horse*. Elizabeth Goudge

1947 *Collected Stories for Children*. Walter De La Mare

1952 *The Borrowers.* Mary Norton

1954 Commended. *The Children of Green Knowe.* L. M. Boston

1954 Commended. *The Horse and His Boy.* C. S. Lewis

1954 Commended. *The Lady of the Linden Tree.* Barbara Picard

1955 *The Little Bookroom.* Eleanor Farjeon

1956 *The Last Battle.* C. S. Lewis

1956 Commended. *The Fairy Doll.* Rumer Godden

1957 *A Grass Rope.* William Mayne

1957 Commended. *The Blue Boat.* William Mayne

1958 *Tom's Midnight Garden.* Philippa Pearce

1958 Commended. *The Chimneys of Green Knowe.* L. M. Boston

1959 Commended. *The Borrowers Afloat.* Mary Norton

1959 Commended. *The Rescuers.* Marjorie Sharp

1961 Commended. *Miss Happiness and Miss Flower.* Rumer Godden

1962 *The Twelve and the Genii.* Pauline Clarke

1962 Commended. *The Summer Birds.* Penelope Farmer

1965 Commended. *Elidor.* Alan Garner

1967 *The Owl Service.* Alan Garner

1967 Commended. *The Piemakers.* Helen Cresswell

1968 *The Moon in the Cloud.* Rosemary Harris

1968 Honour. *The Whispering Mountain.* Joan Aiken

1969 Honour. *The Night Watchmen.* Helen Cresswell

1970 *The God Beneath the Sea.* Leon Garfield & Edward Blishen

1970 Honour. *The Devil's Children.* Peter Dickinson

1971 Highly Commended. *Tristan and Iseult.* Rosemary Sutcliff

1971 Highly Commended. *Up the Pier.* Helen Cresswell

1972 *Watership Down.* Richard Adams

1973 *The Ghost of Thomas Kempe.* Penelope Lively

1973 Commended. *The Bongleweed.* Helen Cresswell

1973 Commended. *The Dark Is Rising.* Susan Cooper

1975 Commended. *Dogsbody.* Diana Wynne Jones

1975 Commended. *The Grey King.* Susan Cooper

1976 Commended. *The Blue Hawk.* Peter Dickinson

1977 Commended. *Charmed Life.* Diana Wynne Jones

1977 Commended. *The Shadow-Cage and Other Tales.* Philippa Pearce

1978 Commended. *The Devil on the Road.* Robert Westall

1981 *The Scarecrows.* Robert Westall

1982 *The Haunting.* Margaret Mahy

    1984   *The Changeover*. Margaret Mahy

    1987   *The Ghost Drum*. Christine Price

    1987   Commended. *Wise Child*. Monica Furlong

    1987   Commended. *The House on the Hill*. Eileen Dunlop

    1987   Commended. *King of the Cloud Forest*. Michael Morpurgo

    1988   *A Pack of Lies*. Geraldine McCaughrean

    1988   Commended. *The Monster Garden*. Vivien Alcock

    1988   Commended. *The Lives of Christopher Chant*. Diana Wynne Jones

Children's Book Council of Australia Book of the Year Award

Awarded by the Children's Book Council of Australia (c/o NSW Branch, P.O. Box 765, Rozelle, NSW 2039, Australia).

    1974   *The Nargun and the Stars*. Patricia Wrightson

    1978   *The Ice Is Coming*. Patricia Wrightson

    1981   *Playing Beatie Bow*. Ruth Park

    1983   *Master of the Grove*. Victor Kelleher

    1984   *A Little Fear*. Patricia Wrightson

    1987   *Pigs Might Fly*. Emily Rodda

    1989   *The Best-Kept Secret*. Emily Rodda

    1991   (for older readers) *Strange Objects*. Gary Crew

    1991   (for younger readers) *Finders Keepers*. Emily Rodda

Margaret A. Edwards Award

Formerly called the YASD/SLJ Young Adult Author Award (1988–1990). Awarded by the Young Adult Library Services Association, American Library Association (50 E. Huron St., Chicago, IL 60611), to an outstanding U.S. author of books for young adults.

    1989   Richard Peck

    1993   M. E. Kerr (pseudonym of Marijane Meaker; uses the pseudonym Mary James for her fantasy novels)

Esther Glen Award

Awarded by the New Zealand Library Association (20 Brandon St., P.O. Box 12-212, Wellington, New Zealand) to a New Zealand children's author of the most distinguished contribution of the year to literature for children.

    1959   *Falter Tom and the Water Boy*. Maurice Duggan

    1983   *The Haunting*. Margaret Mahy

    1985   *The Changeover*. Margaret Mahy

Golden Cat Award

International award given by the Swedish Publishers' Association (Sjostrands Forlag, Hasselby Strandveg 22, S-162 39 Vallingby, Sweden) to an author of any nationality who has created works of distinction and quality in fiction for children and young adults.

1984 Lloyd Alexander (United States)

1985 Leon Garfield (Great Britain)

1986 Patricia Wrightson (Australia)

1988 Philippa Pearce (Great Britain)

1990 Peter Dickinson (Great Britain)

Golden Kite Award

Awarded by The Society of Children's Book Writers (P.O. Box 66296, Mar Vista Station, Los Angeles, CA 90066) to works of fiction, nonfiction, and illustration that exhibit excellence in writing and genuinely appeal to the interests and concerns of children.

1973 Fiction Honor. *McBroom the Rainmaker*. Sid Fleischman

1974 Fiction. *The Girl Who Cried Flowers and Other Tales*. Jane Yolen

1975 Fiction Honor. *The Transfigured Hart*. Jane Yolen

1976 Fiction Honor. *The Moon Ribbon and Other Tales*. Jane Yolen

1980 Fiction Honor. *The Half-a-Moon Inn*. Paul Fleischman

1982 Fiction. *Ralph S. Mouse*. Beverly Cleary

1987 Fiction Honor. *The Great Dimpole Oak*. Janet Taylor Lisle

1988 Fiction Honor. *The Reluctant God*. Pamela F. Service

1993 Fiction Honor. *Owl in Love*. Patrice Kindl

Governor General's Literary Award for Children's Literature

Awarded by the Canada Council (99 Metcalfe St., P.O. Box 1047, Ottawa, ON K1P 5V8, Canada) to outstanding books for young people written in English and in French and/or illustrated by Canadians during the preceding year.

1986 Text. *Shadow in Hawthorn Bay*. Janet Lunn

1988 Text. *The Third Magic*. Welwyn W. Katz

1990 Text. *Redwork*. Michael Bedard

Grand Master of Fantasy Award

Unofficially known as the Galdalf Award, it was presented by the World Science Fiction Society (P.O. Box 1270, Kendall Square Station, Cambridge, MA 02142) at the World Science Fiction Convention Hugo Award ceremonies, for a writer's lifetime contribution to fantasy literature.

    1974 J. R. R. Tolkien

    1976 L. Sprague de Camp

    1977 Andre Norton

    1978 Poul Anderson

    1979 Ursula K. Le Guin

    1980 Ray Bradbury

Kate Greenaway Medal

Awarded by The [British] Library Association (7 Ridgemount St., London WC1E 7AE, UK) to an artist who has produced the most distinguished work in the illustration of a children's book published in the previous year.

    1970 Honors List. *The God Beneath the Sea*. Edward Blishen and Leon Garfield

    1972 Commended. *The Ghost Downstairs*, illus. by Antony Maitland. Leon Garfield

    1976 Highly Commended. *The Church Mice Adrift*. Graham Oakley

    1982 Highly Commended. *The Church Mice in Action*. Graham Oakley

    1985 *Sir Gawain and the Loathly Lady*, illus. by Juan Wijngaard. Selina Hastings

    1987 Commended. *The Enchanter's Daughter*, illus. by Errol LeCain. Antonia Barber

    1988 Highly Commended. *Alice's Adventures in Wonderland*, illus. by Anthony Browne. Lewis Carroll

    1988 Highly Commended. *The Adventures of Pinocchio*, illus. by Roberto Innocenti. Carlo Collodi

    1988 Highly Commended. *Merlin Dreams*, illus. by Alan Lee. Peter Dickinson

    1990 Commended. *A Christmas Carol*, illus. by Roberto Innocenti. Charles Dickens

The Guardian Children's Fiction Award

Awarded by *The Guardian* (Children's Books Editor, 24 Weymouth St., London W1N 3FA, UK) to the best novel for children published in Britain by a British or Commonwealth author.

    1968 *The Owl Service*. Alan Garner

    1969 *The Whispering Mountain*. Joan Aiken

    1973 *Watership Down*. Richard Adams

    1977 *The Blue Hawk*. Peter Dickinson

    1977 Commended. *The Power of Three*. Diana Wynne Jones

    1978 *Charmed Life*. Diana Wynne Jones

    1978 Commended. *The Ice is Coming*. Patricia Wrightson

    1979 *Conrad's War*. Andrew Davies

    1981 Runner-up. *Daggie Dogfoot*. Dick King-Smith

1982 Runner-up. *Playing Beatie Bow*. Ruth Park

1984 *The Sheep-Pig*. Dick King-Smith

1989 *A Pack of Lies*. Geraldine McCaughrean

Nils Holgersson Award

Awarded by the Swedish Library Association (Sveriges Allmanna Biblioteksforening—SAB, Box 3127, 103 62 Stockholm, Sweden) to the best Swedish children's book published during the previous year, or to the collected works of an author.

1953 *Moomin, Mymble and Little My*. Tove Jansson

1965 *The White Stone*. Gunnel Linde

I.R.A. Children's Book Award

Awarded by the International Reading Association (800 Barksdale Rd., P.O. Box 8139, Newark, DE 19714) for an author's first or second work of fiction or nonfiction for children or young adolescents.

1977 *A String in the Harp*. Nancy Bond

1983 *The Darkangel*. Meredith Ann Pierce

1984 *Ratha's Creature*. Clare Bell

Kerlan Award

Awarded by the Kerlan Award Committee, Children's Literature Research Collections, University of Minnesota (109 Walter Library, 117 Pleasant St. S.E., Minneapolis, MN 55455) in recognition of singular attainments in the creation of children's literature.

1975 Elizabeth Coatsworth

1978 Carol Ryrie Brink

1980 Glen Rounds

1985 Eleanor Cameron

1986 Charlotte Zolotow

1988 Jane Yolen

1990 Madeleine L'Engle

1993 Mary Stolz

Coretta Scott King Award

Awarded annually by the American Library Association (50 E. Huron St., Chicago, IL 60611) to an African American author and illustrator whose works "encourage and promote the cause of peace and brotherhood, and inspire children and youth to dedicate their talents and energies to help achieve these goals."

1983 Fiction. *Sweet Whispers, Brother Rush*. Virginia Hamilton

1993 Fiction. *The Dark-Thirty: Southern Tales of the Supernatural*. Patricia C. McKissack

Mythopoeic Fantasy Award

Awarded annually by the Mythopoeic Society (P.O. Box 6707, Altadena, CA 91003), for a book-length work of fantasy in the spirit of the Inklings: J. R. R. Tolkien, C. S. Lewis, and Charles Williams. No awards were given from 1976–1980. The Children's Literature category was created in 1992.

1971 *The Crystal Cave*. Mary Stewart

1972 *Red Moon and Black Mountain*. Joy Chant

1973 *The Song of Rhiannon*. Evangeline Walton

1974 *The Hollow Hills*. Mary Stewart

1975 *A Midsummer Tempest*. Poul Anderson

1981 *Unfinished Tales*. J. R. R. Tolkien

1983 *The Firelings*. Carol Kendall

1984 *When Voiha Wakes*. Joy Chant

1987 *The Folk of the Air*. Peter Beagle

1988 *Seventh Son*. Orson Scott Card

1990 *The Stress of Her Regard*. Tim Powers

1991 *Thomas the Rhymer*. Ellen Kushner

1992 Children's. *Haroun and the Sea of Stories*. Salman Rushdie

National Book Award, Children's Fiction Category

Awarded by the National Book Committee (1969–1974), the American Academy of Arts and Letters (1975–1977), the Association of American Publishers (1978–1979), and the National Book Foundation (1987–) (260 Fifth Ave., 4th floor, New York, NY 10001) to the most distinguished book published in the United States during the preceding year. This award was replaced by The American Book Award (see above) between 1980 and 1986. In 1984 the children's book category was discontinued.

1969 Finalist. *The High King*. Lloyd Alexander

1971 *The Marvelous Misadventures of Sebastian*. Lloyd Alexander

1971 Finalist. *Trumpet of the Swan*. E. B. White

1972 Finalist. *Mrs. Frisby and the Rats of NIMH*. Robert C. O'Brien

1972 Finalist. *The Tombs of Atuan*. Ursula K. Le Guin

1973 *The Farthest Shore*. Ursula K. Le Guin

1973 Finalist. *Dominic*. William Steig

1974 *The Court of the Stone Children*. Eleanor Cameron

1975 Finalist. *The Devil's Storybook.* Natalie Babbitt

1975 Finalist. *The Girl Who Cried Flowers and Other Tales.* Jane Yolen

1979 Finalist. *The First Two Lives of Lukas-Kasha.* Lloyd Alexander

1979 Finalist. *Humbug Mountain.* Sid Fleischman

Nebula Award

Awarded by the Science Fiction Writers of America (P.O. Box 4335, Spartanburg, SC 29305) to the best novel published in the previous year in the field of science fiction, and to a grand master of science fiction writing.

1977 Grand Master. Clifford D. Simak

1979 Grand Master. L. Sprague de Camp

1984 Grand Master. Andre Norton

1987 Grand Master. Isaac Asimov

1988 Best Novel. *The Falling Woman.* Pat Murphy

1989 Grand Master. Ray Bradbury

1990 Best Novel. *The Healer's War.* Elizabeth Ann Scarborough

1991 Best Novel. *Tehanu.* Ursula K. Le Guin

John Newbery Medal

Awarded by the Association for Library Service to Children, American Library Association (50 E. Huron St., Chicago, IL 60611), to the author of the most distinguished contribution to American literature for children published in the United States by a citizen or resident during the preceding year.

1922 *The Old Tobacco Shop.* William A. Bowen

1923 *The Voyages of Doctor Dolittle.* Hugh Lofting

1925 Honor. *The Dream Coach.* Anne and Dilwyn Parrish

1925 Honor. *Nicholas.* Anne Carroll Moore

1926 *Shen of the Sea.* Arthur Bowie Chrisman

1929 Honor. *The Pigtail of Ah Lee Ben Loo.* John Bennett

1930 *Hitty, Her First Hundred Years.* Rachel Lyman Field

1931 *The Cat Who Went to Heaven.* Elizabeth Coatsworth

1931 Honor. *Floating Island.* Anne Parrish

1932 Honor. *The Fairy Circus.* Dorothy P. Lathrop

1938 *The White Stag.* Kate Seredy

1939 Honor. *Mr. Popper's Penguins.* Richard and Florence Atwater

1944 Honor. *Fog Magic.* Julia L. Sauer

1945 *Rabbit Hill.* Robert Lawson

1947   *Miss Hickory*. Carolyn Sherwyn Bailey

1948   *The Twenty-One Balloons*. William Pene Du Bois

1948   Honor. *The Quaint and Curious Quest of Johnny Longfoot*. Catherine Besterman

1949   Honor. *My Father's Dragon*. Ruth Stiles Gannett

1950   Honor. *The Blue Cat of Castle Town*. Catherine Cate Coblentz

1951   Honor. *The Story of Appleby Capple*. Anne Parrish

1953   Honor. *Charlotte's Web*. E. B. White

1960   Honor. *The Gammage Cup*. Carol Kendall

1961   Honor. *The Cricket in Times Square*. George Selden

1962   Honor. *Belling the Tiger*. Mary Stolz

1966   Honor. *The Animal Family*. Randall Jarrell

1966   Honor. *The Black Cauldron*. Lloyd Alexander

1967   Honor. *Zlateh the Goat*. Isaac Bashevis Singer

1968   Honor. *The Fearsome Inn*. Isaac Bashevis Singer

1969   *The High King*. Lloyd Alexander

1970   Honor. *Journey Outside*. Mary Q. Steele

1971   Honor. *Knee-Knock Rise*. Natalie Babbitt

1972   *Mrs. Frisby and the Rats of NIMH*. Robert C. O'Brien

1972   Honor. *The Tombs of Atuan*. Ursula K. LeGuin

1974   Honor. *The Dark Is Rising*. Susan Cooper

1975   Honor. *Figgs and Phantoms*. Ellen Raskin

1975   Honor. *The Perilous Gard*. Elizabeth Pope

1976   *The Grey King*. Susan Cooper

1977   Honor. *Abel's Island*. William Steig

1977   Honor. *A String in the Harp*. Nancy Bond

1981   Honor. *The Fledgling*. Jane Langton

1983   Honor. *The Blue Sword*. Robin McKinley

1983   Honor. *Graven Images*. Paul Fleischman

1983   Honor. *Sweet Whispers, Brother Rush*. Virginia Hamilton

1984   Honor. *The Wish Giver*. Bill Brittain

1985   *The Hero and the Crown*. Robin McKinley

1987   *The Whipping Boy*. Paul Fleischman

1993   Honor. *The Dark-Thirty*. Patricia C. McKissack

Order of New Zealand

New Zealand's highest honor, held by only 20 living people at any one time.

1992   Margaret Mahy, for her internationally acclaimed contribution to children's literature

Phoenix Award

Awarded by the Children's Literature Association (c/o 135 Edgebrook Dr., Battle Creek, MI 49015) to an author of a book for children first published exactly twenty years earlier, which did not win a major literary award at the time of its publication, but which has passed the test of time and is deemed to be of high literary quality.

  1989 *The Night Watchmen.* Helen Cresswell

  1991 Honor. *A Game of Dark.* William Mayne

  1991 Honor. *The Tombs of Atuan.* Ursula K. Le Guin

Smarties Prize for Children's Books

Awarded by the Book Trust (Book House, 45 East Hill, London SW18 2QZ, UK) to a children's book written in English by a citizen or resident of the United Kingdom and published in the United Kingdom to encourage high standards and stimulate interest in books for children. Prizes are given in three age categories, and a Grand Prix is given to one of the three prize winners.

  1986 Grand Prix. *The Snow Spider.* Jenny Nimmo

  1986 Ages 7–11. *The Snow Spider.* Jenny Nimmo

  1987 Ages 6–8. *Tangle and the Firesticks.* Benedict Blathwayt

  1990 Grand Prix. *Midnight Blue.* Pauline Fisk

  1990 Ages 9–11. *Midnight Blue.* Pauline Fisk

  1990 Ages 6–8. *Essio Trott.* Roald Dahl

  1991 Ages 9–11. *Krindlekrax.* Philip Ridley

Tir Na N-Og Award

Awarded by the Welsh Books Council (Castell Brychan, Aberystwyth, Dyfed SY23 2JB, Wales) in three categories: to original Welsh-language novels, stories, and picture books, to other Welsh-language books published during the relevant year, and to the best English-language children's book published in the preceding year with an authentic Welsh background. Fantasy winners in this third category are:

  1976 *The Grey King.* Susan Cooper

  1977 *A String in the Harp.* Nancy Bond

  1978 *Silver on the Tree.* Susan Cooper

  1987 *The Snow Spider.* Jenny Nimmo

Whitbread Literary Award, Children's Novel Category

Awarded by the Booksellers Association of Great Britain and Ireland (Minster House, 272 Vauxhall Bridge Rd., London SW1V 1BA, UK) to books first published in the United Kingdom or Ireland within the previous year, by authors who have lived in Great

Britain or Ireland for three or more years, to promote a high standard of English literature.

1974 *How Tom Beat Captain Najork*. Russell Hoban

1976 *A Stitch in Time*. Penelope Lively

1982 *The Song of Pentecost*. W. J. Corbett

1982 Runner-up. *The Secret World of Polly Flint*. Helen Cresswell

1983 *The Witches*. Roald Dahl

Laura Ingalls Wilder Award

Awarded by the Association for Library Service to Children, American Library Association (50 E. Huron St., Chicago, IL 60611), every five years from 1954 to 1980, and every three years since 1980, to an author or illustrator whose books, published in the United States, have made a substantial and lasting contribution to literature for children.

1965 Ruth Sawyer

1970 E. B. White

1975 Beverly Cleary

1980 Theodor Geisel (Dr. Seuss)

1983 Maurice Sendak

World Fantasy Convention Award

Awarded annually at the World Fantasy convention. Categories include: Best Novel, Best Anthology, and a Life Achievement Award.

1975 Novel. *The Forgotten Beasts of Eld*. Patricia McKillip

1976 Novel. *Bid Time Return*. Richard Matheson

1980 Novel. *Watchtower*. Elizabeth A. Lynn

1980 Anthology. *Amazons!* Ed. by Jessica A. Salmonson

1980 Life Achievement. Manly Wade Wellman

1981 Novel. *The Shadow of the Torturer*. Gene Wolfe

1982 Anthology. *Elsewhere*. Ed. by Terri Windling and Mark Arnold

1983 Life Achievement. Roald Dahl

1984 Life Achievement. L. Sprague de Camp

1984 Life Achievement. Richard Matheson

1984 Life Achievement. Jack Vance

1985 Novel. Mythago Wood. Robert Holdstock

1986 Anthology. *Imaginary Lands*. Ed. by Robin McKinley

1987 Life Achievement. Jack Finney

1989 Anthology. *The Year's Best Fantasy, First Annual Collection*. Ed. by Ellen Datlow and Terri Windling

1989 Life Achievement. Evangeline Walton

1990 Anthology. *The Year's Best Fantasy, Second Annual Collection*. Ed. by Ellen Datlow and Terri Windling

1991 Novel. *Thomas the Rhymer*. Ellen Kushner

1992 Novel. *The White Mists of Power*. Kathryn K. Rusch

YASD/SLJ Young Adult Author Award

See Margaret A. Edwards Award

Young Adult Canadian Book Award

Awarded by the Young Adult Services Interest Group, Canadian Library Association (200 Elgin St., Suite 602, Ottawa, ON K2P 1L5, Canada), to the best Canadian book of the year for young adults.

1989 Runner-up. *Blood Red Ochre*. Kevin Major

PART ONE

ANNOTATED BIBLIOGRAPHY

1
Allegorical Fantasy and Literary Fairy Tales

The books in this chapter are individual tales with both simple and abstract levels of meaning. Literary fairy tales are short stories written by modern authors in the style of traditional folktales, often utilizing such elements as kings, princesses, dragons, and fairies. Modern allegorical fantasies, unlike traditional allegorical fables, frequently involve characters other than animals, and the full significance of the stories may not be obvious. Collections of literary fairy tales are found in Chapter 3, Fantasy Collections. Retellings of legends and myths, which often have allegorical elements, are found in Chapter 5B, Myth Fantasy.

1 **ABELL, Kathleen.** *King Orville and the Bullfrogs.* **Gr. 2–4.**
Three young princes are transformed into frogs and banished after they outdo their father-in-law, King Orville, in a bagpipe contest.
Illus. by Errol Le Cain, Little, 1974, 48 pp., o.p.
(BL 70:871; KR 42:239; LJ 99:1463)

ADAMS, Hazard. *The Truth about Dragons: An Anti-Romance.* See Chapter 5A, Alternate Worlds or Histories.

ADAMS, Richard (George). *Shardik.* See Chapter 5A, Alternate Worlds or Histories.

ADAMS, Richard (George). *Watership Down.* See Chapter 2, Animal Fantasy.

AHLBERG, Allan. *Ten in a Bed.* See Chapter 7, Magic Adventure Fantasy.

AHLBERG, Janet. *Jeremiah in the Dark Woods.* See Chapter 6, Humorous Fantasy.

AIKEN, Joan (Delano). *A Harp of Fishbones and Other Stories.* See Chapter 3, Fantasy Collections.

2   **AIKEN, Joan (Delano).** *The Moon's Revenge.* **Gr. 2–5.**

Young Sep angers the moon when he uses magic in learning to play the fiddle, but his musical ability eventually breaks the moon's curse on his town.

Illus. by Alan Lee, Knopf, 1987, 32 pp., o.p.

(BL 84:929; HB 64:199; KR 55:1623; SLJ Feb 1988 p. 57)

AIKEN, Joan (Delano). *A Necklace of Raindrops and Other Stories.* See Chapter 3, Fantasy Collections.

AIKEN, Joan (Delano). *Past Eight O'Clock: Goodnight Stories.* See Chapter 3, Fantasy Collections.

AIKEN, Joan (Delano). *Smoke from Cromwell's Time and Other Stories.* See Chapter 3, Fantasy Collections.

3   **AIKEN, Joan (Delano).** *Street: A Play for Children.* **Gr. 5–8.**
✓   In the town of Street, the theft of the toll bridge key by the village witch's eldest son causes deep hostilities between the inhabitants of the river side and those of the forest side of Street's only thoroughfare. Only the love between the witch's younger son, Toomy, and Meg, a girl from the other side of the street, can heal the town's animosities and restore safety and justice.

Illus. by Arvis Stewart, Viking, 1978, 128 pp., o.p.

(BL 74:1247, 1251; HB 55:527; KR 46:696; SLJ May 1978 p. 62)

ALDEN, Raymond Macdonald. *Why the Chimes Rang and Other Stories.* See Chapter 3, Fantasy Collections.

ALEXANDER, Lloyd (Chudley). *The Cat Who Wished to Be a Man.* See Chapter 2, Animal Fantasy.

4   **ALEXANDER, Lloyd (Chudley).** *The Remarkable Journey of Prince Jen.* **Gr.**
✓   **5–9.**

Prince Jen wanders from adventure to adventure through the Chinese countryside, accompanied by a flute girl named Voyaging Moon, while learning how to be a good ruler and a good man.

Dutton, 1991, 288 pp. (0-525-44826-8), pap., Dell, 1993 (0-440-40890-3)

(BL 88:696, 865, 872; CC 1992 Suppl. p. 53; CCBB 45:55; HB 68:200; HBG 3[July–Dec 1991]:62; JHC 1992 Suppl. p. 55; KR 60:1219; SLJ Dec 1991 pp. 28, 113; VOYA 14:378)

ALEXANDER, Lloyd. *The Town Cats, and Other Tales.* See Chapter 2, Animal Fantasy.

ALEXANDER, Lloyd. *The Truthful Harp.* See Chapter 5A, Alternate Worlds or Histories.

ALLEN, Judy. *The Lord of the Dance.* See Chapter 5B, Myth Fantasy.

5   **ALLEN, Judy.** *The Spring on the Mountain.* **Gr. 5–8.**

An old woman sends Peter, Emma, and Michael in search of a magical, knowledge-giving spring that she, herself, once found.

Farrar, 1973, 153 pp., o.p.

(BL 70:653; LJ 98:3142; TLS 1973 p. 1114)

AMADO, Jorge. *The Swallow and the Tom Cat: A Grown-Up Love Story.* See Chapter 2, Animal Fantasy.

ANDERSEN, Hans Christian. *Andersen's Fairy Tales.* See Chapter 3, Fantasy Collections.

6 **ANDERSEN, Hans Christian.** *The Emperor's New Clothes.* **Gr. K–4. (Written**
✓ **1837, orig. U.S. pub. as a separate tale, 1848.)**

Thieves pretending to create a magnificent new suit for the vain emperor fool everyone in the kingdom except for one small boy.

Illus. by Virginia Lee Burton, Houghton, 1949, o.p., pap. 1979 (0-395-28594-1); trans. by H. W. Dulcken, adapt. and illus. by Anne Rockwell, Harper, 1982, pap. 1987, o.p.; retold and illus. by Nadine Bernard Westcott, Little, 1984, o.p., pap. (0-316-93124-1); adapt. and illus. by Janet Stevens, Holiday, 1979, o.p.; retold by Anthea Bell, illus. by Dorothée Duntze, North-South, 1986, 24 pp. (1-55858-036-0); retold by Riki Levinson, illus. by Robert Byrd, Dutton, 1991, 40 pp. (0-525-44611-7); retold and illus. by S. T. Mendelson, Stewart, 1992, 32 pp. (1-55670-232-9)

(BL 46:51, 70:336, 78:1155, 81:214, 82:341, 83:346, 88:770; CC:442, 550; CCBB 2[Nov 1949]: 1, 13:25; HB 25:523; HBG 3 [July–Dec 1991]: 23; KR 41:961; LJ 74:1533, 1612, 99:197; SLJ Apr 1982 p. 54, Dec 1984 p. 66, Jan 1987 p. 57, Nov 1991 p. 89, Dec 1992 p. 76; TLS 1973 pp. 384, 1121, Dec 1986 p. 1458)

ANDERSEN, Hans Christian. *Fairy Tales.* See Chapter 3, Fantasy Collections.

7 **ANDERSEN, Hans Christian.** *The Fir Tree.* **Gr. K–4. (Orig. Danish pub. 1837,**
✓ **U.S. 1849.)**

A little fir tree glories in becoming a Christmas tree, and then mourns the fate that awaits him after Christmas.

Illus. by Nancy Ekholm Burkert, Harper, 1970, o.p., 1986, pap., 48 pp. (0-06-443109-6); adapt. and illus. by Bernadette Watts, North-South, 1990, 32 pp. (1-55858-093-X)

(BL 67:375, 87:929; CC:442; CCBB 24:53; Ch&Bks:282; HB 47:66; HBG 2 [July–Dec 1990]: 35; KR 38:1142, 58:1256; LJ 96:3487; Suth: 13; TLS 1971 p. 1343)

8 **ANDERSEN, Hans Christian.** *Little Ida's Flowers.* **Gr. K–3.**

Ida awakens to music and finds cut flowers from the garden waltzing in her playroom, in one of Andersen's lesser known tales.

Illus. by Linda Allen, Putnam, 1989, 32 pp., o.p.

(BL 86:1081; HBG 1[July 1989]:61; SLJ Feb 1990 p. 68)

9 **ANDERSEN, Hans Christian.** *The Little Match Girl.* **Gr. K–5. (Orig. Danish**
✓ **pub. 1846, U.S. 1870.)**

A penniless little match-seller burns the last of her matches to keep warm on Christmas Eve, and sees wondrous visions in the flames.

Illus. by Gustaf Tenggren, Grosset, 1944, o.p.; illus. by Blair Lent, Houghton, 1968, o.p.; illus. by Rachel Isadora, Putnam, 1987, pap., 1990, 30 pp. (0-399-22007-0)

(BL 84:387; CC:442; CCBB 22:121; Ch&Bks:282; HB 63:716, 718; KR 36:1039, 55:1387, 57:1601; LJ 93:3953; SLJ Oct 1987 p. 30; Suth:14; TLS 1987 p. 1284)

10 **ANDERSEN, Hans Christian.** *The Little Mermaid.* **Gr. K–5. (Written 1837,**
✓ **orig. Danish pub. 1846.)**

A young mermaid in love with a human makes the tragic decision to give up her undersea home and live as a mortal. *My Love, My Love, or The Peasant Girl,* by Rosa Guy (Holt, 1985; see Chapter 5B, Myth Fantasy) is a contemporary version of this story, written for young adults.

Trans. by M. R. James, illus. by Pamela Bianco, Holiday, 1935, o.p.; retold and illus. by Dorothy P. Lathrop, Macmillan, 1939, o.p.; trans. by Eva Le Gallienne, illus. by Edward Frascino, Harper, 1971, o.p.; trans. by M. R. James, illus. by Josef Palaček, Faber, 1981, o.p.; adapt. by Anthea Bell, illus. by Chihiro Iwasaki, Picture Book, 1984, 33 pp., o.p., pap., 1991 (0-907234-59-3); adapt. and illus. by Katie Thamer Treherne, Harcourt, 1989, 48 pp. (0-15-246320-8); retold by Deborah Hautzig, illus. by Darcy May, Random, 1991, 48 pp. (0-679-92241-5), pap. (0-679-82241-0); illus. by Charles Santore, Outlet, 1993, 48 pp. (0-517-06495-2); illus. by Michael Hague, Holt, 1994, 48 pp. (0-8050-1010-6)

(BL 32:80, 36:157, 202, 68:468, 81:585, 86:921, 90:149, 90:1814; Bookshelf 1935 p. 2; CCBB 45:116; HB 16:43, 109, 48:142; HBG 1 [July–Dec 1990]:47, 3 [July–Dec 1991]:56, 5 [Jan–June 1994]:298; KR 39:1124, 57:1601; LJ 97:771; Mahony 3:200; SLJ Apr 1982 p. 65, Feb 1985 p. 70, Nov 1989 p. 102, Oct 1993 p. 123, June 1994 p. 124)

11   **ANDERSEN, Hans Christian.** *The Nightingale.* **Gr. K–5. (Written 1844, orig.**
✓   **U.S. pub. 1896.)**

A selfish emperor prefers a bejeweled mechanical bird to the faithful nightingale who loves him. Kara Dalkey's *The Nightingale* (Berkley, 1988; see Chapter 5B, Myth Fantasy) is a novel-length adaptation of this story.

Trans. by Eva Le Gallienne, illus. by Nancy Ekholm Burkert, Harper, 1965, LB(0-06-023781-3), 1985, pap. (0-06-443070-7); trans. by Erik Haugaard, illus. by Lemoine, Schocken, 1981 (entitled: *The Emperor's Nightingale*), o.p.; trans. by Anthea Bell, illus. by Lisbeth Zwerger, Picture Book, 1991 (0-907234-57-7); trans. and adapt. by Alan Benjamin, illus. by Beni Montresor, Crown, 1985, o.p.; adapt. by Anna Bier, illus. by Demi, Harcourt, 1988, 30 pp., pap. (0-15-257428-X); illus. by Alison Claire Darke, Doubleday, 1989, 28 pp. (0-385-26081-4); trans. by Naomi Lewis, illus. by Josef Palaček, North-South, 1990, 40 pp. (1-55858-090-5); adapt. by Michael Bedard, illus. by Regolo Ricci, Houghton, 1992, 32 pp. (0-395-60735-3); retold and illus. by Meilo So, Macmillan, 1992 (entitled *The Emperor and the Nightingale*), 32 pp. (0-02-786045-0)

(BL 31:385, 34:78, 59:113, 61:995, 78:705, 81:585, 82:564, 86:1081, 87:929; CC:442; CCBB 16:89, 18:157, 38:59, 39:41; Ch&Bks:282; HB 38:601, 41:389, 61:172, 62:78; HBG 1 [July–Dec 1989]:83, 2 [July–Dec 1990]:35; KR 33:373, 60:320; LJ 90:2393; Mahony 3:200; SLJ Mar 1982 pp. 116, 126, Feb 1985 p. 61, Oct 1985 p. 166, May 1992 p. 85, Oct 1992, p. 78)

12   **ANDERSEN, Hans Christian.** *The Old House.* **Gr. 2–5. (Orig. pub. in Denmark, orig. British pub. in this edition 1984.)**

The tin soldier once given to a lonely old man by a neighbor boy reappears in a new house built for the now grown-up boy, on the site of the original house.

Trans. and adapt. by Anthea Bell, illus. by Jean Claverie, North-South, 1986, o.p.

(HB 68:364365; SLJ Mar 1987 p. 139)

13   **ANDERSEN, Hans Christian.** *The Red Shoes.* **Gr. 1–4. (Orig. pub. in Denmark, this ed. orig. pub. in Austria.)**

A young girl is punished for her vanity by a stern angel who decrees that she must never stop dancing in her new red shoes.

Trans. by Anthea Bell, illus. by Chihiro Iwasaki, Neugebauer, 1983, 34 pp., o.p.; Oxford, 1983, pap. (0-19-421741-8); Picture Book, 1991, pap., 36 pp. (0-907234-26-7)

(BL 79:1461; SLJ Sept 1983, p. 100)

14   **ANDERSEN, Hans Christian.** *The Snow Queen.* **Gr. 2–5. (Written 1845, orig.**
✓   **U.S. pub. 1849.)**

Gerda faces many perils as she tries to save her friend, Kay, imprisoned in the Snow Queen's ice palace.

Trans. by R. P. Keigwin, illus. by June Corwin, Atheneum, 1968, o.p.; adapt. by Naomi Lewis, illus. by Errol Le Cain, Viking, 1979, o.p.; Puffin, 1982, pap. (0-14-050294-7); adapt. by Amy Ehrlich, illus. by Susan Jeffers, Dial, 1982, 40 pp. (0-8037-8029-X); pap. (0-8037-0692-8); trans. by Eva Le Gallienne, illus. by Arieh Zeldich, Harper, 1985, o.p.;

Macmillan, 1985, o.p.; trans. and adapt. by Anthea Bell, illus. by Bernadette Watts, North-South, 1987, 32 pp. (1-55858-053-0); trans. by Naomi Lewis, illus. by Angela Barrett, Holt, 1988, 42 pp., o.p.; Candlewick, 1993, 32 pp. (1-56402-215-3); illus. by P. J. Lynch, Harcourt, 1994, 48 pp. (0-15-200874-8)

(BL 39:37, 65:650, 69:531, 75:1627, 79:672, 684, 82:977, 84:470, 85:569, 90:521, 91:135; Bookshelf 1921–1922 p. 8; CC:442, 481; CCBB 22:21, 73, 36:121; Ch&Bks:282; HB 49:141; HBG 1 [July–Dec 1989]:82; HBG 5:72, 5 [Jan–June 1998];298; KR 36:820, 40:1307, 47:1205; LJ 67:884, 910, 93:3753, 3964, 98:999; SLJ Jan 1980 p. 64, Mar 1983 p. 154, Jan 1986 p. 53; Oct 1987 p. 109, Feb 1994 p. 76; Suth 3:16; TLS 1968 p. 586)

15
✓ **ANDERSEN, Hans Christian.** *The Steadfast Tin Soldier.* **Gr. K–5. (Written 1838, orig. U.S. pub. 1927.)**

A malevolent jack-in-the-box tries to separate two lovers, a tin soldier and a paper ballerina. The Scribner 1953 edition illustrated by Marcia Brown was awarded a Randolph Caldecott Honor Book Medal in 1954.

Trans. by M. R. James, illus. by Marcia Brown, Scribner, 1953, o.p.; illus. by Monika Laimgruber, Atheneum, 1971 (orig. pub. 1970), o.p.; illus. by Paul Galdone, Houghton, 1979, o.p.; adapt. and illus. by Thomas Di Grazia, Prentice, 1981, 32 pp. (0-13-846295-X); illus. by Alain Vaës, Little, 1983, o.p.; illus. by David Jorgensen, Knopf, 1986, 48 pp., o.p.; trans. by Naomi Lewis, illus. by P. J. Lynch, Harcourt, 1992, 32 pp. (0-15-200599-4); adapt. by Tor Seidler, illus. by Fred Marcellino, Harper, 1992, 32 pp., LB(0-06-205001-X)

(BL 50:18, 76:498, 78:595, 80:853, 89:665; CC:443; CC 1993 suppl. pp. 66, 76; CCBB 7:1; Ch&Bks:282; HB 29:347, 58:151; KR 21:532, 48:61, 60:1138, 1371; LJ 78:1544, 96:2373; SLJ Dec 1979 p. 71, Jan 1982 p. 58, Mar 1984 p. 137, Feb 1993 p. 68; Suth:216)

16
✓ **ANDERSEN, Hans Christian.** *The Swineherd.* **Gr. K–5. (Orig. Danish pub. 1841, U.S. 1924.)**

Scorned by a self-centered princess, a prince decides to make a fool of her by wooing her disguised as a swineherd.

Trans. and illus. by Erik Blegvad, Harcourt, 1958, o.p.; trans. by Anthea Bell, illus. by Lisbeth Zwerger, Morrow, 1982, o.p.; Picture Book, 1986, pap., o.p.; trans. by Naomi Lewis, illus. by Dorothée Duntze, North-South, 1987, 32 pp. (1-55858-038-7); adapt. and illus. by Deborah Hahn, Lothrop, 1991, 32 pp., LB(0-688-10053-8)

(BL 55:27, 78:951, 83:1280; CC:443; CCBB 12:93; HB 34:38, 58:277; HBG 3 [July–Dec 1991]:23; KR 26:605, 59:1085; LJ 55:27, 83:3004; SLJ Mar 1982 p. 127, June/July 1987 p. 75)

17
✓ **ANDERSEN, Hans Christian.** *Thumbelina.* **Gr. K–5. (Written 1835, orig. U.S. pub. Macmillan, 1928.)**

A tiny, thumb-sized girl named Thumbelina is carried off by a frog, saved by a field mouse, and almost married to a mole before reaching the land of the flower people.

Trans. by R. P. Keigwin, illus. by Adrienne Adams, Scribner, 1961, o.p.; adapt. by Amy Ehrlich, illus. by Susan Jeffers, Dial, 1979, LB(0-8037-8814-2), 1985, pap. (0-8037-0232-9); trans. by Richard Winston and Clara Winston, illus. by Lisbeth Zwerger, Morrow, 1980 (entitled: *Thumbeline*), o.p.; trans. by Anthea Bell, illus. by Lisbeth Zwerger, Picture Book, 1985 (entitled: *Thumbeline*), 29 pp. (0-88708-006-5), pap. (0-88708-171-1); adapt. and illus. by Demi, Putnam, 1989, 32 pp., o.p.; retold by Deborah Hautzig, illus. by Kaarina Kaila, Knopf, 1990, 32 pp., LB(0-679-90667-3); illus. by Alison Claire Darke, Doubleday, 1991, o.p.; illus. by Wayne Anderson, retold by James Riordan, Putnam, 1991, 32 pp. (0-399-21756-8)

(BL 58:228, 76:554, 77:112, 82:681, 87:1494, 85:1189; CC:443; CCBB 15:90, 33:145; Ch&Bks:283; HB 4 [Aug 1928]:9, 38:41; HBG 2 [July–Dec 1990]:43, 2 [Jan–June 1991]:241, 3 [July–Dec 1991]:23; KR 29:953, 48:209, 49:55, 58:1332, 59:326; LJ 86:4357; SLJ Jan 1980 p. 53, Mar 1980 p. 116, Sept 1980 p. 55, Feb 1986 p. 70, April 1989 p. 75, Sept 1990 p. 192, June 1991 p. 89, Feb 1992 p. 70)

18   **ANDERSEN, Hans Christian.** *The Tinderbox.* **Gr. K–4. (Orig. Danish pub.**
✓   **1835.)**

A soldier's fortune is made after he steals a magical tinderbox from a witch: striking it
brings three huge dogs to grant their master's wishes. In the edition retold by Moser, the
story is set in the post–Civil War Tennessee mountains, and the witch has been replaced
by a wily mountain man.

Illus. by Warwick Hutton, Macmillan, 1988, 32 pp. (0-689-50458-6); adapt. and illus. by
Barry Moser, Little, Brown, 1990, 32 pp. (0-316-03938-1); adapt. by Peggy Thomson,
illus. by James Warhola, Simon & Schuster, 1991, 40 pp. (0-671-70546-6)

(BL 85:263, 87:438, 971, 88:64; CC:535; HB 64:768, 67:65; HBG 2[July–Dec 1990]:70, 3[July–Dec
1991]:24; KR 56:1145, 58:1165; SLJ Dec 1988 p. 96, Oct 1990 p. 113, Nov 1991 p. 89)

19   **ANDERSEN, Hans Christian.** *The Ugly Duckling.* **Gr. K–5. (Written 1842, orig.**
✓   **U.S. pub. 1850.)**

Mistreated by the other ducks, the "ugly duckling" runs away to spend a terrible winter
on his own, but when spring comes he has grown into a beautiful swan.

Trans. by R. P. Keigwin, illus. by Adrienne Adams, Scribner, 1965, o.p.; retold and illus.
by Lorinda Bryan Cauley, Harcourt, 1979, o.p., 1989, pap. (0-15-692528-1); trans. by
Anne Stewart, illus. by Monika Laimgruber, Greenwillow, 1985, o.p.; adapt. by Joel
Tuber and Clara Stites, illus. by Robert Van Nutt, Knopf, 1986 (0-394-88298-9); adapt.
by Marianna Mayer, illus. by Thomas Locker, Macmillan, 1987, 38 pp. (0-02-765130-4);
illus. by Troy Howell, Putnam, 1990, 38 pp. (0-399-22158-1); illus. by Alan Marks, trans.
by Anthea Bell, Picture Book, 1991, pap., 44 pp. (0-88708-116-9); adapt. by Adrian
Mitchell, illus. by Jonathan Heale, Dorling Kindersley, 1994, 32 pp. (1-56458-557-3)

(BL 62:270, 76:499, 82:681, 83:706, 1280, 86:1337; CC:443; CCBB 5:64, 19:141, 40:141, 43:179;
Ch&Bks:283; HB 41:627, 62:188; HBG [Jan–June 1994]:298; KR 33:899, 47:1206, 54:1719, 55:133,
58:348, 62:839; LJ 90:4602; SLJ Jan 1980 p. 54, Jan 1986 p. 53, Feb 1987 p. 63, Apr 1990 p. 86, July 1994
p. 73; Suth:216)

20   **ANDERSEN, Hans Christian.** *The Wild Swans.* **Gr. K–5. (Orig. pub. in Den**
✓   **mark, orig. U.S. pub. 1922.)**

A young princess tries to break the spell that changed her eleven brothers into swans.
Swan's Wing by Ursula Synge (see this chapter) is an extension of this story written for
young adults.

Trans. by M. R. James, illus. by Marcia Brown, Scribner, 1963, o.p.; adapt. by Amy
Ehrlich, illus. by Susan Jeffers, Dial, 1976 (0-8037-9381-2), 1987, pap. (0-8037-0451-8);
trans. by Naomi Lewis, illus. by Angela Barrett, Bedrick, 1984, 33 pp., o.p.; retold by
Deborah Hautzig, illus. by Kaarina Kaila, Knopf, 1992, 32 pp., LB(0-679-93446-4)

(BL 60:416, 78:646, 81:585; CC:443, 624; CCBB 35:102; Ch&Bks:263; HB 39:601, 40:487; HBG 4
[Spring 1993]:54; SLJ Jan 1982 p. 58, Dec 1984 p. 67)

21   **ANDERSON, Mildred Napier.** *A Gift for Merimond.* **Gr. 4–6 (Orig. pub. in Eng-**
   land.)

Prince Merimond's gift of having all his wishes granted causes him unexpected problems.

Illus. by J. Paget-Fredericks, Oxford, 1953, 84 pp., o.p.

(BL 49:273; CCBB 7:19; HB 29:119; KR 21:114; LJ 78:737)

22   **ANDERSON, Mildred Napier.** *Sandra and the Right Prince.* **Gr. 3–5. (Orig. pub.**
   in England.)

Princess Sandra rules out jousting and dragon-slaying as criteria in selecting her husband.

Illus. by J. Paget-Fredericks, Oxford, 1951, 72 pp., o.p.

(BL 47:369; CCBB 4:40; HB 27:179, 238; LJ 76:781)

23   **ANDERSON, Wayne.** *Dragon.* **Gr. K–4.**

A newly hatched dragon asks creature after creature whether each is his missing parent, until a child uses magic to help him.

Illus. by the author, Simon & Schuster, 1992, 32 pp. (0-671-78397-1)

(BL 89:918; KR 60:1185; SLJ Oct 1992 p. 78)

ANDREWS, Allen. *The Pig Plantagenet.* See Chapter 2, Animal Fantasy.

ARKIN, Alan. *The Lemming Condition.* See Chapter 2, Animal Fantasy.

AULAIRE, Ingri d', and Aulaire, Edgar Parin d'. *D'Aulaire's Trolls.* See Chapter 3, Fantasy Collections.

AULNOY, Marie Catherine Jumelle de Berneville, Comtesse d'. *The Children's Fairyland.* See Chapter 3, Fantasy Collections.

AULNOY, Marie Catherine Jumelle de Berneville, Comtesse d'. *The White Cat and Other Old French Fairy Tales.* See Chapter 3, Fantasy Collections.

24   **BABBITT, Natalie (Zane Moore).** *Knee-Knock Rise.* **Gr. 3–5.**

✓   The people living closest to the hill called Knee-Knock Rise are both proud and fearful of the noisy monster said to live there, until a boy named Egan discovers the real cause of the terrible noise. John Newbery Medal Honor Book, 1971.

Illus. by the author, Farrar, 1970, 117 pp. (0-374-34257-1), 1984, pap. (0-374-44260-6)

(BL 67:99, 659; CC:445; CCBB 24:53; Ch&Bks:262; HB 46:295; KR 38:551; LJ 95:2306; Suth:24)

25   **BABBITT, Natalie (Zane Moore).** *The Search for Delicious.* **Gr. 3–6.**

✓   While polling inhabitants on the exact definition of "delicious," Gaylen uncovers a plot by the queen's brother to take over the kingdom.

Farrar, 1969, 176 pp. (0-374-36534-2); Avon, 1980, pap., o.p.

(BBC:197; BL 66:53; CC:445; CCBB 23:21; HB 45:407; KR 37:373; LJ 95:3603; TLS 1975 p. 365)

BABBITT, Natalie (Zane Moore). *Tuck Everlasting.* See Chapter 5B, Myth Fantasy.

26   **BACH, Richard (David).** *Jonathan Livingston Seagull.* **Gr. 10 up.**

Exiled from his flock for daring to fly for the joy of it, rather than following the dignified Gull family tradition, Jonathan discovers that his purpose in life is to help others find perfection.

Macmillan, 1970, 93 pp. (0-02-504540-7); Avon, 1973, pap. (0-380-01286-3)

(BBS:52; BL 67:553; LJ 95:4187, 97:4093)

BACON, Martha (Sherman). *Moth Manor: A Gothic Tale.* See Chapter 9, Toy Fantasy.

BAKER, Betty (Lou). *Dupper.* See Chapter 2, Animal Fantasy.

27   **BAKER, Betty (Lou).** *Save Sirrushany!* (*Also Agotha, Princess Gwyn and All the Fearsome Beasts*). **Gr. 4–6.**

A dragon, a rare snail, and a girl named Agotha restore the fortunes of the Kingdom of Sirrushany.

Illus. by Erick Ingraham, Macmillan, 1978, 134 pp., o.p.

(CCBB 32:22; KR 46:496; SLJ May 1978 p. 62)

28   **BAKER, Betty (Lou).** *Seven Spells to Farewell.* **Gr. 4–6.**

Orphaned Drucilla runs away from her uncle's inn with a talking raven and a performing pig and crosses the mountain to the town of Farewell to become a sorceress.

Macmillan, 1982, 123 pp., o.p.

(BBC:197; CCBB 35:162; SLJ Apr 1982, p. 65)

29   **BAKER, Margaret.** *The Black Cats and the Tinker's Wife.* **Gr. K–4.**

The tinker's wife works magic with her good wishes.

Illus. by Mary Baker, Dodd, 1939, 1951, 120 pp., o.p.

(BL 20:104; Bookshelf 1923–1924 Suppl., p. 1; CCBB 5:42; LJ 77:71)

30   **BAKER, Margaret.** *Cat's-Cradles for His Majesty.* **Gr. 2–4.**

Pete, his mother, and Cinders the cat introduce the king to the game of cat's cradle.

Illus. by Mary Baker, Dodd, 1933, 115 pp., o.p.

(BL 30:157, Bookshelf 1933 p. 6; HB 9:204; LJ 59:403)

31   **BAKER, Margaret.** *The Lost Merbaby.* **Gr. 2–4.**

The fisherman and his wife adopt a mischievous merbaby placed in the fisherman's basket by the mermaids.

Illus. by Mary Baker, Duffield, 1927, o.p.; Dodd, 1941, 85 pp., o.p.

(BL 23:388; HB 3 [Aug 1927]:2627; Mahony 2:130; Moore:345; TLS 1927 p. 873)

32   **BAKER, Margaret.** *Noddy Goes A-Plowing.* **Gr. 3–4.**

A young man named Noddy wins a plowing match and the hand of the Princess.

Illus. by Mary Baker, Duffield, 1930, 104 pp., o.p.

(BL 27:211; HB 6:319, 7:115; Mahony 3:104; TLS 1930 p. 982)

33   **BANCROFT, Alberta.** *The Goblins of Haubeck.* **Gr. 3–5.**

A mischievous changeling makes trouble for the good goblins who help the housewives of Haubeck.

Illus. by Harold Sichel, McBride, 1925, 1933, 117 pp., o.p.

(BL 22:167; HB 2[Nov 1925]:18; LJ 58:806; Mahony 2:272)

34   **BANKS, Richard.** *The Mysterious Leaf.* **Gr. 2–5.**

A mysterious girl convinces three college professors to care for a tiny leaf that must never touch anything but the flesh of their hands.

Illus. by Irene Haas, Harcourt, 1954, 53 pp., o.p.

(BL 51:251; CCBB 8:74; HB 31:111; KR 22:633; LJ 79:2253)

35   **BARBER, Antonia.** *The Enchanter's Daughter.* **Gr. K–4. (Orig. British pub.**
✓   **1987.)**

The enchanter's beautiful young daughter has vague memories of another life far from the lonely, cold white land at the top of the world. Kate Greenaway Medal Commended Book, 1987.

Illus. by Errol Le Cain, Farrar, 1988, 32 pp. (0-374-32170-1)

(BL 85:478; CCBB 42:64; Ch&Bks:238; KR 56:1319; SLJ Dec 1988 p. 79; Suth 4:21)

BARRETT, Nicholas. *Fledger.* See Chapter 2, Animal Fantasy.

BATO, Joseph. *The Sorcerer.* See Chapter 10, Witchcraft and Sorcery Fantasy.

BAUM, L. Frank. *The Surprising Adventures of the Magical Monarch of Mo and His People.* See Chapter 3, Fantasy Collections.

BAXTER, Lorna. *The Eggchild.* See Chapter 10, Witchcraft and Sorcery Fantasy.

BEAGLE, Peter S(oyer). *The Last Unicorn.* See Chapter 5A, Alternate Worlds or Histories.

36   BEHN, Harry. *The Faraway Lurs.* **Gr. 5–8.**

Heather, a girl from a peaceful forest tribe, falls in love with the son of the enemy chief who plans to cut down the sacred tree of the forest people, in this tragic love story set in prehistoric time.

World, 1963, o.p.; Avon, 1968, pap., 127 pp., o.p.

(BL 59:893, 896; HB 39:165; LJ 88:2140)

37   BENARY-ISBERT, Margot. *The Wicked Enchantment.* **Gr. 5–7. (Orig. pub. in**
✓   Germany.)

Anemone and her dog Winnie run away after an evil spell is cast over their town.

Trans. by Richard Winston and Clara Winston, illus. by Enrico Arno, Harcourt, 1955, o.p.; Ace, 1986, pap., 160 pp., o.p.

(BL 52:18; CCBB 9:18; Eakin:29; HB 31:374; 60:223; Kies:11; KR 23:538; LJ 80:2644)

BENCHLEY, Nathaniel (Goddard). *Feldman Fieldmouse: A Fable.* See Chapter 2, Animal Fantasy.

BENÉT, Stephen Vincent. *The Devil and Daniel Webster.* See Chapter 5B, Myth Fantasy.

38   BENJAMIN, Alan. *Appointment.* **Gr. 4–7. (Adapted from W. Somerset**
Maugham's *Appointment in Samarra,* **from the play** *Sheppey,* **orig. pub. in Eng-**
land in 1934.)

Death, disguised as an old woman, stalks Abdulah, an elderly servant, through the marketplace of Baghdad.

Illus. by Roger Essley, Simon, 1993, 32 pp. (0-671-75887-X)

(BL 89:1692; HBG 4[Fall 1993]:269)

39   BERGER, Barbara Helen. *Gwinna.* **Gr. 4–7.**

The Mother of the Owls grants a childless couple's wish for a baby, but they are horrified when their daughter, Gwinna, grows wings.

Illus. by the author, Putnam, 1980, 127 pp. (0-399-21738-X)

(BL 87:441; CCBB 44:111; HBG 2[July–Dec 1990]:66; KR 58:1391; SLJ Dec 1990 p. 98)

40   BIANCO, Margery (Winifred) Williams. *The House That Grew Smaller.* **Gr.**
2–4.

An uninhabited hillside house blows away and grows steadily smaller until it is just the right size for a special inhabitant.

Illus. by Rachel Lyman Field, Macmillan, 1931, 40 pp., o.p.

(BL 28:107; HB 7:317; Mahony 3:105)

BIANCO, Margery (Winifred) Williams. *The Velveteen Rabbit; or, How Toys Became Real.* See Chapter 9, Toy Fantasy.

41   BIANCO, Pamela. *The Starlit Journey, a Story.* **Gr. 2–4.**

A little princess begins her betrothal journey.

Illus. by the author, Macmillan, 1933, 46 pp., o.p.

(Bookshelf 1933 p. 6; LJ 58:898)

42   BIEGEL, Paul. *The King of the Copper Mountains.* **Gr. 4–6. (Orig. Dutch pub. 1965.)**

While awaiting the arrival of a doctor to save the king's life, several animals tell stories to distract the king.

Trans. by Gillian Hume and Paul Biegel, illus. by Babs Van Wely, Dent, 1977 (repr. of 1968 ed.), 176 pp., o.p.

(CCBB 23:141; LJ 95:1632; Suth:38; TLS 1968 p. 1373)

***Black Water: The Book of Fantastic Literature.* Ed. by Alberto Manguelo.** See Chapter 3, Fantasy Collections.

BLACKWOOD, Gary L. *Beyond the Door.* See Chapter 5C, Travel to Other Worlds.

43   BLISS, Corinne Demas. *Matthew's Meadow.* **Gr. 3–6.**

Matthew returns each summer to a secret meadow cleared by his late grandmother, where he learns from a red-tailed hawk about preserving the natural world.

Illus. by Ted Lewin, Harcourt, 1992, 40 pp. (0-15-200759-8)

(BL 88:1356; HBG 3[Fall 1992]:253; KR 60:250; SLJ Aug. 1992 p. 132)

44   BODECKER, N(iels) M(ogens). *The Lost String Quartet.* **Gr. 2–4.**

The Daffodil String Quartet has a difficult time getting to their next concert: Sidney Periwinkle's cello is crushed by a trash compactor, Marcus Snowdrop's violin gets stuck in a tire, and frozen stringbeans stick to Jerome Crocus's violin.

Illus. by the author, Atheneum, 1981, 28 pp., o.p.

(CCBB 35:6; KR 49:796; SLJ Aug 1981 p. 63)

45   BODGER, Joan (Mercer). *Clever-Lazy, the Girl Who Invented Herself.* **Gr. 5–8.**

Clever-Lazy and her husband flee the Emperor's Court to keep the gunpowder she invented from falling into the wrong hands.

Atheneum, 1979, 201 pp., o.p.

(BL 76:663; HB 56:53; SLJ Jan 1980 p. 77; VOYA 3 [June 1980]:26)

BOMANS, Godfried (Jan Arnold). *The Wily Witch and All the Other Fairy Tales and Fables.* See Chapter 3, Fantasy Collections.

BOURLIAGUET, Léonce. *The Giant Who Drank from His Shoe and Other Stories.* See Chapter 3, Fantasy Collections.

46   BOWEN, Vernon. *The Wonderful Adventures of Ting Ling.* **Gr. 3–5.**

✓   Ting Ling, a juggler's assistant in ancient China, manages to accomplish five impossible tasks set by the cruel emperor and wins the hand of the princess.

Illus. by Kurt Wiese, McKay, 1952, 49 pp., o.p.

(BL 49:18; HB 28:319; KR 20:403; LJ 77:1412)

47   BOYLE, Kay. *The Youngest Camel.* Gr. 3–4. (Orig. pub. 1939.)

A lonely young camel wanders the world until he meets a caravan of white camels that circles the earth.

Illus. by Ronni Solbert, Harper, 1959, 96 pp., o.p.

(HB 15:295, 380, 35:387; LJ 64:870)

BRADBURY, Ray (Douglas). *Something Wicked This Way Comes.* See Chapter 10, Witchcraft and Sorcery Fantasy.

BRADLEY, Marion Zimmer. *Night's Daughter.* See Chapter 5B, Myth Fantasy.

48   BRENTANO, Clemens Maria. *Schoolmaster Whackwell's Wonderful Sons.* Gr. 3–6. (Orig. pub. in Germany.)

The schoolmaster's five sons spend a year seeking their separate fortunes and then join forces to rescue a princess held captive by a giant.

Trans. by Doris Orgel, illus. by Maurice Sendak, Random, 1962, 88 pp., o.p.

(BL 59:490; HB 39:58; LJ 87:4618)

49   BRENTANO, Clemens Maria. *The Tale of Gockel, Hinkel and Gackeliah.* Gr. 4–6. (Orig. German pub. 1838, U.S. Silver, 1914; entitled *Gockel, Hinkel and Gackeleia.*)

A magic ring brings good fortune to Gockel and his family, until his daughter is deceived into giving it to a stranger.

Trans. by Doris Orgel, illus. by Maurice Sendak, Random, 1961, 143 pp., o.p.

(BL 58:444; HB 38:49; KR 29:504; LJ 86:2532)

BRIGGS, K(atharine) M(ary). *Kate Crackernuts.* See Chapter 5B, Myth Fantasy.

BRIGHT, Robert. *Richard Brown and the Dragon.* See Chapter 6, Humorous Fantasy.

BROOKE, William J. *A Telling of the Tales: Five Stories.* See Chapter 3, Fantasy Collections.

50   BROWN, Judith Gwyn. *The Mask of the Dancing Princess.* Gr. 3–6.

Selfish Princess Rosamund spends seven years living with a band of gypsies learning how to be a kind, fair ruler.

Illus. by the author, Macmillan, 1989, 48 pp. (0-689-31427-2)

(BL 86:660; HBG 1[July–Dec 1989]:82; KR 57:1400; SLJ Nov 1989 p. 104)

BRYHER, Winifred. *A Visa for Avalon.* See Chapter 5B, Myth Fantasy.

BUCHWALD, Emilie. *Gildaen: The Heroic Adventures of a Most Unusual Rabbit.* See Chapter 2, Animal Fantasy.

51   BULLA, Clyde Robert. *The Moon Singer.* Gr. 3–5.

Torr, a foundling who sings unearthly songs to the moon, is taken from his foster parents to be raised as a prince.

Illus. by Trina Schart Hyman, Harper, 1969, 48 pp., o.p.

(HB 45:671; KR 37:1111; LJ 95:2307)

52   **BULLA, Clyde Robert.** *My Friend the Monster.* **Gr. 3–5.**

✓   Young Prince Hal rescues a monster named Humbert and the two become fast, but secret, friends.

Illus. by Michele Chessare, Harper, 1980, 75 pp., o.p.

(BL 77:455; CCBB 34:107; HB 56:639; KR 49:6; SLJ Dec 1980 p. 58)

53   **BULLA, Clyde Robert.** *The Sword in the Tree.* **Gr. 3–5.**

✓   Young Shan becomes a knight to avenge his father's loss of all rights to his uncle, Lord Weldon.

Illus. by Paul Galdone, Harper, 1962, 113 pp., LB(0-690-79909-8)

(CC:455; HB 32:184; KR 21:1; LJ 81:764)

54   **BUNYAN, John.** *The Pilgrim's Progress* **(Orig. title:** *The Pilgrim's Progress; from This World to That Which Is to Come,* **1671). Gr. 5 up.**

A simplified retelling of Christian's allegorical journey from the City of Destruction to the Eternal City.

Ed. by Mary Godolphin, illus. by Robert Lawson, Lippincott, 1939, 1976, o.p.; Dent, 1954, 1979 (repr. of 1954 ed.), o.p.; Dodd, 1979, o.p.; adapt. by James Reeves, illus. by Joanna Troughton, Bedrick, 1987, 160 pp. (0-87226-148-4)

(BL 36:76; HB 15:305, 16:17, 26, 126; KR 55:861; LJ 64:712; SHC:672)

BURCH, Robert. *The Jolly Witch.* See Chapter 10, Witchcraft and Sorcery Fantasy.

55   **BURTON, Philip.** *The Green Isle.* **Gr. 2–4.**

After Geraint, a Welsh shepherd, is imprisoned by the Normans as punishment for his love for her, Lady Eleanor escapes with him to a mysterious emerald island.

Illus. by Robert Andrew Parker, Dial, 1974, 32 pp., o.p.

(BL 71:98; KR 42:876; SLJ Jan 1975 p. 37)

BYFIELD, Barbara Ninde. *Andrew and the Alchemist.* See Chapter 10, Witchcraft and Sorcery Fantasy.

56   **CAMERON, Eleanor (Frances Butler).** *The Beast with the Magical Horn.* **Gr. 3–5.**

Alison saves a unicorn and captures seven fabulous creatures for an evil queen.

Illus. by Beth Krush and Joe Krush, Little, 1963, 73 pp., o.p.

(BL 60:313; CCBB 17:75; HB 39:602; LJ 88:4471)

57   **CAMPBELL, Ann.** *Once Upon a Princess and a Pea.* **Gr. K–4.**

In this contemporary retelling of Hans Christian Andersen's tale, independent Princess Esmerelda runs away after refusing to marry a king chosen by her parents, only to fall in love with Prince Hector, who drives a red roadster.

Illus. by Kathy Osborn Young, Stewart, Tabori & Chang, 1993, 32 pp. (1-55670-289-2)

(BL 89:2067; HBG 4[Fall 1993]:252; KR 61:567; SLJ Oct 1993 p. 92)

CAPEK, Karel. *Nine Fairy Tales and One More Thrown in for Good Measure.* See Chapter 3, Fantasy Collections.

58   **CAREW, Jan (Rynveld).** *Children of the Sun.* **Gr. 3–5.**

The two sons of an earth woman and the sun set out to answer their father's query: "Would you like to be good men or great men?"

Illus. by Leo Dillon and Diane Dillon, Little, 1980, 40 pp., o.p.

(BL 76:1122; CCBB 33:187; KR 48:774; SLJ May 1980 p. 65)

CAREY, Valerie Scho. *The Devil and Mother Crump.* See Chapter 6, Humorous Fantasy.

CARROLL, Lewis. *Alice's Adventures in Wonderland.* See Chapter 5C, Travel to Other Worlds.

59 CARTER, Angela. *The Donkey Prince.* **Gr. 1–4.**

Even though he has been transformed into a donkey, Prince Bruno must find a magic apple to save the queen's life.

Illus. by Eros Keith, Simon, 1970, 40 pp., o.p.

(BL 67:662; CCBB 24:103; KR 38:1145; LJ 96:256)

A Cavalcade of Dragons. **Ed. by Roger (Gilbert) Lancelyn Green.** See Chapter 3, Fantasy Collections.

60 CAYLUS, Anne Claude Phillipe, Comte de. *Heart of Ice.* **Gr. 2–3.**

Kidnapped by a vengeful fairy at his christening, a tiny prince manages to scale the slopes of the Ice Mountain to win the hand of Princess Sabella.

Adapt. by Benjamin Appel, illus. by J. K. Lambert, Pantheon, 1977, 58 pp., o.p.

(BL 74:158; CCBB 31:76; KR 45:669; SLJ Oct 1977 p. 109)

61 CERVANTES, Saavedra Miguel de. *The Adventures of Don Quixote de la Man-*
✓ *cha.* **Gr. 5 up. (Orig. Spanish pub. in two parts, 1605 and 1615; first English ed. 1612.)**

Don Quixote and Sancho Panza, knight and page, ride off to defend the poor and rescue ladies in distress.

Adapt. by Leighton Barret, illus. by Warren Chappell, Knopf, 1960, o.p.; illus. by Edward Ardizzone, Walck, 1960, o.p.; Dent, 1983 (repr. of 1953 ed.), o.p.; retold by James Reeves, illus. by Edward Ardizzone, Bedrick, 1985 (entitled: *The Exploits of Don Quixote;* orig. British pub. in this ed. 1959), 219 pp. (0-87226-025-9); adapt. and trans. by Magda Bogin, illus. by Manuel Boix, Stewart, 1991, 144 pp. (1-55670-201-9); adapt. by Margaret Hodges, illus. by Stephen Marchesi, Macmillan, 1992, 72 pp. (entitled: *Don Quixote and Sancho Panza*) (0-684-19235-7); retold and illus. by Marcia Williams, Candlewick, 1993, 32 pp. (1-56402-174-2)

(BL 46:47, 57:130, 88:758; Bookshelf 1932 p.8; CCBB 11:51, 46:171; HB 36:308, 69:227; HBG 4[Spring 1993]:66, 4[Fall 1993]:285; JHC:341; KR 28:621; LJ 85:3869; SHC:674; SLJ Jan 1981 p. 67, Jan 1992 p. 108, Nov 1992 p. 92, May 1993 p. 103; TLS Dec 4, 1951 p. xii, 1980 p. 1032)

CHARLES, Prince of Wales. *The Old Man of Lochnagar.* See Chapter 6, Humorous Fantasy.

CHERRYH, C. J. *The Dreamstone.* See Chapter 5B, Myth Fantasy.

62 CLÉMENT, Claude. *The Man Who Lit the Stars.* **Gr. 3–5. (Orig. pub. in Belgium and France, 1992.)**

A lonely orphan follows a mysterious man who claims to be a star polisher up a great ladder into the heavens.

Illus. by John Howe, Little, Brown, 1992, 32 pp. (0-316-14741-9)

(BL 89:984; KR 60:987; SLJ Oct 1992 p. 114)

63   **CLÉMENT, Claude.** *The Voice of the Wood.* **Gr. 2–5. (Orig. Belgian and French pub. 1988.)**

A cello made by a master craftsman from the wood of a beloved tree can be played only by an extraordinary but unpretentious musician in this tale set in Renaissance Venice.

Trans. by Lenny Hort, illus. by Frédéric Clément, Dial, 1989, 32 pp. (0-8037-0635-9); Puffin, 1993, pap. (0-14-054594-8)

(BL 85:1644; CCBB 42:245; SLJ June 1989 p. 86; KR57:46)

64   **COATSWORTH, Elizabeth (Jane).** *The Cat Who Went to Heaven.* **Gr. 4–6.**
✓   **(Orig. pub. 1930.)**

When a poor Japanese artist paints his little white cat into a picture of the dying Buddha, he lets his pet into heaven. John Newbery Medal, 1931.

Illus. by Lynd Ward, Macmillan, 1967, 62 pp. (0-02-719710-7), pap., 1990 (0-689-71433-5)

(BL 27:107, 55:191; Bookshelf 1932 p.8; CC:469; CCBB 12:60; Ch&Bks:264; HB 6:214, 7:119, 36:146, 62:344; LJ 56:279, 598; Moore:409, 431)

65   **COATSWORTH, Elizabeth (Jane).** *Cricket and the Emperor's Son.* **Gr. 3–6.**
✓   **(Orig. pub. 1932.)**

A little prince with insomnia is entertained each night by Cricket, an apprentice with an endless number of stories to tell.

Illus. by Juliette Palmer, Norton, 1965, 126 pp., o.p.

(BL 29:118, 61:873; Bookshelf 1933 p. 6; CCBB 18:144; Eakin:77; HB 8:157, 41:275; KR 33:310; LJ 58:899, 90:2042)

COATSWORTH, Elizabeth (Jane). *Marra's World.* See Chapter 5B, Myth Fantasy.

66   **COATSWORTH, Elizabeth (Jane).** *The Princess and the Lion.* **Gr. 4–6.**
✓   After the king surprises his court by naming Prince Michael heir to the throne, Princess Miriam journeys to the Prison of Princes to prevent Michael's escape.

Illus. by Evaline Ness, Pantheon, 1963, 77 pp. o.p.

(BL 60:39; Eakin: 77; HB 39:281; LJ 88:2549)

67   **COATSWORTH, Elizabeth (Jane).** *Pure Magic* **(pap. title:** *The Werefox***). Gr. 4–5.**

Johnny's new friend, Giles, has a secret: He can change into a fox, which proves dangerous when fox-hunting season begins.

Illus. by Ingrid Fetz, Macmillan, 1973, 68 pp., o.p.

(BL 70:385; HB 49:464; KR 41:642; LJ 98:2649)

68   **COEHLO, Paulo.** *The Alchemist: A Fable About Following Your Dream.* **Gr. 10 up. (Orig. Brazilian pub. 1988.)**

After a seer advises young shepherd Santiago to follow his dream about hidden treasure by leaving Spain for Egypt, he travels to Tangier and joins a caravan bound for the East.

Trans. by Alan R. Clark and Paulo Coehlo, Harper, 1993, 192 pp. (0-06-250217-4)

(BL 89:1547, 1548; KR 61:545; LJ June 15, 1993 p. 94; SLJ July 1993 p. 110)

COLE, Joanna. *Bony-Legs.* See Chapter 10, Witchcraft and Sorcery Fantasy.

COLE, Joanna. *Dr. Orange.* See Chapter 10, Witchcraft and Sorcery Fantasy.

COLLINS, Meghan. *The Willow Maiden.* See Chapter 5B, Myth Fantasy.

COLLODI, Carlo. *The Adventures of Pinocchio.* See Chapter 9, Toy Fantasy.

COLUM, Padraic. *The Boy Apprenticed to an Enchanter.* See Chapter 10, Witchcraft and Sorcery Fantasy.

69 **COLUM, Padraic.** *The Girl Who Sat by the Ashes.* **Gr. 3–5. (Orig. U.S. pub.**
✓ **1919, 1939.)**
An expanded version of the traditional "Cinderella" story.
Illus. by Imero Gobbato, Macmillan, 1968, 117 pp., o.p.
(BL 16:174; Bookshelf 1923–1924 p. 8; KR 36:336; LJ 45:980; Mahony 1:25, 2:134)

70 **COLUM, Padraic.** *The King of Ireland's Son.* **Gr. 5–7. (Orig. pub. Holt 1916.)**
The king's son falls in love with the daughter of Fedelma, the Enchanter.
Illus. by Willy Pogány, Macmillan, 1962, 275 pp., o.p.
(BL 13:269, 18:95, 59:84; HB 39:75; Mahony 2:277)

COLUM, Padraic. *The Stone of Victory and Other Tales.* See Chapter 3, Fantasy Collections.

71 **COOKE, Donald Edwin.** *The Firebird.* **Gr. 3–5.**
A magical firebird helps the Red Prince pass through an enchanted land and defeat the evil Black Prince. This tale is taken from the same Russian source as Stravinski's "Firebird Suite."
Illus. by the author, Winston, 1939, 144 pp., o.p.
(BL 36:347; LJ 65:37)

72 **COOMBS, Patricia.** *Molly Mullett.* **Gr. K–3.**
Molly becomes a knight after she and her pet blackbird outwit an ogre.
Illus. by the author, Lothrop, 1975, 32 pp., o.p.
(CCBB 29:24; KR 43:69; SLJ Apr 1975 p. 43)

73 **COOPER, Gale.** *Unicorn Moon.* **Gr. 3–5.**
A princess must solve the riddle of true love before she can separate the young man imprisoned in her dreams from a real man she can love.
Illus. by the author, Dutton, 1984, 32 pp., o.p.
(BL 81:786; CCBB 38:103; SLJ Dec 1984 p. 79)

74 **COOPER, Margaret.** *The Ice Palace.* **Gr. 3–5.**
Princess Kasha is given a palace of ice, especially built to keep her cool.
Illus. by Harold Leland Goodwin, Macmillan, 1966, 50 pp., o.p.
(CCBB 20:136; KR 34:574; LJ 91:4329)

75 **COOPER, Paul Fenimore.** *Dindle.* **Gr. 3–5.**
A rug-weaver named Dindle longs to rid the kingdom of the terrible white dragon whose tail turns living things to stone.
Illus. by Marion Cooper, Putnam, 1963, 64 pp., o.p.
(HB 40:174; LJ 89:951)

COOPER (Grant), Susan (Mary). *The Selkie Girl.* See Chapter 5B, Myth Fantasy.

COOPER, Susan. *Tam Lin.* See Chapter 5B, Myth Fantasy.

CORBETT, W(illiam) J(esse). *The Song of Pentecost.* See Chapter 2, Animal Fantasy.

76 **CRESSWELL (Rowe), Helen. *The Night Watchmen.* Gr. 4–6. (Orig. British pub.**
✓ **1969.)**

Two tramps named Josh and Caleb tell Henry the secret of the Night Train. Carnegie Medal Honour Book, 1969; Phoenix Award, 1989.

Illus. by Gareth Floyd, Macmillan, 1970, 122 pp., o.p., pap. 1989, o.p.

(BL 67:371; CCBB 24:121; HB 46:615; KR 38:1146; LJ 96:2128; Suth:94)

CRESSWELL (Rowe), Helen. *Up the Pier.* See Chapter 8, Time Travel Fantasy.

77 **CRESSWELL (Rowe), Helen. *The Winter of the Birds.* Gr. 5–8. (Orig. British**
✓ **pub. 1975.)**

Neighbors unite when old Mr. Rudge foretells the coming of "terrible steel birds" that kill live birds and bring evil to the town.

Macmillan, 1976, 243 pp. o.p.

(BL 72:1404; CCBB 30:80; Ch&Bks:262; HB 52:404; KR 44:482; SLJ Sept 1976 p. 130; TLS 1975 p. 1457)

78 **CROTHERS, Samuel McChord. *Miss Muffet's Christmas Party.* Gr. 4–6. (Written 1891, orig. U.S. pub. 1902.)**

Miss Muffet and the spider invite all of her favorite literary characters to their Christmas party.

Illus. by Olive M. Long, Houghton, 1929, 106 pp., o.p.

(BL 25:401; LJ 53:810; Mahony 2:278)

CUMMINGS, e(dward) e(stlin). *Fairy Tales.* See Chapter 3, Fantasy Collections.

79 **CUNNINGHAM, Julia (Woolfolk). *Come to the Edge.* Gr. 5–7.**

Unable to trust adults after his father's betrayal and the loss of his friend, Gravel Winter continually runs away from foster homes.

Pantheon, 1977, 79 pp., o.p.; Avon, 1985, pap., o.p.

(BL 74:37; CCBB 31:11; HB 53:449; KR 45:4; SLJ May 1977 p. 60)

80 **CUNNINGHAM, Julia (Woolfolk). *Dorp Dead.* Gr. 5 up. (Orig. pub. Pantheon**
✓ **1965.)**

Gilly is taken from an unhappy life in an orphanage to an even more miserable foster home, from which he escapes to avoid being kept in a cage.

Illus. by James J. Spanfeller, Pantheon, 1965, LB(0-394-91089-3); Knopf, 1993, pap., 96 pp. (0-679-84718-9)

(CCBB 19:30; Ch&Bks:280; Eakin:87; JHC:351; LJ 90:2018)

CUNNINGHAM, Julia (Woolfolk). *Maybe, a Mole.* See Chapter 2, Animal Fantasy.

81 **CUNNINGHAM, Julia (Woolfolk). *Oaf.* Gr. 4–6.**

Oaf, who has inherited three magic gifts, shares a dangerous adventure with a crow, a dog, a cat, and a rat.

Illus. by Peter Sis, Knopf, 1986, 86 pp., o.p.

(BBC:201; BL 82:1016; CCBB 39:144; KR 54:544; SLJ Apr 1986 p. 86)

82 **CUNNINGHAM, Julia (Woolfolk).** *Tuppenny.* **Gr. 5–8.**

✓ The appearance of a young girl named Tuppenny changes the lives of three families: one whose daughter ran away from home, one whose retarded daughter is institutionalized, and one whose daughter was murdered.

Dutton, 1978, o.p.; Avon, 1981, pap., 96 pp., o.p.

(BL 75:371; CCBB 32:112; HB 55:639; KR 46:1309; SLJ Nov 1978 p. 72; Suth 2:111)

CUNNINGHAM, Julia (Woolfolk). *Viollet.* See Chapter 2, Animal Fantasy.

83 **CUNNINGHAM, Julia (Woolfolk).** *Wolf Roland.* **Gr. 6–8.**

A medieval peddler hunts down the huge yellow-eyed wolf that devoured his donkey friend, and the talking wolf agrees to take the donkey's place.

Pantheon, 1983, 108 pp., o.p.

(BBJ:69; BL 79:1214; KR 51:522; SLJ May 1983 p. 80)

CURLEY, Daniel. *Ann's Spring.* See Chapter 5B, Myth Fantasy.

CURLEY, Daniel. *Billy Beg and the Bull.* See Chapter 5B, Myth Fantasy.

84 **CURRY, Jane Louise.** *Little Little Sister.* **Gr. K–3.**

✓ A forgetful older brother is saved three times by a sister so tiny that she can stow away in his pocket.

Illus. by Erik Blegvad, Macmillan, 1989, 32 pp., o.p.

(BL 86:741; CCBB 43:53; HB 65:767; HBG 1[July–Dec 1989]:81; KR 57:1472; SLJ Nov 1989 p. 78)

85 **DAHL, Roald.** *Two Fables.* **Gr. 10 up. (Orig. British pub. 1986.)**

Two adult fairy tales: "The Princess and the Poacher" and "Princess Mammalia," the former about a man rewarded by a king with the choice of any woman in the kingdom, and the latter about a plain princess turned pretty who misuses her power.

Illus. by Graham Dean, Farrar, 1987, 61 pp. (0-374-28018-5)

(BBS 55; BL 84:26, 54)

DALKEY, Kara. *The Nightingale.* See Chapter 5B, Myth Fantasy.

86 **DAMJAN, Mischa (pseud.).** *December's Travels.* **Gr. 2–4. (Orig. German pub. 1986.)**

The North Wind gives the boy, December, the magic gift of being able to visit March, June, and October. These visits give him a new appreciation of his winter home.

Illus. by Dušan Kállay, trans. by Anthea Bell, Dial, 1986, 32 pp. (0-8037-0257-4)

(BBC:202; BL 83:127, 138; CCBB 40:103; SLJ Nov 1986 p. 74)

87 **DANK, Gloria Rand.** *The Forest of App.* **Gr. 4–6.**

A young Rhymer, or storyteller, named Nob runs away and gets lost in an enchanted forest, where he helps the creatures recover their lost magic.

Greenwillow, 1983, 154 pp., o.p.

(BBJ:70; CCBB 37:84; KR 51:202; SLJ Feb 1984 p. 67)

DANN, Colin (Michael). *The Animals of Farthing Wood.* See Chapter 2, Animal Fantasy.

88 **DAVIES, Valentine.** *The Miracle on 34th Street.* **Gr. 4–7. (Orig. pub. 1947.)**

Old Mr. Kringle tries to convince skeptics that he is Santa Claus, and gets a job as Macy's Christmas Santa to prove it.

Harcourt, 1947 (0-15-160239-5); illus. by Tomie dePaola, Harcourt, 1984, 116 pp. (0-15-254526-3), 1987, pap. (0-15-254528-X)

(BBJ:70; BL 43:359, 81:190, 211, 245, 247; CCBB 38:43; KR 15:316; LJ 72:1033; SLJ Oct 1984 p. 175)

89 **DAY, David.** *The Emperor's Panda.* **Gr. 3–5. (Orig. Canadian pub. 1986.)**

Wise and magical Lord Beishung, the Master Panda, helps young Kung, a poor flute player, gain wisdom, a princess, and an empire.

Illus. by Eric Beddows, Dodd, 1987, 111 pp., o.p.

(BBC:202; BL 83:1599; SLJ Aug 1987 p. 81)

DEAN, Pamela. *Tam Lin.* See Chapter 5B, Myth Fantasy.

90 **DE FELICE, Cynthia.** *The Strange Night Writing of Jessamine Colter.* **Gr. 5–8.**

✓ Jessie Colter's calligraphic talent has enabled her to record most of her home town's important events over the years, but even she is surprised that she can see into the future, and that what she involuntarily writes at night will actually come to pass.

Calligraphy by Leah Palmer Preiss, Macmillan, 1988, 51 pp. (0-02-726451-3)

(BBJ:70; BL 85:264; CCBB 42:5; KR 56:1058; SLJ Nov 1988 p. 124; VOYA 12:26)

DE LA MARE, Walter (John). *The Three Royal Monkeys.* See Chapter 2, Animal Fantasy.

DE LINT, Charles. *Dreams Underfoot: The Newford Collection.* See Chapter 5A, Alternate Worlds or Histories.

DE LINT, Charles. *Jack the Giant-Killer.* See Chapter 5B, Myth Fantasy.

DELL, Joan. *The Missing Boy.* See Chapter 5C, Travel to Other Worlds.

DE MORGAN, Mary (Augusta). *The Necklace of Princess Fiorimonde; and Other Stories.* See Chapter 3, Fantasy Collections.

DE REGNIERS, Beatrice Schenk (Freedman). *The Boy, the Rat, and the Butter-fly.* See Chapter 7, Magic Adventure Fantasy.

91 **DE REGNIERS, Beatrice Schenk (Freedman).** *Penny.* **Gr. 1–4. (Orig. pub.,**
✓ **illus. by Marvin Bileck, Viking, 1966, o.p.)**

Penny is a tiny girl "no bigger than a penny" who is adopted and raised by an elderly couple, marries a young man just her size, and goes to live in the land of tiny people.

Illus. by Betsy Lewin, Lothrop, 1987, 59 pp., o.p.

(BL 83:1204; CCBB 20:107; HB 42:705; KR 34:1096, 55:135; LJ 91:6184)

92 **DIAMOND, Donna (adapt.).** *Swan Lake.* **Gr. 3 up.**

Prince Siegfried falls in love with the Swan Queen Odette but is fooled by a sorcerer into pledging his love to her lookalike, Odille.

Illus. by the adaptor, Holiday, 1981, 32 pp., o.p.

(BL 76:1289; KR 48:1082; SLJ May 1980 p. 66)

93 **DICKENS, Charles (John Huffam).** *A Christmas Carol.* **Gr. 3 up. (Orig. British**
✓ **pub. 1843.)**

Mean old Ebenezer Scrooge is cured of his miserliness when he is visited by the ghosts of Christmases Past, Present, and Yet to Come.

Illus. by Arthur Rackham, Lippincott, 1952, o.p.; illus. by John Groth, Macmillan, 1963, o.p.; illus. by Michael Foreman, Dial, 1983, 128 pp. (0-8037-0032-6); illus. by Trina

Schart Hyman, Holiday, 1983, 128 pp. (0-8234-0486-2); illus. by Greg Hildebrandt, Simon, 1983, 122 pp. (0-671-45599-0); illus. by Lisbeth Zwerger, Picture Book, 1988, pap., 65 pp. (0-88708-069-3); illus. by Roberto Innocenti, Stewart, 1990, 152 pp. (1-55670-161-6)

(BL 49:147, 58:194, 80:169, 406, 630, 633, 87:817; Bookshelf 1928 p. 35; CC:479; CCBB 37:46; HB 59:731, 64:762, 67:198; HBG 2[July–Dec 1990]:65; HBG 5:64,65; KR 29:564; LJ 86:4046; SLJ Oct 1983 p. 179, Mar 1984 p. 172, Oct 1990 p. 36)

94   **DICKENS, Charles (John Huffam).** *The Magic Fishbone.* **Gr. 3–5. (Orig.**
✓   **British pub. 1868.)**

Exhausted from caring for her nineteen brothers and sisters, Princess Alice is given a magic fishbone that will grant one wish.

Illus. by Louis Slobodkin, Vanguard, 1953, 36 pp., o.p.

(Bookshelf 1923–1924 p. 8; Eakin:99; HB 1[June 1925]:45; LJ 78:2226; Mahony 1:38; TLS 1971 p. 774)

DICKINSON, Peter (pseud. of Malcolm de Brissac). *The Blue Hawk.* See Chapter 5A, Alternate Worlds or Histories.

95   **DICKINSON, Peter (pseud. of Malcolm de Brissac).** *Giant Cold.* **Gr. 4–6. (Orig. British pub. 1983.)**

Giant Cold has awakened and turned tropical Apple Island to ice; when "you" try to stop the Giant, "you" are reduced to Lilliputian size.

Illus. by Alan E. Cober, Dutton, 1984, 69 pp., o.p.

(BCC:202; CCBB 37:184; HB 60:50; SLJ Apr 1984 p. 122; TLS May 1984 p. 558)

96   **DICKINSON, Peter (pseud. of Malcolm de Brissac).** *The Iron Lion.* **Gr. 2–4.**
✓   Princess Yasmin challenges Prince Mustapha to bring her the Iron Lion of Ferdustan, in order to win her hand in marriage.

Illus. by Marc Brown, Little, 1972, o.p.; illus. by Pauline Baynes, Bedrick, 1984 (orig. British pub. in this ed. 1983), 32 pp., o.p.

(CCBB 25:120; HB 60:591; KR 40:135; LJ 97:1594; SLJ Nov 1984 p. 106; TLS 1973 p. 1431)

97   **DOBBS, Rose.** *The Discontented Village.* **Gr. 4–6.**

A thick fog of gloom hangs over a pleasant town until a mysterious stranger teaches the villagers about contentment.

Illus. by Beatrice Tobias, Coward, 1946, 31 pp., o.p.

(BL 43:173; HB 23:108; LJ 71:1466)

98   **DOBBS, Rose.** *No Room: An Old Story Retold.* **Gr. 3–5.**
✓   An old man who wishes to avoid sharing his house with his daughter's family, is given some unexpected advice.

Illus. by Fritz Eichenberg, McKay, 1944, 44 pp., o.p.

(BL 41:61; HB 20:375; KR 12:429; LJ 69:763, 865)

DOLBIER, Maurice (Wyman). *A Lion in the Woods.* See Chapter 6, Humorous Fantasy.

99   **DOLBIER, Maurice (Wyman).** *Torten's Christmas Secret.* **Gr. 2–4.**
✓   Torten, one of Santa's elves, decides to make his own gifts for the not-so-good children overlooked by Santa.

Illus. by Robert Henneberger, Little, 1951, 61 pp., o.p.

(BL 48:51; CCBB 5:28; HB 27:401, 415; KR 19:388; LJ 76:1342)

100   **DONEHOWER, Bruce.** *Miko, Little Hunter of the North.* **Gr. 3–5.**

Young Miko takes his reindeer through the freezing winter-long night to rescue Ravna, daughter of the sun and the moon, whose release will bring the sun back to Lapland.

Illus. by Tom Pohrt, Farrar, 1990, 89 pp., o.p.

(BL 86:1799, 87:637; CCBB 43:236; HBG 1[Jan–June 1990]:257; SLJ Aug 1990 p. 146)

DONOVAN, John. *Family: A Novel.* See Chapter 2, Animal Fantasy.

***Don't Bet on the Prince: Contemporary Feminist Fairy Tales in North America and England.* Ed. by Jack Zipes.** See Chapter 3, Fantasy Collections.

101   **DRUON, Maurice (Samuel Roger Charles).** *Tistou of the Green Thumbs.* **Gr.**
✓   **4–6. (Orig. French pub. 1957; British title:** *Tistou of the Green Fingers.***)**

Tistou makes flowers bloom, bringing beauty and happiness into the world and stopping a war.

Trans. by Humphrey Hare, illus. by Jacqueline Duhème, Scribner, 1958, 178 pp., o.p.

(BL 55:221; CCBB 12:130; HB 34:382, 61:84; KR 26:659; LJ 83:3006; TLS Nov 21, 1958 p. x)

DU BOIS, William (Sherman) Pène. *Lazy Tommy Pumpkinhead.* See Chapter 6, Humorous Fantasy.

DU BOIS, William (Sherman) Pène. *Otto and the Magic Potatoes.* See Chapter 6, Humorous Fantasy.

102   **DUNBAR, Aldis.** *Once There Was a Prince.* **Gr. 5–7. (Orig. pub. in England.)**

Opposed to the oppression of his people, a young prince escapes in disguise to a neighboring land to learn how to rule fairly and wisely.

Illus. by Maurice Day, Little, 1928, 302 pp., o.p.

(BL 25:216; HB 4:27)

DUNSANY, Lord (pseud. of Edward John Morton Drax Plunkett). *The Charwoman's Shadow.* See Chapter 10, Witchcraft and Sorcery Fantasy.

DUNSANY, Lord (pseud. of Edward John Morton Drax Plunkett). *The King of Elfland's Daughter.* See Chapter 5A, Alternate Worlds or Histories.

EDMONDS, Walter D. *Beaver Valley.* See Chapter 2, Animal Fantasy.

EHRLICH, Amy. *Lucy's Winter Tale.* See Chapter 7, Magic Adventure Fantasy.

103   **ELIOT, Ethel (Augusta) Cook.** *The Wind Boy.* **Gr. 5–6. (Orig. pub. 1923.)**
✓   A winged boy from the Clear Land comes to play with two refugee children awaiting their father's return from war.

Illus. by Robert Hallock, Viking, 1945, 244 pp., o.p.

(BL 20:105, 42:61; Bookshelf 1927 p. 7; HB 22:213; KR 13:370; LJ 70:980; Mahony 2:278)

***The Enchanter's Spell: Five Famous Tales.* Adapt. by Gennady Spirin.** See Chapter 3, Fantasy Collections.

ENDE, Michael. *Momo.* See Chapter 5A, Alternate Worlds or Histories.

104   **ENRIGHT, Elizabeth (Wright).** *Tatsinda.* **Gr. K–4.**
✓   In love with an outcast girl named Tatsinda, Prince Tackatan of Tatrajan determines to rescue her from the horrible giant who has kidnapped her.

Illus. by Irene Haas, Harcourt, 1963, 80 pp., o.p.; illus. by Katie Thamer Treherne, Harcourt, 1991, 64 pp. (0-15-284280-2)

(BL 59:896, 89:1830; CCBB 16:159; Ch&Bks:285; Eakin:109; HB 39:382; HBG 2[Fall 1991]:257; KR 61:454; LJ 88:2774; SLJ July 1991 p. 56; TLS 1964 p. 1081)

105   **ERSHOV, Petr Pavlovich.** *The Little Hump-backed Horse: A Russian Tale.* **Gr.**
✓   **3–5. (Orig. U.S. pub. Harper, 1931, entitled** *Humpy,* **o.p.; Macmillan, 1942, entitled** *Little Magic Horse,* **o.p.; Putnam, 1942, entitled** *The Little Hunchback Horse,* **o.p.)**

Ivan the Fool's magical horse helps him defeat his enemies, win a bride, and become tsar of Russia.

Adapt. by Margaret Hodges from a poem by Petr Pavlovich Ershov, trans. by Gina Kovarsky, illus. by Chris Conover, Farrar, 1980, 25 pp., o.p., 1987, pap., 32 pp. (0-374-44495-1)

(BL 28:354, 39:298, 77:513; CCBB 34:172; HB 19:34, 57:61; KR 48:1461; LJ 56:1058, 67:883, 68:38, 173; SLJ Dec 1980 p. 44)

106   **ESSEX, Rosamund (Sibyl).** *Into the Forest.* **Gr. 5–7. (Orig. British pub. 1963.)**

Five children abandoned during the Great Destruction undertake a dangerous journey through the forest in search of a better world.

Coward-McCann, 1965, 156 pp., o.p.

(BL 62:716; KR 33:907; LJ 90:5512)

EUSTIS, Helen. *Mr. Death and the Redheaded Woman.* See Chapter 6, Humorous Fantasy.

Faery! **Ed. by Terri Windling.** See Chapter 3, Fantasy Collections.

107   **FALKBERGET, Johan (Petter).** *Broomstick and Snowflake.* **Gr. 2–4. (Orig. pub. in Norway.)**

Broomstick, the tanner's son, meets the North Mountain Giant's daughter, Snowflake.

Illus. by Helen Sewell, Macmillan, 1933, 88 pp., o.p.

(BL 30:123; Bookshelf 1933 p. 5; HB 9:205; Mahony 3:172)

The Fantastic Imagination: An Anthology of High Fantasy, **vol. I. Ed. by Robert H. Boyer and Kenneth J. Zohorski.** See Chapter 5A, Alternate Worlds or Histories.

FARBER, Norma. *Six Impossible Things Before Breakfast.* See Chapter 3, Fantasy Collections.

FARJEON, Eleanor. *The Glass Slipper.* See Chapter 5B, Myth Fantasy.

FARJEON, Eleanor. *The Little Bookroom: Eleanor Farjeon's Short Stories for Children Chosen by Herself.* See Chapter 3, Fantasy Collections.

108   **FARJEON, Eleanor.** *Martin Pippin in the Apple Orchard.* **Gr. 5–7. (Orig. British pub. 1921, U.S., Stokes, 1922.)**

A minstrel named Martin Pippin frees an imprisoned farm girl by entertaining her six guards with his tales. The sequel is *Martin Pippin in the Daisy Field* (1937, 1963).

Illus. by Richard Kennedy, Lippincott, 1949, 1961, 305 pp., o.p.

(BL 19:53, 58:112; HB 37:557; KR 29:670; Mahony 2:279)

FARJEON, Eleanor. *The Silver Curlew.* See Chapter 5B, Myth Fantasy.

FARMER (Mockridge), Penelope. *A Castle of Bone.* See Chapter 5B, Myth Fantasy.

FARMER (Mockridge), Penelope. *The Summer Birds.* See Chapter 7, Magic Adventure Fantasy.

FAST, Howard (Melvin). *The General Zapped an Angel: New Stories of Fantasy and Science Fiction.* See Chapter 3, Fantasy Collections.

109   **FENTON, Edward.** *The Nine Questions.* **Gr. 5–7.**

✓   Willy and Gabriella use a magical silver whistle and hunting cap to rescue the king, Willy's father.

Illus. by C. Walter Hodges, Doubleday, 1959, 235 pp., o.p.

(BL 56:125; HB 36:129; KR 27:495; LJ 85:1302)

110   **FENWICK, Elizabeth.** *Cockleberry Castle.* **Gr. 3–5.**

When the prince throws a banquet for the other palace children, they are afraid they are about to be punished.

Illus. by Fabio Rieti, Pantheon, 1963, 74 pp., o.p.

(KR 32:3; LJ 88:2550)

111   **FLEISCHMAN, Paul (Taylor).** *The Birthday Tree.* **Gr. 3–4.**

✓   An ex-sailor and his wife try to avoid losing a fourth son to the sea by moving inland and planting a Birthday Tree in honor of his birth.

Illus. by Marcia Sewall, Harper, 1979, 32 pp., LB(0-06-021916-5), pap. (0-06-443246-7)

(BBC:203; BL 75:1535; CC:484; KR 47:573; SLJ Sept 1979 p. 110)

112   **FLEISCHMAN, Paul (Taylor).** *Coming-and-Going Men: Four Tales.* **Gr. 6–9.**

✓   Four interconnected stories involving artisans and tradesmen passing through the town of New Canaan, Vermont, in 1800: a silhouette cutter who battles the devil, a poet who saves a man's soul, three artists whose works are destroyed, and a peddler who gives a woman back her life.

Illus. by Randy Gaul, Harper, 1985, 160 pp., LB(0-06-021884-3)

(BL 81:1390, 1399; CCBB 39:7; HB 61:315; KR 53:J32; SLJ 31[Aug 1985]:75; Suth 4:117; VOYA 8:184)

FLEISCHMAN, Paul (Taylor). *Finzel the Farsighted.* See Chapter 6, Humorous Fantasy.

FLEISCHMAN, Paul (Taylor). *The Half-a-Moon Inn.* See Chapter 10, Witchcraft and Sorcery Fantasy.

113   **FLEISCHMAN, (Albert) Sid(ney).** *The Hey Hey Man.* **Gr. 2–4.**

✓   A wood spirit called the Hey Hey Man magically punishes a thief who has stolen a farmer's gold.

Illus. by Nadine Bernard Westcott, Atlantic, 1979, 32 pp., o.p.

(BL 76:42; HB 55:527; KR 47:1141; SLJ Sept. 1979 p. 135)

FLEISCHMAN, (Albert) Sid(ney). *The Whipping Boy.* See Chapter 5A, Alternate Worlds or Histories.

FLORA, James (Royer). *Wanda and the Bumbly Wizard.* See Chapter 10, Witchcraft and Sorcery Fantasy.

114 **FLORY, Jane Trescott.** *The Lost and Found Princess.* **Gr. 2–4.**

Clues dropped by three robbers enable a cat, a dragon, and an old woman to rescue a captive princess.

Illus. by the author, Houghton, 1979, 48 pp., o.p.

(BL 75:1156; KR 47:518; SLJ Apr 1979 p. 42)

115 **FOLLETT, Barbara Newhall.** *The House Without Windows and Eepersip's Life There.* **Gr. 4–6.**

In this story written by a 9-year-old, a lonely little girl runs away to the woods, where she becomes a dryad.

Knopf, 1927, 166 pp., o.p.

(BL 23:347; HB 3:41; Mahony 2:279; Moore:427)

FORD, Richard. *Quest for the Faradawn.* See Chapter 2, Animal Fantasy.

116 **FORST, S.** *Pipkin.* **Gr. 1–4.**

Pipkin, the lost prince of the gnomes, is cared for by an old woman until he is able to find his way back into the Ladybug Kingdom.

Illus. by Robin Jacques, Delacorte, 1970, 144 pp., o.p.

(HB 46:476; LJ 96:1007)

117 **FOSTER, Malcolm (Burton).** *The Prince with a Hundred Dragons.* **Gr. 2–4.**

A gentle dragon agrees to help Prince Guy fool his father into thinking that Guy is a fearless dragon slayer.

Illus. by Barbara Remington, Doubleday, 1963, 60 pp., o.p.

(CCBB 17:138; KR 31:656; LJ 88:4083)

FOX (Greenberg), Paula. *The Little Swineherd and Other Tales.* See Chapter 3, Fantasy Collections.

FRANCE, Anatole. *Bee, the Princess of the Dwarfs.* See Chapter 5C, Travel to Other Worlds.

FRANKO, Ivan, and MELNYK, Bohdan. *Fox Mykyta.* See Chapter 2, Animal Fantasy.

118 **FREEMAN, Barbara C(onstance).** *Broom-Adelaide.* **Gr. 4–6. (Orig. British pub. 1963.)**

No one at the castle suspects that the governess, Madame Crowberry, is actually a witch.

Illus. by the author, Little, 1965, 124 pp., o.p.

(BL 62:219; HB 41:490; KR 33:626; LJ 90:3790; TLS 1963 p. 980)

119 **FRENCH, Fiona.** *The Magic Vase.* **Gr. 2–5.**

Maria, a Native American potter, teaches a greedy art dealer a lesson with the help of a talking snake, a bear, a rabbit, birds, and fish.

Illus. by the author, Oxford Univ. Pr., 1991, 32 pp. (0-19-279875-8)

(CCBB 45:124; HBG 3[Spring 1992]:33; KR 59:1342; SLJ April 1992 p. 91)

GACKENBACH, Dick. *Beauty, Brave and Beautiful.* See Chapter 2, Animal Fantasy.

120   GALLICO, Paul. *The Snow Goose.* **Gr. 6–12. (Orig. pub. 1940.)**

The wounded snow goose he nursed back to health watches over Rhayader as he braves the German bombardment to rescue English soldiers from the sea during the Battle of Dunkirk.

Knopf, 1941, 57 pp. (0-394-44593-7); illus. by Beth Peck, 1992, 32 pp. (0-679-80683-0)
(BL 89:137; HBG 4[Spring 1993]:68; SLJ Feb 1993 p. 93)

GARDNER, John (Champlin) (Jr.). *Dragon, Dragon, and Other Timeless Tales.* See Chapter 3, Fantasy Collections.

GARDNER, John (Champlin) (Jr.). *In the Suicide Mountains.* See Chapter 5A, Alternate Worlds or Histories.

GARFIELD, Leon. *The Wedding Ghost.* See Chapter 5B, Myth Fantasy.

GARNER, Alan. *Alan Garner's Fairytales of Gold.* See Chapter 3, Fantasy Collections.

GARNER, Alan. *Once Upon a Time: Though It Wasn't in Your Time, and It Wasn't in My Time, and It Wasn't in Anybody Else's Time....* See Chapter 3, Fantasy Collections.

GARNETT, David. *Two by Two: A Story of Survival.* See Chapter 5B, Myth Fantasy.

GATE, Ethel May. *The Fortunate Days.* See Chapter 3, Fantasy Collections.

GERRARD, Roy. *Sir Cedric.* See Chapter 6, Humorous Fantasy.

GERSTEIN, Mordicai. *The Seal Mother.* See Chapter 5B, Myth Fantasy.

121   GIBSON, Katharine. *Cinders.* **Gr. 3–5.**

Overlooked when Cinderella's fairy-godmother turned the other servants back into animals, Cinders the coachman decides to go into service to the king.

Illus. by Vera Bock, Longman, 1939, 133 pp., o.p.
(BL 36:17; HB 15:296; LJ 64:712)

122   GIBSON, Katharine. *Jock's Castle.* **Gr. 4–5.**

The hunter rescued by Jock the miller turns out to be Crown Prince Henry.

Illus. by Vera Bock, Longman, 1940, 139 pp., o.p.   ♦
(BL 37:18; HB 16:343; LJ 65:714, 849)

123   GIFALDI, David. *The Boy Who Spoke Colors.* **Gr. K–4.**

Imprisoned by a greedy king who wants to profit from young Felix's gift of speaking in colors, the boy and a servant girl try to escape.

Illus. by Shana C. Greger, Houghton, 1993, 32 pp. (0-395-65025-9)
(BL 89:1603; HBG 4[Fall 1993]:285; SLJ June 1993 p. 74)

GILMAN, Dorothy. *The Maze in the Heart of the Castle.* See Chapter 5C, Travel to Other Worlds.

124   GODDEN (Dixon), (Margaret) Rumer. *The Dragon of Og.* **Gr. 3–5. (Orig. pub.**
✓   in England.)

The stubborn new lord of Og wants to get rid of the gentle local dragon, against the advice of his wife and chief minister.

Illus. by Pauline Baynes, Viking, 1981, 60 pp., o.p.

(BBC:203; BL 78:706; CCBB 55:106; Ch&Bks:286; SLJ Nov 1981 p. 75; Suth 3:154)

125 **GODDEN (Dixon), (Margaret) Rumer.** *The Mousewife.* **Gr. 2–4. (Orig. British**
✓ **pub. 1951.)**

A little mouse sets a caged dove free, in return for wondrous descriptions of the outside world.

Illus. by William Pène du Bois, Viking, 1951, o.p.; illus. by Heidi Holder, Viking, 1982, 31 pp., o.p.

(BBC:204; BL 47:297, 79:777; CCBB 4:50, 36:46; Eakin:143; HB 27:93, 102; KR 19:61; LJ 76:781; TLS 1951 p. 9)

GOGOL, Nikolai. *The Nose.* See Chapter 6, Humorous Fantasy.

GOLDMAN, William W. *The Princess Bride.* See Chapter 5A, Alternate Worlds or Histories.

GOLDSTEIN, Lisa. *The Red Magician.* See Chapter 10, Witchcraft and Sorcery Fantasy.

GOODWIN, Harold Leland. *Magic Number.* See Chapter 2, Animal Fantasy.

126 **GOUDGE, Elizabeth (de Beauchamp).** *The Valley of Song.* **Gr. 5–8. (Orig.**
✓ **British pub. 1951.)**

Tabitha lifts the spirits of her town's disheartened shipbuilders by leading them into the Valley of Song.

Illus. by Richard Floethe, Coward, 1952, 281 pp., o.p.

(BL 49:92; CCBB 6:67; HB 28:395, 405; KR 20:552; LJ 77:1822; TLS 1951 p. 15)

127 **GRAHAME, Kenneth.** *The Reluctant Dragon.* **Gr. 4–6. (Orig. British pub. 1898**
✓✓ **in** *Dream Days;* **U.S. pub. 1938.)**

St. George and his young friend find a dragon that is not at all like the one they had intended to slay.

Illus. by Ernest Shepard, Holiday, 1938, 58 pp. (0-8234-0093-X), pap. (0-8234-0755-1); illus. by Michael Hague, Holt, 1983, 48 pp. (0-8050-1112-9); Holiday, 1989, pap., 48 pp. (0-8050-0802-0)

(BL 35:143, 80:680; CC:492; CCBB 7:29; Ch&Bks:286; Eakin:146; HB 15:29; LJ 64:118; SLJ Nov 1983 p. 77)

GRAHAME, Kenneth. *The Wind in the Willows.* See Chapter 2, Animal Fantasy.

GRAY, Nicholas Stuart. *Mainly in Moonlight: Ten Stories of Sorcery and the Supernatural.* See Chapter 3, Fantasy Collections.

GRAY, Nicholas Stuart. *A Wind from Nowhere.* See Chapter 3, Fantasy Collections.

128 **GREAVES, Margaret.** *A Net to Catch the Wind.* **Gr. 2–4.**

A king uses his young daughter to trap a unicorn, causing both the girl and the unicorn to fall ill.

Illus. by Stephen Gammell, Harper, 1979, 40 pp., o.p.

(BBC:204; BL 75:1438; KR 47:451; SLJ Sept 1979 p. 110)

GREENE, Jacqueline Dembar. *The Leveller.* See Chapter 5B, Myth Fantasy.

129   **GREGORY, Philippa.** *Florizella and the Wolves.* **Gr. 3–5. (Orig. British pub.**
✓   **1991.)**

Princess Florizella's parents insist that her four orphaned wolf cubs must be returned to
the wild, but one keeps finding its way back to the palace.

Illus. by Patrice Aggs, Candlewick, 1993, 80 pp. (1-56402-126-2)

(BL 89:1588; HBG 4[Fall 1993]:285; KR 61:371; SLJ May 1993 p. 105)

130   **GREGORY, Valiska.** *Through the Mickle Woods.* **Gr. 2–5.**

Despondent after the death of his queen, a king follows his wife's written instructions to
find a bear in the snowy mickle woods, give him her ring, and listen to the three stories he
tells.

Illus. by Barry Moser, Little, Brown, 1992, 32 pp. (0-316-32779-4)

(BL 89:675; HB 69:202; HBG 4[Spring 1993]:57; KR 60:1130; SLJ Dec 1992 p. 113)

GRIPARI, Pierre. *Tales of the Rue Broca.* See Chapter 3, Fantasy Collections.

GRIPE, Maria. *The Glassblower's Children.* See Chapter 10, Witchcraft and Sorcery Fantasy.

GRIPE, Maria. *In the Time of the Bells.* See Chapter 5A, Alternate Worlds or Histories.

GRIPE, Maria. *The Land Beyond.* See Chapter 5C, Travel to Other Worlds.

131   **GUILLOT, René.** *The Three Hundred Ninety-seventh White Elephant.* **Gr. 3–6.**
✓   **(Orig. pub. in France. British title:** *The Elephants of Sargabal.***)**

The young king is cured of his illness by Hong-Mo the Magnificent, a mysterious white
elephant who becomes leader of the royal herd. Two British sequels are *Master of the
Elephants* and *Great Land of the Elephant.*

Trans. by Gwen Marsh, illus. by Moyra Leatham, Phillips, 1957, 94 pp. (0-87599-043-6)

(BL 53:434; HB 33:221; KR 25:176; LJ 82:1102)

GUY, Rosa. *My Love, My Love, or the Peasant Girl.* See Chapter 5B, Myth Fantasy.

132   **HACKETT, Walter Anthony.** *The Swans of Ballycastle.* **Gr. 3–5.**
✓   Three children who were driven from home by their stepmother are changed into swans
and find refuge on an island where time stands still.

Illus. by Bettina, Ariel, 1954, 63 pp., o.p.

(BL 51:179; CCBB 8:51; HB 30:435; KR 22:479; LJ 79:2491)

133   **HALEY, Gail E(inhart).** *Sea Tale.* **Gr. K–4.**

Captain Tom O'Shaunessy falls in love with Princess Falilah, a mermaid in the Lovelorn
Islands, but must return to his crew, not knowing whether they will ever be reunited.

Illus. by the author, Dutton, 1990, 32 pp. (0-525-44567-6)

(BL 86:1343; HB 66:199; HBG 1[Jan–June 1990]:237; KR 58:104; SLJ Feb 1990 p. 74)

134   **HALLOWELL, Priscilla.** *The Long-Nosed Princess: A Fairy Tale.* **Gr. 3–5.**
✓   No one notices Princess Felicity's long nose until her self-centered fiancé brings it up.

Illus. by Rita Fava, Viking, 1959, 61 pp., o.p.

(BL 55:633; CCBB 12:168; HB 35:299; KR 27:88; LJ 84:2086)

HAMILTON, Virginia (Esther). *The Magical Adventures of Pretty Pearl.* See Chapter 5B, Myth Fantasy.

HAMLEY, Dennis. *Hare's Choice.* See Chapter 2, Animal Fantasy.

HANCOCK, Neil. *Dragon Winter.* See Chapter 2, Animal Fantasy.

HANSEN, Ron. *The Shadowmaker.* See Chapter 7, Magic Adventure Fantasy.

HASELEY, Dennis. *Ghost Catcher.* See Chapter 4, Ghost Fantasy.

135 **HAUFF, Wilhelm.** *The Adventures of Little Mouk.* **Gr. 3–4. (Orig. pub. in Germany.)**

Even Little Mouk's magic shoes and walking stick can't keep him out of the king's dungeon.

Trans. and adapt. by Elizabeth Shub, illus. by Monika Laimgruber, Macmillan, 1975, 36 pp., o.p.

(BL 71:866; CCBB 29:10; HB 51:257; KR 43:18; SLJ Apr 1975 p. 53)

HAUFF, Wilhelm. *The Caravan.* See Chapter 3, Fantasy Collections.

136 **HAUFF, Wilhelm.** *Dwarf Long-Nose.* **Gr. 3–5. (Orig. pub. in Germany; orig.**
✓ **U.S. pub. 1881, 1916.)**

Transformed into an ugly dwarf by a wicked fairy, Long-Nose becomes a chef in the Duke's kitchen and searches for a special herb to break the spell.

Trans. by Doris Orgel, illus. by Maurice Sendak, Random, 1960, 60 pp., o.p.

(BL 57:128; Eakin:151; HB 36:510; LJ 85; 3862)

HAUFF, Wilhelm. *The Fairy Tales of Wilhelm Hauff.* See Chapter 3, Fantasy Collections.

137 **HAUGAARD, Erik Christian.** *Prince Boghole.* **Gr. K–4.**
✓ King Desmond sends the three suitors for the hand of Princess Orla on a quest for the most magnificent of birds.

Illus. by Julie Downing, Macmillan, 1987, 32 pp. (0-02-743440-0).

(BL 83:1205; CCBB 40:146; Ch&Bks:256; KR 55:301; SLJ May 1987 p. 87)

138 **HAUGAARD, Erik Christian.** *Princess Horrid.* **Gr. K–5.**

A spoiled princess learns how to behave properly after she is transformed into a cat and adopted by the scullery maid.

Illus. by Dawson Hearn, Macmillan, 1990, 48 pp. (0-02-743445-1)

(BL 87:855; HBG 2[July–Dec 1990]:65; KR 58:1085; SLJ Nov 1990 p. 93)

HAWDON, Robin. *A Rustle in the Grass.* See Chapter 2, Animal Fantasy.

139 **HAWTHORNE, Julian.** *Rumpty-Dudget's Tower: A Fairy Tale.* **Gr. K–4. (Orig. pub. in** *St. Nicholas Magazine* **1879; orig. pub. in book form, illus. by George W. Hood, Stokes, 1924, o.p.)**

An evil dwarf named Rumpty-Dudget kidnaps Prince Henry and locks him in a tower in order to turn the world into a desert, in this story written by Nathaniel Hawthorne's son.

Adapt. and illus. by Diane Goode, Knopf, 1987, 48 pp., o.p.

(BL 21:237, 84:862; Bookshelf 1924–1925 Suppl. p. 1; HB 1[Nov 1924]:7; KR 55:1515; LJ 50:803; Mahony 2:281)

HAWTHORNE, Nathaniel. *The Snow Image.* See Chapter 3, Fantasy Collections.

140   **HAYWOOD, Carolyn.** *A Valentine Fantasy.* **Gr. 2–4.**

Valentine's refusal to shoot the golden-hearted bluebird causes the king to imprison him, but the bird sets him free.

Illus. by Glenys Ambrus and Victor Ambrus, Morrow, 1976, 32 pp., o.p.

(BL 72:1113; KR 44:316; SLJ Apr 1976 p. 60)

HAZEL, Paul. *Yearwood.* See Chapter 5A, Alternate Worlds or Histories.

HEARNE, Betsy. *South Star.* See Chapter 5A, Alternate Worlds or Histories.

141   **HEATH, W(illiam) L.** *The Earthquake Man.* **Gr. 4–6.**

Sinn Fein, a troll-catching tinsmith, convinces Rafe and Ansel O'Grady that he can rid their farm of the troll living under the footbridge.

Beaufort, 1980, 95 pp., o.p.

(KR 49:213; SLJ Jan 1981, p. 61)

142   **HELAKISA, Kaarina.** *The Journey of Pietari and His Wolf.* **Gr. 7 up. (Orig. Swedish pub. 1984.)**

Young Pietari leaves his beloved Meadow to restore hope and purity to a damaged and corrupted world.

Trans. by Michael Rollerson, illus. by Saara Tikka, Simon & Schuster, 1985, 72 pp., o.p., 1991, pap. (0-88138-043-1)

(BBJ:71; SLJ Oct 1985 p. 182)

HELPRIN, Mark. *Swan Lake.* See Chapter 5B, Myth Fantasy.

HELPRIN, Mark. *Winter's Tale.* See Chapter 5A, Alternate Worlds or Histories.

HESSE, Hermann. *Pictor's Metamorphoses and Other Fantasies.* See Chapter 3, Fantasy Collections.

HEWETT, Anita. *The Bull Beneath the Walnut Tree and Other Stories.* See Chapter 3, Fantasy Collections.

143   **HILGARTNER, Beth.** *A Necklace of Fallen Stars.* **Gr. 6–8.**

Princess Kaela runs away rather than marry the man her father has chosen for her.

Illus. by Michael R. Hague, Little, 1979, 209 pp., o.p.

(BL 76:558; KR 48:222; SLJ Oct 1979 p. 150)

144   **HOBAN, Russell C(onwell).** *The Marzipan Pig.* **Gr. 3–5.**

After a marzipan pig falls behind the sofa, his sweetness and loving thoughts are absorbed by the mouse that eats him, and by the owl that eats the mouse, in this gentle and whimsical tale.

Illus. by Quentin Blake, Farrar, 1987, 40 pp. (0-374-34859-6), 1989, pap. (0-374-44750-0)

(CCBB 40:210; KR 55:719; SLJ Sept 1987 p. 164; TLS Apr 3, 1987 p. 356)

145   **HOBAN, Russell C(onwell).** *The Mouse and His Child.* **Gr. 4 up.**

✓✓   A broken windup mouse and his son set out to find happiness but are pursued by an evil rat intent on enslaving them. This story can also be read as a satire on American society.

Illus. by Lillian Hoban, Harper, 1967, LB(0-06-022378-2); Dell, 1990, pap., 181 pp. (0-440-40293-X)

(BBC:205; BL 64:593; CC:502; CCBB 21:143; Ch&Bks:271; KR 35:1134; LJ 92:4612; Suth:185; TLS 1969 p. 357)

HOBAN, Russell C(onwell). *The Sea-Thing Child.* See Chapter 2, Animal Fantasy.

146 **HODGES, Elizabeth Jamison.** *The Three Princes of Serendip.* Gr. 4–6.

The King of Serendip's sons search throughout India and Persia for a dragon-killing potion to save their kingdom. The sequel is *Serendipity Tales* (1966).

Illus. by Joan Berg, Atheneum, 1964, 158 pp., o.p.

(BL 60:1002; HB 40:281; KR 32:108; LJ 89:2219)

HOFFMANN, E(rnst) T(heodor) A(madeus). *The Nutcracker.* See Chapter 9, Toy Fantasy.

147 **HOFFMANN, E(rnst) T(heodor) A(madeus).** *The Strange Child.* Gr. 4–6. (Orig. German pub. as part of a collection, 1857, orig. Austrian pub. in this edition, 1981.)

A mysterious child, the daughter of the queen of fairies, helps two human children get rid of their evil tutor.

Trans. and adapt. by Anthea Bell, illus. by Lisbeth Zwerger, Picture Book, 1984, 31 pp., o.p., 1991, 28 pp. (0-907234-60-7)

(BL 81:520; CC:433; CCBB 38:87; HB 61:177; SLJ Apr 1985 p. 88)

HOLDSTOCK, Robert. *The Emerald Forest.* See Chapter 5C, Travel to Other Worlds.

148 **HOLLANDER, John.** *The Quest of the Gole.* Gr. 6–8.

✓ Three princes search for the "Gole" to break the curse of darkness on their kingdom.

Illus. by Reginald Pollack, Atheneum, 1966, 116 pp., o.p.

(BL 63:418; HB 42:562; KR 34:982; LJ 91:4352)

HOLMAN (Valen), Felice. *The Blackmail Machine.* See Chapter 6, Humorous Fantasy.

149 **HOLT, Isabella.** *The Adventures of Rinaldo.* Gr. 4–6.

✓ Knight Rinaldo wins a bear, a stag, and a pig while searching for a wife and a castle.

Illus. by Erik Blegvad, Little, 1959, 142 pp., o.p.

(BL 55:458; HB 35:131; KR 27:7; LJ 84:643)

150 **HOOKS, William H(arris).** *The Ballad of Belle Dorcas.* Gr. 2–5.

✓ A conjure woman turns Belle's husband into a cedar tree to avoid his being sold to another master in this retelling of an African-American slave tale from the Carolina coast.

Illus. by Brian Pinkney, Knopf, 1990, 40 pp. LB(0-394-94645-6)

(BL 87:51; CC:504; CCBB 44:87; HB 67:208; HBG 2[July–Dec 1990]:101; KR 58:1087; SLJ Oct 1990 p. 116; Suth 4:184)

151 **HOOKS, William H(arris).** *Moss Gown.* Gr. K–4.

✓ Candace, disowned by her father and cast out by her older sisters, returns to their home as a scullery maid after she has been befriended by a witch. This rendition of a traditional southern tale contains elements of "King Lear" and "Cinderella."

Illus. by Donald Carrick, Houghton, 1987, 48 pp. (0-89919-460-5), 1990, pap. (0-395-54793-8)

(BL 83:1206; CCBB 40:127; HB 63:599; KR 55:638; SLJ May 1987 p. 87, Dec 1987 p. 37)

152   HOPE, Christopher. *The Dragon Wore Pink.* **Gr. K–3. (Orig. British pub. 1985.)**

A dragon and a little girl, both rejected by their peers for being different, make friends and fly away to find a new home.

Illus. by Angela Barrett, Macmillan, 1985, 32 pp., o.p.

(CCBB 39:87; SLJ Aug 1986 p. 83; TLS Nov 29, 1985 p. 1359)

HORWITZ, Elinor Lander. *The Strange Story of the Frog Who Became a Prince.* See Chapter 10, Witchcraft and Sorcery Fantasy.

HORWOOD, William. *Duncton Wood.* See Chapter 2, Animal Fantasy.

153   HOUSMAN, Laurence. *Cotton-Wooleena.* **Gr. 2–4. (Orig. British pub. in this format, 1967.)**

A newly crowned king discovers that a haughty fairy named Cotton-Wooleena has been ruling his country for the past 300 years.

Illus. by Robert Binks, Doubleday, 1974, 58 pp., o.p.

(BL 70:1056; KR 42:425; LJ 99:2270)

HOUSMAN, Laurence. *The Rat-Catcher's Daughter: A Collection of Stories.* See Chapter 3, Fantasy Collections.

154   HOWARD, Alice Woodbury. *Ching-Li and the Dragons.* **Gr. 2–4.**

Young King Ching Wong's magical jade flute sends him off to rescue a mighty dragon.

Illus. by Lynd Ward, Macmillan, 1931, 55 pp., o.p.

(BL 28:265; HB 7:322; Mahony 3:205)

HUDSON, W(illiam) H(enry). *Green Mansions: A Romance of the Tropical Forest.* See Chapter 5C, Travel to Other Worlds.

155   HUDSON, W(illiam) H(enry). *A Little Boy Lost: A Tale for Children.* **Gr. 4–6.**
✓   (Orig. British pub. 1905; U.S. Knopf, 1918.)

A little boy following a mirage becomes lost in the wilds of South America, much to his delight.

Illus. by A. D. McCormick, Knopf, 1923, 1946, 1951, o.p.; illus. by Dorothy P. Lathrop, Knopf, 1920, 1939, o.p.; AMS (repr. of 1923 ed.), 222 pp. (0-440-03403-9)

(BL 15:15, 35:70; Bookshelf 1932 p. 8; HB 14:147; LJ 63:817, 847, 76:660; Mahony 2:281)

HUGHES, Ted (Edward James). *How the Whale Became.* See Chapter 2, Animal Fantasy.

156   HUGHES, Ted (Edward James). *The Iron Giant: A Story in Five Nights* **(British title:** *The Iron Man***). Gr. 3–6.**

The people ask the Iron Giant for help against the hungry space-bat-angel-dragon who is terrorizing them.

Illus. by Robert Nadler, Harper, 1968, 1988, 58 pp., LB(0-06-022639-0), 1987, pap., 66 pp. (0-06-440214-2)

(BBC:205; BL 65:496; CCBB 41:208; KR 36:114; Suth 4:194; TLS 1968 p. 256)

157   HUNTER, Mollie (pseud. of Maureen Mollie Hunter McVeigh McIlwraith).
✓   *The Kelpie's Pearls.* **Gr. 4–6. (Orig. British pub. 1964, U.S. Funk, 1966.)**

The pearl necklace that a water sprite gives to Morag MacLeod causes the old woman to be accused of witchcraft.

Harper, 1976, 112 pp., o.p.

(BBC:205; BL 63:451; CC:507; CCBB 20:109; Ch&Bks:287; HB 42:710; KR 34:688; LJ 91:5231; TLS 1964 p. 1081)

158 **HUNTER, Mollie (pseud. of Maureen Mollie Hunter McVeigh McIlwraith).**
✓ ***The Knight of the Golden Plain.* Gr. 1–4.**

Daydreaming, a young boy is transformed into Sir Dauntless, Knight of the Golden Plain, who battles dragons, witches, and a nasty wizard to save the maiden Dorabella. The sequels are *The Three-Day Enchantment* (1985) and *Day of the Unicorn* (1994).

Illus. by Marc Simont, Harper, 1983, 48 pp., LB(0-06-022686-2)

(BBC:205; BL 80:86; CCBB 37:51; Ch&Bks:268; HB 60:54; KR 51:162; SLJ Sept 1983 p. 108)

159 **INGRAM, Tom (Thomas Henry).** *Garranane.* **Gr. 4–6. (British title:** *The Hungry Cloud,* **1971.)**

Prince Kai and Princess Flor flee after discovering that the mysterious Miss Fenrir has trapped the King and Queen within her drawings.

Illus. by Bill Geldart, Bradbury, 1972, 191 pp., o.p.

(BL 69:302; KR 40:623; LJ 98:261; TLS 1971 p. 767)

IPCAR, Dahlov (Zorach). *The Queen of Spells.* See Chapter 5B, Myth Fantasy.

IPCAR, Dahlov (Zorach). *The Warlock of Night.* See Chapter 10, Witchcraft and Sorcery Fantasy.

IRVING, Washington. *The Legend of Sleepy Hollow.* See Chapter 5B, Myth Fantasy.

IRVING, Washington. *Rip Van Winkle.* See Chapter 5B, Myth Fantasy.

***Isaac Asimov's Magical Worlds of Fantasy: Faeries.* Ed. by Isaac Asimov, Martin H. Greenberg, and Charles G. Waugh.** See Chapter 3, Fantasy Collections.

ISH-KISHOR, Sulamith. *The Master of Miracle: A New Novel of the Golem.* See Chapter 5B, Myth Fantasy.

JACQUES, Brian. *Redwall.* See Chapter 2, Animal Fantasy.

160 **JARRELL, Randall.** *The Animal Family.* **Gr. 4–6.**
✓ A lonely hunter and a mermaid fall in love and acquire a family consisting of a bear cub, a lynx kitten, and a shipwrecked boy. John Newbery Medal Honor Book, 1966.

Illus. by Maurice Sendak, Pantheon, 1965, 1985, 200 pp. (0-685-10494-X)

(BBC:206; BL 62:487; CC:510; CCBB 19:100; Ch&Bks:264; Eakin:171; HB 42:45, 61:714716, 737; LJ 90:5516; TLS 1976 p. 392)

161 **JOHNSON, Elizabeth.** *The Little Knight.* **Gr. 3–5.**
✓ To avoid marrying a stranger, Princess Lenora dons armor and sets out to win the contest to determine the bravest knight in the land.

Illus. by Ronni Solbert, Little, 1957, 56 pp., o.p.

(BL 54:28; HB 33:400; KR 25:412; LJ 82:2191)

162 **JOHNSON, Elizabeth.** *The Three-in-One Prince.* **Gr. 3–4.**
✓ All three of King Frederick's sons enter the competition for Princess Alicia Anastasia Alfreda Anne's hand, but only Prince John, the middle son, can prove he is "three in one."

Illus. by Ronni Solbert, Little, 1961, 58 pp., o.p.

(BL 57:498; HB 37:261; KR 29:102; LJ 86:1689)

JONES, Adrienne. *The Hawks of Chelney.* See Chapter 5A, Alternate Worlds or Histories.

JONES, David Lee. *Unicorn Highway.* See Chapter 7, Magic Adventure Fantasy.

JONES, Diana Wynne. *Cart and Cwidder.* See Chapter 5A, Alternate Worlds or Histories.

JONES, Terry. *Fantastic Stories.* See Chapter 6, Humorous Fantasy.

163   **JONES, Terry.** *The Saga of Erik the Viking.* **Gr. 4–6. (Orig. British pub. 1983.)**

A band of Vikings has a series of fantastic adventures while searching for the land where the sun goes at night.

Illus. by Michael Foreman, Schocken, 1983, o.p.; Puffin, 1983, pap., 144 pp. (0-14-032261-2)

(BBC:206; CCBB 37:149; SLJ Jan 1984 p. 78)

JUSTER, Norton. *Alberic the Wise and Other Journeys.* See Chapter 3, Fantasy Collections.

JUSTER, Norton. *The Phantom Tollbooth.* See Chapter 5C, Travel to Other Worlds.

164   **KARPIN, Florence.** *The Prince in the Golden Tower.* **Gr. 1–4.**

Nurvah, the god of creation and destruction, punishes a miserly emperor who reneged on a promise to give his gold to the poor in return for a son, by kidnapping the boy.

Illus. by David Palladini, Viking, 1989, 32 pp., o.p.

(BL 86:1005; HBG 1[July 1989]:59; KR 57:1530; SLJ Mar 1990 p. 194)

KÄSTNER, Erich. *The Animal's Conference.* See Chapter 2, Animal Fantasy.

165   **KAVANAUGH, James.** *A Fable.* **Gr. 6 up.**

A parable about the effect of greed on the contented villagers of Harmony after a stranger seduces them with gold.

Illus. by Daniel Biamonte, Dutton, 1980, 64 pp., o.p.

(BBS:59; BL 77:394, 400; KR 48:1179; SLJ Mar 1981 p. 157)

166   **KAYE, M(argaret) M(ary).** *The Ordinary Princess.* **Gr. 3–6. (Orig. British pub.**
✓   **1981.)**

Tired of suitors who consider her too ordinary to marry, Princess Amy runs away to find a prince who will like her just the way she is.

Illus. by the author, Doubleday, 1984, o.p.; Pocket, 1989, pap. (0-671-69013-2)

(BL 81:641; CCBB 38:8; HB 60:758; SLJ Mar 1985 p. 168; TLS 1980 p. 1326)

167   **KELLER, Beverly (Lou).** *A Small, Elderly Dragon.* **Gr. 4–6.**
✓   Terrorized by a feeble old dragon named Blystfylyl, the peasants of Minervia enlist the aid of the King, a princess, the Black Knight of Doum, and a sorceror whose sister turns the dragon into a parrot.

Illus. by Nola Langner Malone, Lothrop, 1984, 144 pp. (0-688-02553-6)

(BCC:30; BL 80:1248; CCBB 37:188; HB 60:466; SLJ May 1984 p. 81; VOYA 7:147)

KENDALL, Carol (Seeger). *The Gammage Cup.* See Chapter 5A, Alternate Worlds or Histories.

168   **KENNEDY, (Jerome) Richard.** *The Blue Stone.* **Gr. 3–6.**

✓   The blue stone that fell from the sky brings magic into the peaceful lives of Bertie and Jack by turning people into animals, making poems come true, and changing a sparrow into a baby angel.

Illus. by Ronald Himler, Holiday, 1976, 93 pp., o.p.

(BL 73:323; CCBB 30:127; KR 44:1094; SLJ Nov 1976 p. 60)

169   **KENNEDY, (Jerome) Richard.** *The Boxcar at the Center of the Universe.* **Gr. 7–10.**

An elderly bum who calls himself Ali meets a lost sixteen-year-old boy aboard a traveling boxcar and tells him the fabulous story of his search for the center of the universe.

Illus. by Jeff Kronen, Harper, 1982, 89 pp., o.p.

(BL 78:1307, 1314; CCBB 36:70; KR 50:496; SLJ Aug 1982 p. 126; VOYA 5[Aug 1982]:33)

170   **KENNEDY, (Jerome) Richard.** *Come Again in the Spring.* **Gr. 4–6.**

✓   Old Hark is afraid to die and leave his birds to fend for themselves in midwinter, so he strikes a bargain with Death: If Hark can answer three questions, Death will wait until spring to take him.

Illus. by Marcia Sewall, Harper, 1976, 47 pp., o.p.

(BL 73:253; HB 53:154; KR 44:904; SLJ Feb 1977 p. 56)

171   **KENNEDY, (Jerome) Richard.** *The Dark Princess.* **Gr. 5–7.**

A princess's blinding beauty serves as a test for prospective suitors and prevents her from finding love, until the court fool risks blindness to declare his love.

Illus. by Donna Diamond, Holiday, 1978, 32 pp., o.p.

(HB 55:641; KR 46:1137; SLJ Dec 1978 p. 53)

172   **KENNEDY, (Jerome) Richard.** *Inside My Feet: The Story of a Giant.* **Gr. 4–6.**

✓   A boy whose parents have been carried off by a giant frantically prepares for the giant's return.

Illus. by Ronald Himler, Harper, 1991, 80 pp., pap. (0-06-440409-9)

(BBC:207; BL 76:449; CCBB 33:155; Ch&Bks:287; KR 47:1210; SLJ Sept 1979 p. 141)

173   **KENNEDY, (Jerome) Richard.** *The Leprechaun's Story.* **Gr. K–4.**

A crafty leprechaun spins tale after tale to keep a man from winning his pot of gold.

Illus. by Marcia Sewall, Dutton, 1979, 40 pp., o.p.

(HB 56:47; KR 47:1141; SLJ Dec 1979 p. 75)

174   **KENNEDY, (Jerome) Richard.** *The Lost Kingdom of Karnica.* **Gr. 2–4.**

In spite of the wise man's warning not to dig out a huge precious stone, the greedy king of Karnica orders his men to unearth it.

Illus. by Uri Shulevitz, Sierra Club, 1979, 32 pp., o.p.

(BL 76:44; CCBB 33:155; KR 47:998; SLJ Oct 1979 p. 142)

KENNEDY, (Jerome) Richard. *The Mouse God.* See Chapter 2, Animal Fantasy.

KENNEDY, (Jerome) Richard. *Richard Kennedy: Collected Stories.* See Chapter 3, Fantasy Collections.

KILWORTH, Garry. *The Foxes of Firstdark.* See Chapter 2, Animal Fantasy.

175 **KINGSLEY, Charles.** *The Water Babies: A Fairy Tale for a Land Baby.* **Gr. 4–6.**
✓ **(Orig. British pub. 1863, U.S. 1864.)**

An apprentice chimney sweep named Tom runs away from his cruel master and is taken in by fairies who change him into a tiny water baby.

Illus. by Rosalie K(ingsmill) Fry, Dutton, 1905, 1957, o.p.; illus. by Jessie Willcox Smith, Dodd, 1910, 1937, o.p.; illus. by W. Heath Robinson, Houghton, 1915, 1923, o.p.; illus. by Maria L. Kirk, Lippincott, 1917, o.p.; adapt. by Kathleen Lines, illus. by Harold Jones, Watts, 1961, o.p.; illus. by Linley Sambourne, Garland, 1976 (repr. of 1864 ed.), o.p.; Peter Smith, 1979, o.p.; Dent, 1982 (repr. of 1863 ed.), o.p.; Puffin, 1986, pap., 192 pp. (0-14-035035-7)

(BL 1:74, 5:63, 10:253, 12:204, 14:141, 53:538, 58:352; Bookshelf 1928 p. 10; Ch&Bks: 256; HB 1[June 1925]:32, 37:549; LJ 45:980; Mahony 2:282)

176 **KIPLING, (Joseph) Rudyard.** *The Beginning of the Armadilloes.* **Gr. 1–4 (Orig.**
✓ **British pub. in** *Just So Stories,* **1902; in this edition 1982.)**

In this tale from the *Just So Stories* (1897–1902) a hedgehog and a tortoise turn into armadillos while tricking a young jaguar out of his dinner.

Illus. by Charles Keeping, Bedrick, 1983, o.p.; illus. by Lorinda Bryan Cauley, Harcourt, 1985, 43 pp. (0-15-206380-3), 1990, pap. (0-15-206381-1)

(BL 80:859, 82:262; CC:516; HB 60:357; SLJ Feb 1984 p. 60, Dec 1985 p. 75)

177 **KIPLING, (Joseph) Rudyard.** *The Butterfly That Stamped.* **Gr. 2–4. (Orig.**
British pub. in *Just So Stories,* **1902; in this edition 1982.)**

This tale from Kipling's *Just So Stories* (1897–1902) explains the nature of butterflies.

Illus. by Alan Baker, Bedrick, 1983, 31 pp., o.p.

(BL 80:859; CC:516; SLJ Feb 1984 p. 60)

178 **KIPLING, (Joseph) Rudyard.** *The Cat That Walked by Himself.* **Gr. 2–4. (Orig.**
British pub. in *Just So Stories,* **1902; in this edition 1982.)**

A tale from Kipling's *Just So Stories* (1897–1902), in which cats learn to be independent.

Illus. by William Stobbs, Bedrick, 1983, 31 pp., o.p.

(BL 80:859; CC:516; SLJ Feb 1984 p. 60)

179 **KIPLING, (Joseph) Rudyard.** *The Crab That Played with the Sea.* **Gr. 2–4.**
✓ **(Orig. British pub. in** *Just So Stories,* **1902; in this edition 1982.)**

One of Kipling's *Just So Stories* (1897–1902), in which Eldest Magician creates huge ocean creatures that come into conflict with human beings.

Illus. by Michael Foreman, Bedrick, 1983, 31 pp., o.p.

(BL 80:859; CC:517; HB 60:358; SLJ Feb 1984 p. 60)

180 **KIPLING, (Joseph) Rudyard.** *The Elephant's Child.* **Gr. K–4. (Orig. British**
✓ **pub. in** *Just So Stories,* **1902.)**

The familiar tale from the *Just So Stories* (1897–1902) that explains how the elephant got his long trunk.

Illus. by Leonard Weisgard, Walker, 1971; illus. by Lorinda Bryan Cauley, Harcourt, 1983, 44 pp. (0-15-225385-8); illus. by Louise Brierly, Bedrick, 1985, 31 pp., o.p.; illus. by Jan Mogensen, Crocodile, 1989 (orig. pub. in Denmark), 48 pp. (0-940793-41-5); illus. by Emily Bolam, Dutton, 1992, 24 pp. (0-525-44862-4)

(BL 80:87, 82:496; CC:517; CCBB 37:130; Ch&Bks:265; HBG 1[Jan–June 1990]:237; KR 58:660; LJ 96:258; SLJ Oct 1983 p. 150, Feb 1986 p. 76, Jan 1992 p. 92, Feb 1992 p. 74)

181   KIPLING, (Joseph) Rudyard. *How the Camel Got His Hump.* Gr. K–4. (Orig. British pub. in *Just So Stories,* 1902; in this edition 1984.)

A lazy camel who refuses all work with a "Humph!" is given a hump on his back by the magical Djinn in charge of all deserts.

Illus. by Quentin Blake, Bedrick, 1985, 32 pp., o.p.

(BL 82:496; CC:517; SLJ Feb 1986 p. 76)

182   KIPLING, (Joseph) Rudyard. *How the Leopard Got His Spots.* Gr. 1–4. (Orig.
✓   British pub. in *Just So Stories,* 1902.)

The leopard and the Ethiopian change their skins to improve their hunting abilities, in this tale from the *Just So Stories* (1897–1902).

Illus. by Leonard Weisgard, Walker, 1973, o.p.; illus. by Caroline Ebborn, Bedrick, 1986, 32 pp., o.p.; illus. by Lori Loestoeter, Picture Book, 1991 (0-88708-111-8)

(BL 69:948; KR 41:381; LJ 98:3139; TLS 1972 p. 1333)

183   KIPLING, (Joseph) Rudyard. *How the Rhinoceros Got His Skin.* Gr. 2–4. (Orig.
✓   British pub. in *Just So Stories,* 1902.)

A cake-thieving rhinoceros is punished by the Parsee who puts itchy cake crumbs inside the rhino's skin.

Illus. by Leonard Weisgard, Walker, 1974, o.p.; illus. by Jenny Thorne, Bedrick, 1987 (British pub. 1985), 31 pp., o.p.; illus. by Tim Raglin, Picture Book, 1991, 28 pp. (0-88708-078-2)

(BL 70:1154, 83:1749; CCBB 28:45; LJ 99:2250; Suth 2:257; TLS 1973 p. 1431)

184   KIPLING, (Joseph) Rudyard. *How the Whale Got His Throat.* Gr. 2–4. (Orig. British pub. in *Just So Stories,* 1902; in this edition 1983.)

A shipwrecked mariner swallowed by a whale convinces the creature to take him home.

Illus. by Pauline Baynes, Bedrick, 1987, 32 pp., o.p.

(BL 83:1749)

KIPLING, (Joseph) Rudyard. *Just So Stories.* See Chapter 2, Animal Fantasy.

KOONTZ, Dean R. *Oddkins: A Fable for All Ages.* See Chapter 9, Toy Fantasy.

KORTUM, Jeanie. *Ghost Vision.* See Chapter 10, Witchcraft and Sorcery Fantasy.

KOTZWINKLE, William. *Doctor Rat.* See Chapter 2, Animal Fantasy.

KOTZWINKLE, William. *Hearts of Wood: And Other Timeless Tales.* See Chapter 3, Fantasy Collections.

185   KRENSKY, Stephen (Alan). *A Big Day for Scepters.* Gr. 4–6.

A boy named Corey teams up with Calandar, a magician, to oppose the villainous Prince Grogol in a race for possession of a powerful evil scepter.

Illus. by Bruce Degen, Atheneum, 1977, 112 pp., o.p.

(BL 73:1576; KR 45:352; SLJ Apr 1977 p. 68)

KRENSKY, Stephen (Alan). *Castles in the Air and Other Tales.* See Chapter 3, Fantasy Collections.

186   KRENSKY, Stephen (Alan). *The Perils of Putney.* Gr. 4–6.

A peace-loving giant, pressed into a search for a missing Fair Damsel and captured by a band of dwarfs, encounters a dragon, a witch, and a wizard.

Illus. by Jürg Obrist, Atheneum, 1978, 116 pp., o.p.

(BL 75:477; KR 46:1189; SLJ Oct 1978 p. 146)

187   KRENSKY, Stephen (Alan). *A Troll in Passing.* **Gr. 4–6.**

✓   Morgan, dissatisfied with troll life, saves his people from a band of giant trolls and sets off to see the world.

Atheneum, 1980, 128 pp., o.p.

(BL 76:1424; CCBB 33:175; KR 48:440; SLJ May 1980 p. 68; Suth 3:245)

KROPP, Lloyd. *The Drift.* See Chapter 5C, Travel to Other Worlds.

KUMIN, Maxine (Winokur), and SEXTON, Anne. *The Wizard's Tears.* See Chapter 10, Witchcraft and Sorcery Fantasy.

188   KUSHNER, Donn. *Uncle Jacob's Ghost Story.* **Gr. 6–10. (Orig. Canadian pub. 1980.)**

Uncle Jacob is reunited with the ghosts of his best friends, Simon and Esther, who died of typhus long ago, in this touching and sophisticated story. Canadian Library Association Best Book of the Year for Children, 1980.

Holt, 1986, 132 pp., o.p.

(BL 82:1605, 1614; CCBB 39:170; KR 54:550; SLJ May 1986 p. 94)

189   KUSHNER, Donn. *The Violin-Maker's Gift.* **Gr. 5–7. (Orig. Canadian pub.**

✓   **1981.)**

Gaspard the violin-maker rescues a beautiful bird and sets it free. As a reward, the bird tells him a secret that causes all of Gaspard's instruments to sing as though they had souls. Canadian Library Association Best Book of the Year for Children, 1981.

Illus. by Doug Panton, Farrar, 1982, 74 pp., o.p.

(BBC:207; BL 78:1145; CCBB 35:191; SLJ Sept 1982 p. 123; Suth 3:246)

190   LA MOTTE FOUQUÉ, Baron Friedrich Heinrich Karl de. *Undine.* **Gr. 5 up. (Written in 1811, orig. U.S. pub. 1908.)**

Huldbrand, a knight married to the water nymph Undine, is threatened with death if he should ever betray her.

Trans. by Edmund Gosse, illus. by Arthur Rackham, R. West, 1978, o.p.; Hyperion, 1985 (repr. of 1912 ed.), 136 pp. (0-88355-558-1)

(BL 5:195; Bookshelf 1923–1924 p. 15; CCBB 25:5; KR 39:236; Mahony 2:283; TLS 1929 p. 180; Tymn:105)

191   LAGERLÖF, Selma. *The Changeling.* **Gr. K–4. (Orig. Swedish pub. in this ed.**

✓   **1989.)**

A grieving mother risks her life and her marriage to protect the ugly troll baby left in exchange for her own stolen baby.

Trans. by Susanna Stevens, illus. by Jeanette Winter, Knopf, 1992, 40 pp. (0-679-81035-8)

(BL 88:826; CC 1993 Suppl. p. 72; CCBB 45:183; HB 68:337; HBG 3[Fall 1992]:257; KR 60:53; SLJ April 1992 p. 118)

192   LAMORISSE, Albert (Emmanuel). *The Red Balloon.* **Gr. 1–4. (Orig. French**

✓   **pub. 1956.)**

A young Parisian boy has trouble keeping his magical balloon safe from a gang of older boys.

Illus. with photographs from the movie, Doubleday, 1967, 45 pp. (0-685-01494-0)
(BL 54:82; CC:519; KR 25:581; LJ 82:2187; TLS Nov 15, 1957 p. xix)

193 **LANCASTER, Osbert.** *The Saracen's Head; or, the Reluctant Crusader.* **Gr. 4–6. (Orig. British pub. 1948.)**

Cowardly Sir William de Littlehampton becomes a hero after he fights El Babooni.

Illus. by the author, Houghton, 1949, 67 pp., o.p.
(BL 46:101; CCBB 3:7; HB 25:533; KR 17:302; LJ 74:1466; TLS 1948 p. 712)

194 **LANG, Andrew.** *Prince Prigio and Prince Ricardo: The Chronicles of Pantouflia.*
✓ **Gr. 4–6. (Orig. British pub. 1889, 1893; orig. U.S. pub. in** *My Own Fairy Book,* **McKay, 1895, 1927.)**

Prince Prigio and its sequel, *Prince Ricardo,* were originally published separately. *Prince Prigio,* the lighter of the two tales, is the story of an overly clever prince cursed by a fairy not invited to his christening. *Tales of a Fairy Court* (1906) is a related work.

Illus. by Robert Lawson, Little, 1942, o.p.; illus. by Gordon Browne, Garland, 1976, o.p.; illus. by Jeanne Titherington, Godine, 1981 (entitled *The Chronicles of Pantouflia: Prince Prigio and Prince Ricardo of Pantouflia*), 1984, 191 pp., pap. (0-89190-088-8)
(BL 24:75, 39:144; HB 18:423, 60:613; LJ 67:1069; SLJ Nov 1981 p. 94; TLS 1982 p. 795)

195 **LARSON, Jean (Russell).** *The Silkspinners.* **Gr. 3–5.**
✓ Li Po battles a sea monster and a sorcerer while searching for the lost silk spinners of China.

Illus. by Uri Shulevitz, Scribner, 1967, 93 pp., o.p.
(BL 64:448; CCBB 21:112; KR 35:1047; LJ 92:3852; Suth:239)

LATHROP, Dorothy P(ulis). *The Colt from Moon Mountain.* See Chapter 7, Magic Adventure Fantasy.

196 **LATHROP, Dorothy P(ulis).** *The Fairy Circus.* **Gr. 2–4.**

The fairies and the small woodland creatures stage a circus. John Newbery Medal Honor Book, 1932.

Illus. by the author, Macmillan, 1931, 66 pp., o.p.
(BL 28:205; HB 7:315; Mahony 3:107)

197 **LATTIMORE, Deborah Nourse.** *The Dragon's Robe.* **Gr. 2–5.**

Kwan Yin, an orphaned weaver, saves her country after the Chinese emperor puts her in charge of the dragon shrine, and she looses the dragon's magic to defeat an invading army.

Illus. by the author, Harper, 1990, 32 pp. (0-06-023719-8); 1993, pap. (0-06-443321-8)
(BL 86:1556; CC:520; CCBB 43:246; HBG 1[Jan.–June 1990]:238; SLJ May 1990 p. 87)

LAURENCE, Margaret (Wemyss). *Jason's Quest.* See Chapter 2, Animal Fantasy.

LAWRENCE, Ann (Margaret). *The Half Brothers.* See Chapter 5A, Alternate Worlds or Histories.

LAWSON, Amy. *Star Baby.* See Chapter 7, Magic Adventure Fantasy.

198 **LAWSON, John S(hults).** *You Better Come Home with Me.* **Gr. 5 up.**
✓ The lyrical tale of an orphaned boy searching for love, and the scarecrow who takes him home to stay.

Illus. by Arnold Spilka, Crowell, 1966, 125 pp., o.p.; Harper, 1990, 136 pp, o.p.

(BL 63:419; CCBB 20:92; HB 42:711; LJ 91:5232; Suth:241)

199   LAWSON, Julie. *The Dragon's Pearl.* **Gr. K–5. (Orig. Canadian pub. 1993.)**

✓   When young Xiao Sheng foils robbers by swallowing a magical pearl that has produced food for his starving family, he is transformed into a huge dragon. 1994 Canadian Library Association Amelia Frances Howard-Gibbon Award for Illustration to Paul Morin.

Illus. by Paul Morin, Houghton, 1993, 32 pp. (0-395-63623-X)

(BL 89:1513; CCBB 46:287; HBG 4[Fall 1993]:265; KR 61:230; SLJ July 1993 p. 62)

200   LAWSON, Marie (Abrams). *Dragon John.* **Gr. 2–4.**

A small, unhappy dragon turns out to be an enchanted prince.

Illus. by the author, Viking, 1943, 52 pp., o.p.

(BL 40:64; HB 19:409; LJ 68:894)

201   LEE, Tanith. *Animal Castle.* **Gr. 2–4.**

Prince Rimtheed invites animals to live in his kingdom, but regrets his invitation when they take advantage of their hosts.

Illus. by Helen Craig, Farrar, 1972, 37 pp., o.p.

(BL 69:948; KR 40: 1094; LJ 97:3797; TLS 1972 p. 808)

LEE, Tanith. *The Dragon Hoard.* See Chapter 5A, Alternate Worlds or Histories.

LEE, Tanith. *Princess Hynchatti and Some Other Surprises.* See Chapter 3, Fantasy Collections.

LEE, Tanith. *Red as Blood: or Tales from the Sisters Grimmer.* See Chapter 5B, Myth Fantasy.

202   LE GUIN, Ursula K(roeber). *Fish Soup.* **Gr. 1–3.**

The children imagined by the Thinking Man and the Writing Woman come to life, but they are not quite as their parents had pictured them.

Illus. by Patrick Wynne, Macmillan, 1992, 32 pp. (0-689-31733-6)

(HBG 4[Spring 1993]:59; KR 60:1257; SLJ Jan 1993 p. 80)

203   LE GUIN, Ursula K(roeber). *A Ride on the Red Mare's Back.* **Gr. K–4.**

✓   A brave girl fills her pockets with treasures, including a small red wooden horse, and sets off through the snowy woods to rescue the little brother who was stolen by trolls.

Illus. by Julie Downing, Orchard, 1992, 48 pp. LB(0-531-08591-0)

(BL 88:1847; CC 1993 Suppl. p. 72; CCBB 46:47; HB 69:204; HBG 4[Spring 1993]:59; KR 60:851; SLJ Sept. 1992 p. 207)

LE GUIN, Ursula K(roeber). *A Wizard of Earthsea.* See Chapter 5A, Alternate Worlds or Histories.

L'ENGLE, Madeleine. *Many Waters.* See Chapter 8, Time Travel Fantasy.

204   LESKOV, Nikolai. *The Steel Flea, a Story.* **Gr. 3–5. (Orig. U.S. pub. 1943.)**

The Czar challenges his friend Platov to create something even more ingenious than the dancing steel flea sent as a gift from England.

Adapt. by Babette Deutsch and Avrahm Yarmolinsky, illus. by Janina Domanska, Harper, 1964 (rev. ed.), 56 pp., o.p.

(BL 40:167, 60:1004, CCBB 19:65; HB 40:178; LJ 69:73, 89:1452)

205   **LE VERT, John.** *The Flight of the Cassowary.* **Gr. 8–12.**

✓   John's high school classmates label him as crazy after he tells them about the intense moments during which he feels as though he has turned into an animal.

Atlantic, 1986, 288 pp., o.p.; Bantam, 1988, pap., 304 pp. (0-553-27389-2)

(BL 82:1136, 1142, 83:1592; CCBB 39:172; HB 62:332; KR 54:869; SLJ May 1986 p. 105, Mar 1987 p. 120; TLS 1987 p. 1028; VOYA 9:80)

206   **LEVIN, Meyer.** *The Spell of Time: A Tale of Love in Jerusalem.* **Gr. 10 up.**

Two scientists working at an Israeli research institute fall in love with a young French colleague, and make a mystical pact to exchange bodies but retain their own personalities in order to test the young woman's ability to find her true love.

Praeger, 1974, 127 pp., o.p.

(BL 71:268, 285; HB 51:77; KR 42:829; LJ 99:2620)

207   **LEWIS, Beth (pseud. of Beth Lipkin).** *The Blue Mountain.* **Gr. 2–4.**

Prince Desmond agrees to hold a mountain-climbing contest to choose his bride, even though he is in love with Princess Noreen.

Illus. by Adrienne Adams, Knopf, 1956, 59 pp., o.p.

(CCBB 10:52; HB 32:351; KR 24:519)

LEWIS, C(live) S(taples). *The Lion, the Witch, and the Wardrobe.* See Chapter 5C, Travel to Other Worlds.

208   **LEWIS, J. Patrick.** *The Moonbow of Mr. B. Bones.* **Gr. K–3.**

✓   Tommy Morgan refuses to believe in the power of the magical moonbows that old Bartholomew Bones sells as he wanders through the Kentucky mountains.

Illus. by Dirk Zimmer, Knopf, 1992, 32 pp. (0-394-85365-2), LB(0-394-95365-7)

(BL 88:952; CC 1993 Suppl. p. 87; CCBB 45:269; HBG 3[Fall 1992]:238; KR 60:186; SLJ March 1992 p. 216, Dec 1992 p. 21)

209   **LEY, Madeleine.** *The Enchanted Eve.* **Gr. 3 up. (Orig. French pub. 1935.)**

On Saint Sylvain's Eve, Barbara, the crippled daughter of a Flemish painter, is granted her wish for freedom—she is able to skate wherever she wishes to go.

Trans. by Willard Trask, illus. by Edy LeGrand, Howell, 1946, 48 pp., o.p.

(HB 23:263, 438; LJ 72:894)

LEZRA, Giggy (Grizzella Paull). *The Cat, the Horse, and the Miracle.* See Chapter 2, Animal Fantasy.

210   **LIFTON, Betty Jean (Kirschner).** *The Dwarf Pine Tree.* **Gr. 3–5.**

✓   To save the dying princess's life, a young pine tree agrees to undergo painful binding in order to become a dwarf-sized tree.

Illus. by Fuku Akino, Atheneum, 1963, 37 pp., o.p.

(BL 60:262; Eakin:210; HB 39:499; LJ 88:116)

LINDGREN, Astrid. *The Brothers Lionheart.* See Chapter 5C, Travel to Other Worlds.

211   **LISLE, Janet Taylor.** *Forest.* **Gr. 4–7.**

✓   Twelve-year-old Amber and a squirrel named Woodbine are branded as traitors because they want to prevent a war between the humans of Lower Forest and the squirrels of Upper Forest.

Orchard, 1993, 150 pp. (0-531-06803-X)

(BL 90:443; CCBB 47:160; HB 70:199; HBG 5:79; KR 61:1205; SLJ Nov 1993 p. 109)

212   LISLE, Janet Taylor. *The Great Dimpole Oak.* **Gr. 4–7.**

The majestic old oak in the town of Dimpole has a mythic presence that draws both local inhabitants and the followers of a swami in India. Golden Kite Award Honor Book, 1987.

Illus. by Stephen Gammell, Orchard, 1987, 144 pp., LB(0-531-08316-0)

(BL 84:150, 873; CCBB 41:121; HB 64:64; KR 55:1518; SLJ Dec 1987 p. 86)

LIVELY, Penelope (Margaret Low). *Astercote.* See Chapter 5B, Myth Fantasy.

213   LLOYD, (Mary) Norris. *The Desperate Dragons.* **Gr. 2–4.**

✓   A young cowherd puts the knights of Rondo to shame by ridding the kingdom of the last twelve dragons on earth.

Illus. by Joan Balfour Payne, Hastings, 1960, 64 pp., o.p.

(CCBB 13:151; HB 36:289; KR 28:88; LJ 85:2041)

214   LLYWELYN, Morgan. *The Elementals.* **Gr. 10 up.**

Four stories whose main characters, Kesair, Meriones, Annie, and George, live in different times and places, but whose respect for the earth helps them and their people to survive.

Tor, 1993, 304 pp. (0-312-85568-0)

(BL 89:1678, 1682; KR 61:493; LJ June 15, 1993 p. 104; VOYA 16:311)

LOVETT, Margaret (Rose). *The Great and Terrible Quest.* See Chapter 5A, Alternate Worlds or Histories.

215   LOWREY, Janette Sebring. *The Lavender Cat.* **Gr. 4–6.**

✓   The little wild cat tamed by a lost boy named Jemmy eventually leads the boy home.

Illus. by Rafaello Busoni, Harper, 1944, 180 pp., o.p.

(BL 41:127; HB 21:33; KR 12:431; LJ 69:1050)

LUENN, Nancy. *Arctic Unicorn.* See Chapter 10, Witchcraft and Sorcery Fantasy.

216   LUENN, Nancy. *The Ugly Princess.* **Gr. 3–5.**

The veiled Princess Saralinde has difficulty choosing between handsome but vain Prince Phillip, and the kind but unattractive Dragonlord.

Illus. by David Wiesner, Little, 1981, 27 pp., o.p.

(CCBB 35:90; HB 57:659; KR 50:201; SLJ Oct 1981 p. 144)

LUENN, Nancy. *Unicorn Crossing.* See Chapter 7, Magic Adventure Fantasy.

217   LYNCH, Patricia (Nora). *Brogeen Follows the Magic Tune.* **Gr. 4–6. (Orig. British pub. 1952.)**

Brogeen the leprechaun is determined to retrieve the fairies' magic tune, stolen by a human fiddler. This story is preceded by *Brogeen and the Lost Castle* (British), *Brogeen and the Black Enchanter* (British), and *Brogeen and the Little Wind* (1963), and the sequels are *Brogeen and the Bronze Lizard* (1970), *Brogeen and the Red Fez* (British), and *Guests at the Beech Tree* (British).

Illus. by Ralph Pinto, Macmillan, 1968, 165 pp., o.p.

(BL 65:837; KR 36:1163; LJ 94:302)

218 **MACAULAY, David.** *BAAA.* **Gr. 6 up.**

✓   After humans disappear from the earth, sheep take up human clothing, possessions, and thoughts, become consumers, and eventually destroy themselves, rioting over inequities.

Illus. by the author, Houghton, 1985, 64 pp. (0-395-38948-8), pap. (0-395-39588-7)

(BBC:209; BBS:61; BL 82:53; CCBB 31:13; Ch&Bks:289; SLJ Oct 1985 p. 183)

219 **MacDONALD, George.** *At the Back of the North Wind.* **Gr. 5–8. (Orig. British**
✓   **pub. 1871, U.S. 1875.)**

A beautiful lady takes a boy named Diamond on fabulous journeys. The final journey is to the land at the back of the North Wind.

Illus. by Maria L. Kirk, Lippincott, 1909, o.p.; illus. by Jessie Willcox Smith, McKay, 1919, o.p.; illus. by D. Bedford, Macmillan, 1924, o.p.; illus. by Gertrude A. Kay, McKay, 1926, 1934, o.p.; illus. by George Hauman and Doris Hauman, Macmillan, 1950, 1964, o.p.; Garland, 1976 (repr. of 1871 ed.), o.p.; Schocken, 1978, pap. (0-8052-0595-0); Puffin, 1985, pap., 336 pp. (0-14-35030-6); illus. by Jessie Willcox Smith, Morrow, 1989 (facsimile of 1919 ed.), 347 pp. (0-688-07808-7)

(BBC: 209; BL 6:146, 47:162; Bookshelf 1923–1924 p. 15; CC:528; CCBB 11:61; Ch&Bks:256; HB 1[Nov 1924]:7, 26:490, 34:122; LJ 26[no. 8]:67, 45:980, 50:803; Mahony 2:286, SLJ Feb 1989 p. 119; Tymn:132)

220 **MacDONALD, George.** *The Fairy Fleet.* **Gr. 2–4. (Orig. title:** *The Carasoyn,*
        Light Princess and Other Fairy Tales.)

Young Colin rescues a changeling child from the fairy fleet.

Illus. by Stuyvesant Van Veen, Holiday, 1936, 52 pp., o.p.

(BL 33:30; HB 12:289; LJ 61:733)

221 **MacDONALD, George.** *The Golden Key.* **Gr. 4 up. (Orig. British and U.S. pub.**
        in *Dealings with the Fairies,* **1867; as a separate tale, 1906.)**

After Tangle discovers the key to the door at the end of the rainbow, he and his sister search for the mystical land beyond the door.

Crowell, 1906, o.p.; illus. by Maurice Sendak, Farrar, 1976, rev. ed. 1984, 96 pp. (0-374-32706-8), pap. (0-374-42590-6)

(HB 43:464; KR 35:609; LJ 92:3187)

222 **MacDONALD, George.** *The Light Princess.* **Gr. 3–6. (Orig. British pub. in** *Deal-*
✓   *ings with the Fairies,* **1867; orig. British pub. as a separate tale, 1872; U.S. 1926.)**

Angry Aunt Makemnort's curse removes all of the princess's gravity, leaving her to laugh but never cry and to float but never walk on the ground.

Illus. by Dorothy P. Lathrop, Macmillan, 1926, 1940, 1952, o.p.; illus. by William Pène du Bois, Crowell, 1962, o.p.; illus. by Maurice Sendak, Farrar, 1969, rev. ed. 1984, 120 pp. (0-374-34455-8), pap. (0-374-44458-7); adapt. by Robin McKinley, illus. by Katie Thamer Treherne, Harcourt, 1988, 44 pp. (0-15-245300-8)

(BL 59:499, 66:623, 84:1838; Bookshelf 1926–1927 Suppl. p. 3; CC:528; CCBB 23:162; Ch&Bks:289; HB 2[Nov 1928]:45, 28:422, 38:605, 46:41; KR 37:1257, 56:365, LJ 87:427, 95:1640; Mahony 2:288; SLJ Aug 1988 p. 83; Suth:262)

223 **MacDONALD, George.** *Little Daylight.* **Gr. 3–6.**

Princess Daylight was cursed at her christening to sleep all day and remain awake all night, while her youth and beauty waxed and waned with the moon. This story was adapted from a chapter in *At the Back of the North Wind* (1871; see above).

Illus. by Erick Ingraham, Morrow, 1988, 40 pp. LB(0-68806301-2); adapt. by Anthea Bell, illus. by Dorothée Duntze, North-South, 1987, 26 pp., o.p.

(BL 84:787, 85:81; CCBB 42:47; SLJ Nov 1988 p. 92)

224   **MacDONALD, George.** *The Princess and the Goblin.* **Gr. 5–7. (Orig. British**
✓✓   **and U.S. pub. 1872.)**

Curdie, a miner's son, overhears a plot by Goblins to flood the mines and take over the kingdom. The sequel is *The Princess and Curdie* (Orig. British pub. 1882; U.S. 1883; Macmillan, 1954, o.p.; Dell, 1987, pap.).

Illus. by Maria L. Kirk and Arthur Hughes, Lippincott, 1907, 1910, 1913, 1934, o.p.; illus. by Jessie Willcox Smith, McKay, 1920, 1934, o.p.; illus. by F. D. Bedford, Macmillan, 1926, 1930, o.p.; illus. by Elizabeth MacKinstry, Doubleday, 1928, 1937, o.p.; illus. by Nora S. Unwin, Macmillan, 1951, o.p.; Zondervan, 1980, o.p.; Dell, 1985, pap. (0-440-47189-3); illus. by Jessie Willcox Smith, Morrow, 1986, 208 pp. (0-688-06604-6); ed. by Oliver Hunkin, illus. by Alan Parry, Eerdmans, 1987, 93 pp. (0-8028-5014-6)

(BL 5:64, 83:354, 84:67; Bookshelf 1932 p. 8; CCBB 4:45; Ch&Bks:256; HB 27:261, 63:84; LJ 26:67; Mahony 2:287; Moore:290; SLJ Oct 1987 p. 116; Tymn:133)

225   **MacDONALD, George.** *The Wise Woman and Other Fantasy Stories.* **Gr. 5–7. (Orig. British and U.S. pub. 1875; retitled** *The Lost Princess: A Double Story,* **1895.)**

The paths of two little girls, a princess and a shepherd's daughter, converge at the home of the wise woman, who changes both their lives.

Harcourt, 1924 (entitled *The Lost Princess: A Double Story*), o.p.; Dutton, 1966 (entitled *The Lost Princess*), o.p.; Eerdmans, 1980, pap., 176 pp. (0-8028-1860-9); illus. by D(enys) J(ames) Watkins-Pitchford, Zondervan, 1981, o.p.; ed. by Glenn Edward Sadler, illus. by Bernhard Oberdieck (entitled: *The Lost Princess: A Double Story*), Eerdmans, 1992, pap., 148 pp. (0-8028-5070-7)

(BL 89:908; HB 42:306; HBG 1[Jan–June 1990]:239, 4[Spring 1993]:73; SLJ Apr 1981 p. 129; TLS 1965 p. 1150)

226   **McGINLEY, Phyllis (Louise).** *The Plain Princess.* **Gr. 2–4.**
✓   Dame Goodwit teaches a selfish young princess to be kind and helpful.

Illus. by Helen Stone, Lippincott, 1945, 64 pp., o.p.

(BL 42:133; Ch&Bks:289; HB 21:454, 447; KR 13:297; LJ 70:950, 1138)

227   **McGOWEN, Tom (Thomas E.).** *Dragon Stew.* **Gr. 1–3.**
✓   Gluttonous King Chubby holds a contest for the most unusual recipe, and dragon stew wins the prize.

Illus. by Trina Schart Hyman, Follett, 1969, 32 pp., o.p.

(BL 65:1177; CCBB 23:114; HB 45:397; KR 37:171; LJ 94:1770; Suth:264)

228   **McHARGUE, Georgess.** *The Mermaid and the Whale.* **Gr. K–3.**

A mermaid asks Ichabod Paddock, the great whalemaster, to help her tame Long John, the whale she loves.

Illus. by Robert Andrew Parker, Holt, 1973, 34 pp., o.p.

(HB 50:46; KR 41:1157; LJ 99:883)

229   **McKENZIE, Ellen Kindt.** *The King, the Princess, and the Tinker.* **Gr. 2–5.**
✓   None of his subjects recognize the king after his crown falls off, because, unlike the beloved Princess Rosilla, he has spent his entire life inside his mirrored throne room, watching his own reflection and that of his treasure.

Illus. by William Low, Henry Holt, 1992, 70 pp. (0-8050-1773-9), 1993, pap., 64 pp. (0-8050-2951-6)

(BL 88:1280; CCBB 45:168; HBG 3[Fall 1992]:267; KR 60:54; SLJ May 1992 p. 91)

McKILLIP, Patricia A(nne). *The Forgotten Beasts of Eld.* See Chapter 5A, Alternate Worlds or Histories.

McKINLEY, (Jennifer Carolyn) Robin. *Beauty: A Retelling of the Story of Beauty and the Beast.* See Chapter 5B, Myth Fantasy.

McKINLEY, Robin. *The Door in the Hedge.* See Chapter 3, Fantasy Collections.

MacLACHLAN, Patricia. *Tomorrow's Wizard.* See Chapter 10, Witchcraft and Sorcery Fantasy.

230   MAETERLINCK, Maurice. *The Children's Blue Bird.* Gr. 3–5. (Orig. title: *The Blue Bird: A Fairy Play in Five Acts,* 1909; prose version, 1913.)

Two children search for the blue bird of happiness.

Adapt. by Georgette Leblanc (Maeterlinck), trans. by Alexander De Mattos, illus. by Herbert Paus, Dodd, 1962, o.p.; Philos, 1985 (entitled *The Blue Bird,* bound with *The Betrothal*), 304 pp., o.p.

(BL 5:174, 10:163; Bookshelf 1927 Suppl. p. 26; Mahony 1:34; Mahony 2:26; Mahony 3:37)

MAGUIRE, Gregory. *The Dream Stealer.* See Chapter 10, Witchcraft and Sorcery Fantasy.

MAHY, Margaret. *The Door in the Air and Other Stories.* See Chapter 7, Magic Adventure Fantasy.

231   MAUGHAM, W. Somerset. *Princess September.* Gr. 3–5. (Orig. pub. as part of *The Gentleman in the Parlour,* 1930.)

A nightingale caged by Princess September nearly dies.

Illus. by Jacqueline Ayer, Harcourt, 1969, 33 pp., o.p.

(CCBB 22:31; HB 45:308; LJ 94:2104; TLS 1970 p. 420)

MAYER, Marianna. *The Black Horse.* See Chapter 5B, Myth Fantasy.

232   MAYER, Marianna. *The Little Jewel Box.* Gr. K–3.

✓   Isabel proves herself to be "brave, outspoken, and intelligent besides," as she performs the arduous tasks needed to win John for her husband.

Illus. by Margot Tomes, Dial, 1968, 32 pp. (0-8037-0148-9), 1990, pap. (0-8037-0737-1)

(BL 82:1086; CCBB 39:154; HB 62:443; KR 54:793; SLJ May 1986 p. 82)

MAYER, Marianna. *Noble-Hearted Kate: A Celtic Tale.* See Chapter 5B, Myth Fantasy.

MAYER, Marianna. *The Sorcerer's Apprentice; A Greek Fable.* See Chapter 5B, Myth Fantasy.

233   MAYER, Marianna. *The Unicorn and the Lake.* Gr. 1–4.

A powerful unicorn battles an evil serpent and restores a poisoned lake, bringing peace and good health to all of the other animals.

Illus. by Michael Hague, Dial, 1982, LB(0-8037-9338-3), 1987, pap., 32 pp. (0-8037-0436-4)

(BL 79:779; CC:676; SLJ Nov 1982 p. 70)

MAYHAR, Ardath. *The Saga of Grittel Sundotha.* See Chapter 5A, Alternate Worlds or Histories.

234   **MAYNE, William (James Carter).** *The Mouldy.* **Gr. 2–4. (Orig. British pub. 1983.)**

After the king's daughter, Talitha, goes underground to battle Mouldy, a mole who is destroying the kingdom, Mouldy announces that he wants to marry her.

Illus. by Nicola Bayley, Knopf, 1983, 30 pp., o.p.

(CCBB 37:73; Ch&Bks:289; SLJ Feb 1984 p. 61)

235   **MAYNE, William (James Carter).** *A Year and a Day.* **Gr. 4–6. (Orig. British**
✓   **pub. 1976.)**

Sara and Rebecca find a fairy changeling boy who brings happiness to their family, but only for a year and a day.

Dutton, 1976, 86 pp., o.p.; Peter Smith, 1989 (0-8446-6431-6)

(BL 72:1528; Ch&Bks:256; CCBB 29:178; HB 52:398, 60:223; KR 44:391; SLJ Apr 1976 p. 76; TLS 1976 p. 1241)

236   **MAZER, Anne.** *The Oxboy.* **Gr. 4–7.**

Oxboy, the mixed-blood son of a human mother and a banished ox father, is forced to pretend to be a "pure-blood human," and hide his friendship with an otter.

Knopf, 1993, 109 pp. (0-679-84191-1)

(BL 90:523; CCBB 47:52; HBG 5:80; KR 61:1526; SLJ Nov 1993 p. 110)

MEIGS, Cornelia. *The Kingdom of the Winding Road.* See Chapter 3, Fantasy Collections.

237   **MELLECKER, Judith.** *Randolph's Dream.* **Gr. K–4.**

Seven-year-old Randolph, staying with relatives during World War II while his father fights in North Africa, flies in his dreams to the desert where his father lies wounded and leads him to safety.

Illus. by Robert Andrew Parker, Knopf, 1991, 40 pp. (0-679-91115-4)

(BL 87:1037, 1128; CCBB 44:269; HBG 2[Fall 1991]:257; KR 58:1741; SLJ May 1991 p. 81)

MENOTTI, Gian Carlo. *Amahl and the Night Visitors.* See Chapter 5B, Myth Fantasy.

238   **MENUHIN, Yehudi, and HOPE, Christopher.** *The King, the Cat, and the Fiddle.* **Gr. 1–4.**

As an economy measure, the King fires his fiddlers, bringing on rebellion from his countrymen, who miss hearing music.

Illus. by Angela Barrett, Holt, 1983, 31 pp., o.p.

(CCBB 37:33; KR 51:J153; SLJ Jan 1984 p. 79)

MERRILL, Jean (Fairbanks). *The Black Sheep.* See Chapter 2, Animal Fantasy.

MERRILL, Jean (Fairbanks). *The Pushcart War.* See Chapter 6, Humorous Fantasy.

239   **MERRILL, Jean (Fairbanks).** *The Superlative Horse: A Tale of Ancient China.*
✓   **Gr. 4–6.**

After Hankan, the lowly stable boy, finds a wonderful horse for Duke Mu, he is made chief groom.

Illus. by Ronni Solbert, Addison-Wesley, 1961, 79 pp., o.p.

(BL 58:287; Eakin:234; HB 38:48; LJ 87:334)

240   **MILES, (Mary) Patricia.** *The Gods in Winter.* **Gr. 5–8.**

✓   Strange things begin happening after Mrs. Korngold moves in as the Brambles' house-keeper. She changes cousin Crispin into a lizard, saves Lottie's life, and seems to be the cause of an extremely severe winter.

Dutton, 1978, 140 pp., o.p.

(BL 75:51; CCBB 32:48; HB 55:518; KR 46:750; SLJ Oct 1978 p. 147; Suth 2:319; TLS 1978 p. 764)

241   **MILNE, A(lan) A(lexander).** *Once on a Time.* **Gr. 5–7. (Orig. British and U.S.**
✓   **pub. 1917.)**

After the kings go to war, the Kingdoms of Euralia and Barodia are ruled by women.

Illus. by Charles Robinson, Putnam, 1922, o.p.; illus. by Susan Perl, New York Graphic Society, 1962, 242 pp., o.p.

(BL 19:87; Bookshelf 1928 p. 23; HB 2[Nov 1928]:45; KR 29:1086; LJ 87:842)

242   **MILNE, A(lan) A(lexander).** *Prince Rabbit and the Princess Who Could Not Laugh.* **Gr. 2–4.**

Two humorous tales about an enchanted prince in rabbit-form, and a contest to make a princess laugh.

Illus. by Mary Shepard, Dutton, 1966, 72 pp., o.p.

(CCBB 20:61; LJ 92:329)

MODESITT, L. E. *The Magic of Recluce.* See Chapter 5A, Alternate Worlds and Histories.

243   **MOERI, Louise.** *Star Mother's Youngest Child.* **Gr. 2 up.**

✓✓   A crochety old woman and Star Mother's Ugly Child spend Christmas together, turning their otherwise lonely day into a warm and memorable one.

Illus. by Trina Schart Hyman, Houghton, 1980, 48 pp. (0-395-21406-8), 1980, pap. (0-395-29929-2)

(BL 72:304; CC:682; CCBB 29:115; HB 51:582; KR 43:1180; SLJ Oct 1975 p. 81)

244   **MOERI, Louise.** *The Unicorn and the Plow.* **Gr. 2–4.**

A unicorn plows a starving farmer's field, turning it into a flourishing vegetable garden overnight.

Illus. by Diane Goode, Dutton, 1982, 31 pp., o.p.

(BL 78:1527; CCBB 36:16; KR 50:419; SLJ Apr 1982 p. 60)

MOLESWORTH, Mary Louise (Stewart). *Fairy Stories.* See Chapter 3, Fantasy Collections.

MONSELL, Mary Elise. *Toohy and Wood.* See Chapter 2, Animal Fantasy.

MONTROSE, Anne. *The Winter Flower and Other Fairy Stories.* See Chapter 3, Fantasy Collections.

MOON, Sheila. *Knee-Deep in Thunder.* See Chapter 5C, Travel to Other Worlds.

MOORCOCK, Michael (John). *The Ice Schooner: A Tale.* See Chapter 5A, Alternate Worlds or Histories.

245   MOORCOCK, Michael (John). *The War Hound and the World's Pain: A Fable.* **Gr. 10 up.**

Heartsick at the atrocities he has seen perpetrated in the name of God during the Thirty Years' War (1618–1648), Captain Von Beck is sent by Satan to find the "Cure for the World's Pain," in order to free his soul from the Devil's grip. The sequel is *The City in the Autumn Stars* (1987).

Simon, 1981, o.p.; Ultramarine, 1981, 239 pp. (0-671-43708-9)

(BBS:62; KR 49:1100; LJ 106:2052; SLJ Jan 1982 p. 92)

246   MORGAN, Robin. *The Mer-Child: A Legend for Children and Other Adults.* **Gr. 4–6.**

A lonely mer-child, scorned because he is half-human, begins a lifelong friendship with a paralyzed biracial girl who, because of his friendship, grows up to become an oceanographer.

Illus. by Jesse Spicer Zerner, Feminist Pr., 1991, 55 pp. (1-55861-054-5)

(HBG 3[Spring 1992]:70; KR 59:1537; SLJ Aug 1992 p. 156)

247   MORPURGO, Michael. *Jo-Jo the Melon Donkey.* **Gr. 3–5. (Orig. British pub. 1987.)**

A little donkey who longs for a better life saves the citizens of 16th-century Venice by braying loudly to warn them that the sea is coming in.

Illus. by Chris Molan, Prentice-Hall, 1988, 32 pp., o.p.

(KR 55:1677; SLJ April 1988 p. 87)

248   MOZART, Wolfgang Amadeus. *The Magic Flute.* **Gr. 3–6.**

✓   Mozart's well-known opera retold in story form for children. *Night's Daughter* by Marion Zimmer Bradley (Ballantine, 1985; see Chapter 5B, Myth Fantasy) is a contempory version of this story, written for young adults.

Adapt. and illus. by John Updike and Warren Chappell, Knopf, 1962, o.p.; adapt. by Stephen Spender, illus. by Beni Montresor, Putnam, 1966, 40 pp., o.p.

(BL 59:615; HB 43:196; LJ 87:3896, 92:337)

249   MULLER, Robin. *The Magic Paintbrush.* **Gr. 3–5.**

A magic paintbrush that brings to life whatever Nib paints becomes especially useful after the king imprisons Nib.

Illus. by the author, Viking, 1990, 32 pp. (0-670-83167-0)

(BL 86:1634, 2000; HBG 1[Jan 1990]:229; KR 58:344; SLJ July 1990 p. 79)

250   MULOCK, Diana (pseud. of Dinah Craik). *The Little Lame Prince and His*
✓   *Travelling Cloak.* **Gr. 4–6. (Orig. British pub. 1874.)**

Prince Dolor, lame from an accident he had as a baby, uses magic to escape his greedy uncle and to gain his rightful throne.

Grossett, 1948, o.p.; Garland, 1977 (repr. of 1874 ed., bound with *The Adventures of a Brownie*), o.p.; adapt. and illus. by Rosemary Wells, Dial, 1990 (entitled: *The Little Lame Prince*), 32 pp., LB(0-8037-0788-6)

(BL 6:142, 45:145, 87:174: Bookshelf 1932 p. 8; CCBB 2[Jan 1949]:2; HB 7:116; LJ 26 [no. 8]:67, 74:69; Mahony 2:278)

251   MURPHY, Shirley Rousseau. *Silver Woven in My Hair.* **Gr. 4–6.**

✓   In an extended version of the Cinderella story, orphaned Thursey is ill-treated by her stepmother and stepsisters until her friend, the goatherd, turns out to be a long-lost prince.

Illus. by Alan Tiegreen, Atheneum, 1977, 121 pp., o.p.; Macmillan, 1992, pap., 128 pp. (0-689-71525-0)

(BL 73:1355; CCBB 31:51, 44:19; HB 53:316; KR 45:224; SLJ Sept 1977 p. 134)

252   **MURPHY, Shirley Rousseau.** *Valentine for a Dragon.* **Gr. K–4.**

A shy demon's gifts to a lovey lady dragon keep going up in smoke, until he finds the perfect gift and wins her heart.

Illus. by Kay Chorao, Atheneum, 1984, 48 pp., o.p.

(BL 80:1550, 83:360; CCBB 37:171; SLJ Aug 1984 p. 63)

253   **MYERS, Walter Dean.** *The Golden Serpent.* **Gr. 3–5.**

A wise man finds the answer to the mystery of the golden serpent, but the king does not understand this answer.

Illus. by Alice Provensen and Martin Provensen, Viking, 1980, 40 pp., o.p.

(BL 77:575; CCBB 34:157; HB 56: 636; SLJ Jan 1981 p. 53; TLS 1981 p. 343)

254   **NATHAN, Robert (Gruntal).** *Portrait of Jennie.* **Gr. 10 up.**

Each time a struggling artist meets Jennie, she has mysteriously grown older "in order to catch up with him," but tragedy intervenes after they fall in love.

Knopf, 1929, 1940, 1949, 212 pp. (0-394-44093-5)

(BL 36:198; Kies:125; SHC:709; TLS 1940 p. 85)

NESBIT (Bland), E(dith). *The Complete Book of Dragons.* See Chapter 3, Fantasy Collections.

255   **NESBIT (Bland), E(dith).** *The Last of the Dragons.* **Gr. 4–6. (Orig. British and U.S. pub. in** *The Book of Dragons,* **1901; as a separate tale, 1925.)**

Faced with a Cornish princess and her suitor, England's last dragon reveals that he wants only to be loved.

Illus. by Peter Firmin, McGraw-Hill, 1980, 25 pp., o.p.

(CCBB 34:115; SLJ Feb 1981 p. 69)

NESBIT (Bland), E(dith). *The Magic World.* See Chapter 7, Magic Adventure Fantasy.

256   **NESBIT (Bland), E(dith).** *Melisande.* **Gr. K–4. (Orig. British pub. in** *Nine*
✓   *Unlikely Tales,* **1901.)**

A spell of baldness is cast over Princess Melisande by a fairy who was not invited to her christening party, but when she grows up and makes a wish, Melisande suddenly has hair that will not stop growing.

Illus. by P. J. Lynch, Harcourt, 1989, 48 pp. (0-15-253164-5)

(BL 86:353; CC:112; HB 65:763; HBG 1[July–Dec 1989]:81; KR 57:1478; SLJ Jan 1990 p. 87)

257   **NESS, Evaline (Michelow).** *The Girl and the Goatherd, or This and That and*
✓   *Thus and So.* **Gr. 1–4.**

A girl made beautiful after completing a witch's tasks can't understand why she is still unhappy.

Dutton, 1970, 32 pp., o.p.

(BL 67:270; HB 47:159; KR 38:944; LJ 95:4038)

NEWMAN, Robert (Howard). *Merlin's Mistake.* See Chapter 5B, Myth Fantasy.

NORTH, Joan. *The Cloud Forest.* See Chapter 7, Magic Adventure Fantasy.

NYE, Robert. *The Mathematical Princess and Other Stories.* See Chapter 3, Fantasy Collections.

258   **NYE, Robert.** *Wishing Gold.* **Gr. 3–5. (Orig. British pub. 1970.)**

Wishing Gold, the lost son of the King of Ireland, battles an evil queen and her three sons, and saves his father's life.

Illus. by Helen Craig, Hill, 1971, 109 pp., o.p.

(KR 39:52; LJ 96:1507; TLS 1970 p. 714)

259   **NYGREN, Tord.** *Fiddler and His Brothers.* **Gr. K–3. (Orig. Swedish pub. 1986; British title:** *Fiddler and the Witches,* **1987.)**

Fiddler, the youngest of three brothers seeking their fortunes, uses his courage, wit, and common sense to accomplish three impossible tasks.

Illus. by the author, Morrow, 1987, 32 pp., o.p.

(KR 55:1160; SLJ Nov 1987 p. 95)

OAKLEY, Graham. *Henry's Quest.* See Chapter 6, Humorous Fantasy.

O'BRIEN, Robert C. *Mrs. Frisby and the Rats of NIMH.* See Chapter 2, Animal Fantasy.

Once upon a Time: A Treasury of Modern Fairy Tales. **Ed. by Lester Del Rey and Risa Kessler.** See Chapter 3, Fantasy Collections.

ORWELL, George. *Animal Farm.* See Chapter 2, Animal Fantasy.

OSBORNE, Maurice. *Ondine: The Story of a Bird Who Was Different.* See Chapter 2, Animal Fantasy.

The Oxford Book of Modern Fairy Tales. **Ed. by Alison Lurie.** See Chapter 3, Fantasy Collections.

260   **PAGE, P(atricia) K(athleen) (pseud. of Patricia Kathleen Page Irwin).** *A Flask*
✓   *of Sea Water.* **Gr. 2–5. (Orig. Canadian pub. 1989.)**

A goatherd in love with a princess may win her hand only by bringing the king a flask of special seawater.

Illus. by Laszlo Gal, Oxford Univ. Pr., 1989, 32 pp. (0-19-540704-0)

(BL 86:834, 87:178; CC:509; HB 66:60, 367; HBG 1[July–Dec 1989]:81; KR 57:1675)

261   **PAGET, (Reverend) F(rancis) E(dward) (used the pseud. William Churne of Staffordshire).** *The Hope of the Katzekopfs; or, the Sorrow of Selfishness: A Fairy Tale.* **Gr. 3–6. (Orig. British pub. 1844.)**

Abracadabra, the uninvited fairy guest at the christening of the Fairy King and Queen's son, gives him the gift of "self-will," causing him to become selfish and mischievous. When the fairy is called back to take charge of him, she draws him out into a long elastic string, turns him into a ball, and bounces him all over the country. According to *The Oxford Companion to Children's Literature* (Oxford, 1984) and Roger Lancelyn Green in *Tellers of Tales: British Authors of Children's Books from 1800–1964* (Watts, 1965), this book is generally regarded as the first English children's fantasy, and had a direct influence on Thackeray's *The Rose and the Ring* (1855) and Kipling's *Rewards and Fairies* (1910).

(Adapt. and retitled: *The Self-Willed Prince; or, The Hope of the Katzekopfs, a Fairy Tale*

Retold in Short Words), illus. by J. L. Gilmour, Stokes, 1917, o.p.; Johnson, 1968 (repr. of 1844 ed.), 211 pp., o.p.

262 PALMER, Mary. *The Magic Knight.* **Gr. 3–5.**

Prince Gillian's page, Quist, helps him slay a dragon and tame a sea serpent.

Illus. by Bill Sokol, Hale, 1964, 93 pp., o.p.

(CCBB 18:91; KR 32:955; LJ 90:382)

263 PARKER, (James) Edgar (Jr.). *The Enchantress.* **Gr. 3–5.**

✓ The enchantress-princess decides to help the young knight she loves to accomplish the three impossible tasks she set for prospective suitors.

Illus. by the author, Pantheon, 1960, 36 pp., o.p.

(BL 57:249; CCBB 14:99; HB 36:407; KR 28:816; LJ 85:3866)

PARKER, (James) Edgar (Jr.). *The Flower of the Realm.* See Chapter 2, Animal Fantasy.

264 PATERSON, Katherine. *The King's Equal.* **Gr. 2–5.**

✓ A wolf transforms Rosamund the goatherd into the perfect wife for a king, but she refuses the arrogant king's hand and sends him off to learn humility while she rules the land.

Illus. by Vladimir Vagin, Harper, 1992, 64 pp. LB(0-06-022497-5)

(BL 88:1944; CC 1993 Suppl. p. 74; CCBB 46:154; HB 68:583; HBG 4[Spring 1993]:60; KR 60:1066; SLJ Sept 1992 p. 255)

PATON WALSH, Jill. *Birdy and the Ghosties.* See Chaper 4, Ghost Fantasy.

265 PATON WALSH, Jill. *Matthew and the Sea Singer.* **Gr. 2–5. (Orig. British pub.**
✓ **1992.)**

Orphaned Matthew is stolen by the seal-queen who carries him to the bottom of the sea to teach her child how to sing beautifully. This is a companion story to *Birdy and the Ghosties* (1990; see Chapter 4, Ghost Fantasy).

Illus. by Alan Marks, Farrar, 1993, 46 pp. (0-374-34869-3)

(BL 89:1518; CCBB 46:297; HBG 4[Fall 1993]:292; KR 61:535; SLJ May 1993 p. 90)

266 PEARCE, (Ann) Philippa. *The Squirrel Wife.* **Gr. 2–4. (Orig. British pub. 1971.)**

✓ Jealous of Jack's magic ring and fairy wife, Jack's brother has him imprisoned.

Illus. by Derek Collard, Crowell, 1972, 61 pp., o.p.

(BL 68:822; CCBB 26:14; HB 48:265; KR 40:194, 1412; LJ 97:2479; Suth: 307)

267 PELGROM, Els. *Little Sophie and Lanky Flop.* **Gr. 3–6. (Orig. Dutch pub. 1987.)**

Confined to bed by a serious illness, Sophie becomes a cast member of a play performed by her cat and toys, entitled "What Life Has to Offer," in this rather dark vision of life.

Trans. by Arnold Pomerans, illus. by The Tjong Khing, Farrar, 1988, 88 pp., o.p.

(CCBB 42:131; KR 56:1744; SLJ Feb 1989 p. 81)

268 PENDERGRAFT, Patricia. *The Legend of Daisy Flowerdew.* **Gr. 6–9.**

Daisy is sold into an unhappy marriage by her selfish mother and cruel stepfather, but she is rescued by the wish-granting traveling salesman who once gave her some magical paper dolls. This book could be read as a tragic realistic novel with a fantasy ending, or as a contemporary fairy tale.

Putnam, 1990, 192 pp. (0-399-22176-X)

(BBJ:74; BL 86:1694, 1709; CCBB 44:42; HBG 1[Jan–June 1990]:252; JHC 1991 Suppl. p. 78; KR 58:801; SLJ Dec 1990 p. 106; VOYA 13:109)

269 **PHIPSON, Joan (pseud. of Joan Margaret Fitzhardinge).** *The Watcher in the Garden.* **Gr. 6–9. (Orig. Australian pub. 1982.)**

Blind Mr. Lovett's beautiful hilltop garden seems to sense the peaceful intentions of 15-year-old Kitty, as well as the violent plans of 17-year-old Terry toward its elderly owner, in this story told from both young people's points of view.

Macmillan, 1982, 203 pp., o.p.

(BBC:211; BBJ:74; BL 79:199, 248; CCBB 36:75; HB 58: 522; KR 50:1159; SLJ Nov 1982 p. 89)

PICARD, Barbara Leonie. *The Faun and the Woodcutter's Daughter.* See Chapter 3, Fantasy Collections.

PICARD, Barbara Leonie. *The Goldfinch Garden: Seven Tales.* See Chapter 3, Fantasy Collections.

PICARD, Barbara Leonie. *The Lady of the Linden Tree.* See Chapter 3, Fantasy Collections.

PICARD, Barbara Leonie. *The Mermaid and the Simpleton.* See Chapter 3, Fantasy Collections.

270 **PIERCE, Meredith Ann.** *Where the Wild Geese Go.* **Gr. 1–4.**

Truzjka must go on a magical search for the wild geese in order to save her grandmother's life.

Illus. by Jamichael Henterly, Dutton, 1988, 64 pp., o.p.

(HB 64:349; KR 56:205; SLJ June 1988 p. 94)

271 **PIKE, Christopher.** *Sati.* **Gr. 10 up.**

After truck driver Michael meets Sati, a girl who claims to be God reborn, in the Arizona desert, he struggles to decide whether he believes her story or not.

Tor, 1990, 256 pp., o.p., 1991, pap. (0-8125-1035-6)

(BL 87:601, 610; KR 58:1198; SLJ April 1991 p. 154)

POLLAND, Madeleine A(ngela Cahill). *Deirdre.* See Chapter 5B, Myth Fantasy.

POPE, Elizabeth. *The Perilous Gard.* See Chapter 5C, Travel to Other Worlds.

272 **POSTGATE, Oliver, and FIRMIN, Peter.** *King of the Nogs.* **Gr. 2–4. (Orig. British pub. 1965.)**

Noggin battles the wicked Nogbad to gain a throne and a bride. The American sequels are *Noggin and the Whale* (1967), *The Ice Dragon* (1968), *Nogbad and the Elephants* (1967), and *Noggin and the Moon Mouse* (1967). The British sequels are *The Blackwash; The Flowers; The Game; The Icebergs; The Monster; Nogbad Comes Back; Noggin and the Dragon; Noggin and the Money; Noggin and the Storks; Noggin the King; Nogmania;* and *The Pie.*

Illus. by the authors, Holiday, 1968, 48 pp., o.p.

(KR 36:1220; LJ 94:1772; TLS 1965 p. 1149)

PRICE, Susan. *The Ghost Drum.* See Chapter 10, Witchcraft and Sorcery Fantasy.

The Princesses: Sixteen Stories About Princesses. **Ed. by Sally Patrick Johnson.** See Chapter 3, Fantasy Collections.

Princesses and Peasant Boys: Tales of Enchantment. **Ed. by Phyllis Reid Fenner.** See Chapter 3, Fantasy Collections.

PUSHKIN, Alexander Sergeevich. *The Golden Cockerel and Other Stories.* See Chapter 3, Fantasy Collections.

273   **PUSHKIN, Alexander Sergeevich.** *The Tale of Czar Saltan, or the Prince and the Swan Princess.* **Gr. 3–5. (Orig. pub. in Russia; British title:** *The Tale of Tsar Saltan,* **1974.)**

Abandoned in a foreign land, Czar Saltan's son is reunited with his family by an enchanted swan.

Trans. by Patricia Lowe, illus. by I. Bilbin, Crowell, 1975, 24 pp., o.p.

(BL 72:167; SLJ Nov 1975 p. 82; TLS 1974 p. 1382)

274   **PUSHKIN, Alexander Sergeevich.** *The Tale of the Golden Cockerel.* **Gr. 3–5.**
✓   **(Orig. pub. in Russia; Orig. U.S. pub. 1938.)**

The czar's magic cockerel warns him of enemy invasions, but cannot save him from the wiles of an enchantress.

Trans. and retold by Patricia Tracy Lowe, illus. by I. Bilbin, Crowell, 1975, 24 pp., o.p.

(BL 35:51, 72:167; CCBB 29:18; HB 14:298, 51:455; SLJ Oct 1975 p. 101; Suth 2:372)

275   **PYLE, Howard.** *The Garden Behind the Moon: A Real Story of the Moon Angel.* **Gr. 3–6. (Orig. U.S. pub. 1895.)**

The mysterious Moon Angel convinces Davy to follow the moonpath all the way up to the moon.

Illus. by the author, Scribner, 1929, o.p.; Parabola, 1988 (repr. of 1895 ed.), 192 pp. (0-930407-06-7), pap., 176 pp. (0-930407-22-9)

(BBC:212; BL 85:713; Bookshelf 1921–1922 p. 15; Mahony 2:292; SLJ Feb 1989 p. 119)

PYLE, Howard. *King Stork.* See Chapter 10, Witchcraft and Sorcery Fantasy.

276   **PYLE, Howard.** *Twilight Land.* **Gr. 4–6. (Orig. U.S. pub. 1894.)**

The narrator visits Mother Goose's Inn, where he meets a number of well-known fairy tale characters, each of whom tells a tale.

Illus. by the author, Harper, 1922, o.p.; Peter Smith, 1968 (repr. of 1894 ed.), 437 pp., o.p.

(Mahony 2:292; TLS 1968 p. 1120)

PYLE, Howard. *The Wonder Clock; or, Four & Twenty Marvelous Tales.* See Chapter 3, Fantasy Collections.

277   **RAMACHANDER, Akumal.** *Little Pig.* **Gr. 4–6. (Orig. British pub. 1992.)**

Mary, a pig farmer who tricks Little Pig onto a van bound for the slaughterhouse, finds the tables are turned when she herself is transformed into a pig, in this disturbing story illustrated with eerie photographs of masks held in place by human hands.

Illus. by Stasys Eidrigevicius, Viking, 1992, 32 pp. (0-670-84350-4)

(BL 89:593; CCBB 46:85; SLJ Jan 1993 p. 102)

REEVES, James (pseud. of John Morris Reeves). *The Cold Flame.* See Chapter 5A, Alternate Worlds or Histories.

REEVES, James (pseud. of John Morris Reeves). *Maildun the Voyager.* See Chapter 5B, Myth Fantasy.

REEVES, James (pseud. of John Morris Reeves). *Sailor Rumbelow and Other Stories.* See Chapter 3, Fantasy Collections.

278   REID, Alastair. *Fairwater.* **Gr. 3–5.**

A stone-cutter named Garth is barred from the Kingdom of Fairwater after he tries to rescue an enchanted princess. In the sequel, *Allth* (1958), a young minstrel named Prin attempts to rescue Princess Ailin and recover the stolen Song of Allth.

Illus. by Walter Lorraine, Houghton, 1957, 47 pp., o.p.

(CCBB 11:85; Eakin: 269; HB 33:222; KR 25:330; LJ 82:2192)

REID BANKS, Lynne. *The Fairy Rebel.* See Chapter 7, Magic Adventure Fantasy.

279   REID BANKS, Lynne. *The Farthest-Away Mountain.* **Gr. 5–7. (Orig. British pub. 1976.)**

Dakin and a prince-turned-frog set off for an unreachable mountain in order to break a witch's spell.

Illus. by Victor Ambrus, Doubleday, 1977, 140 pp., o.p.; illus. by Dave Henderson, Doubleday, 1991, 128 pp. (0-385-41534-6)

(BL 74:809; CCBB 31:122; HBG 2:270; KR 46:2; SLJ Feb 1978 p. 54, Mar 1991 p. 192; TLS 1976 p. 1553)

REID BANKS, Lynne. *The Magic Hare.* **Chapter 2, Animal Fantasy.**

280   RIORDAN, James. *The Three Magic Gifts.* **Gr. K–4.**

Ivan the Rich manages to steal two of his poor brother's magic gifts, but the third time, Ivan the Poor outwits his brother and retrieves all of them.

Illus. by Errol Le Cain, Oxford, 1980, 29 pp., o.p.

(BL 77:967; CCBB 34:179; KR 99:210; SLJ Mar 1981 p. 136)

ROBINSON, Joan (Mary) G(ale Thomas). *When Marnie Was There.* See Chapter 4, Ghost Fantasy.

ROCCA, Guido. *Gaetano the Pheasant: A Hunting Fable.* See Chapter 2, Animal Fantasy.

RODDA, Emily. *The Best-Kept Secret.* See Chapter 8, Time Travel Fantasy.

ROSS, Ramon Royal. *Prune.* See Chapter 2, Animal Fantasy.

ROSS, Tony. *A Fairy Tale.* See Chapter 7, Magic Adventure Fantasy.

RUSHDIE, Salman. *Haroun and the Sea of Stories.* See Chapter 5A, Alternate Worlds and Histories.

281   RUSKIN, John. *The King of the Golden River, or the Black Brothers: A Legend*
✓   *of Stiria.* **Gr. 2–5. (Written 1841, orig. British pub. 1951, U.S. 1900.)**

Little Gluck's cruel older brothers torment him until the King of the Golden River and the South-West Wind come to his aid.

Illus. by Richard Doyle, Dover, 1974 (repr. of 1889 ed.), pap. (0-486-20066-3); illus. by Krystyna Turska, Greenwillow, 1978, 40 pp., o.p.; Putnam, 1988, o.p.

(BBC:212; BL 42:304; Bookshelf 1921–1922 p. 9; CCBB 13:120; Ch&Bks:290; HB 22:213, 28:422, 55:520; KR 46:1017; Mahony 2:296; SLJ Oct 1978 p. 138; Tymn:155)

282   **SAINT-EXUPÉRY, Antoine (Jean-Baptiste-Marie-Roger) de.** *The Little Prince.*
✓   **Gr. 5 up. (Orig. pub. in France; orig. U.S. pub. 1943.)**

A pilot stranded in the Sahara meets a strange boy who tells him about his travels through the universe.

Trans. by Katherine Woods, illus. by the author, Harcourt, 1943, 91 pp. (0-15-246503-0), 1982, pap. (0-15-646511-6), 1993, 126 pp. (0-15-243820-3)

(BBC:212; BBJ:75; BL 39:354; CC:552; Ch&Bks:264; HB 70:95; HBG 5:74; JHC:409; LJ 68:248; SHC:716)

283   **SANCHEZ-SILVA, José.** *The Boy and the Whale.* **Gr. 3–5. (Orig. Spanish pub. 1962.)**

An imaginary whale helps a young boy deal with his grandmother's approaching death.

Trans. by Michael Heron, illus. by Margery Gill, McGraw-Hill, 1964, 80 pp., o.p.

(HB 40:376; KR 32:453; LJ 89:2662)

284   **SANDERSON, Ruth.** *The Enchanted Wood: An Original Fairy Tale.* **Gr. K–5.**

Galen, the youngest of the king's three sons, succeeds in finding the Heart of the World, needed to end the drought holding their kingdom in its grip.

Illus. by the author, Little, Brown, 1991, 32 pp. (0-316-77018-3)

(HBG 3[Spring 1992]:47; KR 59:1232; SLJ Oct 1991 p. 103)

SAN SOUCI, Robert D. *Feathertop: Based on the Tale by Nathaniel Hawthorne.* See Chapter 10, Witchcraft and Sorcery Fantasy.

SARGENT, Sarah. *Watermusic.* See Chapter 5B, Myth Fantasy.

SCARBOROUGH, Elizabeth Ann. *The Harem of Aman Akbar; or The Djinn Decanted.* See Chapter 6, Humorous Fantasy.

285   **SCHLEIN, Miriam.** *The Raggle Taggle Fellow.* **Gr. 2–4.**
✓   Dick's father disapproves of his third and youngest son's ambition to become a minstrel.

Illus. by Harvey Weiss, Abelard-Schuman, 1959, 62 pp., o.p.

(BL 55:544; Eakin: 286; HB 35:286; KR 27:134; LJ 84:1690)

286   **SCHMIDT, Werner (Felix).** *The Forests of Adventure.* **Gr. 3–6.**

Eric's adventure-filled search for his missing guardian, Black Otto, includes archery battles with outlaws, escape from imprisonment, the rescue of a fair lady, and a king's coronation.

Illus. by Artur Marokvia, Little, 1963, 161 pp., o.p.

(HB 39.174, LJ 88.2554)

287   **SCHRANK, Joseph.** *The Plain Princess and the Lazy Prince.* **Gr. 2–4.**

In an attempt to marry off their unattractive daughter, the king and queen advertise for a dragon, but it is the princess who ends up rescuing the prince.

Illus. by Mircea Vasiliu, Day, 1958, 57 pp., o.p.

(CCBB 12:74; KR 26:498; LJ 83:3012)

288   **SCHWARZ, Eugene M.** *Two Brothers.* **Gr. 1–4. (Orig. pub. in the Soviet Union.)**

After he locks Little Brother out in the cold, Big Brother must save him from Great-grandfather Frost.

Trans. by Elizabeth Hapgood, illus. by Gabriel Lisowski, Harper, 1973, 44 pp., o.p.

(KR 41:559; LJ 98:2644)

SCIESZKA, Jon. *The Stinky Cheese Man and Other Fairly Stupid Tales.* See Chapter 6, Humorous Fantasy.

SCIESZKA, Jon. *The True Story of the 3 Little Pigs: By A. Wolf.* See Chapter 6, Humorous Fantasy.

289 **SÈGUR, Comtesse Sophie (Rostopchine) de.** *The Enchanted Forest.* **Gr. 2–4.**
✓ **(Orig. French pub. 1856, U.S. 1869 in** *Fairy Tales for Little Folks.***) (Other editions: Penn,** *Old French Fairy Tales,* **1920, o.p.; Macrae Smith,** *Princess Rosette and Other Fairy Tales,* **1930, o.p.; British Book Service,** *Blondine and Bear-Cub,* **1957, o.p.; Harlin Quist,** *Forest of Lilacs,* **1969, illus. by Nicole Claveloux, o.p.)**

A wicked queen banishes little Princess Blondine to the enchanted Forest of Lilacs where she is imprisoned by wicked fairies and rescued by good fairies and a young prince.

Adapt. by Beatrice Schenk de Regniers, illus. by Gustave Doré, Atheneum, 1974, 87 pp., o.p.

(BL 17:127; Bookshelf 1932 p. 23; HB 51:54; KR 42:1251; LJ 83:649; SLJ Mar 1975 p. 86; TLS 1970 p. 419)

290 **SELFRIDGE, Oliver.** *The Trouble with Dragons.* **Gr. 4–6.**

Although her older sisters' attempts at dragon slaying failed, Princess Celia succeeds and wins a prince's love in the bargain.

Illus. by Shirley Hughes, Addison-Wesley, 1978, 86 pp., o.p.

(BL 74:1556; CCBB 31:184; SLJ Sept 1978 p. 148; Suth 2:402)

291 **SENDAK, Philip.** *In Grandpa's House.* **Gr. 4 up. (Orig. written in Yiddish.)**

A young boy flying on the back of a large bird encounters giants, monsters, and wild beasts while searching for his parents.

Trans. and adapt. by Seymour Barofsky, illus. by Maurice Sendak, Harper, 1985, 42 pp. LB(0-06-025463-7)

(HB 62:60; SLJ Oct 1985 p. 177; TLS 1986 p. 389)

292 **SEREDY, Kate.** *Lazy Tinka.* **Gr. 3–4.**

After Tinka is befriended by the forest animals, she learns to be more helpful at home.

Illus. by the author, Viking, 1962, 56 pp., o.p.

(BL 59:450; KR 62:683; LJ 88:98; TLS 1964 p. 605)

SEREDY, Kate. *The White Stag.* See Chapter 5B, Myth Fantasy.

293 **SEUSS, Dr. (pseud. of Theodor Seuss Geisel).** *The 500 Hats of Bartholomew*
✓ *Cubbins.* **Gr. 1–4.**

Even the king of Didd's most able wise men and sorcerers cannot take off all 500 of Bartholomew's hats. In the sequel, *Bartholomew and the Oobleck* (Random, 1949), Bartholomew saves the kingdom from sticky green oobleck that falls from the sky. *Bartholomew and the Oobleck* was a Randolph Caldecott Medal Honor Book, 1950.

Illus. by the author, Random, 1938, 45 pp., LB(0-394-84484-X)

(BL 35:102; CC:710; Ch&Bks:273; HB 14:365, 377; LJ 63:818, 890)

294 **SHAPIRO, Irwin.** *Twice upon a Time.* **Gr. 2–4.**

Since the King of Gib-Gib has decreed that everything must be twice as much or twice as many, ought there be two kings?

Illus. by Adrienne Adams, Scribner, 1973, 35 pp., o.p.

(CCBB 27:86; HB 50:40; KR 41:1032; LJ 98:3703)

295   **SHARMA, Partap.** *The Surangini Tales.* **Gr. 4–6.**

✓   Beautiful Surangini refuses to reappear from within the carpet woven by her suitor, Kalu, until seventeen tales have been told.

Illus. by Demi Hitz, Harcourt, 1973, 125 pp., o.p.

(BL 70:125; CCBB 26:176; HB 49:463; KR 41:386, 1351; LJ 98:2657; TLS 1974 p. 716)

296   **SHURA, Mary Francis (pseud. of Mary Francis Craig).** *The Nearsighted Knight.* **Gr. 4–6.**

After learning that his sister must marry before he can leave home, Prince Todd decides to help the Knight Before Glasses kill a dragon and win his sister's hand.

Illus. by Adrienne Adams, Knopf, 1964, 111 pp., o.p.

(CCBB 17:130; HB 40:284; KR 32:61; LJ 89:1454)

297   **SILVERMAN, Maida.** *The Magic Well.* **Gr. K–4.**

The Fairy Queen lures young Janet down into the fairy realm, but her mother saves her on the night of the Fairy Ride, in this story reminiscent of the ballad "Tam Lin."

Illus. by Manuel Boix, Simon & Schuster, 1989, 40 pp., o.p.

(HBG 1[July 1989]:100; KR 57:1537; SLJ Feb 1990 p. 79)

SIMAK, Clifford D(onald). *Enchanted Pilgrimage.* See Chapter 5A, Alternate Worlds or Histories.

298   **SINGER, Isaac Bashevis.** *Alone in the Wild Forest.* **Gr. 4–6.**

Orphaned Joseph dreams of meeting and winning Princess Chassidah, but wicked Bal Makane plots against him.

Trans. by the author and Elizabeth Shub, illus. by Margot Zemach, Farrar, 1971, 79 pp., o.p.

(BBC:213; CCBB 25:97; KR 39:1015; LJ 97:285)

299   **SINGER, Isaac Bashevis.** *The Fearsome Inn.* **Gr. 4–6.**

✓   With his piece of magic chalk, Liebel, a young Cabala student, rescues three young girls held by a witch and a devil. John Newbery Medal Honor Book, 1968.

Trans. by the author and Elizabeth Shub, illus. by Nonny Hogrogian, Scribner, 1967, 45 pp., o.p.

(BL 64:338; CCBB 21:67; Ch&Bks:291; HB 43:751, 61:595; KR 35:880; LJ 92:3190; Suth:367)

300   **SINGER, Isaac Bashevis.** *A Tale of Three Wishes.* **Gr. 2–4.**

Three children make wishes that cause unexpected problems on the night of Hoshanah Rabbah.

Illus. by Irene Lieblich, Farrar, 1976, 30 pp., o.p.

(BL 72:1118; CCBB 30:18; KR 44:201; SLJ Apr 1976 p. 65)

SINGER, Isaac Bashevis. *Zlateh the Goat and Other Stories.* See Chapter 3, Fantasy Collections.

301   **SINGER, Marilyn.** *The Golden Heart of Winter.* **Gr. 1–4.**

A raven gives young Half a riddle to help him find the Golden Heart of Winter, which ensures that life will return to the earth each spring, but Half's older brothers try to steal the treasure.

Illus. by Robert Rayevsky, Morrow, 1991, 40 pp. LB(0-688-07718-8)

(BL 88:166; HBG 3[July–Dec 1991]:61; KR 59:861; SLJ Dec 1991 p. 102)

302   SLOBODKIN, Louis. *The Amiable Giant.* **Gr. 1–3.**

A wizard tries to frighten the villagers with terrifying tales about the friendly local giant, but Gwendolyn discovers the truth.

Illus. by the author, Macmillan, 1955, 36 pp., o.p.; Vanguard, 1966 (c. 1955), 36 pp., o.p.

(BL 52:173; HB 32:27; KR 23:784)

303   SLOBODKIN, Louis. *The Little Mermaid Who Could Not Sing.* **Gr. 1–3.**

A young mermaid named Cynthia discovers that her gigantic voice becomes vitally important whenever fog covers the Blue Rocks in the great Southern Sea.

Macmillan, 1956, 38 pp., o.p.

(BL 53:253; HB 32:330; KR 24:783

304   SMITH, Agnes. *An Edge of the Forest.* **Gr. 5–9. (Orig. pub. Viking, 1959.)**

✓   An orphaned lamb who accidentally wanders into the forest is saved from death and adopted by a black leopardess.

Illus. by Roberta Moynihan, Westwind, 1974, 202 pp., o.p.

(BL 55:578; CCBB 13:21; Eakin:301; HB 35:10; KR 27:91; LJ 84:1700)

SNYDER, Zilpha Keatley. *Below the Root.* See Chapter 5A, Alternate Worlds or Histories.

305   SNYDER, Zilpha Keatley. *The Changing Maze.* **Gr. 2–4.**

✓   A shepherd boy lost in a maze created by an evil wizard searches for his stray pet lamb, ignoring the gold at the heart of the maze.

Illus. by Charles Mikolaycak, Macmillan, 1985, o.p., 1992, 32 pp., pap. (0-689-71618-4)

(BBC:213; BL 82:269; CC:559; CCBB 39:57; HB 62:52; JHC:559; SLJ Dec 1985 p. 83)

SOYER, Abraham. *The Adventures of Yemina.* See Chapter 3, Fantasy Collections.

306   STANLEY, Diane. *Fortune.* **Gr. K–4.**

✓   Omar, a poor farmer's son whose dancing tiger makes him wealthy, learns about humility when the princess he wants to marry rejects him for love of a man who disappeared due to a witch's spell.

Illus. by the author, Morrow, 1990, 32 pp. (0-688-07210-0)

(BL 86:1172; CC:716; CCBB 43:228; HB 66:598; HBG 1[Jan 1990]:215; KR 58:185; SLJ April 1990 p. 97)

STANTON, Mary. *The Heavenly Horse from the Outermost West.* See Chapter 2, Animal Fantasy.

STEARNS, Pamela (Fujimoto). *The Fool and the Dancing Bear.* See Chapter 5A, Alternate Worlds or Histories.

307   STEARNS, Pamela (Fujimoto). *The Mechanical Doll.* **Gr. 4–6.**

Jealous of the life-sized mechanical doll that has captured the king's fancy, Hulon, the court musician, breaks it and is banished from the court.

Illus. by Trina Schart Hyman, Houghton, 1979, 45 pp., o.p.

(BL 75:1160; CCBB 32:184; KR 47:519; SLJ Nov 1979 p. 82)

STEELE, Mary Q(uintard Govan). *Journey Outside.* See Chapter 5A, Alternate Worlds or Histories.

STEELE, Mary Q(uintard Govan). *The Owl's Kiss: Three Stories.* See Chapter 3. Fantasy Collections.

STEELE, Mary Q(uintard Govan). *The True Men.* See Chapter 5A, Alternate Worlds or Histories.

308 **STEIN, Gertrude.** *The World Is Round.* **Gr. 1–4. (Orig. pub. 1939.)**

A reissue of famed writer/philosopher Gertrude Stein's children's story about Rose, Willie, and Willie's pet lion. In this story the author experimented with rhythm and word patterns.

Illus. by Clement Hurd, Young Scott, 1966, o.p.; Arion, 1986, 94 pp. (0-910457-16-6)

(BL 36:180; HB 15:294; LJ 92:330; TLS 1939 p. 758)

STEINER, Jörg. *Rabbit Island.* See Chapter 2, Animal Fantasy.

309 **STEINER, Jörg.** *The Sea People.* **Gr. 3–6. (Orig. German pub. 1981.)**

Two neighboring island communities with vastly different lifestyles must learn to cooperate after one island is virtually destroyed by its people's greed for gold.

Trans. by Victor Gollancz, illus. by Jörg Müller, Schocken, 1982, 35 pp., o.p.

(CCBB 36:135; SLJ April 1983 p. 119; TLS 1982 p. 1305)

310 **STEPHENS, James.** *The Crock of Gold.* **Gr. 6–9. (Orig. U.S. pub. Macmillan, 1912, 1960.)**

Seumas and Brigid, children of two philosophers, meet extraordinary creatures in the woods, including leprechauns and the god Pan.

Illus. by Thomas MacKenzie, Telegraph Books, 1980 (repr. of 1912 ed.), 312 pp., o.p.

(BL 10:245; TLS 1981 p. 348)

STEVENS, Eden Vale. *Abba.* See Chapter 2, Animal Fantasy.

311 **STEWART, Mary (Florence Elinor).** *Ludo and the Star Horse.* **Gr. 5–8. (Orig. British pub. 1974.)**

Ludo and his old horse fall into a hidden pit and journey through the twelve houses of the zodiac.

Illus. by Gino D'Achille, Morrow, 1975, 191 pp., o.p.

(BL 71:967; KR 43:376; SLJ Sept 1975 p. 112; TLS 1974 p. 1380)

312 **STOCKTON, Frank (Francis) R(ichard).** *The Bee-Man of Orn.* **Gr. 4–6. (Orig.**
✓ **pub. in *Fanciful Tales* 1884; as a separate tale, Holt, 1964.)**

An old beekeeper, told by a sorcerer that he was transformed from another sort of being, decides to find out what he was originally.

Illus. by Maurice Sendak, Harper, 1987, 48 pp., LB(0-06-025818-7)

(BL 61:528; CC:563; Ch&Bks:291; Eakin:312; HB 40:611, 63:491; LJ 89:4643; Mahony 1:27; TLS 1976 p. 376)

313 **STOCKTON, Frank (Francis) R(ichard).** *The Griffin and the Minor Canon.* **Gr.**
✓ **3–5. (Orig. pub. in *Fanciful Tales*, 1884; as a separate tale, Holt, 1963.)**

The last of the griffins threatens to stay in a terrified village because it so admires its likeness carved above the church door.

Illus. by Maurice Sendak, Harper, 1986, 56 pp., LB(0-06-025816-0), 1987, pap. (0-06-443126-6)

(BBC:214; BL 59:900, 83:357; CC:563; Eakin:313; HB 39:384, 63:84; LJ 88:2555)

STOCKTON, Frank (Francis) R(ichard). *The Queen's Museum and Other Fanciful Tales.* See Chapter 3, Fantasy Collections.

314   STOLP, Hans. *The Golden Bird.* **Gr. 3 up. (Orig. Dutch pub. 1987.)**

✓   Three birds teach Daniel, who is dying of cancer, that he will blossom like the cherry tree—which blooms after a deathlike winter season—when he is reunited with his father in heaven.

Illus. by Lidia Postma, Dial, 1990, 56 pp., o.p.; Dell, 1992, pap. (0-440-40611-0)

(BL 56:1639; HBG 1[Jan 1990]246; KR 58:432; SLJ April 1990 p. 124; VOYA 13:35)

315   STOLZ, Mary (Slattery). *The Cuckoo Clock.* **Gr. 4–6.**

✓   Ula, the old clockmaker, makes one final marvelous cuckoo clock before he dies, as part of a magical legacy for his assistant, a young foundling named Erich.

Illus. by Pamela Johnson, Godine, 1986, 84 pp. (0-87923-653-1)

(BBC:214; BL 83:652; CC:563; CCBB 40:179; Ch&Bks:291; KR 55:376; SLJ Apr 1987 p. 105; Suth 4:399)

316   STOLZ, Mary (Slattery). *The Leftover Elf.* **Gr. 3–5.**

✓   The survival of the last elf in the world depends on his finding someone who believes in him.

Illus. by Peggy Bacon, Harper, 1952, 57 pp., o.p.

(CCBB 5:69; HB 28:172; KR 20:188; LJ 77:653)

317   STOLZ, Mary (Slattery). *The Scarecrows and Their Child.* **Gr. 3–5.**

Two unemployed scarecrows, Handy and Blossom, marry and live peacefully with their cat child, Bohel, until they are kidnapped, whereupon Bohel sets out to find them.

Illus. by Amy Schwartz, Harper, 1987, 67 pp., o.p.

(BBC:214; BL 54:572; CCBB 41:77; KR 53:1467; SLJ Jan 1988 p. 76)

318   STRANGER, Joyce (pseud. of Joyce Muriel Judson Wilson). *The Fox at Drummer's Darkness.* **Gr. 6–9. (Orig. British pub. 1976.)**

Poisoned by toxic chemicals in the water, a night watchman's ghost rises from his grave to warn the townspeople.

Illus. by William Geldart, Farrar, 1977, 108 pp., o.p.

(BL 73:1731; HB 53:534; KR 45:540; SLJ May 1977 p. 72)

319   SUTCLIFF, Rosemary. *Chess-Dream in a Garden.* **Gr. 3 up. (Orig. British pub. 1993.)**

A sophisticated illustrated tale combining chess and fable, about a queen who goes into battle to save her kingdom from the enemy Red Horde.

Illus. by Ralph Thompson, Candlewick, 1993, 48 pp. (1-56402-192-0)

(BL 90:52; CCBB 47:102; HBG 5:70; KR 61:943; SLJ Nov 1993 p. 110)

320   SUTCLIFF, Rosemary. *The Minstrel and the Dragon Pup.* **Gr. K–4. (Orig.**
✓   **British pub. 1993.)**

A wandering minstrel must cure a young prince's illness to win back the baby dragon stolen from him.

Illus. by Emma Chichester Clark, Candlewick, 1993, 45 pp. (1-56402-098-3)

(BL 89:1238; CCBB 46:226; HB 69:455; HBG 4[Fall 1993]:292; KR 61:380; SLJ Apr 1993 p. 103)

SUTCLIFF, Rosemary. *The Sword and the Circle: King Arthur and the Knights of the Round Table.* See Chapter 5B, Myth Fantasy.

SWIFT, Jonathan. *Gulliver's Travels.* See Chapter 5C, Travel to Other Worlds.

SYNGE, (Phyllis) Ursula. *Swan's Wing.* See Chapter 5B, Myth Fantasy.

TASSIN, Algernon de Vivier. *The Rainbow String.* See Chapter 3, *Fantasy Collections.*

321   **TAZEWELL, Charles.** *The Littlest Angel.* Gr. K–3. (Orig. pub. 1946.)

The newest angel in Paradise is lonely among the well-behaved adult angels, until he is befriended by the Understanding Angel.

Illus. by Sergio Leone, Childrens, 1946, LB(0-516-03533-9); Ideals, 1985 (repr. of 1964 ed.), pap., 32 pp. (0-89542-923-3); illus. by Paul Micich, Ideals, 1991, 32 pp. (0-89542-923-3)

(HBG 3[July–Dec 1991]:62; KR 14:592; LJ 71:1810; SLJ Oct 1991 p. 34)

322   **TENNYSON, Noel.** *The Lady's Chair and the Ottoman.* Gr. 1–4.

✓   True love and loyalty win out in the end, after an ottoman becomes separated from the lady's chair he loves when their owner's home is sold.

Illus. by the author, Lothrop, 1987, 32 pp. (0-688-04098-5)

(BL 84:324; CCBB 41:79; KR 56:1326; SLJ Sept 1987 p. 183)

TEPPER, Sheri S. *Beauty: A Novel.* See Chapter 5B, Myth Fantasy.

323   **TERLOUW, Jan (Cornelis).** *How to Become King.* Gr. 6–8. (Orig. British pub. 1976.)

Seventeen-year-old Stark demands to know how he can become king, so the Ministers of Katoren devise seven impossible tasks for him, including silencing the Birds of Decibel, destroying the Dragon of Smog, and outwitting the Wizard of Equilibrium.

Hastings, 1977, 128 pp., o.p.

(BL 74:1111; CCBB 31:135; SLJ Mar 1978 p. 134; Suth 2:445; VOYA 1 [Apr 1978]:65)

324   **THACKERAY, William Makepeace.** *The Rose and the Ring; or the History of*
✓   *Prince Giglio and Prince Bulbo: A Fireside Pantomime for Great and Small Children.* Gr. 5–8. (Orig. British pub. 1855.)

Princess Rosealba and Prince Giglio are restored to their rightful thrones through the good offices of Fairy Blackstick.

Illus. by the author, John Gilbert, and Paul Hogarth, Pierpont Morgan, 1947, 212 pp., o.p.

(BL 5:124, 6:230, 20:65; Bookshelf 1932 p. 23; HB 23:14, 35:480; Mahony 1:38)

325   **THEROUX, Paul.** *A Christmas Card.* Gr. 5 up.

Lost in a blizzard on Christmas Eve, Marcel and his family are welcomed into the house of a man called Pappy, whose magic helps them find their way home.

Illus. by John Lawrence, Houghton, 1978, 96 pp., o.p.

(BL 75:227; KR 46:1358; SLJ Oct 1978 p. 113)

326   **THURBER, James (Grover).** *The Great Quillow.* Gr. 3–4.

✓   Quillow the toymaker saves the town by outwitting an unruly giant named Hunder.

Illus. by Doris Lee, Harcourt, 1944, o.p.; Peter Smith, n.d., o.p.

(BL 41:95; Ch&Bks:251; HB 20:469, 482; KR 12:449; LJ 69:866, 1004)

327   THURBER, James (Grover). *Many Moons.* **Gr. K–4.**

✓   Only the court jester is wise enough to cure Princess Lenore's illness by "giving" her the moon. Randolph Caldecott Medal for Illustration, 1944.

Illus. by Louis Slobodkin, Harcourt, 1943, 46 pp. (0-15-251873-8); illus. by Marc Simont, Harcourt, 1990, 48 pp. (0-15-251872-X)

(BL 40:20, 87:174; CC:566; Ch&Bks:252; HB 19:318, 422, 20:21, 67:60; HBG 2[July–Dec 1990]:29; KR 58:1096; LJ 68:672, 818; SLJ Jan 1991 p. 82)

328   THURBER, James (Grover). *The 13 Clocks.* **Gr. 5 up.**

To marry the princess, Prince Zorn must find a thousand jewels to start all of the stilled clocks in the land.

Illus. by Marc Simont, Simon, 1950, 124 pp., o.p.; Fine, 1990 (1-55611-188-6); Dell, 1992, pap. (0-440-40582-3)

(BL 47:174; Ch&Bks:291; Tymn:161)

329   THURBER, James (Grover). *The White Deer.* **Gr. 5 up.**

✓   Since he once married a princess who appeared from the enchanted forest in the guise of a white deer, King Clode and his three sons are tempted to hunt in the forest when another white deer is sighted.

Illus. by the author and Don Freeman, Harcourt, 1945, o.p., pap., 1968, 115 pp. (0-15-696264-0)

(BL 42:57; HB 21:447; KR 13:43; Tymn:161)

330   THURBER, James (Grover). *The Wonderful O.* **Gr. 5 up.**

✓   Wicked Black and his pirate crew decide to destroy everything spelled with the letter "O."

Illus. by Marc Simont, Simon, 1957, 72 pp., o.p.; Fine, 1990 (1-55611-189-4); Dell, 1992, pap. (0-440-40579-3)

(BL 53:559; Ch&Bks:291; KR 25:308; LJ 82:1780)

331   TILLSTROM, Burr. *The Dragon Who Lived Downstairs.* **Gr. 2–4.**

A friendly dragon releases the princess and her parents from an enchantment, and helps a nonroyal knight win the princess's hand.

Illus. by David Small, Morrow, 1984, 44 pp., o.p.

(CCBB 37:157; Ch&Bks:292; SLJ Aug 1984 p. 66)

332   TOLKIEN, J(ohn) R(onald) R(euel). *Farmer Giles of Ham.* **Gr. 5–8. (Orig. pub.**
✓   **1949.)**

Farmer Giles leads a simple life until the day he finds himself protecting his village from dragons.

Illus. by Pauline Baynes, Houghton, 1978, 78 pp. (0-395-07121-6); illus. by Roger Garland, Houghton, 1991, 82 pp. (0-395-57645-8)

(CCBB 4:23; HB 26:287; HBG 2:267; LJ 75:2084; Tymn:166)

TOLKIEN, J(ohn) R(onald) R(euel). *Fellowship of the Ring.* See Chapter 5A, Alternate Worlds or Histories.

TOLKIEN, J(ohn) R(onald) R(euel). *The Hobbit; Or, There and Back Again.* See Chapter 5A, Alternate Worlds or Histories.

333   TOLKIEN, J(ohn) R(onald) R(euel). *Smith of Wootton Major.* **Gr. 5–8. (Orig. pub. 1967.)**

After the blacksmith's son finds a magical star buried in a piece of cake, his life is completely changed.

Illus. by Pauline Baynes, Houghton, 1978, o.p.; illus. by Roger Garland, Houghton, 1991, 96 pp. (0-395-57646-6)

(HB 44:63; HBG 2:267; KR 35:1164; LJ 92:4175; TLS 1967 p. 1153)

334   **TORREY, Marjorie (Chanslor Hood).** *Artie and the Princess.* **Gr. 2–4.**

Artie the lonely dragon child searches for a playmate and finds a princess.

Illus. by the author, Howell, 1945, 107 pp., o.p.

(BL 41:344; KR 13:181; LJ 70:343, 492)

335   **TURKLE, Brinton (Cassaday).** *The Fiddler of High Lonesome.* **Gr. 3–6.**

When the magic of Lysander's fiddle-playing draws wild animals into a moonlight dance, his cruel cousins attempt to hunt the helpless creatures down.

Illus. by the author, Viking, 1968, 47 pp., o.p.

(BL 64:1189; CCBB: 21:166; HB 44:424; KR 36:338; LJ 93:2117)

336   **TWAIN, Mark (pseud. of Samuel Clemens).** *Legend of Sagenfeld.* **Gr. 2–8. (Orig. Australian pub. in this edition, 1987.)**

In an attempt to avoid the disaster prophesied for his kingdom, King Hubert chooses a donkey as the animal whose music sounds the sweetest.

Illus. by George Molnar, Publishers Group, 1988, 26 pp., o.p.

(BBC:215; BL 84:1531; KR 55:1739; SLJ Mar 1988 p. 177)

337   **URQUHART, Elizabeth.** *Horace.* **Gr. 3–5.**

A little girl named Miriam and a young dragon named Horace save the dragon's father from St. George.

Illus. by Rosita Pastor, Dutton, 1951, 116 pp., o.p.

(BL 48:38; CCBB 5:25; HB 27:325; KR 19:387; LJ 76:1433)

338   **VAN ALLSBURG, Chris.** *The Stranger.* **Gr. K–4.**

✓   It seems that autumn will never come, the year Farmer Bailey brings home a leather-clad stranger who has lost his memory.

Illus. by the author, Houghton, 1986, 32 pp. (0-395-42331-7)

(BL 83:276; CC:726; CCBB 40:59; HB 62:741; KR 54:1452; SLJ Nov 1986 p. 84)

339   **VAN ALLSBURG, Chris.** *The Sweetest Fig.* **Gr. 3 up.**

✓   Despite self-centered Monsieur Bibot's mistreatment of his dog, the Parisian dentist's dreams literally come true, after he eats one of two magic figs given to him by a poor old woman.

Illus. by the author, Houghton, 1993, 32 pp. (0-395-67346-1)

(BL 90:343; CCBB 47:104; HBG 5:58; KR 61:1339; SLJ Nov 1993 p. 110)

VAN ALLSBURG, Chris. *The Widow's Broom.* See Chapter 10, Witchcraft and Sorcery Fantasy.

340   **VAN ALLSBURG, Chris.** *The Wreck of the Zephyr.* **Gr. 2–5.**

✓   An old sailor tells a young boy about the wondrous night he learned to fly his sailboat through the skies.

Illus. by the author, Houghton, 1983, 28 pp. (0-395-33075-0)

(BBC:215; BL 79:1273, 1279, 1284; CC:726; CCBB 36:220; HB 59:295; KR 51:305; SLJ May 1983 pp. 33, 67)

341   **VAN ALLSBURG, Chris.** *The Wretched Stone.* **Gr. K–4.**

✓   After the crew of the ship *Rita Ann* finds a strange glowing stone on an uncharted island, they begin turning into monkeys.

Illus. by the author, Houghton, 1991, 32 pp. (0-395-53307-4)

(BL 88:338; CC 1992 Suppl. p. 84; CCBB 45:78; HB 68:62; HBG 3[Spring 1992]:51; KR 59:1228; SLJ Nov 1991 p. 108)

***Visions of Wonder: An Anthology of Christian Fantasy.* Ed. by Robert H. Boyer and Kenneth J. Zahorski.** See Chapter 3, Fantasy Collections.

VOEGELI, Max. *The Wonderful Lamp.* See Chapter 5B, Myth Fantasy.

342   **WAECHTER, Friedrich, and EILERT, Bernd.** *The Crown Snatchers.* **Gr. 4–6. (Orig. German pub. 1972.)**

Three children who help bring about the downfall of the Pig King are disappointed to find that the new king is also a tyrant.

Trans. by Edite Kroll, illus. by the authors, Pantheon, 1975, 160 pp., o.p.

(BL 71:697; KR 43:377; SLJ Apr 1975 p. 60)

343   **WAHL, Jan (Boyer).** *How the Children Stopped the Wars.* **Gr. 4–6.**

A shepherd boy envisions terrible wars, gathers children from all the surrounding villages, and marches them to the battlefield to stop the fighting.

Illus. by Mitchell Miller, Farrar, 1969, o.p.; Avon, 1983, pap., 96 pp., o.p.

(CCBB 23:136; HB 46:164; KR 37:1260; LJ 95:782, 3610)

344   **WANGERIN, Walter, Jr.** *The Book of the Dun Cow.* **Gr. 8 up.**

✓   In this complex Christian allegory, Chaunticleer the rooster and Mundo Cani Dog save the world from the evils of the giant Wyrm and his "minion" Cockatrice. The American Book Award, Science Fiction Category, 1980. The sequel is *The Book of Sorrows* (1985).

Harper, 1978, 241 pp., o.p., pap., 1982 (0-06-250937-3)

(BBJ:76; BL 75:927; CCBB 32:92; KR 46:1255; SLJ Oct 1978 p. 160; Suth 2:469; TLS 1980 p. 368; VOYA 1[Feb 1979]:43, 3[Oct 1980]:49)

345   **WANGERIN, Walter, Jr.** *Elisabeth and the Water-Troll.* **Gr. 3–5.**

Elisabeth's despair over her mother's death awakens the sympathy of a water troll who hopes to make her happy at the bottom of his well.

Illus. by Deborah Healy, Harper, 1991, 64 pp. (0-06-026353-9)

(BL 87:1800; HBG 2:272; KR 59:325; SLJ May 1991 p. 96)

346   **WANGERIN, Walter, Jr.** *Potter, Come Fly to the First of the Earth.* **Gr. 4–6.**

An oriole takes a boy named Potter out of his sickbed on a journey that helps him come to terms with his best friend's death.

Illus. by Daniel San Souci, Cook, 1985, 52 pp., o.p.

(BBC:215; BL 82:874; SLJ April 1986 p. 93)

347   **WANGERIN, Walter, Jr.** *Thistle.* **Gr. 2–4.**

Thistle, the youngest child, saves her family from being eaten by a giant potato, by daring to kiss an ugly witch.

Illus. by Marcia Sewall, Harper, 1983, 47 pp., o.p.

(BBC:215; CCBB 37:80; KR 51:J156; SLJ Nov 1983 p. 84)

WARBURG, Sandol Stoddard. *On the Way Home.* See Chapter 5A, Alternate Worlds or Histories.

348   **WEIR, Rosemary (Green).** *Albert the Dragon.* **Gr. 4–6.**

As a favor for a friend, Albert the vegetarian dragon pretends to let a knight defeat him in battle. The sequels are *Further Adventures of Albert the Dragon* (1964), *Albert the Dragon and the Centaur* (1968), and *Albert and the Dragonettes* (British).

Illus. by Quentin Blake, Abelard-Schuman, 1961, 107 pp., o.p.

(CCBB 15:68; KR 29:669; LJ 86:4043)

349   **WERSBA, Barbara.** *Let Me Fall Before I Fly.* **Gr. 3–5.**

A young boy finds a two-inch-high circus giving daily performances in his garden.

Illus. by Mercer Mayer, Atheneum, 1971, o.p.; illus. by James Hoys, Creative, 1986, 48 pp., LB(0-88682-057-X)

(CCBB 26:66; HB 47:616; KR 39:1124; LJ 97:1611)

350   **WERSBA, Barbara.** *A Song for Clowns.* **Gr. 4–6.**

Humphrey the minstrel resents the fact that the king has abolished sheriffs, the color blue, love, hope, puddings, and minstrels.

Illus. by Mario Rivoli, Atheneum, 1965, 100 pp., o.p.

(CCBB 19:53; HB 41:629; KR 33:677; LJ 90:3797; TLS 1966 p. 1087)

351   **WESTON, John (Harrison).** *The Boy Who Sang the Birds.* **Gr. 4–6.**

Two boys try to stop a flock of strange birds from causing a catastrophic winter in their village.

Illus. by Donna Diamond, Scribner, 1976, 106 pp., o.p.

(BL 72:1272; KR 44:257; SLJ Apr 1976 p. 79)

352   **WETTERER, Margaret K.** *The Giant's Apprentice.* **Gr. 2–4.**

When Liam McGowen, apprentice blacksmith, is kidnapped by a giant, only his uncle can save him.

Illus. by Elise Primavera, Atheneum, 1982, 40 pp., o.p.

(BL 78:1261; HB 58:410; KR 50:492; SLJ May 1982 p. 67)

353   **WETTERER, Margaret K.** *The Mermaid's Cape.* **Gr. 2–4.**

A mermaid, trapped into marriage and human form by a lonely fisherman, is freed when their beloved young son finds her magical cape.

Illus. by Elise Primavera, Atheneum, 1981, 32 pp., o.p.

(BL 77:1302; HB 57:427; KR 49:506; SLJ May 1981 p. 60)

WHITE, E(lwyn) B(rooks). *Charlotte's Web.* See Chapter 2, Animal Fantasy.

WHITE, Eliza Orne. *The Enchanted Mountain.* See Chapter 5C, Travel to Other Worlds.

WHITE, T(erence) H(anbury). *The Sword in the Stone.* See Chapter 5B, Myth Fantasy.

354   **WIGGIN, Kate Douglas (Smith).** *The Bird's Christmas Carol.* **Gr. 3–5. (Orig. pub. 1888.)**

Carol Bird saves the Ruggles's Christmas. The sequel is *Polly Oliver's Problem* (1896).

Illus. by Jessie Gillespie, Houghton, 1941, 84 pp., o.p.

(BL 38:137; Bookshelf 19251926 p. 4; CC:572)

WILDE, Oscar (pseud. of Fingal O'Flahertie Wills). *The Birthday of the Infanta and Other Tales.* See *The Fairy Tales of Oscar Wilde* in Chapter 3, Fantasy Collections.

355 **WILDE, Oscar (pseud. of Fingal O'Flahertie Wills).** *The Happy Prince.* **Gr. 3–5.**
✓ **(Orig. British pub. in** *The Happy Prince and Other Tales,* **1888.)**

A bejeweled statue of a prince, unhappy at the misery of the people around him, persuades a swallow to carry his riches to the needy.

Illus. by Kaj Beckman, Methuen, 1977, o.p.; illus. by Jean Claverie, Oxford, 1981, 40 pp. (0-19-279750-6); illus. by Ed Young, Simon, 1989, pap., 32 pp. (0-671-77819-6)

(BL 78:444; Bookshelf 1932 p. 24; HB 41:630; KR 45:1320; LJ 91:430; Mahony 1:37; SLJ Jan 1978 p. 92, Mar 1982 p. 153, July 1989 p. 78; TLS 1981 p. 343)

WILDE, Oscar (pseud. of Fingal O'Flahertie Wills). *The Happy Prince and Other Tales.* See *The Fairy Tales of Oscar Wilde* in Chapter 3, Fantasy Collections.

356 **WILDE, Oscar (pseud. of Fingal O'Flahertie Wills).** *The Picture of Dorian*
✓ *Gray.* **Gr. 10 up. (Orig. British pub. 1891, orig. U.S. pub. in an unauthorized ed. 1890.)**

Granted eternal youth, Dorian Gray lives a wild, dissipated life while his portrait grows old and haggard.

Putnam 1909, 1916, 337 pp., o.p.; Random, 1926, 1954, 1985, 1992, 248 pp. (0-679-60001-9); Dutton, 1930, 186 pp., o.p.; Harper, 1965, o.p.; Oxford, 1974, 1981, pap. (0-19-281553-9); Puffin, 1986, pap. (0-14-043187-X); ed. by Isobel Murray, Oxford Univ. Press, 1974, 249 pp., o.p.

(BL 28:113; Kies:186; Kliatt 16 [Spring 1982]:18; SHC:730; TLS 1974 p. 811)

357 **WILDE, Oscar (pseud. of Fingal O'Flahertie Wills).** *The Selfish Giant.* **Gr. 1–4.**
✓ **(Orig. British pub. in** *The Happy Prince and Other Tales,* **1888.)**

A giant has a change of heart, allows children to play in his garden, and assures himself a place in heaven.

Illus. by Gertrude Reiner and Walter Reiner, Harvey, 1967, 72 pp., o.p.; illus. by Michael Foreman and Freire Wright, Methuen, 1978, 30 pp., o.p.; illus. by Lisbeth Zwerger, Picture Book, 1984, pap., 28 pp. (0-907234-30-5); Scholastic, 1991, pap. (0-590-44460-3); illus. by Dom Mansell, Prentice, 1986, 32 pp. (0-13-803586-5); Simon, 1986, pap. (0-671-66847-1)

(BL 75:551, 80:1631; CC:572; CCBB 8:56, 37:196; Ch&Bks:292; HB 60:463; KR 46:1242; LJ 93:2117; SLJ Jan 1979 p. 49, Jan 1980 p. 63, Sept 1984 p. 122, Apr 1987 p. 91; Suth 3:444; TLS 1967 p. 1137)

358 **WILDE, Oscar (pseud. of Fingal O'Flahertie Wills).** *The Star Child: A Fairy Tale.* **Gr. 2–4. (Orig. British pub. 1891, U.S. 1906 in** *A House of Pomegranates.***)**

A selfish orphaned boy, searching for his mother, learns compassion and self-sacrifice before he learns his true identity.

Adapt. by Jennifer Westwood, illus. by Fiona French, Macmillan, 1979, 30 pp., o.p.

(BL 76:670; CCBB 33:123; SLJ Jan 1980 p. 63)

359 **WILKINS (Freeman), Mary E(leanor).** *Princess Rosetta and the Popcorn Man.* **Gr. 2–4. (Orig. pub. in** *The Pot of Gold,* **1892, 1970.)**

After the infant Princess of Romalia disappears during the annual bee festival, a wandering popcorn man finds her in a neighboring kingdom.

Adapt. by Ellin Greene, illus. by Trina Schart Hyman, Lothrop, 1971, 40 pp., o.p.

(KR 39:94; LJ 97:1174)

360 **WILKINS (Freeman), Mary E(leanor).** *The Pumpkin Giant.* **Gr. 2–4. (Orig.**
✓ **pub. in *The Pot of Gold,* 1892, 1970.)**

A brave father kills the dreadful pumpkin-headed giant so that his plump son can marry
the king's plump daughter, and they all feast on pumpkin pie.

Retold by Ellin Greene, illus. by Trina Schart Hyman, Lothrop, 1970, 40 pp., o.p.

(BL 67:192; CCBB 24:68; HB 46:607; KR 38:870)

WILLARD, Nancy (Margaret). *Beauty and the Beast.* See Chapter 5B, Myth
Fantasy.

361 **WILLARD, Nancy (Margaret).** *The Marzipan Moon.* **Gr. 4–5.**

A hungry parish priest wishes for a marzipan moon to appear in his old crock every
morning. When his wish is granted, an officious bishop steps in and tries to take charge of
this miracle.

Illus. by Marcia Sewall, Harcourt, 1981 (0-15-252962-4), pap., 46 pp. (0-15-252963-2)

(BBC:215; BL 77:1302; HB 57:418; KR 49:428; SLJ Aug 1981 p. 72)

WILLARD, Nancy (Margaret). *Sailing to Cythera, and Other Anatole Stories.*
See Chapter 5C, Travel to Other Worlds.

WILLARD, Nancy (Margaret). *The Sorcerer's Apprentice.* See Chapter 10,
Witchcraft and Sorcery Fantasy.

362 **WILLARD, Nancy (Margaret).** *Things Invisible to See.* **Gr. 10 up.**
✓ Ruth and young neighborhood baseball star Ben fall in love after a ball hit by Ben strikes
Ruth in the head and paralyzes her; she subsequently saves his life.

Knopf, 1984, 263 pp. (0-394-54058-1); Bantam, 1985, 1989, pap., 272 pp. (0-553-
27652-2)

(BBS:67; BL 81:484, 82:753, 86:907; Kies:187; Kliatt 20 [Spring 1986]:26; KR 52:1020; LJ 109:2301, Jan
1986 p. 50; SLJ May 1985 p. 115, Apr 1986 p. 31; VOYA 8:190)

WILLETT, John. *The Singer in the Stone.* See Chapter 5A, Alternate Worlds or
Histories.

363 **WILLIAMS, Anne.** *Secret of the Round Tower.* **Gr. 4–6.**

Melisande and Galpin must keep their discovery of a pure white unicorn secret from the
king.

Illus. by J. C. Kocsis, Random, 1968, 87 pp., o.p.

(HB 45:47; KR 36:820; LJ 94:880)

364 **WILLIAMS, Jay.** *Petronella.* **Gr. 2–4.**

On her way to seek her fortune, Princess Petronella rescues an enchanted prince. This
story has been republished in *The Practical Princess and Other Liberating Fairy Tales*
(1978).

Illus. by Friso Henstra, Parents, 1973, 33 pp., o.p.

(BL 70:176; KR 41:454; LJ 98:2646)

365 **WILLIAMS, Jay.** *The Practical Princess.* **Gr. 2–4.**

The fairy gift of common sense helps a princess defeat a dragon and find her own prince.
This story has been republished in *The Practical Princess and Other Liberating Fairy
Tales* (1978).

Illus. by Friso Henstra, Parents, 1969, 40 pp., o.p.

(BL 65:1129; CCBB 23:68; KR 37:1774, 2073, and 4583)

WILLIAMS, Jay. *The Practical Princess and Other Liberating Fairy Tales.* See Chapter 3, Fantasy Collections.

366 **WILLIAMS, Kit.** *Masquerade.* **Gr. 4–6. (Orig. British pub. 1979.)**

The moon, in love with the sun, gives him the gift of a jeweled hare. This book contains clues that touched off a three-year real-life treasure hunt in England.

Illus. by the author, Schocken, 1980, o.p.

(BL 77:6; CCBB 34:103; SLJ Nov 1980 p. 80)

WILLIAMS, Tad. *Tailchaser's Song.* See Chapter 2, Animal Fantasy.

WILLIAMS (John), Ursula Moray. *Adventures of a Little Wooden Horse.* See Chapter 9, Toy Fantasy.

WILSON, A. N. *Stray.* See Chapter 2, Animal Fantasy.

WILSON, David Henry. *The Coachman Rat.* See Chapter 5B, Myth Fantasy.

WILSON, Willie. *Up Mountain One Time.* See Chapter 2, Animal Fantasy.

367 **WISNIEWSKI, David.** *Elfwyn's Saga.* **Gr. 3–5.**

✓ Intricate paper-cuts illustrate this Viking saga-inspired tale about blind Elfwyn, who ends the curse on her father's family by defeating Gorm the Grim.

Lothrop, 1990, 32 pp. LB(0-688-09590-9)

(BL 87:520; CC:738; HB 66:737; HBG 2[July–Dec 1990]:34; KR 58:1093; SLJ Oct 1990 p. 120)

368 **WISNIEWSKI, David.** *The Warrior and the Wise Man.* **Gr. 2–5.**

✓ Twin sons of the Japanese emperor fulfill their quest to find five magical elements of the world in diametrically opposite ways—one by theft and violence, and the other by healing and repair—in this folktale-like story illustrated with intricate, full-color paper-cuts.

Illus. by the author, Lothrop, 1989, 32 pp. (0-688-07889-3)

(BL 85:1556; CC:738; CCBB 42:286; HB 65:479; KR 57:632; SLJ April 1989 p. 93)

A *Wizard's Dozen: Stories of the Fantastic.* **Ed. by Michael Stearns.** See Chapter 3, Fantasy Collections.

WOLITZER, Meg. *The Dream Book.* See Chapter 7, Magic Adventure Fantasy.

369 **WOOD, Douglas.** *Old Turtle.* **Gr. K up.**

Old Turtle narrates this religious fable about how human beings learned to stop destroying the earth and began to see God in each other.

Illus. by Cheng-Khee Chee, Pfeifer-Hamilton, 1991, 48 pp. (0-938586-48-3)

(KR 59:1541; VOYA 15:38)

WREDE, Patricia C(ollins). *Snow White and Rose Red.* See Chapter 5B, Myth Fantasy.

WRIGGINS, Sally. *The White Monkey King: A Chinese Fable.* See Chapter 5B, Myth Fantasy.

WRIGHTSON, (Alice) Patricia (Furlonger). *Moon Dark.* See Chapter 2, Animal Fantasy.

YEP, Laurence (Michael). *Dragon of the Lost Sea.* See Chapter 5A, Alternate Worlds or Histories.

YOLEN (Stemple), Jane H(yatt). *The Acorn Quest.* See Chapter 2, Animal Fantasy.

370 **YOLEN (Stemple), Jane H(yatt).** *The Bird of Time.* **Gr. 2–4.**

Pieter uses the magic of the Bird of Time to rescue a captive princess from a giant.

Illus. by Mercer Mayer, Crowell, 1971, 32 pp., o.p.

(BL 68:509; CCBB 25:83; LJ 97:770)

371 **YOLEN (Stemple), Jane H(yatt).** *The Boy Who Had Wings.* **Gr. K–4.**

Aetos uses his forbidden wings to rescue his father from a mountain blizzard.

Illus. by Helga Aichinger, Crowell, 1974, 25 pp., o.p.

(BL 71:296; HB 50:687; LJ 99:3270)

YOLEN (Stemple), Jane H(yatt). *Briar Rose.* See Chapter 5B, Myth Fantasy.

372 **YOLEN (Stemple), Jane H(yatt).** *Dove Isabeau.* **Gr. 3–6.**

Her jealous stepmother turns Princess Dove Isabeau into a huge dragon forced to eat her 99 suitors to survive.

Illus. by Dennis Noland, Harcourt, 1989, 32 pp. (0-15-224131-0)

(BL 86:750; HBG 1[July–Dec 1989]:83; KR 57:1483; SLJ July 1990 p. 79)

YOLEN (Stemple), Jane H(yatt). *Dragonfield and Other Stories.* See Chapter 3, Fantasy Collections.

YOLEN (Stemple), Jane H(yatt). *The Giants' Farm.* See Chapter 6, Humorous Fantasy.

YOLEN (Stemple), Jane H(yatt). *The Girl Who Cried Flowers and Other Tales.* See Chapter 3, Fantasy Collections.

373 **YOLEN (Stemple), Jane H(yatt).** *The Girl Who Loved the Wind.* **Gr. 1–4.**

✓ A wealthy merchant tries to protect his beautiful daughter from unhappiness by keeping her a prisoner in their palace, but a whispering wind makes the girl discontented with her life.

Illus. by Ed Young, Harper, 1972, 1982, 32 pp., LB(0-690-33101-0), pap., 1987 (0-06-443088-X)

(BL 69:575; CCBB 26:100; HB 48:585; KR 40:1353; LJ 98:998; TLS 1973 p. 1431)

YOLEN (Stemple), Jane H(yatt). *Greyling: A Picture Story from the Islands of Shetland.* See Chapter 5B, Myth Fantasy.

YOLEN (Stemple), Jane H(yatt). *Here There Be Dragons.* See Chapter 3, Fantasy Collections.

YOLEN (Stemple), Jane H(yatt). *The Hundredth Dove and Other Tales.* See Chapter 3, Fantasy Collections.

YOLEN (Stemple), Jane H(yatt). *Merlin's Booke.* See Chapter 5B, Myth Fantasy.

YOLEN (Stemple), Jane H(yatt). *The Moon Ribbon and Other Tales.* See Chapter 3, Fantasy Collections.

374 **YOLEN (Stemple), Jane H(yatt).** *The Seventh Mandarin.* **Gr. 2–4.**

✓ The youngest mandarin must recover the lost kite containing the king's soul, or be put to death.

Illus. by Ed Young, Seabury, 1970, 36 pp., o.p.
(BL 67:343; CCBB 24:84; KR 38:1142; LJ 96:1112; Suth:432; TLS 1971 p. 388)

YOLEN (Stemple), Jane H(yatt). *Sleeping Ugly.* See Chapter 6, Humorous Fantasy.

YOLEN (Stemple), Jane H(yatt). *Tam Lin: An Old Ballad.* See Chapter 5B, Myth Fantasy.

375   YOLEN (Stemple), Jane H(yatt). *The Transfigured Hart.* **Gr. 5–7.**

Richard and Heather discover an albino hart living near a pool in the woods and protect it from her hunter brothers. Golden Kite Award Honor Book, 1975.

Illus. by Donna Diamond, Crowell, 1975, 96 pp., o.p.
(KR 43:662; SLJ Sept 1975 p. 115)

YOUNG, Ella. *The Unicorn with Silver Shoes.* See Chapter 5C, Travel to Other Worlds.

376   ZARING, Jane T(homas). *The Return of the Dragon.* **Gr. 3–6.**

Caradoc, the last Welsh dragon, decides to go home to Wales, in spite of the fact that the people do not want him to return.

Illus. by Polly Broman, Houghton, 1981, 146 pp., o.p.
(HB 57:541; SLJ Feb 1982 p. 84)

377   ZEMACH, Harve(y Fischtrom). *The Tricks of Master Dabble.* **Gr. 1–3.**

✓   Playing upon the vanity of the castle inhabitants, Master Dabble tricks them into believing he is a painter and that his mirror is a masterpiece.

Illus. by Margot Zemach, Holt, 1965, 32 pp., o.p.
(BL 62:164; HB 41:166; KR 33:3; LJ 90:1546)

ZIMNIK, Reiner. *The Bear and the People.* See Chapter 5A, Alternate Worlds or Histories.

ZINDEL, Paul. *Let Me Hear You Whisper: A Play.* See Chapter 2, Animal Fantasy.

ZOLOTOW, Charlotte. *The Man with Purple Eyes.* See Chapter 7, Magic Adventure Fantasy.

2

Animal Fantasy

There is sometimes only a fine line between realistic and fantastic portrayal of animals in literature. Thus, any tales in which the animal characters think or talk in a humanlike manner have been included in this chapter. For ease of access in this edition of *Fantasy Literature for Children and Young Adults,* all animal fantasy stories, whether they are "Beast Tales" (more serious stories about "realistic" animals fleeing human evils) or "Talking Animal Stories" (lighter in tone, featuring dressed-up, anthropomorphic animals) have been interfiled in one list.

ADAMS, Hazard. *The Truth about Dragons.* See Chapter 1, Allegorical Fantasy and Literary Fairy Tales.

378 **ADAMS, Richard (George).** *The Plague Dogs.* **Gr. 10 up.**

After escaping from an animal research lab, two dogs run free in England's Lake District. They are befriended by a fox, but are hunted by humans as possible carriers of bubonic plague.

Knopf, 1978, 390 pp., o.p.; Fawcett, 1986, pap. (0-449-21182-7)

(BBS:51; BL 74:975; Kliatt 13 [Spring 1979]:4; KR 46:54, 115; LJ 103:773; SLJ Sept 1978 p. 168)

ADAMS, Richard (George). *Shardik.* See Chapter 1, Allegorical Fantasy and Literary Fairy Tales.

379 **ADAMS, Richard (George).** *Watership Down.* **Gr. 6 up. (Orig. British pub.**
✓✓ **1972.)**

Premonitions of destruction drive a small band of rabbits from their peaceful hillside warren into the wilderness. Carnegie Medal, 1972. Guardian Award for Children's Fiction, 1973.

Macmillan, 1974, 429 pp. (0-02-700030-3); Avon, 1976, pap. (0-380-00293-0)

(BBC: 196; BBJ: 68; BBS: 51; BL 70:852, 71:747, 72:1096, 1107, 80:351; CC:438; CCBB 27:121; Ch&Bks:268; HB 50:365, 405; JHC:330; LJ 99:1148, 1235; SHC:665; Suth 2:2)

AIKEN, Joan (Delano). *The Kingdom and the Cave.* See Chapter 5A, Alternate Worlds or Histories.

AIKEN, Joan (Delano). *A Necklace of Raindrops and Other Stories.* See Chapter 3, Fantasy Collections.

AINSWORTH (Gilbert), Ruth (Gallard). *The Bear Who Liked Hugging People and Other Stories.* See Chapter 3, Fantasy Collections.

380   ALEXANDER, Lloyd (Chudley). *The Cat Who Wished to Be a Man.* **Gr. 4–6.**

✓   Lionel nags the wizard Stephanus to change him from a cat into a human. Stephanus grants his wish, only to find that he cannot reverse the process.

Dutton, 1973, 107 pp., o.p.; Dell, 1992, pap. (0-440-40580-7)

(BBC:67; BL 70:168; CC:441; CCBB 27:21; HB 49:463; KR 41:639; LJ 98:2647; Suth 2:8)

381   ALEXANDER, Lloyd (Chudley). *The Town Cats, and Other Tales.* **Gr. 4–6.**

✓   Eight fairy tales about wise and heroic cats.

Illus. by Laszlo Kubinyi, Dutton, 1977, 144 pp., o.p.; Dell, 1981, pap., o.p.

(BL 74:472; CC:577; CCBB 31:89; HB 54:42; KR 45:1096; SLJ Nov 1977 p. 52; Suth 2:9)

382   ALLAN, Ted. *Willie the Squowse.* **Gr. 3–5. (Orig. British pub. 1977.)**

Willie, the son of a mouse and a squirrel, gives a poor family the money stored in their wealthy neighbors' walls.

Illus. by Quentin Blake, Hastings, 1991, 57 pp. (0-8038-9341-8)

(BBC:197; CCBB 32:57; SLJ Nov 1978 p. 39; TLS 1977 p. 1414)

ALTON, Andrea I. *Demon of Undoing.* See Chapter 5A, Alternate Worlds or Histories.

383   AMADO, Jorge. *The Swallow and the Tom Cat: A Grown-Up Love Story.* **Gr. 10 up. (Written 1952.)**

A fable by a major Brazilian novelist about star-crossed lovers: a swallow and a tom cat, whose families force them to marry others.

Trans. by Barbara Shelby Merello, illus. by Carybé, Delacorte, 1982, 96 pp., o.p.

(BL 79:90, 104; KR 50:943; LJ 107:1767)

ANDERSEN, Hans Christian. *Thumbelina.* See Chapter 1, Allegorical Fantasy and Literary Fairy Tales.

ANDERSEN, Hans Christian. *The Ugly Duckling.* See Chapter 1, Allegorical Fantasy and Literary Fairy Tales.

384   ANDERSON, Mary. *F*T*C* Superstar.* **Gr. 4–6.**

Freddie the cat dreams of becoming an actor, but when Emma, his pigeon friend, helps him attain his dream, stardom goes to his head. The sequel is *F*T*C* & Company* (1979).

Illus. by Gail Owens, Atheneum, 1976, 156 pp., o.p.

(BL 73:140; KR 44:320; SLJ Apr 1976 p. 68)

385   ANDREWS, Allen. *The Pig Plantagenet.* **Gr. 10 up. (Adapted from the French**
✓   *Le Roman de Fulbert* **by Michel Héloin.)**

A domesticated thirteenth-century French pig becomes embroiled in a plot to save a family of wild boars from a massacre by the lord of the chateau. The sequel is *Castle Crespin* (1984).

Illus. by Michael Foreman, Viking, 1980, 188 pp., o.p.

(BL 77:286, 287; KR 48:1406; LJ 105:2513; TLS 1980 p. 1329; VOYA 4 [June 1981]:27)

386 **ANNETT (Pipitone Scott), Cora.** *How the Witch Got Alf.* **Gr. 3–5.**

Alf, the old folks' donkey, feels unloved and decides to run away.

Illus. by Steven Kellogg, Watts, 1975, 47 pp., o.p.

(BL 71:864; CCBB 29:1; KR 43:70; SLJ Mar 1975 p. 84; Suth 2:16)

387 **ANNETT (Pipitone Scott), Cora.** *When the Porcupine Moved In.* **Gr. 1–4.**

Porcupine disrupts Rabbit's comfortable life by moving into Rabbit's house and bringing all of his relatives with him.

Illus. by Peter Parnall, Watts, 1971, 40 pp., o.p.

(BL 68:626; CCBB 25:70; LJ 97:1593)

388 **ANNIXTER, Paul (pseud. of Howard Allison Sturtzel).** *The Cat That Clumped.* **Gr. 1–4.**

Unhappy as a cat, Herbert decides to become a horse.

Illus. by Brinton Turkle, Holiday, 1966, 35 pp., o.p.

(CCBB 19:157; KR 34:240; LJ 91:1694)

389 **ARKIN, Alan (Wolf).** *The Lemming Condition.* **Gr. 4–5.**
✓

Bubber's family and friends undertake their unquestioning journey toward the sea and death. In order to live, Bubber must fight not only the other lemmings, but his own instincts as well. The sequel is *The Clearing* (1986).

Illus. by Joan Sandin, Harper, 1976, 64 pp., LB(0-06-020133-9), pap., 1989 (0-06-250048-1)

(BBC:197; BL 72:1182; CC:444; HB 52:394; KR 44:389; SLJ Apr 1976 p. 68)

390 **ARUNDEL, Honor.** *The Amazing Mr. Prothero.* **Gr. 3–5. (Orig. British pub. 1968.)**

Scamp, a dog who prefers to be called Mr. Prothero, rescues Julia's baby brother from a runaway carriage.

Illus. by Jane Paton, Nelson, 1972, 80 pp., o.p.

(BL 69:200; CCBB 26:101; KR 40:30; LJ 97:2928)

391 **ASCH, Frank.** *Pearl's Promise.* **Gr. 3–5.**

Pearl mouse is horrified when her little brother, Tony, is given to the Pet Shop's new python, and she vows to rescue him. The sequel is *Pearl's Pirates* (1987).

Illus. by the author, Delacorte, 1984, 160 pp., LB(0-385-29321-6); Dell, 1984, pap. (0-440-46863-9)

(BBC:197; BL 81:60; CCBB 37:160; HB 60:193; SLJ Apr 1984 p. 111)

392 **ATTWOOD, Frederic.** *Vavache, the Cow Who Painted Pictures.* **Gr. 3–5.**

A young American boy visiting Normandy meets Vavache, a talking cow who paints with her tail.

Illus. by Roger Duvoisin, Aladdin, 1950, 77 pp., o.p.

(BL 46:291; CCBB 3:39; HB 26:193; LJ 75:632, 1054)

393 **AVERILL, Esther (Holden).** *Captains of the City Streets: A Story of the Cat Club.* **Gr. 3–4.**

Two tramp cats named Sinbad and the Duke move to New York City and become involved in a club run by the local cats. This is the sequel to *The Cat Club* (1944), *The School for Cats* (1947), *Jenny's First Party* (1948), *Jenny's Moonlight Adventure* (1949), *How the Brothers Joined the Cat Club* (1953), and *The Hotel Cat* (1969), and is followed by *Jenny and the Cat Club* (1973).

Illus. by the author, Harper, 1972, 147 pp., o.p.

(BL 69:809; CCBB 26:149; HB 48:47; KR 40:1354; LJ 98:1678)

394 AYMÉ, Marcel (André). *The Wonderful Farm.* **Gr. 4–6. (Orig. pub. in France.)**

Marinette and Delphine don't know how to get around their parents' strict rules until the farm animals begin to talk to the girls and give them some unusual ideas. The sequel is *The Magic Pictures: More about the Wonderful Farm* (1954, British title: *Return to the Wonderful Farm,* 1954).

Trans. by Norman Denny, illus. by Maurice Sendak, Harper, 1951, 182 pp., o.p.

(BL 48:161; CCBB 5:35; HB 27:406; LJ 76:2009)

BABCOCK, Betty. *The Expandable Pig.* See Chapter 7, Magic Adventure Fantasy.

BACH, Richard (David). *Jonathan Livingston Seagull.* See Chapter 1, Allegorical Fantasy and Literary Fairy Tales.

BACON, Peggy. *The Ghost of Opalina, or Nine Lives.* See Chapter 4, Ghost Fantasy.

395 BACON, Peggy. *The Lion-Hearted Kitten and Other Stories.* **Gr. 3–4.**

A collection of short, humorous, folktalelike animal stories.

Illus. by the author, Macmillan, 1927, 102 pp., o.p.

(BL 24:124; Bookshelf 1929 p. 9; HB 3[Nov 1927]:19; LJ 53:484)

396 BACON, Peggy. *Mercy and the Mouse and Other Stories.* **Gr. 2–4.**

In the first of these animal stories, an ambitious young cellar cat becomes a household pet.

Illus. by the author, Macmillan, 1928, 85 pp., o.p.

(BL 25:289; HB 4[Aug 1928]:20, 4[Nov 1928]:76; Mahony 2:117; Moore:35)

397 BAILEY, Carolyn Sherwin. *Finnegan II: His Nine Lives.* **Gr. 4–6.**

Finnegan the cat proves to have more than nine lives.

Illus. by Kate Seredy, Viking, 1953, 95 pp., o.p.

(BL 50:150; HB 29:455, 64:516; LJ 78:2225)

398 BAKER, Betty (Lou). *Danby and George.* **Gr. 3–4.**

A wood rat and a deer mouse make a home for themselves at the zoo.

Illus. by Adrienne Lobel, Greenwillow, 1981, 64 pp., o.p.

(BL 77:1025; CCBB 35:4; KR 49:283; SLJ Jan 1982 p. 72)

399 BAKER, Betty (Lou). *Dupper.* **Gr. 5–7.**

Dupper is an outcast in the prairie dog world until his search for the Great Ants leads to a solution to the killer rattlesnake problem.

Illus. by Chuck Eckart, Greenwillow/Morrow, 1976, 147 pp., o.p.

(BL 73:140; CCBB 30:38; KR 44:684; SLJ Feb 1977 p. 60; Suth 2:24)

400 BAKER, Elizabeth Whitemore. *Sonny-Boy Sim.* **Gr. 1–4.**

The woodland animals decide to turn the tables on Sonny-Boy Sim and his hound dog.

Illus. by Susanne Suba, Rand, 1948, 31 pp., o.p.

(BL 45:320; CCBB 2[May 1949]:1; HB 25:285; KR 17:177; LJ 74:666)

401 BAKER, Margaret. *Three for an Acorn.* **Gr. 1–4.**

✓ Mrs. Squirrel's shop sells dandelion lollipops, three for an acorn.

Illus. by Mary Baker, Dodd, 1935, 96 pp., o.p.

(BL 32:45; Bookshelf 1935 p. 2; HB 11:289; LJ 60:857; Mahony 3:78)

402 **BAKER, Margaret Joyce.** *Homer the Tortoise* **(British title: *"Nonsense!" Said the Tortoise*, 1949). Gr. 4–6.**

Homer the educated tortoise comes to live with the Brown family. The sequels are *Homer Goes to Stratford* (1958) and *Homer Sees the Queen* (British).

Illus. by Leo Bates, McGraw-Hill, 1950, 149 pp., o.p.

(BL 46:278; CCBB 3:33; KR 18:97; LJ 75:629, 986)

BAKER, Margaret Joyce. *Porterhouse Major.* See Chapter 7, Magic Adventure Fantasy.

BAKER, Olaf. *Bengey and the Beast.* See Chapter 7, Magic Adventure Fantasy.

403 **BALABAN, John.** *The Hawk's Tale.* **Gr. 4–6.**

Glister the water snake, Mirais the toad, and Mr. Trembly the deermouse search for the fierce White Eagle in order to rescue a boy named James and Mr. Trembly's niece Lilac.

Illus. by David Delamare, Harcourt, 1988, 148 pp., o.p.

(BBC:198; BL 84:1918; KR 51:614; SLJ Sept 1988 p. 182)

404 **BARKLEM, Jill.** *Autumn Story* **(Brambly Hedge series, book 1). Gr. K–3. (Orig. British and U.S. pub. 1980.)**

The mice of Brambly Hedge plan a surprise birthday party for Wilfred Toadflax in this book set in a cozy world of elaborately dressed mice. The sequels are *Winter Story* (1980, 1986), *Spring Story* (1980, 1982, 1989), *Summer Story* (1980, 1989), *The Secret Staircase* (1983, 1986), *The High Hills* (1986), and *Sea Story* (1990, 1991). The first four books have been combined in *The Four Seasons of Brambly Hedge* (1988, 1990).

Illus. by the author, Putnam, 1986, c. 1980, 32 pp. (0-399-21754-1)

(BL 77:695; SLJ Mar 1981 p. 128; TLS Sept 19, 1980, p. 1029)

405 **BARRETT, Nicholas.** *Fledger.* **Gr. 10 up.**

Goldie, a young puffin, leads his flock's fight against the deadly island rats who have destroyed their breeding grounds.

Macmillan, 1985, 207 pp., o.p.

(KR 53:647; LJ Oct 1, 1985 p. 110; SLJ Jan 1986 p. 83; VOYA 9:37)

BAUER, Marion Dane. *Ghost Eye.* See Chapter 4, Ghost Fantasy.

BEAGLE, Peter S(oyer). *A Fine and Private Place.* See Chapter 4, Ghost Fantasy.

406 **BECHDOLT, Jack (pseud. of John Ernest Bechdolt).** *Bandmaster's Holiday.* **Gr. 2–4.**

Barko the circus sea lion decides to try living in the ocean.

Illus. by Decie Merwin, Oxford, 1938, 71 pp., o.p.

(HB 14:159; LJ 63:284, 690)

BEEKS, Graydon. *Hosea Globe and the Fantastical Peg-Legged Chu.* See Chapter 6, Humorous Fantasy.

407 **BEHN, Harry.** *Roderick.* **Gr. 4–6.**

A thoughtful, loving crow named Roderick unexpectedly becomes the leader of his flock.

Illus. by Mel Silverman, Harcourt, 1961, 64 pp., o.p.

(HB 37:340; LJ 86:2353)

BELL, Clare E. *The Jaguar Princess.* See Chapter 5A, Alternate Worlds or Histories.

408 **BELL, Clare E.** *Ratha's Creature.* **Gr. 7–12.**

✓✓ Ratha, a yearling from a clan of intelligent cats living in an alternate prehistoric time, is exiled for learning to handle fire, and then caught up in a war between her clan and the Un-Named, a band of hunter cats. International Reading Association Children's Book Award, 1984. The sequels are *Clan Ground* (1984, 1987) and *Ratha and Thistle-Chaser* (1990), in which Ratha is forced to confront Thistle-Chaser, the maimed daughter she abandoned as a cub.

Atheneum, 1983, 248 pp., o.p.; Dell, 1987, pap. (0-440-97298-1)

(BL 79:956, 962; CCBB 36:202; SHC:669; SLJ Sept 1983 p. 130; VOYA 6:196)

409 **BELL, Clare E.** *Tomorrow's Sphinx.* **Gr. 7–12.**

✓ Kichebo, a black and gold cheetah living in a post-ecological-disaster future time, is able to link minds with an ancient Egyptian cheetah who teaches her to accept a young human companion.

Atheneum, 1986, 312 pp., o.p.; Dell, 1988, pap. (0-440-20124-1)

(BBJ:69, BL 83:344, 346, 83:776; CCBB 40:42; KR 54:1372; SHC: 1988 Suppl. p 62; SLJ Nov 1986 p. 96)

BENCHLEY, Nathaniel (Goddard). *Demo and the Dolphin.* See Chapter 5B, Myth Fantasy.

410 **BENCHLEY, Nathaniel (Goddard).** *Feldman Fieldmouse: A Fable.* **Gr. 3–6.**

✓ Uncle Feldman's lessons in wild mouse survival are quite a change for Fendall, after his pampered life as a household pet.

Illus. by Hilary Knight, Harper, 1971, 96 pp., o.p.

(BL 68:55; CC:450; CCBB 25:54; HB 47:285; KR 39:500; LJ 96:2128; Suth:33)

411 **BENCHLEY, Nathaniel (Goddard).** *Kilroy and the Gull.* **Gr. 5–7.**

Kilroy the killer whale and a seagull friend escape from an aquarium after frustrating attempts to communicate with humans, and search the sea for Kilroy's family.

Illus. by John Schoenherr, Harper, 1977, 118 pp., o.p., pap., 1978 (0-06-440090-5)

(BL 73:1086; CCBB 30:138; Ch&Bks:268; HB 53:309; KR 45:3; SLJ Oct 1977 p. 109; Suth 2:41)

412 **BERESFORD, Elizabeth.** *The Wombles.* **Gr. 4–6. (Orig. pub. in England.)**

Wombles are furry, subterranean creatures who survive by "collecting" things from human beings. The British sequels are *MacWomble's Pipe Band; The Invisible Womble; The Snow Womble; The Wandering Wombles; The Wombles at Work; The Wombles Book; The Wombles Go Round the World; The Wombles in Danger; The Wombles Make a Clean Sweep; The Wombles of Wimbledon;* and *The Wombles to the Rescue.*

Illus. by Margaret Gordon, Meredith, 1968, 183 pp., o.p.

(KR 37:1147; LJ 95:1192; TLS 1968 p. 1376, 1973 p. 386)

BERGRENGREN, Ralph Wilhelm. *David the Dreamer: His Book of Dreams.* See Chapter 5C, Travel to Other Worlds.

413 **BEST, (Oswald) Herbert.** *Desmond's First Case.* **Gr. 3–5.**

A dog detective named Desmond and his boy, Gus, solve the mystery of a missing banker. The sequels are *Desmond the Dog Detective: The Case of the Lone Stranger* (1962), *Desmond and the Peppermint Ghost: The Dog Detective's Third Case* (1965), and *Desmond and Dog Friday* (1968), all o.p.

Illus. by Ezra Jack Keats, Viking, 1961, 96 pp., o.p.

(KR 29:55; LJ 86:1980)

414   **BESTERMAN, Catherine.** *The Quaint and Curious Quest of Johnny Longfoot, the Shoe King's Son.* **Gr. 4–6.**

Johnny Longfoot and a group of animals search for buried treasure. John Newbery Medal Honor Book, 1948. The sequel is *The Extraordinary Education of Johnny Longfoot in His Search for the Magic Hat* (1949).

Bobbs-Merrill, 1947, 147 pp., o.p.

(BL 44:116; HB 23:435; 24:36; LJ 72:1618)

BETHANCOURT, T(homas) Ernesto (pseud. of Tom Paisley). *The Dog Days of Arthur Cane.* See Chapter 7, Magic Adventure Fantasy.

415   **BIANCO, Margery (Winifred) Williams.** *The Good Friends.* **Gr. 4–6.**

The animals on Farmer Hicks's farm must care for themselves after he goes into the hospital.

Illus. by Grace Paull, Viking, 1934, 142 pp., o.p.

(BL 31:67; Bookshelf 1934–1935 p. 5; HB 10:296; LJ 60:304; Mahony 3:200)

BIANCO, Margery (Winifred) Williams. *Poor Cecco; the Wonderful Story of a Wonderful Wooden Dog Who Was the Jolliest Toy in the House Until He Went Out to Explore the World.* See Chapter 9, Toy Fantasy.

BIANCO, Margery (Winifred) Williams. *The Velveteen Rabbit; or, How Toys Became Real.* See Chapter 9, Toy Fantasy.

BIEGEL, Paul. *The King of the Copper Mountains.* See Chapter 1, Allegorical Fantasy and Literary Fairy Tales.

416   **BLACKWOOD, Algernon (Henry).** *The Adventures of Dudley and Gilderoy* **(Orig. British and U.S. title:** *Dudley and Gilderoy: A Nonsense,* **1929). Gr. 1–4.**

An aristocratic parrot and a ginger cat travel to London in search of adventure.

Adapt. by Marion Cothren, illus. by Feodor Rojankovsky, Dutton, 1941, 32 pp., o.p.

(BL 26:159; HB 17:99; TLS 1929 p. 1030)

417   **BLADOW, Suzanne Wilson.** *The Midnight Flight of Moose, Mops and Marvin.* **Gr. 1–4.**

Three mice from Mrs. Santa's kitchen stow away on Santa's sleigh.

Illus. by Joseph Mathieu, McGraw-Hill, 1975, 40 pp., o.p.

(BL 72:448; CCBB 29:91; KR 43:1118; SLJ Oct 1975 p. 78)

418   **BLAISDELL, Mary Frances.** *Bunny Rabbit's Diary.* **Gr. 2–4. (Orig. pub. 1915.)**

Eight tales about Bunny Rabbit and his friends, as recorded by Bunny Rabbit in his maple-leaf book.

Illus. by Anne Jauss, Little, 1960 (rev. ed.), 92 pp., o.p.

(KR 28:29; LJ 85:2025; Mahony 2:162)

419   **BLATHWAYT, Benedict.** *Stories from Firefly Island.* **Gr. 2–4. (Orig. British**
✓   **pub. 1992.)**

Storyteller Tortoise explains the mysteries of life to the other animal inhabitants of Firefly Island.

Illus. by the author, Greenwillow, 1993, 120 pp. (0-688-12487-9)

(BL 90:935; HBG 5:73; KR 61:1269; SLJ Dec 1993 p. 80)

420 **BLATHWAYT, Benedict.** *Tangle and the Firesticks.* **Gr. 1–3. (Orig. British pub. 1987.)**

Tangle, a small, furry inhabitant of the northwoods, learns about matches from a friendly human, and uses this knowledge to save his tribe. Smarties Prize for Children's Books, Ages 6–8, 1987.

Illus. by the author, Knopf, 1987, 32 pp., o.p.

(SLJ Feb 1988 p. 57; TLS 1987 p. 1120)

BLISS, Corinne Demas. *Matthew's Meadow.* See Chapter 1, Allegorical Fantasy and Literary Fairy Tales.

BLUNT, Wilfrid (Jasper Walter). *Omar; a Fantasy for Animal Lovers.* See Chapter 6, Humorous Fantasy.

421 **BODECKER, N(iels) M(ogens).** *The Mushroom Center Disaster.* **Gr. 2–4.**

When the insect inhabitants of Mushroom Center find their peaceful community threatened by littering humans, William Beetle creates a "Garbage Emergency Plan" to recycle the debris.

Illus. by Erik Blegvad, Atheneum, 1974, 48 pp., o.p., 1979, pap., o.p.

(BL 70:1054; CCBB 28:24; KR 42:421; LJ 99:1464)

422 **BOND, (Thomas) Michael.** *A Bear Called Paddington.* **Gr. 3–5. (Orig. British**
✓✓ **pub. 1958.)**

The Brown family decides to adopt a little Peruvian bear they find at Paddington railroad station, but life with Paddington isn't always easy. The sequels are *Paddington Helps Out* (1961), *More about Paddington* (1962), *Paddington at Large* (1963), *Paddington Marches On* (1965), *Paddington at Work* (1967), *Paddington Goes to Town* (1968), *Paddington Takes the Air* (1971), *Paddington Abroad* (1972), *Paddington's Garden* (Random, 1973), *Paddington at the Circus* (Random, 1974), *Paddington's Lucky Day* (1974), *Paddington Takes to TV* (1974), *Paddington on Top* (1975), *Paddington on Stage* (1977), *Paddington at the Seaside* (Random, 1978), *Paddington at the Tower* (Random, 1978), *Paddington Takes the Test* (1980), and *Paddington on Screen* (1982). *Paddington's Storybook* (1984) is a collection of stories from eight of the books. The British sequels are *The Adventures of Paddington; Fun and Games with Paddington; Paddington Bear; Paddington Does It Himself; Paddington Goes Shopping; Paddington Goes to the Sales; Paddington Hits Out; Paddington in the Kitchen;* and *Paddington's Birthday Party.*

Illus. by Peggy Fortnum, Houghton, 1960, o.p.; Dell, 1968, pap., 128 pp. (0-440-40483-5)

(BL 80:95; CC 452; CCBB 14:106; Ch&Bks:268; HB 37:53; KR 28:676; LJ 85:3856; Suth:42; TLS Nov 21, 1958 p. xiv)

423 **BOND, (Thomas) Michael.** *Here Comes Thursday.* **Gr. 3–5. (Orig. British pub. 1966.)**

The "Help Yourself" sign posted by Thursday Mouse almost puts his family's store out of business. The sequels are *Thursday Rides Again* (1969), *Thursday Ahoy!* (1970), and *Thursday in Paris* (British).

Illus. by Daphne Rowles, Lothrop, 1967, 126 pp., o.p.

(BL 64:541; CCBB 21:106; HB 43:748; KR 35:1204; LJ 93:1301; TLS 1966 p. 1087)

424 **BOND, (Thomas) Michael.** *Tales of Olga Da Polga.* **Gr. 3–5. (Orig. British pub.**
✓ **1971.)**

Olga the guinea pig thinks very highly of herself, especially after she wins a pet show prize: Fattest Guinea Pig in the Show. The sequels are *Olga Meets Her Match* (Hastings,

1975), *Olga Carries On* (Hastings, 1977), *Olga Counts Her Blessings* (EMC, 1977, pap.), *Olga Makes a Friend* (EMC, 1977, pap.), *Olga Makes Her Mark* (EMC, 1977, pap.), *Olga Takes a Bite* (EMC, 1977, pap.), *Olga's New Home* (EMC, 1977, pap.), *Olga's Second Home* (EMC, 1977, pap.), *Olga's Special Day* (EMC, 1977, pap.), *Olga Makes a Wish* (EMC, 1977, pap.), and *The Complete Adventures of Olga Da Polga* (Delacorte, 1983).

Illus. by Hans Helweg, Macmillan, 1972, 1989, 113 pp. (0-02-711731-6)

(BL 69:987, 70:826; CC:452; CCBB 27:38; Ch&Bks:283; HB 49:268; KR 41:60, 1349; LJ 98:1384; SLJ Feb 1989 p. 118; Suth 2:52)

BONTEMPS, Arna, and CONROY, Jack. *The Fast Sooner Hound.* See Chapter 6, Humorous Fantasy.

425 **BOSHINSKI, Blanche.** *Aha and the Jewel of Mystery.* **Gr. 4–6.**

Self-centered Aha the cat learns the value of friendship after he is rescued by an Egyptian slave who is searching for his true identity.

Illus. by Shirley Pulido, Parents, 1968, 155 pp., o.p.

(HB 45:168; LJ 94:868)

BOYLE, Kay. *The Youngest Camel.* See Chapter 1, Allegorical Fantasy and Literary Fairy Tales.

426 **BRENNER, Barbara (Johnes).** *Hemi: A Mule.* **Gr. 4–6.**

Hemionus, ex-farm mule and official mascot of West Point, runs away from army life to look for a farmhand who once befriended him.

Illus. by J(effrey) Winslow Higginbottom, Harper, 1973, 120 pp., o.p.

(BL 70:539; KR 41:1263; LJ 98:3142)

BRENTANO, Clemens Maria. *The Tale of Gockel, Hinkel and Gackeliah.* See Chapter 1, Allegorical Fantasy and Literary Fairy Tales.

427 **BRO, Margueritte (Harmon).** *The Animal Friends of Peng-U.* **Gr. 1–4.**

Chickens, a fox, and a rabbit help farmer Peng-U find a wife.

Illus. by Seong Moy, Doubleday, 1965, 96 pp., o.p.

(BL 61:956; HB 41:274; KR 33:173)

428 **BROOKS, Walter Rollin.** *Freddy Goes to Florida* (Orig. title: *To and Again,*
✓   1927; British title: *Freddy's First Adventure*). **Gr. 4–6.**

Charles the Rooster suggests migration to avoid the cold, and Freddy the Pig goes along with the other farmyard animals. The other books in this series are *Freddy Goes to the North Pole* (1951; orig. title: *More To and Again,* 1930), *Freddy the Detective* (1932, 1987), *The Story of Freginald* (1936), *The Clockwork Twin* (1937), *Freddy the Politician* (1948, 1986, orig. title: *Wiggins for President,* 1939), *Freddy's Cousin Weedly* (1940), *Freddy and the Ignormus* (1941), *Freddy and the Perilous Adventure* (1942, 1986), *Freddy and the Bean Home News* (1943), *Freddy and Mr. Camphor* (1944), *Freddy and the Popinjay* (1945), *Freddy the Pied Piper* (1946), *Freddy the Magician* (1947), *Freddy Goes Camping* (1948, 1986), *Freddy Plays Football* (1949), *Freddy Rides Again* (1951), *Freddy the Cowboy* (1951, 1987), *Freddy and Freginald* (1952), *Freddy the Pilot* (1952, 1986), *Collected Poems of Freddy the Pig* (1953), *Freddy and the Space Ship* (1953), *Freddy and the Men from Mars* (1954), *Freddy and the Baseball Team from Mars* (1955, 1987), *Freddy and the Dragon* (1955), *Freddy and Simon the Dictator* (1956), and *Freddy and the Flying Saucer Plans* (1958).

Illus. by Kurt Wiese, Knopf, 1949, 196 pp., o.p.

(BL 24:30, 45:248; Bookshelf 1933 p. 8; CC:454; CCBB 2[Sept 1949]:1; Ch&Bks:283; HB 3[Aug 1927]:46, 3[Nov 1927]: 11, 7:116, 25:115; KR 17:58; LJ 74:559; Mahony 2:112; TLS 1927 p. 883)

429   BROWN, Palmer. *Hickory.* Gr. 3–5.

Hickory the field mouse's youth spent inside a grandfather clock does not prepare him for life in the fields, but a friendly grasshopper helps him overcome his loneliness.

Illus. by the author, Harper, 1978, 42 pp., o.p.

(HB 55:513; KR 46:1137: SLJ Sept 1978 p. 104)

430   BROWN, Rita Mae and BROWN, Sneaky Pie. *Wish You Were Here.* Gr. 10 up.

Small town postmistress Mary ("Harry") Haristeen and her unusually intelligent cat, Mrs. Murphy, and dog, Tee Tucker, solve a number of grisly murders, each preceeded by a strange postcard.

Illus. by Wendy Wray, Bantam, 1990, 243 pp., o.p., 1991, pap. (0-553-28753-2) .

(BL 87:258, 321; KR 58:1269; LJ Nov 1, 1990 p. 128; SLJ Apr 1991 p. 153)

431   BUCHWALD, Emilie. *Floramel and Esteban.* Gr. 3–5.

Lonely Floramel, a Caribbean cow, gets all her news from her friend, Esteban, a cattle egret. After she learns to play music on conch shells, the President makes her a National Treasure.

Illus. by Charles Robinson, Harcourt, 1982, 72 pp., o.p.

(BBC:199; BL 79:976; CCBB 36:3; SLJ Sept 1982 p. 104)

432   BUCHWALD, Emilie. *Gildaen: The Heroic Adventures of a Most Unusual Rab-
✓   **bit.* Gr. 4–6.**

Gildaen Rabbit sets out on a quest to save the kingdom and to restore the memory of his friend, who changes from an owl to a prince to a peasant woman.

Illus. by Barbara Flynn, Harcourt, 1973, 189 pp., o.p.; Milkweed, 1993, 184 pp. (0-915943-38-7)

(BL 69:1019; CCBB 26:167; HBG [Jan–June 1994]:307; KR 41:455; LJ 98:2191; Suth 2:63)

433   BURGESS, Thornton W(aldo). *Old Mother West Wind.* Gr. 2–4. (Orig. pub. 1910.)

Tales of Johnny Chuck, Reddy Fox, and the other animals living near the Green Meadows, the Smiling Pool, the Laughing Brook, and the Lone Little Path through the woods. Other books in the series are *Mother West Wind's Children* (1911; Little, 1962), *Mother West Wind's Animal Friends* (1912; Grosset, 1940), *Mother West Wind's Neighbors* (1913; Little, 1968), *The Adventures of Johnny Chuck* (1913; Grosset, 1952), *The Adventures of Reddy Fox* (1913; Grosset, 1950), *Mother West Wind's "Why" Stories* (1915; Grosset, 1941), *Mother West Wind's "How" Stories* (1916; Grosset, 1941), *The Adventures of Buster Bear* (1916; Grosset, 1941), *Mother West Wind's "When" Stories* (1917; Grosset, 1941), *Mother West Wind's "Where" Stories* (1918; Grosset, 1941), *The Adventures of Old Granny Fox* (Grosset, 1943), *The Adventures of Lightfoot the Deer* (Grosset, 1944), *The Adventures of Whitefoot the Woodmouse* (Grosset, 1944), *The Adventures of Chatterer the Red Squirrel* (Grosset, 1949), *The Adventures of Prickly Porky* (Grosset, 1949), *The Adventures of Sammy Jay* (Grosset, 1949), *The Adventures of Danny Meadowmouse* (Grosset, 1950), *The Adventures of Peter Cottontail* (Grosset, 1950), *The Adventures of Jerry Muskrat* (Grosset, 1951), *The Adventures of Unc' Billy Possum* (Grosset, 1951), *The Adventures of Grandfather Frog* (Grosset, 1952), *The Adventures of Old Man Coyote* (Grosset, 1952), *The Adventures of Poor Mrs. Quack* (Grosset, 1953), *The Adventures of Bob White* (Grosset, 1954), *The Adventures of Bobby Coon* (Grosset, 1954), *The Adventures of Jimmy Skunk* (Grosset, 1954), and *The Adventures of Ol' Mistah Buzzard* (Grosset, 1957).

Illus. by Harrison Cady, Little, 1960, 1985, 140 pp. (0-316-11648-3), pap. (0-316-11655-6); illus. by Harrison Cady and George Kerr, Grossett, 1976, o.p.; illus. by Harrison Cady, Grossett, 1990 (entitled: *Thorton W. Burgess Animal Tales*), 96 pp., o.p.; illus. by Michael Hague, Holt, 1990, 90 pp. (0-8050-1005-X)

(BL 7:168, 86:1976; HB 36:526; HBG 1[Jan–June 1990]:234)

434 **BURMAN, Ben Lucien.** *High Water at Catfish Bend.* **Gr. 5–7.**

The animals of Catfish Bend persuade the Army Corps of Engineers to build levees along the Mississippi River. The sequels are *Seven Stars for Catfish Bend* (1956, 1977), *The Owl Hoots Twice at Catfish Bend* (1961, 1977), *Blow a Wild Bugle for Catfish Bend* (1967, 1979), and *High Treason at Catfish Bend* (Vanguard, 1977). A collection called *Three from Catfish Bend* was published by Taplinger in 1967.

Illus. by Alice Caddy, Messner, 1952, 121 pp., o.p.

(BL 48:344; HB 28:174; KR 20:224; LJ 77:1018)

435 **BUTTERS, Dorothy G(ilman).** *Papa Dolphin's Table.* **Gr. 4–6.**

It was crowded enough in the Dolphin's apartment, without the enormous table Papa brought home.

Illus. by Kurt Werth, Knopf, 1955, 88 pp., o.p.

(BL 52:171; CCBB 9:82; Eakin:56; KR 23:597; LJ 80:2640)

436 **BUZZATI, Dino.** *The Bears' Famous Invasion of Sicily.* **Gr. 4–6.**

King Leander's bear army conquers the island of Sicily.

Trans. by Frances Loeb, illus. by the author, Pantheon, 1947, 146 pp., o.p.

(BL 44:189; CCBB 1[Mar 1948]:2; HB 24:36; KR 15:625; LJ 72:1473)

437 **CAIRE, Helen.** *Señor Castillo, Cock of the Island.* **Gr. 3–4.**

Castillo the old rooster boards a fishing boat to fulfill his dream of seeing the sea.

Illus. by Christine Price, Rinehart, 1948, 76 pp., o.p.

(HB 24:195; LJ 73:604, 656)

CALLANDER, Don. *Aquamancer.* **Chapter 10, Witchcraft and Sorcery Fantasy.**

438 **CAMPBELL, Hope.** *Peter's Angel: A Story about Monsters* (pap. title: *The Monster's Room*, Scholastic, 1979, o.p.). **Gr. 3–5.**

After the monster posters in Peter's room come to life, his two mouse friends decide that an angel is needed to exorcise the creatures.

Illus. by Lilian Obligado, Four Winds, 1976, 151 pp., o.p.

(BL 72:1525; KR 44:467; SLJ Sept 1976 p. 112)

CARLSON, Natalie Savage. *Alphonse, That Bearded One.* See Chapter 6, Humorous Fantasy.

439 **CARLSON, Natalie Savage.** *Evangeline, Pigeon of Paris* (British title: *Pigeon of Paris*). **Gr. 4–6.**
✓

Evangeline and her mate, Gabriel, become separated when the Parisian chief of police orders all pigeons trapped and deported.

Illus. by Nicolas Mordvinoff, Harcourt, 1960, 72 pp., o.p.

(BL 56:632; HB 36:215; KR 28:184; LJ 85:2475)

CARRIS, Joan Davenport. *Witch-Cat.* See Chapter 10, Witchcraft and Sorcery Fantasy.

440   **CASSERLEY, Anne Thomasine.** *Barney the Donkey.* **Gr. 3–5.**

Twelve humorous tales about a mischievous Irish donkey.

Illus. by the author, Harper, 1938, 145 pp., o.p.

(BL 34:304; HB 14:163; LJ 63:385)

441   **CASSERLEY, Anne Thomasine.** *Roseen.* **Gr. 2–4.**

Twelve Irish tales about a little black pig named Roseen, a wild goat, Brock the badger, and Kerry the cow. The sequel is *Brian of the Mountain* (1931).

Illus. by the author, Harper, 1929, 152 pp., o.p.

(BL 26:165; HB 5:44–45, 49, 7:115; Mahony 3:105)

CASSERLEY, Anne Thomasine. *The Whins on Knockattan.* See Chapter 3, Fantasy Collections.

442   **CAUFIELD, Don and CAUFIELD, Joan.** *The Incredible Detectives.* **Gr. 4–6.**

Reginald Bulldog, Madam Chang the Siamese cat, and Hennessy Crow solve their master's mysterious kidnapping.

Illus. by Kiyo Komoda, Harper, 1966, 75 pp., o.p.

(CCBB 20:71; HB 42:708; KR 343:830; LJ 91:5771; Suth:67)

CHASE, Mary. *Harvey, a Play.* See Chapter 6, Humorous Fantasy.

443   **CHEKHOV, Anton.** *Kashtanka.* **Gr. 3–5. (Orig. Russian pub. 1889.)**

✓   Accidentally separated from her master, a dog named Kashtanka is adopted by a circus clown and the pig, goose, and cat who perform in his trained animal act.

Trans. by Richard Pevear, illus. by Barry Moser, Putnam, 1991, 48 pp. (0-399-21905-6)

(CCBB 45:85; HBG 3[Spring 1992]:63; KR 59:1468; SLJ Nov 1991 p. 116)

444   **CHENOWETH, Russ.** *Shadow Walkers.* **Gr. 5–7.**

Brother and sister water rats Peter and Sara travel across Cape Cod to deliver insulin to needy relatives.

Macmillan, 1993, 176 pp. (0-684-19447-3)

(BL 89:1965; HBG 4[Fall 1993]:295; KR 61:526; SLJ May 1993 p. 103)

CHRISTIAN, Mary Blount. *Sebastian [Super-Sleuth] and the Crummy Yummies Caper.* See Chapter 6, Humorous Fantasy.

CHRISTOPHER, Matt(hew F.). *The Dog That Stole Football Plays.* See Chapter 7, Magic Adventure Fantasy.

445   **CLARK, Ann Nolan.** *Looking-for-Something: The Story of a Stray Burro of Ecuador.* **Gr. 1–4.**

Grey Burro searches for someone to belong to.

Illus. by Leo Politi, Viking, 1952, 53 pp., o.p.

(BL 48:236; HB 28:96; KR 20:123; LJ 77:725)

446   **CLEARY, Beverly (Bunn).** *The Mouse and the Motorcycle.* **Gr. 2–4.**

✓✓   A boy named Keith shows a mouse named Ralph the joys of cycling on a toy motorcycle. The sequels are *Runaway Ralph* (1970; Avon, pap., 1991) and *Ralph S. Mouse* (1982; Avon, 1993, pap.). *Ralph S. Mouse* won the Golden Kite Award in 1982.

Illus. by Louis Darling, Morrow, 1965, 158 pp., LB(0-688-31698-0); Avon, 1990, pap. (0-380-70924-4)

(BL 62:270; CC:466; CCBB 19:60; Ch&Bks:268; Eakin:76; HB 41:628; KR 33:905; LJ 90:5510)

447 **CLEARY, Beverly (Bunn).** *Socks.* **Gr. 3–5.**

The Brickers's new baby deprives a kitten named Socks of the family's undivided attention.

Illus. by Beatrice Darwin, Morrow, 1973, 160 pp., LB(0-688-30067-7); Avon, 1990, pap. (0-380-70926-0)

(CC:467; CCBB 27:23; KR 41:599; LJ 98:2185)

448 **CLEMENT, Aeron.** *The Cold Moons.* **Gr. 10 up. (Orig. British pub. 1988.)**

A clan of badgers flees human extermination toward a safe haven called Elysia.

Delacorte, 1989, 336 pp. (0-440-50112-1); Dell, 1990, pap. (0-440-50331-0)

(BBS:54; BL 85:898, 899; KR 57:142; LJ Mar 15, 1989 p. 84; SLJ Nov 1989 p. 136, Dec 1990 p. 216; VOYA 12:273)

449 **CLIFFORD, Eth.** *Flatfoot Fox and the Case of the Missing Eye* **(Flatfoot Fox Mystery series, book 1). Gr. 1–4.**

Fat Cat's glass eye is missing, and the smartest detective in the world, Flatfoot Fox, is called in to crack the case. The sequels are *Flatfoot Fox and the Case of the Noisy Otter* (1992) and *Flatfoot Fox and the Case of the Missing Whoooo* (1993).

Illus. by Brian Lies, Houghton, 1990, 48 pp. (0-395-51945-4); Scholastic, 1992, pap. (0-590-45812-4)

(BL 87:861; HBG 2[July 1990]:69; SLJ Mar 1991, p. 170)

450 **CLIFFORD, Sandy.** *The Roquefort Gang.* **Gr. 2–4.**

Nicole mouse joins forces with the Roquefort Gang to rescue hundreds of mice destined for laboratory experiments.

Illus. by the author, Parnassus, 1981, 79 pp., o.p.

(BL 77:1251; CCBB 34:189; KR 49:283; SLJ Apr 1981 p. 122)

451 **CLINE, Linda.** *The Miracle Season.* **Gr. 10 up.**

Crow discovers that mercury poisoning is the cause of his friends' mysterious deaths.

Berkley, 1976, 182 pp., o.p.

(Kliatt 11 [Fall 1977]:4; KR 44:748; LJ 101:2084; SLJ Dec 1976 p. 74)

452 **COATES, Anna.** *Dog Magic.* **Gr. 3–6.**

Matt and Katie's dog, Toby, tells them that his pups have been adopted by someone bad, and they find the pups in an illegal cosmetics testing laboratory.

Bantam, 1991, pap., 135 pp. (0-553-15910-0)

(BL 88:829; SLJ Jan 1992, p. 108)

453 **COATSWORTH, Elizabeth (Jane).** *The Cat and the Captain.* **Gr. 2–4. (Orig.**
✓ **pub. 1927.)**

The captain's cat saves his master's house from burglary and earns a place in the housekeeper's heart.

Illus. by Bernice Loewenstein, Macmillan, 1974, 95 pp., o.p.

(BL 24:210; CCBB 28:40; HB 3[Nov 1927]:12, 28:421, 50:395; KR 42:364; LJ 53:484, 99:2242)

COATSWORTH, Elizabeth (Jane). *The Cat Who Went to Heaven.* See Chapter 1, Allegorical Fantasy and Literary Fairy Tales.

COATSWORTH, Elizabeth (Jane). *The Enchanted: An Incredible Tale.* See Chapter 5B, Myth Fantasy.

COATSWORTH, Elizabeth (Jane). *Pure Magic.* See Chapter 1, Allegorical Fantasy and Literary Fairy Tales.

COBLENTZ, Catherine Cate. *The Blue Cat of Castle Town.* See Chapter 7, Magic Adventure Fantasy.

454   COLEMAN, Janet Wyman. *Fast Eddie.* **Gr. 3–6.**

Fast Eddie Raccoon's friends, a squirrel, dog, and cat, try to save him from the wrath of Mr. Plotkin, whose family has intruded into raccoon territory.

Illus. by Alec Gillman, Macmillan, 1993, 144 pp. (0-02-722815-0)

(HBG 4[Fall 1993]:296; KR 61:595; SLJ June 1993 p. 104)

455   COLOMA, Padre Luis. *Perez, the Mouse.* **Gr. 1–4. (Orig. pub. in Spain, U.S. pub. 1915.)**

King Bube and Perez the Mouse travel throughout the kingdom.

Adapt. by Lady Moreton, illus. by George Howard Vyse, Dodd, 1950, 63 pp., o.p.

(BL 46:206; HB 26:99, 112; Mahoney 2:112)

456   COLUM, Padraic. *The Boy Who Knew What the Birds Said.* **Gr. 3–5.**

After an old crow teaches the Boy how to speak with the birds, each has a story to tell him.

Illus. by Dugald Stewart Walker, Macmillan, 1918, 176 pp., o.p.

(BL 15:113; HB 1[June 1925]:30; Mahony 1:39)

457   COLUM, Padraic. *Where the Winds Never Blew and the Cocks Never Crew.* **Gr. 3–5.**

Tibbie the cat and seven other animals live peacefully by the old woman's hearth until a beautiful swan's song lures each of them away.

Illus. by Richard Bennett, Macmillan, 1940, 96 pp., o.p.

(BL 37:157; HB 16:429, 17:31)

458   COLUM, Padraic. *The White Sparrow* **(British title:** *Sparrow Alone***). Gr. 3–5. (Orig. pub. 1933.)**

Rescued from a street vendor, Jimmy the sparrow goes to work for a crocodile.

Illus. by Joseph Low, McGraw-Hill, 1972, 61 pp., o.p.

(BL 29:344; Bookshelf 1933 p. 6; KR 40:1097; LJ 58:805, 98:259)

459   CONLY, Jane Leslie. *Racso and the Rats of NIMH* **(The Rats of NIMH series,
✓   book 2). Gr. 5–8.**

Two young rodents, Timothy Frisby mouse and Racso rat, meet on their way to begin their education with the rats of NIMH, and quickly become involved in the rats' plan to destroy the dam that threatens their valley. This is the sequel to Robert C. O'Brien's *Mrs. Frisby and the Rats of NIMH* (1971) (see this chapter). Jane Conly is Robert C. O'Brien's daughter. In Conly's second sequel, *R-T, Margaret, and the Rats of NIMH* (1990), Artie and Margaret, two human children lost in the North Woods, are rescued by Christopher Rat, and soon become involved in the lives of the residents of Thorn Valley.

Illus. by Leonard Lubin, Harper, 1986, 278 pp., o.p., pap., 1988 (0-06-440245-2)

(BBC:200; BL 82:1458; 83:794, 84:1441; CC 473; CCBB 39:182; HB 62:588; SLJ Apr 1986 p. 85; TLS 1986 p. 1042; VOYA 9:86, 10:23)

460   COOK, Glen. *Doomstalker* **(Darkwar trilogy, vol. 1). Gr. 10 up.**

Marika, a young female member of an intelligent, canine-like race, survives the massacre of her tribe by nomads, only to be captured by the Silth Witches who want to use her psychic powers for their own battles with the nomads. The sequels are *Warlock* (1985) and *Ceremony* (1986).

Warner, 1985, pap., 272 pp., o.p.; Fawcett, 1989, pap. (0-449-14577-8)

(BBS:54; BL 82:31, 52; VOYA 8:393)

COOPER, Paul Fenimore. *Tal: His Marvelous Adventures with Noom-Zor-Noom.* See Chapter 5C, Travel to Other Worlds.

461 CORBALIS, Judy. *Porcellus, the Flying Pig.* **Gr. K–4.**

Porcellus single-handedly defeats Al Porcone's bank-robbing gang and becomes a hero, after two magnificent wings sprout from the ugly bumps on his back.

Illus. by Helen Craig, Dial, 1988, 32 pp., o.p.

(BL 85:406; SLJ June 1989 p. 86)

462 CORBETT, W(illiam) J(esse). *The Song of Pentecost.* **Gr. 5–9. (Orig. British**
✓ **pub. 1982.)**

A clan of harvest mice and their leader, Pentecost, leave their polluted home in search of utopia and truth. Whitbread Literary Award, Children's Book Category, 1982. The sequel is *Pentecost and the Chosen One* (1987).

Illus. by Martin Ursell, Dutton, 1983, 216 pp., o.p.; Dell, 1985, pap., o.p.

(BBC:201; BBJ:69; BL 79:1463, 84:1441; CC:475; CCBB 37:3; HB 59:450; SLJ Aug 1983 p. 63; TLS 1982 p. 1302)

463 CREGAN, Maírín. *Old John.* **Gr. 4–6. (Orig. pub. in Ireland.)**

A fairy doctor disguised as a cat comes to live with the old shoemaker of Tir Aulin.

Illus. by Helen Sewell, Macmillan, 1936, 184 pp., o.p.

(BL 32:330; HB 12:153; LJ 61:457, 809)

464 CROWLEY, Maude. *Azor and the Blue-Eyed Cow: A Christmas Story.* **Gr. 1–4.**
✓ **(Orig. U.S. pub. Oxford, 1951.)**

A young boy named Azor decides to prove the existence of Santa Claus. This is the sequel to *Azor* (1948) and *Azor and the Haddock* (1949); it is followed by *Tor and Azor* (1955).

Illus. by Helen Sewell, Gregg, 1980, 70 pp., o.p.

(BL 48:70; CCBB 5:13; HB 27:414; KR 19:530; LJ 76:2120)

465 CULLEN, Countee (Porter). *The Lost Zoo (A Rhyme for the Young, but Not Too*
✓ *Young) by Christopher Cat and Countee Cullen.* **Gr. 3–6. (Orig. pub. Harper,**
1940.)

Christopher Cat tells a tale in verse about some extraordinary beasts that Noah forgot to take on his ark. *My Lives and How I Lost Them, by Christopher Cat and Countee Cullen* (1942, 1964) is Christopher's second literary effort.

Illus. by Joseph Low, Follett, 1969, 95 pp., o.p.; illus. by Brian Pinkney, Silver Burdett, 1991, 95 pp., LB(0-382-24255-6)

(BL 37:292, 66:140; CCBB 23:157, 45:292; HB 45:542, 62:78; LJ 94:4276)

466 CUNNINGHAM, Julia (Woolfolk). *Candle Tales.* **Gr. 3–4.**

Six animals tell a kind old man stories for his birthday.

Illus. by Evaline Ness, Pantheon, 1964, 57 pp., o.p.

(BL 60:876; HB 40:376; KR 32:51; LJ 89:1448)

467   CUNNINGHAM, Julia (Woolfolk). *Macaroon.* **Gr. 3–5.**

Macaroon, a raccoon who spends his winters in children's homes, decides one winter to choose the home of a selfish, surly child so that it won't be so hard to leave in the spring.

Illus. by Evaline Ness, Pantheon, 1962, 63 pp., o.p.

(BL 59:288; HB 38:480; LJ 87:4266; TLS 1963 p. 980)

468   CUNNINGHAM, Julia (Woolfolk). *Maybe, a Mole.* **Gr. 3–5.**

Five episodes about a mole named Maybe who is rejected by his own kind because he is not blind, but is befriended by a fox, a mouse, and a turtle.

Illus. by Cyndy Szekeres, Pantheon, 1974, 81 pp., o.p.

(BL 71:506; CCBB 28:109; HB 51:51; KR 42:1303)

CUNNINGHAM, Julia (Woolfolk). *OAF.* See Chapter 1, Allegorical Fantasy and Literary Fairy Tales.

469   CUNNINGHAM, Julia (Woolfolk). *Viollet.* **Gr. 4–6.**

Oxford the dog, Warwicke the fox, and Viollet the thrush band together to save the life of Oxford's master.

Illus. by Alan E. Cober, Pantheon, 1966, 82 pp., o.p.

(CCBB 20:86; Ch&Bks:285; KR 34:1054; LJ 91:6190)

470   CUNNINGHAM, Julia (Woolfolk). *The Vision of Francois the Fox.* **Gr. 1–4.**

Francois is inspired by a vision to give up his greedy ways and become a saint.

Illus. by Nicholas Angelo, Houghton, 1960, 35 pp., o.p.

(HB 36:406; KR 28:617)

CUNNINGHAM, Julia (Woolfolk). *Wolf Roland.* See Chapter 1, Allegorical Fantasy and Literary Fairy Tales.

471   DAHL, Roald. *The Enormous Crocodile.* **Gr. K–3.**

✓   The other jungle animals thwart the ferocious crocodile's plans to eat some "nice juicy children" for lunch.

Illus. by Quentin Blake, Knopf, 1978, 1991, 32 pp. (0-394-83594-8); Puffin, 1993, pap. (0-14-036556-7); Bantam, 1984, pap. (0-553-15243-2)

(BL 75:684; CCBB 32:134; HB 55:186; HBG 3[July–Dec 1991]:57; KR 45:2; SLJ Feb 1979 p. 40; TLS Sept 29, 1978 p. 1087)

472   DAHL, Roald. *Fantastic Mr. Fox.* **Gr. 3–5. (Orig. British and U.S. pub. 1970.)**

Mr. Fox, his wife, and four children out-fox three of the meanest and stupidest farmers around.

Illus. by Donald Chaffin, Knopf, 1986, 72 pp., LB(0-394-90497-4); Bantam, 1978, pap. (0-553-15390-0); Puffin, 1988, pap. (0-14-032872-6)

(BBC:201; BL 82:1538; CCBB 24:89; LJ 96:1106)

DAHL, Roald. *James and the Giant Peach: A Children's Story.* See Chapter 7, Magic Adventure Fantasy.

DAHL, Roald. *The Twits.* See Chapter 6, Humorous Fantasy.

DAHL, Tessa. *Gwenda & the Animals.* See Chapter 7, Magic Adventure Fantasy.

DAHL, Tessa. *School Can Wait.* See Chapter 6, Humorous Fantasy.

473   **DALLAS-SMITH, Peter.** *Trouble for Trumpets.* **Gr. 2–4. (Orig. British pub. 1982.)**

Pod, a little animal called a Trumpet, tells the story of the Trumpets' war against the hostile Grumpets. The sequel is *Trumpets in Grumpetland* (1985).

Illus. by Peter Cross, Random, 1984, 30 pp., o.p.

(CCBB 38:104; Ch&Bks:285; SLJ Jan 1985 p. 73; Suth 3:112)

474   **DANA, Barbara.** *Rutgers and the Watersnouts.* **Gr. 3–5.**

Rutgers the bulldog and his friends search for more of the prickly creatures he found on the beach.

Illus. by Fred Brenner, Harper, 1969, 149 pp., o.p.

(BL 65:1075; KR 37:53; LJ 94:1324)

475   **DANA, Barbara.** *Zucchini.* **Gr. 3–5.**

✓   Zucchini, a runaway ferret from the Bronx Zoo, is caught by the ASPCA. There, he meets Billy, a boy who loves him, and the ferret has to choose between escape and a real home.

Illus. by Eileen Christelow, Harper, 1982, 128 pp. (0-06-021395-7); Bantam, 1984, pap., 160 pp. (0-553-15437-0)

(BBC:202; BL 79:443; CCBB 36:64; KR 50:1105; SLJ Oct 1982 p. 150)

476   **DANN, Colin (Michael).** *The Animals of Farthing Wood.* **(Orig. British pub. 1979.) Gr. 7–10.**

Led by Fox and Toad, the animal inhabitants of Farthing Wood unite and flee to a safer life in a nature preserve. The British sequels are: *Escape from Danger* (1979), *The Way to White Deer Park* (1979), *In the Grip of Winter* (1982), and *Siege of White Deer Park* (1985; U.S. pub. 1986).

Elsevier, 1980, 255 pp., o.p.

(BL 77:110; LJ 105:2104)

DAVIES, Andrew (Wynford). *Marmalade and Rufus.* See Chapter 6, Humorous Fantasy.

477   **DAVIS, Mary Gould.** *The Handsome Donkey.* **Gr. 3–4.**

Baldasarre the donkey becomes famous, in this story told through the eyes of a dachshund named Tedesco.

Illus. by Emma Brock, Harcourt, 1933, 67 pp., o.p.

(BL 30:51; HB 9:205; Mahony 3:242)

478   **DAVIS, Robert.** *Padre Porko: The Gentlemanly Pig.* **Gr. 4–6. (Orig. pub. 1939.)**

Twelve tales about a pig who helps people and animals in distress.

Illus. by Fritz Eichenberg, Holiday, 1948, 197 pp., o.p.

(BL 36:308; 45:17; CCBB 1[Oct 1948]:2; HB 24:379; LJ 65:123, 74:134)

479   **DE LA MARE, Walter (John).** *Mr. Bumps and His Monkey.* **Gr. 4–6. (Orig. British pub. as "The Old Lion," in the children's annual *Joy Street* [1923–1938].)**

Jasper the English-speaking monkey is stolen from Mr. Bumps.

Illus. by Dorothy P. Lathrop, Holt, 1942, 69 pp., o.p.

(BL 39:73; HB 18:426; LJ 67:884, 955)

480   **DE LA MARE, Walter (John).** *The Three Royal Monkeys.* **(Orig. title:** *The*
✓   *Three Mula Mulgars,* **1910; orig. British pub. with this title, 1927.) Gr. 5–7.**

Three Mulgars, or monkeys, search for their father, the Prince, using a magic wonder-stone.

Illus. by Mildred Eldridge, Knopf, 1919, 1941, 1948, 1966, 277 pp., o.p.

(BL 45:110; CCBB 2[Apr 1949]:3; HB 14:143; LJ 74:69; Mahony 2:278)

DELANEY, M. C. *Henry's Special Delivery.* See Chapter 6, Humorous Fantasy.

DE LEEUW, Adele Louise. *Nobody's Doll.* See Chapter 9, Toy Fantasy.

DE REGNIERS, Beatrice Schenk (Freedman). *The Boy, the Rat, and the Butter-fly.* See Chapter 7, Magic Adventure Fantasy.

481   **DIGGS, Lucy.** *Selene Goes Home.* **Gr. 2–4.**

Angry at her owner for moving to a houseboat, a cat named Selene talks a gull into flying her back home, where an unpleasant surprise is waiting.

Illus. by Emily Arnold McCully, Macmillan, 1989, 64 pp. (0-689-31464-7)

(BBC:202; BL 85:1721; CCBB 42:192; HB 65:368; KR 57:122; SLJ June 1989 p. 87)

DOLBIER, Maurice (Wyman). *A Lion in the Woods.* See Chapter 6, Humorous Fantasy.

482   **DONOVAN, John.** *Family: A Novel.* **Gr. 6–9.**
✓   Four apes escape from a scientific laboratory only to find that survival in the wild is impossible for them.

Harper, 1976, 1986, 128 pp., o.p.

(BL 72:112, 80:95; CCBB 29:173; Ch&Bks:285; HB 52:404; KR 44:405; SLJ Sept 1976 p. 131; Suth 2:127)

483   **DRURY, Roger W(olcott).** *The Champion of Merrimack County.* **Gr. 3–5.**

O Crispin is the champion mouse bicyclist until a sliver of soap on the Berryfields' bath-tub causes a bicycle wreck and a dislocated tail.

Illus. by Fritz Wegner, Little, 1976, 198 pp., o.p.

(BBC:202; BL 73:1265; CCBB 30:104; HB 53:50; KR 44:1092; SLJ Jan 1977 p. 91)

DU BOIS, William (Sherman) Pène. *Elisabeth the Cow Ghost.* See Chapter 4, Ghost Fantasy.

DU BOIS, William (Sherman) Pène. *The Forbidden Forest.* See Chapter 6, Humorous Fantasy.

DU BOIS, William (Sherman) Pène. *The Great Geppy.* See Chapter 6, Humorous Fantasy.

DU BOIS, William (Sherman) Pène. *Otto and the Magic Potatoes.* See Chapter 6, Humorous Fantasy.

DU BOIS, William (Sherman) Pène. *The Squirrel Hotel.* See Chapter 6, Humorous Fantasy.

484   **DUFFEY, Betsy.** *A Boy in the Doghouse.* **Gr. 2–4.**

In alternating chapters, George and his new puppy, Lucky, describe their ultimately suc-cessful master- and pet-training program.

Illus. by Leslie Morrill, Simon & Schuster, 1991, 84 pp. (0-671-73618-3); 1993, pap. (0-671-86698-2)

(BL 88:703; HBG 3[Spring 1992]:58; SLJ Sept 1991 p. 232)

485 **DUFFY, James.** *The Revolt of the Teddy Bears* **(May Gray Mystery series, book 1). Gr. 3–5.**

May Gray, poodle detective, comes out of retirement to solve a rash of attacks by teddy bears on the animal inhabitants of Paris. The sequel is *The Christmas Gang* (1989).

Illus. by Barbara McClintock, Macmillan, 1985, 80 pp., o.p.

(BBC:202; BL 81:949; SLJ May 1985, p. 109)

486 **DUGGAN, Alice.** *Violet's Finest Hour.* **Gr. 2–5.**

A magical purple cape that enables a cat named Violet to fly and to make a new friend, helps the cats foil a bank robbery.

Illus. by Harvey Stevenson, Lothrop, 1991, 64 pp. (0-6880-9456-2)

(BL 88:438; HBG 3[Spring 1992]:58; KR 59:1294; SLJ Jan 1992 p. 109)

487 **DUMAS, Gerald J.** *Rabbits Rafferty.* **Gr. 4–6.**

Rabbits Rafferty stumbles into a fight with Mink Mumsey's tough gang who wants to tear down the other animals' homes.

Illus. by Wallace Tripp, Houghton, 1968, 196 pp., o.p.

(CCBB 22:25; KR 36:510; LJ 93:2733; TLS 1970 p. 414)

DURRELL, Gerald. *The Talking Parcel.* See Chapter 5C, Travel to Other Worlds.

488 **EAGER, Edward (McMaken).** *Mouse Manor.* **Gr. 2–4.**

✓ Myrtilla, a poor but genteel country mouse, travels to London to see the Queen.

Illus. by Beryl Bailey-Jones, Ariel, 1952, 50 pp., o.p.

(BL 49:19; CCBB 6:4; HB 28:399; KR 20:451; LJ 77:1310)

489 **EDMONDS, Walter D(umaux).** *Beaver Valley.* **Gr. 4–6**

A young deermouse watches helplessly as the dams built by an ambitious beaver family destroy or displace the other wild creatures of the valley.

Illus. by Leslie Morrill, Little, 1971, 70 pp., o.p.

(BL 67:797; HB 47:286; KR 39:432; LJ 96:2363)

490 **EDMONDS, Walter D(umaux).** *Time to Go House.* **Gr. 4–6.**

After her family's move to a vacant human house, Smalleata the field-mouse falls in love with Raffles the house-mouse.

Illus. by Joan Victor, Little, 1969, 137 pp., o.p.

(BL 66:296; HB 45:535; KR 37:776; LJ 94:4284)

EDMONDSON, Madeline. *The Witch's Egg.* See Chapter 10, Witchcraft and Sorcery Fantasy.

491 **ELISH, Dan.** *The Great Squirrel Uprising.* **Gr. 4–6.**

The squirrels and other wild animals of New York City's Central Park unite to keep humans out of their territory permanently.

Illus. by Denys Cazet, Orchard, 1992, 128 pp. LB(0-531-08515-3)

(BL 88:1277; CCBB 45:203; HBG 3[Fall 1992]:262; KR 60:252)

492   ELISH, Dan. *Jason and the Baseball Bear.* **Gr. 3–6.**

The coach of Jason's Little League baseball team is Whitney, an elderly polar bear from the zoo, and only Jason can communicate with him.

Illus. by John Stadler, Orchard, 1990, 131 pp., o.p.

(BL 86:1548; HB 66:600; HBG 1[Jan–June 1990]:255; KR 58:422; SLJ June 1990 p. 118)

493   EMSHWILLER, Carol. *Carmen Dog.* **Gr. 10 up.**

In some future time, the men of the world are astounded when women begin turning into animals, and animals into women, including Pooch, a golden setter who longs to become an opera singer.

Mercury, 1990, 161 pp. (0-916515-77-X)

(BL 86:1070, 1078; KR 58:7; LJ Apr 15, 1990 p. 122)

ENDE, Michael. *The Night of Wishes, or The Satanarcheolidealcohellish Notion Potion.* See Chapter 6, Humorous Fantasy.

494   ERICKSON, Russell E(verett). *A Toad for Tuesday.* **Gr. 3–4.**

✓✓   Captured by an owl, Warton the toad becomes his housekeeper to avoid being eaten as birthday dinner. The sequels are *Warton and Morton* (1976), *Warton's Christmas Eve Adventure* (1977), *Warton and the King of the Skies* (1978), *Warton and the Traders* (1979), *Warton and the Castaways* (1982) and *Warton and the Contest* (1986).

Illus. by Lawrence Di Fiori, Lothrop, 1974, 64 pp., LB(0-688-51569-X)

(BL 71:98; CC:482; CCBB 28:76; HB 51:48; KR 42:681; LJ 99:2244)

495   ESTES, Eleanor (Ruth Rosenfeld). *Miranda the Great.* **Gr. 3–5.**

A Roman cat named Miranda, lost by her human family, gathers other strays and proclaims herself Queen of the Colosseum.

Illus. by Edward Ardizzone, Harcourt, 1967, 79 pp., o.p.

(BL 63:948; CCBB 20:120; HB 43:201; KR 35:130; LJ 92:1315)

496   EVANS, Sanford. *Naomi's Geese.* **Gr. 5–7.**

✓   A story told alternately from the points of view of a girl named Naomi and a pair of Canada geese she is trying to protect from environmental poisoning.

Simon, 1993, 192 pp. (0-671-75623-0)

(BL 90:690; CCBB 47:43; HBG 5:75; KR 61:1328; SLJ Nov 1993 p. 106; VOYA 17:26)

497   EZO (pseud.). *Avril.* **Gr. 4–6. (Orig. pub. in France.)**

When Avril runs away from her foster family, she is accompanied by a lamb, a cat, a bear, and a baby ghost.

Trans. by John Buchanan-Brown, illus. by Douglas Bissot, Abelard-Schuman, 1967, 94 pp., o.p.

(KR 35:1046; LJ 92:4612)

EZO (pseud.). *My Son-in-Law, the Hippopotamus.* See Chapter 6, Humorous Fantasy.

FARALLA, Dana. *The Singing Cupboard.* See Chapter 7, Magic Adventure Fantasy.

FAST, Howard (Melvin). *The General Zapped an Angel: New Stories of Fantasy and Science Fiction.* See Chapter 3, Fantasy Collections.

498 **FEAGLES, Anita MacRae.** *Casey, the Utterly Impossible Horse.* **Gr. 2–4.**

Mike is not exactly pleased that Casey the talking horse has chosen him as a pet.

Illus. by Dagmar Wilson, Addison-Wesley, 1960, 95 pp., o.p.; Shoe String, 1989, LB(0-208-02239-2)

(CCBB 14:78; LJ 85:4566)

499 **FIELD, Rachel (Lyman).** *Little Dog Toby.* **Gr. 3–5.**

Toby performs in a Punch and Judy show during a Christmas party at Buckingham Palace.

Illus. by the author, Macmillan, 1928, 1952, 116 pp., o.p.

(BL 25:127, 49:147; Bookshelf 1929 p. 18; HB 4[Aug 1928]:9, 4[Nov 1928]:78, 7:115, 28:421; Mahony 2:118)

FIENBERG, Anna. *The Marvelous Nose and Other Marvels.* See Chapter 7, Magic Adventure Fantasy.

500 **FINE, Anne.** *The Chicken Gave It to Me.* **Gr. 4–6. (Orig. British pub. 1992.)**

"The True Story of Harrowing Farm," a book written by a chicken, reveals to Gemma and Andrew that people-eating aliens are taking over the world.

Illus. by Cynthia Fisher, Little, Brown, 1993, 78 pp. (0-31628316-9)

(BL 89:1966; CCBB 46:343; HBG 4[Fall 1993]:297; KR 61:660; SLJ Aug 1993 p. 163)

501 **FLACK, Marjorie.** *Walter the Lazy Mouse.* **Gr. 2–4. (Orig. pub. 1937.)**

Left behind during his family's move, Walter is befriended by Turtle and the three Frogs while he searches for his family.

Illus. by Cyndy Szekeres, Doubleday, 1963, 95 pp., o.p.

(HB 13:284; LJ 62:782)

FLORY, Jane (Trescott). *The Lost and Found Princess.* See Chapter 1, Allegorical Fantasy and Literary Fairy Tales.

502 **FOOTE, Timothy (Gilson).** *The Great Ringtail Garbage Caper.* **Gr. 4–6.**

Oldest Raccoon and his gang heist a garbage truck to keep their friends in food.

Illus. by Normand Chartier, Houghton, 1980, 66 pp., o.p.

(BBC:203; BL 76:1363, 84:1441; HB 56:294; KR 48:583; SLJ May 1980 p. 66)

FORBUS, Ina B(ell). *The Magic Pin.* See Chapter 7, Magic Adventure Fantasy.

503 **FORD, Richard.** *Quest for the Faradawn.* **Gr. 10 up.**

Abandoned in the woods by his parents, a human baby is taken in by badgers who raise him in fulfilment of a legend that foretold his becoming the savior of the world.

Illus. by Owain Bell, Delacorte, 1982, o.p.

(BL 78:1068, 1082; KR 50:374; LJ 107:1014; SLJ Sept 1982 p. 148; VOYA 5[Aug 1982]:39)

FORST, S. *Pipkin.* See Chapter 1, Allegorical Fantasy and Literary Fairy Tales.

504 **FORT, John.** *June the Tiger.* **Gr. 4–6.**

✓ Mrs. Pinckney's feisty dog, June, and her friend, Billy the Bull, declare war on a bear named Scratch who has ravaged Mrs. Pinckney's house.

Illus. by Bernice Loewenstein, Little, 1975, 59 pp., o.p.

(BL 72:855, 84:1441; CCBB 29:143; HB 52:48; KR 43:1397; SLJ Mar 1976 p. 102)

FOSBURGH, Liza. *Bella Arabella.* See Chapter 7, Magic Adventure Fantasy.

505   FOX, Denise P. *Through Tempest Trails.* Gr. 3–5.

Burr the raccoon, Minkley the mink, a peacock, and three shrews escape from outlaws and journey to Harbor Town, only to be captured by pirates.

Illus. by Judith Gwyn Brown, Atheneum, 1987, 116 pp., o.p.

(BBC:203; BL 84:705, 1441; KR 55:1574; SLJ Dec 1987 p. 85)

506   FOX (Greenberg), Paula. *Dear Prosper.* Gr. 3–5.

A dog named Chien writes his life story in a letter to the boy who was his first master.

Illus. by Steve McLachlin, White, 1968, 67 pp., o.p.

(KR 36:393; LJ 93:2733)

FOX (Greenberg), Paula. *The Little Swineherd and Other Tales.* See Chapter 3, Fantasy Collections.

507   FRANKO, Ivan, and MELNYK, Bohdan. *Fox Mykyta.* Gr. 4–5. (Orig. Ukrainian pub. 1890.)

The animals in Lion's court never manage to hurt wiley Fox Mykyta.

Trans. by Bodhan Melnyk, illus. by William Kurelek, Tundra, 1978, 148 pp., o.p.

(BL 75:933; HB 55:191)

508   FREDDI, Cris. *Pork, and Other Stories.* Gr. 10 up.

A collection of connected animal tales set in a forest ruled by a magical stag.

Knopf, 1981, o.p.; Dutton, 1983, pap., 224 pp., o.p.

(BL 78:28, 36; KR 49:819; LJ 106:2048; SLJ Dec 1981 p. 88)

FREEMAN, Barbara C(onstance). *Broom-Adelaide.* See Chapter 1, Allegorical Fantasy and Literary Fairy Tales.

509   FREMLIN, Robert. *Three Friends.* Gr. 1–3.

The friendship of Cat, Pig, and Squirrel is tested in three stories about Pig threatening to run away, demonstrating his acrobatic "tricks," and giving Squirrel bad advice on a new suit.

Illus. by Wallace Tripp, Little, Brown, 1975, 64 pp., o.p.

(BL 71:965; CCBB 29:44; KR 43:374; SLJ Oct 1975, p. 90)

FRENCH, Fiona. *The Magic Vase.* See Chapter 1, Allegorical Fantasy and Literary Fairy Tales.

510   FRESCHET, Bernice (Louise Speck). *Bernard of Scotland Yard.* Gr. 2–3.

✓   Bernard the mouse helps his cousin Foster of Scotland Yard break up a gang of robber moles who are planning a heist of the crown jewels. This is the sequel to *Bernard Sees the World* (1976) and is followed by *Bernard and the Catnip Caper* (1981).

Illus. by Gina Freschet, Scribner, 1978, 48 pp., o.p.

(BL 75:750; CCBB 32:135; KR 47:3; SLJ Mar 1979 p. 121; Suth 2:156)

511   FRY, Rosalie K(ingsmill). *The Wind Call.* Gr. 2–4.

Mother Blackcap finds a lost baby of the Little People, names him Pierello, and raises him along with her three baby birds.

Illus. by the author, Dutton, 1955, 115 pp., o.p.

(CCBB 10:50; HB 32:30; LJ 80:2916)

512 **GACKENBACH, Dick.** *Beauty, Brave and Beautiful.* **Gr. 2–4.**

A homeless, ugly little mutt finds a loving home with two children after she saves them from an attack by a bear.

Illus. by the author, Houghton, 1990, 48 pp. (0-395-52000-2)

(BL 86:1341; HBG 1[Jan 1990]:237; SLJ May 1990 p. 84)

513 **GALLICO, Paul (William).** *The Abandoned* **(British title:** *Jennie***). Gr. 8 up.**
✓ Injured in an automobile accident, Peter imagines his transformation into a homeless cat.

Knopf, 1950, o.p.; International Polygonics, 1987, 1991, pap., 250 pp. (1-55882-097-3)

(BL 47:2, 39; HB 26:501; KR 18:394; LJ 75:2161)

514 **GANGLOFF, Deborah.** *Albert and Victoria.* **Gr. 3–5.**

Albert misses his best friend and fellow insect, Victoria, after she climbs to the top of the Empire State Building for the winter months, so he undertakes a perilous journey to follow her.

Illus. by Bill Woodman, Crown, 1989, 80 pp., o.p.

(BL 85:1294; KR 56:1810; SLJ July 1989 p. 64)

515 **GATES, Doris.** *The Cat and Mrs. Cary.* **Gr. 5–7.**

Mrs. Cary is able to solve a mystery because she can understand cat language.

Illus. by Peggy Bacon, Viking, 1962, 216 pp., o.p.

(Eakin:135; HB 38:598; LJ 88:864)

516 **GAUNT, Michael (pseud. of [James] Dennis Robertshaw).** *Brim's Boat.* **Gr. 4–6. (Orig. British pub. 1964.)**

A terrier named Brim finds an abandoned boat and decides to become a sailor. The sequels are *Brim Sails Out* (1966) and *Brim's Valley* (British).

Illus. by Stuart Tresilian, Coward, 1966, 128 pp., o.p.

(BL 62:831; HB 42:305; KR 34:56; LJ 91:1063)

517 **GAUTIER, (Louise) Judith.** *The Memoirs of a White Elephant.* **Gr. 5–6. (Orig. pub. in France.)**

A royal Indian elephant tells how he once saved his master's life and became the guardian of the baby princess of Golconda.

Illus. by L. H. Smith and S. B. Kite, trans. by S. A. B. Harvey, Duffield, 1916, 233 pp., o.p.

(BL 13:269; Bookshelf 1921–1922 p. 13; Mahony 2:343)

GIFALDI, David. *Gregory, Maw and the Mean One.* See Chapter 6, Humorous Fantasy.

518 **GODDEN (Dixon), (Margaret) Rumer.** *Mouse House.* **Gr. K–3. (Orig. pub. in**
✓ **England.)**

Mary makes sure that her miniature house gets the right kind of tenants: a family of mice.

Illus. by Adrienne Adams, Viking, 1957, 63 pp., o.p.

(BL 54:28; CCBB 11:80; HB 33:483; KR 25:480; LJ 82:2693)

GODDEN (Dixon), (Margaret) Rumer. *The Mousewife.* See Chapter 1, Allegorical Fantasy and Literary Fairy Tales.

519 **GOLDMAN, Kelly and DAVIDSON, Ronnie.** *Sherlick Hound and the Valentine Mystery.* **Gr. 2–4.**

Who stole Princess Penelope Poodle's new ruby-studded collar? "Dog-Honest Detective" Sherlick Hound and his friend, reporter Scoop Schnauzer, solve the case.

Illus. by Don Madden, Whitman, 1989, 40 pp. (0-8075-7335-3)

(BL 85:1466; SLJ June 1989 p.88)

520 **GOODWIN, Harold Leland.** *Magic Number.* **Gr. 4–6.**

In a bid for equal rights, the garden-dwelling animals declare war on the house pets at a veterinarian's home.

Illus. by the author, Bradbury, 1969, 97 pp., o.p.

(BL 66:206; CCBB 23:8; KR 37:559; LJ 95:3603)

521 **GOODWIN, Murray.** *Alonzo and the Army of Ants.* **Gr. 4–6.**

Alonzo the anteater must save his village from an invasion of army ants.

Illus. by Kiyo Komoda, Harper, 1966, 104 pp., o.p.

(KR 34:419; LJ 91:3258)

522 **GRAHAME, Kenneth.** *Bertie's Escapade.* **Gr. 1–3. (Orig. U.S. pub. in this for-**
✓ **mat, Lippincott, 1949.)**

Bertie Pig and Peter and Benjie Rabbit's Christmas caroling efforts disturb Mr. Stone, who sets his dogs on them. This story was first published as part of *First Whispers of the Wind in the Willows* (1944 in England; 1945 in the U.S.).

Illus. by Ernest Shepard, Harper, 1977, 28 pp., o.p.

(BL 41:223; CCBB 2[Nov 1949]:4; HB 21:200, 25:413, 552; KR 13:31, 45:1094; LJ 70:264, 74:1533, 1681; TLS 1944 p. 369)

523 **GRAHAME, Kenneth.** *The Wind in the Willows.* **Gr. 4–8. (Orig. British pub.**
✓✓ **1907, U.S. 1908.)**

Ratty, Mole, and Toad battle the weasels and stoats that have taken over Toad Hall. A. A. Milne used this story as a basis for a play entitled *Toad of Toad Hall* (Scribner, 1929, 1957; Avon, 1982, pap.). Picture-book versions of four chapters from the novel have been published by Scribner—*The River Bank* (1977), *The Open Road* (1980), *Wayfarers All* (1981), and *Mole's Christmas, or, Home Sweet Home* (1983, pap., 1986). Dixon Scott (see this section) has written a sequel for a slightly older audience entitled *A Fresh Wind in the Willows* (orig. British pub. 1983, Dell, 1987, pap.).William Horwood has written a sequel for adults entitled *The Willows in Winter* (orig. British pub. 1993; St. Martin's, 1994).

Illus. by Arthur Rackham, Heritage, 1940, o.p.; illus. by Ernest H. Shepard, Macmillan, 1933, 1983, 1991, 264 pp. (0-684-19345-0), 1989, pap. (0-689-71310-X); illus. by Michael Hague, Ariel, 1982, o.p.; illus. by John Burningham, Viking, 1983, 240 pp. (0-670-77120-1); Puffin, 1984, pap. (0-14-031544-6); Macmillan, 1989, pap. (0-689-71310-X)

(BBC:204; BL 50:20, 77:1250, 80:85, 680, 85:1188; CC:493; CCBB 7:4, 34:111, 36:209; Ch&Bks:266; HB 1[June 1925]:34, 46, 7:118, 9:205, 30:83, 59:733, 60:357; Mahony 2:280; SLJ Nov 1980 p. 74, Sept 1983 p. 122; Suth 3:158, 159)

GRAY, Nicholas Stuart. *Grimbold's Other World.* See Chapter 5C, Travel to Other Worlds.

GREGORY, Valiska. *Through the Mickle Woods.* See Chapter 1, Allegorical Fantasy and Literary Fairy Tales.

GUILLOT, René. *Nicolette and the Mill.* See Chapter 7, Magic Adventure Fantasy.

GUILLOT, René. *The Three Hundred Ninety-seventh White Elephant.* See Chapter 1, Allegorical Fantasy and Literary Fairy Tales.

524 **HAAS, Dorothy F. (Dee Francis).** *The Bears Up Stairs.* **Gr. 5–7.**

Wendy befriends Otto and Ursula Ma'am, two bears hiding in her apartment building while they wait for transportation to the planet Brun.

Greenwillow, 1978, 192 pp., o.p.

(BL 75:49; CCBB 32:44; KR 46:1248; SLJ Oct 1978 p. 144)

525 **HAHN, Harriet.** *James, the Connoisseur Cat.* **Gr. 10 up.**

An American fine arts agent in London is befriended by James, a large gray art expert cat, who manages to unmask forgeries, find stolen jewels, impersonate an Egyptian cat goddess, and star in a TV show. The sequel is *James, Fabulous Feline: Further Adventures of a Connoisseur Cat* (1993).

St. Martin, 1991, 169 pp. (0-8161-5443-0), 1992, pap., 176 pp. (0-312-08228-2)

(BL 88:120, 131; KR 59:1031)

HALL, Lynn. *The Mystery of the Caramel Cat.* See Chapter 4, Ghost Fantasy.

526 **HAMILTON, Carol.** *The Dawn Seekers.* **Gr. 4–6.**

Nocturnal young Quentin, a Kangaroo rat, joins forces with a bossy jerboa and a poetic centipede to venture out into the desert by day.

Illus. by Jeremy Guitar, Whitman, 1987, 160 pp., LB(0-8075-1480-2)

(BBC:204; BL 83:1446, 84:1441; KR 55:56; SLJ Mar 1987 p. 160)

527 **HAMLEY, Dennis.** *Hare's Choice.* **Gr. 4–6. (Orig. British pub. 1988.)**

A dead hare is given the choice of going to an eternally peaceful valley to become the Queen of Hares, or living on eternally by becoming a character in a children's story.

Illus. by Meg Rutherford, Delacorte, 1990, 88 pp., o.p.; Dell, 1992, pap. (0-440-40698-6)

(CCBB 43:214; HBG 1[Jan–June 1990]:257; KR 58:424; SLJ May 1990 p. 106)

528 **HANCOCK, Neil (Anderson).** *Dragon Winter.* **Gr. 8–12.**

A mysterious voice unites a group of otters, beavers, squirrels, badgers, a muskrat, and a mole, all of whom have been driven from their homes. The voice convinces them to go on a magic quest to find a great silver bear. The sequel is *The Fires of Windameir* (Warner, 1985), and both books are related to Hancock's "The Wilderness of Four" series (1982).

Popular Library, 1978, 351 pp., o.p.

(Kliatt 12 [Spring 1978]:7; VOYA 7: 56)

HARPER, Tara K. *Wolfwalker.* See Chapter 5A, Alternate Worlds or Histories.

529 **HARRIS, Dorothy Joan.** *The House Mouse.* **Gr. K–2.**

All winter long, Jonathan shares cookies and conversation with the mouse who lives in his sister's dollhouse. The sequel is *The School Mouse* (1977).

Illus. by Barbara Cooney, Warne, 1973, 48 pp., o.p.

(CCBB 27:27; KR 41:559; LJ 98:2640)

HARVEY, Dean. *The Secret Elephant of Harlan Kooter.* See Chapter 7, Magic Adventure Fantasy.

530 **HASS, E. A.** *Incognito Mosquito, Private Insective.* **Gr. 3–5.**

A mosquito detective describes five of his most serious cases, including the capture of the "bug napper" of baseball star Mickie Mantis. The sequels are *Incognito Mosquito Flies Again* (1985; pap., 1990) and *Incognito Mosquito Takes to the Air* (1986).

Illus. by the author, Lothrop, 1982, 96 pp. (0-688-01434-8)

(CCBB 36:108; KR 50:1105; SLJ Dec 1982 p. 79)

531 **HATCH, Richard Warren.** *The Lobster Books* **(Orig. title:** *The Curious Lobster,* **Harcourt, 1937; and** *The Curious Lobster's Island,* **Dodd, 1939). Gr. 4–6.**

An old lobster meets a badger and a bear while exploring unknown territory up river.

Illus. by Marion Freeman Wakeman, Houghton, 1951, 347 pp., o.p.

(BL 34:132; CCBB 4:50; HB 13:288, 15:383, 27:260; LJ 62:809, 881, 64:840, 904; TLS 1937 p. 948)

532 **HAWDON, Robin.** *A Rustle in the Grass.* **Gr. 10 up. (Orig. British pub. 1984.)**
✓ A young soldier ant named Dreamer, struggling to work out his purpose in life, scouts the brutal red ant army and plays a key role in the war to defend his territory and his queen.

Dodd, 1985, 244 pp., o.p.; Tor, 1989, pap., 244 pp. (0-8125-0068-7)

(BL 81:1029, 1050; KR 53:150; LJ Apr 1, 1985 p. 158; SLJ Aug 1985 p. 86; VOYA 8:394, 10:23)

533 **HAWKINS, Laura.** *Figment, Your Dog, Speaking.* **Gr. 3–6.**

A talking dog plays an important role in the lives of three unrelated people: lonely ten-year-old Marcella; her frightened, developmentally delayed neighbor, Benny; and an elderly judge with a guilty secret.

Houghton, 1991, 155 pp. (0-395-57032-8), pap. (0-395-60473-7)

(BL 88:1029; CCBB 45:63; HBG 3[July–Dec 1991]:66; KR 59:1403; SLJ Mar 1992 p. 237)

534 **HAYES, Geoffrey.** *The Alligator and His Uncle Tooth: A Novel of the Sea.* **Gr. 3–5.**

Uncle Tooth's adventure-filled tales convince the old sea captain to sail again, with Corduroy as mate. Two sequels written for younger readers are: *The Mystery of the Pirate Ghost* (Random, 1985) and *The Secret of Foghorn Island* (Random, 1988).

Illus. by the author, Harper, 1977, 88 pp., o.p.

(BBC:204; BL 73:1420; CCBB 31:33; HB 53:441; KR 45:350; SLJ Sept 1977 p. 109; TLS 1977 p. 1414)

HAYES, Sarah. *Crumbling Castle.* See Chapter 10, Witchcraft and Sorcery Fantasy.

HEAL, (Berrien) Edith. *What Happened to Jenny.* See Chapter 7, Magic Adventure Fantasy.

HENDRY, Diana. *A Camel Called April.* See Chapter 7, Magic Adventure Fantasy.

HESS, Fjeril. *The Magic Switch.* See Chapter 7, Magic Adventure Fantasy.

HEWETT, Anita. *The Bull Beneath the Walnut Tree and Other Stories.* See Chapter 3, Fantasy Collections.

HILLER, Catherine. *Abracatabby.* See Chapter 7, Magic Adventure Fantasy.

535 **HIMLER, Ronald (Norbert), and HIMLER, Ann.** *Little Owl, Keeper of the Trees.* **Gr. K–3.**

Although Little Owl is afraid of high places, his favorite spot is the highest branch of the Old Sycamore Tree, where he dreams of being the mighty guardian of the forest.

Illus. by Ronald Himler, Harper, 1974, 63 pp., o.p.

(BL 71:570; CCBB 28:148; KR 42:1103; SLJ Jan 1975 p. 39)

536   HOBAN, Lillian. *It's Really Christmas.* **Gr. K–3.**

The family of a lame baby mouse named Gamey Joe cheers him up while he recovers from a bad fall by creating Christmas in July.

Illus. by the author, Greenwillow, 1982, 39 pp., o.p.

(BL 79:116; CCBB 36:27; KR 50:995; SLJ Oct 1982 p. 165)

537   HOBAN, Russell C(onwell). *Jim Hedgehog and the Lonesome Tower.* **Gr. 2–4.**

Heavy-metal fan Jim Hedgehog accidently drops his recorder into a stream and follows it to a mysterious castle, where he teaches a female singer to read music. The sequel is *Jim Hedgehog's Supernatural Christmas* (1992).

Illus. by Betsy Lewin, Houghton, 1992, 44 pp. (0-395597609)

(BL 88:1680; HBG 3[Fall 1992]:256; KR 60:256; SLJ June 1992 p. 95)

538   HOBAN, Russell C(onwell). *Dinner at Alberta's.* **Gr. 2–4.**

✓   Arthur Crocodile decides to learn table manners in preparation for dinner at Alberta Saurian's house. The sequel is *Arthur's New Power* (1978).

Illus. by James Marshall, Crowell, 1975, 40 pp., LB(0-690-23993-9); Dell, 1980, pap., 48 pp. (0-440-41864-X)

(BL 72:302; CCBB 29:98; HB 52:46; KR 42:993; SLJ Dec 1975 pp. 31, 64; Suth 2:216)

HOBAN, Russell C(onwell). *The Mouse and His Child.* See Chapter 1, Allegorical Fantasy and Literary Fairy Tales.

539   HOBAN, Russell C(onwell). *The Sea-Thing Child.* **Gr. 2–4.**

Friendly shore creatures help a newborn sea-thing overcome its fear of flying.

Illus. by Abrom Hoban, Harper, 1972, 35 pp., o.p.

(CCBB 26:92; KR 40:1188, 1412; LJ 98:644; TLS 1972 p. 1323)

HOFFMAN, Mary. *The Four-Legged Ghosts.* See Chapter 7, Magic Adventure Fantasy.

HOFFMANN, E(rnst) T(heodor) A(madeus). *The Nutcracker.* See Chapter 9, Toy Fantasy.

540   HOFFMANN, Eleanor. *The Four Friends.* **Gr. 3–5.**

✓   To avoid becoming Christmas dinner, a pig runs away in a rental car, along with a dog, a parrot, and a hen.

Illus. by Kurt Wiese, Macmillan, 1946, 105 pp., o.p.

(BL 43:173; HB 22:349; KR 14:422; LJ 71:1808)

541   HOLMAN (Valen), Felice. *The Cricket Winter.* **Gr. 3–5.**

A boy and a cricket communicate in Morse code to save a mouse family from a thieving rat.

Illus. by Ralph Pinto, Norton, 1967, 107 pp., o.p.

(BL 64:784; CCBB 21:111; LJ 92:3849; Suth:193)

542   HOŘEJS, Vít. *Pig and Bear.* **Gr. 1–4.**

Pig and Bear open a pawn shop, but run into trouble because they have no idea how to run such a business.

Illus. by Friso Henstra, Macmillan, 1989, 40 pp. (0-02744421-X)

(CCBB 43:60; HBG 1[July 1989]:66; KR 57:1246; SLJ Feb 1990 p. 75)

HORNE, Richard Henry. *The Good-Natured Bear: A Story for Children of All Ages.* See Chapter 6, Humorous Fantasy.

543   **HORNE, Richard Henry.** *King Penguin: A Legend of the South Sea Isles.* **Gr.**
✓   **3–5. (Orig. British pub. 1848, U.S. 1925.)**

A remorseful sailor sets out to free the captive King of the Penguins.

Illus. by James Daugherty, Macmillan, 1952, 68 pp., o.p.

(BL 22:122; HB 2[Nov 1925]:19, 28:421; LJ 51:836; Mahony 2:148; Moore: 42)

HORWITZ, Elinor Lander. *The Strange Story of the Frog Who Became a Prince.* See Chapter 10, Witchcraft and Sorcery Fantasy.

544   **HORWOOD, William.** *Duncton Wood.* **Gr. 10 up.**

The moles of Duncton Wood, and all of southern England, are saved by a pair of star-crossed lovers and a epic battle between the forces of good and evil.

McGraw-Hill, 1980, o.p.

(BL 76:1410, KR 48:152; LJ 105:1409; VOYA 4[Oct 1980]:32, 4[Aug 1981]:48)

HOUGH, (Helen) Charlotte (Woodyatt). *Red Biddy and Other Stories.* See Chapter 3, Fantasy Collections.

545   **HOWARD, Joan (pseud. of Patricia Gordon).** *The Taming of Giants.* **Gr. 1–4.**

A field mouse searching for a new home encounters a classroom full of "giants."

Illus. by Garry MacKenzie, Viking, 1950, 57 pp., o.p.

(BL 47:16; CCBB 4:3; HB 26:375; KR 18:512)

546   **HOWARD, Joan (pseud. of Patricia Gordon).** *Uncle Sylvester.* **Gr. 2–4.**

In order to save their homes from destruction by erosion, Uncle Sylvester mole and his nephew, Digger, move the entire colony across the river to the Green Forest.

Illus. by Garry MacKenzie, Oxford, 1950, 48 pp., o.p.

(CCBB 3:35; HB 26:194; KR 18:176; LJ 75:629, 987)

547   **HOWE, Deborah and HOWE, James.** *Bunnicula: A Rabbit Tale of Mystery.* **Gr.**
✓   **3–5.**

Family pets Chester and Harold suspect that the bunny rabbit brought home from a Dracula movie is really a vampire. The sequels, all written by James Howe, are *Howliday Inn* (1982), *The Celery Stalks at Midnight* (1983), *Nighty-Nightmare* (1987), *Harold and Chester in the Fright Before Christmas* (1988), *Scared Silly: A Halloween Treat* (Morrow, 1989), *Harold and Chester in Hot Fudge* (1990), *Return to Howliday Inn* (1992), and *Rabbit-Cadabra!* (1993).

Illus. by Alan Daniel, Atheneum, 1979, 112 pp. (0-689-30700-4); Avon, 1989, pap., 100 pp. (0-380-51094-4)

(BL 75:1439; CC:505; CCBB 32:192; Ch&Bks:287; KR 47:741; SLJ May 1979 p. 81; Suth 3:200)

548   **HOWE, James.** *Morgan's Zoo.* **Gr. 3–5.**

Morgan the zookeeper, two children, and all of the animals join forces to save their zoo from closing.

Illus. by Leslie Morrill, Atheneum, 1984, 192 pp. (0-689-31046-3); Avon, 1986, pap., 192 pp. (0-380-69994-X)

(BBC :205; BL 81:448; SLJ Sept 1984 p. 119)

549 HUGHES, Ted (Edward James). *How the Whale Became.* Gr. 2–5. (Orig. British
✓ pub. 1963.)

A collection of stories describing how the whale, the owl, the hare, the polar bear, and the hyena developed their individual personalities.

Illus. by Rick Schreiter, Atheneum, 1964, 100 pp., o.p.

(BL 61:482; HB 40:498; KR 32:650; LJ 89:4196)

550 JACQUES, Brian. *Redwall* (Redwall Saga, book 1). Gr. 5–9. (Orig. British pub.
✓ 1986.)

Young Matthias Mouse helps defend Redwall Abbey against marauding rats bent on enslaving the peaceful mice who have taken refuge there. In *Mossflower* (1988), the prequel to *Redwall,* Martin the Warrior battles the evil wildcat Tsarmina to bring peace to the Mossflower Woodlands. In *Mattimeo* (1990), Matthias's son, Mattimeo, is enslaved by Slager the Fox and Matthias attempts a rescue, while Mattimeo's mother, Cornflower, defends Redwall Abbey from other enemies. In *Mariel of Redwall* (1992), set between *Mossflower* and *Redwall* in time, Mariel, the daughter of Joseph the bellmaker, becomes a warrior after Gabool the Wild, a pirate rat, steals the Joseph Bell and tries to drown her. In *Salamandastron* (1993), Martin's sword has been stolen and Salamandastron Castle is attacked by Ferahgo the Assassin. *Martin the Warrior* (1994), set in a time preceding *Redwall* and *Mossflower,* describes the early life of Redwall's founder.

Illus. by Gary Chalk, Putnam, 1987, 351 pp. (0-399-21424-0); Avon, 1990, pap. (0-380-70827-2)

(BBC:206; BL 83:1519, 1522, 84:1248, 1441; CC:510; CCBB 40:211; HB 64:71; KR 55:858; SLJ Aug 1987 p. 96, Dec 1987 p. 37)

551 JAMES, Mary (pseud. of Marijane Meaker, a.k.a. M. E. Kerr). *Shoebag.* Gr.
✓ 3–7.

After his sudden transformation from Shoebag the cockroach into a little boy named Stewart Bagg, Shoebag is adopted by the Biddle family and must deal with a school bully, a TV commercial-star sister, and the increasing hostility of his cockroach father.

Scholastic, 1990, 144 pp. (0-5904-3029-7), 1992, pap. (0-5904-3030-0)

(BL 86:1632; CC:510; CCBB 43:164; HBG 1[Jan–June 1990]:255; KR 58:264; SLJ June 1990, p. 124, Dec 1990 p. 22; VOYA 13:219)

552 JARRELL, Randall. *The Bat-Poet.* Gr. 3–5.

A young bat writes poetry about day-creatures to convince his nocturnal friends to stay awake during the day.

Illus. by Maurice Sendak, Macmillan, 1964, 44 pp. (0-02-747640-5)

(BBC:206; CC:510; Ch&Bks:268; LJ 89:2210)

JARRELL, Randall. *Fly by Night.* See Chapter 7, Magic Adventure Fantasy.

553 JEFFRIES, (John) Richard. *Wood Magic; a Fable.* Gr. 7 up. (Orig. British pub.
1881.)

The animal inhabitants of an English meadow battle over dwelling rights, dominance, and survival, and are observed by a little boy named Bevis. This book is considered to be the first animal fantasy novel written for children. The sequel is *Bevis: The Story of a Boy* (orig. British pub. 1882, U.S. Puffin, 1974).

Introduction by Richard Adams, Third, 1974, 271 pp., o.p.

(BL 71:792; LJ 100:409; SLJ Apr 1975 p. 74)

554   JEKEL, Pamela. *The Third Jungle Book.* **Gr. 5 up.**

Ten further adventures of Mowgli the wolf-boy and his friends Baloo the bear, Bagheera the panther, and Akela the wolf, in this sequel to Rudyard Kipling's *The Jungle Book* (1894; see entry below) and *The Second Jungle Book* (1895).

Illus. by Nancy Malick, Rinehart, 1992, 219 pp. (1-879373-22-X)

(HBG 4[Spring 1993]:71; SLJ Nov 1992, p. 94)

555   JOHANSEN, Hanna. *7 X 7 Tales of a Sevensleeper.* **Gr. 2–4. (Orig. Swiss pub. 1985.)**

Sevensleepers are squirrel-like animals that hibernate for seven months of the year, eat things in multiples of seven, and like seven of anything.

Trans. by Christopher Franceschelli, illus. by Käthi Bhend, Dutton, 1989, 95 pp., o.p.

BL 86:1344; CC:510; HBG 1[July–Dec 1989]:84; SLJ July 1990 p. 61)

556   JOHANSEN, Hanna. *A Tomcat's Tale.* **Gr. 4–7. (Orig. Swiss pub. 1987.)**

✓   Felis, an orange tabby cat, runs away from home chasing a female cat, and lives a dangerous life in the out-of-doors.

Trans. by Susanna Fox, illus by Käthi Bhend, Dutton, 1991, 142 pp. (0-525-44583-8)

(BL 87:1967; CCBB 45:13; KR 59:605; HBG 2:266; SLJ Jan 1991 p. 113)

557   JOHNSON, Annabel. *I Am Leaper.* **Gr. 3–5.**

A talking kangaroo mouse named Leaper tries to contact laboratory scientists to warn them that a monster is destroying her territory in the California desert.

Illus. by Stella Ormai, Scholastic, 1990, 128 pp. (0-5904-3400-4), 1992, pap. (0-5904-3399-7)

(BL 87:657, 1037; HBG 2[July 1990]:81; KR 58:1326; SLJ Jan 1991 p. 92)

558   JOHNSTON, Johanna. *Great Gravity the Cat.* **Gr. 3–5.**

Gravity's jealousy of the new baby in the house causes him to run away to seek his fortune.

Illus. by Kurt Wiese, Knopf, 1958, 66 pp., o.p.; illus. by Melissa Bay Mathis, Linnet, 1989, 64 pp., LB(0-208-02223-6)

(CCBB 111:120; HB 34:195; KR 26:74; LJ 83:1602; SLJ Oct 1989 p. 89)

JONES, Diana Wynne. *Dogsbody.* See Chapter 5C, Travel to Other Worlds.

559   KARAZIN, Nikolaí Nikoleavich. *Cranes Flying South.* **Gr. 4–6. (Orig. pub. in the Soviet Union.)**

A young Russian crane describes his summer of training with Longnose the Wise One, before his first flight south.

Trans. by M. Pokrovsky, illus. by Vera Bock, Doubleday, 1931, 235 pp., o.p.

(BL 27:506; HB 7:237, 238; Mahony 3:206)

560   KÄSTNER, Erich. *The Animal's Conference.* **Gr. 4–6. (Orig. Swiss pub. 1949.)**

The animals of the world unite and force the humans to make peace.

Trans. by Zita de Schauensee, illus. by Walter Trier, McKay, 1953, 62 pp., o.p.

(BL 49:380; CCBB 7:5; HB 29:271; KR 21:333)

561   KATZ, Welwyn Wilton. *Whalesinger.* **Gr. 7–10.**

✓   Shy Marty, spending the summer as an au pair on the California coast, discovers that she can communicate telepathically with a gray whale swimming offshore, in this complicated story involving environmental research, sunken treasure, and suspense.

Macmillan, 1990, 212 pp. (0-689-50511-6); Dell, 1993, pap. (0-440-21419-X)

(BL 87:1125; CCBB 44:144; HBG 2[Fall 1991]:266; KR 59:47; SLJ May 1991 p. 111; VOYA 14:31)

562   KAUFMAN, Charles. *The Frog and the Beanpole.* **Gr. 5–6.**

Wesley, an invisible research laboratory frog, and a girl named Holly run away to join a traveling circus.

Illus. by Troy Howell, Lothrop, 1980, 189 pp., o.p.

(BL 76:1608; CCBB 33:174; KR 48:836; SLJ Aug 1980 p. 64)

KELLER, Gottfried. *The Fat of the Cat and Other Stories.* See Chapter 3, Fantasy Collections.

563   KELLEY, True Adelaide and LINDBLOM, Steven (Winther). *The Mouses' Terrible Christmas.* **Gr. 2–3.**

Santa gets into a sticky situation after he falls through a hole in the Mouse family's roof and lands on last year's recycled Christmas tree. The sequel is *The Mouses' Terrible Halloween* (1980).

Illus. by True Adelaide Kelley, Lothrop, 1978, 63 pp., o.p.

(BL 75:552; CCBB 32:64; KR 46:1187; SLJ Oct 1978 p. 114)

KENEALLY, Thomas (Michael). *Ned Kelly and the City of the Bees.* See Chapter 5C, Travel to Other Worlds.

564   KENNEDY, (Jerome) Richard. *The Mouse God.* **Gr. 2–5.**

✓   Too lazy to catch his own meals, a cat dresses up like a mouse god and convinces the mice to enter a special cage (mouse church) so he can catch them at his leisure.

Illus. by Stephen Harvard, Atlantic-Little, 1979, 32 pp., o.p.

(BL 75:1440; HB 55:407; KR 47:385; SLJ May 1979 p. 52)

KENNEDY, X. J. (pseud. of Joseph Charles Kennedy). *The Owlstone Crown.* See Chapter 5C, Travel to Other Worlds.

565   KESEY, Ken. *Little Tricker the Squirrel Meets Big Double the Bear.* **Gr. 3–6.**

✓   Little Tricker the tree squirrel cuts horrible, huge, hairy, hateful, and hungry Big Double the bear down to size.

Illus. by Barry Moser, Viking, 1990, 32 pp. (0-670-81136-X); Puffin, 1992, pap. (0-14-050623-3)

(BL 87:924, 1484; CC 1992 Suppl., p. 58; CCBB 44:34; HBG 2[July 1990]:65; KR 58:1457; SLJ Dec 1990 p. 104; Suth 4:215)

566   KILWORTH, Garry. *The Foxes of Firstdark.* **Gr. 10 up. (Orig. British pub. 1989.)**

After O-ha, the vixen, sees her first love killed in a fox hunt, she makes a family with Camio, another male fox, and tries to rear their three cubs in the face of food shortages and human cruelty.

Doubleday, 1990, 304 pp. (0-385-26427-5)

(BL 86:1526, 1540; KR 58:294; LJ May 15, 1990 p. 99)

KINDL, Patrice. *Owl in Love.* See Chapter 10, Witchcraft and Sorcery Fantasy.

567   KING, (David) Clive. *The Town That Went South.* **Gr. 4–6.**

A great storm sends the town of Ramsley drifting off across the ocean toward the South Pole.

Illus. by Maurice Bartlett, Macmillan, 1959, 117 pp., o.p.

(HB 36:130; LJ 85:1305; TLS May 20, 1960 p. xv, 1969 p. 352)

568   **KING-SMITH, Dick.** *Ace: The Very Important Pig.* **Gr. 4–6. (Orig. British pub.**
✓   **1990, entitled *Ace*.)**

The great-grandson of *Babe: The Gallant Pig* (1983, 1985; see below), Ace understands human speech and becomes famous after he appears on a television show.

Illus. by Lynette Hemmant, Crown, 1990, 134 pp. (0-517-57832-8); Knopf, 1992, pap. (0-679-81931-2)

(BL 87:442; CC 1992 Suppl. p. 59; CCBB 44:88; HB 66:602; HBG 2[July–Dec 1990]:70; KR 58:1004; SLJ Nov 1990 p. 115, Dec 1990 p. 23; Suth 4:218)

569   **KING-SMITH, Dick.** *Babe: The Gallant Pig* **(Orig. British title: *The Sheep-Pig*,**
✓   **1983). Gr. 4–6.**

Farmer Hogget's sheep dog, Fly, trains Babe the pig to become a champion sheepherder. Guardian Award for Children's Fiction, 1984.

Illus. by Mary Rayner, Crown, 1985, 1993, 176 pp. (0-517-55556-5)

(BBC:207; BL 81:1666, 82:1232; CC:515; HB 61:449, 70:345; HBG 5:78; SLJ Aug 1985 p. 66)

570   **KING-SMITH, Dick.** *The Cuckoo Child.* **Gr. 3–6. (Orig. British pub. 1991.)**
✓

The ostrich egg Jack steals from Wildlife Park and hides under the barnyard goose hatches into a chick named Oliver, who grows to be nine feet tall.

Illus. by Leslie W. Bowman, Hyperion, 1993, 128 pp. (1-56282-350-7)

(BL 89:1514; HBG 4[Fall 1993]:300; KR 61:229; SLJ Apr 1993 p. 121)

571   **KING-SMITH, Dick.** *The Fox-Busters.* **Gr. 3–6. (Orig. British pub. 1978.)**
✓

Three high-flying chickens strike back when four young foxes raid the chicken coop.

Illus. by Jon Miller, Delacorte, 1988, 117 pp., o.p.

(BBC:207; BL 85:711; CC:515; CCBB 42:43; Ch&Bks:268; HB 65:210; KR 56:1605; SLJ Dec 1988 p. 104; Suth 4:218)

KING-SMITH, Dick. *Harry's Mad.* See Chapter 6, Humorous Fantasy.

572   **KING-SMITH, Dick.** *The Jenius.* **Gr. 2–4. (Orig. British pub. 1988.)**

Judy's parents find her stories about the amazing tricks she has taught her baby guinea pig, Jenius, hard to believe.

Illus. by Peter Firmin, Trafalgar Sq./David & Charles, 1990, 44 pp., o.p.

(CCBB 44:10; KR 58:877; SLJ Sept 1990 p. 206)

573   **KING-SMITH, Dick.** *Magnus Powermouse.* **Gr. 4–6. (Orig. British pub. 1982.)**
✓

Life with Magnus, the giant-sized mouse baby, proves to be somewhat difficult for his parents, in spite of his victory over a local cat and his father's liberation from a steel trap.

Illus. by Mary Rayner, Harper, 1984, 120 pp., o.p.

(BBC:207; BL 80:1191; CC:515; CCBB 37:207; Ch&Bks:288; HB 60:329; KR 52:40; SLJ Aug 1984 p. 74; Suth 3:235)

574   **KING-SMITH, Dick.** *Martin's Mice.* **(Orig. British pub. 1988.)**
✓

After Martin, a barn cat who would rather keep mice as pets than eat them, captures Drusilla Mouse, he is kept busy protecting her and her twelve children from his relatives.

Illus. by Jez Alborough, Crown, 1988, 122 pp. (0-517-57113-7); Dell, 1990, (0-440-40380-4)

(BBC:207; BL 85:939; CC:515; HB 65:71; KR 56:1740; SLJ Jan 1989 p. 78, Dec 1989 p. 39)

575 **KING-SMITH, Dick.** *The Mouse Butcher.* **Gr. 4–6. (Orig. British pub. 1981.)**

✓   A cat named Tom Plug is hired by a wealthy Persian cat family to be their mouse butcher, but his life is endangered by a killer cat named Great Mog.

Illus. by Margot Apple, Viking, 1982, 132 pp., o.p.; Puffin, 1982, pap., 144 pp. (0-14-031457-1)

(BL 78:1526; CCBB 36:71; HB 58:404; KR 50:605; SLJ Apr 1982 p. 71; Suth 3:236)

576 **KING-SMITH, Dick.** *Pigs Might Fly* **(Orig. British title:** *Daggie Dogfoot,* **1980).**
✓   **Gr. 4–6.**

Daggie, the dog-footed runt of the pig litter, learns to swim and rescues the other pigs during a flash flood. Runner-up, Guardian Award for Children's Fiction, 1981.

Illus. by Mary Rayner, Viking, 1982, o.p.; Puffin, 1990, pap. (0-14-034537-X)

(BBC:207; BL 78:1368, 79:685, 978, 84:1441; CC:515; CCBB 36:29; HB 58:405; KR 50:419; SLJ Aug 1982 p. 99; Suth 3:236)

KING-SMITH, Dick. *Pretty Polly.* See Chapter 6, Humorous Fantasy.

577 **KING-SMITH, Dick.** *The Toby Man.* **Gr. 3–5. (Orig. British pub. 1989.)**

✓   Tod fulfills his dream of becoming a highway robber like his father with the help of a · talking donkey named Matilda, a mastiff named Digby, Loudmouth the magpie, and Evil the ferret, in this story set in 18th-century England.

Illus. by Lynette Hemmant, Crown, 1991, 83 pp. (0-517-58134-5)

(BL 88:440; CC 1992 Suppl. p. 59; CCBB 45:14; HB 68:736; HBG 3[July–Dec 1991]:68; KR 59:1224; SLJ Sept 1991 p. 254)

578 **KIPLING, (Joseph) Rudyard.** *All the Mowgli Stories.* **Gr. 4–7.**

Mowgli is a human boy raised by jungle animals. His stories were originally told in *The Jungle Books* (1893, 1895).

Illus. by Kurt Wiese, Doubleday, 1936, 299 pp., o.p.

(BL 32:333; HB 12:158; LJ 61:733)

KIPLING, (Joseph) Rudyard. *The Beginning of the Armadilloes.* See Chapter 1, Allegorical Fantasy and Literary Fairy Tales.

KIPLING, (Joseph) Rudyard. *The Elephant's Child.* See Chapter 1, Allegorical Fantasy and Literary Fairy Tales.

KIPLING, (Joseph) Rudyard. *How the Camel Got His Hump.* See Chapter 1, Allegorical Fantasy and Literary Fairy Tales.

KIPLING, (Joseph) Rudyard. *How the Leopard Got His Spots.* See Chapter 1, Allegorical Fantasy and Literary Fairy Tales.

KIPLING, (Joseph) Rudyard. *How the Rhinoceros Got His Skin.* See Chapter 1, Allegorical Fantasy and Literary Fairy Tales.

579 **KIPLING, (Joseph) Rudyard.** *The Jungle Book.* **Gr. 3–7. (Orig. British and U.S.**
✓   **pub. 1894.)**

Tales of Mowgli, a boy adopted by wolves; Kotik the seal, Rikki-Tikki-Tavi, the mongoose; and other jungle animals. The sequel is *The Second Jungle Book* (Scribner, 1895; Doubleday, 1923; Puffin, 1987). Pamela Jekel has written a contemporary sequel entitled: *The Third Jungle Book* (Roberts, 1992).

Illus. by John Lockwood Kipling, Doubleday, 1928, o.p.; illus. by Kurt Wiese, Doubleday, 1932, o.p.; illus. by Fritz Eichenberg, Grosset, 1950, o.p.; illus. by Robert Shore, Macmillan, 1964, o.p.; Schocken, 1984, o.p.; adapt. by Robin McKinley, Random, 1985 (entitled *Tales from "The Jungle Book"*), 64 pp., LB(0-394-96940-5); Random, 1986 (0-394-96940-5); Puffin, 1987, pap. (0-14-035074-8); illus. by Gregory Alexander, Arcade, 1991, 128 pp. (1-55970-127-7); illus. by Inga Moore, Simon, 1992, 98 pp. (entitled: *The Favorite Mowgli Stories from The Jungle Book*), o.p.

(BBJ:72; BL 47:162, 82:135, 89:737; Bookshelf 1933 p. 9; CC:579; CCBB 5:15; Ch&Bks:266, 288; HB 1[June 1925]:34; HBG 4[Spring 1993]:72; JHC:432; KR 32:1014; LJ 75:2085; SLJ Nov 1991 p. 118)

580 **KIPLING, (Joseph) Rudyard.** *Just So Stories.* **Gr. 1–5. (Orig. British pub.**
✓ **1897–1902.)**

Twelve animal tales, including "How the Camel Got His Hump," "How the Leopard Got His Spots," and "How the Rhinoceros Got His Skin."

Illus. by the author, Doubleday, 1902, o.p.; illus. by Feodor Rojankovsky, Doubleday, 1942, o.p.; illus. by Etienne Delessert, Doubleday, 1946 (anniversary ed.), o.p.; NAL, 1974, pap. (0-451-52433-0); illus. by Victor G. Ambrus, Rand, 1982, o.p.; Schocken, 1986, o.p.; illus. by Meg Rutherford, Silver, 1986, o.p.; Puffin, 1987, pap. (0-14-035075-6); illus. by Safaya Salter, Holt, 1987, 96 pp. (0-8050-0439-4); illus. by Michael Foreman, Viking, 1987, 127 pp. (0-670-80242-5); illus. by David Frampton, Harper, 1991, 122 pp., LB(0-06-023294-3); illus. by the author, Knopf, 1992, 192 pp. (0-679-41797-4); illus. by Isabelle Brent, Viking, 1993 (entitled *The Complete Just So Stories*), 160 pp. (0-670-85196-5)

(BL 77:327, 79:778, 83:512, 84:709, 88:625, 90:755; Bookshelf 1928 p. 9; CC:579; CCBB 6:17, 26:93; Ch&Bks:265; Eakin:188; HB 1[June 1925]:45, 58:565, 68:97, 70:199; HBG 3[July–Dec 1991]:68, 5:78; KR 40:940, 1413, 54:1450, 55:1159, 59:1412, KR 61:1393; LJ 98:1682; SLJ Nov 1987 p. 105, Nov 1991 p.118, Dec 1993 p. 112)

581 **KIPLING, (Joseph) Rudyard.** *Rikki-Tikki-Tavi.* **Gr. 1–4. (Orig. British pub. as part of** *The Jungle Book,* **1894.)**

Rikki-Tikki-Tavi, a young mongoose who adopts an English family living in India, saves their little boy's life by killing poisonous snakes in their garden, in this story from *The Jungle Book* (1894; see entry above).

Illus. by Lambert Davis, Harcourt, 1992, 37 pp. (0-15-267015-7)

(BL 89:155; HBG 4[Spring 1993]:58; KR 60:1131; SLJ Dec 1992 p. 85)

582 **KIRBY, Mansfield.** *The Secret of Thut-Mouse III; or Basil Beandesert's Revenge.* **Gr. 3–5. (Orig. Dutch pub. 1983.)**

A group of educated mice living in an art museum take revenge on the museum director for buying a cat, by producing fake Egyptian artifacts that look so real the director writes a book on his fabulous find.

Illus. by Mance Post, Farrar, 1985, 64 pp. (0-374-36677-2)

(BL 82:496; CCBB 39:70; SLJ Dec 1985 p. 90)

KORSCHUNOW, Irina. *Small Fur.* See Chapter 7, Magic Adventure Fantasy.

583 **KOTZWINKLE, William.** *Doctor Rat.* **Gr. 10 up.**

The free animals of the world unite to liberate those trapped in scientific laboratories by human researchers and Doctor Rat, a rodent collaborator. World Fantasy Award, 1976.

Knopf, 1976, 243 pp., o.p.

(BL 72:1570; KR 44:273, 336; LJ 101:1556; TLS 1976 p. 815)

KOTZWINKLE, William. *Trouble in Bugland: A Collection of Inspector Mantis Mysteries.* See Chapter 6, Humorous Fantasy.

584 **KOVACS, Deborah.** *Brewster's Courage.* **Gr. 3–6.**

Having fallen in love with bayou music, Brewster, a black-footed ferret from South Dakota, decides to move to the Moustafaya Swamp in Louisiana and set up a bicycle messenger service.

Illus. by Joe Mathieu, Simon & Schuster, 1992, 104 pp. (0-671-74016-4)

KR 60:780; HBG 3[Fall 1992]:266; SLJ Sept 1992 p. 254)

585 **KRENSKY, Stephen (Alan).** *Woodland Crossings.* **Gr. 3–5.**

Five tales about a proud Flower King brought low, a worm who fools his blackbird captor, and other forest creatures.

Illus. by Jan Brett Bowler, Macmillan, 1978, 43 pp., o.p.

(KR 46:497; SLJ May 1978 p. 69)

586 **KRÜSS, James (Jacob Hinrich).** *Eagle and Dove.* **Gr. 3–5. (Orig. German pub. 1963.)**

Trapped by an eagle, a dove distracts him by telling stories while she digs an escape hole.

Trans. by Edelgard von Heydekampf Brühl, illus. by Pat Kent, Atheneum, 1965, 69 pp., o.p.

(BL 62:364; KR 33:624; LJ 90:3792)

KRÜSS, James (Jacob Hinrich). *The Happy Islands Behind the Winds.* See Chapter 5C, Travel to Other Worlds.

587 **KWITZ, Mary DeBall.** *Shadow Over Mousehaven Manor.* **Gr. 3–5.**

Minabel Mouse makes a treacherous journey across snow-covered prairies to rescue her elderly Aunt Pitty Pat from gang leader Magnus Rat. The sequel is *The Bell Tolls at Mousehaven Manor* (1991).

Illus. by Stella Ormai, Scholastic, 1989, 160 pp., o.p., 1990, pap. (0-590-42033-X)

(BL 86:743; HBG 1[July–Dec 1989]:83; KR 57:1672; SLJ Nov 1989 p. 112)

LAGERLÖF, Selma (Ottiliana Lovisa). *The Wonderful Adventures of Nils.* See Chapter 7, Magic Adventure Fantasy.

LAMPMAN, Evelyn Sibley. *The City under the Back Steps.* See Chapter 5C, Travel to Other Worlds.

588 **LANDSMAN, Sandy.** *Castaways on Chimp Island.* **Gr. 6–8.**

Exiled to an island with other "unteachable" laboratory chimps, Danny and three friends hatch a plan for getting home.

Atheneum, 1986, 202 pp., o.p.

(BBC:207; BL 82:1614; CCBB 39:171; HB 62:597; KR 54:869; SLJ Aug 1986 p. 94; VOYA 9:220)

589 **LANIER, Sterling E(dmund).** *The War for the Lot: A Tale of Fantasy and Terror.* **Gr. 4–6.**

Alec helps the woodland creatures living around his grandfather's farm to fight off the tyrannical rats.

Illus. by Robert Baumgartner, Follett, 1969, 256 pp., o.p.

(BL 66:928; CCBB 24:61; HB 46:162; LJ 95:1945, 3603)

LATHROP, Dorothy P(ulis). *The Fairy Circus.* See Chapter 1, Allegorical Fantasy and Literary Fairy Tales.

LATHROP, Dorothy P(ulis). *The Little White Goat.* See Chapter 7, Magic Adventure Fantasy.

590 **LATHROP, Dorothy P(ulis).** *The Snail Who Ran.* **Gr. 3–4.**

A moonbeam fairy gives one wish each to a mouse and a snail.

Illus. by the author, Stokes, 1934, 57 pp., o.p.

(BL 31:177; Bookshelf 1935 p. 2; HB 10:357; LJ 59:854; Mahony 3:80)

591 **LAUBER, Patricia (Grace).** *Home at Last! A Young Cat's Tale.* **Gr. 2–4.**

Two kittens raised in a library set off to find a new home, fortified for their adventures by reading heroic books.

Illus. by Mary Chalmers, Coward, 1980, 47 pp., o.p.

(BL 77:406; HB 57:47; KR 49:7; SLJ Feb 1981 p. 58)

592 **LAURENCE, Margaret (Wemyss).** *Jason's Quest.* **Gr. 5–7. (Orig. British pub. 1970.)**

Searching for a cure for his hometown's illness, Jason Mole travels to the city of Londinium and is captured by a gang of rats.

Illus. by Staffen Torell, Knopf, 1970, 211 pp., o.p.

(CCBB 24:29; LJ 96:3050; Suth:240; TLS 1970 p. 1458)

LAWSON, John S(hults). *You Better Come Home with Me.* See Chapter 1, Allegorical Fantasy and Literary Fairy Tales.

593 **LAWSON, Robert.** *Ben and Me: A New and Astonishing Life of Benjamin*
✓ *Franklin as Written by His Good Mouse, Amos: Lately Discovered.* **Gr. 4–7. (Orig. pub. 1939.)**

Amos Mouse discloses the fact that most of Ben Franklin's inventions were actually Amos's ideas, and describes their adventures together.

Illus. by the author, Little, 1951, 1988, 114 pp. (0-316-51732-1), pap. (0-316-51730-5); Dell, 1973, pap. (0-440-42038-5)

(BL 36:117; CC:520; Ch&Bks:266; HB 15:388, 16:28; LJ 65:125)

594 **LAWSON, Robert.** *Captain Kidd's Cat: Being the True and Dolorous Chronicle*
✓ *of Wm. Kidd, Gentleman and Merchant of New York; Late Captain of the Adventure Galley; Of the Vicissitudes Attending His Unfortunate Cruise in Eastern Waters, Of His Unjust Trial and Execution, as Narrated by His Faithful Cat, McDermot, Who Ought to Know.* **Gr. 4–7.**

McDermot doesn't think Captain Kidd deserves to be called a pirate.

Illus. by the author, Little, 1956, 151 pp., o.p.

(BL 52:282; CCBB 9:115; Eakin:203; HB 32:121, 61:78; KR 24:3; LJ 81:767)

595 **LAWSON, Robert.** *Edward, Hoppy and Joe.* **Gr. 3–5.**

Father Rabbit struggles to educate his son Edward and friends Hoppy Toad and Joe Possum.

Illus. by the author, Knopf, 1952, 122 pp., o.p.

(BL 48:303; HB 28:107; KR 20:224; LJ 77:907)

596 **LAWSON, Robert.** *I Discover Columbus: A True Chronicle of the Great Admiral and His Finding of the New World, Narrated by the Venerable Parrot Aurelio, Who Shared in the Glorious Venture.* **Gr. 4–7.**

It is Aurelio, a Caribbean parrot stranded in Spain, who convinces Columbus to make his voyage to the New World.

Illus. by the author, Little, 1941, 110 pp., o.p.

(BL 38:58; HB 17:366, 453; LJ 66:908)

597 **LAWSON, Robert.** *Mr. Revere and I: Being an Account of Certain Episodes in*
✓ *the Career of Paul Revere, Esq., as Recently Revealed by His Horse, Scheherazade, Late Pride of His Royal Majesty's 14th Regiment of Foot.* **Gr. 5–7.**

Scheherazade, a former cavalry horse rescued by Sam Adams from the glue factory, tells of her subsequent life with Paul Revere's family.

Illus. by the author, Little, 1953, 152 pp. (0-316-51739-9); Dell, 1973, pap. (0-440-45897-8)

(BL 50:84; CC:520; CCBB 7:31; Ch&Bks:288; Eakin:204; HB 29:464; KR 21:357; LJ 78:1858)

598 **LAWSON, Robert.** *Mr. Twigg's Mistake.* **Gr. 4–6.**
✓ Super-vitamin-laced cereal transforms Mr. Twigg's pet mole.

Illus. by the author, Little, 1947, 141 pp., o.p.

(BL 44:117; CCBB 2[Jan 1949]:4; KR 15:467; LJ 72:1543)

599 **LAWSON, Robert.** *Rabbit Hill.* **Gr. 3–6.**
✓ Although they are happy that a new family is moving into the empty farmhouse, the animals on Rabbit Hill fear the newcomers may bring traps and guns. John Newbery Medal, 1945. The sequels are *Robbut: A Tale of Tails* (1948; Shoe String, 1990) and *The Tough Winter* (1954).

Illus. by the author, Viking, 1944, 127 pp. (0-670-58675-7); Puffin, 1977, pap. (0-14-031010-X)

(BBC:208; BL 41:62; CC:520; Ch&Bks:266; HB 20:487, 66:481; KR 12:403; LJ 69:866, 886)

LAZARUS, Keo Felker. *The Shark in the Window.* See Chapter 6, Humorous Fantasy.

LEE, Tanith. *Animal Castle.* See Chapter 1, Allegorical Fantasy and Literary Fairy Tales.

600 **LE GUIN, Ursula K(roeber).** *Buffalo Gals and Other Animal Presences.* **Gr. 10**
✓ **up.**

Ten stories and 19 poems, many of which have been published previously, on the theme of the oneness of life, told mainly from the point of view of animals attempting to open the eyes of humans to the larger community of life.

Illus. by Margaret Chodos-Irvine, Capra, 1987, 196 pp. (0-88496-270-9); NAL, 1988, pap., 236 pp. (0-452-26480-4), 1990, pap. (0-451-45049-3)

(Kliatt Jan 1991 p. 22; LJ Nov 1, 1987 p. 112; TLS 1990 p. 534; VOYA 13:364)

601 **LE GUIN, Ursula K(roeber).** *Catwings.* **Gr. K–4.**
✓ Four winged kittens escape from a dangerous city neighborhood to a forest where they find friends and a safe home. In *Catwings Return* (1989), two of the kittens fly back to the city in hopes of rescuing their mother and a sister they've never met. *Wonderful Alexander and the Cat Wings* (1994) continues the series.

Illus. by S. D. Schindler, Orchard, 1988, 40 pp. (0-531-05759-3); Scholastic, 1992, pap. (0-5904-6072-2)

(BBC:208; BL 84:1928; CC:521; CCBB 42:13; Ch&Bks:255; HB 64:781; KR 56:976; SLJ Nov 1988 p. 91; Suth 4:240)

602   LE GUIN, Ursula K(roeber). *Lesse Webster.* **Gr. 1–4.**

When Lesse Webster's palace is turned into a museum, her artistic spider webs are put on public display.

Illus. by James Brunsman, Atheneum, 1979, 26 pp., o.p.

(CCBB 34:14; KR 47:998; SLJ Nov 1979 p. 66)

603   LE GUIN, Ursula K(roeber). *Solomon Leviathan's Nine Hundred and Thirty-First Trip Around the World.* **Gr. 3–5.**

Two philosopher friends, a giraffe and a boa constrictor, are swallowed by a whale named Simon Leviathan after they set off across the sea in search of the horizon.

Illus. by Alicia Austin, Putnam, 1988, 32 pp. (0-941826-03-1)

(KR 56:1676; SLJ Dec 1988 p. 88)

604   LEONARD, Nellie Mabel. *The Graymouse Family.* **Gr. 4–6. (Orig. pub. 1916; retitled:** *The Mouse Book,* **1926.)**

Mother Graymouse and her six children live in the walls of a human family's house. The sequel is *Grandfather Whiskers, M.D., a Graymouse Story* (1953; orig. title: *Grand-Daddy Whiskers, M. D.,* 1919).

Illus. by Barbara Cooney, Crowell, 1950, 209 pp., o.p.

(CCBB 4:44; KR 18:330; LJ 75:2162)

LEROE, Ellen. *Ghost Dog.* See Chapter 4, Ghost Fantasy.

605   LEROY, Gen. *Taxi Cat and Huey.* **Gr. 3–6.**

Life changes dramatically for Huey, the Walton family basset hound, after Taxi, a part-Siamese cat who thinks he's a Ninja warrior, moves in.

Illus. by Karen Ritz, Harper, 1992, 140 pp. LB(0-06-021769-3)

(BL 88:1451; HBG 3[Fall 1992]:266; KR 60:721; SLJ July 1992 p. 73)

LEWIS, C(live) S(taples). *The Lion, the Witch, and the Wardrobe.* See Chapter 5C, Travel to Other Worlds.

606   LEZRA, Giggy (Grizzella Paull). *The Cat, the Horse, and the Miracle.* **Gr. 4–6.**

A lady in blue gives an unhappy cat and horse a golden thread that will lead them into their future.

Illus. by Zena Bernstein, Atheneum, 1967, 114 pp., o.p.

(CCBB 20:155; KR 35:198; LJ 92:1317; Suth:250)

LIFTON, Betty Jean (Kirschner). *The Cock and the Ghost Cat.* See Chapter 4, Ghost Fantasy.

607   LINDOP, Audrey E. *The Adventures of the Wuffle.* **Gr. 4–6. (Orig. British pub. 1966.)**

Wuffle's grandmother advises him to become important; so he and his friend, Norrie the tortoise, decide to become lawyers.

Illus. by William Stobbs, McGraw-Hill, 1968, 126 pp., o.p.

(KR 36:150; LJ 93:2730; TLS 1966 p. 1087)

LINDSAY, Norman (Alfred William). *The Magic Pudding: Being the Adventures of Bunyip Bluegum and His Friends Bill Barnacle and Sam Sawnoff.* See Chapter 6, Humorous Fantasy.

LISLE, Janet Taylor. *Forest.* See Chapter 1, Allegorical Fantasy and Literary Fairy Tales.

LITTLE, Jane. *Sneaker Hill.* See Chapter 10, Witchcraft and Sorcery Fantasy.

608 **LIVELY, Penelope (Margaret Low).** *A House Inside Out.* **Gr. 3–6.**
✓ The Dixon family shares their home with thirty-nine animals and several thousand insects. Each chapter of this book is told through the eyes of one of the nonhuman inhabitants of 54 Pavilion Road.

Illus. by David Parkins, Dutton, 1987, 127 pp., o.p.

(BL 84:1265, 1441; CCBB 41:95; Ch&Bks:262; KR 55:1630; SLJ Feb 1988 p. 73; Suth 4:250; TLS 1987 p. 1176)

609 **LIVELY, Penelope (Margaret Low).** *The Voyage of Q V 66.* **Gr. 6–8. (Orig.**
✓ **British pub. 1978.)**

In a future time when animals are the only survivors of a great flood, six creatures travel to London in hope of discovering Stanley's true identity.

Illus. by Harold Jones, Dutton, 1979, 172 pp., o.p.

(BL 75:1627; CCBB 32:195; Ch&Bks:262; HB 55:415; KR 47:637; SLJ Dec 1979 p. 152; Suth 3:269)

LOFTING, Hugh. *The Story of Doctor Dolittle.* See Chapter 6, Humorous Fantasy.

610 **LOFTING, Hugh.** *The Story of Mrs. Tubbs.* **Gr. 2–4. (Orig. pub. 1923.)**

A dog, a duck, and a pig care for old Mrs. Tubbs until she is strong enough to go home to her farm.

Illus. by the author, Lippincott, 1968, 91 pp., o.p.

(BL 20:63; Bookshelf 1927 p. 7; KR 36:393)

611 *The Lonely Little Pig and Other Animal Tales.* **Ed. by Wilhelmina Harper. Gr. 2–4.**

Thirteen short humorous animal stories.

Illus. by Vera Neville, McKay, 1938, 108 pp., o.p.

(BL 35:160; HB 15:31)

LOWREY, Janette Sebring. *The Lavender Cat.* See Chapter 1, Allegorical Fantasy and Literary Fairy Tales.

MACAULAY, David. *BAAA.* See Chapter 1, Allegorical Fantasy and Literary Fairy Tales.

612 **McCOY, Neely.** *The Tale of the Good Cat Jupie.* **Gr. 2–4.**

A talking cat and a little girl set up housekeeping together. The sequels are *Jupie Follows His Tale* (1928) and *Jupie and the Wise Old Owl* (1931).

Illus. by the author, Macmillan, 1926, 1932, 99 pp., o.p.

(BL 23:276; HB 2[Nov 1926]:45; LJ 53:484)

613 **McGOWEN, Tom (Thomas E.).** *Odyssey from River Bend.* **Gr. 4–6.**
✓ Kip the badger leads a group of animals from River Bend into the Haunted Land to search for the secrets of the ancients.

Little, 1975, 166 pp., o.p.

(BL 72:44; CCBB 29:82; KR 43:513; SLJ Sept 1975 p. 107; Suth 2:300)

614   McHUGH, Elizabet. *Beethoven's Cat.* **Gr. 3–6.**

After the Carter's cat, Wiggie, becomes convinced that he is the direct descendant of Beethoven's cat, Ludwig, only a visit to an animal psychiatrist can relieve his haunted spirit. The sequel is *Wiggie Wins the West* (1989).

Illus. by Anita Riggio, Macmillan, 1988, 53 pp., o.p.; Dell, 1991, pap. (0-440-40398-7)

(BBC:209; BL 84:1265; CCBB 41:162; KR 56:541; SLJ Apr 1988 p. 103; VOYA 11:133)

615   McINERNEY, Judith Whitelock. *Judge Benjamin: Superdog.* **Gr. 4–6.**

The O'Rileys' St. Bernard, Judge Benjamin, describes his busy life as family protector. The sequels are *Judge Benjamin: The Superdog Secret* (1983), *Judge Benjamin: The Superdog Rescue* (1984), *Judge Benjamin: The Superdog Surprise* (1985; 1990), *Judge Benjamin: The Superdog Gift* (1986), and *Judge Benjamin and the Purloined Sirloin* (1986).

Illus. by Leslie Morrill, Holiday, 1982, 142 pp., o.p.

(BL 78:1315; SLJ Aug 1982 p. 118)

McINERNY, Ralph M. *Quick As a Dodo.* See Chapter 6, Humorous Fantasy.

616   McPHAIL, (Michael) David. *Henry Bear's Park.* **Gr. 2–4.**

During the long wait for his balloonist father's return, Henry Bear devotes himself to beautifying their park. Stanley Raccoon's life story is told in the companion volume, *Stanley, Henry Bear's Friend* (1979).

Illus. by the author, Little, 1976, 48 pp., LB(0-316-56315-3)

(BL 72:1408; KR 44:589; SLJ Sept 1976 p. 102)

617   *Magicats!* Ed. by Jack Dann and Gardner Dozois. Gr. 10 up.

✓   Eighteen fantasy and science fiction tales involving cats, whose authors include Ursula K. Le Guin, Pamela Sargent, and Gene Wolfe.

Ace, 1984, pap., 270 pp., o.p.

(BL 80:1599, 1609; Kliatt 18 [Fall 1984]:25; SLJ Sept 1984 p. 140; VOYA 7:267)

618   MAJOR, Beverly. *Porcupine Stew.* **Gr. 2–4.**

Thomas gives up his favorite silver whistle for admission to the Perpetu-annual Porcupine Parade and Picnic, where he watches a quill-throwing contest and eats "porcupine stew."

Illus. by Erick Ingraham, Morrow, 1982, 39 pp., o.p.

(BBC:209; BL 79:724, 1283; CCBB 36:93; KR 50:1057; SLJ Nov 1982 p. 70)

MANES, Stephen. *Some of the Adventures of Rhode Island Red.* See Chapter 6, Humorous Fantasy.

619   MARSHALL, James (Edward). *Rats on the Roof and Other Stories.* **Gr. 1–5.**

✓   Seven humorous stories about a near-sighted goose who doesn't recognize a wolf masquerading as a canary, a tall mouse bride who saves the wedding party from a cat, and a dog couple who hire a very ratlike cat to rid their house of mice. The sequel, *Rats on the Range and Other Stories* (1993), contains eight more humorous animal stories.

Illus. by the author, Dial, 1991, 80 pp. LB(0-803-70835-1)

(BL 87:1879; CC 1992 Suppl. p. 65; CCBB 44:244; HB 67:453; HBG 2:257; KR 59:790; SLJ July 1991 p. 61)

620 **MARSHALL, James (Edward).** *A Summer in the South.* **Gr. 2–4.**

Eleanor Owl, famous detective, solves the case of the ghostly figure frightening Marietta Chicken.

Illus. by the author, Houghton, 1977, 97 pp. (0-395-25840-5)

(KR 45:1144; SLJ Dec 1977 p. 61)

621 **MARSHALL, James (Edward).** *Taking Care of Carruthers.* **Gr. 3–4.**

Carruthers the bear, Eugene the turtle, and Emily the pig take a sightseeing trip downriver in a rowboat, traveling through skunk country to Stupendousberg where Carruthers stars in a production of "Goldilocks." This is the sequel to the picture book *What's the Matter with Carruthers?* (1972).

Illus. by the author, Houghton, 1981, 128 pp. (0-395-28593-3)

(BL 78:598; KR 50:3; SLJ Jan 1981 p. 80)

MASEFIELD, John (Edward). *The Midnight Folk: A Novel.* See Chapter 7, Magic Adventure Fantasy.

622 **MASON, Miriam E(vangeline).** *Hoppity.* **Gr. 2–4. (Orig. pub. 1947.)**

Hoppity the goat eats everything from crayons to ladies' hats, until the day he tastes the bee on a baby's nose.

Illus. by Cyndy Szekeres, Macmillan, 1962, 66 pp., o.p.

(BL 44:117; HB 23:34; KR 15:427)

623 **MATTHIESSEN, Peter.** *The Seal Pool.* **Gr. 3–5.**

While being transported to the Bronx Zoo, a Great Auk escapes and hides near the seal pool in Central Park.

Illus. by William Pène Du Bois, Doubleday, 1972, 78 pp., o.p.

(CCBB 25:80; KR 40:724; LJ 98:645)

MAYNE, William (James Carter). *Antar and the Eagles.* See Chapter 5A, Alternate Worlds or Histories.

MAYNE, William (James Carter). *The Blue Boat.* See Chapter 7, Magic Adventure Fantasy.

MAYNE, William (James Carter). *The Mouldy.* See Chapter 1, Allegorical Fantasy and Literary Fairy Tales.

MAZER, Anne. *The Oxboy.* See Chapter 1, Allegorical Fantasy and Literary Fairy Tales.

MENUHIN, Yehudi, and HOPE, Christopher. *The King, the Cat, and the Fiddle.* See Chapter 1, Allegorical Fantasy and Literary Fairy Tales.

624 **MERRILL, Jean (Fairbanks).** *The Black Sheep.* **Gr. 4–6.**

A black sheep born into a community of white ones refuses to conform: Instead of knitting sweaters, he wears his own shaggy coat and spends his time gardening.

Illus. by Ronni Solbert, Pantheon, 1969, 73 pp., o.p.

(CCBB 23:131; LJ 95:1641, 1912, 3603; Suth:279)

625 **MICHELS, Tilde.** *Rabbit Spring.* **Gr. 2–4. (Orig. Swiss pub. 1986.)**

Two litters of babies are born in the spring, one to wild rabbits Silla and Rahn in the meadow, and the other to the hares in the field.

Trans. by J. Alison James, illus. by Käthi Bhend, Harcourt, 1988, 96 pp. (0-15-200568-4); McKay, 1990, pap. (0-679-80153-7)

(BBC:209; BL 84:1352, 1441; HB 64:491; SLJ Sept 1988 p. 184)

MILNE, A(lan) A(lexander). *Prince Rabbit and the Princess Who Could Not Laugh.* See Chapter 1, Allegorical Fantasy and Literary Fairy Tales.

MOLESWORTH, Mary Louisa (Stewart). *The Cuckoo Clock.* See Chapter 5C, Travel to Other Worlds.

MOLESWORTH, Mary Louisa (Stewart). *The Tapestry Room: A Child's Romance.* See Chapter 7, Magic Adventure Fantasy.

626   **MONSELL, Mary Elise.** *Crackle Creek.* **Gr. 2–5.**

Douglas and Rosemary Mouse run rival newspapers in Crackle Creek, until a storm destroys much of the community and they are forced to work together.

Illus. by Kathleen Garry McCord, Macmillan, 1990, 56 pp. (0-689-31564-3)

(BL 86:1900; HBG 1[Jan 1990]:245; KR 58:267; SLJ July 1990 p. 63)

627   **MONSELL, Mary Elise.** *The Mysterious Cases of Mr. Pin* **(Mr. Pin Mystery series, book 1). Gr. 2–4.**

Mr. Pin, a penguin detective, solves his cases from the back room of the Smiling Sally diner in Chicago. The sequels are *Mr. Pin: The Chocolate Files* (1990), *The Spy Who Came North from the Pole* (1993), and *A Fish Named Yum* (1994).

Illus. by Eileen Christelow, Macmillan, 1989, 53 pp. (0-689-31435-3); Pocket, 1992, pap. (0-671-74084-9)

(BL 85:1652; KR 57:627; SLJ June 1989 p. 91)

628   **MONSELL, Mary Elise.** *Toohy and Wood.* **Gr. 3–5.**

✓   Wood, a poetic turtle, helps lizard Toohy accept the death of his best friend, a dove named Pearl.

Illus. by Leslie Tryon, Macmillan, 1992, 80 pp. (0-689-31721-2)

(BL 89:327; CCBB 46:117; HBG 4[Spring, 1993]:74; KR 60:1064; SLJ Oct 1992 p. 118)

MOON, Sheila (Elizabeth). *Knee-Deep in Thunder.* See Chapter 5C, Travel to Other Worlds.

629   **MOORE, Lilian.** *I'll Meet You at the Cucumbers.* **Gr. 2–5.**

✓   Adam Mouse comes to the city to meet Amanda Mouse on her birthday, and during the course of a day of wondrous discovery, he realizes that he is a poet. In the sequel, *Don't Be Afraid, Amanda* (1992), Amanda visits her pen pal, Adam, in the country, despite her fears about life outside the city. *Adam Mouse's Book of Poems* (1992) is a related work.

Illus. by Sharon Wooding, Atheneum, 1988, 72 pp. (0-689-31243-1)

(BBC:210; BL 84:1266, 1441; CCBB 41:142; Ch&Bks:268; HB 64:492; KR 51:622; SLJ Apr 1988 p. 82; Suth 4:296)

630   **MOORE, Margaret Eileen.** *Willie Without.* **Gr. 1–4. (Orig. British pub. 1951.)**

Willy the poetic worm makes many new friends as he searches for a new hat.

Illus. by Nora S. Unwin, Coward, 1952, 85 pp., o.p.

(CCBB 5:81; HB 28:108; KR 20:124; LJ 77:444)

631   **MORGAN, Alison (Mary Raikes).** *River Song.* **Gr. 4–6.**

Timothy Wagtail adopts a young Flycatcher who has lost his family.

Illus. by John Schoenherr, Harper, 1975, 160 pp., o.p.

(BL 72:457; HB 52:52; KR 43:1131; SLJ Sept 1975 p. 108)

MURPHY, Shirley Rousseau. *The Catswold Portal.* See Chapter 5C, Travel to Other Worlds.

632   **MURPHY, Shirley Rousseau.** *Flight of the Fox.* **Gr. 5–7.**

A kangaroo rat and a pet lemming ask a boy named Charlie to help them pilot a motorized model airplane.

Illus. by Donald Sibley, based on original designs by Richard Cuffari, Atheneum, 1978, 164 pp., o.p.

(BL 75:384; CCBB 32:142; KR 46:1358; SLJ Jan 1979 p. 56)

MURPHY, Shirley Rousseau. *Nightpool.* See Chapter 5A, Alternate Worlds or Histories.

MURPHY, Shirley Rousseau. *The Pig Who Could Conjure the Wind.* See Chapter 10, Witchcraft and Sorcery Fantasy.

NAPOLI, Donna Jo. *The Prince of the Pond: Otherwise Known as De Fawg Pin.* See Chapter 6, Humorous Fantasy.

633   **NAYLOR, Phyllis Reynolds.** *The Grand Escape.* **Gr. 4–7.**

Marco and Polo, house cats who set off to find adventure, must solve three "Great Mysteries" in order to join the neighborhood Cats' Club of Mysteries.

Illus. by Alan Daniel, Macmillan, 1993, 148 pp. (0-689-31722-0).

(BL 89:1967; HBG 4[Fall 1993]:302; KR 61:534; SLJ Aug 1993 p. 166)

634   **NEWELL, Averil.** *The Fly-By-Nights.* **Gr. 2–4.**

A mouse family sets up housekeeping in a vacant house conveniently located between a toy shop and a bakery.

Illus. by Kathleen Hiken, Macmillan, 1948, 48 pp., o.p.

(BL 44:253; CCBB 2[Jan 1949]:5; HB 24:190; KR 16:109; LJ 73:485)

NEWMAN, Robert (Howard). *The Shattered Stone.* See Chapter 5A, Alternate Worlds or Histories.

635   **NICKLESS, Will.** *Owlglass.* **Gr. 4–6. (Orig. British pub. 1964.)**

Old Beak and Claws the owl is losing his vision, so the forest animals steal the villagers' eyeglasses for him. The British sequel is *Dotted Lines.*

Illus. by the author, Day, 1966, 158 pp., o.p.

(BL 62:833; HB 42:307; LJ 91:2696)

636   **NIXON, Joan Lowery.** *Magnolia's Mixed-Up Magic.* **Gr. 2–4.**

Magnolia Possum and her grandmother try out a few spells from an old magic book, but can't seem to undo them after Magnolia begins flying around the house, and the mailman disappears.

Illus. by Linda Bucholtz-Ross, Putnam, 1983, 43 pp., o.p.

(BL 79:1403; CCBB 37:14; KR 51:618; SLJ Oct 1983 p. 152)

NORTON, André (pseud. of Alice Mary Norton). *Fur Magic.* See Chapter 7, Magic Adventure Fantasy.

NORTON, André (pseud. of Alice Mary Norton). *The Mark of the Cat.* See Chapter 5A, Alternate Worlds and Histories.

637   NYGAARD, Jacob Bech. *Tobias the Magic Mouse.* **Gr. 2–4. (Orig. Danish pub. 1961.)**

Elected to the position of magic mouse, Tobias travels to the moon to eat magic cheese, in preparation for solving animal and human problems on Earth.

Trans. by Edith Joan McCormick, illus. by Ib Spang Olsen, Harcourt, 1968, 52 pp., o.p.

(KR 36:1049; HB 45:167; LJ 94:288)

638   OAKLEY, Graham. *The Church Mouse.* **Gr. 2–4.**

✓   Despite his friendship with Sampson the cat, Arthur the church mouse was lonely. So he decided to fill the church with friendly mice. The sequels are *The Church Cat Abroad* (1973), *The Church Mice and the Moon* (1974), *The Church Mice Spread Their Wings* (1976), *The Church Mice Adrift* (1977; a Kate Greenaway Medal Highly Commended Book, 1976), *The Church Mice at Bay* (1979), *The Church Mice at Christmas* (1980), *The Church Mice in Action* (1983; a Kate Greenaway Medal Highly Commended Book, 1982), *Diary of a Churchmouse* (1987), and *The Church Mice and the Ring* (1992).

Illus. by the author, Atheneum, 1972, 33 pp., o.p.

(CC:685; CCBB 26:130; HB 49:132; LJ 98:1675; KR 40:1187; TLS 1972 p. 1327)

639   O'BRIEN, Robert C. (pseud. of Robert Leslie Conly). *Mrs. Frisby and the Rats*
✓✓   *of NIMH* **(The Rats of NIMH series, book 1). Gr. 4–7.**

Mrs. Frisby, a field mouse with a problem, is befriended by a group of superintelligent laboratory rats and manages to save their lives. John Newbery Medal, 1972. Boston Globe Horn Book Award Honor Book, 1971; National Book Award finalist, 1972. O'Brien's daughter, Jane Leslie Conly, has written two sequels entitled *Racso and the Rats of NIMH* (Harper, 1986) (see this chapter), and *R-T, Margaret, and the Rats of NIMH* (Harper, 1990).

Illus. by Zena Bernstein, Atheneum, 1971, 240 pp. (0-689-20651-8); Scholastic, 1982 (entitled *The Secret of NIMH*), pap. (0-590-33894-3); Aladdin, 1975, pap., 240 pp. (0-689-71068-2)

(BBC:211; BL 67:955, 68:670, 80:96; CC:538; CCBB 25:29; Ch&Bks:267; HB 47:385; LJ 96:4159, 4186; Suth:298; TLS 1972 p. 1317)

640   ORMONDROYD, Edward. *Broderick.* **Gr. 1–4. (Orig. pub. Parnassus, 1969.)**

✓   Broderick mouse stops chewing up library books long enough to read one about surfing, and is inspired to become a champion surfer.

Illus. by John Larrecq, Houghton, 1975 (0-686-86580-4), 1984, pap. (0-395-36170-2)

(BL 66:459; CCBB 23:104; HB 46:37; KR 37:1252; LJ 95:2303)

641   O'ROURKE, Frank. *Burton and Stanley.* **Gr. 3–6.**

After two Kenyan marabou storks named Burton and Stanley arrive via tornado at his midwestern railroad station in 1935, Mr. Kraft discovers that they can communicate in morse code, and helps them return to Africa.

Illus. by Jonathan Allen, Godine, 1993, 64 pp. (0-87923-824-0)

(BL 89:1693; HBG 4[Fall 1993]:302; KR 61:151; SLJ May 1993 p. 108)

642   ORWELL, George (pseud. of Eric Hugh Blair). *Animal Farm.* **Gr. 7 up. (Orig.**
✓✓   **British pub. 1945, U.S. 1946, 1954.)**

At Farmer Jones's farm, the pigs lead a revolt to drive out the humans and put themselves in charge of the new totalitarian state, in this classic satire of communism.

Illus. by Joy Batchelor and John Halas, Harcourt, 1954, 160 pp. (0-15-107252-3); Buccaneer, 1982 (repr. of 1945 ed.), LB(0-89966-369-9); NAL, 1974, 1983, pap., 128 pp. (0-452-26490-1)

(BBS:63; BL 43:18, 83:1592; JHC:398; KR 14:351; LJ 7:1048; SHC:711; TLS 1945 p. 401)

643 **OSBORNE, M(aurice) M(achado) (Jr.).** *Ondine: The Story of a Bird Who Was*
✓ *Different.* **Gr. 4–6.**

Ondine, a nonconformist sandpiper, is befriended by a seagull, an owl, and a hermit.

Illus. by Evaline Ness, Houghton, 1960, 75 pp., o.p.

(BL 56:690; Eakin:251; HB 36:290; LJ 85:2683)

644 **OSBORNE, M(aurice) M(achado) (Jr.).** *Rudi and the Mayor of Naples.* **Gr. 2–4.**

It takes a very special cake to make Rudi the donkey get up and pull his cart again.

Illus. by Joseph Low, Houghton, 1958, 48 pp., o.p.

(HB 35:33; LJ 84:641)

645 **OSBORNE, Mary Pope.** *Spider Kane and the Mystery Under the May Apple.* **Gr.**
✓ **3–5.**

After the kidnapping of his true love, Mimi, butterfly Leon Leafwing and detective Spider Kane follow her into the Dark Swamp, realm of the evil Emperor Moth. The sequel is *Spider Kane and the Mystery at Jumbo Nightcrawler's* (1993).

Illus. by Victoria Chess, Knopf, 1992, 28 pp. (0-679-80855-8), 1993, pap. (0-679-84174-1)

(BL 88:1602; CC 1993 Suppl. p. 74; CCBB 45:244; HBG 3[Fall 1992]:268; KR 60:541; SLJ Apr 1992 p. 118)

646 **OTTO, Margaret G(lover).** *The Tiny Man.* **Gr. 3–4.**

Two sea gulls find a tiny man carved from the heart of an oak tree, and help him to find a home.

Illus. by Peter Burchard, Holt, 1955, 122 pp., o.p.

(KR 23:647; LJ 81:240)

647 **PAINE, Albert Bigelow.** *The Hollow Tree and Deep Woods Book.* **Gr. 4–6. (Orig. pub. separately as** *The Hollow Tree,* **1898 and** *In the Deep Woods,* **1899.)**

A Coon, a Possum, and a Big Black Crow live together in a hollow tree. The sequels are *Hollow Tree Nights and Days* (1916), *The Hollow Tree Snowed-In Book* (1910, 1937, 1938), *How Mr. Dog Got Even* (1915), *How Mr. Rabbit Lost His Tail* (1910, 1915), *Making Up with Mr. Dog* (1915), *Mr. Crow and the Whitewash* (1917), *Mr. Possum's Great Balloon Trip* (1915), *Mr. Rabbit's Big Dinner* (1901, 1915), *Mr. Rabbit's Wedding* (1917), *Mr. Turtle's Flying Adventure* (1917), and *When Jack Rabbit Was a Little Boy* (1910, 1915).

Illus. by J. M. Conde, Harper, 1898–1900, 1929, 1938, 272 pp., o.p.

(Bookshelf 1928 p. 9; HB 7:116; Mahony 2:113)

648 **PALMER, Robin (Riggs).** *Wise House.* **Gr. 3–5.**

A cat and a crow move a family of children and their house to a pirate's island.

Illus. by Decie Merwin, Harper, 1951, 138 pp., o.p.

(KR 19:387; LJ 76:2124)

649 **PARKER, (James) Edgar (Jr.).** *The Dream of the Dormouse.* **Gr. 2–4.**

Hibernating Dormouse is sure he must be dreaming when he is kidnapped by a pirate bulldog.

Illus. by the author, Houghton, 1963, 48 pp., o.p.

(CCBB 17:144; HB 39:286; KR 3:53; LJ 88:2553)

650 **PARKER, (James) Edgar (Jr.).** *The Duke of Sycamore.* **Gr. 1–4.**

When the Lion King announces an upcoming visit, a group of forest friends search frantically for a castle to borrow.

Illus. by the author, Houghton, 1959, 38 pp., o.p.

(BL 55:488; CCBB 12:154; HB 35:214; KR 27:264; LJ 84:1699)

651 **PARKER, (James) Edgar (Jr.).** *The Flower of the Realm.* **Gr. 3–5.**

Sir Stephen Stag and Baron Roebuck duel for the love of a beautiful doe.

Illus. by the author, Houghton, 1966, 60 pp., o.p.

(HB 42:564; KR 34:831; LJ 91:5236)

652 **PARKER, (James) Edgar (Jr.).** *The Question of a Dragon.* **Gr. 3–5.**

A raccoon, a cat, and a frog are commanded to rid the forest of a dreadful dragon.

Illus. by the author, Pantheon, 1964, 43 pp., o.p.

(CCBB 19:16; HB 40:283; KR 32:232; LJ 89:2661)

PARKER, (James) Edgar (Jr.). *Rogue's Gallery.* See Chapter 6, Humorous Fantasy.

PARRISH, Anne, and PARRISH, Dillwyn. *Knee-High to a Grasshopper.* See Chapter 7, Magic Adventure Fantasy.

653 **PAYNE, Joan Balfour (Dicks).** *Ambrose.* **Gr. 2–4.**

A spoiled dog named Ambrose searches for a family with children to adopt him.

Illus. by the author, Hastings, 1956, 48 pp., o.p.

(CCBB 11:17; HB 32:445; KR 24:627)

654 **PAYNE, Joan Balfour (Dicks).** *The Piebald Princess.* **Gr. 3–5.**

A Siamese cat claiming to be a princess makes life difficult for witch Molly Pippin.

Illus. by the author, Farrar, 1954, 79 pp., o.p.

(BL 50:327; CCBB 7:77; HB 30:95; KR 22:229; LJ 79:702, 865)

655 **PEABODY, Paul.** *Blackberry Hollow.* **Gr. 1–4.**

It's always springtime in Blackberry Hollow, home of Jeremy fieldmouse, Major the horse, Tom McPaddy the Scottish frog, Mr. Kip the raccoon, and Parnassus the bear.

Illus. by the author, Putnam, 1993, 147 pp. (0-399-22500-5)

(BL 90:833; HBG 5:81; KR 61:938; SLJ Jan 1994 p. 96)

656 **PEET, Bill (William Bartlett).** *Big Bad Bruce.* **Gr. 2–4.**

Bruce the bear bully is put in his place by a witch named Roxy, who shrinks him to chipmunk size.

Illus. by the author, Houghton, 1977, 38 pp., o.p., 1978, pap., o.p.

(BL 73:1172; CCBB 30:163; HB 53:302; KR 45:163)

657 **PEET, Bill (William Bartlett).** *The Whingdingdilly.* **Gr. 2–4.**

✓ Wishing to become a famous horse, Orvie's dog Scamp changes into a creature that is part elephant, camel, zebra, rhinoceros, and giraffe.

Illus. by the author, Houghton, 1970, 60 pp. (0-395-24729-2), 1982, pap. (0-395-31381-3)

(BL 66:1280; HB 46:291; KR 38:317; LJ 95:2309; TLS 1971 p. 1515)

658   **PINKWATER, D(aniel) Manus.** *Blue Moose.* **Gr. 1–4.**

✓   The maitre d' of Mr. Breton's gourmet restaurant in the wild is a talking blue moose. The sequels are *Return of the Moose* (1979) and *The Moospire* (1986).

Illus. by the author, Dodd, 1975, 47 pp., o.p.; Knopf, 1993, pap. (0-679-84717-0)

(BL 72:45; CC:546; CCBB 29:84; HB 52:46; KR 43:661; SLJ Sept 1975 p. 88; Suth 2:365)

PINKWATER, D(aniel) Manus. *The Hoboken Chicken Emergency.* See Chapter 6, Humorous Fantasy.

PINKWATER, D(aniel) Manus. *Jolly Roger: A Dog of Hoboken.* See Chapter 6, Humorous Fantasy.

PINKWATER, D(aniel) Manus. *Lizard Music.* See Chapter 6, Humorous Fantasy.

659   **PLENN, Doris.** *The Green Song.* **Gr. 4–6. (Orig. pub. 1954.)**

Pepe, a green tree frog from Puerto Rico, comes to New York City.

Illus. by Paul Galdone, McKay, 1969, 126 pp., o.p.

(HB 30:137; KR 22:152; LJ 79:1238)

660   **POCHOCKI, Ethel.** *The Attic Mice.* **Gr. 3–5.**

A mouse family who live in an old doll farmhouse stored in the attic have a number of adventures.

Illus. by David Catrow, Henry Holt, 1990, 113 pp. (0-8050-1298-2); Dell, 1993, pap. (0-440-40745-1)

(BL 87:743; HBG 2[July–Dec 1990]:80; KR 58:459; SLJ Oct 1990 p. 118)

661   **POLLOCK, Penny.** *Stall Buddies.* **Gr. 3–4.**

Scarlett, a filly whose skittish behavior brought about her sale to a young man who desperately needs her to win races, is befriended by Rufus rooster and Merabel goat, who boost her self-confidence.

Putnam, 1984, 63 pp., o.p.

(BBC:211; BL 81:848; CCBB 38:115; SLJ Mar 1985 p. 170)

662   **POTTER, (Helen) Beatrix (Heelis).** *The Fairy Caravan.* **Gr. 4–6. (Orig. British**
✓   **and U.S. pub. 1929.)**

The animal caravan traveling through the English countryside includes Tuppeny the long-haired guinea pig, Pony Billy, Jenny Ferret, and Princess Xarifa the dormouse.

Warne, 1951, 1985, 225 pp., o.p.

(BBC:211; BL 47:278; CCBB 4:37; HB 5:9, 47–49, 28:163; LJ 76:660; Mahony 3:209; Moore: 120)

663   **POTTER, (Helen) Beatrix (Heelis).** *The Tale of Little Pig Robinson.* **Gr. K–4.**

Sent to market by his aunts Dorcas and Porcas, Little Pig Robinson becomes lost and ends up aboard a ship bound for Robinson Crusoe's island.

Illus. by the author, Warne, 1930, 1987, 123 pp. (0-7232-3503-1)

(BL 27:266; TLS Nov 1930 p. 986)

664   **POTTER, (Helen) Beatrix (Heelis).** *The Tale of the Faithful Dove.* **Gr. 2–4. (Orig. British and U.S. pub. 1955.)**

A mother dove fleeing a falcon becomes trapped in a chimney, but a mouse family and a boy help her to escape.

Illus. by Marie Angel, Warne, 1970 (2nd ed.), 47 pp., o.p.

(CCBB 24:112; HB 46:604; KR 38:1141; LJ 96:1498; TLS 1971 p. 768)

PRICE, Susan. *The Ghost Drum: A Cat's Tale.* See Chapter 10, Witchcraft and Wizardry Fantasy.

PRICE, Susan. *Ghost Song.* See Chapter 10, Witchcraft and Sorcery Fantasy.

PUSHKIN, Alexander Sergeevich. *The Tale of Czar Saltan, or the Prince and the Swan Princess.* See Chapter 1, Allegorical Fantasy and Literary Fairy Tales.

665 **QUACKENBUSH, Robert M(ead).** *Express Train to Trouble: A Miss Mallard Mystery* **(Miss Mallard Mystery series, book 1). Gr. 2–4.**

A humorous takeoff on Agatha Christie's *Murder on the Orient Express,* in which all of the characters are animals, including the detective, Miss Mallard. The sequels are *Dig to Disaster* (1982), *Stairway to Doom* (1983), *Gondola to Danger* (1983), *Rickshaw to Horror* (1984), *Taxi to Intrigue* (1984), *Stage Door to Terror* (1985), *Bicycle to Treachery* (1985), *Dogsled to Dread* (1987), *Danger in Tibet* (Pippen, 1989), *Lost in the Amazon* (1990), and *Evil Under the Sea* (1992).

Illus. by the author, Prentice, 1981, 48 pp. (0-13-298067-3)

(BL 78:758; CC:547; SLJ Aug 1982 p. 104)

666 **RAYNER, Mary (Yoma, neé Grigson).** *Mrs. Pig Gets Cross; and Other Stories.*
✓ **Gr. K–3.**

Seven short, humorous stories about Mrs. Pig and her untidy but clever piglets, who always manage to outwit fox and wolf. This is the sequel to four books for a slightly younger audience: *Mr. and Mrs. Pig's Evening Out* (Atheneum, 1976), *Garth Pig and the Ice-Cream Lady* (Atheneum, 1977), *Mrs. Pig's Bulk Buy* (Atheneum, 1981), and *Garth Pig Steals the Show* (1993).

Illus. by the author, Dutton, 1987, 64 pp. (0-525-44280-4), 1991, pap. (0-525-44705-9)

(BL 83:1209, 84:873; CCBB 40:154; HB 58:338; KR 55:137; SLJ Mar 1987 p. 149, Dec 1987 p. 39)

667 **RAZZI, Jim (James), and RAZZI, Mary.** *The Search for King Pup's Tomb.* **Gr. 3–5.**

Sherluck Bones, master canine detective, finds the lost treasure of King Pup's tomb, in this, his first full-length exploit. There are six short-mystery-episode books in the related Sherluck Bones Mystery-Detective Book series published by Bantam.

Illus. by Ted Enik, Bantam, 1985, 64 pp., pap. (0-553-15312-9)

(BL 81:1337; SLJ May 1985 p. 110)

REID BANKS, Lynne. *The Farthest-Away Mountain.* See Chapter 1, Allegorical Fantasy and Literary Fairy Tales.

668 **REID BANKS, Lynne.** *I Houdini: The Autobiography of a Self-Educated Hamster.* **Gr. 3–6. (Orig. British pub. 1978.)**

Houdini the hamster takes after his namesake in his unrelenting attempts to escape from his cage to explore the out-of-doors and find himself a wife.

Illus. by Terry Riley, Doubleday, 1988, 127 pp. (0-385-24482-7); Avon, 1989, pap. (0-380-70649-0)

(BBC:198; BL 85:70; HB 64:493; KR 56:688; SLJ June 1988 p. 100)

669 **REID BANKS, Lynne.** *The Magic Hare.* **Gr. 3–6. (Orig. British pub. 1993.)**
✓ Ten contemporary fables about a magic hare's encounters with a dragon, a witch, a selfish queen, a prince with hiccups, and two giants.

Illus. by Barry Moser, Morrow, 1993, 49 pp. (0-688-10895-4)

(BL 90:149; CCBB 47:37; HB 69:743; HBG 5:63; KR 61:930; SLJ Nov 1993 p. 104)

670   **ROACH, Marilynne K(athleen).** *Presto: Or, the Adventures of a Turnspit Dog.* **Gr. 5–7.**

Rescued by a traveling puppeteer, a dog named Presto finds adventure in the streets of eighteenth-century London.

Illus. by the author, Houghton, 1979, 148 pp., o.p.

(BL 76:560; CCBB 33:117; HB 56:56; Suth 3:361)

671   **ROBERTSON, Mary Elsie.** *Jemimalee.* **Gr. 4–6.**

Jemimalee, an internationally acclaimed cat poet, types inspiring verses on her master's typewriter, watches out for the family by night, and defends her family's farm from rats by day.

Illus. by Judith Gwyn Brown, McGraw-Hill, 1977, 122 pp., o.p.

(BBC:212; KR 45:991; SLJ Dec 1977 p. 50)

672   **ROBINSON, Mabel L(ouise).** *Back-Seat Driver.* **Gr. 3–5.**

A wirehair terrier who delights in giving his master backseat driving tips is given a car of his own. The sequels are *Skipper Riley* (1955) and *Riley Goes to Obedience School* (1956).

Illus. by Leonard Shortall, Random, 1949, 68 pp., o.p.

(CCBB 3:18; KR 17:360; LJ 74:1918)

673   **ROBINSON, Marileta.** *Mr. Goat's Bad Good Idea.* **Gr. 2–4.**

Three Navajo tales concerning Mr. Goat, Grandfather Sheep, and Jerry the prairie dog.

Illus. by Arthur Getz, Crowell, 1979, 39 pp., o.p.

(BL 75:1160; CCBB 33:17; KR 47:329; SLJ Apr 1979 p. 47)

674   **ROCCA, Guido.** *Gaetano the Pheasant: A Hunting Fable.* **Gr. 3–5. (Orig. pub.**
✓   **1961.)**

Gaetano and his mate decide to escape from the threat of hunters' guns.

Illus. by Giulio Cingoli and Giancarlo Carloni, Harper, 1966, 60 pp., o.p.

(CCBB 20:115; HB 42:431; KR 34:418; LJ 91:3252; Suth:335)

675   **ROGERS, Mark E.** *The Adventures of Samurai Cat* **(Samurai Cat trilogy, book 1). Gr. 10 up.**

A satirical fantasy starring Miaowara Tomokato, the Samurai Cat, who embarks on a quest for vengeance against the killers of his master. The sequels are: *More Adventures of Samurai Cat* (1986), *Samurai Cat in the Real World* (1989), and *Samurai Cat Goes to the Movies* (1994).

Illus. by the author, Tor, 1984, pap., o.p.

(BL 81:483; SLJ Feb 1985 p. 91)

676   **ROSS, Ramon Royal.** *Prune.* **Gr. 5–7.**

Two lonely animals, a magpie and a muskrat, befriend a talking prune who desperately wished to return to his orchard.

Atheneum. 1984, 175 pp. o.p.

(BBC:212; BL 81:848, 84:1441; KR 52:98; SLJ Dec 1984 p. 94)

677   **RUCH, Sandi Barrett.** *Junkyard Dog.* **Gr. 2–4.**

Toad, living under an old stove in the junkyard, describes Slobber the junkyard watchdog's rescue of five-year-old Huey, son of the junkman.

Illus. by Marjorie Wunsch, Orchard, 1990, 96 pp. (0-531-05842-5)

(BL 87:162; HB 66:451; HBG 1[Jan 1990]:236; KR 58:802; SLJ Aug 1990, p. 149)

RUFF, Matt. *Fool on the Hill.* See Chapter 7, Magic Adventure Fantasy.

678 SAINTSBURY (Green), Dana. *The Squirrel That Remembered.* **Gr. 2–4.**

Grandma Nutcracker, an English squirrel living in New York's Central Park, tries to help a homesick English girl.

Illus. by the author, Viking, 1951, 60 pp., o.p.

(CCBB 5:54; HB 27:331; KR 19:388; LJ 76:1572)

SANCHEZ-SILVA, José. *The Boy and the Whale.* See Chapter 1, Allegorical Fantasy and Literary Fairy Tales.

679 SAYERS, Frances Clarke. *Mr. Tidy Paws.* **Gr. 2–4.**

A cat named Mr. Tidy Paws comes to the deserted village of Bear Blossom to help Christopher and his grandmother.

Illus. by Zhenya Gay, Viking, 1935, 64 pp., o.p.

(BL 32:78; Bookshelf 1935 p. 3; HB 11:197, 351; LJ 61:35; Mahony 3:209)

680 SCHEFFLER, Ursel. *Rinaldo, the Sly Fox.* **Gr. 2–4. (Orig. Swiss pub. 1992.)**

Rinaldo the fox is a thieving, swindling trickster whose nemesis, Bruno the Duck, is always one step behind him. The sequel is *The Return of Rinaldo, the Sly Fox* (1993).

Trans. by J. Alison James, illus. by Iskender Gider, North-South, 1992, 62 pp. (1-55858-181-2)

(BL 89:1061; HBG 4[Spring 1993]:62; KR 60:1193; SLJ Nov 1992 p. 78)

SCHOLES, Katherine. *The Landing: A Night of Birds.* See Chapter 7, Magic Adventure Fantasy.

681 SCHWED, Antonia Holding. *Noah and Me: A Novel.* **Gr. 10 up.**

All psychotherapist Nathaniel Danzon's patients are animals, including a butterfly with multiple personality disorder and a praying mantis who feels guilty about eating her mate.

Evans, 1991, 168 pp. (0-87131-664-1)

(BL 88:241, 311; KR 59:967; LJ Oct 1991 p. 122)

SCIESZKA, Jon. *The Frog Prince, Continued.* See Chapter 6, Humorous Fantasy.

SCIESZKA, Jon. *The True Story of the Three Little Pigs: By A. Wolf.* See Chapter 6, Humorous Fantasy.

682 SCOTT, Dixon. *A Fresh Wind in the Willows.* **Gr. 5–7. (Orig. British pub. 1983.)**

The inhabitants of Riverbank still find Toad's misbehavior to be trying, in this contemporary sequel to Kenneth Grahame's *The Wind in the Willows* (1908) (see this section), written for a slightly older audience.

Illus. by Jonathon Coudrille, Dell, 1987, pap., 111 pp. (0-440-42741-X)

(Kliatt 21[Sept 1987]:29; SLJ Nov 1987 p. 107)

683 SEEMAN, Elizabeth (Brickel). *The Talking Dog and the Barking Man.* **Gr. 3–5.**

Candido the talking dog runs away from home and joins a traveling ventriloquist's show.

Illus. by James (Royer) Flora, Watts, 1960, 186 pp., o.p.

(HB 36:291; LJ 85:2043)

684 SEIDLER, Tor. *A Rat's Tale.* **Gr. 4–6.**

✓ An artistic young rat named Montague earns a fortune, brings honor to his family, and wins his girl friend's heart, all by selling his miniature shell paintings.

Illus. by Fred Marcellino, Farrar, 1986, 187 pp. (0-374-36185-1)

(BBC:212; BL 83:788, 84:1441; CCBB 40:118; HB 63:212; KR 54:1511; SLJ Jan 1986 p. 79)

685   SEIDLER, Tor. *The Wainscott Weasel.* **Gr. 4–6.**

✓   In this romantic tale set at the weasels' First Spring Cotillion, Zeke Whitebelly falls in love with newcomer Wendy Blackish, who falls for the dashing Bagley Brown, Jr., who falls in love with a beautiful fish, whose life is threatened by an osprey.

Illus. by Fred Marcellino, Harper, 1993, 193 pp. (0-06-205032-X)

(BL 90:519; CCBB 47:99; HBG 5:82; KR 61:1151; SLJ Dec 1993 p. 116)

686   SELDEN (Thompson), George. *The Cricket in Times Square.* **Gr. 3–6.**

✓   Chester Cricket's beautiful music (as managed by Tucker Mouse) brings fame to Chester and fortune to the subway-station newspaper stand where they live. John Newbery Medal Honor Book, 1961. The sequels are *Tucker's Countryside* (1969), *Harry Cat's Pet Puppy* (1974), *Chester Cricket's Pigeon Ride* (1981), *Chester Cricket's New Home* (1983), *Harry Kitten and Tucker Mouse* (1986), and *The Old Meadow* (1987).

Illus. by Garth Williams, Farrar, 1960, 160 pp. (0-374-31650-3); Dell, 1970, pap. (0-440-41563-2)

(BBC:212; BL 57:250, 80:96; CC:553; CCBB 14:86; Ch&Bks:268; Eakin:288; HB 36:407; LJ 85:4570; TLS 1982 p. 798)

687   SELDEN (Thompson), George. *Irma and Jerry.* **Gr. 4–6.**

Newly arrived in Greenwich Village, a proper cocker spaniel named Jerry meets a runaway cat named Irma, and the two manage to prevent a robbery and become actors in an off-Broadway play.

Illus. by Leslie Morrill, Avon, 1982, pap., 207 pp., o.p.

(BL 79:780; HB 59:167; SLJ Nov 1982 p. 104)

688   SELDEN (Thompson), George. *Oscar Lobster's Fair Exchange* **(orig. title:** *The Garden under the Sea,* **Viking, 1957). Gr. 3–5.**

Oscar Lobster and his friends decide to retaliate for the humans' annual thievery of shells and rocks by making their own undersea garden using items stolen from the humans.

Illus. by Peter Lippman, Harper, 1966, o.p.; Avon, 1974, pap., 174 pp., o.p.

(BL 53:508; CCBB 11:85; KR 25:37; LJ 82:1802, 91:3538)

689   SENDAK, Maurice (Bernard). *Higglety Pigglety Pop! Or, There Must Be More*
✓   *to Life.* **Gr. 2–4.**

Bored by life at home, a sheepdog named Jenny packs her bag and sets off to find happiness as the leading lady in the World Mother Goose Theater.

Illus. by the author, Harper, 1967, 80 pp. (0-06-025487-4)

(BBC:213; BL 64:451; CC:554; CCBB 21:66; Ch&Bks:261; HB 44:151, 161; KR 35:1209; LJ 92:4618; Suth:354)

SEREDY, Kate. *Lazy Tinka.* See Chapter 1, Allegorical Fantasy and Literary Fairy Tales.

690   SHACHTMAN, Tom. *Driftwhistler: A Story of Daniel au Fond* **(Daniel au Fond trilogy, book 3). Gr. 5–8.**

Sea-lion Daniel au Fond gathers together members of the 13 tribes of seagoing mammals and finds the legendary island of Pacifica where humans and sea mammals once lived harmoniously, but he realizes that he must also teach humans to respect all life by ceasing their pollution of the environment. This is the sequel to *Beachmaster* (1988) and *Wavebender* (1989).

Henry Holt, 1991, 176 pp. (0-8050-1285-0)

(BL 88:698; HBG 3[July–Dec 1991]:73; KR 59:1475; SLJ Feb 1992 p. 89)

691   **SHARP (Castle), Margery.** *The Rescuers.* **Gr. 3–6.**

✓✓   Miss Bianca and two other mice go on a dangerous mission to rescue a human poet from imprisonment in a deep dungeon. Carnegie Medal Commended Book, 1959. The sequels are *Miss Bianca* (1962), *The Turret* (1963), *Miss Bianca in the Salt Mines* (1966), *Miss Bianca in the Orient* (1970), *Miss Bianca in the Antarctic* (1971), *Miss Bianca and the Bridesmaid* (1972), *Bernard the Brave* (1977), *Bernard into Battle* (1978), and *Miss Bianca in the Arctic* (British).

Illus. by Garth Williams, Little, 1959 (0-316-78314-5), 1994, pap. (0-316-78355-2); Peter Smith, 1989 (0-8446-6412-X)

(BBC:213; BL 56:274; CC:555; CCBB 13:105; Ch&Bks:268; Eakin:295; HB 36:38; KR 27:617; LJ 84:3153; TLS Dec 4, 1959 p. xv)

692   **SHEEDY, Alexandra E.** *She Was Nice to Mice: The Other Side of Elizabeth I's Character Never Before Revealed by Previous Historians.* **Gr. 3–5.**

Esther Long Whiskers Gray Hair Wallgate the 42nd, a mouse with a literary mind, finds the memoirs of one of her ancestors who lived at the court of Queen Elizabeth I, in this story written and illustrated by two young adolescents.

Illus. by Jessica Levy, McGraw-Hill, 1975, 95 pp., o.p.

(CCBB 29:86; KR 43:849; SLJ Oct 1975 p. 108)

693   **SHEEHAN, Carolyn, and SHEEHAN, Edmond.** *Magnifi-Cat.* **Gr. 6 up.**

The arrival of a small grey cat with a saint's halo at the Pearly Gates jams Heaven's soul-processing computer.

Doubleday, 1972, 229 pp., o.p.

(BL 69:551, 570, 767; KR 40:887; LJ 97:2756)

694   **SHULEVITZ, Uri.** *The Strange and Exciting Adventures of Jeremiah Hush.* **Gr. 3–6.**

A middle-aged monkey named Jeremiah Hush leaves his quiet home to visit the Shake 'n' Roll Dancin' Hole, and to enter a chocolate-banana-pecan-cream pie eating contest.

Illus. by the author, Farrar, 1986, 90 pp. (0-374-33656-3)

(BBC:213; BL 83:846; CCBB 40:135; KR 54:1795; SLJ Feb 1987 p. 84)

695   **SHURA, Mary Francis (pseud. of Mary Francis Craig).** *A Tale of Middle* ✓   *Length.* **Gr. 3–6.**

Dominic and Alec mouse discover that the strange object near the mouse colony is a mouse trap.

Illus. by Peter Parnall, Atheneum, 1966, 105 pp., o.p.

(BL 63:268; CCBB 20:48; HB 42:566; KR 34:687; LJ 91:4343)

SILVERSTEIN, Shel. *Uncle Shelby's Story of Laficadio, the Lion Who Shot Back.* See Chapter 6, Humorous Fantasy.

696   **SIMONT, Marc.** *Mimi.* **Gr. 3–5.**

A mouse named Mimi is secretly trained to run across the stage every time a famous concert singer needs to hit a high note.

Illus. by the author, Harper, 1954, 56 pp., o.p.

(HB 31:111; KR 22:726; LJ 80:193)

697 **SINCLAIR, Tom.** *Tales of a Wandering Warthog.* **Gr. 4–6.**

Wart the warthog flees his African homeland to New York City, where he and his teenaged friends solve numerous local and world crises.

Illus. by John C. Wallner, Whitman, 1985, 134 pp., o.p.

(BBC:213; BL 81:1404; SLJ Aug 1985 p. 69)

SINGER, Marilyn. *Charmed.* See Chapter 5C, Travel to Other Worlds.

698 **SINGER, Marilyn.** *The Fido Frame-Up* **(The Sam Spayed series). Gr. 4–6.**

In this detective novel spoof, Samantha Spayed, dog detective, is the brains behind her master, Philip Barlowe's solutions to his dangerous cases. The sequels are *A Nose for Trouble* (1985) and *Where There's a Will, There's a Wag* (1986).

Illus. by Andrew Glass, Warne, 1983, 90 pp., o.p.

(BL 80:576; HB 59:712; SLJ Dec 1983 p. 83)

699 **SISSON, Rosemary Anne.** *The Adventures of Ambrose.* **Gr. 2–4. (Orig. British pub. 1951.)**

Ambrose and Simon mouse travel to London to meet the king and queen.

Illus. by Astrid Walford, Dutton, 1952, 118 pp., o.p.

(HB 28:406; KR 20:598; LJ 77:1662)

SLEIGH, Barbara (de Riemer). *Carbonel: The King of the Cats.* See Chapter 7, Magic Adventure Fantasy.

SMITH, Agnes. *An Edge of the Forest.* See Chapter 1, Allegorical Fantasy and Literary Fairy Tales.

700 **SMITH, Alison.** *Come Away Home.* **Gr. 3–5.**

Trapped in a Scottish loch by a storm and unable to get back to the ocean, a young sea monster named Angus is befriended by Fiona and her dog, James.

Illus. by Deborah Haeffele, Macmillan, 1991, 105 pp. (0-684-19283-7)

(BL 87:1800; CCBB 44:276; HBG 2:271; KR 59:539; SLJ July 1991 p. 74)

701 **SMITH, Dodie (Dorothy Gladys).** *The Hundred and One Dalmatians.* **Gr. 4–6.**
✓ **(Orig. British pub. 1956.)**

Pongo and Missis rescue their fifteen puppies from Cruella DeVil, who dognapped them to make into fur coats. The sequel is *The Starlight Barking* (1967).

Illus. by Janet Grahame-Johnstone and Anne Grahame-Johnstone, Viking, 1957, o.p.; Avon, 1976, pap., 208 pp. (0-380-00628-6); Buccaneer, 1981, LB(0-89966-420-2); illus. by Michael Dooling, Viking, 1989, pap., 184 pp. (0-670-82660-X)

(BBC:213; BL 53:588; HB 33:222; KR 25:75; LJ 82:1802)

702 **SMITH, Emma.** *Emily: The Traveling Guinea Pig.* **Gr. 3–5.**

Emily Guinea Pig sets off to see the ocean, leaving behind her brother Arthur to look after her tidy little house. The sequel is *Emily's Voyage* (Harcourt, 1966).

Illus. by Katherine Wigglesworth, Astor-Honor, 1960, 76 pp. (0-8392-3007-9)

(HB 36:287; KR 28:232)

703   STANTON, Mary. *The Heavenly Horse from the Outermost West.* **Gr. 10 up.**

✓   The Appaloosa breed faces extinction because of an evil bargain made by the Lead Mare, until the horse god, Dancer, gives up his immortality and returns from the land of the Outermost West. The sequel is *Piper at the Gate* (1989).

Baen, 1988, pap., 344 pp. (0-671-65410-1)

(BBS:64; BL 84:1575, 1598, 86:907; Kliatt Sept 1988 p. 27; LJ June 15, 1988 p. 71; VOYA 11:296, 12:14)

STEARNS, Pamela (Fujimoto). *Into the Painted Bear Lair.* See Chapter 5C, Travel to Other Worlds.

704   STEFANEC-OGREN, Cathy. *Sly, P. I.: The Case of the Missing Shoes.* **Gr. 1–4.**

Sly Fox, private investigator, solves his first case when his old friend ballerina Loretta Oink's toe shoes disappear on the opening night of "Sleeping Beauty."

Illus. by Priscilla Posey Circolo, Harper, 1989, 48 pp., o.p.

(BL 85: 1554; CCBB 42: 206; SLJ Jan 1989 p. 95)

705   STEIG, William. *Abel's Island.* **Gr. 3–6.**

✓✓   A storm sweeps Abel the mouse away from his new bride, Amanda, to a deserted island, where he develops a talent for sculpting. John Newbery Medal Honor Book, 1977.

Illus. by the author, Farrar, 1976, 128 pp. (0-374-30010-0), 1985, pap. (0-374-40016-4)

(BBC:214; BL 73:181, 80:46; CC:562; CCBB 30:33; Ch&Bks:268; HB 52:500; KR 44:686; SLJ Oct 1976 p. 101; Suth 2:429; TLS 1977 p. 1248)

706   STEIG, William. *Dominic.* **Gr. 4–6.**

✓   An adventurous dog named Dominic finds an enchanted garden, is given a fortune by an old pig, and helps fight the Doomsday Gang. National Book Award Finalist, 1973.

Illus. by the author, Farrar, 1972, 145 pp., o.p., 1984, pap. (0-374-41826-8)

(BBC:214; BL 69:531; CC:562; CCBB 26:31; Ch&Bks:291; HB 48:470; KR 40:1414; LJ 97:2954; SLJ Aug 1992 p. 99; Suth 378; TLS 1973 p. 386)

707   STEIG, William. *The Real Thief.* **Gr. 2–5.**

✓   Angry over the theft of his jewels, the king accuses his loyal guard, Gawain the goose, in spite of Gawain's pleas of innocence.

Illus. by the author, Farrar, 1976, 64 pp. (0-374-36217-3), 1991, pap. (0-374-46208-9)

(BBC:214; BL 70:242, 827; CC:562; CCBB 27:102; HB 49:595; KR 41:756; LJ 98:3446; Suth 2:431)

708   STEINER, Jörg. *Rabbit Island.* **Gr. 3–5. (Orig. Swiss pub. 1977.)**

Big Gray and Little Brown escape from the rabbit factory where they are being fattened for slaughter. Mildred L. Batchelder Award, 1978.

Trans. by Ann Conrad Lammers, illus. by Jörg Müller, Harcourt, 1978, 32 pp., o.p.; Bergh, 1984 (repr. of 1978 ed.), o.p.

(HB 54:634; KR 46:1135; SLJ Oct 1978 p. 139; TLS 1978 p. 763)

709   STEVENS, Eden Vale. *Abba.* **Gr. 3–6.**

Abba, an orphaned elephant, searches for Einhorn, the Great White Buffalo, to help him rescue another elephant held captive by hunters.

Illus. by Anthony Stevens, Atheneum, 1962, 116 pp., o.p.

(BL 59:576; LJ 87:190)

710   STEVENSON, James. *Here Comes Herb's Hurricane!* **Gr. 2–4.**

Herb Rabbit develops a hurricane warning system that refuses to work until a real hurricane comes along.

Illus. by the author, Harper, 1973, 149 pp., o.p.

(CCBB 27:150; KR 41:1310, 1351; LJ 98:3709)

711 **STEVENSON, James.** *Oliver, Clarence, and Violet.* **Gr. 2–4.**

Oliver Beaver's round-the-world boat trip is complicated by the numerous friends who decide to go with him, including a toad, a turkey, a turtle, and two bats.

Illus. by the author, Greenwillow, 1982, 96 pp., o.p.

(BL 78:1370; KR 50:347; SLJ May 1952 p. 65)

712 **STEVENSON, James.** *The Supreme Souvenir Factory.* **Gr. 2–4.**

✓ Chester the dog and his bat friend, Wendy, join forces to save the factory from the weasely plans of Mr. Sashwayte.

Illus. by the author, Greenwillow, 1988, 56 pp. (0-688-07782-X)

(BL 85:487; HB 65:206; KR 56:1408; SLJ Dec 1989 p. 94)

STOLP, Hans. *The Golden Bird.* See Chapter 1, Allegorical Fantasy and Literary Fairy Tales.

713 **STOLZ, Mary (Slattery).** *Belling the Tiger.* **Gr. 2–4.**

✓ Asa and Rambo mouse are selected to put a bell on Siri, the tigerlike housecat, bringing about an unexpected trip to the land of elephants and real tigers. John Newbery Medal Honor Book, 1962. The sequels are *The Great Rebellion* (1961), *Siri the Conquistador* (1963), and *Maximilian's World* (1966). These three sequels have been published together as *Tales at the Mousehole* (Godine, 1992, see entry below) with new illustrations and renamed main characters.

Illus. by Beni Montresor, Harper, 1961, 1989, 64 pp., o.p.

(BL 57:644; CCBB 14:149; Ch&Bks:291; Eakin:314; HB 37:339; KR 29:326; LJ 86:1989)

714 **STOLZ, Mary (Slattery).** *Cat Walk.* **Gr. 3–6.**

✓ A six-toed black barn kitten runs away from the home where a little girl has dressed him up and named him Tootsie Wootsie, and searches for a home where he will be loved for himself.

Illus. by Erik Blegvad, Harper, 1983, 120 pp., o.p.; Harper, 1985, pap. (0-06-440155-3)

(BL 79:1223; CC:563; CCBB 36:218; Ch&Bks:291; HB 59:306; KR 51:307; SLJ Aug 1983 p. 71; Suth 3:412)

715 **STOLZ, Mary (Slattery).** *Deputy Shep.* **Gr. 2–5.**

✓ Slow-moving Jack Shep, deputy sheriff, reluctantly tries to solve the rash of robberies at canine homes throughout Canoville in this humorous animal detective story.

Illus. by Pamela Johnson, Harper, 1991, 96 pp. LB(0-06-026040-8)

(BL 87:2148; CC 1992 Suppl. p. 63; CCBB 45:51; HBG 3[July–Dec 1991]:74; KR 59:1094; SLJ Oct 1991 p. 105)

716 **STOLZ, Mary (Slattery).** *Frédou.* **Gr. 4–6.**

✓ Runaway Paul is taken in by a hotel-owning Parisian cat.

Illus. by Tomi Ungerer, Harper, 1962, 118 pp., o.p.

(BL 59:84; CCBB 15:166; HB 38:370; KR 30:386; LJ 87:2625)

717 **STOLZ, Mary (Slattery).** *Pigeon Flight.* **Gr. 2–4.**

Mr. and Mrs. Pigeon decide to leave New York City and move to New England.

Illus. by Murray Tinkelman, Harper, 1962, 54 pp., o.p.

(CCBB 16:16; Eakin:317; HB 38:607; LJ 87:3206)

718   STOLZ, Mary (Slattery). *Quentin Corn.* **Gr. 4–6.**

✓   Bored with life as a pig, Quentin Corn decides to live as a man; but while he is accepted by adults, the children are not all so accepting.

Illus. by Pamela Johnson, Godine, 1985, 128 pp. (0-87923-553-5)

(BBC:214; BL 82:270, 84:1441; CC:563; CCBB 39:80; HB 61:737; SLJ Sept 1985 p. 140, Dec 1985 p. 34; Suth 4:401)

719   STOLZ, Mary (Slattery). *Tales at the Mousehole.* **Gr. 3–5.**

These three stories about the adventures of two tiny house mice were originally published separately as *The Great Rebellion* (Harper, 1961), *Siri the Conquistador* (Harper, 1963), and *Maximillian's World* (Harper, 1966). The names of the main characters have been changed in this edition. This is the sequel to *Belling the Cat* (Harper, 1961; 1989; see entry above).

Illus. by Pamela Johnston, Godine, 1992, 102 pp. (0-87923-789-9)

(BL 89:671; HBG 4[Spring 1993]:77)

720   STONG, Phil(ip Duffield). *Prince and the Porker.* **Gr. 4–6.**

✓   A boy and a pig help a harness trotter named Prince to win blue ribbons.

Illus. by Kurt Wiese, Dodd, 1950, 67 pp., o.p.

(BL 47:226; CCBB 3:71; HB 26:477; LJ 75:2083)

721   SYMONDS, John. *Elfrida and the Pig.* **Gr. 2–4. (Orig. British pub. 1959.)**

Elfrida's secret friend, the pig next door, helps her find a doll of her very own.

Illus. by Edward Ardizzone, Watts, 1959, 48 pp., o.p.

(CCBB 14:18; HB 36:292; LJ 85:2044; TLS Dec 4, 1959 p. xv)

TARN, Sir William Woodthorpe. *The Treasure of the Isle of Mist: A Tale of the Isle of Skye.* See Chapter 7, Magic Adventure Fantasy.

722   TITUS, Eve. *Basil of Baker Street.* **Gr. 3–5.**

✓   Basil, an English mouse detective who idolizes Sherlock Holmes, solves one of Mousedom's most baffling and mysterious kidnapping cases. The sequels are *Basil and the Lost Colony* (1964), *Basil and the Pygmy Cats* (1971; 1989, pap.), *Basil in Mexico* (1975), and *Basil in the Wild West* (1982).

Illus. by Paul Galdone, McGraw-Hill, 1958, 128 pp., LB(0-07-064907-3); Pocket, 1988, pap. (0-318-37408-0)

(BBC:214; BL 54:593; CC:566; CCBB 11:124; Ch&Bks:292; HB 34:266; KR 26:335; LJ 83:1947)

723   TODD, Ruthven. *Space Cat.* **Gr. 3–5.**

Flyball the cat not only makes an important scientific discovery on his way to the moon, but also saves the pilot's life. The sequels are *Space Cat Visits Venus* (1955), *Space Cat Meets Mars* (1957), and *Space Cat and the Kittens* (1959).

Illus. by Paul Galdone, Scribner, 1952, 69 pp., o.p.; Peter Smith, 1992 (0-8446-6561-4)

(CCBB 6:28; HB 28:320; KR 20:657; LJ 77:1819)

724   TOMLINSON, Jill. *Hilda the Hen Who Wouldn't Give Up.* **Gr. 2–4.**

Hilda the hen is so enamored of her Aunt Emma's chicks that she decides to have a brood of her own, against Farmer Biddick's wishes.

Illus. by Fernando Krahn, Harcourt, 1967, 1980, 96 pp., o.p.

(BL 76:1612; KR 48:838; SLJ Aug 1980 p. 58)

725 **TREVOR, Elleston.** *Deep Wood.* **Gr. 4–6.**

Five friends, Badger, Otter, Owl, Squirrel, and Fox, live along the Wild River in Deep Wood. The sequels are *Heather Hill* (1948) and *Badger's Wood* (1958, 1959).

Illus. by Stephen Voorhis, Longman, 1947, 282 pp., o.p.

(BL 44:138; CCBB 1[Dec 1947]:7; HB 23:358; KR 45:394; LJ 73:126)

TURKLE, Brinton (Cassaday). *Mooncoin Castle; or Skulduggery Rewarded.* See Chapter 4, Ghost Fantasy.

726 **UNWIN, Nora S(picer).** *Two Too Many.* **Gr. 2–4.**

On Halloween night, two lost kittens are taken for a ride on a witch's broom.

Illus. by the author, McKay, 1962, 54 pp., o.p.

(Eakin:339; HB 38:473; LJ 87:4615; TLS 1965 p. 1141)

UPENSKY, Eduard. *Uncle Fedya, His Dog, and His Cat.* See Chapter 7, Magic Adventure Fantasy.

727 **UTTLEY, Alison.** *Foxglove Tales.* **Gr. K–3. (Orig. British pub. 1984.)**

Cozy animal stories from Uttley's British books *Moonshine and Magic* (1932), *Candlelight Tales* (1936), and *Lavender Shoes* (1970).

Chosen by Lucy Meredith, illus. by Shirley Felts, Faber, 1984, 107 pp., o.p.

(BL 81:1671; SLJ Feb 1985 p. 69)

VAMBA. *The Prince and His Ants.* See Chapter 7, Magic Adventure Fantasy.

728 **VAN ALLSBURG, Chris.** *Two Bad Ants.* **Gr. K–4.**

✓ Two ants who decide to stay behind in the sugar bowl after a crystal-gathering expedition are nearly drowned in a cup of coffee, roasted in a toaster, and blown apart in a garbage disposal before they find their way home again.

Illus. by the author, Houghton, 1988, 32 pp. (0-395-48668-8)

(BL 85:328; CC:726; CCBB 42:110; HB 65:61; KR 56:1410; SLJ Nov 1988 p. 97)

729 **VAN DE WETERING, Janwillem.** *Hugh Pine.* **Gr. 2–4.**

Hugh Porcupine decides to walk upright and wears a hat and coat in order to cross roads safely. The sequels are *Hugh Pine and the Good Place* (1986), and *Hugh Pine and Something Else* (1989).

Illus. by Lynn Munsinger, Houghton, 1980, 96 pp. (0-395-29459-2)

(BL 77:122; CCBB 34:102; KR 48:1518; SLJ Mar 1981 p. 152)

730 **VAN LEEUWEN, Jean.** *The Great Christmas Kidnapping Caper.* **Gr. 3–5.**

✓ The disappearance of Santa Claus mobilizes Marvin the Magnificent Mouse and his gang to the rescue. This is the sequel to *The Great Cheese Conspiracy* (Random, 1969) and is followed by *The Great Rescue Operation* (1982), and *The Great Summer Camp Catastrophe* (1992).

Illus. by Steven Kellogg, Dial, 1975, 133 pp., o.p.; Puffin, 1990, pap. (0-14-034287-7)

(BL 72:169; CC:569; CCBB 29:54; KR 43:778; SLJ Oct 1975 p. 81; Suth 2:459)

731 **WABER, Bernard.** *Dear Hildegarde.* **Gr. 2–4.**

Hildegarde Owl is an advice columnist who tries to solve the problems of her fellow creatures.

Illus. by the author, Houghton, 1980, 64 pp., o.p.

(CCBB 34:141; HB 57:54; KR 49:4; SLJ Feb 1981 p. 60)

732   WABER, Bernard. *Mice on My Mind.* **Gr. 2–5.**

Suffering from an obsession with mice, a cat finally finds a cure for his malady.

Illus. by the author, Houghton, 1977, 48 pp., o.p.

(CCBB 31:103; HB 53:526; KR 45:1045; SLJ Sept 1977 p. 117; Suth 2:464)

WAECHTER, Friedrich, and EILERT, Bernd. *The Crown Snatchers.* See Chapter 1, Allegorical Fantasy and Literary Fairy Tales.

733   WAHL, Jan (Boyer). *Pleasant Fieldmouse.* **Gr. 2–4.**

Pleasant Fieldmouse becomes a firefighter and courageously rescues Anxious Squirrel's mother and Mrs. Worrywind Hedgehog. The sequels are *The Six Voyages of Pleasant Fieldmouse* (Delacorte, 1971), *Pleasant Fieldmouse's Halloween Party* (Putnam, 1974), *The Pleasant Fieldmouse Storybook* (Prentice, 1977), and *Pleasant Fieldmouse's Valentine Trick* (Dutton, 1977).

Illus. by Maurice Sendak, Harper, 1964, 80 pp., LB(0-06-026331-8)

(CCBB 18:94; HB 40:373; LJ 89:3477; TLS 1969 p. 1387)

734   WALLACE, Barbara Brooks. *Palmer Patch.* **Gr. 4–6.**

Thinking they are no longer wanted, the Patch family's pets run away from home.

Illus. by Lawrence Di Fiori, Follett, 1976, 128 pp., o.p.

(BL 73:671; CCBB 30:116; SLJ Apr 1977 p. 72)

735   WALLACE, Bill. *Snot Stew.* **Gr. 3–5.**

Adopted by a farm family, brother and sister kittens Kikki and Toby enjoy the cuddling and good food but try to avoid Butch, the family's dangerous dog.

Illus. by Lisa McCue, Holiday, 1989, 81 pp. (0-8234-0745-4); Pocket, 1990, pap. (0-671-69335-2)

(BBC:215; BL 85:1657; SLJ Apr 1989 p. 109)

WANGERIN, Walter, Jr. *The Book of the Dun Cow.* See Chapter 1, Allegorical Fantasy and Literary Fairy Tales.

736   WATKINS, Will. *Sid Seal, Houseman.* **Gr. 3–5.**

Sid Seal, waiter, musician, and companion to young Waltham de Swine, enlivens the stuffy and wealthy de Swine family's existence.

Illus. by Toni Goffe, Orchard, 1989, 89 pp. (0-531-00384-5)

(BL 85:1908; CCBB 42:285; SLJ Sept 1989 p. 235)

737   WATSON, Wendy. *Tales for a Winter's Eve.* **Gr. K–3.**

✓   Freddie Fox's family and friends cheer him up after a skiing accident by telling stories.

Illus. by the author, Farrar, 1988, 32 pp. (0-374-37373-6), 1991, pap. (0-374-47419-2)

(BL 85:588, 880; CCBB 42:88; HB 65:64; KR 56:1746; SLJ Feb 1989 p. 76)

738   WEIR, Rosemary (Green). *Pyewacket.* **Gr. 3–5.**

Pyewacket leads the neighborhood cats in revolt against their owners.

Illus. by Charles Pickard, Abelard-Schuman, 1967, 123 pp., o.p.

(KR 35:1210; LJ 93:297; TLS 1967 p. 1153)

739   WENNING, Elisabeth. *The Christmas Mouse* **(British title:** *The Christmas Churchmouse***). Gr. K–4.**

Hungry little Kaspar Kleinmause helps Herr Gruber write the carol "Silent Night."

Illus. by Barbara Remington, Holt, 1959, 44 pp., o.p.

(BL 56:225; HB 35:471; KR 27:756; LJ 84:3627)

WESTALL, Robert (Atkinson). *The Cats of Seroster.* See Chapter 5A, Alternate Worlds or Histories.

740 **WHAYNE, Susanne Santoro.** *Watch the House.* **Gr. 2–5.**

The family pets—a guinea pig, two cats, a dog, a canary, and two guppies—decide to explore the outdoor world while their masters are away.

Illus. by Leslie Morrill, Simon & Schuster, 1992, 80 pp. (0-671-75886-1), 1993, pap. (0-671-86700-8)

(BL 88:1940; HBG 3[Fall 1992]:272; KR 60:856; SLJ July 1992 p. 66)

741 **WHITE, Anne Hitchcock.** *Junket.* **Gr. 4–6.**

✓ It takes an entire summer for an airedale named Junket to teach his new owners about farm life.

. Illus. by Robert McCloskey, Viking, 1955, 183 pp., o.p.

(BL 51:287; CCBB 9:31; Eakin:348; HB 31:114; KR 23:81; LJ 80:1259)

742 **WHITE, Anne Hitchcock.** *The Story of Serapina.* **Gr. 3–5.**

✓ Serapina the cat adopts the Salinas family, although they are not sure they want her.

Illus. by Tony Palazzo, Viking, 1951, 128 pp., o.p.

(BL 47:333; CCBB 4:47; Eakin:348; HB 27:180; LJ 76:970)

743 **WHITE, E(lwyn) B(rooks).** *Charlotte's Web.* **Gr. 3 up.**

✓✓ Wilbur the pig is destined for the annual fall slaughtering, but his resourceful friend, a spider named Charlotte, tries to save him. John Newbery Medal Honor Book, 1953.

Illus. by Garth Williams, Harper, 1952, 184 pp., LB(0-06-026385-7), pap. (0-06-440055-7)

(BBC:215; BL 49:2, 80:96; CC:572; CCBB 6:36; Ch&Bks:267; Eakin:348; HB 28:394, 407; KR 20:501; LJ 77:2185; TLS 1952 p. 7)

745 **WHITE, E(lwyn) B(rooks).** *Stuart Little.* **Gr. 4–6.**

Stuart Little is the second son of a normal American family—except that Stuart turns out to be a mouse instead of a boy.

Illus. by Garth Williams, Harper, 1945, 131 pp., LB(0-06-026395-4), pap. (0-06-440056-5)

(CC:572; Ch&Bks:267; HB 21:455; KR 13:314)

745 **WHITE, E(lwyn) B(rooks).** *The Trumpet of the Swan.* **Gr. 4–6.**

✓ Lewis's father buys him a trumpet to overcome his speech defect and starts the young swan on a career as a nightclub entertainer. Finalist, National Book Award, 1971.

Illus. by Edward Frascino, Harper, 1970, 210 pp., LB(0-06-026397-0), pap. (0-06-440048-4)

(BBC:215; BL 67:59, 661; CCBB 24:35; Ch&Bks:267; HB 46:391; KR 38:455; LJ 95:2537, 4327; TLS 1970 p. 1458)

746 **WHITELAW, Stella, GARDINER, Judith, and RONSON, Mark.** *Grimalkin's Tales.* **Gr. 10 up.**

Twelve tales about cats, some of which are fantasy, including one about Leopold, a large cat who can fly.

St. Martin, 1985, 160 pp., o.p.

(KR 53:830; SLJ Jan 1986 p. 84)

WIGGIN, Kate. *The Bird's Christmas Carol.* See Chapter 1, Allegorical Fantasy and Literary Fairy Tales.

WILDE, Oscar (pseud. of Fingal O'Flahertie Wills). *The Happy Prince.* See Chapter 1, Allegorical Fantasy and Literary Fairy Tales.

747   **WILLIAMS, Garth (Montgomery).** *The Adventures of Benjamin Pink.* **Gr. 2–4.**

A rabbit named Benjamin Pink is shipwrecked while on a fishing trip.

Illus. by the author, Harper, 1952, 152 pp., o.p.

(HB 27:400; 28:27; KR 19:347; LJ 76:1710)

748   **WILLIAMS, Tad.** *Tailchaser's Song.* **Gr. 10 up.**

The quest saga of a young ginger cat, Fritti Tailchaser, who is captured and enslaved by an evil cat-god while on a journey to find his lost mate.

NAL, 1985, o.p.; DAW, 1986, pap., 320 pp. (0-88677-374-1)

(BBS:67; BL 82:317, 332, 86:907; KR 53:980; LJ Nov 15, 1985 p. 112; SLJ Nov 1985 p. 106)

749   **WILLIAMS (John), Ursula Moray.** *Bogwoppit.* **Gr. 5–7. (Orig. British pub.**
✓   **1978.)**

Samantha's crusade to save the furry creatures who live in the drains of her aunt's mansion takes a new turn when her aunt is kidnapped by the Bogwoppits.

Nelson, 1978, 128 pp., o.p.

(BL 75:54; CCBB 32:128; Ch&Bks:292; KR 46:879; SLJ Sept 1978 p. 152; Suth 2:481; TLS 1978 p. 765)

750   **WILLIAMS (John), Ursula Moray.** *The Nine Lives of Island MacKenzie* **(Orig.**
✓   **U.S. title:** *Island MacKenzie***). Gr. 4–6. (Orig. British pub. 1959.)**

MacKenzie the cat and a cat-hating woman named Miss Pettifer survive shipwreck, sharks, and crocodiles to be cast up together on a desert island.

Illus. by Edward Ardizzone, Morrow, 1960, o.p.; Chatto, 1980, 128 pp., o.p.

(BL 57:157; CCBB 14:88; HB 36:503, 56:664; KR 28:498; LJ 85:3228; TLS Dec 4, 1959 p. xv)

WILLIAMS (John), Ursula Moray. *Tiger Nanny.* See Chapter 6, Humorous Fantasy.

WILLIS, Paul J. *No Clock in the Forest.* See Chapter 5C, Travel to OtherWorlds.

751   **WILSON, A. N.** *Hazel the Guinea Pig.* **Gr. 1–4. (Orig. British pub. 1989.)**

Three stories about Hazel, the pet guinea pig, getting stuck in a rubber boot, finding a mate named Tobacco, and starting a family.

Illus. by Jonathan Heale, Candlewick, 1992, 92 pp. (1-56402-013-4)

(CCBB 45:250; HBG 3[Fall 1992]:259; KR 60:473; SLJ June 1992 p. 104)

752   **WILSON, A. N.** *Stray.* **Gr. 6–10. (Orig. British pub. 1987.)**

Pufftail, an independent cat, tells his grandkitten the story of his adventurous life trying to find love and to understand human behavior. *Tabitha* (U.K. 1988, U.S. 1989; see below) is a children's book about Pufftail's daughter.

Orchard, 1989, 256 pp., o.p.

(BL 86:902, 922; HBG 1[July 1989]:79; KR 57:1170; SLJ Oct 1989 p. 138; VOYA 12:285)

753   **WILSON, A. N.** *Tabitha.* **Gr. 1–4. (Orig. British pub. 1988.)**

The daughter of Pufftail the alleycat who told his story in the young adult book *Stray* (U.K. 1987, U.S. 1988; see above), Tabitha describes her life with a family of "two-footers."

Illus. by Sarah Fox-Davies, Orchard, 1989, 48 pp. (0-531-05813-1)

(HB 56:480; KR 57:218; SLJ Aug 1989 p. 133)

WILSON, David Henry. *The Coachman Rat.* See Chapter 5B, Myth Fantasy.

754   **WILSON, Gahan.** *Harry the Fat Bear* **(Orig. title:** *Harry the Fat Bear Spy***). Gr. 4–6.**

Harry would rather be a chef or a tap dancer than the bumbling spy he is, but he does manage to solve the case of the great Bearmania macaroons. The sequel is *Harry and the Sea Serpent* (1976).

Illus. by the author, Scribner, 1973, o.p.

(KR 41:698; LJ 99:2281)

755   **WILSON, Willie.** *Up Mountain One Time.* **Gr. 4–7.**

A young shantytown-dwelling mongoose named Viggo decides to search for a better life in the bush country that his late mother longingly described to him.

Illus. by Karen Bertrand, Orchard, 1987, 133 pp., o.p.

(BBC:216; BL 84:154, 1442; CCBB 41:40; KR 55:1076; SLJ Sept 1987 p. 184)

WOOD, Douglas. *Old Turtle.* See Chapter 1, Allegorical Fantasy and Literary Fairy Tales.

WOOD, James Playsted. *An Elephant in the Family.* See Chapter 6, Humorous Fantasy.

WRIGGINS, Sally. *The White Monkey King: A Chinese Fable.* See Chapter 5B, Myth Fantasy.

756   **WRIGHTSON, (Alice) Patricia (Furlonger).** *Moon–Dark.* **Gr. 5–8. (Orig. Aus-**
✓   **tralian pub. 1987.)**

One dark night, a dog named Blue and the other animal inhabitants of a remote section of Australia call on Keeting, an ancient moon spirit, to save their territory from encroaching human beings who have upset the natural balance.

Illus. by Noela Young, Macmillan, 1988, 163 pp. (0-689-50451-9)

(BBC:216; CCBB 41:194; Ch&Bks:293; HB 64:637; KR 56:462; SLJ Apr 1988 p. 106; Suth 4:447; VOYA 11:92)

757   **WYNDHAM, Lee (pseud. of Jane Andrews Hyndman).** *Mourka, the Mighty Cat.* **Gr. 2–4.**

Mourka the village cat pretends to be the mighty ruler of the forest.

Illus. by Charles Mikolaycak, Parents, 1969, 41 pp., o.p.

(HB 45:529; LJ 95:1192)

758   **YEP, Laurence M(ichael).** *The Curse of the Squirrel.* **Gr. 2–4.**

Farmer Johnson's hunting dog, Howie, is cursed by Shag, the monster squirrel, into becoming a squirrel by night so that he can understand how it feels to be "treed like a possum."

Illus. by Dirk Zimmer, Random, 1987, 45 pp., LB(0-394-98200-2), pap. (0-394-88200-8)

(BL 84:325; CCBB 41:60, KR 55:1582; SLJ Dec 1987 p. 76)

759   **YOLEN (Stemple), Jane H(yatt).** *The Acorn Quest.* **Gr. 3–5.**
✓   King Earthor Owl of Woodland sends his wizard Squirrelin and his knights, a groundhog, a turtle, a rabbit, and a mouse, on a quest for the Golden Acorn, in this takeoff on an Arthurian legend.

Illus. by Susanna Natti, Crowell, 1981, 57 pp., o.p.

(BBC:216; BL 78:444; HB 58:48; KR 49:1346; SLJ Dec 1981 p. 59)

760 **YOLEN (Stemple), Jane H(yatt).** *Hobo Toad and the Motorcycle Gang.* **Gr. 3–5.**

Hobo and his gang foil an attempted bank robbery and kidnapping.

Illus. by Emily McCully, Collins + World, 1970, 62 pp., o.p.

(BL 67:149; HB 46:391; KR 38:455; LJ 95:3056)

761 **YOLEN (Stemple), Jane H(yatt).** *Piggins.* **Gr. K–3.**

✓✓ Mr. and Mrs. Reynard's butler, Piggins, solves the mystery of Mrs. Reynard's stolen diamond lavaliere. The sequels are *Picnic with Piggins* (1988), and *Piggins and the Royal Wedding* (1989).

Illus. by Jane Dyer, Harcourt, 1987, 32 pp. (0-15-261685-1), 1992, pap. (0-15-261686-1)

(BL 83:1132; CC:741; CCBB 40:160; HB 63:459; KR 55:304; SLJ Apr 1987 p. 91; Suth 4:449)

ZARING, Jane T(homas). *The Return of the Dragon.* See Chapter 1, Allegorical Fantasy and Literary Fairy Tales.

ZIMNIK, Reiner. *The Bear and the People.* See Chapter 1, Allegorical Fantasy and Literary Fairy Tales.

762 **ZINDEL, Paul.** *Let Me Hear You Whisper: A Play.* **Gr. 7 up.**

A short but moving play about a laboratory cleaning woman who discovers that the experimental subject, a dolphin, can talk, and tries to save him from being killed.

Illus. by Stephen Gammell, Harper, 1974, 44 pp., o.p.

(CCBB 27:188; KR 42:124; LJ 99:1234)

763 *Zoo 2000: Twelve Stories of Science Fiction and Fantasy Beasts.* **Ed. by Jane H. Yolen. Gr. 6–9.**

A collection of twelve science fiction and fantasy tales about animals of the future, including James Thurber's "Interview with a Lemming," and André Norton's "All Cats Are Grey."

Seabury, 1973, 224 pp., o.p.

(BL 70:538, 546; CCBB 27:167; KR 41:1162; LJ 98:3715)

3
Fantasy Collections

Collections of fantastic tales in the form of short stories are listed in this chapter. These tales often resemble traditional folktales in style.

764 *After the King: Stories in Honor of J. R. R. Tolkien.* **Ed. by Martin H. Greenberg. Gr. 10 up.**

An anthology of fantasy stories written in honor of the 100th anniversary of J. R. R. Tolkien's birth by 19 authors, including Jane Yolen, Emma Bull, Judith Tarr, Charles de Lint, Terry Pratchett, and André Norton.

Tor, 1992, 448 pp. (0-312-85175-8), 1993, pap. (0-312-85353-X)

(BL 88:915, 921; KR 59:1503; LJ Dec 1991 p. 203; VOYA 15:171, 16:9)

AHLBERG, Allan. *The Clothes Horse and Other Stories.* See Chapter 6, Humorous Fantasy.

765 **AIKEN, Joan (Delano).** *The Faithless Lollybird.* **Gr. 5–8. (Orig. British pub. ✓ 1977.)**

These thirteen modern fairy tales include stories about a witch, a haunted tower, and a mermaid.

Illus. by Eros Keith, Doubleday, 1978, 255 pp., o.p.

(BL 74:1614; CCBB 31:153; HB 54:281; KR 46:594; SLJ Apr 1978 p. 90; Suth 2:6; TLS 1977 p. 863)

766 **AIKEN, Joan (Delano).** *The Far Forests: Tales of Romance, Fantasy and Suspense.* **Gr. 8 up. (Orig. British pub. 1977.)**

Fifteen sophisticated tales touched with humor, magic, and the macabre, including "As Gay as Cheese," "A Taxi to Solitude," "Furry Night," and "The Cold Flame."

Viking, 1977, 154 pp., o.p.

(CCBB 31:25; HB 53:536; KR 45:233, 363; LJ 102:827; Suth 2:6)

AIKEN, Joan (Delano). *A Foot in the Grave.* See Chapter 4, Ghost Fantasy.

767 **AIKEN, Joan (Delano).** *Give Yourself a Fright: Thirteen Stories of the Supernatural.* **Gr. 7 up. (Stories originally published in England in 1980, 1984, 1985, 1987, and 1988.)**

Thirteen tales of ghosts, magic, the devil, and the macabre.

Delacorte, 1989, 192 pp. (0-440-50120-2)

(CCBB 42:141; HB 65:213; JHC:428; KR 57:119; SLJ Apr 1989 p. 116; VOYA 12:113)

768 **AIKEN, Joan (Delano).** *The Green Flash and Other Tales of Horror, Suspense, and Fantasy.* **Gr. 6–9. (Orig. British pubs. 1957, 1969.)**

Fourteen tales, including "Marmalade Wine," "The Dead Language Master," and "The Windshield Weepers."

Holt, 1971, 163 pp., o.p.

(BL 68:428; HB 48:54; KR 39:1131; LJ 96:4200)

769 **AIKEN, Joan (Delano).** *A Harp of Fishbones and Other Stories.* **Gr. 5 up. (Orig. British pub. 1972.)**

Thirteen fantasy tales, including "The Boy with a Wolf's Foot," "The Lost Five Minutes," and "The Prince of Darkness."

Puffin, 1975, pap., o.p.

(TLS 1972 p. 474; Tymn:39)

770 **AIKEN, Joan (Delano).** *The Last Slice of Rainbow: And Other Stories.* **Gr. 3–6.**
✓ **(Orig. British pub. 1985.)**

Nine short fantasy stories, including one about a boy who wants to keep a rainbow.

Illus. by Alix Berenzy, Harper, 1988, 144 pp. (0-06-020043-X), pap., 1989 (0-06-440334-3)

(BBC:196; BL 84:1338; CCBB 41:129; KR 56:613; SLJ May 1988 p. 94; TLS 1985 p. 1360)

771 **AIKEN, Joan (Delano).** *A Necklace of Raindrops and Other Stories.* **Gr. 3–5. (Orig. British pub. 1968.)**

Eight stories including "There's Some Sky in This Pie," "The Elves in the Shelves," and "The Patchwork Quilt."

Illus. by Jan Pienkowski, Doubleday, 1969, 96 pp., o.p.

(CCBB 23:37; HB 45:530; KR 37:631; LJ 95:238)

772 **AIKEN, Joan (Delano).** *Not What You Expected: A Collection of Short Stories.*
✓ **Gr. 6–9. (Orig. British pub. 1974.)**

Twenty-one tales, including "The Boy with a Wolf's Foot," "The Lost Five Minutes," and "The Third Wish." These stories were published in Great Britain in three collections: *A Small Pinch of Weather* (1969), *A Harp of Fishbones* (1971), and *All and More* (1971).

Doubleday, 1974, 320 pp., o.p.

(BL 71:377; CCBB 28:73; Ch&Bks:282; HB 51:151; KR 42:1258; SLJ Jan 1975 p. 42; TLS 1969 p. 689)

773 **AIKEN, Joan (Delano).** *Past Eight O'Clock: Goodnight Stories.* **Gr. 3–5. (Orig. British pub. 1986.)**

Eight magical tales about dreams, sleep, and the night.

Illus. by Jan Pienkowski, Viking, 1987, 128 pp., ,o.p.; Puffin, 1991, pap. (0-14-032355-4)

(CC:577; CCBB 40:201; SLJ Oct 1987 p. 124)

774 **AIKEN, Joan (Delano).** *Smoke from Cromwell's Time and Other Stories.* **Gr. 4–7**
✓ **(Orig. British pubs. 1959, 1966, 1969.)**

Fourteen tales, including "The King Who Stood All Night," "The Wolves and the Mermaids," and "The Parrot Pirate Princess."

Doubleday, 1970, 163 pp., o.p.

(BL 67:142; CCBB 24:37; HB 46:476; KR 38:742; LJ 95:3044)

AIKEN, Joan (Delano). *A Touch of Chill: Tales for Sleepless Nights.* See Chapter 4, Ghost Fantasy.

AIKEN, Joan (Delano). *Up the Chimney Down and Other Stories.* See Chapter 6, Humorous Fantasy.

AIKEN, Joan (Delano). *A Whisper in the Night: Tales of Terror and Suspense.* See Chapter 4, Ghost Fantasy.

775 **AINSWORTH (Gilbert), Ruth (Gallard).** *The Bear Who Liked Hugging People and Other Stories.* **Gr. K–4. (Orig. British pub. 1976.)**

Thirteen stories about witches, animals, and magic.

Illus. by Antony Maitland, Crane Russak, 1978, 102 pp., o.p.

(BL 74:1487; SLJ Oct 1978 p. 141)

AINSWORTH (Gilbert), Ruth (Gallard). *The Phantom Carousel and Other Ghostly Tales.* See Chapter 4, Ghost Fantasy.

776 *The Air of Mars; and Other Stories of Time and Space.* **Ed. by Mirra Ginsburg.**
✓ **Gr. 6–9. (Orig. Soviet Union pub. 1964–1972.)**

Nine fantasy and science fiction tales from the former Soviet Union, including one about a woman whose husband turns into a garden.

Trans. by the editor, Macmillan, 1976, 141 pp., o.p.

(BL 72:1592; HB 52:410; KR 44:204; SLJ Apr 1976 p. 74)

ALCOCK, Vivien (Dolores). *Ghostly Companions: A Feast of Chilling Tales.* See Chapter 4, Ghost Fantasy.

777 **ALDEN, Raymond Macdonald.** *Why the Chimes Rang and Other Stories.* **Gr. 3–6. (Orig. pub. 1908.)**

Eleven tales of kings, knights, giants, and magic.

Illus. by Rafaello Busoni, Bobbs-Merrill, 1954, 146 pp., o.p.

(BL 42:170; LJ 80:188; Mahony 2:269)

778 **ALDISS, Brian W(ilson).** *Seasons in Flight.* **Gr. 10 up.**

Ten tales about the impact of modern cultures on ancient ones, including "The Other Side of the Lake," "The Gods in Flight," and "Incident in a Far Country." Some stories are related to Aldiss's Helliconia trilogy: *Helliconia Spring* (1982), *Helliconia Summer* (1983), and *Helliconia Winter* (1985).

Atheneum, 1986, 157 pp., o.p.

(82:733, 750; KR 53:1293)

Alternative Histories: Eleven Stories of the World as It Might Have Been. **Ed. by Charles G. Waugh and Martin H. Greenberg.** See Chapter 5A, Alternate Worlds or Histories.

Amazons! **Ed. by Jessica Amanda Salmonson.** See Chapter 5A, Alternate Worlds or Histories.

779   **ANDERSEN, Hans Christian.** *Fairy Tales.* **Gr. 3 up. (Orig. Danish pub.**
✓✓   **1835–1845; orig. English trans. by Mary Howitt, entitled:** *Wonderful Stories for*
     Children, **1846.)**

Andersen was the first great writer of original fantasy for children, and his tales are still among the best loved of all children's stories. There have been numerous editions of Andersen's stories published in English, under various titles. These include the following, listed first in alphabetical order, then by publication date:

Andersen's Fairy Tales. Illus. by W. Heath Robinson, Houghton, 1931, 355 pp., o.p.

Andersen's Fairy Tales. Putnam, 1958, 352 pp., o.p.

Andersen's Fairy Tales. Wanderer, 1983, 300 pp., o.p.

✓✓   *Ardizzone's Hans Andersen: Fourteen Classic Tales.* Illus. by Edward Ardizzone, Atheneum, 1979, ©1978, 191 pp., o.p.

The Complete Fairy Tales and Stories. Doubleday, 1974, 1101 pp., o.p.

✓✓   *Dulac's The Snow Queen and Other Stories from Hans Andersen.* Illus. by Edmund Dulac, Doubleday, 1976, 143 pp. (0-385-11678-0)

Eighty Fairy Tales. Pantheon, 1983, pap., 394 pp. (0-394-71055-X)

Fairy Tales. Illus. by W. Heath Robinson, Holt, 1913, 288 pp., o.p.

✓   *Fairy Tales.* Illus. by Kay Nielsen, Garden City, 1924, 1932, o.p.; Viking/Metropolitan Museum of Art, 1981, 155 pp., o.p.

✓   *Fairy Tales.* Illus. by Arthur Rackham, McKay, 1932, 287 pp., o.p.

Fairy Tales. Illus. by Fritz Kredel, Heritage, 1942, 297 pp., o.p.

Fairy Tales. Illus. by Vilhelm Pedersen, Scribner, 1950, 394 pp., o.p.

Fairy Tales from Hans Christian Andersen. (Orig. British pub. 1901.) Illus. by Thomas H. Robinson, Charles Robinson, and W. Heath Robinson, Dutton, 1903, 1930, o.p.

Fairy Tales from Hans Christian Andersen. Adapt. by Russell Ash and Bernard Higton, illus. by nine artists, Chronicle, 1992, 128 pp. (0-8118-0230-2)

Favorite Tales of Hans Andersen. Illus. by Robin Jacques, Faber, 1986 (orig. British pub., 1978), 168 pp., o.p.

✓✓   *Hans Andersen: His Classic Fairy Tales.* Illus. by Michael Foreman, Doubleday, 1978, 196 pp. (0-395-13364-2)

Hans Andersen's Fairy Tales. Illus. by Maria L. Kirk and E. A. Lehmann, Lippincott, 1911, 219 pp., o.p.

Hans Andersen's Fairy Tales. Illus. by W. Heath Robinson, Doran, 1924, 319 pp., o.p.

Hans Andersen's Fairy Tales. Illus. by Ernest H. Shepard, Walck, 1962, © 1959, 327 pp., o.p.

Hans Andersen's Fairy Tales. Retold by E. Jean Robertson and Caroline Peachey, illus. by Shirley Hughes, Schocken, 1979 (repr. of 1961 Scottish ed.), 264 pp. pap., o.p.

Hans Andersen's Fairy Tales. Illus. by Sumiko, Schocken, 1980, 96 pp., o.p.

Hans Andersen's Fairy Tales. Illus. by Philip Gough, Penguin, 1981, pap., 176 pp., o.p.

Hans Andersen's Fairy Tales: A Selection. Illus. by Lorenz Frolich and Vilhelm Pedersen, Oxford, pap., 493 pp. (0-19-281699-3)

✓ *Hans Christian Andersen Fairy Tales.* Trans. by Anthea Bell, illus. by Lisbeth Zwerger, Picture Book, 1992, 68 pp. (0-88708-182-7)

It's Perfectly True, and Other Stories. Illus. by Richard Bennett, Harcourt, 1938, 305 pp., o.p.

The Mermaid, and Other Fairy Tales. Illus. by Maxwell Armfield, Dutton, 1914, 1916, 127 pp., o.p.

✓✓ *Michael Hague's Favorite Hans Christian Andersen Fairy Tales.* Illus. by Michael Hague, Holt, 1981, 176 pp. (0-8050-0659-1)

✓✓ *Seven Tales.* Adapt. by Eva Le Gallienne, illus. by Maurice Sendak, Harper, 1959, 127 pp., LB(0-06-023790-2), pap., 1991 (0-06-443172-X)

Stories from Hans Andersen. Illus. by Edmund Dulac, Hodder, 1911, 1922; Doran, 1923, 1927, 1930, 250 pp., o.p.

The Stories of Hans Andersen. Illus. by Robin Lawrie, Silver, 1985, 80 pp., o.p.

Tales and Stories by Hans Christian Andersen. University of Washington Press, 1982, 316 pp., o.p., pap. (0-295-95936-3)

Twelve Tales. Adapt. and illus. by Erik Blegvad, Macmillan, 1994, 96 pp. (0-689-50584-1)

(BL 20:109, 233, 28:110, 396, 34:303, 40:324, 47:241, 55:512, 58:797, 70:738, 73:1159, 74:1730, 75:1216, 78:241, 493, 89:745, 91:328; Bookshelf 1933 p. 5; CC:577; CCBB 27:122, 35:101; Ch&Bks:250, 282; HB 1[Nov 1924]:6; 7:187–189, 9:152, 10:37, 13:25, 14:153, 20:46, 164, 27:93, 35:297, 50:269, 55:408, 58:539, 67:223; HGB 2[July–Dec 1990]:64, 4[Spring 1993]:63, 78; KR 27:264, 30:111, 42:12, 46:879, 47:519, 49:1411, 60:1499, 62:1263; LJ 58:1050, 63:284, 69:72, 76:530, 84:1692, 87:2409, 99:568; Mahony 2:271; SLJ Feb 1977 p. 60, Nov 1978 p. 54, Apr 1979 p. 52, Dec 1981 p. 59, Feb 1993 p. 92; SHC:733; Suth 2:14; Suth 3:15, 16; TLS Dec 1, 1961 p. xii, 1974 p. 1377, 1981 p. 1360)

780 ANDERSON, Poul (William). *Fantasy.* **Gr. 10 up.**

A collection of Anderson's short fantasy fiction and essays, plus an introductory essay on Anderson's work by Sandra Miesel.

Tor, 1981, pap., 334 pp., o.p.

(BL 78:425, 434; LJ 106:2409; SLJ Mar 1982 p. 162)

ANDERSON, Poul (William). *The Time Patrol.* See Chapter 8, Time Travel Fantasy.

781 *Another World; Adventures in Otherness: A Science Fiction Anthology.* Ed. by Gardner Dozois. Gr. 7–12.

Eleven tales of science fiction and fantasy written by Gene Wolfe, Ursula K. Le Guin, and Robert Silverberg, among others.

Follett, 1977, 282 pp., o.p.

(BL 73:1568; SLJ Oct 1977 p. 122)

782 ANTHONY, Piers (pseud. of Piers A. D. Jacob). *Alien Plot.* **Gr. 10 up.**

Eighteen fantasy and science fiction stories plus an essay.

Tor, 1992, 256 pp. (0-312-85394-7), 1993, pap. (0-8125-3072-1)

(BL 89:129, 133; KR 60:1094; LJ Oct 15 19921 p. 104; SLJ Apr 1993 p. 149)

The April Witch and Other Strange Tales. **Ed. by Barbara Ireson.** See Chapter 4, Ghost Fantasy.

783 *Arabesques 2.* **Ed. by Susan Shwartz. Gr. 10 up.**

✓ Eighteen fantasy stories with Arabian settings and themes, written by Judith Tarr, Diana Paxson, Tanith Lee, and others. This is a companion volume to *Arabesques: More Tales of the Arabian Nights* (1988).

Avon, 1989, pap., 384 pp. (0-380-75570-X)

(BL 85:1783; Kliatt Sept 1989, p. 22; LJ June 15, 1989 p. 83; VOYA 12:218)

ASIMOV, Isaac. *Azazel.* See Chapter 7, Magic Adventure Fantasy.

784 *Atlantis.* **Ed. by Isaac Asimov, Martin H. Greenberg, and Charles G. Waugh. Gr. 7 up.**

Short stories about the legend of Atlantis written during the past 50 years by Ursula K. Le Guin, Manly Wade Wellman, L. Sprague de Camp, and others.

NAL, 1988, pap., 349 pp., o.p.

(BL 84:541, 555; VOYA 11:137)

785 **AULAIRE, Ingri Mortenson d', and AULAIRE, Edgar Parin d'.** *D'Aulaires'*
✓ *Trolls.* **Gr. 3–5.**

In the mountains, forests, and waterways of Norway live bands of little creatures called trolls, gnomes, and hulder-people.

Illus. by the authors, Doubleday, 1972, 62 pp., o.p.

(BL 69:404; CCBB 26:37; HB 48:592; KR 40:1415; Suth:22)

786 **AULNOY, Marie Catherine Jumelle de Berneville, Comtesse d'.** *The Children's Fairy Land.* **Gr. 4–6.**

Eight illustrated fairy tales.

Illus. by Harriet Mead Olcott, Holt, 1919, 189 pp., o.p.

(BL 16:62; Bookshelf 1928 p. 10; LJ 45:980)

787 **AULNOY, Marie Catherine Jumelle de Berneville, Comtesse d'.** *The White Cat*
✓ *and Other Old French Fairy Tales.* **Gr. 3–5. (Orig. pub. in France; orig. British title:** *Fairy Tales by the Countess D'Aulnoy,* **1855; orig. U.S. title:** *D'Aulnoy's Fairy Tales,* **1858; McKay, 1923, o.p.; orig. U.S. pub. with this title, 1928.)**

A collection of old French folk tales, embroidered and adapted to take place in a palace, including "The Blue-Bird," "The Hind in the Wood," and "The Yellow Dwarf."

Adapt. by Rachel Field, illus. by Elizabeth MacKinstry, Macmillan, 1967, 150 pp., o.p.

(BL 20:303, 25:253; HB 4[Aug 1928]:11; LJ 53:811, 93:866; Mahony 2:195–197; Moore:290, 434.)

BABBITT, Natalie (Zane Moore). *The Devil's Storybook.* See Chapter 6, Humorous Fantasy.

BACON, Peggy. *The Lion-Hearted Kitten and Other Stories.* See Chapter 2, Animal Fantasy.

BACON, Peggy. *Mercy and the Mouse and Other Stories.* See Chapter 2, Animal Fantasy.

788 **BAILEY, Margery.** *The Little Man with One Shoe.* **Gr. 3–6.**

Six magical fairy tales told by a fairy shoemaker.

Illus. by Alice Bolan Preston, Little, 1921, 227 pp., o.p.

(BL 18:88; Bookshelf 1923–1924 p. 7; LJ 47:869; Mahony 2:271)

789 **BAILEY, Margery.** *Seven Peas in the Pod.* **Gr. 3–6.**

Seven stories; one for each day of the week.

Illus. by Alice Bolan Preston, Little, 1919, 201 pp., o.p.

(BL 16:137; Bookshelf 1923–1924 p. 7; LJ 45:980; Mahony 1:39; Mahony 2:272)

790 **BAILEY, Margery.** *Whistle for Good Fortune, in Which It Is Shown How Six from Six Makes Six and One to Carry, with Other Riddles Here and There Along the Way.* **Gr. 4–6.**

Six original fairy tales told in folktale-style.

Illus. by Alice Bolan Preston, Little, 1940, 237 pp., o.p.

(BL 36:308; LJ 65:260)

791 **BAKER, Margaret.** *Fifteen Tales for Lively Children.* **Gr. 2–4. (Orig. British pub. 1938. New British title:** *The Goose Feather Gown,* **1982.)**

This collection of humorous tales is a companion volume to *Tell Them Again Tales* (1934).

Illus. by Mary Baker, Dodd, 1939, 144 pp., o.p.

(BL 35:292; LJ 64:380; TLS 1938 p. 789)

792 **BAKER, Margaret.** *Tell Them Again Tales.* **Gr. 2–4.**

Eighteen tales about kings, animals, and princesses. *Fifteen Tales for Lively Children* (1939) is a companion volume.

Illus. by Mary Baker, Dodd, 1934, 143 pp., o.p.

(BL 31:67; Bookshelf 1934–1935 p. 4; HB 10:296; LJ 60:403; Mahony 3:85)

793 *A Baker's Dozen: Thirteen Stories to Tell and to Read Aloud.* **Comp. by Mary Gould Davis. Gr. 4–6.**

A collection that includes stories by Laurence Housman, Carl Sandburg, Mary E. Wilkins, Frank R. Stockton, and Gottfried Keller.

Illus. by Emma Brock, Harcourt, 1930, 207 pp., o.p.

(BL 27:108; HB 6:329; LJ 55:736; Mahony 3:158)

794 **BAUM, L(yman) Frank.** *The Surprising Adventures of the Magical Monarch of Mo and His People.* **Gr. 3–6. (Orig. titles:** *A New Wonderland,* **Russell, 1900;** *The Magical Monarch of Mo,* **Bobbs-Merrill, 1901, 1947.)**

Fourteen stories of princes, giants, wizards, and a dragon, set in the magical land of Mo where anything one wants can be picked from a tree.

Dover, 1968, pap. (0-486-21892-9); Amereon, n.d. (0-88411-771-5); Peter Smith (entitled *The Magical Monarch of Mo*), n.d. (0-8446-1609-5)

(LJ 72:1620; TLS 1969 p. 352)

795 **BEAGLE, Peter S(oyer).** *The Fantasy Worlds of Peter S. Beagle.* **Gr. 10 up.**

This collection includes *A Fine and Private Place* and *The Last Unicorn,* plus two short stories, "Lila the Werewolf" and "Come, Lady Death."

Viking, 1978, 430 pp., o.p.

(BL 75:598, 606; KR 46:977)

BENNETT, John. *The Pigtail of Ah Lee Ben Loo, with Seventeen Other Laughable Tales.* See Chapter 6, Humorous Fantasy.

BENSON, E. F. *The Collected Ghost Stories of E. F. Benson.* See Chapter 4, Ghost Fantasy.

796 *Bestiary!* **Ed. by Jack Dann and Gardner Dozois. Gr. 10 up.**

An anthology of tales about dragons, giants, unicorns and other mythical creatures, written by Tanith Lee, Manly Wade Wellman, Gene Wolfe, and others. This is a companion volume to *Unicorns!* (1982) and *Magicats!* (1984).

Ace, 1985, pap., 304 pp., o.p.

(BBS:55; BL 82:195, 216)

797 **BESTON, Henry B. (pseud. of Henry Beston Sheahan).** *Henry Beston's Fairy*
✓ *Tales.* **Gr. 4–6.**

Contains many of the stories from *The Firelight Fairy Book* (1919) and *The Starlight Wonder Book* (1923) including "The Seller of Dreams," "The Lost Half-Hour," and "The City Under the Sea."

Illus. by Fritz Kredel, Aladdin, 1952, 353 pp., o.p.

(BL 16:174, 20:62, 37:364, 49:76; Bookshelf 1932 p. 8; HB 28:311, 420; KR 20:546; LJ 77:1820; Mahony 1:39; Mahony 2:273; Moore:426)

Beware! Beware! Chilling Tales. **Ed. by Jean Richardson.** See Chapter 4, Ghost Fantasy.

798 **BIANCO, Margery (Winifred) Williams.** *A Street of Little Shops.* **Gr. 3–5.**

Seven tales about a street of shops in a small country town, including one about a Cigar Store Indian who runs away.

Illus. by Grace Paull, Doubleday, 1932, o.p.; Gregg, 1981, 111 pp., o.p.

(Bookshelf 1932 p. 10; HB 21:191; LJ 58:899)

799 *Black Water: The Book of Fantastic Literature.* **Ed. by Alberto Manguelo. Gr. 10 up. (Orig. Canadian pub. 1983.)**

Seventy-two stories of fantasy and horror drawn primarily from England, the United States, and Latin America, whose authors include Henry James, D. H. Lawrence, and Tennessee Williams.

Crown, 1984, pap., 992 pp. (0-517-55269-8)

(HB 60:634; LJ 109:824; VOYA 7:262)

800 *The Blue Rose; a Collection of Stories for Girls.* **Ed. by Eulalie Steinmetz Ross.**
✓ **Gr. 4–6.**

Stories by Hans Christian Andersen, Laurence Housman, Howard Pyle, Walter de la Mare, Eleanor Farjeon, George MacDonald, and Ruth Sawyer.

Illus. by Enrico Arno, Harcourt, 1966, 186 pp., o.p.

(BL 63:186; HB 42:566; KR 34:106; LJ 91:4342; TLS 1966 p. 1092)

801 **BOMANS, Godfried (Jan Arnold).** *The Wily Witch and All the Other Fairy Tales*
✓ *and Fables.* **Gr. 3–5. (An earlier Dutch ed. of selected tales pub. 1969; this ed. pub. 1975.)**

Forty-five fairy tales, including "The Rich Blackberry Picker," "The Princess with Freckles," and "The Curse." Twenty-four of these tales were originally published in *The Wily Wizard and the Wicked Witch and Other Weird Stories* (Watts 1969).

Trans. by Patricia Crampton, illus. by Wouter Googendijk, Stemmer, 1977, 205 pp., o.p.
(BL 73:1726; CCBB 23:156, 31:6; LJ 95:777; SLJ Sept 1977 p. 121; Suth 2:51; TLS 1969 p. 3521)

***Boo! Stories to Make You Jump.* Compiled by Laura Cecil.** See Chapter 4, Ghost Fantasy.

802 **BORGES, Jorge Luis, with GUERRERO, Margarita.** *The Book of Imaginary Beings.* **Gr. 10 up. (Orig. Mexican pub. 1957.)**

A treasury of carefully researched descriptions of one hundred and twenty legendary creatures from all over the world.

Rev., enlarged, and trans. by Norman Thomas di Giovanni in collaboration with the author, Dutton, 1969, 256 pp., o.p.
(HB 46:186; LJ 94:4526; TLS 1971 p. 149)

803 **BOUCHER, Anthony (pseud. of William Anthony Parker White).** *The Compleat Werewolf; and Other Stories of Fantasy and Science Fiction.* **Gr. 10 up.**

Ten short stories and novellas about a werewolf, a demon, ogres, and a ghost.

Simon, 1969, 256 pp., o.p.
(BL 66:823, 837; KR 37:955; LJ 94:3665, 3839, 95:1913)

804 **BOURLIAGUET, Léonce.** *The Giant Who Drank from His Shoe and Other Stories.* **Gr. 4–6. (Orig. pub. in France.)**

Humorous tales about French villagers, giants, and animals.

Trans. by John Buchanan Brown, illus. by Gerald Rose, Abelard-Schuman, 1966, 93 pp., o.p.
(KR 34:1979; LJ 91:3531; TLS 1965 p. 1140)

805 **BOURLIAGUET, Léonce.** *A Sword to Slice Through Mountains and Other Stories.* **Gr. 3–5. (Orig. pub. in France.)**

Tales about two smiths who can make a sword capable of slicing mountains in half, but fail to win a princess; a stutterer who gets his revenge on some unkind villagers; and a scarecrow who wants to be rewarded with a medal.

Trans. by John Buchanan-Brown, illus. by Gerald Rose, Abelard-Schuman, 1967, 96 pp., o.p.
(KR 36:117; LJ 93:2732)

806 **BRADBURY, Ray (Douglas).** *Dinosaur Tales.* **Gr. 10 up.**

A collection of Bradbury's stories and poems about dinosaurs, including "Tyrannosaurous Rex," "The Fog Horn," and "Besides a Dinosaur, Whatta Ya Wanna Be When You Grow Up?"

Illus. by Kenneth Smith, William Stout, Steranko, Moebius, Gahan Wilson, and David Wiesner, Bantam, 1983, pap., 144 pp., o.p.
(Kliatt 17[Fall 1983]:21; KR 51:339)

807 **BRADBURY, Ray (Douglas).** *The Illustrated Man.* **Gr. 9 up.**

Eighteen short stories of science fiction, the supernatural, and fantasy.

Doubleday, 1951 (0-553-27449-X); Bantam, 1969, 1983, pap., 251 pp. (0-553-25483-9)
(BBS:53; BL 47:255; HB 27:197; KR 18:740)

808 **BRADBURY, Ray (Douglas).** *A Medicine for Melancholy.* **Gr. 10 up.**

Twenty-two short stories, ranging from fantasy to science fiction and horror.

Doubleday, 1959, 240 pp., o.p.; Bantam, 1990, pap. (0-553-28638-2)
(BBS:53; BL 55:394; KR 26:883)

809   BRADBURY, Ray (Douglas). *R Is for Rocket.* **Gr. 8 up.**

Seventeen science fiction and science-fantasy short stories originally published in magazines, including stories about sea serpents and time travel.

Doubleday, 1962, 233 pp., o.p.; Bantam, 1969, pap. (0-553-25040-X)
(BBS:53; BL 59:488; LJ 88:350)

810   BRADBURY, Ray (Douglas). *The Stories of Ray Bradbury.* **Gr. 10 up.**

✓   One hundred of Bradbury's science fiction, fantasy, horror, and midwestern short stories.

Knopf, 1980, 884 pp. (0-394-51335-5)
(BL 77:4, 7; KR 48:1120; LJ 105:1883; SLJ Dec 1980 p. 79; VOYA 4[June 1981]:36)

811   BRADBURY, Ray (Douglas). *The Toynbee Convector.* **Gr. 10 up.**

A collection of 23 fantasy, horror, and science fiction stories, including a number involving ghosts.

Knopf, 1988, 295 pp. (0-394-54703-9); Turner, 1992 (1-878685-15-6); Bantam, 1989, pap. (0-553-27957-2)
(BBS:53; BL 84:1458; KR 56:573; LJ June 15, 1988 p. 71; VOYA 11:246)

BRÖGER, Achim. *Bruno.* See Chapter 6, Humorous Fantasy.

812   BROOKE, William J. *A Telling of the Tales: Five Stories.* **Gr. 3–6.**

✓   Five well-known tales expanded and retold from new points of view: "Sleeping Beauty," "Paul Bunyan," "Cinderella," "John Henry," and "Jack and the Beanstalk." This is a companion volume to *Untold Tales* (1992).

Illus. by Richard Egielski, Harper, 1990, 32 pp. (0-06-020688-8), 1993, pap. (0-06-440467-6)
(BL 86:1699; CCBB 43:208; HBG 1[Jan 1990]:242; KR 58:496; SLJ June 1990 p. 116; Suth 4:43)

BROWNE, Frances. *Granny's Wonderful Chair and Its Tales of Fairy Times.* See Chapter 7, Magic Adventure Fantasy.

BUCHAN, John. *The Watcher by the Threshold and Other Tales.* See Chapter 5B, Myth Fantasy.

BURGESS, Thornton W(aldo). *Old Mother West Wind.* See Chapter 2, Animal Fantasy.

The Camelot Chronicles. **Ed. by Mike Ashley.** See Chapter 5B, Myth Fantasy.

813   CANFIELD, Dorothy (pseud. of Dorothea Frances [Canfield] Fisher). *Made-to-Order Stories.* **Gr. 4–6.**

The author's ten-year-old son chose the elements used in these humorous stories.

Illus. by Dorothy P. Lathrop, Harcourt, 1925, 263 pp., o.p.
(BL 22:75; Bookshelf 1932 p. 12; HB 2[Nov 1925]:21, 14:208; LJ 51:836; Mahony 2:606)

814   CAPEK, Karel. *Nine Fairy Tales and One More Thrown In for Good Measure.* **Gr. 5–9. (Orig. Czech pub. 1932.)**

Ten modern tales containing humor, wordplay, mythical creatures, and magic.

Trans. by Dagmar Herrmann, illus. by Josef Capek, Northwestern Univ. Pr., 1990, 180 pp. (0-8101-0864-X), 1990, pap. (0-8101-0865-8)
(BL 86:2166, 2170; Kliatt Jan 1991 p. 25; TLS 1990 p. 1036)

815   **CARD, Orson Scott.** *Maps in a Mirror: The Short Fiction of Orson Scott Card.* **Gr. 10 up.**

Forty-six fantasy, science fiction, and horror stories by this well-known writer.

Tor, 1990, 512 pp., o.p., 1993, pap. (0-8125-2367-9)

(BL 87:143, 148; LJ Nov 15, 1990 p. 95; VOYA 14:40, 15:10)

816   **CASSERLEY, Anne Thomasine.** *Michael of Ireland.* **Gr. 4–6. (Orig. British pub. 1926.)**

The animals tell Michael stories about the fairy people.

Illus. by the author, Harper, 1927, 139 pp., o.p.

(BL 24:124; Bookshelf 1932 p. 8; HB 3[Nov 1927]:9–10; LJ 53:484, 1033; Mahony 2:132)

817   **CASSERLEY, Anne Thomasine.** *The Whins on Knockattan.* **Gr. 2–4.**

Pandeen and his grandmother share the whin-covered hillside of Knockattan with Little Black Lamb and Shaughran the red fox.

Illus. by the author, Harper, 1928, 178 pp., o.p.

(BL 25:215; Bookshelf 1929 p. 11; HB 4[Nov 1928]:30–32; Mahony 2:133; TLS 1929 p. 475)

818   *Catfantastic: Nine Lives and Fifteen Tales.* **Ed. by André Norton and Martin H. Greenberg. Gr. 10 up.**

Fantasy and science fiction stories about cats, whose authors include Clare Bell, Elizabeth H. Boyer, Mercedes Lackey, and Ardath Mayhar. *Catfantastic II* (1991) and *Catfantastic III* (1994) are companion volumes.

DAW, 1989, pap., 320 pp. (0-88677-355-5)

(BL 85:1873, 1891; VOYA 12:370)

819   *A Cavalcade of Dragons* **(British title:** *The Hamish Hamilton Book of Dragons,*
✓   **1970). Ed. by Roger (Gilbert) Lancelyn Green. Gr. 4–7.**

Folktales, fantasy, and poetry about dragons, including "The Lady Dragonissa" by Andrew Lang, "The Fiery Dragon" by E. Nesbit, "The Hoard" by J. R. R. Tolkien, and "The Dragon Speaks" by C. S. Lewis.

Illus. by Krystyna Turska, Walck, 1970, 256 pp., o.p.

(BL 68:108; HB 47:283; Kies:209; KR 39:297; LJ 96:2130; TLS 1971 p. 388)

820   *A Cavalcade of Goblins* **(British title:** *The Hamish Hamilton Book of Goblins***).**
✓   **Ed. by Alan Garner. Gr. 4–6.**

A collection of myths, folktales, poems, and literary fairy tales about goblins and other fearsome creatures.

Illus. by Krystyna Turska, Walck, 1969, 227 pp., o.p.

(BL 66:129; CCBB 23:58; HB 45:531; LJ 94:4604; Suth:142)

A Cavalcade of Magicians. **Ed. by Roger (Gilbert) Lancelyn Green.** See Chapter 10, Witchcraft and Sorcery Fantasy.

821   *A Cavalcade of Queens* **(British title:** *Hamish Hamilton Book of Queens,* **1965).**
✓   **Ed. by Eleanor Farjeon and William Mayne. Gr. 4–6.**

A companion volume to *A Cavalcade of Kings* (1965), this collection includes stories by Andrew Lang, Nathaniel Hawthorne, and Rudyard Kipling.

Illus. by Victor Ambrus, Walck, 1965, 243 pp., o.p.

(BL 62:875; HB 42:193; LJ 91:1698; TLS 1965 p. 1136)

CHANT, Joy (pseud. of Eileen Joyce Rutter). *The High Kings.* See Chapter 5B, Myth Fantasy.

822 **CHESNUTT, Charles Waddell.** *Conjure Tales.* **Gr. 5–7.**

✓ Seven tales of magic and witchcraft drawn from nineteenth-century African American slave life.

Retold by Ray Shepard, illus. by John Ross and Clare Romano, Dutton, 1973, 99 pp., o.p.

(CCBB 27:126; HB 50:48; KR 41:1035, 1152; LJ 98:3689, 3705; Suth 2:82)

823 **CHRISMAN, Arthur Bowie.** *Shen of the Sea: Chinese Stories for Children.* **Gr.**
✓ **5–8.**

A collection of humorous Chinese fairy tales. John Newbery Medal, 1926. *The Wind That Wouldn't Blow: Stories of the Merry Middle Kingdom for Children and Myself* (1927) is a companion volume.

Illus. by Else Hasselriis, Dutton, 1926, 1968 (redesigned), 221 pp. (0-525-39244-0)

(BL 22:167; Bookshelf 1932 p. 8; Ch&Bks:284; HB 2[Nov 1925]:20; LJ 51:836; Mahony 2:277; TLS 1969 p. 1193

824 **CHRISMAN, Arthur Bowie.** *The Wind That Wouldn't Blow: Stories of the Merry Middle Kingdom for Children and Myself.* **Gr. 5–7.**

A collection of stories that tell how things came to be as they are in China. This is a companion volume to *Shen of the Sea: Chinese Stories for Children* (1926, 1968).

Illus. by Else Hasselriis, Dutton, 1927, 355 pp., o.p.

(BL 24:71; Bookshelf 1927 Suppl. p. 5; HB 3[Nov 1927]:47; Mahony 2:277)

825 *Christmas Forever.* **Ed. by David G. Hartwell. Gr. 10 up.**

Twenty-eight fantasy and science fiction Christmas stories written by Joan Aiken, Charles de Lint, Roger Zelazny, and others.

Tor, 1993, 416 pp. (0-312-85576-1)

(BL 90:258, 262; KR 61:1107; LJ Oct 15, 1993, p. 93)

Christmas Ghosts. **Ed. by Kathryn Cramer and David G. Hartwell.** See Chapter 4, Ghost Fantasy.

Christmas Ghosts: An Anthology. **Ed. by Seon Manley and Gogo Lewis.** See Chapter 4, Ghost Fantasy.

826 **COATSWORTH, Elizabeth (Jane).** *The Snow Parlor and Other Bedtime Stories.* **Gr. 3–4.**

Five tales about talking animals, toys that come to life, a walking pine tree, and a boy who enters a mountain to find out where snow comes from.

Illus. by Charles Robinson, Grosset, 1971, 64 pp., o.p.

(CCBB 25:137; KR 39:1011; LJ 97:2476)

COHEN, Daniel. *Great Ghosts.* See Chapter 4, Ghost Fantasy.

827 **COLUM, Padraic.** *The Big Tree of Bunlahy: Stories of My Own Countryside.* **Gr. 3–5.**

A combination of Irish legends and original tales, including "Our Hen" and "The Three Companions."

Illus. by Jack B. Yeats, Macmillan, 1933, 166 pp., o.p.

(BL 30:87; HB 10:33–36; LJ 59:482; Mahony 3:166)

COLUM, Padraic. *The Boy Who Knew What the Birds Said.* See Chapter 2, Animal Fantasy.

828   **COLUM, Padraic.** *The Fountain of Youth; Stories to Be Told.* **Gr. 4–6.**

Seventeen of Colum's tales chosen from several of his collections as being particularly good for storytelling.

Illus. by Jay Van Everen, Macmillan, 1927, 206 pp., o.p.

(BL 24:251; LJ 53:485)

829   **COLUM, Padraic.** *The Peep-Show Man.* **Gr. 1–3.**

A peep-show man traveling the roads of Ireland tells a little boy three stories, one each for midsummer-day, Halloween, and Easter.

Illus. by Lois Lenski, Macmillan, 1924, 65 pp., o.p.

(BL 21:71; Bookshelf 1924–1925 Suppl. p. 1; Mahony 3:85)

830   **COLUM, Padraic.** *The Stone of Victory and Other Tales.* **Gr. 4–6.**

✓   Irish tales drawn from Colum's previously published collections, including "The Twelve Silly Sisters," "The Wizard Earl," and "Kat Mary Ellen and the Fairies."

Illus. by Judith Gwyn Brown, McGraw-Hill, 1966, 121 pp., o.p.

(BL 63:794; HB 43:200; KR 34:980; LJ 91:5746; Suth:85)

The Crafters. **Ed. by Christopher Stasheff and Bill Fawcett.** See Chapter 10, Witchcraft and Sorcery Fantasy.

831   **CUMMINGS, e(dward) e(stlin).** *Fairy Tales.* **Gr. K–3.**

Four whimsical tales, originally written for the poet's young daughter, including "The House That Ate Mosquito Pie," "The Old Man Who Said "Why,"" "The Elephant & the Butterfly," and "The Little Girl Named I."

Illus. by John Eaton, Harcourt, 1950, 1965, 1975 (0-15-227080-9), 1975, pap. (0-15-629895-3)

(HB 42:52; KR 33:899; LJ 90:4604)

CUNNINGHAM, Julia (Woolfolk). *Candle Tales.* See Chapter 2, Animal Fantasy.

832   **DAHL, Roald.** *The Wonderful Story of Henry Sugar and Six More.* **Gr. 5–9. (Orig. British pub. 1977.)**

Six short stories including two with fantasy elements, plus an autobiographical essay.

Knopf, 1977 (0-394-83604-9); Bantam, 1977, 1979, pap. (0-553-15445-1); Viking, 1988 (c. 1977), 225 pp. (0-14-032874-2)

(BBC:202; KR 45:1148; HB 54:52)

DAVIS, Robert. *Padro Porko: The Gentlemanly Pig.* See Chapter 2, Animal Fantasy.

833   **DE LA MARE, Walter (John).** *Broomsticks and Other Tales.* **Gr. 5–7. (Orig.**
✓   **British pub. 1925.)**

Twelve stories including "The Lovely Myfanwy," "Alice's Godmother," and "Maria-Fly."

Knopf, 1942, 334 pp., o.p.

(BL 22:252; HB 2[Nov 1925]:20, 18:180; LJ 67:892; TLS 1925 p. 797; Tymn:72)

834   **DE LA MARE, Walter (John).** *The Dutch Cheese.* **Gr. 3–5. (Orig. British pub. 1925.)**

Two stories from *Broomsticks and Other Tales* (1925, 1942): "The Dutch Cheese" and "The Lovely Myfanwy."

Illus. by Dorothy P. Lathrop, Knopf, 1931, 75 pp., o.p.

(BL 28:156; HB 7:223; Mahony 3:204)

835   DE LA MARE, Walter (John). *The Lord Fish.* **Gr. 5–7.**

Seven stories: "The Lord Fish," "A Penny a Day," "The Jacket," "Dick and the Beanstalk," "Hodmadod," "The Old Lion," and "Sambo and the Snow Mountains."

Illus. by Rex Whistler, Faber, 1933, 289 pp., o.p.

(HB 10:232; Mahony 3:204)

836   DE LA MARE, Walter (John). *The Magic Jacket and Other Stories.* **Gr. 5–7.**
✓   **(Orig. British pub. 1943.)**

Ten tales of magic, including "The Magic Jacket," "The Riddle," and "Broomsticks."

Illus. by Paul Kennedy, Knopf, 1962, 277 pp., o.p.

(BL 58:689; CCBB 16:93; Eakin:97; HB 38:276; KR 30:180; LJ 87:1316)

837   DE LA MARE, Walter (John). *A Penny a Day.* **Gr. 4–7. (Orig. British pub.**
✓   **1925.)**

Six stories, including "The Three Sleeping Boys of Warwickshire," "Dick and the Beanstalk," and "The Lord Fish."

Illus. by Paul Kennedy, Knopf, 1960, 209 pp., o.p.

(BL 57:219; CCBB 14:78; Eakin:98; HB 36:503; LJ 85:4565)

838   DE LA MARE, Walter (John). *Tales Told Again* **(Orig. title:** *Told Again; Old*
✓   *Tales Told Again,* **Knopf, 1927, 1943). Gr. 2–5.**

This book contains all of the tales from *Broomsticks and Other Tales* (1942), *A Penny a Day* (1960), and *Animal Stories* (1940), including both traditional and modern fairy tales. One of these tales, "The Turnip," has been published separately as *The Turnip* (Godine, 1992).

Scribner, 1940, o.p.; Knopf, 1946, o.p.; Faber, 1980, 208 pp., o.p.

(BL 24:324, 55:459; CCBB 12:130; HB 35:298; LJ 84:1694; TLS 1927 p. 873, Dec 4, 1959 p. xvi)

DE LINT, Charles. *Dreams Underfoot: The Newford Collection.* See Chapter 5A, Alternate Worlds or Histories.

839   DE MORGAN, Mary (Augusta). *The Complete Fairy Tales of Mary De Morgan.* **Gr. 4–7.**

Contains the stories from three of de Morgan's collections: *On a Pincushion* (orig. British pub. 1876, U.S. 1891), *The Necklace of Princess Fiorimonde* (orig. British pub. 1880, U.S. 1922), and *The Windfairies* (orig. British pub. 1900, U.S. 1901). A facsimile edition of *On a Pincushion* and *The Necklace of Princess Fiorimonde* was published by Garland, 1977, o.p.

Illus. by William de Morgan, Walter Crane, and Olive Cockerell, Watts, 1963, 412 pp., o.p.

(LJ 88:4081)

840   DE MORGAN, Mary (Augusta). *The Necklace of Princess Fiorimonde; and Other Stories.* **Gr. 4–6. (Orig. British pub. in this ed. 1990.)**

Six Victorian fairy tales, including "The Wanderings of Arasmon," "The Rain Maiden," and the title story, "The Necklace of Princess Fiorimonde."

Illus. by Sylvie Monti, Trafalgar Sq., 1992, 96 pp. (0-09-174077-0)

(BL 88:1675; CCBB 45:233; SLJ July 1992 p. 81)

DERMAN, Martha. *Tales from Academy Street.* See Chapter 7, Magic Adventure Fantasy.

DICKINSON, Peter (pseud. of Malcolm de Brissac). *Merlin Dreams.* See Chapter 5B, Myth Fantasy.

841 **DICKSON, Gordon R(upert).** *The Last Dream.* **Gr. 7–12.**

An anthology of fantasy and science fiction stories about dragons, witches, and magical transformations.

Baen, 1986, pap., 263 pp. (0-671-65559-0)

(BBS:55; VOYA 9:236)

842 **DOLBIER, Maurice (Wyman).** *The Half-Pint Jinni, and Other Stories.* **Gr. 4–7.**

Eight magical tales set in Baghdad.

Illus. by Allan Thomas, Random, 194, 242 pp., o.p.

(BL 45:36; CCBB 1[Sept 1948]:2; KR 16:280; LJ 73:1097, 1457)

DONALDSON, Stephen R(upert). *Daughter of Regals and Other Tales.* See Chapter 5A, Alternate Worlds or Histories.

843 *Don't Bet on the Prince: Contemporary Feminist Fairy Tales in North America and England.* **Ed. by Jack Zipes. Gr. 10 up.**

An anthology of sixteen feminist fairy tales written for children and adults, whose authors include Jane Yolen, Judith Viorst, and Tanith Lee, followed by four critical essays about the impact of fairy tales on children.

Routledge, 1986, 270 pp. (0-416-01371-6), pap. (0-415-90263-0)

(BL 83:468, 496; KR 54:1199; SLJ Feb 1987 p. 36; TLS Nov 28, 1986 p. 1348)

Don't Give Up the Ghost: The Delacorte Book of Original Ghost Stories. **Ed. by David Gale.** See Chapter 4, Ghost Fantasy.

844 *Dragon Fantastic.* **Ed. by Rosalind M. Greenberg and Martin H. Greenberg. Gr. 6–12.**

Sixteen dragon stories, some set in alternate worlds and others in our contemporary world.

DAW, 1992, pap., 299 pp. (0-88677-511-6)

(LJ Apr 15, 1992 p. 125; VOYA 15:236)

845 *Dragon Tales.* **Ed. by Isaac Asimov, Charles G. Waugh, and Martin H. Green-**
✓ **berg. Gr. 7 up.**

Twelve stories about dragons, including Anne McCaffrey's "Weyr Search" and Gordon Dickson's "The Dragon and the George."

Fawcett, 1982, pap., 318 pp., o.p.

(BL 79:294, 304; JHC:430; SLJ Dec 1982 p. 86; VOYA 5[Dec 1982]:36)

Dragons and Dreams: A Collection of New Fantasy and Science Fiction Stories. **Ed. by Jane Yolen, Martin H. Greenberg, and Charles G. Waugh.** See Chapter 7, Magic Adventure Fantasy.

846 *Dream Time: New Stories by Sixteen Award Winning Authors.* **Ed. by Toss Gascoigne, Jo Goodman, and Margot Tyrell. Gr. 6–9. (Orig. Australian pub. 1989.)**

Sixteen stories loosely tied to the theme of Australian Aboriginal "Dream Time," written by Patricia Wrightson, Victor Kelleher, Mary Steele, Lee Harding, and others.

Houghton, 1991, 184 pp. (0-395-57434-X)

(CCBB 45:89; HBG 3[Spring 1992]:119; KR 59:930; SLJ Nov 1991, p. 117; VOYA 14:370)

847   **EDGEWORTH, Maria.** *Simple Susan and Other Tales.* **Gr. 3–5. (Orig. U.S. pub. 1819.)**

Eight of the author's best-known stories, including "The Cherry Orchard," "The Orange Man," and "The Purple Jar."

Dutton, 1907, o.p.; illus. by Clara Burd, Macmillan, 1929, 216 pp., o.p.

(BL 26:169; HB 5:53)

Elsewhere, vol. I. **Ed. by Terri Windling and Mark Alan Arnold.** See Chapter 5A, Alternate Worlds or Histories.

848   *Elsewhere, Elsewhen, Elsehow.* **Ed. by Miriam Allen De Ford. Gr. 10 up.**

Eighteen fantasy, science fiction, and horror stories, including "The Old Woman" and "The Monster."

Walker, 1971, 180 pp., o.p.

(KR 39:465, 567; LJ 96:3641, 4205)

849   *The Enchanted Book.* **Ed. by Alice Dalgliesh. Gr. 3–5.**

Twenty-one stories of magical enchantment whose authors include Hans Christian Andersen and Marie d'Aulnoy.

Illus. by Concetta Cacciola, Scribner, 1947, 246 pp., o.p.

(BL 44:137; CCBB 1[Feb 1948]:2; HB 24:37; LJ 72:1436, 1690)

850   *The Enchanter's Spell: Five Famous Tales.* **Adapt. by Gennady Spirin. Gr. 3–7.**
✓   **(Orig. German pub. 1986.)**

This collection of literary fairy tales contains Hans Christian Andersen's "The Emperor's New Clothes," Miguel de Cervantes' "The Beautiful Kitchen Maid," E. T. A. Hoffmann's "The Nutcracker," George MacDonald's "Little Daylight," and Alexander Pushkin's "The Princess and the Seven Brothers."

Illus. by the adaptor, Dial, 1988, 96 pp. (0-8037-0320-1)

(BL 84:1608; CCBB 41:170; KR 56:128; SLJ Apr 1988 p. 100; Suth 4:391)

851   **ESTES, Eleanor (Ruth Rosenfeld).** *The Sleeping Giant and Other Stories.* **Gr.**
✓   **2–5.**

Three tales: "The Sleeping Giant," "The Lost Shadow," and "A Nice Room for Giraffes."

Illus. by the author, Harcourt, 1948, 101 pp., o.p.

(BL 45:123; CCBB 1[Nov 1948]4; HB 25:35; KR 16:571; LJ 73:1825)

852   **EWING, Juliana (Horatia Gatty).** *The Brownies and Other Stories* **(orig. British title:** *The Brownies and Other Tales,* **1870). Gr. 4–6. (Orig. U.S. pub. Macmillan, 1910.)**

Seven tales, including "The Brownies," "Amelia and the Dwarfs," and "The Land of Lost Toys."

Illus. by Ernest H. Shepard, Dent, 1975 (repr. of 1954 ed.), 250 pp., o.p.

(3L 7:85, 51:210; CCBB 9:44; Mahony 2:279)

853   *The Faber Book of Modern Fairy Tales.* **Ed. by Sara Corrin and Stephen Corrin. Gr. 4–6. (Orig. British pub. 1981.)**

Fifteen original tales by E. Nesbit, Laurence Housman, James Thurber, A. A. Milne, Philippa Pearce, and others.

Illus. by Ann Strugnell, Faber, 1982, 312 pp., o.p.

(CCBB 36:6; Ch&Bks:284; Suth 3:103; TLS 1981 p. 1356)

854 *Faery!* **Ed. by Terri Windling. Gr. 10 up.**

An anthology of 23 stories involving the Kingdom of Faery written by Jane Yolen, Patricia McKillip, Sherri Tepper, Robin McKinley, and others.

Ace, 1985, pap., 308 pp., o.p.

(BBS:67; BL 81:927, 945)

855 *Famous Tales of the Fantastic.* **Ed. by Herbert Maurice Van Thal. Gr. 10 up.**

Eleven American and British short stories whose authors include Ray Bradbury, Nathaniel Hawthorne, Washington Irving, and Robert Louis Stevenson.

Illus. by Edward Pagram, Hill, 1965, 208 pp., o.p.

(BL 62:525; LJ 90:5303; TLS 1966 p. 29)

856 *Fantastic Creatures: An Anthology of Fantasy and Science Fiction.* **Ed. by Isaac Asimov, Martin H. Greenberg, and Charles G. Waugh. Gr. 7–10.**

A combination of eight fantasy and science fiction stories, including Anne McCaffrey's "The Smallest Dragonboy."

Watts, 1981, 155 pp., o.p.

(BL 78:434, 438; CCBB 35:142; SLJ Aug 1982 p. 123)

The Fantastic Imagination: An Anthology of High Fantasy, **vol. 1. Ed. by Robert H. Boyer and Kenneth J. Zahorski.** See Chapter 5A, Alternate Worlds or Histories.

857 *Fantasy Annual V.* **Ed. by Terry Carr. Gr. 10 up.**

A sampling of the best short fantasy of 1981, most of which are stories based in reality with a psychological rather than supernatural basis for the fantasy elements. Other books in the series are *The Year's Finest Fantasy, 1978* (Berkley 1978), *The Year's Finest Fantasy,* vol. 2 (1979), *Fantasy Annual III* (1981), and *Fantasy Annual IV* (1981).

Pocket, 1982, 240 pp., o.p.

(BL 79:601; LJ 107:2192)

858 *Fantasy Hall of Fame.* **Ed. by Robert Silverberg and Martin H. Greenberg. Gr. 10 up.**

Twenty-three stories chosen as the best of modern fantasy by the 1982 and 1983 world fantasy conventions. The authors range from Edgar Allan Poe to Ursula K. Le Guin.

Arbor House, 1983, 414 pp., o.p.

(BL 80:397; LJ 108:1976)

859 **FARBER, Norma (Holzman).** *Six Impossible Things Before Breakfast.* **Gr. 3–5.**

Four poems and two short stories about magic, a unicorn, and a princess, each illustrated by a different artist.

Illus. by Tomie dePaola, Trina Schart Hyman, Hilary Knight, Friso Henstra, Lydia Dabcovich, and Charles Mikolaycak, Addison-Wesley, 1977, 43 pp., o.p.

(CCBB 30:123; HB 53:307; SLJ Apr 1977 p. 66)

860 **FARJEON, Eleanor.** *Italian Peepshow and Other Tales.* **Gr. 3–5. (Orig. U.S. pub. 1926.)**

Three children visiting Italy listen to a number of stories, including "Oranges and Lemons" and "Nella's Dancing Shoes."

Illus. by Edward Ardizzone, Walck, 1960, 96 pp., o.p.

(BL 24:125, 57:274; Bookshelf 1928 p. 16; HB 3:18, 36:406; KR 28:904; LJ 85:4566; TLS Nov 25, 1960 p. vii)

861   **FARJEON, Eleanor.** *Jim at the Corner* **(Orig. title:** *The Old Sailor's Yarn Box,*
✓   **Stokes, 1934). Gr. 3–5.**

Old Jim the sailor tells a young boy named Derry eight tales of the sea. This is a companion volume to *The Old Nurse's Stocking Basket* (1931, 1965).

Illus. by Edward Ardizzone, Walck, 1958, 102 pp., o.p.

(BL 31:244, 55:192; Bookshelf 1935 p. 2; Eakin:113; HB 10:355; 34:473; LJ 60:403)

862   **FARJEON, Eleanor.** *The Little Bookroom: Eleanor Farjeon's Short Stories for*
✓   *Children, Chosen by Herself.* **Gr. 4–7. (Orig. British pub. 1931, U.S. Walck, 1956.)**

Twenty-seven stories, including "The Giant and the Mite," "The Seventh Princess," and "The Glass Peacock." Carnegie Medal, 1955.

Illus. by Edward Ardizzone, Oxford, 1979 (repr. of 1931 ed.), o.p.

(BL 52:415; CCBB 10:5; HB 32:179, 270, 61:77; LJ 81:1719)

FARJEON, Eleanor. *Martin Pippin in the Apple Orchard.* See Chapter 1, Allegorical Fantasy and Literary Fairy Tales.

863   **FARJEON, Eleanor.** *The Old Nurse's Stocking Basket.* **Gr. 3–5. (Orig. British pub. 1931.)**

The Old Nurse tells stories about caring for Hercules, the Princess of China, and the Spanish Infanta. A companion to *Jim at the Corner* (1958, orig. title: *The Old Sailor's Yarn Box* 1934).

Illus. by Edward Ardizzone, Walck, 1965, 102 pp., o.p.

(HB 42:193; LJ 91:2209; Mahony 3:86)

864   **FARJEON, Eleanor.** *One Foot in Fairyland: Sixteen Tales.* **Gr. 4–6.**

A collection of original fantasy tales and retellings of fairy tales.

Illus. by Robert Lawson, Stokes, 1938, 261 pp., o.p.

(BL 35:121; HB 14:381; LJ 63:978; TLS 1938 p. 789)

865   **FAST, Howard (Melvin).** *The General Zapped an Angel: New Stories of Fantasy and Science Fiction.* **Gr. 10 up.**

Nine short stories of allegorical fantasy and science fiction.

Morrow, 1970, 160 pp., o.p.

(BL 66:955, 968; LJ 95:1047)

866   **FAST, Howard (Melvin).** *A Touch of Infinity: Thirteen New Stories of Fantasy and Science Fiction.* **Gr. 10 up.**

Thirteen satirical fantasy and science fiction tales, including one about a gnat-sized man on the back porch, and another about plucking breakfast rolls from the air.

Morrow, 1973, 182 pp., o.p.

(BL 70:473, 484; KR 41:659; LJ 98,:2339, 2678)

Festival Moon. **Ed. by C. J. Cherryh.** See Chapter 5A, Alternate Worlds or Histories.

FIELD, Rachel (Lyman). *Eliza and the Elves.* See Chapter 5C, Travel to Other Worlds.

FIENBERG, Anna. *The Magnificent Nose and Other Marvels.* See Chapter 7, Magic Adventure Fantasy.

FINNEY, Jack (pseud. of Walter Branden Finney). *About Time: Twelve Stories.* See Chapter 8, Time Travel Fantasy.

867 *Fires of the Past: Thirteen Contemporary Fantasies about Hometowns.* **Ed. by Anne Devereaux Jordan. Gr. 10 up.**

Twelve fantasy and science fiction stories and one poem on the theme of hometowns.

St. Martin's, 1991, 208 pp. (0-312-05433-5)

(BL 87:1322, 1374; LJ Mar 15, 1991 p. 119; VOYA 14:179, 15:9)

FLEISCHMAN, Paul (Taylor). *Graven Images: Three Stories.* See Chapter 4, Ghost Fantasy.

FLEISCHMAN, (Albert) Sid(ney). *Jim Bridger's Alarm Clock, and Other Tall Tales.* See Chapter 6, Humorous Fantasy.

FLORA, James (Royer). *Grandpa's Ghost Stories.* See Chapter 4, Ghost Fantasy.

868 **FOX (Greenburg), Paula.** *The Little Swineherd and Other Tales.* **Gr. 3–6.**

✓ Five tales: four fables about a rooster, a pony, an alligator, and a raccoon and one story about an abandoned swineherd.

Illus. by Leonard Lubin, Dutton, 1978, 104 pp., o.p.

(BL 75:292; CCBB 32:43; HB 55:516; KR 46:1071; SLJ Oct 1978 p. 144)

FRANKO, Ivan, and MELNYK, Bohdan. *Fox Mykyta.* See Chapter 2, Animal Fantasy.

FREDDI, Cris. *Pork, and Other Stories.* See Chapter 2, Animal Fantasy.

Fun Phantoms: Tales of Ghostly Entertainment. **Ed. by Seon Manley and Gogo Lewis.** See Chapter 4, Ghost Fantasy.

869 **FYLEMAN, Rose (Amy).** *Forty Good-Night Tales.* **Gr. K–4. (Orig. British pub. 1923.)**

Humorous tales and fairy stories to read aloud to young children at bedtime. *Forty Good-Morning Tales* (Doubleday 1929, 1938) is a companion volume.

Illus. by Thelma Cudlipp Grosvenor, Doran, 1924, 131 pp., o.p.

(BL 21:200; HB 1[Oct 1924]:4; Mahony 2:57)

870 **FYLEMAN, Rose (Amy).** *Tea Time Tales.* **Gr. 3–5.**

Twenty humorous short stories to be read aloud.

Illus. by Erick Berry, Doubleday, 1930, 246 pp., o.p.

(BL 26:401; HB 6:210; LJ 55:995; Mahony 3:86)

871 **GARDNER, John (Champlin) (Jr.).** *Dragon, Dragon, and Other Timeless Tales.* **Gr. 5–7.**

Four fairy-tale spoofs about dragons, giants, and magic.

Illus. by Charles Shields, Knopf, 1975, 75 pp., o.p.

(BL 72:684; CCBB 29:109; HB 52:154; KR 43:1129)

872 **GARNER, Alan.** *Alan Garner's Fairytales of Gold.* **Gr. 3–5. (Orig. pub. separately in England in 1979.)**

Four original tales in the fairy-tale tradition: "The Golden Brothers," "The Girl of the

Golden Gate," "The Three Golden Heads of the Well," and "The Princess and the Golden Mane."

Philomel, 1980, 200 pp., o.p.

(BL 77:963; CCBB 34:132; KR 49:357; SLJ Mar 1981 p. 132)

873   **GARNER, Alan.** *Once Upon a Time: Though It Wasn't in Your Time, and It*
✓   *Wasn't in My Time, and It Wasn't in Anybody Else's Time . . .* **Gr. K–3. (Orig. British pub. 1993.)**

Three stories written in folktale style: "The Fox, the Hare, and the Cock," "The Girl and the Geese," and "Battibeth."

Illus. by Norman Messenger, Dorling, 1993, 32 pp. (1-56458-381-3)

(BL 90:694; CCBB 47:153; KR 61:1523; SLJ Mar 1994 p. 215)

874   **GATE, Ethel May.** *The Fortunate Days.* **Gr. 3–5.**

Nine fairy tales about a tailor in Constantinople who follows his Persian cat through its nine lives.

Illus. by Vianna Knowlton, Yale University Press, 1922, 127 pp., o.p.

(BL 19:127; Bookshelf 1923–1924 p. 8; LJ 45:980; Mahony 2:280)

875   **GATE, Ethel May.** *Tales from the Enchanted Isles.* **Gr. 3–5.**

Seven fairy tales modeled on traditional folklore.

Illus. by Dorothy P. Lathrop, Yale University Press, 1927, 118 pp., o.p.

(BL 23:235; HB 2[Nov 1925]:44; Mahony 2:280)

876   **GATE, Ethel May.** *Tales from the Secret Kingdom.* **Gr. 2–4.**

Nine original fairy stories.

Illus. by Katherine Buffum, Yale University Press, 1919, 93 pp., o.p.

(BL 16:138; LJ 45:980; Mahony 1:40)

The Ghost Story Treasury. **Sel. by Linda Sonntag.** See Chapter 4, Ghost Fantasy.

The Ghost's Companion: A Haunting Anthology. **Ed. by Peter Haining.** See Chapter 4, Ghost Fantasy.

Ghosts: An Anthology. **Ed. by William Mayne.** See Chapter 4, Ghost Fantasy.

Ghosts for Christmas. **Ed. by Richard Dalby.** See Chapter 4, Ghost Fantasy.

GODDEN (Dixon), (Margaret) Rumer. *Four Dolls.* See Chapter 9, Toy Fantasy.

GORDON, John (William). *The Burning Baby and Other Ghosts.* See Chapter 4, Ghost Fantasy.

877   **GOROG, Judith.** *In a Messy, Messy Room, and Other Strange Stories.* **Gr. 3–6.**

Five eerie stories including "The Smelly Sneakers Contest," in which Todd wins the championship but loses his feet.

Illus. by Kimberly Bulcken Root, Putnam, 1990, 48 pp. (0-399-22218-9)

(BL 86:1897; CCBB 43:240; HBG 1[Jan–June 1990]:246; KR 58:648; SLJ July 1990 p. 76)

GOROG, Judith. *No Swimming in Dark Pond: And Other Chilling Tales.* See Chapter 4, Ghost Fantasy.

GOROG, Judith. *On Meeting Witches at Wells.* See Chapter 4, Ghost Fantasy.

GOROG, Judith. *Please Do Not Touch.* See Chapter 4, Ghost Fantasy.

GOROG, Judith. *A Taste for Quiet, and Other Disquieting Tales.* See Chapter 4, Ghost Fantasy.

878 **GOROG, Judith.** *Three Dreams and a Nightmare, and Other Tales of the Dark.* **Gr. 5–9.**

✓ A companion volume to Gorog's *A Taste for Quiet* (1983; see Chapter 4, Ghost Fantasy) and *No Swimming in Dark Pond* (1987; see Chapter 4, Ghost Fantasy), this is a collection of fourteen fantasy and horror stories.

Putnam, 1988, 156 pp. (0-399-21578-6); Troll, 1989, pap. (0-81671822-9)

(BBC:204; BBJ:71; BL 85:258, 318; CC:579; CCBB 42:71; KR 56:974; SLJ Nov 1988 p. 125; VOYA 12:16, 42)

GOULART, Ron(ald Joseph). *The Chameleon Corps and Other Shape Changers.* See Chapter 5A, Alternate Worlds or Histories.

879 **GRAHAME, Kenneth.** *The Golden Age.* **Gr. 5–7. (Orig. British and U.S. pub. 1895.)**

Five orphaned children take turns telling the stories in this book, and its companion volume, *Dream Days* (orig. pub. 1898; Garland, 1976; Beaufort, 1976; Ten Speed, 1993). *Dream Days* includes the story "The Reluctant Dragon."

Illus. by Maxfield Parrish, Garland, 1976 (repr. of 1900 ed.), o.p.; Avon, 1975, pap., o.p.; Beaufort, 1985 (repr. of 1898 ed.), 288 pp., o.p.; Ten Speed, 1993, 252 pp. (0-89815-545-2)

(BL 25:176, 26:77; CCBB 18:129; HB 1[June 1925]:46, 7:324, 30:66; HBG 5:86)

880 **GRAY, Nicholas Stuart.** *Mainly in Moonlight: Ten Stories of Sorcery and the*
✓ *Supernatural.* **Gr. 4–6. (Orig. British pub. 1965.)**

Tales of wizards, princes, and princesses, including "The Sorcerer's Apprentices," "The Reluctant Familiar," and "The Man Who Sold Magic."

Illus. by Charles Keeping, Meredith, 1967, 181 pp., o.p.

(HB 43:462; KR 35:207; LJ 92:2449; SLJ Feb 1980 p. 55; TLS 1965 p. 1130)

881 **GRAY, Nicholas Stuart.** *A Wind from Nowhere.* **Gr. 5–7.**

Humorous fairy tales of dragons, princes, wizards, and demons.

Faber, 1979, 155 pp., o.p.

(HB 56:55; SLJ Dec 1979 p. 85)

882 **GREEN, Kathleen.** *Leprechaun Tales.* **Gr. 3–5.**

Irish-inspired tales of leprechauns, foolish human beings, pookas, and banshees.

Illus. by Victoria de Larrea, Lippincott, 1968, 127 pp., o.p.

(BL 64:1042; HB 44:172; KR 36:340; LJ 93:1310)

883 **GREEN, Kathleen.** *Philip and the Pooka and Other Irish Fairy Tales.* **Gr. 4–6.**

Ten tales about Irish fairy folk: the little people, pookas, Lochrimeh, and witches.

Illus. by Victoria de Larrea, Lippincott, 1966, 93 pp., o.p.

(BL 62:831; CCBB 20:25; HB 42:305; LJ 91:2210)

884 **GRIPARI, Pierre.** *Tales of the Rue Broca.* **Gr. 5–7. (Selections from French pub. 1967.)**

Six imaginative tales from France, including three about a good devil, a pair of shoes in love, and a hero with a ridiculous name.

Trans. by Doriane Grutman, illus. by Emily McCully, Bobbs-Merrill, 1969, 111 pp., o.p.

(CCBB 23:128; LJ 95:1942; KR 37:1112; Suth:159)

HALDANE, J(ohn) B(urdon) (Sanderson). *My Friend Mr. Leakey.* See Chapter 10, Witchcraft and Sorcery Fantasy.

HALE, Lucretia P(eabody). *The Complete Peterkin Papers.* See Chapter 6, Humorous Fantasy.

HAMILTON (Adoff), Virginia (Esther). *The All Jahdu Storybook.* See Chapter 6, Humorous Fantasy.

885 **HARRIS, Rosemary (Jeanne).** *Sea Magic and Other Stories of Enchantment*
✓ **(British title: *The Lotus and the Grail: Legends from East to West,* 1974, includes eight additional stories). Gr. 6–8.**

Ten tales of magic and superstition, including "The Graveyard Rose" and "White Orchid, Red Mountain."

Macmillan, 1974, 178 pp., o.p.

(BL 70:819; CCBB 28:9; HB 50:145; KR 42:192; LJ 99:2290; Suth 2:203)

886 **HARRISON, David Lee.** *The Book of Giant Stories.* **Gr. K–4.**

Three tales about boys who use their wits either to escape or to befriend a giant.

Illus. by Philippe Fix, McGraw-Hill, 1972, 44 pp., o.p.

(KR 40:1021; LJ 98:253; TLS 1972 p. 1332)

887 **HAUFF, Wilhelm.** *The Caravan.* **Gr. 6 up. (Orig. pub. in Germany; orig. U.S. pub. Appleton, 1850, entitled *The Caravan: A Collection of Popular Tales;* Stokes, 1912, entitled *Caravan Tales and Some Others.*)**

Six suspenseful tales told by merchants traveling in a caravan across the desert.

Trans. by Alma Overholt, illus. by Burt Silverman, Crowell, 1964, 220 pp., o.p.

(BL 9:303, 61:656; HB 41:57; KR 32:1011; LJ 90:379)

888 **HAUFF, Wilhelm.** *The Fairy Tales of Wilhelm Hauff.* **Gr. 5–7. (Orig. pub. in Germany; orig. U.S. pub. McKay, 1895; Dutton, 1910, entitled *Fairy Tales.*)**

Magical adventure tales with an "Arabian Nights" flavor, including "Snout the Dwarf" and "The Inn in the Forest."

Trans. by Anthea Bell, illus. by Ulrik Schramm, Abelard-Schuman, 1969, 223 pp., o.p.

(BL 66:1045; KR 37:1199; LJ 95:1638; Mahony 1:21; TLS 1969 p. 688)

The Haunted and the Haunters: Tales of Ghosts and Other Apparitions. **Ed. by Kathleen Lines.** See Chapter 4, Ghost Fantasy.

Haunting Tales. **Ed. by Barbara Ireson.** See Chapter 4, Ghost Fantasy.

889 **HAWTHORNE, Nathaniel.** *The Snow Image.* **Gr. 4 up. (Orig. U.S. pub. 1851, 1899.)**

A collection of allegorical and supernatural tales.

Illus. by Dorothy P. Lathrop, Macmillan, 1930, 1944, 69 pp., o.p.; Ohio State University Press, 1974 (entitled *The Snow Image and Uncollected Tales*), o.p.; Ayer, 1975 (entitled *The Snow Image and Other Twice-Told Tales*) repr. of 1899 ed. (0-8369-3457-1); Reprint Services, 1992 (repr. of 1851 ed.) (entitled *The Snow Image and Other Twice-Told Tales*) (0-7812-3044-6)

(Bookshelf 1932 p. 23)

Hecate's Cauldron. **Ed. by Susan M. Shwartz.** See Chapter 10, Witchcraft and Sorcery Fantasy.

890 **HESSE, Hermann.** *Pictor's Metamorphoses, and Other Fantasies.* **Gr. 10 up.**
✓ **(Orig. German pub. 1923, 1975.)**

Nineteen allegorical fairy tales written by the German Nobel laureate between 1900 and 1951, including "Lulu," "The Merman," and "Conversation with the Stove."

Trans. by Rika Lesser, illus. by the author, ed. by Theodore Ziolkowski, Farrar, 1982, 225 pp., o.p., pap. (0-374-51723-1)

(BBS:58; BL 78:537; LJ Jan 1, 1982 p. 108; SHC:738; TLS Sept 10, 1982 p. 965)

891 **HEWETT, Anita.** *The Bull Beneath the Walnut Tree and Other Stories.* **Gr. K–4.**
✓ **(Orig. British pub. 1966.)**

Eighteen short tales including "The Singing Witch" and "The Galloping Hedgehog."

Illus. by Imero Gobbato, McGraw-Hill, 1967, 155 pp., o.p.

(BL 64:501; HB 43:588; KR 35:804; LJ 92:3178; TLS 1966 p. 1092)

892 *Hidden Turnings: A Collection of Stories Through Time and Space.* **Ed. by Diana**
✓ **Wynne Jones. Gr. 7–12. (Orig. British pub. 1989.)**

Twelve tales about strange occurrences in everyday life, written by Helen Cresswell, Diana Wynne Jones, Tanith Lee, and others.

Greenwillow, 1990, 182 pp. (0-688-09163-6)

(BBJ:72; BL 86:1693, 1704; CCBB 43:242; HBG 1[Jan–June 1990]:255; KR 58:730; SLJ Aug 1990 p. 148; VOYA 13:296)

893 **HOUGH, (Helen) Charlotte (Woodyatt).** *Red Biddy and Other Stories.* **Gr. 4–5.**
✓ **(Orig. British pub. 1966.)**

Ten stories about princesses, dragons, giants, witches, and fairies.

Illus. by the author, Coward, 1967, 127 pp., o.p.

(CCBB 22:8; HB 43:463; KR 35:413; LJ 92:2450)

894 **HOUSMAN, Laurence.** *A Doorway in Fairyland.* **Gr. 4–7.**

Twelve tales from *A Farm in Fairyland* (1894), *The House of Joy* (1895), *The Field of Clover* (1898), and *The Blue Moon* (1904) including "The Bound Princess" and "The Rat-Catcher's Daughter."

Illus. by the author and Clemence Housman, Harcourt, 1905, 1922, 219 pp., o.p.

(BL 20:24; Mahony 2:281)

895 **HOUSMAN, Laurence.** *Moonshine and Clover.* **Gr. 4–7. (Orig. British pub. 1922.)**

Eighteen stories from *A Farm in Fairyland* (1894), *The House of Joy* (1895), *The Field of Clover* (1898), and *The Blue Moon* (1904), including "A Capful of Moonshine" and "The White Doe."

Illus. by the author and Clemence Housman, Harcourt, 1923, 220 pp., o.p.

(BL 20:24; Mahony 2:281)

896 **HOUSMAN, Laurence.** *The Rat-Catcher's Daughter: A Collection of Stories.* **Gr.**
✓ **4–7.**

Twelve tales of princesses, magic, and little people, including "The White Doe" and "The Cloak of Friendship."

Ed. by Ellin Greene, illus. by Julia Noonan, Atheneum, 1974, 169 pp., o.p.

(BL 70:874; HB 50:379; KR 42:244; LJ 99:1451, 1473)

HOWE, Deborah, and HOWE, James. *Teddy Bear's Scrapbook.* See Chapter 9, Toy Fantasy.

897   **HUGHES, Richard (Arthur Warren).** *Don't Blame Me!* **Gr. 3–5. (Orig. British pub. 1940.)**

Humorous stories with a touch of the supernatural, including "The Doll and the Mermaid" and "Don't Blame Me."

Illus. by Fritz Eichenberg, Harper, 1940, 159 pp., o.p.

(LJ 65:849, 926; TLS 1940 p. 634)

898   **HUGHES, Richard (Arthur Warren).** *The Wonder-Dog: The Collected Stories of Richard Hughes* **(Orig. titles:** *The Spider's Palace and Other Stories,* **1932 [British pub. 1931], and** *Don't Blame Me!* **1940). Gr. 4–6.**

Thirty illogical tales about a doll who owns a child, talking animals, and an evil motorbike.

Illus. by Antony Maitland, Greenwillow, 1977, 180 pp., o.p.

(Bookshelf 1932 p. 10; HB 37:53; KR 45:1197; LJ 65:849, 926; Mahony 3:206; SLJ Apr 1978 p. 84; TLS 1931 p. 957, 1940 p. 634, 1977 p. 1273)

HUGHES, Ted (Edward James). *How the Whale Became.* See Chapter 2, Animal Fantasy.

899   **HUGHES, Ted (Edward James).** *Tales of the Early World.* **Gr. 4 up. (Orig.**
✓   **British pub. 1988.)**

Ten stories about God's creation of the world's creatures, written by England's Poet Laureate in a variety of styles, ranging from Kiplingesque to Native American myth.

Illus. by Andrew Davidson, Farrar, 1991, 128 pp. (0-374-37377-9)

(BL 87:1646; CCBB 44:240; HBG 2[Fall 1991]:275; KR 59:248; SLJ May 1991 p. 93; VOYA 14:124)

900   **HUNTER, Mollie (pseud. of Maureen Mollie Hunter McVeigh McIlwraith).** *A*
✓   *Furl of Fairy Wind: Four Stories.* **Gr. 2–4.**

Four Scottish tales involving the fairy world: "The Brownie," "The Enchanted Boy," "Hi Johnny," and "A Furl of Fairy Wind."

Illus. by Stephen Gammell, Harper, 1977, 58 pp., o.p.

(BBC:205; BL 74:613; CC:579; CCBB 31:142; Ch&Bks:287; HB 54:47; KR 45:1097; SLJ Sept 1977 p. 109; Suth 2:233)

HUNTER, Norman (George Lorimer). *The Incredible Adventures of Professor Branestawm.* See Chapter 6, Humorous Fantasy.

Imaginary Lands. **Ed. by Robin McKinley.** See Chapter 5A, Alternate Worlds or Histories.

901   *Imagine That! Fifteen Fantastic Tales.* **Ed. by Sara Corrin and Stephen Corrin. Gr. 4–6.**

Twelve folk tales, plus three original tales written by James Reeves, E. Nesbit, and William Hauff.

Illus. by Jill Bennett, Faber, 1986, 175 pp., o.p.

(BL 83:648; KR 54:1648; SLJ Apr 1987 p. 93; TLS 1986 p. 1346)

902   *Into the Unknown: Eleven Tales of Imagination.* **Ed. by Terry Carr. Gr. 7–9.**

This collection of tales about unusual phenomena includes Ray Bradbury's "McGillahee's Brat" and Robert Silverberg's "As Is."

Nelson, 1973, 192 pp., o.p.

(BL 70:649, 654; KR 41:691; LJ 99:216)

903 *Isaac Asimov Presents the Best Fantasy of the 19th Century.* **Ed. by Isaac Asimov, Charles G. Waugh, and Martin H. Greenberg. Gr. 10 up.**

Fourteen tales whose authors include Charles Dickens, Washington Irving, Sir Arthur Conan Doyle, Oscar Wilde, and H. G. Wells.

Beaufort, 1982, 368 pp., o.p.

(LJ 107:2355)

904 *Isaac Asimov's Magical Worlds of Fantasy: Faeries.* **Ed. by Isaac Asimov, Martin H. Greenberg, and Charles G. Waugh. Gr. 10 up.**

Eighteen stories about fairies, elves, and visits to fairyland, written by André Norton, Poul Anderson, Lord Dunsany, and others.

Penguin, 1991, pap., 374 pp., o.p.

(Kliatt Apr 1992 p. 12; VOYA 14:383)

JACQUES, Brian. *Seven Strange and Ghostly Tales.* See Chapter 4, Ghost Fantasy.

JEKEL, Pamela. *The Third Jungle Book.* See Chapter 2, Animal Fantasy.

905 **JENNINGS, Paul.** *Unreal! Eight Surprising Stories.* **Gr. 4–8. (Orig. Australian pub. 1985.)**

Eight humorous and supernatural stories, each told from a boy's point of view, including one about magic underwear which leaves the protagonist naked at school, and another about a pair of ghostly lighthouse keepers who scare visitors away. There are three companion volumes: *Uncanny! Even More Surprising Stories* (1991), *Unmentionable! More Amazing Stories* (1993), and *Unbelievable! More Surprising Stories* (published in England).

Viking, 1991, 112 pp. (0-670-84175-7); Puffin, 1993, pap. (0-14-034910-3)

(BL 87:2147; CCBB 45:13; HBG 3[Spring 1992]:67; KR 59:1344; SLJ Dec 1991 p. 117)

JONES, Diana Wynne. *Stopping for a Spell: Three Fantasies.* See Chapter 7, Magic Adventure Fantasy.

JONES, Diana Wynne. *Warlock at the Wheel and Other Stories.* See Chapter 10, Witchcraft and Sorcery Fantasy.

JONES, Louis C(lark). *Things That Go Bump in the Night.* See Chapter 4, Ghost Fantasy.

JONES, Terry. *Fairy Tales.* See Chapter 6, Humorous Fantasy.

JONES, Terry. *Fantastic Stories.* See Chapter 6, Humorous Fantasy.

906 **JUSTER, Norton.** *Alberic the Wise and Other Journeys.* **Gr. 4–8.**

✓ Three tales about a hero searching for wisdom, a boy who enters a painting, and two kings searching for happiness.

Illus. by Domenico Gnoli, Pantheon, 1965, 67 pp., o.p.; illus. by Leonard Baskin, Picture Book, 1992, 28 pp. (0-88708-243-2)

(BL 89:908; CCBB 19:150, 46:180; HB 42:54, 69:231; HBG 4[Spring 1993]:71; KR 60:1504; LJ 91:1064; SLJ Mar 1993 p. 198)

907 **KELLER, Gottfried.** *The Fat of the Cat and Other Stories.* **Gr. 4–6.**

✓ Adaptations of Swiss legends and folktales about animals and witches.

Adapt. by Louis Untermeyer, illus. by Albert Sallak, Harcourt, 1925, 283 pp., o.p.

(BL 22:122; Bookshelf 1928 p. 10; HB 2(Nov 1925):20; LJ 51:836; Mahony 2:198; Moore:435)

908 **KENNEDY, (Jerome) Richard.** *Richard Kennedy: Collected Stories.* **Gr. 4–9.**

✓ Sixteen stories originally published separately, including "The Porcelain Man," "The Leprechaun's Story," and "The Dark Princess."

Illus. by Marcia Sewall, Harper, 1987, 274 pp. (0-06-023256-0)

(BL 84:625, 635; CC:579; HB 64:359; KR 55:1629; SLJ Nov 1987 p. 105; VOYA 10:235)

Kingdoms of Sorcery. **Ed. by Lin Carter.** See Chapter 5A, Alternate Worlds or Histories.

KIPLING, (Joseph) Rudyard. *All the Mowgli Stories.* See Chapter 2, Animal Fantasy.

KIPLING, (Joseph) Rudyard. *The Jungle Book.* See Chapter 2, Animal Fantasy.

KIPLING, (Joseph) Rudyard. *Just So Stories.* See Chapter 2,Animal Fantasy.

909 **KIPLING, (Joseph) Rudyard.** *Kipling's Fantasy.* **Gr. 6–12.**

Twelve fantasy and horror stories, many of which involve Indian mythology.

Ed. by John Bruner. Tor, 1992, 224 pp. (0-312-85354-8), 1993, pap. (titled *Kipling's Fantasy Stories*) (0-8125-2002-5)

(BL 89:402, 412; VOYA 16:41, 17:8)

KIPLING, (Joseph) Rudyard. *Phantoms and Fantasies: Twenty Tales.* See Chapter 4, Ghost Fantasy.

910 **KOTZWINKLE, William.** *Hearts of Wood: And Other Timeless Tales.* **Gr. 4–6.**

Five original fairy tales including stories about carousel animals that come to life, a man who becomes a butterfly, and a woodsman who becomes King of the fairies. Four of these tales were originally published as *The Oldest Man and Other Timeless Stories* (Pantheon, 1971).

Illus. by Joe Servello, Godine, 1986, 128 pp. (0-87923-648-5)

(CCBB 26:27, 40:129; KR 39:1013; LJ 97:1914; SLJ May 1987 p. 101)

911 **KRENSKY, Stephen (Alan).** *Castles in the Air and Other Tales.* **Gr. 4–6.**

Five humourous fairy tales based on familiar phrases: "Castles in the Air," "A Fine Kettle of Fish," "The Last Straw," "Too Clever for Words," and "A Barrel of Fun."

Illus. by Warren Lieberman, Macmillan, 1979, 66 pp., o.p.

(CCBB 33:50; KR 47:637; SLJ Sept 1979 p. 142)

KRENSKY, Stephen (Alan). *Woodland Crossings.* See Chapter 2, Animal Fantasy.

KRÜSS, James (Jacob Hinrich). *Eagle and Dove.* See Chapter 2, Animal Fantasy.

LEACH, Maria. *The Thing at the Foot of the Bed and Other Scary Tales.* See Chapter 4, Ghost Fantasy.

912 **LEAMY, Edmund.** *The Fairy Minstrel of Glenmalure, and Other Stories for Children.* **Gr. 3–5. (Orig. pub. Warne, 1913.)**

Three fanciful tales set in Ireland.

Fitzgerald, 1913, o.p.; illus. by Vera Casseau, Roth, 1976, 92 pp. (0-8486-0210-2)

(BL 27:216, 34:271; HB 14:106; Mahony 1:22)

913 **LEAMY, Edmund.** *The Golden Spears and Other Fairy Tales.* **Gr. 3–5. (Orig. pub. 1890, entitled** *Irish Fairy Tales, a Collection of Seven Fairy Tales.***)**

Seven tales set in Ireland, including "The Enchanted Cave," "The Fairy Tree of Dooros," and "Princess Finola and the Dwarf."

Fitzgerald, 1911, 1930, o.p.; illus. by Corinne Turner, Roth, 1976, 180 pp. (0-8486-0211-0)

(BL 8:278, 27:216, 35:33; HB 10:299; LJ 63:798; Mahony 3:206)

914 **LEBERMANN, Norbert.** *New German Fairy Tales.* **Gr. 3–6. (Orig. pub. in Germany.)**

A combination of traditional and modern tales including one about an inventor-hero who conquers the goblins of electricity and steam.

Illus. by Margaret Freeman, Knopf, 1930, 247 pp., o.p.

(HB 6:331; LJ 55:1023; Mahony 3:206)

915 **LEE, Tanith.** *Dreams of Dark and Light: The Great Short Fiction of Tanith Lee.* **Gr. 10 up.**

Twenty-three previously published tales written between 1977 and 1984, including "Because Our Skins Are Finer," "Tamastara," and "The Gorgon."

Arkham, 1986, 507 pp., o.p.

(BL 82:1667; KR 54:978; VOYA 9:164, 10:22)

916 **LEE, Tanith.** *Princess Hynchatti and Some Other Surprises.* **Gr. 4–6. (Orig.**
✓ **British pub. 1972.)**

A collection of twelve humorous fairy tales including one about a prince who accidentally falls in love with a witch, and another about a beautiful swan who is transformed into an awkward, yellow-eyed princess.

Illus. by Velma Ilsley, Farrar, 1973, 183 pp., o.p.

(BL 69:1021; HB 69:948; KR 41:457; LJ 98:2195; TLS 1972 p. 1332)

LEE, Tanith. *Red as Blood; or Tales from the Sisters Grimmer.* See Chapter 5B, Myth Fantasy.

LEE, Tanith. *Tamastara; or the Indian Nights.* See Chapter 5B, Myth Fantasy.

LE GUIN, Ursula K(roeber). *Buffalo Gals and Other Animal Presences.* See Chapter 2, Animal Fantasy.

917 **LE GUIN, Ursula K(roeber).** *The Wind's Twelve Quarters: Short Stories.* **Gr. 8**
✓ **up.**

Seventeen stories of fantasy and science fiction, including "Winter's King" and "The Day Before the Revolution."

Harper, 1975, 303 pp., o.p.

(BBS:60; BL 72:615; KR 43:942; LJ 100:1950; SLJ Mar 1976 p. 120; TLS 1976 p. 950; Tymn:112)

Liavek. **Ed. by Will Shetterly and Emma Bull.** See Chapter 5A, Alternate Worlds or Histories.

918 *The Lifted Veil: The Book of Fantastic Literature by Women, 1800–World War II.* **Ed. by A. Susan Williams. Gr. 10 up. (Orig. British pub. 1992.)**

An anthology of English, American, Australian, Irish, Canadian, South African, Indian, West Indian, and New Zealander stories written by women between 1806 and 1992.

Carroll & Graf, 1992, 952 pp. (0-88184-913-8)

(BL 89:579, 586; LJ Nov 1, 1992, p. 120; TLS Dec 18, 1992 p. 17)

919 *Listen to This.* **Ed. by Laura Cecil. Gr. K–4. (Orig. British pub. 1987.)**

A collection meant to be shared aloud: familiar folk tales plus stories by Margaret Mahy, Rudyard Kipling, and Philippa Pearce, with lively watercolor illustrations.

Illus. by Emma Chichester Clark, Greenwillow, 1988, 92 pp. (0-688-07617-3)

(BL 84:1183; KR 56:198; SLJ June 1988 p. 84; TLS 1987 p. 1361)

The Literary Ghost: Great Contemporary Ghost Stories. **Ed. by Larry Dark.** See Chapter 4, Ghost Fantasy.

LIVELY, Penelope (Margaret Low). *Uninvited Ghosts and Other Stories.* See Chapter 6, Humorous Fantasy.

The Lonely Little Pig and Other Animal Tales. See Chapter 2, Animal Fantasy.

920 *The Lost Half-Hour: A Collection of Stories.* **Ed. by Eulalie Steinmetz Ross. Gr. 4–6.**

Stories by Rudyard Kipling, Ruth Sawyer, Howard Pyle, Barbara Freeman, Oscar Wilde, Kate Seredy, and others.

Illus. by Enrico Arno, Harcourt, 1963, 191 pp., o.p.

(BL 60:210; HB 39:604; LJ 88:4088)

Lost Worlds, Unknown Horizons: Nine Stories of Science Fiction. **Ed. by Robert Silverberg.** See Chapter 5C, Travel to Other Worlds.

921 **LYNN, Elizabeth A.** *The Woman Who Loved the Moon, and Other Stories.* **Gr. 10 up.**

This collection of sixteen fantasy and horror short stories includes "Wizard's Domain" and "The Woman Who Loved the Moon," a World Fantasy Award, 1980, winning story.

Berkley, 1981, pap., 197 pp., o.p.

(BL 78:427, 435; Kliatt 16[Winter 1982]:22, VOYA 4[Dec 1981]:39)

922 **MacDONALD, George.** *The Complete Fairy Tales of George MacDonald* **(Orig.**
✓ **U.S. title:** *The Light Princess and Other Fairy Tales,* **1893). Gr. 4–8.**

Eight tales, including "The Light Princess," "The Giant's Heart," "The Golden Key," and "The Day Boy and the Night Girl."

Illus. by Arthur Hughes, Watts, 1961 (entitled: *The Light Princess and Other Tales, Being the Complete Fairy Stories of George MacDonald*), 288 pp., o.p.; illus. by Arthur Hughes, Schocken, 1979, o.p.

(BL 58:446, 74:1014; CC:580; CCBB 32:196; HB 38:177, 55:441)

923 **McKINLEY, (Jennifer Carolyn) Robin (Turrell).** *The Door in the Hedge.* **Gr. 5–7.**

Two original tales, "The Hunting of the Hind" and "The Stolen Princess," and two traditional folk tales, "The Princess and the Frog" and "The Twelve Dancing Princesses."

Greenwillow, 1981 (0-688-00312-5); Ace, 1984, pap., 224 pp. (0-441-15315-1)

(BBJ:73; BL 77:810; CCBB 35:33; HB 57:433; JHC:432; Kies:114; KR 49:876; SLJ Aug 1981 p. 77)

McKISSACK, Patricia C. *The Dark-Thirty: Southern Tales of the Supernatural.* See Chapter 4, Ghost Fantasy.

924 **MACOUREK, Miloš.** *Curious Tales.* **Gr. 3–5. (Orig. Czech pubs. 1966, 1971.)**

Fourteen imaginative tales, including three about a turkey-eating plant, an alarm clock revolt, and an operatic kitchen sink.

Trans. by Marie Burg, illus. by Adolf Born, Oxford, 1980, 88 pp., o.p.

(BL 77:45; SLJ Sept 1981 p. 111; TLS Nov 21, 1980 p. 1325)

Magic in Ithkar. **Ed. by André Norton and Robert Adams.** See Chapter 5A, Alternate Worlds or Histories.

Magicats! **Ed. by Jack Dann and Gardner Dozois.** See Chapter 2, Animal Fantasy.

MAHY, Margaret (May). *Bubble Trouble and Other Poems and Stories.* See Chapter 6, Humorous Fantasy.

MAHY, Margaret (May). *The Chewing-Gum Rescue and Other Stories.* See Chapter 6, Humorous Fantasy.

MAHY, Margaret (May). *The Door in the Air and Other Stories.* See Chapter 7, Magic Adventure Fantasy.

MAHY, Margaret (May). *The Girl with the Green Ear: Stories About Magic in Nature.* See Chapter 7, Magic Adventure Fantasy.

MAHY, Margaret (May). *Nonstop Nonsense.* See Chapter 6, Humorous Fantasy.

MAHY, Margaret (May). *A Tall Story and Other Tales.* See Chapter 7, Magic Adventure Fantasy.

MAMIN-SIBERIAK. *Verotchka's Tales.* See Chapter 2, Animal Fantasy.

MANLEY, Seon. *The Ghost in the Far Garden and Other Stories.* See Chapter 4, Ghost Fantasy.

MARSHALL, James (Edward). *Rats on the Roof: and Other Stories.* See Chapter 2, Talking Animal Fantasy.

925 *Masterpieces of Fantasy and Enchantment.* **Compiled by David G. Hartwell and Kathryn Cramer. Gr. 10 up.**

This collection includes tales written both before and after Tolkein's work appeared, including excerpts and stories by Charles Dickens, Nathaniel Hawthorne, Ursula K. Le Guin and Michael Moorcock.

St. Martin's, 1988, 622 pp. (0-312-02250-6)

(BBS:58; BL 84:1984, 1915; SHC:740; VOYA 12:44)

Masters of Shades and Shadows: An Anthology of Great Ghost Stories. **Ed. by Seon Manley and Gogo Lewis.** See Chapter 4, Ghost Fantasy.

MAYNE, William (James Carter). *The Green Book of Hob Stories.* See Chapter 7, Magic Adventure Fantasy.

926 **MEIGS, Cornelia (Lynde).** *The Kingdom of the Winding Road.* **Gr. 5–7.**

Twelve tales in which the same wandering man with bright blue eyes plays on his silver pipe, summoning those he meets to adventure before he vanishes down the winding road.

Illus. by Frances White, Macmillan, 1915, 238 pp., o.p.

(BL 12:296; Bookshelf 1920–21 p. 15; HB 7:117)

MENDOZA, George. *Gwot! Horribly Funny Hairticklers.* See Chapter 6, Humorous Fantasy.

MILNE, A(lan) A(lexander). *Prince Rabbit and the Princess Who Could Not Laugh.* See Chapter 1, Allegorical Fantasy and Literary Fairy Tales.

927 *Modern Fairy Stories.* **Ed. by Roger (Gilbert) Lancelyn Green. Gr. 5–7. (Orig. British pub. 1955.)**

Sixteen stories written by Lewis Carroll, Juliana Horatia Ewing, Andrew Lang, Mary Louise Molesworth, Oscar Wilde, E. Nesbit, John Ruskin, and others.

Illus. by Ernest Shepard, Dutton, 1956, 270 pp., o.p.

(BL 52:369; HB 30:121)

Modern Ghost Stories by Eminent Women Writers. **Ed. by Richard Dalby.** See Chapter 4, Ghost Fantasy.

928 **MOLESWORTH, Mary Louisa (Stewart).** *Fairy Stories.* **Gr. 4–6.**

Eight tales of magic and enchantment including "The Reel Fairies" and "The Weather Maiden."

Illus. by Edna Cooke, Duffield, 1922, 353 pp. (entitled: *Stories by Mrs. Molesworth*), o.p.; ed. by Roger (Gilbert) Lancelyn Green, Roy, 1958, 159 pp., o.p.

(BL 19:95; HB 34:478; KR 26:659; LJ 83:3002; Mahony 2:291)

929 *Monsters, Ghoulies and Creepy Creatures: Fantastic Stories and Poems.* **Compiled by Lee Bennett Hopkins. Gr. 4–6.**

Stories by Natalie Babbitt, John Gardner, Natalie Savage Carlson, Tom McGowen, and Lee Bennett Hopkins, about devils, dragons, monsters, and demons.

Illus. by Vera Rosenberry, Whitman, 1977, 128 pp., o.p.

(BL 74:1110; CCBB 31:178)

930 **MONTROSE, Anne.** *The Winter Flower, and Other Fairy Stories.* **Gr. 4–6.**

Thirteen tales of princesses, magic, witches, and a dragon.

Illus. by Mircea Vasiliu, Viking, 1964, 143 pp., o.p.

(HB 40:611; LJ 89:4642)

931 *Moonsinger's Friends: In Honor of André Norton.* **Ed. by Susan M. Shwartz. Gr.**
✓ **10 up.**

Fourteen fantasy tales by such well-known authors as Marion Zimmer Bradley, C. J. Cherryh, Katherine Kurtz, Tanith Lee, Anne McCaffrey, Nancy Springer, and Jane Yolen.

Bluejay, 1985, 342 pp., o.p.

(BBS:64; BL 81:1637, 1657; KR 53:561; LJ Aug 1985 p. 121; SLJ Nov 1985 p. 106; VOYA 8:326)

MÜNCHAUSEN, Karl. *The Adventures of Baron Münchausen.* See Chapter 6, Humorous Fantasy.

932 **MURPHY, Pat.** *Points of Departure.* **Gr. 10 up.**

Nineteen powerful fantasy and science fiction stories, including many about lonely women who escape from abusive relationships, including one about time travel ("Orange Blossom Time"), two about selkies ("Sweetly the Waves Call to Me" and "In the Islands"), and one about a witch's black magic ("With Four Hounds").

Bantam, 1990, 336 pp. (0-553-28615-3)

(BL 86:2077, 2083; VOYA 14:46, 15:10)

933 **NESBIT (Bland), E(dith).** *The Complete Book of Dragons.* **Gr. 4–6. (Written in**
✓ **England, 1899, orig. U.S. pub. 1901, entitled** *The Book of Dragons.*)

Nine tales about children confronting dragons, including "The Ice Dragon," "The Dragon
Tamers," and "The Last of the Dragons."

Illus. by Erik Blegvad, Macmillan, 1973, 198 pp., o.p.

(BL 69:911; CCBB 26:142; HB 49:272; Kies:126; KR 41:6; LJ 26:167)

934 **NORTON, André (pseud. of Alice Mary Norton).** *Moon Mirror.* **Gr. 10 up.**

These nine stories include one from Norton's Witch World saga (see Chapter 5C, Travel
to Other Worlds) and two reworkings of traditional fairy tales.

Tor, 1988, 250 pp. (0-312-93098-4), 1990, pap. (0-8125-0303-1)

(BBS:62; BL 85:754, 780; KR 56:1646; VOYA 12:116, 13:258)

NORTON, André (pseud. of Alice Mary Norton). *Wizards' Worlds.* See Chapter
10, Witchcraft and Sorcery Fantasy.

935 **NYE, Robert.** *The Mathematical Princess and Other Stories.* **Gr. 4–6. (British
title:** *Poor Pumpkin,* **1971.)**

Six stories, including the tale of a princess who puts all of her suitors to sleep with her
lectures on Euclid.

Illus. by Paul Bruner, Hill, 1972, 125 pp., o.p.

(HB 48:468; KR 40:673; LJ 98:646)

936 *Once Upon a Time: A Treasury of Modern Fairy Tales.* **Ed. by Lester Del Rey
and Risa Kessler. Gr. 10 up.**

Ten tales written by Anne McCaffrey, Barbara Hambly, C. J. Cherryh, Katherine Kurtz,
and other contemporary authors of fantasy.

Illus. by Michael Pangrazio, Ballantine, 1991, 352 pp. (0-345-36263-2)

(BL 88:608, 611; KR 59:1122; LJ Oct 15 1991 p. 127)

937 *100 Great Fantasy Short Stories.* **Ed. by Isaac Asimov, Terry Carr, and Martin
H. Greenberg. Gr. 10 up.**

The stories chosen for inclusion here were written by Roger Zelazny, Gene Wolfe, and
Marion Zimmer Bradley, among others.

Doubleday, 1984, 311 pp., o.p.

(KR 52:114; LJ 109:600; SHC:732; TLS 1984 p. 1359; VOYA 7:207)

The Other Side of the Clock: Stories Out of Time, Out of Place. **Ed. by Philip Van
Doren Stern.** See Chapter 8, Time Travel Fantasy.

938 *The Oxford Book of Modern Fairy Tales.* **Ed. by Alison Lurie. Gr. 10 up. (Orig.
British pub. 1993.)**

An anthology of fantasy short stories written for children and adults, by such renowned
British and American authors as Joan Aiken, L. Frank Baum, Charles Dickens, Nathaniel
Hawthorne, Richard Hughes, Ursula K. Le Guin, E. Nesbit, Isaac Bashevis Singer, James
Thurber, Oscar Wilde, and Jay Williams.

Oxford Univ. Pr., 1993, 480 pp. (0-19-214218-6)

(BL 89:1572, 1576; TLS July 30, 1993 p. 7)

PAINE, Albert Bigelow. *The Hollow Tree and Deep Woods Book.* See Chapter 2, Animal Fantasy.

PARK, Ruth. *Things in Corners.* See Chapter 4, Ghost Fantasy.

939 **PARRISH, Anne, and PARRISH, Dillwyn.** *The Dream Coach.* **Gr. 3–5.**

Each night a dream coach travels across the sky, leaving dream stories along its way. John Newbery Medal Honor Book, 1925.

Illus. by the authors, Macmillan, 1924, 143 pp., o.p.

(BL 21:158; HB 1(Nov 1924):12, 7:61–67)

PEARCE, (Ann) Philippa. *Lion at School: And Other Stories.* See Chapter 7, Magic Adventure Fantasy.

PEARCE, (Ann) Philippa. *The Shadow-Cage and Other Tales of the Supernatural.* See Chapter 4, Ghost Fantasy.

PEARCE, (Ann) Philippa. *Who's Afraid? And Other Strange Stories.* See Chapter 4, Ghost Fantasy.

The Pendragon Chronicles: Heroic Fantasy from the Time of King Arthur. **Ed. by Mike Ashley.** See Chapter 5B, Myth Fantasy.

940 *Phantasmagoria: Tales of Fantasy and the Supernatural.* **Ed. by Jane Mobley. Gr. 10 up.**

An anthology of English and American fantastic and supernatural tales whose authors include Lord Dunsany, George MacDonald, Ursula K. Le Guin, André Norton, and Peter Beagle.

Doubleday, 1977, pap., 439 pp., o.p.

(BL 74:463, 470; Kliatt 12[Winter 1978]:14)

941 *Phoenix Feathers: A Collection of Mythical Monsters.* **Ed. by Barbara Silverberg. Gr. 6–10.**

Tales of dragons, griffons, unicorns, and the phoenix.

Illus. with old prints, Dutton, 1973, 206 pp., o.p.

(BL 70:737; KR 41:820; LJ 98:3457)

The Phoenix Tree: An Anthology of Myth Fantasy. **Ed. by Robert H. Boyer and Kenneth J. Zahorski.** See Chapter 5B, Myth Fantasy.

942 **PICARD, Barbara Leonie.** *The Faun and the Woodcutter's Daughter.* **Gr. 5–7.**
✓ **(Orig. British pub. 1951.)**

This collection of fourteen fairy tales begins with the story of a woodcutter's daughter who meets a faun in the woods and cannot live without him.

Illus. by Charles Stewart, Abelard-Schuman, 1964, 255 pp., o.p.

(BL 61:436; CCBB 18:168; Eakin:261; HB 41:57; LJ 89:5010)

943 **PICARD, Barbara Leonie.** *The Goldfinch Garden: Seven Tales.* **Gr. 4–6. (Orig.**
✓ **British pub. 1963.)**

Seven original fairy tales about mortals who become involved with a witch, a water sprite, a fairy maiden, and other creatures.

Illus. by Anne Linton, Criterion, 1965, 121 pp., o.p.

(BL 62:532; HB 42:55; KR 33:1042)

944 **PICARD, Barbara Leonie.** *The Lady of the Linden Tree.* **Gr. 5–7. (Orig. British**
✓ **pub. 1954.)**

Twelve tales of knights, princes, princesses, and enchantment, including "Findings Are
Keepings," "The Castle in the Cornfield," and "The Piper with the Hoofs of a Goat."
Carnegie Medal Commended Book, 1954.

Illus. by Charles Stewart, Criterion, 1962, 214 pp., o.p.

(BL 58:694; CCBB 16:14; Eakin:261; HB 38:276; KR 30:176; LJ 87:2027)

945 **PICARD, Barbara Leonie.** *The Mermaid and the Simpleton.* **Gr. 5–7. (Orig.**
✓ **British pub. 1949.)**

Fifteen tales of princesses, witches, and magic, including "Heart of the Wind," "The Ivory
Box," and "Three Wishes."

Illus. by Philip Gough, Criterion, 1970, 253 pp., o.p.

(BL 47:225, 67:150; CCBB 4:15; HB 26:488; KR 18:642, 38:454; LJ 16:55, 95:2535, 4326)

946 **PORTE, Barbara Ann.** *Jesse's Ghost and Other Stories.* **Gr. 4–6.**
✓ A collection of thought-provoking stories told by a storyteller who "sits where three
worlds meet, before and now and after."

Greenwillow, 1983, 105 pp. (0-688-02301-0)

(BBC:211; BL 80:366; CC:581; CCBB 37:134; KR 51:J164; SLJ Nov 1983 p. 82)

PREUSSLER, Otfried. *The Wise Men of Schilda.* See Chapter 6, Humorous Fantasy.

947 *The Princesses: Sixteen Stories about Princesses.* **Ed. by Sally Patrick Johnson.**
✓ **Gr. 4–6. (British title:** *The Book of Princesses.***)**

One tale each by sixteen authors, including Hans Christian Andersen, Mary de Morgan,
Somerset Maugham, Walter de la Mare, Eleanor Farjeon, Ruth Sawyer, and Rudyard
Kipling. *The Harper Book of Princes* (1964) is the companion volume, containing stories
by A. A. Milne, E. Nesbit, Frank R. Stockton, Laurence Housman, and Oscar Wilde.

Illus. by Beni Montresor, Harper, 1962, 318 pp., o.p.

(BL 59:396; CCBB 16:96; Eakin:178; HB 38:603; LJ 87:187)

948 *Princesses and Peasant Boys: Tales of Enchantment.* **Ed. by Phyllis Reid Fenner.**
Gr. 4–6.

Included in this collection are stories by Hans Christian Andersen, Howard Pyle, and
Margery Williams Bianco.

Illus. by Henry C. Pitz, Knopf, 1944, 188 pp., o.p.

(BL 41:126; KR 12:430; LJ 69:1049)

949 *The Provensen Book of Fairy Tales.* **Ed. by Alice Provensen. Gr. 3–6.**

Stories by Hans Christian Andersen, Henry Beston, Ruth Manning-Sanders, A. A. Milne,
Barbara Picard, Howard Pyle, and Oscar Wilde.

Illus. by Alice Provensen and Martin Provensen, Random, 1971, 140 pp., o.p.

(CCBB 25:96; KR 39:1130; LJ 97:1916)

950 **PUSHKIN, Alexander Sergeevich.** *The Golden Cockerel and Other Stories.* **Gr.**
3–7. (Orig. pub. in Russia.)

Five poetic retellings of Russian folktales, including "The Tale of Tsar Saltan" and "The
Tale of the Fisherman and the Little Golden Fish."

Trans. by James Reeves, illus. by Ján Lebiš, Watts, 1969, 110 pp., o.p.; trans. by Jessie

Wood, illus. by Boris Zvorykin, Doubleday, 1990 (orig. pub. in France, 1925), 112 pp. (entitled: *The Golden Cockerel and Other Fairy Tales*) (0-385-26252-3)

(BL 87:1125; HB 46:384; KR 58:1605; LJ 95:3631; TLS 1970 p. 420)

951 **PYLE, Howard.** *Pepper and Salt; or, Seasoning for Young Folk.* **Gr. 4–7. (Orig.**
✓ **British pub. 1886.)**

Eight tales, including "The Skillful Huntsman," "Clever Peter and the Two Bottles," and "The Apple of Contentment."

Illus. by the author, Harper, 1923, 109 pp., o.p.

(BL 20:384; Bookshelf 1932 p. 8; Ch&Bks:290; HB 1[June 1925]:29; Mahony 1:37)

PYLE, Howard. *Twilight Land.* See Chapter 5C, Travel to Other Worlds.

952 **PYLE, Howard.** *The Wonder Clock; or, Four and Twenty Marvelous Tales, Being*
✓ *One for Each Hour of the Day.* **Gr. 5–7. (Orig. British pub. 1887.)**

Twenty-four tales, including "One Good Turn Deserves Another," "The Princess Golden Hair and the Great Black Raven," and "King Stork."

Verses by Katharine Pyle, illus. by the author, Harper, 1943, o.p.; Peter Smith, n.d., 318 pp. (0-8446-2767-4); Dover, n.d., pap. (0-486-21446-X)

(Bookshelf 1932 p. 8; CC:115; Ch&Bks:290; HB 1[June 1925]:31, 19:48; Mahony 2:292)

The Random House Book of Ghost Stories. **Ed. by Susan Hill.** See Chapter 4, Ghost Fantasy.

953 **REEVES, James (pseud. of John Morris Reeves).** *Sailor Rumbelow and Other Stories.* **Gr. 4–6. (Orig. British pub. in two volumes:** *Sailor Rumbelow and Britannia,* **1962 and** *Pigeons and Princesses,* **1956.)**

Two retellings of traditional tales, plus nine original stories, including "The Stonemason of Elphinstone."

Illus. by Edward Ardizzone, Dutton, 1962, 223 pp., o.p.

(BL 59:498; HB 38:605; LJ 87:3898)

REID BANKS, Lynne. *The Magic Hare.* See Chapter 2, Animal Fantasy.

954 *A Ring of Tales.* **Ed. by Kathleen Lines. Gr. 4–7. (Orig. British pub. 1958.)**
✓ Tales by Alison Uttley, A. A. Milne, Hans Christian Andersen, Walter de la Mare, Eleanor Farjeon, and Selma Lagerlöf.

Illus. by Harold Jones, Watts, 1959, 239 pp., o.p.

(BL 55:488; HB 35:299; LJ 84:1698; TLS Nov 21, 1958 p. xvi)

955 **RITCHIE, Alice.** *The Treasure of Li-Po.* **Gr. 4–7. (Orig. British pub. 1948.)**

Six magical stories set in ancient China.

Illus. by T. Ritchie, Harcourt, 1949, 154 pp., o.p.

(BL 46:17; CCBB 2[Sept 1949]:4; HB 25:416, 436; KR 17:393; LJ 74:1208, 1542)

956 **ROACH, Marilynne K(athleen).** *Encounters with the Invisible World; Being Ten*
✓ *Tales of Ghosts, Witches, and the Devil Himself in New England.* **Gr. 6–10.**

Ten supernatural tales set in New England, about ghosts, piracy, witchcraft, and the devil.

Illus. by the author, Crowell, 1977, 131 pp., o.p.; Amereon, n.d. (0-89190-874-9)

ROBINSON, Marileta. *Mr. Goat's Bad Good Idea.* See Chapter 2, Animal Fantasy.

ROUNDS, Glen (Harold). *Mr. Yowder, The Peripatetic Sign Painter: Three Tall Tales.* See Chapter 6, Humorous Fantasy.

SANDBURG, Carl. *Rootabaga Stories.* See Chapter 6, Humorous Fantasy.

SCIESZKA, Jon. *The Stinky Cheese Man and Other Fairly Stupid Tales.* See Chapter 6, Humorous Fantasy.

Shades of Dark: Stories. **Ed. by Aidan Chambers.** See Chapter 4, Ghost Fantasy.

957 **SHANNON, Monica.** *California Fairy Tales.* **Gr. 5–7. (Orig. pub. Doubleday, 1926.)**

Tales of the elves, fairies, and goblins living in California's orchards, gardens, and forests. *More Tales from California* (1960; orig. title: *Eyes for the Dark,* 1928) is the companion volume.

Illus. by C. E. Millard, Stephen Daye, 1957, 298 pp., o.p.

(BL 23:348; 54:310; HB 2[Nov 1926]:42, 344:124; Mahony 2:297; Moore:429)

958 *Shape Shifters: Fantasy and Science Fiction Tales about Humans Who Can Change Their Shapes.* **Ed. by Jane H(yatt) Yolen (Stemple). Gr. 6–9.**

Twelve tales about people who change into animals, monsters, and machines, including "The Boy Who Would Be a Wolf," "The Enchanted Village," and "Judas Fish."

Seabury, 1978, 182 pp., o.p.

(BL 74:1259; CCBB 32:40; KR 46:552; SLJ Sept 1978 p. 167)

SHARMA, Partap. *The Surangini Tales.* See Chapter 1, Allegorical Fantasy and Literary Fairy Tales.

The Silent Playmate: A Collection of Doll Stories. **Ed. by Naomi Lewis.** See Chapter 9, Toy Fantasy.

959 **SINGER, Isaac Bashevis.** *Naftali the Storyteller and His Horse, Sus, and Other* ✓ *Stories.* **Gr. 4–7.**

Eight tales, including stories about the foolish people of Chelm and an imp called the lantuch.

Trans. by Joseph Singer, Ruth Finkel, and the author, illus. by Margot Zemach, Farrar, 1976, pap., 129 pp. (0-374-45487-6); Dell, 1979, pap. (0-440-46642-3)

(BL 73:670; CC:581; CCBB 30:98; HB 53:162; KR 44:1139; SLJ Dec 1976 p. 56; Suth 2:415)

960 **SINGER, Isaac Bashevis.** *Stories for Children.* **Gr. 4–7.**
✓ A collection of most of Singer's children's stories, including those about the fools of Chelm, "Zlateh the Goat" and "Mazel and Shlimazel."

Farrar, 1984, 337 pp., o.p., pap., 1985 (0-374-46489-8)

(BL 81:592; CCBB 38:73; HB 61:183; Suth 3:395; SLJ Dec 1984 p. 86)

961 **SINGER, Isaac Bashevis.** *Zlateh the Goat and Other Stories.* **Gr. 4–7.**
✓ Seven stories, including three tall tales about the foolish people of Chelm, two about the devil, and an allegorical tale about a young boy and his goat who are lost in a blizzard. John Newbery Medal Honor Book, 1967.

Illus. by Maurice Sendak, Harper, 1966, 90 pp. (0-06-025698-2), pap., 1984 (0-06-440147-2)

(BL 63:378; CCBB 20:79; HB 42:712; KR 34:1045; LJ 91:6197; Suth:368)

962 **SLEIGH, Barbara (de Riemer).** *Stirabout Stories, Brewed in Her Own Cauldron* **(British title:** *West of Widdershins,* **1971). Gr. 4–6.**

Fourteen tales of magic, fairies, witches, and sea monsters.

Illus. by Victor Ambrus, Bobbs-Merrill, 1971, 143 pp., o.p.

(CCBB 26:49; LJ 97:3808; TLS 1971 p. 1321)

Small Shadows Creep. **Ed. by André Norton.** See Chapter 4, Ghost Fantasy.

Smart Dragons, Foolish Elves. **Ed. by Alan Dean Foster and Martin H. Greenberg.** See Chapter 6, Humorous Fantasy.

SOMMER-BODENBURG, Angela. *If You Want to Scare Yourself.* See Chapter 4, Ghost Fantasy.

963 **SOYER, Abraham.** *The Adventures of Yemima.* **Gr. 4–6. (Orig. pub. in Palestine, 1939.)**

Six fables, including tales about a gift of flying money, greedy animals, and a brave little girl.

Trans. from Hebrew by Rebecca Beagle and Rebecca Soyer, illus. by Raphael Soyer, Viking, 1979, 80 pp., o.p.

(BL 75:1298; HB 55:305; KR 47:518; SLJ Apr 1979 p. 49)

964 *Spaceships and Spells: A Collection of New Fantasy and Science-Fiction Stories.* **Ed. by Jane Yolen, Martin H. Greenberg, and Charles G. Waugh. Gr. 5–8.**

Thirteen fantasy and science fiction tales whose authors include Bruce Coville, Robert Lawson, Jane Yolen, and Charles de Lint.

Harper, 1987, 182 pp., o.p.

(BL 84:868; CCBB 41:40; SLJ Dec 1987 p. 89; VOYA 10:292)

965 **STEELE, Mary Q(uintard Govan).** *The Owl's Kiss: Three Stories.* **Gr. 6–8.**

In these three tales, a little girl fears owls will kill her for stealing her grandmother's fruit, an older girl longs to become a witch, and a man is falsely accused of theft.

Greenwillow/Morrow, 1978, 99 pp., o.p.

(BL 75:53; HB 55:522; KR 46:878; SLJ Dec 1978 p. 57)

966 **STOCKTON, Frank (Francis) R(ichard).** *The Queen's Museum and Other Fanciful Tales.* **Gr. 5–7. (Orig. pub. 1887.)**

Ten stories, including "The Griffin and the Minor Canon," "The Bee-Man of Orn," and "Old Pipes and the Dryad."

Illus. by Frederick Richardson, Scribner, 1906, 219 pp., o.p.

(BL 3:23; Bookshelf 1921–1922 p. 15; HB 1[June 1925]:45; Mahony 2:297)

967 **STOCKTON, Frank (Francis) R(ichard).** *The Reformed Pirate: Stories from The Floating Prince, Ting-a-Ling Tales and the Queen's Museum.* **Gr. 5–7. (Orig. pub. 1881.)**

Twelve imaginative tales about fairies, dragons, pirates, and kings.

Illus. by Reginald B. Birch, Scribner, 1936, 342 pp., o.p.

(BL 33:94; HB 13:36; LJ 62:126)

968 **STOCKTON, Frank (Francis) R(ichard).** *The Storyteller's Pack, a Frank R.*
✓ *Stockton Reader* **(Orig. title:** *A Story-Teller's Pack,* **1897). Gr. 5–7.**

Seventeen stories, including "The Bee-Man of Orn," "The Griffin and the Minor Canon," and "The Lady or the Tiger."

Illus. by Bernarda Bryson, Scribner, 1968, 358 pp., o.p.

(BL 65:1019; HB 45:60; LJ 94:891; Tymn:159)

969 **STOCKTON, Frank (Francis) R(ichard).** *Ting-a-Ling Tales* **(Orig. title:** *Ting-a-ling,* **1870). Gr. 4–7.**

A collection of fanciful tales.

Illus. by Richard Floethe, Scribner, 1955, 161 pp., o.p.

(BL 52:110; CCBB 11:86; HB 31:445, 466)

970 *Stories for Nine-Year-Olds and Other Young Readers.* **Ed. by Sara Corrin and Stephen Corrin. Gr. 4 up.**

A combination of myths and modern fantasy by such authors as Helen Cresswell, Rudyard Kipling, Joan Aiken, Saki, and James Thurber, all appropriate for reading aloud.

Illus. by Shirley Hughes, Faber, 1979, 160 pp., pap. (0-571-12931-5)

(BL 76:452; SLJ Apr 1980 p. 122; TLS 1979 p. 129)

STORR, Catherine (Cole). *Cold Marble and Other Ghost Stories.* See Chapter 4, Ghost Fantasy.

971 *Strange Dreams: Unforgettable Fantasy.* **Ed. by Stephen R. Donaldson. Gr. 10**
✓ **up.**

Twenty-eight short fantasy and science fiction stories by Rudyard Kipling, C. J. Cherryh, Orson Scott Card, and others.

Bantam, 1993, pap., 544 pp. (0-553-37103-7)

(BL 89:1678; Kliatt Sept 1993 p. 16; LJ May 15 1993 p. 100; VOYA 16:313)

Supernatural Stories: 13 Tales of the Unexpected. **Ed. by Jean Russell.** See Chapter 4, Ghost Fantasy.

Sword and Sorceress: An Anthology of Heroic Fantasy. **Ed. by Marion Zimmer Bradley.** See Chapter 5A, Alternate Worlds or Histories.

Tales out of Time. **Ed. by Barbara Ireson.** See Chapter 8, Time Travel Fantasy.

972 **TASSIN, Algernon de Vivier.** *The Rainbow String.* **Gr. 4–6.**

Six humorous adventure tales about the romances of six princesses.

Illus. by Anna Richards Brewster, Macmillan, 1921, 1929, 114 pp., o.p.

(BL 18:291; Bookshelf 1923–1924 p. 8; Mahony 1:40)

Things That Go Bump in the Night: A Collection of Original Stories. **Ed. by Jane Yolen and Martin H. Greenberg.** See Chapter 4, Ghost Fantasy.

973 *Told Under the Magic Umbrella: Modern Fanciful Stories for Young Children.* **Ed. by The Association for Childhood Education Literature Committee. Gr. 3–5.**

Thirty-three fantasy stories written by Marjorie Williams Bianco, Carl Sandburg, Monica Shannon, Laurence Housman, Eleanor Farjeon, Ted Hughes, Anne Thomasine Casserley, Carol Ryrie Brink, and Betty Brock.

Illus. by Elizabeth Orton Jones, Macmillan, 1939, 1955, 248 pp., o.p.

(BL 35:312; HB 15:166; LJ 64:380)

974 *Tomorrow's Children: 18 Tales of Fantasy and Science Fiction.* **Ed. by Isaac Asi-**
✓ **mov. Gr. 7–12.**

Eighteen fantastic tales whose authors include Ray Bradbury and Clifford Simak.

Illus. by Emanuel Schoengut, Doubleday, 1966, 431 pp., o.p.

(BL 63:843; CCBB 20:69; HB 43:69; KR 34:993; LJ 91:6198)

***Trips in Time: Nine Stories of Science Fiction.* Ed. by Robert Silverberg.** See Chapter 8, Time Travel Fantasy.

975 ***The Unicorn Treasury: Stories, Poems and Unicorn Lore.* Ed. by Bruce Coville. Gr. 5–8.**

Unicorn stories by Jane Yolen, C. S. Lewis, Madeleine L'Engle, and others.

Illus. by Tim Hildebrandt, Doubleday, 1988, 166 pp. (0-385-24000-7), 1991, pap. (0-385-41930-9)

(BBC:201; BL 85:942; KR 56:1057; SLJ Nov 1988 p. 118)

976 ***Unicorns!* Ed. by Jack Dann and Gardner Dozois. Gr. 10 up.**

An anthology of humorous, mythic, and horror tales about unicorns, written by Roger Zelazny, Ursula K. Le Guin, Gene Wolfe, Stephen R. Donaldson, and others.

Ace, 1982, pap., 310 pp., o.p.

(BL 79:95, 106; Kies:205; VOYA 5[Oct 1982]:50)

UTTLEY, Alison. *Foxglove Tales.* See Chapter 2, Animal Fantasy.

***Victorian Ghost Stories: An Oxford Anthology.* Sel. by Michael Cox and R. A. Gilbert.** See Chapter 4, Ghost Fantasy.

977 ***Visions of Wonder: An Anthology of Christian Fantasy.* Ed. by Robert H. Boyer and Kenneth J. Zahorski. Gr. 10 up.**

A collection of fables, fairy tales, legends, allegories, and satires drawn from Christian concepts, including material by George MacDonald.

Avon, 1981, 1986, pap., 240 pp., o.p.

(BL 78:538, 546; Kliatt 16[Winter 1982]:20)

978 **VIVELO, Jackie.** *A Trick of the Light: Stories to Read at Dusk.* **Gr. 5–8.**

Six of these nine stories involve magical events, including "The Fireside Book of Ghost Stories," in which people disappear after reading stories that affect their lives.

Putnam, 1987, 124 pp., o.p.; Beyond Words, 1989, pap. (0-941831-34-5)

(BL 84:638; CCBB 41:104; SLJ Feb 1988 p. 76; VOYA 10:284)

979 ***Wandering Stars: An Anthology of Jewish Fantasy and Science Fiction.* Ed. by Jack Dann. Gr. 10 up.**

Thirteen humorous science fiction and fantasy stories, whose authors include Robert Silverberg, Isaac Asimov, and Isaac Bashevis Singer.

Harper, 1974, 239 pp., o.p.

(BL 70:906, 932; KR 41:1287)

980 **WATT-EVANS, Lawrence.** *Crosstime Traffic.* **Gr. 10 up.**

Twenty fantasy and science fiction stories about alternate worlds, demons, and dragons.

Ballantine, 1992, pap., 247 pp. (0-345-37395-2)

(BL 89: 407, 412; Kliatt Jan 1993 p. 20)

WEAVER, Jack. *Mr. O'Hara.* See Chapter 6, Humorous Fantasy.

981 **WELLS, H(erbert) G(eorge).** *The Door in the Wall and Other Stories.* **Gr. 10 up. (Orig. British and U.S. pub. 1911; 1925, 1939.)**

Eight short stories, including "The Door in the Wall," "A Moonlight Fable," and "The Country of the Blind."

Photos by Alvin Langdon Coburn, Godine, 1980, 157 pp., o.p.

(BL 77:199, 206; Kliatt 15[Winter 1981]:19)

WESTALL, Robert (Atkinson). *The Call and Other Stories.* See Chapter 4, Ghost Fantasy.

WESTALL, Robert (Atkinson). *Demons and Shadows: The Ghostly Best Stories of Robert Westall.* See Chapter 4, Ghost Fantasy.

WESTALL, Robert (Atkinson). *The Haunting of Chas McGill and Other Stories.* See Chapter 4, Ghost Fantasy.

WESTALL, Robert (Atkinson). *In Camera and Other Stories.* See Chapter 4, Ghost Fantasy.

982 **WESTALL, Robert (Atkinson).** *Rachel and the Angel and Other Stories.* **Gr.**
✓ **8–12. (Orig. British pub. 1986.)**

Seven fantasy and science fiction stories, including the title story, in which a vicar's daughter tricks the angel of death into sparing the townspeople, in spite of their faults.

Greenwillow, 1987, 187 pp., o.p.

(BL 84:139, 154; CCBB 41:39; HB 64:74; KR 55:1399; SLJ Dec 1987 p. 106; VOYA 10:239)

What Did Miss Darrington See? An Anthology of Feminist Supernatural Fiction.
Ed. by Jessica Amanda Salmonson. See Chapter 4, Ghost Fantasy.

983 **WHITCHER, Susan.** *Real Mummies Don't Bleed: Friendly Tales for October Nights.* **Gr. 3–6.**

Five humorous scarey stories, including "Annie's Pet Witch," "The Paper Bag Genie," and "Toad Meets Frankenstein."

Illus. by Andrew Glass, Farrar, 1993, 119 pp. (0-374-36213-0)

(CCBB 47:135; KR 61:1082; SLJ Feb 1994 p. 104)

WHITELAW, Stella, GARDINER, Judith, and RONSON, Mark. *Grimalkin's Tales.* See Chapter 2, Animal Fantasy.

984 **WILDE, Oscar (pseud. of Fingal O'Flahertie Wills).** *The Fairy Tales of Oscar Wilde.* **Gr. 4 up. (Orig. British pub. in** *The Happy Prince and Other Tales,* **1888.)**

There have been many editions of Wilde's collected fairy tales for children, which include such well-known stories as "The Happy Prince" and "The Selfish Giant." The following collections are arranged alphabetically by title:

The Birthday of the Infanta and Other Tales. Illus. by Beni Montresor, Macmillan, 1982, 73 pp., o.p.

Complete Fairy Tales of Oscar Wilde. NAL, 1990, pap., 221 pp. (0-451-52435-7)

Fairy Tales of Oscar Wilde. (Orig. British pub. in *The Happy Prince and Other Tales,* 1888; *The House of Pomegranates,* 1991, 1906; and *Fairy Tales,* 1913.) Illus by Charles Mozley, Watts, 1960, o.p.; illus. by Craig P. Russell, Nantier, 1992, 48 pp., (1-

56163056-X); illus. by Michael Hague (Orig. British pub. in this ed. 1991), Holt, 1993, 184 pp., (0-805010092)

The Happy Prince and Other Fairy Stories. Putnam, 1909, 1911, o.p.

The Happy Prince and Other Fairy Tales. (Orig. British pub. 1888.) Illus. by Charles Robinson, Putnam, 1913, o.p.; illus. by Charles Robinson, Brentanos, 1920, o.p.; illus. by Charles Robinson, Morrow, 1991, 136 pp. (0-688-10390-1)

The Happy Prince and Other Tales. Illus. by Peggy Fortnum, Dent, 1977, o.p.

Stories for Children. (Orig. British pub. in this ed. 1990.) Illus. by P. J. Lynch, Macmillan, 1991, 96 pp. (0027927652)

(BL 37:222, 79:782, 88:153, 89:985, 1425; Bookshelf 1921–1922 p. 15; CC:582; CCBB 36:139; Ch&Bks:292; HBG 2[Jan–June 1991]:257, 3[July–Dec 1991]:75, 4[Fall 1993]:306; Kies:186; Kliatt Sept 1990 p. 5; KR 36:826, 59:1170; SLJ Oct 1980 p. 152, Dec 1991 p. 119, Apr 1993 p. 125, Aug 1993 p. 162; TLS 1977 p. 352)

985 **WILHELM, Kate (Katie Gertrude).** *And the Angels Sing: Stories.* **Gr. 10 up.**

✓ Twelve fantasy and horror stories, including "The Dragon Seed," "The Look Alike," and "Forever Yours, Anna."

St. Martin's, 1992, 320 pp. (0-3120-6898-0)

(BL 88:1092, 1095; KR 60:76; LJ Feb 15, 1992 p. 200; SLJ July 1992 p. 98; VOYA 15:49)

986 **WILHELM, Kate (Katie Gertrude).** *Children of the Wind: Five Novellas.* **Gr. 10**
✓ **up.**

One of these five novellas, "The Girl Who Fell into the Sky," which won the 1986 Nebula Award for the best novelette, is about an old player piano that transports two people 100 years into the past where they become involved in a murder.

St. Martin's, 1989, 256 pp. (0-3120-3303-6), 1991, pap. (0-3120-5400-9)

(BL 86:147, 165; KR 57:1288; LJ Oct 15, 1989 p. 105; VOYA 13:11, 40)

987 **WILHELM, Kate (Katie Gertrude).** *The Downstairs Room, and Other Specula-*
tive Fiction. **Gr. 10 up.**

Fourteen fantastic, realistic, and science fiction short stories, including "The Unbirthday Party," "Baby You Were Great," and "The Downstairs Room."

Doubleday, 1968, 215 pp., o.p.

(BL 65:440, 445; KR 36:719)

WILLARD, Nancy (Margaret). *Sailing to Cythera, and Other Anatole Stories.*
See Chapter 5C, Travel to Other Worlds.

988 *William Mayne's Book of Giants* **(English title:** *The Hamish Hamilton Book of*
✓ *Giants,* **1968). Ed. by William (James Carter) Mayne. Gr. 4–6.**

Nineteen tales whose authors include Oscar Wilde, Eleanor Farjeon, and Janet McNeill.

Illus. by Raymond Briggs, Dutton, 1969, 215 pp., o.p.

(BL 65:1078; CCBB 22:179; HB 45:313; KR 37:181; LJ 94:2105; TLS 1968 p. 1373)

989 **WILLIAMS, Jay.** *The Practical Princess and Other Liberating Fairy Tales.* **Gr.**
✓ **3–5.**

Six lively tales originally published separately: "The Practical Princess," "Stupid Marco," "The Silver Whistle," "Forgetful Fred," "Petronella," and "Philbert the Fearful."

Illus. by Rick Schreiter, Parents, 1978, 99 pp., o.p.

(BL 75:937; CCBB 32:166; Ch&Bks:292; KR 47:7; SLJ Sept 1979 p. 124)

Witches. **Ed. by Isaac Asimov, Martin H. Greenberg, and Charles G. Waugh.** See Chapter 10, Witchcraft and Sorcery Fantasy.

Witches, Witches, Witches. **Ed. by Helen Hoke.** See Chapter 10, Witchcraft and Sorcery Fantasy.

With Cap and Bells: Humorous Stories to Tell and to Read Aloud. **Ed. by Mary Gould Davis.** See Chapter 6, Humorous Fantasy.

990　*A Wizard's Dozen: Stories of the Fantastic.* **Ed. by Michael Stearns. Gr. 6 up.**

✓　Thirteen short fantasy tales whose authors include Vivian Vande Velde, Will Shetterly, Bruce Coville, and Patricia Wrede.

Harcourt, 1993, 192 pp. (0-15-200965-5)

(BL 90:748; CCBB 47:169; SLJ Dec 1993 p. 138; VOYA 17:42)

991　*Worlds Near and Far: Nine Stories of Science Fiction.* **Ed. by Terry Carr. Gr. 7 up.**

Nine science-fantasy tales, including Fritz Lieber's "Four Ghosts from Hamlet," Robert Silverberg's "Dybbuk of Mazel Tov IV," and Gene Wolfe's "Feather Tigers."

Nelson, 1974, 224 pp., o.p.

(BL 71:34; KR 42:808; LJ 99:2744)

992　*Xanadu.* **Ed. by Jane Yolen. Gr. 10 up.**

✓　An anthology of contemporary fantasy stories and poetry written by Ursula K. Le Guin and others. *Xanadu 2* (1994) is the second collection in the series.

Tor, 1993, 288 pp. (0-312-85367-X), 1994, pap. (0-8125-2082-3)

(BL 89:872, 885; KR 60:1412; LJ Dec 1992 p. 191; SLJ Aug 1993 p. 206; VOYA 16: 172)

993　*The Year's Best Fantasy: First Annual Collection.* **Ed. by Ellen Datlow and Terri Windling. Gr. 10 up.**

This anthology, which includes stories by Ursula K. Le Guin, Charles de Lint, and Jane Yolen, won the World Fantasy Convention Award, 1989. The succeeding volumes are: *The Year's Best Fantasy: Second Annual Collection* (1989), *The Year's Best Fantasy and Horror: Third Annual Collection* (1990), *The Year's Best Fantasy and Horror: Fourth Annual Collection* (1991), *The Year's Best Fantasy and Horror: Fifth Annual Collection* (1992), *The Year's Best Fantasy and Horror: Sixth Annual Collection* (1993), and *The Year's Best Fantasy and Horror: Seventh Annual Collection* (1994).

St. Martin's, 1988, 512 pp. (0-3120-1851-7)

(BL 85:43; KR 56:1019; LJ Dec 1988 p. 113; VOYA 11:296, 12:16)

994　*The Year's Best Fantasy Stories, 6.* **Ed. by Lin Carter. Gr. 10 up.**

This annual anthology of fantasy contains tales by Roger Zelazny, Tanith Lee, and others. There have been thirteen annual volumes in this series, published between 1975 and 1987. Volumes 10–13, edited by Arthur W. Saha, are still in print.

DAW, 1980, pap., 192 pp., o.p.

(BL 77:561; LJ 105:2437; VOYA 4[Apr 1981]:41; Tymn:191–193)

995　**YOLEN (Stemple), Jane H(yatt).** *Dragonfield and Other Stories.* **Gr. 10 up.**

Twenty stories and seven poems about dragons, angels, shapeshifters, mermen, selchies, princesses, and magic.

Ace, 1985, pap., 241 pp., o.p.

(BL 81:1638, 1657; VOYA 8:397)

996   **YOLEN (Stemple), Jane H(yatt).** *Dream Weaver.* **Gr. 5–8.**

Seven tales told by a blind old woman to passers-by. Two are somewhat lighter in tone, and the other five are more somber.

Illus. by Michael R. Hague, Collins, 1979, 80 pp., o.p.; Putnam, 1989 (rev. ed.), 80 pp. (0-399-22152-2)

(BBJ:76; BL 75:1582, 86:1012: CCBB 33:84; HBG 1[July–Dec 1989]:85; KR 47:742)

997   **YOLEN (Stemple), Jane H(yatt).** *The Faery Flag: Stories and Poems of Fantasy*
✓   *and the Supernatural.* **Gr. 5–10.**

Five poems and nine fantasy and horror stories, including "The Face in the Cloth," "The Boy Who Drew Unicorns," and "Words of Power."

Illus. by Trina Schart Hyman, Orchard, 1989, 128 pp. (0-531-08438-8)

(BBJ:76; BL 86:838; CC:583; CCBB 43:73; HB 66:90; HBG 1[July–Dec 1989]:82; JHC 1991 Suppl. p. 83; KR 57:1172; SLJ Sept 1989 p. 258; VOYA 12:229)

998   **YOLEN (Stemple), Jane H(yatt).** *The Girl Who Cried Flowers and Other Tales.*
✓   **Gr. 4–6.**

Five tales, including one about a girl who cries flowers instead of tears. Golden Kite Award, 1974; National Book Award finalist, 1975.

Illus. by David Palladini, Crowell, 1974, 64 pp., LB(0-690-00216-5)

(BL 71:48, 768; CCBB 28:88; KR 42:741; LJ 99:2744; SLJ Dec 1978 p. 33)

999   **YOLEN (Stemple), Jane H(yatt).** *Here There Be Dragons.* **Gr. 4 up.**

Eight stories and five poems about dragons, including one story Yolen later developed into *The Dragon's Boy* (Harper, 1990; see Chapter 5B, Myth Fantasy), and another that formed the basis for her Pit Dragons trilogy (Delacorte, 1982–1987; see Chapter 5A, Alternate Worlds or Histories).

Illus. by David Wilgus, Harcourt, 1993, 160 pp. (0-15-20988-7)

(KR 61:1532; SLJ Dec 1993 p. 118 and Jan 1994 p. 117)

1000   **YOLEN (Stemple), Jane H(yatt).** *The Hundredth Dove and Other Tales.* **Gr. 2–5.**

Seven stories including "The Lady and the Merman," "The White Seal Maid," and "The Wind Cap."

Illus. by David Palladini, Harper, 1977, o.p.; Schocken, 1980, pap., 80 pp. (0-8052-0659-0)

(BL 74:817; CCBB 31:168; KR 45:1198; SLJ Jan 1978 p. 83)

1001   **YOLEN (Stemple), Jane H(yatt).** *The Moon Ribbon and Other Tales.* **Gr. 3–5.**

Six tales, including "The Moon Child," "Somewhen," "Rosechild," and "Honey-Stick Boy." Golden Kite Award Honor Book, 1976.

Illus. by David Palladini, Crowell, 1976, 54 pp., o.p.

(BL 73:328; KR 44:792; SLJ Feb 1977 p. 70)

YOLEN (Stemple), Jane H(yatt). *The Wizard Islands.* See Chapter 4, Ghost Fantasy.

Young Ghosts. **Ed. by Isaac Asimov, Martin H. Greenberg, and Charles G. Waugh.** See Chapter 4, Ghost Fantasy.

Young Witches and Warlocks. **Ed. by Isaac Asimov, Martin H. Greenberg, and Charles G. Waugh.** See Chapter 10, Witchcraft and Sorcery Fantasy.

1002 **ZELAZNY, Roger (Joseph Christopher).** *Frost and Fire.* **Gr. 10 up.**

Eleven fantasy and science fiction short stories, plus two essays on writing science fiction.

Morrow, 1989, 224 pp. (0-688-08942-9); Avon, 1990, pap. (0-380-75775-3)

(BL 85:1873, 1895; Kliatt Sept 1990 p. 25; KR 57:804; LJ Jan 15, 1989 p. 84)

1003 **ZELAZNY, Roger (Joseph Christopher).** *The Last Defender of Camelot.* **Gr. 10 up.**

Fourteen short stories and two novellas, including "He Who Shapes," "The Last Defender of Camelot," and "For Breath of Tarny." Some of the stories were originally published under the pseudonym Harrison Denmark.

Simon, 1980, pap., 308 pp., o.p.; Avon, 1988, pap. (0-380-70316-5)

(BL 77:376, 377; LJ 105:2436; SLJ Mar 1981 p. 162; VOYA 4[June 1981]:55)

Zoo 2000. **Ed. by Jane H. Yolen.** See Chapter 2, Animal Fantasy.

4

Ghost Fantasy

Tales about ghosts fascinate readers of all ages. Many, although not all, of the tales listed here have an element of humor, and most are only mildly chilling. Horror stories have not been included in this bibliography, unless they are part of an anthology containing fantasy stories. Novels about contemporary protagonists who become involved with ghosts from the past are listed in this chapter. If the human characters travel back into the past with ghosts, however, the books are listed in Chapter 8, Time Travel Fantasy.

1004   ADLER, C(arole) S(chwerdtfeger). *Footsteps on the Stairs.* **Gr. 5–7.**

✓   Dodie, thirteen, and her stepsister, Anne, solve a mystery concerning the ghosts of two teenaged girls who haunt their summer house.

Delacorte, 1982 (0-385-28303-2); Dell, 1984, pap., 160 pp. (0-440-42654-5)

(BBC:135; BL 78:1091; Kies:1; SLJ May 1982 p. 83; VOYA 5[Oct 1982]:39)

1005   ADLER, David A. *Jeffrey's Ghost and the Leftover Baseball Team.* **Gr. 3–5.**

Jeffrey's baseball team isn't doing very well until Bradford, the baseball-playing ghost who lives in Jeffrey's house, joins the team, building up their skills and confidence. The sequels are: *Jeffrey's Ghost and the Fifth-Grade Dragon* (1985) and *Jeffrey's Ghost and the Ziffel Fair Mystery* (1987).

Illus. by Jean Jenkins, Holt, 1984, 58 pp., o.p.

(BBC:135; BL 80:1546; CCBB 38:39; SLJ Oct 1984 p. 153)

1006   AIKEN, Joan (Delano). *A Foot in the Grave.* **Gr. 6–10. (Orig. British pub. 1989.)**

✓   A collection of eight ghostly tales including "Amberland," "Beezlebub's Baby," and the title story, "A Foot in the Grave."

Illus. by Jan Pienkowski, Viking, 1993, 128 pp. (0-670-84169-2)

(BL 88:1349; CC 1993 Suppl. p. 77; CCBB 45:197; HB 68:449; HBG 3[Fall 1992]:260; JHC 1993 Supp. p. 83; KR 60:249; SLJ May 1992 p. 130)

AIKEN, Joan (Delano). *Give Yourself a Fright: Thirteen Stories of the Supernatural.* See Chapter 3, Fantasy Collections.

AIKEN, Joan (Delano). *The Green Flash and Other Tales of Horror, Suspense, and Fantasy.* See Chapter 3, Fantasy Collections.

1007 **AIKEN, Joan (Delano).** *The Haunting of Lamb House.* **Gr. 10 up. (Orig. British pub. 1992.)**

Three interrelated novellas about three eighteenth- and nineteenth-century inhabitants of Lamb house in Sussex: Toby Lamb, who leaves a manuscript about his haunted life, and the authors Henry James and E. F. Benson.

St. Martin, 1993, 208 pp. (0-31209060-9)

(BL 89:466; LJ Dec 15, 1992 p. 184; SLJ May 1993 p. 141)

1008 **AIKEN, Joan (Delano).** *Return to Harken House.* **Gr. 5–8. (Orig. British pub. 1988, entitled** *Voices.***)**

Sent to live with her stepmother after her own mother's remarriage, eleven-year-old Julia begins hearing angry voices from the past: that of Joshua Harken, a seventeenth-century alchemist who died tragically, and of her own parents arguing before their divorce.

Delacorte, 1990, 128 pp. (0-385-29975-3)

(BL 86:996; CCBB 43:152; HBG 1[Jan 1990]:246; JHC 1991 Suppl. p. 67; KR 57:1821; SLJ Mar 1990 p. 215; VOYA 13:349)

1009 **AIKEN, Joan (Delano).** *The Shadow Guests.* **Gr. 6–8. (Orig. British pub. 1980.)**

✓ Cosmo learns of a family curse that may explain the mysterious disappearance of his mother and older brother. According to his cousin, Eunice, the eldest sons of the family are fated to die in battle, and their mothers to die of grief.

Delacorte, 1980, 150 pp. (0-385-28889-1); Dell, 1986, pap. (0-440-48226-7)

(BBC:196; BBJ:68; BL 77:41; CC:439; CCBB 34:85; HB 56:644; JHC:343; Kies:2; SLJ Oct 1980 p. 140; Suth 3:7; TLS 1980 p. 357; VOYA 3[Feb 1981]:27)

1010 **AIKEN, Joan (Delano).** *A Touch of Chill: Tales for Sleepless Nights.* **Gr. 8 up.**
✓ **(Orig. British pub. 1979.)**

Fifteen short stories combining realism, comedy, and fantasy, including "The Cat Flap and the Apple Pie" and "Listening."

Delacorte, 1980, 183 pp. (0-385-29310-0)

(BL 76:1416; CCBB 34:25; JHC:428; Kies:2; SHC:732; SLJ May 1980 p. 73; TLS 1979 p. 123)

1011 **AIKEN, Joan (Delano).** *A Whisper in the Night: Tales of Terror and Suspense.*
✓ **Gr. 6–12. (Orig. British pub. 1982.)**

Thirteen stunning stories of fantasy and horror, including "Snow Horse," "Miss Spitfire," and "Lob's Girl."

Delacorte, 1984, 203 pp., o.p.; Peter Smith, 1989, o.p.

(BL 81:582, 585; CCBB 38:59; JHC:428; Kies:2; KR 52:J102; SHC:732; SLJ Dec 1984 p. 87; TLS 1982 p. 788; VOYA 7:321, 8:46)

1012 **AINSWORTH (Gilbert), Ruth (Gallard).** *The Phantom Carousel and Other Ghostly Tales* **(British title:** *The Phantom Roundabout and Other Ghostly Tales,* **1977). Gr. 4–6.**

Ten stories about children who meet ghosts.

Illus. by Shirley Hughes, Follett, 1978, 176 pp., o.p.

(BL 74:1489; Kies:2; KR 46:176; SLJ Feb 1978 p. 62; TLS 1977 p. 1414)

1013   ALCOCK, Vivien (Dolores). *Ghostly Companions: A Feast of Chilling Tales.* **Gr.**
✓   **6–10. (Orig. British pub. 1984.)**

Ten ghostly tales with young protagonists, including "The Sea Bride," "Qwertyuiop," and "The Whisperer."

Delacorte, 1987, 132 pp., o.p.

(BL 83:1596; CC:577; Ch&Bks:259; CCBB 40:161; HB 63:460; JHC:428; Kies:3; KR 55:789; SLJ Sept 1987 p. 194; VOYA 10:118)

1014   ALCOCK, Vivien (Dolores). *The Haunting of Cassie Palmer.* **Gr. 6–8. (Orig.**
✓   **British pub. 1980.)**

A ghost named Deverill, who is accidentally raised from the dead by Cassie, makes Cassie's life very difficult.

Delacorte, 1982, 149 pp., o.p., pap. (0-385-28402-0)

(BBC:196; BL 78:1305, 1308; CCBB 35:161; Ch&Bks:259; HB 58:294, 62:616; Kies:3; KR 50:421; SLJ Apr 1982 p. 78; Suth 3:9)

1015   ALPHIN, Elaine Marie. *The Ghost Cadet.* **Gr. 4–7.**

Hugh, the ghost of a military cadet killed during The War between the States, is befriended by Benjy, a boy visiting his grandmother, Miss Leota, in contemporary Virginia.

Henry Holt, 1991, 182 pp. (0-8050-1614-7); Scholastic, 1992, pap. (0-590-45244-4)

(BL 87:1714; CCBB 44:184; HBG 2[Fall,1991]:267; KR 59:667; SLJ May 1991 p. 91)

1016   ANASTASIO, Dina. *A Question of Time.* **Gr. 4–6.**

After her unwanted move from Manhattan to Minnesota, Syd discovers a connection between her new friend, Laura, some antique dolls, and an all-but-forgotten tragedy.

Illus. by Dale Payson, Dutton, 1978, 90 pp., o.p.

(BBC:197; BL 75:287; CCBB 32:109; KR 46:1246; SLJ Dec 1978 p. 68)

1017   ANDERSON, Margaret J(ean). *The Ghost Inside the Monitor.* **Gr. 4–6.**

The ghost of Pascale, a girl who lived in Sarah's town nearly a century ago, appears on Sarah's computer screen asking for help in finding her lost home.

Knopf, 1990, 119 pp. LB(0-679-90359-3)

(BL 87:1059; HBG 2[July–Dec 1990]:73; KR 58:1001; SLJ Oct 1990 p. 113)

1018   *The April Witch and Other Strange Tales* (Orig. British title: *Fantasy Tales,* 1977). Ed. by Barbara Ireson. Gr. 7–9.

Fourteen eerie stories by such well-known authors as Ray Bradbury, H. G. Wells, and Nicholas Stuart Gray.

Illus. by Richard Cuffari, Scribner, 1978, 238 pp., o.p.

(BL 74:1676; KR 46:599; SLJ Sept 1978 p. 159)

1019   ARTHUR, Ruth M(abel). *The Autumn People.* **Gr. 6–10. (Orig. pub in England.)**

Ghosts from the year 1901 reveal the truth about the death of Romilly's great-grandmother's suitor.

Illus. by Margery Gill, Atheneum, 1973, 166 pp., o.p.

(BL 69:1071; CCBB 27:21; HB 49:375; KR 41:122; LJ 98:1702; TLS 1973 p. 680)

1020   ARTHUR, Ruth M(abel). *Miss Ghost.* **Gr. 5–7. (Orig. pub. in England.)**

The ghost that Elphie meets in the tower room of her boarding school encourages her to make real friends.

Atheneum, 1979, 119 pp., o.p.

(BL 76:116; HB 55:53; KR 47:1262; SLJ Nov 1979 p. 73)

1021 **ARTHUR, Ruth M(abel).** *The Whistling Boy.* **Gr. 6–9. (Orig. pub. in England.)**

Deeply unhappy over her father's remarriage, Kristy falls in love with a young man haunted by visions of a suicidal ancestor.

Illus. by Margery Gill, Atheneum, 1969, 200 pp., o.p.

(BL 65:1173; HB 45:310; KR 37:244; LJ 94:1789; TLS 1969 p. 1199)

AVI. *Something Upstairs: A Tale of Ghosts.* See Chapter 8, Time Travel Fantasy.

BACON, Martha (Sherman). *Moth Manor: A Gothic Tale.* See Chapter 9, Toy Fantasy.

1022 **BACON, Peggy.** *The Ghost of Opalina, or Nine Lives.* **Gr. 4–7.**

The talkative ghost of a Persian cat named Opalina haunts Philip, Ellen, and Jeb's new home.

Illus. by the author, Little, 1967, 243 pp., o.p.

(BL 64:866; KR 35:648; LJ 92:4608)

BARBER, Antonia. *The Ghosts.* See Chapter 8, Time Travel Fantasy.

1023 **BAUER, Marion Dane.** *Ghost Eye.* **Gr. 3–6.**

Former showcat Purrloom Popcorn resents becoming Melinda's home-bound pet after the death of her elderly owner, despite the companionship of the many feline ghosts who live in Melinda's old house.

Illus. by Trina Schart Hyman, Scholastic, 1994, 64 pp. (0-590-45298-3)

(BL 89:148; HBG 4[Spring 1993]:55; KR 60:1184; SLJ Oct 1992 p. 112)

1024 **BAUER, Marion Dane.** *A Taste of Smoke.* **Gr. 5–8.**

✓ Angry that her older sister is paying so much attention to her boyfriend on their camping trip, thirteen-year-old Caitlin discovers that she can commmunicate with the one hundred-year-old ghost of a young boy orphaned by a forest fire.

Houghton, 1993, 106 pp. (0-395-64341-4)

(BL 90:440; CCBB 47:147; HB 70:68; HBG 5:72; KR 61:1326; SLJ Dec 1993 p. 111; VOYA 16:364)

1025 **BEAGLE, Peter S(oyer).** *A Fine and Private Place, A Novel.* **Gr. 10 up.**

✓ Michael Morgan and Laura Durand, two ghosts in the Yorkchester Cemetery, decide to force themselves to remember what it was like to be alive, in order to circumvent the oblivious forgetfulness of Death.

Viking, 1960, o.p.; NAL, 1992, pap., 304 pp. (0-451-45096-5)

(BBS:52; BL 56:601; Kies:10; KR 28:243; LJ 85:1822; Tymn:50)

BEDARD, Michael. *A Darker Magic.* See Chapter 10, Witchcraft and Sorcery Fantasy.

1026 **BELLAIRS, John.** *The House with a Clock in Its Walls.* **Gr. 5–7.**

Lewis is impressed by his warlock uncle's magic abilities, but when he tries some magic himself, he unwittingly summons up a sinister ghost. The sequels are *The Figure in the Shadows* (1975), *The Letter, the Witch and the Ring* (1977), *The Ghost in the Mirror* (1993), which was completed by Brad Strickland after John Bellairs's death, and *The Vengeance of the Witch-Finder* (1993), also by Bellairs and Brad Strickland.

Illus. by Edward Gorey, Dial, 1984, LB(0-8037-3821-8); Dell, 1974, pap., 192 pp. (0-440-43742-3)

(BL 70:227; CC:449; CCBB 27:37; Kies:11; KR 41:514; LJ 98:1701)

1027   BENDICK, Jeanne. *The Goodknight Ghost.* **Gr. 3–5.**

Karen and Mike meet a ghostly knight and dragon when they are accidentally locked inside a museum overnight.

Illus. by the author, Watts, 1956, 51 pp., o.p.

(CCBB 10:62; HB 32:446; KR 24:432; LJ 82:584)

1028   BENSON, E. F. *The Collected Ghost Stories of E. F. Benson.* **Gr. 10 up. (Orig. pub. in England.)**

Fifty-four British ghost stories written between 1890 and 1940.

Carroll & Graf, 1992, pap., 624 pp. (0-88184-857-3)

(BL 89:578, 586; VOYA 16:98)

1029   *Beware! Beware! Chilling Tales.* Ed. by Jean Richardson. Gr. 6–9.

✓   Nine tales about ghosts and witches, written by Peter Dickinson, Adèle Geras, Vivian Alcock, Jan Mark, and others.

Viking, 1989, 120 pp., o.p.

(BL 85:1717, 1719; CCBB 42:155; HB 65:379; KR 57:127; SLJ Mar 1989 p. 202; VOYA 13:36)

BLAYLOCK, James P(aul). *Land of Dreams.* See Chapter 5C, Travel to Other Worlds.

BLAYLOCK, James P(aul). *The Paper Grail.* See Chapter 5B, Myth Fantasy.

1030   *Boo! Stories to Make You Jump.* Compiled by Laura Cecil. Gr. 2–4. (Orig.
✓   **British pub. 1990.)**

A collection of familiar and not so familiar stories by Margaret Mahy, Diana Wynne Jones, and others.

Illus. by Emma Chichester Clark, Greenwillow, 1990, 93 pp. (0-688-09842-8)

(BL 87:922; CCBB 44:80; HBG 2[July 1990]:133; SLJ Mar 1991 p. 200)

1031   BOSTON, L(ucy) M(aria Wood). *The Children of Green Knowe.* **Gr. 4–7. (Orig.**
✓✓   **British pub. 1954.)**

With the help of three of his ancestors, Tolly lifts the curse on his family's ancient home, Green Knowe. Carnegie Medal Commended Book, 1954. Tolly searches for lost family treasure in *The Treasure of Green Knowe* (British title: *The Chimneys of Green Knowe*; Carnegie Medal Commended Book, 1958) (1958; Peter Smith, 1987), and battles a witch in *An Enemy at Green Knowe* (1964; Peter Smith, n.d.). *The Stones of Green Knowe* (Atheneum, 1976), *The River at Green Knowe* (1959; Peter Smith, n.d.), and *A Stranger at Green Knowe* (1961) are related stories, although the latter is not a fantasy.

Illus. by Peter Boston, Harcourt, 1955, 1967, 157 pp., o.p.; Peter Smith, 1988 (0-8446-6288-7); Harcourt, 1990, pap. (0-15-217151-7)

(BBC:199; BL 52:37, 80:95; CC:452; CCBB 9:33; Ch&Bks:258; Eakin:40; HB 31:375; KR 23:357; LJ 80:1965)

BRADBURY, Ray (Douglas). *The Toynbee Convector.* See Chapter 3, Fantasy Collections.

1032 **BRENNER, Anita.** *The Timid Ghost: Or What Would You Do with a Sackful of Gold?* **Gr. 3–5.**

A man and his wife demand gold in exchange for answering a ghost's questions.

Illus. by Jean Charlot, Addison-Wesley, 1966, 48 pp., o.p.

(BL 62:954; HB 42:193; KR 34:179; LJ 91:2206)

1033 **BRITTAIN, Bill (William).** *Who Knew There'd Be Ghosts?* **Gr. 4–6.**

✓ Tommy Donahue and his friends find allies in two ghosts, Essie and Horace, as they try to save the vacant Parnell mansion from destruction and recover a mysterious treasure. In the sequel, *The Ghost from Beneath the Sea* (1992, 1994), Tommy and his friends try to save their ghostly friends' historic house by attempting to prove that a poker game played on *The Titanic* the night it sank was rigged.

Illus. by Michele Chessare, Harper, 1985, 128 pp., LB(0-06-020700-0), pap., 1988 (0-06-440224-X)

(BL 81:1392, 83:585; HB 61:448; JHC:337; KR 53:31; SLJ May 1985 p. 108)

1034 **BROCK, Betty.** *The Shades.* **Gr. 3–5.**

✓ In an old walled garden, Hollis meets the Shade family, ghosts of previous visitors to the garden.

Illus. by Victoria de Larrea, Harper, 1971, 128 pp., o.p.

(BL 68:290; HB 48:47; KR 39:1069; LJ 96:4198; TLS 1973 p. 386)

1035 **BROW, Thea J.** *The Secret Cross of Lorraine.* **Gr. 5–7.**

Twyla is unable to return a medallion to the elusive old man who lost it, until she finds a secret passageway in the former Second World War-era bunker where her family lives.

Illus. by Allen Say, Houghton, 1981, 177 pp., o.p.

(BL 77:925, 81:1405; CCBB 34:208; HB 57:299; SLJ Apr 1981 p. 121)

BUFFIE, Margaret. *The Haunting of Frances Rain.* See Chapter 8, Time Travel Fantasy.

BUFFIE, Margaret. *The Warnings.* See Chapter 7, Magic Adventure Fantasy.

1036 **BUNTING, (Anne) Eve(lyn Bolton).** *Ghost Behind Me.* **Gr. 6–9.**

Sixteen-year-old Cinnamon's depression after the deaths of her mother and sister in a plane crash causes her to think she's only imagining the ghostly young man she sees in their rented summer house.

Pocket, 1984, 1986, pap., 69 pp. (0-671-62211-0)

(BL 80:1547; Kies 23; VOYA 7:143)

1037 **BUNTING, (Anne) Eve(lyn Bolton).** *The Ghosts of Departure Point.* **Gr. 7–9.**

Vicki and Ted, the ghosts of two teenaged auto accident victims, meet and fall in love while they attempt to prove to the town that a safer highway must be built.

Lippincott, 1982, 113 pp., o.p.; Scholastic, 1984, pap. (0-590-33116-7)

(BL 79:362, 365; CCBB 36:43; Kies:23; KR 50:1109; SLJ Apr 1983 p. 110)

1038 **BURGESS, Barbara Hood.** *Oren Bell.* **Gr. 5–9.**

✓ Seventh-grade twins Oren and Latonya hope that the ghost of the man who built their condemned house will show them his hidden gold so that they and their family can escape from the drug dealing and danger of their Detroit neighborhood. The non-fantasy sequel is *The Fred Field* (1994).

Delacorte, 1991, 192 pp. (0-385-30325-4); Dell, 1993, pap. (0-440-40747-8)

(BL 87:1791; CCBB 44:259; HB 67:196; HBG 2[Fall 1991]:262; KR 59:602; SLJ Apr 1991 p. 116; VOYA 14:26)

1039   BYFIELD, Barbara Ninde. *The Haunted Spy.* Gr. K–4.

The spy discovers that his peaceful retirement home is haunted. The sequels are *The Haunted Churchbell* (1971), *The Haunted Ghost* (1973), and *The Haunted Tower* (1976).

Illus. by the author, Doubleday, 1969, 48 pp., o.p.

(CCBB 23:39; KR 37:923; LJ 94:3809; Suth:62)

1040   CALIF, Ruth. *The Over-the-Hill Ghost.* Gr. 4–6.

Mystery, buried treasure, and a haunted house become part of Jamie's life after his family's move to the country, where he helps a ghost find the murderer of his house's previous owner.

Illus. by Jean Holub, Pelican, 1988, 144 pp. (0-88289-667-9)

(BBC:199; BL 84:1832; SLJ Dec 1988 p. 102)

1041   CAMERON, Eleanor (Frances Butler). *The Court of the Stone Children.* Gr.
✓✓ **5–8.**

The ghost of a nineteenth-century French girl whose father was executed for treason begs Nina Harmsworth to help prove her father's innocence. National Book Award, 1974.

Dutton, 1973, 191 pp., o.p.; Puffin, 1990, pap., 191 pp. (0-14-034289-3)

(BBC:199; BL 70:486, 826, 80:95; CC:460; CCBB 27:75; Ch&Bks:284; HB 50:151; Kies:26; KR 41:1159, 1349; LJ 98:3718; Suth 2:74)

1042   CARLSON, Natalie Savage. *The Ghost in the Lagoon.* Gr. 2–4.
✓ Timmy Hawkins uses an old scarecrow to frighten off the pirate ghost guarding the treasure in the swamp. This is the sequel to *Spooky Night* (1982), a book for younger children.

Illus. by Andrew Glass, Lothrop, 1984, 40 pp., o.p.

(BL 81:842; Ch&Bks:284; CCBB 38:143; SLJ Feb 1985 p. 71)

1043   CARRIS, Joan Davenport. *A Ghost of a Chance.* Gr. 5–7.

Punch and his two new friends decide to search for buried treasure in Blackbeard's home, now rumored to be haunted.

Little, Brown, 1992, 144 pp. (0-316-13016-8)

(CCBB 45:256; HBG 3[Fall 1992]:261; VOYA 15:221)

1044   CASSEDY, Sylvia. *Behind the Attic Wall.* Gr. 6–8.
✓✓ Twelve-year-old Maggie's life with her two unwelcoming great-aunts proves to be as lonely as her previous stays in foster homes and boarding schools, until voices draw her to a forgotten attic room where she finds a family of dolls who have lived there since a mysterious tragedy one hundred years before.

Harper, 1983, 320 pp., LB(0-690-04337-6); Avon, 1985, pap. (0-380-69843-9)

(BBC:200; BL 80:566; CC:462; CCBB 37:45; HB 60:49; Kies:29; KR 51:J200; SLJ Oct 1983 p. 156; Suth 3:80; TLS May 1984 p. 506)

1045   CATES, Emily. *The Ghost in the Attic* (Haunting with Louisa trilogy, book 1). Gr. 4–6.

After her mother dies, Dee is sent to spend the winter on Misty Island, where she meets Louisa, a ghostly girl who died in 1897 but must help four living relatives before she can rest peacefully. The sequels are *The Mystery of Misty Island Inn* (1990) and *The Ghost Ferry* (1991).

Bantam, 1990, pap., 160 pp. (0-553-15826-0)

(BL 87:1502; SLJ Oct 1990, p. 113)

CAVANAGH, Helen. *Panther Glade.* See Chapter 5B, Myth Fantasy.

CHASE, Mary (Coyle). *The Wicked Pigeon Ladies in the Garden.* See Chapter 8, Time Travel Fantasy.

CHERRYH, C. J. (pseud. of Carolyn Janice Cherry). *Rusalka.* See Chapter 10, Witchcraft and Sorcery Fantasy.

1046 *Christmas Ghosts.* **Ed. by Kathryn Cramer and David G. Hartwell. Gr. 10 up.**

Seventeen classic nineteenth- and twentieth-century ghost stories written by British and American authors.

Arbor House, 1987, 283 pp., o.p.

(BL 84:26, 52; Kies:201; VOYA 10:278)

1047 *Christmas Ghosts: An Anthology.* **Ed. by Seon Manley and Gogo Lewis. Gr. 7 up.**

Eleven short stories involving ghosts and Christmas, whose authors include Charles Dickens and Lord Dunsany.

Doubleday, 1978, 227 pp., o.p.

(BL 75:53; CCBB 32:68; SLJ Oct 1978 p. 113)

1048 **CHRISTOPHER, Matt(hew F.).** *Favor for a Ghost.* **Gr. 4–6.**

Lennie is haunted by the ghost of Billy Marble, a former school bully, who wants Lennie to dig up Billy's dog's grave and move it next to his own.

Westminster, 1983, 107 pp., o.p.

(BL 80:966; 83:585; SLJ Feb 1984 p. 67)

CHRISTOPHER, Matt(hew F.). *The Kid Who Only Hit Homers.* See Chapter 7, Magic Adventure Fantasy.

CHRISTOPHER, Matt(hew F.). *Skateboard Tough.* See Chapter 7, Magic Adventure Fantasy.

1049 **CHURCH, Richard (Thomas).** *The French Lieutenant: A Ghost Story.* **Gr. 5–7. (Orig. British pub. 1971.)**

Robert doesn't believe in the eighteenth-century ghost said to haunt the castle near his home, until he actually sees the ghost himself.

Day, 1972, 153 pp., o.p.

(BL 69:44; KR 40:398; LJ 97:1927; TLS 1971 p. 766)

1050 **CLAPP, Patricia.** *Jane-Emily.* **Gr. 5–9.**

✓ No one believes Jane's explanation that the frightening episodes occurring at her grandmother's house are caused by Emily, the ghost of her grandmother's daughter who died at age twelve.

Lothrop, 1969, 160 pp., o.p.; Morrow, 1993, pap., 160 pp. (0-688-04592-8)

(BBC:200; BL 65:1224; CC:465; CCBB 22:172; HB 45:538; Kies:33; LJ 94:2508)

1051 **CLIMO, Shirley.** *T.J.'s Ghost.* **Gr. 4–6.**

On foggy days at the beach, T. J. always meets a strange boy searching for a lost gold ring and slowly comes to understand that the boy is a ghost who drowned in a shipwreck in 1866.

Harper, 1989, 151 pp., o.p.

(BL 85:1721; KR 57:460; SLJ Nov 1989 p. 105; VOYA 12:156)

1052   COBALT, Martin (pseud. of William Mayne). *Pool of Swallows* **(British title:**
✓   *Swallows,* **1972). Gr. 5–8.**

A family of ghosts causes the ponds on Martin's farm to become an ocean that swallows up a herd of cattle and Martin's father as well.

Nelson, 1974, 139 pp., o.p.

(BL 70:999; CCBB 28:26; Ch&Bks:284; LJ 99:2286; Suth 2:91)

1053   COHEN, Daniel. *Great Ghosts.* **Gr. 3–5.**

Nine ghostly encounters from England, the Netherlands, Greece, and the Middle East.

Illus. by David Linn, Dutton, 1990, 48 pp. (0-525-65039-3); Scholastic, 1992, pap. (0-590-45734-9)

(BL 87:329; HBG 2[July 1990]:90; SLJ Nov 1990, p. 121)

CONRAD, Pam. *Stonewords: A Ghost Story.* See Chapter 8, Time Travel Fantasy.

1054   COOKSON, Catherine (McMullen). *Mrs. Flannagan's Trumpet.* **Gr. 6–8.**

A ghostly figure and Eddy's stubborn Granny help rescue Eddy's younger sister from white slavers.

Lothrop, 1980, 192 pp., o.p.

(BL 76:1124; CCBB 34:5; KR 48:364; SLJ Oct 1980 p. 144)

COOPER (Grant), Susan (Mary). *Jethro and the Jumbie.* See Chapter 7, Magic Adventure Fantasy.

1055   CORBETT, Scott. *Captain Butcher's Body.* **Gr. 4–6.**
✓   The ghost of the legendary pirate Captain Butcher is due to make its once-every-hundred-years appearance—and George and Leo don't want to miss seeing it.

Little, 1976, 168 p., o.p.

(BL 73:1010, 75:305; CCBB 30:139; KR 44:973; SLJ Dec 1976 p. 68)

1056   CORBETT, Scott. *The Discontented Ghost.* **Gr. 5–7.**
✓   The ghost of Sir Simon de Canterville retells the Oscar Wilde tale *The Canterville Ghost* (orig. pub. 1906; Picture Book, 1986; see this chapter) and sets the record straight about his attempts to rid his home of its new American owners.

Dutton, 1978, 180 pp., o.p.

(BBC:201; BL 75:859, 865, 928; CC:475; HB 55:190; KR 46:1307; SLJ Feb 1979 p. 62)

1057   CRESSWELL (Rowe), Helen. *A Game of Catch.* **Gr. 4–6. (Orig. British pub.**
✓   **1969.)**

Kate and Hugh's games of ice skating, tag, and catch near an old castle bring to life the children who played there long ago.

Illus. by Ati Forberg, Macmillan, 1977, 48 pp., o.p.

(BL 73:895; CC:457; CCBB 30:173; Ch&Bks:262; HB 53:312; KR 45:4; SLJ Feb 1977 p. 62; Suth 2:109; TLS 1969 p. 1388)

CRESSWELL (Rowe), Helen. *Moondial.* See Chapter 8, Time Travel Fantasy.

1058   CROSS, Gilbert B. *A Witch Across Time.* **Gr. 6–10.**

The ghost of a Puritan girl who was unjustly hanged as a witch haunts fifteen-year-old Hannah, depressed after her mother's death.

Macmillan, 1990, 192 pp. (0-689-31602-X)

(BL 86:1276, 1338; CCBB 43:134; HBG 1[Jan–June 1990]:257; KR 58:103; SLJ Mar 1990 p. 234; VOYA 13:27)

1059 **CROSS, Gillian (Clare Arnold).** *The Dark Behind the Curtain.* **Gr. 6–9. (Orig.**
✓ **British pub. 1982.)**

Only Colin and Ann realize that their rehearsals for the school play, "Sweeney Todd, the Demon Barber of Fleet Street," have called up miserable ghosts intent on reenacting the old legend.

Illus. by David Parkins, Oxford, 1987, 159 pp. (0-19-271457-0); Dell, 1988, pap. (0-440-20207-8)

(CCBB 42:118; Ch&Bks:284; HB 60:596; Kliatt Jan 1989 p.20; SLJ Aug 1984 p. 83; Suth 4:87; TLS 1982 p. 788; VOYA 7:263)

1060 **CULLEN, Lynn.** *The Backyard Ghost.* **Gr. 5–7.**

In the face of rejection by her new school's popular crowd, twelve-year-old Eleanor becomes obsessed with the ghost of a Confederate bugle boy who appears in her back yard.

Houghton, 1993, 149 pp. (0-395-64527-1)

(BL 89:1830; CCBB 46:342; HBG 4[Fall 1993}:296; KR 61:526; SLJ May 1993 p. 104)

1061 **CURRY, Jane Louise.** *The Bassumtyte Treasure.* **Gr. 5–7.**
✓ Clues to the lost family treasure lie in a cryptic riddle, two ancestral portraits, and an old medallion, but it is a sixteenth-century ghost named Lady Margaret who helps Tommy solve the family mystery.

Atheneum, 1978, 129 pp., o.p.

(BL 74:1347; CCBB 32:6; HB 54:393; KR 46:243; SLJ May 1978 p. 84; TLS 1978 p. 1396)

1062 **CURRY, Jane Louise.** *Poor Tom's Ghost.* **Gr. 6–9.**
✓ A hidden staircase is not the only secret held by the old house Roger's father inherits—ghostly sobbings and footsteps prove to be caused by Tom Garland, a seventeenth-century actor who involves Roger's family in danger.

Atheneum, 1977, 178 pp., o.p.

(BL 73:1413, 1419; CCBB 31:12; HB 53:439; KR 45:426; SLJ May 1977 p. 67; TLS 1977 p. 864)

1063 **DEXTER, Catherine.** *The Gilded Cat.* **Gr. 5–9.**

The ghost of a boy pharaoh tells Maggie that the little cat figure she bought at a yard sale is the stolen mummy of his pet kitten, and that his magician uncle murdered him and has pursued his spirit into the twentieth century.

Morrow, 1992, 199 pp. (0-688-09425-2)

(BL 88:1357; CCBB 45:292; HB 68:584; HBG 3[Fall 1992]:262; KR 60:535; SLJ Apr 1992 p. 113; VOYA 15:222)

DICKENS, Charles. *A Christmas Carol.* See Chapter 1, Allegorical Fantasy and Literary Fairy Tales.

1064 *Don't Give Up the Ghost: The Delacorte Book of Original Ghost Stories.* **Ed. by**
✓ **David Gale. Gr. 4–8.**

Twelve tales written by well-known children's book authors including Constance Greene, Joanna Hurwitz, Walter Dean Myers, and Mary Downing Hahn.

Delacorte, 1993, pap., 144 pp. (0-385-31109-5)

(BL 89:2062; KR 61:1200; SLJ Sept 1993 p. 232; VOYA 16:308, 17:7)

1065   **DU BOIS, William (Sherman) Pène.** *Elisabeth the Cow Ghost* **(Orig. title:** *Elizabeth the Cow Ghost,* **1936). Gr. 3–5.**

The ghost of Elisabeth the cow returns to haunt her former master.

Illus. by the author, Viking, 1964, 41 pp., o.p.

(HB 12:28, 40:120; KR:32:108; LJ 89:2208)

1066   **DUNLOP, Eileen (Rhona).** *Green Willow.* **Gr. 5–8. (Orig. British pub. 1993, entitled** *Green Willow's Secret.***)**

Kojima, the ghostly gardener Kit meets near her mother's rented flat, helps Kit and her mother to recover from the death of her sister, Juliet.

Holiday, 1993, 160 pp. (0-8234-1021-8)

(BL 90:684; HBG 5:75; KR 61:1328; SLJ Jan 1994 p. 114; VOYA 17:24)

1067   **DUNLOP, Eileen (Rhona).** *The House on the Hill.* **Gr. 6–9. (Orig. British pub.**
✓   **1987.)**

Two cousins, Susan and Philip, uncover the cause of the mysterious light in their Great Aunt Jane's old house. Carnegie Medal Commended Book, 1987.

Holiday, 1987, 147 pp. (0-8234-0658-X)

(BL 84:392, 1276; CCBB 41:63; Ch&Bks:285; KR 55:1461; SLJ Nov 1987 p. 115; Suth 4:105; TLS 1987 p. 529; VOYA 11:22)

1068   **ERWIN, Betty K.** *Who Is Victoria?* **Gr. 4–6.**

No one seems to know Victoria, the elusive girl in old-fashioned clothes who helps Margaret, Polly, and Emilie solve their problems.

Illus. by Kathleen Anderson, Little, 1973, 134 pp., o.p.

(BL 70:385; KR 41:1035; LJ 99:208)

EUBANK, Judith. *Crossover.* See Chapter 8, Time Travel Fantasy.

EZO (pseud.). *Avril.* See Chapter 2, Animal Fantasy.

1069   **FARMER (Mockridge), Penelope.** *Thicker Than Water.* **Gr. 5–9. (Orig. British**
✓   **pub. 1989.)**

Becky's cousin Will is haunted by the voice of a ghostly boy trapped in the shaft of a coal mine near their home.

Candlewick, 1993, 205 pp. (1-56402-178-5)

(BL 89:1229; CCBB 46:209; HBG 4[Fall 1993]:309; KR 61:659; SLJ Apr 1993 p. 118; TLS Nov 24, 1989 p. 1311)

1070   **FEIL, Hila.** *Blue Moon.* **Gr. 7–9.**

Working as a summer au pair on Cape Cod, sixteen-year-old Julia comes to believe that the ghost of her charge's dead mother is trying to protect the house and her daughter from Molly's stepmother.

Macmillan, 1990, 193 pp. (0-689-31607-0)

(BL 86:1792; CCBB 43:108; HBG 1[Jan–June 1990]:256; KR 58:178; SLJ Mar 1990 p. 235; VOYA 13:29)

1071   **FINNEY, Jack (pseud. of Walter Branden Finney).** *Marion's Wall: A Novel.* **Gr. 10 up.**

Marion Marsh, the ghost of a promising young actress from the 1920s, returns to inhabit Jan Cheyney's body, after Jan and her husband uncover a message Marion left on the wall of their San Francisco apartment.

Simon, 1973, 187 pp., o.p.

(BL 70:221; KR 41:137; LJ 98:563)

1072 FLEISCHMAN, Paul (Taylor). *Graven Images: Three Stories.* **Gr. 7–9.**

✓ In the only fantasy story of the three, "The Man of Influence," a poor but arrogant sculptor accepts a ghost's commission to carve a statue of himself committing an infamous murder. John Newbery Medal Honor Book, 1983.

Illus. by Andrew Glass, Harper, 1982, 85 pp., LB(0-06-021906-8), pap., 96 pp. (0-06-440186-3)

(BL 79:368, 980; CC:578; CCBB 36:125; HB 58:656; JHC:431; KR 50:937; SLJ Sept 1982 p. 137; Suth 3:135)

1073 FLEISCHMAN, (Albert) Sid(ney). *The Ghost in the Noonday Sun.* **Gr. 4–7.**

✓ Pirates kidnap Oliver Finch in the hope that he will be able to see the ghost of Gentleman Jim, guardian of buried treasure.

Illus. by Warren Chappell, Little, 1965, 173 pp., o.p.; illus. by Peter Sis, Greenwillow, 1989, 131 pp. (0-688-08410-9)

(BL 62:54; CCBB 19:43, 42:222; Ch&Bks:274; Eakin:121; HB 41:490; KR 33:245, 472; LJ 90:3790; SLJ Feb 1989 p. 118)

1074 FLEISCHMAN, (Albert) Sid(ney). *The Midnight Horse.* **Gr. 3–6.**

✓✓ Orphaned Touch and his ghostly friend, the Great Chuffalo, work together to foil the dastardly plots of Touch's uncle, Judge Henry Wigglesforth.

Illus. by Peter Sis, Greenwillow, 1990, 84 pp. (0-688-09441-4); Dell, 1992, pap. (0-440-40614-5)

(BL 86:2171; CC:486; CCBB 44:83; HB 66:744; HBG 2[July–Dec 1990]:71; KR 58:1003; SLJ Sept 1990 p. 226, Dec 1990 p. 22; Suth 4:119)

1075 FLORA, James (Royer). *Grandpa's Ghost Stories.* **Gr. 2–4.**

✓ Grandpa has scary tales to tell: about a screaming skeleton, a ghost, a witch, and a werewolf. The sequel is *Grandpa's Witched-Up Christmas* (1982).

Illus. by the author, Atheneum, 1978, 32 pp. (0-689-50112-9)

(BL 75:216; HB 55:510; KR 46:1066; SLJ Oct 1978 p. 132, Apr 1982 p. 31)

1076 FREEMAN, Barbara C(onstance). *A Haunting Air.* **Gr. 5–7. (Orig. British pub. 1976.)**

Melissa and her neighbor search old letters and newspapers to discover why they keep hearing the ghostly singing of a Victorian child named Hanny.

Illus. by the author, Dutton, 1977, 158 pp., o.p.

(BL 74:811; CCBB 31:141; HB 54:163; KR 45:1270; SLJ Feb 1978 p. 57; Suth 2:155)

1077 FREEMAN, Barbara C(onstance). *A Pocket of Silence.* **Gr. 7–9. (Orig. British pub. 1977.)**

Zilia spins a tale of romance, kidnapping, and murder for Caroline, who discovers that Zilia has come from two hundred years in the past to help solve a mystery.

Decorations by the author, Dutton, 1978, 171 pp., o.p.

(BL 75:804, 809; HB 55:192; KR 42:132; SLJ Apr 1979 p. 55; TLS 1977 p. 864)

1078 *Fun Phantoms: Tales of Ghostly Entertainment.* **Ed. by Seon Manley and Gogo Lewis. Gr. 6–10.**

Twelve humorous ghost stories by such authors as Frank Stockton, Philippa Pearce, Oscar Wilde, Saki, and James Thurber.

Morrow, 1979, 192 pp., o.p.

(BL 75:860; KR 47:267; SLJ Mar 1979 p. 142)

1079 GAGE, Wilson (pseud. of Mary Q[uintard] Govan Steele). *The Ghost of Five*
✓ *Owl Farm.* Gr. 4–6.

Ted's attempts to liven up the summer by creating "ghostly" visitations backfire when a
real ghost appears.

Illus. by Paul Galdone, World, 1966, 127 pp., o.p.; Pocket, 1986, pap. (0-671-56085-9)

(BBC 203; BL 62:1049; CCBB 20:9; HB 42:435; KR 34:245; LJ 91:2716)

1080 GARFIELD, Leon. *The Empty Sleeve.* Gr. 6–9. (Orig. British pub. 1988.)
✓ As predicted at his birth, twin Peter Gannet is haunted by ghostly apparitions in this Dickensian tale set in eighteenth-century England.

Delacorte, 1988, 216 pp. (0-385-29817-X); Dell, pap. (0-440-50049-4)

(BL 85:149, 158, 879; CCBB 42:34; Ch&Bks:286; HB 65:78; JHC:361; KR 56:972; SLJ Oct 1988 p.161;
Suth 4:130; TLS 1988 p. 716)

1081 GARFIELD, Leon. *The Ghost Downstairs.* Gr. 7–9. (Orig. pub in England.)

Dennis Fast eagerly gives up seven years of his life in exchange for a million pounds, but
finds, to his dismay, that he is haunted by the ghost of himself as a child because he'd
unwittingly given away the *first* seven years of his life. Kate Greenaway Medal Commended Book, 1972.

Illus. by Antony Maitland, Pantheon, 1972, 107 pp., o.p.

(CCBB 25:168; HB 48:599; KR 40:623; LJ 97:4056, 4087)

1082 GARFIELD, Leon. *Mister Corbett's Ghost.* Gr. 5–8. (Orig. pub. in England.)
✓ The ghost of his former master, Mr. Corbett, returns to haunt Benjamin after his idle wish
for the man's death is fulfilled.

Pantheon, 1968, 87 pp., o.p.; Viking, 1988, o.p.

(BL 65:450, 84:1189; CCBB 22:92; HB 4:560; Kies:63; KR 36:824; LJ 73:8; Suth:141; TLS 1969 p. 350)

1083 GARFIELD, Leon. *The Restless Ghost: Three Stories.* Gr. 5–7. (Orig. pub. in
✓ England.)

In the title story, a ghost returns to haunt his imitator.

Illus. by Saul Lambert, Pantheon, 1969, 132 pp., o.p.

(CCBB 23:143; Ch&Bks:286; HB 46:45; KR 37:1122; LJ 94:4295; Suth:142)

GARFIELD, Leon. *The Wedding Ghost.* See Chapter 5B, Myth Fantasy.

1084 GATES, Susan P. *The Burnhope Wheel.* Gr. 6–9. (Orig. British pub. 1989.)

Fifteen-year-old Ellen and her new friend, Dave, are drawn into replaying a tragedy that
occurred one hundred years previously at the bottom of the Burnhope lead mine in this
suspenseful story.

Holiday, 1989, 174 pp. (0-8234-0767-5)

(BBJ:70; BL 86:735, 742; CCBB 43:84; HBG 1[July–Dec 1989]:83; KR 57:1747; SLJ Dec 1989 p. 118;
VOYA 13:290)

1085 *The Ghost Story Treasury.* Sel. by Linda Sonntag. Gr. 5–8.

Fifteen ghostly stories and poems by such authors as Virginia Hamilton and Judith
Gorog.

Illus. by Annabel Spenceley, Putnam, 1987, 87 pp. (0-399-21477-1)

(KR 55:1325; SLJ Mar 1988 p. 200)

1086 *Ghosts: An Anthology.* Ed. by William (James Carter) Mayne. Gr. 6–9.

Twenty-five stories and poems about ghosts and goblins, including works by Rudyard Kipling, Robert Louis Stevenson, and Walter de la Mare.

Nelson, 1971, 187 pp., o.p.

(BL 68:430, 434; CCBB 25:12; HB 47:491; LJ 96:3478)

1087 *The Ghost's Companion: A Haunting Anthology.* Ed. by Peter Haining. Gr. 10 up.

Fifteen ghostly and supernatural tales whose authors include Ray Bradbury, M. R. James, and Rudyard Kipling.

Taplinger, 1976, 191 pp., o.p.

(BL 72:1090, 1103; KR 44:159; TLS 1976 p. 561)

1088 *Ghosts for Christmas.* Ed. by Richard Dalby. Gr. 10 up. (Orig. British pub. 1988.)

Thirty ghostly tales set during the Christmas season, written in the nineteenth and twentieth centuries, whose authors include Charles Dickens and Robert Louis Stevenson.

Carroll & Graf, 1989, 339 pp., o.p.; Book Sales, 1992, pap. (1-55521-805-9)

(BL 86:525, 540; TLS 1988 p. 1351; VOYA 13:38)

1089 GODDEN (Dixon), (Margaret) Rumer. *Take Three Tenses; A Fugue in Time* (orig. British title: *A Fugue in Time,* 1945). Gr. 10 up.

Ninety-nine years of Dane family history come to life for an American girl visiting her eighty-year-old great-uncle's London home.

Little, 1945, 252 pp., o.p.

(BL 41:225; KR 13:38; TLS 1945 p. 245)

1090 GORDON, John (William). *The Burning Baby and Other Ghosts.* Gr. 8–12.
✓ (Orig. British pub. 1992.)

Five tales about ghosts seeking revenge on those who killed them, including "Under the Ice," "The Eels," and "The Burning Baby."

Candlewick, 1993, 112 pp. (1-56402-067-3)

(BL 90:430; CCBB 47:44; HBG 5:86; KR 61:1273; SLJ Nov 1993 p. 122)

1091 GORDON, John (William). *The Ghost on the Hill.* Gr. 8 up. (Orig. British pub. 1976.)

The ghost of Tom Goodchild becomes entangled in the lives of three young villagers, Ralph, Jenny, and Joe.

Viking, 1977, 171 pp., o.p.

(CCBB 31:32; Kies:68; KR 45:290; SLJ May 1977 p. 78)

GOROG, Judith. *In a Messy, Messy Room, and Other Strange Stories.* See Chapter 3, Fantasy Collections.

1092 GOROG, Judith. *No Swimming in Dark Pond: And Other Chilling Tales.* Gr. 6–10.

Thirteen shiver-producing tales, including "Flawless Beauty," "The Sufficient Prayer," and "No Swimming in Dark Pond."

Putnam, 1987 (entitled: *No Swimming in Dark Pond and Other Stories*), 112 pp. (0-399-21418-6)

(BL 83:1590, 1601; CCBB 40:207; KR 55:227; SLJ Mar 1987 p. 158; VOYA 10:120)

1093 **GOROG, Judith.** *On Meeting Witches at Wells.* **Gr. 5–8.**

Three teachers and some ghostly visitors tell stories to a group of eighth graders, including "An Old, Often Retold, Story of Revenge," "The Silver Skier," and the title story, "On Meeting Witches at Wells."

Putnam, 1991, 119 pp. (0-399-21803-3)

(BL 88:758; CCBB 45:156; HBG 3[July–Dec 1991]:65; KR 59:1222; SLJ Jan 1992 p. 109)

1094 **GOROG, Judith.** *Please Do Not Touch.* **Gr. 5–9.**

Touching an exhibit at an interactive museum sends visitors into the worlds of eleven eerie stories, including three about a shape-shifting brother-in-law, an overbearing teapot that takes over its owner's life, and a young DJ whose thoughts are broadcast on the air.

Scholastic, 1993, 144 pp. (0-590-46682-8)

(BL 90:51; CCBB 47:10; HBG 5:86; KR 61:1001; SLJ Sept 1993 p. 251; VOYA 16 290)

1095 **GOROG, Judith.** *A Taste for Quiet, and Other Disquieting Tales.* **Gr. 6–10.**

Twelve eerie tales, some in fairy-tale style and others in contemporary settings, including "Those Three Wishes," "A Story about Death," and "Critch."

Illus. by Jeanne Titherington, Putnam, 1982, 128 pp., o.p.

(BL 79:906; HB 59:170; KR 50:1295; SLJ Mar 1983 p. 192)

1096 **GRAY, Genevieve S(tuck).** *Ghost Story.* **Gr. 3–5.**

A ghost family is kept busy haunting the vagrants who moved into their house.

Illus. by Greta Matus, Lothrop, 1975, 46 pp., o.p.

(BL 71:690; CCBB 28:177; KR 43:122; SLJ Apr 1975 p. 52; Suth 2:77)

1097 **GRIPE, Maria (Kristina).** *Agnes Cecilia.* **Gr. 6–10. (Orig. Swedish pub. 1981.)**

✓ Lonely Nora's beautiful old doll reveals some sad family secrets involving other orphaned or unloved children from the past.

Trans. by Rika Lesser, Harper, 1990, 288 pp. (0-06-022282-4)

(BL 86:1890,1898; CCBB 43:161; HBG 1[Jan 1990]:250; KR 58:727; SLJ Apr 1990 p. 140, Dec 1990 p. 22; VOYA 13:103)

HAHN, Mary Downing. *The Doll in the Garden: A Ghost Story.* See Chapter 8, Time Travel Fantasy.

1098 **HAHN, Mary Downing.** *Wait Till Helen Comes: A Ghost Story.* **Gr. 5–7.**

Molly and Michael's miserable stepsister, Heather, threatens them with punishment by Helen, a ghost only the children can perceive, in this suspenseful story.

Houghton, 1986, 184 pp. (0-89919-453-2); Avon, 1987, pap. (0-380-70442-0)

(BBC:204; BL 83:60; CC:496; CCBB 40:27; HB 62:744; KR 54:1204; SLJ Oct 1986, p. 176)

HALL, Lynn. *Dagmar Schultz and the Angel Edna.* See Chapter 6, Humorous Fantasy.

1099 **HALL, Lynn.** *The Mystery of the Caramel Cat.* **Gr. 3–4.**

The ghost of a caramel cat has haunted an abandoned mansion, formerly a stop on the underground railroad, ever since it accidentally caused the capture of two runaway slaves.

Illus. by Ruth Sanderson, Garrard, 1981, o.p.

(BBC:204; BL 78:438; SLJ Dec 1981 p. 82)

1100 **HAMILTON (Adoff), Virginia (Esther).** *Sweet Whispers, Brother Rush.* **Gr.**
✓   **7–10.**

Fifteen-year-old Tree (Teresa) has ghostly visions of the past that enable her to piece together the tragic history of her mother's family. John Newbery Medal Honor Book, 1983. Boston Globe/Horn Book Award, 1983. Coretta Scott King Fiction Award, 1983.

Putnam, 1982, 224 pp. (0-399-20894-1); Avon, 1983, pap. (0-380-65193-9)

(BL 78:1518, 1525; 79:685, 980, 80:352, 86:790; CCBB 35:207; Ch&Bks:286; HB 58:505, 59:330; JHC:366; Kies:75; KR 50:801; SHC:688; SLJ Sept 1982 p. 138; Suth 3:172; VOYA 5 [Aug 1982]:31, [Feb 1983]:36)

1101 **HARRIS, Christie (Lucy Irwin).** *Secret in the Stlalakum Wild.* **Gr. 4–7. (Orig. pub. in Canada.)**

Spirits of the Northwest Coast Salish Indians send a little girl named Morann into the wilderness alone on a quest for treasure.

Illus. by Douglas Tait, Atheneum, 1972, 186 pp., o.p.

(BL 68:908; CCBB 25:169; KR 40:478; LJ 97:1913)

HARRIS, Rosemary (Jeanne). *Sea Magic and Other Stories of Enchantment.* See Chapter 3, Fantasy Collections.

HARRIS, Rosemary (Jeanne). *The Seal-Singing.* See Chapter 5B, Myth Fantasy.

1102 **HASELEY, Dennis.** *Ghost Catcher.* **Gr. 3–6.**

This is an allegorical tale about a man who snatches loved ones back from the land of the dead to give them a second chance at happiness, until the day he himself becomes trapped in the land of the ghosts.

Illus. by Lloyd Bloom, Harper, 1991, 40 pp. LB(0-06-022247-6)

(BL 88:327; HBG 3[Spring 1992]:34; KR 59:1160; SLJ Nov 1991 p. 117)

1103 *The Haunted and the Haunters: Tales of Ghosts and Other Apparitions.* **Ed. by Kathleen Lines. Gr. 7–10.**

Spine-tingling tales by Lucy Boston, Joan Aiken, and Walter de la Mare, among others. A companion volume to *The House of the Nightmare and Other Eerie Stories* (1968).

Farrar, 1975, 275 pp., o.p.

(BL 72:358; HB 52:60; KR 43:1194; SLJ Dec 1975 p. 68)

1104 *Haunting Tales.* **Ed. by Barbara Ireson. Gr. 6–9. (Orig. British pub. 1973.)**

Ghostly tales by E. Nesbit, Joan Aiken, Ray Bradbury, and Eleanor Farjeon.

Illus. by Freda Woolf, Dutton, 1974, 279 pp., o.p.

(BL 71:570; HB 50:697; KR 42:1161)

HAYES, Sarah. *Crumbling Castle.* See Chapter 10, Witchcraft and Sorcery Fantasy.

1105 **HAYNES, Betsy.** *The Ghost of the Gravestone Hearth.* **Gr. 4–6.**

Charlie spends the summer searching for buried treasure after an encounter with the ghosts of a drowned boy and his pirate enemies.

Nelson, 1977, 160 pp., o.p.

(BBC:204; BL 74:41; CCBB 31:60; KR 45:351; SLJ May 1977 p. 77)

1106   **HEARNE, Betsy (Gould).** *Eli's Ghost.* **Gr 4–7.**

A young boy named Eli runs away from his mean father to search for his mother, almost drowns in a whirlpool, and releases a mischievous ghost.

Illus. by Ronald Himler, Macmillan, 1987, 104 pp. (0-689-50420-9)

(BL 83:1205; CCBB 40:126; Ch&Bks:287; HB 63:612; KR 55:56; SLJ Apr 1987 p. 94; Suth 4:170)

HENDRICH, Paula (Griffith). *Who Says So?* See Chapter 7, Magic Adventure Fantasy.

1107   **HENRY, Maeve.** *A Gift for Gift: A Ghost Story.* **Gr. 6–9. (Orig. British pub.**
✓   **1990.)**

Michael, a ghostly creature from "the gap between the worlds," promises to take fifteen-year-old Fran away from her squalid home and make all her wishes come true, if she agrees to become his eternal companion.

Delacorte, 1992, 106 pp. (0-385-305-62-1)

(BL 88:1825; CCBB 45:181; HBG 3[Fall 1992]:274; KR 60:670; SLJ Mar 1992 p. 256; VOYA 15:28)

1108   **HILDICK, E(dmund) W(allace).** *The Ghost Squad Breaks Through* **(The Ghost Squad series, book 1). Gr. 5–7.**
✓   Four ghosts and two live teenagers band together to solve crimes. The sequels are: *The Ghost Squad and the Halloween Conspiracy* (1985), *The Ghost Squad Flies Concorde* (1985), *The Ghost Squad and the Ghoul of Grünberg* (1986), *The Ghost Squad and the Prowling Hermits* (1987), and *The Ghost Squad and the Menace of the Malevs* (1988).

Dutton, 1984, 112 pp. (0-525-44097-6)

(BL 80:1398, 85:585; CC:502; JHC:369; Kies:79; SLJ 30 [May 1984]:101)

HOFFMAN, Mary. *The Four-Legged Ghosts.* See Chapter 7, Magic Adventure Fantasy.

1109   **HOTZE, Sollace.** *Acquainted with the Night.* **Gr. 7–12.**
✓   The ghost of Evaline Bloodsworth, a young woman who died on Plum Cove Island in 1824, appears to Molly, seventeen, and her Vietnam veteran cousin, Caleb, throughout the summer they spend together on the Maine island.

Houghton, 1992, 230 pp. (0-395-61576-3)

(BL 89:666; CCBB 46:75; KR 60:1377; SLJ Nov 1992 p. 123; VOYA 15:292)

HOWARD, Joan (pseud. of Patricia Gordon). *The Witch of Scrapfaggot Green.* See Chapter 10, Witchcraft and Sorcery Fantasy.

1110   **HOYLAND, John.** *The Ivy Garland.* **Gr. 4–6. (Orig. British pub. 1982.)**

Linda, Diane, and Jamie feel compelled to solve the mystery of the ghostly boy in old-fashioned clothes whom they meet in a mountain cave.

Illus. by Richard Vicary, Schocken, 1983, 1987, 96 pp. (0-8052-8137-1)

(BBC:205; CCBB 36:211; SLJ Mar 1984 p. 160)

1111   **HUGHES, Dean.** *Nutty's Ghost.* **Gr. 5–7.**

The ghost of a Shakespearean actor whose career was ruined by his appearance in a mediocre film haunts Nutty Nutsell as he prepares for a part in a movie by the same director. This is the sequel to the non-fantasy, *Nutty, the Movie Star* (1989).

Macmillan, 1993, 136 pp. (0-689-31743-3)

(BL 89:1054; HBG 4[Fall 1993]:299; KR 61:148; SLJ May 1993 p. 106)

1112   **IBBOTSON, Eva.** *The Great Ghost Rescue.* **Gr. 5–7.**

So many of England's great mansions have become unhauntable that Humphrey the Horrible appeals to the prime minister for help.

Illus. by Giulio Maestro, Walck, 1975, 135 pp., o.p.

(HB 51:593; Kies:86; KR 43:605; SLJ May 1975 p. 70)

IRVING, Washington. *The Legend of Sleepy Hollow.* See Chapter 5B, Myth Fantasy.

1113   **JACQUES, Brian.** *Seven Strange and Ghostly Tales.* **Gr. 5–7. (Orig. British pub. 1991.)**

Humorous and shivery stories set in present-day English neighborhoods and schools, involving ghosts, vampires, and the devil.

Putnam, 1991, 137 pp. (0-399-22103-4); Avon 1993, pap. (0-380-71906-1)

(BL 88:524; CCBB 45:93; HB 68:341; HBG 3[Spring 1992]:82; SLJ Dec 1991 p. 116)

JAMES, M(ontague) R(hodes). *The Five Jars.* See Chapter 7, Magic Adventure Fantasy.

JENNINGS, Paul. *Unreal! Eight Surprising Stories.* See Chapter 3, Fantasy Collections.

1114   **JENSEN, Dorothea.** *The Riddle of Penncroft Farm.* **Gr. 5–7.**

Lars' oddly dressed new friend, Geordie, tells him about meeting General George Washington and taking part in the Revolutionary War encampment at Valley Forge, Pennsylvania.

Harcourt, 1989, 180 pp. (0-15-200574-9), 1991, pap. (0-15-266908-6)

(BL 86:351; CCBB 43:62; HBG 1[July 1989]:p. 87; KR 57:1328; SLJ Oct 1989 p.120)

JOHNSON, Charles. *Pieces of Eight.* See Chapter 8, Time Travel Fantasy.

1115   **JONES, Louis C(lark).** *Things That Go Bump in the Night.* **Gr. 5–8.**

Tales of ghosts, witches, and haunted houses.

Illus. by Erwin Austin, Hill, 1959, 208 pp., o.p.

(BL 55:559; KR 27:205; LJ 84:1275)

1116   **KEHRET, Peg.** *Horror at the Haunted House.* **Gr. 5–7.**

✓   Lydia Clayton, the ghost of the original owner of the historic Clayton house, keeps appearing to Ellen whenever she examines Mrs. Clayton's priceless collection of Wedgewood china. This is the sequel to *Terror at the Zoo* (1992), which is not a fantasy.

Dutton, 1992, 144 pp. (0-525-65106-3)

(BL 89:56; HBG 4[Spring 1993]:71; JHC 1993 Suppl. p. 77; KR 60:991; SLJ Sept 1992 p. 254; VOYA 15:224)

1117   **KELLEHER, Victor (pseud. of Michael Kitchener).** *Baily's Bones.* **Gr. 6–10. (Orig. Australian pub. 1988.)**

Dee and Alex's mentally disabled brother Kenny is taken over by the vengeful ghost of Frank Baily, in the remote Australian valley where their mother is doing historical research.

Dial, 1989, 182 pp., o.p.

(BL 86:670; CCBB 43:140; HB 66:204; HBG 1[July 1989]:86; KR 57:1594; SLJ Nov 1989 p. 111; VOYA 13:30)

1118 **KEMP, Gene.** *Jason Bodger and the Priory Ghost.* **Gr. 4–7. (Orig. British pub.**
✓ **1985.)**

A medieval ghost that only Jason can see convinces this tough boy to cooperate with his timid teachers.

Illus. by Elaine McGregor Turney, Faber, 1985, 140 pp., o.p.

(BBC:206; BL 82:810; CCBB 39:169; Ch&Bks:287; SLJ Sept 1986 p. 136; Suth 4:211; TLS 1985 p. 1460)

1119 **KINSELLA, W(illiam) P(atrick).** *Shoeless Joe.* **Gr. 10 up.**

✓ Baseball fanatic Ray Kinsella joins forces with J. D. Salinger in resurrecting the long-deceased members of the Chicago Black Sox team, including Shoeless Joe Jackson.

Houghton, 1982, o.p.; Ballantine, 1983, pap., 265 pp. (0-345-34256-9)

(BL 78:941; Kies:95; KR 50:159; LJ 107:745; SLJ Aug 1982 p. 131, Dec 1982 p. 291)

1120 **KIPLING, (Joseph) Rudyard.** *Phantoms and Fantasies: Twenty Tales.* **Gr. 6–8.**

Twenty ghostly stories set in India and England.

Illus. by Burt Silverman, Doubleday, 1965, 302 pp., o.p.

(KR 33:533; LJ 90:3133)

1121 **KLAVENESS, Jan O'Donnell.** *The Griffin Legacy.* **Gr. 6–9.**

✓ Amy's resemblance to an eighteenth-century ancestor, Lucy Griffin, enables her to speak with apparitions of Lucy and of Seth Howes, a Loyalist shot to death by Lucy's father. With the help of friends, Amy solves the mystery of a lost family legacy, and brings peace to the souls of Lucy and Seth.

Macmillan, 1983, 184 pp., o.p.; Dell, 1985, pap. (0-440-43165-4)

(BBC:207; BL 80:297; CC:517; CCBB 37:110; HB 60:61; JHC:377; Kies:95; SLJ Dec 1983 p. 85; Suth 3:236; VOYA 7:32)

1122 **KNOWLES, Anne.** *The Halcyon Island.* **Gr. 5–7.**

✓ A ghostly boy named Giles teaches twelve-year-old Ken to overcome his fear of the water.

Harper, 1981, 120 pp., o.p.

(BL 77:1300; CCBB 34:213; HB 57:302; KR 49:571; SLJ Apr 1981 p. 128; Suth 3:240)

KONIGSBURG, E(laine) L(obl). *Up from Jericho Tel.* See Chapter 7, Magic Adventure Fantasy.

KUSHNER, Donn. *Uncle Jacob's Ghost Story.* See Chapter 1, Allegorical Fantasy and Literary Fairy Tales.

LACKEY, Mercedes, and DIXON, Larry. *Born to Run.* See Chapter 10, Witchcraft and Sorcery Fantasy.

1123 **LAMPMAN, Evelyn Sibley.** *Captain Apple's Ghost.* **Gr. 5–7.**

The ghost of Captain Apple returns to save his former home.

Illus. by Ninon MacKnight, Doubleday, 1952, 249 pp., o.p.

(HB 28:406; KR 20:405; LJ 77:1739, 78:70)

LASKY, Kathryn. *Home Free.* See Chapter 8, Time Travel Fantasy.

1124 **LAWRENCE, Louise (pseud. of Elizabeth Rhoda Holden).** *Sing and Scatter Daisies.* **Gr. 8–10.**

Seventeen-year-old Nicky Hennessy's jealousy of the love between his favorite aunt,

Anna, and a ghost named John Hollis nearly blinds him to the fact that Anna is dying. This is the sequel to *The Wyndcliffe* (1975).

Harper, 1977, 256 pp., o.p.

(BL 73:1084, 1092; CCBB 30:162; HB 53:450; KR 45:358; SLJ Apr 1977 p. 77)

LAWSON, John S(hults). *The Spring Rider.* See Chapter 8, Time Travel Fantasy.

1125 LEACH, Christopher. *Rosalinda.* **Gr. 7–9.**

Rosalinda died in the 1700s at the age of seventeen, but anguish over a thwarted romance causes her to reach into the twentieth century to control the life of Anne, daughter of the curator of the Warrender estate.

Warne, 1978, 124 pp., o.p.

(BL 74:1552; CCBB 32:12; SLJ Sept 1978 p. 142; TLS 1978 p. 765)

1126 LEACH, Maria (pseud. of Alice Mary Doanne Leach). *The Thing at the Foot of the Bed and Other Scary Tales.* **Gr. 5–7.**

A collection of ghost and witch tales, including "The Thing at the Foot of the Bed," "Wait til Martin Comes," and "The Golden Arm."

Illus. by Kurt Werth, Putnam, 1959, 1987, 126 pp. LB(0-389-21496-8)

(BBC:208; BL 55:543; Eakin:204; KR 27:265; LJ 84:1697)

1127 LEROE, Ellen. *Ghost Dog.* **Gr. 2–4.**

Ghost Dog helps nine-year-old Artie protect his grandpa's valuable baseball card from a thief.

Hyperion, 1993, 64 pp. (1-56282-268-3)

(BL 89:1431; HBG 4[Fall 1993]:300; SLJ June 1993 p. 78)

1128 LEVIN, Betty (Lowenthal). *A Binding Spell.* **Gr. 6–8.**

✓   Only Wren and an extremely reclusive neighbor, Axel Pederson, can see the ghostly horse that appears in the countryside near their homes.

Dutton, 1984, 179 pp., o.p.

(BL 81:449; CCBB 38:151; HB 60:759; SLJ Dec 1984 p. 101)

1129 LIFTON, Betty Jean (Kirschner). *The Cock and the Ghost Cat.* **Gr. 1–4.**

✓   Koko the rooster saves his master from the ghost of a huge cat.

Illus. by Fuku Akino, Atheneum, 1965, 32 pp., o.p.

(BL 62:162; CCBB 19:35; Eakin:210; HB 41:492; KR 33:672; LJ 90:4618)

1130 LILLINGTON, Kenneth (James). *Full Moon.* **Gr. 8–12. (Orig. pub. in England.)**

The unhappy ghosts of two sisters possess two teenaged girls who have come to live in an old house and an antique shop inherited from their Great-Aunt Clara.

Faber, 1986, 136 pp., o.p.

(BL 82:1455, 1462; KR 54:1022)

1131 LILLINGTON, Kenneth (James). *What Beckoning Ghost?* **Gr. 7–10. (Orig. British pub. 1983.)**

The sobbing ghost of a young woman appears only to women who have refused to marry men chosen by their parents. Sixteen-year-old Emma Nash tries to understand the ghost's sadness, in this suspenseful tale.

Faber, 1983, 156 pp., o.p.

(BL 80:338, 360; CCBB 37:111; SLJ Dec 1983 p. 85)

1132   **LINDBERGH, Anne Spencer.** *The People in Pineapple Place.* **Gr. 4–6.**

Lonely after his move to a new home, August makes friends with a group of invisible people from the past who take him on wonderful expeditions. The sequel is *The Prisoner of Pineapple Place* (1988, pap., 1990).

Harcourt, 1982, 156 pp. (0-15-260517-7); Avon, 1990, pap. (0-380-70766-7)

(BBC:208; BL 79:116; CCBB 36:30; HB 58:650; KR 50:1106; SLJ Oct 1982 p. 153; Suth 3:265)

1133   **LINDGREN, Astrid.** *The Ghost of Skinny Jack.* **Gr. K–4. (Orig. Swedish pub. 1987.)**

Two children are frightened by their grandmother's story about a farmhand who pretended to be a ghost and ended up scaring himself into becoming one.

Illus. by Ilon Wikland, Viking, 1988, 25 pp., o.p.

(BL 85:791; CCBB 42:78; SLJ Mar 1989 p. 166)

1134   *The Literary Ghost: Great Contemporary Ghost Stories.* **Ed. by Larry Dark. Gr. 10 up.**

Twenty-eight ghost stories from Great Britain, the United States, South Africa, India and Canada, whose authors include Isaac Bashevis Singer, Nadine Gordimer, and Joyce Carol Oates.

Atlantic, 1991, 384 pp. (0-87113-483-7)

(BL 88:408, 423; SHC 1993 Suppl. p. 86)

1135   **LIVELY, Penelope (Margaret Low).** *The Driftway.* **Gr. 5–7. (Orig. British pub.**
✓   **1972.)**

While running away from their father and his new wife, Paul and his sister have visions of a Viking raid, a Civil War battle, and an eighteenth-century highway robbery along the "driftway."

Dutton, 1973, 140 pp., o.p.

(BL 69:813; CCBB 26:172; HB 49:271; Kies:106; KR 41:188; LJ 98:2003; Suth 2:288; TLS 1972 p. 812)

1136   **LIVELY, Penelope (Margaret Low).** *The Ghost of Thomas Kempe.* **Gr. 4–6.**
✓✓   **(Orig. British pub. 1973.)**

James Harrison becomes the unwilling apprentice of a seventeenth-century sorcerer and ends up taking the blame for the mischief caused when Thomas Kempe decides to start life anew in the twentieth century. Carnegie Medal, 1973.

Dutton, 1973, 186 pp. (0-525-30495-9); Berkley, 1986, pap., 192 pp., o.p.

(BBC:208; BL 70:388, 80:96; CC:525; CCBB 27:81; Ch&Bks:262; HB 49:591; Kies:106; KR 41:883; LJ 99:211; Suth 2:288; TLS 1973 p. 380)

1137   **LIVELY, Penelope (Margaret Low).** *The Revenge of Samuel Stokes.* **Gr. 5–7.**
✓   **(Orig. British pub. 1981.)**

Enraged at finding a housing development on the estate he landscaped centuries before, the ghost of Samuel Stokes returns to haunt the residents.

Dutton, 1981, 122 pp., o.p.

(BBC:208; BL 78:549, 550; CCBB 35:175; Ch&Bks:289; HB 58:44; Kies:107; SLJ Oct 1981 p. 144; Suth 3:269; TLS 1982 p. 345)

1138   **LIVELY, Penelope (Margaret Low).** *A Stitch in Time.* **Gr. 4–7. (Orig. British**
✓   **pub. 1976.)**

Maria is convinced that Harriet, the girl in a hundred-year-old photograph hanging in Maria's summer house, still lives in the house.

Dutton, 1976, 140 pp., o.p.

(BL 73:610; CCBB 30:129; Ch&Bks:262; HB 53:52; Kies:107; KR 44:1169; SLJ Jan 1977 p. 94; Suth 2:289; TLS 1976 p. 885)

LIVELY, Penelope (Margaret Low). *Uninvited Ghosts and Other Stories.* See Chapter 6, Humorous Fantasy.

LIVELY, Penelope (Margaret Low). *The Wild Hunt of the Ghost Hounds.* See Chapter 5B, Myth Fantasy.

1139 **LUNN, Janet (Louise Swoboda).** *Shadow in Hawthorn Bay.* **Gr. 6–10. (Orig.**
✓ **Canadian pub. 1986.)**

Her cousin's ghost "calls" fifteen-year-old Mary Urquhart to make the difficult voyage from Scotland to Canada in 1815, only to find that he is summoning her into the lake where he committed suicide. Governor General's Literary Award for Children's Literature, 1986. Canadian Library Association Best Book of the Year for Children, 1987.

Scribner, 1987, 180 pp., o.p.; Puffin, 1988, pap. (0-14-032436-4)

(BL 83:1525; CCBB 40:192; HB 63:618, 641; KR 55:796; SLJ Sept 1987 p. 197; VOYA 10:122)

1140 **LUNN, Janet (Louise Swoboda).** *Twin Spell* **(Orig. Canadian title:** *Double Spell,* **1968). Gr. 5–7.**

An antique doll gives twins Jane and Elizabeth identical nightmares and intertwines their lives with a pair of twins from the past.

Illus. by Emily McCully, Harper, 1969, 158 pp., o.p.; Puffin, 1986 (entitled *Double Spell*), pap., 144 pp. (0-14-031858-5)

(CCBB 23:101; HB 45:675; KR 37:1064; LJ 94:3821)

1141 **LYKKEN, Laurie.** *Little Room of Terror.* **Gr. 6–8.**

The ghost of a young girl appears to Diane in the tower room of the old house her recently remarried father is renovating.

Willowisp Pr., 1991, 156 pp., o.p.

(BL 87:1976; Kliatt Apr 1991 p. 10; VOYA 14:173)

1142 **McBRATNEY, Sam.** *The Ghosts of Hungryhouse Lane.* **Gr 4–6.**

A crisis occurs for the ghosts of Hungryhouse Lane after their friend, Mercia Porterhouse, dies and her house is inherited by the Sweet family and their rambunctious children.

Illus. by Lisa Thiesing, Henry Holt, 1989, 118 pp. (0-8050-0985-X)

(BBC:209; BL 85:1387; CCBB 42:231; KR 57:380; SLJ May 1989 p. 110)

1143 **McGINNIS, Lila S(prague).** *The Ghost Upstairs.* **Gr. 3–6.**

Albert Shook has trouble explaining his unusually good grades and tidy room, because they've been caused by Otis White, the ghost of a boy who died seventy-five years earlier.

Illus. by Amy Rowen, Hastings, 1982, 119 pp., o.p.

(BBC:209; BL 79:314, 83:586; SLJ Sept 1983 p. 124)

McGOWEN, Tom (Thomas E.). *Sir Machinery.* See Chapter 10, Witchcraft and Sorcery Fantasy.

1144 **McGRAW, Eloise Jarvis.** *A Really Weird Summer.* **Gr. 6–8.**
✓ While trying to cope with his parents' imminent divorce, Nels's secret friendship with Alan, a mysterious boy from the past, hurts his younger brother's feelings.

Atheneum, 1977, 218 pp., o.p.; Macmillan, 1990, pap. (0-02-044483-4)

(BL 73:1421; CCBB 31:62; HB 53:532; KR 45:427; SLJ Oct 1977 p. 126; VOYA 14:33)

1145 McGRAW, Eloise Jarvis. *The Trouble with Jacob.* **Gr. 5–8.**

Andy and his twin, Kat, help the ghost of Jacob, a boy who died in 1876, go to his eternal rest.

Macmillan, 1988, 288 pp. (0-689-5047-0)

(BBC:209; BL 84:1435; KR 56:365; SLJ Apr 1988 p. 102; VOYA 11:96)

1146 MacKELLAR, William. *Alfie and Me and the Ghost of Peter Stuyvesant.* **Gr. 5–7.**

Peter Stuyvesant's ghost gives Billy and Alfie a map directing them to treasure buried beneath Times Square.

Illus. by David Stone, Dodd, 1974, 150 pp., o.p.

(KR 42:877; LJ 99:3268)

1147 MacKELLAR, William. *A Ghost Around the House.* **Gr. 4–6.**

While exploring Strowan Castle on Halloween night, Jasper meets a 250-year-old ghost.

Illus. by Marilyn Miller, McKay, 1970, 117 pp., o.p.

(KR 38:876; LJ 95:4352)

1148 MacKELLAR, William. *The Ghost in the Castle.* **Gr. 4–6.**

✓ A ghost tells Angus Campbell the truth about Bonnie Prince Charlie's secret mission to Dunnach.

Illus. by Richard Bennett, McKay, 1960, 86 pp., o.p.

(BL 57:500; HB 36:396; KR 28:624; LJ 85:4568)

MacKELLAR, William. *The Witch of Glen Gowrie.* See Chapter 10, Witchcraft and Sorcery Fantasy.

1149 McKILLIP, Patricia A(nne). *The House on Parchment Street.* **Gr. 5–7.**

Carol's cousins don't believe that she has seen ghosts from the seventeenth century in their cellar.

Illus. by Charles Robinson, Atheneum, 1973, 190 pp., o.p.

(BL 69:1093; CCBB 26:173; Kies:113; KR 41:115; LJ 98:1701)

1150 McKISSACK, Patricia C(arwell). *The Dark-Thirty: Southern Tales of the Super-*
✓ *natural.* **Gr. 4–8.**

Ten ghostly stories written in the style of traditional folk tales, using themes from African-American history and folklore. Newbery Honor Book, 1993. Coretta Scott King Award, 1993.

Illus. by Brian Pinkney, Knopf, 1992, 122 pp. LB(0-679-91863-9)

(BL 89:738; CC Suppl. p. 77; CCBB 46:117; HB 69:209; HBG 4[Spring 1993]:173; KR 60:1313; SLJ Dec 1992 p. 113)

1151 McMULLAN, Kate. *Under the Mummy's Spell.* **Gr. 5–8.**

On a dare, twelve-year-old Peter kisses the mummy mask of Egyptian Princess Nephia, thus fulfilling an ancient prophecy by awakening her ghost, who begs him to bring her the mummy of her pet cat before her sorceress aunt finds it.

Farrar, 1992, 214 pp. (0-374-38033-3)

(BL 88:1936; HBG 3[Fall 1992]:267; KR 60:781; SLJ July 1992 p. 74; VOYA 15:226)

MAHY, Margaret (May). *Dangerous Spaces.* See Chapter 5C, Travel to Other Worlds.

MAHY, Margaret (May). *A Tall Story and Other Tales.* See Chapter 7, Magic Adventure Fantasy.

1152 **MAHY, Margaret (May).** *The Tricksters.* **Gr. 9 up. (Orig. New Zealand pub.**
✓✓ **1986.)**

Harry (Araidne) Hamilton accidentally calls up the spirit of Teddy Carnival, a former inhabitant of their vacation home, who appears in the form of triplet brothers claiming to be long-lost Carnival relations.

Macmillan, 1987, 272 pp. (0-689-50400-4)

(BBS:61; BL 83:1008, 84:1248; CCBB 40:131; HB 63:471; KR 55:60; SLJ Mar 1987 p. 172, Dec 1987 p. 38; TLS 1988 p. 370; VOYA 10:80)

1153 *The Mammoth Book of Ghost Stories 2.* **Ed. by Richard Dalby. Gr. 7–12.**

Fifty-nine British and American stories whose authors include Charles Dickens, Rudyard Kipling, E. Nesbit, and Washington Irving. This is a companion volume to *The Mammoth Book of Ghost Stories* (1990).

Carroll & Graf, 1991, pap., 672 pp. (0-88184-701-1)

(BL 87:2099, 2111; LJ Sept 1, 1991 p. 233; VOYA 14:384)

1154 **MANLEY, Seon.** *The Ghost in the Far Garden and Other Stories.* **Gr. 6–9.**

Eleven original ghost stories based on legends, including "The Mistress of Montauk Point," "The Cats Here Speak Only Spanish," and "Evil One."

Illus. by Emanuel Schoengut, Morrow, 1977, 128 pp., o.p.

(BL 74:1094, 1109; KR 45:1049; SLJ Jan 1978 p. 96)

1155 **MARTIN, Bill (William Ivan), and ARCHAMBAULT, John.** *The Ghost-Eye*
✓ *Tree.* **Gr. 2–3.**

A boy's older sister teases him about his fear of a ghostly tree, until she sees the ghost herself while out on an evening errand.

Illus. by Ted Rand, Holt, 1985, 30 pp., o.p.

(BL 83:586; CCBB 39:114; HB 62:51; SLJ Feb 1986 p. 76)

1156 *Masters of Shades and Shadows: An Anthology of Great Ghost Stories.* **Ed. by Seon Manley and Gogo Lewis. Gr. 7 up.**

Sixteen ghost stories arranged chronologically, from Charles Dickens to Ray Bradbury.

Doubleday, 1978, 216 pp., o.p.

(BL 74:608; CCBB 31:164; KR 46:112; SLJ Dec 1977 p. 62)

1157 **MAYNE, William (James Carter).** *It.* **Gr. 6–9. (Orig. British pub. 1977.)**

The ghost of a witch's familiar alerts Alice to other supernatural occurrences.

Greenwillow, 1978, 189 pp., o.p.

(CCBB 32:84; HB 55:646; KR 46:1017; SLJ Dec 1978 p. 62; TLS 1978 p. 376; VOYA 1[Feb 1979]:40)

MIAN, Mary. *Take Three Witches.* See Chapter 10, Witchcraft and Sorcery Fantasy.

1158 **MILLER, Judi.** *Ghost in My Soup.* **Gr. 3–5.**

A ghost living in Scottie's hundred-year-old house helps the boy make friends in his new neighborhood.

Bantam, 1985, pap. 86 pp. (0-553-15622-5)

(BBC:210; BL 82:811; SLJ Nov 1985 p. 88)

1159   *Modern Ghost Stories by Eminent Women Writers.* **Ed. by Richard Dalby. Gr. 10 up.**

Twenty-seven chilling ghost stories whose authors include Joan Aiken, E. Nesbit, and Penelope Lively. A companion volume to Dalby's *Victorian Ghost Stories by Eminent Women Writers* (1989).

Carroll & Graf, 1992, 318 pp. (0-88184-864-6)

(LJ Oct 15, 1992 p. 102; VOYA 16:44, 17:10)

MURPHY, Pat. *The Falling Woman: A Fantasy.* See Chapter 5B, Myth Fantasy.

MYERS, Walter Dean. *The Black Pearl and the Ghost; or, One Mystery after Another.* See Chapter 6, Humorous Fantasy.

1160   **NATHAN, Robert (Gruntal).** *Mia.* **Gr. 10 up.**

✓ The ghost of a middle-aged woman's lost youth comes between her and a would-be lover, the retired novelist who tells this story.

Knopf, 1970, 179 pp., o.p.

(BL 67:38; HB 46:502; KR 38:346; LJ 95:2181, 3080)

1161   **NAYLOR, Phyllis Reynolds.** *Bernie and the Bessledorf Ghost* **(Bessledorf Mys-**
✓ **tery series, book 3). Gr. 4–6.**

Bernie discovers that the hotel his father manages is haunted by the ghost of a young boy-named Jonathan Bessledorf. This is the sequel to two nonfantasies: *The Mad Gasser of Bessledorf Street* (1983) and *The Bodies in the Bessledorf Hotel* (1986), and is followed by *The Face in the Bessledorf Funeral Parlor* (1993).

Macmillan, 1990, 144 pp. (0-689-31499-X); Avon, 1992, pap. (0-380-71351-9)

(BL 86:1635; CC:536; HBG 1[Jan–June, 1990]:259; KR 58:582; SLJ July 1990 p. 78)

NAYLOR, Phyllis Reynolds. *Shadows on the Wall.* See Chapter 8, Time Travel Fantasy.

1162   **NIXON, Joan Lowery.** *Haunted Island.* **Gr. 4–6.**

While renovating an island inn, Chris Holt and his family discover that the island is haunted by the ghost of Amos Corley who died 175 years before.

Scholastic, 1987, pap., 123 pp. (0-590-40203-X)

(BL 83:1132; Kliatt 21[Spring 1987]:24; SLJ May 1987 p. 102)

1163   **NORTON, André, and MILLER, Phyllis.** *House of Shadows.* **Gr. 5–7.**

Mike, Susan, and Tucker Whelan's frightening dreams seem to be connected to an old set of paper dolls and the deaths of three of their ancestors in their two hundred-year-old house.

Macmillan, 1984, 201 pp., o.p.; Tor, 1985, pap. (0-8125-4743-8)

(BBC:210; BL 80:1118; CCBB 37:171; HB 60:331; JHC 394; Kies:129; SLJ May 1984, p. 92)

1164   **ORMONDROYD, Edward.** *Castaways on Long Ago.* **Gr. 5–7.**

Richard, Linda, and Dudley explore the forbidden Long Ago Island and meet its ghostly inhabitant.

Illus. by Ruth Robbins, Parnassus, 1973, 182 pp., o.p.; Bantam, 1983, pap. (0-553-15457-5)

(BBC:211; CCBB 27:99; HB 50:150; LJ 99:575; Suth 2:346)

1165 **PARK, Ruth.** *Things in Corners.* **Gr. 5–8. (Orig. Australian pub. 1989.)**

✓ Five supernatural stories set in Australia, including one about a fur collar that comes alive and bites at night, and another about an old car haunted by the ghost of a man who drowned his family in it.

Viking, 1991, 197 pp. (0-670-82225-6); Puffin, 1993, pap. (0-14-032713-4)

(BL 87:1194, 1195; CC 1992 Suppl. p. 65; CCBB 44:174; HBG 2:266; KR 59:109; SLJ May 1991 p. 112; VOYA 14:112)

PASSEY, Helen K. *Speak to the Rain.* See Chapter 5B, Myth Fantasy.

1166 **PATON WALSH, Jill.** *Birdy and the Ghosties.* **(Orig. British pub. 1989.) Gr. 1–4.**

✓ Birdy's "second sight" doesn't seem extraordinary until the day her Papa is asked to ferry three "ghosties" across the sea to a mysterious island. *Matthew and the Sea Singer* (1993; see Chapter 1, Allegorical Fantasy and Literary Fairy Tales) is a companion story.

Illus. by Alan Marks, Farrar, 1989, 46 pp. (0-374-30716-4)

(BL 86:1096; CCBB 43:149; HBG 1[July–Dec 1989]:84; KR 57:1675; SLJ Feb 1990 p. 80)

PAYNE, Joan Balfour (Dicks). *The Leprechaun of Bayou Luce.* See Chapter 7, Magic Adventure Fantasy.

1167 **PEARCE, (Ann) Philippa.** *The Shadow-Cage and Other Tales of the Supernat-*
✓ *ural.* **Gr. 5–8.**

Ten tales of ghostly encounters, including "The Shadow Cage," "The Dog Got Them," and "The Strange Illness of Mr. Arthur Cook." Carnegie Medal Commended Book, 1977.

Illus. by Ted Lewin, Crowell, 1977, 144 pp., o.p.

(BL 74:554; Kies:134; KR 45:934; SLJ Dec 1977 p. 50; TLS 1977 p. 864)

1168 **PEARCE, (Ann) Philippa.** *Who's Afraid? And Other Strange Stories.* **Gr. 5–9.**

✓ Eleven strange tales of ghosts and the supernatural.

Greenwillow, 1987, 152 pp. (0-688-06895-2)

(BL 83:1208; CCBB 40:152; Ch&Bks:259; HB 58:344; JHC:433; KR 55:375; SLJ May 1987 p. 116; Suth 4:320: VOYA 10:206)

1169 **PECK, Richard (Wayne).** *The Ghost Belonged to Me: A Novel.* **Gr. 5–9.**

✓✓ Encounters with the ghost of a girl named Inez Dumaine convince Alexander Armsworth that he has second sight. In *Ghosts I Have Been* (1977; 1979; Peter Smith, 1992), Alexander's friend, Blossom Culp's second sight involves her with a child who drowned on the *Titanic,* and earns her a visit to the Queen of England. In *The Dreadful Future of Blossom Culp* (Delacorte, 1983, 1987), Blossom makes an accidental trip from 1918 into the future world of the 1980s. In *Blossom Culp and the Sleep of Death* (Delacorte, 1986, 1987) the angry ghost of Egyptian Princess Sat-Hathor demands that Blossom and Alexander find the missing items plundered from her tomb and protect it from any future defilement.

Viking, 1975, pap. (0-670-33767-6); Dell, 1987, pap., 192 pp. (0-440-42861-0); ABC-CLIO, 1989 (repr.), o.p.

(BBC:211: BL 71:1129, 80:96; CC:544; CCBB 28:182; Ch&Bks:290; HB 51:471; JHC:401; Kies:135; KR 43:456; SLJ Sept 1975 p. 109, Dec 1976 p. 32; TLS 1977 p. 348)

1170 **PEYTON, K. M. (pseud. of Kathleen Wendy Peyton).** *A Pattern of Roses.* **Gr.**
✓ **7–9. (Orig. British pub. 1972.)**

The old drawings Tim finds signed with his own initials enable him to see the ghost of a young man whose death was never explained.

Illus. by the author, Crowell, 1973, 186 pp., o.p.

(BL 70:124, 827; CCBB 27:49; Ch&Bks:290; HB 49:473, 60:361–364; KR 41:819; LJ 98:2667, 3691; Suth 2:361)

***Phantasmagoria: Tales of Fantasy and the Supernatural.* Ed. by Jane Mobley.** See Chapter 3, Fantasy Collections.

POPE, Elizabeth Marie. *The Sherwood Ring.* See Chapter 8, Time Travel Fantasy.

PORTE, Barbara Ann. *Jesse's Ghost and Other Stories.* See Chapter 3, Fantasy Collections.

POSTMA, Lidia. *The Witch's Garden.* See Chapter 7, Magic Adventure Fantasy.

1171   **PREUSSLER, Otfried.** *The Little Ghost.* **Gr. 4–6. (Orig. pub. in Germany.)**

A little ghost disregards the advice of his friend, Toowhoo the owl, and makes a daylight appearance at Town Hall.

Trans. by Anthea Bell, Abelard-Schuman, 1967, 126 pp., o.p.

(KR 35:1271; LJ 92:4617; TLS 1967 p. 445)

PRICE, Susan. *The Ghost Drum: A Cat's Tale.* See Chapter 10, Witchcraft and Wizardry Fantasy.

1172   **RABINOWITZ, Ann.** *Knight on Horseback.* **Gr. 6–8.**

While on a tour of England, Eddy Newby meets the ghost of Richard III, who mistakes the thirteen-year-old American boy for his son, Edward.

Macmillan, 1987, 187 pp., o.p.

(BL 84:572; CCBB 41:73; SLJ Oct 1987 p. 142; VOYA 10:245)

RADFORD, Ken. *The Cellar.* See Chapter 8, Time Travel Fantasy.

1173   **RADFORD, Ken.** *Haunting at Mill Lane.* **Gr. 5–7. (Orig. British pub. 1983.)**

Sally-Anne, the ghost of a young Welsh girl, uses a rag doll to lure twelve-year-old Sarah into her own time.

Holiday, 1988, 153 pp. (0-8234-0676-8)

(BBC:212; BL 84:1437; SLJ June 1988 p. 106)

1174   ***The Random House Book of Ghost Stories.* Ed. by Susan Hill. Gr. 5–8. (Orig. British pub. 1990, entitled *The Walker Book of Ghost Stories.*)**

Sixteen ghost stories by well-known English children's book authors, including Joan Aiken, Leon Garfield, Penelope Lively, and Philippa Pearce.

Illus. by Angela Barrett, Random, 1991, 223 pp. LB(0-679-91234-7)

(BL 88:698; CCBB 45:92; HBG 3[Spring 1992]:119; JHC 1992 Suppl. p. 70)

REISS, Kathryn. *Dreadful Sorry.* See Chapter 8, Time Travel Fantasy.

ROACH, Marilynne K(athleen). *Encounters with the Invisible World; Being Ten Tales of Ghosts, Witches, and the Devil Himself in New England.* See Chapter 3, Fantasy Collections.

1175   **ROBINSON Joan (Mary) G(ale Thomas).** *When Marnie Was There.* **Gr. 5–7. (Orig. British pub. 1967.)**

Anna, a lonely foster child, becomes friends with Marnie, an elusive girl from the house at the edge of the marsh.

Coward, 1968, 256 pp., o.p.
(CCBB 22:163; HB 45:56; KR 36:979; TLS 1967 p. 1141)

1176 RODOWSKY, Colby F. *The Gathering Room.* Gr. 4–7.

✓ Angered by hints of an impending family move away from their cemetery gatehouse home, Mudge realizes that he will miss the friendship of the cemetery's ghostly inhabitants.

Farrar, 1981, 185 pp. (0-374-32520-0)
(BBC:212; BL 78:394; CCBB 35:157; HB 57:537; KR 49:1297; SLJ Oct 1981 p. 146; Suth 3:363)

1177 SARGENT, Sarah. *Jerry's Ghosts and the Mystery of the Blind Tower.* Gr. 5–7.

In a story told alternately by a twelve-year-old ghost named Mattie and by Jerry, a contemporary eleven-year-old, Mattie warns Jerry to stay away from her Uncle Ezekiel's apparatus in an old mansion-turned-museum, or he may be used in an immortality experiment.

Macmillan, 1992, 134 pp. (0-02-778035-X)
(BL 88:1380; CCBB 45:277; HBG 3[Fall 1992]:270; KR 60:398; SLJ Mar 1992 p. 242)

1178 SEFTON, Catherine (pseud. of Martin Waddell). *The Ghost and Bertie Boggin.* Gr. 3–5. (Orig. British pub. 1980.)

Bertie Boggin meets Ghost in his coal cellar, and is overjoyed to have made a friend at last.

Illus. by Jill Bennett, Faber, 1982, 64 pp., o.p.
(BL 78:1261; SLJ Aug 1982 p. 105)

1179 SEVERN, David (pseud. of David Unwin). *The Girl in the Grove.* Gr. 7–9.

✓ Jonquil becomes jealous when her friend Paul spends more and more time with a ghostly girl named Laura.

Harper, 1974, 266 pp., o.p.
(BL 71:93, 102; KR 42:1111; LJ 99:3277; TLS 1974 p. 717)

1180 *Shades of Dark: Stories.* Ed. by Aidan Chambers. Gr. 7 up. (Orig. British pub.
✓ **1984.)**

Eight ghost stories by British authors including Vivian Alcock, Helen Cresswell, and Jan Mark.

Harper, 1986, 126 pp., o.p.
(BL 83:571, 581; CCBB 40:83; HB 63:215; KR 54:1514)

1181 SHECTER, Ben. *The Whistling Whirligig.* Gr. 4–6.

✓ While staying with his history teacher, Josh meets Matthew Hubbard, the hundred-year-old ghost of a runaway slave, who has been hiding since the Civil War.

Harper, 1974, 143 pp., o.p.; Scholastic, pap. (entitled *The Ghost and the Whistling Whirligig*), o.p.
(BL 71:463; CCBB 28:138; HB 50:693; KR 42:1253; LJ 99:2721)

1182 SHURA, Mary Francis (pseud. of Mary Francis Craig). *Happles and Cinnamunger.* Gr. 3–5.

The Taggert children's new housekeeper, Ilsa, is haunted by a ghost, and it is up to the children to free her from it.

Illus. by Bertram M. Tormey, Dodd, 1981, 157 pp., o.p.
(BL 78:655; CCBB 35:116; HB 58:169; SLJ Jan 1982 p. 82)

1183   **SHURA, Mary Francis (pseud. of Mary Francis Craig).** *Simple Spigott.* **Gr. 3–5.**

Simple Spigott is a small ghost searching for lost Irish treasure.

Illus. by Jacqueline Tomes, Knopf, 1960, 90 pp., o.p.

(BL 56:609; CCBB 13:169; Eakin:299; HB 36:291; LJ 85:2043)

1184   **SILVERSTEIN, Herma.** *Mad, Mad Monday.* **Gr. 5–8.**

✓   Miranda Taylor accidentally conjures up the ghost of Monday Newberry, who returns after thirty years to seek revenge on a former girl friend who married someone else after his death.

Dutton, 1988, 120 pp., o.p.; Pocket, 1989, pap. (0-671-67403-X)

(BBJ:75; BL 84:1337, 1353; CCBB 41:76; Kies:156; Kliatt Apr 1989 p. 17; KR 55:1738; SLJ Feb 1988 p. 74, VOYA 11:184)

1185   **SINGER, Marilyn.** *Ghost Host.* **Gr. 5–9.**

High school football star Bart Hawkins enlists the help of a friendly ghost and Arvie, a bright classmate, to deal with Stryker, a poltergeist inhabiting Bart's home.

Harper, 1987, 182 pp., o.p.; Scholastic, 1993, pap. (0-590-44505-7)

(BBJ:75; CCBB 40:218; KR 55:1076; SLJ Sept 1987 p. 182; VOYA 10:83)

1186   *Small Shadows Creep.* **Ed. by André Norton. Gr. 6–10.**

✓   Nine ghostly tales involving children or teenagers, including M. R. James's "Lost Hearts" and Eleanor Farjeon's "Faithful Jenny Dove."

Dutton, 1974, 195 pp., o.p.

(BL 71:687, 694; HB 51:279; KR 43:24; SLJ Apr 1975 p. 56)

1187   **SNYDER, Zilpha Keatley.** *Eyes in the Fishbowl.* **Gr. 6–9.**

Dion thinks the strange girl he meets in the Alcott-Simpson Department Store might be a ghost.

Illus. by Alton Raible, Atheneum, 1968, 1970, 168 pp., o.p.

(BL 64:1097; CCBB 21:181; HB 44:182; KR 36:124; LJ 93:1804)

1188   **SNYDER, Zilpha Keatley.** *The Truth about Stone Hollow.* **Gr. 6–8.**

Jason, new in school, takes Amy to a strange valley where loops of time come together, enabling them to see ghosts from the past.

Illus. by Alton Raible, Atheneum, 1974, 211 pp., o.p.; Dell, 1985, pap. (0-440-48846-X)

(BL 70:825; CCBB 27:164; HB 50:380; KR 42:245; LJ 99:576, 1451)

1189   **SOMMER-BODENBURG, Angela.** *If You Want to Scare Yourself.* **Gr. 3–5. (Orig. German pub. 1984.)**

Freddy's parents and grandmother tell him eerie stories about ghosts and vampires when he is bored with being sick in bed, and he writes a few of his own.

Trans. by Renée Vera Cafiero, illus. by Helga Speiss, Harper, 1989, 105 pp. LB(0-397-32210-0)

(BL 86:464; HBG 1[July 1989]:87; KR 57:1333; SLJ Dec 1989 p. 103)

1190   **SPEARING, Judith (Mary Harlow).** *The Ghosts Who Went to School.* **Gr. 5–7.**

Bored with haunting the house, Wilbur and Mortimer Temple decide to go to school. The sequel is *The Museum House Ghosts* (1969).

Illus. by Marvin Glass, Atheneum, 1966, 186 pp., o.p.

(BL 62:920; HB 42:308; Kies:163; LJ 91:1710)

SPRINGER, Nancy. *The Friendship Song.* See Chapter 5C, Travel to Other Worlds.

1191 ST. JOHN, Wylly Folk. *The Ghost Next Door.* **Gr. 4–6.**

Lindsey and Tammy discover that their neighbor, Sherry, can communicate with the ghost of her dead half-sister, Miranda.

Illus. by Trina Schart Hyman, Harper, 1971, 178 pp., o.p.

(BBC:212; BL 68:395; HB 48:147; Kies:148; KR 39:1014; LJ 96:4198)

1192 STAHL, Ben(jamin). *Blackbeard's Ghost.* **Gr. 5–8.**

J.D. and Hank accidentally summon up the ghost of Blackbeard the pirate, who discovers that the tavern he built 300 years earlier is about to be torn down. The sequel is *The Secret of Red Skull* (1971).

Illus. by the author, Houghton, 1965, 184 pp., o.p.

(HB 41:393; Kies:163; KR 33:244; LJ 90:2897)

1193 STORR, Catherine (Cole). *Cold Marble and Other Ghost Stories.* **Gr. 6–10. (Orig. British pub. 1985.)**

Eleven poignant and humorous ghost stories, including "How to Be a Ghost," "Pale Marble," and "Bill's Ghost."

Faber, 1985, 101 pp., o.p.

(BL 82:861, 871; SLJ Mar 1986 p. 179)

STRANGER, Joyce. *The Fox at Drummer's Darkness.* See Chapter 1, Allegorical Fantasy and Literary Fairy Tales.

STRAUB, Peter (Francis). *Shadowland.* See Chapter 10, Witchcraft and Sorcery Fantasy.

STRICKLAND, Brad. *Dragon's Plunder, or, The Last Voyage of Captain Deadmon: A Fantasy Adventure.* See Chapter 7, Magic Adventure Fantasy.

1194 SUDBERY, Rodie (Tutton). *The Silk and the Skin.* **Gr. 6–8. (Orig. British. pub.** ✓ **1976.)**

Guy Carmichael reluctantly joins the class bully's gang. They try to call up the spirit of a long-dead wizard's bat and succeed by tricking Guy's developmentally delayed younger brother into doing the summoning.

Deutsch, 1982, 144 pp., o.p.

(BBC:214; BL 79:316; HB 58:523; SLJ Nov 1982 p. 91; TLS 1976 p. 1554)

1195 *Supernatural Stories: 13 Tales of the Unexpected.* Ed. by Jean Russell. **Gr. 5–8** ✓

Thirteen "pleasantly eerie" stories whose authors include Joan Aiken, Joan Phipson, Patricia Miles, and Catherine Storr. Many of these stories were previously published in England.

Orchard, 1987, 156 pp., o.p.

(BL 84:55, 74; CCBB 41:75; HB 63:745; SLJ Sept 1987 p. 182; VOYA 10:283)

SYKES, Pamela. *Mirror of Danger.* See Chapter 8, Time Travel Fantasy.

1196 TAPP, Kathy Kennedy. *The Scorpio Ghosts and the Black Hole Gang.* **Gr. 4–7.**

Ryan, Josh, Carrie, and Brooke help a ghostly bus and its inhabitants break through the time barrier.

Harper, 1987, 192 pp., o.p.

(BL 83:1057; CCBB 40:136; KR 55:225; SLJ Apr 1987 p. 105)

1197   THESMAN, Jean. *Appointment with a Stranger.* **Gr. 7–10.**

✓   Embarrassed by her asthma, Keller Parish avoids making friends at her new high school and becomes involved instead with Tom, the ghost of a boy who drowned forty years earlier in an isolated pond.

Houghton, 1989, 155 pp. (0-395-49215-7); Avon, 1990, pap. (0-380-70864-7)

(BL 85:1657; CCBB 43:22; HB 65:380; KR 57:470; SLJ Feb 1989 p. 103; VOYA 12:108)

1198   *Things That Go Bump in the Night: A Collection of Original Stories.* Ed. by Jane
✓   **Yolen and Martin H. Greenberg. Gr. 5–8.**

Eighteen scary stories by Diana Wynne Jones, William Sleator, Jane Yolen, and others.

Harper, 1989, 288 pp. (0-06-26802-6)

(BL 86:356; CC:582; CCBB 43:23; HB 66:73; HBG 1[July–Dec 1989]:82; JHC 1991 Suppl. p. 83; KR 57:1171; SLJ Oct 1989 p. 139)

1199   TOMALIN, Ruth. *Gone Away.* **Gr. 5–7. (Orig. British pub. 1979.)**

✓   Francie becomes convinced that her secret friend is actually the ghost of a girl who lived in her house during the Middle Ages.

Faber, 1979, 158 pp., o.p.

(BL 76:452; CCBB 33:83; KR 47:933; SLJ Dec 1979 p. 89)

1200   TURKLE, Brinton (Cassaday). *Mooncoin Castle; or Skulduggery Rewarded.* **Gr. 4–6.**

A ghost, a witch, and a jackdaw join forces to save an Irish castle from demolition.

Viking, 1970, 141 pp., o.p.

(BL 67:149; KR 38:554; LJ 95:3054)

1201   *Victorian Ghost Stories: An Oxford Anthology.* Selected by Michael Cox and R. A. Gilbert. Gr. 10 up. (Orig. British pub. 1991.)

Thirty-five nineteenth-century British ghost stories by such authors as Rudyard Kipling, Charles Dickens, and Robert Louis Stevenson.

Oxford Univ. Pr., 1991, 497 pp. (0-19-214202-X)

(SHC 1993 Suppl. p. 87; SLJ Mar 1992 p. 270; TLS Nov 22 1991 p. 8)

VIVELO, Jackie. *A Trick of the Light: Stories to Read at Dusk.* See Chapter 3, Fantasy Collections.

1202   WALLIN, Luke. *The Slavery Ghosts.* **Gr. 5–7.**

Jake and Livy pass through a time gate into a world where Mrs. Ruffin, the ghost of a former plantation slaveholder, holds captive the ghosts of her former slaves.

Bradbury, 1983, 121 pp., o.p.

(CCBB 37:20; Ch&Bks:292; SLJ Dec 1983 p. 70; Suth 3:439; VOYA 6:209)

WESLEY, Mary. *Haphazard House.* See Chapter 8, Time Travel Fantasy.

1203   WESTALL, Robert (Atkinson). *The Call and Other Stories.* **Gr. 7–12. (Orig.**
✓   **British pub. 1989.)**

Six spooky stories including "The Badger," "The Red House Clock," "The Call," and "Woman and Home."

Viking, 1993, 120 pp. (0-670-82484-4)

(BL 89:802; CCBB 46:159; HB 69:468; HBG 4[Fall 1993]:313; KR 61:69; SLJ Jan 1993 p. 134; VOYA 15:343)

1204 **WESTALL, Robert (Atkinson).** *Demons and Shadows: The Ghostly Best Stories of Robert Westall.* **Gr. 7–12. (Orig. British pub. 1993.)**

Eleven ghostly supernatural and horror stories, including "The Death of Wizards," "Graveyard Shift," and "A Walk on the Wild Side." The companion volume is *Shades of Darkness: More of the Ghostly Best Stories of Robert Westall* (1994).

Farrar, 1993, 288 pp. (0-37431768-2)

(BL 90:332; HBG 5:92; SLJ Oct 1993 p. 158; VOYA 16:315)

1205 **WESTALL, Robert (Atkinson).** *Ghost Abbey.* **Gr. 5–9. (Orig. British pub. 1988.)**
✓ The old abbey that Maggie's father is restoring exerts a ghostly and dangerous hold on her family and on Ms. MacFarlane, the owner.

Scholastic, 1989, 169 pp. (0-5904-1692-8); 1990, pap. (0-5904-1693-6)

(BBC:215; BL 85:943; CC:571; CCBB 42:161; Ch&Bks:292; HB 65:221, JHC:424; Kies:184; KR 56:1817; SLJ Mar 1989 p. 202; Suth 4:434; VOYA 12:108)

1206 **WESTALL, Robert (Atkinson).** *The Haunting of Chas McGill and Other Sto-*
✓ **ries. Gr. 7–12. (Orig. British pub. 1983.)**

A collection of eerie stories including "The Haunting of Chas McGill," in which the hero of Westall's realistic novel, *The Machine Gunners* (1976; 1990), meets the ghost of a World War I army deserter just at the outbreak of World War II.

Greenwillow, 1983, 181 pp., o.p.

(BL 80:490; CCBB 37:120; HB 60:66; KR 51:209; SLJ Jan 1984 p. 90; Suth 3:447; VOYA 7:98)

1207 **WESTALL, Robert (Atkinson).** *In Camera and Other Stories.* **Gr. 7–12. (Orig.**
✓ **British pub. 1992.)**

Five stories about supernatural occurrences that lurk behind daily life.

Scholastic, 1993, 152 pp. (0-590-45920-1)

(BL 89:2050; HB 69:468; HBG 4[Fall 1993]:313; KR 61:236; SLJ Apr 1993 p. 144; VOYA 16:96)

1208 **WESTALL, Robert (Atkinson).** *The Promise.* **Gr. 6–10. (Orig. British pub.**
✓ **1990.)**

Fourteen-year-old Bob, in love with frail Valerie, promises to find her if she ever gets lost, and her ghost returns after her death to demand that he keep his promise.

Scholastic, 1991, 176 pp. (0-5904-3760-7)

(BL 87:1378; CCBB 44:207; HB 67:207; KR 59:179; SLJ Mar 1991 p. 220; VOYA 14:104)

1209 **WESTALL, Robert (Atkinson).** *The Scarecrows.* **Gr. 6–9. (Orig. British pub.**
✓ **1981.)**

Angry and jealous about his mother's second marriage, thirteen-year-old Simon realizes that scarecrows wearing the clothes of three people once involved in a murderous love triangle are slowly advancing across the field toward his new home. Carnegie Medal, 1981. Boston Globe Horn Book Award Honor Book, 1982.

Greenwillow, 1981, 185 pp., o.p.

(BBJ:76; CCBB 35:19; HB 57:546; Kies:184; KR 49:1166; SLJ Aug 1981 p. 80; TLS 1981 p. 339)

1210 **WESTALL, Robert (Atkinson).** *The Watch House.* **Gr. 7–9. (Orig. British pub.**
✓ **1977.)**

Ghosts from the past haunt a museum of shipwreck salvage and ensnare Anne in their quest for vengeance.

Greenwillow, 1978, 218 pp., o.p.; Knopf, 1990, pap. (entitled: *The Watch Tower*), o.p.

(BL 74:1356; CCBB 31:187; HB 54:405; Kies:184; KR 46:381; SLJ Apr 1978 p. 99, May 1978 p. 36; Suth 2:478; TLS 1977 p. 1408; VOYA 13:233)

1211   *What Did Miss Darrington See? An Anthology of Feminist Supernatural Fiction.* **Ed. by Jessica Amanda Salmonson. Gr. 10 up.**

Twenty-four stories from the United States, England, and Latin America, written between 1850 and 1988 by Vita Sackville-West, Mary E. Watkins Freeman, Anne Sexton, and others.

Feminist Pr., 1989, 263 pp. (1-55861-005-7), pap. (1-55861-006-5)

(BL 86:38, 56; KR 57:960)

1212   **WHITNEY, Phyllis A(yame).** *The Island of Dark Woods.* **Gr. 5–7.**

While visiting their Aunt Serena on Staten Island, Laurie and Celia Kane see the legendary phantom stagecoach, said to stop at the house next door where a young woman once died.

Illus. by Philip Wishnefsky, Westminster, 1951, 191 pp., o.p.; Westminster, 1967 (entitled *Mystery of the Strange Traveller*), 192 pp., o.p.

(Kies:186; KR 35:1136; LJ 92:4271)

1213   **WIBBERLEY, Leonard (Patrick O'Connor).** *The Quest of Excalibur.* **Gr. 10 up. (Orig. pub. Putnam, 1959.)**

King Arthur's ghost appears in twentieth-century England to search for Excalibur, and manages to save Princess Pamela from abdicating to marry an American.

Borgo Press, 1979, 190 pp., LB(0-89370-131-9), pap. (0-89370-231-5)

(BL 56:120, 246; HB 36:59; KR 27:612; LJ 84:3060)

1214   **WILDE, Nicholas.** *Into the Dark.* **Gr. 5–8. (Orig. British pub. 1987.)**

✓   After Roly, a local boy, befriends blind twelve-year-old Matthew during his holiday on the English coast, Matthew comes to understand that Roly is actually the ghost of a boy who lived a century earlier.

Scholastic, 1990, 201 pp. (0-5904-3424-1), 1992, pap. (0-5904-3423-3)

(BL 87:925; CCBB 44:74; HBG 2[July–Dec 1990]:76; KR 58:1254; SLJ Nov 1990, p. 121; VOYA 13:292)

1215   **WILDE, Oscar (pseud. of Fingal O'Flahertie Wills).** *The Canterville Ghost.* **Gr. 7 up. (Orig. pub. 1906.)**

After Virginia's American family buys a home in England, the resident ghost is outraged that they are not afraid of him. Scott Corbett's *The Discontented Ghost* (see this chapter) is a related work.

Illus. by Lisbeth Zwerger, Picture Book, 1986 (0-88708-027-8); Oxford, 1988, o.p.

(SLJ Jan 1986 p. 85)

1216   **WILLIAMS (John), Ursula Moray.** *Castle Merlin.* **Gr. 4–6.**

✓   While vacationing at Castle Merlin, Susie and Bryan meet two medieval ghosts.

Nelson, 1972, 142 pp., o.p.

(BL 69:765; HB 48:471; KR 40:1029, 1414; LJ 98:265; TLS 1972 p. 474)

1217   **WINDSOR, Patricia (Frances).** *How a Weirdo and a Ghost Can Change Your Entire Life.* **Gr. 4–6.**

A Ouija board helps Martha and Teddy contact ghosts, who solve a number of neighborhood mysteries.

Illus. by Jacqueline Rogers, Dell, 1988, pap., 123 pp. (0-440-40094-5)
(KR 54:1371; SLJ Nov 1986 p. 94)

WISEMAN, David. *Jeremy Visick.* See Chapter 8, Time Travel Fantasy.

Worlds Near and Far: Nine Stories of Science Fiction. **Ed. by Terry Carr.** See Chapter 3, Fantasy Collections.

1218 **WRIGHT, Betty Ren.** *Christina's Ghost.* **Gr. 4–6.**

Christina's uncle refuses to believe that she has seen a ghost in a nearby haunted house, until he meets the ghost himself.

Holiday, 1985, 105 pp. (0-8234-0581-8); Scholastic, 1987, pap. (0-590-42709-1)
(BBC:216; BL 82:815, 83:586; CCBB 39:120; SLJ Dec 1985 p. 96)

WRIGHT, Betty Ren. *The Dollhouse Murders.* See Chapter 9, Toy Fantasy.

1219 **WRIGHT, Betty Ren.** *A Ghost in the House.* **Gr. 4–8.**

✓ Sarah discovers that her family's house is haunted by a vengeful ghost, after her Great-Aunt Margaret moves back into what was once her childhood bedroom.

Scholastic, 1991, 160 pp. (0-5904-3606-6)
(BL 88:523; CC 1992 Suppl. p. 63; CCBB 45:79; HB 67:202; HBG 3[July–Dec 1991]:75; KR 59:1477; SLJ Nov 1991 p. 125; VOYA 14:39)

1220 **WRIGHT, Betty Ren.** *The Ghost of Ernie P.* **Gr. 4–7.**

The ghost of a former class bully tries to exert power over Jeff to get revenge on a local witch.

Holiday, 1990, 130 pp. (0-8234-0835-3); Scholastic, 1992, pap. (0-5904-5073-5)
(BL 87:857; CCBB 44:133; HB 67:202; HBG 2[July 1990]:73; KR 58:1537; SLJ Oct 1990 p. 122; VOYA 14:39)

1221 **WRIGHT, Betty Ren.** *The Ghost of Popcorn Hill.* **Gr. 2–5.**

✓ Martin and Peter try to understand the connection between the ghostly man who visits their cabin at night and the mysterious sheepdog who romps on Popcorn Hill.

Illus. by Karen Ritz, Holiday, 1993, 81 pp. (0-8234-1009-9)
(BL 89:1061; CCBB 46:333; HB 69:463; HBG 4[Fall 1993]:293; KR 61:606; SLJ May 1993 p. 111)

1222 **WRIGHT, Betty Ren.** *The Ghost Witch.* **Gr. 3–5.**

After Jenny realizes that her home is haunted by the ghostly witch of Willowby Lane, she tries to find a different house for the ghost to haunt.

Illus. by Ellen Eagle, Holiday, 1993, 103 pp. (0-8234-1036-6)
(BL 90:931; CCBB 47:123; HBG 5:84; SLJ Dec 1993 p. 118)

1223 **WRIGHT, Betty Ren.** *Ghosts Beneath Our Feet.* **Gr. 4–6.**

No one will believe Katie's hunch that warnings brought by a young woman's ghost portend a new tragedy in the abandoned iron mines below her uncle's Upper Peninsula Michigan town.

Holiday, 1984, 137 pp. (0-8234-0538-9); Scholastic, 1986, pap. (0-5904-3444-6)
(BBC:216; BL 81:593; Kies:191; SLJ Apr 1985 p. 95)

1224 **WRIGHT, Betty Ren.** *The Ghosts of Mercy Manor.* **Gr. 4–7.**

✓ Only Gwen's foster brother, Jason, believes that she has met the unhappy ghost of a young girl who disappeared near their house many years ago.

Scholastic, 1993, 172 pp. (0-590-43601-5)

(BL 90:152; CCBB 47:27; HBG 5:84; KR 61:944; SLJ Sept 1993 p. 236; VOYA 16:305)

1225   WRIGHT, Betty Ren. *The Pike River Phantom.* **Gr. 4–7.**

The strange woman Charlie meets in an abandoned house near his grandparents' home is a ghost whose death had something to do with his grandmother and his cousin Rachel.

Holiday, 1988, 153 pp. (0-8234-0721-7); Scholastic, 1990, pap. (0-5904-2808-X)

(BBC:216; BL 85:715; CCBB 42:112; KR 56:1536; SLJ Oct 1988 p. 149; Suth. 4:446)

1226   WRIGHT, T. M. *Goodlow's Ghosts.* **Gr. 10 up.**

After a client unexpectedly kills him, Detective Sam Goodlow finds it hard to believe that he has become a ghost.

Tor, 1993, 224 pp. (0-312-85466-8)

(BL 89:718, 722; KR 60:1405; VOYA 16:107)

WRIGHTSON, (Alice) Patricia (Furlonger). *Balyet.* See Chapter 5B, Myth Fantasy.

WRIGHTSON, (Alice) Patricia (Furlonger). *An Older Kind of Magic.* See Chapter 7, Magic Adventure Fantasy.

1227   WYSS, Thelma Hatch. *A Stranger Here.* **Gr. 6–12.**

✓ Jada Sinclair, sixteen, falls in love with Starr Freeman, the ghost of a World War II pilot killed in action on the day Jada was born.

Harper, 1993, 132 pp. (0-06-021438-4)

(BL 89:1582; CCBB 46:361; HBG 4[Fall 1993]:313; KR 61:236; SLJ May 1993 p. 130; VOYA 16:220)

1228   YOLEN (Stemple), Jane H(yatt). *The Wizard Islands.* **Gr. 4–7.**

A collection of legends about islands, some of which involve ghosts and pirate treasure.

Illus. by Robert M. Quackenbush, Crowell, 1973, 115 pp., o.p.

(CCBB 27:167; HB 50:162; KR 41:1368; LJ 99:1224)

1229   *Young Ghosts.* Ed. by Isaac Asimov, Martin H. Greenberg, and Charles G. Waugh. Gr. 6–9.

Twelve tales about the ghosts of children, written by Arthur Quiller-Couch, M. R. James, and Ray Bradbury, among others.

Harper, 1985, 210 pp., o.p.

(BL 82:862, 874; JHC:435; SLJ Dec 1985 p. 96)

5

High Fantasy
(Heroic or Secondary World
Fantasy)

This chapter lists books about worlds other than our own. J. R. R. Tolkien suggested that these otherworlds be called "Secondary Worlds" and that the term "Primary World" be used for our own everyday world. It was his feeling that the only true fantasy stories are those involving a Secondary World. More recently, critics have used the terms "High Fantasy" and "Heroic Fantasy" for these works.

The books listed here are subdivided into three sections: Alternate Worlds or Histories (stories that take place entirely in a Secondary World), Myth Fantasy (retellings of myth or legend, as well as stories in which contemporary protagonists are drawn into the mythic struggle of good versus evil), and Travel to Other Worlds (tales involving travel between our world and another).

Although true science-fiction stories have not been included here, "science-fantasy" tales, in which science is used to explain the existence of the Secondary World and magic is used thereafter, are included in the Alternate Worlds or Histories section.

A. Alternate Worlds or Histories

1230   ABBEY, Lynn (pseud. of Marilyn Lorraine Abbey). *The Black Flame.* Gr. 10 up.

Exiled warrior-priestess Rifkind rides her horse Turin across the swamps of the Felmargue to find the Black Flame. At the Well of Knowledge she becomes involved in a magical battle of the gods. This is the sequel to *Daughter of the Bright Moon* (1979, 1985), which won Abbey the John W. Campbell Award for best new science fiction writer of 1979.

Ace, 1980, 1985, pap., 376 pp., o.p.

(BL 77:29, 38; Kliatt 14[Fall 1980]:12; VOYA 3[Feb 1981]: 40)

1231   ADAMS, Hazard. *The Truth about Dragons: An Anti-Romance.* **Gr. 10 up.**

Firedrake, an intellectual dragon living in California after an earthquake has severed the state from the rest of the United States, describes how Man ruined the Earth.

Harcourt, 1971, 179 pp., o.p.

(BL 67:685, 741; KR 39:15; LJ 96:653, 2938, 4160)

1232   ADAMS, Richard (George). *Shardik.* **Gr. 8 up. (Orig. British pub. 1974.)**

In Ortelga, a giant bear found by a young hunter is proclaimed Lord Shardik, the sacred messenger of God.

Simon, 1975, 525 pp., o.p.

(BL 71:892, 905; KR 43:251, 322; LJ 100:688)

1233   AIKEN, Joan (Delano). *The Kingdom and the Cave.* **Gr. 4–6. (Orig. British pub. 1960.)**

Prince Michael's cat is kidnapped after Michael uncovers the invasion plans of the people Down Under

Illus. by Victor Ambrus, Doubleday, 1974, 160 pp., o.p.

(BL 70:871; HB 50:146; KR 42:108; LJ 99:2258)

1234   AIKEN, Joan (Delano). *The Whispering Mountain.* **Gr. 5–8. (Orig. British pub.**
✓   **1968.)**

Orphaned Owen is falsely accused of stealing the legendary Golden Harp of Teirtu. Carnegie Medal Honour Book, 1968. Guardian Award for Children's Fiction, 1969.

Illus. by Frank Bozzo, Doubleday, 1969, 240 pp., o.p.

(BL 66:563; CCBB 23:123; Ch&Bks:274; HB 46:39; KR 37:1146; LJ 94:4610; Suth:5)

1235   AIKEN, Joan (Delano). *The Wolves of Willoughby Chase* **(Wolves Chronicles,**
✓✓   **book 1). Gr. 5–7. (Orig. British pub. 1962.)**

In this, the first of five action-filled spoofs of Victorian melodrama set in an England that never was, Bonnie and her cousin Sylvia run away from their sinister governess, are chased by wolves, and end up in an orphanage. With the help of a boy named Simon, they escape and thwart the plans of the evil Miss Slighcarp. In *Black Hearts in Battersea* (1964; 1987, pap.; Peter Smith, 1988), orphaned Simon and his friends, Dido and Justin, are kidnapped and shipwrecked before they uncover the true facts of their births. In *Nightbirds on Nantucket* (1966; 1981, pap.; Peter Smith, 1988), Dido is rescued from the sea, only to be put into the care of an evil woman who is plotting against King James of England. In *The Cuckoo Tree* (1971; Peter Smith, 1989), Dido foils a plot to put St. Paul's Cathedral on rollers and push it into the Thames to disrupt the royal coronation ceremony. In *The Stolen Lake* (1981; Peter Smith, 1989), Dido is sent on a dangerous diplomatic mission to New Cambria in Roman South America, to help England's Queen Ginerva recover a stolen lake. And in *Dido and Pa* (1986), Dido and Simon are reunited in an attempt to stop Dido's wicked Pa from putting a Hanoverian pretender on England's throne. In *Is Underground* (1993) Dido's sister, Is, searches for her missing cousin, Arun, and discovers that she and many other London children lured aboard a train to "Playland," have ended up laboring in the undersea mines of Holdernesse.

Illus. by Pat Marriott, Doubleday, 1962, 1989, 168 pp. (0-385-03594-2); Dell, 1987, pap., 176 pp. (0-440-49603-9); Peter Smith, 1989, o.p.

(CC:439; Ch&Bks:274; Eakin:3; LJ 88:4076; TLS 1962 p. 901; VOYA 4[Dec 1981]:58)

1236   ALEXANDER, Lloyd (Chudley). *The Book of Three* **(The Chronicles of Pry-**
✓   **dain, book 1). Gr. 5–8.**

In this, the first volume of the Chronicles of Prydain, a young pig keeper named Taran and a warrior named Gwydion set out to battle the Horned King. In *The Black Cauldron* (Holt, 1965; Dell, 1985, pap.), Taran and Prince Gwydion plan to destroy the Black Cauldron of the Lord of the Land of Death. *The Black Cauldron* was a John Newbery Medal Honor Book, 1966. In *The Castle of Llyr* (Holt, 1966; Dell, 1985, pap.), Taran and Prince Gwydion rescue the obstreperous Princess Eilonwy, who was kidnapped by the wicked Chief Steward. In *Taran Wanderer* (Holt, 1967; Dell, 1985, pap.), Taran has grown into a young man, journeying throughout Prydain in search of his true identity. In the final volume of the series, *The High King* (Holt, 1968; Dell, 1985, pap.), Taran plays a leading role in the final struggle of the people of Prydain against the Land of Death. *The High King* won the John Newbery Medal, 1969, and was a finalist for the National Book Award, 1969. *Coll and His White Pig* (1965), *The Truthful Harp* (1967), and *The Foundling and Other Tales of Prydain* (1973) are also set in the land of Prydain.

Holt, 1964, 224 pp. (0-8050-0874-8); Dell, 1980, pap., 192 pp. (0-440-90702-0)

(BBC:196; BL 61:344, 346, 80:95; CC:440; CCBB 18:157; Ch&Bks:253; Eakin:4; HB 40:496; KR 32:818; LJ 89:3465; TLS 1966 p. 1089)

1237 ALEXANDER, Lloyd (Chudley). *Coll and His White Pig*. Gr. 2–4.

✓ The theft of his magical pig, Henwen, by Arawan, Lord of the Land of Death, drives Coll to attempt a dangerous rescue.

Illus. by Evaline Ness, Holt, 1965, 26 pp., o.p.

(BL 62:407; CCBB 19:77; Eakin:4; HB 41:619; KR 33:115; LJ 90:5506)

1238 ALEXANDER, Lloyd (Chudley). *The Foundling and Other Tales of Prydain*.
✓ **Gr. 4–7.**

Six tales set in the land of Prydain before the birth of Taran, Assistant Pig Keeper, who is the main character of *The Book of Three* (1964) and its sequels.

Illus. by Margot Zemach, Holt, 1973, 87 pp., o.p.

(BBJ:68; BL 70:594, 826; CCBB 27:122; HB 50:278; KR 41:1308; LJ 98:3688, 3704; Suth 2:9)

1239 ALEXANDER, Lloyd (Chudley). *The Marvelous Misadventures of Sebastian:*
✓ ***Grand Extravaganza, Including a Performance by the Entire Cast of the Galli-***
***maufry Theatricus*. Gr. 4–6.**

Caught in a revolution, Sebastian saves a cat from a witch, rescues a princess, and kills the regent by playing a magical violin. National Book Award, 1971.

Dutton, 1973, 204 pp. (0-525-34739-9); Dell, 1991, pap. (0-440-40549-1)

(BBC:197; BL 67:266, 659; CC:441; CCBB 24:85; Ch&Bks:254; HB 46:628; KR 38:949; LJ 95:4040, 4324; Suth:7)

1240 ALEXANDER, Lloyd (Chudley). *The Truthful Harp*. Gr. 2–4.

✓ Whenever King Fflewddar tells a lie, one of his harp strings breaks.

Illus. by Evaline Ness, Holt, 1967, 32 pp., o.p.

(CCBB 21:89; HB 44:58; KR 35:1268; LJ 92:4608; Suth:7)

1241 ALEXANDER, Lloyd (Chudley). *Westmark* (Westmark trilogy, book 1). Gr.
✓✓ **5–10.**

Theo and Mickle, an orphaned boy and a runaway girl, turn the tables on the King's evil minister, Cabbarus, when he tries to use them in a plot to gain the throne for himself. National Book Award for Children's Fiction, 1982. In *The Kestrel* (Dutton, 1982; Dell, 1983, pap.), Theo becomes a blood-thirsty warrior known as the Kestrel, defending his love, Queen Mickle of Westmark. In *The Beggar Queen,* (Dutton, 1984; Dell, 1985, pap.), the government of Westmark is violently overthrown by ex-prime minister Cabbarus, forcing Mickle and Theo to engineer a bloody resistance movement.

Dutton, 1981 (0-525-42335-4); Dell, 1982, pap., 192 pp. (0-440-99731-3)

(BL 77:1095, 80:351, 86:789; CC:441; CCBB 34:185; Ch&Bks:254; HB 57:428; JHC:331; KR 49:934; SLJ May 1981 pp. 23, 62; Suth 3:10; VOYA 4[Oct 1981]:41)

ALEXANDER, Lloyd (Chudley). *The Wizard in the Tree.* See Chapter 10, Witchcraft and Sorcery Fantasy.

1242 *Alternative Histories: Eleven Stories of the World as It Might Have Been.* **Ed. by Charles G. Waugh and Martin H. Greenberg. Gr. 10 up.**

Eleven stories of historical speculation, including one about black ex-slaves who form a nation called New Africa after the Civil War, and another about American colonists who fail to win their independence from the British.

Garland, 1986, 363 pp., o.p.

(BBS:66; BL 83:686, 704)

1243 **ALTON, Andrea I.** *Demon of Undoing.* **Gr. 10 up.**

Although a deformed leg has kept Fenobar from becoming an Imkaira warrior, he joins forces with a legendary human "Demon" to defeat a rival clan.

Baen, 1988, pap., 308 pp. (0-671-65413-6)

(BBS:51; VOYA 11:292)

1244 *Amazons!* **Ed. by Jessica Amanda Salmonson. Gr. 10 up.**

An anthology of stories on the theme of women warriors written by a number of fantasy writers including André Norton and C. J. Cherryh. Winner of the World Fantasy Convention Award, Anthology/Collection category, 1980. A related work is *Amazons II* (1986).

DAW, 1979, 1986, pap., 206 pp., o.p.

(BL 76:932, LJ 104:2488; VOYA 3[Aug 1980]:51)

1245 **ANDERSON, Poul (William).** *The Merman's Children.* **Gr. 10 up.**

Two young merpeople of the dying faerie race who were driven from the coasts of Denmark by the rise of Christianity, fall in love and search together for a new home.

Putnam, 1979, 258 pp., o.p.

(BL 76:216; Kliatt 15[Winter 1981]:11; KR 47:823; LJ 104:1592; SLJ Nov 1979 p. 96)

1246 **ANDERSON, Poul (William).** *A Midsummer Tempest.* **Gr. 10 up.**

In an alternate seventeenth-century England, faery King Oberon and Queen Titania help King Charles I in his final battle against Cromwell and the Puritans, by giving the Royalists a magical wand and book to awaken the sleeping powers of the land. Mythopoeic Fantasy Award, 1975. This is the sequel to *Three Hearts and Three Lions* (1953, 1961, 1963, 1978, o.p.) and *Operation Chaos* (1971, o.p.).

Doubleday, 1974, 207 pp., o.p.; Tor, 1984, pap., 320 pp. (0-8125-3079-9)

(BL 70:1080, 1098; KR 42:74; LJ 99:1733; Tymn:45)

ANDERSON, Poul (William). *The Time Patrol.* See Chapter 8, Time Travel Fantasy.

1247 **ANDERSON, Poul, and ANDERSON, Karen.** *Gallicenae* **(The King of Ys series, book 2). Gr. 10 up.**

King Gratillonius of Ys, a mythical city-state in Britanny, across the Channel from Roman Britain, must defend Ys from invading barbarians and from the Roman Empire. This is the sequel to *Roman Mater* (1986) and is followed by *Dahut* (1988) and *The Dog and the Wolf* (1988).

Baen, 1987, pap., 384 pp. (0-671-65342-3)

(BBS:51; VOYA 10:174)

1248 **ANTHONY, Piers (pseud. of Piers A. D. Jacob).** *Blue Adept* **(The Apprentice Adept series, book 2). Gr. 10 up.**

Stile searches for an unknown enemy menacing him in both the magic world of Phaze and the science-fictional world of Proton. While in Phaze he is helped by a unicorn, kills a dragon, is given a magic flute, and gains the love of Lady Blue. This is the sequel to *Split Infinity* (1980) and is followed by *Juxtaposition* (1981), *Out of Phaze* (1987, 1988), *Robot Adept* (1988, 1989), *Unicorn Point* (1989, 1990), and *Phaze Doubt* (1990).

Ballantine, 1987, pap., 336 pp. (0-345-35245-9)

(Kliatt 16[Fall 1982]:17; KR 49:390; LJ 106:1325)

1249 **ANTHONY, Piers (pseud. of Piers A. D. Jacob).** *On a Pale Horse* **(Incarnations of Immortality series, book 1). Gr. 10 up.**

When Zane's unsuccessful suicide attempt kills Death instead of himself, the young man finds that he must take over Death's job. The sequels are *Bearing an Hourglass* (1984), *With a Tangled Skein* (1985), *Wielding a Red Sword* (1986), *Being a Green Mother* (1987), *For Love of Evil* (1988), and *And Eternity* (1990).

Ballantine, 1983, 249 pp., o.p., pap., 1986, 336 pp. (0-345-33858-8)

(BL 80:666, 676, 86:782, 903; KR 51:1020; SHC: 666; VOYA 7:37)

1250 **ANTHONY, Piers (pseud. of Piers A. D. Jacob).** *A Spell for Chameleon* **(Magic**
✓ **of Xanth series, book 1). Gr. 10 up.**

Exiled to Mundania from the magical land of Xanth for failing to demonstrate any magical talents, Bink and his friend Chameleon eventually discover that Bink's unique talent is that magic cannot harm him. *A Spell for Chameleon* won the British Fantasy Society Award, Best Novel, 1977. The sequels are *The Source of Magic* (1979), *Castle Roogna* (1979), *Centaur Aisle* (1981), *Ogre, Ogre* (1982), *Night Mare* (1982), *Dragon on a Pedestal* (1983), *Crewel Lye* (1984), *Golem in the Gears* (1986), *Vale of the Vole* (1987), *Heaven Scent* (1988), *Man from Mundania* (1989), *Isle of View* (1990), *Question Quest* (1991), *The Color of Her Panties* (1992), *Demons Don't Dream* (1993), and *Harpy Thyme* (1994).

Ballantine, 1977, pap., 352 pp., o.p., 1982 (entitled *The Magic of Xanth,* [3 vols.]), pap., o.p., 1987, pap. (0-345-34753-6)

(BBS:51; BL 86:903; Kliatt 12[Winter 1978]:12; LJ 102:2083; SHC:666; Tymn:43)

1251 **ANTHONY, Piers, and LACKEY, Mercedes.** *If I Pay Thee Not in Gold.* **Gr. 10 up.**

The queen of Mazonia challenges her magically talented rival, Xylina, to undertake a dangerous quest in search of a powerful shard of crystal, in this story for mature readers.

Baen, 1993, 416 pp. (0-671-72175-5)

(BL 89:1470, 1471; KR 61:561; LJ June 15, 1993 p. 104; VOYA 16:305)

ASPRIN, Robert L. *Hit or Myth.* See Chapter 10, Witchcraft and Sorcery Fantasy.

1252 **AVI.** *Bright Shadow.* **Gr. 5–8.**

Morwenna becomes enmeshed in the conflict between an evil king and his subjects after a dying wizard leaves her the kingdom's last five magic wishes.

Macmillan, 1985, 144 pp. (0-02-707750-0), 1994, pap., 176 pp. (0-689-71783-0)

(BBJ:68; CCBB 39:102; SLJ Dec 1985 p. 86; VOYA 9:37)

1253   **B. B. (pseud. of D(enys) J(ames) Watkins-Pitchford).** *The Little Grey Men*
✓   **(British title:** *The Little Grey Men: A Story for the Young in Heart,* **1942). Gr. 4–6.**

Three gnomes search the length of Folly Brook for their lost brother, Cloudberry. Carnegie Medal winner, 1942. The sequel is *Down the Bright Stream* (British pub. 1948).

Illus. by the author, Scribner, 1949, 249 pp., o.p.

(BL 46:105; CCBB 2 [Nov 1949]:8; HB 25:533; KR 17:28; LJ 74:1541, 1919)

1254   **BABBITT, Lucy Cullyford.** *The Oval Amulet.* **Gr. 6–9.**

Disguised as a boy, seventeen-year-old Paragrin escapes from a restrictive settlement with her only treasure, an oval amulet, determined to find the mysterious woman who once gave it to her. The sequel is *Children of the Maker* (1988).

Harper, 1985, 244 pp., o.p.

(BL 81:1249, 1250; CCBB 38:180; SLJ Sept 1985 p. 141; VOYA 8:191)

1255   **BABBITT, Lucy Cullyford.** *Where the Truth Lies.* **Gr. 7–12.**

Sanctuary-born atheist Kira, seventeen, is chosen to help Lillen and Eli, young representatives of the monotheistic Godsland and the polytheistic Tribes, resolve their peoples' often violent conflicts over which religion is "true."

Orchard, 1993, 199 pp. (0-531-05473-X)

(BL 89:1424; CCBB 46:239; HBG 4[Fall 1993]:307; KR 61:592; SLJ Mar 1993 p. 218; VOYA 16:98)

1256   **BAKKEN, Harald.** *The Fields and the Hills* **(The Journey Once Begun series, book 1). Gr. 5–9.**

After orphaned 13-year-old Weyr runs away from his Tam village and joins a traveling band of Agari performers, his paranormal abilities become very useful.

Houghton, 1992, 228 pp. (0-395-59397-2)

(BL 89:595; CCBB 46:67; HBG 4[Spring 1993]:79; KR 60:1057; SLJ Dec 1992 p. 108)

1257   **BALL, Margaret.** *Changeweaver* **(Flameweaver series, book 2). Gr. 10 up.**

Tamai Flameweaver uses magic to guide British explorer Charles Carrington into the forbidden Chin empire, where they become part of a revolutionary uprising against the corrupt Red Hat Buddhist monks who control the boy emperor. This is the sequel to *Flameweaver* (1991).

Baen, 1993, pap., 298 pp. (0-671-72173-9)

(Kliatt Sept 1993 p. 15; VOYA 16:222, 17:8)

1258   **BARKER, M(uhammad) A(bd-Al-) R(ahman).** *The Man of Gold.* **Gr. 10–12.**

Harsan, a young priest of the god Thumis, becomes expert at deciphering the ancient language of Llayni, leading him to search for the legendary Man of Gold who is powerful enough to save the Empire.

DAW, 1984, pap., 367 pp. (0-88677-082-3)

(BBS 52; LJ 109:1470; VOYA 7:335)

1259   **BAUDINO, Gael.** *Strands of Starlight.* **Gr. 7–12.**

In an alternate fourteenth-century Europe terrorized by the Inquisition, a young healer named Miriam, fleeing accusations of witchcraft, is taken in by elves after she is almost killed by a man she healed.

NAL, 1989, pap., 371 pp. (0-451-16371-0)

(Kliatt Apr 1990 p. 22; VOYA 13:36)

BAXTER, Lorna. *The Eggchild.* See Chapter 10, Witchcraft and Sorcery Fantasy.

1260 **BEAGLE, Peter S(oyer).** *The Innkeeper's Song.* **Gr. 10 up.**

Tikat refuses to accept the drowning death of his sweetheart, Lukassa, and vows to rescue her from the wizard beneath the riverbed.

NAL, 1993, 368 pp. (0-451-45288-7)

(BL 90:394, 395, 866; LJ Oct 15, 1993 p. 93)

1261 **BEAGLE, Peter S(oyer).** *The Last Unicorn.* **Gr. 10 up.**

✓ A magician and a very old but beautiful unicorn travel the world in search of others of her species.

Viking, 1968, 218 pp., o.p.; NAL, 1991, pap., 218 pp. (0-451-45052-3)

(BBJ:68; BBS:52; BL 64:824; KR 36:19; LJ 93:2131; SHC:669; Tymn:50)

1262 **BELL, Clare E.** *The Jaguar Princess.* **Gr. 10 up.**

Mixcatl, apprentice scribe to the Aztec Priests, discovers that she can transform herself into a jaguar and right ancient wrongs.

Tor, 1993, 448 pp. (0-312-09704-2)

(BL 90:417, 427; KR 61:1034; VOYA 16:377, 17:10)

BELL, Clare E. *Ratha's Creature.* See Chapter 2, Animal Fantasy.

1263 **BEMMANN, Hans.** *The Stone and the Flute.* **Gr. 10 up. (Orig. German pub. 1983.)**

Two powerful talismans guide young Listener, son of the chieftain of Fraglund, on his quest to find his grandfather, the legendary Gentle Fluter, and the woman whose eye he sees in his magical stone.

Trans. by Anthea Bell, Viking, 1987, 855 pp., o.p., 1988, pap. (0-14-007445-7)

(BBS:52; BL 83:946, 949; KR 55:397; LJ May 15 1987 p. 101)

1264 **BETANCOURT, John Gregory.** *The Blind Archer.* **Gr. 10 up.**

Ker's rebellious attempts to test his magical talents result in his being sent on a quest to the world of the Faceless Demons.

Avon, 1988, pap., 233 pp. (0-380-75146-1)

(BL 84:1316, 1334; Kliatt Apr 1988 p. 18)

1265 **BISSON, Terry.** *Fire on the Mountain.* **Gr. 10 up.**

An alternate history of the southern United States told from two points of view: that of Dr. Abraham, an ex-slave who witnessed John Brown's defeat of the Virginia militia at Harpers Ferry, thereby averting the Civil War and resulting in an independent, black, socialist South known as Nova Africa; and that of his twentieth-century granddaughter, Yasmin Odinga, whose astronaut husband has died on an African expedition to Mars.

Arbor, 1988, 192 pp., o.p.; Avon, 1990, pap. (0-380-75369-3)

(BBS:53; BL 84:1786, 1818; KR 56:797)

BLATHWAYT, Benedict. *Tangle and the Firesticks.* See Chapter 2, Animal Fantasy.

1266 **BLAYLOCK, James P(aul).** *The Stone Giant* **(The Elfin Sequence, book 3). Gr. 10–12.**

Theophile Escargot, exiled from Twoxbly Town for stealing his wife's pie, becomes a surprised hero in this humorous sequel to *The Elfin Ship* (Ballantine, 1982) and *The Disappearing Dwarf* (Ballantine, 1983).

Ace, 1989, pap., 264 pp., o.p.

(BBS:53; BL 85:1613; VOYA 12:369 & 13:16)

1267   BODECKER, N(iels) M(ogens). *Quimble Wood.* **Gr. 2–4.**

Four miniature people called Quimbles are forced to set up housekeeping in a forest.

Illus. by Branka Starr, Atheneum, 1981, 26 pp., o.p.

(BL 77:1296, KR 49:431; SLJ Sept 1981 p. 104)

1268   *Borderland, No. 1.* Ed. by Terri Windling and Mark Arnold. Gr. 7–12.

Four short stories written by Steven R. Boyett, Bellamy Bach, Charles de Lint, and Ellen Kushner, all set in the magical world of Borderland, surrounded by other warring worlds. The sequel is *Bordertown* (1986). Will Shetterly's *Elsewhere* (1991; see Chapter 5C, Travel to Other Worlds) is also set in the world of Borderland. *Finder* by Emma Bull (Tor, 1994) is set in Borderland as well.

NAL, 1986, pap., 252 pp., o.p.; Tor, 1992, pap., 256 pp. (0-8125-2261-3)

(BL 82:1184; Kliatt 20[Fall 1986]:30; VOYA 9:233, 10:21)

1269   BRADLEY, Marion Zimmer. *Hawkmistress!* **(Darkover series). Gr. 10 up.**

✓   Sixteen-year-old Romilly MacAran gives up her priviledged life by refusing to marry the man her father has chosen and runs away to develop her unusual gift of mind-control over hawks. This novel from the Darkover series (see *The Shattered Chain,* below) can stand on its own.

DAW, 1982, 1988, pap., 336 pp. (0-88677-239-7)

(BL 79:294; LJ 107:1722; VOYA 5:42)

1270   BRADLEY, Marion Zimmer. *The Shattered Chain: A Darkover Novel* **(Darkover series, book 1). Gr. 10 up.**

Lady Rohana of Ardais and a female band of Free Amazons arrive in the Dry Towns of Darkover where all women are kept in chains, in order to free a royal captive and her slave-born daughter. The sequels are *Thendara House* (1983, 1988) and *City of Sorcery* (1984). *The Shattered Chain* has also been published in one volume with *Thendara House,* entitled *Oath of the Renunciates* (Doubleday, 1983). Bradley has written twenty-two novels set in the alternate world of Darkover. *Darkover Landfall* (1972) is the first in terms of internal chronology, but they need not be read in any specific order. The others in the series are: *The Sword of Aldones* (Ace, 1962), *The Planet Savers* (Ace, 1962), *The Bloody Sun* (Ace, 1964, 1969), *Star of Danger* (Ace, 1965), *Winds of Darkover* (Ace, 1970), *The World Wreckers* (Ace, 1971), *The Spell Sword* (1974, 1988), *The Heritage of Hastur* (1975, 1988), *The Forbidden Tower* (1977, 1988), *Stormqueen* (1978, 1989), *Two to Conquer* (1980), *Shaara's Exile* (1981, 1988), *Sword of Chaos and Other Stories* (1982), *Hawkmistress!* (1982, 1988), *Free Amazons of Darkover* (1985), *The Heirs of Hammerfell* (1990), *Leroni of Darkover* (1991), *Rediscovery: A Novel of Darkover* (1993), and *Towers of Darkness* (1993). *The Keeper's Price and Other Stories* (1980), *The Other Side of the Mirror: And Other Darkover Stories* (DAW, 1987), *Red Sun of Darkover* (1987), *Four Moons of Darkover* (1988), *Spells of Wonder* (1989), *Domains of Darkover* (1990), *Renunciates of Darkover* (1991), *Marion Zimmer Bradley's Darkover* (1993), and *Snows of Darkover* (1994), contain Darkover tales written by Bradley and by members of the Friends of Darkover.

DAW, 1976, pap., 287 pp. (0-88677-308-3)

(BL 73:22; LJ 101:1227)

1271   BRADLEY, Marion Zimmer, MAY, Julian, and NORTON, André. *Black Trillium* **(Trillium saga, book 1). Gr. 10 up.**

✓   An evil sorcerer has taken over the Kingdom of Ruwenda and murdered the king and queen, forcing the three princesses, each wearing a magic amulet, to flee. The three co-authors have each written a story of one princess's quest to defeat the sorcerer. The sequels are *Blood Trillium* (1992) written by Julian May and *Golden Trillium* (1993) written by André Norton.

Doubleday, 1990, 410 pp., o.p.; Bantam, 1991, pap. (0-553-29079-7)

(BBS:54; BL 86:1931, 1933, 87:967; KR 58:842; LJ Aug 1990 p. 147; SLJ Nov 1990 p. 156; VOYA 13:224, 14:9)

1272   BRADSHAW, Gillian (Marucha). *The Dragon and the Thief.* **Gr. 5–10.**

✓   Seventeen-year-old Prahotep, attempting the trade of tomb-robbing, accidentally enters the cave of Hathor, the last dragon in ancient Thebes, and agrees to help transport her treasure down the Nile to Nubia while she searches for others of her kind. In the sequel, *The Land of Gold* (1992), Prahotep and Hathor rescue Kandaki, a Nubian princess, from death as a sacrifice to a terrifying water dragon, and she joins their crew, intending to regain her stolen throne.

Greenwillow, 1991, 154 pp. (0-688-10575-0)

(BL 87:2039; CCBB 45:85; HBG 3[July–Dec 1991]:63; JHC 1992 Suppl. p. 56; KR 59:928; SLJ Oct 1991 p. 119)

1273   BROOKS, Terry. *The Sword of Shannara* **(Shannara series, book 1). Gr. 10 up.**

✓   A band of elves, dwarfs, and trolls, reluctantly led by orphaned Shea, set off to find the legendary Sword of Shannara and defeat the forces of evil. The sequels are *The Elfstones of Shannara* (1982), *The Wishsong of Shannara* (1985), *The Scions of Shannara* (1990), *The Druids of Shannara (1991), The Elf Queen of Shannara* (1992), and *The Talismans of Shannara* (1993). The latter four are called The Heritage of Shannara series.

Illus. by the Brothers Hildebrandt, Random, 1977, o.p.; Ballantine, 1978, 1983, pap., 726 pp. (0-345-31425-5), 1991, pap., 736 pp. (0-345-37143-7)

(BL 73:1147, 1155, 78:593, 86:904; KR 45:108; LJ 102:946; SHC 672; SLJ Sept 1977 p. 152; Tymn:55; VOYA 2[Apr 1979]:49)

1274   BRUST, Steven K. (Zoltan). *The Phoenix Guards.* **Gr. 10 up.**

Khaavren and his three companions—Lady Tazendra, Aerich, and Pel—are the Phoenix Guards, who serve the emperor while they engage in duels, fight battles, and search for adventure. This book takes place in an earlier period on Dragaera, the setting for Brust's Vlad Taltos series (1983–1988; see *Taltos* below). The sequel is *Five Hundred Years After* (1994).

Tor, 1991, 320 pp. (0-312-85157-X), 1992, pap. (0-8125-0689-8)

(BL 87:2108, 2110; KR 59:1121; LJ Sept 15, 1991 p. 117; VOYA 15:40)

1275   BRUST, Steven K. (Zoltan). *Taltos* **(Vlad Taltos series, vol. 1). Gr. 10 up.**

The sorcerers of Dragaera keep its citizens in thrall, but Taltos has been able to practice his professions of detective, assassin, and witch in spite of them. The sequels are *Jhereg* (1983, 1987), *Yendi* (1984, 1987), *Tekla* (1987), and *Phoenix* (1990). *The Phoenix Guards* (1991; see above) takes place in an earlier period on Dragaera.

Ace, 1988, pap., 181 pp. (0-441-18200-3)

(BL 84:1098; VOYA 11:137,12:16)

1276   BUJOLD, Lois McMaster. *The Spirit Ring.* **Gr. 10 up.**

A sculptor's daughter battles a sorcerer for her father's soul after the sculptor agrees to animate the sorcerer's spirit ring, in this fantasy set in an alternate Renaissance Italy.

Baen, 1992, 369 pp. (0-671-72142-9)

(BL 89:37, 42; VOYA 16:36, 17:8)

1277　CALDECOTT, Moyra. *The Tall Stones* **(The Sacred Stones series, book 1). Gr. 10 up.**

Karne and his sister Kyra are trained by Maal, the old priest of their Bronze-Age British village, in the powers and secrets held by the Circle of Stones, but their lives are threatened by an evil new priest. The sequels are *The Temple of the Sun* (1978) and *Shadow on the Stones* (1979).

Farrar, 1977, 234 pp., o.p.

(BL 74:1174; KR 45:1057; LJ 103:383; SLJ May 1978 p. 89; TLS 1977 p. 864)

CALLANDER, Don. *Aquamancer.* See Chapter 10, Witchcraft and Sorcery Fantasy.

1278　CARD, Orson Scott. *Hart's Hope.* **Gr. 10 up.**

Black sorcery practiced by young Princess Asineth of Burland, who had been forced into an unloving marriage to her country's conquerer, brings centuries of despair to the kingdom and its rulers.

Berkley, 1983, pap., 272 pp., o.p.; Tor, 1988, 1992, pap. (0-8125-2135-8)

(BL 79:1013; VOYA 6:212)

1279　CARD, Orson Scott. *Seventh Son* **(Tales of Alvin Maker, book 1). Gr. 10 up.**

✓　Something or someone is determined that young Alvin Miller, the seventh son of a seventh son, will never grow up to use his powerful magic, in this novel set on the frontier of an alternate early nineteenth-century America. Mythopoeic Fantasy Award, 1988. The sequels are *Red Prophet* (1988) and *Prentice Alvin* (1989).

Tor, 1987, 241 pp. (0-312-93019-4), 1988, pap., 256 pp. (0-8125-3353-4), 1993, pap. (0-8125-3305-4)

(BBS:54; BL 8 3:1314, 84:838, 855, 1246, 86:904; KR 55:895; LJ June 15, 1987 p. 89; SHC:674; SLJ Dec 1987 p. 109; VOYA 10:243, 11:13)

1280　CARD, Orson Scott. *Songmaster.* **Gr. 10 up.**

Because nine-year-old Ansset's beautiful singing voice has captivated and tamed the formerly tyrannical Emperor Mikal the Terrible, the emperor's jealous advisors kidnap the boy and involve him in a plot to murder the emperor.

Dial, 1980, 320 pp., o.p.; Tor, 1987, 1992, 384 pp., pap. (0-8125-2486-1)

(KR 48:739; SLJ Oct 1980 p. 166; VOYA 3[Oct 1980]:31, 11:13)

1281　CARLYON, Richard. *The Dark Lord of Pengersick.* **Gr. 5–9.**

After young Mabby steals the sorcerer Pengersick's magic ring, her friend Jago goes on a hazardous quest to learn the powers of enchantment so that he can fight the evil enchanter and restore the land of Kernow to the people.

Farrar, 1980, 176 pp., o.p.

(BL 77:39, 42; SLJ Aug 1980 p. 61)

1282　CARTER, Lin. *Mandricardo: New Adventures of Terra Magica* **(Terra Magica series, book 3). Gr. 7–12.**

A knight and his amazon companion encounter magic, monsters, and wizards in the lands of Terra Magica. The preceeding books in the series are *Kesrick* (1982) and *Dragonrouge* (1984), and the sequel is *Callipygia* (1988).

DAW, 1987, pap., 223 pp., o.p.

(Kliatt 21[Spring 1987]:20; VOYA 10:89, 11:13)

1283 **CARVER, Jeffrey A(llan).** *Dragon Rigger* **(Star-Rigger series, book 3). Gr. 10 up.**

In this science fantasy, Star-Rigger Jael LeBrae is called upon to help dragon friends by entering The Flux, an alternate reality, and battling evil forces threatening the Realm. This is the sequel to *Star Rigger's Way* (Doubleday, 1978) and *Dragons in the Stars* (Tor, 1992).

Tor, 1993, 475 pp. (0-312-85061-1)

(BL 89:1793, 1797; LJ June 15, 1993 p. 104; VOYA 16:306)

1284 **CHANT, Joy (pseud. of Eileen Joyce Rutter).** *The Grey Mane of Morning* **(Vandarei series). Gr. 10 up. (Orig. British pub. 1977.)**

In this story set in an earlier period of the history of Vandarei than *Red Moon and Black Mountain* (1970, 1976, see Chapter 5C, Travel to Other Worlds), the nomadic Alnei tribe of Khentor and the Golden People of the Walled Towns come into deadly conflict, and young Mor'anh emerges as an Alnei hero. *When Voiha Wakes* (1983) is set in the same world, and won the Mythopoetic Fantasy Award, 1984.

Illus. by Martin White, Unwin, 1977, 262 pp., o.p.

(BL 77:504; LJ 103:388; Tymn:62)

1285 **CHASE, Carol.** *Hawk's Flight.* **Gr. 10 up.**

Taverik the merchant and his fellow traveler, Marco, a woman in disguise, are chosen to help the forces of Zojikam battle evil in their own world and in the spirit world.

Baen, 1991, pap., 437 pp., o.p.

(Kliatt Sept 1991 p. 20; VOYA 14:237)

1286 **CHERRYH, C. J. (pseud. of Carolyn Janice Cherry).** *Angel with the Sword.* **Gr.**
✓ **10 up.**

Seventeen-year-old Altair Jones rescues an unconscious man named Mondragon from a canal, falls in love with him, and becomes determined to protect him from his powerful enemies in the city of Merovingen. The books in the Merovingen Nights series, edited by Cherryh, are set in the same world: *Festival Moon* (1987; see this section), *Fever Season* (1987), *Troubled Waters* (1988), *Smuggler's Gold* (1988), *Divine Right* (1989), *Flood Tide* (1990), and *Endgame* (1991).

DAW, 1985, 293 pp., o.p., 1987, pap., 304 pp. (0-88677-143-9)

(BL 81:1596, 1599; LJ Sept 15, 1985 p. 96; SHC:584; SLJ Nov 1985 p. 105)

1287 **CHERRYH, C. J. (pseud. of Carolyn Janice Cherry).** *Exile's Gate* **(The Quest**
✓ **of Morgaine, book 4). Gr. 10 up.**

In this, the fourth volume of the Morgaine series, white-haired Morgaine and her leigeman, Vanye, discover that Skarrin, the ruler of their world, is an exiled member of the same ancient race to which Morgaine may belong. This is the sequel to *Gate of Ivrel* (1976), *The Well of Shiuan* (1978), and *The Fires of Azeroth* (1979). *Visible Light* (1986) contains one story set in Morgaine's world.

DAW, 1988, pap., 416 pp. (0-88677-254-0)

(BBS:54; BL 84:417, 418; Kliatt 22[Apr 1988]:18; LJ Dec 1, 1987 p. 131; Tymn:65–66; VOYA 11:94, 12:14)

1288 **CHERRYH, C. J. (pseud. of Carolyn Janice Cherry).** *The Goblin Mirror.* **Gr. 10 up.**

Left behind after his two older brothers travel beyond the mountains with the king's magician to battle the evil goblin queen, Prince Yuri decides to follow them. The author's

Rusalka trilogy—*Rusalka* (1989; see Chapter 10, Witchcraft and Sorcery Fantasy), *Chernevog* (1990), and *Vgenie* (1991)—is set in the same world.

Ballantine, 1992, 304 pp. (0-345-37278-6)

(BL 89:242, 247; KR 60:953; LJ Sept 15 1992 p. 97; VOYA 16:100)

1289   CHERRYH, C. J. (pseud. of Carolyn Janice Cherry) and ASIRE, Nancy. *Wizard Spawn* (Sabis trilogy, vol. 2). Gr. 7–12.

In this volume of a shared-world trilogy about the beleaguered people of Sabis who have been ruled by Ancar wizardry since their empire was conquered five hundred years previously, Duran, an Ancarn wizard, leaves the royal court to work with the poor, angering his Ancar neighbors by befriending some of the Sabirn. This is the sequel to *A Dirge for Sabis* (1989) written by C. J. Cherryh and Leslie Fish, and is followed by *Reap the Whirlwind* written by C. J. Cherryh and Mercedes Lackey (1989).

Baen, 1989, pap., 275 pp. (0-671-69838-9)

(BBS:54; VOYA 13:37)

1290   CHETWIN, Grace. *Child of the Air.* Gr. 5–8.
✓   Orphaned Myl and Brevan, eleven and twelve, are forced into servitude after their grandfather's death, but are able to escape their harsh life after they discover they can fly.

Illus. by the author, Macmillan, 1991, 256 pp. (0-02-718317-3)

(BL 87:1868; CCBB 44:234; HBG 2:275; JHC 1992 Suppl. p. 57; KR 59:469; SLJ June 1991 p. 100; VOYA 14:178)

1291   CHETWIN, Grace. *The Chimes of Alyafaleyn.* Gr. 5–9.
✓   Caidy is furious that her talents with the magical "heynim," chimes controlling weather and healing, have been suppressed by Tamborel, the master tuner.

Macmillan, 1993, 234 pp. (0-02-718222-3)

(BL 90:339; CCBB 47:117; HBG 5:85; KR 61:1387; SLJ Nov 1993 p. 104; VOYA 16:378)

1292   CHETWIN, Grace. *Gom on Windy Mountain: From Tales of Gom* (Tales of
✓   **Gom series, vol. 1). Gr. 6–8.**

The strange runestone left him by his mother, Harga, leads fatherless young Gom into mountain caves where he discovers the truth about his mother's disappearance on the day he was born. In the first sequel, *The Riddle and the Rune: From Tales of Gom in the Legends of Ulm* (1987), Gom travels across Ulm in search of Harga, making both friends and enemies while he struggles to solve a mysterious riddle. In *The Crystal Stair* (1988) Gom prepares for his seven-year wizardry apprenticeship by undertaking a dangerous journey back to Pen'langoth to find a mentor. In *The Starstone* (1989), Gom finishes his apprenticeship with Folgen and is called to fight against the wicked Katak.

Lothrop, 1986, 224 pp. (0-688-05767-5); Dell, 1990, pap. (0-440-20543-3)

(BBC:200; BL 82:1308; CC:464; HB 62:743; JHC 431; SLJ May 1986 p. 89; VOYA 9:234)

1293   CHRISTOPHER, John (pseud. of Christopher Samuel Youd). *The Prince in*
✓✓   ***Waiting* (The Winchester trilogy, vol. 1). Gr. 6–9.**

After our world is destroyed by earthquakes, Luke is rescued by a seer who involves the youth in a struggle for power over the medieval civilization that has arisen. In *Beyond the Burning Lands* (1971, 1989, pap.) Luke must battle his half-brother, Peter, for the throne of Winchester. In the final volume of this trilogy, *The Sword of the Spirits* (1972, 1989, pap., Peter Smith, 1984), Luke's battle accomplishments have made him a hero, but he has become a lonely man, resigned to the fact that he will continually need to fight more battles.

Macmillan, 1970, o.p.; Peter Smith, 1984 (0-8446-6157-0); Macmillan, 1989, pap., 224 pp. (0-02-042573-2)

(BL 67:306; CCBB 24:154; Ch&Bks:284; HB 47:54; KR 38:1160; LJ 95:4051; Suth 2:72; TLS 1970 p. 1460)

1294 **CLAYTON, Jo.** *A Bait of Dreams: A Five Summer Quest.* **Gr. 10 up.**

A jester, a dancer, and a young girl search out the source of the Ranga Eye jewels, deadly gems that drain the soul.

DAW, 1985, pap., 404 pp., o.p.

(BBS:54; Kliatt 19[Spring 1985]:24; LJ Feb 15, 1985 p. 182; VOYA 8:192)

1295 **CLAYTON, Jo.** *The Magic Wars* **(Wild Magic trilogy, book 3). Gr. 10 up.**

While Faan and her three companions travel in search of Faan's real mother, they battle shape shifters, ghosts, and gods. This is the sequel to *Wild Magic* (1991) and *Wildfire* (1992).

DAW, pap., 1993, 367 pp. (0-88677-547-7)

(Kliatt May 1993 p. 13; VOYA 16:100)

1296 **CLAYTON, Jo.** *Moongather* **(Duel of Sorcery triology, book 1). Gr. 10 up.**

Serroi excapes from a wizard who tries to exploit her magic powers and becomes a fugitive woman warrior. The sequels are *Moonscatter* (1983) and *Changer's Moon* (1985). *Dancer's Rise* (1993) is the first book of The Dancer trilogy, in which Serroi is also the heroine.

DAW, pap., 1982, 240 pp., o.p.

(Kliatt Fall 1982 p. 18; LJ June 15, 1982 p. 1245)

1297 **CLAYTON, Jo.** *Shadowspeer* **(Shadow series, book 1). Gr. 10 up.**

Vowing revenge for their imprisonment by Ginbiryol Seyirshi, Shadith, Kikun, and Rohant set a trap for the diabolical filmmaker whose "Limited Editions" destroy entire worlds, with the help of a roving Karintepe female street gang. This is the sequel to *Shadowplay* (1990) and is followed by *Shadowkill* (1991).

DAW, 1990, pap., 342 pp., o.p.

(Kliatt Jan 1991 p. 20; VOYA 14:41)

1298 **COLE, Adrian.** *A Place among the Fallen.* **Gr. 10 up.**

A young girl has a vision that comes true when Korbillian, a man with great magical powers, arrives in Omara to save it from catastrophe.

Arbor House, 1987, 352 pp., o.p.; Avon, 1990, pap., 384 pp. (0-380-70556-7)

(BL 83:1655, 1672; VOYA 10:174)

1299 **COLE, Allan, and BUNCH, Chris.** *The Far Kingdoms.* **Gr. 10 up.**

Almaric, son of a merchant, and Janos, captain in the royal guard, search for the Far Kingdoms and battle an evil wizard threatening the future of their city, Orissa, in this story for mature readers.

Ballantine, 1993, 409 pp. (0-345-38055-X)

(KR 61:1034; VOYA 16:378)

COOK, Glen. *Doomstalker.* See Chapter 2, Animal Fantasy.

1300 **COOK, Glen.** *Tower of Fear.* **Gr. 10 up.**

The city of Qushmarrah is under occupation by the Herodians and their conquering army of Dartars, but a group of revolutionaries hopes to bring Nakar the sorcerer back to life to liberate the city.

Tor, 1989, 320 pp., o.p., 1991, pap. (0-8125-1933-7)

(BL 86:148, 163; KR 57:1287; LJ Sept 15, 1989 p. 138)

COOK, Hugh. *The Wizards and the Warriors.* See Chapter 10, Witchcraft and Sorcery Fantasy.

1301 COOKE, Catherine. *Mask of the Wizard.* **Gr. 7–12.**

The First Priestess of the Three-Fold Goddess leads an army consisting of a young priestess, a guardsman, a renegade wizard, and the Crown Prince and Princess across the Eleven Kingdoms to battle the evil Wizards of Akesh.

Tor, 1985, pap., 384 pp., o.p.

(BBS:55; VOYA 8:192)

1302 COOPER, Louise. *The Master* **(The Time Master trilogy, book 3). Gr. 7–12.**

The confrontation between the gods of Order and the gods of Chaos forces Tarod to decide which side he will follow. To understand this story, it would be helpful to have read the preceding volumes, *The Initiate* (1986) and *The Outcast* (1987).

Tor, 1987, pap., 285 pp., o.p.

(Kliatt Sept 1987 p. 24; VOYA 10:286)

1303 COOPER, Louise. *Nemesis* **(Indigo series, vol. 1). Gr. 7–12.**

To save the world, Princess Indigo must recapture the Seven Demons she accidentally released from the Tower of Regrets. The sequels are *Inferno* (1989), *Infanta* (1990), *Nocturne* (1990), *Troika* (1991), *Avatar* (1992), and *Revenant* (1993).

Tor, 1989, pap., 294 pp. (0-8125-3401-8)

(Kliatt Sept 1989 p. 17, VOYA 12:287, 13:14)

1304 COOPER, Louise. *The Sleep of Stone.* **Gr. 7–12.**

✓   A tragic story of unrequited love about Glysla, a winged shape-shifter, who tries to make Prince Anyr fall in love with her, first by assuming the shapes of various animals he befriends, and finally by kidnapping his betrothed, Sivorne, and imprisoning her in a "sleep of stone."

Illus. by John Collier, Macmillan, 1991, 138 pp. (0-689-31572-4); DAW, 1993, pap. (0-88677-555-8)

(BL 88:819; HBG 3[July–Dec 1991]:77; KR 59:1531; SLJ Mar 1992 p. 256; VOYA 15:41)

1305 COSTIKYAN, Greg. *By the Sword: Magic of the Plains* **(Magic of the Plains series, vol. 1). Gr. 10 up.**

Plains warrior Nijon, banished from his tribe, travels to the City with his mongoose companion, Brother, where they fight their way to fortune.

Tor, 1993, 256 pp. (0-312-85489-7), 1994, pap. (0-8125-2268-0)

(BL 89:1678, 1682; KR 61:492; VOYA 16:307)

1306 COWPER, Richard (pseud. of John Middleton-Murray). *The Road to Corlay.* **Gr. 10 up.**

The death of a boy named Thomas, whose magical piping charmed both beasts and men, brings about the formation of the cult of the White Bird, in this haunting story set in a post-technological thirtieth century. The sequel is *A Dream of Kinship* (1981).

Pocket, 1979, 1986, pap., 239 pp., o.p.

(BL 76:435, 438; Kliatt 14[Winter 1980]:16)

1307 COX, Palmer. *The Brownies: Their Book.* **Gr. 3–5. (Stories written 1883–1887; orig. pub. 1887.)**

Twenty-four stories in verse about tiny creatures who go ice-skating, take a ballon ride, go to school, and put on a circus. The sequels are *Another Brownie Book* (1890, 1941, 1967), *The Brownies at Home* (1891, 1938), *The Brownies around the World* (1892, 1937), *The Brownies through the Union* (1894), *The Brownies Abroad* (1898, 1934), *The Brownies' Latest Adventure* (1900), *The Brownies in the Philippines* (1903, 1939), *The Brownies Many More Nights* (1912, 1939), and *The Brownies and Prince Florimel* (1918).

Illus. by the author, McGraw-Hill, 1967, 144 pp., o.p.

(BBC:200; HB 41:406)

1308 CURRY, Jane Louise. *The Wolves of Aam.* **Gr. 7–9.**

An orphan named Runner and his friends, Cat and Fith, journey north through the Land of Tiddi to the mountain citadel of Ozel, in search of Runner's lost stone of power. The sequel is *Shadow Dancers* (1983).

Atheneum, 1981, 186 pp., o.p.

(BL 77:1084, 1097; HB 57:196; SLJ Apr 1981 p. 124; VOYA 4[Oct 1981]:63)

1309 DALEY, Brian. *A Tapestry of Magics.* **Gr. 10 up.**

The heroic exploits of the reluctant young knight, Crassmor, include courting the Lady Willow, whose tapestry controls the future of this alternate world.

Ballantine, 1983, pap., 304 pp., o.p.

(BL 79:1013, 1020; LJ 108:416)

1310 DE CAMP, L(yon) Sprague. *The Honorable Barbarian.* **Gr. 10 up.**

Kerin, the younger brother of Jorian from the author's Reluctant King trilogy (*The Goblin Tower,* 1968; *The Clocks of Iraz,* 1971, and *The Unbeheaded King,* 1983) is sent to a country reminiscent of China to study clock mechanisms. In this humorous story he rescues and marries a princess and battles sorcerers and demons.

Ballantine, 1989, 256 pp. (0-345-36091-5), 1990, pap. (0-345-36652-2)

(BBS:55; BL 85:1783, 1816; Kliatt Sept 1990 p. 20; KR 57:803; LJ June 15, 1989 p. 83; VOYA 12:370)

1311 DE CAMP, L(yon) Sprague, and DE CAMP, Catherine Crook. *The Incorporated Knight.* **Gr. 10 up.**

A bumbling knight named Sir Eudoric sets off on a series of adventures that eventually help to prove him worthy of his title. *The Pixilated Peeress* (Ballantine, 1991; see below) is set in the same world.

Phantasia Press, 1987, 256 pp. (0-932096-46-8); Baen, 1991, pap. (0-671-72045-7)

(BL 84:437, 466; LJ Oct 15, 1987 p. 95)

1312 DE CAMP, L(yon) Sprague, and DE CAMP, Catherine Crook. *The Pixilated Peeress.* **Gr. 10 up.**

Sergeant Thorolf rescues fugitive Countess Yvette in a forest, only to see her transformed into an octopus by one inept sorcerer and taken prisoner by another. This story is set in the same world of Rhaetia as *The Incorporated Knight* (Phantasia, 1987; see entry above).

Ballantine, 1991, 208 pp. (0-345-36732-4), 1992, pap. (0-345-36733-2)

(BL 87:2108, 2110; KR 59: 764; VOYA 14:380, 15:10)

DE CHANCIE, John. *Castle Kidnapped.* See Chapter 10, Witchcraft and Sorcery Fantasy.

DEITZ, Tom. *The Gryphon King.* See Chapter 5B, Myth Fantasy.

1313   **DELANY, Samuel R.** *Tales of Nevèryön.* Gr. 10 up.

An adventure-filled tale of the life of Gorgik, a youth in the prehistoric empire of Nevèryön, who rises from mine slave to courtier to hero. The sequels are *Nevèryöna: Or, The Tale of Signs and Cities* (1983, o.p.; 1994), *Flight from Nevèryön* (1985, o.p.; 1994), and *The Bridge of Lost Desire* (1987), retitled *Return to Nevèryön* (1994).

Bantam, 1979, pap., 272 pp., o.p.; Wesleyan Univ. Press, 1994, pap., 240 pp. (0-8195-6270-X)

(BL 76:435; LJ 104:1593; VOYA 3[Apr 1980]:48)

1314   **DE LARRABEITI, Michael.** *The Borribles.* Gr. 6–9. (Orig. British pub. 1975.)

After eight Borribles (violent street urchins who look like children) successfully raid a group of enemy creatures called Rumbles, they return home to find betrayal and disillusionment. *The Borribles Go for Broke* is the British sequel.

Macmillan, 1978, 239 pp., o.p.

(BBS:55; BL 74:1420, 1429; CCBB 31:174; KR 46:182; SLJ May 1978 p. 76; Suth 2:120; TLS 1976 p. 1547)

1315   **DE LINT, Charles.** *Dreams Underfoot: The Newford Collection.* Gr. 10 up.
✓   A collection of interconnected short stories set in the magical city of Newford, where Jilly, Geordie, and others meet ghosts, goblins, and mermaids.

Tor, 1993, 448 pp. (0-312-85205-3)

(BL 89:1301, 1308; KR 61:189; LJ Mar 15, 1993 p. 111; SLJ Dec 1993 p. 149; VOYA 16:225)

1316   **DE LINT, Charles.** *Into the Green.* Gr. 10 up.

The Lords of the Green, or Faerie, select young harper-witch Angharad to destroy a powerful puzzle-box found in the desert.

Tor, 1993, 256 pp. (0-312-08087-5)

(BL 90: 258, 262; KR 61:1105; LJ Oct 15, 1993 p. 93; VOYA 17:36)

1317   **DERESKE, Jo.** *Glom Gloom.* Gr. 5–7.

After Raymond's hated adversary, Gillus, is captured by the evil Weeuns, Raymond and his friends set out to free Gillus and to save their world.

Atheneum, 1985, 195 pp., o.p.

(BBC:202; BL 82:335; SLJ Oct 1985 p. 171)

1318   **DICKINSON, Peter (pseud. of Malcolm de Brissac).** *The Blue Hawk.* Gr. 7–12.
✓✓   (Orig. British pub. 1976.)

In what could be ancient Egypt, a boy named Tron defies the high priests by saving a sacrificial hawk, hides in the dead king's coffin, and joins the new king's fight to rule his own land. Carnegie Medal Commended Book, 1976; Guardian Award for Children's Fiction, 1977.

Little, 1976, 229 pp., o.p.; Peter Smith, 1991 (0-8446-6478-2)

(BL 72:1584, 1595; HB 52:503; KR 44:490, 549; LJ 101:1142; SLJ Nov 1976 p. 74; TLS 1976 p. 375)

1319   **DICKINSON, Peter (pseud. of Malcolm de Brissac).** *The Devil's Children* (The
✓   Changes trilogy, book 1). Gr. 6–9. (Orig. British pub. 1970.)

Nicky Gore becomes separated from her parents during the panic and confusion of The

Changes and is taken in by Sikhs suspected of witchcraft. Carnegie Medal Honour Book, 1970. *Heartsease* (1969; see below) and *The Weathermonger* (1968; see below) are set later during The Changes in England.

Little, 1970, o.p.; Delacorte, 1986, 188 pp. (0-385-29450-6); Dell, 1988, pap. (0-440-20082-2)

(BBJ:70; BL 67:262, 267, 82:1604, 1611; CCBB 24:72; Ch&Bks:277; HB 46:616, 63:82; LJ 95:4347; Suth:102; TLS 1970 p. 417; VOYA 9:236)

1320 **DICKINSON, Peter (pseud. of Malcolm de Brissac).** *Heartsease* **(The Changes**
✓ **trilogy, book 2). Gr. 6–9. (Orig. British pub. 1969.)**

Four young people and a foreign "witch" with mechanical know-how escape from an England immersed in The Changes and flee to Ireland. *The Devil's Children* (1970; see above) is set earlier during The Changes, and *The Weathermonger* (1968; see below) is set during a later part of The Changes in England.

Illus. by Nathan Goldstein, Little, 1969, o.p.; Delacorte, 1986, 235 pp. (0-385-29451-4); Dell, 1988, pap. (0-440-20096-2)

(Ch&Bks:277; HB 46:159; 63:82; KR 37:1111; LJ 95:1638; TLS 1969 p. 687; VOYA 9:236)

1321 **DICKINSON, Peter (pseud. of Malcolm de Brissac).** *The Weathermonger* **(The**
✓ **Changes trilogy, book 3). Gr. 6–9. (Orig. British pub. 1968.)**

Able to control the weather through magic, Geoffrey Tinker returns to an England that has reverted to the Middle Ages in hope of uncovering the cause of the enchantment. *The Devil's Children* (1970; see above) and *Heartsease* (1969; see above) are set earlier during The Changes in England.

Little, 1969, o.p.; Delacorte, 1986, 190 pp. (0-385-29450-6); Dell, 1988, pap. (0-440-20003-2)

(BBC:202; BL 65:1075; CCBB 22:156; Ch&Bks:277; HB 63:82; KR 37:501; LJ 94:2499; Suth:103; VOYA 9:236)

1322 **DICKSON, Gordon R(upert).** *The Dorsai Companion* **(Childe Cycle, book 8).**
Gr. 10 up.

Four short stories that fill in the gaps of Dickson's Dorsai series by explaining occurances in Dorsai history. The other books in the series are *Necromancer* (1962; republished as *No Room for Men,* 1963), *Tactics of Mistake* (1971), *Soldier, Ask Not* (1967, 1980), *The Genetic General* (1960; expanded into *Dorsai!,* 1976, 1980, 1993), *The Spirit of Dorsai* (1979, 1993), *Lost Dorsai* (1980), and *The Final Encyclopedia* (1984). *Necromancer, Tactics of Mistake,* and *Dorsai!* were also published together as *Three to Dorsai!* (1976).

Ace, 1986, pap., 231 pp., o.p.

(BBS:55; VOYA 9:236)

1323 **DONALDSON, Stephen R(upert).** *Daughter of Regals and Other Tales.* **Gr. 10**
up.

Eight short stories of fantasy, adventure, and horror, including one left out (for space reasons) of *The Illearth War* (1977) (see Chapter 5C, Travel to Other Worlds).

Ballantine, 1985, pap., 304 pp. (0-345-31443-3)

(BBS:55; BL 80:1081, 1083; KR 52:173; LJ 109:825; VOYA 7:205)

DOUGLAS, Carole Nelson. *Exiles of the Rynth.* See Chapter 10, Witchcraft and Sorcery Fantasy.

1324 **DOWNER, Ann.** *The Spellkey* **(Caitlin and Badger series, book 1). Gr. 7 up.**
✓ Two young people journey unwillingly to far-off Ninthistile together: Caitlin, exiled on

suspicion of witchcraft because she has one blue eye and one green, and Badger, an illegitimate stable boy. Their journey is full of strange adventures that are inexplicably involved with a spellkey that "unlocks all doors." In the sequel, *The Glass Salamander* (1989), Caitlin searches the subterranean Otherworld for Myrrhlock the necromancer after her son (and Badger's) is stolen in exchange for a goblin baby. In *The Books of the Keepers* (1993), Caitlin tries to find the four magical "Books of the Keepers," which are intertwined with the fate of her son, Bram, kidnapped seven years earlier.

Atheneum, 1987, 208 pp., o.p.

(BBJ:70; BL 84:384, 392, 86:904; HB 63:742; KR 55:1068; SLJ Sept 1987 p. 194; VOYA 10:176)

1325   DOYLE, Debra, and MacDONALD, James D. *Knight's Wyrd.* **Gr. 6–9.**

✓   Newly knighted, young Will learns that his wyrd, or fate, will not include becoming Lord of Restonbury after his father, but will be to meet Death after experiencing adventures involving a sea hag, ghostly knights, a man-eating troll, and an immortal ogre.

Harcourt, 1992, 176 pp. (0-15-200764-4)

(BL 89:589; CCBB 46:173; HB 69:89; HBG 4[Spring 1993]:80; KR 60:1253; SLJ Nov 1992 p. 90; VOYA 16:102)

Dragon Tales. **Ed. by Isaac Asimov, Charles G. Waugh, and Martin Harry Greenberg.** See Chapter 3, Fantasy Collections.

1326   DRAKE, David. *The Sea Hag* **(World of Crystal Walls series, vol. 1). Gr. 10 up.**

Promised at birth to the fearsome Sea Hag, sixteen-year-old Dennis runs away to become a hero and find true love in this science-fantasy.

Baen/Simon & Schuster, 1988, pap., 352 pp. (0-671-65424-1)

(BBS:56; BL 84:1894, 1914; VOYA 12:4)

DUANE, Diane (Elizabeth). *The Door into Fire.* See Chapter 10, Witchcraft and Sorcery Fantasy.

DUANE, Diane (Elizabeth). *So You Want to Be a Wizard.* See Chapter 10, Witchcraft and Sorcery Fantasy.

1327   DUNCAN, Dave. *The Cutting Edge* **(Handful of Men tetralogy, vol. 1). Gr. 10 up.**

King Rap, once a kitchen boy with magic powers, becomes involved in a battle for the succession of the throne of the Impire, of which his small kingdom is a part. The sequels are *Upland Outlaws* (1993), *The Stricken Field* (1993), and *The Living God* (1994). Set fifteen years later in the same world of Pandemia as the author's Man of his Word duo: *Magic Casement* (1990) and *Faery Lands Forlorn* (1991).

Ballantine, 1992, 400 pp. (0-345-37896-2), 1993, pap. (0-345-38167-X)

(BL 89:38, 42; KR 60:886; LJ Aug 1992 p. 155)

1328   DUNSANY, Lord (pseud. of Edward John Morton Drax Plunkett). *The King of Elfland's Daughter.* **Gr. 10 up.**

Prince Alveric of Erl crosses into Fairyland where, after many adventures, he wins the hand of Princess Lirazel; but their happiness is short-lived because the King of Elfland uses magic to bring his daughter back to him.

Putnam, 1924, 301 pp., o.p.; Ballantine, 1969, o.p.

(BL 21:111; TLS 1924 pp. 402, 466; Tymn:78)

1329 **EASTON, M. Coleman.** *The Fisherman's Curse* **(Glass Mistress series, book 2). Gr. 10 up.**

Kyala, the only girl ever apprenticed to a Master of Glass, maker of protective glass talismans, returns home to battle three gigantic monsters. This is the sequel to *Masters of Glass* (1985, 1987).

Warner, 1987, pap., 236 pp. (0-445-20332-3)

(BBS:56; BL 83:686; Kliatt 21[Spring 1987]:22)

1330 **EASTON, M. Coleman.** *Spirits of Cavern and Hearth.* **Gr. 10 up.**

Yarkol Dolmi, an exiled Hakhan physician, and his Chirudak companions must battle subterranean spirits to save his people from destruction.

St. Martin's, 1988, 294 pp., o.p.

(KR 56:1572; LJ Dec 1988 p. 138; VOYA 12:40)

1331 **EDDINGS, David.** *The Diamond Throne* **(The Elenium Saga, vol. 1) Gr. 10 up.**

A warrior, a wizard, and a child search for a way to prevent the death of Queen Ehlana. The sequels are *The Ruby Knight* (1991) and *The Sapphire Rose* (1992). *Domes of Fire* (1993; see below), *The Shining Ones* (1993), and *The Hidden City* (1994) comprise the Tamuli trilogy, which is a related series.

Ballantine, 1989, 464 pp. (0-345-35691-9), 1990, pap. (0-345-36769-3)

(BBS:56; BL 85:1218, 1219; KR 57:508; LJ Apr 15, 1989 p. 102; VOYA 12:286)

1332 **EDDINGS, David.** *Domes of Fire* **(The Tamuli trilogy, book 1). Gr. 10 up.**

Prince Sparhawk, Queen Ehlana, and their daughter, Danae, travel to Tamul in hopes of foiling a coup against the Tamulian throne. The sequels are *The Shining Ones* (1993) and *The Hidden City* (1994). This trilogy continues the saga begun in the Elenium trilogy (1989–1992; see *The Diamond Throne,* above).

Ballantine, 1993, 496 pp. (0-345-37321-9), 1993, pap. (0-345-38327-3)

(BL 89:379, 380; KR 60:1389; LJ Dec 1992 p. 191; VOYA 16:102)

1333 **EDDINGS, David.** *Guardians of the West* **(Malloreon series, book 1). Gr. 10 up.**

King Garion and his wife attempt to save their son from the evil sorcerer, Zandramas, in this first volume of a new series that is a sequel to his Belgariad saga (see Chapter 10). The sequels are *King of the Murgos* (1988), *Demon Lord of Karanda* (1988), *Sorceress of Darshiva* (1989), and *The Seeress of Kell* (1991).

Ballantine, 1987, 460 pp. (0-345-33000-5), 1988, pap., 416 pp. (0-345-35266-1)

(BBS:56; BL 83:947, 86:904; KR 55:259; LJ Apr 15, 1987 p. 102)

EDDINGS, David. *Queen of Sorcery.* See Chapter 10, Witchcraft and Sorcery Fantasy.

1334 **EDDISON, E(rik) R(ucker).** *The Worm Ouroboros, a Romance.* **Gr. 10 up. (Orig. British pub. 1922; U.S. Boni, 1926.)**

In this classic fantasy tale, the King of Demonland embarks on a heroic quest to find and free his greatest warrior, who has been enchanted by the sorcerer King of Witchland. The books of the Zimiamvian trilogy are related: *The Menzian Gate* (British pub. 1958; Ballantine, 1969), *A Fish Dinner in Memison* (Dutton, 1941, 1942; Ballantine, 1968), and *Mistress of Mistresses* (Dutton, 1935; Ballantine, 1967, 1978).

Illus. by Keith Henderson, Dutton, 1952, o.p.; Crown, 1962, o.p.; Ballantine, 1967, 1977, 1981, pap., 520 pp. (0-345-27122-X); Dell, 1991, pap. (0-440-50299-3)

(BL 23:38; TLS 1926 p. 676; Tymn:84)

EDGERTON, Teresa. *Child of Saturn.* See Chapter 10, Witchcraft and Sorcery Fantasy.

EDGERTON, Teresa. *Goblin Moon.* See Chapter 10, Witchcraft and Sorcery Fantasy.

1335   EGAN, Doris. *The Gate of Ivory* **(Ivory series, book 1). Gr. 10 up.**

✓   A science-fantasy about Theodora, an anthropology student who becomes stranded on the magic-ruled planet of Ivory, where she works as a fortune teller until she is hired by a local sorcerer to help him battle his enemies. The sequels are *Two-Bit Heroes* (1992) and *Guilt-Edged Ivory* (1992).

DAW, 1989, 320 pp., o.p.

(BL 85:1095, 1129; Kliatt Apr 1989 p. 24; LJ Feb 15, 1989 p. 179; VOYA 12:164, 13:12)

1336   EISENSTEIN, Phyllis. *In the Red Lord's Reach.* **Gr. 7–12.**

Fifteen-year-old minstrel Alaric escapes the bloody tyranny of the Red Lord's castle by magically vanishing and reappearing in the North, where he joins a peaceful nomadic tribe. This is the sequel to *Born to Exile* (Arkham, 1978; NAL, 1989).

NAL, 1989, pap., 268 pp. (0-451-16073-8)

(LJ June 15, 1989 p. 83; VOYA 13:37)

1337   EISENSTEIN, Phyllis. *Sorcerer's Son.* **Gr. 10 up.**

A gentle sorceress's son named Cray searches for the father he has never met, only to discover that his father is, in fact, the demon Gildrum. The sequel is *The Crystal Palace* (NAL, 1988).

Ballantine, 1979, pap., 387 pp., o.p.; NAL, 1989, pap., 384 pp. (0-451-15683-8)

(BBS:56; BL 75:1482, 1485, 78:594; VOYA 2[Dec 1979]:53)

1338   ELDRIDGE, Roger. *The Shadow of the Gloom-World.* **Gr. 6–9. (Orig. British pub. 1977.)**

Exiled from their subterranean worlds, Fernfeather and Harebell search for a better world above the ground.

Dutton, 1978, 191 pp., o.p.

(HB 54:401; SLJ May 1978 p. 76)

1339   ELGIN, (Patricia Anne) Suzette Haden. *Twelve Fair Kingdoms* **(The Ozark trilogy, book 1). Gr. 10 up.**

A fourteen-year-old girl sets out to rally the Twelve Kingdoms in hopes of defeating a magician threatening her world. The sequels are *The Grand Jubilee* (1981, Berkley, 1982, pap.) and *And Then There'll Be Fireworks* (1981, Berkley, 1983, pap.).

Doubleday, 1981, 183 pp., o.p.

(BL 77:1433, 1444, 78:594; KR 49:390; LJ 106:1326)

1340   *Elsewhere, vol. 1.* Ed. by Terri Windling and Mark Alan Arnold. Gr. 10 up.

An anthology of fantasy tales about other worlds, by such authors as Ursula K. Le Guin, Michael Moorcock, and Janny Wurts. World Fantasy Convention Award, Best Anthology, 1982. The companion volumes are *Elsewhere, vol. 2* (1982) and *Elsewhere, vol. 3* (1984).

Ace, 1981, pap., 366 pp., o.p.

(BL 78:634; SLJ Apr 1982 p. 88; VOYA 4[Dec 1981]: 38)

1341   ENDE, Michael. *Momo.* **Gr. 10 up. (Orig. German pub. 1973; British title: *The**
✓   **Grey Gentlemen, 1975.)***

A girl named Momo who lives in a ruined amphitheater is befriended by the poor people because she listens so carefully that everyone is able to think great thoughts. When her friends' lives are threatened by the "men in grey," who live off of others' spare time, only Momo can save them from the plague of deadly tedium.

Trans. by J. Maxwell Brownjohn, Doubleday, 1985, 228 pp., o.p.

(BBS:56; BL 81:602; KR 52:1168; Kliatt 20[Spring 1986]:57; LJ Jan 1985 p. 100; TLS July 11, 1975 p. 767; VOYA 8:192)

1342   ENGH, M(ary) J(ane). *The House in the Snow.* Gr. 4–6.

Cloaks of invisibility help Benjamin lead a rebellion against a gang of robbers who enslave boys.

Illus. by Leslie Bowman, Orchard, 1987, 192 pp., o.p.; Scholastic, 1990, pap., 144 pp. (0-590-42658-3)

(BL 84:476; CCBB 41:6; KR 55:990; SLJ Sept 1987 p. 179)

1343   *The Fantastic Imagination: An Anthology of High Fantasy,* vol. 1. Ed. by Robert H. Boyer and Kenneth J. Zahorski. Gr. 10 up.

Sixteen "high fantasy" short stories whose authors include George MacDonald, C. S. Lewis, J. R. R. Tolkien, Lloyd Alexander, Peter S. Beagle, Ursula K. Le Guin, Lord Dunsany, John Buchan, Frank R. Stockton, and Sylvia Townsend Warner. *The Fantastic Imagination,* vol. 2 (1978) is a companion volume.

Avon, 1977, pap., 325 pp., o.p.

(BL 73:1338; Kliatt 11[Spring 1977]:9; Tymn:185)

1344   FEIST, Raymond E. *Silverthorn* (Riftwar saga, book 2). Gr. 10 up.

✓   Prince Arutha and former bandit Jimmy the Hand set out on a perilous journey in search of the mythical silverthorn plant, needed to awaken the Prince's betrothed from an enchanted slumber. This book is preceded by *Magician* (1982, 1984), and the sequels are *A Darkness at Sethanon* (1986), *Prince of the Blood* (1989, 1992), and *The King's Buccaneer* (1992). *Daughter of the Empire* (1987; see below), written by Feist and Janny Wurts, takes place in the same universe as this saga, as does *Shadow of a Dark Queen* (Morrow, 1994), which is volume 1 of Feist's Serpent War saga.

Doubleday, 1985, 1992, 360 pp. (0-385-19210-X); Bantam, 1986, pap., 336 pp. (0-553-25928-8)

(BBS:57; BL 81:1519, 86:905; KR 53:450; LJ June 15, 1985 p. 74; VOYA 8:324)

1345   FEIST, Raymond E., and WURTS, Janny. *Daughter of the Empire* (Empire trilogy, vol. 1). Gr. 10 up.

Queen Mara of Acoma vows to avenge the deaths of her brother and father, even if it means killing her own husband. The sequels are *Servant of the Empire* (1990, 1992) and *Mistress of the Empire* (1992). These books are set in the same universe as Feist's Riftwar saga (see previous entry, this section), and his Serpent War saga (see previous entry, this section).

Doubleday, 1987, 394 pp., o.p.; Bantam, 1988, pap. (0-553-27211-X)

(BL 83:1564; KR 55:755; LJ June 15, 1987 p. 88; VOYA 10:244, 287)

1346   *Festival Moon* (Merovingen Nights, no. 1). Ed. by C. J. Cherryh. Gr. 10 up.

An anthology of stories by Cherryh, Lynn Abbey, Mercedes Lackey, and others, set in Merovin, the world of Cherryh's *Angel with the Sword* (1985; see above). The sequels are *Smuggler's Gold* (1988), *Divine Right* (1989), *Flood Tide* (1990), and *Endgame* (1991).

DAW, 1987, pap., 300 pp., o.p.

(BL 83:1180, 1198; LJ Mr. 15, 1987 p. 93; VOYA 10:178)

1347 **FINCH, Sheila.** *Infinity's Web.* **Gr. 10 up.**

Anastasia Valerie Stein is confronted with four different possible lives, due to a leak between parallel universes: in one she is a witch in a Nazi-ruled England, and in the others she is an unhappy housewife, a teacher, and an aging hippie.

Bantam, 1985, pap., 230 pp., o.p.

(BL 82:317; LJ Aug 1985 p. 120; VOYA 8:365)

1348 **FISHER, Paul R.** *The Ash Staff* **(Mole and Arien trilogy, book 1). Gr. 6–9.**

An irrepressible boy named Mole becomes the leader of a group of orphans fighting the evil powers of the enchanter Ammar. The sequels are *The Hawks of Fellheath* (1980) and *The Princess and the Thorn* (1981).

Atheneum, 1979, 179 pp., o.p.

(BBS:57; BL 76:448; CCBB 33:151; KR 47:1067; SLJ Jan 1980 p. 68)

1349 **FISHER, Paul R.** *Mont Cant Gold.* **Gr. 7–10.**

Rhian Mont Cant struggles to win the approval of each of the seven guardian fates to become High King of Rhewar.

Atheneum, 1981, 251 pp., o.p.

(BL 77:1191; SLJ Apr 1981 p. 126; VOYA 4[Oct 1981]:63)

1350 **FLEISCHMAN, (Albert) Sid(ney).** *The Whipping Boy.* **Gr. 4–6.**

✓✓ Prince Brat decides to run away from home, taking his much-abused whipping boy, Jemmy, with him, but their roles are reversed when the boys are captured by the villians Cut-Water and Hold-Your-Nose-Billy. John Newbery Award, 1987.

Illus. by Peter Sis, Greenwillow, 1986, 96 pp., LB(0-688-06216-4); Troll, 1987, pap. (0-8167-1038-4)

(BL 82:1018, 83:1135; CC:486; CCBB 39:126; HB 62:325; JHC:359; KR 54:715; SLJ May 1986 p. 90; Suth 4:120)

1351 **FLETCHER, Susan.** *Dragon's Milk.* **Gr. 5–9.**

✓✓ Kaeldra becomes foster mother to three orphaned young dragons after she is sent in search of dragon's milk to cure her younger sister's illness. The prequel is *Flight of the Dragon Kyn* (1993; see below).

Macmillan, 1989, 242 pp. (0-689-31579-1), 1992, pap. (0-689-71623-0)

(BBJ:70; BL 86:547; HB 66:69; HBG 1[July–Dec 1990]:81; KR 57:1592; SLJ Nov 1989 p. 106; VOYA 12:288)

1352 **FLETCHER, Susan.** *Flight of the Dragon Kyn.* **Gr. 5–10.**

✓ After the King tricks Kara into using her bird-calling powers to call down dragons to be killed, she escapes and vows to protect the dragons. This is the prequel to *Dragons' Milk* (1991; see above).

Macmillan, 1993, 213 pp. (0-689-31880-4)

(BL 90:931; CCBB 47:153; HB 70:73; HBG 5:86; KR 61:1329; SLJ Nov 1993 p. 108; VOYA 16:380)

1353 **FORD, John M.** *The Dragon Waiting: A Masque of History.* **Gr. 10 up.**

A Welsh wizard recruits a band of Italian warriors to fight the spread of the Byzantine Empire in England, in this historical fantasy set in an alternate fifteenth-century Europe ruled by magic. World Fantasy Award, 1983.

Timescape, 1983, 368 pp., o.p.; Avon, 1985, pap. (0-380-69887-0)

(BL 80:468; KR 51:976; LJ 108:2174; SLJ Mar 1984 p. 178; VOYA 7:101)

1354   FRIEDMAN, C. S. *Black Sun Rising* **(Cold Fire trilogy, vol. 1). Gr. 10 up.**

In the future world of Erna, where magic has been revived to deal with volcanic activity, a priest and a sorcerer join forces to battle evil. The sequel is *When True Night Falls* (1993).

DAW, 1991, 496 pp., o.p., 1992, pap. (0-88677-527-2)

(BL 88:34, 39; LJ Nov 15 1991 p. 110)

1355   FRIESNER, Esther M. *Druid's Blood.* **Gr. 10 up.**

A humorous tale set in an alternate England ruled by Celtic magic, where Queen Victoria's reign may be cut short by a treasonous conspiracy.

NAL, 1988, pap., 279 pp., o.p.

(BL 85:42; LJ June 15, 1988 p. 70)

FRIESNER, Esther M. *Majyk by Accident.* See Chapter 10, Witchcraft and Sorcery Fantasy.

1356   FRIESNER, Esther M. *Spells of Mortal Weaving* **(The Twelve Kingdoms series, vol. 2). Gr. 10 up.**

Prince Alban finds his curse of unrequited love fulfilled, when his quest for Lady Ursula takes him into the realm of the deadly Morgeld. This is the sequel to *Mustapha and His Wise Dog* (1985).

Avon, 1986, pap., 224 pp. (0-380-75001-5)

(BL 82:1360, 1388; LJ May 15, 1986 p. 81)

1357   FRIESNER, Esther M. *Wishing Season.* **Gr. 6–10.**

✓   After genie school star student Khalid forgets to limit a young merchant's wishes during his trial run in a lamp, they are stuck with each other.

Illus. by Frank Kelly Freas, Macmillan, 1993, 144 pp. (0-689-31574-0)

(BL 89:2049; HBG 5:86; KR 61:1389; SLJ Sept 1993 p. 229; VOYA 16:226, 17:9)

FURLONG, Monica. *Wise Child.* See Chapter 10, Witchcraft and Sorcery Fantasy.

GARD, Joyce (pseud. of Joyce Reeves). *The Mermaid's Daughter.* See Chapter 10, Witchcraft and Sorcery Fantasy.

GARDNER, Craig Shaw. *A Disagreement with Death.* See Chapter 10, Witchcraft and Sorcery Fantasy.

1358   GARDNER, John (Champlin) (Jr.). *In the Suicide Mountains.* **Gr. 7 up.**

A dwarf, a blacksmith's daughter, and a crown prince, all bent on suicide, meet in the mountains and find happiness together.

Illus. by Joe Servello, Knopf, 1977, 159 pp., o.p.

(BL 74:22, 32; CCBB 31:126; HB 54:194; KR 45:868; LJ 102:1677; SLJ Dec 1977 p. 54)

1359   GARRETT, Randall. *Lord Darcy Investigates* **(Lord Darcy series). Gr. 10 up.**

Four stories set in an alternate Anglo-French empire ruled by magic, where a detective named Lord Darcy solves mysteries. The sequels are *Murder and Magic* (Ace, 1979, 1982) and *Too Many Magicians* (Ace, 1967, 1983). Michael Jurland has written another sequel: *Ten Little Wizards* (Berkley/Ace, 1988).

Ace, 1981, 1983, 229 pp., o.p.

(BBS:57; BL 78:426, 435)

1360 **GENTLE, Mary.** *Rats and Gargoyles.* **Gr. 10 up.**

In a magical Renaissance-like world, human beings are slaves to human-sized Ratlords and devil-like Decan Overlords, and the slaves are preparing to revolt, in this complex multicharacter story. The sequel is *The Architecture of Desire* (1993).

Viking, 1991, 414 pp. (0-451-45106-6); NAL, 1992, pap. (0-451-45173-2)

(BL 87:1627, 1630; KR 59:291; LJ Mar 15, 1991 p. 119)

GILLILAND, Alexis A. *Wizenbeak.* See Chapter 10, Witchcraft and Sorcery Fantasy.

1361 **GILLULY, Sheila.** *Greenbriar Queen.* **Gr. 10 up.**

After her father the king's death, a princess comes out of hiding to battle her evil uncle for control of the kingdom.

NAL, 1988, 330 pp., o.p.

(BL 84:831, 855; Kliatt Apr 1988 p. 20; VOYA 11:192, 12:14)

1362 **GLOSS, Molly.** *Outside the Gates.* **Gr. 6–9.**

✓ Exiled beyond the High Gates because of their magic abilities, Vren, a young boy, and a man called Rusche live peacefully until Rusche is kidnapped by the evil Spellbinder.

Atheneum, 1986, 120 pp., o.p.

(BBC:203; BBJ:70; BL 83:270; CCBB 40:26; HB 68:209; KR 54:1207; SLJ Mar 1987 p. 158; VOYA 10:38)

1363 **GOLDIN, Stephen.** *Crystals of Air and Water* **(The Parsina Saga, vol. 3). Gr. 6–12.**

Prince Ahmad and apprentice wizard Jaffar al-Sharif search a desert country far from their home for the three missing pieces of the Crystal of Oromasd, needed to save the world from domination by demons. This is the sequel to *Shrine of the Desert Mage* (1988) and *The Storyteller and the Jann* (1988).

Bantam, 1989, 292 pp. (0-553-27711-1)

(BBS:57; VOYA 12:1654, 13:12)

1364 **GOLDMAN, William W.** *The Princess Bride: S. Morgenstern's Classic Tale of True Love and High Adventure.* **Gr. 8 up.**

In this parody of heroic fairy tales, Westley, the masked hero, tries to reclaim his beloved Buttercup from the evil Prince Humperdink of Florin, while Inigo Montoya, the great swordsman, continues his lifelong search for his father's murderer.

Harcourt, 1973, 320 pp., o.p.; Ballantine, 1987, pap. (0-345-34803-6); Buccaneer, 1991, 290 pp., LB(0-89966-809-7)

(BBS:57; KR 41:704; LJ 98:2570; Tymn:91)

1365 **GOULART, Ron(ald Joseph).** *The Chameleon Corps and Other Shape Changers* **(The Chameleon Corps series, book 2). Gr. 10 up.**

Five of these eleven humorous science fiction and fantasy tales concern Ben Jolson, a shape-changing lieutenant in the Chameleon Corps. These stories are preceded by *The Sword Swallower* (Doubleday, 1968), and the sequels are *Flux* (DAW, 1974), *Spacehawk Inc.* (DAW, 1974), and *A Whiff of Madness* (DAW, 1976).

Macmillan, 1972, 216 pp., o.p.

(BL 68:976, 998; KR 40:283, 341; LJ 97:1742, 3472)

1366 **GOULART, Ron(ald Joseph).** *The Prisoner of Blackwood Castle.* **Gr. 8–12.**

A humorous science fantasy set in 1897, featuring detective Harry Challange, a conjurer called the Great Lorenzo, and Princess Alicia of Orlandia, held prisoner by a vampire in Blackwood Castle.

Avon, 1984, pap., 174 pp., o.p.

(Kliatt 18[Sept 1984]:28; VOYA 7:266)

1367 GREEN, Simon. *Blue Moon Rising.* **Gr. 7–12.**

The Darkwood, filled with demons, is creeping ever closer to King John's castle, destroying Forest Land as it comes, and it is up to the king's younger son, Prince Rupert, and sword-wielding Princess Julia to save the kingdom.

NAL, 1991, pap., 476 pp. (0-451-45095-7)

(Kliatt Sept 1991 p. 23; VOYA 14:242)

1368 GREENO, Gayle. *Finders-Seekers* **(The Ghatti's Tale, book 1). Gr. 10 up.**

Doyce, a seeker, and her telepathic feline ghatti, Khar, are assigned to find the murderers of her lover and his ghatti companion. The sequel is *Mind-Speaker's Call* (1994).

DAW, 1993, 496 pp. (0-88677-550-7)

(Kliatt July 1993 p. 16; LJ Apr 15, 1993 p. 130; VOYA 16:164, 17:10)

1369 GRIMSHAW, Nigel (Gilroy). *Bluntstone and the Wildkeepers.* **Gr. 5–7. (Orig. British pub. 1974.)**

When the Wildkeepers are threatened by a builder named Bluntstone and his "yellow soil-eating monsters," the little people call on dark magic to save themselves. The sequel is *The Wildkeepers' Guest* (1978).

Faber, 1978, 152 pp., o.p.

(BL 75:1090; TLS 1974 p. 721)

1370 GRIPE, Maria (Kristina). *In the Time of the Bells.* **Gr. 5–9. (Orig. Swedish pub.**
✓ **1965.)**

Young Prince Arvid's disregard for his royal duties bodes ill for the kingdom, until the astrologers discover that his "whipping boy" is his brother and true heir to the throne.

Trans. by Sheila La Farge, illus. by Harold Gripe, Delacorte, 1976, 208 pp., o.p.

(BL 73:600, 606; CCBB 30:76; HB 53:51; KR 44:982; SLJ Jan 1977 p. 92; TLS 1978 p. 767)

1371 HALAM, Ann (pseud. of Gwyneth A. Jones). *The Daymaker.* **Gr. 7–10. (Orig.**
✓ **British pub. 1987.)**

While studying magic at Covenant School, ten-year-old Zanne discovers a hidden cache of forgotten machines and searches for the legendary Daymaker, which can make machines run without magic. In the sequel, *Transformations* (1988), Zanne, now a covener, is sent to investigate a community infected with black magic by a relic from a long-dead technological world.

Orchard, 1987, 173 pp., o.p.

(BL 84:466, 478; CCBB 41:28; HB 64:70; KR 55:992; SLJ Oct 1987 p. 138; Suth 4:155; TLS 1987 p. 1205; VOYA 10:287)

HALE, F. J. *Ogre Castle.* See Chapter 10, Witchcraft and Sorcery Fantasy.

HAMBLY, Barbara. *Dragonsbane.* See Chapter 10, Witchcraft and Sorcery Fantasy.

1372 HAMBLY, Barbara. *The Ladies of Mandrigyn.* **Gr. 10 up.**

The women of Mandrigyn trick Sun Wolf, a mercenary captain, into rescuing their men from the wizard who has conquered their city. The sequels are *The Witches of Wenshar*

(1987) and *The Dark Hand of Magic* (1990). The first two titles have been published together as *The Unschooled Wizard* (Doubleday, 1984–1987).

Ballantine, 1984, pap., 320 pp. (0-345-30919-7)

(BL 80:1378; LJ 109:599)

HAMBLY, Barbara. *The Time of the Dark.* See Chapter 5C, Travel to Other Worlds.

HARDY, Lyndon. *Secret of the Sixth Magic.* See Chapter 10, Witchcraft and Sorcery Fantasy.

1373   HARPER, Tara K. *Wolfwalker.* **(Tales of the Wolves, book 1). Gr. 7–12.**

Healer and wolfwalker Dion, her wolf companion Gray Hishn, and her twin brother, Rhom, join Aranur's band in an adventurous journey to rescue Aranur's sister and cousins from slave raiders. The sequels are *Shadow Leader* (1991) and *Storm Runner* (1993).

Ballantine, 1990, pap., 310 pp. (0-345-36539-9)

(Kliatt Sept 1990 p. 21; LJ May 15, 1990 p.99; VOYA 13:297, 14:13)

HARRIS, Deborah Turner. *The Burning Stone.* See Chapter 10, Witchcraft and Sorcery Fantasy.

1374   HARRIS, Geraldine (Rachel). *Prince of the Godborn* **(Seven Citadels quartet,**
✓   book 1). Gr. 7–10. (Orig. British pub. 1982.)

Prince Kerish of Galkis is chosen to journey to the seven citadels of the sorcerers to find seven keys that will save his land from its enemies. *The Children of the Wind* (1983), *The Dead Kingdom* (1983), and *The Seventh Gate* (1984) complete the quartet.

Greenwillow, 1983, 186 pp., o.p.; Dell, 1987, pap. (0-440-95407-X)

(BBJ:71; BL 79:770, 777, 86:905; CCBB 36:127; HB 59:312; KR 50:1335; SLJ Nov 1983 p. 93; Suth 3:175; VOYA 6:215)

HARRIS, Rosemary (Jeanne). *The Moon in the Cloud.* See Chapter 5B, Myth Fantasy.

1375   HARRISON, Harry. *The Hammer and the Cross.* **Gr. 10 up.**

Shef, half Christian Norman and half pagan Norse, develops his own religion in an attempt to free an alternate ninth-century England from both sets of invaders.

Tor, 1993, 480 pp. (0-312-85439-0)

(BL 90:132, 140; KR 61:1035)

1376   HARRISON, M(ichael) John. *The Pastel City* **(Virconium series, book 1). Gr. 10**
up. (Orig. British pub. 1971.)

Poet and swordsman Cromis vows to help Queen Methret of Virconium in her battle against the Northern Barbarians who have released powerful ancient golems. The sequels are: *A Storm of Wings* (1979), *The Floating Gods* (Pocket, 1983; British title: *In Virconium,* 1982), and *Virconium Nights* (Ace, 1984).

Doubleday, 1972, 158 pp., o.p.

(BL 69:620, 644; KR 40:1164; LJ 97:3932)

1377   HAZEL, Paul. *Yearwood* **(Finnbranch trilogy, book 1). Gr. 10 up.**

Finn, the bastard son of a Kell sorceress, sets out to find his birthfight and discovers that his father was actually the High King. The sequels are: *Undersea* (1982) and *Winter King* (1985). *The Wealdwife's Tale* (Avon, 1993) is also set in West Redding.

Little, 1980, 276 pp., o.p.

(HB 56:448; KR 48:150; SLJ Apr 1980 p. 124; VOYA 3[June 1980]:28, 3[Oct 1980]:32, 4[Aug 1981]:48)

1378 HEARNE, Betsy (Gould). *South Star.* **Gr. 4–7.**

After her parents' murder, Megan, a girl giant, flees the Screamer and follows the South Star across a vast plain and plateau toward a colony of giants. The sequel is *Home* (1979).

Illus. by Trina Schart Hyman, Atheneum, 1977, 84 pp., o.p.

(BL 74:375; CCBB 31:78; HB 53:662; KR 45:990; SLJ Oct 1977 p. 112)

1379 HELPRIN, Mark. *Winter's Tale.* **Gr. 10 up.**

Peter Lake escapes from a gang of murderous Manhattan thugs on the back of a flying milk-wagon horse, in this fast-moving Dickensian tale of romance, comedy, and adventure set in the year 2000.

Harcourt, 1983, 608 pp. (0-15-197203-6); Pocket, 1990, pap., 704 pp. (0-671-72707-9)

(BBS:58; BL 79:1421; HB 60:229; KR 51:717; LJ 108:1502)

1380 HENRY, Maeve. *The Witch King.* **Gr. 3–6. (Orig. British pub. 1987.)**

Fifteen-year-old Robert dreams that he must go to the City, where, according to prophesy, a Witch King will come from the sea to destroy it.

Orchard, 1985, 126 pp., o.p.

(BBC:25; BL 84:1609; CCBB 41:206; KR 56:363; SLJ June–July 1988 p. 104)

1381 HILL, Douglas (Arthur). *Blade of the Poisoner.* **Gr. 6–10.**

Three disciples of the good sorcerer Cyrl rescue 12-year-old Jarral from the malevolent Mephtik, who has cursed the boy with a deadly wound, and the four travel to find Cyrl and undo the curse. The sequel is *Master of Fiends* (1988).

Macmillan, 1987, 192 pp., o.p.; Bantam, 1989, pap., 224 pp. (0-553-27717-0)

(BL 84:466, 480; KR 55:1240; SLJ Oct 1987 p. 139; VOYA 10:178)

HOBAN, Russell C(onwell). *The Mouse and His Child.* See Chapter 1, Allegorical Fantasy and Literary Fairy Tales.

1382 HODGELL, P(atricia) C(hristine). *God Stalk.* **Gr. 10 up.**

In flight after her home is destroyed, Jame, one of the last of the magical race of Kencyrs, finds refuge and new friends in Taitastigon, where she becomes involved in political, religious, and magical intrigues. The sequel is *Dark of the Moon* (1985).

Macmillan, 1982, 293 pp., o.p.

(BL 79:189, 198; LJ 107:1772)

1383 HOFFMAN, Lee. *Change Song.* **Gr. 10 up.**

Young Dorey joins forces with a Nightman named Ryik, whose job it is to control the elements with magic, in an attempt to save the world from destruction by uncontrollable natural forces.

Doubleday, 1972, 203 pp., o.p.

(BL 68:931, 940; KR 40:15; LJ 97:217, 98:660)

1384 HUGHART, Barry. *Bridge of Birds: A Novel of an Ancient China That Never Was* **(Master Li series, book 1). Gr. 10 up.**

After young Lu Yu and the great sage Lio Kao set off in search of a magic root to cure the mysterious illness suffered by the children of the village of Ku-Fu, they encounter ghosts and danger along the way. World Fantasy Award, 1984. The sequels are *The Story of the Stone* (1988) and *Eight Skilled Gentlemen* (1991).

St. Martin's, 1984, 256 pp., o.p.; Ballantine, 1985, pap., 278 pp. (0-345-32138-3)

(Kliatt Fall 1985 p. 22; KR 52:314; LJ 109:997)

1385 HUGHES, Monica. *Sandwriter.* **Gr. 6–9. (Original Canadian pub. 1986.)**

Spoiled Princess Antia matures during her visit to the desert kingdom of Roshan, whose prince is rumored to be her future husband. The sequel is *The Promise* (1992).

Henry Holt, 1988, 159 pp., o.p.

(BBC:205; BBJ:71; BL 84:576, 1241, 1259; CCBB 41:138; KR 56:55; SLJ Mar 1988 p. 214; VOYA 11:139)

HUGHES, Robert Don. *The Faithful Traitor.* See Chapter 10, Witchcraft and Sorcery Fantasy.

1386 *Imaginary Lands.* Ed. by Robin McKinley. Gr. 7 up.

✓   Nine tales about imaginary worlds written by Peter Dickinson, P. C. Hodgell, Patricia McKillip, Robin McKinley, Joan D. Vigne, Robert Westall, and Jane Yolen. World Fantasy Convention Award, 1986.

Berkley, 1985, pap., o.p.; Greenwillow, 1986, 160 pp., LB(0-688-05213-4)

(BBS:61; BL 82:609, 621, 628; CCBB 39:152; HB 62:459; KR 54:870; SLJ May 1986 p. 106; TLS 1987 p. 857; VOYA 9:162)

1387 JAMES, Betsy. *Long Night Dance.* **Gr. 7 up.**

✓   Kat finds the rigid Upslope customs of her father's people too confining, but not until the night she rescues a wounded Rigi man from across the sea does she begin to declare her independence. In the sequel, *Dark Heart* (1992), Kat has chosen to live among her dead mother's people, but fails the ritual ceremony that would allow her to join the Women's Circle.

Dutton, 1989, 170 pp. (0-525-44485-8)

(BBS:59; BL 85:1894, 1903; CCBB 42:277; HB 65:775; HBG 1[July–Dec 1989]:81; KR 57:917; SLJ Aug 1989 p. 140; VOYA 12:226, 13:14)

1388 JANSSON, Tove (Marika). *Finn Family Moomintroll* **(Moomintroll series, book**
✓   **1). Gr. 4–6. (Orig. Finnish pub. 1949, orig. U.S. pub. Walck, 1951, entitled *The Happy Moomins;* retitled *Finn Family Moomintroll,* 1958.)**

Trouble comes to Moominvalley, home of the gnomelike Moomins, when Moomintroll, Sniff, and Snufkin bring home a hobgoblin's hat. The sequels are *Moominsummer Madness* (1961; Farrar, 1991), *Moominland Midwinter* (1962; Farrar, 1992), *Tales from Moominvalley* (1964), *The Exploits of Moominpappa* (1966), *Moominpappa at Sea* (1967; Farrar, 1993), *A Comet in Moominland* (1959, 1968; Farrar, 1991), *Moominvalley in November* (1971), *Moomin, Mymble and Little My* (published in Sweden; Nils Holgersson Award, Best Swedish Children's Book, 1953), and *Moominpappa's Memoirs* (1994).

Trans. by Elizabeth Portch, illus. by the author, Walck, 1958, 1965, 170 pp., o.p.; Farrar, 1989, 174 pp., o.p.

(CCBB 5:74; Ch&Bks:275; HBG 1(July–Dec 1989):81; LJ 77:653)

1389 JONES, Adrienne. *The Hawks of Chelney.* **Gr. 7–9.**

✓   In this haunting tale, a lonely boy named Siri is persecuted by superstitious village elders because of his friendship with the ospreys, "the Devil's servants."

Illus. by Stephen Gammell, Harper, 1978, 245 pp., o.p.

(BL 74:1108; CCBB 32:45; HB 54:283; KR 46:640; SLJ Apr 1978 p. 94; VOYA 1[Aug 1978]:35)

1390 **JONES, Diana Wynne.** *Cart and Cwidder* **(The Dalemark trilogy). Gr. 6–9.**
✓   **(Orig. British pub. 1975.)**

Moril inherits an ancient cwidder, a lutelike instrument, whose mystical powers save Moril and his family from the murderous Southern warriors. *Drowned Ammet* (1978; see below) and *The Spellcoats* (1979; see below) are also set in the land of Dalemark.

Atheneum, 1977, 193 pp., o.p.

(BL 73:1014; CCBB 30:161; HB 53:443; KR 45:224; SLJ May 1977 p. 70; TLS 1975 p. 764; VOYA 13:229)

1391 **JONES, Diana Wynne.** *Castle in the Air.* **Gr. 6–9. (Orig. British pub. 1990.)**
✓   Abdulla the carpet merchant's daydreams about a princess, a genie, and a villain become reality after he flies off on a shabby magic carpet. This story is related to *Howl's Moving-Castle* (1986; see Chapter 10, Witchcraft and Sorcery Fantasy).

Greenwillow, 1991, 208 pp. (0-688-09686-7)

(BL 87:1502, 88:873, 932; CC 1992 Suppl., p. 58; CCBB 44:143; HB 67:206; HBG 2:274; JHC 1992 Suppl. p. 61; KR 59:249; SLJ Apr 1991 p. 141)

JONES, Diana Wynne. *Charmed Life.* See Chapter 8, Time Travel Fantasy.

1392 **JONES, Diana Wynne.** *Drowned Ammet* **(The Dalemark trilogy). Gr. 6–9. (Orig.**
✓   **British pub. 1977.)**

Mitt's plot to revenge his father's death misfires, and he escapes by ship to the Holy Islands. *Cart and Cwidder* (1977; see above) and *The Spellcoats* (1979; see below) are also set in the land of Dalemark.

Atheneum, 1978, 255 pp., o.p.

(BL 74:1255; CCBB 31:161; HB 54:403; KR 46:177; SLJ Apr 1978 p. 85; TLS 1978 p. 377)

1393 **JONES, Diana Wynne.** *The Homeward Bounders.* **Gr. 6–9. (Orig. British pub.**
✓   **1981.)**

When Jamie accidentally stumbles on the headquarters of "Their" war games, "They" discard him to the worlds on the Bounds. There he joins other Homeward Bounders in a battle to banish "Them."

Greenwillow, 1981, 224 pp. (0-688-00678-7)

(BL: 78:98, 108; CCBB 35:12; HB 57:542; JHC:374, KR 49:1164; SLJ Sept 1981 p. 137; TLS 1981 pp. 339, 1361)

JONES, Diana Wynne. *The Magicians of Caprona.* See Chapter 10, Witchcraft and Sorcery Fantasy.

JONES, Diana Wynne. *The Power of Three.* See Chapter 5B, Myth Fantasy.

1394 **JONES, Diana Wynne.** *The Spellcoats* **(The Dalemark trilogy). Gr. 6–10. (Orig. British pub. 1979.)**

Tanaqui and her orphaned brother and sisters must flee their village because they look like the enemy Heathen. During their voyage, Tanaqui weaves their story into rugcoats, which prove to have magical powers. This story is set in the prehistory of Dalemark, the setting for *Cart and Cwidder* (1979; see above) and *Drowned Ammet* (1978; see above).

Atheneum, 1979, 249 pp., o.p.

(CCBB 33:111; HB 55:669; KR 47:1072; SLJ Nov 1979 p. 89; VOYA 2[Feb 1980]:30)

1395 **JONES, McClure.** *Cast Down the Stars.* **Gr. 7–10.**

Glory and her friend, Honor, must repair a gap in the ancient serpent line to keep out barbarian invaders.

Holt, 1978, 186 pp., o.p.

(BL 75:178; CCBB 32:100; HB 55:68; SLJ Dec 1978 p. 53)

1396   **JORDAN, Robert.** *The Eye of the World* **(The Wheel of Time Saga, book 1). Gr.**
✓   **10 up.**

Rand, Matrim, and Perrin leave their farming village with a saidar, or witch, after it
becomes clear that the Dark One has marked them for death. The sequels are *The Great
Hunt* (1990), *The Dragon Reborn* (1991), *The Shadow Rising* (1992), *The Fires of
Heaven* (1993), and *Lord of Chaos* (1994).

Tor, 1990, 670 pp., o.p., pap., 1990 (0-8125-1181-6)

(BBS:59; BL 86:218, 220, 87:968, 1478; KR 57:1791; LJ Feb 15, 1990 p. 215; VOYA 13:116, 14:10, 73)

1397   **JORDAN, Sherryl.** *Winter of Fire.* **Gr. 7–12. (Orig. New Zealand pub. 1992.)**
✓   After Elsha rises from slave labor in the Quelled mines to become the powerful firelord,
she speaks out against the dehumanizing Chosen enslavement of the Quelled.

Scholastic, 1993, 336 pp. (0-590-45288-6)

(BL 90: 1358; CCBB 46:214; HBG 4[Fall 1993]:309; JHC 1993 Suppl. p. 77; KR 61:62; SLJ Mar 1993 p.
221; VOYA 16:41)

1398   **KAY, Guy Gavriel.** *A Song for Arbonne.* **Gr. 10 up. (Orig. Canadian pub. 1992.)**

While the neighboring kingdoms of Arbonne, ruled by courtly love, and Gorhaut, ruled
by ambition, prepare for war, young Blaise flees Gorhaut and allies himself with the powerful Arbonnian troubadour, Bertran.

Crown, 1993, 513 pp. (0-51759312-2); NAL, 1994, pap. (0-451-45332-8)

(BL 89:878, 886; KR 60:1339)

1399   **KELLEHER, Victor (pseud. of Michael Kitchener).** *Brother Night.* **Gr. 6–9.**
✓   **(Orig. Australian pub. 1991.)**

Rabon learns that Lal, the ugly swamp creature, is his twin brother, and that both are destined to rule the land.

Illus. by Peter Clarke, Walker, 1991, 179 pp (0-8027-8100-4)

(BL 87:1955; CCBB 44:241; HBG 2:275; JHC 1992 Suppl., p. 62; SLJ May 1991 p. 111; VOYA 14:244,
15:9)

1400   **KELLEHER, Victor (pseud. of Michael Kitchener).** *The Red King.* **Gr. 6–9.**
✓   **(Orig. Australian pub. 1989.)**

Timkin, a young acrobat and slave, joins an old thief named Petie, a huge bear named
Bruno, and a monkey named Crystal in their efforts to dethrone the evil Red King.

Dial, 1990, 185 pp., o.p.; Oxford Univ. Pr., 1991, pap. (0-19-506976-5)

(BBJ:72; BL 86:1540, 1555; CC:513; CCBB 43:269; HBG 1[Jan–June 1990]: 256; JHC1991 Suppl. p. 74;
KR 58:650; SLJ July 1990 p. 89; VOYA 13:116, 14: 12)

1401   **KENDALL, Carol (Seeger).** *The Firelings.* **Gr. 7–9. (Orig. British pub. 1981.)**
✓   Marked by his fellow Firelings as a sacrifice to appease the Volcano, a boy named Tacky-
obbie runs away and manages to fulfill an old prophecy. Mythopoetic Fantasy Award,
1983.

Atheneum, 1982, 252 pp., o.p.

(BL 78:1161; CCBB 35:151; HB 58:299; SLJ May 1982 p. 70; TLS 1981 p. 1065; VOYA 5[Oct 1982]:49)

1402   **KENDALL, Carol (Seeger).** *The Gammage Cup* **(British title: *The Minnipins*).**
✓✓   **Gr. 4–7.**

Four nonconformists banished to the mountains by their fellow Minnipins risk their lives
to save the country when it is invaded by the Mushroom People. John Newbery Medal

Honor Book, 1960. *The Whisper of Glocken* (1965; see below) takes place in the same land at a later time period.

Illus. by Erik Blegvad, Harcourt, 1959, o.p., 1990, pap., 283 pp. (0-15-230575-0); Peter Smith, 1992 (0-8446-6564-9)

(BBC:207; BL 56:248; CC:513; Ch&Bks:287; Eakin:187; HB 34:477; LJ 85:845; Tymn:99–100)

1403 **KENDALL, Carol (Seeger).** *The Whisper of Glocken.* **Gr. 5–7.**

✓ Five Minnipins become heroes in the course of adventures forced on them when flooding drives them from their homes. This story is set in a later time period than *The Gammage Cup* (1959; see above).

Illus. by Imero Gobbato, Harcourt, 1965, o.p., 1986, pap., 256 pp. (0-15-295699-9); Peter Smith, 1992 (0-8446-6574-6)

(BL 62:331; CCBB 19:84; Eakin:187; HB 42:54; KR 33:1042; LJ 90:5097)

1404 **KENNEALY (Morrison), Patricia.** *The Copper Crown* **(Tales of Aeron trilogy, book 1). Gr. 10 up.**

High Queen Aeron of Keltia proposes an alliance with Earth, precipitating a war with two hostile planetary systems, fought with magic as well as technology, in this blend of science fiction and fantasy. The sequel is *The Throne of Scone: A Novel of the Keltiad* (1986). *The Silver Branch: A Novel of the Keltiad* (NAL, 1988) is a prequel to both books. Kennealy's Tales of Arthur series (see *The Hawk's Gray Feather* [NAL, 1990] in Chapter 5B, Myth Fantasy) is set in the same world, 1,500 years earlier.

Bluejay, 1984, o.p.; NAL, 1986, pap., 432 pp. (0-451-45050-7)

(KR 52:936; LJ 109:2301; VOYA 8:364)

KENNEALY (Morrison), Patricia. *The Hawk's Gray Feather: A Book of the Keltiad.* See Chapter 5B, Myth Fantasy.

KERR, Katharine. *Daggerspell.* See Chapter 10, Witchcraft and Sorcery Fantasy.

1405 **KERR, Katharine.** *A Time of Exile: A Novel of the Westlands* **(Westlands series, vol. 1). Gr. 10 up.**

Half-elven Lord Rhodry grows to accept his elven heritage with the help of Wizard Aderyn and Master Wizard Nevyn. The sequels are *A Time of Omens* (1992), *Days of Blood and Fire* (1993), and *Days of Air and Darkness* (1994). Kerr's Deverry series is set in the same world: *Daggerspell* (1986; see Chapter 10, Witchcraft and Sorcery Fantasy), *Darkspell* (1987), *The Bristling Wood* (1989), and *Dragon Revenant* (1990).

Doubleday, 1991, 416 pp., o.p.; Bantam, 1992, pap. (0-553-29813-5)

(BL 87:1282, 1283; KR 59:510; LJ Mar 15, 1991 p. 119; VOYA 14.323)

1406 **KING, Stephen.** *The Eyes of the Dragon.* **Gr. 9 up.**

✓ After old King Roland mysteriously dies by poison, his eldest son, Peter, is imprisoned for the crime. Thomas, the younger son, assumes the throne, with the evil magician, Flagg, as his advisor.

Illus. by David Palladini, Viking, 1987, 336 pp. (0-670-81458-X); NAL, 1987, pap. (0-451-16658-2)

(BBS:59; BL 83:370, 84:856; LJ Dec 1, 1986 p. 141; SLJ June–July 1987 p. 116; VOYA 10:121)

1407 **KING, Stephen.** *The Gunslinger* **(The Dark Tower trilogy, vol. 1). Gr. 10 up.**

A young gunslinger stalking a man in black befriends a boy with amnesia, and together they travel across a vast desert and into a long tunnel through the mountains. The sequels are *The Drawing of the Three* (1989) and *The Wastelands* (1992). This story was originally serialized in *The Magazine of Fantasy and Science Fiction* between 1978 and 1981 and was published in a limited edition in 1982.

Illus. by Michael Whelan, NAL, 1988, pap., 224 pp. (0-451-16052-5)

(BBS:59; BL 84:1755, 1757; KR 56:1019; SHC:698)

1408 *Kingdoms of Sorcery.* **Ed. by Lin Carter. Gr. 10 up.**

Sixteen British and American tales of heroic fantasy, whose authors include J. R. R. Tolkien and Richard Adams.

Doubleday, 1976, 218 pp., o.p.

(BL 72:1393; KR 43:1308)

1409 **KIRWAN-VOGEL, Anna.** *The Jewel of Life.* **Gr. 5–8.**

Apprenticed to old Master Crowe the apothecary, Duffy is thrilled to discover that his new job involves magic and travel to other worlds in search of the Philosopher's stone, or Jewel of Life.

Illus. by David Wilgus, Harcourt, 1991, 128 pp. (0-15-200750-4)

(BL 87:1956; CCBB 44:241; HBG 2:269; KR 59:605; SLJ June 1990 p. 110; VOYA 14:45)

1410 **KISLING, Lee.** *The Fools' War.* **Gr. 5–9.**

✓ Clemmy, fifteen, is asked to intercede with a blind miracle man to convince God to make Lady Libby fall in love with King Fernholtz, and ends up saving Mulberia from Turkish invaders.

Harper, 1992, 166 pp., LB(0-06-020837-6)

(BL 89:418; CCBB 46:181; HBG 4[Spring. 1993]:72; KR 60:1379; SLJ Oct 1992 p. 118)

1411 **KOLLER, Jackie French.** *The Dragonling.* **Gr. 2–4.**

Nine-year-old Derek befriends an orphaned dragonling after its mother is killed by village hunters, and vows to help the baby dragon find his home in the valley of dragons. The sequel is *A Dragon in the Family* (1993).

Illus. by Judith Marshall, Little, Brown, 1990, 60 pp. (0-316-50148-4)

(BL 87:1059; HBG 2[July–Dec 1990]:67; KR 58:1674; SLJ Feb 1991 p. 71)

1412 **KURTZ, Katherine.** *The Bishop's Heir* **(Histories of King Kelson, vol. 1). Gr. 10**
✓ **up.**

King Kelson of Gwynedd must deal with a resurgence of the ancient conflict between the human and Deryni races. The sequels are *The King's Justice* (1985) and *The Quest for Saint Camber* (1986). The Chronicles of Deryni (see *The Deryni Archives,* below) is a related series.

Ballantine, 1984, 1985, 1987, pap., 384 pp. (0-345-34761-7)

(BL 86:905; KR 52:829; LJ 109:2162; SLJ Jan 1985 p. 92; VOYA 8:55, 364)

1413 **KURTZ, Katherine.** *The Deryni Archives* **(The Chronicles of Deryni). Gr. 10 up.**

✓ Nine stories about the magical Deryni, including "Lords of Sorandor," an unpublished novella written in 1965, which served as the basis for *Deryni Rising* (1970). The series includes *Deryni Rising* (1970, 1976), *Deryni Checkmate* (1972, 1976), *High Deryni* (1973, 1982), and *Deryni Magic* (1991). These books are related to three other series: The Legends of Camber of Culdi, which includes *Camber of Culdi* (1976), *Saint Camber* (1978), and *Camber the Heretic* (1980), The Histories of King Kelson, which includes *The Bishop's Heir* (1984) (see this section), *The King's Justice* (1985), and *The Quest for Saint Camber* (1986); and The Heirs of Saint Camber trilogy, which includes *The Harrowing of Gwynned* (1989; see this section), *King Javin's Year* (1992), and *The Bastard Prince* (1994).

Ballantine, 1986, pap., 325 pp. (0-345-32678-4)

(BBS:59; BL 82:1667, 1683; LJ Aug 1986 p. 174; SLJ Nov 1986 p. 116; Tymn:101–104; VOYA 9:238)

1414   KURTZ, Katherine. *The Harrowing of Gwynedd* **(The Heirs of Saint Camber trilogy, book 1). Gr. 10 up.**

In an earlier period of Gwynedd's history than the author's Histories of King Kelson trilogy—*The Bishop's Heir* (1984; see above), *The King's Justice* (1985), and *The Quest for Saint Camber* (1986)—three young friends try to save the outlawed race of Deryni, humans with magical powers, from extinction. The sequels are *King Javin's Year* (1992) and *The Bastard Prince* (1994).

Ballantine, 1989, 400 pp. (0-345-33259-8), pap (0-345-36314-0)

(BBS:60; BL 85:730, 731; KR 56:1781; LJ Feb 15, 1989 p. 179; VOYA 12:166)

1415   LACKEY, Mercedes. *Arrows of the Queen* **(The Heralds of Valdemar trilogy, book 1). Gr. 7 up.**

Talia, a runaway Holdgirl, is chosen to become a trainee herald in the queen's elite guard and to care for young Princess Elspeth, heir to the throne. The sequels are *Arrow's Flight* (1987) and *Arrow's Fall* (1988). The author's Last Herald Mage series (*Magic's Pawn*, 1989; see below; *Magic's Price*, 1990; and *Magic's Promise*, 1990), and her Mage Winds trilogy (*Winds of Fate*, 1991; see below; *Winds of Change*, 1992; and *Winds of Fury*, 1993) are set in the same world. *The Black Gryphon* (1994), written by Lackey and Larry Dixon, is set in Valdemar 1,000 years earlier. *Storm Warning* (1994) is the first book in the author's Mage Storms trilogy, also set in Valdemar.

DAW, 1987, 1991, pap., 320 pp. (0-88677-378-4)

(BL 86:905; VOYA 10:131)

1416   LACKEY, Mercedes. *By the Sword.* **Gr. 10–12.**

Kerowyn, granddaughter of a sorceress, chases bandits who used sorcery to kidnap her future sister-in-law. This story connects the author's Heralds of Valdemar trilogy (*Arrows of the Queen*, 1987; see above; *Arrow's Flight*, 1987; and *Arrow's Fall*, 1988), with her Oaths series (*Oathbound*, 1988; and *Oathbreakers*, 1989), and is related to both her Last Herald Mage series (*Magic's Pawn*, 1989; see below; *Magic's Price*, 1990; and *Magic's Promise*, 1990) and her Mage Winds trilogy (*Winds of Fate*, 1991; see below; *Winds of Change*, 1992; and *Winds of Fury*, 1993).

DAW, 1991, pap., 492 pp. (0-88677-463-2)

(Kliatt Apr 1991 p. 20; VOYA 14:110)

1417   LACKEY, Mercedes. *Magic's Pawn* **(The Last Herald Mage trilogy, book 1).**
✓ **Gr. 10 up.**

Vanyel, the last of Valdemar's Herald Mages, grows to accept his homosexuality but is grief stricken when his lover is killed in a blood feud, in this fantasy for mature readers. The sequels are *Magic's Price* (1990) and *Magic's Promise* (1990). This series is set in the same world as the author's Heralds of Valdemar trilogy (*Arrows of the Queen*, 1987; see above; *Arrow's Flight*, 1987; and *Arrow's Fall*, 1988) and her Mage Winds trilogy (*Winds of Fate*, 1991; see below; *Winds of Change*, 1992; and *Winds of Fury*, 1993). *The Black Gryphon* (1994), written by Lackey and Larry Dixon, is set in Valdemar 1,000 years earlier.

DAW, 1989, pap., 349 pp. (0-88677-352-0)

(BL 85:1783, 1817; Kliatt Sept 1989, p. 18; LJ June 15, 1989 p. 83; VOYA 13:14, 38)

1418   LACKEY, Mercedes. *Winds of Fate* **(The Mage Winds trilogy, vol. 1). Gr. 10 up.**
✓ Darkwind, the Tayledras scout, meets Princess Elspeth while she searches for a mage

who can save the realm of Valdemar from the wizardry of Ancar of Hardorn. The sequels are *Winds of Change* (1992) and *Winds of Fury* (1993). This trilogy follows the author's Heralds of Valdemar (1987–1988; see above) and Last Herald Mage (1989–1990; see above) trilogies. *Storm Warning* (1994) is the first book in the author's Mage Storms trilogy, also set in Valdemar.

NAL, 1991, pap., 384 pp. (0-88677-489-6); DAW, 1992, pap. (0-88677-516-7)

(BL 87:2108, 2111; LJ Oct 15, 1991 p. 126; SLJ May 1992, p. 152; VOYA 14:384)

LACKEY, Mercedes, and EMERSON, Ru. *Fortress of Frost and Fire.* See Chapter 10, Witchcraft and Sorcery Fantasy.

1419 **LAUMER, (John) Keith.** *The Shape Changer: A Science Fiction Novel.* **Gr. 10 up.**

After examining a mysterious treasure, Lafayette O'Leary suddenly finds himself changing from shape to shape and traveling from world to world.

Putnam, 1972, 189 pp., o.p.

(BL 68:753, 766; LJ 97:790)

1420 **LAWHEAD, Stephen R.** *In the Hall of the Dragon King* **(The Dragon King trilogy, vol. 1). Gr. 6–12**

An evil sorcerer has kidnapped Dragon King Eskevar in order to put Prince Jaspin on the throne, and it is up to young Quentin to warn the queen and rescue the king. The sequels are *The Warlords of Nin* (1983, 1989) and *The Sword and the Flame* (1984).

Crossway, 1982, 1982, 1989, pap., 351 pp., o.p.; Good News, 1990, pap. (0-89107-563-1); Avon, 1992, pap. (0-380-71629-1)

(KR 50:651; SLJ Nov 1982 p. 101; VOYA 13:230)

1421 **LAWRENCE, Ann (Margaret).** *The Half Brothers.* **Gr. 5–8.**

✓ All three of Duchess Ambra's cousins want to marry her, but only one is willing to let her be herself.

Walck, 1973, 172 pp., o.p.

(BL 70:341; CCBB 27:97; HB 50:51; LJ 99:891; Suth 2:274; TLS 1973 p. 685)

1422 **LAWRENCE, Louise (pseud. of Elizabeth Rhoda Holden).** *The Warriors of Taan.* **Gr. 7–11. (Orig. British pub. 1986.)**

Elana, destined to become the Reverend Mother of the Sisterhood of Taan, and Khian, heir to the throne, meet by chance and fall in love, after their world has been overrun by the Otherworlders.

Harper, 1988, 249 pp., o.p.

(BL 84:993, 1001; HB 64:789; KR 56:56; SLJ Feb 1988 p. 84; VOYA 10:289)

1423 **LEE, John.** *The Unicorn Quest.* **Gr. 7–12.**

Jarrod and Marianna are sent in search of a unicorn needed to save their world from an enemy invasion. The sequel is *The Unicorn Dilemma: A Saga of War and Magic* (1988).

Tor, 1986, 381 pp., o.p., 1992, pap. (0-8125-2055-6)

(Kliatt Spring 1986 p. 22; VOYA 9:163)

1424 **LEE, Tanith.** *Anackire* **(The Wars of Vis trilogy). Gr. 10 up.**

Young Prince Kesarh's ambitions for power over the land of Karmiss are complicated by his daughter, whose mother is an incarnation of the goddess Anackire, and by the appearance of a long-lost hero's son. This is the sequel to *The Storm Lord* (1978, 1986) and is followed by *The White Serpent* (1988).

DAW, 1983, pap., 414 pp., o.p.

(BBS:60; BL 80:469; VOYA 7:38)

1425 **LEE, Tanith.** *Black Unicorn.* **Gr. 7 up. (Orig. pub. in England.)**

✓ Tanaquil has always been able to mend anything, in spite of her sorceress mother's disappointment in her inability to perform magic, so when her catlike peeve finds some strange golden bones, Tanaquel reconstructs them into a unicorn.

Macmillan, 1991, 144 pp. (0-689-31575-9); Tor, 1993, pap. (0-8125-24599-4)

(BL 88:428; CCBB 45:67; HB 68:746; HBG 3[July–Dec 1991]:79; JHC 1992 Suppl. p. 62; KR 59:1288; SLJ Nov 1991 p. 134; VOYA 14:324, 15:9)

1426 **LEE, Tanith.** *Companions on the Road: Two Novellas.* **Gr. 10 up. (Orig. British pub. separately as** *Companions on the Road,* **1975, and** *The Winter Players,* **1976.)**

In "Companions on the Road," two soldiers and a "snatch purse" set off with the fabled cup of Avillis, but are pursued by three mysterious "undead": the evil Lord of Avillis, his son, and his daughter. In "The Winter Players," a wicked priest-lord uses a young man named Cyrdin and a seventeen-year-old priestess named Oaive as pawns in his attempt to gain power over a magical relic.

St. Martin, 1977, 256 pp., o.p.

(KR 45:1014; TLS 1976 p. 1242; Tymn:107, 108)

1427 **LEE, Tanith.** *Cyrion.* **Gr. 10 up. (Orig. pub. in England.)**

Seven short stories and a novella about a wanderer named Cyrion who uses logic to outwit sorcery.

DAW, 1982, pap., 304 pp. o.p.

(BL 79:483; LJ 107:1772; VOYA 6:45)

1428 **LEE, Tanith.** *Dark Castle, White Horse.* **Gr. 10 up. (Orig. British pub. separately as** *The Castle of Dark,* **1978 and** *Prince on a White Horse,* **1982.)**

In the first novella, "The Castle of Dark," a young harper must fight a fearsome creature to rescue a maiden; and in "Prince on a White Horse," a prince is puzzled by the angry maidens he meets and the useless battles he has fought.

DAW, 1986, pap., 302 pp., o.p.

(Kliatt 20 [Fall 1986]:26; LJ Apr 15, 1986 p. 98; TLS July 23, 1982 p. 794; VOYA 9:164)

1429 **LEE, Tanith.** *The Dragon Hoard.* **Gr. 4–6. (Orig. pub. in England.)**

The witch Maligna's angry gift to Prince Jasleth—that he become a raven for one hour every day—comes in handy after he joins a quest for the Dragon Hoard treasure.

Illus. by Graham Oakley, Farrar, 1971, 162 pp., o.p.

(HB 48:49; KR 39:1120; TLS 1971 p. 1511)

1430 **LEE, Tanith.** *East of Midnight.* **Gr. 10 up. (Orig. British pub. 1977.)**

Dekteon, a young slave, escapes through a Vortex Gate into a parallel world where he is tricked into exchanging lives with Zaister, the doomed Sun King-consort of the ruling Daughter of Night.

St. Martin, 1978, 175 pp., o.p.

(KR 46:334; TLS 1977 p. 1246; Tymn:109)

1431 **LEE, Tanith.** *A Heroine of the World.* **Gr. 10 up. (Orig. pub. in England.)**

Fourteen-year-old noblewoman Ara must escape from captivity by her country's invaders before she can fulfill a prophecy predicting her great powers.

DAW, 1989, pap., 448 pp. (0-88677-362-8)

(BL 85:1949, 1969; LJ Aug 1989 p. 167; VOYA 12:372)

1432 LEE, Tanith. *Sung in Shadow.* **Gr. 10 up. (Orig. pub. in England.)**

This love story about Romulan and Iuletta is a retelling of "Romeo and Juliette," set in a magical alternate Renaissance Italy.

DAW, 1983, pap., 349 pp., o.p.

(BL 79:1448; LJ 108:1019; VOYA 6:283)

1433 LE GUIN, Ursula K(roeber). *A Wizard of Earthsea* **(Earthsea quartet, vol. 1).**
✓✓ **Gr. 6 up.**

In this, the first volume of the Earthsea quartet, young Ged, studying the art of wizardry, accidentally conjures up a terrifying creature that threatens the existence of the entire world of Earthsea. Boston Globe Horn Book Award, 1969. In *The Tombs of Atuan* (Atheneum, 1971, 1985; Bantam, 1984, pap.), Ged, now a wizard, invades the forbidden undertomb and labyrinth of Atuan, forcing Tenar to choose between remaining as High Priestess to the Dark Ones or escaping from Atuan. *The Tombs of Atuan* was a John Newbery Medal Honor Book, 1972, a National Book Award finalist, 1972, and a Phoenix Award Honor Book, 1991. In *The Farthest Shore* (Atheneum, 1972, 1985; Bantam, 1984, pap.), Ged, now Archmage of Roke, and Prince Arren of Enlad make an arduous journey into the Shadow Kindgom of the dead to confront an evil mage who has upset the balance between life and death. *The Farthest Shore* won the National Book Award, 1973. In *Tehanu: The Last Book of Earthsea* (1990, 1991), Tenar, now a middle-aged widow, takes on the tasks of healing both an abused child named Therru, and Ged, who lost his magical powers in a battle to save the world. Nebula Award, Best Novel, 1991.

Illus. by Ruth Robbins, Parnassus, 1968, o.p.; Bantam, 1975, 1984, pap., 192 pp. (0-553-26250-5); Macmillan, 1991, 208 pp. (0-689-31720-4)

(BBJ:73; BL 65:546, 901, 80:95; CC:521; CCBB 22:144; Ch&Bks:254; HB 45:59; JHC:380; LJ 94:2073, 2104, 4582; TLS 1973 p. 379, 1977 p. 863; Tymn:110, 111)

1434 LEVIN, Betty (Lowenthal). *The Ice Bear.* **Gr. 6–8.**
✓ After the evil Lord Uris orders the absent king's great white bear and her keeper killed, young Wat, a baker's assistant, helps the keeper's daughter, Kaila, escape with the last bear cub.

Greenwillow, 1986, 192 pp., LB(0-688-06431-0)

(BBC:208; BBJ:73; BL 83:580; CCBB 40:91; HB 63:56; KR 54:1207; SLJ Oct 1986 p. 192; TLS 1987 p. 804; VOYA 9: 220)

1435 *Liavek.* Ed. by Will Shetterly and Emma Bull. Gr. 10 up.

Eleven tales set in the trading city of Liavek, at the mouth of the Cat River. Each story was written by a different author, including Gene Wolfe and Jane Yolen. *Liavek: The Players of Luck* (1986), *Liavek: Wizard's Row* (1987), and *Liavek: Spells of Binding* (1988) are companion works.

Berkley, 1985, pap., 288 pp., o.p.

(BBS:64; BL 81:1637, 1657; VOYA 8:325)

LINDGREN, Astrid. *The Brothers Lionheart.* See Chapter 1, Allegorical Fantasy and Literary Fairy Tales.

1436 LINDGREN, Astrid. *Ronia, the Robber's Daughter.* **Gr. 4–6. (Orig. Swedish**
✓ **pub. 1981.)**

Ronia and Birk, offspring of two rival robber chieftains, fall in love and run off together into the goblin and harpy-infested forest. Mildred L. Batchelder Award, 1984.

Viking, 1983, 176 pp., o.p.; Puffin, 1985, pap., 176 pp. (0-14-031720-1); Peter Smith, 1993 (0-8446-6649-1)

(BBC:208; BL 79:1095, 86:790; CC:523; Ch&Bks:274; HB 59:304; KR 51:459; SLJ Aug 1983 p. 67)

1437   LINDHOLM, Megan. *Luck of the Wheels* **(Ki series, book 4). Gr. 10 up.**

Ki and Vandien take on the challenge of transporting an unlikable youth with telepathic powers to a distant city, where they become involved in a rebel plot to seize the throne. This is the sequel to *Harpy's Flight* (1983), *The Windsingers* (1984), and *The Limbreth Gate* (1984).

Ace, 1989, pap., 256 pp., o.p.

(BBS: 60; BL 86:726, 736)

1438   LISLE, Janet Taylor. *The Lampfish of Twill.* **Gr. 5–7.**

✓   The fishcatchers of Twill believe all their problems are caused by huge lampfish, which they hunt and occasionally kill, but when old Zeke and young Eric are pulled down by the underwhirl into the lampfish's undersea world, they discover the truth about the creatures.

Illus. by Wendy Anderson Halperin, Orchard, 1991, 161 pp. LB(0-531-08563-5)

(CCBB 45:43; HB 68:72; HBG 3[July–Dec 1991]:69; KR 59:1288; SLJ Sept 1991 p. 256)

1439   LOGSTON, Anne. *Shadow* **(Shadow series, book 1). Gr. 7–12.**

After Shadow, a 500-year-old elf, steals a beautiful bracelet from a young nobleman in the medieval town of Allanmere, she is caught up in the intrigue brewing between the Council of Churches and the Guild of Thieves. The sequels are *Shadow Hunt* (1992) and *Shadow Dance* (1992).

Ace, 1991, pap., 185 pp. (0-441-75989-0)

(Kilatt Jan 1992 p. 18; VOYA 15:111)

1440   LONGYEAR, Barry B(rookes). *The God Box.* **Gr. 10 up.**

The gift of a magical many-drawered box that grants Korvas whatever he needs, but not whatever he wants, propels the former flying-carpet merchant on a perilous journey to fulfill a prophecy.

NAL, 1989, pap., 235 pp., o.p.

(BL 85:1435, 1456; LJ Apr 15, 1989 p. 102)

1441   LOVETT, Margaret (Rose). *The Great and Terrible Quest.* **Gr. 5–7. (Orig.**
✓✓   **British pub. 1967.)**

A runaway boy and a wounded knight join forces to search for the true heir to the throne.

Holt, 1967, 187 pp., o.p.

(BL 64:546; CCBB 21:30; HB 43:597; KR 35:879; LJ 92:4614; TLS 1967 p. 451)

1442   LUENN, Nancy. *Goldclimbers.* **Gr. 6–9.**

Fifteen-year-old apprentice goldsmith Aracco, who secretly longs for the adventurous life of the gold climbers who scale the mountainous cliffs above his village, decides, after his best friend's death in a climbing accident, to climb the mountains alone in search of the legendary golden city of Terenger.

Macmillan, 1991, 184 pp. (0-689-31585-6)

(BL 87:1869; CCBB 44:169; HBG 2:276; KR 59: 473; SLJ June 1991 p. 127; VOYA14:111, 15:10)

1443   LUKEMAN, Tim. *Witchwood.* **Gr. 10 up.**

In hopes of escaping from her life in the workhouse, orphaned Fiona attempts to revive the magic fading from the land of Therrilyn.

Pocket, 1984, 192 pp., o.p.

(BL 80:944, 965; KR 51:1150; LJ 108:2346)

1444   LYNN, Elizabeth A. *Watchtower* **(The Chronicles of Tornor, book 1). Gr. 10 up.**

Princess Sorren, disguised as a messenger, helps her brother, Errel, and his chief warrior, Ryke, to escape from imprisonment by the southern invaders who have captured their castle. They travel to Vanima, a utopian mountain community, where they learn the skills they need to defeat their enemies. World Fantasy Convention Award, Best Novel, 1980. The sequels are *The Dancers of Arun* (1979) and *The Northern Girl* (1980).

Ace, 1979, 1986, pap., 240 pp., o.p.

(BL 75:1203, 1212; KR 46:1346; SLJ Apr 1979 p. 75)

1445   MacAVOY, R(oberta) A(nn). *Lens of the World* **(Nazhuret Saga, vol. 1) Gr. 10**
✓   **up.**

Orphaned and undersized Nazhuret grows up in a military school, learns the trade of lens making, and eventually becomes a warrior who will save the king's life, in this story for mature readers. The sequels are *King of the Dead* (1991) and *The Belly of the Wolf* (1994).

Morrow, 1990, 288 pp. (0-688-09484-8); Avon, 1991, pap. (0-380-71016-1)

(BBS:61; BL 86:1666, 1668; KR 58:696; LJ May 15, 1990 p. 98; SLJ Dec 1990 p. 135)

1446   McCAFFREY, Anne (Inez). *Crystal Singer.* **Gr. 10 up.**
✓   Killashandra Ree uses her musical talent to become one of the most successful crystal miners on the planet of Ballybran. The sequels are *Killashandra* (1985) and *Crystal Line* (1992).

Ballantine, 1982, 1985, pap., 320 pp. (0-345-32786-1)

(BL 78:1394; LJ 107:1487; SHC:706; SLJ Nov 1982 p. 106; VOYA 5[Feb 1983]:45)

1447   McCAFFREY, Anne (Inez). *Dragonflight* **(The Dragonriders of Pern, vol. 1). Gr. 10 up. (Orig. British pub. 1968.)**

In this first volume of McCaffrey's series set on the dragon-filled planet of Pern, a young woman named Lessa joins the riders of the great winged dragons as they battle the deadly threads that periodically fall from the sky. The prequel is *Dragonsdawn* (1988). The sequels are *Dragonquest* (orig. British pub. 1971; Ballantine, 1979, 1981, pap.), *The White Dragon* (orig. British pub. 1978; Ballantine, 1979, 1980, pap.; Ultramarine, 1981), *Moreta: Dragon Lady of Pern* (Ballantine, 1983, 1984, pap.), *Nerilka's Story: A Pern Adventure* (Ballantine, 1986), *The Renegades of Pern* (1989), *All the Weyrs of Pern* (1991), *The Dolphins of Pern* (1994), and three books for younger readers: *Dragonsong* (1976; see below), *Dragonsinger* (1977), and *Dragondrums* (1979). *The Chronicles of Pern: First Fall* (1993) is a short story collection about the history of Pern. The story collection *The Girl Who Heard Dragons* (Tor, 1994) contains one Pern novella.

Walker, 1969, 309 pp., o.p.; Ballantine, 1978, 1981, 1986, pap., 303 pp. (0-345-33546-5)

(JHC:388; SHC:706; TLS 1969 p. 1215)

1448   McCAFFREY, Anne (Inez). *Dragonsong* **(The Harper-Hall trilogy, vol. 1). Gr.**
✓✓   **5–10.**

Menolly, angered by her people's refusal to let a "mere woman" become a Harper, runs away to make her home with a family of fire dragons. In *Dragonsinger* (1977, 1978, pap.) Menolly struggles through her first year of Harper training and continues to care for her brood of fire lizards. In *Dragondrums* (1979, 1980, pap.) Piemer, a friend of Menolly, is trained as a drummer and sent on a mysterious journey by the Masterharper of Pern. All three books were collected in *The Harper Hall of Pern* (Doubleday, 1979).

Macmillan, 1976, 204 pp. (0-689-30507-9); Bantam, 1977, 1986, pap., 192 pp. (0-553-23460-9)

(BL 72:1253, 1266, 80:353; CC:531; CCBB 29:177; Ch&Bks:263; HB 52:406; KR 44:391; SHC:706; SLJ Apr 1976 p. 91; Suth 2:294)

McGOWEN, Tom (Thomas E.). *The Magician's Apprentice.* See Chapter 10, Witchcraft and Sorcery Fantasy.

1449   McKENZIE, Ellen Kindt. *A Bowl of Mischief.* **Gr. 5–8.**

After the death of his wise adopted father, the fakir Phufadia, mischievous young Ranjii travels to the kingdom of Superus, whose people are starving while the selfish king gorges himself.

Henry Holt, 1992, 134 pp. (0-8050-2090-X)

(BL 89:598; HBG 4[Spring 1993]:73; KR 60:1446; SLJ Nov 1992 p. 95)

1450   McKENZIE, Ellen Kindt. *Taash and the Jesters.* **Gr. 5–7.**

An orphan named Taash and two court jesters attempt to foil the Duke of Xon's plot to take over the kingdom. The sequel is *Kashka* (1987).

Holt, 1968, 233 pp., o.p.; 1992, 245 pp. (0-8050-2381-X)

(BL 65:451, 901; HBG 4[Spring 1993]:83; KR 36:1048)

1451   McKIERAN, Dennis L. *Dragondoom.* **Gr. 10 up.**

A story in two parts about the dragon-slaying quests of twins Elgo and Elwyn, warrior prince and princess of Jord, and their mortal enemy, the dwarf lord Thork. This book is set in the same world as the author's Iron Tower trilogy: *The Dark Tide* (1984), *Shadows of Doom* (1984), and *The Darkest Day* (1984). His Silver Call duology, *Trek to Kaggen-Cor* (1986; see below) and *The Brega Path* (1986), is set several hundred years later.

Bantam, 1990, 485 pp. (0-553-28337-5)

(BBS:61; LJ Feb 15, 1990 p. 215; VOYA 13:118)

1452   McKIERNAN, Dennis L. *Trek to Kraggen-Cor* **(Silver Call duology, book 1). Gr. 6–12.**

Peregrin Fairhill and Cotton Buckleburr, two Warrow wee-folk, join a band of dwarves and the human Lord Kian to battle the evil spawn and regain the dwarf homeland. The sequel is *The Brega Path* (1986), and this duology is set several hundred years later in the same world as the author's Iron Tower trilogy: *The Dark Tide* (1984), *Shadows of Doom* (1984), and *The Darkest Day* (1984), as well as *Dragondoom* (1990; see above). *Tales of Mithgar* (Penguin, 1994) is a collection of stories set in the same world.

Doubleday, 1986, 188 pp., o.p.; NAL, 1989, pap. (0-451-15563-7)

(KR 54:429; Kliatt Sept 1987, p. 29; LJ May 15, 1986 p. 81; VOYA 9:239)

1453   McKILLIP, Patricia A(nne). *The Changeling Sea.* **Gr. 7 up.**

✓   Periwinkle curses the sea after her father's drowning, only to become enmeshed in an evil sea queen's curse on two princes switched at birth.

Macmillan, 1988, 139 pp. (0-689-31436-1); Ballantine, 1989, pap. (0-345-36040-0)

(BBJ:73; BL 85:151, 162; CCBB 42:15; HB 64:790; JHC:388; KR 56:1153; SLJ Nov1988 p. 127; VOYA 11:247, 12:13)

1454   McKILLIP, Patricia A(nne). *Cygnet and the Firebird.* **Gr. 10 up.**

Sorceress Nyx Ro and her cousin Meguet, guardian of the Cygnet, must protect Ro Holding from a powerful dragon-born mage. This book is related to *The Sorceress and the Cygnet* (1991; see below).

Ace, 1993, 240 pp. (0-441-12628-6)

(BL 90:132, 140; KR 61:898; SLJ May 1994 p. 143; VOYA 16:311)

1455   McKILLIP, Patricia A(nne). *The Forgotten Beasts of Eld.* **Gr. 6–9.**

✓✓   Sybel, a sorceress, lovingly raises an abandoned baby named Tam, only to discover that his real father is the greatest enemy of the man she loves. First World Fantasy Award, Best Novel, 1975.

Atheneum, 1974, 217 pp., o.p.

(BL 71:173, 767; CCBB 28:82; Ch&Bks:289; KR 42:743; LJ 99:2748)

1456   McKILLIP, Patricia A(nne). *Moon-Flash.* **Gr. 7–10.**

✓✓   Kyreol and her friend Terje set off in a boat to explore the world outside the boundaries of Riverworld, and in doing so, make some astonishing discoveries about the fate of Kyreol's mother and the true nature of their world. The sequel is *The Moon and the Face* (1985).

Atheneum, 1984, 150 pp., o.p.

(BL 81:636, 642; CCBB 38:10; Ch&Bks:289; HB 60:763; JHC:389; SLJ Dec 1984 p. 92; Suth 3:287; VOYA 8:56)

1457   McKILLIP, Patricia A(nne). *The Riddle-Master of Hed* **(The Star-Bearer tril-**
✓   **ogy, vol. 1). Gr. 6–9.**

Morgan, the peace-loving ruler of Hed, is driven to uncover the meaning of the three stars on his forehead. In *Heir of Sea and Fire* (1977, 1978, pap.), Raederle, Morgan's love, uses her magical powers to search for Morgan, who is inexplicably missing. In the final volume of this trilogy, *Harpist in the Wind* (1979, 1980, pap.), Morgan and Raederle battle numerous enemies during his struggle to become heir to the throne of the High One. All three books were collected in *Riddle of the Stars* (Science Fiction Book Club, 1979).

Atheneum, 1976, 240 pp., o.p.; Ballantine, 1978, 1985, pap. (0-345-33104-4)

(BBC:209; BL 73:468, 475; CC:532; CCBB 30:109; HB 52:625; JHC:389; Kliatt 12[Spring 1975]:13; KR 44:1044; SLJ Oct 1976 p. 119; Tymn:136–138)

1458   McKILLIP, Patricia A(nne). *The Sorceress and the Cygnet.* **Gr. 10 up.**

✓   Corleu crosses a forbidden threshold between the real world and legend in search of the mythical Cygnet, needed to rescue his people, the Wayfolk, who have become lost between worlds. *The Cygnet and the Firebird* (1993; see above) is a related story.

Ace, 1991 (0-441-77564-0), 1992, pap. (0-441-77567-5)

(BL 87:1458, 1461; Kliatt Apr 1992, p. 16; KR 59:444; LJ May 15, 1991 p. 111; SHC:707; SLJ Oct 1991 p. 160; VOYA 14:112)

1459   McKILLIP, Patricia A(nne). *The Throme of the Erril of Sherill.* **Gr. 4–6.**

Before permitting his daughter to wed Cnite Caerles, King Magnus orders the young man to bring him the Throme, an ancient magical document.

Illus. by Julia Noonan, Atheneum, 1973, 68 pp., o.p.

(BBS:61; CCBB 27:82; KR 41:686; LJ 98:2654; Tymn:135)

1460   McKINLEY, (Jennifer Carolyn) Robin (Turrell). *The Blue Sword* **(Damar**
✓✓   **series). Gr. 6–12.**

Harry Crewe is kidnapped by Corlath, King of the Damarians, and comes reluctantly to realize that they possess the same mysterious powers. John Newbery Medal Honor Book, 1983. The prequel is *The Hero and the Crown* (1984; see below), and *Deerskin* (1993; see Chapter 5B, Myth Fantasy) is a story for mature readers set at a later time. *A Knot in the Grain and Other Stories* (1994) contains four stories set in the world of Damar.

Greenwillow, 1982, 288 pp. (0-688-00938-7); Ace, 1982, pap. (0-441-06880-4)

(BBJ:73; BL 79:198, 247, 671, 980, 80:353, 86:785, 905; CCBB 36:112; Ch&Bks:249; HB 58:660, 59:330; JHC:389; SLJ Jan 1983 p. 86; Suth 3:287; VOYA 6:46)

McKINLEY, (Jennifer Carolyn) Robin (Turrell). *Deerskin.* See Chapter 5B, Myth Fantasy.

1461 **McKINLEY, (Jennifer Carolyn) Robin (Turrell).** *The Hero and the Crown*
✓✓ **(Damar series). Gr. 6–12.**

Princess Aerin of Damar becomes a legendary dragonslayer, fulfilling her destiny as savior of her kingdom, in this prequel to *The Blue Sword* (1982; see above) and *Deerskin* (1993; see Chapter 5B, Myth Fantasy). John Newbery Medal, 1985.

Greenwillow, 1984, 256 pp., LB(0-688-02593-5); Ace, 1987, pap. (0-441-32809-1)

(BL 81:211, 250, 86:905; CC:532; CCBB 38:30; Ch&Bks:289; HB 61:59; JHC:390; SLJ Oct 1984 p. 169; Suth 3:287; TLS 1985 p. 958; VOYA 7:388)

1462 **MACE, Elisabeth.** *Out There* **(British title:** *Ransome Revisited,* **1975). Gr. 7–10.**

An unnamed man undertakes a fearsome journey to escape his unhappy life and to find the legendary "Colony." *The Travelling Man* is the British sequel.

Greenwillow, 1978, 181 pp., o.p.

(BL 74:807; CCBB 31:145; KR 46:111; SLJ Mar 1978 p. 138)

1463 *Magic in Ithkar.* **Ed. by André Norton and Robert Adams. Gr. 10 up.**
✓ Thirteen tales set in the magical kingdom of Ithkar, each written by a different author, including André Norton and C. J. Cherryh. *Magic in Ithkar 2* (1985), *Magic in Ithkar 3* (1986), and *Magic in Ithkar 4* (1987) are companion works.

Tor, 1988, pap., 320 pp. (0-8125-4715-2)

(BL 81:1436, 1448; Kliatt 19[Fall 1985]:24; SLJ Aug 1985 p. 88; VOYA 8:268)

1464 **MARK, Jan (pseud. of Janet Marjorie Brisland).** *Aquarius.* **Gr. 7–10. (Orig.**
✓ **British pub. 1982.)**

Because Viner's water-divining skills have made him an outcast in his rain-soaked land, he runs away in search of someone who can bring dryness and sunshine to his world.

Atheneum, 1984, 223 pp., o.p.

(CCBB 37:209; Ch&Bks:289; HB 60:598; SLJ Apr 1985 p. 98; Suth 3:295; TLS 1982 p. 791)

1465 **MARK, Jan (pseud. of Janet Marjorie Brisland).** *Divide and Rule.* **Gr. 8 up.**
✓ **(Orig. British pub. 1979.)**

Hanno spends a frightening year in the power of the temple priests, only to learn that he will be sacrificed if he does not join them.

Crowell, 1980, 264 pp., o.p.

(BL 76:1522; CCBB 33:196; HB 56:415; KR 48:516; SLJ Aug 1980 p. 77; TLS 1979 p. 122)

1466 **MARTIN, Graham Dunstan.** *Giftwish.* **Gr. 5–8. (Orig. British pub. 1978.)**

Ewan is tricked into going to the Castle Midnight to fight the wicked Necromancer in order to fulfill an ancient prophecy. The sequel is *Catchfire* (1982), in which Ewan, newly crowned King of Feydom, and Catchfire, the witch girl, struggle to break the enchantment wrought by the wizard Hoodwill.

Houghton, 1981, 202 pp., o.p.

(BL 77:1191, 1197; HB 57:197; SLJ Apr 1981 p. 129)

1467 **MAYHAR, Ardath.** *Lords of the Triple Moons.* **Gr. 7–9.**

Sixteen-year-old Johab, one of the last of the Old Lords of Rehannoth, uses his mental powers to escape from prison and to free his land from the evil ones who murdered his family.

Atheneum, 1983, 141 pp., o.p.

(BBJ:73; BBS:61; BL 79:1059, 1096; SLJ Sept 1983 p. 137; VOYA 6:148)

1468   MAYHAR, Ardath. *Makra Choria.* **Gr. 7–9.**

Choria uses her inherited powers to dethrone her older sister who gained the throne of Makraitis by having their father killed.

Atheneum, 1987, 193 pp., o.p.

(BBS:61; HB 58:347; KR 55:58; SLJ Apr 1987 p. 112; VOYA 10:92)

1469   MAYHAR, Ardath. *Runes of the Lyre.* **Gr. 7–12.**

A science fantasy about Yinri, a runaway girl who discovers the secret gateway into the Kingdom of Hasyih, where she meets both her real and her foster fathers, becomes "The Queen Who Was to Come," and gathers her forces to battle the evil Hasyisi.

Atheneum, 1982, 214 pp., o.p.

(BBS:61; HB 58:520; SLJ Sept 1982 p. 141; VOYA 5[Feb 1983]:45)

1470   MAYHAR, Ardath. *The Saga of Grittel Sundotha.* **Gr. 7–10.**

Seven-foot-tall Grittel wanders the land of Garetha using her magical powers to rescue the helpless, as she searches for her true destiny.

Atheneum, 1985, 204 pp., o.p.

(BL 81:1051, 1060; SLJ 31[Aug 1985]:79)

1471   MAYHAR, Ardath. *Soul-Singer of Tyrnos.* **Gr. 6–9.**

Trained as a Soul-Singer to keep goodness and justice in the souls of the people, Yeleeve is chosen to fight the evil that is corrupting the land of Tyrnos. *Runes of the Lyre* (1982) is a related work.

Atheneum, 1981, 195 pp., o.p.

(BL 78:98, 110; CCBB 35:91; SLJ Feb 1982 p. 90)

1472   MAYNE, William (James Carter). *Antar and the Eagles.* **Gr. 5–8. (Orig. British**
✓✓   **pub. 1989.)**

In this suspenseful story, a boy named Antar is stolen by eagles, who teach him to communicate and to fly so that he can rescue a golden egg containing the future Great Eagle.

Delacorte, 1990, 166 pp., o.p.

(BL 86:1803; CCBB 43:169; HB 66:457; HBG 1[Jan–June, 1990]:254; JHC 1991 Suppl. p. 76; KR 58:267; SLJ June 1990 p. 124; Suth 4:247; VOYA 13:365, 14:9)

1473   MICHAELS, Melisa C. *Far Harbor.* **Gr. 7–12.**

Having run away from her abusive Terran foster family, "Ugly" finds a shard of crystal at an abandoned shrine that shows her visions of Hawke, a young prince searching for the partner he needs to save his people from their Terran masters.

Tor, 1989, pap., 248 pp. (0-8125-4581-8)

(BBS:62; Kliatt Sept 1989, p. 20; VOYA 12:290, 13:12)

1474   MIRRLEES, Hope. *Lud-in-the-Mist.* **Gr. 10 up. (Orig. British pub. 1926.)**

Master Chanticleer, the mayor of the seaport town of Mist, sets out to discover the identity of the smuggler bringing fairy fruits over the border from Fairyland into the sober land of Dorimare.

Knopf, 1927, o.p.; Ballantine, 1970, 1977, pap., 273 pp., o.p.

(BL 23:384; TLS Jan 13, 1927 p. 26; Tymn:141)

1475   **MODESITT, L(eland) E(xton Jr.).** *The Magic of Recluce* **(Recluce series, book 1). Gr. 10 up.**

Lerris feels that his woodworking apprenticeship and life in general on the orderly island of Recluce are boring, so he undertakes a "dangergeld" or quest that leads to his participation in the battle between the forces of order and chaos. The sequels are *Towers of the Sunset* (1992) and *The Magic Engineer* (1994).

Tor, 1991, 448 pp. (0-312-85116-2), 1993, pap. (0-8125-0518-2)

(BL 87:1698 & 1702; KR 59:510; LJ Apr 15, 1991, p. 129; SLJ Sept 1991 p. 294; VOYA 14:247)

1476   **MOON, Elizabeth.** *Surrender None: The Legacy of Gird.* **Gr. 10 up.**

Gird, a peace-loving farmer's son, leads a peasant uprising against the tyrannical overlords. This is the prequel to *The Deed of Paksenarrion* (1992), which was originally published separately as *Sheepfarmer's Daughter* (1988), *Divided Allegiance* (1988), and *Oath of Gold* (1989). *The Deed of Paksenarrion* trilogy tells the story of a sheepfarmer's daughter named Paksenarrion who becomes a soldier, protected by her holy St. Gird medallion, and is eventually transformed into a Paladin, or warrior chosen by the gods.

Baen, 1990, 530 pp. (0-671-69878-8)

(BL 86:1960, 1971; Kliatt Sept 1990, p. 22; VOYA 13:300)

1477   **MOORCOCK, Michael (John).** *The Dragon in the Sword* **(The Eternal Champion Saga, book 3). Gr. 10 up.**

Erehose sets sail to search for his lost love, Ermizhad, and meets Count Von Bek, a refugee from the Third Reich. This is the sequel to *The Eternal Champion: A Fantastic Romance* (Dell, 1970, 1978, 1987) and *Phoenix in Obsidian* (Mayflower, 1970; retitled *The Silver Warrior,* Dell, 1973, 1985).

Ace, 1986, 298 pp., o.p.

(BL 83:34, 52; KR 54:1072; LJ Sept 15, 1986 p. 102; VOYA 9:292, 11:12)

1478   **MOORCOCK, Michael (John).** *The Fortress of the Pearl* **(The Elric Saga, vol. 8). Gr. 10 up.**

Elric, the albino sorcerer and heir to the kingdom of Melnibone, is tricked into helping an evil lord of Quarzhasaat search for the Pearl at the Heart of the World. The sequel is *The Revenge of the Rose* (1991). The preceding volumes in the saga are *Elric of Melnibone* (1972, 1986, 1992; abridged as *The Dreaming Jewels,* 1972); *The Sailor on the Seas of Fate* (1976, 1987, 1989); *The Weird of the White Wolf* (1977, 1983, 1989); *The Vanishing Tower* (1970, 1977, 1983; also titled: *The Sleeping Sorceress,* 1971); *The Bane of the Black Pearl* (1977, 1984); *Stormbringer* (1965; rev. ed. 1977, 1984); and *Elric at the End of Time* (1985, 1986). Two related titles are *The Stealer of Souls and Other Stories* (1965) and *Elric, the Return to Melnibone* (1973)

Ace, 1989, 240 pp., o.p., 1990, pap. (0-441-24866-7)

(BL 86:148; KR 57:1206; LJ Sept 15, 1989 p. 138; VOYA 12:373, 13:12)

1479   **MOORCOCK, Michael (John).** *The Ice Schooner: A Tale.* **Gr. 10 up. (Orig. British and U.S. pub. 1969.)**

An ice-schooner captain, living at the end of a future ice age, makes an ill-fated pilgrimage to the sacred city of New York.

Berkley, 1969, pap., 208 pp., o.p.; Harper, 1977, 192 pp., o.p.

(BL 73:1485, 1490; KR 45:509; LJ 102:1868)

1480   **MORRIS, William.** *The Well at the World's End.* **Gr. 10 up. (Orig. British and U.S. pub. 1896.)**

A boy named Ralph grows to manhood while undertaking an adventure-filled quest to find the well at the world's end. According to Tymn, Zahorski, and Boyer in *Fantasy Literature: A Core Collection and Reference Guide* (Bowker, 1979), Morris could be called the father of modern high fantasy, and this work is his most significant. His work influenced many others, including Lord Dunsany, J. R. R. Tolkien, and C. S. Lewis.

Longman, 1903, 1913, 496 pp., o.p.; Ballantine, 1970, 1978, o.p.

(HB 3[May 1927]:20–22; Tymn:146)

1481 **MURPHY, Shirley Rousseau.** *Nightpool* **(Dragonbards trilogy, book 1). Gr.**
✓ **7–10.**

Young Prince Tebriel, badly injured by his father's murderer, is nursed by a colony of intelligent otters, until he is strong enough to seek out the legendary singing dragon and avenge his father's death. In *The Ivory Lyre* (1987; 1988) Tebriel and his telepathic dragon, Seastrider, join the resistance against the evil ones bent on taking over their world. In *The Dragonbards* (1988; pap., 1989) Teb and the other dragonbards challenge the dark lord Quazelzeg and his army of the unliving.

Harper, 1985, 250 pp., LB(0-06-024361-9), 1987, pap., 256 pp. (0-06-447041-5)

(BBJ:74; BL 82:53, 67, 86:905; CCBB 39:33; SLJ Dec 1985 p. 104; VOYA 8:326)

1482 **MURPHY, Shirley Rousseau.** *The Ring of Fire* **(The Children of Ynell series). Gr. 7–9.**

Zephy and Thorn search for a lost jade runestone that will protect them from the tyrants of Kubal. *The Wolf Bell* (1979) is set in a previous time, and the sequels are *The Castle of Hape* (1980), *Caves of Fire and Ice* (1980), and *The Joining of the Stone* (1981).

Atheneum, 1977, 232 pp., o.p.

(BL 74:368, 378; KR 45:791; SLJ Oct 1977 p. 116; VOYA 3 [June 1980]:46)

1483 **MYRA, Harold.** *The Shining Face.* **Gr. 12 up.**

Despite a prophecy foretelling the coming of a blind princess who will free her people, Mela resists her fate. This is the sequel to *Children in the Night* (1991), and is the second book in a proposed trilogy.

Zondervan, 1993, 256 pp. (0-310-58771-9)

(BL 89:852; VOYA 16:312, 17:19)

1484 **NEWMAN, Robert (Howard).** *The Shattered Stone.* **Gr. 6–8.**

In fulfillment of an ancient prophecy, two children without memories search for part of a stone inscription that will bring peace to their land.

Illus. by John Gretzer, Atheneum, 1975, 231 pp., o.p.

(BL 72:305; HB 51:465; KR 43:1186; SLJ Nov 1975 p. 81)

NICHOLS, (Joanna) Ruth. *The Left-Handed Spirit.* See Chapter 10, Witchcraft and Sorcery Fantasy.

1485 **NIVEN, Larry.** *The Magic Goes Away* **(Magic trilogy, vol. 1). Gr. 10 up.**

A quest to replenish the earth's source of magic is undertaken by four magicians and a Greek swordsman. The sequels are *Magic May Return* (1983) and *More Magic* (1984).

Illus. by Esteban Maroto, Ace, 1978, 1985, pap., 213 pp. (0-441-51554-1)

(BBS:62; BL 75:856, 861; SLJ Mar 1979 p. 153)

1486 **NORTON, André (pseud. of Alice Mary Norton).** *The Crystal Gryphon*
✓ **(Kerovan and Joisan books, vol. 1) . Gr. 7–10.**

Kerovan and his wife, Joisan, fight foreign invaders and the Dark Powers to regain the throne of Ulm. *The Jargoon Pard* (1974; see below) is a companion volume, and *Gryphon in Glory* (1981) and *Gryphon's Eyrie* (1985, 1989) are the sequels. These books are related to Norton's Witch World series (see Chapter 5C, Travel to Other Worlds).

Atheneum, 1972, o.p.; Tor, 1985, pap., 256 pp. (0-8125-4738-1)

(BL 69:192, 204; Ch&Bks:289; KR 40:948; LJ 97:4080; TLS 1973 p. 1114; Tymn:152)

1487 **NORTON, André (pseud. of Alice Mary Norton).** *The Jargoon Pard.* **Gr. 7–9.**

Kethan's magical powers save him from being used as a pawn in the power struggle for the throne of the House of Car Do Prawn. This is a companion volume to *The Crystal Gryphon* (1972; see above) and is related to Norton's Witch World series (see Chapter 5C, Travel to Other Worlds).

Atheneum, 1974, 194 pp., o.p.

(BL 71:46; HB 51:153; LJ 99:2748; TLS 1975 p. 1052)

1488 **NORTON, André (pseud. of Alice Mary Norton).** *The Mark of the Cat.* **Gr. 10**
✓ **up.**

After he is left alone in the desert wilderness to complete his "solo," Hynkkel and the fierce desert sandcats becomes blood brothers, and he follows his fate toward the emperor's palace.

Ace, 1992, 248 pp. (0-441-52020-0)

(BL 88:1316; LJ Apr 15, 1992 p. 125; SLJ Feb 1993 p. 126; VOYA 15:178, 16:10)

NORTON, André (pseud. of Alice Mary Norton). *Quag Keep.* See Chapter 5B, Myth Fantasy.

NORTON, André (pseud. of Alice Mary Norton). *Witch World.* See Chapter 5C, Travel to Other Worlds.

1489 **NORTON, André, and GRIFFIN, P. M.** *Storms of Victory* **(Witch World: The Turning trilogy, book 1). Gr. 10 up.**

Two novellas set in Witchworld after the Turning, a huge magical war. In "Port of Dead Ships" a woman faces an evil sea creature, and in "Sea Keep" another woman struggles to protect her Dale. The sequels are *Flight of Vengeance* (1992) by Norton, Griffin, and Mary Schaub, and *On Wings of Magic* (1994) by Norton, Sacha Miller, and Patricia Matthews. This trilogy is related to Norton's Witch World series (see Chapter 5C, Travel to Other Worlds).

Tor, pap. 1991, 432 pp., (0-312-93171-9)

(BL 87:1180; KR 59:219; VOYA 14:182)

NORTON, André, and LACKEY, Mercedes. *The Elvenbane: An Epic Fantasy of the Halfblood Chronicles.* See Chapter 10, Witchcraft and Sorcery Fantasy.

ORR, A. *The World in Amber.* See Chapter 10, Witchcraft and Sorcery Fantasy.

PALMER, David R. *Threshold.* See Chapter 6, Humorous Fantasy.

1490 **PATON WALSH, Jill.** *Torch.* **Gr. 6–10. (Orig. British pub. 1987.)**
✓ Cal and Dio make a deathbed promise to the old Guardian to care for his magical torch and to search for the "games" for which he had been guarding it, in this story set in what could be Greece in a future time.

Farrar, 1988, 176 pp. (0-374-37684-0)

(BBJ:76; BL 84:1420, 1439; CCBB 41:191; Ch&Bks:292; KR 56:371; SLJ May 1988 p. 111; TLS 1989 p. 648; VOYA 11:139)

1491   PAXON, Diana L. *Lady of Light* (The First Book of Westria). Gr. 10 up.

King Jehan of Westria searches for a wife who will be able to use the jewels of the four natural elements to better the Kingdom. The sequels are *Lady of Darkness* (1983) and *Silverhair the Warrior* (1986).

Pocket, 1982, pap., 261 pp., o.p.

(Kliatt 17[Spring 1983]:16; LJ 107:2355)

1492   PIERCE, Meredith Ann. *Birth of the Firebringer.* Gr. 7–10.

The son of the prince of unicorns discovers that he is Firebringer, destined to save his race from their enemies, the gryphons. The sequel is *Dark Moon* (1992).

Macmillan, 1985, 234 pp., o.p.

(BBJ:74; BL 82:861, 870; CCBB 39:94; KR 53:1090; SLJ Jan 1986 p. 70)

1493   PIERCE, Meredith Ann. *The Darkangel* (The Darkangel trilogy, vol. 1). Gr.
✓   **6–10.**

Even though she is falling in love with him, Aeriel must slay the beautiful but horrifying Darkangel vampire. I.R.A. Children's Book Award, 1983. In *A Gathering of Gargoyles* (1984, 1985, pap.), Aeriel makes a hazardous journey to gather five gargoyles in preparation for a final battle with the White Witch who enslaved her lover. In *The Pearl of the Soul of the World* (1990), Ariel attempts to destroy the White Witch by bringing her a pearl containing all the Ancientlady's knowledge of the world.

Little, 1982, 223 pp., o.p.

(BL 78:1236, 1260, 80:353, 86:785, 905; CCBB 35:213; Ch&Bks:290; HB 58:416; JHC:404; KR 50:376; SHC:713; SLJ Mar 1982 p. 160; VOYA 5[June 1982]:40)

1494   PIERCE, Meredith Ann. *The Woman Who Loved Reindeer.* Gr. 7–12.
✓   A young girl named Caribou and the magical reindeer she raised, lead her tribe on a dangerous journey to a new home.

Little, 1985, 242 pp., o.p.; Tor, 1989, pap. (0-8125-0305-8)

(BBJ:74; BL 82:330, 340; CCBB 39:75; HB 62:208; KR 53:992; SLJ Dec 1985 p. 104; VOYA 9:41, 13:138)

1495   PIERCE, Tamora. *Alanna: The First Adventure* (Song of the Lioness, book 1).
✓   **Gr. 6–10.**

Alanna and her twin brother, Alan, secretly change places as they are sent away from home for training: she is determined to ignore her magical powers and become a knight, while he wants to become a sorcerer, not a knight. In *In the Hand of the Goddess* (1984; pap., 1990), Alanna has reached the level of squire to Prince Jonathan when she becomes suspicious that a sorcerer, Duke Roger, is plotting against the royal family. In *The Woman Who Rides Like a Man* (1986; pap., 1990) Alanna, now a knight, proves her prowess as a warrior by aiding a tribe of desert raiders, who declare her their shaman. *Lioness Rampant* (1988; pap., 1990) completes the series, and *Wild Magic: The Immortals* (1992; see below) is set in the same world.

Macmillan, 1983, 252 pp. (0-689-30994-5); Knopf, 1989, pap., 256 pp. (0-679-80114-6)

(BL 78:1236, 1260, 80:353; CCBB 35:213; Ch&Bks:290; HB 58:416; KR 50:376; SLJ Mar 1982 p. 160; VOYA 5[June 1982]:40)

1496   PIERCE, Tamora. *Wild Magic: The Immortals* (The Immortals, book 1). Gr.
✓   **6–10.**

Shy assistant horsemistress Daine begins to accept her gift of wild magic and learns from the Wizard Numain (trapped in the form of a hawk) how valuable her powers will be to the kingdom's future. This story is related to the author's Song of the Lioness quartet

(1984–1988; see *Alanna: The First Adventure,* above). The sequel is *Wolf-Speaker* (1994).

Macmillan, 1992, 208 pp. (0-689-31761-1)

(BL 89:419; CCBB 46:188; HB 69:93; HBG 4[Spring 1993]:83; KR 60:1314; SLJ Nov 1992 p. 98; VOYA 15:356, 16:16)

1497 **PINI, Wendy, and PINI, Richard.** *ElfQuest: The Novel, Journey to Sorrow's End* **(ElfQuest Saga, book 1). Gr. 6–12.**

A wolf-riding Elf tribe driven from its home by humans crosses a desert in search of a new home. This novel was originally published in comic book format. The sequels are *ElfQuest, Book 2* (1983), *ElfQuest, Book 3* (1984), and *ElfQuest, Book 4* (1985). The Blood of Ten Chiefs books are shared-world anthologies dealing with the history of the ElfQuest characters, written by well-known fantasy authors including C. J. Cherryh, Piers Anthony, Nancy Garden, and Diana Paxon. They are *The Blood of Ten Chiefs,* vol. 1 (Tor, 1986), *Wolfsong,* vol. 2 (Tor, 1988), *Winds of Change,* vol. 3 (Tor, 1989), and *Against the Wind,* vol. 4 (Tor, 1990).

Playboy, 1983, pap., 320 pp., o.p.

(BBS:63; BL 79:602, 606; VOYA 6:46)

1498 **POWERS, Tim.** *The Stress of Her Regard.* **Gr. 10 up.**

Young Doctor Michael Crawford entreats the poets Shelley, Byron, and Keats for help in getting rid of the evil spirits that killed his wife and are haunting his life. 1990 Mythopoeic Fantasy Award.

Ace, 1989, 392 pp. (0-92738901-0); 1991, pap. (0-441-79097-6)

(BL 86:42; VOYA 12:373, 13:16)

1499 **PRATCHETT, Terry.** *Truckers* **(The Bromeliad trilogy, book 1). Gr. 5–9. (Orig.**
✓ **British pub. 1989.)**

The secure world of the miniature people or "nomes" whose lives have flourished beneath the floorboards of the Arnold Brothers Department Store seems fated for extinction when they learn of the imminent demolition of their home, until Masklin shows them a way to escape. In *Diggers* (1991) the nomes have fled to a deserted rural quarry, but life in the country proves difficult, especially after human beings return. In *Wings* (1991) the nomes stow away on the Concorde from England to Florida and attempt to use a communication satellite to summon a ship to take them away from earth.

Delacorte, 1990, 246 pp. (0-385-29984-2)

(BBJ:75; BL 86:1432, 1457; HB 66:202; HBG 1[Jan–June, 1990]:254; KR 58:49; VOYA 13:366, 14:13)

1500 **PRATT, (Murray) Fletcher.** *The Well of the Unicorn.* **Gr. 10 up.**

Airar Alvarson leads the rebels of the Iron Ring in their battle against the Vulking invaders of Dalarna.

Sloane, 1948, 338 pp., o.p.

(KR 15:628; LJ 72:1685; Tymn:154)

1501 **PREISS, Byron (Cary), and REAVES, J. Michael.** *Dragonworld.* **Gr. 10 up.**

Falsely accused of being a spy for the murderous neighboring kingdom of Simballa, Amsel of Fandora travels to the land of the Dragons to discover who is killing both countries' children.

Bantam, 1979, 1983 (rev. ed.), pap., 560 pp. (0-553-25857-5)

(BBS:63; BL 76:544, 550, 78:594; SLJ Jan 1980 p. 82)

1502 RAWN, Melanie. *Dragon Prince* (Dragon Prince trilogy, vol. 1). Gr. 10 up.

Peace seems almost within grasp because of the approaching arranged marriage between Sioned of Goddess Keep and Prince Rohan of Stronghold, until political intrigue touches off war again. The sequels are *The Star Scroll* (1989) and *Sunrunner's Fire* (1990). This trilogy is followed by the Dragon Star trilogy (1990–1993; see below).

DAW, 1988, pap., 574 pp. (0-88677-312-1)

(BBS:63; LJ Nov 15, 1988 p. 88; VOYA 12:186)

1503 RAWN, Melanie. *Stronghold* (Dragon Star trilogy, book 1). Gr. 10 up.

Crown Prince Pol and his cousin, Lord Andry of Goddess Keep, come into conflict over the use of ancient magic to fight a seemingly invincible invasion force that has arrived on their shores, in this story that will be best understood by readers of the author's Dragon Prince trilogy: *Dragon Prince* (1988; see above), *The Star Scroll* (1989), and *Sunrunner's Fire* (1990). The sequels are *The Dragon Token* (1992) and *Skybowl* (1993).

DAW, 1990, 487 pp. (0-88677-440-3), 1991, pap. (0-88677-492-9)

(KR 58:1431; LJ Nov 15, 1990 p. 95; VOYA 14:47)

1504 RAY, Mary (Eva Pedder). *The Golden Bees.* Gr. 7–9. (Orig. British pub. 1984.)

Young Kenofer journeys across the oceans and mountains of Ancient Greece to retrieve a Princess's lost golden earring. This is the sequel to *Song of Thunder* (1978, o.p.).

Faber, 1984, 152 pp., o.p.

(CCBB 37:211; HB 60:477; SLJ Aug 1984 p. 86)

1505 REEVES, James (pseud. of John Morris Reeves). *The Cold Flame.* Gr. 5–7.

A soldier uses a witch's unquenchable blue flame to win himself a kingdom and a princess.

Illus. by Charles Keeping, Meredith, 1967, 137 pp., o.p.

(HB 45:419; LJ 94:1799; TLS 1967 p. 1142)

1506 REICHERT, Mickey Zucker. *The Last of the Renshai* (Renshai trilogy, vol. 1). Gr. 10 up.

Rache, the lone survivor of a fearless warrior race, works as a gladiator trainer until he reluctantly agrees to join forces with the wizards to prevent a Great War ordained by the gods. The sequels are *The Western Wizard* (1992) and *Child of Thunder* (1993).

DAW, 1992, pap., 629 pp. (0-88677-503-5)

(BL 88:684, 686; Kliatt Apr 1992, p. 16; LJ Dec 1991 p. 203; VOYA 15:114)

1507 REYNOLDS, Alfred. *Kiteman of Karanga.* Gr. 6–9.

Having used his Kitewing glider to escape from Karanga after being banished for cowardice, Karl discovers enemy forces plotting to invade his country.

Knopf, 1985, 217 pp., o.p.; Bantam, 1987, pap. (entitled: *Kiteman*), 208 pp. (0-553-26036-7)

(BBJ:75; BL 82:217; Kliatt Jan 1987 p. 18; SLJ Nov 1985 p. 90)

1508 REYNOLDS, Susan Lynn. *Strandia.* (Orig. Canadian pub. 1991.) Gr. 7 up.

Rejected by her people after she pretends to lack the telepathic "talent" of dolphin-calling in order to avoid an unwanted marriage, Sand is taken in by the Midislanders on Strandia.

Farrar, 1991, 277 pp. (0-374-37274-8)

(CCBB 45:20; HBG 3[July–Dec 1991]:80; KR 59:933; SLJ Sept 1991 p. 284; VOYA 14:325)

1509 **ROBERSON, Jennifer.** *A Pride of Princes* **(Chronicles of the Cheysuli, book 5). Gr. 10 up.**

The Cheysuli princes Brennan, Hart, and Corin, shape-shifting warriors who become animals at will, must fulfill a prophecy and battle evil sorcery before they can rule their kingdoms in Homana., The other books in the series are *Shapeshifters* (1984), *The Song of Homana* (1985), *Legacy of the Sword* (1986), *Track of the White Wolf* (1987), *Daughters of Lion* (1989), and *Flight of the Raven* (1990).

DAW, 1988, pap., 453 pp. (0-88677-261-3)

(Kliatt Apr 1988 p. 24, Apr 1989 p. 26; VOYA 11:196, 12:15, 167)

1510 **ROBERSON, Jennifer.** *Sword-Breaker* **(Tiger and Del series). Gr. 7–12.**

Tiger and Del, two sword-dancers, search for the sorcerer Shaka Obre, who can exorcise the spirit of his evil brother from one of their swords. This is the sequel to *Sword Dancer* (1986), *Sword-Singer* (1988), and *Sword-Maker* (1989).

DAW, 1991, 460 pp. (0-88677-476-4)

(Kliatt Sept 1991 p. 28; VOYA 14:325, 15:11)

1511 **ROBERTS, Keith (John Kingston).** *Pavane.* **Gr. 10 up.**

In an alternate Britain where Queen Elizabeth I was assassinated, the Armada triumphed, and the nonindustrial world is ruled by the Pope, a revolution of the oppressed is brewing.

Doubleday, 1968, 288 pp., o.p.

(KR 36:930; LJ 93:4580, 94:1347)

ROHAN, Michael Scott. *The Anvil of Ice.* See Chapter 10, Witchcraft and Sorcery Fantasy.

1512 **ROSENBERG, Joel.** *D'Shai.* **Gr. 10 up.**

When Kami, a clumsy young acrobat, ignores the laws of D'Shai by falling in love with a nobleman's daughter, he is punished with an accusation of murder. The sequel is *Hour of the Octopus* (1994).

Ace, 1991, pap., 327 pp. (0-441-15751-3)

(BL 87:1115, 1120; Kliatt Apr 1991 p. 21; VOYA 14:47)

RUCKER, Rudy. *The Hollow Earth: The Narrative of Mason Algiers Reynolds of Virginia.* See Chapter 5C, Travel to Other Worlds.

1513 **RUSCH, Kristine Kathryn.** *The White Mists of Power.* **Gr. 7–12.**

Before Byron, abandoned as a child, can prove his claim to be the long-lost Prince Adric, his father the king is assassinated, and only the mysterious and magical Cache Enos is left to identify him. World Fantasy Award, 1992.

NAL, 1991, pap., 302 pp. (0-451-45120-1)

(LJ Nov 15, 1991 p. 111; VOYA 15:46, 16:16)

1514 **RUSHDIE, Salman.** *Haroun and the Sea of Stories.* **Gr. 10 up. (Orig. British pub. 1990.)**

Storyteller Rashid Khalifa loses his tale-spinning powers after his wife runs away with another man, so he and his son Haroun travel into the Twilight Strip in an attempt to regain his abilities, only to find that a war is raging over the eternal damming up of the polluted Stream of Stories. 1992 Mythopoeic Fantasy Award for Children's Literature.

Viking, 1991, 210 pp. (0-670-83804-7), 1991, pap. (0-14-15737-9)

(BL 87:203; Kliatt Jan 1992 p. 12; LJ Nov 1, 1990 p. 127, Sept 15, 1990 p. 67; TLS Sept 28, 1990 p. 1036, Dec 15, 1991 p. 13)

1515   **RUSSELL, Sean.** *The Initiate Brother.* **Gr. 7–12.**

Set in an alternate ancient Japan, this is the story of Shuyun, the mysterious and powerful spiritual advisor to the emperor's most feared and hated enemy, Lord Shonto, told from many points of view, including that of the Black Tiger, the emperor's martial arts expert, and Lady Nishima, Lord Shonto's adopted daughter.

DAW, 1991, pap., 480 pp. (0-88677-466-7)

(Kliatt Sept 1991 p. 28; VOYA 14:249)

1516   **SABERHAGEN, Fred.** *Empire of the East.* **Gr. 10 up.**

After the wizard's troops murder the boy's parents and kidnap his sister, sixteen-year-old Rolf is recruited by a rebel band to battle Ominor, the wizard Emperor of the East.

Ace, 1979, 1983, pap., 558 pp., o.p.; Baen, 1990, pap., 576 pp. (0-671-69871-0)

(Kliatt 14[Winter 1980]:18; SLJ Mar 1980 p. 147)

1517   **SABERHAGEN, Fred.** *The First Book of Lost Swords: Woundhealer's Story* **(The Lost Swords series, book 1). Gr. 10 up.**

Prince Mark of Tasavalta seeks the magical sword, Woundhealer, to cure his blind and epileptic son. The sequels are *The Second Book of Lost Swords: Sightblinder's Story* (1987), *The Third Book of Lost Swords: Stonecutter's Story* (1988), *The Fourth Book of Lost Swords: Farslayer's Story* (1989), *The Fifth Book of Lost Swords: Coinspinner's Story* (1989), *The Sixth Book of Lost Swords: Mindsword's Story* (1990), *The Seventh Book of Lost Swords: Wayfinder's Story* (1992), and *The Last Book of Lost Swords: Shieldbreaker's Story* (1994). This is a companion series to Saberhagen's *The Book of Swords* trilogy (Tor, 1984–1985; see below), which was also collected in one volume entitled: *The Complete Book of Swords* (Science Fiction Book Club, 1985).

Tor, 1986, 1991, pap. 281 pp. (0-8125-2058-0)

(BL 82:1667, 1683, 86:905; KR 54:1330; LJ Oct 15, 1986 p. 114; VOYA 9:293, 10:22)

1518   **SABERHAGEN, Fred.** *The Second Book of Swords* **(Book of Swords trilogy, vol. 2). Gr. 10 up.**

Mark manages to enter the treasure trove of the Blue Temple in search of the 12 swords of power to aid Sir Andrew in his battle against magical foes. This is the sequel to *The First Book of Swords* (1983), and is followed by *The Third Book of Swords* (1984). The Lost Swords series (1986–1994; see above) is a companion series.

Tor, 1983, 1991, pap., 313 pp. (0-8125-1934-5)

(BL 80:667, 677; Kliatt Winter 1984 p. 24)

1519   **SALSITZ, R. A. V.** *The Unicorn Dancer.* **Gr. 10 up.**

Princess Sharlin, her companion, Dar, and Turiana the golden dragon, search for the power to bring peace to the land of Rangard.

NAL, 1986, pap., 256 pp., o.p.

(Kliatt 20[Fall 1986]:28; LJ Dec 1986 p. 142; VOYA 9:293, 10:24, 40)

1520   **SALSITZ, R. A. V.** *Where Dragons Lie* **(Dragons trilogy, book 1). Gr. 10 up.**

Soldier's son Dar and Princess Sharlin join a wizard and a dwarf on an adventure-filled trek across deserts to find the place where dragons go to die. The sequels are *Where Dragons Rule* (1987) and *Night of Dragons* (1990).

NAL, 1985, pap., 255 pp., o.p.

(BBS:64; Kliatt Spring 1986 p. 25; VOYA 9:90)

1521 **SCARBOROUGH, Elizabeth Ann.** *Bronwyn's Bane* **(The Aragonia series, vol. 3). Gr. 10 up.**

Cursed at birth with an inability to tell the truth, amazonian Princess Bronwyn is sent away to her cousin Carol's for the duration of a war, whereupon the two young women attempt to lift Bronwyn's curse and end the war on their own. This book is preceded by *Song of Sorcery* (1982) and *The Unicorn Creed* (1983), and is followed by *The Christening Quest* (1985).

Bantam, 1983, pap., 352 pp., o.p.

(BL 80:847; LJ 108:2346; SLJ Apr 1984 p. 130)

SHERMAN, Josepha. *Child of Faerie, Child of Earth.* See Chapter 5B, Myth Fantasy.

1522 **SHERMAN, Josepha.** *The Shining Falcon.* **Gr. 10 up.**

While his sorcerer cousin plots a takeover of his kingdom, a wounded prince who has taken the form of a falcon is nursed back to health by a banished noblewoman who does not suspect his true identity. *The Horse of Flame* (1990) is set in the same world.

Avon, 1989, pap., 342 pp. (0-380-75436-3)

(BBS:64; BL 86:528, 541; LJ Nov 15, 1989 p. 108)

1523 **SHERMAN, Josepha.** *Windleaf.* **Gr. 6–9.**

✓ Count Thierry, eighteen, must recover three Faerie objects lost in the mortal world to win his true love, Glinfinial, the half-human daughter of the Faerie Lord.

Walker, 1993, 128 pp. (0-80278259-0)

(BL 90:519; KR 61:1529; SLJ Dec 1993 p. 138; VOYA 16:385, 17:8)

1524 **SHWARTZ, Susan.** *Silk Roads and Shadows.* **Gr. 10 up. (Orig. British pub. 1988.)**

Alexandria, sister of the emperor of Byzantium, undertakes a desperate journey to the Empire of Chin to steal silkworms that could save the vitally important silk industry of Byzantium.

Tor, 1990, pap., 337 pp., o.p.

(Kliatt Sept 1990, p. 24; VOYA 13:258)

1525 **SILVERBERG, Robert.** *The Gate of Worlds.* **Gr. 7–10.**

✓ If the Great Plague had killed three-quarters of the European population during the Middle Ages, perhaps North America today would be ruled by the Aztecs, South America by the Incas, and Europe by the Turks. It is in this version of the twentieth century that Dan Beauchamp sets sail from Turkish England to Aztec North America. *Beyond the Gate of Worlds* (Tor, 1991) is a related collection of stories by Robert Silverberg and other authors.

Holt, 1967, 244 pp., o.p.; Tor, 1984, 1991, pap., 256 pp. (0-8125-1439-4)

(BL 64:250; CCBB 21:18; KR 35:609; LJ 92:3204; TLS 1978 p. 1396)

1526 **SILVERBERG, Robert.** *Kingdoms of the Wall.* **Gr. 10 up.**

Young Poilar is chosen to lead forty pilgrims on a dangeous sacred quest over a huge wall near their village.

Bantam, 1993 (c. 1992), 320 pp. (0-553-09304-6)

(BL 89:795, 800; LJ Feb 15, 1993 p. 196; VOYA 16:170)

1527   SILVERBERG, Robert. *Lord Valentine's Castle* **(Majipoor trilogy, book 1). Gr.**
✓   **10 up.**

Young Lord Valentine, ruler of Majipoor, wanders his land as an amnesiac juggler until he realizes that his mind and personality have been transferred to someone else's body, and that an imposter is ruling his kingdom. The sequels are: *The Majipoor Chronicles* (Arbor, 1982) and *Valentine Pontifex* (Arbor, 1983).

Harper, 1980, o.p.; Bantam, 1981, pap., 480 pp. (0-553-25097-3)

(BL 76:1110, 77:622, 1148, 78:594; Kliatt 15[Fall 1981]:23; KR 48:247; LJ 105:1008; SLJ Sept 1980 p. 93; TLS 1980 p. 1265; VOYA 3[Aug 1980]:53)

1528   SIMAK, Clifford D(onald). *Enchanted Pilgrimage.* **Gr. 10 up.**
✓   Mark and his traveling companions are set upon by witches, trolls, and other fearful creatures during their journey through the wildlands on search of "the old ones."

Putnam, 1975, o.p.; Ballantine, 1983, pap., 256 pp., LB(0-89968-411-4)

(BL 71:863; 72:1038; KR 43:203; LJ 100:783; SLJ May 1975 p. 75; Tymn:156)

1529   SIMAK, Clifford D(onald). *Where the Evil Dwells.* **Gr. 10 up.**

In an alternate Roman Middle Ages, a nobleman's son named Harcourt, the Abbot Guy, the maiden Yolanda, and the gruff thousand-year-old Knurly Man set off on a quest for the soul of a legendary saint.

Ballantine, 1983, pap., 256 pp. (0-345-33438-8)

(BL 79:484, 490; KR 50:956; VOYA 5[Feb 1983]:46)

1530   SMITH, Sherwood. *Wren to the Rescue.* **Gr. 5–9.**
✓   Soon after Wren's best friend, Tess, reveals that she is actually a princess hiding in their orphanage from the evil Wizard Andreus, Tess is abducted, and Wren sets out to rescue her. In the sequel, *Wren's Quest* (1993), Wren leaves magician school to search for her true parents, accompanied by Connor, while Princess Tess is kidnapped in a plot against the royal family.

Harcourt, 1990, 216 pp. (0-15-200975-2); Dell, 1993, pap. (0-440-40773-7)

(BL 87:857; HB 67:202; HBG 2[July–Dec 1990]:72; KR 58:1092; SLJ Nov 1990 p. 140; VOYA 13:302, 14:13)

1531   SMITH, Stephanie A. *Snow-Eyes.* **Gr. 6–9.**

Amarra, or Snow-Eyes, is taken from her family to become a "servitor" of the Lake Mother, where she learns occult skills from the other women servitors. The sequel is *The Boy Who Was Thrown Away* (1987).

Atheneum, 1985, 184 pp., o.p.

(BBJ:75; CCBB 39:37; SLJ Oct 1985 p. 187; VOYA 9:42)

1532   SNYDER, Zilpha Keatley. *Below the Root* **(Green-Sky trilogy, vol. 1). Gr. 5–8.**
✓   Raamo D'Ok's curiosity about the dreaded land beneath his treetop world of Green-Sky leads him to rescue a girl named Terra and uncover the secret of the world below. In *And All Between* (1976, 1985), Terra escapes from the underworld of Erd to Green-Sky, where she is rescued by Raamo and Neric, who plan to free all of the Erdlings. In *Until the Celebration* (1977, 1985), the Kindar and the Erdlings are finally about to be united, but plans for the celebration are disrupted by dissidents within each tribe, and by the disappearance of Pomma and Terra.

Illus. by Alton Raible, Atheneum, 1975, 231 pp., o.p.; Dell, 1992, pap., 244 pp. (0-440-21266-9)

(BL 71:764; CC:559; CCBB 28:186; Ch&Bks:248; KR 43:239; SLJ Sept 1975 p. 112; Suth 2:424)

1533 **SNYDER, Zilpha Keatley.** *Song of the Gargoyle.* **Gr. 5–9.**

✓ A boy named Tymmon and a doglike gargoyle travel the country together entertaining in villages and towns while they search for Tymmon's kidnapped father.

Delacorte, 1991, 232 pp. (0-385-30301-7); Dell, 1994, pap. (0-440-40898-9)

(BL 87:1127; CC 1992 Suppl. p. 62; CCBB 44:177; HBG 2:278; JHC 1992 Suppl. p. 66; KR 59:323; SLJ Feb 1991 p. 8; VOYA 14:358)

1534 **SNYDER, Zilpha Keatley.** *Squeak Saves the Day and Other Tooley Tales.* **Gr. 3–6.**

The Tiddlers are miniature people who avoid human STOMPERS, in these seven stories about Nipper and Trinket Tooley and their parents.

Illus. by Leslie Morrill, Delacorte, 1988, 192 pp. (0-385-29661-4); Dell, 1992, pap. (0-440-40585-8)

(CCBB 41:189; Ch&Bks:291; KR 51:625; SLJ Aug 1988 p. 98)

1535 *Spells of Wonder.* **Ed. by Marion Zimmer Bradley. Gr. 10 up.**

Sixteen tales about strong heroines who use magic to battle the dangers they find in their alternate worlds. This is a companion volume to the *Sword and Sorceress* books (1984–1994; see below).

DAW, 1989, pap., 288 pp., o.p.

(BL 86:149, 165; LJ Sept 15, 1989 p. 139; VOYA 12:375)

1536 **SPRINGER, Nancy.** *Chains of Gold.* **Gr. 10 up.**

✓ Arlen, the "Summer-King," destined to be sacrificed to bring fertility to the fields of Catena, falls in love with his "bride," Cerilla, refuses to go through with the annual ritual, and flees with her.

Arbor House, 1986, 230 pp., o.p.

(BBS:64; BL 82:1667; KR 54:1074; LJ Aug 1986 p. 174; VOYA 9:241, 10:21)

1537 **SPRINGER, Nancy.** *Madbond* **(The Sea King trilogy, book 1). Gr. 10 up.**

Two young men, Dannoc and Rad Korridun, become blood brothers and set out to find their parents, the Kings of the Seal Kindred and the Red Hart tribes, in order to fight the evil that has come to their land. The sequels are *Mindbond* (1987) and *Godbond* (1988).

Tor, 1987, pap., 214 pp., o.p.

(BBS:64; BL 84:31, 55; Kliatt 21[Sept 1987]:29; VOYA 10:180)

1538 **SPRINGER, Nancy.** *The Sable Moon* **(The Chronicles of Isle, book 3). Gr. 10 up.**

Crown Prince Trevyn completes a quest during which he is enslaved and freed, studies to become a sorcerer, visits the land of elves, and returns home to save his kingdom. This book is preceded by *The White Hart* (1979) and *The Silver Sun* (1980, 1983, revised from *The Book of Suns,* 1977). It is followed by *The Black Beast* (1982, 1986) and *The Golden Swan* (1983). The latter two books were published together as *The Book of Vale* (1985).

Pocket, 1981, 1986, pap., 264 pp. (0-671-44378-X)

(BL 77:1188; VOYA 4[Oct 1981]:64)

1539 **SPRINGER, Nancy.** *Wings of Flame.* **Gr. 10 up.**

The orphan girl Seda saves Prince Kyrem of Devan after he is attacked by an evil wizard.

Tor, 1985, 1986, pap., 256 pp., o.p.

(BL 81:1297, 1327; KR 53:117; LJ Mar 15, 1985 p. 75)

1540   STEARNS, Pamela (Fujimoto). *The Fool and the Dancing Bear.* **Gr. 5–7.**

Only a dancing bear can revive King Rolf's kingdom after its enchantment by a queen. who is jealous of the king's love for her younger sister.

Illus. by Ann Strugnell, Little, 1979, 167 pp., o.p.

(BL 75:1581; CCBB 33:57; HB 55:416; KR 47:742; SLJ Sept 1979 p. 148; Suth 3:408)

1541   STEELE, Mary Q(uintard Govan). *Journey Outside.* **Gr. 5–8.**

✓   Dilar escapes the subterranean life of the Raft People and finds his way up to an unfamiliar sunlit world. John Newbery Medal Honor Book, 1970.

Illus. by Rocco Negri, Viking, 1969, 143 pp., o.p.; Puffin, 1979, pap. (0-14-030588-2); Peter Smith, 1984 (0-8446-6169-4).

(BBC:213; BL 65:1276; CCBB 23:119; HB 45:309; KR 37:506; LJ 94:3227; TLS 1970 p. 1264)

1542   STEELE, Mary Q(uintard Govan). *The True Men.* **Gr. 5–7.**

Driven from his home with the True Men because his skin has begun to glow in the dark, Ree is taken in by two weavers.

Greenwillow, 1976, 144 pp., o.p.

(BBC:214; CCBB 30:82; HB 53:55; KR 44:1045; SLJ Jan 1977 p. 97)

1543   STEUSSY, Marti. *Forest of the Night.* **Gr. 10 up.**

A young woman named Hashti ventures alone into the wilds of New Lebanon seeking the highly intelligent feathered tigers said to roam this world.

Ballantine, 1987, pap., 265 pp., o.p.

(BBS:64; BL 83:1564, 1591; LJ May 15, 1987 p. 101, VOYA 11:12)

1544   STEVENSON, Laura C(aroline). *The Island and the Ring.* **Gr. 7–12.**

✓   Princess Tania escapes from her beloved father's burning castle with a sapphire ring that is the source of her enemy's power, which she vows to use to save her people and destroy him.

Houghton, 1991, 304 pp. (0-395-56401-8); Avon, 1992, pap. (0-380-71915-0)

(BL 88:690; CCBB 45:50; HBG 3[July 1992]:73; KR 59:1409; SLJ Sept 1991 p. 284; VOYA 14:327)

STEVENSON, Robert Louis. *The Touchstone.* See Chapter 1, Allegorical Fantasy and Literary Fairy Tales.

1545   STIRLING, S. M., and MEIER, Shirley. *The Cage.* **Gr. 10 up.**

Sold into slavery by Habiku, the man who ruined her trading business, Megan and her warrior companion, Shkai'ra, return seeking vengeance.

Baen, 1989, 1991, pap., 402 pp. (0-671-72047-3)

(BL 85:1950; VOYA 13:40)

1546   SUCHARITKUL, Somtow. *Utopia Hunters: Chronicles of the High Inquest* **(The Inquestor trilogy, book 3). Gr. 10 up.**

Young Jenjen, a light-weaver who has been unwillingly appointed to the clan of Darkweavers, listens to an ancient Rememberer's tales of the Dispersal of Man, and overcomes her fear of Darkness. This is the sequel to *Light on the Sound* (Pocket, 1982) and *The Throne of Madness* (Pocket, 1983).

Bantam, 1984, pap., 255 pp., o.p.

(LJ 109:2301; VOYA 8:140)

1547 *Sword and Sorceress: An Anthology of Heroic Fantasy* (Sword and Sorceress series). Ed. by Marion Zimmer Bradley. Gr. 10 up.

Fifteen tales of magical and warlike women, whose authors include Diana Paxon and Phyllis Ann Karr. *Spells of Wonder* (1989; see entry above) is a companion volume. The other books in this series are: *Sword and Sorceress II* (1985), *Sword and Sorceress III* (1986), *Sword and Sorceress IV* (1987), *Sword and Sorceress V* (1988), *Sword and Sorceress VI* (1990), *Sword and Sorceress VII* (1990), *Sword and Sorceress VIII* (1991), *Sword and Sorceress IX* (1992), *Sword and Sorceress X* (1993), and *Sword and Sorceress XI* (1994).

DAW, 1986, pap., 256 pp. (0-88677-359-8)

(BBS:53; BL 80:1601, 1610; Kliatt 18[Fall 1984]:24; LJ 109:998)

1548 **TARR, Judith.** *Alamut* (The Hounds of God cycle, book 4). Gr. 10 up.

✓ Prince Aidan of Rhiyana attempts to avenge the murder of his nephew, Gereint, in medieval Jerusalem, but falls in love with the assassin, the immortal Morgiana. The sequel, *The Dagger and the Cross: A Novel of the Crusades* (1991), completes the five-book cycle which began with The Hound and the Falcon trilogy (1985–1986; see *The Isle of Glass* below).

Doubleday, 1989, 480 pp. (0-385-24720-6); Bantam, 1990, pap., 393 pp. (0-553-28786-9)

(BBS:65; BL 86:895, 902; KR 57:1568; LJ Dec 1989 p. 176; VOYA 13:120, 14:9)

1549 **TARR, Judith.** *Ars Magica.* Gr. 10 up.

Young Gerbert of Aurillac's knowledge of the magical arts fuels his rise from French peasant to archbishop of Rheims and Ravenna, to become Pope Sylvester II.

Bantam, 1989, pap., 276 pp. (0-553-28145-3)

(BBS:65; VOYA 12:375, 13:11)

1550 **TARR, Judith.** *The Hall of the Mountain King* (Avaryan Rising, vol. 1). Gr. 10 up.

Prince Mirain's claim to the throne of Ianon is disputed by his treacherous mortal relatives, in this first volume of the Avaryan Rising series. In the sequel, *The Lady of Han-Gilen* (1987), warrior princess Elian rejects her royal suitors and runs away disguised as a boy, to search for her childhood love, Mirain, son of the Sun god. In *A Fall of Princes* (1988; pap. 1989) Elian and Mirain's son, twenty-one-year-old Prince Sarevan of Avaryan, and his hated enemy, fifteen-year-old Prince Hirel of Asanion, meet by chance, grow into a close friendship, and vow to end the conflict between their kingdoms. The fourth book in the series is *Arrows of the Sun* (1993).

Bluejay, 1986, 288 pp., o.p.

(BBS:65; BL 83:192, 220; KR 54:1332; VOYA 9:293, 11:12)

1551 **TARR, Judith.** *The Isle of Glass* (The Hounds of God cycle, vol. 1). Gr. 10 up.

✓ Brother Alfred, torn between his pursuits of healing and scholarship, and the secret knowledge of his elven blood, abandons his life at St. Ruan's Abbey after a seriously wounded ambassador of the elven King Gwydion places the fate of three fueding kingdoms in his hands. In the sequel, *The Golden Horn* (1985), Alfred and his elven companion, Thea, travel to Constantinople during the Fourth Crusade, but Thea disappears when the crusaders sack the city. In *The Hounds of God* (1986), the elven kingdom of Rhiyana is attacked by the Hounds of God, who kill the king's son and kidnap Thea and her newborn twins. *Alamut* (1989; see above), and *The Dagger and the Cross* (1991) are related works that complete the cycle. The first three books in the cycle are called The Hounds and the Falcon trilogy.

Bluejay, 1985, 288 pp., o.p.; Tor, 1986, pap., 288 pp. (0-8125-5600-3)

(BL 81:824, 838; Kies:171; Kliatt 20[Fall 1986]:30; KR 52:1172; LJ Feb 15, 1985 p. 182; VOYA 8:141, 194, 365)

1552   TEPPER, Sheri S. *Jinian Footseer* (Jinian trilogy). Gr. 10 up.

Young Jinian seeks out "sevens" of wizardly women to unleash her own magical powers in order to save the beings from the elder times. The sequels are *Dervish Daughter* (1986) and *Jinian Star-Eye* (1986). This trilogy is related to the Mavin Manyshaped trilogy (see below) and the True Game trilogy (1983–1984).

Tor, 1985, pap., 284 pp., o.p.

(BBS:65; BL 82:380, 398, 86:906; Kliatt 20[Winter 1986]:22; VOYA 8:366, 397)

1553   TEPPER, Sheri S. *Northshore* (The Awakeners, vol. 1). Gr. 10 up.

Pamra, a young woman escaping from life in a priesthood that enslaves the bodies of "awakened" dead, is rescued by Thrasne, a boatman who hides her from creatures bent on killing her. The sequel is *Southshore* (1987, pap., 1988).

Tor, 1988, 256 pp. (0-8125-5617-8)

(BL 83:530; KR 55:267; LJ Feb 15, 1987 p. 164; VOYA 10:93, 11:13)

1554   TEPPER, Sheri S. *The Song of Mavin Manyshaped* (Mavin Manyshaped trilogy). Gr. 10 up.

Mavin Manyshaped flees Danderbat Keep with her brother Mertin, and calls upon her shapeshifting talents to save a plague-stricken city. The sequels are *The Flight of Mavin Manyshaped* (1985) and *The Search of Mavin Manyshaped* (1985). There are two companion trilogies, the Jinian trilogy: *Jinian Footseer* (1985), *Dervish Daughter* (1986), and *Jinian Star-Eye* (1986); and the True Game trilogy: *Kings Blood Four* (1983), *Necromancer Nine* (1983), and *Wizard's Eleven* (1984).

Ace, 1985, pap., 183 pp., o.p.

(BBS:65; BL 81:1297, 1327, 86:906; VOYA 8:195)

TOLKIEN, J(ohn) R(onald) R(euel). *Farmer Giles of Ham.* See Chapter 1, Allegorical Fantasy and Literary Fairy Tales.

1555   TOLKIEN, J(ohn) R(onald) R(euel). *The Fellowship of the Ring* (Lord of the
✓✓   Rings trilogy, vol. 1). Gr. 8 up. (Orig. British and U.S. pub. 1954.)

In this, the first volume of the trilogy set in Middle-Earth, as was *The Hobbit* (1938; see this section), Frodo Baggins inherits a magic ring from his uncle Bilbo and begins a journey to protect it from the evil powers who seek it. In *The Two Towers* (orig. British pub. 1954; U.S. 1955; Houghton, 1967; Ballantine, 1985, pap.), Frodo and Sam take the ring to the borders of the Dark Kingdom while the members of the Company of the Ring battle the wizard Saruman and his goblin army. In *The Return of the King* (orig. British and U.S. pub. 1955; Houghton, 1967; Ballantine, 1985, pap.) Frodo and Sam bring the Ring to Mount Doom where it is destroyed to help the forces of good win their struggle against the Dark Lord. *The Adventures of Tom Bombadil and Other Verses from "The Red Book"* (1962, 1963, 1991) is a related work. Tolkien's son, Christopher Tolkien, has edited seven volumes of previously unpublished legends about the history of Middle-Earth: *The Silmarillion* (1979), *Unfinished Tales of Numenor and Middle-Earth* (1980, 1982; Mythopoetic Fantasy Award, 1981), *The Book of Lost Tales* (1983, 1984, 1986), *The Book of Lost Tales, Volume 2* (1984), *The Lays of the Beleriad* (1985), *The Shaping of*

Middle-Earth: The Quenta, the Ambrakanta, and the Annals (1986), and *The Treason of Isengard* (1989).

Houghton, 1967, 1992, 440 pp. (0-395-64738-X), 1988, pap. (0-395-27223-8); Ballantine, 1986, pap. (0-345-33970-3)

(BBS:65; BL 51:204; HB 31:104, 43:491; JHC:418; KR 22:598; SHC:723; TLS 1954 p. 541; Tymn:153–166)

1556 **TOLKIEN, J(ohn) R(onald) R(euel).** *The Hobbit; Or, There and Back Again.* **Gr.**
✓✓ **5 up. (Orig. British pub. 1937.)**

A wizard tricks a peace-loving Hobbit named Bilbo Baggins into going on a hazardous quest to recover stolen dwarf treasure from the dragon, Smaug. *Bilbo's Last Song* (1990) is a picture book version of one of Bilbo's poems, describing his preparations for leaving home. The Lord of the Rings trilogy (see this section) continues the saga of Middle-Earth.

Houghton, 1938, 1966 (rev. ed.) 317 pp. (0-395-07122-4); illus. by Michael Hague, Houghton, 1984 (collector's ed.), 320 pp. (0-395-36290-3), 1989, pap. (0-395-52021-5)

(BBC:214; BBS:65; BL 34:304, 80:52, 528; CC:566; CCBB 38:96; Ch&Bks:252; HB 14:92, 94, 174; JHC:417; LJ 63:385, 819; SHC:722; SLJ Dec 1984 p. 86; TLS 1937 p. 714; Tymn:162)

TOLKIEN, J(ohn) R(onald) R(euel). *Smith of Wooton Major.* See Chapter 1, Allegorical Fantasy and Literary Fairy Tales.

1557 **TOWNSEND, John Rowe.** *The Fortunate Isles.* **Gr. 7–10. (Orig. British pub.**
✓ **1989.)**

Eleni's friend Andreas convinces her that her unusual blue eyes and dark hair mean that she is the Messenger, bound by prophecy to seek out the Living God, and they run away together to Gold Island.

Harper, 1989, 248 pp., o.p.

(BBJ:76; BL 86:446, 465; CCBB 43:98; HB 66:211; HBG 1[July 1989]:77; JHC 1991 Suppl. p. 80; KR 57:1410; SLJ Oct 1989 p. 138; Suth 4:414; VOYA 12:292, 13:12)

1558 **TURNBULL, Ann (Christine).** *The Wolf King.* **Gr. 5–7. (Orig. British pub. 1975.)**

Grayla and Coll search the wolf-infested forest for their father and brother, aided by the Dark People and the magical Elder Folk.

Seabury, 1976, 141 pp., o.p.

(BL 72:1339; KR 44:473; SLJ Sept 1976 p. 126; TLS 1975 p. 1450)

1559 **VANCE, Jack (pseud. of John Holbrook Vance).** *Cugel's Saga* **(The Dying**
✓ **Earth Saga, book 3). Gr. 10 up.**

Cugel the Clever travels across half a world seeking vengeance against the sorcerer Iucounu. This book is preceded by *The Dying Earth* (Lancer, 1950; Pocket, 1982), *The Eyes of the Overworld* (Ace, 1966, 1980), and *A Quest for Simbils* (written by Michael Shea, DAW, 1974). It is followed by *Rhialto the Marvellous* (1984).

Simon, 1983, 334 pp., o.p.

(BL 80:185; KR 51:979; LJ 108:2173; VOYA 7:102)

1560 **VANCE, Jack (pseud. of John Holbrook Vance).** *Suldrun's Garden* **(Lyonesse trilogy, book 1). Gr. 10 up.**

Imprisoned by her father for refusing to help him gain control of the Elder Isles, Princess Suldren manages to find a lover and escape. The sequels are *The Green Pearl* (1985, 1986), and *Madouc* (Underwood-Miller, 1989; Ace, pap., 1990).

Underwood-Miller, 1983, o.p.

(BBS:65; BL 79:1263, 1269, 86:906; KR 51:213; VOYA 6:218)

1561   VANDE VELDE, Vivian. *Dragon's Bait.* **Gr. 6–10.**

✓   Left as dragon's bait by fellow villagers who want her father's shop, fifteen-year-old Alys is amazed to discover that the huge dragon can transform himself into a young man who agrees to take revenge on her former neighbors.

Harcourt, 1992, 144 pp. (0-15-200726-1)

(BL 89:139; CCBB 46:126; HB 69:213; HBG 4[Spring 1993]:84; KR 60:994; SLJ Sept 1992 p. 261; VOYA 16:48)

1562   VAN SCYOC, Sydney J(oyce). *Bluesong* **(The Darkchild trilogy, vol. 2). Gr. 10 up.**

In this second volume of the science-fantasy trilogy that began with *Darkchild* (1982, 1985) and is followed by *Starsilk* (1984), Darkchild's son, Danior, and niece, Keva, search for her father among a tribe of desert dwellers. All three books have been published in one volume entitled *Daughters of the Sunstone* (Science Fiction Book Club, 1985, o.p.).

Berkley, 1983, 1985, pap., 261 pp., o.p.

(BL 79:1450, 1458; KR 51:272; VOYA 6:218)

1563   VAN SCYOC, Sydney J(oyce). *Drowntide.* **Gr. 10 up.**

Prince Keiris enters a world beneath the sea to search for his long-lost twin sister.

Berkley, 1987, pap., 220 pp., o.p.

(BL 83:1412, 1436; VOYA 10:181)

1564   VOIGT, Cynthia. *Jackaroo.* **Gr. 6–10.**

✓   Independent-minded Gwyn, the innkeeper's daughter, takes on the role of the legendary Jackaroo, the masked rider who inspires hope in the poor and oppressed. *On Fortune's Wheel* (1990; see below) takes place at a later time in the same world, and *The Wings of a Falcon* (Scholastic, 1993; see below) is also set in this world.

Macmillan, 1985, 291 pp. (0-689-31123-0); Fawcett, 1986, pap. (0-44970-187-5)

(BL 82:126; CCBB 39:19; JHC:422; SLJ Dec 1985 p. 96; Suth 4:423)

1565   VOIGT, Cynthia. *On Fortune's Wheel.* **Gr. 6–12.**

✓✓   Birle, the granddaughter of Gwyn in *Jackaroo* (1985; see above), falls in love with a young runaway earl and travels downriver to the sea with him, encountering adventure, shipwreck, capture by pirates, slavery, and freedom. *The Wings of a Falcon* (Scholastic, 1993; see below) is also set in this world.

Macmillan, 1990, 276 pp. (0-689-31636-4); Fawcett, 1991, pap. (0-44970-391-6)

(BL 86:1156; CCBB 43:276; HB 66:341; HBG 1[Jan–June 1990]:254; JHC 1991 Suppl. p. 80; Kliatt Sept 1991 p. 18; KR 58:187; SLJ Mar 1990 p. 240; VOYA 13:40, 14:12)

1566   VOIGT, Cynthia. *The Wings of a Falcon.* **Gr. 7–12.**

✓   After Oriel and Griff escape from slavery on the Damall's Island, they travel to the kingdom to compete for the hand of Princess Merlis. This story is set in the same world as *Jackaroo* (1985; see above) and *On Fortune's Wheel* (1990; see above).

Scholastic, 1993, 480 pp. (0-590-46712-3)

(CCBB 47:25; HB 70:207; HBG 5:91; KR 61:1009; SLJ Oct 1993 p. 156; VOYA 16:314, 17:9)

1567   VOLSKY, Paula. *The Luck of Relian Kru.* **Gr. 10 up.**

Relian Kru's lifelong bad luck is compounded when he is kidnapped by a sorcerer who wants to use Relian's special powers for his own ends.

Ace, 1987, pap., 304 pp., o.p.
(BBS:66; BL 83:1412, 1437)

1568 **VOLSKY, Paula.** *The Wolf of Winter.* **Gr. 10 up.**

✓ When Varis, younger brother of Rhazaulle's ruler, uses necromancy to gain the throne, his niece, Shalindra, is sent into exile to escape a sentence of death.

Bantam, 1993, pap., 368 pp. (0-553-37210-6)
(BL 90:505, 509; KR 61:1233; LJ Nov 15, 1993 p. 103; VOYA 17:102)

WAECHTER, Friedrich, and EILERT, Bernd. *The Crown Snatchers.* See Chapter 1, Allegorical Fantasy and Literary Fairy Tales.

WANGERIN, Walter, Jr. *The Book of the Dun Cow.* See Chapter 1, Allegorical Fantasy and Literary Fairy Tales.

1569 **WARBURG, Sandol Stoddard (pseud. of Sandol Stoddard).** *On the Way Home.* **Gr. 6–9.**

Alexi, his friend Bear, and Alexi's double, Twain, rescue a fair maiden, kill an ice-worm monster, and escape from the Monkey King.

Illus. by Daniel Stolpe, Houghton, 1973, 137 pp. o.p.
(BL 70:546; KR 41:1202, 1351; LJ 99:578)

1570 **WARNER, Sylvia Townsend.** *Kingdoms of Elfin.* **Gr. 10 up.**

✓ A collection of haunting, interconnected tales about the winged inhabitants of ancient Elfin Kingdoms beneath various European hillsides.

Viking, 1976, 222 pp., o.p.
(Kies:180; KR 44:1179, 1112; LJ 102:220; TLS 1977 p. 25; Tymn:172)

1571 **WATSON, Ian.** *Queenmagic, Kingmagic.* **Gr. 10 up.**

The game is ending in a land where life is a chess game played with human pieces, and two young pawn-squires from opposing kingdoms who have fallen in love realize they must escape to another world if they want to stay together.

St. Martin's, 1988, 205 pp., o.p.
(BL 84:908, 926; KR 57:26; LJ Feb 15, 1988 p. 181; VOYA 11:98)

WATT-EVANS, Lawrence. *Crosstime Traffic.* See Chapter 3, Fantasy Collections.

WATT-EVANS, Lawrence. *With a Single Spell.* See Chapter 10, Witchcraft and Sorcery Fantasy.

1572 **WATT-EVANS, Lawrence, and FRIESNER, Esther M.** *Split Heirs.* **Gr. 9 up.**

A humorous tale set in the Kingdom of Hydrangea whose triplet heirs must be kept apart to protect their mother's life.

Tor, 1993, 320 pp. (0-312-85320-3); 1994, pap. (0-8125-2029-7)
(BL 89:1950, 1953; VOYA 16:314, 17:8)

1573 **WEIS, Margaret.** *The Prophet of Akhian* **(Rose of the Prophet trilogy, vol. 3).** **Gr. 10 up.**

Four companions who have restored life to two gods on the Isle of Galos must rally the nomadic tribes to rescue the women and children held captive by the Priests of Kich. This is the sequel to *The Will of the Wanderer* (1989) and *The Paladin of the Night* (1989).

Bantam, 1989, 390 pp., o.p.
(BBS:66; VOYA 12:376)

1574   WEIS, Margaret, and HICKMAN, Tracy. *Dragon Wing* **(The Death Gate cycle, vol. 1). Gr. 10 up.**

Hugh the Hand is recruited to kill the prince of the Volkaran Isles, an assignment that he feels is unjust, while the dwarves plot insurrection deep beneath the earth. The sequels are *Elvin Star* (1990), *Fire Sea* (1991), *Serpent Mage* (1992), *The Hand of Chaos* (1993), *Into the Labyrinth* (1993), and *The Seventh Gate* (1994).

Bantam, 1990, 448 pp. (0-553-28639-0)

(BBS:66; BL 86:619, 621; KR 57:1713; LJ Dec 1989 p. 177; VOYA 13:120,398)

1575   WEIS, Margaret, and HICKMAN, Tracy. *DragonLance Chronicles.* **Gr. 7–12.**

Tanis, half human, half elf, leads his band through numerous battles and adventures related to the fantasy game Dungeons and Dragons. This collection contains three books originally published separately: *Dragons of Autumn Twilight* (1984), *Dragons of Winter Night* (1985), and *Dragons of Spring Dawning* (1985). It is followed by *DragonLance Legends* (1986, 1988; see below).

TSR, 1988, 1,032 pp. (0-88038-543-X)

(BBS: 66; VOYA 12:46)

1576   WEIS, Margaret, and HICKMAN, Tracy. *DragonLance Legends.* **Gr. 7–12.**

These stories involve characters from the fantasy game Dungeons and Dragons, particularly the ingenious Kender thief, Tasslehoff Burrfoot, and the twins, Caramon the warrior and Raistlin the wizard. This collection is the sequel to *The DragonLance Chronicles* (TSR, 1988; see above) and contains *Time of the Twins* (1986), *Test of the Twins* (1986), and *War of the Twins* (1986), originally issued as separate paperbacks.

TSR, 1988, 905 pp. (0-88038-610-X)

(BBS:66; VOYA 12:118, 13:12)

1577   WEIS, Margaret, and HICKMAN, Tracy. *Forging the Darksword* **(Darksword trilogy, vol. 1). Gr. 10 up.**

Earth's witches have fled to Merilon, where they are no longer persecuted for practicing magic; but Joram, born without magical powers, decides to join a secret society that practices science. The sequels are *Doom of the Darksword* (1988) and *Triumph of the Darksword* (1988).

Bantam, 1988, pap., 391 pp. (0-553-26894-5)

(BBS:66; BL 84:831, 855; LJ Dec 1987 p. 130; VOYA 11:141)

1578   WESTALL, Robert (Atkinson). *The Cats of Seroster.* **Gr. 7–12.**

✓   Gentle Cam becomes possessed by his magic dagger, which, with the help of some large, power-wielding cats, turns him into the Seroster, a legendary hero destined to lead his people against their enemies.

Greenwillow, 1984, 349 pp., o.p.

(BL 81:362, 86:907; CCBB 38:75; HB 61:188; Kies:183; KR 52:108; SLJ Jan 1985 p. 88; TLS 1984 p. 1375; VOYA 8:58)

1579   WILDER, Cherry (pseud. of Cherry Barbara Lockett Grimm). *A Princess of*
✓   *the Chameln* **(The Rulers of Hylor trilogy, vol. 1). Gr. 8–12.**

After Princess Aidris Am Firn's parents are assassinated, she flees to Athion where she becomes a cavalry soldier living under a false name until she can return to Chameln as Queen. In *Yorath the Wolf* (1984) young Yorath has been brought up in secret by the court magician because, as heir to the throne of Hylor, he is under a decree of death. In *The*

Summer's King (1986), vain young King Sharn Am Zor is tricked by the sorcerer Rosmer into undergoing a deadly ordeal of trickery and magic.

Atheneum, 1984, 272 pp., o.p.

(BBS:67; BL 80:1111; HB 60:479; SLJ May 1984 p. 95; VOYA 7:269)

1580 WILLETT, John (William Mills). *The Singer in the Stone.* **Gr. 5–7.**

Angelina is the only one who cares enough to help Rubythroat, the last of the Dreamers, bring back storytelling, song, and dance into the world of the Plain People.

Houghton, 1981, 86 pp., o.p.

(BL 77:1342, 1348; CCBB 35:19; KR 49:636; SLJ Sept 1981 p. 132)

1581 WILLEY, Elizabeth. *The Well-Favored Man: The Tale of the Sorcerer's Nephew.* **Gr. 10 up.**

Young sorcerer-prince Gwydion has inherited the throne after the mysterious disappearances of his father and uncle, and is kept busy defending the kingdom from dragons, monsters, diplomatic intrigue, and a woman who may be his long-lost sister.

Tor, 1993, 448 pp. (0-312-85590-7)

(BL 90:422, 428; KR 61:1036; LJ Sept 15, 1993 p. 109; VOYA 17:41)

1582 WILLIAMS, Jay. *The Time of the Kraken.* **Gr. 7–10.**

✓   In this science-fantasy, two warring tribes unite in the face of the coming of monstrous beasts called Kraken, while Thorgeir, his bride, and his blood brother set out for the legendary Temple of Arveid in search of help against the destructive beasts.

Macmillan, 1977, 168 pp., o.p.

(BL 74:609; CCBB 31:120; SLJ Sept 1977 p. 150; TLS 1978 p. 377)

1583 WILLIAMS, Tad. *The Dragonbone Chair* **(Memory, Sorrow and Thorn trilogy, book 1). Gr. 10 up.**

In thrall to the black magician Pyrates, King Elias of Osten Ard decides to destroy his brother, Josua, and a kitchen helper named Simon rises to become a hero after he joins Josua's forces. The sequels are *Stone of Farewell* (1990) and *To Green Angel Tower* (1993).

DAW, 1988, 672 pp. (0-8099-0003-3), 1989, pap. (0-88677-384-9)

(BBS:67; BL 84:906, 1866, 1868; KR 56:1199; LJ Sept 15, 1988 p. 95; SLJ Apr 1989 p. 128; VOYA 11:296, 12:14)

1584 WILLIAMS, Tad, and HOFFMAN, Nina Kiriki. *Child of an Ancient City.* **Gr. 6–12.**

The surviving travelers of a caravan pillaged by bandits must tell stories around the camp fire all night long to keep away a bloodthirsty Vampyr.

Illus. by Greg Hildebrandt, Macmillan, 1992, 137 pp. (0-689-31577-5)

(BL 89:662; HBG 4[Spring 1993]:85; SLJ Jan 1993 p. 134; VOYA 16:48, 17:8)

1585 WOLFE, Gene (Rodman). *The Shadow of the Torturer* **(The Book of the New Sun, vol. 1). Gr. 10 up.**

In this first volume of a tetralogy that combines fantasy and science fiction, Severian, an exiled apprentice of the Torturer's Guild, travels across a future Earth immersed in winter due to its dying sun. As he travels toward his new appointment, his mysterious sword involves him in a duel with poisonous weapons, and he is given a strange jewel. World Fantasy Convention Award, 1981. The sequels are *The Claw of the Conciliator* (1981), *The Sword of the Lictor* (1981, 1982; British Fantasy Society Best Novel Award, 1982),

The Citadel of the Autarch (Ultramarine, 1983), and *The Urth of the New Sun* (1987). *Nightside the Long Sun* (Tor, 1993) is also set in Whorl.

Simon, 1980, 304 pp., o.p.

(BBS:67; BL 76:1594; KR 48:400; LJ 105:1192; SLJ Sept 1980 p. 93)

1586   WOLFE, Gene (Rodman). *Soldier of the Mist.* **Gr. 10 up.**

✓ A head injury causes Latro, a young Greek soldier in 479 B.C., to lose his memory and wander the land, meeting gods, goddesses, and other supernatural beings. The sequel is *Soldier of Arete* (1989).

Tor, 1987, 352 pp. (0-8125-5815-4)

(BBS:67; BL 82:1475, 86:906; Kies:184; KR 54:1324; LJ Nov 15, 1986 p. 112; VOYA 9:294, 10:23)

1587   WREDE, Patricia C(ollins). *Caught in Crystal.* **Gr. 7–12.**

Once a member of the Sisterhood of Stars and now a widowed innkeeper and mother of two, Kayl is called back into service to fight the evil influence of the Magicseekers by destroying a magic crystal hidden within the Twisted Tower.

Ace, 1987, 293 pp., o.p.

(BBS:67; VOYA 10:133)

1588   WREDE, Patricia C(ollins). *Dealing with Dragons* **(Enchanted Forest Chroni-**
✓ **cles, book 1). Gr. 6–9.**

Princess Cimorene vows that she would rather be eaten by a dragon than act like a "proper" princess and marry a dull prince, so she volunteers to be captured by the powerful dragon Kazul. In *Searching for Dragons* (1991), Cimorene and young King Morwen set off on a flying carpet in search of Kazul, who has disappeared. In *Calling on Dragons* (1993), Queen Cimorene sets out to retrieve King Mendanbar's stolen magic sword, accompanied by a witch, a magician, and the dragon king, Kazul. In the concluding volume, *Talking to Dragons* (1985; rev. ed., 1993), set sixteen years later, Cimorene's son, Daystar, faces wizards and monsters when he tries to rescue his father, King Mendanbar.

Harcourt, 1990, 192 pp. (0-15-222900-0); Scholastic, 1992, pap. (0-5904-5722-5)

(BL 87:331, 969; CC:574; HBG 2[July–Dec 1990]: 86; KR 58:1094; SLJ Dec 1990 pp. 25, 112; VOYA 13:370, 14:10)

1589   WREDE, Patricia C(ollins). *The Harp of Imach Thyssel* **(Lyra series, book 2). Gr. 10 up.**

The legendary harp found by Emereck, a young minstrel, must be guarded from sorcerers who seek it and must never be played. This is the sequel to *Shadow Magic* (1982) and is set in the same world as *Daughter of Witches* (1983).

Ace, 1985, pap., 234 pp., o.p.

(BBS:67; BL 81:1374, 1390, 86:907)

1590   WREDE, Patricia C(ollins). *Mairelon the Magician.* **Gr. 10 up.**

✓ Sixteen-year-old Kim, a proficient pickpocket disguised as a boy in an alternate Regency London, travels across England with a magician who is trying to clear his name. This book is set in the same world as Wrede's and Caroline Stevermer's *Sorcery and Cecilia* (1988; see below).

Tor, 1991, 288 pp. (0-312-85041-7), 1992, pap. (0-8125-0896-3)

(BL 87:1783, 1788, 88:872; KR 59:572; LJ May 15, 1991 p. 111; SLJ Feb 1992, p. 122; VOYA 14:327)

1591   WREDE, Patricia C(ollins). *The Seven Towers.* **Gr. 10 up.**

Jermain flees the Sevairn court and takes over command of the armies of the wizard King

Carachel, in an attempt to preserve the Seven Kingdoms and destroy their monstrous enemy.

Ace, 1984, pap., 264 pp., o.p.

(BBS:67; BL 80:1154, 1161; VOYA 7:148)

1592 **WREDE, Patricia C(ollins), and STEVERMER, Caroline.** *Sorcery and Cecilia.* **Gr. 9 up.**

Two cousins in an alternate Regency England exchange letters about their gentlemen friends and magical exploits in this humorous spoof of a Regency romance. *Mairelon the Magician* (1991; see above) is set in the same world, as is *A College of Magics* (1994), written by Stevermer.

Ace, 1988, pap., 197 pp., o.p.

(BBS:67; BL 84:1575, 1598; VOYA 11:248, 12: 16)

1593 **WURTS, Janny.** *The Master of White Storm.* **Gr. 10 up.**

Korendir, a mysterious soldier-for-hire, leads a galley slave revolt after a life spent battling wizards and rescuing princesses.

NAL, 1992, pap., 413 pp. (0-451-45167-8)

(BL 88:1344, 1348; LJ Mar 15, 1992 p. 129)

1594 **WURTS, Janny.** *Sorcerer's Legacy.* **Gr. 10 up.**

A sorcerer who appears in the pregnant Queen Eleinne's dungeon after the murder of her husband convinces the queen to travel to the world of Pendaire and save the life of Prince Darion by marrying him and bearing him a child.

Bantam, 1989, pap., 246 pp. (0-553-27846-0)

(BBS:68; VOYA 12:229, 13:15)

WURTS, Janny. *Stormwarden.* See Chapter 10, Witchcraft and Sorcery Fantasy

1595 **YEP, Laurence M(ichael).** *Dragon of the Lost Sea* **(Dragon Quartet, book 1). Gr.**
✓ **5–8.**

Shimmer, banished princess of the Dragon Clan, joins forces with a thirteen-year-old boy named Thorn to win back the Lost Sea of the dragons from the enchantress Civit. In *Dragon Steel* (1985), Shimmer and Thorn escape imprisonment in her undersea kingdom and fight numerous battles to restore the kingdom of the Inland Sea to the dragon clan. In *Dragon Cauldron,* (1991) Shimmer and Thorn continue their quest for the magic cauldron that will bring back the sea. In *Dragon War* (1992), Shimmer, Monkey, and Indigo attempt to rescue Thorn from the Boneless King's palace, where his soul has been imprisoned in the powerful cauldron.

Harper, 1982, 224 pp., o.p.; 1988, pap. (0-06-440227-4)

(BBC:216; BL 79:250, 978; CCBB 36:59; Ch&Bks:251; KR 50:1107; SLJ Nov 1982 p. 93; Suth 3:464; VOYA 5[Feb 1983]:47)

1596 **YOLEN (Stemple), Jane H(yatt).** *Dragon's Blood.* **(Pit Dragons trilogy, book 1).**
✓ **Gr. 7–10.**

Jakkin steals and trains a young dragon to earn the money to buy his freedom. In *Heart's Blood* (1984), Jakkin oversees the hatching of his beloved Dragon's first clutch, is drawn into a terrorist plot, and is forced to flee with Akki, the daughter of his former master. In *A Sending of Dragons* (1987, 1989), Jakkin and Akki enter a subterranean labyrinth populated by a primitive race who practice sacrificial rituals.

Delacorte, 1982, 256 pp. (0-385-28226-5); Dell, 1984, pap. (0-440-91802-2)

(BL 78:1236, 1262, 86:906; CCBB 35:220; Ch&Bks:293; HB 58:418; JHC:427; SLJ Sept 1982 p. 146; Suth 3:466; VOYA 5[Oct 1982]:51)

YOLEN (Stemple), Jane H(yatt). *Here There Be Dragons.* See Chapter 3, Fantasy Collections.

1597 YOLEN (Stemple), Jane H(yatt). *The Magic Three of Solatia.* **Gr. 5–7.**

✓ A wisewoman named Sianna and her son, Lann, use three magic buttons to keep out of danger's way and to rescue an enchanted bird-girl from a wizard-king.

Illus. by Julia Noonan, Crowell, 1974, 172 pp., o.p.

(BL 71:574; CCBB 28:172; KR 42:1207; SLJ Jan 1975 p. 51; Suth 2:490; Tymn:180)

1598 YOLEN (Stemple), Jane H(yatt). *Sister Light, Sister Dark.* **Gr. 10 up.**

Raised in a mountainous community of women warriors who worship the white goddess, Alta, orphaned Jenna discovers that she is vitally important to the future of this warrior tribe. The sequel is *White Jenna* (1989).

Tor, 1988, 252 pp., o.p., 1989, pap. (0-8125-0249-3)

(BBS:68; BL 85:220, 259; KR 56:1367; SLJ Dec 1988 p. 132; VOYA 12:16, 48)

YOLEN (Stemple), Jane H(yatt). *Wizard's Hall.* See Chapter 10, Witchcraft and Sorcery Fantasy.

ZAMBRENO, Mary Frances. *A Plague of Sorcerers.* See Chapter 10, Witchcraft and Sorcery Fantasy.

ZELAZNY, Roger (Joseph Christopher). *Jack of Shadows.* See Chapter 10, Witchcraft and Sorcery Fantasy.

ZELAZNY, Roger (Joseph Christopher). *Madwand.* See Chapter 10, Witchcraft and Sorcery Fantasy.

1599 ZELAZNY, Roger (Joseph Christopher). *Nine Princes in Amber* **(Amber series, book 1). Gr. 10 up.**

Although he has lost all memory of his life in the land of Amber, Corwin slowly begins to recover his special powers and to fight for his princely birthright. The sequels are *The Guns of Avalon* (1972, 1974), *The Sign of the Unicorn* (1975, 1976), *The Hand of Oberon* (1976, 1977), *The Courts of Chaos* (1978, 1979), *Trumps of Doom* (1985), *Blood of Amber* (1986), *Sign of Chaos* (1987), *Knight of Shadows* (1989), and *Prince of Chaos* (1991, 1992). *Roger Zelazny's Visual Guide to Castle Amber* (Avon, 1988) is an illustrated guide to the Amber lore written by Zelazny and Neil Randall.

Doubleday, 1970, o.p.; Avon, 1977, pap. (0-380-01430-0); Gregg Press, 1979 (repr. of 1970 ed.), 188 pp., o.p.

(BBS:68; BL 67:84, 142, 86:906; KR 38:484; LJ 95:2513; Tymn:180–184)

1600 ZETTNER, Pat. *The Shadow Warrior.* **Gr. 7 up.**

✓ Llyndreth accepts the aid of Angborn the giant and the goblin Zorn when she sets out to find her brother, missing since he left to fight the goblin Shadow Warriors.

Macmillan, 1990, 220 pp. (0-689-31486-8)

(3BS:68; BBJ:77; BL 86:1892, 1903; HB 66:341; HBG 1[Jan–June 1990]: 254; KR 58: 189; SLJ May 1990 p. 129; VOYA 13:122, 14:12)

1601 ZIMNIK, Reiner. *The Bear and the People.* **Gr. 4–7. (Orig. German pub. 1956.)**

✓ Dearman and his talking bear, Brown One, entertain throughout the countryside, until jealous villagers attack them.

Trans. by Nina Ignatowicz, illus. by the author, Harper, 1971, 78 pp., o.p.

(BL 68:670; KR 39:436; LJ 96:2367, 4160; TLS 1972 p. 1328)

B. Myth Fantasy

1602 **ABBEY, Lynn (pseud. of Marilyn Lorraine Abbey).** *Unicorn and Dragon.* **Gr.**
✓ **10 up.**

The conflict between Alison, the last of the Druidic Saxon priestesses, and her foster-sister, Wildecent, a Norman sorceress, embodies the theme of an old culture reluctantly giving way before a new one, in this novel set in eleventh-century Saxon England.

Avon, 1987, pap., 240 pp. (0-380-75567-X)

(Kies:1; Kliatt 21[Spring 1987]:19, LJ Feb 15, 1987 p. 165; SLJ June–July 1987 p. 115)

1603 **AIKEN, Joan (Delano).** *Winterthing: A Play for Children.* **Gr. 6–8.**

Upon their arrival on mysterious Winter Island, four children and their peculiar old "aunt" take in a foundling baby. As the years go by, they realize that only the baby is aging.

Illus. by Arvis Stewart, Holt, 1972, 79 pp., o.p.

(BL 69:490; CCBB 26:85; HB 49:149; KR 40:1314; LJ 97:4075; TLS 1973 p. 681)

1604 **ALCOCK, Vivien (Dolores).** *Singer to the Sea God.* **Gr. 6–10. (Orig. British pub.**
✓✓ **1992.)**

Slave singer Phaidon escapes by ship after the legendary hero Perseus uses Medusa's bloody head to turn the king and his courtiers to stone.

Delacorte, 1993, 208 pp. (0-385-30866-3)

(BL 89:1578; CCBB 46:168; HB 69:463; HBG 4[Fall 1993]:307; KR 60:1567; SLJ Mar 1993 p. 196; VOYA 16:33)

1605 **ALCOCK, Vivien (Dolores).** *The Stonewalkers.* **Gr. 5–8.**

✓ Lightning strikes the old metal bracelet Poppy has placed on the arm of a garden statue, and the statue comes to life, with frightening consequences.

Delacorte, 1983, 192 pp. (0-385-29233-3)

(BBC:196; BL 79:962; CCBB 36:181; Ch&Bks:282; HB 59:299; JHC:440; Kies:3; KR 51:120; SLJ May 1983 pp. 31, 68; Suth 3:9; TLS 1981 p. 1354; VOYA 6:144)

ALEXANDER, Lloyd (Chudley). *The Book of Three.* See Chapter 5A, Alternate Worlds or Histories.

1606 **ALLEN, Judy.** *The Lord of the Dance.* **Gr. 6–8. (Orig. British pub. 1976.)**

In the rubble of a collapsed building, Mike meets the Sun King and the Earth Queen.

Dutton, 1977, 124 pp., o.p.

(CCBB 31:25; HB 53:536; KR 45:580; SLJ Sept 1977 p. 139; TLS 1976 p. 1544)

Atlantis. **Ed. by Isaac Asimov, Martin H. Greenberg, and Charles G. Waugh.**
See Chapter 3, Fantasy Collections.

1607 **ATTANASIO, A(lfred) A(ngelo).** *Kingdom of the Grail.* **Gr. 10 up.**

A dying Welsh baroness on a twelfth-century crusade to the Holy Land recruits a young Jewish girl to impersonate her, rule Wales, and take revenge on her enemies, in this story involving the legend of the Holy Grail.

Harper, 1992, 512 pp. (0-06-017965-1), 1992, pap, (0-06-109979-1)

(BL 88:1086, 1095; KR 60:3; LJ Feb 15, 1992 p. 200; SLJ July 1992 p. 96)

1608   **BABBITT, Natalie (Zane Moore).** *Tuck Everlasting.* **Gr. 4–7.**

✓✓   After a sinister stranger uncovers the Tuck family secret—their discovery of the fountain of youth—it is left to a little girl named Winnie Foster to save her friends from his evil plan.

Farrar, 1975, 139 pp. (0-374-37848-7), 1985, pap. (0-374-48009-5); ABC-Clio, 1987 (repr. of 1975 ed.), o.p.

(BBC:197; BL 72:510, 80:95; CC:445; Ch&Bks:261; HB 52:47; KR 43:1181; SLJ Dec 1975 p. 50; Suth 2:22; Tymn:48)

1609   **BAKER, (Robert) Michael (Graham).** *The Mountain and the Summer Stars: An*
✓   *Old Tale Newly Ended.* **Gr. 4–6. (Orig. British pub. 1968.)**

Owen Morgan, son of a Welsh farmer and a fairy, enters the land under Black Mountain to search for his mother.

Illus. by Erika Weihs, Harcourt, 1969, 124 pp., o.p.

(BL 65:1122; CCBB 23:21; HB 45:303; KR 37:303; LJ 94:1178; TLS 1968 p. 1113)

1610   **BEAGLE, Peter S(oyer).** *The Folk of the Air.* **Gr. 10 up.**

Itinerant lutenist Joe Farrell, staying with old friends in California, becomes involved in acting out fantasy role-playing games, but things turn nasty when a young witch unleashes an evil, destructive power. Mythopoeic Fantasy Award, 1987.

Ballantine, 1987, 336 pp., o. p.

(BBS:52; BL 83:370; KR 54:1738)

BEAR, Greg. *The Infinity Concerto.* See Chapter 5C, Travel to Other Worlds.

1611   **BENCHLEY, Nathaniel (Goddard).** *Demo and the Dolphin.* **Gr. 3–4.**

Demo travels into the legendary past on a talking dolphin, where he meets Odysseus and other figures from Greek mythology.

Illus. by Stephen Gammell, Harper, 1981, 88 pp., o.p.

(BBC:198; KR 49:1344; HB 57:663; SLJ Jan 1982 p. 72)

1612   **BENÉT, Stephen Vicent.** *The Devil and Daniel Webster.* **Gr. 9 up.**
✓   Daniel Webster battles the devil for the soul of a poor New Hampshire farmer, in this version of the Faust legend.

Illus. by Harold Denison, Farrar, 1937, 61 pp., o.p.

(BBS:52; BL 34:107; Kies:11; TLS 1938 p. 91)

1613   **BERGER, Thomas (Louis).** *Arthur Rex: A Legendary Novel.* **Gr. 10 up.**
✓   In this often humorous contemporary reworking of Thomas Malory's legend of Camelot, Arthur invents knightly conduct because of his guilt over Excalibur's invincibility, Guinevere is a liberated woman, and Launcelot is an anguished failure.

Delacorte, 1978, o.p., Dell, 1979, pap., 512 pp. (0-385-28005-X)

(BL 75:275; Kies:12; KR 46:701; LJ 103:2260)

1614   **BERRY, James R.** *The Magicians of Erianne.* **Gr. 6–10.**

Having lost all memory of his past life, Ronan is asked by the Master Mage of the dragons to travel from Erianne to King Arthur's England to find Arthur's stolen sword.

Harper, 1988, 256 pp., o.p.

(BBJ:69; BL 84:1730, 1733; KR 56:1056; SLJ Sept 1988 p. 105; VOYA 11:94, 12:15)

1615   **BISSON, Terry.** *Talking Man.* **Gr. 10 up.**

According to this contemporary extrapolation of the Book of Genesis, God ("Talking

Man,") was so pleased with his creation of our world that he decided to stay here, marry a mortal woman, and have a daughter named Crystal who rides to his rescue in a '62 Chrysler after her father disappears.

Arbor House, 1986, o.p.; Avon, 1987, pap., 192 pp. (0-380-75141-0)

(BBS:53; BL 83:191, 217, 83:777, 86:906; Kies:14; KR 54:1325; LJ Oct 15, 1986 p. 114; VOYA 9:290, 11:14)

1616 BLAYLOCK, James P(aul). *The Paper Grail.* **Gr. 10 up.**

While young museum curator Howard Barton searches for a valuable and magical ancient Japanese sketch whose mysterious owner has disappeared, Howard discovers that a witch also wants this Hokusai drawing.

Ace, 1991, 384 pp. (0-441-65126-7), 1992, pap. (0-441-65127-5)

(BL 87:1698, 1700; KR 59:570; LJ Apr 15, 1991 p. 129)

BOND, Nancy (Barbara). *A String in the Harp.* See Chapter 8, Time Travel Fantasy.

1617 BRADLEY, Marion Zimmer. *The Firebrand.* **Gr. 10 up.**

In this retelling of the legendary fall of Troy, King Priam's daughter, Kassandra, is cursed by the god Apollo, who decrees that her prophetic visions will be regarded as the ravings of a madwoman.

Simon, 1987, 590 pp., o.p.; Pocket, 1991, pap., 624 pp. (0-671-74406-2)

(BBS:53; BL 84:90, 92; KR 55:1177; LJ Oct 15, 1987 p. 90)

1618 BRADLEY, Marion Zimmer. *The Mists of Avalon.* **Gr. 10 up.**

✓ Morgaine, Viviane, and Guinevere, King Arthur's sister, aunt, and wife, alternately tell the story of Arthur's rise to the throne, his betrayal, and his death.

Knopf, 1982, o.p.; Ballantine, 1985, pap., 396 pp. (0-345-33385-3)

(BL 79:409, 410, 86:906; Kies:19; KR 50:1200; LJ 107:2351; SHC:670)

1619 BRADLEY, Marion Zimmer. *Night's Daughter.* **Gr. 10 up.**

A reinterpretation of Mozart's tale, "The Magic Flute," in which Prince Tamion and Princess Pamina face ordeals of earth, air, water, and fire as they try to unravel the conflict between the Queen of the Night and Sarastro, in order to rule their world in peace.

Ballantine, 1985, pap., 249 pp., o.p.

(BL 81:1159, 1177; Kliatt 19[Spring 1985]:24; VOYA 8:366)

1620 BRADSHAW, Gillian (Marucha). *Beyond the North Wind.* **Gr. 5–9.**

✓ Aristeas, a young poet given magical powers by Apollo, is captured by gigantic one-eyed monsters, and befriended by telepathic griffins who help him to escape.

Greenwillow, 1993, 192 pp. (0-688-11357-5)

(BL 89:1312; HBG 4[Fall 1993]:307; KR 61:297; SLJ Apr 1993 p. 117; VOYA 16:223, 17:8)

1621 BRADSHAW, Gillian (Marucha). *Hawk of May* **(King Arthur trilogy, book 1).**
✓ **Gr. 10 up.**

Young Gwalchmai, the son of evil Queen Morgawse, struggles for acceptance at King Arthur's court after Arthur rejects his offer of allegiance. The sequels are *Kingdom of Summer* (1981; NAL, 1982, pap.) and *In Winter's Shadow* (1982).

Simon, 1980, 313 pp., o.p.

(BL 76:1656, 1669, 77:1148, 86:904; KR 48:378; LJ 105:1008; SLJ Aug 1980 p. 81)

1622   BRENNAN, J. H. *Shiva: An Adventure of the Ice Age* **(Shiva trilogy, book 1). Gr. 5–8.**

To her clan's horror, Shiva, an orphaned 12-year-old Cro-Magnon girl, befriends a young Neanderthal boy named Doban, but their friendship helps defuse the hatred between the two peoples after Shiva finds her tribe's totem, a magical saber-toothed tiger skull. The sequels are *Shiva Accused* (1991) and *Shiva's Challenge* (1992).

Harper, 1990, 184 pp., o.p., 1992, pap. (0-06-440392-0)

(BL 87:855; HBG 2[July 1990]:77; KR 58:1453; SLJ Dec 1990 p. 100)

1623   BRIGGS, K(atharine) M(ary). *Hobberdy Dick.* **Gr. 6–8. (Orig. British pub.**
✓   **1955.)**

A hobgoblin named Hobberdy Dick uses his magic to help the children of the manor.

Greenwillow, 1977, 239 pp., o.p.

(BL 73:1417; CC:438; CCBB 31:7; HB 53:311; KR 45:166; SLJ May 1977 p. 59)

1624   BRIGGS, K(atharine) M(ary). *Kate Crackernuts.* **Gr. 6–9. (Orig. British pub.**
✓   **1963; rev. ed. 1979.)**

Jealousy of her new stepdaughter, Katherine, drives Kate Maxwell's mother to bewitch the girl, and the two Kates run away together. A retelling of the folktale of the same name.

Greenwillow, 1980, 224 pp. (0-688-80240-0)

(BL 76:1360; CC:454; HB 56:304; KR 48:369; SLJ May 1980 p. 73; VOYA 3[June 1980]:26)

1625   BRINDEL, June Rachuy. *Ariadne.* **Gr. 10 up.**

Two narrators, Ariadne, the young high priestess of Crete, and Daedalus, the Greek refugee physician at the Cretan court, tell this exciting tale of Ariadne's love for Theseus of Athens and the end of matriarchal rule in the Western world.

St. Martin, 1980, o.p., 1981, pap., 246 pp. (0-312-04912-9)

(KR 48:1094; LJ 105:2229; SLJ Jan 1981 p. 74)

BROOKE, William J. *A Telling of the Tales: Five Stories.* See Chapter 3, Fantasy Collections.

1626   BRUST, Steven K. (Zoltan). *Brokedown Palace.* **Gr. 10 up.**

A miraculous tree grows in Fenario, a land ruled by four brothers, in this tale adapted from Hungarian folklore.

Ace, 1986, pap., 270 pp., o.p.

(BBS:54; BL 82:851; VOYA 9:86)

1627   BRUST, Steven K. (Zoltan). *To Reign in Hell.* **Gr. 10 up.**

God and his angels battle Satan for control of the universe in this fantasy about the creation of the world.

SteelDragon, 1984, 258 pp. (0-916595-00-5)

(Kies:22; VOYA 8:393)

1628   BRYHER, Winifred (pseud. of Annie Winifred Ellerman). *A Visa for Avalon.*
✓   **Gr. 8–10.**

Six people whose world is engulfed in revolution escape to the legendary island of Avalon.

Harcourt, 1965, 119 pp., o.p.

(BL 61:980; CCBB 18:143; KR 33:198; LJ 90:1929)

1629 BUCHAN, John. *The Watcher by the Threshold and Other Tales.* **Gr. 10 up. (Orig. British pub. 1902.)**

Three of the five stories in this collection are fantasies: "The Far Islands," "The Watcher by the Threshold," and "The Outgoing of the Tide." "The Far Islands" is about a young man's tragic involvement with the Celtic legend of the Isle of the Apple-Trees.

Doran, 1918, o.p.; Nelson, 1922, 264 pp., o.p.; Scholarly Press, 1971 (repr. of 1918 ed.), 312 pp. (0-403-00880-8)

(BL 15:265; Tymn:56)

1630 BULL, Emma. *War for the Oaks.* **Gr. 10 up.**

Rock guitarist Eddi McCandry is drawn into a war between two Fairy Courts, in this fantasy set in contemporary Minneapolis.

Ace, 1989, pap., 309 pp. (0-441-87073-2)

(BL 84:112, 132, 1246; 86:906; Kies:23; VOYA 10:286)

1631 BURNFORD, Sheila (Philip [née Every] Cochrane). *Mr. Noah and the Second Flood.* **Gr. 5 up. (Orig. Canadian pub. 1973.)**

After Mr. Noah rebuilds the ark to escape a pollution-caused flood, he is shocked to discover how many animals have become extinct.

Illus. by Michael Foreman, Washington Square, 1974, pap., 64 pp., o.p.

(CCBB 27:59; KR 41:753; LJ 98:3474; TLS 1973 p. 386)

1632 *The Camelot Chronicles: Heroic Adventures from the Time of King Arthur.* Ed. by Mike Ashley. Gr. 10 up. (Orig. British pub. 1992.)

A collection of 18 Arthurian stories and novellas written by Jane Yolen, Vera Chapman, Howard Pyle, Phyllis Ann Karr, and others. *The Pendragon Chronicles* (1989, 1990; see below) is a companion volume.

Carroll, 1992, 432 pp. (0-88184-912-X)

(LJ Sept 1, 1992; VOYA 16:36, 17:10)

CAMERON, Eleanor (Frances Butler). *Time and Mr. Bass: A Mushroom Planet Book.* See Chapter 8, Time Travel Fantasy.

1633 CANNING, Victor. *The Crimson Chalice.* **Gr. 10 up.**

This retelling of the Arthurian epic concentrates on the Celtic chieftain Arturo's battles against the Saxon invaders of Roman Britain.

Morrow, 1978, 540 pp., o.p.

(BL 74:1717, 1726; KR 46:649; LJ 103:1529)

1634 CAVANAGH, Helen. *Panther Glade.* **Gr. 4–8.**

Stranded overnight on a Florida island, Bill is forced to confront his fears of the Everglades and ancient Indian spirits.

Simon, 1993, 148 pp. (0-671-75617-6)

(BL 89:1808; CCBB 46:278; HBG 4[Fall 1993]:295; KR 61:717; SLJ June 1993 p. 104; VOYA 16:214)

1635 CHANT, Joy (pseud. of Eileen Joyce Rutter). *The High Kings.* **Gr. 10 up.**

Retellings of tales about the Celtic heroes who ruled the British Isles before Arthur came to power.

Bantam, 1983, 1985, pap., 244 pp. o.p.

(Kies:30; Kliatt 20[Spring 1986]:19)

CHANT, Joy (pseud. of Eileen Joyce Rutter). *Red Moon and Black Mountain: The End of the House of Kendreth.* See Chapter 5C, Travel to Other Worlds.

1636   CHAPMAN, Vera. *The Green Knight* **(The Three Damosels trilogy, book 2). Gr. 10 up. (Orig. British pub. 1975.)**

This retelling of "Sir Gawain and the Green Knight" is told through the eyes of fifteen-year-old Vivian, niece of the sorceress Morgan Le Fay, and eighteen-year-old Gawain, whose knightly chastity is reluctantly tested by Vivian, at her aunt's insistence. The first book in this series, *The King's Damosel* (1976, 1978) describes the adventures of Lady Lynett, who is forced into an unwanted marriage, and then becomes King Arthur's damosel, or royal messenger to his Knights. In the final book, *King Arthur's Daughter* (1976, 1978), Lady Lynett comes to the aid of Ursulet, Arthur and Guinevere's daughter and proclaimed heir to the throne, who is forced into hiding after Arthur's defeat and the breaking up of the Round Table.

Avon, 1978, pap., 173 pp., o.p.

(Kies:30; Kliatt 12[Spring 1978]:5; Tymn:64)

1637   CHERRYH, C. J. (pseud. of Carolyn Janice Cherry). *The Dreamstone* **(Arafel's Saga, book 1). Gr. 10 up. (Revised and expanded from the novella, "Ealdwood," 1981.)**

Arafel, the last of the guardian spirits of Ealdwood, narrates this haunting tale of the last stand of faerie and magic against humanity and iron. The sequel is *The Tree of Swords and Jewels* (1983, pap., 1991).

DAW, 1983, 1987, pap., 192 pp. (0-88677-013-0)

(BBS:54; BL 79:1075, 1084; LJ 108:603; VOYA 6:148)

CHERRYH, C. J. (pseud. of Carolyn Janice Cherry). *Rusalka.* See Chapter 10, Witchcraft and Sorcery Fantasy.

1638   CHRISTIAN, Catherine. *The Pendragon.* **Gr. 10 up.**

Bedivere, Arthur's boyhood friend and lifelong companion, narrates this story of Artus's life from age twelve through his initiation rites with Celidon the Merlin, his tragic love for Vivian (Ygern), his betrayal, and his death.

Warner, 1978, 607 pp., o.p.

(Kies:33; KR 46:1260; LJ 104:126)

1639   CLARKE, Pauline (pseud. of Pauline [Clarke] Hunter Blair). *The Two Faces of Silenus.* **Gr. 5–7.**

Drusilla and Rufus's wish at an Italian fountain brings the ancient god, Silenus, to life.

Coward, 1972, 160 pp., o.p.

(CCBB 26:73; HB 48:594; KR 40:1244; TLS 1972 p. 1325)

1640   COATSWORTH, Elizabeth (Jane). *The Enchanted: An Incredible Tale.* **Gr. 7–9.**
✓   David Ross doesn't believe the Indian legends that the animals of the Enchanted Forest can assume human form, so he buys an abandoned farm on the very edge of the forest.

Pantheon, 1951, 157 pp., o.p.; illus. by Mary Frank, Pantheon, 1968, 151 pp., o.p.; Blackberry, 1992, pap., 156 pp. (0-942396-65-0)

(BL 47:381; HB 27:316; KR 19:233, 36:343; LJ 76:1236, 93:2119)

1641   COATSWORTH, Elizabeth (Jane). *Marra's World.* **Gr. 3–5.**
✓   Marra doesn't understand her grandmother's hatred or her father's disinterest until she discovers that her mother was a selkie, or seal-woman, who went back to live in the sea.

Pantheon, 1951, 157 pp., o.p.;, illus. by Krystyna Turska, Greenwillow, 1975, 83 pp., o.p.

(BL 72:448; CCBB 29:107; HB 52:48; KR 43:1129; SLJ Apr 1976 p. 70; Suth 2:90)

1642 COATSWORTH, Elizabeth (Jane). *Silky: An Incredible Tale.* **Gr. 7–10.**

Silky, a young girl with strange powers, appears one day and helps Cephas Hewes control his temper and end his shiftless ways.

Illus. by John Carroll, Pantheon, 1953, 144 pp., o.p.

(HB 29:229; LJ 78:1164; TLS 1953 p. 813)

1643 COCHRAN, Molly, and MURPHY, Warren. *The Forever King.* **Gr. 10 up.**

✓ In this contemporary version of the Arthurian legend, King Arthur has been reincarnated as a ten-year-old boy named Arthur Blessing, who joins forces with Merlin and the reincarnated Sir Galahad to fight terrorists and a psychotic killer.

Tor, 1992, 368 pp. (0-312-85227-4), 1993, pap. (0-8125-1716-4)

(BL 88:1925, 1929; KR 60:625; LJ June 15, 1992 p. 100; SLJ Dec 1992 pp. 24, 146; VOYA 15:291, 16:10)

1644 COHEN, Barbara. *Roses.* **Gr. 7–10.**

Talented high school senior Isabel's relationships with a middle-aged florist and her would-be boyfriend, Rob, help her to overcome a fear of closeness with anyone but her father, in this modern version of "Beauty and the Beast."

Lothrop, 1984, 224 pp., o.p.

(BL 80:963; CCBB 37:163; SLJ Aug 1984 p. 82)

1645 COHEN, Barbara. *Unicorns in the Rain.* **Gr. 7–9.**

✓ Nikki falls in love with a young man whose family has been told by God to build an ark to save themselves and their animals (including two unicorns) from a disastrous flood.

Atheneum, 1980, 164 pp., o.p.; Macmillan, 1988 (repr.), pap., 176 pp. (0-02-042210-5); Peter Smith, 1992 (0-8446-6484-7)

(BL 77:1148; CCBB 34:29; SLJ Sept 1980 p. 80; VOYA 3[Oct 1980]:31)

COLE, Joanna. *Bony-Legs.* See Chapter 10, Witchcraft and Sorcery Fantasy.

1646 COLLINS, Meghan. *The Willow Maiden.* **Gr. 1–4.**

A young man deeply in love with a Willow Maiden learns that he must let her go back to her willow tree every Spring or their love will not survive.

Illus. by Laszlo Gal, Dial, 1985, 40 pp., LB(0-8037-0218-3), 1988, pap. (0-8037-0558-1)

(BL 82:625; SLJ Jan 1986 p. 55)

1647 CONEY, Michael Greatrex. *The Celestial Steam Locomotive* **(Song of the Earth**
✓ **series, vol. 1). Gr. 10 up.**

In this science-fantasy set in the far future, three humans—Manuel, Zozula, and the Girl-with-No-Name—are chosen by the god Starquin to become the Triad who will change the course of history by going on a quest to find the True Humans aboard the Celestial Steam Locomotive. The sequels are *Gods of the Greatway* (1984), *Fang, the Gnome* (NAL,1988), and *King of the Scepter'd Isle* (NAL, 1989).

Houghton, 1983, 302 pp., o.p.

(KR 51:790; LJ Sept 15, 1983 p. 1811; SLJ Dec 1983 p. 89; VOYA 7:205)

1648 COOLIDGE, Olivia E(nsor). *The King of Men.* **Gr 7 up.**

✓ This retelling of Greek legends follows the life of King Agamemnon from his childhood to his marriage to Clytemnestra, alternating with scenes of the gods quarreling on Mount Olympus and affecting the fates of the mortals.

Illus. by Ellen Raskin, Houghton, 1966, 230 pp., o.p.

(BL 63:37; CCBB 20:106; HB 42:438; KR 34:311; LJ 91:3264)

1649   COONTZ, Otto. *Isle of the Shape-Shifters.* **Gr. 5–8.**

Theo's summer on Nantucket takes on frightening proportions when she discovers that the descendants of local Indian tribes plan to use her in their ancient shape-shifting rites to regain the island for themselves.

Houghton, 1983, 209 pp., o.p.

(BL 80:856; CCBB 37:124; Kies:37; SLJ Mar 1984 p. 157)

1650   COOPER (Grant), Susan (Mary). *Over Sea, Under Stone* **(The Dark Is Rising**
✓✓   **sequence, vol. 1). Gr. 5–8. (Orig. British pub. 1965.)**

Simon, Jane, and Barney Drew set out to find King Arthur's grail, touching off a struggle between good and evil forces, the Light and the Dark. In *The Dark Is Rising* (Atheneum, 1973; Macmillan, 1986, pap.), a boy named Will Stanton travels into the past in search of six magic signs needed by the forces of the Light to hold back the forces of Darkness. Boston Globe Horn Book Award, 1973; Carnegie Medal Commended Book, 1973; John Newbery Medal Honor Book, 1974. In *Greenwitch* (Atheneum, 1974; Macmillan, 1986, pap.), it falls to Jane, Simon, and Barney to retrieve from the sea creature, Greenwitch, a manuscript needed to interpret the inscription on King Arthur's grail. In *The Grey King* (Atheneum, 1975; Macmillan, 1986, pap.), Will and an albino boy named Bran Davies search for the golden harp needed to waken King Arthur's knights for the final battle against the Dark. Carnegie Medal Commended Book, 1975; John Newbery Medal, 1976; Tir na n-Og Award, 1976. In the final volume of this series, *Silver on the Tree* (Atheneum, 1977; Macmillan, 1986, pap.), all five children are summoned to a Welsh mountainside where Will and Bran search for the crystal sword, Eiras, while the Drews meet King Arthur and prepare for the ultimate battle against the forces of Darkness. Tir na n-Og Award, 1978.

Illus. by Margery Gill, Harcourt, 1966, 252 pp. (0-15-259034-X); 1989, pap., 256 pp. (0-02-042785-9)

(BBJ:69; BL 63:118; CC:474; Ch&Bks:255; JHC:348; Kies:38; TLS 1965 p. 513; Tymn:67–71)

1651   COOPER (Grant), Susan (Mary). *The Selkie Girl.* **Gr. K–4.**
✓   A young selkie, or seal-woman, is forced to live with her human husband, Donallan, for twenty years until her youngest son finds her seal-skin, freeing her to return to the sea.

Illus. by Warwick Hutton, Macmillan, 1986, 32 pp. (0-689-50390-3); Macmillan, 1991, pap. (0-689-71467-X)

(BL 83:127; CCBB 40:46; Ch&Bks:255; HB 62:731; KR 54:1443; SLJ Nov 1986 p. 74; Suth 4:83)

1652   COOPER (Grant), Susan (Mary). *Tam Lin.* **Gr. 1–6.**
✓   Margaret, daughter of the king, falls in love with Tam Lin and saves him from the elfin queen in this retelling of the Scottish ballad.

Illus. by Warwick Hutton, Macmillan, 1991, 32 pp. (0-689-50505-1)

(BL 87:1191; CC 1992 Suppl. p. 10; HB 67:340; HBG 2:289; KR 59:43; SLJ May 1991 p. 88)

1653   CREW, Gary. *Strange Objects.* **Gr. 8–12. (Orig. Australian pub. 1990.)**

Alternately told through sixteen-year-old Stephen's notebook entries and various anthropological publications, this is a fantasy-mystery about the strange events that follow Stephen's discovery of a mummfied hand and a three-hundred-year-old journal written by murderers. Children's Book Council of Australia Book of the Year Award, 1991.

Simon, 1993, 224 pp. (0-671-79759-X)

(BL 89:1812; CCBB 47:7; HBG 4[Fall 1993]:308; KR 61:658; SLJ May 1993 p. 124; VOYA 16:162, 17:19)

CROSS, Gillian. *The Dark Behind the Curtain.* See Chapter 4, Ghost Fantasy.

1654 CURLEY, Daniel. *Ann's Spring.* **Gr. 4–6.**

Spring reverts to winter when neighborhood boys lock Mother Nature's children in an old truck and prevent them from supervising the changing of the seasons.

Illus. by Donna Diamond, Crowell, 1977, 48 pp., o.p.

(CCBB 31:12; KR 45:46; SLJ Jan 1977 p. 90)

1655 CURLEY, Daniel. *Billy Beg and the Bull.* **Gr. 3–5.**

Billy Beg flees his wicked stepmother and, with his friend the bull, sets out on an adventure-filled journey from Ireland to China. A retelling of tales from Irish folklore.

Illus. by Frank Bozzo, Crowell, 1978, 127 pp., o.p.

(BL 74:1677; HB 54:289; KR 46:243; SLJ May 1978 p. 65)

1656 CURRY, Ann. *The Book of Brendan.* **Gr. 5–7. (Orig. British pub. 1989.)**

Two children and some magical beasts that have come to life from an illuminated manuscript thwart an evil sorcerer's plot to take over King Arthur's kingdom.

Holiday, 1990, 170 pp. (0-8234-0003-5)

(BL 86:1445; CCBB 43:156; HBG 1[Jan–June 1990]:256; SLJ May 1990 p. 103; VOYA 13:226)

1657 CURRY, Jane Louise. *Beneath the Hill.* **Gr. 5–8.**

✓   When strip mining threatens the mountain home of the Fair Folk, Miggle, Dub, and Stevie help them return to their ancestral land. This is the sequel to *The Change Child* (1969).

Illus. by Imero Gobbato, Harcourt, 1967, 255 pp., o.p.

(BL 63:1146; CCBB 21:25; HB 43:461; LJ 92:2020; KR 35:61; TLS 1968 p. 1113)

CURRY, Jane Louise. *The Daybreakers.* See Chapter 8, Time Travel Fantasy.

1658 CURRY, Jane Louise. *The Sleepers.* **Gr. 5–8.**

✓   Four English young people meet Myrdain the Sorcerer who asks their help in foiling a plot to murder King Arthur and his knights in their sleep.

Illus. by Gareth Floyd, Harcourt, 1968, 255 pp., o.p.

(BL 65:61; HB 44:427; KR 36:459; TLS 1969 p. 351)

CURRY, Jane Louise. *The Watchers.* See Chapter 8, Time Travel Fantasy.

CUTT, W. Towrie. *Seven for the Sea.* See Chapter 8, Time Travel Fantasy.

1659 DALKEY, Kara. *The Nightingale.* **Gr. 6 up.**

In this novelized version of the Hans Christian Andersen story (see Chapter 1, Allegorical Fantasy and Literary Fairy Tales), the nightingale is a beautiful flute player in love with the emperor in tenth-century Japan.

Ace, 1988, 221 pp., o.p.

(BL 84:1786; VOYA 11:192, 12:15)

1660 DAVID, Peter. *Knight Life.* **Gr. 10 up.**

King Arthur escapes from his cave to New York City in the late 1980s, ready to run for mayor, but his "totally honest" campaign attracts the attention of both Merlin and his enemy, Morgan Le Fey, in this spoof of Arthurian legend.

Ace, 1987, 193 pp., o.p.

(BBS:55; VOYA 10:176)

1661 DEAN, Pamela. *Tam Lin.* **Gr. 10 up.**

✓ In this updated version of the sixteenth-century Scottish ballad set on a twentieth-century Minnesota college campus, Janet Carter, an English literature major, discovers that she must defy the Faerie Queen to rescue her own true love.

Tor, 1991, 288 pp. (0-312-85137-5), 1992, pap. (0-8125-4450-1)

(BL 87:1627, 1630; KR 59:365; LJ Mar 15, 1991 p. 119; VOYA 14:238)

1662 DEITZ, Tom. *The Gryphon King.* **Gr. 10 up.**

Two medieval English artifacts, a sword and a manuscript, arrive at the University of Georgia and entangle faculty and students in a deadly magical battle between two mythical worlds.

Avon, 1989, pap., 406 pp. (0-380-75506-8)

(BL 85:1873, 1894, 86:906; LJ May 15, 1989 p. 92)

DEITZ, Tom. *Windmaster's Bane.* See Chapter 5C, Travel to Other Worlds.

DE LINT, Charles. *The Dreaming Place.* See Chapter 5C, Travel to Other Worlds.

1663 DE LINT, Charles. *Jack the Giant-Killer.* **Gr. 10 up. (Orig. pub. in Canada.)**

A young Canadian named Jacky Rowan finds herself caught up in a Scottish fairy tale in which she becomes Jack the Giant-Killer. Canadian Science Fiction and Fantasy Award, 1988. In the sequel, *Drink Down the Moon* (1990), Jacky is kidnapped by a wizard who has stolen the fairy power of the moon.

Ace, 1987, 202 pp., o.p.

(BL 84:752, 775, 86:906; KR 55:1425; VOYA 11:38)

1664 DE LINT, Charles. *Moonheart.* **Gr. 10 up. (Orig. pub. in Canada.)**

Sara Kendell is caught up in an ancient battle between good and evil after she finds four mysterious objects and meets Kieran Foy, apprentice to an ancient Welsh mage. The sequel is *Spiritwalk* (Tor, 1992).

Ace, 1984, pap., 496 pp., o.p.; Tor, 1994, pap. (0-312-89004-4)

(BBS:55; BL 81:558, 582; Kies:45; VOYA 7:335)

DEXTER, Catherine. *The Oracle Doll.* See Chapter 9, Toy Fantasy.

1665 DICKINSON, Peter (pseud. of Malcolm de Brissac). *Merlin Dreams.* **Gr. 6–12.**
✓ **(Orig. British pub. 1988.)**

While Merlin sleeps through his enchantment, his nine dreams become the stories in this book—dreams of dragons, unicorns, damsels, and knights. Kate Greenaway Medal Highly Commended Book, 1988.

Illus. by Alan Lee, Delacorte, 1988, 167 pp. (0-440-50067-2)

(BBC:202; BBJ:70; BL 85:934, 938; CC:479; CCBB 42:96; HB 65:210; KR 56:1525; SLJ Dec 1988 p. 120; TLS 1988 p. 1323; VOYA 11:293)

1666 DIXON, Marjorie (Mack). *The Forbidden Island.* **Gr. 5–7. (Orig. pub. in Eng-**
✓ **land.)**

Libby makes a forbidden visit to the Irish Island of Thunder, and finds it to be inhabited by an ancient race who live by violent, age-old laws.

Illus. by Richard Kennedy, Criterion, 1960, 201 pp., o.p.

(HB 36:515; KR 28:760; LJ 86:4223; TLS May 20, 1960 p. iv)

DONNEHOWER, Bruce. *Miko, Little Hunter of the North.* See Chapter 1, Allegorical Fantasy and Literary Fairy Tales.

1667 DUNLOP, Eileen (Rhona). *Clementina.* **Gr. 6–10. (Orig. British pub. 1985.)**

✓ Spending a month visiting a friend at a Scottish estate, Daisy finds herself caught up in frightening events surrounding twentieth-century Clementina and her ties to a young woman who lived on the estate in 1746 and was involved in the death of a young man.

Holiday, 1987, 156 pp. (0-8234-0642-3)

(BL 83:1286, 1687; CCBB 40:186; HB 63:466; KR 55:635; SLJ May 1987 p. 109; Suth 4:104; VOYA 10:119)

1668 ESTEY, Dale. *A Lost Tale.* **Gr. 10 up.**

Brigid falls in love with a wounded German soldier and enlists the aid of druids and a unicorn to protect him from the British authorities.

St. Martin, 1980, 208 pp., o.p.

(BL 76:1490, 1520, 77:621, 78:594, 86:906; KR 48:305; LJ 105:1000; SLJ Dec 1980 p. 78)

1669 FARJEON, Eleanor. *The Glass Slipper.* **Gr. 5–7. (Orig. British pub. 1946 and**
✓ **1955.)**

A humorous retelling of the Cinderella story.

Illus. by Ernest Shepard, Viking, 1956, 187 pp., o.p.; Buccaneer, 1981 (repr.), LB(0-89967-034-2); Harper, 1986, 213 pp., o.p.

(BBJ:70; BL 52:282, 83:350; CC:483; HB 32:120, 63:84; KR 24:43; LJ 81:1309)

1670 FARJEON, Eleanor. *The Silver Curlew.* **Gr. 3–6. (Orig. British pub. 1953.)**

✓ A young queen must give up her child unless she can guess the Spindle-Imp's name, in this novel-length version of "Rumplestiltskin."

Illus. by Ernest Shepard, Viking, 1954, 162 pp., o.p.

(BL 50:345; CCBB 8:29; HB 30:174; KR 22:114; LJ 79:1064)

1671 FARMER (Mockridge), Penelope. *A Castle of Bone.* **Gr. 5–8. (Orig. British pub.**
✓ **1972.)**

Hugh panics when his friend, Penn, enters a magic cupboard and is changed into a baby.

Atheneum, 1972, 151 pp., o.p.

(BL 69:572; CCBB 26:153; HB 49:52; KR 40:1201; LJ 98:652; TLS 1972 p. 802)

1672 FARMER (Mockridge), Penelope. *Eve: Her Story.* **Gr. 10 up. (Orig. British pub.**
1986.)

A retelling of the biblical creation story from Eve's point of view, that of an intelligent woman determined to learn all she can about her world.

Mercury, 1988, 188 pp. (0-916515-25-7)

(BL 84:604 & 625; KR 55:1594; LJ Dec 1987 p. 127)

1673 FARMER (Mockridge), Penelope. *Year King.* **Gr. 10 up. (Orig. British pub.**
1977.)

Jealous of his twin brother's academic and social successes, Lan, 18, finds that he can enter his brother Lew's body and share his life, but these transformations make him feel even more inadequate and resentful of his twin.

Atheneum, 1977, 232 pp., o.p.

(CCBB 31:125; Ch&Bks:260; HB 54:76; KR 45:1205; SLJ Jan 1978 p. 94; TLS 1977 p. 1246)

1674 FINNEY, Charles G(randison). *The Circus of Dr. Lao.* **Gr. 10 up.**

The mysterious Dr. Lao brings his magical menagerie of mythical beasts and legendary figures to a small Arizona town.

Illus. by Boris Artzybasheff, Viking, 1935, 154 pp., o.p.; Lightyear, 1993, LB(0-89968-402-5)

(Kies:59; Kliatt 11[Winter 1977]:9)

FISK, Pauline. *Midnight Blue.* See Chapter 5C, Travel to Other Worlds.

1675 FLINT, Kenneth C. *Cromm.* **Gr. 10 up.**

Colin McMahon discovers he is the reincarnation of a fourth-century Celtic warrior who once fought an ancient god named Cromm, revived in the twentieth century by a secret cult.

Doubleday, 1990, 387 pp., o.p.; Bantam, 1991, pap. (0-553-28851-2)

(BBS:57; BL 86:1267, 1276; KR 58:69; LJ Feb 15, 1990 p. 215)

1676 FLINT, Kenneth C. *The Dark Druid.* **Gr. 10 up.**

The Dark Druid is angered when legendary Irish hero Finn MacCumhal rescues a young woman from an evil enchantment. This is the sequel to *Challenge of the Clans* (1986) and *The Storm Shield* (1987).

Bantam, 1987, pap., 326 pp. (0-553-26715-9)

(BBS:57; LJ Aug 1987 p. 147; VOYA 10:287)

1677 FLINT, Kenneth C. *The Riders of the Sidhe* **(The Sidhe trilogy, vol. 1). Gr. 10 up.**

Lugh of the Long Arm and his companions, Aine, the sea-god's sister, and Gilla the jester, battle the Formorian invaders of ancient Ireland, in this retelling of a Celtic legend. The sequels are *Champion of the Sidhe* (1984) and *Master of the Sidhe* (1984).

Bantam, 1984, pap., 272 pp., o.p.

(LJ 109:1253; VOYA 7:206)

1678 FLYNN, Casey. *Most Ancient Song* **(The Gods of Ireland series, book 1). Gr. 7–12.**

In a reworking of Ireland's Celtic myths of gods and heroes, this is the story of the peaceful Nemedians who are forced to take up arms to defend themselves from the evil Fomor after crossing the sea to find a new home on a beautiful green island.

Bantam, 1991, pap., 261 pp. (0-553-28832-6)

(Kliatt Apr 1991 p. 18; VOYA 14:179)

1679 FORREST, Elizabeth. *Phoenix Fire.* **Gr. 7 up.**

Chinese archeologists excavating the grave of Ch'in Dynasty Emperor Huang unwittingly wake two long-buried mythical creatures, the Phoenix and a huge and terrible Demon, who eventually clash at the edge of the La Brea Tar Pits in contemporary Los Angeles.

DAW, 1992, pap., 364 pp. (0-88677-515-9)

(LJ Mar 15, 1992 p. 129; VOYA 15:173)

1680 FRIEDMAN, Michael Jan. *The Seekers and the Sword.* **Gr. 10 up.**

In this retelling of Norse mythology, Vidar, one of the immortal but not invulnerable race of the Aesir, must find the lost Sword of Frey to restore peace to Alfheim. This is the sequel to *The Hammer and the Horn* (1985) and is followed by *The Glove of Maiden's Hair* (1987).

Warner, 1985, pap., 263 pp., o.p.

(BL 82:733; LJ Dec 1985 p. 129)

FRIESNER, Esther M. *Gnome Man's Land.* See Chapter 5C, Travel to Other Worlds.

1681 **FRIESNER, Esther M.** *Yesterday We Saw Mermaids.* **Gr. 10 up.**

As three other ships leave Spain to search for the Indies in 1492, a fourth ship, once a tiny brass model, sets sail with an unusual mixture of passengers: two officials of the Inquisition, a gypsy, a sorceress, and a pregnant Jewish virgin.

Tor, 1992, 157 pp. (0-312-85352-1), 1993, pap. (0-8125-1345-2)

(SLJ June 1993 p. 142; VOYA 15:348)

1682 **FRY, Rosalie K(ingsmill).** *The Secret of the Ron Mor Skerry* **(British title:** *Child*
✓ *of the Western Isles,* **1957). Gr. 4–6.**

Fiona McConville searches the Western Isles for her little brother, Jamie, whose mysterious disappearance is connected to local legends about the selkies of Ron Mor Skerry.

Illus. by the author, Dutton, 1959, 95 pp., o.p.

(BL 55:513; HB 35:214; KR 27:39; LJ 84:1696)

1683 **GARD, Joyce (pseud. of Joyce Reeves).** *Talargain.* **Gr. 6–8. (Orig. British pub.**
✓ **1964.)**

A seventh-century orphan, fascinated by the seals near his Farne Island home, appears in modern England and describes his life and attempts to aid King Aldfrith in uniting the British tribes.

Holt, 1965, 251 pp., o.p.

(BL 61:1029; CCBB 19:8; Eakin:134; HB 41:175; KR 33:243; LJ 90:1558)

1684 **GARDEN, Nancy.** *Fours Crossing.* **Gr. 6–8.**

Melissa and her friend, Jed, are kidnapped by a hermit who has kept spring from coming to their New Hampshire town, Fours Crossing. *Watersmeet* (1983) and *The Door Between* (1987) are the sequels in this trilogy involving Celtic mythology.

Farrar, 1981, 199 pp. (0-374-32451-4)

(BBC:203; BL 77:1252; CCBB 34:170; HB 57:431; SLJ May 1981 p. 72)

1685 **GARDNER, Craig Shaw.** *The Other Sinbad* **(Arabian Nights trilogy, book 1).**
Gr. 7 up.

Sinbad the Porter undertakes the eighth voyage of his namesake, Sinbad the Sailor, and is haunted by the creatures his namesake encountered on his first seven adventures. The sequels to this humorous story are *A Bad Day for Ali Baba* (1992) and *The Last Arabian Night* (1993).

Ace, 1991, pap., 248 pp. (0-441-76720-6)

(Kliatt Apr 1992, p. 14; VOYA 14:382, 15:10)

1686 **GARDNER, John (Champlin) (Jr.).** *Grendel.* **Gr. 10 up.**
✓ This version of the Anglo-Saxon legend of Beowulf is told from the point of view of Grendel, the marauding monster whom Beowulf sets out to destroy.

Illus. by Emil Antonucci, Knopf, 1971 (0-394-47143-1); Ballantine, 1972, 1975, 1979, pap., 140 pp. (0-345-28865-3)

(BBS:57; BL 68:353; KR 39:762; LJ 96:2670, 97:1180; TLS 1972 p. 793; Tymn:87)

1687 **GARFIELD, Leon.** *The Wedding Ghost.* **Gr. 7 up. (Orig. British pub. 1985.)**

✓ Jack and Jill open a strange wedding gift; a mysterous map that leads Jack through foggy London into a demonic forest where a dust-covered Sleeping Beauty lies in a golden mansion.

Illus. by Charles Keeping, Oxford, 1987, 66 pp. (0-19-79779-4), pap., 1992 (0-19-272246-8)

(BBS:57; BL 83:1275; CCBB 40:144; Ch&Bks:256; HB 63:611; KR 55:637; SLJ June–July 1987 p. 106; Suth 4:130; TLS 1985 p. 350)

1688 **GARFIELD, Leon, and BLISHEN, Edward.** *The God Beneath the Sea.* **Gr. 8**
✓ **up. (Orig. British pub. 1970.)**

This story poetically weaves together the legends of Greek mythology, including those about Prometheus, Pandora, and Persephone. Carnegie Medal, 1970; Kate Greenaway Medal, Honors List, 1970.

Illus. by Zevi Blum, Pantheon, 1971, 212 pp., o.p.

(BL 68:144, 150; CCBB 25:56; HB 47:477; LJ 96:2137; TLS 1970 p. 1254)

1689 **GARFIELD, Leon, and BLISHEN, Edward.** *The Golden Shadows: A Recre-*
✓ *ation of Greek Legends.* **Gr. 7 up.**

An old bard travels through ancient Greece collecting stories, which are woven into this powerful retelling of the myths surrounding the life of Heracles.

Illus. by Charles Keeping, Pantheon, 1973, 159 pp., o.p.

(BL 70:592; CCBB 27:78; HB 50:45; KR 41:1370, LJ 99:1226; TLS 1973 p. 675)

GARNER, Alan. *Elidor.* See Chapter 5C, Travel to Other Worlds.

1690 **GARNER, Alan.** *The Owl Service.* **Gr. 6–9. (Orig. British pub. 1967.)**

✓✓ A curse on the set of owl-decorated dishes found by Gwyn, Alison, and Roger turns the two boys against each other and threatens Alison's life. Carnegie Medal, 1967; Guardian Award for Children's Fiction, 1968.

Walck, 1968, 202 pp., o.p.; Philomel, 1979, 156 pp., o.p.; ABC-CLIO, repr., 1987, o.p.; Dell, 1992, pap., 160 pp. (0-440-40735-4)

(BBC:203; BL 65:310, 900; CCBB 22:58; Ch&Bks:255; HB 44:563; Kies:63; KR 36:1058; LJ 93:3980; Suth:143; TLS 1967 p. 1134, 1969 p. 1384; Tymn:89)

1691 **GARNER, Alan.** *The Weirdstone of Brisingamen.* **Gr. 5–8. (Orig. British pub.**
✓ **1960.)**

The stone on Susan's bracelet is the key to power over 140 knights who lie in an enchanted sleep within a nearby mountain. When this weirdstone is stolen, two dwarfs help Susan and her brother, Colin, make a torturous journey to recover and return it to its rightful owner. In the sequel, *The Moon of Gomrath* (orig. British pub. 1963; U.S. 1967, 1981), Susan's bracelet brings Morrigan the witch and her evil moon spirits into the twentieth century to battle the good dwarfs and elves.

Walck, 1961, 253 pp., o.p.; Philomel, 1979, 224 pp., o.p.

(BL 76:718; CCBB 15:29; Ch&Bks:255; HB 46:45; Kies:63; KR 37:940; LJ 95:786; SLJ May 1980 p. 90; Tymn:87–88)

1692 **GARNETT, David.** *Two by Two: A Story of Survival.* **Gr. 8 up. (Orig. British pub. 1963.)**

Two girls disguise themselves as monkeys and stow away on Noah's ark in order to survive the flood.

Atheneum, 1964, 143 pp., o.p.

(BL 60:489; LJ 89:653; TLS 1963 p. 781)

1693 GEAR, W. Michael, and GEAR, Kathleen O'Neal. *People of the Fire.* **Gr. 10 up.**

In this fantasy saga based on Native American folklore and mysticism, young Little Dancer, destined to become a powerful dreamer, is the Red Hand people's only hope against the machinations of a brutal chief who is draining the power from the sacred Wolf Bundle. This is the sequel to *People of the Wolf* (1990), and is followed by *People of the Earth* (1992) and *People of the River* (1992).

Tor, 1991, pap., 467 pp. (0-8125-2150-1)

(BL 87:1011, 1049; VOYA 14:95)

1694 GEMMELL, David. *Lion of Macedon.* **Gr. 10 up. (Orig. British pub. 1990.)**

Parmenion, a half-Spartan, half-Macedonian warrior in pre-Alexandrian Greece, rises to become second in command to Philip of Macedonia. The sequel is *Dark Prince* (1993).

Ballantine, 1992, pap., 560 pp. (0-345-37911-X)

(LJ Sept 15, 1992 p. 97; Kliatt Mar 1993 p. 16)

1695 GERSTEIN, Mordicai (adapt.). *The Seal Mother.* **Gr. K–4.**

✓ A fiddler playing to the seals on Midsummer's Eve tells a young boy the story of a seal who shed her skin to marry a human, bore a son, and eventually returned to her home in the sea.

Illus. by the adapt., Dial, 1986, 32 pp., LB(0-8037-0303-1), pap., 1990 (0-8037-0743-6)

(BL 83:128; CCBB 40:48; HB 63:200; KR 54:1445; SLJ Nov 1986 p. 76; Suth 4:136)

1696 GODWIN, Parke. *Beloved Exile* **(The Camelot trilogy, book 2). Gr. 10 up.**

King Arthur's widow, Queen Guenevere, narrates this story of her expulsion from Camelot after her husband's death, her enslavement, and her dream of returning to her homeland. This is the sequel to *Firelord* (Doubleday, 1980, o.p.). In *The Last Rainbow* (1985), an injured priest named Patrick falls in love with the Faerie queen, who wants him to save her people.

Bantam, 1984, pap., 422 pp. (0-553-24924-X)

(BL 80:1273, 1274; KR 52:367; LJ 109:1253; SLJ Nov 1984 p. 145)

1697 GODWIN, Parke. *Sherwood* **(Robin Hood duology, book 1). Gr. 10 up.**

A retelling of the Robin Hood legend set 100 years earlier than usual, during the Norman Conquest of Britain in 1066, with Robin as an Anglo-Saxon leader resisting William the Conquerer, and the Sheriff of Nottingham as a sympathetic young Norman knight. The sequel is *Robin and the King* (1993).

Morrow, 1991, 384 pp. (0-688-05264-9)

(BL 87:1842, 1843; KR 59:748; LJ July 1991 p. 134)

1698 GOLDSTEIN, Lisa. *Strange Devices of the Sun and Moon.* **Gr.10 up.**

Widowed bookseller Alice Wood discovers that the exiled fairy folk have returned to Elizabethan London, and that her missing son, Arthur, is to become their king.

Tor, 1993, 304 pp. (0-312-85460-9)

(BL 89:1041, 1045; KR 60:1471; LJ Dec 1992 p. 191; VOYA 16:164)

1699 GORDON, John (William). *The Giant under the Snow: A Story of Suspense.* **Gr. 5–7. (Orig. British pub. 1968.)**

An ancient brooch gives Jonquil, Bill, and Arthur the ability to fly in order to protect the Seal of Power from a huge Green Man.

Illus. by Rocco Negri, Harper, 1970, 200 pp., o.p.

(BL 67:492; Kies:68; KR 38:1037; LJ 95:4374)

1700   **GORDON, John (William).** *The House on the Brink: A Story of Suspense.* **Gr. 8 up. (Orig. British pub. 1970.)**

At "the house on the brink," Dick and Helen are drawn into a strange game involving divining for water and the lost treasure of King John.

Harper, 1971, 217 pp., o.p.

(HB 47:489; KR 39:683; LJ 96:4199; TLS 1970 p. 1251)

1701   **GOROG, Judith.** *Winning Scheherazad.* **Gr. 5–9.**

In this sequel to the fairy tale about the girl who saves her own life by telling her captor 1001 stories, Scheherazad, now Storyteller of the Kingdom, tries to escape from an unwanted suitor by running away to the desert.

Macmillan, 1991, 112 pp. (0-689-31648-8)

(BL 87:1193; CCBB 44:218; HBG 2:290; KR 59:392; SLJ Apr 1991 p. 118; VOYA 14:170)

1702   **GREELEY, Andrew M(oran).** *The Magic Cup: An Irish Legend.* **Gr. 10 up.**

King Cormac of Ireland falls in love with the slave girl, Brigid, while searching for the holy grail.

McGraw-Hill, 1979, o.p.; Warner, 1985, 304 pp., o.p.

(BBS:57; BL 76:540, 548; Kies:71; Kliatt 19[Spring 1985]:10; KR 47:1081; LJ 104:2118)

1703   **GREEN, Roger J(ames).** *The Fear of Samuel Walton* **(The Stone Cycle, vol. 1). Gr. 10 up. (Orig. British pub. 1984.)**

Having found an old book which reveals that a Stone on the hill above the Walton farm becomes powerful every thousand years and takes human lives on Midsummer Day, Samuel feels powerless to protect his family from the evil of the Stone. The sequels are *The Lengthening Shadow* (1986), *The Devil Finds Work* (1987), and *They Watched Him Die* (1988).

Illus. by David Parkins, Oxford Univ. Pr., 1984, 235 pp., o.p.

(BL 81:982; HB 61:315; SLJ May 1985 p. 101; TLS Feb 22, 1985 p. 101)

1704   **GREENE, Jacqueline Dembar.** *The Leveller.* **Gr. 6–8.**

Tom Cook is a young man who steals from the rich to help the poor, despite the fact that his mother signed his soul over to the devil to save him from death as a child.

Walker, 1984, 128 pp. (0-8027-6521-1)

(BBC:204; BL 80:1549; CCBB 37:146; HB 60:474; SLJ Apr 1984 p. 114)

1705   **GUARD, David.** *Deirdre: A Celtic Legend.* **Gr. 10 up.**

A druidic prophecy that Deirdre's beauty would bring death and destruction to the land of Ulster, causes the King to imprison her, but she falls in love with a young knight and flees the country, bringing about war and their deaths.

Celestial Arts, 1981, o.p.; Tricycle, 1993 (repr. 1977 ed.), 120 pp. (1-883672-05-8)

(BL 74:375; SLJ Nov 1977 p. 79)

1706   **GUY, Rosa (Cuthbert).** *My Love, My Love, or, the Peasant Girl.* **Gr. 9 up.**

✓ This touching story about the ill-fated love of a Caribbean peasant girl for a rich young man she rescued from a car crash, is based on Hans Christian Andersen's "The Little Mermaid."

Holt, 1985, pap., 119 pp. (0-8050-1659-7)

(BL 82:108, 124; KR 53:891; LJ Oct 15, 1985 p. 101; SLJ Jan 1986 p. 84; VOYA 9:30)

1707   **HALDEMAN, Linda (Wilson).** *Esbae: A Winter's Tale.* **Gr. 10 up.**

In order to pass his college finals, a lazy young man makes a bargain with the demon

Asmodeas, which involves the sacrifice of a coed who has come under the protection of the exiled sprite, Esbae.

Avon, 1981, 1984, pap., 224 pp., o.p.

(BL 78:537, 545, 594; Kliatt 16[Winter 1982]:21; VOYA 5[Apr 1982]:39)

1708   HALDEMAN, Linda (Wilson). *The Lastborn of Elvinwood.* **Gr. 10 up.**

Ian James is captured by fairies in a local forest, reduced to fairy size, and becomes a reluctant participant in their plot to exchange a fairy for a female human child.

Doubleday, 1978, 237 pp., o.p.

(BL 75:860, 78:594; KR 46:962, 1077; TLS 1981 p. 1375)

HAMILTON (Adoff), Virginia (Esther). *The All Jahdu Storybook.* See Chapter 6, Humorous Fantasy.

1709   HAMILTON (Adoff), Virginia (Esther). *The Magical Adventures of Pretty Pearl.*
✓   **Gr. 7–10.**

Young Pretty Pearl is transformed from a god-child into a human as she helps relieve the suffering of the black slaves in the pre-Civil War South.

Harper, 1983, 320 pp., LB(0-06-022187-9), 1986, pap. (0-06-440178-2)

(BL 79:1020, 1034; CC:497; CCBB 36:167; Ch&Bks:286; HB 59:312; Kies:75; KR 51:380; SLJ Apr 1983 p. 123, May 1983 p. 32; Suth 3:172; VOYA 6:215)

1710   HAMLETT, Christina. *The Enchanter.* **Gr. 10 up.**

Merlin travels to twentieth-century Washington, D.C., to find his true love, Catherine, now a newspaper reporter, and to ask her help in retrieving Excalibur.

Evans, 1990, 220 pp., o.p.

(BBS:58; BL 87:26, 36; LJ Aug 1990 p. 141)

HAMLEY, Dennis. *Pageants of Despair.* See Chapter 8, Time Travel Fantasy.

1711   HARRIS, Rosemary (Jeanne). *The Moon in the Cloud* **(The Nile trilogy, book**
✓✓   **1). Gr. 6–8. (Orig. British pub. 1968.)**

In this, the first volume of a trilogy, Reuben agrees to go to Egypt in search of a pair of lions and a royal cat, in order to pay for his family's passage on Noah's Ark. *The Moon in the Cloud* was awarded the Carnegie Medal, 1968. In *The Shadow on the Sun* (1970) the young king of Egypt disguises himself to court the Chamberlain's daughter, Meri-Mekhmet. She is kidnapped, and he sends his friend Reuben to rescue her. In *The Bright and Morning Star* (1972), Reuben and Thamar arrive in Egypt to find a cure for their son's illness, and become enmeshed in a power struggle between the Prince and Princess's advisors.

Macmillan, 1968, 182 pp., o.p.; Peter Smith, 1989 (0-8446-6429-4); Faber, 1990, pap., 176 pp. (0-571-15338-0)

(BL 66:982; CCBB 23:159; Ch&Bks:256; HB 46:167, 64:236; KR 38:7; LJ 95:1911, 1953, 4325; Suth:169)

1712   HARRIS, Rosemary (Jeanne). *The Seal-Singing.* **Gr. 7–10. (Orig. British pub.**
✓   **1971.)**

Miranda's eerie resemblance to an infamous Scottish ancestor portends her own supernatural power over the seals.

Macmillan, 1971, 245 pp., o.p.

(BL 68:364; CCBB 25:57; Ch&Bks:286; HB 48:57; KR 39:954; LJ 96:4190; Suth:169; TLS 1971 p. 1318)

1713   **HASTINGS, Selina.** *Sir Gawain and the Green Knight.* **Gr. 3 up. (Orig. British**
✓   **pub. 1981.)**

A retelling of the Arthurian tale of young Gawain's testing by the Green Knight. *Sir Gawain and the Loathly Lady* (1985), a companion volume, won the Kate Greenaway Medal for its illustrations by Juan Wijngaard, 1985.

Illus. by Juan Wijngaard, Lothrop, 1981, 32 pp. (0-688-00592-6)

(BL 78:44; CC:100; Ch&Bks:288; CCBB 39:47; HB 57:673; KR 49:1298; SLJ Oct 1981 p. 142; Suth 4:66; TLS 1981 p. 1360)

1714   **HELPRIN, Mark.** *Swan Lake.* **Gr. 6 up.**
✓

An elderly royal tutor tells the tragic love story of Prince Siegfried and the swan maiden Odette to their daughter, in this beautifully illustrated novelization of the ballet.

Illus. by Chris Van Allsburg, Houghton, 1989, 80 pp. (0-395-49858-9), 1992, pap. (0-395-64647-2)

(BL 86:274, 349; CCBB 43:85; HB 66:63; HBG 1[July 1989]:72; KR 57:1530; SLJ Dec 1989 p 125; VOYA 12:356)

1715   **HIEATT, Constance B(artlett).** *The Knight of the Cart.* **Gr. 5–7.**
✓

Sir Lancelot rescues Queen Guinevere from the evil Sir Malagant, in this Arthurian retelling from medieval sources. *Sir Gawain and the Green Knight* (1967), *The Knight of the Lion* (1968), *The Joy of the Court* (1971), *The Sword and the Grail* (1972), *The Castle of the Ladies* (1973), and *The Minstrel Knight* (1974) are companion volumes.

Illus. by John Gretzer, Crowell, 1969, 85 pp., o.p.

(BL 66:516; CCBB 23:129; Ch&Bks:245; HB 45:671; KR 37:1067; LJ 95:242)

1716   **HODGES, Margaret, adapt.** *The Kitchen Knight: A Tale of King Arthur.* **Gr. 3–5.**
✓

Sir Gareth spends a year scrubbing pots in King Arthur's kitchen and then helps Lady Linesse rescue her sister from the Red Knight.

Illus. by Trina Schart Hyman, Holiday, 1990, 52 pp. (0-8234-0787-X)

(BL 87:660, 970; CC 1992 Suppl. p. 11; CCBB 44:62; Ch&Bks:238; HB 67:77; HBG 2[July–Dec 1990]:101; KR 58:1324; SLJ Jan 1991 p. 101; Suth 4:18; TLS July 12, 1991 p. 21)

1717   **HOLDSTOCK, Robert (P.) (pseud. of Robert Faulcon).** *Mythago Wood.* **Gr. 10**
✓   **up. (Orig. British pub. 1984.) (Ryhope Woods series, book 1.)**

Upon his return from battle in World War II, Steven Huxley and his brother Christian are inexorably drawn into a horrifying world within the forest near their home, a world where mythical creatures actually exist. World Fantasy Convention Award, Best Novel, 1985. The sequels are *Lavondyss* (Morrow, 1989) and *The Hollowing* (Penguin, 1994).

Arbor House, 1985, 252 pp., o.p.; Berkley, 1986, pap., o.p.; Avon, 1991, pap., 288 pp. (0-380-76276-5)

(BL 82:468, 482; Kies:81; KR 53:1048; LJ Nov 15, 1985 p. 112; TLS 1985 p. 284; VOYA 9:40)

1718   **HOLT, Tom.** *Who's Afraid of Beowulf?* **Gr. 10 up. (Orig. British pub. 1988.)**

By removing a brooch from a Viking ship found at a Scottish archeological dig, Hildy Frederiksen awakens a Norse king, his wizard, and his warriors, who need her help to fight their old enemy, an evil sorcerer.

St. Martin's, 1989, 208 pp., o.p.; Ace, 1991, pap. (0-441-88591-8)

(BBS:58; BL 85:835, 861; KR 56:1781; VOYA 12:116, 13:16)

1719   **HOOVER, H(elen) M(ary).** *The Dawn Palace: The Story of Medea.* **Gr. 7–12.**

A retelling of the Greek legend of Jason and Medea, portraying Medea as a beautiful, intelligent woman betrayed by her love for handsome, arrogant Jason, who takes her away from her home in Colchis to a life in Greece where she is despised and feared.

Dutton, 1988, 244 pp., o.p.

(BL 84:1667, 1676; CCBB 41:207; KR 56:539; SLJ Sept 1988 p. 198; VOYA 11:238)

1720   HUDDY, Delia. *Time Piper.* Gr. 6–9. (Orig. British pub. 1976.)
✓   While assisting a young scientist in building a time machine, Luke falls in love with a mysterious girl called Hare who is somehow connected to the missing children of twelfth-century Hamelin.

Greenwillow, 1979, 237 pp., o.p.

(CCBB 33:29; HB 55:309; KR 47:580; Kies:84; SLJ Mar 1979 p. 140; TLS Dec 10, 1976 p. 1547)

1721   HUFF, Tanya. *Gate of Darkness, Circle of Light.* Gr. 10 up.

Although almost no one on earth believes in magic, Rebecca and Roland realize they must find an Adept of Light to stop an Adept of Darkness's Midsummer's Night sacrifice that will loose Darkness across the world.

DAW, 1989, pap., 272 pp., o.p.

(BBS:59; BL 86:528, 540; LJ Nov 15, 1989 p. 108; VOYA 13:38, 14:11)

1722   HUNTER, Mollie (pseud. of Maureen Mollie Hunter McVeigh McIlwraith). *A*
✓   ***Stranger Came Ashore.* Gr. 6–8. (Orig. pub. in England.)**

No one but Robbie suspects that the handsome stranger who wishes to marry his sister may actually be the Great Selkie, a legendary seal-man who carries young girls off to the bottom of the sea. Boston Globe Horn Book Award Honor Book for Fiction, 1976.

Harper, 1975, 192 pp., o.p., pap., 1977 (0-06-440082-4)

(BBJ:71; BL 72:303, 80:95; CC:507; CCBB 29:79; Ch&Bks:256; HB 51:592; KR 43:1067; SLJ Dec 1975 p. 31; Suth 2:233; TLS 1975 p. 1053)

HUNTER, Mollie (pseud. of Maureen Mollie Hunter McVeigh McIlwraith). *The Walking Stones: A Story of Suspense.* See Chapter 10, Witchcraft and Sorcery Fantasy.

INGRAM, Tom (Thomas Henry). *The Night Rider.* See Chapter 8, Time Travel Fantasy.

1723   IPCAR, Dahlov (Zorach). *The Queen of Spells.* Gr. 6–9.
✓   In this retelling of the ballad of Tam Lin, Janet is able to enter the Green World to save her lover, Tom, but only on Halloween night.

Viking, 1973, 128 pp., o.p.

(BL 70:51; CCBB 27:45; KR 41:396; LJ 98:2665)

1724   IRVING, Washington. *The Legend of Sleepy Hollow.* Gr. 4 up. (Orig. U.S. pub.
✓   **in *The Sketch-Book of Geoffrey Crayon, Gent.*, 1819; as a separate tale, 1849.)**

Ichabod Crane, a superstitious schoolmaster courting a wealthy farmer's beautiful daughter, is frightened off by his rival Brom Bones, masquerading as the legendary headless horseman.

Illus. by Arthur Rackham, McKay, 1928, o.p.; illus. by Leonard Everett Fisher, Watts, 1966, o.p.; Buccaneer, 1982 (repr. of 1849 ed.), LB(0-89966-410-5); retold by Robert D. San Souci, illus. by Daniel San Souci, Doubleday, 1986, 32 pp., LB(0-385-23397-3); illus. by Barry Moser, Harcourt, 1986 (entitled *Two Tales: Rip Van Winkle and The Legend of Sleepy Hollow*), o.p.; adapt. by Diane Wolkstein, illus. by R. W. Alley, Morrow, 1987, 32 pp., o.p.; illus. by Arthur Rackham, Morrow. 1990, 112 pp. (0-688-05276-2);

illus. by Gary Kelley, Stewart, 1990, 64 pp. (1-55670-046-6); illus. by Michael Garland, Boyds Mills, 1992, 62 pp. (1-56397-027-9)

(BBC:205; BL 25:174, 83:623, 641, 87:1125, 89:513; Bookshelf 1929 p. 21; HB 67:224; HBG 2[July–Dec 1990]:72, 75, 4[Spring 1993]:71; JHC:374; LJ 91:2210; Mahony 2:260; SLJ Nov 1992 p. 94)

1725   **IRVING, Washington.** *Rip Van Winkle.* **Gr. 4–7. (Orig. pub. in** *The Sketch-Book*
✓   ***of Geoffrey Crayon, Gent.,* 1819; as a separate tale in 183?.)**

After a drinking bout with some strange little men, Rip falls asleep for twenty years.

Illus. by Arthur Rackham, Doubleday, 1905, o.p.; illus. by Maria L. Kirk, Stokes, 1908, o.p.; illus. by Charles Robinson, Stokes, 1915, o.p.; illus. by N. C. Wyeth, McKay, 1921, o.p.; illus. by Arthur Rackham, Harper, 1967, o.p.; Buccaneer, 1983 (repr.) (0-89966-411-3); retold by Catherine Storr, illus. by Peter Wingham, Raintree, 1984 (0-8172-2108-5); adapt. by Morrell Gipson, illus. by Daniel San Souci, Doubleday, 1984, 1987, pap. (0-385-23965-3); illus. by Barry Moser, Harcourt, 1986 (entitled *Two Tales: Rip Van Winkle and The Legend of Sleepy Hollow*), o.p.; illus. by N. C. Wyeth, Morrow, 1987, 110 pp. (0-688-07459-6); Puffin, 1987, pap. (0-14-035051-9); adapt. and illus. by Thomas Locker, Dial, 1988, LB(0-8037-0521-2); retold and illus. by John Howe, Little, 1988, 32 pp. (0-316-37578-0), pap. (0-316-37584-5); illus. by Arthur Rackham, Dial, 1992, 124 pp. (0-8037-1264-2); illus. by Gary Kelley, Creative, 1993, 62 pp. LB(0-88682-631-4)

(BBC:205; BL 18:65, 63:586, 81:589, 791, 84:64, 85:408; CC:509; CCBB 38:150; HBG 4[Spring 1993]:71, 5:77; JHC:374; Kies:86; KR 56:1241; LJ 47:869, 92:350; Mahony 2:260; SLJ Mar 1985 p. 154, Nov 1987 p. 92, Dec 1993 p. 112)

1726   **ISH-KISHOR, Sulamith.** *The Master of Miracle: A New Novel of the Golem.* **Gr.**
✓   **5–8.**

A huge clay being created by the Rabbi of Prague to protect the Jews from anti-Semitic attacks goes on a rampage when its creator tries to destroy it.

Illus. by Arnold Lobel, Harper, 1971, 108 pp., o.p.

(BL 68:394, 669; HB 47:611; KR 39:1120; LJ 96:3902)

1727   **JAMES, J. Alison.** *Runa.* **Gr. 6–9.**

American thirteen-year-old Runa is drawn into an ancient family curse while visiting her Swedish grandfather.

Macmillan, 1993, 138 pp. (0-689-31708-5)

(BL 89:1958; CCBB 47:12; HBG 4[Fall 1993]:299; KR 61:662: SLJ July 1993 p. 101; VOYA 16:228)

1728   **JOHNSON, Dorothy M(arie).** *Witch Princess.* **Gr. 6–9.**

The enchantress Medea creates the illusion of evil occurrences to escape from Corinth with her sons and save her father's land from the Argonauts, in this retelling of a Greek legend.

Illus. by Carolyn Cather, Houghton, 1967, 192 pp., o.p.

(BL 64:681, 700; KR 35:1145; LJ 92:3850)

1729   **JOHNSTON, Norma.** *Pride of Lions: The Story of the House of Atreus.* **Gr. 8–12.**

A powerful retelling of the tragic story of Queen Clytemnestra and King Agamemnon: the father who sacrifices his daughter, Iphigenia, to aid the cause of the Trojan War, and the mother whose revenge on her husband curses the lives of their other children, Electra and Orestes.

Atheneum, 1979, 156 pp., o.p.

(BL 76:110; HB 56:180; SLJ Nov 1979 p. 88)

1730 **JOHNSTON, Norma.** *Strangers Dark and Gold.* **Gr. 7–12.**

✓ A poetic retelling of the tragic Greek myth of Jason and Medea, the young sailor questing for the golden fleece who wins the love of the virgin priestess of Hecate, the princess of Colchis.

Atheneum, 1975, 240 pp., o.p.

(BL 71:1070, 1075; CCBB 29:12; KR 43:245; SLJ Apr 1975 p. 66)

1731 **JONES, Courtway.** *In the Shadow of the Oak King* **(Story of the Dragon's Heirs trilogy, book 1). Gr. 10 up.**

In this retelling of Arthurian lore, Arthur's older half-brother, Pelleas, helps Myrddin raise his younger brother, Arthur, from childhood to his marriage to Guinevere. The sequel is *Witch of the North* (1992).

Pocket, 1991, 320 pp. (0-671-73404-0)

(KR 59:687; LJ Aug 1991 p. 150; SLJ Apr 1992 p. 163)

1732 **JONES, Diana Wynne.** *Eight Days of Luke.* **Gr. 7–9. (Orig. British pub. 1975.)**

✓ Orphaned David's miserable life changes dramatically after he recites a curse releasing a fire-loving boy named Luke from an other-world prison.

Greenwillow, 1988, 150 pp. (0-688-08006-5); Knopf, 1990, pap. (0-394-84339-8)

(BBJ:71; BL 85:320; CC:511; CCBB 42:11; Ch&Bks:287; HB 64:789; KR 56:1061; SLJ Sept, 1988 p. 184; Suth. 4:206; TLS 1975 p. 365; VOYA 11:295)

JONES, Diana Wynne. *Fire and Hemlock.* See Chapter 10, Witchcraft and Sorcery Fantasy.

1733 **JONES, Diana Wynne.** *The Power of Three.* **Gr. 6–9. (Orig. British pub. 1976.)**

An ancient curse is revived and entangles three psychic children, a race of giants, and a group of shape-shifting Dorig in a struggle for water. Commended Book, Guardian Award for Children's Fiction, 1977.

Greenwillow, 1977, 250 pp., o.p.

(BBC:206: BL 74:298; KR 45:790; SLJ Nov 1977 p. 58; TLS 1976 p. 383)

1734 **KARR, Phyllis Ann.** *The Idylls of the Queen.* **Gr. 10 up.**

After one of the knights of Arthur's Round Table dies of poisoning, Sir Kay must conduct an investigation to clear Queen Guinevere of the suspicion of murder.

Ace, 1982, pap., 352 pp., o.p.

(BBS:59; BL 79:92, 105; VOYA 5[Dec 1982]:38)

1735 **KATZ, Welwyn Wilton.** *False Face.* **Gr. 6–9. (Orig. Canadian pub. 1987.)**

Two Iroquois false-face masks exude an evil power that exacerbates the tensions between thirteen-year-old Laney and her divorced mother, eventually threatening Laney's life.

Macmillan, 1988, 200 pp. (0-689-50456-X)

(BBJ:72; BL 85:399, 410; KR 56:1151; SLJ Nov 1988 p. 126, VOYA 11:286)

KATZ, Welwyn Wilton. *The Third Magic.* See Chapter 5C, Travel to Other Worlds.

1736 **KEANEY, Brian.** *No Need for Heroes.* **Gr. 5–8. (Orig. British pub. 1989.)**

Princess Ariadne of Crete rejects both her mad father, King Minos, and the new male cult of the Bull, in favor of the goddess-cult of the Great Mother and her own independence, in this retelling of the Greek myth of the Minotaur.

Oxford Univ. Pr., 1989, 114 pp., o.p.

(CCBB 42:253; KR 57:838; SLJ July 1989, p. 91; VOYA 12:166)

1737 **KENNEALY (Morrison), Patricia.** *The Hawk's Gray Feather: A Book of the Keltiad* **(The Tales of Arthur, vol. 1). Gr. 10 up.**

The bard Taliesin, foster brother of Arthur, heir to the throne of Keltia, narrates this story of Arthur's rebellion against Edeyrn, the tyranical Death-druid who overthrew the Royal House of Don and has ruled Keltia through sorcery and bloodshed for the past two hundred years. The sequel is *The Oak Above the Kings* (NAL, 1994). This series is set 1500 years earlier in the same world as Kennealy's Tales of Aeron series (1984–1988): *The Copper Crown* (1984; see Chapter 5A, Alternate Worlds or Histories), *The Throne of Scone* (1986, 1987), and *The Silver Branch* (1988).

NAL, 1990, 400 pp. (0-451-45053-1)

(Kliatt Apr 1991 p. 20; LJ Mar 15, 1990 p. 116; VOYA 13:229, 14:142)

1738 **KESEY, Ken.** *The Sea Lion: A Story of the Sea Cliff People.* **Gr. 3–6.**

✓   Only orphaned, crippled Eemook recognizes the true identity of the evil sea spirit who appears among his Pacific Northwest coastal people, and he saves his tribe from destruction.

Illus. by Neil Waldman, Viking, 1991, 48 pp. (0-670-83916-7)

(BL 88:328; CCBB 45:95; HBG 3[Spring 1992]:67; KR 59:1161; SLJ Nov 1991 p. 101)

1739 **KING, Bernard.** *Starkadder.* **Gr. 10 up.**

The legendary Norse warrior Starkadder has been cursed with immortality by the Fates and will be allowed to die only after committing three terrible betrayals. The sequel is *Vargr-Moon* (1988).

St. Martin, 1987, 244 pp., o.p.

(KR 55:1355; LJ Oct 15, 1987 p. 95; VOYA 10:288)

KIPLING, (Joseph) Rudyard. *Kipling's Fantasy.* See Chapter 3, Fantasy Collections.

1740 **KUSHNER, Ellen.** *Thomas the Rhymer.* **Gr. 10 up.**

✓   After the Queen of Elfland captures wandering minstrel Thomas the Rhymer, she enslaves him for seven years and then casts him back, cursed with a tongue that can speak only the truth, in this novelization of an English folk tale. 1991 Mythopoeic Fantasy Award. 1991 World Fantasy Convention Award, Best Novel.

Morrow, 1990, 224 pp. (1-557-10046-2); Tor, 1991, pap. (0-8125-1445-9)

(BBS:60; BL 86:1420, 1430; KR 58:211; LJ Mar 15, 1990 p. 116)

LA MOTTE FOUQUÉ, Friedrich Heinrich Karl baron de. *Undine.* See Chapter 1, Allegorical Fantasy and Literary Fairy Tales.

1741 **LATTIMORE, Deborah Nourse.** *The Winged Cat: A Tale of Ancient Egypt.* **Gr. 2–5.**

When Merit, a serving girl to the pharaoh, reports that she has seen the high priest, Waha, accidentally kill Bast, the sacred cat, the pharaoh orders them both to travel to the Netherworld's Hall of Judgment.

Illus. by the author, Harper, 1992, 32 pp. LB(0-06-023636-1)

(BL 89:60; HBG 3[Fall 1992]:237; KR 60:720; SLJ Apr 1992 p. 94)

1742 **LAUBENTHAL, Sanders Anne.** *Excalibur.* **Gr. 10 up.**

Inspired by the legendary twelfth-century voyage of King Arthur's descendant, Madoc, to the New World, this story describes the renewal of the battle between good and evil after the Holy Grail and Arthur's sword, Excalibur, are discovered in twentieth-century Mobile, Alabama.

Ballantine, 1973, pap., 236 pp., o.p.

(Kies:100; Tymn:107)

1743 LAWHEAD, Stephen R. *The Silver Hand* **(Song of Albion series, book 2). Gr. 10 up.**

Llew of the Silver Hand vows revenge against the false High King who cut off his hand and blinded the royal bard, in this reworking of Celtic lore. This is the sequel to *The Paradise War* (1991; Avon, 1993, pap.).

Lion, 1992, 400 pp. (0-7459-2230-9), 1993, pap. (0-7459-2245-7)

(BL 88:1749, 1752; KR 60:54)

1744 LAWHEAD, Stephen R. *Taliesin* **(Pendragon Cycle, book 1). Gr. 10 up.**

A retelling of an Arthurian legend about the bard Taliesin and his love for Charis, the princess of Atlantis. The sequels are *Merlin* (1988, 1990), *Arthur* (1989, 1990), and *Pendragon* (1994).

Good News, 1987, pap., 452 pp. (0-89107-407-4); Avon, 1990, pap. (0-380-70613-X)

(BL 84:31, 54; KR 55:965; LJ Aug 187 p. 146)

1745 LAWRENCE, Louise (pseud. of Elizabeth Rhoda Holden). *The Earth Witch.* **Gr. 7–12.**

The belligerent old woman to whom young Owen is drawn becomes increasingly younger as Spring approaches. He falls in love with her and is devastated when she leaves him.

Harper, 1981, 214 pp., o.p.

(BBJ:72; BL 77:1296; CCBB 35:33; HB 57:310: Kies:100; KR 49:745; SLJ May 1981 p. 74; VOYA 4[June 1981]:30)

1746 LAWRENCE, Louise (pseud. of Elizabeth Rhoda Holden). *Star Lord.* **Gr. 8–10.**

✓✓ A young Star Lord crashes into the Welsh mountains and is hidden from the British Security by Rhys Williams and his family.

Harper, 1978, 176 pp., o.p.

(BL 75:369; CCBB 32:65; HB 55:525; KR 46:1310; SLJ Oct 1978 p. 156; Suth 2:274; VOYA 1[Dec 1978]:33)

LAWSON, John S(hults). *The Spring Rider.* See Chapter 8, Time Travel Fantasy.

1747 LEE, Tanith. *Red as Blood; or Tales from the Sisters Grimmer.* **Gr. 10 up. (Orig.**
✓ **pub. in England.)**

A collection of well-known fairy tales such as "Snow White," "Cinderella," and "The Pied Piper of Hamelin," reworked with strange and original twists.

DAW, 1983, 1986, pap., 208 pp., o.p.

(BL 79:715, 719; LJ 108:147; Kies:102; VOYA 7:206)

LEE, Tanith. *Sung in Shadow.* See Chapter 5A, Alternate Worlds or Histories.

1748 LEE, Tanith. *Tamastara; or the Indian Nights.* **Gr. 10 up. (Orig. British pub.,**
1983.)

Seven supernatural tales set in India, drawn from the Hindu tradition, including "Foreign Skins," "Tamastara," and "Oh, Shining Star."

DAW, 1984, pap., 174 pp., o.p.

(BL 80:1294, 1339; LJ 109:826; VOYA 7:206)

LE GUIN, Ursula K(roeber). *A Wizard of Earthsea.* See Chapter 5A, Alternate Worlds or Histories.

L'ENGLE, Madeleine. *Many Waters.* See Chapter 8, Time Travel Fantasy.

1749   LEVIN, Betty (Lowenthal). *Landfall.* **Gr. 7–10.**

New Hampshire-born Liddy becomes convinced that she has spoken with a selkie, and uncovers a terrible crime against the seals during a visit to the Scottish island of Kelda.

Atheneum, 1979, 216 pp., o.p.

(CCBB 33:98; HB 55:669; KR 47:1005; SLJ Nov 1979 p. 89)

LEVIN, Meyer. *The Spell of Time: A Tale of Love in Jerusalem.* See Chapter 1, Allegorical Fantasy and Literary Fairy Tales.

1750   LILLINGTON, Kenneth (James). *Selkie.* **Gr. 7–9. (Orig. British pub. 1985.)**

Saved from drowning by a selkie or seal-woman, Cathy is determined to find her new friend's magical skin and return it, in spite of the villagers' hatred and superstition.

Faber, 1985, 145 pp., o.p.

(BL 81:1179, 1196; SLJ May 1985 p. 111; TLS Feb 1985 p. 214; VOYA 8:325)

1751   LIVELY, Penelope (Margaret Low). *Astercote.* **Gr. 6–8. (Orig. British pub. 1970.)**

Mair and Peter Jenkins attempt to recover a missing medieval chalace said to have kept the Black Plague away from their town.

Dutton, 1971, 154 pp., o.p.

(HB 47:172; Kies:106; TLS 1970 p. 421)

1752   LIVELY, Penelope (Margaret Low). *The Whispering Knights.* **Gr. 4–7. (Orig.**
✓   **British pub. 1971.)**

William, Martha, and Susie inadvertently bring the sorceress Morgan le Fay to life. Whitbread Literary Award, Children's Book Category, 1976.

Illus. by Gareth Floyd, Dutton, 1976, 160 pp., o.p.; Chivers, 1990 (large type ed.), (0-7451-1153-X)

(BL 72:1467; CCBB 30:13; HB 52:499; Kies:107; KR 44:593; SLJ Sept 1976 p. 121; Suth 2:289; TLS 1971 p. 774)

1753   LIVELY, Penelope (Margaret Low). *The Wild Hunt of the Ghost Hounds*
✓   **(British title:** *The Wild Hunt of Hagworthy,* **1971). Gr. 5–8.**

Lucy uses magic to save her friend Kester from the ghostly horned riders who endanger his life when he takes part in an ancient stag-hunting dance.

Dutton, 1972, 141 pp., o.p.

(BL 68:1004; CCBB 26:28; HB 48:376; Kies:107; KR 40:402; LJ 97:2964)

1754   LLYWELYN, Morgan. *Bard: The Odyssey of the Irish.* **Gr. 10 up.**

Amergin, a visionary Celtic bard, inspires his Warrior clan, the Gaels, to cross the ocean from the Iberian peninsula to Ierne (Ireland), where they conquer the gentle inhabitants by force, in this retelling of fourth-century Irish history.

Houghton, 1984, 463 pp., o.p.

(BL 81:3, 5; KR 52:706; LJ 109:1863; SLJ Sept 1985 p. 154)

1755 LLYWELYN, Morgan. *Druids*. Gr. 10 up. (Orig. British pub. 1991.)

Fifteen-year-old Ainvar, protégé of the chief druid of the Order of the Wise, leads his Celtic Carnute tribe against Caesar's Roman legions who are attempting to conquer Gaul.

Morrow, 1991, 448 pp. (0-688-08819-8); Ivy, 1993, pap. (0-8041-0844-7)

(BL 87:692, 693; KR 58:1631; LJ Jan 1991 p. 154; SLJ July 1991 p. 97)

LLYWELYN, Morgan. *The Horse Goddess*. See Chapter 10, Witchcraft and Sorcery Fantasy.

1756 LLYWELYN, Morgan. *The Isles of the Blest*. Gr. 10 up.

Connla the Irish warrior soon regrets his bargain with the fairy woman who transported him to the Isles of the Blest, where he finds eternal peace.

Ace, 1989, pap., 176 pp., o.p.

(BBS:60; BL 85:1614, 1638; VOYA 12:290, 13:13)

1757 LLYWELYN, Morgan. *Lion of Ireland: The Legend of Brian Boru*. Gr. 10 up.

A spellbinding retelling of the rise of Brian Boru, warrior and King of tenth-century Ireland.

Houghton, 1979, 522 pp., o.p.

(BL 76:757, 765; KR 47:1451; LJ 105:225)

1758 LLYWELYN, Morgan. *Red Branch*. Gr. 10 up.

Young Setanta grows up to join the King's Red Branch warrior band and becomes the legendary warrior, Cuchulain, a hero in the Irish feud with the Kingdom of Connaught.

Morrow, 1989, 600 pp., o.p.; Ivy, 1990, pap. (0-8041-0591-X)

(BL 85:818, 819; KR 57:79)

1759 LOCKLEY, Ronald Mathias. *The Seal-Woman*. Gr. 8 up. (Orig. British pub. 1974.)

Convinced that she is a seal-princess, an Irish girl named Shian lives alone in the wild, awaiting the coming of her seal-prince.

Bradbury, 1975, 178 pp., o.p.

(BL 72:228, 1038; KR 43:869; SLJ Nov 1975 p. 96; TLS 1974 p. 1405)

1760 LOGAN, Carolyn F. *The Power of the Rellard*. Gr. 5–7. (Orig. Australian pub.
✓ **1986.)**

After recovering from an illness that has left her with a withered arm, Lucy discovers that she's been endowed with an ancient magical power that endangers her life and those of her older brother and sister.

Angus and Robertson, 1987, o.p.; Macmillan, 1988, 278 pp., o.p.

(BBC:209; BL 83:1749, 84:1183; KR 56:281; SLJ Nov 1987 p. 105; VOYA 11:88)

1761 MacAVOY, R(oberta) A(nn). *Tea with the Black Dragon*. Gr. 10 up.
✓

Searching for her missing daughter, Martha Macnamara seeks the help of Mayland Long, an oriental gentleman who claims to have the magical powers of a 1000-year-old Imperial Chinese black dragon. The sequel is *Twisting the Rope* (1986).

Bantam, 1984, pap., 192 pp. (0-553-27992-0)

(BBS:61; BL 79:1448, 1458, 86:907; Kies:111; LJ 108:1018; VOYA 6:216)

1762   McDONALD, Ian. *King of Morning, Queen of Day.* **Gr. 10 up.**

Three separate stories about three generations of young Irish women tempted to use their elfin magic—Emily, Jessica, and Enye—one of whom was abused as a child.

Bantam, 1991, pap., 400 pp. (0-553-29049-5)

(BL 87:1937; LJ Jan 15, 1991 p. 109; VOYA 14:324)

1763   McKINLEY, (Jennifer Carolyn) Robin (Turrell). *Beauty: A Retelling of the*
✓✓   *Story of Beauty and the Beast.* **Gr. 5–9.**

A beautiful girl marries a Beast and grows to love him in this novel-length version of the old French tale written by Madame le Prince de Beaumont.

Harper, 1978, 245 pp., LB(0-06-024150-0), 1993, pap., 256 pp. (0-06-440477-3)

(BBJ:73; BBS:61; BL 75:222; 80:96, 353; CC:532; CCBB 32:67; Ch&Bks:249; HB 55:201, 59:71; JHC:389; Kies:113; KR 46:1307; SLJ Nov 1978 p. 65; Suth 2:301; TLS 1983 p. 1312; VOYA 1[Feb 1979]:40)

1764   McKINLEY, (Jennifer Carolyn) Robin (Turrell). *Deerskin.* **Gr. 10 up.**
✓

Princess Lissar escapes into the mountains with her beloved fleethound, Ash, after being beaten and raped by her royal father, in this dark retelling of Perrault's fairytale, "Donkeyskin," for mature readers. This story is set in the world of *The Blue Sword* (1982; see Chapter 5A, Alternate Worlds or Histories) and *The Hero and the Crown* (1984; see Chapter 5A, Alternate Worlds or Histories), but at a later time.

Ace, 1993, 320 pp. (0-44114226-5)

(BL 89:1416, 1420; CCBB 47:16; KR 61:494; LJ Apr 15, 1993 p. 130; SLJ Sept 1993 p. 261; VOYA 16:168, 17:8)

1765   MacLEISH, Roderick. *Prince Ombra.* **Gr. 10 up.**

Eight-year-old Bentley Ellicott finds a secret stone used by famous heroes throughout history in their battles against Prince Ombra, and realizes that it is his turn to fight the evil Prince of Darkness.

Cogdon, 1982, 305 pp., o.p.

(BBS:61; KR 50:1069; LJ 107:2191)

1766   MAJOR, Kevin (Gerald). *Blood Red Ochre.* **Gr. 7–9. (Orig. Canadian pub.
1989.)**

In alternating chapters set in two different periods, Dauoodaset, the last member of a Canadian Indian tribe, and David, a fifteen-year-old contemporary Canadian, tell their stories. The link between their lives is Nancy, a new girl in David's class, who becomes Sanawdithit, the lost love of Dauoodaset, after she and David canoe out to Red Ochre Island. Young Adult Canadian Book Award Runner Up, 1989.

Delacorte, 1989, 147 pp. (0-385-29794-7); Dell, 1990, pap. (0-440-20730-4)

(BL 87:178; CCBB 42:200; HB 65:659; KR 57:297; SLJ Apr 1989 p. 119; VOYA 12:104)

1767   MALORY, Sir Thomas. *La Morte D'Arthur.* **Gr. 6 up. (Written in 1485; orig.
✓   British pub. 1634, orig. U.S. pub. Macmillan, 1879.)**

This medieval masterpiece, which combined the many legends about the reign of King Arthur and the quest for the Holy Grail, is the primary source used for contemporary retellings of the Arthurian legends.

There have been numerous adaptations of Malory's tales published over the years, with various titles. The following are arranged alphabetically by title:

The Acts of Arthur and His Noble Knights from the Winchester Manuscripts of Thomas Malory and Other Sources.

Retold by John (Ernst) Steinbeck. Farrar, 1976, 363 pp., o.p.

Arthur Pendragon of Britain.

Ed. by John W. Donaldson, illus. by Andrew Wyeth, Putnam, 1943, o.p.

The Book of King Arthur and His Noble Knights.

Adapt. by Nancy MacLeod, illus. by Henry C. Pitz, Lippincott, 1949, 325 pp., o.p.

✓✓ *The Boy's King Arthur.*

Retold by Sidney Lanier, illus. by N. C. Wyeth, Scribner, 1917, 1952, o.p.

King Arthur and His Knights.

Illus. by Mead Schaeffer and John Rea Neill, Rand, 1924, 1936, o.p.; retold by Mary MacLeod, illus. by Howard Pyle, Parents, 1966, © 1964, o.p.; ed. by Eugene Vinaver, Oxford, 1975, pap. (0-19-501905-9)

King Arthur and the Legends of Camelot.

Adapt. by Molly Perham, illus. by Julek Heller, Viking, 1993, 176 pp. (0-670-84990-1)

King Arthur: The Sword in the Stone.

Adapt. and illus. by Hudson Talbott, Morrow, 1991, 56 pp., LB(0-688-09404-X)

The Legend of King Arthur.

Adapt. by Robin Lister, illus. by Alan Baker, Doubleday, 1990 (orig. British pub. 1988), 96 pp. (0-385-26369-4)

Of Swords and Sorcerers: The Adventures of King Arthur and His Knights.

Ed. by Margaret Hodges and Margery Evernden, illus. by David Frampton, Macmillan, 1993, 112 pp. (0-684-19437-6)

The Romance of King Arthur and His Knights of the Round Table.

Ed. by Alfred W. Pollard, illus. by Arthur Rackham, Macmillan, 1917, 1927, o.p.

Stories of King Arthur.

Adapt. by U. Waldo Cutler, illus. by Elinore Blaisdell, Crowell, 1941, o.p.

Stories of King Arthur and His Knights.

Retold by Barbara Leonie Picard, illus. by Roy Morgan, Walck, 1955, o.p.

The Story of Idylls of the King.

Adapt. by Lord Alfred Tennyson and Inez N(ellie) (Canfield) McFee, illus. by Maria L. Kirk, Stokes, 1912, o.p.

✓✓ *The Story of King Arthur and His Knights.*

Adapt. by Howard Pyle, Macmillan, 1903, 1933, 1984, 320 pp. (0-684-14814-5)

✓✓ *The Sword and Circle: King Arthur and Knights of the Round Table.*

Retold by Rosemary Sutcliff, Dutton, 1981, 261 pp. (0-525-40585-2)

Tales of King Arthur.

Ed. and abridged by Michael Senior, Schocken, 1981, © 1980, o.p.

Macmillan, 1900, pap., 1986, 768 pp. (0-02-022560-1); Dutton, 1908, 1941, o.p., pap., 1962 (0-451-62567-6); ed. by Ernest Rhys, Dent, 1972 (2 vols.), o.p.; ed. by R. M. Lumiansky, Scribner, 1982, o.p.

(BL 9:215, 14:142, 39:460, 46:18, 58:646, 73:294, 78:694, 79:654, 80:1392, 86:1990, 88:528, 89:1963;

CC:115; CCBB 44:12, 45:75, 47:12, 20; Ch&Bks:238, 245; HB 25:544, 53:561, 60:359; HBG 1[Jan–June 1990]:277, 3[July–Dec 1991]:93; Kies:164; Kliatt Fall 1986 p. 28; KR 30:82, 44:1025, 58:800, 59:1094, 61:598, 939; LJ 66:798, 101:2178, 107:459, 108:208; SHC:154, 155; SLJ Apr 1977 p. 84, Oct 1990 p. 136, Sept 1991 p. 273, Aug 1993 p. 174; TLS 1917 p. 613, 1967 p. 1126, 1977 p. 536; VOYA 3[Dec 1980]:55)

1768   MAYER, Marianna. *The Black Horse.* Gr. 2–4.

In this retelling of a Celtic myth, Tim, a poor king's son, joins forces with a magical black horse to rescue a princess, defeat an evil king, and break the enchantment holding the princess's brother.

Illus. by Katie Thamer, Dial, 1984, 39 pp. LB(0-8037-0076-8), 1987, pap., 42 pp. (0-8037-0181-0)

(BL 81:526; SLJ Jan 1985 p. 78)

1769   MAYER, Marianna. *Noble-Hearted Kate: A Celtic Tale.* Gr. 4–6.

In this adaptation and expansion of the Scottish fairy tales "Kate Crackernuts" and "Tam Lin," Kate frees her stepsister Meghan from a witch's spell and rescues a prince from the fairy realm.

Illus. by Winslow Pels, Bantam, 1990, 64 pp. (0-553-07049-5)

(BL 87:1194; CCBB 44:171; HBG 2[July–Dec 1990]:75)

1770   MAYER, Marianna. *The Sorcerer's Apprentice: A Greek Fable.* Gr. 3–5.

Apprentice enchanter Alex casts a spell of his own while Bleise the sorcerer is away, but has no idea how to cancel it when things get out of hand.

Illus. by David Wiesner, Bantam, 1989, 64 pp. (0-553-05844-4)

(BL 86:1093; HBG 1[July–Dec 1989]:82; KR 57:1751; SLJ May 1990 p. 107)

1771   MAYNE, William (James Carter). *Earthfasts.* Gr. 6–8. (Orig. British pub. 1966.)

✓✓   A curious cold-flamed candle, powerful enough to reverse time, endangers the lives of David and Keith when it brings King Arthur and his knights back to life.

Dutton, 1967, 154 pp., o.p.; Peter Smith, 1989 (0-8446-6430-8)

(BL 68:1050; CCBB 20:172; Ch&Bks:256; HB 43:343; KR 35:508; LJ 92:1750; Suth 274; TLS 1966 p. 1080; Tymn:139)

1772   MEANY, Dee Morrison. *Iseult: Dreams That Are Done.* Gr. 10 up.

A retelling of the tragic love story of Tristan and Iseult.

Ace, 1985, pap., 229 pp., o.p.

(BBS:62; BL 82:195, 216; Kies:53; VOYA 9:41)

1773   MENDEZ, Phil. *The Black Snowman.* Gr. K–4.

A magic Kente, or African shawl, brings Jacob and Pee Wee Miller's snowman to life, and he tells the boys about some ancestral African heroes before helping Jacob save his younger brother's life.

Illus. by Carole Byard, Scholastic, 1989, 48 pp. (0-5904-0552-7), 1991, pap. (0-5904-4873-0)

(BL 86:352; CCBB 43:65; HBG 1[July 1989]:67; KR 57:1478; SLJ Sept 1989 p. 230)

1774   MENOTTI, Gian Carlo. *Amahl and the Night Visitors.* Gr. 1–5. (Orig. Italian
✓   **pub. 1938.)**

A narrative version of the Menotti opera about the crippled shepherd boy who leads the Three Kings to the Christ Child's manger and leaves his own special gift.

Adapt. by Frances Frost, illus. by Roger Duvoisin, McGraw-Hill, 1952, 1962, o.p.; illus. by Michele Lemieux, Morrow, 1986, 64 pp., LB(0-688-05427-7)

(BL 49:112, 83:274, 1138; CC:532; CCBB 6:40, 40:54; HB 28:310, 402, 61:762, 62:725–727; KR 20:550; LJ 77:1747, 2184; SLJ Oct 1986 p. 113)

1775 MINOT, Stephen. *Surviving the Flood.* **Gr. 10 up.**

Noah's youngest son, Ham, decides to set the offical record straight, in this humorous report about what really happened aboard Noah's ark.

Atheneum, 1981, o.p.; Second Chance, 1987 (repr. of 1981 ed.), 306 pp. (0-933256-63-9)

(BL 78:178, 188; KR 49:895; LJ 106:2049)

1776 MOORE, John. *Slay and Rescue.* **Gr. 10 up.**

A bawdy parody of novelized fairy tales about seventeen-year-old Prince Charming whose raging hormones lead him to court Cinderella, Sleeping Beauty, and Snow White, while slaying dragons, battling evil sorcerers, and rescuing princesses.

Baen, 1993, pap., 226 pp. (0-671-72152-6)

(Kliatt May 1993 p. 18; VOYA 16:168)

1777 MORPURGO, Michael. *King of the Cloud Forests.* **Gr. 6–9. (Orig. British pub.**
✓ **1987.)**

Fourteen-year-old Ashley Anderson escapes the World War II-era Japanese invasion of China by crossing the Himalayas on foot, where he is rescued by a band of yeti, or abominable snowmen, who believe he is a god. Carnegie Medal Commended Book, 1987.

Viking, 1988, 146 pp. (0-670-87069-5); Puffin, 1991, pap. (0-14-032586-7)

(BL 84:1820, 1840 & 85:879; CCBB 41:234; HB 64:634; KR 56:764; SLJ Sept 1988 p. 200; Suth 4:296; TLS 1988 p. 200)

1778 MORRIS, Kenneth. *The Book of the Three Dragons.* **Gr. 10 up.**

In this retelling of the fourth branch of the Welsh *Mabinogion,* the immortal hero, Manawyddan embarks on numerous adventures as he seeks to recover two treasures stolen from the gods: a magical breastplate and the divine harp of Alawn. This is the sequel to *The Fates of the Princes of Dyfed* (1913, 1914, 1978, 1980), which retells the first three branches of the *Mabinogion.*

Longman, 1930, o.p.; ed. by R. Reginald and Douglas Melville, illus. by Ferdinand Huszti Horvath, Longman, 1930, 206 pp., o.p.; Ayer, 1978 (repr. of 1930 ed.), 206 pp., o.p.

(BL 27:266; Tymn:143)

1779 MURPHY, Pat (pseud. of E[mmet] Jefferson Murphy). *The Falling Woman: A*
✓ *Fantasy.* **Gr. 10 up.**

While excavating an ancient Mayan city, archeologist Elizabeth Butler conjures up the ghost of a Mayan priestess who offers to revive the Mayan gods if Elizabeth will sacrifice the life of her estranged daughter. Nebula Award, Best Novel, 1988.

Tor, 1986, 288 pp. (0-312-93230-8), 1993, pap. (0-312-85406-4)

(BBS:62; BL 83:34, 52; Kies:125; KR 54:1319; LJ Oct 15, 1986 p. 114; VOYA 10:40)

MURPHY, Shirley Rousseau, and SUGGS, Welch. *Medallion of the Black Hound.* See Chapter 5C, Travel to Other Worlds.

MYERS, Bernice. *Sidney Rella and the Glass Sneaker.* See Chapter 6, Humorous Fantasy.

MYERS, John Myers. *Silverlock.* See Chapter 5C, Travel to Other Worlds.

1780 **MYERS, Walter Dean.** *The Legend of Tarik.* **Gr. 7–9.**

Armed with a magic sword and the Crystal of Truth, Tarik seeks revenge against the murderous El Muerte, in this saga set in medieval North Africa.

Viking, 1981, 185 pp., o.p.; Scholastic, 1982, pap. (0-5904-4426-3)

(BBJ:74; BL 77:1444, 1449; HB 57:434; SLJ May 1981 p. 76; VOYA Oct 1981 p. 36)

NAPOLI, Donna Jo. *The Magic Circle.* See Chapter 10, Witchcraft and Sorcery Fantasy.

NAPOLI, Donna Jo. *The Prince of the Pond: Otherwise Known as De Fawg Pin.* See Chapter 6, Humorous Fantasy.

1781 **NATHAN, Robert (Gruntal).** *The Elixir.* **Gr. 10 up.**

An American historian and the mysterious girl he meets at Stonehenge travel back and forth through time, reliving the Arthurian legend of Merlin and Nimue.

Knopf, 1971, 177 pp., o.p.

(BL 68:183; KR 39:608; LJ 96:2544, 3915, 4161)

1782 **NEWMAN, Robert (Howard).** *Merlin's Mistake.* **Gr. 5–8.**

Tertius's knowledge of the future hampers Merlin's attempts to free himself from the bonds of Nimue. The sequel is *The Testing of Tertius* (1973, 1985).

Illus. by Richard Lebenson, Atheneum, 1970, 237 pp., o.p.; Peter Smith, 1985 (0-8446-6187-2)

(BBC:210; BL 66:1162; HB 46:298, 60:223, 63:491; KR 38:174; LJ 95:2309; TLS 1971 p. 390)

NEWMAN, Robert (Howard). *The Shattered Stone.* See Chapter 5A, Alternate Worlds or Histories.

1783 **NEWMAN, Sharan.** *Guinevere* **(Guinevere trilogy, book 1). Gr. 10 up.**

✓ This is the story of Queen Guinevere's childhood love for a unicorn. The sequels are *The Chessboard Queen* (1983) and *Guinevere Evermore* (1985, 1986).

St. Martin, 1981, o.p., pap., 1984, 296 pp. (0-312-35321-9)

(BBS:62: BL 77:796, 806; Kies:127; Kliatt 18[Fall 1984]:29; KR 48:1482; LJ 106:815; SLJ Apr 1981 p. 146)

NIMMO, Jenny. *The Snow Spider.* See Chapter 7, Magic Adventure Fantasy.

1784 **NIMMO, Jenny.** *Ultramarine.* **Gr. 5–8. (Orig. British pub. 1990.)**

Arion, a mysterious new friend who rescues sea creatures, helps two lonely children, Ned and Nell, unravel the secret about their heritage and their connection to the sea.

Dutton, 1992, 192 pp. (0-525-44869-1)

(BL 88:1593; CCBB 45:301; HBG 3[Fall, 1992]:276; KR 60:327; SLJ May 1992 p. 116; VOYA 15:113)

1785 **NORMAN, Roger.** *Albion's Dream: A Novel of Terror.* **Gr. 6–10. (Orig. British** ✓ **pub. 1990.)**

English boarding-school student Edward discovers that whatever happens on the board of an old game called Albion's Dream also happens in real life.

Delacorte, 1992, 209 pp. (0-385-30533-8)

(BL 89:48; CCBB 46:84; HB 68:724; HBG 4[Spring 1993]:75; KR 60:923; SLJ Oct 1992 p. 120; VOYA 15:241)

NORTON, André (pseud. of Alice Mary Norton). *Here Abide Monsters.* See Chapter 5C, Travel to Other Worlds.

1786 **NORTON, André (pseud. of Alice Mary Norton).** *Huon of the Horn.* **Gr. 6–9.**

An exciting retelling of the legend of the Duke of Bordeaux from the Charlemagne saga.

Illus. by Joe Krush, Harcourt, 1951, 208 pp., o.p.

(KR 19:632; LJ 76:2126)

1787 **NORTON, André (pseud. of Alice Mary Norton).** *Quag Keep.* **Gr. 7–10.**

✓ With identical bracelets locked to their wrists, seven strangers journey to the lair of the powerful being who has enslaved them.

Atheneum, 1978, 224 pp., o.p.

(BL 74:1176; HB 54:285; JHC:394; SLJ Mar 1978 p. 139; VOYA 1[June 1978]:42, 2[Dec 1979]:58)

NORTON, André (pseud. of Alice Mary Norton). *Steel Magic.* See Chapter 5C, Travel to Other Worlds.

1788 **NORTON, André, and SHWARTZ, Susan.** *Imperial Lady: A Fantasy of Han China.* **Gr. 10 up.**

Exiled from the Chinese emperor's court to the barbaric land of the Hsiung-nu, Silver Snow uses her wits and magic skills to protect herself and her husband from the tribal shaman.

Tor, 1980, 320 pp., o.p., 1990, pap. (0-8125-0722-3)

(BBS:62; BL 85:1950, 1969; Kliatt Sept 1990 p. 22; KR 57:959; LJ Aug 1989 p. 117; VOYA 13:119)

1789 **NYE, Robert.** *Beowulf; a New Telling.* **Gr. 5–8.**

A modernized version of the Anglo-Saxon epic about the hero, Beowulf's conquest of the monsters Grendel, She, and the Firedrake.

Illus. by Alan E. Cober, Hill, 1968, 116 pp., o.p.

(BBS:63; BL 65:839; HB 45:49)

1790 **OGIWARA, Noriko.** *Dragon Sword and Wind Child.* **Gr. 7–12. (Orig. Japanese**
✓ **pub. 1992.)**

A complex and adventure-filled saga drawn from Japanese mythology, about Saya, a village girl chosen by the mythical son of the God of Light to be the reincarnation of the handmaiden to the Goddess of Darkness.

Trans. by Cathy Hirano, Farrar, 1993, 329 pp. (0-374-30466-1)

(BL 89:2050; CCBB 46:355; HBG 4[Fall 1993]:311; KR 61:666; SLJ Sept 1993 p. 252; VOYA 16:169)

1791 **OPPENHEIM, Shulamith (Levey).** *The Selchie's Seed.* **Gr. 4–6.**

✓ Marian never suspected that her ancestors were seal people until the night she is drawn to a white whale in the ocean near her island home.

Illus. by Diane Goode, Bradbury, 1975, 83 pp., o.p.

(BL 72:580; CCBB 29:129; KR 43:1287; SLJ Jan 1976 p. 49; Suth 2:345)

1792 **ORLOCK, Carol (Ellen).** *The Goddess Letters: The Demeter-Persephone Myth Retold.* **Gr. 10 up.**

After her daughter's abduction by Hades, Demeter exchanges a series of letters with Persephone chronicling the decline of goddess worship on earth, in this unusual feminist retelling of Greek myth.

St. Martin, 1987, 220 pp., o.p.

(KR 55:415; SLJ Feb 1988 p. 95)

1793 O'SHEA, Pat. *The Hounds of the Morrigan.* **Gr. 6–9. (Orig. British pub. 1985.)**

✓ The ancient book Pidge found brings the evil Queen Morrigan and her two witchlike assistants to his door, threatening the future of the world.

Holiday, 1986, 469 pp. (0-8234-0595-8)

(BBC:211; BBJ:74; BL 82:1144; CCBB 39:215; HB 62:451; KR 54:870; SLJ Mar 1986 p. 169, Feb 1987 p. 34, Apr 1987 p. 48; Suth 4:308; TLS Nov 1985 p. 1358; VOYA 10:22)

1794 PARK, Ruth. *My Sister Sif.* **Gr. 6–9. (Orig. Australian pub. 1986.)**

Fourteen-year-old Riko and her sister, Sif, run away from their school in Sydney and return to the island home where their mother and brother live beneath the sea.

Viking, 1991, 180 pp. (0-670-83924-8)

(BL 87:1560; CCBB 44:201; HBG 2:278; JHC 1992 Suppl. p. 64; KR 59:675; SLJ May 1991 p. 94; TLS Sept 4, 1987 p. 964; VOYA 14:100)

1795 PASSEY, Helen K. *Speak to the Rain.* **Gr. 6–10.**

Grief over their mother's death seems to be drawing Janna's younger sister into a spirit world connected with a Northwest Indian totem pole near an isolated lake.

Macmillan, 1989, 160 pp. (0-689-31489-2)

(BL 86:736, 746; HBG 1[July–Dec 1989]:83; KR 57:1595; SLJ Sept 1989 p. 256; VOYA 12:280)

1796 PATTOU, Edith. *Hero's Song.* **Gr. 6–10.**

Young Colun is joined on his search for his missing sister, Nessa, by his friend, the bard Talisen, a master archer, and one of the Fair Folk.

Harcourt, 1991, 320 pp. (0-15-233807-1)

(BL 88:429; CCBB 45:102; HBG 3[Spring 1992]:71; KR 59:1406; SLJ Jan 1992 p. 137; VOYA 14:385)

1797 PAXON, Diana L. *The Serpent's Tooth.* **Gr. 10 up.**

King Lear's youngest daughter tells the story of his marriage to three captive queens, the birth of his three daughters, and his betrayal by the older two, in this retelling of the King Lear legend set in Iron Age Britain.

Morrow, 1991, 394 pp. (0-688-08339-0); Avon, 1993, pap. (0-380-75680-3)

(BL 87:2034, 2037; KR 59:628)

1798 PAXON, Diana L. *The Wolf and the Raven* **(Sigfrid and Brunahild trilogy, vol.**
✓ **1). Gr. 10 up.**

This story sets the scene for the tragic love affair between Brunahild, a fifth-century Hun princess studying sorcery, and Sigfrid, a royal youth apprenticed to a smith.

Morrow, 1993, 320 pp. (0-688-01821-0)

(BL 89:1298, 1308; KR 61:89; LJ Mar 19, 1993 p. 111; SLJ Sept 1993 p. 263)

1799 PAXON, Diana L., and MARTINE-BARNES, Adrienne. *Master of Earth and Water* **(Finn MacCool trilogy, vol. 1). Gr. 10 up.**

Fionn mac Cumhal (Finn MacCool), raised in the forest by a sorceress and a warrior, discovers his magical powers and royal blood, in this first volume of a trilogy based on Celtic mythology. The sequel is *The Shield Between the Worlds* (1994).

Morrow, 1993, 416 pp. (0-68812505-0)

(BL 89:1410, 1420; KR 61:266; LJ Apr 15, 1993 p. 130)

PEARCE, (Ann) Philippa. *The Squirrel Wife.* See Chapter 1, Allegorical Fantasy and Literary Fairy Tales.

1800 **PECK, Sylvia.** *Seal Child.* **Gr. 4–6.**

✓ Molly's vacation friend, Meara, on an island off the coast of Maine, has a sadness about her that Molly can't understand, until the day Meara saves Molly from drowning.

Illus. by Robert Andrew Parker, Morrow, 1989, 208 pp. (0-688-08682-9); Bantam, 1991, pap. (0-553-15868-6)

(BL 86:188; CCBB 43:91; HB 66:65; HBG 1[July–Dec 1989]:81; KR 57:1479; SLJ Nov 1989 p. 112; Suth 4:321)

1801 *The Pendragon Chronicles: Heroic Fantasy from the Time of King Arthur.* **Ed. by**
✓ **Mike Ashley. Gr. 10 up. (Orig. British pub. 1989.)**

A collection of Arthurian stories whose authors include Jane Yolen, André Norton, and John Steinbeck. *The Camelot Chronicles* (1992; see entry earlier in this section) is a companion volume.

Bedrick, 1990, 417 pp. (0-87226-335-5), 1991, pap. (0-87226-228-6)

(BBS:52; BL 86:1688, 1694; Kliatt Sept 1991 p. 19; LJ Apr 15, 1990 p. 127; SLJ Aug 1990 p. 174; VOYA 13:232, 14:12)

1802 **PHILIP, Neil.** *The Tale of Sir Gawain.* **Gr. 6–10.**

Elderly and wounded, Sir Gawain tells his young squire old tales of the Round Table, tales of magic, love, adventure, and betrayal.

Illus. by Charles Keeping, Putnam, 1987, 112 pp. (0-399-21488-7)

(BL 84:774 787; CCBB 41:73; Ch&Bks:245; HB 64:78; TLS 1987 p. 1261)

1803 **PHILLIPS, Ann.** *The Oak King and the Ash Queen.* **Gr. 6–8. (Orig. British pub. 1984.)**

Twelve-year-old English twins, Dan and Daisy, are reluctantly drawn into the battle between the Oak King and the Ash Queen, living trees who are fighting to preserve the natural balance of the forest.

Oxford, 1985, 171 pp., o.p.

(BBJ:74; BL 82:68; HB 61:458; SLJ Nov 1985 p. 100; VOYA 8:269)

1804 *The Phoenix Tree: An Anthology of Myth Fantasy.* **Ed. by Robert H. Boyer and Kenneth J. Zahorski. Gr. 10 up.**

Sixteen short story retellings of myths, whose authors include Lord Dunsany, Richard Adams, Evangeline Walton, and Vera Chapman.

Avon, 1980, pap., 279 pp., o.p.

(BL 77:309, 322; Kliatt 15[Winter 1981]:20)

1805 **POLLAND, Madeleine A(ngela Cahill).** *Deirdre.* **Gr. 7–9.**

Even though the old king keeps his daughter, Deirdre, imprisoned in a castle, he is unable to hide her from her tragic fate.

Illus. by Seon Morrison, Doubleday, 1967, 166 pp., o.p.

(BL 63:1050; CCBB 21:16; HB 43:465; KR 35:424; TLS 1967 p. 1133)

POOLE, Josephine. *The Visitor: A Story of Suspense.* See Chapter 10, Witchcraft and Sorcery Fantasy.

1806 **PRICE, Susan.** *The Devil's Piper.* **Gr. 6–9. (Orig. British pub. 1973.)**

✓ In this novel written by a sixteen-year-old, the parents of four children spirited off by a sly luchorpan ask the Devil for help in finding them.

Greenwillow, 1976, 216 pp., o.p.

(BL 72:981; HB 52:292; KR 44:392; SLJ Apr 1976 p. 92; TLS 1973 p. 1429)

PRICE, Susan. *The Ghost Drum.* See Chapter 10, Witchcraft and Sorcery Fantasy.

PRICE, Susan. *Ghost Song.* See Chapter 10, Witchcraft and Sorcery Fantasy.

1807 **PURTILL, Richard.** *Enchantment at Delphi.* **Gr. 7–9.**

Visiting Greece to further her studies of Greek mythology, Alice Grant is transported into ancient times by a strange mist, and becomes involved in the struggle by the gods Apollo, Athena, and Dionysius to protect the Delphic oracle from the Dark Powers.

Harcourt, 1986, 149 pp. (0-15-200447-5)

(BBJ:75; CCBB 40:74; KR 54:1375; SLJ Nov 1986 p. 107)

1808 **PYLE, Howard.** *The Story of King Arthur and His Knights.* **Gr. 5–12.**

✓✓ This is the first of a classic four-volume retelling of the Arthurian legends. The three companion volumes are *The Story of the Champions of the Round Table* (1905, 1968, 1984), *The Story of Sir Launcelot and His Companions* (1907, 1985), and *The Story of the Grail and the Passing of Arthur* (1910, 1985).

Illus. by the author, Scribner, 1903, 1933, 312 pp., o.p.; Dover, 1965, pap., 312 pp. (0-486-21445-1); illus. by the author, Macmillan, 1984 (repr. of 1903 ed.), 320 pp. (0-684-14814-5); NAL, 1986, pap. (0-451-52488-8)

(BL 80:1392, 1401; CC:115; Ch&Bks:245; HB 60:359; Kliatt 20[Fall 1986]:28; SHC:155)

1809 **RAYNER, William.** *Stag Boy.* **Gr. 7–10. (Orig. British pub. 1972.)**

✓ Whenever Jim Hooper puts on an ancient stag-horn helmet, he enters the body of a huge black stag.

Harcourt, 1973, 160 pp., o.p.

(BL 69:902, 909; HB 49:387; KR 4:259; LJ 98:1692; TLS 1972 p. 1318; Tymn:155)

1810 **REAVES, Michael.** *Street Magic.* **Gr. 10 up.**

Danny Thayer, a sixteen-year-old runaway living on the San Francisco streets, discovers he is actually a fairy changeling, after he meets the scatterlings, who are runaways from Faerie.

Tor, 1991, 320 pp. (0-312-85125-1), 1992, pap. (0-8125-1112-3)

(BL 87:2034, 2037; KR 59:640; LJ June 15, 1991 p. 109; SLJ Apr 1991 p. 164)

1811 **REEVES, James (pseud. of John Morris Reeves).** *Maildun the Voyager.* **Gr. 4–6. (Orig. British pub. 1971.)**

A retelling of an Irish legend about a young man who sails beyond the Western Isles to avenge his father's murder.

Illus. by Rocco Negri, Walck, 1972, 104 pp., o.p.

(HB 48:464; KR 40:1104; LJ 97:4074)

1812 **REID BANKS, Lynne.** *Melusine: A Mystery.* **Gr. 7–12. (Orig. British pub. 1988.)**

✓ Roger discovers, to his horror, that the owner of the decaying French chateau where his family is vacationing is sexually abusing his daughter, Melusine, who is named for a legendary creature who was both woman and snake.

Harper, 1989, 248 pp., o.p., 1991, pap. (0-06-447054-7)

(3BS:52; BL 86:273, 343; CCBB 43:1; HB 65:626; HBG 1[July 1989]:76; KR 57:1071; SLJ Nov 1989 p. 124; TLS 1988 p. 1322; VOYA 12:340)

1813 **RENAULT, Mary (pseud. of Mary Challans).** *The King Must Die.* **Gr. 10 up.**

✓ Seventeen-year-old King Theseus joins a group of young people conscripted to become bull-dancers on the island of Crete. There he becomes renowned at the dangerous sport, and eventually manages to overthrow the Cretan Kingdom. The sequel is *The Bull from the Sea* (1962).

Pantheon, 1958, 1980 (0-394-43195-2); Bantam, 1974, 1985, pap., 416 pp. (0-553-26065-0)

(BL 54:574, 587; Kies:141; KR 26:341; LJ 83:2053; SHC:715; TLS 1958 p. 528)

1814 RICE, Robert. *The Last Pendragon.* **Gr. 10 up.**

Eleven years after King Arthur's death, Bedwyr, the last of his knights, travels through Britain giving aid to the tribes who are battling the Saxons and completing Arthur's final request to find his sword, Caliburn, and cast it into the lake.

Walker, 1991, 209 pp. (0-8027-1180-4)

(KR 59:1428; SLJ May 1992 p. 152)

1815 ROBBINS, Ruth. *Taliesin and King Arthur.* **Gr. 3–5.**

✓ When the young poet Taliesin tells the magical story of his birth at the Grand Contest of Poets, King Arthur proclaims him the greatest bard of all.

Illus. by the author, Parnassus, 1970, 31 pp., o.p.

(BL 67:452; CCBB 24:98; HB 47:166; KR 38:1288; LJ 96:1119)

1816 ROBERSON, Jennifer. *Lady of the Forest.* **Gr. 10 up.**

A romantic adventure based on the legends of Robin Hood, set in thirteenth-century England.

Zebra, 1992, 608 pp. (0-8217-3919-0)

(BL 88:1899, 1900; KR 60:876; LJ Aug 1992 p. 152)

1817 ROOT, Phyllis. *The Listening Silence.* **Gr. 4–7.**

Orphaned thirteen-year-old Kiri, raised by Mali the village healer, goes into the wilderness on a vision quest to understand her ability to send her spirit "within" other people and animals.

Harper, 1992, 106 pp. LB(0-06-025093-3)

(BL 88:1380; CCBB 45:191; HBG 3[Fall 1992]:269; KR 60:616; SLJ June 1992 p. 125)

1818 RUSH, Alison. *The Last of Danu's Children.* **Gr. 7–10.**

Matt and Kate enter the Otherworld, battle the forces of evil who have bewitched Kate's sister Anna, and call forth the Lord of Light to help save their world.

Houghton, 1982, 240 pp., o.p.

(BBS:63; BL 79:364, 373; CCBB 36:96; Kies:146; Kliatt 18[Spring 1984]:22; SLJ Jan 1983 p. 87)

1819 SALSITZ, Rhodi Vilott. *The Twilight Gate.* **Gr. 6–10.**

While their mother undergoes chemotherapy, George, fifteen, Leigh, thirteen, and Mindy, five, spend the summer with their mother's ex-husband, and accidentally unleash magical forces of good and evil.

Illus. by Alan M. Clark, Walker, 1993, 181 pp. (0-8027-8213-2)

(BL 89:1506; CCBB 46:357; HBG 4[Fall 1993]:312; KR 61:379; SLJ May 1993 p. 108; VOYA 16:104, 170)

1820 SAN SOUCI, Robert D. *Young Guinevere.* **Gr. 2–5.**

A shape-changing wolf-boy helps Guinevere escape her father's besieged castle, save herself from a dragon, and find her way to the court of her future husband, King Arthur.

Illus. by Jamichael Henterly, Doubleday, 1993, 32 pp. (0-385-41623-7)

(HBG 4[Fall 1993]:329; KR 61:305; SLJ May 1993 p. 120)

1821 SAN SOUCI, Robert D. *Young Merlin.* **Gr. 2–5.**

This is the story of Merlin's childhood and youth, culminating in his creation of Stonehenge and his vision of Arthur's future greatness.

Illus. by Daniel R. Horne, Doubleday, 1990, 32 pp. (0-385-248000-8)

(BL 86:1990; HBG 1[Jan 1990]:276; KR 58:880; SLJ Sept 1990 p. 220)

1822 SARGENT, Sarah. *Lure of the Dark.* **Gr. 7–10.**

Fourteen-year-old Ginny's empty home life with an alcoholic mother and an indifferent father leaves her vulnerable to the dark forces of Loki, the Norse god in wolf-form, who tempts her toward suicide.

Four Winds, 1984, 118 pp., o.p.

(BBJ:75; BL 80:1551; CCBB 37:191; SLJ Aug 1984 p. 86; VOYA 7:332)

1823 SARGENT, Sarah. *Watermusic.* **Gr. 6–9.**

A haunting story in which Laura's flute-playing brings a huge white bat and a female ogre to life, and their battle symbolizes the struggle between love and intellect.

Clarion, 1986, 120 pp., o.p.

(BBJ:75; BL 82:1087; CCBB 39:195; SLJ May 1986 p. 109)

1824 SCARBOROUGH, Elizabeth Ann. *The Healer's War: A Fantasy Novel of Vietnam.* **Gr. 10 up.**

Army nurse Kitty McCully is given an amulet by an old Vietnamese mystic that enables her to see people's auras, understand their true motives, and heal them, in this novel for mature readers set during the Vietnam War. Nebula Award, Best Novel, 1990.

Doubleday, 1988, 303 pp., o.p.; Bantam, 1989, pap., 312 pp. (0-553-28252-2)

(BBS:64; BL 85:450, 471; KR 56:1366; VOYA 12:118, 13:72)

1825 SCHILLER, Barbara, adapt. *Erec and Enid.* **Gr. 3–5.**

✓ A retelling based on Arthurian legend from the French of Chretien de Troyes, in which Erec, a knight of Arthur's court, battles a cruel knight who mistreated Guinevere's attendants, and wins the hand of Enid.

Trans. by the adaptor, illus. by Ati Forberg, Dutton, 1970, 48 pp., o.p.

(BL 67:423; CCBB 24:144; HB 46:612; KR 38:1158; LJ 95:4326, 4355)

1826 SCHILLER, Barbara. *The Kitchen Knight.* **Gr. 3–4.**

✓ King Arthur's nephew, Gareth, proves himself worthy of becoming a knight by laboring for a year as a palace kitchen boy. *The Wandering Knight* (Dutton, 1971) retells the story of young Lancelot.

Illus. by Nonny Hogrogian, Holt, 1965, 64 pp., o.p.

(Ch&Bks:245; HB 41:277; KR 33:374; LJ 90:3122)

1827 SCHILLER, Barbara, adapt. *The Wandering Knight.* **Gr. 4–6.**

Sir Lancelot du Lac battles and bests many knights in his search for adventure, in this story adapted from Sir Thomas Malory's *Le Morte d'Arthur.*

Illus. by Herschel Levit, Dutton, 1971, 55 pp., o.p.

(CCBB 25:163; KR 39:880; LJ 96:3470)

1828 SEREDY, Kate. *The White Stag.* **Gr. 5–8.**

The white stag and the red eagle help guide Hunor, Magyar, Bendeguz, Attila, and their people to found the land of Hungary. John Newbery Medal, 1938.

Illus. by the author, Viking, 1937, 94 pp. (0-670-76375-6); Puffin, 1979, pap. (0-14-031258-7)

(BL 34:197; CC:554; HB 13:366, 378; LJ 62:807, 63:34, 691)

1829   SERRAILLIER, Ian (Lucien). *The Challenge of the Green Knight.* **Gr. 6–9.**

✓   Gawain of Camelot is tested by a huge green knight who allows Gawain to behead him, then picks up his head and vows to return in twelve months to strike an exchange blow.

Illus. by Victor G. Ambrus, Walck, 1976, 56 pp., o.p.

(BL 64:275, 329; CCBB 21:84; HB 43:466; KR 35:653; LJ 92:3204; TLS 1966 p. 1078)

1830   SERVICE, Pamela F. *Weirdos of the Universe, Unite!* **Gr. 5–7.**

✓   Researching an English paper on mythology, Mandy and Owen accidentally bring to life the mythical figures Baba Yaga, Coyote, the Horned King, Siegfried, and Lung Nu the Chinese Dragon Princess, all of whom enlist Mandy and Owen's aid in saving the earth from alien invaders.

Macmillan, 1992, 160 pp. (0-689-31746-8)

(BL 88:1603; CCBB 45:278; HBG 3[Fall 1992]:270; KR 60:260; SLJ June 1992 p. 125; VOYA 15:179)

SERVICE, Pamela F. *When the Night Wind Howls.* See Chapter 10, Witchcraft and Sorcery Fantasy.

1831   SERVICE, Pamela F. *Winter of Magic's Return.* **Gr. 5–8.**

✓   Welly and Heather befriend a young man who has lost his memory, and become embroiled in a struggle to awaken King Arthur and save Britain from evil. In *Tomorrow's Magic* (1987, 1988) a youthful Merlin and King Arthur appear from the past and join Heather and Welly in an attempt to use magic to unite Britain.

Atheneum, 1985, 192 pp., o.p.; Fawcett, 1986, pap. (0-449-70202-2)

(BL 82:269; CCBB 39:56; HB 61:742; Kliatt 21[Spring 1987]:25; SLJ Dec 1985 p. 94)

1832   SERVICE, Pamela F. *Wizard of Wind and Rock.* **Gr. K–4.**

Growing up in Wales, Merlin was a lonely boy fathered by an unknown wizard, but Merlin's own magic springs to life when he is almost murdered by a greedy warlord.

Illus. by Laura Marshall, Macmillan, 1990, 32 pp. (0-689-31600-3)

(BL 86:1559; HBG 1[Jan 1990]:276; KR 58:107; SLJ Apr 1990 p. 111)

1833   SEYMOUR, Miranda (pseud. of Miranda Sinclair). *Medea.* **Gr. 10 up.**

Three narrators: Jason, Aegeus, and Medea, herself, tell this dramatic story of the king's daughter who agrees to become the priestess of Hecate, goddess of death, in exchange for promised political power, falls in love with Jason, and finally loses all chance for love or power.

St. Martin, 1982, 248 pp., o.p.

(KR 50:299; LJ 107:1013; SLJ Dec 1982 p. 88)

1834   SHERMAN, Josepha. *Child of Faerie, Child of Earth.* **Gr. 6–10.**

Mistreated by her father, the Count d'Aulnoy, and his toadlike new wife, Graciosa is tempted to return the love of Percinet, half-mortal son of the Queen of Faerie, and flee with him to the Faerie realm, in this adaptation of one of Madame d'Aulnoy's French fairy tales.

Illus. by Rick Farley, Walker, 1992, 176 pp. (0-8027-8112-8)

(BL 88:1107; HBG 3[Fall 1992]:277; KR 60:398; SLJ May 1992 p. 134; VOYA 15:47)

1835   SILVERBERG, Robert. *Gilgamesh the King.* **Gr. 10 up.**

✓   Young Gilgamesh grows to manhood, is crowned king, and must eventually face his own mortality, in this powerful retelling of the 5,000-year-old Sumerian epic.

Arbor House, 1984, 290 pp., o.p.

(BL 81:3, 5; KR 52:874; LJ 109:1980)

SILVERMAN, Maida. *The Magic Well.* See Chapter 1, Allegorical Fantasy and Literary Fairy Tales.

1836   SINGER, Isaac Bashevis. *The Golem.* **Gr. 5–7.**

✓   A clay giant named Joseph is brought to life to protect the endangered Jews of Prague.

Illus. by Uri Shulevitz, Farrar, 1982, 96 pp., o.p.

(BL 79:504, 980; CCBB 36:97; HB 59:48, 331; KR 50:1237; SLJ Dec 1982 p. 68; Suth 3:394; TLS 1983 p. 776)

1837   SKURZYNSKI, Gloria (Joan). *What Happened in Hamelin.* **Gr. 5–7.**

✓   A charismatic stranger with a silvery flute lures the rats and then the children out of the village of Hamelin, in this retelling of the legend, as seen through the eyes of Geist, an orphaned baker's apprentice.

Four Winds, 1979, 177 pp., o.p.; Random, 1993, pap., 192 pp. (0-679-83645-4)

(BL 76:669; CCBB 33:119; HB 56:57; KR 47:1376; SLJ Jan 1980 p. 75)

1838   SLOAN, Carolyn. *The Sea Child.* **Gr. 5–7. (Orig. British pub. 1987.)**

Jessie's father knows that her mother, Mara, will soon call ten-year-old Jessie to her from their isolated seaside home, so he tries to introduce his daughter, who swims like a mermaid and doesn't feel the cold, to other mainland children in hopes of keeping her with him.

Holiday, 1988, 128 pp. (0-8234-0723-3)

(BBC:213; BL 85:942; CCBB 42:84; HB 65:75; KR 56:1328; SLJ Oct 1988 p. 148; Suth 4:385)

1839   SMITH, Doris Buchanan. *Voyages.* **Gr. 5–8.**

✓   Twelve-year-old Janessa retreats from the terrifying memories of her abduction and injuries during a robbery, by traveling on an origami boat from her hospital bed to Asgard, home of the Norse gods.

Viking, 1980, 176 pp., o.p., 1991, pap. (0-14-032224-8)

(BL 86:558; CCBB 43:148; HB 66:203; HBG 1[July–Dec 1989]:81; KR 57:1332; SLJ Nov 1989 p. 114)

SMITH, L(isa) J. *Night of the Solstice.* See Chapter 5C, Travel to Other Worlds.

SNYDER, Zilpha Keatley. *The Truth about Stone Hollow.* See Chapter 4, Ghost Fantasy.

SPRINGER, Nancy. *The Friendship Song.* See Chapter 5C, Travel to Other Worlds.

✓   **STEINBECK, John (Ernst), reteller.** *The Acts of King Arthur and His Noble Knights from the Winchester Manuscripts of Thomas Malory and Other Sources.* See: Malory, Sir Thomas. *La Morte D'Arthur,* this section.

1840   STEPHENS, James. *Deirdre.* **Gr. 8 up. (Orig. British and U.S. pub. Macmillan,**
✓   **1923.)**

King Conachur raises Deirdre in exile to evade a fateful prophecy, but his jealousy of

Deirdre's love for another man brings about the very tragedy he had sought to avoid. A retelling of an Irish legend.

Illus. by Nonny Hogrogian, Macmillan, 1970, 202 pp., o.p.; Arden, 1977 (repr of 1924 ed.), o.p.

(BL 20:103; HB 46:395; KR 38:331; LJ 95:1957; TLS 1923 p. 618)

1841 **STEWART, Mary (Florence Elinor).** *The Crystal Cave* **(Merlin trilogy, vol. 1).**
✓✓ **Gr. 10 up. (Orig. British pub. 1970.)**

In this first volume of Stewart's Arthurian trilogy, young Merlin has a difficult childhood at the court of the King of Wales. He is trained in magic by a learned wizard and eventually becomes involved in efforts to unite all of Britain. Mythopoetic Fantasy Award, 1971. In *The Hollow Hills* (Morrow, 1973; Fawcett, 1984, pap.), Merlin brings up young Arthur and helps him search for the magical sword, Caliburn. Mythopoetic Fantasy Award, 1974. *The Last Enchantment* (Morrow, 1979; Fawcett, 1984, pap.) deals with Arthur's reign and Merlin's death. *The Wicked Day* (orig. British pub. 1983; Morrow, 1984) is a related work in which Arthur's illegitimate son, Mordred, brings about the prophesied "wicked day," after he is left in charge of the kingdom while Arthur battles the Romans in Brittany.

Morrow, 1970, o.p.; Fawcett, 1984, pap., 521 pp. (0-449-20644-0); also pub. in *Mary Stewart's Merlin Trilogy*, Morrow, 1980, 919 pp. (0-688-00347-8)

(BBS:64; BL 67:287, 305, 655; HB 46:503; JHC:415; Kies:166; KR 38:528; LJ 95:2830, 3082, 4328; SHC:720; Tymn:158)

1842 **STORR, Catherine (Cole).** *Thursday.* **Gr. 7–10. (Orig. British pub. 1971.)**

Bee Earnshaw believes that it was Thursday Townsend's involvement with the fairy folk, and not a nervous breakdown, that has made him so lonely and withdrawn.

Harper, 1972, 274 pp., o.p.

(BL 69:295, 303; HB 49:148; KR 40:730; LJ 97:3465)

1843 **SUTCLIFF, Rosemary.** *The Sword and the Circle: King Arthur and the Knights*
✓✓ *of the Round Table.* **Gr. 6–10. (Orig. British pub. 1981.)**

Thirteen Arthurian stories retold mainly from Sir Thomas Malory's *La Morte d'Arthur* (see Malory, this section), involving King Arthur, Merlin, Sir Lancelot, and Morgan la Fay. Sutcliff's trilogy of Arthurian retellings continues with *The Light Beyond the Forest: The Quest for the Holy Grail* (orig. British pub. 1979; U.S. 1980) and *The Road to Camlann* (orig. British pub. 1981; U.S. 1982). *The Light Beyond the Forest* retells the adventures of Gawain, Bors, Percival, Lancelot, and Galahad as they search for the Holy Grail. In *The Road to Camlann,* Mordred, Arthur's illegitimate son, undermines the relationships between Arthur, Guenevere, and Lancelot, to bring about the tragic end of the company of the Round Table. Boston Globe Horn Book Award Honor Book in Fiction, 1983.

Dutton, 1981, 261 pp. (0-525-40585-2)

(BL 78:644, 655, 86:906; CCBB 35:96; Ch&Bks:238; HB 58:59; Kies:170; KR 50:141; SLJ Jan 1981 p. 90; Suth 3: 416; TLS 1981 p. 341)

1844 **SUTCLIFF, Rosemary.** *Sword at Sunset.* **Gr. 10 up. (Orig. British pub. 1963.)**
✓

Artos the Bear leads his people in thrusting back the barbarian invaders of Britain, in this version of the Arthurian legend.

Coward, 1963, 495 pp., o.p.

(BL 59:814, 822; HB 39:634; LJ 88:2786, 2930; TLS 1963 p. 473)

1845 **SUTCLIFF, Rosemary.** *Tristan and Iseult.* **Gr. 5–9.**
✓

A poetic retelling of the legendary love story of Tristan and Iseult. Carnegie Medal Highly Commended Book, 1971. Boston Globe Horn Book Award, 1972.

Dutton, 1971, 150 pp., o.p.; Farrar, 1991, pap. (0-374-47982-8)

(BL 68:431, 435, 670; CCBB 25:129; Ch&Bks:245; HB 47:620; KR 39:1015; TLS 1971 p. 764)

1846   SYNGE, (Phyllis) Ursula. *Land of Heroes: A Retelling of the Kalevala* (British
✓   title: *Kalevala, 1977*). Gr. 6 up.

Three magician-heroes: Vainamoinen the singer, Ilmarinen the smith, and Lemminkainen
the rogue, vie for the hand of the beautiful daughter of the sorceress, Mistress Louhi, in
this retelling of Finnish folklore.

Atheneum, 1978, 222 pp., o.p.

(BL 74:1342, 1355; CCBB 32:55; HB 54:289; SLJ Sept 1978 p. 150; TLS 1977 p. 1410)

1847   SYNGE, (Phyllis) Ursula. *Swan's Wing.* Gr. 7 up. (Orig. British pub. 1981.)

In this extension of Hans Christian Anderson's story, "The Wild Swans," Lothar, the self-
centered eleventh Prince who retained a swan's wing instead of one arm, Gerda, a goose-
girl who loves him, and Matthew, a tormented sculptor in love with Gerda, travel the land
in search of a cure for Lothar's affliction.

Bodley, 1984, 155 pp., o.p.

(BBS:65; BL 81:436, 451; SLJ Mar 1985 p. 183; VOYA 8:366)

1848   SYNGE, (Phyllis) Ursula. *Weland, Smith of the Gods.* Gr. 5–8. (Orig. British
pub. 1972.)

Crippled Weland and his brothers ignore their mother's warnings and leave home to find
the Valkyries, in this retelling of Norse myth from the Icelandic poetic Edda.

Illus. by Charles Keeping, Phillips, 1973, 94 pp. (0-87599-200-5)

(BL 70:335, 343; LJ 99:577; TLS 1972 p. 1322)

1849   *Tales from the Mabinogion.* Gr. 5–9. (Orig. British pub. 1984.)

These medieval Welsh heroic fantasy tales form the basis of the works of many well-
known authors of contemporary fantasy, including Alan Garner, Lloyd Alexander, and
Susan Cooper.

Trans. by Thomas Gwyn and Kevin Crossley-Holland, illus. by Margaret Jones, Overlook, 1985, 88 pp. (0-87951-987-8)

(BL 81:1123; CCBB 38:190)

1850   TARR, Judith. *Lord of the Two Lands.* Gr. 10 up.

When Alexander the Great sets out to conquer the world, Meriamon, priestess daughter
of the Pharaoh of Egypt, becomes his trusted advisor.

Tor, 1993, 320 pp. (0-312-85362-9), 1994, pap. (0-8125-2078-5)

(BL 89:1036, 1045; KR 60:1533; VOYA 16:171, 17:10)

1851   TEMPEST, John. *Vision of the Hunter.* Gr. 10 up.

Banished from his adopted tribe in a time of food scarcity, Finn develops a plan to
domesticate the vital reindeer herds and liberate his people from their harsh new leaders.

Harper, 1989, 288 pp., o.p.; Pocket, 1991, pap. (0-671-69409-X)

(BL 85:1250, 1276, 86:995; KR 57:16; LJ Mar 15, 1989 p. 88)

1852   TENNY, Dixie. *Call the Darkness Down.* Gr. 7–12.

American-born Morfa Owen's research into her Welsh heritage uncovers her family's ties
to ancient Druidic powers, and almost costs her her life.

Atheneum, 1984, 185 pp., o.p.

(BL 80:1111, 1122; CCBB 37:175; KR 52[Mar 1, 1984]:J23; SLJ May 1984 p.104; VOYA 7:198)

1853 **TEPPER, Sheri S.** *Beauty: A Novel.* **Gr. 10 up.**

✓ The diary of a half-mortal, half-fairy fifteen-year-old girl named Beauty, written in 1347, describes the magical and frightening course of her life, in this retelling of the fairy tale "Sleeping Beauty."

Doubleday, 1991, 432 pp. (0-385-41939-2); Bantam, 1992, pap. (0-553-29527-6)

(BL 87:2012 & 88:872; KR 59:701; LJ Aug 1991 p. 150; SHC 1993 Suppl. p. 84; SLJ Feb 1992 p. 121; VOYA 14:327)

1854 **TOLSTOY, Nikolai.** *The Coming of the King: The First Book of Merlin* **(Merlin** ✓ **trilogy, book 1). Gr. 10 up. (Orig. British pub. 1988.)**

Merlin the sorcerer tells King Ceneu of Prydein the story of his life and the history of the ancient land of Prydein.

Bantam, 1989, 640 pp. (0-553-05269-1), 1990, pap. (0-553-28395-2)

(BL 85:1250; Kliatt Sept 1990 p. 24; KR 57:249; LJ Apr 1, 1989 p. 115; VOYA 12:292, 13:12)

1855 **TREGARTHEN, Enys (pseud. of Nellie Sloggett).** *The White Ring.* **Gr. 4–6.**

✓ In this retelling of a Cornish legend, the King and Queen of Fairyland take on the forms of an old man and a little girl until they are able to return to their own world.

Ed. by Elizabeth Yates, illus. by Nora S. Unwin, Harcourt, 1949, 65 pp., o.p.

(BL 45:286; CCBB 2[June 1949]:6; HB 25:210; KR 17:150; LJ 74:557)

TWAIN, Mark (pseud. of Samuel Clemens). *A Connecticut Yankee in King Arthur's Court.* See Chapter 8, Time Travel Fantasy.

1856 **VALENCAK, Hannelore.** *When Half-Gods Go.* **Gr. 8–12. (Orig. Austrian pub. 1974.)**

Tired of her lover Andreas's contemptuous treatment during an archaeological tour of Greece, Barbara strikes out on her own and is befriended by a young Greek named Alexander, who may be the god, Hermes, come to life.

Trans. by Patricia Crampton, Morrow, 1976, 192 pp., o.p.

(BL 73:316, 327; CCBB 30:84; HB 52:630; KR 44:910; SLJ Oct 1976 p. 121)

VAN ALLSBURG, Chris. *The Stranger.* See Chapter 1, Allegorical Fantasy and Literary Fairy Tales.

Visions of Wonder: An Anthology of Christian Fantasy. **Ed. by Robert H. Boyer and Kenneth J. Zahorski.** See Chapter 3, Fantasy Collections.

1857 **VOEGELI, Max.** *The Wonderful Lamp.* **Gr. 5–7. (Orig. German pub. 1952.)**

In legendary Baghdad, Ali the beggar-boy searches for Aladdin's magic lamp and ends up aboard the ship of Sinbad the sailor. The sequel is *The Prince of Hindustan* (1961).

Trans. by E. M. Prince, illus. by Felix Hoffman, Oxford, 1955, 228 pp., o.p.

(BL 51:455; CCBB 9:13; HB 31:260; KR 23:358)

1858 **WALKER, Kenneth Macfarlane, and BOUMPHREY, Geoffrey.** *The Log of the Ark* **(British title:** *The Log of the Arc,* **1923; orig. U.S. title:** *What Happened in the Arc?* **Dutton, 1926). Gr. 5–7.**

A humorous retelling of the story of Noah.

Pantheon, 1960, 214 pp., o.p.

(BL 23:139, 57:33; HB 36:217)

1859 WALKER, Mary Alexander. *The Scathach and Maeve's Daughters*. Gr. 6–9.

A shapeshifter and female warrior from Celtic folklore, the Scathach uses her supernatural powers to aid four related women named Maeve: in 8th-century Scotland, 12th-century England, 17th-century Canada, and New York City in the year 2000. The story is marred by its stereotypical depiction of Canadian Iroquois people.

Macmillan, 1990, 119 pp. (0-689-31638-0)

(BL 87:328; HBG 2[July–Dec 1990]:86; KR 58:1537; SLJ Dec 1990 p. 125; VOYA 13:304)

1860 WALTON, Evangeline (pseud. of Evangeline Ensley). *The Prince of Annwn* (The Mabinogion tetralogy, book 1). Gr. 10 up.

In this retelling of the first branch of the Welsh *Mabinogion*, Prince Pwyll of Dyfed (in Wales) battles Havgan, a ruler in the Kingdom of Death, and then travels into the Bright World in search of a bride, Rhiannon of the Birds. The sequels are *The Children of Llyr* (1971, 1978), *The Song of Rhiannon* (1972, 1978), Mythopoetic Fantasy Award, 1973, and *The Virgin and the Swine* (Willett, 1936; repr. as *The Island of the Mighty*, 1970, 1979).

Random, 1971, 179 pp., o.p.

(Kies:180; Tymn:169; VOYA 2[Apr 1979]:48)

WANGERIN, Walter, Jr. *The Book of the Dun Cow*. See Chapter 1, Allegorical Fantasy and Literary Fairy Tales.

1861 WEIN, Elizabeth E. *The Winter Prince*. Gr. 6–12.

✓✓ Medraut, High King Artos's eldest, but illegitimate son, describes his love for and rivalry with his half brother, Lleu, a relationship complicated by the sorcery of Medraut's mother, Morgause, who is also Artos's sister.

Macmillan, 1993, 202 pp. (0-689-31747-6)

(BL 90:615; HB 70:208; HBG 5:91; KR 61:1153; SLJ Oct 1993 p. 158; VOYA 16:314)

1862 WELLMAN, Manly Wade. *Cahena*. Gr. 10 up.

A retelling of the story of the Cahena, a legendary female warrior-priestess in eighth-century North Africa, who fought to her death against the Moslem conquest.

Doubleday, 1986, 182 pp., o.p.

(BL 83:625, 642; LJ Dec 1986 p. 141)

1863 WELLMAN, Manly Wade. *The Old Gods Waken* (Silver John series, book 3).
✓ **Gr. 10 up.**

Only John, a wandering minstrel with a silver-stringed guitar, realizes the danger posed to his Appalachian home by the sinister revival of a druidic cult. This book is preceded by *Who Fears the Devil?* (1963) and *Worse Things Waiting* (1973). The sequels are *After Dark* (1980, 1984), *The Lost and the Lurking* (1981, 1984), *The Hanging Stones* (1982, 1984), *The Voice of the Mountain* (1984), and *The Valley So Low* (1987). *John the Balladeer* (Baen, 1988) is a collection of related short stories. In 1984 Manly Wade Wellman was given a British Fantasy Society Special Award.

Doubleday, 1979, 186 pp., o.p.

(BL 76:758; Kies:181; KR 47:1292; LJ 104:2666)

WESTALL, Robert (Atkinson). *The Devil on the Road*. See Chapter 8, Time Travel Fantasy.

1864 WHITE, T(erence) H(anbury). *The Once and Future King*. Gr. 10 up.
✓✓ A revised omnibus edition of White's retelling of Arthurian legends. The first three sec-

tions of this book were originally published separately: *The Sword in the Stone* (1939; see below), *The Witch in the Wood* (1939; here called "The Queen of Air and Darkness"), *The Ill-Made Knight* (1940), and the previously unpublished section, "The Candle in the Wind." *The Book of Merlyn,* written in 1941, was originally intended as the fifth and final book of the saga. It was first published by the University of Texas Press in 1977 and reissued by Berkley, 1978 (pap.).

Putnam, 1958, 677 pp. (0-399-10597-2); Ace, pap. (0-441-62740-4)

(BBS:67; BL 55:48; Ch&Bks:238; JHC:425; Kies:186; KR 26:429; LJ 83:2184; SHC:730; TLS 1958 p. 224; Tymn:174)

1865   **WHITE, T(erence) H(anbury).** *The Sword in the Stone* **(Camelot series, book 1).**
✓   **Gr. 5–8. (Orig. British pub. 1938.)**

Merlyn the sorcerer teaches young King Arthur about magic and history. This story and its sequel, *The Witch in the Wood* (1939), were revised to become the first two parts of *The Once and Future King* (1958; see above).

Illus. by the author, Putnam, 1939, o.p.; illus. by Dennis Nolan, 1993, 256 pp. (0-399-22502-1); Dell, 1978, pap. (0-440-98445-9)

(BBJ:76; BBS:67; BL 35:191; HBG 5:83; KR 61:1082; TLS 1938 p. 571)

WIBBERLEY, Leonard (Patrick O'Connor). *The Quest of Excalibur.* See Chapter 4, Ghost Fantasy.

1866   **WIESEL, Elie(zer).** *The Golem; the Story of a Legend.* **Gr. 10 up.**
✓   An old gravedigger in sixteenth-century Prague tells this story of Yossel, the huge clay figure created by Rabbi Yehuda Loew to protect the Jews from persecution.

Trans. by Anne Borchardt, illus. by Mark Podwal, Summit, 1983, 105 pp., o.p.

(BL 80:847, 853; LJ 109:510)

1867   **WIGNELL, Edel.** *Escape by Deluge.* **Gr. 5–8. (Orig. Australian pub. 1989.)**
✓   Water-loving Shelley discovers that only a huge rainstorm and flood can free the mythical bunyip trapped for decades in the underground pipes beneath their apartment building.

Holiday, 1990, 142 pp. (0-8234-0802-7)

(BL 86:2096; HB 66:337; HBG 1[Jan–June 1990]:255; KR 58:657; SLJ May 1990 p. 114; VOYA 13:233, 14:10)

WILDE, Oscar (pseud. of Fingal O'Flahertie Wills). *The Picture of Dorian Gray.* See Chapter 1, Allegorical Fantasy and Literary Fairy Tales.

1868   **WILHELM, Kate (Katie Gertrude).** *Cambio Bay.* **Gr. 10 up.**

The suspenseful story of six guests whose lives become intertwined with legends about the Native American family who once lived on the site of Miss Luisa's huge Victorian guesthouse overlooking Cambio Bay, California.

St. Martin's, 1990, 294 pp., o.p.

(BL 86:1122, 1124; KR 58:230; LJ Mar 15, 1990 p. 116)

1869   **WILLARD, Nancy (Margaret).** *Beauty and the Beast.* **Gr. 2–6.**
✓   Beauty's family moves to the woods after her father, a wealthy New York City merchant, goes bankrupt, in this retelling of the French fairytale set in the United States in 1900.

Illus. by Barry Moser, Harcourt, 1992, 274 pp. (0-15-206052-9)

(BL 89:504; CC 1993 Suppl. p. 18; CCBB 46:80; HB 68:734; HBG 4[Spring 1993]:99; JHC 1993 Suppl. p. 21; KR 60:1318; SLJ Oct 1992 p. 123, Dec 1992 p. 23)

WILLIAMS, Thomas. *Tsuga's Children.* See Chapter 5C, Travel to Other Worlds.

1870   WILSON, David Henry. *The Coachman Rat.* **Gr. 10 up. (Orig. German pub.**
✓   **1985.)**

Robert the rat gets his wish to become human when a fairy godmother transforms him
into a coachman to chauffeur Amadea to the ball, but trouble starts when the spell ends at
midnight, in this Cinderella story told from an unusual point of view.

Carroll & Graf, 1989, 171 pp. (0-88184-508-6); Baen, 1990, pap., 218 pp (0-671-72030-
9)

(BBS:67; BL 86:38, 56, 907, 995; Kies:188; KR 57:1120; LJ Oct 15 1989 p. 105; VOYA 12:376, 13:12)

1871   WOLF, Joan. *The Road to Avalon.* **Gr. 10 up.**

Arthur's love for his childhood friend and aunt, Morgan, threatens his marriage to Gwen-
hyfar and the future of his reign.

NAL, 1988, 368 pp., o.p.; Onyx, 1989, pap. (0-451-40138-7)

(KR 56:858; LJ Oct 15, 1988 p. 105; VOYA 13:138)

1872   WOLFE, Gene. *Castleview.* **Gr. 10 up.**
✓   The mysterious medieval castle for which Castleview, Illinois, was named turns out to be
the property of King Arthur's nemesis, Morgan Le Fay.

Tor, 1990, 400 pp., o.p., 1991, pap. (0-8125-0625-1)

(BL 86:866, 869; Kliatt Apr 1991 p. 60; KR 58:230; LJ Mar 15, 1990 p. 116)

1873   WOOLLEY, Persia. *Child of the Northern Spring* **(Guinevere trilogy, book 1).
Gr. 10 up.**

This Arthurian legend is retold through the eyes of young Gwen, soon to become Queen
Guinevere. The sequels are *Queen of the Summer Stars* (1990), and *Guinevere: The Legend in Autumn* (1991).

Poseidon, 1987, 418 pp., o.p.; Pocket, 1988, pap., 480 pp. (0-671-62199-8)

(BL 83:1410, 1437, 84:1250; KR 55:422; LJ June 1, 1987 p. 131)

1874   WREDE, Patricia C(ollins). *Snow White and Rose Red.* **Gr. 10 up.**

In this novelization of the Grimm fairy tale "Snow White and Rose Red" set in Elizabethan England on the edge of the Faerie Kingdom, the bear befriended by the two sisters
is actually the enchanted son of Queen Elizabeth.

Tor, 1989, 224 pp. (0-312-93180-8), 1990, pap. (0-8125-5825-1)

(BBS:67; BL 85:1511, 1540, 86:907, 995; KR 57:510; VOYA 12:294)

1875   WRIGGINS, Sally. *The White Monkey King: A Chinese Fable.* **Gr. 4–6.**

In ancient China, a monkey prankster with magical powers meets his match when he
challenges the Buddha.

Illus. by Ronni Solbert, Pantheon, 1977, 113 pp., o.p.

(CCBB 31:104; HB 53:529; KR 45:487; SLJ Mar 1978 p. 135; Suth 2:487)

1876   WRIGHTSON, (Alice) Patricia (Furlonger). *Balyet.* **Gr. 6–9. (Orig. Australian**
✓   **pub. 1989.)**

Rebellious fourteen-year-old Jo ignores the frantic warnings of her Granny Willet to stay
away from Balyet, a dangerous wild aboriginal spirit who was banished from her tribe a
thousand years earlier.

Macmillan, 1989, 144 pp. (0-689-50468-3); Puffin, 1990, pap. (0-14-034339-3)

(BL 85:1370, 1393; CC:574; Ch&Bks:253; CCBB 42:161; HB 56:493; KR 57:632; SLJ Apr 1989 p. 120;
Suth 4:446; VOYA 12:119, 13:11)

1877 **WRIGHTSON, (Alice) Patricia (Furlonger).** *The Ice Is Coming* **(Wirrun tril-**
✓✓ **ogy, book 1). Gr. 6–9. (Orig. Australian pub. 1977.)**

Wirrun, a young Aborigine, discovers that the ancient ice people, or Ninya, are on the march, forming ice all over the land. He realizes that it is up to him to find the most ancient Nargun, or rock monster, to stop them. Australian Children's Book of the Year Award, 1978; Guardian Award Commended Book, 1978. In *The Dark Bright Water* (1978, 1979), Wirrun uses magic to fight an enemy deep within the earth. In *Journey Behind the Wind* (1981) the evil Wulgaru, master of a mysterious death-bringing thing, causes Wirrun's water-spirit wife to disappear, and Wirrun must confront Wulgaru to save the land.

Atheneum, 1977, 222 pp., o.p.

(BL 74:559; CCBB 31:104; Ch&Bks:253; HB 54:57; Kies:192; KR 45:996; SLJ Nov 1977 p. 65; Suth 2:487)

WRIGHTSON, (Alice) Patricia (Furlonger). *Moon Dark.* See Chapter 2, Animal Fantasy.

1878 **WRIGHTSON, (Alice) Patricia (Furlonger).** *The Nargun and the Stars.* **Gr. 5–8.**
✓ **(Orig. Australian pub. 1973.)**

The lives of Simon Brent and his elderly cousins are threatened by the Nargun, a rocklike monster from the past. Australian Children's Book of the Year Award, 1974.

Atheneum, 1974, 1986, 184 pp., o.p.; Puffin, 1988, pap. (0-14-030780-X)

(BBC:216; BBJ:76; BL 70:1108, 71:768; 83:415; CC:575; CCBB 28:72; Ch&Bks:253; HB 50:382, 63:84; KR 42:302; LJ 99:2300; Suth 2:488; TLS 1973 p. 1434; Tymn:179; VOYA 9:292)

YEP, Laurence. *Dragon of the Lost Sea.* See Chapter 5A, Alternate Worlds or Histories.

1879 **YOLEN (Stemple), Jane H(yatt).** *Briar Rose.* **Gr. 10 up.**

After the death of the beloved grandmother who told her variations on "Sleeping Beauty" throughout her childhood, Becca discovers the truth about her family's involvement in the Holocaust.

Tor, 1992, 192 pp. (0-312-85135-9), 1993, pap. (0-8125-5862-6)

(BL 89:125, 133; KR 60:888; LJ Sept 15, 1992 p. 97; SHC 1993 Suppl. p. 85; SLJ Apr 1993 p. 150)

1880 **YOLEN (Stemple), Jane H(yatt).** *The Dragon's Boy.* **Gr. 5–7.**

✓ Artos, a young kennel boy, learns wisdom from an old dragon hidden in a secret cave, in this retelling of the lore about King Arthur's boyhood.

Harper, 1990, 120 pp. LB(0-06-026790-9)

(BL 87:165; CC:576; CCBB 44:134; HB 67:72; HBG 2[July–Dec 1990]:73; JHC 1991 Suppl. p. 81; KR 58:1175; SLJ Oct 1990 p. 122)

1881 **YOLEN (Stemple), Jane H(yatt).** *Greyling: A Picture Story from the Islands of*
✓ *Shetland.* **Gr. 2–4.**

A selchie, or seal-boy, raised by a fisherman and his wife, reverts to his seal form to save his foster father's life.

Illus. by William Stobbs, Philomel, 1968, 29 pp., o.p.; illus by David Ray, Putnam, 1991, 40 pp. (0-399-22262-6)

(BL 87:1975; CC 1992 Suppl. p. 86; CCBB 22:151; HB 45:44; KR 59:733; LJ 94:2096; SLJ Aug 1991 p. 158; Suth:342; TLS 1969 p. 695)

1882   YOLEN (Stemple), Jane H(yatt). *Merlin's Booke.* **Gr. 7–12.**

Ten stories and poems about the Arthurian wizard, Merlin, beginning with a ballad prophesying his birth and ending with an "Epitaph" in which an archaeological team proclaims the finding of Merlin's body to a group of skeptical journalists.

Illus. by Thomas Canty, SteelDragon, 1986, 178 pp. (0-916595-03-X)

(Kies:193; LJ Feb 1, 1987 p. 80; VOYA 9:242)

1883   YOLEN (Stemple), Jane H(yatt). *Tam Lin: An Old Ballad.* **Gr. 3-7.**

✓   Jennet MacKenzie rescues her true love, Tam Lin, from fairy bondage in this retelling of the Scottish ballad.

Illus. by Charles Mikolaycak, Harcourt, 1990, 32 pp. (0-15-284261-6)

(BL 87:158; HB 67:78; HBG 2[July–Dec 1990]:101; KR 58:1255; SLJ Jan 1991 p. 109)

1884   YOUNG, Robert F. *The Vizier's Second Daughter.* **Gr. 7–12.**

Sent into the past to kidnap Scheherazade for duplication by a supplier of wax museum figures, Bill Billings grabs her younger sister, Dunyzad, by mistake, and meets up with Ali Baba when he tries to escape.

DAW, 1985, pap., 203 pp., o.p.

(Kliatt 19[Spring 1985]:30; VOYA 8:196)

ZELAZNY, Roger, and SHECKLEY, Robert. *If at Faust You Don't Succeed.* See Chapter 8, Time Travel Fantasy.

C. Travel to Other Worlds

1885   AAMODT, Donald. *A Name to Conjure With.* **Gr. 10 up.**

Sandy MacGregor is reluctantly transported to the world of Zarathandra, where he becomes involved in a battle between a god and a goddess.

Avon, 1989, pap., 272 pp. (0-380-75137-2)

(BBS:51; BL 85:1949, 1967; LJ June 15, 1989 p. 84; VOYA 12:218)

1886   ADAIR, Gilbert. *Alice Through the Needle's Eye: The Further Adventures of*
✓   *Lewis Carroll's "Alice."* **Gr. 4–7. (Orig. British pub. 1984, entitled** *Alice Through the Needle's Eye: A Third Adventure for Lewis Carroll's Alice.)*

In this contemporary sequel to Lewis Carroll's *Alice's Adventures in Wonderland* (see this section) and *Through the Looking Glass,* Alice slips through the eye of her needle and sets off on adventures with a Country Mouse, Jack and Jill, and the Red and White Queens.

Illus. by Jenny Thorne, Dutton, 1985, 184 pp., o.p.

(BL 81:1188; KR 53:1; LJ Apr 15, 1985 p. 84; TLS Jan 4, 1985 p. 18)

AIKEN, Joan (Delano). *Winterthing: A Play for Children.* See Chapter 5B, Myth Fantasy.

1887   ALEXANDER, Lloyd (Chudley). *The First Two Lives of Lukas-Kasha.* **Gr. 5–8.**

✓✓   Lukas volunteers to participate in a magic act and unexpectedly ends up in the land of Abadan, where he is made king despite the objection of the Grand Vizier. National Book Award Finalist, Children's Book Category, 1979.

Dutton, 1978, 224 pp. (0-525-29748-0); Dell, 1982, pap. (0-440-42784-3)

(BBC:197; BBJ:68; BL 75:42; CC:441; CCBB 32:57; Ch&Bks:254; HB 55:513; KR 46:878; SLJ Oct 1978 p. 141; Suth 2:8)

1888 **ALEXANDER, Lloyd (Chudley).** *The Illyrian Adventure* **(Vesper Holly Adven-**
✓ **ture series, book 1). Gr. 5–9.**

In this adventure-filled romp set in the 1870s, young Vesper Holly travels to the kingdom of Illyria to continue her late father's research on Illyria's legendary magical warriors. In *The El Dorado Adventure* (1987) Vesper goes to the Central American country of El Dorado, where she is in constant danger from numerous villains as she attempts to save the homelands of the Chirica Indians. *The Drackenberg Adventure* (1988), *The Jedera Adventure* (1989), and *The Philadelphia Adventure* (1990) continue Vesper's exploits.

Dutton, 1986, 160 pp. (0-525-44250-2); Dell, 1987, 1990, pap. (0-440-40297-2)

(BL 82:1134, 1137, 83:794, 1136; CC:44; CCBB 39:142; HB 62:447; JHC:331; Kliatt 21[Spring 1987]:19; KR 54:543; SLJ May 1986 p. 99; VOYA 9:232, 10:22)

ALLEN, Judy. *The Lord of the Dance.* See Chapter 5B, Myth Fantasy.

ANDERSEN, Hans Christian. *The Snow Queen.* See Chapter 1, Allegorical Fantasy and Literary Fairy Tales.

1889 **ANTHONY, Piers (pseud. of Piers A. D. Jacob).** *Virtual Mode* **(Mode series,**
✓ **book 1). Gr. 10 up.**

Darius, King of Hlanter, brings fourteen-year-old Colene home with him after he falls in love with the suicidal girl during a visit to our world. The sequels are *Fractal Mode* (1992) and *Chaos Mode* (1994).

Putnam, 1991, 323 pp. (0-399-13661-4); Ace, 1991, pap. (0-441-86503-8)

(BL 87:890, 891; Kliatt Apr 1992 p. 12; KR 58:1715; LJ Feb 15, 1991 p. 224; SLJ Nov 1991 p. 115; VOYA 15:38)

1890 **ANTHONY, Piers, and FARMER, Philip Jose.** *The Caterpillar's Question.* **Gr. 10 up.**

After an art student named Jack begins driving Tappy, a nearly catatonic girl, across country to a clinic, they find themselves in another world, where Tappy is transformed into a powerful spirit.

Ace, 1992, 272 pp. (0-441-09488-0)

(BL 89:37, 42; LJ Sept 15, 1992 p. 97; SHC 1993 Suppl. p. 77; SLJ Apr 1993 p. 149; VOYA 15:289)

1891 **ANTHONY, Piers, and KORNWISE, Robert Ian.** *Through the Ice.* **Gr. 6–12.**

Set upon by punkers who try to drown him under the ice, Seth awakens in another world where he and his three companions attempt to defeat Nefarious, an enchanter bent on destroying the world.

Illus. by Daniel Horne, Underwood-Miller, 1989, 199 pp. (0-88733-071-1); Baen, 1993, pap. (0-671-72113-5)

(HB 66:67; HBG 1[July–Dec 1989]:82; KR 57:1367; VOYA 12:369)

1892 **ASKOUNIS, Christina.** *The Dream of the Stone.* **Gr. 7–12.**

A mysterious stone sent by her missing brother helps fifteen-year-old Sarah and her new friend, Angel, escape from villainous CIPHER agents into another world.

Farrar, 1993, 304 pp. (0-374-31877-8)

(BL 89:1806; CCBB 46:307; HBG 4[Fall 1993]:307; KR 61:656; SLJ June 1993 p. 126; VOYA 16:160)

BAKER, Michael. *The Mountain and the Summer Stars: An Old Tale Newly Ended.* See Chapter 5B, Myth Fantasy.

1893　BALL, Brian. *The Quest for Queenie.* **Gr. 2–5.**

Harry pulls the magical sword Sigismund out of a pile of trash and travels to Mandragora to rescue his dog, Queenie, who was kidnapped by the Bad Wizard.

Illus. by Lisa Thiesing, Little, Brown, 1991, 88 pp. (0-316-07961-8)

(BL 87:1965; HBG 2[Fall 1991]:257; KR 59:668; SLJ June 1991 p. 100)

1894　BALL, Margaret. *The Shadow Gate.* **Gr. 10 up.**

An illustration in a rare fantasy book draws a young woman into Elfland, where she is proclaimed its long-lost queen.

Baen, 1991, pap., 352 pp. (0-671-72032-5)

(BL 87:910, 917, 88:872; SLJ Sept 1991 p. 297, Oct 1991 p. 172; VOYA 14:105)

1895　BARKER, Clive. *The Thief of Always: A Fable.* **Gr. 10 up.**

Bored at home, ten-year-old Harvey follows a con man named Rictus to Mr. Hood's Holiday House at the edge of a strange black lake filled with huge, sad-eyed fish, a place where children can do anything they want.

Harper, 1992, 240 pp. (0-06-017724-1)

(BL 89:379; KR 60:1144; SHC 1993 Suppl. p. 78; VOYA 16:34)

1896　**BARRIE, Sir J(ames) M(atthew).** *Peter Pan.* **Gr. 4 up. (Orig. British pub. as a**
✓　**play entitled;** *Peter Pan; or, The Boy Who Wouldn't Grow Up,* **1904; U.S. pub.**
　1905. The novel, entitled *Peter and Wendy,* **was published in 1911.)**

Peter Pan teaches three children to fly to Never Never Land, but a jealous fairy betrays them to Captain Hook's pirate band. *Peter Pan in Kensington Gardens* (abridged from *The Little White Bird,* 1892; orig. British pub. in this format, 1906; U.S. pub. Scribner, 1906, 1937, o.p.) is a related work that describes Peter's infant adventures with the birds and fairies of Kensington Gardens. Barrie also wrote a sequel play entitled *When Wendy Grew Up: An Afterthought* (Nelson, 1957).

Illus. by F. D. Bedford, Scribner, 1918 (entitled *Peter and Wendy*), o.p.; illus. by Mabel Lucie Attwell, Scribner, 1921 (entitled *Peter Pan and Wendy*), o.p.; illus. by Nora S. Unwin, Scribner, 1950, 242 pp., o.p.; illus. by Trina Schart Hyman, Macmillan, 1980, 184 pp. (0-684-16611-9); ed. by Josette Frank, illus. by Diane Goode, Random, 1983, 1987, 65 pp. (0-394-89226-7); Bantam, 1985, pap. (0-685-00704-9); Puffin, 1986, pap. (0-14-035066-7); illus. by Michael Hague, Holt, 1987, 159 pp. (0-8050-0276-6); NAL, 1987, pap. (0-451-52088-2); illus. by Jan Omerod, Viking, 1987, 204 pp., o.p.; illus. by Scott Gustafson, Viking, 1991, 192 pp. (0-670-84180-3)

(BBC:198; BL 8:171, 47:18, 77:807, 79:1140, 84:700, 858; Bookshelf 1923–1924 p. 15; CC:444, 1992 Suppl. p. 53; CCBB 3:66, 6:12, 11:66, 34:125, 36:162; Ch&Bks:256, 283; HB 26:387, 56:661; KR 59:1466; Mahony 1:35; SLJ Dec 1980 p. 57, Aug 1983 p. 48, Jan 1992 p. 108; Suth 3:40; TLS 1981 p. 1363)

1897　BARTHOLOMEW, Barbara. *The Time Keeper* **(The Timeways trilogy, book 1)**
　(British title: *The Timekeeper,* **1986). Gr. 6–10.**

Jeanette and her brother Neil are transported into a world with two moons where they are befriended by a boy named Jesse and his unicorn. The sequels are *Child of Tomorrow* (1985) and *When Dreamers Cease to Dream* (1985).

Signet, 1985, pap., 191 pp., o.p.

(Kliatt 19[Fall 1985]:20; SLJ Dec 1985 p. 97; VOYA 8:323)

1898　**BAUM, L(yman) Frank.** *The Wizard of Oz* **(Orig. title:** *The Wonderful Wizard of*
✓　*Oz,* **1900). Gr. 3–6.**

A cyclone blows Dorothy from Kansas to the Land of Oz. The price of her trip home is the death of the Wicked Witch of the West. There are fifty-three Oz sequels. Baum wrote the first fourteen: *The Land of Oz* (retitled *The Marvellous Land of Oz*) (1904), *Ozma of Oz* (1907; Peter Smith, 1985; Morrow, 1989), *Dorothy and the Wizard in Oz* (1908; Peter Smith, 1984; Morrow, 1990), *The Road to Oz* (1909; Peter Smith, n.d.; Morrow, 1991), *The Emerald City of Oz* (1910; Peter Smith, 1989; Morrow, 1993), *The Patchwork Girl of Oz* (1913), *Tik-Tok of Oz* (1914), *The Scarecrow of Oz* (1915), *Rinki-tink of Oz* (1916), *The Lost Princess of Oz* (1917), *The Tin Woodman of Oz* (1918), *The Magic of Oz* (1919), *Glinda of Oz* (1920), and *The Visitors from Oz* (Reilly, 1960). Baum also wrote *Little Wizard Stories of Oz* (1913; Schocken, 1985; Bantam, 1988; Morrow, 1994). The series was continued by Ruth Plumly Thompson, Frank Joslyn Baum, John Rea Neill, Jack Snow, Rachel R. Cosgrove, Eloise Jarvis McGraw, and Lauren McGraw Wagner. Thompson wrote *The Royal Book of Oz* (1921), *Kabumpo in Oz* (1922), *The Cowardly Lion of Oz* (1923), *Grampa in Oz* (1924), *The Lost King of Oz* (1925), *The Hungry Tiger of Oz* (1926), *The Gnome King of Oz* (1927), *The Giant Horse of Oz* (1928), *Jack Pumpkinhead of Oz* (1929), *The Yellow Knight of Oz* (1930), *Pirates in Oz* (1931), *The Purple Prince of Oz* (1932), *Ojo in Oz* (1933), *Speedy in Oz* (1934), *The Wishing Horse of Oz* (1935), *Captain Salt in Oz* (1936), *Handy Mandy in Oz* (1937), *The Silver Princess in Oz* (1938), *Ozoplaning with the Wizard of Oz* (1939), *Yankee in Oz* (Oz Club, 1972), and *The Enchanted Island of Oz* (Oz Club, 1976). Frank Joslyn Baum wrote *The Laughing Dragon of Oz* (Whitman, 1934). Neill wrote *The Wonder City of Oz* (1940), *The Scalawagons of Oz* (1941; Morrow, 1991), and *Lucky Bucky in Oz* (1942; Morrow, 1992). Snow wrote *The Magical Mimics in Oz* (1946), *The Shaggy Man of Oz* (1949), and *Who's Who in Oz* (1954). Cosgrove wrote *The Hidden Valley of Oz* (1951), and McGraw and Wagner coauthored *Merry-Go-Round in Oz* (1963; Morrow, 1990) and *The Forbidden Fountain of Oz* (Reilly, 1980). Recent additions to the series include *A Barnstormer in Oz* by Philip Jose Farmer (Berkley, 1982), *Ozma and the Wayward Wand* by Polly Berends (Random, 1985), *Dorothy and the Seven-Leaf Clover* by Dorothy F. Haas (Random, 1985), *Mister Tinker in Oz* by James Howe (Random, 1985), *Dorothy and the Magic Belt* by Susan Saunders (Random, 1985), *Return to Oz* by Joan D. Vinge (Ballantine, 1985), *Dorothy of Oz* by Roger S. Baum (Morrow, 1989), and *How the Wizard Came to Oz* (Books of Wonder, 1991, 1993) by Donald Abbott.

Illus. by Evelyn Copelman, adapted from the illus. of W. W. Denslow, Putnam, 1956, deluxe ed., 206 pp. (0-448-06026-4); illus. by W. W. Denslow, Peter Smith, n.d., o.p.; illus. by Michael Hague, Holt, 1982, 219 pp. (0-8050-0221-9); Puffin, 1983, pap. (0-14-035001-2); adapt. by Deborah Hautzig, illus. by Joseph A. Smith, Random, 1984, 56 pp., LB(0-394-95331-2); illus. by Barry Moser, Univ. of California/Penroyal, 1986, 268 pp., o.p.; illus. by W. W. Denslow, Morrow, 1987 (entitled *The Wonderful Wizard of Oz*), 316 pp. (0-688-06944-4); illus. by Charles Santore, Outlet, 1991, 96 pp., LB(0-517-06655-6)

(BBC:198; BL 79:673, 82:1661, 1682, 84:470; CC:447; CCBB 4:10, 36:21; Ch&Bks:279, 283; HB 63:82; SLJ Oct 1982 p. 148, Dec 1991 p. 78, Suth 3.43, TLS 1982 p. 1308; Tymn:49)

1899 **BEAR, Greg(ory Dale).** *The Infinity Concerto.* **Gr. 10 up.**

An old house is the gateway to another world entered by sixteen-year-old Michael Perrin, who meets the powerful Sidhe of Celtic legend. The sequel is *The Serpent Mage* (1986).

Berkley, 1984, pap., 352 pp., o.p.

(BBS:52; BL 81:557, 582, 86:904; VOYA 8:54, 365)

1900 **BEATON-JONES, Cynon.** *The Adventures of So Hi.* **Gr. 4–6. (Orig. British pub. 1951.)**

The wind carries a Chinese boy named So Hi and his kite across the sea, where he meets a lovable dragon and embarks on a series of adventures. The sequel is *So Hi and the White Horse* (1952, 1957).

Illus. by John Ward, Vanguard, 1956, 178 pp., o.p.

(BL 53:228; CCBB 10:114; HB 32:445; LJ 82:224)

1901   BENSON, E(dward) F(rederic). *David Blaize and the Blue Door.* **Gr. 4–6. (Orig. British pub. 1918.)**

Six-year-old David locks the shining blue door to the real world behind him and escapes into a topsy-turvy nonsense world. *David Blaize* (1916) and *David Blaize of Kings* (1924; British title: *David of Kings*) are related stories but not fantasies.

Illus. by H. J. Ford, Doubleday, 1919, 217 pp., o.p.

(BL 16:100; HB 3[May 1927]:17–23; LJ 45:980; Mahony 1:38; TLS 1918 p. 642)

1902   BERGENGREN, Ralph Wilhelm. *David the Dreamer: His Book of Dreams.* **Gr. 2–4.**

David and his dog, Fido, share many strange adventures in Dreamland.

Illus. by Tom Freud, Atlantic, 1922, 67 pp., o.p.

(BL 19:90; Bookshelf 1923–1924 p. 7; HB 3[May 1927]:18,21)

1903   BERTON, Pierre. *The Secret World of Og.* **Gr. 3–5. (Orig. Canadian pub. 1961.)**

Five children are imprisoned in the subterranean world of Og, whose small green inhabitants learned to speak from comic books.

Illus. by William Winter, Little, 1962, 146 pp., o.p.

(BL 58:688; HB 38:176; KR 30:181; LJ 87:2020)

BIANCO, Pamela. *Little Houses Far Away.* See Chapter 9, Toy Fantasy.

1904   BLACKWOOD, Gary L. *Beyond the Door.* **Gr. 5–9.**

Scott and his friend Tully go through a doorway in the library stacks into the pastoral world of Gale'tin, where an evil wizard wants them to bring him modern technology to increase his power.

Macmillan, 1991, 144 pp. (0-689-31645-3)

(BL 87:1125; CCBB 44:159; HBG 2:270; KR 59:171; SLJ Mar 1991 p. 192; VOYA 14:105)

1905   BLAYLOCK, James P(aul). *Land of Dreams.* **Gr. 10 up.**

During Solstice, when visits to strange lands become possible, Skeezix and Jack find a boat-sized shoe on a California beach and travel to the "land of dreams."

Morrow, 1987, 272 pp. (0-87795-898-X)

(Kies:16; KR 55:895; LJ Aug 1987 p. 146; VOYA 10:242)

BOSTON, L(ucy) M(aria Wood). *The Castle of Yew.* See Chapter 7, Magic Adventure Fantasy.

1906   BOSTON, L(ucy) M(aria Wood). *The Guardians of the House.* **Gr. 4–6. (Orig.
✓   British pub. 1974.)**

A collection of peculiar masks and carved heads in an old mansion lures Tom Morgan to a jungle temple, a submerged Roman villa, and an Indian cave.

Illus. by Peter Boston, Atheneum, 1975, 52 pp., o.p.

(CCBB 29:3; HB 51:265; KR 43:121; SLJ May 1975 p. 52; TLS 1974 p. 1373)

BOSTON, L(ucy) M(aria Wood). *The Sea Egg.* See Chapter 7, Magic Adventure Fantasy.

1907   **BOWEN, William A(lvin).** *Merrimeg.* **Gr. 3–5.**

On her way to do some errands, a little girl named Merrimeg finds herself in strange places, meeting chimney imps, starlight fairies, appleseed elves, and gnomes.

Illus. by Emma Brock, Macmillan, 1923, 1938, 166 pp., o.p.

(BL 20:143; Bookshelf 1923–1924 Suppl. p. 1; Mahony 2:132)

1908   **BOYER, Elizabeth H.** *The Troll's Grindstone* **(The Wizard's War trilogy, book 1). Gr. 10 up.**

A man named Leif, kidnapped by elves to impersonate the enemy of the sorcerer Sorkvir, saves himself by stealing a magic sword. The sequels are: *The Curse of Slagfid* (1989) and *The Dragon's Carbuncle* (1990).

Ballantine, 1986, pap., 342 pp., o.p.

(BBS:53; BL 82:1587, 1604; VOYA 10:35)

1909   **BRADLEY, Marion Zimmer.** *The House Between the Worlds.* **Gr. 10 up.**

Cameron Fenton enters the faerie world while conducting an ESP experiment and stays to help battle an evil threat to the world.

Doubleday, 1980, 244 pp., o.p.

(BBS:53; BL 76:1409, 78:593; KR 48:397; LJ 105:1192)

1910   **BRIN, David.** *The Practice Effect.* **Gr. 10 up.**

Dennis Nuel, a young physicist, is transported to a magical alternate world where he discovers that he is a wizard.

Bantam, 1984, 1985, pap., 288 pp. (0-553-26981-X)

(BL 80:1377, 1391; LJ 109:600; VOYA 8:54)

BRYHER, Winifred. *A Visa for Avalon.* See Chapter 5B, Myth Fantasy.

BURTON, Philip. *The Green Isle.* See Chapter 1, Allegorical Fantasy and Literary Fairy Tales.

1911   **CARLSEN, Ruth Christoffer.** *Ride a Wild Horse.* **Gr. 4–6.**

Julie pretends to be suffering from memory loss while she searches for an escape hatch into her own world.

Illus. by Beth Krush and Joe Krush, Houghton, 1970, 164 pp., o.p.

(BL 67:338; KR 38:1145; LJ 96:264)

1912   **CARPENTER, Christopher.** *The Twilight Realm.* **Gr. 7–12.**

Five teenagers engaged in a fantasy role-playing game are suddenly pulled into the world of Xhandarre where they become warriors and enchanters fighting an evil sorcerer who is plotting to enter our world.

Putnam, 1986, 237 pp., o.p.

(BL 82:1387, 1392; KR 54:549; SLJ Aug 1986 p. 99; VOYA 9:160)

1913   **CARROLL, Lewis (pseud. of Charles Ludwidge Dodgson).** *Alice's Adventures*
✓✓   *in Wonderland* **(orig. title:** *Alice's Adventures Underground,* **written 1863; orig. pub. 1865). Gr. 5–8.**

Alice has two adventures: First she follows a rabbit into a curious world where she meets the Mad Hatter and the Queen of Hearts. In *Through the Looking Glass and What Alice Found There* (written 1870; orig. U.S. pub. 1899; St. Martin, 1977; Knopf, 1986; Schocken, 1987; Morrow, 1993), she steps through a mirror into a backward world. *Davy and the Goblin, or What Followed Reading "Alice's Adventures in Wonderland,"* is a related story, written by Charles Edward Carryl (Houghton, 1909, 1920; see this section). *Alice Through the Needle's Eye* is a contemporary sequel written by Gilbert Adair (Dutton, 1985; see this section). Barry Moser's illustrations for the 1982 edition were awarded the American Book Award for Pictorial Design, 1983. Anthony Browne's illustrations for the 1988 edition were Highly Commended by the Kate Greenaway Medal, 1989.

Dover, 1965, 128 pp. (0-486-21482-6); illus. by Arthur Rackham, Watts, 1966, 161 pp., o.p.; Oxford, 1973, pap. (0-19-580713-8); illus. by Tove Jansson, Delacorte, 1977, 120 pp., o.p.; illus. by John Spiers, Messner, 1982 (bound with *Through the Looking Glass*), o.p.; illus. by Barry Moser, Univ. of California Press, 1982, 146 pp., o.p; illus. by Barry Moser, Harcourt, 1991, 145 pp. (0-15-104230-6), pap. (0-15-604426-9); illus. by Michelle Wriggins, Knopf, 1983, 143 pp., o.p.; illus. by Justin Todd, Outlet, 1984 (0-517-55591-3); illus. by Michael Hague, Holt, 1985, 122 pp. (0-8050-0212-X); Puffin, 1985, pap. (0-14-035038-1); illus. by John Tenniel, Bantam, 1985, 256 pp. (0-553-21173-0); Scholastic, 1988, pap. (0-590-42035-6); Holt, 1986 (entitled *Alice's Adventures Under Ground,* facsimile ed.), 112 pp., o.p.; illus. by Anthony Browne, Knopf, 1988, 118 pp., o.p.; illus. by Peter Weevers, Putam, 1989, 126 pp., o.p.; illus. by Markéta Prachatická, Wellington, 1989 (Orig. Czech pub. 1982), 165 pp. (entitled: *Alice's Adventures in Wonderland and Through the Looking Glass*), o.p.; comp. by Cooper Edens, with illus. from more than 25 classic editions, Bantam, 1989, 208 pp. (entitled: *Alice's Adventures in Wonderland: The Ultimate Illustrated Edition*) (0-553-05385-X); Knopf, 1992 (entitled *Alice's Adventures in Wonderland and Through the Looking Glass*), 336 pp. (0-679-41795-8); illus. by John Tenniel, Morrow, 1992, 208 pp. (0-688-11087-8); adapt. and trans. by Nancy Sheppard, illus. by Donna Leslie, Ten Speed, 1992 (Orig. Australian pub. 1975) (entitled: *Alitji in Dreamland/Alitjinya Ngura Tjukurmankuntjala: An Aboriginal Version of Lewis Carroll's "Alice's Adventures in Wonderland"* (0-89815-478-2); adapt. and illus. by Tony Ross, Macmillan, 1994, 93 pp. (0-689-31864-2)

(BBC:199; BL 4:119, 51:210, 63:189, 79:76, 80:678, 81:646, 1552, 82:682, 85:480, 1188, 86:544, 1086, 1158, 87:1172; Bookshelf 1932 p. 8; CC:462; CCBB 3:11, 5:21, 36, 9:66, 38:162, 43:106; Ch&Bks:256, 1993 Suppl. p. 67; HB 1[June 1925]:34; HB 5:48, 42:76, 326, 49:284, 56:80, 59:73, 59:732, 61:74, 62:344, 65:208, 68:604; HBG 1[July–Dec 1989]:82, 3[Fall 1992]:261, 5[Jan–June 1994]:307; KR 56:1401, 57:1823; LJ 91:5258; Mahony 2:276; SLJ Jan 1984 p. 73, Aug 1985 p. 62, Nov 1985 p. 82, Nov 1988 p. 110, Jan 1990 p. 98, May 1990 p. 102, Aug 1992 p. 99; Suth 4:61; TLS 1972 p. 1525, 1985 p. 18; Tymn:60)

1914 CARRYL, Charles Edward. *The Admiral's Caravan.* Gr. 4–6. (Orig. pub. in *St. Nicholas* magazine, 1891–1892.)

A little girl visits a land inhabited by the animals from Noah's ark.

Illus. by Reginald B. Birch, Houghton, 1909, 1920, 140 pp., o.p.

(Bookshelf 1928 p. 11; HB 3[May 1927]:21; Mahony 2:276)

1915 CARRYL, Charles Edward. *Davy and the Goblin, or What Followed Reading "Alice's Adventures in Wonderland."* Gr. 3–5. (Reprint of 1885 ed.; orig. pub. in *St. Nicholas* magazine, 1884, 1885.)

After reading *Alice in Wonderland* (see Carroll, this section), Davy sets off on a voyage with a goblin.

Houghton, 1909, 1920, o.p.; illus. by E. B. Bensell and Herman I. Bacharach, Houghton, 1909, 1920, 198 pp., o.p.; University Microfilms, 1967, 160 pp., o.p.

(BL 25:173; Bookshelf 1932 p. 8; HB 3[May 1927]:18, 21, 7:115; Mahony 2:276)

**1916 CHANT, Joy (pseud. of Eileen Joyce Rutter). *Red Moon and Black Mountain:*
✓✓ *The End of the House of Kendreth* (Vandarei series). Gr. 6–10. (Orig. British pub. 1970.)**

A prophecy calls three children into Vandarei, the Starlit Land—Nick and Penelope to the

Black Mountain lair of the sorcerer Fendarl, and Oliver to join a warrior band battling the Black Lord. Mythopoetic Fantasy Award, 1972. *The Grey Mane of Morning* (1977, see Chapter 5A, Alternate Worlds or Histories) and *When Voiha Wakes* (1983; Mythopoetic Fantasy Award, 1984) are set in the same world.

Ballantine, 1971, pap., o.p.; Dutton, 1976, 227 pp., o.p.; Peter Smith, 1991, o.p.

(BL 72:1584, 1594; CCBB 30:22; KR 44:600; SLJ Sept 1976 p. 130; TLS 1970 p. 1449; Tymn:61)

1917   CHARNAS, Suzy McKee. *The Kingdom of Kevin Malone.* **Gr. 7 up.**

Amy chases neighborhood bully Kevin Malone through Central Park into the magical world of Fayre Farre, where they become princess and prince and are menaced by the White One.

Harcourt, 1993, 224 pp. (0-15-200756-3)

(BL 89:1808; HBG 4[Fall 1993]:308; KR 61:594; SLJ Jan 1994 p. 132; VOYA 16:162)

1918   CHASE, Mary (Coyle). *Loretta Mason Potts.* **Gr. 4–6.**

✓   Bewitched for seven years, Loretta refuses to live with her real family and draws her brother, Colin, into the enchantment with her.

Illus. by Harold Berson, Lippincott, 1958, 221 pp., o.p.; Peter Smith, 1989 (0-8446-6428-6)

(BL 55:189; KR 26:711; LJ 84:248)

1919   CHETWIN, Grace. *Out of the Dark World.* **Gr. 5–8.**

Nightmares filled with cries for help convince Meg that she must enter the Dark World to rescue a young cousin whose spirit has been taken over by the forces of evil.

Lothrop, 1985, 160 pp. (0-688-04272-4)

(CCBB 39:105; SLJ Jan 1986 p. 64)

1920   CHEW, Ruth. *Do-It-Yourself Magic.* **Gr. 3–5.**

A magic double-headed hammer, which enables Rachel and Scott to make objects larger or smaller, helps them prevent a burglary and takes them inside a medieval castle.

Illus. by the author, Hastings, 1988, 127 pp., o.p.

(BBC:200; BL 84:932; CCBB 41:113; KR 55:1731; SLJ Mar 1988 p. 188)

1921   CHRISTOPHER, John (pseud. of Christopher Samuel Youd). *Fireball.* **Gr. 5–8.**

✓   British Simon and his American cousin Brad are sent into the parallel world of twentieth-century Roman Britain, where they take part in a Christian revolution against the Romans, and escape on a ship bound for the New World. In *New Found Land* (1983), Brad, Simon, and their Roman friends, Bos and Curtius, make a dangerous journey across the North American continent, battling Algonquins and Vikings, and arrive at an Aztec settlement on the Pacific Coast. In *Dragon Dance* (1986), Simon and Brad are kidnapped by slavers and taken to China, where they learn the secret of the fireball that began their adventures.

Elsevier/Dutton, 1981, 148 pp., o.p.

(BBJ:69; BL 77:1083, 1097; CC:464; CCBB 35:7; Ch&Bks:277; HB 57:307; SLJ Apr 1981 p. 122; Suth 3:85; TLS 1981 p. 1069; VOYA 4[Dec 1981]:38)

1922   CLEMENTS, Bruce. *Two Against the Tide.* **Gr. 5–7.**

Tom and Sharon are kidnapped and taken to an island where the inhabitants have found the secret of everlasting youth.

Farrar, 1967, 199 pp., o.p., 1987, pap., 224 pp. (0-374-48016-8)

(BL 64:542; HB 43:587; KR 35:966, 1444; SLJ 93:289)

1923 **COATSWORTH, Elizabeth (Jane).** *Knock at the Door.* **Gr. 3–5.**

A half-fairy, half-mortal boy named Stephen helps his mortal father escape from imprisonment in Fairyland to the Outer World.

Illus. by F(rancis) D. Bedford, Macmillan, 1931, 73 pp., o.p.

(BL 28:155; HB 7:311; LJ 57:865; Mahony 3:202)

1924 **COOK, Rick.** *Wizardry Compiled* **(Wizardry trilogy, vol. 2). Gr. 7–12.**

After Wiz (William Irving Zumwalt), a computer programmer turned wizard, is magically "summoned" into another world to battle the Dark League and captured by evil forces, his wife, Moira, travels to our world to enlist the aid of Wiz's computer-operator friends to free him. This is the sequel to *Wizard's Bane* (1989) and is followed by *Wizardry Cursed* (1991).

Baen, 1990, pap., 307 pp. (0-671-69856-7)

(BBS:55; VOYA 13:114, 14:13)

COOMBS, Patricia. *The Lost Playground.* See Chapter 9, Toy Fantasy.

1925 **COOPER, Paul Fenimore.** *Tal: His Marvelous Adventures with Noom-Zor-Noom.* **Gr. 4–6.**

Tal's journey to the kingdom of Troom ends with the discovery that he is the king's long-lost son.

Illus. by Ruth Reeves, Ungar, 1929, 305 pp., o.p.

(BL 26:285; HB 5:45, 49, 14:143, 34:124; Mahony 3:203; Moore 51:427; TLS 1930 p. 979)

1926 **COOPER (Grant), Susan (Mary).** *Seaward.* **Gr. 6–9.**

✓   West and Cally become traveling companions after being wrenched into an unnamed world. Their treacherous journey takes them ever seaward, in search of parents they fear are dead.

Macmillan, 1983, 180 pp. (0-689-50275-3), 1987, pap. (0-02-042190-7)

(BBC:201; BBJ:69; BL 80:158, 168, 169; CC:474; CCBB 37:65; HB 60:59; JHC:348; KR 51:202; SLJ Oct 1983 p. 157; Suth 3:100; TLS 1983 p. 1317; VOYA 7:37)

1927 **CORBETT, Scott.** *The Mysterious Zetabet.* **Gr. 1–3.**

Zachary Zwicker finds Zyxland to be the perfect place for him: All the important places and things begin with Z.

Illus. by John McIntosh, Little, 1979, 48 pp., o.p.

(BBC:201; CCBB 33:4; KR 47:576; SLJ Sept 1979 p. 107)

1928 **COVILLE, Bruce.** *The Dark Abyss* **(The Dungeon series, vol. 2). Gr. 10 up.**

When Clive Folliot leaves England in 1868 to search the African jungle for his missing twin brother, Neville, he and his companions never expect to find themselves in a multi-layered world called The Dungeon. The idea for this series was developed by Philip Jose Farmer. The first book is *The Black Tower* by Richard A. Lupoff (1988), and the sequels are *Valley of Thunder* by Charles de Lint (1989), *The Lake of Fire* by Robin W. Bailey (1989), *The Hidden City* by Charles de Lint (1990), and *Final Battle* by Richard A. Lupoff (1990).

Illus. by Robert Gould, Bantam, 1989, pap., 311 pp., o.p.

(BBS:55; VOYA 12:221)

1929 **CROSS, John Kier.** *The Other Side of Green Hills* **(British title: *The Owl and the Pussycat,* 1946). Gr. 5–7.**

Five children exploring a world on the other side of their old house meet the Moon Folk and an evil sorcerer.

Illus. by Robin Jacques, Coward, 1947, 190 pp., o.p.

(CCBB 1[Dec 1947]:2; HB 23:443; LJ 72:1473)

DAHL, Roald. *James and the Giant Peach: A Children's Story.* See Chapter 7, Magic Adventure Fantasy.

1930 **DAHL, Roald.** *The Minpins.* **Gr. K–4. (Orig. British pub. 1991.)**

✓ When Billy goes exploring in the Forest of Sin, he meets the Minpins, tiny people who live high in the trees and are terrified of the Terrible Bloodsucking Toothplucking Stone Chuckling Spittler.

Illus. by Patrick Benson, Viking, 1991, 48 pp. (0-670-84168-4)

(BL 88:447; CCBB 45:61; HB 68:64; HBG 3[July–Dec 1991]:57; KR 59:1285; SLJ Nov 1991 p. 92; TLS Nov 22, 1991 p. 23)

1931 **DALTON, Annie.** *Out of the Ordinary.* **Gr. 6–10. (Orig. British pub. 1988.)**

✓ Molly's ability to see and hear things that others cannot qualifies her to care for Floris, a mute child from another world whose enemies are trying to find him.

Harper, 1990, 256 pp., o.p., 1992, pap., 273 pp. (0-06-447081-4)

(BL 87:436; CCBB 44:113; HBG 2[July–Dec 1990]:85; KR 58:1083; SLJ Oct 1990 p. 140; VOYA 13:295, 14:12)

1932 **DAVIDSON, Lionel.** *Under Plum Lake.* **Gr. 7 up.**

A twelve-year-old boy exploring a smugglers' cave on the Cornwall coast enters the netherworld of Egon, an advanced civilization.

Knopf, 1980, 136 pp., o.p.

(KR 48:1097; LJ 105:2236; TLS 1980 p. 1325; VOYA 4[June 1981]:54)

1933 **DE HAVEN, Tom.** *Walker of Worlds* **(The Chronicles of the King's Tramp, vol.**
✓ **1). Gr. 10 up.**

Pursued by sorcerers and monsters from another world, Jack comes to Earth and tries to expose a drug company's research scandal, in this violent story for mature readers. The sequels are *The End-of-Everything Man* (1991) and *The Last Human* (1992).

Doubleday, 1990, 341 pp., o.p.; Bantam, 1991, pap. (0-553-29011-6)

(BL 86:2076; KR 58:748; LJ May 15, 1990 p. 99; VOYA 13:228, 14:13)

1934 **DEITZ, Tom.** *Windmaster's Bane.* **Gr. 10 up.**

David Sullivan enters the fairy kingdom through a crack in the world and becomes enmeshed in a power struggle between the Sidhe of Celtic myth and the Windmaster. The sequels are *Fireshaper's Doom* (1987), *Darkthunder's Way* (1989), and *Sunshaker's War* (1990).

Avon, 1986, pap., 279 pp. (0-380-75029-5)

(BBS:55; BL 83:475, 502, 86:904)

1935 **DE LINT, Charles.** *The Dreaming Place.* **Gr. 7 up. (Orig. Canadian pub. 1990.)**

✓ Nina and Ashley, sixteen-year-old cousins, alternately narrate this tale in which Nina is kidnapped by a manitou, or Native American earth spirit, and Ash enters the spirit world to offer herself in her cousin's place.

Illus. by Brian Froud, Macmillan, 1990, 138 pp. (0-689-31571-6); Warner, 1992, pap. (0-446-36287-5)

(BL 87:734; CCBB 44:114; HBG 2[July 1990]:89; KR 58:1454; SLJ Feb 1991, p. 93; VOYA 13:362, 14:10)

DE LINT, Charles. *Moonheart.* See Chapter 5B, Myth Fantasy.

1936 **DE LINT, Charles.** *Yarrow: An Autumn Tale.* **Gr. 10 up. (Orig. pub. in Canada.)**

Canadian fantasy author Caitlin Midhir discovers that the only way to escape from the vampire who is feasting on her dreams is to enter an alternate world populated by gnomes and elves.

Ace, 1986, pap., 244 pp., o.p.

(BL 83:625, 641; Kies:45; VOYA 9:291)

1937 **DELL, Joan.** *The Missing Boy.* **Gr. 4–6.**

A young cockney girl named Deborah puts on a pair of magical 3-D glasses and is transported into a five-dimensional world where she helps a young boy to see again.

Illus. by Sheila Greenwald, Putnam, 1958, 192 pp., o.p.

(HB 35:130; KR 26:819; LJ 84:249)

DE REGNIERS, Beatrice Schenk (Freedman). *Penny.* See Chapter 1, Allegorical Fantasy and Literary Fairy Tales.

1938 **DICKINSON, Peter (pseud. of Malcolm de Brissac).** *A Box of Nothing.* **Gr. 4–8.**
✓ **(Orig. British pub. 1985.)**

A magical box filled with ancient nothing takes James to a future world dump patrolled by a vicious organization of rats, where he is befriended by a creature called the Burra.

Illus. by Ian Newsham, Delacorte, 1988, 110 pp. (0-385-29664-9)

(CCBB 41:153; Ch&Bks:285; HB 54:630; KR 56:691; SLJ June–July 1988, p. 103; TLS 1985 p. 347)

1939 **DICKSON, Gordon R(upert).** *The Dragon and the George* **(Dragon series, book**
✓ **1). Gr. 10 up.**

Jim Eckert finds himself transplanted into the body of a dragon in an alternate world where his fiance is being held captive. British Fantasy Society Award, Best Novel, 1976. This story was based in part on Dickson's novelette "St. Dragon and the George" published in *The Magazine of Fantasy and Science Fiction* (Sept 1957). The story was also published in *Dragon Tales,* ed. by Isaac Asimov (Fawcett, 1982; see Chapter 3, Fantasy Collections). The sequels are *The Dragon Knight* (Tor, 1990), *The Dragon on the Border* (1992), and *Dragon at War* (1992).

Ballantine, 1976, pap., 279 pp., o.p., 1987 (0-345-35050-2)

(BL 73:994, 1001, 78:594; Kliatt 11[Spring 1977]: 10; Tymn:73; VOYA 1[Feb 1979]:54)

1940 **DONALDSON, Stephen R(upert).** *Lord Foul's Bane* **(The Chronicles of**
✓ **Thomas Covenant, the Unbeliever, vol. 1). Gr. 10 up.**

In this first volume of a complex and powerful fantasy trilogy, Thomas Covenant, a successful author shunned by family and friends because he has leprosy, is struck by a car and awakens in The Land, where he reluctantly agrees to help the Lords of Revelstone recover the Staff of Law, needed to thwart Lord Foul's destructive plans. The sequels are *The Illearth War* (1977, 1978) and *The Power That Preserves* (1977, 1979), which have been published in a three-volume boxed set entitled *The Chronicles of Thomas Covenant* (Ballantine, 1982). British Fantasy Society Best Novel Award, 1978. This trilogy is succeeded by a second trilogy called The Second Chronicles of Thomas Covenant: *The Wounded Land* (1981), *The One Tree* (1983), and *White Gold Wielder* (1983).

Holt, 1977, 369 pp., o.p.; Ballantine, 1987, pap. (0-345-34865-6)

(BBS:55; BL 74:600, 606, 78:594, 86:904; KR 45:865; LJ 102:2184; SHC:680; Tymn:74)

1941 **DONALDSON, Stephen R(upert).** *The Mirror of Her Dreams* **(Mordant's Need series, book 1). Gr. 10 up.**

Gerarden, a bumbling young sorcerer, is sent into our world to search for a champion to save the Kingdom of Mordant. He stumbles across Terisa Morgan, who makes the impulsive decision to return to Mordant with the sorcerer. The sequel is *A Man Rides Through* (1987).

Ballantine, 1986, 535 pp. (0-345-33298-9), 1987, pap. (0-345-34697-1)

(BBS:55; BL 82:1633, 1636, 83:761; KR 54:1326; LJ Nov 15, 1986 p. 112)

1942 DOUGLAS, Carole Nelson. *Cup of Clay* **(Taliswoman trilogy, vol. 1). Gr. 10 up.**

Alison Carver, a Minnesota journalist, is transported to the land of Veil, where she is given the task of guarding a magical cup that safeguards the existence of her new world. The sequel is *Seed upon the Wind* (1992).

Tor, 1991, 352 pp. (0-312-85146-4), 1992, pap. (0-8125-1248-0)

(BL 88:34, 38; KR 59:975; LJ Sept 15, 1991 p. 116; VOYA 14:380)

DOUGLAS, Carole Nelson. *Exiles of the Rynth.* See Chapter 10, Witchcraft and Sorcery Fantasy.

1943 DRAGT, Tonke. *The Towers of February: A Diary By an Anonymous (for the Time Being) Author with Added Punctuation and Footnotes.* **Gr. 5–9. (Orig. pub. in the Netherlands.)**

In this science-fantasy, Tim convinces his scientist friend, Mr. Avla, to take him along on a travel experiment to a coexisting world. Once there, however, Tim realizes that he has lost his memory and his name.

Trans. by Maryka Rudnik, Morrow, 1975, 251 pp., o.p.

(BL 72:572, 577; CCBB 29:109; HB 52:163; KR 43:1192; SLJ Jan 1976 p. 45)

DUANE, Diane (Elizabeth). *So You Want to Be a Wizard.* See Chapter 10, Witchcraft and Sorcery Fantasy.

1944 DUGGAN, Maurice (Noel). *Falter Tom and the Water Boy.* **Gr. 3–5. (Orig. pub. in New Zealand, 1958.)**

A sea-boy invites an old sailor named Falter Tom to come and live in the realm of the sea kings. Esther Glen Award, 1959.

Illus. by Kenneth Rowell, Phillips, 1959, 61 pp., o.p.

(CCBB 13:112; HB 36:128; LJ 84:3925; TLS 1975 p. 365)

1945 DURRELL, Gerald (Malcolm). *The Talking Parcel.* **Gr. 4–6. (Orig. British pub. 1974.)**

A parrot, a spider, and a toad enlist the help of three children to save Mythologia after fire-breathing Cockatrices steal the books of magic.

Illus. by Pamela Johnson, Lippincott, 1975, 191 pp., o.p.

(BBC:202; BL 71:1127; HB 51:268; KR 43:453; SLJ May 1975 p. 54; TLS 1974 p. 1380)

1946 EAGER, Edward (McMaken). *Knight's Castle.* **Gr. 4–6.**

✓ Roger, Ann, Jack, and Eliza find their way into a mixed-up medieval world where they become knights and battle giants. In the sequel *Time Garden* (1958; Peter Smith, 1985), they return to the past, and in *Half Magic* (1954; see Chapter 7, Magic Adventure Fantasy) and *Magic by the Lake* (1957), their parents have magic adventures as children.

Illus. by N. M. Bodecker, Harcourt, 1956, 183 pp., 1985, 1989, pap. (0-15-243105-5); Peter Smith, 1985 (0-8446-6232-1)

(BBC:202; BL 52:281; HB 32:120; KR 23:859; LJ 81:766)

1947 **ECKERT, Allan W.** *The Dark Green Tunnel* **(Mesmerian Annals, book 1). Gr. 5–7.**

The dark-green tunnel near their cousin William's Everglades home ends at a turnstile through which he and twins Lara and Barbaby enter Mesmeria, a kingdom enslaved by its evil king. The sequel is *The Wand: The Return to Mesmeria* (1985).

Illus. by David Wiesner, Little, Brown, 1984, 256 pp., o.p.

(BL 80:1114; CCBB 37:185; SLJ Aug 1984, p. 72)

1948 **EMERSON, Ru.** *Night Threads: The Calling of the Three* **(Night Threads series, vol. 1). Gr. 10 up.**

Threads of magic pull three Californians, Jennifer, a young attorney, her older sister, Robyn, and Robyn's teenage son, into a medieval world to help an exiled nobleman regain his throne. The sequels are *The Two in Hiding* (1991), *One Land, One Duke* (1992), and *The Craft of Light* (1993).

Ace, 1990, 256 pp., o.p.

(BL 87:421, 430; Kliatt Jan 1991 p. 20; LJ Sept 15, 1990 p. 104; VOYA 14:42)

1949 **ENDE, Michael.** *The Neverending Story.* **Gr. 5 up. (Orig. German pub. 1979.)**

✓ A boy named Bastian becomes so engrossed in reading a book about young Atreyu's quest to find a cure for the ailing Empress of Fantasiana, that he enters the book himself, saves Fantasiana, and sets off on his own adventures.

Trans. by Ralph Mannheim, illus. by Roswitha Quadflieg, Doubleday, 1983, 396 pp., o.p.; Puffin, 1984, 1993, pap. (0-14-031793-7); Buccaneer, 1991, 400 pp. (0-89966-807-0)

(BBS:56; BL 80:488, 496; HB 60:228; KR 51:844; TLS 1983 p. 1317)

1950 **ESTES, Rose.** *The Name of the Game* **(Saga of the Lost Lands trilogy, vol. 1). Gr. 7–12.**

Mike dreams about Princess Linnea Tsurin and is transported to Perrenland, where he helps the princess wage war against the monsters of Tusmit and a powerful board game. The sequels are *Brother to the Lion* (Bantam, 1988) and *Spirit of the Hawk* (Bantam, 1988).

TSR, 1988, pap., 311 pp., o.p.

(BBJ:70; VOYA 11:294)

FARMER (Mockridge), Penelope. *A Castle of Bone.* See Chapter 5B, Myth Fantasy.

1951 **FARMER (Mockridge), Penelope.** *William and Mary: A Story.* **(Orig. British**
✓ **pub. 1974.) Gr. 5–7.**

Mary and William find that a rare shell has the power to carry them into an aquarium, back to the fall of Atlantis, and to a world beneath the sea.

Atheneum, 1974, 160 pp., o.p.

(BL 71:168; CCBB 28:93; HB 50:690; KR 42:1160; LJ 99:3052; Suth 2:141; TLS 1974 p. 1380)

1952 **FARTHING, Alison.** *The Mystical Beast.* **Gr. 4–6. (Orig. British pub. 1976.)**

Sara and Henry enter the Other Side after meeting Lavinia, daughter of the Hereditary Keeper of the Mystical Beast, and organize a hectic search for the Beast, to avert a "terrible" occurrence.

Illus. by Anne Mieke, Hastings, 1978, 123 pp., o.p.

(CCBB 32:42; SLJ Oct 1978 p. 144; TLS 1976 p. 882)

FEYDY, Anne. *Osprey Island.* See Chapter 7, Magic Adventure Fantasy.

1953 **FIELD, Rachel (Lyman).** *Eliza and the Elves.* **Gr. 2–4.**

Tales and rhymes about elfin life and the possibility of stumbling into their green land.

Illus. by Elizabeth MacKinstry, Macmillan, 1926, 96 pp., o.p.

(BL 23:136; HB 2[Nov 1925]:42; Mahony 2:279; Moore:130)

FIELD, Rachel (Lyman). *The Magic Pawnshop; a New's Year Eve Fantasy.* See Chapter 7, Magic Adventure Fantasy.

1954 **FISCHER, Marjorie.** *Red Feather.* **Gr. 3–5.**

When the Queen of Fairyland needs a new mortal child to be her maid, she commands that a fairy child be exchanged for baby Rosemary, but the two babies look identical and no one can tell them apart.

Illus. by Davine, Modern Age, 1937, 151 pp., o.p.; illus. by Davine, Messner, 1950, 149 pp., o.p.

(BL 34:112; CCBB 3:68; LJ 75:1756, 2085)

1955 **FISK, Pauline.** *Midnight Blue.* **Gr. 6–9. (Orig. British pub. 1990.)**

✓✓ Bonnie escapes life with her hateful grandmother and ineffectual mother by stowing away on a hot air balloon to an alternate version of her own unhappy world. Smarties Grand Prix for Children's Books, 1990.

Lion, 1990, 217 pp., o.p., 1992, pap. (0-7459-1925-1)

(BL 87:1464; HBG 1[Jan–June 1990]:255)

1956 **FLECKER, (Herman) James Elroy.** *The King of Alsander.* **Gr. 6 up. (Orig. British pub. 1914; U.S., Putnam, 1914.)**

In this tale written by an English poet, Norman Price walks out of a grocer's shop one day and steps into the legendary white city of Alsander.

Knopf, 1926, 286 pp., o.p.

(HB 3[May 1927]:18–22)

1957 **FRANCE, Anatole (pseud. of Jacques Anatole François Thibault).** *Bee, the Princess of the Dwarfs* **Gr. 5–7. (Orig. pub. in France; orig. U.S. title *Honey-Bee*, 1911, 1924.)**

After she is spirited away by nixies, Honey-Bee is crowned princess of the dwarfs, but she longs for her home and her playmate, George.

Trans. by Peter Wright, illus. by Charles Robinson, Dutton, 1912, 127 pp., o.p.

(BL 9:40; Mahony 1:25)

1958 **FRIESNER, Esther M.** *Gnome Man's Land* **(Tim Desmond trilogy, book 1). Gr. 10 up.**

After ancient mythical creatures escape from the Faerie world into ours through a leak in a Brooklyn delicatessen, high school student Tim Desmond finds himself under the "protection" of a banshee. The sequels are *Harpy High* (1991) and *Unicorn U* (1992).

Ace, 1991, pap., 235 pp., o.p.

(BL 87:805, 817; VOYA 14:42)

1959 **FRY, Rosalie K(ingsmill).** *The Mountain Door.* **Gr 4–6. (Orig. British pub. 1960.)**

Fenella returns to the fairies who once exchanged her for a human baby, and meets Nell, the girl whose place she took.

Illus. by the author, Dutton, 1961, 128 pp., o.p.

(BL 57:612; HB 37:269; KR 29:163; LJ 86:1983; TLS Nov 25, 1960 p. x)

1960   GALL, Alice (Crew), and CREW, Fleming. *The Royal Mimkin.* **Gr. 3–5.**

Binney and Mr. Tidd board a flying boat to another world.

Illus. by Camille Masline, Oxford, 1934, 128 pp., o.p.

(BL 31:99; Bookshelf 1934–1935 p. 5; HB 10:298; LJ 60:213; Mahony 3:205)

GARFIELD, Leon. *The Wedding Ghost.* See Chapter 5B, Myth Fantasy.

1961   GARNER, Alan. *Elidor.* **Gr. 6–8. (Orig. British pub. 1965.)**

✓   Roland, Helen, Nicholas, and David unexpectedly stumble into the medieval kingdom of Elidor, where they promise to protect four treasures from evil beings able to follow them back into twentieth-century England. Carnegie Medal Commended Book, 1965.

Walck, 1967, 186 pp., o.p.; Philomel, 1979, 148 pp., o.p.; Dell, 1993, pap. (0-440-40763-X)

(BL 63:1099; HB 43:462; Kies:63; KR 35:269; LJ 92:2449; TLS 1965 p. 1131; Tymn:89)

1962   GEE, Maurice (Gough). *The Halfmen of O.* **Gr. 5–8. (Orig. pub. in New Zealand, 1982.)**

Susan and her cousin Nick are chosen to set things right in the Land of O, a country in turmoil ever since the invasion of the murderous Halfmen.

Oxford, 1983, 204 pp., o.p.

(BL 79:1400; SLJ Sept 1983 p. 134; TLS 1982 p. 1302)

1963   GEE, Maurice (Gough). *The World Around the Corner.* **Gr. 3–6. (Orig. pub. in New Zealand, 1981.)**

An old woman tells Caroline that she must keep her magical antique spectacles away from the evil Mr. Grimble.

Illus. by Gary Hebley, Oxford, 1984, 72 pp., o.p.

(CCBB 38:25; SLJ Oct 1981 p. 141, Apr 1985 p. 87)

1964   GENTLE, Mary. *A Hawk in Silver.* **Gr. 7–9. (Orig. British pub. 1978.)**

A strange silver coin takes fifteen-year-olds Holly and Chris out of their tension-filled lives at an English school ruled by an abusive gang of girls, and draws them into a magical world where a unicorn helps them stop a bitter war between the hill-dwellers and the sea-people.

Lothrop, 1985, 240 pp., o.p.

(BL 81:1050, 1058; CCBB 38:125; SLJ May 1985 p. 100; TLS 1978 p. 376; VOYA 8:138)

1965   GILMAN (Butters), Dorothy. *The Maze in the Heart of the Castle.* **Gr. 6–10.**

The sudden deaths of his beloved parents compel sixteen-year-old Colin to undertake a perilous journey through a maze, deep within the castle atop Rheembeck Mountain.

Doubleday, 1983, 230 pp., o.p.; Fawcett, 1991, pap. (0-449-70398-3)

(BL 79:1138, 1143; CCBB 36:16; SLJ Dec 1983 p. 66; VOYA 6:214)

1966   GOLDS, Cassandra. *Michael and the Secret War.* **Gr. 6–9. (Orig. Australian pub. 1985.)**

When the Secret War between Good and Evil seeps into our world through Michael's cracked mirror, he and his sister, Sarah Jane, are enlisted to aid the forces of Good.

Macmillan, 1989, 184 pp., o.p.

(HBG 1[July–Dec 1989]:83; KR 57:1326; SLJ Oct 1989 p. 133; VOYA 12:289, 13:14)

1967 **GORDON, John (William).** *The Edge of the World.* **Gr. 7–9. (Orig. British pub.**
✓ **1983.)**

Tension and horror predominate as Tekker and Kit slip back and forth between the fens near their home and a bewitched land at the edge of the world, where they attempt to rescue a woman imprisoned by Ma Grist.

Atheneum, 1983, 186 pp., o.p.

(HB 59:581; KR 51:175; SLJ Jan 1984 p. 75; TLS 1983 p. 1047; VOYA 6:343)

GOUDGE, Elizabeth (de Beauchamp). *The Valley of Song.* See Chapter 1, Allegorical Fantasy and Literary Fairy Tales.

1968 **GOULD, Joan.** *Otherborn.* **Gr. 6–9.**

Shipwrecked on a tropical island called the Land of Light, Mark and Allegra discover the inhabitants' secret: The young people are the tribal elders and the old people are the newborn children.

Coward, 1980, 160 pp., o.p.

(CCBB 34:53; HB 57:190; SLJ Sept 1980 p. 71; Suth 3:157)

1969 **GRAY, Nicholas Stuart.** *Grimbold's Other World.* **Gr. 5–7. (Orig. British pub. 1963.)**

A goatherd named Muffler gets himself into trouble when he returns to a world of darkness shown him by Grimbold the cat.

Illus. by Charles Keeping, Meredith, 1968, 184 pp., o.p.

(BL 64:1185; KR 36:114; TLS 1963 p. 427)

1970 **GREAVES, Margaret.** *The Dagger and the Bird: A Story of Suspense.* **Gr. 4–7.**
✓ **(Orig. British pub. 1971.)**

When Bridget and Luke discover that their brother, Simon, is actually a fairy changeling, they journey to the Kingdom of the Good People to find their real brother.

Illus. by Laszlo Kubinyi, Harper, 1975, 144 pp., o.p.

(BL 71:618; HB 51:147; KR 43:374; SLJ May 1975 p. 70)

1971 **GREGORIAN, Joyce Ballou.** *The Broken Citadel.* **Gr. 7–9.**

A shaft of sunlight in an abandoned house takes Sibby into the lands of Tredana and Treclere, where she joins Prince Leron in his fight against Queen Simirimia. The sequels are *Castledown* (1977) and *The Great Wheel* (Tor, 1987).

Illus. by the author, Atheneum, 1975, 373 pp., o.p.

(BL 72:235; HB 52:154; KR 43:782; SLJ Nov 1975 p. 90; Tymn:92)

GRIFFIN, Peni R(ae). *Otto from Otherwhere.* See Chapter 7, Magic Adventure Fantasy.

1972 **GRIPE, Maria (Kristina).** *The Land Beyond.* **Gr. 5–8. (Orig. Swedish pub. 1967.)**

An explorer, a young king, and a princess travel to a world not found on any map.

Trans. by Sheila La Farge, illus. by Harald Gripe, Delacorte, 1974, 214 pp., o.p.

(HB 51:152; KR 42:949; LJ 99:3045; TLS 1975 p. 1457)

1973 **GURNEY, James.** *Dinotopia: A Land Apart from Time.* **Gr. 4 up.**

Shipwrecked on an uncharted island, Boston biologist Arthur Denison and his son, Will, discover Dinotopia, a land where dinosaurs and humans live together in a harmonious society.

Illus. by the author, Turner, 1992, 159 pp. (1-878685-23-6)

(BL 89:329; KR 60:921; SLJ Dec 1992 p. 110)

HACKETT, Walter Anthony. *The Swans of Ballycastle.* See Chapter 1, Allegorical Fantasy and Literary Fairy Tales.

1974 HAMBLY, Barbara. *The Silent Tower* **(Windrose Chronicles, book 1). Gr. 10 up.**

Kidnapped and taken into an alternate world where magic works, Joanna, a young computer programmer, becomes embroiled in the intrigues of the Empire of Perryth. The sequels are *Search the Seven Hills* (1987), *The Silicon Mage* (1988), and *Dog Wizard* (1993). *Stranger at the Wedding* (1994) is set in the same world.

Ballantine, 1988, pap., 369 pp. (0-345-33764-6)

(BBS:58; BL 83:550, 571, 86:905; LJ Dec 1986 p. 142)

1975 HAMBLY, Barbara. *The Time of the Dark* **(Darwath trilogy, book 1). Gr. 10 up.**

Gil is forced to fight for her life after she travels to the city of Karst and joins a wizard's battle against the Dark Ones. The sequels are *The Walls of Air* (1983) and *The Armies of Daylight* (1983).

Ballantine, 1982, pap., 156 pp. (0-345-31965-6)

(BBS:58; LJ 107:1014)

1976 HARDING, Lee. *Misplaced Persons.* **Gr. 7–9. (Orig. pub. in *Science Fantasy* magazine, 1961; orig. Australian pub. 1979, entitled *Displaced Person*)**

Graeme is horrified to discover that he has become invisible in his own world and has slipped into a dim gray parallel world.

Harper, 1979, 149 pp., o.p.

(BBS:58; CCBB 32:174; KR 47:580)

HENRY, Jan. *Tiger's Chance.* See Chapter 7, Magic Adventure Fantasy.

1977 HILGARTNER, Beth. *Colors in the Dreamweaver's Loom.* **Gr. 6–10.**

✓ Zan Scarsdale becomes lost in the woods after her father's death and ends up in another world, where she becomes a warrior hero of the gentle Orathi tribe. In the sequel, *The Feast of the Trickster* (1991), five of Zan's Orathi companions are sent to our world to search for Zan after the Trickster pulls her back through the void and erases her memories.

Houghton, 1989, 256 pp. (0-395-50214-4)

(BBJ:71; BL 86:53, 772, 906, 994.; HB 65:775; HBG 1[July–Dec 1989]:81; JHC 1991 Suppl. p. 73; KR 57:1403; SLJ Oct 1989 p. 119; VOYA 12:224)

HILL, Elizabeth Starr. *Ever-After Island.* See Chapter 7, Magic Adventure Fantasy.

1978 HILTON, James. *Lost Horizon.* **Gr. 8 up. (Orig. British pub. 1933.)**

✓ Four survivors of a plane crash in Tibet find their way to the lamasery of Shangri-La, an oasis of eternal youth, but they long to return home.

Morrow, 1933, 1936, 218 pp., o.p.; Pocket, 1981, pap. (0-671-42243-X); Buccaneer, 1983, 231 pp., LB(0-89966-450-4)

(BBS:58; BL 30:79; Kies:80; SHC:692; TLS 1933 p. 648)

HOFFMANN, E(rnst) T(heodor) A(madeus). *The Nutcracker.* See Chapter 9, Toy Fantasy.

1979 **HOLDSTOCK, Robert (P.) (pseud. of Robert Faulcon).** *The Emerald Forest.* **Gr. 10 up.**

Tommy Markham, a young boy lost in the Brazilian jungle, lives for ten years as the adopted son of the leader of a tribe of "the Invisible People," while his American father continues to search for him.

Zoetrope, 1985 (from the film script by Rospo Pallenberg), pap., 192 pp., o.p.

(BL 82:28; Kies:81)

1980 **HOUGHTON, Eric.** *Gates of Glass.* **Gr. 6–8. (Orig. British pub. 1987.)**

A piece of yellow crystal draws Julia through her mirror into an underground world ruled by the Wizard Quorgrun, who wants to destroy all life on Earth.

Oxford Univ. Pr., 1987, 136 pp., o.p.

(BBJ:71; SLJ Jan 1988 p. 85)

1981 **HOWARD, Joan (pseud. of Patricia Gordon).** *The Oldest Secret.* **Gr. 6–8.**

Clues in an ancient book lead Hugh to an island populated by legendary beings.

Illus. by Garry MacKenzie, Viking, 1953, 128 pp., o.p.

(BL 50:84; CCBB 7:62; HB 29:362; KR 21:429)

HOWARD, Joan (pseud. of Patricia Gordon). *The Thirteenth Is Magic.* See Chapter 7, Magic Adventure Fantasy.

1982 **HOWE, James.** *Babes in Toyland.* **Gr. 3–5.**

In this story based on the libretto of Victor Herbert's 1903 operetta, Jane and Alan survive a shipwreck arranged by their greedy Uncle Barnaby, and escape to Toyland, where they meet Mother Goose characters and are reunited with their true loves.

Illus. by Allen Atkinson, Harcourt, 1986, 96 pp., o.p., 1988, pap. (0-15-200410-6)

(BL 83:352; KR 54:1370; SLJ Oct 1986 p. 112)

1983 **HUDSON, W(illiam) H(enry).** *Green Mansions: A Romance of the Tropical Forest.* **Gr. 10 up. (Orig. British pub. 1893, U.S. Putnam, 1904.)**

The romance between a magical girl of the forest and an Amazon jungle adventurer ends tragically after he introduces her to the outside world and her paradise is destroyed.

Illus. by E. McKnight Kauffer, Knopf, 1916, 1943, o.p.; illus by Keith Henderson, World, 1931, o.p.; illus. by E. McKnight Kauffer, Random, 1944, 303 pp., o.p.; Airmont, 1966, © 1965, pap., 191 pp., pap. (0-8049-0087-6); AMS (repr. of 1923 ed.) (0-404-03402-0)

(BBS:58; BL 12:482, 22:428, 27:417, 41:304, 46:201; SHC:693)

1984 **HUNTER, Mollie (pseud. of Maureen Mollie Hunter McVeigh McIlwraith).**
✓ *The Haunted Mountain: A Story of Suspense.* **Gr. 4–7. (Orig. British pub. 1972.)**

A stubborn Highlander named MacAllister, enslaved by the fairy folk for refusing to pay a tithe, is rescued by his dog and his son.

Illus. by Laszlo Kubinyi, Harper, 1972, 144 pp., o.p.

(BBC:205; BL 68:909; CC:506; CCBB 26:9; HB 48:269; Kies:84; KR 40:401; LJ 97:1928; Suth:203; TLS 1972 p. 1323)

1985 **INGELOW, Jean.** *Mopsa the Fairy.* **Gr. 4–6. (Orig. British and U.S. pub. 1869.)**

A boy named Jack crawls into the hollow of an old thorn tree and finds himself in Fairyland.

Illus. by Dora Curtis and Diana Stanley, Dutton, 1964, 142 pp., o.p.; Garland, 1976 (repr.), o.p.

(BL 60:882; Bookshelf 1923–1924, p. 15; HB 3[Aug 1927]:48, 40:377; LJ 26[no. 8]:67; Mahony 2:281; Tymn:98)

1986   IPCAR, Dahlov (Zorach). *A Dark Horn Blowing.* **Gr. 7–10.**

Nora is unwillingly drawn into an unknown world to care for the infant son of a dying queen.

Viking, 1978, 228 pp., o.p.

(BL 74:1610; KR 46:510; SLJ Nov 1978 p. 82; VOYA 1[Dec 1978]:42, 3[Aug 1980]:55)

IPCAR, Dahlov (Zorach). *The Queen of Spells.* See Chapter 5B, Myth Fantasy.

1987   JAMES, Mary (pseud. of Maryjane Meaker; a.k.a. M. E. Kerr). *The Shuteyes.* **Gr. 4–7.**

Chester Dumbello's wish to escape his small Mississippi town is granted when a one-eyed parrot takes him to Alert, where he is imprisoned in the Tower of Loathing.

Scholastic, 1993, 176 pp. (0-590-45069-7)

(HBG 4[Fall 1993]:299; KR 61:62; SLJ Apr 1993 p. 120)

1988   JONES, Adrienne. *The Mural Master.* **Gr. 5–7.**

Four children follow Til Pleeryn, the mural master, through one of his murals into the land of Pawthania, on a mission to free the captive king.

Illus. by David White, Houghton, 1974, 249 pp., o.p.

(CCBB 28:44; HB 50:283; LJ 99:2271)

1989   JONES, Diana Wynne. *Dogsbody.* **Gr. 6–8. (Orig. British pub. 1976.)**

✓   Visiting Earth in search of a sacred object that fell from the sky, Sirius, the Dog Star, takes on a dog's form and befriends a lonely human girl. Carnegie Medal Commended Book, 1975.

Greenwillow, 1977, 1988, 256 pp. (0-688-08191-6); Knopf, 1990, pap. (0-394-82031-2)

(BBJ:71; BL 73:1414, 1421; CC:511; CCBB 30:176; HB 53:319; KR 45:95; SLJ May 1977 p. 62; TLS 1976 p. 383; VOYA 2[Aug 1979]:57, 11:294, 12:13)

1990   JONES, Diana Wynne. *The Lives of Christopher Chant* **(Chrestomanci series,**
✓✓   **book 1). Gr. 5–9. (Orig. British pub. 1988.)**

After Christopher discovers that his dreams are so realistic that he can actually visit other worlds and bring things back from them, he must decide whether his beloved uncle's encouragement of these expeditions is altruistic or part of a frightening illegal scheme. Carnegie Medal Commended Book, 1988. This book is a prequel to *Charmed Life* (1978; see Chapter 8, Time Travel Fantasy), *The Magicians of Caprona* (1980; see Chapter 10, Witchcraft and Sorcery Fantasy), and *Witch Week* (1982; see Chapter 10, Witchcraft and Sorcery Fantasy).

Greenwillow, 1988, 230 pp. (0-688-07806-0); Knopf, 1990, pap. (0-394-82205-6)

(BBJ:72; BL 84:1523, 1529, 85:879; CCBB 41:140; Ch&Bks:260; HB 64:208; JHC:395; KR 51:619; SLJ May 1988 p. 98; Suth 4:207; TLS 1989 p. 378; VOYA 11:96, 12:14)

1991   JONES, Diana Wynne. *A Tale of Time City.* **Gr. 6 up. (Orig. British pub. 1987.)**

✓   After eleven-year-old Vivian Smith is kidnapped by time travelers who mistake her for the "Time Lady," she plunges from 1939 London to Time City, where she helps her kidnappers thwart a wicked plot to alter history.

Greenwillow, 1987, 288 pp. (0-688-07315-8); Knopf, 1989, pap. (0-394-82030-4)

(BL 84:569; CCBB 41:31; Ch&Bks:260; HB 64:71; KR 55:1158; SLJ Sept 1987 p. 196; TLS 1987 p. 1283; VOYA 10:288, 11:14)

JONES, Terry. *Nicobobinus.* See Chapter 6, Humorous Fantasy.

1992   **JUSTER, Norton.** *The Phantom Tollbooth.* **Gr. 5–7.**

✓   Finding a boy-sized car and tollbooth in his bedroom, Milo drives off to rescue the lost princesses, Rhyme and Reason, aided by the Spelling Bee and a watchdog named Tock.

Illus. by Jules Feiffer, Knopf, 1961, 1972, 255 pp. (0-394-81500-9), 1993, pap. (0-394-82037-1)

(BBC:206; CC:513; CCBB 15:112; Ch&Bks:280; LJ 87:332; TLS 1962 p. 892)

1993   **KATZ, Welwyn Wilton.** *The Third Magic.* **Gr. 7–10. (Orig. Canadian pub. 1988.)**

In this complex Arthurian fantasy, Morgan, a twentieth-century Canadian teenager, is transported to the Celtic kingdom of Nwm, where she becomes Morgan Le Fay, twin sister of Arddu, or Arthur. Governor General's Literary Award for Children's Literature, 1988. Runner-Up, Canadian Library Association Best Book of the Year for Children, 1989.

Macmillan, 1989, 208 pp. (0-689-50480-2)

(BBJ:72; BL 85:1274, 1300; CCBB 42:150; KR 57:294; SLJ May 1989 p. 126; VOYA 12:116)

1994   **KAY, Guy Gavriel.** *The Summer Tree.* **(Fionavar Tapestry trilogy, book 1). Gr. 10 up. (Orig. Canadian pub. 1984.)**

Five Canadian college students are summoned into the alternate world of Fionavar, just as the evil Unraveller escapes its 1,000-year imprisonment. These young people are destined to play legendary roles in the coming war against the Dark. The sequels are *The Wandering Fire* (1986; Canadian Science Fiction and Fantasy Award, 1987) and *The Darkest Road* (1986).

Arbor House, 1985, 324 pp., o.p.; NAL, 1992, pap., 400 pp. (0-451-45138-4)

(BL 82:4, 86:905, 88:1092, 1095; KR 53:984; LJ Oct 15, 1985 p. 104)

1995   **KAYE, Marvin.** *The Incredible Umbrella.* **Gr. 10 up.**

A magic umbrella transports a young Pennsylvania college professor into a number of alternate literary worlds, including the London of Charles Dickens and Sir Arthur Conan Doyle, the Cornwall of Gilbert and Sullivan, and the worlds of the Arabian Nights, Frankenstein, and Flatland. The sequel is *The Amorous Umbrella* (1981).

Doubleday, 1979, 218 pp., o.p.

(BL 75:853, 860; LJ 104:213)

1996   **KENEALLY, Thomas (Michael).** *Ned Kelly and the City of the Bees.* **Gr. 5–7. (Orig. British pub. 1978.)**

Miniaturized by a kindly bee named Apis, Ned Kelly spends his summer recuperating from appendicitis, inside a bee hive.

Illus. by Stephen Ryan, Godine, 1981, 120 pp., o.p.

(BBC:207; HB 57:535; KR 49:1160; SLJ Nov 1981 p. 93; TLS 1978 p. 1396)

1997   **KENNEDY, X. J. (pseud. of Joseph Charles Kennedy).** *The Owlstone Crown.*
✓   **Gr. 4–6.**

Twins Timothy and Verity Tibb enter the world of Owlstonia in search of their lost grandparents, and, with the help of talking animal friends, manage to overthrow the villainous dictator.

Illus. by Michele Chessare, Atheneum, 1983, 210 pp., o.p.; Bantam, 1985, pap., 224 pp. (0-553-15349-8)

(BBC:207; BL 80:992; CC:514; KR 51:192; SLJ Jan 1984 p. 78)

1998   **KEY, Alexander (Hill).** *The Forgotten Door.* **Gr. 5–7.**

✓   Falling from another world into a remote mountain town, Jon's mind-reading ability generates fear and greed in the villagers who find him.

Westminster, 1965, 126 pp., o.p.; Scholastic, 1968, 1986, pap., 144 pp. (0-590-43130-7)
(CC:515; CCBB 18:151; HB 41:392; KR 33:117; LJ 90:972; TLS 1966 p. 449)

1999   **KING, Stephen, and STRAUB, Peter.** *The Talisman.* **Gr. 10 up.**

As twelve-year-old Jack Sawyer travels cross-country from California, searching for a magic stone to save his mother's life, he visits the Territories, an alternate-past world where another woman's life is in danger.

Viking, 1984 (0-670-69199-2); Berkley, 1985, pap., 784 pp. (0-425-10533-4)
(BBS:59; BL 81:686, 708; KR 52:771; LJ 109:2080; SLJ Jan 1985 p. 92; VOYA 8:49)

KINGSLEY, Charles. *The Water Babies: A Fairy Tale for a Land Baby.* See Chapter 1, Allegorical Fantasy and Literary Fairy Tales.

2000   **KROPP, Lloyd.** *The Drift.* **Gr. 10 up.**

Becalmed in the Sargasso Sea, Peter Sutherland discovers an unknown ship-dwelling community called The Drift, whose inhabitants welcome him lovingly and urge him to stay.

Doubleday, 1969, 240 pp., o.p.; Dorchester, 1979, pap. (0-8439-0658-8)
(BL 65:997, 1069; LJ 94:1162; TLS 1969 p. 910)

2001   **KRÜSS, James (Jacob Hinrich).** *The Happy Islands Behind the Winds.* **Gr. 3–6. (Orig. German pub. 1959.)**

Captain Madirankowitsch and his crew discover an island paradise governed by talking animals. The sequel is *Return to the Happy Islands* (1967).

Trans. by Edelgard Brühl, illus. by Eberhart Binder-Strassfurt, Atheneum, 1966, 153 pp., o.p.
(KR 34:1097; LJ 91:5750)

KUSHNER, Ellen. *Thomas the Rhymer.* See Chapter 5B, Myth Fantasy.

2002   **KUTTNER, Henry.** *The Startling Worlds of Henry Kuttner.* **Gr. 10 up.**

Three novellas about people who travel to alternate worlds: "The Portal in the Picture," "Valley of the Flame" (orig. pub. Ace, 1964), and "The Dark World."

Warner, 1987, pap., 368 pp. (0-445-20328-5)
(BL 83:550, 571; VOYA 10:130)

2003   **LACKEY, Mercedes, and LISLE, Holly.** *When the Bough Breaks.* **Gr. 10 up.**

A tale for mature readers about Lianne, a teacher who falls in love with a humanlike elf named Maclyn, and Amanda, an unhappy little girl whose fate is tied to the survival of the world of Faerie.

Baen, 1993, pap., 279 pp. (0-671-72154-2)
(Kliatt May 1993 p. 16; VOYA 16:166)

2004   **LAMPMAN, Evelyn Sibley.** *The City Under the Back Steps.* **Gr. 4–6.**

After they insult the Queen ant, Craig and Jill dwindle to insect size and are put to work in the ant colony.

Illus. by Honoré Valintcourt, Doubleday, 1960, 210 pp., o.p.
(HB 36:510; KR 28:816; LJ 85:4567)

LANGTON, Jane (Gillson). *The Diamond in the Window.* See Chapter 7, Magic Adventure Fantasy.

LATTIMORE, Deborah Nourse. *The Winged Cat: A Tale of Ancient Egypt.* See Chapter 5B, Myth Fantasy.

LAWRENCE, Louise (pseud. of Elizabeth Rhoda Holden). *Star Lord.* See Chapter 5B, Myth Fantasy.

2005 **LE GUIN, Ursula K(roeber).** *The Beginning Place.* **Gr. 8 up. (British title:** *The* ✓ *Threshold,* **1980.)**

Irene resents Hugh's intrusion into the otherworld she has found, but the two unhappy young people are drawn together on their quest to destroy a terrible beast.

Harper, 1980, 183 pp. (0-06-012573-X), 1990, 1991, pap. (0-06-100148-1)

(BBS:60; BL 76:756, 77:621, 1148, 86:907; CCBB 34:14; Ch&Bks:269; HB 56:333; JHC:379; KR 47:1393, 1437; LJ 105:227; SLJ Apr 1980 p. 132; Suth 3:259; TLS Dec 12, 1980 p. 1408; VOYA 3[Feb 1981]:38)

2006 **LEVY, Robert.** *Escape from Exile.* **Gr. 6–8.**

Struck by lightning, thirteen-year-old Daniel awakens in a strange world where he can communicate with animals, a skill that makes him a valuable asset to both sides in the ongoing civil war.

Houghton, 1993, 176 pp. (0-395-64379-1)

(BL 89:1314; HBG 4[Fall 1993]:301; SLJ May 1993 p. 106; VOYA 16:166)

2007 **LEWIS, C(live) S(taples).** *The Lion, the Witch, and the Wardrobe* **(The Chroni-** ✓✓ **cles of Narnia, book 1). Gr. 4–7. (Orig. British pub. 1950.)**

The White Witch casts a spell over the land of Narnia, ensnaring Edmund, and drawing Susan, Peter, and Lucy into Narnia too, where they join the great lion Aslan's struggle to break the witch's enchantment. Lewis felt that the Narnia series ought to be read in the following order: first, *The Magician's Nephew* (1955; 1970; pap., 1986), in which young Digory and Polly borrow his sorcerer-uncle's magic rings and are transported to Narnia, just as Aslan is singing it into existence. Many years later, four children exploring the now-elderly Digory's house stumble through a magic wardrobe into Narnia, in *The Lion, the Witch, and the Wardrobe* (1951, 1983, pap., 1986). In *The Horse and His Boy* (1954; Carnegie Medal Commended Book, 1954; pap., 1986), two children and their talking horses flee into Narnia: Shasta to escape imprisonment and Aravis to avoid an unwanted marriage. In *Prince Caspian: The Return to Narnia* (1951; pap., 1986) Lucy, Edmund, Susan, and Peter help Aslan save Prince Caspian from his murderous uncle and restore him to the throne of Narnia. In *The Voyage of the Dawn Treader* (1952; pap., 1986), Edmund, Lucy, their cousin Eustace, and Prince Caspian sail to World's End aboard the Dawn Treader, in search of seven missing noblemen. In *The Silver Chair* (1953; pap., 1986) Aslan sends Eustace and Jill on a quest to free King Caspian's missing son, Prince Rilian, from an enchantment, and bring him back to Narnia. In the final volume of this series, *The Last Battle* (1956; pap., 1986), Aslan calls on all creatures who believe in and love Narnia to return for the final battle against the forces of evil. *The Last Battle* won the Carnegie Medal, 1956.

Illus. by Pauline Baynes, Macmillan, 1951, 1988, 154 pp. (0-02-758120-9); pap., 1970 (0-02-044220-3); illus. by Michael Hague, Macmillan, 1983, 183 pp. (0-02-758200-0)

(BBC:208; BBJ:73; BL 47:208, 80:96, 683; CC:522; CCBB 4:35; Ch&Bks:252; HB 27:54; JHC:382; KR 18:514; LJ 75:1756; SLJ Jan 1984 p. 79; Tymn:120–126)

2008 **LILLINGTON, Kenneth (James).** *Jonah's Mirror.* **Gr. 6 up. (Orig. British pub. 1988.)**

Jonah Sprockett invents a mirror that sends him into a world of knights, wizards, and damsels in distress. Then he begins to wonder whether he really wants to spend the rest of his life there.

Faber, 1988, 148 pp., o.p.

(BBJ:73; SLJ Oct 1988 p. 162; TLS 1988 p. 369)

2009 **LINDBERGH, Anne Spencer.** *Bailey's Window.* **Gr. 4–6.**

Anna, Carl, and their friend, Ingrid, are astonished to be able to step through a picture drawn by Anna's obnoxious cousin, Bailey, and have magical adventures visiting the past, a forest, and a carnival.

Illus. by Kinuko Craft, Harcourt, 1984, 115 pp. (0-15-205642-4); Avon, 1991, pap., 144 pp. (0-380-70767-5)

(BBC:208; BL 80:1250; CCBB 37:208; SLJ May 1984 p. 82)

2010 **LINDGREN, Astrid.** *The Brothers Lionheart.* **Gr. 6–8. (Orig. Swedish pub. 1973.)**

Two brothers, Jonathan and Karl, are reunited after death in an land called Nangiyala, where they fight a vicious tyrant and his dragon to liberate the other inhabitants.

Trans. by Joan Tate; illus. by J. K. Lambert, Viking, 1975, o.p.; Puffin, 1985, pap., 184 pp. (0-14-031955-7)

(BBC:208; HB 51:594; KR 43:777; SLJ Oct 1975 p. 100)

2011 **LINDGREN, Astrid.** *Mio, My Son.* **Gr. 4–6. (Orig. pub. in Sweden.)**

After a genii carries Mio away from his unhappy foster home, he is adopted by the King of Faraway Land.

Trans. by Marianne Turner, illus. by Ilon Wikland, Viking, 1956, 179 pp., o.p.

(BL 53:304; KR 24:868; LJ 82:588)

2012 **LINKLATER, Eric (Robert Russell).** *The Pirates in the Deep Green Sea.* **Gr. 5–7. (Orig. British pub. 1949.)**

Two boys travel beneath the sea to enlist the aid of Davy Jones in their battle with pirates.

Illus. by William Reeves, Macmillan, 1949, 398 pp., o.p.

(BL 46:52; HB 25:411; KR 17:324; LJ 74:1105, 1542; TLS July 15, 1949 p. iii)

LITTLE, Jane. *Sneaker Hill.* See Chapter 10, Witchcraft and Sorcery Fantasy.

LOFTING, Hugh. *The Story of Doctor Dolittle.* See Chapter 6, Humorous Fantasy.

2013 *Lost Worlds, Unknown Horizons: Nine Stories of Science Fiction.* **Ed. by Robert**
✓ **Silverberg. Grade 10 up.**

Nine stories of adventure in other-worlds, whose authors include Jack Finney, Edgar Allan Poe, H. G. Wells, and Robert Silverberg.

Nelson, 1978, 192 pp., o.p.

(BL 75:745; KR 46:976, 1077; SLJ Apr 1979 p. 72; VOYA 2[June 1979]:48)

LOVEJOY, Jack. *The Rebel Witch.* See Chapter 10, Witchcraft and Sorcery Fantasy.

MacDONALD, George. *At the Back of the North Wind.* See Chapter 1, Allegorical Fantasy and Literary Fairy Tales.

MacDONALD, George. *The Golden Key.* See Chapter 1, Allegorical Fantasy and Literary Fairy Tales.

McGOWEN, Tom (Thomas E.). *Odyssey from River Bend.* See Chapter 2, Animal Fantasy.

2014 McGOWEN, Tom (Thomas E.). *The Shadow of Fomor.* **Gr. 4–7.**

On a visit to Ireland, Rick and his cousin Moira suddenly find themselves in the Great Forest of the Middle Kingdom, battling to save the Old Magic.

Dutton, 1990, 128 pp., o.p.

(BL 86:1634; HBG 1[Jan–June1990]:255; SLJ May 1990 p. 107; VOYA 13:39)

2015 McHARGUE, Georgess. *Elidor and the Golden Ball.* **Gr. 3–4.**

Elidor breaks the Faeries' trust when he steals a magic ball to prove to his mother that he really had lived with them.

Illus. by Emanuel Schoengut, Dodd, 1973, 61 pp., o.p.

(BL 70:388; KR 41:1036; LJ 99:201)

2016 McKENZIE, Ellen Kindt. *Drujienna's Harp.* **Gr. 5–8.**

A San Francisco curio shop is the entrance to the terror-ridden land of T'Pahl, where Tha and Duncan attempt to topple a tyrant from power.

Dutton, 1971, 305 pp., o.p.

(BL 67:908; CCBB 25:12; HB 47:614; KR 39:434; LJ 96:1814)

2017 McNEILL (Alexander), Janet. *Tom's Tower.* **Gr. 5–7. (Orig. British pub. 1965.)**

Tom is unexpectedly summoned into an unfamiliar world where he must protect the king's treasure from two corrupt courtiers.

Illus. by Mary Russon, Little, 1967, 182 pp., o.p.

(HB 43:464; KR 35:132; TLS 1965 p. 513)

2018 MACE, Elisabeth. *Under Siege.* **Gr. 7–10. (Orig. British pub. 1988.)**

Sixteen-year-old Morris becomes a giant in his uncle's room-sized computerized fantasy game, complete with castle, and discovers he can actually communicate with two of the tiny people.

Orchard, 1990, 224 pp. LB(0-531-08471-X); Trafalgar Sq., 1990, pap. (0-233-98345-7)

(BL 86:1970, 1993; HBG 1[Jan–June 1990]:256; KR 58:501; SLJ Apr 1990 p. 144; VOYA 13:107)

2019 MAGUIRE, Gregory. *The Daughter of the Moon.* **Gr. 5–7.**

Unhappy living with her stepmother in Chicago, Erikka is drawn into a watercolor painting of Canaan Lake, New York.

Farrar, 1980, 257 pp., o.p.

(CCBB 33:219; HB 56:299; KR 48:585; SLJ May 1980 p. 69)

2020 MAHY, Margaret (May). *Dangerous Spaces.* **Gr. 5–8. (Orig. New Zealand pub.**
✓ 1991.)

Anxious to escape from her cousin Flora's chaotic home after the deaths of her parents, Anthea, eleven, is drawn into the dreamworld of Viridian, where the ghost of her great-uncle begs her to accompany him on the "journey beyond."

Viking, 1991, 160 pp. (0-670-83734-2); Puffin, 1993, pap. (0-14-036362-9)

(BL 87:1799; CC 1992 Suppl. p. 59; CCBB 44:222; HB 67:330; HBG 2:262; JHC 1992 Suppl. p. 63; KR 59:319; SLJ Apr 1991 p. 121; TLS July 12, 1991, p. 20; VOYA 14:111, 15:9)

MASEFIELD, John (Edward). *The Midnight Folk: A Novel.* See Chapter 7, Magic Adventure Fantasy.

2021   MAYNE, William (James Carter). *All the King's Men.* **Gr. 5 up. (Orig. British**
✓   **pub. 1982.)**

Three unusual stories, including one fantasy: "Boy to Island," about two people captured by fairies in the west of Scotland.

Delacorte, 1988, 192 pp. (0-385-29626-6)

(CCBB 41:142; Ch&Bks:289; HB 64:633; KR 56:203; SLJ Apr 1988 p. 103; TLS 1982 p. 788; VOYA 11:96)

2022   MERRITT, A(braham P.). *The Ship of Ishtar.* **Gr. 10 up.**

An ancient Babylonian stone sends John Kenton from New York City into an alternate world aboard the magical ship of Ishtar, where he falls in love with the princess Sharane and helps her to battle the Ruler of the Dead.

Illus. by Virgil Finlay, Borden, 1924, 1949, 1990, 309 pp. (0-87505-355-6); Macmillan, 1991, pap., 304 pp. (0-02-022871-6)

(TLS 1926 p. 397; Tymn:140)

2023   MIESEL, Sandra. *Shaman.* **Gr. 10 up.**

Two shamans, human and otter, summon professor Ria Legarde into their alternate world to develop her magic powers. This is an expanded and revised version of *Dreamrider* (Ace, 1982).

Baen, 1989, pap., 320 pp., o.p.

(BBS:62; BL 79:190, 199, 86:42, 54; VOYA 5[Dec 1982]:39)

2024   MOLESWORTH, Mary Louisa (Stewart). *The Cuckoo Clock.* **Gr. 4–6. (Orig.**
British pub. 1877; U.S., Dutton, 1954.)

The cuckoo in Griselda's new home takes her through its clock into a magical land. The sequel is *A Christmas Child* (1880).

Illus. by Ernest Shepard, Dutton, 1954, 165 pp., o.p.; Dent, 1974 (repr. of 1954 ed.), o.p.; Garland, 1976 (bound with *The Tapestry Room*), o.p.; illus. by Ernest Shepard, Peter Smith, 1980, 208 pp., o.p.; Dell, 1987, pap. (0-440-41618-3)

(BL 18:95, 22:77, 27:216, 36:118, 51:48; Bookshelf 1932 p. 2; HB 1[June 1925]:32, 2[Nov 1925]:29; HB 3[May 1927]:17–22, 30:324, 344; 38:66; Mahony 2:291)

2025   MONACO, Richard. *Journey to the Flame.* **Gr. 10 up.**

British and German forces set out to discover the secrets of the lost city of Kôr, while World War I begins in Europe. This is a contemporary sequel to Sir H(enry) Rider Haggard's *She* (1886, 1911, 1961, 1976), *Ayesha, the Return of She* (1905, 1912), *She and Allan* (1920, 1931), and *Wisdom's Daughter* (1923).

Bantam, 1985, pap., 203 pp., o.p.

(Kies:124; LJ Nov 15, 1985, p. 112)

2026   MOON, Sheila (Elizabeth). *Knee-Deep in Thunder.* **Gr. 6–9.**
✓   A blue-green stone takes Maris to the Great Land, where she and her animal companions capture savage beasts that were terrifying the people. Maris returns to the Great Land in *Hunt Down the Prize* (1971).

Illus. by Peter Parnall, Atheneum, 1967, o.p.; Guild for Psychological Studies, 1986, pap., 307 pp. (0-917479-08-4)

(BL 64:503; CCBB 21:98; HB 43:589; KR 35:968; LJ 92:3853; Suth:285)

2027 MUNDY, Talbot (pseud. of William Lancaster Gribbon). *OM, The Secret of Abhor Valley* (The Jingrim/Ramsden series, book 6). Gr. 10 up.

A young English adventurer in India during the 1920s sets out to find a piece of jade with supernatural powers and the hidden valley inhabited by a holy lama who can reveal the secrets of the universe. The 23 books in this series, published between 1916 and 1939, are all somewhat related, although they may have different main characters. In order of publication they are: *King—of the Khybers* (1916; aka *King of the Kyber Rifles*), *The Winds of the World* (1916), *Hira Singh's Tale* (1918), *Guns of the Gods* (1921), *The Caves of Terror* (1924), *The Nine Unknown* (1924), *Ramsden* (1926; aka *The Devil's Guard*), *The Woman Ayisha* (1930), *The Hundred Days* (1930), *Jingrim* (1931; aka *Jingrim Sahib*, 1953), *The Lost Trooper* (1931), *C. I. D.* (1932), *Jungle Jest* (1932), *The Lion of Petra* (1932), *The King in Check* (1933; aka *Affair in Araby*, 1953), *The Gunga Sahib* (1933), *The Mystery of Khufu's Tomb* (1933), *Jingrim and Allah's Peace* (1933), *The Red Flame of Erinpura* (1934), *The Seventeen Thieves of El-Kalil* (1935), *The Thunder Dragon Gate* (1937), and *Old Ugly Face* (1939).

Crown, 1924, o.p.; Amereon, repr. of 1924 ed., n.d. (0-89190-490-5); Carroll, 1984, pap., 400 pp. (0-88184-045-9)

(BL 21:234; Kies:125; TLS 1925 p. 57)

2028 MURPHY, Shirley Rousseau. *The Catswold Portal.* Gr. 10 up.

Queen Siddonie transforms Melissa, rightful heir to the throne of the Netherworld, into a calico cat left to die along a highway on earth in 1957, but Melissa is taken in by an artist named Branden West.

Penguin, 1992, 416 pp. (0-451-45146-5)

(BL 88:1509, 1516, 89:842; KR 60:147; LJ Mar 15, 1992 p. 129; SLJ Aug 1992 p. 189, Dec 1992 p. 24)

2029 MURPHY, Shirley Rousseau, and SUGGS, Welch. *Medallion of the Black Hound.* Gr. 5–8.

A magic medallion transports David to the land of Meryn, where he joins a band of warriors battling the evil Balcher, who is attempting to take control of both worlds.

Harper, 1989, 182 pp., o.p.

(BL 86:462; HBG 1[July–Dec 1989]:84; SLJ Oct 1989 p. 120)

2030 MYERS, John Myers. *Silverlock.* Gr. 10 up.

A young man shipwrecked in a land called the Commonwealth finds it to be populated by characters from classical literature, including Beowulf, Robin Hood, and Don Quixote. The sequel is *The Moon's Fire-Eating Daughter* (Donning, 1981).

Lippincott, 1949, 314 pp., o.p.; Lightyear, 1993, LB(0-89968-409-2)

(BBS:62; BL 46:48; KR 17:310; LJ 74:1095)

NASTICK, Sharon. *Mr. Radagast Makes an Unexpected Journey.* See Chapter 6, Humorous Fantasy.

NATHAN, Robert (Gruntal). *The Snowflake and the Starfish.* See Chapter 10, Witchcraft and Sorcery Fantasy.

2031 NESBIT (Bland), E(dith). *The Magic City.* Gr. 5–7. (Orig. British pub. 1910.)

Awakening in the middle of the night, Philip finds himself in a city made of books, blocks, and toys.

Illus. by H. R. Millar, Coward, 1958, 333 pp., o.p.; Gregg, 1981, 333 pp., o.p.

(BL 57:32; HB 36:309; LJ 85:3224)

NESBIT (Bland), E(dith). *Wet Magic.* See Chapter 7, Magic Adventure Fantasy.

2032 **NICHOLS, (Joanna) Ruth.** *The Marrow of the World.* **Gr. 5–7. (Orig. Canadian pub. 1972.)**

Summoned into another world by her dying half-sister, Linda is ordered to bring back the essence of life, in exchange for her freedom. Canadian Library Association Best Book of the Year for Children, 1973.

Illus. by Trina Schart Hyman, Atheneum, 1972, 168 pp., o.p.

(BL 69:717; KR 40:1191; LJ 98:262; Tymn:148)

2033 **NICHOLS, (Joanna) Ruth.** *A Walk out of the World.* **Gr. 5–7. (Orig. Canadian** ✓ **pub. 1969.)**

Judith and her brother, Tobit, follow a strange light into a world once ruled by their ancestors, where they mastermind a plot to overthrow the hated King Hagerrak.

Illus. by Trina Schart Hyman, Harcourt, 1969, 192 pp., o.p.

(BBC:210; BL 65:1178; CCBB 22:180; HB 45:412; KR 37:304; LJ 94:2677)

2034 **NORTH, Joan.** *The Light Maze.* **Gr. 6–9.**
✓ Kit Elting uses a circular medieval ornament called a Lightstone to enter the light maze and set Tom Nancarrow free.

Farrar, 1971, 185 pp., o.p.

(BL 68:392; CCBB 26:12; HB 48:156; KR 39:1132; LJ 96:4192; Suth:297; TLS 1972 p. 1329)

2035 **NORTON, André (pseud. of Alice Mary Norton).** *Here Abide Monsters.* **Gr. 7–9.**
Nick and Linda stumble into legendary Avalon where they become fugitives hunted by dangerous demons and mythical beasts.

Atheneum, 1974, o.p.; Tor, 1985, pap., 256 pp. (0-8125-4732-2)

(BBJ:74; BL 70:485; JHC:394; KR 41:760; LJ 98:3708)

2036 **NORTON, André (pseud. of Alice Mary Norton).** *Knave of Dreams.* **Gr. 7 up.**
After crossing into a parallel world called Ulad, Ramsey Kimble becomes Kaskar, doomed son of the late emperor.

Viking, 1975, 252 pp., o.p.

(BL 72:294; KR 43:856; SLJ Nov 1975 p. 94; TLS 1976 p. 1242)

2037 **NORTON, André (pseud. of Alice Mary Norton).** *Operation Time Search.* **Gr. 7–10.**
Ray Osborne is caught up in the conflict between the peoples of Atlantis and Mu after he steps from 1980s America through a time-space opening into an alternate world.

Harcourt, 1967, 224 pp., o.p.; Fawcett, 1981, pap. (0-449-24370-2)

(BL 64:442; HB 43:760; KR 35:747; LJ 92:3202)

2038 **NORTON, André (pseud. of Alice Mary Norton).** *Steel Magic.* **Gr. 5–7.**
✓ Eric, Sara, and Greg Lowry enter Avalon through a miniature castle, and search for Arthur's sword and Merlin's ring in order to save the land from evil.

Illus. by Robin Jacques, World, 1965, 155 pp., o.p.

(CCBB 19:151; HB 41:629; LJ 90:5519; TLS 1967 p. 451; Tymn:152)

2039 **NORTON, André (pseud. of Alice Mary Norton).** *Witch World* **(Witch World** ✓ **series, vol. 1; Simon Tregarth sequence, book 1). Gr. 8 up.**
Simon Tregarth escapes from his post-World War II pursuers through a dimension portal

into Estcarp, where the Witches use magic to battle their enemies. This book and the first five sequels listed here are called the Simon Tregarth sequence: *Web of the Witch World* (Ace, 1964; Gregg, 1977), *Three Against the Witch World* (Ace, 1965, pap.; Gregg, 1977), *Warlock of the Witch World* (Ace, 1967, pap.; Gregg, 1977), *Sorceress of the Witch World* (Ace, 1968, pap.; Gregg, 1977), and *Spell of the Witch World* (DAW, 1972, pap.; Gregg, 1977). The following are related books: *Year of the Unicorn* (Ace, 1965, pap.; Gregg, 1977), *The Crystal Gryphon* (Atheneum, 1972; Tor, 1985; see Chapter 5A, Alternate Worlds or Histories); *The Jargoon Pard* (Atheneum, 1974; Fawcett, 1978, pap.; Ballantine, 1986, pap.; see Chapter 5A, Alternate Worlds or Histories), *Trey of Swords* (Grosset, 1977; Ace, 1983, pap.), *Zarsthor's Bane* (Ace, 1978), *Horn Crown* (DAW, 1981, 1985, pap.), *Gryphon in Glory* (Atheneum, 1981; Ballantine, 1983, pap.), *'Ware Hawk* (Atheneum, 1983; Ballantine, 1984, pap.), *Gryphon's Eyrie* (Tor, 1984; 1985, 1989, pap.) by André Norton and A(nn) C(arol) Crispin, *Lore of the Witch World* (DAW, 1987), and *The Gate of the Cat* (Ace, 1987). *Tales of the Witch World* (St. Martin, 1987), *Tales of the Witch World, 2* (St. Martin, 1988), *Four from the Witch World* (Tor, 1989), *Tales of the Witch World, 3* (Tor, 1990), and *Songsmith* (Tor, 1992) are anthologies of short stories by authors other than Norton. Witch World: The Turning series includes *Storms of Victory* (Tor, 1991; see Chapter 5A, Alternate Worlds or Histories), *Flight of Vengeance* (Tor, 1992) and *On the Wings of Magic* (1994).

Ace, 1963, pap. o.p.; Gregg, 1977, 222 pp., o.p.

(BBS:62; JHC:394; SHC:711; SLJ 1977 p. 153; Tymn:149–152)

2040   **NORTON, André (pseud. of Alice Mary Norton).** *Wraiths of Time.* **Gr. 7–12.**

Radiation from a curious artifact thrusts Tallahassee Mitford into the Nubian kingdom of Meroë, where she takes on the memories and powers of Princess Ashake to battle evil forces from another world.

Atheneum, 1976, 210 pp., o.p.; Fawcett, 1987, pap. (0-449-23532-7); Tor, 1992, pap., 256 pp. (0-8125-4752-7)

(BL 73:138, 180; CCBB 30:96; Ch&Bks:290; KR 44:740; SLJ Oct 1976 p. 120; Suth 2:338)

2041   **NORTON, Mary (Pearson).** *Are All the Giants Dead?* **Gr. 4–6.**

James goes on a guided tour of fairy-tale land where he battles a giant to save Princess Dulcibel from an ill-fated marriage to a frog.

Illus. by Brian Froud, Harcourt, 1975, 123 pp., o.p., 1978, pap. (0-15-607888-0)

(BBC:210; BL 72:627; CCBB 29:129; HB 51:465; KR 43:1131; SLJ Sept 1975 p. 107; TLS 1975 p. 1053)

2042   **O'BRIEN, Robert C. (pseud. of Robert Leslie Conly).** *The Silver Crown.* **Gr. 5–8.**

Ellen's bejeweled crown saves her from death by fire but endangers her life because of its potential for overthrowing the terrible Hieronymus Machine.

Illus. by Dale Payson, Atheneum, 1968, o.p.; Macmillan, 1988, pap., 272 pp. (0-02-044651-9)

(HB 44:174; LJ 93:1802; TLS 1973 p. 1115)

2043   **O'HANLON (Meek), Jacklyn.** *The Door.* **Gr. 5–8.**

Rachel steps through "The Door" into a frightening world populated by the captives of Burt Pelf.

Dial, 1978, 76 pp., o.p.

(CCBB 32:49; KR 46:498; SLJ Apr 1978 p. 87)

2044   **PALMER, Mary.** *The Dolmop of Dorkling.* **Gr. 3–5.**

On Dorkling Island, Stafford trains the watermelon-armed navy and is proclaimed king.

Illus. by Fen Lasell, Houghton, 1967, 155 pp., o.p.

(BL 64:335; CCBB 21:31; KR 35:652; LJ 92:2454)

PATON WALSH, Jill. *Matthew and the Sea Singer.* See Chapter 1, Allegorical Fantasy and Literary Fairy Tales.

PATTEN, Brian. *Mr. Moon's Last Case.* See Chapter 7, Magic Adventure Fantasy.

PAYNE, Joan Balfour (Dicks). *Magnificent Milo.* See Chapter 7, Magic Adventure Fantasy.

PINKWATER, D(aniel) Manus. *Lizard Music.* See Chapter 6, Humorous Fantasy.

2045 POPE, Elizabeth Marie. *The Perilous Gard.* **Gr. 6–9.**

✓✓ The centuries-old spell surrounding the castle of Perilous Gard envelops Kate Sutton when she is enslaved by the Fairy Folk. John Newbery Medal Honor Book, 1975.

Illus. by Richard Cuffari, Houghton, 1974, 272 pp. (0-395-18512-2); Puffin, 1991, pap. (0-14-034912-X)

(BBS:63; BL 70:1201; CC:547; HB 50:287; Kies:137; KR 42:433; LJ 99:1484)

2046 POSTMA, Lidia. *The Stolen Mirror.* **Gr. 1–4. (Orig. pub. in the Netherlands.)**

A magical bicycle takes Michael into a world of wizards, fairies, and a dragon.

Illus. by the author, McGraw-Hill, 1976, 26 pp., o.p.

(BL 72:1468; CCBB 30:29; KR 44:532; SLJ Feb 1977 p. 58)

PYLE, Howard. *The Garden Behind the Moon: A Real Story of the Moon Angel.* See Chapter 1, Allegorical Fantasy and Literary Fairy Tales.

PYLE, Howard. *Twilight Land.* See Chapter 1, Allegorical Fantasy and Literary Fairy Tales.

2047 REEVES, James (pseud. of John Morris Reeves). *The Strange Light.* **Gr. 4–6. (Orig. British pub. 1964.)**

Christina finds her way into a land whose occupants are characters in as yet unwritten books.

Illus. by J. C. Kocsis, Rand, 1966, 152 pp., o.p.

(BL 63:491; CCBB 20:97; KR 34:689; LJ 91:5237; TLS 1964 p. 602)

2048 RHYS, Mimpsey. *Mr. Hermit Crab: A Tale for Children by a Child.* **Gr. 4–6.**

In this story written by a fourteen-year-old girl, ten-year-olds Lucia and Louisa enter a world of danger and enchantment.

Illus. by Helen Sewell, Macmillan, 1929, 190 pp., o.p.

(BL 26:208; HB 5[Nov 1929]:52–53; Mahony 3:413; Moore:30, 427)

2049 RILEY, Louise. *Train for Tiger Lily.* **Gr. 4–6. (Orig. Canadian pub. 1954.)**

A magical train takes five children to Tiger Lily, where wishes are granted by a Master of Magic. Canadian Library Association Best Book of the Year for Children, 1956. The sequel is *A Spell at Scoggin's Crossing* (1960).

Illus. by Christine Price, Viking, 1954, 186 pp., o.p.

(BL 51:117; KR 22:485; LJ 79:916, 80:192)

2050 RODDA, Emily. *Finders Keepers.* **Gr. 4–7. (Orig. Australian pub. 1990.)**

✓ Computer game-loving Patrick is transported through his television screen into another world, where he becomes a contestant on the quiz show "Finders Keepers" and searches for lost objects belonging to the three Seekers. Children's Book Council of Australia Book of the Year Award for Younger Readers, 1991. The sequel is *The Timekeeper* (1993).

Illus. by Noela Young, Greenwillow, 1991, 184 pp. (0-688-10516-5)

(BL 88:625; CC 1992 Suppl. p. 61; CCBB 45:104; HBG 3[July–Dec 1991]:72; KR 59:1349; SLJ Aug 1991 p. 168)

2051 **ROSENBERG, Joel.** *The Sleeping Dragon* **(The Guardians of the Flame series, book 1). Gr. 10 up.**

Seven students engaged in a role-playing board game are transferred into their game world and must find their way home. The series continues with *The Sword and the Chain* (1984, 1987), *The Silver Crown* (1985), *Heir Apparent* (1987), *The Warrior Lives* (1990), and *The Road to Ehvenor* (1991).

NAL, 1983, 1986, pap., 256 pp. (0-451-14833-9)

(BBS:63; Kliatt 18[Winter 1984]:24; LJ 108:1976; VOYA 7:102)

2052 **RUBIN, Amy Kateman.** *Children of the Seventh Prophecy.* **Gr. 5–7.**

Alice and Bernard are recruited by Klig, a troll prince-child, to help outwit the evil Unking who is plotting to take control of both human and troll worlds.

Warne, 1981, 178 pp., o.p.

(BL 77:1449; CCBB 35:56; KR 49:801; SLJ Sept 1981 p. 129; VOYA 4[Oct 1981]:44)

2053 **RUCKER, Rudy.** *The Hollow Earth: The Narrative of Mason Algiers Reynolds of Virginia.* **Gr. 10 up.**

Fifteen-year-old Mason, his slave companion, Atha, and Edgar Allan Poe travel from the pre-Civil War South to the center of the earth and back again, in this science-fantasy suggested for mature readers.

Morrow, 1990, 288 pp., o.p.; Avon, 1992, pap. (0-380-75535-1)

(BL 87:32, 38; KR 58:972; LJ Aug 1990 p. 147)

2054 **RUFFELL, Ann.** *Pyramid Power.* **Gr. 6–9.**

The mail-order pyramid with "magical powers" transports Martin into a dream world where he learns to cope with a potential stepfather he dislikes.

Watts, 1981, 159 pp., o.p.

(CCBB 35:36; SLJ Feb 1983 p. 82; TLS 1982 p. 345)

RUSH, Alison. *The Last of Danu's Children.* See Chapter 5B, Myth Fantasy.

2055 **SABERHAGEN, Fred.** *Pyramids.* **Gr. 10 up.**

Tom Scheffler is transported to an alternate ancient Egypt whose gods are living beings. The sequel is *After the Fact* (1987).

Baen, 1987, pap., 311 pp., o.p.

(BBS:64; BL 83:550, 571; VOYA 10:93)

SAINT-EXUPÉRY, Antoine de. *The Little Prince.* See Chapter 1, Allegorical Fantasy and Literary Fairy Tales.

2056 **SALVATORE, R. A.** *The Woods Out Back* **(Spearwielder's Tale, vol. 1). Gr. 10 up.**
✓

Gary Leger, bored with his job in a plastics factory, takes a walk in the woods and awakens in another world, where he becomes a warrior for the Land of Faerie, fighting an evil witch. The sequel is *The Dragon's Dagger* (1994).

Ace, 1993, pap., 290 pp. (0-441-90872-1)

(BL 90:422, 428; Kliatt Mar 1994 p. 20; LJ Oct 15, 1993 p. 93; VOYA 16:385)

2057   SHELLEY, Rick. *Son of the Hero* **(Varayan Memoir series, book 1). Gr. 7–12.**

Home from college on vacation, Gil Tyner finds a secret basement room that leads into the kingdom of Varay, where he must take up his dead father's quest to defeat the enemies besieging the kingdom. The sequel is *The Hero of Varay* (1991).

Viking, 1990, 256 pp., o.p.

(Kliatt Jan 1991 p. 24; VOYA 13:367)

2058   SHERMAN, Josepha. *Strange and Ancient Name.* **Gr.10 up.**

Half-human, half-Faerie Prince Hauberin is forced to make a dangerous journey into the human world to discover the secret of his human heritage.

Baen, 1993, pap., 386 pp. (0-671-72151-8)

(Kliatt May 1993 p. 19; VOYA 16:104)

2059   SHETTERLY, Will. *Elsewhere.* **Gr. 8–12.**

✓ In Bordertown, on the boundary between the real world and Faerie, Ron searches for his brother, Tony, and finds gangs of runaway elves, humans, and "halfies" living violent lives in abandoned buildings. This book is set in the Bordertown/Borderlands world of Terri Winding's adult anthology, *Borderland* (NAL, 1986, Tor, 1992; see Chapter 5A, Alternate Worlds or Histories). In the sequel, *Nevernever* (1993), set several months later, Wolfboy, formerly called Ron, is unable to protect young Florida, the missing heir of Faerie, who is kidnapped by the River Rats. *Finder* by Emma Bull (Tor, 1994), is also set in Bordertown.

Harcourt, 1991, 224 pp. (0-15-200731-8); Tor, 1992, pap. (0-8125-2003-3)

(BL 88:430; CCBB 45:74; HBG 3[July–Dec 1991]:80; KR 59:1409; SLJ Nov 1991, p. 134; VOYA 14:326)

SILVERMAN, Maida. *The Magic Well.* See Chapter 1, Allegorical Fantasy and Literary Fairy Tales.

SIMAK, Clifford D(onald). *Enchanted Pilgrimage.* See Chapter 1, Allegorical Fantasy and Literary Fairy Tales.

2060   SINGER, Marilyn. *Charmed.* **Gr. 5–8.**

Twelve-year-old Miranda and her invisible cat friend, Bastable, battle the evil Charmer, who has used mind control and drugs to conquer other worlds.

Macmillan, 1990, 224 pp. (0-689-31619-4)

(BL 87:922; CC:555; HBG 2[July–Dec 1990]:80; JHC 1991 Suppl. p. 79; KR 58:1536; SLJ Dec 1990 p. 111; VOYA 13:302, 14:10)

2061   SINGER, Marilyn. *Horsemaster.* **Gr. 6–9.**

After dreaming of flight on a winged horse, Jessica is thrust into another world to become the protector of an ancient tapestry needed by the next Horsemaster to rule the war-torn land.

Atheneum, 1985, 179 pp., o.p.

(BBJ:75; BL 81:1390, 1406; SLJ Sept 1985 p. 149; VOYA 8:194)

SLEATOR, William. *Among the Dolls.* See Chapter 9, Toy Fantasy.

SMITH, Doris Buchanan. *Voyages.* See Chapter 5B, Myth Fantasy.

2062 **SMITH, L(isa) J.** *Night of the Solstice.* **Gr. 5–8.**

Claudia, Alys, Charles, and Janie travel into the Wildworld to free the sorceress Morgana and battle an evil magician bent on enslaving our world. The sequel is *Heart of Valor* (1990).

Macmillan, 1987, 231 pp. (0-02-785840-5); Harper, 1993, pap. (0-06-106172-7)

(CCBB 41:125; HB 64:212; KR 55:1397; SLJ Jan 1988 p. 76; VOYA 10:292)

2063 **SPRINGER, Nancy.** *The Friendship Song.* **Gr. 5–7.**

Sixth-grade friends Harper and Rawnie both love the rock group Neon Shadow, so when Nico, the lead singer, collapses during a performance, the girls enter a spirit world of dead musicians and attempt to bring him back to life, in this story with parallels to the Orpheus legend.

Macmillan, 1992, 114 pp. (0-689-31727-1)

(BL 88:941; KR 60:120; HBG 3[Fall 1992]:270; KR 60:120; SLJ Apr 1992 p. 125)

2064 **SPRINGER, Nancy.** *Red Wizard.* **Gr. 5–8.**

Unhappy at home, Ryan runs away to the hut of a bumbling wizard in another world, inadvertantly bringing with him a red crayon talisman that may help him get home.

Macmillan, 1990, 138 pp. (0-689-31485-X)

(BBJ:75; HBG 1[Jan–June 1990]:255; KR 58:270; SLJ July 1990 p. 79; VOYA 13:40)

2065 **STASHEFF, Christopher.** *Her Majesty's Wizard* **(A Wizard in Rhyme series, book 1). Gr. 10 up.**

Reading a runic verse plunges Matt into an alternate world where he helps Princess Alisande to regain her throne. The sequels are *The Oathbound Wizard* (1993) and *The Witch Doctor* (1994).

Ballantine, 1986, 1993, pap., 342 pp. (0-345-27456-3)

(BL 83:192, 220; LJ Oct 15, 1986 p. 114)

2066 **STEARNS, Pamela (Fujimoto).** *Into the Painted Bear Lair.* **Gr. 4–6.**

A visit to a toy store takes Gregory into a fairy-tale kingdom where a hungry bear and a knight help him rescue a princess from a dragon and awaken an enchanted prince.

Illus. by Ann Strugnell, Houghton, 1976, 153 pp., o.p.

(BL 73:670; CCBB 30:133; HB 53:164; KR 44:1170; SLJ Dec 1976 p. 56)

STEWART, Mary (Florence Elinor). *Ludo and the Star Horse.* See Chapter 1, Allegorical Fantasy and Literary Fairy Tales.

STORR, Catherine (Cole). *Thursday.* See Chapter 5B, Myth Fantasy.

2067 **STRAUSS, Victoria.** *Worldstone.* **Gr. 7–12.**

Alexina Taylor, orphaned and unhappy in her exile from New York City, discovers that she has psychic powers when a thief from another world links minds with her, enabling his escape into our world.

Macmillan, 1985, 324 pp., o.p.

(BBJ:76; BL 82:398, 415; CCBB 39:159; SLJ Jan 1986 p. 75)

2068 **SWAHN, Sven.** *The Island Through the Gate.* **Gr. 6–8. (Orig. pub. in Sweden.)**

Stranded on the isolated island of Oberair, Michael is prevented from leaving by the superstitious islanders and their leader, Gourven the sorcerer.

Trans. by Patricia Crampton, Macmillan, 1974, 183 pp., o.p.

(BL 70:1059; HB 50:154; KR 42:187; LJ 99:2279)

2069 **SWIFT, Jonathan.** *Gulliver's Travels into Several Remote Nations of the World.*
✓ **Gr. 5 up. (Orig. British pub. 1726.)**

In these editions adapted for young people, Gulliver is shipwrecked on an island of miniature people called Lilliput and then travels to Brobdingnag, Land of Giants. A contemporary sequel is *Castaways in Lilliput* by Henry Winterfeld (Harcourt, 1960; see this section).

Illus. by Arthur Rackham, Dutton, 1957, 210 pp., o.p.; adapt. by Padraic Colum, illus. by Willy Pogany, Macmillan, 1962, 260 pp., o.p.; ed. by Ronald Storer, Oxford, 1972, pap. (0-19-421764-7); illus. by David Small, Morrow, 1983, 94 pp., o.p.; adapt. by James Riordan, illus. by Victor G. Ambrus, Oxford, 1992, 96 pp. (0-19-279897-9); adapt. by Ann Keay Beneduce, illus. by Gennady Spirin, Philomel, 1993, 32 pp. (entitled: *Gulliver's Adventures in Lilliput*) (0-399-22021-6)

(BBC:214; BL 44:118, 45:145, 80:817, 89:599, 90:71; Bookshelf 1932 p. 23; CCBB 2[May 1949]:6, 3:19; HB 1[Nov 1924]:8, 39:604; HBG 4[Spring 1993]:77, 5:70; JHC 416; KR 60:1316, 61:1338; Mahony 2:297; SHC:721; SLJ Jan 1984 p. 82, Oct 1993 p. 132)

. **TARN, Sir William Woodthorpe.** *The Treasure of the Isle of Mist: A Tale of the Isle of Skye.* See Chapter 7, Magic Adventure Fantasy.

2070 **TEPPER, Sheri S.** *Marianne, the Magus, and the Manticore.* **Gr. 10 up.**

Marianne, an American college student from the tiny principality of Alphenlicht, finds herself in an alternate world battling a magus, or sorcerer, and a deadly manticore.

Ace, 1985, pap., 185 pp., o.p.

(BBS:65; BL 82:662, 677; VOYA 9:91)

2071 **THOMPSON, Julian F(rancis).** *Gypsyworld.* **Gr. 7–12.**

Five teenagers bought or kidnapped by the king and queen of Gypsyworld are taken into this parallel world to convince the inhabitants to help Earth solve its environmental problems.

Henry Holt, 1992, 227 pp. (0-8050-1907-3); Puffin, 1993, pap. (0-14-036531-1)

(BL 89:49; CCBB 46:24; HBG 4[Sept 1993]:84; KR 60:994; SLJ Sept 1992 p. 280; VOYA 16:96)

TOLKIEN, J(ohn) R(onald) R(euel). *Smith of Wootton Major.* See Chapter 1, Allegorical Fantasy and Literary Fairy Tales.

TOWNE, Mary. *Goldenrod.* See Chapter 7, Magic Adventure Fantasy.

TREGARTHEN, Enys. *The White Ring.* See Chapter 5B, Myth Fantasy.

2072 **TROTT, Susan.** *The Sea Serpent of Horse.* **Gr. 4–6.**

A young girl must choose between staying forever in an undersea world or returning to her unhappy life on land.

Illus. by Irene Burns, Little, 1973, 117 pp., o.p.

(BL 70:546; KR 41:1045, 1358; LJ 99:577)

URE, Jean. *The Wizard in the Woods.* See Chapter 10, Witchcraft and Sorcery Fantasy.

2073 **WALKER, Gwen.** *The Golden Stile.* **Gr. 4–6.**

On the Golden Stile leading to the moon, Noel meets a little man who grants his wishes for adventure.

Illus. by C. Walter Hodges, Day, 1958, 188 pp., o.p.

(HB 34:479; KR 26:606; LJ 83:3304)

2074   **WERSBA, Barbara.** *The Land of Forgotten Beasts.* **Gr. 3–5.**

Scientifically minded Andrew is magically transported to a land of mythical beasts who are doomed because people no longer believe in them.

Illus. by Margot Tomes, Atheneum, 1964, 88 pp., o.p.

(HB 40:499; KR 32:651; LJ 89:3477; TLS 1965 p. 1130)

2075   **WHEELER, Thomas.** *Loose Chippings.* **Gr. 7–10.**

Stranded after his car breaks down in the village of Loose Chippings, Bob Vickery finds the town to be full of secrets.

Phillips, 1969, 190 pp. (0-87599-152-1)

(BL 66:50; KR 37:247; LJ 94:1802)

2076   **WHEELER, Thomas.** *Lost Threshold: A Novel.* **Gr. 8–10.**

His father's disappearance brings James MacGregor into another world, where he leads an uprising against the tyrants in power and finds himself a wife.

Phillips, 1968, 189 pp. (0-87599-140-8)

(BL 65:167; KR 36:467; LJ 93:3328)

2077   **WHITE, Eliza Orne.** *The Enchanted Mountain.* **Gr. 3–5.**

Four children are taken to an enchanted mountain where they learn to be polite and industrious.

Illus. by E. Pollak Ottendorff, Houghton, 1911, 107 pp., o.p.

(BL 8:183; HB 3:17–22)

2078   **WICKENDEN, Dan.** *The Amazing Vacation.* **Gr. 5–7.**
✓   Cousin Emmeline sends Ricky and Joanna through a magic window to search for her lost turquoise gem stone.

Illus. by Erik Blegvad, Harcourt, 1956, 216 pp., o.p.

(BL 53:230; HB 32:352; KR 24:475; LJ 82:230)

2079   **WILLARD, Nancy (Margaret).** *Sailing to Cythera, and Other Anatole Stories* *(Anatole trilogy, book 1).* **Gr. 3–5.**

Three stories about a boy named Anatole and his journeys to magical lands, including one tale in which he enters the wallpaper of his bedroom to meet the Blimlim. The sequels are *The Island of the Grass King: The Further Adventures of Anatole* (1979) and *Uncle Terrible: More Adventures of Anatole* (1982).

Illus. by (Michael) David McPhail, Harcourt, 1974, o.p., 1985, pap., 72 pp. (0-15-269961-9)

(BL 71:573; KR 43:19; LJ 99:2281)

2080   **WILLIAMS, Jay.** *The Hero from Otherwhere.* **Gr. 5–7.**

Jesse and Rich, sent to the principal's office for fighting, end up instead in the kingdom of Gwyliath, charged with finding a magic rope to shackle the fiendish wolf, Fenris.

Walck, 1972, 175 pp., o.p.

(BL 69:407; CCBB 26:99; KR 40:1193; LJ 98:1399)

2081   **WILLIAMS, Thomas (Alonzo).** *Tsuga's Children.* **Gr. 10 up.**
✓   Arn and Jen are two young children who find their way into a mythical valley beyond a waterfall, where they are taken in by Tsuga, leader of a peace-loving tribe.

Random, 1977, 239 pp., o.p.

(BL 73:1327; KR 45:245; LJ 102:1046; SLJ Oct 1977 p. 130)

2082 **WILLIS, Paul J.** *No Clock in the Forest.* **Gr. 7–12**

Grace and Lance, two runaway campers on Queen's Mountain, are rescued from a bog by Lady Lira and imprisoned in the caverns below the mountains of the Three Queens.

Good News, 1991, pap., 219 pp. (0-89107-599-2)

(LJ Nov 1, 1991 p. 66; VOYA 14:250)

2083 **WILSON, Robert Charles.** *Gypsies.* **Gr. 10 up.**

Karen has always repressed her childhood memories of making doors into other worlds with her brother and sister, until she sees that her teenaged son, Michael, has similar powers and is haunted by the same Gray Man of her own nightmares.

Doubleday, 1989, 240 pp. (0-385-24933-0); Bantam, 1990, pap., 311 pp. (0-553-28304-9)

(BL 85:837, 863, 86:907, 995; KR 56:1646; VOYA 12:293, 13:258)

2084 **WINTERFELD, Henry.** *Castaways in Lilliput.* **Gr. 5–7. (Orig. German pub. 1958.)**

Two hundred and fifty years after Gulliver's visit, the Lilliputians are again alarmed by the appearance of giants: three human children whose raft accidentally drifted to Lilliput.

Trans. by Kyrill Schabert, illus. by William Hutchinson, Harcourt, 1960, 188 pp., o.p., 1990, pap., 220 pp. (0-15-214822-1)

(BL 56:577; Eakin:355; HB 36:292; LJ 85:2484)

2085 **WINTHROP (Mahony), Elizabeth.** *The Castle in the Attic.* **Gr. 4–6.**

✓ Angry at his lifelong baby-sitter for planning to leave him, ten-year-old William uses a magic token to shrink her and himself small enough to enter the world inside an elaborate toy castle. In the sequel, *The Battle for the Castle* (1993), William, now 12, and his friend Jason, are given a magic coin that takes them and their bicycles back in time to the Middle Ages.

Illus. by Trina Schart Hyman, Holiday, 1985, 192 pp. (0-8234-0579-6); Bantam, 1986, pap. (0-553-15601-2)

(BBC:216; BL 82:761; CC:573; CCBB 39:40; HB 62:204; SLJ Feb 1986 p. 91; VOYA 9:37)

2086 **WOOD, Marcia.** *The Secret Life of Hilary Thorne.* **Gr. 4–6.**

Hilary Thorne has the ability to enter the worlds of her favorite books and make friends with the characters, but her family's move to a new town forces her to pay more attention to the real world.

Macmillan, 1988, 128 pp., o.p.

(BL 84:1932; KR 56:1412; SLJ Oct 1988 p. 149)

2087 **YOUNG, Ella.** *The Unicorn with Silver Shoes.* **Gr. 5–7.**

Ballor's Son and Flame of Joy escape to the Land of the Ever Young.

Illus. by Robert Lawson, McKay, 1932, 213 pp., o.p.

(BL 29:80, Bookshelf 1933 p. 6; CCBB 11:104; HB 34:124; LJ 58:43; Mahony 3:213; TLS 1932 p. 893)

YOUNG, Robert F. *The Vizier's Second Daughter.* See Chapter 5B, Myth Fantasy.

6

Humorous Fantasy

Listed here are a variety of humorous and exaggerated tales, including those with fast-paced comic plots, tales of people with bizarre pets, tall tales, and amusing stories of inanimate objects that come to life.

ABELL, Kathleen. *King Orville and the Bullfrogs.* See Chapter 1, Allegorical Fantasy and Literary Fairy Tales.

ADLER, David A. *Jeffrey's Ghost and the Leftover Baseball Team.* See Chapter 4, Ghost Fantasy.

2088 **AHLBERG, Allan.** *The Clothes Horse and Other Stories.* **Gr. 1–4. (Orig. British pub. 1987.)**

Six short, humorous stories about people who take everyday expressions literally, including "The Jack Pot," in which a giant collects boys named Jack and keeps them in a pot.

Illus. by Janet Ahlberg, Viking, 1988, 32 pp., o.p.; Puffin, 1992, pap., 32 pp. (0-14-032907-2)

(KR 56:119; SLJ Apr 1988 p. 77)

AHLBERG, Allan. *Ten in a Bed.* See Chapter 7, Magic Adventure Fantasy.

2089 **AHLBERG, Janet.** *Jeremiah in the Dark Woods.* **Gr. 2–4. (Orig. British pub. 1977.)**

Who has stolen Jeremiah Obadiah Jackenory Jones's auntie's tarts: three hungry bears, a wolf with a craving for grandmas, a Mad Hatter, a crocodile with a clock in his stomach, or a girl named Goldilocks?

Illus. by Allan Ahlerg, Viking, 1978, 47 pp. o.p.; Puffin, 1990, pap. (0-14-032811-4)

(BL 74:1426; CC:439; KR 46:237; SLJ May 1978 p. 49)

2090 **AIKEN, Joan (Delano).** *Arabel's Raven.* **Gr. 4–7. (Orig. British pub. 1972, entitled *Tales of Arabel's Raven.*)**

Life in the Jones's house just isn't the same after Mr. Jones brings home a raven named

355

Mortimer who enjoys eating stairs and sleeping in the refrigerator. The sequels are *Arabel and Mortimer* (1981), *Mortimer's Cross* (1984), and *Mortimer Says Nothing* (1987).

Illus. by Quentin Blake, Doubleday, 1974, 118 pp., o.p.

(CC:439; CCBB 28:1; Ch&Bks:274; HB 50:278; KR 42:478; LJ 99:2258)

2091   AIKEN, Joan (Delano). *Armitage, Armitage, Fly Away Home.* **Gr. 4–7. (Orig.**
✓ **British pub. 1965.)**

Harriet and Mark's parents are proud of their unusual children's incredible adventures.

Illus. by Betty Fraser, Doubleday, 1968, 214 pp., o.p.

(BL 65:183; CCBB 22:1; HB 44:558; KR 36:603; LJ 93:3296)

AIKEN, Joan (Delano). *The Faithless Lollybird.* See Chapter 3, Fantasy Collections.

AIKEN, Joan (Delano). *A Foot in the Grave.* See Chapter 4, Ghost Fantasy.

AIKEN, Joan (Delano). *The Kingdom and the Cave.* See Chapter 5A, Alternate Worlds or Histories.

2092   AIKEN, Joan (Delano). *Up the Chimney Down and Other Stories.* **Gr. 5–8. (Orig.**
✓ **British pub. 1984.)**

Eleven eerie and humorous tales, including "The Missing Heir," "The Midnight Rose," and "The Happiest Sheep in London."

Harper, 1985, 248 pp., o.p.

(BBC:196; BBJ:68; BL 82:807; CC:577; CCBB 39:121; HB 62:205; JHC:428; KR 53:1139; SLJ Dec 1985 p. 85; TLS May 1984 p. 558; VOYA 8:323)

AIKEN, Joan (Delano). *The Whispering Mountain.* See Chapter 5A, Alternate Worlds or Histories.

AIKEN, Joan (Delano). *The Wolves of Willoughby Chase.* See Chapter 5A, Alternate Worlds or Histories.

ALEXANDER, Lloyd (Chudley). *The Cat Who Wished to Be a Man.* See Chapter 2, Animal Fantasy.

ALEXANDER, Lloyd (Chudley). *The Illyrian Adventure.* See Chapter 5C, Travel to Other Worlds.

ANDERSON, Mary. *F*T*C Superstar.* See Chapter 2, Animal Fantasy.

ANDERSON, Mildred Napier. *A Gift for Merimond.* See Chapter 1, Allegorical Fantasy and Literary Fairy Tales.

ANDREWS, Allen. *The Pig Plantagenet.* See Chapter 2, Animal Fantasy.

2093   ANDREWS, Frank (Emerson). *The Upside-Down Town.* **Gr. 3–5.**

Anne and Rickie visit a town where everything is done backward.

Illus. by Louis Slobodkin, Little, 1958, 60 pp., o.p.

(BL 54:449; CCBB 11:106; KR 26:34; LJ 83:1282)

ANGELL, Judie. *The Weird Disappearance of Jordan Hall.* See Chapter 7, Magic Adventure Fantasy.

ANNETT (Pipitone Scott), Cora. *When the Porcupine Moved In.* See Chapter 2, Animal Fantasy.

ANTHONY, Piers (pseud. of Piers A. D. Jacob). *A Spell for Chameleon.* See Chapter 5A, Alternate Worlds or Histories.

ANTHONY, Piers, and LACKEY, Mercedes. *If I Pay Thee Not in Gold.* See Chapter 5A, Alternate Worlds or Histories.

ASIMOV, Isaac. *Azazel.* See Chapter 7, Magic Adventure Fantasy.

ASPRIN, Robert L. *Hit or Myth.* See Chapter 10, Witchcraft and Sorcery Fantasy.

2094 **ATWATER, Richard (Tupper), and ATWATER, Florence (Hasseltine Carroll).**
✓ *Mr. Popper's Penguins.* **Gr. 3–5.**

A paperhanger named Mr. Popper is given a penguin as a gift, but before he knows it, his problems multiply into twelve penguins. John Newbery Medal Honor Book, 1939.

Illus. by Robert Lawson, Little, 1938 (0-316-05842-4), 1992, pap., 151 pp. (0-316-05843-2); Dell, 1978, 1986, 1992, pap., 144 pp. (0-440-21370-3)

(BL 35:86; CC:444; Ch&Bks:274; HB 14:370; LJ 63:818)

2095 **AVI (pseud. of Avi Wortis).** *Emily Upham's Revenge: Or, How Deadwood Dick*
✓ *Saved the Banker's Niece: A Massachusetts Adventure.* **Gr. 4–6.**

Emily and her friend Seth need money to escape to Boston. Their plans to rob a bank go awry, but Emily triumphs in the end.

Illus. by Paul O. Zelinsky, Pantheon, 1978, 172 pp., o.p.; Morrow, 1992, 172 pp. (0-688-11898-4), pap. (0-688-11899-2)

(BL 74:1098; CCBB: 31:170; HBG 4[Spring 1993]:63; KR 46:304; SLJ Mar 1978 p. 24)

2096 **BABBITT, Natalie (Zane Moore).** *The Devil's Storybook.* **Gr. 4–6.**
✓✓ Ten tales about Satan's battles with humans. National Book Award Finalist, Children's Fiction Category, 1975. *The Devil's Other Storybook* (1987, 1989) is a companion volume.

Illus. by the author, Farrar, 1974, 102 pp. (0-374-31770-4), 1984, pap. (0-374-41708-3)

(BBC:197; BL 71:37, 765; CC:577; CCBB 28:58; Ch&Bks:262; HB 50:134; KR 42:679; Suth 2:22; TLS 1976 p. 882)

2097 **BABBITT, Natalie (Zane Moore).** *Goody Hall.* **Gr. 4–6.**
✓ The mystery surrounding the death of young Willet Goody's father is solved after a seance visitation by Shakespeare and a nighttime visit to Mr. Goody's tomb.

Illus. by the author, Farrar, 1971, 1991, 176 pp., o.p., 1991, pap., 192 pp. (0-374-42767-4)

(BL 67:954; CCBB 25:21; HB 47:380; KR 39:431; LJ 96:1780, 1820; SLJ Aug 1992 p. 99; Suth:23)

BABCOCK, Betty. *The Expandable Pig.* See Chapter 7, Magic Adventure Fantasy.

BAKER, Betty (Lou). *Save Sirrushany! (Also Agotha, Princess Gwyn and All the Fearsome Beasts).* See Chapter 1, Allegorical Fantasy and Literary Fairy Tales.

BAKER, Margaret. *Fifteen Tales for Lively Children.* See Chapter 3, Fantasy Collections.

BAKER, Margaret Joyce. *Porterhouse Major.* See Chapter 7, Magic Adventure Fantasy.

BALL, Brian. *The Quest for Queenie.* See Chapter 5C, Travel to Other Worlds.

BEAGLE, Peter S(oyer). *A Fine and Private Place, A Novel.* See Chapter 4, Ghost Fantasy.

2098   BEEKS, Graydon. *Hosea Globe and the Fantastical Peg-Legged Chu.* **Gr. 4–6.**

Hosea and his talking dog are ordered to bring a scientist able to control cyclones and typhoons to their secret island home.

Illus. by Carol Nicklaus, Atheneum, 1974, 170 pp., o.p.

(BL 71:813; KR 43:305; SLJ Oct 1975 p. 94)

2099   BELL, Norman (Edward). *The Weightless Mother.* **Gr. 4–6.**

After Mrs. Flipping accidentally swallows weightlessness pills, she floats out of the house and off into the sky.

Illus. by W. T. Mars, Follett, 1967, 144 pp., o.p.

(BL 64:384; HB 43:459; KR 35:339; LJ 92:2647)

2100   BENDICK, Jeanne. *The Blonk from Beneath the Sea.* **Gr. 3–5.**

Peter and his uncle, Professor Pokeberry, discover a prehistoric sea creature (half-fish, half-seal), nickname it the Blonk, and put it on display at the oceanarium.

Illus. by the author, Watts, 1958, 55 pp., o.p.

(CCBB 11:90; HB 34:265; KR 26:133; LJ 83:1940)

2101   BENNETT, John. *The Pigtail of Ah Lee Ben Loo, with Seventeen Other Laughable Tales.* **Gr. 3–5.**

This collection of humorous stories and poems was a John Newbery Medal Honor Book, 1929.

Illus. by the author, Longmans, 1928, 298 pp., o.p.

(BL 25:126; HB 4[Nov 1928]:82; Mahony 2:273; Moore:47, 430)

BERGER, Thomas. *Arthur Rex: A Legendary Novel.* See Chapter 5B, Myth Fantasy.

BEST, Herbert. *Desmond's First Case.* See Chapter 2, Animal Fantasy.

BETHANCOURT, T(homas) Ernesto (pseud. of Tom Paisley). *The Dog Days of Arthur Cane.* See Chapter 7, Magic Adventure Fantasy.

BLACKWOOD, Algernon. *The Adventures of Dudley and Gilderoy.* See Chapter 2, Animal Fantasy.

BLAYLOCK, James P(aul). *The Stone Giant.* See Chapter 5A, Alternate Worlds or Histories.

2102   BLUNT, Wilfrid (Jasper Walter). *Omar; a Fantasy for Animal Lovers.* **Gr. 10 up.**

Omar, the rare talking bander-snatch, is given to Rose Bavistock for her fiftieth birthday.

Illus. by John Verney, Doubleday, 1968, 192 pp., o.p.

(BL 65:866, 875; KR 36:836; SLJ Dec 15, 1968 p. 4740)

2103   BODECKER, N(iels) M(ogens). *Carrot Holes and Frisbee Trees.* **Gr. 3–5.**

The Plumtree family's love of gardening produces carrots big enough to "grow" post-holes, bringing them unexpected business opportunities.

Illus. by Nina Winters, Macmillan, 1983, 48 pp. (0-689-50097-1)

(BBC:199; BL 80:404; HB 60:49; SLJ Jan 1984 p. 72)

BODECKER, N(iels) M(ogens). *The Lost String Quartet.* See Chapter 1, Allegorical Fantasy and Literary Fairy Tales.

BOND, (Thomas) Michael. *A Bear Called Paddington.* See Chapter 2, Animal Fantasy.

BOND, (Thomas) Michael. *Here Comes Thursday.* See Chapter 2, Animal Fantasy.

BOND, (Thomas) Michael. *Tales of Olga Da Polga.* See Chapter 2, Animal Fantasy.

2104 **BONTEMPS, Arna (Wendell), and CONROY, Jack.** *The Fast Sooner Hound.*
✓ **Gr. 1–4.**

Sooner, the hound dog who would rather run than eat, can outrun any train to stay near his master, the Boomer railroad fireman.

Illus. by Virginia Lee Burton, Houghton, 1942, 28 pp., o.p.

(BL 39:73; Ch&Bks:283; HB 18:417; LJ 67:882, 954)

BOUCHER, Anthony. *The Compleat Werewolf.* See Chapter 3, Fantasy Collections.

BOURLIAGUET, Léonce. *The Giant Who Drank from His Shoe and Other Stories.* See Chapter 3, Fantasy Collections.

BOURLIAGUET, Léonce. *A Sword to Slice Through Mountains and Other Stories.* See Chapter 3, Fantasy Collections.

BOWEN, Vernon. *The Wonderful Adventures of Ting Ling.* See Chapter 1, Allegorical Fantasy and Literary Fairy Tales.

2105 **BRELIS, Nancy (Burns).** *The Mummy Market.* **Gr. 5–7.**
✓ The Martin children visit the Mummy Market to select a new mother.

Illus. by Ben Shecter, Harper, 1966, 145 pp., o.p.; Peter Smith, 1991, o.p.

(CCBB 20:38; HB 42:707; KR 34:757; LJ 91:5222; Suth:50)

BRENNAN, Herbie. *Emily and the Werewolf.* See Chapter 10, Witchcraft and Sorcery Fantasy.

2106 **BRIGHT, Robert.** *Richard Brown and the Dragon.* **Gr. 2–4.**
✓ Richard Brown uses a fire extinguisher to battle a dragon and win the hand of Princess Rosalie, in this story retold from an anecdote by Samuel Clemens.

Illus. by the author, Doubleday, 1952, 81 pp., o.p.

(BL 49:18; CCBB 6:13; HB 28:319; KR 20:498; LJ 77:1661)

2107 **BRINK, Carol Ryrie.** *Andy Buckram's Tin Men.* **Gr. 5–7.**

A bolt of lightning brings Andy's tin-can robots to life in time to help him rescue two children from a flood.

Illus. by W. T. Mars, Viking, 1966, 192 pp., o.p.

(BL 62:774; CCBB 19:143; Ch&Bks:278; KR 34:245; LJ 91:3255)

2108 **BRINK, Carol Ryrie.** *Baby Island.* **Gr. 3–5.**

Two little girls and two babies are shipwrecked on a desert island off the coast of Australia.

Illus. by Helen Sewell, Macmillan, 1937, 1954, 172 pp., o.p., 1973, 1993, pap. (0-689-71751-2); Lightyear, 1992, LB(0-89968-304-5)

(BL 34:196; HB 13:284; LJ 62:811, 881)

2109 **BRITTAIN, Bill (William).** *All the Money in the World.* **Gr. 3–6.**

A group of friends who find all the money in the world deposited in their backyard are sought out by the army, kidnappers, and the President of the United States.

Illus. by Charles Robinson, Harper, 1979, 160 pp., LB(0-06-020676-4), 1982, pap., 160 pp. (0-06-440128-6)

(BBC:199; CC:454; CCBB 32:170; KR 47:328; SLJ Mar 1979 p. 135)

BRITTAIN, Bill (William). *The Fantastic Freshman.* See Chapter 7, Magic Adventure Fantasy.

2110 **BRÖGER, Achim.** *Bruno.* **Gr. 4–6. (Orig. German pub. 1973.)**

Amazing things keep happening to Bruno: A dinosaur comes for dinner, snowmen and statues talk to him, and he meets forty-two doubles of himself. The sequel is *Bruno Takes a Trip* (1978).

Trans. by Hilda Van Stockum, illus. by Ronald Himler, Morrow, 1975, 160 pp., o.p.

(BL 72:622; KR 43:1128; SLJ Nov 1975 p. 71)

2111 **BRÖGER, Achim.** *Little Harry.* **Gr. 3–5. (Orig. German pub. 1979.)**

Seventeen tales from Little Harry's imagination, in which he meets a vacuum cleaner-witch, a human alarm clock, and learns to fly.

Trans. by Elizabeth Crawford, illus. by Judy Morgan, Morrow, 1979, 189 pp., o.p.

(BL 75:1153; KR 47:451; SLJ May 1979 p. 50)

2112 **BROOKS, Terry.** *Magic Kingdom for Sale—Sold!* **(The Magic Kingdom of Lan-**
✓ **dover series, book 1). Gr. 10 up.**

The magic kingdom bought by Ben Holliday for a million dollars turns out to be possessed by a demon prince who has defeated all previous human rulers. The sequels are *The Black Unicorn* (1987), *Wizard at Large* (1988), and *The Tangle Box* (1994).

Ballantine, 1986, 324 pp. (0-345-31757-2), 1987, pap. (0-345-31758-0)

(BL 82:913, 83:1117, 86:904; KR 54:254; LJ Apr 15, 1986 p. 97; SHC:672)

BROOKS, Walter Rollin. *Freddy Goes to Florida.* See Chapter 2, Animal Fantasy.

2113 **BROWN, Jeff.** *Flat Stanley.* **Gr. 2–4.**
✓ Stanley Lambchop, squashed flat as a pancake after a huge bulletin board falls on him, is lowered through sidewalk gratings, mailed to California, and disguised as a framed painting to capture art thieves. The sequel is *A Lamp for the Lambchops* (1983).

Illus. by Tomi Ungerer, Harper, 1964, 64 pp., LB(0-06-020681-0), 1989, pap., 48 pp. (0-06-440293-2)

(BL 60:875; CC:599; HB 40:274; LJ 89:1850; TLS 1968 p. 583)

BUCHWALD, Emilie. *Floramel and Esteban.* See Chapter 2, Animal Fantasy.

BUFFIE, Margaret. *The Warnings.* See Chapter 7, Magic Adventure Fantasy.

BURMAN, Ben Lucien. *High Water at Catfish Bend.* See Chapter 2, Animal Fantasy.

2114 **BURN, Doris.** *The Tale of Lazy Lizard Canyon.* **Gr. 2–4.**

The longstanding feud between the Hokums and the Burleys is settled by the marriage between Lafe Hokum and Mattie Mae Burley.

Illus. by the author, Putnam, 1977, 48 pp., o.p.

(BL 73:1495; KR 45:425; SLJ Sept 1977 p. 103)

BUTTERS, Dorothy G. *Papa Dolphin's Table.* See Chapter 2, Animal Fantasy.

2115 **BUTTERWORTH, Oliver.** *The Enormous Egg.* **Gr. 4–6.**

✓ Nate Twitchell's new pet hatches from a leatherlike egg and turns out to be a baby Triceratops. In *The Narrow Passage* (1973), Nate and Nicol meet a prehistoric man.

Illus. by Louis Darling, Little, 1956, 187 pp. (0-316-11904-0), 1993, pap., 188 pp. (0-316-11920-2); Dell, 1987, pap. (0-440-42337-6)

(BL 52:298; CC:456; CCBB 9:91; Ch&Bks:274; Eakin:56; HB 32:187; KR 24:45; LJ 81:1042)

2116 **BUTTERWORTH, Oliver.** *The Trouble with Jenny's Ear.* **Gr. 4–6.**

✓ After Jenny discovers that one of her ears is sensitive enough to hear other people's thoughts, her brothers concoct an ingenious money-making scheme.

Illus. by Julian de Miskey, Little, 1960, 275 pp., o.p., 1993, pap. (0-316-11922-9)

(BL 56:546; CCBB 13:143; Ch&Bks:284; Eakin:56; HB 36:215; KR 28:184; LJ 85:2034)

BUZZATI, Dino. *The Bears' Famous Invasion of Sicily.* See Chapter 2, Animal Fantasy.

BYFIELD, Barbara Ninde. *The Haunted Spy.* See Chapter 4, Ghost Fantasy.

2117 **CALLEN, Larry (Lawrence Willard, Jr.).** *Pinch.* **Gr. 5–8.**

✓ Pinch Grimball trains his pet pig, Homer, to be the best bird-hunting pig in Four Corners, Louisiana.

Illus. by Marvin Friedman, Little, 1976, 179 pp. (0-316-12495-8)

(BL 72:1260, 73:1425; CCBB 30:5; HB 52:394; KR 44:134; SLJ Apr 1976 p. 70, May 1976 p. 34)

CAMPBELL, Ann. *Once Upon a Princess and a Pea.* See Chapter 1, Allegorical Fantasy and Literary Fairy Tales.

CANFIELD, Dorothy. *Made-to-Order Stories.* See Chapter 3, Fantasy Collections.

CAPEK, Karel. *Nine Fairy Tales and One More Thrown in for Good Measure.* See Chapter 3, Fantasy Collections.

2118 **CAREY, Valerie Soho.** *The Devil and Mother Crump.* **Gr. 2–4.**

Old Mother Crump is so mean that she defeats both the Devil and Death.

Illus. by Arnold Lobel, Harper, 1987, o.p., 1992, pap., 40 pp. (0-06-443278-5)

(BL 84:257; HB 64:50; KR 55:1316; SLJ Nov 1987 p. 87)

2119 **CARKEET, David.** *I Been There Before.* **Gr. 10 up.**

Halley's comet has brought Mark Twain back to life in 1985, and the literary world begins to doubt that he was the true author of his famous works.

Harper, 1985, 384 pp. (0-06-015426-8)

(BL 82:307, 327; KR 53:801; SLJ Sept 1986 p. 152)

2120 **CARLSEN, Ruth Christoffer.** *Henrietta Goes West.* **Gr. 4–6.**

The Nelson family travels westward in their automobile, Henrietta.

Illus. by Wallace Tripp, Houghton, 1966, 185 pp., o.p.

(CCBB 19:175; KR 34:475; LJ 91:3256)

CARLSEN, Ruth Christoffer. *Mr. Pudgins.* See Chapter 7, Magic Adventure Fantasy.

CARLSEN, Ruth Christoffer. *Sam Bottleby.* See Chapter 7, Magic Adventure Fantasy.

2121 **CARLSON, Natalie Savage.** *Alphonse, That Bearded One.* **Gr. 3–5.**

✓ Trained to take a clever woodsman's place as a soldier, Alphonse the bear causes chaos in the French-Canadian army.

Illus. by Nicolas Mordvinoff, Harcourt, 1954, 78 pp., o.p.

(BL 50:325; CCBB 7:70; Eakin:59; HB 30:174; KR 22:197; LJ 79:783)

CARLSON, Natalie Savage. *Evangeline, Pigeon of Paris.* See Chapter 2, Animal Fantasy.

2122 **CARLSON, Natalie Savage.** *Hortense, the Cow for a Queen.* **Gr. 4–6.**

A French cow named Hortense is kidnapped by pirates and shipwrecked on the coast of Africa.

Illus. by Nicolas Mordvinoff, Harcourt, 1957, 95 pp., o.p.

(BL 53:458; CCBB 11:92; HB 33:208, 298; KR 25:274; LJ 82:1684)

CARTER, Lin. *Mandricardo.* See Chapter 5A, Alternate Worlds or Histories.

CASSERLEY, Anne Thomasine. *Barney the Donkey.* See Chapter 2, Animal Fantasy.

CATLING, Patrick Skene. *The Chocolate Touch.* See Chapter 7, Magic Adventure Fantasy.

CAUFIELD, Don, and CAUFIELD, Joan. *The Incredible Detectives.* See Chapter 2, Animal Fantasy.

2123 **CHARLES, Prince of Wales.** *The Old Man of Lochnagar.* **Gr. K–4. (Written, 1969; orig. British pub. 1980.)**

Six humorous episodes about a very old Scotsman's adventures, which include meeting a merman, being carried off by an eagle, and drinking a shrinking formula.

Illus. by Hugh Casson, Farrar, 1980, 46 pp., o.p.

(BL 77:807; CCBB 34:147; KR 49:209; SLJ Feb 1981 p. 55)

2124 **CHASE, Mary (Coyle).** *Harvey, a Play* (orig. title: *Harvey, a Comedy in Three Acts,* **1944). Gr. 6 up.**

Elwood Down has an invisible rabbit friend named Harvey, in this humorous story adapted from the 1943 play, *The White Rabbit.*

Illus. by R. O. Blechman, Oxford, 1953, 89 pp., o.p.

(BL 49:234; LJ 8:525)

CHASE, Mary (Coyle). *Mrs. McThing: A Play.* See Chapter 10, Witchcraft and Sorcery Fantasy.

CHRISMAN, Arthur Bowie. *Shen of the Sea: Chinese Stories for Children.* See Chapter 3, Fantasy Collections.

2125 **CHRISTIAN, Mary Blount.** *Sebastian [Super Sleuth] and the Crummy Yummies Caper.* **Gr. 3–4.**

Sebastian the dog detective uncovers a dognapping plot, saves Chummy the Wonder Dog, and captures the would-be thief, although his master manages to take all the credit. The sequels are *Sebastian [Super Sleuth] and the Hair of the Dog Mystery* (1982), *Sebastian*

[*Super Sleuth*] *and the Bone to Pick Mystery* (1983), *Sebastian* [*Super Sleuth*] *and the Case of the Santa Claus Caper* (1984), *Sebastian* [*Super Sleuth*] *and the Secret of the Skewered Skier* (1984), *Sebastian* [*Super Sleuth*] *and the Clumsy Cowboy* (1985), *Sebastian* [*Super Sleuth*] *and the Purloined Sirloin* (1986), *Sebastian* [*Super Sleuth*] *and the Stars-in-His-Eyes Mystery* (1987, 1990), *Sebastian* [*Super Sleuth*] *and the Egyptian Connection* (1988), *Sebastian* [*Super Sleuth*] *and the Time Capsule Caper* (1989), *Sebastian* [*Super Sleuth*] *and the Baffling Bigfoot* (1990), *Sebastian* [*Super Sleuth*] *and the Mystery Patient* (1991), *Sebastian* [*Super Sleuth*] *and the Impossible Crime* (1992), and *Sebastian* [*Super Sleuth*] *and the Copycat Crime* (1993).

Illus. by Lisa McCue, Macmillan, 1983, 64 pp. (0-02-718430-7)

(BL 79:1272; KR 51:375; SLJ May 1983 p. 91)

CHRISTOPHER, Matt(hew F.). *The Dog That Stole Football Plays.* See Chapter 7, Magic Adventure Fantasy.

CLARK, Douglas W. *Alchemy Unlimited.* See Chapter 10, Witchcraft and Sorcery Fantasy.

CLEARY, Beverly (Bunn). *The Mouse and the Motorcycle.* See Chapter 2, Animal Fantasy.

CLIFFORD, Eth. *Flatfoot Fox and the Case of the Missing Eye.* See Chapter 2, Animal Fantasy.

COBALT, Martin. *Pool of Swallows.* See Chapter 4, Ghost Fantasy.

COONTZ, Otto. *Hornswoggle Magic.* See Chapter 7, Magic Adventure Fantasy.

COOPER (Grant), Susan (Mary). *The Boggart.* See Chapter 7, Magic Adventure Fantasy.

COOPER (Grant), Susan (Mary). *Jethro and the Jumbie.* See Chapter 7, Magic Adventure Fantasy.

2126 **CORBALIS, Judy.** *The Ice Cream Heroes.* Gr. 4–7.

Oscar and Henrietta travel to the Himalayas to bring an ice pick to Oscar's mountain-climbing mother, but they are imprisoned by a villain bent on stealing all the ice cream in the world.

Illus. by David Parkins, Little, Brown, 1989, 160 pp., o.p.

(HB 66:61; HBG 1[July–Dec 1989]:82; KR 57:1745)

CORBALIS, Judy. *Porcellus, the Flying Pig.* See Chapter 2, Animal Fantasy.

CORBETT, Scott. *The Discontented Ghost.* See Chapter 4, Ghost Fantasy.

2127 **CORBETT, Scott.** *Ever Ride a Dinosaur?* Gr. 4–6.

Bronson the talking brontosaurus visits his old friends at the Museum of Natural History.

Illus. by Mircea Vasiliu, Holt, 1969, 128 pp., o.p.

(CCBB 23:41; Ch&Bks:274; HB 45:409; KR 37:558; LJ 94:2111; Suth:91)

CORBETT, Scott. *The Great Custard Pie Panic.* See Chapter 10, Witchcraft and Sorcery Fantasy.

CORBETT, Scott. *The Lemonade Trick.* See Chapter 7, Magic Adventure Fantasy.

2128 COREN, Alan. *Arthur the Kid.* **Gr. 3–5. (Orig. British pub. 1977.)**

✓ Ten-year-old Arthur's career as leader of a gang of bank-robbing gunslingers takes an about-face when they save the bank from another gang. The sequels are *Buffalo Arthur* (1978), *The Lone Arthur* (1978), *Railroad Arthur* (1978), *Klondike Arthur* (1979), *Arthur's Last Stand* (1979), *Arthur and the Great Detective* (1980), *Arthur and the Purple Panic* (1984), *Arthur versus the Rest* (1985), and *Arthur and the Bellybutton Diamond* (British).

Illus. by John Astrop, Little, 1978, o.p.; Bantam, 1984, pap., 80 pp. (0-553-15169-X)

(BL 74:1616; CC:476; CCBB 32:26; KR 46:594; SLJ Sept 1978 p. 133; Suth 2:103)

COSTIKYAN, Greg. *By the Sword: Magic of the Plains.* See Chapter 5A, Alternate Worlds or Histories.

COUNSEL, June. *A Dragon in Class 4.* See Chapter 7, Magic Adventure Fantasy.

COVILLE, Bruce. *Jennifer Murdley's Toad.* See Chapter 7, Magic Adventure Fantasy.

COVILLE, Bruce. *Jeremy Thatcher, Dragon Hatcher.* See Chapter 7, Magic Adventure Fantasy.

CRESSWELL (Rowe), Helen. *Almost Goodbye.* See Chapter 7, Magic Adventure Fantasy.

CRESSWELL (Rowe), Helen. *The Bongleweed.* See Chapter 7, Magic Adventure Fantasy.

2129 CRESSWELL (Rowe), Helen. *The Piemakers.* **Gr. 4–6. (Orig. British pub.**
✓ **1967.)**

A family of bakers, competing with their cousins for the king's prize, concocts a meat pie big enough to serve 2,000 people. Carnegie Medal Commended Book, 1967.

Illus. by W. T. Mars, Lippincott, 1967, 142 pp., o.p.; illus. by Judith Gwyn Brown, Macmillan, 1980, 117 pp., o.p.

(BL 64:1041, 77:404; Ch&Bks:262; HB 56:662, 57:215; KR 36:261; LJ 93:2536; SLJ Sept 1980 p. 68; TLS 1967 p. 445)

CRESSWELL (Rowe), Helen. *Time Out.* See Chapter 8, Time Travel Fantasy.

2130 CRETAN, Gladys. *Joey's Head.* **Gr. 1–4.**

Angry at his little brother for messing up his baseball cards, Mike mixes up a magic brew, wishes that Joey would disappear, and is astonished to find that only Joey's head has vanished.

Illus. by Blanche Sims, Simon & Schuster, 1991, 48 pp. (0-671-73201-3), 1993, pap. (0-671-86699-0)

(BL 87:2155; HBG 3[Spring 1992]:57; SLJ Dec 1991 p. 84)

2131 CUYLER, Margery. *Weird Wolf.* **Gr. 2–5.**

Nine-year-old Harry Walpole is desparate to cure a condition he inherited from his grandfather—every night with a full moon he turns into a werewolf.

Illus. by Dirk Zimmer, Henry Holt, 1989, 72 pp. (0-8050-0835-7), 1991, pap. (0-8050-1643-0)

(BL 86:743; CCBB 43:107; HBG 1[July–Dec 1989]:84; KR 57:1602; SLJ Apr 1990 p. 116)

2132 **DAHL, Roald.** *The BFG.* **Gr. 4–6. (Orig. British pub. 1982.)**

Kidnapped by the BFG (big friendly giant) and taken to Giant Country, orphaned Sophie and her vegetarian giant friend are horrified that the other giants eat "human beans," and ask the Queen of England to put a stop to it.

Illus. by Quentin Blake, Farrar, 1982, 221 pp. (0-374-30471-8); Puffin, 1989, pap. (0-14-034019-X); Knopf, 1993 (0-679-42813-5)

(BBC:201; BL 79:608, 685; CCBB 36:86; HB 59:165; KR 50:1153; SLJ Dec 1982 p. 43; TLS 1982 p. 1303)

DAHL, Roald. *Charlie and the Chocolate Factory.* See Chapter 7, Magic Adventure Fantasy.

DAHL, Roald. *The Enormous Crocodile.* See Chapter 2, Animal Fantasy.

2133 **DAHL, Roald.** *Esio Trot.* **Gr. 2–5. (Orig. British pub. 1990.)**

Mr. Hoppy keeps substituting ever-larger tortoises for Mrs. Silver's pet Alfie, in hopes of convincing her to marry him. Smarties Prize for Children's Books, Ages 6–8, 1990.

Illus. by Quentin Blake, Viking, 1990, 64 pp. (0-670-83451-3); Puffin, 1992, pap. (0-14-036099-9)

(BL 87:442; CCBB 44:82; HBG 2[July–Dec 1990]:66; KR 58:1393; SLJ Nov 1990, p. 113; Suth 4:90; TLS 1990 p. 509)

DAHL, Roald. *Fantastic Mr. Fox.* See Chapter 2, Animal Fantasy.

DAHL, Roald. *George's Marvelous Medicine.* See Chapter 7, Magic Adventure Fantasy.

DAHL, Roald. *The Magic Finger.* See Chapter 7, Magic Adventure Fantasy.

2134 **DAHL, Roald.** *Matilda.* **Gr. 3–7. (Orig. British pub. 1988.)**
✓✓ Brilliant first-grader Matilda triumphs over her book-hating parents and Miss Trunchbull, the odious school principal.

Illus. by Quentin Blake, Viking, 1988, 240 pp. (0-670-82439-9); Puffin, 1990, pap. (0-14-034294-X)

(CC:477; CCBB 42:30; HB 65:68; KR 56:1237; SLJ Oct 1988 p. 143; Suth 4:90; TLS 1988 p. 573)

2135 **DAHL, Roald.** *The Twits.* **Gr. 3–6. (Orig. British pub. 1980.)**

The terrible Twit family keeps the Muggle-Wump monkeys in a cage until the local birds free them and take revenge on the Twits.

Illus. by Quentin Blake, Knopf, 1981, 76 pp. (0-394-84599-4); Puffin, 1991, pap. (0-14-034640-6)

(CCBB 34:149; HBG 3[July–Dec 1991]:64; KR 49:356; SLJ May 1981 p. 63; TLS Nov 21, 1980 p. 1330)

2136 **DAHL, Roald.** *The Vicar of Nibbleswicke.* **Gr. 4–6. (Orig. British pub. 1991.)**

The shy vicar's parishioners are shocked by his colorful language, caused by "Back-to-Front Dyslexia," in this story written to benefit the British Dyslexia Institute.

Illus. by Quentin Blake, Viking, 1992, 24 pp. (0-670-84384-9)

(BL 88:939; CC 1993 Suppl. p. 68; HBG 3[Fall 1992]:254; KR 60:51; SLJ May 1992 p. 112)

DAHL, Roald. *The Witches.* See Chapter 10, Witchcraft and Sorcery Fantasy.

2137 **DAHL, Tessa.** *School Can Wait.* **Gr. 3–5. (Orig. British pub. 1990.)**

Jack and his parents head for the North Pole after they find Blitzen, one of Father Christmas's reindeer, lost in their back yard.

Illus. by Korky Paul, Viking, 1991, 64 pp. (0-670-84170-6)

(BL 88:940; HBG 3[July–Dec 1991]:64; KR 59:1341; SLJ Jan 1992 p. 108)

DANA, Barbara. *Zucchini.* See Chapter 2, Animal Fantasy.

DAVID, Peter. *Knight Life.* See Chapter 5B, Myth Fantasy.

DAVIES, Andrew (Wynford). *Conrad's War.* See Chapter 8, Time Travel Fantasy.

2138 DAVIES, Andrew (Wynford). *Marmalade and Rufus.* **Gr. 3–5. (Orig. British pub. 1979; 2nd ed. entitled** *Marmalade Atkins' Dreadful Deeds.***)**

Marmalade Atkins, the worst-behaved girl in the world, joins forces with an ornery talking donkey named Rufus to wreak havoc at the El Poco Nightclub, the Midnight Steeplechase, and a Christmas pageant. The British sequels are *Danger—Marmalade at Work, Marmalade Atkins Hits the Big Time, Marmalade Atkins in Space,* and *Educating Marmalade.*

Illus. by Bert Dodson, Crown, 1983, 84 pp., o.p.

(BL 80:82; CCBB 37:46; HB 59:572; KR 51:659; SLJ Sept 1983 p. 121)

2139 DAVIES, Valentine. *It Happens Every Spring.* **Gr. 7 up.**

A secret formula developed by a college professor enables him to pitch St. Louis to a World Series victory.

Farrar, 1949, 224 pp., o.p.

(BL 45:359; KR 17:238; LJ 74:955, 1031)

DAVIES, Valentine. *The Miracle on 34th Street.* See Chapter 1, Allegorical Fantasy and Literary Fairy Tales.

DE CAMP, L(yon) Sprague. *The Honorable Barbarian.* See Chapter 5A, Alternate Worlds or Histories.

DE CAMP, L(yon) Sprague, and DE CAMP, Catherine Crook. *The Incorporated Knight.* See Chapter 5A, Alternate Worlds or Histories.

DE CAMP, L(yon) Sprague, and DE CAMP, Catherine Crook. *The Pixilated Peeress.* See Chapter 5A, Alternate Worlds or Histories.

2140 DELANEY, M. C. *Henry's Special Delivery.* **Gr. 3–6.**

Armed with a knapsack full of junk food, Henry sets out for the house of his secret love, Heather, determined to win her heart with the gift of a live, talking panda, ordered with two proof-of-purchase seals from his favorite cereal.

Illus. by Lisa McCue, Dutton, 1984, 138 pp., o.p.

(BL 80:1547; CCBB 37:202; SLJ Oct 1984 p. 156)

2141 DE WEESE, (Thomas Eugene) Gene. *The Adventures of a Two Minute Werewolf.* **Gr. 5–7.**

One incredible day, fourteen-year-old Walt Cribbens discovers that he has turned into a werewolf.

Illus. by Ronald Fritz, Doubleday, 1983, 132 pp., o.p.

(BL 79:1274; SLJ May 1983 p. 91)

DICKINSON, Peter (pseud. of Malcolm de Brissac). *The Iron Lion.* See Chapter 1, Allegorical Fantasy and Literary Fairy Tales.

DILLON, Barbara. *A Mom by Magic.* See Chapter 7, Magic Adventure Fantasy.

DILLON, Barbara. *Mrs. Tooey and the Terrible Toxic Tar.* See Chapter 10, Witch-craft and Sorcery Fantasy.

DILLON, Barbara. *My Stepfather Shrank!* See Chapter 7, Magic Adventure Fantasy.

DILLON, Barbara. *What's Happened to Harry?* See Chapter 10, Witchcraft and Sorcery Fantasy.

2142   DOLBIER, Maurice (Wyman). *A Lion in the Woods.* **Gr. 4–6.**

A newspaper reporter makes up a story about a lion at large in Forest Park.

Illus. by Robert Henneberger, Little, 1955, 115 pp., o.p.

(BL 51:301; CCBB 8:77; HB 31:111; LJ 80:999)

DRURY, Roger W(olcott). *The Champion of Merrimack County.* See Chapter 2, Animal Fantasy.

2143   DRURY, Roger W(olcott). *The Finches Fabulous Furnace.* **Gr. 4–6.**

✓   The Finch family tries to keep the volcano in their basement a secret, yet safeguard their town.

Illus. by Erik Blegvad, Little, 1971, 149 pp., o.p.

(BL 67:907; CCBB 25:4; HB 47:382; LJ 97:1169; Suth:108)

2144   DU BOIS, William (Sherman) Pène. *The Alligator Case.* **Gr. 3–5.**

✓   A case involving a circus alligator and three suspicious strangers is solved by a boy detective even before the crime is committed. *The Horse in the Camel Suit* (1967) is the sequel.

Illus. by the author, Harper, 1965, 63 pp., o.p.

(BL 62:330; CCBB 19:31; Eakin:103; HB 41:497; KR 33:827; LJ 90:3788)

2145   DU BOIS, William (Sherman) Pène. *Call Me Bandicoot.* **Gr. 3–5.**

A young con artist named Ermine Bandicoot is responsible for the color of New York Harbor's tobacco-brown water.

Illus. by the author, Harper, 1970, 63 pp., o.p.

(CCBB 24:105; KR 38:1095; LJ 95:4326, 4354; Suth:109)

2146   DU BOIS, William (Sherman) Pène. *The Flying Locomotive.* **Gr. 1–4.**

A fairy godmother gives a special wish to a Swiss locomotive.

Illus. by the author, Viking, 1941, 48 pp., o.p.

(HB 17:356, 381; LJ 66:878)

2147   DU BOIS, William (Sherman) Pène. *The Forbidden Forest.* **Gr. 3–5.**

✓   Lady Adelaide the kangaroo, Buckingham the bulldog, and Spider Max the champion boxer are hailed as heroes for stopping World War I.

Illus. by the author, Harper, 1978, 56 pp., o.p.

(BL 75:215; CCBB 32:78; Ch&Bks:257; HB 55:515; KR 46:946; SLJ Sept 1978 p. 122; Suth 2:130; TLS 1978 p. 1397)

2148   DU BOIS, William (Sherman) Pène. *The Giant.* **Gr. 4–6.**

✓   A gigantic eight-year-old boy named El Muchacho, whose toys are live wild animals and real trains and trucks, makes a visit to Paris.

Illus. by the author, Viking, 1954, 124 pp., o.p.; Dell, 1987, pap. (0-440-42994-3); Peter Smith, 1989, o.p.

(BL 51:114; CCBB 8:98; Eakin:103; HB 30:434; KR 22:529; LJ 80:190; Suth:212)

2149   **DU BOIS, William (Sherman) Pène.** *The Great Geppy.* **Gr. 4–6.**

A red and white striped horse detective called The Great Geppy is hired to investigate problems at the Bolt Bros. Circus.

Illus. by the author, Viking, 1940, 1946, 92 pp., o.p.

(BL 36:368; HB 16:166, 175, 60:223; LJ 65:502, 847)

2150   **DU BOIS, William (Sherman) Pène.** *Lazy Tommy Pumpkinhead.* **Gr. 2–4.**

✓   Tommy is so lazy that every day he slides from his automatic bed into an automatic bath, to be automatically dressed and fed, until the day the electricity fails.

Illus. by the author, Harper, 1966, 32 pp., o.p.

(CCBB 20:87; Ch&Bks:257; HB 43:61; KR 34:1095; LJ 91:6190)

2151   **DU BOIS, William (Sherman) Pène.** *Otto and the Magic Potatoes.* **Gr. 2–4.**

✓   In this sequel to *Otto at Sea* (1936, 1958, 1964), *Otto in Texas* (1959), and *Otto in Africa* (1961), Otto, a lovable giant-sized dog, is kidnapped by Baron Backgammon, who is trying to grow gigantic potatoes and roses.

Illus. by the author, Viking, 1970, 48 pp., o.p.

(BL 66:1406; CCBB 24:57; KR 38:238; LJ 95:1940)

2152   **DU BOIS, William (Sherman) Pène.** *Peter Graves.* **Gr. 5–7.**

Peter uses a retired inventor's antigravity alloy to try such feats as tightrope walking upside down and the Indian rope trick.

Illus. by the author, Viking, 1950, 168 pp., o.p.

(BL 47:140; CCBB 4:19; HB 26:375; KR 18:518)

2153   **DU BOIS, William (Sherman) Pène.** *The Squirrel Hotel.* **Gr. 3–6.**

✓   A retired toy dealer and bee-orchestra conductor describes his hotel for squirrels, equipped with all the modern conveniences.

Illus. by the author, Viking, 1952, 48 pp., o.p.; Gregg, 1980. o.p.

(BL 48:269; HB 28:106; KR 20:71; LJ 77:727)

2154   **DU BOIS, William (Sherman) Pène.** *The Three Policemen, or Young Bottsford of Farbe Island.* **Gr. 4–6.**

The mystery of the stolen fishing nets on the fabulous island of Farbe is solved by three policemen, with the help of young Bottsford.

Illus. by the author, Viking, 1938, 1960, 95 pp., o.p.

(BL 57:190; HB 14:365, 375, 36:485; LJ 63:818, 978)

2155   **DU BOIS, William (Sherman) Pène.** *The Twenty-One Balloons.* **Gr. 5–7.**

✓   Professor William Waterman Sherman is tired of teaching arithmetic. He sails off in a balloon to see the world and lands on the volcanic island of Krakatoa. John Newbery Medal, 1948.

Illus. by the author, Viking, 1947 (0-670-73441-1); Puffin, 1986, pap., 184 pp. (0-14-032097-0)

(BL 43:296; CC:480; Ch&Bks:257; HB 23:214; LJ 72:819)

DUFFEY, Betsy. *A Boy in the Doghouse.* See Chapter 2, Animal Fantasy.

DUGGAN, Alice. *Violet's Finest Hour.* See Chapter 2, Animal Fantasy.

DUTTON, Sandra. *The Magic of Myrna C. Waxweather.* See Chapter 7, Magic Adventure Fantasy.

2156 EDMONDS, Walter D(umaux). *Uncle Ben's Whale.* **Gr. 3–5.**

A canal skipper named Uncle Ben harpoons a whale and sets up a museum inside it.

Illus. by William Gropper, Dodd, 1931, 1955, 90 pp., o.p.

(BL 52:60; KR 23:646; LJ 80:2641)

EDMONDSON, Madeline. *Anna Witch.* See Chapter 10, Witchcraft and Sorcery Fantasy.

2157 EGNER, Thorbjørn. *The Singing Town.* **Gr. 1–4. (Orig. Norwegian pub. 1955.)**

A musical comedy about three robbers and a pet lion who frighten the villagers of Kardemomma. Awarded first prize by the Norwegian Ministry of Church and Education, 1955.

Trans. by Evelyn Ramsden and Leila Berg, illus. by the author, Macmillan, 1959, 105 pp., o.p.

(HB 35:387; LJ 84:3630; TLS Dec 4, 1959 p. iv)

ELISH, Dan. *Jason and the Baseball Bear.* See Chapter 2, Animal Fantasy.

2158 ELISH, Dan. *The Worldwide Dessert Contest.* **Gr. 4–6.**

John Appleteller and his culinary team long to wrest the gold medal in the Worldwide Dessert Contest away from sly Sylvester Sweet, the self-proclaimed King of Dessert.

Illus. by John Steven Gurney, Orchard, 1988, 224 pp. (0-531-05752-6); Bantam, 1990, pap. (0-553-15820-1)

(BL 84:1735; KR 56:760; SLJ May 1988 p. 96)

EMSHWILLER, Carol. *Carmen Dog.* See Chapter 2, Animal Fantasy.

2159 ENDE, Michael. *The Night of Wishes, or The Satanarcheolidealcohellish Notion Potion.* **Gr. 7–9. (Orig. German pub. 1989.)**

Two secret agents from the High Council of Animals, a tomcat and a raven, have been assigned to stop Shadow Sorcery Minister Beelzebub Preposteror and his Aunt Tyrannia Vampirella's wicked plans to make ten species of animals extinct, kill 10,000 trees, and bring a new plague into the world before New Year's Day.

Trans. by Heike Schwarzbauer and Rick Takvorian, Farrar, 1992, 244 pp. (0-374-19594-3)

(BL 88:2004; CCBB 46:174; HBG 4[Spring 1993]:67; KR 60:847; SLJ Aug 1992 p. 154; VOYA 15:291)

ERWIN, Betty K. *Aggie, Maggie, and Tish.* See Chapter 7, Magic Adventure Fantasy.

2160 EUSTIS, Helen. *Mr. Death and the Redheaded Woman.* **Gr. 5 up. (Orig. pub. in the *Saturday Evening Post,* 1950.)**

Redheaded Maud Applegate sets out to convince Mr. Death to restore the life of her own true love, Billy-Be-Damn Bangtry.

Illus. by Reinhard Michl, Green Tiger Press, 1983, pap., 32 pp., o.p.

(BL 80:170; HB 60:50; SLJ Jan 1984 p. 84)

2161 EVARTS, Hal G. *Jay-Jay and the Peking Monster.* **Gr. 6–9.**

Aunt Hattie's experiments on ancient human bones bring a boy named Zurria to life, and involve Jay-Jay with the Marines, a Chinese attaché, and gangsters.

Scribner, 1978, 185 pp., o.p.; Peter Smith, 1984 (0-8446-6166-X)

(BL 74:1492; HB 54:401; KR 46:500; SLJ May 1978 p. 86)

2162   EZO (pseud.). *My Son-in-Law, the Hippopotamus.* **Gr. 4–6. (Orig. pub. in France.)**

Madame Hournarette's wild tales about her son-in-law, Baldomer the hippo, inspire two Parisian children to go to Africa in search of him.

Trans. by Hugh Shelley, illus. by Quentin Blake, Abelard-Schuman, 1962, 160 pp., o.p.

(HB 38:602; LJ 87:3201)

FARJEON, Eleanor. *The Glass Slipper.* See Chapter 5B, Myth Fantasy.

FAST, Howard (Melvin). *A Touch of Infinity: Thirteen New Stories of Fantasy and Science Fiction.* See Chapter 3, Fantasy Collections.

FEAGLES, Anita M. *Casey, the Utterly Impossible Horse.* See Chapter 2, Animal Fantasy.

FIENBERG, Anna. *The Magnificent Nose and Other Marvels.* See Chapter 7, Magic Adventure Fantasy.

2163   FIENBERG, Anna. *Wiggy and Boa.* **Gr. 3–7. (Orig. Australian pub. 1988.)**

✓   Boa and her friend, Wiggy, struggle to save her sea captain uncle from the savage pirates she magically summoned from their island prison. Australian Children's Book of the Year Award, Runner-up, 1988.

Illus. by Ann James, Houghton, 1990, 112 pp., o.p.

(CCBB 43:158; HB 66:454; HBG 1[Jan–June 1990]:254; KR 58:575; SLJ May 1990 p. 104)

FINE, Anne. *The Chicken Gave It to Me.* See Chapter 2, Animal Fantasy.

FINNEY, Jack (pseud. of Walter Branden Finney). *Marion's Wall; A Novel.* See Chapter 4, Ghost Fantasy.

FISHER, Leonard Everett. *Noonan: A Novel about Baseball, ESP, and Time Warps.* See Chapter 8, Time Travel Fantasy.

2164   FLEISCHMAN, Paul (Taylor). *Finzel the Farsighted.* **Gr. 2–4.**

✓   Although Finzel the fortune teller can barely see, his predictions enable him to outwit his greedy brother, Osip.

Illus. by Marcia Sewall, Dutton, 1983, 48 pp. (0-525-44057-7)

(BL 80:484; CC:484; CCBB 37:86; Ch&Bks:274; KR 51:147; SLJ Dec 1983 p. 65; Suth 3:134)

FLEISCHMAN, Paul (Taylor). *Graven Images: Three Stories.* See Chapter 4, Ghost Fantasy.

2165   FLEISCHMAN, (Albert) Sid(ney). *By the Great Horn Spoon.* **Gr. 4–6.**

✓   Jack Flagg runs away from his Boston home to make his fortune in the California gold fields, accompanied by Praiseworthy, his butler.

Illus. by Eric Von Schmidt, Little, 1963, 1988, 193 pp. (0-316-28577-3), pap. (0-316-28612-5)

(BL 60:207; CC:485; CCBB 17:110; Ch&Bks:274; HB 39:598; LJ 88:3348)

2166   FLEISCHMAN, (Albert) Sid(ney). *Chancy and the Grand Rascal.* **Gr. 4–6.**

✓   Chancy, orphaned and searching for his long-lost sister, Indiana, meets a tall-tale-telling uncle and a sly villain named Colonel Plugg.

Illus. by Eric Von Schmidt, Little, 1966, 1989, 190 pp. (0-316-28575-7), pap. (0-316-26012-6)

(BL 63:119; CC:485; CCBB 20:41; Ch&Bks:274; HB 42:569; KR 34:625; LJ 91:5226; Suth:126; TLS 1967 p. 1145)

FLEISCHMAN, (Albert) Sid(ney). *The Ghost in the Noonday Sun.* See Chapter 4, Ghost Fantasy.

2167 FLEISCHMAN, (Albert) Sid(ney). *The Ghost on Saturday Night.* **Gr. 3–5.**

✓ Opie becomes a town hero when he exposes Dr. Pepper's traveling ghost-raising show as a front for bank robberies.

Illus. by Eric Von Schmidt, Little, 1974, 64 pp. (0-316-28583-8)

(BL 70:1252; CC:485; CCBB 28:61; HB 50:379; KR 42:535; LJ 99:2267; Suth 2:148; TLS 1975 p. 770)

FLEISCHMAN, (Albert) Sid(ney). *The Hey Hey Man.* See Chapter 7, Magic Adventure Fantasy.

2168 FLEISCHMAN, (Albert) Sid(ney). *Humbug Mountain.* **Gr. 4–6.**

✓ Grandpa Flint's "property" in the boom town of Sunshine, Dakota, turns out to be no more than an abandoned riverboat in the ghost town of Sunshine, Nevada, but the family makes the best of it by setting off a gold rush. Boston Globe Horn Book Award, 1979. National Book Award Finalist, Children's Fiction Category, 1979.

Illus. by Eric Von Schmidt, Little, 1978, 149 pp., o.p., pap., 1988 (0-316-28613-3)

(BL 75:477, 80:95; CC:485; CCBB 32:113; HB 55:640; KR 46:1071; SLJ Sept 1978 p. 136; Suth 2:149)

2169 FLEISCHMAN, (Albert) Sid(ney). *Jim Bridger's Alarm Clock, and Other Tall* ✓ *Tales.* **Gr. 2–4.**

Three tall tales about an army scout and mountain man named Jim Bridger, including one in which he uses the echo of fireworks to outwit bank robbers.

Illus. by Eric Von Schmidt, Dutton, 1978, 56 pp., o.p.

(BL 75:808; HB 55:191; KR 42:124; SLJ Apr 1979 p. 55)

2170 FLEISCHMAN, (Albert) Sid(ney). *Jingo Django.* **Gr. 4–6.**

✓ Orphaned Jingo Hawks and his benefactor, Mr. Peacock-Hemlock-Jones, travel from Boston to Mexico trying their hands at horse trading, river piloting, portrait painting, and treasure hunting.

Illus. by Eric Von Schmidt, Little, 1971, 172 pp., o.p.

(BL 67:954, 68:669; CC:468; HB 47:383, 63:439; KR 39:432; LJ 96:2916; TLS 1971 p. 1509)

2171 FLEISCHMAN, (Albert) Sid(ney). *McBroom Tells the Truth* **(British title:** *Mc-* ✓ *Broom's Wonderful One Acre Farm).* **Gr. 3–5.**

Farmer McBroom's crops grow so fast that his eleven children can ride on the pumpkins and use the cornstalks for pogo sticks. The sequels, all published by Little, are *McBroom and the Big Wind* (1967; rev. ed. 1982), *McBroom's Ear* (1969), *McBroom's Ghost* (1971; rev. ed. 1981), *McBroom's Zoo* (1972; rev. ed. 1982), *McBroom the Rainmaker* (1973; Golden Kite Award Honor Book, 1973; rev. ed. 1982), *McBroom Tells a Lie* (1976; British title: *Here Comes McBroom!*), *McBroom and the Beanstalk* (1978), *McBroom and the Great Race* (1980), and *McBroom's Almanac* (1984). *McBroom's Wonderful One-Acre Farm: Three Tall Tales* (Greenwillow, 1992) contains "McBroom Tells the Truth," "McBroom and the Big Wind," and "McBroom's Ear." *Here Comes McBroom! Three More Tall Tales* (Greenwillow, 1992) contains "McBroom in the Rain," "McBroom's Ghost," and "McBroom's Zoo."

Illus. by Walter Lorraine, Grosset, 1966, o.p.; Little, 1981 (repr. of 1966 ed.), 48 pp. (0-

316-28550-1); published in *McBroom's Wonderful One-Acre Farm: Three Tall Tales,* Greenwillow, 1992 (0-688-11159-9)

(BL 62:662; CC:485, 1993 Suppl. p. 69; CCBB 19:129; Ch&Bks:275; HB 42:193; HBG 4[Spring 1993]:56; KR 33:1187; LJ 91:424; SLJ Aug 1992 p. 99; Suth:1 27)

2172 **FLEISCHMAN, (Albert) Sid(ney).** *Me and the Man on the Moon-Eyed Horse.*
✓ **Gr. 3–5.**

The circus train's visit to Furnace Flats is almost ruined by a desperado named Step-and-a-half Jackson, but young Clint saves the day.

Illus. by Eric Von Schmidt, Little, 1977, 57 pp., o.p.

(BL 73:1652; HB 53:553; KR 45:46; SLJ May 1977 p. 61)

FLEISCHMAN, (Albert) Sid(ney). *The Midnight Horse.* See Chapter 4, Ghost Fantasy.

2173 **FLEISCHMAN, (Albert) Sid(ney).** *Mister Mysterious and Company.* **Gr. 4–6.**
✓ Mr. Mysterious and his magician family travel across the country in a covered wagon, entertaining people with wonderful feats of magic.

Illus. by Eric Von Schmidt, Little, 1962, 151 pp., o.p.

(BL 58:728; CC:486; HB 38:279; LJ 87:1318)

2174 **FLEMING, Ian (Lancaster).** *Chitty-Chitty Bang Bang: The Magical Car.* **Gr.**
✓ **4–6. (Orig. British pub. 1964.)**

The Pott family's rattletrap auto can both fly and float, and it takes them across the English Channel to the underground hideout of England's worst gangster.

Illus. by John Burningham, Random, 1964, o.p.; Amereon Pr., 1976 (repr. of 1964 ed.), 159 pp., LB(0-88411-983-1); Knopf, 1989, pap. (0-394-81948-9)

(BBC:203; BL 61:435; CC:486; CCBB 18:73, 22:77; Ch&Bks:286; HB 41:167; LJ 89:4646)

FLORA, James (Royer). *Grandpa's Ghost Stories.* See Chapter 4, Ghost Fantasy.

FLORA, James (Royer). *Wanda and the Bumbly Wizard.* See Chapter 10, Witchcraft and Sorcery Fantasy.

FOOTE, Timothy. *The Great Ringtail Garbage Caper.* See Chapter 2, Animal Fantasy.

2175 **FORESTER, C(ecil) S(cott).** *Poo Poo and the Dragons.* **Gr. 3–5.**

Harold "Poo Poo" Brown brings home a dragon named Horatio.

Illus. by Robert Lawson, Little, 1942, 142 pp., o.p.

(HB 18:332; LJ 67:682; TLS 1942 p. 573)

2176 **FOSTER, John T(homas).** *Marco and the Tiger.* **Gr. 4–6.**
✓ Marco concocts wild schemes to protect the aging Bengal tiger he met while delivering newspapers.

Illus. by Lorence Bjorklund, Dodd, 1967, 128 pp., o.p.

(BL 64:273; HB 43:462; KR 35:57; LJ 92:2020)

FRESCHET, Bernice. *Bernard of Scotland Yard.* See Chapter 2, Animal Fantasy.

2177 **FRIESNER, Esther M.** *Elf Defense.* **Gr. 10 up.**

A small Connecticut town is overrun with Faerie creatures after the human wife of the king of American elves announces that she wants a divorce.

NAL, 1988, pap., 224 pp., o.p.

(BBS:57; BL 84:1223, 1241, 86:906; LJ Feb 15, 1988 p. 180)

FRIESNER, Esther M. *Gnome Man's Land.* See Chapter 5C, Travel to Other Worlds.

2178   FRIESNER, Esther M. *Hooray for Hellywood* **(Demon trilogy, book 3). Gr. 10 up.**

Melisan Cardiff uses demonic magic to stop an evil demon disguised as a television evangelist from opening the gates of Hell. This is the sequel to *Here Be Demons* (1988) and *Demon Blues* (1989).

Ace, 1990, pap., 224 pp., o.p.

(BBS:57; BL 86:1072, 1078)

FRIESNER, Esther M. *Majyk by Accident.* See Chapter 10, Witchcraft and Sorcery Fantasy.

FRIESNER, Esther M. *Wishing Season.* See Chapter 5A, Alternate Worlds or Histories.

FROMAN, Elizabeth Hull. *Eba, the Absent-Minded Witch.* See Chapter 10, Witchcraft and Sorcery Fantasy.

Fun Phantoms: Tales of Ghostly Entertainment. **Ed. by Seon Manley and Gogo Lewis.** See Chapter 4, Ghost Fantasy.

FYLEMAN, Rose (Amy). *Tea Time Tales.* See Chapter 3, Fantasy Collections.

GAGE, Wilson (pseud. of Mary Q[uintard] Govan Steele). *The Ghost of Five Owl Farm.* See Chapter 4, Ghost Fantasy.

2179   GANNETT (Kahn), Ruth Stiles. *The Wonderful House-Boat-Train.* **Gr. 2–4.**

A retired railroad engineer and his grandchildren move to a house in the country that looks like a train and floats like a boat.

Illus. by Fritz Eichenberg, Random, 1949, 64 pp., o.p.

(BL 46:161; HB 26:37; KR 17:653; LJ 75:112)

GARDNER, Craig Shaw. *A Disagreement with Death.* See Chapter 10, Witchcraft and Sorcery Fantasy.

GARDNER, Craig Shaw. *The Other Sinbad.* See Chapter 5B, Myth Fantasy.

GARNETT, David. *Two by Two: A Story of Survival.* See Chapter 5B, Myth Fantasy.

2180   GATHORNE-HARDY, Jonathan. *Operation Peeg* **(British title:** *Jane's Adventures on the Island of Peeg,* **1968). Gr. 4–6.**
✓

After a rocket explosion sets the island of Peeg adrift in the Atlantic Ocean, two little girls and a housekeeper are caught up in a power struggle between two long-lost World War II soldiers and an evil billionaire. The sequels are *The Airship Ladyship Adventure* (1977) and *Jane's Adventures In and Out of the Book* (Overlook, 1981).

Illus. by Glo Coalson, Lippincott, 1974, 192 pp., o.p.

(CCBB 28:77; HB 51:147; KR 42:1060, 43:6; LJ 99:2740; TLS 1968 p. 1377)

2181 GERRARD, Roy. *Sir Cedric.* **Gr. 1–4.**

✓ Balding Sir Cedric battles bullying Black Ned to free captive princess Fat Matilda, in this spoof of the age of chivalry. The sequel is *Sir Cedric Rides Again* (1986).

Illus. by the author, Farrar, 1984, 32 pp. (0-374-36959-3), 1986, pap. (0-374-46659-9)

(BL 81:246; CCBB 38:83; KR 52:J61; SLJ Jan 1985 p. 74; TLS 1984 p. 1139)

GIBSON, Katharine. *Cinders.* See Chapter 1, Allegorical Fantasy and Literary Fairy Tales.

2182 GIFALDI, David. *Gregory, Maw and the Mean One.* **Gr. 4–6.**

Twelve-year-old Gregory, raised by a crow, avoids a disastrous encounter with mean and smelly Norbert Meaney by offering to take Norbert back through time to find his missing heart.

Illus. by Andrew Glass, Houghton, 1992, 136 pp. (0-395-60821-X)

(HBG 4[Spring 1993]:68; KR 60:1060; SLJ Nov 1992, p. 91)

GILLILAND, Alexis A. *Wizenbeak.* See Chapter 10, Witchcraft and Sorcery Fantasy.

GILMORE, Kate. *Enter Three Witches.* See Chapter 10, Witchcraft and Sorcery Fantasy.

2183 GOGOL, Nikolai. *The Nose.* **Gr. 3 up. (Orig. Russian pub. as a short story.)**

Kovaliov searches St. Petersburg for his missing nose, only to be told that it has become an "independent individual."

Illus. by Gennady Spirin, Godine, 1993, 28 pp. (0-87923-963-8)

(BL 89:1814; HBG 4[Fall 1993]:285; SLJ Aug 1993 p. 163)

GOLDMAN, William W. *The Princess Bride: S. Morgenstern's Classic Tale of True Love and High Adventure.* See Chapter 5A, Alternate Worlds or Histories.

GORMLEY, Beatrice. *Best Friend Insurance.* See Chapter 7, Magic Adventure Fantasy.

GORMLEY, Beatrice. *Fifth Grade Magic.* See Chapter 7, Magic Adventure Fantasy.

GORMLEY, Beatrice. *Paul's Volcano.* See Chapter 7, Magic Adventure Fantasy.

GOULART, Ron(ald Joseph). *The Chameleon Corps and Other Shape Changers.* See Chapter 5A, Alternate Worlds or Histories.

GOULART, Ron(ald Joseph). *The Prisoner of Blackwood Castle.* See Chapter 5A, Alternate Worlds or Histories.

GRAVES, Robert. *The Big Green Book.* See Chapter 7, Magic Adventure Fantasy.

GRAY, Nicholas Stuart. *The Apple Stone.* See Chapter 7, Magic Adventure Fantasy.

GRAY, Nicholas Stuart. *A Wind from Nowhere.* See Chapter 3, Fantasy Collections.

GREEN, Phyllis. *Eating Ice Cream with a Werewolf.* See Chapter 7, Magic Adventure Fantasy.

2184 GREENBURG, Dan. *Young Santa.* **Gr. 4–7.**

Young Santa spends an ordinary childhood in Sioux City, Iowa, until his father is transferred to the North Pole, where Santa gets a job talking to children in a department store.

Illus. by Warren Miller, Viking, 1991, 89 pp. (0-670-83905-1)

(BL 88:313; KR 59:930; SLJ Oct 1991, p. 30)

GREER, Gery, and RUDDICK, Bob. *Max and Me and the Time Machine.* See Chapter 8, Time Travel Fantasy.

GRIFFITH, Helen V(irginia). *Emily and the Enchanted Frog.* See Chapter 7, Magic Adventure Fantasy.

GROSSER, Morton. *The Snake Horn.* See Chapter 8, Time Travel Fantasy.

HAHN, Harriet. *James, the Connoisseur Cat.* See Chapter 2, Animal Fantasy.

HALE, F. J. *Ogre Castle.* See Chapter 10, Witchcraft and Sorcery Fantasy.

2185 HALE, Lucretia P(eabody). *The Complete Peterkin Papers* **(British titles:** *The*
✓   *Peterkin Papers* **and** *The Last of the Peterkins***). Gr. 5–8. (Orig. pub. 1880.)**

The Peterkin family's problems are solved by the common sense of the Lady from Philadelphia. *The Lady Who Put Salt in Her Coffee* (Harcourt, 1989) is an illustrated version of the first of the Peterkin stories, adapted by Amy Schwartz for children in grades 3–5.

Illus. by the author, Houghton, 1960, 302 pp., o.p.

(BL 57:190; Bookshelf 1932 p. 12; Ch&Bks:272; HB 1[Nov 1924]:4–7, 1[June 1925]:44; KR 28:905; LJ 50:803, 85:4567)

2186 HALL, Lynn. *Dagmar Schultz and the Angel Edna* **(Dagmar Schultz series,**
✓   **book 3). Gr. 5–8.**

Thirteen-year-old Dagmar's guardian angel, long-dead Aunt Edna, disapproves of Dagmar's resolve to find a boyfriend, until Aunt Edna falls in love herself. This is the sequel to *The Secret Life of Dagmar Schultz* (1988; not a fantasy), and *Dagmar Schultz and the Powers of Darkness* (1989). It is followed by *Dagmar Schultz and the Green-Eyed Monster* (1991).

Macmillan, 1989, 86 pp. (0-6841-9097-4), 1992, pap. (0-689-71615-X)

(BL 86:457; CC:496; HB 65:770; HBG 1[July 1989]:70; KR 57:1245; SLJ Sept 1989 p. 250; VOYA 12:276)

2187 HAMILTON (Adoff), Virginia (Esther). *The All Jahdu Storybook.* **Gr. 3–6.**

Fifteen stories about the magical shape-shifting trickster Jahdu, of which four are new and eleven are from *Jahdu* (Greenwillow, 1980), *The Time-Ago Tales of Jahdu* (1969), and *Time-Ago Lost: More Tales of Jahdu* (1973).

Illus. by Barry Moser, Harcourt, 1991, 108 pp. (0-15-239498-2)

(BL 88:697; CC 1992 Suppl. p. 65; CCBB 45:127; HBG 3[July–Dec 1991]:66; KR 59:1402; SLJ Jan 1992 p. 109)

HARVEY, Dean. *The Secret Elephant of Harlan Kooter.* See Chapter 7, Magic Adventure Fantasy.

2188 HARVEY, Jayne. *Great-Uncle Dracula.* **Gr. 2–4.**

New at school after her family's move to Transylvania to live with her Great-Uncle Dracula, Emily discovers that her classmates are all werewolves, ghosts, witches, or vampires. The sequel is *Great-Uncle Dracula and the Dirty Rat* (1993).

Illus. by Abby Carter, Random, 1992, 79 pp. (0-679-92448-5)

(CCBB 46:113; HBG 4[Spring 1993]:57; SLJ Sept 1992 p. 204)

2189 HASELEY, Dennis. *Doctor Gravity.* **Gr. 7 up.**

The two hundred and seven townspeople of Avebury, Ohio, find themselves 4.2 miles up in the air after Dr. Gravity sells them his Formula #2 to cure the heaviness of gravity.

Farrar, 1992, 322 pp. (0-374-31842-5)

(CCBB 46:147; HB 69:211; HBG 4[Spring 1993]:81; KR 60:1376; SLJ Dec 1992 p. 133; VOYA 15:292, 16: 10)

HASS, E. A. *Incognito Mosquito, Private Insective.* See Chapter 2, Animal Fantasy.

2190 HAUFF, Wilhelm. *A Monkey's Uncle.* **Gr. 4–6. (Orig. pub. in Germany.)**

A newcomer decides to introduce an orangutan as his nephew.

Retold by Doris Orgel, illus. by Mitchell Miller, Farrar, 1969, 74 pp., o.p.

(KR 37:1109; LJ 95:241)

HAYES, Geoffrey. *The Alligator and His Uncle Tooth: A Novel of the Sea.* See Chapter 2, Animal Fantasy.

HAYNES, Betsy. *The Ghost of the Gravestone Hearth.* See Chapter 4, Ghost Fantasy.

2191 HEIDE, Florence Parry. *The Shrinking of Treehorn.* **Gr. 2–4.**

✓ No one believes that Treehorn is growing smaller and smaller every day. The sequels are *Treehorn's Treasure* (1981) and *Treehorn's Wish* (1984).

Illus. by Edward Gorey, Holiday, 1971, 64 pp., LB(0-8234-0189-8), pap. (0-8234-0975-9); Dell, 1983, pap. (entitled *The Adventures of Treehorn;* also includes *Treehorn's Treasure*), 128 pp. (0-440-40045-7)

(BL 68:564, 669; CC:499; CCBB 25:156; Ch&Bks:287; HB 48:45; KR 39:1118; LJ 97:763, 1884)

HELPRIN, Mark. *Winter's Tale.* See Chapter 5A, Alternate Worlds or Histories.

HENDRY, Diana. *A Camel Called April.* See Chapter 7, Magic Adventure Fantasy.

HEWETT, Anita. *The Bull Beneath the Walnut Tree and Other Stories.* See Chapter 3, Fantasy Collections.

HILDICK, E(dmund) W(allace). *The Case of the Dragon in Distress: A McGurk Fantasy.* See Chapter 8, Time Travel Fantasy.

2192 HILDICK, E(dmund) W(allace). *The Dragon That Lived Under Manhattan.* **Gr. 3–4.**

Jimmy tries to convince the mayor of New York to allow a shy vegetarian dragon to live beneath the city.

Illus. by Harold Berson, Crown, 1970, 62 pp., o.p.

(BL 67:420; KR 38:1143; LJ 95:4337)

HISER, Constance. *No Bean Sprouts, Please!* See Chapter 7, Magic Adventure Fantasy.

HITE, Sid. *Dither Farm.* See Chapter 7, Magic Adventure Fantasy.

HOBAN, Russell C(onwell). *Dinner at Alberta's.* See Chapter 2, Animal Fantasy.

2193 **HOBAN, Russell C(onwell).** *How Tom Beat Captain Najork and His Hired*
✓ *Sportsmen.* **Gr. 3–5. (Orig. British pub. 1974.)**

Tom's Aunt Fidget Wonkham-Strong hires Captain Najork to teach Tom a lesson about foolish behavior, but even that doesn't stop him. Whitbread Literary Award, Children's Books Category, 1974. The sequel is *A Near Thing for Captain Najork* (1976).

Illus. by Quentin Blake, Atheneum, 1974, 32 pp., o.p.

(BL 71:766; CCBB 28:78; Ch&Bks:287; HB 51:138; KR 42:1299, 43:2; LJ 99:2733; Suth 2:216; TLS 1974 p. 718)

HOBAN, Russell C(onwell). *Jim Hedgehog and the Lonesome Tower.* See Chapter 2, Animal Fantasy.

2194 **HOBAN, Russell C(onwell).** *The Twenty-Elephant Restaurant.* **Gr. K–4.**

A wobbly table, strengthened enough for an elephant to dance on, inspires an old man to build a restaurant featuring twenty dancing elephants.

Illus. by Emily McCully, Atheneum, 1978, 37 pp., o.p.

(BL 74:1494; CCBB 32:10; KR 46:299; SLJ May 1978 p. 56)

2195 **HODGES, C(yril) Walter.** *Sky High: The Story of a House That Flew* **(British title:** *The Flying House***). Gr. 3–5.**

Uncle Ben's latest invention, super-inflating gas, causes Nicky and Linda's house to float off into the sky.

Illus. by the author, Coward, 1947, 112 pp., o.p.

(BL 44:189; HB 23:436; LJ 72:1543)

HOFFMANN, Eleanor. *The Four Friends.* See Chapter 2, Animal Fantasy.

2196 **HOLMAN (Valen), Felice.** *The Blackmail Machine.* **Gr. 4–6.**
✓ A flying treehouse enables Murk and Arabella to "blackmail" the government into preserving wildlife and bringing peace to the world.

Illus. by Victoria de Larrea, Macmillan, 1968, 182 pp., o.p.

(BL 64:995; CCBB 21:129; HB 44:173; KR 35:1472; LJ 93:870; TLS 1968 p. 1112)

2197 **HOLMAN (Valen), Felice.** *The Escape of the Giant Hogstalk.* **Gr. 3–6.**

A national emergency is declared after a gigantic plant at the Royal Botanic Gardens grows out of control.

Illus. by Ben Shecter, Scribner, 1974, 96 pp., o.p.

(CCBB 28:28; HB 50:283; KR 42:363; LJ 99:2270; Suth 2:223)

2198 **HOLMAN (Valen), Felice.** *The Future of Hooper Toote.* **Gr. 5–7.**

Hooper Toote can walk on air.

Illus. by Gahan Wilson, Scribner, 1972, 138 pp., o.p.

(BL 69:529; CCBB 25:171; KR 40:259; LJ 97:2951; Suth:193)

HOLMAN (Valen), Felice. *The Witch on the Corner.* See Chapter 10, Witchcraft and Sorcery Fantasy.

2199 **HOOKS, William H(arris).** *Mean Jake and the Devils.* **Gr. 3–5.**
✓ Mean old Jake manages to outwit three generations of devils, in these three tales told to a boy by his grandmother.

Illus. by Dirk Zimmer, Dial, 1981, 64 pp., o.p.

(BBC:205; BL 78:756; CCBB 35:172; HB 58:164; KR 50:202; SLJ Jan 1982 p. 77)

HÖREJS, Vít. *Pig and Bear.* See Chapter 2, Animal Fantasy.

2200 **HORNE, Richard Henry.** *The Good-Natured Bear: A Story for Children of All Ages.* **Gr. 4–6. (Orig. British pub. 1846; U.S. 1854.)**

A good-natured uncle, disguised as a bear, tells the Littlepump children moralistic and humorous tales about his wandering life.

Illus. by Lisl Hummel, Macmillan, 1927, 159 pp., o.p.

(BL 24:168; HB 3[Nov 1927]:44; LJ 53:484, 1033; Mahony 2:147)

HORWITZ, Elinor Lander. *The Strange Story of the Frog Who Became a Prince.* See Chapter 10, Witchcraft and Sorcery Fantasy.

HOWE, Deborah, and HOWE, James. *Bunnicula: A Rabbit Tale of Mystery.* See Chapter 2, Animal Fantasy.

HUGHART, Barry. *Bridge of Birds: A Novel of an Ancient China That Never Was.* See Chapter 5A, Alternate Worlds or Histories.

HUGHES, Dean. *Nutty's Ghost.* See Chapter 4, Ghost Fantasy.

HUGHES, Frieda. *Getting Rid of Aunt Edna.* See Chapter 10, Witchcraft and Sorcery Fantasy.

HUGHES, Richard (Arthur Warren). *Don't Blame Me!* See Chapter 3, Fantasy Collections.

HUGHES, Ted (Edward James). *Tales of the Early World.* See Chapter 3, Fantasy Collections.

2201 **HUNTER, Mollie (pseud. of Maureen Mollie Hunter McVeigh McIlwraith).**
✓ *The Smartest Man in Ireland* **(British title: *Patrick Kentigen Keenan,* 1963). Gr. 4–6.**

Patrick's boastful claim of being the smartest man in Ireland tempts the fairy folk to test him.

Illus. by Charles Keeping, Funk, 1965, 95 pp., o.p.

(BL 62:487; HB 41:629; KR 33:821; TLS 1963 p. 427)

HUNTER, Mollie (pseud. of Maureen Mollie Hunter McVeigh McIlwraith). *Thomas and the Warlock.* See Chapter 10, Witchcraft and Sorcery Fantasy.

2202 **HUNTER, Norman (George Lorimer).** *The Incredible Adventures of Professor Branestawm.* **Gr. 5–7. (Orig. British pub. 1933.)**

Professor Branestawm's zany inventions include a clock that strikes thirteen and a time machine. The sequels are *The Best of Branestawm* (1981), *Professor Branestawm's Building Bust-Up* (1982), *Professor Branestawm's Mouse War* (1982), *The Peculiar Triumph of Professor Branestawm* (British), *Professor Branestawm up the Pole* (British), *Professor Branestawm's Great Revolution* (British), and *Professor Branestawm's Treasure Hunt* (British).

Illus. by W. Heath Robinson, Bodley Head, 1979, 203 pp., o.p.

(BL 76:558; SLJ Aug 1980 p. 64; TLS 1970 p. 1458)

HUTCHINS, Hazel (J.). *The Three and Many Wishes of Jason Reid.* See Chapter 7, Magic Adventure Fantasy.

2203 **HUTCHINS, Pat (Goundry).** *Follow That Bus!* **Gr. 2–4.**

✓ After their teacher and schoolbus are hijacked by robbers, Miss Beaver's second-grade class rescues her and captures the bandits. The sequel is *The Mona Lisa Mystery* (1981).

Illus. by Laurence Hutchins, Greenwillow, 1977, 102 pp., o.p.; Knopf, 1988 (repr. of 1977 ed.), pap., 112 pp. (0-394-80792-8); Peter Smith, 1992 (0-8446-6557-6)

(BL 73:1498; CCBB 31:48; HB 53:442; KR 45:351; SLJ Apr 1977 p. 55; TLS 1977 p. 1412)

2204 **HUTCHINS, Pat (Goundry).** *The House That Sailed Away.* **Gr. 4–6.**

✓ A house that floats out to sea, a battle with pirates, a landing on a cannibal island, and the discovery of buried treasure are just some of the adventures in store for Morgan and his family.

Illus. by Laurence Hutchins, Greenwillow, 1975, 150 pp. (0-688-84013-2)

(BL 72:303; CCBB 29:64; HB 51:593; KR 43:777; SLJ Sept 1975 p. 84; TLS 1976 p. 882)

IBBOTSON, Eva. *The Great Ghost Rescue.* See Chapter 4, Ghost Fantasy.

2205 **IRVING, Washington.** *Knickerbocker's History of New York* **(Orig. title:** *A History of New York, from the Beginning of the World to the End of the Dutch Dynasty . . . ,* **1812). Gr. 8 up.**

A shortened version of Irving's comic history of New York City.

Ed. by Anne Carroll Moore, illus. by James Daugherty, Doubleday, 1928, 1940, o.p.; Continuum, 1959, o.p., 1983, pap., 441 pp. (0-8044-6291-7)

(BL 12:302, 25:174, 56:359, 450; HB 4[Aug 1928]:77; Moore:138, 431)

JACQUES, Brian. *Seven Strange and Ghostly Tales.* See Chapter 4, Ghost Fantasy.

JAMES, Mary. *Shoebag.* See Chapter 2, Animal Fantasy.

JAMES, Mary. *The Shuteyes.* See Chapter 5C, Travel to Other Worlds.

2206 **JANEWAY, Elizabeth (Hall).** *Ivanov Seven.* **Gr. 5–8.**

✓ Stepan's curiosity and independence cause problems after he joins the Czar's army.

Illus. by Eros Keith, Harper, 1967, 176 pp., o.p.

(BL 64:502; HB 43:750; KR 35:1145; LJ 92:4261)

JENNINGS, Paul. *Unreal! Eight Surprising Stories.* See Chapter 3, Fantasy Collections.

2207 **JETER, K. W.** *Infernal Devices: A Mad Victorian Fantasy.* **Gr. 10 up.**

✓ A witty, adventure-filled romp about the owner of a clock repair shop in Victorian London who becomes involved with a mechanical man, a pair of con men, a gentleman bent on blowing up the world, and the peculiar fishlike inhabitants of Wetwick.

St. Martin, 1987, 282 pp., o.p.

(BL 83:1253, 1275; KR 55:261; LJ Apr 15, 1987 p. 103; VOYA 10:130)

JONES, Diana Wynne. *Archer's Goon.* See Chapter 10, Witchcraft and Sorcery Fantasy.

JONES, Diana Wynne. *Castle in the Air.* See Chapter 5A, Alternate Worlds or Histories.

JONES, Diana Wynne. *Howl's Moving Castle.* See Chapter 10, Witchcraft and Sorcery Fantasy.

JONES, Diana Wynne. *The Ogre Downstairs.* See Chapter 7, Magic Adventure Fantasy.

JONES, Diana Wynne. *Stopping for a Spell: Three Fantasies.* See Chapter 7, Magic Adventure Fantasy.

JONES, Diana Wynne. *A Tale of Time City.* See Chapter 5C, Travel to Other Worlds.

2208 **JONES, Terry.** *Fairy Tales.* **Gr. 3–5. (Orig. British pub. 1981.)**

An oversized book containing thirty short, humorous tales for reading aloud.

Illus. by Michael Foreman, Schocken, 1983, 127 pp., o.p.; Puffin, 1986, 1993, pap., 160 pp. (0-14-032262-0)

(CCBB 36:169; Ch&Bks:287; Suth 3:222; TLS 1981 p. 1360)

2209 **JONES, Terry.** *Fantastic Stories.* **Gr. 3–6. (Orig. British pub. 1993.)**

Twenty-one humorous tales, including "The Improving Mirror," "The Slow Ogre," and "The Flying King."

Illus. by Michael Foreman, Viking, 1993, 128 pp. (0-670-84899-9); Chivers (large type ed.), 1993, 128 pp. (0-7451-1908-5)

(BL 89:2070; CCBB 46:284; HBG 4[Fall 1993]:299; SLJ Jan 1994 p. 114)

2210 **JONES, Terry.** *Nicobobinus.* **Gr. 5–7. (Orig. British pub. 1985.)**

Nicobobinus and his friend Rosie make a madcap journey to the Land of Dragons seeking a cure for Nicobobinus's enchanted golden foot.

Illus. by Michael Foreman, Bedrick, 1986, 176 pp. (0-87226-065-8)

(BBC:206; BL 82:1613; SLJ Aug 1986 p. 94; TLS 1986 p. 174)

2211 **JONSSON, Runer.** *Viki Viking* **(British title:** *Vike the Viking***). Gr. 4–6. (Orig. Swedish pub. 1963.)**

Chief Halvar's son, Viki, hates fighting but still manages to rescue his father's troops.

Trans. by Birgit Rogers and Patricia Lowe, illus. by Ewert Karlsson, World, 1968, 143 pp., o.p.

(BL 64:1094; CCBB 21:129; HB 44:324; KR 35:1473; LJ 93:2114; TLS 1969 p. 689)

JUSTER, Norton. *The Phantom Tollbooth.* See Chapter 5C, Travel to Other Worlds.

KARR, Kathleen. *Gideon and the Mummy Professor.* See Chapter 7, Magic Adventure Fantasy.

2212 **KÄSTNER, Erich.** *The Little Man.* **Gr. 4–6. (Orig. Swiss pub. 1963.)**

✓ Two-inch-tall Maxie Pichelsteiner gains fame by becoming Professor Hokus Von Pokus's Invisible Right-Hand Man. Mildred L. Batchelder Award, 1968. The sequels are *The Little Man and the Big Thief* (1970) and *The Little Man and the Little Miss* (British).

Trans. by James Kirkup, illus. by Rick Schreiter, Knopf, 1966, 183 pp., o.p.

(BBC:206; BL 63:728; CCBB 20:124; Ch&Bks:287; KR 34:1101; LJ 91:6192; Suth:220; TLS 1966 p. 1077)

KAUFMAN, Charles. *The Frog and the Beanpole.* See Chapter 2, Animal Fantasy.

KAYE, Marvin. *The Incredible Umbrella.* See Chapter 5C, Travel to Other Worlds.

2213 **KEELE, Luqman, and PINKWATER, D(aniel) Manus.** *Java Jack.* **Gr. 4–8.**

Jack travels from Missouri to Indonesia in search of his missing parents. En route, he is kidnapped, pilots an airplane, acquires a magic needle, fights a gang of pirates, and voyages out of the universe.

Harper, 1980, 152 pp., o.p.

(HB 56:297; KR 48:584; SLJ May 1980 p. 68)

KEMP, Gene. *Jason Bodger and the Priory Ghost.* See Chapter 4, Ghost Fantasy.

2214 **KENNEDY, William, and KENNEDY, Brendan.** *Charlie Malarkey and the Belly-Button Machine.* **Gr. 2–4.**

Charlie Malarkey and Iggy Gowalowicz wake up to discover that their belly buttons have been stolen by a salesman named Ben Bubie and his mysterious machine. William Kennedy is a Pulitzer Prize-winning author and Brendan Kennedy is his son. The sequel is *Charlie Malarkey and the Singing Moose* (1994).

Illus. by Glen Baxter, Little, 1986, 40 pp., o.p.; Puffin, 1990, pap. (0-14-054239-6)

(KR 54:1728; SLJ Dec 1986 p. 90)

KESEY, Ken. *Little Tricker the Squirrel Meets Big Double the Bear.* See Chapter 2, Animal Fantasy.

KINDL, Patrice. *Owl in Love.* See Chapter 10, Witchcraft and Sorcery Fantasy.

KING, Clive. *The Town That Went South.* See Chapter 2, Animal Fantasy.

KING-SMITH, Dick. *Ace: The Very Important Pig.* See Chapter 2, Animal Fantasy.

KING-SMITH, Dick. *The Cuckoo Child.* See Chapter 2, Animal Fantasy.

KING-SMITH, Dick. *The Fox-Busters.* See Chapter 2, Animal Fantasy.

2215 **KING-SMITH, Dick.** *Harry's Mad.* **Gr. 3–6. (Orig. British pub. 1986.)**

✓ Just after Harry discovers that Madison, the parrot he inherited from a great-uncle, can talk like a human, Mad is stolen by a burglar.

Illus. by Jill Bennet, Crown, 1988, 123 pp. (0-517-56254-5); Dell, 1988, pap. (0-440-40112-7)

(BL 83:1680, 84:1274; CC:515; CCBB 40:171; Ch&Bks:268; HB 63:463; KR 55:221; SLJ May 1987 p. 101, Dec 1987 p. 37; Suth 4:218; TLS Nov 1986 p. 1347)

KING-SMITH, Dick. *The Jenius.* See Chapter 2, Animal Fantasy.

KING-SMITH, Dick. *Martin's Mice.* See Chapter 2, Animal Fantasy.

2216 **KING-SMITH, Dick.** *Pretty Polly.* **Gr. 3–5. (Orig. British pub. 1992.)**

✓ Abigail names her chicken Polly and procedes to teach Polly to talk because she can't afford to buy a parrot from a pet shop.

Illus. by Marshall Peck, Crown, 1992, 120 pp. LB(0-517-58607-X); Random, 1994, pap. (0-679-85396-0)

(BL 89:327; CCBB 46:45; HB 69:85; HBG 4[Spring 1993]:71; KR 60:921; SLJ Sept 1992 p. 254)

KISLING, Lee. *The Fools' War.* See Chapter 5A, Alternate Worlds or Histories.

2217 **KLEIN, Robin.** *Thing.* **Gr. 1–4. (Orig. British pub. 1982.)**

Emily's pet rock hatches into a baby stegosaurus, who grows to the size of a small rhinoceros and prevents a robbery in their landlady's apartment.

Illus. by Alison Lester, Oxford, 1983, 32 pp., o.p.

(BL 79:1402; CCBB 37:52; SLJ Mar 1984 p. 146)

KONIGSBURG, E(laine) L(obl). *Up From Jericho Tel.* See Chapter 7, Magic Adventure Fantasy.

2218 **KOTZWINKLE, William.** *Trouble in Bugland: A Collection of Inspector Mantis*
✓ *Mysteries.* **Gr. 7 up.**

Five short mystery tales starring Inspector Mantis and his grasshopper sidekick, characters modeled on Sir Arthur Conan Doyle's Sherlock Holmes and Dr. Watson.

Illus. by Joe Servello, Godine, 1983, o.p., pap., 1986, 160 pp. (0-87923-555-1)

(BL 80:469, 490, 498; HB 60:196; KR 51:1022; SLJ Feb 1984 p. 74)

KOVACS, Deborah. *Brewster's Courage.* See Chapter 2, Animal Fantasy.

KRENSKY, Stephen (Alan). *Castles in the Air and Other Tales.* See Chapter 3, Fantasy Collections.

KRÜSS, James (Jacob Hinrich). *The Happy Islands Behind the Winds.* See Chapter 5C, Travel to Other Worlds.

LAMPMAN, Evelyn Sibley. *Captain Apple's Ghost.* See Chapter 4, Ghost Fantasy.

2219 **LAMPMAN, Evelyn Sibley.** *The Shy Stegosaurus of Cricket Creek.* **Gr. 5–7.**

Joey, Joan, and a shy dinosaur named George capture a thief. The sequel is *The Shy Stegosaurus of Indian Springs* (1962).

Illus. by Hubert Buel, Doubleday, 1955, 218 pp., o.p.

(BL 52:150; HB 31:377; LJ 80:2386)

LAUMER, Keith. *The Shape Changer: A Science Fiction Novel.* See Chapter 5A, Alternate Worlds or Histories.

LAWSON, Robert. *Ben and Me: A New and Astonishing Life of Benjamin Franklin as Written by His Good Mouse, Amos: Lately Discovered.* See Chapter 2, Animal Fantasy.

LAWSON, Robert. *Captain Kidd's Cat: Being the True and Dolorous Chronicle of Wm. Kidd, Gentleman and Merchant of New York; Late Captain of the Adventure Galley; Of the Vicissitudes Attending His Unfortunate Cruise in Eastern Waters, Of His Unjust Trial and Execution, as Narrated by His Faithful Cat, McDermot, Who Ought to Know.* See Chapter 2, Animal Fantasy.

LAWSON, Robert. *The Fabulous Flight.* See Chapter 7, Magic Adventure Fantasy.

LAWSON, Robert. *I Discover Columbus: A True Chronicle of the Great Admiral and His Finding of the New World, Narrated by the Venerable Parrot Aurelio, Who Shared in the Glorious Venture.* See Chapter 2, Animal Fantasy.

2220 **LAWSON, Robert.** *McWhinney's Jaunt.* **Gr. 3–5.**

Professor McWhinney flies off to Hollywood on his z-gas powered bicycle.

Illus. by the author, Little, 1951, 77 pp., o.p.

(BL 48:16; CCBB 5:6; KR 19:294; LJ 76:1341)

LAWSON, Robert. *Mr. Revere and I: Being an Account of Certain Episodes in the Career of Paul Revere, Esq., as Recently Revealed by His Horse, Scheherazade, Late Pride of His Royal Majesty's 14th Regiment of Foot.* See Chapter 2, Animal Fantasy.

LAWSON, Robert. *Mr. Twigg's Mistake.* See Chapter 2, Animal Fantasy.

2221 LAWSON, Robert. *Smeller Martin.* **Gr. 4–6.**

✓   Davy Martin's extraordinary sense of smell helps the police solve a crime and makes him a celebrity at school.

Illus. by the author, Viking, 1950, 157 pp., o.p.

(BL 47:104; CCBB 4:5; HB 26:474; KR 18:470; LJ 75:2084)

2222 LAZARUS, Keo Felker. *The Shark in the Window.* **Gr. 4–6.**

Shelly's new pet shark can swim through the air.

Illus. by Laurel Schindelman, Morrow, 1972, 159 pp., o.p.

(BL 69:357; CCBB 26:45; KR 40:940; LJ 97:3806; Suth:241)

2223 LEE, Robert C. *The Iron Arm of Michael Glenn.* **Gr. 5–8.**

After Mike's pitching arm is accidentally exposed to Professor Von Heiner's experiment, he moves up from Little League baseball to pitching for the San Francisco Giants. The sequel is *The Day It Rained Forever* (1968).

Illus. by Al Fiorentino, Little, 1965, 153 pp., o.p.

(KR 33:752; LJ 90:4636)

LEE, Tanith. *Princess Hynchatti and Some Other Surprises.* See Chapter 3, Fantasy Collections.

2224 LEESON, Robert (Arthur). *Genie on the Loose.* **Gr. 6–8.**

Keeping wily Abdul the genie in check proves to be more difficult than Alec Bowden bargained for. This is the sequel to the British book *The Third Class Genie* (1975).

Hamish Hamilton, 1984, 127 pp., o.p.

(BBC:208; BL 81:524; SLJ Jan 1985 p. 87)

2225 LE GRAND (Henderson). *How Baseball Began in Brooklyn.* **Gr. 3–5.**

It seems that baseball was accidentally invented in New Amsterdam by ten Dutch colonial boys and a Native American.

Illus. by the author, Abingdon, 1958, 58 pp., o.p.

(BL 54:540; CCBB 11:97; Eakin:205; HB 34:108; LJ 83:1604)

2226 LE GRAND (Henderson). *How Space Rockets Began.* **Gr. 3–5.**

Windwagon Smith invents a steam wagon that flies to the moon.

Illus. by the author, Abingdon, 1960, 64 pp., o.p.

(HB 36:289; KR 28:89; LJ 85:2040)

2227 LE GRAND (Henderson). *Matilda.* **Gr. 4–6.**

A goat named Matilda becomes a student at Columbia University.

Illus. by the author, Abingdon, 1956, 63 pp., o.p.

(BL 53:52; Eakin:205; KR 24:353; LJ 81:2041)

LE GUIN, Ursula K(roeber). *Solomon Leviathan's Nine Hundred and Thirty First Trip Around the World.* See Chapter 2, Animal Fantasy.

LEROE, Ellen. *Leap Frog Friday.* See Chapter 7, Magic Adventure Fantasy.

LEROY, Gen. *Taxi Cat and Huey.* See Chapter 2, Animal Fantasy.

LE VERT, John. *The Flight of the Cassowary.* See Chapter 1, Allegorical Fantasy and Literary Fairy Tales.

2228   LEVITIN, Sonia (Wolff). *Jason and the Money Tree.* **Gr. 4–6.**

The ten-dollar bill Jason's grandfather gave him sprouts into a money tree, but leaves him with the problem of accounting for his sudden wealth.

Illus. by Pat Porter, Harcourt, 1974, 121 pp., o.p.

(BL 70:1057; CCBB 27:180; KR 42:300; LJ 99:2274)

LEVOY, Myron. *The Magic Hat of Mortimer Wintergreen.* See Chapter 10, Witchcraft and Sorcery Fantasy.

2229   LIFTON, Betty Jean (Kirschner). *The One-Legged Ghost.* **Gr. 1–4.**

✓   The villagers decide that the strange bamboo object that fell from the sky must be a god.

Illus. by Fuku Akino, Atheneum, 1968, 37 pp., o.p.

(BL 65:314; CCBB 22:63; KR 36:1163; LJ 93:4396; Suth:251)

LILLINGTON, Kenneth (James). *An Ash-Blond Witch.* See Chapter 10, Witchcraft and Sorcery Fantasy.

LILLINGTON, Kenneth (James). *Jonah's Mirror.* See Chapter 5C, Travel to Other Worlds.

LINDENBAUM, Pija. *Else-Marie and Her Seven Little Daddies.* See Chapter 7, Magic Adventure Fantasy.

2230   LINDGREN, Astrid. *Pippi Longstocking.* **Gr. 4–6. (Orig. Swedish pub. 1945.)**

✓   Life is never dull for Annika and Tommy after the strongest child in the world moves in next door with her pet monkey and horse. The sequels are *Pippi Goes on Board* (1957; British title: *Pippi Goes Abroad*), *Pippi in the South Seas* (1959), and *Pippi on the Run* (1976).

Trans. by Florence Lamborn, illus. by Louis Glanzman, Viking, 1950, 158 pp. (0-670-55745-5); Buccaneer, 1981 (repr. of 1950 ed.), LB(0-89966-338-9); Puffin, 1988, pap. (0-14-032772-X)

(BL 47:208; CC:523; CCBB 4:21; Ch&Bks:273; HB 26:376; KR 18:515; LJ 75:1754)

2231   LINDSAY, Norman (Alfred William). *The Magic Pudding: Being the Adventures of Bunyip Bluegum and His Friends Bill Barnacle and Sam Sawnoff.* **Gr. 3–5. (Orig. Australian pub. 1918.)**

A koala, a sailor, and a penguin find a magic pudding.

Illus. by the author, Farrar, 1936, 159 pp., o.p.

(LJ 61:809, 62:38; TLS 1936 p. 974)

LINKLATER, Eric (Robert Russell). *The Pirates in the Deep Green Sea.* See Chapter 5C, Travel to Other Worlds.

2232   **LISLE, Janet Taylor.** *The Dancing Cats of Applesap.* **Gr. 4–6.**

Ten-year-old Melba vows to save the drugstore home of Miss Toonie's fabulous dancing cats.

Illus. by Joelle Shefts, Bradbury, 1984, 169 pp., o.p.; Bantam, 1985, pap. (0-553-15348-X); Macmillan, 1993, pap., 176 pp. (0-689-71687-7)

(BBC:208; BL 80:1550; CCBB 37:208; SLJ Oct 1984 p. 159)

LISLE, Janet Taylor. *The Great Dimpole Oak.* See Chapter 1, Allegorical Fantasy and Literary Fairy Tales.

2233   **LIVELY, Penelope (Margaret Low).** *Uninvited Ghosts and Other Stories.* **Gr.**
✓   **4–6. (Orig. British pub. 1984.)**

Eight hilarious tales about ghosts, a dragon, and a Martian who invade ordinary family life.

Illus. by John Lawrence, Dutton, 1985, 119 pp., o.p.

(BBC:208; BL 81:1459; CC:580; CCBB 38:189; Ch&Bks:262; HB 61:450; KR 53:34; SLJ Aug 1985 p. 68; Suth 4:251; TLS 1984 p. 1381)

LOBE, Mira. *The Grandma in the Apple Tree.* See Chapter 7, Magic Adventure Fantasy.

LOCKE, Angela. *Mr. Mullett Owns a Cloud.* See Chapter 7, Magic Adventure Fantasy.

2234   **LOFTING, Hugh.** *The Story of Doctor Dolittle.* **Gr. 3–6.**
✓   When a great plague strikes the animals of Africa, Doctor Dolittle, the best animal doctor in the world, travels to Africa to save them. Lofting's depiction of black Africans has been criticized as racist; the Delacorte revised editions have changed or eliminated the prejudicial passages. The sequels are *The Voyages of Doctor Dolittle* (1922; John Newbery Medal, 1923; rev. ed., 1988), *Doctor Dolittle's Post Office* (1923), *Doctor Dolittle's Circus* (1924; Delacorte, 1988; Peter Smith, 1989), *Doctor Dolittle and the Green Canary* (1924, 1950, 1989), *Doctor Dolittle's Zoo* (1925), *Doctor Dolittle's Caravan* (1926), *Doctor Dolittle's Garden* (1927), *Doctor Dolittle in the Moon* (1928), *Gub-Gub's Book: An Encyclopedia of Food* (1932), *Doctor Dolittle's Return* (1933), *Doctor Dolittle and the Secret Lake* (1948), and *Doctor Dolittle's Puddleby Adventures* (1952). *Doctor Dolittle: A Treasury* (Dell, 1986, pap.) is a collection of tales.

Illus. by the author, Lippincott, 1920, 172 pp., o.p.; Delacorte, 1988 (rev. ed.) (0-385-29662-2), pap. (0-685-18953-8)

(BBC:209; BL 19:193, 84:1838; Bookshelf 1932 p. 8; Ch&Bks:279; HB 24:341; Mahony 2:284; Moore:426)

LORD, Beman. *The Perfect Pitch.* See Chapter 7, Magic Adventure Fantasy.

McBRATNEY, Sam. *The Ghosts of Hungryhouse Lane.* See Chapter 4, Ghost Fantasy.

2235   **MacDONALD, Betty (Campbell Bard).** *Mrs. Piggle-Wiggle.* **Gr. 2–5.**

Mrs. Piggle-Wiggle has magical cures for all children's ailments, including the won't-pick-up-toys cure, the answer-backer cure, and the selfishness cure. The sequels are *Mrs. Piggle-Wiggle's Farm* (1954), *Hello, Mrs. Piggle-Wiggle* (1957), and *Mrs. Piggle-Wiggle's Magic* (1957).

Lippincott, 1947, illus. by Richard Bennett, 118 pp., o.p.; illus. by Hilary Knight, Harper, 1957 (rev. ed.), 118 pp. (0-397-31712-3), 1985, pap. (0-06-440148-0)

(BBC:209; BL 43:260; CC:528; HB 23:213; KR 15:127; LJ 72:590, 739)

McHUGH, Elizabet. *Beethoven's Cat.* See Chapter 2, Animal Fantasy.

2236 McINERNY, Ralph M. *Quick As a Dodo.* **Gr. 6 up.**

Dormer, a literate dodo who hatches from a strange Easter egg, decides to free a caged rabbit and escape from his owner's home.

Illus. by Pam Butterworth, Juniper, 1977, o.p.; Vanguard, 1978, 116 pp., o.p.

(BL 75:27, 39; LJ 103:973)

MacKELLAR, William. *Alfie and Me and the Ghost of Peter Stuyvesant.* See Chapter 4, Ghost Fantasy.

2237 McNAUGHTON, Colin. *Jolly Roger and the Pirates of Abdul the Skinhead.* **Gr. 3–5.**

Roger joins a pirate band to escape the demands of his mother, who retaliates by enslaving the entire band, in this Gilbert and Sullivanesque melodrama.

Illus. by the author, Simon & Schuster, 1988, 48 pp., o.p.

(BL 85:940; CCBB 42:129; SLJ Mar 1989 p 166)

MACOUREK, Milos. *Max and Sally and the Phenomenal Phone.* See Chapter 7, Magic Adventure Fantasy.

2238 **MAHY, Margaret (May).** *The Birthday Burglar & A Very Wicked Headmistress.*
✓ **Gr. 2–6. (Orig. New Zealand pub. 1984.)**

In the first of these two wacky tales, young Bassington decides to steal other people's birthdays; in the second, evil Miss Taffeta opens a boarding school for wealthy children, and to save money she pretends to be all of the teachers.

Illus. by Margaret Chamberlain, Godine, 1988, 137 pp. (0-87923-720-1); Morrow, 1993, pap. (0-688-12470-4)

(BL 85:580; CCBB 42:47; KR 56:1244; SLJ Dec 1989 p. 109; TLS 1984 p. 1458)

2239 **MAHY, Margaret (May).** *The Blood-and-Thunder Adventure on Hurricane*
✓ *Peak.* **Gr. 4–6. (Orig. New Zealand pub. 1989.)**

Huxley and Zaza Hammond are new students at the Unexpected School atop Hurricane Peak, run by a magician named Mr. Warlock whose true love, Belladonna Doppler, is being pursued by the nefarious Sir Quincey Judd-Sprockett. *The Pirates' Mixed-Up Voyage: Dark Doings in the Thousand Islands* (Dial, 1993; see below) is also set in Hookywalker.

Illus. by Wendy Smith, Macmillan, 1989, 144 pp. (0-689-50488-8); Dell, 1991, pap. (0-440-40422-3)

(BL 86:460; CC:529; CCBB 43:38; HB 65:772; HBG 1[July–Dec 1989]:81; KR 57:1162; SLJ Oct 1989 p. 120; TLS 1989 p. 37)

2240 **MAHY, Margaret (May).** *Bubble Trouble and Other Poems and Stories.* **Gr. 3–6.**
✓ **(Orig. New Zealand pub. 1991.)**

Two silly stories and three funny poems, including "The Gargling Gorilla" and "Bubble Trouble."

Illus. by the author, MacMillan, 1992, 80 pp. (0-689-50557-4)

(BL 89:664; CCBB 46:80; HBG 4[Spring 1993]:59; KR 60:1258; SLJ Oct 1992 p. 118)

2241 **MAHY, Margaret (May).** *The Chewing-Gum Rescue and Other Stories.* **Gr. 3–5.**
(Orig. New Zealand pub. 1982.)

Eleven whimsical short stories, including "The Devil and the Corner Grocer" and "The World's Highest Tray Cloth."

Illus. by Jan Omerod, Overlook, 1991, 141 pp. (0-87951424-8)

(HBG 3[Fall 1992]:267; KR 59:1595; SLJ Feb 1992 p. 87)

MAHY, Margaret (May). *The Door in the Air and Other Stories.* See Chapter 7, Magic Adventure Fantasy.

2242 **MAHY, Margaret (May).** *The Great Piratical Rumbustification, and The Librar-*
✓ *ian and the Robbers.* **Gr. 3–6. (Orig. pub. in New Zealand, 1978.)**

Two humorous stories about a pirate babysitter and a beautiful librarian who rescues herself from kidnappers.

Illus. by Quentin Blake, Godine, 1986, 64 pp. (0-87923-629-9); Morrow, 1993, pap. (0-688-12469-0)

(CC:529; CCBB 40:92; KR 54:1584; SLJ Mar 1987 p. 163; Suth 4:262; TLS 1978 p. 1398)

2243 **MAHY, Margaret (May).** *The Great White Man-Eating Shark: A Cautionary*
✓✓ *Tale.* **Gr. K–4. (Orig. New Zealand pub. 1989.)**

Norvin's shark costume and sharklike behavior clear the Caramel Cove waters of human swimmers but attract a love-struck female shark.

Illus. by Jonathan Allen, Dial, 1990, 32 pp. (0-8037-0749-5)

(BL 86:1168; CC:673; HB 66:193; HBG 1[Jan 1990]:211; KR 58:181; SLJ Jan 1990 p. 86, Dec 1990 p. 23)

2244 **MAHY, Margaret (May).** *Nonstop Nonsense.* **Gr. 4–7. (Orig. New Zealand pub.**
✓ **1977.)**

Humorous stories and nonsense verse about book ghosts, a poetic cat, a word witch, and a green-toothed good-hearted monster.

Illus. by Quentin Blake, Macmillan, 1989, 120 pp. (0-689-50483-7)

(BL 85:1551; CCBB 42:257; HB 56:496; SLJ May 1989 p. 110)

2245 **MAHY, Margaret (May).** *The Pirates' Mixed-Up Voyage: Dark Doings in the*
✓ *Thousand Islands.* **Gr. 4–6. (Orig. New Zealand pub. 1983.)**

Lionel Wafer and his Ye Olde Pirate Shippe Tea Shoppe staff decide to become real pirates, bent on stealing a huge diamond doorknob owned by a legendary millionaire. This story, like *The Blood and Thunder Adventure on Hurricane Peak* (McElderry, 1989; see above) is set in Hookywalker.

Illus. by Margaret Chamberlain, Dial, 1993, 180 pp. (0-80371350-9)

(BL 89:908; HB 69:334; HBG 4[Fall 1993]:301; KR 61:461; SLJ Apr 1993 p. 124)

2246 **MAHY, Margaret (May).** *Raging Robots and Unruly Uncles.* **Gr. 4–6. (Orig.**
✓ **New Zealand pub. 1981.)**

Prudence detests Lilly Rose Blossom, the blond, blue-eyed robot gift from her seven virtuous cousins, and sends them a crime-minded robot named Nadger in return.

Illus. by Peter Stevenson, Overlook, 1993, 94 pp. (0-87951-469-8)

(BL 89:1230; HBG 4[Fall 1993]:301; KR 61:65: SLJ Mar 1993 p. 214; TLS Nov 20, 1981 p. 1357)

2247 **MANES, Stephen.** *Chicken Trek: The Third Strange Thing That Happened to Oscar Noodleman.* **Gr. 4–6.**

Oscar and his cousin, Dr. Prechtwinkle, attempt to win a prize offered by the Bagful O' Chicken Company, using a Picklemobile that can travel in a matter of seconds to any spot on Earth. This is the sequel to two humorous science fiction tales: *That Game from Outer Space* (1983) and *The Oscar J. Noodleman Television Network* (1984).

Illus. by Ron Barrett, Dutton, 1987, 128 pp., o.p.; Bantam, 1989, pap. (0-553-15716-7)

(BL 83:1750; CCBB 41:13; KR 55:860; SLJ Aug 1987 p. 86)

MANES, Stephen. *Monstra vs. Irving.* See Chapter 7, Magic Adventure Fantasy.

2248   MANES, Stephen. *Some of the Adventures of Rhode Island Red.* **Gr. 3–6.**

Folk-hero Rhode Island Red is an egg-sized boy who was raised by chickens, can out-smart foxes, and aims to marry the mayor's daughter.

Illus. by William Joyce, Harper, 1990, 117 pp. LB(0-397-32348-4), 1993, pap. (0-06-440358-0)

(BL 86:1994; CCBB 43:272; HBG 1[Jan–June 1990]:255; SLJ July 1990 p. 77)

2249   MANNING, Rosemary (Joy). *Dragon in Danger.* **Gr. 4–6. (Orig. British pub. 1959.)**

The first dragon to appear in five hundred years, R. Dragon is offered a starring role in the town's annual pageant. This is the sequel to *Green Smoke* (1957), and is followed by *The Dragon's Quest* (1962) and *Dragon in Summer* (British).

Illus. by Constance Marshall, Doubleday, 1960, 169 pp., o.p.

(KR 28:775; LJ 85:4569; TLS May 29, 1959 p. xiii)

MARSHALL, James (Edward). *Rats on the Roof: And Other Stories.* See Chapter 2, Animal Fantasy.

MARSHALL, James (Edward). *A Summer in the South.* See Chapter 2, Animal Fantasy.

MARSHALL, James (Edward). *Taking Care of Carruthers.* See Chapter 2, Animal Fantasy.

2250   MARTIN, Ann M(atthews). *Ma and Pa Dracula.* **Gr. 3–6.**

After Jonathan Primave discovers that his parents are vampires, he demands to be allowed to stay awake during the day and go to school like other children.

Illus. by Dirk Zimmer, Holiday, 1989, 112 pp. (0-8234-0781-0); Scholastic, 1991, pap. (0-5904-3828-X)

(BL 86:672; CCBB 43:142; HBG 1[July–Dec 1989]:84; KR 57:1330; SLJ Sept. 1989 p. 256)

2251   MELENDEZ, Francisco. *The Mermaid and the Major: or, The True Story of the Invention of the Submarine.* **Gr. 4 up. (Orig. Spanish pub. 1987.)**

Major Monday falls in love with a mermaid and invents a submarine to follow her into the depths of the sea. Awarded Spain's Ministry of Culture National Prize for Illustration, 1987.

Illus. by the author, adapt. by Robert Morton, trans. by William Dyckes, Abrams, 1991, 64 pp. (0-8109-3619-4)

(HBG 3[Spring 1992]:70; KR 59:1231; SLJ Jan 1992 p. 114)

2252   MENDOZA, George. *Gwot! Horribly Funny Hairticklers.* **Gr. 3–5.**

Three ghastly tales: a huge black snake that grows bigger each time its head is chopped off, an old woman who eats a hairy toe, and the hunt for the horrible Gumberoo.

Illus. by Steven Kellogg, Harper, 1967, 41 pp., o.p.

(KR 35:1048; LJ 92:4615)

2253   MERRILL, Jean (Fairbanks). *The Pushcart War.* **Gr. 5–7.**

✓   Traffic congestion in New York City brings on a war between the truck drivers and the pushcart owners.

Illus. by Ronni Solbert, Harper, 1964, 1992, 222 pp., LB(0-06-020822-8); Dell, 1987, pap., 224 pp. (0-440-47147-8); Peter Smith, 1988, o.p.

(BL 61:219, 80:96; CC:532; Ch&Bks:248; Eakin:223; HB 40:378; LJ 89:2828)

2254 **MERRILL, Jean (Fairbanks).** *The Toothpaste Millionaire.* **Gr. 4–5.**

✓ Eleven-year-old Lucas starts his own toothpaste factory to compete with the higher-priced name-brand toothpastes.

Houghton, 1974, 96 pp. (0-395-18511-4), 1993, pap. (0-395-66954-5)

(BL 70:1254; CC:533; CCBB 28:49; HB 50:137; KR 42:480; Suth 2:316)

MILLER, Judi. *Ghost in My Soup.* See Chapter 4, Ghost Fantasy.

MILNE, A(lan) A(lexander). *Prince Rabbit and the Princess Who Could Not Laugh.* See Chapter 1, Allegorical Fantasy and Literary Fairy Tales.

MILNE, A(lan) A(lexander). *Winnie-the-Pooh.* See Chapter 9, Toy Fantasy.

MINOT, Stephen. *Surviving the Flood.* See Chapter 5B, Myth Fantasy.

MONSELL, Mary Elise. *Crackle Creek.* See Chapter 2, Animal Fantasy.

MONSELL, Mary Elise. *The Mysterious Cases of Mr. Pin.* See Chapter 2, Animal Fantasy.

MOORE, John. *Slay and Rescue.* See Chapter 5B, Myth Fantasy.

MOORE, Margaret Eileen. *Willie Without.* See Chapter 2, Animal Fantasy.

MORRESSY, John. *A Voice for Princess.* See Chapter 10, Witchcraft and Sorcery Fantasy.

MORRISON, Dorothy Nafus. *Vanishing Act.* See Chapter 7, Magic Adventure Fantasy.

2255 **MÜNCHAUSEN, Karl.** *The Adventures of Baron Münchausen.* **Gr. 3–6. (Orig. German pub. 1781–1783; U.S. pub. 1813.)**

These tales were originally printed anonymously in Germany, 1781–1783, and are sometimes attributed to Karl Friedrich Hieronymus, Baron Von Münchausen. They were translated into English and edited by Rudolf Erich Raspé in 1786, and first published in the U.S. (1813), entitled *Gulliver Redivivus; or the Curious and Entertaining Travels and Adventures by Sea and by Land of the Renowned Baron Munchausen; Including a Tour to the United States of America in the Year 1803; and the First Chapters of a Second Tour in 1816.* In *The Baron Rides Out* (Putnam, 1985, 1986), the fabulous Baron Münchausen travels to a Ceylonese jungle where he meets a gigantic alligator, a huge lion, and an enormous giant called Peter the Great. Two companion volumes, both edited by Adrian Mitchell, are: *The Baron on the Island of Cheese* (1986), and *The Baron All at Sea* (1987).

Illus. by W. Heath Robinson, Dutton, 1903 (entitled *The Surprising Travels and Adventures of Baron Münchausen*), o.p.; retold by John Martin (pseud. of Morgan Shepard), illus. by Gordon Ross, Houghton, 1921 (entitled *The Children's Münchausen*), o.p.; illus. by Gustave Doré, Pantheon, 1944, o.p.; retold by Erich Kästner, trans. by Richard Wilson and Clara Wilson, illus. by Walter Trier, Messner, 1951, 1957 (entitled *Baron Münchausen, His Wonderful Travels and Adventures*), o.p.; illus. by Fritz Kredel, Heritage, 1952 (entitled *The Singular Adventures of Baron Münchausen*), o.p.; retold by Angelita von Münchhausen, illus. by Harry Carter, Devin-Adair, 1960 (entitled: *The Real Münchhausen: Authentic Tales of the Fabulous Baron of Bodenwerder*), 224 pp. (0-8159-6701-2); ed. and illus. by Brian Robb, Deutsch, 1979 (orig. British pub. 1947; entitled *12 Adventures of the Celebrated Baron Münchausen*), o.p.; ed. by Adrian Mitchell, illus. by Patrick Benson, Putnam, 1986 (orig. British pub. 1985, entitled *The Baron Rides Out: A Baron Münchausen Tall Tale*), 28 pp., o.p.; adapt. by Peter Nickl, trans. by Elizabeth B.

Taylor, illus. by Binette Schroeder, North-South, 1992 (orig. Swiss pub. in this ed., 1977), (entitled: *The Wonderful Travels and Adventures of Baron Münchhausen*), 56 pp. (1-55858-134-0)

(BL 18:162, 25:87, 41:157; Bookshelf 1924–1925 p. 15, 1932 p. 23; HB 55:536; KR 12:483, 54:1451; LJ 69:1006, 86:575, 96:3470; SLJ Feb 1980 p. 60, May 1986 p. 82, Jan 1987 p. 76; TLS 1985 pp. 355, 1435)

2256 MURPHY, Jill. *Jeffrey Strangeways*. Gr. 3–6.

✓ Clumsy Jeffrey longs to become a knight, so he tells his mother he has been offered a job by Sir Walter of Winterwood and sets off to seek his dream.

Illus. by the author, Candlewick, 1992, 140 pp. (1-56402-018-5)

(BL 88:1840; CCBB 46:20; HBG 3[Fall 1992]:268; KR 60:673; SLJ May 1992 p. 114)

MURPHY, Jill. *The Worst Witch*. See Chapter 10, Witchcraft and Sorcery Fantasy.

2257 MYERS, Bernice. *Sidney Rella and the Glass Sneaker*. Gr. 2–4.

✓ In this Cinderella spoof, Sydney dreams of becoming a football hero, until his fairy god-mother magically takes over his household chores and provides a new uniform and a pair of glass sneakers.

Illus. by the author, Macmillan, 1985, 32 pp. (0-02-767790-7)

(BBC:210; BL 82:340; CCBB 39:155; Ch&Bks:289; SLJ Mar 1986 p. 150; Suth 4:300)

2258 MYERS, Walter Dean. *The Black Pearl and the Ghost; or, One Mystery after Another*. Gr. 2–4.

Two humorous mystery stories, one involving a stolen pearl and the other a haunted manor house.

Illus. by Robert M. Quackenbush, Viking, 1980, 40 pp., o.p.

(BL 76:1297; CCBB 33:180; HB 56:301; KR 48:514; SLJ May 1980 p. 85)

2259 NAPOLI, Donna Jo. *The Prince of the Pond: Otherwise Known as De Fawg Pin*.

✓ **Gr. 3–6.**

A female frog is mystified by the unfroglike behavior of a male she finds one day, tangled in a pile of human clothing, in this humorous version of "The Frog Prince."

Illus. by Judith Byron Schachner, Dutton, 1992, 151 pp. (0-525-44976-0)

(BL 89:909; CCBB 46:153; KR 60:1259; SLJ Oct 1992 p. 118)

2260 NASH, Mary (Hughes). *While Mrs. Coverlet Was Away*. Gr. 4–6.

✓ After their father and their housekeeper are both called out of town, Molly, Malcolm, and Todd manage on their own. The sequels are *Mrs. Coverlet's Magicians* (1961) and *Mrs. Coverlet's Detectives* (1965).

Illus. by Garrett Price, Little, 1958, 133 pp., o.p.

(BL 55:137; CCBB 12:52; Eakin:243; HB 34:386; KR 26:380; LJ 83:2502)

2261 NASTICK, Sharon. *Mr. Radagast Makes an Unexpected Journey*. Gr. 4–7.

A seventh grade class is amazed to find that their experiment in immaterialism has made their teacher, Mr. Radagast, disappear.

Illus. by Judy Glasser, Crowell, 1981, 85 pp., o.p.

(BL 77:1346; KR 49:504; SLJ May 1981 p. 67)

NAYLOR, Phyllis Reynolds. *Bernie and the Bessledorf Ghost*. See Chapter 4, Ghost Fantasy.

NAYLOR, Phyllis Reynolds. *The Grand Escape*. See Chapter 2, Animal Fantasy.

NESBIT (Bland), E(dith). *The Last of the Dragons.* See Chapter 1, Allegorical Fantasy and Literary Fairy Tales.

NIXON, Joan Lowery. *Magnolia's Mixed-Up Magic.* See Chapter 2, Animal Fantasy.

2262 **NÖSTLINGER, Christine.** *Konrad* **(British title:** *Conrad: The Hilarious Adven-*
✓✓ *tures of a Factory-made Child,* **1976). Gr. 4–6. (Orig. Austrian pub. 1975.)**

Despite his unexpected arrival, a canned, mail-order child named Konrad is allowed to move in with Mrs. Bartolotti, but his perfect behavior disturbs his new mother and angers his classmates. Mildred L. Batchelder Award, 1978.

Trans. by Anthea Bell, illus. by Carol Nicklaus, Watts, 1977, 135 pp., o.p.

(BL 74:482; CCBB 31:98; Ch&Bks:290; HB 53:665; SLJ Nov 1977 p. 60; Suth 2:339; TLS 1977 p. 348)

2263 **OAKLEY, Graham.** *Henry's Quest.* **Gr. 5 up.**
✓
Sometime in a future post-technology England, the king sends shepherd Henry off on a quest for the magical substance "gasoline," in order to win the hand of Princess Isolde.

Illus. by the author, Atheneum, 1986, 32 pp., o.p.

(BL 83:893, 902; CCBB 40:133; KR 54:1374; SLJ Dec 1986 p. 107; TLS 1986 p. 1345)

OLSON, Helen Kronberg. *The Strange Thing That Happened to Oliver Wendell Iscovitch.* See Chapter 7, Magic Adventure Fantasy.

ORMONDROYD, Edward. *Broderick.* See Chapter 2, Animal Fantasy.

ORMONDROYD, Edward. *David and the Phoenix.* See Chapter 7, Magic Adventure Fantasy.

OSBORNE, Mary Pope. *Dinosaurs Before Dark.* See Chapter 8, Time Travel Fantasy.

PAGET, F. E. *The Hope of the Katzekopfs; or, the Sorrow of Selfishness: A Fairy Tale.* See Chapter 1, Allegorical Fantasy and Literary Fairy Tales.

2264 **PALMER, David R.** *Threshold.* **Gr. 10 up.**
✓
Peter Cory is recruited as the savior of the universe by a beautiful witch who looks like Tinkerbell without wings, in this spoof of heroic fantasy. Two sequels are planned.

Bantam, 1985, pap., 274 pp. (0-553-24878-2)

(BBS:63; BL 82:468, 482; Kliatt 20[Spring 1986]:24; LJ Dec 1985 p. 130; VOYA 9:89)

PALMER, Mary. *The Dolmop of Dorkling.* See Chapter 5C, Travel to Other Worlds.

PALMER, Robin. *Wise House.* See Chapter 2, Animal Fantasy.

PARKER, (James) Edgar (Jr.). *The Dream of the Dormouse.* See Chapter 2, Animal Fantasy.

PARKER, (James) Edgar (Jr.). *The Question of a Dragon.* See Chapter 2, Animal Fantasy.

2265 **PARKER, (James) Edgar (Jr.).** *Rogue's Gallery.* **Gr. 4–6.**

A crime story spoof starring master criminal Hoimie-the-stoat, Reynolds the policefox, and Matou, a tomcat gone straight.

Illus. by the author, Pantheon, 1969, 63 pp., o.p.

(CCBB 23:104; KR 37:1113)

2266   PARKER, Nancy Winslow. *The Spotted Dog: The Strange Tale of a Witch's Revenge.* **Gr. 2–4.**

A witch turns the Cruikshank-Jones's baby, Eileen, into a dog, but the family doesn't seem to mind—they enjoy winning ribbons at dog shows.

Illus. by the author, Dodd, 1980, 46 pp., o.p.

(BL 77:407; KR 48:1395; SLJ Dec 1980 p. 54)

2267   PARRISH, Anne. *The Story of Appleby Capple.* **Gr. 3–5.**

✓   A boy has alphabetical adventures while searching for a rare zebra moth. John Newbery Medal Honor Book, 1951.

Illus. by the author, Harper, 1950, 184 pp., o.p.

(BL 47:225; CCBB 4:22; HB 26:457, 467, 27:20; KR 18:512; LJ 75:1745, 76:338)

PASCAL, Francine. *Hangin' Out with Cici.* See Chapter 8, Time Travel Fantasy.

PEABODY, Paul. *Blackberry Hollow.* See Chapter 2, Animal Fantasy.

PECK, Richard. *The Ghost Belonged to Me: A Novel.* See Chapter 4, Ghost Fantasy.

PEET, Bill (William Bartlett). *Big Bad Bruce.* See Chapter 2, Animal Fantasy.

PEET, Bill (William Bartlett). *The Whingdingdilly.* See Chapter 2, Animal Fantasy.

2268   PETRIE, Stuart. *The Voyage of Barracks.* **Gr. 4–6. (Orig. British pub. 1967.)**

An English family ties their house to a hot-air balloon and soars off around the world.

Illus. by the author, Meredith, 1968, 120 pp., o.p.

(BL 65:754; KR 36:643; LJ 93:3308; TLS 1967 p. 1133)

PINKWATER, D(aniel) Manus. *Blue Moose.* See Chapter 2, Animal Fantasy.

2269   PINKWATER, D(aniel) Manus. *The Frankenbagel Monster.* **Gr. 2–5.**

✓   Harold Frankenbagel creates Bagelnuculus in his quest to become the greatest bagel maker in history, but Harold must stop the monster bagel when it goes mad and heads off towards a lox warehouse.

Illus. by the author, Dutton, 1986, 24 pp., o.p.

(BL 83:356; HB 62:742; KR 54:1584; SLJ Oct 1986 p. 165)

2270   PINKWATER, D(aniel) Manus. *The Hoboken Chicken Emergency.* **Gr. 3–5.**

✓   Arthur Bobowicz's adoption of a 266-pound chicken meets with opposition from his parents, the mayor, and the townspeople.

Illus. by the author, Prentice-Hall, 1977, 1984, 83 pp. (0-13-392514-5), pap. (0-13-392499-8); Simon, 1990, pap., 94 pp. (0-671-66447-6)

(BL 73:1268; CC:546; CCBB 30:163; HB 53:316, 61:755; KR 45:166; SLJ Sept 1977 p. 134)

2271   PINKWATER, D(aniel) Manus. *Jolly Roger: A Dog of Hoboken.* **Gr. 3–5.**

Jolly Roger (half husky, half chow chow) is befriended by The Kid, but soon becomes the leader of the Hoboken dock dogs.

Illus. by the author, Lothrop, 1984, 64 pp. (0-688-03898-0)

(BL 82:69; HB 61:559; KR 53:35; SLJ Sept 1985 p. 138)

2272   PINKWATER, D(aniel) Manus. *The Last Guru.* **Gr. 5–7.**

After twelve-year-old Harold Blatz invests his racetrack winnings in a hamburger chain and becomes a billionaire, the Blatz family tries to escape their newfound fame by moving to a castle in the Bavarian Alps and then to a village in India.

Illus. by the author, Dodd, 1978, 115 pp., o.p.

(BL 75:548; CCBB 32:124; KR 46:1189; SLJ Nov 1978 p. 66)

2273   PINKWATER, D(aniel) Manus. *Lizard Music.* **Gr. 4–6.**

✓   Victor can't understand why lizards and the Chicken Man turn up wherever he goes, until he is taken to an invisible, lizard-run island.

Illus. by the author, Dodd, 1976, 157 pp., o.p.; Bantam, 1988, pap., 160 pp. (0-553-15605-5)

(BL 73:41, 80:96; CC:546; CCBB 30:112; HB 53:161; KR 44:846; SLJ Oct 1976 p. 110)

2274   PINKWATER, D(aniel) Manus. *The Muffin Fiend.* **Gr. 3–5.**

Inspector Charles LeChat tracks down an extraterrestrial muffin thief who needs thousands of muffins to fuel a rocket for his trip home.

Illus. by the author, Lothrop, 1986, 48 pp., LB(0-688-04275-9)

(CCBB 39:156; HB 62:324, KR 54:475; SLJ Aug 1986 p. 97)

2275   PINKWATER, D(aniel) Manus. *The Worms of Kukumlima.* **Gr. 5–8.**

Ronald Donald Almandotter, his grandfather, Seumas Finneganstein, and Sir Charles Pelicanstein go on a safari into wildest Kukumlima to capture a huge, intelligent worm.

Illus. by the author, Elsevier-Dutton, 1981, 152 pp., o.p.

(BL 77:1034; CCBB 35:35; KR 49:571; SLJ May 1981 p. 68; VOYA 5[Apr 1982]:41)

2276   PINKWATER, D(aniel) Manus. *Yobgorgle: Mystery Monster of Lake Ontario.* **Gr. 5–7.**

Only a corned beef sandwich will remove the curse on the captain of the "Flying Piggie" submarine.

Illus. by the author, Houghton, 1979, 138 pp., o.p.

(BL 76:126; KR 47:1068; SLJ Nov 1979 p. 80)

POCHOCKI, Ethel. *The Attic Mice.* See Chapter 2, Animal Fantasy.

2277   POMERANTZ, Charlotte. *Detective Poufy's First Case: Or the Missing Battery-Operated Pepper Grinder.* **Gr. 3–5.**

A lonely dragon named Dragobert turns out to be the robber who broke into Rosie Maloon's house and left all the electrical gadgets running.

Illus. by Marty Norman, Addison-Wesley, 1976, 64 pp., o.p.

(BL 73:476; KR 44:796; SLJ Dec 1976 p. 65)

POMERANTZ, Charlotte. *The Downtown Fairy Godmother.* See Chapter 7, Magic Adventure Fantasy.

2278   POPHAM, Hugh. *The Fabulous Voyage of the Pegasus.* **Gr. 4–6.**

Lee-O! sets sail on the Pegasus in search of a Narwhal and the sea god, Poseidon.

Illus. by Graham Oakley, Phillips, 1959, 150 pp., o.p.

(HB 35:301; KR 27:176; LJ 84:1700)

2279   PORTER, David Lord. *Help! Let Me Out!* **Gr. 2–5.**

✓   Hugo learns ventriloquism and throws his voice, only to have the voice take off for a life of its own.

Illus. by David Macaulay, Houghton, 1982, 32 pp., o.p.

(BL 79:315; CCBB 36:75; KR 50:676; SLJ Sept 1982 p. 110)

POSTGATE, Oliver, and FIRMIN, Peter. *King of the Nogs.* See Chapter 1, Allegorical Fantasy and Literary Fairy Tales.

2280 PREUSSLER, Otfried. *The Robber Hotzenplotz.* Gr. 5–7. (Orig. pub. in Germany.)

Kasperl and Seppel are trapped in the hideout of the notorious bandit, Hotzenplotz. The sequels are *Further Adventures of the Robber Hotzenplotz* (1971), and *The Final Adventures of the Robber Hotzenplotz* (British).

Trans. by Anthea Bell, illus. by F. J. Tripp, Abelard-Schuman, 1965, 126 pp., o.p.

(KR 33:107; LJ 90:2409; TLS 1964 p. 1081)

2281 PREUSSLER, Otfried. *The Wise Men of Schilda.* Gr. 4–6. (Orig. pub. in Germany.)

The foolish inhabitants of Schilda try to prove their cleverness to the rest of the world.

Trans. by Anthea Bell, illus. by F. J. Tripp, Abelard-Schuman, 1963, 185 pp., o.p.

(BL 60:44; CCBB 17:128; HB 39:286; LJ 88:2553)

2282 PULLMAN, Philip. *Spring-Heeled Jack.* Gr. 3–7. (Orig. British pub. 1989.)

✓ Rose, Lily, and Ned escape from an orphanage in Victorian England, only to be captured by Mack the Knife's gang, and saved by the hero Spring-Heeled Jack.

Illus. by David Mostyn, Knopf, 1991, 112 pp. (0-679-91057-3), pap. (0-679-81057-9)

(CCBB 45:46; HBG 3[July–Dec 1991]:72; KR 59:793; SLJ Dec 1991 p. 117)

QUACKENBUSH, Robert M. *Express Train to Trouble: A Miss Mallard Mystery.* See Chapter 2, Animal Fantasy.

2283 RASKIN, Ellen. *Figgs and Phantoms.* Gr. 5–7.

✓ Mona Lisa Newton does not appreciate her kooky relatives—her tapdancing mother, twin brothers Romulus and Remus, contortionist Truman Figg, and cousin Fido Figg—until her beloved uncle dies. John Newbery Medal Honor Book, 1975.

Illus. by the author, Dutton, 1974, 1977, 160 pp. (0-525-29680-8); Puffin, 1989, pap. (0-14-032944-7)

(BBC:212: BL 71:46; CC:548; CCBB 28:98; HB 50:138; KR 42:425; LJ 99:1451, 1475, 3247; Suth 2:374)

2284 RASKIN, Ellen. *The Mysterious Disappearance of Leon (I Mean Noel).* Gr. 5–7.

✓ Married at five and seven years of age to solve their parents' business problems, Caroline (Little Dumpling) and Leon (Noel) Carillon don't see each other again for fourteen clue-, puzzle-, and secret code-filled years.

Illus. by the author, Dutton, 1971, 1977, 149 pp., o.p.; Puffin, 1989, pap. (0-14-032945-5)

(BL 68:394, 670; CC:548; CCBB 25:79; HB 48:51; KR 39:1122; LJ 96:4160; Suth:323)

2285 RASKIN, Ellen. *The Tattooed Potato and Other Clues.* Gr. 5–7.

✓ Dickory Dock's detective work leads her to the blackmailers of a brilliant artist and the murderer of her parents.

Dutton, 1975, 170 pp. (0-525-40805-3)

(BL 71:967; CC:520; CCBB 29:52; HB 51:271; KR 43:457; SLJ Apr 1975 p. 69, Dec 1975 p. 32; Suth 2:374; TLS 1976 p. 1548)

RAYNER, Mary. *Mrs. Pig Gets Cross; and Other Stories.* See Chapter 2, Animal Fantasy.

RAZZI, Jim, and RAZZI, Mary. *The Search for King Pup's Tomb.* See Chapter 2, Animal Fantasy.

REID BANKS, Lynne. *The Magic Hare.* See Chapter 1, Allegorical Fantasy and Literary Fairy Tales.

2286   REIT, Seymour. *Benvenuto.* **Gr. 3–5.**

Paolo brings home a baby dragon from summer camp.

Illus. by Will Winslow, Addison-Wesley, 1974, 126 pp., o.p.

(BL 70:878; KR 42:301; LJ 99:2276)

RICHEMONT, Enid. *The Magic Skateboard.* See Chapter 7, Magic Adventure Fantasy.

2287   RICHLER, Mordecai. *Jacob Two-Two Meets the Hooded Fang.* **Gr. 3–5. (Orig. Canadian pub. 1975.)**

Jacob is teased for his habit of saying everything twice, but he proves to be courageous after his capture by the Slimers and their chief, the Hooded Fang. Winner, Canadian Library Association Best Book of the Year for Children, 1976. The sequel is *Jacob Two-Two and the Dinosaur* (1987).

Illus. by Fritz Wegner, Knopf, 1975, 87 pp., o.p.; Bantam, 1987, pap. (0-317-64199-9)

(CCBB 28:184; KR 43:568; SLJ Sept 1975 p. 90; TLS 1976 p. 376)

2288   RIDLEY, Philip. *Krindlekrax; or, How Ruskin Splinter Battled a Horrible Monster and Saved His Entire Neighborhood.* **Gr. 3–6. (Orig. British pub. 1991.)**

Nine-year-old Ruskin, afraid of the local bully, has dreams of becoming a hero. They come true after he climbs down into the dark sewer and tames Krindlekrax, the dragon who lives in the depths. Smarties Prize for Children's Books, 1991.

Illus. by Gary Hovland, Knopf, 1992, 144 pp., LB(0-679-91764-0)

(BL 88:1280; HBG 3[Fall 1992]:269; KR 60:471; SLJ Mar 1992 p. 241)

2289   RINKOFF, Barbara (Jean). *Elbert, the Mind Reader.* **Gr. 4–6.**

Elbert's new filling enables him to tune in on people's thoughts, a talent he uses to impress the football coach so that he can join the team.

Illus. by Paul Galdone, Lothrop, 1967, 112 pp., o.p.

(BL 64:594; CCBB 21:65; KR 35:809; LJ 92:3855)

2290   RIOS, Tere (Teresa). *The Fifteenth Pelican.* **Gr. 4–6.**

On the windy island of San Juan, Sister Bertrille's large white headpiece enables her to fly like a pelican.

Illus. by Arthur King, Doubleday, 1965, 118 pp., o.p.

(KR 33:782; LJ 90:4076)

ROBERTS, Willo Davis. *The Magic Book.* See Chapter 7, Magic Adventure Fantasy.

RODDA, Emily. *The Pigs Are Flying!* See Chapter 7, Magic Adventure Fantasy.

2291   RODGERS (Guettel), Mary. *Freaky Friday.* **Gr. 5–7.**

✓✓   One morning, Annabel Adams awakens to discover that she has turned into her mother, and that her mother has taken over Annabel's own body. In *A Billion for Boris* (1974, 1976), a television set that broadcasts tomorrow's programs gives Annabel the urge to do good deeds, but inspires her friend Boris to make a fortune at the racetrack. In *Summer*

Switch (1982), Annabel's brother, Ben, inadvertently trades bodies with his father while Ben is at summer camp and his father is on a business trip in Hollywood.

Harper, 1972, 155 pp., LB(0-06-025049-6), 1977, pap. (0-06-080392-4)

(BL 68:910, 80:96; CC:550; Ch&Bks:290; CCBB 26:15; HB 48:378; JHC:407; Kies:143; KR 40:267; LJ 97:1608)

ROGERS, Mark E. *The Adventures of Samurai Cat.* See Chapter 2, Animal Fantasy.

2292 ROUNDS, David. *Cannonball River Tales.* **Gr. 3–6.**

Five tall-tale episodes about North Dakotan Tom Terry, including one about finding a dragon's silver.

Illus. by Alix Berenzy, Sierra, 1992, 104 pp. (0-87156-577-3)

(BL 89:909; KR 60:1447; SLJ Dec 1992 p. 113)

2293 ROUNDS, Glen (Harold). *The Day the Circus Came to Lone Tree.* **Gr. 3–4.**

✓   The townspeople of Lone Tree are treated to some unwelcome entertainment when a circus lion and his trainer stampede all of the town's livestock. The sequels are *Mr. Yowder and the Lion Roar Capsules* (1976), *Mr. Yowder and the Steamboat* (1977), *Mr. Yowder and the Giant Bull Snake* (1978), *Mr. Yowder and the Train Robbers* (1981), and *Mr. Yowder and the Windwagon* (1983). Three of the sequels have been published in a single volume entitled *Mr. Yowder, the Peripatetic Sign Painter* (1980; see below).

Illus. by the author, Holiday, 1973, 39 pp., o.p.

(BL 70:545; CCBB 27:85; Ch&Bks:290; HB 52:393; KR 41:1155; LJ 99:203; Suth 2:387)

2294 ROUNDS, Glen (Harold). *Mr. Yowder, the Peripatetic Sign Painter: Three Tall Tales.* **Gr. 3–5.**

Three tall tales about Mr. Yowder, now published in one volume, in which he sells canned lion roars, travels through Manhattan via steamboat, and hunts buffalo on a giant bull snake.

Holiday, 1980, 126 pp., o.p.

(BL 76:1132; KR 48:912; SLJ Sept 1980 p. 63)

RUFF, Matt. *Fool on the Hill.* See Chapter 7, Magic Adventure Fantasy.

RUSHDIE, Salman. *Haroun and the Sea of Stories.* See Chapter 5A, Alternate Worlds or Histories.

SABERHAGEN, Fred. *Empire of the East.* See Chapter 5A, Alternate Worlds or Histories.

2295 SACHAR, Louis. *Wayside School Is Falling Down.* **Gr. 3–6.**

Thirty wacky episodes about the children in Mrs. Jewls's classroom on the top floor of the thirty-story-high Wayside School. This is the sequel to *Sideways Stories from Wayside School* (Follett, 1978; Knopf, 1990). *Sideways Arithmetic from Wayside School* (Scholastic, 1989) is a related nonfiction work.

Illus. by Joel Schick, Lothrop, 1989, 192 pp. (0-688-07868-8); Avon, 1990, pap. (0-380-75484-3)

(BL 85:1553; KR 57:127; SLJ May 1989 p. 111)

2296 SANDBURG, Carl (August). *Rootabaga Stories.* **Gr. 4 up. (Orig. pub. 1922.)**

✓   A collection of forty-nine humorous tales written by the well-known poet. *Rootabaga Pigeons* (1923, 1974) and *Potato Face* (1930) are companion volumes. An omnibus volume was published in 1936. *More Rootabagas* (Knopf, 1993) contains ten previously unpublished tales.

Illus. by Maud Petersham and Miska Petersham, Harcourt, 1951, 218 pp., o.p.; illus. by Michael Hague, Harcourt, 1988, (entitled: *Rootabaga Stories: Part One*), 192 pp. (0-15-269061-1), 1990, pap. (0-15-269065-4); illus. by Michael Hague, Harcourt, 1989 (entitled: *Rootabaga Stories: Part Two*), 179 pp. (0-15-269062-X), 1990, pap. (0-15-269063-8)

(BL 19:92, 85:580; CC:581; Ch&Bks:290; HB 27:129; Moore:426; SLJ Feb 1989 p. 82)

SCARBOROUGH, Elizabeth Ann. *Bronwyn's Bane.* See Chapter 5A, Alternate Worlds or Histories.

2297 **SCARBOROUGH, Elizabeth Ann.** *The Drastic Dragon of Draco, Texas.* **Gr. 10 up.**

Even after she is captured by Indians and sold to the infamous Frank Drake, journalist Pelagia Harper never imagines she would meet a fire-breathing dragon in the Wild West.

Bantam, 1986, pap., 247 pp., o.p.

(Kies:66; LJ May 15, 1986 p. 81)

2298 **SCARBOROUGH, Elizabeth Ann.** *The Harem of Aman Akbar; or The Djinn Decanted.* **Gr. 10 up.**

A nobleman turned into an ass while searching for a fourth wife is forced to rely on his other three wives and his mother to rescue him.

Bantam, 1984, pap., 215 pp., o.p.

(BL 81:561, 583; LJ 109:1775)

SCHEFFLER, Ursel. *Rinaldo: The Sly Fox.* See Chapter 2, Animal Fantasy.

SCHWED, Antonia Holding. *Noah and Me: A Novel.* See Chapter 2, Animal Fantasy.

2299 **SCIESZKA, Jon.** *The Frog Prince, Continued.* **Gr. 1–4.**

✓ The former frog and the princess whose kiss transformed him into a prince are not happily married, so the prince decides to find someone who can change him back.

Illus. by Steve Johnson, Viking, 1991, 32 pp. (0-670-83421-1)

(BL 87:1880, 88:1367, 1369; CCBB 44:225; HB 67:451; HBG 2[Fall 1991]:230; KR 59:732; SLJ May 1991 p. 83)

SCIESZKA, Jon. *Knights of the Kitchen Table.* See Chapter 8, Time Travel Fantasy.

2300 **SCIESZKA, Jon.** *The Stinky Cheese Man and Other Fairly Stupid Tales.* **Gr. 2–8.**

✓ Raucous retellings of familiar fairy tales, including "The Gingerbread Boy" transformed into "The Stinky Cheese Man," "The Ugly Duckling" who grows up to be an ugly duck, and "Little Red Running Shorts" who outruns the wolf. Caldecott Medal Honor Book, 1993.

Illus. by Lane Smith, Viking, 1992, 56 pp. (0-670-84487-X)

(BL 89:56, 844; CC 1993 Suppl. p. 92; CCBB 46:33, 53; HB 68:720; HBG 4[Spring 1993]:62; KR 60:1193; SLJ Sept 1992, p. 210, Dec 1992 p. 23)

2301 **SCIESZKA, Jon.** *The True Story of the 3 Little Pigs: By A. Wolf.* **Gr. K–3.**

✓ Mr. A. Wolf has been terribly misunderstood: he was only trying to borrow some sugar to make a cake for his dear old granny when his cold caused those huge sneezes which accidentally blew down the pigs' houses, and now he's in jail and wants everyone to know that he was framed.

Illus. by Lane Smith, Viking, 1989, 32 pp. (0-670-82759-2)

(BL 86:74; CCBB 43:19; HB 66:58; HBG 1[July 1989]:46; KR 57:1167; SLJ Oct 1989 p. 108, Mar 1990 p. 153)

2302 **SCULLARD, Sue.** *Miss Fanshawe and the Great Dragon Adventure.* **Gr. K–4. (Orig. British pub. 1986.)**

Renowned Victorian explorer, Miss Fanshawe, captures a dragon in Patagonia, brings it back to London, and then chases down a thief who steals the dragon's egg.

Illus. by the author, St. Martin, 1987, 32 pp. (0-312-00510-5)

(BBC:212; BL 83:1526; KR 55:472)

SEEMAN, Elizabeth. *The Talking Dog and the Barking Man.* See Chapter 2, Animal Fantasy.

SEIDLER, Tor. *The Wainscott Weasel.* See Chapter 2, Animal Fantasy.

SELDEN (Thompson), George. *The Cricket in Times Square.* See Chapter 2, Animal Fantasy.

SELDEN (Thompson), George. *The Genie of Sutton Place.* See Chapter 7, Magic Adventure Fantasy.

SELDEN (Thompson), George. *Irma and Jerry.* See Chapter 2, Animal Fantasy.

SENDAK, Maurice (Bernard). *Higglety Pigglety Pop! Or, There Must Be More to Life.* See Chapter 2, Animal Fantasy.

SEUSS, Dr. (pseud. of Theodor Seuss Geisel). *The 500 Hats of Bartholomew Cubbins.* See Chapter 1, Allegorical Fantasy and Literary Fairy Tales.

Shape Shifters: Fantasy and Science Fiction Tales about Humans Who Can Change Their Shapes. **Ed. by Jane H. Yolen.** See Chapter 3, Fantasy Collections.

2303 **SHARMAT, Marjorie Weinman.** *The Trolls of Twelfth Street.* **Gr. 1–3.**

A troll family who arrives in Manhattan to spend a few hundred years above ground has problems dealing with human landlords, housewives, and children.

Illus. by Ben Shecter, Coward, 1979, 64 pp., o.p.

(BL 76:838; CCBB 33:142; KR 48:214; SLJ May 1980 p. 84; Suth 3:387)

SHEEHAN, Carolyn, and SHEEHAN, Edmond. *Magnifi-Cat.* See Chapter 2, Animal Fantasy.

SHUSTERMAN, Neal. *The Eyes of Kid Midas.* See Chapter 7, Magic Adventure Fantasy.

2304 **SILVERSTEIN, Shel(by).** *Uncle Shelby's Story of Laficadio, the Lion Who Shot Back.* **Gr. 3–5.**

Laficadio the lion teaches himself to shoot a hunting rifle and becomes a famous circus star.

Illus. by the author, Harper, 1963, 112 pp., LB(0-06-025676-1)

(CCBB 17:85; LJ 88:4858)

SIMAK, Clifford D(onald). *The Goblin Reservation.* See Chapter 8, Time Travel Fantasy.

2305 **SIMONT, Marc.** *The Contest at Paca.* **Gr. 3–5.**

✓ The feuding soldiers and university students of Paca challenge each other to a stew-eating contest.

Illus. by the author, Harper, 1959, 60 pp., o.p.

(BL 55:634; HB 35:301; KR 27:300; LJ 84:2084; TLS Nov 25, 1960 p. iv)

SIMONT, Marc. *Mimi.* See Chapter 2, Animal Fantasy.

SINGER, Isaac Bashevis. *Naftali the Storyteller and His Horse, Sus, and Other Stories.* See Chapter 3, Fantasy Collections.

SINGER, Isaac Bashevis. *Stories for Children.* See Chapter 3, Fantasy Collections.

SINGER, Isaac Bashevis. *Zlateh the Goat and Other Stories.* See Chapter 3, Fantasy Collections.

SINGER, Marilyn. *The Fido Frame-Up.* See Chapter 2, Animal Fantasy.

2306 **SLOTE, Alfred.** *My Robot Buddy.* **Gr. 2–4.**

Jack is mistaken for his robot by a gang of robotnappers, but the robot rescues him from his captors.

Illus. by Joel Schick, Harper, 1975, 1991, 80 pp. (0-397-32505-3), 1986, pap. (0-06-440165-0)

(BL 72:460; CCBB 29:102; KR 43:999; SLJ Oct 1975 p. 92)

2307 *Smart Dragons, Foolish Elves.* **Ed. by Alan Dean Foster and Martin H. Greenberg. Gr. 10 up.**

Nineteen contemporary humorous fantasy stories written by Robert Silverberg, Roger Zelazny, Esther M. Friesner, and others.

Ace, 1991, 352 pp. (0-441-18481-2)

(BL 87:1458, 1461; VOYA 14:113)

SNYDER, Zilpha Keatley. *Black and Blue Magic.* See Chapter 7, Magic Adventure Fantasy.

2308 **SOMMER-BODENBURG, Angela.** *My Friend the Vampire* **(Vampire series, book 1). Gr. 3–5. (Orig. German pub. 1982.)**

Nine-year-old Tony makes friends with Rudolf, the young vampire he finds on his window sill, but worries about keeping his parents and his new friend's family apart. The sequels are *The Vampire Moves In* (1984), *The Vampire Takes a Trip* (1985), *The Vampire on the Farm* (1989, 1990), and *The Vampire in Love* (1991).

Illus. by Amelie Glienke, Dial, 1984, 160 pp., LB(0-8037-0046-6)

(BBC:213; CCBB 38:56; HB 60:333; SLJ Aug 1984 p. 78)

SPEARING, Judith. *The Ghosts Who Went to School.* See Chapter 4, Ghost Fantasy.

2309 **SPURR, Elizabeth.** *Mrs. Minetta's Car Pool.* **Gr. 1–3.**

Trips to school in Mrs. Minetta's car pool turn into fantastic adventures when the children fly off into the sky in her red convertible.

Illus. by Blanche Sims, Macmillan, 1985, 32 pp. (0-689-31103-6), 1990, pap. (0-689-71430-0)

(BL 81:1463; CCBB 38:195; SLJ Sept 1985 p. 126)

STAHL, Ben. *Blackbeard's Ghost.* See Chapter 4, Ghost Fantasy.

STASHEFF, Christopher. *Her Majesty's Wizard.* See Chapter 5C, Travel to Other Worlds.

2310 **STEELE, William O(wen).** *Andy Jackson's Water Well.* **Gr. 4–6.**

✓ Andy Jackson and Chief Ticklepitcher are traveling to East Tennessee to fetch a water well for drought-stricken Nashville, but Andy can't control his temper.

Illus. by Michael Ramos, Harcourt, 1959, 80 pp., o.p.

(BL 55:426; Ch&Bks:291; Eakin:307; HB 35:214; KR 27:224; LJ 84:1700)

2311 **STEELE, William O(wen).** *Daniel Boone's Echo.* **Gr. 3–5.**

Daniel Boone helps Aaron Adamsale overcome his fear of the Sling-Tailed Galootis and the One-Horned Sumpple.

Illus. by Nicolas Mordvinoff, Harcourt, 1957, 79 pp., o.p.

(BL 54:146; HB 33:490; KR 25:771; LJ 82:2976)

2312 **STEELE, William O(wen).** *Davy Crockett's Earthquake.* **Gr. 3–5.**

✓ Davy Crockett meets up with a comet while out shooting bears in Tennessee.

Illus. by Nicolas Mordvinoff, Harcourt, 1956, 64 pp., o.p.

(BL 52:346; Eakin:308; HB 32:188; KR 24:242; LJ 81:2045)

2313 **STEELE, William O(wen).** *The No-Name Man of the Mountain.* **Gr. 4–6.**

✓ A young man outwits his trick-playing older brothers.

Illus. by Jack Davis, Harcourt, 1964, 79 pp., o.p.

(BL 61:805; CCBB 18:110; Eakin:308; HB 41:58; KR 32:894; LJ 89:4642)

STEFANEC-OGREN, Cathy. *Sly, P.I.: The Case of the Missing Shoes.* See Chapter 2, Animal Fantasy.

STERMAN, Betsy, and STERMAN, Samuel. *Backyard Dragon.* See Chapter 7, Magic Adventure Fantasy.

STEVENSON, James. *Here Comes Herb's Hurricane!* See Chapter 2, Animal Fantasy.

STEVENSON, James. *Oliver, Clarence, and Violet.* See Chapter 2, Animal Fantasy.

STEVENSON, James. *The Supreme Souvenir Factory.* See Chapter 2, Animal Fantasy.

2314 **STOCKTON, Frank (Francis) R(ichard).** *The Casting Away of Mrs. Lecks and Mrs. Aleshine.* **Gr. 7 up. (Orig. pub. 1886; bound with its sequel, *The Dusantes*, 1888.)**

The humorous adventures of two New England widows.

Illus. by George Richards, Appleton-Century, 1933, 290 pp., o.p.

(BL 30:23; Bookshelf 1933 p. 9; HB 9:155; LJ 58:804; Mahony 3:484)

STOLZ, Mary (Slattery). *Deputy Shep.* See Chapter 2, Animal Fantasy.

STOLZ, Mary (Slattery). *Quentin Corn.* See Chapter 2, Animal Fantasy.

STOLZ, Mary (Slattery). *Tales at the Mousehole.* See Chapter 2, Animal Fantasy.

2315 **STORR, Catherine (Cole).** *Clever Polly and the Stupid Wolf.* **Gr. 3–5. (Orig. British pub. 1955; U.S. 1970, entitled** *The Adventures of Polly and the Wolf.***)**

In spite of the wolf's attempts to disguise himself as a fox and as Father Christmas, he never manages to capture Polly. The British sequels are *Polly and the Wolf Again* (1970) and *Tales of Polly and the Hungry Wolf* (1980).

Illus. by Marjorie-Ann Watts, Faber, 1979, 95 pp., o.p; Chivers (large type ed.), 1992, 117 pp. (0-7451-1623-X)

(LJ 95:3054; SLJ Jan 1980 p. 62)

STRUGATSKII, Arkadii Natanovich, and STRUGATSKII, Boris Natanovich. *Monday Begins on Saturday.* See Chapter 10, Witchcraft and Sorcery Fantasy.

2316 **SWAYNE, Samuel, and SWAYNE, Zoa.** *Great Grandfather in the Honey Tree.*
✓ **Gr. 1–4.**

With one round of ammunition and a net, Great-Grandfather captures a bear, a fish, twenty-four geese, a partridge, a deer, twelve turkeys, and a barrel of wild honey.

Illus. by the authors, Viking, 1949, 54 pp., o.p.

(BL 46:86; CCBB 3:10; HB 25:411; KR 17:465; LJ 74:1531, 75:51)

2317 **TANNEN, Mary.** *Huntley Nutley and the Missing Link.* **Gr. 4–6.**

Huntley decides that the apelike creature he found is an Australopithecus, or "missing link" between apes and humans, and discovers that the creature loves TV and video games and helps him win over a gang of bullies.

Illus. by Rob Sauber, Knopf, 1983, 121 pp., o.p.

(BBC:214; BL 79:1405; CCBB 36:219; KR 51:525; SLJ Sept 1983 p. 128)

2318 **THOMPSON, Julian.** *Herb Seasoning.* **Gr. 9–12.**

Herbie Hertzman visits the Castles in the Air counseling agency after high school graduation, where he whirls a giant wheel of fortune and is transported into numerous zany situations as he investigates his possible destinies.

Scholastic, 1990, 272 pp. (0-5904-3023-8), 1991, pap. (0-5904-3024-6)

(BL 86:1792, 1794; CCBB 43:149; HBG 1[Jan 1990]:258; KR 58:271; SLJ Mar 1990 p. 240; VOYA 13:111)

THURBER, James (Grover). *The Wonderful O.* See Chapter 1, Allegorical Fantasy and Literary Fairy Tales.

TITUS, Eve. *Basil of Baker Street.* See Chapter 2, Animal Fantasy.

2319 **TODD, Barbara Euphan (pseud. of Barbara Euphan [Todd] Bower).** *Worzel Gummidge, the Scarecrow of Scatterbrook Farm* **(British titles:** *Worzel Gummidge,* **1936, and** *Worzel Gummidge Again,* **1937). Gr. 3–6.**

Worzell Gummidge is a scarecrow who comes alive. The British sequels are *More about Worzel Gummidge* (1938), *Worzel Gummidge and Saucy Nancy* (1947), *Worzel Gummidge Takes a Holiday* (1949), *Earthy Mangold and Worzel Gummidge* (1949), *Worzel Gummidge and the Railway Scarecrows* (1955), *Worzel Gummidge at the Circus* (1956), and *Worzel Gummidge and the Treasure Ship* (1958).

Illus. by Ursula Koering, Putnam, 1947, 200 pp., o.p.

(KR 15:190; LJ 72:595)

TODD, Ruthven. *Space Cat.* See Chapter 2, Animal Fantasy.

TOLLE, Jean Bashor. *The Great Pete Penney.* See Chapter 7, Magic Adventure Fantasy.

TRAVERS, P. L. *Mary Poppins.* See Chapter 7, Magic Adventure Fantasy.

UPENSKY, Eduard. *Uncle Fedya, His Dog and His Cat.* See Chapter 7, Magic Adventure Fantasy.

VAN ALLSBURG, Chris. *The Sweetest Fig.* See Chapter 1, Allegorical Fantasy and Literary Fairy Tales.

VAN LEEUWEN, Jean. *The Great Christmas Kidnapping Caper.* See Chapter 2, Animal Fantasy.

2320 VAN STOCKUM, Hilda (Gerarda). *Kersti and Saint Nicholas.* **Gr. 2–5.**

Naughty Kersti convinces St. Nicholas to leave gifts for the bad children instead of the good ones.

Illus. by the author, Viking, 1940, 72 pp., o.p.

(BL 37:328; HB 16:435; LJ 65:849, 928)

2321 VASILIU, Mircea. *Hark, the Little Angel.* **Gr. 2–4.**

A mischievous little angel spends a few days on earth disguised as a little boy.

Illus. by the author, Day, 1965, 48 pp., o.p.

(CCBB 19:71; KR 33:979; LJ 90:4530)

2322 VAUGHAN, Agnes Carr. *Lucian Goes A-Voyaging.* **Gr. 3–5.**

Tall tales in a similar vein as the Baron Münchausen tales (see this chapter), adapted from the Greek of Lucian.

Illus. by Harrie Wood, Knopf, 1930, 139 pp., o.p.

(BL 27:68; HB 6:127–130, 146, 7:117; LJ 55:465; Mahony 3:213; TLS 1930 p. 717)

WABER, Bernard. *Dear Hildegarde.* See Chapter 2, Animal Fantasy.

WABER, Bernard. *Mice on My Mind.* See Chapter 2, Animal Fantasy.

WAECHTER, Friedrich, and EILERT, Bernd. *The Crown Snatchers.* See Chapter 1, Allegorical Fantasy and Literary Fairy Tales.

WALKER, Kenneth Macfarlane, and BOUMPHREY, Geoffrey. *The Log of the Ark.* See Chapter 5B, Myth Fantasy.

WALLACE, Barbara Brooks. *Miss Switch to the Rescue.* See Chapter 10, Witchcraft and Sorcery Fantasy.

Wandering Stars: An Anthology of Jewish Fantasy and Science Fiction. **Ed. by Jack Dann.** See Chapter 3, Fantasy Collections.

WATKINS, Will. *Sid Seal, Houseman.* See Chapter 2, Animal Fantasy.

WATT-EVANS, Lawrence. *Crosstime Traffic.* See Chapter 3, Fantasy Collections.

WATT-EVANS, Lawrence. *With a Single Spell.* See Chapter 10, Witchcraft and Sorcery Fantasy.

WATT-EVANS, Lawrence, and FRIESNER, Esther. *Split Heirs.* See Chapter 5A, Alternate Worlds or Histories.

WEALES, Gerald. *Miss Grimsbee Is a Witch.* See Chapter 10, Witchcraft and Sorcery Fantasy.

2323 WEAVER, Jack. *Mr. O'Hara.* **Gr. 4–6.**

Mr. O'Hara entertains the customers in his general store with tall tales about his life in Ireland.

Illus. by the author, Viking, 1953, 160 pp., o.p.

(CCBB 7:34; HB 29:221; KR 21:115; LJ 78:705)

2324 WEISS, Ellen, and FRIEDMAN, Mel. *The Adventures of Ratman.* **Gr. 2–5.**

Eight-year-old Tod dons his new rat costume and is instantaneously transformed into the comic book-style superhero, Ratman, who rescues neighbors from danger before his powers disappear.

Illus. by Dirk Zimmer, Random, 1990, 64 pp., o.p., pap. (0-679-00531-1)

(BL 86:2183; CCBB 44:18; HBG 2[July–Dec 1990]:68)

2325 WERSBA, Barbara. *The Brave Balloon of Benjamin Buckley.* **Gr. 2–4.**
✓ Benjamin and his cat stow away aboard a hot-air balloon.

Illus. by Margot Jones, Atheneum, 1963, 66 pp., o.p.

(BL 60:632; CCBB 17:102; HB 39:500; LJ 88:122)

WHITCHER, Susan. *Real Mummies Don't Bleed: Friendly Tales for October Nights.* See Chapter 3, Fantasy Collections.

WHITE, Anne Hitchcock. *Junket.* See Chapter 2, Animal Fantasy.

WHITE, Anne Hitchcock. *The Story of Serapina.* See Chapter 2, Animal Fantasy.

WHITE, E(lwyn) B(rooks). *Stuart Little.* See Chapter 2, Animal Fantasy.

WHITE, E(lwyn) B(rooks). *The Trumpet of the Swan.* See Chapter 2, Animal Fantasy.

2326 WIBBERLEY, Leonard (Patrick O'Connor). *McGillicuddy McGotham.* **Gr. 4–6.**

Timothy Patrick Fegus Kevin Sean Desmond McGillicuddy is the first leprechaun diplomat posted to America.

Illus. by Aldren A. Watson, Little, 1956, 111 pp., o.p.

(BL 52:312; KR 24:55; LJ 81:833)

2327 WIBBERLEY, Leonard (Patrick O'Connor). *The Mouse That Roared* **(The**
✓ **Grand Fenwick series, book 2). Gr. 7 up.**

Attempting to revive its national economy, the tiny duchy of Grand Fenwick declares war on the United States, hoping for a quick defeat and large war reparations. But its twenty-three longbowmen not only win the war, they capture the top secret Q-Bomb! The prequel is *Beware of the Mouse* (1958), and the sequels are *The Mouse on the Moon* (1962), *The Mouse on Wall Street* (1969), and *The Mouse That Saved the West* (Morrow, 1981).

Little, 1955, o.p.; Bantam, 1971, pap., 279 pp. (0-553-24969-X); Buccaneer, 1992, LB(0-89966-887-9)

(BL 51:190, 83:1593; JHC:425; KR 22:788; LJ 79:1506)

WIBBERLEY, Leonard (Patrick O'Connor). *The Quest of Excalibur.* See Chapter 4, Ghost Fantasy.

2328   **WIEMER, Rudolf Otto.** *The Good Robber, Willibald.* **Gr. 2–4. (Orig. German pub. 1965.)**

Willibald the robber steps out of Manni's storybook, ready for trouble.

Trans. by Barbara Kowall Gollob, illus. by Marie Marcks, Atheneum, 1968, 65 pp., o.p.

(CCBB 21:167; KR 36:181; TLS 1969 p. 699)

WILKINS (Freeman), Mary E(leanor). *The Pumpkin Giant.* See Chapter 1, Allegorical Fantasy and Literary Fairy Tales.

WILLARD, Barbara. *Spell Me a Witch.* See Chapter 10, Witchcraft and Sorcery Fantasy.

WILLARD, Nancy (Margaret). *The Marzipan Moon.* See Chapter 1, Allegorical Fantasy and Literary Fairy Tales.

WILLEY, Elizabeth. *The Well-Favored Man: The Tale of the Sorcerer's Nephew.* See Chapter 5A, Alternate Worlds or Histories.

WILLIAMS, Jay. *The Practical Princess and Other Liberating Fairy Tales.* See Chapter 3, Fantasy Collections.

2329   **WILLIAMS (John), Ursula Moray.** *The Cruise of the Happy-Go-Gay.* **Gr. 3–5.**
✓   **(Orig. British pub. 1967.)**

Aunt Hegarty and her five nieces sail off in search of buried treasure.

Illus. by Gunvor Edwards, Meredith, 1968, 151 pp., o.p.

(BL 64:1046; CCBB 22:87; HB 44:424; KR 35:1474; LJ 93:298; Suth:424)

WILLIAMS (John), Ursula Moray. *The Nine Lives of Island Mackenzie.* See Chapter 2, Animal Fantasy.

2330   **WILLIAMS (John), Ursula Moray.** *Tiger Nanny* **(British title:** *Johnnie Tigerskin,* **1964). Gr. 4–6.**

A tiger cub becomes the perfect nanny for the Harper children.

Illus. by Gunvor Edwards, Nelson, 1974, 128 pp., o.p.

(CCBB 28:140; HB 51:151; KR 42:805; SLJ Jan 1975 p. 42)

WILSON, A. N. *Hazel the Guinea Pig.* See Chapter 2, Animal Fantasy.

WILSON, Gahan. *Harry the Fat Bear.* See Chapter 2, Animal Fantasy.

WINDSOR, Patricia. *How a Wierdo and a Ghost Can Change Your Entire Life.* See Chapter 4, Ghost Fantasy.

2331   *With Cap and Bells: Humorous Stories to Tell and to Read Aloud.* **Ed. by Mary Gould Davis. Gr. 4–6.**

Humorous tales by Carl Sandburg, Frank R. Stockton, Mary Eleanor Wilkins, and others.

Illus. by Richard Bennett, Harcourt, 1937, 246 pp., o.p.

(BL 34:12; HB 13:286; LJ 62:782)

2332   **WOOD, James Playsted.** *An Elephant in the Family.* **Gr. 2–4.**

Three children and their parents adopt a talking elephant. The sequels are *The Elephant in the Barn* (Harper, 1961), *The Elephant on Ice* (Seabury, 1965), and *The Elephant Tells* (Reilly, 1968).

Illus. by Kurt Werth, Nelson, 1957, 64 pp., o.p.

(CCBB 11:32; HB 33:223; LJ 82:1803)

2333 **WORK, Rhoda O.** *Mr. Dawson Had a Farm.* **Gr. 1–4.**

✓ A lazy farmer gets himself into humorous predicaments. The sequels are *Mr. Dawson Had an Elephant* (1959) and *Mr. Dawson Had a Lamb* (1963).

Illus. by Dorothy Maas, Bobbs-Merrill, 1951, 131 pp., o.p.

(BL 47:386; CCBB 4:47; HB 27:247; LJ 76:880)

WREDE, Patricia C(ollins). *Dealing with Dragons.* See Chapter 5A, Alternate Worlds or Histories.

WREDE, Patricia C(ollins). *Mairelon the Magician.* See Chapter 5A, Alternate Worlds or Histories.

WREDE, Patricia C(ollins)., and STEVERMER, Caroline. *Sorcery and Cecilia.* See Chapter 5A, Alternate Worlds or Histories.

WRIGHT, Betty Ren. *The Ghost of Ernie P.* See Chapter 4, Ghost Fantasy.

WRIGHT, T. M. *Goodlow's Ghosts.* See Chapter 4, Ghost Fantasy.

WRIGHTSON, (Alice) Patricia (Furlonger). *An Older Kind of Magic.* See Chapter 7, Magic Adventure Fantasy.

WYSS, Thelma Hatch. *A Stranger Here.* See Chapter 4, Ghost Fantasy.

YEP, Laurence. *The Curse of the Squirrel.* See Chapter 2, Animal Fantasy.

YOLEN (Stemple), Jane H(yatt). *The Acorn Quest.* See Chapter 2, Animal Fantasy.

2334 **YOLEN (Stemple), Jane H(yatt).** *The Giants' Farm.* **Gr. 1–4.**

Five humorous stories about the giants who run Fe-Fi-Fo-Farm, Grizzle, Stout, Grab, Grub, and Dab. The sequel is *The Giants Go Camping* (1979).

Illus. by Tomie dePaola, Houghton, 1977, 48 pp., o.p.

(BL 74:382; KR 45:849; SLJ Dec 1977 p. 57)

YOLEN (Stemple), Jane H(yatt). *Hobo Toad and the Motorcycle Gang.* See Chapter 2, Animal Fantasy.

YOLEN (Stemple), Jane H(yatt). *Piggins.* See Chapter 2, Animal Fantasy.

2335 **YOLEN (Stemple), Jane H(yatt).** *Sleeping Ugly.* **Gr. 1–3.**

✓ A beautiful but nasty princess named Miserella gets her comuppance when Prince Charming kisses awake homely but virtuous Plain Jane and forgets all about sleeping Miserella.

Illus. by Diane Stanley, Putnam, 1981, 64 pp., o.p.; pap., 1981, 64 pp. (0-698-20617-7)

(BL 78:656; CC:576; CCBB 35:99; KR 49:1158; SLJ Dec 1981 p. 75; Suth 3:467)

YOLEN (Stemple), Jane H(yatt). *Wizard's Hall.* See Chapter 10, Witchcraft and Sorcery Fantasy.

2336 **YORK, Carol Beach.** *Pudmuddles.* **Gr. 2–4.**

The Pudmuddle family does everything backward, including bathing fully clothed, and eating breakfast at night and dinner in the morning.

Harper, 1993, 44 pp. (0-06-020436-2)

(BL 89:1435; HBG 4[Fall 1993]:292; KR 61:606; SLJ May 1993 p. 92)

YOUNG, Robert F. *The Vizier's Second Daughter.* See Chapter 5B, Myth Fantasy.

ZELAZNY, Roger, and SHECKLEY, Robert. *If at Faust You Don't Succeed.* See Chapter 8, Time Travel Fantasy.

ZEMACH, Harve. *The Tricks of Master Dabble.* See Chapter 1, Allegorical Fantasy and Literary Fairy Tales.

7

Magic Adventure Fantasy

The majority of these books are about ordinary people who either gain magical powers or come in contact with magical objects, creatures, or events. A lighthearted tone usually prevails in this type of fantasy. Most tales involving extrasensory perception (ESP) or the occult have been excluded.

ADAIR, Gilbert. *Alice Through the Needle's Eye: The Further Adventures of Lewis Carroll's "Alice."* See Chapter 5C, Travel to Other Worlds.

2337   ADLER, C. S. *Eddie's Blue-Winged Dragon.* **Gr. 4–7.**

Eddie's angry longing for revenge against the school bully who taunts him because he has cerebral palsy brings a glass dragon to life to fight Eddie's battle with fire.

Putnam, 1988, 144 pp., o.p.; Avon, 1990, pap. (0-380-70768-3)

(BL 85:704; Ch&Bks:282; KR 56:1399; SLJ Jan 1989, p. 72; Suth 4:2)

2338   AHLBERG, Allan. *Ten in a Bed.* **Gr. 3–6. (Orig. British pub. 1983.)**

✓ Every night at bedtime, Dinah Price finds her bed occupied by a new fairy tale character, none of whom will let her go to sleep.

Illus. by André Amstutz, Viking, 1989, 95 pp. (0-670-82042-3); Puffin, 1991, pap. (0-14-032531-X)

(BL 86:446; CC:439; CCBB 43:25; HBG 1[July–Dec 1989]:82; KR 57:1153; Suth 4:4)

AHLBERG, Janet. *Jeremiah in the Dark Woods.* See Chapter 6, Humorous Fantasy.

AIKEN, Joan (Delano). *The Faithless Lollybird.* See Chapter 3, Fantasy Collections.

AIKEN, Joan (Delano). *Smoke from Cromwell's Time and Other Stories.* See Chapter 3, Fantasy Collections.

AIKEN, Joan (Delano). *Up the Chimney Down and Other Stories.* See Chapter 6, Humorous Fantasy.

2339 **ALCOCK, Vivien (Dolores).** *The Monster Garden.* **Gr. 5–9. (Orig. British pub.**
✓ **1988.)**

After the experimental cell-matter she stole from her father's laboratory grows into a
monster, Frankie tries to hide it from her family. Carnegie Medal Commended Book,
1988.

Delacorte, 1988, 144 pp. (0-440-50053-2); Dell, 1990, pap. (0-440-40257-3)

(BL 85:263; CCBB 42:24; HB 64:781; KR 56:1235; SLJ Oct 1988 p. 138; Suth 4:6; TLS 1988 p. 433;
VOYA 11:292, 12:15)

ALCOCK, Vivien (Dolores). *The Stonewalkers.* See Chapter 5B, Myth Fantasy.

ALLEN, Judy. *The Spring on the Mountain.* See Chapter 1, Allegorical Fantasy
and Literary Fairy Tales.

2340 **ANCKARSVÄRD, Karin (Inez Maria).** *Bonifacius the Green.* **Gr. 3–5. (Orig.**
Swedish pub. 1952.)

Bonifacius the dragon helps children to gain self-confidence.

Trans. by C. M. Anckarsvärd and K. H. Beales, illus. by Ingrid Rossell, Abelard-Schuman, 1961, 95 pp., o.p.

(HB 38:314; KR 30:7; LJ 87:1314; TLS Dec 4, 1961 p. vii)

2341 **ANDERSON, Joy.** *Juma and the Magic Jinn.* **Gr. 2–4.**
✓ Hoping to solve his problems at school, Juma calls up his family's magic jinn, who grants
his wishes in unexpected ways.

Illus. by Charles Mikolaycak, Lothrop, 1986, 32 pp., LB(0-688-05444-7)

(BBC:197; BL 83:266; HB 62:729; KR 54:1123; SLJ Dec 1986 p. 78)

ANDREWS, Frank. *The Upside-Down Town.* See Chapter 6, Humorous Fantasy.

2342 **ANGELL, Judie.** *The Weird Disappearance of Jordan Hall.* **Gr. 5–8.**

Hired as an assistant in his girlfriend's father's magic shop, Jordan Hall follows a black
cat into the "disappearing box" and becomes invisible.

Watts, 1987, 121 pp., o.p.

(BBJ:68; BL 84:52, 57; HB 64:61; SLJ Nov 1987 p. 102)

2343 **ANSA, Tina McElroy.** *Baby of the Family.* **Gr. 10 up.**   .

Lena, born with a caul over her face, has the ability to predict the future, in this story
about a loving African-American family in rural Georgia.

Harcourt, 1989, 263 pp. (0-15-110431-X), 1991, pap. (0-15-610150-5)

(BL 86:524, 539, 994; KR 57:1265; SLJ June 1990 p. 144)

2344 **ARNOLD, Tim.** *The Winter Mittens.* **Gr. 2–4.**

Addie's magic mittens make it snow whenever she wears them, but when she can't get
them off, on Christmas a blizzard threatens to bury the town.

Illus. by the author, Macmillan, 1988, 32 pp. (0-689-50419-7)

(BL 85:704; HB 64:761; KR 56:1463; SLJ Jan 1989 p. 58)

2345 **ASIMOV, Isaac.** *Azazel.* **Gr. 10 up.**

A tiny demon named Azazel grants George a number of wishes, and he describes the
results of his wishing in these short stories.

Doubleday, 1988, 216 pp. (0-385-24410-X); Bantam, 1990, pap. (0-553-28339-1)

(BBS:52; BL 85:367; KR 56:1364; LJ Nov 15, 1988 p. 88; VOYA 12:39, 13:138)

ASKOUNIS, Christina. *The Dream of the Stone.* See Chapter 5C, Travel to Other Worlds.

BABBITT, Natalie (Zane Moore). *Tuck Everlasting.* See Chapter 5B, Myth Fantasy.

2346 BABCOCK (Thompson), Betty (Elizabeth S.). *The Expandable Pig.* **Gr. 3–5.**

Pig suddenly expands like a balloon and takes Gary and his three dogs on a trip to England.

Illus. by the author, Scribner, 1949, 114 pp., o.p.

(CCBB 2[Oct 1949]:1; HB 25:410, 436; KR 17:323; LJ 74:1541, 1760)

BACON, Martha (Sherman). *The Third Road.* See Chapter 8, Time Travel Fantasy.

BACON, Peggy. *The Ghost of Opalina, or Nine Lives.* See Chapter 4, Ghost Fantasy.

2347 BACON, Peggy. *The Magic Touch.* **Gr. 3–4.**

Recipes from a witch's cookbook transform Ben, Esther, and Ted into animals.

Illus. by the author, Little, 1968, 112 pp., o.p.

(BL 63:183; HB 44:556; KR 36:690; LJ 94:292)

2348 BAKER, Margaret. *Patsy and the Leprechauns.* **Gr. 2–4. (Orig. British pub. 1932.)**

Patsy decides that the quickest way to make money is to steal a leprechaun's gold.

Illus. by Mary Baker, Duffield, 1933, 109 pp., o.p.

(BL 29:208; Bookshelf 1933 p. 6; LJ 58:710; Mahony 3:103; TLS 1932 p. 894)

2349 BAKER, Margaret. *Pollie Who Did as She Was Told.* **Gr. 3–4.**

Pollie accidentally washes out all of the magic potion-containing bottles when she tidies up the Wise Woman's house.

Illus. by Mary Baker, Dodd, 1934, 100 pp., o.p.

(LJ 60:304; Mahony 3:104; TLS 1934 p. 838)

2350 BAKER, Margaret. *The Water Elf and the Miller's Child.* **Gr. 2–4.**

A mischievous young water elf plays tricks on the frogs, cranes, and fish living at the mill pond.

Illus. by Mary Baker, Duffield, 1928, 84 pp., o.p.

(BL 25:126; HB 4[Nov 1928]:76; Mahony 2:131)

BAKER, Margaret Joyce. *Homer the Tortoise.* See Chapter 2, Animal Fantasy.

2351 BAKER, Margaret Joyce. *The Magic Sea Shell.* **Gr. 3–5. (Orig. British pub. 1959.)**

Three children find a magic sea shell and meet a wish-granting mermaid.

Illus. by Susan Elson, Holt, 1960, 122 pp., o.p.

(KR 28:6, LJ 85:2033; TLS Dec 4, 1959 p. xxii)

2352 BAKER, Margaret Joyce. *Porterhouse Major.* **Gr. 4–6. (Orig. British pub. 1967.)**

Rory uses her mother's magic books to create a gigantic cat named Porterhouse.

Illus. by Shirley Hughes, Prentice-Hall, 1967, 116 pp., o.p.

(CCBB 21:105, 121; Suth:26; TLS 1967 p. 451)

2353 **BAKER, Olaf.** *Bengey and the Beast.* **Gr. 5–7.**

Bengey uses magic to destroy the horrible Gunderbust.

Illus. by Victor J. Dowling, Dodd, 1947, 243 pp., o.p.

(BL 43:260; HB 23:212; LJ 72:466, 597)

2354 **BALL, Duncan.** *Emily Eyefinger.* **Gr. 2–4.**

Emily was born with an extra eye on the end of her left index finger, which comes in handy against a school bully and a bank robber.

Illus. by George Ulrich, Simon & Schuster, 1992, 82 pp. (0-671-74618-9)

(BL 88:1599; HBG 3[Fall 1992]:253; SLJ July 1992, p. 56)

BARRIE, Sir J. M. *Peter Pan.* See Chapter 5C, Travel to Other Worlds.

BARZINI, Luigi. *The Little Match Man.* See Chapter 9, Toy Fantasy.

BATTLES, Edith. *The Witch in Room 6.* See Chapter 10, Witchcraft and Sorcery Fantasy.

2355 **BAUER, Marion Dane.** *Touch the Moon.* **Gr. 4–6.**

✓ Jennifer's tiny china horse turns into Moonseeker, a talking palomino stallion, who teaches her how to ride, while she teaches him courage.

Illus. by Alix Berenzy, Houghton, 1987, 96 pp. (0-89919-526-1)

(BBC:198; BL 84:144; CCBB 41:2; HB 63:608; KR 55:1388; SLJ Nov 1987 p. 102)

BEACHCROFT, Nina. *Well Met by Witchlight.* See Chapter 10, Witchcraft and Sorcery Fantasy.

2356 **BEACHCROFT, Nina.** *The Wishing People.* **Gr. 4–6. (Orig. British pub. 1980.)**

Released from a spell that imprisoned them inside a barometer, Tom and Mrs. Tom grant ten wishes to Martha and her friend, Jonathan.

Dutton, 1982, 181 pp., o.p.

(BBC:198; BL 78:954; KR 50:553; SLJ Apr 1982 p. 65)

BEATON-JONES, Cynon. *The Adventures of So Hi.* See Chapter 5C, Travel to Other Worlds.

2357 **BECKER, Eve.** *Thirteen Means Magic.* **Gr. 5–7.**

On her thirteenth birthday, Dawn discovers that if she arches her left eyebrow, she can cause things to happen. The sequel is *The Love Potion* (1989).

Bantam, 1989, pap., 144 pp. (0-553-15730-2)

(BBJ:68; BL 86:839; SLJ Nov 1989 p. 125)

BEDARD, Michael. *A Darker Magic.* See Chapter 10, Witchcraft and Sorcery Fantasy.

2358 **BELDEN, Wilianne Schneider.** *Frankie!* **Gr. 4–6.**

All of the O'Rileys have magical powers, but Frankie also happens to be a griffin.

Illus. by Stewart Daniels, Harcourt, 1987, 163 pp. (0-15-229380-9)

(SLJ Dec 1987 p. 83; VOYA 11:36)

2359 **BELL, Thelma Harrington.** *Take It Easy.* **Gr. 5–7.**

Thirteen-year-old Margie rubs her brass elephant and an invisible genie comes forth.

Illus. by Corydon Bell, Viking, 1953, 172 pp., o.p.

(KR 21:428; LJ 78:2042)

2360 **BELLAIRS, John.** *The Dark Secret of Weatherend* **(Anthony Munday series,**
✓ **book 2). Gr. 5–8.**

Anthony suspects that their exceptionally harsh Minnesota winter has been caused by J.
K. Borkman, a dead millionaire who once plotted to destroy the world. This is the sequel
to *The Treasure of Alpheus Winterborn* (1978) and is followed by *The Lamp from the
Warlock's Tomb* (1988) and *The Mansion in the Mist* (1992).

Dial, 1984, 182 pp. (0-8037-0072-5); Bantam, 1986, pap. (0-553-15375-7)

(BBC:198; BL 80:1186; HB 60:326; JHC:334; KR 52:J36; SLJ May 1984 p. 103; VOYA 8:46)

BELLAIRS, John. *The House with the Clock in Its Walls.* See Chapter 4, Ghost
Fantasy.

2361 **BENCHLEY, Nathaniel (Goddard).** *The Magic Sled* **(British title:** *The Magic
Sledge***). Gr. 3–5.**

No snow for his new sled? Fred finds that magic can make more snow than he ever
dreamed of.

Illus. by Mel Furukawa, Harper, 1972, 44 pp., o.p.

(BL 68:1002; CCBB 25:134; KR 40:68; LJ 97:1593)

BENDICK, Jeanne. *The Goodknight Ghost.* See Chapter 4, Ghost Fantasy.

2362 **BENNETT, Rodney.** *Eagle Boy.* **Gr. 6–9. (Orig. British pub. 1986.)**

Abandoned by his parents, who feared that the other villagers would blame him for their
crop failures, lame and mute Stephan is raised by a golden eagle who teaches him to fly.

Deutsch, 1989, 163 pp., o.p.

(SLJ Aug 1989 p. 138; VOYA 12:211)

BENSON, E. F. *David Blaize and the Blue Door.* See Chapter 5C, Travel to Other
Worlds.

BERESFORD, Elisabeth. *Invisible Magic.* See Chapter 8, Time Travel Fantasy.

BERESFORD, Elisabeth. *Travelling Magic.* See Chapter 8, Time Travel Fantasy.

2363 **BERGENGREN, Ralph Wilhelm.** *Susan and the Butterbees.* **Gr. 4–6.**

Fairy Maud grants Susan's wish for forty-seven Butterbee uncles to appear whenever she
needs entertainment or help.

Illus. by Anne Vaughan, Longmans, 1947, 175 pp., o.p.

(HB 23:212; KR 15:163; LJ 72:643)

2364 **BETHANCOURT, T(homas) Ernesto (pseud. of Tom Paisley).** *The Dog Days of
Arthur Cane.* **Gr. 6–9.**

Arthur is changed into a stray mutt by a classmate he has ridiculed.

Holiday, 1976, 160 pp., o.p.

(BBC:199; BBJ:69; HB 53:157; KR 44:848; SLJ Jan 1977 p. 99; TLS 1978 p. 1082)

2365 **BIANCO, Margery (Winifred) Williams.** *The Hurdy-Gurdy Man.* **Gr. 2–4.**

The magical music of the hurdy-gurdy man changes the lives of the prim inhabitants of
an overly tidy town.

Illus. by Robert Lawson, Oxford, 1933, 55 pp., o.p.; Gregg, 1980, 56 pp., o.p.

(BL 30:184; HB 9:204; LJ 58:897)

2366 **BINNS, Archie (Fred).** *The Radio Imp.* **Gr. 4–7.**

Jim Tompkins's second-hand Irish radio reports on the future as well as the past. The sequel is *Secret of the Sleeping River* (1952).

Illus. by Rafaello Busoni, Winston, 1950, 216 pp., o.p.

(BL 46:266; CCBB 3:49; HB 26:193; KR 18:69; LJ 75:706)

2367 **BONHAM, Frank.** *The Friends of the Loony Lake Monster.* **Gr. 4–6.**

A baby dinosaur hatches from an orange egg and adopts Gussie as its mother.

Dutton, 1972, 135 pp., o.p.

(BBC:199; BL 69:711; CCBB 26:71; KR 40:1097; LJ 97:3803)

2368 **BOSTON, L(ucy) M(aria Wood).** *The Castle of Yew.* **Gr. 3–5. (Orig. British pub.**
✓ **1965.)**

Two boys peer into a castle-shaped yew bush and find that they have shrunken to only a few inches in height and are inside the castle.

Illus. by Margery Gill, Harcourt, 1965, 58 pp., o.p.

(BL 62:327; CCBB 19:42; HB 42:192; KR 33:903; LJ 90:4609; TLS 1965 p. 513)

BOSTON, L(ucy) M(aria Wood). *The Children of Green Knowe.* See Chapter 4, Ghost Fantasy.

2369 **BOSTON, L(ucy) M(aria Wood).** *The Fossil Snake.* **Gr. 4–6. (Orig. British pub.**
1975.)

The fossilized prehistoric snake that Rob hid under his radiator comes to life and begins to grow.

Illus. by Peter Boston, Atheneum, 1976, 53 pp., o.p.

(BL 72:1259; HB 52:287; KR 44:199; SLJ May 1976 p. 56; TLS 1975 p. 1060)

BOSTON, L(ucy) M(aria Wood). *The Guardians of the House.* See Chapter 5C, Travel to Other Worlds.

2370 **BOSTON, L(ucy) M(aria Wood).** *Nothing Said.* **Gr. 3–5. (Orig. British pub.**
✓ **1971.)**

Libby meets a small, weeping dryad and promises to find her a new tree to replace the one felled by a storm.

Illus. by Peter Boston, Harcourt, 1971, 64 pp., o.p.

(BL 67:746; CCBB 25:2; HB 47:286; LJ 96:2128; TLS 1971 p. 1317)

2371 **BOSTON, L(ucy) M(aria Wood).** *The River at Green Knowe.* **Gr. 5–7.**
✓ While canoeing on the river near Green Knowe, Ping, Oskar, and Ida meet a hermit, a giant, and winged horses. Ping's adventures continue in *An Enemy at Green Knowe* (1964) and in a nonfantasy story, *A Stranger at Green Knowe* (1961).

Illus. by Peter Boston, Harcourt, 1959, o.p., 1966, pap., 153 pp., o.p.; Peter Smith, 1984 (0-8446-6153-8); Harcourt, 1989, pap. (0-15-267450-0)

(CCBB 13:27; KR 27:701; LJ 84:3318; TLS Dec 4, 1959 p. xvii)

2372 **BOSTON, L(ucy) M(aria Wood).** *The Sea Egg.* **Gr. 4–5.**
✓ Toby and Joe find a green, egg-shaped stone that hatches into a sea boy.

Illus. by Peter Boston, Harcourt, 1967, 94 pp. (0-15-271050-7)

(BBC:199; BL 63:1045; CC:553; CCBB 21:1; HB 43:460; KR 35:498; LJ 92:2647; Suth:47; TLS 1967 p. 1133)

BOWEN, William A(lvin). *Merrimeg.* See Chapter 5C, Travel to Other Worlds.

2373 **BOWEN, William A(lvin).** *The Old Tobacco Shop: A True Account of What Befell a Little Boy in Search of Adventure.* **Gr. 5–7.**

Tales told by the old tobacco shop owner involve Freddie in thrilling pirate adventures. John Newbery Medal Honor Book, 1922.

Macmillan, 1921, 236 pp., o.p.

(BL 18:159; Bookshelf 1923–1924 p. 8; LJ 47:869; Mahony 1:39; Moore:426)

BRADBURY, Ray (Douglas). *The Halloween Tree.* See Chapter 8, Time Travel Fantasy.

2374 **BRAND, (Mary) Christianna (Milne Lewis).** *Nurse Matilda.* **Gr. 2–5.**

It takes only one stamp of Nurse Matilda's big black stick to straighten out the Browns' naughty children. The sequels are *Nurse Matilda Goes to Town* (1967) and *Nurse Matilda Goes to the Hospital* (British).

Illus. by Edward Ardizzone, Dutton, 1964, o.p.; Gregg, 1980, 128 pp., o.p.

(BL 61:436; HB 40:497; KR 32:732; LJ 89:3468; TLS 1964 p. 589)

2375 **BRENNER, Barbara.** *The Flying Patchwork Quilt.* **Gr. 2–4.**

Five-year-old Ellen, determined to fly, tries paper wings, balloons, and an umbrella before she succeeds with a magical patchwork quilt.

Illus. by Fred Brenner, Young Scott, 1965, 42 pp., o.p.

(CCBB 20:4; KR 33:749; LJ 90:3778)

2376 **BRITTAIN, Bill (William).** *The Fantastic Freshman.* **Gr. 5–9.**

Stanley Muffet's daydreams of football stardom, becoming student council president, and dating the head cheerleader suddenly all come true, but this magical good luck also creates a few problems.

Harper, 1988, 154 pp. (0-06-020718-3), 1990, pap. (0-06-447016-4)

(BBJ:69; BL 85:67, 72; KR 56:1056; SLJ Sept 1988 p. 182; VOYA 11:235)

2377 **BRITTAIN, Bill (William).** *Wings.* **Gr. 6–7.**

Everyone is shocked when twelve-year-old Ian grows wings, especially his father, who fears they will put a damper on his political career.

Harper, 1991, 135 pp. LB(0-06-020649-7)

(BL 88:519; CCBB 45:57; HBG 3[July–Dec 1991]:63; KR 59:1007; SLJ Oct 1991 p. 119; VOYA 14:320)

2378 **BROCK, Betty.** *No Flying in the House.* **Gr. 3–5.**

Annabel, a half-mortal, half-fairy child, is tempted by a wicked fairy to misuse her magic powers.

Illus. by Wallace Tripp, Harper, 1970, 139 pp., 1982, pap., 144 pp. (0-06-440130-8)

(BL 66:1340; CCBB 24:38; KR 38:450; LJ 95:2531; Suth:52)

BROCK, Betty. *The Shades.* See Chapter 4, Ghost Fantasy.

2379 **BROOKE, William J.** *A Brush with Magic.* **Gr. 4–7.**

✓ Liang, found as a baby clutching a paintbrush, discovers that the pictures he paints come to life, in this story based on a Chinese folktale.

Illus. by Michael Koelsh, Harper, 1993, 137 pp. (0-06-022973-X)

(BL 90:827; CCBB 47:148; HBG 5:73; KR 61:1458; SLJ Jan 1994 p. 112; VOYA 17:7, 34)

2380 **BROWN, Palmer.** *Beyond the Pawpaw Trees: The Story of Anna Lavinia.* **Gr. 4–6.**

Anna Lavinia has a number of strange adventures during a trip to her aunt's house, culminating in the discovery of her long-lost father. In the sequel, *The Silver Nutmeg* (1956), Anna Lavinia discovers another world on the other side of the dew pond near her house.

Illus. by the author, Harper, 1954, 121 pp., o.p.

(CCBB 8:66; HB 30:343; KR 22:385; LJ 79:2254)

2381 **BROWNE, Frances.** *Granny's Wonderful Chair and Its Tales of Fairy Times.* **Gr.**
✓ **4–6. (Orig. British pub. 1856; repr. 1887, retitled:** *The Story of the Lost Fairy Book;* **orig. U.S. pub. 1892.)**

Snowflower's magical chair tells wondrous stories and helps her find the king's long-lost brother.

Illus. by Clara E. Atwood, Heath, 1900, 1930 (entitled: *The Wonderful Chair and the Tales It Told*), o.p.; illus. by Katherine Pyle, Dutton, 1916, 1925, 1933, o.p.; illus. by Emma L. Brock, Macmillan, 1924 (entitled: *Granny's Wonderful Chair*), o.p.; illus. by D(enys) J(ames) Watkins-Pitchford, Dutton, 1963, 150 pp., o.p.

(BL 21:74, 59:859; Bookshelf 1928 p. 10; HB 1[June 1925]:30, 39:402; LJ 26:67, 50:803; Mahony 2:274)

2382 **BRUÈRE, Martha (Bensley).** *Sparky-for-Short.* **Gr. 3–4.**

An electric spark released from the radio is really a radio photograph of a lost boy.

Illus. by the author, Coward, 1930, 85 pp., o.p.

(LJ 55:995; Mahony 3:132; Moore 131, 431)

2383 **BUCHAN, John.** *The Magic Walking-Stick.* **Gr. 5–7. (Orig. Canadian pub. 1932.)**

Bill's magic walking stick takes him to the South Pacific and to darkest Africa, where it helps him restore a prince to his throne.

Illus. by Arthur E. Becher, Houghton, 1932, 215 pp., o.p.

(Bookshelf 1933: 11; LJ 58:806; TLS 1932 pp. 840, 867)

BUFFETT, Jimmy and BUFFETT, Savannah Jane. *Trouble Dolls.* See Chapter 9, Toy Fantasy.

2384 **BUFFIE, Margaret.** *The Warnings.* **Gr. 7 up. (Orig. Canadian title:** *The*
✓ *Guardian Circle,* **1989.)**

Fifteen-year-old Rachel and her new friend, Will, discover that her Aunt Irene and the elderly Fossils who live with her aunt have special magical powers, and need Rachel's help to keep an ancient spirit from seizing their stone of power.

Scholastic, 1991, 256 pp. (0-5904-3665-1)

(BL 87:1464; CCBB 44:160; HBG 2[Fall 1991]:275; KR 59:105; SLJ Apr 1991 p. 141; VOYA 14:93)

BULLETT, Gerald W. *The Happy Mariners.* See Chapter 8, Time Travel Fantasy.

2385 **BURNETT (Townsend), Frances (Elizabeth) Hodgson.** *Racketty-Packetty House, as Told by Queen Crosspatch.* **Gr. 3–5. (Orig. British and U.S. pub. 1906.)**

When Cynthia replaces her tumbledown doll house with an elegant new one, Queen Crosspatch of the fairies steps in to save the old discarded dolls. This is the sequel to *Queen Silverbell* (Century, 1906), and was followed by *Spring Cleaning, as Told by Queen Crosspatch* (1908).

Illus. by Harold Berson, Scribner, 1961 (entitled: *Racketty Packetty House and Other Sto-*

ries), o.p.; illus. by Harrison Caddy, Dodd, 1961, o.p.; Outlet, 1992, 72 pp. (0-517-07249-1); illus. by Holly Johnson, Lippincott, 1975, 60 pp., o.p.

(BL 2:249, 58:111, 203, 72:362; HB 37:549; KR 43:1065; LJ 95:1192; Mahony 1:40; Mahony 2:127; SLJ Nov 1975 p. 42; TLS 1968 p. 589)

BUTTERWORTH, Oliver. *The Enormous Egg.* See Chapter 6, Humorous Fantasy.

2386 BYARS, Betsy (Cromer). *The Winged Colt of Casa Mia.* **Gr. 5–7.**

The colt Charles is given when he comes to live on his Uncle Coot's ranch is special—it has wings!

Illus. by Richard Cuffari, Viking, 1973, 128 pp., o.p.; Avon, 1981, pap., 132 pp. (0-380-00201-9)

(BBC:199; CCBB 27:107; HB 50:47; LJ 98:3448; Suth 2:71)

2387 CALHOUN, Mary (pseud. of Mary Huiskamp Wilkins). *Magic in the Alley.* **Gr. 4–6.**

Cleery buys a box of magic items in an alley junk shop.

Illus. by Wendy Watson, Atheneum, 1970, 167 pp., o.p.

(BL 67:55; HB 46:295; KR 38:242; LJ 95:1939)

2388 CALHOUN, Mary (pseud. of Mary Huiskamp Wilkins). *Ownself.* **Gr. 4–6.**

Laurabelle summons up a joyful fairy who convinces the girl to defy her stern father.

Harper, 1975, 160 pp., o.p.

(CCBB 29:59; HB 51:265; KR 43:371; SLJ Apr 1975 p. 50)

2389 CAMERON, Eleanor (Frances Butler). *The Terrible Churnadryne.* **Gr. 4–6.**

✓ Few people believe the stories of a tremendous beast seen near Redwood Cove, so Tom and Jennifer decide to track it down themselves.

Illus. by Beth Krush and Joe Krush, Little, 1959, 125 pp., o.p.

(BL 56:247; Eakin:58; HB 35:481; KR 27:701; LJ 84:3629)

2390 CARLSEN, Ruth Christoffer. *Mr. Pudgins.* **Gr. 3–6.**

When Mr. Pudgins baby-sits for John's family, the faucets run with soda pop and the bathtubs fly.

Illus. by Margaret Bradfield, Houghton, 1951, 163 pp., o.p.

(BL 47:240; CCBB 4:26; HB 27:1; LJ 76:415)

2391 CARLSEN, Ruth Christoffer. *Sam Bottleby.* **Gr. 4–6.**

A fairy godfather cares for Trygve and Solveig after they are stranded at the airport.

Illus. by Wallace Tripp, Houghton, 1968, 151 pp., o.p.

(KR 36:1282; LJ 94:1324)

CARROLL, Lewis (pseud. of Charles Ludwidge Dodgson). *Alice's Adventures in Wonderland.* See Chapter 5C, Travel to Other Worlds.

CASSEDY, Sylvia. *Behind the Attic Wall.* See Chapter 4, Ghost Fantasy.

2392 CATLING, Patrick Skene. *The Chocolate Touch.* **Gr. 3–5.**

John Midas transforms everyone, even his mother, into chocolate statues because of his insatiable craving for chocolate. The sequel is *John Midas in the Dreamtime* (1986).

Illus. by Mildred Coughlin McNutt, Morrow, 1952, 95 pp., o.p.; illus. by Margot Apple,

Morrow, 1979, 126 pp. (revision of 1952 ed.), LB(0-688-32187-9); Bantam, 1981, pap., 96 pp. (0-553-15479-6), 1984 (0-553-15639-X)
(BBC:200; BL 49:18, 75:1579; KR 20:369; SLJ Sep 1979 p. 131)

CHARLES, Prince of Wales. *The Old Man of Lochnagar.* See Chapter 6, Humorous Fantasy.

CHARNAS, Suzy McKee. *The Bronze King.* See Chapter 10, Witchcraft and Sorcery Fantasy.

CHARNAS, Suzy McKee. *The Kingdom of Kevin Malone.* See Chapter 5C, Travel to Other Worlds.

CHASE, Mary. *Loretta Mason Potts.* See Chapter 5C, Travel to Other Worlds.

CHESNUTT, Charles Waddell. *Conjure Tales.* See Chapter 3, Fantasy Collections.

CHETWIN, Grace. *Out of the Dark World.* See Chapter 5C, Travel to Other Worlds.

CHEW, Ruth. *Do-It-Yourself Magic.* See Chapter 5C, Travel to Other Worlds.

2393 **CHEW, Ruth.** *Mostly Magic.* **Gr. 3–4.**

Emily and her younger brother, Dick, are given a miniature ladder that can take them anywhere, and a pencil that causes anything it writes to happen.

Illus. by the author, Holiday, 1982, 126 pp., o.p.
(BBC:200; BL 78:1521; SLJ Dec 1982 p. 64)

CHEW, Ruth. *No Such Thing as a Witch.* See Chapter 10, Witchcraft and Sorcery Fantasy.

CHEW, Ruth. *The Would-Be Witch.* See Chapter 10, Witchcraft and Sorcery Fantasy.

2394 **CHRISTOPHER, Matt(hew F.).** *The Dog That Stole Football Plays.* **Gr. 2–4.**

Mike can communicate with his Airedale, Harry, who advises him on football plays after listening to the opposing team's coaches. The sequels are *The Dog That Called the Signals* (1982) and *The Dog That Pitched a No-Hitter* (1988).

Illus. by Bill Ogden, Little, Brown, 1980, 1993, 48 pp. (0-316-14082-1)
(CCBB 34:4; KR 48:909; SLJ May 1980 p. 84)

2395 **CHRISTOPHER, Matt(hew F.).** *The Kid Who Only Hit Homers.* **Gr. 3–5.**

Syl's dream of winning the Best Athlete Ever trophy comes true, all because of his mysterious baseball coach, George Baruth. The sequel is *Return of the Home Run Kid* (1992).

Illus. by Harvey Kidder, Little, Brown, 1972, 151 pp. (0-316-13918-1); 1986, pap. (0-316-13987-4)
(KR 40:34; LJ May 15, 1972 p. 1929)

2396 **CHRISTOPHER, Matt(hew F.).** *Skateboard Tough.* **Gr. 4–6.**

The glorious skateboard Brett unearths enables him to perform incredibly difficult tricks, but he discovers that the skateboard's previous owner was killed while riding it.

Illus. by Paul Casale, Little, Brown, 1991, 162 pp. (0-316-14247-6)
(BL 87:1797; CCBB 44:212; HBG 2[Fall 1991]:268; KR 59:728; SLJ June 1991 p. 74)

2397 **CLAPP, Patricia.** *King of the Doll House.* **Gr. 3–4.**

Tiny King Borra Borra and his family of twelve move into Ellie's doll house for the summer.

Illus. by Judith Gwyn Brown, Lothrop, 1974, 94 pp., o.p.

(CCBB 28:74; KR 42:680; LJ 99:2738)

CLARKE, J(udith). *Teddy B. Zoot.* See Chapter 9, Toy Fantasy.

CLARKE, Pauline (pseud. of Pauline [Clarke] Hunter Blair). *The Return of the Twelves.* See Chapter 9, Toy Fantasy.

CLARKE, Pauline (pseud. of Pauline [Clarke] Hunter Blair). *The Two Faces of Silenus.* See Chapter 5B, Myth Fantasy.

COATES, Anna. *Dog Magic.* See Chapter 2, Animal Fantasy.

COATSWORTH, Elizabeth (Jane). *Pure Magic.* See Chapter 1, Allegorical Fantasy and Literary Fairy Tales.

2398 **COATSWORTH, Elizabeth (Jane).** *Troll Weather.* **Gr. 2–4.**

Selma sees the trolls' golden castles on the mountainside above her Norwegian village.

Illus. by Ursula Arndt, Macmillan, 1967, 41 pp., o.p.

(BL 63:944; HB 43:198; KR 35:3; LJ 92:1309)

2399 **COBLENTZ, Catherine Cate.** *The Blue Cat of Castle Town.* **Gr. 4–6.**

A blue cat steps out of a rug and wanders through the town of Castleton. John Newbery Medal Honor Book, 1950.

Illus. by Janice Holland, McKay, 1949, o.p.; Countryman, 1983, pap., 124 pp. (0-914378-05-8)

(BBC:200; BL 46:15; CCBB 2[July 1949]:1; HB 25:412; LJ 74:1105)

COLE, Joanna. *Bony-Legs.* See Chapter 10, Witchcraft and Sorcery Fantasy.

COLE, Joanna. *Doctor Change.* See Chapter 10, Witchcraft and Sorcery Fantasy.

COLLODI, Carlo. *The Adventures of Pinocchio.* See Chapter 9, Toy Fantasy.

2400 **CONFORD, Ellen.** *Genie with the Light Blue Hair.* **Gr. 6–9**

✓ A cigar-smoking genie named Arthur appears after fifteen-year-old Jean lights her seemingly useless birthday present lamp, but her wishes never turn out as planned.

Bantam, 1989, 160 pp, (0-553-05806-1), 1990, pap., 150 pp. (0-553-28484-3)

(BL 85:1000; CC:472; CCBB 42:145; HB 65:215; JHC:347; Kies:37; KR 57:47; SLJ Feb. 1989 p. 100; VOYA 12:26)

2401 **COONTZ, Otto.** *Hornswoggle Magic.* **Gr. 3–5.**

Jenny the shopping-bag lady uses magical coins, or hornswoggles, to jam up the new vending machine and save Mr. Wiseman's newsstand from going out of business.

Illus. by the author, Little, 1981, 88 pp., o.p.

(BL 78:705; SLJ Feb 1982 p. 73)

2402 **COOPER (Grant), Susan (Mary).** *The Boggart.* **Gr. 4–7.**

✓ After Emily accidentally releases a mischievous Boggart from an ancient Scottish desk, he makes himself at home in modern-day Toronto, causing problems for the Volnik family.

Macmillan, 1993, 196 pp. (0-689-50576-0)

(BL 89:908, 90:869; CCBB 46:208; HB 69:330; HBG 4[Fall 1993]:296; KR 60:1570; SLJ Jan 1993 p. 96)

2403 **COOPER (Grant), Susan (Mary).** *Jethro and the Jumbie.* **Gr. 2–4.**

✓ Furious with his elder brother who has broken a promise to take him fishing, eight-year-old Jethro marches off into the bush and has a series of magical adventures.

Illus. by Ashley Bryan, Atheneum, 1979, 28 pp., o.p.

(BBC:201; BL 76:610; CCBB 33:91; Ch&Bks:255; HB 56:51; KR 48:120; SLJ Feb 1980 p. 44)

COOPER (Grant), Susan (Mary). *Over Sea, Under Stone.* See Chapter 5B, Myth Fantasy.

CORBETT, Scott. *Ever Ride a Dinosaur?* See Chapter 6, Humorous Fantasy.

CORBETT, Scott. *The Great Custard Pie Panic.* See Chapter 10, Witchcraft and Sorcery Fantasy.

2404 **CORBETT, Scott.** *The Lemonade Trick.* **Gr. 4–6.**

✓ Kirby's new chemistry set can change a person's character, but the fun ends when it changes his friend, Bumps, into a bully. The sequels are *The Mailbox Trick* (1961), *The Disappearing Dog Trick* (1963), *The Limerick Trick* (1964), *The Turnabout Trick* (1967), *The Hairy Horror Trick* (1969), *The Hateful Plateful Trick* (1971), *The Home Run Trick* (1973), and *The Black Mask Trick* (1976).

Illus. by Paul Galdone, Little, 1960, o.p.; Scholastic, 1988, pap., 96 pp. (0-590-32197-8)

(BL 56:633; CC:475; CCBB 13:128; HB 36:128; KR 28:90; LJ 85:2035)

2405 **COUNSEL, June.** *A Dragon in Class 4.* **Gr. 3–5. (Orig. British pub. 1984.)**

An omniscient and vain young dragon named Scales adopts Sam as his boy and secretly manages to help him and his classmates with their school assignments.

Illus. by Jill Bennett, Faber, 1984, 102 pp., o.p.

(BBC:201; CCBB 38:21; SLJ Dec 1984 p. 79)

2406 **COVILLE, Bruce.** *Jennifer Murdley's Toad* **(Magic Shop books, vol. 2). Gr. 3–6.**

✓ After her worst fifth-grade enemy turns into a toad, Jennifer realizes that the talking toad she bought at Mr. Elives's magic shop transforms anyone who kisses it. *The Monster's Ring* (Pantheon, 1982; see below) and *Jeremy Thatcher, Dragon Hatcher* (Harper, 1991; see below) involve the same magic shop.

Illus. by Gary A. Lippincott, Harcourt, 1992, 160 pp. (0-15-200745-8); Pocket, 1993, pap. (0-671-79401-9)

(BL 88:1357; CC 1993 Suppl. p. 68; CCBB 45:292; HBG 3[Fall 1992]:262; KR 60:462; SLJ Sept 1992 p. 250)

2407 **COVILLE, Bruce.** *Jeremy Thatcher, Dragon Hatcher* **(Magic Shop books, vol. 1). Gr. 5–7.**

✓ The small marbled ball Jeremy buys at Mr. Elives's magic shop turns out to be a dragon egg that hatches into a scaly red dragon named Tiamat, invisible except to Jeremy and one friend. *The Monster's Ring* (Pantheon, 1982; see below) and *Jennifer Murdley's Toad* (Harcourt, 1992; see above) involve the same magic shop.

Illus. by Gary A. Lippincott, Harcourt, 1991, 160 pp. (0-15-200748-2); Pocket, 1992, pap. (0-671-74782-7)

(BL 87:1798; CC 1992 Suppl. p. 56; HBG 2:265; KR 59:246; SLJ May 1991 p. 91; VOYA 14:106)

2408   **COVILLE, Bruce.** *The Monster's Ring.* **Gr. 4–6.**

At Elives's Magic Supply Store, Russell finds a ring that can turn him into a monster—but can he turn himself back? *Jeremy Thatcher, Dragon Hatcher* (Harper, 1991; see above) and *Jennifer Murdley's Toad* (Harcourt, 1992, see above) also involve Mr. Elives's magic shop.

Illus. by Katherine Coville, Pantheon, 1982, 87 pp. (0-394-85320-2); Pocket, 1989, pap. (0-671-69389-1)

(BBS:201; BL 79:498; SLJ Feb 1983 p. 75)

2409   **CRESSWELL (Rowe), Helen.** *Almost Goodbye.* **Gr. 2–4. (Orig. British pub. 1990.)**

Gumball Gumford is granted his wish for invisiblity after he and Susie Potts find a genie in a magic lamp while collecting "white elephants" for their school sale.

Illus. by Judy Brown, Dutton, 1992, 62 pp. (0-525-44858-6)

(CCBB 46:8; HBG 3[Fall 1992]:253; SLJ Sept 1992 p. 202)

2410   **CRESSWELL (Rowe), Helen.** *The Beachcombers.* **Gr. 5–8. (Orig. British pub.**
✓   **1972.)**

On holiday at the coast, Ned is caught in a feud between the beachcombing Pickerings and the scavenging Dallakers, distant cousins searching for their lost family treasure.

Macmillan, 1972, 133 pp., o.p.

(BL 69:646; CCBB 26:74; HB 49:52; TLS 1972 p. 1312)

2411   **CRESSWELL (Rowe), Helen.** *The Bongleweed.* **Gr. 5–7. (Orig. British pub.**
✓   **1973.)**

The magic seeds Becky plants change neatly manicured Pew Gardens into a jungle of bongleweed. Carnegie Medal Commended Book, 1973.

Macmillan, 1973, 138 pp., o.p.

(BL 70:540; CCBB 27:174; Ch&Bks:262; KR 41:1159; LJ 98:3143; Suth 2:109; TLS 1973 p. 1428)

2412   **CRESSWELL (Rowe), Helen.** *The Secret World of Polly Flint.* **Gr. 5–7. (Orig.**
✓   **British pub. 1982.)**

Banished to live with her Aunt Em during her father's recuperation from a mine accident, fanciful Polly Flint senses the magic surrounding an ancient maypole and becomes involved with the Time Gypsies, people who have "slipped the net of time" between Polly's world and the centuries-old village of Grimstone, which disappeared from that very site. Runnerup, Whitbread Literary Award, Children's Book Category, 1982.

Illus. by Shirley Felts, Macmillan, 1984, o.p., pap., 1991, 176 pp. (0-689-71532-3)

(BBC:201; BL 80:1624; CC:476; CCBB 37:183; Ch&Bks:284; HB 60:465; KR 52[May 1, 1984]:J38; SLJ Aug 1984 p. 70; Suth 3:107)

2413   **CRESSWELL (Rowe), Helen.** *The White Sea Horse.* **Gr. 3–5. (Orig. British pub. 1964.)**

Six donkeys mysteriously disappear after the mayor of Piskerton takes away the tiny white horse Molly's fisherman father drew up in his net.

Illus. by Robin Jacques, Lippincott, 1964, 64 pp., o.p.

(KR 33:904; LJ 90:5511; TLS 1964 p. 605)

CRETAN, Gladys. *Joey's Head.* See Chapter 6, Humorous Fantasy.

CREW, Gary. *Strange Objects.* See Chapter 5B, Myth Fantasy.

2414 **CROSS, Gillian (pseud. of Claire Arnold).** *Twin and Super-Twin.* **Gr. 4–6. (Orig. British pub. 1990.)**

Cornered by a neighborhood gang, twins Ben and David discover that if Ben concentrates hard enough, he can transform David's right arm into amazing things, including a hissing snake.

Illus. by Maureen Bradley, Holiday, 1990, 176 pp. (0-8234-0840-X)

(BL 87:521; CCBB 44:113; HBG 2[July 1990]:74; KR 58:1248; SLJ Jan 1991 p. 88)

CROSS, John Kier. *The Other Side of Green Hills.* See Chapter 5C, Travel to Other Worlds.

CROTHERS, Samuel McChord. *Miss Muffet's Christmas Party.* See Chapter 1, Allegorical Fantasy and Literary Fairy Tales.

CURLEY, Daniel. *Ann's Spring.* See Chapter 5B, Myth Fantasy.

CURRY, Jane Louise. *Beneath the Hill.* See Chapter 5B, Myth Fantasy.

2415 **CURRY, Jane Louise.** *Mindy's Mysterious Miniature* **(Scholastic pap. title:** *The*
✓ *Mysterious Shrinking House,* **o.p.; British title:** *The Housenapper***). Gr. 3–5.**

Mindy and her neighbor, Mrs. Bright, are captured and shrunk to miniature size by Mr. Putt's miniaturizing machine. The "reducer" strikes again in *The Lost Farm* (1974), when Pete McCubbin and his family's entire farm are miniaturized by the unscrupulous Professor Lilliput.

Illus. by Charles Robinson, Harcourt, 1970, 157 pp., o.p.; Peter Smith, 1989 (0-8446-6433-2)

(BL 67:340; CCBB 24:104; HB 46:616; KR 38:1146; LJ 95:4374; Suth:96; TLS 1971 p. 774)

CUYLER, Margery. *Weird Wolf.* See Chapter 6, Humorous Fantasy.

2416 **DAHL, Roald.** *Charlie and the Chocolate Factory.* **Gr. 3–6. (Orig. British pub. 1964.)**

Charlie Bucket is one of five lucky children who win a tour of Wonka's wonderful chocolate factory. The sequel is *Charlie and the Great Glass Elevator* (1972, 1991). Dahl's depiction of Wonka's helpers as mischievous, music loving, chocolate-colored pygmies has been judged derogatory toward African Americans.

Illus. by Joseph Schindelman, Knopf, 1964, 161 pp., LB(0-394-91011-7); Bantam, 1984, pap., 176 pp. (0-553-15454-0); Puffin, 1988, pap. (0-14-032869-6)

(BBC:201; CCBB 18:115; Ch&Bks:280; HBG 3[July–Dec 1991]:64; KR 32:1009; LJ 89:5004; TLS 1978 p. 1398)

2417 **DAHL, Roald.** *George's Marvelous Medicine.* **Gr. 3–5. (Orig. British pub. 1981.)**

Eight-year-old George mixes up a batch of "medicine" which causes his grouchy grandmother to grow so tall that she bursts through the roof.

Illus. by Quentin Blake, Knopf, 1982, 1990, 89 pp., o.p.; Puffin, 1991, pap. (0-14-034641-4)

(BBC:201; CCBB 35:166; HBG 3[July–Dec 1991]:57; SLJ Apr 1982 p. 57; TLS 1981 p. 839)

2418 **DAHL, Roald.** *James and the Giant Peach: A Children's Story.* **Gr. 3–5. (Orig. British pub. 1961.)**

A magic potion enables James to escape from his cruel aunts and travel across the ocean in a huge peach, with human-sized insects as traveling companions. Richard R. George has turned this story into a play entitled: *Roald Dahl's James and the Giant Peach: A Play* (Penguin, 1983, pap.).

Illus. by Nancy Ekholm Burkert, Knopf, 1961, 118 pp., LB(0-394-91282-9); Bantam, 1984, pap. (0-553-15317-X); Puffin, 1988, pap. (0-14-032871-8)

(BBC:201; CC:477; CCBB 15:57; KR 29:727; LJ 86:4036)

2419   **DAHL, Roald.** *The Magic Finger.* **Gr. 2–4. (Orig. British pub. 1966.)**

✓   Zak puts the Magic Finger on her teacher and her duck-hunting neighbors, changing the former into a cat and the latter into bird-sized people hunted by huge ducks.

Illus. by William Pène Du Bois, Harper, 1966, 46 pp., LB(0-06-021382-5); Puffin, 1993, pap., 64 pp. (0-14-036303-3)

(BBC:201; BL 63:264; Ch&Bks:280; KR 34:830; LJ 91:5224)

2420   **DAHL, Tessa.** *Gwenda & the Animals.* **Gr. 2–5. (Original British pub. 1989.)**

Gwenda takes revenge on an uncle who teases the zoo animals after she finds she can understand their speech.

Illus. by Anthony Carnabuci, Viking, 1990, 48 pp., o.p.

(BL 87:1059; HBG 2[July 1990]:67; KR 58:1248; SLJ Dec 1990 p. 75)

DALTON, Annie. *Out of the Ordinary.* See Chapter 5C, Travel to Other Worlds.

DANK, Gloria Rand. *The Forest of App.* See Chapter 1, Allegorical Fantasy and Literary Fairy Tales.

DAVIES, Valentine. *The Miracle on 34th Street.* See Chapter 6, Humorous Fantasy.

DAWSON, Carley. *Mr. Wicker's Window.* See Chapter 8, Time Travel Fantasy.

2421   **DAWSON, Mitchell.** *The Magic Firecrackers.* **Gr. 4–6.**

✓   Uncle Dick brings the Carsons some six-hundred-year-old wish-granting Chinese firecrackers.

Illus. by Kurt Wiese, Viking, 1949, 192 pp., o.p.

(BL 46:144; CCBB 3:14; HB 26:36; KR 17:510)

DE FELICE, Cynthia. *The Strange Night Writing of Jessamine Colter.* See Chapter 1, Allegorical Fantasy and Literary Fairy Tales.

2422   **DE LA MARE, Walter (John).** *Crossings: A Fairy Play.* **Gr. 4–6. (Orig. British pub. 1921.)**

Four children spend their winter holiday at an old English country house inhabited by fairies.

Illus. by Dorothy P. Lathrop, Knopf, 1923, 170 pp., o.p.

(BL 20:221; Mahony 2:383)

DE LA MARE, Walter (John). *The Magic Jacket.* See Chapter 3, Fantasy Collections.

DE LINT, Charles. *The Little Country.* See Chapter 10, Witchcraft and Sorcery Fantasy.

2423   **DE REGNIERS, Beatrice Schenk (Freedman).** *The Boy, the Rat, and the Butterfly.* **Gr. 2–4.**

After he finds a jar of wish-granting bubble solution, Peter can stop worrying about his butterfly friend's short lifespan.

Illus. by Haig Shekerjian and Regina Shekerjian, Atheneum, 1971, 40 pp., o.p.

(CCBB 25:104; HB 47:475; KR 39:805)

2424   DERMAN, Martha. *Tales from Academy Street.* Gr. 5–7.

Eight stories set in the houses along Academy Street during one school year involving talking sneakers, a gardener who may be a mallard duck, and some ghostly spiders who take over a computer.

Scholastic, 1991, 103 pp. (0-5904-3703-8), 1992, pap. (0-590-43704-6)

(CCBB 45:7; HBG 3[Spring 1992]:65; KR 59:930; SLJ Aug 1991 p. 164; VOYA 14:238)

DEXTER, Catherine. *The Gilded Cat.* See Chapter 4, Ghost Fantasy.

DEXTER, Catherine. *The Oracle Doll.* See Chapter 9, Toy Fantasy.

DICKINSON, Peter (pseud. of Malcolm de Brissac). *A Box of Nothing.* See Chapter 5C, Travel to Other Worlds.

2425   DILLON, Barbara. *The Good-Guy Cake.* Gr. 2–4.

A "good-guy" cake baked in a magic oven turns Marvin into a suspiciously polite and helpful little boy.

Illus. by Alan Tiegreen, Morrow, 1980, 64 pp., o.p.

(BL 77:458; CCBB 34:91; KR 48:1163; SLJ Mar 1981 p. 130)

2426   DILLON, Barbara. *A Mom by Magic.* Gr. 4–6.

Jessica's department store wishing well-wish transforms mannequin Amalie Evans into Jessica's mom until Christmas day.

Illus. by Jeffrey Lindberg, Harper, 1990, 144 pp. (0-397-32450-2), 1991, (0-06-440388-2)

(BL 87:742; CCBB 44:27; HBG 2[July–Dec 1990]:77; SLJ Sept 1990 p. 224)

DILLON, Barbara. *Mrs. Tooey and the Terrible Toxic Tar.* See Chapter 10, Witchcraft and Sorcery Fantasy.

2427   DILLON, Barbara. *My Stepfather Shrank!* Gr. 3–6.

After her new stepfather eats some "weight-reduction" candy and shrinks to four and one-half inches in height, it is up to nine-year-old Mallory to reverse the magic before her mother comes home.

Illus. by Paul Casale, Harper, 1992, 128 pp. LB(0-06-021581-X); 1994, pap., 128 pp. (0-06-440459-5)

(BL 89:596; CCBB 46:109; HBG 4[Sept 1993] 66; KR 60:1374; SLJ Sept 1992 p. 250)

DILLON, Barbara. *What's Happened to Harry?* See Chapter 10, Witchcraft and Sorcery Fantasy.

DIXON, Marjorie. *The Forbidden Island.* See Chapter 5B, Myth Fantasy.

DOLBIER, Maurice (Wyman). *The Half-Pint Jinni, and Other Stories.* See Chapter 3, Fantasy Collections.

2428   DOLBIER, Maurice (Wyman). *The Magic Shop.* Gr. 3–5.

✓   Dick and Denise buy their father a magic wand as a birthday gift.

Illus. by Fritz Eichenberg, Random, 1946, 74 pp., o.p.

(BL 43:19; HB 22:350, 456; KR 14:324; LJ 71:1054)

2429 *Dragons & Dreams: A Collection of New Fantasy and Science Fiction Stories.* **Ed.**
✓ **by Jane Yolen, Martin H. Greenberg, and Charles G. Waugh. Gr. 5–9.**

Ten imaginative tales by Patricia McKillip, Jane Yolen, Diana Wynne Jones, Diane
Duane, Patricia MacLachlan, Zilpha Keatley Snyder, and others.

Harper, 1986, 180 pp., o.p.

(BBJ:76; BL 82:1219; CCBB 39:200; HB 62:459; JHC:431; SLJ May 1986 p. 99; VOYA 9:87, 10:21)

DRUON, Maurice. *Tistou of the Green Thumbs.* See Chapter 1, Allegorical Fantasy and Literary Fairy Tales.

DUANE, Diane (Elizabeth). *So You Want to Be a Wizard.* See Chapter 10, Witchcraft and Sorcery Fantasy.

2430 **DUNLOP, Eileen (Rhona).** *The House on Mayferry Street* (Orig. British title: *A
Flute in Mayferry Street,* 1976). **Gr. 7–10.**

Mysterious flute music and the search for hidden treasure bring excitement into the lives
of Colin and his invalid sister, Marion.

Illus. by Phillida Gili, Holt, 1977, 204 pp., o.p.

(BL 74:611; CCBB 31:91; HB 54:54; KR 45:990; SLJ Dec 1977 p. 62)

2431 **DURRELL, Gerald.** *The Fantastic Flying Journey.* **Gr. 3–6.** (Orig. British pub.
1987.)

When their scientist Great-Uncle Lancelot takes twins Conrad and Ivan and their sister
Emma on a hot-air balloon trip around the world, he gives them the magical ability to
communicate with any animal.

Illus. by Graham Percy, Simon & Schuster, 1989, 152 pp., o.p.; Sterling, 1990, pap. (0-
80697460-5)

(BL 85:1973; HBG 1[July–Dec 1989]:83; KR 57:915; SLJ July 1989 p. 82)

2432 **DUTTON, Sandra.** *The Magic of Myrna C. Waxweather.* **Gr. 3–5.**

Ten-year-old Bertha Zuchelli's fairy godmother appears with three magical items to help
overcome her reputation as teacher's pet: a fan, a boa, and a black satin camisole.

Illus. by Matthew Clark, Macmillan, 1987, 96 pp. (0-689-31273-3); Bantam, 1990, pap.
(0-553-15788-4)

(BL 83:1745; CCBB 40:186; KR 55:372; SLJ Apr 1987 p. 93)

2433 **EAGER, Edward (McMaken).** *Half Magic.* **Gr. 3–6.**
✓✓ Jane, Mark, Katharine, and Martha find a coin that grants half of every wish they make.
The sequel is *Magic by the Lake* (1957; Peter Smith, 1991), and two related books,
Knight's Castle (1956; Peter Smith, n.d.; see Chapter 5C, Travel to Other Worlds) and
Time Garden (1958; Peter Smith, n.d.), describe the magical adventures of their children.

Illus. by N. M. Bodecker, Harcourt, 1954, 217 pp. (0-15-233078-X), 1989, pap., 192 pp.
(0-15-233081-X)

(BL 50:363; CC:481; CCBB 7:86; Ch&Bks:280; HB 30:174; KR 22:232; LJ 79:784; TLS Nov 19, 1954 p.
vii)

EAGER, Edward (McMaken). *Knight's Castle.* See Chapter 5C, Travel to Other
Worlds.

2434 **EAGER, Edward (McMaken).** *Magic or Not?* **Gr. 4–6.**
✓ Did Laura, James, Lydia, and Kip's wishes come true because of magic, or was it only
coincidence? The sequel is *The Well-Wishers* (1960; Peter Smith, 1989).

Illus. by N. M. Bodecker, Harcourt, 1959, o.p., 1989, pap., 197 pp. (0-15-251160-1); Peter Smith, 1984 (0-8446-6154-6)

(BL 55:424; CCBB 12:131; Ch&Bks:280; HB 35:213; KR 26:906; LJ 84:1332; TLS Dec 4, 1959 p. xiv)

2435   EAGER, Edward (McMaken). *Seven-Day Magic.* **Gr. 4–6.**

✓ The main characters in Susan's library book turn out to be Susan, herself, and the friends who share her seven magic adventures.

Illus. by N. M. Bodecker, Harcourt, 1962, 156 pp., o.p., 1989, pap., 190 pp. (0-15-272916-X); Peter Smith, 1984 (0-8446-6381-6)

(BBC:203; CC:481; CCBB 16:78; Ch&Bks:280; HB 38:602; LJ 88:863; TLS 1963 p. 427)

ECKERT, Allan W. *The Dark Green Tunnel.* See Chapter 5C, Travel to Other Worlds.

EDWARDS, Dorothy. *The Witches and the Grinnygog.* See Chapter 10, Witchcraft and Sorcery Fantasy.

2436   EHRLICH, Amy. *Lucy's Winter Tale.* **Gr. K–4.**

A juggler from a traveling carnival awakens Lucy and convinces her to help him find his lost sweetheart, a high-wire artist.

Illus. by Troy Howell, Dial, 1992, 32 pp. LB(0-8037-0661-8)

(BL 88:1942; CCBB 46:144; KR 60:1060; SLJ Sept 1992 p. 202)

2437   ELIOT, Ethel (Augusta) Cook. *Buttercup Days.* **Gr. 4–6.**

Fairy Tim appears from Fairyland to spend the summer with the parsonage children.

Illus. by Julia Daniels, Doubleday, 1924, 188 pp., o.p.

(BL 21:30; Bookshelf 1924–1925 Suppl. p. 1; Mahony 2:135; HB 1[Oct 1924]:4)

ELISH, Dan. *Jason and the Baseball Bear.* See Chapter 2, Animal Fantasy.

2438   ELKIN, Benjamin. *Al and the Magic Lamp.* **Gr. 2–4.**

Every time Al tries to wish on Aladdin's magic lamp, something goes wrong.

Illus. by William Wiesner, Harper, 1963, 31 pp., o.p.

(BL 60:207; CCBB 16:125; HB 39:280; LJ 88:2550)

ENDE, Michael. *The Neverending Story.* See Chapter 5C, Travel to Other Worlds.

2439   ENRIGHT, Elizabeth (Wright). *Zeee.* **Gr. 2–4.**

✓ Pandora Smith gives a temperamental fairy a safe new home in her dollhouse.

Illus. by Irene Haas, Harcourt, 1965, 46 pp., o.p.; illus. by Susan Gaber, Harcourt, 1993, 48 pp. (0-15-299958-2)

(BL 89:1830; CCBB 18:127; HB 41:276; HGB 4[Fall 1993]:285; KR 33:309, 61:454; LJ 90:2883; SLJ June 1993 p. 73)

2440   ERWIN, Betty K. *Aggie, Maggie, and Tish.* **Gr. 3–5.**

Three elderly sisters bring magic into the lives of the four Eliot children. The sequel is *Where's Aggie?* (1967).

Illus. by Paul Kennedy, Little, 1965, 154 pp., o.p.

(BL 62:330; HB 41:628; KR 33:626; LJ 90:4615)

ESTERN, Anne Graham. *The Picolinis and the Haunted House.* See Chapter 9, Toy Fantasy.

ESTES, Eleanor (Ruth Rosenfeld). *The Witch Family.* See Chapter 10, Witchcraft and Sorcery Fantasy.

2441 **EWING, Juliana (Horatia Gatty).** *The Brownies.* **Gr. 4–6. (Orig. British pub. 1865; U.S., 1901, in** *The Brownies and Other Tales.***)**

Lazy children become helpful brownies, in this story that gave rise to the Brownie Scout name.

Illus. by Katherine Milhous, Scribner, 1946, 50 pp., o.p.; illus. by Ernest H. Shepard, Dutton, 1954, o.p.

(BL 43:140; KR 14:523; LJ 72:83)

2442 **FARALLA, Dana.** *The Singing Cupboard.* **Gr. 3–5. (Orig. British pub. 1962.)**

A magical mouse takes Nils and Ulla on a journey from Denmark to England.

Illus. by Edward Ardizzone, Lippincott, 1963, 94 pp., o.p.

(BL 60:630; HB 40:174; LJ 88:4852; TLS 1962 p. 900)

2443 **FARALLA, Dana.** *The Wonderful Flying-Go-Round.* **Gr. 4–6. (Orig. pub. in**
✓ **England.)**

Mr. and Mrs. Florabella drift across the town dump in a red balloon and decide to create a playground complete with a Flying-Go-Round.

Illus. by Harold Berson, World, 1965, 94 pp., o.p.

(BL 62:528; CCBB 20:24; HB 42:52; KR 33:905; LJ 90:5076)

FARBER, Norma. *Six Impossible Things before Breakfast.* See Chapter 3, Fantasy Collections.

2444 **FARJEON, Eleanor.** *Mr. Garden.* **Gr. 3–5. (Orig. British pub. in this format 1965.)**

A tiny man works wonders in Harry and Angela's garden.

Illus. by Jane Paton, Walck, 1966, 39 pp., o.p.

(CCBB 20:139; HB 42:429; LJ 91:4312; TLS 1966 p. 448)

2445 **FARMER (Mockridge), Penelope.** *The Magic Stone.* **Gr. 5–7. (Orig. British pub. 1964.)**

Caroline and Alice's obsession with a magic stone blinds them to the growing rivalry between their younger brothers' gangs.

Illus. by John Kaufmann, Harcourt, 1964, 223 pp., o.p.

(CCBB 18:53; HB 41:52; KR 32:898; LJ 89:4646; TLS 1965 p. 513)

2446 **FARMER (Mockridge), Penelope.** *The Summer Birds.* **Gr. 4–7. (Orig. British**
✓✓ **pub. 1962.)**

A strange boy spends the summer teaching Charlotte, Emma, and their friends to fly, but the magic ends when they learn his true identity. Carnegie Medal Commended Book, 1962. The sequels are *Charlotte Sometimes* (1969, see Chapter 8, Time Travel Fantasy) and *Emma in Winter* (1966).

Illus. by James J. Spanfeller, Harcourt, 1962, 155 pp., o.p.; Dell, 1987, pap. (0-440-47737-9); Peter Smith, 1991, o.p.

(BL 58:728; CCBB 15:124 Ch&Bks:260; HB 38:176; KR 30:58; LJ 87:2032; TLS 1985 p. 348)

FARMER (Mockridge), Penelope. *William and Mary: A Story.* See Chapter 5C, Travel to Other Worlds.

FARTHING, Alison. *The Mystical Beast.* See Chapter 5C, Travel to Other Worlds.

2447 **FAULKNER, William (Cuthbert).** *The Wishing Tree.* **Gr. 4 up. (Written 1927.)**

A strange red-headed boy leads a birthday-girl and her friends on a magical hunt for the wishing tree, in this story by the Nobel Prize-winning author.

Illus. by Don Bolognese, Random, 1967, 81 pp. (0-394-45222-4)

(BL 63:1132; LJ 92:1176; TLS Nov 1967 p. 1133)

2448 **FEYDY, Anne (Lindbergh Sapieyevski).** *Osprey Island.* **Gr. 4–6.**

Through magic, Lizzie, Charles, and Amy enter identical paintings of their houses and meet on an island called Carmar-Ogali-Retne.

Illus. by Maggie Smith, Houghton, 1974, 164 pp., o.p.

(CCBB 28:128; HB 51:146; KR 42:1201; LJ 98:3045)

2449 **FIELD, Rachel (Lyman).** *The Magic Pawnshop; a New Year's Eve Fantasy.* **Gr. 3–5.**

While tending Minerva MacLoon's shop on New Year's Eve, Prinda Bassett uses magic to spark a romance between Rose Martha and Christopher Marlowe Green.

Illus. by Elizabeth MacKinstry, Dutton, 1927, 125 pp., o.p.

(BL 24:125; HB 3[Nov 1927]:47; LJ 53:484)

2450 **FIENBERG, Anna.** *The Magnificent Nose and Other Marvels.* **Gr. 2–4. (Orig. Australian pub. 1991.)**

Aristan, a golden spider, gives the children in these five whimsical stories advice about discovering their special talents and putting them to good use.

Illus. by Kim Gamble, Little, Brown, 1992, 48 pp. (0-316-28195-6)

(BL 89:438; HB 68:582; KR 60:920; SLJ Jan 1993 p. 74)

FIENBERG, Anna. *Wiggy and Boa.* See Chapter 6, Humorous Fantasy.

FINNEY, Charles G(randison). *The Circus of Dr. Lao.* See Chapter 5B, Myth Fantasy.

FLEISCHMAN, (Albert) Sid(ney). *The Hey Hey Man.* See Chapter 1, Allegorical Fantasy and Literary Fairy Tales.

2451 **FORBUS, Ina B(ell).** *The Magic Pin.* **Gr. 4–6.**

Neelie, the seventh grand-daughter of a seventh grand-daughter, inherits a broach enabling her to speak to animals.

Illus. by Corydon Bell, Viking, 1956, 138 pp., o.p.

(CCBB 10:135; KR 24:435; LJ 81:2726)

2452 **FOSBURGH, Liza.** *Bella Arabella.* **Gr. 3–5.**

Lonely Arabella's wish to become a cat is granted by her talking feline, Miranda, but Arabella finds that life as a cat is not quite what she imagined.

Illus. by Catherine Stock, Macmillan, 1985, 102 pp. (0-02-735430-X); Bantam, 1987, pap. (0-553-15484-2)

(BBC:203; BL 82:756; CCBB 39:127; SLJ Mar 1986 p. 162)

FOSTER, Elizabeth. *Gigi: The Story of a Merry-Go-Round Horse.* See Chapter 9, Toy Fantasy.

FRANCHI, Anna. *The Little Lead Soldier.* See Chapter 9, Toy Fantasy.

2453 FRAZIER, Neta Lohnes. *The Magic Ring.* **Gr. 4–6.**

Fairy child gives sensible Rebecca Osborn a magic ring and three wishes.

Illus. by Kathleen Voute, Longmans, 1959, 149 pp., o.p.

(BL 56:247; HB 35:382; KR 27:402; LJ 84:3926)

2454 FRITZ, Jean (Guttery). *Magic to Burn.* **Gr. 4–6.**

On a ship bound for America, Stephen and Ann meet a stowaway boggart named Blaze.

Illus. by Beth Krush and Joe Krush, Coward, 1964, 255 pp., o.p.

(BL 61:711; CCBB 18:74; LJ 89:3470)

2455 FROST, Frances. *Then Came Timothy.* **Gr. 4–6.**

Kathy and her grandparents have an eventful three-day visit from an Irish leprechaun.

Illus. by Richard Bennett, Whittlesey, 1950, 155 pp., o.p.

(BL 47:47; HB 26:375; KR 18:418; LJ 75:1834)

FRY, Rosalie K(ingsmill). *The Mountain Door.* See Chapter 5C, Travel to Other Worlds.

2456 FRY, Rosalie K(ingsmill). *Mungo.* **Gr. 3–5.**

Richie's summer adventures with a sea monster take him to an uncharted isle inhabited by a shipwrecked sailor.

Illus. by Velma Ilsley, Farrar, 1972, 123 pp., o.p.

(BL 68:1004; HB 48:370; KR 40:324)

2457 **GAGE, Wilson (pseud. of Mary Q[uintard] Govan Steele).** *Miss Osborne-the-*
✓ *Mop.* **Gr. 4–6.**

Jody's magic abilities bring a dust mop to life, but she soon regrets her actions.

Illus. by Paul Galdone, Philomel, 1963, 156 pp., o.p.

(BL 59:747; CCBB 16:110; Eakin:133; HB 39:382; LJ 88:2143)

GALL, Alice (Crew), and CREW, Fleming. *The Royal Mimkin.* See Chapter 5C, Travel to Other Worlds.

2458 GALLICO, Paul (William). *The House That Wouldn't Go Away.* **Gr. 5–7.**

Visions of the Victorian mansion that once stood on the site of their apartment building enable Miranda and her brothers to delve into the lives of their neighbors.

Delacorte, 1980, 234 pp., o.p.

(BL 76:1290; CCBB 32:189; HB 56:406; SLJ Aug 1980 p. 64)

2459 GANNETT (Kahn), Ruth Stiles. *My Father's Dragon.* **Gr. 3–5.**
✓ When a stray alley cat tells him about a captive baby dragon, Elmer Elevator decides to run away and rescue it. John Newbery Medal Honor Book, 1949. The sequels are *Elmer and the Dragon* (1950, 1987) and *The Dragons of Blueland* (1951, 1987).

Illus. by Ruth Chrisman Gannett, Random, 1948, 1986, 88 pp., LB(0-394-91438-4); Knopf, 1987, pap., 96 pp. (0-394-89048-5)

(BL 44:320, 83:708; CC:488; CCBB 1[June 1948]:2; HB 26:266, 63:82; KR 16:194; LJ 73:604, 824)

GARDEN, Nancy. *Fours Crossing.* See Chapter 5B, Myth Fantasy.

GEE, Maurice (Gough). *The World Around the Corner.* See Chapter 5C, Travel to Other Worlds.

GENTLE, Mary. *A Hawk in Silver.* See Chapter 5C, Travel to Other Worlds.

GODDEN (Dixon), (Margaret) Rumer. *Fu-Dog.* See Chapter 9, Toy Fantasy.

GOLDS, Cassandra. *Michael and the Secret War.* See Chapter 5C, Travel to Other Worlds.

GORDON, John (William). *The Giant under the Snow: A Story of Suspense.* See Chapter 5B, Myth Fantasy.

2460   GORMLEY, Beatrice. *Best Friend Insurance.* **Gr. 4–6.**

Maureen's purchase of "best friend insurance" from mysterious Mr. Costue results in her mother's transformation into a girl named Kitty who expects Maureen to run the household.

Illus. by Emily Arnold McCully, Dutton, 1983, 147 pp. (0-525-44066-6); Avon, 1985, pap. (0-380-69854-4)

(BBC:204; BL 80:813; CCBB 37:87; SLJ Feb 1984 p. 70)

2461   GORMLEY, Beatrice. *Fifth Grade Magic.* **Gr. 4–6.**

A delinquent apprentice-fairy godmother named Errora does a bungled job of granting fifth-grader Gretchen's wish to be the lead in the class play. The sequel is *More Fifth Grade Magic* (1989, 1990).

Illus. by Emily Arnold McCully, Dutton, 1982, o.p.; Avon, 1983, pap., 136 pp. (0-380-67439-4)

(BBC:204; BL 79:564; HB 58:516; SLJ Oct 1982 p. 152)

2462   GORMLEY, Beatrice. *Mail-Order Wings.* **Gr. 4–6.**

Andrea finds she can actually fly using her Wonda-Wings Kit, but she becomes frightened when the wings won't come off. The sequel is *The Ghastly Glasses* (1985).

Illus. by Emily Arnold McCully, Elsevier-Dutton, 1981, 164 pp., o.p.; Avon, 1984, pap., 164 pp. (0-380-67421-1)

(BBC:204; BL 78:235; CCBB 35:107; SLJ Dec 1981 p. 63; Suth 3:157)

2463   GORMLEY, Beatrice. *Paul's Volcano.* **Gr. 4–7.**

Paul and Adam's science project, a paper-mâché volcano, begins to grow during the night, and they fear that they've summoned up an ancient volcano god.

Illus. by Cat Bowen Smith, Houghton, 1987, 144 pp. (0-395-43079-8); Avon, 1988, pap., 160 pp. (0-380-70562-1)

(BL 83:1445; KR 55:552; SLJ Mar 1987 p. 158)

GOROG, Judith. *On Meeting Witches at Wells.* See Chapter 4, Ghost Fantasy.

2464   GOUDGE, Elizabeth (de Beauchamp). *Linnets and Valerians.* **Gr. 5–7. (Orig.**
✓   **pub. in England.)**

After Mrs. Valerian takes in the runaway Linnet children, they decide to repay her kindness by searching for her long-lost son. On the way, they encounter a witch, giants, and magic cats.

Illus. by Ian Ribbons, Coward, 1946, o.p.; Gregg, 1981, 290 pp., o.p.; Dell, 1992, pap. (0-440-40590-4)

(BL 61:578; CCBB 18:74; Eakin:145; HB 40:615; TLS 1964 p. 1077)

2465   GOUDGE, Elizabeth (de Beauchamp). *The Little White Horse.* **Gr. 5–8. (Orig.**
✓   **British pub. 1946.)**

Magical creatures help Maria Merryweather fight the evil Black Men of the forest. Carnegie Medal, 1946.

Illus. by C. Walter Hodges, Coward, 1947, o.p.; Gregg, 1980, 280 pp., o.p.; Dell, 1992, pap., 272 pp. (0-440-40734-6)

(BL 43:349; HB 23:212; KR 15:167; LJ 72:738)

2466 **GOUDGE, Elizabeth (de Beauchamp).** *Smoky-House.* **Gr. 5–8. (Orig. British pub. 1940.)**

Fairies help the Trequddick children save their father from betrayal as a smuggler.

Illus. by Richard Floethe, Coward, 1940, o.p.; Buccaneer, 1983 (repr.), 391 pp. (0-89966-108-4)

(BL 37:94; HB 16:343, 430; LJ 65:849, 878; TLS 1940 p. 634)

2467 **GRAVES, Robert.** *The Big Green Book.* **Gr. 2–3.**

Jack uses spells from a big green magic book to fool his overprotective aunt and uncle into letting him have more freedom.

Illus. by Maurice Sendak, Crowell-Collier, 1962, 1968, o.p.; Macmillan, 1985, 61 pp. (0-02-736810-6), 1988, pap. (0-689-71402-5)

(BL 81:1333; HB 61:437)

2468 **GRAY, Genevieve S(tuck).** *The Seven Wishes of Joanna Peabody.* **Gr. 3–5.**

Joanna is granted seven wishes by Aunt Thelma, a Special Spirit who appears on Joanna's TV screen.

Illus. by Elton Fax, Lothrop, 1972, 61 pp., o.p.

(BL 69:493; CCBB 26:154; KR 40:939; LJ 97:3806)

2469 **GRAY, Nicholas Stuart.** *The Apple Stone.* **Gr. 5–7. (Orig. British pub. 1965.)**

A golden Apple Stone brings a stuffed bird, a model rocket, a leopard-skin rug, and a stone gargoyle to life.

Illus. by Charles Keeping, Hawthorn, 1969, 230 pp., o.p.

(BL 66:408; CCBB 23:128; KR 37:777; LJ 94:4582, 4606; TLS 1965 p. 1131)

2470 **GREEN, Phyllis.** *Eating Ice Cream with a Werewolf.* **Gr. 4–6.**

When Brad and Nancy's wacky baby-sitter decides to try out her new hobby, witchcraft, the chicken that turns up in Nancy's bed is only one of many strange results.

Illus. by Patti Stern, Harper, 1983, 121 pp., o.p.; Dell, 1985, pap. (0-440-42182-9)

(BL 79:1465; CCBB 36:189; HB 59:302)

2471 **GREEN, Susan.** *Self-Portrait with Wings.* **Gr. 5–7.**

After the wings Jennifer drew on her self-portrait appear in real life, she is able to do a fabulous "Jennifer Jump" on ice skates.

Little, Brown, 1989, 206 pp., o.p.

(BBC:204; BL 85:1649; CCBB 42:275; HB 65:620; KR 57:762; SLJ May 1989 p. 109)

2472 **GRIFFIN, Peni R(ae).** *Hobkin.* **Gr. 5–8.**

Running away from their stepfather's abuse, Liza and Kay Frandlin take over an abandoned farmhouse. While Kay works in a nearby store, Liza does the household chores with the help of Hobkin, a brownie who traveled to West Texas from England with the farm's former owner.

Macmillan, 1992, 202 pp. (0-689-50539-6); Puffin, 1993, pap. (0-14-036356-4)

(BL 88:1378; CCBB 45:261; HBG 3[Fall 1992]:263; KR 60:537; SLJ June 1992 p. 136; VOYA 15:94)

2473 **GRIFFIN, Peni R(ae).** *Otto from Otherwhere.* **Gr. 4–6.**

A science-fantasy about Paula and Peter, who find an odd-looking alien with a beautiful singing voice, name him Otto, try to pass him off as their cousin, and help him find his way home.

Macmillan, 1990, 192 pp. (0-689-50500-0); Knopf, 1992, pap. (0-679-81571-6)

(BL 86:1702; CCBB 43:264; HBG 1[Jan–June 1990]:258; KR 58:499; SLJ Aug 1990 p. 146)

GRIFFITH, Helen V(irginia). *Caitlin's Holiday.* See Chapter 9, Toy Fantasy.

2474 GRIFFITH, Helen V(irginia). *Emily and the Enchanted Frog.* **Gr. 1–3.**

✓ In these three stories Emily meets an unwilling frog prince, a wish-granting elf, and a hermit crab that thinks it's a mermaid.

Illus. by Susan Condie Lamb, Greenwillow, 1989, 32 pp., o.p.

(BL 86:180; CCBB 43:33; HBG 1[July 1989]:49; KR 57:989; SLJ Sept 1989 p. 226)

2475 GRIMBLE, Rosemary. *Jonothon and Large.* **Gr. 2–4. (Orig. British pub. 1965.)**

The sea-serpent that Jonothon raised returns to save him and his father from a hurricane at sea.

Illus. by the author, Bobbs-Merrill, 1966, 88 pp., o.p.

(KR 38:340; LJ 92:2014; TLS 1965 p. 1131)

GROSSER, Morton. *The Snake Horn.* See Chapter 8, Time Travel Fantasy.

2476 GUILLOT, René. *Nicolette and the Mill.* **Gr. 2–4. (Orig. pub. in France.)**

An emerald fairy ring enables Nicolette to understand the language of animals.

Trans. by Gwen Marsh, illus. by Charles Mozley, Abelard-Schuman, 1960, 79 pp., o.p.

(KR 28:949; LJ 86:373; TLS May 20, 1960 p. vii)

GURNEY, James. *Dinotopia: A Land Apart from Time.* See Chapter 5C, Travel to Other Worlds.

HAAS, Dorothy. *The Bears Up Stairs.* See Chapter 2, Animal Fantasy.

HACKETT, Walter Anthony. *The Swans of Ballycastle.* See Chapter 1, Allegorical Fantasy and Literary Fairy Tales.

HALAM, Ann. *The Daymaker.* See Chapter 5A, Alternate Worlds or Histories.

HAMILTON (Adoff), Virginia (Esther). *The All Jadhu Storybook.* See Chapter 6, Humorous Fantasy.

2477 HAMLEY, Dennis. *Blood Line.* **Gr. 9–12. (Orig. British pub. 1989.)**

A strange television saga comes to life in television-obsessed Rory's home, causing the high school loner to become haunted by questions about his family's past.

Deutsch, 1990, pap., 160 pp, o.p.

(BBS:58; BBJ:71; BL 87:46; SLJ Sept 1990 p. 250)

2478 HANLEY, Eve. *The Enchanted Toby Jug.* **Gr. 3–5. (Orig. British pub. 1964.)**

A Toby jug comes to life and tells stories to four children.

Illus. by Nora S. Unwin, Washburn, 1965, 134 pp., o.p.

(KR 33:6; LJ 90:960; TLS 1964 p. 602)

2479 HANSEN, Ron. *The Shadowmaker.* **Gr. 3–6.**

✓ Drizzle, the poorest child in town, manages to outwit the Shadowmaker, a mysterious man who sells shadows of people's secret dreams.

Illus. by Margot Tomes, Harper, 1987, 80 pp., LB(0-06-022203-4), 1989, pap. (0-06-440287-8)

(BBC:204; BL 83:1446; CCBB 40:125; HB 63:605; KR 55:719; SLJ Aug 1987 p. 83)

HARRIS, Rosemary (Jeanne). *Sea Magic and Other Stories of Enchantment.* See Chapter 3, Fantasy Collections.

2480 HARVEY, Dean. *The Secret Elephant of Harlan Kooter.* **Gr. 3–5.**

Harlan's problems with bullies and managing his solo paper route are solved after he finds Hannibal the talking elephant hiding in his garage.

Illus. by Mark Richardson, Houghton, 1992, 130 pp. (0-395-62523-8)

(CCBB 46:113; HB 68:724; HBG 4[Spring 1993]:69; KR 60:1187; SLJ Nov 1992 p. 91)

HASELEY, Dennis. *Doctor Gravity.* See Chapter 6, Humorous Fantasy.

HAUFF, Wilhelm. *The Adventures of Little Mouk.* See Chapter 1, Allegorical Fantasy and Literary Fairy Tales.

HAWKINS, Laura. *Figment, Your Dog, Speaking.* See Chapter 2, Animal Fantasy.

HAWTHORNE, Julian. *Rumpty-Dudget's Tower: A Fairy Tale.* See Chapter 1, Allegorical Fantasy and Literary Fairy Tales.

2481 HEAL (Berrien), Edith. *What Happened to Jenny.* **Gr. 3–5.**

Neighborhood dogs take Jenny on a tour of the city although she is supposed to be in bed recovering from the measles.

Illus. by Abbi Giventer, Atheneum, 1962, 62 pp., o.p.

(HB 39:53, 76; KR 30:559)

2482 HENDRICH, Paula (Griffith). *Who Says So?* **Gr. 4–6.**

Lucinda conjures up an apparition and decides to use it as her science project at the county fair.

Illus. by Trina Schart Hyman, Lothrop, 1972, 160 pp., o.p.

(CCBB 26:56; KR 40:259; LJ 98:644)

2483 HENDRY, Diana. *A Camel Called April.* **Gr. 2–3. (Orig. British pub. 1990.)**

When the animals from Harry's dreams begin appearing in the park next door he tries to dream them away, but one camel refuses to leave.

Illus. by Thor Wickstrom, Lothrop, 1991, 48 pp. (0-688-10193-3)

(HBG 2[Fall 1991]:255; SLJ Aug 1991 p. 150)

2484 HENRY, Jan. *Tiger's Chance.* **Gr. 3–5.**

✓ A tiger rug with magic whiskers takes Jennifer and her cat, Midnight, to his jungle home.

Illus. by Hilary Knight, Harcourt, 1957, 138 pp., o.p.

(BL 53:460; CCBB 10:130; Eakin:156; HB 33:222; KR 25:218; LJ 82:2190)

HENRY, Maeve. *A Gift for a Gift: A Ghost Story.* See Chapter 4, Ghost Fantasy.

2485 HESS, Fjeril. *The Magic Switch.* **Gr. 2–4.**

Marenka's magic birch switch enables her to talk to animals, trees, and flowers.

Illus. by Neva Kanaga Brown, Macmillan, 1929, 74 pp., o.p.

(BL 26:166; HB 5:46, 49; Mahony 3:173)

2486   HILL, Douglas. *Penelope's Pendant.* **Gr. 4–6. (Orig. British pub. 1990.)**

The tarnished pendant Perry finds on the beach proves to have magic powers when she is threatened by a gang of older boys.

Doubleday, 1991, 112 pp. (0-385-41641-5)

(BL 87:1493; HBG 2:270; KR 59:107; SLJ Mar 1991 p. 193)

2487   HILL, Elizabeth Starr. *Ever-After Island.* **Gr. 4–6.**

Ryan and Sara search the Cavern of the Winds for the magic jewel needed to break the spell that binds their father.

Dutton, 1977, 160 pp., o.p.

(BL 73:1497; CCBB 31:34; Kr 45:575; SLJ Sept 1977 p. 130)

2488   HILLER, Catherine. *Abracatabby.* **Gr. 2–4.**

Although Adam's black kitten, Abracatabby, can do magic and grant wishes, the cat doesn't want anyone else to know his secret.

Illus. by Victoria de Larrea, Coward, 1981, 62 pp., o.p.

(BL 77:1350; KR 49:799; SLJ Nov 1981 p. 77)

HISER, Constance. *The Missing Doll.* See Chapter 9, Toy Fantasy.

2489   HISER, Constance. *No Bean Sprouts, Please!* **Gr. 2–4.**

The lunch box James's Uncle Wesley sends for his ninth birthday turns James's health-food lunches into delicious cheeseburgers and fries.

Illus. by Carolyn Ewing, Holiday, 1989, 57 pp. (0-8234-0760-8); Pocket, 1991, pap. (0-671-72325-1)

(BL 86:743; HBG 1[July 1989]:75; KR 57:1826; SLJ Nov 1989 p. 83)

2490   HITE, Sid. *Dither Farm.* **Gr. 6–10.**

✓   The Dither family's quiet life on the farm is transformed after their world-traveling Great-Aunt Emma leaves orphaned eleven-year-old Warren and a magic carpet in their care.

Henry Holt, 1992, 216 pp. (0-8050-1871-9)

(BL 88:1676; CC 1993 Suppl. p. 70; HBG 3[Fall 1992]:274; KR 60:719; SLJ May 1992 p. 133; VOYA 16:90)

2491   HOFFMAN, Mary. *The Four-Legged Ghosts.* **Gr. 2–5. (Orig British title:** *The*
✓   *Ghost Menagerie,* **1992.)**

Alex and Carrie's pet mouse, Cedric, can magically summon the ghosts of all the pets who ever lived in the Brodie's house.

Illus. by Laura L. Seeley, Dial, 1993, 96 pp. (0-8037-1466-1)

(BL 90:60; CCBB 47:156; HBG 5:66; KR 61:1002; SLJ Aug 1993 p. 164)

HOFFMANN, E(rnst) T(heodor) A(madeus). *The Nutcracker.* See Chapter 9, Toy Fantasy.

2492   HOFFMANN, Eleanor. *Mischief in Fez.* **Gr. 4–6.**

Mousa's new stepmother brings evil Djinns to disrupt the household, but a desert fox flies the boy over the mountains to find a magical solution to his problems.

Illus. by Fritz Eichenberg, Holiday, 1943, 109 pp., o.p.

(BL 39:373; HB 19:170; LJ 68:433, 825)

HOLT, Tom. *Who's Afraid of Beowulf?* See Chapter 5B, Myth Fantasy.

2493 HOPP, Zinken. *The Magic Chalk.* **Gr. 3–5. (Orig. Norwegian pub. 1948.)**

John uses a witch's magic chalk to draw a boy who comes to life.

Trans. by Suzanne Bergensdahl, illus. by Malvin Neset, McKay, 1959, 127 pp., o.p.

(KR 27:492; LJ 85:844; TLS Nov 25, 1960 p. x)

HOUGH, (Helen) Charlotte (Woodyatt). *Red Biddy and Other Stories.* See Chapter 3, Fantasy Collections.

HOUSMAN, Laurence. *The Rat-Catcher's Daughter: A Collection of Stories.* See Chapter 3, Fantasy Collections.

2494 HOWARD, Alice (Woodbury). *Sokar and the Crocodile: A Fairy Story of Egypt.* **Gr. 3–5.**

A young Egyptian boy named Sokar finds himself inside a fairy story and goes on a quest in search of the magic lotus bud.

Illus. by Coleman Kubinyi, Macmillan, 1928, 1948, 58 pp., o.p.

(BL 25:170; HB 4[Nov 1928]:79, 4[Aug 1928]:19, 7:115; Mahony 2:424)

HOWARD, Joan (pseud. of Patricia Gordon). *The Oldest Secret.* See Chapter 5C, Travel to Other Worlds.

2495 HOWARD, Joan (pseud. of Patricia Gordon). *The Thirteenth Is Magic.* **Gr. 4–6.**

A black cat takes Ronnie and Gillian up to the magical thirteenth floor of their apartment building. The sequel is *The Summer Is Magic* (1952).

Illus. by Adrienne Adams, Lothrop, 1950, 170 pp., o.p.

(BL 47:224; CCBB 4:20; HB 27:31; KR 18:725; LJ 76:338)

HOYLAND, John. *The Ivy Garland.* See Chapter 4, Ghost Fantasy.

HUFF, Tanya. *Gate of Darkness, Circle of Light.* See Chapter 5B, Myth Fantasy.

2496 HUGHES, Dean. *Theo Zephyr.* **Gr. 5–7.**

Sixth-grader Brad's imaginary hero, Theo Zephyr, comes to life and exacts revenge on the school bully.

Macmillan, 1987, 128 pp., o.p.

(CCBB 40:210; KR 55:1071; SLJ Oct 1987 p. 126; VOYA 10:201)

2497 HUNT, Marigold. *Hester and the Gnomes.* **Gr. 2–5.**

Hester discovers that a group of gnomes have set up housekeeping in a hollow tree on her father's farm.

Illus. by Jean Charlot, Whittlesey, 1955, 124 pp., o.p.

(HB 31:376; KR 23:417; LJ 80:2645)

2498 HUNTER, Mollie (pseud. of Maureen Mollie Hunter McVeigh McIlwraith). *The Ferlie.* **Gr. 4–6. (Orig. pub. in England.)**

Hob the herd boy enters into a battle of wits with a ferlie over some stolen cattle.

Illus. by Joseph Cellini, Funk, 1968, 128 pp., o.p.

(BL 65:498; CCBB 22:95; HB 45:55)

2499 HUNTER, Mollie (pseud. of Maureen Mollie Hunter McVeigh McIlwraith).
✓   *The Mermaid Summer.* **Gr. 4–7. (Orig. British pub. 1988.)**

Anna and Jon try to tame the mermaid who has power over their Scottish fishing village, in order to bring home their banished grandfather.

Harper, 1988, 128 pp. (0-06-022627-7), 1990, pap. (0-06-440344-0)

(BBC:205; BBJ:71; BL 84:1676, 85:879; CC:507; CCBB 41:180; HB 65:70; KR 54:828; SLJ June–July 1988 p. 105; Suth 4:195)

2500 **HUNTER, Mollie (pseud. of Maureen Mollie Hunter McVeigh McIlwraith).**
✓ *The Wicked One.* **Gr. 5–8. (Orig. pub. in England.)**

Scottsman Colin Grant moves his family to America to avoid the devilish tricks of the Grollican, only to find that the demon has followed them.

Harper, 1977, 128 pp., o.p.; 1980, pap., 136 pp. (0-06-440117-0)

(BBC:205; BL 73:1339, 1352; CC:507; CCBB 30:160; HB 53:442; KR 45:426; SLJ May 1977 pp. 36, 62; Suth 2:234)

2501 **HURLBUTT, Isabelle B.** *Little Heiskell.* **Gr. 3–4.**

Little Heiskell, a soldier-shaped weather-vane, descends from the market-house roof to bring Christmas cheer to the children of Hagerstown.

Illus. by Alida Conover, Dutton, 1928, 59 pp., o.p.

(BL 25:127; Bookshelf 1929 p. 12; HB 4[Nov 1928]:80); Mahony 2:716)

2502 **HUTCHINS, Hazel (J.).** *Anastasia Morningstar.* **Gr. 3–5. (Orig. Canadian title:**
Anastasia Morningstar and the Crystal Butterfly, **1984.)**

Sarah wants to use Anastasia Morningstar's magical talents as a science project after she watches her neighbor turn an annoying boy into a frog.

Illus. by Julie Tennent, Viking, 1989, 88 pp., o.p.; Puffin, 1992, pap. (0-14-034343-1)

(BL 86:2090; HBG 1[Jan–June 1990]:256; SLJ Aug 1990 p. 148)

2503 **HUTCHINS, Hazel (J.).** *The Three and Many Wishes of Jason Reid.* **Gr. 2–5.**
✓ **(Orig. Canadian pub. 1983.)**

Jason convinces leprechaun-like Quicksilver to grant him a wish that won't just make him a better baseball player, but will make a difference in the world.

Illus. by Julie Tennent, Viking, 1988, 89 pp., o.p.; Puffin, 1990, pap. (0-14-032178-0)

(BBC:205; BL 84:1926; CCBB 41:208; KR 56:279; SLJ May 1989 p. 97; Suth 4:197)

INGELOW, Jean. *Mopsa the Fairy.* See Chapter 5C, Travel to Other Worlds.

IRVING, Washington. *Rip Van Winkle.* See Chapter 5B, Myth Fantasy.

2504 **JAMES, M(ontague) R(hodes).** *The Five Jars.* **Gr. 7 up.**

The magical contents of five jars discovered by an Englishman reveal the fairy world all around him.

Longman, 1922, 172 pp., o.p.; Ayer, 1976 (repr. of 1922 ed.), o.p.

(BL 19:224; HB 3[May 1927]:22)

JAMES, Mary. *Shoebag.* See Chapter 2, Animal Fantasy.

JAMES, Mary. *The Shuteyes.* See Chapter 5C, Travel to Other Worlds.

JANE, Pamela. *Noelle of the Nutcracker.* See Chapter 9, Toy Fantasy.

2505 **JARRELL, Randall.** *Fly by Night.* **Gr. 3–4.**
✓ A young boy floats out into the night, sees into dreams, listens to animals talking, and visits an owl's nest to hear a bedtime poem-story.

Illus. by Maurice Sendak, Farrar, 1969, 1976, 1985, 40 pp. (0-374-32348-8), pap., 1986 (0-374-42350-4)

(BL 73:474; CCBB 30:92; HB 53:52, 62:616; KR 44:1137; SLJ Nov 1976 p. 59; Suth 2:241)

JENNINGS, Paul. *Unreal! Eight Surprising Stories.* See Chapter 3, Fantasy Collections.

2506 **JOHNSON, Elizabeth.** *Break a Magic Circle.* **Gr. 3–5.**

An invisible boy asks Tilly to help break the magical spell over him.

Illus. by Trina Schart Hyman, Little, 1971, 70 pp., o.p.

(BL 68:109; CCBB 25:27; HB 47:482; KR 39:676)

2507 **JOHNSON, Elizabeth.** *No Magic, Thank You.* **Gr. 3–4.**

Gordon and Debbie's belief in magic helps them win a contest against the Unlucks, bringing more good luck into the world.

Illus. by Garrett Price, Little, 1964, 55 pp., o.p.

(CCBB 18:119; HB 40:499; KR 32:550)

2508 **JOHNSON, Elizabeth.** *Stuck with Luck.* **Grade 3–5.**

✓ Tom wishes for a dog but gets a powerless leprechaun instead.

Illus. by Trina Schart Hyman, Little, 1967, 88 pp., o.p.

(BL 64:198; HB 43:589; KR 35:740; LJ 92:3187)

JONES, Adrienne. *The Mural Master.* See Chapter 5C, Travel to Other Worlds.

2509 **JONES, David Lee.** *Unicorn Highway.* **Gr. 6–12.**

After Thaddy Williams discovers that his neighbor, Mr. Tucker, is growing wheat for a unicorn, Thaddy comes to believe that if he could only ride the unicorn all his dreams would come true.

Avon, 1992, pap., 339 pp. (0-380-76506-3)

(Kliatt Sept 1992 p. 22; VOYA 15:44, 16:16)

JONES, Diana Wynne. *Aunt Maria.* See Chapter 10, Witchcraft and Sorcery Fantasy.

JONES, Diana Wynne. *Eight Days of Luke.* See Chapter 5B, Myth Fantasy.

JONES, Diana Wynne. *The Lives of Christopher Chant.* See Chapter 5C, Travel to Other Worlds.

2510 **JONES, Diana Wynne.** *The Ogre Downstairs.* **Gr. 5–8. (Orig. British pub. 1974.)**

✓✓ Amazing things happen when Johnny and Malcolm use the chemistry sets given to them by "The Ogre," their new stepfather.

Dutton, 1975, 191 pp., o.p.; Greenwillow, 1990, 182 pp. (0-688-09195-4); Knopf, 1991, pap. (0-679-81839-1)

(BBJ:72; BL 71:1075; CC 1992 Suppl. p. 58; CCBB 28:179; HB 51:464, 66:480; HBG 1[Jan–June 1990]:254; KR 43:453; SLJ Sept 1975 p. 105; Suth 2:246; VOYA 13:116)

2511 **JONES, Diana Wynne.** *Stopping for a Spell: Three Fantasies.* **Gr. 3–6. (Orig.**
✓ **British titles:** *Chair Person,* **1989,** *The Four Grannies,* **1980, and "The Fearsome Friend," 1975.)**

Three fantasy novellas about a boy who magically transforms four grannies into one, an unwelcome visitor driven away by furniture he has insulted, and an old armchair that comes to life as an obnoxious person.

Illus. by Joseph A. Smith, Greenwillow, 1993, 148 pp. (0-688-11367-2)

(CCBB 46:348; HBG 4[Fall 1993]:299; KR 61:663; SLJ July 1993 p. 85)

JONES, Diana Wynne. *Warlock at the Wheel and Other Stories.* See Chapter 10, Witchcraft and Sorcery Fantasy.

2512   JONES, Elizabeth Orton. *Twig.* **Gr. 3–5.**

A little girl named Twig finds a fairy living in a tomato can.

Illus. by the author, Macmillan, 1942, 152 pp., o.p.

(BL 39:256; HB 19:102; LJ 67:884, 68:173)

JUSTER, Norton. *The Phantom Tollbooth.* See Chapter 5C, Travel to Other Worlds.

2513   KARR, Kathleen. *Gideon and the Mummy Professor.* **Gr. 5–8.**

✓   After twelve-year-old Gideon's con-artist father tries to sell a valuable scarab found in the wrappings of their ancient Egyptian mummy, they are pursued by other thieves and a voodoo queen, in this fast-moving tale set in 1885 New Orleans.

Farrar, 1993, 137 pp. (0-37432563-4)

(BL 89:1958; CCBB 47:12; HB 69:599; HBG 4:300; KR 61:663; SLJ June 1993 p. 107)

KATZ, Welwyn Wilton. *The Third Magic.* See Chapter 5C, Travel to Other Worlds.

KAYE, Marvin. *The Incredible Umbrella.* See Chapter 5C, Travel to Other Worlds.

KEELE, Luqman, and PINKWATER, D(aniel) Manus. *Java Jack.* See Chapter 6, Humorous Fantasy.

KEMP, Gene. *Mr. Magus Is Waiting for You.* See Chapter 10, Witchcraft and Sorcery Fantasy.

KENNEDY, (Jerome) Richard. *Amy's Eyes.* See Chapter 9, Toy Fantasy.

2514   KENNEDY, (Jerome) Richard. *Crazy in Love.* **Gr. 3–5.**

Kindness to an old woman gains Diana a husband who worries that Diana is a "crazy wife" because she talks to a donkey.

Illus. by Marcia Sewall, Elsevier, 1980, 57 pp., o.p.

(BBC:207; BL 77:625; HB 57:51; KR 49:7; SLJ Jan 1981 p. 62)

KENNEDY, William, and KENNEDY, Brendan. *Charlie Malarkey and the Belly-Button Machine.* See Chapter 6, Humorous Fantasy.

KINDL, Patrice. *Owl in Love.* See Chapter 10, Witchcraft and Sorcery Fantasy.

KING-SMITH, Dick. *Harry's Mad.* See Chapter 6, Humorous Fantasy.

KING-SMITH, Dick. *Lady Daisy.* See Chapter 9, Toy Fantasy.

2515   KING-SMITH, Dick. *Paddy's Pot of Gold.* **Gr. 2–5. (Orig. British pub. 1990.)**

✓   Eight-year-old Brigid meets Paddy, a tiny 174-year-old leprechaun who lives on her father's farm.

Illus. by David Perkins, Crown, 1992, 114 pp. LB(0-517-58137-X)

(BL 88:1379; CC 1993 Suppl. p. 71; CCBB 45:266; HBG 3[Fall 1992]:265; KR 60:325; SLJ May 1992 p. 90)

2516   KING-SMITH, Dick. *The Queen's Nose.* **Gr. 3–6. (Orig. British pub. 1983.)**

✓   A mysterious coin grants Harmony Parker seven wishes.

Illus. by Jill Bennett, Harper, 1985, 111 pp., o.p.

(BBC:207; BL 82:262; CCBB 38:209; Ch&Bks:288; HB 61:555; SLJ Aug 1985 p. 66)

KING-SMITH, Dick. *The Toby Man.* See Chapter 2, Animal Fantasy.

2517 KOFF, Richard M(yram). *Christopher.* **Gr. 5–8.**

The mysterious "Headmaster" shows Christopher how to use his supernatural powers to read minds, change his size, and make himself invisible.

Illus. by Barbara Reinertson, Celestial Arts, 1981, 128 pp. (0-89742-050-0); Bantam, 1985, pap., 160 pp. (0-553-15363-3)

(BBJ:72; CCBB 35:110; SLJ Feb 1982 p. 78; VOYA 4[Feb 1982]:34)

2518 KOLLER, Jackie French. *If I Had One Wish. . . .* **Gr. 5–7.**

Alec's wish that his little brother had never been born comes true, with disastrous results for their family.

Little, Brown, 1991, 161 pp. (0-316-50150-6)

(BL 88:506; CCBB 45:96; HBG 3[Spring 1992]:68; KR 59:1471; SLJ Nov 1991 p. 120)

2519 KONIGSBURG, E(laine) L(obl). *Up from Jericho Tel.* **Gr. 5–9.**

✓   Jeanmarie and Malcolm are summoned into ghostly Tallulah's underground boudoir, where they are made invisible in order to recover Tallulah's missing Regina Stone necklace.

Macmillan, 1986, 192 pp. (0-689-31194-X)

(BBJ:72; BL 82:1304, 1312, 1313, 83:794, 1136; CCBB 39:131; Ch&Bks:288; HB 62:327; KR 54:209; SLJ May 1986 p. 93, Apr 1987 p. 48; Suth 4:224; VOYA 9:219)

KOOIKER, Leonie. *The Magic Stone.* See Chapter 10, Witchcraft and Sorcery Fantasy.

2520 KORSCHUNOW, Irina. *Adam Draws Himself a Dragon.* **Gr. 1–4. (Orig. German pub. 1978; British pub. 1982, entitled** *Johnny's Dragon.***)**

✓   Adam's imaginary dragon friend gives him the confidence to do better at school, to make friends, and to lose some excess weight.

Trans. by James Skofield, illus. by Mary Rahn, Harper, 1986, 57 pp., o.p.

(BL 82:1312; CCBB 40:11; HB 62:587; KR 54:638; SLJ Sept 1986 p. 123)

2521 KORSCHUNOW, Irina. *Small Fur.* **Gr. K–4. (Orig. Swiss pub. 1984.)**

Lonely after his best friend moves away from the forest, a furry human-faced creature named Small Fur passes through a magic green gate and meets an elf who teaches him to fly. The sequel is *Small Fur Is Getting Bigger* (1990).

Trans. by James Skofield, illus. by Reinhard Michl, Harper, 1988, 72 pp., o.p.

(BBC:207; BL 85:321; CCBB 41:209; KR 54:829; SLJ Nov 1988 p. 90)

2522 KRENSKY, Stephen (Alan). *The Dragon Circle.* **Gr. 4–6.**

The Wynd children are kidnapped by five dragons who plan to use the children's magic powers to search for treasure. The sequels are *The Witching Hour* (1981, 1990) and *A Ghostly Business* (1984, 1990).

Illus. by A. Delaney, Atheneum, 1977, 116 pp., o.p.

(BL 74:477; CCBB 31:97; KR 45:728; SLJ Oct 1977 p. 115)

2523 KUSHNER, Donn. *A Book Dragon.* **Gr. 6–10. (Orig. Canadian pub. 1987.)**

✓   A six-hundred-year-old dragon emerges in present-day Canada to protect his treasure, a medieval illuminated book, from an unscrupulous land developer threatening to demolish the bookstore where the book is hidden.

Henry Holt, 1988, 197 pp., o.p.; Avon, 1991, pap. (0-380-70769-1)

(BBJ:72; BL 84:1820, 1837; HB 64:627; KR 56:659; SLJ June–July 1988 p. 118)

LACKEY, Mercedes, and DIXON, Larry. *Born to Run.* See Chapter 10, Witchcraft and Sorcery Fantasy.

2524   LAGERLÖF, Selma (Ottilliana Lovisa). *The Wonderful Adventures of Nils.* **Gr.**
✓   **5–7. (Orig. Swedish pub. 1906–1907; U.S. 1908.)**

An elf turns a boy named Nils into a Thumbling, smaller than the animals he once mistreated. *The Further Adventures of Nils* (1907) is included in this edition.

Doubleday, 1925, o.p.; trans. by Velma Swanston Howard, illus. by H. Baumhauer, Pantheon, 1947, 539 pp., o.p.; Buccaneer, 1992, 540 pp., LB(0-89966-936-0)

(BL 4:22, 22:171, 44:118; Bookshelf 1932 p. 8; CCBB 1[Feb 1948]:4; HB 1[June 1925]:30, 7:118, 23:451; LJ 72:1544; Mahony 2:283)

LAMORISSE, Albert (Emmanuel). *The Red Balloon.* See Chapter 1, Allegorical Fantasy and Literary Fairy Tales.

LAMPMAN, Evelyn Sibley. *The Shy Stegosaurus of Cricket Creek.* See Chapter 6, Humorous Fantasy.

2525   LANCASTER, Clay. *Periwinkle Steamboat.* **Gr. 2–4.**

Nothing ever happens on Pennypacker Square until the night a flying-ferry-boat takes Timmy and his friends to the other side of the world.

Illus. by the author, Viking, 1961, 54 pp., o.p.

(HB 37:261; LJ 86:1984)

2526   LANGTON, Jane (Gillson). *The Diamond in the Window.* **Gr. 5–7.**
✓   The mysterious disappearance of two children and an Indian prince intrigues Eleanor and Eddie, who decide to find the key to the mystery: the Star of India Diamond. In *The Swing in the Summerhouse* (1967) Eleanor and Eddie go on magic adventures by swinging out through each of the summerhouse's six sides. In *The Astonishing Stereoscope* (1971), an optical toy sends Eleanor into the past. *The Fledgling* (1980) (see below) is a related work.

Illus. by Erik Blegvad, Harper, 1962, o.p., 1973, pap., 256 pp. (0-06-440042-5); Peter Smith, 1989 (0-8446-6414-6)

(CCBB 16:30; Ch&Bks:263; HB 38:481; LJ 87:3895; Tymn:106)

2527   LANGTON, Jane (Gillson). *The Fledgling.* **Gr. 5–7.**
✓✓   Georgie's parents fear for her safety after an old Canada goose teaches the little girl to fly. John Newbery Medal Honor Book, 1981. *The Fragile Flag* (1984) is a non-fantasy sequel. Georgie's cousins, Eleanor and Eddie, have their own magic adventures in *The Diamond in the Window* (1962), *The Swing in the Summerhouse* (1967), and *The Astonishing Stereoscope* (1971).

Harper, 1980, 192 pp., LB(0-06-023679-5), 1981, pap. (0-06-440121-9)

(BBC:207; BL 76:1365, 80:95; CC:520; CCBB 33:218; Ch&Bks:263; HB 56:408; KR 48:513; SLJ Sept 1980 p. 73)

2528   LATHROP, Dorothy P(ulis). *The Colt from Moon Mountain.* **Gr. 3–5. (Orig. pub. 1941.)**

Cynthy befriends an elusive snow-white colt who runs wild on Moon Mountain.

Illus. by the author, Macmillan, 1956, 62 pp., o.p.

(BL 38:162; HB 17:460; LJ 66:879, 67:42)

2529 **LATHROP, Dorothy P(ulis).** *The Dog in the Tapestry Garden.* **Gr. 2–4.**

The dog in the tapestry on Maria's wall comes to life.

Illus. by the author, Macmillan, 1962, 40 pp., o.p.

(CCBB 16:83; HB 38:481; LJ 87:3203)

2530 **LATHROP, Dorothy P(ulis).** *The Little White Goat.* **Gr. 2–4.**

On May Day Eve, a magical goat leads Debby and Pats into the forest, where they play with the forest creatures.

Illus. by the author, Macmillan, 1933, 58 pp., o.p.

(BL 30:185; HB 9:206; LJ 59:321; Mahony 3:80)

2531 **LATHROP, Dorothy P(ulis).** *The Lost Merry-Go-Round.* **Gr. 3–5.**

Each child has a magic adventure while riding merry-go-round animals through Flittermouse Wood at night.

Illus. by the author, Macmillan, 1934, 104 pp., o.p.

(BL 31:177; Bookshelf 1934–1935 p. 6; HB 10:360; Mahony 3:107)

2532 **LAWRENCE, Ann (Margaret).** *Tom Ass: Or the Second Gift.* **Gr. 4–6. (Orig. British pub. 1972.)**

Two elfin gifts bring fortune and adventure to Tom and his wife, Jennifer.

Illus. by Mila Lazarevich, Walck, 1973, 132 pp., o.p.

(BL 70:173; CCBB 27:46; HB 49:378; KR 41:600)

2533 **LAWSON, Amy.** *Star Baby.* **Gr. 3–5.**

✓ Allie's ninth birthday wish for a baby brother comes true when a Star Baby falls from the sky into her father's arms.

Illus. by Margot Apple, Harcourt, 1992, 72 pp. (0-15-200905-1)

(BL 88:1762; CCBB 45:268; HBG 3[Fall 1992]:266; KR 60:467; SLJ May 1992, p 114)

2534 **LAWSON, Robert.** *The Fabulous Flight.* **Gr. 4–6.**

Seven-year-old Peter Peabody Pepperell III shrinks to four inches in height and flies off on a seagull's back.

Illus. by the author, Little, 1949, o.p., 1984, pap., 152 pp. (0-316-51731-3)

(BBC:208; BL 46:37; CCBB 2[Nov 1949]:5; HB 25:410, 61:77; KR 17:394; LJ 74:1542, 1682)

LE GUIN, Ursula K(roeber). *Catwings.* See Chapter 2, Animal Fantasy.

2535 **LEROE, Ellen.** *Leap Frog Friday.* **Gr. 2–4.**

After an argument with his older brother, Ollie uses the magic rocks he got for his birthday to turn Danny into a frog.

Illus. by Dee de Rosa, Dutton, 1992, 64 pp. (0-525-67370-9)

(BL 89:60; KR 60:1311; SLJ Nov 1992 p. 72)

LEWIS, C(live) S(taples). *The Lion, the Witch, and the Wardrobe.* See Chapter 5C, Travel to Other Worlds.

LEWIS, Hilda (Winifred). *The Ship That Flew.* See Chapter 8, Time Travel Fantasy.

LEWIS, J. Patrick. *The Moonbow of Mr. B. Bones.* See Chapter 1, Allegorical Fantasy and Literary Fairy Tales.

LINDBERGH, Anne Spencer. *Bailey's Window.* See Chapter 5C, Travel to Other Worlds.

LINDBERGH, Anne Spencer. *The Hunky-Dory Dairy.* See Chapter 8, Time Travel Fantasy.

LINDBERGH, Anne Spencer. *The Shadow on the Dial.* See Chapter 8, Time Travel Fantasy.

2536   LINDBERGH, Anne Spencer. *Travel Far, Pay No Fare.* **Gr. 5–8.**

✓ Owen and his cousin Parsley use a magic bookmark from the library's summer reading club to travel into their favorite books and bring back whatever they can carry—until they find out that Owen's divorced mom is planning to marry Parsley's widowed dad.

Harper, 1992, 192 pp. LB(0-06-021776-6)

(BL 89:513; CCBB 46:78; HBG 4[Spring 1993]:72; JHC 1993 Suppl. p. 77; KR 60:1380; SLJ Dec 1992 p. 113; VOYA 16:26)

2537   LINDE, Gunnel (Geijerstam). *The White Stone.* **Gr. 4–6. (Orig. Swedish pub. 1964.)**

Fia and Hampus are transformed into fearless Fideli and Prince Perilous. Nils Holgersson Award for best Swedish children's book, 1965.

Trans. by Richard Winston and Clara Winston, illus. by Imero Gobbato, Harcourt, 1966, 185 pp., o.p.

(BL 63:734; CCBB 20:156; HB 42:717; KR 34:1053; LJ 91:5232)

2538   LINDENBAUM, Pija. *Else-Marie and Her Seven Little Daddies.* **Gr. K–3. (Orig.**
✓ **Swedish pub. 1991.)**

Else-Marie is embarrassed that her seven tiny daddies must pick her up after school on the day her mother works late, but no one seems to notice anything out of the ordinary.

Adapt. by Gabrielle Charbonnet, illus. by the author, Henry Holt, 1991, 32 pp. (0-8050-1752-6)

(BL 88:952; CCBB 45:161; HBG 3[Spring 1992] 39; KR 59:1535; SLJ Mar 1992 p. 216)

2539   LINDGREN, Astrid. *Karlsson-on-the-Roof.* **Gr. 3–5. (Orig. Swedish pub. 1955; British pub. 1958.)**

No one believes Eric's story that a small, mischievous flying man is living on his roof. *Karlson Flies Again, Erik and Karlson on the Roof,* and *The World's Best Karlson* are the British sequels.

Trans. by Marianne Turner, illus. by Jan Pyk, Viking, 1971, 128 pp., o.p.

(CCBB 26:28; KR 39:1156; LJ 97:1168; TLS 1975 p. 373)

LINDGREN, Astrid. *Mio, My Son.* See Chapter 5C, Travel to Other Worlds.

2540   LINKLATER, Eric (Robert Russell). *The Wind on the Moon.* **Gr. 5–7.**

A magical wind from the moon turns two girls into kangaroos and helps them rescue their father. Carnegie Medal, 1944.

Illus. by Nicolas Bentley, Macmillan, 1944, 323 pp., o.p.

(BL 41:140; HB 21:112; KR 12:458; TLS 1944 p. 574)

2541 **LOBE, Mira.** *The Grandma in the Apple Tree.* **Gr. 2–4. (Orig. Austrian pub.**
✓ **1965.)**

Andi's imaginary grandma takes him on tiger hunts and voyages to pirate-infested seas.

Trans. by Doris Orgel, illus. by Judith Gwyn Brown, McGraw-Hill, 1970, 95 pp., o.p.

(BL 67:703; CCBB 24:126; HB 47:163; LJ 96:1109)

2542 **LOCKE, Angela.** *Mr. Mullett Owns a Cloud.* **Gr. 3–5. (Orig. British pub. 1982.)**

A shepherd named Mr. Mullett is given a small cloud named Napoleon as a gift, but the
cloud proves to be quite vain and impulsive.

Illus. by Ian Newsham, Chatto, 1983, 128 pp., o.p.

(HB 60:196; SLJ Feb 1984 p. 75)

2543 **LOFTING, Hugh.** *The Twilight of Magic.* **Gr. 5–7.**

Anne and Giles learn about magic from Agnes the wise woman, who is believed to be a
witch.

Illus. by Lois Lenski, Stokes, 1930, 303 pp., o.p.; Harper, 1967 (repr. of 1930 ed.), 303
pp., o.p.; illus. by Tatsuro Kiuchi, Simon, 1993, pap., 246 pp. (0-671-78358-0)

(BL 27:367; HBG 5:79; KR 35:60; LJ 56:278; VOYA 16:383)

LOGAN, Carolyn F. *The Power of the Rellard.* See Chapter 5B, Myth Fantasy.

2544 **LORD, Beman.** *The Perfect Pitch.* **Gr. 2–4.**

Mr. Watts, the new local wish-granter, has trouble granting Tommy's wish to become a
super baseball pitcher.

Illus. by Harold Berson, Walck, 1965, 55 pp., o.p.; Gregg, 1981, 55 pp., o.p.

(CCBB 19:85; KR 33:823; LJ 90:4636, 4637)

LORING, Selden M. *Mighty Magic: An Almost-True Story of Pirates and Indians.* See Chapter 8, Time Travel Fantasy.

LOVEJOY, Jack. *The Rebel Witch.* See Chapter 10, Witchcraft and Sorcery Fantasy.

2545 **LUENN, Nancy.** *Unicorn Crossing.* **Gr. 3–5.**

Jenny longs to see a unicorn while staying at Unicorn Crossing, but only her family's
elderly hostess, Mrs. Donovan, takes her wish seriously.

Illus. by Peter E. Hanson, Macmillan, 1987, 64 pp. (0-689-31384-5); Troll, 1988, pap. (0-
8167-1321-9)

(BL 84:67; CCBB 41:12; KR 55:1395; SLJ Oct 1987 p. 126)

2546 **LYNCH, Patricia (Nora).** *The Turf-Cutter's Donkey: An Irish Story of Mystery
and Adventure.* **Gr. 4–6. (Orig. British pub. 1934.)**

Eileen, Seamus, and Long Ears the Donkey meet a leprechaun and travel through ancient
Ireland. The sequels are *The Turf-Cutter's Donkey Goes Visiting* (1936) and *The Turf-Cutter's Donkey Kicks Up His Heels* (1939).

Illus. by Jack B. Yeats. Dutton, 1935, 245 pp., o.p.

(BL 32:22; Bookshelf 1935 p. 3; HB 11:295; LJ 61:115; Mahony 3:207)

2547 **MacALPINE, Margaret H(esketh Murray).** *The Black Gull of Corie Lachan.*
Gr. 4–6. (Orig. British pub. 1964.)

When Morag and Rory search for their missing father, rumored to have been abducted by
the wee folk, they are followed by a strange black gull.

Illus. by James Armstrong, Prentice-Hall, 1965, 105 pp., o.p.

(CCBB 19:102; KR 33:627; LJ 91:427; TLS 1964 p. 602)

2548 **McCAUGHREAN, Geraldine (Jones).** *A Pack of Lies.* **Gr. 6–10. (Orig. British**
✓ **pub. 1988.)**

Business in their used-furniture store improves dramatically after a strange young man moves into Ailsa and her widowed mother's house and charms potential customers with elaborate stories about the objects they are considering. Carnegie Medal, 1988. Guardian Award for Children's Fiction, 1989.

Oxford Univ. Pr., 1989, 168 pp. (0-19-271612-3)

(BBC:209; BL 85:1718; CCBB 42:232; KR 57:839; SLJ May 1989 p. 126; TLS 1988 p. 1322)

MacDONALD, Betty. *Mrs. Piggle-Wiggle.* See Chapter 6, Humorous Fantasy.

2549 **MacDONALD, Greville.** *Billy Barnicoat: A Fairy Romance for Young and Old.*
Gr. 5–8. (Orig. British pub. 1922.)

In this story written by George MacDonald's son, a boy cast up by the sea onto the Cornish coast searches for his inheritance while battling smugglers, storms, and a witch. The sequel is *Count Billy* (1928).

Illus. by Francis D. Bedford, Dutton, 1923, 230 pp., o.p.

(BL 20:146; Bookshelf 1932 p. 8; Mahony 2:290; Moore:426)

2550 **McGRAW, Eloise Jarvis.** *Joel and the Great Merlini.* **Gr. 3–5.**

The Great Merlini teaches Joel how to perform real magic.

Illus. by Jim Arnosky, Pantheon, 1979, 59 pp., o.p.

(BBC:209; CCBB 33:156; SLJ Feb 1980 p. 58)

2551 **McHARGUE, Georgess.** *Beastie.* **Gr. 4–7.**
✓ Mary, Theo, and Scott discover that the "beastie" their scientist parents are stalking in a Scottish loch is in danger of dying because of their expedition.

Delacorte, 1992, 192 pp. (0-385-30589-3)

(BL 88:1029; CC 1993 Suppl. p. 73; CCBB 45:216; HBG 3[Fall 1992]:267; KR 60:540; SLJ July 1992 p. 74)

2552 **McHARGUE, Georgess.** *Stoneflight.* **Gr. 5–7.**
✓ When Jane's home life becomes unbearable, she discovers the joys of night flight on the back of a stone griffin come to life.

Illus. by Arvis Stewart, Viking, 1975, 222 pp., o.p.

(BBC:209; BBJ:73; BL 71:762; CCBB 29:50; HB 51:268; KR 43:239; SLJ Mar 1975 p. 98)

McKEAN, Thomas. *The Secret of the Seven Willows.* See Chapter 8, Time Travel Fantasy.

2553 **MacKELLAR, William.** *The Smallest Monster in the World.* **Gr. 3–5.**

A kelpie introduces Wullie Watson to Maggie the sea monster.

Illus. by Ursula Koering, McKay, 1969, 113 pp., o.p.

(BL 66:621; HB 46:36; KR 37:1064; LJ 95:1628)

MacLEITH, Roderick. *Prince Ombra.* See Chapter 5B, Myth Fantasy.

MacLEOD, Charlotte. *The Curse of the Giant Hogweed.* See Chapter 8, Time Travel Fantasy.

McMULLAN, Kate. *Under the Mummy's Spell.* See Chapter 4, Ghost Fantasy.

2554 McNEILL (Alexander), Janet. *A Monster Too Many.* **Gr. 3–5.**

Sam and Joe circumvent their sea monster's incarceration in a zoo by returning it to the sea.

Illus. by Ingrid Fetz, Little, 1972, 60 pp., o.p.

(BL 68:1004; KR 40:136; LJ 97:2232)

McNEILL, Janet. *Tom's Tower.* See Chapter 5C, Travel to Other Worlds.

MACE, Elisabeth. *Under Siege.* See Chapter 5C, Travel to Other Worlds.

2555 MACOUREK, Milos. *Max and Sally and the Phenomenal Phone.* **Gr. 2–4. (Orig. Czech. pub. 1980.)**

A magical telephone changes the lives of third-graders Max Blair and Sally Chase, whose adventures include transforming a neighbor's dog into a boy.

Trans. by Dagmar Herrmann, illus. by Adolf Born, Wellington, 1989, 84 pp., o.p.

(BL 86:745; CCBB 43:142; SLJ Feb. 1990 p. 76)

MAETERLINCK, Maurice. *The Children's Blue Bird.* See Chapter 1, Allegorical Fantasy and Literary Fairy Tales.

Magicats! **Ed. by Jack Dann and Gardner Dozois.** See Chapter 2, Animal Fantasy.

MAGUIRE, Gregory. *The Daughter of the Moon.* See Chapter 5C, Travel to Other Worlds.

MAGUIRE, Gregory. *Lightning Time.* See Chapter 8, Time Travel Fantasy.

MAHY, Margaret (May). *The Blood-and-Thunder Adventure on Hurricane Peak.* See Chapter 6, Humorous Fantasy.

2556 MAHY, Margaret (May). *The Door in the Air and Other Stories.* **Gr. 6–10. (Orig.**
✓ **New Zealand pub. 1988.)**

Nine humorous magical stories about princes, witchcraft, and magic in the contemporary world.

Illus. by Diana Catchpole, Delacorte, 1991, 112 pp. (0-385-30252-5); Dell, 1993, pap. (0-440-40774-5)

(BL 87:1125; CC 1992 Suppl. p. 65; CCBB 44:170; HB 67:201; HBG 2:263; JHC 1992 Suppl. p. 69; KR 59:474; SLJ Apr 1991 p. 121; VOYA 14:246, 15:9)

2557 MAHY, Margaret (May). *The Girl with the Green Ear: Stories About Magic in*
✓ *Nature.* **Gr. 3–6. (Orig. New Zealand pub. in four collections: 1972, 1973, 1975, 1986.)**

Nine magical stories with ecological themes, originally published in New Zealand in *The First Margaret Mahy Storybook* (1972), *The Second Margaret Mahy Storybook* (1973), *The Third Margaret Mahy Storybook* (1975), and *The Downhill Crocodile Whizz and Other Stories* (1986).

Illus. by Shirley Hughes, Knopf, 1992, 102 pp. (0-679-82231-3), 1993, pap. (0-679-84000-1)

(BL 88:1280; CC 1993 Suppl. p. 77; CCBB 45:270; HBG 3[Fall 1992]:267; KR 60:468; SLJ July 1992 p. 61)

MAHY, Margaret (May). *The Haunting.* See Chapter 10, Witchcraft and Sorcery Fantasy.

2558 MAHY, Margaret (May). *A Tall Story and Other Tales.* **Gr. 2–5. (Orig. New Zealand pub. in three collections: 1972, 1973, 1975; orig. British pub. 1991.)**

Eleven short stories about magical happenings in everyday life, involving ghosts, witches, and monsters; originally published in New Zealand in *The First Margaret Mahy Story Book* (1972), *The Second Margaret Mahy Storybook* (1973), and *The Third Margaret Mahy Storybook* (1975).

Illus. by Jan Nesbitt, Macmillan, 1992, 88 pp. (0-689-50547-7)

(BL 88:1029; HBG 3[Fall 1992]:267; KR 60:117; SLJ Mar 1992 p. 238)

MAJOR, Kevin. *Blood Red Ochre.* See Chapter 5B, Myth Fantasy.

MANES, Stephen. *Chicken Treck: The Third Strange Thing That Happened to Oscar Noodleman.* See Chapter 6, Humorous Fantasy.

2559 MANES, Stephen. *Monstra vs. Irving.* **Gr. 2–4.**

When Irving's little sister, Claire, drinks the Monster-Ade formula he ordered from a monster magazine, she is transformed into Monstra, with fangs, claws, a horn, and bat wings.

Illus. by Michael Sours, Henry Holt, 1989, 74 pp. (0-8050-0836-5), 1991, pap. (0-8050-1642-2)

(BL 86:1006; CCBB 43:115; HBG 1[July–Dec 1989]:84; KR 57:1681; SLJ Jan 1990 p. 106)

2560 MASEFIELD, John (Edward). *The Midnight Folk: A Novel.* **Gr. 5–7. (Orig.**
✓ **British pub. 1927.)**

Five animals help Kay solve the mystery of his great-grandfather's stolen treasure. This story has been said to contain the first feisty girl character in children's literature. In the sequel, *The Box of Delights: Or, When the Wolves Were Running* (1935, 1984), Kay battles evil forces to save the magical Box of Delights.

Illus. by Rowland Hilder, Macmillan, 1932, o.p.; Dell, 1985, pap., 176 pp. (0-440-45631-2)

(BBC:209; BL 24:264, 287, 28:396, 401; Bookshelf 1932 p. 24; LJ 53:856; Moore: 332, 427; TLS 1927 p. 906)

2561 MASON, Arthur. *The Wee Men of Ballywooden.* **Gr. 4–7.**
✓ Times were hard for Danny Fay and the others until the Wee Men returned to their Irish village. The sequel is *From the Horn of the Moon* (1931).

Illus. by Robert Lawson, Doubleday, 1930, 266 pp., o.p.; Viking, 1952, 214 pp., o.p.

(BL 27:167; CCBB 6:34; HB 6:331, 7:121, 29:62; LJ 56:452, 77:1747; Mahony 3:207; Moore:435)

2562 MAXWELL, William (Keepers). *The Heavenly Tenants.* **Gr. 3–5.**
✓ The constellations descend from the sky to care for the Marvells' farm.

Illus. by Ilonka Karasz, Harper, 1946, 56 pp., o.p.; Parabola, 1992, 60 pp. (0-930407-25-3)

(BL 43:90, 277; HB 22:455; KR 14:455; LJ 71:1412, 1720; SLJ Aug 1992 p. 99)

2563 MAYNE, William (James Carter). *The Blue Boat.* **Gr. 4–6. (Orig. British pub.**
✓ **1957.)**

Christopher and Hugh meet a goblin and a giant while exploring a magical lake. Carnegie Medal Commended Book, 1957.

Illus. by Geraldine Spence, Dutton, 1960, 173 pp., o.p.

(BL 56:609; CCBB 14:178; KR 28:49; LJ 85:2479)

2564 **MAYNE, William (James Carter).** *The Glass Ball.* **Gr. 3–5. (Orig. pub. in Eng-**
✓ **land.)**

Max and Niko follow a rolling glass ball.

Illus. by Janet Duchesne, Dutton, 1962, 63 pp., o.p.

(BL 58:796; Eakin:228; HB 38:374; LJ 87:2026)

2565 **MAYNE, William (James Carter).** *A Grass Rope.* **Gr. 4–6. (Orig. British pub.**
✓ **1957.)**

Four children weave a special rope to capture a unicorn. Carnegie Medal, 1957.

Illus. by Lynton Lamb, Dutton, 1962, 166 pp., o.p.

(Eakin:224; HB 38:600; LJ 87:4622)

2566 **MAYNE, William (James Carter).** *The Green Book of Hob Stories.* **Gr. 2–3.**
✓ **(Orig. British pub. 1984.)**

Five tales about an invisible two-foot-tall man who magically smooths out household problems. Hob's adventures continue in *The Blue Book of Hob Stories* (1984), *The Yellow Book of Hob Stories* (1984), *The Red Book of Hob Stories* (1984), and *Hob and the Goblins* (Dorling Kindersley, 1994).

Illus. by Patrick Benson, Putnam, 1984, 25 pp., o.p.

(BL 80:1550; CC:677; CCBB 38:32; Ch&Bks:289; HB 60:468; SLJ Oct 1984 p. 160; Suth 3:298; TLS Mar 3, 1984 p. 338)

2567 **MEIGS, Cornelia (Lynde).** *The Wonderful Locomotive.* **Gr. 3–5.**

A little boy named Peter takes old engine number 44 for its last exciting cross-country run.

Illus. by Berta Hader and Elmer Hader, Macmillan, 1928, 104 pp., o.p.

(BL 25:171; Bookshelf 1932 p. 8; HB 4[Aug 1928]:13, 32–33, 4[Nov 1928]:76, 7:115, 20:347–349; Mahony 2:141)

MELLICKER, Judith. *Randolph's Dream.* See Chapter 1, Allegorical Fantasy and Literary Fairy Tales.

MENDEZ, Phil. *The Black Snowman.* See Chapter 5B, Myth Fantasy.

MILES, Patricia. *The Gods in Winter.* See Chapter 1, Allegorical Fantasy and Literary Fairy Tales.

MOERI, Louise. *Star Mother's Youngest Child.* See Chapter 1, Allegorical Fantasy and Literary Fairy Tales.

MOLESWORTH, Mary Louisa (Stewart). *The Cuckoo Clock.* See Chapter 5C, Travel to Other Worlds.

2568 **MOLESWORTH, Mary Louisa (Stewart).** *The Tapestry Room: A Child's*
Romance. **Gr. 4–6. (Orig. British and U.S. pubs., 1879.)**

A family of French children living in an old chateau have wonderful dreams and adventures.

Illus. by Walter Crane, Random, 1961, 217 pp., o.p.; Garland, 1976 (bound with *The Cuckoo Clock,* 1877, 1954), o.p.

(HB 38:66; Mahony 2:291)

2569   MONATH, Elizabeth. *Topper and the Giant.* **Gr. 3–5.**

Mat and his dog, Topper, are given a magic charm by a giant whom they rescued from an avalanche.

Illus. by the author, Viking, 1960, 60 pp., o.p.

(HB 36:216; KR 28:144; LJ 85:2029)

2570   MOON, Grace Purdie, and MOON, Carl. *Lost Indian Magic: A Mystery Story of the Red Man as He Lived Before the White Men Came.* **Gr. 5–7.**

A brave young Indian boy must recover his tribe's magic jewel, a turquoise elephant stolen long ago.

Illus. by Carl Moon, Stokes, 1918, 301 pp., o.p.; Gordon, 1977, LB(0-8490-2185-5)

(BL 15:1512; Mahony 2:538)

2571   MOORE, Annie Carroll. *Nicholas: A Manhattan Christmas Story.* **Gr. 4–6.**

An eight-inch-tall Dutch boy arrives in New York City on Christmas Eve, determined to see everything of interest, past and present. John Newbery Medal Honor Book, 1925. The sequel is *Nicholas and the Golden Goose* (1932).

Illus. by Jay Van Everen, Putnam, 1924, 331 pp., o.p.

(BL 21:158; Bookshelf 1927 p. 10; HB 1[Nov 1924]:13; LJ 50:803; Mahony 2:717)

2572   MORGAN, Helen (Gertrude Louise Axford). *Satchkin Patchkin.* **Gr. 2–4. (Orig. British pub. 1966.)**

Satchkin Patchkin is a small green man who lives in an apple tree. *Mother Farthing's Luck* is the British sequel.

Illus. by Shirley Hughes, M. Smith, 1970, 64 pp., o.p.

(CCBB 24:63; LJ 95:4340; TLS 1966 p. 1092)

MORGAN, Robin. *The Mer-Child: A Legend for Children and Other Adults.* See Chapter 1, Allegorical Fantasy and Literary Fairy Tales.

2573   MORRISON, Dorothy Nafus. *Vanishing Act.* **Gr. 5–8.**

Joanna performs magic tricks at her school's talent show, and impresses everyone in the audience, including some crooks, when she uses a device called a transmuter to make herself invisible.

Macmillan, 1989, 202 pp. (0-689-31513-9)

(BL 86:188; HBG 1[July–Dec 1989]:72; KR 57:1248; SLJ Nov 1989 p. 112)

2574   MULOCK, Diana (pseud. of Dinah Craik). *The Adventures of a Brownie as Told to My Child.* **Gr. 3–5. (Orig. British pub. 1872.)**

Six tales in which only children can see the brownie work his mischief.

Illus. by Mary Seaman, Macmillan, 1952, 122 pp., o.p.; Garland, 1977 (bound with *The Little Lame Prince*, 1874, 1948), o.p.

(BL 15:153, 20:224; HB 28:422; LJ 50:803; Mahony 1:36)

MYERS, Bernice. *Sidney Rella and the Glass Sneaker.* See Chapter 6, Humorous Fantasy.

NABB, Magdalen. *The Enchanted Horse.* See Chapter 9, Toy Fantasy.

NASTICK, Sharon. *Mr. Radagast Makes an Unexpected Journey.* See Chapter 6, Humorous Fantasy.

NESBIT (Bland), E(dith). *The Complete Book of Dragons.* See Chapter 3, Fantasy Collections.

2575 **NESBIT (Bland), E(dith).** *The Deliverers of Their Country.* **Gr. 3–5. (Orig.**
✓ **British pub. in** *Strand Magazine,* **1899; U.S. pub. in** *The Book of Dragons,* **1901, 1973; this ed. orig. pub. in Austria, 1985.)**

Harry and Effie awaken a marble statue of St. George to ask his advice on fighting the plague of dragons infesting England.

Illus. by Lisbeth Zwerger, Picture Book Studio, 1985, 32 pp. (0-88708-005-7)

(BBC:210; BL 82:759; CCBB 39:93; HB 62:195; SLJ Apr 1986 p. 91; TLS July 1986 p. 789)

2576 **NESBIT (Bland), E(dith).** *The Enchanted Castle.* **Gr. 5–7. (Orig. British pub.**
✓ **1907.)**

A magical ring transports Gerald, Jimmy, and Cathy to a garden of stone monsters surrounding a castle.

Illus. by H. R. Millar, Coward, 1933, o.p.; illus. by Cecil Leslie, Dutton, 1964, o.p.; Dent, 1968 (repr. of 1964 ed.), 231 pp., o.p.; Puffin, 1986, pap. (0-14-035057-8); illus. by Paul O. Zelinsky, Morrow, 1992, 304 pp. (0-688-05435-8)

(BL 30:24, 60, 89:738; Bookshelf 1933 p. 9; HB 8:153, 214; HBG 69:232; HBG 4[Spring 1993]:75; KR 32:293, 60:1263; LJ 58:1052; Mahony 3:208)

2577 **NESBIT (Bland), E(dith).** *Five Children and It.* **Gr. 5–7. (Orig. British pub.**
✓ **1902.)**

Anthea, Jane, Robert, Cyril, and the Baby uncover a Psammead or Sand Fairy, who reluctantly agrees to grant their wishes. In *The Phoenix and the Carpet* (1904, 1949, 1960, 1987; Peter Smith, 1989) a magic carpet carrying a phoenix egg takes the children on magical journeys to Persia. In *The Story of the Amulet* (orig. British pub. 1906; U.S. 1907, 1949, 1960, 1987; Peter Smith, 1989), which was the first time travel fantasy ever written for children, the Sand Fairy helps the children travel to ancient Egypt, Babylon, and Rome. All three books were published in one volume entitled *The Five Children; Containing Five Children and It; The Phoenix and the Carpet; The Story of the Amulet* (Coward, 1930).

Illus. by J. S. Goodall, Looking Glass, 1905, 1948, 1959, 255 pp., o.p.; illus. by H. R. Millar, Coward, 1949, 1963, 223 pp., o.p.; Puffin, 1985, pap. (0-14-035061-6); illus. by J. S. Goodall, Buccaneer, 1981, 253 pp. (0-89966-362-1); Dell, 1986, pap. (0-440-42586-7); Scholastic, 1988, pap. (0-590-42146-8); Peter Smith, 1989, o.p.; ed. by Sandra Kemp, Oxford Univ. Pr., 1994, pap. (0-19-283163-1)

(BBC:210; BL 27:215; HB 6:332, 25:297, 579; LJ 74:618; Mahony 2:291)

NESBIT (Bland), E(dith). *The House of Arden.* See Chapter 8, Time Travel Fantasy.

NESBIT (Bland), E(dith). *The Magic City.* See Chapter 5C, Travel to Other Worlds.

2578 **NESBIT (Bland), E(dith).** *The Magic World.* **Gr. 5–7. (Orig. British pub. 1912.)**

Twelve fantasy tales including "The Cat-hood of Maurice," "Accidental Magic," and "The Magician's Heart."

Illus. by H. R. Millar and Spencer Pryse, Coward, 1960, o.p.; British Book Center, 1974 (repr. of 1912 ed.), 280 pp., o.p.

(BL 57:32; HB 36:309; LJ 85:3224; TLS 1981 p. 348)

2579   NESBIT (Bland), E(dith). *Wet Magic.* **Gr. 5–7. (Orig. British pub. 1913.)**

Four children rescue a mermaid and are taken on an undersea adventure.

Illus. by H. R. Millar, Coward, 1938, 1960, 244 pp., o.p.

(BL 57:32; HB 13:378, 36:309; LJ 62:881, 63:691, 85:3224)

2580   NESBIT (Bland), E(dith). *The Wonderful Garden; or the Three C's.* **Gr. 5–7. (Orig. British pub. 1911.)**

Carolyn, Charlotte, and Charles find an old book of magic and a magical garden.

Illus. by H. R. Millar, Coward, 1960, o.p.; British Book Center, 1974 (repr. of 1911 ed.), 293 pp., o.p.

(BL 32:80, 57:32; Bookshelf 1935 p. 2; HB 11:296, 36:309, 61:196; LJ 60:830, 85:3224; Mahony 3:209)

2581   NIMMO, Jenny. *The Snow Spider* **(Gwyn Griffiths trilogy, book 1). Gr. 4–7.**
✓   **(Orig. British pub. 1986.)**

On his tenth birthday, Gwyn's grandmother gives him five magic gifts to help solve the mystery of his sister's disappearance in the Welsh mountains. Smarties Grand Prix for Children's Books, 1986. Tir na n-Og Award, 1987. In the sequel, *Orchard of the Crescent Moon* (1989; British title: *Emlyn's Moon,* 1987), Gwyn's magic and the friendship of a little girl named Nia save Gwyn's cousin Emlyn from the evil creatures that took Gwyn's sister away. The third book in the trilogy is *The Chestnut Soldier* (1991).

Dutton, 1987, 144 pp. (0-525-44306-1); Troll, 1990, pap., 136 pp. (0-8167-2264-1)

(BBC:210; BL 83:1751; CCBB 40:216; HB 63:613; Kies:128; KR 55:861; SLJ Aug 1987 p. 87; Suth 4:304)

2582   NIXON, Joan Lowery. *The Gift.* **Gr. 4–6.**

Brian's Irish grandfather enchants him with tales of pookas, fairies, and leprechauns, and he resolves to bring a real leprechaun home with him.

Illus. by Andrew Glass, Macmillan, 1983, 96 pp. (0-02-768160-2), 1988, pap. (0-689-71217-0)

(BL 79:1036; CCBB 36:214; KR 51:524; SLJ May 1983 p. 74)

NIXON, Joan Lowery. *Magnolia's Mixed-Up Magic.* See Chapter 2, Animal Fantasy.

NORMAN, Roger. *Albion's Dream: A Novel of Terror.* See Chapter 5B, Myth Fantasy.

2583   NORTH, Joan. *The Cloud Forest.* **Gr. 5–8. (Orig. British pub. 1965.)**

The Annerlie Ring causes Andrew to have disturbing dreams of the Cloud Forest.

Farrar, 1966, 180 pp., o.p.

(BL 63:326; CCBB 20:96; HB 42:564; Suth:297; TLS 1965 p. 1133)

2584   NORTON, André (pseud. of Alice Mary Norton). *Fur Magic.* **Gr. 5–7.**

Corey is afraid of everything on his foster uncle's ranch until the Changer, part-coyote and part-man, turns him into a beaver named Yellow Shell.

Illus. by John Kaufmann, World, 1968, 174 pp., o.p.

(HB 45:172; KR 36:1164; LJ 94:877; TLS 1969 p. 689)

NORTON, André (pseud. of Alice Mary Norton). *Lavender Green Magic.* See Chapter 8, Time Travel Fantasy.

2585 NORTON, André (pseud. of Alice Mary Norton), and MILLER, Phyllis. *Seven Spells to Sunday.* Gr. 5–7.

Gifts and spells found in a purple and silver mailbox bring hope into the lives of two foster children named Monnie and Bim.

Atheneum, 1979, 144 pp., o.p.

(BL 75:1219; KR 47:741; SLJ Mar 1979 p. 143)

2586 NORTON, Mary (Pearson). *Bedknob and Broomstick.* Gr. 4–6. (Orig. pub. sepa-
✓✓ rately in England as *The Magic Bedknob or; How to Become a Witch in Ten Easy Lessons,* 1943, and *Bonfires and Broomsticks,* 1946.)

In this two-part story, a witch gives Paul, Carey, and Charles a magical bedknob, enabling their bed to fly through time.

Illus. by Erik Blegvad, Harcourt, 1957, 189 pp., o.p., 1990, pap., 229 pp. (0-15-206231-9)

(BBC:210; BL 54:177; CC:538; CCBB 11:98; HB 33:489; KR 25:638; LJ 69:355, 82:3248; TLS Nov 15, 1957 p. iii)

2587 NORTON, Mary (Pearson). *The Borrowers* (The Borrowers series, book 1). Gr.
✓✓ 4–7. (Orig. British pub. 1952.)

Pod, Homily, and Arrietty Clock, a family of tiny people who live by "borrowing" from humans, must flee for their lives after Arrietty makes friends with a human boy. Carnegie Medal, 1952. In *The Borrowers Afield* (1955), the Clocks live precariously outdoors in an old boot, until they are rescued from the winter snows by Arietty's friend, the gamekeeper's son. In *The Borrowers Afloat* (1959), a young Borrower named Spiller guides the family on an exciting trip through the drains to the river, where they settle in a tea kettle, only to be washed away by a flood. Carnegie Medal Commended Book, 1959. In *The Borrowers Aloft* (1961), the Clocks' safe, happy life in a miniature railway village is interrupted when they are kidnapped by greedy Mr. and Mrs. Platter. In *Poor Stainless* (1971), Homily tells Arrietty about Stainless, a young Borrower who spent a glorious week in a candy store, while his worried family searched for him. In *The Borrowers Avenged* (1982, Peter Smith, 1988), the Clocks move into a rectory and rid themselves forever of the money-hungry Platters and their plot to put the Borrowers on display. The first four books were published together as *The Borrowers Omnibus* (Dent, 1966).

Illus. by Beth Krush and Joe Krush, Harcourt, 1953, 180 pp. (0-15-209987-5), 1989, pap., 200 pp. (0-15-209990-5); illus. by Michael Hague, Harcourt, 1991, 177 pp. (0-15-209991-3)

(BBC:211; BL 50:4, 40, 80:96; CC:538; CCBB 7:25; Ch&Bks:258; Eakin:249; HB 29:456; HBG 3[July–Dec 1991]:70; KR 21:483; LJ 78:1699)

ODGERS, Sally Farrell. *Drummond: The Search for Sarah.* See Chapter 9, Toy Fantasy.

2588 O'FAOLÁIN, Eileen (Gould). *The Little Black Hen; An Irish Fairy Story.* Gr. 4–6. (Orig. pub. in Ireland.)

Garret and Julie lift a spell laid on a changeling hen by Cliona, the fairy queen. Garret has other magic adventures in *King of the Cats* (Morrow, 1942), *Miss Pennyfeather and the Pooka* (Random, 1946), and *Miss Pennyfeather in the Springtime* (pub. in Ireland, 1946).

Illus. by Aldren A. Watson, Random, 1940, 135 pp., o.p.

(BL 37:20; HB 16:339, 342; LJ 65:715, 848; TLS 1940 p. 633)

2589 OLSON, Helen Kronberg. *The Strange Thing That Happened to Oliver Wendell Iscovitch.* Gr. 1–4.

Oliver Wendell's fat cheeks enable him to hold his breath and float through the air.

Illus. by Betsy Lewin, Dodd, 1983, 62 pp., o.p.

(BL 79:1221; CCBB 37:14; SLJ Sept 1938 p. 110; Suth 3:328)

OPPENHEIM, Shulamith. *The Selchie's Seed.* See Chapter 5B, Myth Fantasy.

2590 ORMONDROYD, Edward. *David and the Phoenix.* **Gr. 4–6.**

✓ David meets the Phoenix on a mountain ledge and helps him outwit a scientist bent on capturing the mythical creature.

Illus. by Joan Raysor, Follett, 1957, 173 pp., o.p.

(BL 54:113; CCBB 11:38; HB 33:401; KR 25:583; LJ 82:3249)

ORMONDROYD, Edward. *Time at the Top.* See Chapter 8, Time Travel Fantasy.

OSBORNE, Mary Pope. *Dinosaurs Before Dark.* See Chapter 8, Time Travel Fantasy.

2591 OUIDA (pseud. of [Marie] Louise de la Ramée). *The Nürnberg Stove.* **Gr. 4–6. (Orig. British pub. 1882, in** *Stories for Children;* **U.S. pub. in** *The Nürnberg Stove and Other Stories,* **1901, 1928.)**

A boy named August hides inside his family's porcelain stove and goes on a journey when the stove is sold.

Illus. by Maria L. Kirk, Lippincott, 1905, 1916, o.p.; illus. by Frank Boyd, Macmillan, 1928, 1952, 122 pp., o.p.

(BL 12:392, 21:160, 25:253, 49:209; HB 4[Aug 1928]:9, 28:421; Mahony 2:296)

2592 PALMER, Mary. *The Teaspoon Tree.* **Gr. 3–5.**

A girl named Andulasia searches for the magical Teaspoon Tree.

Illus. by Carlota Dodge, Houghton, 1963, 114 pp., o.p.

(CCBB 16:115; HB 39:174; LJ 88:1769)

2593 PARKER, Richard. *M for Mischief.* **Gr. 3–5. (Orig. British pub. 1965.)**

Andrew and Milly find an old-fashioned stove with a magical dial that cooks foods that cause invisibility and change people into animals.

Illus. by Charles Geer, Hawthorn, 1966, 90 pp., o.p.

(HB 42:307; KR 34:57; LJ 91:2697; TLS 1965 p. 513)

PARKER, Richard. *The Old Powder Line.* See Chapter 8, Time Travel Fantasy.

2594 PARKER, Richard. *Spell Seven.* **Gr. 3–5. (Orig. British pub. 1971.)**

Carolyn gives her brother, Norman, a magic wand.

Illus. by Trevor Ridley, Nelson, 1971, 127 pp., o.p.

(HB 47:385; LJ 96:2920; TLS 1971 p. 774)

2595 PARRISH, Anne, and PARRISH, Dillwyn. *Knee-High to a Grasshopper.* **Gr. 4–6.**

Little Man "ungrows" to the size of a meadow mouse.

Illus. by the authors, Macmillan, 1923, 209 pp., o.p.

(BL 20:107; Bookshelf 1923–1924 Suppl. p. 2; HB 7:61–67; LJ 50:803; Mahony 2:291)

PASCAL, Francine. *Hangin' Out with Cici.* See Chapter 8, Time Travel Fantasy.

PATON WALSH, Jill. *Matthew and the Sea Singer.* See Chapter 1, Allegorical Fantasy and Literary Fairy Tales.

2596 **PATTEN, Brian.** *Mr. Moon's Last Case.* **Gr. 5–8. (Orig. British pub. 1975.)**

A leprechaun called Nameon, who accidentally entered the human world, is pursued by a detective named Mr. Moon and aided by the members of the Secret Society for the Protection of Leprechauns as he desperately tries to get home.

Illus. by Mary Moore, Scribner, 1976, 158 pp., o.p.

(BL 73:410; CCBB 30:111; HB 52:626; KR 44:974; SLJ Feb 1977 p. 67)

2597 **PAYNE, Joan Balfour (Dicks).** *The Leprechaun of Bayou Luce.* **Gr. 3–5.**

✓ Josh helps a leprechaun win back gold stolen by pirate ghosts.

Illus. by the author, Hastings, 1957, 60 pp., o.p.

(BL 54:208; CCBB 11:39; HB 33:489; KR 25:689; LJ 83:240)

2598 **PAYNE, Joan Balfour (Dicks).** *Magnificent Milo.* **Gr. 3–5.**

A young centaur named Milo accidentally falls from his mountain home into the world of men, where he joins a traveling circus and tries to find his way home again.

Illus. by the author, Hastings, 1958, 64 pp., o.p.

(BL 55:137; HB 34:478; KR 26:605; LJ 84:253)

2599 **PEARCE, (Ann) Philippa.** *A Dog So Small.* **Gr. 4–6. (Orig. British pub. 1962.)**

Ben's powerful imaginary chihuahua comes to life whenever Ben closes his eyes.

Illus. by Antony Maitland, Lippincott, 1963, 142 pp., o.p.

(BL 59:946; CCBB 16:131; HB 39:284, 60:499; LJ 88:2149; TLS 1962 p. 397)

2600 **PEARCE, (Ann) Philippa.** *Lion at School: And Other Stories.* **Gr. 3–5. (Orig.**
✓ **British pub. 1985.)**

Nine tales, including "The Lion at School," "The Executioner," and "The Crooked Little Finger."

Illus. by Caroline Sharpe, Greenwillow, 1986, 122 pp., o.p.

(BBC:211; BL 82:1616; CCBB 39:177; KR 54:716; SLJ Sept 1986 p. 138; Suth 4:320)

2601 **PEARCE, (Ann) Philippa.** *Mrs. Cockle's Cat.* **Gr. 2–4. (Orig. British pub. 1961.)**

✓ The wind sweeps a balloon-seller named Mrs. Cockle off in search of her lost cat.

Illus. by Antony Maitland, Lippincott, 1962, 32 pp., o.p.

(BL 58:694; CCBB 15:130; HB 38:172; LJ 87:2026; TLS Dec 1, 1961 p. xiv)

PEARCE, (Ann) Philippa. *Tom's Midnight Garden.* See Chapter 8, Time Travel Fantasy.

PEASE, Howard. *The Gypsy Caravan.* See Chapter 8, Time Travel Fantasy.

PENDERGRAFT, Patricia. *The Legend of Daisy Flowerdew.* See Chapter 1, Allegorical Fantasy and Literary Fairy Tales.

PFEFFER, Susan Beth. *Rewind to Yesterday.* See Chapter 8, Time Travel Fantasy.

PHILLIPS, Ann. *The Oak King and the Ash Queen.* See Chapter 5B, Myth Fantasy.

PIKE, Christopher. *Sati.* See Chapter 1, Allegorical Fantasy and Literary Fairy Tales.

2602 **PINKWATER, D(aniel) Manus.** *Magic Camera.* **Gr. 2–3.**

Charles's antique camera can make real things disappear and imaginary things become real.

Illus. by the author, Dodd, 1974, 35 pp., o.p.

(BL 70:878; KR 42:53)

PINKWATER, D(aniel). Manus. *Wingman.* See Chapter 8, Time Travel Fantasy.

2603 POLESE, Carolyn. *Something about a Mermaid.* **Gr. 2–4.**

The mermaid Janie finds at the beach does not adjust well to life in an apartment.

Illus. by Gail Owens, Dutton, 1978, 27 pp., o.p.

(BL 75:867; KR 47:66; SLJ Mar 1979 p. 129)

2604 POMERANTZ, Charlotte. *The Downtown Fairy Godmother.* **Gr. 3–5.**

Olivia's fairy godmother turns out to be an amateur who needs a lot of practice to perfect her wish-granting abilities.

Illus. by Susanna Natti, Addison-Wesley, 1978, 45 pp., o.p.

(CCBB 32:70; Ch&Bks:290; KR 46:1190; SLJ Nov 1978 p. 67)

PORTE, Barbara Ann. *Jesse's Ghost and Other Stories.* See Chapter 3, Fantasy Collections.

POSTMA, Lidia. *The Stolen Mirror.* See Chapter 5C, Travel to Other Worlds.

2605 POSTMA, Lidia. *The Witch's Garden.* **Gr. 1–3. (Orig. pub. in the Netherlands.)**

Seven children exploring the garden of a tumbledown house meet some elves and see circus ghosts dancing in a magic tree.

Illus. by the author, McGraw-Hill, 1979, 23 pp., o.p.

(CCBB 33:54; SLJ Sept 1979 p. 119; Suth 3:352)

2606 POTTER, Miriam (S.) Clark. *Sally Gabble and the Fairies.* **Gr. 3–5.**

Old Sally Gabble makes friends with the fairies after she catches a particularly troublesome one in a trap.

Illus. by Helen Sewell, Macmillan, 1929, 87 pp., o.p.

(BL 26:237; HB 5:49; Mahony 3:109)

2607 PROYSEN, Alf. *Little Old Mrs. Pepperpot and Other Stories.* **Gr. 3–5. (Orig. Swedish pub. 1957; British pub. 1959.)**

Twelve stories, mostly about a woman who can shrink to the size of a pepper shaker. The sequels are *Mrs. Pepperpot Again* (1961; republished as *Mrs. Pepperpot and the Moose,* Farrar, 1991), *Mrs. Pepperpot to the Rescue* (Pantheon, 1964), *Mrs. Pepperpot in the Magic Wood* (Pantheon, 1968), and *Mrs. Pepperpot's Outing* (Pantheon, 1971). Three British sequels are *Mrs. Pepperpot's Busy Day, Mrs. Pepperpot's Christmas,* and *Mrs. Pepperpot's Year.*

Trans. by Marianne Helwig, illus. by Bjorn Berg, Astor-Honor, 1960, 95 pp. (0-8392-3021-4)

(BBC:211; HB 36:216; KR 28:235; LJ 85:2042; SLJ Feb 1992 p. 77; TLS May 29, 1959 p. xiii)

PULLMAN, Philip. *Spring-Heeled Jack.* See Chapter 6, Humorous Fantasy.

PYLE, Howard. *King Stork.* See Chapter 10, Witchcraft and Sorcery Fantasy.

2608 RAWLINGS (Baskin), Marjorie Kinnan. *The Secret River.* **Gr. 2–4.**

✓   Calpurnia stumbles upon a beautiful river, but when she tries to find it again, it has disappeared.

Illus. by Leonard Weisgard, Scribner, 1955, 56 pp., o.p; San Marco (repr. of 1955 ed.), 57 pp., LB(0-935259-02-3)

(CCBB 9:12; BL 51:436; HB 31:254, 258; KR 23:327; LJ 80:1508)

2609 **REID BANKS, Lynne.** *The Fairy Rebel.* **Gr. 3–6. (Orig. British pub. 1985.)**

The queen of the fairies is angered when Tiki uses her fairy powers to help a human couple, Jan and Charles, have a baby.

Illus. by William Geldart, Doubleday, 1988, 125 pp., o.p.; Avon, 1989, pap. (0-380-70650-4)

(BL 85:642; KR 56:1319; SLJ Oct 1988 p. 143)

2610 **REID BANKS, Lynne.** *The Indian in the Cupboard.* **Gr. 4–7. (Orig. British pub.**
✓ **1980.)**

An old wall cupboard turns Patrick and Omri's toy cowboy and Indian into miniature people named Boone and Little Bear, who immediately begin to fight. This series has been criticized for its sterotypical representation of the Native American characters. In *The Return of the Indian* (1986), Omri and Patrick reinstitute the magic after Little Bear is gravely wounded in the French and Indian Wars. In *The Secret of the Indian* (1989, 1990), Patrick uses the key to the magic cupboard to travel back in time to the Old West, but accidentally brings a tornado with him to present-day England. In *The Mystery of the Cupboard* (1993), Omri uncovers the connection between the cupboard's magical origins and his family's tragic history.

Illus. by Brock Cole, Doubleday, 1981, 1985, 181 pp. (0-385-17051-3); Avon, 1982, pap. (0-380-60012-9)

(BBC:198; CC:549; CCBB 35:22; HB 57:662; SLJ Dec 1981 p. 59; TLS 1980 p. 1326)

REIT, Seymour. *Benvenuto.* See Chapter 6, Humorous Fantasy.

RENDALL, Justine. *A Child of Their Own.* See Chapter 9, Toy Fantasy.

RHYS, Mimpsey. *Mr. Hermit Crab: A Tale for Children by a Child.* See Chapter 5C, Travel to Other Worlds.

2611 **RICHEMONT, Enid.** *The Glass Bird.* **Gr. 3–4. (Orig. British pub. 1990.)**

Wishing on a magic chestnut brings Adam a beautiful glass bird and a new friend.

Illus. by Caroline Anstey, Candlewick, 1993, 108 pp. (1-56402-195-5)

(BL 90:443; HBG 5:81; SLJ Oct 1993 p. 128)

2612 **RICHEMONT, Enid.** *The Magic Skateboard.* **Gr. 3–5. (Orig. British pub. 1992.)**

Danny can hardly believe that an old woman has given his skateboard the magical power to transport him wherever he wishes.

Illus. by Jan Ormerod, Candlewick, 1993, 80 pp. (1-56402-132-7)

(HBG 4[Fall 1993]:303; KR 61:378; SLJ May 1993 p. 108)

RIDLEY, Philip. *Krindlekrax; or, How Ruskin Splinter Battled a Horrible Monster and Saved His Entire Neighborhood.* See Chapter 6, Humorous Fantasy.

RILEY, Louise. *Train for Tiger Lily.* See Chapter 5C, Travel to Other Worlds.

2613 **ROBERTS, Willo Davis.** *The Magic Book.* **Gr. 4–6.**

Alex is hopeful that a book called *Magic Spells and Potions for the Beginner,* will help disarm Norm, the neighborhood bully.

Macmillan, 1986, 156 pp. (0-689-31120-6), 1988, pap. (0-689-71284-7)

(BBC:212; BL 82:1400; CCBB 39:195; KR 54:866; SLJ May 1986 p. 97)

2614   ROCKWELL, Thomas. *Tin Cans.* **Gr. 5–7.**

The police begin searching for David and Jane after a magical soup can makes them wealthy.

Illus. by Saul Lambert, Bradbury, 1975, 70 pp., o.p.

(BL 72:240; KR 43:714; SLJ Oct 1975 p. 101)

RODDA, Emily. *The Best-Kept Secret.* See Chapter 8, Time Travel Fantasy.

RODDA, Emily. *Finders Keepers.* See Chapter 5C, Travel to Other Worlds.

2615   RODDA, Emily. *The Pigs Are Flying!* **Gr. 4–6. (Orig. Australian pub. 1986, entitled** *Pigs Might Fly.***)**

After a boring day at home with a cold, Rachel wakes to find herself flying on a unicorn's back through a sky full of pigs. Australian Children's Book of the Year Award, 1987.

Illus. by Noela Young, Greenwillow, 1988, 144 pp. (0-688-08130-4); Avon, 1989, pap. (0-380-70555-9); Puffin (entitled *Pigs Might Fly*), 1990, pap. (0-14-034637-X)

(BBC:212; BL 85:326, 424, 460, 880, 1845; HB 64:784; SLJ Sept 1988 p. 185)

2616   RODDA, Emily. *Something Special.* **Gr. 3–5. (Orig. Australian pub. 1984.)**

Samantha's imaginary re-creations of past owners of the rummage-sale clothing she is sorting are startlingly accurate portraits of the shoppers who buy the clothes.

Illus. by Noela Young, Henry Holt, 1989, 74 pp., o.p., 1991, pap. (0-8050-1641-4)

(BL 86:1009; HBG 1[July 1989]:67; KR 57:1597; SLJ Jan 1990 p. 106)

RODGERS, Mary. *Freaky Friday.* See Chapter 6, Humorous Fantasy.

2617   ROSS, Tony. *A Fairy Tale.* **Gr. 2–5. (Orig. British pub. 1991.)**

Mrs. Leaf, young Bessie's elderly neighbor in an ugly English mill town, tells her that fairyland could be all around them, like a reverse image just below the surface, so neither one thinks it odd that they remain fast friends as the years go by, while Bessie grows older and Mrs. Leaf grows younger.

Illus. by the author, Little, Brown, 1992, 28 pp. (0-316-75750-0)

(BL 88:1602; HBG 3[Fall 1992]:258; KR 60:543; SLJ Aug 1992 p. 147)

2618   RUFF, Matt. *Fool on the Hill.* **Gr. 10 up.**

The ordinary life of a Cornell University writer-in-residence is transformed into a romantic saga after he learns to write without paper, finds true love, and slays a dragon.

Atlantic Monthly, 1988, 400 pp., o.p.; Warner, 1989, pap. (0-446-35772-3)

(BBS:63; KR 56:1271; LJ Oct 15, 1988 p. 104; VOYA 12:14, 45)

RUFFELL, Ann. *Pyramid Power.* See Chapter 5C, Travel to Other Worlds.

SACHAR, Louis. *Wayside School Is Falling Down.* See Chapter 6, Humorous Fantasy.

SALSITZ, Rhodi Vilott. *The Twilight Gate.* See Chapter 5B, Myth Fantasy.

2619   SARGENT, Sarah. *Jonas McFee, A. T. P.* **Gr. 4–7.**

Lonely Jonas, new kid in fifth grade, is given a mysterious blue marble-sized ball by a frightened girl—a ball with tremendous powers that enable its possessor to take over the world.

Macmillan, 1989, 112 pp., o.p., 1992, pap. (0-689-71579-X)

(BL 85:1471; CCBB 42:180; KR 57:553; SLJ May 1989 p. 112)

2620 · SARGENT, Sarah. *Weird Henry Berg.* **Gr. 4–6.**

✓ Millie Levenson wants to help a Welsh dragon recover its lost baby, but Henry Berg does not want to give up his pet "lizard."

Crown, 1980, 113 pp., o.p.; Dell, 1988, pap. (0-440-79346-7); Knopf, 1993, pap., 120 pp. (0-679-80703-9)

(BBC:212; BL 77:48; CC:553; CCBB 34:20; Ch&Bks:290: HB 56:642; KR 48:1164; SLJ Sept 1980 p. 78; Suth 3:375)

SAUER, Julia L(ina). *Fog Magic.* See Chapter 8, Time Travel Fantasy.

2621 SAWYER, Ruth. *The Enchanted Schoolhouse.* **Gr. 4–6.**

A leprechaun's magic helps Lobster Cove build a new school.

Illus. by Hugh Troy, Viking, 1956, 128 pp., o.p.

(BL 53:182; HB 32:450; KR 24:70)

2622 SAWYER, Ruth. *The Year of the Christmas Dragon.* **Gr. 3–5.**

✓ A little boy and an ancient Chinese dragon enliven a Mexican Christmas fiesta.

Illus. by Hugh Troy, Viking, 1960, 88 pp., o.p.

(BL 57:249; Eakin:283; HB 36:504; KR 28:556; LJ 85:4570)

2623 SCHAEFFER, Susan Fromberg. *The Dragons of North Chittendon.* **Gr. 5–7.**

Arthur, a dragon who can communicate through dreams with a boy named Patrick, battles the Moon and her Dark Angels while attempting to win the Queen of Dragons for his wife.

Illus. by Darcy May, Simon & Schuster, 1986, 208 pp., o.p., 1986, pap. (0-685-14462-3)

(BBC:212; BL 82:1694; SLJ Sept 1986 p. 139)

2624 SCHEIDL, Gerda Marie. *Loretta and the Little Fairy.* **Gr. 2–4. (Orig. Swiss pub. 1992.)**

Loretta tries to help a little girl who says she was exiled from fairyland for naughtiness, and can make herself invisible.

Illus. by Christa Unzer-Fischer, trans. by J. Alison James, North-South, 1993, 64 pp. (1-55858-185-5)

(HBG 4[Fall 1993]:290; KR 61:464; SLJ June 1993 p. 88)

2625 SCHOLES, Katherine. *The Landing: A Night of Birds.* **Gr. 4–6. (Orig. Australian pub. 1987.)**

Annie listens in on the nightime conversations among dozens of sea birds who have taken shelter from an ocean storm inside her grandfather's boathouse.

Illus. by David Wong, Doubleday, 1989, 65 pp. (0-385-26191-8)

(BL 86:1349; HBG 1[July–Dec 1989]:83)

SCIESZKA, Jon. *Knights of the Kitchen Table.* See Chapter 8, Time Travel Fantasy.

2626 SEABROOKE, Brenda. *The Dragon That Ate Summer.* **Gr. 3–6**

Alistair's scientist Uncle George helps convince the boy's parents that Alistair should be allowed to keep the baby dragon he found.

Putnam, 1992, 110 pp. (0-399-22115-8)

(BL 88:1281; HBG 3[Fall 1992]:270; KR 60:544; SLJ Apr 1992 p. 125)

2627 **SEFTON, Catherine (pseud. of Martin Waddell).** *The Emma Dilemma.* **Gr. 3–5. (Orig. British pub. 1982.)**

A bump on the head brings a mischievous transparent twin into Emma's life.

Illus. by Jill Bennett, Faber, 1983, 96 pp., o.p.

(BBC:212; BL 79:1098; CCBB 37:37; SLJ May 1983 p. 77)

2628 **SELDEN (Thompson), George.** *The Genie of Sutton Place.* **Gr. 5–7.**

✓ Nothing is quite the same for Tim after Abdulla, the genie, is released from 1,000 years of captivity in an Arabian carpet.

Farrar, 1973, o.p., 1994, pap., 175 pp. (0-374-42530-2)

(BBC:213; BL 69:861; CC:553; CCBB 26:176; HB 49:382; KR 41:116; LJ 98:1398, 1656)

2629 **SELZNICK, Brian.** *The Houdini Box.* **Gr. 2–5.**

✓ Ten-year-old Victor dreams of duplicating the incredible escapes of his idol, Harry Houdini.

Illus. by the author, Knopf, 1991, 64 pp. (0-679-81429-9); Random, pap., 1994 (0-679-85448-7)

(BL 87:1875; CC 1992 Suppl. p. 62; CCBB 44:250; HBG 2[Fall 1991]:261; KR 59:538; SLJ Sept 1991 p. 241, Oct 1991 p. 104)

2630 **SENDAK, Maurice (Bernard).** *Kenny's Window.* **Gr. 1–4. (Orig. pub. 1956.)**

✓ Kenny must find the answers to seven difficult questions asked by a four-legged rooster.

Illus. by the author, Harper, 1964, 1989, 64 pp., LB(0-06-025495-5), pap. (0-06-443209-2)

(BL 52:393; CCBB 10:13; HB 32:108; KR 24:242; LJ 81:1546)

SEREDY, Kate. *Lazy Tinka.* See Chapter 1, Allegorical Fantasy and Literary Fairy Tales.

2631 **SERVICE, Pamela F.** *Being of Two Minds.* **Gr. 5–8.**

Because Connie, a fourteen-year-old Midwestern girl, and Crown Prince Rudolph of Thulgaria were born at the exact same moment, they have always been able to communicate telepathically during so-called fainting episodes.

Macmillan, 1991, 169 pp. (0-689-31524-4); Fawcett, 1992, pap. (0-44970-415-7)

(BL 88:521; CCBB 45:74; HBG 3[July–Dec 1991]:72; KR 59:1349; SLJ Oct 1991 p. 128; VOYA 14:387)

SERVICE, Pamela F. *The Reluctant God.* See Chapter 8, Time Travel Fantasy.

Shape Shifters. **Ed. by Jane H. Yolen.** See Chapter 3, Fantasy Collections.

2632 **SHOWELL, Ellen Harvey.** *Cecelia and the Blue Mountain Boy.* **Gr. 4–6.**

Long ago, the townspeople of Chester began holding an annual music festival to cheer up a girl named Cecelia who had been enchanted by a fiddler on Blue Mountain.

Illus. by Margot Tomes, Lothrop, 1983, 76 pp., o.p.

(BL 79:1468; CCBB 36:178; SLJ Aug 1983 p. 70)

SHURA, Mary Francis (pseud. of Mary Francis Craig). *Happles and Cinnamunger.* See Chapter 4, Ghost Fantasy.

2633 **SHURA, Mary Francis (pseud. of Mary Francis Craig).** *A Shoe Full of Shamrock.* **Gr. 3–5.**

✓ Davie O'Sullivan's secret wish comes true after he returns a pouch of fairy gold to a leprechaun.

Illus. by N. M. Bodecker, Atheneum, 1965, 64 pp., o.p.

(BL 62:222; CCBB 19:68; Eakin:299; HB 41:500; KR 33:677; LJ 90:4622)

2634 **SHUSTERMAN, Neal.** *The Eyes of Kid Midas.* **Gr. 5–9.**

The sunglasses Kevin finds at the top of a mountain are saturated with magic and will grant him any wish.

Little, Brown, 1992, 185 pp. (0-316-77542-8)

(CCBB 46:157; HBG 4[Spring 1993]:76; KR 60:1508; SLJ Dec 1992 p. 133; VOYA 15:358)

SHYER, Marlene Fanta. *Ruby, the Red Hot Witch at Bloomingdale's.* See Chapter 10, Witchcraft and Sorcery Fantasy.

SILVERSTEIN, Herma. *Mad, Mad Monday.* See Chapter 4, Ghost Fantasy.

SINGER, Isaac Bashevis. *A Tale of Three Wishes.* See Chapter 1, Allegorical Fantasy and Literary Fairy Tales.

SINGER, Marilyn. *California Demon.* See Chapter 10, Witchcraft and Sorcery Fantasy.

SINGER, Marilyn. *Charmed.* See Chapter 5C, Travel to Other Worlds.

2635 **SLATER, Jim.** *Grasshopper and the Unwise Owl.* **Gr. 3–5. (Orig. British pub. 1979.)**

Magic candy makes Graham Hooper small enough to thwart Mr. Groll's plot to cheat the boy's widowed mother out of her home.

Illus. by Babette Cole, Holt, 1980, 88 pp., o.p.

(BL 77:812; CCBB 34:161; SLJ Mar 1981 p. 152)

2636 **SLEIGH, Barbara (de Riemer).** *Carbonel: The King of the Cats* **(British title:**
✓ *Carbonel,* **1955). Gr. 4–7.**

Rosemary tries to break the spell on the witch's cat that came with her new broom. The sequels are *The Kingdom of Carbonel* (1960) and *Carbonel and Calidor* (British).

Illus. by V. H. Drummond, Bobbs-Merrill, 1956, 253 pp., o.p.

(BL 54:30; CCBB 11:40; Eakin:300; HB 33:408; LJ 82:2702; TLS 1978 p. 765)

SLEPIAN, Jan. *Back to Before.* See Chapter 8, Time Travel Fantasy.

SMITH, Alison. *Come Away Home.* See Chapter 2, Animal Fantasy.

SMITH, L(isa) J. *Night of the Solstice.* See Chapter 5C, Travel to Other Worlds.

2637 **SNYDER, Dianne.** *George and the Dragon Word.* **Gr. 1–4.**

George's "angry word" makes his sister cry and turns Great Aunt Agatha into a dragon.

Illus. by Brian Lies, Houghton, 1991, 56 pp. (0-395-55129-3)

(BL 88:533; HBG 3[July–Dec 1991]:61; KR 59:1227; SLJ Jan 1992 p. 98)

2638 **SNYDER, Zilpha Keatley.** *Black and Blue Magic.* **Gr. 5–7.**

✓ Mr. Mazzeek's magic lotion causes Harry Houdini Marco to sprout wings.

Illus. by Gene Holtan, Macmillan, 1966, 1972, 192 pp. (0-689-30075-1); Dell, 1988, 1994, pap. (0-440-40053-8); Peter Smith, 1989, o.p.

(BBC:213; BL 62:878; CCBB 20:48; HB 42:308; KR 34:108; LJ 91:2214; Suth:371)

2639 **SNYDER, Zilpha Keatley.** *A Season of Ponies.* **Gr. 5–7.**

Her father's amulet enables Pamela to make friends with a beautiful pastel pony and escape from the pig woman in the swamp.

Illus. by Alton Raible, Macmillan, 1964, 133 pp., o.p.; Dell, 1988, pap. (0-440-40006-6); Peter Smith, 1989, o.p.

(BBC:213; CCBB 18:20; HB 40:284; KR 32:108; LJ 89:1862)

SOMMER-BODENBURG, Angela. *My Friend the Vampire.* See Chapter 6, Humorous Fantasy.

SOMTOW, S. P. (pseud. of Somtow Sucharitkul). *The Wizard's Apprentice.* See Chapter 10, Witchcraft and Sorcery Fantasy.

Spaceships & Spells: A Collection of New Fantasy and Science-Fiction Stories. **Ed. by Jane Yolen, Martin H. Greenberg, and Charles G. Waugh.** See Chapter 3, Fantasy Collections.

SPRINGER, Nancy. *The Friendship Song.* See Chapter 5C, Travel to Other Worlds.

SPRINGER, Nancy. *The Hex Witch of Seldom.* See Chapter 10, Witchcraft and Sorcery Fantasy.

SPRINGER, Nancy. *Red Wizard.* See Chapter 5C, Travel to Other Worlds.

SPURR, Elizabeth. *Mrs. Minetta's Car Pool.* See Chapter 6, Humorous Fantasy.

2640 **STEELE, Mary Q(uintard Govan).** *Wish, Come True.* **Gr. 4–6.**

The magic ring that Meg finds while she and her brother are staying at Great-Aunt Louise's enables them to miniaturize themselves, breathe under water, and search for treasure.

Illus. by Muriel Batherman, Greenwillow, 1979, 160 pp., o.p.

(BL 76:47, 1545; KR 48:128; SLJ Sept 1979 p. 148)

2641 **STERMAN, Betsy, and STERMAN, Samuel.** *Backyard Dragon.* **Gr. 3–5.**

Owen and his friends are saddled with a hungry medieval Welsh dragon, after the wizard who accidentally brought the dragon to New Jersey finds he can't work his magic in the twentieth century.

Illus. by David Wenzel, Harper, 1993, 192 pp. (0-06-020783-3)

(BL 90:346; HBG 4[Fall 1993]:305; KR 61:792; SLJ Aug 1993 p. 166)

2642 **STERMAN, Betsy, and STERMAN, Samuel.** *Too Much Magic.* **Gr. 3–6.**

Bill and his younger brother, Jeff, find a magic wish-granting cube, but discover that the consequences are difficult to handle.

Illus. by Judy Glasser, Harper, 1987, 160 pp., 1994, pap. (0-06-440404-8)

(BL 83:1130; KR 54:1796; SLJ Feb 1987 p. 86)

2643 **STEVENSON, Jocelyn.** *O'Diddy.* **Gr. 2–4.**

Boon's outgrown imaginary friend, O'Diddy, is determined not to be forgotten.

Illus. by Sue Truesdell, Random, 1988, 64 pp. (0-394-99609-7), pap. (0-394-89609-2)

(BBC:214; BL 84:1842; SLJ Oct 1988 p. 129)

STOLZ, Mary (Slattery). *The Cuckoo Clock.* See Chapter 1, Allegorical Fantasy and Literary Fairy Tales.

2644 **STORR, Catherine (Cole).** *The Magic Drawing Pencil* (British title: *Marianne Dreams*, 1958). Gr. 5–7.

Everything that Marianne draws comes to life in her dreams, including a boy named Mark.

Illus. by Marjorie-Ann Watts, Barnes, 1960, 191 pp., o.p.

(Kies:168; LJ 86:378; TLS 1958 p. 355)

STORR, Catherine (Cole). *Thursday.* See Chapter 5B, Myth Fantasy.

STOVER, Marjorie Filley. *When the Dolls Woke.* See Chapter 9, Toy Fantasy.

2645 **STRICKLAND, Brad.** *Dragon's Plunder, or, The Last Voyage of Captain Deadmon: A Fantasy Adventure.* Gr. 6–8.

In this suspenseful adventure story, twelve-year-old cabin boy Jamie Falconer uses magic to free Captain Deadmon from a vow to roam the high seas until he captures a dragon's treasure.

Illus. by Wayne Barlow, Macmillan, 1992, 154 pp. (0-689-31573-2)

(BL 89:892; SLJ Apr 1993 p. 125; VOYA 16:47)

SYKES, Pamela. *Mirror of Danger.* See Chapter 8, Time Travel Fantasy.

2646 **TAPP, Kathy Kennedy.** *Moth-Kin Magic.* Gr. 3–5.

Six tiny people, or Moth-Kins, who were captured by "giants" and imprisoned in a classroom terrarium, carry out a daring escape. The sequel is *Flight of the Moth-Kin* (1987).

Illus. by Michele Chessare, Atheneum, 1983, 122 pp., o.p.

(BBC:214; BL 80:685; CCBB 37:98; KR 51:166; SLJ Mar 1984 p. 166)

2647 **TARN, (Sir) W(illiam) W(oodthorpe).** *The Treasure of the Isle of Mist: A Tale of the Isle of Skye.* Gr. 4–7. (Written 1913–1914; orig. British pub. 1919.)

Fiona's search for lost treasure becomes a frantic hunt for a friend held captive in an elfin cave on the Isle of Mist. This story has been said to contain the first real-world villain in children's fantasy literature.

Putnam, 1920, 192 pp. o.p.; illus. by Robert Lawson, Putnam, 1934, 192 pp., o.p.

(BL 17:119, 31:38; HB10:236, 14:143; LJ 47:814; Mahony 2:298; TLS 1919 p. 740)

THEROUX, Paul. *A Christmas Card.* See Chapter 1, Allegorical Fantasy and Literary Fairy Tales.

THOMPSON, Julian. *Herb Seasoning.* See Chapter 6, Humorous Fantasy

2648 **TOLLE, Jean Bashor.** *The Great Pete Penney.* Gr. 3–5.

A leprechaun gives Pete (short for Priscilla) Penney a magic ring, enabling her to throw a curve ball well enough to be called up from Little League to major league baseball.

Atheneum, 1979, 90 pp., o.p.

(BL 76:358; CCBB 33:121; KR 47:1002; SLJ Dec 1979 p. 100)

2649 **TOWNE, Mary (pseud. of Mary Spelman).** *Goldenrod.* Gr. 5–7.

Goldenrod, the baby-sitter, can magically transport the Madder children anywhere they choose to go.

Atheneum, 1977, 180 pp., o.p.

(CCBB 31:149; KR 45:852; SLJ Nov 1977 p. 64)

2650 **TOWNSEND, John Rowe.** *The Persuading Stick.* **Gr. 4–6. (Orig. British pub.**
✓ **1986.)**

Quiet Sarah, the youngest sister of an angry and depressed older brother, finds a small magical stick that forces people to do whatever she wishes.

Lothrop, 1987, 96 pp., o.p.

(BBC:214; BL 84:486; CCBB 41:38; Ch&Bks:292; HB 64:205; KR 55:1398; SLJ Sept 1987 p. 184; Suth 4:414; TLS 1986 p. 1344)

2651 **TRAVERS, P(amela) L(yndon).** *Mary Poppins.* **Gr. 3–6. (Orig. British and U.S.**
✓ **pub. 1934.)**

Mary Poppins blows in on an East Wind and becomes the Banks children's nanny, bringing hilarious and magical adventures. These adventures continue in *Mary Poppins Comes Back* (1935, 1963), *Mary Poppins Opens the Door* (1943), *Mary Poppins in the Park* (1952; Peter Smith, 1988), *Mary Poppins from A to Z* (1962), *Mary Poppins in Cherry Tree Lane* (1982), and *Mary Poppins and the House Next Door* (Delacorte, 1989).

Illus. by Mary Shepard, Harcourt, 1962, 1981 (rev. ed), 206 pp. (0-15-252408-8); Buccaneer, 1981 (reprint) (0-89966-390-7); Dell, 1991, pap. (0-440-40406-1)

(BL 31:178, 78:709; Bookshelf 1935 p. 3; CC:567; Ch&Bks:272; Mahony 3:212; SLJ Feb 1982 p. 82; TLS 1934 p. 637)

TURNER, Ann. *Rosemary's Witch.* See Chapter 10, Witchcraft and Sorcery Fantasy.

TWOHILL, Maggie. *Jeeter, Mason and the Magic Headset.* See Chapter 9, Toy Fantasy.

2652 **UPDIKE, David.** *An Autumn Tale.* **Gr. K–4.**

One Halloween night, Homer puts a real jack-o-lantern on as a mask and joins a mysterious procession of walking trees who call him Mr. Pumpkin and won't believe he is a human boy.

Illus. by Robert Andrew Parker, Pippin, 1988, 40 pp. (0-945912-02-1)

(BL 85:416; CCBB 42:160; SLJ Nov 1988 p. 96)

2653 **UPENSKY, Eduard.** *Uncle Fedya, His Dog, and His Cat.* **Gr. 2–4. (Orig. Russian pub. 1989.)**

After his parents refuse to let him keep pets, Fedya and his talking cat run away to the country and set up housekeeping with a talking dog.

Illus. by Vladimir Shpitalnik, trans. by Michael Henry Heim, Knopf, 1993, 136 pp. (0-679-82064-7)

(CCBB 47:61; HBG 5:83; KR 61:1530; SLJ Nov 1993 p. 95)

URE, Jean. *The Wizard in the Woods.* See Chapter 10, Witchcraft and Sorcery Fantasy.

2654 **VAMBA (pseud. of Luigi Bertelli).** *The Prince and His Ants.* **Gr. 4–6. (Orig. pub. in Italy.)**

A little Italian boy learns all about the lives of ants, bees, and wasps after he is transformed into an ant.

Trans. by S. F. Woodruff, Holt, 1911, o.p.; trans. by Nicola di Pietro, illus. by the author, Crowell, 1935 (entitled *Emperor of the Ants*), 239 pp., o.p.

(BL 7:81; Bookshelf 1921–1922 p. 9, 1935 p. 3; LJ 61:116; Mahony 2:107)

2655 **VAN ALLSBURG, Chris.** *Ben's Dream.* **Gr. 2–4.**

✓ Ben and his friend, Margaret, find they have had the same dream: sailing across a flooded world in their half-submerged houses.

Illus. by the author, Houghton, 1982, 32 pp. (0-395-32084-4)

(BL 78:1371; CC:725; CCBB 35:217; HB 58:396; KR 50:487; SLJ May 1982 p. 66; Suth 3:429)

2656 **VAN ALLSBURG, Chris.** *The Garden of Abdul Gasazi.* **Gr. 1–5.**

✓ Alan chases Miss Hester's dog, Fritz, into a magician's garden where he finds Fritz changed into a duck. Boston Globe Horn Book Award for Illustration, 1980. Randolph Caldecott Medal Honor Book, 1980.

Illus. by the author, Houghton, 1979, 32 pp. (0-395-27804-X)

(BL 76:510; CC:725; CCBB 33:121; HB 56:49; SLJ Jan 1980 pp. 40, 62; Suth 3:429; TLS 1981 p. 1067)

2657 **VAN ALLSBURG, Chris.** *Jumanji.* **Gr. 1–5.**

✓✓ A frightening jungle world is unleashed as Peter and Judy play the magical board game they brought home from the park. Boston Globe Horn Book Award Honor Book for Illustration, 1981. Randolph Caldecott Medal, 1982. National Book Award for Graphic Design, 1982.

Illus. by the author, Houghton, 1981, 28 pp. (0-395-30448-2)

(BL 77:1258, 86:790; CC:725; CCBB 35:18; HB 57:416; KR 49:737; SLJ May 1981 pp. 24, 60; Suth 3:430)

VAN ALLSBURG, Chris. *The Sweetest Fig.* See Chapter 1, Allegorical Fantasy and Literary Fairy Tales.

VAN ALLSBURG, Chris. *The Widow's Broom.* See Chapter 10, Witchcraft and Sorcery Fantasy.

VAN ALLSBURG, Chris. *The Wreck of the Zephyr.* See Chapter 1, Allegorical Fantasy and Literary Fairy Tales.

VAN ALLSBURG, Chris. *The Wretched Stone.* See Chapter 1, Allegorical Fantasy and Literary Fairy Tales.

VAN STOCKUM, Hilda. *Kersti and Saint Nicholas.* See Chapter 6, Humorous Fantasy.

VIVELO, Jackie. *A Trick of the Light: Stories to Read at Dusk.* See Chapter 3, Fantasy Collections.

WALKER, Gwen. *The Golden Stile.* See Chapter 5C, Travel to Other Worlds.

2658 **WALLACE, Barbara Brooks.** *The Barrel in the Basement.* **Gr. 3–5.**

✓ After their protector, an elderly man named Noah, disappears, three elves living in his house face danger in the form of an inquisitive nine-year-old boy.

Illus. by Sharon Wooding, Atheneum, 1985, 127 pp., o.p.

(BBC:215; BL 81:1260; CCBB 38:177; HB 61:561; KR 53:14; SLJ Sept 1985 p. 140)

2659 **WALLACE, Barbara Brooks.** *The Interesting Thing That Happened at Perfect Acres, Inc.* **Gr. 4–6.**

Perfecta and her friend Puck use invisibility to outwit the nasty owner of the Perfect Acres housing development.

Illus. by Blanche Sims, Atheneum, 1988, 144 pp., o.p.

(BBC:215; BL 84:1269; CCBB 41:172; KR 56:287; SLJ Apr 1988 p. 105)

WANGERIN, Walter, Jr. *Elisabeth and the Water-Troll.* See Chapter 1, Allegorical Fantasy and Literary Fairy Tales.

WANGERIN, Walter, Jr. *Potter, Come Fly to the First of the Earth.* See Chapter 1, Allegorical Fantasy and Literary Fairy Tales.

2660 **WARD, Patricia A(nn).** *The Secret Pencil* **(British title:** *The Silver Pencil,* **1959). Gr. 5–7.**

Spending the summer with her uncle on the coast of Wales, Anna finds a magical silver pencil.

Illus. by Nicole Hornby, Random, 1960, 277 pp., o.p.

(HB 36:217; KR 28:90; LJ 85:2045)

2661 **WEBB, Clifford (Cyril).** *The North Pole Before Lunch.* **Gr. 2–4. (Orig. U.S. pub. 1936.)**

Michael and Jennifer make a fast trip to the North Pole.

Illus. by the author, Warne, 1951, 63 pp., o.p.

(HB 2:349, 27:261; LJ 61:808)

WEISS, Ellen, and FRIEDMAN, Mel. *The Adventures of Ratman.* See Chapter 6, Humorous Fantasy.

WESLEY, Mary. *Haphazard House.* See Chapter 8, Time Travel Fantasy.

2662 **WHITE, Stewart Edward.** *The Magic Forest: A Modern Fairy Story.* **Gr. 4–6. (Orig. pub. Macmillan, 1923.)**

Jimmy Ferris steps off a Canadian Pacific Railroad car into an enchanted forest where he lives with an Ojibway Indian tribe.

Lightyear, 1976, 146 pp., LB(0-89968-126-3); Buccaneer, 1990, (0-89966-663-9)

(BL 20:303, 49:209; Bookshelf 1932 p. 12; HB 1[June 1925]:32, 28:422)

2663 **WHITE, T(erence) H(anbury).** *Mistress Masham's Repose.* **Gr. 5–7.**

✓ Maria discovers a group of Lilliputians living on her rundown estate and resolves to save them from her greedy governess, who is plotting to sell them to a circus.

Illus. by Fritz Eichenberg, Putnam, 1946, 255 pp., o.p.; Gregg, 1980, 255 pp., o.p.

(BL 43:36; HB 57:565; KR 14:529; LJ 71:2107; Tymn:173)

WHITEHEAD, Victoria. *The Chimney Witches.* See Chapter 10, Witchcraft and Sorcery Fantasy.

WICKENDEN, Dan. *The Amazing Vacation.* See Chapter 5C, Travel to Other Worlds.

WIGNELL, Edel. *Escape by Deluge.* See Chapter 5B, Myth Fantasy.

WILLARD, Barbara. *Spell Me a Witch.* See Chapter 10, Witchcraft and Sorcery Fantasy.

2664 **WILLARD, Nancy (Margaret).** *The High Rise Glorious Skittle Skat Roarious* ✓ *Sky Pie Angel Food Cake.* **Gr. 2–5.**

A magic spell and some angelic help are the missing ingredients needed to make the glorious angel-food cake a young girl's mother requested for her birthday.

Illus. by Richard Jesse Watson, Harcourt, 1990, 64 pp. (0-15-234332-6)

(BL 87:52; CCBB 44:105; HBG 2[July–Dec 1990]:66; KR 58:1009; SLJ Nov 1990 p. 100)

2665 **WILLARD, Nancy (Margaret).** *The Mountains of Quilt.* **Gr. 1–4.**

✓ After the narrator's grandmother accidentally sews the magic carpet belonging to the Magician of the Mountains of Cleveland into her crazy quilt, the carpet flies her up into the clouds to have lunch with four Magicians.

Illus. by Tomie dePaola, Harcourt, 1987, 32 pp. (0-15-256010-6)

(BL 84:325; CCBB 41:105; HB 63:732; KR 55:1399; SLJ Oct 1987 p. 119)

WILLARD, Nancy (Margaret). *Things Invisible to See.* See Chapter 1, Allegorical Fantasy and Literary Fairy Tales.

WILLIAMS, Jay. *The Hero from Otherwhere.* See Chapter 5C, Travel to Other Worlds.

2666 **WILLIAMS, Jay.** *The Magic Grandfather.* **Gr. 4–6.**

Sam and his cousin, Sarah, experiment with magic to bring back their missing grandfather.

Illus. by Gail Owens, Macmillan, 1979, 149 pp., o.p.

(BL 75:1631; HB 55:418; SLJ Sept 1979 p. 151)

WILLIAMS, Ruth L. *The Silver Tree.* See Chapter 8, Time Travel Fantasy.

WILLIAMS (John), Ursula Moray. *Castle Merlin.* See Chapter 4, Ghost Fantasy.

2667 **WILLIAMS (John), Ursula Moray.** *The Moonball.* **Gr. 3–5. (Orig. British pub.**
✓ **1958.)**

The children who find a strange, furry, round creature decide to protect it from scientific investigations.

Illus. by Jane Paton, Hawthorn, 1967, 138 pp., o.p.

(BL 63:1194; CCBB 21:19; HB 43:344; KR 35:201; LJ 92:2024; Suth:425)

WINDSOR, Patricia. *How a Weirdo and a Ghost Can Change Your Entire Life.* See Chapter 4, Ghost Fantasy.

WINTHROP, Elizabeth. *The Castle in the Attic.* See Chapter 5C, Travel to Other Worlds.

2668 **WISEMAN, David.** *Blodwen and the Guardians.* **Gr. 5–7. (Orig. pub. in England.)**

Blodwen, ten, and Tiddy, her six-year-old brother, join forces with the fairy "Guardians" of the ancient Grove to save their home from a road-construction project.

Houghton, 1983, 163 pp., o.p.

(BBC:216; BL 80:504; HB 60:58; SLJ Jan 1982 p. 82; VOYA 7:102)

WOLF, Joyce. *Between the Cracks.* See Chapter 10, Witchcraft and Sorcery Fantasy.

2669 **WOLITZER, Meg.** *The Dream Book.* **Gr. 5–7.**

Eleven-year-olds Claudia Lemmon and Mindy (Danger) Roth attempt to share each other's dreams in order to find Claudia's missing father.

Greenwillow, 1986, 148 pp., o.p.

(CCBB 40:59; KR 54:1018; SLJ Nov 1986 p. 94; VOYA 9:224)

WOOD, Marcia. *The Secret Life of Hilary Thorne.* See Chapter 5C, Travel to Other Worlds.

2670 **WOODRUFF, Elvira.** *Awfully Short for the Fourth Grade.* **Gr. 3–6.**

Magic powder makes Noah's wish come true: to shrink to the size of his action figures in order to share their adventures. The sequel is *Back in Action* (1991).

Illus. by Will Hillenbrand, Holiday, 1989, 142 pp. (0-8234-0785-3); Dell, 1990, pap. (0-440-40366-9)

(BL 86:922; HBG 1[July–Dec 1989]:85; KR 57:1831; SLJ Nov 1989 p. 116)

WOODRUFF, Elvira. *The Disappearing Bike Shop.* See Chapter 8, Time Travel Fantasy.

2671 **WOODRUFF, Elvira.** *The Summer I Shrank My Grandmother.* **Gr. 3–6.**

To Nelly's shock, the anti-aging formula she secretly applies to her grandmother turns the elderly woman into a baby.

Illus. by Katherine Coville, Holiday, 1990, 153 pp. (0-8234-0832-9); Dell, 1992, pap. (0-440-40640-4)

(BL 87:1059; HBG 2[July–Dec 1990]:76; SLJ Dec 1990 p. 112)

WRIGHT, Betty Ren. *The Ghost of Ernie P.* See Chapter 4, Ghost Fantasy.

2672 **WRIGHTSON, (Alice) Patricia (Furlonger).** *A Little Fear.* **Gr. 6 up. (Orig. Aus-**
✓ **tralian pub. 1983.)**

Mrs. Tucker escapes from a nursing home to set up an independent life in a rural cottage, but her peace is disturbed by a mischievous Njimbin, or forest gnome, who wants the cottage for himself. Australian Children's Book of the Year, 1984.

Atheneum, 1983, 111 pp., o.p.

(BBC:216; BBJ:76; BL 80:404, 422, 86:907; Ch&Bks:293; CCBB 37:60; HB 60:66; JHC:426; Kies:192; KR 51:210; SLJ Nov 1983 p. 98; Suth 3:462; VOYA 7:36)

2673 **WRIGHTSON, (Alice) Patricia (Furlonger).** *An Older Kind of Magic* **(Aus-**
tralian title: *An Older Form of Magic,* **1972). Gr. 4–7.**

On the night a comet streaks through the sky, aboriginal spirits appear and Rupert, Selina, and Benny save the Botanical Gardens by using ancient spells.

Illus. by Noela Young, Harcourt, 1972, 186 pp., o.p.

(BL 69:247; CCBB 26:35; Ch&Bks:253; HB 48:472; KR 40:1100; LJ 97:3458; TLS 1972 p. 1325)

2674 **WUORIO, Eva-Lis.** *Tal and the Magic Barruget.* **Gr. 3–5.**
✓ Tal conjures up a bottle-imp, or barruget, to help with the housework.

Illus. by Bettina, World, 1965, 76 pp., o.p.

(BL 62:414; HB 41:630; KR 33:981; LJ 91:430)

YOLEN (Stemple), Jane H(yatt). *The Faery Flag: Stories and Poems of Fantasy and the Supernatural.* See Chapter 3, Fantasy Collections.

2675 **YOLEN (Stemple), Jane H(yatt).** *The Mermaid's Three Wisdoms.* **Gr. 4–6.**

Jess comes to terms with her deafness with the help of Melusina, an exiled mermaid who is unable to speak.

Illus. by Laura Rader, Collins + World, 1978, o.p.; Philomel, 1981, 112 pp., o.p.

(BL 74:1738; KR 46:638; SLJ Nov 1978 p. 71)

YOLEN (Stemple), Jane H(yatt). *The Wizard of Washington Square.* See Chapter 10, Witchcraft and Sorcery Fantasy.

2676   **YORK, Carol Beach.** *Miss Know-It-All; A Butterfield Square Story.* **Gr. 3–4.**

Miss Know-It-All's box of magic chocolates and her marvelous memory create quite a stir in the orphanage at number 18 Butterfield Square. The sequels are *The Christmas Dolls* (1967) and *Miss Know-It-All Returns* (1972).

Illus. by Victoria de Larrea, Watts, 1966, 87 pp., o.p.

(CCBB 20:52; LJ 91:4345)

2677   **ZOLOTOW, Charlotte S(hapiro).** *The Man with Purple Eyes.* **Gr. 2–4.**

The odd-looking seed Anna is given grows into a beautiful purple plant that helps her invalid father recover from his illness.

Illus. by Joe Lasker, Abelard-Shuman, 1961, 60 pp., o.p.

(CCBB 15:152; HB 37:340; LJ 86:2361)

8

Time Travel Fantasy

Stories about people who step into another time can be the most memorable of fantasy tales. This chapter includes books about travel from our time to the past and future, and stories in which travelers from the past or future visit the twentieth century. A few stories deal with two time periods that somehow touch, permitting glimpses into the past or future without any actual traveling. In fantasy, the means of time travel must be magical, not scientific. Tales of travelers to other worlds, rather than other times, are found in Chapter 5C, Travel to Other Worlds. Stories about people who meet ghosts from the past have been placed in Chapter 4, Ghost Fantasy, if the ghosts, not the human protagonists, do the time traveling.

2678 ADKINS, Jan. *Solstice: A Mystery of the Season.* **Gr. 6 up.**

Charlie and his father are welcomed into Vern Filson's cabin after their motorboat engine fails near his remote Maine island on Winter Solstice night, only to discover on their return home that Vern and his family died more than fifty years before.

Illus. by the author, Walker, 1990, 128 pp. (0-8027-6970-5)

(HBG 2[July–Dec 1990]:84; KR 58:1389; SLJ Oct 1990 p. 33; VOYA 13:275)

2679 ADKINS, Jan. *A Storm Without Rain.* **Gr. 6–9.**

After sailing to an island off the coast of Cape Cod, fifteen-year-old Jack is caught in a storm and finds himself in the year 1904, where he is befriended by young John Swain, his own grandfather.

Little, 1983, 179 pp., o.p.; Morrow, 1993, pap., 192 pp. (0-688-11852-6)

(BBJ:68; BL 79:1089; HB 59:448; KR 51:662; SLJ Oct 1983 p. 155; VOYA 6:212)

AIKEN, Joan (Delano). *The Shadow Guests.* See Chapter 4, Ghost Fantasy.

2680 ALEXANDER, Lloyd (Chudley). *Time Cat: The Remarkable Journeys of Jason and Gareth.* **Gr. 5–7. (British title:** *Nine Lives.***)**

Jason's magic cat, Gareth, takes him back through time to visit the nine historical periods of his previous lives.

Illus. by Bill Sokol, Henry Holt, 1963, 191 pp., o.p.; Peter Smith, n.d. (0-8446-6237-2)

(BBC:197; LJ 88:2548; TLS 1963 p. 980)

2681   ALLAN, Mabel E(sther). *Romansgrove*. Gr. 5–7.

Wandering through the ruins of the old manor house called Romansgrove, Clare and Richard find themselves in the year 1902, attempting to save Emily Roman and her family from death by fire.

Illus. by Gail Owens, Atheneum, 1975, 192 pp., o.p.

(BL 72:295; CCBB 29:89; HB 52:54; KR 43:776; SLJ Oct 1975 p. 93)

2682   ALLAN, Mabel E(sther). *Time to Go Back*. Gr. 5–8.

Sarah reads her late Aunt Larke's poetry and finds herself living in the year 1942, where her friend, Larke, has a tragic wartime love affair.

Abelard-Schuman, 1972, 134 pp., o.p.

(CCBB 26:70; KR 40:1105; LJ 98:257)

ALLEN, Judy. *The Spring on the Mountain*. See Chapter 1, Allegorical Fantasy and Literary Fairy Tales.

2683   ANDERSON, Margaret J(ean). *The Druid's Gift*. Gr. 6–9.

✓   Caitlin, a rebellious girl living on a Scottish isle during the time of the Druids, has visions of herself in three future times as Cathan, Catie, and Catriona.

Knopf, 1989, 192 pp. (0-394-81936-5)

(BBJ:68; BL 85:1967, 1970; CCBB 42:188; HB 56:481; KR 57:288; SLJ Mar 1989 p. 175; Suth 4:13)

2684   ANDERSON, Margaret J(ean). *In the Circle of Time* (The Time trilogy, book 2). Gr. 5–8.

A strange fog swirling around an ancient Scottish stone circle sweeps Jennifer and Robert into the year 2179, where they attempt to help a peace-loving tribe escape enslavement by the mechanized Barbaric Ones. This is the sequel to *In the Keep of Time* (Random, 1977) and is followed by *The Mists of Time* (Knopf, 1984).

Knopf, 1979, 181 pp., o.p.

(BBJ:68; BL 75:1533; CCBB 32:185; KR 47:635; SLJ Apr 1979 p. 52)

2685   ANDERSON, Margaret J(ean). *To Nowhere and Back*. Gr. 5–7.

On a path near her home, Elizabeth travels 100 years into the past and becomes a girl named Ann.

Knopf, 1975, 141 pp., o.p.

(BL 71:961; CCBB 28:157; HB 51:379; KR 43:181; SLJ Mar 1975 p. 91)

2686   ANDERSON, Poul (William). *The Time Patrol* (The Time Patrol series). Gr. 10
✓   **up.**

Nine science-fantasy short stories and novellas about Manse Everard, a member of the Time Patrol, which travels through time correcting problems in the past to ensure their own future time's safety. This is the sequel to *The Shield of Time* (1990) and is related to *Guardians of Time* (1960, 1976, 1988) and *Time Patrolman* (1983).

Tor, 1991, 458 pp. (0-312-85231-2)

(BL 88:416, 421; KR 59:1188; LJ Oct 15, 1991 p. 127; SLJ Apr 1992 p. 170; VOYA 15:38)

2687   ANDREWS, J(ames) S(ydney). *The Green Hill of Nendrum* (British title: *The Bell of Nendrum*, 1969). Gr. 6–8.

Nial Ross is caught in a storm while sailing and transported 1,000 years back through time to the island monastery of Nendrum.

Hawthorn, 1970, 214 pp., o.p.

(BL 67:266; HB 46:613; TLS 1969 p. 690)

2688   APPEL, Allen. *Time After Time* **(Alex Balfour series, book 1).** *Gr. 10 up.*

Alex Balfour, a young history professor, travels back in time to Petrograd in 1917, determined to rescue Czar Nicholas and his family from assassination. In the sequel, *Twice Upon a Time* (1988), Alex helps two Native Americans on display at the 1876 Philadelphia Centennial Exposition escape from their captors, and then finds himself in South Dakota on the eve of the Battle of Little Bighorn. The third book in the series is *Till the End of Time* (Doubleday, 1990).

Carroll & Graf, 1985, 373 pp. (0-88184-182-X); Dell, 1987, pap. (0-440-59116-3)

(BL 82:179, 215, 83:1117; Kies:7)

ARTHUR, Ruth M(abel). *The Autumn People.* See Chapter 4, Ghost Fantasy.

2689   ARTHUR, Ruth M(abel). *On the Wasteland.* **Gr. 5–7. (Orig. British pub. 1975.)**

When Betony travels into the past, she is transformed from a friendless orphan into Estrith, a Viking chief's daughter engaged to a Saxon prince.

Illus. by Margery Gill, Atheneum, 1975, 159 pp., o.p.

(BL 72:163; HB 51:459; KR 43:710; SLJ Oct 1975 p. 94; TLS 1975 p. 1455)

2690   ARTHUR, Ruth M(abel). *Requiem for a Princess.* **Gr. 6–9. (Orig. British pub. 1967.)**

Willow Forrester's upsetting discovery that she is adopted brings on nightmares, in which she becomes a sixteenth-century Spanish girl fated to die by drowning.

Illus. by Margery Gill, Atheneum, 1967, 182 pp., o.p.

(BL 63:1098; CCBB 21:138; HB 43:211; KR 35:61; LJ 92:1744; TLS 1967 p. 1141)

2691   AVI. *Something Upstairs: A Tale of Ghosts.* **Gr. 5–9.**

✓   The ghost of Caleb, a young black slave murdered nearly two hundred years ago in the attic of Kenny's house, convinces Kenny to travel back through time to eighteenth-century Providence, Rhode Island, to change Caleb's fate.

Orchard, 1988, 120 pp. (0-531-05782-8); Avon, 1990, pap. (0-380-70853-1)

(BL 85:476; CCBB 42:2; HB 65:65; JHC:332; Kies:8; KR 56:1145; SLJ Oct 1988 p. 138; VOYA 11:293, 12:16)

2692   BACON, Martha (Sherman). *The Third Road.* **Gr. 5–8.**

A twentieth-century girl named Fox becomes stranded in seventeenth-century Spain.

Illus. by Robin Jacques, Little, 1971, 188 pp., o.p.

(KR 39:943; LJ 96:4182)

2693   BARBER, Antonia (pseud. of Barbara Anthony). *The Ghosts.* **Gr. 5–7.**

✓   Lucy and Jamie move to an old country house where they meet two ghostly children, and make a frightening journey into the past to save the ghosts from a fiery death.

Farrar, 1969, 189 pp., o.p.; Pocket, 1982, 1989, pap., 224 pp. (0-671-70714-0)

(BBC:198; BL 66:563; CCBB 23:92; HB 45:532; Kies:9; KR 37:854; LJ 95:777; TLS 1969 p. 689)

2694   BARRON, T(homas) A. *The Ancient One.* **Gr. 6–9.**

When thirteen-year-old Kate visits an old-growth redwood forest in the fog-shrouded Lost Crater of Oregon, her owl-headed walking stick takes her hundreds of years into the past, where a long-vanished Indian tribe is fighting to save the forest. This is the sequel to the science-fiction book *Heartlight* (1990).

Putnam, 1992, 368 pp. (0-685-10268-8)

(BL 89:46; CCBB 46:139; HBG 4[Spring 1993]:79; KR 60:918; SLJ Nov 1992 p. 88; VOYA 15:290, 16:9)

2695 BELLAIRS, John. *The Trolley to Yesterday* **(Johnny Dixon series, book 6). Gr. 5–8.**

Professor Childermass takes Johnny and Fergie on a trolley back through time to Constantinople, in an attempt to change history by preventing a massacre. The eight other stories in this series are more horror than fantasy: *The Mummy, the Will and the Crypt* (1983), *The Curse of the Blue Figurine* (1983), *The Spell of the Sorcerer's Skull* (1984), *The Revenge of the Wizard's Ghost* (1985), *The Eyes of the Killer Robot* (1986), *The Chessmen of Doom* (1989), *The Secret of the Underground Room* (1990), and *The Drum, the Doll and the Zombie* (1994, written by Bellairs and Brad Strickland).

Dial, 1989, 183 pp. (0-8037-0581-6); Bantam, 1990, pap. (0-553-15795-7)

(BL 85:1719; CCBB 42:217; KR 57:686; SLJ June 1989 p. 102; VOYA 12:219)

2696 BELLAMY, Edward. *Looking Backward: 2000–1887.* **Gr. 10 up. (Orig. U.S. pub. 1888.)**

Wealthy nineteenth-century Bostonian Julian West awakens in the year 2000, in a Massachusetts that has become a cooperative utopia, where he falls in love with his fiancé's great-granddaughter. The sequel is *Equality* (1897, 1924, 1970, 1985).

Houghton, 1915, 1941, 276 pp., o.p.; Harvard Univ. Pr., 1967, 314 pp., o.p.; Amereon (repr. of 1888 ed.), o.p.; Random, 1966, 1982, pap., 275 pp. (0-685-04266-9)

(BL 25:403, 39:141, 42:59; SHC:669)

2697 BERESFORD, Elizabeth. *Invisible Magic.* **Gr. 4–6. (Orig. British pub. 1975.)**

Princess Elfrida-of-the-Castle decides she likes life in the twentieth century better than in her own time, and welcomes the chance to trade places with Mr. Patrick.

Illus. by Reg Gray, Hart-Davis/Granada, 1977, 158 pp., o.p.

(BL 74:1185; CCBB 32:23; TLS 1975 p. 763)

2698 BERESFORD, Elizabeth. *Travelling Magic.* **Gr. 4–6. (Orig. British pub. 1965.)**

Kate and Marcus meet a magician from Ancient Britain who has come to the twentieth century as part of his studies.

Illus. by Judith Valpy, Granada, 1977, 163 pp., o.p.

(BL 74:1185; TLS 1965 p. 1130)

2699 BETHANCOURT, T(homas) Ernesto (pseud. of Tom Paisley). *Tune in Yesterday.* **Gr. 8–10.**

A love for jazz propels two friends into the past to 1942, but racial prejudice and Nazi plots make life more complicated than they had anticipated. In *The Tomorrow Connection* (1984), Richie and Matty escape their problems by traveling to 1912 and then 1906, but Matty is forced to endure more racial prejudice while they search for a tomorrow gate to take them home.

Holiday, 1978, 156 pp., o.p.

(BL 74:1420, 80:351; HB 54:400; KR 46:311; SLJ May 1978 p. 73)

2700 BOND, Nancy (Barbara). *Another Shore.* **Gr. 8–12.**

✓ One day she is a summer employee of a Nova Scotia historical park, playing the role of an eighteenth-century girl, and the next day Lyn Paget awakens to find that she has actually become her "character," seventeen-year-old Elisabeth Bernard living in the year

1744. This story is disturbing because it ends with Lyn helplessly stranded in a past life she has grown to detest.

Macmillan, 1988, 308 pp. (0-689-50463-2)

(BBS:53; BL 85:67, 70; CCBB 42:26; Ch&Bks:283; HB 65:214; JHC:335; KR 56:1400; SLJ Oct 1988 p. 159; Suth 4:39; VOYA 11:246, 12:13)

2701   BOND, Nancy (Barbara). *A String in the Harp.* **Gr. 6–8.**

✓   Unhappy over his mother's recent death and the family's move to Wales, Peter Morgan is drawn into the sixth-century period of Taliesin by the tuning key of an ancient harp. Boston Globe Horn Book Award Honor Book for Fiction, 1976. John Newbery Medal Honor Book, 1977. I.R.A. Children's Book Award, 1977. Tir na n-Og Award, 1977.

Macmillan, 1976, 384 pp. (0-689-50036-X)

(BBJ:69; BL 72:1108, 80:95; CC:452; CCBB 29:171; Ch&Bks:283; HB 52:287; JHC:349; KR 44:255; SLJ Apr 1976 p. 84; Suth 2:52; Tymn:54)

2702   BOSSE, Malcolm J(oseph). *Cave Beyond Time.* **Gr. 7–9.**

Bitten by a rattlesnake while on an Arizona archaeological dig, Ben travels back in time for a series of encounters with two Native American tribes. His experiences in the past help him adjust to the recent loss of his parents.

Harper, 1980, 187 pp., o.p

(BBJ:69; BL 77:400, 402; CCBB 34:66; HB 57:57; SLJ Nov 1980 p. 83; VOYA 3[Dec 1980]:37)

BOSTON, L(ucy) M(aria Wood). *The Children of Green Knowe.* See Chapter 4, Ghost Fantasy.

2703   BOSTON, L(ucy) M(aria Wood). *The Stones of Green Knowe.* **Gr. 4–6.**

✓   In the year 1120, a boy named Roger discovers two magical stones at the building site of Green Knowe manor house, and is sent into the future to meet Toby, Linnet, Susan, and Tolly, the protagonists in *The Children of Green Knowe* (1954, 1967; see Chapter 4, Ghost Fantasy).

Illus. by Peter Boston, Atheneum, 1976, 118 pp., o.p.

(BL 73:141; CCBB 30:39; Ch&Bks:259; HB 52:623; KR 44:845; SLJ Jan 1977 p. 87; Suth 2:53; TLS 1976 p. 881)

2704   BRADBURY, Ray (Douglas). *The Halloween Tree.* **Gr. 5–8.**

✓   Eight Halloween-costumed boys search through ancient Egypt, druidic Britain, medieval Europe, and some Mexican catacombs for a friend who vanished from a haunted house.

Illus. by Joseph Mugnaini, Knopf, 1972, 1988, 160 pp., LB(0-394-92409-6); Bantam, 1982, 1984, pap. (0-553-25823-0)

(BBS:53; BL 69:404; JHC:336; KR 40:801; Kies:18; LJ 97:4086; VOYA 12:39)

2705   BRANDEL, Marc (pseud. of Marcus Beresford). *The Mine of Lost Days.* **Gr.**
✓   **4–7.**

Deep inside an abandoned Irish copper mine, Henry discovers four people who have lived without aging for over one hundred years, but who would die if they emerged into the modern world.

Illus. by John Verling, Harper, 1974, 185 pp., o.p.

(BL 71:241; KR 42:876; LJ 99:2738)

2706   BUCHAN, John. *Lake of Gold.* **Gr. 5–7. (Orig. Canadian pub. 1941; British title:** *The Long Traverse,* **1941.)**

Bored by his history lessons, a young boy on a camping trip is given the chance to take part in Canadian history.

Illus. by S. Levenson, Houghton, 1941, 190 pp., o.p.

(HB 17:367, 476; LJ 66:737)

2707 **BUFFIE, Margaret.** *The Haunting of Frances Rain.* **Gr. 6–9. (Orig. Canadian**
✓ **title:** *Who Is Frances Rain?*, **1987.)**

The old spectacles Lizzie finds on Rain Island allow her to glimpse the past life of a reclusive woman named Francis Rain. YA Canadian Book Award, 1988.

Scholastic, 1989, 192 pp. (0-5904-2034-9)

(BBJ:69; BL 86:273, 344; HBG 1[July–Dec 1989]:82; KR 57:1471; SLJ Sept 1989 p. 272; VOYA 12:286)

2708 **BURFORD, Lolah.** *The Vision of Stephen: An Elegy.* **Gr. 7 up.**

Fleeing a sentence of execution, Prince Stephen escapes from the seventh-century Anglo-Saxon period into Victorian England.

Illus. by Bill Greer, Macmillan, 1972, 192 pp., o.p.

(BL 69:26, 292, 299; KR 40:344; LJ 97:2640, 3473)

2709 **BUTLER, Octavia E.** *Kindred.* **Gr. 10 up.**

Dana, a young black writer living in Los Angeles in 1976, undertakes a series of unexpected and dangerous trips into the year 1819 to rescue Rufus, the young son of a Maryland slaveholder.

Doubleday, 1979, 264 pp., o.p.; Beacon, 1988, pap. (0-8070-8305-4)

(KR 47:587; LJ 104:1585; VOYA 2[Feb 1980]:28, 4[Aug 1981]:47)

2710 **CAMERON, Eleanor (Frances Butler).** *Beyond Silence.* **Gr. 6–10.**
✓ Andy is plagued by nightmares and unsettling visits to the past when he and his father visit their ancestral home in Scotland, following his brother's death.

Dutton, 1980, 208 pp. (0-525-26463-9)

(BBC:199; BL 77:205, 207; CC:460; CCBB 34:88; HB 56:646, 62:616; Kies:26; KR 49:78; SLJ Jan 1981 p. 67; VOYA 4[Dec 1981]:28)

CAMERON, Eleanor (Frances Butler). *The Court of the Stone Children.* See Chapter 4, Ghost Fantasy.

2711 **CAMERON, Eleanor (Frances Butler).** *Time and Mr. Bass: A Mushroom Planet*
✓ *Book.* **Gr. 4–6.**

Forces of evil reach through Mycetian history to ensnare Tyco Bass and his friends, Chuck and David, after they visit ancient Wales to translate an old scroll. *The Wonderful Flight to the Mushroom Planet* (1954), *Stowaway to the Mushroom Planet* (1956), *Mr. Bass's Planetoid* (1958), and *A Mystery for Mr. Bass* (1960) are science-fiction stories that precede this book in the Mushroom Planet series.

Illus. by Fred Meise, Little, 1967, 247 pp., o.p.

(BL 63:988; HB 43:460; KR 35:56; LJ 92:1314)

CARKEET, David. *I Been There Before.* See Chapter 6, Humorous Fantasy.

2712 **CHASE, Mary (Coyle).** *The Wicked Pigeon Ladies in the Garden.* **Gr. 4–6.**
✓ Maureen Swanson, trespassing at the Old Messerman Place, finds a strange bracelet and meets seven evil ghosts who try to trap her in the past.

Illus. by Don Bolognese, Knopf, 1968, 115 pp., o.p.; Peter Smith, 1985 (0-8446-6192-9)

(BL 65:493, 82:682; CCBB 22:90; HB 45:52, 63:491; KR 36:1162; LJ 94:293; Suth:69)

2713 **CHETWIN, Grace.** *Friends in Time.* **Gr. 4–7.**

Emma Gibson has always had trouble making friends because her family has moved so often, so she is overjoyed when her heartfelt wish for one true friend brings Abigail Bently to the twentieth century from the year 1846.

Macmillan, 1992, 132 pp. (0-02-718318-1)

(BL 88:1936; HBG 3[Fall 1992]:261; KR 60:716; SLJ July 1992 p. 72; VOYA 15:236)

CHURCH, Richard. *The French Lieutenant: A Ghost Story.* See Chapter 4, Ghost Fantasy.

2714   CONRAD, Pam. *Stonewords: A Ghost Story.* **Gr. 5–9.**

✓✓   Zoe's grandparents think Zoe Louise is only an imaginary friend, but Zoe knows Zoe Louise is the ghost of a little girl who died in a fire on her eleventh birthday, and she decides to go back in time to save her. Boston Globe Horn Book Award Honor Book, 1990.

Harper, 1990, 130 pp. (0-06-021315-9), 1991, pap. (0-06-440354-8)

(BL 86:1338; CC:474; CCBB 43:211; HB 66:600; HBG 1[Jan–June 1990]:254; JHC 1991 Suppl. p. 69; KR 58:339; SLJ May 1990 p. 103; Suth 4:81; VOYA 13:10)

COOPER (Grant), Susan (Mary). *Over Sea, Under Stone.* See discussion of *The Dark Is Rising* and *Silver on the Tree* in Chapter 5B, Myth Fantasy.

CRESSWELL (Rowe), Helen. *A Game of Catch.* See Chapter 4, Ghost Fantasy.

2715   CRESSWELL (Rowe), Helen. *Moondial.* **Gr. 5–8. (Orig. British pub. 1987.)**

✓   Minty Kane feels compelled to travel back through time to rescue the ghosts of two abused children she meets while spending the summer near an old English manor house.

Macmillan, 1987, 208 pp. (0-02-725370-8)

(BBC:201; BL 84:317, 873; CCBB 41:86; Ch&Bks:262; HB 66:68; KR 55:1238; SLJ Nov 1987 p. 104; TLS 1987 p. 1285; VOYA 10:243)

CRESSWELL (Rowe), Helen. *The Secret World of Polly Flint.* See Chapter 7, Magic Adventure Fantasy.

2716   CRESSWELL (Rowe), Helen. *Time Out.* **Gr. 3–6. (Orig. British pub. 1990.)**

✓   Wilks the butler takes his family on an amazing vacation to the future: from London in 1887 to 1987, where they are astonished by television and automobiles.

Illus. by Peter Ewell, Macmillan, 1990, 80 pp. (0-02-725425-9)

(BL 86:1089; HBG 1[Jan–June 1990]:256; KR 58:261; SLJ June 1990 p. 118)

2717   CRESSWELL (Rowe), Helen. *Up the Pier.* **Gr. 4–6. (Orig. British pub. 1971.)**

✓   Lonely Carrie meets the invisible Pontifex family, who were unwillingly transported from 1921 to 1971 and need Carrie's help to break the spell that holds them in the wrong time. Carnegie Medal Highly Commended Book, 1971.

Illus. by Gareth Floyd, Macmillan, 1971, 144 pp., o.p.

(BL 68:1002; CCBB 26:40; HB 48:368; KR 40:477; LJ 97:4070; Suth:94; TLS 1971 p. 1516)

CURRY, Jane Louise. *The Bassumtyte Treasure.* See Chapter 4, Ghost Fantasy.

2718   CURRY, Jane Louise. *The Daybreakers.* **Gr. 5–7.**

Researching the history of Apple Lock, Callie, Liss, and Harry are drawn back through time to Abáloc, a primitive village whose people need the children's help to defeat their enemies. The sequel is *The Birdstones* (1977). Both stories are related to *Over the Sea's Edge* (1971) (see this chapter).

Illus. by Charles Robinson, Harcourt, 1970, 191 pp., o.p.

(BL 66:1406; HB 46:296; KR 38:452; LJ 95:3626; TLS 1970 p. 1251)

2719 **CURRY, Jane Louise.** *Over the Sea's Edge.* **Gr. 5–7.**

✓ An ancient medallion causes Dave Reese to exchange places with a twelfth-century Welsh boy named Dewi. He accompanies the exiled Prince Maduac to the legendary island of Antillia where they are drawn into a struggle between the fairy people of Abáloc and a Native American civilization. *The Daybreakers* (1970, see above) and *The Birdstones* (1977) are related stories.

Illus. by Charles Robinson, Harcourt, 1971, 182 pp., o.p.

(BL 68:333; HB 47:610; KR 39:1079; LJ 96:3474; TLS 1971 p. 1510)

2720 **CURRY, Jane Louise.** *Parsley, Sage, Rosemary and Time.* **Gr. 3–6.**

An herb from her aunt's garden sends Rosemary into Pilgrim times, where she helps a woman accused of witchcraft. The sequel is *The Magical Cupboard* (1976).

Illus. by Charles Robinson, Atheneum, 1975, 108 pp., o.p.

(KR 43:306; SLJ Apr 1975 p. 51)

CURRY, Jane Louise. *Poor Tom's Ghost.* See Chapter 4, Ghost Fantasy.

CURRY, Jane Louise. *The Sleepers.* See Chapter 5B, Myth Fantasy.

2721 **CURRY, Jane Louise.** *The Watchers.* **Gr. 6–8.**

✓ Ray Silver joins the family battle against a coal company threatening their land, and when a stone splinter sends him sixteen hundred years into the past, he becomes involved in a tragedy surrounding his ancestors.

Illus. by Trina Schart Hyman, Atheneum, 1975, 235 pp., o.p.

(BL 72:451; CCBB 29:108; KR 43:988; SLJ Nov 1975 p. 73; Suth 2:112; TLS 1976 p. 392)

2722 **CUTT, W(illiam) Towrie.** *Seven for the Sea.* **Gr. 6–8. (Orig. British pub. 1972.)**

Two cousins travel 100 years into the past to investigate rumors of Selkie ancestors. This is the sequel to the British book *Message from Arkmae* (1972).

Follett, 1974, 96 pp., o.p.

(BL 71:507; HB 50:690; LJ 99:3276)

2723 **DAVIES, Andrew (Wynford).** *Conrad's War.* **Gr. 5–8. (Orig. British pub. 1978.)**

✓✓ The tank and the model plane Conrad built allow his "leak" through time to World War II, where he becomes a pilot imprisoned in a German POW camp. Guardian Award for Children's Fiction, 1978. Boston Globe Horn Book Award for Fiction, 1980.

Crown, 1980, 120 pp., o.p.; Dell, 1986, pap., 144 pp. (0-440-91452-3); Knopf, 1991, pap., 128 pp. (0-679-80434-X)

(BL 76:883; CCBB 33:130; HB 56:171; JHC:352; KR 48:364; SLJ Apr 1980 p. 107; Suth 3·113)

2724 **DAWSON, Carley.** *Mr. Wicker's Window.* **Gr. 5–7.**

Chris travels from an antique shop into the Revolutionary War period, where he is sent on a dangerous mission to China. The sequels are *The Sign of the Seven Seas* (1954) and *Dragon's Run* (1955).

Illus. by Lynd Ward, Houghton, 1952, 272 pp., o.p.

(BL 49:160; CCBB 6:31; HB 29:53; LJ 78:68)

2725 **DEXTER, Catherine.** *Mazemaker.* **Gr. 5–8.**

✓ After a spray-painted sidewalk maze takes Winnie Brown into the past to Crescent Ridge, she realizes she may be trapped there forever unless she can find the missing maze painter.

Morrow, 1989, 202 pp. (0-688-07383-2)

(BL 85:1820; CCBB 42:192; HB 56:504; KR 57:461; SLJ May 1989 p. 103; VOYA 12:115, 13:14)

2726 **DOTY, Jean Slaughter.** *Can I Get There by Candlelight?* **Gr. 5–7.**

Gail's horse, Candlelight, takes her through a long-unused gate to Babylon, a nineteenth-century estate, where she befriends a girl named Hilary.

Illus. by Ted Lewin, Macmillan, 1980, 111 pp., o.p.

(BBC:202; BL 76:980; HB 56:405; KR 48:364; SLJ Mar 1980 p. 130)

2727 **DUNLOP, Eileen (Rhona).** *Elizabeth, Elizabeth* **(British title:** *Robinsheugh,*
✓ **1975). Gr. 6–9.**

On a lonely visit to her aunt at the Melville manor house, Elizabeth escapes through an old looking glass into the eighteenth century, but she soon fears for her life.

Illus. by Peter Farmer, Holt, 1977, 185 pp., o.p.

(BL 73:1349; CCBB 30:174; Ch&Bks:285; HB 53:314; Kies:53; SLJ May 1977 p. 67; Suth 2:131; TLS 1975 p. 733)

2728 **DUNLOP, Eileen (Rhona).** *The Maze Stone.* **Gr. 6–10. (Orig. British pub. 1982.)**
✓ After Fanny's suspicions about their new drama teacher are aroused by the unusual pendant he wears, she must take quick action to save her sister from a terrifying fate.

Coward, 1983, 159 pp., o.p.

(BBC:202; BL 80:337, 356; CCBB 37:85; KR 51[Sept 1, 1983]:J173; SLJ Dec 1983 p. 84; TLS 1982 p. 1302; VOYA 7:29)

2729 **DUNLOP, Eileen (Rhona).** *The Valley of Deer.* **Gr. 5–8. (Orig. British pub. 1989.)**
✓ A crystal charm once owned by a deformed eighteenth-century herbal healer allows Anne Farrar glimpses into the past of the rural Scottish town where her archeologist parents are excavating a burial mound.

Holiday, 1989, 139 pp. (0-8234-0766-7)

(BL 86:456; CCBB 43:54; HB 66:201; HBG 1[July 1989]:86; KR 57:1473; SLJ Jan 1990 103; TLS 1989 p. 560)

2730 **EAGAR, Frances.** *Time Tangle.* **Gr. 5–7.**

Beth spends a lonely Christmas at boarding school until she meets a boy from the sixteenth century who involves her in a plot to save a hidden cleric.

Nelson, 1977, 172 pp., o.p.

(CCBB 31:45; KR 45:539; SLJ Oct 1977 p. 88)

2731 **EISENBERG, Lawrence B(enjamin).** *The Villa of the Ferromonte.* **Gr. 10 up.**

While visiting his elderly Aunts Elizabeth and Amy in their run-down Manhattan apartment, Norman Dickens realizes that both he and they can travel into the past.

Simon, 1974, 191 pp., o.p.

(BL 71:22, 34; KR 42:443; LJ 99:1847)

2732 **EUBANK, Judith.** *Crossover.* **Gr. 10 up.**

Ghostly sightings of the Victorian family who once lived in the seventeenth-century English manor house, now a university dormitory, distract American graduate student Meredith Blake from her studies.

Carroll & Graf, 1992, 224 pp. (0-88184-746-1)

(BL 88:907, 923; KR 59:1436; LJ Dec 1991 p. 196)

EVARTS, Hal G. *Jay-Jay and the Peking Monster.* See Chapter 6, Humorous Fantasy.

FARMER (Mockridge), Penelope. *A Castle of Bone.* See Chapter 5B, Myth Fantasy.

2733 **FARMER (Mockridge), Penelope.** *Charlotte Sometimes.* **Gr. 5–7. (Orig. British**
✓✓ **pub. 1969.)**

Charlotte Makepeace discovers that she has a double named Claire who slept in the same boarding school bed in the year 1918, and that she and Claire can exchange places in time. This is the sequel to *The Summer Birds* (1962, see Chapter 7, Magic Adventure Fantasy) and *Emma in Winter* (1966, see below).

Illus. by Chris Conor, Harcourt, 1969, 192 pp., o.p.; Dell, 1987, pap. (0-440-41261-7); Peter Smith, 1993 (0-8446-6673-4)

(BL 66:457; CCBB 23:158; Ch&Bks:260; HB 45:675, 60:223; KR 37:1121; LJ 94:4604; Suth:120; TLS 1969 p. 1190, 1985 p. 348)

2734 **FARMER (Mockridge), Penelope.** *Emma in Winter.* **Gr. 5–7. (Orig. British pub.**
1966.)

Lonely Emma and Bobby find themselves sharing a dream in which they travel so far back through time that they are in danger of not being able to return to the real world. This is the sequel to *The Summer Birds* (1962, see Chapter 7, Magic Adventure Fantasy) and is followed by *Charlotte Sometimes* (1969, see above).

Illus. by James J. Spanfeller, Harcourt, 1966, 160 pp., o.p.; Dell, 1987, pap. (0-440-42308-2)

(BL 63:488: Ch&Bks:260; KR 34:835; LJ 91:5747; TLS 1966 p. 1071)

2735 **FINNEY, Jack (pseud. of Walter Branden Finney).** *About Time: Twelve Stories.*
Gr. 10 up. (Orig. pub. separately, 1950–1969.)

Twelve witty and romantic stories about time and time travel, including "Second Change," "Of Missing Persons," and "I'm Scared."

Simon, 1986, pap., 224 pp. (0-671-62887-9)

(BL 83:34, 52, 83:777; Kliatt 21[Winter 1987]:16; KR 54:1078)

2736 **FINNEY, Jack (pseud. of Walter Branden Finney).** *Time and Again.* **Gr. 10 up.**
✓

Simon Morley agrees to move into the Dakota apartment building in Manhattan, where he will travel back to the year 1882 as part of a U.S. government project, but he balks at altering historical events after he falls in love with Julia, a nineteenth-century girl.

Simon, 1970, 399 pp., o.p., 1978, pap., 1986 (0-671-24295-4)

(BL 67:36, 95, 654; HB 46:502; KR 38:272, 473; LJ 95:3304, 3649)

2737 **FISHER, Leonard Everett.** *Noonan: A Novel about Baseball, ESP, and Time*
Warps. **Gr. 6–9.**

In 1896, young hopeful Johnny Noonan, a baseball pitcher, is hit by a foul ball and sent one hundred years into the future, where his psychokinetic ability to control a baseball leads to stardom.

Doubleday, 1978, 125 pp., o.p.

(BBJ:70; BL 74:1733; CCBB 32:60; KR 46:749; SLJ May 1978 p. 87)

2738 **FREEMAN, Barbara C(onstance).** *The Other Face.* **Gr. 5–8. (Orig. British pub.**
1975.)

A miniature china cottage transports Betony 150 years into the past where she becomes involved in an ancestor's romance.

Illus. by the author, Dutton, 1976, 151 pp., o.p.

(BL 73:832; KR 44:1169; SLJ Jan 1977 p. 91; TLS 1975 p. 733)

FREEMAN, Barbara C(onstance). *A Pocket of Silence.* See Chapter 4, Ghost Fantasy.

2739 GABALDON, Diana. *Outlander: A Novel* **(Claire Randall and Jamie Fraser**
✓   **series, book 1). Gr. 10 up.**

Touching an ancient Scottish stone circle transports former battlefield nurse Claire Randall back through time from 1945 to 1743, where her medical knowledge draws accusations of witchcraft. The sequels are: *A Dragonfly in Amber* (1992) and *Voyager* (1994).

Delacorte, 1991, 640 pp. (0-385-30230-4); Dell, 1992, pap. (0-440-21256-1)

(BL 87:2029; KR 59:686; LJ July 1991 p. 134; VOYA 14:311)

GARD, Joyce (pseud. of Joyce Reeves). *Talargain.* See Chapter 5B, Myth Fantasy.

2740 GARNER, Alan. *The Red Shift.* **Gr. 8 up. (Orig. British pub. 1973.)**
✓   The lives of three British teenagers from different time periods—the Roman occupation, the Civil War, and contemporary Britain—are linked by an ancient stone ax.

Macmillan, 1973, 197 pp., o.p.

(BL 70:801; CCBB 27:142; HB 49:580; Kies:63; KR 41:989; TLS 1973 p. 1112; Tymn:90)

GARNER, Alan. *The Weirdstone of Brisingamen.* See discussion of *The Moon of Gomrath* in Chapter 5B, Myth Fantasy.

GATES, Susan P. *The Burnhope Wheel.* See Chapter 4, Ghost Fantasy.

2741 GERROLD, David. *The Man Who Folded Himself.* **Gr. 10 up.**

Danny Eakins's timebelt shows him numerous versions of himself, occupying many different time lines.

Random, 1973, 148 pp., o.p.; Amereon, 1976 (repr. of 1973 ed.), LB(0-88411-191-1)

(BL 69:835; KR 40:1445; LJ 98:436; TLS 1974 p. 163)

GIFALDI, David. *Gregory, Maw and the Mean One.* See Chapter 6, Humorous Fantasy.

2742 GOLDSTEIN, Lisa. *The Dream Years.* **Gr. 10 up.**
✓   A young Parisian surrealist painter living during the 1920s is transported in his dreams to the future of 1968, where he falls in love with a student named Solange and becomes involved in the student protests.

Bantam, 1985, 181 pp., pap., 1989 (0-553-27657-3)

(BL 81:1637; Kies:68; Kliatt 20[Fall 1986]:24; KR 53:678; LJ Aug 1985 p. 120; SLJ Dec 1985 p. 110)

2743 GOODWIN, Marie D. *Where the Towers Pierce the Sky.* **Gr. 6–9.**

Lizzie Patterson is drawn from South Bend, Indiana, to fifteenth-century France by an astrologer attempting to see Jeanne D'Arc's future.

Macmillan, 1989, 192 pp. (0-02-736871-8)

(BBJ:70; BL 86:742; CCBB 43:57; HBG 1[July–Dec 1989]:82; KR 57:1403; SLJ Nov 1989 p. 126; VOYA 12:289)

2744 GREAVES, Margaret. *Cat's Magic.* **Gr. 5–7. (Orig. British pub. 1980.)**

An Egyptian cat goddess rewards Louise for rescuing a drowning kitten by enabling her to travel through time to visit ancient Egypt and Victorian England.

Harper, 1981, 183 pp., o.p.

(BBC:204; BL 77:1028; CCBB 35:9; KR 49:633; SLJ Apr 1981 p. 127; TLS 1980 p. 360; VOYA 3[June 1981]:38)

2745 GREER, Gerry, and RUDDICK, Bob. *Max and Me and the Time Machine.* **Gr.**
✓   **4–7.**

Max's doubts about his friend Steve's time machine are dispelled after they find themselves in medieval England: Steve inside the body of a famous knight, and Max inside his horse. The sequel is *Max and Me and the Wild West* (1988).

Harcourt, 1983, 140 pp. (0-15-253134-3); Harper, 1988, pap., 128 pp. (0-06-440222-3)

(BBC:204; BL 79:1465; CC:495; CCBB 37:28; HB 59:443; KR 51:660; SLJ May 1983 pp. 32, 71; VOYA 6:214)

2746   GRIFFIN, Peni R(ae). *A Dig in Time.* **Gr. 4–7.**

Artifacts found by Nan and Tim in their grandmother's San Antonio home allow them to travel into the past to witness their family history first-hand.

Macmillan, 1991, 208 pp. (0-689-50525-6); Puffin, 1992, pap. (0-14-036001-8)

(BL 87:1965; CCBB 45:38; HBG 2:270; KR 59:471; SLJ June 1991 p. 104; VOYA 14:180)

2747   GRIFFIN, Peni R(ae). *Switching Well.* **Gr. 5–9.**

✓   A wishing well enables twelve-year-olds Ada and Amber to trade lives in 1891 and 1991 San Antonio, Texas, but both girls soon long for their own familiar worlds.

Macmillan, 1993, 224 pp. (0-689-50581-7)

(BL 89:1812; CCBB 46:345; HBG 4[Fall 1993]: 309; KR 61:529; SLJ June 1993 p. 106; VOYA 16:164; 17:7)

2748   GROSSER, Morton. *The Snake Horn.* **Gr. 5–7.**

When Danny blows his antique horn, a seventeenth-century music-master appears and teaches the boy's father music that makes him famous.

Illus. by David Stone, Atheneum, 1973, 131 pp., o.p.

(BL 70:50; CCBB 26:171; KR 41:114; LJ 98:1387; Suth 2:193)

2749   HAHN, Mary Downing. *The Doll in the Garden: A Ghost Story.* **Gr. 4–7.**

✓   Ashley finds an old china doll buried in her landlady's rose garden, and follows a ghostly cat through a hedge eighty years into the past, where she meets the little girl from whom the doll was stolen.

Houghton, 1989, 128 pp. (0-89919-848-1); Avon, 1990, pap. (0-380-70865-5)

(BBC:204; BL 85:1296; CC:496; CCBB 42:171; HB 65:370; KR 57:546; SLJ May 1989 p. 109)

HAMILTON (Adoff), Virginia (Esther). *Sweet Whispers, Brother Rush.* See Chapter 4, Ghost Fantasy.

HAMLETT, Christina. *The Enchanter.* See Chapter 5B, Myth Fantasy.

2750   HAMLEY, Dennis. *Pageants of Despair.* **Gr. 6–8. (Orig. British pub. 1974.)**

Giles helps the Pageant Master of a medieval English town fight off the devil's influence on the annual miracle plays.

Phillips, 1974, 180 pp. (0-87599-205-6)

(BL 71:618; KR 42:1065; SLJ Jan 1975 p. 54; TLS 1974 p. 717)

2751   HANLON, Emily. *Circle Home.* **Gr. 5–7.**

A Stone Age girl named Mai finds herself in the twentieth century, trapped inside the body of a nine-year-old girl who is recovering from a near-fatal automobile accident.

Bradbury, 1981, 237 pp., o.p.

(BL 78:706; CCBB 35:130; KR 50:208; SLJ May 1982 p. 70; VOYA 5[Apr 1982]:39)

HAYNES, Betsy. *The Ghost of the Gravestone Hearth.* See Chapter 4, Ghost Fantasy.

2752 **HILDICK, E(dmund) W(allace).** *The Case of the Dragon in Distress: A McGurk Fantasy* **(McGurk Fantasy series, book 1). Gr. 4–6.**

Jack and the other five members of his McGurk Detective Agency are sent to England in the year 1175 to rescue knights held captive by the literally bloodthirsty Princess Melisande. The sequel is *The Case of the Weeping Witch* (1992), and both books are related to the author's nonfantasy series of McGurk Mysteries.

Macmillan, 1991, 153 pp. (0-02-743931-3)

(BL 87:1716; CCBB 44:264; HBG 2:266; SLJ June 1991 p. 106)

2753 **HOPPE, Joanne.** *Dream Spinner.* **Gr. 6–10.**

After Mary, fifteen, her father, and her new stepfamily move into an old Victorian house, she realizes that in her dreams she can visit this house at the turn of the century, where she becomes a girl called Christabel whose uncle has fallen in love with her.

Morrow, 1992, 240 pp. (0-688-08559-8)

(BL 89:321; CCBB 46:74; HB 69:92; HBG 4[Spring 1993]:81; KR 60:1309; SLJ Dec 1992 p. 277)

2754 **HOUGHTON, Eric.** *Steps Out of Time.* **Gr. 5–8.**

✓ New in town and lonely, Jonathan is able to step through the dense fog into another time, where he lives in the same house but seems to have a sister who calls him Peter.

Lothrop, 1980, 128 pp., o.p.

(BBC:205; BL 77:405; CCBB 34:12; SLJ Sept 1980 p. 72; Suth 2:119; VOYA 3[Feb 1981]:38)

2755 **HURMENCE, Belinda.** *A Girl Called Boy.* **Gr. 6–8.**

✓ Blanch Overtha Yoncey learns about the hardships of slavery firsthand when she goes back through time to become one of her ancestors, a slave girl named Overtha, in North Carolina during the 1850s.

Houghton, 1982, 180 pp. (0-395-31022-9), 1990, pap. (0-395-55698-8)

(BBC:205; BL 78:1445; CCBB 36:12; KR 50:490; HB 58:404; SLJ May 1982 p. 63)

2756 **INGRAM, Tom (Thomas Henry).** *The Night Rider.* **Gr. 5–8.**

A cursed golden bracelet lures Laura to pre-Roman Britain where she becomes a girl called Merta, desperate to find the matching necklace and destroy it before the curse kills her.

Bradbury, 1975, 176 pp., o.p.

(BL 71:1128; CCBB 29:47; KR 43:521; SLJ Sept 1975 p. 105)

2757 **JAMES, J. Alison.** *Sing for a Gentle Rain.* **Gr 7–10.**

✓ Spring Rain, a thirteenth-century Anasazi Indian girl, fears for her tribe's survival during an endless drought, and hopes that the unexpected arrival of James, a twentieth-century teenager, is a good omen for her cliff-dwelling community.

Macmillan, 1990, 211 pp. (0-689-31561-9)

(BL 87:1476; CCBB 44:88; HB 67:74; HBG 2[July 1990]:83; KR 58:1456; SLJ Jan 1991 p. 110; VOYA 13:298)

2758 **JOHNSON, Charles.** *Pieces of Eight.* **Gr. 5–7.**

A sea captain's ghost grants David and Mitchell's wish to meet Blackbeard the pirate by transporting them to 1716, where they join the Brothers of the Coast for an action-filled shipboard adventure.

Illus. by Jennie Ann Nelson, Discovery, 1989, 110 pp. (0-944770-00-2)

(BBC:206; BL 85:1300)

JONES, Diana Wynne. *Aunt Maria.* See Chapter 10, Witchcraft and Sorcery Fantasy.

2759 **JONES, Diana Wynne.** *Charmed Life* **(Chrestomanci series). Gr. 5–8. (Orig.**
✓ **British pub. 1977.)**

After Cat and Gwen Chant are adopted by the mysterious Chrestomanci, Gwen uses witchcraft to change places with a twentieth-century girl, leaving Cat to fend for himself. Carnegie Medal Commended Book, 1977. Guardian Award for Children's Fiction, 1978. The prequel is *The Lives of Christopher Chant* (1988; see Chapter 5C, Travel to Other Worlds). *The Magicians of Caprona* (1980; see Chapter 10, Witchcraft and Sorcery Fantasy) and *Witch Week* (1982; see Chapter 10, Witchcraft and Sorcery Fantasy) are related works, and there are short stories about Chrestomanci in *Warlock at the Wheel* (1985; see Chapter 10, Witchcraft and Sorcery Fantasy) and *Dragons and Dreams* (Ed. by Jane Yolen, Harper, 1986; see Chapter 7, Magic Adventure Fantasy).

Greenwillow, 1978, 217 pp., o.p.; Knopf, 1989, pap. (0-394-82032-0); Peter Smith, 1993 (0-8446-6668-8)

(BBC:206; BL 74:1009; CCBB 31:113; HB 54:396; KR 46:177; SLJ Apr 1978 p. 94; Suth 2:45; TLS 1977 p. 348)

JONES, Diana Wynne. *A Tale of Time City.* See Chapter 5C, Travel to Other Worlds.

2760 **JORDAN, Sherryl.** *The Juniper Game.* **Gr. 7–10. (Orig. New Zealand pub. 1991.)**

When Dylan agreed to take part in a telepathic experiment with Juniper, he had no idea she would take him back in time to the fifteenth century to befriend a young woman accused of witchcraft.

Scholastic, 1991, 240 pp. (0-5904-4728-9)

(BL 88:617; HBG 3[July–Dec 1991]:79; KR 59:1011; SLJ Oct 1991, p. 145; VOYA 14:313)

2761 **JORDAN, Sherryl.** *A Time of Darkness.* **Gr. 7 up. (Orig. New Zealand pub. 1990.)**

Rocco's nightmares of life in a cave plagued by wolf attacks become reality when he finds himself in a primitive world struggling to be accepted by a cave-dwelling clan.

Scholastic, 1990, 224 pp. (0-5904-3363-6), 1992, pap. (0-5904-3362-8)

(BL 87:734; HBG 2[July–Dec 1990]:85; KR 58:1251; SLJ Jan 1991 p. 110; VOYA 13:298, 14:13)

2762 **KENNEMORE, Tim.** *Changing Times.* **Gr. 7–10. (Orig. British pub. 1984.)**

✓ After a junk-shop-purchased 24-hour alarm clock propels Victoria back into her own past, at ages fourteen, eight, and fifteen months, she begins to understand the roots of her parents' miserable marriage.

Faber, 1984, 149 pp., o.p.

(BL 81:436, 449; CCBB 38:110; HB 61:58; SLJ Sept 1984 p. 129; Suth 3:229; TLS Nov 1984 p. 1383)

2763 **KEY, Alexander (Hill).** *The Sword of Aradel.* **Gr. 5–7.**

Brian and Merra escape from medieval England into twentieth-century Manhattan, searching for the magic sword of Aradel.

Westminster, 1977, 144 pp., o.p.

(BL 73:1728; CCBB 31:35; SLJ Sept 1977 p. 146)

2764   KIPLING, (Joseph) Rudyard. *Puck of Pook's Hill.* **Gr. 5–8. (Orig. British pub.**
✓   **1906.)**

Puck, the last of the English fairies, takes Don and Una into the past to meet well-known figures from England's history. The sequel is *Rewards and Fairies* (1910).

Illus. by Arthur Rackham, Doubleday, 1906, 1946, 275 pp., o.p.; Scribners, 1906, 1925, 305 pp., o.p.; Puffin, 1987, pap. (0-14-035077-2)

(BL 2:216; HB 61:84; Kies:95; LJ 32:260; TLS 1906 p. 536)

2765   KITTLEMAN, Laurence R. *Canyons Beyond the Sky.* **Gr. 6–8.**

While visiting his archaeologist father on a dig, Evan Ferguson falls off a cliff and awakens 5,000 years in the past, where he is befriended by a Native American boy and his people.

Atheneum, 1985, 212 pp., o.p.

(BBJ:72; BL 82:810; CCBB 39:111; SLJ Nov 1985 p. 86)

2766   LAHEY, Michael. *Quest for Apollo.* **Gr. 7–12.**

Dell, an American tourist, travels into the past to ancient Rome with the poet Virgil, searching for the trapped spirit of Apollo, whose freedom can prevent the world's destruction.

DAW, 1989, pap., 255 pp., o.p.

(BBS:60; LJ Aug 19 89 p. 167; VOYA 12:371, 13:15)

2767   LAMPLUGH, Lois. *Falcon's Tor.* **Gr. 7–10. (Orig. British pub. 1984.)**

Aiden Westleigh awakens after a riding accident to find that it is 1915 and he has become Arthur Morchand, son of a wealthy British family experiencing the difficulties of wartime life.

Andre Deutsch, 1984, 121 pp., o.p.

(BL 81:130; CCBB 38:9; SLJ Dec 1984 p. 91; TLS 1984 p. 335)

LAMPMAN, Evelyn Sibley. *Captain Apple's Ghost.* See Chapter 4, Ghost Fantasy.

LANGTON, Jane (Gillson). *The Diamond in the Window.* See discussion of *The Astonishing Stereoscope* in Chapter 7, Magic Adventure Fantasy.

2768   LASKI, Marghanita. *The Victorian Chaise Longue.* **Gr. 10 up.**
✓   Twentieth-century Melanie Langdon falls asleep on her antique Victorian chaise longue and awakens in 1864, inside the body of Milly Baines, the consumptive young mother of an illegitimate child.

Houghton, 1953, 1954, o.p.; Academy Chicago, 1984, pap., 119 pp. (0-89733-097-8)

(BL 50:420; Kies:100; Kliatt 18[Fall 1984]:14; KR 22:249; TLS 1953 p. 705)

2769   LASKY (Knight), Kathryn. *Home Free.* **Gr. 7 up.**

An eagle takes fifteen-year-old Sam and his supposedly autistic friend, Lucy, into the past to the time before four Massachusetts towns were abandoned and flooded to create the huge Quabbin Reservoir, in this story about conservation of wilderness areas and endangered species.

Macmillan, 1985, 244 pp., o.p.; Dell, 1988, pap. (0-440-20038-5)

(BBJ:72; BL 82:751, 758; CCBB 39:112; KR 53:1198; SLJ Mar 1986, p. 176; VOYA 9:145)

LAWRENCE, Louise (pseud. of Elizabeth Rhoda Holden). *Sing and Scatter Daisies.* See Chapter 4, Ghost Fantasy.

2770 LAWSON, John S(hults). *The Spring Rider.* **Gr. 5–8.**

✓ Jacob and his sister, Gray, meet the ghost of a Union soldier whose bugle call brings a Civil War battle to life once more. Boston Globe Horn Book Award, 1968.

Crowell, 1968, 147 pp., o.p.; Harper, 1990, 160 pp., o.p.

(BL 65:254; HB 44:564; KR 36:699; Suth:240)

2771 LEE, Robert C. *Once upon Another Time.* **Gr. 7–9.**

After a car accident propels Bob Crawford back through time to 1942 when he was fifteen, he dates the girl he'd once been too shy to approach and draws attention from the military with his knowledge of the future.

Nelson, 1977, 160 pp., o.p.

(CCBB 31:35; KR 45:436; SLJ Mar 19 77, p. 152)

2772 LEE, Robert C. *Timequake.* **Gr. 6–8.**

Caught in a "timequake" while on a canoe trip, Randy and his cousin Morgan are thrown forward in time to the year 2027. They discover a United States run by state police, where rationed food, computer designated death, and cannibalism are all part of daily life.

Westminster, 1982, 151 pp., o.p.

(BL 79:907; CCBB 36:128; SLJ Feb 1983 p. 79; VOYA 6:148)

2773 L'ENGLE, Madeleine. *An Acceptable Time.* **Gr. 7–10.**

While visiting her grandparents, Dr. and Dr. Murry, in rural Connecticut, Polly O'Keefe suddenly finds herself in a prehistoric time where she is mistaken for a goddess by two warring tribes. This is the sequel to L'Engle's nonfantasy mystery stories *The Arm of the Starfish* (1965), *Dragons in the Waters* (1976), and *A House Like a Lotus* (1984). Polly is the daughter of Meg Murry and Calvin O'Keefe from L'Engle's science fiction books *A Wrinkle in Time* (1962), *A Wind in the Door* (1973), *A Swiftly Tilting Planet* (1978), and *Many Waters* (1986, see below).

Farrar, 1989, 342 pp. (0-374-30027-5); Dell, 1990, pap. (0-440-20814-9)

(BBJ:73; BL 86:902, 918; CCBB 43:87; HBG 1[July–Dec 1989]:84; KR 57:1672; SLJ Jan 1990 p. 120; VOYA 13:11, 38)

2774 L'ENGLE, Madeleine. *Many Waters.* **Gr. 6–10.**

Twins Sandy and Dennys Murry are stranded in Biblical times, where they become involved in a struggle surrounding Noah and his ark. This is the sequel to *A Wrinkle in Time* (1962), *A Wind in the Door* (1973), and *A Swiftly Tilting Planet* (1978), three "science fantasies" that tend more toward science fiction than fantasy. *A Wrinkle in Time* was the John Newbery Medal winner, 1962.

Farrar, 1986, 310 pp. (0-374-34796-4); Dell, 1987, pap. (0-440-95252-2)

(BL 82:1633, 1636, 84:1248; CCBB 40:54; Ch&Bks:288; JHC:380; KR 54:1374; SLJ Nov 1986 p. 104; VOYA 9:238)

2775 LEVIN, Betty (Lowenthal). *Mercy's Mill.* **Gr. 6–9.**

After her mother and stepfather move to the country to renovate an old mill, Sarah meets a boy named Jethro who was a slave before the Civil War and is searching for his friend Mercy, the daughter of a woman accused of witchcraft in the 1600s.

Greenwillow, 1992, 256 pp. (0-688-11122-X)

(BL 89:670; CCBB 46:182; HB 69:92; HBG 4[Spring 1993]:72; KR 60:1064; SLJ Dec 1992 p. 278)

2776 LEVIN, Betty (Lowenthal). *The Sword of Culann.* **Gr. 6–9.**

Claudia and Evan are transported from coastal Maine to Iron Age Ireland where they become involved in terrifying mythic battles. The sequels are *A Griffon's Nest* (1975) and *The Forespoken* (1976).

Macmillan, 1973, 288 pp., o.p.

(KR 41:1212; LJ 98:3156)

2777 LEVY, Elizabeth. *Running Out of Magic with Houdini.* **Gr. 4–6.**

Three young joggers are swept back in time by a mysterious fog to 1912, where they help save Harry Houdini's life. This is the sequel to *Running Out of Time* (1980), in which the fog takes them back to Ancient Rome.

Illus. by Blanche Sims and Jenny Rutherford, Knopf, 1981, 121 pp., o.p.

(BBC:208; BL 78:390; SLJ Dec 1981 p. 86)

2778 LEWIS, Hilda (Winifred). *The Ship That Flew.* **Gr. 5–7. (Orig. British pub. 1939.)**

A dwarf-made toy Viking ship takes four modern children to Ancient Egypt, Norman Britain, and Sherwood Forest.

Illus. by Nora Levrin, Phillips, 1958, 246 pp. (0-87599-067-3)

(BL 54:509; CCBB 11:121; HB 34:109; KR 26:77; LJ 83:1286)

2779 LINDBERGH, Anne Spencer. *The Hunky-Dory Dairy.* **Gr. 4–6.**

Zannah's old-fashioned horse and buggy dairy wagon enables her to enter a small town "removed" by witchcraft from the nineteenth to the twentieth century, where she befriends a girl named Utopia Graybeal.

Illus. by Julie Brinkloe, Harcourt, 1986, 147 pp. (0-15-237449-3); Avon, 1987, pap. (0-380-70320-3)

(BBC:208; BL 82:1143; CCBB 40:12; KR 54:865; SLJ Aug 1986 p. 95)

LINDBERGH, Anne Spencer. *The People in Pineapple Place.* See Chapter 4, Ghost Fantasy.

2780 LINDBERGH, Anne Spencer. *The Shadow on the Dial.* **Gr. 5–7.**

Marcus and Dawn find a coupon that promises to deliver their heart's desire. They use it to travel back and forth in time trying to fulfill their uncle's dream of becoming a flautist.

Harper, 1987, 160 pp., o.p.; Avon, 1988, pap. (0-380-70545-1)

(BL 83:1680; CCBB 40:191; HB 63:463; KR 55:927; SLJ June–July 1987 p. 97; VOYA 10:90)

2781 LINDBERGH, Anne Spencer. *Three Lives to Live.* **Gr. 5–8.**

✓ Resentful of her grandmother's easy acceptance of the mysterious arrival of her "twin," Daisy, Garet discovers that Daisy has actually come from the past.

Little, Brown, 1992, 183 pp. (0-316-52628-2)

(BL 88:1523; CCBB 45:269; HBG 3[Fall 1992]:266; JHC 1993 Suppl. p. 77; KR 60:672; SLJ June 1992 p. 121)

2782 LISSON, Deborah. *The Devil's Own.* **Gr. 5–9. (Orig. Australian pub. 1990.)**

Bored with cruising on her family's boat, fifteen-year-old Julie is swept back through time to the year 1629, where she becomes a shipwrecked passenger struggling to survive.

Holiday, 1991, 169 pp. (0-8234-0871-X)

(BL 87:1956; CCBB 45:15; HBG 2[Fall 1991]:278; KR 59:319; SLJ Apr 1991 p. 120)

2783 LITTLE, Jane. *The Philosopher's Stone.* **Gr. 4–6.**

When a sorcerer named Nyvrem needs a rock from Stephen's collection to convert copper into gold, he accidentally transports Stephen from Indiana to the twelfth-century Castle Mordemagne.

Illus. by Robin Hall, Atheneum, 1971, 123 pp., o.p.

(BL 68:367; KR 39:1121; LJ 96:2918)

LIVELY, Penelope (Margaret Low). *The Driftway.* See Chapter 4, Ghost Fantasy.

LIVELY, Penelope (Margaret Low). *The Ghost of Thomas Kempe.* See Chapter 4, Ghost Fantasy.

2784 **LIVELY, Penelope (Margaret Low).** *The House in Norham Gardens.* **Gr. 6–9.**
✓ **(Orig. British pub. 1974.)**

A New Guinean ceremonial shield brought home by Clare Mayfield's great-grandfather has the power to transport Clare from present-day England to the primitive jungles of New Guinea.

Dutton, 1974, 154 pp., o.p.

(BL 71:767; CCBB 28:96; HB 51:55; Kies:107; KR 42:1161; LJ 99:3273; Suth 2:289; TLS 1974 p. 717)

LIVELY, Penelope (Margaret Low). *A Stitch in Time.* See Chapter 4, Ghost Fantasy.

LIVELY, Penelope (Margaret Low). *The Whispering Knights.* See Chapter 5B, Myth Fantasy.

2785 **LORING, Selden M(elville).** *Mighty Magic: An Almost-True Story of Pirates and Indians.* **Gr. 3–5. (Orig. pub. 1937.)**

Granny Matten gives Jack Hollis a magic Indian drum.

Illus. by Brinton Turkle, Holiday, 1964, 126 pp., o.p.

(HB 13:151; KR 32:738; LJ 62:564)

Lost Worlds, Unknown Horizons. **Ed. by Robert Silverberg.** See Chapter 5C, Travel to Other Worlds.

2786 **LUNN, Janet (Louise Swoboda).** *The Root Cellar.* **Gr. 5–7. (Orig. Canadian pub.**
✓ **1981.)**

Orphaned Rose escapes from her adoptive relatives by hiding in an old root cellar. There, she travels back in time to 1860 and helps a young woman search for her missing lover, a soldier in the American Civil War. Canadian Library Association Best Book of the Year for Children, 1982.

Macmillan, 1983, 256 pp. (0-684-17855-9); Puffin, 1985, pap., 230 pp. (0-14-031835-6)

(BBC:209; BBJ:73; BL 79:1402; CC:527; HB 59:575; KR 51:661; SLJ Sept 1983 p. 124)

LUNN, Janet (Louise Swoboda). *Twin Spell.* See Chapter 4, Ghost Fantasy.

LYNCH, Patricia (Nora). *The Turf-Cutter's Donkey.* See Chapter 7, Magic Adventure Fantasy.

2787 **MacAVOY, R(oberta) A(nn).** *The Book of Kells.* **Gr. 10 up.**
✓

A professor of Irish history and an unemployed Canadian artist are pulled back through time by the spirals of a Celtic cross to tenth-century Ireland, where the survivors of a Viking raid are yearning for vengeance.

Bantam, 1985, pap., 352 pp. (0-553-25260-7)

(BL 82:195; Kies:110; LJ Aug 1985 p. 120; VOYA 8:364, 394)

2788   MacDONALD, Reby Edmond. *The Ghosts of Austwick Manor.* Gr. 5–7.

✓   Hilary and Heather MacDonald travel into the past through an exact model of their old family homestead in England and uncover a family curse that threatens their brother's life.

Atheneum, 1982, 144 pp., o.p.

(BL 78:961; HB 58:406; SLJ May 1982 p. 85; VOYA 5[Aug 1982]:34)

McGRAW, Eloise Jarvis. *A Really Weird Summer.* See Chapter 4, Ghost Fantasy.

2789   McKEAN, Thomas. *The Secret of the Seven Willows* (**Doors into Time trilogy, book 1**). **Gr. 4–6.**

A magic ring enables Martha and Tad to save their ancestral home by traveling into the past to the year 1771. The sequel is *The Haunted Circus* (1993).

Simon, 1991, 151 pp. (0-671-72997-7), 1993, pap. (0-671-86690-7)

(HBG 3[Spring 1992]:69; Kliatt Sept 1993 p. 20; SLJ Oct 1991 p. 125)

MacKELLAR, William. *Alfie and Me and the Ghost of Peter Stuyvesant.* See Chapter 4, Ghost Fantasy.

MacKELLAR, William. *The Ghost in the Castle.* See Chapter 4, Ghost Fantasy.

McKILLIP, Patricia A(nne). *The House on Parchment Street.* See Chapter 4, Ghost Fantasy.

2790   MacLEOD, Charlotte (Matilda Hughes). *The Curse of the Giant Hogweed.* Gr. 10 up.

Three Massachusetts horticultural professors suddenly find themselves in medieval Wales battling a plant that is taking over the countryside.

Doubleday, 1985, 1986, o.p.; Avon, 1986, pap., 176 pp. (0-380-70051-4)

(BBS:61; BL 81:823, 838; Kies:114; KR 52:1170)

2791   MACE, Elisabeth. *The Ghost Diviners.* Gr. 5–7. (Orig. British pub. 1977.)

Martin's sister, Jackie, travels back in time to the turn of the century, where she witnesses a murder on the future site of their house.

Nelson, 1977, 160 pp., o.p.

(BL 74:299; KR 46:3; SLJ Sept 1977 p. 132; TLS 1977 p. 864)

2792   MACE, Elisabeth. *The Rushton Inheritance.* Gr. 5–7. (Orig. British pub. 1978.)

Two generations of Rushtons search for treasure after Steve visits the nineteenth century.

Nelson, 1978, 173 pp., o.p.

(BL 75:1093; CCBB 32:179; HB 55:195; KR 42:126; SLJ Dec 1978 p. 54; TLS 1978 p. 1083)

2793   MAGUIRE, Gregory. *Lightning Time.* Gr. 6–8.

Daniel is distressed to learn of construction plans for the mountain where his grandmother lives and where magic occurs whenever lightning strikes. The sequel is *Lights on the Lake* (1981).

Farrar, 1978, 256 pp., o.p.

(BL 74:1680; HB 55:517; KR 46:750; SLJ Sept 1978 p. 143)

2794   MARZOLLO, Jean. *Halfway Down Paddy Lane.* Gr. 7–10.

Kate awakens to discover that she has gone back in time to 1850 and become Kate O'Hara, daughter of Irish immigrants who work exhausting twelve-hour days in the New England cotton mills.

Dial, 1981, 178 pp. (0-8037-3329-1); Scholastic, 1984, pap. (entitled: *Out of Time, Into Love*), o.p.

(BBS:61; BL 77:1198; Kies:118; KR 49:1165; SLJ May 1981 p. 76; VOYA 4[Dec 1981]:33)

2795   MATHESON, Richard (Burton). *Bid Time Return.* **Gr. 10 up.**

✓   Knowing that he is about to die, Richard Collier manages to pull himself back through time from 1971 to 1896 to search for a beautiful girl he once saw in an old photograph. World Fantasy Award, Best Novel, 1976.

Viking, 1975, o.p.; Ballantine, 1976, pap. (entitled: *Somewhere in Time*), o.p.; Buccaneer, 1986, 280 pp., LB(0-89966-514-4)

(BL 71:1008; Kies:120; KR 42:1320; LJ 100:410; SLJ May 1975 p. 36, Dec 1975 p. 32)

MAYNE, William (James Carter). *Earthfasts.* See Chapter 5B, Myth Fantasy.

2796   MAYNE, William (James Carter). *A Game of Dark.* **Gr. 7–10. (Orig. British**
✓   **pub. 1971.)**

Feeling increasingly helpless and guilty over his father's critical illness, Donald finds himself traveling into the past to a land menaced by a huge man-eating worm, or dragon, that only he can destroy. Phoenix Award Honor Book, 1991.

Dutton, 1971, 143 pp., o.p.

(BL 68:629; CCBB 25:61; HB 48:58; KR 39:1022; LJ 97:2490; Suth:274; TLS 1971 p. 1319)

2797   MAYNE, William (James Carter). *The Hill Road* **(British title:** *Over the Hills and Far Away,* **1968). Gr. 5–7.**

Sara, Dolly, and Andrew ride their ponies back through time to post-Roman Britain, where Sara is mistaken for an accused witch.

Dutton, 1968, 144 pp., o.p.

(CCBB 22:161; HB 45:171; KR 37:55; LJ 94:1783)

2798   MAZER, Norma Fox. *Saturday, the Twelfth of October.* **Gr. 6–9.**

✓   Furious at her family, Zan Ford wishes so intensely to be elsewhere that she crosses the "river of time" into the Stone Age and is adopted by a tribe of cave dwellers.

Delacorte, 1975, 247 pp., o.p.

(BBJ:73; BL 72:44; CCBB 29:67; KR 43:1195; SLJ Nov 1975 p. 93; Suth 2:312)

2799   MELLING, O(rla) R. *The Singing Stone.* **Gr. 6–9. (Orig. Canadian pub. 1986.)**

Eighteen-year-old Kay Warrick, abandoned at birth, visits Ireland in hopes of discovering her true identity. There, she is swept back through time to ancient Ireland where she meets an amnesiac young woman named Ahorne and learns that their destinies are intertwined.

Viking, 1987, 206 pp., o.p.

(BBJ:74; BL 84:135, 150, 576; CCBB 41:71; SLJ Sept 1987 p. 198)

2800   MILLER (Mandelkorn), Eugenia. *The Sign of the Salamander.* **Gr. 5–7. (Orig. British pub. 1982.)**

After he plunges through a French castle floor, twentieth-century Henry Carter finds himself inside the body of a sixteenth-century would-be apprentice to Leonardo Da Vinci.

Holt, 1967, 233 pp., o.p.

(HB 43:464; KR 35:600; LJ 92:2022)

2801   MOONEY, Bel. *The Stove Haunting.* **Gr. 5–8. (Orig. British pub. 1986.)**

An old stove in the house Daniel's family is renovating calls him into the past to 1835, where he becomes another Daniel, a kitchen boy during an era of conflict between rising agricultural unions and privileged English land owners.

Houghton, 1988, 125 pp., o.p.

(BBC:210; BL 83:1677; CCBB 41:185; KR 56:281; SLJ May 1988 p. 99; TLS 1986 p. 898; VOYA 11:96)

2802 **MOORE, Katherine (Davis).** *The Little Stolen Sweep.* **Gr. 4–6. (Orig. British pub. 1982.)**

Staying with relatives in his father's boyhood village, Daniel makes a series of journeys into the past. There he befriends a child chimney sweep named Jim, and offers to change places in order to help the boy escape his cruel master.

Illus. by Pat Marriott, Allison, 1982, 121 pp., o.p.

(CCBB 36:131; SLJ Mar 1983 p. 181; TLS 1982 p. 345)

2803 **MOSKIN, Marietta D(unston).** *Dream Lake.* **Gr. 5–8.**

Spending an unhappy summer with her great aunt, Hilary is drawn to a lake she has seen in nightmares, where she is transformed into Margaret Mooney, an eighteenth-century servant girl.

Atheneum, 1981, 156 pp., o.p.

(BL 77:1024, 1032, 81:1408; CCBB 35:51; KR 49:635; SLJ Mar 1981 p. 149)

MURPHY, Pat. *Points of Departure.* See Chapter 3, Fantasy Collections.

NATHAN, Robert (Gruntal). *The Elixer.* See Chapter 5B, Myth Fantasy.

2804 **NAYLOR, Phyllis Reynolds.** *Shadows on the Wall* **(The York trilogy, book 1).**
✓ **Gr. 6–10.**

Visiting England with his parents, Dan Roberts makes two disturbing discoveries: that he may have a hereditary illness, Huntington's disease, and that he can see ghostly soldiers from Roman times. In *Faces in the Water* (1981), Dan and his family have returned home to Pennsylvania, where he continues to worry about his father's illness, and is unexpectedly sent back through time to fourteenth-century Britain. In *Footprints at the Window* (1981), Dan returns to fourteenth-century Britain, where he tries to help the gypsy girl Orlenda elude the Black Death.

Atheneum, 1980, 165 pp., o.p.

(BL 77:118; CCBB 34:115; HB 56:649; KR 48:1465; SLJ Jan 1981 p. 71; VOYA 4[Apr 1981]:35)

2805 **NESBIT (Bland), E(dith).** *The House of Arden.* **Gr. 5–7. (Orig. British pub. 1908.)**

In the ruins of Arden Castle lives a magical creature called Mouldiwarp with the power to send Edred and Elfrida into the past in search of lost Arden treasure. The sequel is *Harding's Luck* (Orig. British pub. 1909; U.S. 1910, 1960).

Illus. by H. R. Millar, Coward, 1960, o.p.; illus. by Clarke Hutton, Dutton, 1968, 244 pp., o.p.; Puffin, 1986, pap. (0-14-035073-X)

(BL 57:32; HB 36:309; LJ 85:3224)

2806 **NESBIT (Bland), E(dith).** *The Story of the Amulet.* **Gr. 5–7. (Orig. British pub. 1906, U.S. 1907.)**

In this, the first time-travel fantasy written with children as protagonists, Cyril, Robert, Anthea, and Jane make journeys to ancient Egypt, Babylon, and Rome with the help of their old friend, the Sand Fairy. This is the sequel to *Five Children and It* (1902, see Chapter 7, Magic Adventure Fantasy) and *The Phoenix and the Carpet* (1904).

Illus. by J. S. Goodall, Coward, 1949, o.p.; Looking Glass Lib., 1960, o.p.; illus. by H. R. Millar, Puffin, 1965, 1986, pap., 281 pp. (0-14-035063-2)

(BL 3:206, 27:215, 46:146; CCBB 3:21)

2807 **NICHOLS, (Joanna) Ruth.** *Song of the Pearl.* **Gr. 7–10. (Orig. Canadian pub. 1976.)**

Margaret Redmond, a withdrawn and troubled young woman, dies in 1900 at the age of seventeen, only to regain consciousness and health on a silent island where she learns about her three previous lives: as the wife of an Elizabethan explorer, as an Indian slave girl, and as a young Sumerian prince.

Macmillan, 1976, 158 pp., o.p.

(CCBB 30:110; HB 53:59; KR 44:740; SLJ Oct 1976 p. 120; VOYA 2[Oct 1979]:63)

NICHOLS, (Joanna) Ruth. *A Walk out of the World.* See Chapter 5C, Travel to Other Worlds.

2808 **NORTON, André (pseud. of Alice Mary Norton).** *Dragon Magic.* **Gr. 5–7.**

Each of four boys who complete a dragon puzzle are sent into a different era of the past.

Illus. by Robin Jacques, Crowell, 1972, 213 pp., o.p.

(BL 68:1004; CCBB 25:160; HB 48:373; KR 40:485; LJ 97:2244)

2809 **NORTON, André (pseud. of Alice Mary Norton).** *Lavender Green Magic.* **Gr. 5–7.**
✓

A maze at their grandparents' home causes Holly Wade and her brother and sister to travel into the past and meet two witches, one good and one evil.

Illus. by Judith Gwyn Brown, Crowell, 1974, 241 pp., o.p.

(BBC:210; BL 71:101; Ch&Bks:290; HB 50:137; LJ 99:2275)

2810 **NORTON, André (pseud. of Alice Mary Norton).** *Octagon Magic.* **Gr. 5–7.**

Lorrie enters a doll-sized replica of Octagon House and goes back in time to the Civil War period where she takes part in the Underground Railroad rescue of escaped slaves.

Illus. by Mac Conner, World, 1967, 189 pp., o.p.

(KR 35:610; LJ 92:2656; TLS 1968 p. 584)

2811 **NORTON, André (pseud. of Alice Mary Norton).** *Red Hart Magic.* **Gr. 5–7.**

Mutual dreams of an old English inn draw Charles and Nan, step-brother and sister, together, as they travel through history and learn to deal with problems in their own lives.

Illus. by Donna Diamond, Crowell, 1976, 179 pp., o.p.

(BBC:210; BBJ:74; BL 73:610; CCBB 30:110; HB 53:160; KR 44:974; SLJ Nov 1976 p. 61)

NORTON, Mary (Pearson). *Bedknob and Broomstick.* See Chapter 7, Magic Adventure Fantasy.

2812 **ORMONDROYD, Edward.** *Time at the Top.* **Gr. 4–6.**
✓

Susan Shaw takes the elevator to the top floor of her apartment building and steps out into the world of 1881, where she helps two children search for lost treasure. The sequel, *All in Good Time* (1975), describes what happens after Susan's father follows her into the past.

Illus. by Peggie Bach, Parnassus, 1963, 176 pp., o.p.; Bantam, 1990, pap. (0-553-15420-6)

(BBC:211; BL 60:262; Ch&Bks:290; Eakin:251; HB 39:603; LJ 88:4478; TLS 1976 p. 392)

2813 **OSBORNE, Mary Pope.** *Dinosaurs Before Dark* **(Magic Tree House series, book 1). Gr. 1–3.**

The books in their magic tree house take Jack and his sister, Annie, sixty-five million years into the past for adventures in a world of dinosaurs and volcanoes. The sequels are *Knight at Dawn* (1993), and *Mummies in the Morning* (1994).

Illus. by Sal Murdocca, Random, 1992, 68 pp. (0-679-92411-6), 1992, pap. (0-679-82411-1)

(BL 89:339; HBG 4[Spring 1993]:60; KR 60:993; SLJ Sept 1992 p. 209)

2814 *The Other Side of the Clock: Stories Out of Time, Out of Place.* **Ed. by Philip Van Doren Stern. Gr. 10 up.**

Twelve stories speculating on the nature of time, whose authors include H. G. Wells and Jack Finney.

Van Nostrand Reinhold, 1969, 192 pp., o.p.

(BL 66:1139, 1157; CCBB 23:152; KR 37:1089; LJ 95:1661)

2815 **PARDOE, M(argaret Mary).** *Curtain of Mist* **(British title: *Argyle's Mist*, 1956). Gr. 6–8.**

Three twentieth-century children step through a "curtain of mist" into Celtic Britain. The British sequels are *Argyle's Causeway* and *Argyle's Oracle*.

Illus. by Leslie Atkinson, Funk, 1957, 246 pp., o.p.

BB 11:73; HB 34:38; KR 25:485; LJ 83:652)

2816 **PARK, (Rosina) Ruth (Lucia).** *Playing Beatie Bow.* **Gr. 5–8. (Orig. Australian**
✓✓ **pub. 1980.)**

Angry at her parents' upcoming remarriage and move to Norway, Abigail follows a waif-like girl named Beatie Bow one hundred years into the past. Best Australian Children's Book of the Year Award, 1981. Boston Globe Horn Book Award, 1982. Guardian Award, Runnerup, 1982.

Macmillan, 1982, 204 pp. (0-689-30889-2); Puffin, 1984, pap. (0-14-031460-1)

(BBJ:74; BL 78:1307, 1315, 79:685, 980, 86:790; CC:541; CCBB 35:156; Ch&Bks:290; HB 58:487, 59:331; JHC:398; SLJ May 1982 p. 64; Suth 3:336; TLS 1981 p. 1354; VOYA 5[Aug 1982]:35)

2817 **PARKER, Richard.** *The Old Powder Line.* **Gr. 5–8. (Orig. British pub. 1971.)**
✓ Brian Kane embarks on a dangerous journey when he boards an antiquated steam train to rescue his friend, Mr. Mincing, trapped somewhere in the past.

Nelson, 1971, 143 pp., o.p.; Peter Smith, 1989, (0-8446-6432-4)

(BL 68:676; CCBB 25:78; KR 39:677; Suth:306; TLS 1971 p. 744)

2818 **PARKER, Richard.** *A Time to Choose: A Story of Suspense.* **Gr. 6–9. (Orig.**
✓ **British pub. 1973.)**

Stephen and Mary are given the choice of staying in a peaceful, unpolluted future world or returning to their unhappy twentieth-century lives.

Harper, 1974, 151 pp., o.p.

(CCBB 27:183; HB 50:385; KR 42:309; LJ 99:1488; TLS 1973 p. 1434)

2819 **PASCAL, Francine.** *Hangin' Out with Cici.* **Gr. 7–9.**
✓ After Victoria's disruptive behavior gets her expelled from school, a bump on the head transports her to 1944 where she makes friends with a strangely familiar girl.

Viking, 1977, 152 pp., o.p.; Dell, 1986, pap. (0-440-93364-1); Puffin, 1991, pap. (0-14-034885-9)

(BBC:211; BBJ:74; BL 73:1355; CC:542; HB 53:541; JHC:398; Kies:133; KR 45:99; SLJ Sept 1977 p. 134)

2820 **PATON WALSH, Jill (Gillian Bliss).** *A Chance Child.* **Gr. 6–9. (Orig. pub. in**
✓ **England.)**

Abused by his twentieth-century mother, Creep enters an even crueler time, that of the nineteenth century before child labor laws, where he and two runaways must work to survive.

Farrar, 1978, o.p., 1990, pap. 192 pp. (0-374-41174-3); Avon, 1980, pap., 144 pp. (0-380-48561-3)

(BBJ:76; BBS:66; BL 75:1215, 1222; CCBB 32:147; HB 55:64; Kies:179; KR 46:1359; SLJ Jan 1979 p. 63)

2821 **PAYNE, Bernal C., Jr.** *It's About Time.* **Gr. 5–7.**

Chris and Gail Davenport travel back in time to the day in 1955 that their parents first met, but they soon discover their appearance has altered the past, and they must spend the day trying to ensure their own future existence.

Macmillan, 1982, 170 pp., o.p.; Pocket (entitled: *Trapped in Time*), 1984, pap., o.p.

(CCBB 37:210; Kies:134; SLJ Sept 1984 p. 121; VOYA 7:330)

2822 **PEARCE, (Ann) Philippa.** *Tom's Midnight Garden.* **Gr. 5–8. (Orig. British pub.**
✓✓ **1958; U.S. Lippincott, 1959.)**

When the grandfather clock strikes thirteen, Tom Long is able to enter an old-fashioned garden to meet Hatty, a mysterious girl who seems to have grown older each time he visits her. Carnegie Medal, 1958.

Illus. by Susan Einzig, Harper, 1984, 1992, 240 pp., LB(0-397-30477-3), pap. (0-06-440445-5)

(BBC:211; BL 56:126; CC:544; CCBB 13:18; Ch&Bks:259; Eakin:254; HB 35:478; KR 27:492; LJ 84:3930; TLS Nov 21, 1958 p. x)

2823 **PEARSON, Kit.** *A Handful of Time.* **Gr. 5–8. (Orig. Canadian pub. 1987.)**
✓ Spending a lonely summer with unfamiliar cousins while her parents get divorced, twelve-year-old Patricia finds an old pocket watch that transports her to the time her mother was twelve. Canadian Library Association Best Book of the Year for Children, 1988.

Viking, 1988, 186 pp., o.p.; Puffin, 1991, pap. (0-14-032268-X)

(BBJ:74; BL 84:576, 1677; CCBB 41:186; HB 64:391, 497; KR 56:282; SLJ May 1988 p. 100)

2824 **PEASE, (Clarence) Howard.** *The Gypsy Caravan; Being the Merry Tale of the*
Travels of Betty and Joe With the Gypsies—Their Amazing Adventures with Robin
Hood—with Richard-the-Lion-Hearted—with Roland—and Sundry Other Great
and Famous Persons. **Gr. 5–7.**

Two children join a gypsy caravan and embark on a series of adventures with heroes from their history books.

Illus. by Harrie Wood, Doubleday, 1930, 1946, 254 pp., o.p.

(HB 6:331; LJ 56:179; Mahony 3:209)

PECK, Richard. *The Ghost Belonged to Me.* See discussion of *Ghosts I Have Been*, in Chapter 4, Ghost Fantasy.

2825 **PECK, Richard.** *Voices After Midnight.* **Gr. 5–9.**
✓ After Heidi, Chad, and Luke discover they are able to enter the past in the one-hundred-

year-old house their family is renting in Manhattan, they try to change history by averting a tragedy that occurred on the night of March 12, 1888.

Delacorte, 1989, 181 pp. (0-385-29779-3); Dell, 1990, pap. (0-440-40378-2)

(BBJ:74; BL 86:274, 353; CCBB 43:41; HB 65:776; HBG 1[July–Dec 1989]:81; JHC 1991 Suppl. p. 77; KR 57:1249; SLJ Sept 1989 p. 276; VOYA 12:346)

PEYTON, K. M. *A Pattern of Roses.* See Chapter 4, Ghost Fantasy.

2826   PFEFFER, Susan Beth. *Rewind to Yesterday.* **Gr. 4–7.**

After their grandfather is shot in a robbery, twins Kelly and Scott attempt to change history using a VCR that sends them twenty-four hours back in time. The sequel is *Future Forward* (1989).

Illus. by Andrew Glass, Delacorte, 1988, 137 pp., o.p.; Dell, pap. (0-440-40474-6)

(BBJ:74; CCBB 42:49; KR 56:1154; SLJ Oct 1988 p. 147; VOYA 11:247)

2827   PHIPSON, Joan (pseud. of Margaret Fitzhardinge). *The Way Home.* **Gr. 5–7.**

Prue, Peter, and Richard are thrown over a cliff during a car accident and swept downstream into a world of enormous monsters and volcanic eruptions.

Atheneum, 1973, 184 pp., o.p.

(HB 50:52; KR 41:760; LJ 98:2656; TLS 1973 p. 1114)

2828   PINKWATER, D(aniel) Manus. *Wingman.* **Gr. 4–6.**

Wingman flies truant Daniel Chen off of the George Washington Bridge and into ancient China.

Illus. by the author, Dodd, 1975, 63 pp., o.p.

(KR 43:375; SLJ Sept 1975 p. 109)

2829   POPE, Elizabeth Marie. *The Sherwood Ring.* **Gr. 6 up.**

✓   The American Revolutionary period comes alive for Peggy when she meets the ghost of her ancestor, Barbara Grahame, and sympathizes with Barbara's forbidden love affair with a British soldier.

Illus. by Evaline Ness, Houghton, 1958, 266 pp., o.p.; Peter Smith, 1989 (0-8446-6416-2); Puffin, 1992, pap. (0-14-034911-1)

(BL 54:567; CCBB 11:22; Eakin:265; HB 34:112, 613, 35:399; Kies:137; KR 26:38; LJ 83:2073)

PURTILL, Richard. *Enchantment at Delphi.* See Chapter 5B, Myth Fantasy.

RABINOWITZ, Ann. *Knight on Horseback.* See Chapter 4, Ghost Fantasy.

2830   RADFORD, Ken. *The Cellar.* **Gr. 5–8.**

While working at an isolated house in northern Wales, orphaned Sian finds the diary of a girl who was cruelly mistreated by her guardian after the death of her mother, and Sian travels into the past to find out what happened to Sarah Jane.

Holiday, 1989, 171 pp. (0-8234-0744-6)

(BBC:212; BL 85:1654; CCBB 42:282; SLJ Mar 1989 p. 200; VOYA 12:216)

RADFORD, Ken. *Haunting at Mill Lane.* See Chapter 4, Ghost Fantasy.

REID BANKS, Lynne. *The Indian in the Cupboard.* See Chapter 7, Magic Adventure Fantasy.

2831   REISS, Kathryn. *Dreadful Sorry.* **Gr. 7–12.**

✓   Haunted by nightmares in which she becomes a girl named Clementine who died in

1912, sixteen-year-old Molly fears that she and her new friend, Jared, are re-living a tragic love story.

Harcourt, 1993, 272 pp. (0-15-224213-9)

(BL 89:1959; CCBB 46:293; HBG 4[Fall 1993]:312; KR 61:603; SLJ June 1993 p. 132; VOYA 16: 157)

2832 REISS, Kathryn. *Time Windows.* **Gr. 5–9.**

✓ When Miranda looks out through the windows of a dollhouse in her attic, she can watch scenes from the lives of three past inhabitants of her house: eight-year-old Dorothy in 1904 and two brothers in the 1940s, all of whom have abusive mothers. The sequel is *Pale Phoenix* (1994).

Harcourt, 1991, 192 pp. (0-15-288205-7)

(BL 88:507; CCBB 45:47; HBG 3[July–Dec 1991]:72; KR 59:1407; SLJ Oct 1991 p. 126; VOYA 14:325, 15:11)

2833 REYNOLDS, Mack, and ING, Dean. *The Other Time.* **Gr. 10 up.**

Don Fielding, an archeologist who finds himself in sixteenth-century Mexico just before the landing of Hernando Cortez, tries to organize the Aztecs to fight against the Spanish.

Baen, 1984, pap., 308 pp., o.p.

(BBS:63; VOYA 8:140)

2834 RICHEMONT, Enid. *The Time Tree.* **Gr. 4–7. (Orig. British pub. 1989.)**

✓ After Anne, a deaf girl from the sixteenth century, appears in their secret hideaway in a tall tree, Rachel and Joanna teach her to read and write, thus improving her previously unhappy life when she returns to Elizabethan England.

Little, Brown, 1990, 96 pp., o.p.

(BL 86:2179; CCBB 43:224; HBG 1[Jan–June 1990]:255; KR 58:654; SLJ June 1990 p. 125; VOYA 13:119)

ROBINSON, Joan (Mary) G(ale Thomas). *When Marnie Was There.* See Chapter 4, Ghost Fantasy.

2835 RODDA, Emily. *The Best-Kept Secret.* **Gr. 3–6. (Orig. Australian pub. 1988.)**

✓ A mysterious carousel takes Jo and some neighbors seven years into the future, and what they see during their one-hour visit affects the choices they make for the rest of their lives.

Illus. by Noela Young, Henry Holt, 1990, 119 pp. (0-8050-0936-1)

(BL 87:52; CC:550; HBG 1[Jan–June 1990]:255; KR 58:802; SLJ Jan 1991 p. 79)

2836 RODOWSKY, Colby F. *Keeping Time.* **Gr. 6–9.**

Drew Wakeman is drawn back into the past to Elizabethan London, where he is befriended by an apprentice minstrel, Symon Ives, who helps the youth learn to communicate with his taciturn father.

Farrar, 1983, 137 pp. (0-374-34061-7)

(BBJ:75; BL 80:419; CCBB 37:116; HB 60:203; SLJ Jan 1984 p. 85)

SABERHAGEN, Fred. *Pyramids.* See Chapter 5C, Travel to Other Worlds.

2837 SAUER, Julia L(ina). *Fog Magic.* **Gr. 4–6.**

✓ While searching for a friend her own age, Greta Addington wanders through the Nova Scotia fog and enters Blue Cove, a village from one hundred years in the past. John Newbery Medal Honor Book, 1944.

Viking, 1943, o.p.; Puffin, 1986, pap., 128 pp. (0-14-032163-2); Peter Smith, 1988 (0-8446-6344-1)

(BL 40:83; HB 19:405, 422, 56:548–551; Kies:149; LJ 68:822, 963; TLS 1977 p. 1409)

2838 SCIESZKA, Jon. *Knights of the Kitchen Table* (Time Warp Trio series, book 1).
✓ Gr. 3–5.

The Time Warp Trio—Joe, Fred, and Sam—travel through time using a magical book given to Joe by his magician uncle and save Camelot from a smelly giant. In *The Not-So-Jolly Roger* (1991), the Trio tangles with bloodthirsty Bluebeard the pirate. The third book in this wacky series is *The Good, the Bad and the Goofy* (1992). *Your Mother Was a Neanderthal* (1993) continues the series.

Illus. by Lane Smith. Viking, 1991, 64 pp. (0-670-83622-2)

(BL 87:1716; CC 1992 Suppl. p. 62; CCBB 44:274; HBG 2[Fall 1991]:259; KR 59:609; SLJ Aug 1991 p. 168)

SELDEN (Thompson), George. *The Genie of Sutton Place.* See Chapter 7, Magic Adventure Fantasy.

2839 SERVICE, Pamela F. *The Reluctant God.* Gr. 6–9.

After Ameni, a young ancient Egyptian king, comes back to life in the twentieth century when his body is discovered by apprentice achaeologist Lorna, they undertake a dangerous journey to England to recover two sacred urns. Golden Kite Award Honor Book, 1988.

Macmillan, 1988, 206 pp. (0-689-31404-3); Fawcett, 1989, pap. (0-44970-339-8)

(BBJ:75; BL 84:1186; CCBB 41:167; SLJ June 1988 p. 106; VOYA 11:97, 12:15)

2840 SERVICE, Pamela F. *Vision Quest.* Gr. 5–8.
✓ Two time periods overlap in this story set in Nevada about Kate, whose ancient Indian charm stone brings her visions of Wadat, a Native American shaman from long ago whose sacred relic has disappeared.

Macmillan, 1989, 160 pp. (0-689-31498-1); Fawcett, 1990, pap. (0-44970-372-X)

(BBC:213; BL 85:1471; CCBB 42:236; HB 56:506; Kliatt Sept 1990 p. 24; KR 57:383; SLJ Mar 1989 p. 202)

2841 SEVERN, David (pseud. of David Unwin). *Dream Gold.* Gr. 6–8. (Orig. British pub. 1949.)

Peter and Guy have frightening experiences involving pirates and their "dream gold," while vacationing in Cornwall.

Illus. by Isami Kashiwagi, Viking, 1952, 192 pp., o.p.

(HB 29:53; KR 20:412; LJ 77:2079)

SEVERN, David (pseud. of David Unwin). *The Girl in the Grove.* See Chapter 4, Ghost Fantasy.

SHECTER, Ben. *The Whistling Whirligig.* See Chapter 4, Ghost Fantasy.

2842 SHERBURNE, Zoa (Morin). *Why Have the Birds Stopped Singing?* Gr. 5–7.

An epileptic seizure at an ancestor's birthplace sends Katie into the nineteenth century where she becomes Kathryn, a girl imprisoned by her uncle.

Morrow, 1974, 189 pp., o.p.

(BL 70:1202; LJ 99:1488)

2843 SIEGEL, Robert (Harold). *Alpha Centauri.* Gr. 7–9.

Rebecca finds herself in pre-Druid Britain, where she must complete a dangerous quest to save the half-horse, half-human centaurs who have befriended her.

Illus. by Kurt Mitchell, Good News, 1980, 256 pp., o.p.

(BL 77:40, 48; LJ 105:1665)

2844 SILVERBERG, Robert. *Letters from Atlantis.* **Gr. 6–12.**

✓ Roy, a twenty-first-century time-traveler, takes over the mind of Crown Prince Ram on the legendary continent of Atlantis in an attempt to learn its secret history.

Illus. by Robert Gould, Macmillan, 1990, 136 pp. (0-689-31570-8); Warner, 1992, pap. (0-446-36286-7)

(BL 87:660, 1123; HBG 2[July–Dec 1990]:88; JHC 1991 Suppl. p 79; KR 58:1460; SLJ Mar 1991 p. 218; VOYA 13:367, 14:11)

2845 SIMAK, Clifford D(onald). *The Goblin Reservation.* **Gr. 10 up.**

Time travel permits goblins, trolls, Shakespeare, a Neanderthal man, and a ghost to live together on The Reservation.

Putnam, 1968, 192 pp., o.p.

(BL 65:484, 492; KR 36:722; LJ 94:1164, 2074; SLJ Dec 15, 1968 p. 4740)

2846 SLEATOR, William. *The Green Futures of Tycho.* **Gr. 5–8.**

✓ Tycho's visits to his past and future lives, using an egg-shaped metal object, become frightening as he begins to realize what kind of person his older self has become.

Dutton, 1981, 133 pp., o.p.; Puffin, 1991, pap. (0-14-034581-7)

(BBC:213; BL 77:1108; CC:556; CCBB 35:58; HB 57:426; KR 49:440; SLJ Apr 1981 p. 133, May 1981 p. 24)

2847 SLEIGH, Barbara (de Riemer). *Jessamy.* **Gr. 5–7. (Orig. British pub. 1967.)**

✓ Jessamy travels to the period of World War I to solve a mystery surrounding a rare, missing book.

Bobbs-Merrill, 1967, 246 pp., o.p.

(BL 63:1195; CCBB 21:33; HB 43:343; KR 35:416; LJ 92:2024; TLS 1967 p. 451)

2848 SLEPIAN, Jan. *Back to Before.* **Gr. 5–7.**

Two cousins get their wish to travel one year back through time to the period before Linny's mother's death and Hilary's father leaves his family, in hopes of making things turn out differently.

Putnam, 1993, 170 pp. (0-399-22011-9)

(BL 90:58; CCBB 47:24; HBG 5:82; KR 61:728; SLJ Oct 1993 p. 130)

SNYDER, Zilpha Keatley. *The Truth about Stone Hollow.* See Chapter 4, Ghost Fantasy.

2849 ST. GEORGE, Judith. *The Mysterious Girl in the Garden.* **Gr. 3–5.**

Led back through time into 1805 by a small white dog, Terrie meets Princess Charlotte Augusta. Both girls miss their mothers' companionship and a friendship develops, culminating in a plan to exchange places in time.

Illus. by Margot Tomes, Putnam, 1981, 64 pp., o.p.

(BL 78:599; 81:1408; KR 50:7; SLJ Dec 1981 p. 68)

2850 ST. GEORGE, Judith. *Who's Scared? Not Me!* **Gr. 7–10.**

Since the old house Micki finds in New York's Central Park was torn down years ago, she knows she must have gone into the past to visit naturalist John James Audubon at home.

Putnam, 1987, 174 pp., o.p.

(BBJ:75; BL 84:555, 572; KR 55:1397; SLJ Dec 1987 p. 105; VOYA 10:283)

2851 **STEWART, Mary (Florence Elinor).** *A Walk in Wolf Wood.* **Gr. 5–8. (Orig.**
✓ **British pub. 1980.)**

John and Margaret help Mardian, a man forced to become a ferocious wolf each night, to
defeat the enchanter who has taken Mardian's place as the king's adviser.

Illus. by Emanuel Schoengut, Morrow, 1980, 1984, 160 pp., o.p.

(BL 77:40, 49; CCBB 34:42; Ch&Bks:291; Kies:166; KR 48:1300; SLJ Sept 1980 p. 78; TLS 1980 p.
806)

2852 **STOLZ, Mary (Slattery).** *Cat in the Mirror.* **Gr. 5–7.**

✓ Difficulties in coping with a disinterested mother and unfriendly classmates lead to two
lives for Erin Gandy, one in the twentieth century and the other in ancient Egypt.

Harper, 1975, 199 pp., o.p.

(BBC:214; BBJ:76; BL 72:628; CCBB 29:70; HB 51:597; KR 45:999; SLJ Oct 1975 p. 103; Suth 2:434)

2853 **SYKES, Pamela.** *Mirror of Danger* **(British title:** *Come Back, Lucy,* **1973). Gr.**
✓ **5–7.**

Orphaned Lucy comes to live with distant cousins and is befriended by Alice, the ghost of
a Victorian girl, who tries to trap Lucy permanently in the past. The sequel is *Lucy
Beware!* (1984).

Nelson, 1974, 175 pp., o.p.

(BBJ:76; BL 70:1007; Kies:170; LJ 99:2742; TLS 1973 p. 1117)

2854 **SYMONS, (Dorothy) Geraldine.** *Crocuses Were Over, Hitler Was Dead* **(British
title:** *Now and Then,* **1977). Gr. 5–7.**

Jassy travels back in time to the period of World War II, where she helps a British solider
accomplish a secret mission behind German lines.

Harper, 1978, 158 pp., o.p.

(BL 75:550; CCBB 32:145; KR 46:1308; SLJ Oct 1978 p. 151; TLS 1977 p. 864)

2855 *Tales out of Time.* **Ed. by Barbara Ireson. Gr. 7 up.**

Fourteen fantasy and science-fiction time-travel tales written by John Rowe Townsend,
Ray Bradbury, H. G. Wells, and others.

Putnam, 1981, 247 pp., o.p.

(BL 77:1342; CCBB 35:11; SLJ Sept 1981 p. 136)

2856 **TANNEN, Mary.** *The Wizard Children of Finn.* **Gr. 5–7.**

Magic brings Fiona and Bran into ancient Ireland where they help Finn McCool claim his
kingdom. The sequel is *The Lost Legend of Finn* (1982).

Illus. by John Burgoyne, Knopf, 1981, 214 pp., o.p.

(BBC:214; BBJ:76; BL 77:1157; Kies:171; KR 49:505; SLJ Sept 1981 p. 131)

TAPP, Kathy Kennedy. *The Scorpio Ghosts and the Black Hole Gang.* See Chapter 4, Ghost Fantasy.

2857 **THOMAS, Jane Resh.** *The Princess in the Pigpen.* **Gr. 4–6.**

Ill with a fever, Elizabeth, daughter of the Duke of Umberland, is transported from England in 1591 to a twentieth-century Iowa farm where the McCormick family take her in,
but don't believe her time-travel story.

Houghton, 1989, 128 pp. (0-395-51587-4); Avon, 1993, pap. (0-380-71194-X)

(BL 86:190; CCBB 43:46; HBG 1[July–Dec 1989]:83; KR 57:1537; SLJ Nov 1989 p. 115)

2858 TOWNSEND, John Rowe. *The Visitors* **(British title:** *The Xanadu Manuscript,*
✓ **1977). Gr. 6–10.**

Katherine Wyatt and her parents are sent from the world of 2149 A.D. back into the twentieth century, but they need John Dunham's help to survive and stay out of trouble.

Lippincott, 1977, 221 pp. (0-397-31752-2)

(BL 74:34, 45; CCBB 31:87; HB 53:671; JHC:418; KR 45:856; SLJ Nov 1977 p. 75; Suth 2:454)

2859 *Trips in Time: Nine Stories of Science Fiction.* **Ed. by Robert Silverberg. Gr. 9 up.**

Nine time-travel tales by Poul Anderson, Roger Zelazny, Robert Silverberg, and others.

Nelson, 1977, 192 pp., o.p.

(BL 74:369; KR 45:884, 941)

2860 TWAIN, Mark (pseud. of Samuel Clemens). *A Connecticut Yankee in King*
✓ *Arthur's Court* **(British title:** *A Connecticut Yankee at the Court of King Arthur***).
Gr. 8 up. (Orig. pub. Harper, 1889.)**

An accidental blow on the head sends Hank Morgan 1,300 years back through time to King Arthur's court, where he uses his knowledge of history and modern technology to replace Merlin as Court Magician.

Harper, 1925, 450 pp., o.p.; Puffin, 1972, pap. (0-14-043064-4); Buccaneer, 1982 (repr.) (0-89966-381-8); illus. by Daniel C. Beard, University of California Press, 1983, 482 pp. (0-520-05089-4); Bantam, 1983, pap. (0-553-21143-9); illus. by Trina Schart Hyman, Morrow, 1988, 384 pp. (0-688-06346-2)

(BBC:215; BL 22:170, 85:1005; HB 2[Nov 1925]:30, 60:359; JHC:419; Kies:175; SHC:724)

2861 UTTLEY, Alison (pseud. of Alice Jane [Taylor] Uttley). *A Traveler in Time.* **Gr.**
✓ **6–8. (Orig. British pub. 1939, entitled:** *A Traveller in Time.***)**

While visiting her family's ancient country home, Penelope Cameron is drawn back through time to Elizabethan England, where she becomes involved in an ill-fated plot to save Mary, Queen of Scots.

Illus. by Phyllis Bray, Putnam, 1940, 306 pp., o.p.; illus. by Christine Price, Viking, 1964, 287 pp., o.p.; Faber, 1981, 331 pp., o.p.

(BL 61:581; HB 40:612, 58:721; Kies:176; LJ 65:923, 89:4653; SLJ Oct 1981 p. 154; TLS 1939 p. 667)

2862 VICK, Helen Hughes. *Walker of Time.* **Gr. 6–10.**

A flash of lightning throws Walker, a fifteen-year-old Hopi, and Tag, the twelve-year-old son of an archeologist, seven-hundred-fifty years into the past to save an endangered Sinagua Indian settlement.

Harbinger, 1993, 192 pp. (0-943173-84-1), pap. (0-943173-80-9)

(BL 90:52; Kliatt Sept 1993 p. 24)

2863 VOIGT, Cynthia. *Building Blocks.* **Gr. 4–7.**

✓ A fortress made of children's blocks takes Brann Connell back into the time of his father's boyhood, where he comes to better understand the man he had thought of as a loser.

Macmillan, 1984, 132 pp. (0-689-31035-8); Fawcett, 1985, pap., 128 pp. (0-449-70130-1); Scholastic, pap., 1994 (0-590-47732-3)

(BBC:215; BBJ:76; BL 80:1350; CCBB 37:157; Ch&Bks:292; HB 60:470; JHC:421; Kies:177; KR 52:24; SLJ May 1984 p. 85; Suth 3:435)

WALKER, Mary Alexander. *The Scathach and Maeve's Daughters.* See Chapter 5B, Myth Fantasy.

WALLIN, Luke. *The Slavery Ghosts.* See Chapter 4, Ghost Fantasy.

2864   **WELCH, Ronald (pseud. of Ronald Oliver Felton).** *The Gauntlet.* **Gr. 7–9. (Orig. British pub. 1951.)**

A medieval gauntlet sends Peter Staunton into the fourteenth century where he lives in his ancestors' castle and takes part in their battles.

Illus. by T. R. Freeman, Oxford, 1952, 248 pp., o.p.

(BL 49:53; HB 29:53; KR 20:456; LJ 77:1522)

2865   **WELDRICK, Valerie.** *Time Sweep.* **Gr. 5–7. (Orig. Australian pub. 1976.)**

Laurie's bed is the means by which he travels from twentieth-century Sydney, Australia, to 1862 London, where he and his new friend, Frank, avert a robbery.

Illus. by Ron Brooks, Lothrop, 1978, 157 pp., o.p.

(CCBB 32:127; HB 55:196; KR 47:7; SLJ Jan 1978 p. 58; Suth 2:474)

2866   **WESLEY, Mary.** *Haphazard House.* **Gr. 6–9. (Orig. British pub. 1983.)**

A Panama hat causes the eccentric Fuller family to move from London to an old country house in a village that seems to be outside of time.

Overlook, 1993, 144 pp. (0-87951-470-1)

(BL 90:828; CCBB 47:61; HBG 5:92; KR 61:793; SLJ Aug 1993 p. 190)

2867   **WESTALL, Robert (Atkinson).** *The Devil on the Road.* **Gr. 8 up. (Orig. British**
✓   **pub. 1978.)**

John Webster becomes convinced of the innocence of Johanna, a seventeenth-century girl accused of witchcraft, and makes the mistake of bringing her into the twentieth century. Carnegie Medal Commended Book, 1978.

Greenwillow, 1979, 256 pp., o.p.

(BBJ:76; BL 75:1532, 76:1199; CCBB 32:204; Ch&Bks:292; HB 55:541; KR 47:860; Kies:183; SLJ May 1979 pp. 36, 76)

WESTALL, Robert (Atkinson). *The Haunting of Chas McGill and Other Stories.* See Chapter 4, Ghost Fantasy.

WESTALL, Robert (Atkinson). *The Watch House.* See Chapter 4, Ghost Fantasy.

2868   **WESTALL, Robert (Atkinson).** *The Wind Eye.* **Gr. 6–9. (Orig. British pub.**
✓✓   **1976.)**

A boat that once belonged to a medieval monk carries Mike, Beth, and Sally across time into the seventh century, where St. Cuthbert changes both their lives and those of their parents.

Greenwillow, 1977, 213 pp., o.p.

(BL 74:370, 381; CCBB 31:103; HB 54:56; Kies:184; KR 45:1104; SLJ Nov 1977 p. 77; Suth 2:248; TLS 1976 p. 1547)

2869   **WIBBERLEY, Leonard (Patrick O'Connor).** *The Crime of Martin Coverly.* **Gr.**
✓   **6–8.**

Nick Ormsby is drawn into the eighteenth century for shipboard adventures with his ancestor, pirate Martin Coverly.

Farrar, 1980, 167 pp., o.p.

(BBJ:76; BL 76:1538; HB 56:418; KR 48:986; SLJ May 1980 p. 80; VOYA 3[June 1981]:34)

2870 WILDE, Nicholas. *Down Came a Blackbird.* **Gr. 6–9. (Orig. British pub. 1991.)**

Angry at his alcoholic mother and his probation officer for sending him to live with his great-uncle, thirteen-year-old James has vivid dreams about the uncle's tragic childhood.

Henry Holt, 1992, 182 pp. (0-8050-2001-2)

(BL 89:662; CCBB 46:197; KR 60:1450; SLJ Feb 1993 p. 109; VOYA 16:96)

2871 WILLIAMS, Ruth L. *The Silver Tree.* **Gr. 5–8.**

A beautiful dollhouse in an old toy museum transports Micki Silver one-hundred years into the past to become her cousin, Michelle DeSilver.

Harper, 1992, 243 pp. (0-06-020296-3)

(BL 89:62; HBG 3[Fall 1992]:272; KR 60:786; SLJ June 1992 p. 126; VOYA 15:116)

WILLIAMS (John), Ursula Moray. *Castle Merlin.* See Chapter 4, Ghost Fantasy.

2872 WILLIS, Connie. *Doomsday Book.* **Gr. 10 up.**

After Kivrin Engles, a twenty-first century Oxford University history student, is accidentally sent back through time to medieval England during the time of the Black Death, she becomes stranded in the past.

Bantam, 1992, 448 pp. (0-553-08131-4)

(BL 88:1811, 1817, 89:842; KR 60:434; LJ May 15, 1992 p. 123)

2873 WILLIS, Connie. *Lincoln's Dreams.* **Gr. 10 up.**

Historical researcher Jeff Johnston attempts to help a young woman named Annie who is haunted by the Civil War—ravaged dreams of Robert E. Lee.

Bantam, 1987 (0-553-05197-0), pap., 1992, 224 pp. (0-553-27025-7)

(BBS:67; BL 83:1098, 1117; KR 55:519; LJ Apr 15, 1987 p. 102; VOYA 10:182)

2874 WILSON, Robert Charles. *A Bridge of Years.* **Gr. 10 up.**

✓ The tunnel beneath the abandoned cottage Tom Winter buys after his divorce leads back in time to Manhattan in 1962, but he must take care to avoid the murderous twenty-first-century soldier who patrols the tunnel.

Doubleday, 1991, 348 pp. (0-385-41936-8); Bantam, 1992, pap. (0-553-29892-5)

(BL 87:2108, 2112; KR 59:829; LJ Aug 1991 p. 150; VOYA 14:388)

2875 WISEMAN, David. *Adam's Common.* **Gr. 5–7. (Orig. pub. in England.)**

Peggy uses her ability to glimpse townspeople from the past to solve a mystery and protect the town common from a proposed transformation into a shopping mall.

Houghton, 1984, 175 pp., o.p.

(BBJ:76; BL 81:592; CCBB 38:97; KR 52:98; SLJ Nov 1984 p. 129)

2876 WISEMAN, David. *Jeremy Visick* **(British title:** *The Fate of Jeremy Visick,* **1981).**
✓✓ **Gr. 5–8.**

Having learned about a twelve-year-old boy named Jeremy who died in the Cornish mines in 1852, Matthew begins visiting Jeremy's time in an attempt to save his life.

Houghton, 1981, 170 pp. (0-395-30449-0), pap., 1990 (0-395-56153-1)

(BBC:216; BL 77:1397, 80:96; CC:574; CCBB 35:20; HB 57:193; KR 49:741; SLJ Apr 1981 p. 134, May 1981 p. 25; Suth 3:456)

2877 WISEMAN, David. *Thimbles.* **Gr. 5–7. (Orig. pub. in England.)**

Two old thimbles propel Cathy into Manchester, England, in the year 1819, where she becomes, alternately, two girls involved in a dangerous demonstration by thousands of workers pleading for the right to vote.

Houghton, 1982, 134 pp., o.p.

(BBC:216; BL 78:965, 980; CCBB 35:219; KR 50:556; SLJ Mar 1982 p. 153; TLS 1983 p. 1318)

2878 **WISEMAN, David.** *A Tie to the Past.* **Gr. 5–9. (Orig. British pub. 1989.)**

Plagued by guilt at having stolen a box of mementos from an elderly friend, Mary has frightening dreams in which she becomes Gladys Mayhew, a militant suffragette in 1909 London.

Houghton, 1989, 160 pp., o.p.

(BL 86:191; CCBB 43:23; HBG 1[July 1989]:74; KR 57:1482; SLJ Sept 1989 p. 258; VOYA 12:285)

2879 **WOODRUFF, Elvira.** *The Disappearing Bike Shop.* **Gr. 3–6.**

Tyler and Freckles suspect that Quentin Quigley, a mysterious bike-shop owner, may actually be the Renaissance genius Leonardo da Vinci, especially after one of his inventions sends them into the past.

Holiday, 1992, 103 pp. (0-8234-0933-3)

(BL 88:1380; HBG 3[Fall 1992]:272; SLJ May 1992 p. 117)

2880 **YOLEN (Stemple), Jane H(yatt).** *The Devil's Arithmetic.* **Gr. 5–9.**

✓ Twelve-year-old Hannah, bored by the stories of her Holocaust-survior relatives, suddenly finds herself in Poland during World War II, within the body of Chaya, a Jewish girl on her way to a death camp.

Viking, 1988, 160 pp. (0-670-81027-4); Puffin, 1990, pap. (0-14-034535-3)

(BBJ:76; BL 85:69, 86; CC:576; CCBB 42:23, 59; JHC:427; KR 56:1248; SLJ Nov 1988 p. 114)

2881 **ZELAZNY, Roger, and SHECKLEY, Robert.** *If at Faust You Don't Succeed.* **Gr.**
✓ **10 up.**

A burgler-monk mistaken for Johann Faust is sent back and forth through history to compete in a contest between Light and Dark to determine whether humanity's fortunes will be shaped by Good or by Evil. This is the sequel to *Bring Me the Head of Prince Charming* (1991).

Bantam, 1993, pap., 336 pp. (0-553-37141-X)

(BL 89:972, 975; KR 60:1542; LJ Feb 15, 1993 p. 196; VOYA 16:172)

9

Toy Fantasy

Tales of toys that talk or exhibit other magical abilities are listed in this chapter. Most of the main characters are dolls, but there are a few stories about carousel horses, stuffed animals, toy soldiers, and windup toys.

2882 AHLBERG, Janet, and AHLBERG, Allan. *The Bear Nobody Wanted.* **Gr. 2–6. (Orig. British pub. 1992.)**

A snobbish teddy bear's adventures teach him to be more tolerant and compassionate.

Illus. by Janet Ahlberg, Viking, 1993, 143 pp. (0-670-83982-5)

(CCBB 46:307; HB 69:456; HBG 4[Fall 1993]:293; KR 61:141; SLJ Sept 1993 p. 248)

2883 ALBRECHT, Lillie Vanderveer. *Deborah Remembers.* **Gr. 4–6.**

Deborah describes to the other museum dolls the events she witnessed during the American Revolution.

Illus. by Rita Newton, Hastings, 1959, 111 pp., o.p.

(BL 56:246; HB 38:381; KR 27:548)

ANASTASIO, Dina. *A Question of Time.* See Chapter 4, Ghost Fantasy.

ANDERSEN, Hans Christian. *The Steadfast Tin Soldier.* See Chapter 1, Allegorical Fantasy and Literary Fairy Tales.

2884 AVERILL, Esther (Holden). *The Adventures of Jack Ninepins.* **Gr. 3–4.**

Jack Ninepins, Charlotte's favorite toy, is determined to follow her across the ocean to France.

Harper, 1944, 63 pp., o.p.

(HB 20:471, 480; KR 12:399; LJ 69:863, 1104)

2885 BACON, Martha (Sherman). *Moth Manor: A Gothic Tale.* **Gr. 5–7.**

A ghostly moth sparks Monica's interest in the mystery surrounding her great-aunt's doll-house.

Illus. by Gail Burroughs, Little, 1978, 160 pp., o.p.

(BL 75:42; CCBB 32:93; KR 46:1188; SLJ Sept 1978 p. 130)

2886   BAILEY, Carolyn Sherwin. *Miss Hickory.* **Gr. 3–5.**

✓   Miss Hickory, a doll with a hickory-nut head, is forgotten by her family and has a winter full of adventure. John Newbery Medal, 1947.

Illus. by Ruth Chrisman Gannett, Viking, 1946, 123 pp. (0-670-47940-3); Puffin, 1977, pap. (0-14-030956-X)

(BBC:197; BL 43:74; CC:446; Ch&Bks:271; HB 22:465; KR 14:387; LJ 71:1412, 1544)

2887   BAKER, Margaret. *Victoria Josephine* **(British title:** *The Roaming Doll,* **1936). Gr. 2–4.**

Freed after seventy years in a box, Victoria Josephine is determined to travel.

Illus. by Mary Baker, Dodd, 1936, 95 pp., o.p.

(HB 12:350; LJ 62:217)

2888   BAKER, Margaret Joyce. *The Shoe Shop Bears.* **Gr. 3–5. (Orig. British pub. 1963.)**

Three Teddy bears leave the shoe shop in search of a truly loving home. The sequels are *Hannibal and the Bears* (1966), *Bears Back in Business* (1967), and *Hi Jinks Joins the Bears* (1969).

Illus. by C. Walter Hodges, Ariel, 1965, 96 pp., o.p.

(CCBB 19:41; LJ 90:3785; TLS 1964 p. 605)

2889   BARRINGER, Marie. *Martin the Goose Boy.* **Gr. 3–5.**

Only Gustel knew that his wooden goose-boy doll, Martin, could talk.

Illus. by Maud Petersham and Miska Petersham, Doubleday, 1932, 1936, 188 pp., o.p.

(BL 29:77; Bookshelf 1932 p. 6; LJ 58:711; Mahony 3:53)

BEAUMONT, Cyril W(illiam). *The Mysterious Toyshop: A Fairy Tale.* See Chapter 7, Magic Adventure Fantasy.

2890   BEMELMANS, Ludwig. *The Happy Place.* **Gr. 2–4.**

Unsold by Easter, Winthrop the toy rabbit is turned loose in Central Park, where the zoo animals befriend him.

Illus. by the author, Little, 1952 (c. 1951), 58 pp., o.p.

(KR 20:499; LJ 77:1661)

2891   BIANCO, Margery (Winifred) Williams. *The Little Wooden Doll.* **Gr. 2–4.**

A lonely doll found in the attic is transformed into a princess doll.

Illus. by Pamela Bianco, Macmillan, 1925, 65 pp., o.p.

(BL 22:121; Bookshelf 1928 p. 9; HB 2[Nov 1925]:18; LJ 51:836; Moore:426)

2892   BIANCO, Margery (Winifred) Williams. *Poor Cecco: The Wonderful Story of a*
✓   *Wonderful Wooden Dog Who Was the Jolliest Toy in the House Until He Went Out to Explore the World.* **Gr. 3–5. (Orig. U.S. and British pubs. 1925.)**

Cecco the wooden dog and his friends, Jensina the doll and Bulka the toy rabbit, leave their home in the toy cupboard to search for adventure.

Illus. by Arthur Rackham, Doubleday, 1945, 175 pp., o.p.

(BL 22:121; Bookshelf 1926–1927 p. 5; HB 2[Nov 1925]:13, 19, 20; Mahony 2:122; Moore:426; TLS 1925 p. 809)

2893 **BIANCO, Margery (Winifred) Williams.** *The Velveteen Rabbit; or, How Toys*
✓✓ *Became Real.* **Gr. K–4. (Orig. British and U.S. pub. 1922.)**

A well-loved toy is transformed into a real rabbit after it is worn out and discarded. This story is considered to be the first toy animal fantasy novel. The sequel is *The Skin Horse* (orig. British pub. 1927, 1978).

Illus. by William Nicholson, Doubleday, 1958, 1991, 44 pp. (0-385-00913-5); Dell, 1992, pap. (0-440-40722-2); illus. by Michael Hague, Holt, 1983, 33 pp., (0-8050-0209-X); illus. by Allen Atkinson, Knopf, 1983, 40 pp. (0-394-53221-X); Avon, 1982, pap. (0-380-58156-6); illus. by Ilsa Plume, Harcourt, 1987, 32 pp. (0-15-293500-2)

(BBC:216; BL 77:137, 79:1337, 1443, 82:632, 84:401; Bookshelf 1923–1924 p. 7; CC:450; CCBB 37:2, 39:59; Ch&Bks:283; HBG 2:257; KR 51:374; Moore:426; SLJ Dec 1981 p. 58, Aug 1983 p. 60; Jan 1986 p. 62)

2894 **BIANCO, Pamela.** *Little Houses Far Away.* **Gr. 1–4.**

Paula explores the teddy-bear and doll world she saw from a train window.

Illus. by the author, Oxford, 1951, 87 pp., o.p.

(BL 48:174; CCBB 5:26; HB 27:324; KR 19:614; LJ 76:2009)

2895 **BIANCO, Pamela.** *Toy Rose.* **Gr. 3–5.**

A talking doll named Toy Rose comes between Joy and Jessica, twins who had always been best friends.

Illus. by the author, Lippincott, 1957, 91 pp., o.p.

(CCBB 11:77; HB 33:398; KR 25:479; LJ 82:3241)

2896 **BLOCH, Marie Halun.** *The Dollhouse Story.* **Gr. 3–5.**

Three dollhouse dolls come to life to get rid of a cat who frightened away their friend, Mouse.

Illus. by Walter Erhard, Walck, 1961, 63 pp., o.p.

(BL 58:488; HB 38:176; LJ 87:329)

BRINK, Carol Ryrie. *Andy Buckram's Tin Men.* See Chapter 6, Humorous Fantasy.

2897 **BROWN, Abbie Farwell.** *The Lonesomest Doll.* **Gr. 3–5. (Orig. U.S. pub. 1901.)**

The porter's daughter teaches a princess how to play with her lonesome doll.

Illus. by Arthur Rackham, Houghton, 1928, 80 pp., o.p.

(BL 25:173; Bookshelf 1923–1924 p. 12; HB 4[Nov 1928]:76; Mahony 1:40; Mahony 2:127)

2898 **BUCK, David.** *The Small Adventures of Dog.* **Gr. 3–5. (Orig. British pub. 1968.)**

A discarded leather pig called "Dog" finds he can talk with both toys and real animals.

Illus. by the author, Watts, 1969, 76 pp., o.p.

(CCBB 24:5; LJ 95:778; TLS 1968 p. 1376)

2899 **BUFFETT, Jimmy, and BUFFETT, Savannah Jane.** *Trouble Dolls.* **Gr. K–4.**

Lizzy's tiny Guatemalan Trouble Dolls help her rescue her father, who has become lost in the Florida Everglades.

Illus. by Lambert Davis, Harcourt, 1991, 32 pp. (0-15-290790-4)

(BL 87:1496; HBG 2[Fall 1991]:260; SLJ June 1991 p. 72)

BURNETT, Frances Hodgson. *Racketty-Packetty House.* See Chapter 7, Magic Adventure Fantasy.

2900 **BYARS, Betsy (Cromer).** *Clementine.* **Gr. 3–4.**

Clementine, a dragon made from an old green sock, grows dissatisfied with her toy-shelf home and insists on moving to a cave in the country.

Illus. by Charles Wilton, Houghton, 1962, 72 pp., o.p.

(KR 30:280; LJ 87:3199)

CASSEDY, Sylvia. *Behind the Attic Wall.* See Chapter 4, Ghost Fantasy.

2901 **CLARKE, J(udith).** *Teddy B. Zoot.* **Gr. 2–4.**

When Sarah forgets to bring home her math assignment, her teddy bear braves a rainstorm and a vicious dog to find the worksheet and bring it home to her.

Illus. by Margaret Hewitt, Henry Holt, 1990, 58 pp. (0-8050-1452-7), 1992, pap. (0-8050-2210-4)

(BL 87:1130; HBG 2[July 1990]:69; SLJ Jan 1991 p. 70)

2902 **CLARKE, Pauline (pseud. of Pauline [Clarke] Hunter Blair).** *Five Dolls in a House.* **Gr. 3–5. (Orig. British pub. 1961.)**

After she shrinks to doll-size, Elizabeth sees what life is like for her own five dolls. The sequels are *Five Dolls in the Snow* (1967), *Five Dolls and Their Friends* (British), *Five Dolls and the Duke* (British), and *Five Dolls and the Monkey* (British).

Illus. by Aliki (Brandenberg), Prentice-Hall, 1965, 143 pp., o.p.

(CCBB 19:145; HB 41:627; LJ 91:1696; TLS 1961 p. 451)

2903 **CLARKE, Pauline (pseud. of Pauline [Clarke] Hunter Blair).** *The Return of the*
✓ *Twelves* **(British title:** *The Twelve and the Genii,* **1962). Gr. 4–7.**

Max Morley discovers that his twelve toy soldiers are alive, and he helps them return to their ancestral home. Carnegie Medal, 1962.

Illus. by Bernarda Bryson, Coward, 1963, o.p.; Gregg, 1981, 251 pp., o.p.; Buccaneer, 1990 (0-89966-675-2)

(BL 60:701; Ch&Bks:271; Eakin:74; HB 39:602, 60:223; LJ 89:390; TLS 1962 p. 901)

2904 **COATSWORTH, Elizabeth (Jane).** *All-of-a-Sudden Susan.* **Gr. 3–5.**

Susan finds that her doll, Emelida, can speak, after they are accidentally left behind when her family abandons their house during a flood.

Illus. by Richard Cuffari, Macmillan, 1974, 74 pp., o.p.

(BL 71:506; CCBB 28:128; KR 42:1303; SLJ Mar 1975 p. 86)

2905 **COLLODI, Carlo (pseud. of Carlo Lorenzini).** *The Adventures of Pinocchio.* **Gr.**
✓ **4–7. (Written 1880; pub. serially beginning in 1881; orig. Italian pub. in book form, 1883, U.S. pub. 1892.)**

A wooden puppet named Pinocchio longs to become a real boy. Five sequels were written by authors other than Collodi and published in the U.S.: *Pinocchio in Africa* (Ginn, 1911) by Eugenio Cherubini, *Pinocchio under the Sea* (Macmillan, 1913) by Gemma Mongiardini Rembadi, *The Heart of Pinocchio* (Harper, 1919) by Paolo Lorenzini, *Pinocchio in America* (Doubleday, 1928) by Angelo Patri, and *Puppet Parade* (Longmans, 1932) by Carol(yn M.) Della Chiesa. Roberto Innocenti's illustrations for the 1988 edition won the Kate Greenaway Highly Commended Medal, 1989.

Trans. by Carol(yn M.) Della Chiesa, illus. by Atillo Mussino, Macmillan, 1969, 1978, 1989, 310 pp. (0-02-722821-5); adapt. by Neil Morris, illus. by Frank Baber, Macmillan, 1982, 83 pp., o.p.; illus. by Fritz Kredel, Putnam, 1982, 239 pp. (0-448-06001-9); trans. by M. L. Rosenthal, illus. by Troy Howell, Lothrop, 1983, o.p.; adapt. by Stephanie Spinner, illus. by Diane Goode, Random, 1983, o.p.; trans. by James T. Teahan, illus. by Alexa Jaffurs, Schocken, 1985, o.p.; trans. and illus. by Francis Wainwright, Holt, 1986, 96 pp., o.p.; trans. by E. Harden, illus. by Roberto Innocenti, Knopf, 1988, 144 pp. (0-394-82110-6); adapt. by James Riordan, illus. by Victor G. Ambrus, Oxford, 1988, 96 pp. (entitled: *Pinocchio*) (0-19-279855-3); adapt. and illus. by Chris McEwan, Doubleday, 1990, 32 pp. (0-385-41327-0); illus. by Lorenzo Mattotti, Lothrop, 1993, 40 pp., LB(0-688-12451-8)

(BBC:200; BL 12:299, 21:238, 60:307, 79:674; 80:856, 85:573, 87:1135, 90:339; Bookshelf 1928 p. 9; CC:471, 508; CCBB 2[Jan 1949]:4, 4:45, 11:67, 37:105, 144; Ch&Bks:269; HB 2[Nov 1925]:29, 27:260, 59:70, 60:357, 61:588, 65:209; HBG 2[July–Dec 1990]:54; KR 37:719; LJ 95:258, June 15, 1985 p. 71; Mahony 2:286; SLJ Feb 1984 p. 56, Feb 1986 p. 72, Mar 1987 p. 156, Feb 1989 p. 68, Jan 1991 p. 78; Suth 3:97)

2906   COOMBS, Patricia. *The Lost Playground.* **Gr. 1–4.**

Accidentally left in the park, Mostly, June's home-made stuffed animal, floats off to the Lost Playground where all lost toys go.

Illus. by the author, Lothrop, 1963, 46 pp., o.p.

(CCBB 17:153; HB 39:380)

2907   DE LEEUW, Adele Louise. *Nobody's Doll.* **Gr. 2–5.**

Susan Araminta is rescued from the trash by Mr. McHugh, a Scottie who helps her find a new owner.

Illus. by Anne Vaughan, Little, 1946, 85 pp., o.p.

(BL 42:319; HB 22:268; LJ 71:827)

2908   DEXTER, Catherine. *The Oracle Doll.* **Gr. 5–8.**

When Gabriella, Lucy's talking doll, begins saying things she was not programmed to say, Lucy and her sister realize that Gabby can predict the future, like the ancient Oracle at Delphi.

Macmillan, 1985, 195 pp., o.p.; Dell, 1988, pap. (0-440-40114-3); Morrow, pap., 1994 (entitled: *The Doll Who Knew the Future*), 208 pp. (0-688-13117-4).

(BBJ:70; BL 82:403; CCBB 39:145; SLJ Feb 1986 p. 84)

2909   DIAZ, Abby (Morton). *Polly Cologne.* **Gr. 3–5. (Orig. pub. 1881.)**

A rag doll named Polly Cologne goes for a ride in a dog's mouth and gets lost.

Illus. by Morgan J. Sweeney, Lothrop, 1930, 215 pp., o.p.

(BL 27:215; HB 6:332, 7:116; Mahony 1:14)

2910   DICKS, Terrance. *Sally Ann on Her Own* **(Sally Ann series, book 1). Gr. 2–4.**

Sally Ann, a spunky rag doll, mobilizes the other toys at Mrs. Foster's day-care center to expose the crooked inspectors attempting to close the school down. The sequels are *Sally Ann and the School Show* (1992), *Sally Ann and the Mystery Picnic* (1993), and *Nurse Sally Ann* (1994).

Illus. by Blanche Simms, Simon & Schuster, 1992, 64 pp. (0-671-74512-3)

(BL 88:1680; HBG 3[Fall 1992]:254; KR 60:776; SLJ July 1992 p. 58)

2911   DILLON, Barbara. *The Teddy Bear Tree.* **Gr. 3–5.**

Bertine buries a worn-out teddy bear's glass eye, and a tree full of teddy bears grows there.

Illus. by David S. Rose, Morrow, 1982, 79 pp., o.p.; Pocket, 1990, pap. (0-671-68432-9)

(BL 79:244; KR 50:734; SLJ Oct 1982 p. 150)

2912 DILLON, Barbara. *Who Needs a Bear?* **Gr. 2–4.**

Three old toys leave the safety of their attic home, searching for new owners who really care about them.

Illus. by Diane de Groat, Morrow, 1981, 63 pp., o.p.

(BL 78:104; CCBB 35:84; KR 49:1159; SLJ Nov 1981 p. 90)

2913 DU BOIS, William (Sherman) Pène. *Gentleman Bear.* **Gr. 4–6.**

Bayard the gentleman teddy bear accompanies his owner, Sir Billy Browne-Browne, from age four through adulthood.

Illus. by the author, Farrar, 1985, 80 pp. (0-374-32533-2), pap., 1988 (0-374-42536-1)

(BBC:202; BL 82:1080; CCBB 39:145; SLJ Apr 1986 p. 86; Suth 4:103)

DUFFY, James. *The Revolt of the Teddy Bears.* See Chapter 2, Animal Fantasy.

2914 ESTERN, Anne Graham. *The Picolinis and the Haunted House.* **Gr. 4–6.**

The Picolini circus doll family helps Jessica and Peter solve a mystery surrounding the haunted house their parents want to buy.

Illus. by Hal Frenck, Bantam, 1989, pap., 128 pp. (0-553-15771-X)

(BL 86:1467; SLJ Mar 1990 p. 217)

ESTES, Eleanor (Ruth Rosenfeld). *The Witch Family.* See Chapter 10, Witchcraft and Sorcery Fantasy.

2915 FAIRSTAR, Mrs. (pseud. of Richard Henry Horne). *Memoirs of a London Doll,*
✓ *Written by Herself.* **Gr. 4–6. (Orig. British pub. 1846, U.S. 1852.)**

Maria Poppet describes her harrowing experiences as she is passed from owner to owner. This story is considered to be the first talking doll fantasy, and has been reprinted in *The Silent Playmate* (Macmillan, 1979, 1981), ed. by Naomi Lewis (see this chapter).

Illus. by Emma L. Brock, Macmillan, 1922, 1944, 1951, o.p.; illus. by Margaret Gillies and Richard Smith, Macmillan, 1968, 143 pp., o.p.

(BL 65:257; Bookshelf 1928 p. 16; CCBB 22:79; HB 44:560; KR 36:642; TLS 1967 p. 1143)

2916 FANCIULLI, Guiseppe. *The Little Blue Man.* **Gr. 4–6. (Orig. pub. in Italy.)**

The story of the adventures of a small blue puppet-man.

Trans. by May M. Sweet, illus. by H(erman) I. Bacharach, Houghton, 1926, 198 pp., o.p.

(BL 23:234; HB 2[Nov 1926]:42; Mahony 2:123)

2917 FIELD, Rachel (Lyman). *Hitty, Her First Hundred Years.* **Gr. 4–6. (Orig. pub.**
✓ **1929.)**

The adventures of a carved-wood doll named Hitty include being shipwrecked while traveling from Maine to the South Seas. John Newbery Medal, 1930.

Illus. by Dorothy P. Lathrop, Macmillan, 1937, 1969, 207 pp. (0-02-734840-7); Dell, 1990, pap. (0-440-40337-5)

(BBC:203; BL 26:125; Bookshelf 1932 p. 12; CC:483; Ch&Bks:271; HB 5:53, 6:22; LJ 54:986, 55:603, 996; Moore:235, 427)

2918 FOSTER, Elizabeth. *Gigi: The Story of a Merry-Go-Round Horse.* **Gr. 4–6.**

A merry-go-round horse has many adventures while traveling from Vienna to Paris, London, and America. The sequel is *Gigi in America: Further Adventures of a Merry-Go-Round Horse* (1946, 1983).

Illus. by Ilse Bischoff, Houghton, 1943, o.p.; North Atlantic Books, 1983, 124 pp. (0-913028-55-X)

(BBC:203; BL 40:116; HB 19:319; LJ 68:820, 1008)

2919 **FYLEMAN, Rose (Amy).** *The Dolls' House.* **Gr. 2–4. (Orig. British pub. 1930.)**

The doll house family has a number of adventures while their owner is gone.

Illus. by Erick Berry, Doubleday, 1931, 99 pp., o.p.

(BL 28:66; HB 7:220; LJ 56:958; TLS 1930 p. 986)

2920 **GARDAM, Jane (Pearson).** *Through the Dolls' House Door.* **Gr. 4–8. (Orig.**
✓ **British pub. 1987.)**

Forgotten for many years after their playmates have moved away, the "creatures" living in an antique doll house (a Dutch doll, a rag doll, a soldier, a little girl doll, and a china cat) despair that they will never be found and played with again.

Greenwillow, 1987, 128 pp. (0-688-07447-2); Dell, 1991, pap. (0-440-40433-9)

(BBC:203; BL 84:318; CCBB 41:48; Ch&Bks:286; KR 55:1155; SLJ Oct 1987 p. 125; TLS 1987 p. 751; VOYA 11:39)

2921 **GODDEN (Dixon), (Margaret) Rumer.** *Candy Floss.* **Gr. 1–4. (Orig. British**
✓ **pub. 1959.)**

A spoiled little girl named Clementina decides to steal Jack's doll, Candy Floss. This story has been reprinted in *Four Dolls* (Greenwillow, 1984; see this chapter).

Illus. by Adrienne Adams, Viking, 1959, 63 pp., o.p.; illus. by Nonny Hogrogian, Putnam, 1991, 64 pp. (0-399-21807-6)

(BL 56:633, 88:532; CC 1993 Suppl. p. 69; CCBB 13:147; Ch&Bks:271; Eakin:141; HB 36:212; HBG 3[July–Dec 1991]:58; KR 28:144; LJ 85:247; SLJ Dec 1991 p. 90; TLS Nov 25, 1960 p. iv)

2922 **GODDEN (Dixon), (Margaret) Rumer.** *The Dolls' House.* **Gr. 3–5. (Orig. British**
✓ **pub. 1947.)**

Life in a Victorian dollhouse changes drastically when a haughty new doll arrives.

Illus. by Tasha Tudor, Viking, 1948, 1962, 136 pp., o.p.; Puffin, 1976, pap. (0-14-030942-X)

(BL 45:53, 59:292; CC:492; CCBB 2[Jan 1949]:3, 13:147; Ch&Bks:271; Eakin:141; HB 24:347, 457, 39:75; KR 16:363; LJ 73:1097; TLS 1947 p. 636)

2923 **GODDEN (Dixon), (Margaret) Rumer.** *The Fairy Doll.* **Gr. 2–4. (Orig. British**
✓ **pub. 1955.)**

The fairy doll atop the Christmas tree helps Elizabeth to gain self-confidence. Carnegie Medal Commended Book, 1956. This story has been reprinted in *Four Dolls* (Greenwillow, 1984; see this chapter).

Illus. by Adrienne Adams, Viking, 1956, 67 pp., o.p.

(BL 53:51; HB 34:453; KR 24:431; LJ 81:2720; TLS Nov 23, 1956 p. xv)

2924 **GODDEN (Dixon), (Margaret) Rumer.** *Four Dolls* **(Orig. titles:** *Impunity Jane,*
✓ **Viking, 1954 [see below];** *The Fairy Doll,* **Viking, 1956 [see above];** *The Story of*
Holly and Ivy, **Viking, 1958 [see below]; and** *Candy Floss,* **Viking, 1960 [see**
above].) Gr. 3–5. (Orig. British pub. in this edition 1983.)

Four timeless tales about spirited little dolls and their resourceful owners.

Illus. by Pauline Baynes, Greenwillow, 1984 (0-688-02801-2); Dell, 1986, pap., 206 pp. (0-440-42568-9)

(BBC:204; BL 81:306; CC:579; HB 60:615; SLJ Nov 1984 p. 124)

2925 **GODDEN (Dixon), (Margaret) Rumer.** *Fu-Dog.* **Gr. 1–4. (Original British pub.**
✓ **1989.)**

The embroidered satin Fu-Dog her great-uncle sends her from London's Chinatown enables Li-la to find her Chinese relatives and reconcile the English and Chinese sides of her family.

Illus. by Valerie Littlewood, Viking, 1990, 64 pp. (0-670-82300-7)

(BL 86:1897; CC:492; HBG 1[Jan–June 1990]:237; KR 58:727; SLJ May 1990 p. 86)

2926 GODDEN (Dixon), (Margaret) Rumer. *Home Is the Sailor.* **Gr. 3–5. (Orig.**
✓ **British pub. 1964.)**

A Welsh doll named Curley sets sail for France to search for his older brother, Thomas.

Illus. by Jean Primrose, Viking, 1964, 128 pp., o.p.

(CCBB 18:86; Eakin:141; HB 41:56; LJ 90:960; TLS 1964 p. 1081)

2927 GODDEN (Dixon), (Margaret) Rumer. *Impunity Jane: The Story of a Pocket*
✓ *Doll.* **Gr. 2–4. (Orig. British pub. 1954.)**

Impunity Jane grows bored sitting on a dollhouse cushion all day, and longs to take a ride in someone's pocket. This story has been reprinted in *Four Dolls* (Greenwillow, 1984; see this chapter).

Illus. by Adrienne Adams, Viking, 1954, 47 pp., o.p.

(BL 51:47; CCBB 9:23; Eakin:142; HB 30:330; KR 22:383; LJ 79:1913, 2018)

2928 GODDEN (Dixon), (Margaret) Rumer. *Miss Happiness and Miss Flower.* **Gr.**
✓ **3–5. (Orig. British pub. 1960.)**

Nona and her cousins build a Japanese-style house for her two Japanese dolls. Carnegie Medal Commended Book, 1961. The sequel is *Little Plum* (1962, 1963).

Illus. by Jean Primrose, Viking, 1961, o.p.; Puffin, 1987, pap., 88 pp. (0-14-030273-5)

(BL 57:580; CCBB 14:143; Ch&Bks:271; Eakin:142; HB 37:269; KR 29:328; LJ 86:1983; TLS May 19, 1961 p. iv)

2929 GODDEN (Dixon), (Margaret) Rumer. *The Story of Holly and Ivy.* **Gr. 2–4.**
✓ **(Orig. British pub. 1957.)**

The Christmas wishes of an orphaned girl named Ivy, a doll named Holly, and a lonely woman named Mrs. Jones, are all granted. This story can also be found in *Four Dolls* (Greenwillow, 1984; see this chapter).

Illus. by Adrienne Adams, Viking, 1958, o.p.; illus. by Barbara Cooney, Viking, 1985, 32 pp. (0-670-80622-6); Puffin, 1987, pap. (0-14-050723-X)

(BL 55:53, 82:261, 417; CC:633; CCBB 12:47, 39:27; Eakin:143; HB 34:461; KR 26:453; LJ 83:3572; SLJ Oct 1985 p. 190; TLS Nov 21, 1958 p. xv)

2930 GREENWALD, Sheila (pseud. of Sheila Green). *The Secret Museum.* **Gr. 3–5.**

Jennifer comes upon some antique dolls who agree to take part in plays to earn money to help Jennifer's parents.

Illus. by the author, Lippincott, 1974, 127 pp., o.p.

(BL 70:1104; CCBB 27:177; KR 42:424; LJ 99:1473)

2931 GRIFFITH, Helen V(irginia). *Caitlin's Holiday.* **Gr. 3–5.**
✓ Something compels Caitlin to trade her favorite doll for Holiday, a beautiful teenage doll who walks, talks, complains, sulks, and throws tantrums. In the sequel, *Doll Trouble* (1993), Caitlin and Jennifer's friendship is tested after Holiday is accused of stealing Jennifer's missing doll clothes.

Illus. by Susan Condie Lamb, Greenwillow, 1990, 96 pp. (0-688-69470-8)

(BL 86:2172; CC 1992 Suppl. p. 57; CCBB 44:29; HBG 2[July–Dec 1990]:74; KR 58:931; SLJ Oct 1990 p. 92

GRIPE, Maria (Kristina). *Agnes Cecilia.* See Chapter 4, Ghost Fantasy.

2932 HISER, Constance. *The Missing Doll.* **Gr. 3–4.**

Abby and Heather find a missing classmate using rhyming clues supplied by Abby's talking doll.

Illus. by Marcy Ramsey, Holiday, 1993, 104 pp. (0-8234-1046-3)

(BL 90:623; CCBB 47:123; HBG 5:77; SLJ Feb 1994 p. 102)

HOBAN, Russell C(onwell). *The Mouse and His Child.* See Chapter 1, Allegorical Fantasy and Literary Fairy Tales.

2933 HOFFMANN, E(rnst) T(heodor) A(madeus). *The Nutcracker.* **Gr. 2 up. (Orig.**
✓✓ **German pub. 1819; U.S. pub. 1853, entitled:** *Nutcracker and Mouse-King.***)**

In a little girl's Christmas Eve dream, her toy nutcracker comes to life and takes her to a magical world.

Whitman, 1930, o.p.; adapt. and illus. by Warren Chappell, Knopf, 1958, o.p.; adapt. by Janet Schulman, illus. by Kay Chorao, Knopf, 1988 (repr. of 1978 ed.), 64 pp. (0-394-82018-5); illus. by Rachel Isadora, Macmillan, 1981, o.p.; trans. and adapt. by Anthea Bell, illus. by Lisbeth Zwerger, Picture Book Studio, 1983, 1987, 28 pp., o.p., 1991, pap. (0-88708-156-8); trans. by Ralph Manheim, illus. by Maurice Sendak, Crown, 1991, pap., 120 pp. (0-517-58659-2)

(BL 35:139, 55:78, 56:225, 72:791, 76:452, 78:304, 80:417, 81:146; CC:449, 502; CCBB 32:153, 37:30, 38:67; HB 6:329, 34:460, 35:487, 61:53; HBG 2[July–Dec 1990]:46; KR 26:606, 27:597, 49:1292, 52:75; LJ 55:924; SLJ Oct 1979 p. 118, Oct 1981 p. 155, Feb 1984 p. 73, Nov 1984 p. 125, Oct 1987 p. 31; Suth 3:194, 195; TLS 1985 p. 75)

2934 HOWE, Deborah, and HOWE, James. *Teddy Bear's Scrapbook.* **Gr. 2–4.**

Teddy tells his owner seven adventure-filled tales. His exploits include visiting the abominable snowman and becoming a cowboy, a circus performer, and a movie star.

Illus. by David S. Rose, Macmillan, 1980, 73 pp., o.p., 1988, pap., 80 pp. (0-689-71168-9)

(BL 76:1424; CCBB 34:13; KR 48:911; SLJ Sept 1980 p. 60)

2935 JANE, Pamela. *Noelle of the Nutcracker.* **Gr. 3–5.**

A ballerina doll who dreams of a dancing career is desperately desired by second-graders Ilyana Ingram and her arch-rival, wealthy Mary Jane Igoe.

Illus. by Jan Brett, Houghton, 1986, 64 pp. (0-395-39969-6); Bantam, 1988, pap. (0-553-15673-X)

(BBC:206; BL 83:132; CCBB 40:28; KR 54:1125; SLJ Oct 1986 p. 112)

2936 JOHNSON, Crockett (pseud. of David Leisk). *Ellen's Lion: Twelve Stories.* **Gr. 2–4.**

Ellen and her talking toy lion go on twelve adventures together.

Illus. by the author, Harper, 1959, 62 pp., o.p.

(HB 35:379; KR 27:370; LJ 84:3625)

2937 JONES, Elizabeth Orton. *Big Susan.* **Gr. 2–4. (Orig. pub. 1947.)**
✓ Big Susan helps the Doll family come to life on Christmas Eve.

Illus. by the author, Macmillan, 1967, 82 pp., o.p.

(BL 44:138, CCBB 1[Dec 1947]:3; HB 24:39; KR 15:547; LJ 72;1692)

2938 KENNEDY, (Jerome) Richard. *Amy's Eyes.* **Gr. 5–7.**
✓ Orphaned Amy's love for her sailor doll, Captain, causes him to grow into a real sailor who runs away from the Home for Girls, vowing to return for Amy once he has made his fortune.

Illus. by Richard Egielski, Harper, 1985, 448 pp. (0-06-023219-6), pap., 1988 (0-06-440220-7)

(BBC:207; BL 81:1254, 82:1234; CC:514; CCBB 38:150; Ch&Bks:271; HB 61:554; KR 53:42; SLJ May 1985 p. 90; Suth 4:212; VOYA 8:193)

2939   **KING-SMITH, Dick.** *Lady Daisy.* **Gr. 3–6. (Orig. British pub. 1992.)**

✓   Hidden away for eighty-nine years, a beautiful Victorian doll is reluctantly "adopted" by nine-year-old Ned, who is teased about her at school before she is stolen.

Illus. by Naimo Jones, Delacorte, 1993, 144 pp. (0-385-30891-4)

(BL 89:1590; CCBB 46:215; HBG 4[Fall 1993]:300; KR 61:458; SLJ July 1993 p. 62)

2940   **KNIGHT, Marjorie.** *Alexander's Christmas Eve.* **Gr. 2–4.**

Three Christmas toys escape from Santa's pack and set out to see the world and find their own home. The sequels are *Alexander's Birthday* (1940), and *Alexander's Vacation* (1943).

Illus. by Howard Simon, Dutton, 1938, 93 pp., o.p.

(HB 14:413; LJ 63:798)

2941   **KOONTZ, Dean R(ay).** *Oddkins: A Fable for All Ages.* **Gr. 7–12.**

A stuffed bear and his toy friends battle an evil jack-in-the-box to preserve the toys' magical ability to help children cope with their problems.

Illus. by Phil Parks, Warner, 1988, 180 pp., o.p.

(BL 85:220, 258; KR 56:1200)

2942   **KROEBER, Theodora (Kracow).** *Carrousel.* **Gr. 2–4.**

When Pegason the winged horse falls into a giant city, his friends Gryphon and Pyggon must rescue him.

Illus. by Douglas Tait, Atheneum, 1977, 91 pp., o.p.

(CCBB 31:97; HB 53:664; KR 45:1198; SLJ Nov 1977 p. 49)

LAMORISSE, Albert (Emmanuel). *The Red Balloon.* See Chapter 1, Allegorical Fantasy and Literary Fairy Tales.

2943   **LATHROP, Dorothy P(ulis).** *An Angel in the Woods.* **Gr. 2–4. (Orig. pub. 1947.)**

A toy Christmas angel brings the Christmas spirit to the forest animals.

Illus. by the author, Macmillan, 1955, 42 pp., o.p.

(BL 44:156; HB 24:37; KR 15:578; LJ 72:1784)

LATHROP, Dorothy P(ulis). *The Lost Merry-Go-Round.* See Chapter 7, Magic Adventure Fantasy.

MARIA, Consort of Ferdinand, King of Rumania. *The Magic Doll of Rumania.* See Chapter 7, Magic Adventure Fantasy.

2944   **MILNE, A(lan) A(lexander).** *Winnie-the-Pooh.* **Gr. 2–4. (Orig. British and U.S.**
✓✓   **pub. 1926.)**

The adventures of Christopher Robin and his friends, Winnie-the-Pooh, Tigger, Eeyore, Piglet, Rabbit, Owl, Kanga, and Baby Roo, include Pooh's tangles with honeybees, and Piglet's encounter with a Heffalump. The sequels are *The House at Pooh Corner* (1961; orig. pub. 1928) and *The Hums of Pooh* (1930). Collections of tales about Pooh include *The World of Pooh* (1957), *The Pooh Story Book* (1965), *The Christopher Robin Story Book* (1966) and *Pooh's Bedtime Book* (1980).

Illus. by Ernest H. Shepard, Dutton, 1954, 1988 (0-525-44443-2); Dell, 1988, pap. (0-440-40116-X); Puffin, 1992, pap., 176 pp. (0-14-036121-9)

(BBC:210; BL 23:137; Bookshelf 1928 p. 9; CC:534; Ch&Bks:270; HB 2[Nov 1925]:42, 34:122; KR 39:1213; LJ 52:1017; Moore:427; TLS 1926 p. 861, 1971 p. 1614)

2945 NABB, Magdalen. *The Enchanted Horse.* **Gr. 3–6. (Orig. British pub. 1992.)**

✓ Lonely Irina's love for Bella, a shabby wooden rocking horse, transforms Bella into a beautiful wild horse who takes Irina on midnight rides.

Illus. by Julek Heller, Orchard, 1993, 90 pp. (0-53106805-6)

(BL 90:623; HB 69:744; HBG 5:80; KR 61:1333; SLJ Oct 1993 p. 126)

NESBIT (Bland), E(dith). *The Magic City.* See Chapter 5C, Travel to Other Worlds.

2946 O'CONNELL, Jean S. *The Dollhouse Caper.* **Gr. 4–6.**

✓ Although the Dollhouse family is unable to warn the Humans about an upcoming robbery, they manage to scare the burglars off by themselves.

Illus. by Erik Blegvad, Harper, 1988 (repr. of 1976 ed.), 96 pp. (0-06-440236-3)

(BBC:211; BL 72:1049; CCBB 29:149; Ch&Bks:271; HB 52:291; KR 44:70; SLJ Apr 1976 p. 63; Suth 2:341)

2947 ODGERS, Sally Farrell. *Drummond: The Search for Sarah.* **Gr. 2–4. (Orig. Australian pub. 1990.)**

Drummond, a teddy bear bought at a garage sale, tells Sarah and Nicholas that he'd like to be reunited with his original owner.

Illus. by Carol Jones, Holiday, 1990, 112 pp., o.p.

(BL 87:58; HB 66:775; HBG 2[July 1990]:65; SLJ Mar 1991 p. 177)

2948 PARRISH, Anne. *Floating Island.* **Gr. 3–5.**

✓ The adventures of a family of dolls who are shipwrecked on a deserted island. John Newbery Medal Honor Book, 1931. This book has been criticized for its sterotypical depiction of Dinah, the black cook doll.

Illus. by the author, Harper, 1930, 265 pp., o.p.

(BL 27:214; Bookshelf 1932 p. 12; HB 6:331, 7:60, 116; Moore: 280, 427; TLS 1930 p. 1043)

PELGROM, Els. *Little Sophie and Lanky Flop.* See Chapter 1, Allegorical Fantasy and Literary Fairy Tales.

PENDERGRAFT, Patricia. *The Legend of Daisy Flowerdew.* See Chapter 1, Allegorical Fantasy and Literary Fairy Tales.

2949 PHILLIPS, Ethel Calvert. *Little Rag Doll.* **Gr. 3–5.**

Mrs. Thimbletop, the doll fairy, befriends a neglected rag doll named Dilly and they go to live with a cat named Grandma Reddy, inside a child's playhouse.

Illus. by Lois Lenski, Houghton, 1930, 174 pp., o.p.

(BL 27:214; HB 6:322; LJ 55:955, 56:279; Mahony 3:56)

2950 PHILLIPS, Ethel Calvert. *The Popover Family.* **Gr. 2–4.**

Ellen meets the Popover doll family who live in her Aunt Amelia's old red dollhouse.

Illus. by E. F. Butler, Houghton, 1927, 132 pp., o.p.

(BL 24:73; HB 3[Nov 1927]:43; LJ 53:1033; Mahony 2:128)

REID BANKS, Lynne. *The Indian in the Cupboard.* See Chapter 7, Magic Adventure Fantasy.

2951   RENDAL, Justine. *A Child of Their Own.* Gr. 3–6. (Orig. British pub. 1990.)

The Darling doll family and two less-elegant dolls, Amanda and Johnsley, are bought in England and shipped to America, where they dream of being loved and played with by real children.

Viking, 1992, 96 pp. (0-670-84418-7)

(BL 88:2014; CCBB 45:276; HBG 4[Spring 1993]:75; KR 60:854; SLJ Aug 1992 p. 158)

2952   SHECTER, Ben. *The Stocking Child.* Gr. 2–4.

Sam and his friend, Epaphroditus, search far and wide for a missing button eye, and wind up at Sam's own house.

Illus. by the author, Harper, 1976, 32 pp. o.p.

(BL 73:669; CCBB 30:114; KR 44:1038; SLJ Jan 1977 p. 85)

2953   SIEBE, Josephine. *Kasperle's Adventures.* Gr. 3–5. (Orig. German pub. 1928.)

Kasperle, a mischievous wooden doll, comes to life after Master Friedolm finishes carving him.

Trans. by Florence Geiser, illus. by Frank Dobias, Macmillan, 1929, 1939, 199 pp., o.p.

(BL 26:126; Bookshelf 1930–1931 p. 9; HB 5:46–47, 49, 7:117; Mahony 3:56)

2954   *The Silent Playmate: A Collection of Doll Stories.* Ed. by Naomi Lewis. Gr. 4–6. (Orig. British pub. 1979.)

Doll stories from various sources, including Mrs. Fairstar's *Memoirs of a London Doll* (1846, 1852; see this chapter).

Illus. by Harold Jones, Macmillan, 1981, 223 pp., o.p.

(BL 78:589; CCBB 35:89; HB 58:44; SLJ Feb 1982 p. 78)

2955   SLEATOR, William (Warner III). *Among the Dolls.* Gr. 3–5.

✓   Vicky learns a painful lesson when she shrinks to doll size and must suffer the ill-temper of the dolls she had mistreated.

Illus. by Trina Schart Hyman, Dutton, 1975, 70 pp. (0-525-25563-X); Knopf, 1991, pap. (0-679-80347-5)

(BBC:213; BL 72:628; CC:555; CCBB 29:118; HB 52:53; KR 43:1186; SLJ Dec 1975 p. 55)

2956   SLOBODKIN, Louis. *The Adventures of Arab.* Gr. 3–5. (Orig. pub. 1946.)

Arab is not happy as a merry-go-round horse, so he changes places with a coach horse.

Illus. by the author, Vanguard, 1967, 123 pp., o.p.

(BL 43:148; HB 22:349; KR 14:386; LJ 72:167)

STEARNS, Pamela (Fujimoto). *The Mechanical Doll.* See Chapter 1, Allegorical Fantasy and Literary Fairy Tales.

2957   STOVER, Marjorie Filley. *When the Dolls Woke.* Gr. 3–6.

Great-Great-Aunt Abigail's dollhouse holds a treasure, if only the doll family can remember where it is hidden in time to help Abigail, now a destitute old woman. The sequel is *Midnight in the Dollhouse* (1990).

Illus. by Karen Loccisano, Whitman, 1985, 128 pp., LB(0-8075-8882-2); Scholastic, 1993, pap. (0-590-44624-X)

(BBC:214; BL 82:814; SLJ Jan 1986 p. 71)

2958 **SYMONDS, John.** *Away to the Moon.* **Gr. 2–4.**

Two dollhouse dolls named Hetty and Betty set off to visit the moon.

Illus. by Pamela Bianco, Lippincott, 1956, 64 pp., o.p.

(BL 53:101; HB 32:349; KR 24:571; LJ 81:2723)

2959 **TREGARTHEN, Enys (pseud. of Nellie Sloggett).** *The Doll Who Came Alive.* **Gr. 3–5. (Orig. U.S. pub. 1942.)**

A little girl's great love for her wooden doll brings it to life.

Ed. by Elizabeth Yates, illus. by Nora S. Unwin, Day, 1972 (repr. of 1942 ed.), 75 pp., o.p.

(BL 69:911; CCBB 4:51, 26:33; HB 48:596; KR 40:860; LJ 67:884, 98:1009; TLS 1973 p. 387)

2960 **TWOHILL, Maggie.** *Jeeter, Mason and the Magic Headset.* **Gr. 3–5.**

Ten-year-old Jeeter's Cabbage Patch doll, Morgan, suddenly begins talking to Jeeter through her radio headphones.

Bradbury, 1985, 103 pp., o.p.; Dell, 1986, pap. (0-440-44220-6)

(CCBB 39:18; SLJ Sept 1985 p. 140)

2961 **WILLIAMS (John), Ursula Moray.** *The Toymaker's Daughter.* **Gr. 4–6. (Orig.**
✓ **British pub. 1968.)**

A doll-girl named Marta escapes from Malkin, the evil toymaker, and crosses the mountains, hoping to become a real girl. The sequels are *The Three Toymakers* (1970, 1971) and *Malkin's Mountain* (Nelson, 1971, 1972).

Illus. by Shirley Hughes, Meredith, 1969, 134 pp., o.p.

(CCBB 23:68; HB 45:538; KR 37:507; LJ 94:3209; TLS 1968 p. 1377)

WOODRUFF, Elvira. *Awfully Short for the Fourth Grade.* See Chapter 7, Magic Adventure Fantasy.

2962 **WRIGHT, Betty Ren.** *The Dollhouse Murders.* **Gr. 4–7.**
✓ A miniature version of her great-grandparents' house, complete with dolls, leads Amy to the conclusion that her great-grandparents were murdered and that the dolls know who the killer was.

Holiday, 1983, 149 pp. (0-8234-0497-8); Scholastic, 1985, pap. (0-590-43461-6)

(BL 80:301; CC:574; HB 59:713; SLJ Nov 1983 p. 84)

YOUNG, Miriam. *The Witch Mobile.* See Chapter 10, Witchcraft and Sorcery Fantasy.

10
Witchcraft and Sorcery Fantasy

These books are tales of magic as practiced by witches and wizards, enchanters and enchantresses, sorceresses, sorcerers, and magicians. Most have a lighthearted quality that distinguishes them from the darker, more terrifying tales of the occult called horror fiction. Horror fiction has not been included in this book.

AAMODT, Donald. *A Name to Conjure With.* See Chapter 5C, Travel to Other Worlds.

AIKEN, Joan (Delano). *The Faithless Lollybird.* See Chapter 3, Fantasy Collections.

AIKEN, Joan (Delano). *The Kingdom and the Cave.* See Chapter 5A, Alternate Worlds or Histories.

AIKEN, Joan (Delano). *Smoke from Cromwell's Time and Other Stories.* See Chapter 3, Fantasy Collections.

AINSWORTH (Gilbert), Ruth (Gallard). *The Bear Who Liked Hugging People and Other Stories.* See Chapter 3, Fantasy Collections.

ALCOCK, Vivien (Dolores). *The Haunting of Cassie Palmer.* See Chapter 4, Ghost Fantasy.

ALEXANDER, Lloyd (Chudley). *The Cat Who Wished to Be a Man.* See Chapter 2, Animal Fantasy.

ALEXANDER, Lloyd (Chudley). *The Marvelous Misadventures of Sebastian.* See Chapter 5A, Alternate Worlds or Histories.

2963 ALEXANDER, Lloyd (Chudley). *The Wizard in the Tree.* Gr. 4–6.

✓ A firm belief in magic helps Mallory, an overworked, orphaned servant girl, to release a crotchety old wizard from imprisonment in an oak tree.

Illus. by Laszlo Kubinyi, Dutton, 1974, 144 pp. (0-525-43128-4); Dell, 1981, pap. (0-440-49556-3)

(BBC:197; BBJ:68; BL 71:813; CCBB 28:173; Ch&Bks:254; HB 51:377; KR 43:451; SLJ May 1975 pp. 34, 45; Suth 2:9)

2964 AMOSS, Berthe. *Lost Magic.* **Gr. 5–9.**

Ceridwen, a herbal healer, is accused of witchcraft after she fails to save the life of Lord Robert's wife.

Hyperion, 1993, 184 pp. (1-56282573-9)

(BL 90:514; HBG 5:72; KR 61:1139; SLJ Sept 1993 p. 248)

ANDERSEN, Hans Christian. *The Snow Queen.* See Chapter 1, Allegorical Fantasy and Literary Fairy Tales.

ANTHONY, Piers (pseud. of Piers A. D. Jacob). *A Spell for Chameleon.* See Chapter 5A, Alternate Worlds or Histories.

ANTHONY, Piers, and KORNWISE, Robert Ian. *Through the Ice.* See Chapter 5C, Travel to Other Worlds.

2965 ASPRIN, Robert L(ynn). *Hit or Myth* **(Myth Adventure series, book 4). Gr. 10 up.**

In this, the fourth book of Asprin's pun-filled Myth Adventure series, Skeeve, a bumbling apprentice wizard, is left without the aid of his demon-mentor Aahz to fight off numerous magical enemies. The other books in the series are: *Another Fine Myth* (1978), *Myth Conceptions* (1980), *Myth Directions* (1982, 1986), *Myth-ing Persons* (1984), *Little Myth Marker* (1985, 1987), *M.Y.T.H. Inc. Link* (1986), and *Myth-Nomers and Im-Perfections* (1987).

Ed. by Kay Reynolds, Donning, 1983, 172 pp., LB(0-89865-339-8); Ace, 1986, pap. (0-441-33851-8)

(BL 80:715; LJ 108:2174)

AVI. *Bright Shadow.* See Chapter 5A, Alternate Worlds or Histories.

BACON, Peggy. *The Magic Touch.* See Chapter 7, Magic Adventure Fantasy.

BALL, Brian. *The Quest for Queenie.* See Chapter 5C, Travel to Other Worlds.

BALL, Margaret. *Changeweaver.* See Chapter 5A, Alternate Worlds or Histories.

BARBER, Antonia. *The Enchanter's Daughter.* See Chapter 1, Allegorical Fantasy and Literary Fairy Tales.

BARKER, Clive. *The Thief of Always: A Fable.* See Chapter 5C, Travel to Other Worlds.

2966 BATO, Joseph. *The Sorcerer.* **Gr. 7–10.**

Cro-Magnon Ao'h's sorcery brings him power, but eventually causes his downfall.

Ed. by Katherine Donnelly, illus. by the author, McKay, 1976, 171 pp., o.p.

(BL 73:890, 893; HB 53:165; KR 44:1174; SLJ Nov 1976 p. 65)

2967 BATTLES, Edith. *The Witch in Room 6.* **Gr. 4–6.**

Sean triumphs over his fifth-grade rival with the help of the new girl, an apprentice witch named Cheryl Suzanne.

Harper, 1987, 151 pp., o.p.

(CCBB 40:203; KR 55:854; SLJ June–July 1987 p. 92; VOYA 10:118)

BAUDINO, Gael. *Strands of Starlight.* See Chapter 5A, Alternate Worlds or Histories.

BAUM, L(yman) Frank. *The Wizard of Oz.* See Chapter 5C, Travel to Other Worlds.

2968 BAXTER, Caroline. *The Stolen Telesm.* **Gr. 4–6 (Orig. British pub. 1975.)**

David and Lucy escape on a winged colt from the evil magic of Marada the sorceress.

Lippincott, 1976, 192 pp., o.p.

(KR 44:794; SLJ Oct 1976 p. 104; TLS 1975 p. 1457)

2969 BAXTER, Lorna. *The Eggchild.* **Gr. 5–7. (Orig. British pub. 1978.)**

Two children with magic powers try to rescue a baby able to transform itself into a glowing egg, from Doppel the Enchanter.

Dutton, 1979, 157 pp., o.p.

(BL 76:663; CCBB 33:126; KR 47:1325; SLJ Jan 1980 p. 65; TLS 1978 p. 1089)

2970 BEACHCROFT, Nina. *Well Met by Witchlight.* **Gr. 4–6. (Orig. British pub. 1972.)**

Three children help a good witch fight the evil power of Mrs. Black.

Atheneum, 1973, 137 pp., o.p.

(BL 70:595; KR 41:1199; LJ 99:205)

BEAGLE, Peter S(oyer). *The Folk of the Air.* See Chapter 5B, Myth Fantasy.

BEAGLE, Peter S(oyer). *The Innkeeper's Song.* See Chapter 5A, Alternative Worlds or Histories.

2971 BEDARD, Michael. *A Darker Magic.* **Gr. 6–9. (Orig. Canadian pub. 1987.)**

✓ Emily and her elderly teacher, Miss Potts, attempt to thwart the evil plans of Professor Mephisto, whose magic show was responsible for the death of one of Miss Potts's friends, back in 1936. In the sequel, *Painted Devil* (1994), the sinister magician reappears twenty-eight years later and tries to ensnare Emily's niece, Alice, in his evil plans.

Macmillan, 1987, 208 pp. (0-689-31342-X); Avon, 1989, pap. (0-380-70611-3)

(BBJ:68; BL 84:59; CCBB 41:2; KR 55:1235; SLJ Sept 1987 p. 177; VOYA 10:242)

2972 BEDARD, Michael. *Redwork.* **Gr. 6–10. (Orig. Canadian pub. 1990.)**

All the neighborhood children are frightened of Cass's landlord, Mr. Magus, and even Cass thinks his vivid dreams of trench warfare, pain, and fear are somehow connected to the strange old man. Governor General's Literary Award for Children's Literature, 1990. Canadian Library Association Best Book of the Year for Children, 1991.

Macmillan, 1990, 261 pp. (0-689-31622-4); Avon, 1992, pap. (0-380-71612-7)

(BL 87:734; HBG 2[July–Dec 1990]:87; KR 58:1528; SLJ Oct 1990 p. 139; VOYA 13:1293, 16:34)

BEHN, Harry. *The Faraway Lurs.* See Chapter 1, Allegorical Fantasy and Literary Fairy Tales.

BELLAIRS, John. *The Dark Secret of Weatherend.* See Chapter 7, Magic Adventure Fantasy.

2973   **BELLAIRS, John.** *The Face in the Frost.* **Gr. 8 up.**

Two bumbling wizards search for the powerful being causing eerie dreams, terrifying gray shadows, and frost faces on the windows of their land.

Illus. by Marilyn Fitschen, Macmillan, 1969, o.p., pap., 1991, 224 pp. (0-02-016581-1)

(BBS:52; BL 65:1209; KR 36:1395; LJ 94:776; Tymn:51)

BELLAIRS, John. *The House with a Clock in Its Walls.* See Chapter 4, Ghost Fantasy.

BENARY-ISBERT, Margot. *The Wicked Enchantment.* See Chapter 1, Allegorical Fantasy and Literary Fairy Tales.

2974   **BENNETT, Anna Elizabeth.** *Little Witch.* **Gr. 3–5.**

✓   Even though she can perform all kinds of exciting and unusual feats, Miniken does not want to be a witch. She wants to go to school like a real little girl.

Illus. by Helen Stone, Harper, 1953, o.p., 1981, pap., 128 pp. (0-06-440119-7)

(BBC:199; CC:450; CCBB 7:51; HB 29:356; LJ 78:1855)

BERESFORD, Elizabeth. *Travelling Magic.* See Chapter 8, Time Travel Fantasy.

BERRY, James R. *The Magicians of Erianne.* See Chapter 5B, Myth Fantasy.

Beware! Beware! Chilling Tales. **Ed. by Jean Richardson.** See Chapter 4, Ghost Fantasy.

BLACKWOOD, Gary L. *Beyond the Door.* See Chapter 5C, Travel to Other Worlds.

BLAYLOCK, James P(aul). *The Paper Grail.* See Chapter 5B, Myth Fantasy.

BOMANS, Godfried (Jan Arnold). *The Wily Witch and All the Other Fairy Tales and Fables.* See Chapter 3, Fantasy Collections.

BOSTON, L(ucy) M(aria Wood). *An Enemy at Green Knowe.* See discussion under *The Children of Green Knowe* in Chapter 4, Ghost Fantasy.

BOYER, Elizabeth H. *The Troll's Grindstone.* See Chapter 5C, Travel to Other Worlds.

2975   **BRADBURY, Ray (Douglas).** *Something Wicked This Way Comes.* **Gr. 8 up.**

✓   Two boys attending a carnival freak show become the targets of an evil magician who imprisons them in the Wax Museum.

Simon, 1962, 317 pp., o.p.; Bantam, 1983, pap. (0-553-25774-9); Knopf, 1983 (0-394-53041-1)

(BBS:53; BL 59:163; JHC:336; Kies:18; SHC:670; TLS 1963 p. 189)

BRADLEY, Marion Zimmer. *The Mists of Avalon.* See Chapter 5B, Myth Fantasy.

2976   **BRADLEY, Marion Zimmer, and McINTYRE, Vonda.** *Lythande.* **Gr. 10 up.**

Six tales about the journeys of the magician Lythande.

DAW, 1986, pap., 240 pp. (0-88677-291-5)

(BL 82:1667; VOYA 9:290)

BRADLEY, Marion Zimmer, MAY, Julian, and NORTON, André. *Black Trillium.* See Chapter 5A, Alternate Worlds or Histories.

2977 BRENNAN, Herbie. *Emily and the Werewolf.* **Gr. 3–6. (Orig. British pub. 1993.)**

Emily tries to learn enough about magic from her grandmother, a witch, to enable her to confront an angry werewolf.

Illus. by David Pace, Macmillan, 1993, 96 pp. (0-689-50593-0)

(HBG 5:73; KR 61:1387; SLJ Nov 1993 p. 76)

BRIGGS, K(atherine) M(ary). *Hobberdy Dick.* See Chapter 5B, Myth Fantasy.

BRIGGS, K(atherine) M(ary). *Kate Crackernuts.* See Chapter 5B, Myth Fantasy.

BRIN, David. *The Practice Effect.* See Chapter 5C, Travel to Other Worlds.

2978 BRITTAIN, Bill (William). *The Devil's Donkey* **(Coven Tree Saga, book 1). Gr.**
✓ **3–6.**

Turned into a donkey by Old Magda for stealing wood from the witches' tree, Dan'l must confront the devil himself to be freed of the curse. In *The Wish Giver: Three Tales of Coven Tree* (1983) a stranger offers to grant the wishes of four young people from Coven Tree. John Newbery Medal Honor Book, 1984. In *Doctor Dredd's Wagon of Wonders* (1987) orphaned Calvin escapes from bondage to the mysterious rain-maker called Dr. Dredd in time to keep townspeople from trading away their souls. In *Professor Popkin's Prodigious Polish: A Tale of Coven Tree* (1990) Luther Gilpin, a farmer's son, dreams of becoming a salesman for a product that literally brings things to life.

Illus. by Andrew Glass, Harper, 1981, 128 pp., LB(0-06-020683-7), pap., 1982 (0-06-440129-4)

(BBC:199; BL 77:1097, 86:790; CC:354; HB 57:420; KR 49:503; SLJ Mar 1981 p. 141, May 1981 p. 23)

BROOKS, Terry. *Magic Kingdom for Sale—Sold!* See Chapter 6, Humorous Fantasy.

2979 BROWN, Mary. *The Unlikely Ones.* **Gr. 10 up.**

Seven human and animal companions, all under a witch's curse, set out to break their enchantment.

McGraw-Hill, 1986, o.p.; Baen, 1987, pap., 432 pp. (0-671-65361-X)

(BBS:54; BL 83:191, 217; KR 54:1223; LJ Oct 15, 1986 p. 114)

BRUST, Steven K. (Zoltan). *Taltos.* See Chapter 5A, Alternate Worlds or Histories.

BUCHWALD, Emilie. *Gildaen: The Heroic Adventures of a Most Unusual Rabbit.* See Chapter 1, Allegorical Fantasy and Literary Fairy Tales.

BUJOLD, Lois McMaster. *The Spirit Ring.* See Chapter 5A, Alternate Worlds or Histories.

2980 BURCH, Robert. *The Jolly Witch.* **Gr. 2–3.**

Cheerful Cluny uses witchcraft to change the lives of an old woman and her son.

Illus. by Leigh Grant, Dutton, 1975, 32 pp., o.p.

(BL 72:512; CCBB 29:92; SLJ Jan 1976 p. 35)

2981 BUTLER, Beverly. *Witch's Fire.* **Gr. 5–7.**
✓ Confined to a wheelchair since the automobile accident that killed her mother and sister,

thirteen-year-old Kirsty resents moving with her father's new family to a house previously owned by a witch.

Dutton, 1993, 135 pp. (0-525-65132-2)

(BL 89:2056; CCBB 47:40; HBG 5:73; KR 61:998; SLJ Sept 1993 p. 228; VOYA 16:306)

2982 BYFIELD, Barbara Ninde. *Andrew and the Alchemist.* **Gr. 4–6.**

✓ Andrew's "easy" job as apprentice to an alchemist goes wrong after he is accused of misusing his power to steal the king's treasure.

Illus. by Deanne Hollinger, Doubleday, 1976, 129 pp., o.p.

(BL 73:128; CCBB 30:172; HB 53:312; KR 44:1264; SLJ Jan 1977 p. 88; Suth 2:71)

CALHOUN, Mary (pseud. of Mary Huiskamp Wilkins). *Magic in the Alley.* See Chapter 7, Magic Adventure Fantasy.

2983 CALLANDER, Don. *Aquamancer* **(Pyromancer series, book 2). Gr. 10 up.**

Journeyman fire adept Douglas Brightglade and his sea otter companion, Marbleheart, face goblins and black magic while he tries to prove himself worthy of becoming a master magician. This is the sequel to *Pyromancer* (1992) and is followed by *Geomancer* (1994).

Berkley, 1993, pap., 304 pp. (0-441-02816-0)

(BL 89:718, 722; VOYA 16:36)

CARD, Orson Scott. *Hart's Hope.* See Chapter 5A, Alternate Worlds or Histories.

CARD, Orson Scott. *Seventh Son.* See Chapter 5A, Alternate Worlds or Histories.

CARLYON, Richard. *The Dark Lord of Pengersick.* See Chapter 5A, Alternate Worlds or Histories.

CARPENTER, Christopher. *The Twilight Realm.* See Chapter 5C, Travel to Other Worlds.

2984 CARRIS, Joan Davenport. *Witch-Cat.* **Gr. 4–6.**

Rosetta the witch-cat has trouble making her new mistress understand that she's a witch.

Illus. by Beth Peck, Harper, 1984, 160 pp., o.p.

(BL 80:1236; SLJ Sept 1984 p. 114)

Catfantastic: Nine Lives and Fifteen Tales. **Ed. by André Norton and Martin H. Greenberg.** See Chapter 3, Fantasy Collections.

2985 *A Cavalcade of Magicians.* Ed. by Roger (Gilbert) Lancelyn Green. (British
✓ **title:** *A Book of Magicians,* **1973). Gr. 5–7.**

Legends, folktales, and original tales about magic and magicians, including "The Sorcerer's Apprentice" and the story of Merlin.

Illus. by Victor Ambrus, Walck, 1973, 274 pp., o.p.

(BL 70:291; HB 49:461; KR 41:645; LJ 98:2664; TLS 1973 p. 1115)

CAYLUS, Anne Claude Philippe, Comte de. *Heart of Ice.* See Chapter 1, Allegorical Fantasy and Literary Fairy Tales.

CHANT, Joy (pseud. of Eileen Joyce Rutter). *Red Moon and Black Mountain: The End of the House of Kendreth.* See Chapter 5C, Travel to Other Worlds.

CHAPMAN, Vera. *The Green Knight.* See Chapter 5B, Myth Fantasy.

2986   **CHARNAS, Suzy McKee.** *The Bronze King* **(Sorcery Hall trilogy, book 1). Gr. 5–8.**

An elderly man with magical powers needs Tina and Joel's help to defeat a monster hiding in the depths of Manhattan's subway system. The sequels are *The Silver Glove* (Bantam, 1988) and *The Golden Thread* (Bantam, 1989).

Houghton, 1985, o.p.; Bantam, 1988, pap., 208 pp. (0-553-27104-0)

(BBJ:69; CCBB 39:82; Kies:31; KR 53:1087; SLJ Nov 1985 p. 94)

2987   **CHASE, Mary (Coyle).** *Mrs. McThing: A Play.* **Gr. 5 up.**

A witch punishes a wealthy woman who objected to her son's friendship with the witch's daughter.

Illus. by Madeleine Gekiere and Helen Sewell, Oxford, 1952, 141 pp., o.p.

(BL 49:101, 111; CCBB 6:37; HB 28:310, 418; LJ 77:1814)

CHERRYH, C. J. (pseud. of Carolyn Janice Cherry). *The Goblin Mirror.* See Chapter 5A, Alternate Worlds or Histories.

2988   **CHERRYH, C. J. (pseud. of Carolyn Janice Cherry).** *Rusalka* **(Rusalka trilogy, book 1). Gr. 10 up.**

Sasha and Pyetr try to convince a wizard to bring a Rusalka, the ghost of a murdered girl, back to life in this story steeped in Russian legends. The sequels are *Chernevog* (1990) and *Yvgenie* (1991).

Ballantine, 1989, 374 pp. (0-345-35953-4), 1990, pap. (0-345-36934-3)

(BBS:54; BL 86:2, 6, 906; KR 57:1205; LJ Sept 15, 1989 p. 138; VOYA 13:37)

CHESNUTT, Charles Waddell. *Conjure Tales.* See Chapter 3, Fantasy Collections.

CHETWIN, Grace. *Gom on Windy Mountain.* See Chapter 5A, Alternate Worlds or Histories.

2989   **CHEW, Ruth (Silver).** *No Such Thing as a Witch.* **Gr. 2–4. (Orig. pub. Scholastic, 1972, pap.)**

Fudge made by Nora and Tad's neighbor, Maggie, turns people into animals.

Illus. by the author, Hastings, 1980, 112 pp. (0-8038-5073-5)

(CCBB 33:168; SLJ May 1980 p. 52)

2990   **CHEW, Ruth (Silver).** *The Would-Be Witch.* **Gr. 3–5.**

Miniaturized by a magic cream, Robin and Andy take midnight flights and rescue their friend Zelda from a witches' coven.

Illus. by the author, Hastings, 1977, 112 pp., o.p.

(BBC:200; BL 74:745; SLJ Dec 1977 p. 43)

2991   **CLARK, Douglas W.** *Alchemy Unlimited.* **Gr. 10 up.**

Puns in both English and French abound in this humorous story set in an alternate fifteenth-century France about a sorcerer and a young would-be scholar who discover that foreign-financed water pollution is causing a plague.

Avon, 1990, pap., 310 pp. (0-380-75726-5)

(LJ Aug 1990 p. 147; VOYA 13:294)

CLAYTON, Jo. *Moongather.* See Chapter 5A, Alternate Worlds or Histories.

2992 **COLE, Joanna.** *Bony-Legs.* **Gr. 1–4.**

Sasha uses a magical mirror and comb to escape from Bony-Legs, the witch with the iron teeth, in this adaptation of a Russian Baba Yaga tale.

Illus. by Dirk Zimmer, Macmillan, 1984, 48 pp. (0-02-722970-X); Scholastic, 1986, pap. (0-590-40516-0)

(CCBB 37:123; HB 60:47; SLJ Dec 1983 p. 79)

2993 **COLE, Joanna.** *Doctor Change.* **Gr. K–4.**

✓ Young Tom learns the tricks of magical transformation in order to escape from his mysterious employer, Doctor Change.

Illus. by Donald Carrick, Morrow, 1986, 32 pp., LB(0-688-06136-2)

(BBC:200; BL 83:127; CCBB 40:46; HB 62:730; KR 54:934; SLJ Oct 86 p. 158)

2994 **COLUM, Padraic.** *The Boy Apprenticed to an Enchanter.* **Gr. 4–6. (Orig. pub. 1920.)**

Merlin the magician and a girl called Bird of Gold help Eean escape from a wicked enchanter.

Illus. by Edward Leight, Macmillan, 1966, 150 pp., o.p.

(BL 63:493; HB 42:708; LJ 92:333; Mahony 1:39; Tymn: 67)

COLUM, Padraic. *The Stone of Victory and Other Tales.* See Chapter 3, Fantasy Collections.

COOK, Glen. *Doomstalker.* See Chapter 2, Animal Fantasy.

COOK, Glen. *Tower of Fear.* See Chapter 5A, Alternate Worlds or Histories.

2995 **COOK, Hugh.** *The Wizards and the Warriors* **(Chronicles of an Age of Darkness, no. 1). Gr. 10 up. (Orig. pub. in New Zealand, 1986.)**

Miphon and the other members of the Confederation of Wizards form an uneasy alliance with their ancient enemies, the Warriors of Rovac, to battle a renegade sorcerer threatening to end the world. The sequels are *The Women and the Warlords* (1987) *The Wordsmiths and the Warguild* (1988), and *The Walrus and the Warwolf* (1993).

Dufour, 1987, 352 pp. (0-86140-244-8)

(BBS:54; BL 83:1252, 1273; LJ Apr 15, 1987 p. 102)

COOK, Rick. *Wizardry Compiled.* See Chapter 5C, Travel to Other Worlds.

COOKE, Catherine. *Mask of the Wizard.* See Chapter 5A, Alternate Worlds or Histories.

2996 **COOMBS, Patricia.** *Dorrie and the Blue Witch.* **Gr. 2–4.**

✓ Shrinking powder enables young Dorrie witch to capture the bad blue witch and win first prize for witch-catching. Other titles in this series are *Dorrie's Magic* (1962), *Dorrie's Play* (1965), *Dorrie and the Weather-Box* (1966), *Dorrie and the Witch Doctor* (1967), *Dorrie and the Wizard's Spell* (1968), *Dorrie and the Haunted House* (1970), *Dorrie and the Birthday Eggs* (1971), *Dorrie and the Goblin* (1972), *Dorrie and the Fortune Teller* (1973), *Dorrie and the Amazing Magic Elixir* (1974), *Dorrie and the Witch's Imp* (1975), *Dorrie and the Halloween Plot* (1976), *Dorrie and the Dreamyard Monsters* (1977), *Dorrie and the Screebit Ghost* (1979), *Dorrie and the Witchville Fair* (1980), *Dorrie and the Witches' Camp* (1983), *Dorrie and the Museum Case* (1986), *Dorrie and the Pin Witch* (1989), and *Dorrie and the Haunted Schoolhouse* (1992).

Illus. by the author, Lothrop, 1964, o.p.; Dell, 1980, pap., 48 pp. (0-440-42210-8)

(BL 61:217; CCBB 18:51; HB 40:488; KR 32:595; LJ 89:3458)

COOPER, Gale. *Unicorn Moon.* See Chapter 1, Allegorical Fantasy and Literary Fairy Tales.

COOPER, Louise. *The Sleep of Stone.* See Chapter 5A, Alternate Worlds or Histories.

2997 CORBETT, Scott. *The Great Custard Pie Panic.* **Gr. 2–4.**

Nick thwarts Dr. Merlin's diabolical plot to use Nick's dog's brain to create the smartest dog in the world. This is the sequel to *Dr. Merlin's Magic Shop* (1973) and is followed by *The Foolish Dinosaur Fiasco* (1978).

Illus. by Joseph Mathieu, Little, 1974, 47 pp., o.p.

(BL 70:1252; CCBB 28:26; KR 42:580)

2998 *The Crafters* **(The Crafters series, book 1). Ed. by Christopher Stasheff and Bill Fawcett. Gr. 10 up.**

Shared world stories concerning a family of chemists called the Crafters, set in various historical periods from Puritan Massachusetts to nineteenth-century Ireland, written by Katherine Kurtz, Morgan Llewelyn, Ru Emerson, and others. The sequel is *The Crafters, vol. 2: Blessings and Curses* (1992).

Ace, 1991, pap., 246 pp. (0-441-12130-6)

(BL 88:606, 610; Kliatt Apr 1992 p. 16; VOYA 14:380)

CROSS, Gilbert B. *A Witch Across Time.* See Chapter 4, Ghost Fantasy.

CURLEY, Daniel. *Billy Beg and the Bull.* See Chapter 5B, Myth Fantasy.

CURRY, Jane Louise. *The Sleepers.* See Chapter 5B, Myth Fantasy.

DAHL, Roald. *George's Marvelous Medicine.* See Chapter 7, Magic Adventure Fantasy.

2999 DAHL, Roald. *The Witches.* **Gr. 4–6. (Orig. British pub. 1983.)**

✓ A boy and his grandmother thwart the plans of England's witches to turn all children into mice. Whitbread Literary Award, Children's Book Category, 1983.

Illus. by Quentin Blake, Farrar, 1983, 202 pp. (0-374-38458-4); Puffin, 1985, 1989, pap. (0-14-034020-3)

(BBC:201; BL 80:567; CCBB 37:105; HB 60:194; KR 51:190; SLJ Jan 1984 p. 74)

DAWSON, Carley. *Mr. Wicker's Window.* See Chapter 8, Time Travel Fantasy.

3000 DE CHANCIE, John. *Castle Kidnapped* **(Castle series, book 3). Gr. 10 up.**

One by one, the wizards of Castle Perilous are being kidnapped by the Hosts of Hell, and those who are left use magic, a time machine, and a computer to save the universe in this science-fantasy. This is the sequel to *Castle Perilous* (1985) and *Castle for Rent* (1989) and is followed by *Castle War!* (1990), *Castle Murders* (1991), and *Castle Dreams* (1992).

Ace, 1989, pap., 208 pp. (0-441-09408-2)

(BL 86:265, 273; Kliatt Jan 1990 p. 18)

DE HAVEN, Tom. *Walker of Worlds.* See Chapter 5C, Travel to Other Worlds.

DE LINT, Charles. *Into the Green.* See Chapter 5A, Alternate Worlds or Histories.

3001 **DE LINT, Charles.** *The Little Country.* **Gr. 10 up.**

A rare magical book owned by folk musician Janey Little and her grandfather draws John Madden and his henchmen to their Cornish village, while inside the book, a witch transforms a girl named Jodi into a six-inch-high Small and imprisons her.

Morrow, 1991, 544 pp. (0-688-10366-9); Tor, 1993, pap. (0-8125-2248-6)

(BL 87:1011, 1049; KR 59:23; LJ Feb 15, 1991 p. 224)

DIAMOND, Donna, adapt. *Swan Lake.* See Chapter 1, Allegorical Fantasy and Literary Fairy Tales.

DICKINSON, Peter (pseud. of Malcolm de Brissac). *Merlin Dreams.* See Chapter 5B, Myth Fantasy.

DICKINSON, Peter (pseud. of Malcolm de Brissac). *The Weathermonger.* See Chapter 5A, Alternate Worlds or Histories.

DICKSON, Gordon R(upert). *The Last Dream.* See Chapter 3, Fantasy Collections.

3002 **DILLON, Barbara.** *Mrs. Tooey and the Terrible Toxic Tar.* **Gr. 3–6.**

While two witches battle over the fate of their town, Margo and Craig Saunders help destroy a bottle of Terrible Toxic Tar.

Harper, 1988, 96 pp. LB(0-397-32277-1)

(BBC:202; BL 84:1734; KR 56:759; SLJ Aug 1988 p. 92)

3003 **DILLON, Barbara.** *What's Happened to Harry?* **Gr. 3–5.**

A mischievous witch captures Harry on Halloween, changes him into a poodle, and takes over his real body.

Illus. by Chris Conover, Morrow, 1982, 125 pp., o.p.

(BL 78:1255; CCBB 36:7; HB 58:399; SLJ Aug 1982, p. 114)

3004 **DOUGLAS, Carole Nelson.** *Exiles of the Rynth* **(Irissa and Kendric trilogy, book 2). Gr. 10 up.**

Propelled through a magic gate into the Rynth, Irissa, the last of the Torloc sorceresses, is captured by the wizard Sofistron, and her lover, Kendric, joins a band of outlaws. This is the sequel to *Six of Swords* (1982) and is followed by *Keepers of Edanvant* (Tor, 1987), in which Irissa and Kendric return to Edanvant as a war is beginning between males and females. The latter book also begins a second trilogy about Irissa and Kendric, called Sword & Circlet. The other books in this newer trilogy are: *Heir of Rengarth* (1988) and *Seven of Swords* (1989).

Ballantine, 1984, pap., 193 pp. (0-345-30836-0)

(BL 80:1586, 1608, 86:904; LJ 109:1253)

3005 **DUANE, Diane (Elizabeth).** *The Door into Fire* **(The Epic Tales of the Five series, book 1). Gr. 10 up.**

Herewiss Hearn's son, a young sorcerer, has difficulty controlling the extra portion of Fire within him, until the Goddess helps him to better understand himself. The sequels are *The Door into Shadow* (Bluejay, 1984) and *The Door into Sunset* (1993).

Dell, 1979, 304 pp., o.p.; Tor, 1985, 288 pp., pap. (0-8125-3671-1)

(BL 75:1482; VOYA 2[Oct 1979]:58)

3006 **DUANE, Diane (Elizabeth).** *So You Want to Be a Wizard* **(The Wizard Sequence, book 1). Gr. 5–8.**

Two novice wizards, Nita and Kit, journey into a frightening alternate Manhattan full of evil machines and terrified people, where they attempt to fight the powers of darkness who are destroying the world. The sequels are *Deep Wizardry* (1985, 1992) and *High Wizardry* (1990). *Dragons and Dreams* (Harper, 1986; see Chapter 7, Magic Adventure Fantasy) contains a related story.

Delacorte, 1983, 288 pp. (0-385-29305-4); Dell, 1992, pap., 226 pp. (0-440-40638-2)

(BBC:202; BBJ:70; CCBB 37:106; HB 59:716; JHC:366; Kliatt 18[Fall 1984]:26; SLJ Jan 1984 p. 74; VOYA 6:342)

DUNLOP, Eileen (Rhona). *The Valley of Deer.* See Chapter 8, Time Travel Fantasy.

3007 **DUNSANY, Lord (pseud. of Edward John Morton Drax Plunkett).** *The Charwoman's Shadow.* **Gr. 10 up.**

Having sold his shadow to the Magician in exchange for the magical secrets needed to create a dowry and a love potion for his sister, Ramon attempts to use his new-found knowledge to regain his shadow and that of the Magician's kindly charwoman.

Putnam, 1926, 294 pp., o.p.

(BL 23:38; TLS 1926 p. 262; Tymn:79)

ECKERT, Allan W. *The Dark Green Tunnel.* See Chapter 5C, Travel to Other Worlds.

3008 **EDDINGS, David.** *Queen of Sorcery* **(Belgariad Saga, book 2). Gr. 10 up.**

A Sorcerer, his daughter, and a young wizard struggle to keep the Orb of Aldur from being used to revive an evil god. This book is preceded by *Pawn of Prophecy* (1982, 1984), and followed by *Magician's Gambit* (1983, 1984), *Castle of Wizardry* (1984), and *Enchanter's End Game* (1984). This series is related to the Malloreon series, which begins with *Guardians of the West* (1987; see Chapter 5A, Alternate Worlds or Histories).

Ballantine, 1982, 1986, pap., 327 pp. (0-345-33565-1)

(BL 79:714, 86:904; Kliatt Winter 1983 p. 17; SLJ Jan 1983 p. 90)

3009 **EDGERTON, Teresa.** *Child of Saturn* **(Green Lion trilogy, vol. 1). Gr. 10 up.**

Young apprentice wizard Teleri and the queen's knight, Ceilyn, join forces against the king's sister, Princess Diaspad, who plans to make her own son the heir to the throne. The sequels are *The Moon in Hiding* (1989) and *The Work of the Sun* (1990).

Ace, 1989, pap., 288 pp (0-441-10401-0)

(BL 85:1095, 1129; VOYA 12:164)

3010 **EDGERTON, Teresa.** *Goblin Moon.* **Gr. 10 up.**

A coffin containing a sorcerer and all his magical books comes into the possession of a group of river scavengers in this tale of magic, intrigue, trolls in disguise, goblins, fairies, and romance. The sequel is *The Gnome's Engine* (1991).

Ace, 1991, pap., 293 pp., o.p.

(BL 87:1011; VOYA 14:41, 15:10)

3011 **EDMONDSON, Madeline.** *Anna Witch.* **Gr. 2–4.**

Angry at her mother's disappointment in her daughter's lack of magical prowess, Anna surprises herself by turning her mother into a frog.

Illus. by William Pène Du Bois, Doubleday, 1982, 88 pp., o.p.

(BL 79:608; CCBB 36:24; SLJ Dec 1982 p. 64)

3012 EDMONDSON, Madeline. *The Witch's Egg.* **Gr. 2–4.**

A crabby witch named Agatha who is living in an abandoned eagle's nest becomes the foster mother of a baby bird.

Illus. by Kay Chorao, Seabury, 1974, 47 pp., o.p.

(BL 70:939; KR 42:182; LJ 99:1465)

3013 EDWARDS, Dorothy (Brown). *The Witches and the Grinnygog.* **Gr. 5–7. (Orig. British pub. 1981.)**

Seven children who uncover the history of the last three witches to live in their village bring the old magic to life in time for the Midsummer's Eve festival.

Faber, 1983, 176 pp., o.p.

(BL 79:1400; CCBB 37:47; KR 51:4; SLJ Sept 1983 p. 132)

EGAN, Doris. *The Gate of Ivory.* See Chapter 5A, Alternate Worlds or Histories.

EISENSTEIN, Phyllis. *Sorcerer's Son.* See Chapter 5A, Alternate Worlds or Histories.

ELGIN, Suzette Haden. *Twelve Fair Kingdoms.* See Chapter 5A, Alternate Worlds or Histories.

3014 EMBRY, Margaret (Jacob). *The Blue-Nosed Witch.* **Gr. 2–4.**

✓ On her way to the witches' Halloween flight meeting, a young witch named Blanche joins a group of trick-or-treating children.

Illus. by Carl Rose, Holiday, 1956, 45 pp., o.p.; Bantam, 1984, pap. (0-553-15435-4)

(BL 53:154; CCBB 11:23; HB 32:366, 63:495; KR 24:514; LJ 81:2720)

ENDE, Michael. *The Night of Wishes, or The Satanarcheolidealcohellish Notion Potion.* See Chapter 6, Humorous Fantasy.

ERWIN, Betty K. *Aggie, Maggie and Tish.* See Chapter 7, Magic Adventure Fantasy.

3015 ESTES, Eleanor (Ruth Rosenfeld). *The Witch Family.* **Gr. 3–5.**

✓ Two girls drawing witches are amazed when their drawings come to life. Amy has another magic adventure in *The Curious Adventures of Jimmy McGee* (1987).

Illus. by Edward Ardizzone, Harcourt, 1960, 1990, pap., 223 pp. (0 15 298572 7); Peter Smith, 1992 (0-8446-6504-5)

(BBC:203; BL 57:329; CC:483; CCBB 14:57; Ch&Bks:285; HB 36:395; KR 28:817; LJ 85:4558; TLS 1962 p. 393)

FARTHING, Alison. *The Mystical Beast.* See Chapter 5C, Travel to Other Worlds.

FEIST, Raymond E. *Silverthorn.* See Chapter 5A, Alternate Worlds or Histories.

3016 FLEISCHMAN, Paul (Taylor). *The Half-a-Moon Inn.* **Gr. 4–6.**

✓ Sinister Miss Grackle, thieving innkeeper and dream reader, holds a mute boy named Aaron prisoner after he wanders away from home in search of his mother. Golden Kite Award Honor Book, 1980.

Illus. by Kathy Jacobi, Harper, 1980, 96 pp., LB(0-06-021918-1), pap., 1991 (0-06-440364-5)

(BBJ:70; BL 76:1531; CC:485; HB 56:294; KR 48:513; SLJ Oct 1980 p. 145)

FLORA, James (Royer). *Grandpa's Ghost Stories.* See Chapter 4, Ghost Fantasy.

3017   **FLORA, James (Royer).** *Wanda and the Bumbly Wizard.* **Gr. 2–4.**

An inept wizard and an orphaned girl named Wanda tame a giant and save the queen's castle.

Illus. by the author, Atheneum, 1980, 32 pp., o.p.

(BL 76:1056; KR 48:511; SLJ Mar 1980 p. 120)

FREEMAN, Barbara C(onstance). *Broom-Adelaide.* See Chapter 1, Allegorical Fantasy and Literary Fairy Tales.

3018   **FRIESNER, Esther M.** *Majyk by Accident.* **Gr. 8–12.**

Kendar Gangle, an accident-prone student wizard, needs the help of his wisecracking feline familiar, Scandal, to handle his newly acquired majyk.

Ace, 1993, pap., 288 pp. (0-441-51376-X)

(BL 89:1949, 1953; Kliatt Jan 1994 p. 16; VOYA 16:309)

FRIESNER, Esther M. *Yesterday We Saw Mermaids.* See Chapter 5B, Myth Fantasy.

3019   **FROMAN, Elizabeth Hult.** *Eba, the Absent-Minded Witch.* **Gr. 3–5.**

Eba the witch is so absent-minded that she has forgotten how to fly.

Illus. by Dorothy Maas, World, 1965, 64 pp., o.p.

(CCBB 20:24; HB 41:491; KR 33:824; LJ 90:5514; TLS 1968 p. 256)

3020   **FURLONG, Monica (Navis).** *Wise Child.* **Gr. 6–8. (Orig. British pub. 1987.)**

✓   Wise Child, a headstrong young orphan, is taken in by Juniper, a mysterious healer, who teaches the girl the arts of witchcraft. Carnegie Medal Commended Book, 1987. In the prequel, *Juniper* (1991; orig. British pub. 1990) a girl named Juniper leaves her comfortable castle life to study herb-lore and spell-casting with a harsh mentor named Euny.

Knopf, 1987, 228 pp., LB(0-394-99105-2), pap., 1989 (0-394-82598-5)

(BL 84:632, 1276, 88:1768; CCBB 41:116; Ch&Bks:286; HB 64:206; Kies:61; KR 55:1461; SLJ Sept 1987 p. 195; Suth 4:128; TLS 1987 p. 964)

3021   **GABHART, Ann.** *The Gifting.* **Gr. 6–8.**

An old woman passes on her healing powers to thirteen-year-old Ginny in this otherwise realistic family story.

Simon & Schuster, 1987, pap., 155 pp. (0-373-98008-6)

(BBJ:70; BL 84:714; VOYA 10 234)

3022   **GARD, Joyce (pseud. of Joyce Reeves).** *The Mermaid's Daughter.* **Gr. 7–9.**

Astria, High Priestess of a mystical cult of woman worshippers, travels from the Scilly Islands to Britain to defeat a Roman plot to destroy her cult.

Holt, 1969, 319 pp., o.p.

(BL 66:564; CCBB 23:176; HB 46:166; LJ 95:1202; Suth:139; TLS 1969 p. 690)

3023   **GARDNER, Craig Shaw.** *A Disagreement with Death* **(Ballad of Wuntvor trilogy, book 3). Gr. 7–12. (Orig. Britsh pub. 1989.)**

Death has kidnapped the wizard Ebenezum, causing his apprentice, Wuntvor, to set out with a witch, three demons, a brownie, a dragon, a unicorn, a giant, and seven dwarves to save his master in this humorous conclusion to the trilogy. The preceding volumes are *A Difficulty with Dwarves* (1989) and *An Excess of Enchantment* (1989).

Ace, 1989, pap. (0-441-14924-3)

(BBS:57; VOYA 12:222)

GARNER, Alan. *The Weirdstone of Brisingamen.* See Chapter 5B, Myth Fantasy.

3024   GILLILAND, Alexis A(rnaldus). *Wizenbeak.* **Gr. 10 up.**

Wizard Wizenbeak, sent into the outlands to establish a new settlement, is asked by the Witch-Queen Shaia to protect her two children from their royal half-brother, and to help them take control of the throne of Cymdulock. The sequels are *The Shadow Shaia* (1987) and *Lord of the Troll-Bats* (1992).

Bluejay, 1986, 288 pp., o.p.

(BL 82:1361, 1388; KR 54:587; VOYA 9:237)

GILLULY, Sheila. *Greenbriar Queen.* See Chapter 5A, Alternate Worlds or Histories.

GILMAN, Dorothy. *The Maze in the Heart of the Castle.* See Chapter 5C, Travel to Other Worlds.

3025   GILMORE, Kate. *Enter Three Witches.* **Gr. 6–10.**
✓✓   Sixteen-year-old Bren has a problem: how to keep his new girl friend from discovering that his mother and grandmother are practicing witches.

Houghton, 1990, 210 pp. (0-395-50213-6); Scholastic, 1992, pap. (0-590-44494-8)

(BBJ:70; BL 86:1430, 1446, 87:459, 1476; CCBB 43:159; HBG 1[Jan–June 1990]:255; JHC 1991 Suppl. p. 72; KR 58:341; SLJ Apr 1990 p. 139; Suth 4:140; VOYA 13:29)

GLOSS, Molly. *Outside the Gates.* See Chapter 5A, Alternate Worlds or Histories.

3026   GOLDSTEIN, Lisa. *The Red Magician.* **Gr. 10 up.**
✓   Young Kicsi describes the battle between a wonder-working rabbi and a traveling magician who fortells the Holocaust, in this tale set in a small Hungarian Jewish village. American Book Award, Original Paperback Category, 1983.

Pocket, 1982, pap., 1983, 156 pp., o.p.; Tor, 1993, 192 pp. (0-312-85462-5)

(BL 78:1004, 1014; Kies:68; VOYA 6:342, 17:19)

GORDON, John (William). *The Edge of the World.* See Chapter 5C, Travel to Other Worlds.

GORDON, John (William). *The Giant Under the Snow.* See Chapter 5B, Myth Fantasy.

GOUDGE, Elizabeth (de Beauchamp). *Linnets and Valerians.* See Chapter 7, Magic Adventure Fantasy.

GRAY, Nicholas Stuart. *Mainly in Moonlight: Ten Stories of Sorcery and the Supernatural.* See Chapter 3, Fantasy Collections.

GREEN, Kathleen. *Philip and the Pooka and Other Irish Fairy Tales.* See Chapter 3, Fantasy Collections.

GREEN, Phyllis. *Eating Ice Cream with a Werewolf.* See Chapter 7, Magic Adventure Fantasy.

3027   GREGORY, Philippa. *The Wise Woman.* **Gr. 10 up. (Orig. British pub. 1992.)**

Orphaned Alys, trained in the arts of healing and magic by a healer and witch named Morach, tries to hide in a convent to avoid persecution in sixteenth-century England.

Pocket, 1993, 438 pp. (0-671-79274-1)

(BL 90:195; LJ Oct 15, 1993 p. 87)

3028   GRIPE, Maria (Kristina). *The Glassblower's Children.* **5–7. (Orig. Swedish pub.**
✓ **1964.)**

Klaus and Klara, kidnapped and imprisoned by the Lord of All Wishes Town, lose all hope of rescue until a sorceress named Flutter Mildweather arrives to help them.

Trans. by Sheila LaFarge, illus. by Harald Gripe, Delacorte, 1973, 170 pp., o.p.

(BL 70:170; CCBB 27:9; Ch&Bks:286; HB 62:756; KR 41:515, 1350; LJ 98:2194; Suth 2:192; TLS 1975 p. 365)

3029   HAHN, Mary Downing. *The Time of the Witch.* **Gr. 5–7.**
✓ Laura convinces an old woman with witch powers to cast a spell that will reunite her parents, but the spell goes wrong and makes Laura's younger brother very ill.

Houghton, 1982, 160 pp. (0-89919-115-0); Avon, 1991, pap. (0-380-71116-8)

(BBC:204; BL 79:311; HB 59:44; Kies:74; SLJ Nov 1982 p. 84)

3030   HALDANE, J(ohn) B(urdon) S(anderson). *My Friend Mr. Leakey.* **Gr. 3–5. (Orig. British pub. 1937.)**

A collection of eerie tales, many of which concern a magician named Mr. Leakey.

Illus. by L. H. Rosoman, Harper, 1938, 179 pp., o.p.

(HB 14:382)

HALDEMAN, Linda (Wilson). *The Lastborn of Elvinwood.* See Chapter 5B, Myth Fantasy.

3031   HALE, F. J. *Ogre Castle* **(After the Spell Wars trilogy, book 1). Gr. 10 up.**

An itinerant wizard hired to exorcise some ghostly spells from a castle ends up pursuing a horrible ogre who has kidnapped a princess. The sequel is *In the Sea Nymph's Lair* (1982, 1989).

Crown, 1988, pap., 224 pp., o.p.

(BBS:58; BL 85:42, 68; LJ Sept 15, 1988 p. 96)

3032   HAMBLY, Barbara. *Dragonsbane.* **Gr. 10 up.**
✓✓ Mage Jenny Waynest unites her powers with those of the Black Dragon that her lover, John Aversin, has pledged to destroy, in order to defeat an evil sorceress threatening the kingdom.

Ballantine, 1987, pap., 352 pp. (0-345-34939-3)

(BBS:58; BL 82:851, 860, 83:777, 1118, 86:906; LJ Feb 15, 1986 p. 196, SLJ Sept 1986 p. 152; VOYA 9:162, 10:21)

HAMBLY, Barbara. *The Ladies of Mandrigyn.* See Chapter 5A, Alternate Worlds or Histories.

HAMBLY, Barbara. *The Silent Tower.* See Chapter 5C, Travel to Other Worlds.

HAMLETT, Christina. *The Enchanter.* See Chapter 5B, Myth Fantasy.

HANSEN, Ron. *The Shadowmaker.* See Chapter 7, Magic Adventure Fantasy.

3033 HARDY, Lyndon. *Secret of the Sixth Magic.* **(The Principles of Magic, book 2). Gr. 10 up.**

A bumbling apprentice magician, attempting to master the five magics that govern his world, stumbles upon a demonic sixth magic controlled by the evil Melazar. This is the sequel to *Master of the Five Magics* (1980).

Ballantine, 1986, pap., 384 pp. (0-345-34500-2)

(BL 81:25, 58; LJ 109:1776; SLJ Jan 1985 p. 92)

3034 HARRIS, Deborah Turner. *The Burning Stone* **(Mages of Garillon, book 1). Gr. 10 up.**
✓

Young Carodoc Penlluathe seeks revenge against Borthen Berigeld, the man responsible for expelling the young mage from his order. The sequels are *The Gauntlet of Malice* (1988), and *Spiral of Fire* (1989).

Tor, 1987, pap., 307 pp., o.p.

(BL 83:1097, 1116; Kliatt 21[Spring 1987]:22; SLJ Sept 1987 p. 204; VOYA 10:90; 11:12)

3035 HAYES, Sarah. *Crumbling Castle.* **Gr. 2–5. (Orig. British pub. 1989.)**

Three stories describing how the newest residents of Crumbling Castle—a wizard named Zeb and a talking crow named Jason—learn to live with the ghost, the baby dragon, the mice, the toads, and the beetles already in residence.

Illus. by Helen Craig, Candlewick, 1992, 76 pp. (0-56402-108-4)

(BL 89:737; HBG 4[Spring 1993]:57; KR 60:989; SLJ Oct 1992 p. 88)

3036 *Hecate's Cauldron.* Ed. by Susan M. Shwartz. Gr. 10 up.

An anthology of fantasy stories based on European, African, and Japanese tales of witchcraft, written by Katherine Kurtz, C. J. Cherryh, Tanith Lee, and André Norton, among others.

DAW, 1982, pap., 256 pp., o.p.

(BL 78:1299, 1307; Kliatt 16[Spring 1982]:29; VOYA 5[Aug 1982]:39)

3037 HENDRY, Frances Mary. *Quest for a Maid.* **Gr. 6–9. (Orig. British pub. 1988.)**
✓

Meg, a thirteenth-century ship-builder's daughter, accompanies an eight-year-old Norwegian princess on a voyage to Scotland to marry Prince Edward, but the ship is wrecked in a storm caused by Meg's sorceress older sister, Inge, in this historical novel with just a touch of the supernatural.

Farrar, 1990, 273 pp., o.p., 1992, pap. (0-374-46155-4)

(BL 86:2083, 2089, 87:1229, 1476, 1488; CCBB 44:9; HB 66:601; HBG 2[July-Dec 1990]:83; KR 58:875; JHC 1991 Suppl p. 73; SLJ Dec 1990 p. 121; Suth 4:173; VOYA 13:218)

HENRY, Maeve. *The Witch King.* See Chapter 5A, Alternate Worlds or Histories.

HEWETT, Anita. *The Bull beneath the Walnut Tree and Other Stories.* See Chapter 3, Fantasy Collections.

HILL, Douglas. *Blade of the Poisoner.* See Chapter 5A, Alternate Worlds or Histories.

HILL, Elizabeth Starr. *Ever-After Island.* See Chapter 7, Magic Adventure Fantasy.

HOFFMANN, Eleanor. *Mischief in Fez.* See Chapter 7, Magic Adventure Fantasy.

3038 **HOLMAN (Valen), Felice.** *The Witch on the Corner.* **Gr. 3–5.**

✓ Miss Pinchon tries to fly on a broomstick, but realizes that her magic is meant for gardening.

Illus. by Arnold Lobel, Norton, 1966, 88 pp., o.p.

(CCBB 20:108; KR 34:1101; LJ 92:335; TLS 1967 p. 1133)

HOLT, Tom. *Who's Afraid of Beowulf?* See Chapter 5B, Myth Fantasy.

HOOKS, William H(arris). *Moss Gown.* See Chapter 1, Allegorical Fantasy and Literary Fairy Tales.

HOPP, Zinken. *The Magic Chalk.* See Chapter 7, Magic Adventure Fantasy.

3039 **HOROWITZ, Anthony.** *The Devil's Door-Bell* **(Martin Hopkins trilogy, book 1). Gr. 6–8. (Orig. British pub. 1983.)**

The ancient power of a Druidic stone circle, now the site of an abandoned nuclear power plant, awakens orphaned thirteen-year-old Martin's magical powers to the possibility that his guardian is planning to use black magic to murder him. The sequels are *The Night of the Scorpion* (Pacer, 1984) and *The Silver Citadel* (1986).

Henry Holt, 1984, 159 pp., o.p.

(BL 80:814, 1070; Kliatt Spring 1985 p. 26; KR 52:J15; SLJ Apr 1984 p. 124)

3040 **HORWITZ, Elinor Lander.** *The Strange Story of the Frog Who Became a Prince.* **Gr. 1–4.**

A witch changes a happy frog into a prince and can neither understand his dissatisfaction, nor remember how to change him back.

Illus. by John Heinly, Delacorte, 1971, 45 pp., o.p.

(HB 47:282; KR 39:428; LJ 96:2906)

HOUGH, (Helen) Charlotte (Woodyatt). *Red Biddy and Other Stories.* See Chapter 3, Fantasy Collections.

HOUGHTON, Eric. *Gates of Glass.* See Chapter 5C, Travel to Other Worlds.

3041 **HOUSTON, James A(rchibald).** *Spirit Wrestler.* **Gr. 10 up.**

Shoonah, an orphaned Eskimo boy, longs to become a hunter and lead a normal life, rather than follow in his adoptive mother's footsteps and become the tribal shaman.

Harcourt, 1980, 288 pp., o.p.

(BL 76:700, 713; Kies:38; KR 47:1342, 1382; LJ 10:120)

3042 **HOWARD, Joan (pseud. of Patricia Gordon).** *The Witch of Scrapfaggot Green.* **Gr. 3–5.**

A witch's ghost brings trouble to a small English village.

Illus. by William Pène Du Bois, Viking, 1948, 78 pp., o.p.

(BL 44:228; CCBB 1[May 1948]:2; HB 24:191; KR 16:49; LJ 73:609, 657)

3043 **HUFF, Tanya.** *The Last Wizard.* **Gr. 10 up.**

Crystal, a wizard formed from seven goddesses who fused themselves together to defeat evil, joins two brothers searching for the tower of the ancient wizard Aryalan.

DAW, 1989, pap., 288 pp. (0-88677-331-8)

(BBS:59; VOYA 12:224, 13:14)

3044 HUGHES, Frieda. *Getting Rid of Aunt Edna.* **Gr. 3–5. (Orig. British pub. 1986.)**

The peaceful lives of apprentice witch Miranda and her Aunt Agatha are disrupted by the arrival of the third witch in the family, Aunt Edna.

Illus. by Ed Levine, Harper, 1986, 74 pp., o.p.

(BL 82:1612; CCBB 39:211; KR 54:715; SLJ Oct 1986 p. 177; TLS Aug 1, 1986 p. 850)

3045 HUGHES, Robert Don. *The Faithful Traitor* **(Wizard and Dragon series, book 2). Gr. 7–12.**

After the two-headed dragon he was ordered to create begins destroying the countryside, powershaper Seagryn is branded a traitor. This is the sequel to *The Forging of the Dragon* (1989).

Ballantine, 1992, pap, 277 pp. (0-345-36090-7)

(Kliatt Sept 1992 p. 20; VOYA 15:174)

HUNTER, Mollie (pseud. of Maureen Mollie Hunter McVeigh McIlwraith). *The Ferlie.* See Chapter 7, Magic Adventure Fantasy.

HUNTER, Mollie (pseud. of Maureen Mollie Hunter McVeigh McIlwraith). *The Kelpie's Pearls.* See Chapter 1, Allegorical Fantasy and Literary Fairy Tales.

HUNTER, Mollie (pseud. of Maureen Mollie Hunter McVeigh McIlwraith). *A Stranger Came Ashore.* See Chapter 5B, Myth Fantasy.

3046 **HUNTER, Mollie (pseud. of Maureen Mollie Hunter McVeigh McIlwraith).**
✓ *Thomas and the Warlock.* **Gr. 4–6. (Orig. British pub. 1967.)**

Thomas, the village blacksmith, manages to rescue his wife from an angry warlock and drive all of the witches out of the Scottish lowlands.

Illus. by Joseph Cellini, Funk, 1967, o.p.; Peter Smith, 1986, 128 pp. (0-8446-6243-7)

(BL 64:450; CCBB 21:60; HB 43:749, 61:84, 63:492; KR 35:808; LJ 92:3850; Suth:204; TLS 1967 p. 451)

3047 **HUNTER, Mollie (pseud. of Maureen Mollie Hunter McVeigh McIlwraith).**
✓ *The Walking Stones: A Story of Suspense* **(British title:** *The Bodach,* **1970). Gr. 4–6.**

An elderly Bodach, or sorcerer, lets Donald Campbell take over his magical powers in order to save his stone circle from the waters of a new hydroelectric plant.

Illus. by Trina Schart Hyman, Harper, 1970, 143 pp., o.p.

(BL 67:228; CCBB 24:157; Ch&Bks:256; HB 47:51; KR 38:800; LJ 95:4375; Suth:204; TLS 1970 p. 1251)

IPCAR, Dahlov (Zorach). *The Queen of Spells.* See Chapter 5B, Myth Fantasy.

3048 IPCAR, Dahlov (Zorach). *The Warlock of Night.* **Gr. 5–7.**

A young apprentice to the dreaded Warlock of the Land of Night tries to use magic to save his country.

Viking, 1969, 159 pp., o.p.

(KR 37:1195; LJ 95:789, 1911)

JOHNSON, Dorothy M. *Witch Princess.* See Chapter 5B, Myth Fantasy.

3049 JONES, Diana Wynne. *Archer's Goon.* **Gr. 6–9. (Orig. British pub. 1984.)**
✓✓ Howard Sykes and his sister, Awful, are determined to discover how their father's writ-

ings have kept the mysterious and powerful Archer from leaving their town to rule the world. Boston Globe Horn Book Award Honor Book in Fiction, 1984.

Greenwillow, 1984, 241 pp. (0-688-02582-X)

(BBJ:71; BL 80:1060; CC:511; CCBB 37:167; Ch&Bks:260; HB 60:202; JHC:374; SLJ Mar 1984 p. 160; Suth 3:220; TLS 1984 p. 1198; VOYA 7:101)

3050   **JONES, Diana Wynne.** *Aunt Maria.* **Gr. 6–9. (Orig. British title:** *Black Maria,*
✓   **1991.)**

Meg seeks help from a magician buried alive for twenty years, after Aunt Maria turns Meg's mother into a virtual slave and transforms her brother into a wolf, encouraging the villagers to hunt him down.

Greenwillow, 1991, 224 pp. (0-688-10611-0)

(BL 88:316; CCBB 45:41; HBG 3[July–Dec 1991]:79; KR 59:1223; SLJ Oct 1991 p. 142; TLS July 12, 1991 p. 20; VOYA 15:44, 16:9)

JONES, Diana Wynne. *Charmed Life.* See Chapter 8, Time Travel Fantasy.

3051   **JONES, Diana Wynne.** *Fire and Hemlock.* **Gr. 7–12. (Orig. pub. in England.)**
✓✓   When Polly's vague memories of the year that she was ten and first met Thomas Lynn become clearer, she is horrified to realize that someone has erased Tom's existence from both her memory and that of the world at large, and that his life is in her hands.

Greenwillow, 1984, 352 pp. (0-688-03942-1)

(BBJ:72; BL 81:300, 307, 86:906; CCBB 38:68; HB 61:58; JHC:374; Kies:90; SLJ Oct 1984 p. 167; Suth 3:221; VOYA 7:266, 8:365)

3052   **JONES, Diana Wynne.** *Howl's Moving Castle.* **Gr. 7–12. (Orig. British pub.**
✓✓   **1986.)**

After a witch turns Sophie into an old woman, she moves into Wizard Howl's moving castle and attempts to tame him, even as she is falling in love with him. Boston Globe Horn Book Award Honor Book in Fiction, 1986. This story is related to *Castle in the Air* (1991; see Chapter 5A, Alternate Worlds or Histories).

Greenwillow, 1986, 224 pp. (0-688-06233-4)

(BBJ:72; BL 82:1455, 1461, 83:777, 1118, 1138, 1274, 1592, 86:907; CC:511; CCBB 39:187; Ch&Bks:260; HB 62:331; JHC:575; KR 54:868; SLJ Aug 1986 p. 101, Apr 1987 p. 48; Suth 4:207; TLS 1986 p. 1410)

JONES, Diana Wynne. *The Lives of Christopher Chant.* See Chapter 5C, Travel to Other Worlds.

3053   **JONES, Diana Wynne.** *The Magicians of Caprona* **(Chrestomanci series). Gr.**
✓   **5–7. (Orig. British pub. 1980.)**

When an evil enchantress tries to destroy Caprona by dividing its two families of magicians, two young children and the wizard, Chrestomanci, join forces to defeat her. This book is related to *Charmed Life* (1978; see Chapter 8, Time Travel Fantasy), *Witch Week* (1982; see below) and *The Lives of Christopher Chant* (1988; see Chapter 5C, Travel to Other Worlds), which is a prequel to this story. Two collections contain short stories about Chrestomanci: *Dragons and Dreams* ed. by Jane Yolen (Harper, 1986; see Chapter 7, Magic Adventure Fantasy) and *Warlock at the Wheel* by Diana Wynne Jones (Greenwillow, 1985; see below).

Greenwillow, 1980, 223 pp., o.p.

(BBJ:72; BL 76:1676; CCBB 33:216; Ch&Bks:287; HB 56:407; KR 48:1163; SLJ Oct 1980 p. 147; Suth 3:221; TLS 1980 p. 360)

3054 **JONES, Diana Wynne.** *A Sudden Wild Magic.* **Gr. 10 up. (Orig. pub. in England.)**

A young woman named Zillah, unaware of her powerful wild magic abilities, stows away on the Witches' Council mission to the pirate world of Arth, whose all-male society is sending environmental disasters, wars, and plagues to Earth.

Morrow, 1992, 416 pp. (0-688-11882-8)

(BL 89:492, 496, 842; KR 60:1024; SLJ Mar 1993 p. 234)

JONES, Diana Wynne. *A Tale of Time City.* See Chapter 5C, Travel to Other Worlds.

3055 **JONES, Diana Wynne.** *Warlock at the Wheel and Other Stories.* **Gr. 6–8. (Orig.**
✓ **British pub. 1984.)**

Eight stories of fantasy and magic, warlocks and wizards, including one about Chrestomanci (see *The Magicians of Caprona,* this chapter).

Greenwillow, 1985, 156 pp., o.p.

(BBC:206; BBJ:72; BL 81:1196; CCBB 38:129; Ch&Bks:287; HB 61:453; JHC:432; SLJ Apr, 1985 p. 97; Suth 4:207; TLS 1984 p. 1198; VOYA 8:139)

3056 **JONES, Diana Wynne.** *Witch Week.* **Gr. 5–7. (Orig. British pub. 1982.)**
✓ Magical chaos fills Class 6B when a group of witch orphans begins playing magic tricks. This book is related to *Charmed Life* (1978; see Chapter 8, Time Travel Fantasy) and *The Magicians of Caprona* (1980; see above).

Greenwillow, 1982, 1993, 224 pp. (0-688-12374-0); Knopf, 1988, pap. (0-394-80600-X)

(BL 79:246; CCBB 36:49; HB 59:44, 70:345; HBG 5:87; Kies:90; KR 50:938; SLJ Nov 1982 p. 86; Suth 3:221; TLS 1982 p. 797; VOYA 6:38, 16:382, 17:8)

3057 **JONES, Diana Wynne.** *Witch's Business* **(British title:** *Wilkin's Tooth,* **1973). Gr. 5–7.**

Jess and Frank's "revenge business" runs into competition from a nasty local witch.

Dutton, 1974, 168 pp., o.p.

(KR 42:186; LJ 99:1220; TLS 1973 p. 387)

JORDAN, Robert. *The Eye of the World.* See Chapter 5A, Alternate Worlds or Histories.

3058 **KATZ, Welwyn Wilton.** *Come Like Shadows.* **Gr. 9–12. (Orig. Canadian pub. 1993.)**

Macbeth's witches seem to have cast an evil spell involving sixteen-year-old Stratford Festival Theater production assistant, Kinny, and an ancient mirror.

Viking, 1993, 304 pp. (0-670-84861-1)

(BL 90:685; HBG 5:87; KR 61:1203; SLJ Dec 1993 p. 134; VOYA 16:228)

KAY, Guy Gavriel. *The Summer Tree.* See Chapter 5C, Travel to Other Worlds.

3059 **KELLEHER, Victor (pseud. of Michael Kitchener).** *Master of the Grove.* **Gr. 6–8. (Orig. Australian pub. 1982.)**

Derin, fourteen, follows Marna of the Witch people on a dangerous journey to rescue the father he does not remember. Australian Children's Book of the Year Award, 1983.

Puffin, 1983, 1988, pap., 183 pp. (0-317-69634-3)

(BL 85:423; TLS 1982 p. 344)

KELLER, Beverly. *A Small, Elderly Dragon.* See Chapter 1, Allegorical Fantasy and Literary Fairy Tales.

KELLER, Gottfried. *The Fat of the Cat and Other Stories.* See Chapter 3, Fantasy Collections.

3060 KEMP, Gene. *Mr. Magus Is Waiting for You.* **Gr. 4–7. (Orig. British pub. 1987.)**

Four young people's lives are endangered after they enter an ancient house surrounded by a strangely beautiful garden.

Illus. by Alan Baker, Faber, 1987, 91 pp., o.p.

(SLJ Sept 1987 p. 180; TLS May 1987 p. 529)

3061 KERR, Katharine. *Daggerspell* **(Deverry series, book 1). Gr. 10 up.**

Nevyn, an ancient sorcerer who has become immortal in order to right the wrong he once did to a certain woman, must follow her through several incarnations. The sequels are *Darkspell* (1987), *The Bristling Wood* (1989), and *The Dragon Reverant* (1990). The Westlands series is also set in Deverry: *A Time of Exile* (1991; see Chapter 5A, Alternate Worlds or Histories), *A Time of Omens* (1992), *Days of Blood and Fire* (1993), and *Days of Air and Darkness* (1994).

Doubleday, 1986, o.p.; Ballantine, 1987, pap., 384 pp. (0-345-34430-8)

(BL 82:1667, 1683, 86:905; KR 54:1071; LJ Aug 1986 p. 174; VOYA 9:237, 10:21)

KERR, Katharine. *A Time of Exile.* See Chapter 5A, Alternate Worlds or Histories.

3062 KIMMEL, Margaret Mary. *Magic in the Mist.* **Gr. 2–4.**

✓ Although he is studying to be a wizard, young Thomas's spells cannot even warm his own hut until his pet toad, Jeremy, leads him to a tiny dragon.

Illus. by Trina Schart Hyman, Macmillan, 1975, 32 pp. (0-689-50026-2)

(BL 71:867; CC:515; CCBB 29:28; HB 51:139; KR 43:119; SLJ Apr 1975 p. 46)

3063 KINDL, Patrice. *Owl in Love.* **Gr. 5–10.**

✓✓ Owl, a shape-shifting fourteen-year-old, tries to understand the connection between the science teacher she has a crush on, the starving boy she finds camping in the woods, and the inexperienced young owl she has befriended.

Houghton, 1993, 208 pp. (0-395-66162-5)

(BL 90:51; CCBB 47:35, 49; HBG 5:88; KR 61:1276; SLJ Aug 1993 p. 186; VOYA 16:310)

KING, Stephen. *The Gunslinger.* See Chapter 5A, Alternate Worlds or Histories.

KIRWAN-VOGEL, Anna. *The Jewel of Life.* See Chapter 5A, Alternate Worlds or Histories.

3064 KOOIKER, Leonie (pseud. of Johanna Maria Kooyker-Romijn). *The Magic* ✓ *Stone.* **Gr. 4–6. (Orig. Dutch pub. 1974.)**

Frank's grandmother's magic stone enables his friend, Chris, to control other people's behavior, but when the witch's association wants the stone back, she is determined that he keep it. In *Legacy of Magic* (orig. Dutch pub. 1979; U.S. 1981) Chris, now a witch's apprentice, thinks that his friend Alec's book of magic may help them find buried treasure.

Trans. by Richard Winston and Clara Winston, illus. by Carl Hollander, Morrow, 1978, 224 pp., o.p.

(BBC:207; BL 74:1494; CCBB 32:65; Ch&Bks:288; HB 54:396; KR 46:595; SLJ May 1978 p. 68; Suth 2:263)

3065 KORTUM, Jeanie. *Ghost Vision.* Gr. 5–8.

A young Greenland Eskimo named Panipaq's visions teach him that he is becoming an *angakok,* or wise one, with special powers allowing him to see into other worlds.

Illus. by Dugald Stermer, Sierra Club, 1983, 144 pp., LB(0-685-42977-6)

(BBC:207; BL 80:814; CCBB 37:110; SLJ Jan 1984 p. 78)

KRENSKY, Stephen (Alan). *A Big Day for Scepters.* See Chapter 1, Allegorical Fantasy and Literary Fairy Tales.

KRENSKY, Stephen (Alan). *The Dragon Circle.* See Chapter 7, Magic Adventure Fantasy.

KRENSKY, Stephen (Alan). *The Perils of Putney.* See Chapter 1, Allegorical Fantasy and Literary Fairy Tales.

**3066 KUMIN, Maxine (Winokur), and SEXTON, Anne (Harvey). *The Wizard's*
✓ *Tears.* Gr. 1–3.**

The new young wizard of Drocknock goes too far with his magical powers and is rescued by the former wizard and a dalmation.

Illus. by Evaline Ness, McGraw-Hill, 1975, 48 pp., o.p.

(CCBB 29:99; HB 51:587; KR 43:911; SLJ Nov 1975 p. 64, Dec 1975 p. 31; Suth 2:266)

3067 KURTZ, Katherine. *Lammas Night.* Gr. 10 up.

On Lammas night in 1940, a coven of witches gathers to use the "old religion" to keep Hitler from invading England.

Ballantine, 1983, pap., 438 pp., o.p.

(BBS:60; BL 80:846, 853; Kies:98)

3068 KURTZ, Katherine, and HARRIS, Deborah. *The Adept* (The Adept series, book 1). Gr. 10 up.

Evil magic has been revived in Scotland, causing Sir Adam Sinclair, psychiatrist and police assistant, to assume his true identity of Adept, a magician guarding the Light from the forces of Darkness. In the sequel, *The Lodge of the Lynx* (1992), Sir Adam and his apprentice, Peregrine Lovat, hunt down a brotherhood of sorcerers using Hitler's book of black spells. The third book in the series is *The Templar Treasure* (1993).

Ace, 1991, pap., 336 pp (0-441-00343-5); Severn, 1992 (0-7278-4378-8)

(BL 87:1322, 1374, 88:1670; LJ Mar 15, 1991 p. 119; SLJ Sept 1991 p. 298; VOYA 14:110)

LACKEY, Mercedes. *By the Sword.* See Chapter 5A, Alternate Worlds or Histories.

LACKEY, Mercedes. *Magic's Pawn.* See Chapter 5A, Alternate Worlds or Histories.

3069 LACKEY, Mercedes, and DIXON, Larry. *Born to Run* (The Serrated Edge series, book 1). Gr. 10 up.

Tania, a teenaged runaway, meets a young mage named Tannim, and both become involved in a battle between good and evil elves.

Baen, 1992, pap., 319 pp. (0-671-72110-0)

(BL 88:1344, 1348; VOYA 15:176)

3070 **LACKEY, Mercedes, and EMERSON, Ru.** *Fortress of Frost and Fire* **(The Bard's Tale series, book 2). Gr. 7–12.**

Having foresworn the use of dark sorcery, former necromancer Naitachel, his apprentice bard, Gawaine, and their traveling companions search for an enchanted valley guarded by an invincible Snow Dragon. This is the sequel to *Castle of Deception* (1992, written by Lackey and Josepha Sherman). The third book in the series is *Prison of Souls* (1993, written by Lackey).

Baen, 1993, pap., 297 pp. (0-671-72162-3)

(Kliatt Sept 1993 p. 18; VOYA 16:166, 230)

LARSON, Jean. *The Silkspinners.* See Chapter 1, Allegorical Fantasy and Literary Fairy Tales.

3071 **LAUGHLIN, Florence (Young).** *The Little Leftover Witch.* **Gr. 2–4.**

When Felina witch's broomstick breaks in midair, she falls out of the sky and is stranded on earth for an entire year.

Illus. by Sheila Greenwald, Macmillan, 1960, 1971, o.p., pap., 1973, 1988, 96 pp. (0-689-71273-1)

(BL 57:362; CCBB 14:82; HB 36:396; KR 28:496; LJ 85:4226; TLS 1967 p. 1153)

LAWHEAD, Stephen R. *In the Hall of the Dragon King.* See Chapter 5A, Alternate Worlds or Histories.

LAWRENCE, Louise (pseud. of Elizabeth Rhoda Holden). *The Earth Witch.* See Chapter 5B, Myth Fantasy.

LEACH, Maria. *The Thing at the Foot of the Bed and Other Scary Tales.* See Chapter 4, Ghost Fantasy.

3072 **LEE, Josephine.** *Joy Is Not Herself.* **Gr. 5–7. (Orig. British pub. 1962.)**

Melisanda Montgomery discovers that she is part witch.

Illus. by Pat Marriott, Harcourt, 1963, 154 pp., o.p.

(HB 39:174; LJ88:1768; TLS 1962 p. 393)

LEE, Tanith. *Black Unicorn.* See Chapter 5A, Alternate Worlds or Histories.

LEE, Tanith. *Cyrion.* See Chapter 5A, Alternate Worlds or Histories.

LEE, Tanith. *The Dragon Hoard.* See Chapter 1, Allegorical Fantasy and Literary Fairy Tales.

LEE, Tanith. *Princess Hynchatti and Some Other Surprises.* See Chapter 1, Allegorical Fantasy and Literary Fairy Tales.

LE GUIN, Ursula K(roeber). *A Wizard of Earthsea.* See Chapter 5A, Alternate Worlds or Histories.

3073 **LEVOY, Myron.** *The Magic Hat of Mortimer Wintergreen.* **Gr. 4–7.**

Orphaned Joshua and Amy Bains are rescued from the clutches of evil Aunt Vootch by the magic hat of Wizard Mortimer Q. Wintergreen.

Illus. by Andrew Glass, Harper, 1988, 211 pp., LB(0-06-023842-9)

(BL 84:1001; CCBB 41:121; KR 55:1734; SLJ Mar 1988 p. 197)

LEWIS, C(live) S(taples). *The Lion, the Witch, and the Wardrobe.* See Chapter 5C, Travel to Other Worlds.

3074 **LIFTON, Betty Jean (Kirschner).** *Jaguar, My Twin.* **Gr. 4–6.**

Two shamans battle for the soul of young Shun and his twin animal spirit, a jaguar, in this Zinacantec Indian tale set in Mexico.

Illus. by Ann Legett, Macmillan, 1976, 114 pp., o.p.

(CCBB 30:44; HB 52:625; KR 44:732; SLJ Oct 1976 p. 108)

3075 **LILLINGTON, Kenneth (James).** *An Ash-Blond Witch.* **Gr. 7 up. (Orig. British pub. 1987.)**

A young woman from the twenty-second century "beyond the mountains," arrives in the old-fashioned village of Urstwhile and becomes the rival of the local witch.

Faber, 1987, 138 pp., o.p.

(BBS:60; BL 83:776, 1274, 1592; KR 55:60)

LITTLE, Jane. *The Philosopher's Stone.* See Chapter 8, Time Travel Fantasy.

3076 **LITTLE, Jane.** *Sneaker Hill.* **Gr. 3–5.**

After Matthew's mother, a witch-in-training, forgets to take her owl with her, Matthew and Susan follow her into a magic land.

Illus. by Nancy Grossman, Atheneum, 1967, 176 pp., o.p.

(CCBB 21:29; LJ 92:1738)

3077 **LITTLE, Jane.** *Spook.* **Gr. 3–5.**

Grimalda the witch is allergic to cats and tries to make do with a small dog named Spook, but a boy named Jamie wants Spook too.

Illus. by Suzanne Larsen, Atheneum, 1965, 110 pp., o.p.

(CCBB 19:35; HB 41:492; LJ 90:3812)

LIVELY, Penelope (Margaret Low). *The Ghost of Thomas Kempe.* See Chapter 4, Ghost Fantasy.

LIVELY, Penelope (Margaret Low). *The Whispering Knights.* See Chapter 5B, Myth Fantasy.

3078 **LLYWELYN, Morgan.** *The Horse Goddess.* **Gr. 10 up.**
✓ Destined from birth to become the Shaman of her father's Celtic tribe, Epona runs away with Kazhak, leader of a nomadic band of horsemen from Asia Minor.

Houghton, 1982, 417 pp., o.p.

(BL 78:1483, 1485, 86:907; Kies:107; KR 50:818; LJ 107:1170; SLJ Dec 1982 p. 87)

LOFTING, Hugh. *The Twilight of Magic.* See Chapter 7, Magic Adventure Fantasy.

3079 **LOVEJOY, Jack.** *The Rebel Witch.* **Gr. 4–6.**

A magic wand enables Suzie, an apprentice witch, to enter the witch world of Veneficon to search for her teacher, Madame Mengo.

Illus. by Judith Gwyn Brown, Morrow, 1978, 201 pp., o.p.

(BL 75:50; KR 46:1248; SLJ Dec 1978 p. 54)

3080 **LUENN, Nancy.** *Arctic Unicorn.* **Gr. 6–10.**

Kala, a thirteen-year-old Eskimo girl, is torn between her attraction to a young hunter who could become her husband, and her visions of arctic unicorns that beckon her to accept her magical powers and become an *angakok,* or shaman.

Atheneum, 1986, 168 pp., o.p.

(BBJ:73; CCBB 39:188; KR 54:869; SLJ Oct 1986 p. 179; VOYA 10:38)

3081 **MacAVOY, R(oberta) A(nn).** *Damiano* **(Damiano series, book 1). Gr. 10 up.**

✓ Damiano, a fourteenth-century Italian wizard, is forced by marauders to flee with his wise dog, Macchiata. His determination for vengeance leads him on an adventurous quest. The sequels are *Damiano's Lute* (1984) and *Raphael* (1984). All three books were collected in *A Trio for Lute* (Science Fiction Book Club, 1985).

Bantam, 1983, pap., 243 pp. (0-553-25347-6)

(BBS:61; BL 80:1099, 1110, 86:905; Kies:111; SLJ Nov 1984 p. 146; VOYA 7:101)

3082 **MacAVOY, R(oberta) A(nn).** *The Grey Horse.* **Gr. 10 up.**

✓ The Irish village of Carraroe is thrown into turmoil upon the arrival of Ruairi MacEibhir, a faerie in search of the woman he loves.

Bantam, 1987, pap., 247 pp. (0-553-26557-1)

(BBS:61; BL 83:1655, 1672; Kies:111; LJ Apr 15, 1987 p. 103; VOYA 10:179)

MacDONALD, Greville. *Billy Barnicoat: A Fairy Romance for Young and Old.* See Chapter 7, Magic Adventure Fantasy.

3083 **McGOWEN, Tom (Thomas E.).** *The Magical Fellowship* **(The Age of Magic tril-**
✓ **ogy, book 1). Gr. 5–9.**

Two wizards, one troll and one human, try to convince the warring races of trolls, dragons, elves, and humans to join forces to fend off an impending attack on Earth by forces from another world. In the sequel, *A Trial of Magic* (1992), a powerful mage uses black magic to disrupt the other mages' unity plan so that his race will inherit the Earth after the Earthdoom. The final book in the trilogy is *A Question of Magic* (1993).

Dutton, 1991, 133 pp. (0-525-67339-3)

(BL 87:1377; HBG 2:266; KR 59:396; SLJ Apr 1991 p. 120; VOYA 14:46)

3084 **McGOWEN, Tom (Thomas E.).** *The Magician's Apprentice* **(The Magician tril-**
✓ **ogy, book 1). Gr. 5–7.**

A wily street urchin named Tigg is befriended by the magician Armindor, who takes him to the Wild Lands in search of magical artifacts from an earlier civilization. In *The Magician's Company* (1988) Tigg, Armindor, and a girl named Jilla bring two treasures from the Wild Lands to the counsel of sages and warn the counsel about a threat to world security. In *The Magician's Challenge* (1989) Tigg and Jilla are captured by the ratlike Reen, who want to destroy human kind.

Dutton, 1987, 119 pp., o.p.

(BBC:209; BL 83:580, 84:873; CCBB 40:113; KR 54:1649; SLJ Jan 1987 p. 76)

3085 **McGOWEN, Tom (Thomas E.).** *Sir Machinery.* **Gr. 3–6.**

✓ Merlin the wizard joins forces with a physicist to battle an ancient race of demons bent on taking over the world.

Illus. by Trina Schart Hyman, Follett, 1971, 155 pp., o.p.

(BL 68:367; HB 48:49; KR 39:1071; LJ 96:4191)

3086 **MacKELLAR, William.** *The Witch of Glen Gowrie.* **Gr. 5–7.**

Old Meg's ghost keeps everyone but young Gavin Fraser from finding her treasure.

Illus. by Ted Lewin, Dodd, 1978, 134 pp., o.p.

(BL 74:1109; CCBB 32:34; SLJ May 1978 p. 85)

McKENZIE, Ellen Kindt. *Taash and the Jesters.* See Chapter 5A, Alternate Worlds or Histories.

McKILLIP, Patricia A(nne). *The Changeling Sea.* See Chapter 5A, Alternate Worlds or Histories.

McKILLIP, Patricia A(nne). *The Cygnet and the Firebird.* See Chapter 5A, Alternate Worlds or Histories.

McKILLIP, Patricia A(nne). *The Forgotten Beasts of Eld.* See Chapter 5A, Alternate Worlds or Histories.

McKILLIP, Patricia A(nne). *The Riddle-Master of Hed.* See Chapter 5A, Alternate Worlds or Histories.

McKILLIP, Patricia A(nne). *The Sorceress and the Cygnet.* See Chapter 5A, Alternate Worlds or Histories.

3087 MacLACHLAN, Patricia. *Tomorrow's Wizard.* **Gr. 3–5.**

Tomorrow's Wizard and his apprentice, Murdoch, travel the kingdom solving problems and fulfilling the wishes of the inhabitants.

Illus. by Kathy Jacobi, Harper, 1982, 80 pp., o.p.

(BBC:209; CC:580; HB 58:290; SLJ Apr 1982 p. 72)

3088 McLEOD, Emilie Warren. *Clancy's Witch.* **Gr. 2–4.**

✓ Clancy's next-door neighbor is a witch.

Illus. by Lisl Weil, Little, 1959, 38 pp., o.p.

(BL 55:543; Eakin:224; HB 35:131; KR 26:905; LJ 84:1686)

McMULLAN, Kate. *Under the Mummy's Spell.* See Chapter 4, Ghost Fantasy.

McNEILL, Janet. *Tom's Tower.* See Chapter 5C, Travel to Other Worlds.

3089 MAGUIRE, Gregory. *The Dream Stealer.* **Gr. 3–5.**

Pasha and Lisette set out to consult the fearsome hag Baba Yaga about their encounter with a Firebird and rumors of a marauding demon wolf called the Blood Prince.

Harper, 1983, 118 pp., o.p.

(BL 80:299; HB 59:576; KR 51:164; SLJ Feb 1984 p. 75)

3090 MAHY, Margaret (May). *The Changeover: A Supernatural Romance.* **Gr. 6–10.**
✓✓ **(Orig. pub. in New Zealand, 1984.)**

Laura Chant must undergo a changeover to become a witch in order to save the life of her brother Jacko, who has been bewitched by a demon. Carnegie Medal, 1984. New Zealand Library Association Esther Glen Award, 1985. Boston Globe Horn Book Award Honor Book in Fiction, 1985.

Macmillan, 1984, 224 pp. (0-689-50303-2); Puffin, 1994, pap. (0-14-036599-0)

(BBS:61; BL 81:122, 132, 86:790; CCBB 38:11; Ch&Bks:289; HB 60:764; JHC:385; Kies:115; KR 52:81; SLJ Sept 1984 p. 132; Suth 3:292; TLS 1984 p. 794; VOYA 8:50, 364)

3091 MAHY, Margaret (May). *The Haunting.* **Gr. 5–8. (Orig. pub. in New Zealand,**
✓✓ **1982.)**

Eight-year-old Barney's frightening messages from a long-lost uncle bring to light a secret family curse. Carnegie Medal, 1982. New Zealand Library Association Esther Glen Award, 1983.

Macmillan, 1982, 144 pp. (0-689-50243-5)

(BBC:209; BL 79:117; CC:530; CCBB 36:31; Ch&Bks:289; HB 59:46; JHC:385; Kies:115; KR 50:1155; SLJ Aug 1982 p. 119; Suth 3:293; TLS 1982 p. 1001)

MAHY, Margaret (May). *A Tall Story and Other Tales.* See Chapter 7, Magic Adventure Fantasy.

MARTIN, Graham Dunstan. *Giftwish.* See Chapter 5A, Alternate Worlds or Histories.

MASEFIELD, John (Edward). *The Midnight Folk: A Novel.* See Chapter 7, Magic Adventure Fantasy.

MAYER, Marianna. *The Sorcerer's Apprentice: A Greek Fable.* See Chapter 5B, Myth Fantasy.

MAYNE, William (James Carter). *The Hill Road.* See Chapter 8, Time Travel Fantasy.

3092   MIAN, Mary (Lawrence Shipman). *Take Three Witches.* **Gr. 6–8.**

Three sixth-graders, three witches, and a ghost join forces to prevent their town from spraying bird-killing insecticide. The sequel is *The Net to Catch War* (1975).

Illus. by Eric Von Schmidt, Houghton, 1971, 279 pp., o.p.

(HB 47:485; LJ 96:2133)

MIESEL, Sandra. *Shaman.* See Chapter 5C, Travel to Other Worlds.

MONTROSE, Anne. *The Winter Flower, and Other Fairy Stories.* See Chapter 3, Fantasy Collections.

3093   MORRESSY, John. *A Voice for Princess* **(Kedrigern series, book 1). Gr. 10 up.**

Disgruntled because the wizards' guild has decided to admit alchemists, Kedrigern quits, sets off to see the world, and meets a mute princess under an enchantment. The sequels are *The Questing of Kedrigern* (1987), *Kedrigern in Wanderland* (1988), *A Remembrance for Kedrigern* (1990), and *Kedrigern and the Charming Couple* (1990).

Ace, 1987, pap., 213 pp., o.p.

(BBS:62; BL 83:1181, 1199, 1592)

MOZART, Wolfgang Amadeus. *The Magic Flute.* See Chapter 1, Allegorical Fantasy and Literary Fairy Tales.

3094   MURPHY, Jill. *The Worst Witch* **(The Worst Witch trilogy, book 1). Gr. 2–5. (Orig. British pub. 1974.)**

Mildred is the worst student at Miss Cackle's Academy for witches, but she runs away and becomes a heroine by turning a coven of evil witches into snails. The sequels are *The Worst Witch Strikes Again* (1981, 1989) and *A Bad Spell for the Worst Witch* (1982, 1989).

Illus. by the author, Allison, 1980, 1987, 71 pp. (0-8052-8019-7); Avon, 1982, pap. (0-380-60665-8); Viking, 1988, 106 pp., o.p.; Puffin, 1991, pap. (0-14-031108-4)

(BBC:216; CCBB 34:38; HBG 1[July-Dec 1989]:85; KR 57:1163; SLJ Sept 1980 p. 62)

MURPHY, Pat. *Points of Departure.* See Chapter 3, Fantasy Collections.

MURPHY, Shirley Rousseau. *The Catswold Portal.* See Chapter 5C, Travel to Other Worlds.

3095 **MURPHY, Shirley Rousseau.** *The Pig Who Could Conjure the Wind.* **Gr. 2–4.**

Miss Folly, a flying witch pig, rescues the wind demon's victims.

Illus. by Mark Lefkowitz, Atheneum, 1978, 58 pp., o.p.

(BL 74:1436; HB 54:278; KR 46:239; SLJ Apr 1978 p. 73)

3096 **NAPOLI, Donna Jo.** *The Magic Circle.* **Gr. 7–12.**

✓ A midwife/sorceress called Ugly One, haunted by demons she summoned to help with her healing, hides in the forest, decorating her cottage with candies in memory of her beloved daughter. This is a reworking of the German folktale, "Hansel and Gretel," told from the point of view of the witch.

Dutton, 1993, 118 pp. (0-525-45127-7)

(BL 89:1957, 90:868; CCBB 46:260; HBG 4[Fall 1993]:311; KR 61:789; SLJ Aug 1993 p. 186; VOYA 16:169)

3097 **NATHAN, Robert (Gruntal).** *The Snowflake and the Starfish.* **Gr. 3–4.**

A lonely sea-witch takes Vicky and Thomas into the sea with her.

Illus. by Leonard Weisgard, Knopf, 1959, 68 pp., o.p.

(HB 35:478; LJ 84:3930)

NESS, Evaline. *The Girl and the Goatherd, or This and That and Thus and So.* See Chapter 1, Allegorical Fantasy and Literary Fairy Tales.

NEWMAN, Robert (Howard). *Merlin's Mistake.* See Chapter 5B, Myth Fantasy.

NEWMAN, Robert (Howard). *The Shattered Stone.* See Chapter 5A, Alternate Worlds or Histories.

3098 **NICHOLS, (Joanna) Ruth.** *The Left-Handed Spirit.* **Gr. 8–10.**

Kidnapped by the Chinese ambassador to the Roman Empire, Mariana is expected to use her healing powers to save the life of the ambassador's twin brother.

Atheneum, 1978, 260 pp., o.p.

(BL 75:469; CCBB 32:85; KR 46:1254; SLJ Oct 1978 p. 158; VOYA 1[Dec 1978]:43)

NICHOLS, (Joanna) Ruth. *The Marrow of the World.* See Chapter 5C, Travel to Other Worlds.

NIVEN, Larry. *The Magic Goes Away.* See Chapter 5A, Alternate Worlds or Histories.

NORTON, André (pseud. of Alice Mary Norton). *Lavender Green Magic.* See Chapter 8, Time Travel Fantasy.

NORTON, André (pseud. of Alice Mary Norton). *Witch World.* See Chapter 5C, Travel to Other Worlds.

3099 **NORTON, André (pseud. of Alice Mary Norton).** *Wizards' Worlds.* **Gr. 10 up.**

Thirteen of Norton's favorites, mostly fantasy stories, six of which appeared in *Lore of the Witchworld* (1980).

Tor, 1989, 288 pp., o.p.

(BL 86:149, 164; KR 57:1437; VOYA 12:373, 13:16)

3100 **NORTON, André, and LACKEY, Mercedes.** *The Elvenbane: An Epic Fantasy of the Halfblood Chronicles* **(The Halfblood Chronicles, book 1). Gr. 10 up.**

Half human, half elven Shana, raised by dragons, grows up to become The Elvenbane, a legendary wizard powerful enough to defeat the tyrannical elves who have enslaved the humans of the world.

Tor, 1991, 384 pp. (0-312-85106-5), 1993, pap. (0-8125-1175-1)

(BL 88:416, 423; KR 59:1123; LJ Oct 15, 1991 p. 127; VOYA 15:45)

NORTON, André, and SCHWARTZ, Susan. *Imperial Lady: A Fantasy of Han China.* See Chapter 5B, Myth Fantasy.

NORTON, Mary (Pearson). *Bedknob and Broomstick.* See Chapter 7, Magic Adventure Fantasy.

O'HANLON, Jacklyn. *The Door.* See Chapter 5C, Travel to Other Worlds.

3101 ORR, A. *The World in Amber.* **Gr. 10 up.**

Court sorcerer Judah Hila transports complacent King Ambrose and his minstrel son Isme to magical locations, and transforms Queen Maldive into a palace cat, all in an attempt to improve their ability to rule the land of Phar-Tracil. The sequel is *In the Ice King's Palace* (1986).

Bluejay, 1985, 214 pp., o.p.

(KR 53:679; VOYA 10:105)

O'SHEA, Pat. *The Hounds of the Morrigan.* See Chapter 5B, Myth Fantasy.

PALMER, David R. *Threshold.* See Chapter 6, Humourous Fantasy.

PARKER, (James) Edgar (Jr.). *The Enchantress.* See Chapter 1, Allegorical Fantasy and Literary Fairy Tales.

PARKER, Nancy Winslow. *The Spotted Dog: The Strange Tale of a Witch's Revenge.* See Chapter 6, Humorous Fantasy.

PAYNE, Joan Balfour (Dicks). *The Piebald Princess.* See Chapter 2, Animal Fantasy.

PEET, Bill (William Bartlett). *Big Bad Bruce.* See Chapter 2, Animal Fantasy.

PEET, Bill (William Bartlett). *The Whingdingdilly.* See Chapter 2, Animal Fantasy.

PICARD, Barbara Leonie. *The Goldfinch Garden: Seven Tales.* See Chapter 3, Fantasy Collections.

PICARD, Barbara Leonie. *The Mermaid and the Simpleton.* See Chapter 3, Fantasy Collections.

PIERCE, Meredith Ann. *The Darkangel.* See Chapter 5A, Alternate Worlds or Histories.

PIERCE, Tamora. *Alanna: The First Adventure.* See Chapter 5A, Alternate Worlds or Histories.

PIERCE, Tamora. *Wild Magic: The Immortals.* See Chapter 5A, Alternate Worlds or Histories.

3102 PLACE, Marian T(empleton). *The Resident Witch.* **Gr. 3–5.**

Living with her aunt while her mother is away, Witcheena is working hard at becoming a Junior Witch when she makes the mistake of befriending some earthlings.

Illus. by Marilyn Miller, Washburn, 1970, 119 pp., o.p.

(CCBB 24:65; KR 38:244; LJ 95:2309)

3103 PLACE, Marian T(empleton). *The Witch Who Saved Halloween.* **Gr. 4–6.**

When pollution threatens both witches and humans, Witchard comes up with a plan to save them.

Illus. by Marilyn Miller, Washburn, 1971, 150 pp., o.p.

(BL 75:306; CCBB 25:1281; KR 39:1072; LJ 97:284)

3104 POOLE, Josephine. *The Visitor: A Story of Suspense.* **Gr. 6–9. (Orig. British pub. 1965.)**

Fifteen-year-old Harry's tutor, Mr. Bogle, exerts a strange power over the villagers of Cormundy, and this strangeness is tied to the ancient Fury Wood surrounding Harry's house.

Harper, 1972, 148 pp., o.p.

(BBJ:75; BL 69:352, 358; KR 40:1153; LJ 97:4087)

POSTMA, Lidia. *The Witch's Garden.* See Chapter 7, Magic Adventure Fantasy.

3105 PRANTERA, Amanda. *The Cabalist.* **Gr. 10 up. (Orig. British pub. 1985.)**

Joseph Kestler, a modern-day Cabalist with a terminal illness, searches for someone to inherit his magical powers.

Atheneum, 1986, 192 pp., o.p.

(BL 82:1663, 1683; KR 54:966; LJ Aug 1986 p. 172; TLS 1985 p. 1266)

3106 PREUSSLER, Otfried. *The Little Witch.* **Gr. 3–5. (Orig. pub. in Germany.)**

Little Witch plots revenge on the older witches who took away her magic broomstick on Walpurgis Night.

Trans. by Anthea Bell, illus. by Winnie Gayler, Abelard-Schuman, 1961, 127 pp., o.p.

(BL 58:450; CCBB 15:84; KR 29:843; LJ 86:4040; TLS May 19, 1961 p. iv)

PREUSSLER, Otfried. *The Robber Hotzenplotz.* See Chapter 6, Humorous Fantasy.

3107 PREUSSLER, Otfried. *The Satanic Mill.* **Gr. 6–9. (Orig. German pub. 1971.)**

✓✓ Krabat thinks he has been apprenticed to a miller, but discovers that the mill is actually a school of black magic run by an evil magician.

Trans. by Anthea Bell, Macmillan, 1973, o.p., pap., 1991 (0-02-044775-2); Peter Smith, 1985, 250 pp. (0-8446-6196-1)

(BBC:211; BL 69:1073, 70:827, 82:677, 686; CCBB 26:143; Ch&Bks:290; HB 49:147; 61:84, 63:492; KR 41:61, 1351; LJ 98:1398, 1655; Suth 2:369; TLS 1972 p. 1489)

3108 PRICE, Susan. *The Ghost Drum: A Cat's Tale.* **Gr. 5–9. (Orig. British pub.**
✓ **1987.)**

A cat tells the story of the friendship between Chingis, a shaman who lives in a house on chicken legs, and Safa, the Czar's son, who has been imprisoned in a windowless room since birth. Carnegie Medal, 1987. The companion volume is *Ghost Song* (1992; see below).

Farrar, 1987, 167 pp. (0-374-32538-3), 1989, pap. (0-374-42547-7)

(BBC:211; BL 84:152; CC:547; CCBB 41:36; KR 55:929; SLJ Sept 1987 p. 182, Dec 1987 p. 38; TLS 1987 p. 248; VOYA 10:245)

3109   PRICE, Susan. *Ghost Song.* **Gr. 6–12. (Orig. British pub. 1992.)**

✓   The fates of two young men become entangled in this Russian story: Ambrosi, beloved son of two slaves to the czar, but claimed as an apprentice by Kuzma, a shaman from the Ghost World; and Fox, a son of the reindeer people who have been transformed by Kuzma into wolves. This is a companion story to *The Ghost Drum* (1987; see above).

Farrar, 1992, 160 pp. (0-374-32544-8)

(BL 89:147; CCBB 46:155; HB 69:87; HBG 4[Spring 1993]:75; KR 60:1133; SLJ Jan 1993 p. 102; VOYA 15:356)

PUSHKIN, Alexander Sergeevich. *The Golden Cockerel and Other Stories.* See Chapter 3, Fantasy Collections.

3110   PYLE, Howard. *King Stork.* **Gr. 2–4. (Orig. pub. in *The Wonder Clock,* 1887.)**

✓   A beautiful but wicked witch is tamed and won by a poor drummer and King Stork's magic. Boston Globe Horn Book Award for Illustration, 1973.

Illus. by Trina Schart Hyman, Little, 1973, 48 pp., o.p.

(BL 70:174; CC:114; HB 49:373; KR 41:455; LJ 98:2643)

RAWN, Melanie. *Stronghold.* See Chapter 5A, Alternate Worlds or Histories.

3111   REAVES, Michael. *The Shattered World.* **Gr. 10 up.**

While master-wizard Pandrogas tries to put the world back together 1000 years after it was shattered by an evil sorcerer's spell, his former protege, Ardatha, sends a master-thief to steal Pandrogas's runestone in order to raise the Necromancer from the dead.

Simon & Schuster, 1984, 349 pp., o.p.; Pocket, pap., 1984 (0-671-49942-4)

(BBS:63; KR 52:66; LJ 109:599; VOYA 8:212)

REEVES, James (pseud. of John Morris Reeves). *The Cold Flame.* See Chapter 1, Allegorical Fantasy and Literary Fairy Tales.

REICHERT, Mickey Zucker. *The Last of the Renshai.* See Chapter 5A, Alternate Worlds or Histories.

REID, Alastair. *Fairwater.* See Chapter 1, Allegorical Fantasy and Literary Fairy Tales.

REID BANKS, Lynne. *The Farthest-Away Mountain.* See Chapter 1, Allegorical Fantasy and Literary Fairy Tales.

ROACH, Marilynne K(athleen). *Encounters with the Invisible World.* See Chapter 3, Fantasy Collections.

ROBERSON, Jennifer. *Sword-Breaker.* See Chapter 5A, Alternate Worlds or Histories.

3112   ROHAN, Michael Scott. *The Anvil of Ice* **(Winter of the World trilogy, vol. 1). Gr. 10 up.**

A young magesmith defies his master and attempts to use his growing magical powers to battle the evil Ice Age threatening to destroy the world.

Morrow, 1986, 344 pp., o.p.

(KR 54:1330; LJ Oct 15, 1986 p. 112; SLJ Feb 1987 p. 99)

RUSCH, Kristine Kathryn. *The White Mists of Power.* See Chapter 5A, Alternate Worlds or Histories.

RUSH, Alison. *The Last of Danu's Children.* See Chapter 5B, Myth Fantasy.

SABERHAGEN, Fred. *Empire of the East.* See Chapter 5A, Alternate Worlds or Histories.

SALSITZ, R. A. V. *The Unicorn Dancer.* See Chapter 5A, Alternate Worlds or Histories.

SALSITZ, R. A. V. *Where Dragons Lie.* See Chapter 5A, Alternate Worlds or Histories.

SALVATORE, R. A. *The Woods Out Back.* See Chapter 5C, Travel to Other Worlds.

3113 SAN SOUCI, Robert D., reteller. *Feathertop: Based on the Tale by Nathaniel Hawthorne.* **Gr. 2–4.**

A witch named Old Mother Rigby transforms her scarecrow into a gentleman to play a trick on Judge Gookin by courting his daughter.

Illus. by Daniel San Souci, Doubleday, 1992, 132 pp. (0-385-42044-7)

(HBG 4[Spring 1993]:61; SLJ Dec 1992 p. 90)

SAN SOUCI, Robert D. *Young Merlin.* See Chapter 5B, Myth Fantasy.

3114 SCARBOROUGH, Elizabeth Ann. *Phantom Banjo* **(The Songkiller Saga, vol. 1). Gr. 10 up.**

After devils discover that humans can use music as a weapon against them, they target folk songs as the first type of music to be expunged from the world, begin killing major folksingers, and destroy recording archives. The sequels are *Picking the Ballad's Bones* (1991) and *Strum Again?* (1992).

Bantam, 1991, pap., 272 pp. (0-553-28761-3)

(BL 87:1937; VOYA 14:326)

3115 SENDAK, Jack. *The Second Witch.* **Gr. 3–5.**

Andrew tries to save Vivian, an unpopular witch, from the wrath of the villagers of Platzenhausen, in this story written by Maurice Sendak's brother.

Illus. by Uri Shulevitz, Harper, 1965, 94 pp., o.p.

(KR 33:751; LJ 90:4620)

3116 SERVICE, Pamela F. *When the Night Wind Howls.* **Gr. 6–8.**

Sid and Joel suspect that Sid's mother's new boyfriend, the star of a local theater group, is actually a warlock.

Macmillan, 1987, 153 pp., o.p., Fawcett, 1988, pap. (0-449-70279-0)

(BL 83:1607; CCBB 40:178; KR 55:224; SLJ Apr 1987 p. 113; VOYA 10:82)

SERVICE, Pamela F. *Winter of Magic's Return.* See Chapter 5B, Myth Fantasy.

SERVICE, Pamela F. *Wizard of Wind and Rock.* See Chapter 5B, Myth Fantasy.

SHERMAN, Josepha. *Child of Faerie, Child of Earth.* See Chapter 5B, Myth Fantasy.

SHERMAN, Josepha. *The Shining Falcon.* See Chapter 5A, Alternate Worlds or Histories.

3117 SHYER, Marlene Fanta. *Ruby, the Red Hot Witch at Bloomingdale's.* **Gr. 4–6.**

Newly arrived in New York City after their parents' separation, Petra and Thomas meet red-headed Ruby, who claims to be a good witch, on the sixth floor of Bloomingdale's department store.

Viking, 1991, 151 pp. (0-670-83473-4); Puffin, 1993, pap. (0-14-034510-8)

(BL 88:54; CCBB 44:275; HB 67:598; HBG 3[July–Dec 1991]:73; KR 59:861; SLJ Oct 1991 p. 130)

SINGER, Isaac Bashevis. *Alone in the Wild Forest.* See Chapter 1, Allegorical Fantasy and Literary Fairy Tales.

SINGER, Isaac Bashevis. *The Fearsome Inn.* See Chapter 1, Allegorical Fantasy and Literary Fairy Tales.

3118 SINGER, Marilyn. *California Demon.* **Gr. 4–6.**

Rosy Rodriquez, daughter of a practitioner of "the craft" of white magic, accidentally lets loose a demon who stows away to California and makes life difficult for Danny and Laura Pauling.

Hyperion, 1992, 149 pp. LB(1-56282-299-3)

(BL 89:671; CCBB 46:191; HBG 4[Spring 1993]:76)

SLEIGH, Barbara (de Riemer). *Carbonel: The King of the Cats.* See Chapter 7, Magic Adventure Fantasy.

SLEIGH, Barbara (de Riemer). *Stirabout Stories, Brewed in Her Own Cauldron.* See Chapter 3, Fantasy Collections.

SLOBODKIN, Louis. *The Amiable Giant.* See Chapter 1, Allegorical Fantasy and Literary Fairy Tales.

SMITH, L(isa) J. *Night of the Solstice.* See Chapter 5C, Travel to Other Worlds.

SMITH, Sherwood. *Wren to the Rescue.* See Chapter 5A, Alternate Worlds or Histories.

SMITH, Stephanie A. *Snow-Eyes.* See Chapter 5A, Alternate Worlds or Histories.

SNYDER, Zilpha Keatley. *The Changing Maze.* See Chapter 1, Allegorical Fantasy and Literary Fairy Tales.

SNYDER, Zilpha Keatley. *A Season of Ponies.* See Chapter 7, Magic Adventure Fantasy.

3119 SOMTOW, S. P. (pseud. of Somtow Sucharitkul). *The Wizard's Apprentice.* **Gr. 7–10.**

Aaron's summer plans are limited to skateboarding, girls, and the mall, until the wizard Anazagoras offers to train Aaron to become hs apprentice.

Illus. by Nicholas Jainschigg, Macmillan, 1993, 144 pp. (0-689-31576-7)

(HBG 5:91; KR 61:1398; SLJ Aug 1993 p. 189; VOYA 16:235)

Spells of Wonder. **Ed. by Marion Zimmer Bradley.** See Chapter 5A, Alternate Worlds or Histories.

3120 SPRINGER, Nancy. *The Hex Witch of Seldom.* **Gr. 7–12.**

The powerful black mustang stallion bought for Bobbi Yandro by her grandfather is actually Shane, the Dark Rider, who has been enslaved within the body of a horse.

Baen, 1988, 276 pp., o.p.

(BBS:64; BL 84:908, 962, 85:863, 86:907; KR 56:169; VOYA 11:196, 12:14)

SPRINGER, Nancy. *Red Wizard.* See Chapter 5C, Travel to Other Worlds.

STASHEFF, Christopher. *Her Majesty's Wizard.* See Chapter 5C, Travel to Other Worlds.

STEARNS, Pamela (Fujimoto). *The Fool and the Dancing Bear.* See Chapter 1, Allegorical Fantasy and Literary Fairy Tales.

STEELE, Mary Q(uintard Govan). *The Owl's Kiss: Three Stories.* See Chapter 3, Fantasy Collections.

STEELE, Mary Q(uintard Govan). *Wish, Come True.* See Chapter 7, Magic Adventure Fantasy.

STERMAN, Betsy, and STERMAN, Samuel. *Backyard Dragon.* See Chapter 7, Magic Adventure Fantasy.

STEWART, Mary (Florence Elinor). *The Crystal Cave.* See Chapter 5B, Myth Fantasy.

3121 STEWART, Mary (Florence Elinor). *The Little Broomstick.* **Gr. 3–5. (Orig. British pub. 1971.)**

Mary goes to witch school to learn enough magic to rescue her black cat.

Illus. by Shirley Hughes, Morrow, 1972, 192 pp., o.p.

(BL 68:822; CCBB 25:146; HB 48:271; KR 40:5; LJ 97:1610; Suth:382)

3122 STEWART, Mary (Florence Elinor). *Thornyhold.* **Gr. 10 up. (Orig. British pub. 1988.)**

Gilly suspects that the animals and people living near her old country house are behaving strangely because they are under a witch's spell cast by her late cousin Geillis.

Fawcett, 1989, pap., 192 pp. (0-449-21712-4)

(BL 85:186; KR 56:1274; LJ Nov 15, 1988 p. 86)

STEWART, Mary (Florence Elinor). *A Walk in Wolf Wood.* See Chapter 8, Time Travel Fantasy.

STOCKTON, Frank (Francis) R(ichard). *The Bee-Man of Orn.* See Chapter 1, Allegorical Fantasy and Literary Fairy Tales.

3123 STRAUB, Peter (Francis). *Shadowland.* **Gr. 10 up.**

Tom and Del, two high school students drawn together by an interest in magic, visit Shadowland, home of renowned magician, Coleman Collins, who wants Tom to be his successor in the practice of black magic.

Coward, 1980, o.p.; Berkley, 1981, 1985, pap., 480 pp. (0-425-09726-9)

(Kies:168; KR 48:1187; LJ 105:2235; SLJ Feb 1981 p. 82; TLS 1981 p. 430)

3124 STRUGATSKII, Arkadii Natanovich, and STRUGATSKII, Boris Natanovich. *Monday Begins on Saturday.* **Gr. 10 up.**

A computer scientist studying witchcraft and magic in a secret laboratory produces a time-traveling sofa, an unspendable coin, a talking cat, and a house on hen's legs, in this satire of Russian scientific research.

Trans. by Leonid Renen, DAW, 1977, pap., 220 pp., o.p.

(BL 74:899, 905; Kliatt Winter 1978 p. 11)

SWAHN, Sven. *The Island through the Gate.* See Chapter 5C, Travel to Other Worlds.

Sword and Sorceress. **Ed. by Marion Zimmer Bradley.** See Chapter 5A, Alternate Worlds or Histories.

SYNGE, (Phyllis) Ursula. *Land of Heroes: A Retelling of the Kalevala.* See Chapter 5B, Myth Fantasy.

3125 **TARR, Judith.** *His Majesty's Elephant.* **Gr. 6–10.**

A stable boy and a princess join forces with Emperor Charlemagne's enchanted elephant to defeat the magic of a Byzantine sorcerer and save her father's life.

Harcourt, 1993, 193 pp. (0-15-200737-7)

(BL 90:817; HBG 5:91; CCBB 47:170; HB 70:76; KR 61:1398; VOYA 16:387)

TENNY, Dixie. *Call the Darkness Down.* See Chapter 5B, Myth Fantasy.

TEPPER, Sheri S. *Jinian Footseer.* See Chapter 5A, Alternate Worlds or Histories.

TEPPER, Sheri S. *Marianne, the Magus, and the Manticore.* See Chapter 5C, Travel to Other Worlds.

TEPPER, Sheri S. *The Song of Mavin Manyshaped.* See Chapter 5A, Alternate Worlds or Histories.

TERLOUW, Jan. *How to Become King.* See Chapter 1, Allegorical Fantasy and Literary Fairy Tales.

TOLKIEN, J(ohn) R(onald) R(euel). *The Hobbit; or There and Back Again.* See Chapter 5A, Alternate Worlds or Histories.

TOLSTOY, Nikolai. *The Coming of the King: The First Book of Merlin.* See Chapter 5B, Myth Fantasy.

TURKLE, Brinton (Cassaday). *Mooncoin Castle; or Skulduggery Rewarded.* See Chapter 4, Ghost Fantasy.

3126 **TURNBULL, Ann (Christine).** *The Frightened Forest.* **Gr. 4–6. (Orig. British**
✓ **pub. 1974.)**

Responsible for releasing a witch from an abandoned tunnel, Gillian and her cousins make a midnight attempt to recapture the malevolent creature.

Illus. by Gillian Gaze, Seabury, 1975, 125 pp., o.p.

(BL 71:1018; HB 51:385; KR 43:460; SLJ May 1975 p. 59; TLS 1974 p. 714)

3127 **TURNER, Ann.** *Rosemary's Witch.* **Gr. 4–8.**
✓ Told alternately from the points of view of Mathilda, a witch who was an unloved little girl one-hundred-fifty years ago, and of Rosemary, a contemporary nine-year-old whose family has moved into Mathilde's house, this is the story of an empathetic little girl who reaches out to a lonely, mean, sad old woman.

Harper, 1991, 164 pp. LB(0-06-026128-5), 1994, pap., 176 pp. (0-06-440494-3)

(BL 87:1569; CC 1992 Suppl. p. 63; CCBB 44:230; HBG 2:267; KR 59:400; SLJ May. 1991 p. 95)

UNWIN, Nora S. *Two Too Many.* See Chapter 2, Animal Fantasy.

3128 **URE, Jean.** *The Wizard in the Woods.* **Gr. 3–5. (Orig. British pub. 1990.)**

After his wizard's exam spell goes awry, Ben-Muzzy ends up in our world, where twins Joel and Gemma try to help him get home. The sequel is *Wizard in Wonderland* (1993).

Illus. by David Anstey, Candlewick, 1992, 176 pp. (1-56402-110-6)

(BL 89:671; HBG 4[Spring '93]:78; KR 60:1136; SLJ Oct 1992 p. 122)

VAN ALLSBURG, Chris. *The Garden of Abdul Gasazi.* See Chapter 7, Magic Adventure Fantasy.

3129 **VAN ALLSBURG, Chris.** *The Widow's Broom.* **Gr. K–3.**

✓ A witch gives her broomstick to Widow Shaw, and it proves to be talented at housekeeping, wood-chopping, and even piano playing, to the horror of her neighbors.

Illus. by the author, Houghton, 1992, 32 pp. (0-395-64051-2)

(BL 89:147, 846; CCBB 46:56; HB 69:79; KR 60:1136; SLJ Nov 1992 p. 144, Dec 1992 p. 23)

VANCE, Jack (pseud. of John Holbrook Vance). *Cugel's Saga.* See Chapter 5A, Alternate Worlds or Histories.

3130 **VINGE, Joan D(ennison).** *Ladyhawke.* **Gr. 10 up. (Orig. British pub. 1985.)**

✓ Orphaned Phillipe escapes death in the Bishop's prison and goes into the service of the mysterious Navarre, whose beautiful lover, Isabeau, has been transformed into a hawk by the evil Bishop.

NAL, 1985, pap., 252 pp., o.p.

(Kies:177; Kliatt 19[Fall 1985]:27; TLS 1985 p. 345; VOYA 8:195)

VOLSKY, Paula. *The Luck of Relian Kru.* See Chapter 5A, Alternate Worlds or Histories.

VOLSKY, Paula. *The Wolf in Winter.* See Chapter 5A, Alternate Worlds or Histories.

3131 **WALLACE, Barbara Brooks.** *Miss Switch to the Rescue.* **Gr. 3–6.**

Miss Switch saves the day after a witch turns Rupert, Amelia, and their entire fifth-grade class into toads. This is the sequel to *The Trouble with Miss Switch* (1981).

Illus. by Kathleen Garry McCord, Abingdon, 1981, 158 pp., o.p.

(BBC:215; BL 78:760; SLJ Mar 1982 p. 152)

WANGERIN, Walter, Jr. *Thistle.* See Chapter 1, Allegorical Fantasy and Literary Fairy Tales.

3132 **WARNER, Sylvia Townsend.** *Lolly Willowes: or, the Loving Huntsman.* **Gr. 10 up. (Orig. pub. Viking, 1926, 1928.)**

Laura Willowes leads an uneventful, spinsterly life until the age of forty-seven, when she decides to take up witchcraft, and makes a pact with the devil.

Academy Chicago, 1978, 1979, pap., 252 pp. (0-915864-91-6); Charles River Books, pap. (0-7043-3824-6)

(BL 22:332, 25:83; Kies:180; TLS 1926 p. 78, 1978 p. 273)

3133 **WATT-EVANS, Lawrence (pseud. of Richard Watt Evans).** *With a Single Spell.* **Gr. 10 up.**

An inexperienced wizard's apprentice joins a dragon hunt and comes across a magical tapestry linked to another world. This book is set in the same world as *Misenchanted Sword* (1985).

Ballantine, 1987, pap., 263 pp. (0-345-32616-4)

(BBS:66; BL 83:983, 1009; LJ Mar 15, 1987 p. 93)

3134 **WEALES, Gerald (Clifford).** *Miss Grimsbee Is a Witch.* **Gr. 3–5.**

Jimmy is the only one who believes that Miss Grimsbee is a real witch. The sequel is *Miss Grimsbee Takes a Vacation* (1965).

Illus. by Lita Scheel, Little, 1957, 123 pp., o.p.

(BL 53:435; CCBB 10:138; HB 33:140; KR 25:74; LJ 82:884)

WEIN, Elizabeth E. *The Winter Prince.* See Chapter 5B, Myth Fantasy.

WEIS, Margaret, and HICKMAN, Tracy. *Forging the Darksword.* See Chapter 5A, Alternate Worlds or Histories.

WHITCHER, Susan. *Real Mummies Don't Bleed: Friendly Tales for October Nights.* See Chapter 3, Fantasy Collections.

WHITE, T(erence) H(anbury). *The Once and Future King.* See Chapter 5B, Myth Fantasy.

3135 **WHITEHEAD, Victoria.** *The Chimney Witches.* **Gr. 4–6. (Orig. British pub. 1986.)**

On Halloween Eve, Lucy finally meets the witches she suspected of living in her chimney: Weird Hannah and her bumbling son, Rufus. The sequel is *Chimney Witch Chase* (1988).

Illus. by Linda North, Orchard, 1987, 117 pp., o.p.

(BL 84:154; CCBB 41:59; SLJ Nov 1987 p. 107)

WICKENDEN, Dan. *The Amazing Vacation.* See Chapter 5C, Travel to Other Worlds.

WILDE, Oscar (pseud. of Fingal O'Flahertie Wills). *The Happy Prince.* See Chapter 1, Allegorical Fantasy and Literary Fairy Tales.

3136 **WILLARD, Barbara.** *Spell Me a Witch.* **Gr. 3–5. (Orig. British pub. 1979.)**

Belladonna Agrimony, headmistress of the Academy for Young Witches, and Betony, a star student, rescue another young witch who has been transformed into a pig.

Harcourt, 1981, 142 pp., o.p.

(BL 78:313; KR 49:1410; SLJ Nov 1981 p. 99)

WILLARD, Nancy (Margaret). *The Mountains of Quilt.* See Chapter 7, Magic Adventure Fantasy.

3137 **WILLARD, Nancy (Margaret).** *The Sorcerer's Apprentice.* **Gr. K–5.**

✓ In this retelling of the traditional tale, sorcerer Tottibo assigns his new apprentice, Sylvia, the task of using a magic sewing machine to make clothing for his menagerie of fantastical creatures.

Illus. by Leo Dillon and Diane Dillon, Scholastic, 1993, 32 pp. (0-590-47329-8)

(BL 90:529; CCBB 47:170; HB 70:193; KR 61:1470; SLJ Jan 1994 p. 116)

WILLEY, Elizabeth. *The Well-Favored Man: The Tale of the Sorcerer's Nephew.* See Chapter 5A, Alternate Worlds or Histories.

WILLIAMS, Anne. *Secret of the Round Tower.* See Chapter 1, Allegorical Fantasy and Literary Fairy Tales.

WILLIAMS, Jay. *The Magic Grandfather.* See Chapter 7, Magic Adventure Fantasy.

WILLIAMS, Jay. *Petronella.* See Chapter 1, Allegorical Fantasy and Literary Fairy Tales.

WILLIAMS (John), Ursula Moray. *The Toymaker's Daughter.* See Chapter 9, Toy Fantasy.

3138 *Witches.* **Ed. by Isaac Asimov, Martin H. Greenberg, and Charles G. Waugh. Gr. 10 up.**

Thirteen fantasy and science fiction tales about female witchcraft, including Schmitz's "Witches of Karres" and L'Engle's "Poor Little Saturday." The companion volume is *Wizards* (1983).

NAL, 1984, pap., 350 pp. (0-451-12882-6)

(BL 80:1228, 1234; Kliatt Fall 1984 p. 24; VOYA 7:269)

3139 *Witches, Witches, Witches.* **Ed. by Helen Hoke. Gr. 5–8. (Orig. British pub. 1958.)**

Twenty-five tales about folktale and fantasy witches, whose authors include Oscar Wilde and Andrew Lang.

Illus. by W. R. Lohse, Watts, 1966, 230 pp., o.p.

(BL 55:190; KR 26:663; LJ 83:3572)

A Wizard's Dozen: Stories of the Fantastic. **Ed. by Michael Stearns.** See Chapter 3, Fantasy Collections.

3140 **WOLF, Joyce.** *Between the Cracks.* **Gr. 6–8.**

Eighth-grader Bentley saves her friend Charles from the corrupting influence of Mordicus the magician.

Dial, 1992, 176 pp. (0-8037-1270-7)

(BL 89:432; HBG 4[Spring 1992]:78; KR 60:1195; SLJ Dec 1992 p. 262; VOYA 15:296)

WREDE, Patricia C(ollins). *The Harp of Imach Thyssel.* See Chapter 5A, Alternate Worlds or Histories.

WREDE, Patricia C(ollins). *The Seven Towers.* See Chapter 5A, Alternate Worlds or Histories.

WRIGGINS, Sally. *The White Monkey King: A Chinese Fable.* See Chapter 5B, Myth Fantasy.

WRIGHT, Betty Ren. *The Ghost of Ernie P.* See Chapter 4, Ghost Fantasy.

WRIGHT, Betty Ren. *The Ghost Witch.* See Chapter 4, Ghost Fantasy.

WRIGHTSON, (Alice) Patricia (Furlonger). *An Older Kind of Magic.* See Chapter 7, Magic Adventure Fantasy.

WURTS, Janny. *Sorcerer's Legacy.* See Chapter 5A, Alternate Worlds or Histories.

3141 **WURTS, Janny.** *Stormwarden* **(Cycle of Fire series, book 1). Gr. 10 up.**

A brother and sister named Emien and Taen and a young scholar named Jaric are caught up in a battle between opposing sorceresses. The sequels are *Keeper of the Keys* (1988) and *Shadowfane* (1988).

Berkley, 1984, pap., 325 pp., o.p.

(BL 81:484, 520; VOYA 8:141)

YOLEN (Stemple), Jane H(yatt). *Dove Isabeau.* See Chapter 1, Allegorical Fantasy and Literary Fairy Tales.

YOLEN (Stemple), Jane H(yatt). *The Magic Three of Solatia.* See Chapter 1, Allegorical Fantasy and Literary Fairy Tales.

YOLEN (Stemple), Jane H(yatt). *Merlin's Booke.* See Chapter 5B, Myth Fantasy.

3142 YOLEN (Stemple), Jane H(yatt). *The Wizard of Washington Square.* Gr. 4–6.

A tiny wizard is distressed to discover how many children have forgotten that he exists.

Illus. by Ray Cruz, Collins + World, 1969, 126 pp., o.p.

(CCBB 23:170; KR 37:1150; LJ 95:783)

3143 YOLEN (Stemple), Jane H(yatt). *Wizard's Hall.* Gr. 4–7.

✓   Eleven-year-old novice wizard Henry, renamed Thornmallow, means well but can't seem to do spell-casting and transformations, even though Wizard's Hall needs all the help it can get to defeat the evil Master and his Quilted Beast.

Harcourt, 1991, 134 pp. (0-15-298132-2)

(BL 87:1494; CCBB 44:280; HBG 2:270; KR 59:611; SLJ July 1991 p. 75; VOYA 14:184, 15:11)

3144 YOUNG, Miriam. *The Witch Mobile.* Gr. 2–4.

Nanette, the smallest witch in the toy shop, does not want to work revengeful spells like her older sisters.

Illus. by Victoria Chess, Lothrop, 1969, 48 pp., o.p.

(KR 37:995; LJ 95:1192)

3145 *Young Witches and Warlocks.* Ed. by Isaac Asimov, Martin H. Greenberg, and
✓   **Charles G. Waugh. Gr. 6–9.**

Ten stories about adolescents with unusual abilities, including "Teregram," "The Entrance Exam," and two by Ray Bradbury and Elizabeth Coatsworth.

Harper, 1987, 207 pp., o.p.

(BL 83:1673, 1683; CCBB 40:202; JHC:435; KR 55:921; SHC:747; SLJ Jan 1988 p. 83; VOYA 10:93)

3146 ZAMBRENO, Mary Frances. *A Plague of Sorcerers.* Gr. 6–10.

✓   A skunk named Delia becomes apprentice wizard Jermyn's familiar, and the two try to save the city's sorcerers, most of whom have been struck down by a mysterious plague. In the sequel, *Journeyman Wizard: A Magical Mystery* (1994), Jermyn is accused of the murder of his teacher, spell-master Lady Jean.

Harcourt, 1991, 224 pp. (0-15-262430-9)

(BL 88:626; CCBB 45:53; HBG 3[July–Dec 1991]:75; JHC 1992 Suppl. p. 69; KR 59:1230; SLJ Oct 1991 p. 150; VOYA 14:328, 15:10)

3147 ZELAZNY, Roger (Joseph Christopher). *Jack of Shadows.* Gr. 10 up.

Jack, a shadow magician from the dark side of the world who was unjustly punished for thievery, is determined to have vengeance.

Walker, 1971, 207 pp., o.p.; NAL, 1985, pap. (0-451-15976-4)

(BL 68:320; LJ 97:217; Tymn:184)

3148 ZELAZNY, Roger (Joseph Christopher). *Madwand* (The Changeling Saga, book 2). Gr. 10 up.

Pol Detson must use his newly learned magician's skills to battle a sorcerer bent on ruling the world. This is the sequel to *Changeling* (Ace, 1980). Both books were published together in *Wizard World* (Baen, 1989).

Phantasia Press, 1981, 254 pp., o.p.

(BL 78:850; VOYA 5:41)

PART TWO

RESEARCH
GUIDE

11

Bibliographical and Reference Sources on Fantasy Literature

The works listed here include bibliographies of fantasy (such as Naomi Lewis's *Fantasy Books for Children*), indexes to fantasy criticism (such as Tymn's *The Year's Scholarship in Fantastic Literature*), biographical directories (such as *Something About the Author*), and atlases and dictionaries of the faerie world (such as J. B. Post's *An Atlas of Fantasy*). Multivolume reference works and those works commonly known by title (such as *Children's Catalog*) have been listed by title, rather than by editor.

The Preface contains a list of sources from which the information in Chapters 11 through 14 was drawn.

American Library Association Best of the Best for Children. Edited by Denise Perry Donavin. New York: Random, 1992. "Fractured Fairy Tales," pp. 53–55; "Fantasy Fiction," pp. 90–92.

American Writers for Children Before 1900 (*Dictionary of Literary Biography,* vol. 42). Edited by Glenn E. Estes. Detroit: Gale, 1985.

American Writers for Children, 1900–1960 (*Dictionary of Literary Biography,* vol. 22). Edited by John Cech. Detroit: Gale, 1983.

American Writers for Children Since 1960: Fiction (*Dictionary of Literary Biography,* vol. 52). Edited by Glenn E. Estes. Detroit: Gale, 1986.

Anderson, Hugh, ed. *The Singing Roads: A Guide to Australian Children's Authors and Illustrators.* Sydney: Wentworth Press, 1965.

Andronik, C. M. "More About King Arthur." *Book Report* 9 (Jan–Feb 1991): 37–38. (bibliographic essay)

Ashley, Mike. *Who's Who in Horror and Fantasy Literature.* London: Elm Tree Books, 1977.

Becker, M. R. "The Year in Young Adult Science Fiction, Fantasy and Horror: 1989." *Science Fiction and Fantasy Book Review Annual,* 1990, pp. 119–138. New York: Greenwood, 1991. (bibliographic essay)

Belden, E. A., and J. M. Beckman. "Dragons, Dystopias and Time Travel: Fantasy and Science Fiction for Everyone." *English Journal* 80 (Jan 1991): 78–81.

Bell, John. "Time Voyageurs: An Annotated Checklist of Juvenile Books Involving Fantastic Journeys in Canadian History." *Canadian Children's Literature* 38 (1985): 26–28.

Best Books for Children: Preschool Through Grade 6. 5th ed. Edited by John T. Gillespie and Corinne J. Naden. New Providence, NJ: Bowker, 1994. "Fantasy," pp. 300–327. (bibliography)

Best Books for Junior High Readers. Edited by John T. Gillespie. New Providence, NJ: Bowker, 1991. "Fantasy," pp. 67–76. (bibliography)

Best Books for Senior High Readers. Edited by John T. Gillespie. New Providence, NJ: Bowker, 1991. "Fantasy," pp. 51–68. (bibliography)

"[Best] Science Fiction and Fantasy for Young Adults [1984–1985]." *VOYA* 8 (Feb 1986): 363–367.

"Best Science Fiction/Fantasy [1985–1986]." *VOYA* 10 (Apr 1987): 21–24. (bibliography)

"Best Science Fiction/Fantasy [1987]." *VOYA* 11 (Apr 1988): 11–14. (bibliography)

"Best Science Fiction/Fantasy [1988]." *VOYA* 12 (Apr 1989): 13–16.

"Best Science Fiction/Fantasy and Horror [1989]." *VOYA* 13 (Apr 1990): 11–16.

"Best Science Fiction, Fantasy, and Horror [1990]." *VOYA* 14 (Apr 1991): 9–13.

"Best Science Fiction, Fantasy, and Horror [1991]." *VOYA* 15 (Apr 1992): 9–13.

"Best Science Fiction, Fantasy, and Horror [1992]." *VOYA* 16 (Apr 1993): 9–10, 16.

"Best Science Fiction, Fantasy, and Horror [1993]." *VOYA* 17 (Apr 1994): 7–10, 19. (bibliography)

"Bibliography: The Year's Work in Children's Literature Studies: 1987." *Children's Literature Association Quarterly* 14 (Summer 1989): 81–96.

"Bibliography: The Year's Work in Children's Literature Studies: 1988." *Children's Literature Association Quarterly* 15 (Summer 1990): 58–107.

"Bibliography: The Year's Work in Children's Literature Studies: 1989." *Children's Literature Association Quarterly* 16 (Fall 1991): 97–216.

"Bibliography: The Year's Work in Children's Literature Studies: 1990." *Children's Literature Association Quarterly* 17 (Summer 1992): 1–47.

"Bibliography: The Year's Work in Children's Literature Studies: 1991." *Children's Literature Association Quarterly* 18 (Summer 1993).

Bingham, Jane, ed. *Writers for Children: Critical Surveys of Major Authors Since the Seventeenth Century.* New York: Scribner, 1988.

A Biographical Dictionary of Science Fiction and Fantasy Artists. Edited by Robert Weinberg. New York: Greenwood, 1988.

Bleiler, Everett Franklin. *The Checklist of Fantastic Literature: A Bibliography of Fantasy, Weird and Science Fiction Published in the English Language.* Chicago: Shasta, 1948. 2nd ed. Mercer Island, WA: Fax, 1972.

Books for You: A Booklist for Senior High Students. 10th ed. Edited by Richard F. Abrahamson and Betty Carter. Urbana, IL: National Council of Teachers of English, 1988. "Fantasy," pp. 181—201.

Briggs, Katharine M. *An Encyclopedia of Fairies: Hobgoblins, Brownies, Bogies, and Other Supernatural Creatures.* New York: Pantheon, 1976.

Briney, Robert E., and Edward Wood. *Science Fiction Bibliographies: An Annotated Bibliography of Bibliographic Works on Science Fiction and Fantasy Fiction.* Chicago: Advent, 1972.

Broderick, Kathryn. "Flights of Fancy." *Book Links* 2 (Jan 1993): 48–52. (bibliographic essay: books about flying)

Burgess, Michael. *Reference Guide to Science Fiction, Fantasy, and Horror.* Englewood, CO: Libraries Unlimited, 1992.

Caywood, C. "Stories from the Dawn of Time." *VOYA* 14 (Dec 1991): 297. (bibliography)

Chang, Margaret. "Fantasy Literature: Encounters in the Globe of Time." *School Library Journal* 36 (Sept 1990): 163–164.

Children's Authors and Illustrators: An Index to Biographical Dictionaries. 4th ed. Edited by Joyce Nakamura. Detroit: Gale, 1986.

Children's Catalog. 16th ed. Edited by Juliette Yaakov. New York: Wilson, 1991 (Suppl., 1992, 1993, 1994).

Children's Literature Abstracts. Rowys, Wales: The Children's Libraries Section of the International Federation of Library Associations, 1973–Mar 1991; Austin, TX: International Federation of Library Associations: Children's Libraries Section and Round Table of Children's Literature Documentation Centers, June 1991–Sept 1993. (bibliography of children's literature studies)

Children's Literature Review: Excerpts from Reviews, Criticism and Commentary on Books for Children and Young People. Edited by Carolyn Riley. Detroit: Gale, 1976–.

Clareson, Thomas D. *Science Fiction Criticism: An Annotated Checklist.* Kent, OH: Kent State Univ. Press, 1972.

Contemporary Authors. Edited by Hal May and Susan M. Trosky. Detroit: Gale, 1962–.

Contemporary Literary Criticism. Edited by Daniel J. Marowski and Roger Matuz. Detroit: Gale, 1973–.

Cooper, Ilene. "Popular Reading—After *The Borrowers.*" *Booklist* 81 (Nov 15, 1984): 452–453. (bibliography)

Currey, L. W. *Science Fiction and Fantasy Authors: A Bibliography of First Printings of Their Fiction and Selected Non-Fiction.* Boston: G. K. Hall, 1979.

Davidson, Don Adrian. "Sword and Sorcery Fiction: An Annotated Book List." *English Journal* 61 (1972): 43–51.

Dictionary of Literary Biography. Detroit: Gale, 1981–. Each volume has its own editor and subject matter; vols. 22, 42, and 52 are devoted to children's literature.

Dooley, Patricia. "Finding Fantasy." *School Library Journal* 27 (Dec 1980): 32–33. (bibliographic essay)

Doyle, Brian. *The Who's Who of Children's Literature.* New York: Schocken, 1968.

Eaglen, Audrey B. "Alternatives: A Bibliography of Books and Periodicals on Science Fiction and Fantasy." *Top of the News* 39 (Fall 1982): 96–103.

Eakin, Mary, ed. *Good Books for Children, 1950–1965.* 3rd ed. Chicago: Univ. of Chicago Press, 1966.

Elleman, Barbara. "The Days of Camelot." *Book Links* 1 (Sept 1991): 23–27.

———. "Popular Reading: Animal Fantasy." *Booklist* 76 (Feb 15, 1980): 839–841. (bibliography)

———. "Popular Reading—Animal Fantasy: Update." *Booklist* 84 (Apr 15, 1988): 1441–1442. (bibliography)

———. "Popular Reading—Ghosts, Witches, and Such: Update." *Booklist* 83 (Dec 1, 1986): 585–586. (bibliography)

———. "Popular Reading: Time Fantasy." *Booklist* 74 (June 1, 1978): 1558–1560. (bibliography)

———. "Popular Reading—Time Fantasy: Update." *Booklist* 81 (June 1, 1985): 1407–1408. (bibliography)

The Encyclopedia of Science Fiction and Fantasy. 3 vols. Edited by Donald Henry Tuck. Chicago: Advent, 1974–1983. Previous edition entitled *A Handbook of Science Fiction and Fantasy.* Hobart, Tasmania, Australia, 1959.

Estes, Sally. "Fantastic Reading: Selected Fantasy for Young Adults." *Booklist* 78 (Jan 1, 1982): 593–594.

———. "Fantasy: Highlights of the '80s." *Booklist* 86 (Jan 1, 1990): 903–907.

———, ed. *Genre Favorites for Young Adults: A Collection of "Booklist" Columns.* Chicago: American Library Association, 1993. "Fantasy Highlights of the 1980's," pp. 36–45.

———. "Science Fiction/Fantasy in Series." Speech given at the Young Adult Books Open

Forum at the ALA Conference, July 1985. *Booklist* 82 (Nov 1, 1985): 393–396. (bibliography)

Fantasy Literature: A Readers' Guide. Edited by Neil Barron. New York: Garland, 1990. "From Baum to Tolkien, 1900–1956," pp. 116–222; "Modern Fantasy for Young Adults, 1950–1988," pp. 305–350.

"Fiction for Children 1970–1980: Myth and Fantasy." *Children's Literature in Education* 12 (Autumn 1981): 119–139.

Fifth Book of Junior Authors and Illustrators. Edited by Sally Holmes Holtze. New York: Wilson, 1983.

Forrest, Linda A. "Young Adult Fanatsy and the Search for Gender-Fair Genres." *Journal of Youth Services in Libraries* 7 (Fall 1993): 37–42. (annotated bibliography)

Fourth Book of Junior Authors and Illustrators. Edited by Doris de Montreville and Elizabeth D. Crawford. New York: Wilson, 1978.

Gallo, Donald R. *Books for You: A Booklist for Senior High Students.* Urbana, IL: National Council of Teachers of English, 1985. "Fantasy," pp. 121–132.

A Ghoul at Your Fingertips: Supernatural Fiction for Teens. Englewood, CO: Libraries Unlimited, 1992.

Gillispie, John T. *The Elementary School Paperback Collection.* Chicago: American Library Association, 1985. "Fantasy." pp. 126–139.

———. *The Junior High School Paperback Collection.* Chicago: American Library Association, 1985. "Fantasy," pp. 30–37; "Science Fiction," pp. 95–107.

———. *The Senior High School Paperback Collection.* Chicago: American Library Association, 1986. "Fantasy and Science Fiction," pp. 55–94.

Greene, David L. "Children's Literature Periodicals on Individual Authors, Dime Novels, Fantasy." *Phaedrus* 3, no. 1 (Spring 1976): 22–25.

Grudzien, P. "The Matter of Britain: Publications Concerning the Arthurian Legend." *Serials Review* 15 (1989): 67–70.

Hall, H. W., ed. *Science Fiction Book Review Index, 1921–1973.* Detroit: Gale, 1975.

Handbook of American Popular Culture. Edited by M. Thomas Inge. Westport, CT: Greenwood, 1988. "Fantasy" by Roger C. Schlobin, pp. 139–155.

Hannabus, Stuart, Barry Litherland, and Stephanie Morland, comps. "Fiction for Children, 1970–1980. 1. Myth and Fantasy." *Children's Literature in Education* 12 (Autumn 1981): 119–139. (bibliography)

Helbig, Alethea K., and Agnes R. Perkins. *Dictionary of American Children's Fiction, 1859–1959: Books of Recognized Merit.* Westport, CT: Greenwood, 1985.

———. *Dictionary of American Children's Fiction, 1960–1984.* Westport, CT: Greenwood, 1986.

———. *Dictionary of American Children's Fiction, 1985–1989.* New York: Greenwood, 1993.

———. *Dictionary of Children's Fiction from Australia, Canada, India, New Zealand, and Selected African Countries: Books of Recognized Merit.* New York: Greenwood, 1992.

Hendrickson, Linnea. *Children's Literature: A Guide to the Criticism.* Boston: G. K. Hall, 1987. "Fantasy," pp. 402–411.

Hepler, Susan, and Susan Steinberg. "Here There Be Dragons." *Book Links* 3 (Nov 1993): 5–7. (bibliography)

Hoffman, Miriam, and Eva Samuels. *Authors and Illustrators of Children's Books: Writings of Their Lives and Works.* New York: Bowker, 1972, pp. 56–61, 70–107, 165–171, 186–192, 256–267, 280–301, 340–342, 364–393, 407–411. Essays on Carlson, Cleary, Coatsworth, Hamilton, Lawson, Lewis, Lindgren, M. Norton, Seuss, Sendak, Seredy, and E. B. White.

Hopkins, Lee Bennett. "Fantasy Flights Circa 1976." *Teacher* 93 (Apr 1976): 34+. (bibliography)

Hutchinson, Tom. *British Science Fiction and Fantasy.* London: National Book League and the British Council, 1975. "Children's Books," pp. 39–45. (bibliography)

The Junior Book of Authors. 2nd rev. ed. Edited by Stanley J. Kunitz and Howard Haycraft. New York: Wilson, 1951.

Junior High School Library Catalog. 6th ed. Edited by Juliette Yaakov. New York: Wilson, 1990 (Suppl., 1991, 1992, 1993).

Kies, Cosette N. *Supernatural Fiction for Teens: More Than 1,300 Good Paperbacks to Read for Wonderment, Fear, and Fun.* 2nd ed. Englewood, CO: Libraries Unlimited, 1992.

Lacy, Norris J. *The Arthurian Encyclopedia.* New York: Garland, 1986.

Lehan, Terri, and Peggy Murray. "Fantasy: A Reader's List." *VOYA* 5, no. 4 (Oct 1982): 28–34.

Leif, Irving P. *Children's Literature: A Historical and Contemporary Bibliography.* Troy, New York: Whitson, 1977.

Levin, Betty, Gregory Maguire, and Martha Walke. "Worlds Apart." Watertown, MA: The Foundation for Children's Books: *The Children's Book Bag,* vol. III (Fall 1992). (bibliographic essay)

Lewis, Naomi. *Fantasy Books for Children.* rev. ed. London: National Book League, 1975, 1977. (bibliography)

Los Angeles Fantasy Society, Children's Literature Committee. "Recommended Reading List." North Hollywood, CA: Los Angeles Fantasy Society, 1993. (bibliography)

"Luck, Wishes and Spells." *School Librarians Workshop* 10 (Oct 1989): 9–10. (bibliography)

Lukenbill, W. Bernard, and Sharon Lee Stewart. *Youth Literature: An Interdisciplinary, Annotated Guide to North American Dissertation Research, 1930–1985.* New York: Garland, 1988.

Lurker, Manfred, ed. *Dictionary of Gods and Goddesses, Devils and Demons.* New York: Routledge, 1987.

Lynn, Ruth Nadelman. "'There Is Another Kind of Real: Fantasy Literature for Children." Watertown, MA: The Foundation for Children's Books: *The Children's Book Bag,* Spring 1991. (bibliographic essay)

McGeehon, C. "I Have Read Everything by Tolkien." *Unabashed Librarian* 50 (1980): 25. (bibliography)

McGhan, Barry, ed. *Science Fiction and Fantasy Pseudonyms.* rev. ed. Dearborn, MI: Misfit Press, 1979.

Mahony, Bertha E. *Books for Boys and Girls: A Suggestive Purchase List.* Boston: Women's Educational and Industrial Union, Bookshop for Boys and Girls, 1916. "Modern Fairy Tales," pp. 23–27. (2nd ed. 1917, pp. 15, 23–27; 3rd ed. 1919, pp. 14, 23–26; 4th rev. ed. 1922, pp. 35–40)

Mahony, Bertha E., and Elinor Whitney. *Five Years of Children's Books 1930–1935: A Supplement to Realms of Gold.* Garden City, NY: Doubleday, 1936. "Creations of Fancy—Modern Fairy Tales," pp. 195–214.

———. *Realms of Gold in Children's Books* (5th ed. of *Books for Boys and Girls—A Suggestive Purchase List,* previously published by the Bookshop for Boys and Girls, Women's Educational and Industrial Union, Boston). Garden City, NY: Doubleday, 1929. "Creations of Fancy—Modern Fairy Tales," pp. 263–298.

Major Authors and Illustrators for Children and Young Adults: A Selection of Sketches from "Something About the Author." Edited by Laurie Collier and Joyce Nakamura. 6 vols. Detroit: Gale, 1993.

Manguel, Alberto, and Gianni Guadalupi. *The Dictionary of Imaginary Places.* Expanded ed. San Diego: Harcourt, 1987.

Masterworks of Children's Literature: 1550–1900. 9 vols. Edited by Jonathan Cott. New

York: Stonehill/Chelsea House, 1983–1986. Vol. VI: *The Victorian Era, 1837–1900.* Edited by Robert Lee Wolf. Includes Thackeray, Browne, Ruskin, Kingsley. Vol. VIII: *The Twentieth Century.* Edited by William T. Moynihan and Mary E. Shaner. Includes a chapter on contemporary fantasy.

Means, H. J. "Books for Young Adults: Science Fiction, Fantasy, and the Occult." *English Journal* 62 (Oct 1973): 1059–1060. (bibliographic essay)

Miller, C. "Science Fiction, Fantasy, and Horror: The Year in Review." *AB Bookman's Weekly* 80 (Oct 26, 1987): 1576–1578. (bibliography)

More Junior Authors. Edited by Muriel Fuller. New York: Wilson, 1963.

Muller, Al, and C. W. Sullivan III. "Science Fiction and Fantasy Series Books." *English Journal* 69 (Oct 1980): 71–74. (bibliography)

Nelms, Beth, and Ben Nelms. "The Farfaring Imagination: Recent Fantasy and Science Fiction." *English Journal* 74 (Apr 1985): 83–86. (bibliography)

Olcott, F. J. "Fairy Tales for Children: Bibliography No. 13." *New York Special Library Report,* 1898.

The Oxford Companion to Children's Literature. Edited by Humphrey Carpenter and Mari Prichard. New York: Oxford Univ. Press, 1984. "Fantasy," pp. 181–182.

Page, Michael, and Robert Ingpen. *Encyclopedia of Things That Never Were: Creatures, Places and People.* New York: Viking, 1987 (orig. British pub. 1985).

Parish, M. "Children's Fantasy for Young Adults." *English Journal* 66 (Oct 1977): 92–93. (bibliography)

"The Pendragon Chroniclers: A Survey of Arthurian Fiction." In *The Pendragon Chronicles: Heroic Fantasy from the Time of King Arthur,* ed. by Mike Ashley. New York: Bedrick, 1990, pp. 402–416. (bibliography)

Pflieger, Pat, and Helen M. Hill. *A Reference Guide to Modern Fantasy for Children.* Westport, CT: Greenwood, 1984.

Phillips, R. A. "Discovering New Worlds." *Curriculum Review* 19 (Sept 1980): 336–337. (bibliographic essay)

Post, J. B. *An Atlas of Fantasy.* rev. ed. New York: Ballantine, 1979. Expanded edition of articles published in *Special Library Association Geography and Map Division Bulletin* 75 (Mar 1969): 11–13, and 101 (Sept 1975): 12–14.

Raburn, Josephine. "Ghost Stories." *School Library Journal* 31 (Nov 1984): 25–27. (bibliography)

———. "Shuddering Shades! A Ghostly Book List." *Top of the News* 41 (Spring 1985): 275–281.

Rahn, Suzanne. *Children's Literature: An Annotated Bibliography of the History and Criticism.* New York: Garland, 1981. "Fantasy," pp. 83–92.

Recommended Reading List for Young People Ages Nine and Up. North Hollywood, CA: Los Angeles Science Fantasy Society, 1991.

Richards, George M. *The Fairy Dictionary.* New York: Macmillan, 1932.

Roginski, Jim, ed. *Newbery and Caldecott Medalists and Honor Book Winners: Bibliographies and Resource Material Through 1977.* Littleton, CO: Libraries Unlimited, 1982.

Rosenberg, Betty. *Genreflecting: A Guide to Reading Interests in Genre Fiction.* Littleton, CO: Libraries Unlimited, 1982. "Fantasy," pp. 210–221.

Ross, Jan. "Small Is Tall—Children and Self-Esteem." *Book Links* 2 (Jan 1993): 53–59. (bibliographic essay: miniature worlds)

Rovin, Jeff. *The Fantasy Almanac.* New York: Dutton, 1979.

Sanborn, L. "Fractured Folk and Fairy Tales for All Ages." *School Library Media Activities Monthly* 7 (June 1991): 43–44+.

Schacterle, Lance, and Jeanne Welcher. "A Checklist of Secondary Studies on Imaginary Voyages." *Bulletin of Bibliography* 31 (1974): 99–100, 106.

Schlobin, Roger C. *The Literature of Fantasy: An Annotated Bibliography of Modern Fantasy Fiction.* New York: Garland, 1979.

Schlobin, Roger C., and Marshall B. Tymn. "The Year's Scholarship in Science Fiction and Fantasy: 1974." *Extrapolation* 18 (Dec 1976): 73–96.

―――. "The Year's Scholarship in Science Fiction and Fantasy, 1975." *Extrapolation* 19 (May 1978): 156–199.

―――. "The Year's Scholarship in Science Fiction and Fantasy, 1976." *Extrapolation* 20 (Spring 1979): 60–99.

―――. "The Year's Scholarship in Science Fiction and Fantasy, 1977." *Extrapolation* 20 (Fall 1979): 238–287.

―――. "The Year's Scholarship in Science Fiction and Fantasy, 1978." *Extrapolation* 21 (Spring 1980): 45–89.

―――. "The Year's Scholarship in Science Fiction and Fantasy, 1979." *Extrapolation* 22 (Spring 1981): 25–91.

"Science Fiction and Fantasy for Young Adults." *VOYA* 8 (Feb 1986): 363–367. (bibliography)

Science Fiction and Fantasy Literature: A Checklist from 1700–1974 (bound with *Contemporary Science Fiction Authors. II*). 2 vols. Edited by Robert Reginald. Detroit: Gale, 1979.

Science Fiction and Fantasy Literature, 1975–1991: A Bibliography of Science Fiction, Fantasy and Horror Fiction Books and Nonfiction Monographs. Edited by Robert Reginald. Detroit: Gale, 1992.

Science Fiction and Fantasy Reference Index: 1878–1985: An International Author and Subject Index to History and Criticism. 2 vols. Edited by H. W. Hall. Detroit: Gale, 1987. Updates and will be followed by the annual *Science Fiction and Fantasy Research Index* published by Borgo Press. More emphasis on science fiction than fantasy. Includes children's writers who have also written for adults.

Science Fiction and Fanatsy Reference Index, 1985–1991: An International Author and Subject Index to History and Criticism. Edited by Hal W. Hall. Englewood, CO: Libraries Unlimited, 1993.

Science Fiction and Fantasy Series and Sequels: A Bibliography. Vol. 1: *Books.* Edited by Tim Cottrill, Martin H. Greenberg, and Charles G. Waugh. New York: Garland, 1986.

Science Fiction Writers: Critical Studies of the Major Authors from the Early Nineteenth Century to the Present Day. Edited by E. F. Bleiler. New York: Scribner, 1982.

Searles, Baird, Beth Meacham, and Michael Franklin. *A Reader's Guide to Fantasy.* New York: Avon, 1982. Includes both children's and adult books. (bibliography)

Seattle (Washington) Public Library. "After *Mary Poppins:* Book List." *Top of the News* 23 (Nov 1966): 31–34.

Senior High School Library Catalog. 14th ed. Edited by Brenda Smith and Juliette Yaakov. New York: Wilson, 1992. (suppl., 1993)

Shapiro, Lillian I. *Fiction for Youth: A Guide to Recommended Books.* New York: Neal-Schuman, 1992. "Fantasies" indexed, p. 236.

Sixth Book of Junior Authors and Illustrators. Edited by Sally Holmes Holtze. New York: Wilson, 1988.

Sleigh, Bernard. *An Ancient Mappe of Fairyland, with a Guide to the Map of Fairyland; Newly Discovered and Set Forth.* rev. ed. New York: Dutton, 1920, 1925. Originally published in England, 1920.

Something About the Author: Autobiography Series. Edited by Adele Sarkissian. Detroit: Gale, 1985–.

Something About the Author: Facts and Pictures About Authors and Illustrators of Books for Young People. Edited by Anne Commire. Detroit: Gale, 1971–.

South, Malcolm. *Mythical and Fabulous Creatures: A Source Book and Research Guide.* Westport, CT: Greenwood, 1987.

Speaking for Ourselves: Autobiographical Sketches by Notable Authors of Books for Young

Adults. Edited by Donald R. Gallo. Urbana, IL: National Council of Teachers of English, 1990.

Stott, John C. *Children's Literature from A to Z: A Guide for Parents and Teachers.* New York: McGraw-Hill, 1984. "Fantasy," pp. 104–108.

Supernatural Fiction Writers: Fantasy and Horror. 2 vols. Edited by E. F. Bleiler. New York: Scribner, 1985.

Survey of Modern Fantasy Literature. 5 vols. Edited by Frank N. Magill. Englewood Cliffs, NJ: Salem Press, 1983.

Sutherland, Zena, ed. *The Best in Children's Books, 1966–1972.* Chicago: Univ. of Chicago Press, 1973.

———. *The Best in Children's Books, 1973–1978.* Chicago: Univ. of Chicago Press, 1980.

———. *The Best in Children's Books: The University of Chicago Guide to Children's Literature, 1979–1984.* Chicago: Univ. of Chicago Press, 1986.

Third Book of Junior Authors. Edited by Doris de Montreville and Donna Hill. New York: Wilson, 1972.

"Time Zones [Ventures into the Past, Present, or Parallel World]." *School Librarians' Workshop* 12 (Sept 1991): 13–14. (bibliography)

Twentieth-Century Children's Writers. 3rd ed. Edited by Tracy Chevalier and D. L. Kirkpatrick. Chicago: St. James, 1989.

Twentieth Century Literary Criticism. Edited by Dennis Poupard and James E. Persorn, Jr. Detroit: Gale, 1978–.

Twentieth Century Science Fiction Writers. 3rd ed. Edited by Noelle Watson and Paul E. Schellinger. Chicago: St. James, 1991. Original publication, St. Martin, 1981. "Major Fantasy Writers," pp. 863–870.

Tymn, Marshall B. *American Fantasy and Science Fiction: Toward a Bibliography of Works Published in the United States, 1948–1973.* San Bernardino, CA: Borgo Press, 1980.

———. "An Annotated Bibliography of Critical Studies and Reference Works on Fantasy." *CEA Critic* 40 (Jan 1978): 43–47. Expanded version: *Recent Critical Studies on Fantasy Literature: An Annotated Checklist, Exchange Bibliography #1522.* Chicago: Council of Planning Librarians, 1978.

———. "Bibliography of Fantastic Scholarship: History and Culture, Themes and Motifs, Author Studies, Children's Literature." In *The Scope of Fantastic—Culture, Biography, Themes, Children's Literature: Selected Essays from the First International Conference on the Fantastic in Literature and Film.* Edited by Robert A. Collins and Howard D. Pearce. Westport, CT: Greenwood, 1985, pp. 267–270.

———. "Fantasy Literature: A Survey." *Analytical & Enumerative Bibliography* 5 (1981): 25–34.

———. "Guide to Science Fiction and Fantasy Scholarship: 1980–1982." In *Science Fiction Dialogues.* Edited by Gary K. Wolfe. Chicago: Academy Chicago, 1982, pp. 215–227.

———. "Modern Critical Studies and Reference Works on Fantasy." In *The Aesthetics of Fantasy Literature and Art.* Edited by Roger C. Schlobin. South Bend, IN: Univ. of Notre Dame Press, 1982, pp. 262–270.

———. "Science Fiction and Fantasy in the School Curriculum: Part I: A Checklist of Articles, 1967–1975." *English Language Arts Bulletin* 21 (Fall/Winter 1981): 24–27.

———. "Science Fiction and Fantasy Scholarship, 1982: The Year in Review." *Fantasy Review* 64 (1984): 52–54.

———. "The Year's Scholarship in Fantastic Literature: 1986." *Extrapolation* 28 (Fall 1987): 201–254.

———. *The Year's Scholarship in Science Fiction, Fantasy, and Horror Literature, 1980.* Kent, OH: Kent State Univ. Press, 1983.

———. *The Year's Scholarship in Science Fiction, Fantasy, and Horror Literature, 1981.* Kent, OH: Kent State Univ. Press, 1984.

————. *The Year's Scholarship in Science Fiction, Fantasy, and Horror Literature, 1982.* Kent, OH: Kent State Univ. Press, 1985.

————. "The Year's Scholarship in Science Fiction, Fantasy, and Horror Literature, 1983." *Extrapolation* 26 (Summer 1985): 85–142.

————. "The Year's Scholarship in Science Fiction, Fantasy, and Horror Literature: 1984." *Extrapolation* 26 (Winter 1985): 316–377.

————. "The Year's Scholarship in Science Fiction, Fantasy, and Horror Literature: 1985." *Extrapolation* 27 (Summer 1986): 123–173.

————. "The Year's Scholarship in Fantastic Literature: 1987." *Extrapolation* 29, 3 (1988): 235–284.

Tymn, Marshall B., and Roger C. Schlobin. "Checklist of American Critical Works on Science Fiction: 1972–1973." *Extrapolation* 17 (Dec 1975): 78–96.

————, eds. *The Year's Scholarship in Science Fiction and Fantasy, 1972–1975.* Kent, OH: Kent State Univ. Press, 1979. Followed by *The Year's Scholarship in Science Fiction and Fantasy: 1976 to 1979.* Kent, OH: Kent State Univ. Press, 1983. Compilations of annual checklists published between 1974 and 1981 in *Extrapolation: A Science-Fiction Newsletter.*

Tymn, Marshall B., Roger C. Schlobin, and L. W. Currey. *A Research Guide to Science Fiction Studies: An Annotated Checklist of Primary and Secondary Materials on Fantasy and Science Fiction.* New York: Garland, 1977.

Tymn, Marshall B., Kenneth J. Zahorski, and Robert H. Boyer. *Fantasy Literature: A Core Collection and Reference Guide.* New York: Bowker, 1979. Mainly lists adult books, except for a "core collection" of children's books. (bibliography)

Waggoner, Diana. *The Hills of Faraway: A Guide to Fantasy.* New York: Atheneum, 1978. Lists both adult and children's books. (bibliography)

Ward, Martha E., and Dorothy A. Marquardt. *Authors of Books for Young People.* 2nd ed. Metuchen, NJ: Scarecrow Press, 1971.

Weinberg, Robert. *A Biographical Dictionary of Science Fiction and Fantasy Artists.* Westport, CT: Greenwood, 1988.

Werner, Nancy. *Flights of Fancy. Resources in Education.* ED 025-401. Washington, DC: U.S. Office of Education, 1968. (bibliography)

Wolf, Gary K. *Critical Terms for Science Fiction and Fantasy: A Glossary and Guide to Scholarship.* Westport, CT: Greenwood, 1986.

Writers for Young Adults: Biographies Master Index. 2nd ed. Edited by Adele Sarkissian. Detroit: Gale, 1984.

Yates, J. "50 Years of Fantasy." *Books for Keeps* (Sept 1987): 4–7.

————. "Recent Fantasy for Children." *British Book News Children's Books* (Sept 1987): 40—43.

Yesterday's Authors of Books for Children: Facts and Pictures About Authors and Illustrators of Books for Young People, from Early Times to 1960. 2 vols. Edited by Anne Commire. Detroit: Gale, 1977–1978.

Your Reading: A Book List for Junior High and Middle School Students. 8th ed. Edited by Alleen Pace Nilsen. Urbana, IL: National Council of Teachers of English, 1991. "Imagining What If: Science Fiction and Fantasy," pp. 153–173.

12

Critical and Historical Studies of Fantasy Literature

This chapter lists general studies of children's and young adult fantasy, such as Brian Atte-bery's "Fantasy for American Children" and James E. Higgins's *Beyond Words: Mystical Fancy in Children's Literature.* Works about children's and young adult literature that dis-cuss fantasy, like Sheila Egoff's *Thursday's Child* and Cornelia Meigs's *A Critical History of Children's Literature,* are found here as well, with citations to the particular chapters or pages devoted to fantasy.

Also listed are collections of interviews and critical studies by and/or about children's and young adult fantasists, such as Edward Blishen's *The Thorny Paradise* and Sheila Egoff's *Only Connect.* Books on fantastic illustration have been included here, as well.

The Preface contains a list of sources from which the information in this chapter was drawn.

Articles and studies on the educational or psychological uses of fantasy, like Bruno Bet-telheim's *The Uses of Enchantment* and Marshall Tymn's *Teacher's Guide to Fantasy Litera-ture,* as well as audiovisual materials on fantasy literature, are located in Chapter 13, Teaching Resources.

For information about individual fantasists, see Chapter 14, Author Studies.

AB Bookman's Weekly. "Special Issue: Science Fiction, Fantasy, and Horror." 28 (Aug 1989).

AB Bookman's Weekly. "Special Issue: Science Fiction, Fantasy, and Horror." 29 (Oct 22, 1990).

Abbey, K. "Science Fiction and Fantasy: A Collection Proposal." *Wilson Library Bulletin* 55 (Apr 1981): 584–588.

Adams, Bess Porter. *About Books and Children: Historical Survey of Children's Literature.* New York: Holt, 1953, pp. 456–460, 473–477, 495–497, 534–535.

Adams, John. "Linkages: Science Fiction and Science Fantasy." *School Library Journal* 26 (May 1980): 23–28, and 27 (Nov 1980): 3.

After "Alice": Exploring Children's Literature. Edited by Morag Styles, Eve Bearne, and Victor Watson. Fort Lauderdale, FL: Cassell, 1992.

ALAN Review. "Special Issue: Fantasy and Science Fiction." 15 (Winter 1988).

Alberghene, Janice Marie. "From Alcott to *Abel's Island:* The Image of the Artist in American Children's Literature." Ph.D. diss., Brown University, 1980.

Alcorn, Noeline. "Fantasy and Family Life: Children's Books from Northern Europe." *Children's Literature Association Yearbook.* Auckland, New Zealand: Children's Literature Association, 1976, pp. 29–42. Discusses Astrid Lindgren, Maria Gripe, Christine Nöstlinger, Otfried Preussler, and Paul Biegel.

Alderson, Brian, ed. *Children's Books in England: Five Centuries of Social Life.* Orig. pub. 1932, ed. by F. J. Harvey Darton. 3rd ed. New York: Cambridge Univ. Press, 1982, pp. 252–266, 281–285, 308–315. Discusses Kinsley, Carroll, Potter, Kipling, and Barrie.

Alexander, Lloyd. "Fantasy and the Human Condition." *The New Advocate* 1 (Spring 1988): 75–83.

———. "Fantasy as Images: A Literary View." *Language Arts* 55 (1978): 440–446.

———. "Substance and Fantasy." *Library Journal* 91 (Dec 15, 1966): 6157–6159.

———. "The Truth About Fantasy." *Top of the News* 24 (Jan 1968): 168–174.

———. "Wishful Thinking—Or Hopeful Dreaming?" *Horn Book* 44 (Aug 1968): 383–390.

Alpers, Hans Joachim. "Loincloth, Double Ax, and Magic: 'Heroic Fantasy' and Related Genres." *Science–Fiction Studies* 5 (1978): 19–32.

Anderson, William, and Patrick Groff. *A New Look at Children's Literature.* Belmont, CA: Wadsworth, 1972. "Fantasy," pp. 66–93, 254–266.

Andronik, Catherine M. "More About King Arthur." *Book Report* 9 (Jan–Feb 1991): 37–38.

———. *Quest for a King: Searching for the Real King Arthur.* New York: Atheneum, 1989.

Antczak, Janice. *Science Fiction: The Mythos of a New Romance.* New York: Neal-Schuman, 1985. "Science Fantasy," pp. 184–189.

Anthony, Piers. "In Defense of Fantasy." *Isaac Asimov's Science Fiction Magazine,* Dec 1983, pp. 71–87.

Apter, T. E. *Fantasy Literature.* Bloomington: Indiana Univ. Press, 1972.

Aquino, John. *Fantasy in Literature.* Washington, DC: National Education Association, 1977, "Fantasy Literature," pp. 13–19, 23–26, 28–29, 40–47.

Arbuthnot, May Hill, and Mark Taylor, eds. *Time for New Magic.* Glenview, IL: Scott, Foresman, 1971.

"Are Fairy Tales Outgrown?" *Literary Digest* 63 (1919): 32.

Armstrong, Judith. "Ghost Stories: Exploiting the Convention." *Children's Literature in Education* 11 (Autumn 1980): 117–123.

Arrowsmith, Nancy, and George Moorse. *A Field Guide to the Little People.* New York: Hill, 1977.

Ashe, Geoffrey. *The Discovery of King Arthur.* New York: Henry Holt, 1987. (Orig. pub 1985.)

———. *King Arthur: In Fact and Legend.* New York: Nelson, 1971.

———, et al. *The Quest for Arthur's Britain.* Chicago: Academy, 1987. (Reprint of Praeger, 1968 ed.)

Asker, David Barry Desmond. "The Modern Bestiary: Animal Fiction from Hardy to Orwell." Ph.D. diss., University of British Columbia, 1978.

Astbury, E. A. "Other and Deeper Worlds." *Junior Bookshelf* 39 (Oct 1975): 301–305.

Attebery, Brian L. "America and the Materials of Fantasy." Ph.D. diss., Brown University, 1979.

———. *The Fantasy Tradition in American Literature: From Irving to Le Guin.* Bloomington: Indiana Univ. Press, 1980. "Fantasy for American Children," pp. 59–108, 134–153.

———. "Science Fantasy and Myth." In *Intersections: Science Fiction and Fantasy,* ed. by George E. Slusser and Eric S. Rabkin. Carbondale: Southern Illinois Univ. Press, 1987.

———. "Women's Coming of Age in Fantasy." *Extrapolation* 28 (Spring 1987): 10–22.

Auerbach, Mina, and U. C. Knoepflmacher, eds. *Forbidden Journeys: Fairy Tales and Fan-*

tasys by Victorian Women Writers. Chicago: Univ. of Chicago Press, 1992. Discusses Frances Hodgson Burnett, Juliana Ewing, Jean Ingelow, Mary Louisa Molesworth, and E. Nesbit.

Auerbach, N. "Falling Alice, Fallen Women, and Victorian Dream Children." *English Language Notes* 20 (Dec 1982): 46–64.

Avery, Gillian. "American Distaste for Fairy Tales." *Horn Book* 62 (July–Aug 1986): 486–489.

———. "The Quest for Fairyland." *Quarterly Journal of the Library of Congress* 38 (Fall 1981): 220–227.

Avery, Gillian, and Julia Briggs, eds. *Children and Their Books.* Oxford: Clarendon, 1989.

Babbitt, Natalie. "Metamorphosis." *Magpies* 3 (Nov 1988).

———. "The Purposes of Fantasy." In *Proceedings of the Ninth Annual Conference of the Children's Literature Association.* University of Florida, March 1982. Ypsilanti, MI: Children's Literature Association, 1983, pp. 22–29.

Bailey, W. L. "Fairy Tales as Character-Builders." *Libraries* 31 (1926): 44–46.

Bainton, George, ed. *The Art of Authorship: Literary Reminiscences, Methods of Work, and Advice to Young Beginners, Personally Contributed by Leading Authors of the Day.* London: James Clarke, 1890.

Baker, F. T. "Old and Modern Fairy Tales." *Teachers College Record* 9 (Jan 1908): 9–23.

Barnes, Myra Edwards. "Linguistics and Languages in Science Fiction–Fantasy." Ph.D. diss., East Texas State University, 1971. Reprinted. New York: Arno Press, 1975.

Barth, Melissa Ellen. "Problems in Generic Classification: Toward a Definition of Fantasy Fiction." Ph.D. diss., Purdue University, 1981.

Baswell, Christopher, and William Sharpe, eds. *The Passing of Arthur: New Essays in Arthurian Tradition.* New York: Garland, 1988.

Bator, Robert. *Signposts to Criticism of Children's Literature.* Chicago: American Library Association, 1983. "Fantasy," pp. 240–264.

Beard, Patten. "Why Punish the Fairy Tale?" *Libraries* 34 (1929): 457–459.

Becker, May Lamberton. *First Adventures in Reading: Introducing Children to Books.* New York: Stokes, 1936. "The Fairy-Tale Age," pp. 43–66; "Animals in Books," pp. 67–87.

Belert, Keld. "Fantasi och Barnlitteratur [Fantasy and Children's Literature]." *Barnkultur* 1 (1981): 10–12.

Berman, Ruth. "A Note on the Mythopoeic Holdings in the Kerlan Collection." *Mythlore* 6 (Fall 1979): 32, 42. Survey of the holdings of the Children's Literature Collection of the University of Minnesota of works by Bellairs, Lewis, MacDonald, Coatsworth, Ipcar, Nichols, Pope, and Yolen.

———. "Victorian Dragons: The Reluctant Brood." *Children's Literature in Education* 15 (Winter 1984): 220–233.

Billman, Carol. "Reading and Mapping: Directions in Children's Fantasy." In *Proceedings of the Ninth Annual Conference of the Children's Literature Association.* University of Florida, March 1982. Ypsilanti, MI: Children's Literature Association, 1983, pp. 40–46.

Bisenieks, Dainis. "Children, Magic and Choices." *Mythlore* 6 (Winter 1979): 13–16. Discussion of Le Guin, Alexander, Garner, Cooper, and Lewis.

———. "Welsh Myth in Modern American Fantasy." *Anglo-Welsh Review* 24 (1974): 130–134.

Blackham, H. J. *The Fable as Literature.* Dover, NH: Athlone Press, 1985.

Blishen, Edward, ed. *The Thorny Paradise: Writers on Writing for Children.* Boston: Horn Book, 1975, pp. 25–52, 58–61, 65–76, 81–92, 103–116, 123–145, 163–173. Originally published in Great Britain in 1975. Articles written by Storr, Gordon, Aiken, Walsh, Hoban, Garfield, Le Guin, Farmer, Cresswell, Peyton, Hunter, Pearce, and Adams.

Blount, Margaret. *Animal Land: The Creatures of Children's Fiction.* New York: Morrow, 1975. "Animal Fantasy," pp. 95–244, 258–324.

Borges, Jorge Luis, with Margarita Guerreo. *The Book of Imaginary Beings.* New York: Dutton, 1969. Revised and enlarged from original Mexican publication in 1957.

Boyer, Robert H., and Kenneth J. Zahorski, eds. *Fantasists on Fantasy: A Collection of Critical Reflections by Eighteen Masters of the Art.* New York: Avon, 1984.

Bradley, Marion Zimmer. "Fantasy and the Contemporary Occult Novel: Social and Intellectual Approaches." *Fantasy Review* 80 (1985): 10–12.

———. "Fantasy and the Contemporary Occult Novel: Social and Intellectual Approaches II." *Fantasy Review* 81 (1985): 31–32.

Branham, Robert J. "Fantasy and Ineffability: Fiction at the Limits of Language." *Extrapolation* 24 (Spring 1983): 66–79.

A Bridge to Magic Realms. Fourth Biennial Conference on Literature and Hawaii's Children. Honolulu/Kamuela, June 23–28, 1988. A Humanities Guide.

Briggs, Katherine Mary. *The Fairies in Tradition and Literature.* London: Routledge & Kegan Paul, 1967.

———. *The Vanishing People: Faery Lore and Legends.* Illus. by Mary I. French. New York: Pantheon, 1978.

Britton, J. "The Role of Fantasy." *English in Education* 5, no. 3 (Winter 1971): 39–44.

Brooke-Rose, Christine. *A Rhetoric of the Unreal: Studies in Narrative and Structure, Especially of the Fantastic.* New York: Cambridge Univ. Press, 1983.

Buechner, Frederick. "If Not God, Old Scratch." *New York Times Book Review,* sect. 7, pt. II, May 6, 1973, pp. 3, 14–16.

Burns, Linda Lattin. "High Fantasy: A Definition." Ph.D. diss., University of Missouri-Columbia, 1979.

Burns, Marjorie Jean. "Victorian Fantasists from Ruskin to Lang: A Study in Ambivalence." Ph.D. diss., University of California at Berkeley, 1978.

Butler, Francelia, and Richard Rotert, eds. *Reflections on Literature for Children: Selected from the Annual "Children's Literature."* Hamden, CT: Shoe String Press, 1984. Essays on Baum, Milne, Potter, Singer, Travers, E. B. White, Collodi, MacDonald, Ruskin, Barrie, Nesbit, Grahame, Lewis, and Sendak.

———, eds. *Triumphs of the Spirit in Children's Literature.* Hamden, CT: Shoe String Press, 1986. Anderson, pp. 122–126; Sendak, pp. 142–149; Collodi, pp. 171–179.

Butts, Dennis, ed. *Good Writers for Young Readers.* St. Albans, England: Hart-Davis, 1977, pp. 12–49, 57–66, 79–128. Articles about Aiken, Boston, Garfield, Garner, Hoban, Mayne, M. Norton, Pearce, Peyton, Adams, and Le Guin.

Cadogan, Mary, and Patricia Craig. *You're a Brick, Angela! A New Look at Girls' Fiction from 1839 to 1975.* London: Gollancz, 1976.

Cameron, Eleanor. "The Dearest Freshness Deep Down Things." *Horn Book* 40 (Oct 1964): 459–472.

———. "The Eternal Moment." *Children's Literature Association Quarterly* 9 (Winter 1984/1985): 157–164.

———. "Fantasy." In *The Green and Burning Tree.* 2nd ed. Boston: Little, Brown, 1985, pp. 3–134, 258–274.

———. "The Inmost Secret." *Horn Book* 59 (Feb 1983): 17–24.

———. "Into Something Rich and Strange: Of Dreams, Art, and the Unconscious." *Quarterly Journal of the Library of Congress* 5 (1978): 92–107. Reprinted in *The Openhearted Audience.* Washington, DC: Library of Congress, 1980, pp. 152–176.

———. "On Fantasy." In *The Seed and the Vision: On the Writing and Appreciation of Children's Books.* New York: Dutton, 1993, pp. 149–204.

Campbell, Margaret. "Children in Time." *British Book News* (June 1979): 472–473.

Campbell, P. "Young Adult Perplex: Adult Fantasy Illustration." *Wilson Library Bulletin* 54 (Feb 1980): 392–393.

Canadian Children's Literature: A Journal of Criticism and Review. "A Double Issue on Fantasy," nos. 15 and 16 (1980).

Canadian Children's Literature. "Special Issue: Time Slip Fantasies." 67 (1992).

Carpenter, Humphrey. *Secret Gardens: A Study of the Golden Age of Children's Literature.* Boston: Houghton Mifflin, 1985. Discusses Kingsley, Carroll, MacDonald, Grahame, Nesbit, Potter, Barrie, Milne, Jeffries.

Cart, Michael. "A Light in the Darkness: Humor Returns to Children's Fantasy." *School Library Journal* 33 (Apr 1987): 48–49.

Carter, Lin. *Imaginary Worlds: The Art of Fantasy.* New York: Ballantine, 1973.

Chambers, Aidan. *Booktalk: Occasional Writing on Literature and Children.* New York: Harper, 1986. Original British publication, Bodley Head, 1985.

———. "Letter from England: Magical Thinking." *Horn Book* 58 (Feb 1982): 94–105.

Chambers, Nancy, ed. *The Signal Approach to Children's Books.* Metuchen, NJ: Scarecrow Press, 1980.

Chang, Margaret. "Fantasy Literature: Encounters in the Globe of Time." *School Library Journal* 36 (Sept 1990): 163–164. (bibliographic essay)

The Child and the Family: Selected Papers from the 1988 International Conference of the Children's Literature Association. Edited by Susan R. Gannon and Ruth Ann Thompson. New York: Pace University, 1990.

Children and Books. 7th ed. Edited by Zena Sutherland and May Hill Arbuthnot. Glenview, IL: Scott, Foresman, 1985. "Modern Fantasy," pp. 226–272.

Children and Their Books. Edited by Gillian Avery and Julia Briggs. Oxford: Clarendon, 1989.

Children's Literature. Annual of the Modern Language Association Seminar on Children's Literature and the Children's Literature Association. Vols. 1–21. New Haven, CT: Yale Univ. Press, 1980–1993.

Chubb, Percival. "The Value and Place of Fairy Stories in the Education of Children." *National Education Association Journal* (1905): 871–879.

Chukovskii, Kornei. *From Two to Five.* Translated and edited by Miriam Morton. Berkeley: Univ. of California Press, 1963. Originally published in Russia, 1925. "The Battle for the Fairy Tale," pp. 114–139.

Cianciolo, Patricia Jean. "A Look at Modern Fantasy Currently Available to Young Readers." Syracuse, NY: ERIC Clearinghouse on Information Resources, 1977.

Clancy, Joseph P. *Pendragon: Arthur and His Britain.* New York: Praeger, 1971.

Clark, Rosalind Elizabeth. "Goddess, Fairy Mistress, and Sovereignty: Women of the Irish Supernatural." Ph.D. diss., University of Massachusetts, 1985.

Cline, Ruth K. J. *A Guide to Literature for Young Adults: Background, Selection, and Use.* Glenview, IL: Scott, Foresman, 1983.

Cloud, A. "Once Upon a Legend." *Indiana Media Journal.* 10 (Fall 1988): 5–7. (bibliographic essay)

Cohen, John Arthur. "An Examination of Four Key Motifs Found in High Fantasy for Children." Ph.D. diss., Ohio State University, 1975.

Collings, Michael R., ed. *Reflections on the Fantastic: Selected Essays from the Fourth International Conference on the Fantastic in the Arts.* Westport, CT: Greenwood, 1986.

Collins, Robert A., and Howard D. Pearce, eds. *The Scope of the Fantastic—Culture, Biography, Themes, Children's Literature: Selected Essays from the First International Conference on the Fantastic in Literature and Film.* Westport, CT: Greenwood, 1985. "Fantasy and Children's Literature," pp. 221–270.

———. *The Scope of the Fantastic—Theory, Technique, Major Authors: Selected Essays from the First International Conference on the Fantastic in Literature and Film.* Westport, CT: Greenwood, 1985.

Cook, Elizabeth. *The Ordinary and the Fabulous.* New York: Cambridge Univ. Press, 1969.

Cooper, Susan. "Escaping into Ourselves." In Betsy Hearne and Marilyn Kaye. *Celebrating Children's Books.* New York: Lothrop, 1981, pp. 14–23.

―――. "Fantasy in the Real World." *Horn Book* 66 (May–June 1990): 304–316.

Cornwell, Charles Landrum. "From Self to the Shire: Studies in Victorian Fantasy." Ph.D. diss., University of Virginia, 1972. Discusses George MacDonald, Lewis Carroll, Oscar Wilde, Kenneth Grahame, and J. R. R. Tolkien.

Costello, Matthew J., and Piers Anthony. "The Six Magical Elements of Fantasy Fiction," *Writers Digest* 71 (Jan 1991): 30.

Cott, Jonathan. *Pipers at the Gates of Dawn: The Wisdom of Children's Literature.* New York: Random, 1983. Interviews with Sendak, Lindgren, Seuss, Steig, and Travers.

―――, ed. *Beyond the Looking Glass: Extraordinary Works of Fantasy and Fairy Tales.* New York: Stonehill, 1973. Anthology of ten Victorian children's tales by Ruskin, de Morgan, MacDonald, and others.

Coville, B. "Magic Mirrors." (New York State Library) *Bookmark* 49 (Fall 1990): 35–36.

Cox, Harvey. *The Feast of Fools: A Theological Essay on Festivity and Fantasy.* Cambridge, MA: Harvard Univ. Press, 1969, pp. 59–97.

Crago, Hugh. "Faintly from Elfland: How This Column Originated." *Children's Literature Association Quarterly* 13 (Fall 1988): 145–148.

―――. "Faintly from Elfland: A Strange, Dark Shop." *Children's Literature Association Quarterly* 16 (Spring 1991): 33–37.

―――. "Terra Incognita, Cognita." In Margaret Trask. *Fantasy, Science Fiction, Science Materials.* Kensington, NSW, Australia: Univ. of New South Wales, School of Librarianship, 1972, pp. 41–68.

Crago, Hugh, and Maureen Crago. "A Cupful of Diamond Juice." *Growing Point* 10 (1972): 1866–1869.

―――. "A World Beneath the Waves." *Signal* 11 (1973): 74–87; continued in 12 (1973): 123–132.

Crisler, Jesse. "Fantasy: A Welcome Alternative." *Canadian Children's Literature* 67 (1992): 69–75.

Cross-Culturalism in Children's Literature. Selected Papers from the 1987 International Conference of the Children's Literature Association. New York: Pace University, 1987.

Crouch, Marcus S. "Experiments in Time." *Junior Bookshelf* 20 (Jan 1956): 5–11. Discusses Kipling, Nesbit, H. Lewis, Uttley, others.

―――. "Guest Essay, New Faces, New Directions in Britain." *Children's Literature Review,* vol. 11. Edited by Gerard J. Senick. Detroit: Gale, 1986, pp. 11–18.

―――. *The Nesbit Tradition: Children's Novels 1945–1972.* Totowa, NJ: Rowman & Littlefield, 1972. "Laughter," pp. 101–111; "Magic Casements," pp. 112–141.

―――. *Treasure Seekers and Borrowers: Children's Books in Britain, 1900–1960.* London: The Library Association, 1961, amended ed. 1970, pp. 15–21, 36, 43–49, 61–67, 91–92, 101–103, 115–118.

Crouch, Marcus, and Alec Ellis, eds. *Chosen for Children: An Account of the Books Which Have Been Awarded the Library Association Carnegie Medal, 1936–1975.* 3rd ed. London: The Library Association, 1977, pp. 30–49, 66–69, 78–99, 117–123, 141–149, 164–172. B. B., Linklater, Goudge, de la Mare, M. Norton, Farjeon, C. S. Lewis, Mayne, Pearce, Clarke, Garner, R. Harris, Adams, and Lively.

Cullinan, B. E. "Fantasy and Science Fiction." In *Literature and the Child,* 2nd ed., edited by B. E. Cullinan. San Diego: Harcourt, 1989, pp. 278–337.

―――. *Literature and the Child.* New York: Harcourt Brace Jovanovich, 1981. "Fantasy and Science Fiction," pp. 209–245.

Cunningham, Michael Henry. "The Triumph of Fantasy: Childhood and Children's Literature in Victorian England." Ph.D. diss., New School for Social Research, 1978.

Curry, Jane Louise. "On the Elvish Craft." *Signal* 2 (May 1970): 42–49. Reprinted in Aidan

Chambers. *Signal Approach to Children's Books.* Metuchen, NJ: Scarecrow Press, 1971, pp. 83–93.

Dalgliesh, Alice. *First Experiences with Literature.* New York: Scribner, 1932, pp. 87–99, 148–152.

Dalphin, Marcia. "I Give You the End of a Golden String." *Horn Book* 14 (Apr 1938): 143–149.

Dankert, B. "Phantastiche Kinder—Und Jugend—Literatur und Märchen [Fantastic Children's and Youth Books and Fairy Tales]." *Buch und Bibliothek* 34 (June 1982): 496–498+.

Darton, F. J. Harvey. "Battles Long Ago: War against Fairyland." *Cornhill Magazine* (London) 68 (Mar 1930): 330–337.

De Camp, L. Sprague. *Blond Barbarians and Noble Savages.* Baltimore: T-K Graphics, 1975.

———. *Lost Continents: The Atlantis Theme in History, Science, and Literature.* New York: Gnome Press, 1954.

De Camp, L. Sprague, and Willy Ley. *Lands Beyond.* New York: Rinehart, 1952.

DeLuca, Geraldine, and Roni Natov. "The State of the Field in Children's Fantasy: An Interview with George Woods." *The Lion and the Unicorn* 1, no. 2 (Fall 1977): 4–16.

Dibiasio, Becky Lynn McCan. "The Path of Metamorphosis: Patterns in the Literary Fairy Tale Tradition." Ph.D. diss., Purdue University, 1984.

Dickinson, Peter. "Fantasy: The Need for Realism." *Children's Literature in Education* 17 (Spring 1986): 39–51. Paper given at the Fourth *Bookquest* Conference, Brighton Polytechnic, Spring 1984.

———. *The Flight of Dragons.* Illus. by Wayne Anderson. New York: Harper, 1979.

Digg, Sandra Elizabeth. "The Identification and Analysis of Contemporary and Universal Themes in Selected Books of Children's Literary Fantasy, Published between 1965 and 1970." Ph.D. diss., University of Chicago, 1971.

Di Lauro, Stephen. "100 Years of Fantasy Illustrations." *TZM* (June 1981): 36–41.

Disney, Walt. "Children Love Fantasy." *Instructor* 64 (Jan 1955): 42.

Donaldson, Stephen R. *Epic Fantasy in the Modern World: A Few Observations.* Kent, OH: Kent State Univ. Libraries, 1986.

Donelson, Kenneth L., and Alleen Pace Nilsen. *Literature for Today's Young Adults.* Glenview, IL: Scott, Foresman, 1980. "Fantasy," pp. 265–272.

Dooley, Patricia, ed. *The First Steps: Articles and Columns from the "Children's Literature Association Newsletter/Quarterly,"* vols. I–VI. West Lafayette, IN: Children's Literature Association Publications, 1984.

Dowd, Frances A., and Lisa C. Tayor. "Is There a Typical Young Adult Fantasy? A Content Analysis." *Journal of Youth Services in Libraries* 5 (Winter 1992): 175–184.

Drury, Roger W. "Realism Plus Fantasy Equals Magic." *Horn Book* 78 (Apr 1972): 113–119. Reprinted in Paul Heins. *Crosscurrents of Criticism.* Boston: Horn Book, 1977, pp. 178–184.

DuMont, Mary J. "Images of Women in Young Adult Science Fiction and Fantasy, 1970, 1980, and 1990: A Comparative Content Analysis." *VOYA* 16 (Apr 1993): 11–15, 21.

Eaton, Anne. "Extensions of Reality." *Horn Book* 3 (May 1927): 17–22.

———. *Reading with Children.* New York: Viking, 1940, pp. 13–23, 78–106, 310–330.

———. *Treasure for the Taking: A Book List for Boys and Girls.* rev. ed. New York: Viking, 1957. Original publication 1946. "Talking Beasts and Other Fanciful Creatures," pp. 28–33; "Modern Wonder Stories," pp. 72–86.

Ebert, G. "Zwischen Phantasie und Personlichkeit: Neue Tendenzen Sozialisatischer Kinderliteratur [Between Fantasy and Reality: New Trends in Socialist Children's Literature]." *Bibliothekar* 35 (Mar 1981): 133–137.

Edwards, Malcolm, and Robert Holdstock. *Realms of Fantasy.* Garden City, NY: Doubleday, 1983. Tolkien, pp. 11–22; Hilton, pp. 27–31; Le Guin, pp. 87–97.

Egoff, Sheila A. "Beyond the Garden Wall: Some Observations on Current Trends in Children's Literature." May Hill Arbuthnot Lecture. *Top of the News* 35 (Spring 1979): 257–271.

———. *The New Republic of Childhood: A Critical Guide to Canadian Children's Literature in English.* Toronto: Oxford Univ. Press, 1990. "Fantasy," pp. 229–272.

———. *The Republic of Childhood: A Critical Guide to Canadian Children's Literature in English.* New York: Oxford Univ. Press, 1967, 1975. "Books of Fantasy," pp. 131–149, 157–159.

———. *Thursday's Child: Trends and Patterns in Contemporary Children's Literature.* Chicago: American Library Association, 1981. "The New Fantasy," pp. 80–129.

———. *Worlds Within: Children's Fantasy from the Middle Ages to Today.* Chicago: American Library Association, 1988.

Egoff, Sheila, G. T. Stubbs, and L. F. Ashley, eds. *Only Connect: Readings on Children's Literature.* 2nd ed. New York: Oxford Univ. Press, 1980, pp. 106–120, 133–175, 183–220, 233–243, 337–355. Articles written by Tolkien, Travers, and Lewis; others about Baum, Lewis, Andersen, and Carroll.

Elgin, Don D. *The Comedy of the Fantastic: Ecological Perspectives on the Fantasy Novel.* Westport, CT: Greenwood, 1985.

Elleman, Barbara. "A Game of Catch." Speech given at the 1985 Children's Books Open Forum at the ALA Annual Conference, July 1985. *Booklist* 82 (Nov 15, 1985): 494–496. (time travel)

Ellis, Alec. "Little Folk and Young People." *Junior Bookshelf* 30, no. 2 (Apr 1966): 97–102. Discusses Andersen, Carroll, Clarke, M. Norton, Swift, Tolkien, and T. H. White.

Ellis, Sarah. "News from the North." *Horn Book* 64 (May–June 1988): 390–394. Discusses Canadian time travel novels by Cora Taylor, Kit Pearson, and Margaret Buffie.

Emerson, Caroline D. "The Contemporaneous in Fairy Lore." *Horn Book* 3 (Nov 1927): 38–41.

Epstein, Connie C. "Young Adult Books." *Horn Book* 63 (Nov–Dec 1987): 774–777. Contemporary fantasy and science fiction.

Esmonde, Margaret P. "Beyond the Circles of the World: Death and the Hereafter in Children's Literature." In *Webs and Wardrobes: Humanist and Religious World Views in Children's Literature,* ed. by Joseph O'Beirne Milner and Lucy Floyd Morcock Milner. Lanham, MD: University Press of America, 1987, pp. 33–45.

———. "Death and Deathlessness in Children's Fantasy." *Fantasiae* 7 (Apr 1979): 8–11.

Evans, Gwyneth. "Harps and Harpers in Contemporary Fantasy." *The Lion and the Unicorn* 16 (Dec 1992): 199–209.

———. "'Nothing Odd *Ever* Happens Here': Landscape in Canadian Fantasy." *Canadian Children's Literature* 15–16 (1980): 15–30.

Evans, W. D. Emrys. "The Welsh Mabinogion: Tellings and Retellings." *Children's Literature in Education* 28, no. 9 (Spring 1978): 17–33. Discusses Alexander and Garner.

Extrapolation. "Special Issue: Fantasy and Science Fiction." 28 (Spring 1987).

Eyre, Frank. *British Children's Books in the 20th Century.* New York: Dutton, 1971. "Fantasy," pp. 115–147.

———. "Twentieth Century British Fantasy Writers." In Margaret Trask. *Fantasy Science Fiction, Science Materials.* Kensington, NSW, Australia: Univ. of New South Wales, School of Librarianship, 1972, pp. 177–204.

"Fantasy and Creativity in Children's Literature." *The Lion and the Unicorn* 1 (Fall 1977): 1–115.

Farmer, Penelope. "'Jorinda and Jorindel' and Other Stories." *Children'sLiterature in Education* 7 (Mar 1972): 23–37. Reprinted in Fox. *Writers, Critics and Children.* New York: Agathon, 1976, pp. 55–72.

Farrell, Eleanor M. "'And Clove the Wind from Unseen Shores': The Sea Voyage Motif in Imaginative Literature." *Mythlore* 45 (1986): 43–47, 60.

Field, Elinor Whitney, comp. *Horn Book Reflections on Children's Books and Reading, 1949–1966.* Boston: Horn Book, 1969, pp. 6–13, 49–53, 203–249, 260–275, 286–290. Articles written by Coatsworth, Pearce, Eager, and Alexander; others about MacDonald, Nesbit, Lofting, C. S. Lewis, P. F. Cooper, Lynch, de la Mare, Grahame, and Carroll.

Filmer-Davies, Kath. "Welsh Myth and Contemporary Literature." *Mythlore* 73 (Summer 1993): 53–58. Discusses Susan Cooper, Nikolai Tolstoi, Lloyd Alexander, Madeleine L'Engle, Brian Caswell, Jay Ashton, and Nancy Bond.

Finch-Reyner, S. "The Unseen Shore: Thoughts on the Popularity of Fantasy." *Journal of Popular Culture* 18 (Spring 1985): 127–134.

Fisher, Leona W. "Mythical Fantasy for Children: Silence and Community." *The Lion and the Unicorn* 14 (Dec 1990): 37–57.

Fisher, Margery. *Intent upon Reading: A Critical Appraisal of Modern Fiction for Children.* New York: Watts, 1962. "Fantasy," pp. 36–169.

Fleming, William. "Perilous Realms: Towards an Understanding of Fantasy." *Review* (Australia) 8 (Dec 1980): 12–14.

Ford, Boris, ed. *Young Writers, Young Readers: An Anthology of Children's Writing and Reading.* London: Hutchinson, 1960.

Forrest, Linda A. "Young Adult Fantasy and the Search for Gender-Fair Genres." *Journal of Youth Services in Libraries* 7 (Fall 1993): 37–42. (annotated bibliography)

Fox, Geoff P., et al., eds. *Writers, Critics and Children: Articles from "Children's Literature in Education."* New York: Agathon, 1976, pp. 15–26, 55–124, 211–223. Articles written by Aiken, Farmer, Dickinson, Hughes, and Hoban; others about E. B. White, C. S. Lewis, and Le Guin.

Frank, Josette. *Your Child's Reading Today.* rev. ed. Garden City, NY: Doubleday, 1969, pp. 81–86, 97–98, 243–246, 265–268, 272–273. Original title: *What Books for Children?* 1937.

Frey, Charles, and John Griffiths. *The Literary Heritage of Childhood: An Appraisal of Children's Classics in the Western Tradition.* Westport, CT: Greenwood, 1987.

Frongia, Terri. "Good Wizard/Bad Wizard: Merlin and Faust Archetypes in Contemporary Children's Literature." In *Contending Archetypes in Western Culture,* ed. by Charlotte Spivak. Lewiston, NY: Mellen, 1992, pp. 65–93. Discusses Ursula K. Le Guin and Pamela Service.

———. "Merlin's Fathers: The Sacred and the Profane." *Children's Literature Association Quarterly* 18 (Fall 1993): 120–125. Discusses Peter Dickinson, Pamela Service, Rosemary Sutcliff, and Jane Yolen.

Fryatt, Norma R. *A Horn Book Sampler: On Children's Books and Reading (1924–1948).* Boston: Horn Book, 1959, pp. 4–7, 50–54, 133–139, 146–149.

Gagnon, Laurence. "Philosophy and Fantasy." In *Children's Literature: The Great Excluded,* vol. 1. Storrs, CT: Journal of the Modern Language Association, 1972, pp. 98–103.

Gardner, Emelyn E., and Eloise Ramsey. *A Handbook of Children's Literature: Methods and Materials.* Darby, PA: Arden Library, 1981. Original publisher Scott, Foresman, 1927. "Modern Fairy Tales," pp. 82–83, 209–213.

Garner, Barbara Carman. "Lost and Found in Time: Canadian Time-Slip Fantasies for Children." *Children's Literature Association Quarterly* 15 (Winter 1990): 206–211. Discusses Margaret Buffie and Janet Lunn.

Garthwaith, Marion. "The Acid Test." *Horn Book* 39 (Aug 1963): 408–411. Discusses witchcraft and sorcery fantasy.

Geer, Caroline. "Land of Faerie: The Disappearing Myth." *Mythlore* 5 (Autumn 1978): 3–5.

Georgiou, Constantine. *Children and Their Literature.* Englewood Cliffs, NJ: Prentice-Hall, 1969. "Fantasy in Children's Literature," pp. 240–301.

Giblin, James Cross. "Forum: Does It Have to Be Fantasy to Be Imaginative?" *Children's Literature in Education* 30, no. 9 (Autumn 1978): 151–155. Reply from Göte Klingberg. *Children's Literature in Education* 10 (Spring 1979): 49–51.

Gilead, Sarah. "Magic Abjured: Closure in Children's Fantasy Fiction." *Publications of the Modern Language Association of America* 106 (Mar 1991): 277–293.

Gillespie, Margaret C., and John W. Conner. *Creative Growth through Literature for Children and Adolescents.* Columbus, OH: Merrill, 1975. "Fantasy," pp. 11–14.

Glassman, Peter. "Juvenile Fantasy—An Overview." *AB Bookman's Weekly* 76 (Oct 28, 1985): 3108–3113. (bibliographic essay)

Glazer, Joan I., and Gurney Williams. *Introduction to Children's Literature.* New York: McGraw-Hill, 1979. "Modern Fantasy," pp. 256–301.

Goldthwaite, John. "The Black Rabbit: Part One." *Signal* 47 (May 1985): 86–111; "The Black Rabbit: Part Two." *Signal* 48 (Sept 1985): 148–167. Reprinted in Goldthwaite. *The Natural History of Make-Believe: A Study of Imaginative Children's Literature from Perrault to Sendak.* London: Oxford Univ. Press, 1987.

Goodrich, Norma Lorre. *Guinevere.* New York: Harper, 1991.

———. *King Arthur.* New York: Watts, 1986.

———. *Merlin.* New York: Watts, 1987.

Goodrich, Peter Hampton. "Merlin: The Figure of the Wizard in English Fiction." Ph.D. diss., University of Michigan, 1983.

Gose, Elliott. *Mere Creatures: A Study of Modern Fantasy Tales for Children.* Toronto: Univ. of Toronto Press, 1988. Articles on Rudyard Kipling, A. A. Milne, Kenneth Grahame, E. B. White, L. Frank Baum, Russell Hoban, Richard Adams, J. R. R. Tolkien.

Gottzmann, Carola L. *Artursdichtung.* Stuttgart: Metzler, 1989. Comparative study of Arthurian literature from the 12th through 17th centuries in France, Germany, and England.

Gove, Philip Babcock. *The Imaginary Voyage in Prose Fiction: A History of Its Criticism and a Guide to Its Study.* New York: Columbia Univ. Press, 1941; New York: Arno, 1975.

Graham, Eleanor. "Nonsense in Children's Literature." *Junior Bookshelf* 9 (July 1945): 61–68.

Gray, Irene. "The Shadow Line between Reality and Fantasy: The Development of Fantasy in Australian Children's Literature." M. Ed. diss., University of Tasmania, 1985.

Green, Carole. "Australian Fantasy." *Orana* (Australia) 15 (May 1979): 74–76.

Green, Roger Lancelyn. *Tellers of Tales: British Authors of Children's Books from 1800–1964.* New York: Watts, 1965, pp. 23–39, 49–73, 97–115, 202–224, 238–257, 269–279.

Greene, Ellin. "Literary Uses of Traditional Themes: From 'Cinderella' to *The Girl Who Sat by the Ashes* and *The Glass Slipper.*" *Children's Literature Association Quarterly* 11 (Fall 1986): 128–132.

Grieve, Ann. "The Psychotic State in Fantasy for Post-Primary Readers." *School Library Bulletin* (Australia) 10 (Aug 1978): 3–10. Discusses Penelope Farmer's *The Year King* and Catherine Storr's *Marianne Dreams.*

Hafer-Drescher, B. "Phantastik mit 'Hartem Kern' [Fantasy with a 'Hard Core']." *Buch und Bibliothek* (Munich) 38 (July–Aug 1986): 664+.

Hallowell, Lillian. *A Book of Children's Literature.* New York: Farrar, 1938. "Modern Fairy Tales," pp. 177–282.

Hambleton, A. "Canadian Fantasy." *British Columbia Library Quarterly* 26 (Oct 1962): 11–13.

Hannabuss, Stuart. "Fantasy: A Genre on the Edge." *Bookmark* (Edinburgh) 15 (1988): 26–32.

Hannabus, Stuart, Barry Litherland, and Stephanie Morland, comps. "Fiction for Children, 1970–1980. 1. Myth and Fantasy." *Children's Literature in Education* 12, no. 3 (Autumn 1981): 119–139.

Harmes, Jean McLain. "Children's Responses to Fantasy in Relation to Their Stages of Intellectual Development." Ph.D. diss., Ohio State University, 1972.

Hartmann, Waltraut. "Identification and Projection in Folk Fairy Tales and in Fantastic Stories for Children." *Bookbird* 7, no. 2 (1969): 8–17.

Hartwell, David G. "Dollars and Dragons: The Truth About Fantasy." *The New York Times Book Review* 29 (Apr 29, 1990): 1, 40–41.

Hathaway, Nancy. *The Unicorn.* New York: Viking, 1980; Outlet Book Co., 1984.

Haviland, Virginia. *Children and Literature: Views and Reviews.* Glenview, IL: Scott, Foresman, 1973, pp. 50–63, 71–77, 140–159, 220–249. Articles written by de la Mare, E. B. White, Aiken, Babbitt, Buchan, C. S. Lewis, Alexander, and Travers.

———. "Fairy Tales and Creativity." In *How Can Children's Literature Meet the Needs of Modern Children?* 15th IBBY Conference, 1976, pp. 56–61.

Hazard, Paul. *Books, Children, and Men.* 4th ed. Boston: Horn Book, 1960, pp. 92–105, 111–118, 135–141, 157–165. Originally published in France, 1932.

Hearne, Betsy. *Beauties and Beasts.* Phoenix: Oryx, 1993.

Hedges, Ned Samuel. "The Fable and the Fabulous: The Use of Traditional Forms in Children's Literature." Ph.D. diss., University of Nebraska, 1968.

Heins, Paul. "Mythic Journeys." In *Innocence & Experience.* Edited by Barbara Harrison and Gregory Maguire. New York: Lothrop, 1987, pp. 129–137.

———, ed. *Crosscurrents of Criticism: Horn Book Essays 1968–1977.* Boston: Horn Book, 1977, pp. 3–6, 98–125, 169–204, 226–233, 277–282, 311–314, 333–348. Articles written by Lindgren, Cameron, Dahl, Le Guin, Alexander, Drury, Langton, Fleischman, and Lively; others about Andersen, Adams, Le Guin, and Lively.

Helson, Ravenna. "The Creative Spectrum of Authors of Fantasy." *Journal of Personality* 45 (June 1977): 310–326. An examination of 98 books for 8-to-12-year olds written between 1930 and 1972.

———. "Experiences of Authors in Writing Fantasy: Two Relationships Between Creative Process and Product." *Altered States of Consciousness* 3, no. 3 (1977–1978): 235–248.

———. "Fantasy and Self-Discovery." *Horn Book* 46 (Apr 1970): 121–134. Reprinted in M. L. White. *Children's Literature.* Columbus, OH: Merrill, 1976, pp. 117–125.

———. "From Magical Woman to Wizard: Comparisons of Literary Fantasy in the Nineteenth and Twentieth Centuries." In *Proceedings of the XVIIth International Congress of Applied Psychology.* Brussels: Editest, 1972, pp. 1515–1519.

———. "Heroic and Tender Modes in Women Authors of Fantasy." *Journal of Personality* 41 (Dec 1973): 493–512. Twenty-eight women authors of children's fantasy written since 1930.

———. "The Heroic, the Comic, and the Tender: Patterns of Literary Fantasy and Their Authors." *Journal of Personality* 41 (June 1973): 163–184. Twenty-seven male authors of children's fantasy written since 1930.

———. "The Imaginative Process in Children's Literature: A Quantitative Appraisal." *Poetics* 7 (1978): 135–153.

———. "Sex-Specific Patterns in Creative Literary Fantasy." *Journal of Personality* 38, no. 3 (Sept 1970): 344–363.

———. "Through the Pages of Children's Books." *Psychology Today,* 7, no. 6 (Nov 1973): 107–117.

———. "Women Authors of Fantasy." *Multicultural Children's Literature.* (India) 3, no. 3 (1984): 53–77.

———, and Alf Proysen. "The Psychological Origins of Fantasy for Children in Mid-Victorian England." In *Children's Literature,* vol. 3. Storrs, CT: Journal of the Modern Language Association, 1974, pp. 66–75.

Hendrix, Miriam Jenson. "Flight to Fantasy." *Christianity Today,* 18 (Sept 13, 1974): 29–32.

Hennelly, Mark M., Jr. "Alice's Big Sister: Fantasy and the Adolescent Dream." *Journal of Popular Culture* 16 (Summer 1982): 72–87.

Hibbert, Christopher. *The Search for King Arthur.* New York: Harper, 1969.

Hickman, Janet, and Bernice E. Cullinan. Children's Literature in the Classroom: Weaving "Charlotte's Web." Needham Heights, MA: Christopher-Gordon, 1989. "Fantasy," pp. 109–134.

Hieatt, Constance B. "Analyzing Enchantment: Fantasy after Bettelheim." *Canadian Children's Literature* 15–16 (1980): 6–14.

Higgens, Regina. *Magic Kingdoms: Discovering the Joys of Childhood Classics with Your Child.* New York: Simon, 1992. Includes books by A. A. Milne, Beatrix Potter, Kenneth Grahame, Rudyard Kipling, J. M. Barrie, P. L. Travers, C. S. Lewis, and J. R. R. Tolkien.

Higgins, James E. *Beyond Words: Mystical Fantasy in Children's Literature.* New York: Teachers College Press, Columbia Univ., 1970.

———. "Five Authors of Mystical Fantasy for Children: A Critical Study." Ed.D. diss., Columbia University, 1965. Discusses Hudson, C. S. Lewis, Saint-Exupéry, MacDonald, and Tolkien.

Hiller, Claire. "The World of Fantasy—The World Where Anything Can Happen." *English in Australia* 86 (Dec 1988): 54–59. Examines E. B. White's *Charlotte's Web,* Ursula K. Le Guin's *A Wizard of Earthsea,* Philippa Pearce's *Tom's Midnight Garden* and Penelope Lively's *The Ghost of Thomas Kempe.*

Hoffield, Laura. "Where Magic Begins." *The Lion and the Unicorn* 3 (Spring 1979): 4–13.

Holdstock, Robert, and Malcolm Edwards. *Lost Realms.* Englewood Cliffs, NJ: Salem Press, 1985. Illustrated landscapes of fantasy fiction.

Hollinger, V. "Deconstructing the Time Machine." *Science Fiction Studies* 14 (July 1987): 201–221. Discusses time travel in literature.

Honig, Edith Lazaros. *Breaking the Angelic Image: Woman Power in Victorian Children's Fantasy.* Westport, CT: Greenwood, 1988.

———. "A Quiet Rebellion: The Portrait of the Female in Victorian Children's Fantasy." Ph.D. diss., Fordham University, 1986.

Hopkins, Lee Bennett. *Books Are by People: Interviews with 104 Authors and Illustrators of Books for Young Children.* New York: Citation Press, 1969, pp. 107–120, 125–127, 226–229, 250–258, 289–291, 299–302. Interviews with Ipcar, Lathrop, Raskin, Sendak, Seuss, Turkle, and Warburg.

———. *More Books by More People: Interviews with Sixty-five Authors of Books for Children.* New York: Citation Press, 1974, pp. 10–17, 24–28, 35–40, 68–77, 88–99, 105–114, 138–140, 147–152, 199–207, 303–307, 312–322, 343–350, 355–362, 375–380. Interviews with Alexander, Babbitt, M. Bond, Byars, Carlson, Cleary, Coatsworth, Cunningham, Dahl, Edmonds, Estes, Hamilton, Selden, Singer, Snyder, Stolz, Travers, and E. B. White.

Hughes, Felicity A. "Children's Literature: Theory and Practice, Part 2." *English Literary History* 45 (1978): 552–561. Reprinted in Robert Bator. *Signposts to Criticism of Children's Literature.* Chicago: American Library Association, 1983, pp. 242–248.

———. "Value for Sixpence: An Essay on Fantasy and Criticism." *Reading Time* (Australia) 78 (Jan 1981): 16–21.

Hume, Kathryn. *Fantasy and Mimesis: Responses to Reality in Western Literature.* New York: Methuen, 1984.

Hunt, Caroline. "Form as Fantasy—Fantasy as Form." *Children's Literature Association Quarterly* 12 (Spring 1987): 7–11.

Hunt, Peter. "Landscapes and Journeys, Metaphors and Maps: The Distinctive Feature of English Fantasy." *Children's Literature Association Quarterly* 12 (Spring 1987): 11–15.

Hunter, Mollie. "One World." *Horn Book* 51 (Dec 1975): 557–563; continued in 52 (Jan 1976): 32–38.

Hürlimann, Bettina. "Fantasy and Reality." In *Three Centuries of Children's Books in Europe.* Cleveland: World, 1968, pp. 76–92.

Huygen, Wil. *Gnomes.* New York: Abrams, 1977. Illus. by Rien Poortvliet. New York: Bantam, 1979. A companion volume is *Faeries* by Brian Froud and Alan Lee. New York: Abrams, 1978.

Inglis, Fred. *The Promise of Happiness: Value and Meaning in Children's Fiction.* New York: Cambridge Univ. Press, 1981.

Innocence & Experience: Essays & Conversations on Children's Literature. Edited by Barbara Harrison and Gregory Maguire. New York: Lothrop, 1987. "Mythic Patterns," pp. 87–164; "Fantasy: The Perilous Realm," pp. 165–210.

Issayeva, Alexandra. "The Contemporary Children's Tale: Images and Intent." *Bookbird* (Denmark) 3 (1984): 18–32.

Jackson, Rosemary. *Fantasy: The Literature of Subversion.* London: Methuen, 1981. "Victorian Fantasies," pp. 141–156.

Jan, Isabelle. *On Children's Literature.* Edited by Catherine Storr. New York: Schocken, 1974, pp. 42–89. Originally published in France, 1969.

Jarvis, Sharon, ed. *Inside Outer Space: Science Fiction Professionals Look at Their Craft.* New York: Ungar, 1985.

Jenkins, Sue. "'I Will Take the Ring': Responsibility and Maturity in Modern Fantasy Fiction for Young People." In Peter Hunt. *Further Approaches to Research in Children's Literature.* Cardiff: Univ. of Wales, 1982.

Johnson, Diana L. *Fantastic Illustration and Design in Britain, 1850–1930.* Providence: Museum of Art, Rhode Island School of Design, 1979.

Johnson, Edna, Evelyn R. Sickels, and Frances Clark Sayers. *Anthology of Children's Literature.* Originally published 1959, 4th ed. Boston: Houghton Mifflin, 1970. "Fantasy," pp. 607–750.

Jones, Cornelia, and Olivia R. Way. *British Children's Authors: Interviews at Home.* Chicago: American Library Association, 1976, pp. 3–10, 31–40, 49–100, 127–154. Interviews with Aiken, Arthur, M. Bond, Boston, Clarke, Farmer, Gard, Garner, Peyton, Picard, and Sutcliff.

Jones, Gwyneth. "Perceptions of Children's Fiction." *Vector* 140 (1987): 11–13.

Jones, Kathleen. "The Use and Misuse of Fantasy." *Mallorn* 23 (1986): 5–9.

Jordan, Alice M. "Animals in Fairyland." *Horn Book* 17 (Nov–Dec 1941): 439–444. Reprinted in Norma Fryatt. *A Horn Book Sampler.* Boston: Horn Book, 1959, pp. 146–149.

Kan, Katharine. "Science Fiction and Fantasy Graphic Novels." *VOYA* 16 (June 1993): 83–94.

Keightley, Thomas. *The World Guide to Gnomes, Fairies, Elves and Other Little People.* New York: Avenel, 1978. Originally published in 1880 as *The Fairy Mythology.*

Kellogg, Judith L. "The Dynamics of Dumbing: The Case of Merlin." *The Lion and the Unicorn* 17 (June 1993): 57–72. Discusses Heyer's *Excalibur,* White's *The Sword in the Stone,* Talbott's *King Arthur,* and Yolen's *Merlin's Booke.*

———. "Fantasy: A Gift of Childhood." In *A Bridge to Magic Realms.* Fourth Biennial Conference on Literature and Hawaii's Children. Honolulu/Kamuela, June 23–28, 1988. A Humanities Guide, pp. 4, 10.

Kiefer, Barbara. "Wales as a Setting for Children's Fantasy." *Children's Literature in Education* 13 (Summer 1982): 95–102.

Killheffer, Robert K. J. "Exploring Alternate Worlds." *Publishers Weekly* (Aug 2, 1993): 53–56. "A user's guide to publishers' subgenres of science fiction and fantasy."

Kilworth, Garry. "On Animal Fantasy." *Million* (U.K.) 11 (1992): 11–15.

Kincaid, Paul. "The Realms of Fantasy." *Vector* 117 (1983): 10–14.

Kingman, Lee, ed. *Newbery and Caldecott Medal Books: 1966–1975, with Acceptance Papers, Biographies and Related Material Chiefly from the Horn Book Magazine.* Boston: Horn Book, 1975. Alexander, O'Brien, pp. 45–55, 79–92.

———. *Newbery and Caldecott Medal Books, 1976–1985.* Boston: Horn Book, 1986. Cooper, McKinley, and Van Allsburg.

Kinney, Thomas L. "Arthurian Romances." In *Supernatural Fiction Writers*, vol. 1. Edited by E. F. Bleiler. New York: Scribner, 1985, pp. 11–18.

Kirsch, Hans-Christian. "Die Frage nach dem Sinn: Sinnbeduerfnis und Sinnsuche in der Modernen Fantasy-Literatur [The Question of Taste: Needs and Demands in Modern Fantasy Literature]." *Informationen des Arbeitskreises für Jugend Literatur* (Germany) 2 (1983): 30–47.

Klingberg, Göte. "The Fantastic and the Mythical as Reading for Modern Children and Young People." In *How Can Children's Literature Meet the Needs of Modern Children?* 15th IBBY Conference, 1976, pp. 32–35.

———. *The Fantastic Tale for Children: A Genre Study from the Viewpoints of Literary and Educational Research.* LIGRU Monograph no. 2. Gothenburg, Sweden: Gothenburg School of Education, 1970.

———. "The Fantastic Tale for Children: Its Literary and Educational Problems." *Bookbird* 5, no. 3 (1967): 13–20.

Kloet, Christine A. "Fantasy: A Personal View." *School Bookshop News* 9 (Spring 1978): 29–31.

Knoblauch, C. J. "Recent Trends in Fantasy in Children's Literature." Research paper. Kent, OH: Kent State Univ. Press, 1975.

Knoepflmacher, U. C. "The Balancing of Child and Adult: An Approach to Victorian Fantasies for Children." *19th Century Fiction* 37 (Mar 1983): 497–530.

———. "The Doubtful Marriage: A Critical Fantasy." *Children's Literature* 18 (1990): 131–134.

Kobil, Daniel T. "The Elusive Appeal of the Fantastic." *Mythlore* 4 (June 1977): 17–19.

Kondratiev, Alexei. "Tales Newly Told." *Mythlore* 71, no. 19 (Winter 1993): 15, 21.

Kroeber, Karl. *Romantic Fantasy and Science Fiction.* New Haven: Yale Univ. Press, 1988. Discusses J. R. R. Tolkien, Lord Dunsany, and E. T. A. Hoffmann.

Kulling, E. "Das Fremde Kind: Beobachtungen Zu Einem Motiv in der Phantastischen Kinder-und-Jugendliteratur [The Strange Child: Observations on a Motif in Fantasy Literature for Children and Young People]." *Jugendliteratur* (Switzerland) 4 (1984): 21–27.

Kurth, R. J. "Realism in Children's Books of Fantasy." *California Librarian* 39 (July 1978): 39–40.

Kuznets, Lois R. "Games of Dark: Psychofantasy in Children's Literature." *The Lion and the Unicorn* 1 (Fall 1977): 17–24.

———. "'High Fantasy' in America: A Study of Lloyd Alexander, Ursula Le Guin, and Susan Cooper." *The Lion and the Unicorn* 9 (1985): 19–35.

Lacy, Norris J., ed. *The Arthurian Encyclopedia.* New York: Garland, 1986.

Lacy, Norris J., and Geoffrey Ashe. *The Arthurian Handbook.* New York: Garland, 1988.

Ladden, Arlene. "Merlin's Mind: A Study of Merlin in Literature." Ph.D. diss., New York University, 1987.

Landow, G. P. "And the World Became Strange: Realms of Literary Fantasy." *Georgia Review* 33 (Spring 1979): 7–42. Reprinted in Diana Johnson. *Fantastic Illustration and Design in Britain 1850–1930.* Providence: Rhode Island School of Design, 1979, pp. 28–43; and in Roger Schlobin. *The Aesthetics of Fantasy Literature and Art.* Notre Dame, IN: Univ. of Notre Dame Press, 1982, pp. 105–142.

Landsberg, Michele. *Reading for the Love of It: Best Books for Young Readers.* New York: Prentice Hall, 1987. "Fantasy," pp. 157–182; "Traveling in Time," pp. 183–200.

Lane, Daryl, William Vernon, and David Carlson. *The Sound of Wonder: Interviews from "The Science Fiction Radio Show."* 2 vols. Phoenix: Oryx, 1985.

Lanes, Selma. *Down the Rabbit Hole: Adventures and Misadventures in the Realm of Children's Literature.* New York: Atheneum, 1976. "America as Fairy Tale," pp. 91–111.

———. "Fantasy and Reality: Where Do They Meet?" *Reading Time* (Australia) 62 (Jan 1977): 2–7.

Langton, Jane. "The Weak Place in the Cloth: A Study of Fantasy for Children." *Horn Book*

49 (Oct 1973): 433–441; continued in 49 (Dec 1973): 570–578. Reprinted in Paul Heins, ed. *Crosscurrents of Criticism.* Boston: Horn Book, 1977, pp. 185–196.

"A Large Youthful Appetite for Magic and Fantasy." *London Times Literary Supplement,* Sept 9, 1960, pp. xxi–xxii.

Larkin, David. *The Fantastic Kingdom: A Collection of Illustrations from the Golden Days of Storytelling.* New York: Ballantine, 1974.

Laughlin, Jeannine L., and Sherry Laughlin. *Children's Authors Speak.* Libraries Unlimited, 1993.

Laurence, M. J. P. "Animals and Dressed Animals." *Junior Bookshelf* 21 (Dec 1957): 289–294.

———. "Fantasy and Fashion." *Junior Bookshelf* 18 (Oct 1954): 169–174.

Lavender, Ralph. "Other Worlds: Myth and Fantasy, 1970–1980." *Children's Literature in Education* 12, no. 3 (Autumn 1981): 140–150.

Lawrence, Jane. "A World of Their Own." *Junior Education* 7 (Apr 1983): 21–22.

Le Guin, Ursula K. *From Elfland to Poughkeepsie.* Portland, OR: Pendragon, 1973.

———. "In Defense of Fantasy." *Horn Book* 49 (June 1973): 239. Reprinted in Paul Heins. *Crosscurrents of Criticism.* Boston: Horn Book, 1977, p. 169.

———. *The Language of the Night: Essays on Fantasy and Science Fiction.* New York: Putnam, 1979.

Lehnert-Rodiek, Gertrud. "Fantastic Children's Literature and Travel in Time." *Phaedrus 13* (1988): 61–72. Discusses Philippa Pearce, E. Nesbit, Robert Westall, Alison Uttley, and Susan Cooper.

Lehr, Susan. "Fantasy: Inner Journeys for Today's Child." *Publishing Research Quarterly* 7 (Fall 1991): 91–101.

Leiby, David A. "The Tooth That Gnaws: Reflections on Time Travel." In *Intersections: Science Fiction and Fantasy,* ed. by George E. Slusser and Eric S. Rabkin. Carbondale: Southern Illinois Univ. Press, 1987.

L'Engle, Madeleine. "What Is Real?" *Language Arts* 55 (1977): 447–451.

Lenz, Millicent. "Fantasy and Survival." *Catholic Library World* 48 (Sept 1976): 56–61.

Lenz, Millicent, and Ramona M. Mahood, comps. *Young Adult Literature: Background and Criticism.* Chicago: American Library Association, 1980, pp. 415–445.

Lepage, Francoise. "Pour une Rhetorique de la Representation Fantastique. [In Search of a Theory of Illustration of Fantastic Literature]." *Canadian Children's Literature* 60 (1990): 97–107.

Lerner, Fred. "Tell the Old Stories Again." *VOYA* 15 (Aug 1992): 159, 162.

Lesser, Wendy. *The Life Below the Ground: A Study of the Subterranean in Literature and History.* London: Faber, 1988. Discusses Lewis Carroll, George MacDonald, and C. S. Lewis.

Levin, Betty, Gregory Maguire, and Martha Wolke. "Worlds Apart." Watertown, MA: The Foundation for Children's Books: *The Children's Book Bag,* vol. III (Fall 1992). (bibliographic essay)

Lewis, Naomi. "The Road to Fantasy." In *Children's Literature,* vol. 11. New Haven, CT: Yale Univ. Press, 1983, pp. 201–210.

Lind, Dianne. "The Importance of Fantasy in Young Adult Literature." *ALAN Review* 15 (1988): 13–14. Discusses Susan Cooper, C. S. Lewis, and J. R. R. Tolkien.

Lindskold, Jane M. "The Elements of Fantastic Fiction." *The Writer* 106 (Nov 1993): 18.

Lindskoog, John, and Kay Lindskoog. *How to Grow a Young Reader.* Elgin, IL: Cook, 1978. "Flights of Fancy: Fantastic Tales Today," pp. 62–88.

Literature and Hawaii's Children. Proceedings of the Third Biennial Conference on Literature and Hawaii's Children, 1986. Honolulu: Literature and Hawaii's Children, 1988.

Literature and Hawaii's Children. Edited by Christina Bacchilega and Steven Curry. Proceedings of the Fifth Biennial Conference on Literature and Hawaii's Children, 1988. Honolulu: Literature and Hawaii's Children, 1990.

Literature and Hawaii's Children. Spirit, Land, and Storytelling: The Heritage of Childhood. Edited by Stephen Canham. Proceedings of the Sixth Biennial Conference on Literature and Hawaii's Children, 1990. Honolulu: University of Hawaii at Manoa, 1992.

Lochhead, Marion. *Renaissance of Wonder: The Fantasy Worlds of J. R. R. Tolkien, C. S. Lewis, George MacDonald, E. Nesbit and Others.* New York: Harper, 1980. Originally published in England in 1977 as *The Renaissance of Wonder in Children's Literature.* Major chapters on MacDonald, Nesbit, Kipling, Masefield, de la Mare, Stephens, Lynch, C. S. Lewis, and Tolkien.

Loder Reed, Elizabeth. "Personal Identity Concepts in the Context of Children's Fantasy Literature." Ph.D. diss., Boston University, 1979.

Lourie, Helen. "Where Is Fancy Bred?" *New Society,* Dec 6, 1962. Reprinted in Sheila A. Egoff. *Only Connect.* New York: Oxford Univ. Press, 1980, pp. 106–110.

Lowentrout, Peter. "The Rags of Lordship: Science Fiction, Fantasy, and the Reenchantment of the World." *Mythlore* 41 (1985): 47–51, 57.

Lukens, Rebecca J. *A Critical Handbook of Children's Literature.* 3rd ed. Glenview, IL: Scott, Foresman, 1986. "Fantasy," pp. 18–19, 95–97, 106–107, 140–141, 161, 167–168.

Lupak, Alan C. "Modern Arthurian Novelists on the Arthurian Legend." *Studies in Medievalism* 2 (Fall 1983): 79–88.

Lüthi, Max. *Once upon a Time: On the Nature of Fairy Tales.* New York: Ungar, 1970.

Lynn, Ruth Nadelman. "'There Is Another Kind of Real:' Fantasy Literature for Children." Watertown, MA: The Foundation for Children's Books: *The Children's Book Bag* (Spring 1991). (bibliographic essay)

MacCann, Donnarae. "Wells of Fancy, 1865–1965." *Wilson Library Bulletin* 40 (Dec 1965): 334–343. Reprinted in Sheila A. Egoff. *Only Connect.* New York: Oxford Univ. Press, 1980, pp. 133–149.

McClintock, Michael W. "High Tech and High Sorcery: Some Discriminations Between Science Fiction and Fantasy." In *Intersections: Science Fiction and Fantasy,* ed. by George E. Slusser and Eric S. Rabkin. Carbondale: Southern Illinois Univ. Press, 1987.

MacDonald, Ruth. "The Tale Retold: Feminist Fairy Tales." *Children's Literature Association Quarterly* 7 (Summer 1982): 18–20.

McDonough, Irma, ed. *Profiles.* rev. ed. Ottawa: Canadian Library Association, 1975.

———. *Profiles 2: Authors and Illustrators, Children's Literature in Canada.* Ottawa: Canadian Library Association, 1982.

McGillis, Roderick. "Fantasy as Adventure: 19th Century Children's Fiction." *Children's Literature Association Quarterly* 8 (Fall 1983): 18–22.

McHargue, Georgess. "Leaping into Fantasy." *American Libraries* 5 (Dec 5, 1974): 610–611.

MacIlroy, Barry. "Those Magical Time-Slip Stories." *Souvenir* (U.K.) 21 (1992): 14–15. Discusses Violet Needham, David Severn, Mabel Esther Allan, and Alison Uttley.

Macneice, Louis. *Varieties of Parable.* New York: Cambridge Univ. Press, 1965, pp. 82–102.

MacRae, Cathi. "Timescapes in Cambridge." *Wilson Library Bulletin* 64 (Nov 1989): 22–28. Discusses a conference on time travel in children's books.

MacVeagh, Charles Peter, and Frances Shands. "Fairy Stories: Fantasy, Fact, or . . . Forecast?" *Language Arts* 59 (1982): 328–335.

McVitty, Walter. *Innocence and Experience: Essays on Contemporary Australian Children's Writers.* Melbourne, Australia: Nelson, 1981.

———. "A Taste of the Best: A Gourmet Guide to Children's Books." *Reading Time* 82 (Jan 1982): 7–22. Discusses Kenneth Grahame, A. A. Milne, and Norman Lindsay.

Maddox, Donald. *The Arthurian Romances of Chretien de Troyes: Once and Future Fictions.* Cambridge: Cambridge Univ. Press, 1992.

Maguire, Gregory. "Belling the Cat: Heroism and the Little Hero." *The Lion and the Unicorn* 13 (June 1989): 102–119.

————. "Themes in English Language: Fantastic Literature for Children, 1938–1988." Ph.D. diss., Tufts University, 1990.

Mahon, R. L. "The Epic Tradition in Science Fiction and Fantasy." *Teaching in a Two-Year College* 14 (Fall 1987): 47–51.

Malmgren, C. D. "Toward a Definition of Science Fantasy." *Science Fiction Studies* 15 (Nov 1988): 259–281.

Mamula, I. "Festival der Fantasy und Science Fiction (Munich, 1987)." *Buch und Bibliothek* 40 (Mar 1988): 273–274.

Manlove, Colin N. *Christian Fantasy: From 1200 to the Present.* Notre Dame, IN: Univ. of Notre Dame Press, 1991.

————. "Comic Fantasy." *Extrapolation* 28 (Spring 1987): 37–44.

————. "The Elusiveness of Fantasy." *Fantasy Review* 90 (1986): 13–14+.

————. *The Impulse of Fantasy Literature.* Kent, OH: Kent State Univ. Press, 1983, pp. 7–14, 31–114. Major chapters on Thackeray, Le Guin, Nesbit, MacDonald, and T. H. White.

————. *Modern Fantasy: Five Studies.* New York: Cambridge Univ. Press, 1975. "On the Nature of Fantasy," pp. 1–12. Reprinted in Roger Schlobin. *The Aesthetics of Fantasy Literature and Art.* Notre Dame, IN: Univ. of Notre Dame Press, 1982, pp. 16–35. Discusses Kingsley, MacDonald, C. S. Lewis, and Tolkien.

Manuel, Diane. "The Realm of the Imagination: Enduring Fantasy." *Christian Science Monitor* (Nov 6, 1987): B1–2.

Mappin, Alf. "A Core List VIII: Fantasy." *Literature Base* (Australia) 3 (June 1992): 16–17.

————. "Defining Fantasy." *Literature Base* (Australia) 3 (June 1992): 12–15.

May, Jill P., ed. *Children and Their Literature: A Readings Book.* West Lafayette, IN: Children's Literature Association Publications, 1983. Includes articles on MacDonald and Aiken.

Meek, Margaret. "Speaking of Shifters." In *Changing English: Essays for Harold Rosen.* London: Heinemann, 1984. Reprinted in *Signal* 45 (Sept 1984): 152–167.

Meek, Margaret, Aidan Warlow, and Griselda Barton. *The Cool Web: The Pattern of Children's Reading.* New York: Atheneum, 1978, pp. 76–79, 103–105, 120–128, 157–158, 166–187, 196–200, 216–221, 265–271, 284–293, 314–330. Articles by C. S. Lewis, Storr, Aiken, Pearce, Garner, and Boston.

Meigs, Cornelia, Anne Thaxter Eaton, Elizabeth Nesbitt, and Ruth Hill Viguers. *A Critical History of Children's Literature: A Survey of Children's Books in English* (originally published 1953), rev. ed. New York: Macmillan, 1969, pp. 165–174, 182–183, 186–202, 278–284, 310–348, 446–483, 512–513.

Merla, Patrick. "'What Is Real?' Asked the Rabbit One Day: Realism vs. Fantasy in Children's and Adult Literature." *Saturday Review,* Nov 4, 1972, pp. 43–50. Reprinted in Sheila A. Egoff. *Only Connect.* New York: Oxford Univ. Press, 1980, pp. 337–355.

Michalson, Karen Ann. "Victorian Fantasy Literature and the Politics of Canon-Making." Ph.D. diss., University of Massachusetts, 1990. Discusses John Ruskin, George MacDonald, Charles Kingsley, H. Rider Haggard, and Rudyard Kipling.

Millar, John Hepburn. "On Some Books for Boys and Girls." In *A Peculiar Gift: Nineteenth Century Writings on Books for Children.* Edited by Lance Salway. Harmondsworth, England: Penguin, 1976, pp. 154–161. Reprinted from *Blackwood's Magazine* 159 (Mar 1896): 389–395.

Miller, Bertha Mahony, and Elinor Whitney Field, eds. *Newbery Medal Books: 1922–1955.* Boston: Horn Book, 1957. Lofting, pp. 17–27; Chrisman, pp. 39–43; Field, pp. 74–88; Coatsworth, pp. 89–98; Seredy, pp. 157–165; Lawson, pp. 255–267; Bailey, pp. 288–299; Du Bois, pp. 300–317.

Miller, Joseph D. "Parallel Universes: Fantasy or Science Fiction?" In *Intersections: Science Fiction and Fantasy,* ed. by George E. Slusser and Eric S. Rabkin. Carbondale: Southern Illinois Univ. Press, 1987.

Miller, Patricia. "The Importance of Being Earnest: The Fairy Tale in 19th Century England." *Children's Literature Association Quarterly* 7 (Summer 1982): 11–14.

Milne, Rosemary. "Fantasy in Literature for Early Childhood." In *Readings in Children's Literature: Proceedings of the National Seminar on Children's Literature,* ed. by Moira Robinson. Frankston, Australia: Frankston State College, 1975.

Milnes, P. C. "Analysis of British and American Fantasy in Children's Literature." Research paper. Long Island University, 1969.

Milosh, Joseph E., Jr. "Reason and Mysticism in Fantasy and Science Fiction." In *Young Adult Literature: Background and Criticism,* ed. by Millicent Lenz and Ramona M. Mahood. Chicago: American Library Association, 1980, pp. 433–439.

Mobley, Jane. "Magic Is Alive: A Study of Contemporary Fantasy Fiction." Ph.D. diss., University of Kansas, 1974.

———. "Toward a Definition of Fantasy Fiction." *Extrapolation* 15 (May 1974): 117–128. Reprinted in Robert Bator. *Signposts to Criticism of Children's Literature.* Chicago: American Library Association, 1983, pp. 249–260.

———, ed. *Phantasmagoria: Tales of Fantasy and the Supernatural.* New York: Anchor Press, 1977. "Preface," pp. 13–18; "The Wondrous Fair: Magical Fantasy," pp. 21–35.

Moeller, Joachim, ed. *Imagination on a Long Rein: English Literature Illustration.* Marburg: Jonas Verlag, 1988.

Møller, H. H. "What Is Fantastic Literature?" *Bogens Verden* (Denmark) 69 (1987): 477–483.

Molson, Francis J. *Children's Fantasy.* Mercer Island, WA: Starmont House, 1989.

———. "Children's Fantasy and Science Fiction." In *The Science Fiction Reference Book,* ed. by Marshall Tymn. Mercer Island, WA: Starmont House, 1981.

———. "Ethical Fantasy for Children." In Roger Schlobin. *The Aesthetics of Fantasy Literature and Art.* Notre Dame, IN: Univ. of Notre Dame Press, 1982, pp. 82–104.

Montgomery, Catherine J. "The Dialectical Approach of Writers of Children's Arthurian Retellings." *Arthurian Interpretations* 3 (Fall 1988): 79–88.

Montgomery, Marion. "The Prophetic Poet and the Loss of Middle-Earth." *Georgia Review* 33 (Spring 1979): 63–88.

Moorcock, Michael. "The Heroes in Heroic Fantasy." *Dragonfields* 3 (1980): 50–61.

———. *Wizardry and Wild Romance: A Study of Epic Fantasy.* London: Gollancz, 1988.

Moore, Anne Carroll. *The Three Owls: A Book About Children's Books, Their Authors, Artists and Critics.* New York: Macmillan, 1925. Followed by *The Three Owls: Second Book. Contemporary Critics of Children's Books.* New York: Coward-McCann, 1928; and *The Three Owls, Third Book.* New York: Coward-McCann, 1931.

Moore, Annie E. *Literature Old and New for Children: Materials for a College Course.* Boston: Houghton Mifflin, 1934. "The Modern Fanciful Tale," pp. 352–387.

Morris, John S. "Fantasy in a Mythless Age." In *Children's Literature,* vol. 2. Storrs, CT: Journal of the Modern Language Association, 1973, pp. 77–86.

Morse, Donald E., ed. *The Fantastic in World Literature and the Arts.* New York: Greenwood, 1987. Discusses Lewis Carroll, Astrid Lindgren, and J. R. R. Tolkien.

Moss, Anita West. "Children and Fairy Tales: A Study in Nineteenth Century British Fantasy." Ph.D. diss., Indiana University, 1979.

———. "Crime and Punishment—Or Development—In Fairy Tales and Fantasy." *Mythlore* 8 (Spring 1981): 26–28, 42.

———. "Varieties of Literary Fairy Tale." *Children's Literature Association Quarterly* 7 (Summer 1982): 15–17.

Moss, Elaine. *Part of the Pattern: A Personal Journey through the World of Children's Books, 1960–1985.* New York: Greenwillow Press, 1986.

Mountjoy, Harry W. "The Comic Fantasy in English Fiction of the Victorian Period." Ph.D. diss., University of Pennsylvania, 1934.

Muir, Percival Horace. *English Children's Books, 1600–1900.* Original U.S. publication,

Praeger, 1954. North Pomfret, VT: David and Charles, 1979, pp. 105–107, 136–143, 153–160.

Mulderig, Gerald P. "Alice and Wonderland: Subversive Elements in the World of Victorian Children's Fiction." *Journal of Popular Culture* 11 (1978): 320–329.

Muta, Orie. "The Development of Fantasy in Australian Children's Literature." Master's diss., University of Sydney (Australia), 1983.

Natov, Roni, and Geraldine Deluca. "Current Trends in Children's Books: Fantasy and Realism." *U.S.A. Today* 109 (July 1980): 42–47.

Newman, Anne Royall. "Images of the Bear in Children's Literature." *Children's Literature in Education* 18 (Fall 1987): 131–138. Milne, Bond, Kipling, and Stearns.

Nikolajeva, Maria. "Fantasy: Atervandsgrand Eller Framtidsperspektiv [Fantasy: Dead End or Future Perspective]." *Opsis Kalopsis* (Sweden) 3 (1988): 25–27.

——. *The Magic Code: The Use of Magical Patterns in Fantasy for Children.* Stockholm: Almquist, 1988.

——. "Mod, Vanskap och Uppfuyllda Onskemal: Nagra Milstolpar i den Ryska Fantasilitteraturen [Courage, Friendship and Wishes Realized: Some Milestones in Russian Fantasy Literature]." *Barnboken* (Stockholm) 2 (1984): 15–18.

Nodelman, Perry. "Defining Children's Literature." In *Children's Literature,* vol. 8. New Haven, CT: Yale Univ. Press, 1980, pp. 184–190.

——. "Interpretation and the Apparent Sameness of Children's Novels." *Studies in Literary Imagination* 18 (Fall 1985): 5–20. (time travel)

——. *The Pleasures of Children's Literature.* New York: Longman, 1992. "Literary Fairy Tales," pp. 171–172; "Stories About Toys, Dolls, and Other Small Things," pp. 198–200; "Time Fantasies," pp. 202–203.

——. "Some Presumptuous Generalizations About Fantasy." *Children's Literature Association Quarterly* 4 (Summer 1979): 5–6, 18. Reprinted in *Festschrift: A Ten Year Retrospective,* ed. by Perry Nodelman and Jill P. May. West Lafayette, IN: Children's Literature Association Publications, 1983, pp. 26–27; and in *The First Steps,* ed. by Patricia Dooley. West Lafayette, IN: Children's Literature Association Publications, 1984, pp. 15–16.

——, ed. *Touchstones: Reflections on the Best in Children's Literature,* vol. 1. West Lafayette, IN: Children's Literature Association Publications, 1985.

Nodelman, Perry, and Jill P. May. *Festschrift: A Ten Year Retrospective.* West Lafayette, IN: Children's Literature Association Publications, 1983. "Fantasy," pp. 26–35.

Noel, Roberta Christine. "The Borrowed Cup of Courage: A Descriptive Comparison of Archetypes Presented by Male and Female Authors in Fantasy for Adolescents." Ed.D. diss., Gonzaga University (Washington), 1987.

Norton, Donna E. *Through the Eyes of a Child: An Introduction to Children's Literature.* 2nd ed. Columbus, OH: Merrill, 1987. "Modern Fantasy," pp. 264–324.

Norton, Eloise D., ed. *Folk Literature of the British Isles: Readings for Librarians, Teachers and Those Who Work with Children and Young Adults.* Metuchen, NJ: Scarecrow Press, 1978.

Nugent, Susan Monroe. "Quests for Self-Awareness." *ALAN Review* 15 (1988): 43–44. Discusses Susan Cooper, Anne McCaffrey, Patricia McKillip, and Robin McKinley.

Olcott, Frances Jenkins. *The Children's Reading.* rev. ed. Boston: Houghton Mifflin, 1927. "Fables, Myths and Fairy Tales," p. 90.

The Openhearted Audience: Ten Authors Talk About Writing for Children. Washington, DC: Library of Congress, 1980. P. L. Travers, pp. 3–24; Maurice Sendak, pp. 25–46; Joan Aiken, pp. 47–68; Ursula Le Guin, pp. 101–114; Virginia Hamilton, pp. 115–132; John Rowe Townsend, pp. 133–152; Eleanor Cameron, pp. 153–176; and Jill Paton Walsh, pp. 177–198.

Osborne, E. "Fairy Tales and Fantasy." *Library Association Record* 45 (Dec 1943): 211–212.

Owen, Helen Hammet. "In Defense of Fairy Tales." *Horn Book* 7 (Aug 1931): 131–139.

Parish, Helen Rand. "Children's Books in Latin America: Part II. Fantasy and Other Modern Trends." *Horn Book* 24 (July–Aug 1948): 257–262.

Paton Walsh, Jill. "Realism, Fantasy and History: Facts in Fiction." *Canadian Children's Literature* 48 (1987): 7–14.

Pawling, Christopher, ed. *Popular Fiction and Societal Changes.* New York: St. Martin, 1984.

Paxon, Diana. "The Tolkien Tradition." *Mythlore* 39 (1984): 23–27, 37. Includes Adams, Alexander, Brooks, Le Guin, Lewis.

Peel, Doris. "Books That Enchant." *Horn Book* 25 (May 1949): 242–247. Grahame and St. Exupéry.

The Pendragon Chronicles: Heroic Fantasy from the Time of King Arthur. Edited by Mike Ashley. New York: Bedrick, 1990. "The Pendragon Chroniclers: A Survey of Arthurian Fiction," pp. 402–416. (anthology and bibliography)

Peppin, Brigid. *Fantasy: Book Illustration 1860–1920.* London: Thames and Hudson, 1977.

———. *Fantasy: The Golden Age of Fantastic Illustration.* Original British publication, 1975. New York: New American Library, 1976.

Pernicone, Celeste. "Homecomings: Fantasy and Horror." In *Intersections: Science Fiction and Fantasy,* ed. by George E. Slusser and Eric S. Rabkin. Carbondale: Southern Illinois Univ. Press, 1987.

Peterson, Linda Kauffman, and Marilyn Leathers Solt. "The Newbery Medal and Honor Books, 1922–1981: Fantasy." *Children's Literature Association Quarterly* 6 (Fall 1981): 23.

Petrich, Shirley. "A Note on Contemporary Soviet Fantasies." In *Children's Literature,* vol. 2. Storrs, CT: Journal of the Modern Language Association, 1973, pp. 221–223.

Philip, Neil. "Fantasy: Double Cream or Instant Whip?" *Signal* 35 (May 1981): 82–90.

Pierce, Tamora. "Fantasy: Why Kids Read It, Why Kids Need It." *School Library Journal* 39 (Oct 1993): 50–51.

Plank, Robert. "The Golem and the Robot." *Literature and Psychology* 13–15 (1963–1965): 12–27.

Platt, Charles. *Dream Makers: Science Fiction and Fantasy Writers at Work.* New York: Ungar, 1987. Interviews.

———. "In Defense of the Real World." *Isaac Asimov's Science Fiction Magazine,* Nov 1983, pp. 53–66.

Ponnau, Gwenhail. *La Folie dans la Litterature Fantastique [Madness in Fantasy Literature].* Paris: Editions du Centre National de la Recherche Scientifique, 1987. Discusses E. T. A. Hoffmann, Nathaniel Hawthorne, Robert Louis Stevenson, and H. G. Wells.

Popatov, N. "Is Fantasy Needed in Children's Literature?" *Soviet Studies in Literature* 24 (Winter 1987–1988): 49–54.

Poskanzer, Susan Cornell. "A Case for Fantasy." *Elementary English* 52 (Apr 1975): 472–475.

Post, J. B. "Cartographic Fantasy." *Bulletin of the Geography and Map Division, Special Libraries Association* 101 (1975): 12–14.

Prickett, Stephen. "Religious Fantasy in the Nineteenth Century." In Frank N. Magill. *Survey of Modern Fantasy Literature,* vol. 5. Englewood Cliffs, NJ: Salem Press, 1983, pp. 2369–2382.

———. *Victorian Fantasy.* Bloomington: Indiana Univ. Press, 1979. Discusses Carroll, Kingsley, MacDonald, Kipling, and Nesbit.

Pringle, David. *Modern Fantasy: The Hundred Best Novels: An English Language Selection, 1946–1987.* New York: Peter Bedrick, 1989.

Quayle, Eric. *The Collector's Book of Children's Books.* New York: Crown, 1971. "Fairy, Folk Tales and Fantasy," pp. 36–46.

———. *Early Children's Books: A Collector's Guide.* New York: Barnes and Noble, 1983, pp. 74–88, 176–181.

Rabkin, Eric S. "The Appeal of the Fantastic: Old Worlds for New." In *The Scope of the Fantastic—Theory, Technique, Major Authors,* ed. by Robert A. Collins and Howard D. Pearce. Westport, CT: Greenwood, 1985.

————. *The Fantastic in Literature.* Princeton: Princeton Univ. Press, 1975.

————. *Fantastic Worlds: Myths, Tales, and Stories.* New York: Oxford Univ. Press, 1979. Anthology plus critical essay.

Radu, Kenneth. "Canadian Fantasy." *Canadian Children's Literature* 1, no. 2 (Summer 1975): 73–79.

Rahn, Suzanne. "The Expression of Religious and Political Concepts in Fantasy for Children." Ph.D. diss., University of Washington, 1986. Discusses C. S. Lewis, Eleanor Farjeon, Kenneth Grahame, Walter De La Mare, E. Nesbit, Beatrix Potter, K. M. Briggs, and Diana Wynne Jones.

Rausch, Helen Martha. "The Debate over Fairy Tales." Ph.D. diss., Columbia University Teachers College, 1977.

Rawlinson, Eleanor. *Introduction to Literature for Children.* rev. ed. New York: Norton, 1937. "Fanciful Tales," pp. 337–340.

Ray, Sheila G. *Children's Fiction: A Handbook for Librarians.* rev. ed. London: Brockhampton, 1972. "Fantasy," pp. 23–33.

Rees, David. *The Marble in the Water: Essays on Contemporary Writers of Fiction for Children and Young Adults.* Boston: Horn Book, 1980, pp. 1–13, 36–89, 185–198. Articles on Farmer, Pearce, Garner, E. B. White, Le Guin, and Lively.

————. *Painted Desert, Green Shade: Essays on Contemporary Writers of Fiction for Children and Young Adults.* Boston: Horn Book, 1984. Includes Boston, Dickinson, Hamilton, Hoban, T. Hughes, Mark, Langton, Townsend, and Westall.

————. *"What Do Draculas Do?" Essays on Contemporary Writers of Fiction for Children and Young Adults.* Metuchen, NJ: Scarecrow Press, 1990. Articles on Susan Cooper, Roald Dahl, Helen Cresswell, Maurice Sendak, Leon Garfield, Margaret Mahy, William Mayne, Patricia Wrightson, Mary Norton, Joan Aiken, Madeleine L'Engle, and Jane Gardam.

"Reflections on Fantasy and Science Fiction." *Top of the News* 39 (Fall 1982): 39–96. Issue on fantasy.

Reginald, R. *Science Fiction and Fantasy Literature, 1975–1991: A Bibliography of Science Fiction, Fantasy, and Horror Fiction Books and Nonfiction Monographs.* Detroit: Gale, 1992.

Richardson, A. "Reluctant Lords and Lame Princes: Engendering the Male Child in Nineteenth-Century Juvenile Fiction." *Children's Literature 21.* New Haven: Yale Univ. Press, 1993, pp. 3–19.

Richardson, Carmen C. "The Reality of Fantasy." *Language Arts* 53 (1976): 549–551, 563.

Robinson, Evelyn R., ed. *Readings About Children's Literature.* New York: McKay, 1966, pp. 302–312.

Robinson, Moira, ed. *Readings in Children's Literature: Proceedings of the National Seminar on Children's Literature.* Frankston, Australia: Frankston State College, 1975.

Rochelle, Larry. "Quest: The Search for Meaning Through Fantasy." *English Journal* 66 (October 1977): 54–55.

Rogers, S. "It's Only a Game . . . or Is It?" *School Library Journal* 38 (Mar 1992): 176–177.

Roginski, Jim. *Behind the Covers: Interviews with Authors and Illustrators of Books for Children and Young Adults.* Littleton, CO: Libraries Unlimited, 1985.

Ross, Meredith Jane. "The Sublime to the Ridiculous: Restructuring of Arthurian Materials in Selected Modern Novels." Ph.D. diss., University of Wisconsin, 1985.

Rottensteiner, Franz. "European Theories of Fantasy." In Frank N. Magill. *Survey of Modern Fantasy Literature,* vol. 5. Englewood Cliffs, NJ: Salem Press, 1983, pp. 2235–2246.

————. *The Fantasy Book: An Illustrated History from Dracula to Tolkien.* New York: Macmillan, 1978, pp. 96–98, 108–115.

Roy, Kuldip Kumar. "The Fantastic Concept in Children's Literature of India." *Multicultural Children's Literature* (India) 4, no. 1 (1987): 1–13.

Rustin, Margaret. "Deep Structures of Fantasy in Modern British Children's Books." *The Lion and the Unicorn* 10 (1986): 60–82.

Rustin, Margaret, and Michael Rustin. *Narratives of Love and Loss: Studies in Modern Children's Fiction.* London: Verso, 1987; New York: Routledge, 1988. Articles on Philippa Pearce, C. S. Lewis, E. Nesbit, E. B. White, Russell Hoban, Mary Norton, Lynne Reid Banks, Rumer Godden, and Paula Fox.

Ryan, John S. *Australian Fantasy and Folklore.* Armidale, NSW, Australia: Univ. of New England, 1981.

———. "Australian Fantasy and Folklore." *Orana* (Australia) 17 (May 1981): 65–79.

———. "Australian Fantasy and Folklore: Part 2." *Orana* (Australia) 17 (Aug 1981): 112–133.

———. "Australian Fantasy and Folklore: Part 3." *Orana* (Australia) 17 (Nov 1981): 164–177.

Safford, Barbara Ripp. "High Fantasy: An Archetypal Analysis of Children's Literature." D.L.S. diss., Columbia University, 1983.

Saint Paul, Therese. "The Magical Mantle, the Drinking Horn, and the Chastity Test: A Study of a 'Tale' in Arthurian Celtic Literature." Ph.D. diss., University of Edinburgh, 1987.

Sale, Roger. "The Audience in Children's Literature." In George Slusser, Eric Rabkin, and Robert Scholes. *Bridges to Fantasy.* Carbondale: Southern Illinois Univ. Press, 1982, pp. 78–89.

———. *Fairy Tales and After: From Snow White to E. B. White.* Cambridge, MA: Harvard Univ. Press, 1978. Discusses Carroll, Grahame, Kipling, Baum, Brooks, and E. B. White.

Salway, Lance, ed. *A Peculiar Gift: Nineteenth Century Writings on Books for Children.* Harmondsworth, Middlesex: Kestrel, 1976. "Fairy Tale Never Dies," pp. 111–167, 173–194. Articles by Dickens, Ruskin, Lang, Molesworth, MacDonald, and Horne.

Sammons, Martha C. *"A Better Country": The Worlds of Religious Fantasy and Science Fiction.* Westport, CT: Greenwood, 1988. Discusses Madeleine L'Engle, Ursula K. Le Guin, C. S. Lewis, George MacDonald, and J. R. R. Tolkien.

Sargent, Abby L. "Books for Children: Fairy Tales. *Library Journal* 26, no. 8 (1901): 66–69. Discusses Browne, Ingelow, Craik, MacDonald, and Nesbit.

Saxby, H. M., and Marjorie Cotton. *A History of Australian Children's Literature, 1941–1970.* Sydney: Wentworth Books, 1971. "Fantasy," pp. 139–154.

Saxby, Maurice. "Over the Rim of Reality." *Magpies* (Australia) 3 (Mar 1988): 4–8.

Sayers, Frances Clarke. "Walt Disney Accused. An Interview with Frances Clarke Sayers." *Horn Book* 41 (Dec 1965): 602–611.

Schaafsma, Karen. "Beyond the Between: The Paradoxical Journey of Fantasy Literature." Ph.D. diss., University of California, Davis, 1990.

———. "The Demon Lover: Lilith and the Hero in Modern Fantasy." *Extrapolation* 28(1987): 52–61.

Schadewinkel, K. "Fantasy—Literatur, Mode oder Was? [Fantasy—Literature, Fashion or Something Else?]" *Buch und Bibliothek* (Munich) 38 (July–Aug 1986): 676–680.

Scherf, Walter. "Magic Tales as an Invitation to a Child's Necessary Scaling Off." In *How Can Children's Literature Meet the Needs of Modern Children?* 15th IBBY Conference, 1976, pp. 36–41.

Schlobin, Roger C., ed. *The Aesthetics of Fantasy Literature and Art.* Notre Dame, IN: Univ. of Notre Dame Press, 1982.

Schlobin, Roger C. "Fantasy." In *Handbook of American Popular Literature,* ed. by M. Thomas Inge. Westport, CT: Greenwood, 1988, pp. 139–155.

———. "Fantasy Versus Horror." In Frank N. Magill. *Survey of Modern Fantasy Literature,* vol. 5. Englewood Cliffs, NJ: Salem Press, 1983, pp. 2259–2266.

————. "In the Looking Glasses: The Popular and Cultural Fantasy Response." In *The Scope of the Fantastic—Culture, Biography, Themes, Children's Literature,* ed. by Robert A. Collins and Howard D. Pearce. Westport, CT: Greenwood, 1985.

Schmidt, Nancy J. *Children's Fiction About Africa in English.* New York: Conch Magazine, 1981.

Scholes, Robert. "Boiling Roses: Thoughts on Science Fantasy." In *Intersections: Science Fiction and Fantasy,* ed. by George E. Slusser and Eric S. Rabkin. Carbondale: Southern Illinois Univ. Press, 1987.

Schorr, Karl. "The Rewards of Reading Fantasy." *Mythlore* 41 (1985): 9–15.

Schwarcz, H. Joseph. "Machine Animism in Modern Children's Literature." In Sara Fenwick. *A Critical Approach to Children's Literature.* Chicago: Univ. of Chicago Press, 1967, pp. 78–95. Originally published in *The Library Quarterly,* 37 (Jan 1967): 78–95.

Searles, Baird, Beth Meacham, and Michael Franklin. *A Reader's Guide to Fantasy.* New York: Avon, 1982.

Sebesta, Sam Leaton, and William J. Iverson. *Literature for Thursday's Child.* Palo Alto, CA: Science Research Associates, 1975. "Fanciful Fiction," pp. 177–242.

Shaner, Mary E. "Twentieth Century Fantasy." In *Masterworks of Children's Literature,* vol. VIII. New York: Chelsea House, 1986, pp. 119–158.

Shannon, George. "All Times in One." *Children's Literature Association Quarterly* 10 (Winter 1986): 178–181. Discusses time travel.

Shapiro, Lillian L. *Fiction for Youth: A Guide to Recommended Books.* 2nd ed. New York: Neal-Schuman, 1985.

Shinn, Thelma J. *Worlds Within Women: Myth and Mythmaking in Fantastic Literature by Women.* New York: Greenwood, 1986.

Shippey, Tom. "The Golden Bough and the Incorporation of Magic in Science Fiction." *Foundation* 11/12 (1977): 119–134.

Shochet, Lois. "Fantasy and English Children." *Top of the News* 24 (Apr 1968): 311–320.

Singh, Michael J. "Law and Emotion in Fantasy." *Orana* 18 (May 1982): 49–54.

Slusser, George, and Eric S. Rabkin. *Intersections: Fantasy and Science Fiction.* Carbondale: Southern Illinois Univ. Press, 1987. Discusses L. Frank Baum, Lewis Carroll, Ursula K. Le Guin, Dr. Seuss, and J. R. R. Tolkien.

Slusser, George, Eric Rabkin, and Robert Scholes, eds. *Bridges to Fantasy.* Carbondale: Southern Illinois Univ. Press, 1982. Children's literature, pp. 78–89; Twain, pp. 130–141.

Smaridge, Norah. *Famous Modern Storytellers for Young People.* New York: Dodd, 1969. Brink, Coatsworth, Enright, Farjeon, Godden, Lindgren, Lofting, Milne, M. Norton, Travers, and E. B. White.

Smedman, M. Sarah. "Springs of Hope: Recovery of Primordial Time in 'Mythic' Novels for Young Readers." *Children's Literature* 16 (1988): 91–108.

Smith, Curtis S., ed. *Twentieth-Century Science Fiction Writers.* 2nd ed. Chicago: St. James Press, 1986.

Smith, James Steel. *A Critical Approach to Children's Literature.* New York: McGraw-Hill, 1967. "Sensibility," pp. 171–202.

Smith, Karen Patricia. "The English Psychological Fantasy Novel: A Bequest of Time." *School Library Journal* 31 (May 1985): 44–45.

————. *The Fabulous Realm: A Literary-Historical Approach to British Fantasy, 1780–1990.* Metuchen, NJ: Scarecrow, 1993.

————. "The Keys to the Kingdom: From Didacticism to Dynamism in British Children's Fantasy, 1780–1979." Ed.D. diss., Columbia University, 1982.

Smith, Lillian. *The Unreluctant Years: A Critical Approach to Children's Literature.* Chicago: American Library Association, 1953. "Fantasy," pp. 149–162.

Snyman, K. "Imaginary Worlds: Fantasy, Fairy Tale, Myth and Science Fiction. Part 1." *Skolmediasentrum* (South Africa) 1 (1988): 31–33.

————. "Imaginary Worlds: Myth, Fairy Tale, Fantasy, and Science Fiction. Part 2." *Skol-*

mediasentrum (South Africa) 2 (1988): 46–51. Discusses Alan Garner's *The Owl Service,* Robin McKinley's *Beauty,* and Ursula K. Le Guin's *Earthsea* books.

South, Malcolm, ed. *Mythical and Fabulous Creatures: A Sourcebook and Research Guide.* Westport, CT: Greenwood, 1987.

"Special Issue: Fantasy and Science Fiction." *ALAN Review* 15 (Winter 1988).

"Special Issue: Fantasy and Science Fiction." *Extrapolation* 28 (Spring 1987).

"Special Issue: Science Fiction, Fantasy, and Horror." *AB Bookman's Weekly* 28 (Aug 1989).

"Special Issue: Science Fiction, Fantasy, and Horror." *AB Bookman's Weekly* 29 (Oct 22, 1990).

"Special Issue: Time Slip Fantasies." *Canadian Children's Literature* 67 (1992).

Spencer, Kathleen Louise. "The Urban Gothic in British Fantastic Fiction, 1880–1930." Ph.D. diss., University of California, Los Angeles, 1987.

Spivak, Charlotte. *Merlin's Daughters: Contemporary Women Writers of Fantasy.* New York: Greenwood, 1987. "Fantasy and the Feminine," pp. 3–15. Includes essays on Susan Cooper and Ursula K. Le Guin.

Stableford, Brian. "The Mythology of Faerie." In Frank N. Magill. *Survey of Modern Fantasy Literature,* vol. 5. Englewood Cliffs, NJ: Salem Press, 1983, pp. 2283–2298.

Stewig, John Warren. *Children and Literature.* Skokie, IL: Rand McNally, 1980, pp. 396–449, 452–461.

Stibbs, Andrew. "For Realism in Children's Fiction." *Use of English* 32 (Autumn 1980): 18–24.

Stohler, Sara L. "The Mythic World of Childhood." *Children's Literature Association Quarterly* 12 (Spring 1987): 28–32.

Stokes, Kathy Jo. "Children's Journey Stories as an Epic Subgenre." Ph.D. diss., University of Nebraska, Lincoln, 1988.

Stone, Grant. "Looking into the Other." *Magpies* (Australia) 3 (July 1988): 5–10.

Stott, Jon C. "Midsummer Night's Dream: Fantasy and Self-Realization in Children's Fiction." *The Lion and the Unicorn* 1 (Fall 1977): 25–39.

———. "Of Time and the Prairie: Canadian Fantasies and the Search for Self-Worth." *Children's Literature Association Bulletin* 16 (Fall 1990): 2–6.

Sullivan, C. W., III. "Fantasy." In *Story and Society: Children's Literature in Its Social Context,* ed. by Dennis Butts. London: Macmillan, 1992, pp. 97–111.

———. "The Influence of Celtic Myth and Legend on Modern Imaginative Fiction." Ph.D. diss., University of Oregon, 1976.

———. "Traditional Ballads and Modern Children's Fantasy: Some Comments on Structure and Intent." *Children's Literature Association Quarterly* 11 (Fall 1986): 145–147.

———. "Traditional Welsh Materials in Modern Fantasy." *Dragon's Tale* (The Journal of the Welsh National Centre for Children's Literature) 2 (1985): 2–12. Reprinted in *Extrapolation* 28 (Spring 1987): 87–97. Discusses Evangeline Walton, Alan Garner, Kenneth Morris, Nancy Bond, Lloyd Alexander, and Susan Cooper.

———. *Welsh Celtic Myth in Modern Fantasy.* Westport, CT: Greenwood, 1989.

———. "Women of Power: Mythic and Cultural Sources." *Fantasy Review* 91 (1986): 7–8, 42.

———, ed. "Special Section: Fantasy." *Children's Literature Association Quarterly* 12 (Spring 1987): 6–32.

Summerfield, Geoffrey. *Fantasy and Reason: Children's Literature in the 18th Century.* Athens: Univ. of Georgia Press, 1985.

Survey of Modern Fantasy Literature. 5 vols. Edited by Frank N. Magill. Englewood Cliffs, NJ: Salem Press, 1983. Five hundred essay-reviews.

Susina, Jan Christopher. "Victorian Kunstmärcher: A Study in Children's Literature, 1840–1875." Ph.D. diss., Indiana University, 1986. Discusses F. E. Paget, John Ruskin, Charles Kingsley, George MacDonald, Lewis Carroll, and Jean Ingelow.

Svenson, Asfrid. "Opening Windows onto Unreality, Some Elements of Fantasy in Scandinavian Children's Literature." *International Review of Children's Literature and Librarianship* 2 (Spring 1987): 1–9. (bibliographic essay)

Svensson, Sonja. "Saga, Realism, Sanning. Om Barnlitteraturens Forvandlingar [Fairy Tale, Realism, Truth. On the Transformations of Children's Literature]." *Bonniers Litterara Magisin* (Stockholm) 49 (Sept 1980): 203–211.

Swan, Ann M. "An Analysis of Selected Pseudoscientific Phenomena in Children's Literature." Ph.D. diss., University of Akron, 1991. Discusses ghost stories.

Swinfen, Ann. *In Defense of Fantasy: A Study of the Genre in English and American Literature Since 1945.* Boston: Routledge, 1984. Animal fantasy, pp. 12–43; time fantasy, pp. 44–74; secondary worlds, pp. 75–99; allegory, pp. 100–122; magical powers, pp. 123–146.

———. "The Sub-Creative Art: An Examination of Some Aspects of the Use of Fantasy, Principally in English Children's Literature, 1945–1975." Ph.D. diss., University of Dundee (Scotland), 1979.

Tatar, Maria. *Off with Their Heads! Fairytales and the Culture of Childhood.* Princeton, NJ: Princeton Univ. Press, 1992.

Taylor, Robert. "'Wishful Thinking' or 'Hopeful Dreaming'?" *Horn Book* 59 (Aug 1983): 398–399.

Taylor, Una Ashworth. "Fairy Tales as Literature." *Signal* 21 (Sept 1976): 123–138; continued in 22 (Jan 1977): 48–56.

Terry, June S. "To Seek and to Find: Quest Literature for Children." *School Librarian* 18 (Dec 1970): 399–404. Reprinted in M. L. White. *Children's Literature.* Columbus, OH: Merrill, 1976, pp. 138–143. Discusses Garner, de la Mare, Andersen, Tolkien, MacDonald, and C. S. Lewis.

Thompson, Hilary. "Doorways to Fantasy." *Canadian Children's Literature* 21 (1981): 8–16.

Thompson, Raymond H. "Arthurian Legend and Modern Fantasy." In Frank N. Magill. *Survey of Modern Fantasy Literature,* vol. 5. Englewood Cliffs, NJ: Salem Press, 1983, pp. 2299–2315.

———. "Commentary: King Arthur in Modern Fantasy." *Fantasy Review* 86 (Dec 1985): 12–13.

———. "The Enchanter Awakes: Merlin in Modern Fantasy." In *Death and the Serpent: Immortality in Science Fiction and Fantasy,* ed. by Carl B. Yoke and Donald M. Hassler. Westport, CT: Greenwood, 1985, pp. 49–56.

———. "Modern Fantasy and Medieval Romance. A Comparative Study." In Roger Schlobin. *The Aesthetics of Fantasy Literature and Art.* Notre Dame, IN: Univ. of Notre Dame Press, 1982, pp. 211–225.

———. *The Return from Avalon: A Study of the Arthurian Legend in Modern Fiction.* Westport, CT: Greenwood, 1985.

Thwaite, Mary F. *From Primer to Pleasure in Reading.* Boston: Horn Book, 1963. "Fairy Lore and Fantasy," pp. 106–125.

Timmerman, John H. *Other Worlds: The Fantasy Genre.* Bowling Green, OH: Bowling Green Univ., 1983.

Toijer-Nilsson, Ving. *Fantasins Underland. Myt Och Ide I Den Fantastika Berättelsen [The Wonderland of Fantasy. Myth and Ideology in Fantasy Literature].* Stockholm: Efs-Förlaget, 1981.

———. "Fantasykongress i Montreal [Congress on Fantasy Literature in Montreal]." *Barn och Kultur* (Sweden) 32, no. 1 (1986): 18–20.

Tolkien, J. R. R. "On Fairy-Stories." In *Tree and Leaf.* Boston: Houghton Mifflin, 1965, pp. 3–84.

Tolstoy, Nikolai. *The Quest for Merlin.* Boston: Little, Brown, 1985.

Townsend, John Rowe. "Border Country." *Canadian Children's Literature* 48 (1987): 29–41.

————. "Guest Essay: Heights of Fantasy." *Children's Literature Review,* vol. 5. Detroit: Gale, 1983, pp. 7–12.

————. *A Sense of Story: Essays on Contemporary Writers for Children.* Philadelphia: Lippincott, 1971, pp. 9–27, 39–47, 57–67, 97–119, 130–153, 163–181, 204–214. Essays on Aiken, Boston, Christopher, Cresswell, Estes, Garfield, Garner, Mayne, M. Norton, Pearce, Peyton, and Wrightson.

————. *A Sounding of Storytellers: New and Revised Essays on Contemporary Writers for Children.* Philadelphia: Lippincott, 1979, pp. 41–55, 66–110, 125–178, 194–206. Essays on Dickinson, Garfield, Garner, Hamilton, Lively, Mayne, Walsh, Peyton, and Wrightson.

————. "Travellers in Time." *Times Educational Supplement* (Aug 4, 1989): 17.

————. *Written for Children: An Outline of English Language Children's Literature.* 4th ed. New York: Harper, 1992. "Fantasy", pp. 76–84, 94–102, 127–140, 211–245.

A Track to Unknown Water: Proceedings of the Second Pacific Rim Conference on Children's Literature. Edited by Stella Lees. Metuchen, NJ: Scarecrow, 1987. Articles by Betsy Byars, Margaret Mahy, and Patricia Wrightson.

Trask, Margaret. "Fantasy and the Young Child—A Personal View." In Margaret Trask. *Fantasy, Science Fiction, Science Materials.* Kensington, NSW, Australia: Univ. of New South Wales School of Librarianship, 1972, pp. 117–138.

Travelers in Time: Past, Present and to Come. Proceedings of Children's Literature New England, Summer Institute, 1989. Cambridge, England: Green Bay, 1990.

Trease, Geoffrey. *Tales Out of School.* 2nd ed. London: Heinemann, 1964. "Fancy Free," pp. 40–52.

Valdman, Bertrand Andre. "The Metaphor of Commerce and the Quest of the Self in Arthurian Romance Literature." Ph.D. diss., Stanford University, 1987.

Valli, Luigi. "Shakespeare and Fantasy: Modern Theories and Interpretations of the Genre." Ph.D. diss., Bowling Green University, 1981.

Varlejs, Jana, ed. *Young Adult Literature in the Seventies: A Selection of Readings.* Metuchen, NJ: Scarecrow Press, 1978.

Veglahn, Nancy. "Images of Evil: Male and Female Monsters in Heroic Fantasy." In *Children's Literature,* vol. 15. New Haven, CT: Yale Univ. Press, 1987, pp. 106–119.

Viguers, Ruth Hill. "Out of the Abundance." *Horn Book* 34 (Oct 1958): 341. Reprinted in Elinor Field. *Horn Book Reflections.* Boston: Horn Book, 1969, pp. 248–249.

Vogel, Bruce. "Science, Magic, and the Test of Luck." In *Webs and Wardrobes: Humanist and Religious World Views in Children's Literature,* ed. by Joseph O'Beirne Milner and Lucy Floyd Morcock Milner. Lanham, MD: University Press of America, 1987, pp. 111–122.

The Voice of the Narrator in Children's Literature: Insights from Writers and Critics. Edited by Charlotte F. Otten and Gary D. Schmidt. New York: Greenwood, 1989.

Wagenknecht, Edward. "The Little Prince Rides the White Deer: Fantasy and Symbolism in Recent Literature." *College English* 7, no. 8 (May 1946): 431–437.

Watson, Ian. "The Author as Torturer." *Foundation* 40 (1987): 11–25.

Watt, Lois Belfield. "Fantasy," *Selection* 2, no. 1 (Autumn 1982): 9–10.

Webber, Rosemary. "Folklore and Fantasy—Mix or Match." Syracuse, NY: ERIC Clearinghouse on Information Resources, 1978.

Webs and Wardrobes: Humanist and Religious World Views in Children's Literature. Edited by Joseph O'Beirne Milner and Lucy Floyd Morcock Milner. Lanham, MD: University Press of America, 1987.

Weinberg, R. "Collecting Fantasy and Science Fiction." *AB Bookman's Weekly* 76 (Oct 28, 1985): 3101–3107.

West, Mark I., ed. *Before Oz: Juvenile Fantasy Stories from Nineteenth-Century America.* Hamden, CT: Shoe String Press, 1989. Discusses Christopher P. Cranch, Nathaniel Hawthorne, and Charles Edward Carryl.

West, Mark I. "Imagination Defended: Nineteenth-Century Critics of Fanciful Children's Literature." In *Proceedings of the Eighth Annual Conference of the Children's Literature Association.* University of Minnesota, March 1981. Ypsilanti, MI: Children's Literature Association, 1982, pp. 126–131.

———. "In Defense of Fantasy." *Use of English* 32 (Summer 1981): 70–73. Response to Andrew Stibbs. "For Realism in Children's Fiction." *Use of English* 32 (Fall 1980): 18–24.

———. *A Wondrous Menagerie: Animal Fantasy Stories from American Children's Literature.* Hamden, CT: Shoe String, 1994.

Where Rivers Meet: Confluence and Concurrents. Proceedings of the 1989 Conference of the Children's Literature Association. Edited by Susan R. Gannon and Ruth Anne Thompson. New York: Pace University, 1991.

Whetton, Betty B. "In This Year of the Dragon: An Invitation to a Retrospective of Fantasy Literature, or a New Look at an Age-Old Genre Many Thought to Have Been Replaced by Realistic Fiction." *Arizona English Bulletin* 18 (Apr 1976): 110–115.

Whitaker, Muriel A. "Swords at Sunset and Bag-Puddings: Arthur in Modern Fiction." *Children's Literature in Education* 27, no. 8 (Winter 1977): 143–153. Discusses Mayne and T. H. White.

White, Dorothy M. *About Books for Children.* New York: Oxford Univ. Press, 1949. Originally published in New Zealand by Whitcombe and Tombs, 1946."Modern Fairy Tales," pp. 51–67.

White, Mary Lou. *Children's Literature: Criticism and Response.* Columbus, OH: Merrill, 1976, pp. 56–68, 75–77, 112–130, 138–143, 191–201. Articles on Garner, Collodi, Travers, Alexander, and C. S. Lewis.

Williams, Madawc. "Cock and Bull About Epic Fantasy." *Mallorn* 26 (1989): 5–15.

Wilson, Andrew J. "If It's Wednesday This Must Be Narnia: Exploring the Links Between Phantasy and Reality." *Dark Horizons* 24 (1981): 19–23.

Wilson, Anne. *The Magical Quest: The Use of Magic in Arthurian Romance.* Manchester: Manchester Univ. Press, 1988; New York: St. Martin, 1990.

———. *Magical Thought in Creative Writing: The Distinctive Roles of Fantasy and Imagination in Fiction.* Stroud, Gloucestershire: Thimble Press, 1983.

———. "Magical Thought in Story." *Signal* 36 (Sept 1981): 138–151.

———. "What Is Magic?" *Signal* 57 (Sept 1988): 170–180.

Wintle, Justin, and Emma Fisher. *The Pied Pipers: Interviews with the Influential Creators of Children's Literature.* London: Paddington Press, 1974, pp. 20–24, 101–170, 192–248, 263–294. Interviews with Sendak, Dahl, Seuss, E. B. White, Adams, Gray, Aiken, Garfield, Alexander, Garner, Townsend, Peyton, Boston, and Godden.

Witucke, Virginia. "The Treatment of Fantasy and Science Fiction in Juvenile and Young Adult Literature Texts." *Top of the News* 39 (Fall 1982): 77–91.

Wolfe, Gary Kent. "Contemporary Theories of Fantasy." In Frank N. Magill. *Survey of Modern Fantasy Literature,* vol. 5. Englewood Cliffs, NJ: Salem Press, 1983, pp. 2220–2234.

———. *Critical Terms for Science Fiction and Fantasy: A Glossary and Guide to Scholarship.* Westport, CT: Greenwood, 1986.

———. "The Encounter with Fantasy." In *The Aesthetics of Fantasy Literature and Art,* ed. by Roger Schlobin. Notre Dame, IN: Univ. of Notre Dame Press, 1982, pp. 1–15.

———. "Fairy Tales, Märchen, and Modern Fantasy." In Frank N. Magill. *Survey of Modern Fantasy Literature,* vol. 5. Englewood Cliffs, NJ: Salem Press, 1983, pp. 2267–2282.

———. "Symbolic Fantasy." *Genre* 8 (1975): 194–209.

———. "The Symbolic Fantasy in England." Ph.D. diss., University of Chicago, 1972.

Woolsey, Dan. "Dreams and Wishes: Fantasy Literature for Children." In *Children's Literature in the Classroom: Weaving Charlotte's Web,* ed. by Janet Hickman and Bernice E. Cullinan. Needham Heights, MA: Christopher-Gordon, 1989, pp. 109–120.

Work and Play in Children's Literature. Selected Papers from the 1990 International Con-

ference of the Children's Literature Association. Edited by Susan R. Gannon and Ruth Anne Thompson. New York: Pace University, 1992. Articles on Lewis Carroll, Rudyard Kipling, and Sylvia Cassedy.

Wortley, John, ed. "Faerie, Fantasy and Pseudo-Mediavalia in 20th Century Literature." Special issue of *Mosaic* 10, no. 2 (Winter 1977): 1–195.

Wrightson, Patricia. "The Nature of Fantasy." In Moira Robinson, ed. *Readings in Children's Literature.* Frankston, Australia: Frankston State College, 1975.

———. "The Slippery Stuff of Fantasy." *Educational Magazine* (Australia) 33 no. 6 (1976): 22–25.

Writers for Children: Critical Studies of Major Authors Since the Seventeenth Century. Edited by Jane M. Bingham. New York: Scribner, 1988.

Writers on Writing for Young Adults. Edited by Patricia E. Freehan and Pamela Petrick Barron. Detroit: Omnigraphics, 1991.

Wynne Jones, Pat. "Exploring the Extra Dimension: The Occult and the Supernatural in Children's Fiction." *Christian Librarian* 7 (1983): 28–38.

Yates, Jessica. "Adventures and Parables: Recent Fantasy for Children." *British Book News Children's Books* (Sept 1987): 40–43.

———. "50 Years of Fantasy." *Books for Keeps* 46 (1987): 4–7.

———. "In Defense of Fantasy." *Use of English* 32 (Summer 1981):70–73. Response to Andrew Stibbs. "For Realism in Children's Fiction." *Use of English* 32 (Fall 1980): 18–24.

Yep, Laurence. "Fantasy and Reality." *Horn Book* 54 (Apr 1978): 137–143.

Yoke, Carl B., and Donald M. Hassler, eds. *Death and the Serpent: Immortality in Science Fiction and Fantasy.* Westport, CT: Greenwood, 1985.

Yolen, Jane. "An Experiential Act [The Time Travel Story]." *Language Arts* 66 (Mar 1989): 246–251.

———. "Here There Be Dragons." *Top of the News* 39 (Fall 1982): 54–56.

———. "The Literary Underwater World." *Language Arts* 57 (1980): 403–412. Stories of merfolk and selchies.

———. *Touch Magic: Fantasy, Faerie and Folklore in the Literature of Childhood.* New York: Philomel, 1992.

———. "The Voice of Fantasy." *Advocate* 3 (Fall 1983): 50–56.

———. "The Wood Between the Worlds." *Mythlore* 41 (1985): 5–7. Fifteenth mythopoetic conference guest of honor speech on fantasy.

Zahorski, Kenneth J., and Robert H. Boyer. "The Secondary Worlds of High Fantasy." In Roger C. Schlobin. *The Aesthetics of Fantasy Literature and Art.* Notre Dame, IN: Univ. of Notre Dame Press, 1982, pp. 56–81.

Zanger, Jules. "Goblins, Warlocks, and Weasels: Classic Fantasy and the Industrial Revolution." *Children's Literature in Education* 8 (Winter 1977): 154–162.

Zelazny, Roger. "Fantasy and Science Fiction: A Writer's View." In *Intersections: Science Fiction and Fantasy,* ed. by George E. Slusser and Eric S. Rabkin. Carbondale: Southern Illinois Univ. Press, 1987.

The Zena Sutherland Lectures, 1983–1992. Edited by Betsy Hearne. New York: Clarion, 1993. Lectures by Maurice Sendak, Lloyd Alexander, Katherine Paterson, Virginia Hamilton, Paula Fox, Jean Fritz, and Besty Byars.

Zipes, Jack. "The Age of Commodified Fanaticism: Reflections of Children's Literature and the Fantastic." *Children's Literature Association Quarterly* 9 (Winter 1984–85): 187–190.

———. *Breaking the Magic Spell: Radical Theories of Folk and Fairy Tales.* Austin: Univ. of Texas Press, 1979; reprinted New York: Methuen, 1984.

———. *Don't Bet on the Prince: Contemporary Feminist Fairy Tales in North America and England.* New York: Methuen, 1986. Sixteen tales, including four by Tanith Lee, Jay Williams, Angela Carter, and Jane Yolen, plus four essays of feminist literary criticism.

————. "The Potential of Liberating Fairy Tales for Children." *New Literary History* 13 (1982): 309–325.

————, ed. *Spells of Enchantment: The Wondrous Fairy Tales of Western Culture.* New York: Viking, 1991.

————. "Towards a Social History of the Literary Fairy Tale for Children." *Children's Literature Association Quarterly* 7 (Summer 1982): 23–25.

————, ed. *Victorian Fairy Tales: The Revolt of the Fairies and Elves.* New York: Methuen, 1987. Anthology of fairy tales written between 1830 and 1902, including tales by Dickens, Wilde, and Carroll.

13

Educational Resources on Fantasy Literature

This chapter lists articles and studies on the educational and psychological uses of fantasy literature, as well as audiovisual materials on fantasy literature in general. Audiovisual materials on individual fantasists are also listed in Chapter 14, Author Studies.

The Preface contains a list of sources from which the information in this chapter was drawn.

Abramson, R. F. "Classroom Uses for the Books of William Steig." *Reading Teacher* 32 (Dec 1978): 307–311.

Alberghene, Janice M. "The Writing in *Charlotte's Web.*" *Children's Literature in Education* 16 (Spring 1985): 32–44.

Allen, A. T. "On Keeping the Sense of Wonder: Fantasy for Children." *The Record* 69 (Feb 1968): 513–516.

Aquino, John. *Fantasy in Literature.* Washington, DC: National Education Association, 1977, pp. 13–19, 23–26, 28–29, 40–47.

Bailey, W. L. "Fairy Tales as Character-Builders." *Libraries* 31 (1926): 44–46.

Bernagozzi, T. "Curriculum Adventures with Chris Van Allsburg." *Learning '93* 21 (Apr–May 1993): 42–44.

Bettelheim, Bruno. *The Uses of Enchantment.* New York: Knopf, 1976, pp. 143–147.

Bingham, Jane M., and Grayce Scholt. "Enchantment Revisited: Or, Why Teach Fantasy?" *The CEA Critic* 39 (Jan 1978): 11–15. Reprinted in Robert Bator. *Signposts to Criticism of Children's Literature.* Chicago: American Library Association, 1983, pp. 261–264.

Bodem, Marguerite M. "The Role of Fantasy in Children's Reading." *Elementary English* 52 (Apr 1975): 470–471, 538.

Bortolussi, Marisa. "Fantasy, Realism and the Dynamics of Reception: The Case of the Child Reader." *Canadian Children's Literature* 41 (1986): 32–43.

Boyer, Robert H., and Kenneth J. Zahorski. "Science Fiction and Fantasy Literature: Clarification Through Juxtaposition." *Wisconsin English Journal* 18 (1976): 2–8.

Chubb, Percival. "The Value and Place of Fairy Stories in the Education of Children." *N.E.A. Journal* (1905): 871–879.

Chukovskii, Kornei. *From Two to Five.* Translated and edited by Miriam Morton. Berkeley: Univ. of California Press, 1963. Originally published in Russia in 1925. "The Battle for the Fairy Tale," pp. 114–139.

Clark, Beverly Lyon. "Crossword Puzzle: *The Hobbit.*" *Children's Literature Association Quarterly* 9 (Summer 1984): 76, 95.

Cooper, Ilene. "Popular Reading—After *The Borrowers.*" *Booklist* 81 (Nov 15, 1984): 452–453. (bibliography)

Crossley, Robert. "Education and Fantasy." *College English* 37 (1975): 281–293.

———. "Teaching the Course in Fantasy: An Elvish Counsel." *Extrapolation* 22 (Fall 1981): 242–251.

Davidson, D. A. "Sword and Sorcery Fiction: An Annotated Booklist." *English Journal* 61 (Jan 1972): 43–51.

Derby, J. "Anthropomorphism in Children's Literature; Or, Mom, My Doll's Talking Again." *Elementary English* 47 (Fall 1970): 190–192.

Domo, Marlene Anne. "Seventh and Eighth Graders' Response to a Moral Dilemma Across Three Genres in a Classroom Setting." Ph.D. diss., Ohio State University, 1989.

Donelson, Kenneth L., and Alleen Pace Nilsen. *Literature for Today's Young Adults.* 3rd ed. Scott, Foresman, 1989. "Fantasy," pp. 187–199.

Dyson, Anne Haas. "Research Currents: The Space/Time Travels of Story Writers." *Language Arts* 66 (Mar 1989): 150–156.

Elleman, Barbara. "Popular Reading—Animal Fantasy Update." *Booklist* 84 (Apr 15, 1988): 1441–1442. (bibliography)

———. "Popular Reading—Time Fantasy Update." *Booklist* 81 (Jan 1, 1985): 1407–1408. (bibliography)

Elleman, Barbara, and Natalie Babbitt. "Natalie Babbitt's *The Search for Delicious.*" *Book Links* 2 (Sept 1992): 18–21.

Epstein, S. "Animals: Fantasy Roles and Science Facts." *School Library Media Activities Monthly* 9 (Jan 1993): 20–21.

Fantasy and Reality. North Hollywood, CA: Center for Cassette Studies, 1972. (audiocassette)

"Fantasy and Science Fiction; by Children." *Elementary English* 52 (May 1975): 620–630.

Fantasy Literature. Peoria, IL: Thomas S. Klise, 1981. (filmstrip and audiocassette)

Fortuna, Mary Ann. "A Descriptive Evaluative Study of Children's Modern Fantasy and Children's Science Fiction Using a Well-Known Example of Each." Ed.D. diss., Temple University, 1988. Discusses C. S. Lewis and Madeleine L'Engle.

Gallagher, Mary Elizabeth. *Young Adult Literature: Issues and Perspectives.* Rev. ed. Haverford, PA: Catholic Library Association, 1991. "Science Fiction and Fantasy," pp. 127–143.

George Orwell. Peoria, IL: Thomas S. Klise, 1985. (filmstrip and audiocassette)

Getting Hooked on Fantasy. White Plains, NY: Guidance Associates, 1976. (filmstrip and audiocassette) Contains Juster's *The Phantom Tollbooth;* Lewis's *The Lion, the Witch, and the Wardrobe;* Boston's *The Treasure of Green Knowe;* Lindgren's *Pippi Longstocking;* White's *Charlotte's Web;* Selden's *The Genie of Sutton Place;* Eager's *Half Magic;* Butterworth's *The Enormous Egg;* Norton's *The Borrowers;* Babbitt's *The Search for Delicious;* and Alexander's *The Book of Three.*

Getting Hooked on Science Fiction. White Plains, NY: Guidance Associates, 1976. (filmstrip and audiocassette) Includes O'Brien's *Mrs. Frisby and the Rats of NIMH.*

Gillespie, John T. *The Elementary School Paperback Collection.* Chicago: American Library Association, 1985. "Fantasy," pp. 126–139.

———. *The Junior High School Paperback Collection.* Chicago: American Library Association, 1985. "Fantasy," pp. 30–37.

———. *More Juniorplots: A Guide for Teachers and Librarians.* New York: Bowker, 1977. Books by Rogers, Aiken, Garner, and Peck.

————. *The Senior High School Paperback Collection.* Chicago: American Library Association, 1986. "Fantasy and Science Fiction," pp. 55–94.

Gillespie, John T., and Diana Lembo. *Introducing Books: A Guide for the Middle Grades.* New York: Bowker, 1970. Books by Brelis, Corbett, Dahl, Aiken, Benary-Isbert, Robert Lawson, Clarke, Clements, Lampman, Mayne, Merrill, Alexander, Jarrell, Lewis, Pearce, Travers, E. B. White, Butterworth, Du Bois, Lindgren, Mary Norton, Sharp, and Anne White.

————. *Juniorplots: A Book Talk Manual for Teachers and Librarians.* New York: Bowker, 1967. Books by Behn, Juster, Agnes Smith, Tolkien, E. B. White, and T. H. White.

Gillespie, John T., and Corinne J. Naden. *Juniorplots 3: A Book Talk Guide for Use with Readers Ages 12–16.* New York: Bowker, 1987. Books by Alexander, Diana Wynne Jones, Mahy, Hamilton, McCaffrey, Le Guin, McKinley, Park, Pascal, Yolen, and Westall.

————. *Juniorplots 4: A Book Talk Guide for Use with Readers Ages 12–16.* New Providence, NJ: Bowker, 1993. Books by Reid Banks, Alexander, Bell, Conford, Gilmore, Jones, and Garfield.

Gillespie, Margaret C., and John W. Conner. *Creative Growth Through Literature for Children and Adolescents.* Columbus, OH: Merrill, 1975. "Fantasy," pp. 11–14.

Golden, Joanne Marie. "A Scheme for Analyzing Response to Literature Applied to the Responses of 5th and 8th Graders to Realistic and Fantasy Short Stories." Ph.D. diss., Ohio State University, 1978.

Goodwin, P. "Elements of Utopias in Young Adult Literature." *English Journal* 74 (Oct 1985): 66–69.

Green, Roland J. "Modern Science Fiction and Fantasy: A Frame of Reference." *Illinois Schools Journal* 57 (Fall 1977): 45–53.

Greene, Ellin. "A Peculiar Understanding: Recreating the Literary Fairy Tale." *Horn Book* 59 (June 1983): 270–278. Discusses Alexander, Cooper, McKillip, Murphy, Yolen and Hodgell.

Greenlaw, M. Jean. "Books in the Classroom." *Horn Book* 64 (Nov–Dec 1988): 820–822.

Guthrie, John T. "Research Views: Fantasy as Purpose." *Reading Teacher* 32 (1978): 106–108.

Harms, Jean McLain. "Children's Responses to Fantasy in Literature." *Language Arts* 52 (Oct 1975): 942–946.

————. "Children's Responses to Fantasy in Relation to Their Stages of Intellectual Development." Ph.D. diss., Ohio State University, 1972.

Harrell, P. "Hooray for Fantasy!" *Elementary English* 39 (Nov 1962): 710–712.

Hartmann, Waltraut. "Identification and Projection in Folk Fairy Tales and in Fantastic Stories for Children." *Bookbird* 7, no. 2 (1969): 8–17.

Haviland, Virginia. "Fairy Tales and Creativity." In *How Can Children's Literature Meet the Needs of Modern Children?* 15th IBBY Conference, 1976, pp. 56–61.

Helson, Ravenna. "Fantasy and Self-Discovery." *Horn Book* 46 (Apr 1970): 121–34. Reprinted in M. L. White. *Children's Literature.* Columbus, OH: Merrill, 1976, pp. 117–125.

Hickman, Janet, and Bernice E. Cullinan. *Children's Literature in the Classroom: Weaving Charlotte's Web.* Norwood, MA.: Christopher-Gordon, 1989. Woolsey, Dan. "Dreams and Wishes: Fantasy Literature for Children," pp. 109–120; Stelk, Virginia. "Fantasy in the Classroom," pp. 121–128; L'Engle, Madeleine. "Fantasy Is What Fantasy Does," pp. 129–134.

"The Hobbit": Reading Motivation Unit. Wilton, CT: Current Affairs, 1977. (filmstrip and audiocassette)

Hopkins, Lee Bennett. "Fantasy Flights Circa 1976." *Teacher* 93 (Apr 1976): 34+. (bibliography)

An Hour with Katherine Kurtz: An Introduction to the Author and Her Work. Garden Grove, NY: Hourglass Productions, 1979. (audiocassette)

An Hour with Marion Zimmer Bradley: A Personal Note. Garden Grove, NY: Hourglass Productions, 1979. (audiocassette)

Huck, Charlotte S. "Modern Fantasy." *Elementary English* 41 (May 1964): 473–474, 515.

Huck, Charlotte S., Susan Hepler, and Janet Hickman. *Children's Literature in the Elementary School.* 4th ed. New York: Holt, 1987. "Modern Fantasy," pp. 335–377.

Hughes, M. "Confessions of a Science Fiction Reader: Notes upon Values Taught to Adolescents by Fantasy and Science Fiction." In *Reaching Young People Through Media.* Littleton, CO: Libraries Unlimited, 1983, pp. 69–80.

Hunter, C. Bruce. "Generating Magic in the English Classroom." *Curriculum Review* 21 (Feb 1982): 41–43.

Jacobs, James S. "The Focus of Fantasy." *Arizona English Bulletin* 18 (Apr 1976): 199–202.

Klingberg, Göte. *The Fantastic Tale for Children: A Genre Study from the Viewpoints of Literary and Educational Research.* LIGRU Monograph, no. 2. Gothenburg, Sweden: Gothenburg School of Education, 1970.

———. "The Fantastic Tale for Children: Its Literary and Educational Problems." *Bookbird* 5, no. 3 (1967): 13–20.

Koss, H. G. "Relevancy and Children's Literature." *Elementary English* 49 (Nov 1972): 991–992.

Latshaw, Jessica Louise. "An In-Depth Examination of Four Pre-Adolescents' Responses to Fantasy Literature." Ph.D. diss., University of Saskatchewan, 1986.

The Legend of Arthur. Princeton, NJ: Films for the Humanities, 1986. (videocassette)

Le Guin, Ursula K. "Why are Americans Afraid of Dragons?" *Pacific Northwest Library Association Quarterly* 38, no. 2 (1974): 14–18.

L'Engle, Madeleine. "What Is Real?" *Language Arts* 55 (1977): 447–451.

Lewis, Claudia. "Fairy Tales and Fantasy in the Classroom." *Childhood Education* 49 (Nov 1972): 64–67.

Liddell, Sharon. "Recommended: Anne McCaffrey." *English Journal* 73 (Nov 1984): 89.

Lind, Dianne. "The Importance of Fantasy in Young Adult Literature." *ALAN Review* 15 (1988): 13–14. Discusses Susan Cooper, C. S. Lewis, and J. R. R. Tolkien.

Loder Reed, Elizabeth. "Personal Identity Concepts in the Context of Children's Fantasy Literature." Ph.D. diss., Boston University, 1979.

McGeehon, C. "I Have Read Everything by Tolkien." *Unabashed Librarian* 50 (1984): 25. (bibliography)

McIntosh, Margaret E., and M. Jean Greenlaw. "Ladies First: Teaching Characterization Through Strong Female Protagonists in High Fantasy Literature." *ALAN Review* 15 (1988): 47–51. Discusses Robin McKinley and Meredith Ann Pierce.

Mahon, R. L. "The Epic Tradition in Science Fiction and Fantasy." *Teaching English in the Two-Year College* 14 (Feb 1987): 47–51.

Mappin, Alf. "A Core List VIII: Fantasy." *Literature Base* (Australia) 3 (June 1992): 16–17.

———. "Defining Fantasy." *Literature Base* (Australia) 3 (June 1992): 12–15.

Marshall, Sybil. "Dragons or Pterodactyls?" *School Bookshop News* (U.K.) (Mar 4, 1976): 3–6.

May, Jill. "The American Literary Fairy Tale and Its Classroom Uses." *Journal of Reading* 22 (Nov 1978): 148–152.

Means, H. J. "Books for Young Adults: Science Fiction, Fantasy, and the Occult." *English Journal* 62 (Oct 1973): 1059–1060. (bibliography)

Meek, Margaret, Aidan Warlow, and Griselda Barton. *The Cool Web: The Pattern of Children's Reading.* New York: Atheneum, 1978.

Meraklis, Michael. "Fairy Tales and Their Pedagogical Content." In *How Can Children's Literature Meet the Needs of Modern Children?* 15th IBBY Conference, 1976, pp. 53–55.

Michaels, Wendy. "At the Dark Edge of Vision." *Orana* 17 (Nov 1981): 145–148. Discusses Patricia Wrightson.

Miller, A. I. "My Eighth Graders Like Fantasy." *Journal of Education* 124 (Sept 1941): 199–201.

Montgomery, J. W. "*The Chronicles of Narnia* and the Adolescent Reader." *Religious Education* 54 (Sept 1959): 418–428.

Muller, Al, and C. W. Sullivan III. "Science Fiction and Fantasy Series Books." *English Journal* 69 (Oct 1980): 71–74. (bibliography)

Mura, J. "Pern Puzzle." *VOYA* 9 (June 1986): 69; erratum *VOYA* 9 (Aug–Oct 1986): 133. (Anne McCaffrey)

Nelms, Beth, and Ben Nelms. "The Farfaring Imagination: Recent Fantasy and Science Fiction." *English Journal* 74 (Apr 1985): 83–86. (bibliography)

Nissel, Marva J. Goldstein. "The Oral Responses of Three Fourth Graders to Realistic Fiction and Fantasy." Ph.D. diss., Fordham University, 1987.

Noel, Roberta Christine. "The Borrowed Cup of Courage: A Descriptive Comparison of Archetypes Presented by Male and Female Authors in Fantasy for Adolescents." Ed.D. diss., Gonzaga University (Washington), 1987.

Norman, Felicity. "J. R. R. Tolkien's *The Hobbit.*" *The Literature Base* (Australia) 3, no. 3 (Aug 1992): 12–13.

Norton, Donna E. *Through the Eyes of a Child: An Introduction to Children's Literature.* 2nd ed. Columbus, OH: Merrill, 1987. "Modern Fantasy," pp. 264–324.

O'Donnell, H. "Once upon a Time in the Classroom. ERIC/RCS Report." *Language Arts* 55 (Apr 1978): 534–537.

Olson, Miken Rae. "Exposure to Fantasy Literature, Related Activities, and Creativity in Kindergarten." Ph.D. diss., Arizona State University, 1977.

"Other Worlds: Fantasy and Science Fiction [symposium]." *English Journal* 79 (Mar 1990): 17–22.

Ovens, C. "Coming to a Sticky End." *Child Education* (U.K.) 69 (Oct 1992): 52–53. Roald Dahl in the classroom.

Owen, Linda. "Dragons in the Classroom." *English Journal* 73 (Nov 1984): 76–77.

Page, T. "Project File: *The Iron Man.*" *Childhood Education* (Jan 1990): 19–26. Discusses Ted Hughes.

Parish, Margaret. "Children's Fantasies for Young Adults." *English Journal* 66 (Nov 1977): 92–93. (bibliography)

Petersen, Vera D. "Dragons in General." *Elementary English* 39 (Jan 1962): 3–6.

Phillips, R. A. "Discovering New Worlds." *Curriculum Review* 19 (Sept 1980): 336–337. (bibliography)

Polette, N. "Responding to the Novel: Reading, Writing and Research." *School Library Media Activities Monthly* [Baltimore, MD], 1991. Activities for *The Wolves of Willoughby Chase* by Joan Aiken.

Poskanzer, Susan Cornell. "A Case for Fantasy." *Elementary English* 52 (Apr 1975): 472–475

———. "Thoughts on C. S. Lewis and *The Chronicles of Narnia.*" *Language Arts* 53 (1976): 523–526.

Pritchard, A. "A Week of Roald Dahl." *Language and Learning* (U.K.) (Dec 1992): 27–30.

Rausch, Helen Martha. "The Debate over Fairy Tales." Ph.D. diss., Columbia University Teachers College, 1977.

Ray Bradbury as Philosopher. North Hollywood, CA: Center for Cassette Studies, 1974. (audiocassette)

Read, Arthea J. S. *Reaching Adolescents: The Young Adult Book and the School.* New York: Holt, 1985. "Fantasy and Science Fiction," pp. 86–95, 108–111.

Richardson, Carmen C. "The Reality of Fantasy." *Language Arts* 53 (May 1976): 549–551, 563.

Robert Silverberg. North Hollywood, CA: Center for Cassette Studies, 1974. (audiocassette)

Roberts, Thomas J. "Before You Dump Those 'Junk' Books." *Media & Methods* 15 (May–June 1979): 27–28, 46.

Rochelle, Larry. "Quest: The Search for Meaning Through Fantasy." *English Journal* 66 (Oct 1977): 54–55.

Rollin, L. W. "Exploring Earthsea: A Sixth Grade Literature Project." *Children's Literature in Education* 16 (Winter 1985): 195–202. (Ursula K. Le Guin)

Rosenfeld, Judith B. "Books in the Classroom: Tales of King Arthur." *Horn Book* 68 (July–Aug 1992): 501–506.

Rupert, Pamela Rae. "Analysis of the Need Fulfillment Imagery in Fantasy Literature for Children." Ph.D. diss., University of Akron, 1979.

Salisi, Rosemary A. "Fanciful Literature and Reading Comprehension." Syracuse, NY: ERIC Clearinghouse on Information Resources, 1978.

Sams, Edwin Boyer. "Studies in Experiencing Fantasy." *Teaching English in the Two-Year College* 5 (1979): 235–237.

Scherf, Walter. "Magic Tales as an Invitation to a Child's Necessary Scaling Off." In *How Can Children's Literature Meet the Needs of Modern Children?* 15th IBBY Conference, 1976, pp. 36–41.

Science Fiction and Fantasy. Pleasantville, NY: Educational Audio-Visual, 1975. (filmstrip and audiocassette)

"Science Fiction and Fantasy: Symposium." *Media and Methods* 16 (Nov 1979): 18–20+.

Science Fiction and Time Fiction. Tarrytown, NY: Prentice-Hall Media, 1977. (filmstrip and audiocassette)

Sellers, F. E. "Fantasy." *New Jersey School Librarian* 14 (Spring 1960): 2–5.

Shackelford, Lisa. "Science Fiction and Fantasy Books Prepare Teens for Life's Realities." *Unabashed Librarian* 77 (1990): 9–11.

Sloane, B. L. "The Real World of the Imagination." *English Journal* 67 (Feb 1978): 74–75.

Spirt, Diana L. *Introducing Bookplots 3: A Book Talk Guide for Use with Readers Ages 8–12.* New York: Bowker, 1988. Books by Sid Fleischman, Brittain, Godden, Hastings, Cooper, Pinkwater, and Stewart.

———. *Introducing More Books: A Guide for the Middle Grades.* New York: Bowker, 1978. Books by Steig, Donovan, Peck, Babbitt, Hunter, Lively, and Pinkwater.

Stein, R. M. "Changing Styles in Dragons: From Fáfnir to Smaug." *Elementary English* 45 (Feb 1968): 179–183+.

Stelk, Virginia. "Fantasy in the Classroom." In *Children's Literature in the Classroom: Weaving Charlotte's Web,* ed. by Janet Hickman and Bernice E. Cullinan. Needham Heights, MA: Christopher-Gordon, 1989, pp. 121–128.

Stott, Jon C. "'Will the Real Dragon Please Stand Up?' Convention and Parody in Children's Stories." *Children's Literature in Education* 21 (Dec 1990): 219–228.

Studier, Catherine Elizabeth. "A Comparison of the Responses of Fifth Grade Students to Modern Fantasy and Realistic Fiction." Ed.D. diss., University of Georgia, 1978.

Sullivan, F. "Boggarts and Such: Books of Fantasy for Children." *P.T.A. Magazine* 62 (Mar 1968): 34–35.

Thomas, Rebecca L. *Primaryplots 2: A Book Talk Guide for Use with Readers Ages 4–8.* New Providence, NJ: Bowker, 1993. Books by Scieszka, Van Allsburg, Wisniewski.

Thomason, Maggie. "Unicorn Club: A Drama Workshop on *The Hobbit.*" *Amon Hen* 78 (1986): 6–7. Discusses J. R. R. Tolkien.

Toothaker, Roy E. "What's Your Fantasy I.Q.?" *Language Arts* 54 (1976): 11–24.

The True Legend of King Arthur. Princeton, NJ: Films for the Humanities, 1986. (videocassette)

Tunnell, Michael. "Books in the Classroom." *Horn Book* 63 (July–Aug 1987): 509–511. Discusses Natalie Babbitt's *Tuck Everlasting.*

Tunnell, Michael, and James S. Jacobs. "*The Prydain Chronicles* by Lloyd Alexander." *Book Links* 3 (Mar 1994): 30–39.

Tymn, Marshall B. "A Guide to Audio-Visual Resources in Science Fiction and Fantasy." *Media and Methods* 16 (Nov 1979): 40–42, 56–57.

———. "Guide to Resource Materials for Science Fiction and Fantasy Teachers." *English Journal* 68 (Jan 1979): 68–74.

———. "Resource Materials for Science Fiction and Fantasy Teachers." *Arizona English Bulletin* 19 (1977): 54–58.

———. "Science Fiction and Fantasy in the School Curriculum: Part I: A Checklist of Articles, 1967–1975." *English Language Arts Bulletin* 21 (Fall/Winter 1981): 24–27.

———. *A Teacher's Guide to Fantastic Literature.* Mercer Island, WA: Starmont, 1986.

Tyre, Richard H. "You Can't Teach Tolkien." *Media and Methods* 15 (Nov 1978): 18–20, 54.

The Unexpected: Stories of Humor and Fantasy. Pleasantville, NY: Educational Audio Visual, 1979. (filmstrip and audiocassette)

Ursula Le Guin: Woman of Science Fiction. North Hollywood, CA: Center for Cassette Studies, 1973. (audiocassette)

Watanabe, S. "Study of Children's Literature, Syllabus II: Fantasy." *Library and Information Science* 7 (1969): 67–78.

"Who Is Your Favorite Writer of Science Fiction or Fantasy?" *English Journal* 82 (Oct 1993): 166. (discussion)

Wilkinson, G. "On the Bulletin Board: Enchant Yourself—Read [Fantasy or Magic Books]!" *School Librarian's Workshop* 9 (May 1989): 15–16.

Wilson, Doreen. "Experiments with *NIMH*." *About Books for Children* (U.K.) 2 (Apr 1981): 17–18. Discusses Robert C. O'Brien.

Winfield, Evelyn T. "Fantasy Stories: A Passport to Lands of Enchantment." *PTA Today* 10 (Feb 1985): 12.

Wolf, Virginia L. "Readers of *Alice:* My Children, Meg Murry and Harriet M. Welsch." *Children's Literature Association Quarterly* 13 (Fall 1988): 135–136.

Yolen, Jane. "An Experiential Act." *Language Arts* 66 (Mar 1989): 246–251.

Zipes, Jack. "The Liberating Potential of the Fantastic Projection in Fairy Tales for Children." In *The Scope of the Fantastic—Culture, Biography, Themes, Children's Literature,* ed. by Robert A. Collins and Howard D. Pearce. Westport, CT: Greenwood, 1985, pp. 257–266.

———. "The Use and Abuse of Folk and Fairy Tales with Children." In Jill P. May. *Children and Their Literature.* West Lafayette, IN: Children's Literature Association Publications, 1983, pp. 14–33.

Zuck, J. E. "Religion and Fantasy." *Religious Education* 70 (Nov 1975): 586–604.

14

Fantasy Literature Author Studies

The resources in this chapter are arranged alphabetically by fantasy author. These resources include books, articles, dissertations, and biographical information by and about a particular fantasist, as well as interviews with them, bibliographies of their work, the published texts of their speeches, and audiovisual materials about them. The Preface lists the sources used to compile the information in this chapter.

Additional information regarding individual fantasists can be found in the following Gale Research publications: *Children's Literature Review, Contemporary Authors, Contemporary Authors Autobiography Series, Contemporary Literary Criticism, Dictionary of Literary Biography, Something about the Author, Something about the Author: Autobiography Series, Twentieth Century Literary Criticism,* and *Yesterday's Authors of Books for Children.*

Adams, Richard (George)

Adams, Gillian. *"Watership Down* as a Double Journey." *Proceedings of the 13th Annual Conference of The Children's Literature Association, 1986.* New York: Pace University, 1988, pp. 106–111.

Adams, Richard. "The Bowdlerization of Children's Books—Where Will It Stop?" *Sunday Times Books* (Mar 6, 1988): G.4.

———. *The Day Gone By: An Autobiography.* London: Hutchinson, 1990; New York: Knopf, 1991.

———. "Musings on *Watership Down." Books for Your Children* (U.K.) 8 (Aug 1973).

———. "Some Ingredients of *Watership Down." Children's Book Review* 4 (Autumn 1974): 92–95. Reprinted in Edward Blishen. *The Thorny Paradise.* Boston: Horn Book, 1975, pp. 163–173.

———. "To the Order of Two Little Girls: The Oral and Written Versions of *Watership Down."* In *The Voice of the Narrator in Children's Literature: Insights from Writers and Critics,* edited by Charlotte F. Otten and Gary D. Schmidt. Westport, CT: Greenwood, 1989, pp. 115–122.

———. "Watership Days." (London) *Sunday Telegraph* (May 6, 1990): xxi–xxii.

Anderson, Celia. "Troy, Carthage, and *Watership Down." Children's Literature Association Quarterly* 8 (Spring 1983): 12–13.

Chambers, Aidan. "Letter from England: Great Leaping Lapins!" *Horn Book* 49 (June 1973): 253–255.

Chapman, Edgar L. "The Shaman as Hero and Spiritual Leader: Richard Adams' Mythmaking in *Watership Down* and *Shardik.*" *Mythlore* 5, 18 (1978).

Fritz, Jean. "An Evening with Richard Adams." *Children's Literature in Education* 9, no. 29 (Summer 1975): 67–72.

Gentle, Mary. "Godmakers and Worldshapers: Fantasy and Metaphysics." *Vector* 106 (1982): 8–14.

Gose, Elliott. *Mere Creatures: A Study of Modern Fantasy Tales for Children.* Toronto: Univ. of Toronto Press, 1988, pp. 122–147.

Green, Timothy. "Richard Adams' Long Journey from *Watership Down.*" *Smithsonian* 10, no. 4 (July 1979): 76–83.

Hammond, Graham. "Trouble with Rabbits." *Children's Literature in Education* 12 (Sept 1973): 48–63.

Heins, Paul. "*Watership Down,* a Review." *Horn Book* 50 (Aug 1974): 365.

Hunt, Peter. "Landscapes and Journeys, Metaphors and Maps: The Distinctive Feature of English Fantasy." *Children's Literature Association Quarterly* 12 (Spring 1987): 11–15.

Inglis, Fred. *The Promise of Happiness: Value and Meaning in Children's Fiction.* New York: Cambridge Univ. Press, 1981, pp. 201–210.

———. "Spellbinding and Anthropology: The Work of Richard Adams and Ursula Le Guin." In Dennis Butts. *Good Writers for Young Readers.* St. Albans, England: Hart-Davis, 1977, pp. 114–128.

Jordan, Tom. "Breaking Away from the Warren." In Douglas Street. *Children's Novels and the Movies.* New York: Ungar, 1985, pp. 227–235.

King, Catherine. "Catherine King Interviews . . . Richard Adams." *Education Library Service Bulletin* (Australia) 17 (Feb–Mar 1979): 14–18.

Kitchell, Kenneth. "The Shrinking of the Epic Hero: From Homer to Richard Adams's *Watership Down.*" *Classical and Modern Literature* 7 (1986): 13–30.

Morgan, Chris. "Shardik." In Frank N. Magill. *Survey of Modern Fantasy Literature,* vol. 3. Englewood Cliffs, NJ: Salem Press, 1983, pp. 1387–1391.

Nelson, Marie. "Non-Human Speech in the Fantasy of C. S. Lewis, J. R. R. Tolkien and Richard Adams." *Mythlore* 5, 17 (1978): 37–39.

The Oxford Companion to Children's Literature. Edited by Humphrey Carpenter and Mari Prichard. New York: Oxford Univ. Press, 1984, pp. 3, 563.

Paul, Lissa. "Dumb Bunnies: A Re-Visionist Re-Reading of *Watership Down.*" *Signal* 56 (May 1988): 113–122.

Pawling, Christopher. "*Watership Down:* Rolling Back the 1960's." In *Popular Fiction and Social Change.* New York: St. Martin, 1984.

Paxon, Diana. "The Tolkien Tradition." *Mythlore* 39 (1984): 23, 27, 37.

Petzold, Dieter. "Fantasy Out of Myth and Fable: Animal Stories in Rudyard Kipling and Richard Adams." *Children's Literature Association Quarterly* 12 (Spring 1987): 15–19.

Pflieger, Pat, and Helen M. Hill. *A Reference Guide to Modern Fantasy for Children.* Westport, CT: Greenwood, 1984, pp. xv, 4–6, 582–583.

Reed, Julia R. "*The Plague Dogs.*" In *Survey of Modern Fantasy Literature,* vol. 3. Edited by Frank N. Magill. Englewood Cliffs, NJ: Salem Press, 1983, pp. 1268–1270.

Rees, Jenny. "*Watership Down* and the Irresistible Rise of Richard Adams." (London) *Times* (Nov 8, 1974): 12.

Schmoll, Edward A. "Homeric Reminiscence in *Watership Down.*" *Classical and Modern Literature* 10 (Fall 1989): 21–26.

Searles, Baird, Beth Meacham, and Michael Franklin. *A Reader's Guide to Fantasy.* New York: Avon, 1982, pp. 19–20.

Shippey, T. A. *"Watership Down."* In Frank N. Magill. *Survey of Modern Fantasy Literature,* vol. 5. Englewood Cliffs, NJ: Salem Press, 1983, pp. 2079–2083.

Stone, James S. "The Rabbitness of *Watership Down." English Quarterly* 13 (Spring 1980): 37–46.

Stott, Jon C. *Children's Literature from A to Z.* New York: McGraw-Hill, 1984, p. 3.

Swinfen, Ann. *In Defense of Fantasy.* London: Routledge, 1984, pp. 37–42, 218–229. Discusses *Watership Down.*

Thomas, Jane Resh. "Old Worlds and New: Anti-Feminism in *Watership Down." Horn Book* 50 (Aug 1974): 405–408. Reprinted in Paul Heins. *Crosscurrents of Criticism.* Boston: Horn Book, 1977, pp. 311–314.

Twentieth-Century Children's Writers. 3rd ed. Edited by Tracy Chevalier and D. L. Kirkpatrick. Chicago: St. James, 1989, pp. 3–5.

Vine, Phillip. "Richard Adams." *Words* (U.K.) 2 (1985): 20–29.

———. "Richard Adams: A Personal View." *Words* (U.K.) 1, no. 2 (July 1985): 14–18.

"Watership Down." In M. Crouch and A. Ellis. *Chosen for Children.* 3rd ed. London: The Library Association, 1977, pp. 164–167.

Welch, Randy C. *"Watership Down:* The Individual and Society." *Mythlore* 50 (1987): 48–50.

Wintle, Justin, and Emma Fisher. "Richard Adams." In *The Pied Pipers,* New York: Paddington Press, 1974, pp. 32–46.

Adkins, Jan

Fifth Book of Junior Authors and Illustrators. Edited by Sally Holmes Holtze. New York: Wilson, 1983, pp. 2–4.

Adler, C. S.

Helbig, Alethea, and Agnes Regan Perkins. *Dictionary of American Children's Fiction, 1985–1989.* Westport, CT: Greenwood, 1993, p. 4.

Ahlberg, Janet, and Ahlberg, Allan

Ahlberg, Janet, and Allan Ahlberg. "Where Do Your Ideas Come From?" *Books for Your Children* 14 (U.K.) (Spring 1979): 7.

"Authorgraph no. 14: Janet and Allan Ahlberg." *Books for Keeps* (U.K.) 14 (May 1982): 14–15.

Charlton, Hannah. "A Day in the Life of Allan Ahlberg." (London) *Sunday Times Magazine* (Dec 15, 1991): 82.

Cruickshank, Mary. "Happy Family Man." *Times Educational Supplement* (Aug 25, 1989): p. 18.

"Janet Ahlberg." *Books for Keeps* (U.K.) 52 (Sept 1988): 20–21.

Mackey, M. "Metafiction for Beginners: Allan Ahlberg's *Ten in a Bed." Children's Literature in Education* 21 (Sept 1990): 179–187.

Moss, Elaine. "A Certain Particularity: An Interview with Janet and Allan Ahlberg." *Signal* 61 (Jan 1990): 20–26.

Stephens, Catherine. "Peepo Ergo Sum? Anxiety and Pastiche in the Ahlbergs' Picture Books." *Children's Literature in Education* 21 (Sept 1990): 165–177.

Twentieth-Century Children's Writers. 3rd ed. Edited by Tracy Chevalier and D. L. Kirkpatrick. Chicago: St. James, 1989, pp. 7–9.

Aiken, Joan (Delano)

Aers, Lesley. "Joan Aiken's Historical Fantasies." In Dennis Butts. *Good Writers for Young Readers.* St. Albans, England: Hart-Davis, 1977, pp. 12–24. Originally published in *Use of English* 22 (Summer 1971): 336–344, entitled "Writers for Children—Joan Aiken."

Aiken, Joan. "Any Moral Is Incidental." *Federation of Children's Book Groups Yearbook* 9 (1977–1978): 44–49.

———. "Between Family and Fantasy: An Author's Perspectives on Children's Books." *Quarterly Journal of the Library of Congress* 29 (Oct 1972): 308–326. Reprinted in *The Openhearted Audience.* Washington, DC: Library of Congress, 1980, pp. 46–67.

———. "'Bred an Bawn in a Briar-Patch'—Dialect and Language in Children's Books." *Children's Literature in Education* 9 (Nov 1972): 7–23.

———. "A Free Gift." In Edward Blishen. *The Thorny Paradise.* Boston: Horn Book, 1975, pp. 36–52.

———. "Hope Is the Spur." *Signal* 45 (Sept 1984): 146–151.

———. "In and Out of Wonderland." *Times Educational Supplement* (Jan 15, 1988): 27.

———. "International Children's Book Day Message." *Horn Book* 50 (Apr 1974): 229.

———. "Interpreting the Past." *Children's Literature in Education* 16 (Summer 1985): 67–83.

———. "A Letter to a Boy in Leicester." *London Times Saturday Review* 14 (Apr 1973): 7. Reprinted in *Horn Book* 49 (Oct 1973): 450–452.

———. "On Imagination." *Horn Book* 60 (Nov–Dec 1984): 735–741. Reprinted in *Innocence & Experience.* Edited by Barbara Harrison and Gregory Maguire. New York: Lothrop, 1987, pp. 45–58.

———. "Plot and Character in Suspense Fiction." *The Writer* (May 1989): 9–13.

———. "Purely for Love." *Books* (London, National Book League) 2 (Winter 1970). Reprinted in Margaret Meek. *The Cool Web.* New York: Atheneum, 1978, pp. 166–181; and in Virginia Haviland. *Children and Literature.* Glenview, IL: Scott, Foresman, 1973, pp. 141–154.

———. "A Thread of Mystery." *Children's Literature in Education* 2 (July 1970): 30–47. Reprinted in Geoff Fox. *Writers, Critics and Children.* New York: Agathon Press, 1976, pp. 15–26, entitled "Writing for Enjoyment."

———. "Using History to Create Fiction." In *Prelude, Series 6; Mini-Seminars on Using Books Creatively.* New York: Children's Book Council, 1982. Cassette-taped lecture plus bibliography.

———. "Using Imagination in Plotting." *Freelance Writing and Photography* (U.K.) (Spring 1988).

———. "Vom Erzahlen Phantastischer Geschichten [On the Telling of Fantasy Stories]." *IJB Report* (Germany) 3 (1988): 4–9.

———. *The Way to Write for Children.* New York: St. Martin, 1983.

Alderson, Brian. "Books for Love, Rather Than Respect." (London) *Times* (May 31, 1978).

Apseloff, Marilyn. "Joan Aiken: Literary Dramatist." *Children's Literature Association Quarterly* 9 (Fall 1984): 116–118.

Cadogan, Mary, and Patricia Craig. *You're a Brick, Angela! A New Look at Girls' Fiction from 1839 to 1975.* London: Gollancz, 1976, pp. 357–360.

Crouch, Marcus. *The Nesbit Tradition: The Children's Novel in England 1945–1970.* London: Benn, 1972, pp. 38–39.

Eccleshare, Julia. "Out of the Ordinary." *Times Educational Supplement* (Nov 27, 1987): 43. (interview)

Ellis, A. "Writers for Children: Joan Aiken." *School Librarian* 18 (June 1970): 147–151.

Evans, Gwyenth. "Harps and Harpers in Contemporary Fantasy." *The Lion and the Unicorn* 16 (Dec 1992): 199–209.

Gellert, James H. "Family Disintegration and Self-Realization: The Heroine in the Historical Romances of Joan Aiken." In *The Child and the Family: Selected Papers from the 1988 International Conference of the Children's Literature Association,* ed. by Susan R. Gannon and Ruth A. Thompson. New York: Pace University, 1990, p. 78. (abstract)

Gillespie, John T. *More Juniorplots: A Guide for Teachers and Librarians.* New York: Bowker, 1977, pp. 75–78.

Gillespie, John T., and Diana Lembo. *Introducing Books: A Guide for the Middle Grades.* New York: Bowker, 1970, pp. 106–108.

Jones, Cornelia, and Olivia R. Way. "Joan Aiken." In *British Children's Authors.* Chicago: American Library Association, 1976, pp. 3–10.

McGillis, Rod. "'A Fair Amount of Chaos.' The World of Joan Aiken." *World of Children's Books* 6 (1981): 3–9.

Nicholls, Stan. "Aiken to Write." *Million* (U.K.) 2 (1991): 25–28.

Nuttell, Stephanie. "Authorgraph no. 39: Joan Aiken." *Books for Keeps* (U.K.) 39 (1986): 12–13.

The Oxford Companion to Children's Literature. Edited by Humphrey Carpenter and Mari Prichard. New York: Oxford Univ. Press, 1984, pp. 10, 577.

Polette, N. "Responding to the Novel: Reading, Writing, and Research [Activities for *The Wolves of Willoughby Chase* by Joan Aiken]." *School Library Media Activities Monthly* (Baltimore, Md.), 1991.

Rees, David. "The Virtues of Improbability: Joan Aiken." *Children's Literature in Education* 19 (Spring 1988): 32–41. Reprinted in *"What Do Draculas Do?" Essays on Contemporary Writers of Fiction for Children and Young Adults.* Metuchen, NJ: Scarecrow Press, 1990, pp. 30–46.

Rose, Anne. "Profile: Joan Aiken." *Language Arts* 66 (Nov 1989): 784–790.

Searles, Baird, Beth Meacham, and Michael Franklin. *A Reader's Guide to Fantasy.* New York: Avon, 1982, pp. 20–21.

Speaking for Ourselves; Autobiographical Sketches by Notable Authors of Books for Young Adults. Edited by Donald R. Gallo. Urbana, IL: National Council of Teachers of English, 1990, pp. 1–4.

Stott, Jon C. *Children's Literature from A to Z.* New York: McGraw-Hill, 1984, p. 5.

Stroud, Daphne. "Aiken's England." *Junior Bookshelf* 55 (1991): 3–8.

Third Book of Junior Authors. Edited by Doris De Montreville and Donna Hill. New York: Wilson, 1972, pp. 4–5.

Townsend, John Rowe. "Joan Aiken." In *A Sense of Story.* Philadelphia: Lippincott, 1971, pp. 9–16.

———. "Joan Aiken." *Signal* 5 (May 1971): 72–77.

Twentieth-Century Children's Writers. 3rd ed. Edited by Tracy Chevalier and D. L. Kirkpatrick. Chicago: St. James, 1989, pp. 9–11.

Usrey, Malcolm. "America's Gift to British Children: The Tall Tales of Joan Aiken." In *Proceedings of the Sixth Annual Conference of the Children's Literature Association,* Univ. of Toronto, March 1979. Ypsilanti, MI: Children's Literature Association, 1981, pp. 196–203. Reprinted in Jill P. May. *Children and Their Literature.* West Lafayette, IN: Children's Literature Association Publications, 1983, pp. 58–64.

Wintle, Justin, and Emma Fisher. "Joan Aiken." In *The Pied Pipers.* New York: Paddington Press, 1974, pp. 161–170.

Ainsworth (Gilbert), Ruth (Gallard)

Doyle, Brian. *The Who's Who of Children's Literature.* New York: Schocken, 1968, pp. 3–4.

Twentieth-Century Children's Writers. 3rd ed. Edited by Tracy Chevalier and D. L. Kirkpatrick. Chicago: St. James, 1989, pp. 11–13.

Alcock, Vivien (Dolores)

English, George. "Drama and Laughter: The Work of Vivien Alcock."*Books for Your Children* (U.K.) 26 (1991): 2.
Helbig, Alethea K., and Agnes Regan Perkins. *Dictionary of American Children's Fiction, 1960–1984.* Westport, CT: Greenwood, 1986, pp. 7–8.
Sixth Book of Junior Authors and Illustrators. Edited by Sally Holmes Holtze. New York: Wilson, 1989, pp. 8–9.
Smith, A. "Of Ghosts and History." *Publishers Weekly* 234 (Sept 30, 1988): 28+.
Twentieth-Century Children's Writers. 3rd ed. Edited by Tracy Chevalier and D. L. Kirkpatrick. Chicago: St. James, 1989, pp. 13–14.

Alexander, Lloyd (Chudley)

Alexander, Lloyd. "The Alchemical Experience." *Library News Bulletin* 37 (Jan 1970): 28–29.
———. "The American Book Award Acceptance." *Horn Book* 58 (Oct 1982): 571–583.
———. "Books Remembered." *The Calendar* (now *CBC* [Children's Book Council] *Features*) 38 (Mar–Oct 1981).
———. "Fantasy and the Human Condition. In *Prelude, Series 2; Mini-Seminars on Using Books Creatively.* New York: Children's Book Council, 1977. Cassette-taped lecture plus bibliography.
———. "Fantasy and the Human Condition." *The New Advocate* 1 (Spring 1988): 75–83.
———. "Fantasy as Images: A Literary View." *Language Arts* 55 (Apr 1978): 440–446.
———. "The Flat-Heeled Muse." *Horn Book* 41 (Apr 1965): 141–146. Reprinted in Elinor Field. *Horn Book Reflections.* Boston: Horn Book, 1969, pp. 242–247; and in Virginia Haviland. *Children and Literature.* Glenview, IL: Scott, Foresman, 1973, pp. 241–245.
———. "Flights of Fancy . . . and Welsh History." *Fontana Booknews* (U.K.) 1985/1986, p. iv.
———. "Foreword." In Marshall B. Tymn, Kenneth J. Zahorski, and Robert H. Boyer. *Fantasy Literature: A Core Collection and Reference Guide.* New York: Bowker, 1979, pp. vii–x.
———. "Foreword." In John Gillespie and Diana Lembo. *Introducing Books: A Guide for the Middle Grades.* New York: Bowker, 1970, pp. xi–xiv.
———. "Future Conditional." *Children's Literature Association Quarterly* 10 (Winter 1986): 164–166.
———. "High Fantasy and Heroic Romance." *Horn Book* 47 (Dec 1971): 577–584. Reprinted in Paul Heins. *Crosscurrents of Criticism.* Boston: Horn Book, 1977, pp. 170–177.
———. "How Does the Author View His Relationship to His Audience?" *Elementary English* 45 (Nov 1968): 932–933.
———. "Identification and Identities." *Wilson Library Bulletin* 45 (Oct 1970): 144–148.
———. "Literature, Creativity, and Imagination." *Childhood Education* 47 (Mar 1971): 307–310. Reprinted in Patricia Maloney Markun. *Association for Childhood Education International.* Wheaton, MD: Association for Childhood Education International, 1973, pp. 3–6.
———. "A Manner of Speaking." In *The Voice of the Narrator in Children's Literature: Insights from Writers and Critics,* edited by Charlotte F. Otten and Gary D. Schmidt. Westport, CT: Greenwood, 1989, pp. 123–131.
———. "Meet the Newbery Author—A Series." New York: Random/Miller-Brody, 1974. (filmstrip and audiocassette)
———. "Newbery Award Acceptance." *Horn Book* 45 (Aug 1969): 378–381.

————. "1986 Regina Medal Acceptance." *Catholic Library World* 58, no. 1 (1986): 14–15.

————. "No Laughter in Heaven." *Horn Book* 46 (Feb 1970): 11–19.

————. "Notes on the Westmark Trilogy." *Advocate* 4 (Fall 1984): 1–6.

————. "On Responsibility and Authority." *Horn Book* 50 (Aug 1974): 363–364. Reprinted in *Michigan Librarian* 41 (Summer 1974): 14–15; and in *Nebraska Library Association Quarterly* 5 (Fall 1974): 17–19.

————. "Outlooks and Insights." In Helen W. Painter. *Reaching Children and Young People through Literature.* Newark, DE: International Reading Association, 1971, pp. 19–29.

————. "A Recorded Message to Loughborough '83." In *Loughborough '83: Proceedings.* Welsh National Centre for Children's Literature, 1984, pp. 77–78.

————. "A Second Look: *Five Children and It.*" *Horn Book* 61 (May–June 1985): 354–355.

————. "Seeing with the Third Eye." *English Journal* 63 (May 1974): 35–40.

————. "Substance and Fantasy." *School Library Journal* 13 (Dec 1966): 19–21; *Library Journal,* 91 (Dec 15, 1966): 6157–6159.

————. "Travel Notes." In *Innocence & Experience.* Edited by Barbara Harrison and Gregory Maguire. New York: Lothrop, 1987, pp. 59–65.

————. "The Truth about Fantasy." *Texas Library Journal* 43 (Fall 1967): 101–102. Reprinted in *Top of the News* 24 (Jan 1968): 168–174.

————. "Where the Novel Went." *Saturday Review,* 52 (Mar 22, 1969): 62.

————. "Wishful Thinking—Or Hopeful Dreaming?" *Horn Book* 44 (Aug 1968): 383–390. Reprinted in *Bookbird* 7 (1969): 3–9; and in Boyer and Zahorski. *Fantasists on Fantasy.* New York: Avon, 1984, pp. 137–150.

Anon. "NBA Winner Stresses Seriousness of Fantasy." *Library Journal,* Apr 15, 1971, pp. 1412–1413.

Bagnall, Norma. "An American Hero in Welsh Fantasy." *New Welsh Review* 2, no. 4 (1990): 25–29.

Bisenieks, Dainis. "Children, Magic and Choices." *Mythlore* 6 (Winter 1979): 13–16.

————. "Tales from the 'Perilous Realm.'" Good News for the Modern Child." *Christian Century* 91 (June 5, 1974): pp. 617–620.

Carr, Marion G. "Classic Hero in a New Mythology." *Horn Book* 47 (Oct 1971): 508–513. Reprinted in White. *Children's Literature.* Columbus, OH: Merrill, 1976, pp. 112–116.

Colbath, Mary Lou. "Worlds as They Should Be: Middle-Earth, Narnia and Prydain." *Elementary English* 48 (Dec 1971): 937–945.

Deitz, Thomas F. "The Foundling and Other Tales of Prydain." In Frank N. Magill. *Survey of Modern Fantasy Literature,* vol. 2. Englewood Cliffs, NJ: Salem Press, 1983, pp. 571–574.

Durell, Ann. "Lloyd Alexander: Newbery Winner." *Library Journal* 94 (May 15, 1969): 2066–2068.

————. "Who's Lloyd Alexander?" *Horn Book* 45 (Aug 1969): 382–384.

Evans, Gwyneth. "Harps and Harpers in Contemporary Fantasy." *The Lion and the Unicorn* 16 (Dec 1992): 199–209.

Evans, W. D. Emrys. "The Welsh Mabinogion: Tellings and Retellings." *Children's Literature in Education* 28, no. 9 (Spring 1978): 17–33.

Filmer-Davies, Kath. "Welsh Myth and Contemporary Literature." *Mythlore* 73 (Summer 1993): 53–58. Discusses Susan Cooper, Nikolai Tolstoi, Lloyd Alexander, Madeleine L'Engle, Brian Caswell, Jay Ashton, and Nancy Bond.

Fisher, Margery. "A Quintet of Old Favourites." *Growing Point* (U.K.) 27, no. 4 (1988): 5056–5057.

Gillespie, John T. *Juniorplots 4: A Book Talk Guide for Use with Readers Ages 12–16.* New Providence, NJ: Bowker, 1993, pp. 183–187.

Gillespie, John T., and Diana Lembo. *Introducing Books: A Guide for the Middle Grades.* New York: Bowker, 1970, pp. 234–238.

Gillespie, John T., and Corinne J. Naden. *Juniorplots 3: A Book Talk Guide for Use with Readers Ages 12–16.* New York: Bowker, 1987, pp. 161–165.

Glass, Rona. "*A Wrinkle in Time* and *The High King:* Two Couples, Two Perspectives." *Children's Literature Association Quarterly* 6 (Fall 1981): 15–18. Reprinted in Patricia Dooley. *The First Steps.* West Lafayette, IN: Children's Literature Association Publications, 1984, pp. 119–121.

Greenlaw, M. Jean. "Books in the Classroom." *Horn Book* 64 (Nov/Dec 1988): 820–822.

———— "Profile: Lloyd Alexander." *Language Arts* 61 (Apr 1984): 406–413.

Heins, Paul. "*The Marvelous Misadventures of Sebastian,* a Review." *Horn Book* 46 (Dec 1970): 628.

Helbig, Alethea, and Agnes Regan Perkins. *Dictionary of American Children's Fiction, 1985–1989.* Westport, CT: Greenwood, 1993, pp. 9–10, 108–109, 272.

————. *Dictionary of American Children's Fiction, 1960–1984.* Westport, CT: Greenwood, 1986, pp. 8, 56–57, 67–68, 98, 101, 213–214, 286–287, 354–355, 404, 644, 709–710.

"The High King." In Lee Kingman. *Newbery and Caldecott Medal Books: 1966–1975.* Boston: Horn Book, 1975, pp. 45–55.

Hopkins, Lee Bennett. "Lloyd Alexander." In *More Books by More People.* New York: Citation Press, 1974, pp. 10–17.

Ingram, Laura. "Lloyd Alexander." In *American Writers for Children since 1960: Fiction. Dictionary of Literary Biography,* vol. 52. Detroit: Gale, 1986, pp. 3–21.

Jacobs, James Swenson. "Lloyd Alexander: A Critical Biography." Ed.D. diss., University of Georgia, 1978.

————. "A Personal Look at Lloyd Alexander." *Advocate* 4 (Fall 1984): 8–18.

Kuznets, Lois R. "'High Fantasy' in America: Alexander, Le Guin and Cooper." An unpublished paper delivered at the Conference on Fantasy and Social Values in German and American Children's Literature, Humanities Institute of Brooklyn College, March 1984.

————. "'High Fantasy' in America: A Study of Lloyd Alexander, Ursula Le Guin, and Susan Cooper." *The Lion and the Unicorn* 9 (1985): 19–35.

Lane, Elizabeth. "Lloyd Alexander's *Chronicles of Prydain* and the Welsh Tradition." *Orcrist* 7 (1973): 25–29.

Livingston, Myra C. *Tribute to Lloyd Alexander.* Philadelphia: Drexel Institute, 1976.

McGovern, John Thomas. "Lloyd Alexander—Bard of Prydain: A Study of the Prydain Cycle." Ph.D. diss., Temple University, 1980.

May, Jill P. *Lloyd Alexander.* Boston: Twayne, 1991.

————. "Lloyd Alexander's Truthful Harp." *Children's Literature Association Quarterly* 10 (Spring 1985): 37–38.

Miklovic, J. "Biography-Bibliography of Lloyd Alexander, with an Analysis of Some of His Fantasy Works." Research paper. Kent, OH: Kent State University, 1973.

Miller, Francis A. "Humor, Humility, Humanity and Hope: The Prydain Chronicles of Lloyd Alexander." *Orana* (Australia) 15 (Feb 1979): 35–39.

Molson, Francis J. "The Chronicles of Prydain." In Frank N. Magill. *Survey of Modern Fantasy Literature,* vol. 1. Englewood Cliffs, NJ: Salem Press, 1983, pp. 256–261.

Omdal, Marsha de Prez. "For Wayfarers Still Journeying: *Taran Wanderer.*" *Language Arts* 55 (Apr 1978): 501–502.

The Oxford Companion to Children's Literature. Edited by Humphrey Carpenter and Mari Prichard. New York: Oxford Univ. Press, 1984, pp. 14, 428.

Painter, Helen W. "Lloyd Alexander: The Man and His Books for Children." In Helen W. Painter. *Reaching Children and Young People through Literature.* Newark, DE: International Reading Association, 1971, pp. 30–36.

Patterson, Nancy-Lou. "Homo Monstrous: Lloyd Alexander's Gurgi and Other Shadow Figures of Fantastic Literature." *Mythlore* 3, 11 (1976): 24–28.

Paxon, Diana. "The Tolkien Tradition." *Mythlore* 39 (1984): 23–27, 37.

"The Perilous Realms: A Colloquy." In *Innocence & Experience*. Edited by Barbara Harrison and Gregory Maguire. New York: Lothrop, 1987, pp. 195–210.

Pflieger, Pat, and Helen M. Hill. *A Reference Guide to Modern Fantasy for Children*. Westport, CT: Greenwood, 1984, pp. xiii–xvi, 8–11, 61–62, 71–73, 97–99, 100–101, 186–187, 240–243, 350–351, 522–524, 533–535, 609–611.

Roginski, Jim, ed. *Newbery and Caldecott Medalists and Honor Book Winners*. Littleton, CO: Libraries Unlimited, 1982, pp. 29–30.

Rossman, Douglas A., and Charles E. Rossman, eds. *Pages from 'The Book of Three': A Prydain Glossary*. Baltimore: T-K Graphics, 1975.

Searles, Baird, Beth Meacham, and Michael Franklin. *A Reader's Guide to Fantasy*. New York: Avon, 1982, pp. 21–22.

"*SLJ* Meets Lloyd Alexander." *School Library Journal* 18 (Apr 1971): 23–25; *Library Journal* 96 (Apr 15, 1971): 1421–1423.

Speaking for Ourselves: Autobiographical Sketches by Notable Authors of Books for Young Adults. Edited by Donald R. Gallo. Urbana, IL: National Council of Teachers of English, 1990, pp. 5–7.

Stott, Jon C. *Children's Literature from A to Z*. New York: McGraw-Hill, 1984, p. 9.

———. "Lloyd Alexander's *Chronicles of Prydain*: The Nature of Beginnings." In *Touchstones*. Edited by Perry Nodelman. West Lafayette, IN: Children's Literature Association Publications, 1985, pp. 21–29.

Stuart, Dee, ed. "An Exclusive Interview with Lloyd Alexander." *Writer's Digest* 53 (Apr 1973): 32–35, 58–59.

Sullivan, Charles Williams, III. "The Influence of Celtic Myth and Legend on Modern Imaginative Fiction." Ph.D. diss., University of Oregon, 1976.

———. "Traditional Welsh Materials in Modern Fantasy." *Extrapolation* 28 (Spring 1987): 87–97.

———. *Welsh Celtic Myth in Modern Fantasy*. Westport, CT: Greenwood, 1989, pp. 55–65+.

Swinfen, Ann. *In Defense of Fantasy*. London: Routledge, 1984. Prydain series, pp. 77–78, 80, 83–85, 88, 94–95, 101–103.

Third Book of Junior Authors. Edited by Doris De Montreville and Donna Hill. New York: Wilson, 1972, pp. 6–7.

Townsend, John Rowe. "Guest Essay: Heights of Fantasy." In *Children's Literature Review*, vol. 5. Detroit: Gale, 1983, pp. 8–9.

Trautman, Patricia Ann. "Welsh Mythology and Arthurian Legend in the Novels of Lloyd Alexander and Susan Cooper: Parallels of Motif, Character, and Other Elements." Ph.D. diss., Vanderbilt University, 1984.

Tunnell, Michael O'Grady. "An Analytical Companion to Prydain." Ph.D. diss., Brigham Young University, 1986.

———. "An Interview with Lloyd Alexander." *The New Advocate* 2 (Spring 1989): 83–95.

———. "Profile: Eilonwy of the Red-Gold Hair." *Language Arts* 66 (1989): 558–563.

———. *The Prydain Companion: A Reference Guide to Lloyd Alexander's "Prydain Chronicles."* Westport, CT: Greenwood, 1989.

Tunnell, Michael O., and James S. Jacobs. "Alexander's *Chronicles of Prydain*: Twenty Years Later." *School Library Journal* 34 (Apr 1988): 27–31.

———. "Fantasy at Its Best: Alexander's *Chronicles of Prydain*." *Children's Literature in Education* 21 (Winter 1990): 229–236.

———. "*The Prydain Chronicles* by Lloyd Alexander." *Book Links* 3 (Mar 1994): 30–39.

Twentieth-Century Children's Writers. 3rd ed. Edited by Tracy Chevalier and D. L. Kirkpatrick. Chicago: St. James, 1989, pp. 16–18.

Waggoner, Diana. "Lloyd Alexander." In *Supernatural Fiction Writers*, vol. 2. Edited by E. F. Bleiler. New York: Scribner, 1985, pp. 965–972.

West, Richard C. "The Tolkienians." *Orcrist* 2 (1967): 4–15.

Whetton, Betty B. "Who Will Read Prydain?" *Arizona English Bulletin* 14 (Apr 1972): 51–53.

Wing, Susan. "The Politics of *The Black Cauldren:* Disney's Confused Adaptation of Alexander's *The Chronicles of Prydain.*" In *Literature and Hawaii's Children.* Proceedings of the Third Biennial Conference on Literature and Hawaii's Children. Honolulu: Literature and Hawaii's Children, 1988, pp. 33–38.

Wintle, Justin, and Emma Fisher. "Lloyd Alexander." In *The Pied Pipers.* New York: Paddington Press, 1974, pp. 208–220.

Zahorski, Kenneth J., and Robert H. Boyer. *Lloyd Alexander, Evangeline Walton Ensley, Kenneth Morris: A Primary and Secondary Bibliography.* Boston: G. K. Hall, 1981, pp. 1–110.

The Zena Sutherland Lectures, 1983–1992. Edited by Betsy Hearne. New York: Clarion, 1993, pp. 26–43.

Ziefer, Barbara Z. "Wales as a Setting for Children's Fantasy." *Children's Literature in Education* 13 (Summer 1982): 95–102.

Allan, Mabel E(sther)

Allan, Mabel Esther. *The Background Came First: My Books and Places. Pt. 1: Britain and Ireland; Pt. 2: Other Countries.* Heswall, Wirral, England: Mabel Esther Allan, 1988.

———. *More About Being an Author.* Heswall, Wirral, England: Mabel Esther Allan, 1985.

———. *The Road to the Isles and Other Places.* Heswall, Wirral, England: Mabel Esther Allan, 1989.

MacIlroy, Barry. "'Those Magical Time-Slip Stories.'" *Souvenir* (U.K.) 21 (1992): 14–15. Discusses Violet Needham, David Severn, Mabel Esther Allan, and Alison Uttley.

Sixth Book of Junior Authors and Illustrators. Edited by Sally Holmes Holtze. New York: Wilson, 1989, pp. 10–11.

Twentieth-Century Children's Writers. 3rd ed. Edited by Tracy Chevalier and D. L. Kirkpatrick. Chicago: St. James, 1989, pp. 18–20.

Andersen, Hans Christian

Alderson, Brian. "Andersen and the English." *Books for Keeps* (U.K.) 25 (Mar 1984): 18–19.

American-Scandinavian Review 18, no. 4 (Apr 1930). Hans Christian Andersen Anniversary issue.

Andersen, Hans Christian. *The Fairy Tale of My Life: An Autobiography.* Translated by Horace E. Scudder. London: Hurd & Houghton, 1871, reprinted London: Paddington Press, 1975.

Anderson, Celia Catlett. "Andersen's Heroes and Heroines: Relinquishing the Reward." In *Triumphs of the Spirit in Children's Literature.* Edited by Francelia Butler and Richard Rotert. Hamden, CT: Shoe String Press, 1986, pp. 122–126.

Auden, W. H. "Grimm and Andersen." In W. H. Auden. *Forewords and Afterwords.* New York: Random, 1973, pp. 198–208.

Bianco, Margery. "Four Tales from Andersen." *Horn Book* 12 (Mar–Apr 1936): 89–90.

———. *"It's Perfectly True*—A New Andersen." *Horn Book* 14 (May 1938): 153–155.

———. "The Mackinstry Andersen." *Horn Book* 10 (Jan 1934): 37.

———. "The Real Andersen." *Horn Book* 7 (Aug 1931): 187–189

———. "The Stories of Hans Andersen." *Horn Book* 3 (May 1927): 29–34. Reprinted in

Anne Carroll Moore and Bertha Mahony Miller. *Writing and Criticism.* Boston: Horn Book, 1951, pp. 58–62.

———. "The Story of a Storyteller." *Horn Book* 19 (May 1934): 186–189.

Blegvad, Erik. *Hans Christian Andersen: From an Artist's Point of View.* [A lecture for International Children's Book Day, presented on May 1, 1987.] Edited by Sybille A. Jagush and Margaret N. Coughlan. Washington, DC: Library of Congress, 1988.

Böök, Fredrik. *Hans Christian Andersen: A Biography.* Translated by George C. Schoolfield. Norman: Univ. of Oklahoma Press, 1962.

Bredsdorff, Elias. "A Critic's Guide to the Literature on Hans Christian Andersen." *Scandinavica* 6, no. 2 (Nov 1967): 108–125.

———. "Hans Christian Andersen: A Bibliographic Guide to His Works." *Scandinavica* 6, no. 1 (May 1967): 26–42.

———. *Hans Christian Andersen: The Story of His Life and Work, 1805–1875.* New York: Scribner, 1975.

Catalog of the Jean Hersholt Collection of Hans Christian Andersen. Washington, DC: Library of Congress, 1954.

"Cem Anos de Andersen. [A Hundred Years of Andersen]." *Jornal de Tarde* (Brazil) (Aug 4, 1975): 23.

Cimino, Maria. "Children Illustrate Andersen's Tales." *Horn Book* 30 (Oct 1954): 318–324.

Clausen, Julius. "Hans Christian Andersen Abroad and at Home." *American-Scandinavian Review* 18 (Apr 1930): 228–234.

Conroy, Patricia, and Sven H. Rossel, eds. *The Diaries of Hans Christian Andersen.* Seattle: Univ. of Washington Press, 1989.

Dahl, Svend, and H. G. Topsöe-Jensen, eds. *A Book on the Danish Writer Hans Christian Andersen, His Life and Work, Published on the 150th Anniversary of His Birth.* Translated by W. Glyn Jones. Copenhagen: Det Berlingske Bogtry Kkeri, 1955.

Dahlerup, Pil, et al. "Splash! Six Views of 'The Little Mermaid.'" *Scandinavian Studies* 62 (1990): 403–428.

Dal, Erik. "Hans Christian Andersen's Tales and America." *Scandinavian Studies* 40, no. 1 (Feb 1968): 1–25.

———. "Research on Hans Christian Andersen: Trends, Results, and Desiderata." *Orbis Litterarum* 17 (1962): 166–183.

Dooley, Patricia. "Porcelain, Pigtails, Pagodas: Images of China in 19th and 20th Century Illustrated Editions of 'The Nightingale.'" In *Proceedings of the Sixth Annual Conference of the Children's Literature Association.* Univ. of Toronto, March 1979. Ypsilanti, MI: Children's Literature Association, 1981, pp. 94–105.

Doyle, Brian. *The Who's Who of Children's Literature.* New York: Schocken, 1968, pp. 7–8.

Ellwood, Gracia Fay. "Matters of Grave Import." *Mythlore* 8, 28 (1981).

Fell, Christine E. "Symbolic and Satiric Aspects of Hans Andersen's Fairy-Tales." *Leeds Studies in English.* n.s. 1 (1967): 83–91.

Freeman, Ann. "A Comparative Study of Hans Christian Andersen and Charles Dickens: The Relationship between Spiritual and Material Value Systems as Defined by Their Treatment of the Child." Ph.D. diss., University of California, Berkeley, 1979.

Frey, Charles, and John Griffiths. *The Literary Heritage of Childhood: An Appraisal of Children's Classics in the Western Tradition.* Westport, CT: Greenwood, 1987, pp. 41–50.

Friederich, Reinhard. "Dis-Enchantment: Some Tales by Andersen." In *Literature and Hawaii's Children,* ed. by Cristina Bacchilega and Steven Curry. Honolulu: Literature and Hawaii's Children, 1990, pp. 18–24.

Fullam, Victoria Ann. "Mermaid." Ph.D. diss., University of Minnesota, 1984. An original opera adapted from "The Little Mermaid."

Godden, Rumer. "Hans Andersen, Writer." *Horn Book* 66 (Sept–Oct 1990): 554–562.

———. *Hans Christian Andersen: A Great Life in Brief.* New York: Knopf, 1955.

Grabowski, Simon. "The Refrigerated Heart: A Comparative Study of Novalis' 'Marchen von Hyacinth und Rosenblute' and Hans Christian Andersen's 'Sneedronninger' ['The Snow Queen']." *Scandinavica* 10, no. 1 (May 1971): 43–58.

Griffith, John. "Personal Fantasy in Andersen's Fairy Tales." *Kansas Quarterly* 16 (Summer 1984): 81–88.

Grønbech, Bo. *Hans Christian Andersen.* Boston: Twayne, 1980.

"Hans Christian Andersen Museum Dedicated." *AB Bookman's Weekly* 16 (Apr 1990): 1636–1637.

Hastings, A. Walter. "Moral Simplification in Disney's *The Little Mermaid.*" *The Lion and the Unicorn* 17 (June 1993): 83–92.

Haugaard, Erik Christian. "Hans Christian Andersen." In *Writers for Children: Critical Studies of Major Authors since the Seventeenth Century.* Edited by Jane M. Bingham. New York: Scribner, 1988, pp. 7–14.

———. "Hans Christian Andersen, 1805–1875." *Books for Keeps* (U.K.) 25 (Mar 1984): 18–19.

———. "Hans Christian Andersen: A Twentieth Century View." *Scandinavian Review* 63 (Dec 1975): 4–12.

———. "The Poet Who Lives." *Horn Book* 51 (Oct 1975): 443–448.

———. *Portrait of a Poet: Hans Christian Andersen and His Fairy Tales.* Washington, DC: Library of Congress, 1973. Reprinted in *The Openhearted Audience.* Washington, DC: Library of Congress, 1980, pp. 68–81.

———. "Random Thoughts by a Translator of Andersen." *Horn Book* 48 (Dec 1972): 557–562. Reprinted in Paul Heins. *Crosscurrents of Criticism.* Boston: Horn Book, 1977, pp. 277–282.

———. "The Simple Truth." *Signal* 11 (May 1973): 69–73.

———. "A Translator's Opinions." *Quarterly Journal of the Library of Congress* 30 (Apr 30, 1973): 89–94.

Hazard, Paul. "Hans Christian Andersen." *Junior Bookshelf* 4 (Dec 1939): 65–77.

———. "Prince of Story-Tellers." *Horn Book* 19 (May–June 1943): 141–147. Reprinted in Paul Hazard. *Books, Children, and Men.* Boston: Horn Book, 1960, pp. 92–105.

Hearn, Michael Patrick. "Afterword." In Kate Greenway. *Original Drawings for "The Snow Queen" by Hans Christian Andersen.* New York: Schocken, 1981, pp. 53–58.

Heins, Paul. "*Hans Christian Andersen: The Complete Fairy Tales and Stories,* a Review." *Horn Book* 50 (June 1974): 269.

Hersholt, Jean. "Hans Andersen Fairy Tales Published First in America." *The Colophon* 1, no. 4 (Feb 1940): 5–12.

———. "Hans Christian Andersen's First Book." *The New Colophon* 3 (1950): 44–48.

Holbek, Bengt. "Hans Christian Andersen's Use of Folktales." *Merveilles & Contes* (Boulder CO) 4 (Dec 1990): 220–232.

Hürlimann, Bettina. "Hans Christian Andersen." In *Three Centuries of Children's Books in Europe.* Edited by Brian W. Alderson. Cleveland: World, 1968, pp. 42–52.

Jan, Isabelle. "Hans Christian Andersen or Reality." In *On Children's Literature.* New York: Schocken, 1974, pp. 45–55.

The Junior Book of Authors. 2nd rev. ed. Edited by Stanley J. Kunitz and Howard Haycraft. New York: Wilson, 1951, pp. 5–6.

Kate, Lynn. "The Ugly Duckling Who Wanted to Be a Swan." *Listener* (London) (Jan 2, 1986): 13–14.

Kromann-Kelly, I. "Hans Christian Andersen's Tales: Alive and Well in Denmark?" *Top of the News* 36 (Summer 1980): 381–383.

Lanes, Selma. "A Literary Correspondance Between H. E. Scudder and H. C. Andersen. [Pt. I] *Horn Book* 65 (Jan–Feb 1989): 39–47.

Lavender, R. "Hans Christian Andersen and Erik Christian Haugaard." *School Librarian* 23 (June 1975): 113–119.

Lederer, Wolfgang. *The Kiss of "The Snow Queen": Hans Christian Andersen and Man's Redemption by Woman.* Berkeley and Los Angeles: Univ. of California Press, 1986.

Lowry, Betty. "An Andersen Anniversary." *Horn Book* 62 (May–June 1986): 378–379.

McNulty, Faith. "Children's Books for Christmas." *The New Yorker* (Dec 12, 1988): 148–153.

Meynell, Esther. *Story of Hans Andersen.* New York: H. Schuman, 1950.

Misheff, Sue. "Redemptive Journey: The Storytelling Motif in Andersen's *The Snow Queen.*" *Children's Literature in Education* 20 (Mar 1989): 1–7.

Mishler, William. "Hans Christian Andersen's 'Tin Soldier' in a Freudian Perspective." *Scandinavian Studies* 50, no. 4 (Autumn 1975): 389–395.

Molesworth, Mary. "Hans Christian Andersen." In Lance Salway. *A Peculiar Gift.* Harmondsworth, Middlesex: Kestrel, 1976, pp. 137–145.

Möller, Kai Friis. "The Poet and the Fair Sex." *American-Scandinavian Review* 18 (Apr 1930): 220–227.

The Oxford Companion to Children's Literature. Edited by Humphrey Carpenter and Mari Prichard. New York: Oxford Univ. Press, 1984, pp. 20–23, 166, 317, 378, 427, 489, 495, 509–510, 528, 549, 571.

Piehl, Kathy. "Under the Sea—and Above: Picture Books That Link the Human World to Other Realms." *CLA Bulletin* 17 (Spring 1991): 18–22.

Pizzocoli, G. "Il Favolista Andersen fu Anche un Buon Disegnatore" [Hans Christian Andersen, Storyteller and Illustrator]." *Specchio del Libro per Ragazzi* (Italy) 75 (Mar–Apr 1976): 21–23.

Potter, R. A. "The World of Hans Christian Andersen." *AB Bookman's Weekly* 80 (Dec 7, 1987): 2237–2242.

Robb, Nesca A. "Hans Andersen." In *Four in Exile.* Stroudsburg, PA: Hutchinson Ross, 1945, pp. 120–158.

Roy, Kuldip Kumar. "Andersen and Indian Children's Literature." *Multicultural Children's Literature* (India) 3, no. 4 (1987): 61–72.

Rubeck, Mary Ann. "Annotations Documenting and Interpreting the Reflections of Hans Christian Andersen's Life in His Fairy Tales." Ph.D. diss., State University of New York at Buffalo, 1981.

Rubow, Paul V. "Hans Andersen and His Fairy Tales." *Life and Letters* (London) 53 (May 1947): 92–98.

————. "Idea and Form in Hans Christian Andersen's Fairy Tales." In *A Book on the Danish Writer Hans Christian Andersen: His Life and Work.* Edited by Svend Dahl and H. G. Topsöe-Jensen. Copenhagen: Det Berlingske Bogtrykkeri, 1955, pp. 97–135.

Sale, Roger. *Fairy Tales and After.* Cambridge, MA: Harvard Univ. Press, 1978, pp. 63–73.

Scudder, Horace E. "Andersen's Short Stories." *Atlantic Monthly* 36 (Nov 1875): 598–602.

————. "Hans Christian Andersen." *Atlantic Monthly* 36 (Nov 1875): 203–234. Reprinted in Horace E. Scudder. *Childhood in Literature and Art.* Boston: Houghton Mifflin, 1894; reprinted, Folcroft, 1978, pp. 201–216; and in Virginia Haviland. *Children and Literature.* Glenview, IL: Scott, Foresman, 1973, pp. 50–56.

Searles, Baird, Beth Meacham, and Michael Franklin. *A Reader's Guide to Fantasy.* New York: Avon, 1982, p. 22.

Sicherman, Ruth. "Time to Tell an Andersen Tale." *Top of the News* 30 (Jan 1974): 161–168.

Smith, Janet. "Hard Times." *The New York Review of Books* (June 27, 1991): 26–31.

Spink, Reginald. *Hans Christian Andersen and His World.* New York: Putnam, 1972.

Stirling, Monica. *The Wild Swan: The Life and Times of Hans Christian Andersen.* New York: Harcourt Brace Jovanovich, 1965.

Stott, Jon C. *Children's Literature from A to Z.* New York: McGraw-Hill, 1984, p. 12.

Sutherland, Zena. "Hans Christian Andersen." In *Children and Books.* 7th ed. Edited by Zena Sutherland and May Hill Arbuthnot. Glenview, IL: Scott, Foresman, 1985, pp. 228–230.

Toksvig, Signe. "Good News for Lovers of Andersen." *Horn Book* 12 (Mar–Apr 1936): 87–88.

————. *The Life of Hans Christian Andersen.* New York: Harcourt Brace Jovanovich, 1934.

Topsöe-Jensen, Helge, and Paul V. Rubow. "Hans Christian Andersen the Writer." *American-Scandinavian Review* 18 (Apr 1930): 205–212.

Trapp, F. "'The Emperor's Nightingale': Some Aspects of Mimesis." *Critical Inquiry* 4 (Aug 1977): 85–103.

Tucker, Alan. "Andersen Complete." *Signal* 16 (Jan 1975): 12–17.

Williams, Alan Moray. "Hans Christian Andersen." *Time and Tide* (Feb 1963): 9–13. Reprinted in Sheila A. Egoff. *Only Connect.* 2nd ed. New York: Oxford Univ. Press, 1980, pp. 233–237.

Yolen, Jane. "The Literary Underwater World." *Language Arts* 57 (1980): 403–412.

Anderson, Margaret J(ean)

Fifth Book of Junior Authors and Illustrators. Edited by Sally Holmes Holtze. New York: Wilson, 1983, pp. 7–9.

Anderson, Poul (William)

Anderson, Poul. "Concerning Future Histories." *Bulletin of the Science Fiction Writers of America* 14 (1979): 7–14.

————. *Fantasy.* New York: Pinnacle, 1981.

————. "Star-Flights and Fantasies: Sagas Still to Come." In *The Craft of Science Fiction.* Edited by Reginald Bretnor. New York: Harper, 1976.

Brenner, Malcolm. "Interview: Poul Anderson." *Future Life* 109 (1981): 26–28.

Clark, Judith A. *"A Midsummer Tempest."* In *Survey of Modern Fantasy Literature,* vol. 2. Edited by Frank N. Magill. Englewood Cliffs, NJ: Salem Press, 1983, pp. 1025–1028.

Dean, John. "A Curious Note in the Wind: The New Literary Genre of Heroic Fantasy." *New Mexico Humanities Review* 2 (Summer 1979): 34–41.

De Camp, L. Sprague, ed. *The Blade of Conan.* New York: Ace, 1979.

Dietz, Thomas F. *"The Merman's Children."* In *Survey of Modern Fantasy Literature,* vol. 2. Edited by Frank N. Magill. Englewood Cliffs, NJ: Salem Press, 1983, pp. 1021–1024.

Elliot, Jeffrey M. *Science Fiction Voices #2.* San Bernardino, CA: Borgo Press, 1979.

Elliott, Elton T. "An Interview with Poul Anderson." *Science Fiction Review* 7 (May 1978): 32–37.

McGuire, Patrick L. *"Operation Chaos."* In *Survey of Modern Fantasy Literature,* vol. 3. Edited by Frank N. Magill. Englewood Cliffs, NJ: Salem Press, 1983, pp. 1160–1163.

Miesel, Sandra. *Against Time's Arrow: The High Crusade of Poul Anderson.* San Bernardino, CA: Borgo Press, 1978.

Morgan, Chris. "The Short Fiction of Anderson." In *Survey of Modern Fantasy Literature,* vol. 3. Edited by Frank N. Magill. Englewood Cliffs, NJ: Salem Press, 1983, pp. 1417–1419.

————. *"Three Hearts and Three Lions."* In *Survey of Modern Fantasy Literature,* vol. 2. Edited by Frank N. Magill. Englewood Cliffs, NJ: Salem Press, 1983, pp. 1913–1917.

Pierce, Hazel Beasley. *A Literary Symbiosis: Science Fiction/Fantasy Mystery.* Westport, CT: Greenwood, 1983.

Platt, Charles. *Dream Makers II: The Uncommon Men and Women Who Write Science Fiction.* New York: Berkley, 1983, pp. 151–158.

Shippey, Tom. "The Golden Bough and the Incorporation of Magic in Science Fiction." *Foundation* 11/12 (1977): 119–134.

Tweet, Roald D. "Poul Anderson." In *Supernatural Fiction Writers,* vol. 2. Edited by E. F. Bleiler. New York: Scribner, 1985, pp. 973–980.

Twentieth-Century Science Fiction Writers. 3rd ed. Edited by Noelle Watson and Paul E. Schellinger. Chicago: St. James Press, 1991, pp. 9–12.

Walker, Paul. *Speaking of Science Fiction.* Oradell, NJ: Luna, 1978, pp. 107–120. Interview.

Andrews, J(ames) S(ydney)

Taylor, Anne. "Traveling in Time—Towards a Project." *Children's Literature in Education* 13 (1974): 68–79.

Twentieth-Century Children's Writers. 3rd ed. Edited by Tracy Chevalier and D. L. Kirkpatrick. Chicago: St. James, 1989, p. 27.

Annett (Pipitone Scott), Cora

Helbig, Alethea K., and Agnes Regan Perkins. *Dictionary of American Children's Fiction, 1960–1984.* Westport, CT: Greenwood, 1986, pp. 19, 300–301.

Anthony, Piers (pseud. of Piers A[nthony] D[illingham] Jacob)

Anthony, Piers. *Bio of an Ogre: An Autobiography of Piers Anthony to Age 50.* New York: Ace, 1988.

———. "In Defense of Fantasy." *Isaac Asimov's Science Fiction Magazine,* Dec 1983, pp. 71–87.

Biggers, Cliff. "An Interview with Piers Anthony." *Science Fiction Review* 6 (Nov 1977): 56–62.

Clark, Judith A. "The Xanth Novels." In *Survey of Modern Fantasy Literature,* vol. 5. Edited by Frank N. Magill. Englewood Cliffs, NJ: Salem Press, 1983, pp. 2185–2191.

Collings, Michael R. *Reader's Guide to Piers Anthony.* Mercer Island, WA: Starmont, 1983.

———. "Words and Worlds: The Creation of a Fantasy Universe in Zelazny, Lee and Anthony." In *The Scope of the Fantastic—Theory, Technique, Major Authors.* Edited by Robert A. Collins and Howard D. Pearce. Westport, CT: Greenwood, 1985, pp. 173–182.

Collins, Robert A. "Piers Anthony: A Twenty-Year Trek to the Top." *Fantasy Newsletter* 59 (1983): 12–16.

Costello, Mathew J., and Peirs Anthony. "The Six Magical Elements of Fantasy Fiction." *Writers Digest* 71 (Jan 1991): 30.

Lane, Daryl, William Vernon, and David Carlson. *The Sound of Wonder: Interviews from "The Science Fiction Radio Show,"* vol 2. Phoenix, AZ: Oryx Press, 1985, pp. 1–28.

"Piers Anthony: Bard in a Gilded Cage." *Locus* 319 (1987): 4+.

Platt, Charles. *Dream Makers.* New York: Ungar, 1987, pp. 221–230. Interview.

———. "Profile: Piers Anthony." *Science Fiction Review* 49 (1983): 35–38.

Scarborough, John. "Piers Anthony." In *Supernatural Fiction Writers,* vol. 2. Edited by E. F. Bleiler. New York: Scribner, 1985, pp. 981–986.

Searles, Baird, Beth Meacham, and Michael Franklin. *A Reader's Guide to Fantasy.* New York: Avon, 1982, pp. 24–25.

Smith, Scott S. "Interview with Piers Anthony." *Thrust* 25 (1986): 9–13.

Twentieth-Century Science Fiction Writers. 3rd ed. Edited by Noelle Watson and Paul E. Schellinger. Chicago: St. James Press, 1991, pp. 12–14.

Wiater, Stanley. "Piers Anthony." *Twilight Zone* 5 (1987): 26–27.

Arthur, Ruth M(abel)

Crouch, Marcus. *The Nesbit Tradition.* London: Benn, 1972, pp. 205–206, 218.
————. "The Painful Art of Growing Up: The Novels of Ruth M. Arthur." *Junior Bookshelf* 42 (Oct 1978): 239–244.
Fifth Book of Junior Authors and Illustrators. Edited by Sally Holmes Holtze. New York: Wilson, 1983, pp. 13–14.
Gough, John. "Rivalry, Rejection and Recovery: Variations of the 'Cinderella' Story." *Children's Literature in Education* 21 (June 1990): 99–108.
Jones, Cornelia, and Olivia R. Way. "Ruth M. Arthur." In *British Children's Authors.* Chicago: American Library Association, 1976, pp. 31–40.
Twentieth-Century Children's Writers. 3rd ed. Edited by Tracy Chevalier and D. L. Kirkpatrick. Chicago: St. James, 1989, pp. 34–35.

Arundel (McCrindle), Honor (Morfydd)

Boyd, Celia. "Growing Pains: A Survey of Honor Arundel's Novels." *Signal* 4 (Jan 1973): 38–51.
Fourth Book of Junior Authors and Illustrators. Edited by Doris De Montreville and Elizabeth D. Crawford. New York: Wilson, 1978, pp. 16–17.
Russell, J. "Honor Arundel." *Junior Bookshelf* 37 (Dec 1973): 367–369.
Twentieth Century Children's Writers. 3rd ed. Edited by Tracy Chevalier and D. L. Kirkpatrick. New York: St. Martin, 1989, pp. 35–36.

Asch, Frank

Fourth Book of Junior Authors and Illustrators. Edited by Doris De Montreville and Elizabeth D. Crawford. New York: Wilson, 1978, pp. 17–18.

Asimov, Isaac

Ingersoll, Earl G., ed. "A Conversation with Isaac Asimov." *Science-Fiction Studies* 14 (1987): 68–77.

Asprin, Robert L(ynn)

Searles, Baird, Beth Meacham, and Michael Franklin. *A Reader's Guide to Fantasy.* New York: Avon, 1982, pp. 25–26.
Twentieth-Century Science Fiction Writers. 3rd ed. Edited by Noelle Watson and Paul E. Schellinger. Chicago: St. James Press, 1991, pp. 25–26.

Atwater, Richard (Tupper), and Atwater, Florence (Hasseltine Carroll)

Helbig, Alethea K., and Agnes Regan Perkins. *Dictionary of American Children's Fiction, 1859–1959.* Westport, CT: Greenwood, 1985, pp. 28, 360–361.
Jameyson, Karen. "A Second Look: *Mr. Popper's Penguins.*" *Horn Book* 64 (Mar–Apr 1988): 186–187.

More Junior Authors. Edited by Muriel Fuller. New York: Wilson, 1963, pp. 3–4.

The Oxford Companion to Children's Literature. Edited by Humphrey Carpenter and Mari Prichard. New York: Oxford Univ. Press, 1984, p. 366.

Roginski, Jim, ed. *Newbery and Caldecott Medalists and Honor Book Winners.* Littleton, CO: Libraries Unlimited, 1982, p. 36.

Twentieth-Century Children's Writers. 3rd ed. Edited by Tracy Chevalier and D. L. Kirkpatrick. Chicago: St. James, 1989, pp. 40–41.

Aulaire, Edgar Parin d', and Aulaire, Ingri (Mortenson) d'

Bader, Barbara. "Ingri and Edgar Parin D'Aulaire." In *American Picturebooks: From Noah's Ark to the Beast Within.* New York: Macmillan, 1976, pp. 42–46.

Children's Literature Review Board. "Review." In MacCann. *Cultural Conformity in Books for Children.* Metuchen, NJ: Scarecrow Press, 1977, pp. 144–145.

Crago, Hugh. "Ingri and Edgar D'Aulaire." In *American Writers for Children, 1900–1960. Dictionary of Literary Biography,* vol. 22. Detroit: Gale, 1983, pp. 102–109.

D'Aulaire, Ingri, and Edgar Parin D'Aulaire. "Working Together on Books for Children." *Horn Book* 16 (July 1940): 247–256.

Farquhar, M. C. "The Magic Rug of Ingri and Edgar Parin D'Aulaire." *Elementary English* 30 (Apr 1953): 197–201.

Mahony, Bertha E., and Marguerite M. Mitchell. "Ingri and Edgar Parin D'Aulaire." *Horn Book* 16 (July 1940): 257–264.

Stott, Jon C. *Children's Literature from A to Z.* New York: McGraw-Hill, 1984, p. 89.

Twentieth-Century Children's Writers. 3rd ed. Edited by Tracy Chevalier and D. L. Kirkpatrick. Chicago: St. James, 1989, pp. 265–266.

Aulnoy, Countess Marie Catherine de Berneville d'

Chartrand, Claudine Denise. "Fairyland Revisited: A Gynocentric Reading of Selected English, French, and German Folk and Fairy Tales." Ph.D. diss., Pennsylvania State University, 1990.

Degraff, Amy Vanderlyn. "The Tower and the Well: A Study of Form and Meaning in Mme. d'Aulnoy's Fairy Tales." Ph.D diss., University of Virginia, 1979.

Doyle, Brian. *The Who's Who of Children's Literature.* New York: Schocken, 1968, p. 69.

Farrell, Michele L. "Celebration and Representation of Feminine Desire in Madame d'Aulnoy's Fairy Tale: 'La Chatte Blanche.'" *L'Esprit Createur* 29 (Fall 1989): 52–64.

Filstrup, Jane Merrill. "Individuation in 'La Chatte Blanche.'" *Children's Literature,* vol. 6. Philadelphia: Temple University Press, 1977, pp. 77–92.

Hearn, Michael Patrick. "Preface." In Marie Catherine, Comtesse d'Aulnoy. *The Tales of the Fairies in Three Parts, Compleat.* New York: Garland, 1977.

McLeod, Glenda. "Writer of Fantasy: Madame d'Aulnoy." In *Women Writers of the Seventeenth Century,* ed. by Katharina M. Wilson and Frank J. Warnke. Athens: Univ. of Georgia Press, 1989.

Marin, Catharine. "Faerie ou Sorcellerie? Les Contes de Fées de Madame d'Aulnoy." *Merveilles & Contes* 6 (May 1992): 45–58.

Mitchell, Jane. "Thematic Analysis of Mme. Comtesse d'Aulnoy's *Contes de Fées.*" Ph.D. diss., University of North Carolina at Chapel Hill, 1973.

The Oxford Companion to Children's Literature. Edited by Humphrey Carpenter and Mari Prichard. New York: Oxford Univ. Press, 1984, pp. 35–36, 67, 568–569, 583.

Palmer, Melvin Delmar. "Madame d'Aulnoy in England." Ph.D. diss., University of Maryland, 1969.

Palmer, Nancy, and Melvin D. Palmer. "English Editions of French Contes de Fées Attributed to Mme. d'Aulnoy." *Studies in Bibliography* 27 (1974): 227–232.

———. "The French 'Conte de Fée' in England." *Studies in Short Fiction* 11, no. 1 (Winter 1974): 35–44.

Sale, Roger. *Fairy Tales and After.* Cambridge, MA: Harvard Univ. Press, 1978, pp. 54–58.

Seifert, Lewis Carl. "The Time That (N)ever Was: Women's Fairy Tales in Seventeenth-Century France." Ph.D. diss., University of Michigan, 1989.

Williams, Elizabeth Detering. "The Fairy Tales of Madame d'Aulnoy." Ph.D. diss., Rice University, 1982.

Averill, Esther (Holden)

The Junior Book of Authors. 2nd rev. ed. Edited by Stanley J. Kunitz and Howard Haycraft. New York: Wilson, 1951, pp. 13–14.

Twentieth-Century Children's Writers. 3rd ed. Edited by Tracy Chevalier and D. L. Kirkpatrick. Chicago: St. James, 1989, pp. 41–42.

Avi (pseud. of Avi Wortis)

Avi. "All That Glitters." *Horn Book* 63 (Sept–Oct 1987): 569–576.

———. "I Can Read, I Can Read!" *Horn Book* 70 (Mar–Apr 1994): 166–169.

———. "The Child in Children's Literature." *Horn Book* 69 (Jan–Feb 1993): 40–50.

———. "Seeing Through the I." *The ALAN Review* 20 (Spring 1993): 2–7.

———. "Some Thoughts on the Young Adult World." *VOYA* 7 (Oct 1984): 183–184.

———. "Young People, Books and the Right to Read." *Journal of Youth Services in Libraries* 6 (Spring 1993): 245–256.

Fifth Book of Junior Authors and Illustrators. Edited by Sally Holmes Holtze. New York: Wilson, 1983, pp. 15–16.

Helbig, Alethea, and Agnes Regan Perkins. *Dictionary of American Children's Fiction, 1985–1989.* Westport, CT: Greenwood, 1993, pp. 16–17, 236–237.

———. *Dictionary of American Children's Fiction, 1960–1984.* Westport, CT: Greenwood, 1986, pp. 31–32, 191.

Marinak, B. A. "Author Profile: Avi." *Book Report* 10 (Mar–Apr 1992): 26–28.

Roginski, Jim. *Behind the Covers: Interviews with Authors and Illustrators of Books for Children and Young Adults.* Littleton, CO: Libraries Unlimited, 1985, pp. 33–41.

Stan, Susan. "Conversations: Avi." *Five Owls* 3, no. 3 (1990): 45.

Twentieth-Century Children's Writers. 3rd ed. Edited by Tracy Chevalier and D. L. Kirkpatrick. Chicago: St. James, 1989, pp. 45–46.

Aymé, Marcel (André)

Brand, Patricia Petrus. "The Modern French Fairy Tale: Aspects of 'Le Merveilleux' in Aymé, Supervielle, Saint-Exupéry and Sabatier." Ph.D. diss., Univ. of Colorado at Boulder, 1983.

Loy, J. R. "The Reality of Marcel Aymé's World." *French Review* 28 (Dec 1954): 115–127.

Voorhees, R. J. "Marcel Aymé: Neglected Novelist." *Midwest Quarterly* 25 (Autumn 1983): 74–89.

Babbitt, Natalie (Zane Moore)

Aippersbach, Kim. "*Tuck Everlasting* and the Tree at the Center of the World." *Children's Literature in Education* 21 (June 1990): 83–98.

Anderson, Celia Catlett. "Journey to Forever and Back: Clements and Babbitt." *Proceedings of the 13th Annual Conference of The Children's Literature Association, 1986.* New York: Pace University, 1988, pp. 64–68.

Babbitt, Natalie. "Beacons of Light." *Horn Book* 70 (Sept–Oct 1994): 546–554.

———. "Between Innocence and Maturity." *Horn Book* 48 (Dec 1972): 33–37. Reprinted in Varlejs. *Young Adult Literature in the Seventies.* Metuchen, NJ: Scarecrow Press, 1978.

———. "Drawing on the Child Within." *Horn Book* 69 (May–June 1993): 284–290.

———. "Easy Does It." *Top of the News* 43 (Summer 1987): 376–382.

———. "The Fantastic Voyage." *The Five Owls* (July–Aug 1987).

———. "Fantasy." *Language Arts* 62, no. 8 (1985): 824–825.

———. "Fantasy and the Classic Hero." In *Innocence & Experience.* Edited by Barbara Harrison and Gregory Maguire. New York: Lothrop, 1987, pp. 148–155. Reprinted in *School Library Journal* 34 (Oct 1987): 25–29.

———. "The Great American Novel for Children—And Why Not." *Horn Book* 50 (Apr 1974): 176–185.

———. "Happy Endings? Of Course, and Also Joy." *New York Times Book Review,* pt. II, Nov 8, 1970, pp. 1, 50. Reprinted in Virginia Haviland. *Children and Literature.* Glenview, IL: Scott, Foresman, 1973, pp. 155–159.

———. "How Can We Write Children's Books If We Don't Know Anything about Children?" *Publishers Weekly* 200 (July 19, 1971): 64–66.

———. "The Mad Tea Party Maxim: or, How Books Don't Always Mean What the Writer Intended." *Children's Literature in Education* 22 (June 1991): 89–96.

———. "Metamorphosis." *Horn Book* 64 (Sept–Oct 1988): 582–590; *Magpies* (Australia) 3 (Nov 1988).

———. "Protecting Children's Literature." *Horn Book* 66(Nov/Dec 1990): 696–703.

———. "The Purpose of Literature: Who Cares?" *School Library Journal* 36 (Mar 1990): 150–152.

———. "The Purposes of Fantasy." In *Proceedings of the Ninth Annual Conference of the Children's Literature Association.* University of Florida, March 1982. Ypsilanti, MI: Children's Literature Association, 1983, pp. 22–29. Reprinted in *Innocence & Experience.* Edited by Barbara Harrison and Gregory Maguire. New York: Lothrop, 1987, pp. 174–181.

———. "The Rhinoceros and the Pony: Disputing the Tame Nature of Writers for Children." *Horn Book* 65 (Nov–Dec 1989): 728–731.

———. "Saying What You Think." *Quarterly Journal of the Library of Congress* 39 (Spring 1982): 80–89.

———. "Something Has to Happen." *The Lion and the Unicorn* 9 (1985): 7–10.

———. "What Makes a Book Worth Reading?" *Language Arts* 52 (Oct 1975): 924–927ff.

———. "Who Is the Child?" *Horn Book* 62 (Mar–Apr 1986): 161–166.

De Luca, Geraldine. "Extensions of Nature: The Fantasies of Natalie Babbitt." *The Lion and the Unicorn* 1, no. 2 (Fall 1977): 47–70.

Elleman, Barbara, and Natalie Babbitt. "Natalie Babbitt's *The Search for Delicious.*" *Book Links* 2 (Sept 1992): 18–21.

Fourth Book of Junior Authors and Illustrators. Edited by Doris De Montreville and Elizabeth D. Crawford. New York: Wilson, 1978, pp. 22–23.

Hartvigsen, M. Kip, and Christen Brog Hartvigsen. "'Rough and Soft, Both at Once': Winnie Foster's Initiation in *Tuck Everlasting.*" *Children's Literature in Education* 18 (Fall 1987): 176–183.

Helbig, Alethea K., and Agnes Regan Perkins. *Dictionary of American Children's Fiction, 1960–1984.* Westport, CT: Greenwood, 1986, pp. 35, 248, 364, 579–580, 680–681.

Hirsch, Corinne. "Toward Maturity: Natalie Babbitt's Initiatory Journeys." In *Proceedings of the Seventh Annual Conference of the Children's Literature Association.* Baylor Univ., March 1980. Ypsilanti, MI: Children's Literature Association, 1982, pp. 107–113.

Hopkins, Lee Bennett. "Natalie Babbitt." In *More Books by More People.* New York: Citation Press, 1974, pp. 24–28.

Lanes, Selma G. "A Second Look: *The Devil's Storybook.*" *Horn Book* 64 (May–June 1988): 329–331.

———. "A Talk with Natalie Babbitt." *New York Times Book Review,* Nov 14, 1982, pp. 44, 54.

Levy, Michael. *Natalie Babbitt.* Boston: Twayne, 1991.

Lynch, Catherine M. "Winnie Foster and Peter Pan: Facing the Dilemma of Growth." In *Proceedings of the Ninth Annual Conference of the Children's Literature Association.* Univ. of Florida, March 1982. Ypsilanti, MI: Children's Literature Association, 1983, pp. 107–111.

Meeker, Amy. "*PW* Interviews Natilie Babbitt." *Publishers Weekly* 241 (Feb 21, 1994): 229–230.

Mercier, J. "Natalie Babbitt, Admired Author-Illustrator for Children." *Publishers Weekly* 208 (July 28, 1975): 66–67.

Moss, Anita. "Crime and Punishment—Or Development—In Fairy Tales and Fantasy." *Mythlore* 8 (Spring 1981): 26–28, 42.

———. "Natalie Babbitt." In *American Writers for Children since 1960: Fiction. Dictionary of Literary Biography,* vol. 52. Detroit: Gale, 1986, pp. 22–29.

———. "Pastoral and Heroic Patterns: Their Uses in Children's Fantasy." In *The Scope of the Fantastic—Culture, Biography, Themes, Children's Literature.* Edited by Robert A. Collins and Howard D. Pearce. Westport, CT: Greenwood, 1985, pp. 231–238.

———. "A Second Look: *The Search for Delicious.*" *Horn Book* 60 (Nov–Dec 1984): 779–783.

The Oxford Companion to Children's Literature. Edited by Humphrey Carpenter and Mari Prichard. New York: Oxford Univ. Press, 1984, p. 40.

"The Perilous Realms: A Colloquy." In *Innocence & Experience.* Edited by Barbara Harrison and Gregory Maguire. New York: Lothrop, 1987, pp. 195–210.

Pflieger, Pat, and Helen M. Hill. *A Reference Guide to Modern Fantasy for Children.* Westport, CT: Greenwood, 1984, pp. xii, 33–35, 485–486, 555–556.

Ragsdale, W. "Presentation of the Recognition of Merit to Natalie Babbitt." *Claremont Reading Conference Yearbook* 43 (1979): 199–203.

Raymond, A. "Natalie Babbitt: The Critics' Choice." *Teaching Pre K–8* 21 (Aug–Sept 1990): 42–44.

Roginski, Jim, ed. *Newbery and Caldecott Medalists and Honor Book Winners.* Littleton, CO: Libraries Unlimited, 1982, p. 36.

Sherman, S. "Babbitt Has Strong Words for 'Star System.'" *Publishers Weekly* 240 (Apr 19, 1993): 24.

Spirt, Diana L. *Introducing More Books: A Guide for the Middle Grades.* New York: Bowker, 1978, pp. 194–196.

Stott, Jon C. *Children's Literature from A to Z.* New York: McGraw-Hill, 1984, p. 22.

Tunnell, Michael D. "Books in the Classroom." *Horn Book* 63 (July–Aug 1987): 509–511. *Tuck Everlasting.*

Twentieth-Century Children's Writers. 3rd ed. Edited by Tracy Chevalier and D. L. Kirkpatrick. Chicago: St. James, 1989, pp. 48–49.

Veglahn, Nancy. "Images of Evil: Male and Female Monsters in Heroic Fantasy." *Children's Literature* 15 (1987): 106–119.

Bach, Richard (David)

Watson, Christine. "*Jonathan Livingston Seagull.*" In *Survey of Modern Fantasy Literature,* vol. 2. Edited by Frank N. Magill. Englewood Cliffs, NJ: Salem Press, 1983, pp. 808–810.

Bacon, Martha (Sherman)

Helbig, Alethea K., and Agnes Regan Perkins. *Dictionary of American Children's Fiction, 1960–1984.* Westport, CT: Greenwood, 1986, pp. 35–36.

Twentieth Century Children's Writers. 2nd ed. Edited by D. L. Kirkpatrick. New York: St. Martin, 1983, pp. 49–50.

Bailey, Carolyn Sherwin

Bailey, Carolyn Sherwin. "*Miss Hickory:* Her Genealogy. The Newbery Acceptance Paper." *Horn Book* 23 (July–Aug 1947): 239–242.

Davis, Dorothy R. *Carolyn Sherwin Bailey, 1876–1961: Profile and Bibliography.* Bloomington, IN: Eastern Press, 1967.

————. *Carolyn Sherwin Bailey Historical Collection of Children's Books: A Catalog.* New Haven: Southern Connecticut State College, 1966.

Helbig, Alethea K., and Agnes Regan Perkins. *Dictionary of American Children's Fiction, 1859–1959.* Westport, CT: Greenwood, 1985, pp. 33, 34, 348.

The Junior Book of Authors. 2nd rev. ed. Edited by Stanley J. Kunitz and Howard Haycraft. New York: Wilson, 1951, pp. 14–15.

Kuznets, Lois R. "Two Newbery Medal Winners and the Feminine Mystique: *Hitty, Her First Hundred Years* and *Miss Hickory.*" *The Lion and the Unicorn* 15 (Dec 1991): 1–14.

Lindquist, Jennie. "Books and an Apple Orchard." *Horn Book* 23 (July–Aug 1947): 243–249.

"*Miss Hickory.*" In Bertha Miller and Elinor Field. *Newbery Medal Books: 1922–1955.* Boston: Horn Book, 1957, pp. 288–299.

Pflieger, Pat, and Helen M. Hill. *A Reference Guide to Modern Fantasy for Children.* Westport, CT: Greenwood, 1984, pp. xii–xvi, 37–40, 369–370.

Roginski, Jim, ed. *Newbery and Caldecott Medalists and Honor Book Winners.* Littleton, CO: Libraries Unlimited, 1982, pp. 37–39.

Twentieth-Century Children's Writers. 3rd ed. Edited by Tracy Chevalier and D. L. Kirkpatrick. Chicago: St. James, 1989, pp. 51–53.

Baker, Betty (Lou)

Helbig, Alethea K., and Agnes Regan Perkins. *Dictionary of American Children's Fiction, 1960–1984.* Westport, CT: Greenwood, 1986, p. 36.

Third Book of Junior Authors. Edited by Doris De Montreville and Donna Hill. New York: Wilson, 1972, pp. 24–25.

Twentieth-Century Children's Writers. 3rd ed. Edited by Tracy Chevalier and D. L. Kirkpatrick. Chicago: St. James, 1989, pp. 53–54.

Baker, Margaret

The Junior Book of Authors. 2nd rev. ed. Edited by Stanley J. Kunitz and Howard Haycraft. New York: Wilson, 1951, pp. 15–17.

Baker, Margaret J(oyce)

Baker, Margaret J. "Beginning of *The Shoe Shop Bears.*" *Junior Bookshelf* 34 (Dec 1970): 337–340.

More Junior Authors. Edited by Muriel Fuller. New York: Wilson, 1963, pp. 6–7.

Twentieth-Century Children's Writers. 3rd ed. Edited by Tracy Chevalier and D. L. Kirkpatrick. Chicago: St. James, 1989, pp. 54–56.

Baker, Olaf

The Junior Book of Authors. 2nd rev. ed. Edited by Stanley J. Kunitz and Howard Haycraft. New York: Wilson, 1951, p. 17.

Barrie, Sir J(ames) M(atthew)

Alderson, Brian, ed. *Children's Books in England.* 3rd ed. New York: Cambridge Univ. Press, 1982, pp. 309–312.

Aller, Susan. "The Search for *Peter Pan:* Never Never Land's Ambassador Has Assumed a Variety of Shapes and Styles." *Five Owls* 4, no. 4 (Mar–Apr 1990): 67–68.

Asquith, Lady Cynthia. *Portrait of Barrie.* New York: Dutton, 1955.

Barrie, J(ames) M. "Captain Hook at Eton." *M'Connachie and J. M. B. The Works of J. M. Barrie—Peter Pan Edition,* vol. 35. New York: Scribner, 1940, pp. 108–121.

Birkin, Andrew. *J. M. Barrie and the Lost Boys: The Love Story That Gave Birth to Peter Pan.* London: Constable, 1979, 1986. New York: Potter, 1979.

———. "The Tragedy of *Peter Pan.*" *Folio* (London) (Autumn 1992): 3–9.

Blackburn, William. "*Peter Pan* and the Contemporary Adolescent Novel." In *Proceedings of the Ninth Annual Conference of the Children's Literature Association.* University of Florida, March 1982. Ypsilanti, MI: Children's Literature Association, 1983, pp. 47–53.

———. "The Quest for Values in Contemporary Adolescent Fiction." Syracuse, NY: ERIC Clearinghouse on Information Resources, 1982.

Blake, Kathleen. "The Sea-Dream: *Peter Pan* and *Treasure Island.*" In *Children's Literature,* vol. 6. Philadelphia: Temple Univ. Press, 1977, pp. 165–181. Reprinted in *Reflections on Literature for Children.* Hamden, CT: Shoe String Press, 1984, pp. 215–228.

Burg, B. R. "*Peter Pan* and His 'Bieber Mom.'" *Connecticut Review* 10 (Summer 1987): 13–21.

Burson, Linda. "Fantasy Components of Sir James Matthew Barrie: A Study through Selected Plays." Ph.D. diss., University of Georgia, 1983.

Carpenter, Humphrey. "J. M. Barrie and *Peter Pan:* 'That Terrible Masterpiece.'" In *Secret Gardens: A Study of the Golden Age of Children's Literature.* Boston: Houghton Mifflin, 1985, pp. 170–187.

———, et al. "Children's Books." *Times Educational Supplement* (Feb 5, 1988): 56–60.

———. "Neverland Unlimited." *Times Educational Supplement* (Feb 5, 1988): 53.

Chalmers, Patrick R. *The Barrie Inspiration.* London: Davies, 1938.

Clayton, Walter. "An Interrupted Pan Resumes His Piping." *Forum* 41 (Jan 1909): 83–85.

Doyle, Brian. *The Who's Who of Children's Literature.* New York: Schocken, 1968, pp. 20–22.

Dunbar, Janet. *J. M. Barrie: The Man behind the Image.* Boston: Houghton Mifflin, 1970.

Egan, Michael. "The Neverland of Id: Barrie, *Peter Pan,* and Freud." In *Children's Literature,* vol. 10. New Haven, CT: Yale Univ. Press, 1982, pp. 37–55.

Foster, Michael A. "Peter Pan: The Lost Last Act." *Mythlore* 54 (1988): 53–60. An unpublished and generally unknown last act from Barrie's first draft manuscript of the play, in Indiana Univerity's Lilly Library manuscript collection.

Fraser, Morris. "Narcissus and the Lost Boys." *New Society* (London) 46 (Oct 19, 1978): 144–145.

Frey, Charles, and John Griffiths. *The Literary Heritage of Childhood: An Appraisal of Children's Classics in the Western Tradition.* Westport, CT: Greenwood, 1987, pp. 181–188.

Garland, Herbert. *A Bibliography of the Writings of Sir James Matthew Barrie Bart., OM.* London: Bookman's Journal, 1928.

Gibson, Lois Rauch. "Beyond the Apron: Archetypes, Stereotypes, and Alternative Portrayals of Mothers in Children's Literature." *Children's Literature Association Quarterly* 13 (1988): 177–181.

Gilead, S. "Magic Abjured: Closure in Children's Fantasy Fiction." *Publications of the Modern Language Association* 106 (Mar 1991): 277–293.

Green, Martin. "The Charm of *Peter Pan.*" In *Children's Literature,* vol. 9. New Haven, CT: Yale Univ. Press, 1981, pp. 19–27.

Green, Roger Lancelyn. "Barrie and *Peter Pan.*" *Junior Bookshelf* 24 (Oct 1960): 197–204.

———. *Fifty Years of Peter Pan.* London: Davies, 1954.

———. *J. M. Barrie.* New York: Walck, 1961. Reprinted in Edward Blishen, Margaret Meek, and Roger Lancelyn Green. *Hugh Lofting/Geoffrey Trease/J. M. Barrie.* London: Bodley Head, 1968.

Griffith, John. "Making Wishes Innocent: *Peter Pan.*" *The Lion and the Unicorn* 3 (Spring 1979): 28–37.

Haill, Catherine. *Dear Peter Pan.* Winchester, MA: Faber, 1984.

Hanson, Bruce K. *The Peter Pan Chronicles: The Nearly 100-Year History of the "Boy Who Wouldn't Grow Up."* New York: Carol Publishing Group, 1993.

Higgens, Regina. *Magic Kingdoms: Discovering the Joys of Childhood Classics with Your Child.* New York: Simon, 1992.

Hodges, J. M. "J. M. Barrie." In *Writers for Children: Critical Studies of Major Authors Since the Seventeenth Century.* Edited by Jane M. Bingham. New York: Scribner, 1988, pp. 29–36.

Hollindale, Peter. "*Peter Pan:* The Text and the Myth." *Children's Literature in Education* 24 (Mar 1993): 19–30.

Honig, Edith Lazaros. *Breaking the Angelic Image: Woman Power in Victorian Children's Fantasy.* Westport, CT: Greenwood, 1988.

———. "A Quiet Rebellion: The Portrait of the Feminine in Victorian Children's Fantasy." Ph.D. diss., Fordham University, 1985.

Hunter, Lynette. "J. M. Barrie: The Rejection of Fantasy." *Scottish Literary Journal* 5 (1978): 39–52.

———. "J. M. Barrie's Islands of Fantasy." *Modern Drama* 23 (1980): 65–74.

Jack, R. D. S. "The Manuscript of *Peter Pan.*" *Children's Literature* 18 (1990): 101–113.

———. *The Road to the Never Land: A Reassessment of J. M. Barrie's Dramatic Art.* Aberdeen: Aberdeen Univ. Press, 1991.

James, Brian. "We are Truly the Lost Children." (London) *Times Saturday Review* (Dec 22, 1990): 4–6.

Karpe, Marietta. "The Origins of Peter Pan." *Psychoanalytic Review* 43, no. 1 (Jan 1956): 104–110.

Kissel, Susan S. "'But When at Last She Really Came, I Shot Her': *Peter Pan* and the Drama of Gender." *Children's Literature in Education* 19 (Spring 1988): 32–41.

Last, Richard. "Subtle Study of Barrie and His Lost Boys." *Daily Telegraph* (London) 38369 (Oct 17, 1978): 8.

Lurie, Alison. "The Boy Who Couldn't Grow Up." *New York Review of Books,* vol. XXII, 1 (Feb 6, 1975): 11–15.

Lynch, Catherine M. "Winnie Foster and Peter Pan: Facing the Dilemma of Growth." In *Proceedings of the Ninth Annual Conference of the Children's Literature Association.* Univ. of Florida, March 1982. Ypsilanti, MI: Children's Literature Association, 1983, pp. 107–111.

MacAskill, Hilary. "The Battle for *Peter*'s Rich Legacy." *Guardian* (Dec 21, 1987): 8.

McGowan, Maureen Ann. "An Analysis of the Fantasy Plays of James M. Barrie Utilizing

Vladimir Propp's Structural Model of the Fairy Tale." Ph.D. diss., New York University, 1984.

Mackail, Denis. *Barrie: The Story of J. M. B.* New York: Scribner, 1941.

McPherson, Kay. "The Lost Boy Who Wrote *Peter Pan.*" *School Library Journal* 35 (Jan 1989): 32–33.

Margraf, Carl. *J. M. Barrie: An Annotated Secondary Bibliography.* Greensboro, NC: ELT Press, 1989.

Marsh, Corinna. "Eleven Little Girls and *Peter Pan.*" *Horn Book* 31 (June 1955): 199–206.

Master, Helen. "Peter's Kensington." *Horn Book* 10 (Sept 1934): 316–321.

Meisel, Frederick L. "The Myth of Peter Pan." *Psychoanalytic Study of the Child* 32 (1977): 545–563.

Mobley, Valerie. "The Retelling of *Peter Pan.*" *S. M. M. A. R. T. Journal* (Australia) 2 (1977): 2–7.

Murray, Thomas J. "J. M. Barrie and the Search for Self." Ph.D. diss., Harvard University, 1988.

The Oxford Companion to Children's Literature. Edited by Humphrey Carpenter and Mari Prichard. New York: Oxford Univ. Press, 1984, pp. 45–48, 320–321, 403–407.

Pflieger, Pat, and Helen M. Hill. *A Reference Guide to Modern Fantasy for Children.* Westport, CT: Greenwood, 1984, pp. xii–xiii, 42–46, 432–436.

Philip, Neil. "Letters." *Signal* 38 (May 1982): 129–132. A response to Tucker, below.

Rotert, Richard. "The Kiss in a Box." *Children's Literature* 18 (1990): 114–123.

Roy, James A. *James Matthew Barrie: An Appreciation.* New York: Scribner, 1938.

Russell, Patricia Read. "Parallel Romantic Fantasies: Barrie's *Peter Pan* and Spielberg's *E. T.: The Extraterrestrial.*" *Children's Literature Association Quarterly* 8 (Winter 1983): 28–30.

Sims, George. "James Barrie and the Boy Castaways." *Antiquarian Book Monthly Review* (U.K.) XIV (Dec 1987): 452–461.

Skinner, John. "James M. Barrie, or the Boy Who Wouldn't Grow Up." *American Imago* 14 (Summer 1947): 111–141.

Smith, Louisa A. "*Peter Pan.*" In Frank N. Magill. *Survey of Modern Fantasy Literature,* vol. 3. Englewood Cliffs, NJ: Salem Press, 1983, pp. 1230–1233.

Stableford, Brian M. "J. M. Barrie." In *Supernatural Fiction Writers,* vol. 1. Edited by E. F. Bleiler. New York: Scribner, 1985, pp. 405–410.

Stevenson, Lionel. "A Source for Barrie's *Peter Pan.*" *Philological Quarterly* 8, no. 2 (Apr 1929): 210–214.

Storr, Catherine. "*Peter Pan.*" *Children's Literature in Education* 23 (Mar 1992): 15–26.

Stott, Jon C. *Children's Literature from A to Z.* New York: McGraw-Hill, 1984, p. 23.

Tucker, Nicholas. "Enchanted Chronicle." *New Society* (London) 18 (Dec 25, 1980): 568–569.

———. "Fly Away, Peter?" *Signal* 37 (Jan 1982): 43–49.

———. "*Peter Pan* Goes Public." *Books for Keeps* (U.K.) (Jan 1988): 4–5.

Twentieth-Century Children's Writers. 3rd ed. Edited by Tracy Chevalier and D. L. Kirkpatrick. Chicago: St. James, 1989, pp. 62–65.

Bauer, Marion Dane

Helbig, Alethea K., and Agnes Regan Perkins. *Dictionary of American Children's Fiction, 1960–1984.* Westport, CT: Greenwood, 1986, p. 40.

Baum, L(yman) Frank

Abraham, Paul M., and Stuart Kenter. "Tik-Tok and the Laws of Robotics." *Science-Fiction Studies* 5 (Mar 1978): 67–80.

Algeo, John. *"Oz* and Kansas: A Theosophical Quest." *Proceedings of the 13th Annual Conference of The Children's Literature Association, 1986.* New York: Pace University, 1988, pp. 135–139.

Alitzer, Nell. "Peonies, *Petites Madeleines,* and the Past." In *A Bridge to Magic Realms.* Fourth Biennial Conference on Literature and Hawaii's Children. Honolulu/Kamuela, June 23–28, 1988. A Humanities Guide, p. 6.

———. "The Wicked Witch of the West, the Wicked Witch of the East." In *Literature and Hawaii's Children,* ed. by Cristina Bacchilega and Steven Curry. Honolulu: Literature and Hawaii's Children, 1990, pp. 11–17.

The American Book Collector. Special issue on Baum 13, no. 4 (Dec 1962).

Anderson, Celia Catlett. "The Comedians of *Oz." Studies in American Humor* 5 (Winter 1986–1987): 229–242.

Attebery, Brian. "The Oz Books." In Frank N. Magill. *Survey of Modern Fantasy Literature,* vol. 3. Englewood Cliffs, NJ: Salem Press, 1983, pp. 1196–1208.

Baughman, Roland. "L. Frank Baum and the 'Oz Books.'" *Columbia Library Columns* 4 (May 1955): 15–35.

Baum, Frank Joslyn, and Russell P. McFall. *To Please a Child: A Biography of L. Frank Baum.* Chicago: Reilly and Lee, 1961.

Baum, Harry Neal. "How My Father Wrote the Oz Books." *American Book Collector* 13 (Dec 1962): 17.

Baum, Joan, and Roland Baughman. *L. Frank Baum: The Wonderful Wizard of Oz. An Exhibition of His Published Writings, in Commemoration of the Centenary of His Birth, May 15, 1856.* New York: Columbia Univ. Libraries, 1956.

Baum, L. Frank. "Modern Fairy Tales." *The Advance,* Aug 19, 1909.

———. *The Wizard of Oz.* Edited by Michael Patrick Hearn. New York: Schocken, 1983. Complete text plus 20 critical essays.

The Baum Bugle: A Journal of Oz. Kinderhook, IL: International Wizard of Oz Club, 1957–.

Beckwith, Osmond. "The Oddness of Oz." In *Children's Literature,* vol. 5. Philadelphia: Temple Univ. Press, 1976, pp. 74–91.

Bewley, Marius. "The Land of Oz: America's Great Good Place." *New York Review of Books,* Dec 3, 1964. Reprinted in Marius Bewley. *Masks and Mirrors: Essays in Criticism.* New York: Atheneum, 1970, pp. 255–267.

Billman, Carol. "'I've Seen the Movie': Oz Revisited." In Douglas Street. *Children's Novels and the Movies.* New York: Ungar, 1983, pp. 92–100.

Brotman, Jordan. "A Late Wanderer in Oz." *Chicago Review* 18, no. 2 (1965): 63–73. Reprinted in Sheila A. Egoff. *Only Connect.* New York: Oxford Univ. Press, 1980, pp. 156–169.

Callahan, Jean. "I Have the Feeling We're Not in Kansas Any More." *American Film* 10 (May 1985): 24.

Callary, Edward, ed. *From Oz to the Onion Patch.* DeKalb, IL: North Central Name Society, 1986.

Carpenter, Lynette. "There's No Place Like Home: *The Wizard of Oz* and American Isolationism." *Film and History* 15 (1985): 37–45.

Cath, Stanley H., and Claire Cath. "On the Other Side of Oz: Psychoanalytic Aspects of Fairy Tales." *Psychoanalytic Study of the Child* 33 (1978): 621–639.

Chadwick, Joseph. "The Politics of Action and Magic in *The Wonderful Wizard of Oz.*" In *Literature and Hawaii's Children.* Proceedings of the Third Biennial Conference on Literature and Hawaii's Children. Honolulu: Literature and Hawaii's Children, 1988, pp. 45–49.

Collins, Robert G. *"Star Wars:* The Pastiche of Myth and the Yearning for a Past Future." *Journal of Popular Culture* 11 (Summer 1977): 1–10.

Culver, Stuart. "What Manikins Want: *The Wonderful Wizard of Oz* and *The Art of Decorating Dry Goods Windows." Representations* 21 (1988): 97–116.

De Luca, Geraldine, and Roni Natov. "Researching Oz: An Interview with Michael Patrick Hearn." *The Lion and the Unicorn* 11 (Oct 1987): 51–62.

Dempsey, David. "The Wizardry of L. Frank Baum." In William Targ. *Bibliophile in the Nursery.* Chicago: World, 1957, pp. 387–391.

Donovan, Ann. "*Alice* and Dorothy: Reflections from Two Worlds." In *Webs and Wardrobes: Humanist and Religious World Views in Children's Literature,* ed. by Joseph O'Beirne Milner and Lucy Floyd Morcock Milner. Lanham, MD: University Press of America, 1987, pp. 25–31.

Downing, David C. "Waiting for Godoz: A Post-Nasal Deconstruction of the Wizard of Oz." *Christianity and Literature* 33 (Winter 1984): 28–30.

Doyle, Brian. *The Who's Who of Children's Literature.* New York: Schocken, 1968, pp. 22–26.

Elms, Alan C. "Oz in Science Fiction Film." *The Baum Bugle* 27 (Winter 1983): 2–7.

Erisman, Fred. "L. Frank Baum and the Progressive Dilemma." *American Quarterly* 20 (Fall 1968): 616–623.

Eyles, Allen. *The World of Oz: An Historical Expedition Over the Rainbow, 1900–1985.* Harmondsworth: Viking, 1985.

Fisher, Eugene J. "Gopher Prairie and the Emerald City: A Comparison of Themes and Techniques of Sinclair Lewis and L. Frank Baum." *The Baum Bugle* 26 (Winter 1982): 14–16.

Ford, Alla T., and Dick Martin. *The Musical Fantasies of L. Frank Baum.* Torrance, CA: Wizard Press, 1958.

Frey, Charles, and John Griffiths. *The Literary Heritage of Childhood: An Appraisal of Children's Classics in the Western Tradition.* Westport, CT: Greenwood, 1987, pp. 169–174.

Gardner, Martin. "A Child's Garden of Bewilderment: *Alice's Adventures in Wonderland* and *The Wonderful Wizard of Oz* Compared." *Saturday Review,* July 17, 1965, pp. 18–19, and Aug 14, 1965, p. 26. Reprinted in Sheila A. Egoff. *Only Connect.* New York: Oxford Univ. Press, 1980, pp. 150–155.

———. "The Enchanted Isle of Yew: Baum's Adult Children's Books." *Baum Bugle* 34 (Spring 1990): 13–14, 29–30.

———. "John Dough and the Cherub." *Children's Literature,* vol. 2. Storrs, CT: Journal of the Modern Language Association, 1973, pp. 110–118.

———. "Librarians in Oz." *Saturday Review* 42 (Apr 11, 1959): 18–19.

———. "Why Librarians Dislike Oz." *Library Journal* 88 (Feb 1963): 834–836; *School Library Journal* 10 (Feb 1963): 22–24. Reprinted from *American Book Collector* 13 (Dec 1962): 14–16.

Gardner, Martin, and Russell B. Nye. *The Wizard of Oz and Who He Was.* East Lansing: Michigan State Univ. Press, 1957.

Gessel, Michael. "The Other Father of *Oz* [W. W. Denslow]." *Baum Bugle* 36 (Autumn 1992): 3–4.

Gilead, S. "Magic Abjured: Closure in Children's Fantasy Fiction." *Publications of the Modern Language Association* 106 (Mar 1991): 277–293.

Glassman, P. "The Wonderful World of Oz." *A.B. Bookman's Weekly* 72 (Nov 14, 1983): 3329–3334. (bibliographic essay)

———. "The World of Oz Lives On." *A.B. Bookman's Weekly* 76 (Aug 19–26, 1985): 1198–1203.

Gose, Elliott. *Mere Creatures: A Study of Modern Fantasy Tales for Children.* Toronto: Univ. of Toronto Press, 1988, pp. 90–107.

Greene, David L. "Collecting *Oz* and L. Frank Baum: Then and Now." *AB Bookman's Weekly* 92 (Nov 8, 1993): 1860+. Bibliographic essay.

——— "The Concept of Oz." In *Children's Literature,* vol. 3. Storrs, CT: Journal of the Modern Language Association, 1974, pp. 173–176.

————. "L. Frank Baum: Science Fiction and Fantasy." *Children's Literature Association Quarterly* 5 (Winter 1981): 13–16. Reprinted in Patricia Dooley. *The First Steps.* West Lafayette, IN: Children's Literature Association Publications, 1984, pp. 60–61.

Greene, David L., and Dick Martin. *The Oz Scrapbook.* New York: Random, 1977.

Greene, Douglas G. "Bibliographical Baumania." *The Baum Bugle* 29 (Autumn 1985): 20–21.

Griswold, Jerry. *Audacious Kids: Coming of Age in America's Classic Children's Books.* New York: Oxford Univ. Press, 1992. *The Wizard of Oz,* pp. 29–41.

————. "There's No Place But Home: *The Wizard of Oz.*" *Antioch Review* 45 (Fall 1987): 462–475.

Hamilton, Margaret. "There's No Place Like Oz." In *Children's Literature,* vol. 10. New Haven, CT: Yale Univ. Press, 1982, pp. 153–158.

Hanff, Peter E., and Douglas G. Greene. *Bibliographia Oziana: A Concise Bibliographical Checklist of the Oz Books by L. Frank Baum and His Successors.* Demorest, GA: International Wizard of Oz Club, 1976.

Harmetz, Aljean. *The Making of "The Wizard of Oz."* New York: Knopf, 1977; reprinted New York: Limelight, 1984, #1060.

Hearn, Michael Patrick. "Charles Santore's Journey to the Great Oz." *Baum Bugle* 34 (Winter 1990): 6–7.

————. "Discovering Oz (The Great and Terrible) at the Library of Congress." *Quarterly Journal of the Library of Congress* 39 (Spring 1982): 70–79.

————. "L. Frank Baum." In *American Writers for Children, 1900–1960. Dictionary of Literary Biography,* vol. 22. Detroit: Gale, 1983, pp. 13–36.

————. "L. Frank Baum." In *Writers for Children: Critical Studies of Major Authors Since the Seventeenth Century.* Edited by Jane M. Bingham. New York: Scribner, 1988, pp. 37–48.

————. "L. Frank Baum and the Modernized Fairy Tale." *Children's Literature in Education* 33 (Summer 1979): 57–67.

————. "The Mantle of *Oz* Is Passed." *Baum Bugle* 55, no. 2 (Autumn 1991): 3–6.

————. "When L. Frank Baum was 'Laura Bancroft.'" *American Book Collector* 8 (May 1987): 11–16.

————. "The Wizard of Oz." Unpublished paper. Presented at the meeting of the Modern Language Association, 1974.

————, ed. *The Annotated Wizard of Oz.* New York: Potter, 1973.

————, ed. *The Wizard of Oz: The Critical Heritage.* New York: Schocken, 1983.

Helbig, Alethea K., and Agnes Regan Perkins. *Dictionary of American Children's Fiction, 1859–1959.* Westport, CT: Greenwood, 1985, pp. 37, 576–577.

Hudlin, Edward W. "The Mythology of Oz: An Interpretation." *Papers on Language and Literature* 25 (Fall 1989): 443–464.

Indick, Ben P. "L. Frank Baum: The Wonderful Wizard of Oz." *Anduril* 7 (1979): 7–14.

Jackson, Shirley. "The Lost Kingdom of Oz." *The Reporter,* Dec 10, 1959, pp. 42–43.

Jones, Alan. "*Return to Oz.*" *Cinefantastique* 15 (July 1985): 27–31.

Jones, Vernon H. "The Oz Parade." *New Orleans Review* 3 (1973): 375–378.

Keller, Karl. "L. Frank Baum: The Wizard of Coronado." *Seacoast* 2 (Feb 1981): 52–55.

Knoepflmacher, U. C. "Roads Half Taken: Travel, Fantasy and Growing Up." *Proceedings of the 13th Annual Conference of The Children's Literature Association, 1986.* New York: Pace University, 1988, pp. 48–59.

Koelle, Barbara. "After *The Wizard:* The Influence of America's Best Loved Fairy Tales on Other Fantasies for Children." *Baum Bugle* 33 (Spring 1989): 16–21.

Kopp, Sheldon. "The Wizard of Oz behind the Couch." *Psychology Today* 3, no. 10 (Mar 1970): 70.

Laumer, March. "*Oz* in Russia: *The Yellow Fog* [by Alexander Volkov]." *Baum Bugle* 32 (1988): 8–11.

Littlefield, Henry M. "The Wizard of Oz: Parable on Populism." *American Quarterly* 16 (Spring 1964): 47–58.

Luehrs, R. B. "Nineteenth-Century Profile: L. Frank Baum and the Land of Oz: A Children's Author as Social Critic." *Nineteenth Century* 6, no. 3 (Aug 1980): 55–57.

MacFall, Russell P. "L. Frank Baum—Shadow and Substance." *American Book Collector* 13 (Dec 1962): 9, 11.

McGraw, Eloise Jarvis. "On Wearing Well." *Baum Bugle* 34 (Winter 1990): 3–5.

McGuire, Willam. *From Tolkien to Oz.* Parsippany, NJ: Unicorn, 1985. The Art of Greg Hildebrandt.

McMaster, Juliet. "The Trinity Archetype in *The Jungle Books* and *The Wizard of Oz.*" *Children's Literature* 20 (1992): 90–110.

Mannix, Daniel P. "The Annotated *Road to Oz* (Part II)" *Baum Bugle* 34 (Winter 1990): 10–14.

———. "The Father of *The Wizard of Oz.*" *American Heritage* 16 (Dec 1964): 36–47, 108–109.

Martin, Dick. "The First Edition of *The Wonderful Wizard.*" *American Book Collector* 13 (Dec 1962): 26–27.

Maund, Patrick. "*American Fairy Tales* (1901)." *Baum Bugle* 34 (Spring 1990): 19–20.

Moore, Raylyn. *Wonderful Wizard, Marvelous Land.* Bowling Green, OH: Bowling Green Univ. Press, 1974.

Nye, Russell B. "The Wizardess of Oz—And Who She Is." In *Children's Literature,* vol. 2. Storrs, CT: Journal of the Modern Language Association, 1973, pp. 119–122.

The Oxford Companion to Children's Literature. Edited by Humphrey Carpenter and Mari Prichard. New York: Oxford Univ. Press, 1984, pp. 50–51, 578–579.

Pattrick, Robert B. *Unexplored Territory in Oz: An Excursion through Hitherto Uncharted Regions.* Demorest, GA: International Wizard of Oz Club, 1975.

Perry, George. "Back on the Road to *Oz.*" *Sunday Times Magazine* (May 5, 1985): 26–28, 31.

Philip, Neil. "Follow the Yellow Brick Road." *Times Educational Supplement* (Dec 29, 1989): 16.

Prentice, Ann E. "Have You Been to See the Wizard: Oz Revisited." *Top of the News* 27 (Nov 1970): 32–44.

Rakestrow, Mary. "The Mystery of Dr. Nikikik and Dr. Pipt." *Baum Bugle* 34 (Spring 1990): 9–10.

Reckford, Kenneth. "Allegiance to Utopia." *Baum Bugle* 32 (1988): 11–13.

Rowe, David. "The L. Frank Baum Collection at the Alexander Mitchell Library." *Baum Bugle* 34 (Spring 1990): 11–12.

Rushdie, Salman. "Out of Kansas." *New Yorker* 11 (May 1992): 93–103.

Sackett, S. J. "The Utopia of Oz." *Georgia Review* 14 (Fall 1960): 275–291.

Salc, Roger. "Baum's Magic Powder of Life." *Children's Literature,* vol. 8. New Haven: Yale University Press, 1980, pp. 157–163.

———. "Child Reading and Man Reading: Oz, Babar and Pooh." In *Children's Literature,* vol. 1. Storrs, CT: Journal of the Modern Language Association, 1972, pp. 162–172. Reprinted in *Reflections on Literature for Children,* ed. by Francelia Butler and Richard Rotert. Hamden, CT: Shoe String Press, 1984, pp. 19–31.

———. *Fairy Tales and After: From Snow White to E. B. White.* Cambridge, MA: Harvard Univ. Press, 1978, pp. 223–244.

———. "L. Frank Baum and Oz." *Hudson Review* 25 (Winter 1972–1973): 571–592.

Schuman, Samuel. "Out of the Fryeing Pan and Into the Pyre: Comedy, Myth and *The Wizard of Oz.*" *Journal of Popular Culture* 7 (Fall 1973): 302–304. Reprinted as "Comic Mythos and Children's Literature—Or, Out of the Fryeing Pan and Into the Pyre." In *It's a Funny Thing, Humor.* Edited by Antony J. Chapman and Hugh C. Foot. Elmsford, NY: Pergamon Press, 1977, pp. 119–121.

Searles, Baird, Beth Meacham, and Michael Franklin. *A Reader's Guide to Fantasy.* New York: Avon, 1982, pp. 26–27.

Shepherd, Kenneth R. "Communications and Oz." *Baum Bugle* 32 (1988): 6–7.

———. "Restoration of Oz." *Baum Bugle* 34 (Winter 1990): 19–20.

Shippey, Tom. "Darling Children." *Times Literary Supplement* (Apr 17, 1992): 18.

Smyers, R. P. "A Librarian Looks at Oz." *Library Occurrent* (Indiana State University) 21 (Dec 1964): 190–192.

Snow, Jack. *Who's Who in Oz.* Chicago: Reilly and Lee, 1954; New York: Bedrick, 1988.

Stott, Jon C. *Children's Literature from A to Z.* New York: McGraw-Hill, 1984, p. 25.

Street, Douglas. "The Wonderful Wiz That Was: The Curious Transformation of *The Wizard of Oz.*" *Kansas Quarterly* 16 (Summer 1984): 91–98.

Third Book of Junior Authors. Edited by Doris De Montreville and Donna Hill. New York: Wilson, 1972, pp. 28–29.

Thurber, James. "The Wizard of Chitenago." *New Republic* 21 (Dec 12, 1934): 141–142. Reprinted in Boyer and Zahorski. *Fantasists on Fantasy.* New York: Avon, 1984, pp. 59–66.

Tuerk, Richard. "Dorothy's Timeless Quest." *Mythlore* 17 (Autumn 1990): 20–24.

Twentieth-Century Children's Writers. 3rd ed. Edited by Tracy Chevalier and D. L. Kirkpatrick. Chicago: St. James, 1989, pp. 66–69.

Vander Noot, Jim. "Establishing Ozian Geography." *Baum Bugle* 35 (Spring 1991): 13–16.

Veglahn, Nancy. "Images of Evil: Male and Female Monsters in Heroic Fantasy." *Children's Literature* 15 (1987): 106–119.

Vidal, Gore. "On Rereading the Oz Books." *New York Review of Books,* Oct 13, 1977, pp. 38–42.

———. "The Wizard of *The Wizard.*" *New York Review of Books,* Sept 29, 1977, pp. 10–15.

Vogel, Carl S. "The Amazonia of Oz." *The Baum Bugle* 26 (Autumn 1982): 4–8.

Wagenknecht, Edward. *Utopia America.* Seattle: Univ. of Washington Press, 1929; rev. ed. entitled "The Yellow Brick Road." In *As Far as Yesterday: Memories and Reflections.* Stillwater: Univ. of Oklahoma Press, 1968, pp. 63–79.

———. "'Utopia America' A Generation Afterwards." *American Book Collector* 13 (Dec 1962): 12–13.

"*The Wonderful Wizard of Oz.*" *Literature Base* (Australia) 1, no. 4 (Oct 1990): 15–20.

Watkins, Tony. "Cultural Studies, New Historicism and Children's Literature." In *Literature for Children: Contemporary Criticism,* ed. by Peter Hunt. London: Routledge, 1992, pp. 173–195.

West, Mark I. "The Dorothys of Oz: A Heroine's Unmasking." In *Story and Society: Children's Literature in Its Social Context,* ed. by Dennis Butts. London: Macmillan, 1992, pp. 125–131.

"Why *The Wizard of Oz* Is So Popular." *Unabashed Librarian* 85 (1992): 27. Reprinted from the *New York Times,* Nov 28, 1991.

B. B. (pseud. of D[enys] J[ames] Watkins-Pitchford)

Crouch, Marcus. "B. B. at 80." *Junior Bookshelf* 49, no. 4 (1985): 165–168.

Doyle, Brian. *The Who's Who of Children's Literature.* New York: Schocken, 1968, pp. 284–285.

Driver, Christopher. "A Wildfowler with a Delicate Eye for the Detail of County Life." *Guardian* (Sept 13, 1990): 39.

Fisher, Marjorie T. "B. B. As a Writer for Young People." *Bookbird* 5, no. 3 (1967): 21–27.

"*The Little Grey Men.*" In M. Crouch and A. Ellis. *Chosen for Children.* 3rd ed. London: The Library Association, 1977, pp. 30–34.

McEwen, John. "A Hunter Home from the Hills." (London) *Daily Telegraph* (Dec 2, 1989): xi.

Moorehead, Caroline. "Cry for a Vanished World." *Books for Your Children* (U.K.) 14 (Spring 1979): 15.

Oakes, Philip. "A Long Dream of England." *Sunday (London) Times* (Aug 20, 1978): 35.

The Oxford Companion to Children's Literature. Edited by Humphrey Carpenter and Mari Prichard. New York: Oxford Univ. Press, 1984, p. 52.

Ringrose, Christopher. "Getting Lost in a Book: The Gnomes and the Reader in B. B.'s *Little Grey Men* Novels." *Children's Literature in Education* 21 (Sept 1990): 145–154.

Ryan, J. S. "'B. B.'—Delineator of England's Natural Glories." *Orana* 19 (Feb 1983): 11–24.

Third Book of Junior Authors. Edited by Doris De Montreville and Donna Hill. New York: Wilson, 1972, pp. 32–33.

Twentieth-Century Children's Writers. 3rd ed. Edited by Tracy Chevalier and D. L. Kirkpatrick. Chicago: St. James, 1989, pp. 1017–1018.

Watkins-Pitchford, D. J. "Writing for Young People." *Federation of Children's Book Groups Year Book* (U.K.) 7 (1975–1976): 44–45.

Beachcroft, Nina

Thomson, Pat. "Meet Nina Beachcroft." *Books for Keeps* (U.K.) (July 21, 1983): 26.

Twentieth-Century Children's Writers. 3rd ed. Edited by Tracy Chevalier and D. L. Kirkpatrick. Chicago: St. James, 1989, p. 71.

Beagle, Peter S(oyer)

Foust, R. E. "Fabulous Paradigm: Fantasy, Meta-Fantasy, and Peter S. Beagle's *The Last Unicorn.*" *Extrapolation* 21 (1980): 5–20.

Hark, I. R. "The Fantasy Worlds of Peter Beagle." In *Survey of Modern Fantasy Literature,* vol. 2. Edited by Frank N. Magill. Englewood Cliffs, NJ: Salem Press, 1983, pp. 526–534.

Manlove, C. N. *The Impulse of Fantasy Literature.* Kent, OH: Kent State Univ. Press, 1983, pp. 148–154.

"'A Myth, a Memory, a Will-O' the-Wish': Peter Beagle's Funny Fantasy." In *Reflections on the Fantastic.* Edited by Michael R. Collings. Westport, CT: Greenwood, 1986.

Norford, Don Parry. "Reality and Illusion in Peter Beagle's *The Last Unicorn.*" *Critique: Studies in Modern Fiction* 19 (1987): 93–104.

Olsen, Alexandra Hennessey. "The *Anti-Consolatio*: Boethius and *The Last Unicorn.*" *Mosaic* 13 (Spring/Summer 1980): 133–144.

Pennington, John. "Innocence and Experience and the Imagination in the World of Peter S. Beagle." *Mythlore* 15 (Summer 1989): 10–16.

Samuelson, David N. "Peter S. Beagle." In *Supernatural Fiction Writers,* vol. 2. Edited by E. F. Bleiler. New York: Scribner, 1985, pp. 987–992.

Schlobin, Roger C. "The Fool and the Fantastic." *Fantasy Newsletter* 43 (1981): 6–9, 29.

Searles, Baird, Beth Meacham, and Michael Franklin. *A Reader's Guide to Fantasy.* New York: Avon, 1982, pp. 28–29.

Stevens, David. "Incongruity in a World of Illusion: Patterns of Humor in Peter Beagle's *The Last Unicorn.*" *Extrapolation* 20 (1979): 230–237.

Tobin, Jean. "Introduction." By Peter S. Beagle. *The Last Unicorn.* Boston: Gregg, 1978, pp. v–xxiv.

Van Becker, David. "Time, Space, and Consciousness in the Fantasy of Peter S. Beagle." *San José Studies* 1 (1975): 52–61.

Bear, Greg(ory Dale)

Bear, Greg. "Beneath the Dream: Tomorrow through the Past." *Bulletin of the Science Fiction Writers of America* 14 (1979): 38–40.
Klein, Jay Kay. "Greg Bear." *Analog* (June 1983): 37.
Twentieth-Century Science Fiction Writers. 3rd ed. Edited by Noelle Watson and Paul E. Schellinger. Chicago: St. James Press, 1991, pp. 41–42.
Thomas, Pascal J. "Interview with Greg Bear." *Thrust* 27 (1987): 8–10.
Vorda, Allan. "The Forging of Science Fiction: An Interview with Greg Bear." *Extrapolation* 31 (Fall 1990): 197–215.

Beaumont, Madame le Prince de

Barchilon, J. "A Note on the Original Text of 'Beauty and the Beast.'" *Modern Language Review* 56 (Jan 1961): 81–82.
Mintz, Thomas. "The Meaning of Rose in 'Beauty and the Beast.'" *Psychoanalytic Review* 56 (1969–1970): 615–620.
Zipes, Jack. "The Dark Side of 'Beauty and the Beast': The Origins of the Literary Fairy Tale for Children." In *Proceedings of the Eighth Annual Conference of the Children's Literature Association.* University of Minnesota, March 1981. Ypsilanti, MI: Children's Literature Association, 1982, pp. 119–125.

Bedard, Michael

Ellis, Sarah. "News from the North." *Horn Book* 68 (Jan–Feb 1992): 109–111.
Jenkinson, Dave H. "Portraits: Michael Bedard." *Emergency Librarian* 19 (Nov–Dec 1991): 66–70.

Behn, Harry

Behn, Harry. "A Definition Implied." *Horn Book* 43 (Oct 1967): 561–564.
———. "The Golden Age." *Horn Book* 36 (Apr 1960): 109–115.
———. "Poetry, Fantasy, and Reality." *Elementary English* 43 (Apr 1965): 355–361.
———. "Poetry for Children." *Horn Book* 42 (Apr 1966): 163–175.
Gillespie, John T., and Diana Lembo. *Juniorplots: A Book Talk Manual for Teachers and Librarians.* New York: Bowker, 1967, pp. 12–13.
Helbig, Alethea K., and Agnes Regan Perkins. *Dictionary of American Children's Fiction, 1960–1984.* Westport, CT: Greenwood, 1986, pp. 46, 204.
More Junior Authors. Edited by Muriel Fuller. New York: Wilson, 1963, pp. 12–13.
Richardson, Carmen C. "Harry Behn: Wizard of Childhood." *Elementary English* 51 (Oct 1974): 975–976, 1002.
Roop, Peter. "Profile: Harry Behn." *Language Arts* 62 (Jan 1985): 92–94.
Twentieth-Century Children's Writers. 3rd ed. Edited by Tracy Chevalier and D. L. Kirkpatrick. Chicago: St. James, 1989, pp. 74–75.
Viguers, Ruth H. "*The Faraway Lurs,* a Review." *Horn Book* 39 (Apr 1963): 164.

Bell, Thelma Harrington

Gillespie, John T. *Juniorplots 4: A Book Talk Guide for Use with Readers Ages 12–16.* New Providence, NJ: Bowker, 1993, pp. 188–192.
Helbig, Alethea K., and Agnes Regan Perkins. *Dictionary of American Children's Fiction, 1960–1984.* Westport, CT: Greenwood, 1986, pp. 46, 543–544.

Third Book of Junior Authors. Edited by Doris De Montreville and Donna Hill. New York: Wilson, 1972, pp. 35–36.

Bellairs, John

Burgess, Mary A. "*The Face in the Frost.*" In Frank N. Magill. *Survey of Modern Fantasy Literature,* vol. 1. Englewood Cliffs, NJ: Salem Press, 1983, pp. 508–510.

Fifth Book of Junior Authors and Illustrators. Edited by Sally Holmes Holtz. New York: Wilson, 1983, pp. 26–27.

Helbig, Alethea, and Agnes Regan Perkins. *Dictionary of American Children's Fiction, 1985–1989.* Westport, CT: Greenwood, 1993, pp. 22, 137–138.

Schmidt, Gary D. "See How They Grow: Character Development in Children's Series Books." *Children's Literature in Education* 18 (1987): 34–44.

Searles, Baird, Beth Meacham, and Micahel Franklin. *A Reader's Guide to Fantasy.* New York: Avon, 1982, p. 30.

Stasio, Marilyn. "Under the Spell of Scary Stuff." *New York Times Book Review* (June 9, 1991): 53.

Bellamy, Edward

Gies, Joseph. "Looking Forward to Utopia." *Vocational Education* 57 (Jan–Feb 1982): 30–31.

James, Max H. "The Polarity of Individualism and Conformity, a Dynamic of the Dream of Freedom, Examinied in *Looking Backward.*" *Christianity and Literature* 35 (1985): 17–59.

Jehmlich, Reimer. "Cog-Work: The Organization of Labor in Edward Bellamy's *Looking Backward* and in Later Utopian Fiction." In *Clockwork Worlds.* Edited by Richard D. Erlich and Thomas P. Dunn. Westport, CT: Greenwood, 1983.

Kerr, Howard, John W. Crowley, and Charles W. Crowley, eds. *The Haunted Dusk: American Supernatural Fiction, 1820–1920.* Athens: Univ. of Georgia Press, 1983.

Michaels, Walter Benn. "An American Tragedy; or, the Promise of American Life: Classes and Individuals." *Representation* 25 (Winter 1989): 71–98.

Pfaelzer, Jean. "A State of One's Own: Feminism as Ideology in American Utopias 1880–1915." *Extrapolation* 24 (Winter 1983): 311–328.

Rosemont, Franklin. "Free Play and No Limit: An Introduction to Edward Bellamy's Utopia." In *Popular Culture in America,* ed. by Paul Buhle. Minneapolis: Univ. of Minnesota Press, 1987, pp. 26–37.

Thomas, W. K. "The Underside of Utopias." *College English* 38 (1976): 356–372.

Twentieth-Century Science Fiction Writers. 3rd ed. Edited by Noelle Watson and Paul E. Schellinger. Chicago: St. James Press, 1991, pp. 43–44.

Widdicombe, Richard Toby. "Edward Bellamy's Utopian Vision: An Annotated Checklist of Reviews." *Extrapolation* 29 (Spring 1988): 5–20.

Williams, Raymond. "Utopia and Science Fiction." *Science Fiction Studies* 5 (1978): 203–214.

Winters, Donald E. "The Utopianism of Survival: Bellamy's *Looking Backward* and Twain's *A Connecticut Yankee.*" *American Studies* 21 (1980): 23–28.

Bemelmans, Ludwig

More Junior Authors. Edited by Muriel Fuller. New York: Wilson, 1963, pp. 14–15.

Benary-Isbert, Margot

Benary-Isbert, Margot. "An Author's Reflections." *Library Journal* 82 (May 15, 1957): 1329–1334.
———. "Editorial: The Light in the Darkness." *Horn Book* 34 (Dec 1958): 443.
———. "The Need of Understanding in Our Shrinking World." *Horn Book* 31 (June 1955): 167–176.
———. "On Words, Singleness of Mind, and the Genius Loci." *Horn Book* 40 (Apr 1964): 202–208.
Gillespie, John T., and Diana Lembo. *Introducing Books: A Guide for the Middle Grades.* New York: Bowker, 1970, pp. 109–111.
More Junior Authors. Edited by Muriel Fuller. New York: Wilson, 1963, p. 15.

Benchley, Nathaniel (Goddard)

Fourth Book of Junior Authors and Illustrators. Edited by Doris De Montreville and Elizabeth D. Crawford. New York: Wilson, 1978, pp. 36–37.
Helbig, Alethea K., and Agnes Regan Perkins. *Dictionary of American Children's Fiction, 1960–1984.* Westport, CT: Greenwood, 1986, pp. 47–48.
Twentieth-Century Children's Writers. 3rd ed. Edited by Tracy Chevalier and D. L. Kirkpatrick. Chicago: St. James, 1989, pp. 80–81.

Bendick, Jeanne

More Junior Authors. Edited by Muriel Fuller. New York: Wilson, 1963, p. 16.

Benét, Stephen Vincent

Bromley, Robin. "Stephen Vincent Benét." In *Supernatural Fiction Writers: Fantasy and Horror,* vol. 2. Edited by E. F. Bleiler. New York: Scribner, 1985, pp. 797–804.
Bennett, John. "The Love of Grotesquerie." *Horn Book* 4 (Aug 1928): 67–70.
Bennett, M. "Youth in Pleasant Places." *Horn Book* 36 (June 1960): 245–247.
Coyle, William, ed. *Ohio Authors and Their Books.* Cleveland: World, 1962.
Gunterman, Bertha. "The Astrologer's Tower." *Horn Book* 4 (Aug 1928): 63–66.
The Junior Book of Authors. 2nd rev. ed. Edited by Stanley J. Kunitz and Howard Haycraft. New York: Wilson, 1951, pp. 27–28.
Roginski, Jim, ed. *Newbery and Caldecott Medalists and Honor Book Winners.* Littleton, CO: Libraries Unlimited, 1982, pp. 44–45.
Smith, Janie M. "Author for Children in the South." *Horn Book* 18 (Mar 1942): 83–87.
———. "John Bennett of Chillicothe." *Horn Book* 19 (Jan 1943): 427–433.

Benson, E(dward) F(rederic)

Morgan, Chris. "E. F. Benson." In *Supernatural Fiction Writers,* vol. 1. Edited by E. F. Bleiler. New York: Scribner, 1985, pp. 491–496.
The Oxford Companion to Children's Literature. Edited by Humphrey Carpenter and Mari Prichard. New York: Oxford Univ. Press, 1984, p. 142.
Searles, A. L. "The Short Fiction of Benson." In *Survey of Modern Fantasy Literature,* vol. 3. Edited by Frank N. Magill. Englewood Cliffs, NJ: Salem Press, 1983, pp. 1433–1435.

Beresford, Elisabeth

Beresford, Elisabeth. "Growing Up with *The Wombles." Federation of Children's Book Groups Yearbook* (U.K.) 6 (1974–1975): 44.

————. "Ten Years with *The Wombles." Federation of Children's Book Groups Yearbook* (U.K.) 10 (1978–1979): 29.

Twentieth-Century Children's Writers. 3rd ed. Edited by Tracy Chevalier and D. L. Kirkpatrick. Chicago: St. James, 1989, pp. 83–85.

Berger, Thomas (Louis)

Chapman, Edgar L. "*Arthur Rex.*" In *Survey of Modern Fantasy Literature,* vol. 1. Edited by Frank N. Magill. Englewood Cliffs, NJ: Salem Press, 1983, pp. 57–60.

Evans, Gwyneth. "Harps and Harpers in Contemporary Fantasy." *The Lion and the Unicorn* 16 (Dec 1992): 199–209.

Thompson, Raymond H. "Humor and Irony in Modern Arthurian Fantasy: Thomas Berger's *Arthur Rex.*" *Kansas Quarterly* 16 (Summer 1984): 45–49.

Berton, Pierre

Hambleton, A. "Canadian Fantasy." *British Columbia Library Quarterly* 26 (Oct 1962): 11–13.

Sigman, Joseph. "Pierre Berton and the Romantic Tradition." *Canadian Children's Literature* 7 (1977): 21–27.

Stott, Jon C. "An Interview with Pierre Berton." *Canadian Children's Literature* 23/24 (1981): 4–19.

Best, (Oswald) Herbert

The Junior Book of Authors. 2nd rev. ed. Edited by Stanley J. Kunitz and Howard Haycraft. New York: Wilson, 1951, pp. 32–33.

Twentieth-Century Children's Writers. 3rd ed. Edited by Tracy Chevalier and D. L. Kirkpatrick. New York: St. Martin, 1989, pp. 87–88.

Besterman, Catherine

Helbig, Alethea K., and Agnes Regan Perkins. *Dictionary of American Children's Fiction, 1859–1959.* Westport, CT: Greenwood, 1985, pp. 46, 417.

Beston, Henry B.

The Junior Book of Authors. 2nd rev. ed. Edited by Stanley J. Kunitz and Howard Haycraft. New York: Wilson, 1951, pp. 33–34.

Bethancourt, T. Ernesto (pseud. of Tom Paisley)

Fifth Book of Junior Authors and Illustrators. Edited by Sally Holmes Holtze. New York: Wilson, 1983, pp. 31–32.

Speaking for Ourselves: Autobiographical Sketches by Notable Authors of Books for Young

Adults. Edited by Donald R. Gallo. Urbana, IL: National Council of Teachers of English, 1990, pp. 19–21.

Bianco, Margery (Winifred) Williams [Prior to 1925, she wrote as Margery Williams.]

Bechtel, Louise Seaman. "A Tribute to Margery Bianco." *Elementary English Review* 12 (June 1935): 147–149, 165.

Bianco, Margery Williams. "Easter Rabbits—And Others." *Horn Book* 27 (Mar–Apr 1951): 131–134.

———. "Our Youngest Critics." In Anne Carroll Moore and Bertha Mahony Miller. *Writing and Criticism.* Boston: Horn Book, 1951, pp. 47–57.

———. "Writing Books for Boys and Girls." *Elementary English Review* 14 (May 1937): 161–164.

Daniels, Steven V. "*The Velveteen Rabbit:* A Kleinian Perspective." *Children's Literature* 18 (1990): 17–30.

———. "*The Velveteen Rabbit:* Fragment of an Analysis." *The Psychoanalytic Study of the Child* 45 (1990): 295–315.

Doyle, Brian. *The Who's Who of Children's Literature.* New York: Schocken, 1968, pp. 28–29.

Helbig, Alethea K., and Agnes Regan Perkins. *Dictionary of American Children's Fiction, 1859–1959.* Westport, CT: Greenwood, 1985, p. 47.

The Junior Book of Authors. 2nd rev. ed. Edited by Stanley J. Kunitz and Howard Haycraft. New York: Wilson, 1951, pp. 34–36.

Moore, Anne Carroll. "Margery Williams Bianco, 1881–1944." *Horn Book* 21 (May–June 1945): 157–164.

Moore, Anne Carroll, and Bertha Mahony Miller, eds. *Writing and Criticism: A Book for Margery Bianco.* Boston: Horn Book, 1951.

The Oxford Companion to Children's Literature. Edited by Humphrey Carpenter and Mari Prichard. New York: Oxford Univ. Press, 1984, pp. 59–60.

Roginski, Jim, ed. *Newbery and Caldecott Medalists and Honor Book Winners.* Littleton, CO: Libraries Unlimited, 1982, pp. 48–50.

Ryan, J. S. "The Young Child as Sub–Creator: A Theology of Toys." *Orana* 18 (Nov 1982): 117–119.

Seaman, Louise. "About the Biancos." *Horn Book* 2 (Mar 1926): 17–25.

Stott, Jon C. *Children's Literature from A to Z.* New York: McGraw-Hill, 1984, p. 34.

Twentieth-Century Children's Writers. 3rd ed. Edited by Tracy Chevalier and D. L. Kirkpatrick. Chicago: St. James, 1989, pp. 90–91.

Whalen-Levitt, Peggy. "Margery Williams Bianco." In *Writers for Children: Critical Studies of Major Authors Since the Seventeenth Century.* Edited by Jane M. Bingham. New York: Scribner, 1988, pp. 63–68.

Bianco, Pamela

Helbig, Alethea K., and Agnes Regan Perkins. *Dictionary of American Children's Fiction, 1859–1959.* Westport, CT: Greenwood, 1985, pp. 47, 301–302.

Seaman, Louise. "About the Biancos." *Horn Book* 2 (Mar 1926): 17–25.

Biegel, Paul

Alcorn, Noeline. "Fantasy and Family Life: Children's Books from Northern Europe." *Children's Literature Association Yearbook.* Auckland, New Zealand: Children's Literature

Association, 1976, pp. 29–42. Discusses Astrid Lindgren, Maria Gripe, Christine Nöstlinger, Otfried Preussler, and Paul Biegel.

Biegel, Paul. "Tell Me a Story." *Horn Book* 58 (Feb 1982): 87–93.

"State Prize for Paul Biegel: Report of the Jury Presented to the Minister of Culture, Recreation and Social Work." *Junior Bookshelf* 39 (Feb 1975): 9–11. Translation from the Dutch journal *En Nu Over Jeugdliteratuur* 2, no. 1 (1975): 1–2.

Binns, Archie (Fred)

Helbig, Alethea K., and Agnes Regan Perkins. *Dictionary of American Children's Fiction, 1859–1959.* Westport, CT: Greenwood, 1985, p. 51.

Blackwood, Algernon (Henry)

Ashley, Mike. *Algernon Blackwood: A Bio-Bibliography.* New York: Greenwood, 1987.

Columbo, John Robert. *Blackwood's Books: A Bibliography Devoted to Algernon Blackwood.* Toronto: Hounslow, 1981.

Hudson, Derek. "A Study of Algernon Blackwood." In *Essays and Studies for 1961.* Edited by Derek Hudson. London: Murray, 1961, pp. 102–114.

Letson, Russell Francis. "The Approaches to Mystery: The Fantasies of Arthur Machen and Algernon Blackwood." Ph.D. diss., Southern Illinois University, 1975.

Punter, David. "Algernon Blackwood." In *Supernatural Fiction Writers: Fantasy and Horror,* vol. 1. Edited by E. F. Bleiler. New York: Scribner, 1985, pp. 463–469.

Searles, Baird, Beth Meacham, and Michael Franklin. *A Reader's Guide to Fantasy.* New York: Avon, 1982, pp. 31–32.

Stevenson, Lionel. "Purveyors of Myth and Magic." In *Yesterday and After: The History of the English Novel.* Totowa, NJ: Barnes and Noble, 1967, pp. 111–154.

Blishen, Edward

Blishen, Edward, ed. *The Thorny Paradise: Writers on Writing for Children.* Boston: Horn Book, 1975; Harmondsworth, Middlesex: Kestrel, 1975.

Garfield, Leon, Edward Blishen, and Charles Keeping. "Greek Myths and the Twentieth Century Reader." *Children's Literature in Education* 3 (Nov 1970): 48–65.

Bloch, Marie Halun

Fourth Book of Junior Authors and Illustrators. Edited by Doris De Montreville and Elizabeth D. Crawford. New York: Wilson, 1978, pp. 44–46.

Helbig, Alethea K., and Agnes Regan Perkins. *Dictionary of American Children's Fiction, 1960–1984.* Westport, CT: Greenwood, 1986, p. 59.

Bodecker, N(iels) M(ogens)

Twentieth-Century Children's Writers. 3rd ed. Edited by Tracy Chevalier and D. L. Kirkpatrick. Chicago: St. James, 1989, pp. 110–111.

Bond, (Thomas) Michael

Ash, Russell, and Michael Bond. *The Life and Times of Paddington Bear.* New York: Viking, 1989.

Blount, Margaret. "Animals Are Equal: A Bear in a London Family." In *Animal Land: The Creatures of Children's Fiction.* New York: Morrow, 1975, pp. 307–322.

Bond, Karen. "A Marmalade Paw on the Till." *Bookseller* (Feb 19, 1983): 574–575.

Bond, Michael. "Jumping In at the Deep End: On Writing for Children." *Horn Book* 56 (June 1980): 335–339.

———. "One Day . . . ." *School Bookshop News* (U.K.) 5 (Autumn 1976): 30–32.

Carter, Angela. "In the Bear Garden." *New Society* (London) 39 (Feb 24, 1977): 403–404.

Doyle, Brian. *The Who's Who of Children's Literature.* New York: Schocken, 1968, pp. 32–33.

Hopkins, Lee Bennett. "Michael Bond." In *More Books by More People.* New York: Citation Press, 1974, pp. 35–40.

Jones, Cornelia, and Olivia R. Way. "Michael Bond." In *British Children's Authors.* Chicago: American Library Association, 1976, pp. 49–54.

Khan, Naseem. "The Bear Truth." *Radio Times* (London) 225 (Oct 20–26, 1979). (interview)

The Oxford Companion to Children's Literature. Edited by Humphrey Carpenter and Mari Prichard. New York: Oxford Univ. Press, 1984, pp. 70, 393.

Stott, Jon C. *Children's Literature from A to Z.* New York: McGraw-Hill, 1984, p. 44.

Third Book of Junior Authors. Edited by Doris De Montreville and Donna Hill. New York: Wilson, 1972, pp. 40–41.

Twentieth-Century Children's Writers. 3rd ed. Edited by Tracy Chevalier and D. L. Kirkpatrick. Chicago: St. James, 1989, pp. 111–113.

Bond, Nancy (Barbara)

Bond, Nancy. "Conflict in Children's Literature." *Horn Book* 60 (June 1984): 297–306.

———. "Landscape of Fiction." In *Loughborough '83: Proceedings.* Welsh National Centre for Children's Literature, 1984, pp. 91–99.

———. "On Not Teaching Creative Writing." In *Innocence & Experience.* Edited by Barbara Harrison and Gregory Maguire. New York: Lothrop, 1987, pp. 445–446.

———. "A Writer's Freedom." *Catholic Library World* 56 (Nov 1984): 169–171.

Elleman, Barbara. "The *Booklist* Interview: Nancy Bond." *Booklist* 86 (June 15, 1990): 188–190.

Evans, Gwyneth. "Harps and Harpers in Contemporary Fantasy." *The Lion and the Unicorn* 16 (Dec 1992): 199–209.

Fifth Book of Junior Authors and Illustrators. Edited by Sally Holmes Holtze. New York: Wilson, 1983, pp. 38–40.

Filmer-Davies, Kath. "Welsh Myth and Contemporary Literature." *Mythlore* 73 (Summer 1993): 53–58. Discusses Susan Cooper, Nikolai Tolstoi, Lloyd Alexander, Madeleine L'Engle, Brian Caswell, Jay Ashton, and Nancy Bond.

Helbig, Alethea, and Agnes Regan Perkins. *Dictionary of American Children's Fiction, 1985–1989.* Westport, CT: Greenwood, 1993, pp. 27–28.

———. *Dictionary of American Children's Fiction, 1960–1984.* Westport, CT: Greenwood, 1986, pp. 65, 630–631.

Sullivan, C. W., III. "Nancy Bond and Welsh Traditions." *Children's Literature Association Quarterly* 11 (Spring 1986): 33–37.

———. "*A String in the Harp.*" In Frank N. Magill. *Survey of Modern Fantasy Literature,* vol. 4. Englewood Cliffs, NJ: Salem Press, 1983, pp. 1851–1853.

———. "Traditional Welsh Materials in Modern Fantasy." *Extrapolation* 28 (Spring 1987): 87–97.

———. *Welsh Celtic Myth in Modern Fantasy.* Westport, CT: Greenwood, 1989, pp. 45–54+.

Twentieth-Century Children's Writers. 3rd ed. Edited by Tracy Chevalier and D. L. Kirkpatrick. Chicago: St. James, 1989, pp. 113–114.

Bonham, Frank

Third Book of Junior Authors. Edited by Doris De Montreville and Donna Hill. New York: Wilson, 1972, pp. 42–43.

Bontemps, Arna (Wendell)

Bontemps, Arna. "The *Lonesome Boy* Theme." *Horn Book* 42 (Dec 1966): 672–680.
———. "Sad-Faced Author." *Horn Book* 15 (Jan–Feb 1939): 7–12.
The Junior Book of Authors. 2nd rev. ed. Edited by Stanley J. Kunitz and Howard Haycraft. New York: Wilson, 1951, pp. 39–40.
Ryder, Ione Morrison. "Arna Bontemps." *Horn Book* 15 (Jan–Feb 1939): 13–20.

Borges, Jorge Luis

Balderston, Daniel. *The Literary Universe of Jorge Luis Borges: An Index to References and Allusions to Persons, Titles, and Places in His Writings.* Westport, CT: Greenwood, 1986.
Barnstone, Willis, ed. *Borges at Eighty: Conversations.* Bloomington: Indiana Univ. Press, 1982.
Bell-Villada, Gene H. *Borges and His Fiction: A Guide to His Mind and Art.* Chapel Hill: Univ. of North Carolina Press, 1981.
Foster, David William. *Jorge Luis Borges: An Annotated Primary and Secondary Bibliography.* New York: Garland, 1984.
Fulton, Patricia Teague. "Borges, Hawthorne, and Poe: A Study of Significant Parallels in Their Theories and Methods of Short Story Writing." Ph.D. diss., Auburn University, 1979.
Gordon, Ambrose, Jr. "A Quiet Betrayal: Some Mirror Work in Borges." *Texas Studies in Literature and Language* 17 (1975): 207–218.
Hager, Stanton. "Places of the Looking Glass: Borges's Deconstruction of Metaphysics." In *The Scope of the Fantastic.* Edited by Robert A. Collins and Howard D. Pearce. Westport, CT: Greenwood, 1985, pp. 231–238.
Menton, S. "Jorge Luis Borges, Magic Realist." *Hispanic Review* 50 (Autumn 1982): 411–426.
Philmus, Robert M. "Wells and Borges and the Labyrinths of Time." *Science Fiction Studies* 1, pt. 4 (1974): 237–248.

Bosse, Malcolm J(oseph)

Fifth Book of Junior Authors and Illustrators. Edited by Sally Holmes Holtze. New York: Wilson, 1983, pp. 40–42.

Boston, L(ucy) M(aria Wood)

Bamber, B. "The Spirit of Green Knowe." *Country Living* (July 1992): 66–71.
Blatt, G. T. "Profile: Lucy M. Boston." *Language Arts* 60 (Fall 1983): 220–225.

Boston, Diana. *A Literary Guide to Green Knowe.* Huntingdon, Cambridgeshire, England: Diana Boston, 1992.

———. "Lucy Boston and Her Home." *Children's Books History Society Newsletter* (U.K.) 46 (1993): 2–5.

Boston, Lucy M. "Christmas at Green Knowe." *Horn Book* 31 (Dec 1955): 473.

——— *Memories: Incorporating "Perverse and Foolish" and "Memory in a House."* Cambridge: Colt, 1992.

———. *Memory in a House.* New York: Macmillan, 1974.

———. "A Message from Green Knowe." *Horn Book* 39 (June 1963): 259–264. Originally published as "The Place That Is Green Knowe." *Junior Bookshelf* 26 (Dec 1962): 295–301. Reprinted in Margaret Meek et al. *The Cool Web.* New York: Atheneum, 1978, pp. 216–221.

———. *Perverse and Foolish: A Memoir of Childhood and Youth.* New York: Atheneum, 1979.

Campbell, Alastair K. D. "Children's Writers: Lucy Boston." *School Librarian* 26 (Sept 1978): 212–217.

Chambers, Aidan. *Booktalk: Occasional Writing on Literature and Children.* New York: Harper, 1986, pp. 19, 49–58. Original British publication, 1985.

———. "The Reader in the Book." *Signal* 23 (May 1977): 64–68. Reprinted in Aidan Chambers. *Signal Approach to Children's Books.* Metuchen, NJ: Scarecrow Press, 1980, pp. 267–275.

Crouch, Marcus S. "Another Ghost for Green Knowe." *Junior Bookshelf* 54, 3(1990): 159–161.

———. "Lucy Boston at 80." *Junior Bookshelf* 36 (Dec 1972): 355–357.

———. "A Visit to Green Knowe." *Junior Bookshelf* 26 (Dec 1962): 302–305.

Doyle, Brian. *The Who's Who of Children's Literature.* New York: Schocken, 1968, pp. 33–34.

Drower, George. "Built By Conquerers." *Traditional Homes* (London) (May 1991): 15–18.

Elleman, Barbara, and Margaret K. McElderry. "The Inside Story: Lucy Boston, 1892–1990." *Book Links* 87 (Nov 15, 1990): 628–632.

Gilbert, Jenny. "Boston Tea-Party." *Times Educational Supplement* (Nov 14, 1986): 42.

Hatch, Jane. "Lucy M. Boston." *Wilson Library Bulletin* 37 (Oct 1962): 188.

Hollindale, Peter. "Lucy Boston, Storyteller." *Signal* 64 (Jan 1991): 3–6.

———. "The Novels of L. M. Boston." In Butts. *Good Writers for Young Readers.* St. Albans, England: Hart-Davis, 1977, pp. 25–33.

Jones, Cornelia, and Olivia R. Way. "L. M. Boston." In *British Children's Authors.* Chicago: American Library Association, 1976, pp. 55–64.

Lenander, David. "Crosscurrents in *The River at Green Knowe* by L. M. Boston." In *Where Rivers Meet: Confluence and Concurrents: Proceedings of the 1989 Conference of the Children's Literature Association,* ed. by Susan R. Gannon and Ruth A. Thompson. New York: Pace University, 1991, pp. 47–54.

Lively, Penelope. "The World of Green Knowe." *Books for Your Children* 5, no. 2 (Winter 1969–1970).

Livo, Norma J. "Lucy Boston at 80." *Junior Bookshelf* 36 (Dec 1972): 355–357.

Meek, Margaret. "A Private House." *Times Literary Supplement,* June 15, 1973, p. 676. Reprinted in Margaret Meek. *The Cool Web.* New York: Atheneum, 1978, pp. 325–330.

The Oxford Companion to Children's Literature. Edited by Humphrey Carpenter and Mari Prichard. New York: Oxford Univ. Press, 1984, pp. 76–77, 473.

Perrin, Noel. "Magic That Endures: Two Classic Children's Spellbinders Turn 40." *New York Times Book Review* 98 (Nov 14, 1993): 54.

Pflieger, Pat, and Helen M. Hill. *A Reference Guide to Modern Fantasy for Children.* Westport, CT: Greenwood, 1984, pp. 79–82, 108–112, 175–176, 476–477, 504–505.

Rees, David. "Green Thought in Green Shade—L. M. Boston." In *Painted Desert, Green Shade.* Boston: Horn Book, 1984, pp. 1–16.

Robbins, Sidney. "A Nip of Otherness, Like Life: The Life of Lucy Boston." *Children's Literature in Education* 6 (Nov 1971): 6–16.

Rose, Jasper. *Lucy Boston.* New York: Walck, 1966.

Rosenthal, Lynne. "The Development of Consciousness in Lucy Boston's *The Children of Green Knowe.*" In *Children's Literature,* vol. 8. New Haven, CT: Yale Univ. Press, 1980, pp. 53–67.

Small, Moira. "Dinner at Green Knowe." *Books for Your Children* (U.K.) 18 (Spring 1983): 18.

Stott, Jon C. *Children's Literature from A to Z.* New York: McGraw-Hill, 1984, p. 46.

———. "From Here to Eternity: Aspects of Pastoral in the Green Knowe Series." In *Children's Literature,* vol. 11. New Haven, CT: Yale Univ. Press, 1983, pp. 145–155.

Swinfen, Ann. *In Defense of Fantasy.* London: Routledge, 1984, pp. 49, 55–56.

Third Book of Junior Authors. Edited by Doris De Montreville and Donna Hill. New York: Wilson, 1972, pp. 44–45.

Townsend, John Rowe. "L. M. Boston." In *A Sense of Story.* Philadelphia: Lippincott, 1971, pp. 17–27.

Townsend, John Rowe, et al. "Mrs. Oldknow Ever Young: Obituary for Lucy Boston." *Guardian* (May 31, 1990): 39.

Travers, P. L. "World Beyond World." *Book Week* (May 7, 1967): 4–5. Reprinted in Haviland. *Children and Literature.* Glenview, IL: Scott, Foresman, 1973, pp. 246–249.

Twentieth-Century Children's Writers. 3rd ed. Edited by Tracy Chevalier and D. L. Kirkpatrick. Chicago: St. James, 1989, pp. 119–121.

Wintle, Justin, and Emma Fisher. "L. M. Boston." In *The Pied Pipers.* New York: Paddington Press, 1974, pp. 277–284.

Boucher, Anthony (pseud. of W[illiam] A[nthony] P[arker] White)

Boucher, Anthony. "The Publishing of Science Fiction." In *Modern Science Fiction: Its Meaning and Its Future.* 2nd ed. Edited by Reginald Bretnor. Chicago: Advent, 1979.

Fredericks, Casey. *The Future of Eternity: Mythologies of Science Fiction and Fantasy.* Bloomington: Indiana Univ. Press, 1982.

Pierce, Hazel Beasley. *A Literary Symbiosis: Science Fiction/Fantasy Mystery.* Westport, CT: Greenwood, 1983.

Twentieth-Century Science Fiction Writers. 3rd ed. Edited by Noelle Watson and Paul E. Schellinger. Chicago: St. James Press, 1991, pp. 63–65.

Bourliaguet, Leonce

Fourth Book of Junior Authors and Illustrators. Edited by Doris De Montreville and Elizabeth D. Crawford. New York: Wilson, 1978, pp. 51–52.

Bowen, William (Alvin)

Helbig, Alethea K., and Agnes Regan Perkins. *Dictionary of American Children's Fiction, 1859–1959.* Westport, CT: Greenwood, 1985, pp. 61, 379–380.

Bradbury, Ray (Douglas)

Albright, Donn. "Ray Bradbury Index: Part I." *Xenophile* 13 (May 1975).

———. "Ray Bradbury Index: Part II." *Xenophile* 26 (Sept 1976): 4–10.

———. "Ray Bradbury Index: Part III." *Xenophile* 36 (1977): 2–7.

Ash, Lee. "WLB Biography—Ray Bradbury." *Wilson Library Bulletin* 39 (Nov 1964): 268, 280.

Atkins, T. R. "Illustrated Man: Interview." *Sight & Sound* 43 (Spring 1974): 96–100.

Bradbury, Ray. "How, Instead of Being Educated in College, I Was Graduated from Libraries, or, Thoughts from a Chap Who Landed on the Moon in 1932." *Wilson Library Bulletin* 45 (May 1971): 842–851.

———. "Rationale for Bookburners: A Further Word from Ray Bradbury." *ALA Bulletin* 55 (May 1961): 403–404.

———. "Science Fiction as Modern Romance." *Intellect* 104 (1976): 490. Summary of speech.

———. "The Secret Mind." In David Wingrove, ed. *The Science Fiction Source Book.* New York: Van Nostrand Reinhold, 1984, pp. 72–74.

———. *Yestermorrow: Obvious Answers to Impossible Futures.* Santa Barbara, CA: Capra, 1992.

———. *Zen in the Art of Writing.* Santa Barbara, CA: Capra, 1990.

Dimeo, Richard Steven. "The Mind and Fantasies of Ray Bradbury." Ph.D. diss., University of Utah, 1970.

Elliot, Jeffrey M. "The Bradbury Chronicles." *Future* 5 (1978): 22–26. Interview.

———. "An Interview with Ray Bradbury." *Science Fiction Review* 6 (Nov 1977): 48–50. Reprinted from *San Francisco Review of Books,* June 1977.

———. *Science Fiction Voices #2.* San Bernardino, CA: Borgo Press, 1979.

Fantasy and Reality. North Hollywood, CA: Center for Cassette Studies, 1972. (audiocassette)

Foster, Mark Anthony. "Write the Other Way: The Correlation of Style and Theme in Selected Prose Fiction of Ray Bradbury." Ph.D. diss., Florida State University, 1973.

Grabowski, William J. "Whales, Libraries, and Dreams: Ray Bradbury." *Fantasy Review* 93 (1986): 11, 16.

Jacobs, Robert. *"The Writer's Digest* Interview: Bradbury." *Writer's Digest* (Feb 1976): 18–25.

Johnson, Wayne L. *Ray Bradbury.* New York: Ungar, 1980.

Kilworth, Garry. "The Profession of Science Fiction 31: Confessions of a Bradbury Eater." *Foundation* 29 (1983): 5–10.

Linkfield, Thomas P. "The Fiction of Ray Bradbury: Universal Themes in Midwestern Settings." *Midwestern Miscellany* 8 (1980): 44–101.

McNelly, Willis E. "Bradbury Revisited." *CEA Critic* 31 (Mar 1969): 4, 6.

———. "Ray Bradbury." In *Science Fiction Writers.* Edited by E. F. Bleiler. New York: Scribner, 1982, pp. 171–178.

———. "Ray Bradbury." In *Supernatural Fiction Writers,* vol. 2. Edited by E. F. Bleiler. New York: Scribner, 1985, pp. 917–924.

———. "Ray Bradbury—Past, Present and Future." In *Voices for the Future: Essays on Major Science Fiction Writers,* vol. 1. Edited by Thomas D. Clareson. Bowling Green, OH: Bowling Green Univ. Popular Press, 1976.

McReynolds, Douglas J. "The Short Fiction of Bradbury." In *Survey of Modern Fantasy Literature,* vol. 3. Edited by Frank N. Magill. Englewood Cliffs, NJ: Salem Press, 1983, pp. 1471–1481.

Mogen, David. *Ray Bradbury.* Boston: Twayne, 1986.

Moskowitz, Sam. *Seekers of Tomorrow; Masters of Modern Science Fiction.* New York: Ballantine, 1967, pp. 352–375.

Nolan, William F. *The Ray Bradbury Companion: A Life and Career History, Photolog, and Comprehensive Checklist of Writings with Facsimiles from Ray Bradbury's Unpublished and Uncollected Work in All Media.* Detroit: Gale, 1975. Originally published in *Xenophile,* May 1975. (For the continuation of this index, see: Albright, Donn, above.)

Orlander, Joseph D., and Martin Harry Greenberg, eds. *Ray Bradbury.* New York: Taplinger, 1979.

Plank, R. "Expedition to the Planet of Paranoia." *Extrapolation* 22 (Summer 1981): 171–185.

Platt, Charles. "Ray Bradbury." In *Dream Makers: The Uncommon People Who Write Science Fiction.* New York: Berkley, 1980; rev. ed. New York: Ungar, 1987, pp. 161–172. Interview.

Ray Bradbury as Philosopher; the Science Fiction Writer Talks about Man, Evil and the Future. North Hollywood, CA: Center for Cassette Studies, 1974. (audiocassette)

Reilly, Robert. "The Artistry of Ray Bradbury." *Extrapolation* 13 (Dec 1971): 64–74.

Searles, Baird, Beth Meacham, and Michael Franklin. *A Reader's Guide to Fantasy.* New York: Avon, 1982, pp. 36–37.

Slusser, George Edgar. *The Bradbury Chronicles.* San Bernardino, CA: Borgo Press, 1977.

Stupple, A. James. "The Past, the Future and Ray Bradbury." In *Voices for the Future: Essays on Major Science Fiction Writers,* vol. 1. Edited by Thomas D. Clareson. Bowling Green, OH: Bowling Green Univ. Popular Press, 1976.

Sullivan, Anita T. "Ray Bradbury and Fantasy." *English Journal* 61 (1972): 1309–1314.

Touponce, William Ferdinand. "Laughter and Freedom in Ray Bradbury's *Something Wicked This Way Comes.*" *Children's Literature Association Quarterly* 13 (Spring 1988): 17–21.

———. *Ray Bradbury and the Poetics of Reverie: Fantasy, Science Fiction and the Reader.* Ph.D. diss., University of Massachusetts, 1981; Ann Arbor, MI: University of Michigan Research Press, 1984.

Twentieth-Century Science Fiction Writers. 3rd ed. Edited by Noelle Watson and Paul E. Schellinger. Chicago: St. James Press, 1991, pp. 69–72.

Wolfe, Gary K. "*Something Wicked This Way Comes.*" In Frank N. Magill. *Survey of Modern Fantasy Literature,* vol. 4. Englewood Cliffs, NJ: Salem Press, 1983, pp. 1769–1773.

Bradley, Marion Zimmer

Arbur, Rosemarie. "*Darkover.*" In *Survey of Modern Fantasy Literature,* vol. 1. Edited by Frank N. Magill. Englewood Cliffs, NJ: Salem Press, 1983, pp. 488–492.

———. *Leigh Brackett, Marion Zimmer Bradley, Anne McCaffrey: A Primary and Secondary Bibliography.* Boston: G. K. Hall, 1982.

———. *Reader's Guide to Marion Zimmer Bradley.* Mercer Island, WA: Starmont, 1985.

Aygun, Ayla. "The Romantic Shadows of Avalon." *Children's Literature Association Quarterly* 17 (Winter 1992–1993): 38.

Bradley, Marion Zimmer. "An Evolution of Consciousness: Twenty-five Years of Writing about Women in Science Fiction." *Science Fiction Review* 6 (Aug 1977): 34–45.

———. "Experiment Perilous: The Art and Science of Anguish in Science Fiction." In *Experiment Perilous: Three Essays on Science Fiction.* Edited by Andrew Porter. New York: Algol Press, 1976.

———. "Fandom: It's Value to the Professional." In *Inside Outer Space.* Edited by Sharon Jarvis. New York: Ungar, 1985.

———. "Fantasy and the Contemporary Occult Novel: Social and Intellectual Approaches." *Fantasy Review* 80 (1985): 10–12. Part II. *Fantasy Review* 81 (1985): 31–32.

———. "Introduction." *The Bloody Sun and "To Keep the Oath."* Boston: Gregg, 1979.

———. "Introduction." *The Forbidden Tower.* Boston: Gregg, 1979.

———. "Introduction." *The Shattered Chain.* Boston: Gregg, 1979.

————. "Introduction." *The Spell Sword.* Boston: Gregg, 1979.

————. "Introduction." *Star of Danger.* Boston: Gregg, 1979.

————. "Introduction." *Stormqueen!* Boston: Gregg, 1979.

————. "Introduction." *The Winds of Darkover.* Boston: Gregg, 1979.

————. "Introduction." *The World Wreakers.* Boston: Gregg, 1979.

————. "The Maverick View." *Bulletin of the Science Fiction Writers of America* 14 (1979): 17–21.

————. *Men, Halflings and Hero Worship.* Baltimore: T-K Graphics, 1973. Discusses Tolkien.

————. "My Trip through Science Fiction." *Algol* 15 (Winter 1978): 10–20.

————. "Responsibilities and Temptations of Women Science Fiction Writers." In *Women Worldwalkers: New Dimensions of Science Fiction and Fantasy,* ed. by Jane B. Weedman. Lubbock: Texas Tech Press, 1985.

————. "Two Worlds of Fantasy." *Haunted: Studies in Gothic Fiction* 1 (June 1968): 82–85.

————. "Why Did My Story Get Rejected?" In *The Writer's Handbook.* Edited by Sylvia K. Burack. Boston: The Writer, 1985.

Breen, Walter. *The Darkover Concordance: A Reader's Guide.* Berkeley, CA: Pennyfarthing Press, 1979.

————. *The Gemini Problem: A Study in Darkover.* New York: Berkley, 1973; reprinted Baltimore: T-K Graphics, 1976.

Day, Phyllis J. "Earthmother/Witchmother: Feminism and Ecology Renewed." *Extrapolation* 23 (1982): 12–21.

De Camp, L. Sprague, ed. *The Blade of Conan.* New York: Ace, 1979. pap.

Fry, Carol L. "'What God Doth the Wizard Pray To': Neo-Pagan Witchcraft and Fantasy Fiction." *Extrapolation* 31 (Winter 1990): 333–346.

Godwin, Parke. "The Road to Camelot: A Conversation with Marion Zimmer Bradley." *Science Fiction and Fantasy Review* 66 (1984): 6–9.

Hanna, Judith. "Though He Was No Arthur." *Vector* 123 (1984): 20–21.

Heldreth, L. M. "The Darkover Novels." In *Survey of Modern Fantasy Literature,* vol. 1. Edited by Frank N. Magill. Englewood Cliffs, NJ: Salem Press, 1983, pp. 341–346.

Herbert, Rosemarie. "The Authors' Visions." *Publishers Weekly,* 203 (May 23, 1986): 42–45.

Hornum, Barbara. "Wife/Mother, Sorceress/Keeper, Amazon/Renunciate: Status Ambivalence and Conflicting Roles on the Planet Darkover." In *Women Worldwalkers: New Dimensions of Science Fiction and Fantasy,* ed. by Jane B. Weedman. Lubbock: Texas Tech Press, 1985.

An Hour with Marion Zimmer Bradley: A Personal Note. Garden Grove, NY: Hourglass Productions, 1979. (audiocassette)

Kimpel, R. "*The Mists of Avalon/Die Nebel Von Avalon:* Marion Zimmer Bradley's German Best Seller." *Journal of American Culture* 9 (Fall 1986): 25–28.

Lacy, N. J. *The Arthurian Encyclopedia.* New York: Garland, 1986, pp. 59–60.

Leith, Linda. "Marion Zimmer Bradley and Darkover." *Science-Fiction Studies* 7 (1980): 28–35.

Lupoff, Richard A. "Introduction." In Marion Zimmer Bradley. *The Sword of Aldones.* Boston: Gregg, 1977.

"Marion Zimmer Bradley." In Daryl Lane, William Vernon, and David Carlson. *The Sound of Wonder: Interviews from "The Science Fiction Radio Show,"* vol. 2. Phoenix, AZ: Oryx Press, 1985, pp. 111–132.

Roberts, Thomas J. "Before You Dump Those 'Junk' Books." *Media and Methods* 15 (May–June 1979): 27–28, 46.

Russ, Joanna. "Recent Feminist Utopias." In *Future Females.* Edited by Marleen S. Barr. Bowling Green, OH: Bowling Green Univ. Press, 1984, pp. 71–87.

Shwartz, Susan M. "Marion Zimmer Bradley's Ethic of Freedom." In *The Feminine Eye:*

Science Fiction and the Women Who Write It. Edited by Tom Staicar. New York: Ungar, 1982, pp. 73–88.

———. "Other Worlds: By the Light of the Bloody Sun." *Fantasy Newsletter* 32 (1981): 12–15.

Sturgeon, Theodore. "Introduction." In Marion Zimmer Bradley. *Darkover Landfall.* Boston: Gregg, 1978.

Twentieth-Century Science Fiction Writers. 3rd ed. Edited by Noelle Watson and Paul E. Schellinger. Chicago: St. James Press, 1991, pp. 72–74.

Wise, S. *The Darkover Dilemma: Problems of the Darkover Series.* Baltimore: T-K Graphics, 1976.

Wood, Diane S. "Gender Roles in the Darkover Novels of Marion Zimmer Bradley." In *Women Worldwalkers: New Dimensions of Science Fiction and Fantasy,* ed. by Jane B. Weedman. Lubbock: Texas Tech Press, 1985.

Wood, Susan. "Introduction." In Marion Zimmer Bradley. *The Heritage of Hastur.* Boston: Gregg, 1977.

Bradshaw, Gillian (Marucha)

Spivack, Charlotte. *Merlin's Daughters: Contemporary Women Writers of Fantasy.* New York: Greenwood, 1987.

Brand, Christianna (pseud. of Mary [Christianna Milne] Lewis)

The Oxford Companion to Children's Literature. Edited by Humphrey Carpenter and Mari Prichard. New York: Oxford Univ. Press, 1984, p. 80.

Twentieth-Century Children's Writers. 3rd ed. Edited by Tracy Chevalier and D. L. Kirkpatrick. Chicago: St. James, 1989, pp. 122–123.

Brelis, Nancy (Burns)

Gillespie, John T., and Diana Lembo. *Introducing Books: A Guide for the Middle Grades.* New York: Bowker, 1970, pp. 1–3.

Brenner, Barbara (Johnes)

Fourth Book of Junior Authors and Illustrators. Edited by Doris De Montreville and Elizabeth D. Crawford. New York: Wilson, 1978, pp. 55–56.

Briggs, K(atherine) M(ary)

Briggs, K. M. "Fairies in Children's Books." Lecture given at Mississippi University for Women, 1977. In *Folk Literature of the British Isles.* Metuchen, NJ: Scarecrow Press, 1978, pp. 11–21.

Davidson, H. R. Ellis. *Katherine Briggs: Storyteller.* Cambridge: Lutterworth Press, 1986.

Fifth Book of Junior Authors and Illustrators. Edited by Sally Holmes Holtze. New York: Wilson, 1983, pp. 49–50.

Hodges, Margaret. "Katherine M. Briggs: A Memoir." *Children's Literature in Education* 43, no. 4 (Winter 1981): 209–213.

Moss, Elaine. "K. M. Briggs, Novelist." *Signal* 30 (Sept 1979): 133–139.

The Oxford Companion to Children's Literature. Edited by Humphrey Carpenter and Mari Prichard. New York: Oxford Univ. Press, 1984, pp. 82–83.

Philip, Neil. "The Goodwill of Our Hearts: K. M. Briggs as Novelist." *Folklore* 92 (1981): 155–159.

Rahn, Suzanne. "The Expression of Religious and Political Concepts in Fantasy for Children." Ph.D. diss., University of Washington, 1986.

Searles, Baird, Beth Meacham, and Michael Franklin. *A Reader's Guide to Fantasy.* New York: Avon, 1982, pp. 37–38.

Twentieth-Century Children's Writers. 3rd ed. Edited by Tracy Chevalier and D. L. Kirkpatrick. Chicago: St. James, 1989, pp. 128–129.

Bright, Robert

More Junior Authors. Edited by Muriel Fuller. New York: Wilson, 1963, pp. 28–29.

Twentieth-Century Children's Writers. 3rd ed. Edited by Tracy Chevalier and D. L. Kirkpatrick. New York: St. Martin, 1989, pp. 131–132.

Brin, David

Klein, Jay Kay. "David Brin." *Analog* (Nov 1983): 119.

Brink, Carol Ryrie

Brink, Carol Ryrie. "*Caddy Woodlawn:* Newbery Medal Winner 1936: Her History." *Horn Book* 12 (July–Aug 1936): 248–250.

———. "Keep the Bough Green." *Horn Book* 43 (Aug 1967): 447–452.

Hadlow, Ruth M. "*Caddie Woodlawn.*" *Elementary English* 37 (Apr 1960): 221–226, 237.

Helbig, Alethea K. "Carol Ryrie Brink." In *Writers for Children: Critical Studies of Major Authors Since the Seventeenth Century.* Edited by Jane M. Bingham. New York: Scribner, 1988, pp. 85–90.

Helbig, Alethea K., and Agnes Regan Perkins. *Dictionary of American Children's Fiction, 1859–1959.* Westport, CT: Greenwood, 1985, pp. 69–70.

Hopkins, Lee Bennet. *More Books by More People: Interviews with Sixty-five Authors of Books for Children.* New York: Citation Press, 1974, pp. 53–59.

The Junior Book of Authors. 2nd rev. ed. Edited by Stanley J. Kunitz and Howard Haycraft. New York: Wilson, 1951, pp. 45–46.

Orland, Norine. "Carol Ryrie Brink and *Caddie Woodlawn.*" *Elementary English* 45 (Apr 1968): 425–428, 451.

The Oxford Companion to Children's Literature. Edited by Humphrey Carpenter and Mari Prichard. New York: Oxford Univ. Press, 1984, pp. 83–84.

Reed, M. E. "Carol Ryrie Brink: Legacy of an Idaho Childhood." *Idaho Librarian* 34 (Oct 1982): 142–147.

Roginski, Jim, ed. *Newbery and Caldecott Medalists and Honor Book Winners.* Littleton, CO: Libraries Unlimited, 1982, pp. 54–55.

Smaridge, Norah. *Famous Modern Storytellers for Young People.* New York: Dodd, 1969, pp. 52–56.

Twentieth-Century Children's Writers. 3rd ed. Edited by Tracy Chevalier and D. L. Kirkpatrick. New York: St. Martin, 1989, pp. 132–133.

Brittain, Bill (William)

Brittain, Bill. "The Plotting of *Dr. Dredd.*" *The New Advocate* 2 (Spring 1988): 81–91.
Fifth Book of Junior Authors and Illustrators. Edited by Sally Holmes Holtze. New York: Wilson, 1983, pp. 50–51.
Helbig, Alethea K., and Agnes Regan Perkins. *Dictionary of American Children's Fiction, 1960–1984.* Westport, CT: Greenwood, 1986, pp. 75, 730–731.
Spirt, Diana L. *Introducing Bookplots 3: A Book Talk Guide for Use with Readers Ages 8–12.* New York: Bowker, 1988, pp. 65–67.
Twentieth-Century Children's Writers. 3rd ed. Edited by Tracy Chevalier and D. L. Kirkpatrick. Chicago: St. James, 1989, pp. 135–136.

Bro, Marguerite (Harmon)

More Junior Authors. Edited by Muriel Fuller. New York: Wilson, 1963, pp. 30–31.

Bröger, Achim

Bröger, A. "Lügt Nicht—Ihr Lest Nicht! ["Don't Lie—You Don't Read!]." *Buch und Bibliothek* (Munich) 40 (Feb 1988): 161–163.

Brooks, Terry

Paxon, Diana. "The Tolkien Tradition." *Mythlore* 39 (1984): 23–27, 37.
Searles, Baird, Beth Meacham, and Michael Franklin. *A Reader's Guide to Fantasy.* New York: Avon, 1982, p. 38.
Watson, Christine. "*The Sword of Shannara.*" In *Survey of Modern Fantasy Literature,* vol. 4. Edited by Frank N. Magill. Englewood Cliffs, NJ: Salem Press, 1983, pp. 1866–1868.

Brooks, Walter R(ollin)

Cart, Michael. "Fanfare for *Freddy:* A Classic Neglected No Longer." *School Library Journal* 32 (Feb 1986): 25–27.
———. "Freddy, St. Peter, and Me." *Children's Literature in Education* 14 (Autumn 1983): 142–148.
———. "What's So Funny? Humor in the Writing of Walter R. Brooks." *The Lion and the Unicorn* 13 (Dec 1989): 131–140.
The Junior Book of Authors. 2nd rev. ed. Edited by Stanley J. Kunitz and Howard Haycraft. New York: Wilson, 1951, pp. 51–52.
Kurth, Ruth Justine. "Realism in Children's Books of Fantasy." *California Librarian* 39 (July 1978): 39–40.
Sale, Roger. *Fairy Tales and After: From Snow White to E. B. White.* Cambridge, MA: Harvard Univ. Press, 1978, pp. 245–258.
Speth, Lee. "The Pig in the Widow's Shawl." *Mythlore* 6, 22 (Fall 1979): 7–8.
Twentieth-Century Children's Writers. 3rd ed. Edited by Tracy Chevalier and D. L. Kirkpatrick. Chicago: St. James, 1989, pp. 136–137.

Brown, Abbie Farwell

"Abbie Farwell Brown." *Horn Book* 3 (May 1927): 15–16.

Brown, Palmer

Bader, Barbara. *American Picturebooks, From Noah's Ark to the Beast Within.* New York: Macmillan, 1976, pp. 492–494.

Fifth Book of Junior Authors and Illustrators. Edited by Sally Holmes Holtze. New York: Wilson, 1983, pp. 55–56.

Twentieth-Century Children's Writers. 3rd ed. Edited by Tracy Chevalier and D. L. Kirkpatrick. Chicago: St. James, 1989, p. 142.

Browne, Frances

Doyle, Brian. *The Who's Who of Children's Literature.* New York: Schocken, 1968, pp. 39–40.

"Frances Browne: *Granny's Wonderful Chair.*" In *Masterworks of Children's Literature,* vol. VI. New York: Stonehill/Chelsea House, 1984, pp. 137–162.

The Oxford Companion to Children's Literature. Edited by Humphrey Carpenter and Mari Prichard. New York: Oxford Univ. Press, 1984, p. 219.

Buchan, John

Blackburn, William. "John Buchan's *Lake of Gold:* A Canadian Imitation of Kipling." *Canadian Children's Literature* 14 (1979): 5–13.

Buchan, John. "The Novel and the Fairy Tale." In *Children and Literature: Views and Reviews.* Edited by Virginia Haviland. New York: Lothrop, 1973, pp. 220–229.

Morgan, Chris. "The Short Fiction of John Buchan." In *Survey of Modern Fantasy Literature,* vol. 3. Edited by Frank N. Magill. Englewood Cliffs, NJ: Salem Press, 1983, pp. 1482–1484.

The Oxford Companion to Children's Literature. Edited by Humphrey Carpenter and Mari Prichard. New York: Oxford Univ. Press, 1984, p. 87.

Buffie, Margaret

Buffie, Margaret. "Back on This Side of the Door." *School Libraries in Canada* 11 (Spring 1991): 29–34.

———. "Reflections on a Personal Case of Censorship." *Canadian Children's Literature* 68 (1992): 43–49.

Ellis, Sarah. "News from the North." *Horn Book* 64 (May–June 1988): 390–394. Three Canadian time travel novels.

Garner, Barbara Carman. "Lost and Found in Time: Canadian Time-Slip Fantasies for Children." *Children's Literature Association Quarterly* 15 (Winter 1990): 206–211.

Stanbridge, Joanne. "Out of the Blue: Coping with the Book-Banners." *The New Advocate* 6 (Winter 1993): 36–42

Stott, Jon C. "Of Time and the Prairie: Canadian Fantasies and the Search for Self-Worth." *Children's Literature Association Bulletin* 16 (Fall 1990): 2–6.

Bulla, Clyde Robert

Bulla, Clyde Robert. *A Grain of Wheat: A Writer Begins.* Boston: Godine, 1985.

Griese, Arnold A. "Clyde Robert Bulla: Master Story Weaver." *Elementary English* 48 (Nov 1971): 766–778. Reprinted in *Authors and Illustrators of Children's Books.* Edited by Miriam Hoffman and Eva Samuels. New York: Bowker, 1972, pp. 28–40.

Helbig, Alethea K., and Agnes Regan Perkins. *Dictionary of American Children's Fiction, 1859–1959.* Westport, CT: Greenwood, 1985, pp. 73, 504.

———. *Dictionary of American Children's Fiction, 1960–1984.* Westport, CT: Greenwood, 1986, pp. 78–79.

More Junior Authors. Edited by Muriel Fuller. New York: Wilson, 1963, p. 34.

Twentieth-Century Children's Writers. 3rd ed. Edited by Tracy Chevalier and D. L. Kirkpatrick. Chicago: St. James, 1989, pp. 151–152.

Bunting, (Anne) Eve(lyn Bolton)

Fifth Book of Junior Authors and Illustrators. Edited by Sally Holmes Holtze. New York: Wilson, 1983, pp. 60–61.

Twentieth-Century Children's Writers. 3rd ed. Edited by Tracy Chevalier and D. L. Kirkpatrick. Chicago: St. James, 1989, pp. 152–154.

Bunyan, John

Bator, Robert. "John Bunyan." In *Writers for Children: Critical Studies of Major Authors Since the Seventeenth Century.* Edited by Jane M. Bingham. New York: Scribner, 1988, pp. 97–102.

Batson, E. Beatrice. *John Bunyan, Allegory and Imagination.* Totowa, NJ: Barnes and Noble, 1984.

Collmer, Robert, ed. *Bunyan in Our Time.* Kent, OH: Kent State Univ. Press, 1989.

Hill, Christopher. "John Bunyan and His Public." *History Today* 38 (Oct 1988): 13–19.

———. *A Tinker and a Poor Man: John Bunyan and His Church, 1628–1688.* New York: Knopf, 1988.

———. *A Turbulent, Seditious and Factious People: John Bunyan and His Church.* Oxford: Clarendon, 1988.

MacDonald, Ruth K. "The Case for *The Pilgrim's Progress.*" *Children's Literature Association Quarterly* 10 (Spring 1985): 29–30.

———. *Christian's Children: The Influence of John Bunyan's "The Pilgrim's Progress" on American Children's Literature.* New York: Lang, 1989.

Simmons, Carl. "The Works (and Grace) of John Bunyan." *AB Bookman's Weekly* (Jan 14, 1991): 97–101.

White, Alison. "*Pilgrim's Progress* as Fairy Tale." In *Children's Literature,* vol. 1. Storrs, CT: Journal of the Modern Language Association, 1972, pp. 42–45.

Burgess, Thornton Waldo

Agosta, Lucien L. "Thornton W. Burgess." In Cech. *American Writers for Children, 1900–1960. Dictionary of Literary Biography,* vol. 22. Detroit: Gale, 1983, pp. 71–87.

Bixler, Phyllis, and Lucien L. Agosta. "Formula Fiction and Children's Literature: Thornton Waldo Burgess and Frances Hodgson Burnett." *Children's Literature in Education* 15 (Summer 1984): 63–72.

Burgess, Thornton W. *Now I Remember: Autobiography of an Amateur Naturalist.* Boston: Little, Brown, 1960.

Doyle, Brian. *The Who's Who of Children's Literature.* New York: Schocken, 1968, pp. 42–43.

Fox, Dorothea Magdalene. "A 90-Year Romance with Nature." *Audubon Magazine* 66, no. 5 (Sept–Oct 1964): 312–313.

Goldthwaite, John. "The Black Rabbit: Part One." *Signal* 47 (May 1985): 86–111; "The

Black Rabbit: Part Two." *Signal* 48 (Sept 1985): 148–167. Reprinted in Goldthwaite. *The Natural History of Make-Believe.* New York: Oxford Univ. Press, 1987.

The Junior Book of Authors. 2nd rev. ed. Edited by Stanley J. Kunitz and Howard Haycraft. New York: Wilson, 1951, pp. 60–61.

Lovell, Russell A., Jr. *The Cape Cod Story of Thornton W. Burgess.* Thornton W. Burgess Centennial Committee 1874–1974, in conjunction with William S. Sullwold Publishing (Taunton, MA), 1974.

O'Neil, Paul. "Fifty Years in the Green Meadow." *Life,* Nov 14, 1960, p. 112.

The Oxford Companion to Children's Literature. Edited by Humphrey Carpenter and Mari Prichard. New York: Oxford Univ. Press, 1984, p. 386.

Stott, Jon C. *Children's Literature from A to Z.* New York: McGraw-Hill, 1984, p. 57.

Twentieth-Century Children's Writers. 3rd ed. Edited by Tracy Chevalier and D. L. Kirk-patrick. Chicago: St. James, 1989, pp. 155–158.

Burman, Ben Lucien

Burman, Ben Lucien. "A Message from Catfish Bend." *School Bookshop News* (U.K.) 12 (Spring 1979): 13–14.

Hamilton, Alex. "Raccoonteur." *Guardian* (May 31, 1978): 7.

Helbig, Alethea K., and Agnes Regan Perkins. *Dictionary of American Children's Fiction, 1859–1959.* Westport, CT: Greenwood, 1985, pp. 74, 462–463.

Twentieth-Century Children's Writers. 3rd ed. Edited by Tracy Chevalier and D. L. Kirk-patrick. Chicago: St. James, 1989, pp. 158–159.

Burnett (Townsend), Frances (Elizabeth) Hodgson

Auerbach, Mina, and U. C. Knoepflmacher, eds. *Forbidden Journeys: Fairy Tales and Fantasys by Victorian Women Writers.* Chicago: Univ. of Chicago Press, 1992, pp. 164–176, 361.

Baker, Margaret J. "Mrs. Burnett of Maytham Hall." *Junior Bookshelf* 13 (Oct 1949): 126–136.

Bixler, Phyllis. "The Oral-Formulaic Training of a Popular Fiction Writer: Frances Hodgson Burnett." *Journal of Popular Culture* 15 (Spring 1982): 44–52.

Bixler, Phyllis, and Lucien Agosta. "Formula Fiction and Children's Literature: Thornton Waldo Burgess and Frances Hodgson Burnett." *Children's Literature in Education* 15 (Summer 1984): 63–72.

Burnett, Constance Buel. "Frances Hodgson Burnett: Episodes in Her Life." *Horn Book* 41 (Feb 1965): 86–94.

Burnett, Frances Hodgson. *The One I Knew Best of All: A Memory of the Mind of a Child.* New York: Scribner, 1893.

Burnett, Vivian. *The Romantick Lady (Frances Hodgson Burnett): The Life Story of an Imagination.* New York: Scribner, 1927.

Doyle, Brian. *The Who's Who of Children's Literature.* New York: Schocken, 1968, pp. 43–45.

Laski, Marghanita. *Mrs. Ewing, Mrs. Molesworth, and Mrs. Hodgson Burnett.* New York: Oxford Univ. Press, 1951.

Molson, Francis J. "Frances Hodgson Burnett (1848–1924)." *American Literary Realism 1870–1910* 8, no. 1 (Winter 1975): 35–41.

Stott, Jon C. *Children's Literature from A to Z.* New York: McGraw-Hill, 1984, p. 58.

Thwaite, Ann. *Waiting for the Party: The Life of Frances Hodgson Burnett 1849–1924.* New York: Scribner, 1974; Boston: Godine, 1991.

Twentieth-Century Children's Writers. 3rd ed. Edited by Tracy Chevalier and D. L. Kirkpatrick. Chicago: St. James, 1989, pp. 159–161.

Burnford, Sheila (Philip [née Every] Cochrane)

Fourth Book of Junior Authors and Illustrators. Edited by Doris De Montreville and Elizabeth D. Crawford. New York: Wilson, 1978, pp. 63–65.
Hughes, Catherine. "Sheila Burnford." *Publishers Weekly* 213 (Mar 27, 1978): 6–7. (interview)
Stott, Jon C. *Children's Literature from A to Z.* New York: McGraw-Hill, 1984, p. 60.
Twentieth-Century Children's Writers. 3rd ed. Edited by Tracy Chevalier and D. L. Kirkpatrick. Chicago: St. James, 1989, pp. 161–162.

Butler, Octavia E(stelle)

Barr, Marleen S., et al. *Reader's Guide to Suzy McKee Charnas, Octavia Butler and Joan Vinge.* Mercer Island, WA: Starmont, 1985.
Beal, Frances M. "Black Women and the Science Fiction Genre: Interview with Octavia Butler." *Black Scholar* 17 (1986): 14–18.
Elliot, Jeffrey. "Interview with Octavia Butler." *Thrust* 12 (Summer 1979): 19–22.
Foster, Frances Smith. "Octavia Butler's Black Female Future Fiction." *Extrapolation* 23 (1982): 37–49.
Friend, Beverly. "Time Travel as a Feminist Didactic in Works by Phyllis Eisenstein, Marlys Millhiser and Octavia Butler." *Extrapolation* 23 (1982): 50–55.
Govan, Sandra Y. "Connections, Links, and Extended Networks: Patterns in Octavia Butler's Science Fiction." *Black American Literature Forum* 18 (1984): 82–87.
Salvaggio, Ruth. "Octavia Butler and the Black Science Fiction Heroine." *Black American Literature Forum* 18 (1984): 78–81.
Twentieth-Century Science Fiction Writers. 3rd ed. Edited by Noelle Watson and Paul E. Schellinger. Chicago: St. James Press, 1991, pp. 109–110.
Weinkauf, Mary S. "So Much for the Gentle Sex." *Extrapolation* 20 (1985): 231–239.
Weixlmann, Joe. "An Octavia E. Butler Bibliography." *Black American Literature Forum* 18 (1984): 88–89.

Butterworth, Oliver

Fourth Book of Junior Authors and Illustrators. Edited by Doris De Montreville and Elizabeth D. Crawford. New York: Wilson, 1978, pp. 65–66.
Gillespie, John T., and Diana Lembo. *Introducing Books: A Guide for the Middle Grades.* New York: Bowker, 1970, pp. 263–265.
Helbig, Alethea K., and Agnes Regan Perkins. *Dictionary of American Children's Fiction, 1859–1959.* Westport, CT: Greenwood, 1985, pp. 75, 149.
———. *Dictionary of American Children's Fiction, 1960–1984.* Westport, CT: Greenwood, 1986, pp. 83, 677–678.
Twentieth-Century Children's Writers. 3rd ed. Edited by Tracy Chevalier and D. L. Kirkpatrick. Chicago: St. James, 1989, pp. 165–166.

Byars, Betsy (Cromer)

"Authorgraph no. 15: Betsy Byars." *Books for Keeps* (U.K.) 15 (July 1982): 14–15.
Byars, Betsy. "Authoress Betsy Byars Tells It Like It Is." *West Virginia Libraries* (Fall 1971).

————. "Beginnings, 'Human Things' and the Magical Moments." *Proceedings of the Eighth Annual Conference of the Children's Literature Association.* Ypsilanti, MI: Children's Literature Association, 1982, pp. 4–8.

————. ["Betsy Byars."] *Books for Your Children* (U.K.) 10, no. 2 (Mar 1975): 4–5.

————. "Ladders and Authority: Creating the Craft." *Journal of Youth Services in Libraries* 7 (Winter 1994): 141–145.

————. "The Lure of the Chapter." *CBC Features* 41, no. 3 (1988): 2.

————. "Newbery Award Acceptance." *Horn Book* 47 (Aug 1971): 354–358.

————. "Oak Leaves and Spider Webs and Other Debts of Gratitude [Where a Children's Author Gets Her Ideas]." In *Pacific Rim Conference on Children's Literature.* Melbourne, Australia: Melbourne State College, 1979. Reprinted in *A Track to Unknown Water.* Metuchen, NJ: Scarecrow Press, 1987, pp. 372–378.

————. "Spinning Straw into Gold." *School Librarian* 34 (Mar 1986): 6–13. Shortened transcript of talk given at 1985 SLA Course, Christ Church College.

————. "Writing for Children." *Signal* 37 (Jan 1982): 3–10.

Byars, Edward F. "Betsy Byars." *Horn Book* 47 (Oct 1971): 459–462.

Chambers, Aidan. "Letter from England: Arrows—All Pointing Upward." *Horn Book* 54 (Dec 1978): 680–684.

Cooper, Ilene. "The *Booklist* Interview: Betsy Byars." *Booklist* 89 (Jan 15, 1993): 906–907.

Hansen, I. V. "A Decade of Betsy Byars' Boys." *Children's Literature in Education* 15 (Spring 1984): 3–11.

Helbig, Alethea K., and Agnes Regan Perkins. *Dictionary of American Children's Fiction, 1960–1984.* Westport, CT: Greenwood, 1986, pp. 83–84.

Hopkins, Lee Bennett. *More Books by More People: Interviews with Sixty-five Authors of Books for Children.* New York: Citation Press, 1974, pp. 68–72.

Kingman, Lee, ed. *Newbery and Caldecott Medal Books: 1966–1975.* Boston: Horn Book, 1975, pp. 66–75.

Kuznets, Lois T. "Betsy Byars' Slice of 'American Pie.'" *Children's Literature Association Quarterly* 5 (1981): 31–33.

Laski, Audrey. "On the Side of Life, When Three Is Company." *Times Educational Supplement* (June 11, 1982): 39.

The Oxford Companion to Children's Literature. Edited by Humphrey Carpenter and Mari Prichard. New York: Oxford Univ. Press, 1984, p. 91.

Rees, David. "Little Bit of Ivory—Betsy Byars." In *Painted Desert, Green Shade.* Boston: Horn Book, 1984, pp. 33–46.

Robertson, Ina. "Profile: Betsy Byars—Writer for Today's Child." *Language Arts* 57 (Mar 1980): 328–334.

Roginski, Jim, ed. *Newbery and Caldecott Medalists and Honor Book Winners.* Littleton, CO: Libraries Unlimited, 1982, pp. 59–60.

Segel, Elizabeth. "Betsy Byars." In *American Writers for Children since 1960: Fiction. Dictionary of Literary Biography,* vol. 52. Detroit: Gale, 1986, pp. 52–65.

————. "Betsy Byars: An Interview." *Children's Literature in Education* 13 (Winter 1984): 171–179.

Stott, Jon C. *Children's Literature from A to Z.* New York: McGraw-Hill, 1984, p. 66.

Third Book of Junior Authors. Edited by Doris De Montreville and Donna Hill. New York: Wilson, 1972, p. 55.

Twentieth-Century Children's Writers. 3rd ed. Edited by Tracy Chevalier and D. L. Kirkpatrick. Chicago: St. James, 1989, pp. 166–168.

Watson, Ken. "The Art of Betsy Byars." *Orana* (Australia) 16 (Feb 1980): 3–5.

The Zena Sutherland Lectures, 1983–1992. Edited by Betsy Hearne. New York: Clarion, 1993, pp. 206–227.

Caldecott, Moyra

Searles, Baird, Beth Meacham, and Michael Franklin. *A Reader's Guide to Fantasy.* New York: Avon, 1982, pp. 40–41.

Calhoun, Mary (pseud. of Mary Huiskamp Wilkins)

Barnett, D. "Mary Calhoun Visits Green River Schools." *Wyoming Library Roundup* 39 (Winter 1984): 66–67.

Batman, G. "Interview with Mary Calhoun." *Colorado Libraries* 9 (Dec 1983): 36–39.

Calhoun, Mary. "Tracking Down Elves in Folklore." *Horn Book* 45 (June 1969): 278–281.

Third Book of Junior Authors. Edited by Doris De Montreville and Donna Hill. New York: Wilson, 1972, pp. 56–57.

Callen, Larry (Lawrence Willard, Jr.)

Fifth Book of Junior Authors and Illustrators. Edited by Sally Holmes Holtze. New York: Wilson, 1983, pp. 63–64.

Cameron, Eleanor (Frances Butler)

Cameron, Eleanor. "Art and Morality." In *Proceedings of the Seventh Annual Conference of the Children's Literature Association.* Baylor University, March 1980. Ypsilanti, MI: Children's Literature Association, 1982, pp. 30–44. Reprinted in *Festschrift: A Ten Year Retrospective.* Edited by Perry Nodelman and Jill P. May. West Lafayette, IN: Children's Literature Association Publications, 1983, pp. 28–35.

———. "Books Remembered." *CBC (Children's Book Council) Features* 41 (Jan–Aug 1987).

———. "Characterization—Some Unforgettables." In *A Sea of Upturned Faces: Proceedings of the Third Pacific Rim Conference on Children's Literature,* ed. by Winifred Ragsdale. Metuchen, NJ: Scarecrow Press, 1989, pp. 79–100.

———. "The Dearest Freshness Deep Down Things." *Horn Book* 40 (Oct 1964): 459–472.

———. "The Eternal Moment." *Children's Literature Association Quarterly* 9 (Winter 1984–1985): 157–163.

———. "Fantasy, Science Fiction and the *Mushroom Planet* Books." *Children's Literature Association Quarterly* 5 (Winter 1981): 1, 5–9. Reprinted in *Signposts to Criticism of Children's Literature.* Edited by Robert Bator. Chicago: American Library Association, 1983, pp. 294–300; and in *The First Steps.* Edited by Patricia Dooley. West Lafayette, IN: Children's Literature Association Publications, 1984, pp. 55–57.

———. *The Green and Burning Tree: On the Writing and Enjoyment of Children's Books.* Boston: Little, Brown, 1969. "Fantasy," pp. 3–134.

———. "The Inmost Secret." *Horn Book* 59 (Feb 1983): 17–23.

———. "Into Something Rich and Strange: Of Dreams, Art and the Unconscious." *Quarterly Journal of the Library of Congress* 35 (Apr 1978): 92–107. Reprinted in *The Openhearted Audience.* Washington, DC: Library of Congress, 1980, pp. 152–176.

———. "McLuhan, Youth, and Literature." *Horn Book* 48 (Oct 1972): 433–440, (Dec 1972): 572–579, and 49 (Feb 1973): 79–85. Reprinted in Paul Heins. *Crosscurrents of Criticism.* Boston: Horn Book, 1977, pp. 98–120.

———. "Of Style and the Stylist." *Horn Book* 40 (Feb 1964): 25–32.

———. "On Fantasy." In *The Seed and the Vision: On the Writing and Appreciation of Children's Books.* New York: Dutton, 1993.

————. "One Woman as Writer and Feminist." *Children's Literature Association Quarterly* 7 (Winter 1982–1983): 3-6ff.

————. "A Question of Taste: A Reply to Anne Merrick." *Children's Literature in Education* 21 (Summer 1976): 59–63.

————. "A Reply to Perry Nodelman's 'Beyond Explanation.'" In *Children's Literature,* vol. 12. New Haven, CT: Yale Univ. Press, 1984, pp. 134–146.

————. "An Unforgettable Glimpse." *Wilson Library Bulletin* 37 (Oct 1962): 147–153. Revised for *The Green and Burning Tree.* Boston: Little, Brown, 1969, pp. 3–47.

————. "Why *Not* for Children?" *Horn Book* 42 (Feb 1966): 21–33.

————. "With Wrinkled Brow and Cool Fresh Eye. Part I." *Horn Book* 61 (May–June 1985): 280–288; "Part II." *Horn Book* 61 (July–Aug 1985): 426–431.

————. "Write What You Care About." *School Library Journal* 35 (June 1989): 50–51.

————. "A Writer's Journey." In *Innocence & Experience.* Edited by Barbara Harrison and Gregory Maguire. New York: Lothrop, 1987, pp. 30–44.

————. "Writing from Experience." *Five Owls* 5 (Jan–Feb 1991): 45–47.

Elleman, Barbara, and Eleanor Cameron. "Eleanor Cameron's *Court of the Stone Children.*" *Book Links* 3 (July 1994): 30–32.

Helbig, Alethea K., and Agnes Regan Perkins. *Dictionary of American Children's Fiction, 1859–1959.* Westport, CT: Greenwood, 1985, p. 84.

————. *Dictionary of American Children's Fiction, 1960–1984.* Westport, CT: Greenwood, 1986, pp. 90–91, 133, 661–662.

Nodelman, Perry. "Beyond Explanation, and Beyond Inexplicability, in Eleanor Cameron's *Beyond Silence.*" Abstract. In *Proceedings of the Ninth Annual Conference of the Children's Literature Association.* University of Florida, March 1982. Ypsilanti, MI: Children's Literature Association, 1983, pp. 128–129. Reprinted in *Children's Literature,* vol. 12. New Haven, CT: Yale Univ. Press, 1984, pp. 122–133.

————. "The Depths of All She Is: Eleanor Cameron." *Children's Literature Association Quarterly* 4 (Winter 1980): 6–8.

Pflieger, Pat, and Helen M. Hill. *A Reference Guide to Modern Fantasy for Children.* Westport, CT: Greenwood, 1984, pp. 93–95, 127–129.

Stott, Jon C. *Children's Literature from A to Z.* New York: McGraw-Hill, 1984, p. 71.

Sulerud, Grace, and Sue Garness. "Eleanor Cameron." In *American Writers for Children since 1960: Fiction. Dictionary of Literary Biography,* vol. 52. Detroit: Gale, 1986, pp. 66–74.

Third Book of Junior Authors. Edited by Doris De Montreville and Donna Hill. New York: Wilson, 1972, pp. 57–58.

Twentieth-Century Children's Writers. 3rd ed. Edited by Tracy Chevalier and D. L. Kirkpatrick. Chicago: St. James, 1989, pp. 168–169.

Card, Orson Scott

Abdullah, Cheryl. "Orson Scott Card." *Book Report* 8 (Sept–Oct 1989): 31–34.

Brown, C. N. "Orson Scott Card: Jack of Many Trades." *Locus* 317 (1987): 5+.

Card, Orson Scott. "Adolescence and Adulthood in Science Fiction." *Amazing Stories* (Nov 1987): 49–58.

————. *How to Write Science Fiction and Fantasy.* Cincinnati: Writers Digest, 1990.

————. "On Sycamore Hill: A Personal View." *Science Fiction Review* 55 (1985): 6–11.

————. "The Well-Ground Axe: On Themes." *Bulletin of the Science Fiction Writers of America* 73 (1980): 10–12.

————. "The Well-Ground Axe: Using Criticism." *Bulletin of the Science Fiction Writers of America* 73 (1980): 43–45.

Collings, Michael R. *Card Catalogue: The Science Fiction and Fantasy of Orson Scott Card.* Eugene, OR: Hypatia, 1987.

Moser, Cliff. "An Interview with Orson Scott Card." *Science Fiction Review* 8 (Aug 1979): 32–35.

Schaafsma, Karen. "The Demon Lover: Lilith and the Hero in Modern Fantasy." *Extrapolation* 28 (1987): 52–61.

Twentieth-Century Science Fiction Writers. 3rd ed. Edited by Noelle Watson and Paul E. Schellinger. Chicago: St. James, 1991, pp. 119–121.

Watson, Ian. "The Author as Torturer." *Foundation* 40 (1987): 11–25.

Carlson, Natalie Savage

Carlson, Julie McAlpine. "Family Unity in Natalie Savage Carlson's Books for Children." *Elementary English* 45 (Feb 1968): 214–217. Reprinted in Miriam Hoffman and Eva Samuels. *Authors and Illustrators of Children's Books.* New York: Bowker, 1972, pp. 56–61.

Helbig, Alethea K., and Agnes Regan Perkins. *Dictionary of American Children's Fiction, 1960–1984.* Westport, CT: Greenwood, 1986, pp. 94–95.

Hopkins, Lee Bennett. "Natalie Savage Carlson." In *More Books by More People.* New York: Citation Press, 1974, pp. 73–77.

McAlpine, Julie Carlson. "Fact and Fiction in Natalie Savage Carlson's Autobiographical Stories." *Children's Literature,* vol. 5. Philadelphia: Temple Univ. Press, 1976, pp. 157–161.

More Junior Authors. Edited by Muriel Fuller. New York: Wilson, 1963, pp. 34–35.

Roginski, Jim, ed. *Newbery and Caldecott Medalists and Honor Book Winners.* Littleton, CO: Libraries Unlimited, 1982, pp. 60–61.

Twentieth-Century Children's Writers. 3rd ed. Edited by Tracy Chevalier and D. L. Kirkpatrick. Chicago: St. James, 1989, pp. 172–173.

Carroll, Jonathan

Rottensteiner, Franz. "Jonathan Carroll: The Wonder and the Threat of Existence." *Fantasy Review* 97 (1986): 10–13.

Carroll, Lewis (pseud. of Charles Lutwidge Dodgson)

Adams, Gillian. "Student Responses to *Alice's Adventures in Wonderland* and *At the Back of the North Wind.*" *Children's Literature Association Quarterly* 10 (Spring 1985): 6–9.

Adelman, Richard Parker. "Comedy in Lewis Carroll's *Alice's Adventures in Wonderland* and *Through the Looking Glass.*" Ph.D. diss., Temple University, 1979.

Alderson, Brian, ed. *Children's Books in England.* 3rd ed. New York: Cambridge Univ. Press, 1982, pp. 255–261.

Alexander, Peter. *Logic and the Humor of Lewis Carroll.* London: Chorley and Pickersgill, 1951. Originally published in the *Proceedings of the Leeds Philosophy and Literature Society* 6 (May 1951): 551–566.

Amadio, M. "Un Libro Chiave per L. Carroll e la Sua *Alice* [Cluebook for L. Carroll and His *Alice*]." *Schedario* (Italy) 136 (July–Aug 1975): 28–29.

Armstrong, Nancy. "The Occidental *Alice.*" *Differences* [Bloomington, IN] 2, no. 2 (1990): 3–40.

Arnoldi, Richard. "Parallels between *Our Mutual Friend* and the *Alice* Books." In *Children's Literature,* vol. 1. Storrs, CT: Journal of the Modern Language Association, 1972, pp. 54–57.

Auden, W. H. "Lewis Carroll." In W. H. Auden. *Forewords and Afterwords.* New York: Random, 1973, pp. 283–293.

Auerbach, Nina. "Alice and Wonderland: A Curious Child." *Victorian Studies* 17 (Sept 1973): 31–47.

———. "Falling *Alice,* Fallen Women, and Victorian Dream Children." *English Language Notes* 20 (Dec 1982): 46–64.

———. *Romantic Imprisonment: Women and Other Glorified Outcasts.* New York: Columbia Univ. Press, 1985. Includes two essays on *Alice's Adventures in Wonderland.*

Ayres, Harry Morgan. *Carroll's Alice.* New York: Columbia Univ. Press, 1936.

Bacon, Deborah. "The Meaning of Non-Sense: A Psychoanalytic Approach to Lewis Carroll." Ph.D. diss., Columbia University, 1950.

Baker, Margaret J. "Jo Meets the Reverend C. L. Dodgson." *Junior Bookshelf* 8 (July 1944): 45–54.

Baldwin, Honor. "*Alice* and Louise Stimson." *Horn Book* 24 (May 1948): 181–188.

Barry, Georgina. "Lewis Carroll's Mock Heroic in *Alice's Adventures in Wonderland* and *The Hunting of the Snark.*" *Jabberwocky* (London) 8, no. 4 (Autumn 1979): 79–93.

Bartley, William Warren, III. "Lewis Carroll's Lost Book on Logic." *Scientific American* 227 (July 1972): 38–46.

———, ed. *Lewis Carroll's Symbolic Logic.* New York: Potter, 1977.

Bassett, Lisa. *Very Truly Yours, Charles L. Dodgson, Alias Lewis Carroll.* New York: Lothrop, 1987.

Batchelor, John. "Dodgson, Carroll, and the Emancipation of Alice." In *Children and Their Books,* ed. by Gillian Avery and Julia Briggs. Oxford: Clarendon, 1989, pp. 181–199.

Batey, Mavis. *The Adventures of Alice: The Stories Behind the Stories Lewis Carroll Told.* London: Macmillan, 1991.

Baum, Alwin L. "Carroll's *Alice:* The Semiotics of Paradox." *American Imago* 34 (1977): 86–108.

Bedinger, Margery. "Guide Books for *Alice* in the Wonderland of Life." *Horn Book* 8 (Feb 1932): 33–40.

Berman, Ruth. "White Knight and Leech Gatherer: The Poet as Boor." *Mythlore* 9 (Autumn 1982): 29–31.

Birns, Margaret Boe. "Solving the Mad Hatter's Riddle." *Massachusetts Review* 25 (1984): 457–468.

Bivona, Daniel. "*Alice* the Child-Imperialist and the Games of Wonderland." *Nineteenth-Century Literature* 41 (1986): 143–171.

———. "Desire and Contradiction: A Nineteenth Century Imperial Mythos and Its Critics." Ph.D. diss., Brown University, 1987.

Blackburn, William. "'A New Kind of Rule': The Subversive Narrator in *Alice's Adventures in Wonderland* and 'The Pied Piper of Hamelin.'" *Children's Literature in Education* 17 (Fall 1986): 181–190.

Blake, Kathleen. *Play, Games, and Sport: The Literary Works of Lewis Carroll.* Ithaca, NY: Cornell Univ. Press, 1974.

———. "The Play Theme in the Imaginative Writing of Lewis Carroll." Ph.D. diss., University of California, San Diego, 1971.

Bloom, Harold, ed. *Lewis Carroll.* New York: Chelsea, 1987.

Bohem, Hilda. "Alice's Adventures with Altemus (and Vice Versa)." *Papers of the Bibliographic Society of America* 73 (1979): 423–442.

Bond, W. H. "The Publication of *Alice's Adventures in Wonderland.*" *Harvard Library Bulletin* 10 (Autumn 1956): 306–324.

Bowman, Isa. *Lewis Carroll As I Knew Him.* London: Dent, 1899; Dover, 1972. Originally published as *The Story of Lewis Carroll.*

Bowman, Isa. *Lewis Carroll As I Knew Him.* London: Dent, 1899; Dover, 1972. Originally published as *The Story of Lewis Carroll.*

Briggs, Elizabeth D. "Lewis Carroll, Friend of Children. 1832–1932." *Elementary English Review* 9 (Jan 1932): 5–7, 11.

Bushnell, John Palmer. "Powerless to Be Born: Victorian Struggles in Romantic Landscapes of Adolescence." Ph.D. diss., Rutgers University, 1983.

Carpenter, Humphrey. "*Alice* and the Mockery of God." In *Secret Gardens: A Study of the Golden Age of Children's Literature.* Boston: Houghton Mifflin, 1985, pp. 44–69.

Carroll, Lewis. "Alice on the Stage." In *The Lewis Carroll Picture Book.* Edited by Stuart Dodgson Collingwood. London: Unwin, 1899, pp. 163–170.

———. *The Annotated Alice: Alice's Adventures in Wonderland and Through the Looking Glass,* ed. by Martin Gardner. New York: Crown, 1960.

———. *More Annotated Alice: Alice's Adventures in Wonderland and Through the Looking Glass,* illus. by Peter Newell. New York: Random, 1990.

Chadwick-Joshua, Jocelyn. "*Alice's Adventures in Wonderland* and *Through the Looking Glass*: A Menippean Assessment and Rhetorical Analysis of Carroll's *Alice* Books." Ph.D. diss., Texas Woman's University, 1987.

Cixous, Helene. "Introduction to Lewis Carroll's *Through the Looking Glass* and *The Hunting of the Snark.*" *New Literary History* 13 (1982): 231–251.

Clark, Anne. *Lewis Carroll: A Biography.* London: Dent, 1979.

———. *The Real Alice: Lewis Carroll's Dream Child.* New York: Stein and Day, 1982.

Clark, Beverly Lyon. "Carroll's Well-Versed Narrative: *Through the Looking Glass.*" *English Language Notes* 20 (Dec 1982): 65–76.

———. "Lewis Carroll's *Alice* Books: The Wonder of Wonderland." In *Touchstones.* Edited by Perry Nodelman. West Lafayette, IN: Children's Literature Association Publications, 1985, pp. 44–52.

———. "The Mirror Worlds of Carroll, Nabokov, and Pynchon: Fantasy in the 1860's and 1960's." Ph.D. diss., Brown University, 1979.

———. *Reflections of Fantasy: The Mirror Worlds of Carroll, Nabokov and Pynchon.* New York: Lang, 1986.

———. "What Went Wrong with Alice?" *Children's Literature Association Quarterly* 11 (Spring 1986): 29–33. Reprinted in *The Fantastic in World Literature and the Arts,* ed. by David E. Morse. Westport, CT: Greenwood, 1987, pp. 87–101.

Cohen, Morton N. "Another Wonderland: Lewis Carroll's *The Nursery 'Alice.'*" *The Lion and the Unicorn* 7/8 (1983–1984): 120–126.

———. "'Curiouser and Curiouser.' The Endurance of Little *Alice.*" *New York Times Book Review* (Nov 11, 1990): 54–55.

———. "Lewis Carroll and the House of Macmillan." *Browning Institute for Studies in Victorian Literature and Cultural History* 7 (1979): 31–70.

———, ed. *Lewis Carroll: Interviews and Recollections.* Iowa City: Univ. of Iowa Press, 1989.

———. "Lewis Carroll's *Memoria Technica.*" *Library Chronicle of the University of Texas* 11 (1979): 77–88.

———, ed. *The Selected Letters of Lewis Carroll.* New York: Pantheon, 1982.

Collingwood, Stuart Dodgson. *The Life and Letters of Lewis Carroll.* New York: Century, 1898; reprinted Detroit: Gale, 1967.

———, ed. *The Lewis Carroll Picture Book.* London: Unwin, 1899.

Colquhoun, Daryl. *The "Alice" Concordance: A Concordance to Lewis Carroll's "Alice's Adventures in Wonderland" and "Through the Looking Glass."* Adelaide: Univ. of Adelaide, 1986.

Cornwell, Charles Landrum. "From Self to the Shire: Studies in Victorian Fantasy." Ph.D. diss., University of Virginia, 1972.

Crawford, T. T. "Making the World Go Round in *Alice in Wonderland.*" *Notes and Queries* 36 (June 1989): 191–192.

Cripps, Elizabeth A. "*Alice* and the Reviewers." In *Children's Literature,* vol. 11. New Haven, CT: Yale Univ. Press, pp. 32–48.

Cunningham, Michael Henry. "The Triumph of Fantasy: Childhood and Children's Literature in Victorian England." Ph.D. diss., New School for Social Research, 1978.

D'Ambrosio, Michael A. *"Alice* for Adolescents." *English Journal* 59 (Nov 1970): 1074–1075, 1085.

Davies, Ivor. "Looking-Glass Chess." *Anglo-Welsh Review* 19 (Autumn 1970): 189–191.

De la Mare, Walter. *Lewis Carroll.* London: Faber, 1932.

———. "Lewis Carroll—A Biography." *Fortnightly Review,* Sept 1, 1930, pp. 319–331. Reprinted in Virginia Haviland. *Children and Literature.* Glenview, IL: Scott, Foresman, 1973, pp. 57–63.

De la Roche, Wayne William. "Privacy and Community in the Writings of Lewis Carroll." Ph.D. diss., Columbia University, 1975.

Dohm, J. H. *"Alice* in America." *Junior Bookshelf* 29 (Oct 1965): 261–267.

Doonan, Jane. "Realism and Surrealism in Wonderland: John Tenniel and Anthony Browne." *Signal* 58 (Jan 1989): 9–30.

Doyle, Brian. *The Who's Who of Children's Literature.* New York: Schocken, 1968, pp. 46–50.

Dreyer, Lawrence M. "The Mathematic References to the Adoption of the Gregorian Calendar in Lewis Carroll's *Alice's Adventures in Wonderland." American Notes and Queries* 19 (1980): 41–44.

Dusinberre, Juliet. *Alice to the Lighthouse: Children's Books and Radical Experimentalism in Art.* New York: St. Martin, 1987.

Ede, L. "The Nonsense Literature of Edward Lear and Lewis Carroll." Ph.D. diss., Ohio State University, 1975.

Edes, Mary Elizabeth. "Alice Liddell of Wonderland." *Publishers Weekly,* 179 (July 2, 1962): 112–115. Reprinted in *Readings about Children's Literature.* Edited by Evelyn R. Robinson. New York: McKay, 1966, pp. 304–312.

Empson, William. *"Alice in Wonderland:* The Child as Swain." In *Some Versions of Pastoral.* London: Chatto, 1935, pp. 251–294.

Engen, Rodney. *Sir John Tenniel: Alice's White Knight.* Aldershot, VT: Scolar, 1991.

Europe. "Special Issue: Lewis Carroll." *Europe* (Paris) 736–737 (Aug–Sept 1990).

Evans, Luther H. "The Return of *Alice's Adventures under Ground." Columbia Library Columns* 15 (Nov 1965): 29–35.

Fisher, John, ed. *The Magic of Lewis Carroll.* New York: Simon, 1973.

Flesher, Jacqueline. "The Language of Nonsense in *Alice." Yale French Studies* 43 (1969): 128–144.

Flieger, Verlyn. "Time and Dream in *The Lost Road* and *The Lord of the Rings." Inklings-Jahrbuch fur Literatur und Asthetik* 10 (1992): 111–133.

Fordyce, Rachel. *Lewis Carroll: A Reference Guide.* Boston: Hall, 1988.

Fortuna, Mary Ann. "A Descriptive Evaluative Study of Children's Modern Fantasy and Children's Science Fiction Using a Well-Known Example of Each." Ed.D. diss., Temple University, 1988.

Frey, Charles, and John Griffiths. *The Literary Heritage of Childhood: An Appraisal of Children's Classics in the Western Tradition.* Westport, CT: Greenwood, 1987, pp. 115–122.

Furniss, Harry. "Recollections of Lewis Carroll." Edited by Lance Salway. *Signal* 19 (Jan 1976): 45–50. Originally published in *Strand Magazine* 35 (Jan 1908): 48–52.

Gabriele, Mark. *"Alice in Wonderland:* Problems of Identity—Aggressive Content and Form Control." *American Imago* 39 (Winter 1982): 369–389.

Garber, Frederick. "Pastoral Spaces." *Texas Studies in Language and Literature* 30 (1988): 431–460.

Gardner, Martin. "An Anniversary for *Alice.* A Child's Garden of Bewilderment [*Alice's Adventures in Wonderland* and *The Wonderful Wizard of Oz* Compared]." *Saturday Review* 48 (July 17, 1965): 18–19, 48 (Aug 14, 1965): 26. Reprinted in Sheila A. Egoff. *Only Connect.* New York: Oxford Univ. Press, 1980, pp. 150–155.

————. "The Games and Puzzles of Lewis Carroll." *Scientific American* 202 (Mar 1960): 172–174ff.

————, ed. *The Annotated Alice.* New York: Potter, 1960.

Gattegno, J. "D'Un Proces à l'Autre, ou de *Pickwick* à *Alice* [From One Trial to Another, from *Pickwick* to *Alice*]." *Études Anglaises* 23 (Apr–June 1970): 208–209.

————. *Lewis Carroll: Fragments of a Looking-Glass.* New York: Crowell, 1976.

Gibson, Lois Rauch. "Beyond the Apron: Archetypes, Stereotypes, and Alternative Portrayals of Mothers in Children's Literature." *Children's Literature Association Quarterly* 13 (1988): 177–181.

Gilbert, Pamela K. "*Alice's Ab-surd-ity: Demon in Wonderland.*" *Victorian Newsletter* 83 (Spring 1993): 17–22.

Gilead, S. "Magic Abjured: Closure in Children's Fantasy Fiction." *Publications of the Modern Language Association* 106 (Mar 1991): 277–293.

Glastonbury, M. "In and Out of Wonderland." *Times Educational Supplement* 3192 (Aug 6, 1976): 16.

Goldthwaite, John. "Do You Admire the View? The Critics Go Looking for Nonsense." *Signal* 67 (Jan 1992): 41–66.

Goodacre, Selwyn H. "The *Alice* Manuscript—from 1928." *Jabberwocky* (London) 8 (Autumn 1978): 85–88.

————. "1865 *Alice:* A New Appraisal and a Revised Census." *English Language Notes* 20 (Dec 1982): 77–96.

Gordon, Jan B., and Edward Guiliano. "From Victorian Textbook to Ready-Made: Lewis Carroll and the Black Art." *English Language Notes* 20 (Dec 1982): 1–25.

Graham, Eleanor. "Nonsense in Children's Literature." *Junior Bookshelf* 9 (July 1945): 61–68.

Gray, Donald J., ed. *Lewis Carroll's "Alice in Wonderland."* New York: Norton, 1971.

Green, David L. "Children's Literature Periodicals on Individual Authors, Dime Novels, Fantasy." *Phaedrus* 3 (1976): 22–24.

Green, Roger Lancelyn. "Bibliographer in Wonderland." *Private Libraries* 4 (Oct 1962): 62–65.

————. *Lewis Carroll.* London: Bodley Head, 1960; New York: Walck, 1962. Reprinted in Green, Bell, and Nesbitt. *Lewis Carroll, E. Nesbit and Howard Pyle.* London: Bodley Head, 1968.

————. "The Lewis Carroll Handbook." New York: Oxford Univ. Press, 1962. Revision of original edition by Sidney Herbert Williams and Falconer Madan.

————. "More Aspects of *Alice.*" *Jabberwocky* 13 (Winter 1972): 9–14.

————. "Picnic in Wonderland." *Junior Books* 26 (July 1962): 110–114.

————, ed. *The Diaries of Lewis Carroll.* 2 vols. New York: Oxford Univ. Press, 1954.

Greenacre, Phyllis. *Swift and Carroll: A Psychoanalytic Study of Two Lives.* New York: International Universities Press, 1955.

Grotjahn, Martin. "About the Symbolization of *Alice's Adventures in Wonderland.*" *American Imago* 4 (Dec 1947): 32–41.

Guiliano, Edward. "Lewis Carroll: A Sesquicentennial Guide to Research." *Dickens Studies Annual* 10 (1982): 263–310.

————. "*Lewis Carroll: An Annotated International Bibliography, 1960–1977.* Charlottesville: Univ. Press of Virginia, 1981.

————. "Lewis Carroll in a Changing World: An Interview with Morton N. Cohen." *English Language Notes* 20 (Dec 1982): 97–108.

————. "150th Anniversary: Lewis Carroll: His Genius Was 'Frabjous.'" *A.B. Bookman's Weekly,* Jan 18, 1982, pp. 355–356ff.

————. "Popular and Critical Responses to Lewis Carroll: A Comparative Survey of Publishers since 1960." Ph.D. diss., State University of New York at Stony Brook, 1978.

————, ed. *Lewis Carroll, a Celebration.* New York: Potter; dist. by Crown, 1981.

————, ed. *Lewis Carroll Observed: A Collection of Unpublished Photographs, Drawings, Poetry, and New Essays.* New York: Potter, 1976.

Hancher, Michael. *"Alice's* Audiences." In *Romanticism and Children's Literature in Nineteenth-Century England,* ed. by James Hold McGavran, Jr. Athens: Univ. of Georgia Press, 1991, pp. 190–207.

————. "The Placement of Tenniel's *Alice* Illustrations." *Harvard Library Bulletin* 30 (July 1982): 237–252.

————. *The Tenniel Illustrations to the 'Alice' Books.* Columbus: Ohio State Univ. Press, 1985.

Hancock, Cecily Raysor. "Musical Notes to *The Annotated Alice." Children's Literature* 16 (1988): 1–29.

Hardyment, Christina. "The Literary Landscape: 2. *Alice* in Oxford." (London) *Daily Telegraph Magazine* (June 23, 1990): 52–56.

Hazard, Paul. *Books, Children and Men,* 4th ed. Boston: Horn Book, 1960, pp. 135–140.

Hearn, Michael Patrick. *"Alice's* Other Parent: John Tenniel as Lewis Carroll's Illustrator." *American Book Collector* 3 (May–June 1984): 11–20.

Heath, Peter. "Carroll through the Pillar-Box." *Virginia Quarterly Review* 56 (1980): 552–558.

Hedberg, Johannes. "Dodgson, Charles Lutwidge = Lewis Carroll." *Artes* 6 (1983): 98–108.

Helson, Ravenna, and Alf Proysen. "The Psychological Origins of Fantasy for Children in Mid-Victorian England." *Children's Literature,* vol. 3. Storrs, CT: Journal of the Modern Language Association, 1974, pp. 66–75.

Hentoff, N. "Looking Backward and Ahead with *Alice." Wilson Library Journal* 45 (Oct 1970): 169–171.

Herson, Flodden W. "The 1866 Appleton *Alice." The Colophon* 1 (Winter 1936): 422–427.

Higgens, Regina. *Magic Kingdoms: Discovering the Joys of Childhood Classics with Your Child.* New York, Simon & Schuster, 1992.

Hilton, Tom. "Drawn into *Wonderland." The Guardian* (Nov 27, 1991): 38.

Hinde, Thomas, ed. *Looking-Glass Letters: The Letters of Lewis Carroll.* London: Collins, 1991.

Holešovsky, František. "Contribution to the Lewis Carroll Jubilee by Illustrators of the BIB." *Bookbird* 1 (1984): 52–55.

Holmes, Roger W. "The Philosopher's *Alice in Wonderland." Antioch Review* 19 (Summer 1959): 133–149.

Honig, Edith Lazaros. *Breaking the Angelic Image: Woman Power in Victorian Children's Fantasy.* Westport, CT: Greenwood, 1988.

————. "A Quiet Rebellion: The Portrait of the Feminine in Victorian Children's Fantasy." Ph.D. diss., Fordham University, 1985.

Hubbell, George Shelton. "Triple *Alice." Sewanee Review* 48, no. 2 (Apr–June 1940): 174–196.

Hudson, Derek. *Lewis Carroll: An Illustrated Biography.* London: Constable, 1954; New York: Potter, 1977.

Imholtz, August A., Jr. "Jam Sempiterne: A Note on Time in *Through the Looking Glass." Jabberwocky* (U.K.) 8 (Winter 1978/1979): 13–15.

"In Honor of the Lewis Carroll Centenary." *Horn Book* 8 (Feb 1932): 41–43.

Inglis, Fred. *The Promise of Happiness.* New York: Cambridge Univ. Press, 1981, pp. 103–109.

Jabberwocky: The Journal of the Lewis Carroll Society. Lewis Carroll Society (British), 1969– .

Jackson, Rosemary. *Fantasy: The Literature of Subversion.* New York: Methuen, 1980.

Johnson, Paula. *"Alice* among the Analysts." *Hartford Studies in Literature* 4 (1972): 114–122.

Jorgens, Jack. "*Alice,* Our Contemporary." In *Children's Literature,* vol. 1. Storrs, CT: Journal of the Modern Language Association, 1972, pp. 152–161.

Kelly, Richard. *Lewis Carroll.* Boston: G. K. Hall, 1977.

Kibel, Alvin C. "Logic and Satire in *Alice in Wonderland.*" *American Scholar* 43, no. 4 (Autumn 1974): 605–629.

Kincaid, James R. "*Alice's* Invasion of Wonderland." *Publications of the Modern Language Association* 33 (Jan 1973): 92–99.

The Knight Letter. Lewis Carroll Society of North America, 1974– .

Knoepflmacher, U. C. "Avenging Alice: Christina Rossetti and Lewis Carroll." *Nineteenth-Century Literature* 41 (Dec 1986): 299–328.

———. "Revisiting Wordsworth: Lewis Carroll's 'The White Knight's Song.'" *Victorians Institute Journal* 14 (1986): 1–20.

Kolbe, Martha Emily. "Three Oxford Dons as Creators of Other Worlds for Children: Lewis Carroll, C. S. Lewis, and J. R. R. Tolkien." Ph.D. diss., University of Virginia, 1981.

Leach, Elsie. "*Alice in Wonderland* in Perspective." *Victorian Newsletter* 25 (Spring 1964): 9–11.

Lebovitz, Richard. "Alice as Eros." *Jabberwocky* 10 (Winter 1981): 72–87.

Lee, Hermione. "Mr. Dodgson and the Little Girls." *New Statesman* (Nov 2, 1979): 684–685.

Lennon, Florence Becker. *The Life of Lewis Carroll.* rev. ed. New York: Collier, 1962. Original title: *Victoria through the Looking-Glass: The Life of Lewis Carroll.* New York: Simon, 1945.

Lesser, Wendy. *The Life Below the Ground: A Study of the Subterranean in Literature and History.* London: Faber, 1988.

Levin, Harry. "Wonderland Revisited." *Kenyon Review* 27 (Autumn 1965): 591–616.

Lewis, Naomi. "Authorgraph no. 71: Lewis Carroll." *Books for Keeps* (U.K.) 71 (1991): 16–17, 19.

Liebs, Elke. "Between *Gulliver* and *Alice*: Some Remarks on the Dialectic of GREAT and SMALL in Literature." *Phaedrus* 13(1988): 56–60.

Little, Edmund. *The Fantasists: Studies in J. R. R. Tolkien, Lewis Carroll, Mervyn Peake, Nikolay Gogol and Kenneth Grahame.* Amersham, England: Avebury, 1984.

Little, Judith. "Liberated *Alice:* Dodgson's Female Hero as Domestic Rebel." *Women's Studies* 3 (1976): 195–205.

Lott, Sandra. "The Evolving Consciousness of Feminine Identity in Doris Lessing's *The Memoirs of a Survivor* and Lewis Carroll's *Alice's Adventures in Wonderland* and *Through the Looking-Glass.*" In *Women Worldwalkers: New Dimensions of Science Fiction and Fantasy,* ed. by Jane B. Weedman. Lubbock: Texas Tech Press, 1985.

Lovett, Charles C. *Alice on Stage: A History of the Earlier Theatrical Productions of "Alice in Wonderland".* Westport, CT: Meckler, 1990.

Lovett, Charles C., and Stephanie B. Lovett. *Lewis Carroll's "Alice": An Annotated Checklist of the Lovett Collection.* Westport, CT: Meckler, 1990.

Luchinsky, Ellen A. "*Alice*: Child or Adult." *Jabberwocky* 6 (Summer 1977): 63–71.

McEwan, Ian. "Thank Heavens." *New Review* (London) IV (Mar 1978): 53–54.

McGillis, Roderick F. "Fantasy as Adventure: Nineteenth Century Children's Fiction." *Children's Literature Association Quarterly* 8 (Fall 1983): 18–22.

———. "Novelty and Roman Cement: Two Versions of *Alice.*" In Douglas Street. *Children's Novels and the Movies.* New York: Ungar, 1983, pp. 15–27.

———. "'What *Is* the Fun?' Said Alice." *Children's Literature in Education* 17 (Spring 1986): 25–36.

McGrath, Robin. "*Alice* of New Moon: The Influence of Lewis Carroll on L. M. Montgomery's Emily Bird Star." *Canadian Children's Literature* 65 (1992): 62–67.

Madeen, William. "Framing the *Alices.*" *PMLA* 101 (1986): 362–373.

Mango, Susan. "*Alice* in Two Wonderlands: Lewis Carroll in German." Ph.D. diss., American University, 1974.

Matthews, Charles. "Satire in the *Alice* Books." *Criticism* 12 (Spring 1970): 105–119.

Meacham, Margaret McKeen Ramsey. "*Alice in Wonderland,* a Chamber Opera in One Act." Original composition. D.M.A. diss., University of Maryland, 1982.

Molson, Francis J. "*Alice's Adventures in Wonderland* and *Through the Looking Glass.*" In *Survey of Modern Fantasy Literature,* vol. 1. Edited by Frank N. Magill. Englewood Cliffs, NJ: Salem Press, 1983, pp. 7–16.

Morse, Donald E., ed. *The Fantastic in World Literature and the Arts.* Westport, CT: Greenwood, 1987.

Morton, Lionel. "Memory in the *Alice* Books." *Nineteenth-Century Fiction* 33 (Dec 1978): 285–308.

Morton, Richard. "*Alice's Adventures in Wonderland* and *Through the Looking-Glass.*" *Elementary English* 37 (Dec 1960): 509–513.

Moss, Anita. "Lewis Carroll." In *Writers for Children: Critical Studies of Major Authors Since the Seventeenth Century.* Edited by Jane M. Bingham. New York: Scribner, 1988, pp. 117–128.

———. "Sacred and Secular Visions of Imagination and Reality in Nineteenth-Century British Fantasy for Children." In *Webs and Wardrobes: Humanist and Religious World Views in Children's Literature,* ed. by Joseph O'Beirne Milner and Lucy Floyd Morcock Milner. Lanham, MD: University Press of America, 1987, pp. 65–78.

Mulderig, G. "*Alice* and *Wonderland:* Subversive Elements in the World of Victorian Children's Fiction." *Journal of Popular Culture* 11 (Fall 1977): 320–329.

Munich, Adrienne Auslander. "Queen Victoria, Empire, and Excess." *Tulsa Studies in Women's Literature* 6 (1987): 265–281.

Myer, Michael Grosvenor. "Some Omissions from Martin Gardner's *The Annotated Alice.*" *Notes and Queries* 30 (Aug 1983): 302–303.

Natov, Roni. "The Persistence of *Alice.*" *The Lion and the Unicorn* 3, no. 1 (Spring 1979): 38–61.

Newman, Cathy. "The Wonderland of Lewis Carroll." *National Geographic* 179 (June 1991): 100–129.

Nicholson, Mervyn. "Food and Power: Homer, Carroll, Atwood and Others." *Mosaic* 20 (1987): 37–55.

Nieres, Isabelle. *Lewis Carroll en France (1870–1985): Les Ambivalences d'une Reception Litteraire.* Ph.D. diss., University of Amiens, 1988.

O'Brien, Hugh B. "Alice's Journey in *Through the Looking-Glass.*" *Notes and Queries* 14 (Oct 1967): 380–382.

Ovenden, Graham. *The Illustrators of "Alice in Wonderland" and "Through the Looking Glass."* New York: St. Martin, 1972; rev. ed. 1980.

———. *Lewis Carroll.* London: Macdonald, 1984.

The Oxford Companion to Children's Literature. Edited by Humphrey Carpenter and Mari Prichard. New York: Oxford Univ. Press, 1984, pp. 15–19, 97–102, 382, 512, 527.

Page, Jane Izzard. "Enduring *Alice.*" Ph.D. diss., University of Washington, 1970.

Pennington, John. "*Alice At the Back of the North Wind,* or the Metafictions of Lewis Carroll and George MacDonald." *Extrapolation* 33 (Spring 1992): 59–72.

Perrot, Jean A. "A Historic Turning Point: *Alice*'s 'Russian Doll.'" *International Review of Children's Literature and Librarianship* 4 (1989): 154–166.

Peterson, Calvin R. "Time and Stress: *Alice in Wonderland.*" *Journal of the History of Ideas* 46 (1985): 427–433.

Pfeiffer, John R. "Lewis Carroll." In *Supernatural Fiction Writers: Fantasy and Horror,* vol. 1. Edited by E. F. Bleiler. New York: Scribner, 1985, pp. 247–254.

Phillips, Robert, ed. *Aspects of "Alice": Lewis Carroll's Dreamchild as Seen through the Critics' Looking-Glasses, 1865–1971.* New York: Vanguard, 1970.

Plackis, Anashia Poulos. "*Alice*: Carroll's Subversive Message of Christian Hope and Love." Ph.D. diss., State University of New York at Stony Brook, 1986.

Platzner, R. L. "Child's Play: Games and Fantasy in Carroll, Stevensen, and Grahame." In *Proceedings of the Fifth Annual Conference of the Children's Literature Association.* Harvard University, March 1978. Ypsilanti, MI: Children's Literature Association, 1979, pp. 78–86.

Potter, Greta Lagro. "Millions in Wonderland." *Horn Book* 41 (Dec 1965): 593–597.

Preston, Michael James. *Concordance to Lewis Carroll's "Alice's Adventures in Wonderland" and "Through the Looking Glass."* New York: Garland, 1986.

———. *A Concordance to the Verse of Lewis Carroll.* New York: Garland, 1985.

———. *A KWIC Concordance to Lewis Carroll's "Alice's Adventures in Wonderland" and "Through the Looking Glass."* New York: Garland, 1986.

Prickett, Stephen. "Religious Fantasy in the Nineteenth Century." In Frank N. Magill. *Survey of Modern Fantasy Literature,* vol. 5. Englewood Cliffs, NJ: Salem Press, 1983, pp. 2369–2382.

———. *Victorian Fantasy.* Bloomington: Indiana Univ. Press, 1979.

Pritchett, V. S. "Lewis Carroll." *The New Yorker* 56 (Mar 3, 1980): 123–128.

Profeta, C. C. "Lewis Carroll: Reflections of His Psyche in His Work." MSLS thesis, University of North Carolina at Chapel Hill, 1991.

Pudney, John. *Lewis Carroll and His World.* New York: Scribner, 1976.

Pycior, Helena M. "At the Intersection of Mathematics and Humor: Lewis Carroll's *Alice* and Symbolical Algebra." *Victorian Studies* 28 (1984): 149–170.

Rackin, Donald. "Alice's Journey to the End of Night." *PMLA* 81 (1966): 313–326. Reprinted in Robert Phillips, ed. *Aspects of Alice.* New York: Vanguard, 1970.

———. "Corrective Laughter: Carroll's Alice and Popular Children's Literature of the 19th Century." *Journal of Popular Culture* 1 (1967): 343–355.

———. "The Critical Interpretation of *Alice in Wonderland:* A Survey and Suggested Reading." Ph.D. diss., University of Illinois, 1964.

———. "Love and Death in Carroll's *Alices.*" *English Language Notes* 20 (Dec 1982): 26–45.

———. "*Through the Looking Glass*: Alice Becomes an 'I'." *Victorians Institute Journal* 15 (1987): 1–16.

———. "What You Always Wanted to Know about Alice but Were Afraid to Ask." *Victorian Newsletter* 44 (Feb 1973): 1–5.

Rahn, Suzanne. "The Expression of Religious and Political Concepts in Fantasy for Children." Ph.D. diss., University of Washington, 1986.

Rapaport, Herman. "The Disarticulated Image: Gazing in Wonderland." *Encomia* 6 (Fall 1982): 57–77.

Reardon, Margaret. "A Present for Alice." *Horn Book* 38 (June 1962): 243–247. Reprinted in Elinor Field. *Horn Book Reflections.* Boston: Horn Book, 1969, pp. 286–290.

Reed, Langford. "The Life of Lewis Carroll." London: Foyle, 1932.

Reichertz, Ronald. "*Alice* Through the Looking Glass Book: Carroll's Use of Children's Literature as a Ground for Reversal in *Through the Looking Glass and What Alice Found There.*" *Children's Literature Association Quarterly* 17 (Fall 1992): 23–26.

———. "Carroll's *Alice in Wonderland.*" *Explicator* 43 (Winter 1985): 21–22.

Reinstein, P. Gila. *Alice in Context.* New York: Garland, 1988.

Richardson, J. "Dodgson in Wonderland." *History Today* 25 (Feb 1975): 110–117.

Rosenbaum, David, ed. *Queen Victoria's "Alice in Wonderland."* San Francisco: Continental Historical Society, 1990.

Rottensteiner, Franz. *The Fantasy Book: An Illustrated History from Dracula to Tolkien.* New York: Macmillan, 1978, pp. 108–111.

Sale, Roger. *Fairy Tales and After: From Snow White to E. B. White.* Cambridge, MA: Harvard Univ. Press, 1978, pp. 101–126.

Sams, Edwin Boyer. "Studies in Experiencing Fantasy." *Teaching English in a Two-Year College* 5 (1979): 235–237.

Sapire, D. "*Alice in Wonderland:* A Work of Intellect." *English Studies in Africa* 15 (Mar 1972): 53–62.

Schaefer, David, and Maxine Schaefer. "The Movie Adventures of Lewis Carroll's *Alice.*" *American Classic Screen* 5 (Sept–Oct 1981): 9–12.

Scott, Carole. "Limits of Otherworlds: Rules of the Game in *Alice's Adventures in Wonderland* and *The Jungle Books.*" In *Work and Play in Children's Literature: Selected Papers from the 1990 International Conference of the Children's Literature Association,* ed. by Susan R. Gannon and Ruth Anne Thompson. New York: Pace University, 1992, pp. 20–24.

Searles, Baird, Beth Meacham, and Michael Franklin. *A Reader's Guide to Fantasy.* New York: Avon, 1982, p. 42.

Sewell, Elizabeth. *The Field of Nonsense.* London: Chatto, 1952.

Shires, Linda M. "Fantasy, Nonsense, Parody, and the Status of the Real: The Example of Carroll." *Victorian Poetry* 26 (Autumn 1988): 267–283.

Sibley, Brian. "Through a Darkling Glass: An Appreciation of Mervyn Peake's Illustrations to *Alice.*" *The Mervyn Peake Review* 6 (1978): 25–29 and 7 (1978): 26–29.

Sircar, Sanjay. "Other *Alices* and Alternative Wonderlands: An Exercise in Literary History." *Jabberwocky* 58 (Spring 1984): 13.

————. "A Select List of Previously Unlisted *Alice* Imitations." *Jabberwocky* (U.K.) (Summer 1984): 59–67.

————. "Tea with Alice of *Alice in Wonderland.*" *Children's Literature* 22 (1994): 127–138.

Skinner, John. "Lewis Carroll's *Adventures in Wonderland.*" *American Imago* 4 (Dec 1947): 3–31.

Spacks, Patricia Meyer. "Logic and Language in *Through the Looking-Glass.*" *ETC* 18, no. 1 (Apr 1961): 91–100.

"Special Issue: Lewis Carroll." *Europe* [Paris] 736–737 (Aug–Sept 1990).

Spink, John. "'A Welly Serious Thing': Carroll's *Sylvie and Bruno.*" *Signal* 63 (Sept 1990): 221–228.

Steveson, Lynn Bradley. "Lewis Carroll's *Through the Looking Glass* as a Kaleidoscope of English History: A Critical Approach to Scripting Interpreters Theatre." Ph.D. diss., Southern Illinois University at Carbondale, 1983.

Stott, Jon C. *Children's Literature from A to Z.* New York: McGraw-Hill, 1984, p. 73.

Stowell, Phyllis. "We're All Mad Here." *Children's Literature Association Quarterly* 8 (Summer 1983): 5–8.

Suchan, James. "Alice's Journey from Alien to Artist." In *Children's Literature,* vol. 7. Storrs, CT: Parousia Press, 1978, pp. 78–92.

Susina, Jan Christopher. "*Respiciendo Prudens:* Lewis Carroll's Juvenilia." *Children's Literature Association Quarterly* 17 (Winter 1992–1993): 10–14.

————. "Victorian Kunstmärcher: A Study in Children's Literature, 1840–1875." Ph.D. diss., Indiana University, 1986.

Sutherland, Robert D. "Language and Lewis Carroll." Ph.D. diss., University of Iowa, 1964.

————. *Language and Lewis Carroll.* The Hague and Paris: Mouton, 1970.

Taylor, Alexander L. *The White Knight: A Study of C. L. Dodgson.* London: Oliver, 1952.

Thomas, Ronald R. "Profitable Dreams in the Marketplace of Desire: *Alice in Wonderland, A Christmas Carol,* and the Interpretation of Dreams." *Nineteenth-Century Contexts* 12 (1988): 34–35.

Thurber, James. "Tempest in a Looking Glass." *Forum* (Apr 1937): 236–238. Reprinted in Boyer and Zahorski. *Fantasists on Fantasy.* New York: Avon, 1985, pp. 67–74.

Twentieth Century Children's Writers. 2nd ed. Edited by D. L. Kirkpatrick. New York: St. Martin, 1983, p. 863.

Veglahn, Nancy. "Images of Evil: Male and Female Monsters in Heroic Fantasy." *Children's Literature* 15 (1987): 106–119.

Warren, A. "Carroll and His *Alice* Books." *Sewanee Review* 88 (Summer 1980): 331–353.

Weaver, Warren. "*Alice's Adventures in Wonderland:* Its Origin and Its Author." *Princeton University Library Chronicle* 13 (Autumn 1951): 1–17.

———. "In Pursuit of Lewis Carroll." *Library Chronicle of the University of Texas* 2 (Nov 1970): 38–45.

Whimperley, Arthur. *Lewis Carroll and Cheshire.* London: Overcoat, 1991.

White, Alison. "*Alice* after a Hundred Years." *Michigan Quarterly Review* 4 (Fall 1965): 261–264.

Williams, Sidney Herbert. *A Bibliography of the Writings of Lewis Carroll.* London: Bookman's Journal, 1924.

Wolf, Virginia L. "Readers of *Alice*: My Children, Meg Murry and Harriet M. Welsch." *Children's Literature Association Quarterly* 13 (Fall 1988): 135–136.

Carryl, Charles E(dward)

Sargent, Constance Carryl. "The Carryls—Father and Son." *Horn Book* 8 (May 1932): 105–113.

Street, Douglas. "Charles E. Carryl." In *American Writers for Children before 1900. Dictionary of Literary Biography,* vol. 42. Detroit: Gale, 1985, pp. 122–126.

West, Mark I., ed. *Before Oz: Juvenile Fantasy Stories from Nineteenth Century America.* Archon, 1989. "Davy and the Goblin," pp. 191–200.

Carter, Angela

Twentieth-Century Science Fiction Writers. 3rd ed. Edited by Noelle Watson and Paul E. Schellinger. Chicago: St. James Press, 1991, pp. 121–126.

Carter, Lin

Twentieth-Century Science Fiction Writers. 3rd ed. Edited by Noelle Watson and Paul E. Schellinger. Chicago: St. James Press, 1991, pp. 126–128.

Cassedy, Sylvia

Cassedy, Sylvia. *In Your Own Words: A Beginner's Guide to Writing.* Garden City, NY: Doubleday, 1979.

Helbig, Alethea, and Agnes Regan Perkins. *Dictionary of American Children's Fiction, 1985–1989.* Westport, CT: Greenwood, 1993, pp. 42–43.

McDonnell, Christine. "Sylvia Cassedy: Valuing the Child's Inner Life." *Horn Book* 67 (Jan–Feb 1990): 101–105.

Sixth Book of Junior Authors and Illustrators. Edited by Sally Holmes Holtze. New York: Wilson, 1989, pp. 49–50.

Twentieth-Century Children's Writers. 3rd ed. Edited by Tracy Chevalier and D. L. Kirkpatrick. Chicago: St. James, 1989, pp. 176–177.

Wolf, Virginia. "Playing and Reality in Sylvia Cassedy's Novels." In *Work and Play in Children's Literature: Selected Papers from the 1990 International Conference of the Children's Literature Association,* ed. by Susan R. Gannon and Ruth A. Thompson. New York: Pace University, 1992, pp. 51–54.

Casserley, Anne Thomasine

Casserley, Anne. "The Home of *Michael of Ireland.*" *Horn Book* 3 (Nov 1927): 28–29.
The Junior Book of Authors. 2nd rev. ed. Edited by Stanley J. Kunitz and Howard Haycraft. New York: Wilson, 1951, pp. 67–68.

Chant, Joy (pseud. of Eileen Joyce Rutter)

"Attracting the Reader." *Times Literary Supplement* 42 (Sept 19, 1980): 1028.
Berman, Ruth. "Discussion Reports." *Mythlore* 7, 24 (1980).
Chant, Joy. *Fantasy and Allegory in Literature for Young Readers.* Student Project no. 2. Aberystwyth, Wales: University College of Wales, 1971.
———. "A Letter from Joy Chant." *Mythlore* 3, 9 (1976).
———. "Niggle and Numenor." *Children's Literature in Education* 19 (Winter 1975): 161–171.
Elgin, Don D. *The Comedy of the Fantastic: Ecological Perspectives on the Fantasy Novel.* Westport, CT: Greenwood, 1985.
Hanna, Judith. "Though He Was No Arthur." *Vector* 123 (1984): 20–21.
Searles, Baird, Beth Meacham, and Michael Franklin. *A Reader's Guide to Fantasy.* New York: Avon, 1982, pp. 44–45.
Stroud, Daphne. "Joy Chant's Starlit Land." *Junior Bookshelf* 52 (Dec 1988): 271–274.
Sullivan, C. W., III. "The Khendiol Novels." In *Survey of Modern Fantasy Literature,* vol. 2. Edited by Frank N. Magill. Englewood Cliffs, NJ: Salem Press, 1983, pp. 839–843.
Swinfen, Ann. *In Defense of Fantasy.* London: Routledge, 1984, pp. 97–98, 106–107.

Chapman, Vera

Chapman, Vera. "The Books of My Childhood." *Amon Hen* 100 (Nov 1989): 36–37.
Miller, M. Y. "The Three Damosels Trilogy." In *Survey of Modern Fantasy Literature,* vol. 4. Edited by Frank N. Magill. Englewood Cliffs, NJ: Salem Press, 1983, pp. 1908–1912.
Spivak, Charlotte. *Merlin's Daughters: Contemporary Women Writers of Fantasy.* New York: Greenwood, 1987, pp. 127–137.

Charnas, Suzy McKee

Barr, Marleen S., et al. *Reader's Guide to Suzy McKee Charnas, Octavia Butler, and Joan Vinge.* Mercer Island, WA: Starmont, 1985.
Bartokowski, Frances. "Toward a Feminist Eros: Readings in Feminist Utopian Fiction." Ph.D. diss., University of Iowa, 1982.
Bogstad, Janice. "Interview: Suzy McKee Charnas." *Janus* 5 (Spring 1979): 20–23.
Charnas, Suzy McKee. "A Woman Appeared." In *Future Females.* Edited by Marleen S. Barr. Bowling Green, OH: Bowling Green Univ. Press, 1981, pp. 103–108.
Charnas, Suzy McKee, and Douglas Winter. "Mostly I Want to Break Your Heart." *Fantasy Review* 7 (Sept 1984): 5–6, 41.
Day, Phyllis J. "Earthmother/Witchmother: Feminism and Ecology Renewed." *Extrapolation* 23 (1982): 12–21.
Howard, Susan E. "*Unicorn Tapestry:* A Modern Romance." *Extrapolation* 27 (1986): 39–48.
Miller, Margaret. "The Ideal Woman in Two Feminist Science Fiction Utopias." *Science Fiction Studies* 10 (July 1983): 191–198.

Russ, Joanna. "Recent Female Utopias." In *Future Females*. Edited by Marleen S. Barr. Bowling Green, OH: Bowling Green Univ. Press, 1981, pp. 71–87.

Twentieth-Century Science Fiction Writers. 3rd ed. Edited by Noelle Watson and Paul E. Schellinger. Chicago: St. James Press, 1991, pp. 133–135.

Wilgus, Neal. "*Algol* Interview: Suzy McKee Charnas." *Algol* 16 (Winter 1979): 21–25.

Cherryh, C. J. (pseud. of Carolyn Janice Cherry)

Brizzi, Mary T. "C. J. Cherryh and Tomorrow's New Sex Roles." In *The Feminine Eye*. Edited by Tom Staicar. New York: Ungar, 1982, pp. 32–47.

Burnick, Gale. "An Interview with C. J. Cherryh." *Science Fiction Review* 7 (Nov–Dec 1978): 14–18.

Cherryh, C. J. "Female Characters in Science Fiction and Fantasy." *Bulletin of the Science Fiction Writers of America* 77 (1982): 22–29.

———. "Goodbye Star Wars. Hello Alley-Oop." In *Inside Outer Space*. Edited by Sharon Jarvis. New York: Ungar, 1985.

———. "Linguistic Sexism in Science Fiction and Fantasy: A Modest Proposal." *Bulletin of the Science Fiction Writers of America* 73 (1980): 7–9, 26.

———. "The Use of Archaeology in Worldbuilding." *Bulletin of the Science Fiction Writers of America* 13 (1978): 5–10. Reprinted in *Glass and Amber*. Cambridge, MA: NESFA, 1987, pp. 123–134.

Lane, Daryl; Vernon, William; and Carlson, David. "C. J. Cherryh." In *The Sound of Wonder: Interviews from "The Science Fiction Radio Show,"* vol. 1. Phoenix, AZ: Oryx Press, 1985, pp. 22–51.

McGuire, Patrick. "Water into Wine: The Novels of C. J. Cherryh." *Starship* 16 (Spring 1979): 47–49.

Twentieth-Century Science Fiction Writers. 3rd ed. Edited by Noelle Watson and Paul E. Schellinger. Chicago: St. James Press, 1991, pp. 135–136.

Vance, Michael. "C. J. Cherryh: The Quiet Berserker." *Science Fiction and Fantasy Review* 65 (1984): 9–10, 22.

Williams, Lynn F. "Women and Power in C. J. Cherryh's Novels." *Extrapolation* 27 (1986): 85–92.

Chetwin, Grace

Lehr, Susan. "Between the Covers: People Behind the Book: Grace Chetwin: Portrait of an Author of Fantasy." *C.L.A. Bulletin* 15 (Fall 1989): 2–4.

Chew, Ruth (Silver)

Sixth Book of Junior Authors and Illustrators. Edited by Sally Holmes Holtze. New York: Wilson, 1989, pp. 56–57.

Chrisman, Arthur Bowie

Chrisman, Arthur Bowie. "The Father of Children's Books." *Horn Book* 3 (Aug 1927): 14–17. (John Newbery)

Jordan, Mrs. Arthur M. "Arthur Chrisman—Newbery Medalist." *Elementary English Review* 3 (Oct 1926): 251, 267.

The Junior Book of Authors. 2nd rev. ed. Edited by Stanley J. Kunitz and Howard Haycraft. New York: Wilson, 1951, pp. 69–70.

Roginski, Jim, ed. *Newbery and Caldecott Medalists and Honor Book Winners.* Littleton, CO: Libraries Unlimited, 1982, p. 65.

"*Shen of the Sea.*" In Bertha Mahony Miller and Elinor Field. *Newbery Medal Books: 1922–1955.* Boston: Horn Book, 1957, pp. 39–43.

Twentieth-Century Children's Writers. 3rd ed. Edited by Tracy Chevalier and D. L. Kirkpatrick. Chicago: St. James, 1989, pp. 194–195.

Christopher, John (pseud. of Christopher Samuel Youd)

Antczak, Janice. *Science Fiction: The Mythos of a New Romance.* New York: Neal-Schuman, 1985, pp. 46–48, 144.

"Authorgraph no. 9: John Christopher." *Books for Keeps* (U.K.) 9 (July 1981): 14–15.

Crago, Hugh, and Maureen Crago. "John Christopher: An Assessment with Reservations." *Children's Book Review* 1 (June 1971): 77–79.

Crouch, Marcus. *The Nesbit Tradition.* Totowa, NJ: Rowman and Littlefield, 1972, pp. 50–52.

Fourth Book of Junior Authors and Illustrators. Edited by Doris De Montreville and Elizabeth D. Crawford. New York: Wilson, 1978, pp. 78–79.

Fraser, John. "The Worlds of John Christopher." *Space Voyager* 9 (1984): 52–54.

Gough, John. "An Interview with John Christopher." *Children's Literature in Education* 15 (Summer 1984): 93–102.

Newsinger, John. "Rebellion and Power in the Juvenile Science Fiction of John Christopher." *Foundation* 47 (Winter 1989–1990): 46.

The Oxford Companion to Children's Literature. Edited by Humphrey Carpenter and Mari Prichard. New York: Oxford Univ. Press, 1984, p. 117.

Ragsdale, W. "Presentation of the Recognition of Merit to John Christopher for the *White Mountains Trilogy.*" *Claremont Reading Conference Yearbook* 41 (1977): 76–79.

Swinfen, Ann. *In Defense of Fantasy.* London: Routledge, 1984, pp. 202–218, 227–229.

Townsend, John Rowe. "John Christopher." In *A Sense of Story.* Philadelphia: Lippincott, 1971, pp. 39–47.

Twentieth-Century Children's Writers. 3rd ed. Edited by Tracy Chevalier and D. L. Kirkpatrick. Chicago: St. James, 1989, pp. 195–196.

Twentieth-Century Science Fiction Writers. 3rd ed. Edited by Noelle Watson and Paul E. Schellinger. Chicago: St. James Press, 1991, pp. 139–141.

Wehmeyer, Lillian B. "The Future of Religion in Junior Novels." *Catholic Library World* 54 (Apr 1983): 366–369.

Williams, Jay. "John Christopher: Allegorical Historian." *Signal* 4 (Jan 1971): 18–23.

Christopher, Matt(hew F.)

Fifth Book of Junior Authors and Illustrators. Edited by Sally Holmes Holtze. New York: Wilson, 1983, pp. 68–69.

Twentieth-Century Children's Writers. 3rd ed. Edited by Tracy Chevalier and D. L. Kirkpatrick. Chicago: St. James, 1989, p. 196.

Church, Richard (Thomas)

Church, Richard. *The Golden Sovereign.* London: Heinemann, 1957.

———. *Over the Bridge.* London: Heinemann, 1955.

———. *The Voyage Home.* London: Heinemann, 1964.

Doyle, Brian. *The Who's Who of Children's Literature.* New York: Shocken, 1968, p. 51.

Hannabuss, Stuart. "The Motive in the Actuality: Richard Church as Writer for Children." *Children's Literature Review* 2 (June 1972): 69–70.

More Junior Authors. Edited by Muriel Fuller. New York: Wilson, 1963, p. 47.

Twentieth-Century Children's Writers. 3rd ed. Edited by Tracy Chevalier and D. L. Kirkpatrick. Chicago: St. James, 1989, pp. 196–198.

Churne of Staffordshire, William *see* Paget, F. E.

Clapp, Patricia

Fifth Book of Junior Authors and Illustrators. Edited by Sally Holmes Holtze. New York: Wilson, 1983, pp. 69–71.

Twentieth-Century Children's Writers. 3rd ed. Edited by Tracy Chevalier and D. L. Kirkpatrick. Chicago: St. James, 1989, pp. 200–202.

Clare, Helen *see* Clarke, Pauline

Clark, Ann Nolan

Bishop, Claire Huchet. "Ann Nolan Clark." *Catholic Library World* 34 (Feb 1963): 280–286, 333.

Clark, Ann Nolan. *Journey to the People.* New York: Viking Press, 1969.

———. "Newbery Award Acceptance." *Horn Book* 29 (Aug 1953): 249–257.

Gilbert, Ophelia. "Ann Nolan Clark." In *American Writers for Children since 1960: Fiction. Dictionary of Literary Biography,* vol. 52. Detroit: Gale, 1986, pp. 75–83.

Griese, Arnold A. "Ann Nolan Clark—Building Bridges of Cultural Understanding." *Elementary English* 49 (May 1972): 648–658.

The Junior Book of Authors. 2nd rev. ed. Edited by Stanley J. Kunitz and Howard Haycraft. New York: Wilson, 1951, p. 71.

Massee, May. "Ann Nolan Clark." *Horn Book* 29 (Aug 1953): 258–262.

Miller, Bertha Mahony, and Elinor Whitney Field. *Newbery Medal Books: 1922–1955.* Boston: Horn Book, 1957, pp. 388–404.

Twentieth-Century Children's Writers. 3rd ed. Edited by Tracy Chevalier and D. L. Kirkpatrick. Chicago: St. James, 1989, pp. 202–203.

Wenzel, Evelyn. "Ann Nolan Clark: 1953 Newbery Award Winner." *Elementary English* 30 (Oct 1953): 327–332. Reprinted in *Authors and Illustrators of Children's Books.* Edited by Miriam Hoffman and Eva Samuels. New York: Bowker, 1972, pp. 62–69.

Clarke, Pauline (pseud. of Pauline [Clarke] Hunter Blair) (a.k.a. Helen Clare)

Clarke, Pauline. "Books Remembered." *C.B.C. Calendar* 34 (Mar–Aug 1975).

———. "Chief Genii Branwell, the Inspiration behind *The Twelve and the Genii.*" *Junior Bookshelf* 27 (July 1963): 119–123.

Doyle, Brian. *The Who's Who of Children's Literature.* New York: Schocken, 1968, pp. 51–52.

Gillespie, John T., and Diana Lembo. *Introducing Books: A Guide for the Middle Grades.* New York: Bowker, 1970, pp. 208–211.

Jones, Cornelia, and Olivia R. Way. "Pauline Clarke." In *British Children's Authors.* Chicago: American Library Association, 1976, pp. 65–76.

Kuznets, Lois. "Good News from the Land of the Brontyfans, or Intertextuality in Clarke's *The Return of the Twelves.*" In *Where Rivers Meet: Confluence and Concurrents: Proceedings of the 1989 Conference of the Children's Literature Association,* ed. by Susan R. Gannon and Ruth A. Thompson. New York: Pace University, 1991, pp. 67–73.

Pflieger, Pat, and Helen M. Hill. *A Reference Guide to Modern Fantasy for Children.* Westport, CT: Greenwood, 1984, pp. xiv, 115–116, 558–559.

Swinfen, Ann. *In Defense of Fantasy.* London: Routledge, 1984, pp. 127–128.

Third Book of Junior Authors. Edited by Doris De Montreville and Donna Hill. New York: Wilson, 1972, p. 67.

"The Twelve and the Genii." In M. Crouch and A. Ellis. *Chosen for Children.* 3rd ed. London: The Library Association, 1977, pp. 117–123.

Twentieth-Century Children's Writers. 3rd ed. Edited by Tracy Chevalier and D. L. Kirkpatrick. Chicago: St. James, 1989, pp. 208–209.

Cleary, Beverly (Atlee Bunn)

"Authorgraph: Beverly Cleary." *Books for Keeps* (U.K.) 7 (Mar 1981): 14–15.

Bauer, Caroline Feller. "Laura Ingalls Wilder Award Presentation." *Horn Book* 51 (Aug 1975): 359–360.

Burns, Paul C., and Ruth Hines. "Beverly Cleary: Wonderful World of Humor." *Elementary English* 44 (Nov 1967): 743–747, 752.

Cleary, Beverly. "Books for 'Kids Like Us.'" *About Books for Children* (U.K.) 1 (Apr 1980): 31–33.

———. "Books Remembered." *The Calendar* (now *CBC Features*) 38 (July 1982–Feb 1983).

———. *A Girl from Yamhill: A Memoir.* New York: Morrow, 1988.

———. "The Laughter of Children." *Horn Book* 58 (Oct 1981): 555–564.

———. "Laura Ingalls Wilder Award Acceptance." *Horn Book* 51 (Aug 1975): 361–364.

———. "Low Man in the Reading Circle: Or, A Blackbird Takes Wing." *Horn Book* 45 (June 1969): 287–293.

———. "Newbery Medal Acceptance." *Horn Book* 60 (Aug 1984): 429–438.

Cooper, Ilene. "The *Booklist* Interview: Beverly Cleary." *Booklist* 87 (Oct 15, 1990): 448–449.

Helbig, Alethea K., and Agnes Regan Perkins. *Dictionary of American Children's Fiction, 1859–1959.* Westport, CT: Greenwood, 1985, pp. 105–106.

———. *Dictionary of American Children's Fiction, 1985–1989.* Westport, CT: Greenwood, 1993, pp. 46–47.

———. *Dictionary of American Children's Fiction, 1960–1984.* Westport, CT: Greenwood, 1986, pp. 117, 435–436, 564–565.

Hopkins, Lee Bennett. "Beverly Cleary." In *More Books by More People.* New York: Citation Press, 1974, pp. 88–94.

Mercier, Jean F. "Beverly Cleary." *Publishers Weekly* 209 (Feb 23, 1976): 54–55. (interview)

More Junior Authors. Edited by Muriel Fuller. New York: Wilson, 1963, pp. 49–50.

Novinger, Margaret. "Beverly Cleary: A Favorite Author of Children." *Southeastern Librarian* 18 (Fall 1968): 194–202. Reprinted in Miriam Hoffman and Eva Samuels. *Authors and Illustrators of Children's Books.* New York: Bowker, 1972, pp. 70–83.

Pflieger, Pat. *Beverly Cleary.* Boston: Twayne, 1991.

Rahn, Suzanne. "Cat-Child: Rediscovering *Socks* and *Island MacKenzie.*" *The Lion and the Unicorn* 12 (1988): 111–120.

Rees, David. "Middle of the Way: Rodie Sudbery and Beverly Cleary." In *Marble in the Water.* Boston: Horn Book, 1980, pp. 90–103.

Reuther, David. "Beverly Cleary." *Horn Book* 60 (Aug 1984): 439–443.

Roggenbuck, Mary June. "Profile: Beverly Cleary—The Children's Force at Work." *Language Arts* 56 (Jan 1979): 55–60.

Roozen, N. "Presentation of the Recognition of Merit Award to Beverly Cleary." *Claremont College Reading Conference Yearbook* (1983): 86–90.

Stan, Susan. "Conversation: Beverly Cleary." *Five Owls* 3 (July–Aug 1989): 87.

Trout, Anita. "Beverly Cleary." In *American Writers for Children since 1960: Fiction. Dictionary of Literary Biography,* vol. 52. Detroit: Gale, 1986, pp. 84–90.

Twentieth-Century Children's Writers. 3rd ed. Edited by Tracy Chevalier and D. L. Kirkpatrick. Chicago: St. James, 1989, pp. 209–210.

Clements, Bruce

Anderson, Celia Catlett. "Journey to Forever and Back: Clements and Babbitt." *Proceedings of the 13th Annual Conference of The Children's Literature Association, 1986.* New York: New York: Pace University, 1988, pp. 64–68.

Fifth Book of Junior Authors and Illustrators. Edited by Sally Holmes Holtze. New York: Wilson, 1983, pp. 71–72.

Gillespie, John T., and Diana Lembo. *Introducing Books: A Guide for the Middle Grades.* New York: Bowker, 1970, pp. 212–214.

Twentieth-Century Children's Writers. 3rd ed. Edited by Tracy Chevalier and D. L. Kirkpatrick. Chicago: St. James, 1989, p. 212.

Coatsworth, Elizabeth (Jane)

Abbott, Barbara. "To Timbuctoo and Back: Elizabeth Coatsworth's Books for Children." *Horn Book* 6 (Nov 1930): 283–289.

Bechtel, Louise Seaman. "Elizabeth Coatsworth: Poet and Writer." *Horn Book* 12 (Jan 1936): 27–31.

"*The Cat Who Went to Heaven.*" In Bertha Miller and Elinor Field. *Newbery Medal Books: 1922–1955.* Boston: Horn Book, 1957, pp. 89–98.

Coatsworth, Elizabeth. *Personal Geography: Almost an Autobiography.* Brattleboro, VT: Stephen Green Press, 1976.

———. "Upon Writing for Children." *Horn Book* 24 (Sept 1948): 389–395. Reprinted in Elinor Field. *Horn Book Reflections.* Boston: Horn Book, 1969, pp. 6–13.

Crouch, Marcus. "Elizabeth Coatsworth: 1893–1986." *Junior Bookshelf* 51 (1987): 68–72.

Doyle, Brian. *The Who's Who of Children's Literature.* New York: Schocken, 1968, pp. 53–54.

Helbig, Alethea K., and Agnes Regan Perkins. *Dictionary of American Children's Fiction, 1859–1959.* Westport, CT: Greenwood, 1985, pp. 89–90, 106–107.

———. *Dictionary of American Children's Fiction, 1960–1984.* Westport, CT: Greenwood, 1986, pp. 121–122.

Hogarth, Grace. "Elizabeth Coatsworth." *Books for Your Children* (U.K.) 10 (May 1975): 8–9.

Hopkins, Lee Bennett. "Elizabeth Coatsworth." In *More Books by More People.* New York: Citation Press, 1974, pp. 95–99.

Jacobs, L. "Elizabeth Coatsworth." *Instructor* 72 (Nov 1962): 100ff.

The Junior Book of Authors. 2nd rev. ed. Edited by Stanley J. Kunitz and Howard Haycraft. New York: Wilson, 1951, pp. 71–73.

Kuhn, Doris Young. "Elizabeth Coatsworth: Perceptive Impressionist." *Elementary English* 46 (Dec 1969): 991–1007. Reprinted in Miriam Hoffman and Eva Samuels. *Authors and Illustrators of Children's Books.* New York: Bowker, 1972, pp. 84–107.

Lukens, Rebecca. "Elizabeth Coatsworth." In *American Writers for Children, 1900–1960. Dictionary of Literary Biography,* vol. 22. Detroit: Gale, 1983, pp. 94–101.

Meigs, Cornelia. "Alice-All-by-Herself." *Horn Book* 14 (Mar 1938): 77–80.

The Oxford Companion to Children's Literature. Edited by Humphrey Carpenter and Mari Prichard. New York: Oxford Univ. Press, 1984, p. 122.

Rice, Mabel F. "The Poetic Prose of Elizabeth Coatsworth." *Elementary English* 31 (Jan 1954): 3–10.

Roginski, Jim, ed. *Newbery and Caldecott Medalists and Honor Book Winners.* Littleton, CO: Libraries Unlimited, 1982, pp. 67–70.

Schmidt, Nancy. *Children's Fiction about Africa in English.* New York: Conch Magazine, 1981, pp. 178–179.

Smaridge, Norah. *Famous Modern Storytellers for Young People.* New York: Dodd, 1969, pp. 57–62.

Twentieth-Century Children's Writers. 3rd ed. Edited by Tracy Chevalier and D. L. Kirkpatrick. Chicago: St. James, 1989, pp. 216–219.

Yolen, Jane. "The Literary Underwater World." *Language Arts* 57 (1980): 403–412.

Cobalt, Martin *see* Wayne, William

Coblentz, Catherine Cate

Coblentz, Catherine Cate. "Through a Diamond Pane." *Horn Book* 19 (Sept 1943): 309–313.

———. "Wading into Yesterday." *Horn Book* 20 (July 1944): 293–298.

Helbig, Alethea K., and Agnes Regan Perkins. *Dictionary of American Children's Fiction, 1859–1959.* Westport, CT: Greenwood, 1985, pp. 57, 107.

The Junior Book of Authors. 2nd rev. ed. Edited by Stanley J. Kunitz and Howard Haycraft. New York: Wilson, 1951, pp. 73–74.

Quimby, Harriet B. "A Second Look: *The Blue Cat of Castle Town.*" *Horn Book* 61 (July–Aug 1985): 481–491.

Roginski, Jim, ed. *Newbery and Caldecott Medalists and Honor Book Winners.* Littleton, CO: Libraries Unlimited, 1982, p. 70.

Cohen, Barbara

Fifth Book of Junior Authors and Illustrators. Edited by Sally Holmes Holtze. New York: Wilson, 1983, pp. 75–76.

Karp, Hazel B., and Sibley Veal. "Point of View." *Advocate* 1 (Winter 1982): 122–125.

Cole, Joanna

Fifth Book of Junior Authors and Illustrators. Edited by Sally Holmes Holtze. New York: Wilson, 1983, pp. 77–78.

Collodi, Carlo (pseud. of Carlo Lorenzini)

Bacon, Martha. "Puppet's Progress: *Pinocchio.*" *Atlantic Monthly* 225 (Apr 1970): 88–90, 92. Reprinted in Virginia Haviland. *Children and Literature.* Glenview, IL: Scott, Foresman, 1973, pp. 71–77.

Beyer, Roland. "*Pinocchio,* Roman Sans Fin [*Pinocchio,* Novel Without an End]." *Janus Bifrons* (France) 8 (1983): 95–112.

Bosetti, G. "Actualité Singuliere et Plurielle de *Pinocchio* [Current Single and Multiple Aspects of Pinocchio]." *Nous Voulons Lire* [France] 49(1983): 1–24.

Cambon, Glauco. "*Pinocchio* and the Problem of Children's Literature." In *Children's Literature,* vol. 2. Storrs, CT: Journal of the Modern Language Association, 1973, pp. 50–60.

Cazelles, Nicolas. "Le Cas de Pinocchio en France." *Revue de Littérature Comparée* 63 (Apr–June 1989): 209–215.

Cech, John. "The Triumphant Transformations of *Pinocchio.*" In *Triumphs of the Spirit in Children's Literature.* Edited by Francelia Butler and Richard Rotert. Hamden, CT: Shoe String Press, 1986, pp. 171–179.

Cro, Stelio. "Collodi: When Children's Literature Becomes Adult." *Merveilles & Contes* 7 (May 1993): 87–111.

Doyle, Brian. *The Who's Who of Children's Literature.* New York: Schocken, 1968, pp. 56–57.

Filimonova, N., and L. Ziman. "Dolagaya Zhinzn' Chelovechka S Dlinnym Nosom [The Long Life of the Little Man with the Long Nose: *Pinocchio* in Illustrations by Foreign Artists]." *Detskaya Literatura* (Moscow) 4 (Apr 1983): 43–53.

Frey, Charles, and John Griffiths. *The Literary Heritage of Childhood: An Appraisal of Children's Classics in the Western Tradition.* Westport, CT: Greenwood, 1987, pp. 99–106.

Gannon, Susan R. "A Note on Collodi and Lucian." In *Children's Literature,* vol. 8. New Haven, CT: Yale Univ. Press, 1980, pp. 98–102.

―――. "*Pinocchio:* The First Hundred Years." *Children's Literature Association Quarterly* 6 (Winter 1981–1982): 1, 5–8. Reprinted in *The First Steps.* Edited by Patricia Dooley. West Lafayette, IN: Children's Literature Association Publications, 1984, pp. 131–133.

Hawkes, Louise Restieaux. *Before and after "Pinocchio": A Study of Italian Children's Books.* Paris: Puppet Press, 1933.

Hazard, Paul. *Books, Children and Men,* 4th ed. Boston: Horn Book, 1960, pp. 111–119. Excerpted in *Horn Book* 19 (Mar–Apr 1943): 119–126.

Heins, Paul. "A Second Look: *The Adventures of Pinocchio.*" *Horn Book* 58 (Apr 1982): 200–204.

Heisig, James. "*Pinocchio:* Archetype of the Motherless Child." In *Children's Literature,* vol. 3. Storrs, CT: Journal of the Modern Language Association, 1974, pp. 23–35. Reprinted in *Reflections on Literature for Children.* Edited by Francelia Butler. Hamden, CT: Shoe String Press, 1984, pp. 155–170.

The Junior Book of Authors. 2nd rev. ed. Edited by Stanley J. Kunitz and Howard Haycraft. New York: Wilson, 1951, pp. 74–76.

Kissel, S. S. " 'But When at Last She Really Came, I Shot Her': *Peter Pan* and the Drama of Gender." *Children's Literature in Education* 19 (Spring 1988): 32–41.

Mareschi, Daniela. "Collodi Sterniano. Da *Un Romanzo in Vapore alle Avventure di Pinocchio.*" *Merveilles & Contes* 7 (May 1993): 51–68.

Mayne, W. G. "*Pinocchio* Turns Fascist." *Living Age* 359, no. 4493 (Feb 1941): 569–571. Reprinted in Mary Lou White. *Children's Literature.* Columbus, OH: Merrill, 1976, pp. 56–58.

Melegari, V. "*Pinocchio, Cuore,* and Other Italian Books." *Junior Bookshelf* 19 (Mar 1955): 71–77.

Morrissey, Thomas J. "Alive and Well but Not Unscathed: A Reply to Susan R. Gannon's '*Pinocchio* at 100.'" *Children's Literature Association Quarterly* 7 (Summer 1982): 37–38.

Morrissey, Thomas J., and Richard Wunderlich. "Death and Rebirth in Pinocchio." In *Children's Literature,* vol. 11. New Haven, CT: Yale Univ. Press, 1983, pp. 64–75.

The Oxford Companion to Children's Literature. Edited by Humphrey Carpenter and Mari Prichard. New York: Oxford Univ. Press, 1984, pp. 123, 413–414.

Patterson, Harriet. "*Pinocchio*'s Growing Nose." *The Age* (Australia) (Feb 9, 1991): 3.

Petrini, E. "Collodi and His Times." *Bookbird* 13, no. 1 (1975): 24–26.
Poesio, Carla. *"Pinocchio's Centenary Celebrations."* Horn Book *58 (Apr 1982): 235–239;* Bookbird *21 (1983): 29–30.*
Redmont, Dennis. "*Pinocchio* Lives at 100." *The Gainsville Sun* (Nov 28, 1980).
Russell, David L. "*Pinocchio* and the Child-Hero's Quest." *Children's Literature in Education* 20 (Dec 1989): 203–214.
Sacchetti, L. "Riscoperta di un *Pinocchio*: Echi di un Congresso: Considerazioni e Interrogativi [*Pinocchio* Is Discovered Again: Report on the First Collodi Congress in Pescia, 1974]." *Schedario* (Italy) 136 (July–Aug 1975): 4–8.
Schroeder, Ida. "Homage to Pinocchio." *Horn Book* 35, no. 5 (Oct 1959): 368–373. Reprinted in Robinson. *Readings about Children's Literature.* New York: McKay, 1966, pp. 302–303.
Segal, Elizabeth. "Beastly Boys: A Century of Mischief." *Children's Literature in Education* 18 (1987): 3–12.
Stott, Jon C. *Children's Literature from A to Z.* New York: McGraw-Hill, 1984, p. 80.
Street, Douglas. "*Pinocchio*—From Picaro to Pipsqueak." In Douglas Street. *Children's Novels and the Movies.* New York: Ungar, 1983, pp. 47–57.
Taylor, David. "Toy Town." *Radio Times* 221 (Dec 2–8, 1978): 4–5.
Teahan, James T. "Carlo Collodi." In *Writers for Children: Critical Studies of Major Authors Since the Seventeenth Century.* Edited by Jane M. Bingham. New York: Scribner, 1988, pp. 129–138.
West, Mark I. "From the Pleasure Principle to the Reality Principle: *Pinocchio's* Psychological Journey." *Proceedings of the 13th Annual Conference of The Children's Literature Association, 1986.* New York: Pace University, 1988, pp. 112–115.
Wunderlich, Richard. "The Tribulations of *Pinocchio*: How Social Change Can Wreck a Good Story." *Poetics Today* 13 (Spring 1992): 197–219.
———, comp. *The Pinocchio Catalogue: Being a Descriptive Bibliography and History of English Language Translations and Other Renditions Appearing in the United States, 1892–1987.* Westport, CT.: Greenwood, 1988.
Wunderlich, Richard, and Thomas J. Morrissey. "Carlo Collodi's *The Adventures of Pinocchio:* A Classic Book of Choices." In *Touchstones.* Edited by Perry Nodelman. West Lafayette, IN: Children's Literature Association Publications, 1985, pp. 53–63.
———. "The Desecration of *Pinocchio* in the United States." In *Proceedings of the Eighth Annual Conference of the Children's Literature Association.* University of Minnesota, March 1981. Ypsilanti, MI: Children's Literature Association, 1982, pp. 106–118. Reprinted in *Horn Book* 58 (Apr 1982): 205–211.
———. "*Pinocchio* before 1920: The Popular and Pedagogical Traditions." *Italian Quarterly* 23 (Spring 1982): 61–72.
Zago, Esther. "Carlo Collodi as Translator; From Fairy Tale to Folk Tale." *The Lion and the Unicorn* 12 (1988): 61–73.

Colum, Padraic

Bechtel, Louise Seaman. "Padraic Colum: A Great Storyteller of Today." *Catholic Library World* 32 (Dec 1960): 159–160.
Bowen, Zackary R. *"Padraic Colum: A Biographical-Critical Introduction.* Carbondale: Southern Illinois Univ. Press, 1970.
Colum, Padraic. "Imagination and the Literature of Children." *Illinois Libraries* 7 (1925): 50–52.
———. "Patterns for the Imagination: Acceptance of the 1961 Regina Medal Award." *Horn Book* 36 (Feb 1962): 82–86.
———. "Storyteller's Story: The Power of Imagination." *New York Public Library Bulletin* 70 (Oct 1966): 528–532.

————. "Storytelling in Ireland." *Horn Book* 10 (May 1934): 190–194.

————. "Storytelling New and Old." In *The Fountain of Youth.* New York: MacMillan, 1927, 1968. Reprinted in *Horn Book* 59 (June 1983): 358–377.

Dolbier, Maurice. "Padraic Colum." *N.Y. Herald Tribune Book Review* (June 9, 1957).

Greene, Ellin. "Literary Uses of Traditional Themes: From 'Cinderella' to *The Girl Who Sat by the Ashes* and *The Glass Slipper.*" *Children's Literature Association Quarterly* 11 (Fall 1986): 128–132.

Helbig, Alethea K., and Agnes Regan Perkins. *Dictionary of American Children's Fiction, 1859–1959.* Westport, CT: Greenwood, 1985, pp. 108–109, 559–560.

The Junior Book of Authors. 2nd rev. ed. Edited by Stanley J. Kunitz and Howard Haycraft. New York: Wilson, 1951, pp. 76–77.

Mahony, Bertha E. "Tir-Nan-Oge and Tir Tairngire." *Horn Book* 10 (Jan 1934): 31–36.

Myers, Andrew. "'In the Wild Earth a Grecian Vace!' For Padraic Colum (1881–1972)." *Columbia Library Columns* 22 (Feb 1973): 11–21.

Nichols, L. "A Talk with Padraic Colum." *New York Times Book Review* 15 (June 23, 1957): 1.

The Oxford Companion to Children's Literature. Edited by Humphrey Carpenter and Mari Prichard. New York: Oxford Univ. Press, 1984, p. 125.

Roginski, Jim, ed. *Newbery and Caldecott Medalists and Honor Book Winners.* Littleton, CO: Libraries Unlimited, 1982, pp. 71–73.

Seaman, Louise H. "Stories Out of the Youth of the World—As Recreated by Padraic Colum." *Horn Book* 1 (Mar 1925): 16–20.

Twentieth-Century Children's Writers. 3rd ed. Edited by Tracy Chevalier and D. L. Kirkpatrick. Chicago: St. James, 1989, pp. 226–228.

Warren, Dorothea C. "Padraic Colum." In *Writers for Children: Critical Studies of Major Authors Since the Seventeenth Century.* Edited by Jane M. Bingham. New York: Scribner, 1988, pp. 139–146.

Conford, Ellen

Gillespie, John T. *Juniorplots 4: A Book Talk Guide for Use with Readers Ages 12–16.* New Providence, NJ: Bowker, 1993, pp. 202–205.

Twentieth-Century Children's Writers. 3rd ed. Edited by Tracy Chevalier and D. L. Kirkpatrick. Chicago: St. James, 1989, pp. 228–229.

Conrad, Pam

Conrad, Pam. "The Last Book." *Horn Book* 68 (May–June 1992): 309–310.

Dietrich, M. A., and B. Longo. "Focus on: Pam Conrad." *School Librarian's Workshop* 13 (Jan 1993): 11–12.

Helbig, Alethea, and Agnes Regan Perkins. *Dictionary of American Children's Fiction, 1985–1989.* Westport, CT: Greenwood, 1993, pp. 50–51.

Micklos, John, Jr. "Connecting with Readers: Pam Conrad's Books Touch Emotions." *Reading Today* (Newark, DE) (Dec 1991–Jan 1992): 14.

Rinn, M. "Author Profile: Pam Conrad." *Book Report* 12 (May–June 1993): 28–30.

Coolidge, Olivia E(nsor)

Helbig, Alethea K., and Agnes Regan Perkins. *Dictionary of American Children's Fiction, 1960–1984.* Westport, CT: Greenwood, 1986, pp. 129–130.

More Junior Authors. Edited by Muriel Fuller. New York: Wilson, 1963, pp. 52–53.

Cooper, Paul F(enimore)

Dalphin, Marcia. "I Give You the End of a Golden String." *Horn Book* 14 (May 1938): 143–149. Reprinted in Norma Fryatt. *A Horn Book Sampler.* Boston: Horn Book, 1959, pp. 133–139.

Jones, Louis C. "Paul Fenimore Cooper and *Tal.*" *Horn Book* 26 (Jan–Feb 1950): 30–32. Reprinted in Elinor Field. *Horn Book Reflections.* Boston: Horn Book, 1969, pp. 238–241.

Cooper (Grant), Susan (Mary)

"Adventure: The Novels of Susan Cooper." *Books for Your Children* (U.K.) 11 (Spring 1976): 9.

Bisenieks, Dainis. "Children, Magic and Choices." *Mythlore* 6 (Winter 1979): 13–16.

Canham, Stephen. "Evil and the High Ethical Fantasy of Susan Cooper's *The Dark Is Rising.*" In *Literature and Hawaii's Children,* ed. by Cristina Bacchilega and Steven Curry. Honolulu: Literature and Hawaii's Children, 1990, pp. 107–111.

Carlson, Dudley Brown. "A Second Look: *Over Sea, Under Stone.*" *Horn Book* 52 (Oct 1976): 522–523.

Cooper, Susan. "Address Delivered at the Children's Round Table Breakfast: Is There Really Such a Species Called Children's Books?" *Texas Library Journal* 52 (May 1976): 52–54.

———. "Creating the Tools." *Youth Library Review* (U.K.) 11 (1991): 6–8, 10–14.

———. "*The Dark Is Rising.*" *School Bookshop News* (U.K.) 7 (Summer 1977): 7–9.

———. "A Dream of Revels." *Horn Book* 55 (Dec 1979): 633–640.

———. "Escaping into Ourselves." In Betsy Hearne and Marilyn Kaye. *Celebrating Children's Books: Essays on Children's Literature in Honor of Zena Sutherland.* New York: Lothrop, 1981, pp. 14–23. Reprinted in Boyer and Zahorski. *Fantasists on Fantasy.* New York: Avon, 1984, pp. 277–287.

———. "Fantasy in the Real World." *Horn Book* 66 (May–June 1990): 304–315.

———. "How I Began." *New Welsh Review* 2, no. 4 (1990): 19–21.

———. "In Defense of the Artist." In *Proceedings of the Fifth Annual Conference of the Children's Literature Association.* Harvard University, March 1978. Ypsilanti, MI: Children's Literature Association, 1979, pp. 20–28. Reprinted in Robert Bator. *Signposts to Criticism of Children's Literature.* Chicago: American Library Association, 1983, pp. 98–108.

———. "A Love Letter to the *Horn Book.*" *Horn Book* 50 (Oct 1974): 182–183.

———. "My Links with Wales." In *Loughborough '83: Proceedings.* Welsh National Centre for Children's Literature, 1984, pp. 79–81.

———. "My Work." *Books for Your Children* (U.K.) 19 (Autumn/Winter 1984): 33.

———. "Nahum Tarune's Book." *Horn Book* 56 (Oct 1980): 497–507. Reprinted in *Innocence & Experience.* Edited by Barbara Harrison and Gregory Maguire. New York: Lothrop, 1987, pp. 76–86.

———. "Newbery Award Acceptance Address." *Horn Book* 52 (Aug 1967): 361–366; *Top of the News* 33 (Fall 1976): 39–43.

———. "Preserving the Light." *Magpies* (Australia) 3 (May 1988): 5–9.

———. "Susan Cooper—A Famous Author from Wales Who Writes about Wales." *Bookbird* 17, no. 4 (1979): 19–21.

———. "Susan Cooper's *The Boggart.*" *Book Links* 3 (Nov 1993): 47–50.

———. [Tir na n-Og Acceptance Speech] *Bookbird* (Denmark) 4 (1979): 19–21.

Dawson, Jean I. "Fantasy in the Post-Christian Era: Some Comments on the Novels of Susan Cooper and Ursula Le Guin." *Orana* 20 (Nov 1984): 161–168.

Esmonde, Margaret. Articles on Susan Cooper's *Dark Is Rising* sequence. *Fantasiae* (Nov 1974): 6–7, (Jan 1975): 7–9, (Feb 1975): 5–6, (Feb 1976): 7–8.

Evans, Emrys. "Children's Novels and Welsh Mythology: Multiple Voices in Susan Cooper and Alan Garner." In *The Voice of the Narrator in Children's Literature: Insights from Writers and Critics,* ed. by Charlotte F. Otten and Gary D. Schmidt. New York: Greenwood, 1989, pp. 92–100.

Evans, Gwyneth. "Harps and Harpers in Contemporary Fantasy." *The Lion and the Unicorn* 16 (Dec 1992): 199–209.

———. "Three Modern Views of Merlin." *Mythlore* 16 (Summer 1990): 17–22.

Filmer-Davies, Kath. "Welsh Myth and Contemporary Literature." *Mythlore* 73 (Summer 1993): 53–58. Discusses Susan Cooper, Nikolai Tolstoi, Lloyd Alexander, Madeleine L'Engle, Brian Caswell, Jay Ashton, and Nancy Bond.

Fourth Book of Junior Authors and Illustrators. Edited by Doris De Montreville and Elizabeth D. Crawford. New York: Wilson, 1978, pp. 98–99.

Gilderdale, B. "Susan Cooper, *The Dark Is Rising,* and the Legends." *Children's Literature Association Yearbook* (Auckland, New Zealand), vol. 7 (1978), pp. 11–23.

Goodrich, Peter. "Magical Medievalism and the Fairy Tale in Susan Cooper's *The Dark Is Rising* Sequence." *The Lion and the Unicorn* 12 (1988): 165–177.

Gough, John. "A Critical View of Susan Cooper's Fantasy Quintet, *The Dark Is Rising.*" *English in Education* (U.K.) 19 (Summer 1985): 55–66.

Greenlaw, M. Jean, "Books in the Classroom." *Horn Book* 64 (Nov/Dec 1988): 820–822.

"*The Grey King.*" In *Newbery and Caldecott Medal Books 1976–1985.* Edited by Lee Kingman. Boston: Horn Book, 1986, pp. 3–17.

Heins, Ethel L. "*The Dark Is Rising,* a Review." *Horn Book* 49 (June 1973): 286.

Helbig, Alethea K., and Agnes Regan Perkins. *Dictionary of American Children's Fiction, 1960–1984.* Westport, CT: Greenwood, 1986, pp. 130, 144–145, 257–258, 496–497.

Hipolito, Jane. "*The Dark Is Rising* Series." In Frank N. Magill. *Survey of Modern Fantasy Literature,* vol. 1. Englewood Cliffs, NJ: Salem Press, 1983, pp. 331–335.

Kuznets, Lois R. "'High Fantasy' in America: Alexander, Le Guin and Cooper." An unpublished paper delivered at the Conference on Fantasy and Social Values in German and American Children's Literature, Humanities Institute of Brooklyn College, March 1984.

———. "'High Fantasy' in America: A Study of Lloyd Alexander, Ursula Le Guin, and Susan Cooper." *The Lion and the Unicorn* 9(1985): 19–35.

———. "Susan Cooper: A Reply." *Children's Literature Association Newsletter* 3 (Spring–Summer 1978): 14–16. Reprinted in Robert Bator. *Signposts to Criticism of Children's Literature.* Chicago: American Library Association, 1983, pp. 109–113.

Lehnert-Rodiek, Gertrud. "Fantastic Children's Literature and Travel in Time." *Phaedrus* 13 (1988): 61–72.

Levin, Betty. "Journey through Mountain and Mist: *The Grey King.*" *Horn Book* 52 (Aug 1976): 443–445.

Lind, Dianne. "The Importance of Fantasy in Young Adult Literature." *ALAN Review* 15 (1988): 13–14.

McElderry, Margaret K. "Susan Cooper." *Horn Book* 52 (Aug 1976): 367–372.

Nugent, Susan Monroe. "Quests for Self-Awareness." *ALAN Review* 15 (1988): 43–44.

The Oxford Companion to Children's Literature. Edited by Humphrey Carpenter and Mari Prichard. New York: Oxford Univ. Press, 1984, pp. 130, 141–142.

Pearson, Maisie K. "High Magic and the Presence of Good and Evil in the Novels of Susan Cooper." Paper presented at the 1982 Popular Culture/American Culture Association Meeting, Louisville, KY, April 1982.

"The Perilous Realms: A Colloquy." In *Innocence & Experience.* Edited by Barbara Harrison and Gregory Maguire. New York: Lothrop, 1987, pp. 195–210.

Pflieger, Pat, and Helen M. Hill. *A Reference Guide to Modern Fantasy for Children.* Westport, CT: Greenwood, 1984, pp. xii–xiv, 122–125, 138–140, 216–218, 414–415, 492–494.

Philip, Neil. "Fantasy: Double Cream or Instant Whip?" *Signal* 35 (May 1981): 82–90.

Plante, Raymond L. "Object and Character in *The Dark Is Rising.*" *Children's Literature Association Quarterly* 11 (Spring 1986): 37–41.

Rees, David. "Children's Writers: Susan Cooper." *School Librarian* 32 (Sept 1984): 197–205.

———. "The Dark Is Risible: Susan Cooper." In *"What Do Draculas Do?" Essays on Contemporary Writers of Fiction for Children and Young Adults.* Metuchen, NJ: Scarecrow Press, 1990, pp. 175–189.

Roginski, Jim, ed. *Newbery and Caldecott Medalists and Honor Book Winners.* Littleton, CO: Libraries Unlimited, 1982, p. 76.

Schmidt, Gary D. "See How They Grow: Character Development in Children's Series Books." *Children's Literature in Education* 18 (1987): 34–44.

Searles, Baird, Beth Meacham, and Michael Franklin. *A Reader's Guide to Fantasy.* New York: Avon, 1982, pp. 47–48.

Speaking for Ourselves: Autobiographical Sketches by Notable Authors of Books for Young Adults. Edited by Donald R. Gallo. Urbana, IL: National Council of Teachers of English, 1990, pp. 54–56.

Spirt, Diana L. *Introducing Bookplots 3: A Book Talk Guide for Use with Readers Ages 8–12.* New York: Bowker, 1988, pp. 215–218.

Spivak, Charlotte. *Merlin's Daughters: Contemporary Women Writers of Fantasy.* New York: Greenwood, 1987, pp. 35–50.

Spraggs, Gillian. "A Lawless World: The Fantasy Novels of Susan Cooper." *Use of English* 33 (Spring 1982): 23–31.

Stott, Jon C. "The Nature of Fantasy: A Conversation with Ruth Nichols, Susan Cooper, and Maurice Sendak." *World of Children's Books* 3, no. 2 (Fall 1978): 32–43.

Sullivan, C. W., III. "Traditional Welsh Materials in Modern Fantasy." *Extrapolation* 28 (Spring 1987): 87–97.

———. *Welsh Celtic Myth in Modern Fantasy.* Westport, CT: Greenwood, 1989, pp. 55, 66–75+.

Swinfen, Ann. *In Defense of Fantasy: A Study of the Genre in English and American Literature since 1945.* Boston: Routledge, 1984, pp. 141–146.

Thompson, Hilary. "Doorways to Fantasy." *Canadian Children's Literature* 21 (1981): 8–16.

Thwaite, Ann. "Gooseflesh and Nameless Longings." *Times Literary Supplement* March 29, 1985, p. 348.

Townsend, John Rowe. "Guest Essay: Heights of Fantasy." *Children's Literature Review,* vol. 5. Detroit: Gale, 1983, pp. 9–10.

Trautmann, Patricia Ann. "Welsh Mythology and Arthurian Legend in the Novels of Lloyd Alexander and Susan Cooper: Parallels of Motif, Character and Other Elements." Ph.D. diss., Vanderbilt University, 1984.

Tucker, Nicholas. "The Work of Susan Cooper." *Books for Your Children* (U.K.) 19 (Autumn–Winter 1984): 32.

Twentieth-Century Children's Writers. 3rd ed. Edited by Tracy Chevalier and D. L. Kirkpatrick. Chicago: St. James, 1989, pp. 231–232.

Veeder, Mary Harris. "Gender and Empowerment in Susan Cooper's *The Dark Is Rising* Series." *Children's Literature Association Quarterly* 16 (Spring 1991): 11–15.

Veglahn, Nancy. "Images of Evil: Male and Female Monsters in Heroic Fantasy." *Children's Literature* 15 (1987): 106–119.

Ziefer, Barbara Z. "Wales as a Setting for Children's Fantasy." *Children's Literature in Education* 13 (Summer 1982): 95–102.

Corbett, Scott

Fourth Book of Junior Authors and Illustrators. Edited by Doris De Montreville and Elizabeth D. Crawford. New York: Wilson, 1978, pp. 99–100.

Gillespie, John T., and Diana Lembo. *Introducing Books: A Guide for the Middle Grades.* New York: Bowker, 1970, pp. 33–35.

Helbig, Alethea K., and Agnes Regan Perkins. *Dictionary of American Children's Fiction, 1960–1984.* Westport, CT: Greenwood, 1986, pp. 130–131.

Twentieth-Century Children's Writers. 3rd ed. Edited by Tracy Chevalier and D. L. Kirkpatrick. Chicago: St. James, 1989, pp. 232–234.

Corbett, W(illiam) J(esse)

Twentieth-Century Children's Writers. 3rd ed. Edited by Tracy Chevalier and D. L. Kirkpatrick. Chicago: St. James, 1989, p. 234.

Cosgrove (Payes), Rachel R.

Hanff, Peter E., and Douglas G. Greene. *Bibliographia Oziana.* Demorest, GA: International Wizard of Oz Club, 1976.

Coville, Bruce

Coville, Bruce. "Magic Mirrors." *Bookmark* [New York State Library] 49 (Fall 1990): 35–36.

Cowper, Richard (pseud. of John Middleton-Murray, Jr.)

Cowper, Richard. "Apropos: The White Bird of Kinship." *Vector* 110 (1982): 6–13.

———. "Is There a Story in It Somewhere?" In *The Science Fiction Sourcebook.* New York: Van Nostrand Reinhold, 1984, pp. 74–75.

———. "The Profession of Science Fiction: X: Backwards Across the Frontier." *Foundation* 9 (1975): 4–21.

Elliot, Jeffrey. "Interview: Richard Cowper." *Fantasy Newsletter* 36 (1981): 17–24, 30.

Twentieth-Century Science Fiction Writers. 3rd ed. Edited by Noelle Watson and Paul E. Schellinger. Chicago: St. James Press, 1991, pp. 163–165.

Cox, Palmer

Cummins, R. W. *Humorous but Wholesome: A History of Palmer Cox and the Brownies.* Watkins Glen, NY: Century, 1973.

The Oxford Companion to Children's Literature. Edited by Humphrey Carpenter and Mari Prichard. New York: Oxford Univ. Press, 1984, p. 132.

Spivak, Charlotte. "Palmer Cox." In *American Writers for Children before 1900. Dictionary of Literary Biography,* vol. 42. Detroit: Gale, 1985, pp. 133–138.

Twentieth Century Children's Writers. 2nd ed. Edited by D. L. Kirkpatrick. New York: St. Martin, 1983, pp. 864–865.

Craik, Dinah *see* Mulock, Diana

Cranch, Christopher P(earse)

Miller, R. DeWolfe. *Christopher Pearse Cranch and His Caricatures of New England Transcendentalism.* Cambridge, MA: Harvard Univ. Press, 1951.

The Oxford Companion to Children's Literature. Edited by Humphrey Carpenter and Mari Prichard. New York: Oxford Univ. Press, 1984, p. 133.

Scott, Leonora Cranch. *The Life and Letters of Christopher Pearse Cranch.* Boston: Houghton, 1917.

West, Mark I., ed. *Before Oz: Juvenile Fantasy Stories from Nineteenth Century America.* Archon, 1989. "The Last of the Huggermuggers," pp. 11–25.

Cregan, Mairin

Patee, Doris. "Mairin Cregan and *Old John.*" *Horn Book* 12 (May 1936): 165–166.

Cresswell (Rowe), Helen

"Authorgraph no. 42: Helen Cresswell." *Books for Keeps* (U.K.) 42 (1986): 12–13.

Cresswell, Helen. "Ancient and Modern and Incorrigibly Plural." In Edward Blishen. *The Thorny Paradise.* Boston: Horn Book, 1975, pp. 108–116.

———. "Dreams Dare." *Books for Your Children* (U.K.) (1972). Reprinted in *School Bookshop News* (U.K.) 12 (Spring 1979): 17–19.

———. "The Great Pie." *Magpies* (Australia) 4 (Mar 1989): 13.

———. "How I Wrote *The Night Watchmen.*" *Puffin Post* (U.K.) 9, no. 4 (1975): 20, 24.

———. "If It's Someone from Porlock, Don't Answer the Door." *Children's Literature in Education* 4 (Mar 1971): 32–39.

———. "Only Negatively Capable." *Books for Your Children* (U.K.) (1971). Reprinted in *School Bookshop News* (U.K.) 12 (Spring 1979): 17–19.

Crouch, Marcus S. "Helen Cresswell, Craftsman." *Junior Bookshelf* 34 (June 1970): 135–139.

Elleman, Barbara. "*A Game of Catch.*" *Booklist* 82 (Nov 15, 1985): 494–496. Speech given at the 1985 Children's Books Open Forum, 1985 ALA Conference.

Fourth Book of Junior Authors and Illustrators. Edited by Doris De Montreville and Elizabeth D. Crawford. New York: Wilson, 1978, pp. 105–106.

Greaves, Margaret. "Warm Sun, Cold Wind: The Novels of Helen Cresswell." *Children's Literature in Education* 5 (July 1971): 51–59.

Kingsley, Madeleine. "Tell Us a Story." *Radio Times* 221 (Dec 2–8, 1978): 4–5. (interview)

Maguire, Gregory. "A Second Look: *The Piemakers.*" *Horn Book* 57 (Apr 1981): 215–217.

Merrick, Anne. "*The Nightwatchmen* and *Charlie and the Chocolate Factory* as Books to Be Read to Children." *Children's Literature in Education* 16 (Spring 1975): 21–30.

The Oxford Companion to Children's Literature. Edited by Humphrey Carpenter and Mari Prichard. New York: Oxford Univ. Press, 1984, p. 134.

Philip, Neil. "Facing into the Light." *Times Educational Supplement* (Mar 27, 1981): 28.

Rees, David. "Persons from Porlock: Helen Cresswell." In "*What Do Draculas Do?*" *Essays on Contemporary Writers of Fiction for Children and Young Adults.* Metuchen, NJ: Scarecrow Press, 1990, pp. 206–221.

Swinfen, Ann. *In Defense of Fantasy: A Study of the Genre in English and American Literature since 1945.* Boston: Routledge, 1984, pp. 72–74.

Townsend, John Rowe. "Helen Cresswell." In *A Sense of Story.* Philadelphia: Lippincott, 1971, pp. 57–67.

Twentieth Century Children's Writers. 3rd ed. Edited by Tracy Chevalier and D. L. Kirkpatrick. New York: St. Martin, 1989, pp. 241–243.

Crew, Gary

Crew, Gary. "New Directions in Fiction" *Magpies* (Australia) 3 (July 1992): 5–8.

Mills, Alice. "Written in Blood: *So Much to Tell You* and *Strange Objects.*" *Papers: Explorations into Children's Literature* (Australia) 4 (Apr 1993): 38–41.

Cross, Gillian (Clare Arnold)

Barker, Keith. *Gillian Cross.* Swindon, U.K.: School Library Association, 1992.
Carter, Margaret, and Gillian Cross. "The Work of Gillian Cross." *Books for Your Children* [U. K.] 19 (Summer 1984): 15–16.
Cross, Gillian. "Carnegie Medal Acceptance Speech." *Youth Library Review* (U.K.) 12 (Autumn 1991): 7–8.
———. "Twenty Things I Don't Believe about Children's Books." *School Librarian* 39, no. 2(1991): 44–46.
Self, D. "First Catch Your Reader." *Times Educational Supplement Review: Children's Books* (Feb 19, 1993): 1.
Sixth Book of Junior Authors and Illustrators. Edited by Sally Holmes Holtze. New York: Wilson, 1989, pp. 66–67.
Twentieth-Century Children's Writers. 3rd ed. Edited by Tracy Chevalier and D. L. Kirkpatrick. Chicago: St. James, 1989, pp. 247–249.
Whitehead, W. "The Novels of Gillian Cross." *Use of English* (U.K.) 43 (1992): 57–66.

Cross, John Keir

Cross, John Keir. *Aspect of Life: An Autobiography of Youth.* London: Selwyn and Blount, 1937.
Doyle, Brian. *The Who's Who of Children's Literature.* New York: Schocken, 1968, pp. 66–67.
Twentieth-Century Science Fiction Writers. 3rd ed. Edited by Noelle Watson and Paul E. Schellinger. Chicago: St. James Press, 1991, pp. 177–178.

Crownfield, Getrude

The Junior Book of Authors. 2nd rev. ed. Edited by Stanley J. Kunitz and Howard Haycraft. New York: Wilson, 1951, p. 83.

Cullen, Countee (Porter)

Cullen, Countee. *My Soul's High Song: The Collected Writings of Countee Cullen, Voice of the Harlem Renaissance,* ed. by Gerald L. Early. New York: Doubleday, 1991.
Fourth Book of Junior Authors and Illustrators. Edited by Doris De Montreville and Elizabeth D. Crawford. New York: Wilson, 1978, pp. 110–112.
Shucard, Alan R. *Countee Cullen.* Boston: Twayne, 1984.

cummings, e. e.

Ostrom, Alan. "*Fairy Tales*: The Other cummings." *The Lion and the Unicorn* 2 (Spring 1978): 65–72.

Cunningham, Julia (Woolfolk)

Cunningham, Julia. "The Creative Spirit and Children's Literature: A Symposium." Paper presented at the University of California, Berkeley, July 1977. *Wilson Library Bulletin* 53 (Oct 1978): 155–160.

———. "Dear Characters." *Horn Book* 43 (Apr 1967): 233–234.

———. "From Another Edge of the Forest." *Horn Book* 42 (June 1966): 291.

Helbig, Alethea K., and Agnes Regan Perkins. *Dictionary of American Children's Fiction, 1960–1984.* Westport, CT: Greenwood, 1986, pp. 82–83, 126, 136, 165, 217–218, 673–674.

Hopkins, Lee Bennett. "Julia Cunningham." In *More Books by More People.* New York: Citation Press, 1974, pp. 105–109.

Jones, Raymond E. "Ironic Journeys in *Dorp Dead.*" *Proceedings of the 13th Annual Conference of The Children's Literature Association, 1986.* New York: Pace University, 1988, pp. 80–83.

Keyser, Elizabeth Lennox. "A Contemporary Gothic for Girls: Julia Cunningham's *Tuppenny.*" *Children's Literature in Education* 17 (Summer 1986): 88–100.

Third Book of Junior Authors. Edited by Doris De Montreville and Donna Hill. New York: Wilson, 1972, pp. 70–71.

Twentieth-Century Children's Writers. 3rd ed. Edited by Tracy Chevalier and D. L. Kirkpatrick. Chicago: St. James, 1989, pp. 252–253.

Curry, Jane L(ouise)

Bridgewater, Sue. "The Sense of Belonging: An Introduction to the Novels of Jane Louise Curry." *International Review of Children's Literature and Librarianship* 3 (Winter 1988): 176–189.

Curry, Jane Louise. "On the Elvish Craft." *Signal* 2 (May 1970): 42–49. Reprinted in Nancy Chambers. *Signal Approach to Children's Books.* Metuchen, NJ: Scarecrow Press, 1981, pp. 83–93.

Fourth Book of Junior Authors and Illustrators. Edited by Doris De Montreville and Elizabeth D. Crawford. New York: Wilson, 1978, pp. 112–113.

Helbig, Alethea K., and Agnes Regan Perkins. *Dictionary of American Children's Fiction, 1960–1984.* Westport, CT: Greenwood, 1986, pp. 38–39, 137, 521–522.

Mills, Marion. "Making Connections: The Novels of Jane Louise Curry." *Bookmark* [Edinburgh] 5 (Autumn 1979): 9–24.

Pflieger, Pat, and Helen M. Hill. *A Reference Guide to Modern Fantasy for Children.* Westport, CT: Greenwood, 1984, pp. xiii–xvi, 47–49, 53–54, 58–60, 105–106, 132–134, 143–145, 323–325, 341–342, 366–367, 415–418, 424–425, 446–448, 495–497, 576–578, 613–614.

Twentieth-Century Children's Writers. 3rd ed. Edited by Tracy Chevalier and D. L. Kirkpatrick. Chicago: St. James, 1989, pp. 253–254.

Cutt, W(illiam) Towrie

Aldritt, Judith Morse. "Profile: W. Towrie Cutt." *In Review* (Canada) 14 (Apr 1980): 12–15.

McDonough, Irma, ed. "William Towrie Cutt." In *Profiles 2: Authors and Illustrators, Children's Literature in Canada.* Ottawa: Canadian Library Association, 1982.

Twentieth-Century Children's Writers. 3rd ed. Edited by Tracy Chevalier and D. L. Kirkpatrick. Chicago: St. James, 1989, pp. 254–255.

Dahl, Roald

Appleyard, B. "Roald and the Promiscuous Girl." *Independent* (London) (Mar 21, 1990): 15.

Bosmajian, Hamida. "*Charlie and the Chocolate Factory* and Other Excremental Visions." *The Lion and the Unicorn* 9 (1985): 36–49.

Bouchard, Lois Kalb. "A New Look at Old Favorites: *Charlie and the Chocolate Factory.*" *Interracial Books for Children, Bulletin* 3 (1970): 3, 8. Reprinted in MacCann. *The Black American in Books for Children.* Metuchen, NJ: Scarecrow Press, 1972, pp. 112–115.

Cameron, Eleanor. "McLuhan, Youth, and Literature." *Horn Book* 48 (Oct 1972): 433–440. Reprinted in Paul Heins. *Crosscurrents of Criticism.* Boston: Horn Book, 1977, pp. 98–125.

―――. "A Question of Taste." *Children's Literature in Education* 21 (Summer 1976): 59–63.

―――. "A Reply to Roald Dahl." *Horn Book* 49 (Apr 1973): 127–128. Reprinted in Paul Heins. *Crosscurrents of Criticism.* Boston: Horn Book, 1977, pp. 123–125.

Campbell, A. K. D. "Children's Writers: Roald Dahl." *School Librarian* 29 (June 1981): 108–114.

"The Children's Book Award 1988, Given by the Federation of Children's Book Groups to Roald Dahl." *School Librarian* 37 (Nov 1989): 131.

Chesterfield-Evans, Jan "Roald Dahl: A Discussion and Comparison of His Stories for Children and Adults." *Orana* 19 (Nov 1983): 165–168.

Corner, Calla. "The Weird Writing World of Roald Dahl." *Writers Digest* 60 (Aug 1980): 40–42, 47.

Culley, Jonathon. "Roald Dahl—'It's about Children and It's for Children'—But Is It Suitable?" *Children's Literature in Education* 22 (Mar 1991): 59–74.

Dahl, Roald. "Books Remembered." *CBC Features* 43, no. 2 (1990): 12.

―――. *Boy: Tales of Childhood.* New York: Farrar, 1984. Autobiography.

―――. "*Charlie and the Chocolate Factory:* A Reply." *Horn Book* 49 (Feb 1973): 77–78. Reprinted in Paul Heins. *Crosscurrents of Criticism.* Boston: Horn Book, 1977, pp. 121–122.

―――. *Going Solo.* New York: Farrar, 1986. Autobiography.

Du Pré, Nicole. "Roald Dahl, Champion Toutes Categories [Roald Dahl, Overall Champion]." *Lire au College* (France) 7 (Jan 1984): 19–22.

Faundez, Anne. [Roald Dahl] *Junior Education* (U.K.) 15, no. 3 (1991): 64.

Fitzpatrick, Christine. "Author Profile no. 3: Roald Dahl." *Review Bulletin* (Australia) 20, no. 3 (1988): 1–6.

Fransson, Birgitta. "Roald Dahl: Haxmastare for Barn Och Vuxna [Roald Dahl: Wizard for Children and Adults]." *Opsis Kalopsis* (Sweden) (Aug 4, 1987): 9–11. (interview)

Gillespie, John T., and Diana Lembo. *Introducing Books: A Guide for the Middle Grades.* New York: Bowker, 1970, pp. 60–62.

Glastonbury, Marion. "Children's Own." *New Society* (London) 30, no. 632 (Nov 14, 1974): 427–428.

Gregg, Alison. "Meeting Roald Dahl." *Orana* (Australia) 21 (May 1985): 82–84.

Haigh, Gerald. "For Non Squiffle Trotters Only." *Times Educational Supplement* 3464 (Nov 19, 1982): 35.

Harris, Martyn. "Children Mourn *Mr. Fox*'s Finale." *Sunday Telegraph* (London) (Nov 25, 1990): 3.

Henderson, Meredith. "Rules and Responsibilities." *Update on Law Related Education* 12 (1988): 14. *Fantastic Mr. Fox* in the classroom.

Hildick, Wallace. "A Vitally Engaging Author." *Growing Point* (U.K.) 30, no. 6 (1992): 5672–5675.

Hopkins, Lee Bennett. "Roald Dahl." In *More Books by More People.* New York: Citation Press, 1974, pp. 110–114.

"Interview." *Words International* (Dec 2, 1987): 26–34.

Itzen, Catherine. "Bewitching the Boys." *Times Educational Supplement* (Dec 27, 1985): 13.

Kettle, Martin. "Roald, *the Champion of the World.*" *Guardian* (May 19–20, 1990): 20–21.

Kjersen Edman, Lena. "Lusten att bli Skramd: Om Roald Dahl [The Desire to Be Frightened: About Roald Dahl]." *Abrakadabra* (Sweden) 1 (1987): 18–22.

Kunnemann, Horst. "Tretminen im Kinderzimmer: Roald Dahl! Du Anarchist!" *Bulletin Jugend + Literatur* (Germany) 22 (1991): 13–20.

Lennon, Peter. "A Bumpy Rise to Fantasy." (London) *Times* (Dec 27, 1983): 8.

Lewis, Naomi. "Charlie Will Always Be Our Darling." *Observer* (London) (Nov 25, 1990): 6.

"Meet a Puffin Person: Roald Dahl." *Puffin Post* (U.K.) 5 (Spring 1985): 11–14.

Merrick, Anne. "*The Nightwatchmen* and *Charlie and the Chocolate Factory* as Books to Be Read to Children." *Children's Literature in Education* 16 (Spring 1975): 21–30.

Moorehead, Caroline. "Roald Dahl: Creating a Fantasy World for Real Children." (London) *Times* (Oct 31, 1976): 16.

Moss, Anita. "*Charlie and the Chocolate Factory* and *James and the Giant Peach.*" In *Part of the Pattern.* New York: Greenwillow, 1986, p. 28.

———. "Crime and Punishment—Or Development—In Fairy Tales and Fantasy." *Mythlore* 8 (Spring 1981): 26–28, 42.

Nudd, Kevin. "The Children's Books of Roald Dahl." *Book and Magazine Collector* (U.K.) 58 (Jan 1989): 12–19.

"*Observer* Profile: Roald and the Revenge Factory." *Observer* (London) (July 30, 1989): 13.

Osborn, M. E. "Roald Dahl: A Giant in Popularity Amongst Child Readers—But Was He Always Friendly to Them?" *Media Focus* (South Africa) 3, no. 1 (1991): 22.

Ovens, C. "Coming to a Sticky End." *Child Education* (U.K.) 69 (Oct 1992): 52–53.

The Oxford Companion to Children's Literature. Edited by Humphrey Carpenter and Mari Prichard. New York: Oxford Univ. Press, 1984, pp. 108, 139.

Petzold, Dieter. "Wish-Fulfilment and Subversion: Roald Dahl's Dickensian Fantasy, *Matilda.*" *Children's Literature in Education* 23 (Dec 1992): 185–194.

Pol, Barber van de. "Je Hebt Geen Idee Hoe Heerlijk het 40, 50 Jaar Geleden was een Teenager te Zijn [Barber van de Pol Interviews Roald Dahl]." *Bulletin* (The Netherlands) 7, no. 59 (1978): 17–25.

Powling, Chris. "The Big Friendly Giant. *Books for Keeps* (U.K.) 17 (Nov 1982): 4–5.

———. "Farewell to the Big Friendly Giant." *Books for Keeps* (U.K.) 66 (Jan 1991): 10–11.

———. *Roald Dahl.* rev. ed. Harmondsworth: Puffin, 1985.

Pritchard, A. "A Week of Roald Dahl." *Language and Learning* (U.K.) (Dec 1992): 27–30.

Rees, David. "Dahl's Chickens: Roald Dahl." *Children's Literature in Education* 19 (Fall 1988): 143–155. Reprinted in "*What Do Draculas Do?*" *Essays on Contemporary Writers of Fiction for Children and Young Adults.* Metuchen, NJ: Scarecrow Press, 1990, pp. 190–205.

Search, Gay. "Tales of the Unexpected: Roald Dahl." *Woman's Journal* (London) (Nov 1979): 74–79.

Seiter, Richard D. "The Bittersweet Journey from *Charlie* to 'Willy Wonka.'" In Douglas Street. *Children's Novels and the Movies.* New York: Ungar, 1983, pp. 191–196.

Stott, Jon C. *Children's Literature from A to Z.* New York: McGraw-Hill, 1984, p. 86.

Third Book of Junior Authors. Edited by Doris De Montreville and Donna Hill. New York: Wilson, 1972, pp. 73–74.

Townsend, John Rowe. "Anarchic Talent That Left Adults Embarrassed." *Times Educational Supplement* (Nov 30, 1990): 5.

Toynbee, Polly. "Mystery Man." *Guardian* (Dec 23, 1985): 8.

Treglown, Jeremy. *Roald Dahl: A Biography.* New York: Farrar, 1994.

Twentieth-Century Children's Writers. 3rd ed. Edited by Tracy Chevalier and D. L. Kirkpatrick. Chicago: St. James, 1989, pp. 255–256.

West, Mark L. "The Grotesque and the Taboo in Roald Dahl's Humorous Writings for Children." *Children's Literature Association Quarterly* 15 (Fall 1990): 115–117.

————. "Interview with Roald Dahl." *Children's Literature in Education* 21 (June 1990): 61–66.

————. "Regression and Fragmentation of the Self in *James and the Giant Peach*." *Children's Literature in Education* 16 (Winter 1985): 219–226.

Wintle, Justin, and Emma Fisher. "Roald Dahl." In *The Pied Pipers*. New York: Paddington Press, 1974, pp. 101–112.

Wood, Michael. "The Confidence Man." *New Society* (London) 50(Dec 1979): xiv–xvi.

Dalgliesh, Alice

Helbig, Alethea K., and Agnes Regan Perkins. *Dictionary of American Children's Fiction, 1859–1959*. Westport, CT: Greenwood, 1985, p. 119.

Dallas-Smith, Peter

Wood, Anne. "Trumpets and Grumpets." *Books for Your Children* (U. K.) 17 (1982): 6–7.

Davies, Andrew (Wynford)

Fifth Book of Junior Authors and Illustrators. Edited by Sally Holmes Holtze. New York: Wilson, 1983, pp. 94–95.

Nettell, Stephanie. "Fathers and Sons." *Guardian* (Mar 29, 1979): 13.

Twentieth-Century Children's Writers. 3rd ed. Edited by Tracy Chevalier and D. L. Kirkpatrick. Chicago: St. James, 1989, pp. 266–267.

Davis, Robert

Helbig, Alethea K., and Agnes Regan Perkins. *Dictionary of American Children's Fiction, 1859–1959*. Westport, CT: Greenwood, 1985, pp. 125–126.

The Junior Book of Authors. 2nd rev. ed. Edited by Stanley J. Kunitz and Howard Haycraft. New York: Wilson, 1951, pp. 95–96.

De Camp, L(yon) Sprague

De Camp, L. Sprague. *Blond Barbarians and Noble Savages*. Baltimore: T-K Graphics, 1975.

————. "Ghost Trouble." *Fantasy Newsletter* 26 (1980): 12–13.

————. "Imaginative Fiction and Creative Fiction." In *Modern Science Fiction*. 2nd ed. Edited by Reginald Bretnor. Chicago: Advent, 1979.

————. *Literary Swordsmen and Sorcerers: The Makers of Heroic Fantasy*. Sauk City, WI: Arkham House, 1976.

————, ed. *The Blade of Conan*. New York: Ace, 1979. Essays on sword-and-sorcery fantasy.

Fredericks, Casey. *The Future of Eternity: Mythologies of Science Fiction and Fantasy*. Bloomington: Indiana Univ. Press, 1982.

Laughlin, Charlotte, and Daniel J. H. Levack. *De Camp: An L. Sprague De Camp Bibliography*. Columbia, PA: Underwood-Miller, 1983.

Moskowitz, Sam. *Seekers of Tomorrow; Masters of Modern Science Fiction*. New York: Ballantine, 1967, pp. 151–166.

Schlobin, Roger C. "The Fool and the Fantastic." *Fantasy Newsletter* 43 (1981): 6–9, 29.

Schuyler, William M., Jr. "Recent Developments in Spell Construction." In *The Aesthetics of*

Fantasy Literature and Art. Edited by Roger C. Schlobin. Notre Dame, IN: Univ. of Notre Dame Press, 1982, pp. 237–248.

Schweitzer, Darrell. *Science Fiction Voices #1.* San Bernardino, CA: Borgo Press, 1979.

———, ed. *Science Fiction Voices.* Baltimore: T-K Graphics, 1976.

Schweitzer, Darrell, and Richard E. Geis. "An Interview with: L. Sprague De Camp." *Science Fiction Review* 4 (1975): 11–14.

Stableford, Brian M. "L. Sprague De Camp and Fletcher Pratt." In *Supernatural Fiction Writers,* vol. 2. Edited by E. F. Bleiler. New York: Scribner, 1985, pp. 925–932.

Twentieth-Century Science Fiction Writers. 3rd ed. Edited by Noelle Watson and Paul E. Schellinger. Chicago: St. James Press, 1991, pp. 190–192.

De La Mare, Walter (John)

Auden, W. H. "Walter de la Mare." In W. H. Auden. *Forewords and Afterwords.* New York: Random, 1973, pp. 384–394.

Bayley, John. "The Child in Walter de la Mare." In *Children and Their Books,* ed. by Gillian Avery and Julia Briggs. Oxford: Clarendon, 1989, pp. 337–349.

Bianco, Margery. "De la Mare." *Horn Book* 18 (May–June 1942): 141–147. Reprinted in Anne Carroll Moore and Bertha Mahony Miller. *Writing and Criticism.* Boston: Horn Book, 1951, pp. 67–77.

Bianco, Pamela. "Editorial: Walter de la Mare." *Horn Book* 29 (June 1953): 173.

———. "Walter de la Mare." *Horn Book* 33 (June 1957): 242–247. Reprinted in Elinor Field. *Horn Book Reflections.* Boston: Horn Book, 1969, pp. 265–270.

Buchan, S. "Walter de la Mare for Children." *Spectator* (London), Aug 24, 1918, pp. 200–201.

Chapman, Vera. "Forerunner to Tolkien? Walter de la Mare's *The Three Royal Monkeys.*" *Mythlore* 8 (Summer 1981): 32–33.

Clark, Keith. "A Child of Mature Years: Walter de la Mare, 1873–1956." *Junior Bookshelf* 37 (Apr 1973): 89–93.

Clark, Leonard. *Walter de la Mare.* New York: Walck, 1960. Reprinted in Hugh Shelley, Rosemary Sutcliff, and Leonard Clark. *Arthur Ransome, Rudyard Kipling and Walter de la Mare.* London: Bodley Head, 1968.

Clute, John. "The Short Fiction of Walter de la Mare." In Frank N. Magill. *Survey of Modern Fantasy Literature,* vol. 3. Englewood Cliffs, NJ: Salem Press, 1983, pp. 1492–1495.

———. "Walter de la Mare." In *Supernatural Fiction Writers: Fantasy and Horror,* vol. 1. Edited by E. F. Bleiler. New York: Scribner, 1985, pp. 497–504.

"Collected Stories for Children." In M. Crouch and A. Ellis. *Chosen for Children.* 3rd ed. London: The Library Association, 1977, pp. 45–49.

Cooper, Susan. "Naham Tarune's Book." *Horn Book* 56 (Oct 1980): 497–507.

Crouch, Marcus S. "Farewell to Walter de la Mare." *Junior Bookshelf* 20 (Oct 1956): 187–191.

———. "Walter de la Mare and His Illustrators." *Junior Bookshelf* 17 (Mar 1953): 51–60.

Dalphin, Marcia. "I Give You the End of a Golden String." *Horn Book* 14 (May 1938): 143–149. Reprinted in Norma Fryatt. *A Horn Book Sampler.* Boston: Horn Book, 1959, pp. 133–139.

Degan, James Nerhood. "The Short Fiction of Walter de la Mare." Ph.D. diss., University of Iowa, 1982.

De la Mare, Walter. "A Sort of Interview." *London Mercury* 35 (Dec 1936): 165–171.

Doyle, Brian. *The Who's Who of Children's Literature.* New York: Schocken, 1968, pp. 73–74.

Farjeon, Eleanor. "Walter de la Mare." *Horn Book* 33 (June 1957): 197–205.

Gardner, Jane E. "Walter De la Mare's Stories for Children: An Analysis of Variant Texts." *Private Library, Third Series* (U.K.) 1, no. 3 (Autumn 1978): 101–118.

Graham, Eleanor. "The Riddle of Walter de la Mare: An Appreciation of His Work for Children." *Junior Bookshelf* 12 (July 1948): 59–65.

Greene, Ellin. "Walter de la Mare." In *Writers for Children: Critical Studies of Major Authors Since the Seventeenth Century.* Edited by Jane M. Bingham. New York: Scribner, 1988, pp. 173–180.

Gulliver, Lucile. "Walter de la Mare: A Godfather Fairy." *Horn Book* 2 (Nov 1925): 36–42.

Hopkins, Kenneth. *Walter de la Mare.* rev. ed. London: Longman, 1957.

Horn Book Magazine. Walter de la Mare special issues 18 (May–June 1942): 139–157, 33 (Oct 1957): 195–247.

The Junior Book of Authors. 2nd rev. ed. Edited by Stanley J. Kunitz and Howard Haycraft. New York: Wilson, 1951, pp. 97–98.

Lathrop, Dorothy P. "Illustrating de la Mare." *Horn Book* 18 (May–June 1942): 188–196.

Lochhead, Marion. *Renaissance of Wonder.* New York: Harper, 1980, pp. 70–76.

McCrosson, Doris Ross. *Walter de la Mare.* Boston: Twayne, 1966.

Megroz, Rodolphe Louis. *Walter de la Mare: A Biographical and Critical Study.* New York: Doran, 1924.

Miller, Bertha E. Mahony, ed. "The Books of Walter de la Mare." *Horn Book* 33 (June 1957): 235–241.

Murphy, Michael William. "The British Tale in the Early 20th Century: Walter de la Mare, A. E. Coppard, and T. F. Powys." Ph.D. diss., University of Wisconsin, 1971.

The Oxford Companion to Children's Literature. Edited by Humphrey Carpenter and Mari Prichard. New York: Oxford Univ. Press, 1984, pp. 145, 526.

Pflieger, Pat, and Helen M. Hill. *A Reference Guide to Modern Fantasy for Children.* Westport, CT: Greenwood, 1984, pp. 146–147, 529–531.

Rahn, Suzanne. "The Expression of Religious and Political Concepts in Fantasy for Children." Ph.D. diss., University of Washington, 1986.

Read, Herbert. "Walter de la Mare." *Horn Book* 33 (June 1957): 209–210.

Reid, Forrest. *Walter de la Mare: A Critical Study.* London: Faber, 1929.

Stott, Jon C. *Children's Literature from A to Z.* New York: McGraw-Hill, 1984, p. 90.

Twentieth-Century Children's Writers. 3rd ed. Edited by Tracy Chevalier and D. L. Kirkpatrick. Chicago: St. James, 1989, pp. 276–278.

Walsh, William. "De la Mare's Small World." In Ford. *Young Writers, Young Readers.* London: Hutchinson, 1960, pp. 107–114.

Zanger, Jules. "*The Three Mulla Mulgars.*" In *Survey of Modern Fantasy Literature,* vol. 4. Edited by Frank N. Magill. Englewood Cliffs, NJ: Salem Press, 1983, pp. 1926–1929.

Delany, Samuel R(ay), Jr.

Barbour, Douglas. "Cultural Invention and Metaphor in the Novels of Samuel R. Delany." *Foundation* 7/8 (1975): 105–121.

———. "Patterns of Meaning in the Science Fiction Novels of Ursula K. Le Guin, Joanna Russ and Samuel R. Delany, 1962–1972." Ph.D. diss., Queen's University (Ontario, Canada), 1976.

———. "Samuel R. Delany, Jr." In *Science Fiction Writers.* Edited by E. F. Bleiler. New York: Scribner, 1982, pp. 329–336.

———. *Worlds Out of Words: The Science Fiction Novels of Samuel R. Delany.* Frome, Somerset, U.K.: Bran's Head, 1978.

Braswell, Laurel. "The Visionary Voyage in Science Fiction and Medieval Allegory." *Mosaic* 14 (Winter 1981): 125–142.

Bravard, Robert S., and Michael W. Peplow. "Through a Glass Darkly: Bibliographing Samuel R. Delany." *Black American Literature Forum* 18 (1984): 69–75.

Canary, Robert H. "Science Fiction as Fictive History." *Extrapolation* 16 (1974): 81–95.

Delany, Samuel R. "Generic Protocols: Science Fiction and Mundane." In *The Technological Imagination: Theories and Fictions.* Edited by Teresa De Laurentis, Andreas Huyssen, and Kathleen Woodward. Madison, WI: Coda Press, 1980, pp. 175–193.

———. "The Profession of Science Fiction: VIII: Shadows—Part 1." *Foundation* 6 (1974): 31–60. "Shadows—Part 2." *Foundation* 7/8 (1975): 122–154.

———. "Reflections on Historical Models of Modern English Language Science Fiction." *Science Fiction Studies* 7 (1980): 135–149.

———. *Starboard Wine: More Notes on the Language of Science Fiction.* Pleasantville, NY: Dragon Press, 1984.

Fox, Robert Elliot. "The Mirrors of Caliban: A Study of the Fiction of LeRoi Jones, Ishmael Reed and Samuel R. Delany." Ph.D. diss., State University of New York at Buffalo, 1976.

Govan, Sandra Y. "The Insistent Presence of Blackfolk in the Novels of Samuel R. Delany." *Black American Literature Forum* 18 (1984): 43–48.

Hausdorff, Don. "Introduction." In Samuel R. Delany. *The Jewels of Aptor.* Boston: Gregg, 1976.

Littlefield, Ralph Emerson. "Character and Language in Eight Novels by Ursula K. Le Guin and Samuel R. Delany." Ph.D. diss., Florida State University, 1984.

McCaffrey, Larry, and Sinda Gregory. "An Interview with Samuel Delany." In *Alive and Writing: Interviews with American Authors of the 1980s.* ed. by Larry McCaffrey and Sinda Gregory. Urbana: Univ. of Illinois Press, 1987, pp. 83–110.

McEvoy, Seth. *Samuel R. Delany.* New York: Ungar, 1984.

Peplow, Michael W. "Meet Samuel Delany: Black Science Fiction Writer." *The Crisis* 86 (Apr 1979): 115–121.

Peplow, Michael W., and Robert S. Bravard. *Samuel R. Delany: A Primary and Secondary Bibliography, 1962–1979.* Boston: G. K. Hall, 1980.

———. "Samuel R. Delany: A Selective Primary and Secondary Bibliography, 1979–1983." *Black American Literature Forum* 18 (1984): 75–77.

Platt, Charles. *Dream Makers: The Uncommon People Who Write Science Fiction.* New York: Berkley, 1980, pp. 69–76. Interview.

Rabkin, Eric S. "Metalinguistics and Science Fiction." *Critical Inquiry* 6 (1979): 79–97.

Samuelson, David N. "Tales of Nevèrÿon." In *Survey of Modern Fantasy Literature,* vol. 4. Edited by Frank N. Magill. Englewood Cliffs, NJ: Salem Press, 1983, pp. 1875–1879.

Schuyler, William M., Jr. "Heroes and History." In *The Intersection of Science Fiction and Philosophy.* Edited by Robert E. Myers. Westport, CT: Greenwood, 1983, pp. 197–210.

Schweitzer, Darrell. "*Algol* Interview: Samuel R. Delany." *Algol* 13 (1976): 16–20.

Searles, Baird, Beth Meacham, and Michael Franklin. *A Reader's Guide to Fantasy.* New York: Avon, 1982, pp. 53–54.

Slusser, George Edgar. *The Delany Intersection: Samuel R. Delany Considered as a Writer of Semi-Precious Words.* San Bernardino, CA: Borgo Press, 1977.

Somay, Bulent. "Towards an Open-Ended Utopia." *Science Fiction Studies* 11 (1984): 25–38.

Spencer, Kathleen L. "Deconstructing *Tales of Nevèrÿon:* Delany, Derrida, and 'The Modular Calculus, Parts I–IV.'" *Essays in Arts and Sciences* 14 (May 1985): 59–89.

Sullivan, C. W., III. "*The Jewels of Aptor.*" In *Survey of Modern Fantasy Literature,* vol. 2. Edited by Frank N. Magill. Englewood Cliffs, NJ: Salem Press, 1983, pp. 798–800.

Twentieth-Century Science Fiction Writers. 3rd ed. Edited by Noelle Watson and Paul E. Schellinger. Chicago: St. James Press, 1991, pp. 194–196.

Watson, Ian. "The Author as Torturer." *Foundation* 401 (1987): 11–25.

Weedman, Jane Branham. "Art and the Artist's Role in Delany's Works." In *Voices for the Future,* vol. 3. Edited by Thomas D. Clareson and Thomas L. Wymer. Bowling Green, OH: Bowling Green Univ. Press, 1984, pp. 151–187.

———. *Reader's Guide to Samuel R. Delany.* Mercer Island, WA: Starmont, 1982.

————. "Samuel R. Delany: Present-Day Cultures in Future Literary Worlds." Ph.D. diss., State University of New York at Buffalo, 1979.

De Larrabeiti, Michael

"Meet the Borribles." *Books for Keeps* (U. K.) 18 (Jan 1983): 20–21.
Newsinger, John. "Don't Get Caught: *The Borribles*: Children's Fantasy Literature in Today's Britain." *Vector* (U. K.) 149 (Apr–May 1989): 7–9.
Zipes, Jack. "The Adventure of Fantasy as Struggle for Survival." *Children's Literature,* vol. 7. Storrs, CT: Parousia Press, 1978, pp. 242–247.

De Leeuw, Adele Louise

The Junior Book of Authors. 2nd rev. ed. Edited by Stanley J. Kunitz and Howard Haycraft. New York: Wilson, 1951, pp. 98–100.

De Lint, Charles

De Lint, Charles. "Bushes and Briars: Women in Fantasy." *Mythlore* 49 (1987): 4–5+.

Denslow, W(illiam) W(allace)

Fourth Book of Junior Authors and Illustrators. Edited by Doris De Montreville and Elizabeth D. Crawford. New York: Wilson, 1978, pp. 113–115.
Hanff, Peter E., and Douglas G. Greene. *Bibliographia Oziana.* Demorest, GA: International Wizard of Oz Club, 1976.

De Regniers, Beatrice Schenk (Freedman)

More Junior Authors. Edited by Muriel Fuller. New York: Wilson, 1963, p. 65.
Twentieth-Century Children's Writers. 3rd ed. Edited by Tracy Chevalier and D. L. Kirkpatrick. Chicago: St. James, 1989, pp. 281–283.

De Weese, (Thomas Eu)Gene

Twentieth-Century Science Fiction Writers. 3rd ed. Edited by Noelle Watson and Paul E. Schellinger. Chicago: St. James Press, 1991, pp. 205–209.

Dickens, Charles (John Huffam)

Adrian, Arthur A. *Dickens and the Parent-Child Relationship.* Athens: Ohio Univ. Press, 1984.
Allen, Michael. *Charles Dickens' Childhood.* London: Macmillan, 1988; New York: St. Martin, 1988.
Bentley, Nicholas, Michael Slater, and Nina Buris. *The Dickens Index.* Oxford: Oxford Univ. Press, 1988.
Chittick, Kathryn. *The Critical Reception of Charles Dickens, 1833–1841.* New York: Garland, 1989.
Coats, Daryl R. "'The Devil Is Loose in London Somewhere': Five Supernatural Figures in the Works of Charles Dickens." Ph.D. diss., University of Mississippi, 1986.

Cohn, Alan M. "The Dickens Checklist." *Dickens Quarterly* 5 (1988): 40–44, 99–103, 166–169, and 204–207.

Davis, Paul. *The Lives and Times of Ebeneezer Scrooge.* New Haven: Yale Univ. Press, 1990.

Dickens, Charles. "Frauds on the Fairies." *Household Words* 8 (Oct 5, 1853): 97–100. Reprinted in *Masterworks of Children's Literature,* vol. VI. New York: Stonehill/Chelsea House, 1984, pp. 55–62; and in Lance Salway. *A Peculiar Gift.* Harmondsworth, Middlesex: Kestrel, 1967, pp. 111–118.

Doyle, Brian. *The Who's Who of Children's Literature.* New York: Schocken, 1968, pp. 75–76.

Fraden, Rena. "The Sentimental Tradition in Dickens and Hawthorne." Ph.D. diss., Yale University, 1983.

Freeman, Ann. "A Comparative Study of Hans Christian Andersen and Charles Dickens: The Relationship between Spiritual and Material Value Systems as Defined by Their Treatment of the Child." Ph.D. diss., University of California, Berkeley, 1979.

Frey, Charles, and John Griffiths. *The Literary Heritage of Childhood: An Appraisal of Children's Classics in the Western Tradition.* Westport, CT: Greenwood, 1987, pp. 71–80.

Gilbert, E. "The Ceremony of Innocence: Charles Dickens' *A Christmas Carol.*" *PMLA* 90 (Jan 1975): 22–31.

Glancy, Ruth R. *Dickens's Christmas Books, Children's Stories, and Other Short Fiction: An Annotated Bibliography.* New York: Garland, 1985.

Guiliano, Edward, and Philip Collins. *The Annotated Dickens.* London: Orbis, 1986. Includes *A Christmas Carol.*

Hearn, Michael Patrick. "Charles Dickens." In *Writers for Children: Critical Studies of Major Authors Since the Seventeenth Century.* Edited by Jane M. Bingham. New York: Scribner, 1988, pp. 181–192.

Hodges, Margaret. "Dickens for Children." *Horn Book* 58 (Dec 1982): 626–635. •

Jackson, Rosemary. *Fantasy: The Literature of Subversion.* New York: Methuen, 1980, pp. 5, 10, 15, 47, 108, 123–124, 126–127, 133, 155, 172, 180.

Kaplan, Fred. *Dickens: A Biography.* London: Hodder, 1988; New York: Morrow, 1988.

Marlow, James E. "Social Harmony and Dickens's Revolutionary Cookery." *Dickens Studies Annual* 17 (1988): 145–178.

Miller, Patricia. "The Importance of Being Earnest: The Fairy Tale in 19th-Century England." *Children's Literature Association Quarterly* 7 (Summer 1982): 11–14.

Sable, Martin H. "The Day of Atonement in Charles Dickens' *A Christmas Carol.*" *Tradition* 22 (1986): 66–76.

Stableford, Brian. "Charles Dickens." In *Supernatural Fiction Writers: Fantasy and Horror,* vol. 1. Edited by E. F. Bleiler. New York: Scribner, 1985, pp. 213–218.

———. "Christmas Stories." In *Survey of Modern Fantasy Literature,* vol. 1. Edited by Frank N. Magill. Englewood Cliffs, NJ: Salem Press, 1983, pp. 242–247.

Stone, Harry. "Dark Corners of the Mind: Dickens' Childhood Reading." *Horn Book* 39 (June 1963): 306–321.

Tremper, Ellen. "Commitment and Escape: The Fairy Tales of Thackeray, Dickens, and Wilde." *The Lion and the Unicorn* 2 (Spring 1978): 38–47.

Dickinson, Peter (pseud. of Malcolm de Brissac)

Alderdice, Kit. "Notes from a Crossover Novelist." *Publishers Weekly* (May 11, 1992): 29–30.

Antczak, Janice. *Science Fiction: The Mythos of a New Romance.* New York: Neal-Schuman, 1985, pp. 53, 162, 186.

"Authorgraph no. 10: Peter Dickinson." *Books for Keeps* (U.K.) 10 (Sept 1981): 16–17.

Crouch, Marcus. *The Nesbit Tradition.* Totowa, NJ: Rowman and Littlefield, 1972, pp. 50–52.

Dickinson, Mike. "*The Blue Hawk.*" In *Survey of Modern Fantasy Literature,* vol. 1. Edited by Frank N. Magill. Englewood Cliffs, NJ: Salem Press, 1983, pp. 132–136.

Dickinson, Peter. "The Burden of the Past." In *Innocence & Experience.* Edited by Barbara Harrison and Gregory Maguire. New York: Lothrop, 1987, pp. 91–101.

———. "The Day of the Tennis Rabbit." *Quarterly Journal of the Library of Congress* 38 (Fall 1981): 203–220.

———. "Fantasy: The Need for Realism." *Children's Literature in Education* 17 (Spring 1986): 39–51. Paper given at the Fourth *Bookquest* Conference, Brighton Polytechnic, Spring 1984.

———. "Masks." *Horn Book* 69 (Mar–Apr 1993): 160–169.

———. "The Oral Voices of *City of Gold.*" In *The Voice of the Narrator in Children's Literature: Insights from Writers and Critics,* ed. by Charlotte F. Otten and Gary D. Schmidt. New York: Greenwood, 1989, pp. 78–80.

Fourth Book of Junior Authors and Illustrators. Edited by Doris De Montreville and Elizabeth D. Crawford. New York: Wilson, 1978, pp. 117–118.

Frongia, Terri. "Merlin's Fathers: The Sacred and the Profane." *Children's Literature Association Quarterly* 18 (Fall 1993): 120–125. Discusses Peter Dickinson, Pamela Service, Rosemary Sutcliff, and Jane Yolen.

Grimshaw, Nigel. "Peter Dickinson's Children's Stories." *School Librarian* 22 (Sept 1974): 219–223.

Hutchison, Joanna. "Peter Dickinson Considered, In and Out of the Classroom." *Children's Literature in Education* 17 (Summer 1975): 88–98.

The Oxford Companion to Children's Literature. Edited by Humphrey Carpenter and Mari Prichard. New York: Oxford Univ. Press, 1984, pp. 148–149.

Rees, David. "Plums and Roughage—Peter Dickinson." In *Painted Desert, Green Shade.* Boston: Horn Book, 1984, pp. 153–167.

Searles, Baird, Meacham, Beth; and Franklin, Michael. *A Reader's Guide to Fantasy.* New York: Avon, 1982, pp. 55–56.

Townsend, John Rowe. "Peter Dickinson." In *A Sounding of Storytellers.* Philadelphia: Lippincott, 1979, pp. 41–54.

Twentieth-Century Children's Writers. 3rd ed. Edited by Tracy Chevalier and D. L. Kirkpatrick. Chicago: St. James, 1989, pp. 287–289.

Twentieth-Century Science Fiction Writers. 3rd ed. Edited by Noelle Watson and Paul E. Schellinger. Chicago: St. James Press, 1991, pp. 209–211.

Williams, Jay. "Very Iffy Books: An Interview with Peter Dickinson." *Signal* 13 (Jan 1974): 21–29.

Dickson, Gordon R(upert)

Clute, John. "Gordon Dickson." In *Science Fiction Writers.* Edited by E. F. Bleiler. New York: Scribner, 1982, pp. 345–350.

Dickson, Gordon R. "Plausibility in Science Fiction." In *Science Fiction Today and Tomorrow.* Edited by Reginald Bretnor. New York: Harper, 1974, pp. 295–308.

Lane, Daryl, William Vernon, and David Carlson. *The Sound of Wonder: Interviews from "The Science Fiction Radio Show,"* vol. 2. Phoenix, AZ: Oryx Press, 1985, pp. 159–173.

McMurry, Clifford. "An Interview with Gordon R. Dickson." *Science Fiction Review* 7 (July 1978): 6–12.

Miesel, Sandra. "*Algol* Interview: Gordon R. Dickson." *Algol* 15 (Spring 1978): 33–38.

———. "The Plume and the Sword; Gordon Dickson: A Biographical Sketch of the Man and His Work." *Destinies* 2 (1980): 116–131.

Schweitzer, Darrell, ed. *Science Fiction Voices.* Baltimore: T-K Graphics, 1976. Interview.

Searles, Baird, Beth Meacham, and Michael Franklin. *A Reader's Guide to Fantasy.* New York: Avon, 1982, pp. 56–57.

Thompson, Raymond H. *Gordon R. Dickson: A Primary and Secondary Bibliography.* Boston: G. K. Hall, 1983.

————. "Gordon R. Dickson: Science Fiction for Young Canadians." *Canadian Children's Literature* 15/16 (Summer 1980): 38–46.

Twentieth-Century Science Fiction Writers. 3rd ed. Edited by Noelle Watson and Paul E. Schellinger. Chicago: St. James Press, 1991, pp. 211–213.

Watson, Christine. "The Dragon and the George." In *Survey of Modern Fantasy Literature,* vol. 1. Edited by Frank N. Magill. Englewood Cliffs, NJ: Salem Press, 1983, pp. 418–422.

Dillon, Barbara

Twentieth-Century Children's Writers. 3rd ed. Edited by Tracy Chevalier and D. L. Kirkpatrick. Chicago: St. James, 1989, pp. 289–291.

Dolbier, Maurice (Wyman)

Helbig, Alethea K., and Agnes Regan Perkins. *Dictionary of American Children's Fiction, 1859–1959.* Westport, CT: Greenwood, 1985, pp. 132–133, 323.

More Junior Authors. Edited by Muriel Fuller. New York: Wilson, 1963, p. 69.

Donaldson, Stephen R.

Bacon, Jonathan. "Interview with Stephen R. Donaldson." *Fantasy Crossroads* 15 (1979): 11–16.

Barkley, Christine. "Donaldson as Heir to Tolkien." *Mythlore* 38 (1984): 50–57.

Clute, John. "The Chronicles of Thomas Covenant the Unbeliever *and* The Second Chronicles of Thomas Covenant." In *Survey of Modern Fantasy Literature,* vol. 1. Edited by Frank N. Magill. Englewood Cliffs, NJ: Salem Press, 1983, pp. 266–274.

Donaldson, Stephen R. *Epic Fantasy in the Modern World: A Few Observations.* Kent, OH: Kent State Univ. Libraries, 1986.

Fiske, Matthew A. "Nature as Supernature: Donaldson's Revision of Spenser." *Mythlore* 18, no. 2 (Spring 1992): 17–20, 22.

Fonstad, Karen Wynn. *The Atlas of the Land.* New York: Del Rey, 1985.

Gentle, Mary. "Godmakers and Worldshapers: Fantasy and Metaphysics." *Vector* 106 (1982): 8–14.

Godfrey, R. J. "Peake and Donaldson: A Comparative Study of Their Fantasies." *The Mervyn Peake Review* 11 (1980): 26–34.

"An Interview with Stephen Donaldson." *Extro Science Fiction* (Feb–Mar 1982): 7–9.

Kress, Nancy, and Paul Ferguson. "The Power of Darkness: A Conversation with Stephen R. Donaldson." *Thrust* 26 (1987): 15–17.

Lane, Daryl; Vernon, William; and Carlson, David. *The Sound of Wonder: Interviews from "The Science Fiction Radio Show,"* vol. 1. Phoenix, AZ: Oryx Press, 1985 pp. 1–21.

Myers, Walter E. "Stephen R. Donaldson." In *Supernatural Fiction Writers: Fantasy and Horror,* vol. 2. Edited by E. F. Bleiler. New York: Scribner, 1985, pp. 1009–1014.

Paulsen, Steven. "An Interview with Stephen Donaldson." *Dark Horizons* 27 (1984): 3–8.

Paxon, Diana. "The Tolkien Tradition." *Mythlore* 39 (1984): 23–27, 37.

Rich, Calvin, and Earl Ingersol. "A Conversation with Stephen R. Donaldson." *Mythlore* 46 (1986): 23–26.

Senior, William A. "Donaldson and Tolkien." *Mythlore* 70 (Autumn 1992): 37–43.

————. "The Significance of Names: Mythopoesis in *The First Chronicles of Thomas Covenant.*" *Extrapolation* 31 (Fall 1990): 258–269.

Slethaug, Gordon E. "No Exit: The Hero as Victim in Donaldson." *Mythlore* 40 (1984): 22–27.

Timmerman, John H. *Other Worlds: The Fantasy Genre.* Bowling Green, OH: Bowling Green Univ. Press, 1983, pp. 103–115.

Vance, Michael. "Interview: Stephen Donaldson." *Fantasy Review* 85 (1985): 8–10, 14.

Wilgus, Neal. "An Interview with Stephen R. Donaldson." *Science Fiction Review* 8 (Mar–Apr 1979): 26–29.

Wilson, Andrew J. "Melding for Beginners: Language and Names in *The Illearth War.*" *Dark Horizons* 24 (1981): 9–13.

Donovan, John

Fifth Book of Junior Authors and Illustrators. Edited by Sally Holmes Holtze. New York: Wilson, 1983, pp. 103–104.

Goldman, Suzy. "John Donovan: Sexuality, Stereotypes and Self." *The Lion and the Unicorn* 2 (Fall 1978): 27–36.

Helbig, Alethea K., and Agnes Regan Perkins. *Dictionary of American Children's Fiction, 1960–1984.* Westport, CT: Greenwood, 1986, pp. 163–164.

Spirt, Diana L. *Introducing More Books: A Guide for the Middle Grades.* New York: Bowker, 1978, pp. 123–125.

Twentieth-Century Children's Writers. 3rd ed. Edited by Tracy Chevalier and D. L. Kirkpatrick. Chicago: St. James, 1989, pp. 294–295.

Drury, Roger W(olcott)

Drury, Roger W. "Realism Plus Fantasy Equals Magic." *Horn Book* 48 (Apr 1972): 113–119. Reprinted in Heins. *Crosscurrents of Criticism.* Boston: Horn Book, 1977, pp. 178–184.

Helbig, Alethea K., and Agnes Regan Perkins. *Dictionary of American Children's Fiction, 1960–1984.* Westport, CT: Greenwood, 1986, pp. 107–108, 171.

Duane, Diane (Elizabeth)

Duane, Diane. "Watching the Sparks Fly Upward: Six Months after *The Door into Fire.*" *Empire* 4 (Sept 1979): 10–12.

Elliot, Jeffrey. "Interview with Diane Duane." *Starship* 40 (1980): 17–24.

Helbig, Alethea, and Agnes Regan Perkins. *Dictionary of American Children's Fiction, 1985–1989.* Westport, CT: Greenwood, 1993, pp. 58–59, 61–62.

Reimer, James D. "Masculinity and Feminist Fantasy Authors." *Science Fiction and Fantasy Review* 66 (1984): 19–21.

Twentieth-Century Science Fiction Writers. 3rd ed. Edited by Noelle Watson and Paul E. Schellinger. Chicago: St. James Press, 1991, pp. 225–226.

Du Bois, William (Sherman) Pène

Bader, Barbara. *American Picturebooks: From Noah's Ark to the Beast Within.* New York: Macmillan, 1976, pp. 175–186.

Burkert, Nancy Ekholm. "A Second Look: *Lion.*" *Horn Book* 56 (Dec 1980): 671–676.

Doyle, Brian. *The Who's Who of Children's Literature.* New York: Schocken, 1968, pp. 81–82.

Du Bois, William Pène. "Animal History Will Bear This Out." In *Contents of the Basket and*

Other Papers on Children's Books and Reading. New York: New York Public Library, 1960, pp. 35–39.

———. "Newbery Acceptance Paper—1947." *Horn Book* 24 (July 1948): 235–244.

Du Bois, Yvonne. "William Pène Du Bois, Boy and Artist." *Horn Book* 24 (July 1948): 245–249.

Gillespie, John T., and Diana Lembo. *Introducing Books: A Guide for the Middle Grades.* New York: Bowker, 1970, pp. 266–268.

Helbig, Alethea K., and Agnes Regan Perkins. *Dictionary of American Children's Fiction, 1859–1959.* Westport, CT: Greenwood, 1985, pp. 139–140, 165–166, 180–181, 539.

———. *Dictionary of American Children's Fiction, 1960–1984.* Westport, CT: Greenwood, 1986, p. 172.

The Junior Book of Authors. 2nd rev. ed. Edited by Stanley J. Kunitz and Howard Haycraft. New York: Wilson, 1951, pp. 102–104.

Miller, Bertha Mahony, and Elinor Whitney Field, eds. *Newbery Medal Books: 1922–1955.* Boston: Horn Book, 1957, pp. 300–317.

The Oxford Companion to Children's Literature. Edited by Humphrey Carpenter and Mari Prichard. New York: Oxford Univ. Press, 1984, pp. 158, 547.

Roginski, Jim, ed. *Newbery and Caldecott Medalists and Honor Book Winners.* Littleton, CO: Libraries Unlimited, 1982, pp. 91–92.

Stott, Jon C. *Children's Literature from A to Z.* New York: McGraw-Hill, 1984, p. 95.

Twentieth-Century Children's Writers. 3rd ed. Edited by Tracy Chevalier and D. L. Kirkpatrick. Chicago: St. James, 1989, pp. 298–300.

Duggan, Maurice (Noel)

Twentieth-Century Children's Writers. 3rd ed. Edited by Tracy Chevalier and D. L. Kirkpatrick. Chicago: St. James, 1989, pp. 300–301.

Dunlop, Eileen

Dunlop, Eileen. "The Growth of the Maker." *Bookmark* (Edinburgh) 3 (Winter 1978): 56–67.

———. "Some Facts, Some Fantasies." *Book Window* (Glasgow) 6 (1979): 1–5.

Dunsany, Lord (pseud. of Edward John Morton Drax Plunkett)

Branham, Robert J. "Fantasy and Inaffability: Fiction at the Limits of Language." *Extrapolation* 24 (1983): 66–79.

Cantrell, Brent. "British Fairy Tradition in *The King of Elfland's Daughter.*" *The Romantist* 4–5 (1980–1981): 51–53.

Clute, John. "*The King of Elfland's Daughter.*" In *Survey of Modern Fantasy Literature,* vol. 2. Edited by Frank N. Magill. Englewood Cliffs, NJ: Salem Press, 1983, pp. 848–851.

De Camp, L. Sprague. *Literary Swordsmen and Sorcerers: The Makers of Heroic Fantasy.* Sauk City, WI: Arkham House, 1976.

De Casseres, Benjamin. "Lord Dunsany." *Studies in Weird Fiction* 1 (Summer 1986): 33–34.

Eckley, Grace. "The Short Fiction of Dunsany." In *Survey of Modern Fantasy Literature,* vol. 3. Edited by Frank N. Magill. Englewood Cliffs, NJ: Salem Press, 1983, pp. 1507–1510.

Gardner, Martin. "Lord Dunsany." In *Supernatural Fiction Writers,* vol. 1. Edited by E. F. Bleiler. New York: Scribner, 1985, pp. 471–478.

Kroeber, Karl. *Romantic Fantasy and Science Fiction.* New Haven: Yale Univ. Press, 1988.

Mahoney, Patrick. "Lord Dunsany's Centennial: A Memoir." *Érie* 14 (1979): 126–130.

Manlove, C. N. *The Impulse of Fantasy Literature.* Kent, OH: Kent State Univ. Press, 1983.

Ringel, Faye Joyce. "Patterns of the Hero and the Quest: Epic, Romance, Fantasy." Ph.D. diss., Brown University, 1979.

Schweitzer, Darrell. "Lord Dunsany: Grand Master of Wonder." *The Eildon Tree* 1, no. 1 (1974): 4–7.

———. "The Novels of Lord Dunsany." *Mythlore* 25 (1980): 39–42. "Part 2." *Mythlore* 26 (1981): 39–41.

———. *Pathways to Elfland: The Writings of Lord Dunsany.* Philadelphia: Owlswick Press, 1989.

Shippey, T. A. "*The Charwoman's Shadow.*" In *Survey of Modern Fantasy Literature,* vol. 1. Edited by Frank N. Magill. Englewood Cliffs, NJ: Salem Press, 1983, pp. 232–235.

Twentieth-Century Science Fiction Writers. 3rd. ed. Edited by Noelle Watson and Paul E. Schellinger. Chicago: St. James, 1991, pp. 228–230.

Eagar, Frances

Leder, Sharon. "Contemporary Adolescent Gothic." *The Lion and the Unicorn* 1 (Fall 1977): 111–115.

Eager, Edward (McMaken)

Chaston, Joel D. "Polistopolis and Torquilstone: Nesbit, Eager, and the Question of Imitation." *The Lion and the Unicorn* 17 (June 1993): 73–82.

Doyle, Brian. *The Who's Who of Children's Literature.* New York: Schocken, 1968, pp. 83–84.

Eager, Edward. "Daily Magic." *Horn Book* 34 (Oct 1958): 349–358.

———. "A Father's Minority Report." *Horn Book* 24 (March 1948): 104–109.

Helbig, Alethea K., and Agnes Regan Perkins. *Dictionary of American Children's Fiction, 1859–1959.* Westport, CT: Greenwood, 1985, pp. 141, 200, 276–277, 322–323.

———. *Dictionary of American Children's Fiction, 1960–1984.* Westport, CT: Greenwood, 1986, pp. 179, 588.

More Junior Authors. Edited by Muriel Fuller. New York: Wilson, 1963, pp. 71–72.

Perrin, Noel. "Magic That Endures: Two Classic Children's Spellbinders Turn 40." *New York Times Book Review* 98 (Nov 14, 1993): 54.

Searles, Baird, Beth Meacham, and Michael Franklin. *A Reader's Guide to Fantasy.* New York: Avon, 1982, pp. 59–60.

Spivack, Charlotte. "Edward Eager." In Cech. *American Writers for Children, 1900–1960. Dictionary of Literary Biography,* vol. 22. Detroit: Gale, 1983, pp. 135–139.

Twentieth-Century Children's Writers. 3rd ed. Edited by Tracy Chevalier and D. L. Kirkpatrick. New York: St. Martin, 1989, pp. 309–310.

Eddings, David

Twentieth-Century Science Fiction Writers. 3rd ed. Edited by Noelle Watson and Paul E. Schellinger. Chicago: St. James, 1991, pp. 233–234.

Eddison, E(rik) R(ucker)

Attebery, Brian. "E. R. Eddison." In *Supernatural Fiction Writers: Fantasy and Horror,* vol. 2. Edited by E. F. Bleiler. New York: Scribner, 1985, pp. 529–534.

————. "The Zimiamvian Trilogy." In *Survey of Modern Fantasy Literature,* vol. 5. Edited by Frank N. Magill. Englewood Cliffs, NJ: Salem Press, 1983, pp. 2206–2213.

De Camp, L. Sprague. *Literary Swordsmen and Sorcerers: The Makers of Heroic Fantasy.* Sauk City, WI: Arkham House, 1976.

————, ed. *The Blade of Conan.* New York: Ace, 1979.

Flieger, Verlyn. "The Man Who Loved Women: Aspects of the Feminine in Eddison's Zimiamvia." *Mythlore* 49 (1987): 29–32.

Fredericks, Casey. *The Future of Eternity: Mythologies of Science Fiction and Fantasy.* Bloomington: Indiana Univ. Press, 1982.

Lewis, C. S. *On Stories and Other Essays on Literature.* Edited by Walter Hooper. New York: Harcourt Brace Jovanovich, 1982.

Manlove, C. N. *The Impulse of Fantasy Literature.* Kent, OH: Kent State Univ. Press, 1983, pp. 137–148.

Paul, Terri. "*The Worm Ouroboros:* Time Travel, Imagination and Entropy." *Extrapolation* 24 (1983): 272–279.

Pesch, Helmut W. "The Sign of the Worm: Images of Death and Immortality in the Fiction of E. R. Eddison." In *Death and the Serpent.* Edited by Carl B. Yoke and Donald M. Hassler. Westport, CT: Greenwood, 1985, pp. 91–102.

Schuyler, William M., Jr. "Recent Developments in Spell Construction." In *The Aesthetics of Fantasy Literature and Art.* Edited by Roger C. Schlobin. South Bend, IN: Univ. of Notre Dame Press, 1982, pp. 237–248.

Stableford, Brian. "*The Worm Ouroboros.*" In *Survey of Modern Fantasy Literature,* vol. 5. Edited by Frank N. Magill. Englewood Cliffs, NJ: Salem Press, 1983, pp. 2180–2184.

Twentieth-Century Science Fiction Writers. 3rd ed. Edited by Noelle Watson and Paul E. Schellinger. Chicago: St. James Press, 1991, p. 234.

Wilson, Andrew J. "If It's Wednesday This Must Be Narnia: Exploring the Links between Phantasy and Reality." *Dark Horizons* 24 (1981): 19–23.

Wilson, Sharon. "The Doctrine of Organic Unity: E. R. Eddison and the Romance Tradition." *Extrapolation* 25 (1984): 12–19.

Edmonds, Walter D(umaux)

Carmer, C. "Walter Edmonds of Black River Valley." *Publishers Weekly* 141 (June 27, 1942): 2346–2348.

Helbig, Alethea K., and Agnes Regan Perkins. *Dictionary of American Children's Fiction, 1859–1959.* Westport, CT: Greenwood, 1985, p. 144.

————. *Dictionary of American Children's Fiction, 1960–1984.* Westport, CT: Greenwood, 1986, p. 185.

Hopkins, Lee Bennett. "Walter D. Edmonds." In *More Books by More People.* New York: Citation Press, 1974, pp. 138–140.

Miller, Bertha Mahony, and Elinor Whitney Field, eds. *Newbery Medal Books, 1922–1955.* Boston: Horn Book, 1957, pp. 208–224.

More Junior Authors. Edited by Muriel Fuller. New York: Wilson, 1963, p. 73.

Roginski, Jim, ed. *Newbery and Caldecott Medalists and Honor Book Winners.* Littleton, CO: Libraries Unlimited, 1982, pp. 98–99.

Twentieth-Century Children's Writers. 3rd ed. Edited by Tracy Chevalier and D. L. Kirkpatrick. Chicago: St. James, 1989, pp. 310–311.

Wyld, Lionel D. *Walter D. Edmonds, Storyteller.* Syracuse, NY: Syracuse Univ. Press, 1982.

Edwards, Dorothy (Brown)

Twentieth-Century Children's Writers. 3rd ed. Edited by Tracy Chevalier and D. L. Kirkpatrick. New York: St. Martin, 1989, pp. 311–312.

Eisenstein, Phyllis (Kleinstein)

Eisenstein, Phyllis. "The Profession of Science Fiction, 28: Science Fiction and Me." *Foundation* 25 (1982): 31–35.

Friend, Beverly. "Time Travel as a Feminist Didactic in Works by Phyllis Eisenstein, Marlys Millhiser, and Octavia Butler." *Extrapolation* 23 (1982): 50–55.

Sanders, Jo. "*Sorcerer's Son.*" In *Survey of Modern Fantasy Literature,* vol. 4. Edited by Frank N. Magill. Englewood Cliffs, NJ: Salem Press, 1983, pp. 1780–1783.

Searles, Baird, Beth Meacham, and Michael Franklin. *A Reader's Guide to Fantasy.* New York: Avon, 1982, pp. 61–62.

Twentieth-Century Science Fiction Writers. 3rd ed. Edited by Noelle Watson and Paul E. Schellinger. Chicago: St. James Press, 1991, pp. 239–241.

Elgin, (Patricia Anne) Suzette Haden

Attebery, Brian. "Women's Coming of Age in Fantasy." *Extrapolation* 28 (Spring 1987): 10–22.

Bray, Mary Kay. "The Naming of Things: Men and Women, Language and Reality in Suzette Haden Elgin's *Native Tongue.*" *Extrapolation* 27 (1986): 49–61.

Chapman, Edgar L. "Sex, Satire, and Feminism in the Science Fiction of Suzette Haden Elgin." In *The Feminine Eye.* Edited by Tom Staicar. New York: Ungar, 1982.

Cristie, Mike. "Giving Tongue." *Vector* 139 (1987): 17–19.

Jakiel, S. James, and Rosandra E. Levinthal. "The Laws of Time Travel." *Extrapolation* 21 (1980): 130–138.

Shinn, Thelma J. "Worlds of Words and Swords: Suzette Haden Elgin and Joanna Russ at Work." In *Women Worldwalkers: New Dimensions of Science Fiction and Fantasy,* ed. by Jane B. Weedman. Lubbock: Texas Tech Press, 1985.

"Suzette Haden Elgin Creates 'Women's Language.'" *Science Fiction Chronicle* 6 (Aug 1985): 4.

Twentieth-Century Science Fiction Writers. 3rd ed. Edited by Noelle Watson and Paul E. Schellinger. Chicago: St. James Press, 1991, pp. 244–246.

Elkin, Benjamin

Fourth Book of Junior Authors and Illustrators. Edited by Doris De Montreville and Elizabeth D. Crawford. New York: Wilson, 1978, pp. 120–122.

Ende, Michael

Beer, Werner. "Michael Ende und sein Jim Knopf." In *Handbuch der Literatur in Bayern: Vom Fruhmittelalter bis zur Gegenwart: Geschichte und Interpretationen,* ed. by Albrecht Weber. Regensburg: Pustet, 1987, pp. 635–649.

Bosmjian, Hamida. "Grief and Its Displacemant Through Fantasy in Michael Ende's *The Neverending Story.*" *Proceedings of the 13th Annual Conference of The Children's Literature Association, 1986.* New York: Pace University, 1988, pp. 120–123.

Filmer, Kath. "Beware the Nothing: An Allegorical Reading of Ende's *The Neverending Story.*" *Mythlore* 46 (1986): 34–36.

———. "Religion and Romanticism in Michael Ende's *The Neverending Story.*" *Mythlore* 18 (Autumn 1991): 59–64.

Fleischer, Leonore. "Talk of the Trade: Off to Fantastica." *Publishers Weekly* 244 (Oct 7, 1983): 95.

Frenkell, Pavel. "Beskonechnaya Energiya Fatasii [The Boundless Energy of Fantasy]." *Detskaya Literatura* (Moscow) (Feb 2, 1982): 43–47.

Huse, Nancy. "The Blank Mirror of Death: Protest as Self-Creation in Contemporary Fantasy." *The Lion and the Unicorn* 12 (1988): 28–43.

Luserke, Uwe. "*The Neverending Story.*" *Space Voyager* 14 (1985): 56–59.

Meier, Ulrike. "Every Culture Needs a Myth: Ende." *Japan Times* (Japan) (Aug 26, 1986): 10.

Neumeyer, Peter F. "An Exhortation: Michael Ende, Father Goose, and the Confusion of Categories." *Journal of Aesthetic Education* 21 (Fall 1987): 45–51.

Nikolajeva, Maria. "How Fantasy Is Made: Patterns and Structures in *The Neverending Story.*" *Marveilles et Contes* 4(May 1990): 34–42.

Rutherford, Leonie. "The Reader in *The Never-Ending Story.*" *Reading Time* (Australia) 36 (Nov 1992): 7–12.

Schueler, Heinz J. "Michael Ende's *Die Unendliche Geschichte* and the Recovery of Myth through Romance." *Seminar* 23 (1987): 355–374.

Enright, Elizabeth (Wright)

Cameron, Eleanor. "The Art of Elizabeth Enright." *Horn Book* 45 (Dec 1969): 641–651; continued in 46 (Feb 1970): 26–30.

Enright, Elizabeth. "Acceptance Speech, Newbery Medal." *Horn Book* 15 (July 1939): 231–236.

———. *Doublefields: Memories and Stories.* New York: Harcourt Brace Jovanovich, 1966.

———. "Realism in Children's Literature." *Horn Book* 43 (Apr 1967): 165–170.

Gendron, Charisse. "Elizabeth Enright." In Cech. *American Writers for Children, 1900–1960. Dictionary of Literary Biography,* vol. 22. Detroit: Gale, 1983, pp. 140–145.

Helbig, Alethea K., and Agnes Regan Perkins. *Dictionary of American Children's Fiction, 1859–1959.* Westport, CT: Greenwood, 1985, p. 150.

———. *Dictionary of American Children's Fiction, 1960–1984.* Westport, CT: Greenwood, 1986, pp. 196–197, 647–648.

Hunt, Caroline. "Elizabeth Enright and the Family Story." *The Lion and the Unicorn* 14 (Dec 1990): 16–29.

The Junior Book of Authors. 2nd rev. ed. Edited by Stanley J. Kunitz and Howard Haycraft. New York: Wilson, 1951, p. 113.

Miller, Bertha Mahony, and Elinor Whitney Field, eds. *Newbery Medal Books: 1922–1955.* Boston: Horn Book, 1957, pp. 166–175.

The Oxford Companion to Children's Literature. Edited by Humphrey Carpenter and Mari Prichard. New York: Oxford Univ. Press, 1984, p. 168.

Roginski, Jim, ed. *Newbery and Caldecott Medalists and Honor Book Winners.* Littleton, CO: Libraries Unlimited, 1982, pp. 103–104.

Smaridge, Norah. *Famous Modern Storytellers for Young People.* New York: Dodd, 1969, pp. 38–43.

Smedman, M. Sarah. "Elizabeth Enright." In *Writers for Children: Critical Studies of Major Authors Since the Seventeenth Century.* Edited by Jane M. Bingham. New York: Scribner, 1988, pp. 215–220.

Twentieth-Century Children's Writers. 3rd ed. Edited by Tracy Chevalier and D. L. Kirkpatrick. Chicago: St. James, 1989, pp. 317–318.

Ensley, Evangeline *see* Walton, Evangeline

Ershov, Petr Pavlovich

The Oxford Companion to Children's Literature. Edited by Humphrey Carpenter and Mari Prichard. New York: Oxford Univ. Press, 1984, pp. 315–316.

Estes, Eleanor (Ruth Rosenfeld)

Altsteter, Mabel F. "Eleanor Estes and Her Books." *Elementary English* 29 (May 1952): 245–251.

Donnelly, E. "The 'Way' of Eleanor Estes." *Ontario Library Review* 40 (May 1956): 93–94.

Estes, Eleanor. "Gathering Honey." *Horn Book* 36 (Dec 1960): 487–494.

————. "Newbery Award Acceptance." *Horn Book* 28 (Aug 1952): 261–270.

————. "What Makes a Good Book?" *Writer* 48 (Nov 1935).

————. "Writing for Children." *Writer* 66 (Apr 1953): 109–111.

Helbig, Alethea K., and Agnes Regan Perkins. *Dictionary of American Children's Fiction, 1859–1959.* Westport, CT: Greenwood, 1985, pp. 150–151.

————. *Dictionary of American Children's Fiction, 1960–1984.* Westport, CT: Greenwood, 1986, pp. 199, 735.

Hopkins, Lee Bennett. "Eleanor Estes." In *More Books by More People.* New York: Citation Press, 1974, pp. 147–152.

The Junior Book of Authors. 2nd rev. ed. Edited by Stanley J. Kunitz and Howard Haycraft. New York: Wilson, 1951, pp. 114–115.

McElderry, Margaret K. "Eleanor Estes, 1906–1988." *Publishers Weekly* 26 (Aug 1988): 60.

Miller, Bertha Mahony, and Elinor Whitney Field, eds. *Newbery Medal Books: 1922–1955.* Boston: Horn Book, 1957, pp. 372–387.

Rice, Mabel R. "Eleanor Estes: A Study in Versatility." *Elementary English* 45 (May 1968): 553–557.

Roginski, Jim, ed. *Newbery and Caldecott Medalists and Honor Book Winners.* Littleton, CO: Libraries Unlimited, 1982, pp. 104–105.

Sayers, Frances Clarke. "The Books of Eleanor Estes." *Horn Book* 28 (Aug 1952): 257–260. Reprinted in Sayers. *Summoned by Books.* New York: Viking Press, 1965, pp. 116–121.

Stott, Jon C. *Children's Literature from A to Z.* New York: McGraw-Hill, 1984, p. 100.

Townsend, John Rowe. *A Sense of Story: Essays on Contemporary Writers for Children.* Philadelphia: Lippincott, 1971, pp. 79–88.

Twentieth-Century Children's Writers. 3rd ed. Edited by Tracy Chevalier and D. L. Kirkpatrick. Chicago: St. James, 1989, pp. 318–319.

Wolf, Virginia L. "Eleanor Estes." In Cech. *American Writers for Children, 1900–1960. Dictionary of Literary Biography,* vol. 22. Detroit: Gale, 1983, pp. 146–156.

Ewing, Juliana (Horatia Gatty)

Auerbach, Mina, and U. C. Knoepflmacher, eds. *Forbidden Journeys: Fairy Tales and Fantasys by Victorian Women Writers.* Chicago: Univ. of Chicago Press, 1992, pp. 105–128, 145–163, 361–362.

Avery, Gillian. "Juliana Horatia Ewing." In *Writers for Children: Critical Studies of Major Authors Since the Seventeenth Century.* Edited by Jane M. Bingham. New York: Scribner, 1988, pp. 221–226.

————. *Mrs. Ewing.* New York: Walck, 1964. Originally published London: Bodley Head, 1961.

Binding, P. M. "Mrs. Ewing: A Critical Appreciation of Her Work." B. Litt. thesis, Oxford University, 1969.

Cashdan, Liz. "Powerful Levers: Margaret Gatty, Juliana Horatia Ewing, and Mary Louisa Molesworth." *Children's Literature in Education* 20 (Dec1989): 215–226.

Downie, Mary Alice. "Mrs. Ewing in Canada." *Horn Book* 43 (Dec 1967): 721–725.

Doyle, Brian. *The Who's Who of Children's Literature.* New York: Schocken, 1968, pp. 90–91.

Fisher, Margery. "Perspectives in Prose: Re-Reading Some of Mrs. Ewing's Stories." *Signal* 59 (May 1989): 118–126.

Gunn, Katharine. "The Children's Books of Juliana Horatia Ewing." *Book and Magazine Collector* (London) 44 (Nov 1987): 22–29.

Hall, Donald E. "'We and the World': Juliana Horatia Ewing and Victorian Colonialism for Children." *Children's Literature Association Quarterly* 16 (Summer 1991): 51–55.

Kent, Muriel. "Juliana Horatia Ewing (1841–1885)." *Junior Bookshelf* 5 (Dec 1941): 123–128.

Kilby, H. T. "Yorkshire Genius: Juliana Horatia Ewing; A Note on Her Popular Children's Books and Their Illustrators." *Apollo* 41 (Apr 1945): 102–103.

Laski, Marghanita. *Mrs. Ewing, Mrs. Molesworth, and Mrs. Hodgson Burnett.* New York: Oxford Univ. Press, 1951.

Maxwell, Christabel. *Mrs. Gatty and Mrs. Ewing.* London: Constable, 1949.

The Oxford Companion to Children's Literature. Edited by Humphrey Carpenter and Mari Prichard. New York: Oxford Univ. Press, 1984, pp. 86, 171–172, 323.

Twentieth Century Children's Writers. 2nd ed. Edited by D. L. Kirkpatrick. New York: St. Martin, 1983, p. 867.

Whitney, Elinor. "Country Tales of Juliana Horatia Ewing." *Horn Book* 2 (Mar 1926): 12–16.

Yates, Elizabeth. "Juliana Horatia Ewing." *Junior Bookshelf* 2 (July 1938): 183–186.

Fairstar, Mrs. *see* Horne, Richard Henry

Farber, Norma (Holzman)

Bagnall, Norma. "Profile: Norma Farber." *Language Arts* 58 (Apr 1981): 481–486.

Harrison, Barbara. "Norma H. Farber 1909–1984." *Horn Book* 60 (June 1984): 404.

Helbig, Alethea K. "Bravura and Skill Yield Kernels of Truth: Norma Farber's Poetry for the Young." *Children's Literature Association Quarterly* 9 (Summer 1984): 79–80.

Twentieth-Century Children's Writers. 3rd ed. Edited by Tracy Chevalier and D. L. Kirkpatrick. Chicago: St. James, 1989, pp. 321–322.

Farjeon, Eleanor

Andrews, Sheryl R. "A Second Look: *The Glass Slipper.*" *Horn Book* 53 (Apr 1977): 193–194.

Blakelock, Denys. *Eleanor: Portrait of a Farjeon.* London: Gollancz, 1966.

———. "In Search of Elsie Piddock: An Echo of Eleanor Farjeon." *Horn Book* 44 (Feb 1968): 17–23; and *Junior Bookshelf* 32, no. 1 (Feb 1968): 17–23.

Cameron, Eleanor. "A Fine Old Gentleman." In *The Green and Burning Tree.* Boston: Little, Brown, 1962, pp. 317–334.

Colwell, Eileen H. *Eleanor Farjeon.* New York: Walck, 1961.

———. "Eleanor Farjeon: A Centenary View." *Horn Book* 57 (July 1981): 280–287.

———. "100 Years Young." *Puffin Post* (U.K.) 15, no. 1 (1981): 10–12.

———. "Our Friend, Eleanor Farjeon." *Junior Bookshelf* 28 (Aug 1965): 205–208.

Crouch, Marcus S. "Eleanor Farjeon." *Junior Bookshelf* 20 (July 1956): 110–114.

Doyle, Brian. *The Who's Who of Children's Literature.* New York: Schocken, 1968, pp. 93–95.

Farjeon, Annabel. *Morning Has Broken: A Biography of Eleanor Farjeon.* New York: Watts, 1986.

Farjeon, Eleanor. "A Comedy in Wax, or Lucy and Their Majesties." *Horn Book* 41 (Aug 1965): 358–363.

———. "A London Letter from Eleanor Farjeon." *Horn Book* 19 (Mar 1941): 90–92.

———. *Magic Casements.* London: Allen & Unwin, 1941.

———. *A Nursery in the Nineties.* rev. ed. New York: Oxford Univ. Press, 1960. Original U.S. title: *Portrait of a Family,* 1934.

———. "A Pepperpot Question." *Horn Book* 18 (May 1942): 149–151.

———. "Regina Award Acceptance." *Horn Book* 35 (Apr 1959): 105–108.

———. "Writing 'for' Children." *Signal* 71 (May 1993): 134–138. Reprinted from *The Writer's Desk Book: A Comprehensive Guide to the Various Aspects of the Writer's Craft* (Black, 1935).

Fish, Helen Dean. "The Spring-Green Lady: Eleanor Farjeon." *Horn Book* 6 (Feb 1930): 10–16.

Fisher, Margery. "Eleanor Farjeon: In Memorium." *Bookbird* 4 (1965): 3–10.

Godden, Rumer. "Tea with Eleanor Farjeon." *Horn Book* 68 (Jan–Feb 1992): 48–53.

Graham, Eleanor. "Eleanor Farjeon—A Study and an Appreciation." *Junior Bookshelf* 5 (July 1941): 81–86.

Greene, Ellin. "Eleanor Farjeon." In *Writers for Children: Critical Studies of Major Authors Since the Seventeenth Century.* Edited by Jane M. Bingham. New York: Scribner, 1988, pp. 227–234.

———. "Eleanor Farjeon: The Shaping of a Literary Imagination." Ed.D. diss., Rutgers University, 1979. Reprinted in *Proceedings of the Ninth Annual Conference of the Children's Literature Association.* University of Florida, March 1983. Ypsilanti, MI: Children's Literature Association, 1983, pp. 61–70.

———. "Literary Uses of Traditional Themes: From 'Cinderella' to *The Girl Who Sat by the Ashes* and *The Glass Slipper.*" *Children's Literature Association Quarterly* 11 (Fall 1986): 128–132.

Harvey, Anne. "Eleanor Farjeon." *Books for Keeps* (U.K.) 8 (May 1981): 30; *Children's Books History Society Newsletter* 41 (1990): 2–6.

The Junior Book of Authors. 2nd rev. ed. Edited by Stanley J. Kunitz and Howard Haycraft. New York: Wilson, 1951, pp. 117–119.

Junior Bookshelf. Eleanor Farjeon special issue 29 (Aug 1965): 195–208.

Lewis, Naomi, comp. *The Eleanor Farjeon Book: A Tribute to Her Life and Work, 1881–1965.* London: Hamish Hamilton, 1966.

"*The Little Bookroom.*" In M. Crouch and A. Ellis. *Chosen for Children.* 3rd ed. London: The Library Association, 1977, pp. 78–82.

Miller, Bertha Mahony. "Editorial: Honour to Eleanor Farjeon." *Horn Book* 32 (Oct 1956): 333.

———. "Little Brother and Sister." *Horn Book* 12 (May 1936): 167–174.

Morgan, M. E. "Eleanor Farjeon: An Evaluation." *Junior Bookshelf* 18 (Oct 1954): 175–179.

The Oxford Companion to Children's Literature. Edited by Humphrey Carpenter and Mari Prichard. New York: Oxford Univ. Press, 1984, pp. 182–183.

Rahn, Suzanne. "The Expression of Religious and Political Concepts in Fantasy for Children." Ph.D. diss., University of Washington, 1986.

Sayers, Frances Clarke. "Eleanor Farjeon's Room with a View." *Horn Book* 32 (Oct 1956): 335–345. Reprinted in *Horn Book* 57 (June 1981): 337–346; and in Frances Clarke Sayers. *Summoned by Books.* New York: Viking Press, 1965, pp. 122–132.

Smaridge, Norah. *Famous Modern Storytellers for Young People.* New York: Dodd, 1969, pp. 21–25.

Twentieth-Century Children's Writers. 3rd ed. Edited by Tracy Chevalier and D. L. Kirkpatrick. Chicago: St. James, 1989, pp. 322–325.

"27 Years Ago: Eleanor Farjeon." *Books and Bookmen* 339 (Dec1993): 12.

Viguers, Ruth Hill, ed. "Eleanor Farjeon." *Horn Book* 41 (Aug 1965): 419–420.

Farmer (Mockridge), Penelope (Jane)

Anderson, Lesley J. "A Consideration of Some of the Fantasy Novels of Penelope Farmer." *School Library Bulletin* (Australia)10 (Aug 1978): 69–75.

Cameron, Eleanor. "Afterword." In Penelope Farmer. *Charlotte Sometimes.* New York: Dell/Yearling, 1987.

Cohen, John. "The God Within: An Examination of *A Castle of Bone* by Penelope Farmer." *Orana* (Australia) 13 (May 1977): 48–50.

Crago, Hugh. "Penelope Farmer's Novels." *Signal* 17 (May 1975): 81–90.

Duguid, Lindsay. "The Terrible Made Tangible." *Times Educational Supplement* (Feb 16, 1990): 59.

Esmonde, Margaret P. "Narrative Methods in Penelope Farmer's *A Castle of Bone.*" *Children's Literature in Education* 14 (Autumn 1983): 171–179.

Farmer, Penelope. "But I'll Ask Them All the Same." *School Library Bulletin Supplement* (Australia) 10, no. 2 (1978): 21–24.

———. "Discovering the Pattern." In Edward Blishen. *The Thorny Paradise.* Boston: Horn Book, 1975, pp. 103–107.

———. "'Jorinda and Jorindel' and Other Stories." *Children's Literature in Education* 7 (Mar 1972): 23–34. Reprinted in Geoff Fox. *Writers, Critics, and Children.* New York: Agathon Press, 1976, pp. 55–72.

———. "On the Effects of Collecting Myth for Children and Others." *Children's Literature in Education* 27, no. 4 (Winter 1977): 176–185.

———. "Patterns on a Wall." *Horn Book* 50 (Oct 1974): 169–176.

Fourth Book of Junior Authors and Illustrators. Edited by Doris De Montreville and Elizabeth D. Crawford. New York: Wilson, 1978, pp. 124–126.

Grieve, Ann. "The Psychotic State in Fantasy for Post-Primary Readers." *School Library Bulletin* (Australia) 10 (Aug 1978): 3–10.

Hewitt, Marion R. "Emergent Authors: Penelope Farmer." *Junior Bookshelf* 27 (Jan 1963): 20–22.

Jones, Cornelia, and Olivia R. Way. "Penelope Farmer." In *British Children's Authors.* Chicago: American Library Association, 1976, pp. 77–84.

McElderry, Margaret K. "Penelope Farmer: The Development of an Author." *Elementary English* 51 (Sept 1974): 799–805.

Meek, Margaret. "Inwardly Adolescent." *Times Literary Supplement* March 29, 1985, p. 348.

Rees, David. "The Marble in the Water: The Real World in Penelope Farmer's Novels." *Horn Book* 52 (Oct 1976): 471–478. Reprinted in David Rees. *The Marble in the Water.* Boston: Horn Book, 1980, pp. 1–13.

Salway, Lance, and Nancy Chambers. "Book Post." *Signal* 25 (Jan 1978): 49–55; "Book Post Returns." *Signal* 26 (May 1978): 92–98.

Swinfen, Ann. *In Defense of Fantasy.* London: Routledge, 1984. *Charlotte Sometimes,* pp. 53, 56–58; *Castle of Bone,* pp. 67–71; *The Magic Stone, The Summer Birds, William and Mary,* pp. 138–141.

Twentieth-Century Children's Writers. 3rd ed. Edited by Tracy Chevalier and D. L. Kirkpatrick. Chicago: St. James, 1989, pp. 326–327.

Fast, Howard (Melvin)

Burgess, E. E. "This Man, Howard Fast." *Top of the News* 21 (Jan 1965): 138–141.
Twentieth-Century Science Fiction Writers. 3rd ed. Edited by Noelle Watson and Paul E. Schellinger. Chicago: St. James Press, 1991, pp. 269–271.

Faulkner, William (Cuthbert)

Brown, Calvin S. "Faulkner's Rowan Oak Tales." *Mississippi Quarterly* 34 (Summer 1981): 367–374.
Ditsky, John. "William Faulkner's *The Wishing Tree:* Maturity's First Draft." *The Lion and the Unicorn* 2 (Spring 1978): 56–64.
Gidley, Mick. "William Faulkner and Children." *Signal* 3 (Sept 1970): 91–102.

Feagles, Anita M(acRae)

Fourth Book of Junior Authors and Illustrators. Edited by Doris De Montreville and Elizabeth D. Crawford. New York: Wilson, 1978, pp. 128–129.

Feist, Raymond E.

Twentieth-Century Science Fiction Writers. 3rd ed. Edited by Noelle Watson and Paul E. Schellinger. Cichago: St. James, 1991, pp. 277–278.

Fenton, Edward

Third Book of Junior Authors. Edited by Doris De Montreville and Donna Hill. New York: Wilson, 1972, pp. 82–83.
Twentieth-Century Children's Writers. 3rd ed. Edited by Tracy Chevalier and D. L. Kirkpatrick. Chicago: St. James, 1989, pp. 331–332.

Field, Rachel (Lyman)

Bechtel, Louise Seaman. "Rachel's Gifts." *Horn Book* 18 (July–Aug 1942): 230–236.
Benét, Laura. "Rachel Field—A Memory." *Horn Book* 18 (July–Aug 1942): 227–229.
Bianco, Margery Williams. "*Hitty, Her First Hundred Years.*" In Anne Carroll Moore and Bertha Mahony Miller. *Writing and Criticism.* Boston: Horn Book, 1951, pp. 63–66.
Field, Rachel Lyman. "How *Hitty* Happened." *Horn Book* 6 (Feb 1930): 22–26.
———. "A Hunt Breakfast—Authors' Symposium." *Horn Book* 2 (Nov 1926): 35–36.
Griffin, Deuel N. "Rachel Field." In Cech. *American Writers for Children, 1900–1960. Dictionary of Literary Biography,* vol. 22. Detroit: Gale, 1983, pp. 170–175.
Hale, Florence M. "Concerning *Hitty: Her First Hundred Years.*" *Grade Teacher* 48 (Nov 1930): 189.
Helbig, Alethea K. "Rachel Lyman Field." In *Writers for Children; Critical Studies of Major Authors Since the Seventeenth Century.* Edited by Jane M. Bingham. New York: Scribner, 1988, pp. 235–240.
Helbig, Alethea K., and Agnes Regan Perkins. *Dictionary of American Children's Fiction, 1859–1959.* Westport, CT: Greenwood, 1985, pp. 160, 220–221.
Horn Book Magazine. A Memorial *Horn Book* for Rachel Field. *Horn Book* 18 (July–Aug 1942).

The Junior Book of Authors. 2nd rev. ed. Edited by Stanley J. Kunitz and Howard Haycraft. New York: Wilson, 1951, pp. 123–126.

Kuznets, Lois R. "Two Newbery Medal Winners and the Feminine Mystique: *Hitty, Her First Hundred Years* and *Miss Hickory.*" *The Lion and the Unicorn* 15 (Dec 1991): 1–14.

Twentieth-Century Children's Writers. 3rd ed. Edited by Tracy Chevalier and D. L. Kirkpatrick. Chicago: St. James, 1989, pp. 334–336.

Fine, Anne

Bierman, Valerie. "Authorgraph no. 69: Anne Fine." *Books for Keeps* (U.K.) 69 (1991): 16–17.

Blaisdale, Julie. "In Touch With the Child: The Novels of Anne Fine." *School Librarian* 39 (1991): 135–136.

Fine, Anne. "A Year Beside Slimy Mallows." *Author* 102 (Summer 1991): 43.

Linklater, Andro. "The Prime of Class 3C." *The Guardian* Supplement (Feb 22, 1993): 13.

Mappin, Alf. "Know the Author: Anne Fine." *Magpies* (Australia) 8 (Mar 1993): 10–13.

Nieuwenhuizen, Agnes. "The Young Ones." *The Age Saturday Extra* (Australia) (May 22, 1993): 8.

Waldron, Murray. "A Fine Line in Fiction." *Australian Weekend Review* (May 29–30, 1993): 7.

Finney, Charles G(randison)

Schlobin, Roger C. "The Fool and the Fantastic." *Fantasy Newsletter* 43 (1981): 6–9, 29.

Smith, Curtis C. "Charles Finney." In *Supernatural Fiction Writers: Fantasy and Horror,* vol. 2, Edited by E. F. Bleiler. New York: Scribner, 1985, pp. 821–826.

Wolfe, Gary K. "*The Circus of Dr. Lao.*" In *Survey of Modern Fantasy Literature,* vol. 1. Edited by Frank N. Magill. Englewood Cliffs, NJ: Salem Press, 1983, pp. 282–286.

Finney, Jack (pseud. of Walter Braden Finney)

Landon, Brooks. "Time and Again." In *Survey of Modern Fantasy Literature,* vol. 4. Edited by Frank N. Magill. Englewood Cliffs, NJ: Salem Press, 1983, pp. 1938–1942.

Searles, Baird, Beth Meacham, and Michael Franklin. *A Reader's Guide to Fantasy.* New York: Avon, 1982, pp. 63–64.

Twentieth-Century Science Fiction Writers. 3rd ed. Edited by Noelle Watson and Paul E. Schellinger. Chicago: St. James Press, 1991, pp. 279–280.

Fischtrom, Harvey *see* Zemach, Harve

Fisher, Dorothy (Frances) Canfield

Maguire, Gregory. "A Second Look: *Understood Betsy.*" *Horn Book* 50 (Oct 1979): 558–560.

Twentieth-Century Children's Writers. 3rd ed. Edited by Tracy Chevalier and D. L. Kirkpatrick. New York: St. Martin, 1989, pp. 342–344.

Washington, Ida H. *Dorothy Canfield Fisher: A Biography.* Shelburne, VT: New England Press, 1982.

Fisher, Leonard Everett

Fisher, Leonard Everett. "The Artist at Work: Creating Non Fiction." *Horn Book* 64 (May–June 1988): 315–323.
Third Book of Junior Authors. Edited by Doris De Montreville and Donna Hill. New York: Wilson, 1972, pp. 84–85.

Flack, Marjorie

Bader, Barbara. *American Picturebooks: From Noah's Ark to the Beast Within.* New York: Macmillan, 1976, pp. 61–64.
Twentieth-Century Children's Writers. 3rd ed. Edited by Tracy Chevalier and D. L. Kirkpatrick. New York: St. Martin, 1989, pp. 348–349.

Flecker, (Herman) James Elroy

Eaton, Anne. "Extensions of Reality." *Horn Book* 3 (May 1927): 17–22.
Speth, Lee. "Cavalier Treatment: James Elroy Flecker's *King of Alsander.*" *Mythlore* 5, 19 (1978), and 6 (Winter 1979): 17.

Fleischman, Paul (Taylor)

Clark, Anne. "Books in the Classroom." *Horn Book* 69 (Mar–Apr 1993): 187–189.
Fifth Book of Junior Authors and Illustrators. Edited by Sally Holmes Holtze. New York: Wilson, 1983, pp. 114–116.
Fleischman, Paul. "1989 Newbery Acceptance Speech." *Journal of Youth Services in Libraries* 2 (Summer 1989): 299–306; and *Horn Book* 65 (July– Aug 1989): 442–451.
———. "Sid Fleischman." *Horn Book* 63 (July–Aug 1987): 429–432.
———. "Sound and Sense." *Horn Book* 62 (Sept–Oct 1986): 551–555.
Fleischman, Sid. "Paul Fleischman." *Horn Book* 65 (July–Aug 1989): 452–455.
Helbig, Alethea, and Agnes Regan Perkins. *Dictionary of American Children's Fiction, 1985–1989.* Westport, CT: Greenwood, 1993, p. 76.
Sorenson, Marilou. "Between the Covers: People Behind the Books: Paul Fleischman." *CLA Bulletin* 15 (Spring 1989): 10.
Twentieth-Century Children's Writers. 3rd ed. Edited by Tracy Chevalier and D. L. Kirkpatrick. Chicago: St. James, 1989, pp. 349–350.

Fleischman, (Albert) Sid(ney)

Dane, C. "Presentation of the Eighth Recognition of Merit to Sid Fleischman for *By the Great Horned Spoon.*" *Claremont Reading Conference Yearbook* 36 (1972): 94–96.
Erol, Sibel. "*Beyond the Divide:* Lasky's Feminist Revision of the Westward Journey." *Children's Literature Association Quarterly* 17 (Spring 1992): 5–8.
Fleischman, Paul. "Sid Fleischman." *Horn Book* 63 (July–Aug 1987): 429–432.
Fleischman, Sid. "Boston Globe-Horn Book Acceptance." *Horn Book* 56 (Feb 1980): 94–96.
———. "Laughter and Children's Literature." *Horn Book* 52 (Oct 1976): 465–470. Reprinted in Paul Heins. *Crosscurrents of Criticism.* Boston: Horn Book, 1977, pp. 199–204; and in *The Claremont Reading Conference Yearbook* 40 (1976): 88–92.
———. "The Magic of Story." *Five Owls* 2 (1988): 81–83.
———. "Newbery Medal Acceptance." *Horn Book* 63 (July–Aug 1987): 423–428.

————. "1987 Newbery Acceptance Speech." *Top of the News* 48 (Summer 1987): 385–390.

————. "Reality on Laughing Gas." *Horn Book* 70 (Mar–Apr 1994): 162–165.

Helbig, Alethea, and Agnes Regan Perkins. *Dictionary of American Children's Fiction, 1985–1989.* Westport, CT: Greenwood, 1993, pp. 77, 273–275.

————. *Dictionary of American Children's Fiction, 1960–1984.* Westport, CT: Greenwood, 1986, pp. 84–85, 108–109, 216, 237–238, 302, 410, 439–440.

Johnson, Emily R. "Profile: Sid Fleischman." *Language Arts* 59 (Oct 1982): 754–759, 772.

Nettell, Stephanie. "Sid Fleischman." *Books for Keeps* (U.K.) 52 (Sept 1988): 14–15.

The Oxford Companion to Children's Literature. Edited by Humphrey Carpenter and Mari Prichard. New York: Oxford Univ. Press, 1984, p. 188.

Spirt, Diana L. *Introducing Bookplots 3: A Book Talk Guide for Use with Readers Ages 8–12.* New York: Bowker, 1988, pp. 40–42.

Third Book of Junior Authors. Edited by Doris De Montreville and Donna Hill. New York: Wilson, 1972, pp. 86–87.

Twentieth-Century Children's Writers. 3rd ed. Edited by Tracy Chevalier and D. L. Kirkpatrick. Chicago: St. James, 1989, pp. 350–351.

Webb, Kaye. "Sid Fleischman, Magic Extraordinary." *Puffin Post* (U.K.) 13, no. 4 (1979): 12–13.

Fleming, Ian (Lancaster)

Fifth Book of Junior Authors and Illustrators. Edited by Sally Holmes Holtze. New York: Wilson, 1983, pp. 116–117.

West, Mark. "Fleming's Flying Flivver Flops on Film." In Douglas Street. *Children's Novels and the Movies.* New York: Ungar, 1983, pp. 197–204.

Flora, James (Royer)

Third Book of Junior Authors. Edited by Doris De Montreville and Donna Hill. New York: Wilson, 1972, pp. 87–89.

Twentieth-Century Children's Writers. 3rd ed. Edited by Tracy Chevalier and D. L. Kirkpatrick. Chicago: St. James, 1989, pp. 351–352.

Follett, Barbara Newhall

Follett, Barbara Newhall. "In Defense of Butterflies." *Horn Book* 9 (Feb 1933): 24–28.

Follett, Helen Thomas. "Education à la Carte." *Pictorial Review* (July 1929): 2+.

Follett, Wilson. "To a Daughter, One Year Lost." *Atlantic Monthly* 167 (1941): 564–567.

————. "Notes on a Junior Author: With a Glance at Precocity." *Horn Book* 4 (May 1928): 6–13.

Grier, Harold, and Helen Follett. *Barbara: The Unconscious Autobiography of a Child Genius.* Chapel Hill: Univ. of North Carolina Press, 1966.

Sadler, David. "Innocent Hearts: The Child Authors of the 1920's." *Children's Literature Association Quarterly* 17 (Winter 1992–1993): 24–30.

Fox (Greenberg), Paula

Bach, Alice. "Cracking Open the Geode: The Fiction of Paula Fox." *Horn Book* 53 (Oct 1977): 514–521.

Baker, Augusta. "Paula Fox." *Horn Book* 50 (Aug 1974): 351–353.

Council on Interracial Books for Children. *"The Slave Dancer:* Critiques of This Year's Newbery Award Winner." *Interracial Books for Children* 5 (1974): 4–6, 8.

Fourth Book of Junior Authors and Illustrators. Edited by Doris De Montreville and Elizabeth D. Crawford. New York: Wilson, 1978, pp. 135–136.

Fox, Paula. "Hans Christian Andersen Medal Acceptance." *Horn Book* 55 (Apr 1979): 222–223.

———. "Newbery Award Acceptance." *Horn Book* 50 (Aug 1974): 345–350.

———. "One Human Heart." In *Innocence & Experience,* ed. by Barbara Harrison and Gregory Maguire. New York: Lothrop, 1987, pp. 250–258.

———. "Other Places [Children and the Complexity of Life]." *Horn Book* 63 (Jan/Feb 1987): 21–27.

———. "To Write Simply." *Horn Book* 67 (Sept–Oct 1991): 552–555.

Heins, Paul. "Editorial: Paula Fox: Hans Christian Andersen Medal Winner." *Horn Book* 54 (Oct 1978): 486–487.

Helbig, Alethea K., and Agnes Regan Perkins. *Dictionary of American Children's Fiction, 1960–1984.* Westport, CT: Greenwood, 1986, pp. 222–223.

Inglis, Fred. *The Promise of Happiness.* New York: Cambridge Univ. Press, 1981, pp. 281–283.

Kingman, Lee, ed. *Newbery and Caldecott Medal Books: 1966–1975.* Boston: Horn Book, 1975, pp. 113–125.

McDonnell, Christine. "A Second Look: *The Stone-Faced Boy.*" *Horn Book* 60 (Apr 1984): 219–222.

Moss, Anita. "Paula Fox." In *American Writers for Children since 1960: Fiction. Dictionary of Literary Biography,* vol. 52. Detroit: Gale, 1986, pp. 143–155.

The Oxford Companion to Children's Literature. Edited by Humphrey Carpenter and Mari Prichard. New York: Oxford Univ. Press, 1984, pp. 189–190.

Parker, Patricia Anne Falstad. "Responses of Adolescents and Librarians to Selected Contemporary Fiction." Ph.D. diss., University of Minnesota, 1974.

Rees, David. "'The Colour of Saying': Paula Fox." In *Marble in the Water.* Boston: Horn Book, 1980, pp. 114–127.

Rustin, Michael. "Finding Oneself Among Strangers: Three Stories by Paula Fox." In Margaret Rustin and Michael Rustin. *Narratives of Love and Loss: Studies in Modern Children's Fiction.* London: Verso, 1987; New York: Routledge, 1988, pp. 215–247.

Speaking for Ourselves: Autobiographical Sketches by Notable Authors of Books for Young Adults. Edited by Donald R. Gallo. Urbana, IL: National Council of Teachers of English, 1990, pp. 69–70.

Townsend, John Rowe. "Paula Fox." In *A Sounding of Storytellers.* New York: Lippincott, 1979, pp. 55–65.

———. *A Sense of Story: Essays on Contemporary Writers for Children.* Philadelphia: Lippincott, 1971, pp. 89–96.

Twentieth-Century Children's Writers. 3rd ed. Edited by Tracy Chevalier and D. L. Kirkpatrick. Chicago: St. James, 1989, pp. 357–358.

The Zena Sutherland Lectures, 1983–1992. Ed. by Betsy Hearne. New York: Clarion, 1993, pp. 111–137.

France, Anatole (pseud. of Jacques Anatole Francois Thibault)

Stableford, Brian M. "Anatole France." In *Supernatural Fiction Writers: Fantasy and Horror,* vol. 1. New York: Scribner, 1985, pp. 67–73.

Freeman, Barbara C(onstance)

Twentieth-Century Children's Writers. 3rd ed. Edited by Tracy Chevalier and D. L. Kirkpatrick. Chicago: St. James, 1989, pp. 358–359.

Freschet, Berniece (Louise Speck)

Fourth Book of Junior Authors and Illustrators. Edited by Doris De Montreville and Elizabeth D. Crawford. New York: Wilson, 1978, pp. 130–139.

Friesner, Esther M.

Lerner, Frederick Andrew. "The Newcomer." [Esther M. Friesner] *VOYA* 14 (Dec 1991): 294.

Fritz, Jean (Guttery)

Alberghene, Janice. "Artful Memory: Jean Fritz, Autobiography and the Child Reader." In *The Voice of the Narrator in Children's Literature: Insights from Writers and Critics,* ed. by Charlotte F. Otten and Gary D. Schmidt. New York: Greenwood, 1989, pp. 362–368.

Ammon, Richard. "Profile: Jean Fritz." *Language Arts* 60 (Mar 1983): 365–369.

Busbin, O. Mell. "Jean Fritz." In *American Writers for Children since 1960: Fiction. Dictionary of Literary Biography,* vol. 52. Detroit: Gale, 1986, pp. 156–167.

Fritz, Jean. "Books Still on My Shelves." *CBC Features* 42, no. 2 (1989): 11.

———. "The Education of an American." *Top of the News* 32 (June 1976): 321–336.

———. "Journeying." In *Innocence & Experience,* ed. by Barbara Harrison and Gregory Maguire. New York: Lothrop, 1987, pp. 45–63.

———. "Making It Real." *Children's Literature in Education* 22 (Autumn 1976): 125–127.

———. "On Writing Historical Fiction." *Horn Book* 43 (Oct 1967): 565–570.

———. "The Role of History in Recreating the Past." In *Literature and Hawaii's Children.* Proceedings of the Third Biennial Conference on Literature and Hawaii's Children. Honolulu: Literature and Hawaii's Children, 1988, pp. 7–16.

———. "The Teller and the Tale." In *Worlds of Childhood,* ed. by William Zinsser, Houghton, 1990, pp. 21–46.

———. "There Once Was." 1986 Laura Ingalls Wilder Award Acceptance Speech. *Top of the News* 42 (Summer 1986): 401–404; *Horn Book* 62 (July–Aug 1986): 432–435.

———. "Turning History Inside Out." *Horn Book* 61 (Jan 1985): 29–34.

———. "The Voice of One Biographer." In *The Voice of the Narrator in Children's Literature: Insights from Writers and Critics,* ed. by Charlotte F. Otten and Gary D. Schmidt. New York: Greenwood, 1989, pp. 337–346.

Heins, Ethel L. "Presentation of the 1986 Laura Ingalls Wilder Medal." *Horn Book* 62 (July/Aug 1986): 430–431.

Helbig, Alethea K., and Agnes Regan Perkins. *Dictionary of American Children's Fiction, 1960–1984; Recent Books of Recognized Merit.* Westport, CT: Greenwood, 1986, pp. 226–227.

Hopkins, Lee Bennett. *More Books by More People.* New York: Citation Press, 1974, pp. 172–177.

Roginski, Jim. *Behind the Covers: Interview with Authors and Illustrators of Books for Children and Young Adults.* Littleton, CO: Libraries Unlimited, 1985, pp. 73–84.

Third Book of Junior Authors. Edited by Doris De Montreville and Donna Hill. New York: Wilson, 1972, pp. 94–95.

Twentieth-Century Children's Writers. 3rd ed. Edited by Tracy Chevalier and D. L. Kirkpatrick. Chicago: St. James, 1989, pp. 363–364.
The Zena Sutherland Lectures, 1983–1992. Edited by Betsy Hearne. New York: Clarion, 1993, pp. 160–182.

Fry, Rosalie K(ingsmill)

Third Book of Junior Authors. Edited by Doris De Montreville and Donna Hill. New York: Wilson, 1972, pp. 95–97.
Twentieth-Century Children's Writers. 3rd ed. Edited by Tracy Chevalier and D. L. Kirkpatrick. Chicago: St. James, 1989, pp. 364–365.

Fyleman, Rose (Amy)

Adams, Lady Agnes. "Rose Fyleman." *Bookman* 77 (Oct 1929): 27–28.
———. "Rose Fyleman, the Fairies' Laureate." *Elementary English Review* 6 (Mar 1929): 61–63.
Doyle, Brian. *The Who's Who of Children's Literature*. New York: Schocken, 1968, pp. 104–105.
Fyleman, Rose. "How I Came to Write for Children." *Horn Book* 5 (Aug 1929): 22–23.
———. "Writing Poetry for Children." *Horn Book* 16 (Jan–Feb 1940): 58–66.
———. "Writing Verse for Children." *Horn Book* 13 (May 1937): 144–146.
The Junior Book of Authors. 2nd ed. rev. Edited by Stanley J. Kunitz and Howard Haycraft. New York: Wilson, 1951, pp. 133–134.
The Oxford Companion to Children's Literature. Edited by Humphrey Carpenter and Mari Prichard. New York: Oxford Univ. Press, 1984, p. 193.
Shippen, Elizabeth P. "Rose Fyleman." *Elementary English* 35 (Oct 1958): 358–365.
Twentieth-Century Children's Writers. 3rd ed. Edited by Tracy Chevalier and D. L. Kirkpatrick. Chicago: St. James, 1989, pp. 367–369.
Whitney, Elinor. "A Pilgrim Fairy." *Horn Book* 5 (Aug 1929): 18–21.

Gage, Wilson *see* Steele, Mary Q.

Gall, Alice Crew, and Crew, Fleming H.

The Junior Book of Authors. 2nd ed. rev. Edited by Stanley J. Kunitz and Howard Haycraft. New York: Wilson, 1951, pp. 136–137.

Gallico, Paul (William)

Searles, Baird, Beth Meacham, and Michael Franklin. *A Reader's Guide to Fantasy*. New York: Avon, 1982, pp. 65–66.

Gannett (Kahn), Ruth Stiles

Fourth Book of Junior Authors and Illustrators. Edited by Doris De Montreville and Elizabeth D. Crawford. New York: Wilson, 1978, pp. 143–144.
Helbig, Alethea K., and Agnes Regan Perkins. *Dictionary of American Children's Fiction, 1859–1959*. Westport, CT: Greenwood, 1985, pp. 174–175, 365.
Roginski, Jim, ed. *Newbery and Caldecott Medalists and Honor Book Winners*. Littleton, CO: Libraries Unlimited, 1982, p. 123.

Twentieth-Century Children's Writers. 3rd ed. Edited by Tracy Chevalier and D. L. Kirkpatrick. Chicago: St. James, 1989, p. 371.

Gard, Joyce (pseud. of Joyce Reeves)

Jones, Cornelia, and Olivia R. Way. "Joyce Gard." In *British Children's Authors.* Chicago: American Library Association, 1976, pp. 85–93.

Twentieth-Century Children's Writers. 3rd ed. Edited by Tracy Chevalier and D. L. Kirkpatrick. Chicago: St. James, 1989, pp. 371–372.

Gardam, Jane (Pearson)

Crouch, Marcus. "The Tragicomedy of Being Young." *Junior Bookshelf* 51 (1987): 260–265.

Gardam, Jane. "Mrs. Hookaneye and I." In Edward Blishen. *The Thorny Paradise.* Boston: Horn Book, 1975, pp. 77–80.

———. "On Writing for Children: Some Wasps in the Marmalade, Part I." *Horn Book* 54 (Oct 1978): 489–496. "Part II." *Horn Book* 54 (Dec 1978): 672–679.

Leech, Michael. "Mum's the Word." *Sunday Times Magazine* (June 14, 1992): 14, 17.

Rees, David. "Caviare to the General: The Novels of Jane Gardam." *School Librarian* 37 (Feb 1989): 5–8. Reprinted in *"What Do Draculas Do?" Essays on Contemporary Writers of Fiction for Children and Young Adults.* Metuchen, NJ: Scarecrow Press, 1990, pp. 160–174.

Twentieth-Century Children's Writers. 3rd ed. Edited by Tracy Chevalier and D. L. Kirkpatrick. Chicago: St. James, 1989, pp. 372–374.

Garden, Nancy

Chelton, Mary K. "Interview with Nancy Garden." *VOYA* 5 (Feb 1983): 15–16.

———. "*VOYA* Interview with Nancy Garden." In *The VOYA Reader.* Metuchen, NJ: Scarecrow Press, 1990, pp. 270–274.

Fifth Book of Junior Authors and Illustrators. Edited by Sally Holmes Holtze. New York: Wilson, 1983, pp. 126–127.

Gardner, John (Champlin, Jr.)

De Luca, Geraldine, and Roni Natov. "Modern Moralities for Children: John Gardner's Children's Books." In *John Gardner: Critical Perspectives.* Edited by Robert A. Morace and Kathryn Van Spanckeren. Carbondale: Southern Illinois Univ. Press, 1982, pp. 89–96.

Evans, W. D. Emrys. "The Welsh Mabinogion: Tellings and Retellings." *Children's Literature in Education* 28, no. 9 (Spring 1978): 17–33.

Fifth Book of Junior Authors and Illustrators. Edited by Sally Holmes Holtze. New York: Wilson, 1983, pp. 127–129.

Foust, R. E. "Monstrous Image: Theory of Fantasy Antagonists." *Genre* 13 (1981): 441–453.

Howell, John M. *John Gardner: A Bibliographic Profile.* Carbondale: Southern Illinois Univ. Press, 1980.

Merrill, Robert. "John Gardner's *Grendel* and the Interpretation of Modern Fables." *American Literature* 56 (1984): 162–180.

Miller, Patricia Ann. "'Balance is Everything': John Gardner and His Fiction." Ph.D. diss., University of Iowa, 1986.

Morace, Robert A. *John Gardner: An Annotated Secondary Bibliography.* New York: Garland, 1984.

Morace, Robert A., and Kathryn Morace, eds. *John Gardner.* Carbondale: Southern Illinois Univ. Press, 1982.

Morris, G. L. *World of Order and Light: The Fiction of John Gardner.* Athens: Univ. of Georgia Press, 1984.

Myers, Walter E. "*Grendel.*" In *Survey of Modern Fantasy Literature,* vol. 2. Edited by Frank N. Magill. Englewood Cliffs, NJ: Salem Press, 1983, pp. 675–679.

Natov, Roni, and Geraldine De Luca. "An Interview with John Gardner." *The Lion and the Unicorn* 2 (Spring 1979): 114–136.

Tuso, Joseph F. "*Grendel:* Chapter I: John Gardner's Perverse Prologue." *College Literature* 12 (1985): 184–186.

Garfield, Leon

"Authorgraph no. 13: Leon Garfield." *Books for Keeps* (U. K.) 13 (Mar 1982): 14–15.

"Bookmark *Talks to Leon Garfield.*" *Bookmark* 10 (1982): 2–17.

Camp, Richard. "Garfield's Golden Net." *Signal* 5 (May 1971): 47–55.

Crouch, Marcus. *The Nesbit Tradition.* London: Benn, 1972, pp. 34–38.

Doyle, Brian. *The Who's Who of Children's Literature.* New York: Schocken, 1968, pp. 105–106.

Fourth Book of Junior Authors and Illustrators. Edited by Doris De Montreville and Elizabeth D. Crawford. New York: Wilson, 1978, pp. 144–145.

Garfield, Leon. "And So It Grows." *Horn Book* 44 (Dec 1968): 668–672. Reprinted from *Children's Book News* (Mar–Apr 1968).

———. "Bookmaker and Punter." In Edward Blishen. *The Thorny Paradise.* Boston: Horn Book, 1975, pp. 81–86.

———. "An Evening with Leon Garfield." In *One Ocean Touching.* Edited by Sheila A. Egoff. Metuchen, NJ: Scarecrow Press, 1979, pp. 110–120.

———. "Historical Fiction for Our Global Times." *Horn Book* 64 (Nov–Dec 1988): 736–742.

———. "The Outlaw." *Horn Book* 66 (Mar–Apr 1990): 164–170.

Garfield, Leon. "A Present for Mr. Patten." *Books for Keeps* (U.K.) 77 (1992): 36–37.

———. "The Uses of Experience." *Canadian Children's Literature* 54 (1989): 37–40.

———. "Writing for Childhood." *Children's Literature in Education* 2 (July 1970): 56–63.

Garfield, Leon, Edward Blishen, and Charles Keeping. "Greek Myths and the Twentieth Century Reader." *Children's Literature in Education* 3 (Nov 1970): 48–65.

Gillespie, John T. *Juniorplots 4: A Book Talk Guide for Use with Readers Ages 12–16.* New Providence, NJ: Bowker, 1993, pp. 248–252.

Holland, Phillip. "Shades of the Prison House: The Fiction of Leon Garfield." *Children's Literature in Education* 9 (Winter 1978): 159–172.

Jones, Rhodri. "Writers for Children—Leon Garfield." *The Use of English* 23 (Summer 1972): 293–299. Reprinted in Dennis Butts. *Good Writers for Young Readers.* St. Albans, England: Hart-Davis, 1977, pp. 34–44.

Ketley, Christopher. "Garfield the Stylist." *Children's Libraries Newsletter* (Australia) 10, no. 4 (Nov 1974): 105–106.

Kingsley, Madeleine. "Tell Us a Story." *Radio Times* 221 (Dec 2–8, 1978): 4–5. (interview)

Natov, Roni. *Leon Garfield.* Boston: Twayne, 1994.

———. "'Not the Blackest of Villains . . . Not the Brightest of Saints.' Humanism in Leon Garfield's Adventure Novels." *Lion and Unicorn* 2 (Fall 1978): 44–71.

———. "Re-Imagining the Past: An Interview with Leon Garfield." *The Lion and the Unicorn* 15 (June 1991): 89–115.

The Oxford Companion to Children's Literature. Edited by Humphrey Carpenter and Mari Prichard. New York: Oxford Univ. Press, 1984, pp. 196–198.

Philip, Neil. "Romance, Sentiment, Adventure." *Times Educational Supplement* (Feb 19, 1982): 23.

Rees, David. "Blood, Thunder, Muck, and Bullets: The Novels of Leon Garfield." *School Librarian* 36 (May 1988): 43–47. Reprinted in Rees' *What Do Draculas Do?" Essays on Contemporary Writers of Fiction for Children and Young Adults.* Metuchen, NJ: Scarecrow Press, 1990, pp. 126–143.

Smith, A. "Of Ghosts and History." *Publishers Weekly* 234 (Sept 30,1988): 28+.

Stephens, John. "Intertextuality and *The Wedding Ghost.*" *Children's Literature in Education* 21 (Mar 1990): 23–36.

Stott, Jon C. *Children's Literature from A to Z.* New York: McGraw-Hill, 1984, p. 120.

Sucher, Mary Wadsworth. "Recommended: Leon Garfield." *English Journal* 72 (Sept 1983): 71–72.

Swinfen, Ann. *In Defense of Fantasy.* London: Routledge, 1984. Discussion of *The Ghost Downstairs,* pp. 55, 116–117, 159–168, 187–189.

Townsend, John Rowe. "Family Likenesses." *Guardian* (May 5, 1976): 11.

———. "Leon Garfield." In *A Sense of Story.* Philadelphia: Lippincott, 1971, pp. 97–107.

———. "Leon Garfield." In *A Sounding of Storytellers.* Philadelphia: Lippincott, 1979, pp. 66–80.

Twentieth-Century Children's Writers. 3rd ed. Edited by Tracy Chevalier and D. L. Kirkpatrick. Chicago: St. James, 1989, pp. 374–376.

Wintle, Justin, and Emma Fisher. "Leon Garfield." In *The Pied Pipers.* New York: Paddington Press, 1974, pp. 192–207.

Wood, Anne. "Portrait of an Author: Leon Garfield." *Books for Your Children* (U.K.) 11 (Summer, 1976): 3.

Garner, Alan

Aers, Lesley. "Alan Garner: An Opinion." *Use of English* 22 (Winter 1978): 141–147, 153.

Alderson, Brian. "A Wizard in His Own Landscape." (London) *Times* (Aug 24, 1977): 16.

Alderson, Valerie. "*Red Shift*—Some Aspects Considered." *Children's Book Review* 4 (Summer 1974): 49.

Archer, Jill, and Lucy Wall. "Alan Garner: Novels from the Edge." *In Brief* (U.K.) 7 (1992): 8–11.

Attebery, Brian. "Alan Garner." In *Supernatural Fiction Writers: Fantasy and Horror,* vol. 2. Edited by E. F. Bleiler. New York: Scribner, 1985, pp. 1023–1030.

Bartle, F. R. "Alan Garner." *Children's Libraries Newsletter* 8 (May 1972): 38–47.

Bennett, David. "Authorgraph no. 77: Alan Garner." *Books for Keeps* (U.K.) 77 (1992): 20–21.

Benton, Michael. "Detective Imagination." *Children's Literature in Education* 13 (1974): 5–12.

Berman, Ruth. "Who's Lleu?" *Mythlore* 4, 16 (June 1977): 20–21.

Bisenieks, Dainis. "Children, Magic and Choices." *Mythlore* 6 (Winter 1979): 13–16.

Blishen, Edward. "Ambiguous Triptych." *Times Educational Supplement* (Oct 12, 1973): 22.

"Books of International Interest: Forum of Children's Books." *Bookbird* 6 (1968): 27–30.

Brewer, Rosemary. "Alan Garner: A Perspective." *Orana* (Australia) 14 (Nov 1978): 127–133.

Bryden, Ronald. "The Man Who Created *The Owl Service.*" *The Observer* (Jan 25, 1970): 30–33.

Cadogan, Mary, and Patricia Craig. *You're a Brick Angela!* London: Gollancz, 1976, pp. 367–371.

Cameron, Eleanor. "*The Owl Service: A Study.*" *Wilson Library Bulletin* 44 (Dec 1969): 425–433. Reprinted in Mary Lou White. *Children's Literature: Criticism and Response.*

Chambers, Aidan. *Booktalk: Occasional Writing on Literature and Children.* London: Bodley Head, 1985; New York: Harper, 1985, pp. 70, 83, 87.

———. "An Interview with Alan Garner." *Signal* 27 (Sept 1978): 119–137. Reprinted in *The Signal Approach to Children's Books,* ed. by Nancy Chambers. London: Kestrel, 1980; Metuchen, NJ: Scarecrow Press, 1981, pp. 276–328.

———. "Letter from England: A Matter of Balance." *Horn Book* 53 (Aug 1977): 479–482.

———. "Letter from England: Literary Crossword Puzzle . . . or Literary Masterpiece?" *Horn Book* 49 (Oct 1973): 494–497. Discussion of *Red Shift.*

Clute, John. *"Elidor."* In *Survey of Modern Fantasy Literature,* vol. 1. Edited by Frank N. Magill. Englewood Cliffs, NJ: Salem Press, 1983, pp. 472–474.

Crosse, Gordon. "Alan Garner—Librettist." *Labrys* (Wales) 7 (Nov 1981): 129–132.

Doyle, Brian. *The Who's Who of Children's Literature.* New York: Schocken, 1968, pp. 106–107.

Elliott, Ralph W. "A Cheshire Voice." *Labrys* (Wales) 7 (Nov 1981): 109–114.

Evans, Emrys. "Children's Novels and Welsh Mythology: Multiple Voices in Susan Cooper and Alan Garner." In *The Voice of the Narrator in Children's Literature: Insights from Writers and Critics,* ed. by Charlotte F. Otten and Gary D. Schmidt. New York: Greenwood, 1989, pp. 92–100.

Farrell, Jacqueline M. "Recommended: Alan Garner." *English Journal* 70 (Sept 1981): 65–66.

Finlayson, Iain. "Myths and Passages." *Books and Bookmen* (London) 23 (Nov 1977): 74–79.

Foss, Peter J. "The Undefined Boundary." *New Welsh Review* 2, no. 4 (1990): 30–35.

Garner, Alan. "Achilles in Altjira." *Children's Literature Association Quarterly* 8 (Fall 1983): 5–10. Reprinted In *Innocence & Experience.* Edited by Barbara Harrison and Gregory Maguire. New York: Lothrop, 1987, pp. 116–128.

———. "A Bit More Practice." *Times Literary Supplement,* June 6, 1968, pp. 577–578. Reprinted in Meek. *The Cool Web.* New York: Atheneum, 1978, pp. 196–200.

———. "Coming to Terms." *Children's Literature in Education* 2 (July 1970): 15–29.

———. "The Death of Myth." *Children's Literature in Education* 3 (1970): 69–71.

———. "The Edge of the Ceiling." *Horn Book* 60 (Sept/Oct 1984): 559–565. Reprinted from *Loughborough 1983: Proceedings.* Welsh National Centre for Children's Literature, 1984, pp. 72–76.

———. "Inner Time." In Peter Nicholl. *Science Fiction at Large.* New York: Harper, 1976, pp. 119–138.

———. "Predel Potolka [The Boundary of the Ceiling]." *Detskya Literatura* (Moscow) 3 (Mar 1991): 56–59.

———. "Real Mandrakes in Real Gardens." *New Statesman,* Nov 1, 1968, pp. 591–592.

———. "Skazka Britantsa [Tales of a British Man]." *Detskya Literatura* (Moscow) 12 (Dec 1985). 41–43.

Gillespie, John T. *More Juniorplots: A Guide for Teachers and Librarians.* New York: Bowker, 1977, pp. 88–91.

Gillies, Carolyn. "Possession and Structure in the Novels of Alan Garner." *Children's Literature in Education* 18 (Fall 1975): 107–117.

Gough, John. "Alan Garner, the Critic and Self-Critic." *Orana* (Australia) 20 (Aug 1984): 110–118.

Gould, Rachel. "For Children from 9–90." *Sunday Express Magazine* (London) (Sept 6, 1981): 18–20.

Heins, Paul. "Off the Beaten Path." *Horn Book* 49 (Dec 1973): 580–581. Reprinted in Paul Heins. *Crosscurrents of Criticism.* Boston: Horn Book, 1977, p. 319. *Discussion of The Jersey Shore.*

Hellings, Carol. "Alan Garner: His Use of Mythology and Dimension in Time." *Orana* (Australia) 15 (may 1979): 66–71.

Herbert, Kathleen. "*The Owl Service* and the Fourth Branch of the Maginogion." *Labrys* 7 (Nov 1981): 115–122.

Hunt, Peter. "Landscapes and Journeys, Metaphors and Maps: The Distinctive Feature of English Fantasy." *Children's Literature Association Quarterly* 12 (Spring 1987): 11–15.

Inglis, Fred. *The Promise of Happiness*. New York: Cambridge Univ. Press, 1981, pp. 242–245.

"An Interview with Alan Garner." *Labrys* (Wales) 7 (Nov 1981): 80–87.

Jones, Cornelia, and Olivia R. Way. "Alan Garner." In *British Children's Authors*. Chicago: American Library Association, 1976, pp. 94–100.

Kemball-Cook, Jessica. "More on Alan Garner's *Red Shift*." *Fantasiae* (Los Angeles) 4 (Nov–Dec 1976): 18–19. Comments on an article by Michael Benton in *Children's Literature in Education* 15 (1974): 67–68.

Kohler, Margaret. "Author Study—Alan Garner." *Orana* (Australia) 16 (May 1980): 39–48.

Lockwood, Michael. "'A Sense of the Spoken': Language in *The Owl Service*." *Children's Literature in Education* 23 (June 1992): 83–92.

Lockyer, Daphne. "Deeply Strange in Darkest Cheshire." *Plus Magazine* (U.K.) 231 (Nov 1990): 8–10.

McMahon, Patricia. "A Second Look—*Elidor*." *Horn Book* 56 (June 1980): 328–331.

McVitty, Walter. "Compact Ideas in a Limited Space." *Reading Time* (Australia) (Apr 1974); *School Bookshop News* (U.K.) 10 (Summer 1978): 21–23.

———. "Response to *Red Shift*." *Labrys* (Wales) 7 (Nov 1981): 133–138.

Mould, G. H. "*Weirdstone of Brisingamen*: A Four-Way Experience with the Novel by Alan Garner." *School Librarian* 15 (July 1967): 146–150.

Nikolajeva, Maria. "The Function of the Charm." *Labrys* (Wales) 7 (Nov 1981): 141–145.

———. "The Insignificance of Time: *Red Shift*." *Children's Literature Association Quarterly* 14 (Fall 1989): 128–131.

Nye, Robert. "*Red Shift*." *Labrys* (Wales) 7 (Nov 1981): 147–148.

"*The Owl Service*." In M. Crouch and A. Ellis. *Chosen for Children*. 3rd ed. London: The Library Association, 1977, pp. 141–145.

The Oxford Companion to Children's Literature. Edited by Humphrey Carpenter and Mari Prichard. New York: Oxford Univ. Press, 1984, pp. 164–165, 198–200, 392, 444–445, 498, 564.

Pearce, Philippa. "*The Owl Service*." *Children's Book News* (1967). Reprinted in Margaret Meek. *The Cool Web*. New York: Atheneum, 1978, pp. 291–293.

Pflieger, Pat, and Helen M. Hill. *A Reference Guide to Modern Fantasy for Children*. Westport, CT: Greenwood, 1984, pp. xiv, 169–171, 199–201, 377–379, 418–420, 585–587.

Philip, Neil. *A Fine Anger: A Critical Introduction to the Work of Alan Garner*. New York: Collins/Philomel, 1981.

———. "Garner and Shamanism." *Labrys* (Wales) 7 (Nov 1981): 99–107.

Plummer, Peter. "The Unlocked Gate." *Labrys* (Wales) 7 (Nov 1981): 91–98.

Rees, David. "Alan Garner: Some Doubts." *Horn Book* 55 (July 1979): 282–289. Reprinted as "Hanging in Their True Shapes." In David Rees. *The Marble in the Water*. Boston: Horn Book, 1980, pp. 56–67.

Scutter, Heather. "*The Owl Service*: A Study of Gwyn as Traditional and Modern Hero.' *Review Bulletin* (Australia) 2 (1987): 10–16.

Searles, Baird, Beth Meacham, and Michael Franklin. *A Reader's Guide to Fantasy*. New York: Avon, 1982, pp. 66–67.

Snyman, K. "Imaginary Worlds: Myth, Fairy Tale, Fantasy, and Science Fiction. Part II." *Skoolmediasentrum* (South Africa) 2 (1988): 46–51.

Speaking for Ourselves: Autobiographical Sketches by Notable Authors of Books for Young Adults. Edited by Donald R. Gallo. Urbana, IL: National Council of Teachers of English, 1990, pp. 71–73.

Stableford, Vivien. "*The Owl Service.*" In *Survey of Modern Fantasy Literature,* vol. 3. Edited by Frank N. Magill. Englewood Cliffs, NJ: Salem Press, 1983, pp. 1188–1190.

———. "*The Weirdstone of Brisingamen* and *The Moon of Gomrath.*" In *Survey of Modern Fantasy Literature,* vol. 5. Edited by Frank N. Magill. Englewood Cliffs, NJ: Salem Press, 1983, pp. 2087–2089.

Stott, Jon C. *Children's Literature from A to Z.* New York: McGraw-Hill, 1984, p. 121.

Stroud, Daphne. "The Wizard of Alderley Edge." *The Junior Bookshelf* 55 (1991): 133–135.

Sullivan, C. W., III. "Traditional Welsh Materials in Modern Fantasy." *Extrapolation* 28 (Spring 1987): 87–97.

———. *Welsh Celtic Myth in Modern Fantasy.* Westport, CT: Greenwood, 1989, pp. 23–33+.

Swinfen, Ann. *In Defense of Fantasy.* London: Routledge, 1984. Discussion of *The Owl Service,* pp. 101, 107–109.

Taylor, Andrew. "Polishing Up the Pattern: The Ending of *The Owl Service.*" *Children's Literature in Education* 23 (June 1992): 93–100.

Third Book of Junior Authors. Edited by Doris De Montreville and Donna Hill. New York: Wilson, 1972, pp. 99–100.

Thompson, Hilary. "Doorways to Fantasy." *Canadian Children's Literature* 21 (1981): 8–16.

Townsend, John Rowe. "Alan Garner." In *A Sense of Story.* Philadelphia: Lippincott, 1971, pp. 108–119.

———. "Alan Garner." In *A Sounding of Storytellers.* Philadelphia: Lippincott, 1979, pp. 81–96.

Twentieth-Century Children's Writers. 3rd ed. Edited by Tracy Chevalier and D. L. Kirkpatrick. Chicago: St. James, 1989, pp. 376–377.

Walsh, Robin. "Alan Garner: A Study." *Orana* 13 (May 1977): 31–39.

Watkins, Tony. "Alan Garner." *The Use of English* 21, no. 2 (Winter 1969): 114–117. Reprinted in Dennis Butts. *Good Writers for Young Readers.* St. Albans, England: Hart-Davis, 1977, pp. 45–49.

———. "Alan Garner's *Elidor.*" *Children's Literature in Education* 7 (Mar 1972): 56–63.

Watson, Victor. "In Defense of Jan: Love and Betrayal in *The Owl Service* and *Red Shift.*" *Signal* 41 (May 1983): 77–87.

West, Richard C. "The Tolkinians." *Orcrist* 2 (1967): 4–15.

Whitaker, Muriel A. "'The Hollow Hills': A Celtic Motif in Modern Fantasy." *Mosaic* 13 (Spring/Summer 1980): 165–178.

White, D. "Welsh Legends Through English Eyes: An American Viewpoint." *School Librarian* (U.K.) 39 (Nov 1991): 130–131+.

Wintle, Justin, and Emma Fisher. "Alan Garner." In *The Pied Pipers.* New York: Paddington Press, 1974, pp. 221–235.

Ziefer, Barbara Z. "Wales as a Setting for Children's Fantasy." *Children's Literature in Education* 13 (Summer 1982): 95–102.

Garnett, David

Clute, John. "David Garnett." In *Supernatural Fiction Writers: Fantasy and Horror,* vol. 2. Edited by E. F. Bleiler. New York: Scribner, 1985, pp. 535–539.

Gates, Doris

Gates, Doris. "Along the Road to Kansas." *Horn Book* 31 (Oct 1955): 382–390.

Helbig, Alethea K., and Agnes Regan Perkins. *Dictionary of American Children's Fiction, 1960–1984.* Westport, CT: Greenwood, 1986, pp. 99, 231.

The Junior Book of Authors. 2nd ed. rev. Edited by Stanley J. Kunitz and Howard Haycraft. New York: Wilson, 1951, pp. 137–138.

Rollins, Charlemae. "The Work of Doris Gates." *Elementary English* 31 (Dec 1954): 459–465. Reprinted in *Authors and Illustrators of Children's Books.* Edited by Miriam Hoffman and Eva Samuels. New York: Bowker, 1972, pp. 157–164.

Twentieth-Century Children's Writers. 3rd ed. Edited by Tracy Chevalier and D. L. Kirkpatrick. New York: St. Martin, 1989, pp. 378–379.

Gee, Maurice (Gough)

Twentieth-Century Children's Writers. 3rd ed. Edited by Tracy Chevalier and D. L. Kirkpatrick. Chicago: St. James, 1989, pp. 379–381.

Gentle, Mary

Barrett, D. V. "Mary Gentle Interviewed." *Vector* 116 (Sept 1983): 7–12.

Twentieth-Century Science Fiction Writers. 3rd ed. Edited by Noelle Watson and Paul E. Schellinger. Chicago: St. James Press, 1991, pp. 309–310.

Gerstein, Mordicai

Sixth Book of Junior Authors and Illustrators. Ed. by Sally Holmes Holtze. New York: Wilson, 1989, pp. 95–96.

Gibson, Katharine (Wicks)

Helbig, Alethea K., and Agnes Regan Perkins. *Dictionary of American Children's Fiction, 1859–1959.* Westport, CT: Greenwood, 1985, pp. 102–103, 181.

The Junior Book of Authors. 2nd ed. rev. Edited by Stanley J. Kunitz and Howard Haycraft. New York: Wilson, 1951, pp. 140–141.

Gilliland, Alexis A(rnaldus)

Lowell, Priscilla. "Interview: Alexis Gilliland." *Thrust* 22 (Spring/Summer 1985): 23–24, 32.

Twentieth-Century Science Fiction Writers. 3rd ed. Edited by Noelle Watson and Paul E. Schellinger. Chicago: St. James Press, 1991, pp. 315–316.

Gilmore, Kate

Gillespie, John T. *Juniorplots 4: A Book Talk Guide for Use with Readers Ages 12–16.* New Providence, NJ: Bowker, 1993, pp. 215–218.

Godden (Dixon), (Margaret) Rumer

De Temple, J. "The Magic of Rumer Godden." *Canadian Library* 18 (July 1961): 23.

Doyle, Brian. *The Who's Who of Children's Literature.* New York: Schocken, 1968, pp. 112–113.

Godden, Rumer. *A House with Four Rooms.* New York: Morrow, 1989. (autobiography)

———. "A Little Tale That Anyone Could Write." *Horn Book* 63 (May–June 1987): 301–307.

———. "Shining Popocatapetl: Poetry for Children." *Horn Book* 64 (May–June 1988): 305–314.

———. *A Time to Dance, No Time to Weep.* New York: Morrow, 1987. Autobiography.

———. "The Writer Must Become as a Child." *Writer* 68 (June 1955): 229.

Godden, Rumer, and Jon Godden. *Two under the Indian Sun.* New York: Knopf, 1966. Autobiography.

Hines, Ruth, and Paul C. Burns. "Rumer Godden." *Elementary English* 44 (Feb 1967): 101–104.

Montgomery-Massingberd, Hugh. "A Spinner of Indian Tales from the Scottish Hills." *Sunday* (London) *Telegraph* (Nov 5, 1989): 49.

More Junior Authors. Edited by Muriel Fuller. New York: Wilson, 1963, pp. 101–102.

Moss, Elaine. "The Lady Who Lives in Mermaid Street." *Puffin Post* (U.K.) 9, no. I (1975): 7–9.

———. "Rumer Godden: Prince of Storytellers." *Signal* 17 (May 1975): 55–60. Reprinted in *Part of the Pattern.* New York: Greenwillow, 1986, pp. 75–80.

The Oxford Companion to Children's Literature. Edited by Humphrey Carpenter and Mari Prichard. New York: Oxford Univ. Press, 1984, pp. 209–210.

Rustin, Michael. "The Life of Dolls: Rumer Godden's Understanding of Children's Imaginative Play." In Margaret Rustin and Michael Rustin. *Narratives of Love and Loss: Studies in Modern Children's Fiction.* London: Verso, 1987; New York: Routledge, 1988, pp. 84–103.

Simpson, Hassell A. *Rumer Godden.* Boston: Twayne, 1973.

Smaridge, Norah. *Famous Modern Storytellers for Young People.* New York: Dodd, 1969, pp. 68–72.

Spirt, Diana L. *Introducing Bookplots 3: A Book Talk Guide for Use with Readers Ages 8–12.* New York: Bowker, 1988, pp. 76–78.

Stott, Jon C. *Children's Literature from A to Z.* New York: McGraw-Hill, 1984, p. 125.

Twentieth-Century Children's Writers. 3rd ed. Edited by Tracy Chevalier and D. L. Kirkpatrick. Chicago: St. James, 1989, pp. 386–387.

Willard, Nancy. "Afterword." In Rumer Godden. *Four Dolls.* New York: Dell, 1987.

Wintle, Justin, and Emma Fisher. "Rumer Godden." In *The Pied Pipers.* New York: Paddington Press, 1974, pp. 285–294.

Godwin, Parke

Godwin, Parke. "There Goes Deuteronomy." In *Inside Outer Space.* Edited by Sharon Jarvis. New York: Ungar, 1985.

Goldman, William (W.)

Walter, E. M. "*The Princess Bride.*" In *Survey of Modern Fantasy Literature,* vol. 3. Edited by Frank N. Magill. Englewood Cliffs, NJ: Salem Press, 1983, pp. 1286–1290.

Goldstein, Lisa

"Lisa Goldstein Wins American Book Award." *Locus* 16 (June 1983): 1.

Gordon, John (William)

Blishen, Edward. "The Bare Pebble: The Novels of John Gordon." *Signal* 3 (May 1972): 62–73.

————. "The Slow Art of John Gordon." *Signal* 40 (Jan 1983): 12–17.

Gordon, John. "Beginnings." *Signal* 58 (Jan 1989): 4–8.

————. "Fenland Connections." *Federation of Children's Book Groups Year Book* (U.K.) 7 (1975–1976): 46.

————. "On Firm Ground." In Edward Blishen. *The Thorny Paradise.* Boston: Horn Book, 1975, pp. 34–35.

————. *Ordinary Seaman: A Teenage Memoir.* London: Walker, 1992.

Twentieth-Century Children's Writers. 3rd ed. Edited by Tracy Chevalier and D. L. Kirkpatrick. Chicago: St. James, 1989, p. 388.

Gordon, Patricia *see* Howard, Joan

Gorog, Judith

Marcus, Leonard. "Night Visions: Conversations with Alvin Schwartz and Judith Gorog." *The Lion and the Unicorn* 12 (1988): 44–62.

Goudge, Elizabeth (De Beauchamp)

Colwell, Eileen H. "Elizabeth Goudge." *Junior Bookshelf* 11 (July 1947): 58–61.

Doyle, Brian. *The Who's Who of Children's Literature.* New York: Schocken, 1968, pp. 115–117.

Goudge, Elizabeth. *The Joy of the Snow.* New York: Coward-McCann, 1974.

————. "Today and Tomorrow." *Junior Bookshelf* 11 (July 1947): 53–57.

————. "West Country Magic." *Horn Book* 23 (Mar 1947): 100–103.

Gough, John. "Rediscovering *The Little White Horse*." *Signal* 48 (Sept 1985): 168–175.

————. "Unicorns and Literature: Elizabeth Goudge's *The Little White Horse*." *Junior Bookshelf* 51 (1987): 113–117.

"*The Little White Horse*." In M. Crouch and A. Ellis. *Chosen for Children.* 3rd ed. London: The Library Association, 1977, pp. 40–44.

Searles, Baird, Beth Meacham, and Michael Franklin. *A Reader's Guide to Fantasy.* New York: Avon, 1982, pp. 68–69.

Third Book of Junior Authors. Edited by Doris De Montreville and Donna Hill. New York: Wilson, 1972, pp. 105–107.

Twentieth-Century Children's Writers. 3rd ed. Edited by Tracy Chevalier and D. L. Kirkpatrick. Chicago: St. James, 1989, pp. 388–390.

Yates, Jessica. "Forty Years On." *Books for Your Children* (U.K.) 20 (Spring 1985): 22.

Goulart, Ron(ald Joseph)

Goulart, Ron. "Historical Hysteria or Humor in Science Fiction." In *Inside Outer Space.* Edited by Sharon Jarvis. New York: Ungar, 1985.

Pierce, Hazel Beasley. *A Literary Symbiosis: Science Fiction/Fantasy Mystery.* Westport, CT: Greenwood, 1983.

Shapiro, David. "Introduction." In Ron Goulart. *After Things Fell Apart.* Boston: Gregg, 1977.

Twentieth-Century Science Fiction Writers. 3rd ed. Edited by Noelle Watson and Paul E. Schellinger. Chicago: St. James Press, 1991, pp. 331–333.

Grahame, Kenneth

Battiscombe, Georgina. "Exile from the Golden City." *Times Literary Supplement,* Mar 13, 1959, p. 144. Reprinted in Margaret Meek. *The Cool Web.* New York: Atheneum, 1978, pp. 284–290.

Berman, R. "Victorian Dragons: The Reluctant Brood." *Children's Literature in Education* 15 (Winter 1984): 220–233.

Braybrooke, Neville. "Kenneth Grahame—1859–1932: A Centenary Study." *Elementary English* 36 (Jan 1959): 11–15.

———. "A Note on Kenneth Grahame." *Horn Book* 46 (Oct 1970): 504–507.

Carpenter, Humphrey. "Kenneth Grahame and the Search for Arcadia." In *Secret Gardens: A Study of the Golden Age of Children's Literature.* Boston: Houghton Mifflin, 1985, pp. 115–125.

———. "*The Wind in the Willows.*" In *Secret Gardens: A Study of the Golden Age of Children's Literature.* Boston: Houghton Mifflin, 1985, pp. 151–169.

Chalmers, Patrick R. *Kenneth Grahame: Life, Letters and Unpublished Work.* London: Methuen, 1933.

Clausen, Christopher. "Home and Away in Children's Fiction." *Children's Literature* 10 (1982): 141–152.

Cornwell, Charles Landrum. "From Self to the Shire: Studies in Victorian Fantasy." Ph.D. diss., University of Virginia, 1972.

Cripps, Elizabeth A. "Kenneth Grahame: Children's Author?" *Children's Literature in Education* 40, no. 12 (Spring 1981): 15–23.

Dempster, Christine. "All Aboard for the River Bank: A Look at the Influx of New Editions of *The Wind in the Willows.*" *Review* (Australia) 12 (Mar 1984): 26–28.

Doyle, Brian. *The Who's Who of Children's Literature.* New York: Schocken, 1968, pp. 118–121.

Fadiman, Clifton. "Professionals and Confessionals: Dr. Seuss and Kenneth Grahame." In Egoff. *Only Connect.* 2nd ed. New York: Oxford Univ. Press, 1980, pp. 277–283.

"A Feeling of Change in the Air." *Teaching and Learning Literature* (Brandon, VT) 6 (Sept–Oct 1992): 35–36.

Fisher, Leona W. "Mythical Fantasy for Children: Silence and Community." *The Lion and the Unicorn* 14 (Dec 1990): 37–57.

Fletcher, D. "The Book That Cannot Be Illustrated: *The Wind in the Willows.*" *Horn Book* 44 (Feb 1968): 87–90.

Forsyth, A. "*The Wind in the Willows*—50 Years Later." *Junior Bookshelf* 22 (Mar 1958): 57–62.

Frey, Charles, and John Griffiths. *The Literary Heritage of Childhood: An Appraisal of Children's Classics in the Western Tradition.* Westport, CT: Greenwood, 1987, pp. 175–180.

Gagnon, Laurence. "Philosophy and Fantasy." *Children's Literature* 1 (1972): 98–103.

Gilead, Sarah. "Grahame's *The Wind in the Willows.*" *Explicator* 46 (Fall 1987): 3–36.

———. "The Undoing of Idyll in *The Wind in the Willows.*" *Children's Literature* 16 (1988): 145–158.

Gillin, Richard. "Romantic Echoes *in the Willows.*" *Children's Literature* 16 (1988): 169–174.

Goldthwaite, John. "The Black Rabbit: Part One." *Signal* 47 (May 1985): 86–111. "Part Two." *Signal* 48 (Sept 1985): 148–167. Reprinted in Goldthwaite. *The Natural History of Make-Believe.* New York: Oxford Univ. Press, 1987.

Gose, Elliott. *Mere Creatures: A Study of Modern Fantasy Tales for Children.* Toronto: Univ. of Toronto Press, 1988, pp. 42–52.

Graham, Eleanor. *Kenneth Grahame.* New York: Walck, 1963.

Grahame, Kenneth. *First Whisper of "The Wind in the Willows."* Edited by Elspeth Grahame. Philadelphia: Lippincott, 1945.

———. "Introduction." In *A Hundred Fables of Aesop.* New York: Dodd, 1924, pp. i–xv. Originally published 1898.

Green, Peter. *Beyond the Wild Wood: The World of Kenneth Grahame, Author of "The Wind in the Willows."* New York: Facts on File, 1983. An abridged version of Green's 1959 biography.

———. *Kenneth Grahame: A Biography.* Chicago: World, 1959.

———. "The Rentier's Rural Dream." *Introduction to The Wind in the Willows.* New York: Oxford Univ. Press, 1983. Reprinted from the *Times Literary Supplement* (Nov 26, 1982): 1299–1301.

Green, Roger Lancelyn. "The Magic of Kenneth Grahame." *Junior Bookshelf* 23 (Mar 1959): 47–58.

Greene, R. "Kenneth Grahame." *Aryan Path* 41 (Feb 1970): 79–83.

Haining, Peter. *Paths to the River Bank: The Origins of The Wind in the Willows, from the Writings of Kenneth Grahame.* London: Blandford, 1983; Fort Lauderdale, FL: Cassell, 1988.

Hardyment, Christina. "The Literary Landscape: 3. Toad Hall on Thames." (London) *Daily Telegraph Magazine* (June 30, 1990): 52–56.

Haynes, Mary. *"The Wind in the Willows*—A Classic for Children?" *International Review of Children's Literature and Librarianship* 4 (1989): 115–129.

Hedges, Ned Samuel. "The Fable and the Fabulous: The Use of Traditional Forms in Children's Literature." Ph.D. diss., University of Nebraska, 1968.

Higgens, Regina. *Magic Kingdoms: Discovering the Joys of Childhood Classics with Your Child.* New York: Simon & Schuster, 1992.

Hodges, M. "Happy Birthday, *The Wind in the Willows.*" *Top of the News* 14 (Mar 1958): 7–10.

Hunt, Peter. "Dialogue and Dialectic: Language and Class in *The Wind in the Willows.*" *Children's Literature* 16 (1988): 159–168.

———. "Landscapes and Journeys, Metaphors and Maps: The Distinctive Feature of English Fantasy." *Children's Literature Association Quarterly* 12 (Spring 1987): 11–15.

Inglis, Fred. *The Promise of Happiness.* New York: Cambridge Univ. Press, 1981, pp. 117–123.

Kuznets, Lois R. "Kenneth Grahame." In *Writers for Children; Critical Studies of Major Authors Since the Seventeenth Century.* Edited by Jane M. Bingham. New York: Scribner, 1988, pp. 247–254.

———. *Kenneth Grahame.* Boston: Twayne, 1987.

———. "Kenneth Grahame and Father Nature, or, Whither Blows *The Wind in the Willows.*" *Children's Literature* 16 (1988): 175–181.

———. "Toad Hall Revisited." *Children's Literature,* vol. 7. Storrs, CT: Parousia Press, 1978, pp. 115–128.

———. "Toad's Journey to Buggleton, or Kenneth Grahame's Trip from Bedside to Back." *Proceedings of the 13th Annual Conference of The Children's Literature Association, 1986.* New York: Pace University, 1988, pp. 75–79.

Lippman, Charles. "All the Comforts of Home." *Antioch Review* 41 (1983): 409–420.

Little, Edmund. *The Fantasts: Studies in J. R. R. Tolkien, Lewis Carroll, Mervyn Peake, Nikolay Gogol, and Kenneth Grahame.* Amersham, England: Avebury, 1984.

Lowe, Elizabeth Cochran. "Kenneth Grahame and the Beast Tale." Ph.D. diss., New York University, 1976.

Luenn, Nancy. "A Visit to Toad Hall and Pooh Forest." *Horn Book* 62 (July–Aug 1986): 507–508.

McGillis, Roderick. "Utopian Hopes: Criticism Beyond Itself." *Children's Literature Association Quarterly* 9 (Winter 1984–1985): 184–186.

MacLeod, Helen. "Kenneth Grahame, Author of *The Wind in the Willows.*" *Book and Magazine Collector* 18 (Aug 1985): 15–24.

McQuire, Elizabeth. "'Home' Versus 'Dulce Domum.'" *Children's Libraries Newsletter* (Australia) 11 (May 1975): 48–52.

McVitty, Walter. "A Taste of the Best: A Gourmet Guide to Children's Books." *Reading Time* 82 (Jan 1982): 7–22.

Macy, George. "Arthur Rackham and *The Wind in the Willows.*" *Horn Book* 16 (May–June 1940): 153–158. Reprinted in Norma Fryatt. *A Horn Book Sampler.* Boston: Horn Book, 1959, pp. 50–54.

Meek, Margaret. "The Limits of Delight." *Books for Keeps* (U.K.) 68 (1991): 24–25.

Mendelson, Michael. "*The Wind in the Willows* and the Plotting of Contrast." *Children's Literature* 16 (1988): 127–144.

Moore, Anne Carroll. "Kenneth Grahame, 1859–1932." *Horn Book* 10 (Mar 1934): 73–81.

Norman, Felicity. "*The Wind in the Willows.*" *Literature Base* (Australia) 1, no. 1 (Feb 1990): 4–6.

The Oxford Companion to Children's Literature. Edited by Humphrey Carpenter and Mari Prichard. New York: Oxford Univ. Press, 1984, pp. 216–219, 573–575.

Pflieger, Pat, and Helen M. Hill. *A Reference Guide to Modern Fantasy for Children.* Westport, CT: Greenwood, 1984, pp. xv, 210–213, 606–607.

Philip, Neil. "Kenneth Grahame's *The Wind in the Willows:* A Companionable Vitality." In *Touchstones.* Edited by Perry Nodelman. West Lafayette, IN: Children's Literature Association Publications, 1985, pp. 96–105.

———. "*The Wind in the Willows*: The Vitality of a Class." In *Children and Their Books,* ed. by Gillian Avery and Julia Briggs. Oxford: Clarendon, 1989, pp. 299–316. Reworking of an essay from *Touchstones,* ed. by Perry Nodelman. West Lafayette, IN: Children's Literature Association, 1985.

Platzner, R. L. "Child's Play: Games and Fantasy in Carroll, Stevenson, and Grahame." In *Proceedings of the Fifth Annual Conference of the Children's Literature Association.* Harvard University, March 1978. Ypsilanti, MI: Children's Literature Association, 1979, pp. 78–86.

Poss, Geraldine D. "An Epic in Arcadia: The Pastoral World of *The Wind in the Willows.*" In *Children's Literature,* vol. 4. Philadelphia: Temple Univ. Press, 1975, pp. 80–90. Reprinted in *Reflections on Literature for Children.* Edited by Francelia Butler and Richard Rotert. Hamden, CT: Shoe String Press, 1984, pp. 237–246.

Price, Juantia. "*The Wind in the Willows:* Kenneth Grahame's Creation of a Wild Wood." *AB Bookman's Weekly* 81 (Jan 25, 1988): 265–266 ff.

Rahn, Suzanne. "The Expression of Religious and Political Concepts in Fantasy for Children." Ph.D. diss., University of Washington, 1986.

Ray, Laura Krugman. "Kenneth Grahame and the Literature of Childhood." *English Literature in Transition* 20 (1977): 3–12.

Ryan, J. S. "The Wild Wood—Place of Dander, Place of Protest." *Orana* 19 (Aug 1983): 133–140.

Sale, Roger. *Fairy Tales and After: From Snow White to E. B. White.* Cambridge, MA: Harvard Univ. Press, 1978, pp. 165–194.

Sayers, Frances Clarke. "Editorial: *The Wind in the Willows.*" *Horn Book* 35 (June 1959): 189.

Searles, Baird, Beth Meacham, and Michael Franklin. *A Reader's Guide to Fantasy.* New York: Avon, 1982, p. 69.

Shepard, Ernest H. "Illustrating *The Wind in the Willows.*" *Horn Book* 30 (Apr 1954): 83–86. Reprinted in Elinor Field. *Horn Book Reflections.* Boston: Horn Book, 1969, pp. 273–275.

Slobodkin, Louis. "Artist's Choice: *Bertie's Escapade.*" *Horn Book* 26 (July 1950): 293–295.

Smith, Kathryn A. "Kenneth Grahame and the Singing Willows." *Elementary English* 45 (Dec 1968): 1024–1035.

Smith, Louisa A. "*The Wind in the Willows.*" In *Survey of Modern Fantasy Literature,* vol. 5. Edited by Frank N. Magill. Englewood Cliffs, NJ: Salem Press, 1983, pp. 2132–2135.

Steig, Michael. "At the Back of *The Wind in the Willows:* An Experiment in Biographical and Autobiographical Interpretation." *Victorian Studies* 24 (Spring 1981): 303–323.

Sterck, Kenneth. "Rereading *The Wind in the Willows.*" *Children's Literature in Education* 12 (Sept 1973): 20–28.

Stott, Jon C. *Children's Literature from A to Z.* New York: McGraw-Hill, 1984, p. 126.

———. "'Will the Real Dragon Please Stand Up?' Convention and Parody in Children's Stories." *Children's Literature in Education* 21 (Winter 1990): 219–228.

Stridsberg, A. B. "On Illustrating Kenneth Grahame." *Yale University Library Gazette* 24 (July 1949): 28–35.

Taylor, S. Keith. "Universal Themes in Kenneth Grahame's *The Wind in the Willows.*" Ph.D. diss., Temple University, 1967.

Thum, Maureen. "Exploring 'The Country of the Mind:' Mental Dimensions of Landscape in Kenneth Grahame's *The Wind in the Willows.*" Children's Literature Association Quarterly *17 (Fall 1992):27–32.*

Townsend, John Rowe. "The Best Bargain I Ever Made." *Books for Keeps* (U.K.) 17 (Nov 1982): 14–15.

Tucker, Nicholas. "The Children's Falstaff." In Nicholas Tucker. *Suitable for Children? Controversies in Children's Literature.* Berkeley: Univ. of California Press, 1976, pp. 160–164. Originally published in *Times Literary Supplement,* June 26, 1969.

Twentieth-Century Children's Writers. 3rd ed. Edited by Tracy Chevalier and D. L. Kirkpatrick. Chicago: St. James, 1989, pp. 395–396.

Waddey, Lucy E. "Home in Children's Fiction: Three Patterns." *Children's Literature Association Quarterly* 8 (Spring 1983): 13–15.

Watkins, Tony. "Cultural Studies, New Historicism and Children's Literature." In *Literature for Children: Contemporary Criticism,* ed. by Peter Hunt. London: Routledge, 1992, pp. 173–195.

———"'Making a Break for the Real England': The River-Bankers Revisited." *Children's Literature Association Quarterly* 9 (Spring 1984): 34–35.

Wilkin, June. "*The Wind in the Willows* and *The Golden Age.*" *Orana* (Australia) 27 (May 1991): 74–81.

Williams, Jay. "Reflections on *The Wind in the Willows.*" *Signal* 21 (Sept 1976): 103–107.

Willis, Lesley. "'A Sadder and Wiser Rat/He Rose the Morrow Morn:' Echoes of the Romantics in Kenneth Grahame's *The Wind in the Willows.*" *Children's Literature Association Quarterly* 13 (Fall 1988): 108–110.

Zanger, Jules. "Goblins, Morlocks, and Weasels: Classic Fantasy and the Industrial Revolution." *Children's Literature in Education* 27, no. 4 (1977): 154–162.

Gray, Nicholas Stuart

Crouch, Marcus. "Revels Ended." *Junior Bookshelf* 45 (June 1981): 101–103.

Twentieth-Century Children's Writers. 3rd ed. Edited by Tracy Chevalier and D. L. Kirkpatrick. Chicago: St. James, 1989, pp. 397–398.

Wintle, Justin, and Emma Fisher. "Nicholas Stuart Gray." In *The Pied Pipers.* New York: Paddington Press, 1974, pp. 147–160.

Greaves, Margaret

Twentieth-Century Children's Writers. 3rd ed. Edited by Tracy Chevalier and D. L. Kirkpatrick. Chicago: St. James, 1989, pp. 398–400.

Green, Roger (Gilbert) Lancelyn

Hobbs, Mary. "Roger Lancelyn Green, 1918–1987." *Junior Bookshelf* 52, no. 1 (1988): 9–13.

Twentieth-Century Children's Writers. 3rd ed. Edited by Tracy Chevalier and D. L. Kirkpatrick. Chicago: St. James, 1989, pp. 400–402.

Yates, Jessica. "Roger Lancelyn Green: A Personal Memoir." *Amon Hen* 90 (1988): 22–24.

Greenwald, Sheila (pseud. of Sheila Ellen Green)

Fifth Book of Junior Authors and Illustrators. Edited by Sally Holmes Holtze. New York: Wilson, 1983, pp. 139–140.

Gripe, Maria (Kristina)

Alcorn, Noeline. "Fantasy and Family Life: Children's Books from Northern Europe." *Children's Literature Association Yearbook.* Auckland, New Zealand: Children's Literature Association, 1976, pp. 29–42. Discusses Astrid Lindgren, Maria Gripe, Christine Nöstlinger, Otfried Preussler, and Paul Biegel.

Gripe, Maria. "A Word and a Shadow." *Bookbird* 12 (1974): 4–10.

Heins, Paul. "*The Glassblower's Children,* a Review." *Horn Book* 49 (Aug 1973): 365.

Hulten, Sonne, Lena Hulten, and Gosta Hulten. "Maria Gripe." *Abrakadabra* (Stockholm) 4 (1991): 3–6. (interview)

Jakobsen, Gunnar. "En Dag Med Maria Gripe [A Day With Maria Gripe]." *Born og Boger* (Denmark) 39, 2 (1986): 6–13.

———. "The Nordic Children's Book Prize." *Bookbird* 4 (1985): 18–23.

Mannheimer, Carin. "Maria Gripe." *Bookbird* 11 (1973): 24–34.

Nettervik, Ingrid. "Maria och Harald Gripe: Konstnarer i Samverkan [Maria and Harald Gripe: Concurrent Artists]." *Svensklararen* (Sweden) 32, 3 (1988): 20–25.

Rydin, Lena. "Maria Gripe: My Childhood." Translated by Sheila La Farge from *Vi Foraldrar* (Stockholm) 2 (1977): 48–51, 65. *U.S. Friends of IBBY Newsletter* 3 (Winter–Spring 1977–1978): 1–6. Adapted version: "Childhood: The Universal Experience." *Books for Your Children* (U.K.) 13 (Summer 1978): 4–5, 7. (interview)

Stanton, Lorraine. "Shadows and Motifs: A Review and Analysis of the Works of Maria Gripe." *Catholic Library World* 51 (May 1980): 447–449.

Svensen, Asfrid. "Opening Windows on to Unreality: Some Elements of the Fantastic in Scandinavian Children's Literature." *The International Review of Children's Literature and Librarianship* 2 (Spring 1987): 1–9.

Third Book of Junior Authors. Edited by Doris De Montreville and Donna Hill. New York: Wilson, 1972, pp. 113–114.

Guillot, René

Crouch, Marcus. *The Nesbit Tradition.* London: Benn, 1972, pp. 39–40.

Doyle, Brian. *The Who's Who of Children's Literature.* New York: Schocken, 1968, pp. 126–127.

Marsh, Gwen. "René Guillot." *Horn Book* 41 (Apr 1965): 192–194.

More Junior Authors. Edited by Muriel Fuller. New York: Wilson, 1963, pp. 104–105.

Schmidt, Nancy J. *Children's Books about Africa in English.* New York: Conch Magazine, 1981, pp. 114–118.

Guy, Rosa (Cuthbert)

Fifth Book of Junior Authors and Illustrators. Edited by Sally Holmes Holtze. New York: Wilson, 1983, pp. 140–141.

Twentieth-Century Children's Writers. 3rd ed. Edited by Tracy Chevalier and D. L. Kirkpatrick. New York: St. Martin, 1989, pp. 412–413.

Haas, Dorothy

Sixth Book of Junior Authors and Illustrators. Edited by Sally Holmes Holtze. New York: Wilson, 1989, pp. 109–110.

Haggard, H. Rider *see:* Monaco, Richard

Hahn, Mary Downing

Helbig, Alethea, and Agnes Regan Perkins. *Dictionary of American Children's Fiction, 1985–1989.* Westport, CT: Greenwood, 1993, pp. 95–96.

Sixth Book of Junior Authors and Illustrators. Edited by Sally Holmes Holtze. New York: Wilson, 1989, pp. 111–113.

Halam, Ann (pseud. of Gwyneth A. Jones)

Jones, Gwyneth. "Riddles in the Dark." *Foundation* (U.K.) 43 (Summer 1988): 50–59.

Twentieth-Century Children's Writers. 3rd ed. Edited by Tracy Chevalier and D. L. Kirkpatrick. Chicago: St. James, 1989, pp. 416–417.

Twentieth-Century Science Fiction Writers. 3rd ed. Edited by Noelle Watson and Paul E. Schellinger. Chicago. St. James, 1991, pp. 417–419.

Haldane, J(ohn) B(urdon) S(anderson)

The Oxford Companion to Children's Literature. Edited by Humphrey Carpenter and Mari Prichard. New York: Oxford Univ. Press, 1984, p. 368.

Twentieth-Century Children's Writers. 3rd ed. Edited by Tracy Chevalier and D. L. Kirkpatrick. Chicago: St. James, 1989, pp. 417–418.

Twentieth-Century Science Fiction Writers. 2nd ed. Edited by Curtis C. Smith. Chicago: St. James Press, 1986, pp. 310–312.

Haldeman, Linda (Wilson)

Searles, Baird, Beth Meacham, and Michael Franklin. *A Reader's Guide to Fantasy.* New York: Avon, 1982, p. 72.

Hale, Lucretia Peabody

Doyle, Brian. *The Who's Who of Children's Literature.* New York: Schocken, 1968, p. 132.

Gay, Carol. "Lucretia Peabody Hale." In *American Writers for Children before 1900. Dictionary of Literary Biography,* vol. 42. Detroit: Gale, 1985, pp. 207–216.

Heins, Paul. "Lucretia P. Hale." In *Writers for Children; Critical Studies of Major Authors*

Since the Seventeenth Century. Edited by Jane M. Bingham. New York: Scribner, 1988, pp. 265–268.

Helbig, Alethea K., and Agnes Regan Perkins. *Dictionary of American Children's Fiction, 1859–1959.* Westport, CT: Greenwood, 1985, pp. 200, 403–404.

The Oxford Companion to Children's Literature. Edited by Humphrey Carpenter and Mari Prichard. New York: Oxford Univ. Press, 1984, pp. 235, 404.

Twentieth-Century Children's Writers. 3rd ed. Edited by Tracy Chevalier and D. L. Kirkpatrick. Chicago: St. James, 1989, pp. 418–419.

Wankmiller, Madelyn C. "Lucretia P. Hale and *The Peterkin Papers.*" *Horn Book* 34 (Apr 1958): 95–103, 137–147. Reprinted in Siri Andrews. *The Hewins Lectures. 1947–1962.* Boston: Horn Book, 1963, pp. 235–249.

White, Eliza Orne. "Lucretia P. Hale: The Author of *The Peterkin Papers.*" *Horn Book* 16 (Sept–Oct 1940): 317–322.

———. "Some New England Authors and Their Stories." *Horn Book* 1 (June 1925): 11–21.

Whitney, Elinor. "The Peterkins Visit the Bookshop." *Horn Book* 2 (Nov 1924): 4–6. Reprinted in *Horn Book* 53 (Apr 1977): 215–216.

Haley, Gail E(inhart)

Haley, Gail E. "Of Mermaids, Myths and Meaning: *A Sea Tale.*" *The New Advocate* 3 (Winter 1990): 1–12.

Hall, Lynn

Fifth Book of Junior Authors and Illustrators. Edited by Sally Holmes Holtze. New York: Wilson, 1983, pp. 145–147.

Twentieth-Century Children's Writers. 3rd ed. Edited by Tracy Chevalier and D. L. Kirkpatrick. Chicago: St. James, 1989, pp. 420–422.

Hambly, Barbara

"Barbara Hambly: Saved by the Ax." *Locus* 305 (1986): 27ff.

Hamilton (Adoff), Virginia (Esther)

Apseloff, Marilyn F. "A Conversation with Virginia Hamilton." *Children's Literature in Education* 14 (Winter 1983): 204–213.

———. "Creative Geography in the Ohio Novels of Virginia Hamilton." *Children's Literature Association Quarterly* 8 (Spring 1983): 17–20.

———. "Virginia Hamilton." In *American Writers for Children since 1960: Fiction. Dictionary of Literary Biography,* vol. 52. Detroit: Gale, 1986, pp. 207–212.

Bishop, Rudine Sims. "Books from Parallel Cultures: Celebration a Silver Anniversary." *Horn Book* 69 (Mar–Apr 1993): 175–180.

Dressel, Janice Hartwick. "The Legacy of Ralph Ellison in Virginia Hamilton's *Justice Trilogy.*" *English Journal* 73 (Nov 1984): 42–48.

Farrell, K. "Virginia Hamilton's *Sweet Whispers, Brother Rush* and the Case for a Radical Existential Criticism." *Contemporary Literature* 31 (Summer 1990): 161–176.

Fourth Book of Junior Authors and Illustrators. Edited by Doris De Montreville and Elizabeth D. Crawford. New York: Wilson, 1978, pp. 162–164.

Garrett, Jeffrey. "Hans Christian Andersen Award Winner, 1992: Virginia Hamilton." *Bookbird* 30 (Sept 1992): 3–6.

————. "Virginia Hamilton: African American Cosmologist." *Bookbird* (Denmark) 30, no. 3 (1992): 3–6.

————. "Virginia Hamilton: 1992 Andersen Winner." *Book Links* 2 (Jan 1993): 22–42.

Gillespie, John T., and Corinne J. Naden. *Juniorplots 3: A Book Talk Guide for Use with Readers Ages 12–16.* New York: Bowker, 1987, pp. 166–169.

Hamilton, Virginia. "Ah, Sweet Rememory!" Based on a paper given at the Simmons College Center for the Study of Children's Literature, March 14, 1981. *Horn Book* 57 (Dec 1981): 633–651. Reprinted in *Innocence & Experience.* Edited by Barbara Harrison and George Maguire. New York: Lothrop, 1987, pp. 6–12.

————. "Boston Globe—Horn Book Award Acceptance." *Horn Book* 60 (Feb 1984): 24–28.

————. "Changing Woman, Working." In Betsy Hearne. *Celebrating Children's Books.* New York: Lothrop, 1981, pp. 54–61.

————. "Coretta Scott King Award Acceptance." *Horn Book* 62 (Nov/Dec 1986): 683–687.

————. "Everything of Value: Moral Realism in Literature for Children [May Hill Arbuthnot Honor Lecture]." *Journal of Youth Services in Libraries* 6 (Summer 1993): 363–377.

————. "Hans Christian Andersen Award Acceptance." *USBBY Newsletter* (Newark, DE) 18 (Fall 1992): 6–8.

————. "High John's Risen Again." *Horn Book* 51 (Apr 1975): 113–121.

————. "Illusion and Reality." In Haviland. *The Openhearted Audience.* Washington, DC: Library of Congress, 1980, pp. 115–131.

————. "The Known, the Remembered, and the Imagined: Celebrating Afro-American Folktales." *Children's Literature in Education* 18 (Summer 1987): 67–76.

————. "The Mind of a Novel: The Heart of the Book." *Children's Literature Association Quarterly* 8 (Fall 1983): 10–14.

————. "Newbery Award Acceptance." *Horn Book* 51 (Aug 1975): 337–343.

————. "On Being a Black Writer in America." *The Lion and the Unicorn* 10 (1986): 15–17.

————. "Planting Seeds." *Horn Book* 68 (Nov–Dec 1992): 674–680.

————. "Portrait of the Author as a Working Writer." *Elementary English* 48 (Apr 1971): 237–240ff. Reprinted in Miriam Hoffman and Eva Samuels. *Authors and Illustrators of Children's Books.* New York: Bowker, 1972, pp. 186–192.

————. [Regina Medal Acceptance] *Catholic Library World* 62 (July–Dec 1990): 296–299.

————. "The Spirit Spins: A Writer's Resolution." *ALAN Review* 15 (1987): 1–4.

————. "A Toiler, a Teller." In *Many Faces, Many Voices: Multicultural Literary Experiences for Youth,* ed. by Anthony L. Manna and Carloyn S. Brodie. Fort Atkinson, WI: Highsmith, 1992, pp. 1–7.

————. "Writing the Source: In Other Words." *Horn Book* 54 (Dec 1978): 609–619.

Hearne, Betsy. "Virginia Hamilton: An Eminent Writer for Children in the USA." *Bookbird* 4 (1980): 22–23.

Heins, Ethel L. "*Sweet Whispers, Brother Rush.*" *Horn Book* 58 (Oct 1982): 505–506. Review.

Heins, Paul. "Virginia Hamilton." *Horn Book* 51 (Aug 1975): 344–348.

Helbig, Alethea, and Agnes Regan Perkins. *Dictionary of American Children's Fiction, 1985–1989.* Westport, CT: Greenwood, 1993, p. 96.

————*Dictionary of American Children's Fiction, 1960–1984; Recent Books of Recognized Merit.* New York: Greenwood, 1986, pp. 269, 639–640.

Hopkins, Lee Bennett. "Virginia Hamilton." *Horn Book* 48 (Dec 1972): 563–569. Reprinted in *More Books by More People.* New York: Citation Press, 1974, pp. 199–207.

Kingman, Lee, ed. *Newbery and Caldecott Medal Books: 1966–1975.* Boston: Horn Book, 1975, pp. 126–140.

Langton, Jane. "Virginia Hamilton the Great." *Horn Book* 50 (Dec 1971): 671–673.

Mikkelsen, Nina. "But Is It a Children's Book? A Second Look at Virginia Hamilton's *The*

Magical Adventures of Pretty Pearl." *Children's Literature Association Quarterly* 11 (Fall 1986); 134–142.

———. "A Conversation with Virgina Hamilton." *Journal of Youth Services in Libraries* 7 (Summer 1994): 392–405.

———. *Virgina Hamilton.* Boston: Twayne, 1994.

Moss, Anita. "Myth Narrative: Virginia Hamilton's *The Magical Adventures of Pretty Pearl.*" *The Lion and the Unicorn* 9 (1985): 50-57.

The Oxford Companion to Children's Literature. Edited by Humphrey Carpenter and Mari Prichard. New York: Oxford Univ. Press, 1984, p. 237.

"Profile of an Author: Virginia Hamilton." *Top of the News* 25 (June 1969): 376–380.

Rees, David. "Ride through a Painted Desert—Virginia Hamilton." In *Painted Desert, Green Shade.* Boston: Horn Book, 1984, pp. 168–184.

Rochman, Hazel. "The *Booklist* Interview: Virginia Hamilton." *Booklist* 88 (Feb 1, 1992): 1020–1021.

Roginski, Jim, ed. *Newbery and Caldecott Medalists and Honor Book Winners.* Littleton, CO: Libraries Unlimited, 1982, p. 136.

Rush, Theresa Gunnell; Myers, Carol Fairbanks; and Arata, Esther Spring, comps. *Black American Writers, Past and Present,* vol. 1. Metuchen, NJ: Scarecrow Press, 1975, pp. 351–352.

Russell, David. "Virginia Hamilton's Symbolic Presentation of the Afro-American Sensibility." In *Cross-Culturalism in Children's Literature: Selected Papers from the 1987 International Conference of the Children's Literature Association,* ed. by Susan R. Gannon and Ruth A. Thompson. New York: Pace University, 1988.

Speaking for Ourselves: Autobiographical Sketches by Notable Authors of Books for Young Adults. Edited by Donald R. Gallo. Urbana, IL: National Council of Teachers of English, 1990, pp. 90–92.

"Special Issue: Virgina Hamilton." *USBBY Newsletter* (Newark, DE) 17, no. 1 (Spring 1992).

Stan, Susan. "Conversations: Virginia Hamilton." *Five Owls* 3 (Mar–Apr 1989): 54–55.

Stott, Jon C. *Children's Literature from A to Z.* New York: McGraw-Hill, 1984, p. 135.

Townsend, John Rowe. "Virginia Hamilton." In *A Sounding of Storytellers.* Philadelphia: Lippincott, 1974, pp. 97–110.

Twentieth-Century Children's Writers. 3rd ed. Edited by Tracy Chevalier and D. L. Kirkpatrick. Chicago: St. James, 1989, pp. 422–424.

Wilson, Geraldine. "Review." *Interracial Books for Children* 1–2 (1983): 32. Review of *Sweet Whispers, Brother Rush.*

The Zena Sutherland Lectures, 1983–1992. Edited by Betsy Hearne. New York: Clarion, 1993, pp. 71–91.

Hancock, Neil (Anderson)

Paxon, Diana. "The Tolkien Tradition." *Mythlore* 39 (1984): 23–27, 37.

Harris, Christie (Lucy Irwin)

Davies, Cory. "Bridge Between Two Realities: An Interview with Christie Harris." *Canadian Children's Literature* 51 (1988): 6–24.

Ellison, Shirley, and Mary Mishra. "Award-Winning Canadian Author Christie Harris." *Bookbird* 19, no. 4 (1981): 19–22.

Fourth Book of Junior Authors and Illustrators. Edited by Doris De Montreville and Elizabeth D. Crawford. New York: Wilson, 1978, pp. 165–167.

Harris, Christie. "Christie Harris on Fantasy." *In Review* 15 (Oct 1981): 5–8.

———. "In Tune with Tomorrow." *Canadian Children's Literature* 10 (Autumn 1978): 26–30.

———. "My Heroine Helped Me." *Horn Book* 41 (Aug 1964): 361–363.

———. "Never Underestimate an Indian Village." *Horn Book* 39 (Apr 1963): 156–161.

———. "The Shift from Feasthouse to Book." *Canadian Children's Literature* 31/32 (1983): 9–11.

McDonough, Irma, ed. "Christie Harris." In *Profiles.* rev. ed. Ottowa: Canadian Library Association, 1975.

Radu, Kenneth. "Canadian Fantasy." *Canadian Children's Literature* 1 (Summer 1975): 75–79.

Stott, Jon C. *Children's Literature from A to Z.* New York: McGraw-Hill, 1984, p. 138.

Twentieth-Century Children's Writers. 3rd ed. Edited by Tracy Chevalier and D. L. Kirkpatrick. Chicago: St. James, 1989, pp. 430–431.

Whitaker, Muriel A. "Monsters from Native Canadian Mythologies." *Canadian Children's Literature* 15/16 (1980): 57–66.

Wood, Susan. "Stories and Stlalakums: Christie Harris and the Supernatural World." *Canadian Children's Literature* 15 and 16 (1980): 47–56.

Harris, Geraldine (Rachel)

Twentieth-Century Children's Writers. 3rd ed. Edited by Tracy Chevalier and D. L. Kirkpatrick. Chicago: St. James, 1989, pp. 431–432.

Harris, Rosemary (Jeanne)

Fourth Book of Junior Authors and Illustrators. Edited by Doris De Montreville and Elizabeth D. Crawford. New York: Wilson, 1978, pp. 167–168.

Harris, Rosemary. "*The Moon in the Cloud.*" *Junior Bookshelf* 33 (Aug 1969): 223–226.

Hastings, Selina. "Meet Rosemary Harris." *Puffin Post* (U.K.) 11, no. 4 (1977): 7–8.

"*The Moon in the Cloud.*" In M. Crouch and A. Ellis. *Chosen for Children.* 3rd ed. London: The Library Association, 1977, pp. 146–149.

The Oxford Companion to Children's Literature. Edited by Humphrey Carpenter and Mari Prichard. New York: Oxford Univ. Press, 1984, p. 242.

Schmidt, Nancy J. *Children's Fiction about Africa in English.* New York: Conch Magazine, 1981, pp. 157–158.

Stroud, D. J. "Nile Trilogy." *Junior Bookshelf* 56, no. 3 (1992): 91–94.

Twentieth-Century Children's Writers. 3rd ed. Edited by Tracy Chevalier and D. L. Kirkpatrick. New York: St. Martin, 1989, pp. 433–434.

Yolen, Jane. "The Literary Underwater World." *Language Arts* 57 (1980): 403–412.

Harrison, M(ichael) John

Darlington, Andy. "M. John Harrison: The Condition of Falling." *Vector* 122 (1984): 3–5.

Fowler, Christopher. "The Last Rebel: An Interview with M. John Harrison." *Foundation* 23 (1981): 5–30.

Twentieth-Century Science Fiction Writers. 3rd ed. Edited by Noelle Watson and Paul E. Schellinger. Chicago: St. James Press, 1991, pp. 361–363.

Hastings, Selina

Spirt, Diana L. *Introducing Bookplots 3: A Book Talk Guide for Use with Readers Ages 8–12.* New York: Bowker, 1988, pp. 79–81.

Hatch, Richard Warren

Doyle, Brian. *The Who's Who of Children's Literature.* New York: Schocken, 1968, p. 138.
Hatch, Richard W. "Too Good to Be Forgotten." *Horn Book* 19 (July 1943): 251–252.

Hauff, Wilhelm

Cobbs, Alfred L. "Wilhelm Hauff." In *Supernatural Fiction Writers: Fantasy and Horror,* vol. 1. Edited by E. F. Bleiler. New York: Scribner, 1985, pp. 107–110.
Doyle, Brian. *The Who's Who of Children's Literature.* New York: Schocken, 1968, pp. 138–139.
The Oxford Companion to Children's Literature. Edited by Humphrey Carpenter and Mari Prichard. New York: Oxford Univ. Press, 1984, p. 242.

Haugaard, Erik Christian

Haugaard, Erik Christian. "A Writer Comments." *Horn Book* 43 (Aug 1967): 444–446.
Kuznets, Lois R. "Other People's Children: Erik Haugaard's 'Untold Tales.'" *Children's Literature in Education* 11 (Summer 1980): 62–68. Reprinted from *Proceedings of the Sixth Annual Conference of the Children's Literature Association,* 1979. Ypsilanti, MI: Children's Literature Association, 1981, pp. 128–135.
Lavender, Ralph. "Hans Christian Andersen and Erik Christian Haugaard." *School Librarian* 23 (June 1975): 113–119.
Nist, Joan. "*Places of Freedom:* Erik Christian Haugaard's Historical Fiction." *Advocate* 2 (Winter 1985): 114–120.
Root, Shelton L., and M. Jean Greenlaw. "Profile: An Interview with Erik Christian Haugaard." *Language Arts* 56 (May 1979): 549–561.
Third Book of Junior Authors. Edited by Doris De Montreville and Donna Hill. New York: Wilson, 1972, pp. 120–121.
Twentieth-Century Children's Writers. 3rd ed. Edited by Tracy Chevalier and D. L. Kirkpatrick. New York: St. Martin, 1989, pp. 434–435.

Hawthorne, Julian

Bassan, Maurice. *Hawthorne's Son: The Life and Literary Career of Julian Hawthorne.* Columbus: Ohio State Univ. Press, 1970.
West, Mark I., ed. *Before Oz: Juvenile Fantasy Stories from Nineteenth-Century America.* Hamden, CT: Shoe String, 1989. "Rumpty-Dudget's Tower," pp. 67–88.

Hawthorne, Nathaniel

Becker, Allienne Rimer. "The Fantastic in the Fiction of Hoffmann and Hawthorne." Ph.D. diss., Pennsylvania State University, 1984.
Billman, Carol. "Nathaniel Hawthorne: 'Revolutionizer' of Children's Literature." *Studies in American Fiction* 10 (1982): 107–114.

Bonney, Agnes Mavis. "Artistic Uses of Supernaturalism in the Fiction of Brown, Irving and Hawthorne." Ph.D. diss., Washington University, 1978.

Burns, Thomas. "More Life-Like Warmth: Reality in Hawthorne's Tales." Ph.D. diss., Ohio University, 1974.

Coleman, A. "Hawthorne's Pragmatic Fantasies." *Children's Literature Association Journal* 31 (Mar 1988): 360–371.

Crisman, William. "'The Snow-Image' as a Key to Hawthorne's Biotechnology Tales." *ATQ: A Journal of New England Writing* 3 (June 1989): 169–187.

Doyle, Brian. *The Who's Who of Children's Literature.* New York: Schocken, 1968, pp. 139–140.

Fraden, Rena. "The Sentimental Tradition in Dickens and Hawthorne." Ph.D. diss., Yale University, 1983.

Fulton, Patricia Teague. "Borges, Hawthorne and Poe: A Study of Significant Parallels in Their Theories and Methods of Short Story Writing." Ph.D. diss., Auburn University, 1979.

Jordan, Alice M. "The Dawn of Imagination in American Books for Children." *Horn Book* 20 (May 1944): 168–175.

Kerr, Howard, John W. Crowley, and Charles W. Crowley, eds. *The Haunted Dusk: American Supernatural Fiction, 1820–1920.* Athens: Univ. of Georgia Press, 1983, pp. 67–98.

Laffrado, Laura. "Delicate Playthings, Granite Rocks: A Study of Hawthorne's Works for Children." Ph.D. diss., State University of New York at Buffalo, 1987.

Lee, A. Robert, ed. *Nathaniel Hawthorne, New Critical Essays.* Totowa, NJ: Barnes and Noble, 1982.

Marks, Alfred H. "Hawthorne, Tiek, and Hoffmann: Adding to the Improbabilities of a Marvelous Tale." *ESQ: A Journal of the American Renaissance* 35 (Spring 1989): 1–21.

Martin, Terence. *Nathaniel Hawthorne.* rev. ed. Boston: Twayne, 1983.

Mattfield, M. "Hawthorne's Juvenile Classics." *Discourse* 12 (Summer 1969): 346–364.

Neilson, Keith. "The Short Fiction of Nathaniel Hawthorne." In *Survey of Modern Fantasy Literature,* vol. 3. Edited by Frank N. Magill. Englewood Cliffs, NJ: Salem Press, 1983, pp. 1536–1543.

The Oxford Companion to Children's Literature. Edited by Humphrey Carpenter and Mari Prichard. New York: Oxford Univ. Press, 1984, pp. 243, 516, 577–578.

Ponnau, Gwenhail. *La Folie Dans la Littérature Fantastique [Madness in Fantasy Literature].* Paris: Editions du Centre National de la Recherche Scientifique, 1987.

Rupprecht, Erich S. "Nathaniel Hawthorne." In *Supernatural Fiction Writers: Fantasy and Horror,* vol. 2. Edited by E. F. Bleiler. New York: Scribner, 1985, pp. 707–716.

Scharnhorst, Gary. *Nathaniel Hawthorne: An Annotated Bibliography of Commentary and Criticism Before 1900.* Metuchen, NJ: Scarecrow Press, 1988.

Stott, Jon C. "Nathaniel Hawthorne." In *Writers for Children; Critical Studies of Major Authors Since the Seventeenth Century.* Edited by Jane M. Bingham. New York: Scribner, 1988, pp. 277–282.

Swann, Charles. *Nathaniel Hawthorne: Tradition and Revolution.* Cambridge: Cambridge Univ. Press, 1991.

Wagenknecht, Edward. *Nathaniel Hawthorne: The Man, His Tales and Romances.* New York: Ungar, 1989.

Zipes, Jack, ed. *Spells of Enchantment: The Wondrous Fairy Tales of Western Culture.* New York: Viking, 1991.

Haywood, Carolyn

Burns, Paul C., and Ruth Hines. "Carolyn Haywood." In *Authors and Illustrators of Chil-*

dren's Books. Edited by Miriam Hoffman and Eva Samuels. New York: Bowker, 1972, pp. 193–196. Reprinted from *Elementary English* 47 (Feb 1970): 172–175.

The Junior Book of Authors. 2nd ed. rev. Edited by Stanley J. Kunitz and Howard Haycraft. New York: Wilson, 1951, pp. 155–156.

Shaken, Grace. "Our Debt to Carolyn Haywood." *Elementary English* 32 (Jan 1955): 3–8.

Twentieth-Century Children's Writers. 3rd ed. Edited by Tracy Chevalier and D. L. Kirkpatrick. New York: St. Martin, 1989, p. 437.

Hazel, Paul

Searles, Baird, Beth Meacham, and Michael Franklin. *A Reader's Guide to Fantasy.* New York: Avon, 1982, p. 73.

Hearne, Betsy (Gould)

Hearne, Betsy. *Beauties and Beasts.* Phoenix: Oryx, 1993.

Sixth Book of Junior Authors and Illustrators. Edited by Sally Holmes Holtze. New York: Wilson, 1989, pp. 119–120.

Heide, Florence Parry

Chambers, Aidan. *Booktalk: Occasional Writing on Literature and Children.* New York: Harper, 1986, pp. 33, 62, 76, 80, 120.

Fourth Book of Junior Authors and Illustrators. Edited by Doris De Montreville and Elizabeth D. Crawford. New York: Wilson, 1978, pp. 172–173.

Herman, Gertrude. "A Picture Is Worth Several Hundred Words." [*The Shrinking of Treehorn*] *Horn Book* 65 (Jan–Feb 1989): 104–105.

Twentieth-Century Children's Writers. 3rd ed. Edited by Tracy Chevalier and D. L. Kirkpatrick. Chicago: St. James, 1989, pp. 438–441.

Helprin, Mark

Twentieth-Century Science Fiction Writers. 2nd ed. Edited by Curtis C. Smith. Chicago: St. James Press, 1986, pp. 328–329.

Hess, Fjeril

The Junior Book of Authors. 2nd ed. rev. Edited by Stanley J. Kunitz and Howard Haycraft. New York: Wilson, 1951, pp. 157–159.

Seaman, Louise. "From California to the Volga with Fjeril Hess." *Horn Book* 10 (Nov 1934): 385–389.

Hewett, Anita

Twentieth-Century Children's Writers. 3rd ed. Edited by Tracy Chevalier and D. L. Kirkpatrick. New York: St. Martin, 1989, pp. 446–447.

Hickman, Tracy *see* Weis, Margaret

Hildick, E(dmund) W(allace)

Doyle, Brian. *The Who's Who of Children's Literature.* New York: Schocken, 1968, pp. 143–144.
Fourth Book of Junior Authors and Illustrators. Edited by Doris De Montreville and Elizabeth D. Crawford. New York: Wilson, 1978, pp. 174–176.
Twentieth-Century Children's Writers. 3rd ed. Edited by Tracy Chevalier and D. L. Kirkpatrick. Chicago: St. James, 1989, pp. 449–451.

Hill, Douglas (Arthur)

Hill, Douglas. "Getting Ideas." *Puffin Post* (U.K.) 9 (Spring 1986): 8.
———. "Ladders and Other Metaphors." *Bookmark* [Edinburgh] 13 (1985): 13–15.
Jenkinson, Dave. "Douglas Hill." *Emergency Librarian* 12 (Mar–Apr 1985): 49–51.
Sawyer, Andy. "Douglas Hill Interviewed." *Vector* (U.K.) 140 (Oct–Nov 1987): 7–8.

Hilton, James

Crawford, John W. "The Utopian Dream Alive and Well." *Cuyahoga Review* 2 (Spring–Summer 1984): 27–33.
Edwards, Malcolm, and Robert Holdstock. "Lost Worlds." In *Realms of Fantasy.* Garden City, NY: Doubleday, 1983, pp. 27–31.
Stableford, Brian. "*Lost Horizon.*" In *Survey of Modern Fantasy Literature,* vol. 2. Edited by Frank N. Magill. Englewood Cliffs, NJ: Salem Press, 1983, pp. 920–923.

Hoban, Russell C(onwell)

Allison, Alida. "Living the Non-Mechanical Life: Russell Hoban's Metaphorical Wind-Up Toys." *Children's Literature in Education* 22 (Sept 1991): 189–194.
———. "Russell Hoban." In *American Writers for Children since 1960: Fiction. Dictionary of Literary Biography,* vol. 52. Detroit: Gale, 1986, pp. 192–201.
———. "Russell Hoban." *Poets and Writer's Magazine* 20 (July–Aug 1992): 27–28.
———, ed. "Russell Hoban Reads Russell Hoban: Children's Books." *The Lion and the Unicorn* 15 (Dec 1991): 96–106.
Archer, John. "Interview with Russell Hoban." *Hard Times* (University College, Cardiff, Wales) 2 (Dec 1974).
"Authorgraph no. 12: Russell Hoban." *Books for Keeps* (U.K.) 12 (Jan 1982): 16–17.
Blount, Margaret. *Animal Land: The Creatures of Children's Fiction.* New York: Morrow, 1975, pp. 186–188.
Bowers, Joan A. "From Badgers to Turtles: The Fantasy World of Russell Hoban." In *Proceedings of the Sixth Annual Conference of the Children's Literature Association.* University of Toronto, March 1979. Ypsilanti, MI: Children's Literature Association, 1981, pp. 86–93. Reprinted in *Children's Literature,* vol. 8. New Haven, CT: Yale Univ. Press, 1980, pp. 80–97.
Branscomb, J. "The Quest for Wholeness in the Fiction of Russell Hoban." *Critique* 28 (Fall 1986): 29–38.
Brooks, David. "Russell Hoban." *Helix* 21, no. 2 (1986): 75–81.
Bunbury, Rhonda M. "'Always a Dance Going On in the Stone': An Interview with Russell Hoban." *Children's Literature in Education* 17 (Fall 1986): 139–149.
De Luca, Geraldine. "'A Condition of Complete Simplicity:' The Toy as Child in *The Mouse and His Child.*" *Children's Literature in Education* 19 (Winter 1988): 211–221.

Gose, Elliott. *Mere Creatures: A Study of Modern Fantasy Tales for Children.* Toronto: Univ. of Toronto Press, 1988, pp. 108–121.

Gough, John. "Rivalry, Rejection and Recovery: Variations of the 'Cinderella' Story." *Children's Literature in Education* 21 (June 1990): 99–108.

Hamilton, Alex. "Interview with Russell Hoban." *The Guardian,* Mar 24, 1975.

Helbig, Alethea K., and Agnes Regan Perkins. *Dictionary of American Children's Fiction, 1960–1984.* Westport, CT: Greenwood, 1986, pp. 291, 434–435.

Hoban, Russell. "Blighter's Rock." *Poets and Writers Magazine* 20 (July–Aug 1992): 27, 29–31.

———. *The Moment Under the Moment.* London: Cape, 1992.

———. "*The Mouse and His Child*—Yes, It's a Children's Book." *Books for Your Children* (U.K.) 12 (Winter 1976): 3.

———. "One Pays Attention." *Puffin Post* (London) 10, no. 2 (1976): 14.

———. "Thoughts on a Shirtless Cyclist, Robin Hood, Johann Sebastian Bach and One or Two Other Things." *Children's Literature in Education* 4 (Mar 1971): 5–23. Reprinted in Geoff Fox. *Writers, Critics and Children.* New York: Agathon Press, 1976, pp. 95–103.

———. "Thoughts on Being and Writing." In Edward Blishen. *The Thorny Paradise.* Boston: Horn Book, 1975, pp. 65–76.

———. "Time Slip, Uphill Lean, Laminar Flow, Place-to-Place Talking and Hearing the Silence." *Children's Literature in Education* 9 (Nov 1972): 33–47.

Hunter, Linnet. "*The Mouse and His Child* by Russell Hoban: Two Exercises in Literary Criticism: Archetypal and Sociological." *Review Bulletin* (Australia) 20 (1988): 11–16.

Inglis, Fred. *The Promise of Happiness.* New York: Cambridge Univ. Press, 1981, pp. 303–304.

Kincaid, Paul. "The Mouse, the Lion and *Ridley Walker:* Russell Hoban Interviewed." *Vector* 124/125 (1985): 5–9.

Knoepflmacher, U. C. "Roads Half Taken: Travel, Fantasy and Growing Up." *Proceedings of the 13th Annual Conference of The Children's Literature Association, 1986.* New York: Pace University, 1988, pp. 48–59.

Krips, Valerie. "Mistaken Identity: Russell Hoban's *Mouse and His Child.*" *Children's Literature 21.* New Haven, CT: Yale Univ. Press, 1993, pp. 92–100.

Lenz, Millicent. "Russell Hoban's *The Mouse and His Child* and the Search to Be Self-Winding." In *Proceedings of the Fifth Annual Conference of the Children's Literature Association.* Harvard University, March 1978. Ypsilanti, MI: Children's Literature Association, 1979, pp. 64–69.

Lynn, Joanne. "Threadbare Utopia: Hoban's Modern Pastoral." *Children's Literature Association Quarterly* 11 (Spring 1986): 19–24.

McCaffrey, Larry, and Sinda Gregory. "An Interview with Russell Hoban." In *Alive and Writing: Interviews with American Authors of the 1980s.* Urbana: Univ. of Illinois Press, 1987, pp. 175–195.

MacKillop, Ian D. "Russell Hoban: Returning to the Sunlight." In Dennis Butts. *Good Writers for Young Readers.* St. Albans, England: Hart-Davis, 1977, pp. 57–66.

McMahon-Hill, Gillian. "A Narrow Pavement Says 'Walk Alone': The Books of Russell Hoban." *Children's Literature in Education* 20 (Spring 1976): 41–55.

Morrissey, Thomas J. "Armageddon from Huxley to Hoban." *Extrapolation* 25 (Fall 1984): 197–213.

The Oxford Companion to Children's Literature. Edited by Humphrey Carpenter and Mari Prichard. New York: Oxford Univ. Press, 1984, pp. 254–255, 365.

Rees, David. "Beyond the Last Visible Dog—Russell Hoban." In *Painted Desert, Green Shade.* Boston: Horn Book, 1984, pp. 138–152.

Rustin, Michael. "Making Out in America: *The Mouse and His Child.*" In Margaret Rustin and Michael Rustin. *Narratives of Love and Loss: Studies in Modern Children's Fiction.* London: Verso, 1987; New York: Routledge, 1988, pp. 181–195.

Singh, Michael J. "Law and Emotion in Fantasy." *Orana* 18 (May 1982): 49–54.

Swinfen, Ann. *In Defense of Fantasy.* London: Routledge, 1984. A discussion of *The Mouse and His Child,* pp. 21, 31–34, 105, 193–202, 228–229.

Third Book of Junior Authors. Edited by Doris De Montreville and Donna Hill. New York: Wilson, 1972, pp. 129–130.

Toomey, Philippa. "An Explorer Who Maps the Continents of His Imagination." (London) *Times* (Nov 15, 1974): 20.

———. "Interview with Russell Hoban." *The* [London] *Times,* Nov 15, 1974.

Townsend, John Rowe. "A Second Look—*The Mouse and His Child.*" *Horn Book* 51 (Oct 1975): 449–451. Reprinted in Paul Heins. *Crosscurrents of Criticism.* Boston: Horn Book, 1977, pp. 330–332.

Twentieth-Century Children's Writers. 3rd ed. Edited by Tracy Chevalier and D. L. Kirkpatrick. Chicago: St. James, 1989, pp. 455–457.

Twentieth-Century Science Fiction Writers. 2nd ed. Edited by Curtis C. Smith. Chicago: St. James Press, 1986, pp. 338–339.

Wilkie, Christine. *Through the Narrow Gate: The Mythological Consciousness of Russell Hoban.* Cranbury, NJ: Farleigh Dickenson Univ. Press, 1990.

Hodgell, P(atricia) C(hristine)

Greenlaw, M. Jean. "Books in the Classroom." *Horn Book* 64 (Nov–Dec 1988): 820–822.

Hodges, C(yril) Walter

Crouch, Marcus S. "Illustrated by C. Walter Hodges." *Junior Bookshelf* 15 (July 1951): 79–84.

Hodges, C. Walter. "Adventures with a Problem." *Horn Book* 16 (Sept–Oct 1940): 331–333.

———. "Children? What Children?" In *The Thorny Paradise: Writers on Writing for Children,* ed. by Edward Blishen. Boston: Horn Book, 1975, pp. 53–57.

———. "On Writing about King Alfred." *Horn Book* 43 (Apr 1967): 179–182; *Junior Bookshelf* 31 (June 1967): 159–163. Reprinted in *Folk Literature of the British Isles.* Edited by Eloise S. Norton. Metuchen, NJ: Scarecrow Press, 1978, pp. 67–70.

Long, Sidney. "A Second Look: *The Namesake.*" *Horn Book* 53 (Aug 1977): 477–482.

Third Book of Junior Authors. Edited by Doris De Montreville and Donna Hill. New York: Wilson, 1972, pp. 130–132.

Twentieth-Century Children's Writers. 3rd ed. Edited by Tracy Chevalier and D. L. Kirkpatrick. Chicago: St. James, 1989, pp. 457–459.

Hodges, Elizabeth Jamison

Hodges, Elizabeth Jamison. "The Magic of Serendipity." *Horn Book* 43 (June 1967): 370–374. "Part II." *Horn Book* 45 (Aug 1969): 436–439.

Hoffmann, Eleanor

Helbig, Alethea K., and Agnes Regan Perkins. *Dictionary of American Children's Fiction, 1859–1959.* Westport, CT: Greenwood, 1985, p. 221.

The Oxford Companion to Children's Literature. Edited by Humphrey Carpenter and Mari Prichard. New York: Oxford Univ. Press, 1984, pp. 256, 384.

Hoffmann, E(rnst) T(heodor) A(madeus)

Becker, Allienne Rimer. "The Fantastic in the Fiction of Hoffmann and Hawthorne." Ph.D. diss., Pennsylvania State University, 1984.

Doyle, Brian. *The Who's Who of Children's Literature.* New York: Schocken, 1968, p. 144.

Duroche, Leonard L. "E. T. A. Hoffmann." In *Writers for Children; Critical Studies of Major Authors Since the Seventeenth Century.* Edited by Jane M. Bingham. New York: Scribner, 1988, pp. 283–288.

Grenz, Dagmar. "E. T. A. Hoffmann as an Author for Children and Adults, or the Child and the Adult as Reader of Children's Literature." *Phaedrus* 13 (1988): 91–96.

Goff, Penrith. "E. T. A. Hoffmann." In *Supernatural Fiction Writers: Fantasy and Horror,* vol. 1. Edited by E. F. Bleiler. New York: Scribner, 1985, pp. 111–120.

Jackson, Rosemary. *Fantasy: The Literature of Subversion.* New York: Methuen, 1980, pp. 14, 37, 43–44, 50, 55, 66–67, 104, 107, 123, 172, 176.

Kranz, Gisbert. "E. T. A. Hoffmann's Einfluss auf George MacDonald [E. T. A. Hoffmann's Influence on George MacDonald].'" *Mitteilungen der E. T. A. Hoffmann-Gesellschaft-Bamberg* 33 (1987): 102–108.

Kroeber, Karl. *Romatic Fantasy and Science Fiction.* New Haven: Yale Univ. Press, 1988.

Marks, Alfred H. "Hawthorne, Tiek and Hoffmann: Adding to the Improbabilities of a Marvelous Tale." *ESQ: A Journal of the American Renaissance* 35 (Spring 1989): 1–21.

Ponnau, Gwenhail. *La Folie Dans la Littérature Fantastique.* [*Madness in Fantasy Literature*]. Paris: Editions du Centre National de la Recherche Scientifique, 1987.

Searles, Baird, Beth Meacham, and Michael Franklin. *A Reader's Guide to Fantasy.* New York: Avon, 1982, pp. 75–76.

Vitt-Maucher, Gisela. "E. T. A. Hoffmann's Märchenshaffen: Kaleidoscop der Verfremdung in Seinen Sieben Märchen." Chapel Hill: Univ. of North Carolina Press, 1989.

Wolfe, Gary K. "The Short Fiction of E. T. A. Hoffmann." In *Survey of Modern Fantasy Literature,* vol. 4. Edited by Frank N. Magill. Englewood Cliffs, NJ: Salem Press, 1983, pp. 1547–1553.

Holdstock, Robert (P.)

Kincaid, Paul. "The Novels of Robert Holdstock." *Arena* 9 (Aug 1979): 27–32.

Rippington, Geoff. "Robert Holdstock Interviewed." *Arena* 9 (Aug 1979): 18–26.

Twentieth-Century Science Fiction Writers. 3rd ed. Edited by Noelle Watson and Paul E. Schellinger. Chicago: St. James Press, 1991, pp. 383–384.

Holman (Valen), Felice

Fourth Book of Junior Authors and Illustrators. Edited by Doris De Montreville and Elizabeth D. Crawford. New York: Wilson, 1978, pp. 182–183.

Helbig, Alethea K., and Agnes Regan Perkins. *Dictionary of American Children's Fiction, 1960–1984.* Westport, CT: Greenwood, 1986, p. 293.

Holman, Felice. "*Slake's Limbo:* In Which a Book Switches Authors." *Horn Book* 52 (Oct 1976): 479–485.

Twentieth-Century Children's Writers. 3rd ed. Edited by Tracy Chevalier and D. L. Kirkpatrick. Chicago: St. James, 1989, pp. 464–465.

Holt, Isabella

Helbig, Alethea K., and Agnes Regan Perkins. *Dictionary of American Children's Fiction, 1859–1959.* Westport, CT: Greenwood, 1985, pp. 7–9, 223.

Hooks, William H(arris)

Sixth Book of Junior Authors and Illustrators. Edited by Sally Holmes Holtze. New York: Wilson, 1989, pp. 133–134.

Hopkins, Lee Bennett

Fifth Book of Junior Authors and Illustrators. Edited by Sally Holmes Holtze. New York: Wilson, 1983, pp. 155–157.

Horne, Richard Henry (Hengist)

Blainey, Ann. *The Farthing Poet: A Biography of Richard Hengist Horne, 1802–1884, a Lesser Literary Lion.* London: Longmans, 1968.

Fisher, Margery. "A Bear in the Nursery: Richard Hengist Horne Writing for Children." *Signal* 61 (Jan 1990): 27–41.

———. "Introduction and Notes" to *Memoirs of a London Doll Written by Herself,* by Mrs. Fairstar. Reproduction of 1846 edition. New York: Macmillan, 1967.

Horne, Richard Henry. "A Witch in the Nursery." *Household Words,* Sept 20, 1851, pp. 601–609. Reprinted in Lance Salway. *A Peculiar Gift.* Harmondsworth, Middlesex: Kestrel, 1976, pp. 173–194.

The Oxford Companion to Children's Literature. Edited by Humphrey Carpenter and Mari Prichard. New York: Oxford Univ. Press, 1984, pp. 261, 348.

Pearl, Cyril. *Always Morning: The Life of Richard Henry "Orion" Horne.* Melbourne, Australia: F. W. Cheshire, 1960.

Horwood, William

Morgan, Chris. "*Duncton Wood.*" In *Survey of Modern Fantasy Literature,* vol. 1. Edited by Frank N. Magill. Englewood Cliffs, NJ: Salem Press, 1983, pp. 436–444.

Hough, (Helen) Charlotte (Woodyatt)

Twentieth-Century Children's Writers. 3rd ed. Edited by Tracy Chevalier and D. L. Kirkpatrick. New York: St. Martin, 1989, pp. 467–468.

Housman, Laurence

The Oxford Companion to Children's Literature. Edited by Humphrey Carpenter and Mari Prichard. New York: Oxford Univ. Press, 1984, p. 262.

Houston, James A(rchibald)

Fourth Book of Junior Authors and Illustrators. Edited by Doris De Montreville and Elizabeth D. Crawford. New York: Wilson, 1978, pp. 183–185.

Howard, Joan (pseud. of Patricia Gordon)

Helbig, Alethea K., and Alice Regan Perkins. *Dictionary of American Children's Fiction, 1859–1959.* Westport, CT: Greenwood, 1985, p. 189.

Howe, Deborah

Sixth Book of Junior Authors and Illustrators. Edited by Sally Holmes Holtze. New York: Wilson, 1989, pp. 134–135.

Howe, James

Brainard, D. "James Howe." *Publishers Weekly* 225 (Feb 24, 1984): 144–145. Interview.
Howe, James. "Writing for the Hidden Child." *Horn Book* 61 (Mar–Apr 1985): 156–161.
———. "Writing Mysteries for Children." *Horn Book* 66 (Mar–Apr 1990): 178–183.
Raymond, A. "James Howe: Corn, Ham, and Punster Cheese." *Teaching K–8* 17 (Feb 1987): 32–34.
Sixth Book of Junior Authors and Illustrators. Edited by Sally Holmes Holtze. New York: Wilson, 1989, pp. 135–137.
Twentieth-Century Children's Writers. 3rd ed. Edited by Tracy Chevalier and D. L. Kirkpatrick. Chicago: St. James, 1989, pp. 470–471.

Hudson, W(illiam) H(enry)

Dalphin, Marcia. "I Give You the End of a Golden String." *Horn Book* 14 (May 1938): 143–149. Reprinted in Norma Fryatt. *A Horn Book Sampler.* Boston: Horn Book, 1959, pp. 133–139.
Higgins, James Edward. "Five Authors of Mystical Fancy for Children: A Critical Study." Ed.D. diss., Columbia University, 1965.
Ronner, Amy D. *W. H. Hudson: The Man, the Novelist, the Naturalist.* New York: AMS Press, 1986.
Stableford, Brian. "Green Mansions." In *Survey of Modern Fantasy Literature*, vol. 2. Edited by Frank N. Magill. Englewood Cliffs, NJ: Salem Press, 1983, pp. 670–674.
Tomalin, Ruth. *W. H. Hudson: A Biography.* London: Faber, 1982.

Hughes, Monica

Hughes, Monica. "The Writer as Mask-Maker and Mask-Wearer." *Horn Book* 68 (Mar–Apr 1992): 178–185.

Hughes, Richard (Arthur Warren)

Doyle, Brian. *The Who's Who of Children's Literature.* New York: Schocken, 1968, pp. 149–150.
Parker, Geoffrey. "Richard Hughes' *The Spider Palace and Other Stories.*" *Children's Literature in Education* 20 (Spring 1976): 32–40.
———. "*The Wonder-Dog:* The Collected Children's Stories of Richard Hughes." *Children's Literature in Education* 27, no. 4 (1977): 163–175.
Stevenson, Lionel. "Purveyors of Myth and Magic." In *Yesterday and After: The History of the English Novel.* Totowa, NJ: Barnes and Noble, 1967, pp. 111–154.
Twentieth-Century Children's Writers. 3rd ed. Edited by Tracy Chevalier and D. L. Kirkpatrick. Chicago: St. James, 1989, pp. 474–475.

Hughes, Ted (Edward James)

Adams, John. "Dark Rainbow: Reflections of Ted Hughes." *Signal* 5 (May 1971): 65–71.

Reprinted in Chambers. *The Signal Approach to Children's Literature.* Metuchen, NJ: Scarecrow Press, 1980, pp. 101–108.

Bradman, T. "Giant Singer: The Children's Books of Ted Hughes." *Junior Bookshelf* 44 (Aug 1980): 163–165.

Bubbers, Lissa Paul. "Telling Stories for Children and Adults: The Writings of Ted Hughes." Ph.D. diss., York University (Canada), 1984.

Hughes, Ted. "The Interpretation of Parables." *Times Educational Supplement* (Mar 20, 1992): 21–22; *Signal* 69 (Sept 1992): 147–152.

———. "Myth and Education." *Children's Literature in Education* 1 (Mar 1970): 55–70. Reprinted in Geoff Fox. *Writers, Critics and Children.* New York: Agathon Press, 1976, pp. 77–94.

Inglis, Fred. *The Promise of Happiness.* New York: Cambridge Univ. Press, 1981, pp. 248–250.

Morris, J. "Iron Manic." *Child Education* (U.K.) 70 (Nov 1993): 25–27.

Nettell, Stephanie. "The Guardian Award." *Books for Keeps* (U.K.) 32 (May 1985): 18.

The Oxford Companion to Children's Literature. Edited by Humphrey Carpenter and Mari Prichard. New York: Oxford Univ. Press, 1984, p. 264.

Page, T. "Project File: *The Iron Man.*" *Child Education* (Jan 1990): 19–26.

Paul, Lissa. "Inside the Lurking-Glass with Ted Hughes." *Signal* 49 (Jan 1986): 52–63.

Ray, Sheila. "Author Notes from Great Britain: Ted Hughes, John Masefield, and Alison Uttley." *Bookbird* 2 (1985): 29–30.

Rees, David. "Hospitals Where We Heal—Ted Hughes." In *Painted Desert, Green Shade.* Boston: Horn Book, 1984, pp. 47–61. Reprinted from *San Jose Studies* (July 1983).

Twentieth-Century Children's Writers. 3rd ed. Edited by Tracy Chevalier and D. L. Kirkpatrick. Chicago: St. James, 1989, pp. 477–480.

Hunter, Mollie (pseud. of Maureen Mollie Hunter McVeigh McIlwraith)

Cook, S. "Children's Writers: Mollie Hunter." *School Librarian* 26 (June 1978): 108–111.

Dooley, Patricia. "Profile: Mollie Hunter." *Children's Literature Association Quarterly* 3 (Autumn 1978): 3–6.

Hickman, J. "Profile: The Person behind the Book: Mollie Hunter." *Language Arts* 56 (Mar 1979): 302–306.

Hoffman, Mary. "Scottish Story Weaver." *Times Educational Supplement* (Jan 13, 1984): 10.

Hollindale, Peter. "World Enough and Time: The Work of Mollie Hunter." *Children's Literature in Education* 26, no. 3 (1977): 109–119.

Hunter, Mollie. "Folklore—One Writer's View." In *Folk Literature of the British Isles.* Edited by Eloise S. Norton. Metuchen, NJ: Scarecrow Press, 1978, pp. 124–133.

———. "Following a Star." *USBBY Newsletter* [Newark, DE] 17, no. 1 (Spring 1993): 4.

———. "If You Can Read." *Horn Book* 54 (June 1978): 257–262.

———. "The Last Lord of Redhouse Castle." In *Children's Books International 1; Proceedings and Book Catalog.* Boston: Boston Public Library, 1976, pp. 26–32. Reprinted from Edward Blishen. *The Thorny Paradise.* Boston: Horn Book, 1975, pp. 128–139.

———. "A Need for Heroes." In *Proceedings of the Sixth Annual Conference of the Children's Literature Association.* University of Toronto, March 1979. Ypsilanti, MI: Children's Literature Association, 1981, pp. 52–66. Reprinted in *Horn Book* 59 (Apr 1983): 146–154.

———. "One World." *Horn Book* 51 (Dec 1975): 557–563, and 52 (Jan 1976): 32–38. Reprinted in Mollie Hunter. *Talent Is Not Enough.* New York: Harper, 1976, pp. 57–77; and in Boyer and Zahorski. *Fantasists on Fantasy.* New York: Avon, 1984, pp. 211–230.

———. *The Pied Piper Syndrome and Other Essays.* New York: Harper, 1992.

————. "Talent Is Not Enough." In *The Arbuthnot Lectures, 1970–1979.* Chicago: American Library Association, 1980, pp. 105–119.

————. *Talent Is Not Enough: Mollie Hunter on Writing for Children.* New York: Harper, 1976. "One World," pp. 57–77; "The Other World," pp. 78–102.

————. "The Third Eye." In *Innocence & Experience.* Edited by Barbara Harrison and Gregory Maguire. New York: Lothrop, 1987, pp. 243–249.

Kaye, Marilyn J. "Mollie Hunter: An Interview." *Top of the News* 41 (Winter 1985): 141–146.

Mutton, Jenny. "Mollie Hunter: Underrated Downunder?" *Orana* (Australia) 24 (Aug 1988): 157–165.

Rowe, M. "Mollie Hunter." Auckland, New Zealand: *Children's Literature Association Yearbook* (1977): 33–38.

Ryan, J. S. "The Spirit of Old Scotland: Tone in the Fiction of Mollie Hunter." *Orana* 20 (May 1984): 93–101; continued in (Aug 1984): 138–145.

Spirt, Diana L. *Introducing More Books: A Guide for the Middle Grades.* New York: Bowker, 1978, pp. 204–207.

Third Book of Junior Authors. Edited by Doris De Montreville and Donna Hill. New York: Wilson, 1972, pp. 140–141.

Twentieth-Century Children's Writers. 3rd ed. Edited by Tracy Chevalier and D. L. Kirkpatrick. Chicago: St. James, 1989, pp. 484–486.

Walker, Margaret. "Window on Mollie Hunter." *Book Window* [Glasgow] 3 (Winter 1975): 9–11.

Welham, H. "Love of Land and Language: The Work of Mollie Hunter." *Bookmark* 16 (1990): 38–41.

Withers, Zoe. "Fact and Fancy." *Children's Libraries Newsletter* (Australia) 12 (Nov 1976): 118–121.

Yolen, Jane. "The Literary Underwater World." *Language Arts* 57 (1980): 403–412.

Hunter, Norman (George Lorimer)

Doyle, Brian. *The Who's Who of Children's Literature.* New York: Schocken, 1968, pp. 151–152.

The Oxford Companion to Children's Literature. Edited by Humphrey Carpenter and Mari Prichard. New York: Oxford Univ. Press, 1984, pp. 266, 427.

Twentieth-Century Children's Writers. 3rd ed. Edited by Tracy Chevalier and D. L. Kirkpatrick. Chicago: St. James, 1989, pp. 486–487.

Hurmence, Belinda

Helbig, Alethea, and Agnes Regan Perkins. *Dictionary of American Children's Fiction, 1985–1989.* Westport, CT: Greenwood, 1993, p. 105.

Hutchins, Pat (Goundry)

Fourth Book of Junior Authors and Illustrators. Edited by Doris De Montreville and Elizabeth D. Crawford. New York: Wilson, 1978, pp. 189–191.

Lehr, Susan. "Between the Covers: People Behind the Books. An Interview with Pat Hutchins." *Children's Literature Association Bulletin* 16 (Fall 1990): 16–20.

Moss, Elaine. "Pat Hutchins: A Natural." *Signal* 10 (Jan 1973): 32–36.

Ricketson, Matthew. "Writing from Experience." *The Age* (Australia) (June 17, 1992): 4.

Thompson, Hillary. "An Interview with Pat Hutchins." *Children's Literature Association Quarterly* 10 (Summer 1985): 57–59.

Twentieth-Century Children's Writers. 3rd ed. Edited by Tracy Chevalier and D. L. Kirkpatrick. Chicago: St. James, 1989, pp. 488–489.

Hyndman, Jane Andrews Lee *see* Wyndham, Lee

Ingelow, Jean

Attebery, Brian. "Women's Coming of Age in Fantasy." *Extrapolation* 28 (Spring 1987): 10–22.

Auerbach, Mina, and U. C. Knoepflmacher, eds. *Forbidden Journeys: Fairy Tales and Fantasys by Victorian Women Writers.* Chicago: Univ. of Chicago Press, 1992, pp. 207–316, 362.

Black, Helen C. "Jean Ingelow." In *Notable Women Authors of the Day: Biographical Sketches.* Glasgow: David Bryce, 1893.

Doyle, Brian. *The Who's Who of Children's Literature.* New York: Schocken, 1968, pp. 152–153.

Lewis, Naomi. "A Lost Pre-Raphaelite." *Times Literary Supplement,* Dec 8, 1972, pp. 1487–1488.

McGillis, Roderick. "Fantasy as Adventure: Nineteenth Century Children's Fiction." *Children's Literature Association Quarterly* 8 (Fall 1983): 18–22.

The Oxford Companion to Children's Literature. Edited by Humphrey Carpenter and Mari Prichard. New York: Oxford Univ. Press, 1984, pp. 271, 357.

Peters, Maureen. *Jean Ingelow: Victorian Poetess.* Ipswich: Boydell Press, 1972.

Pflieger, Pat, and Helen M. Hill, eds. *A Reference Guide to Modern Fantasy for Children.* Westport, CT: Greenwood, 1984, pp. xiii–xvi, 259–261, 380–383.

Some Recollections of Jean Ingelow and Her Early Friends. 1901. Reprinted by Kennikat Press, Port Washington, NY, 1972.

Susina, Jan Christopher. "Victorian Kunstmärcher: A Study in Children's Literature, 1840–1875." Ph.D. diss., Indiana University, 1986.

Twentieth Century Children's Writers. 2nd ed. Edited by D. L. Kirkpatrick. New York: St. Martin, 1983, pp. 873–874.

Ipcar, Dahlov (Zorach)

Hopkins, Lee Bennett. "Dahlov Ipcar." In *Books Are by People.* New York: Citation Press, 1969, pp. 107–120.

Ipcar, Dahlov. "The Artist at Work: Combining Dinobase and Wash on Paper." *Horn Book* 42 (Feb 1966): 83–86.

———. "Making Pictures on the Farm." *Horn Book* 37 (Oct 1961): 460–464.

———. "Two Worlds in Balance." *Bookmark* (Scotland) 7 (Summer 1980): 18–22.

Searles, Baird, Beth Meacham, and Michael Franklin. *A Reader's Guide to Fantasy.* New York: Avon, 1982, pp. 78–79.

Sullivan, C. W., III. "Traditional Ballads and Modern Children's Fantasy: Some Comments on Structure and Intent." *Children's Literature Association Quarterly* 11 (Fall 1986): 145–147.

Third Book of Junior Authors. Edited by Doris De Montreville and Donna Hill. New York: Wilson, 1972, pp. 145–146.

Irving, Washington

Aderman, R. M. "Mary Shelley and Washington Irving Once More." *Keats-Shelley Journal* 31 (1982): 24–28.

Bashore, J. Robert, Jr. "Washington Irving." In *Writers for Children; Critical Studies of Major Authors Since the Seventeenth Century.* Edited by Jane M. Bingham, New York: Scribner, 1988, pp. 303–308.

Bonney, Agnes Mavis. "Artistic Uses of Supernaturalism in the Fiction of Brown, Irving, and Hawthorne." Ph.D. diss., Washington University, 1978.

Bowden, Edwin T., ed. *Washingon Irving Bibliograpy.* Boston: Twayne, 1989.

Brooks-Rose, Christine. *A Rhetoric of the Unreal: Studies in Narration and Structure, Especially of the Fantastic.* New York: Cambridge Univ. Press, 1983, pp. 106–112.

Christensen, Peter. "Washington Irving and the Denial of the Fantastic." In *The Old and New World Romanticism of Washington Irving.* Westport, CT: Greenwood, 1986, pp. 51–60.

Daigrepont, Lloyd M. "*Rip Van Winkle* and the Gnostic Vision of History." *CLIO* 15 (1986): 47–59.

Doyle, Brian. *The Who's Who of Children's Literature.* New York: Schocken, 1968, pp. 153–155.

Eberwein, Jane D. "Transatlantic Contrasts in Irving's *Sketch Book.*" *College Literature* 15 (1988): 153–170.

Fisher, Franklin, IV. "Washington Irving." In *Supernatural Fiction Writers: Fantasy and Horror,* vol. 2. Edited by E. F. Bleiler. New York: Scribner, 1985, pp. 685–692.

Franklin, Bruce H. *Future Perfect: American Science Fiction of the 19th Century.* rev. ed. New York: Oxford Univ. Press, 1978.

Helbig, Alethea K., and Agnes Regan Perkins. *Dictionary of American Children's Fiction, 1859–1959.* Westport, CT: Greenwood, 1985, pp. 237, 287–288, 433–434.

Masiello, Lea. "Speaking of Ghosts: Style in Washington Irving's Tales of the Supernatural." Ph.D. diss., University of Cincinnati, 1983.

Morsberger, Robert E. "The Short Fiction of Washington Irving." In *Survey of Modern Fantasy Literature,* vol. 4. Edited by Frank N. Magill. Englewood Cliffs, NJ: Salem Press, 1983, pp. 1554–1562.

The Oxford Companion to Children's Literature. Edited by Humphrey Carpenter and Mari Prichard. New York: Oxford Univ. Press, 1984, pp. 272, 308, 452.

Steig, Michael. "*Rip Van Winkle* by Washington Irving and Arthur Rackham." In *Imagination on a Long Rein: English Literary Illustation,* ed. by Joachim Moeller. Marburg: Jonas Verlag, 1988, pp. 172–180.

Thompson, G. R. "Washington Irving and the American Ghost Story." In Howard Kerr. *The Haunted Dusk: American Supernatural Fiction, 1820–1920.* Athens: Univ. of Georgia Press, 1983, pp. 11–36.

Ish-Kishor, Sulamith

Fifth Book of Junior Authors and Illustrators. Edited by Sally Holmes Holtze. New York: Wilson, 1983, pp. 160–161.

Helbig, Alethea K., and Agnes Regan Perkins. *Dictionary of American Children's Fiction, 1960–1984.* Westport, CT: Greenwood, 1986, p. 313.

Kingston, Carolyn T. *The Tragic Mode in Children's Literature.* New York: Teacher's College Press, 1974, pp. 46–48.

Roginski, Jim, ed. *Newbery and Caldecott Medalists and Honor Book Winners.* Littleton, CO: Libraries Unlimited, 1982, pp. 145–146.

Twentieth-Century Children's Writers. 3rd ed. Edited by Tracy Chevalier and D. L. Kirkpatrick. New York: St. Martin, 1989, pp. 489–490.

Jacob, Piers A(nthony) D(illingham) *see* Anthony, Piers

Jacques, Brian

Estes, Sally. "The *Booklist* Interview: Brian Jacques." *Booklist* 88 (Nov 1, 1991): 516–517.

James, M(ontague) R(hodes)

Ashley, Mike. "M. R. James." *TZM* (Dec 1981): 55–59.
Donaldson, Norman. "M. R. James." In *Supernatural Fiction Writers: Fantasy and Horror,* vol. 1. Edited by E. F. Bleiler. New York: Scribner, 1985, pp. 429–436.
Holmes, Richard. "Of Ghosts and Kings." (London) *Times* (Nov 23, 1974): 7.
Kidd, A. F. "M. R. James: An English Humorist." *Ghosts and Scholars* 5 (1983): 31–34.
Mason, Michael A. "On Not Letting Them Lie: Moral Significance in the Ghost Stories of M. R. James." *Studies in Short Fiction* 19 (1982): 253–260.
Pardoe, Rosemary. "The Unfinished Ghost Stories of M. R. James." *Ghosts and Scholars* 4 (1982): 37–41.
Pfaff, Richard William. *Montague Rhodes James.* London: Scolar Press, 1980.
Rowlands, David, ed. *Masters of Fantasy 3: M. R. James.* Surrey, England: British Fantasy Society, 1987.

James, Mary *see* Kerr, M. E.

Jansson, Tove (Marika)

Ahola, Suvi. "Towards the Empty Page." *Books from Finland* 3 (1991): 131–137.
Archer, Eileen. "Window on Tove Jansson." *Book Window* (Scotland) 2 (Spring 1975): 9–11.
Bargum, Marianne. "Tove Jansson: The Art of Travelling Light." *Books from Finland* 21 (1987): 136–187.
Blount, Margaret. *Animal Land: The Creatures of Children's Fiction.* New York: Morrow, 1975, pp. 277–279.
Burton, Nina. "Tove Jansson's Mumintrollet [Tove Jansson's Moomintrolls]." *Studiekamrated* (Sweden) 62, no. 7 (1980): 16–18.
Campbell, A. K. D. "Tove Jansson and the Moominvalley Saga." *Books for Your Children* (U.K.) 10 (Sept 1975): 8–9.
Crouch, Marcus S. "Moomin-Sagas, by Tove Jansson." *Junior Bookshelf* 30 (Dec 1966): 352–357.
Doyle, Brian. *The Who's Who of Children's Literature.* New York: Schocken, 1968, pp. 156–157.
"Finnish Twilight." *Times Literary Supplement,* October 22, 1971, pp. 1315–1316.
Fleisher, Frederic, and Boel Fleisher. "Tove Jansson and the Moomin Family." *American-Scandinavian Review* 51 (Mar 1963): 47–54.
Goldthwaite, John. "The Black Rabbit: Part One." *Signal* 47 (May 1985): 86–111. "Part Two." *Signal* 48 (Sept 1985): 148–167. Reprinted in Goldthwaite's *The Natural History of Make-Believe.* London: Oxford Univ. Press, 1987.
Gough, John "Tove Jansson and the *Moomin* Sequence." *Papers* (Australia) 1,1 (Apr 1990): 24–33.
Hallsten, Annika. "Moonintroll Conquers the World." *Scandinavian Review* (Fort Lee, NJ) 80, no. 2 (1992): 57–62.
———. "Tove Jansson." *Abrakadabra* (Stockholm) 2 (1991): 4–7. (interview)

Huse, Nancy Lyman. "The Blank Mirror of Death: Protest as Self-Creation in Contemporary Fantasy." *The Lion and the Unicorn* 12 (1988): 28–43.

———. "Equal to Life: Tove Jansson's Moomintrolls." In *Proceedings of the Eighth Annual Conference of the Children's Literature Association.* University of Minnesota, March 1981. Ypsilanti, MI: Children's Literature Association, 1982, pp. 44–49. Reprinted in *Webs and Wardrobes: Humanist and Religious World Views in Children's Literature,* ed. by Joseph O'Beirne Milner and Lucy Floyd Morcock Milner. Lanham, MD: University Press of America, 1987, pp. 135–146.

———. "Tove Jansson and Her Readers: No One Excluded." *Children's Literature* 19 (1991): 149–161.

Jansson, Tove. "Det Läsande Barnet [The Child Reader]." *Barnboken* (Sweden) 2 (1985): 13–14.

———. "On Winning the Andersen Award." *Top of the News* 23 (Apr 1967): 234–239; *Bookbird* 4 (1966): 3–6.

———. "Once Upon a Time There Was a Moomin." *Books for Your Children* (U.K.) 17, no. 3 (1982): 8–9.

———. *Sculptor's Daughter.* Translated by Kingsley Hart. New York: Avon, 1969.

———. "Security and Fear in the World of Children." Translated title of her acceptance speech for the Hans Christian Andersen Medal, 1966, Finland. *Skolbiblioteket* 13, no. 3 (1967): 102–107.

———. "Tarzan the Incomparable." *Signal* 64 (Jan 1991): 20–24.

Lowe, Virginia. "Snufkin, Sniff and Little My: The 'Reality' of Fictional Characters for the Young Child." *Papers* (Australia) 2 (Aug 1991): 87–91.

Lurie, Alison. "Undiscovered Country." *New York Review of Books* (Dec 17, 1992): 16–20.

MacLean, Rusty. "You've Put an End to the Summer: Tove Jansson's *Moomin* Books." *School Librarian* 35 (Aug 1987): 197–201.

Mitchell, Adrian. "Valley of the Trolls." *Sunday Times* (Dec 6, 1992, section 6): 8.

Neumeyer, Peter F. "Tove Jansson at Eighty." Horn Book 70 (Sept–Oct 1994): 555–561.

Orjasaeter, Tordis. "Humorni Tove Jansson Forfattarskap gor oss Suynliga for Varqandra [The Humor in the Works of Tove Jansson Makes Us Visible to Each Other]." *Barn och Kultur* (Sweden) 32, no. 5 (1986): 116–118.

The Oxford Companion to Children's Literature. Edited by Humphrey Carpenter and Mari Prichard. New York: Oxford Univ. Press, 1984, p. 356.

Searles, Baird, Beth Meacham, and Michael Franklin. *A Reader's Guide to Fantasy.* New York: Avon, 1982, pp. 81–82.

Svensen, Asfrid. "Opening Windows on to Unreality: Some Elements of the Fantastic in Scandinavian Children's Literature." *The International Review of Children's Literature and Librarianship* 2 (Spring 1987): 1–9.

Third Book of Junior Authors. Edited by Doris De Montreville and Donna Hill. New York: Wilson, 1972, pp. 147–149.

Ulfsson, Birgitta. "Min Van Tove [My Friend Tove]." *Opsis Kalopsis* (Sweden) 4 (1987): 20–23.

Welsh, Renata. "Toffle Seen through Childish Eyes." *Bookbird* 5 (1967): 37–38.

Westin, Boel. "Creating a Zest for Life: Feminine, Masculine and Human in Tove Jansson's Moomin World." *Swedish Book Review 1990 Suppplement: Swedish Children's Literature,* pp. 30–36.

Wilson, Anne. "Wanted—Tove Jansson's Cartoon Books!" *Signal* 52 (Jan 1987): 12–23.

Jarrell, Randall

Adams, Charles N. *Randall Jarrell: A Bibliography.* Chapel Hill: Univ. of North Carolina Press, 1958.

Dunn, D. "Affable Misery." *Encounter* 39 (Oct 1972): 42–48.

Ellis, Sarah. "A Second Look: *The Bat-Poet.*" *Horn Book* 57 (Aug 1981): 453–455.

Ferguson, Suzanne. *Critical Essays on Randall Jarrell.* Boston: G. K. Hall, 1983.

———. *Randall Jarrell and the Lost World of Childhood.* Athens: Univ. of Georgia Press, 1990.

Flynn, Richard McDonnell. "Happy Families are All Invented: Randall Jarrell's Fiction for Children." *Children's Literature* 16 (1988): 109–125.

———. "Randall Jarrell and the Lost World of Childhood." Ph.D. diss., George Washington University, 1987.

———. "Randall Jarrell's Mermaid: *The Animal Family* and 'Semifeminine' Poetics." *Children's Literature in Education* 23 (Sept 1992): 167–173.

Getz, Thomas. "Memory and Desire in *Fly by Night.*" In *Children's Literature,* vol. 11. New Haven, CT: Yale Univ. Press, 1983, pp. 125–134.

Gillespie, John T., and Diana Lembo. *Introducing Books: A Guide for the Middle Grades.* New York: Bowker, 1970, pp. 246–247.

Griswold, Jerome J. *The Children's Books of Randall Jarrell,* illus. by Maurice Sendak and Garth Williams. Athens, GA: Univ. of Georgia Press, 1988.

———. "Mother and Child in the Poetry and Children's Books of Randall Jarrell." Ph.D. diss., University of Connecticut, 1979.

———. "Preliminary Minutiae: The Holograph of Jarrell's *The Animal Family.*" *Children's Literature in Education* 22 (Sept 1991): 205–210.

Haegenbuchle, Helen. "Laurels for a Bat: Aesthetic Theories in Randall Jarrell's *The Bat Poet.*" *Literaturwissenschaftliches Jahrbuch im Auftrage der Goerres-Gesellschaft* [Berlin] 28 (1987): 115–131.

Helbig, Alethea K., and Agnes Regan Perkins. *Dictionary of American Children's Fiction, 1960–1984.* Westport, CT: Greenwood, 1986, pp. 16–17, 39, 327.

Holtze, Sally Holmes. "A Second Look: *The Animal Family.*" *Horn Book* 61 (Nov–Dec 1985): 714–716.

Horn, Bernard. "'The Tongue of Gods and Children': Blakean Innocence in Randall Jarrell's Poetry." *Children's Literature,* Vol. 2. Storrs, CT: Journal of the Modern Language Association, 1973, pp. 148–151.

Howell, Pamela R. "Voice Is Voice Whether a Bat or a Poet: Randall Jarrell's *The Bat-Poet.*" In *Proceedings of the Ninth Annual Conference of the Children's Literature Association.* University of Florida, March 1982. Ypsilanti, MI: Children's Literature Association, 1983, pp. 71–76.

Jarrell, Randall. *Randall Jarrell's Letters: An Autobiography and Literary Selection.* Edited by Mary Jarrell. Boston: Houghton Mifflin, 1985.

Lovell, Barbara. "Randall Jarrell." In *American Writers for Children since 1960: Fiction. Dictionary of Literary Biography,* vol. 52. Detroit: Gale, 1986, pp. 209–213.

Lowell, Robert, ed. *Randall Jarrell, 1914–1965.* New York: Farrar, 1968.

Moore, M. "Randall Jarrell." *Atlantic Monthly* 220 (Sept 1967): 96–98.

Neumeyer, Peter F. "Randall Jarrell's *The Animal Family:* New Land and Old." In *Proceedings of the Seventh Annual Conference of the Children's Literature Association.* Baylor University, March 1980. Ypsilanti, MI: Children's Literature Association, 1982, pp. 139–145.

———. "Randall Jarrell's *The Bat-Poet:* An Introduction to the Craft." *Children's Literature Association Quarterly* 9 (Summer 1984): 51–54.

Pflieger, Pat, and Helen M. Hill. *A Reference Guide to Modern Fantasy for Children.* Westport, CT: Greenwood, 1984, pp. 15–16, 268–270.

Pritchard, William H. *Randall Jarrell: A Literary Life.* New York: Farrar, 1990.

Roginski, Jim, ed. *Newbery and Caldecott Medalists and Honor Book Winners.* Littleton, CO: Libraries Unlimited, 1982, pp. 147–148.

Rosenthal, Marie. *Randall Jarrell.* Minneapolis: Univ. of Minnesota Press, 1972.

Sale, Roger. *Fairy Tales and After.* Cambridge, MA: Harvard Univ. Press, 1978, pp. 84–90.

Shapiro, Karl. *Randall Jarrell: A Lecture with a Bibliography of Jarrell Materials in the Library of Congress.* Washington, DC: Library of Congress, 1967.

Third Book of Junior Authors. Edited by Doris De Montreville and Donna Hill. New York: Wilson, 1972, pp. 140–150.

Travers, P. L. "A Kind of Visitation." In *Randall Jarrell, 1914–1965.* Edited by Robert Lowell. New York: Farrar, 1967, pp. 253–256. Reprinted from *New York Times Book Review,* Nov 21, 1965.

Twentieth-Century Children's Writers. 3rd ed. Edited by Tracy Chevalier and D. L. Kirkpatrick. Chicago: St. James, 1989, pp. 492–493.

Updike, John. *"Fly by Night." New York Times Book Review,* Nov 14, 1976, Children's Books Section, pp. 25, 36.

Viguers, Ruth Hill. *"The Animal Family,* a Review." *Horn Book* 42 (Feb 1966): 45–46.

Willard, Nancy. "Radiant Fact." *Field* 35 (1986): 51–54.

Wilson, Robert A., comp. "Randall Jarrell: A Bibliographic Checklist." *American Book Collector* 3 (May–June 1982): 32–40.

Wright, Stuart. *Randall Jarrell: A Descriptive Bibliography: 1929–1983.* Charlottesville, VA: University Press of Virginia, 1986.

Zanderer, Leo. "Randall Jarrell: About and for Children." *The Lion and the Unicorn* 2 (Spring 1978): 73–93.

Jeffries, (John) Richard

Carpenter, Humphrey. "Bevis, the Pioneer." In Carpenter. *Secret Gardens: A Study of the Golden Age of Children's Literature.* Boston: Houghton Mifflin, 1985, pp. 103–114.

Jackson, Brian. *"Bevis:* A Lost Classic." *Use of English* 24 (Autumn 1972): 3–10.

Stoate, Graham. "The Unconscious Teaching of the Country—A Rereading of *Bevis: The Story of a Boy." Children's Literature in Education* 8 (Spring 1977): 30–38.

Twentieth Century Children's Writers. 2nd ed. Edited by D. L. Kirkpatrick. New York: St. Martin, 1983, pp. 874–875.

Johnson, Crockett (pseud. of David Johnson Leisk)

Bader, Barbara. "Crockett Johnson." In *American Picturebooks from Noah's Ark to the Beast Within.* New York: Macmillan, 1976, pp. 434–442.

Third Book of Junior Authors. Edited by Doris De Montreville and Donna Hill. New York: Wilson, 1972, pp. 152–153.

Twentieth-Century Children's Writers. 3rd ed. Edited by Tracy Chevalier and D. L. Kirkpatrick. Chicago: St. James, 1989, p. 499.

Johnston, Johanna

Fourth Book of Junior Authors and Illustrators. Edited by Doris De Montreville and Elizabeth D. Crawford. New York: Wilson, 1978, pp. 201–202.

Johnston, Norma

Fifth Book of Junior Authors and Illustrators. Edited by Sally Holmes Holtze. New York: Wilson, 1983, pp. 162–164.

Jones, Adrienne

Fifth Book of Junior Authors and Illustrators. Edited by Sally Holmes Holtze. New York: Wilson, 1983, pp. 164–166.

Jones, Adrienne. "And All for the Want of a Horseshoe-Nail: The Dilemma of a Writer— And of Us All." *VOYA* 6 (Feb 1984): 316–319.

Jones, Diana Wynne

Alderdice, K. "*Publishers Weekly* Interviews: Diana Wynne Jones." *Publishers Weekly* 238 (Feb 22, 1991): 201–202.

Antczak, Janice. *Science Fiction: The Mythos of a New Romance.* New York: Neal-Schuman, 1985, pp. 187–189.

Bennett, David. "Authorgraph no. 46: Diana Wynne Jones." *Books for Keeps* (U.K.) 46 (1987): 14–15.

Brown, Pauline. "Tooth, *Cwidder* and *Dogsbody*: An Introduction to the Books of Diana Wynne Jones." *Bookmark* [Edinburgh] 1 (May 1978): 34–43.

Cart, Michael. "A Light in the Darkness: Humor Returns to Children's Fantasy." *School Library Journal* 33 (Apr 1987): 48–49.

Croome, Lesley. "Meet Your Author, Diana Wynne Jones." *Puffin Post* (U.K.) 9, no. 2 (1975): 3–4.

Fifth Book of Junior Authors and Illustrators. Edited by Sally Holmes Holtze. New York: Wilson, 1983, pp. 166–167.

Gillespie, John T. *Juniorplots 4: A Book Talk Guide for Use with Readers Ages 12–16.* New Providence, NJ: Bowker, 1993, pp. 223–226.

Gillespie, John T., and Corinne J. Naden. *Juniorplots 3: A Book Talk Guide for Use with Readers Ages 12–16.* New York: Bowker, 1987, pp. 170–173.

Glastonbury, Marion. "Home-Grown Magic." *Times Educational Supplement* (Nov 23, 1984): 38.

Jones, Diana Wynne. "*Dogsbody*." *School Bookshop News* (U.K.) 11 (Autumn 1978): 18–20.

———. "Far Out Fantasy." *Books for Your Children* (U.K.) 16 (Autumn/Winter 1991): 4–5.

———. "The Heroic Ideal—A Personal Odyssey." *The Lion and the Unicorn* 13 (June 1989): 129–140.

———. "Why Don't You Write Real Books?" *Reading Time* (Australia) 37 (May 1993): 9–11.

———. "Why Don't You Write Real Books?" *Vector* (U.K.) 140 (Oct–Nov 1988): 14–16.

Kondratiev, Alexei. "Tales Newly Told." *Mythlore* 72 (Spring 1993): 34, 44.

Lafferty, Fiona. "An Interview with Diana Wynne Jones." *British Book News Children's Books* (Dec 1987): 2–5.

Mappin, Alf. "The Novels of Diana Wynne Jones." *Literature Base* (Australia) 3 (June 1992): 8–11.

Nicholls, Peter. "Children's Writer a Legend Among Adults." *The Age* (Australia) (Sept 30, 1992): 4.

The Oxford Companion to Children's Literature. Edited by Humphrey Carpenter and Mari Prichard. New York: Oxford Univ. Press, 1984, pp. 281–282.

Rahn, Suzanne. "The Espression of Religious and Political Concepts in Fantasy for Children." Ph.D. diss., University of Washington, 1986.

Searles, Baird, Beth Meacham, and Michael Franklin. *A Reader's Guide to Fantasy.* New York: Avon, 1982, pp. 82–84.

Spraggs, Gillian. "True Dreams: The Fantasy Fiction of Diana Wynne Jones." *Use of English* 34 (Summer 1983): 17–22.

Townsend, John Rowe. "Even Nice People Behave Like Wicked Stepmothers." *Guardian* (Apr 27, 1978): 15.

Twentieth-Century Children's Writers. 3rd ed. Edited by Tracy Chevalier and D. L. Kirkpatrick. Chicago: St. James, 1989, pp. 500–501.

Waterhouse, Ruth. "Time for a Ghostly Point of View." *Papers* (Australia) 2 (Dec 1991): 135–142.

———. "Which Way to Encode and Decode Fiction?" *Children's Literature Association Quarterly* 16 (Spring 1991): 2–6.

Yates, Jessica. "The Fantasy of Diana Wynne Jones." *Fantasiae* [Los Angeles] 6 (Sept 1978): 6–8.

———. "In Defense of Fantasy." *Mallorn* 21 (June 1984): 23–28.

Jones, Elizabeth Orton

Duff, Annis. "Our Miss Jones." *Horn Book* 21 (July 1945): 281–288.

Helbig, Alethea K., and Agnes Regan Perkins. *Dictionary of American Children's Fiction, 1859–1959.* Westport, CT: Greenwood, 1985, pp. 259, 539–540.

Jones, Elizabeth Orton. "The Caldecott Medal Acceptance." *Horn Book* 21 (July 1945): 289–294.

The Junior Book of Authors. 2nd ed. rev. Edited by Stanley J. Kunitz and Howard Haycraft. New York: Wilson, 1951, pp. 173–174.

Roginski, Jim, ed. *Newbery and Caldecott Medalists and Honor Book Winners.* Littleton, CO: Libraries Unlimited, 1982, p. 152.

Jones, McClure

Antczak, Janice. *Science Fiction: The Mythos of a New Romance.* New York: Neal-Schuman, 1985, pp. 96–97, 179–181.

Juster, Norton

Doyle, Brian. *The Who's Who of Children's Literature.* New York: Schocken, 1968, p. 160.

Fourth Book of Junior Authors and Illustrators. Edited by Doris De Montreville and Elizabeth D. Crawford. New York: Wilson, 1978, pp. 205–206.

Gillespie, John T., and Diana Lembo. *Juniorplots: A Book Talk Manual for Teachers and Librarians.* New York: Bowker, 1967, pp. 184–187.

Helbig, Alethea K., and Agnes Regan Perkins. *Dictionary of American Children's Fiction, 1960–1984.* Westport, CT: Greenwood, 1986, pp. 346, 511–512.

Moross, Barbara, Sonia Landes, and Molly Flender. "*The Phantom Tollbooth.*" Norwood, MA: Christopher-Gordon, 1989.

The Oxford Companion to Children's Literature. Edited by Humphrey Carpenter and Mari Prichard. New York: Oxford Univ. Press, 1984, p. 409.

Ragsdale, W. "Presentation of the Seventh Recognition of Merit to Norton Juster for *The Phantom Tollbooth.*" *Claremont Reading Conference Yearbook* 35 (1971): 37–40.

Swinfen, Ann. *In Defense of Fantasy.* London: Routledge, 1984, pp. 118–122.

Twentieth-Century Children's Writers. 3rd ed. Edited by Tracy Chevalier and D. L. Kirkpatrick. Chicago: St. James, 1989, pp. 503–504.

Karazin, Nikolai Nikolaevich

Whitney, Elinor. "*Cranes Flying South.*" *Horn Book* 7 (Aug 1931): 237–239.

Kästner, Erich

Doyle, Brian. *The Who's Who of Children's Literature.* New York: Schocken, 1968, pp. 160–161.

Kästner, Erich. "The Natural History of the Author of Children's Books." *Bookbird* 2 (1965): 3–8.

Mathiew, François. "Erich Kästner, un Classique Allemand." *La Revue des Livres Pour Enfants* (France) 150 (Spring 1993): 44–50.

Petri, Walther. "Mein Kästner." *Neue Deutsche Literatur* [Berlin] 37 (1989): 165–168.

Springman, L. "A 'Better Reality': The Enlightenment Legacy in Erich Kästner's Novels for Young People." *German Quarterly* 64 (Fall 1991): 518–530.

Third Book of Junior Authors. Edited by Doris De Montreville and Donna Hill. New York: Wilson, 1972, pp. 157–158.

Weiss, Gerhard H. "Erich Kästner." In *Writers for Children; Critical Studies of Major Authors Since the Seventeenth Century.* Edited by Jane M. Bingham. New York: Scribner, 1988, pp. 317–322.

Katz, Welwyn Wilton

Jenkinson, David H. "Portraits: Welwyn Wilton Katz, Author of Award-Winning Fantasy." *Emergency Librarian* 21 (Nov–Dec 1993): 61–65.

Katz, Welwyn Wilton. "My Own Story: Plain and Coloured." *Canadian Children's Literature* 54 (1989): 31–36.

Micros, Marianne. "When Is a Book Not a Book?: The Novels of Welwyn Wilton Katz" *Canadian Children's Literature* 47 (1987): 23–28.

Twentieth-Century Children's Writers. 3rd ed. Edited by Tracy Chevalier and D. L. Kirkpatrick. Chicago: St. James, 1989, pp. 507–508.

Vandemoer, Jamie. "Welwyn Wilton Katz." *Canadian Author and Bookman* 65 (Summer 1990): 14–16.

Kay, Guy Gavriel

Kincaid, Paul. "The Imperfect Hero: Guy Gavriel Kay." *Vector* 137 (1987): 7–10.

Randall, N. "Shifting Focalization and the Strategy of Delay: The Narrative Weaving of 'The Fionavar Tapestry.'" *Canadian Literature* 129 (Summer 1991): 40–53.

Twentieth-Century Science Fiction Writers. 3rd ed. Edited by Noelle Watson and Paul E. Schellinger. Chicago: St. James, 1991, pp. 427–428.

Kelleher, Victor (Michael Kitchener)

Kelleher, Victor. "Know the Author: Victor Kelleher in His Own Words." *Magpies* (Australia) 1, no. 4 (Sept 1986): 16–18.

———. "Preoccupations in Kelleher's Fantasies." *Magpies* (Australia) 35 (Sept 1988): 5–8; continued in 35 (Nov 1988): 5–8.

———. "Problems and Pleasures." *Reading Time* (Australia) 88 (July 1983): 14–16.

———. "Writing for Children in Australia Today." In *A Sea of Upturned Faces: Proceedings of the Third Pacific Rim Conference on Children's Literature.* Ed. by Winifred Ragsdale. Metuchen, NJ: Scarecrow Press, 1989, pp. 213–235.

Masson, Sophie. "Victor Kelleher—*Brother Night.*" *Reading Time* (Australia) 35, 1 (1991): 5–6.

Sorenson, Meg. "Kids Books (An Interview with Victor Kelleher)." *Australian Book Review* 127 (Dec 1990–Jan 1991): 45–47.

Twentieth-Century Children's Writers. 3rd ed. Edited by Tracy Chevalier and D. L. Kirkpatrick. Chicago: St. James, 1989, pp. 514–515.

Kemp, Gene (Rushton)

Cross, Gillian. "Children Are Real People: The Stories of Gene Kemp." *Children's Literature in Education* 10 (Autumn 1979): 131–140.

King, E. J. "Children's Writers: Gene Kemp." *School Librarian* 34 (Dec 1986): 309–313.

The Oxford Companion to Children's Literature. Edited by Humphrey Carpenter and Mari Prichard. New York: Oxford Univ. Press, 1984, pp. 289–290.

Twentieth-Century Children's Writers. 3rd ed. Edited by Tracy Chevalier and D. L. Kirkpatrick. Chicago: St. James, 1989, pp. 517–518.

Kendall, Carol (Seeger)

Coyle, William, ed. *Ohio Authors and Their Books.* Cleveland: World, 1962.

Helbig, Alethea K., and Agnes Regan Perkins. *Dictionary of American Children's Fiction, 1859–1959.* Westport, CT: Greenwood, 1985, pp. 173–174, 271.

————. *Dictionary of American Children's Fiction, 1960–1984; Recent Books of Recognized Merit.* Westport, CT: Greenwood, 1986, pp. 353, 715.

Kendall, Carol. "My International Journeys in Children's Literature." *Proceedings of the 13th Annual Conference of The Children's Literature Association, 1986.* New York: Pace University, 1988, pp. 20–22.

Roginski, Jim, ed. *Newbery and Caldecott Medalists and Honor Book Winners.* Littleton, CO: Libraries Unlimited, 1982, p. 159.

Russell, David L. "*The Gammage Cup* as Utopian Literature for Children." *Children's Literature in Education* 24 (Dec 1993): 241–250.

Searles, Baird, Beth Meacham, and Michael Franklin. *A Reader's Guide to Fantasy.* New York: Avon, 1982, p. 84.

Swinfen, Ann. *In Defense of Fantasy.* London: Routledge, 1984, pp. 78, 80, 83, 85, 89.

Third Book of Junior Authors. Edited by Doris De Montreville and Donna Hill. New York: Wilson, 1972, pp. 160–161.

Twentieth-Century Children's Writers. 3rd ed. Edited by Tracy Chevalier and D. L. Kirkpatrick. Chicago: St. James, 1989, pp. 518–519.

West, Richard C. "The Tolkinians." *Orcrist* 2 (1967): 4–15.

Keneally, Tom

Hughes, P. J. "Tom Keneally's Recollections of Childhood." *Orana* (Australia) 15 (Aug 1979): 95–97.

Ryan, J. S. "Thomas Keneally's Gentlest Fantasy, *Ned Kelly and the City of Bees.*" *Orana* (Australia) 15 (Aug 1979): 91–95.

Kennedy, (Jerome) Richard

Fifth Book of Junior Authors and Illustrators. Edited by Sally Holmes Holtze. New York: Wilson, 1983, pp. 170–171.

Helbig, Alethea, and Agnes Regan Perkins. *Dictionary of American Children's Fiction, 1985–1989.* Westport, CT: Greenwood, 1993, pp. 11–13, 20–22.

Lanes, Selma G. "Richard Kennedy Aims High [When Writing Children's Books]." *Publishers Weekly* 227 (Feb 22, 1985): 102–103.

Neumeyer, Peter F. *"Amy's Eyes* Examined." *The Lion and the Unicorn* 9 (1985): 58–69.
———. "Introducing Richard Kennedy." *Children's Literature in Education* 15 (Summer 1984): 85–92.
Twentieth-Century Children's Writers. 3rd ed. Edited by Tracy Chevalier and D. L. Kirkpatrick. Chicago: St. James, 1989, pp. 519–520.
Udal, John. "Richard Kennedy and *Pippi Longstocking." Junior Bookshelf* 42 (Apr 1978): 75–77.

Kennedy, X. J. (pseud. of Joseph Charles Kennedy)

Sixth Book of Junior Authors and Illustrators. Edited by Sally Holmes Holtze. New York: Wilson, 1989, pp. 155–156.
Twentieth-Century Children's Writers. 3rd ed. Edited by Tracy Chevalier and D. L. Kirkpatrick. Chicago: St. James, 1989, pp. 520–521.

Kerr, M. E. (also uses: Mary James) (pseud. of Marijane Meaker)

Fourth Book of Junior Authors and Illustrators. Edited by Doris De Montreville and Elizabeth D. Crawford. New York: Wilson, 1978, pp. 210–212.
Graham, Joyce L. "An Interview with M. E. Kerr." *Journal of Youth Services in Libraries* 7 (Fall 1993): 31–36.
Gray, B. Allison. "Her, Her, Her: An Interview With M. E. Kerr." *VOYA* 13 (Feb 1991): 337–342.
Kerr, M. E. "1993 Margaret A. Edwards Award Acceptance Speech." *Journal of Youth Services in Libraries* 7 (Fall 1993): 19–24.
Nilson, Alleen Pace. *Presenting M. E. Kerr.* Boston: Hall, 1986.
Sutton, Roger. "A Conversation with M. E. Kerr." *School Library Journal* 39 (June 1993): 24–29.
Twentieth-Century Children's Writers. 3rd ed. Edited by Tracy Chevalier and D. L. Kirkpatrick. Chicago: St. James, 1989, pp. 523–525.
Wente, E. M. "M. E. Kerr: A Young Adult Author Worthy of Acclaim." MSLS thesis, University of North Carolina at Chapel Hill, 1987.

Key, Alexander (Hill)

Helbig, Alethea K., and Agnes Regan Perkins. *Dictionary of American Children's Fiction, 1960–1984.* Westport, CT: Greenwood, 1986, pp. 220, 335–336.
Twentieth-Century Science Fiction Writers. 3rd ed. Edited by Noelle Watson and Paul E. Schellinger. Chicago: St. James Press, 1991, p. 434.

King, (David) Clive

Twentieth-Century Children's Writers. 3rd ed. Edited by Tracy Chevalier and D. L. Kirkpatrick. Chicago: St. James, 1989, pp. 525–527.

King, Stephen (Edwin)

Beahm, George, ed. *The Stephen King Companion.* Kansas City, MO: Andrews, 1989.
Bleiler, Richard. "Stephen King." In *Supernatural Fiction Writers: Fantasy and Horror,* vol. 2. Edited by E. F. Bleiler. New York: Scribner, 1985, pp. 1037–1044.

Bosky, Bernadette. "Stephen King and Peter Straub: Fear and Friendship." In *Discovering Stephen King.* Edited by Darrell Schweitzer. Mercer Island, WA: Starmont, 1985.

Collings, Michael R. *The Annotated Guide to Stephen King: A Primary and Secondary Bibliography of the Works of America's Premier Horror Writer.* Mercer Island, WA: Starmont, 1986.

————. *The Many Facets of Stephen King.* Mercer Island, WA: Starmont, 1985.

Indick, Ben P. "King as a Writer for Children." In *Kingdom of Fear: The World of Stephen King,* ed. by Tim Underwood and Chuck Miller. New York: NAL, 1986.

King, Stephen. "Dr. Seuss and the Two Faces of Fantasy." *Fantasy Review* 68 (1984): 10–12.

————. "Imagery and the Third Eye." *The Writer* 93 (Oct 1980): 11–14, 44.

Leiber, Fritz. "On Fantasy." *Fantasy Newsletter* 21 (1980): 3–4, 30.

"1990 Winner of the Colorado Blue Spruce Young Adult Award is Stephen King's *The Eye of the Dragon.*" *VOYA* 13 (June 1990): 86.

Platt, Charles. *Dream Makers.* New York: Ungar, 1987, pp. 261–272. Interview.

Smith, Karen Patricia. "A Delicate Balance: The Concept of Good and Evil in Stephen King's *The Eyes of the Dragon.*" *ALAN Review* 16 (1988): 48–50.

Strupp, Peter. "Interview with Stephen King." *Science Fiction Review* 56 (1985): 32.

Tymn, Marshall B. "Stephen King: A Bibliography." In *Discovering Stephen King.* Edited by Darrell Schweitzer. Mercer Island, WA: Starmont, 1985.

Winter, Douglas E. "Some Words with Stephen King." *Fantasy Newsletter* 56 (1983): 11–14.

————. *Stephen King: The Art of Darkness.* New York: Signet, 1986. Updated and expanded from the NAL, 1984 edition.

King-Smith, Dick

Arnold, A. "The Pig—Pet, Pork, or Sacrifice?" *Children's Literature in Education* 19 (Summer 1988): 80–85.

Barker, Keith. *Dick King-Smith.* Swinton (England): The School Library Association, 1991.

Campbell, Alasdair. "Children's Writers 12: Dick King-Smith." *School Librarian* 34, no. 2 (1986): 116–121.

Eccleshare, Julia. "Four Legs Good." *Times Educational Supplement* (Nov 15, 1985): 47.

"Meet a Puffin Person: Dick King-Smith." *Puffin Post* (U.K.) 6 (Summer 1985): 11–13.

Mappin, Alf. "Know the Author: Dick King-Smith." *Magpies* (Australia) 8 (July 1993): 19–21.

Nettell, Stephanie. "Happy Ever After." *Guardian* (Mar 22, 1984): 10.

Powling, Chris. "Authorgraph no. 45: Dick King-Smith." *Books for Keeps* (U.K.) 45 (1987): 12–13.

Sixth Book of Junior Authors and Illustrators. Edited by Sally Holmes Holtze. New York: Wilson, 1989, pp. 156–157.

Thomson, Pat. "Dick King-Smith: Champion of the Underdog." *British Book News Children's Books* (June 1987): 2–5.

Twentieth-Century Children's Writers. 3rd ed. Edited by Tracy Chevalier and D. L. Kirkpatrick. Chicago: St. James, 1989, pp. 527–528.

Kingsley, Charles

Alderson, Brian, ed. *Children's Books in England.* 3rd ed. New York: Cambridge Univ. Press, 1982, pp. 252–255.

Avery, Gillian. "Charles Kingsley." In *Writers for Children; Critical Studies of Major Authors Since the Seventeenth Century.* Edited by Jane M. Bingham. New York: Scribner, 1988, pp. 323–328.

Babbitt, Natalie. "Saying What You Think." *Quarterly Journal of the Library of Congress* 39 (Spring 1982): 80–89.

Baker, Richard; Connolly, John J.; and Zudeck, Ronald. "Notes on Chesterton's Notre Dame Lectures on Victorian Literature." *The Chesterton Review* 4 (1978): 115–143, 285–301.

Barry, James D. "Charles Kingsley." In George H. Ford. *Victorian Fiction: A Second Guide to Research.* Storrs, CT: Modern Language Association of America, 1978, pp. 219–222.

Buckley, Jerome Hamilton. "The Pattern of Conversion." In *The Victorian Temper: A Study in Literary Culture.* Cambridge, MA: Harvard Univ. Press, 1951, pp. 87–108.

Campbell, Robert A. "Charles Kingsley: A Bibliography of Secondary Studies." Pt. I and II. *Bulletin of Bibliographies* 33 (1976): 78–91, 104, 127–130.

Carpenter, Humphrey. "Parson Lot Takes a Cold Bath: Charles Kingsley and *The Water-Babies.*" In Carpenter. *Secret Gardens: A Study of the Golden Age of Children's Literature.* Boston: Houghton Mifflin, 1985, pp. 23–43.

Chitty, Susan. *The Beast and the Monk: A Life of Charles Kingsley.* London: Mason/Charter, 1975.

Coleman, Dorothy. "Rabelais and *The Water-Babies.*" *Modern Language Review* 66, no. 3 (July 1971): 511–521.

Colloms, Brenda. *Charles Kingsley.* Totowa, NJ: Barnes and Noble, 1975.

Cunningham, V. "Soiled Fairy: *The Water-Babies* in Its Time." *Essays in Criticism* 35 (Apr 1985): 121–148.

Doyle, Brian. *The Who's Who of Children's Literature.* New York: Schocken, 1968, pp. 161–163.

Fasick, Laura. "Women's Moral Role in Selected Victorian Religious Novels." Ph.D. diss., Indiana University, 1990.

Harris, Styron. *Charles Kingsley: A Reference Guide.* Boston: G. K. Hall, 1981.

Hawley, John C., S. J. "*The Water Babies* as Catechetical Paradigm." *Children's Literature Association Quarterly* 14 (Spring 1989): 19–21.

Hebblethwaite, Peter. "England Rinsed Clean: Sanitary and Evolutionary Themes in Charles Kinglsey." *Times Educational Supplement* 3237 (June 17, 1977): 22.

Hoagwood, Terence. "Kingsley's Young and Old." *Explicator* 46 (1988): 18–20.

Ison, Mary M. "Things Nobody Ever Heard of: Jessie Willcox Smith Draws *The Water-Babies.*" *Quarterly Journal of the Library of Congress* 39 (Spring 1982): 90–101.

Jackson, Rosemary. *Fantasy: The Literature of Subversion.* New York: Methuen, 1980.

Johnston, Arthur. "*The Water-Babies:* Kingsley's Debt to Darwin." *English* 12, 7 (Autumn 1959): 215–219.

Kingsley, Frances Eliza, ed. *Charles Kingsley: His Letters and Memoirs of His Life, Edited by His Wife.* 2 vols. London: King, 1877.

Leavis, Q. D. "*The Water-Babies.*" *Children's Literature in Education* 23 (Winter 1976): 155–163.

MacLeod, Helen. "Charles Kingsley and *The Water Babies.*" *Book and Magazine Collector* 23 (Jan 1986): 36–43.

Manlove, C(olin) N(icholas). *Modern Fantasy: Five Studies.* New York: Cambridge Univ. Press, 1975.

Martin, R. B. *The Dust of Combat: The Life & Work of Charles Kingsley.* London: Faber, 1959.

Michalson, Karen Ann. "Victorian Fantasy Literature and the Politics of Canon-Making." Ph.D. diss., University of Massachusetts, 1990. Discusses Ruskin, MacDonald, Kingsley, Haggard, and Kipling.

The Oxford Companion to Children's Literature. Edited by Humphrey Carpenter and Mari Prichard. New York: Oxford Univ. Press, 1984, pp. 294–295, 561–563.

Pfeiffer, John R. "*The Water-Babies.*" In *Survey of Modern Fantasy Literature,* vol. 5. Edited by Frank N. Magill. Englewood Cliffs, NJ: Salem Press, 1983, pp. 2074–2078.

Pflieger, Pat, and Helen M. Hill. *A Reference Guide to Modern Fantasy for Children.* Westport, CT: Greenwood, 1984, pp. xiv, xv, 285–287, 579–581.

Pope-Hennessy, Una. *Canon Charles Kingsley: A Biography.* London: Chatto, 1948.

Prickett, Stephen. "Religious Fantasy in the Nineteenth Century." In *Survey of Modern Fantasy Literature,* vol. 5. Edited by Frank N. Magill. Englewood Cliffs, NJ: Salem Press, 1983, pp. 2369–2382.

———. *Victorian Fantasy.* Bloomington: Indiana Univ. Press, 1979.

Rapple, Brendan. "Charles Kinglsey's *The Water Babies*: The Spiritual and Physical Cleansing Properties of Water." In *Where Rivers Meet: Confluence and Concurrents: Proceedings of the 1989 Conference of the Children's Literature Association,* ed. by Susan R. Gannon and Ruth A. Thompson. New York: Pace University, 1991, pp. 42–46.

Stolzenbach, Mary M. "*The Water-Babies:* An Appreciation." *Mythlore* 8, 28 (Summer 1981): 20.

Sullivan, C. W., III. "Fantasy." In *Story and Society: Children's Literature in Its Social Context,* ed. by Dennis Butts. London: Macmillan, 1992, pp. 97–111.

Susina, Jan Christopher. "Victorian Kunstmärcher: A Study in Children's Literature, 1840–1875." Ph.D. diss., Indiana University, 1986.

Tanner, Tony. "Mountains and Depths—An Approach to Nineteenth Century Dualism." *Review of English Literature* 3, no. 4 (Oct 1962): 51–61.

Twentieth Century Children's Writers. 2nd ed. Edited by D. L. Kirkpatrick. New York: St. Martin, 1983, pp. 875–876.

Uffelman, Larry K. "An Evolutionary Fantasy: *The Water-Babies.*" In *Charles Kingsley.* Boston: Twayne, 1979, pp. 67–81.

Kinsella, W(illiam) P(atrick)

Randall, N. "*Shoeless Joe:* Fantasy and the Humor of Fellow-Feeling." *Modern Fiction Studies* 33 (Spring 1987): 173–182.

Kipling, (Joseph) Rudyard

Achar, Radha. "The Child in Kipling's Fiction: An Analysis." *The Literary Criterion* 22 (1987): 46–53.

Alderson, Brian, ed. *Children's Books in England.* 3rd ed. New York: Cambridge Univ. Press, 1982, pp. 305–308.

———. "Just-So Pictures: Illustrated Versions of *The Just So Stories for Little Children.*" *Children's Literature* 20 (1992): 147–174.

Amis, Kingsley. *Rudyard Kipling and His World.* New York: Scribner, 1976.

Anderson, Celia Catlett. "Kipling's Mowgli and *Just So Stories:* The Vine of Fact and Fantasy." In *Touchstones.* Edited by Perry Nodelman. West Lafayette, IN: Children's Literature Association Publications, 1985, pp. 113–122.

———. "'O Best Beloved': Kipling's Reading Instructions in *The Just So Stories.*" In *Proceedings of the Ninth Annual Conference of the Children's Literature Association.* University of Florida, March 1982. Ypsilanti, MI: Children's Literature Association, 1983, pp. 33–39.

Annan, Noel. "Kipling's Place in the History of Ideas." *Victorian Studies* 3, no. 4 (June 1960): 323–348. Reprinted in Andrew Rutherford. *Kipling's Mind and Art: Selected Critical Essays.* Stanford, CA: Stanford Univ. Press, 1964.

Arata, Stephen E. "A Universal Foreignness: Kipling in the Fin-de-Siecle." *English Literature in Transition* 36 (1993): 7–38.

Birkenhead, Lord. *Rudyard Kipling.* New York: Random, 1978.

Birkenhead, Sheila. "The Kipling Mystery." *New Statesman* (May 4, 1979): 627–638.

Bivona, Daniel Edward. "Desire and Contradiction: A Nineteenth Century Imperial Mythos and Its Critics." Ph.D. diss., Brown University, 1987.

Blackburn, William. "Rudyard Kipling." In *Writers for Children; Critical Studies of Major Authors Since the Seventeenth Century.* Edited by Jane M. Bingham. New York: Scribner, 1988, pp. 329–336.

Bloom, Harold, ed. *Rudyard Kipling.* New York: Chelsea, 1987. (critical essays)

Blount, Margaret. "The Tables Turned at the Zoo: Mowgli and Stuart Little." In *Animal Land: The Creatures of Children's Fiction.* New York: Morrow, 1975, pp. 226–244.

Born, Daniel Keith. "The Late Victorian and Edwardian Novel and the Birth of Liberal Guilt." Ph.D. diss., City University of New York, 1990.

Bratton, Jacqueline S. "Kipling's Magic Art." In *Critical Essays on Rudyard Kipling,* ed. by Harold Orel. Boston: Hall, 1989, pp. 45–65.

Carrington, Charles. "The Kipling 'Mystery.'" *New Statesman* (Mar 2, 1979): 298–299.

———. *Rudyard Kipling: His Life and Work.* 3rd rev. ed. London: Macmillan, 1978. Originally published 1955.

Carroll, S. W. "Victorian Boys' Adventure Writers: George Henty, Robert Lewis Stevenson, and Rudyard Kipling." MSLS thesis, University of North Carolina at Chapel Hill, 1990.

Cell, Howard R. "The Socratic Pilgrimage of *The Elephant's Child.*" *Children's Literature* 20 (1992): 132–146.

Chambers, Aidan. "Letter from England: *Just So.*" *Horn Book* 58 (Dec 1982): 565–570.

Colvin, I. D. "This Bore Fruit Afterwards: Kipling's Childhood Reading." *National Review* 110 (Feb 1938): 215–221.

Crook, Nora. *Kipling's Myths of Love and Death.* New York: St. Martin, 1989.

Cushing, David. "Kipling and 'The White Seal.'" *Arlington Quarterly* 3, no. 1 (1970–1971): 171–182.

Dalby, Richard. "Rudyard Kipling's Novels and Stories." *Book and Magazine Collector* 23 (Jan 1986): 4–12.

Davie, Donald. "A Puritan's Empire: The Case of Kipling." *Sewanee Review* 87 (1979): 34–48.

Doyle, Brian. *The Who's Who of Children's Literature.* New York: Schocken, 1968, pp. 164–166.

Fido, Martin. *Rudyard Kipling: An Illustrated Biography.* New York: Peter Bedrick, 1986.

Flynn, Richard. "Kipling and Scouting, or 'Akela, We'll Do Our Best.'" *Children's Literature Association Quarterly* 16 (Summer 1991): 55–58.

Frey, Charles, and John Griffiths. *The Literary Heritage of Childhood: An Appraisal of Children's Classics in the Western Tradition.* Westport, CT: Greenwood, 1987, pp. 189–200.

Gerould, Katherine Fullerton. "The Remarkable Rightness of Rudyard Kipling." *Atlantic Monthly* 123 (Jan 1919): 12–21.

Gilbert, Elliot L. "Three Criticisms of *The Jungle Books.*" *Kipling Journal* 33 (Dec 1966): 6–10.

Goldthwaite, John. "The Black Rabbit: Part One." *Signal* 47 (May 1985): 86–111. "Part Two." *Signal* 48 (Sept 1985): 148–167. Reprinted in Goldthwaite. *The Natural History of Make-Believe.* London: Oxford Univ. Press, 1987.

Gose, Elliott. *Mere Creatures: A Study of Modern Fantasy Tales for Children.* Toronto: Univ. of Toronto Press, 1988, pp. 17–28, 63–82.

Green, Roger Lancelyn. *Kipling and the Children.* London: Elek Books, 1965.

———. "Rudyard Kipling." *Junior Bookshelf* 20 (Dec 1956): 312–319.

———, ed. *Kipling: The Critical Heritage.* Totowa, NJ: Barnes and Noble, 1971.

Haines, Helen E. "The Wisdom of Baloo: Kipling and Childhood." *Horn Book* 12 (May–June 1936): 135–143.

Hardyment, Christina. "The Literary Landscape: 4. *Puck of Pook's* Sussex." (London) *Daily Telegraph Magazine* (July 7, 1990): 48–53.

Harrison, James. "Kipling's Jungle Eden." *Mosaic* 7 (Winter 1974): 151–164. Reprinted in *Critical Essays on Rudyard Kipling,* ed. by Harold Orel. Boston: Hall, 1989, pp. 77–92.

———. *Rudyard Kipling.* Boston: Twayne, 1982.

Havholm, Peter. "Kipling and Fantasy." *Children's Literature* 4 (1975): 91–104. Reprinted in *Critical Essays on Rudyard Kipling,* ed. by Harold Orel. Boston: Hall, 1989, pp. 92–105.

Hedges, Ned Samuel. "The Fable and the Fabulous: The Use of Traditional Forms in Children's Literature." Ph.D. diss., University of Nebraska, 1968.

Herman, Gertrude B. "A Picture is Worth Several Hundred Words." *Horn Book* 64 (July–Aug 1988): 518–521. Discusses *The Just So Stories.*

Higgens, Regina. *Magic Kingdoms: Discovering the Joys of Childhood Classics with Your Child.* New York, Simon & Schuster, 1992.

Hinchcliffe, Peter. "Coming to Terms with Kipling: *Puck of Pook's Hill, Rewards and Fairies,* and the Shape of Kipling's Imagination." *University of Toronto Quarterly* 45 (1975): 75–90. Reprinted in *Critical Essays on Rudyard Kipling,* ed. by Harold Orel. Boston: Hall, 1989, pp. 153–168.

Hindle, Alan. "Rudyard Kipling's *Rewards and Fairies.*" *School Librarian* 21 (Dec 1973): 295–300.

Holt, Marilyn J. "Rudyard Kipling." In *Supernatural Fiction Writers: Fantasy and Horror,* vol. 1. Edited by E. F. Bleiler. New York: Scribner, 1985, pp. 437–442.

Inglis, Fred. *The Promise of Happiness.* New York: Cambridge Univ. Press, 1981, pp. 156–162.

Islam, Shamsul. "Psychological Allegory in *The Jungle Books.*" *Kipling Journal* 40 (Mar 1973): 9–12.

Jarrett-Kerr, M. "The Theology of Rudyard Kipling." *Kipling Journal* 43 (Sept 1976): 4–8.

Kamen, Gloria. *Kipling: Storyteller of East and West.* New York: Atheneum, 1985.

Kemp, Sandra. *Kipling's Hidden Narratives.* Oxford: Blackwell, 1988.

Kilworth, Garry. "On Animal Fantasy." *Million* (U.K.) 11 (1992): 11–15.

The Kipling Journal. Kipling Society, 1927– .

Kipling, Rudyard. "Author's Notes on the Names in *The Jungle Books.*" In *The Burwash Edition of the Complete Works in Prose and Verse of Rudyard Kipling.* Garden City, NY: Doubleday, 1941, pp. 427–433.

———. *Something of Myself and Other Autobiographical Writings,* ed. by Thomas Pinney. Cambridge: Cambridge Univ. Press, 1990.

———. *Something of Myself for My Friends Known and Unknown.* Garden City, NY: Doubleday, 1937.

Knoepflmacher, U. C. "Female Power and Male Self-Assertion: Kipling and the Maternal." *Children's Literature* 20 (1992): 15–35.

Laski, Marghanita. *From Palm to Pine: Rudyard Kipling Abroad and at Home.* New York: Facts on File, 1987.

Lerner, Fred. "Master of Our Art. *VOYA* 16 (Oct 1993): 211–213.

Lesser, Margaret. "Kipling and His Publishers." *Horn Book* 12 (Mar 1936): 128–129.

Lewis, C. S. "Kipling's World." In *They Asked for a Paper.* London: Bles, 1962.

Lochhead, Marion. *Renaissance of Wonder.* New York: Harper, 1980, pp. 70–76.

Lukens, Rebecca. "Kipling's Humor—In All Its Promiscuous Parts." *Studies in American Humor* 5 (Winter 1986–1987): 256–266.

McBratney, John. "Imperial Subjects, Imperial Space in Kipling's *Jungle Book.*" *Victorian Studies* 35 (Spring 1992): 277–293.

McCutchan, Corinne. "Puck and Company: Reading *Puck of Pook's Hill* and *Rewards and Fairies* as a Romance." *Children's Literature* 20 (1992): 69–89.

McMaster, Juliet. "The Trinity Archetype in *The Jungle Books* and *The Wizard of Oz.*" *Children's Literature* 20 (1992): 90–110.

Mallet, Phillip, ed. *Kipling Considered.* New York: St. Martin, 1989.

Mason, Philip. *Kipling: The Glass, the Shadow and the Fire.* New York: Harper, 1975.

Michalson, Karen Ann. "Victorian Fantasy Literature and the Politics of Canon-Making." Ph.D. diss., University of Massachusetts, 1990. Discusses Ruskin, MacDonald, Kingsley, Haggard, and Kipling.

Moss, Robert R. "Adolescence in Kipling." Ph.D. diss., Columbia University, 1973. Published as: *Rudyard Kipling and the Fiction of Adolescence.* New York: St. Martin, 1982.

Murray, John. "The Law of *The Jungle Books.*" *Children's Literature* 20 (1992): 1–14.

Musgrave, P. W. "Kipling's View of Educating Children." *Australian Journal of Education* 25 (Nov 1981): 211–223.

———. ed. *Critical Essays on Rudyard Kipling.* Boston: Hall, 1989.

Orel, Harold. "Hardy, Kipling, and Haggard." *English Literature in Transition* 25 (1982): 232–248.

———. "Kipling and Children's Literature." *English Literature in Transition* 36 (1993): 199–204.

———, ed. *Kipling: Interviews and Recollections.* 2 vols. Totowa, NJ: Barnes and Noble, 1983.

The Oxford Companion to Children's Literature. Edited by Humphrey Carpenter and Mari Prichard. New York: Oxford Univ. Press, 1984, pp. 282–285, 296–297, 428–429, 449.

Pafford, Mark. *Kipling's Indian Fiction.* New York: St. Martin, 1989.

Petzold, Dieter. "Fantasy Out of Myth and Fable: Animal Stories in Rudyard Kipling and Richard Adams." *Children's Literature Association Quarterly* 12 (Spring 1987): 15–19.

Pflieger, Pat, and Helen M. Hill. *A Reference Guide to Modern Fantasy for Children.* Westport, CT: Greenwood, 1984, pp. xv, xvi, 275–278, 287–291.

Prickett, Stephen. *Victorian Fantasy.* Bloomington: Indiana Univ. Press, 1979.

Reid, D. M. "Rudyard Kipling." *Ontario Library Review* 45 (Aug 1961): 157–158.

Rivet, A. L. F. "Rudyard Kipling's Roman Britain." *Kipling Journal* 45 (June 1978): 5–15.

Rogers, T. "Rudyard Kipling." *School Librarian* 10 (Dec 1961): 503–506ff.

"Rudyard Kipling: An Annotated Bibliography of Writings about Him." *English Fiction in Transition* 3–5 (1960): 1–74, 75–148, 149–235.

Rutherford, Andrew. "Officers and Gentlemen." In Andrew Rutherford. *Kipling's Mind and Art: Selected Critical Essays.* Stanford, CA: Stanford Univ. Press, 1964.

Sale, Roger. *Fairy Tales and After: From Snow White to E. B. White.* Cambridge, MA: Harvard Univ. Press, 1978. "Kipling's Boys," pp. 195–222.

Scott, Carole. "Limits of Otherworlds: Rules of the Game in *Alice's Adventures in Wonderland* and *The Jungle Books.*" In *Work and Play in Children's Literature: Selected Papers from the 1990 International Conference of the Children's Literature Association,* ed. by Susan R. Gannon and Ruth Anne Thompson. New York: Pace University, 1992, pp. 20–24.

Scott-Giles, C. W. "Historical Background of Some *Puck* Stories." *Kipling Journal* 28 (June 1961): 15–21.

Searles, Baird, Beth Meacham, and Michael Franklin. *A Reader's Guide to Fantasy.* New York: Avon, 1982, pp. 85–86.

Seymour-Smith, Martin. *Rudyard Kipling: A Biography.* London: Macdonald, 1988; New York: St. Martin,1989.

Shippey, T. A. "*The Jungle Books.*" In *Survey of Modern Fantasy Literature,* vol. 2. Edited by Frank N. Magill. Englewood Cliffs, NJ: Salem Press, 1983, pp. 822–826.

———. "The Short Fiction of Kipling." In *Survey of Modern Fantasy Literature,* vol. 4. Edited by Frank N. Magill. Englewood Cliffs, NJ: Salem Press, 1983, pp. 1586–1588.

"Special Issue on Rudyard Kipling." *Children's Literature, Volume 20.* New Haven: Yale Univ. Press, 1992.

Steward, J. I. M. *Rudyard Kipling.* New York: Dodd, 1966.

Stott, Jon C. *Children's Literature from A to Z.* New York: McGraw-Hill, 1984, p. 156.

Sutcliff, Rosemary. *Rudyard Kipling.* New York: Walck, 1961. Reprinted in Hugh Shelley,

Rosemary Sutcliff, and Leonard Clark. *Arthur Ransome, Rudyard Kipling and Walter de la Mare.* London: Bodley Head, 1968.

Tompkins, Joyce M. S. *The Art of Rudyard Kipling.* 2nd ed. London: Methuen, 1965, pp. 55–64.

———. "Kipling and Nordic Myth and Saga." *English Studies* 52 (Apr 1971): 147–157.

———. "Report on Discussion Meeting—12th April, 1967." *Kipling Journal* 34 (Sept 1967): 11–17.

Tucker, Nicholas. "When the Kipling Had to Stop." *Books for Keeps* (U.K.) 44 (1987): 24–25.

Twentieth-Century Children's Writers. 3rd ed. Edited by Tracy Chevalier and D. L. Kirkpatrick. Chicago: St. James, 1989, pp. 529–533.

Twentieth-Century Science Fiction Writers. 3rd ed. Edited by Noelle Watson and Paul E. Schellinger. Chicago: St. James Press, 1991, pp. 441–445.

Wendelmoot, Thomas Leroy. "Masonic Allusions and Themes in the Works of Rudyard Kipling." Ph.D. diss., University of Southern Florida, 1980.

Wilson, Angus. *The Strange Ride of Rudyard Kipling.* New York: Viking Press, 1978, pp. 122–133.

Wright, H. "Shadows on the Down: Some Influences of Rudyard Kipling on Rosemary Sutcliff." *Children's Literature in Education* 12 (Summer 1981): 90–102.

Klaveness, Jan O'Donnell

Helbig, Alethea K., and Agnes Regan Perkins. *Dictionary of American Children's Fiction, 1960–1984.* Westport, CT: Greenwood, 1986, pp. 258–259, 362.

Konigsburg, E(laine) L(obl)

Callaghan, L. W. "Consistent Focus and Recurring Elements in Books for the Young by Konigsburg, O'Dell, Singer, and Snyder." Master's thesis, University of Chicago, 1979.

Cart, Michael. "A Light in the Darkness: Humor Returns to Children's Fantasy." *School Library Journal* 33 (Apr 1987): 48–49.

Hanks, Dorrel Thomas. *E. L. Konigsburg.* Boston: Twayne, 1992.

Helbig, Alethea, and Agnes Regan Perkins. *Dictionary of American Children's Fiction, 1985–1989.* Westport, CT: Greenwood, 1993, pp. 135, 265–266.

———. *Dictionary of American Children's Fiction, 1960–1984.* Westport, CT: Greenwood, 1986, p. 364.

Hopkins, Lee Bennett. *More Books by More People.* New York: Citation Press, 1974, pp. 234–238.

Jones, L. T. "Profile: Elaine Konigsburg." *Language Arts* 63 (Feb 1986): 177–184. Interview.

Konigsburg, E. L. "Between a Peach and the Universe." In *Innocence & Experience.* Edited by Barbara Harrison and Gregory Maguire. New York: Lothrop, 1987, pp. 464–476.

———. "Book Remembered." *CBC Features* 39, no. 3 (Oct 1984–July 1985): 1.

———. "The Double Image: Language as the Perimeter of Culture." *School Library Journal* 16 (Feb 1970): 31–34. Reprinted in *Issues in Children's Book Selection.* Edited by Lillian Gerhardt. New York: Bowker, 1977, pp. 24–30.

———. "Elaine L. Konigsburg." *Horn Book* 44 (Aug 1968): 396–398.

———. "Newbery Award Acceptance." *Horn Book* 44 (Aug 1968): 391–395.

———. "Of Ariel, Caliban, and Certain Beasts of Mine Own." *Proceedings of the Seventh Annual Conference of the Children's Literature Association,* 1980. Ypsilanti, MI: Children's Literature Association, 1981, pp. 1–16.

————. "Ruthie Brittain and Because I Can." In Betsy Hearne. *Celebrating Children's Books.* New York: Lothrop, 1981, pp. 62–72.

————. "Sprezzatura: A Kind of Excellence." *Horn Book* 52 (June 1976): 253–261.

————. "The Winner of the Newbery Medal for 1968, Says. . . ." *Instructor* 78 (Apr 1969): 67ff.

Nodelman, Perry. "E. L. Konigsburg." In *American Writers for Children since 1960: Fiction. Dictionary of Literary Biography,* vol. 52. Detroit: Gale, 1986, pp. 214–227.

The Oxford Companion to Children's Literature. Edited by Humphrey Carpenter and Mari Prichard. New York: Oxford Univ. Press, 1984, p. 298.

Rees, David. "Your Arcane Novelist—E. L. Konigsburg: An English Viewpoint." *Horn Book* 54 (Feb 1978): 79–85. Reprinted in *Marble in the Water.* Boston: Horn Book, 1980, pp. 14–24.

Third Book of Junior Authors. Edited by Doris De Montreville and Donna Hill. New York: Wilson, 1972, pp. 164–165.

Townsend, John Rowe. *A Sounding of Storytellers.* New York: Lippincott, 1979, pp. 111–124.

Twentieth-Century Children's Writers. 3rd ed. Edited by Tracy Chevalier and D. L. Kirkpatrick. Chicago: St. James, 1989, pp. 541–542.

Kotzwinkle, William

"1977 World Fantasy Award Winners." *Locus* 10 (Nov 1977): 1.

Twentieth-Century Science Fiction Writers. 3rd ed. Edited by Noelle Watson and Paul E. Schellinger. Chicago: St. James Press, 1991, pp. 454–455.

Krensky, Stephen (Alan)

Sixth Book of Junior Authors and Illustrators. Edited by Sally Holmes Holtze. New York: Wilson, 1989, pp. 159–160.

Krüss, James (Jacob Hinrich)

Third Book of Junior Authors. Edited by Doris De Montreville and Donna Hill. New York: Wilson, 1972, pp. 166–167.

Kurtz, Katherine

Elliot, Jeffrey M. *Fantasy Voices: Interviews with American Fantasy Writers.* San Bernardino, CA: Borgo Press, 1982.

————. "Interview: Katherine Kurtz: Tapestries of Medieval Wonder." *Fantasy Newsletter* 24 (1980): 16–21. "Part Two." *Fantasy Newsletter* 25 (1980): 12–17, 31.

Fry, Carol L. "'What God Doth the Wizard Pray To': Neo-Pagan Witchcraft and Fantasy Fiction." *Extrapolation* 31 (Winter 1990): 333–346.

An Hour with Katherine Kurtz: An Introduction to the Author and Her Work. Garden Grove, NY: Hourglass Productions, 1979. (audiocassette)

"Katherine Kurtz: To the Manor Bound." *Locus* 302 (1986): 26, 32.

Kurtz, Katherine. "The Historian as a Myth-Maker and Vice Versa." *Bulletin of the Science Fiction Writers of America* 13 (1978): 16–18.

Kurtz, Katherine, and Jeffrey M. Elliot. "Interview Essay." In *Fantasists on Fantasy.* Edited by Robert H. Boyer and Kenneth J. Zahorski. New York: Avon, 1984, pp. 235–260.

Searles, Baird, Beth Meacham, and Michael Franklin. *A Reader's Guide to Fantasy.* New York: Avon, 1982, pp. 87–88.

Spivack, Charlotte. *Merlin's Daughters: Contemporary Women Writers of Fantasy.* New York: Greenwood, 1987.
Stableford, Brian. "The Deryni Trilogy." In *Survey of Modern Fantasy Literature,* vol. 1. Edited by Frank N. Magill. Englewood Cliffs, NJ: Salem Press, 1983, pp. 360–365.
Twentieth-Century Science Fiction Writers. 3rd ed. Edited by Noelle Watson and Paul E. Schellinger. Chicago: St. James, 1991, pp. 458–459.

Kushner, Donn

Jenkinson, D. H. "Portraits: Donn Kushner; Ghosts and Dragons." *Emergency Librarian* 17 (Nov–Dec 1989): 67–72.

Kuttner, Henry

Blish, James. "Moskowitz on Kuttner." *Riverside Quarterly* 5 (Feb 1972): 140–143.
Bradbury, Ray. "Kuttner Recalled." *Etchings and Odysseys* 4 (1984): 7.
Moskowitz, Sam. *Seekers of Tomorrow.* New York: Ballantine, 1967, pp. 319–334.
Myers, Walter E. "The Short Fiction of Henry Kuttner. In *Survey of Modern Fantasy Literature,* vol. 4. Edited by Frank N. Magill. Englewood Cliffs, NJ: Salem Press, 1983, pp. 1592–1596.
"Recollections of Henry Kuttner by His Friends." *Etchings and Odysseys* 4 (1984): 9–11, 38.
Twentieth-Century Science Fiction Writers. 3rd ed. Edited by Noelle Watson and Paul E. Schellinger. Chicago: St. James Press, 1991, pp. 459–461.

Lackey, Mercedes

Taylor, Rebecca, Gayle Keresey, and Margaret Miles. "Interview with Mercedes Lackey." *VOYA* 15 (Oct 1992): 213–217.

Lagerlöf, Selma (Ottiliana Lovisa)

Afzelius, Nils. "The Scandalous Selma Lagerlöf." *Scandinavica* 5, no. 2 (Nov 1966): 91–99.
Althen, Torbjörn. "Nils Holgersson, den Förargelseväckände [*The Wonderful Adventures of Nils* —The Annoying Book]." *Barn och Kultur* (Sweden) 31, no. 5 (1985): 100–103.
———. "Nils Holgersson och Folkhemmet [*The Wonderful Adventures of Nils* and 'The People's Home']." *Svensklärarföreningens Arsskrift* (Sweden) (1983): 16–37.
Berendsohn, Walter A. *Selma Lagerlöf: Her Life and Work.* Translated and adapted by George F. Timpson. Preface by V. Sackville-West. Port Washington, NY: Kennikat Press, 1968. Reprinted from 1931 edition.
Doyle, Brian. *The Who's Who of Children's Literature.* New York: Schocken, 1968, pp. 170–171.
Edstrom, Vivi. *Selma Lagerlöf.* Translated by Barbara Lide. Boston: Twayne, 1984.
———. "Selma Lagerlöf och Barnet [Selma Lagerlöf and the Child]." *Barn och Kultur* (Sweden) 27 (1981): 104–107.
Grigor'eva, L. "Kak Nils i Dikie Gusi Zagovorili Po-Russki [How Nils and the Wild Geese Started to Speak Russian]." *Detskaya Literatura* (Moscow) 11 (Nov 1983): 33–36.
Heian, Bente. "Skolebok og Diktverk. En Analyses av Pedagogiske mal og Litteraere Virkemidler i Selma Lagerloffs *Nils Holgerssons Underbara Resa Genom Sverige.*" *Edda* (Norway) 88 (1988): 213–226.
Lagerlöf, Selma. "The Christmas Gift Book: A Childhood Memory." *Horn Book* 35 (Dec 1959): 459–464.

————. *Mårbacka.* Translated by Velma Swanston Howard. Garden City, NY: Doubleday, 1925; continued in *Memories of My Childhood: Further Years at Mårbacka.* Garden City, NY: Doubleday, 1934.

Lagerroth, Erland. "Selma Lagerlöf Research, 1900–1964: A Survey and an Orientation." *Scandinavian Studies* 37, no. 1 (Feb 1965): 1–30.

Larsen, Hanna Astrup. *Selma Lagerlöf.* Garden City, NY: Doubleday, 1936.

Lindquist, Jennie D. "Selma Lagerlöf." *Horn Book* 20 (Mar 1944): 115–122.

Maule, Harry E. *Selma Lagerlöf: The Woman, Her Work, Her Message.* 2nd ed. Garden City, NY: Doubleday, 1924.

Miller, Bertha Mahony. "Editorial: Arthur Rackham and Selma Lagerlöf." *Horn Book* 16 (May 1940): 145.

Norberg, Susanne, and Birgit Peters. "Nils Holgerssons Underbara Resa Genom Sverige: En Bok for Dagens Tonåringar? [*The Wonderful Adventures of Nils*: A Book for Today's Teenagers?]." *Svensklaren* (Sweden) 29, no. 1 (1985): 17–23, 31.

The Oxford Companion to Children's Literature. Edited by Humphrey Carpenter and Mari Prichard. New York: Oxford Univ. Press, 1984, pp. 300, 578.

Peters, Birgit. "Nils Holgersson i Tunnelbanen [Nils Holgersson in the Underground]." *Barn Och Kultur* (Sweden) 31, no. 3 (1985): 58–60.

Rahn, Susan. "Rediscovering *Nils.*" *The Lion and the Unicorn* 10 (1986): 158–164.

St. Andrews, Bonnie. *Forbidden Fruit: On the Relationship between Women and Knowledge in Doris Lessing, Selma Lagerlöf, Kate Chopin, Margaret Atwood.* Troy, NY: Whitston, 1986.

Sale, Roger. *Fairy Tales and After.* Cambridge, MA: Harvard Univ. Press, 1978, pp. 90–97.

Lamorisse, Albert (Emmanuel)

Fourth Book of Junior Authors and Illustrators. Edited by Doris De Montreville and Elizabeth D. Crawford. New York: Wilson, 1978, pp. 217–218.

La Motte Fouqué, Baron Friedrich de

Doyle, Brian. *The Who's Who of Children's Literature.* New York: Schocken, 1968, pp. 102–103.

Hoppe, Manfred K. E. "Baron Friedrich de La Motte Fouqué." In *Supernatural Fiction Writers: Fantasy and Horror,* vol. 1. Edited by E. F. Bleiler. New York: Scribner, 1985, pp. 77–106.

The Oxford Companion to Children's Literature. Edited by Humphrey Carpenter and Mari Prichard. New York: Oxford Univ. Press, 1984, pp. 301, 551–552.

Stableford, Brian. "*Undine.*" In *Survey of Modern Fantasy Literature,* vol. 4. Edited by Frank N. Magill. Englewood Cliffs, NJ: Salem Press, pp. 1992–1994.

Lamplugh, Lois

Twentieth-Century Children's Writers. 3rd ed. Edited by Tracy Chevalier and D. L. Kirkpatrick. New York: St. Martin, 1989, pp. 551–552.

Lampman, Evelyn Sibley

Gillespie, John T., and Diana Lembo. *Introducing Books: A Guide for the Middle Grades.* New York: Bowker, 1970, pp. 218–220.

Helbig, Alethea K., and Agnes Regan Perkins. *Dictionary of American Children's Fiction, 1960–1984.* Westport, CT: Greenwood, 1986, pp. 367–368.

More Junior Authors. Edited by Muriel Fuller. New York: Wilson, 1963, p. 131.

Twentieth Century Children's Writers. 2nd ed. Edited by D. L. Kirkpatrick. New York: St. Martin, 1983, pp. 452–453.

Lang, Andrew

Anon. "A Checklist of the Works of Andrew Lang." *Indiana University Bookman* 7 (Apr 1965): 91–101.

———. "Descriptions from the Darlington Collection of Andrew Lang." *Indiana University Bookman* 7 (Apr 1965): 73–90.

Burns, Marjorie Jean. "Victorian Fantasists from Ruskin to Lang: A Study in Ambivalence." Ph.D. diss., University of California, Berkeley, 1978.

Doyle, Brian. *The Who's Who of Children's Literature.* New York: Schocken, 1968, pp. 172–174.

Green, Roger Lancelyn. *Andrew Lang.* New York: Walck, 1962.

———. *Andrew Lang: A Critical Biography with a Short-Title Bibliography of the Works of Andrew Lang.* Leicester: Ward, 1946.

———. "Andrew Lang and the Fairy Tale." *Review of English Studies* 20 (July 1944): 227–231.

———. "Andrew Lang in Fairyland." *Junior Bookshelf* 26 (Oct 1962): 171–180. Reprinted in Egoff. *Only Connect.* New York: Oxford Univ. Press, 1969, pp. 270–278.

———. "Andrew Lang—'The Greatest Bookman of His Age.'" *Indiana University Bookman* 7 (Apr 1965): 10–72.

———. "C. S. Lewis and Andrew Lang." *Notes and Queries* 22 (May 1975): 208–209.

Indiana University Bookman. Andrew Lang issue. 7 (Apr 1965): 10–101.

Lang, Andrew. *Adventures Among Books.* London: Longman, 1905, pp. 3–38.

———. "Modern Fairy Tales." In *A Peculiar Gift,* by Lance Salway. Harmondsworth, Middlesex: Kestrel, 1976, pp. 133–136.

Levitt, Andrew. "Andrew Lang." In *Writers for Children; Critical Studies of Major Authors Since the Seventeenth Century.* Edited by Jane M. Bingham. New York: Scribner, 1988, pp. 337–344.

Montenyohl, Eric Lawrence. "Andrew Lang and the Fairy Tale." Ph.D. diss., Indiana University, 1986.

Moss, Anita. "Crime and Punishment—Or Development—In Fairy Tales and Fantasy." *Mythlore* 8 (Spring 1981): 26–28, 42.

The Oxford Companion to Children's Literature. Edited by Humphrey Carpenter and Mari Prichard. New York: Oxford Univ. Pres, 1984, pp. 302–303, 425–426.

Repplier, Agnes. "Andrew Lang." *Catholic World* 96 (Dec 1912): 289–297.

Stott, Jon C. *Children's Literature from A to Z.* New York: McGraw-Hill, 1984, p. 161.

Twentieth Century Children's Writers. 2nd ed. Edited by D. L. Kirkpatrick. New York: St. Martin, 1983, p. 876.

Langton, Jane (Gillson)

Fifth Book of Junior Authors and Illustrators. Edited by Sally Holmes Holtze. New York: Wilson, 1983, pp. 188–190.

Helbig, Alethea K., and Agnes Regan Perkins. *Dictionary of American Children's Fiction, 1960–1984.* Westport, CT: Greenwood, 1986, pp. 155–156, 215–216, 369.

Langton, Jane. "Down to the Quick: The Use of Reality in Writing Fiction." *Horn Book* 49 (Feb 1973): 24–30.

———. "A Hair's Breadth Aside." In *Innocence & Experience.* Edited by Barbara Harrison and Gregory Maguire. New York: Lothrop, 1987, pp. 167–169.

————. "The Weak Place in the Cloth: A Study of Fantasy for Children." *Horn Book* 49 (Oct 1973): 433–441, and 49 (Dec 1973): 570–578. Reprinted in Paul Heins. *Crosscurrents of Criticism*. Boston: Horn Book, 1977, pp. 185–196; and in Boyer and Zahorski. *Fantasists on Fantasy*. New York: Avon, 1984, pp. 163–180.

Rees, David. "Real and Transcendental—Jane Langton." In *Painted Desert, Green Shade*. Boston: Horn Book, 1984, pp. 75–88.

Twentieth-Century Children's Writers. 3rd ed. Edited by Tracy Chevalier and D. L. Kirkpatrick. Chicago: St. James, 1989, pp. 523–554.

Lanier, Sterling E(dmund)

Schweitzer, Darrell. "Interview: Sterling E. Lanier." *Thrust* 24 (1986); 17–19.

Twentieth-Century Science Fiction Writers. 3rd ed. Edited by Noelle Watson and Paul E. Schellinger. Chicago: St. James Press, 1991, pp. 466–467.

Lasky (Knight), Kathryn

Sixth Book of Junior Authors and Illustrators. Edited by Sally Holmes Holtze. New York: Wilson, 1989, pp. 160–161.

Lathrop, Dorothy P(ulis)

Alberghene, Janice M. "Dorothy P. Lathrop." In Cech. *American Writers for Children, 1900–1960. Dictionary of Literary Biography*, vol. 22. Detroit: Gale, 1983, pp. 222–230.

Bechtel, Louise Seaman. "Dorothy Lathrop: Artist and Author." *Library Journal* 63 (June 15, 1938): 485–487.

Helbig, Alethea K., and Agnes Regan Perkins. *Dictionary of American Children's Fiction, 1859–1959*. Westport, CT: Greenwood, 1985, pp. 153–154, 284.

Hopkins, Lee Bennett. "Dorothy Lathrop." In *Books Are by People*. New York: Citation Press, 1969, pp. 125–127.

The Junior Book of Authors. 2nd ed. rev. Edited by Stanley J. Kunitz and Howard Haycraft. New York: Wilson, 1951, pp. 186–187.

Lathrop, Dorothy P. "Children, Fairies, and Animals." *Horn Book* 11 (May–June 1935): 135–142.

————. "A Hunt Breakfast—Authors' Symposium." *Horn Book* 2 (Nov 1926): 38.

————. "Illustrating De La Mare." *Horn Book* 18 (May 1942): 188–196.

————. "A Test of *Hitty*'s Pegs and Patience." *Horn Book* 6 (Feb 1930): 27–30.

Mahony, Bertha. "Artist's Triumph." *Horn Book* 14 (July 1938): 201–208.

Renwick, Stephen Lee. "Dorothy P. Lathrop, Author and Illustrator of Children's Books." *American Artist* 6 (Oct 1942): 12–15ff.

Roginski, Jim, ed. *Newbery and Caldecott Medalists and Honor Book Winners*. Littleton, CO: Libraries Unlimited, 1982, pp. 164–165.

Lauber, Patricia (Grace)

Third Book of Junior Authors. Edited by Doris De Montreville and Donna Hill. New York: Wilson, 1972, pp. 173–174.

Laumer, (John) Keith

Platt, Charles. *Dream Makers*. New York: Ungar, 1987, pp. 231–240. Interview.

Twentieth-Century Science Fiction Writers. 3rd ed. Edited by Noelle Watson and Paul E. Schellinger. Chicago: St. James Press, 1991, pp. 471–473.

Walker, Paul. *Speaking of Science Fiction.* Oradell, NJ: Luna Publications, 1978. Interview.

Laurence, (Jean) Margaret (Wemyss)

Letson, D. R. "Mother of Manawaka: Margaret Laurence as Author of Children's Stories." *Canadian Children's Literature* 21 (1981): 17–24.

Lawhead, Stephen, R.

Summer, B. "Crossway's Crossover Novelist." *Publishers Weekly* 236 (Oct 6, 1989): 28+.

Lawrence, Ann (Margaret)

Ray, Sheila. "Ann Lawrence, 1942–1987." *Junior Bookshelf* 51, no. 5 (1987): 205–209.

———. "Children's Writers: Ann Lawrence." *School Librarian* 30 (Sept 1982): 196–199.

Twentieth-Century Children's Writers. 3rd ed. Edited by Tracy Chevalier and D. L. Kirkpatrick. Chicago: St. James, 1989, pp. 558–559.

Lawrence, Louise (pseud. of Elizabeth Rhoda Holden)

Antczak, Janice. *Science Fiction: The Mythos of a New Romance.* New York: Neal-Schuman, 1985, pp. 186–187.

Sixth Book of Junior Authors and Illustrators. Edited by Sally Holmes Holtze. New York: Wilson, 1989, pp. 161–163.

Twentieth-Century Children's Writers. 3rd ed. Edited by Tracy Chevalier and D. L. Kirkpatrick. Chicago: St. James, 1989, pp. 559–560.

Lawson, John S(hults)

Helbig, Alethea K., and Agnes Regan Perkins. *Dictionary of American Children's Fiction, 1960–1984; Recent Books of Recognized Merit.* Westport, CT: Greenwood, 1986, pp. 373, 622–623.

Lawson, Robert

Avi. "Robert Lawson." In *Writers for Children; Critical Studies of Major Authors Since the Seventeenth Century.* Edited by Jane M. Bingham. New York: Scribner, 1988, pp. 345–350.

Bader, Barbara. *American Picturebooks from Noah's Ark to The Beast Within.* New York: Macmillan, 1976, pp. 143–147.

Burns, Mary Mehlman. "'There Is Enough for All': Robert Lawson's America." *Horn Book* 48 (Feb 1972): 24–32; 48 (Apr 1972): 120–128; and 48 (June 1972): 295–305.

Cart, Michael. "*Ben, Mr. Popper* and the Rabbits: Remembering Robert Lawson." *New York Times Book Review* (Nov 13, 1988): 59.

Cornell, Robert W. "Robert Lawson: For All Children." *Elementary English* 50 (May 1973): 718–725, 738.

Fish, Helen Dean. "Robert Lawson, Illustrator in the Great Tradition." *Horn Book* 16 (Jan–Feb 1940): 17–26.

Gardner, Frederick R. *Robert Lawson on My Shelves*. Philadelphia: Free Library of Philadelphia, 1977.

Gillespie, John T., and Diana Lembo. *Introducing Books: A Guide for the Middle Grades*. New York: Bowker, 1970, pp. 147–149.

Helbig, Alethea K., and Agnes Regan Perkins. *Dictionary of American Children's Fiction, 1859–1959*. Westport, CT: Greenwood, 1985, pp. 42–43, 286, 361–362, 421–422, 529–530.

Inman, Sue Lile. "Robert Lawson." In Cech. *American Writers for Children, 1900–1960. Dictionary of Literary Biography*, vol. 22. Detroit: Gale, 1983, pp. 231–240.

Jameyson, Karen. "A Second Look: *Mr. Popper's Penguins*." *Horn Book* 64 (Mar–Apr 1988): 186–187.

Jones, Helen L., ed. *Robert Lawson, Illustrator: A Selection of His Characteristic Illustrations*. Boston: Little, Brown, 1972.

The Junior Book of Authors. 2nd ed. rev. Edited by Stanley J. Kunitz and Howard Haycraft. New York: Wilson, 1951, pp. 189–190.

Kurth, Ruth Justine. "Realism in Children's Books of Fantasy." *California Librarian* 39 (July 1978): 39–40.

Lawson, Marie A. "Master of *Rabbit Hill:* Robert Lawson." *Horn Book* 21 (July–Aug 1945): 239–242.

Lawson, Robert. *At That Time*. New York: Viking Press, 1947.

——. "Caldecott Acceptance Speech." *Horn Book* 17 (July 1941): 273–284.

——. "The Genius of Arthur Rackham." *Horn Book* 16 (May 1940): 147–152.

——. "Lo, the Poor Illustrator." *Publishers Weekly* 128 (Dec 17, 1935): 2091.

——. "Make Me a Child Again." *Horn Book* 16 (Nov–Dec 1940): 447–456.

——. "The Newbery Medal Acceptance." *Horn Book* 21 (July 1945): 233–238.

——. *They Were Strong and Good*. New York: Viking Press, 1940.

Lindquist, Jennie D. "The Master of *Rabbit Hill*." *Horn Book* 33 (Aug 1957): 273.

Madsen, Valden. "Classic Americana: Themes and Values in the Tales of Robert Lawson." *The Lion and the Unicorn* 3 (Spring 1979): 89–106.

Miller, Bertha Mahony, and Elinor Whitney Field, eds. *Newbery Medal Books: 1922–1955*. Boston: Horn Book, 1957, pp. 255–267.

The Oxford Companion to Children's Literature. Edited by Humphrey Carpenter and Mari Prichard. New York: Oxford Univ. Press, 1984, pp. 305, 437.

Pflieger, Pat, and Helen M. Hill. *A Reference Guide to Modern Fantasy for Children*. Westport, CT: Greenwood, 1984, pp. xv, xvi, 52–53, 179–180, 297–300, 370–372, 467–468, 545–546.

"Robert Lawson: Biographical Sketch." *Horn Book* 17 (July 1941): 285–288.

"The Robert Lawson Collection of the Rare Book Department of the Free Library of Philadelphia." *Horn Book* 48 (June 1972): 318.

Roginski, Jim, ed. *Newbery and Caldecott Medalists and Honor Book Winners*. Littleton, CO: Libraries Unlimited, 1982, pp. 165–168.

Salway, Lance, and Nancy Chambers. "Book Post." *Signal* 26 (May 1978): 99–107.

Searles, Baird, Beth Meacham, and Michael Franklin. *A Reader's Guide to Fantasy*. New York: Avon, 1982, pp. 89–90.

Sicherman, Ruth. "An Appreciation of Robert Lawson." *Elementary English* 44 (Dec 1967): 866–869.

Stott, Jon C. *Children's Literature from A to Z*. New York: McGraw-Hill, 1984, p. 163.

Twentieth-Century Children's Writers. 3rd ed. Edited by Tracy Chevalier and D. L. Kirkpatrick. Chicago: St. James, 1989, pp. 560–561.

Weston, Annette H. "Robert Lawson: Author and Illustrator." *Elementary English* 47 (Jan 1970): 74–84. Reprinted in Miriam Hoffman and Eva Samuels. *Authors and Illustrators of Children's Books*. New York: Bowker, 1972, pp. 256–267.

Leach, (Alice Mary) Maria (Doanne)

Fourth Book of Junior Authors and Illustrators. Edited by Doris De Montreville and Elizabeth D. Crawford. New York: Wilson, 1978, pp. 220–221.

Lee, Tanith

Ashley, Mike. "The Tanith Lee Bibliography." *Fantasy Macabre* 4 (1983): 27–35.
Collings, Michael R. "Words and Worlds: The Creation of a Fantasy Universe in Zelazny, Lee and Anthony." In *The Scope of the Fantastic—Theory, Technique, Major Authors.* Edited by Robert A. Collins and Howard D. Pearce. Westport, CT: Greenwood, 1985, pp. 173–182.
Holding, Deanne. "A Pen in Her Own Country: Tanith Lee." *Space Voyager* 13 (1985): 16–18.
Kemp, Geoff. "Tanith Lee." *Quartz* 4 (1983): 12–16. Interview.
Saunders, Charles R., Charles De Lint, and Galad Elflandsson. "The Fiction of Tanith Lee: 1971–1983." *Dragonfields* 4 (1983): 21–25.
Schuyler, William M., Jr. "Recent Developments in Spell Construction." In *The Aesthetics of Fantasy Literature and Art.* Edited by Roger C. Schlobin. Notre Dame, IN: Univ. of Notre Dame Press, 1982, pp. 237–248.
Schweitzer, Darrell. "Interview: Tanith Lee." *Fantasy Newsletter* 42 (1981): 12–15.
Searles, Baird, Beth Meacham, and Michael Franklin. *A Reader's Guide to Fantasy.* New York: Avon, 1982, pp. 90–91.
Stroud, Daphne J. "Dark Quintet." *Junior Bookshelf* 54, no. 2 (1990): 63–66.
Twentieth-Century Children's Writers. 3rd ed. Edited by Tracy Chevalier and D. L. Kirkpatrick. Chicago: St. James, 1989, pp. 565–566.
Waggoner, Diana. "Tanith Lee." In *Supernatural Fiction Writers: Fantasy and Horror,* vol. 2. Edited by E. F. Bleiler. New York: Scribner, 1985, pp. 1053–1058.
Weinkauf, Mary S. "So Much for the Gentle Sex." *Extrapolation* 26 (1985): 231–239.

Leeson, Robert (Arthur)

Ashton, Paul. "Old Bottles, New Wine: An Interview with Robert Leeson." *English Magazine* [London] 1 (Spring 1979): 16–17.
Twentieth-Century Children's Writers. 3rd ed. Edited by Tracy Chevalier and D. L. Kirkpatrick. Chicago: St. James, 1989, pp. 566–567.

Le Grand (Henderson)

The Junior Book of Authors. 2nd ed. rev. Edited by Stanley J. Kunitz and Howard Haycraft. New York: Wilson, 1951, pp. 192–193.

Le Guin, Ursula K(roeber)

Algeo, John. "Magic Names: Onomastics in the Fantasies of Ursula Le Guin." *American Name Society* 30, no. 2 (1982): 59–67.
Attebery, Brian. "*The Beginning Place:* Le Guin's Metafantasy." In *Children's Literature,* vol. 10. New Haven, CT: Yale Univ. Press, 1982, pp. 113–123. Reprinted in *Ursula K. Le Guin.* Edited by Harold Bloom. New York: Chelsea House, 1986.
———. "On a Far Shore: The Myth of *Earthsea.*" *Extrapolation* 21 (1980): 268–277.
———. "Women's Coming of Age in Fantasy." *Extrapolation* 28 (Spring 1987): 10–22.

Bailey, E. C., Jr. "Shadows in *Earthsea:* Le Guin's Use of a Jungian Archetype." *Extrapolation* 21 (Fall 1980): 254–261.

Bailey, K. V. "Counter-Landscapes of Fantasy: *Earthsea*/Narnia." *Foundation* (U.K.) 40 (1987): 26–36.

Bain, Dena C. "The *Tao Te Ching* as Background to the Novels of Ursula K. Le Guin." *Extrapolation* 21 (1980): 209–222. Reprinted in *Ursula K. Le Guin.* Edited by Harold Bloom. New York: Chelsea House, 1986.

Barbour, Douglas. "On Ursula Le Guin's *A Wizard of Earthsea.*" *Riverside Quarterly* 6 (Apr 1974): 119–123.

———. "Patterns of Meaning in the Science Fiction Novels of Ursula K. Le Guin, Joanna Russ and Samuel R. Delany, 1962–1972. Ph.D. diss., Queen's University (Ontario, Canada), 1976.

———. "Wholeness and Balance." In *Ursula K. Le Guin.* Edited by Harold Bloom. New York: Chelsea House, 1986.

Barrow, Craig, and Diana Barrow. "Le Guin's *Earthsea*: Voyages into Consciousness." *Extrapolation* 32 (Spring 1991): 20–44.

Berkley, Miriam. "Ursula K. Le Guin." *Publishers Weekly* 228 (May 23, 1986): 72.

Bisenieks, Dainis. "Children, Magic and Choices." *Mythlore* 6 (Winter 1979): 13–16.

———. "Tales from the 'Perilous Realm': Good News for the Modern Child." *Christian Century,* June 5, 1974, pp. 617–620.

Bittner, James W. *Approaches to the Fiction of Ursula K. Le Guin.* Ann Arbor: Univ. of Michigan Research Press, 1984.

———. "Approaches to the Fiction of Ursula Le Guin." Ph.D. diss., University of Wisconsin-Madison, 1979.

Bloom, Harold, ed. *Ursula K. Le Guin.* New York: Chelsea House, 1986.

Bradbury, Margaret. "What's in a Name? Ursula Le Guin's *Earthsea* Trilogy." *School Librarian* 31 (Sept 1983): 205–210.

Braswell, Laurel. "The Visionary Voyage in Science Fiction and Medieval Allegory." *Mosaic* 14 (Winter 1981): 125–142.

Brigg, Peter. "*The Beginning Place.*" In *Survey of Modern Fantasy Literature,* vol. 1. Edited by Frank N. Magill. Englewood Cliffs, NJ: Salem Press, 1983, pp. 81–83.

Bucknell, Barbara J. "Rilke and Le Guin." *Mythlore* 16 (Winter 1989): 62–66.

———. *Ursula K. Le Guin.* New York: Ungar, 1981.

Cameron, Eleanor. "High Fantasy: *A Wizard of Earthsea.*" *Horn Book* 47 (Apr 1971): 129–138. Reprinted in Paul Heins. *Crosscurrents of Criticism.* Boston: Horn Book, 1977, pp. 333–341. Revised for publication in Gerard Senick. *Children's Literature Review,* vol. 3. Detroit: Gale, 1978, pp. 124–125.

Cogell, Elizabeth Cummins. "The Metaphor of Turning and Returning in the Novels of Ursula K. Le Guin, 1968–1974." Ph.D. diss., University of Illinois, 1985.

———. *Ursula K. Le Guin: A Primary and Secondary Bibliography.* Boston: G. K. Hall, 1983.

Crowe, Edith L. "Integration in *Earthsea* and Middle-Earth." *San Jose Studies* 14 (1988): 63–80.

Cummins, Elizabeth. *Understanding Ursula K. Le Guin.* Columbia, SC: Univ. of South Carolina, 1990.

Cunneen, Sheila. "Earthseans and Earthteens." *English Journal* 74 (Feb 1985): 68–69.

Davis, Boyd H. "Childe Reader and the Saussurean Paradox." *Children's Literature Association Quarterly* 7 (Fall 1981): 36–38.

Dawson, Jean I. "Fantasy in the Post-Christian Era: Some Comments on the Novels of Susan Cooper and Ursula Le Guin." *Orana* 20 (Nov 1984): 161–168.

Dean, John. "Uses of the Occult in the *Earthsea* Trilogy." *Fantasy Commentator* 5 (1984): 116–121.

De Bolt, Joe, ed. *Ursula K. Le Guin: Voyager to Inner Lands and to Outer Space.* Port Washington, NY: Kennikat Press, 1979.

Djarv, Hakon, and Pia-Lena Niklasson. "Växandets Lust: Ursula Le Guin's Trilogi on Ovärlden [The Joy of Growing: The Trilogy of Ursula Le Guin]." *Abrakadabra* (Sweden) 2 (1986): 16–21.

Dooley, Patricia. "Earthsea Patterns." *Children's Literature Association Quarterly* 4 (Summer 1979): 1–4. Reprinted in Dooley. *The First Steps.* West Lafayette, IN: Children's Literature Association Publications, 1984, pp. 14–15.

———. "Magic and Art in Ursula Le Guin's *Earthsea Trilogy.*" In *Children's Literature,* vol. 8. New Haven, CT: Yale Univ. Press, 1980, pp. 103–110.

Dunn, Margaret M. "In Defense of Dragons: Imagination as Experience in the *Earthsea Trilogy.*" In *Proceedings of the Ninth Annual Conference of the Children's Literature Association.* University of Florida, March 1982. Ypsilanti, MI: Children's Literature Association, 1983, pp. 54–60.

Edwards, Malcolm, and Robert Holdstock. "Earthsea." In *Realms of Fantasy.* Garden City, NY: Doubleday, 1983, pp. 87–97.

Erlich, Richard D. "The Earthsea Trilogy." In *Survey of Modern Fantasy Literature,* vol. 1. Edited by Frank N. Magill. Englewood Cliffs, NJ: Salem Press, 1983, pp. 447–459.

———. "Ursula K. Le Guin and Arthur C. Clarke on Immanence, Transcendence, and Massacres." *Extrapolation* 28 (1987): 105–129.

Esmonde, Margaret P. "Beyond the Circles of the World: Death and the Hereafter in Children's Literature." In *Webs and Wardrobes: Humanist and Religious World Views in Children's Literature,* ed. by Joseph O'Beirne Milner and Lucy Floyd Morcock Milner. Lanham, MD: University Press of America, 1987, pp. 33–45.

———. "The Master Pattern: The Psychological Journey in *The Earthsea Trilogy.*" In Joseph Olander and Martin Greenberg. *Ursula K. Le Guin.* New York: Taplinger, 1979, pp. 15–35.

Extrapolation. Special issue. 2 (Fall 1980): 195–304.

Fantastes. "Enchantress of Earthsea." *Cambridge Review: Fantasy in Literature,* Nov 23, 1973, pp. 43–45.

Finch, Sheila. "Oath of Fealty: No Thud, Some Blunders." *Science Fiction Review* 57 (1985): 28–30.

———. "Paradise Lost: The Prison at the Heart of Le Guin's Utopia." *Extrapolation* 26 (1985): 240–248.

Fourth Book of Junior Authors and Illustrators. Edited by Doris De Montreville and Elizabeth D. Crawford. New York: Wilson, 1978, pp. 221–223.

Fox, Geoff. "Notes on Teaching *A Wizard of Earthsea.*" *Children's Literature in Education* 11 (May 1973): 58–67. Reprinted in Geoff Fox. *Writers, Critics and Children.* New York: Agathon Press, 1976, pp. 211–223.

Frongia, Terri. "Good Wizard/Bad Wizard: Merlin and Faust Archetypes in Contemporary Children's Literature." In *Contending Archetypes in Western Culture,* ed. by Charlotte Spivak. Lewiston, NY: Mellen, 1992, pp. 65–93.

Galbreath, R. "Taoist Magic in *The Earthsea Trilogy.*" *Extrapolation* 21 (Fall 1980): 262–268.

Gillespie, Bruce. "Ursula Le Guin: Explorer of New Worlds." *Educational Magazine* (Australia) 32, no. 3 (1975): 43–46.

Gillespie, John T., and Corinne J. Naden. *Juniorplots 3: A Book Talk Guide for Use with Readers Ages 12–16.* New York: Bowker, 1987, pp. 174–177.

Greenland, Colin. "Doing Two Things in Opposite Directions." *Interzone* (U.K.) (Mar 1991): 51–61.

Gordon, Andrew. "Ursula K. Le Guin." In *American Writers for Children since 1960: Fiction. Dictionary of Literary Biography,* vol. 52. Detroit: Gale, 1986, pp. 233–240.

Hare, Delmas Edwin. *"In This Land There Be Dragons:* Carl G. Jung, Ursula K. Le Guin, and Narrative Prose Fantasy." Ph.D. diss., Emory University, 1982.

Harris, Mason. "The Psychology of Power in Tolkien's *The Lord of the Rings,* Orwell's *1984,* and Le Guin's *A Wizard of Earthsea." Mythlore* 55 (1988): 46–56.

Haselkorn, Mark P. "An Interview with Ursula K. Le Guin." *Science Fiction Review* 7 (May 1978): 72–74.

Hassler, Donald M. "The Touching of Love and Death in Ursula Le Guin with Comparisons to Jane Austen." *University of Mississippi Studies in English* 4 (1983): 168–177.

Hatfield, Len. "From Master to Brother: Shifting the Balance of Authority in Ursula K. Le Guin's *Farthest Shore* and *Tehanu." Children's Literature 21.* New Haven: Yale Univ. Press, 1993 pp. 43–65.

Helbig, Alethea K., and Agnes Regan Perkins. *Dictionary of American Children's Fiction, 1960–1984; Recent Books of Recognized Merit.* Westport, CT: Greenwood, 1986, pp. 180–181, 207–208, 375, 666–667, 736–737.

Hiller, Claire. "The World of Fantasy—the World Where Anything Can Happen." *English in Australia* 86 (Dec 1988): 54–59.

Holliday, Liz. "War of the Worlds." *Guardian* (Oct 4, 1990): 38.

Hoxmier, Kelly. "A Positive Alternative: The Novels of Ursula K. Le Guin." *ALAN Review* 10 (Fall 1982): 3–7.

Huntington, John. "Public and Private Imperatives in Le Guin's Novels." *Science-Fiction Studies* 2 (1975): 237–243.

Inglis, Fred. *The Promise of Happiness.* New York: Cambridge Univ. Press, 1981, pp. 245–247.

―――. "Spellbinding and Anthropology: The Work of Richard Adams and Ursula Le Guin." In Dennis Butts. *Good Writers for Young Readers.* St. Albans, England: Hart-Davis, 1977, pp. 114–128.

Jackson, Rosemary. *Fantasy: The Literature of Subversion.* New York: Methuen, 1980.

Jago, Wendy. *"A Wizard of Earthsea* and the Charge of Escapism." *Children's Literature in Education* 8 (July 1972): 21–29.

Jameson, Fredric. "World-Reduction in Le Guin: The Emergence of Utopian Narrative." In *Ursula K. Le Guin.* Edited by Harold Bloom. New York: Chelsea House, 1986.

Jameson, Gloria. "Developing Self-Identity Through Religious Consciousness in Stories of George MacDonald, C. S. Lewis, Madeleine L'Engle, Katherine Paterson, Ursula K. Le Guin, and Laura Adams Armer." In *Literature and Hawaii's Children. Proceedings of the Third Biennial Conference on Literature and Hawaii's Children.* Honolulu: Literature and Hawaii's Children, 1988, pp. 143–147.

Jenkins, Sue. "Growing Up in Earthsea." *Children's Literature in Education* 16 (Spring 1985): 21–31.

Kemball-Cook, Jessica. "Earthsea and Others." *New Society* (Nov 11, 1976): 314–315.

Kuznets, Lois R. "'High Fantasy' in America: Alexander, Le Guin and Cooper." An unpublished paper delivered at the Conference on Fantasy and Social Values in German and American Children's Literature, Humanities Institute of Brooklyn College, March 1984. Reprinted as: "'High Fantasy' in America: A Study of Lloyd Alexander, Ursula Le Guin, and Susan Cooper." *The Lion and the Unicorn* 9 (1985): 19–35.

LaBar, Martin. "Slipping the Truth in Edgewise (Taoist Themes in Fantasies of U. K. Le Guin)." *Christianity Today* 25 (Mar 27, 1981): 38–39.

Le Guin, Ursula K. "Books Remembered." *C.B.C. Calendar* 36, no. 2 (Nov–June 1978): 6.

―――. "The Child and the Shadow." *Quarterly Journal of the Library of Congress* 32 (Apr 1975): 139–148. Reprinted in Ursula K. Le Guin. *The Language of the Night.* New York: Putnam, 1979, pp. 59–71; and in *The Openhearted Audience.* Washington, DC: Library of Congress, 1980, pp. 100–113.

―――. "The Creative Spirit and Children's Literature: A Symposium." *Wilson Library Bulletin* 53 (Oct 1978): 166–169.

———. *Dancing at the Edge of the World: Thoughts on Words, Women, and Places.* London: Gollancz, 1988; New York: Grove, 1989.

———. "Dreams Must Explain Themselves." *Algol,* no. 21 (Nov 1973). Reprinted in *Dreams Must Explain Themselves.* New York: Algol Press, 1975, pp. 5–13; *Signal* 19 (Jan 1976): 3–11; Ursula K. Le Guin. *The Language of the Night.* New York: Putnam, 1979, pp. 47–56; and in Boyer and Zahorski. *Fantasists on Fantasy.* New York: Avon, 1984, pp. 181–194.

———. *Earthsea Revisioned: Children, Women, Men, and Dragons.* Madison, NJ: [Norwood Long] Children's Literature New England, Inc., 1992. Transcript of lecture delivered at "Worlds Apart," Children's Literature New England Summer Institute held at Oxford College, August 2–8, 1992.

———. "Fantasy, Like Poetry, Speaks the Language of the Night." *San Francisco Sunday Examiner and Chronicle,* "World," Nov 21, 1976.

———. *From Elfland to Poughkeepsie.* New York: Pendragon Press, 1973. Reprinted in Ursula K. Le Guin. *The Language of the Night.* New York: Putnam, 1979, pp. 83–96; and in Boyer and Zahorski. *Fantasists on Fantasy.* New York: Avon, 1984, pp. 195–210.

———. "In Defense of Fantasy." Excerpts from the acceptance remarks of Ursula Le Guin on receiving the National Book Award in Children's Books for *The Farthest Shore. Horn Book* 49 (June 1973): 239. Reprinted in Paul Heins. *Crosscurrents of Criticism.* Boston: Horn Book, 1977, p. 169.

———. *The Language of the Night: Essays on Fantasy and Science Fiction.* New York: Putnam, 1979.

———. "Legends for a New Land." [Guest of Honor Speech at the 19th Annual Mythopoeic Conference, Summer 1987.] *Mythlore* 56 (1988): 4–10.

———. "Mapping Imaginary Countries." In David Wingrove. *The Science Fiction Source Book.* New York: Van Nostrand Reinhold, 1984, pp. 77–79.

———. "On Writing Science Fiction." *The Writer* 94 (Feb 1981): 11–14. Reprinted in *The Writer's Handbook.* Edited by Sylvia K. Burack. Boston: The Writer, 1985.

———. "Science Fiction and Mrs. Brown." In *Science Fiction at Large: A Collection of Essays.* Edited by Peter Nicholls. New York: Harper, 1976, pp. 13–34.

———. "Talking About Writing." *The Writer* 105 (Dec 1992): 9–11+.

———. "Why Are Americans Afraid of Dragons?" *Pacific North West Library Association Quarterly* 38 (Feb 1974): 14–18. Reprinted in Ursula K. Le Guin. *The Language of the Night.* New York: Putnam, 1979, pp. 39–46; and in Edward Blishen. *The Thorny Paradise.* Boston: Horn Book, 1975, pp. 87–92, entitled "This Fear of Dragons."

Levin, Jeff. "Ursula K. Le Guin: A Select Bibliography." *Science-Fiction Studies* 2 (1975): 204–208.

Littlefield, Ralph Emerson. "Characters and Language in Eight Novels by Ursula K. Le Guin and Samuel R. Delany." Ph.D. diss., Florida State University, 1984.

McCaffrey, Larry, and Sinda Gregory. "An Interview with Ursula Le Guin." *Missouri Review* 7 (1984): 64–85. Reprinted in *Alive and Writing: Interviews with American Authors of the 1980's.* Urbana: Univ. of Illinois Press, 1987, pp. 175–195.

McGuire, Patrick L. "The Short Fiction of Ursula K. Le Guin." In *Survey of Modern Fantasy Literature,* vol. 4. Edited by Frank N. Magill. Englewood Cliffs, NJ: Salem Press, 1983, pp. 1607–1610.

McLean, Susan. "*The Beginning Place:* An Interpretation." *Extrapolation* 24 (Summer 1983): 130–142.

Manlove, C. N. "Conservatism in the Fantasy of Ursula Le Guin." *Extrapolation* 21 (Fall 1980): 287–297. Revised for inclusion in C. N. Manlove. *The Impulse of Fantasy Literature.* Kent, OH: Kent State Univ. Press, 1982, pp. 31–44.

Miles, Margaret. "'*Earthsea* Revisited' Revisited." *VOYA* 14 (Dec 1991): 301–302.

Molson, Francis J. "*The Earthsea Trilogy:* Ethical Fantasy for Children." In Joe De Bolt.

Ursula K. Le Guin: Voyager to Inner Lands and Outer Space. Port Washington, NY: Kennikat Press, 1979.

Moylan, T. "Beyond Negation: The Critical Utopias of Ursula K. Le Guin and Samuel R. Delany." *Extrapolation* 21 (Fall 1980): 236–253.

Neill, Heather. "Strong as Woman's Magic." *Times Educational Supplement* (Nov 9, 1990): R9. Interview.

Nudelman, Rafail. "An Approach to the Structure of Le Guin's Science Fiction." *Science-Fiction Studies* 2 (1975): 210–220.

Olander, Joseph D., and Martin Harry Greenberg, eds. *Ursula K. Le Guin.* New York: Taplinger, 1979.

The Oxford Companion to Children's Literature. Edited by Humphrey Carpenter and Mari Prichard. New York: Oxford Univ. Press, 1984, pp. 162, 308.

Parish, Margaret. "Fantasy." *English Journal* 66 (Nov 1977): 90–93.

Patterson, Richard F. "Le Guin's Earthsea Trilogy: The Psychology of Fantasy." In *The Scope of the Fantastic—Culture, Biography, Themes, Children's Literature.* Edited by Robert A. Collins and Howard D. Pearce. Westport, CT: Greenwood, 1985, pp. 239–248.

Pausacker, Jenny. "Ursula Le Guin—The *Earthsea* Trilogy." *School Library Bulletin* (Australia) 10 (Aug 1973): 61–64; reprinted in *S.M.M.A.R.T. Journal* 2 (1978): 39–42.

Paxon, Diana. "The Tolkien Tradition." *Mythlore* 39 (1984): 23–27, 37.

Pflieger, Pat, and Helen M. Hill. *A Reference Guide to Modern Fantasy for Children.* Westport, CT: Greenwood, 1984, pp. xii–xvi, 181–182, 301–304, 541–542, 611–612.

Plank, Robert. "Ursula K. Le Guin and the Decline of Romantic Love." *Science-Fiction Studies* 3 (1976): 36–43.

Porter, David L. "The Politics of Le Guin's Opus." *Science-Fiction Studies* 2 (1975): 243–248.

Rabkin, Eric S. "Metalinguistics and Science Fiction." *Critical Inquiry* 6 (1979): 79–97.

Rees, David. "*Earthsea* Revisited: Ursula K. Le Guin." In *Marble in the Water.* Boston: Horn Book, 1980, pp. 78–89.

Remington, T. J. "A Time to Live and a Time to Die: Cyclical Renewal in *The Earthsea Trilogy.*" *Extrapolation* 21 (Fall 1980): 278–286.

Roginski, Jim, ed. *Newbery and Caldecott Medalists and Honor Book Winners.* Littleton, CO: Libraries Unlimited, 1982, p. 168.

Rollin, Lucy W. "Exploring Earthsea: A Sixth Grade Literature Project." *Children's Literature in Education* 16 (Winter 1985): 195–202.

Ross, Anthony. "Ursula Le Guin's Last Book of Earthsea: *Tehanu.*" *Papers: Explorations into Children's Literature* (Australia) 4 (Apr 1993): 14–21.

Sammons, Martha C. "*A Better Country*": The Worlds of Religious Fantasy and Science Fiction.* Westport, CT: Greenwood, 1988.

Samuelson, David N. "Ursula Le Guin." In *Science Fiction Writers.* Edited by E. F. Bleiler. New York: Scribner, 1982, pp. 409–418.

———. "Ursula Le Guin." In *Supernatural Fiction Writers: Fantasy and Horror,* vol. 1. Edited by E. F. Bleiler. New York: Scribner, 1985, pp. 1059–1066.

Schlobin, Roger C. "Preparing for Life's Passages: How Fantasy Literature Can Help." *Media and Methods* 16 (Nov 1979): 26–27, 29, 50–51.

Scholes, Robert. "The Good Witch of the West." *Hollins Critic* 11, no. 2 (1974): 1–12. Revised for inclusion in *Structural Fabulation: An Essay on Fiction of the Future.* Notre Dame, IN: Univ. of Notre Dame Press, 1975, pp. 79–87. Reprinted in *Ursula K. Le Guin.* Edited by Harold Bloom. New York: Chelsea House, 1986.

Schuyler, William M., Jr. "Recent Developments in Spell Construction." In *The Aesthetics of Fantasy Literature and Art.* Edited by Roger C. Schlobin. Notre Dame, IN: Univ. of Notre Dame Press, 1982, pp. 237–248.

Searles, Baird, Beth Meacham, and Michael Franklin. *A Reader's Guide to Fantasy.* New York: Avon, 1982, pp. 92–94.

Selinger, Bernard George. "Ursula K. Le Guin and the Paradox of Identity in Contemporary Fiction." Ph.D. diss., York University (Canada), 1984. Published as *Le Guin and Identity in Contemporary Fiction.* Ann Arbor, MI: UMI, 1987.

Sherman, Cordelia. "The Princess and the Wizard: The Fantasy Worlds of Ursula K. Le Guin and George MacDonald." *Children's Literature Association Quarterly* 12 (Spring 1987): 24–28.

Shippey, Tom. "The Golden Bough and the Incorporation of Magic in Science Fiction." *Foundation* 11/12 (1977): 119–134.

———. "The Magic Art and the Evolution of Words: Usula Le Guin's *Earthsea Trilogy.*" *Mosaic* 10, no. 2 (Winter 1976–1977): 147–163. Reprinted in *Ursula K. Le Guin.* Edited by Harold Bloom. New York: Chelsea House, 1986.

Sibley, Kenneth R. "Ursula Le Guin: The Long Rhythm." *Book Report* 7 (Mar–Apr 1989): 26–29.

Slethaug, Gordon E. "The Paradoxical Double in Le Guin's *A Wizard of Earthsea.*" *Extrapolation* 27 (1986): 326–333.

Slusser, George Edgar. *The Farthest Shores of Ursula K. Le Guin.* San Bernardino, CA: Borgo Press, 1976. "*The Earthsea Trilogy,*" pp. 31–46. Reprinted in *Ursula K. Le Guin.* Edited by Harold Bloom. New York: Chelsea House, 1986.

Snyman, K. "Imaginary Worlds: Myth , Fairy Tale , Fantasy and Science Fiction. Part II." *Skoolmediasentrum* (South Africa) 2 (1988): 46–51.

Spivak, Charlotte. *Merlin's Daughters: Contemporary Women Writers of Fantasy.* New York: Greenwood, 1987, pp. 51–66.

———. *Ursula K. Le Guin.* Boston: Twayne, 1984.

Stott, Jon C. *Children's Literature from A to Z.* New York: McGraw-Hill, 1984, p. 168.

Swinfen, Ann. *In Defense of Fantasy.* London: Routledge, 1984. Discusses *The Earthsea Trilogy,* pp. 79, 82, 83, 87–88, 90, 95, 168–189, 232–233.

Taormina, Agatha. "The Hero, the Double, and the Outsider: Images of Three Archetypes in Science Fiction." Ph.D. diss., Carnegie-Mellon University, 1980.

Tavormina, M. Teresa. "A Gate of Horn and Ivory: Dreaming True and False in Earthsea." *Extrapolation* 29 (1988): 338–348.

Taylor, Angus. "The Politics of Space, Time, and Entropy." *Foundation* 10 (1976): 34–44.

Thomason, Sue. "Women Wizards? Yes—Now." *Vector* 139 (1987): 7–8+.

Thompson, Christine K. "Going North and West to Watch the Dragons Dance: Norse and Celtic Elements in Ursula Le Guins's *Earthsea Trilogy.*" *Mythlore* 55 (1988): 19–22.

Timmerman, John H. *Other Worlds: The Fantasy Genre.* Bowling Green, OH: Bowling Green Univ. Press, 1983. Discusses *The Wizard of Earthsea,* pp. 81–90.

Toijer-Nilsson, Ying. "Ursula Le Guin's Jungianska Ovarld [Ursula Le Guin's Jungian *Earthsea*]." *Opsis Kalopsis* [Stockholm] 4 (1989): 26–28.

Townsend, John Rowe. Guest Essay, "Heights of Fantasy." In *Children's Literature Review,* vol. 5. Detroit: Gale, 1983, pp. 10–11.

Twentieth-Century Children's Writers. 3rd ed. Edited by Tracy Chevalier and D. L. Kirkpatrick. Chicago: St. James, 1989, pp. 569–571.

Twentieth-Century Science Fiction Writers. 3rd ed. Edited by Noelle Watson and Paul E. Schellinger. Chicago: St. James Press, 1991, 475–478.

Tymn, Marshall B. "Ursula K. Le Guin: A Bibliography." In Joseph Olander and Martin Greenberg. *Ursula K. Le Guin.* New York: Taplinger, 1979.

Ursula Le Guin: Woman of Science Fiction. North Hollywood, CA: Center for Cassette Studies, 1973. (audiocassette)

Veglahn, Nancy. "Images of Evil: Male and Female Monsters in Heroic Fantasy." *Children's Literature* 15 (1987): 106–119.

Walker, Jeanne Murray. "Rites of Passage Today: The Cultural Significance of *A Wizard of Earthsea.*" *Mosaic* 13 (1980): 179–191.

Walker, Paul. "Ursula Le Guin: An Interview." *Luna Monthly* 63 (1976): 1–7. Reprinted in Walker. *Speaking of Science Fiction.* Oradell, NJ: Luna Publications, 1978, pp. 24–36.

Ward, Jonathon. "Ursula K. Le Guin." *Algol* 12, no. 2 (1975): 7–10.

Welton, Ann. "*Earthsea* Revisited: *Tehanu* and Feminism. *VOYA* 14 (Apr 1991): 14–18.

White, Virginia L. "Bright the Hawk's Flight: The Journey of the Hero in Ursula K. Le Guin's *Earthsea Trilogy.*" *Ball State University Forum* 20, no. 4 (1979): 34–45.

Wickes, George, and Louise Westling. "Dialogue with Ursula K. Le Guin." *Northwest Review* 20 (1982): 147–159.

Wilson, Mary. "The *Earthsea* Series of Ursula Le Guin: A Successful Example of Modern Fantasy." *Papers* (Australia) 3 (Aug 1992): 60–74.

Wood, Susan. "Discovering Worlds: The Fiction of Ursula K. Le Guin." In *Voices for the Future: Essays on Major Science Fiction Writers,* vol. 2. Edited by Thomas D. Clareson. Bowling Green, OH: Bowling Green Univ. Press, 1979. Reprinted in *Ursula K. Le Guin.* Edited by Harold Bloom. New York: Chelsea House, 1986.

Wytenbroek, Jacqueline. "*Always Coming Home:* Pacifism and Anarchy in Le Guin's Latest Utopia." *Extrapolation* 28 (1987): 330–339.

———. "Science Fiction and Fantasy." *Extrapolation* 23 (1982): 321–332.

Yates, Jessica. "In Defense of Fantasy." *Mallorn* 21 (June 1984): 23–28.

L'Engle, Madeleine

Bostian, Frieda F. "Family-Based Fantasy: Parents and Children in L'Engle's Time Series." In *The Child and the Family: Selected Papers from the 1988 International Conference of the Children's Literature Association,* ed. by Susan R. Gannon and Ruth A. Thompson. New York: Pace University, 1990, p. 77. (abstract)

Carter, M. L. "The Cosmic Gospel: Lewis and L'Engle." *Mythlore* 8 (1982): 10–12.

Filmer-Davies, Kath. "Welsh Myth and Contemporary Literature." *Mythlore* 73 (Summer 1993): 53–58. Discusses Susan Cooper, Nikolai Tolstoi, Lloyd Alexander, Madeleine L'Engle, Brian Caswell, Jay Ashton, and Nancy Bond.

Fisher, Leona W. "Mythical Fantasy for Children: Silence and Community." *The Lion and the Unicorn* 14 (Dec 1990): 37–57.

Fortuna, Mary Ann. "A Descriptive Evaluative Study of Children's Modern Fantasy and Children's Science Fiction Using a Well Known Example of Each." Ed. D. diss., Temple University, 1988.

Franklin, Hugh. "Madeleine L'Engle." *Horn Book* 39 (Aug 1963): 356–360.

Glass, Rona. "*A Wrinkle in Time* and *The High King:* Two Couples, Two Perspectives." *Children's Literature Association Quarterly* 6 (Fall 1981): 15–18. Reprinted in Patricia Dooley. *The First Steps.* West Lafayette, IN: Children's Literature Association Publications, 1984, pp. 119–121.

Helbig, Alethea K., and Agnes Regan Perkins. *Dictionary of American Children's Fiction, 1960–1984.* Westport, CT: Greenwood, 1986, pp. 375–376.

Heltinga, Donald R. *Presenting Madleine L'Engle.* Boston: Twaine, 1993.

Hopkins, Lee Bennett. *More Books by More People.* New York: Citation Press, 1974, pp. 257–266.

Jameson, Gloria. "Developing Self-Identity Through Religious Consciousness in Stories of George MacDonald, C. S. Lewis, Madeleine L'Engle, Katherine Paterson, Ursula K. Le Guin, and Laura Adams Armer." In *Literature and Hawaii's Children. Proceedings of the Third Biennial Conference on Literature and Hawaii's Children.* Honolulu: Literature and Hawaii's Children, 1988, pp. 143–147.

Jones, K. "A Pentaperceptual Analysis of Social and Philosophical Commentary in *A Wrinkle in Time* by Madeleine L'Engle." Ph.D diss., University of Mississippi, 1977.

L'Engle, Madeleine. "Before Babel." *Horn Book* 42 (Dec 1966): 661–670.

————. "The Centipede and the Creative Spirit." *Horn Book* 45 (Aug 1969): 373–376.

————. "Childlike Wonder and the Truths of Science Fiction." *Children's Literature,* vol. 10. New Haven, CT: Yale Univ. Press, 1982, pp. 102–110.

————. *A Circle of Quiet.* New York: Farrar, 1972.

————. "The Danger of Wearing Glass Slippers." *Elementary English* 41 (Feb 1964): 105–111ff.

————. "Do I Dare Disturb the Universe?" *Horn Book* 59 (Dec 1983): 673–682.

————. "The Expanding Universe: Newbery Award Acceptance." *Horn Book* 39 (Aug 1963): 351–355.

————. "Extracts from a Tape-Recording." Auckland, New Zealand: *Children's Literature Association Yearbook 1977,* pp. 39–49.

————. "Fantasy Is What Fantasy Does." In *Children's Literature in the Classroom: Weaving Charlotte's Web,* ed. by Janet Hickman and Bernice E. Cullinan. Needham Heights, MA: Christopher-Gordon, 1989, pp. 129–134.

————. *From This Day Forward.* Oxford: Lion, 1989. (autobiography)

————. "The Heroic in Literature and Living." *The Lion and the Unicorn* 13 (June 1989): 120–128.

————. "Kerlan Award Lecture." *Kerlan Collection Newsletter* (Fall 1990):5–7.

————. "The Key, the Door, the Road." *Horn Book* 40 (June 1964): 260–268.

————. "Regina Medal Acceptance Speech." *Catholic Library World* 56, no. 1 (1984): 28–31.

————. "A Sense of Wonder." *Advocate* 2 (Winter 1983): 69–80.

"Madeleine L'Engle: Out of the Pigeonhole." *Locus* 294 (1985): 4ff.

Parker, Marygail G. "Madeleine L'Engle." In *American Writers for Children since 1960: Fiction. Dictionary of Literary Biography,* vol. 52. Detroit: Gale, 1986, pp. 241–248.

Patterson, Nancy-Lou. "Angel and Psycho-Pomp in Madeleine L'Engle's *Wind* Trilogy." *Children's Literature in Education* 14 (Winter 1983): 195–203.

Perry, Barbara. "Profile: Madeleine L'Engle: A Real Person." *Language Arts* 54 (Oct 1977): 812–816.

Rausen, Ruth. "An Interview with Madeleine L'Engle." *Children's Literature in Education* 19 (Winter 1975): 198–206.

Rees, David. "Sunday School Teacher: Madeleine L'Engle." In *"What Do Draculas Do?" Essays on Contemporary Writers of Fiction for Children and Young Adults.* Metuchen, NJ: Scarecrow Press, 1990, pp. 47–63.

Sammons, Martha C. *"A Better Country": The Worlds of Religious Fantasy and Science Fiction.* Westport, CT: Greenwood, 1988.

Samuels, L. A. "Profile: Madeleine L'Engle." *Language Arts* 58 (Sept 1981): 704–712.

Schmidt, Gary D. "The Story as Teller: An Interview with Madeleine L'Engle." *The ALAN Review* 18 (Winter 1991): 10–14.

Schneebaum, Katherine. "Finding a Happy Medium: The Design of Womenhood in *A Wrinkle in Time." The Lion and the Unicorn* 14 (Dec 1990): 30–36.

Speaking for Ourselves: Autobiographical Sketches by Notable Authors of Books for Young Adults. Edited by Donald R. Gallo. Urbana, IL: National Council of Teachers of English, 1990, pp. 116–119.

Thompson, Hilary. "Doorways to Fantasy." *Canadian Children's Literature* 21 (1981): 8–16.

Townsend, John Rowe. *A Sense of Story.* Philadelphia: Lippincott, 1971, pp. 120–129.

Twentieth-Century Children's Writers. 3rd ed. Edited by Tracy Chevalier and D. L. Kirkpatrick. Chicago: St. James, 1989, pp. 571–573.

Twentieth-Century Science Fiction Writers. 3rd ed. Edited by Noelle Watson and Paul E. Schellinger. Chicago: St. James, 1991, pp. 482–484.

Veglahn, Nancy. "Images of Evil: Male and Female Monsters in Heroic Fantasy." *Children's Literature* 15(1987): 106–119.

Wilson, Bruce Alan. "Madeleine L'Engle: Christian Storyteller." *Librarians Christian Fellowship Newsletter* (U.K.) 39 (Spring 1988): 29–33.

Wintle, Justin, and Emma Fisher. *The Pied Pipers.* New York: Two Continents, 1975, pp. 249–262.

Wolf, Virginia L. "Readers of *Alice*: My Children, Meg Murry and Harriet M. Welsch." *Children's Literature Association Quarterly* 13 (Fall 1988): 135–136.

Levin, Betty (Lowenthal)

Levin, Betty. "The Universe and Old MacDonald." In *Innocence & Experience.* Edited by Barbara Harrison and Gregory Maguire. New York: Lothrop, 1987, pp. 102–115.

Sixth Book of Junior Authors and Illustrators. Edited by Sally Holmes Holtze. New York: Wilson, 1989, pp. 169–170.

Twentieth-Century Children's Writers. 3rd ed. Edited by Tracy Chevalier and D. L. Kirkpatrick. Chicago: St. James, 1989, pp. 576–577.

Levitin, Sonia (Wolff)

Twentieth-Century Children's Writers. 3rd ed. Edited by Tracy Chevalier and D. L. Kirkpatrick. Chicago: St. James, 1989, pp. 577–578.

Levoy, Myron

Speaking for Ourselves: Autobiographical Sketches by Notable Authors of Books for Young Adults. Edited by Donald R. Gallo. Urbana, IL: National Council of Teachers of English, 1990, pp. 120–121.

Twentieth-Century Children's Writers. 3rd ed. Edited by Tracy Chevalier and D. L. Kirkpatrick. Chicago: St. James, 1989, pp. 578–579.

Levy, Elizabeth

Fifth Book of Junior Authors and Illustrators. Edited by Sally Holmes Holtze. New York: Wilson, 1983, pp. 193–195.

Lewis, C(live) S(taples)

Arnott, Anne. *The Secret Country of C. S. Lewis.* Grand Rapids, MI: Eerdmans, 1974.

"Authorgraph no. 27: C. S. Lewis." *Books for Keeps* (U.K.) 27 (July 1984): 14–15.

Aveling, Helan A. "The Need for Belief in the *Narnian Chronicles*." *CSL: The Bulletin of the New York C. S. Lewis Society* 15 (Sept 1984): 16–17.

Aymard, E. "On C. S. Lewis and the *Narnian Chronicles*." *Caliban* 5 (1968): 129–145.

Bailey, K. V. "Counter-Landscapes of Fantasy: *Earthsea*/Narnia." *Foundation* (U.K.) 40 (1987): 26–36.

Bailey, Mark. "The Honour and Glory of a Mouse: Reepicheep of Narnia." *Mythlore* 5, 18 (Autumn 1978): 35–36, 46.

Bakke, Jeannette A. "The Lion, the Lamb and the Child. Christian Childhood Education through *The Chronicles of Narnia*." Ph.D. diss., University of Minnesota, 1975.

Barratt, David. *C. S. Lewis and His World.* Grand Rapids, MI: Eerdmans, 1987.

Becker, Joan Quall. "Patterns of Guilt and Grace in the Development and Function of Character in C. S. Lewis's Romances." Ph.D. diss., University of Washington, 1981.

Bell, Albert A., Jr. "Origin of the Name 'Narnia.'" *Mythlore* 7, no. 24 (1980): 29.

Berman, Ruth. "Dragons for Tolkien and Lewis." *Mythlore* 39 (1984): 53–58.

Biggs, R. S. "*The Lion, the Witch* and Plato." [London] *Times* (Apr 20, 1985): 10.

Bisenieks, Dainis. "Children, Magic and Choices." *Mythlore* 6, no. 19 (Winter 1979): 13–16.

Blasdell, Heather L. "... And There Shall the Lilith Repose." *Mythlore* 54 (1988): 4–6.

Blount, Margaret. "Fallen and Redeemed: Animals in the Novels of C. S. Lewis." In *Animal Land: The Creatures of Children's Fiction*. New York: Morrow, 1975, pp. 284–306.

Brady, Charles A. "Finding God in Narnia." *America,* Oct 27, 1956, pp. 103–105. Reprinted in Mary Lou White. *Children's Literature*. Columbus, OH: Merrill, 1976, pp. 126–130.

Brown, Carol Ann. "Once upon a Narnia." *CSL: The Bulletin of the New York C. S. Lewis Society* 8, no. 8 (1977): 1–4.

Burgess, Andrew J. "The Concept of Eden." In *The Transcendent Adventure: Studies of Religion in Science Fiction/Fantasy*. Edited by Robert Reilly. Westport, CT: Greenwood, 1985.

Carnell, Corbin S. "C. S. Lewis: An Appraisal." *Mythlore* 1, no. 4 (1974).

Carpenter, Humphrey. *The Inklings: C. S. Lewis, J. R. R. Tolkien, Charles Williams, and Their Friends*. Boston: Houghton Mifflin, 1979; New York: Ballantine, 1981.

Carter, Margaret L. "A Note on Moral Concepts in Lewis' Fiction." *Mythlore* 5 (1978): 35.

Carter, Margaret R., and Richard A. Carter. "Perpetual Winter in C. S. Lewis and Patricia McKillip." *Mythlore* 16 (Autumn 1989): 35–36.

Cassell, George F. *Clive Staples Lewis*. Chicago: Chicago Literary Club, 1950.

Chapman, Ed. "Images of the Numinous in T. H. White and C. S. Lewis." *Mythlore* 4, no. 16 (June 1978): 3–10.

The Chesterton Review. "Special Issue: C. S. Lewis." 17 (Aug–Nov 1991).

Christopher, Joe R. *C. S. Lewis*. Boston: Twayne, 1986.

———. "An Inklings Bibliography." (2) *Mythlore* 4, no. 1 (1976): 33–38; (3) *Mythlore* 4, no. 2 (1976): 33–38; (4) *Mythlore* 4 (Mar 1977): 33–38; (5) *Mythlore* 4 (June 1977): 40–46; (6) *Mythlore* 5 (May 1978): 40–46; (7) *Mythlore* 5 (Autumn 1978): 43–46; (8) *Mythlore* 6 (Winter 1979): 46–47; (9) *Mythlore* 6 (Spring 1979): 40–46; (10) *Mythlore* 6 (Summer 1979): 38–45; (11) *Mythlore* 6 (Fall 1979): 44–47; (12) *Mythlore* 23 (1980): 41–45; (13) *Mythlore* 24 (1980): 42–47; (14) *Mythlore* 25 (1980): 43–47; (15) *Mythlore* 26 (1981): 42–46; (16) *Mythlore* 27 (1981): 43–47; (17) *Mythlore* 28 (1981): 43–47; (18) *Mythlore* 29 (1981): 43–47; (19) *Mythlore* 30 (1982): 43–47; (20) *Mythlore* 31 (1982): 37–41; (21) *Mythlore* 32 (1982): 42–46; (22) *Mythlore* 33 (1982): 42–46; (23) *Mythlore* 34 (1983): 51–55; (24) *Mythlore* 35 (1983): 51–55; (25) *Mythlore* 36 (1983): 51–55; (26) *Mythlore* 37 (1984): 51–55; (27) *Mythlore* 38 (1984): 58–63; (28) *Mythlore* 39 (1984): 59–63; (29) *Mythlore* 46 (1986): 57–59; (30) *Mythlore* 47 (1986): 51–54; (31) *Mythlore* 50 (1987): 58–62; (33) *Mythlore* 56 (1988): 64–66.

———. "An Introduction to Narnia." *Mythlore* 2, 6–8 (1975) and 3, 9 (1976). (in 4 parts)

———. "The Natural Law Tradition of C. S. Lewis." *The Ring Bearer* (Australia) 4 (1986): 11–16.

———. "The World of Narnia." *Niekas* 32 (Winter 1983): 46–57.

Christopher, Joe R., and Joan K. Ostling. "C. S. Lewis: A Bibliographic Supplement." *CSL: The Bulletin of the New York C. S. Lewis Society* 5, no. 8 (1974): 4–6.

———. *C. S. Lewis: An Annotated Checklist of Writings about Him and His Works*. Kent, OH: Kent State Univ. Press, 1973.

Clute, John. "C. S. Lewis." In *Science Fiction Writers*. Edited by E. F. Bleiler. New York: Scribner, 1982, pp. 243–249.

———. "C. S. Lewis." In *Supernatural Fiction Writers: Fantasy and Horror,* vol. 2. Edited by E. F. Bleiler. New York: Scribner, 1985, pp. 661–666.

Colbath, Mary Lou. "Worlds as They Should Be: Middle Earth, Narnia and Prydain." *Elementary English* 48 (Dec 1971): 937–945.

Collings, Michael R. "Of Lions and Lamp-Posts: C. S. Lewis's *The Lion, the Witch, and the Wardrobe* as Response to Olaf Stapledon's *Sirius.*" *Christianity and Literature* 34 (Summer 1983): 33–38.

Como, James T., ed. *C. S. Lewis at the Breakfast Table and Other Reminiscences.* New York: Macmillan, 1979; Collier, 1985.

Como, James T. "A Look into Narnia." *CSL: The Bulletin of the New York C. S. Lewis Society* 15 (July 1984): 1–6.

———. "Mediating Illusions: Three Studies of Narnia." *Children's Literature,* vol. 10. New Haven, CT: Yale Univ. Press, 1982, pp. 102–110.

Cox, John D. "Epistemological Release in *The Silver Chair.*" In Peter J. Schakel. *The Longing for Form: Essays on the Fiction of C. S. Lewis.* Kent, OH: Kent State Univ. Press, 1977.

Crouch, Marcus. "Chronicles of Narnia." *Junior Bookshelf* 20 (Nov 1956): 245–253.

CSL: The Bulletin of the New York C. S. Lewis Society. New York: C. S. Lewis Society, 1969– .

Daigle, Marsha Ann. "Dante's *Divine Comedy* and the Fiction of C. S. Lewis." Ph.D. diss., University of Michigan, 1984.

Dockery, C. "The Myth of the Shadow in the Fantasies of Williams, Lewis and Tolkien." Ph.D. diss., Auburn University, 1975.

Dorsett, Lyle W. *The Essential C. S. Lewis.* New York: Macmillan, 1988.

Doyle, Brian. *The Who's Who of Children's Literature.* New York: Schocken, 1968, pp. 178–179.

Duriez, Colin. *The C. S. Lewis Handbook.* Grand Rapids, MI: Baker, 1990.

Eastman, Jackie F. "C. S. Lewis's Indebtedness to Edmund Spenser: The Labyrinth Episode as Threshold Symbol in *The Lion, the Witch and the Wardrobe.*" *Proceedings of the 13th Annual Conference of The Children's Literature Association, 1986.* New York: Pace University, 1988, pp. 140–143.

Edwards, Bruce, ed. *The Taste of the Pineapple: Essays on C. S. Lewis as Reader, Critic, and Imaginative Writer.* Bowling Green, OH: Bowling Green Univ., 1988.

Edwards, Bruce L., Jr. "A Rhetoric of Reading: A Study of C. S. Lewis's Approach to the Written Text." Ph.D. diss., University of Texas at Austin, 1981.

———. "Toward a Rhetoric of Fantasy Criticism: C. S. Lewis's Readings of MacDonald and Morris." *Literature and Belief* 3 (Mar 1983): 63–73.

Elgin, Don D. *The Comedy of the Fantastic: Ecological Perspectives on the Fantasy Novel.* Westport, CT: Greenwood, 1985.

Esmonde, Margaret P. "Beyond the Circles of the World: Death and the Hereafter in Children's Literature." In *Webs and Wardrobes: Humanist and Religious World Views in Children's Literature,* ed. by Joseph O'Beirne Milner and Lucy Floyd Morcock Milner. Lanham, MD: University Press of America, 1987, pp. 33–45.

Evans, Murray. "C. S. Lewis' Narnia Books: The Reader in the Myth." In *Touchstones.* Edited by Perry Nodelman. West Lafayette, IN: Children's Literature Association Publications, 1985, pp. 132–145.

"An Evening with Walter Hooper." *CSL: The Bulletin of the New York C. S. Lewis Society* 6, no. 9 (1975): 1–7.

Filmer, Kath. "The Polemic Image: The Role of Metaphor and Symbol in the Fiction of C. S. Lewis." *Seven: An Anglo-American Literary Review* 7 (1986): 61–76.

Fisher, Leona W. "Mythical Fantasy for Children: Silence and Community." *The Lion and the Unicorn* 14 (Dec 1990): 37–57.

Fisher, Margery. "An Old Favorite." *Growing Point* 26 (Mar 1988): 4937–4939. Discusses *The Horse and His Boy.*

Fitzgerald, Dorothy Hobson. "C. S. Lewis' Images." *CSL: The Bulletin of the New York C. S. Lewis Society* 14 (Sept 1983): 1–7.

Forbes, Cheryl. "Narnia: Fantasy, But. . . ." *Christianity Today* 20 (Apr 23, 1976): 6–10.

Ford, Paul F. *Companion to Narnia: A Complete, Illustrated Guide to the Themes, Characters, and Events of C. S. Lewis's Imaginary World.* New York: Harper, 1981; 1983. pap.

Foulon, Jacqueline. "The Theology of C. S. Lewis' Children's Books." Master's thesis, Fuller Theological Seminary, 1962.

Frost, Naomi. "Life after Death: Visions of Lewis and Williams." *CSL: The Bulletin of the New York C. S. Lewis Society* 6 (1975): 2–6.

Futch, Ken. "The Syntax of C. S. Lewis's Style: A Statistical Look at Some Syntactic Features." Ph.D. diss., University of Southern California, 1969.

Gibb, Jocelyn, ed. *Light on C. S. Lewis.* New York: Harcourt Brace Jovanovitch, 1966.

Gibson, Evan K. *C. S. Lewis, Spinner of Tales: A Guide to His Fiction.* Washington, DC: Christian Univ. Press, 1980.

Gilbert, Douglas, and Clyde S. Kilby. *C. S. Lewis: Images of His World.* Grand Rapids, MI: Eerdmans, 1973.

Gillespie, John T., and Diana Lembo. *Introducing Books: A Guide for the Middle Grades.* New York: Bowker, 1970, pp. 248–251.

Glover, Donald E. *C. S. Lewis: The Art of Enchantment.* Athens: Ohio Univ. Press, 1981.

Goodknight, Glen. "A Cosmological Geography in the Works of J. R. R. Tolkien, C. S. Lewis, and Charles Williams." *Mythlore* 1, no. 3 (1974).

Gopman, V. "Volshebnye Miry Klaiva Steplza L'Yuisa [The Enchanted Worlds of C. S. Lewis]." *Detskaya Literatura* [Moscow] 8 (Aug 1983): 33–37.

Gough, John. "C. S. Lewis and the Problem of David Holbrook." *Children's Literature in Education* 8 (Summer 1977): 51–62.

Green, David L. "Children's Literature Periodicals on Individual Authors, Dime Novels, Fantasy." *Phaedrus* 3 (1976): 22–24.

Green, Roger Lancelyn. *C. S. Lewis.* New York: Walck, 1963. Reprinted in Margery Fisher, Roger Lancelyn Green, and Marcus Crouch. *Henry Treese, C. S. Lewis and Beatrix Potter.* London: Bodley Head, 1969.

———. "C. S. Lewis and Andrew Lang." *Notes and Queries* 22 (May 1975): 208–209.

Green, Roger Lancelyn, and Walter Hooper. *C. S. Lewis: A Biography.* London: Collins, 1974. New York: Harcourt Brace Jovanovich, 1974.

Griffin, William. *Clive Staples Lewis: The Drama of a Life.* New York: Harper, 1986. Republished as *C. S. Lewis: The Authentic Voice.* Oxford: Lion, 1988.

Guthrie, Barbara Ann Bowman. "The Spiritual Quest and Health and C. S. Lewis." Ph.D. diss., University of North Texas, 1988.

Haigh, Gerald. "Through the Wardrobe." *Times Educational Supplement* (Feb 6, 1981): 24.

Haigh, John D. "The Fiction of C. S. Lewis." Ph.D. diss., University of Leeds (England), 1962.

Hall, Grace R. W. "Dynamic Life Choices in the Lewis Tapestries." *Webs and Wardrobes* 47 (1988): 47–55.

Hanger, Nancy C. "The Excellent Absurdity: Substitution and Co-Inherence in C. S. Lewis and Charles Williams. *Mythlore* 34 (1983): 14–18.

Hannay, Margaret Patterson. *C. S. Lewis.* New York: Ungar, 1981.

———. "C. S. Lewis' Theory of Mythology." *Mythlore* 1, no. 1 (1974).

———. "'Surprised by Joy': C. S. Lewis' Changing Attitudes toward Women." *Mythlore* 4, 13 no. 1 (1977): 15–20.

Harsh, Donna J. "Aslan in Filmland: The Animation of Narnia." In Douglas Street. *Children's Novels and the Movies.* New York: Ungar, 1983, pp. 163–170.

Hart, Dabney Adams. *Through the Open Door: A New Look at C. S. Lewis.* Birmingham: Univ. of Alabama Press, 1984.

Hartt, Walter F. "Godly Influences: The Theology of J. R. R. Tolkien and C. S. Lewis." *Studies in the Literary Imagination* 14 (Fall 1981): 21–29.

Heald, Tim. "Lewis's Wonderland." *Radio Times* [London] 218 (Jan 28–Feb 3, 1978): 13.

Henthorne, Susan Cassandra. "The Image of Woman in the Fiction of C. S. Lewis." Ph.D. diss., State University of New York at Buffalo, 1985.

Higgens, Regina. *Magic Kingdoms: Discovering the Joys of Childhood Classics with Your Child.* New York: Simon, 1992.

Higgins, James Edward. "Five Authors of Mystical Fancy for Children: A Critical Study." Ed.D. diss., Columbia University, 1965.

———. "A Letter from C. S. Lewis." *Horn Book* 42 (Dec 1966): 533–539. Reprinted in Elinor Field. *Horn Book Reflections.* Boston: Horn Book, 1969, pp. 230–237; and in Margaret Meek. *The Cool Web.* New York: Atheneum, 1976, pp. 157–158.

Hillegas, Mark Robert, ed. *Shadows of the Imagination: The Fantasies of C. S. Lewis, J. R. R. Tolkien and Charles Williams.* Carbondale: Southern Illinois Univ. Press, 1969.

Hindle, Alan. "C. S. Lewis: A Personal View." *Amon Hen* 58 (Aug 1982): 21–22.

Hoey, Mary Amy. "An Applied Linguistic Analysis of the Prose Style of C. S. Lewis." Ph.D. diss., University of Connecticut, 1966.

Holbrook, David. *C. S. Lewis's Fantasies: A Phenomenological Study.* Lewisburg, PA: Bucknell Univ. Press, 1991.

———. "The Problem of C. S. Lewis." *Children's Literature in Education* 10 (Mar 1973): 3–25. Reprinted in Geoff Fox. *Writers, Critics and Children.* New York: Agathon Press, 1976, pp. 116–124.

Hollindale, P. "The Image of the Beast: C. S. Lewis's *Chronicles of Narnia.*" *Use of English* 28 (Spring 1977): 16–21.

Hollowitz, John Charles. "The Mythopoeic Art of C. S. Lewis." Ph.D. diss., Northwestern University, 1980.

Hood, Gwyneth. "Husbands and Gods as Shadowbrutes: 'Beauty and the Beast' from Apuleius to C. S. Lewis." *Mythlore* 56 (1988): 33–43.

Hooper, Walter. "Narnia: The Author, the Critics, and the Tale." *Children's Literature,* vol. 3. Storrs, CT: Journal of the Modern Language Association, 1974, pp. 12–22. Reprinted in Peter J. Schakel. *The Longing for a Form.* Kent, OH: Kent State Univ. Press, 1977; and in *Reflections on Literature for Children.* Edited by Francelia Butler and Richard Rotert. Hamden, CT: Shoe String Press, 1984, pp. 247–259.

———. *Past Watchful Dragons: The Narnia Chronicles of C. S. Lewis.* New York: Macmillan, 1979.

———. "Reminiscences." *Mythlore* 3, no. 12 (1976).

———. *Through Joy and Beyond: A Pictorial Biography of C. S. Lewis.* New York: Macmillan, 1982.

Howard, Thomas. *The Achievement of C. S. Lewis.* Wheaton, IL: Harold Shaw, 1980.

———. "The 'Moral Mythology' of C. S. Lewis." *Modern Age* 22 (1978): 384–392.

Huttar, Charles A. "C. S. Lewis's Narnia and the 'Grand Design.'" In Peter J. Schakel. *The Longing for a Form.*

Hutton, M. "Writers for Children: C. S. Lewis." *School Librarian* 12 (July 1964): 124–126ff.

Hyles, Vernon. "On the Nature of Evil: The Cosmic Myths of Lewis, Tolkien, and Williams." *Mythlore* 50 (1987): 9–13+.

Jameson, Gloria. "Developing Self-Identity Through Religious Consciousness in Stories of George MacDonald, C. S. Lewis, Madeleine L'Engle, Katherine Paterson, Ursula K. Le Guin, and Laura Adams Armer." In *Literature and Hawaii's Children. Proceedings of the Third Biennial Conference on Literature and Hawaii's Children.* Honolulu: Literature and Hawaii's Children, 1988, pp. 143–147.

Jenkins, Sue. "Love, Loss, and Seeking: Material Deprivation and the Quest." *Children's Literature in Education* 15 (Summer 1984): 73–84.

Johnson, William G., and Marcia K. Houtman. "Platonic Shadows in C. S. Lewis' Narnia Chronicles." *Studies in Modern Fiction* 32 (Spring 1986): 75–87.

Jones, Karla Faust. "Girls in Narnia: Hindered or Human." *Mythlore* 49 (1987): 15–19.

Kantar, Maythee Jensen. "Children's Responses to Televised Adaptations of Literature." Ph.D. diss., University of Minnesota, 1990.

Karimipour, Zahra. "A Descriptive Bibliography of C. S. Lewis's Fiction: 1938–1981." Ph.D. diss., Oklahoma State University, 1985.

Karkainen, Paul A. *Narnia Explored.* Old Tappan, NJ: Revell, 1979.

Keefe, Carolyn. "Narnia Tales: A Refracting of Pictures." Syracuse, NY: ERIC Clearinghouse on Information Resources, 1978.

King, Don. "The Childlike in George MacDonald and C. S. Lewis." *Mythlore* 46 (1986): 17–22, 26.

———. "Narnia and the Seven Deadly Sins." *Mythlore* 38 (1984): 14–19.

Kirk, Tim. "A Map of Narnia." *Mythlore* 2, no. 7 (1975).

Kirkpatrick, Hope. "Hierarchy in C. S. Lewis." *CSL: The Bulletin of the New York C. S. Lewis Society* 6, no. 4 (1975): 1–6.

Kirkpatrick, Mary. "An Introduction to the Curdie Books by George MacDonald, including Parallels between Them and the Narnia Chronicles." *CSL: The Bulletin of the New York C. S. Lewis Society* 5, no. 5 (1974): 1–6.

———. "Lewis and MacDonald." *CSL: The Bulletin of the New York C. S. Lewis Society* 5, no. 7 (1974): 2–4.

Koelb, Clayton. *The Incredulous Reader: Literature and the Function of Disbelief.* Ithaca, NY: Cornell Univ. Press, 1984.

Kolbe, Martha Emily. "Three Oxford Dons as Creators of Other Worlds for Children: Lewis Carroll, C. S. Lewis and J. R. R. Tolkien." Ph.D. diss., University of Virginia, 1981.

Kotzin, Michael C. "C. S. Lewis and George MacDonald: *The Silver Chair* and the *Princess* Books." *Mythlore* 8, no. 27 (Spring 1981): 5–15.

———. "Mrs. Moore as the Queen of Underland." *Mythlore* 6 (Summer 1979): 46.

"*The Last Battle.*" In M. Crouch and A. Ellis. *Chosen for Children.* 3rd ed. London: The Library Association, 1977, pp. 83–90.

Lesser, Wendy. *The Life Below the Ground: A Study of the Subterranean in Literature and History.* London: Faber, 1988.

Lewis, C. S. *All My Road Before Me: The Diary of C. S. Lewis, 1922–1927,* ed. by Walter Hooper. London: Harper, 1991.

———. *C. S. Lewis's Letters to Children.* Edited by Lyle W. Dorsett and Marjorie Lamp. New York: Macmillan, 1985.

———. "The Dethronement of Power." *Time and Tide* 36 (Oct 22, 1955): 1373–1374.

———. *The Discarded Image.* New York: Cambridge Univ. Press, 1964, 1967.

———. *An Experiment in Criticism.* New York: Cambridge Univ. Press, 1961. "On Myth," "The Meaning of Fantasy," "On Realism," pp. 40–49, 50–56, 70–73.

———. "The Gods Return to Earth." *Time and Tide* 35 (Aug 1954): 1083.

———. *Of Other Worlds: Essays and Stories.* Edited by Walter Hooper. New York: Harcourt Brace Jovanovich, 1967.

———. "On Stories." In *Of Other Worlds: Essays and Stories.* New York: Harcourt Brace Jovanovich, 1967, pp. 247–259. Reprinted in *Essays Presented to Charles Williams.* Freeport, NY: Books for Libraries Press, 1972, pp. 90–105; and in Margaret Meek. *The Cool Web.* New York: Atheneum, 1978, pp. 76–90.

———. "On Three Ways of Writing for Children." *Horn Book* 39 (Oct 1963): 459–469 (written in 1952). Reprinted in C. S. Lewis. *Of Other Worlds: Essays and Stories.* Edited by Walter Hooper. New York: Harcourt Brace Jovanovich, 1967, pp. 22–34; in Virginia Haviland. *Children and Literature.* Glenview, IL: Scott, Foresman, 1973, pp. 231–240; and in Sheila A. Egoff. *Only Connect.* New York: Oxford Univ. Press, 1980, pp. 207–220.

———. "A Preface to *Paradise Lost.*" New York: Oxford Univ. Press, 1942.

———. "Sometimes Fairy Stories May Say Best What's to Be Said." *New York Times Book Review.* Pt. II. Nov 18, 1956, p. 3. Reprinted in C. S. Lewis. *Of Other Worlds: Essays and*

Stories. New York: Harcourt Brace Jovanovich, 1967, pp. 35–38, and in Boyer and Zahorski. *Fantasists on Fantasy.* New York: Avon, 1984, pp. 111–118.

———. *Surprised by Joy: The Shape of My Early Life.* New York: Harcourt Brace Jovanovich, 1955.

———. *They Asked for a Paper.* London: Bles, 1955.

Lind, Dianne. "The Importance of Fantasy in Young Adult Literature." *ALAN Review* 15 (1988): 13–14.

Lindskoog, Kathryn. "The First Chronicle of Narnia: The Restoring of Names." *Mythlore* 46 (1986): 43–46, 63.

———. *The Lion of Judah in Never-Never Land: The Theology of C. S. Lewis Expressed in His Fantasies for Children.* Grand Rapids, MI: Eerdmans, 1973.

Lively, Penelope. "The Wrath of God: An Opinion of the Narnia Books." *The Use of English* 20, no. 2 (Winter 1968): 126–129.

Lochhead, Marion. *Renaissance of Wonder.* New York: Harper, 1980, pp. 82–100.

Loney, John Douglas. "Reality, Truth and Perspective in the Fiction of C. S. Lewis." Ph.D. diss., McMaster University (Canada), 1983.

Lowentrout, Peter. "The Rags of Lordship: Science Fiction, Fantasy, and the Reenchantment of the World." *Mythlore* 41 (1985): 47–51, 57.

Lundin, Anne. "On the Shores of Lethe: C. S. Lewis and the Romantics." *Children's Literature in Education* 21 (Mar 1990): 53–59.

McKenzie, Patricia Alice. "*The Last Battle:* Violence and Theology in the Novels of C. S. Lewis." Ph.D. diss., University of Florida, 1974.

McMillan, Lex O., III. "C. S. Lewis as Spiritual Autobiography: A Study in the Sacramental Imagination." Ph.D. diss., University of Notre Dame, 1986.

Manlove, Colin. *C. S. Lewis: His Literary Achievement.* New York: St. Martin, 1987.

———. *The Chronicles of Narnia: The Patterning of a Fantastic World.* Boston: Twayne, 1993.

———. *Modern Fantasy: Five Studies.* New York: Cambridge Univ. Press, 1975.

Manna, Anthony L. "'Borrowing' C. S. Lewis: Aurand Harris's Dramatization of *The Magician's Nephew.*" *Children's Literature Association Quarterly* 11 (Fall 1986): 148–150.

Masson, Sophie. "On Re-Reading the Narnia Books." *Orana* 29 (May 1993): 71–75.

Matheson Sue. "C. S. Lewis and the Lion: Primitivism and Arthetype in the *Chronicles of Narnia.*" *Mythlore* 55 (1988): 13–18.

Matthews, Kenneth Ernest. "C. S. Lewis and the Modern World." Ph.D. diss., University of California, Los Angeles, 1983.

Meileander, Gilbert, Jr. "The Social and Ethical Thought of C. S. Lewis." Ph.D. diss., Princeton University, 1976.

———. *The Taste for the Other: The Social and Ethical Thought of C. S. Lewis.* Grand Rapids, MI: Eerdmans, 1978.

Milner, Joseph O'Beirne. "When Worlds Collide: The Humanist-Religious Ethos in Children's Literature." In *Webs and Wardrobes: Humanist and Religious World Views in Children's Literature,* ed. by Joseph O'Beirne Milner and Lucy Floyd Morcock Milner. Lanham, MD: University Press of America, 1987, pp. 1–5.

Montgomery, John W. "The Chronicles of Narnia and the Adolescent Reader." *Religious Education* 54 (Sept 1959): 418–428. Reprinted in Miriam Hoffman and Eva Samuels. *Authors and Illustrators of Children's Books.* New York: Bowker, 1972, pp. 280–296.

———, ed. *Myth, Allegory and Gospel: An Interpretation of J. R. R. Tolkien, C. S. Lewis, G. K. Chesterton, and Charles Williams.* Minneapolis: Bethany, 1974.

Mooreman, Charles W. "Myth and Modern Literature: A Study of the Arhurian Myth in Charles Williams, C. S. Lewis, and T. S. Eliot." Ph.D. diss., Tulane University, 1953.

———. "'Now Entertain Conjectures of a Time'—The Fictive Worlds of C. S. Lewis and J. R. R. Tolkien." In *Shadows of the Imagination.* Edited by Mark R. Hillegas. Carbondale: Southern Illinois Univ. Press, 1969.

————. "Sacramentalism in Charles Williams." *Chesterton Review* 8 (1982): 35–50.

More Junior Authors. Edited by Muriel Fuller. New York: Wilson, 1963, p. 140.

Morrison, John. "The Idea of Covenant in Narnia." *CSL: The Bulletin of the New York C. S. Lewis Society* 10 (Oct 1979): 1–7.

————. "Obedience and Surrender in Narnia." *CSL: The Bulletin of the New York C. S. Lewis Society* 7, no. 12 (1976): 2–4.

Morus, Ivan Rhys. "Comparisons Between *The Chronicles of Narnia* and *The Histories of Middle-Earth.*" *Amon Hen* 54 (Feb 1982): 6–7.

Murphy, Brian. *C. S. Lewis.* Mercer Island, WA: Starmont, 1983. (bibliography)

————. "Enchanted Rationalism: The Legacy of C. S. Lewis." *Christianity and Literature* 25 (Winter 1976): 13–29.

Murrin, Michael. "The Dialectic of Multiple Worlds: An Analysis of C. S. Lewis's Narnia Stories." *Seven: An Anglo-American Literary Review* 3 (1982).

Nardo, Anna K. "Fantasy Literature and Play: An Approach to Reader Response." *Centennial Review* 22 (1978): 201–213.

Nelson, Marie. "Non-Human Speech in the Fantasy of C. S. Lewis, J. R. R. Tolkien and Richard Adams." *Mythlore* 5, no. 17 (May 1978): 37–39.

Nelson, Michael. "C. S. Lewis and His Critics." *Virginia Quarterly Review* 64 (1988): 1–19.

Neuleib, Janice Witherspoon. "The Concept of Evil in the Fiction of C. S. Lewis." Ph.D. diss., University of Illinois, 1974.

————. "Technology and Theocracy: The Cosmic Voyages of Wells and Lewis." *Extrapolation* 16 (May 1975): 130–136.

New York C. S. Lewis Society. *Bibliography of the Works of C. S. Lewis.* New Haven, CT: New York C. S. Lewis Society, 1979.

Nicholson, Mervyn. "What C. S. Lewis Took From E. Nesbit." *Children's Literature Association Quarterly* 16 (Spring 1991): 16–22.

O'Hare, C. "Charles Williams, C. S. Lewis, and J. R. R. Tolkien: Three Approaches to Religion in Modern Fiction." Ph.D. diss., University of Toronto, 1973.

Olsen, D. "First and Second Things: The Theoretical Criticism of C. S. Lewis." Ph.D. diss., Bowling Green State University, 1978.

The Oxford Companion to Children's Literature. Edited by Humphrey Carpenter and Mari Prichard. New York: Oxford Univ. Press, 1984, pp. 309–310, 370.

Patterson, Nancy-Lou. "'Always Winter and Never Christmas': Symbols of Time in Lewis's *Chronicles of Narnia.*" *Mythlore* 18 (Autumn 1991): 10–14.

————. "An Appreciation of Pauline Baynes." *Mythlore* 7, no. 25 (1980).

————. "The Bolt of Tash: The Figure of Satan in C. S. Lewis's *The Horse and his Boy* and *The Last Battle.*" *Mythlore* 16 (Summer 1990): 23–26.

————. "Guardaci Ben: The Visionary Woman in C. S. Lewis' *Chronicles of Narnia* and *That Hideous Strength.*" *Mythlore* 6 (Summer 1979): 6–10, and 6 (Winter 1979): 20–24.

————. "Half Like a Serpent: The Green Witch in *The Silver Chair.*" *Mythlore* 40 (1984): 37–47.

————. "The Host of Heaven, Astrological and Other Images of Divinity in the Fantasies of C. S. Lewis." *Mythlore* 7 (1980): 19–29ff.

————. "Narnia and the North: The Symbolism of Northernness in the Fantasies of C. S. Lewis." *Mythlore* 4, no. 2 (1976): 9–16.

Pauline, Sister, C.S.M. "Secondary Worlds: Lewis and Tolkien." *CSL: The Journal of the New York C. S. Lewis Society* 12 (May 1981): 1–8.

Paxon, Diana. "The Tolkien Tradition." *Mythlore* 39 (1984): 23–27, 37.

————. "What I Did for Love." *Mythlore* 17 (Autumn 1990): 4–8.

Peters, John. *C. S. Lewis: The Man and His Achievement.* Exeter, England: Paternoster Press, 1985.

Pflieger, Pat, and Helen M. Hill. *A Reference Guide to Modern Fantasy for Children.* Westport, CT: Greenwood, 1984, pp. xi–xvi, 249–251, 295–297, 307–311, 313–315, 342–344, 452–454, 470–472, 490–492.

Phelps, Russ A. *"Mother Hubberd's Tale* and *The Last Battle." CSL: The Bulletin of the New York C. S. Lewis Society* 11 (Apr 1980): 9–10.

Philip, Neil, and Brian Sibley. "An Allegory of Love." *Times Educational Supplement* (Nov 10, 1989): 62.

Pietrusz, Jim. "Rites of Passage: *The Chronicles of Narnia* and the Seven Sacraments." *Mythlore* 54 (1988): 61–63.

Pittenger, Norman. "C. S. Lewis: Combative in Defense." *Studies in the Literary Imagination* 14 (1981): 13–20.

Pitts, Mary Ellen. "The Motif of the Garden in the Novels of J. R. R. Tolkien, Charles Williams, and C. S. Lewis." *Mythlore* 8, no. 30 (1981).

Poskanzer, Susan Cornell. "Thoughts on C. S. Lewis and *The Chronicles of Narnia." Language Arts* 53 (May 1976): 523–526.

Presley, Horton. "C. S. Lewis: Mythmaker." In Thomas D. Clareson and Thomas L. Wymer. *Voices for the Future,* vol. 3. Bowling Green, OH: Bowling Green Univ. Press, 1984.

Price, Meredith. "'All Shall Love Me and Despair': The Figure of Lilith in Tolkien, Lewis, Williams, and Sayers." *Mythlore* 9 (1982): 3–7ff.

Purtill, Richard. *Lord of Elves and Eldils: Fantasy and Philosophy in C. S. Lewis and J. R. R. Tolkien.* Grand Rapids, MI: Zondervan, 1974.

Quinn, Dennis B. "The Narnia Books of C. S. Lewis: Fantastic or Wonderful?" In *Children's Literature,* vol. 12. New Haven, CT: Yale Univ. Press, 1984, pp. 105–121.

Reddy, Albert Francis, S.J. "The Else Unspeakable: An Introduction to the Fiction of C. S. Lewis." Ph.D. diss., University of Massachusetts, 1972.

Riga, Frank P. "Mortals Call Their History Fable: Narnia and the Use of Fairy Tale." *Children's Literature Association Quarterly* 14 (Spring 1989): 26–29.

Rigsbee, Sally. "Fantasy Places and Imaginative Belief: *The Lion, the Witch and the Wardrobe* and *The Princess and the Goblin." Children's Literature Association Quarterly* 8 (Spring 1983): 10–12.

Rogers, Deborah Champton Webster. "The Fictitious Characters of C. S. Lewis and J. R. R. Tolkien in Relation to Their Medieval Sources." Ph.D. diss., University of Wisconsin, 1972.

Rossi, Lee D. "The Politics of Fantasy: C. S. Lewis and J. R. R. Tolkien." Ph.D. diss., Cornell University, 1972.

———. *The Politics of Fantasy: C. S. Lewis and J. R. R. Tolkien.* Ann Arbor: Univ. of Michigan Research Press, 1984.

Rustin, Michael. "Narnia: An Imaginary Land as Container of Moral and Emotional Adventure." In Margaret Rustin and Michael Rustin. *Narratives of Love and Loss: Studies in Modern Children's Fiction.* London: Verso, 1987; New York: Rutledge, 1988, pp. 40–58.

Sadler, Glenn Edward. "C. S. Lewis." In *Writers for Children: Critical Studies of Major Authors Since the Seventeenth Century.* Edited by Jane M. Bingham. New York: Scribner, 1988, pp. 357–364.

Sammons, Martha C. *"A Better Country": The Worlds of Religious Fantasy and Science Fiction.* Westport, CT: Greenwood, 1988.

———. *A Guide through Narnia.* Wheaton, IL: Shaw, 1979.

———. "Lewis' Influence on the New Inklings: *The Chronicles of Narnia* and John White's *Tower of Geburah* and *The Iron Sceptre." CSL: The Bulletin of the New York C. S. Lewis Society* 17 (Nov 1985): 1–7.

San José, Pilar, and Gregory Starkey. "Tolkien's Influence on C. S. Lewis." *Mallorn* 17 (Oct 1981): 23–28.

———. "Tolkien's Influence on C. S. Lewis: Epilogue." *Mallorn* 19 (Dec 1982): 29–30.

Sardello, Robert J. "An Empirical-Phenomenological Study of Fantasy, with a Note on J. R. R. Tolkien and C. S. Lewis." *Psycho-Cultural Review* 2 (1978): 203–220.

Saunders, Paulette G. "The Idea of Love in the Writings of C. S. Lewis." Ph.D. diss., Ball State University, 1987.

Sayer, George. *Jack: C. S. Lewis and His Times.* London: Macmillan, 1988; San Francisco: Harper, 1988.

Sayers, Dorothy L. "The Chronicles of Narnia." *Spectator* (July 22, 1955): 123.

Schakel, Peter J. "Dance as Metaphor and Myth in Lewis, Tolkien, and Williams." *Mythlore* 45 (1986): 4–8, 23.

———. *Reading with the Heart: The Way into Narnia.* Grand Rapids, MI: Eerdmans, 1979.

———, ed. *The Longing for a Form: Essays on the Fiction of C. S. Lewis.* Kent, OH: Kent State Univ. Press, 1977.

Schofield, Stephen, ed. *In Search of C. S. Lewis.* South Plainfield, NJ: Bridge Publishers, Inc., 1983.

Searles, Baird, Beth Meacham, and Michael Franklin. *A Reader's Guide to Fantasy.* New York: Avon, 1982, pp. 94–95.

Shippey, Tom A. "*The Chronicles of Narnia.*" In *Survey of Modern Fantasy Literature,* vol. 1. Edited by Frank N. Magill. Englewood Cliffs, NJ: Salem Press, 1983, pp. 248–255.

———. "The Golden Bough and the Incorporation of Magic in Science Fiction." *Foundation* 11/12 (1977): 119–134.

Shoemaker, S. "Beyond the Walls of the World: Practical Theology in the Fantasy Novels of C. S. Lewis." Ph.D. diss., Duke University, 1979.

Sibley, Brian. *The Land of Narnia: Brian Sibley Explores the World of C. S. Lewis.* Illus. by Pauline Baynes. London: Collins, 1989; New York: Harper, 1990.

Simmons, Courtney Lynn, and Joe Simmons. "*The Silver Chair* and Plato's Allegory of the Cave: Archetypes of Spiritual Liberation." *Mythlore* 17, no. 4 (Summer 1991): 12–15.

Smith, Lillian H. "News from Narnia." *Canadian Library Association Bulletin* (July 1958). Reprinted in *Horn Book* 39 (Oct 1963): 470–473; in Elinor Field. *Horn Book Reflections.* Boston: Horn Book, 1969, pp. 225–229; and in Sheila A. Egoff. *Only Connect.* New York: Oxford Univ. Press, 1980, pp. 170–175.

Stott, Jon C. *Children's Literature from A to Z.* New York: McGraw-Hill, 1984, p. 173.

Studies in the Literary Imagination. "Special Issue: C. S. Lewis: A Critic Recriticized." 22 (Fall 1989).

Sullivan, Dale Lee. "A Rhetoric of Children's Literature as Epideictic Discourse." Ph.D. diss., Rensselaer Polytechnic Institute, 1988.

Suthamchai, Phanida. "The Fusion of Christian and Fictional Elements in C. S. Lewis's *Chronicles of Narnia.*" Ph.D. diss., Oklahoma State University, 1985.

Sutherland, S. "From Childhood to Narnia." *Christian Librarian* (Cedarville, OH) 34 (Aug 1991): 124–126.

Swinfen, Ann. *In Defense of Fantasy.* London: Routledge, 1984, pp. 19, 22–23, 79–83, 85–86, 90–91, 103–105, 115, 147–159, 186–189, 231–232.

Terry, June S. "To Seek and to Find: Quest Literature for Children." *School Librarian* 18 (Dec 1970): 399–404. Reprinted in Mary Lou White. *Children's Literature.* Columbus, OH: Merrill, 1976, pp. 138–143.

Thompson, Hilary. "Doorways to Fantasy." *Canadian Children's Literature* 21 (1981): 8–16.

Timmerman, John H. "*The Magician's Nephew:* Mage and Maker." In *Other Worlds: The Fantasy Genre.* Bowling Green, OH: Bowling Green Univ. Press, 1983, pp. 75–81.

Tixier, Elaine. "Imagination Baptized, or 'Holiness' in the *Chronicles of Narnia.*" In Peter J. Schakel. *The Longing for a Form: Essays on the Fiction of C. S. Lewis.* Kent, OH: Kent State Univ. Press, 1977.

Twentieth-Century Children's Writers. 3rd ed. Edited by Tracy Chevalier and D. L. Kirkpatrick. Chicago: St. James, 1989, pp. 580–583.

Twentieth-Century Science Fiction Writers. 3rd ed. Edited by Noelle Watson and Paul E. Schellinger. Chicago: St. James Press, 1991, pp. 489–492.

Unrue, John C. "Beastliness in Narnia: Medieval Echoes." In *Man's "Natural Powers."*

Edited by Raymond P. Tripp, Jr. London: The Society for New Language Study, 1975, pp. 9–16.

Urang, Gunnar. *Shadows of Heaven: Religion and Fantasy in the Writing of C. S. Lewis, Charles Williams and J. R. R. Tolkien.* Ph.D. diss., University of Chicago, 1970. New York: Pilgrim Press, 1971.

Wade, Barrie and John Shepard. "Marx in Narnia." *The Use of English* 40 (Summer 1989): 51–58.

Wain, John. "C. S. Lewis." *The American Scholar* 50 (1980–1981): 73–80.

Walker, Andrew, and James Patrick. *A Christian for All Christians: Essays in Honour of C. S. Lewis.* London: Hodder, 1990.

Walker, Jeanne Murray. "*The Lion, the Witch, and the Wardrobe* as Rite of Passage." *Children's Literature in Education* 16 (1985): 177–188.

Walsh, Chad. *The Literary Legacy of C. S. Lewis.* New York: Harcourt Brace Jovanovich, 1979.

Ward, Samuel Keith. "C. S. Lewis and the Nature-Grace Aesthetic." Ph.D. diss., University of Pittsburgh, 1977.

Watson, James Darrell. "A Reader's Guide to C. S. Lewis: His Fiction." Ed.D. diss., East Texas University, 1981.

Wilcox, Steven Michael. "Reality, Romanticism and Reason: Perspectives on a C. S. Lewis Pedagogy." Ph.D. diss., University of Colorado at Boulder, 1982.

Wilson, A. N. *C. S. Lewis: A Biography.* London: Collins, 1990; New York: Norton, 1990.

Wolfe, Gary Kent. "Symbolic Fantasy." *Genre* 8 (1975): 194–209.

Wood, Doreen Anderson. "Of Time and Eternity: C. S. Lewis and Charles Williams." *CSL: The Bulletin of the New York C. S. Lewis Society* 17 (1986): 1–7.

Wright, Marjorie Evelyn. "The Cosmic Kingdom of Myth: A Study in the Myth-Philosophy of Charles Williams, C. S. Lewis, and J. R. R. Tokien." Ph.D. diss., University of Illinois, 1960.

Wytenbroek, Jacqueline. "Science Fiction and Fantasy." *Extrapolation* 23 (1982): 321–332.

Yandell, Steven. "The Trans-Cosmic Journeys in *The Chronicles of Narnia*." *Mythlore* 43 (1985): 9–23.

Yates, Jessica. "Tolkien's Influence on *The Chronicles of Narnia*." *Mallorn* (June 18, 1982): 31–33.

Ziegler, Mervin. "Imagination as a Rhetorical Factor in the Works of C. S. Lewis." Ph.D. diss., University of Florida, 1973.

Lewis, Hilda (Winifred)

The Oxford Companion to Children's Literature. Edited by Humphrey Carpenter and Mari Prichard. New York: Oxford Univ. Press, 1984, p. 484.

Twentieth-Century Children's Writers. 3rd ed. Edited by Tracy Chevalier and D. L. Kirkpatrick. Chicago: St. James, 1989, p. 584.

Lifton, Betty Jean (Kirschner)

Helbig, Alethea K., and Agnes Regan Perkins. *Dictionary of American Children's Fiction, 1960–1984; Recent Books of Recognized Merit.* Westport, CT: Greenwood, 1986, pp. 176, 380.

Lifton, Betty Jean. "In Search of Kappas." *Horn Book* 37 (Feb 1961): 34–41.

———. "On Children's Literature: A Runcible Symposium." *Horn Book* 46 (June 1970): 255–263.

———. "Report on a Thousand Cranes." *Horn Book* 45 (Apr 1969): 148–151.

————. "A Thousand Cranes." *Horn Book* 39 (Apr 1963): 211–216.
Third Book of Junior Authors. Edited by Doris De Montreville and Donna Hill. New York: Wilson, 1972, pp. 178–199.
Twentieth-Century Children's Writers. 3rd ed. Edited by Tracy Chevalier and D. L. Kirkpatrick. Chicago: St. James, 1989, pp. 586–587.

Lindbergh, Anne

Lindbergh, Anne. "Thoughts in the Rabbit Hole." *The Writer* 97 (Apr 1985): 7–10.
Mercier, J. F. "Anne Lindbergh: Author of Books for Young People." *Publishers Weekly,* 226 (July 27, 1984) 147–148.
Sixth Book of Junior Authors and Illustrators. Edited by Sally Holmes Holtze. New York: Wilson, 1989, pp. 172–173.

Linde, Gunnel (Geijerstam)

Fourth Book of Junior Authors and Illustrators. Edited by Doris De Montreville and Elizabeth D. Crawford. New York: Wilson, 1978, pp. 226–228.
Linde, Gunnel. "Konsrollstankandet Som Iasning [The Limitations of Sex Role Analysis]." *Opsis Kalopsis* [Stockholm] 1 (1991): 38–40.

Lindgren, Astrid

Ahmansson, Gabriella. "Ar det Bara Pojkar Som Kan Radda Variden?" [Can Only Boys Save the World?] *Opsis Kalopsis* (Sweden) 1 (1992): 24–26.
Alcorn, Noeline. "Fantasy and Family Life: Children's Books from Northern Europe." *Children's Literature Association Yearbook.* Auckland, New Zealand: Children's Literature Association, 1976, pp. 29–42. Discusses Astrid Lindgren, Maria Gripe, Christine Nöstlinger, Otfried Preussler, and Paul Biegel.
Andreadis, A. Harriette. "The Screening of Pippi Longstocking." In Douglas Street. *Children's Novels and the Movies.* New York: Ungar, 1983, pp. 151–162.
Auraldsson, K. "Astrid Lindgren" *Bookbird* 25 (Oct 1987): 8–10.
Bamberger, Richard. "Astrid Lindgren and a New Kind of Books for Children." *Bookbird* 5, no. 2 (1967): 3–12.
————. "Astrid Lindgren on the Occasion of Her 70th Birthday." *Bookbird* 15, no. 2 (1977): 17–21.
Berkley, M. "*Pippi Longstocking*—And After." *Publishers Weekly,* 227 (Feb 22, 1985): 96–97.
Bjoran, Lillian. "Pippis og Emils Mor, Astrid Lindgren [Pippi's and Emil's Mother, Astrid Lindgren]." *Foreldre & Barn* (Norway) 6/7 (1978): 6–8.
Cott, Jonathan. "Profiles: Astrid Lindgren: The Astonishment of Being." *The New Yorker,* 59 (Feb 28, 1983): 46–63. Reprinted in Cott. *Pipers at the Gates of Dawn.* New York: Random, 1983, pp. 137–160.
Crampton, Patricia. "Astrid-Trans-Lindgren." *Books for Keeps* (U.K.) 59 (Nov 1989): 21.
Edström, Vivi. "*Pippi Longstocking*: Chaos and Postmodernism." *Swedish Book Review: 1990 Supplement: Swedish Children's Literature,* pp. 22–29.
Gillespie, John T., and Diana Lembo. *Introducing Books: A Guide for the Middle Grades.* New York: Bowker, 1970, pp. 269–271.
Gould, Tony. "Swedish Mischief." *New Society* [London] 44 (May 25, 1978): 436–437.
Hagliden, Sten. "Astrid Lindgren, the Swedish Writer of Children's Books." *Junior Book-*

shelf 23 (July 1959): 113–121. Reprinted in Miriam Hoffman and Eva Samuels. *Authors and Illustrators of Children's Books.* New York: Bowker, 1972, pp. 297–301.

Hoffeld, Laura. "*Pippi Longstocking:* The Comedy of the Natural Girl." *The Lion and Unicorn* 1, no. 1 (Spring 1977): 47–53.

Hürlimann, Bettina. *Three Centuries of Children's Books in Europe.* Translated and edited by Brian W. Alderson. Cleveland: World, 1968, pp. 81–83.

Hurwitz, Johanna. *Astrid Lindgren: Storyteller to the World.* New York: Viking, 1989.

———. "A Special Visit." *Five Owls* 3, no. 3 (1989): 45–46.

Huse, Nancy. "The Blank Mirror of Death: Protest as Self-Creation in Contemporary Fantasy." *The Lion and the Unicorn* 12 (1988): 28–43.

Juncker, Clara. "The Ultimate Fantasy: Astrid Lindgren's *The Brothers Lionheart.*" In *The Fantastic in World Literature and the Arts,* ed. by Donald E. Morse. New York: Greenwood, 1987.

Kvint, Kerstin. "Astrid Lindgrens Lansering Utomlands [The Promotion of Astrid Lindgren Abroad]." *Barn och Kultur* (Sweden) 33, no. 5 (1987): 111–114.

Lindgren, Astrid. "Astrid Lindgren Tells about Herself." *School Library Bulletin Supplement* (Australia) 10, no. 2 (1978): 34–37.

———. "I Remember..." *Signal* 57 (Sept 1988): 155–169.

———. "I Sanning Vedervärdig Busunge Fyller 40 [A Truly Repulsive Rascal Turns 40]." *Barnboken* (Sweden) 2 (1985): 5–6.

———. "Pippi Can Lift a Horse: The Importance of Children's Books." *Quarterly Journal of the Library of Congress* 40 (Summer 1983): 188–201.

———. "A Short Talk with a Prospective Children's Writer." *Horn Book* 49 (June 1973): 248–252. Reprinted in Paul Heins. *Crosscurrents of Criticism.* Boston: Horn Book, 1977, pp. 3–6.

———. "Zachem Pishut Detskie Knigi [Why Write Children's Books]?" *Detskaya Literatura* (Moscow) 11 (Nov 1985): 36–39.

Lindgren, Astrid, and Eva Von Zweigbergk. "The Road to Sunnanang." *Bookbird* 9, no 1 (1971): 37–55.

Lundqvist, Ulla. "The Child of the Century: The Phenomenon of *Pippi Longstocking* and Its Premises." *The Lion and the Unicorn* 13 (Dec 1989): 97–102.

Metcalf, Eva-Maria. "Astrid Lindgren, Rebel for Peace." *Scandinavian Review* 78 (1990): 34–41.

———. "Astrid Lindgren's *Ronia, The Robber's Daughter*: A Twentieth-Century Fairy Tale." *The Lion and the Unicorn* 12 (1988): 151–164.

———. "Tall Tale and Spectacle in *Pippi Longstocking.*" *Children's Literature Association Quarterly* 15 (Fall 1990): 130–135.

More Junior Authors. Edited by Muriel Fuller. New York: Wilson, 1963, pp. 141–142.

Morse, Donald E., ed. *The Fantastic in World Literature and the Arts.* Westport, CT: Greenwood, 1987.

Orvig, Mary, et al. *Duvdrottningen: En Bok Till Astrid Lindgren [To Astrid Lindgren, Queen of the Doves]* Stockholm: Raben, 1987.

The Oxford Companion to Children's Literature. Edited by Humphrey Carpenter and Mari Prichard. New York: Oxford Univ. Press, 1984, pp. 312, 414.

Powling, Chris. "Authorgraph no. 59: Astrid Lindgren." *Books for Keeps* (U.K.) 59 (Nov 1989): 16–17.

Reeder, Kik. "*Pippi Longstocking*—Feminist or Anti-Feminist?" *Interracial Books for Children* 5, no. 4 (1974): 1.

Slayton, Ralph. "The Love Story of Astrid Lindgren." *Scandinavian Review* 63 (Dec 1975): 44–53.

Smaridge, Norah. *Famous Modern Storytellers for Young People.* New York: Dodd, 1969, pp. 105–109.

Söderblom, Harriette. "Astrid Lindgren." Translated by Martin Naylor. *CBC Features* (formerly *The Calendar*) 40 (June–Dec 1986).

Svensen, Asfrid. "Opening Windows onto Unreality: Some Elements of the Fantastic in Scandinavian Children's Literature." *The International Review of Children's Literature and Librarianship* 2 (Spring 1987): 1–9.

Tornqvist, Lena. "Astrid of Smaland—and of the World." *Bookbird* (Denmark) 4 (1992): 5–8.

Udal, John. "Richard Kennedy and *Pippi Longstocking.*" *Junior Bookshelf* 42 (Apr 1978): 75–77.

Wignell, Edel. "*Pippi* at the Mid-Life Crossroad." *Reading Time* (Australia) 98 (Jan 1986): 5–7.

Lindsay, Norman (Alfred William)

Colebatch, Hal. "Norman Lindsay and *The Magic Pudding.*" *Westerly* 1 (Mar 1976): 83–86.

Doyle, Brian. *The Who's Who of Children's Literature.* New York: Schocken, 1968, pp. 180–181.

Hetherington, John. *Norman Lindsay.* Melbourne: Lansdowne Press, 1961.

Lindsay, Norman. *My Mask: For What Little I Know of the Man Behind It: An Autobiography.* Sydney: Argus & Robertson, 1970.

McVitty, Walter. "*The Magic Pudding*: Hors D'Oeuvres and Appetisers." *Reading Time* (Australia) 59 (Apr 1976): 2–12.

———. "A Taste of the Best: A Gourmet Guide to Children's Books" *Reading Time* (Australia) 82 (Jan 1982): 7–22.

The Oxford Companion to Children's Literature. Edited by Humphrey Carpenter and Mari Prichard. New York: Oxford Univ. Press, 1984, p. 334.

Roe, Marjorie. "Forum of Children's Books: A *Magic Pudding* from Australia." *Bookbird* 6, no. 3 (Sept 1968): 28–33.

Twentieth-Century Children's Writers. 3rd ed. Edited by Tracy Chevalier and D. L. Kirkpatrick. Chicago: St. James, 1989, pp. 589–590.

Linklater, Eric (Robert Russell)

Doyle, Brian. *The Who's Who of Children's Literature.* New York: Schocken, 1968, pp. 181–182.

The Oxford Companion to Children's Literature. Edited by Humphrey Carpenter and Mari Prichard. New York: Oxford Univ. Press, 1984, p. 575.

Twentieth-Century Children's Writers. 3rd ed. Edited by Tracy Chevalier and D. L. Kirkpatrick. Chicago: St. James, 1989, pp. 593–594.

"*The Wind on the Moon.*" In M. Crouch and A. Ellis. *Chosen for Children.* 3rd ed. London: The Library Association, 1977, pp. 35–39.

Lisle, Janet Taylor

Cooper, Ilene. "New Voices, New Visions: Janet Taylor Lisle." *Horn Book* 64 (Nov–Dec 1988): 755–758.

Helbig, Alethea, and Agnes Regan Perkins. *Dictionary of American Children's Fiction, 1985–1989.* Westport, CT: Greenwood, 1993, p. 141.

Sixth Book of Junior Authors and Illustrators. Edited by Sally Holmes Holtze. New York: Wilson, 1989, pp. 174–175.

Lively, Penelope (Margaret Low)

Abbs, Peter. "Penelope Lively, Children's Fiction and the Failure of Adult Culture." *Children's Literature in Education* 18 (Fall 1975): 118–124.

Ainsworth, Marlane. "Exceptional Authors: Penelope Lively." *Educational Library Service Bulletin* (Australia) 18 (Aug–Sept 1980): 9–14.

Armstrong, Judith. "Ghosts as Rhetorical Devices in Children's Fiction." *Children's Literature in Education* 29, no. 9 (Summer 1978): 59–66.

"Authorograph no. 2: Penelope Lively." *Books for Keeps* (U.K.) 2 (May 1980): 14–15.

Cleaver, Pamela. "Author by Accident." *Books and Bookmen* [London] 21 (Dec 1974): 66–68.

Fourth Book of Junior Authors and Illustrators. Edited by Doris De Montreville and Elizabeth D. Crawford. New York: Wilson, 1978, pp. 229–231.

"The Ghost of Thomas Kempe." In M. Crouch and A. Ellis. *Chosen for Children.* 3rd ed. London: The Library Association, 1974, pp. 168–172.

Gough, John. "Dreaming of Death and Ancestors: Penelope Lively's Novel *The House in Norham Gardens.*" *Papers* (Australia) 2 (Dec 1991): 108–116.

Hardyment, Christina. "Time Out of Mind.'" *Oxford Today* (U.K.) 2, no. 3 (1990): 30–31.

Hiller, Claire. "The World of Fantasy—The World Where Anything Can Happen." *English in Australia* 86 (Dec 1988): 54–59.

Hoffman, Mary. "Past Mistress: Mary Hoffman Interviews Penelope Lively, Winner of the Whitbread Award for Children's Fiction." *Times Educational Supplement* 3216 (Jan 21, 1977): 37.

Inglis, Fred. *The Promise of Happiness.* New York: Cambridge Univ. Press, 1981, pp. 226–229.

Le Mesurier, Nicholas. "A Lesson in History: The Presence of the Past in the Novels of Penelope Lively." *New Welsh Review* 2, no. 4 (Spring 1990): 36–38.

Lively, Penelope. "Bones in the Sand." Based on a paper given at the Simmons College Center for the Study of Children's Literature, March 14, 1981. *Horn Book* 57 (Dec 1981): 641–651. Reprinted in *Innocence & Experience.* Edited by Barbara Harrison and Gregory Maguire. New York: Lothrop, 1987, pp. 13–21.

———. "Carnegie Medal Acceptance Address." *YLG News* (U.K.) 18, no. 3 (Winter 1974): 10–13.

———. "Children and Memory." *Horn Book* 49 (Aug 1973): 400–407. Reprinted in Paul Heins. *Crosscurrents of Criticism.* Boston: Horn Book, 1977, pp. 226–233.

———. "Children and the Art of Memory, Part I." *Horn Book* 54 (Feb 1978): 17–23. "Part II." *Horn Book* 54 (Apr 1978): 197–203.

———. *"The Driftway."* *School Bookshop News* (U.K.) 5 (Autumn 1976): 22–23; *Puffin Post* (U.K.) 5 (Spring 1985): 20–21.

———. *"The Ghost of Thomas Kempe."* *Junior Bookshelf* 38 (June 1974): 143–145.

———. "Winning Reflections." *Author* [London] 90 (Summer 1979): 70–71.

"Meet a Puffin Person: Penelope Lively." *Puffin Post* (U.K.) 10 (Summer 1986): 11–13.

Moon, Kenneth. "Don't Tell It: Show It." *School Librarian* 31 (Dec 1983): 319–327.

The Oxford Companion to Children's Literature. Edited by Humphrey Carpenter and Mari Prichard. New York: Oxford Univ. Press, 1984, pp. 261–262, 322.

Pflieger, Pat, and Helen M. Hill. *A Reference Guide to Modern Fantasy for Children.* Westport, CT: Greenwood, 1984, pp. xii–xvi, 157–158, 204–205, 316–319, 471–472, 569–570, 591–592, 600–601.

Rees, David. "The Narrative Art of Penelope Lively." *Horn Book* 51 (Feb 1976): 17–25. Reprinted in Paul Heins. *Crosscurrents of Criticism.* Boston: Horn Book, 1977, pp. 342–348; and in David Rees. *The Marble in the Water.* Boston: Horn Book, 1980, pp. 185–198.

————. "Time Present and Time Past: Penelope Lively." In *Marble in the Water.* Boston: Horn Book, 1980, pp. 185–198. Revised from an article in *Horn Book* 51 (Feb 1975): 17–25. Reprinted in Paul Heins. *Crosscurrents of Criticism.* Boston: Horn Book, 1977, pp. 342–348.

Ryan, J. S. "'The Tolkien Formation'—With a Lively Example." *Mallorn* 25 (1988): 20–22.

Salway, Lance, and Nancy Chambers. "Book Post." *Signal* 26 (May 1978): 99–107.

Smith, Amanda. "*PW* Inteviews: Penelope Lively." *Publishers Weekly* 25 (Mar 1988): 47–48.

Smith, Louisa A. "Layers of Language in Lively's *The Ghost of Thomas Kempe.*" *Children's Literature Association Quarterly* 10 (Fall 1985): 114–116.

Spirt, Diana L. *Introducing More Books: A Guide for the Middle Grades.* New York: Bowker, 1978, pp. 208–210.

Townsend, John Rowe. "Penelope Lively." In *A Sounding of Storytellers.* Philadelphia: Lippincott, 1979, pp. 125–138.

Twentieth-Century Children's Writers. 3rd ed. Edited by Tracy Chevalier and D. L. Kirkpatrick. Chicago: St. James, 1989, pp. 600–602.

Ward, David. "Another Time, Another Place." *The Guardian* (Sept 28, 1982): 8.

Lockley, Ronald (Mathias)

Yolen, Jane. "The Literary Underwater World." *Language Arts* 57 (1980): 403–412.

Lofting, Hugh (John)

Blishen, Edward. "Hugh Lofting." In Edward Blishen, Margaret Meek, and Roger Lancelyn Green. *Hugh Lofting/Geoffrey Trease/J. M. Barrie.* London: Bodley Head, 1968, pp. 9–61.

Certain, C. C. "*Dr. Dolittle,* the Children, and the Droll 'Huge' Lofting." *Elementary English Review* 1, no. 3 (May 1924): 90–92.

Chambers, Dewey W. "How, Now, Dr. Dolittle?" *Elementary English* 45 (Apr 1968): 437–439ff.

Colwell, Eileen H. "Hugh Lofting: An Appreciation." *Junior Bookshelf* 11 (Dec 1947): 149–154.

Doyle, Brian. *The Who's Who of Children's Literature.* New York: Schocken, 1968, pp. 182–183.

Fish, Helen Dean. "*Doctor Dolittle*: His Life and Works." *Horn Book* 24 (Oct 1948): 339–346. Reprinted in Elinor Field. *Horn Book Reflections.* Boston: Horn Book, 1969, pp. 218–224.

————. "*Dr. Dolittle*'s Creator." *Saturday Review* 31 (Jan 10, 1948): 28–29.

Helbig, Alethea K., and Agnes Regan Perkins. *Dictionary of American Children's Fiction, 1859–1959.* Westport, CT: Greenwood, 1985, pp. 308, 494–496, 552–554.

"John Dolittle, M.D." *Times Literary Supplement* (London) 23 (Nov 1951): vii.

Jones, M. E. "Connecticut's Puddleby-on-the-Marsh: Hugh Lofting." *Horn Book* 44 (Aug 1968): 463, 475.

The Junior Book of Authors. 2nd ed. rev. Edited by Stanley J. Kunitz and Howard Haycraft. New York: Wilson, 1951, pp. 198–200.

Lanes, Selma G. "Children's Books: *Doctor Dolittle,* Innocent Again." *New York Times Book Review* (Aug 28, 1988): 20.

Lofting, Christopher. "Trouble in Puddleby-on-the-Marsh." *Life Magazine* 61 (Sept 30, 1966): 7.

Lofting, Hugh. "Children and Internationalism." *Nation* 150 (Feb 13, 1924): 172–173.

————. "A Hunt Breakfast—Authors' Symposium." *Horn Book* 2 (Nov 1926): 34–35.

————. "War and Dr. Dolittle." *Junior Bookshelf* 11 (Dec 1947): 155–158.

MacCann, Donnarae. "Hugh Lofting." In *Writers for Children; Critical Studies of Major Authors Since the Seventeenth Century.* Edited by Jane M. Bingham. New York: Scribner, 1988, pp. 365–372.

Mack, Lori. "A Publisher's Perspective." *Horn Book* 64 (May–June 1988): 382–384. Discusses the revision of the *Doctor Dolittle* books.

Miller, Bertha Mahony, and Elinor Whitney Field, eds. *Newbery Medal Books: 1922–1955.* Boston: Horn Book, 1957, pp. 17–27.

The Oxford Companion to Children's Literature. Edited by Humphrey Carpenter and Mari Prichard. New York: Oxford Univ. Press, 1984, pp. 153–155, 324.

Roginski, Jim, ed. *Newbery and Caldecott Medalists and Honor Book Winners.* Littleton, CO: Libraries Unlimited, 1982, pp. 179–180.

Schlegelmilch, W. "From Fairy Tale to Children's Novel: In Honor of *Doctor Dolittle's* Fiftieth Birthday." *Bookbird* 8, no. 4 (1970): 14–21. Reprinted in Margaret Meek. *The Cool Web.* New York: Atheneum, 1978, pp. 265–271.

Schmidt, Gary D. "The Craft of the Cobbler's Son: Tommy Stubbins and the Narrative Form of the *Doctor Dolittle* Series." *Children's Literature Association Quarterly* 12 (Spring 1987): 19–24.

Schmidt, Nancy J. *Children's Fiction about Africa in English.* New York: Conch Magazine, 1981, pp. 175–178.

Searles, Baird, Beth Meacham, and Michael Franklin. *A Reader's Guide to Fantasy.* New York: Avon, 1982, pp. 96–97.

Shackford, J. "Dealing with *Dr. Dolittle:* A New Approach to the -isms." *Language Arts* 55 (Feb 1978): 180–187.

Shenk, Dorothy C. "Hugh Lofting: Creator of *Dr. Dolittle.*" *Elementary English* 32 (Apr 1955): 201–208.

Smaridge, Norah. *Famous Modern Storytellers for Young People.* New York: Dodd, 1969, pp. 32–37.

Suhl, Isabelle. "The 'Real' *Doctor Dolittle.*" *Interracial Books for Children* 2, no. 1–2 (Spring–Summer 1968): 1, 5–7. Reprinted in Donnarae MacCann and Gloria Woodard. *The Black American in Books for Children.* Metuchen, NJ: Scarecrow Press, 1972, pp. 78–88.

Twentieth-Century Children's Writers. 3rd ed. Edited by Tracy Chevalier and D. L. Kirkpatrick. Chicago: St. James, 1989, pp. 608–609.

Lowrey, Janette (Sebring)

Johnston, Leah Carter. "A Texas Author." *Horn Book* 23 (Jan 1947): 56–61.

Lunn, Janet

Gagnon, A. "Janet Lunn, Writer-In-Residence [at the Regina Public Library]." *Emergency Librarian* 11 (Nov–Dec 1983): 21–22.

Garner, Barbara Carman. "Journey as Structural and Thematic Motif in Janet Lunn's *The Root Cellar.*" *Proceedings of the 13th Annual Conference of The Children's Literature Association, 1986.* New York: Pace University, 1988, pp. 69–74.

————. "Lost and Found in Time: Canadian Time-Slip Fantasies for Children." *Children's Literature Association Quarterly* 15 (Winter 1990): 206–211.

Harrison, James. "Janet Lunn's Time/Space Travellers." *Canadian Children's Literature* 46 (1987): 60–63.

Jones, Raymond E. "Border Crossing: Janet Lunn's *The Root Cellar.*" *Children's Literature Association Quarterly* 10 (Spring 1985): 43–44.

Lunn, Janet. "Images of a Literature at Home." Presented at the Canadian Images Canadiennes Conference. *School Libraries in Canada* 7 (Spring 1987): 36–40.

Lunn, Lois. "The *Doppelgaenger* of *Shadow in Hawthorn Bay.*" In *The Voice of the Narrator in Children's Literature: Insights from Writers and Critics,* ed. by Charlotte F. Otten and Gary D. Schmidt. New York: Greenwood, 1989, pp. 276–277.

McDonough, Irma, ed. "Janet Lunn." In *Profiles.* rev. ed. Ottawa: Canadian Library Association, 1975.

Nikolajeva, Maria. "A Typological Approach to the Study of *The Root Cellar.*" *Canadian Children's Literature* 63 (1991): 53–60.

Reimer, Mavis. "Ice Women, Earth Mothers and Fairy Godmothers: Women as Metaphor in Two Recent Canadian Children's Novels." *Canadian Children's Literature* 49 (1988): 6–13.

Sixth Book of Junior Authors and Illustrators. Edited by Sally Holmes Holtze. New York: Wilson, 1989, pp. 179–181.

Thompson, Elizabeth. "Intergenerational Discourse: Collaboration and Time Travel in Canadian Fiction." *Canadian Children's Literature* 67 (1992): 19–31.

Twentieth-Century Children's Writers. 3rd ed. Edited by Tracy Chevalier and D. L. Kirkpatrick. Chicago: St. James, 1989, pp. 611–612.

Lynch, Patricia (Nora)

Crouch, Marcus. *The Nesbit Tradition.* London: Benn, 1972, pp. 182–184.

Deevy, Teresa. "Patricia Lynch: A Study." *Junior Bookshelf* 13 (Mar 1949): 17–27.

Doyle, Brian. *The Who's Who of Children's Literature.* New York: Schocken, 1968, pp. 185–186.

Graham, Eleanor. "Patricia Lynch: An Appreciation." *Junior Bookshelf* 7 (Mar 1943): 2–6.

Lochhead, Marion. *Renaissance of Wonder.* New York: Harper, 1980, pp. 77–81.

Lynch, Patricia. *A Storyteller's Childhood.* London: Dent, 1947.

The Oxford Companion to Children's Literature. Edited by Humphrey Carpenter and Mari Prichard. New York: Oxford Univ. Press, 1984, p. 326.

Twentieth-Century Children's Writers. 3rd ed. Edited by Tracy Chevalier and D. L. Kirkpatrick. Chicago: St. James, 1989, pp. 612–614.

Van Stockum, Hilda. "A Visit with Patricia Lynch." *Horn Book* 29 (Oct 1953): 367–372. Reprinted in Elinor Field. *Horn Book Reflections.* Boston: Horn Book, 1969, pp. 260–264.

Lynn, Elizabeth A.

Card, Orson Scott. "Unities in Digression." *Science Fiction Review* 37 (1980): 36–39.

"1980 World Fantasy Award Winners." *Locus* 13 (Oct 1980): 1, 4.

Notkin, Debbie. "Interview: Elizabeth A. Lynn." *Janus* 5 (Spring 1979): 18–19, 25.

Reimer, James D. "Masculinity and Feminist Fantasy Authors." *Science Fiction Fantasy Review* 66 (1984): 19–21.

Spencer, Kathleen L. "*The Chronicles of Tornor.*" In *Survey of Modern Fantasy Literature,* vol. 1. Edited by Frank N. Magill. Englewood Cliffs, NJ: Salem Press, 1983, pp. 275–281.

Twentieth-Century Science Fiction Writers. 3rd ed. Edited by Noelle Watson and Paul E. Schellinger. Chicago: St. James Press, 1991, pp. 512–513.

Watson, Ian. "The Author as Torturer." *Foundation* 40 (1987): 11–25.

MacAvoy, R(oberta) A(nn)

Twentieth-Century Science Fiction Writers. 3rd ed. Edited by Noelle Watson and Paul E. Schellinger. Chicago: St. James Press, 1991, pp. 515–516.

McCaffrey, Anne (Inez)

Antczak, Janice. *Science Fiction: The Mythos of a New Romance.* New York: Neal-Schuman, 1985, pp. 69–70, 114–115, 126–134, 159–160, 184–185.

Arbur, Rosemarie. *Leigh Brackett, Marion Zimmer Bradley, Anne McCaffrey: A Primary and Secondary Bibliography.* Boston: G. K. Hall, 1981.

Barr, Marleen. "Science Fiction and the Fact of Women's Repressed Creativity: Anne McCaffrey Portrays a Female Artist." *Extrapolation* 23 (Spring 1982): 70–76.

Barrett, David V. "Fire-Lizards Is Cats; Dragons Ain't Horses: Anne McCaffrey." *Vector* 1213 (1984): 3–7.

Brizzi, Mary T. *Anne McCaffrey.* Mercer Island, WA: Starmont, 1986.

"Dearest Ms. McCaffrey: Letters from Andrew Fox." *VOYA* 1 (Oct 1978): 5–6.

Evans, Gwyenth. "Harps and Harpers in Contemporary Fantasy." *The Lion and the Unicorn* 16 (Dec 1992): 199–209.

Fifth Book of Junior Authors and Illustrators. Edited by Sally Holmes Holtze. New York: Wilson, 1983, pp. 206–207.

Fonstad, Karen Wynn. *The Atlas of Pern.* New York: Ballantine, 1984.

Gillespie, John T., and Corinne J. Naden. *Juniorplots 3: A Book Talk Guide for Use with Readers Ages 12–16.* New York: Bowker, 1987, pp. 178–181.

Graham, Wendy. "Dragonlady of Pern: Anne McCaffrey." *Space Voyager* 16 (1985): 19–23.

Helbig, Alethea K., and Agnes Regan Perkins. *Dictionary of American Children's Fiction, 1960–1984.* Westport, CT: Greenwood, 1986, pp. 167, 410.

Heldreth, Lillian M. "Speculations on Heterosexual Equality: Morris, McCaffrey, Le Guin." In *Erotic Universe: Sexuality and Fantastic Literature.* Edited by Donald Palumbo. Westport, CT: Greenwood, 1986.

Liddell, Sharon. "Recommended: Anne McCaffrey." *English Journal* 73 (Nov 1984): 89.

McCaffrey, Anne. "On Pernography." *Algol* 16 (Winter 1979): 27–28.

———. "Romance and Glamour in Science Fiction." In *Science Fiction, Today and Tomorrow.* Edited by Reginald Bretnor. New York: Harper, 1974, pp. 278–294.

Markman, Roberta Hoffman. "The Fairy Tale: An Introduction to Literature and the Creative Process." *College English* 45 (1983): 31–45.

Monaghan, Pat, and Ray Olson. "*The Booklist* Interview: Anne McCaffrey." *Booklist* 90 (Mar 15, 1994): 1300–1301.

Morgan, Chris. "Interview: Anne McCaffrey." *Science Fiction Review* 44 (1983): 20–24.

———. "Science Fiction with Dragons: An Interview with Anne McCaffrey." *Extro Science Fiction* (July–Aug 1982): 18–22.

Mura, J. "Pern Puzzle." *VOYA* 9 (July 1986): 69; "Erratum," *VOYA* 9 (Aug–Oct 1986): 133.

Naha, Ed. "Living with the Dragons: Anne McCaffrey." *Future* 6 (1978): 22–23, 74.

Nugent, Susan Monroe. "Quests for Self-Awareness." *ALAN Review* 15 (1988): 43–44.

Nye, Jody Lynn, and Anne McCaffrey. *The Dragonlover's Guide to Pern.* New York: Ballantine, 1989.

Speaking for Ourselves: Autobiographical Sketches by Notable Authors of Books for Young Adults. Edited by Donald R. Gallo. Urbana, IL: National Council of Teachers of English, 1990, pp. 128–130.

Twentieth-Century Children's Writers. 3rd ed. Edited by Tracy Chevalier and D. L. Kirkpatrick. Chicago: St. James, 1989, pp. 652–653.

Twentieth-Century Science Fiction Writers. 3rd ed. Edited by Noelle Watson and Paul E. Schellinger. Chicago: St. James Press, 1991, pp. 538–540.

Vandergrift, K. E. "Meaning-Making and the Dragons of Pern." *Literature 21—The Best of 1990.* Metuchen, NJ: Scarecrow Press, 1992, pp. 387–404. Reprinted from *Children's Literature Association Quarterly,* 15 (Spring 1990): 27–32.

Walker, Paul. "Anne McCaffrey: An Interview." *Luna Monthly* 56 (1974): 1–5. Reprinted in Paul Walker. *Speaking of Science Fiction.* New York: Luna Publications, 1978, pp. 253–262.

Wytenbroek, J. R. "The Child as Creator in McCaffrey's *Dragonsong* and *Dragonsinger.*" *The Lion and the Unicorn* 16 (Dec 1992): 210–214.

McCaughrean, Geraldine (Jones)

McCaughrean, Geraldine. "Carnegie Medal Acceptance Speech." *Youth Library Review* (U.K.) 8 (1989): 11, 13.

Nettell, Stephanie. "Mother Fiction." *Guardian* (Mar 31, 1989): 25.

Twentieth-Century Children's Writers. 3rd ed. Edited by Tracy Chevalier and D. L. Kirkpatrick. Chicago: St. James, 1989, pp. 653–654.

MacDonald, George

Adams, Gillian. "Student Responses to *Alice in Wonderland* and *At the Back of the North Wind.*" *Children's Literature Association Quarterly* 10 (Spring 1985): 6–9.

Auden, W. H. "Afterword." *Horn Book* 43 (Apr 1967): 176–177. Reprinted in Meek. *The Cool Web.* London: Bodley Head, 1977, pp. 103–104; and in Auden. *Forewords and Afterwords.* New York: Random, 1973, pp. 268–273.

———. "George MacDonald." In Auden. *Forewords and Afterwords.* New York: Random, 1973, pp. 268–273.

Babbitt, Natalie. "Afterword." In George MacDonald. *The Princess and Curdie.* New York: Dell, 1987.

Bergmann, Frank. "The Roots of Tolkien's Tree: The Influence of George MacDonald and German Romanticism upon Tolkien's Essay 'On Fairy Stories.'" *Mosaic* 10 (Winter 1977): 5–14.

Bleeker, Timothy Jonathon. "The Christian Romanticism of George MacDonald: A Study of His Thought and Fiction." Ph.D. diss., Tufts University, 1990.

Blishen, Edward. "Maker of Fairy Tales." *Books and Bookmen* [London] (May 1974): 92–95.

Burns, Marjorie Jean. "Victorian Fantasists from Ruskin to Lang: A Study in Ambivalence." Ph.D. diss., University of California, Berkeley, 1978.

Carpenter, Humphrey. "George MacDonald and the Tender Grandmother." In *Secret Gardens: A Study of the Golden Age of Children's Literature.* Boston: Houghton Mifflin, 1985, pp. 70–85.

Cornwell, Charles Landrum. "From Self to the Shire: Studies in Victorian Fantasy." Ph.D. diss., University of Virginia, 1972.

Douglass, Jane. "Dealings with the Fairies, an Appreciation of George MacDonald." *Horn Book* 37 (Aug 1961): 327–335. Reprinted in Elinor Field. *Horn Book Reflections.* Boston: Horn Book, 1969, pp. 203–210.

Doyle, Brian. *The Who's Who of Children's Literature.* New York: Schocken, 1968, pp. 186–188.

Edwards, Bruce L., Jr. "Toward a Rhetoric of Fantasy Criticism: C. S. Lewis's Readings of MacDonald and Morris." *Literature and Belief* 3 (Mar 1983): 63–73.

Faben, Aline Sidny. "Folklore in the Fantasies and Romances of George MacDonald." Ph.D. diss., State University of New York at Buffalo, 1978.

Fasick, Laura. "Women's Moral Role in Selected Victorian Religious Novels." Ph.D. diss., Indiana University, 1990.

Fisher, Leona W. "Mythical Fantasy for Children: Silence and Community." *The Lion and the Unicorn* 14 (Dec 1990): 37–57.

Frey, Charles, and John Griffiths. *The Literary Heritage of Childhood: An Appraisal of Children's Classics in the Western Tradition.* Westport, CT: Greenwood, 1987, pp. 87–92.

Gough, John. "George MacDonald's Fantastic Imgination." *Orana* 23 (May 1987): 95–96.

Hastings, Albert Waller. "Social Myth and Fictional Reality: The Decline of Fairy Tale Thinking in the Victorian Novel." Ph.D. diss., University of Wisconsin, Madison, 1988.

Hein, Rolland. *The Harmony Within: The Spiritual Vision of George MacDonald.* Grand Rapids, MI: Eerdmans, 1982.

Helson, Revenna, and Alph Proysen. "The Psychological Origins of Fantasy for Children in Mid-Victorian England." *Children's Literature,* Vol. 3. Storrs, CT: Journal of the Modern Language Association, 1974, pp. 66–75.

Higgins, James Edward. "Five Authors of Mystical Fancy for Children: A Critical Study." Ed.D. diss., Columbia University, 1965.

Hines, Joyce Rose. "Getting Home: A Study of Fantasy and the Spiritual Journey in the Christian Supernatural Novels of Charles Williams and George MacDonald." Ph.D. diss., City University of New York, 1972.

Hoffeld, Laura. "Where Magic Begins." *The Lion and the Unicorn* 3, no. 1 (Spring 1979): 4–13.

Holbrook, David. "George MacDonald and Dreams of the Other World." *Seven: An Anglo-American Literary Review* 4 (1983): 27–37.

Honig, Edith Lazaros. *Breaking the Angelic Image: Woman Power in Victorian Children's Fantasy.* Westport, CT.: Greenwood, 1988.

———. "A Quiet Rebellion: The Portrait of the Feminine in Victorian Children's Fantasy." Ph.D. diss., Fordham University, 1985.

Howard, Susan E. "In Search of Spiritual Maturity—George MacDonald's *Phantastes.*" *Extrapolation* 30 (Fall 1989): 280–292.

Hutton, Muriel. "The George MacDonald Collection." *Yale University Library Gazette* 51, no. 2 (Oct 1976): 74–85.

———. "Unfamiliar Libraries XIII: The George MacDonald Collection, Brander Library, Huntly." *Book Collector* 17, no. 1 (Spring 1968): 13–25.

———. "Writers for Children: George MacDonald." *School Librarian* 12 (Dec 1964): 244ff.

Jackson, Rosemary. *Fantasy: The Literature of Subversion.* New York: Methuen, 1980.

Jameson, Gloria. "Developing Self-Identity Through Religious Consciousness in Stories of George MacDonald, C. S. Lewis, Madeleine L'Engle, Katherine Paterson, Ursula K. Le Guin, and Laura Adams Armer." In *Literature and Hawaii's Children. Proceedings of the Third Biennial Conference on Literature and Hawaii's Children.* Honolulu: Literature and Hawaii's Children, 1988, pp. 143–147.

Jenkins, Sue. "Love, Loss, and Seeking: Maternal Deprivation and the Quest." *Children's Literature in Education* 15 (Summer 1984): 73–84.

John, Judith Gero. "Searching for Great Great Grandmother: Powerful Women in George MacDonald's Fantasies." *The Lion and the Unicorn* 15 (Dec 1991): 27–34.

King, Don. "The Childlike in George MacDonald and C. S. Lewis." *Mythlore* 46 (1986): 17–22, 26.

Kirkpatrick, Mary. "An Introduction to the Curdie Books by George MacDonald, Including Parallels between Them and the Narnia Chronicles." *CSL: The Bulletin of the New York C. S. Lewis Society* 5, no. 5 (1974): 1–6.

Kocher, Paul H. "J. R. R. Tolkien and George MacDonald." *Mythlore* 8, 29 (1981); *The Crescent* 8 (1981): 3–4.

Kotzin, Michael C. "C. S. Lewis and George MacDonald: *The Silver Chair* and the *Princess Books.*" *Mythlore* 8, 27 (Spring 1981): 5–15.

Kranz, Gisbert. "E. T. A. Hoffmann's Einfluss auf George MacDonald. [E. T. A. Hoffmann's Influence on George MacDonald]." *Mitteilungen der E. T. A. Hoffmann-Gesellschaft-Bamberg* 33 (1987): 102–108.

Landow, George P. "And the World Became Strange: Realms of Literary Fantasy." In Diane Johnson. *Fantastic Illustration and Design in Britain, 1850–1930.* Providence: Rhode Island School of Design, 1979, pp. 9–43. Reprinted in *Georgia Review* 33 (Spring 1979): 7–42.

Lesser, Wendy. *The Life Below the Ground: A Study of the Subterranean in Literature and History.* London: Faber, 1988.

Lewis, C. S. "Preface." In *George MacDonald: An Anthology.* Edited by C. S. Lewis. London: Bles, 1946, pp. 10–22.

Lochhead, Marion. "George MacDonald and the World of Faery." *Seven: An Anglo-American Literary Review* 3 (1982): 63–71.

———. *Renaissance of Wonder.* New York: Harper, 1980, pp. 1–51. Original title: *The Renaissance of Wonder in Children's Literature.* Edinborough, 1977.

MacDonald, George. "*At the Back of the North Wind.*" In *Masterworks of Children's Literature,* vol. 6. Edited by Robert L. Wolff. New York: Chelsea House, 1984, pp. 171–369.

———. "Fairy Tale in Education." *Contemporary* 103 (1913): 491–499; *Living Age* 277 (1913): 783–790.

———. "The Fantastic Imagination." Original publication 1893. In George MacDonald. *The Gifts of the Christ Child: Fairytales and Stories for the Childlike,* vol. 1. Grand Rapids, MI: Eerdmans, 1974, pp. 23–28. Reprinted in Boyer and Zahorski. *Fantasists on Fantasy.* New York: Avon, 1984, pp. 11–22.

MacDonald, Greville. *George MacDonald and His Wife.* New York: Johnson Reprographics Corporation, 1971. Reprinted from 1924 edition.

McGillis, Roderick F.. "Childhood and Growth: George MacDonald and William Wordsworth." In *Romanticism and Children's Literature in Nineteenth-Century England,* ed. by James Holt McGavran, Jr. Athens: Univ. of Georgia Press, 1991, pp. 150–167.

———. "The Fantastic Imagination: The Prose Romances of George MacDonald." Ph.D. diss., University of Reading (U.K.), 1973.

———. "Fantasy as Adventure: Nineteenth Century Children's Fiction." *Children's Literature Association Quarterly* 8 (Fall 1983): 18–22.

———, ed. *For the Childlike: George MacDonald's Fantasies for Children.* Metuchen, NJ: Scarecrow Press, 1992.

———. "George MacDonald's *Princess* Books: High Seriousness." In *Touchstones.* Edited by Perry Nodelman. West Lafayette, IN: Children's Literature Association Publications, 1985, pp. 146–162.

———. "'If You Call Me Grandmother, That Will Do.'" *Mythlore* 6, 21 (Summer 1979): 27–28.

———. "Language and Secret Knowledge in *At the Back of the North Wind.*" In *Proceedings of the Seventh Annual Conference of the Children's Literature Association.* Baylor University, March 1980. Ypsilanti, MI: Children's Literature Association, 1982, pp. 120–127. Reprinted in *Durham University Journal* 73 (1981): 191–198.

McGregor, D. R. "Myth and Fantasy in Some Late Victorian Novelists with Special Reference to R. L. Stevenson and George MacDonald." Ph.D. diss., Auckland (New Zealand), 1973.

MacLeod, Helen. "The Children's Books of George MacDonald." *Book and Magazine Collector* [London] 43 (Oct 1987): 28–36.

Manlove, C. N. "Circularity in Fantasy: George MacDonald." Revised from an article in *Studies in Scottish Literature,* 1982. In C. N. Manlove. *The Impulse of Fantasy Literature.* Kent, OH: Kent State Univ. Press, 1983, pp. 70–92.

————. "George MacDonald's Fairy Tales: Their Roots in MacDonald's Thought." *Studies in Scottish Literature* 8 (Oct 1970): 97–108.

————. *Modern Fantasy: Five Studies.* New York: Cambridge Univ. Press, 1975.

Mann, Nancy Elizabeth Dawson. "George MacDonald and the Tradition of Victorian Fantasy." Ph.D. diss., Stanford University, 1973.

Marshall, Cynthia. "Allegory, Orthodoxy, Ambivalence: MacDonald's *The Day Boy and the Night Girl.*" *Children's Literature* 16 (1988): 57–75.

————. "Reading *The Golden Key*: Narrative Strategies of Parable." *Children's Literature Association Quarterly* 14 (Spring 1989): 26–29.

May, Jill P. "Symbolic Journeys Toward Death: George MacDonald and Howard Pyle as Fantasists." *Proceedings of the 13th Annual Conference of The Children's Literature Association, 1986.* New York: Pace University, 1988, pp. 129–134.

Mendolson, Michael. "Opening Moves: The Entry into the Other World." *Extrapolation* 25 (1984): 171–179.

Michalson, Karen Ann. "Victorian Fantasy Literature and the Politics of Canon-Making." Ph.D. diss., University of Massachusetts, 1990. Discusses Ruskin, MacDonald, Kingsley, Haggard, and Kipling.

Moss, Anita. "'Felicitous Space' in the Fantasies of George MacDonald and Mervyn Peake." *Mythlore* 30 (1982): 16–17, 42.

————. "Sacred and Secular Visions of Imagination and Reality in Nineteenth-Century British Fantasy for Children." In *Webs and Wardrobes: Humanist and Religious World Views in Children's Literature,* ed. by Joseph O'Beirne Milner and Lucy Floyd Morcock Milner. Lanham, MD: University Press of America, 1987, pp. 65–78.

Mudhenk, Rosemary Karmelich. "Another World: The Mode of Fantasy in the Fiction of Selected Nineteenth Century Writers." Ph.D. diss., University of California, Los Angeles, 1972.

Norton, André. "Afterword." In George MacDonald. *The Princess and the Goblin.* New York: Dell, 1986.

The Oxford Companion to Children's Literature. Edited by Humphrey Carpenter and Mari Prichard. New York: Oxford Univ. Press, 1984, pp. 33–34, 211, 311, 328–329, 426–427.

Pennington, John. "*Alice At the Back of the North Wind,* or the Metafictions of Lewis Carroll and George MacDonald." *Extrapolation* 33 (Spring 1992): 59–72.

————. "*Phantastes* as Metafiction: George MacDonald's Self-Reflexive Myth." *Mythlore* 53 (1988): 26–29.

————. "Thematic and Structural Subversion in the Fairy Tales and Fantasies of George MacDonald." Ph.D. diss., Purdue University, 1987.

Pflieger, Pat, and Helen M. Hill. *A Reference Guide to Modern Fantasy for Children.* Westport, CT: Greenwood, 1984, pp. xiv, 28–29, 330–333, 454–457.

Phillips, Michael R. *George MacDonald: Scotland's Beloved Storyteller.* Minneapolis: Bethany, 1987.

Pierson, Clayton Jay. "Toward Spiritual Fulfillment: A Study of the Fantasy World of George MacDonald." Ph.D. diss., University of Maryland, 1978.

Prickett, Stephen. "*At the Back of the North Wind.*" In *Survey of Modern Fantasy Literature,* vol. 1. Edited by Frank N. Magill. Englewood Cliffs, NJ: Salem Press, 1983, pp. 63–65.

————. "*Phantastes.*" In *Survey of Modern Fantasy Literature,* vol. 3. Edited by Frank N. Magill. Englewood Cliffs, NJ: Salem Press, 1983, pp. 1241–1245.

————. "Religious Fantasy in the Nineteenth Century." In *Survey of Modern Fantasy Literature,* vol. 5. Edited by Frank N. Magill. Englewood Cliffs, NJ: Salem Press, 1983, pp. 2369–2382.

————. "The Short Fiction of George MacDonald." In *Survey of Modern Fantasy Literature,* vol. 4. Edited by Frank N. Magill. Englewood Cliffs, NJ: Salem Press, 1983, pp. 1629–1632.

————. "The Two Worlds of George MacDonald." *North Wind: The Journal of the George MacDonald Society* 2 (1983): 14–23.

————. *Victorian Fantasy.* Bloomington: Indiana Univ. Press, 1979.

Raeper, William. *George MacDonald.* Oxford: Lion, 1988.

————, ed. *The Golden Thread: Essays on George MacDonald.* Edinburgh: Edinburgh Univ. Press, 1990.

Ragg, Laura M. *George MacDonald and His Household: Some Personal Recollections. English* 11, no. 62 (Summer 1956): 59–63.

Reed-Nancarrow, Paula Elizabeth. "Remythologizing the Bible: Fantasy and the Revelatory Hermeneutic of George MacDonald." Ph.D. diss., University of Minnesota, 1988.

Reis, Richard H. *George MacDonald.* New York: Twayne, 1972.

Rigsbee, Sally. "Fantasy Places and Imaginative Belief: *The Lion, the Witch and the Wardrobe* and *The Princess and the Goblin.*" *Children's Literature Association Quarterly* 8 (Spring 1983): 10–12.

Robb, David S. *George MacDonald.* Edinburgh: Scottish Academic Press, 1987.

————. "Realism and Fantasy in the Fiction of George MacDonald." In *The History of Scottish Literature III: Nineteenth Century,* ed. by Douglas Clifford. Aberdeen: Aberdeen Univ. Press, 1988, pp. 275–290.

Robertson, A. "Homage to a Fantastic Giant." *Time Magazine* (Sept 29, 1990): 17.

Sadler, Glenn Edward. "George MacDonald." In *Writers for Children; Critical Studies of Major Authors Since the Seventeenth Century.* Edited by Jane M. Bingham. New York: Scribner, 1988, pp. 373–380.

————. "An Unpublished Children's Story by George MacDonald." In *Children's Literature,* vol. 2. Storrs, CT: Journal of the Modern Language Association, 1973. Reprinted in *Reflections on Literature for Children.* Edited by Francelia Butler and Richard Rotert. Hamden, CT: Shoe String Press, 1984, pp. 171–181.

Saintsbury, Elizabeth. *George MacDonald: A Short Life.* Edinburgh: Canongate, 1987.

Sammons, Martha C. "*A Better Country": The Worlds of Religious Fantasy and Science Fiction.* Westport, CT: Greenwood, 1988.

Searles, Baird, Beth Meacham, and Michael Franklin. *A Reader's Guide to Fantasy.* New York: Avon, 1982, pp. 101–103.

Shaberman, Raphael B. *George MacDonald: A Bibliographical Study.* Detroit: Omnigraphics, 1990.

Sherman, Cordelia. "The Princess and the Wizard: The Fantasy Worlds of Ursula K. Le Guin and George MacDonald." *Children's Literature Association Quarterly* 12 (Spring 1987): 24–28.

Sigman, Joseph. "Death's Ecstasies: Transformation and Rebirth in George MacDonald's *Phantastes.*" *English Studies in Canada* 2 (1976): 203–226.

Sparks, Elisa Kay. "*The Princess and the Goblin* and *The Princess and Curdie.*" In *Survey of Modern Fantasy Literature,* vol. 3. Edited by Frank N. Magill. Englewood Cliffs, NJ: Salem Press, 1983, pp. 1280–1285.

Stott, Jon C. *Children's Literature from A to Z.* New York: McGraw-Hill, 1984, p. 190.

Sullivan, C. W., III. "Fantasy." In *Story and Society: Children's Literature in Its Social Context,* ed. by Dennis Butts. London: Macmillan, 1992, pp. 97–111.

Susina, Jan Christopher. "Victorian Kunstmärcher: A Study in Children's Literature, 1840–1875." Ph.D. diss., Indiana University, 1986.

Tanner, Tony. "Mountains and Depths—An Approach to Nineteenth Century Dualism." *Review of English Literature* 3, no. 4 (Oct 1962): 51–61.

Thorpe, Douglas James. "A Hidden Rime: The World View of George MacDonald." Ph.D. diss., University of Toronto, 1981.

Twentieth Century Children's Writers. 2nd ed. Edited by D. L. Kirkpatrick. New York: St. Martin, 1983, pp. 877–878.

Veglahn, Nancy. "Images of Evil: Male and Female Monsters in Heroic Fantasy." *Children's Literature* 15 (1987): 106–119.

Willard, Nancy. "Goddess in the Belfry." *Parabola* 6 (Summer 1981): 90–94.

———. "The Nonsense of Angels: George MacDonald *At the Back of the North Wind.*" In *Proceedings of the Fifth Annual Conference of the Children's Literature Association.* Harvard University, March 1978. Ypsilanti, MI: Children's Literature Association, 1979, pp. 106–112. Reprinted in Jill P. May. *Children and Their Literature: A Readings Book.* West Lafayette, IN: Children's Literature Association Publications, 1983, pp. 34–40.

Willis, Leslie. "'Born Again': The Metamorphosis of Irene in George MacDonald's *The Princess and the Goblin.*" *Scottish Literary Journal* 12 (May 1985): 24–39.

Wilson, Keith. "The Quest for 'The Truth': A Reading of George MacDonald's *Phantastes.*" *Études Anglaises* 34 (1981): 41–52.

Wolfe, Gary Kent. "George MacDonald." In *Supernatural Fiction Writers: Fantasy and Horror,* vol. 1. Edited by E. F. Bleiler. New York: Scribner, 1985, pp. 239–246.

———. "Symbolic Fantasy." *Genre* 8 (1975): 194–209.

Wolff, R. L. *The Golden Key: A Study of the Fiction of George MacDonald.* New Haven, CT: Yale Univ. Press, 1961.

Wood, Naomi J. "Suffer the Children: The Problem of the Loving Father in *At the Back of the North Wind.*" *Children's Literature Association Quarterly* 18 (Fall 1993): 112–119.

Woods, Robert Michael. "Imagination, Religion, and Morality in the Shorter Imaginative Fiction of George MacDonald." Ph.D. diss., Florida State University, 1990.

Yates, Elizabeth. "George MacDonald." *Horn Book* 14 (Jan 1938): 23–29.

Zanger, Jules. "Goblins, Morlocks and Weasels: Classic Fantasy and the Industrial Revolution." *Children's Literature in Education* 27, no. 4 (1977): 154–162.

McGinley, Phyllis (Louise)

Helbig, Alethea K., and Agnes Regan Perkins. *Dictionary of American Children's Fiction, 1859–1959.* Westport, CT: Greenwood, 1985, pp. 324, 407.

The Junior Book of Authors. 2nd ed. rev. Edited by Stanley J. Kunitz and Howard Haycraft. New York: Wilson, 1951, pp. 205–206.

Stone, Helen. "*The Princess* Goes to Press." *Horn Book* 22 (Jan 1946): 31–34.

Twentieth-Century Children's Writers. 3rd ed. Edited by Tracy Chevalier and D. L. Kirkpatrick. Chicago: St. James, 1989, pp. 659–660.

Wagner, Linda W. *Phyllis McGinley.* New York: Twayne, 1971.

McGraw, Eloise Jarvis

Hanff, Peter E., and Douglas G. Greene. *Bibliographia Oziana.* Demorest, GA: International Wizard of Oz Club, 1976.

Helbig, Alethea K., and Agnes Regan Perkins. *Dictionary of American Children's Fiction, 1859–1959.* Westport, CT: Greenwood, 1985, p. 334.

———. *Dictionary of American Children's Fiction, 1960–1984.* Westport, CT: Greenwood, 1986, p. 411.

McGraw, Eloise Jarvis. "On Wearing Well." *Baum Bugle* 34 (Winter 1990): 3–5.

More Junior Authors. Edited by Muriel Fuller. New York: Wilson, 1963, pp. 147–148.

Roginski, Jim, ed. *Newbery and Caldecott Medalists and Honor Book Winners.* Littleton, CO: Libraries Unlimited, 1982, pp. 185–186.

Twentieth-Century Children's Writers. 3rd ed. Edited by Tracy Chevalier and D. L. Kirkpatrick. Chicago: St. James, 1989, pp. 662–663.

McHargue, Georgess

Fifth Book of Junior Authors and Illustrators. Edited by Sally Holmes Holtze. New York: Wilson, 1983, pp. 209–211.

Kuznets, Lois R. "Games of Dark: Psychofantasy in Children's Literature." *The Lion and the Unicorn* 1, no. 2 (Fall 1977): 17–24.

McHargue, Georgess. "Leaping into Fantasy." *American Libraries* 5 (Dec 5, 1974): 610–611.

Yolen, Jane. "The Literary Underwater World." *Language Arts* 57 (1980): 403–412.

McKillip, Patricia A(nne)

Attebery, Brian. "Women's Coming of Age in Fantasy." *Extrapolation* 28 (Spring 1987): 10–22.

Carter, Margaret R., and Richard A. Carter. "Perpetual Winter in C. S. Lewis and Patricia McKillip." *Mythlore* 16 (Autumn 1989): 35–36.

Fifth Book of Junior Authors and Illustrators. Edited by Sally Holmes Holtze. New York: Wilson, 1983, pp. 211–212.

Geenlaw, M. Jean. "Books in the Classroom." *Horn Book* 64 (Nov–Dec 1988): 820–822.

Haunert, Rita M. "Mythic Female Heroes in the High Fantasy Novels of Patricia McKillip." Ph.D. diss., Bowling Green State University, 1983.

McKillip, Patricia A. "Once Upon A Time Too Often." *The Writer* 105 (Aug 1992): 18.

Nicholls, Peter. "The Star-Bearer Trilogy." In *Survey of Modern Fantasy Literature,* vol. 4. Edited by Frank N. Magill. Englewood Cliffs, NJ: Salem Press, 1983, pp. 1813–1820.

Nugent, Susan Monroe. "Quests for Self-Awareness." *ALAN Review* 15 (1988): 43–44.

Searles, Baird, Beth Meacham, and Michael Franklin. *A Reader's Guide to Fantasy.* New York: Avon, 1982, pp. 104–106.

Sparks, Elisa Kay. "*The Forgotten Beasts of Eld.*" In *Survey of Modern Fantasy Literature,* vol. 2. Edited by Frank N. Magill. Englewood Cliffs, NJ: Salem Press, 1983, pp. 566–570.

Spivack, Charlotte. *Merlin's Daughters: Contemporary Women Writers of Fantasy.* New York: Greenwood, 1987.

Twentieth-Century Children's Writers. 3rd ed. Edited by Tracy Chevalier and D. L. Kirkpatrick. Chicago: St. James, 1989, pp. 666–667.

Wymer, Thomas L. "Patricia McKillip." In *Supernatural Fiction Writers: Fantasy and Horror,* vol. 2. Edited by E. F. Bleiler. New York: Scribner, 1985, pp. 1067–1072.

McKinley, (Jennifer Carolyn) Robin (Turrell)

Altmann, Anna E. "Welding Brass Tits on the Armor: An Examination of the Quest Metaphor in Robin McKinley's *The Hero and the Crown.*'" *Children's Literature in Education* 23 (Sept 1992): 143–156.

Arnold, Mark Alan, and Terri Windling. "Robin McKinley." *Horn Book* 61 (July–Aug 1985): 406–409.

Fifth Book of Junior Authors and Illustrators. Edited by Sally Holmes Holtze. New York: Wilson, 1983, pp. 212–213.

Gillespie, John T., and Corinne J. Naden. *Juniorplots 3: A Book Talk Guide for Use with Readers Ages 12–16.* New York: Bowker, 1987, pp. 182–185.

Helbig, Alethea, and Agnes Regan Perkins. *Dictionary of American Children's Fiction, 1985–1989.* Westport, CT: Greenwood, 1993, pp. 101–102, 152–153, 182–183.

———. *Dictionary of American Children's Fiction, 1960–1984.* Westport, CT: Greenwood, 1986, pp. 42–43, 61–62, 412.

"The Hero and the Crown." In *Newbery and Caldecott Medal Books 1976–1985.* Boston: Horn Book, 1986, pp. 136–152.

Karrenbrock, Marilyn H. "Robin McKinley." In *American Writers for Children since 1960: Fiction. Dictionary of Literary Biography,* vol. 52. Detroit: Gale, 1986, pp. 262–266.

McIntosh, Margaret E., and M. Jean Greenlaw. "Ladies First: Teaching Characterization Through Strong Female Protagonists in High Fantasy Literature." *ALAN Review* 15 (1988): 47–51.

McKinley, Robin. "1985 Newbery Acceptance Speech." *Top of the News* 41 (Summer 1985): 387–394; *Horn Book* 61 (July–Aug 1985): 395–405.

Meek, Margaret. "Happily Ever After." *Times Literary Supplement* (London), November 25, 1983, p. 1212.

Moslander, Charlotte. "An Interview with Robin McKinley." *VOYA* 8 (Feb 1986): 368–369.

Nugent, Susan Monroe. "Quests for Self-Awareness." *ALAN Review* 15 (1988): 43–44.

Searles, Baird, Beth Meacham, and Michael Franklin. *A Reader's Guide to Fantasy.* New York: Avon, 1982, pp. 106–107.

Snyman, K. "Imaginary Worlds: Myth, Fairy Tale, Fantasy and Science Fiction. Part II." *Skoolmediasentrum* (South Africa) 2 (1988): 46–51.

Speaking for Ourselves; Autobiographical Sketches by Notable Authors of Books for Young Adults. Edited by Donald R. Gallo. Urbana, IL: National Council of Teachers of English, 1990, pp. 131–132.

Twentieth-Century Children's Writers. 3rd ed. Edited by Tracy Chevalier and D. L. Kirkpatrick. Chicago: St. James, 1989, pp. 667–668.

Woolsey, Daniel P. "The Realm of Fairy Story: J. R. R. Tolkien and Robin McKinley's *Beauty.*" *Children's Literature in Education* (June 1991): 129–134.

Zipes, Jack, ed. *Spells of Enchantment: The Wondrous Fairy Tales of Western Culture.* New York: Viking, 1991.

MacLachlan, Patricia

Babbitt, Natalie. "Patricia MacLachlan: The Biography." *Horn Book* 62 (July–Aug 1986): 414–416.

Courtney, A. "Profile: Patricia MacLachlan." *Language Arts* 62 (Nov 1985): 783–787. Interview.

"Dialogue Between Charlotte Zolotow and Patricia MacLachlan; an Illumination of an Old-Style Editor-Author Relationship." *Horn Book* 65 (Nov–Dec 1989): 736–745.

Helbig, Alethea K., and Agnes Regan Perkins. *Dictionary of American Children's Fiction, 1960–1984.* Westport, CT: Greenwood, 1986, p. 393.

MacLachlan, Patricia. "1986 Newbery Award Acceptance Speech." *Horn Book* 62 (July–Aug 1986): 407–413; *Top of the News* 42 (Summer 1986): 391–395.

———. "Painting the Air." *The New Advocate* 3 (Fall 1990): 219–226.

MacLachlan, Robert. "A Hypothetical Dilemma." *Horn Book* 62 (July–Aug 1986): 416–419.

Rounds, L. "Cheyenne Native Patricia MacLachlan: 1986 Newbery Winner." *Wyoming Library Roundup* 4 (Spring 1986): 22–24.

Sixth Book of Junior Authors and Illustrators. Edited by Sally Holmes Holtze. New York: Wilson, 1989, pp. 183–184.

Twentieth-Century Children's Writers. 3rd ed. Edited by Tracy Chevalier and D. L. Kirkpatrick. Chicago: St. James, 1989, pp. 622–623.

McNeill (Alexander), Janet

Fourth Book of Junior Authors and Illustrators. Edited by Doris De Montreville and Elizabeth D. Crawford. New York: Wilson, 1978, pp. 245–247.

McNeill, Janet. "Enter Fairies through a Hole in the Hedge." *Junior Bookshelf* 31 (Fall 1967): 23–27.

———. "When the Magic Has to Stop." *Horn Book* 48 (Aug 1972): 337–342.

Moss, Elaine. "'Go On! Go On!': Janet McNeill and *The Battle of St. George Without.*" *Signal* 6 (Sept 1971): 96–101.

Twentieth-Century Children's Writers. 3rd ed. Edited by Tracy Chevalier and D. L. Kirkpatrick. Chicago: St. James, 1989, pp. 668–670.

Maeterlinck, Maurice

The Oxford Companion to Children's Literature. Edited by Humphrey Carpenter and Mari Prichard. New York: Oxford Univ. Press, 1984, pp. 67–68.

Maguire, Gregory

Harrison, Barbara, and Gregory Maguire, eds. *Innocence & Experience: Essays and Conversations on Children's Literature.* New York: Lothrop, 1987.

Maguire, Gregory. "Belling the Cat: Heroism and the Little Hero." *The Lion and the Unicorn* 13 (June 1989): 102–119.

———. "Rememory." *Horn Book* 57 (Dec 1981): 629–631. Reprinted in *Innocence & Experience.* Ed. by Barbara Harrison and Gregory Maguire. New York: Lothrop, 1987. Based on an introductory talk given at the Simmons College Center for the Study of Children's Literature, March 14, 1981.

———. "Themes in English Language: Fantastic Literature for Children, 1938–1988." Ph.D. diss., Tufts University, 1990.

Twentieth-Century Children's Writers. 3rd ed. Edited by Tracy Chevalier and D. L. Kirkpatrick. Chicago: St. James, 1989, pp. 625–626.

Mahy, Margaret (May)

"Authorgraph no. 24: Margaret Mahy." *Books for Keeps* (U.K.) 24 (Jan 1984): 12–13.

Berkin, Adam. "'I Woke Myself': *The Changeover* as a Modern Adaptation of 'Sleeping Beauty.'" *Children's Literature in Education* 21 (Dec 1990): 245–251.

Brownlee, Steven, and Catherine Towers. "Margaret Mahy Reads the World." *In Brief* (U.K.) 7 (1992): 4–5.

Carter, Margaret. "Margaret Mahy." *Books for Your Children* (U.K.) 19 (Spring 1984): 20.

Cutts, Alida von Krogh. "Imagination: The Creative Use of Reality: Margaret Mahy Speaks." *USBBY Newsletter* 12, no. 2 (1987): 3.

Fourth Book of Junior Authors and Illustrators. Edited by Doris De Montreville and Elizabeth D. Crawford. New York: Wilson, 1978, pp. 248–250.

Gillespie, John T., and Corinne J. Naden. *Juniorplots 3: A Book Talk Guide for Use with Readers Ages 12–16.* New York: Bowker, 1987, pp. 132–136.

Gose, Elliott. "Fairy Tale and Myth in *The Changeover* and *The Tricksters.*" *Children's Literature Association Quarterly* 16 (Spring 1991): 6–10.

Gough, John. "Author Profile: Margaret Mahy." *Review Bulletin* (Australia) 21, no. 4 (1998): 1–5.

———. "Rivalry, Rejection and Recovery: Variations of the 'Cinderella' Story." *Children's Literature in Education* 21 (June 1990): 99–108.

Hearne, Betsy. "*The Changeover.*" *Booklist* 82 (Nov 1, 1985): 410–412. Speech given at the 1985 Children's Books Open Forum, 1985 ALA Conference.

Hoffman, M. "The Fabulous in the Ordinary: An Interview with Margaret Mahy." *School Librarian* 34 (Sept 1986): 212–216.

Jones, Nicolette. "Phantoms of Teenage Desire." *Books & Bookmen* [London] (Dec 1986–Jan 1987): 39.

"Know the Author: Margaret Mahy." *Magpies* (Australia) 1, no. 2 (May 1986): 16–17

Lehman, Rebecca L. "Margaret Mahy Mixing the Familiar with the Unfamiliar." *ALAN Review* 17 (Winter 1990): 33–34, 40.

Mahy, Margaret. "Author's Corner: Margaret Mahy." *Review Bulletin* (Australia) 18, no. 3 (1986): 34–36.

———. "Joining the Network." *Signal* 54 (Sept 1987): 151–160.

———. "The Lion, the Magician, the Hero, the Witch: Thoughts about Magic and Reality." *Children's Literature Association Yearbook.* New Zealand: Children's Literature Association, 1976, pp. 9–15.

———. "May Hill Arbuthnot Honor Lecture: 'A Dissolving Ghost: Possible Operations of Truth in Children's Books and the Lives of Children.'" *Journal of Youth Services in Libraries* 2 (Summer 1989): 313–330. Reprinted in *The Arbuthnot Lectures, 1980–1989.* Chicago: American Library Association, 1990, pp. 127–144.

———. "A New Zealand Writer Speaks." In *Brave New World: International Understanding Through Books,* ed. by Wendy Birman and Jon Birman. Perth, Australia: Curtin Univ. of Technology, 1988.

———. "1984 Carnegie Medal Acceptance Speech." *Youth Library Review* (U.K.) 1 (1986): 8–11.

———. "On Building Houses That Face Towards the Sun." In *A Track to Unknown Water: Proceedings of the Second Pacific Rim Conference on Children's Literature,* ed. by Stella Lees. Metuchen, NJ: Scarecrow Press, 1987, pp. 104–118.

———. "There Are No Rules for Writers." *Australian Author* 17, no. 4 (Dec 1985): 7–8.

Marsh, Gwen. "Margaret Mahy and Her Books." *School Bookshop News* (U.K.) 7 (Summer 1977): 15–16.

Nettell, Stephanie. "*Tricksters* and Treats." *Guardian* (July 9, 1986): 9.

The Oxford Companion to Children's Literature. Edited by Humphrey Carpenter and Mari Prichard. New York: Oxford Univ. Press, 1984, p. 334.

Paul, Lissa. "Enigma Variations: What Feminist Theory Knows about Children's Literature." *Signal* 54 (Sept 1987): 186–202. Discusses *The Changeover.*

Raburn, Josephine. "*The Changeover,* a Fantasy of Opposites." *Children's Literature in Education* 23 (Mar 1992): 27–38.

Rees, David. "What Do Draculas Do? Margaret Mahy." In "*What Do Draculas Do?*" *Essays on Contemporary Writers of Fiction for Children and Young Adults.* Metuchen, NJ: Scarecrow Press, 1990, pp. 144–159.

Sheahan, Robyn. "The Use of the Supernatural to Explore Realistic Issues in Margaret Mahy's *The Changeover.*" Papers (Australia) 2 (Apr 1991): 36–47.

Twentieth-Century Children's Writers. 3rd ed. Edited by Tracy Chevalier and D. L. Kirkpatrick. Chicago: St. James, 1989, pp. 626–629.

Worman, Ceri. "From Idealism to Capitalism: Margaret Mahy Talks About the Process of Writing and Her Recent Books." *Youth Library Review* (U.K.) 14 (1992): 5–7.

Major, Kevin (Gerald)

Ellis, Sarah. "News from the North [Kevin Major]." *Horn Book* 65 (Sept–Oct 1989): 659–661.

Jenkinson, D. H. "Portraits: Kevin Major." *Emergency Librarian* 19 (Jan–Feb 1992): 66–70.

Major, Kevin. "Challenged Materials: An Author's Perspective." *School Libraries in Canada* 4 (Spring 1984): 15–16.

———. "My Life and Letters." *Canadian Children's Literature* 54 (1989): 6–25.

Smiley, Barbara. "Proile: Kevin Major." *In Review* (Canada) 13 (Feb 1979): 11–12.

Twentieth-Century Children's Writers. 3rd ed. Edited by Tracy Chevalier and D. L. Kirkpatrick. Chicago: St. James, 1989, pp. 629–631.

Malory, Sir Thomas

Kellogg, Judith L. "The Dynamics of Dumbing: The Case of Merlin." *The Lion and the Unicorn* 17 (June 1993): 57–72. Discusses Heyer's *Excalibur,* White's *The Sword in the Stone,* Talbott's *King Arthur,* and Yolen's *Merlin's Booke.*

Kinney, Thomas L. "Arthurian Romances." In *Supernatural Fiction Writers: Fantasy and Horror,* vol. 1. Edited by E. F. Bleiler. New York: Scribner, 1985, pp. 11–18.

Paxon, Diana. "The Holy Grail." *Mythlore* 3, no. 9 (1976).

Manning, Rosemary (Joy)

"Dragon in No Danger." *About Books for Children.* (U.K.) 2 (Apr 1981): 31–32.

Manning, Rosemary. "Our Dreams Are Tales." *Horn Book* 41 (Feb 1965): 25–26.

Moss, Elaine. "Rosemary Manning's *Arripay: Variation on a Theme." Signal* 2 (May 1970): 31–35.

Twentieth-Century Children's Writers. 3rd ed. Edited by Tracy Chevalier and D. L. Kirkpatrick. Chicago: St. James, 1989, pp. 631–632.

Mark, Jan (pseud. of Janet Marjorie Brisland)

"Authorgraph no. 25: Jan Mark." *Books for Keeps* (U.K.) 25 (Mar 1984): 12–13.

Chambers, Aidan. "Letter from England: A Mark of Distinction." *Horn Book* 60 (Sept–Oct 1984): 665–670.

Duguid, Lindsay. "The Art of Conversation." *Times Educational Supplement* (June 3, 1988): 45.

Fifth Book of Junior Authors and Illustrators. Edited by Sally Holmes Holtze. New York: Wilson, 1983, pp. 201–203.

Hunt, Peter. "Whatever Happened to Jan Mark?" *Signal* 31 (Jan 1980): 11–19.

Mappin, Alf. "Know the Author: Jan Mark." *Magpies* (Australia) 4 (Mar 1989): 20–23.

March-Penny, Robbie. "I Don't Want to Learn Things, I'd Just Rather Find Out." *Children's Literature in Education* 10 (Spring 1979): 18–24.

Mark, Jan "Authors Island." *Books for Keeps* (U.K.) 14 (May 1982): 16–17.

———. "Journeys." *Horn Book* 63 (Mar–Apr 1987): 171–180.

———. "The Short Story." *Horn Book* 64 (Jan–Feb 1988): 42–47.

———. "Something To Be Afraid Of." *English in Education* (U.K.) 15 (Spring 1981): 8–10.

———. "The Story of the Golem." In *Innocence & Experience.* Edited by Barbara Harrison and Gregory Maguire. New York: Lothrop, 1987, pp. 184–187.

———. [untitled] *School Bookshop News* (U.K.) 12 (Spring 1979): 14–18.

Philip, Neil. "Read Mark, Learn." *Times Educational Supplement* (June 3, 1983): 37.

Rees, David. "No Such Thing as Fairness—Jan Mark." In *Painted Desert, Green Shade.* Boston: Horn Book, 1984, pp. 62–74. Revised from *School Librarian* 29 (Sept 1981): 206–212.

Twentieth-Century Children's Writers. 3rd ed. Edited by Tracy Chevalier and D. L. Kirkpatrick. Chicago: St. James, 1989, pp. 635–637.

Whitehead, Winifred. "Jan Mark." *Use of English* 33 (Spring 1982): 32–39.

Marshall, James (Edward)

Alderson, Brian. "Rapscallion Laureate." *Books for Keeps* (U.K.) 80 (1993): 28–29.

Fourth Book of Junior Authors and Illustrators. Edited by Doris De Montreville and Elizabeth D. Crawford. New York: Wilson, 1978, pp. 253–254.

Hale, Robert. "Musings." [James Marshall Remembered] *Horn Book* 69 (Jan–Feb 1993): 110–111.

"James Marshall Remembered." *Publishers Weekly* 231 (Dec 7, 1992): 30–31.

Laughlin, Jeannine L., and Sherry Laughlin. *Children's Authors Speak.* Libraries Unlimited, 1993.

Silvey, Anita. "Editorial: James Marshall (1942–1992)." *Horn Book* 69 (Jan–Feb 1993): 4–5.

———. "James Marshall (1942–1992)." *Horn Book* 69 (Jan–Feb 1993): 4–5.

Stan, Susan. "Conversations: James Marshall." *Five Owls* 4, no. 4 (1990): 56–57.

Twentieth-Century Children's Writers. 3rd ed. Edited by Tracy Chevalier and D. L. Kirkpatrick. Chicago: St. James, 1989, pp. 637–639.

Martin, Bill (William Ivan), Jr.

Larrick, Nancy. "Profile: Bill Martin, Jr." *Language Arts* 59 (May 1982): 490–494.

Masefield, John (Edward)

Alderson, Brian. "The Timeless Quality of Convincing Storytelling." [London] *Times* (July 2, 1975): 11.

Babington Smith, Constance. *John Masefield: A Life.* London: Hamish Hamilton, 1985. Original publisher Oxford Univ. Press, 1978.

Dickinson, Patrick. "John Masefield and *The Midnight Folk.*" *Children's Literature in Education* 21 (Dec 1990): 237–243.

Doyle, Brian. *The Who's Who of Children's Literature.* New York: Schocken, 1968, pp. 193–194.

Fisher, Marjorie. *John Masefield.* London: Bodley Head, 1963.

Hollindale, Peter. "John Masefield." *Children's Literature in Education* 23 (Winter 1976): 187–195.

Kingsley, Madeleine. "A Box Full of Magic." *Radio Times* 244 (Nov 17–23, 1984): 101–103.

L'Engle, Madeleine. "Afterword." In John Masefield. *The Midnight Folk.* New York: Dell, 1985.

Lochhead, Marion. *Renaissance of Wonder.* New York: Harper, 1980.

Masefield, John. *In the Mill.* London: Heinemann, 1941.

———. *New Chum.* London: Heinemann, 1944.

———. *So Long to Learn.* New York: Macmillan, 1952.

The Oxford Companion to Children's Literature. Edited by Humphrey Carpenter and Mari Prichard. New York: Oxford Univ. Press, 1984, pp. 77–78, 342–343, 349.

Ray, Sheila. "Author Notes from Great Britain: Ted Hughes, John Masefield, and Alison Uttley." *Bookbird* 2 (1985): 29–30.

Smith, Constance Babington. *John Masefield: A Life.* London: Hamish Hamilton, 1985.

Spark, Muriel. *John Masefield.* London: Nevill, 1953.

Spernlicht, Sanford. *John Masefield.* Boston: Twayne, 1977.

Strong, L. A. G. *John Masefield.* London: Longman, 1952.

Taylor, J. "John Masefield." *Ontario Library Review* 46 (Feb 1962): 16–19.

Trotman, Felicity. "Meet Your Author: John Masefield." *Puffin Post* (U.K.) 8, no. 4 (1974): 13–15.

Twentieth-Century Children's Writers. 3rd ed. Edited by Tracy Chevalier and D. L. Kirkpatrick. Chicago: St. James, 1989, pp. 643–647.

Mason, Arthur

Mason, Arthur. "*The Wee Men.*" *Horn Book* 6 (Nov 1930): 337–339.

Mason, Miriam E(vangeline)

Burns, P. C., and R. Hines. "Miriam E. Mason: Storytelling Sister." *Elementary English* 43 (Jan 1966): 5–9ff.

Matheson, Richard (Burton)

Blaine, Michael. "A Richard Matheson Update." *Twilight Zone,* June 1986, pp. 22–23, 94.
———. "Richard Matheson's 'Layer-Cake' Career." *Twilight Zone,* June 1986, pp. 24–25, 94.
Lofficier, Randy, and Jean-Marc Lofficier. "Twilight Zone Interview: Richard Matheson." *Twilight Zone,* Sept–Oct 1983, pp. 40–41.
Neilson, Keith. "Richard Matheson." In *Supernatural Fiction Writers: Fantasy and Horror,* vol. 2. Edited by E. F. Bleiler. New York: Scribner, 1985, pp. 1073–1080.
Nicholls, Peter. "Richard Matheson." In *Science Fiction Writers.* Edited by E. F. Bleiler. New York: Scribner, 1982, pp. 425–432.
Rathbun, Mark, and Graeme Flanagan. *Richard Matheson: He Is Legend: An Illustrated Bio-Biography.* Chico, CA: Rathbun, 1984.
Searles, Baird, Beth Meacham, and Michael Franklin. *A Reader's Guide to Fantasy.* New York: Avon, 1982, p. 107.
Sharp, Roberta. "The Short Fiction of Matheson." In *Survey of Modern Fantasy Literature,* vol. 4. Edited by Frank N. Magill. Englewood Cliffs, NJ: Salem Press, 1983, pp. 1645–1651.
Watson, Christine. "*Bid Time Return.*" In *Survey of Modern Fantasy Literature,* vol. 1. Edited by Frank N. Magill. Englewood Cliffs, NJ: Salem Press, 1983, pp. 90–94.

Maxwell, William

Helbig, Alethea K., and Agnes Regan Perkins. *Dictionary of American Children's Fiction, 1859–1959.* Westport, CT: Greenwood, 1985, pp. 209–210, 333.

Mayer, Marianna

Fourth Book of Junior Authors and Illustrators. Edited by Doris De Montreville and Elizabeth D. Crawford. New York: Wilson, 1978, pp. 257–259.

Mayhar, Ardath

Mayhar, Ardath. "Let Us Have Stories in Verse Again!" *Fantasy Review* 76 (1985): 7–41.
Twentieth-Century Science Fiction Writers. 3rd ed. Edited by Noelle Watson and Paul E. Schellinger. Chicago: St. James Press, 1991, pp. 536–537.

Mayne, William (James Carter) (a.k.a. Martin Cobalt)

Alderson, Brian. "On the Littoral: William Mayne's *The Jersey Shore.*" *Children's Literature Review* 3 (Oct 1973): 133–135.

Antczak, Janice. *Science Fiction: The Mythos of a New Romance.* New York: Neal-Schuman, 1985.

Blishen, Edward. "Writers for Children: William Mayne." *The Use of English* 20, no. 2 (Winter 1968): 99–103. Reprinted in Dennis Butts. *Good Writers for Young Readers.* St. Albans, England: Hart-Davis, 1977, pp. 79–85.

Carey, Joanna. "The Mayne Adventure." *The Guardian* Supplement (Mar 25, 1993): 10.

Doyle, Brian. *The Who's Who of Children's Literature.* New York: Schocken, 1968, pp. 194–195.

Gillespie, John T., and Diana Lembo. *Introducing Books: A Guide for the Middle Grades.* New York: Bowker, 1970, pp. 221–223.

"*A Grass Rope.*" In M. Crouch and A. Ellis. *Chosen for Children.* 3rd ed. London: The Library Association, 1977, pp. 91–95.

Heins, Paul. "Off the Beaten Path." *Horn Book* 49 (Dec 1973): 580–581.

Hunt, Peter. "The Mayne Game: An Experiment in Response." *Signal* 28 (Jan 1979): 9–25.

Inglis, Fred. *The Promise of Happiness.* New York: Cambridge Univ. Press, 1981, pp. 12–15, 228–231, 253–257.

Kuznets, Lois R. "Games of Dark: Psychofantasy in Children's Literature." *The Lion and the Unicorn* 1, no. 2 (Fall 1977): 17–24.

Lurie, Alison. "The Children's Books of William Mayne." *New York Review of Books* (Feb 18, 1988): 11–13.

———. "William Mayne." In *Children and Their Books,* ed. by Gillian Avery and Julia Briggs. Oxford: Clarendon, 1989, pp. 369–379.

McVitty, Walter. "Who's Afraid of William Mayne?" *Reading Time* (Australia) 55 (Apr 1975): 31–36. Also in *Australian School Librarian* 12 (Mar 1975): 7–12.

Mayne, William. "A Discussion with William Mayne." *Children's Literature in Education* 2 (July 1970): 48–55.

———. [The *Hob* Books] *Books for Your Children* (U.K.) 19 (Spring 1984): 6–7.

Moon, Kenneth. "Don't Tell It, Show It: The Force of Metaphor in *A Game of Dark.*" *School Librarian* 31 (Dec 1983): 319–327.

Nettell, Stephanie. "Authorgraph no. 63: William Mayne." *Books for Keeps* (U.K.) 63 (1990): 14–15.

The Oxford Companion to Children's Literature. Edited by Humphrey Carpenter and Mari Prichard. New York: Oxford Univ. Press, 1984, pp. 345–347.

Pflieger, Pat, and Helen M. Hill. *A Reference Guide to Modern Fantasy for Children.* Westport, CT: Greenwood, 1984, pp. xiv, 163–165, 358–360.

Rees, David. "Enigma Variations: William Mayne." *Children's Literature in Education* 19 (Summer 1988): 94–105. Reprinted in *"What Do Draculas Do?" Essays on Contemporary Writers of Fiction for Children and Young Adults.* Metuchen, NJ: Scarecrow Press, 1990, pp. 15–29.

Scutter, Heather. "Fantastic Imagery in William Mayne's *Winter Quarters.*" *Papers* (Australia) 1, no. 2 (Aug 1990): 87–94.

Searles, Baird, Beth Meacham, and Michael Franklin. *A Reader's Guide to Fantasy.* New York: Avon, 1982, pp. 107–108.

Stephens, John. "'I Am Where I Think I Am': Imagination and Everyday Wonders in William Mayne's *Hob Stories.*" *Children's Literature in Education* 20 (Mar 1989): 37–50.

———. "'In the Middle of Being Two Places at Once': Perception and Signification in William Mayne's *All the King's Men.*" *Ariel: A Review of International English Literature* 19 (1988): 59–71.

———. "Metaficiton and Interpretation: William Mayne's *Salt River Times, Winter Quarters,* and *Drift.*" *Children's Literature 21.* New Haven: Yale Univ. Press, 1993 pp. 101–117.

———. "Modernism to Post Modernism, or, The Line from Insk to Onsk: William Mayne's *Tiger's Railway.*" *Papers* (Australia) 3 (Aug 1992): 51–59.

Stott, Jon C. *Children's Literature from A to Z.* New York: McGraw-Hill, 1984, p. 183.
Swinfen, Ann. *In Defense of Fantasy.* London: Routledge, 1984, pp. 63–67. Discusses *A Game of Dark.*
Third Book of Junior Authors. Edited by Doris De Montreville and Donna Hill. New York: Wilson, 1972, pp. 189–190.
Thompson, Hilary. "Doorways to Fantasy." *Canadian Children's Literature* 21 (1981): 8–16.
Townsend, John Rowe. "William Mayne." In *A Sense of Story.* Philadelphia: Lippincott, 1971, pp. 130–142.
———. "William Mayne." In *A Sounding of Storytellers.* Philadelphia: Lippincott, 1979, pp. 139–152.
Twentieth-Century Children's Writers. 3rd ed. Edited by Tracy Chevalier and D. L. Kirkpatrick. Chicago: St. James, 1989, pp. 649–651.
Walker, Alastair. "Landscape as Metaphor in the Novels of William Mayne." *Children's Literature in Education* 36 (Spring 1980): 31–42.
Whitaker, Muriel A. "'The Hollow Hills': A Celtic Motif in Modern Fantasy." *Mosaic* 13 (Spring/Summer 1980): 165–178.
———. "Swords at Sunset and Bag-Puddings: Arthur in Modern Fiction." *Children's Literature in Education* 27, no. 8 (Winter 1977): 143–153.

Mazer, Norma Fox

Coyle, Lisa R. "The Creative Use of Stereotypes in the Short Stories of Norma Fox Mazer." *The ALAN Review* 19 (Fall 1991): 2–5.
Fifth Book of Junior Authors and Illustrators. Edited by Sally Holmes Holtze. New York: Wilson, 1983, pp. 204–206.
Helbig, Alethea, and Agnes Regan Perkins. *Dictionary of American Children's Fiction, 1985–1989.* Westport, CT: Greenwood, 1993, p. 152.
———. *Dictionary of American Children's Fiction, 1960–1984.* Westport, CT: Greenwood, 1986, pp. 409, 574–575.
Holtze, Sally Holmes. *Presenting Norma Fox Mazer.* Boston: Hall, 1987.
Mazer, Norma Fox. "Growing Up with Stories." *Top of the News* 41 (Winter 1985): 157–168.
———. "Letters to Me." *ALAN Review* 17 (Spring 1990): 8–11.
———. "Words on a Ketchup Bottle. *The ALAN Review* 19 (Fall 1991): 2–5.
———. "Young Adult Literature: An Inner View." *VOYA* 12 (Aug 1989): 147–148.
Twentieth-Century Children's Writers. 3rd ed. Edited by Tracy Chevalier and D. L. Kirkpatrick. Chicago: St. James, 1989, pp. 651–652.

Meigs, Cornelia (Lynde)

"Cornelia Meigs Accepts Newbery Award." *Horn Book* 10 (July 1934): 217–220.
Helbig, Alethea K., and Agnes Regan Perkins. *Dictionary of American Children's Fiction, 1859–1959.* Westport, CT: Greenwood, 1985, pp. 339–340.
The Junior Book of Authors. 2nd ed. rev. Edited by Stanley J. Kunitz and Howard Haycraft. New York: Wilson, 1951, pp. 217–219.
Meigs, Cornelia. "Following the Sea." *Horn Book* 3 (Feb 1927): 30–38.
———. "How *The Wonderful Locomotive* Happened." *Horn Book* 4 (Aug 1928): 32–33.
———. "Writing for Children Today." *Horn Book* 25 (Sept 1949): 370–374.
Murdoch, Clarissa. "Cornelia Meigs: Chronicler of the Sea." *Elementary English Review* 5 (May 1928): 148–149, 153.
Patee, Doris. "Cornelia Meigs." *Horn Book* 20 (Sept–Oct 1944): 356–362.
Sauer, Julia L. "The Books of Cornelia Meigs." *Horn Book* 20 (Sept–Oct 1944): 347–355.

Twentieth-Century Children's Writers. 3rd ed. Edited by Tracy Chevalier and D. L. Kirkpatrick. New York: St. Martin, 1989, pp. 673–674.

Viguers, Susan T. "Cornelia Meigs." In *Writers for Children: Critical Studies of Major Authors Since the Seventeenth Century.* Edited by Jane M. Bingham. New York: Scribner, 1988, pp. 389–392.

Whitney, Elinor. "The Stories of Cornelia Meigs." *Horn Book* 3 (Feb 1927): 39–40.

Melling, O(rla) R.

Jenkinson, D. H. "O. R. Melling: Award Winning Fantasy Writer." *Emergency Librarian* 16 (Sept–Oct 1988): 60–64.

Keenlyside, David. "An Exile at Home: Conversations with O. R. Melling at the Tyrone Guthrie Center" *Canadian Author and Bookman* 64 (Fall 1988): 2–3.

Melling, Orla. "Ancient Dreams." *Children's Books in Ireland* 7 (1992): 18.

Mendoza, George

Third Book of Junior Authors. Edited by Doris De Montreville and Donna Hill. New York: Wilson, 1972, pp. 192–193.

Merrill, Jean (Fairbanks)

Gillespie, John T., and Diana Lembo. *Introducing Books: A Guide for the Middle Grades.* New York: Bowker, 1970, pp. 227–229.

Helbig, Alethea K., and Agnes Regan Perkins. *Dictionary of American Children's Fiction, 1960–1984.* Westport, CT: Greenwood, 1986, pp. 418, 529, 636.

Third Book of Junior Authors. Edited by Doris De Montreville and Donna Hill. New York: Wilson, 1972, pp. 195–196.

Twentieth-Century Children's Writers. 3rd ed. Edited by Tracy Chevalier and D. L. Kirkpatrick. Chicago: St. James, 1989, pp. 677–679.

Merritt, A(braham P.)

Bleiler, E. F. "A. Merritt." In *Supernatural Fiction Writers: Fantasy and Horror,* vol. 2. Edited by E. F. Bleiler. New York: Scribner, 1985, pp. 835–844.

De Camp, L. Sprague, ed. *The Blade of Conan.* New York: Ace, 1979.

Foust, R. E. "Monstrous Image: Theory of Fantasy Antagonists." *Genre* 13 (1981): 441–453.

Moskowitz, Sam. *A. Merritt: Reflections in the Moon Pool.* Philadelphia: Train, 1985.

Twentieth-Century Science Fiction Writers. 3rd ed. Edited by Noelle Watson and Paul E. Schellinger. Chicago: St. James Press, 1991, pp. 557–558.

Yoke, Carl B. "The Ship of Ishtar." In *Survey of Modern Fantasy Literature,* vol. 3. Edited by Frank N. Magill. Englewood Cliffs, NJ: Salem Press, 1983, pp. 1407–1411.

Middleton-Murray, John, Jr. *see* Cowper, Richard

Milne, A(lan) A(lexander)

Alldahl, Tomas. "A. A. Milne, Varldsberomd for 'en Bisak' [A. A. Milne, World Famous for 'a Side Issue']." *Opsis Kalopsis* (Sweden) 5/6 (1991): 60–65.

Canham, Stephen. "Reassuring Readers: *Winnie-the-Pooh*." *Children's Literature Association Quarterly* 5 (Fall 1980): 1, 25–27.

Carpenter, Humphrey. "A. A. Milne and *Winnie-the-Pooh:* Farewell to the Enchanted Places." In *Secret Gardens: The Golden Age of Children's Literature.* Boston: Houghton Mifflin, 1985, pp. 188–209.

Carter, Angela. "In the Bear Garden." *New Society* (London) 39 (Feb 24, 1977): 403–404.

Cock, Geoffrey. "A. A. Milne: Sources of His Creativity." *American Imago* 34 (1977): 313–326.

Crews, Frederick C. *The Pooh Perplex: A Freshman Casebook.* New York: Dutton, 1963.

Crouch, Marcus. "Pooh Lives—O.K.?" *Junior Bookshelf* 40 (Oct 1976): 252–255. Reprinted in *Bookbird* 15, no. 2 (1977): 14–16.

Doyle, Brian. *The Who's Who of Children's Literature.* New York: Schocken, 1968, pp. 199–201.

Farjeon, Eleanor. "A. A. Milne." *Junior Bookshelf* 20 (Mar 1956): 51–59.

Goldthwaite, John. "The Black Rabbit: Part One." *Signal* 47 (May 1985): 86–111; "The Black Rabbit: Part Two." *Signal* 48 (Sept 1985): 148–167. Reprinted in Goldthwaite. *The Natural History of Make-Believe.* London: Oxford Univ. Press, 1987.

Gose, Elliott. *Mere Creatures: A Study of Modern Fantasy Tales for Children.* Toronto: Univ. of Toronto Press, 1988, pp. 29–41.

Graham, Eleanor. "A. A. Milne." *Junior Bookshelf* 20 (Mar 1956): 51–59.

Gunderson, Ethel, and Agnes G. Gunderson. "A. A. Milne and Today's 7-Year-Olds." *Elementary English* 39 (May 1962): 408–411.

Haring-Smith, Tori. *A. A. Milne: A Critical Biography.* New York: Garland, 1982.

Higgens, Regina. *Magic Kingdoms: Discovering the Joys of Childhood Classics with Your Child.* New York: Simon, 1992.

Holmstrum, John. "Whisper Who Dares." *New Statesman* 12 (Nov 1965): 752.

Hunt, Peter. "A. A. Milne." In *Writers for Children: Critical Studies of Major Authors Since the Seventeenth Century.* Edited by Jane M. Bingham. New York: Scribner, 1988, pp. 397–406.

———. "Oogie-Woogie-Boo!" *Books for Keeps* (U.K.) 81 (1993): 25.

———. "*Winnie-the-Pooh* and Domestic Fantasy." In *Story and Society: Children's Literature in Its Social Context,* ed. by Dennis Butts. London: Macmillan, 1992, pp. 112–124.

The Junior Book of Authors. 2nd ed. rev. Edited by Stanley J. Kunitz and Howard Haycraft. New York: Wilson, 1951, pp. 221–223.

Low, Anthony. "Religious Myth in *Winnie-the-Pooh*." *Greyfriar* 22 (1981): 13–16.

Luenn, Nancy. "A Visit to Toad Hall and Pooh Forest." *Horn Book* 62 (July–Aug 1986): 507–508.

Lurie, Alison. "Back to Pooh Corner." In *Children's Literature,* vol. 2. Storrs, CT: Journal of the Modern Language Association, 1973, pp. 11–17. Reprinted in *Reflections on Literature for Children.* Edited by Francelia Butler and Richard Rotert. Hamden, CT: Shoe String Press, 1984, pp. 32–38.

———. "Now We Are Fifty." *New York Times Book Review,* Nov 14, 1967, p. 27.

McGrath, Charles. "School Days." *The New Yorker* (Apr 8, 1991): 95–99.

McVitty, Walter. "A Taste of the Best: A Gourmet Guide to Children's Books." *Reading Time* (Australia) 82 (Jan 1982): 7–22.

Milne, A. A. *Autobiography.* New York: Dutton, 1939. Original British title: *It's Too Late Now: The Autobiography of a Writer,* 1939.

———. "Children's Books." *Spectator,* December 4, 1926, p. 1011.

———. *When I Was Very Young.* New York: Fountain Press, 1930.

Milne, Christopher. *The Enchanted Places.* New York: Dutton, 1974.

———. *The Path through the Trees.* New York: Dutton, 1979.

Moss, Elaine. "A. A. Milne on 'Books for Children.'" *Signal* 44 (May 1984): 89–92.

Naumann, N. "*Winnie-the-Pooh* Week and a Half." *Teacher* 93 (Apr 1976): 42–44.

Nelson, Claudia. "The Beast Within: *Winnie-the-Pooh* Reassessed." *Children's Literature in Education* 21 (Mar 1990): 17–22.

Nesmith, Mary Ethel. "The Children's Milne." *Elementary English Review* 9 (Sept 1932): 172–173, 192.

Norton, E. "An 'Expotition' to Christopher Robin's Home." *Top of the News* 29 (Jan 1973): 146–150.

Novak, Barbara. "Milne's Poems: Form and Content." *Elementary English* 34 (Oct 1957): 355–361.

O'Neill, C. "The Professor Who Lives in Toad Hall." *Chronicle of Higher Education* 17 (Sept 18, 1978): R6–7.

The Oxford Companion to Children's Literature. Edited by Humphrey Carpenter and Mari Prichard. New York: Oxford Univ. Press, 1984, pp. 261, 350–353, 575–576.

Palmer, Alix. "Hip-Hip *Pooh*-Ray." [London] *Sun* (Oct 7, 1976): 8–9.

Payne, John R. "Four Children's Books by A. A. Milne." *Studies in Bibliography* 23 (1970): 127–139.

Phifer, Kenneth W. "A Bear of Very Little Brain: A Commentary on the *Pooh* Saga." *Religious Humanism* 13 (Winter 1979): 32–38.

Sale, Roger. "Child Reading and Man Reading: Oz, Babar, and Pooh." In *Children's Literature,* vol. 1. Storrs, CT: Journal of the Modern Language Association, 1972, pp. 162–172. Reprinted in *Reflections on Literature for Children.* Edited by Francelia Butler and Richard Rotert. Hamden, CT: Shoe String Press, 1984, pp. 19–31.

————. *Fairy Tales and After.* Cambridge, MA: Harvard Univ. Press, 1978, pp. 15–18.

Shepard, E. H. *The Pooh Sketchbook.* Edited by Brian Sibley. New York: Dutton, 1984.

Siddens, L. "*Winnie-the-Pooh* Goes to School." *Instructor* 84 (Mar 1975): 70–71.

Singer, Dorothy G. "Piglet, Pooh and Piaget." *Psychology Today* 6 (June 1972): 70–74, 96.

Smaridge, Norah. *Famous Modern Storytellers for Young People.* New York: Dodd, 1969, pp. 26–31.

Stanger, Carol A. "*Winnie the Pooh* through a Feminist Lens." *The Lion and the Unicorn* 11 (Oct 1987): 34–50.

Sterck, Kenneth. "The Real Christopher Robin: An Appreciation of A. A. Milne's Children's Verse." *Children's Literature in Education* 37 (Summer 1980): 52–61.

Stott, Jon C. *Children's Literature from A to Z.* New York: McGraw-Hill, 1984, p. 192.

Swabey, Betty. "*Pooh* Appeal." *Books for Your Children* (U.K.) 11 (Autumn 1976): 3; reprint of 2 (Mar 1967) article.

Swann, Thomas Burnett. *A. A. Milne.* Boston: Twayne, 1971.

Thompson, David. "A Bear of Very Little Brain." *Stamps and Printed Matters* (London) 9, no. 3 (1989): 58–61.

Thwaite, Ann. *A. A. Milne: The Man Behind "Winnie-the-Pooh."* New York: Random, 1991. (British title: *A. A. Milne: His Life.* London: Faber, 1990.)

————. *The Brilliant Career of "Winnie-The-Pooh." The Story of A. A. Milne and His Writing for Children.* London: Methuen, 1992, New York: Dutton: 1994.

————. "Childhood in a World That *Pooh* Created." (London) *Daily Telegraph* (June 2, 1990): 1.

————. "On the Road to *Pooh* Corner." *Daily Telegraph* (May 26, 1990): 1–11. Extract from Thwaite's biography of Milne.

Townsend, John Rowe. "A Bear of Very Great Age: John Rowe Townsend Celebrates *Pooh's* Fiftieth Birthday." *Guardian* (Oct 14, 1976): 11.

Tremper, Ellen. "'Instigorating' Winnie-the-Pooh." *The Lion and the Unicorn* 1, no. 1 (Spring 1977): 33–46.

Twentieth-Century Children's Writers. 3rd ed. Edited by Tracy Chevalier and D. L. Kirkpatrick. Chicago: St. James, 1989, pp. 682–684.

Von Schweinitz, Eleanor. *"Pooh* without Milne." *Children's Book News* 2 (Jan–Feb 1967): 5–8.

Werner, Craig. *"Pooh's* Extended Family." In *The Child and the Family: Selected Papers from the 1988 International Conference of the Children's Literature Association,* ed. by Susan R. Gannon and Ruth A. Thompson. New York: Pace University, 1990, p. 84. (abstract)

Wilson, Anita. "Milne's *Pooh* Books: The Benevolent Forest." In *Touchstones.* Edited by Perry Nodelman. West Lafayette, IN: Children's Literature Association Publications, 1985, pp. 163–172.

Woods, George A. "Winnie Was Not Pooh-Poohed." *New York Times Book Review,* June 1968, pp. 7, 28.

Mirrlees, Hope

Chapman, Edgar L. *"Lud-in-the-Mist."* In *Survey of Modern Fantasy Literature,* vol. 2. Edited by Frank N. Magill. Englewood Cliffs, NJ: Salem Press, 1983, pp. 926–931.

Gentle, Mary. "Godmakers and Worldshapers: Fantasy and Metaphysics." *Vector* 106 (1982): 8–14.

Waggoner, Diana. "Hope Mirrlees." In *Supernatural Fiction Writers: Fantasy and Horror,* vol. 2. Edited by E. F. Bleiler. New York: Scribner, 1985, pp. 603–608.

Moeri, Louise

Fifth Book of Junior Authors and Illustrators. Edited by Sally Holmes Holtze. New York: Wilson, 1983, pp. 220–221.

May, Jill P. "Winter Magic: Understanding the Complexities of a Simple Story" *Catholic Library World* 59 (1988): 222–225.

Molesworth, Mary Louisa (Stewart)

Auerbach, Mina, and U. C. Knoepflmacher, eds. *Forbidden Journeys: Fairy Tales and Fantasys by Victorian Women Writers.* Chicago: Univ. of Chicago Press, 1992, pp. 75–104, 363.

Baker, Margaret J. "Mary Louisa Molesworth." *Junior Bookshelf* 12 (Mar 1948): 19–26.

Cashdan, Liz. "Powerful Levers: Margaret Gatty, Juliana Horatia Ewing, and Mary Louisa Molesworth." *Children's Literature in Education* 20 (Dec 1989): 215–226.

Cooper, Jane. "'Just Really What They Do,' or, Re-Reading Mrs. Molesworth." *Signal* 57 (Sept 1988): 181–196.

Crago, Hugh. "Hearing Her Own Story: Morwenna and *The Cuckoo Clock."* *Papers: Explorations into Children's Literature* (Australia) 3 (Dec 1992): 106–125.

Doyle, Brian. *The Who's Who of Children's Literature.* New York: Schocken, 1968, pp. 203–204.

Fox, Paula. "A Second Look: *The Cuckoo Clock."* *Horn Book* 63 (Sept–Oct 1987): 592–593.

Green, Roger Lancelyn. *Mrs. Molesworth.* London: Bodley Head, 1961.

———. "Mrs. Molesworth." *Junior Bookshelf* 21 (July 1957): 101–108.

Honig, Edith Lazaros. *Breaking the Angelic Image: Woman Power in Victorian Children's Fantasy.* Westport, CT: Greenwood, 1988.

———. "A Quiet Rebellion: The Portrait of the Feminine in Victorian Children's Fantasy." Ph.D. diss., Fordham University, 1985.

Keenan, Hugh T. "Mary Louisa Stewart Molesworth." In *Writers for Children: Critical*

Studies of Major Authors Since the Seventeenth Century. Edited by Jane M. Bingham. New York: Scribner, 1988, pp. 407–414.

Laski, Marghanita. *Mrs. Ewing, Mrs. Molesworth, and Mrs. Hodgson Burnett.* New York: Oxford Univ. Press, 1951.

McGillis, Roderick. "Fantasy As Adventure: Nineteenth Century Children's Fiction." *Children's Literature Association Quarterly* 8 (Fall 1983): 18–22.

Molesworth, Mrs. "On the Art of Writing Fiction for Children." *Atalanta* (London) 6 (May 1893): 583–586.

———. "Story-Reading and Story-Writing." *Chambers' Journal* (London), Nov 5, 1898, pp. 772–775.

Moss, Anita. "Mothers, Monsters, and Morals in Victorian Fairy Tales." *The Lion and the Unicorn* 12 (1988): 47–60.

———. "Mrs. Molesworth: Victorian Visionary." *The Lion and the Unicorn* 12 (1988): 105–110.

———. "Sacred and Secular Visions of Imagination and Reality in Nineteenth-Century British Fantasy for Children." In *Webs and Wardrobes: Humanist and Religious World Views in Children's Literature,* ed. by Joseph O'Beirne Milner and Lucy Floyd Morcock Milner. Lanham, MD: University Press of America, 1987, pp. 65–78.

The Oxford Companion to Children's Literature. Edited by Humphrey Carpenter and Mari Prichard. New York: Oxford Univ. Press, 1984, pp. 137, 355, 516.

Pflieger, Pat, and Helen M. Hill. *A Reference Guide to Modern Fantasy for Children.* Westport, CT: Greenwood, 1984, pp. xvi, 131–132, 374–377, 520–521.

Rosenthal, Lynne M. "Writing Her Own Story: The Integration of the Self in the Fourth Dimension of Mrs. Molesworth's *The Cuckoo Clock.*" *Children's Literature Association Quarterly* 10 (Winter 1986): 187–192.

Sircar, Sanjay Kumar. "The Art of Victorian Fantasy: Ambiguity and Unity in *The Cuckoo Clock.*" *Papers* (Australia) 3 (Apr 1992): 3–17.

———. "The Fantasy Fiction of Mrs. Molesworth: Family Resemblances." *Orana* (Australia) 28 (Aug 1992): 186–202.

———. "The Victorian Auntly Narrative Voice and Mrs. Molesworth's *Cuckoo Clock.*" *Children's Literature* 17 (1989): 1–24.

——— "Victorian Children's Fantasy: A Critical Study of Two Works of Fantasy of Mrs. Molesworth." M.A. diss., Australian National University, 1980.

Twentieth Century Children's Writers. 2nd ed. Edited by D. L. Kirkpatrick. New York: St. Martin, 1983, pp. 881–882.

Monaco, Richard

Lawler, Donald L. "The *She* Series." In *Survey of Modern Fantasy Literature,* vol. 3. Edited by Frank N. Magill. Englewood Cliffs, NJ: Salem Press, 1983, pp. 1396–1401.

Michalson, Karen Ann. "Victorian Fantasy Literature and the Politics of Canon-Making." Ph.D. diss., University of Massachusetts, 1990. Discusses Ruskin, MacDonald, Kingsley, Haggard, and Kipling.

Smith, Curtis C. "H. Rider Haggard." In *Supernatural Fiction Writers: Fantasy and Horror,* vol. 1. Edited by E. F. Bleiler. New York: Scribner, 1985, pp. 321–328.

Storr, Catherine. "H. Rider Haggard's *She.*" *Children's Literature in Education* 22 (Sept 1991): 161–167.

Twentieth-Century Science Fiction Writers. 2nd ed. Edited by Curtis C. Smith. Chicago: St. James Press, 1986, pp. 308–310. About H. Rider Haggard.

Moon, Sheila (Elizabeth)

Helbig, Alethea K., and Agnes Regan Perkins. *Dictionary of American Children's Fiction, 1960-1984.* Westport, CT: Greenwood, 1986, pp. 430–431.

Moorcock, Michael (John)

Allen, Paul C. "Of Swords and Sorcery: 5." *Fantasy Crossroads* 13 (1978): 31–40.

"Behold the Man Himself." *Quartz* (Mar 1982): 8–11. Interview.

Bilyeu, Richard. *The Tanlorn Archives: A Primary and Secondary Bibliography of the Works of Michael Moorcock, 1949–1979.* San Bernardino, CA: Borgo Press, 1982.

Butler, Ted. "*Algol* Interviews Michael Moorcock." *Algol* 15 (Winter 1978): 29–32.

Callow, A. J. *The Chronicles of Moorcock.* UK: [privately printed], 1978. (bibliography)

Clute, John. "The Eternal Champion Series." In *Survey of Modern Fantasy Literature,* vol. 1. Edited by Frank N. Magill. Englewood Cliffs, NJ: Salem Press, 1983, pp. 489–496.

Darlington, Andrew. "The Evolution of Michael Moorcock." *Dark Horizons* 22 (1981): 4–10.

Dean, John. "'A Curious Note in the Wind': The New Literary Genre of Heroic Fantasy." *New Mexico Humanities Review* 2 (Summer, 1979): 34–41.

"*The Eildon Tree* Interviews Michael Moorcock." *The Eildon Tree* 1, no. 2 (1976): 4–8.

Glover, David. "Utopia and Fantasy in the Late 1960s: Burroughs, Moorcock, Tolkien." In *Popular Fiction and Social Change.* Edited by Christopher Pawling. New York: St. Martin, 1984.

Harper, Andrew, and George McAulay. *Michael Moorcock: A Bibliography.* Baltimore: T-K Graphics, 1976.

Lupoff, Richard. "*Rigel* Interviews Michael Moorcock." *Rigel Science Fiction* (Spring 1983): 21–25.

McFerran, Dave. "The Celtic Incarnation." *Dark Horizons* 29 (1985): 33–37.

Moorcock, Michael. "Aspects of Fantasy." In *Exploring Fantasy Worlds.* Edited by Darrell Schweitzer. San Bernardino, CA: Borgo Press, 1985.

———. "The Heroes in Heroic Fantasy." *Dragonfields* 3 (1980): 50–61.

———. "*New Worlds:* A Personal History." *Foundation* 15 (1979): 5–18.

———. "Wit and Humor in Fantasy." In *Fantasists on Fantasy.* Edited by Robert H. Boyer and Kenneth J. Zahorski. New York: Avon, 1984, pp. 265–276. Originally published in *Foundation* 16 (1979): 16–22.

———. *Wizardry and Wild Romance: A Study of Epic Fantasy.* London: Gollancz, 1988.

Nicholls, Peter. "Michael Moorcock." In *Supernatural Fiction Writers: Fantasy and Horror,* volume 2. Edited by E. F. Bleiler. New York: Scribner, 1985, pp. 1081–1090.

Platt, Charles. *Dream Makers: The Uncommon People Who Write Science Fiction.* New York: Ungar, 1987, pp. 97–104. Interview.

Powers, Richard. "Introduction." In *The Sword Trilogy* by Michael Moorcock. Boston: Gregg, 1980.

Twentieth-Century Science Fiction Writers. 3rd ed. Edited by Noelle Watson and Paul E. Schellinger. Chicago: St. James Press, 1991, pp. 567–570.

Walker, Paul. "Michael Moorcock: An Interview." *Luna Monthly* 59 (1975): 5–9.

———. *Speaking of Science Fiction: The Paul Walker Interviews.* Oradell, NJ: Luna Publications, 1978, pp. 213–228.

Moore, Anne Carroll

Helbig, Alethea K., and Agnes Regan Perkins. *Dictionary of American Children's Fiction, 1859–1959*. Westport, CT: Greenwood, 1985, pp. 354–355, 373.
Hogarth, Grace. "A Publisher's Perspective." *Horn Book* 58 (May–June 1987): 372–377.
The Junior Book of Authors. 2nd ed. rev. Edited by Stanley J. Kunitz and Howard Haycraft. New York: Wilson, 1951, pp. 225–226.
Twentieth Century Children's Writers. 2nd ed. Edited by D. L. Kirkpatrick. New York: St. Martin, 1983, pp. 562–563.

Moore, Lilian

Glazer, Joan I. "Profile: Lilian Moore." *Language Arts* 62, no. 6 (1985): 647–652.
Helbig, Alethea, and Agnes Regan Perkins. *Dictionary of American Children's Fiction, 1985–1989*. Westport, CT: Greenwood, 1993, pp. 107–108, 160.

Morgan, Alison (Mary Raikes)

Twentieth-Century Children's Writers. 3rd ed. Edited by Tracy Chevalier and D. L. Kirkpatrick. New York: St. Martin, 1989, pp. 699–700.

Morgan, Helen (Gertrude Louise Axford)

Twentieth-Century Children's Writers. 3rd ed. Edited by Tracy Chevalier and D. L. Kirkpatrick. New York: St. Martin, 1989, p. 700.

Morpurgo, Michael

Cruickshank, Mary. "Paradise Glimpsed." *Times Educational Supplement* (July 22, 1988): 15.
Mills, Colin. "Authorgraph no. 79: Michael Morpurgo." *Books for Keeps* (U.K.) 79 (1993): 16–17.
Morpurgo, Michael. "War Horse." *Books for Your Children* (U.K.) 18 (Summer 1983): 2–3.

Morris, Kenneth

Bisenieks, Dainis. "Finder of the Welsh Gods." *Mythlore* 3, no. 11 (1976).
Sullivan, C. W., III. *"The Fates of the Princes of Dyfed* and *Book of the Three Dragons."* In *Survey of Modern Fantasy Literature*, vol. 2. Edited by Frank N. Magill. Englewood Cliffs, NJ: Salem Press, 1983, pp. 539–542.
———. "The Influence of Celtic Myth and Legend on Modern Imaginative Fiction." Ph.D. diss., University of Oregon, 1976.
———. "Kenneth Morris and *The Mabinogian*: The Welsh Influence on Children's Fantasy." In *Cross-Culturalism in Children's Literature: Selected Papers from the 1987 International Conference of the Children's Literature Association*, ed. by Susan R. Gannon and Ruth A. Thompson. New York: Pace University, 1988, pp. 101–106.
———. *Welsh Celtic Myth in Modern Fantasy*. Westport, CT: Greenwood, 1989, pp. 35–44+.
Zahorski, Kenneth J., and Robert H. Boyer. *Lloyd Alexander, Evangeline Walton Ensley, Kenneth Morris: A Primary and Secondary Bibliography*. Boston: G. K. Hall, 1981.

Morris, William

Allen, Elizabeth Estelle. "The Prose Romances of William Morris." Ph.D. diss., Tulane University, 1975.

Bono, Barbara. "The Prose Fictions of William Morris: A Study in the Literary Aesthetic of a Victorian Social Reformer." *Victorian Poetry* 13 (1975): 43–59.

Bradley, Ian. *William Morris and His World.* New York: Scribner, 1978.

Burns, Marjorie Jean. "Victorian Fantasists from Ruskin to Lang: A Study in Ambivalence." Ph.D. diss., University of California, Berkeley, 1978.

Carmassi, Guido Remo. "The Expanding Vision: Changes in the Emphasis in William Morris' Late Prose Romances." Ph.D. diss., University of Notre Dame, 1975.

Currie, Robert. "Had Morris Gone Soft in the Head?" *Essays in Criticism* 29 (1979): 341–356.

De Camp, L. Sprague. *Literary Swordsmen and Sorcerers: The Makers of Heroic Fantasy.* Sauk City, WI: Arkham House, 1976.

Denington, Frances Barbara. "The Complete Book: An Investigation of the Development of William Morris' Aesthetic and Literary Practice." Ph.D. diss., McMaster University, Hamilton, Ont., Canada, 1976.

Edwards, Bruce L. "Toward a Rhetoric of Fantasy Criticism: C. S. Lewis's Readings of MacDonald and Morris." *Literature and Belief* 3 (Mar 1983): 63–73.

Hoare, Dorothy. *The Works of Morris and Yeats in Relation to Early Saga Literature.* New York: Cambridge Univ. Press, 1937; Norwood, PA: Norwood Editions, 1975.

Jackson, Rosemary. *Fantasy: The Literature of Subversion.* New York: Methuen, 1980, pp. 42, 44, 110–112, 153–154, 156.

Keller, Donald G. "William Morris: Dreams and the End of Dreams." *The Eildon Tree* 1 (1974): 5–7.

Kirschhoff, Frederick, ed. *Studies in the Late Prose Romances of William Morris.* New York: William Morris Society, 1976.

Landow, George P. "And the World Became Strange: Realms of Literary Fantasy." In Diane L. Johnson. *Fantastic Illustration and Design in Britain, 1850–1930.* Providence: Rhode Island School of Design, 1979, pp. 9–43. Reprinted in *Georgia Review* 33 (Spring 1979): 7–42.

McCormick, Judith Kay. "Biography and the Pattern of Degeneration in the Late Prose Romances of William Morris." Ph.D. diss., Kansas State University, 1980.

Manlove, C. N. *The Impulse of Fantasy Literature.* Kent, OH: Kent State Univ. Press, 1983.

Mathews, Richard. "The Well at the World's End." In *Survey of Modern Fantasy Literature,* vol. 5. Edited by Frank N. Magill. Englewood Cliffs, NJ: Salem Press, 1983, pp. 2090–2096.

———. *Worlds Beyond the World: The Fantastic Vision of William Morris.* San Bernardino, CA: Borgo Press, 1978.

Mendelson, Michael. "The Modernization of Prose Romance: The Radical Form of William Morris and George MacDonald." Ph.D. diss., Washington State University, 1981.

———. "Opening Moves: The Entry into the Other World." *Extrapolation* 25 (1984): 171–179.

Munn, Nancy D. "Eros and Community in the Fiction of William Morris." *Nineteenth-Century Fiction* 34 (1979): 302–325.

Pfeiffer, John R. "William Morris." In *Supernatural Fiction Writers: Fantasy and Horror,* vol. 1. Edited by E. F. Bleiler. New York: Scribner, 1985, pp. 299–306.

Ringel, Faye Joyce. "Patterns of the Hero and the Quest: Epic, Romance, Fantasy." Ph.D. diss., Brown University, 1979.

Ruby, Dona Lin. "The Late Prose Romances of William Morris." Ph.D. diss., Northern Illinois University, 1979.

Silver, Carole. *The Romance of William Morris.* Athens, OH: Ohio Univ. Press, 1983.

Spatt, Hartley Steven. "William Morris: The Language of History and Myth." Ph.D. diss., Johns Hopkins University, 1975.

Stansky, Peter. *William Morris.* New York: Oxford Univ. Press, 1983.

Sullivan, C. W., III. "Fantasy." In *Story and Society: Children's Literature in Its Social Context,* ed. by Dennis Butts. London: Macmillan, 1992, pp. 97–111.

Taylor, Angus. "Pilgrim of Hope: William Morris on the Way to Utopia." *Foundation* 32 (1984): 15–22.

Twentieth-Century Science Fiction Writers. 3rd. ed. Edited by Noelle Watson and Paul E. Schellinger. Chicago: St. James Press, 1991, pp. 579–583.

Valentine, Kristin Bervig. "Motifs from Nature in the Design Work and Prose Romances of William Morris (1876–1896)." *Victorian Poetry* 13 (1975): 83–98.

———. "A Patterned Imagination: William Morris' Use of Pattern in Decorative Design and the Last Prose Romances, 1883–1896." Ph.D. diss., University of Utah, 1974.

Wolfshohl, Clarence. "William Morris's *The Wood Beyond the World:* The Victorian World vs. the Mythic Eternities." *Mythlore* 6 (Summer 1979): 29–32.

Mulock, Diana (pseud. of Dinah Maria Mulock Craik)

Doyle, Brian. *The Who's Who of Children's Literature.* New York: Schocken, 1968, pp. 204–205.

Fasick, Laura. "Women's Moral Role in Selected Victorian Religious Novels." Ph.D. diss., Indiana University, 1990.

Frey, Charles, and John Griffiths. *The Literary Heritage of Childhood: An Appraisal of Children's Classics in the Western Tradition.* Westport, CT: Greenwood, 1987, pp. 93–98.

McGillis, Roderick. "Fantasy as Adventure: Nineteenth Century Children's Fiction." *Children's Literature Association Quarterly* 8 (Fall 1983): 18–22.

Mitchell, Sally. *Dinah Mulock Craik.* Boston: Twayne, 1983.

Moss, Anita. "Sacred and Secular Visions of Imagination and Reality in Nineteenth-Century British Fantasy for Children." In *Webs and Wardrobes: Humanist and Religious World Views in Children's Literature,* ed. by Joseph O'Beirne Milner and Lucy Floyd Morcock Milner. Lanham, MD: University Press of America, 1987, pp. 65–78.

Mulock, Dinah Maria. *Studies from Life.* New York: Harper, 1861.

The Oxford Companion to Children's Literature. Edited by Humphrey Carpenter and Mari Prichard. New York: Oxford Univ. Press, 1984, pp. 132, 316.

Reade, Aleyn Lyell. *The Mellards and Their Descendants . . . With Memoirs of Dinah Maria Mulock.* London: Arden Press, 1915.

Richardson, Alan. "Reluctant Lords and Lame Princes: Engendering the Male Child in Nineteenth-Century Juvenile Fiction." *Children's Literature 21.* New Haven: Yale Univ. Press, 1993, pp. 3–19.

Showalter, Elaine. "Dinah Mulock Craik and the Tactics of Sentiment: A Case Study in Victorian Female Authorship." *Feminist Studies* 2 (1975): 5–23.

Münchausen, Karl (Friedrich Hieronymus, Baron Von)

Bethnal Green Museum of Childhood. *Tall Stories of Baron Münchausen.* London: The Victoria and Albert Museum, 1985.

The Oxford Companion to Children's Literature. Edited by Humphrey Carpenter and Mari Prichard. New York: Oxford Univ. Press, 1984, p. 368.

Stableford, Brian. "*Baron Münchausen's Narrative of His Marvellous Travels and Campaigns in Russia.*" In *Survey of Modern Fantasy Literature,* vol. 1. Edited by Frank N. Magill. Englewood Cliffs, NJ: Salem Press, 1983, pp. 78–80.

Tall Stories of Baron Münchausen: A Book Accompanying the Exhibition at the Bethnal Green Museum of Childhood. London: Victoria & Albert Museum, 1985.

Mundy, Talbot

Bleiler, E. F. "Talbot Mundy." In *Supernatural Fiction Writers: Fantasy and Horror,* vol. 2. Edited by E. F. Bleiler. New York: Scribner, 1985, pp. 845–852.

Chapman, Edgar L. "OM: The Secret of Abhor Valley." In *Survey of Modern Fantasy Literature,* vol. 3. Edited by Frank N. Magill. Englewood Cliffs, NJ: Salem Press, 1983, pp. 1142–1145.

De Camp, L. Sprague, ed. *The Blade of Conan.* New York: Ace, 1979.

Ellis, Peter Berresford. *The Last Adventurer: The Life of Talbot Mundy 1879–1940.* West Kingston, RI: Grant, 1984.

Grant, Donald M. *Talbot Mundy: Messenger of Destiny.* West Kingston, RI: Grant, 1983.

Murphy, Shirley Rousseau

Esmonde, Margaret P. "Beyond the Circles of the World: Death and the Hereafter in Children's Literature." In *Webs and Wardrobes: Humanist and Religious World Views in Children's Literature,* ed. by Joseph O'Beirne Milner and Lucy Floyd Morcock Milner. Lanham, MD: University Press of America, 1987, pp. 33–45.

Greenlaw, M. Jean. "Books in the Classroom." *Horn Book* 64 (Nov–Dec 1988): 820–822.

Murphy, Shirley Rousseau. "Fantasy for Young Readers." *The Writer* (Sept 1989): 19–20.

———. "The Reality of Magic." *School Media Quarterly* 2 (Fall 1973): 31–35.

Sixth Book of Junior Authors and Illustrators. Edited by Sally Holmes Holtze. New York: Wilson, 1989, pp. 205–206.

Twentieth-Century Children's Writers. 3rd ed. Edited by Tracy Chevalier and D. L. Kirkpatrick. Chicago: St. James, 1989, pp. 706–707.

Myers, John Myers

Dickinson, Mike. "*Silverlock* and *The Moon's Fire-Eating Daughter.*" In *Survey of Modern Fantasy Literature,* vol. 4. Edited by Frank N. Magill. Englewood Cliffs, NJ: Salem Press, 1983, pp. 1749–1753.

Nathan, Robert (Gruntal)

Indick, Ben. "Portrait of Nathan." In *Exploring Fantasy Worlds.* Edited by Darrell Schweitzer. San Bernardino, CA: Borgo Press, 1985.

Meyers, Julia. "Robert Nathan." In *Supernatural Fiction Writers: Fantasy and Horror,* vol. 2. Edited by E. F. Bleiler. New York: Scribner, 1985, pp. 813–820.

Stableford, Brian. "*Portrait of Jenny.*" In *Survey of Modern Fantasy Literature,* vol. 3. Edited by Frank N. Magill. Englewood Cliffs, NJ: Salem Press, 1983, pp. 1276–1279.

Naylor, Phyllis Reynolds

Graham, Joyce L. "An Interview with Phyllis Reynolds Naylor." *Journal of Youth Services in Libraries* 6 (Summer 1993): 392–398.

Helbig, Alethea, and Agnes Regan Perkins. *Dictionary of American Children's Fiction, 1985–1989.* Westport, CT: Greenwood, 1993, p. 171.

————. *Dictionary of American Children's Fiction, 1960–1984.* Westport, CT: Greenwood, 1986, p. 469.

Naylor, Phyllis Reynolds. "Becoming a Writer." *Five Owls* (Nov–Dec 1989): 17–22.

————. "Newbery Acceptance Speech." *Horn Book* 68 (July–Aug 1992): 404–411; and *Journal of Youth Services in Libraries* 5 (Summer 1992): 351–356.

Naylor, Rex. "Phyllis Reynolds Naylor." *Horn Book* 68 (July–Aug 1992): 412–415.

Twentieth-Century Children's Writers. 3rd ed. Edited by Tracy Chevalier and D. L. Kirkpatrick. Chicago: St. James, 1989, pp. 710–712.

Neill, John Rea

Hanff, Peter E., and Douglas G. Greene. *Bibliographia Oziana.* Demorest, GA: International Wizard of Oz Club, 1976.

Nesbit (Bland), E(dith)

Aers, Lesley. "The Treatment of Time in Four Children's Books." *Children's Literature in Education* 2 (July 1970): 69–81.

Alexander, Lloyd. "Afterword." In E. Nesbit's *Five Children and It.* Dell, 1985.

————. "A Second Look: *Five Children and It.*" *Horn Book* 61 (May–June 1985): 354–361.

Armstrong, Dennis Lee. "E. Nesbit: An Entrance to *The Magic City.*" Ph.D. diss., Johns Hopkins University, 1974.

Auerbach, Mina, and U. C. Knoepflmacher, eds. *Forbidden Journeys: Fairy Tales and Fantasys by Victorian Women Writers.* Chicago: Univ. of Chicago Press, 1992, pp. 177–206, 363–364.

Bell, Anthea. *E. Nesbit.* New York: Walck, 1964. Reprinted in Roger Lancelyn Green, Anthea Bell, and Elizabeth Nesbitt. *Lewis Carroll, E. Nesbit, and Howard Pyle.* London: Bodley Head, 1968.

Brandon, Ruth. *The New Women and the Old Men: Love, Sex, and the Woman Question.* London: Secker, 1990.

Briggs, Julia. *A Woman of Passion: The Life of E. Nesbit 1858–1924.* London: Hutchinson, 1987; New York: New Amsterdam, 1987, New York: Penguin, 1989.

Buckley, Mary F. "Words of Power: Language and Reality in the Fantasy Novels of E. Nesbit and P. L. Travers." Ed.D. diss., East Texas State University, 1977.

Carpenter, Humphrey. "E. Nesbit: A Victorian in Disguise." In *Secret Gardens: The Golden Age of Children's Literature.* Boston: Houghton Mifflin, 1985, pp. 126–137.

Chaston, Joel D. "Polistopolis and Torquilstone: Nesbit, Eager, and the Question of Imitation." *The Lion and the Unicorn* 17 (June 1993): 73–82.

Colwell, Eileen H. "E. Nesbit." *Junior Bookshelf* 8 (Nov 1944): 85–89.

Cooper, Susan. "Afterword." In *The Phoenix and the Carpet* by E. Nesbit. New York: Dell, 1987.

Crago, Hugh. "A Strong Dark Shop." *Children's Literature Association Quarterly* 16 (Spring 1991): 33–37.

Crouch, Marcus S. "E. Nesbit in Kent." *Junior Bookshelf* 19, 1 (Jan 1955): 11–21.

————. "The Nesbit Tradition." *Junior Bookshelf* 22 (Oct 1958): 195–198.

————. *The Nesbit Tradition: The Children's Novel in England, 1845–1970.* London: Benn, 1972, p. 16.

Croxon, Mary. "The Emancipated Child in the Novels of E. Nesbit." *Signal* 14 (May 1974): 51–64.

De Alonso, Joan Evans. "E. Nesbit's Well Hall, 1915–1921: A Memoir." In *Children's Literature,* vol. 3. Storrs, CT: Journal of the Modern Language Association, 1974, pp.

147–152. Reprinted in *Reflections on Literature for Children.* Edited by Francelia Butler and Richard Rotert. Hamden, CT: Shoe String Press, 1984, pp. 229–236.

Dusinberre, Juliet. *"Alice" to the Lighthhouse: Children's Books and Radical Experimentalism in Art.* New York: St. Martin, 1987.

Doyle, Brian. *The Who's Who of Children's Literature.* New York: Schocken, 1968, pp. 206–208.

Eager, Edward. "Daily Magic." *Horn Book* 34 (Oct 1958): 349–358. Reprinted in Elinor Field. *Horn Book Reflections.* Boston: Horn Book, 1969, pp. 211–217.

Ellis, Alec. "E. Nesbit and the Poor." *Junior Bookshelf* 38 (Apr 1974): 73–78.

Fromm, Gloria G. "E. Nesbit and the Happy Moralist." *Journal of Modern Literature* 11 (Mar 1984): 45–65.

Gilead, S. "Magic Abjured: Closure in Children's Fantasy Fiction." *Publications of the Modern Language Association* 106 (Mar 1991): 277–293.

Graham, Eleanor. "Places of Enchantment." *Horn Book* 34 (Oct 1958): 364–365.

Green, Roger Lancelyn. "E. Nesbit: Treasure-Seeker." *Junior Bookshelf* 22 (Oct 1958): 175–185.

Hand, Nigel. "The Other E. Nesbit." *The Use of English* 26 (Winter 1974): 108–116.

Honig, Edith Lazaros. *Breaking the Angelic Image: Woman Power in Victorian Children's Fantasy.* Westport, CT.: Greenwood, 1988.

———. "A Quiet Rebellion: The Portrait of the Feminine in Victorian Children's Fantasy." Ph.D. diss., Fordham University, 1985.

Horn Book Magazine. E. Nesbit Special Number. "Magic and the Magician." *Horn Book* 35 (Oct 1958): 341, 347–373.

Inglis, Fred. *The Promise of Happiness.* New York: Cambridge Univ. Press, 1981, pp. 113–117.

Jackson, Rosemary. *Fantasy: The Literature of Subversion.* New York: Methuen, 1980, pp. 145–146, 153.

Jacobs, W. J., and P. L. Jacobs. "E. Nesbit: Storyteller and Victorian Swinger." *Record* 69 (Mar 1968): 621–623.

Junior Bookshelf. E. Nesbit special issue 22, no. 4 (Oct 1958).

Kingsley, Madeleine. "Ageless Enchantress." *Radio Times* 225 (Nov 2–9, 1979).

Knoepflmacher, U. C. "Of Babylands and Babylons: E. Nesbit and the Reclamation of the Fairy Tale." *Tulsa Studies in Women's Literature* 6 (Fall 1987): 299–325.

Krensky, Stephen. "A Second Look: *The Story of the Treasure Seekers.*" *Horn Book* 54 (June 1978): 310–312.

Lansner, Helen. "The Genius of E. Nesbit." *Elementary English* 43 (Jan 1966): 53–55.

Lehnert-Rodiek, Gertrud. "Fantastic Children's Literature and Travel in Time." *Phaedrus* 13 (1988): 61–72.

Lochhead, Marion. *Renaissance of Wonder.* New York: Harper, 1980, pp. 59–69.

Lurie, Alison. "E. Nesbit." In *Writers for Children: Critical Studies of Major Authors Since the Seventeenth Century.* Edited by Jane M. Bingham. New York: Scribner, 1988, pp. 423–430.

Lynch, Patricia. "Remembering E. Nesbit." *Horn Book* 29 (Oct 1953): 342–343.

McCaffrey, Anne. "Afterword." In E. Nesbit's *Book of Dragons.* Dell, 1985.

MacLeod, Helen. "The Children's Books of E. Nesbit." *Book and Magazine Collector* 17 (July 1985): 46–53.

Manlove, C(olin) N. "Fantasy as Witty Conceit: E. Nesbit." *Mosaic* 10, no. 2 (Winter 1976–1977): 109–130.

———. "The Union of Opposites in Fantasy: E. Nesbit." In C. N. Manlove. *The Impulse of Fantasy Literature.* Kent, OH: Kent State Univ. Press, 1983, pp. 46–69. Revised from an article in *Mosaic,* 1977.

Molson, Francis J. *"The Enchanted Castle."* In *Survey of Modern Fantasy Literature,* vol. 3. Edited by Frank N. Magill. Englewood Cliffs, NJ: Salem Press, 1983, pp. 483–485.

────. "The Psammead Trilogy." In *Survey of Modern Fantasy Literature,* vol. 3. Edited by Frank N. Magill. Englewood Cliffs, NJ: Salem Press, 1983, pp. 1297–1300.

Moore, Doris Langley. *E. Nesbit: A Biography,* rev. ed. Radnor, PA: Chilton, 1966. Originally published 1933.

More Junior Authors. Edited by Muriel Fuller. New York: Wilson, 1963, pp. 157–158.

Moss, Anita. "Makers of Meaning: A Structuralist Study of Twain's *Tom Sawyer* and Nesbit's *The Enchanted Castle.*" *Children's Literature Association Quarterly* 7 (Fall 1982): 39–44.

Nesbit, E. *Long Ago When I Was Young* (original title: *The Girl's Own.* London, 1896). New York: Watts, 1966; New York: Dial, 1988.

────. "Pirates and Explorers" *Horn Book* 42 (Feb 1966): 87–91. An excerpt from *Long Ago When I Was Young.* New York: Watts, 1966

────. *Wings and the Child; Or, The Building of Magic Cities.* London: Hodder, 1913.

Nicholson, Mervyn. "What C. S. Lewis Took from E. Nesbit." *Children's Literature Association Quarterly* 16 (Spring 1991): 16–22.

The Oxford Companion to Children's Literature. Edited by Humphrey Carpenter and Mari Prichard. New York: Oxford Univ. Press, 1984, pp. 167, 187, 238, 262, 333, 371–374, 410, 499.

Parent, L. K. "Bibliography of Edith Nesbit (Bland)." M.L.S. thesis, Catholic University of America, 1962.

Pflieger, Pat, and Helen M. Hill. *A Reference Guide to Modern Fantasy for Children.* Westport, CT: Greenwood, 1984, pp. xii–xvi, 63–67, 173–175, 188–190, 231–233, 251–253, 338–341, 439–442, 505–508, 589–591.

Prickett, Stephen. *Victorian Fantasy.* Bloomington: Indiana Univ. Press, 1979.

Rahn, Suzanne. "The Expression of Religious and Political Concepts in Fantasy for Children." Ph.D. diss., University of Washington, 1986.

────. "News from E. Nesbit: *The Story of The Amulet* and the Socialist Utopia." *English Literature in Transition 1880–1920* 28 (1985): 124–144.

Robson, W. W. "E. Nesbit and *The Book of Dragons.*" In *Children and Their Books,* ed. by Gillian Avery and Julia Briggs. Oxford: Clarendon, 1989, pp. 251–270.

Rustin, Michael. "Magic Wishes and the Self Explorations of Children: *Five Children and It.*" In Margaret Rustin and Michael Rustin. *Narratives of Love and Loss: Studies in Modern Children's Fiction.* London: Verso, 1987; New York: Routledge, 1988, pp. 59–83.

Searles, Baird, Beth Meacham, and Michael Franklin. *A Reader's Guide to Fantasy.* New York: Avon, 1982, pp. 116–119.

Smith, Barbara. "The Expression of Social Values in the Writing of E. Nesbit." In *Children's Literature,* vol. 3. Storrs, CT: Journal of the Modern Language Association, 1974, pp. 153–164.

Smith, Louisa A. "The Magician's Conjuror: E. Nesbit's Illustrator, H. R. Millar." In *Proceedings of the Ninth Annual Conference of the Children's Literature Association.* University of Florida, March 1982. Ypsilanti, MI: Children's Literature Association, 1983, pp. 130–136.

Stott, Jon C. *Children's Literature from A to Z.* New York: McGraw-Hill, 1984, p. 201.

────. "'Will the Real Dragon Please Stand Up?' Convention and Parody in Children's Stories." *Children's Literature in Education* 21 (Winter 1990): 219–228.

Strange, Mavis. "E. Nesbit, As I Knew Her." *Horn Book* 34 (Oct 1958): 359–363.

Streatfeild, Noel. *Magic and the Magician: E. Nesbit and Her Children's Books.* New York: Abelard-Schuman, 1958, pp. 90–116, 127–150.

────. "The Nesbit Influence." *Junior Bookshelf* 22 (Oct 1958): 187–193.

────. "Oswald Bastable." *Horn Book* 34 (Oct 1958): 366–373.

Twentieth-Century Children's Writers. 3rd ed. Edited by Tracy Chevalier and D. L. Kirkpatrick. Chicago: St. James, 1989, pp. 713–716.

Walbridge, Earle F. "E. Nesbit." *Horn Book* 29 (Oct 1953): 335–341.
Watkins, G. M. "E. Nesbit: *The Treasure Seeker.*" *Antiquarian Books Monthly Review* (U.K.) XV (May 1988): 174–176.
Yolen, Jane. "The Literary Underwater World." *Language Arts* 57 (1980): 403–412.

Ness, Evaline (Michelow)

Third Book of Junior Authors. Edited by Doris De Montreville and Donna Hill. New York: Wilson, 1972, pp. 206–207.
Twentieth-Century Children's Writers. 3rd ed. Edited by Tracy Chevalier and D. L. Kirkpatrick. New York: St. Martin, 1989, pp. 716–718.

Newman, Robert (Howard)

Helbig, Alethea K., and Agnes Regan Perkins. *Dictionary of American Children's Fiction, 1960–1984.* Westport, CT: Greenwood, 1986, p. 471.
Sixth Book of Junior Authors and Illustrators. Edited by Sally Holmes Holtze. New York: Wilson, 1989, pp. 206–208.
Twentieth-Century Children's Writers. 3rd ed. Edited by Tracy Chevalier and D. L. Kirkpatrick. Chicago: St. James, 1989, pp. 718–719.

Nichols, (Joanna) Ruth

Esmonde, Margaret P. "Beyond the Circles of the World: Death and the Hereafter in Children's Literature." In *Webs and Wardrobes: Humanist and Religious World Views in Children's Literature,* ed. by Joseph O'Beirne Milner and Lucy Floyd Morcock Milner. Lanham, MD: University Press of America, 1987, pp. 33–45.
Evans, Gwyneth. "'Nothing Odd *Ever* Happens Here.' Landscape in Canadian Fantasy." *Canadian Children's Literature* 15–16 (1980): 15–30.
Fourth Book of Junior Authors and Illustrators. Edited by Doris De Montreville and Elizabeth D. Crawford. New York: Wilson, 1978, pp. 274–275.
McDonough, Irma, ed. "Ruth Nichols." In *Profiles,* rev. ed. Ottawa: Canadian Library Association, 1975.
Nichols, Ruth. "Fantasy: The Interior Universe." In *Proceedings of the Fifth Annual Conference of the Children's Literature Association.* Ypsilanti, MI: The Children's Literature Assn., 1980, pp. 41–47.
———. "Fantasy and Escapism." *Canadian Children's Literature* 4 (1976): 20–27.
———. "Something of Myself." In *One Ocean Touching: Papers from the First Pacific Rim Conference on Children's Literature.* Metuchen, NJ: Scarecrow Press, 1979, pp. 189–194.
"Ruth Nichols: An Interview." *Children's Literature Association Quarterly* 2 (Summer 1977): 2–4.
Store, R. E. "Ruth Nichols: An Outstanding Canadian Author." *Orana* (Australia) 14 (Nov 1978): 134–137.
Stott, Jon C. *Children's Literature from A to Z.* New York: McGraw-Hill, 1984, p. 205.
———. "An Interview with Ruth Nichols." *Canadian Children's Literature* 12 (1978): 5–19.
———. "The Nature of Fantasy: A Conversation with Ruth Nichols, Susan Cooper, and Maurice Sendak." *World of Children's Books* 3, no. 2 (Fall 1978): 32–43.
Thompson, Hilary. "Doorways to Fantasy." *Canadian Children's Literature* 21 (1981): 8–16.
Twentieth-Century Children's Writers. 3rd ed. Edited by Tracy Chevalier and D. L. Kirkpatrick. Chicago: St. James, 1989, pp. 719–720.

Nimmo, Jenny

Crouch, Marcus. "Welsh Magic and Jenny Nimmo." *New Welsh Review* 2, no. 4 (1990): 22–24.

Twentieth-Century Children's Writers. 3rd ed. Edited by Tracy Chevalier and D. L. Kirkpatrick. Chicago: St. James, 1989, p. 722.

White, D. "Welsh Legends Through English Eyes: An American Viewpoint." *School Librarian* (U.K.) 39 (Nov 1991): 130–131+.

Nixon, Joan Lowery

Helbig, Alethea K., and Agnes Regan Perkins. *Dictionary of American Children's Fiction, 1960–1984.* Westport, CT: Greenwood, 1986, p. 475.

Hildebrand, S. "Joan Lowery Nixon." *Texas Libraries* 50 (Spring 1989): 10–11.

Twentieth-Century Children's Writers. 3rd ed. Edited by Tracy Chevalier and D. L. Kirkpatrick. Chicago: St. James, 1989, pp. 723–724.

North, Joan

Searles, Baird, Beth Meacham, and Michael Franklin. *A Reader's Guide to Fantasy.* New York: Avon, 1982, pp. 120–121.

Swinfen, Ann. *In Defense of Fantasy.* London: Routledge, 1984, pp. 105–106. Discusses *The Light Maze.*

Norton, André (pseud. of Alice Mary Norton)

Allen, L. David. "André Norton." In *Supernatural Fiction Writers: Fantasy and Horror,* vol. 2. Edited by E. F. Bleiler. New York: Scribner, 1985, pp. 1091–1096.

Allen, Paul. "Of Swords and Sorcery 4." *Fantasy Crossroads* 12 (1977): 21–27.

Boss, Judith E. "Elements of Style in Science Fiction: André Norton Compared with Others." *Extrapolation* 26 (1985): 201–211.

Carter, Lin. "André Norton, a Profile by Lin Carter." Introduction to *The Sioux Spaceman* by André Norton. Boston: Gregg, 1978.

Crouch, Marcus. *The Nesbit Tradition.* London: Benn, 1972, pp. 54–55.

Dohner, Jan "Literature of Change: Science Fiction and Women." *Top of the News* 34 (1978): 261–265.

Elwood, Roger, ed. *The Many Worlds of André Norton.* Dallas: Chilton, 1974.

Fisher, Marjorie T. "Writers for Children: André Norton." *School Librarian* 15 (July 1967): 141–145.

Fraser, Brian M. "Putting the Past into the Future: Interview with André Norton." *Fantastic Science Fiction* (Oct 1980): 4–9.

Hensley, Charlotta Cook. "André Norton's Science Fiction and Fantasy, 1950–1979: An Introduction to the Topics of Philosophy, Reflection, Imaginary Voyages, and Future Prediction in Selected Books for Young Readers." Ph.D. diss., University of Colorado at Boulder, 1980.

Lacy, N. J. *The Arthurian Encyclopedia.* New York: Garland, 1986, p. 408.

McGhan, Barry. "André Norton: Why Has She Been Neglected?" *Riverside Quarterly* 4 (1970): 128–131.

Miesel, Sandra. "Introduction." In *Witch World* by André Norton. Boston: Gregg, 1977.

Molson, Francis J. "André Norton." In *American Writers for Children since 1960: Fiction. Dictionary of Literary Biography,* vol. 52. Detroit: Gale, 1986, pp. 267–277.

More Junior Authors. Edited by Muriel Fuller. New York: Wilson, 1963, pp. 159–160.

Norton, André. *The Book of André Norton.* New York: DAW, 1975. "On Writing Fantasy," pp. 71–79. Reprinted in Boyer and Zahorski. *Fantasists on Fantasy.* New York: Avon, 1984, pp. 151–162.

The Oxford Companion to Children's Literature. Edited by Humphrey Carpenter and Mari Prichard. New York: Oxford Univ. Press, 1984, p. 381.

Peters, B. D. "Bio-Bibliographical Study of André Norton, 1960–1971." Research paper. Kent State University, 1971.

Platt, Charles. *Dream Makers II: The Uncommon Men and Women Who Write Science Fiction.* New York: Berkley, 1983, pp. 95–102. Interview.

Ruse, Gary Alan. "Algol Profile: André Norton." *Algol* 14 (Summer–Fall 1977): 15–17.

Schlobin, Roger C. *André Norton: A Primary and Secondary Bibliography.* Boston: G. K. Hall, 1980.

———. "André Norton: Humanity Amid the Hardware." In *The Feminine Eye.* Edited by Tom Staicar. New York: Ungar, 1982, pp. 25–31.

———. "The *Witch World* Series." In *Survey of Modern Fantasy Literature,* vol. 5. Edited by Frank N. Magill. Englewood Cliffs, NJ: Salem Press, 1983, pp. 2139–2149.

Searles, Baird, Beth Meacham, and Michael Franklin. *A Reader's Guide to Fantasy.* New York: Avon, 1982, pp. 121–122.

Smith, Karen Patricia. "Claiming a Place in the Universe: The Portrayal of Minorities in Seven Works by André Norton." *Top of the News* 42 (Winter 1986): 165–172.

Spivack, Charlotte. *Merlin's Daughters: Contemporary Women Writers of Fantasy.* New York: Greenwood, 1987.

Townsend, John Rowe. *A Sense of Story.* London: Longman, 1971; Philadelphia: Lippincott, 1971, pp. 143–153.

Turner, David G. *The First Editions of André Norton.* Menlo Park, CA: Turner, 1974.

Twentieth-Century Children's Writers. 3rd ed. Edited by Tracy Chevalier and D. L. Kirkpatrick. Chicago: St. James, 1989, pp. 727–729.

Twentieth-Century Science Fiction Writers. 3rd ed. Edited by Noelle Watson and Paul E. Schellinger. Chicago: St. James Press, 1991, pp. 596–599.

Walker, Paul. "André Norton: An Interview." *Luna Monthly* 40 (1972): 1–4. Reprinted in Walker. *Speaking of Science Fiction.* Oradell, NJ: Luna Publications, 1978, pp. 263–270.

Wilson, Andrew J. "If It's Wednesday This Must Be Narnia: Exploring the Links between Phantasy and Reality." *Dark Horizons* 24 (1981): 19–23.

Wolf, Virginia L. "André Norton: Feminist Pied Piper in Science Fiction." *Children's Literature Association Quarterly* 10 (Summer 1985): 66–70.

Yoke, Carl. *Roger Zelazny and André Norton: Proponents of Individualism.* Columbus: State Library of Ohio, 1979.

Norton, Mary (Pearson)

"The Borrowers." In M. Crouch and A. Ellis. *Chosen for Children,* 3rd ed. London: The Library Association, 1977, pp. 66–69.

Cooper, Ilene. "Popular Reading—After *The Borrowers.*" *Booklist* 81 (Nov 15, 1984): 452–453. (bibliography)

Crouch, Marcus. "The End . . . or the Beginning: Mary Norton, 1903–1992." *Junior Bookshelf* (U.K.) 57 (1993): 5–7.

Davenport, Julia. "The Narrative Framework of *The Borrowers:* Mary Norton and Emily Brontë." *Children's Literature in Education* 14 (Summer 1983): 75–79.

Doyle, Brian. *The Who's Who of Children's Literature.* New York: Schocken, 1968, pp. 210–212.

Elkin, Judith. "*The Borrowers* Anew." *Books for Keeps* (U.K.) 17 (Nov 1982): 21–22.

Field, C. "Mary Norton." *School Librarian* 11 (July 1963): 464–469.

Gillespie, John T., and Diana Lembo. *Introducing Books: A Guide for the Middle Grades.* New York: Bowker, 1970, pp. 278–280.

Hand, Nigel. "Mary Norton and *The Borrowers.*" *Children's Literature in Education* 7 (Mar 1972): 38–55.

———. "Mary Norton, Fred Inglis, and the World We Have Lost." In Dennis Butts. *Good Writers for Young Readers.* St. Albans, England: Hart-Davis, 1977, pp. 86–93.

Harbage, Mary. "*The Borrowers* at Home and Afield." *Elementary English* 33 (Feb 1956): 67–75.

Heins, Ethel. "*The Borrowers Avenged.*" *Horn Book* 59 (Apr 1983): 155–156. Review.

Inglis, Fred. *Ideology and Imagination.* New York: Cambridge Univ. Press, 1975.

Jones, Ursula. "Mary Norton." *Puffin Post* (U.K.) 14, no. 3 (1980): 22–23.

Josipovici, G. *The World and the Book.* Boulder, CO: Paladin Press, 1973.

Knowsley, J. "*The Borrowers* Alive." *Times Educational Supplement* (Sept 25, 1992): 10.

Kuznets, Lois R. "Mary Norton's *The Borrowers:* Diaspora in Miniature." In *Touchstones.* Edited by Perry Nodelman. West Lafayette, IN: Children's Literature Association Publications, 1985, pp. 198–203.

———. "Permutations of Frame in Mary Norton's *Borrowers* Series." *Studies in Literary Imagination* 18 (Fall 1985): 65–78.

Laslett, P. *The World We Have Lost.* London: Methuen, 1971.

Marsh, Gwen. "Mary Norton: A Writer of Fantasy." *The Guardian* (Sept 10, 1992): 37.

Middleton, Christopher. "Small World." *Radio Times* (U.K.) (Nov 7–13, 1992): 40–41.

Norton, Mary. "Thoughts on *The Borrowers.*" *School Bookshop News* (U.K.) 9 (Spring 1978): 5–6.

Olson, Barbara V. "Mary Norton and *The Borrowers.*" *Elementary English* 47 (Feb 1970): 185–189.

The Oxford Companion to Children's Literature. Edited by Humphrey Carpenter and Mari Prichard. New York: Oxford Univ. Press, 1984, pp. 54, 76, 381.

Pflieger, Pat, and Helen M. Hill. *A Reference Guide to Modern Fantasy for Children.* Westport, CT: Greenwood, 1984, pp. xii–xvi, 23–24, 69–70, 74–79, 337–338, 401–403.

Philip, Neil. "Careful with Magic." *Times Educational Supplement* 3464 (Nov 19, 1982): 33.

Rees, David. "Freedom and Imprisonment: The Novels of Mary Norton." *School Librarian* 36 (Aug 1988): 83–86. Reprinted in *"What Do Draculas Do?" Essays on Contemporary Writers of Fiction for Children and Young Adults.* Metuchen, NJ: Scarecrow Press, 1990, pp. 1–14.

Rustin, Margaret. "Deep Structures of Fantasy in Modern British Children's Books." *The Lion and the Unicorn* 10 (1986): 60–82.

Rustin, Michael. "Who Believes in '*Borrowers*'?" In Margaret Rustin and Michael Rustin. *Narratives of Love and Loss: Studies in Modern Children's Fiction.* London: Verso, 1987; New York: Routledge, 1988, pp. 163–180.

Smaridge, Norah. *Famous Modern Storytellers for Young People.* New York: Dodd, 1969, pp. 79–85.

Stableford Vivien. "*The Borrowers* Series." In *Survey of Modern Fantasy Literature,* vol. 1. Edited by Frank N. Magill. Englewood Cliffs, NJ: Salem Press, 1983, pp. 164–165.

Stott, Jon C. "Anatomy of a Masterpiece: *The Borrowers.*" *Language Arts* 53, no. 5 (May 1976): 538–544.

———. *Children's Literature from A to Z.* New York: McGraw-Hill, 1984, p. 206.

———. *Mary Norton.* Boston: Twayne, 1994.

Swinfen, Ann. *In Defense of Fantasy.* New York: Routledge, 1984, pp. 127, 130–131, 191.

Third Book of Junior Authors. Edited by Doris De Montreville and Donna Hill. New York: Wilson, 1972, pp. 211–212.

Thomas, Margaret. "The Discourse of the Difficult Daughter: A Feminist Reading of Mary Norton's *Borrowers.*" *Children's Literature in Education* 23 (Mar 1992): 39–48.

Toomey, Philippa. "Reluctant Writer: Mary Norton." *Children's Book Review* 5 (Autumn/Winter 1975): 85–86.

———. "Writing a Timeless 200 Words Forever and a Day." [London] *Times* (Aug 1, 1975): 12. (interview)

Townsend, John Rowe. "Mary Norton." In *A Sense of Story*. Philadelphia: Lippincott, 1971, pp. 143–153.

Twentieth-Century Children's Writers. 3rd ed. Edited by Tracy Chevalier and D. L. Kirkpatrick. Chicago: St. James, 1989, pp. 729–730.

Ulman, Ruth. "WLB Biography: Mary Norton." *Wilson Library Bulletin* 36 (May 1962): 767. Reprinted in Miriam Hoffman and Eva Samuels. *Authors and Illustrators of Children's Books*. New York: Bowker, 1972, pp. 340–342.

Nöstlinger, Christine

Alcorn, Noeline. "Fantasy and Family Life: Children's Books from Northern Europe." *Children's Literature Association Yearbook*. Auckland, New Zealand: Children's Literature Association, 1976, pp. 29–42. Discusses Astrid Lindgren, Maria Gripe, Christine Nöstlinger, Otfried Preussler, and Paul Biegel.

Allmann, Renate. "Die Fran: Kinderliteraturproduzentin Christine Nöstlinger." *Bulletin Jugend + Literatur* (Germany) 12 (1983): 13–20.

Barker, K. "Standing Your Own Company: The Novels of Christine Nöstlinger." *School Librarian* 40 (Feb 1992): 6–7.

Bell, Anthea. "Christine Nöstlinger." *Junior Bookshelf* 48 (Apr 1984): 49–51.

Faerber, Gerda. "An Austrian Elf." *Children's Books in Ireland* 7 (1992): 13.

Fetz, Nancy Tillman. "Christine Nöstlinger's Emancipatory Fantasies." *The Lion and the Unicorn* 10 (1986): 40–53.

Fifth Book of Junior Authors and Illustrators. Edited by Sally Holmes Holtze. New York: Wilson, 1983, p. 231.

Frenkel, Pavel. "A Vzglyad Vsegda Ser' Ezen [But the Author's View Is Always Serious]." *Detskaya Literatura* (Moscow) 8 (Aug 1984): 40–45.

Huse, Nancy. "The Blank Mirror of Death: Protest as Self-Creation in Contemporary Fantasy." *The Lion and the Unicorn* 12 (1988): 28–43.

Libelt, B. "Zur Problematik des Dickseins bei Christine Nöstlinger [The Problems of the Fat in the Work of Christine Nöstlinger]." *Informationen Arbeitskreises für Jugendliteratur* (Germany) 1 (1983): 27–33, 47.

Martinell, Ingegerd. "Vixnas Dusbelmoral Mot Barns Lojlitet [Grown-ups' Double Standards and Children's Loyalty]." *Opsis Kalopsis* (Sweden) 1, no. 1 (1986): 18–19.

Nöstlinger, Christine. "Acceptance Speech for the 1984 Andersen Writers Medal." *Bookbird* 3 (1984): 8–11.

———. "Doing It But Not Knowing It." [Politics and Children's Authors] *Bookbird* 31 (May 1993): 5.

Schmidt, K. "Vom *Maikafer* bis zum *Stundenplan*: Christine Nöstlinger und Ihre Bucher. [From *Maikafer* to *Stundenplan*: Christine Nöstlinger and Her Books.]" *Das Gute Jungendbuch* (Austria) 28, no. 3 (1978): 119–126.

Thomson, Pat. "Christine Nöstlinger." *Books for Keeps* (U.K.) 28 (Sept 1984): 26.

Nye, Robert

Twentieth-Century Children's Writers. 3rd ed. Edited by Tracy Chevalier and D. L. Kirkpatrick. Chicago: St. James, 1989, pp. 731–732.

Oakley, Graham

Fifth Book of Junior Authors and Illustrators. Edited by Sally Holmes Holtze. New York: Wilson, 1983, pp. 232–233.

Twentieth-Century Children's Writers. 3rd ed. Edited by Tracy Chevalier and D. L. Kirkpatrick. Chicago: St. James, 1989, pp. 732–733.

O'Brien, Robert C. (pseud. of Robert Leslie Conly)

Boulanger, Susan. "A Second Look: *The Silver Crown.*" *Horn Book* 61 (Jan–Feb 1984): 95–98.

Crofton, Alison, and Patricia McCall. "*Mrs. Frisby,* Those Rats, N.I.M.H. and the Children of Coniston School." *Bookmark* [Edinburgh] 2 (Sept 1978): 30–41.

Fourth Book of Junior Authors and Illustrators. Edited by Doris De Montreville and Elizabeth D. Crawford. New York: Wilson, 1978, pp. 275–278.

Getting Hooked on Science Fiction. White Plains, NY: Guidance Associates, 1976. Includes *Mrs. Frisby and the Rats of NIMH.* (filmstrip and audiocassette)

Helbig, Alethea K. "Robert C. O'Brien's *Mrs. Frisby and the Rats of NIMH:* Through the Eyes of Small Animals." In *Touchstones.* Edited by Perry Nodelman. West Lafayette, IN: Children's Literature Association Publications, 1985, pp. 204–211.

Helbig, Alethea K., and Agnes Regan Perkins. *Dictionary of American Children's Fiction, 1960–1984.* Westport, CT: Greenwood, 1986, pp. 441–442, 481.

Henke, James T. "Growing Up as Epic Adventure: The Biblical Collage in *Z for Zachariah.*" *Children's Literature in Education* 13 (Summer 1982): 87–94.

Morse, Brian. "The Novels of Robert C. O'Brien." *Signal* 40 (Jan 1983): 30–36.

"*Mrs. Frisby and the Rats of NIMH.*" In Lee Kingman. *Newbery and Caldecott Medal Books: 1966–1975.* Boston: Horn Book, 1975, pp. 79–92.

O'Brien, Robert C. "Newbery Award Acceptance." *Horn Book* 48 (Aug 1972): 343–348.

O'Brien, Sally M. "Robert C. O'Brien." *Horn Book* 48 (Aug 1972): 349–351.

The Oxford Companion to Children's Literature. Edited by Humphrey Carpenter and Mari Prichard. New York: Oxford Univ. Press, 1984, p. 385.

Pflieger, Pat, and Helen M. Hill. *A Reference Guide to Modern Fantasy for Children.* Westport, CT: Greenwood, 1984, pp. xi, xv, 387–388, 405–406.

Roginski, Jim, ed. *Newbery and Caldecott Medalists and Honor Book Winners.* Littleton, CO: Libraries Unlimited, 1982, p. 204.

Stott, Jon C. *Children's Literature from A to Z.* New York: McGraw-Hill, 1984, p. 210.

Swinfen, Ann. *In Defense of Fantasy.* New York: Routledge, 1984, pp. 36–37.

Twentieth-Century Children's Writers. 3rd ed. Edited by Tracy Chevalier and D. L. Kirkpatrick. Chicago: St. James, 1989, pp. 733–734.

Wilson, Doreen. "Experiments with *NIMH.*" *About Books for Children* (U.K.) 2 (Apr 1981): 17–18.

O'Faolin, Eileen (Gould)

Twentieth-Century Children's Writers. 3rd ed. Edited by Tracy Chevalier and D. L. Kirkpatrick. Chicago: St. James, 1989, pp. 736–737.

Ormondroyd, Edward

Helbig, Alethea K., and Agnes Regan Perkins. *Dictionary of American Children's Fiction, 1960–1984.* Westport, CT: Greenwood, 1986, pp. 492, 662–663.

Twentieth-Century Children's Writers. 3rd ed. Edited by Tracy Chevalier and D. L. Kirkpatrick. Chicago: St. James, 1989, pp. 744–745.

Orwell, George (pseud. of Eric Hugh Blair)

Asker, David Harry Desmond. "The Modern Bestiary: Animal Fiction from Hardy to Orwell." Diss., University of British Columbia, 1978.

Boos, Florence, and William Boos. "Orwell's Morris and 'Old Major's' Dream." *English Studies* 71 (Aug 1990): 361–371.

Buckley, David Patrick. "The Novels of George Orwell." Ph.D. diss., Columbia University, 1962.

Burger, Douglas A. "*Animal Farm.*" In *Survey of Modern Fantasy Literature,* Vol. 1. Edited by Frank N. Magill. Englewood Cliffs, NJ: Salem Press, 1983, pp. 45–47.

Byrne, Katherine. "A Different-Looking Orwell." *Commonweal* 11 (Mar 1983): 149–151.

Concannon, Gerald J. "The Development of George Orwell's Art." Ph.D. diss., University of Denver, 1973.

Connelly, Mark. "The Diminished Self: The Loss of Individual Autonomy in Orwell's Novels." Ph.D. diss., University of Wisconsin-Milwaukee, 1984.

Coppard, Audrey, and Bernard Crick, eds. *Orwell Remembered.* New York: Facts on File, 1984.

Crick, Bernard. *George Orwell: A Life.* New York: Little, Brown, 1981; Penguin, 1982. Originally published by Secker and Warburg, 1980.

Davison, Peter. "George Orwell: Dates and Origins." *The Library* 13 (June 1991): 137–150.

Duffey, Paula. "Form and Meaning in the Novels of George Orwell." Ph.D. diss., University of Pennsylvania, 1967.

Edrich, Emmanuel. "Literature, Technology, and Social Temper in the Fiction of George Orwell." Ph.D. diss., University of Wisconsin, 1960.

Elkins, Charles L. "George Orwell." In *Science Fiction Writers.* Edited by E. F. Bleiler. New York: Scribner, 1985, pp. 233–242.

Fiderer, Gerald Lionel. "A Psychoanalytic Study of the Novels of George Orwell." Ph.D. diss., University of Oklahoma, 1967.

Fink, H. K. "George Orwell's Novels in Relation to His Social and Literary Theory." Ph.D. diss., London University (U.K.), 1968.

Fyvel, T. R. *George Orwell: A Personal Memoir.* New York: Macmillan, 1982.

Gardner, Averil. *George Orwell.* Boston: Hall, 1987.

George Orwell. Maltoon, IL: Spectrum Educational Media, 1984. (audiocassette)

George Orwell. Peoria, IL: Thomas S. Klise, 1985. (filmstrip and audiocassette)

Hunter, Jefferson Estock. "George Orwell and the Uses of Literature." Ph.D. diss., Yale University, 1973.

Kearse, Lee Andrew, Jr. "George Orwell: Romantic Utopian." Ph.D. diss., Brown University, 1973.

Knapp, John V. "Dance to a Creepy Minuet: Orwell's *Burmese Days,* Precursor of *Animal Farm.*" *Modern Fiction Studies* 21 (1979): 11–29.

Mellichamp, Leslie R., Jr. "A Study of George Orwell: The Man, His Import and His Outlook." Ph.D. diss., Emory University, 1968.

Meyers, Jeffrey. "George Orwell: A Bibliography." *Bulletin of Bibliography* 31 (1974): 117–121.

―――. "George Orwell: A Selected Checklist." *Modern Fiction Studies* 21 (1975); 133–136.

―――. *A Reader's Guide to George Orwell.* London: Thames, 1975.

―――, ed. *George Orwell: The Critical Heritage.* Boston: Routledge, 1975.

Meyers, Jeffrey, and Valerie Meyers. *George Orwell: An Annotated Bibliography of Criticism.* New York: Garland, 1977.

Mezciems, Jenny. "Swift and Orwell: Utopia as Nightmare." In *Between Dream and Nature: Essays on Utopia and Dystopia,* ed. by Dominic Baker-Smith and C. C. Barfoot. Amsterdam: Rodopi, 1987, pp. 91–112.

Rai, Alok. *Orwell and the Politics of Despair: A Critical Study of the Writings of George Orwell.* Cambridge: Cambridge Univ. Press, 1988.

Reilly, Patrick. *George Orwell: The Age's Adversary.* New York: St. Martin's Press, 1986.

Shelden, Michael. *Orwell: A Biography.* New York: Harper, 1991.

Small, Christopher. *The Road to Miniluv: George Orwell, the State, and God.* Pittsburgh: Univ. of Pittsburgh Press, 1976.

Smith, David, and Michael Mosher. *Orwell for Beginners.* London: Writers and Readers Publishing Cooperative, 1984.

Smyer, Richard I. *"Animal Farm": Pastoralism and Politics.* Boston: Hall, 1988.

———. "Structure and Meaning in the Works of George Orwell." Ph.D. diss., Stanford University, 1968.

Snyder, Phillip John. "Doing the Necessary Task: The Bourgeois Humanism of George Orwell." Ph.D. diss., Case Western Reserve University, 1964.

Stevenson, Lionel. "Purveyors of Myth and Magic." In *Yesterday and After: The History of the English Novel.* Totowa, NJ: Barnes and Noble, 1967, pp. 111–154.

Thompson, John. *Orwell's London.* New York: Schocken, 1985.

Trambling, Victor R. S. "Following in the Footsteps of Jack London: George Orwell, Writer and Critic." *Jack London Newsletter* 11 (1978): 63–70.

Twentieth-Century Science Fiction Writers. 3rd ed. Edited by Noelle Watson and Paul E. Schellinger. Chicago: St. James Press, 1991, pp. 609–611.

The Unexpected: Stories of Humor and Fantasy. Pleasantville, NY: Educational Audio-Visual, 1979. (filmstrip and audiocassette)

Van Dellen, Robert J. "Politics in Orwell's Fiction." Ph.D. diss., Indiana University, 1973.

Voohees, Richard Joseph. "The Paradox of George Orwell." Ph.D. diss., Indiana University, 1958.

Wain, John. "Dear George Orwell: A Personal Letter." *American Scholar* 52 (Winter 1982–1983): 21–37.

Wemyss, Courtney T., and Alexej Ugrinsky. *George Orwell.* New York: Greenwood, 1987.

Williams, Raymond. *George Orwell.* New York: Columbia Univ. Press, 1981. Originally published by Viking, 1971.

———, ed. *George Orwell: A Collection of Critical Essays.* Englewood Cliffs, NJ: Prentice-Hall, 1974.

Woodcock, George. *The Crystal Spirit: A Study of George Orwell.* New York: Schocken, 1984. Originally published by Little, Brown, 1966.

Zehr, David Morgan. "George Orwell: The Novelist's Dilemma." Ph.D. diss., Indiana University, 1977.

O'Shea, Pat

Cart, Michael. "A Light in the Darkness: Humor Returns to Children's Fantasy." *School Library Journal* 33 (Apr 1987): 48–49.

O'Shea, Pat. "Growing a Story." *Books for Keeps* (U.K.) 46 (1987): 10.

Ouida (pseud. of Marie Louise de la Ramée)

Chang, Charity. "*The Nürnberg Stove* as an Artistic Fairy Tale." In *Children's Literature,* vol. 5. Philadelphia: Temple Univ. Press, 1976, pp. 148–156.

The Oxford Companion to Children's Literature. Edited by Humphrey Carpenter and Mari Prichard. New York: Oxford Univ. Press, 1984, p. 390.

Paget, (Reverend) F(rances) E(dward) (used the pseud. William Churne of Staffordshire)

The Oxford Companion to Children's Literature. Edited by Humphrey Carpenter and Mari Prichard. New York: Oxford Univ. Press, 1984, p. 393.

Susina, Jan Christopher. "Victorian Kunstmärcher: A Study in Children's Literature, 1840–1875." Ph.D. diss., Indiana University, 1986.

Paine, Albert Bigelow

Kunitz, S. J., ed. *Twentieth Century Authors.* New York: Wilson, 1942, p. 1067.

Pardoe, M(argot Mary)

Twentieth-Century Children's Writers. 3rd ed. Edited by Tracy Chevalier and D. L. Kirkpatrick. Chicago: St. James, 1989, pp. 750–751.

Park, (Rosina) Ruth (Lucia)

Gascoigne, Toss. "Know the Author: Ruth Park." *Magpies* (Australia) 3 (Mar 1988): 14–15.

Gillespie, John T., and Corinne J. Naden. *Juniorplots 3: A Book Talk Guide for Use with Readers Ages 12–16.* New York: Bowker, 1987, pp. 186–189.

O'Sullivan, Anne M. "Structures and Narrative Point of View in *Playing Beatie Bow.*" *The Literature Base* (Australia) 2 (Feb 1991): 14–16.

Park, Ruth. "A Very Ordinary Girl." *Reading Time* (Australia) 80 (July 1981): 8.

———."A Vision of Continuity." *Agora* 16 (Apr 1982): J57.

Rutherford, Leonie. "'Lineaments of Gratified [Parental] Desire': Romance and Domestication in Some Recent Australian Children's Fiction." *Papers: Explorations into Children's Literature* (Australia) 4 (Apr 1993): 3–17.

Sixth Book of Junior Authors and Illustrators. Edited by Sally Holmes Holtze. New York: Wilson, 1989, pp. 215–216.

Twentieth-Century Children's Writers. 3rd ed. Edited by Tracy Chevalier and D. L. Kirkpatrick. Chicago: St. James, 1989, pp. 752–754.

Parker, (James) Edgar, (Jr.)

Third Book of Junior Authors. Edited by Doris De Montreville and Donna Hill. New York: Wilson, 1972, p. 219.

Parker, Richard

Twentieth-Century Children's Writers. 3rd ed. Edited by Tracy Chevalier and D. L. Kirkpatrick. Chicago: St. James, 1989, pp. 754–756.

Parrish (Tizell), Anne

"Anne Parrish Tizell: With a Catalog of Her Drawings and Paintings She Collected." *Wadsworth Atheneum Bulletin* (Winter, 1958).

Davis, Lavinia R. "Anne Parrish as a Writer of Children's Books." *Horn Book* 36 (Feb 1960): 63–67.
Helbig, Alethea K., and Agnes Regan Perkins. *Dictionary of American Children's Fiction, 1859–1959.* Westport, CT: Greenwood, 1985, pp. 138–139, 165, 395, 493–494.
Miller, Bertha E. Mahony. "Anne Parrish's Memorable Nonsense Story." *Horn Book* 27 (Jan–Feb 1951): 20–22.
———. "The Honey Heart of Earth in the Books of Anne and Dillwyn Parrish." *Horn Book* 7 (Feb 1931): 61–67. Reprinted in Norma Fryatt. *A Horn Book Sampler.* Boston: Horn Book, 1959, pp. 4–7.
Parrish, Anne. "Do You Remember?" *Horn Book* 23 (Jan–Feb 1949): 26–32.
———. "For Dillwyn Parrish." *Horn Book* 36 (Feb 1960): 68.
———. "Writing for Children." *Horn Book* 27 (Mar–Apr 1951): 85–89.
Roginski, Jim, ed. *Newbery and Caldecott Medalists and Honor Book Winners.* Littleton, CO: Libraries Unlimited, 1982, pp. 209–210.
Twentieth-Century Children's Writers. 3rd ed. Edited by Tracy Chevalier and D. L. Kirkpatrick. Chicago: St. James, 1989, p. 756.

Parrish, (George) Dillwyn

Helbig, Alethea K., and Agnes Regan Perkins. *Dictionary of American Children's Fiction, 1859–1959.* Westport, CT: Greenwood, 1985, p. 395.
Miller, Bertha E. Mahony. "'The Honey Heart of Earth' in the Books of Anne and Dillwyn Parrish." *Horn Book* 7 (Mar 1931): 61–67.
Parrish, Anne. "For Dillwyn Parrish." *Horn Book* 36 (Feb 1960): 68.

Pascal, Francine

Fifth Book of Junior Authors and Illustrators. Edited by Sally Holmes Holtze. New York: Wilson, 1983, pp. 235–236.
Gillespie, John T., and Corinne J. Naden. *Juniorplots 3: A Book Talk Guide for Use with Readers Ages 12–16.* New York: Bowker, 1987, pp. 190–193.

Paterson, Katherine (Womeldorf)

American Writers for Children Since 1960: Fiction (Dictionary of Literary Biography, Vol. 52). Ed. by Glenn E. Estes. Detroit: Gale, 1986, pp. 296–314.
"Authorgraph no. 43: Katherine Paterson." *Books for Keeps* (U.K.) 43 (1987): 14–15.
Brady, Veronica. "The Moral Stance in the Books of Paterson and Wheatley." *Magpies* (Australia) 4 (Sept 1989): 5–9.
Christian, Cheryl. "Between the Covers: People Behind the Books." *CLA Bulletin* 15 (Fall 1989): 9–11.
Crisler, Jesse S. "The Miracles of Reading Katherine Paterson." In *A Bridge to Magic Realms.* Fourth Biennial Conference on Literature and Hawaii's Children. Honolulu/Kamuela, 1988, pp. 2, 11.
Field, Carolyn W. "Katherine Paterson: 1988 Regina Medal Recipient." *Catholic Library World* 59 (Mar–Apr 1988): 229.
Fifth Book of Junior Authors and Illustrators. Edited by Sally Holmes Holtze. New York, Wilson, 1983, pp. 236–238.
Gascoigne, Toss. "Know the Author: Katherine Paterson." *Magpies* (Australia) 3 (Nov 1988): 18–20
Goodman, Jo. "An Interview with Katherine Paterson." *Reading Time* (Australia) 32, no. 4 (1988): 15–16.

Harris, Laura. "Katherine Paterson: Interview, March 1993." *Reading Time* 37 (May 1993): 11–12.

Helbig, Alethea, and Agnes Regan Perkins. *Dictionary of American Children's Fiction, 1985–1989.* Westport, CT: Greenwood, 1993, p. 187.

———. *Dictionary of American Children's Fiction, 1960–1984.* Westport, CT: Greenwood, 1986, pp. 501–502.

Jameson, Gloria. "Developing Self-Identity Through Religious Consciousness in Stories of George MacDonald, C. S. Lewis, Madeleine L'Engle, Katherine Paterson, Ursula K. Le Guin, and Laura Adams Armer." In *Literature and Hawaii's Children. Proceedings of the Third Biennial Conference on Literature and Hawaii's Children.* Honolulu: Literature and Hawaii's Children, 1988, pp. 143–147.

Jones, Linda T. "Profile: Katherine Paterson." *Language Arts* 52 (Feb 1981): 189–196.

Kimmel, Eric A. "Trials and Revelations: Katherine Paterson's Heroic Journeys." *The New Advocate* 3 (Fall 1990): 235–245.

Namowicz, Gene Inyart. "Katherine Paterson." *Horn Book* 57 (Aug 1981): 394–399.

Paterson, Katherine. "Books Remembered." *CBC Features* 40, no. 1 (1985): 9.

———. "Hope and Happy Endings." *Catholic Library World* 60 (July–Aug 1988): 14–19. Reprinted in Cristina Bacchilega and Steven Curry, eds. *Literature and Hawaii's Children.* Honolulu: Literature and Hawaii's Children, 1990, pp. 146–155.

———. "Hope Is More Than Happiness." *New York Times Book Review* (Dec 25, 1988): 19.

———. "Living in a Peaceful World." *Horn Book* 67 (Jan–Feb 1991): 32–38.

———. "My Life Based on a True Story." *Magpies* (Australia) 4 (May 1989): 5–10.

———. "National Book Award Acceptance." *Horn Book* 55 (Aug 1979): 402–403.

———. "Sounds in the Heart." *Horn Book* 57 (Dec 1981): 694–702. Reprinted in *Innocence & Experience: Essays & Conversations on Children's Literature,* ed. by Barbara Harrison and Gregory Maguire. New York: Lothrop, 1987, pp. 22–29.

———. *The Spying Heart: More Thoughts on Reading and Writing for Children.* New York: Lodestar, 1988; Dutton, 1989.

———. "Tale of a Reluctant Dragon." *The New Advocate* 2 (Winter 1989): 1–8.

———. "To Give the Enemy a Human Face." *USBBY Newsletter* 16 (Fall 1991): 1.

———. "What Writing Has Taught Me—Three Lessons." *The Writer* (Aug 1990): 9–10.

Peltola, Bette. "Katherine Paterson." *USBBY Newsletter* 15, no. 1 (1990): 3–4.

Schmidt, Gary D. *Katherine Paterson.* Boston: Twayne, 1993.

Smedman, Sarah. "When Literary Works Meet: Allusion in the Novels of Katherine Paterson." In *Where Rivers Meet: Confluence and Concurrents: Proceedings of the 1989 Conference of the Children's Literature Association,* ed. by Susan R. Gannon and Ruth A. Thompson. New York: Pace University, 1991, pp. 59–66.

Twentieth-Century Children's Writers. 3rd ed. Edited by Tracy Chevalier and D. L. Kirkpatrick. Chicago: St. James, 1989, pp. 758–760.

The Zena Sutherland Lectures, 1983–1992. Edited by Betsy Hearne. New York: Clarion, 1993, pp. 44–70.

Paton Walsh, Jill (Gillian Bliss)

Crago, Hugh. "The Readers in the Reader: An Experiment in Personal Response and Literary Criticism." *Signal* 39 (Sept 1982): 172–182. Discusses *A Chance Child.*

Fourth Book of Junior Authors and Illustrators. Edited by Doris De Montreville and Elizabeth D. Crawford. New York: Wilson, 1978, pp. 284–285.

Funnell, John. "'A Dream Upon the Waters': The Novels of Jill Paton Walsh." *Orana* (Australia) 13 (Nov 1977): 110–114.

"Meet a Puffin Person: Jill Paton Walsh." *Puffin Post* (U.K.) 11 (1986): 9–11.

The Oxford Companion to Children's Literature. Edited by Humphrey Carpenter and Mari Prichard. New York: Oxford Univ. Press, 1984, pp. 560–561. (Listed under Walsh.)

Paton Walsh, Jill. "Disturbing the Universe." In *Innocence & Experience.* Edited by Barbara Harrison and Gregory Maguire. New York: Lothrop, 1987, pp. 156–164.

———. "History Is Fiction." *Horn Book* 48 (Feb 1972): 17–23.

———. "The Language of Children's Literature." *Bookquest* (U.K.) 8, no. 1 (1985): 4–9.

———. "The Lords of Time." *Quarterly Journal of the Library of Congress* 36 (Spring 1979): 96–113. Reprinted in *The Openhearted Audience.* Washington DC: Library of Congress, 1980, pp. 177–198.

———. "Realism, Fantasy and History: Facts in Fiction." *Canadian Children's Literature* 48 (1987): 7–14.

———. "Seeing Green." In Edward Blishen. *The Thorny Paradise.* Boston: Horn Book, 1975, pp. 58–61.

———. "What It Was Really Like." *Times Educational Supplement* (Jan 31, 1975): 62.

———. "The Writers in the Writer: A Reply to Hugh Crago." *Signal* 40 (Jan 1983): 3–11.

———. "The Writer's Responsibility." *Children's Literature in Education* 10 (Mar 1973): 30–36.

Pflieger, Pat, and Helen M. Hill. *A Reference Guide to Modern Fantasy for Children.* Westport, CT: Greenwood, 1984, pp. xii–xvi, 103–105, 425–426.

Rees, David. "Types of Ambiguity: Jill Paton Walsh." In *Marble in the Water.* Boston: Horn Book, 1980, pp. 141–154.

Speaking for Ourselves: Autobiographical Sketches by Notable Authors of Books for Young Adults. Edited by Donald R. Gallo. Urbana, IL: National Council of Teachers of English, 1990, pp. 219–221.

Townsend, John Rowe. "Jill Paton Walsh." In *A Sounding of Storytellers.* Philadelphia: Lippincott, 1979, pp. 153–165.

Twentieth-Century Children's Writers. 3rd ed. Edited by Tracy Chevalier and D. L. Kirkpatrick. Chicago: St. James, 1989, pp. 760–762.

"Writers and Critics: A Dialogue Between Jill Paton Walsh and John Rowe Townsend, Part I." *Horn Book* 58 (Oct 1982): 498–504; "Part II." *Horn Book* 58 (Dec 1982): 680–685.

Patten, Brian

Twentieth Century Children's Writers. 3rd ed. Edited by Tracy Chevalier and D. L. Kirkpatrick. New York: St. Martin, 1989, pp. 762–763.

Paxon, Diana L.

Paxon, Diana. "The Holy Grail." *Mythlore* 3, no. 9 (1976).

———. "The Tolkien Tradition." *Mythlore* 39 (1984): 23–27, 37.

———. "What I Did for Love." *Mythlore* 17 (Autumn 1990): 4–8.

———. "Why Write Fantasy?" *Mythlore* 10 (Sept 1984): 23–27.

Payne, Joan Balfour (Dicks)

Payne, Joan Balfour. "Another King for Christmas." *Horn Book* 37 (Dec 1961): 569–585.

Pearce (Christie), (Ann) Philippa

Aers, Lesley. "The Treatment of Time in Four Children's Books." *Children's Literature in Education* 2 (July 1970): 69–81.

"Authorgraph no. 23: Philippa Pearce." *Books for Keeps* (U.K.) 23 (Nov 1983): 14–15.

Billman, Carol. "Young and Old Alike: The Place of Old Women in Two Recent Novels for Children." *Children's Literature Association Quarterly* 8 (Spring 1983): 6–8, 31.

Chambers, Aidan. "Letter from England: Reaching Through a Window." *Horn Book* 57 (Apr 1981): 229–233.

Crouch, Marcus. *The Nesbit Tradition.* London: Benn, 1972, pp. 198–200.

Doyle, Brian. *The Who's Who of Children's Literature.* New York: Schocken, 1968, pp. 214–215.

Evans, David. "The Making of *The Children of the House*." In *Further Approaches to Research in Children's Literature.* Edited by Peter Hunt. Cardiff: Univ. of Wales, 1982, pp. 51–56.

Gillespie, John T., and Diana Lembo. *Introducing Books: A Guide for the Middle Grades.* New York: Bowker, 1970, pp. 252–255.

Hiller, Claire. "The World of Fantasy—The World Where Anything Can Happen." *English in Australia* 86 (Dec 1988): 54–59.

Inglis, Fred. *The Promise of Happiness.* New York: Cambridge Univ. Press, 1981, pp. 257–267.

Jackson, Brian. "Philippa Pearce in the Golden Age of Children's Literature." *The Use of English* 21, no. 3 (Spring 1970): 195–203, 207. Reprinted in Margaret Meek. *The Cool Web.* New York: Atheneum, 1978, pp. 314–324; and in Dennis Butts. *Good Writers for Young Readers.* St. Albans, England: Hart-Davis, 1977, pp. 94–103.

Jones, Raymond E. "Philippa Pearce's *Tom's Midnight Garden:* Finding and Losing Eden." In *Touchstones.* Edited by Perry Nodelman. West Lafayette, IN: Children's Literature Association Publications, 1985, pp. 212–220.

Lehnert-Rodiek, Gertrud. "Fantastic Children's Literature and Travel in Time." *Phaedrus* 13 (1988): 61–72.

Martin, Tony. "Horizons, Themes and Pretensions: How Sally Solved the Mystery of *Tom's Midnight Garden*." *Reading* (U.K.) 19 (Apr 1985): 13–19.

Meek, Margaret. "Speaking of Shifters." *Signal* 45 (Sept 1984): 152–167. Reprinted from Meek's *Changing English: Essays for Harold Rosen.* London: Heinemann, 1984.

Moon, Kenneth. "Don't Tell It: Show It." *School Librarian* 31 (Dec 1983): 319–327.

Natov, Roni, and Geraldine DeLuca. "An Interview with Philippa Pearce." *The Lion and the Unicorn* 9 (1985): 75–88.

The Oxford Companion to Children's Literature. Edited by Humphrey Carpenter and Mari Prichard. New York: Oxford Univ. Press, 1984, pp. 155, 398, 534.

Pearce, Philippa. "Guest Review." *Puffin Post* (London) 14 (Spring 1980): 22–23.

———. "*Robin Hood and His Merry Men:* A Re-Reading." *Children's Literature in Education* 16 (Autumn 1985): 159–164.

———. "*Tom's Midnight Garden*." *School Bookshop News* (U.K.) 7 (Summer 1977): 10–11.

———. "A Writer's View." *Orana* 22, no. 4 (Nov 1986): 166–172.

———. "The Writer's View of Childhood." *Horn Book* 38 (Feb 1962): 74–78. Reprinted in Elinor Field. *Horn Book Reflections.* Boston: Horn Book, 1969, pp. 49–53.

———. "Writing a Book: *A Dog So Small*." *Listening and Writing* (London). BBC Booklet for Schools (Autumn 1962). Reprinted in Margaret Meek. *The Cool Web.* New York: Atheneum, 1978, pp. 182–187; in *Horn Book* 43 (June 1967): 317–321; and in Edward Blishen. *The Thorny Paradise.* Boston: Horn Book, 1975, pp. 140–145.

Pflieger, Pat, and Helen M. Hill. *A Reference Guide to Modern Fantasy for Children.* Westport, CT: Greenwood, 1984, pp. xiii, 427–429, 543–544.

Philip, Neil. "*Tom's Midnight Garden* and the Vision of Eden." *Signal* 37 (Jan 1982): 21–25.

———. "Understanding Children's Thoughts: An Interview with Philippa Pearce." *British Book News Children's Books* (Autumn 1983): 2–4.

Rees, David. "The Novels of Philippa Pearce." *Children's Literature in Education* 4 (Mar 1971): 40–53. Reprinted in David Rees. *The Marble in the Water.* Boston: Horn Book, 1980, pp. 36–55, entitled "Achieving One's Heart's Desires."

Royds, Pam. "Meet Your Author: Philippa Pearce." *Puffin Post* (U.K.) 12, no. 2 (1978): 8–9.

Rustin, Michael. "Animals in Reality and Fantasy: Two Stories by Philippa Pearce." In Margaret Rustin and Michael Rustin. *Narratives of Love and Loss: Studies in Modern Children's Fiction.* London: Verso, 1987; New York: Routledge, 1988, pp. 119–145.

————. "Loneliness, Dreaming and Discovery: *Tom's Midnight Garden.*" In Margaret Rustin and Michael Rustin, *Narratives of Love and Loss: Studies in Modern Children's Fiction.* London: Verso, 1987; New York: Routledge, 1988, pp. 27–39.

Snyder, Zilpha Keatley. "Afterword." In Philippa Pearce's *Tom's Midnight Garden.* Dell, 1985.

Swinfen, Ann. *In Defense of Fantasy.* London: Routledge, 1984, pp. 52, 58–61. Discusses *Tom's Midnight Garden.*

Third Book of Junior Authors. Edited by Doris De Montreville and Donna Hill. New York: Wilson, 1972, pp. 221–222.

"*Tom's Midnight Garden.*" In M. Crouch and A. Ellis. *Chosen for Children,* 3rd ed. London: The Library Association, 1977, pp. 96–99.

Townsend, John Rowe. "Philippa Pearce." In *A Sense of Story.* Philadelphia: Lippincott, 1971, pp. 163–171.

Twentieth-Century Children's Writers. 3rd ed. Edited by Tracy Chevalier and D. L. Kirkpatrick. Chicago: St. James, 1989, pp. 766–767.

Waite, Maggi. "An Afternoon in *Tom's Midnight Garden.*" *Bookquest* (U.K.) 13, no. 1 (1990): 17–18.

Wolf, Virginia L. "Belief in *Tom's Midnight Garden.*" In *Proceedings of the Ninth Annual Conference of the Children's Literature Association.* University of Florida, March 1982. Ypsilanti, MI: Children's Literature Association, 1983, pp. 142–146.

Pearson, Kit

Ellis, Sarah. "News from the North." *Horn Book* 64 (May–June 1988): 390–394. Discusses three Canadian time travel novels.

Stott, Jon C. "Of Time and the Prairie: Canadian Fantasies and the Search for Self-Worth." *Children's Literature Association Bulletin* 16 (Fall 1990): 2–6.

Pease, (Clarence) Howard

Jennings, Shirley May. "A Study of the Creative Genesis of the Twenty-two Published Children's Novels by Howard Pease." Ed.D. diss., University of the Pacific, 1969.

Jennings, Shirley May, and Dewey Chambers. "The Real Ted Moran." *Elementary English* 46 (Apr 1969): 488–491. Reprinted in *Children's Literature: Criticism and Response.* Edited by Mary Lou White. Columbus, OH: Merrill, 1976, pp. 19–25.

The Junior Book of Authors. 2nd rev. ed. Edited by Stanley J. Kunitz and Howard Haycraft. New York: Wilson, 1951, pp. 239–240.

Twentieth-Century Children's Writers. 3rd ed. Edited by Tracy Chevalier and D. L. Kirkpatrick. New York: St. Martin, 1989, pp. 767–768.

Peck, Richard (Wayne)

Blackburn, William. "The Quest for Values in Contemporary Adolescent Fiction." Syracuse, NY: ERIC Clearinghouse on Information Resources, 1982.

Crew, Hilary. "Blossom Culp and Her Ilk: The Independent Female in Richard Peck's Young Adult Fiction." *Top of the News* 43 (Spring 1987): 297–302.

Fifth Book of Junior Authors and Illustrators. Edited by Sally Holmes Holtze. New York: Wilson, 1983, pp. 238–240.

Gillespie, John T. *More Juniorplots: A Guide for Teachers and Librarians.* New York: Bowker, 1977, pp. 140–142.

Hartvigsen, M. Kip, and Christen Brog Hartvigsen. "The Divine Miss Blossom Culp." *ALAN Review* 16 (Winter 1989): 33–35.

Helbig, Alethea, and Agnes Regan Perkins. *Dictionary of American Children's Fiction, 1985–1989.* Westport, CT: Greenwood, 1993, pp. 24–25, 188.

———. *Dictionary of American Children's Fiction, 1960–1984.* Westport, CT: Greenwood, 1986, pp. 503–504.

Peck, Richard. "Coming Full Circle: From Lesson Plans to Young Adult Novels." *Horn Book* 59 (Apr 1983): 208–215.

———. "Communicating with a New Generation: A Challenge to Writers and Teachers." *Illinois Libraries* 57 (May 1975): 305–312.

———. "Communicating with the Pubescent." *Booklist* 90 (June 1 & 15, 1994): 1818–1819.

———. "The Great Library Shelf Witch Hunt." *Booklist* 88 (Jan 1, 1992): 816–817.

———. "Huck Finns of Both Sexes: Protagonists and Peer Leaders in Young-Adult Books." *Horn Book* 69 (Sept–Oct 1993): 554–558.

———. "I Was the First Writer I Ever Met." In *The VOYA Reader.* Metuchen, NJ: Scarecrow Press, 1990, pp. 223–229.

———. "In the Country of Teenage Fiction." *American Libraries* 4 (Apr 1973): 204–207. Reprinted in *Young Adult Literature in the Seventies.* Edited by Jana Varlejs. Metuchen, NJ: Scarecrow Press, 1978, pp. 97–105.

———. "The Invention of Adolescence and Other Thoughts on Youth." *Top of the News* 39 (Winter 1983): 182–190.

———. *Love and Death at the Mall: Teaching and Writing for the Literate Young.* New York: Delacorte, 1994.

———. "Love Is Not Enough." *Journal of Youth Services in Libraries* 4 (Fall 1990): 35–39; and *School Library Journal* 36 (Sept 1990): 153–154.

———. "People of the Word: A Look at Today's Young Adults, and Their Needs." *School Library Media Quarterly* 10 (Fall 1981): 16–21.

———. "The Silver Anniversary of Young Adult Books." *Journal of Youth Services in Libraries* 7 (Fall 1993): 19–24.

———. "Traveling in Time." *ALAN Review* 17 (Winter 1990): 1–3.

———. "Writing for the Young Adult." *Texas Library Journal* 51 (Winter 1975): 191–196.

Speaking for Ourselves: Autobiographical Sketches by Notable Authors of Books for Young Adults. Edited by Donald R. Gallo. Urbana, IL: National Council of Teachers of English, 1990, pp. 165–167.

Spirt, Diana L. *Introducing More Books: A Guide for the Middle Grades.* New York: Bowker, 1978, pp. 187–189.

Sutton, Roger. "A Conversation with Richard Peck." *School Library Journal* 36 (June 1990): 36–40.

Twentieth-Century Children's Writers. 3rd ed. Edited by Tracy Chevalier and D. L. Kirkpatrick. Chicago: St. James, 1989, pp. 768–769.

Vinsonhaler, C. "Children's Book Festival Honors Richard Peck." *Mississippi Libraries* 55 (Summer 1991): 49–50.

Writers on Writing for Young Adults. Edited by Patricia E. Freehan and Pamela Petrick Barron. Detroit: Omnigraphics, 1991.

Peet, Bill (William Bartlett)

Bader, Barbara. *American Picturebooks from Noah's Ark to the Beast Within.* New York: Macmillan, 1976, pp. 38–42.

Twentieth-Century Children's Writers. 3rd ed. Edited by Tracy Chevalier and D. L. Kirkpatrick. Chicago: St. James, 1989, pp. 771–772.

Peyton, K. M. (pseud. of Kathleen Wendy Peyton)

Ainsworth, Marlane. "Exceptional Authors—K. M. Peyton." *Education Library Service Bulletin* (Australia) 18 (Apr–May 1980): 10–14.

Butts, Dennis. "Writers for Children: K. M. Peyton." *The Use of English* 23 (Spring 1972): 195–202. Reprinted in Dennis Butts. *Good Writers for Young Readers.* St. Albans, England: Hart-Davis, 1977, pp. 104–113.

Crouch, Marcus. *The Nesbit Tradition.* London: Benn, 1972, pp. 152–153, 177–179.

———. "Streets Ahead in Experience." *Junior Bookshelf* 33 (June 1969): 153–159.

Hamilton, Alex. "K. M. Peyton." *Puffin Post* (U.K.) 10, no. 3 (1976): 9–11.

Hibbard, Dominic. "The Flambards Trilogy: Objections to a Winner." *Children's Literature in Education* 8 (July 1972): 5–15. Reprinted in Fox. *Writers, Critics and Children.* New York: Agathon, 1976, pp. 125–137. For response, see Ray, below.

Inglis, Fred. *The Promise of Happiness.* New York: Cambridge Univ. Press, 1981, pp. 221–224.

Jones, Cornelia, and Olivia R. Way. "K. M. Peyton." In *British Children's Authors.* Chicago: American Library Association, 1976, pp. 127–136.

Looker, Ann. "Children's Writers: K. M. Peyton." *School Librarian* 25 (Sept 1977): 223–228.

The Oxford Companion to Children's Literature. Edited by Humphrey Carpenter and Mari Prichard. New York: Oxford Univ. Press, 1984, pp. 408–409.

Peyton, K. M. "The Carnegie Medal—A Speech of Acceptance." *Junior Bookshelf* 34 (Oct 1970): 269–271.

———. "On Not Writing a Proper Book." In Edward Blishen. *The Thorny Paradise.* Boston: Horn Book, 1975, pp. 123–127.

———. "The Ponies in My Life." *Puffin Post* (U.K.) 11, no. 1 (1977): 9–10.

Ray, Colin. "*The Edge of the Cloud*—A Reply to Dominic Hibbard." *Children's Literature in Education* 9 (Nov 1972): 5–6.

Third Book of Junior Authors. Edited by Doris De Montreville and Donna Hill. New York: Wilson, 1972, pp. 224–226.

Townsend, John Rowe. "K. M. Peyton." In *A Sense of Story.* Philadelphia: Lippincott, 1971, pp. 172–181.

———. "K. M. Peyton." In *A Sounding of Storytellers.* Philadelphia: Lippincott, 1979, pp. 166–178.

———. "A Second Look: *A Pattern of Roses.*" *Horn Book* 60 (June 1984): 361–364.

Twentieth-Century Children's Writers. 3rd ed. Edited by Tracy Chevalier and D. L. Kirkpatrick. Chicago: St. James, 1989, pp. 775–776.

Wintle, Justin, and Emma Fisher. "K. M. Peyton." In *The Pied Pipers.* New York: Paddington Press, 1974, pp. 263–276.

Yeatman, Linda. "K. M. Peyton, Profile of an Author at Work." *British Book News: Children's Supplement* (Spring 1980): 1–2.

Phillips, Ethel Calvert

The Junior Book of Authors, 2nd rev. ed. Edited by Stanley J. Kunitz and Howard Haycraft. New York: Wilson, 1951, pp. 244–245.

Phillips, Ethel Calvert. "A Hunt Breakfast—Authors' Symposium." *Horn Book* 2 (Nov 1926): 36.

Phipson, Joan (pseud. of Joan Margaret Fitzhardinge)

McVitty, Walter. "Joan Phipson: Archetypal Australian Children's Author." *Reading Time* (Australia) 78 (Jan 1981): 5–15.

———. "Joan Phipson: Archetypal Australian Children's Books." In *Innocence and Experience.* Melborne, Australia: Nelson, 1981, pp. 37–65.

Nieuwenhuizen, Agnes. "Joan Phipson: A Portrait and a Tribute." *Magpies* (Australia) 5 (Mar 1990): 16–18.

Simpson, Anne. "Joan Phipson." *Review* (Australia) 6 (Dec 1978): 27–30.

Third Book of Junior Authors. Edited by Doris De Montreville and Donna Hill. New York: Wilson, 1972, pp. 226–227.

Twentieth-Century Children's Writers. 3rd ed. Edited by Tracy Chevalier and D. L. Kirkpatrick. Chicago: St. James, 1989, pp. 776–778.

Picard, Barbara Leonie

Crouch, Marcus. *The Nesbit Tradition.* London: Benn, 1972, pp. 74–75.

Jones, Cornelia, and Olivia R. Way. "Barbara Leonie Picard." In *British Children's Authors.* Chicago: American Library Association, 1976, pp. 137–145.

Third Book of Junior Authors. Edited by Doris De Montreville and Donna Hill. New York: Wilson, 1972, p. 228.

Twentieth-Century Children's Writers. 3rd ed. Edited by Tracy Chevalier and D. L. Kirkpatrick. Chicago: St. James, 1989, pp. 778–779.

Pierce, Meredith Ann

Helbig, Alethea K., and Agnes Regan Perkins. *Dictionary of American Children's Fiction, 1960–1984.* Westport, CT: Greenwood, 1986, pp. 142–143, 514.

McIntosh, Margaret E., and M. Jean Greenlaw. "Ladies First: Teaching Characterization Through Strong Female Protagonists in High Fantasy Literature." *ALAN Review* 15 (1988): 47–51.

Phillips, Robert, and Branimir Rieger. "The Agony and the Ecstasy: A Jungian Analysis of Two Vampire Novels, Meredith Ann Pierce's *The Darkangel* and Bram Stocker's *Dracula.*" *West Virginia University Philological Papers* 31 (1986): 10–19.

Pierce, Meredith Ann. "A Lion in the Room [Where My Heroines Come From, on Whom They Are Modeled]." *Horn Book* 64 (Jan–Feb 1988): 35–41.

———. "The Magical Moment in Fantasy." *ALAN Review* 15 (1988): 39–42.

———. "On the Making of Monsters." *The New Advocate* 3 (Spring 1990): 101–110.

———. "The Queen of the Night." *The New Advocate* 1 (Fall 1988): 221–229.

Sixth Book of Junior Authors and Illustrators. Edited by Sally Holmes Holtze. New York: Wilson, 1989, pp. 224–225.

Twentieth-Century Children's Writers. 3rd ed. Edited by Tracy Chevalier and D. L. Kirkpatrick. Chicago: St. James, 1989, p. 779.

Pierce, Tamora

Pierce, Tamora. "Fantasy: Why Kids Read It, Why Kids Need It." *School Library Journal* 39 (Oct 1993): 50–51.

Pinkwater, D(aniel) Manus

Antczak, Janice. *Science Fiction: The Mythos of a New Romance.* New York: Neal-Schuman, 1985, pp. 174–178.

Fifth Book of Junior Authors and Illustrators. Edited by Sally Holmes Holtze. New York: Wilson, 1983, pp. 246–247.

Pinkwater, Daniel. *Fish Whistle: Commentaries, Uncommentaries, and Vulgar Excesses.* Reading, MA: Addison-Wesley, 1989.

Spirt, Diana L. *Introducing Bookplots 3: A Book Talk Guide for Use with Readers Ages 8–12.* New York: Bowker, 1988, pp. 301–305.

————. *Introducing More Books: A Guide for the Middle Grades.* New York: Bowker, 1978, pp. 217–220.

Twentieth-Century Children's Writers. 3rd ed. Edited by Tracy Chevalier and D. L. Kirkpatrick. Chicago: St. James, 1989, pp. 781–782.

Plunkett, Edward John Morton Drax *see* Dunsany, Lord

Polland, Madeleine A(ngela Cahill)

Third Book of Junior Authors. Edited by Doris De Montreville and Donna Hill. New York: Wilson, 1972, pp. 229–230.

Twentieth-Century Children's Writers. 3rd ed. Edited by Tracy Chevalier and D. L. Kirkpatrick. Chicago: St. James, 1989, pp. 784–785.

Pomerantz, Charlotte

Sixth Book of Junior Authors and Illustrators. Edited by Sally Holmes Holtze. New York: Wilson, 1989, pp. 229–231.

Pope, Elizabeth Marie

Fifth Book of Junior Authors and Illustrators. Edited by Sally Holmes Holtze. New York: Wilson, 1983, pp. 250–251.

Heins, Ethel L. "A Second Look: *The Sherwood Ring.*" *Horn Book* 21 (Dec 1975): 613.

Helbig, Alethea K., and Agnes Regan Perkins. *Dictionary of American Children's Fiction, 1859–1959.* Westport, CT: Greenwood, 1985, pp. 408, 466–467.

————. *Dictionary of American Children's Fiction, 1960–1984.* Westport, CT: Greenwood, 1986, pp. 115–116, 506–507, 522.

Pope, Elizabeth Marie. "The Attic of Faerie." *Mythlore* 9 (Spring 1982): 8–10.

Porte, Barbara Ann

Sixth Book of Junior Authors and Illustrators. Edited by Sally Holmes Holtze. New York: Wilson, 1989, pp. 231–232.

Postma, Lidia

Thiel-Schoonebeek, Joke. "Lidia Postma—Fantasy as Atmosphere." *Bookbird* 1 (1980): 62–64.

Potter, (Helen) Beatrix (Heelis)

Alderson, Brian. "*The Tailor of Gloucester.*" *Children's Book News* 4 (Nov–Dec 1969): 309–312.

Anderson, Celia Catlett. "The Ancient Lineage of Beatrix Potter's *Mr. Todd.*" *Proceedings of the Seventh Annual Conference of the Children's Literature Association, 1980.* Ypsilanti, MI: Children's Literature Association Publications, 1981, pp. 84–90. Reprinted in *Festschrift.* Edited by Perry Nodelman and Jill P. May. West Lafayette, IN: Children's Literature Association Publications, 1983, pp. 45–47.

Avery, Gillian. "Beatrix Potter and Social Comedy." *Beatrix Potter Society Newsletter* 46 (1992): 3–4.

Banner, D. "Portrait." *Illustrated London News* 243 (Oct 9, 1948): 394.

Battrick, Elizabeth. *The Real World of Beatrix Potter.* London: National Trust, 1986.

Bartlett, Wynne, and Joyce Irene Whalley. *Beatrix Potter's Derwentwater.* London: Warne, 1988.

Bassom, Enid, et al., eds. *Beatrix Potter and Mrs. Heelis: Beatrix Potter Studies IV.* Whitby, North Yorkshire: Beatrix Potter Society, 1991.

Bodin, Madeline. "100 Candles for *Peter Rabbit.*" *Publishers Weekly* 240 (Mar 29, 1993): 19–20.

Boultbee, Winifred W. "Some Personal Recollections of Beatrix Potter." *Horn Book* 47 (Dec 1971): 586–588.

Brandenburger, Barbara. "Leslie Linder." *Horn Book* 42 (Dec 1966): 686–689.

Cameron, Eleanor. "Why Not for Children?" *Horn Book* 42 (Feb 1966): 21–23.

Campbell, A. K. D. "The Stories of Beatrix Potter: A Suggested Order for Reading." *Children's Literature in Education* 5 (July 1971): 12–19.

Carpenter, Humphrey. "Beatrix Potter: The Ironist in Arcadia." In *Secret Gardens: The Golden Age of Children's Literature.* Boston: Houghton Mifflin, 1985, pp. 138–150.

———. "Excessively Impertinent Bunnies: The Subversive Elements in Beatrix Potter." In *Children and Their Books,* ed. by Gillian Avery and Julia Briggs. Oxford: Clarendon, 1989, pp. 271–298.

"Centenary of Beatrix Potter's Birth Marked by Publications and Exhibits." *Library Journal* 91 (Sept 15, 1966): 4240–4241.

Children's Literature Association Newsletter. Special Issue 2 (Winter 1978).

Clark, Keith. *Beatrix Potter's Gloucester.* London: Warne, 1988.

———. "The Linder Collection of the Works and Drawings of Beatrix Potter." *Horn Book* 47 (Oct 1971): 554–555.

Clegg, John. "*The Fairy Caravan* Sale." *Beatrix Potter Society Newsletter* (U.K.) 44 (1992): 4.

Coolidge, Henry P. "A Visit to Beatrix Potter." *Horn Book* 4 (Feb 1928): 48–53.

Cott, Jonathan. "Peter Rabbit and Friends." *New York Times Book Review* (May 1, 1977): 25, 38.

Crouch, Marcus E. *Beatrix Potter.* London: Bodley Head, 1960.

———. "Leslie Linder: He Knew More About Beatrix Than She Knew Herself." *Junior Bookshelf* 37 (Oct 1973): 301–303.

Dalphin, Marcus. "The Tale of Beatrix Potter." *Horn Book* 22 (July–Aug 1946): 431–437.

Davies, Hunter. *Beatrix Potter's Lakeland.* London: Warne, 1988.

Dohm, J. H. "My Beatrix Potter." *Junior Bookshelf* 30 (Aug 1966): 233ff.

Doyle, Brian. *The Who's Who of Children's Literature.* New York: Schocken, 1968, pp. 220–223.

Foote, Timothy. "Beatrix Potter's Artful Escape." *Smithsonian* 19 (Jan 1989): 80–91.

"Free Library of Philadelphia Named Recipient of the Collamore Collection of Beatrix Potter." *Wilson Library Bulletin* 42 (Jan 1968): 450.

Frey, Charles. "Victors and Victims in the Tales of *Peter Rabbit* and *Squirrel Nutkin.*" *Children's Literature in Education* 18 (Summer 1987): 105–112.

Gilpatrick, Naomi. "The Secret Life of Beatrix Potter." *National History* 81 (Oct 1972): 38.

Godden, Rumer. "Beatrix Potter." *Horn Book* 42 (Aug 1966): 390–398.

——. "An Imaginary Correspondence." *Horn Book* 39 (Aug 1963): 369–375. Reprinted in Haviland. *Children and Literature.* Glenview, IL: Scott, Foresman, 1973; and in Egoff. *Only Connect.* 1st ed. Toronto: Oxford Univ. Press, 1969, pp. 62–69.

Goldthwaite, John. "The Black Rabbit: Part One." *Signal* 47 (May 1985): 86–111; "The Black Rabbit: Part Two." *Signal* 48 (Sept 1985): 148–167. Reprinted in Goldthwaite. *The Natural History of Make-Believe.* London: Oxford Univ. Press, 1987.

——. "Sis Beatrix (Part One)." *Signal* 53 (May 1987): 117–137; "Sis Beatrix (Part Two)." *Signal* 54 (Sept 1987): 161–177. Reprinted in Goldthwaite. *The Natural History of Make-Believe.* London: Oxford Univ. Press, 1987.

Grahame, Eleanor. "Beatrix Potter." *Junior Bookshelf* 3 (1939): 171–175.

Greene, Graham. "Beatrix Potter." In *The Lost Childhood and Other Essays.* New York: Viking, 1952. Reprinted in Egoff. *Only Connect.* 2nd ed. New York: Oxford Univ. Press, 1980, pp. 258–268.

——. "Beatrix Potter: A Critical Estimate." *London Mercury* 27 (Jan 1933): 241–245.

Hale, Robert D. "Musings." *Horn Book* 64 (Jan–Feb 1988): 100–101.

Hamer, D. "Journal of Beatrix Potter: Some Corrections." *Notes and Queries* 16 (July 1969): 221.

Hearn, Michael Patrick. "A Second Look: *Peter Rabbit* Redux." *Horn Book* 53 (Oct 1977): 563–566.

Higgens, Regina. *Magic Kingdoms: Discovering the Joys of Childhood Classics with Your Child.* New York: Simon, 1992.

Hobbs, Anne S., comp. *Beatrix Potter's Art: Paintings and Drawings.* New York: Warne, 1990.

Hobbs, Anne S., and Joyce Irene Whalley. *Beatrix Potter: The Victoria and Albert Collection.* London: Warne and The Victoria and Albert Museum, 1985.

Hodges, Margaret. "A Second Look: *The Tailor of Gloucester.*" *Horn Book* 54 (Dec 1978): 659–664.

Hough, Richard. "The Tailors of Gloucester." *Signal* 42 (Sept 1983): 150–154.

Hunt, Peter. "But Don't Go into Mr. McGregor's Garden." *The New Advocate* 1 (1988): 155–161.

Hurwitz, Johanna. "Will the Real *Peter Rabbit* Please Stand Up?" *Library Journal* 94 (Apr 15, 1969): 1687–1688.

Inglis, Fred. *The Promise of Happiness.* New York: Cambridge Univ. Press, 1981, pp. 109–111.

Jordan, Alice M. "*The Fairy Caravan* by Beatrix Potter." *Horn Book* 5 (Nov 1929): 9–11.

The Junior Book of Authors. 2nd ed. rev. Edited by Stanley J. Kunitz and Howard Haycraft. New York: Wilson, 1951, pp. 247–249.

Junior Bookshelf. Special Issue 30 (Aug 1966).

Lane, Margaret. "The Art of Beatrix Potter." *New Statesman and Nation* 27 (Jan 8, 1944): 23–24.

——. *The Magic Years of Beatrix Potter.* New York: Warne, 1978.

——. "On the Writing of Beatrix Potter's Life Story." *Horn Book* 22 (Nov–Dec 1946): 438–445.

——. *The Tale of Beatrix Potter: A Biography.* Originally published, 1946. New York: Warne, 1968; Penguin, 1986.

Lathrop, Dorothy P. "*The Art of Beatrix Potter.*" *Horn Book* 31 (Oct 1955): 331–337.

Linder, Leslie. "*The Art of Beatrix Potter* and How It Came to Be." *Horn Book* 31 (Oct 1955): 338–356.

————. "The Beatrix Potter Centenary Exhibit: 1866–1966." *Top of the News* 22 (June 1966): 367–375.

————. "Beatrix Potter's Code Writing." *Horn Book* 39 (Apr 1963): 141–155.

————, comp. *History of the Writings of Beatrix Potter.* New York: Warne, 1971.

————, ed. *The Journal of Beatrix Potter, 1881–1897.* London: Warne, 1989.

Linder, Leslie, and W. A. Herring, comps. *The Art of Beatrix Potter.* New York: Warne, 1972. Originally edited by Leslie Linder and Enid Linder, 1955.

MacDonald, Ruth K. *Beatrix Potter.* Boston: Twayne, 1986.

————. "Beatrix Potter." In *Writers for Children: Critical Studies of Major Authors Since the Seventeenth Century.* Edited by Jane M. Bingham. New York: Scribner, 1988, pp. 439–446.

————. "Narrative Voice and Narrative View in Beatrix Potter's Books." In *The Voice of the Narrator in Children's Literature: Insights from Writers and Critics,* ed. by Charlotte F. Otten and Gary D. Schmidt. New York: Greenwood, 1989, pp. 54–60.

————. "Why This Is Still 1893: *The Tale of Peter Rabbit* and Beatrix Potter's Manipulations of Timelessness." *Children's Literature Association Quarterly* 10 (Winter 1986): 185–187.

McEwen, John. "Tales from the Dark Side." *Art in America* 76 (June 1988): 45–48.

McKillop, A. "Beatrix Potter Centenary, 1866–1966." *Canadian Library* 23 (Jan 1967): 277–280.

McKinley Carol. "Beatrix Potter, Picture Letters, and *Peter Rabbit.*" *AB Bookman's Weekly* (May 16, 1988): 1065–1068.

Maloney, Margaret Crawford, ed. *Dear Ivy, Dear June: Letters from Beatrix Potter.* Toronto: Other Press, 1977.

Mayer, A. M. "Authors Are People: Beatrix Potter, Author, Artist, Farmer." *Instructor* 82 (Nov 1972): 60–61.

Messer, Persis B. "Beatrix Potter: Classic Novelist of the Nursery: A Bibliographic Essay." *Elementary English* 45 (Mar 1968): 325–333.

Miller, Bertha Mahony. "Beatrix Potter and Her Art." *Horn Book* 31 (Oct 1955): 329.

————. "Beatrix Potter and Her Nursery Classics." *Horn Book* 17 (May 1941): 230–238. Reprinted in Fryatt. *Horn Book Sampler.* Boston: Horn Book, 1959, pp. 228–233.

————. "Beatrix Potter in Letters." *Horn Book* 20 (May 1944): 214–224.

Morse, Jane Crowell, ed. *Beatrix Potter's Americans: Selected Letters.* Boston: Horn Book, 1982.

Naumann, Nancy. "Beatrix Potter: Childhood Magic for Now and September." *Learning* 11 (Aug 1982): 32–34.

Nikola-Lisa, W. "The Cult of *Peter Rabbit*: A Barthesian Analysis." *The Lion and the Unicorn* 15 (Dec 1991): 61–66.

Olson, Kimberly. "Brightening up Beatrix." *Publishers Weekly* 232 (Sept 25, 1987): 25–26.

The Oxford Companion to Children's Literature. Edited by Humphrey Carpenter and Mari Prichard. New York: Oxford Univ. Press, 1984, pp. 176–177, 420–424, 514.

"Peter Rabbit Turns 100." *Orana* (Australia) 29 (May 1993): 132–134.

Potter, Beatrix. *Beatrix Potter's Letters,* sel. by Judy Taylor. London: Warne, 1989; New York: Viking, 1990.

————. *The History of the Tale of Peter Rabbit.* New York: Warne, 1877.

————. *Journal of Beatrix Potter from 1881–1897: Transcribed from Her Code Writing by Leslie Linder.* New York: Warne, 1966.

————. *The Journal of Beatrix Potter, 1881–1897,* rev. ed. Transcribed by Leslie Linder. New York: Viking, 1990.

————. *Letters to Children from Beatrix Potter.* Ed. by Judy Taylor. New York: Warne, 1992.

————. "The Lonely Hills." *Horn Book* 18 (May 1942): 153–156.

————. "Over the Hills and Far Away." *Horn Book* 5 (Feb 1929): 3–10.

————. "The 'Roots' of the Peter Rabbit Tales." *Horn Book* 5 (May 1929): 69–72. Reprinted in Meek. *The Cool Web.* London: Bodley Head, 1977, pp. 188–191.

————. "The Strength That Comes from the Hills." *Horn Book* 20 (Mar–Apr 1944): 77. Reprinted in Fryatt. *Horn Book Sampler.* Boston: Horn Book, 1959, pp. 28–29.

————. "The Tale of the Faithful Dove." *Horn Book* 31 (Dec 1955): 480–492.

————. "Wag-by-Wall." *Horn Book* 20 (May 1944): 199–202.

Pritchard, Jane, and Brian Riddle, eds. *Beatrix Potter Studies, I.* London: Beatrix Potter Society, 1986.

Pritchett, V. S. "Fur and Freedom." *New Statesman* 72 (July 22, 1966): 131–132.

Quinby, Jane. *Beatrix Potter: A Bibliographic Check List.* London: Sawyer, 1954.

Rahn, Suzanne. "The Expression of Religious and Political Concepts in Fantasy for Children." Ph.D. diss., University of Washington, 1986.

————. "Tailpiece: *The Tale of Two Bad Mice.*" *Children's Literature,* vol. 12. New Haven, CT: Yale Univ. Press, 1984, pp. 78–91.

Richardson, Patrick. "Miss Potter and the Little Rubbish." *New Society* (July 7, 1966). Reprinted in Tucker. *Suitable for Children?* London: Chatto, 1976, pp. 173–178.

Riddle, Brian. "Literary Criticism of Beatrix Potter." *Beatrix Potter Society Newsletter* 44 (1992): 7–9.

————, ed. *Beatrix Potter Before "Peter Rabbit." Papers Presented at the Beatrix Potter Society Conference, Perth, July 1988.* London: Beatrix Potter Society, 1989.

Robinson, Lolly. "Beatrix Potter: Artist and Storyteller." *Horn Book* 64 (1988): 408.

Sale, Roger. "Beatrix Potter." In *Fairy Tales and After.* Cambridge, MA: Harvard Univ. Press, 1978, pp. 82–83, 126–163.

Scott, Carole. "Between Me and the World: Clothes as Mediator Between Self and Society in the Work of Beatrix Potter." *The Lion and the Unicorn* 16 (Dec 1992): 199–209.

Sendak, Maurice. "The Aliveness of Peter Rabbit." *Wilson Library Bulletin* 40 (Dec 1965): 345–348.

Shaffer, Ellen. "Beatrix Potter Lives in the Philadelphia Free Library." *Horn Book* 42 (Aug 1966): 401–405.

Sheppard-Conrad, Connie. "The Enduring Appeal of Beatrix Potter." *Emergency Librarian* 16 (May–June 1989): 21–25.

Sicroff, Seth. "Prickles under the Frock: The Art of Beatrix Potter." In *Children's Literature,* vol. 2. Storrs, CT: Journal of the Modern Language Association, 1973. Reprinted in *Reflections on Literature for Children.* Edited by Francelia Butler and Richard Rotert. Hamden, CT: Shoe String Press, 1984, pp. 39–44.

Stevens, Elizabeth H. "A Visit to Mrs. Tiggywinkle." *Horn Book* 34 (Apr 1958): 131–136.

Stott, Jon C. *Children's Literature from A to Z.* New York: McGraw-Hill, 1984, p. 228.

"*The Tailor of Gloucester.*" *Times Literary Supplement* (London), Jan 8, 1944, p. 15.

Taylor, Judy. "Beatrix Potter." *Magpies* (Australia) 5 (Mar 1990): 12–14.

————. *Beatrix Potter: Artist, Storyteller and Countrywoman.* New York: Viking Press, 1987.

————, ed. *Beatrix Potter's Letters.* London: Warne, 1989.

————, ed. *"So I Shall Tell You a Story." Encounters with Beatrix Potter.* New York: Warne, 1993.

————. "The Tale of Peter Rabbit." [Children's Book Council] CBC Features 44 (Jan–June 1991).

Tucker, Nicholas. *The Child and the Book.* New York: Cambridge Univ. Press, 1981, pp. 57–66.

Twentieth-Century Children's Writers. 3rd ed. Edited by Tracy Chevalier and D. L. Kirkpatrick. Chicago: St. James, 1989, pp. 789–791.

Weiner, R. W. "Beatrix Potter: Mrs. William Heelis." *Ontario Library Review* 41 (Aug 1957): 202–204.

Whalley, Joyce Irene. "The Other World of Beatrix Potter." *Natural History* 97 (May 1988): 48–51.

Yoshida, Shin-Ichi. "The World of Beatrix Potter as Seen Through the Eyes of a Japanese Visitor." *International Library Review* 5 (Apr 1973): 225–228.

Pratchett, Terry

Connolly, Ray. "Western Avenue, Road to Damascus." (London) *Times Saturday Review* (July 14, 1990): 62.

Stone, Grant. "Know the Author: Terry Pratchett." *Magpies* (Australia) 8 (Mar 1993): 19.

Pratt, (Murray) Fletcher

De Camp, L. Sprague. *Literary Swordsmen and Sorcerers: The Makers of Heroic Fantasy.* Sauk City, WI: Arkham House, 1976.

Pratt, Fletcher. "A Critique of Science Fiction." In *Modern Science Fiction.* 2nd ed. Edited by Reginal Bretnor. Chicago: Advent, 1979, pp. 73–90.

Schuyler, William M., Jr. "Recent Developments in Spell Construction." In *The Aesthetics of Fantasy Literature and Art.* Edited by Roger C. Schlobin. South Bend, IN: Notre Dame Univ. Press, 1982, pp. 237–248.

Stableford, Brian M. "L. Sprague de Camp and Fletcher Pratt." In *Supernatural Fiction Writers: Fantasy and Horror,* vol. 2. Edited by E. F. Bleiler. New York: Scribner, 1985, pp. 925–932.

Twentieth-Century Science Fiction Writers. 3rd ed. Edited by Noelle Watson and Paul E. Schellinger. Chicago: St. James Press, 1991, pp. 637–638.

Watson, Christine. *"The Well of the Unicorn."* In *Survey of Modern Fantasy Literature,* vol. 5. Edited by Frank N. Magill. Englewood Cliffs, NJ: Salem Press, 1983, pp. 2097–2101.

Preussler, Otfried

Alcorn, Noeline. "Fantasy and Family Life: Children's Books from Northern Europe." *Children's Literature Association Yearbook.* Auckland, New Zealand: Children's Literature Association, 1976, pp. 29–42. Discusses Astrid Lindgren, Maria Gripe, Christine Nöstlinger, Otfried Preussler, and Paul Biegel.

Fourth Book of Junior Authors and Illustrators. Edited by Doris De Montreville and Elizabeth D. Crawford. New York: Wilson, 1978, pp. 290–291.

Frenkel, Pavel. "Beskonechnaya Energiya Fatasii. [The Boundless Energy of Fantasy]" *Detskaya Literatura* (Moscow) 2 (Feb 1982): 43–47.

———. "Yeshcho Razo Babe-Yage [More about the Witch]." *Detskaya Literatura* (Moscow) 9 (Sept 1983): 45–48.

Preussler, Otfried. "My Partner and I." *Bookbird* 10, no. 4 (1972): 22–23.

———. "What You Write for Children: Diversity and Limitations of Children's Literature." *Bookbird* 13, no. 4 (1975): 3–5.

Preussler, Otfreid, and Vladimir Zheleznikov. "Chrevoveshchateli i Kanatokhodtsy [Ventriloquists and Tightrope-Walkers]." *Detskaya Literatura* (Moscow) 4 (Apr 1991): 14–17.

Price, Susan

Price, Susan. "A Letter to Anne Wood." *Books for Your Children* (U.K.) 11 (Autumn 1976): 13.

Twentieth-Century Children's Writers. 3rd ed. Edited by Tracy Chevalier and D. L. Kirkpatrick. Chicago: St. James, 1989, pp. 796–797.

Worpole, Ken. "Susan Price: A Socialist Writer for Teenagers." *Children's Book Bulletin* 6 (Summer 1981): 6–9.

Provensen, Alice, and Provensen, Martin

"The Provensens: Book Artists for Children." *Publishers Weekly* 186 (July 13, 1964): 111–112.

Third Book of Junior Authors. Edited by Doris De Montreville and Donna Hill. New York: Wilson, 1972, pp. 231–232.

Pushkin, Alexander Sergeevich

The Oxford Companion to Children's Literature. Edited by Humphrey Carpenter and Mari Prichard. New York: Oxford Univ. Press, 1984, p. 432.

Pyle, Howard

Abbott, Charles D. *Howard Pyle: A Chronicle.* New York: Harper, 1925.

Agosta, Lucien L. *Howard Pyle.* Boston: Twayne, 1987.

Doyle, Brian. *The Who's Who of Children's Literature.* New York: Schocken, 1968, pp. 225–227.

Elzea, Rowland. "Howard Pyle's Manuscripts: The Delaware Art Museum." *Children's Literature Association Quarterly* 8 (Summer 1983): 10.

Helbig, Alethea K., and Agnes Regan Perkins. *Dictionary of American Children's Fiction, 1859–1959.* Westport, CT: Greenwood, 1985, pp. 415–416.

Kirkus, Virginia. "Howard Pyle: A Backwards Glance." *Horn Book* 5 (Nov 1929): 37–39.

May, Jill P. "Howard Pyle." In *American Writers for Children before 1900. Dictionary of Literary Biography,* vol. 42. Detroit: Gale, 1985, pp. 295–307.

———. "Howard Pyle." In *Writers for Children: Critical Studies of Major Authors Since the Seventeenth Century.* Edited by Jane M. Bingham. New York: Scribner, 1988, pp. 447–454.

———. "Pyle's Fairy Tales: Folklore Remade." *Children's Literature Association Quarterly* 8 (Summer 1983): 19–21.

———. "Special Section: Howard Pyle Commemorative." *Children's Literature Association Quarterly* 8 (Summer 1983): 9–34.

———. "Symbolic Journeys Toward Death: George MacDonald and Howard Pyle as Fantasists." *Proceedings of the 13th Annual Conference of The Children's Literature Association, 1986.* New York: Pace University, 1988, pp. 129–134.

Morse, Willard S., and Gertrude Brincklé, comps. *Howard Pyle: A Record of His Illustrations and Writings* (reproduction of 1921 ed.). Detroit: Singing Tree Press, 1969.

Nesbitt, Elizabeth. *Howard Pyle.* New York: Walck, 1966. Reprinted in Roger Lancelyn Green, Anthea Bell, and Elizabeth Nesbitt. *Lewis Carroll, E. Nesbit, and Howard Pyle.* London: Bodley Head, 1968.

Nodelman, Perry. "Pyle's Sweet, Thin, Clear Tune: *The Garden Behind the Moon.*" *Children's Literature Association Quarterly* 8 (Summer 1983): 22–25.

Oakley, Thornton. "Howard Pyle." *Horn Book* 7 (May 1931): 91–97.

The Oxford Companion to Children's Literature. Edited by Humphrey Carpenter and Mari Prichard. New York: Oxford Univ. Press, 1984, pp. 433–435.

Pitz, Henry C. *Howard Pyle: Writer, Illustrator, Founder of the Brandywine School.* New York: Potter, 1975.

Pyle, Howard. "When I Was a Little Boy." *Woman's Home Companion* 39 (Apr 1912): 5.

Reprinted in Phyllis Reid Fenner. *Something Shared: Children and Books.* New York: John Day, 1959, pp. 6–12.

Stott, Jon C. *Children's Literature from A to Z.* New York: McGraw-Hill, 1984, p. 232.

Twentieth Century Children's Writers. 2nd ed. Edited by D. L. Kirkpatrick. New York: St. Martin, 1983, p. 883.

Yitz, Robert. "Howard Pyle's America." *Children's Literature Association Quarterly* 8 (Summer 1983): 15–16, 34.

Zipes, Jack, ed. *Spells of Enchantment: The Wondrous Fairy Tales of Western Culture.* New York: Viking, 1991.

Quackenbush, Robert M(ead)

Fourth Book of Junior Authors and Illustrators. Edited by Doris De Montreville and Elizabeth D. Crawford. New York: Wilson, 1978, pp. 293–294.

Raskin, Ellen

Bach, Alice. "Ellen Raskin: Some Clues About Her Life." *Horn Book* 61 (Mar–Apr 1985): 162–167.

Flanagan, Dennis. "The Raskin Conglomerate." *Horn Book* 55 (Aug 1979): 392–395.

Helbig, Alethea K., and Agnes Regan Perkins. *Dictionary of American Children's Fiction, 1960–1984.* Westport, CT: Greenwood, 1986, pp. 212, 648.

Herman, Gertrude. "A Picture Is Worth Several Hundred Words." *Horn Book* 62 (July–Aug 1986): 479. Discusses *Figgs and Phantoms.*

Hieatt, Constance B. "The Mystery of *Figgs and Phantoms.*" In *Children's Literature,* vol. 13. New Haven, CT: Yale Univ. Press, 1985, pp. 128–138.

Hopkins, Lee Bennet. "Ellen Raskin." In *Books Are by People.* New York: Citation Press, 1969, pp. 226–229.

Karrenbrock, Marilyn H. "Ellen Raskin." In *American Writers for Children since 1960: Fiction. Dictionary of Literary Biography,* vol. 52. Detroit: Gale, 1986, pp. 314–324.

Olson, Marilynn Strasser. *Ellen Raskin.* Boston: Twayne, 1991.

Raskin, Ellen. "Characters and Other Clues." *Horn Book* 54 (Dec 1978): 620–625.

———. "The Creative Spirit and Children's Literature: A Literary Symposium." *Wilson Library Bulletin* 53 (Oct 1978): 152–154.

———. "Me and Blake, Blake and Me." In *Innocence & Experience.* Edited by Barbara Harrison and Gregory Maguire. New York: Lothrop, 1987, pp. 347–353.

———. "Newbery Medal Acceptance." *Horn Book* 55 (Aug 1979): 385–391.

———. "Profile of an Author: Ellen Raskin." *Top of the News* 28 (June 1972): 394–398.

Roginski, Jim. *Behind the Covers: Interviews with Authors and Illustrators of Books for Children and Young Adults.* Littleton, CO: Libraries Unlimited, 1985, pp. 167–176.

———, ed. *Newbery and Caldecott Medalists and Honor Book Winners.* Littleton, CO: Libraries Unlimited, 1982, pp. 215–216.

Stott, Jon C. *Children's Literature from A to Z.* New York: McGraw-Hill, 1984, p. 236.

Third Book of Junior Authors. Edited by Doris De Montreville and Donna Hill. New York: Wilson, 1972, pp. 235–236.

Twentieth-Century Children's Writers. 3rd ed. Edited by Tracy Chevalier and D. L. Kirkpatrick. Chicago: St. James, 1989, pp. 808–809.

Rawlings (Baskin), Marjorie Kinnan

Bellman, Samuel I. *Marjorie Kinnan Rawlings.* Boston: Twayne, 1974.

————. "Writing Literature for Young People: Marjorie Kinnan Rawlings's '*Secret River*' of the Imagination." *Costerus* 9 (1973): 19–27.

Bigelow, Gordon E. *Frontier Eden: The Literary Career of Marjorie Kinnan Rawlings.* Gainesville: Univ. of Florida, 1966.

————. "Marjorie Kinnan Rawlings's Wilderness." *Sewanee Review* 73 (Spring 1965): 299–310.

Cech, John. "Marjorie Kinnan Rawlings's *The Secret River: A Fairy Tale, a Place, a Life.*" *Southern Studies* 19 (1977): 29–58.

Galbraith, Lachlan N. "Marjorie Kinnan Rawlings's *The Secret River.*" *Elementary English* 52 (Apr 1975): 455–459.

Helbig, Alethea K., and Agnes Regan Perkins. *Dictionary of American Children's Fiction, 1859–1959.* Westport, CT: Greenwood, 1985, p. 425.

Kilgo, Reese Danley. "Marjorie Kinnan Rawlings." In Cech. *American Writers for Children, 1900–1960. Dictionary of Literary Biography,* vol. 22. Detroit: Gale, 1983, pp. 282–285.

Nichols, L. "Talk with Mrs. Rawlings." *New York Times Book Review,* Sect. 7, Feb 1, 1953, p. 1.

Perkins, Agnes Regan. "Marjorie Kinnan Rawlings." In *Writers for Children: Critical Studies of Major Authors Since the Seventeenth Century.* Edited by Jane M. Bingham. New York: Scribner, 1988, pp. 463–468.

Roginski, Jim, ed. *Newbery and Caldecott Medalists and Honor Book Winners.* Littleton, CO: Libraries Unlimited, 1982, pp. 216–217.

Third Book of Junior Authors. Edited by Doris De Montreville and Donna Hill. New York: Wilson, 1972, pp. 237–239.

Twentieth-Century Children's Writers. 3rd ed. Edited by Tracy Chevalier and D. L. Kirkpatrick. Chicago: St. James, 1989, pp. 809–810.

Williams, William Carlos. "To the Ghost of Marjorie Kinnan Rawlings." *Virginia Quarterly Review* 36 (Fall 1960): 579–580.

York, Lamar. "Marjorie Kinnan Rawlings's Rivers." *Southern Literary Journal* 9 (Spring 1977): 91–107.

Ray, Mary (Eva Pedder)

Stroud, Daphne J. "The Road to Glevum." *Junior Bookshelf* 53, no. 3 (1989): 103–107.

Twentieth-Century Children's Writers. 3rd ed. Edited by Tracy Chevalier and D. L. Kirkpatrick. Chicago: St. James, 1989, pp. 810–811.

Rayner, Mary (Yorna, née Grigson)

Fifth Book of Junior Authors and Illustrators. Edited by Sally Holmes Holtze. New York: Wilson, 1983, pp. 254–255.

Rayner, William. "About *Stag Boy.*" *School Bookshop News* (U.K.) 5 (Autumn 1976): 23–24.

————. "A Reading Spree That Lasted for Years." *Federation of Children's Book Groups Yearbook* (U.K.) 9 (1977–1978): 54.

Twentieth-Century Children's Writers. 3rd ed. Edited by Tracy Chevalier and D. L. Kirkpatrick. Chicago: St. James, 1989, p. 811.

Reeves, James (pseud. of John Morris Reeves)

Butts, Dennis. "James Reeves: The Truthful Poet." *Junior Bookshelf* 30 (Dec 1966): 358–363.

Hutton, M. "Writers for Children: James Reeves." *School Librarian* 14 (July 1966): 139–146.

The Oxford Companion to Children's Literature. Edited by Humphrey Carpenter and Mari Prichard. New York: Oxford Univ. Press, 1984, pp. 445–446.

Robbins, Sidney. "Interpreting in Sharing—James Reeves: *The Cold Flame.*" *Children's Literature in Education* 2 (July 1970): 7–14.

Third Book of Junior Authors. Edited by Doris De Montreville and Donna Hill. New York: Wilson, 1972, pp. 240–241.

Twentieth-Century Children's Writers. 3rd ed. Edited by Tracy Chevalier and D. L. Kirkpatrick. Chicago: St. James, 1989, pp. 816–819.

Reid Banks, Lynne

Gillespie, John T. *Juniorplots 4: A Book Talk Guide for Use with Readers Ages 12–16.* New Providence, NJ: Bowker, 1993, pp. 131–134.

Moore, Opal, and Donnarae McCann. "On 'Reading' Institutions." *Children's Literature Association Quarterly* 13, no. 4 (1989): 198–200.

Nettell, Stephanie. "Authorgraph no. 67: Lynne Reid Banks." *Books for Keeps* (U.K.) 67 (1991): 12–13.

Rustin, Michael. "The Maternal Capacities of a Small Boy: *The Indian in the Cupboard.*" In Margaret Rustin and Michael Rustin, *Narratives of Love and Loss: Studies in Modern Children's Fiction.* London: Verso, 1987; New York: Routledge, 1988, pp. 104–118.

Sixth Book of Junior Authors and Illustrators. Edited by Sally Holmes Holtze. New York: Wilson, 1989, pp. 22–24.

Smith, A. "Lynne Reid Banks." *Publishers Weekly* 236 (Oct 27, 1989): 30+.

Twentieth-Century Children's Writers. 3rd ed. Edited by Tracy Chevalier and D. L. Kirkpatrick. Chicago: St. James, 1989, pp. 56–58.

Renault, Mary

Sweetman, David. *Mary Renault: A Biography.* New York: Harcourt, 1993.

Rhys, Mimpsy

Sadler, David. "Innocent Hearts: The Child Authors of the 1920's." *Children's Literature Association Quarterly* 17 (Winter 1992–1993): 24–30.

Seaman, Louise H. "Mimpsy Rhys." *Horn Book* 5 (Nov 1929): 95–99.

Richler, Mordecai

Fisher, Margery. "An Old Favourite: Mordecai Richler's *Jacob-Two-Two and the Dinosaur.*" *Growing Point* 27 (Mar 1989): 5118–5119.

Nodelman, Perry. "*Jacob Two-Two* and the Satisfactions of Paranoia." *Canadian Children's Literature* 15–16 (1980): 31–37.

Parr, John. "Richler Rejuvenated." *Canadian Children's Literature* 1 (Autumn 1975): 96–102.

Richler, Mordecai. "Writing *Jacob Two-Two.*" *Canadian Children's Literature* 78 (Autumn 1978): 6–8.

Stott, Jon C. "Midsummer Night's Dreams: Fantasy and Self-Realization in Children's Fiction." *The Lion and the Unicorn* 1, no. 2 (Fall 1977): 25–39.

Ridley, Philip

Mappin, Alf. "Using *Krindlekrax* to Examine Narrative in Various Forms." *Literature Base* (Australia) 4 (June 1993): 23–26.

Rinkoff, Barbara (Jean)

Helbig, Alethea K., and Agnes Regan Perkins. *Dictionary of American Children's Fiction, 1960–1984.* Westport, CT: Greenwood, 1986, p. 554.

Robbins, Ruth

Third Book of Junior Authors. Edited by Doris De Montreville and Donna Hill. New York: Wilson, 1972, pp. 241–242.

Roberts, Keith (John Kingston)

Hurst, L. J. "A Timeless Dance: Keith Roberts' *Pavane* Re-Examined." *Vector* 124/125 (1985): 17–19.
Kincaid, Paul. "A Mosaic of Worlds." *Vector* 132 (1986): 2–5.
Peek, Bernie. "Exercises in Landscape: An Overview of the Work of Keith Roberts." *Vector* 132 (1986): 12–13.
Roberts, Keith. "The Chalk Giant." *Vector* 132 (1986): 6–8.

Robinson, Joan (Mary) G(ale Thomas)

Crouch, Marcus. *The Nesbit Tradition.* London: Benn, 1972, pp. 208–210.
Doyle, Brian. *The Who's Who of Children's Literature.* New York: Schocken, 1968, pp. 234–235.
Twentieth-Century Children's Writers. 3rd ed. Edited by Tracy Chevalier and D. L. Kirkpatrick. Chicago: St. James, 1989, pp. 833–834.

Rodda, Emily (pseud. of Jennifer Rowe)

Jameyson, Karen. "News from Down Under." *Horn Book* 69 (Nov–Dec 1993): 778–780.
"Know the Author: Emily Rodda." *Magpies* (Australia) 5, no. 3 (July 1990): 19–21.

Rodgers (Guettel), Mary

Fifth Book of Junior Authors and Illustrators. Edited by Sally Holmes Holtze. New York: Wilson, 1983, pp. 267–269.
Gillespie, John T. *More Juniorplots: A Guide for Teachers and Librarians.* New York: Bowker, 1977, pp. 19–21.
Helbig, Alethea K., and Agnes Regan Perkins. *Dictionary of American Children's Fiction, 1960–1984.* Westport, CT: Greenwood, 1986, pp. 53–54, 223–224, 558–559.
Hopkins, Lee Bennett. "*Freaky Friday* from Book to Film." *Teacher* 95 (Oct 1977): 80–82.
Kaye, M. J. "Mary Rodgers: An Interview." *Top of the News* 40 (Winter 1984): 155–162.
Rogers, S. "It's Only a Game . . . or Is It?" *School Library Journal* 38 (Mar 1992): 176–177.
Twentieth-Century Children's Writers. 3rd ed. Edited by Tracy Chevalier and D. L. Kirkpatrick. Chicago: St. James, 1989, pp. 836–837.

Rodowsky, Colby

Sixth Book of Junior Authors and Illustrators. Edited by Sally Holmes Holtze. New York: Wilson, 1989, pp. 245–246.

Rounds, Glen (Harold)

Bader, Barbara. *American Picturebooks from Noah's Ark to the Beast Within.* New York: Macmillan, 1976, pp. 147–151.

Freeman, Russell. "Glen Rounds and Holiday House." *Horn Book* 61 (Mar–Apr 1985): 222–225.

The Junior Book of Authors. 2nd ed. rev. Edited by Stanley J. Kunitz and Howard Haycraft. New York: Wilson, 1951, pp. 261–262.

Twentieth-Century Children's Writers. 3rd ed. Edited by Tracy Chevalier and D. L. Kirkpatrick. Chicago: St. James, 1989, pp. 843–844.

Rubinstein, Gillian

Foster, John. "'Your Part in This Adventure Is Over. You Have Lost': Gillian Rubinstein's Novels for Older Readers." *Children's Literature in Education* 22 (June 1991): 121–127.

Jackson, Adrian. "May We Recommend . . . Gillian Rubinstein." *Books for Keeps* (U.K.) 66 (Jan 1991): 17.

Kroll, Jeri. "The Hazards of Fame: Gillian Rubenstein Talks to Jeri Kroll." *Southerly* (Australia) 4 (1990): 457–459.

Mappin, Alf. "Know the Author: Gillian Rubinstein." *Magpies* (Australia) 4 (June 1989): 18–20.

Mills, Alice. "Dancing *The Labyrinth*: Gillian Rubinstein's Game-Players." *Papers* (Australia) 2 (Apr 1991): 24–29.

Rubinstein, Gillian. "Beyond the Labyrinth." *Reading Time* (Australia) 34, no. 2(1990): 5–6.

———. "A Hero Is a Man. . . .???" *Magpies* (Australia) 8 (May 1993): 5–9.

———. "The World According to Kids." *Island Magazine* (Tasmania) 40 (Spring 1989): 7–10.

Rushdie, Salman

Isaksson, Britt. "*The Sea of Stories* and the Shadow Warriors." *Bookbird* 31, no. 2 (1993): 6–7.

Ruskin, John

Birch, Dinah. *Ruskin's Myths.* Oxford: Oxford Univ. Press, 1988.

Burns, Marjorie Jean. "The Anonymous Fairy Tale: Ruskin's *King of the Golden River.*" *Mythlore* 53 (1988): 38–47.

———. "Victorian Fantasists from Ruskin to Lang: A Study in Ambivalence." Ph.D. diss., University of California, Berkeley, 1978.

Butler, Francelia. "From Fantasy to Reality: Ruskin's *King of the Golden River,* St. George's Guild and Ruskin, Tennessee." In *Children's Literature,* vol. 1. Storrs, CT: Journal of the Modern Language Association, 1972, pp. 62–73.

Cate, George Allan. *John Ruskin: A Reference Guide.* Boston: Hall, 1988.

Coyle, William. "Ruskin's *King of the Golden River:* A Victorian Fairy Tale." In *The Scope of the Fantastic—Culture, Biography, Themes, Children's Literature.* Edited by Robert A. Collins and Howard D. Pearce. Westport, CT: Greenwood, 1985, pp. 85–90.

Doyle, Brian. *The Who's Who of Children's Literature.* New York: Schocken, 1968, pp. 235–236.

Filstrup, James Merrill. "Thirst for Enchanted Views in Ruskin's *The King of the Golden River.*" In *Children's Literature,* vol. 8. New Haven, CT: Yale Univ. Press, 1980, pp. 68–79.

Frey, Charles, and John Griffiths. *The Literary Heritage of Childhood: An Appraisal of Children's Classics in the Western Tradition.* Westport, CT: Greenwood, 1987, pp. 81–86.

Hearn, Michael Patrick. "Mr. Ruskin and Miss Greenaway." *Children's Literature* 8 (1980): 22–34. Reprinted in *Reflections on Literature for Children.* Edited by Francelia Butler and Richard Rotert. Hamden, CT: Shoe String Press, 1984, pp. 182–190.

Helson, Ravenna, and Alf Proysen. "The Psychological Origins of Fantasy for Children in Mid-Victorian England." *Children's Literature,* vol. 3. Storrs, CT: Journal of the Modern Language Association, 1974, pp. 67–76.

Knoepflmacher, U. C. "The Return to Childhood through Fairy Tale in Ruskin's *King of the Golden River.*" In *Children's Literature,* vol. 13. New Haven, CT: Yale Univ. Press, 1985, pp. 3–30.

Landow, George P. "And the World Became Strange: Realms of Literary Fantasy." In Diane L. Johnson. *Fantastic Illustration and Design in Britain, 1850–1930.* Providence: Rhode Island School of Design, 1979, pp. 9–43. Reprinted in *Georgia Review* 33 (Spring 1979): 7–42.

———. "The King of the Golden River." In *Survey of Modern Fantasy Literature,* vol. 2. Edited by Frank N. Magill. Englewood Cliffs, NJ: Salem Press, 1983, pp. 852–854.

Leland, Lowell P. "John Ruskin." In *Writers for Children: Critical Studies of Major Authors Since the Seventeenth Century.* Edited by Jane M. Bingham. New York: Scribner, 1988, pp. 493–496.

Michalson, Karen Ann. "Victorian Fantasy Literature and the Politics of Canon-Making." Ph.D. diss., University of Massachusetts, 1990. Discusses Ruskin, MacDonald, Kingsley, Haggard, and Kipling.

Miller, Patricia. "The Importance of Being Earnest: The Fairy Tale in 19th Century England." *Children's Literature Association Quarterly* 7 (Summer 1982): 11–14.

The Oxford Companion to Children's Literature. Edited by Humphrey Carpenter and Mari Prichard. New York: Oxford Univ. Press, 1984, pp. 293–294, 464.

Ruskin, John. "Fairy Land: Mrs. Allingham and Kate Greenaway." In *The Library Edition of the Works of John Ruskin,* vol. 53. Edited by E. T. Cook and Alexander Wedderburn. London: Longman, 1903–1912, pp. 327–349.

———. "Fairy Stories." In *The Library Edition of the Works of Ruskin,* vol. 19. Edited by E. T. Cook and Alexander Wedderburn. London: Longman, 1903–1912, pp. 233–239. Reprinted in *Signal* 8 (May 1972): 81–86, ed. by Lance Salway; Lance Salway. *A Peculiar Gift.* Harmondsworth, Middlesex: Kestrel, 1976, pp. 127–132; *Masterworks of Children's Literature,* vol. 6. New York: Stonehill/Chelsea House, 1984, pp. 163–169.

———. "The King of the Golden River; or The Black Brothers." In *Masterworks of Children's Literature,* vol. 6. New York: Stonehill/Chelsea House, 1984, pp. 1–25.

———. "Praeterita." In *The Library Edition of the Works of John Ruskin,* vol. 35. Edited by E. T. Cook and Alexander Wedderburn. London: Longman, 1903–1912.

Susina, Jan Christopher. "Victorian Kunstmärcher: A Study in Children's Literature, 1840–1875." Ph.D. diss., Indiana University, 1986.

Saberhagen, Fred (Thomas)

Twentieth-Century Science Fiction Writers. 3rd ed. Edited by Noelle Watson and Paul E. Schellinger. Chicago: St. James Press, 1991, pp. 683–684.

Wilgus, Neal. "An Interview with Fred Saberhagen." *Science Fiction Review* 35 (1980): 15–16.

Saint-Exupéry, Antoine (Jean Baptiste Marie Roger), de

Arnold, James W. "Musical Fantasy: *The Little Prince*." In *Shadows of the Magic Lamp: Fantasy and Science Fiction in Film.* Edited by George Slusser and Eric S. Rabkin. Carbondale: Southern Illinois Univ. Press, 1985.

Brand, Patricia Petrus. "The Modern French Fairy Tale: Aspects of 'Le Merveilleux' in Aymé, Supervielle, Saint-Exupéry and Sabatier." Ph.D. diss., University of Colorado at Boulder, 1983.

Breaux, Adele. *Saint-Exupéry in America, 1942–1943: A Memoir.* Rutherford, NJ: Fairleigh Dickinson Univ. Press, 1971.

Cate, Curtis. *Antoine de Saint-Exupéry: His Life and Times.* New York: G. P. Putnam, 1970.

Dodd, Anne W. "*The Little Prince:* A Study for Seventh Grade in Interpretation of Literature." *Elementary English* 46 (Oct 1969): 772–776.

Fourth Book of Junior Authors and Illustrators. Edited by Doris De Montreville and Elizabeth D. Crawford. New York: Wilson, 1978, pp. 300–302.

Gagnon, Laurence. "Webs of Concern: Heidegger, *The Little Prince,* and *Charlotte's Web.*" In *Children's Literature,* vol. 2. Storrs, CT: Journal of the Modern Language Association, 1973, pp. 61–66.

Harris, John R. "The Elusive Act of Faith: Saint-Exupéry's Sacrifice to an Unknown God." *Christianity and Literature* 39 (Winter 1990): 50–52.

Higgins, James Edward. "Five Authors of Mystical Fancy for Children: A Critical Study." Ed.D. diss., Columbia University, 1965.

———. "*The Little Prince:* A Legacy." *Elementary English* 37 (Dec 1960): 514–515, 572.

Hürlimann, Bettina. "*The Little Prince* from Outer Space: An Attempt to Describe Antoine de Saint-Exupéry's *Le Petit Prince.*" In *Three Centuries of Children's Books in Europe.* Cleveland: World, 1968, pp. 93–98.

Kaminskas, Jurate. "Sur les Traces du *Petit Prince.*" *Canadian Children's Literature* 37 (1985): 29–33.

Mooney, Philip. "*The Little Prince,* a Story for Our Time." *America* 121 (Dec 20, 1969): 610–611, 614.

Murison, D. M. "*The Little Prince* as a Child's Book: A Child's View." *Australian School Librarian* 14 (Mar 1977): 10–13.

The Oxford Companion to Children's Literature. Edited by Humphrey Carpenter and Mari Prichard. New York: Oxford Univ. Press, 1984, pp. 318–319.

Robinson, Joy D. Marie. *Antoine de Saint-Exupéry.* Boston: Twayne, 1984.

Smith, Louisa A. "*The Little Prince.*" In *Survey of Modern Fantasy Literature,* vol. 2. Edited by Frank N. Magill. Englewood Cliffs, NJ: Salem Press, 1983, pp. 891–893.

Salmonson, Jessica Amanda

Salmonson, Jessica Amanda. "Ethics and Editing: Altering Manuscripts." *Bulletin of the Science Fiction Writers of America* 94 (1986): 4–7.

Sánchez-Silva, José Mariá

Hürlimann, Bettina. *Three Centuries of Children's Books in Europe.* Cleveland: World, 1968, pp. 86–87.

Third Book of Junior Authors. Edited by Doris De Montreville and Donna Hill. New York: Wilson, 1972, pp. 244–246.

Sandburg, Carl (August)

Callahan, North. *Carl Sandburg: His Life and Works.* University Park: Penn State Univ. Press, 1987.

Lynn, Joanne L. "Hyacinths and Biscuits in the Village of Liver and Onions: Sandburg's *Rootabaga Stories.*" In *Children's Literature,* vol. 8. New Haven, CT: Yale Univ. Press, 1980, pp. 118–132.

Massee, May. "Carl Sandburg as a Writer for Children." *Elementary English Review* 5 (Feb 1928): 40–42.

Mitgang, Herbert, ed. *The Letters of Carl Sandburg.* New York: Harcourt Brace Jovanovich, 1968.

Niven, Penelope. *Carl Sandburg: A Biography.* Champaign: Univ. of Illinois Press, 1994.

The Oxford Companion to Children's Literature. Edited by Humphrey Carpenter and Mari Prichard. New York: Oxford Univ. Press, 1984, p. 460.

Perkins, Agnes Regan. "Carl Sandburg." In *Writers for Children: Critical Studies of Major Authors Since the Seventeenth Century.* Edited by Jane M. Bingham. New York: Scribner, 1988, pp. 503–510.

Sandburg, Carl. *Always the Young Strangers.* New York: Harcourt Brace Jovanovich, 1952.

Sayers, Frances Clark. "Rootabaga Processional." *Horn Book* 8 (May 1932): 124–130.

Sargent, Pamela

Morrissey, J. J. "Pamela Sargent's Science Fiction for Young Adults: Celebrations of Change." *Science-Fiction Studies* 16 (July 1989): 184–190.

Sixth Book of Junior Authors and Illustrators. Edited by Sally Holmes Holtze. New York: Wilson, 1989, pp. 264–265.

Twentieth-Century Children's Writers. 3rd ed. Edited by Tracy Chevalier and D. L. Kirkpatrick. Chicago: St. James, 1989, pp. 850–851.

Sauer, Julia L(ina)

Elleman, Barbara. "A Second Look: *Fog Magic.*" *Horn Book* 56 (Oct 1980): 548–551.

Helbig, Alethea K., and Agnes Regan Perkins. *Dictionary of American Children's Fiction, 1859–1959.* Westport, CT: Greenwood, 1985, pp. 166, 454.

More Junior Authors. Edited by Muriel Fuller. New York: Wilson, 1963, pp. 174–175.

Roginski, Jim, ed. *Newbery and Caldecott Medalists and Honor Book Winners.* Littleton, CO: Libraries Unlimited, 1982, p. 224.

Sauer, Julia L. "Making the World Safe for the Janey Larkins." In Robinson. *Readings about Children's Literature.* New York: McKay, 1966, pp. 318–327.

———. "So Close to the Gulls." *Horn Book* 25 (Sept–Oct 1949): 361–369.

Twentieth-Century Children's Writers. 3rd ed. Edited by Tracy Chevalier and D. L. Kirkpatrick. Chicago: St. James, 1989, pp. 851–852.

Sawyer (Durand), Ruth

Cecile, Mother Mary, S. H. C. J. "Regina Medal Presentation." *Horn Book* 41 (Oct 1965): 477.

Gilbertson, Irvyn. "Ruth Sawyer, Storyteller." *The Dragon Lode* 10 (Summer 1992): 1–2.

Haviland, Virginia. *Ruth Sawyer.* New York: Walck, 1985.

Helbig, Alethea K. "Ruth Sawyer." In *Writers for Children: Critical Studies of Major Authors Since the Seventeenth Century.* Edited by Jane M. Bingham. New York: Scribner, 1988, pp. 511–518.

Helbig, Alethea K., and Agnes Regan Perkins. *Dictionary of American Children's Fiction, 1859–1959.* Westport, CT: Greenwood, 1985, pp. 148, 454–455.

Horn Book 41 (Oct 1965): 463, 474–486. Special issue.

Jewett, E. "Ruth Sawyer Durand." *Catholic Library World* 36 (Feb 1965): 355–357.

The Junior Book of Authors. 2nd ed. rev. Edited by Stanley J. Kunitz and Howard Haycraft. New York: Wilson, 1951, pp. 266–267.

McCloskey, Margaret Durand. "Our Fair Lady!" *Horn Book* 41 (Oct 1965): 481–486.

Moore, Anne Carroll. "Ruth Sawyer, Storyteller." *Horn Book* 12 (Jan 1936): 34–38.

Mulholland, Marion J. "Ruth Sawyer." In Cech. *American Writers for Children, 1900–1960. Dictionary of Literary Biography,* vol. 22. Detroit: Gale, 1983, pp. 294–298.

Newbery Medal Books: 1922–1955. Edited by Bertha Mahony Miller and Elinor Whitney Field. Boston: Horn Book, 1957, pp. 145–156.

Overton, Jacqueline. *"This Way to Christmas* with Ruth Sawyer." *Horn Book* 20 (Nov–Dec 1944): 447–460.

The Oxford Companion to Children's Literature. Edited by Humphrey Carpenter and Mari Prichard. New York: Oxford Univ. Press, 1984, p. 469.

Robinson, Beryl Y. "Editorial: Ruth Sawyer, 1880–1970." *Horn Book* 46 (Aug 1970): 347.

———. "To Ruth Sawyer." *Horn Book* 41 (Oct 1965): 478–480.

Roginski, Jim, ed. *Newbery and Caldecott Medalists and Honor Book Winners.* Littleton, CO: Libraries Unlimited, 1982, pp. 224–226.

"Ruth Sawyer Durand: A Checklist of Her *Horn Book* Articles, Editorials, Stories, and Poems; Articles and Editorials About Her." *Horn Book* 46 (Aug 1970): 431.

Sawyer, Ruth. "Editorial: The Miracle of the Story Hour." *Horn Book* 34 (Feb 1958): 15.

———. "The Laura Ingalls Wilder Award Acceptance." *Horn Book* 41 (Oct 1965): 474–476.

———. "Newbery Medal Acceptance." *Horn Book* 13 (Sept 1937): 251–255.

———. "On Reading the Bible Aloud." *Horn Book* 21 (Mar–Apr 1945): 99–107.

———. "Remarks Upon Receiving the Newbery Award." *ALA Bulletin* 31 (Oct 15, 1937): 872–874.

———. "Sharers of a Heritage." *Catholic Library World* 37 (Sept 1965): 15–17. Regina Award Acceptance Speech.

———. "Wee Meg Barnileg and the Fairies." *Horn Book* 15 (Sept 1939): 310–318.

Sullivan, Frances. "The Laura Ingalls Wilder Award Presentation." *Horn Book* 41 (Oct 1965): 474.

Sullivan, Sheila R. "Fairy Gold in a Storyteller's Yarns." *Elementary English* 35 (Dec 1958): 502–507.

Twentieth-Century Children's Writers. 3rd ed. Edited by Tracy Chevalier and D. L. Kirkpatrick. Chicago: St. James, 1989, pp. 853–855.

Viguers, Ruth Hill. "Editorial: For Ruth Sawyer." *Horn Book* 37 (Dec 1961): 521.

Sayers, Frances Clarke

Cameron, Eleanor. "The Inimitable Frances." *Horn Book* 67 (Mar–Apr 1991): 180–185.

Heins, Ethel L. "Frances Clarke Sayers: A Legacy." *Horn Book* 66 (Jan–Feb 1990): 31–35.

Helbig, Alethea K., and Agnes Regan Perkins. *Dictionary of American Children's Fiction, 1859–1959.* Westport, CT: Greenwood, 1985, pp. 362–363, 455.

The Junior Book of Authors. 2nd ed. rev. Edited by Stanley J. Kunitz and Howard Haycraft. New York: Wilson, 1951, pp. 267–268.

Sayers, Frances Clarke. "Of Memory and Muchness." *Horn Book* 20 (May 1944): 153–163.

———. "A Skimming of Memory." *Horn Book* 52 (June 1976): 270–275.

———. "A Time to Begin." *Horn Book* 50 (Dec 1974): 674–678.

———. "Walt Disney Accused: An Interview with Frances Clarke Sayers." *Horn Book* 41 (Dec 1965): 602–611.

————. "'You Elegant Fowl': A Reproduction of Frances Clarke Sayers's Last Speech." *Horn Book* 65 (Nov–Dec 1989): 748–749.

Scarborough, Elizabeth Ann

Sullivan, C. W., III. "Traditional Ballads and Modern Children's Fantasy: Some Comments on Structure and Intent." *Children's Literature Association Quarterly* 11 (Fall 1986): 145–147.

Schlein, Miriam

More Junior Authors. Edited by Muriel Fuller. New York: Wilson, 1963, pp. 175–176.

Schrank, Joseph

Ward, Martha E., and Dorothy A. Marquardt. *Authors of Books for Young People.* 2nd ed. Metuchen, NJ: Scarecrow Press, 1971, pp. 455–456.

Scieszka, Jon

Bernstock, N. K. "The Wolf on Trial." *School Library Journal* 39 (Sept 1993): 166.

Raymond, A. "Jon Scieszka: Telling the *True* Story." *Teaching Pre K–8* 22 (May 1992): 38–40.

Smith, A. "*PW* Interviews: Jon Scieszka and Lane Smith, Author/Illustrator Duo." *Publishers Weekly* 238 (July 26, 1991): 220–221.

Thomas, Rebecca L. *Primaryplots 2: A Book Talk Guide for Use with Readers Ages 4–8.* New Providence, NJ: Bowker, 1993. pp. 327–329.

Sefton, Catherine (pseud. of Martin Waddell)

"Authorgraph No. 48—Martin Waddell." *Books for Keeps* (U.K.) (Jan 1988): 12–13.

Gough, John. "Meet Martin Waddell." *Magpies* (Australia) 5 (Nov 1990): 10–13.

Twentieth-Century Children's Writers. 3rd ed. Edited by Tracy Chevalier and D. L. Kirkpatrick. Chicago: St. James, 1989, pp. 1006–1008.

Waddell, Martin. "Catherine Sefton alias Martin Waddell." *Puffin Post* (U.K.) 12, no. 1 (1978): 12–14.

Sègur, Comtesse de (née Rostopchine)

Aiken, Joan. "The Comtesse de Sègur: 1799–1874." *Horn Book* 52 (Dec 1976): 583–600.

Andersen, Ida Anine. "La Grande et la Petite Sophie: Une Approche de la Comtesse de Sègur, née Rostopchine." *(Pre)Publications* 15 (Mar 1989): 3–39.

Beaussant, Claudine. *La Comtesse de Sègur ou L'Enfance de l'Art.* Paris: Laffont, 1988.

Bluche, Francios. *Le Petit Monde de la Comtesse de Sègur.* Paris: Hachette, 1988.

Doray, Marie-France. "Cleanliness and Class in the Countess de Sègur's Novels." *Children's Literature* 17 (1989): 64–80.

————. "Ramoramor et la Comtesse de Sègur." *Notre Librairie* 90 (1987): 79–81.

Lac, Christine Marie Andrée. "A Comparative Study of Louisa May Alcott and Sophie de Sègur (Rostopchine)." Ph.D. diss., University of Nebraska at Lincoln, 1988.

Lastinger, Valerie C. "Of Dolls and Girls in Nineteenth-Century France." *Children's Literature 21.* New Haven: Yale Univ. Press, 1993 pp. 20–42.

Petrini, E. "Countess of Sègur." *Bookbird* 12, no. 3 (1974): 50–51.

Selden (Thompson), George

Fourth Book of Junior Authors and Illustrators. Edited by Doris De Montreville and Elizabeth D. Crawford. New York: Wilson, 1978, pp. 313–314.

Helbig, Alethea K., and Agnes Regan Perkins. *Dictionary of American Children's Fiction, 1960–1984.* Westport, CT: Greenwood, 1986, pp. 134, 233, 586–587, 679–680.

Hopkins, Lee Bennett. "George Selden." In *More Books by More People.* New York: Citation Press, 1974, pp. 303–307.

Potts, Lesley S. "George Selden." In *American Writers for Children since 1960: Fiction. Dictionary of Literary Biography,* vol. 52. Detroit: Gale, 1986, pp. 325–333.

Twentieth-Century Children's Writers. 3rd ed. Edited by Tracy Chevalier and D. L. Kirkpatrick. Chicago: St. James, 1989, pp. 867–868.

Sendak, Maurice (Bernard)

Alderson, Brian. "Maurice Before Max: The Yonder Side of the See-Saw." *Horn Book* 69 (May–June 1993): 291–295.

Bell, Anthea. "An Affectionate Analysis of *Higglety Pigglety Pop!*" *Horn Book* 44 (Apr 1968): 151–154.

Bodmer, George R. "Sendak into Opera: *Wild Things* and *Higglety Pigglety Pop!*" *The Lion and the Unicorn* 16 (Dec 1992): 167–175.

Braun, Saul. "Sendak Raises the Shade on Childhood." *New York Times Magazine,* June 7, 1970, p. 34.

Brenner, C., and Brian Alderson. "Are You Still Sitting Comfortably?" *Times Saturday Review* (May 2, 1992): 30–31.

Cech, John. "Maurice Sendak: Off the Page." *Horn Book* 62 (May–June, 1986): 305–313.

Chambers, Aidan. "Letter from England: Sendak on Show." *Horn Book* 52 (June 1976): 323–326.

Cott, Jonathan. "Maurice Sendak: King of All the Wild Things." In *Pipers at the Gates of Dawn.* New York: Random, 1983, pp. 41–87. Revised version of an interview in *Rolling Stone* 229 (Dec 30, 1976): 55, 59.

De Luca, Geraldine. "Exploring the Levels of Childhood: The Allegorical Sensibility of Maurice Sendak." In *Children's Literature,* vol. 12. New Haven: Yale Univ. Press, 1984, pp. 3–24.

———. "Progression Through Contraries: The Triumphs of the Spirit in the Work of Maurice Sendak." In *Triumphs of the Spirit in Children's Literature.* Edited by Francelia Butler and Richard Rotert. Hamden, CT: Shoe String Press, 1986, pp. 142–149.

Devereaux, E. "In the Studio with Maurice Sendak." *Publishers Weekly* 240 (Nov 1, 1993): 28–29.

Dohm, J. H. "Twentieth Century Illustrators: Maurice Sendak." *Junior Bookshelf* 30 (Apr 1966): 103–111.

Dooley, Patricia. "'Fantasy Is the Core . . . ?'—Sendak." *Children's Literature Association Quarterly Newsletter* 1 (Autumn 1976): 1–4.

Ford, Roger H. "'Let the Wild Rumpus Start!'" *Language Arts* 56, 4 (Apr 1979): 386–393.

Galvin, Dallas. "Maurice Sendak Observes Children's Literature." *Harper's Bazaar* 106 (Dec 1972): 102–103.

Gilead, S. "Magic Abjured: Closure in Children's Fantasy Fiction." *Publications of the Modern Language Association* 106 (Mar 1991): 277–293.

Griffin-Beale, Christopher. "In Search of *The Wild Things'* Pedigree." *Times Educational Supplement* (London), Jan 30, 1976, pp. 44–45.

Harris, Muriel. "Impressions of Sendak." *Elementary English* 48, no. 7 (Nov 1971): 825–832.

Haviland, Virginia, and Maurice Sendak. "Questions to an Artist Who Is Also an Author." *Quarterly Journal of the Library of Congress* 28 (Oct 1971): 263–280. Reprinted, in part, in Miriam Hoffman and Eva Samuels. *Authors and Illustrators of Children's Books.* New York: Bowker, 1972, pp. 364–377; Reprinted in *The Openhearted Audience.* Washington DC: The Library of Congress, 1980, pp. 25–46.

Hentoff, Nat. "Among the Wild Things." *New Yorker* 41 (Jan 22, 1966): 39–40ff. Reprinted in Egoff. *Only Connect.* 1st ed. New York: Oxford Univ. Press, 1969, pp. 323–345.

Hopkins, Lee Bennett. "Maurice Sendak." In *Books Are by People.* New York: Citation Press, 1969, pp. 250–254.

Hürlimann, Benita. "Maurice Sendak." *Graphis* 25 (1969–1970): 252–263ff.

Knoepflmacher, U. C. "Roads Half Taken: Travel, Fantasy and Growing Up." *Proceedings of the 13th Annual Conference of The Children's Literature Association, 1986.* New York: Pace University, 1988, pp. 48–59.

Lanes, Selma G. *The Art of Maurice Sendak.* New York: Abrams, 1980.

———. "The Art of Maurice Sendak: A Diversity of Influences Inform an Art for Children." *Artforum* 9 (May 1971): 70–73.

———. "Sendak at Fifty." *New York Times Book Review,* Apr 29, 1979, pp. 23, 48–49.

Lystad, Mary. "Taming the Wild Things." *Christianity Today* 18 (Mar–Apr 1989): 16–19.

"Maurice Sendak: Doctor of Fine Arts." *Horn Book* 60 (Aug 1984): 515.

May, Jill P. "Sendak's American Hero." *Journal of Popular Culture* 12 (1978): 30–35.

More Junior Authors. Edited by Muriel Fuller. New York: Wilson, 1963, pp. 181–182.

Newbery and Caldecott Medal Books: 1966–1975. Edited by Lee Kingman. Boston: Horn Book, 1975, pp. 246–257.

Nordstrom, Ursula. "Maurice Sendak." *Library Journal* 89 (Mar 15, 1964): 92–94.

O'Doherty, B. "Portrait of the Artist as a Young Alchemist." *New York Times Book Review,* sect. VII, pt. 2, May 12, 1963, p. 3.

Otten, Charlotte F. "An Interview with Maurice Sendak." In *The Voice of the Narrator in Children's Literature: Insights from Writers and Critics,* ed. by Charlotte F. Otten and Gary D. Schmidt. New York: Greenwood, 1989. Reprinted in *Signal* 68 (May 1992): 110–127.

The Oxford Companion to Children's Literature. Edited by Humphrey Carpenter and Mari Prichard. New York: Oxford Univ. Press, 1984, pp. 474–477.

Perrot, Jean. "Maurice Sendak's Ritual Cooking of the Children in Three Tableaux: The Moon, Mother, and Music." *Children's Literature* 18 (1990): 68–86.

Rees, David. "King of Wild Things." *San Jose Studies* 14 (1988): 96–107.

Rochman, Hazel. "The *Booklist* Interview: Maurice Sendak." *Booklist* 88 (June 15, 1992): 1848–1849.

Roginski, Jim, ed. *Newbery and Caldecott Medalists and Honor Book Winners.* Littleton, CO: Libraries Unlimited, 1982, pp. 228–231.

Sadler, Glenn Edward. "Maurice Sendak and Dr. Seuss: A Conversation." *Horn Book* 65 (Sept–Oct 1989): 582–588.

Sendak, Maurice. "[Hans Christian Andersen Award] Acceptance Speech." *Bookbird* 8, no. 2 (1970): 6–7; *Times Literary Supplement,* July 2, 1970, p. 709.

———. *Caldecott & Co.: Notes on Books and Pictures.* New York: Farrar, 1988.

———. "Caldecott Award Acceptance." *Horn Book* 40 (Aug 1964): 345–351.

———. "Enamored of the Mystery." In *Innocence & Experience.* Edited by Barbara Harrison and Gregory Maguire. New York: Lothrop, 1986, pp. 362–374.

———. "Frightened into Being an Artist." *Books for Keeps* (U.K.) 56 (1989): 4–6.

———. "I Don't Write Children's Books—I Just Know What Is in My Head." *Yale Alumni Review* 36 (May 1972).

————. "Maurice Sendak's Narative Images." In *The Voice of the Narrator in Children's Literature: Insights from Writers and Critics,* ed. by Charlotte F. Otten and Gary D. Schmidt. New York: Greenwood, 1989, pp. 7–24.

————. "1983 Laura Ingalls Wilder Award Acceptance Speech." *Top of the News* 39 (Summer 1983): 367–369; *Horn Book* 59 (Aug 1983): 474–477.

————. "On the Importance of Imagination." *Claremont Reading Conference Yearbook* 29 (1965): 53–58.

————. "The Shape of Music." *New York Herald Tribune.* "Book Week Fall Children's Issue." Nov 1, 1964, p. 1.

————. "Visitors from My Boyhood." In *Worlds of Childhood,* ed. by William Zinsser. Boston: Houghton, 1990, pp. 47–70.

Sendak, Maurice, and Virginia Haviland. "Questions to an Artist Who Is Also an Author." *Quarterly Journal of the Library of Congress* 28 (Oct 1971): 263–280. Reprinted in *The Openhearted Audience.* Washington, DC: Library of Congress, 1980, pp. 25–46.

Shaw, Spencer G. "Laura Ingalls Wilder Award Presentation." *Horn Book* 59 (Aug 1983): 471–473.

Sonheim, Amy. *Maurice Sendak.* Boston: Twayne, 1991.

Steig, Michael. "Reading *Outside Over There.*" *Children's Literature,* vol. 13. New Haven, CT: Yale Univ. Press, 1985, pp. 139–153.

Stott, Jon C. *Children's Literature from A to Z.* New York: McGraw-Hill, 1984, p. 246.

————. "The Nature of Fantasy: A Conversation with Ruth Nichols, Susan Cooper, and Maurice Sendak." *World of Children's Books* 3, no. 2 (Fall 1978): 32–43.

Taylor, Mary-Agnes. "In Defense of *The Wild Things.*" *Horn Book* 46 (Dec 1970): 642–646.

————. "Which Way to Castle Yonder?" *Children's Literature Association Quarterly* 12 (Fall 1987): 142–144. Discusses *Higglety Pigglety Pop!*

Twentieth-Century Children's Writers. 3rd ed. Edited by Tracy Chevalier and D. L. Kirkpatrick. Chicago: St. James, 1989, pp. 868–870.

Waller, Jennifer R. "Maurice Sendak and the Blakean Vision of Childhood." In *Children's Literature,* vol. 6. Philadelphia: Temple Univ. Press, 1977, pp. 130–140. Reprinted in Reflections on Literature for Children. Edited by Francelia Butler and Richard Rotert. Hamden, CT: Shoe String Press, 1984, pp. 260–268.

White, David E. "A Conversation with Maurice Sendak." *Horn Book* 56 (Apr 1980): 145–155.

Wintle, Justin. "Where the Wild Things Come From: Interview: Maurice Sendak." *Times Educational Supplement* 3131 (May 30, 1975): 17.

Wintle, Justin, and Emma Fisher. "Maurice Sendak." In *The Pied Pipers.* New York: Paddington Press, 1974, pp. 20–34.

Wolfe, Leo. "Maurice Sendak." *Horn Book* 40 (Aug 1964): 351–354.

The Zena Sutherland Lectures, 1983–1992. Edited by Betsy Hearne. New York: Clarion, 1993, pp. 1–25.

Seredy, Kate

Helbig, Alethea K. "Kate Seredy." In *Writers for Children: Critical Studies of Major Authors Since the Seventeenth Century.* Edited by Jane M. Bingham. New York: Scribner, 1988, pp. 519–524.

Helbig, Alethea K., and Agnes Regan Perkins. *Dictionary of American Children's Fiction, 1859–1959.* Westport, CT: Greenwood, 1985, pp. 461–462.

Higgins, James E. "Kate Seredy: Storyteller." *Horn Book* 44 (Apr 1968): 162–168.

The Junior Book of Authors. 2nd ed. rev. Edited by Stanley J. Kunitz and Howard Haycraft. New York: Wilson, 1951, pp. 270–271.

Kassen, Aileen M. "Kate Seredy: A Person Worth Knowing." *Elementary English* 45 (Mar

1968): 303–315. Reprinted in Miriam Hoffman and Eva Samuels. *Authors and Illustrators of Children's Books.* New York: Bowker, 1972, pp. 378–393.

"Kate Seredy." *Horn Book* 11 (July–Aug 1935): 230–235.

Markey, Lois R. "Kate Seredy's World." *Elementary English* 29 (Dec 1952): 451–457.

Piehl, Kathy. "Kate Seredy." In Cech. *American Writers for Children, 1900–1960. Dictionary of Literary Biography,* vol. 22. Detroit: Gale, 1985, pp. 299–306.

Roginski, Jim, ed. *Newbery and Caldecott Medalists and Honor Book Winners.* Littleton, CO: Libraries Unlimited, 1982, pp. 231–232.

Seredy, Kate. "The Country of *The Good Master.*" *Elementary English Review* 13 (May 1936): 167–168.

———. "Kate Seredy: A Letter about Her Books and Her Life." *Horn Book* (July–Aug 1935): 239–235.

———. "Newbery Medal Acceptance." *Horn Book* 14 (July 1938): 226–229.

———. "A Small Eternal Flame." *Horn Book* 33 (Feb 1957): 59–60.

Sutor, Peggy M. "Kate Seredy: A Bio-Bibliography." Master's thesis, Florida State University, 1955.

Thompson, B. J. "Kate Seredy." *Junior Bookshelf* 10 (July 1946): 49–52.

Twentieth-Century Children's Writers. 3rd ed. Edited by Tracy Chevalier and D. L. Kirkpatrick. New York: St. Martin, 1989, pp. 870–871.

"The White Stag." In Bertha Mahony Miller and Elinor Field. *Newbery Medal Books: 1922–1955.* Boston: Horn Book, 1957, pp. 157–165.

Serraillier, Ian (Lucien)

Crouch, Marcus. *The Nesbit Tradition: The Children's Novel in England, 1974–1970.* London: Benn, 1972.

Third Book of Junior Authors. Edited by Doris De Montreville and Donna Hill. New York: Wilson, 1972, pp. 257–258.

Twentieth-Century Children's Writers. 3rd ed. Edited by Tracy Chevalier and D. L. Kirkpatrick. New York: St. Martin, 1989, pp. 871–873.

Service, Pamela F.

Frongia, Terri. "Good Wizard/Bad Wizard: Merlin and Faust Archetypes in Contemporary Children's Literature." In *Contending Archetypes in Western Culture,* ed. by Charlotte Spivak. Lewiston, NY: Mellen, 1992, pp. 65–93.

———. "Merlin's Fathers: The Sacred and the Profane." *Children's Literature Association Quarterly* 18 (Fall 1993): 120–125. Discusses Peter Dickinson, Pamela Service, Rosemary Sutcliff, and Jane Yolen.

Service, Pamela F. "On Writing Science Fiction and Fantasy for Kids." *ALAN Review* 19 (Spring 1992): 17–18.

Seuss, Dr. (pseud. of Theodor Seuss Geisel)

Arakelian, Paul G. "Minnows into Whales: Integration Across Scales in the Early Styles of Dr. Seuss." *Children's Literature Association Quarterly* 18 (Spring 1993): 18–22.

Bader, Barbara. "Dr. Seuss." In *American Picturebooks from Noah's Ark to the Beast Within.* New York: Macmillan, 1976, pp. 302–312.

Bailey, John P., Jr. "Three Decades of Dr. Seuss." *Elementary English* 42 (Jan 1965): 7–12.

Barber, Michael. "Every Other Page a Cliffhanger." *The Guardian* (Aug 30, 1977): 13.

Barrs, M. "Laughing Your Way Into Literacy; Dr. Seuss Books." *Times Educational Supplement* 3164 (Jan 23, 1976): 20–21.

Butler, Francelia. "Seuss as a Creator of Folklore." *Children's Literature in Education* 20 (Sept 1989): 175–181.

Cohn, R. "The Wonderful World of Dr. Seuss." *Saturday Evening Post* 230 (July 6, 1957): 17–19ff.

Cott, Jonathan. "The Good Dr. Seuss." In *Pipers at the Gates of Dawn.* New York: Random, 1983, pp. 3–40.

Dempsey, D. "The Signature of Dr. Seuss." *The New York Times Book Review,* section 7, May 11, 1958, p. 2.

"Dr. Seuss' Success; Writing for Children." *Times Educational Supplement,* Oct 19, 1962, pp. 2474–2489.

Dohm, Janice H. "The Curious Case of Dr. Seuss: A Minority Report from America." *Junior Bookshelf* 27, no. 6 (Dec 1963): 323–329. Reprinted in *Top of the News* 21 (Jan 1965): 151–155.

Doyle, Brian. *The Who's Who of Children's Literature.* New York: Schocken, 1968, pp. 241–243.

Estes, Glenn E. "Laura Ingalls Wilder Award Presentation." *Horn Book* 56 (Aug 1980): 388–389.

Fadiman, Clifford. "A Party of One." *Holiday* 25 (Apr 1959): 11ff.

———. "Professionals and Confessionals: Dr. Seuss and Kenneth Grahame." In Egoff. *Only Connect.* 2nd ed. New York: Oxford Univ. Press, 1980, pp. 277–283.

Freeman, Donald. "Who Thunk You Up, Dr. Seuss?" *San Jose Mercury News.* "Parade" sect., June 15, 1969, pp. 12–13. Reprinted in Miriam Hoffman and Eva Samuels. *Authors and Illustrators of Children's Books.* New York: Bowker, 1972, pp. 165–171.

Hopkins, Lee Bennett. "Dr. Seuss." In *Books Are by People.* New York: Citation Press, 1969, pp. 255–258.

Jennings, C. R. "Dr. Seuss: What Am I Doing Here?" *Saturday Evening Post* 238 (Oct 23, 1965): 105–109.

Kann, E. J., Jr. "Profiles: Children's Friend." *New Yorker* 36 (Dec 17, 1960): 47–48ff.

Kasindorf, M. "A Happy Accident." *Newsweek* 79 (Feb 21, 1972): 100ff.

King, Stephen. "Dr. Seuss and the Two Faces of Fantasy." *Fantasy Review* 68 (1984): 10–12.

Kuskin, Karla. "Seuss at Seventy-Five." *New York Times Book Review,* Apr 29, 1979, pp. 23, 41–42.

Lanes, Selma. "Seuss for the Goose is Seuss for the Gander." In *Down the Rabbit Hole.* New York: Atheneum, 1971, pp. 79–89.

"The Logical Insanity of Dr. Seuss." *Time* 90 (Aug 11, 1967): 58–59.

Lurie, Alison. "The Cabinet of Dr. Seuss." *New York Review of Books* 20 (Dec 1990): 50–52.

Lystad, M. "The World According to Dr. Seuss." *Childhood Today* 13 (May–June 1984): 19–22.

MacDonald, Ruth K., ed. *Dr. Seuss.* Boston: Twayne, 1988.

Moje, E. B., and W. R. Shyu. "Oh the Places You've Taken Us, Dr. Seuss." *Reading Teacher* 45 (May 1992): 670–676; *Education Digest* 58 (Dec 1992): 26–30.

More Junior Authors. Edited by Muriel Fuller. New York: Wilson, 1963, pp. 182–183.

"Name—Ted Geisel." *Newsweek* 55 (June 20, 1960): 114–115.

Ort, Lorrene Love. "Theodor Seuss Geisel—The Children's Dr. Seuss." *Elementary English* 32 (Mar 1955): 135–142.

The Oxford Companion to Children's Literature. Edited by Humphrey Carpenter and Mari Prichard. New York: Oxford Univ. Press, 1984, pp. 477–478.

Reimer, Mavis. "Dr. Seuss' *500 Hats of Bartholomew Cubbins*: Of Hats and Kings." *Touchstones* 3 (1989): 132–142.

Roginski, Jim, ed. *Newbery and Caldecott Medalists and Honor Book Winners.* Littleton, CO: Libraries Unlimited, 1982, pp. 233–236.

Roth, Rita. "*On Beyond Zebra* with Dr. Seuss." *The New Advocate* 2 (Fall 1989): 213–226.

Sadler, Glenn Edward. "Maurice Sendak and Dr. Seuss: A Conversation." *Horn Book* 65 (Sept–Oct 1989): 582–588.

Sale, Roger. *Fairy Tales and After.* Cambridge, MA: Harvard Univ. Press, 1978, pp. 8–12.

Seuss, Dr. "1980 Laura Ingalls Wilder Award Acceptance Speech." *Top of the News* 36 (Summer 1980): 397–399; *Horn Book* 56 (Aug 1980): 390–391.

Stewart-Gordon, J. "Dr. Seuss: Fanciful Sage of Childhood." *Reader's Digest* 100 (Apr 1972): 141–145.

Stofflet, Mary. *Dr. Seuss from Then to Now.* New York: Random, 1986.

Stott, Jon C. *Children's Literature from A to Z.* New York: McGraw-Hill, 1984, p. 250.

Sullivan, E. P. "Brightening Our Years: A Half Century of Laughter and Learning with Dr. Seuss." *Delta Kappa Gamma Bulletin* 59 (Fall 1992): 47–51.

Twentieth-Century Children's Writers. 3rd ed. Edited by Tracy Chevalier and D. L. Kirkpatrick. Chicago: St. James, 1989, pp. 875–877.

"The Wacky World of Dr. Seuss." *Life Magazine* 46 (Apr 6, 1959): 107–108ff.

Wintle, Justin, and Emma Fisher. "Dr. Seuss." In *The Pied Pipers.* New York: Paddington Press, 1974, pp. 113–123.

Severn, David (pseud. of David S[torr] Unwin)

MacIlroy, Barry. "'Those Magical Time-Slip Stories.'" *Souvenir* (U.K.) 21 (1992): 14–15. Discusses Violet Needham, David Severn, Mabel Esther Allan, and Alison Uttley.

The Oxford Companion to Children's Literature. Edited by Humphrey Carpenter and Mari Prichard. New York: Oxford Univ. Press, 1984, p. 479.

Severn, David. "Why Don't You Write Books About Men Your Own Age?" *Books for Your Children* (U.K.) 10 (May 1975): 12–14.

Twentieth-Century Children's Writers. 3rd ed. Edited by Tracy Chevalier and D. L. Kirkpatrick. Chicago: St. James, 1989, pp. 877–879.

Shannon (Wing), Monica

The Junior Book of Authors. 2nd ed. rev. Edited by Stanley J. Kunitz and Howard Haycraft. New York: Wilson, 1951, pp. 272–273.

Miller, Elizabeth Cleveland. "Monica Shannon: An Appreciation." *Horn Book* 11 (Mar 1935): 73–81.

Roginski, Jim, ed. *Newbery and Caldecott Medalists and Honor Book Winners.* Littleton, CO: Libraries Unlimited, 1982, p. 238.

Shannon, Monica. "The Goat Who Owned Me." *Horn Book* 10 (Mar 1934): 117–119.

———. "A Hunt Breakfast-Authors' Symposium." *Horn Book* 2 (Nov 1926): 37–38.

Twentieth-Century Children's Writers. 3rd ed. Edited by Tracy Chevalier and D. L. Kirkpatrick. Chicago: St. James, 1989, p. 880.

Shapiro, Irwin

The Junior Book of Authors. 2nd ed. rev. Edited by Stanley J. Kunitz and Howard Haycraft. New York: Wilson, 1951, pp. 273–274.

Sharmat, Marjorie Weinman

Fifth Book of Junior Authors and Illustrators. Edited by Sally Holmes Holtze. New York: Wilson, 1983, pp. 282–283.

Twentieth-Century Children's Writers. 3rd ed. Edited by Tracy Chevalier and D. L. Kirkpatrick. New York: St. Martin, 1989, pp. 881–882.

Sharp (Castle), Margery

Blount, Margaret. *Animal Land: The Creatures of Children's Fiction.* New York: Morrow, 1975, pp. 163–169.

Gillespie, John T., and Diana Lembo. *Introducing Books: A Guide for the Middle Grades.* New York: Bowker, 1970, pp. 281–283.

Smith, Louisa A. "The *Miss Bianca* Series." In *Survey of Modern Fantasy Literature,* vol. 3. Edited by Frank N. Magill. Englewood Cliffs, NJ: Salem Press, 1983, pp. 1037–1039.

Third Book of Junior Authors. Edited by Doris De Montreville and Donna Hill. New York: Wilson, 1972, pp. 258–259.

Twentieth-Century Children's Writers. 3rd ed. Edited by Tracy Chevalier and D. L. Kirkpatrick. Chicago: St. James, 1989, pp. 883–884.

Shecter, Ben

Third Book of Junior Authors. Edited by Doris De Montreville and Donna Hill. New York: Wilson, 1972, pp. 259–260.

Sherburne, Zoa (Morin)

Fourth Book of Junior Authors and Illustrators. Edited by Doris De Montreville and Elizabeth D. Crawford. New York: Wilson, 1978, pp. 314–315.

Sherman, Josepha

Sherman, Josepha. "An Open Letter to Fantasy Writers." *The Writer* 106 (May 1993): 13.

Shulevitz, Uri

Shulevitz, Uri. "Caldecott Award Acceptance." *Horn Book* 45 (Aug 1969): 385–388.

———. "Writing with Pictures." *Horn Book* 58 (Feb 1982): 17–22.

Third Book of Junior Authors. Edited by Doris De Montreville and Donna Hill. New York: Wilson, 1972, pp. 263–264.

Zaum, Marjorie. "Uri Shulevitz." *Horn Book* 45 (Aug 1969): 389–391.

Shura, Mary Francis (pseud. of Mary Francis Craig)

Third Book of Junior Authors. Edited by Doris De Montreville and Donna Hill. New York: Wilson, 1972, pp. 264–265.

Toothaker, R. "Profile: Mary Frances Shura; Why She Writes." *Language Arts* 57 (Feb 1980): 193–198.

Shwartz, Susan

Shwartz, Susan. "Critiquing the Critics: The 'Write Stuff.'" *Lan's Lantern* 22 (1987): 4–7.

Silverberg, Robert

Aldiss, Brian W., and Harry Harrison, eds. *Hell's Cartographers: Some Personal Histories of Science Fiction Writers.* New York: Harper, 1976, pp. 7–45.

Canary, Robert H. "Science Fiction as Fictive History." *Extrapolation* 16 (1974): 81–95.

Clareson, Thomas D. "The Fictions of Robert Silverberg." In *Voices for the Future,* vol. 2. Bowling Green, OH: Bowling Green Univ. Press, 1979.

———. *A Reader's Guide to Robert Silverberg.* Mercer Island, WA: Starmont, 1983.

———. *Robert Silverberg: A Primary and Secondary Bibliography.* Boston: G. K. Hall, 1983.

———. "Whose Castle? Speculation as to the Parameters of Science Fiction." *Essays in Arts and Sciences* 9 (1980): 139–143.

Edwards, Malcolm. "Robert Silverberg." In *Science Fiction Writers.* Edited by E. F. Bleiler. New York: Scribner, 1982, pp. 505–512.

Elliot, Jeffrey M. "Robert Silverberg—Next Stop: *Lord Valentine's Castle.*" *P*S*F*Q** 5 (1981): 18–24.

———. "Robert Silverberg Returns." *Future Life* 12 (1979): 25–27.

———. *Science Fiction Voices #2.* San Bernardino, CA: Borgo Press, 1979.

Fredericks, Casey. *The Future of Eternity: Mythologies of Science Fiction and Fantasy.* Bloomington, IN: Indiana Univ. Press, 1982.

Hall, Melissa Mia. "Interview: Robert Silverberg." *Fantasy Newsletter* 60 (1983): 16–17, 46.

Harrison, Harry. "Benford, Wolfe, Silverberg . . . and Literature." *Fantasy Review* 81 (1985): 33.

Klein, Jay Kay. "Robert Silverberg." *Analog,* Mar 1983, p. 88.

Kroitor, Harry P. "The Special Demands of Points of View in Science Fiction." *Extrapolation* 17 (1976): 153–159.

Letson, Russell. "Falling Through Many Trapdoors: Robert Silverberg." *Extrapolation* 20 (1979): 109–117.

Platt, Charles. *Dream Makers: The Uncommon People Who Write Science Fiction.* New York: Berkley, 1980, pp. 261–268. Interview.

Robert Silverberg; The Mind and Method of a Science Fiction Novelist. North Hollywood, CA: Center for Cassette Studies, 1974. (Audio-cassette)

"Robert Silverberg: Up, Up, and Away." *Locus* 289 (1985): 1.

Schweitzer, Darrell, ed. *Science Fiction Voices.* Baltimore: T-K Graphics, 1976. Interview.

Searles, Baird, Beth Meacham, and Michael Franklin. *A Reader's Guide to Fantasy.* New York: Avon, 1982, p. 134.

Silverberg, Robert. "Amazing, Astounding Journeys into the Unknown and Back." *Horizon* 16 (1974): 47–48.

———. "Opinion." *Amazing Stories,* July 1981, pp. 6–7.

———. "Opinion." *Amazing Stories,* May 1985, pp. 4–6.

———. "Opinion." *Amazing Stories,* Sept 1985, p. 4.

———. "The Profession of Science Fiction: IX: Sounding Brass, Tinkling Cymbal." *Foundation* 7/8 (1975): 6–37; *Algol* 13 (1976): 7–18. Reprinted in *Hell's Cartographers: Some Personal Histories of Science Fiction Writers.* Edited by Brian Aldis and Harry Harrison. New York: Harper, 1975.

———. "The Silverberg Papers." *Starship* 37 (1980): 17–21.

———. "The Silverberg Papers." *Science Fiction Chronicle* 64 (1985): 22.

———. "The Silverberg Papers: Part 2." *Starship* 38 (1980): 25–30.

———. "The Silverberg Papers: Part 3." *Starship* 39 (1980): 15–17.

———. "The Silverberg That Was." *Science Fiction Review* 6 (Nov 1977): 8–16.

———. "Thirty Years of Writing." In David Wingrove. *The Science Fiction Source Book.* New York: Van Nostrand Reinhold, 1984, pp. 80–82.

Stableford, Brian M. "The Metamorphosis of Robert Silverberg." In Brian M. Stableford. *Masters of Science Fiction.* San Bernardino, CA: Borgo Press, 1981, pp. 32–42.

Third Book of Junior Authors. Edited by Doris De Montreville and Donna Hill. New York: Wilson, 1972, pp. 265–266.

Tuck, Donald H. "Robert Silverberg: Bibliography." *Fantasy and Science Fiction* 46 (Apr 1974): 81–88.

Twentieth-Century Science Fiction Writers. 3rd ed. Edited by Noelle Watson and Paul E. Schellinger. Chicago: St. James Press, 1991, pp. 728–732.

Walker, Paul. *Speaking of Science Fiction: The Paul Walker Interviews.* Oradell, NJ: Luna Publications, 1978, pp. 281–290.

Silverstein, Shel(by)

Fifth Book of Junior Authors and Illustrators. Edited by Sally Holmes Holtze. New York: Wilson, 1983, pp. 288–289.

Twentieth-Century Children's Writers. 3rd ed. Edited by Tracy Chevalier and D. L. Kirkpatrick. Chicago: St. James, 1989, pp. 886–887.

Simak, Clifford D(onald)

Aiken, Arnold. "An Age Without An Aim?" *Crystal Ship* 7 (1983): 5–19.

Becker, Muriel R. *Clifford D. Simak: A Primary and Secondary Bibliography.* Boston: G. K. Hall, 1980.

A Career in Science Fiction: An Interview With Clifford Simak. Lawrence, KS: Univ. of Kansas, 1975. (Film)

Chapman, Edgar L. "The Fellowship of the Talisman." In *Survey of Modern Fantasy Literature,* vol. 2. Edited by Frank N. Magill. Englewood Cliffs, NJ: Salem Press, 1983, pp. 549–552.

Clareson, Thomas D. "Clifford D. Simak: The Inhabited Universe." In *Voices for the Future: Essays on Major Science Fiction Writers,* vol. 1. Bowling Green, OH: Bowling Green Univ. Press, 1976.

Kroitor, Harry P. "The Special Demands of Point of View in Science Fiction." *Extrapolation* 17 (1976): 153–159.

Lake, Ken. "City in Ashes." *Vector* 129 (1985): 8.

Moskowitz, Sam. *Seekers of Tomorrow: Masters of Modern Science Fiction.* New York: Ballantine, 1967, pp. 266–282.

Pringle, David. "Aliens for Neighbors: A Reassessment of Clifford D. Simak." *Foundation* 11/12 (1979): 15–29.

Schweitzer, Darrell. "Clifford Simak." In *Science Fiction Voices #5.* Edited by Darrell Schweitzer. San Bernardino, CA: Borgo Press, 1981, pp. 48–55.

Simak, Clifford. "'Room Enough for All of Us.'" *Extrapolation* 13 (1972): 102–105.

Tweet, Roald D. "Clifford D. Simak." In *Science Fiction Writers.* New York: Scribner, 1982, pp. 513–518.

Twentieth-Century Science Fiction Writers. 3rd ed. Edited by Noelle Watson and Paul E. Schellinger. Chicago: St. James Press, 1991, pp. 732–734.

Walker, Paul. *Speaking of Science Fiction: The Paul Walker Interviews.* Oradell, NJ: Luna Publications, 1978, pp. 56–67. Originally published in *Luna Monthly* 57 (1975): 1–6.

Simont, Marc

More Junior Authors. Edited by Muriel Fuller. New York: Wilson, 1963, pp. 186–187.

Singer, Isaac Bashevis

Ahnlund, Knut. "De Vuxna Barnen, de Barnsliga Vuxna: Isaac Singer's Barnboksfilosofi [The Grown up Children, the Childlike Adults: The Philosophy of Isaac Singer's Books for Children]." *Barnboken* (Stockholm) 3 (1982): 5–7.

Alexander, Edward. *Isaac Bashevis Singer: A Study of the Short Fiction.* Boston: Twayne, 1990.

Allentuck, Marcia, ed. *The Achievements of Isaac Bashevis Singer.* Carbondale: Southern Illinois Univ. Press, 1969.

Berkley, Miriam. "Isaac Bashevis Singer, His Great Success in Writing Children's Books." *Publishers Weekly* 223 (Feb 18, 1983): 65–66.

Bernheim, Mark A. "Five Hundred Reasons of Isaac Singer." *Bookbird* 20, nos. 1–2 (1982): 31–36.

Blocker, J., and R. Elman. "Interview with Isaac Bashevis Singer." *Commentary* 36 (Nov 1963): 364–372; 37 (Mar 1964): 20.

Bluchen, Irving H. *Isaac Bashevis Singer and the Eternal Past.* New York: New York Univ. Press, 1968.

Burgin, R. "From Conversations with Isaac Bashevis Singer: Interview." *Hudson Review* 31 (Winter 1978): 621–630.

Calaghan, L. W. "Consistent Focus and Recurring Elements in Books for the Young by Konigsburg, O'Dell, Singer, and Snyder." Master's thesis, University of Chicago, 1979.

Deitch, Gene. "Filming 'Zlateh the Goat.'" *Horn Book* 51 (June 1975): 241–249.

Flender, H. "Isaac Bashevis Singer, Interview." *Paris Review* 11 (Fall 1968).

Goldsmith, Arnold L. "Isaac Bashevis Singer and the Legend of the Golem of Prague." *Yiddish* 6 (1986): 39–50.

Haiblum, Isidore. "Isaac Bashevis Singer: Portrait of a Magician." *The Twilight Zone Magazine,* Jan–Feb 1984, pp. 24–27.

———. "*Twilight Zone Magazine* Interview: 'These Hidden Powers are Everywhere.'" *The Twilight Zone Magazine,* Jan–Feb 1984, pp. 28–29.

Hernández, Frances. "Isaac Bashevis Singer and the Supernatural." *CEA Critic* 40 (Jan 1978): 28–32.

Hopkins, Lee Bennett. "Isaac Bashevis Singer." In *More Books by More People.* New York: Citation Press, 1974, pp. 312–317.

Iskander, Sylvia W. "Isaac Bashevis Singer." In *American Writers for Children since 1960: Fiction. Dictionary of Literary Biography,* vol. 52. Detroit: Gale, 1986, pp. 334–352.

Jurich, Marilyn. "Once Upon a *Shtetl*: *Schlimazels, Schlemiels, Schnorrers, Shadchens,* and Sages: Yiddish Humor in Children's Books." *The Lion and the Unicorn* 1 (Spring 1977): 9–25.

Kimmel, Eric. "I. B. Singer's *Alone in the Wild Forest:* A Kabbalistic Parable." *Children's Literature in Education* 18 (Fall 1975): 147–158.

———. "The Wise Men of Chelm." *Horn Book* 50 (Feb 1974): 78–82.

Kresh, Paul. *Isaac Bashevis Singer: The Magician of West 86th Street.* New York: Dial Press, 1979.

———. *Isaac Bashevis Singer: The Story of a Storyteller.* New York: Dutton/Lodestar, 1984.

Leventhal, Naomi Susan. "Storytelling in the Works of Isaac Bashevis Singer." Ph.D. diss., Ohio State University, 1978.

Lottman, H. "Isaac Bashevis Singer, Storyteller." *New York Times Book Review,* sect. 7, Jan 25, 1972, p. 5.

McGregor, Barbara Ruth. "The American Fiction of Isaac Bashevis Singer: Lost and Found in America." Ph.D. diss., Texas Christian University, 1985.

Malin, Irving. *Critical Views of Isaac Bashevis Singer.* New York: New York Univ. Press, 1969.

———. *Isaac Bashevis Singer.* New York: Ungar, 1972.

May, Jill P. "Families Lost, Families Found." In *The Child and the Family: Selected Papers from the 1988 International Conference of the Children's Literature Association,* ed. by Susan R. Gannon and Ruth A. Thompson. New York: Pace University, 1990, p. 80. (abstract)

Menashe, A. "Demons by Choice: An Interview with Isaac Bashevis Singer." *Parabola* 6, no. 4 (Fall 1981): 69–74.

Morse, Naomi S. "Values for Children in the Stories of Isaac Bashevis Singer." In MacLeod. *Children's Literature*. College Park: Univ. of Maryland, 1977.

"A Note on Isaac Bashevis Singer." *Children's Literature in Education* 6 (Fall 1975): 134–135.

The Oxford Companion to Children's Literature. Edited by Humphrey Carpenter and Mari Prichard. New York: Oxford Univ. Press, 1984, pp. 485–486.

Patterson, Sylvia W. "Isaac Singer: Writer for Children." In *Proceedings of the Eighth Annual Conference of the Children's Literature Association*. University of Minnesota, March 1981. Ypsilanti, MI: Children's Literature Association, 1982, pp. 69–76.

Pinsker, S. "Isaac Bashevis Singer: An Interview." *Critique* 11, no. 2 (1969): 16–25.

Pondrom, C. N. "Isaac Bashevis Singer." *Contemporary Literature* 10 (Winter 1969): 1–32; 10 (Summer 1964): 332–351.

Reicheck, M. "Storyteller." *New York Times Magazine,* sect. 6, Mar 23, 1975, p. 16.

Riggio, Thomas P. "The Symbols of Faith: Isaac Bashevis Singer's Children's Books." In *Recovering the Canon: Essays on Isaac Bashevis Singer,* ed. by David Neal Miller. Leiden: Brill, 1986, pp. 133–144.

Roginski, Jim, ed. *Newbery and Caldecott Medalists and Honor Book Winners*. Littleton, CO: Libraries Unlimited, 1982, pp. 241–243.

Rubinstein, Esther Levin. "The Grotesque: Aesthetics of Pictorial Disorder in the Writings of Edgar Allan Poe and Isaac Bashevis Singer." Ph.D. diss., State University of New York at Albany, 1984.

Schlessinger, June H., and June D. Vanderryst. "Supernatural Themes in Selected Children's Stories of Isaac Bashevis Singer." *Journal of Youth Services in Libraries* 2 (Summer 1989): 331–338.

Shub, Elizabeth. "Isaac Bashevis Singer." *C. B. C. Calendar* 34 (Mar–Aug 1975).

Siegel, Ben. *Isaac Bashevis Singer.* Minneapolis: Univ. of Minnesota Press, 1969.

Siegel, Mark. "The Short Fiction of Isaac Bashevis Singer." In *Survey of Modern Fantasy Literature,* vol. 4. Edited by Frank N. Magill. Englewood Cliffs, NJ: Salem Press, 1983, pp. 1686–1691.

Sinclair, Clive. "Conversation with Isaac Bashevis Singer: Interview." *Encounter* 52 (Feb 1979): 21–28.

Sinclair, Clive, and W. J. Weathersby. "Great Works from Small Worlds: Master Storyteller with a Message for Everyone." *The Guardian* (July 26, 1991): 33.

Singer, Isaac Bashevis. "Are Children the Ultimate Literary Critics?" *Top of the News* 29 (Nov 1972): 32–36.

———. "'I See the Child as a Last Refuge.'" *New York Times Book Review,* pt. II, Nov 9, 1969, pp. 1, 66. Reprinted in Robert Bator. *Signposts to Criticism of Children's Literature.* Chicago: American Library Association, 1983, pp. 50–53.

———. "Isaac Bashevis Singer: Interview." In Butler. *Sharing Literature With Children.* New York: McKay, 1977, pp. 155–160.

———. "Isaac Bashevis Singer on Writing for Children." In *Children's Literature,* vol. 6. Philadelphia: Temple Univ. Press, 1977, pp. 9–16. Reprinted in *Reflections on Literature for Children.* Edited by Francelia Butler and Richard Rotert. Hamden, CT: Shoe String Press, 1984, pp. 51–57.

———. *A Little Boy in Search of God: Mysticism in a Personal Light.* Garden City, NY: Doubleday, 1976. Followed by *A Young Man in Search of Love,* Doubleday, 1978; and *Lost in America,* Doubleday, 1978. (autobiographies)

———. "'Our Children Are a Menace to Literature.'" *Horn Book* 50 (Dec 1974): 679.

———. "Ten More Reasons for Loving Children." *Horn Book* 49 (Dec 1973): 579.

Third Book of Junior Authors. Edited by Doris De Montreville and Donna Hill. New York: Wilson, 1972, pp. 266–268.

Twentieth-Century Children's Writers. 3rd ed. Edited by Tracy Chevalier and D. L. Kirkpatrick. Chicago: St. James, 1989, pp. 887–889.

Wolf, H. R. "Singer's Children's Stories and *In My Father's Court:* Universalism and the Rankian Hero." In *The Achievement of Isaac Bashevis Singer.* Edited by Allentuck. Carbondale: Southern Illinois Univ. Press, 1969, pp. 145–158.

Wolkstein, Diane. "The Stories behind the Stories: An Interview with Isaac Bashevis Singer." *Children's Literature in Education* 18 (Fall 1975): 136–146.

Singer, Marilyn

Roginski, Jim. *Behind the Covers: Interviews with Authors and Illustrators of Books for Children and Young Adults.* Littleton, CO: Libraries Unlimited, 1985, pp. 186–193.

Skurzynski, Gloria (Joan)

Fifth Book of Junior Authors and Illustrators. Edited by Sally Holmes Holtze. New York: Wilson, 1983, pp. 294–295.

Helbig, Alethea K., and Agnes Regan Perkins. *Dictionary of American Children's Fiction, 1960–1984.* Westport, CT: Greenwood, 1986, pp. 602, 710.

Sleator, William (Warner III)

Fifth Book of Junior Authors and Illustrators. Edited by Sally Holmes Holtze. New York: Wilson, 1983, pp. 295–296.

Helbig, Alethea, and Agnes Regan Perkins. *Dictionary of American Children's Fiction, 1985–1989.* Westport, CT: Greenwood, 1993, pp. 233–234.

Jenkinson, D. H. "Portraits: William Sleator; Stellar Science Fiction Author." *Emergency Librarian* 17 (Jan–Feb 1990): 67+.

Mappin, Alf. "Know the Author: William Sleator." *Magpies* (Australia) 4 (July 1989): 21–22.

Rogers, S. "It's Only a Game . . . or Is It?" *School Library Journal* 38 (Mar 1992): 176–177.

Roginski, Jim. *Behind the Covers: Interviews with Authors and Illustrators of Books for Children and Young Adults.* Littleton, CO: Libraries Unlimited, 1985, pp. 194–205.

Speaking for Ourselves: Autobiographical Sketches by Notable Authors of Books for Young Adults. Edited by Donald R. Gallo. Urbana, IL: National Council of Teachers of English, 1990, pp. 193–194.

Thorson, A. S. "An Interview with William Sleator." *Book Report* 11 (May–June 1992): 26–30.

Twentieth-Century Children's Writers. 3rd ed. Edited by Tracy Chevalier and D. L. Kirkpatrick. Chicago: St. James, 1989, pp. 889–890.

Sleigh, Barbara (de Riemer)

Doyle, Brian. *The Who's Who of Children's Literature.* New York: Schocken, 1968, pp. 247–248.

Moss, Elaine. "*Signal* Interview: Barbara Sleigh: The Voice of Magic." In *Part of the Pattern.* New York: Greenwillow, 1986, pp. 70–74. Reprinted from *Signal* 8 (May 1972): 43–48.

Twentieth-Century Children's Writers. 3rd ed. Edited by Tracy Chevalier and D. L. Kirkpatrick. Chicago: St. James, 1989, pp. 890–891.

Slobodkin, Louis

Estes, Eleanor. "Louis Slobodkin." *Horn Book* 20 (July–Aug 1944): 299–306.
Hopkins, Lee Bennett. *More Books by More People: Interviews with Sixty-five Authors of Books for Children.* New York: Citation Press, 1974, pp. 270–272.
Roginski, Jim, ed. *Newbery and Caldecott Medalists and Honor Book Winners.* Littleton, CO: Libraries Unlimited, 1982, pp. 245–246.
Slobodkin, Louis. "The Caldecott Medal Acceptance." *Horn Book* 20 (July–Aug 1944): 307–317.
———. "Notes on a Sculptor's Life." *Magazine of Art* 32 (June 1939): 336–338.
Twentieth-Century Children's Writers. 3rd ed. Edited by Tracy Chevalier and D. L. Kirkpatrick. New York: St. Martin, 1989, pp. 891–892.

Slote, Alfred

Fifth Book of Junior Authors and Illustrators. Edited by Sally Holmes Holtze. New York: Wilson, 1983, pp. 298–299.

Smith, Agnes

Gillespie, John T., and Diana Lembo. *Juniorplots: A Book Talk Manual for Teachers and Librarians.* New York: Bowker, 1967, pp. 192–194.
Helbig, Alethea K., and Agnes Regan Perkins. *Dictionary of American Children's Fiction, 1859–1959.* Westport, CT: Greenwood, 1985, pp. 143–144, 477.

Smith, Dodie (Dorothy Gladys)

"Capturing the Theatre with a Quite Uncommon Touch." *The Guardian* (Nov 27, 1990): 39.
Twentieth-Century Children's Writers. 3rd ed. Edited by Tracy Chevalier and D. L. Kirkpatrick. Chicago: St. James, 1989, pp. 896–897.

Smith, Emma

Twentieth-Century Children's Writers. 3rd ed. Edited by Tracy Chevalier and D. L. Kirkpatrick. Chicago: St. James, 1989, pp. 898–899.

Smith, Thorne

Goldin, Stephen. "*Topper* and *Topper Takes a Trip.*" In *Survey of Modern Fantasy Literature,* vol. 4. Edited by Frank N. Magill. Englewood Cliffs, NJ: Salem Press, 1983, pp. 1958–1962.
Neilson, Keith. "Thorne Smith." In *Supernatural Fiction Writers: Fantasy and Horror,* vol. 2. Edited by E. F. Bleiler. New York: Scribner, 1985, pp. 805–812.
Stewart, Robert. "Filmedia: Of Human Badinage." *Starship* 4 (1980): 36–37.

Snow, Jack

Baum Bugle. Special Issue. 32, no. 2 (1988).
Hanff, Peter E., and Douglas G. Greene. *Bibliographia Oziana.* Demorest, GA: International Wizard of Oz Club, 1976.

Snyder, Zilpha Keatley

Calaghan, L. W. "Consistent Focus and Recurring Elements in Books for the Young by Konigsburg, O'Dell, Singer and Snyder." Master's thesis, University of Chicago, 1979.

Helbig, Alethea K., and Agnes Regan Perkins. *Dictionary of American Children's Fiction, 1960–1984; Recent Books of Recognized Merit.* Westport, CT: Greenwood, 1986, pp. 609–610.

Hopkins, Lee Bennett. "Zilpha Keatley Snyder." In *More Books by More People.* New York: Citation Press, 1974, pp. 318–322.

Karl, Jean. "Zilpha Keatley Snyder." *Elementary English* 51 (Sept 1974): 784–789.

Roginski, Jim, ed. *Newbery and Caldecott Medalists and Honor Book Winners.* Littleton, CO: Libraries Unlimited, 1982, pp. 247–248.

Snyder, Zilpha Keatley. "Alternate Worlds." In *Innocence & Experience.* Edited by Barbara Harrison and Gregory Maguire. New York: Lothrop, 1987, pp. 189–190.

———. "The Uses of Magic." *Catholic Library World* 44 (July 1972): 49–56.

Speaking for Ourselves: Autobiographical Sketches by Notable Authors of Books for Young Adults. Edited by Donald R. Gallo. Urbana, IL: National Council of Teachers of English, 1990, pp. 195–197.

Third Book of Junior Authors. Edited by Doris De Montreville and Donna Hill. New York: Wilson, 1972, pp. 270–271.

Twentieth-Century Children's Writers. 3rd ed. Edited by Tracy Chevalier and D. L. Kirkpatrick. Chicago: St. James, 1989, pp. 903–905.

Springer, Nancy

Paxon, Diana. "The Tolkien Tradition." *Mythlore* 39 (1984): 23–27, 37.

Steele, Mary Q(uintard Govan) (a.k.a. Wilson Gage)

Helbig, Alethea K., and Agnes Regan Perkins. *Dictionary of American Children's Fiction, 1960–1984.* Westport, CT: Greenwood, 1986, pp. 341, 426–427, 624.

Roginski, Jim, ed. *Newbery and Caldecott Medalists and Honor Book Winners.* Littleton, CO: Libraries Unlimited, 1982, pp. 252–253.

Steele, Mary Q. "As Far As You Can Bear to See: Excellence in Children's Literature." *Horn Book* 51 (June 1975): 250–255.

———. "Realism, Truth, and Honesty." *Horn Book* 47 (Feb 1971): 17–27.

Third Book of Junior Authors. Edited by Doris De Montreville and Donna Hill. New York: Wilson, 1972, p. 97.

Twentieth-Century Children's Writers. 3rd ed. Edited by Tracy Chevalier and D. L. Kirkpatrick. Chicago: St. James, 1989, pp. 914–915.

Steele, William O(wen)

Burns, P. C., and R. Hines. "Tennessee's Teller of Tall Tales: William O. Steele." *Elementary English* 38 (Dec 1961): 545–548.

Helbig, Alethea K., and Agnes Regan Perkins. *Dictionary of American Children's Fiction, 1859–1959.* Westport, CT: Greenwood, 1985, p. 487.

More Junior Authors. Edited by Muriel Fuller. New York: Wilson, 1963, pp. 192–193.

Steele, William O. "The Last Buffalo Killed in Tennessee." *Horn Book* 45 (Apr 1969): 196–199.

———. "The Long Hunter and the Tall Tale." *Horn Book* 34 (Feb 1958): 54–62.

Twentieth-Century Children's Writers. 3rd ed. Edited by Tracy Chevalier and D. L. Kirkpatrick. Chicago: St. James, 1989, pp. 915–916.

Steig, William

Abrahamson, Richard F. "Classroom Uses for the Books of William Steig." *Reading Teacher* 32 (Dec 1978): 307–311.

Alberghene, Janice Marie. "From Alcott to *Abel's Island:* The Image of the Artist in American Children's Literature." Ph.D. diss., Brown University, 1980.

Allender, D. "William Steig at 80." *Publishers Weekly* 204 (July 24, 1987): 116–118.

Bader, Barbara. *American Picturebooks from Noah's Ark to the Beast Within.* New York: Macmillan, 1976, pp. 563–564.

Bottner, Barbara. "William Steig: The Two Legacies." *The Lion and the Unicorn* 2, no. 1 (Spring 1978): 4–16.

Cott, Jonathan. "William Steig and His Path." In *Pipers at the Gates of Dawn.* New York: Random, 1983, pp. 87–136.

Hearn, Michael Patrick. "Drawing Out William Steig." *Bookbird* 3–4 (1982): 61–65. Interview.

Helbig, Alethea K., and Agnes Regan Perkins. *Dictionary of American Children's Fiction, 1960–1984.* Westport, CT: Greenwood, 1986, pp. 1–2, 162, 545–546, 625.

Higgins, James E. "William Steig: Champion for Romance." *Children's Literature in Education* 28, no. 1 (1978): 3–16.

Kingman, Lee, ed. *Newbery and Caldecott Medal Books: 1966–1975.* Boston: Horn Book, 1975, pp. 66–75.

Kraus, Robert. "William Steig." *Horn Book* 46 (Aug 1970): 361–362.

Kuskin, Karla. ". . . and William Steig." *New York Times Book Review,* Nov 14, 1976, pp. 24, 34.

Lanes, Selma G. "Books: A Reformed Masochist Writes a Sunlit Children's Classic." *Harper's* 245 (Oct 1972): 122–126. Discusses *Dominic.*

Langford, Sondra Gordon. "A Second Look: *The Real Thief.*" *Horn Book* 67 (Jan–Feb 1990): 48–49.

Moss, Anita. "The Spear and the Piccolo: Heroic and Pastoral Dimensions of William Steig's *Dominic* and *Abel's Island.*" In *Children's Literature,* vol. 10. New Haven, CT: Yale Univ. Press, 1982, pp. 124–140.

Roginski, Jim, ed. *Newbery and Caldecott Medalists and Honor Book Winners.* Littleton, CO: Libraries Unlimited, 1982, pp. 254–255.

Spirt, Diana L. *Introducing More Books: A Guide for the Middle Grades.* New York: Bowker, 1978, pp. 66–68.

Steig, William. "The Artist at Work." *Horn Book* 69 (Mar–Apr 1993): 170–174.

———. "Caldecott Award Acceptance." *Horn Book* 46 (Aug 1970): 359–360.

Stott, Jon C. *Children's Literature from A to Z.* New York: McGraw-Hill, 1984, p. 260.

Third Book of Junior Authors. Edited by Doris De Montreville and Donna Hill. New York: Wilson, 1972, pp. 276–277.

Twentieth-Century Children's Writers. 3rd ed. Edited by Tracy Chevalier and D. L. Kirkpatrick. Chicago: St. James, 1989, pp. 916–918.

"William Steig in Three Parts." *American Artist* 7 (Mar 1943): 17–19.

Wilner, Arlene. "'Unlocked by Love': William Steig's Tales of Transformation and Magic." *Children's Literature* 18 (1990): 31–41.

Stein, Gertrude

Bechtel, Louise Seaman. "Gertrude Stein for Children." *Horn Book* 15 (Sept 1939):

287–290. Reprinted in Fryatt. *Horn Book Sampler.* Boston: Horn Book, 1959, pp. 128–132.

Hoffeld, Laura. "Gertrude Stein's Unmentionables: A Reading of *The World Is Round.*" *The Lion and the Unicorn* 2 (Spring 1978): 48–55.

Kellner, Bruce, ed. *A Gertrude Stein Companion: Content with the Example.* New York: Greenwood, 1988.

Neuman, Shirley, and Ira B. Nadel, eds. *Gertrude Stein and the Making of Literature.* Boston: Northeastern Univ. Press, 1988.

O'Hara, J. D. "Gertrude Stein's *The World Is Round.*" In Francelia Butler. *Sharing Literature with Children.* New York: McKay, 1977, pp. 446–449.

Stephens, James

Brown, M. "Leprechaun Out of Costume." *Sewanee Review* 84 (Winter 1976): 190–195.

Clute, John. *"The Crock of Gold."* In *Survey of Modern Fantasy Literature,* vol. 1. Edited by Frank N. Magill. Englewood Cliffs, NJ: Salem Press, 1983, pp. 324–327.

Craig, P. "Rounding Up the Strays." *Times Literary Supplement* 4217 (Jan 27, 1984): 81.

Davison, Edward L. "Three Irish Poets: A. E. Housman, W. B. Yeats, and James Stephens." *English Journal* 15 (May 1926): 327–336.

Douglas, Aileen. "James Stephens." In *Supernatural Fiction Writers: Fantasy and Horror,* vol. 1. Edited by E. F. Bleiler. New York: Scribner, 1985, pp. 485–490.

Lochhead, Marion. *Renaissance of Wonder.* New York: Harper, 1980, pp. 77–81.

Marshall, H. P. "James Stephens." *London Mercury* 12 (Sept 1925): 500–510.

"A Minstrel Comes from Ireland." *Our World Weekly* 2 (Mar 16, 1925): 107.

Morris, L. R. "Four Irish Poets." *Columbia University Quarterly* 18 (Sept 1916): 332–344.

Peake, M. "Portrait." *London Mercury* 38 (May 1938): 606.

"Portrait." *Bookman* 78 (Aug 1930): 316; 82 (Sept 1932): 280.

Schley, Margaret Anne. "The Elfin Craft: Fairytale Elements in James Stephens' Prose." Ph.D. diss., University of North Carolina at Chapel Hill, 1982.

Searles, Baird, Beth Meacham, and Michael Franklin. *A Reader's Guide to Fantasy.* New York: Avon, 1982, pp. 138–139.

Stevenson, James

Fifth Book of Junior Authors and Illustrators. Edited by Sally Holmes Holtze. New York: Wilson, 1983, pp. 303–304.

Stevenson, Robert Louis (Balfour)

Bawer, Bruce. "R. L. S. Meets *TLS.*" *The New Criterion* 6 (1988): 81–86.

Bell, Ian. *Dreams of Exile: Robert Louis Stevenson, a Biography.* Edinburgh: Mainstream, 1992.

Brown, Douglas. "Robert Louis Stevenson: Inspiration and Industry." In *Young Writers, Young Readers.* Edited by Boris Ford. London: Hutchinson, 1960, pp. 123–129.

Butts, Dennis. *Robert Louis Stevenson.* New York: Walck, 1966.

Calder, Janet. *R. L. S.: A Life Study.* Glasgow: Drew, 1990.

Daiches, David. *Robert Louis Stevenson and His World.* London: Thames, 1973.

———. *Robert Louis Stevenson: The Makers of Modern Literature.* Norfolk, CT: New Directions Books, 1947, pp. 32–73.

Doyle, Brian. *The Who's Who of Children's Literature.* New York: Schocken, 1968, pp. 251–253.

Epstein, Joseph. "The Short Happy Life of Robert Stevenson." *The New Criterion* 7 (Nov 1988): 22–33.

Hart, Francis R. "Robert Louis Stevenson in Prose." In *The History of Scottish Literature III: Nineteenth Century,* ed. by Douglas Giffard and Craig Cairnes. Aberdeen: Aberdeen Univ. Press, 1988.

Hodges, Margaret. "Robert Louis Stevenson 1850–1894." In *Writers for Children: Critical Studies of Major Authors Since the Seventeenth Century,* ed. by Jane M. Bingham. New York: Macmillan, 1988, pp. 535–543.

Knight, Allana, ed. *The Robert Louis Stevenson Treasury.* New York: St. Martin 1985.

Knudsen, Grethe. "Off the Beaten Track." *Orana* (Australia) 22 (Nov 1986): 173–174.

McGregor, D. R. "Myth and Fantasy in Some Late Victorian Novels with Special Reference to Robert Louis Stevenson and George MacDonald." Ph.D. diss., Auckland (New Zealand), 1973.

Naugrette, Jean-Pierre. "Robert Louis Stevenson, the Master of Ballantrye." *CVE* 30 (Oct 1989): 177–187.

Noble, Andrew, ed. *Robert Louis Stevenson.* Totowa, NJ: Barnes and Noble, 1983.

The Oxford Companion to Children's Literature. Edited by Humphrey Carpenter and Mari Prichard. New York: Oxford Univ. Press, 1984, pp. 496–497.

Ponnau, Gwenhail. *La Folie Dans la Littérature Fantastique [Madness in Fantasy Literature].* Paris: Editions du Centre National de la Recherche Scientifique, 1987.

Smith, Curtis C. "Robert Louis Stevenson." In *Supernatural Fiction Writers: Fantasy and Horror,* vol. 1. Edited by E. F. Bleiler. New York: Scribner, 1985, pp. 307–315.

Svilpis, J. E. "The Short Fiction of Stevenson." In *Survey of Modern Fantasy Literature,* vol. 4. Edited by Frank N. Magill. Englewood Cliffs, NJ: Salem Press, 1983, pp. 1698–1702.

Twentieth-Century Children's Writers. 3rd ed. Edited by Tracy Chevalier and D. L. Kirkpatrick. Chicago: St. James, 1989, pp. 919–920.

Stewart, Mary (Florence Elinor)

Fries, Maureen. "The Rationalization of the Arthurian Matter in T. H. White and Mary Stewart." *Philological Quarterly* 56 (1977): 258–265.

Herman, Harold J. "The Women in Mary Stewart's Merlin Trilogy." *Interpretations* 15 (Spring 1984): 101–114.

Myers, W. E. "The Merlin Trilogy." In *Survey of Modern Fantasy Literature,* vol. 2. Englewood Cliffs, NJ: Salem Press, 1983, pp. 1010–1014.

The Oxford Companion to Children's Literature. Edited by Humphrey Carpenter and Mari Prichard. New York: Oxford Univ. Press, 1984, p. 497.

Reaves, Monetha Roberta. "The Popular Fiction Tradition and the Novels of Mary Stewart." Ph.D. diss., Middle Tennessee State University, 1978.

Ryan, J. S. "Merlin and the 'Past and Future King': The Stewart Recension." *Orana* (Australia) 13 (Aug 1977): 67–72.

Searles, Baird, Beth Meacham, and Michael Franklin. *A Reader's Guide to Fantasy.* New York: Avon, 1982, p. 139.

Spirt, Diana L. *Introducing Bookplots 3: A Book Talk Guide for Use with Readers Ages 8–12.* New York: Bowker, 1988, pp. 309–314.

Spivack, Charlotte. *Merlin's Daughters: Contemporary Women Writers of Fantasy.* New York: Greenwood, 1987.

Stewart, Mary. "Why Shouldn't One Write 'Escapist' Fiction?" *Australian Author* 9 (Summer–Jan 1977): 5–10.

Whitaker, Muriel A. "'The Hollow Hills': A Celtic Motif in Modern Fantasy." *Mosaic* 13 (Spring-Summer 1980): 165–178.

Stockton, Frank (Francis) R(ichard)

Bell, Joseph. *A Bibliographical List of the Writings of Mr. Stockton.* Toronto: Soft Books, 1986.

Candill, Alma. "The Juvenile Literature of Frank R. Stockton." Master's thesis, George Peabody College for Teachers, 1930.

Eliason, Norman E. "Frank R. Stockton: A Critical Study." Master's thesis, University of Iowa, 1931.

Golemba, Henry L. *Frank R. Stockton.* Boston: Twayne, 1981.

Griffin, Martin I. J. *Frank R. Stockton: A Critical Biography.* Philadelphia: Univ. of Pennsylvania, 1939.

Hearn, Michael Patrick. "Frank R. Stockton." In *Writers for Children; Critical Studies of Major Authors Since the Seventeenth Century.* Edited by Jane M. Bingham. New York: Scribner, 1988, pp. 545–554.

Helbig, Alethea K., and Agnes Regan Perkins. *Dictionary of American Children's Fiction, 1859–1959.* Westport, CT: Greenwood, 1985, pp. 196, 490.

May, Jill P. "Frank R. Stockton." In *American Writers for Children before 1900. Dictionary of Literary Biography,* vol. 42. Detroit: Gale, 1985, pp. 332–337.

The Oxford Companion to Children's Literature. Edited by Humphrey Carpenter and Mari Prichard. New York: Oxford Univ. Press, 1984, p. 497.

Rahn, Suzanne. "Life at the Squirrel Inn: Rediscovering Frank Stockton." *The Lion and the Unicorn* 12 (1988): 224–239.

Twentieth-Century Children's Writers. 2nd ed. Edited by D. L. Kirkpatrick. New York: St. Martin, 1983, pp. 886–887.

Twentieth-Century Science Fiction Writers. 3rd ed. Edited by Noelle Watson and Paul E. Schellinger. Chicago: St. James Press, 1991, pp. 771–772.

Waggoner, Diana. "Frank R. Stockton." In *Supernatural Fiction Writers: Fantasy and Horror,* vol. 2. Edited by E. F. Bleiler. New York: Scribner, 1985, pp. 753–760.

Zipes, Jack, ed. *Fairy Tales of Frank Stockton* New York: Penguin, 1990.

Stoddard, Sandol *see* Warburg, Sandol Stoddard

Stolz, Mary (Slattery)

Haviland, Virginia. "*Cat in the Mirror,* a Review." *Horn Book* 51 (Dec 1975): 597–601.

Helbig, Alethea, and Agnes Regan Perkins. *Dictionary of American Children's Fiction, 1859–1959.* Westport, CT: Greenwood, 1985, pp. 490–491.

———. *Dictionary of American Children's Fiction, 1960–1984.* Westport, CT: Greenwood, 1986, pp. 47, 100, 626–627.

———. *Dictionary of American Children's Fiction, 1985–1989.* Westport, CT: Greenwood, 1993, pp. 201–202, 241–242.

Hopkins, Lee Bennett. "Mary Stolz." In *More Books by More People.* New York: Citation Press, 1974, pp. 343–350.

Jenkins, R. "A Bio-Bibliographical Study of Mary Stolz." Research paper, Kent State University, 1974.

Kaser, Billie F. "The Literary Value and Adolescent Appeal of Mary Stolz's Novels." *Arizona English Bulletin* 14 (Apr 1972): 14–19.

More Junior Authors. Edited by Muriel Fuller. New York: Wilson, 1963, pp. 195–196.

The Oxford Companion to Children's Literature. Edited by Humphrey Carpenter and Mari Prichard. New York: Oxford Univ. Press, 1984, pp. 497–498.

Robinson, J. L. "Presentation of the Recognition of Merit Award to Mary Stolz." *Claremont Reading Conference Yearbook* 46 (1982): 83–87.

Roginski, Jim, ed. *Newbery and Caldecott Medalists and Honor Book Winners.* Littleton, CO: Libraries Unlimited, 1982, pp. 255–256.

Speaking for Ourselves: Autobiographical Sketches by Notable Authors of Books for Young Adults. Edited by Donald R. Gallo. Urbana, IL: National Council of Teachers of English, 1990, pp. 200–202.

Stolz, Mary. "Children's Books, According to an Ex-Child Who Not Only Remembers But Writes Them." *Claremont Reading Conference Yearbook* 31 (1967): 244–249.

———. "An Honorable Profession." *Saturday Review* 47 (Nov 7, 1964): 45–46. Reprinted in Robert Bator. *Signposts to Criticism of Children's Literature.* Chicago: American Library Association, 1983, pp. 46–49.

Twentieth-Century Children's Writers. 3rd ed. Edited by Tracy Chevalier and D. L. Kirkpatrick. Chicago: St. James, 1989, pp. 921–923.

Stong, Phil(ip Duffield)

Helbig, Alethea K., and Agnes Regan Perkins. *Dictionary of American Children's Fiction, 1859–1959.* Westport, CT: Greenwood, 1985, pp. 491–492.

More Junior Authors. Edited by Muriel Fuller. New York: Wilson, 1963, pp. 197–198.

The Oxford Companion to Children's Literature. Edited by Humphrey Carpenter and Mari Prichard. New York: Oxford Univ. Press, 1984, p. 258.

Roginski, Jim, ed. *Newbery and Caldecott Medalists and Honor Book Winners.* Littleton, CO: Libraries Unlimited, 1982, pp. 257–258.

Twentieth-Century Children's Writers. 3rd ed. Edited by Tracy Chevalier and D. L. Kirkpatrick. Chicago: St. James, 1989, pp. 923–924.

Storr, Catherine (Cole)

Farmer, Penelope. "'Jorinda and Jorindel' and Other Stories." *Children's Literature in Education* 7 (Mar 1972): 23–37. Reprinted in Fox. *Writers, Critics, and Children.* New York: Agathon Press, 1976, pp. 55–72.

Grieve, Ann. "The Psychotic State in Fantasy for Post-Primary Readers." *School Library Bulletin* (Australia) 10 (Aug 1978): 3–10.

The Oxford Companion to Children's Literature. Edited by Humphrey Carpenter and Mari Prichard. New York: Oxford Univ. Press, 1984, p. 498.

Storr, Catherine. "Folk and Fairy Tales." *Children's Literature in Education* 17 (Spring 1986): 63–70. Paper given at the Fourth *Bookquest* Conference, Brighton Polytechnic, Spring, 1984.

———. "Things That Go Bump in the Night." *Sunday Times Magazine* (London), Mar 7, 1971. Reprinted in Margaret Meek. *The Cool Web.* New York: Atheneum, 1978, pp. 120–128.

———. "Why Folk Tales and Fairy Stories Live Forever." *Where* 53 (1971): 8–11. Reprinted in Robert Bator. *Signposts to Criticism of Children's Literature.* Chicago: American Library Association, 1983, pp. 177–184.

———. "Why Write? Why Write for Children?" In Edward Blishen. *The Thorny Paradise.* Boston: Horn Book, 1975, pp. 25–33.

Twentieth-Century Children's Writers. 3rd ed. Edited by Tracy Chevalier and D. L. Kirkpatrick. Chicago: St. James, 1989, pp. 925–927.

Stranger, Joyce (pseud. of Joyce Muriel Judson Wilson)

The Oxford Companion to Children's Literature. Edited by Humphrey Carpenter and Mari Prichard. New York: Oxford Univ. Press, 1984, p. 500.

Stranger, Joyce. "The Way I Live." *Junior Bookshelf* (U.K.) 43 (Oct 1979): 259–264.
Twentieth-Century Children's Writers. 3rd ed. Edited by Tracy Chevalier and D. L. Kirkpatrick. New York: St. Martin, 1989, pp. 930–931.

Straub, Peter (Francis)

Bosky, Bernadette. "Stephen King, and Peter Straub: Fear and Friendship." In *Discovering Stephen King.* Mercer Island, WA: Starmont, 1985.
Grant, Charles L. "Many Years Ago, When We All Lived in the Forest . . ." In *Shadowings.* Edited by Douglas E. Winter. Mercer Island, WA: Starmont, 1983, pp. 30–32.
Winter, Douglas E. *Faces of Fear: Encounters with the Creators of Modern Horror.* New York: Berkley, 1985.

Strugatskii, Arkadii Natanovich, and Strugatskii, Boris Natanovich

Csicery-Ronay, Istuan, Jr. "Towards the Last Fairy Tale: On the Fairy-Tale Paradigm in the Strugatsky's Science Fiction, 1963–1972." *Science-Fiction Studies* 13 (1986): 1–41.
Kuczka, Petor. "Fifty Questions: An Interview with the Strugatsky Brothers." *Foundation* 34 (1985): 16–21.
McGuire, Patrick L. "Future History, Soviet Style: The Work of the Strugatsky Brothers." In *Critical Encounters II.* Edited by Tom Staicar. New York: Ungar, 1982, pp. 104–124.
Myers, Alan. "Some Developments in Soviet Science Fiction Since 1966." *Foundation* 19 (1980): 38–47.
Salvestroni, Simonetta. "The Ambiguous Miracle in Three Novels by the Strugatsky Brothers." *Science-Fiction Studies* 11 (1984): 291–303.
Twentieth-Century Science Fiction Writers. 2nd ed. Edited by Curtis C. Smith. Chicago: St. James Press, 1986, pp. 850–852.

Sucharitkul, Somtow

"Interview: Somtow Sucharitkul." *Thrust* 18 (1982): 20–24.
"Somtow Sucharitkul: Clown Prince of Science Fiction." *Locus* 291 (1985): 1ff.
Twentieth-Century Science Fiction Writers. 3rd ed. Edited by Noelle Watson and Paul E. Schellinger. Chicago: St. James Press, 1991, pp. 775–777.

Sudbery, Rodie (Tutton)

Rees, David. "Middle of the Way: Rodie Sudbery and Beverly Cleary." In *Marble in the Water.* Boston: Horn Book, 1980, pp. 90–103.
Twentieth-Century Children's Writers. 3rd ed. Edited by Tracy Chevalier and D. L. Kirkpatrick. Chicago: St. James, 1989, p. 937.

Sutcliff, Rosemary

Adamson, Lynda Gossett. "A Content Analysis of Values in Rosemary Sutcliff's Historical Fiction for Children." Ph.D. diss., University of Maryland, 1981.
Aldridge, J. "Rosemary Sutcliff: A Personal Memoir." *Bookmark* (Scotland) 17 (1992): 35–37.
Atterton, Julian, and Tina Massey. "Rosemary Sutcliff: Warrior Queen." *Books for Your Children* (U.K.) 26, no. 1 (1991): 18–19.

Brown, M. O. "Rosemary Sutcliff." *Ontario Library Review* (May 1958): 84–86.

Colwell, Eileen H. "Rosemary Sutcliff—Lantern Bearer." *Horn Book* 36 (Jan 1960): 200–205.

Corbett, E. V. "Carnegie Medal Goes to Rosemary Sutcliff." [British] *Library Association Record* (Sept 1960): 159–160.

Crouch, Marcus. *The Nesbit Tradition.* London: Benn, 1972, pp. 63–66.

———. "Rosemary Sutcliff, 1920–1992." *Junior Bookshelf* (U.K.) 56 (1992): 181–184.

Frongia, Terri. "Merlin's Fathers: The Sacred and the Profane." *Children's Literature Association Quarterly* 18 (Fall 1993): 120–125. Discusses Peter Dickinson, Pamela Service, Rosemary Sutcliff, and Jane Yolen.

Gardiner, J. "A Suitcase of Dreams." *Times Educational Supplement* (Nov 9, 1990): 22–23.

Gould, Rachel. "For Children from 9–90." *Sunday Express Magazine* (London) (Sept 6, 1981): 18–20.

Inglis, Fred. *The Promise of Happiness.* New York: Cambridge Univ. Press, 1981, pp. 217–221.

———. "Reading Children's Novels: Private Culture and the Politics of Literature." *Children's Literature in Education* 5 (July 1971): 60–75. Reprinted in Fox. *Writers, Critics and Children.* New York: Agathon Press, 1976, pp. 157–173.

Jeffs, Carol. "The High Deeds of Rosemary Sutcliff." *Amon Hen* 57 (Aug 1982): 14, 16–17.

Jones, Cornelia, and Olivia R. Way. *British Children's Authors: Interviews at Home.* Chicago: American Library Association, 1976, pp. 146–154.

Keenan, S. V. "Rosemary Sutcliff." *Wilson Library Bulletin* 35 (Sept 1960): 75.

Lewis, Tom. "An Interview with Rosemary Sutcliff." *Magpies* (Australia) 7 (Mar 1992): 14–16.

MacMurray, Susan E. *Rosemary Sutcliff: A Bibliography.* Johannesburg: Univ. of Witwatersrand, 1972.

Meek, Margaret. "'Of the Minstrel Kind'." *Books for Keeps* (U.K.) 64 (1990): 28–29.

———. *Rosemary Sutcliff.* New York: Walck, 1962.

More Junior Authors. Edited by Muriel Fuller. New York: Wilson, 1963, pp. 200–201.

Moss, Elaine. "Chronicler of Occupied Britannia: Rosemary Sutcliff." *The Guardian* (July 27, 1992): 39.

———. "Rosemary Sutcliff, a Love of Legend." In *Part of the Pattern.* New York: Greenwillow, 1986, pp. 17–19.

Philip, Neil. "Romance, Sentiment, Adventure." *Times Educational Supplement* (Feb 19, 1982): 23.

Potter, Joyce Elizabeth. "Eternal Relic: A Study of Setting in Rosemary Sutcliff's *Dragon Slayer.*" *Children's Literature Association Quarterly* 10 (Fall 1985): 108–112.

Ryan, J. S. "Romance Blighted but Pain Vanquished: Or, the Making of Rosemary Sutcliff." *Orana* (Australia) 19 (May 1983): 61–67.

"The Search for Selfhood: The Historical Novels of Rosemary Sutcliff." *Times Literary Supplement,* June 17, 1965, p. 498. Reprinted in Egoff. *Only Connect.* 1st ed. New York: Oxford Univ. Press, 1969, pp. 249–255.

Speaking for Ourselves: Autobiographical Sketches by Notable Authors of Books for Young Adults. Edited by Donald R. Gallo. Urbana, IL: National Council of Teachers of English, 1990, pp. 206–208.

Stroud, Daphne. "Rosemary Sutcliff and the Matter of Britain." *Junior Bookshelf* 52, no. 2 (1988): 69–72.

Sutcliff, Rosemary. "Acceptance Speech: The Phoenix Award." *Children's Literature Association Quarterly* 10 (Winter 1986): 175–176.

———. "Beginning with Beowulf." *Horn Book* 29 (Feb 1953): 36–38.

———. *Blue Remembered Hills.* London: Oxford, 1988.

———. *Blue Remembered Hills: A Recollection.* London: Bodley Head, 1983.

————. "Lost Summer." In *The Thorny Paradise: Writers on Writing for Children,* ed. by Edward Blishen. Boston: Horn Book, 1975, pp. 93–96.

————. "Novelist's Hat and Minstrel's Bonnet." *Bookmark* (Scotland) 11 (Sept 1983): 12–17.

————. "Rosemary Sutcliff's Thank-You Address to the Children's Literature Association in Ann Arbor, MI, 19th May, 1985, Upon Receipt of the Phoenix Award." *Children's Literature Association Quarterly* 10 (Winter 1986): 176–177.

————. "Still in the Making." *School Bookshop News* (U.K.) (Mar 4, 1976): 21–23.

Townsend, John Rowe. *A Sense of Story.* London: Longman, 1971; Philadelphia: Lippincott, 1971, pp. 193–203.

Twentieth-Century Children's Writers. 3rd ed. Edited by Tracy Chevalier and D. L. Kirkpatrick. Chicago: St. James, 1989, pp. 938–940.

Wintle, Justin, and Emma Fisher. *The Pied Pipers.* New York: Paddington Press, 1974, pp. 182–191.

Wright, Hilary. "Shadows on the Downs: Some Influences of Rudyard Kipling on Rosemary Sutcliff." *Children's Literature in Education* 12 (Summer 1981): 90–102.

Young, Carol C. "Goodbye to Camelot." *English Journal* 74 (Feb 1985): 54–58.

Swift, Jonathan

Basney, Lionel. "*Gulliver* and the Child." In *The Voice of the Narrator in Children's Literature: Insights from Writers and Critics,* ed. by Charlotte F. Otten and Gary D. Schmidt. New York: Greenwood, 1989, pp. 148–158.

Bator, Robert. "Jonathan Swift." In *Writers for Children: Critical Studies of Major Authors Since the Seventeenth Century.* Edited by Jane M. Bingham. New York: Scribner, 1988, pp. 555–560.

Bergin, Mary Washington. "Jonathan Swift and 'The Whole People of Ireland.'" Ph.D. diss., University of Virginia, 1986.

Billingsley, Dale B. "Gulliver, Mandeville and Capital Crime." *Notes and Queries* 30 (1983): 32–33.

Blakeney, Richard. "The Rhetoric of Paradox in *Gulliver's Travels.*" Ph.D. diss., Louisiana State University, 1974.

Bryant, D. C. "Persuasive Uses of Imaginary Literature in Certain Satires of Jonathan Swift." *Southern Speech and Communications Journal* 46 (Winter 1981): 175–183.

Case, A. E. *Four Essays on Gulliver's Travels.* Princeton, NJ: Princeton Univ. Press, 1945.

Cohan, S. M. "*Gulliver's* Fiction." *Studies in the Novel* 6 (Spring 1974): 7–16.

Danchin, Pierre. "The Text of *Gulliver's Travels.*" *Texas Studies in Literature and Language* 2 (1960): 233–250.

Donoghue, Denis. "The Brainwashing of *Gulliver.*" *Listener* [London] 96, no. 2482 (Nov 11, 1976): 578–579.

————. "Swift and the Association of Ideas." *Yearbook of English Studies* 18 (1988): 1–17.

Doyle, Brian. *The Who's Who of Children's Literature.* New York: Schocken, 1968, pp. 261–262.

Fitzgerald, R. P. "The Structure of *Gulliver's Travels.*" *Studies in Philology* 71 (Apr 1974): 247–263.

Greenacre, Phyllis. *Swift and Carroll: A Psychoanalytic Study of Two Lives.* New York: International Universities Press, 1955.

Hazard, Paul. *Books, Children, and Men.* Boston: Horn Book, 1960, pp. 61–69.

Hazenstaub, Steven F. "Swift's *Gulliver's Travels.*" *Explicator* 47 (Winter 1989): 14–16.

Hubbard, Lucius. *Contributions toward a Bibliography of Gulliver's Travels.* Chicago: Hill, 1922.

Irwin, W. R. "Swift and the Novelists." *Philological Quarterly* 45 (Jan 1966): 102–113.

Koch, Robert Allen. "Gulliver and Dr. Swift: The Issue of the Satirist's Identity." Ph.D. diss., Rice University, 1982.

Liebs, Elke. "Between *Gulliver* and *Alice*: Some Remarks on the Dialectic of GREAT and SMALL in Literature." *Phaedrus* 13 (1988): 56–60.

Mezciems, Jenny. "Swift and Orwell: Utopia as Nightmare." In *Between Dream and Nature: Essays on Utopia and Dystopia,* ed. by Dominic Baker-Smith and C. C. Barfoot. Amsterdam: Rodopi, 1987, pp. 91–112.

Mortenson, Robert. "A Note on the Revision of *Gulliver's Travels.*" *University of Pennsylvania Library Chronicle* 28 (Winter 1962): 26–28.

Nuttal, A. D. "*Gulliver* Among the Horses." *Yearbook of English Studies* 18 (1988): 51–57.

The Oxford Companion to Children's Literature. Edited by Humphrey Carpenter and Mari Prichard. New York: Oxford Univ. Press, 1984, pp. 232, 311.

Passmann, Dirk F. "The Lilliputian Utopia: A Revised Focus." *Swift Studies* 2 (1987): 67–76.

Pickering, S. F. "Gulliver and the Lilliputians." *AB Bookman's Weekly* 73 (Jan 9, 1984): 175ff.

Reilly, Edward J., ed. *Approaches to Teaching Swift's "Gulliver's Travels."* New York: Modern Language Association, 1988.

Rodino, Richard. H. "'Splendide Mendax': Authors, Characters, and Readers in *Gulliver's Travels.*" *PMLA* 106 (Oct 1991): 1054–1070.

Sackett, S. "*Gulliver* Four: Here We Go Again." *Rocky Mountain MLA Bulletin* 27 (Dec 1973): 212–218.

Salvaggio, Ruth. "Swift and Psychoanalysis, Language, and Woman." *Women's Studies* 15 (1988): 417–434.

Smith, Frederik N., ed. *The Genres of "Gulliver's Travels."* Newark: Univ. of Delaware Press, 1990.

———. "Science, Imagination and Swift's Brobdingnagians." *Eighteenth-Century Life* 14 (1990): 100–114.

Sullivan, Evelin Elisabeth. "*Gulliver's Travels:* A Study in Meaning." Ph.D. diss., University of California, San Diego, 1981.

Taylor, Sheila. "The 'Secret Pocket': Private Vision and Communal Identity in *Gulliver's Travels.*" *Studies in the Humanities* 6 (1978): 5–11.

Tilton, John W. "Gulliver's Travels as a Work of Art." *Bucknell Review* 8, no. 4: 246–254.

Vessberg, Viveka. "*Gullivers Resor*: En Vuxenbok som Blivit Barnbok [*Gulliver's Travels*: A Book for Adults Which Became a Children's Book]." *Tidskrift for Litteraturvetenskap* [Stockholm] 11 (1982): 185–195.

Washington, E. "The Habsburgs and *Gulliver's Travels.*" *American Notes and Queries* 16 (1977–78): 83 85.

Welcher, Jeanne K. "Eighteenth Century Views of *Gulliver*: Some Contrasts Between Illustrations and Prints." In *Imagination on a Long Rein: English Literary Illustration,* ed. by Joachim Moeller. Marburg: Jonas Verlag, 1988, pp. 82–93.

Williams, Harold. *The Text of Gulliver's Travels.* New York: Cambridge Univ. Press, 1952.

Williams, Kathleen. "Jonathan Swift." In *Dryden to Johnson,* ed. by Roger Lonsdale. New York: Bedrick, 1987, pp. 41–76.

Symons, (Dorothy) Geraldine

Twentieth-Century Children's Writers. 3rd ed. Edited by Tracy Chevalier and D. L. Kirkpatrick. Chicago: St. James, 1989, pp. 945–946.

Tarn, Sir William Woodthrope

Dalphin, Marcia. "I Give You the End of a Golden String." *Horn Book* 14 (May 1938): 143–149. Reprinted in Norma Fryatt. *A Horn Book Sampler.* Boston: Horn Book, 1959, pp. 133–139.

MacAdam, Henry Ines. "Return to *The Island of Mist.*" *The Lion and the Unicorn* 15 (Dec 1991): 67–71.

Searles, Baird, Beth Meacham, and Michael Franklin. *A Reader's Guide to Fantasy.* New York: Avon, 1982, p. 143.

Yates, Elizabeth. *"The Isle of Mist."* *Horn Book* 14 (May 1938): 150–152.

Tepper, Sheri S.

Kondratiev, Alexei. "Tales Newly Told." *Mythlore* 18 (Autumn 1991): 28–29.

Price, Beverly. "Sheri S. Tepper and Feminism's Future." *Mythlore* 18 (Spring 1992): 41–44.

Thackeray, William Makepeace

Burns, Marjorie Jean. "Victorian Fantasists from Ruskin to Lang: A Study in Ambivalence." Ph.D. diss., University of California, Berkeley, 1978.

Doyle, Brian. *The Who's Who of Children's Literature.* New York: Schocken, 1968, p. 264.

Goldfarb, Sheldon. *William Makepeace Thackeray: An Annotated Bibliography, 1976–1987.* New York: Garland, 1989.

McMaster, Juliet. *"The Rose and the Ring:* Quintessential Thackeray." *Mosaic* 9, no. 4 (Summer 1976): pp. 157–165.

Manlove, C. N. "Comments on Thackeray's *The Rose and the Ring.*" In C. N. Manlove. *The Impulse of Fantasy Literature.* Kent, OH: Kent State Univ. Press, 1983, pp. 7–14.

The Oxford Companion to Children's Literature. Edited by Humphrey Carpenter and Mari Prichard. New York: Oxford Univ. Press, 1984, pp. 460–461.

Ritchie, Lady. *Blackstick Papers.* New York: G. P. Putnam, 1908.

Sorenson, Gail D. "Thackeray's *The Rose and the Ring*: A Novelist's Fairy Tale." *Mythlore* 57 (Spring 1989): 37–38.

Thackeray, William Makepeace. *"The Rose and the Ring."* In *Masterworks of Children's Literature,* vol. 6. New York: Stonehill/Chelsea House, 1984, pp. 63–136.

Tremper, Ellen. "Commitment and Escape: The Fairy Tales of Thackeray, Dickens, and Wilde." *The Lion and the Unicorn* 2 (Spring 1978): 38–47.

Zanger, Jules. *"The Rose and the Ring."* In *Survey of Modern Fantasy Literature,* vol. 3. Edited by Frank N. Magill. Englewood Cliffs, NJ: Salem Press, 1983, pp. 1135–1137.

Theroux, Paul

Wright, Ann. "Paul Theroux's Christmas Tales." *Children's Literature in Education* 15 (Autumn 1984): 141–146.

Thompson, Ruth Plumly

Doyle, Brian. *The Who's Who of Children's Literature.* New York: Schocken, 1968, pp. 264–265.

Hanff, Peter E., and Douglas G. Greene. *Bibliographia Oziana.* Demorest, GA: International Wizard of Oz Club, 1976.

Hearn, Michael Patrick. "The Mantle of *Oz* Is Passed." *Baum Bugle* 55, no. 2 (Autumn 1991): 3–6.

————. "Ruth Plumly Thompson." In Cech. *American Writers for Children, 1900–1960. Dictionary of Literary Biography,* vol. 22. Detroit: Gale, 1983, pp. 307–314.

Searles, Baird, Beth Meacham, and Michael Franklin. *A Reader's Guide to Fantasy.* New York: Avon, 1982, pp. 143–144.

Thurber, James (Grover)

Bernstein, Burton. *Thurber: A Biography.* New York: Dodd, 1975.

Bowden, Edwin T. *James Thurber: A Bibliography.* Columbus: Ohio State Univ. Press, 1968.

Ewing, J. "Sharing Thurber with Children." *Elementary English* 32 (Feb 1955): 99–100.

Fensch, Thomas. *Conversations with James Thurber.* Mississippi State: Univ. Press of Mississippi, 1989.

Helbig, Alethea K., and Agnes Regan Perkins. *Dictionary of American Children's Fiction, 1859–1959.* Westport, CT: Greenwood, 1985, pp. 194–195, 518, 523.

Hildebrand, Ann M. "A New Phase of James Thurber's *Many Moons.*" *Children's Literature in Education* 15 (1984): 147–156.

Holmes, Charles S. *The Clocks of Columbus: The Literary Career of James Thurber.* New York: Atheneum, 1972.

————. "James Thurber and the Art of Fantasy." *Yale Review* 55 (Oct 1965): 17–33.

Long, Robert Emmet. *James Thurber.* New York: Crossroad/Ungar/Continuum, 1988.

More Junior Authors. Edited by Muriel Fuller. New York: Wilson, 1963, pp. 204–205.

Morsberger, Robert E. "The Short Fiction of James Thurber." In *Survey of Modern Fantasy Literature,* vol. 4. Edited by Frank N. Magill. Englewood Cliffs, NJ: Salem Press, 1983, pp. 1712–1717.

————. "The Thirteen Clocks." In *Survey of Modern Fantasy Literature,* vol. 4. Edited by Frank N. Magill. Englewood Cliffs, NJ: Salem Press, 1983, pp. 1904–1907.

————. "The White Deer." In *Survey of Modern Fantasy Literature,* vol. 5. Edited by Frank N. Magill. Englewood Cliffs, NJ: Salem Press, 1983, pp. 2118–2121.

————. "The Wonderful O." In *Survey of Modern Fantasy Literature,* vol. 5. Edited by Frank N. Magill. Englewood Cliffs, NJ: Salem Press, 1983, pp. 2159–2161.

Rupprecht, Erich S. "James Thurber." In *Supernatural Fiction Writers: Fantasy and Horror,* vol. 2. Edited by E. F. Bleiler. New York: Scribner, 1985, pp. 827–834.

Searles, Baird, Beth Meacham, and Michael Franklin. *A Reader's Guide to Fantasy.* New York: Avon, 1982, pp. 144–145.

Thurber, James. *Collecting Himself: James Thurber on Writing and Writers, Humor and Himself,* ed. by Michael J. Rosen. New York: Harper, 1989; London: Hamilton, 1989.

Toomes, Sarah Eleanora. *James Thurber: An Annotated Bibliography of Criticism.* New York: Garland, 1987.

Twentieth-Century Children's Writers. 3rd ed. Edited by Tracy Chevalier and D. L. Kirkpatrick. Chicago: St. James, 1989, pp. 929–960.

Vousden, E. Charles. "James Thurber." In Cech. *American Writers for Children, 1900–1960. Dictionary of Literary Biography,* vol. 22. Detroit: Gale, 1985, pp. 315–320.

Zipes, Jack, ed. *Spells of Enchantment: The Wondrous Fairy Tales of Western Culture.* New York: Viking, 1991.

Titus, Eve

Third Book of Junior Authors. Edited by Doris De Montreville and Donna Hill. New York: Wilson, 1972, pp. 283–284.

Twentieth-Century Children's Writers. 3rd ed. Edited by Tracy Chevalier and D. L. Kirkpatrick. Chicago: St. James, 1989, pp. 962–963.

Todd (Bower), Barbara Euphan

Twentieth-Century Children's Writers. 3rd ed. Edited by Tracy Chevalier and D. L. Kirkpatrick. Chicago: St. James, 1989, pp. 963–964.

Todd, Ruthven

Antczak, Janice. *Science Fiction: The Mythos of a New Romance.* New York: Neal-Schuman, 1985, pp. 168, 173.

Helbig, Alethea K., and Agnes Regan Perkins. *Dictionary of American Children's Fiction, 1859–1959.* Westport, CT: Greenwood, 1985, pp. 482, 524–525.

More Junior Authors. Edited by Muriel Fuller. New York: Wilson, 1963, pp. 205–206.

Tolkien, J(ohn) R(onald) R(euel)

Abbot, Joe. "Tolkien's Monsters: Concept and Function in *The Lord of the Rings.*" *Mythlore* 16 (Autumn 1989): 19–26; continued 16 (Winter 1989): 10–17; continued 16 (Spring 1990): 51–59.

Alderson, Brian. *"The Hobbit": 50th Anniversary 1937–1987.* London: Unwin, 1987.

Aldrich, Kevin. "The Sense of Time in J. R. R. Tolkien's *The Lord of the Rings.*" *Mythlore* 55 (1988): 5–9.

Allan, Jim, ed. and comp. *An Introduction to Elvish, and to Other Tongues. . . . in the Published Writings of Professor John Ronald Reuel Tolkien.* Hays, Middlesex: Bran's Head Books, 1978.

Allen, Elizabeth M. "The Fellowship of Merlin: The Role of the Sorcerer in *The Once and Future King* and *The Lord of the Rings.*" Master's thesis, Baylor University, 1978.

―――. "Persian Influences on J. R. R. Tolkien's *The Lord of the Rings.*" In *The Transcendent Adventure.* Edited by Robert Reilly. Westport, CT: Greenwood, 1985, pp. 189–206.

Arda 1987. Special Journal on J. R. R. Tolkien. Upsala, Sweden, 1992.

Arthur, Elizabeth. "Above All Shadows Rides the Sun: Gollum as Hero." *Mythlore* 18 (Autumn 1991): 19–27.

Ashmolean Museum. *Catalogue of an Exhibition of Drawings by J. R. R. Tolkien.* London: Ashmolean Museum and National Book League, in conjunction with Allen & Unwin, 1976.

Barber, Dorothy Elizabeth Klein. "The Structure of *The Lord of the Rings.*" Ph.D. diss., University of Michigan, 1965.

Barnfield, Marie. "Celtic Influences on the History of the First Age." *Mallorn* (U.K.) 28 (1991): 2–6.

―――. "More Celtic Influences: Numemor and the Second Age." *Mallorn* (U.K.) 29 (1992): 6–13.

Barbour, Douglas. "J. R. R. Tolkien." In *Supernatural Fiction Writers: Fantasy and Horror,* vol. 2. Edited by E. F. Bleiler. New York: Scribner, 1985, pp. 675–684.

―――. "The Shadow of the Past: History in Middle Earth." *University of Windsor Review* 8 (Fall 1972): 35–42.

Barkley, Christine. "Donaldson As Heir to Tolkien." *Mythlore* 38 (1984): 50–57.

―――. "Predictability and Wonder: Familiarity and Recovery in Tolkien's Works." *Mythlore* 8 (Spring 1981): 16–18.

Basney, Lionel. "Tolkien and the Ethical Function of 'Escape' Literature." *Mosaic* 13 (Winter 1980): 23–46.

Beagle, Peter S. "Tolkien's Magic Ring." *Holiday,* June 1966, pp. 128–131. Reprinted in *The Tolkien Reader.* New York: Ballantine, 1966, pp. ix–xvi; Boyer and Zahorski. *Fantasists on Fantasy.* New York: Avon, 1984.

Becker, Alida, ed. *The Tolkien Scrapbook.* Philadelphia: Running Press, 1978.

Beetridge, William Edwin. "Tolkien's New Mythology." *Mythlore* 16 (Summer 1990): 27–36.

Bennet, C. "In the Beginning, There Was Bilbo." *Times Literary Supplement* (Aug 2, 1987): 13.

Bergmann, Frank. "The Roots of Tolkien's Tree: The Influence of George MacDonald and German Romanticism Upon Tolkien's Essay 'On Fairy-Stories.'" *Mosaic* 10 (Winter 1977): 5–14.

Berman, Ruth. "Dragons for Tolkien and Lewis." *Mythlore* 39 (1984): 53–58.

———. "Victorian Dragons: The Reluctant Brood." *Children's Literature in Education* 15 (Winter 1984): 220–233.

Bisenieks, Dainis. "Power and Poetry in Middle Earth." *Mythlore* 3, 10 (1976).

Blackburn, William. "'Dangerous as a Guide to Deeds': Politics in the Fiction of J. R. R. Tolkien." *Mythlore* 55 (1988): 62–66.

Blackwelder, Richard E. *Tolkien Phraseology: A Companion to "A Tolkien Thesaurus."* Milwaukee, WI: Tolkien Archives Fund, Marquette University, 1990.

———. *A Tolkien Thesaurus.* New York: Garland, 1990.

Boenig, Robert. "Tolkien and Old Germanic Ethics." *Mythlore* 48 (1986): 9–12, 40.

Bold, Alan. "Hobbit Verse Versus Tolkien's Poem." In *J. R. R. Tolkien: This Far Land.* Totowa, NJ: Barnes and Noble, 1984, pp. 137–153.

Boswell, G. W. "Tolkien as *Litteratur.*" *South Central Bulletin Studies* 32 (Winter 1972): 4188–4197.

Bradley, Marion Zimmer. *Men, Halflings and Hero Worship.* Baltimore: T-K Graphics, 1973.

Bratman, David S. "Books about J. R. R. Tolkien and His Works." *Science Fiction Collector* 5 (1977): 26–28.

Brooks-Rose, Christine. "The Evil Ring: Realism and the Marvellous." *Poetics Today* 1, no. 4 (1980). Reprinted in Christine Brooks-Rose. *A Rhetoric of the Unreal.* New York: Cambridge Univ. Press, 1983, pp. 233–255.

Brown, G. "Pastoralism and Industrialism in *The Lord of the Rings.*" *English Studies in Africa* 19 (Sept 1976): 83–91.

Brunsdale, Mitzi M. "Norse Mythological Elements in *The Hobbit.*" *Mythlore* 34 (1983): 49–50, 55.

Bryce, Lynn. "The Influence of Scandinavian Mythology on the Works of J. R. R. Tolkien." *Edda,* 1983, pp. 113–119.

———. "The Use of Christian Iconography in Selected Marginalia of J. R. R. Tolkien's Lothlórien Chapters." *Extrapolation* 25 (Spring 1984): 51–59.

Bullock, Richard P. "The Importance of Free Will in *The Lord of the Rings.*" *Mythlore* 41 (1985): 29ff.

Burger, Douglas A. "Tolkien's Elvish Craft and Frodo's Mithril Coat." In *The Scope of the Fantastic—Theory, Technique, Major Authors.* Edited by Robert A. Collins and Howard D. Pearce. Westport, CT: Greenwood, 1985, pp. 255–262.

———. "The Uses of the Past in *The Lord of the Rings.*" *Kansas Quarterly* 16 (Summer 1984): 23–28.

Burgess, Michael W. "Of Barghest, Orc, and Ringwraith." *Amon Hen,* Sept 1985, pp. 15–16.

———. "Orome and the Wild Hunt: The Development of a Myth." *Mallorn* 22 (1985): 5–11.

Burns, Marjorie J. "J. R. R. Tolkien and the Journey North." *Mythlore* 15 (Summer 1989): 5–9.

Calabrese, John A. "Continuity with the Past: Mythic Time in Tolkien's *The Lord of the Rings.*" In *The Fantastic in World Literature and the Arts.,* ed. by Donald E. Morse. New York: Greenwood, 1987, pp. 31–45.

———. "Dynamic Symbolism and the Mythic Resolution of Polar Extremes in *The Lord of the Rings.*" In *Spectrum of the Fantastic,* ed. by Doland Palumbo. Westport, CT: Greenwood, 1988.

———. "Elements of Myth in J. R. R. Tolkien's *Lord of the Rings* and Selected Paintings of Paul Klee." Ph.D. diss., Ohio University, 1980.

Callahan, Patrick J. "Animism and Magic in Tolkien's *The Lord of the Rings.*" *Riverside Quarterly* 4 (1971): 240–249.

Callaway, David. "Gollum: A Misunderstood Hero." *Mythlore* 37 (1984): 14–17, 22.

Carpenter, Humphrey. *The Inklings: C. S. Lewis, J. R. R. Tolkien, Charles Williams, and Their Friends.* Boston: Houghton Mifflin, 1979.

———. *J. R. R. Tolkien: A Biography.* London: Grafton, 1992 (orig. pub. 1977).

———. *Tolkien: A Biography.* Boston: Houghton Mifflin, 1977.

Chance, Jane. *"The Lord of the Rings": The Mythology of Power.* Boston: Twayne, 1992.

Chance, Jane, and David D. Day. "Medievalism in Tolkien: Two Decades of Criticism in Review." *Studies in Medievalism* 3 (Winter 1991): 375–388.

Chant, Joy. "Niggle and Numenor." *Children's Literature in Education* 19 (Winter 1975): 161–171.

Chapman, Vera. "Forerunner to Tolkien? Walter de la Mare's *The Three Royal Monkeys.*" *Mythlore* 8, 28 (1981): 32–33.

Christensen, Bonniejean McGuire. *"Beowulf* and *The Hobbit:* Elegy into Fantasy in J. R. R. Tolkien's Creative Technique." Ph.D. diss., University of Southern California, 1969.

———. "Tolkien's Creative Technique: *Beowulf* and *The Hobbit.*" *Mythlore* 15 (Spring 1989): 1–10.

Christopher, Joe R. "An Inklings Bibliography." (2) *Mythlore* 4, no. 1 (1976): 33–38; (3) *Mythlore* 4, no. 2 (1976): 33–38; (4) *Mythlore* 4 (Mar 1977): 33–38; (5) *Mythlore* 4 (June 1977): 40–46; (6) *Mythlore* 5 (May 1978): 40–46; (7) *Mythlore* 5 (Autumn 1978): 43–46; (8) *Mythlore* 6 (Winter 1979): 46–47; (9) *Mythlore* 6 (Spring 1979): 40–46; (10) *Mythlore* 6 (Summer 1979): 38–45; (11) *Mythlore* 6 (Fall 1979): 44–47; (12) *Mythlore* 22 (1980): 41–45; (13) *Mythlore* 24 (1980): 42–47; (14) *Mythlore* 25 (1980): 43–47; (15) *Mythlore* 26 (1981): 42–46; (16) *Mythlore* 27 (1981): 43–47; (17) *Mythlore* 28 (1981): 43–47; (18) *Mythlore* 29 (1981): 43–47; (19) *Mythlore* 30 (1982): 43–47; (20) *Mythlore* 31 (1982): 37–41; (21) *Mythlore* 32 (1982): 42–46; (22) *Mythlore* 33 (1982): 42–46; (23) *Mythlore* 34 (1983): 51–55; (24) *Mythlore* 35 (1983): 51–55; (25) *Mythlore* 36 (1983): 51–55; (26) *Mythlore* 37 (1984): 51–55; (27) *Mythlore* 38 (1984): 58–63; (28) *Mythlore* 39 (1984): 59–63; (29) *Mythlore* 46 (1986): 57–59; (30) *Mythlore* 47 (1986): 51–54; (31) *Mythlore* 50 (1987): 58–62; (33) *Mythlore* 56 (1988): 64–66.

Clark, Beverly Lyon. "Crossword Puzzle: *The Hobbit.*" *Children's Literature Association Quarterly* 9 (Summer 1984): 76, 95.

Clausen, Christopher. "Home and Away in Children's Fiction." *Children's Literature* 10 (1982): 141–152.

———. "*The Lord of the Rings* and 'The Ballad of the White Horse.'" *South Atlantic Bulletin* 39, no. 2 (1974): 10–16.

Cockburn, Paul. "The Lore of the Rings." *Amon Hen* 99 (Sept 1989): 15–16.

Colbath, Mary Lou. "Worlds as They Should Be: Middle Earth, Narnia, and Prydain." *Elementary English* 48 (Dec 1971): 937–945.

Collins, David R. *J. R. R. Tolkien: Master of Fantasy.* Minneapolis: Lerner, 1992.

Cornwell, Charles Landrum. "From Self to the Shire: Studies in Victorian Fantasy." Ph.D. diss., University of Virginia, 1972.

Cox, John. "Tolkien's Platonic Fantasy." *Seven: An Anglo-American Literary Review* 5 (1984): 53–69.

Crabbe, Katharyn F. *J. R. R. Tolkien.* New York: Ungar, 1981.

Crawford, Edward. *Some Light on Middle-Earth.* Pinner, Middlesex: The Tolkien Society, 1985.

Crawford, Ted. "The Geography and Economy of Numenor." *Mallorn* 20 (Sept 1983): 15, 27.

Crossley, Robert. "A Long Day's Dying: The Elves of J. R. R. Tolkien and Sylvia Townsend Warner." In *Death and the Serpent: Immortality in Science Fiction and Fantasy.* Edited by Carl B. Yoke and Donald M. Hassler. Westport, CT: Greenwood, 1985, pp. 57–70.

Crouch, Marcus S. "Another Don in Wonderland." *Junior Bookshelf* 14, no. 2 (Mar 1950): 50–53.

Crowe, Edith L. "Integration in *Earthsea* and Middle-Earth." *San Jose Studies* 14 (1988): 63–80.

———. "The Many Faces of Heroism in Tolkien." *Mythlore* 36 (1983): 5–8.

Curtis, Jared. "On Re-Reading *The Hobbit,* Fifteen Years Later." *Children's Literature in Education* 15 (Summer 1984): 113–120.

Davenport, Guy. "'The Persistence of Light,' an Article on the Fantasy of J. R. R. Tolkien." *National Review* 11 (Apr 20, 1965): 332–334.

Davey, Colin. "Missing Rings—Revisited." *Amon Hen,* Jan 1985, pp. 18–19.

Day, David. *A Tolkien Bestiary.* Illus. by Ian Miller and others. New York: Ballantine, 1979.

———. "The Tolkien Centennial." *Books for Keeps* (U.K.) 72 (1992): 4–5.

———. *Tolkien: The Illustrated Encyclopedia.* London: Mitchell Beazley, 1991.

de Camp, L. Sprague. *Literary Swordsmen and Sorcerers: The Makers of Heroic Fantasy.* Sauk City, WI: Arkham House, 1976.

Deyo, Steven M. "Niggle's Leaves: The Red Book of Westmarch and Related Minor Poetry of J. R. R. Tolkien." *Mythlore* 45 (1986): 28–31ff.

Dockery, C. "The Myth of the Shadow in the Fantasies of Williams, Lewis and Tolkien." Ph.D. diss., Auburn University, 1975.

Dodds, David Llewellyn. "Magic in the Mythos of J. R. R. Tolkien and Charles Williams." *Inklings-Jahrbuch für Literatur und Asthetik* 10 (1992): 37–60.

Donahue, Thomas S. "A Linguist Looks at Tolkien's Elvish." *Mythlore* 37 (1984): 28–34.

Downing, Angelia. "From Quenya to the Common Speech: Linguistic Diversification in J. R. R. Tolkien's *The Lord of the Rings.*" *Revista Caneria de Estudios Ingleses* 4 (Apr 1982): 23–31.

Doxey, William S. "Culture as an Aspect of Style in Fantasy." *West Georgia College Review* 13 (May 1981): 1–7.

Doyle, Brian. *The Who's Who of Children's Literature.* New York: Schocken, 1968, pp. 266–268.

Drury, Roger. "Providence at Elrond's Council." *Mythlore* 7 (1980): 8–9.

Dubbs, Kathleen E. "Providence, Fate, and Chance: Boethian Philosophy in *The Lord of the Rings.*" *Twentieth Century Literature* 27 (1981): 34–42.

Dunsire, Brin. ". . . and the Mabinogion." *Amon Hen* 54 (Feb 1982): 7–10.

———. "Of Ham, and What Became of It." *Amon Hen* 98 (July 1989): 14–16.

Duriez, Colin. "Leonardo, Tolkien, and Mr. Baggins." *Mythlore* 1, 2 (1974).

———. *The Tokien and Middle-Earth Handbook.* Tundbridge Wells (U.K.): Monarch, 1992.

Edmonds, K. L. "Echoes in Age from the World of J. R. R. Tolkien." *Seven* 9 (1988): 67–82.

Edwards, Malcolm, and Robert Holdstock. "Middle Earth." In *Realms of Fantasy.* Garden City, NY: Doubleday, 1983, pp. 11–22.

Eiseley, Loren. "The Elvish Art of Enchantment: An Essay on J. R. R. Tolkien's *Tree and Leaf,* and on Mr. Tolkien's Other Distinguished Contributions to Imaginative Literature." *Horn Book* 41 (Aug 1965): 364–367.

Elgin, Don D. *The Comedy of the Fantastic: Ecological Perspectives on the Fantasy Novel.* Westport, CT: Greenwood, 1985.

Ellison, John A. "From Innocence to Experience: The Naiveté of J. R. R. Tolkien." *Mallorn* 23 (1986): 10–13.

———. "The Legendary War and the Real One: *The Lord of the Rings* and the Climate of Its Times." *Mallorn* 26 (1989): 17–20.

————. "Music in Relation to Tolkien: A Critique." *Amon Hen,* May 1983, pp. 10–11.

————. "The Reality of Middle-Earth." *Amon Hen* 54 (Feb 1982): 14–16.

————. "The Structure of *The Hobbit.*" *Mallorn* 27 (Sept 1990): 29–32.

Esmonde, Margaret P. "Beyond the Circles of the World: Death and the Hereafter in Children's Literature." In *Webs and Wardrobes: Humanist and Religious World Views in Children's Literature,* ed. by Joseph O'Beirne Milner and Lucy Floyd Morcock Milner. Lanham, MD: University Press of America, 1987, pp. 33–45.

Evans, Gwyenth. "Harps and Harpers in Contemporary Fantasy." *The Lion and the Unicorn* 16 (Dec 1992): 199–209.

Evans, Robley. *J. R. R. Tolkien.* New York: Crowell, 1976.

Evans, W. D. Emrys. "Illusion, Tale and Epic." *School Librarian* 21 (Mar 1973): 5–11.

————. *"The Lord of the Rings."* *School Librarian* 16, no. 3 (Dec 1968): 284–287.

Ferguson, S. "Whose Head on the Penny?" *Mallorn* [London] 11 (1978): 48–51.

Fifield, M. "Fantasy in and for the Sixties; *The Lord of the Rings,* by J. R. R. Tolkien." *English Journal* 55 (Oct 1966): 841–844.

Filmer, Kath. "An Allegory Unveiled: A Reading of *The Lord of the Rings.*" *Mythlore* 50 (1987): 19–21.

Flieger, Verlyn Brown. "Medieval Epic and Romance Motifs in J. R. R. Tolkien's *The Lord of the Rings.*" Ph.D. diss., Catholic University of America, 1977.

————. "Missing Person." *Mythlore* 46 (1986): 12–15.

————. "Time and Dream in *The Lost Road* and *The Lord of the Rings.*" *Inklings-Jahrbuch für Literatur und Asthetik* 10 (1992): 111–133.

Fonstad, Karen Wynn. *An Atlas of Middle Earth.* Boston: Houghton Mifflin, 1981.

————. *The Atlas of Middle-Earth,* rev. ed. Boston: Houghton, 1991.

Forbes, Cheryl. "Frodo Decides—Or Does He?" *Christianity Today* 20 (Dec 19, 1975): 10–13.

Foster, Robert. *The Complete Guide to Middle Earth: From "The Hobbit" to "The Silmarillion."* New York: Ballantine, 1985. Revised edition of *A Guide to Middle Earth.* Baltimore: Mirage Press, 1971.

Fraser, K. C. "Whose Ring Is It Anyway?" *Mallorn* 25 (1988): 12–14.

Fry, Carrol L. "Tolkien's Middle Earth and the Fantasy Frame." *Studies in the Humanities* 7 (1978): 35–42.

Gardner, A. "Literary Giant or Monstrous Myth?" (London) *Times Saturday Review* (Dec 28, 1991): 30–31, 33.

Garnett, Irene. "From Genesis to Revelation in Middle Earth." *Mallorn,* Apr 1985, p. 39.

Giddings, Robert, ed. *J. R. R. Tolkien, This Far Land: Essays on New Aspects of Middle Earth.* Totowa, NJ: Barnes and Noble, 1984.

Giddings, Robert, and Elizabeth Holland. *J. R. R. Tolkien: The Shores of Middle-Earth.* Frederick, MD: Altheia Books, 1982.

Gillespie, John T., and Diana Lembo. *Juniorplots: A Book Talk Manual for Teachers and Librarians.* New York: Bowker, 1967, pp. 197–198.

Glover, David. "Utopia and Fantasy in the Late 1960's: Burroughs, Moorcock, Tolkien." In *Popular Fiction and Social Change.* Edited by Christopher Pawling. New York: St. Martin, 1984.

Glover, Willis B. "The Christian Character of Tolkien's Invented World." *Criticism* 13 (Winter 1971): 1, 39–53.

Goodknight, Glen. "A Comparison of Cosmological Geography in the Works of J. R. R. Tolkien, C. S. Lewis, and Charles Williams." *Mythlore* 1, 3 (1974).

————. "J. R. R. Tolkien in Translation." *Mythlore* 69, no. 18 (Summer 1992): 61–69.

Goodwin, Karen. "A Phytogeography of Middle-Earth." *Mallorn* (June 18, 1982): 5–9.

Gose, Elliot. *Mere Creatures: A Study of Modern Fantasy Tales for Children.* Toronto: Univ. of Toronto Press, 1988, pp. 148–168.

Goselin, Peter Damien. "Two Faces of Eve: Galdriel and Shelob as Anima Figures." *Mythlore* 6 (Spring 1979): 3–4, 28.

Gottlieb, S. "An Interpretation of Gollum." *Tolkien Journal* 4 (1970–71): 11–12.

Graff, Eric. S. "The Three Faces of Faerie in Tolkien's Shorter Fiction: Niggle, Smith and Giles." *Mythlore* 69, no. 18 (Summer 1992): 15–189.

Gray, Thomas. "Bureaucratization in *The Lord of the Rings*." *Mythlore* 24 (1980): 3–5.

Green, David L. "Children's Literature Periodicals on Individual Authors, Dime Novels, Fantasy." *Phaedrus* 3 (1976): 22–24.

Green, Roger Lancelyn. "Recollections." *Amon Hen* 44 (May 1980): 6–8.

Green, William Howard. "The Four Part Structure of Bilbo's Education." In *Children's Literature,* vol. 8. New Haven, CT: Yale Univ. Press, 1980, pp. 133–140.

———. "*The Hobbit* and Other Fiction by J. R. R. Tolkien: Their Roots in Medieval Heroic Literature and Language." Ph.D. diss., Louisiana State University, 1969.

———. "Legendary and Historical Time in Tolkien's *Farmer Giles of Ham*." *Notes on Contemporary Literature* 5, no. 3 (1975): 14–15.

———. "The Ring at the Center: Eaca in *The Lord of the Rings*." *Mythlore* 4 (1976): 17–19.

Grotta, Daniel. *The Biography of J. R. R. Tolkien: Architect of Middle Earth.* 2nd ed. Philadelphia: Running Press, 1978.

———. *J. R. R. Tolkien, Architect of Middle-Earth.* Philadelphia: Running Press, 1992.

Hall, Robert A., Jr. "Silent Commands? Frodo and Gollum at the Cracks of Doom." *Mythlore* 37 (1984): 5–7.

———. "Tolkien's Hobbit Tetralogy as 'Anti-Nibelungen.'" *Western Humanities Review* 32 (Autumn 1979): 351–359.

———. "Who Is the Master of the 'Precious'?" *Mythlore* 41 (1985): 34–35.

Hamilton, Meg. "Orphans and One-Parent Families in *Lord of the Rings*." *Amon Hen* 53 (1981): 5–7.

Hammond, Wayne G. "Addenda to 'J. R. R. Tolkien: A Bibliography.'" *Bulletin on Bibliography and Magazine Notes* 34 (1977): 119–127.

———. "All the Comforts: The Image of Home in *The Hobbit* and *The Lord of the Rings*." *Mythlore* 51 (1987): 29–33.

———, ed. *J. R. R. Tolkien: a Descriptive Bibliography.* New Castle, DE: Oak Knoll, 1992.

Hannabus, C. Stuart. "Deep Down: A Thematic and Bibliographical Excursion." *Signal* 6 (Sept 1971): 87–95.

Hardy, Gene. "More Than a Magic Ring." In Douglas Street. *Children's Novels and the Movies.* New York: Ungar, 1983, pp. 131–140.

Hargrove, Gene. "Who Is Tom Bombadil?" *Mythlore* 47 (1986): 20–24.

Harris, Mason. "The Psychology of Power in Tolkien's *The Lord of the Rings,* Orwell's *1984,* and Le Guin's *A Wizard of Earthsea*." *Mythlore* 55 (1988): 46–56.

Harrod, Elizabeth. "Trees in Tolkien, and What Happened under Them." *Mythlore* 39 (1984): 47–52, 58.

Hartt, Walter F. "Godly Influences: The Theology of J. R. R. Tolkien and C. S. Lewis." *Studies in the Literary Imagination* 14 (Fall 1981): 21–29.

Havard, R. E. "Professor J. R. R. Tolkien: A Personal Memoir." *Mythlore* 17 (Winter 1990): 61–62.

Hedges, Ned Samuel. "The Fable and the Fabulous: The Use of Traditional Forms in Children's Literature." Ph.D. diss., University of Nebraska, 1968.

Helms, Randel. "All Tales Need Not Come True." *Studies in the Literary Imagination* 14 (Fall 1981): 31–45.

———. *Tolkien's World* (original British title: *Myth, Magic and Meaning in Tolkien's World.* London: Thames, 1974). Boston: Houghton Mifflin, 1974.

Hennelly, Mark M., Jr. "The Road and the Ring: Solid Geometry in Tolkien's Middle-Earth." *Mythlore* 33 (1982): 3–13.

Higgens, Regina. *Magic Kingdoms: Discovering the Joys of Childhood Classics with Your Child.* New York: Simon, 1992.

Higgins, James Edward. "Five Authors of Mystical Fancy for Children: A Critical Study." Ed.D. diss., Columbia University, 1965.

Hillegas, Mark Robert, ed. *Shadows of the Imagination: The Fantasies of C. S. Lewis, J. R. R. Tolkien, and Charles Williams.* Carbondale: Southern Illinois Univ. Press, 1969.

Ho, Tisa. "The Childlike Hobbit." *Mythlore* 34 (1983): 3–9.

"The Hobbit"; Reading Motivation Unit. Wilton, CT: Current Affairs, 1977. (Filmstrip and audiocassette)

Hodge, James L. "Tolkien: Formulas of the Past." *Mythlore* 8 (1981): 15–18.

Houghton, Joe, Mike Bywater, and Michael Mertins. "Dragons." *Amon Hen,* Feb 1983, pp. 13–15.

Howard, A. "The Tolkien Society." *C. C. B. News* (Aug 1987): 11.

Hyde, Paul Nolan. "J. R. R. Tolkien and Love." *Mythlore* 17 (Autumn 1990): 14–19.

———. "Leaf and Key." *Mythlore* 46 (1986): 27–29, 36.

———. "Linguistic Techniques Used in Character Development in the Works of J. R. R. Tolkien. (Vols. I–III)." Ph.D. diss., Purdue University, 1982.

———. "Translations from the Elvish: The Lingo-Cultural Foundations of Middle Earth." *Publications of the Missouri Philological Association* 8 (1983): 11–16.

Hyles, Vernon. "On the Nature of Evil: The Cosmic Myths of Lewis, Tolkien, and Williams." *Mythlore* 50 (1987): 9–13+.

Inglis, Fred. "Gentility and Powerlessness: Tolkien and the New Class." In *J. R. R. Tolkien: This Far Land.* Totowa, NJ: Barnes and Noble, 1984, pp. 25–41.

———. *The Promise of Happiness.* New York: Cambridge Univ. Press, 1981, pp. 194–200.

Isaacs, Neil D., and Rose A. Zimbardo, eds. *Tolkien: New Critical Perspectives.* Lexington, KY: Univ. Press of Kentucky, 1981.

———. *Tolkien and the Critics: Essays on J. R. R. Tolkien's "The Lord of the Rings."* South Bend, IN: Univ. of Notre Dame, 1968.

Jeffs, Carol. "The Forest." *Mallorn* 22 (Apr 1985): 33–36.

———. *"Lord of the Rings* as Tragedy." *Mallorn* 21 (June 1984): 5–10.

Jenkins, Sue. "Love, Loss and Seeking: Material Deprivation and the Quest." *Children's Literature in Education* 15 (Summer 1984): 73–84.

Johnson, Janice. "The Celeblain of Celeborn and Galadriel." *Mythlore* 32 (1982): 11–19.

Johnson, Judith A. *J. R. R. Tolkien: Six Decades of Criticism.* Westport, CT: Greenwood, 1986.

Jones, Diana Wynne. "The Shape of the Narrative in *The Lord of the Rings.* In *J. R. R. Tolkien: This Far Land.* Totowa, NJ: Barnes and Noble, 1984, pp. 87–107.

Jones, Kathleen. "'Frodo Lives': Long Live Frodo!" *Amon Hen* 64 (Oct 1983): 9–10.

———. "The Use and Misuse of Fantasy." *Mallorn* 23 (1986): 5–9.

J. R. R. Tolkien: Life and Legend. An Exhibition to Commemorate the Centenary of the Birth of J. R. R. Tolkien (1892–1973). Oxford: Bodleian Library, 1992.

Kemball-Cook, Jessica. "Illustration of *The Hobbit.*" *Growing Point* (U.K.) 16 (July 1977): 3144.

———. "Male Chauvinist Lions: Part 1. Sex Discrimination in Tolkien." *Mallorn* 10 (1976): 14–19.

King, Roger. "Recovery, Escape, Consolation: Middle Earth and the English Fairy Tale." In *J. R. R. Tolkien: This Far Land.* Totowa, NJ: Barnes and Noble, 1984, pp. 42–55.

Kobil, Daniel T. "The Elusive Appeal of the Fantastic." *Mythlore* 4 (June 1977): 17–19; *Mythlore* 8, 29 (1981).

Kocher, Paul H. *"The Hobbit."* In *Master of Middle Earth: The Achievement of J. R. R. Tolkien.* Boston: Houghton Mifflin, 1972, pp. 19–33.

———. "Iluvatar and the Secret Fire." *Mythlore* 43 (1985): 36–37.

———. "J. R. R. Tolkien and George MacDonald." *The Crescent* 8, 29 (1981): 3–4.

――――. "The Tale of the Noldor." *Mythlore* 4 (Mar 1977): 3–7.

――――. "Turin Turambar." *Mythlore* 8 (Spring 1981): 22–23.

Kolbe, Martha Emily. "Three Oxford Dons as Creators of Other Worlds for Children: Lewis Carroll, C. S. Lewis, and J. R. R. Tolkien." Ph.D. diss., University of Virginia, 1981.

Kroeber, Karl. *Romantic Fantasy and Science Fiction.* New Haven: Yale Univ. Press, 1988.

Langford, Jonathan D. "The Souring of the Shire as a *Hobbit* Coming of Age." *Mythlore* 18 (Autumn 1991): 4–9.

Lawler, Donald L. *"The Silmarillion."* In *Survey of Modern Fantasy Literature,* vol. 4. Edited by Frank N. Magill. Englewood Cliffs, NJ: Salem Press, 1983, pp. 1733–1743.

Lense, Edward. "Sauron Is Watching *You:* The Role of the Great Eye in *The Lord of the Rings." Mythlore* 4, 13 (1976): 3–6.

Levin, Bernard. "Weaving an Epic Fantasy." (London) *Times* (Jan 30, 1992): 14.

Lewis, Alex. "*Hobbit* Culture 2." *Amon Hen* 84 (1987): 13–14. Follows the article by Gary Savage, listed below.

――――. "The Moving Mountains of Merkwood." *Amon Hen* Jan 1985, pp. 11–12.

Lewis, Gary. "Across the Misty Mountains." *Amon Hen* 82 (1986): 17–18.

Lind, Dianne. "The Importance of Fantasy in Young Adult Literature." *ALAN Review* 15 (1988): 13–14.

Lindsay, Sean. "The Dream System in *The Lord of the Rings." Mythlore* 49 (1987): 7–14.

Little, Edmund. *The Fantasts: Studies in J. R. R. Tolkien, Lewis Carroll, Mervyn Peake, Nikolay Gogol and Kenneth Grahame.* Amersham, England: Avebury, 1984.

Lloyd, Paul M. "The Role of Warfare and Strategy in *The Lord of the Rings." Mythlore* 3, 11 (1976).

Lobdell, Jared. *England and Always: Tolkien's World of the Rings.* Grand Rapids, MI: Eerdmans, 1982.

――――, ed. *A Tolkien Compass: Including J. R. R. Tolkien's Guide to the Names in 'The Lord of the Rings.'* New York: Ballantine, 1980. (Orig. pub. LaSalle, IL: Open Court, 1975.)

Lochhead, Marion. *Renaissance of Wonder.* New York: Harper, 1980, pp. 101–125.

Lowentrout, Peter. "The Evocation of Good in Tolkien." *Mythlore* 38 (1984): 32–33.

Luling, Virginia. "The Genesis of Sub-Creation." *Amon Hen* 50 (1981): 20–22.

Lynch, James. "The Literary Banquet and the Eucharistic Feast: Tradition in Tolkien." *Mythlore* 5 (1978): 13–14.

McComas, Alan. "Negating and Affirming Spirit Through Language: The Integration of Character, Magic and Story in *The Lord of the Rings." Mythlore* 72 (Spring 1993): 4–14; 73 (Summer 1993): 40–49.

McGeehon, C. "'I Have Read Everything by Tolkien.'" *Unabashed Librarian* 50 (1984): 25. (bibliography)

McGuire, Willam. *From Tolkien to Oz.* Parsippany, NJ: Unicorn, 1985. The art of Greg Hildebrandt.

MacIntyre, Jean. "'Time Shall Run Back': Tolkien's *The Hobbit." Children's Literature Association Quarterly* 13 (Spring 1988): 12–16.

Mack, H. C. "A Parametric Analysis of Antithetical Conflict and Irony: Tolkien's *The Lord of the Rings." Word* 31 (1981): 121–149.

McKenzie, Sister Elizabeth. "Above All Shadows Rides the Sun." *Mythlore* 2, 5 (1975).

McKinley, Robin. "J. R. R. Tolkien." In *Writers for Children: Critical Studies of Major Authors Since the Seventeenth Century.* Edited by Jane M. Bingham. New York: Scribner, 1988, pp. 561–572.

McLaughlin, F. *"The Lord of the Rings;* a Fantasy Film." *Media & Methods* 15 (Nov 1978): 14–17.

McLeish, Kenneth. "The Rippingest Yarn of All." In *J. R. R. Tolkien: This Far Land.* Totowa, NJ: Barnes and Noble, 1984, pp. 125–136.

Madsen, Catherine. "Light from an Invisible Lamp: Natural Religion in *The Lord of the Rings.*" *Mythlore* 53 (1988): 43–47.

Manganiello, Dominic. "The Neverending Story: Textual Happiness in *The Lord of the Rings.*" *Mythlore* 69, no. 18 (Summer 1992): 5–14.

Manlove, C. N. *Modern Fantasy: Five Studies.* New York: Cambridge Univ. Press, 1975.

Marchesani, Diane. "Tolkien's Lore: The Songs of Middle Earth." *Mythlore* 23 (1980): 3–5.

Martin, Darrell A. "J. R. R. Tolkien's Calendars, or the Saga of Hader the Incompetent." *Mythlore* 53 (1988): 52–59.

Mathews, Richard. *Lightning from a Clear Sky: Tolkien, the Trilogy, and 'The Silmarillion.'* San Bernardino, CA: Borgo Press, 1978.

———. "The Lord of the Rings." In *Survey of Modern Fantasy Literature,* vol. 2. Edited by Frank N. Magill. Englewood Cliffs, NJ: Salem Press, 1983, pp. 897–915.

Mende, Lisa Anne. "Gondolin, Minas Tirith and the Eucatastrophe." *Mythlore* 48 (1986): 37–40.

Mendelson, M. "Opening Moves: The Entry into the Other World." *Extrapolation* 25 (Summer 1984): 171–179.

Menzies, Janet. "Middle Earth and the Adolescent." In *J. R. R. Tolkien: This Far Land.* Totowa, NJ: Barnes and Noble, 1984, pp. 56–72.

Mercer, Archie. "Here Lies Gandalf." *Mallorn* (London) 11 (1978): 10–15.

Miesel, Sandra. *Myth, Symbol and Religion in 'The Lord of the Rings.'* Baltimore: T-K Graphics, 1973.

Miller, Miriam Youngerman. "The Green Sun: A Study of Color in J. R. R. Tolkien's *The Lord of the Rings.*" *Mythlore* 7, 26 (1980).

———. "The Hobbit, or There and Back Again." In *Survey of Modern Fantasy Literature,* vol. 3. Edited by Frank N. Magill. Englewood Cliffs, NJ: Salem Press, 1983, pp. 732–739.

———. "J. R. R. Tolkien's Merlin: An Old Man with a Staff: Gandalf and the Magus Tradition." In *The Figure of Merlin in the Nineteenth and Twentieth Centuries,* ed. by Jeanie Watson and Maureen Fries. Lewiston, NY: Mellen, 1989.

Miller, Stephen O. *Middle Earth: A World in Conflict.* London: T-K Graphics, 1975.

———. *Mithrandir.* Baltimore: T-K Graphics, 1974.

Milward, Peter. "Perchance to Touch: Tolkien as Scholar." *Mythlore* 22 (1979): 31–32.

Montgomery, John Warwick, ed. *Myth, Allegory and Gospel: An Interpretation of J. R. R. Tolkien/C. S. Lewis/G. K. Chesterton/Charles Williams.* Minneapolis: Bethany Fellowship, 1974.

Moorman, Charles W. "Heroism in *The Lord of the Rings.*" *Southern Quarterly* 11 (1972): 29–39.

———. "'Now Entertain Conjecture of a Time'—The Fictive Worlds of C. S. Lewis and J. R. R. Tolkien." In Mark R. Hillegas, ed. *Shadows of the Imagination.* Carbondale: Univ. of Southern Illinois, 1969.

More Junior Authors. Edited by Muriel Fuller. New York: Wilson, 1963, pp. 206–207.

Morgan, Gwyneth. "The Origin of the Arkenstone." *Amon Hen* Dec 1983, pp. 15–16.

Morris, John S. "Fantasy in a Mythless Age." In *Children's Literature,* vol. 2. Storrs, CT: Journal of the Modern Language Association, 1973, pp. 77–86.

Morrison, Louise D. *J. R. R. Tolkien's 'The Fellowship of the Ring': A Critical Commentary.* New York: Monarch Press, 1976.

Morse, Donald E., ed. *The Fantastic in World Literature and the Arts.* Westport, CT: Greenwood, 1987.

Morse, Robert E. "Rings of Power in Plato and Tolkien." *Mythlore* 7 (1980): 38.

Morus, Ivan Rhys. "Comparisons Between *The Chronicles of Narnia* and *The Histories of Middle-Earth.*" *Amon Hen* 54 (Feb 1982): 6–7.

Moss, Elaine. "*Smith of Wooton Major.*" In *Part of the Pattern.* New York: Greenwillow, 1986, p. 28.

Muirden, Geoff. "Tolkien—Lord of Faerie?" *School Library Bulletin* (Australia) 10 (Aug 1978): 65–68.

Murphy, Paul. "The Dwarfs of the Fourth Age." *Amon Hen,* May 1984, pp. 7–8.

Mythlore 69. "Special Issue: J. R. R. Tolkien." 18 (Summer 1992).

Nardo, Anna K. "Fantasy Literature and Play: An Approach to Reader Response." *Centennial Review* 22 (1978): 201–213.

Naur, Sam. "Errors of Gandalf." *Amon Hen* 82 (1986): 15–16.

Nelson, Marie. "Non-Human Speech in the Fantasy of C. S. Lewis, J. R. R. Tolkien and Richard Adams." *Mythlore* 5, 17 (May 1978): 37–39.

Nitzsche, Jane Chance. "The King under the Mountain: Tolkien's *Hobbit.*" *North Dakota Quarterly* 47 (Winter 1979): 5–18.

———. *Tolkien's Art: A Mythology for England.* New York: St. Martin, 1979.

Nodelman, Perry. "A Tolkien Bibliography." *Children's Literature Association Quarterly* 4 (Summer 1979): 17–18.

Noel, Ruth S. *The Languages of Tolkien's Middle Earth.* Boston: Houghton Mifflin, 1980.

———. *The Mythology of Middle Earth.* Boston: Houghton Mifflin, 1977.

Nored, Gary. "*The Lord of the Rings*—A Textual Inquiry." *Papers of the Bibliographical Society of America* 68 (Jan 1974): 71–74.

Norman, Felicity. "J. R. R. Tolkien's *The Hobbit.*" *The Literature Base* (Australia) 3 (Aug 1992): 12–13.

Norman, Philip. "The Prevalence of Hobbits." *New York Times Magazine,* Jan 15, 1967, pp. 30–31ff.

O'Brien, Donald. "On the Origin of the Name '*Hobbit*'" *Mythlore* 16 (Winter 1989): 32–48.

———. "Studies in the Chronology of Middle-Earth." *Mallorn* 19 (Dec 1982): 9–13.

O'Connor, Gerard W. "The Many Ways to Read an 'Old' Book." *Extrapolation* 15 (1973): 72–74.

———. "Why Tolkien's *The Lord of the Rings* Should *Not* Be Popular Culture." *Extrapolation* 13 (Dec 1971): 48–55.

O'Hare, Coleman. "Charles Williams, C. S. Lewis, and J. R. R. Tolkien: Three Approaches to Religion in Modern Fiction." Ph.D. diss., University of Toronto, 1973.

———. "On Reading an 'Old' Book." *Extrapolation* 14 (1972): 59–63.

O'Neill, Timothy R. *The Individuated Hobbit: Jung, Tolkien and the Archetypes.* Boston: Houghton Mifflin, 1979.

The Oxford Companion to Children's Literature. Edited by Humphrey Carpenter and Mari Prichard. New York: Oxford Univ. Press, 1984, pp. 254–255, 325, 529–531.

Pace, David Paul. "The Influence of Vergil's *Aeneid* on *The Lord of the Rings.*" *Mythlore* 6 (Spring 1979): 37–38.

Page, Gill. "The Wild Hunt." *Amon Hen* 42 (Dec 1979): 7–8.

Parker, Douglass. "Hwaet We Holbytla." *Hudson Review* 9 (1956–57): 598–609.

Partridge, Brenda. "No Sex Please—We're Hobbits: The Construction of Female Sexuality in *The Lord of the Rings.*" In *J. R. R. Tolkien: This Far Land.* Totowa, NJ: Barnes and Noble, 1984, pp. 179–198.

Pauline, Sister, CSM. "Secondary Worlds: Lewis and Tolkien." *CSL* 12 (May 1981): 1–8.

Pawling, Christopher, ed. *Popular Fiction and Social Change.* New York: St. Martin, 1984.

Paxon, Diana. "The Tolkien Tradition." *Mythlore* 39 (1984): 23–27, 37.

———. "What I Did for Love." *Mythlore* 17 (Autumn 1990): 4–8.

Perret, Marion. "Rings Off Their Fingers: Hands in *The Lord of the Rings.*" *Ariel* 6 (Oct 1975): 52–66.

Petty, Anne C. *One Ring to Bind Them All: Tolkien's Mythology.* Tuscaloosa: Univ. of Alabama Press, 1979.

Pfeiffer, J. D. "Tolkien and the Problem of Evil." *Children's Books in Ireland* 7 (1992): 21.

Pflieger, Pat, and Helen M. Hill. *A Reference Guide to Modern Fantasy for Children.* Westport, CT: Greenwood, 1984, pp. xii–xvi, 243–245, 537–540.

Philip, Neil. "The Lore of the Rings." *Times Educational Supplement* (Jan 31, 1992): 26.

Pitts, Mary Ellen. "The Motif of the Garden in the Novels of J. R. R. Tolkien, Charles Williams, and C. S. Lewis." *Mythlore* 8, 30 (1981).

Plimmer, Charlotte, and Denis Plimmer. "The Man Who Understands Hobbits." *Daily Telegraph Magazine* 181 (Mar 22, 1968): 31–32, 35.

Price, Meredith. "'All Shall Love Me and Despair': The Figure of Lilith in Tolkien, Lewis, Williams, and Sayers." *Mythlore* 9 (1982): 3–7ff.

Provost, W. "Language and Myth in the Fantasy Writings of J. R. R. Tolkien." *Modern Age* 33 (Spring 1990): 42–52.

Pugh, Dylan. "Atlantis and Middle Earth." *Amon Hen,* July 1984, pp. 11–12.

Purtill, Richard L. "Heaven and Other Perilous Realms." *Mythlore* 22 (1979): 3–6.

———. *Lord of Elves and Eldils: Fantasy and Philosophy in C. S. Lewis and J. R. R. Tolkien.* Grand Rapids, MI: Zondervan, 1974.

Ratliff, John D. "'And Something Yet Remains to Be Said': Tolkien and Williams." *Mythlore* 45 (1986): 48–54.

———. "*She* and Tolkien." *Mythlore* 8 (1981): 6–8.

Rawls, Melanie. "Arwen, Shadow Bride." *Mythlore* 43 (1985): 24–25, 37.

———. "The Feminine Principle in Tolkien." *Mythlore* 38 (1984): 5–13.

———. "The Rings of Power." *Mythlore* 40 (1984): 29–32.

Ready, William. *Understanding Tolkien and 'The Lord of the Rings.'* New York: Warner Books, 1969.

Reckford, Kenneth J. "'There and Back Again'—Odysseus and Bilbo Baggins." *Mythlore* 53 (1988): 5–9.

Reed, A. K. "The Greatest Problem Is What Lies Ahead. Problems in Media and Mythology—An Analysis of the Rankin/Bass Production of Tolkien's *The Hobbit.*" *Journal of Popular Culture* 17 (Spring 1984): 138–146.

Reynolds, Patricia. "Funeral Customs in Tolkien's Fiction." *Mythlore* 72 (Spring 1993): 45–53.

Ringel, Faye Joyce. "Patterns of the Hero and the Quest: Epic, Romance, Fantasy." Ph.D. diss., Brown University, 1979.

Robinson, Derek. "The Hasty Stroke Goes Oft Astray: Tolkien and Humour." In *J. R. R. Tolkien: This Far Land.* Totowa, NJ: Barnes and Noble, 1984, pp. 108–124.

Rockow, Karen. *Funeral Customs in Tolkien's Trilogy.* Baltimore: T-K Graphics, 1973.

Rogers, Deborah Webster. "The Fictitious Characters of C. S. Lewis and J. R. R. Tolkien in Relation to Their Medieval Sources." Ph.D. diss., University of Wisconsin, 1972.

Rogers, Deborah Webster, and Ivor A. Rogers. *J. R. R. Tolkien.* Boston: Twayne, 1980.

Roos, R. "Middle Earth in the Classroom: Studying J. R. R. Tolkien." *English Journal* 58 (Nov 1969): 1175–1180.

Rosebury, Brian. *Tolkien: A Critical Assessment.* London: Macmillan, 1992.

Rosenberg, Jerome. "The Humanity of Sam Gamgee." *Mythlore* 5, 17 (Mar 1978): 10–11.

Rossi, Lee D. "Politics of Fantasy: C. S. Lewis and J. R. R. Tolkien." Ph.D. diss., Cornell University, 1972.

———. *The Politics of Fantasy: C. S. Lewis and J. R. R. Tolkien.* Ann Arbor, MI: UMI Research Press, 1984.

Rottensteiner, Franz. *The Fantasy Book: An Illustrated History from Dracula to Tolkien.* New York: Macmillan, 1978, pp. 96–98.

Russell, Mariann. "'The Northern Literature' and the Ring Trilogy." *Mythlore* 5 (Autumn 1978): 41–42.

Ryan, John S. "The Barghest as Possible Source for Tolkien's Goblins and Ringwraiths." *Amon Hen,* May 1985, pp. 10–11.

———. "Cultural Name Association: A Tolkien Example from Gilgamesh." *Mallorn* 22 (1985): 21–23.

———. "Entrance to a Smial!" *Amon Hen,* May 1983, pp. 12–13.

———. "Frothi, Frodo—and Dodo and Odo." *Orana* 16 (May 1980): 35–38.

———. "Gollum and the Golem: A Neglected Tolkien Association With Jewish Thought." *Orana* 18 (Aug 1983): 110–113.

———. "Mid-Century Perceptions of the Ancient Celtic Peoples of 'England'" *Seven* 9 (1988): 57–64.

———. "The Mines of Mendip and of Moria." *Mythlore* 17 (Autumn 1990): 25–27.

———. "Origin of the Name 'Wetwang.'" *Amon Hen,* Aug 1983, pp. 10–13.

———. "Saruman, 'Sharkey' and Suruman: Analogous Figures of Eastern Ingenuity and Cunning." *Mythlore* 43 (1985): 43–44, 57.

———. *The Shaping of Middle-Earth's Maker: Influences on the Life and Literature of J. R. R. Tokien.* Highland, MI: American Tolkien Society, 1992.

———. *Tolkien: Cult or Culture?* Armidale, New South Wales: Univ. of New England, 1969.

———. "Tolkien's Sources." *Orana* 13 (Feb 1977): 8–11.

———. "Warg, Wearg, Earg and Werewolf: A Note on a Speculative Tolkien Etymology." *Mallorn* 23 (1986): 25–29.

———. "Woses: Wild Men or 'Remnants of an Older Time'?" *Amon Hen,* Dec 1983, pp. 7–12.

St. Clair, Gloriana. "*The Lord of the Rings* as Saga." *Mythlore* 6 (Spring 1979): 11–16.

Salu, Mary, and Robert T. Farrell, eds. *J. R. R. Tolkien, Scholar and Storyteller: Essays in Memorium.* Ithaca, NY: Cornell Univ. Press, 1979.

Sammons, Margaret. "Tolkien on Fantasy in *Smith of Wooton Major.*" *Mythlore* 43 (1985): 3–7, 37.

Sammons, Martha C. *"A Better Country": The Worlds of Religious Fantasy and Science Fiction.* Westport, CT: Greenwood, 1988.

San José, Pilar, and Gregory Starkey. "Tolkien's Influence on C. S. Lewis." *Mallorn* 17 (1981): 23–28.

———. "Tolkien's Influence on C. S. Lewis: Epilogue." *Mallorn* 19 (Dec 1982): 29–30.

Sams, Edwin Boyer. "Studies in Experimental Fantasy." *Teaching English in the Two-Year College* 5 (1979): 235–237.

Sanders, Joseph Lee. "Fantasy in the 20th Century British Novel." Ph.D. diss., Indiana University, 1972.

Sardello, Robert J. "An Empirical-Phenomenological Study of Fantasy, With a Note on J. R. R. Tolkien and C. S. Lewis." *Psycho-Cultural Review* 2 (1978): 203–220.

Sarjeant, Williams A. S. "Where Did the Dwarfs Come From?" *Mythlore* 71, no. 19 (Winter 1993): 43, 64.

Savage, Gary. "The Culture of the *Hobbit.*" *Amon Hen* 83 (1987): 15–16. Followed by the Alex Lewis article listed above.

Savater, Fernando. *Childhood Regained: The Art of the Storyteller.* New York: Columbia Univ. Press, 1982.

Scafella, Frank. "Tolkien, the Gospel, and the Fairy Story." *Soundings* 64 (1981): 310–325.

Schakel, Peter. "Dance as Metaphor and Myth in Lewis, Tolkien, and Williams." *Mythlore* 45 (1986): 4–8, 23.

Schmiel, Mary Eileen. "In the Forge of Los: Tolkien and the Art of Creative Fantasy." *Mythlore* 35 (1983): 17–22.

Schorr, Karl. "The Nature of Dreams in *The Lord of the Rings.*" *Mythlore* 36 (1983): 21, 46.

Science Fiction and Time Fiction. Tarrytown, NY: Prentice-Hall Media, 1977. (Filmstrip and audiocassette)

Scott, N. C. "War and Pacifism in *The Lord of the Rings.*" *Tolkien Journal* 15 (Summer 1972): 23–25, 27–30.

Scull, Christina. "The Fairy-Tale Tradition." *Mallorn* 23 (1986): 30–36.

———. "The Publishing History of *Farmer Giles of Ham.*" *Amon Hen* 98 (July 1989): 9–10.

———. "Tolkien: The Great Storyteller." *British Philatelic Bulletin* 30 (1992): 32–35. See also: 30 (1992): 6–8.

Searles, Baird, Beth Meacham, and Michael Franklin. *A Reader's Guide to Fantasy.* New York: Avon, 1982, pp. 145–147.

Senior, William. "Donaldson and Tolkien." *Mythlore* 70 (Autumn 1992): 37–43.

Shippey, T. A. *The Road to Middle-Earth.* 2nd ed. London: Grafton, 1992 (orig. pub. 1982).

Shoemaker, D. "A Savvy Animator Finds Perils on the Paths of Middle Earth." *Chronicle of Higher Education* 17 (Nov 27, 1978): 18–20.

Sirridge, Mary. "J. R. R. Tolkien and the Fairy Tale Truth." *The British Journal of Aesthetics* 15 (1975): 81–92.

Sklar, Robert. "Tolkien and Hesse: Tops of the Pops." *Nation* 204 (May 8, 1967): 598–601. Reprinted in Lenz. *Young Adult Literature.* Chicago: American Library Association, 1980, pp. 422–424.

"Special Issue: Tolkien." *Mythlore* 69, no. 18 (Summer 1992).

Speth, Lee. "Cavalier Treatment." *Mythlore* 6 (Summer 1979): 18, 38.

———. "Cavalier Treatment: Once More Round the Cauldron." *Mythlore* 24 (1980): 14–15.

Stevens, C. D. "High Fantasy Versus Low Comedy: Humor in J. R. R. Tolkien." *Extrapolation* 21 (Summer 1980): 122–129.

———. "The Sound Systems of the Third Age of Middle Earth." *Quarterly Journal of Speech* 54 (Oct 1968): 232–240.

Stevens, David. "The Short Fiction of J. R. R. Tolkien." In *Survey of Modern Fantasy Literature,* vol. 4. Edited by Frank N. Magill. Englewood Cliffs, NJ: Salem Press, 1983, pp. 1724–1728.

———. "Trolls and Dragons versus Pocket Handkerchiefs and 'Polite Nothings': Elements of the Fantastic and the Prosaic in *The Hobbit.*" In *The Scope of the Fantastic—Culture, Biography, Themes, Children's Literature.* Edited by Robert A. Collins and Howard D. Pearce. Westport, CT: Greenwood, 1985, pp. 249–256.

Stevens, Simon. "Tolkien's Field of Dreams." *The Ring Bearer* (Australia) 8, no. 2 (Spring 1991): 103–110.

Stevenson, Jeff. "Life After Life." *Amon Hen,* May 1984, pp. 10–11.

Stoddard, William. "A Critical Approach to Fantasy with Application to *The Lord of the Rings.*" *Mythlore* 37 (1984): 8–13.

———. "Law and Institutions in the Shire." *Mythlore* 70, no. 18 (Autumn 1992): 4–8.

Stott, Jon C. *Children's Literature from A to Z.* New York: McGraw-Hill, 1984, p. 270.

Strachey, Barbara. *Journeys of Frodo: An Atlas of J. R. R. Tolkien's "The Lord of the Rings."* New York: Ballantine, 1981.

Sturch, Richard. "The Theology of *The Book of Lost Tales.*" *Amon Hen,* May 1984, pp. 9–10.

Sullivan, C. W., III. "Fantasy." In *Story and Society: Children's Literature in Its Social Context,* ed. by Dennis Butts. London: Macmillan, 1992, pp. 97–111.

———. "J. R. R. Tolkien's *The Hobbit:* The Magic of Words." In *Touchstones.* Edited by Perry Nodelman. West Lafayette, IN: Children's Literature Association Publications, 1985, pp. 253–261.

———. "Name and Lineage Patterns: Aragorn and *Beowulf.*" *Extrapolation* 25 (Fall 1984): 239–246.

———. "Real-izing the Unreal: Folklore in Young Adult Science Fiction and Fantasy." In *Literature for Children: Contemporary Criticism,* ed. by Peter Hunt. London: Routledge, 1992, pp. 141–155.

Swinfen, Ann. *In Defense of Fantasy.* London: Routledge, 1984; New York: Routledge, 1984, pp. 78, 80–81, 84–87, 89, 93–94.

Syme, Margaret Ruth. "Tolkien as Gospel Writer." Ph.D. diss., McGill University (Canada), 1989.

Taylor, W. L. "Frodo Lives; J. R. R. Tolkien's *The Lord of the Rings.*" *English Journal* 56 (Sept 1967): 818–821; Reply: R. M. Stein. *English Journal* 57 (Feb 1968): 252–253.

Terry, June S. "To Seek and to Find: Quest Literature for Children." *School Librarian* 18 (Dec 1970): 399–404. Reprinted in Mary Lou White. *Children's Literature.* Columbus, OH: Merrill, 1976, pp. 138–143.

Thomas, Lew. "J. R. R. Tolkien, Author of *The Lord of the Rings.*" *Book and Magazine Collector* 17 (July 1985): 15–22.

Thompson, George H. "Early Review[s] of Books by J. R. R. Tolkien." *Mythlore* 41 (1985): 59–63.

Thompson, Kristin. "*The Hobbit* as a Part of *The Red Book of Westmarch.*" *Mythlore* 56 (1988): 11–16.

Thomson, Maggie. "Unicorn Club: A Drama Workshop on *The Hobbit.*" *Amon Hen* 78 (1986): 6–7.

Thrope, Wayne. "Fantasy Characterizations: The Example of Tolkien." *Mythlore* 17 (Summer 1991): 37–41, 65.

"A Tolkien Bibliography." *Children's Literature Association Quarterly* 4 (Summer 1979): 17–18.

Tolkien, Christopher. "J. R. R. Tolkien: A Bibliography." *Bulletin of Bibliography* 27 (1970).

Tolkein, J. R. R. *The Annotated Hobbit: The Hobbit or There and Back Again,* ed. by Douglas Anderson. Boston: Houghton, 1988.

––––––. "Beowulf: The Monsters and the Critics." *Proceedings of the British Academy* 22 (1936): 248–295.

––––––. *Bilbo's Last Song.* Illus. By Pauline Baynes. Boston: Houghton, 1990.

––––––. *The Book of Lost Tales* (The History of Middle-Earth, vol. 1). Edited by Christopher Tolkien. Boston: Houghton Mifflin, 1984 (c. 1983), 1986.

––––––. *The Book of Lost Tales,* vol. 2. Edited by Christopher Tolkien. Boston: Houghton Mifflin, 1984.

––––––. "*The Hobbit.*" *Horn Book* 14 (May 1938): 184–188.

––––––. *The Lays of Beleriad* (The History of Middle Earth, vol. 3). Edited by Christopher Tolkien. Boston: Houghton Mifflin, 1985.

––––––. *The Letters of J. R. R. Tolkien.* Edited and selected by Humphrey Carpenter and Christopher Tolkien. Boston: Houghton Mifflin, 1981. Excerpt entitled "To W. H. Auden." Reprinted in Boyer and Zahorski. *Fantasists on Fantasy.* New York: Avon, 1984, pp. 85–94.

––––––. *The Lord of the Rings,* Centenary Volume. Illus. by Alan Lee. Boston: Houghton 1991.

––––––. *The Lost Road and Other Writings,* ed. by Christopher Tolkien. Boston: Houghton, 1987.

––––––. *The Monsters and the Critics, and Other Essays.* Edited by Christopher Tolkien. Boston: Houghton Mifflin, 1984 (c. 1983).

––––––. "On Fairy Tales. In *Essays Presented to Charles Williams* (original publication 1947). Freeport, NY: Books for Libraries Press, 1972, pp. 38–90. Reprinted in *Horn Book* 39 (1963): 457, entitled "Editorial: On Fairy-Stories"; also in J. R. R. Tolkien. *Tree and Leaf.* Boston: Houghton Mifflin, 1965, pp. 3–84, entitled "On Fairy-Stories"; in *The Tolkien Reader.* New York: Ballantine, 1966, 1974, pp. 3–84, entitled "On Fairy Stories"; and in Sheila A. Egoff. *Only Connect.* New York: Oxford Univ. Press, 1980, pp. 111–120, entitled "Children and Fairy Stories." An excerpt entitled "Fantasy" has been reprinted in Boyer and Zahorski. *Fantasists on Fantasy.* New York: Avon, 1984, pp. 75–84.

––––––. *Pictures by J. R. R. Tolkien.* Boston: Houghton, 1992.

––––––. *The Return of the Shadow: The History of "The Lord of the Rings," Pt. 1.* ed. by Christopher Tolkien. Boston: Houghton, 1988.

————. *Sauron Defeated: The History of "The Lord of the Rings," Pt. 4,* ed. by Christopher Tolkien. Boston: Houghton, 1992.

————. *The Shaping of Middle Earth: The Quenta, the Ambrakanta, and the Annals.* (The History of Middle Earth, vol. 4). Edited by Christopher Tolkien. Boston: Houghton Mifflin, 1986.

————. *The Treason of Isengard: The History of "The Lord of the Rings," Pt. 2.* ed. by Christopher Tolkien. Boston: Houghton, 1989.

————. *Unfinished Tales of Numenor and Middle Earth.* Edited by Christopher Tolkien. Boston: Houghton Mifflin, 1980, 1982.

Tolkien, John, and Priscilla Tolkein. *A Tolkien Family Album.* Boston: Houghton, 1992.

Tolkien, Priscilla. "Memories of J. R. R. Tolkien in His Centenary Year." *The Brown Book* [Oxford University] (Dec 1992): 12–14.

————. "News from the North Pole." *Oxford Today* (U.K.) 5, no. 1 (1992): 8–9.

Treloar, John L. "The Middle-Earth Epic and the Seven Capital Vices." *Mythlore* 16 (Autumn 1989): 37–42.

Twentieth-Century Children's Writers. 3rd ed. Edited by Tracy Chevalier and D. L. Kirkpatrick. Chicago: St. James, 1989, pp. 965–968.

Twentieth-Century Science Fiction Writers. 3rd ed. Edited by Noelle Watson and Paul E. Schellinger. Chicago: St. James Press, 1991, pp. 798–801.

Tyler, J. E. A. *The New Tolkien Companion* (originally published London: Macmillan, 1976). rev. ed. New York: St. Martin, 1980.

Unwin, Rayner. "*The Hobbit:* 50th Anniversary." *Bookseller* (Jan 16, 1987): 166–167; *Books for Keeps* (U.K.) 46 (1987): 8–9; *Reading Time* (Australia) 31, no. 2 (1987): 8–10; *Science Fiction Chronicle* 8 (June 1987): 48–50.

————. "Taming *The Lord of the Rings.*" *Bookseller* (U.K.) (Aug 19, 1988): 647–650.

Urang, Gunnar. "Shadows of Heaven: Religion and Fantasy in the Writing of C. S. Lewis, Charles Williams and J. R. R. Tolkien." Ph.D. diss., University of Chicago, 1970. New York: Pilgrim Press, 1971.

Vanhecke, Johan. "Mandala Symbolism in *Lord of the Rings.*" *Mallorn* 17 (Oct 1981): 11–17.

Van Rossenberg, René, ed. *Elrond's Holy Round Table.* Leiden: Tolkien Genootschap Unquendor, 1990.

Walker, R. C. "The Little Kingdom: Some Considerations and a Map." *Mythlore* 37 (1984): 47–48.

Walker, Steven Charles. "The Making of a Hobbit, Tolkien's Tantalizing Narrative Technique." *Mythlore* 7 (1980): 6–7ff.

————. "Narrative Technique in the Fiction of J. R. R. Tolkien." Ph.D. diss., Harvard University, 1973.

————. "Super Natural Supernatural: Tolkien as Realist." In *Proceedings of the Fifth Annual Conference of the Children's Literature Association.* Harvard University, Mar 1978. Ypsilanti, MI: Children's Literature Association Publications, 1979, pp. 100–105.

————. "The War of the Rings Trilogy: An Elegy for Lost Innocence and Wonder." *Mythlore* 5 (May 1978): 3–5.

Wells, Andrew. "Armor in the Third Age." *Amon Hen,* July 1984, pp. 16–17.

West, Richard C. "An Annotated Bibliography of Tolkien Criticism." *Extrapolation* 10 (Dec 1968): 17–49.

————. "The Status of Tolkien Scholarship." *Tolkien Journal* 15 (Summer 1972): 21.

————. *Tolkien Criticism: An Annotated Checklist.* rev. ed. Kent, OH: Kent State Univ. Press, 1981. Originally published in *Tolkien Journal* 4 (1970–1971): 14–31.

Williams, Madawc. "Cock and Bull about Epic Fantasy." *Mallorn* 26 (1989): 5–15.

Wilson, Anne. *Magical Thought in Creative Writing.* Stroud, Gloucestershire: Thimble Press, 1983, pp. 70–81.

Wilson, Colin. "J. R. R. Tolkien." In *The Strength to Dream: Literature and the Imagination.* rev. ed. Westport, CT: Greenwood, 1973, pp. 145–148.

———. *Tree by Tolkien.* Santa Barbara, CA: Capra Press, 1974.

Wilson, Edmund. "Oo, Those Awful Orcs." *Nation* 182 (Apr 14, 1956): 312–313.

Wood, Denis. "Growing Up Among the Stars." *Literary/Film Quarterly* 6 (1978): 327–341.

Wood, Michael. "Tolkien's Fictions." In Nicholas Tucker. *Suitable for Children? Controversies in Children's Literature.* Berkeley: Univ. of California Press, 1976, pp. 165–172. Originally published in *New Society,* Mar 27, 1969.

Woolsey, Daniel P. "The Realm of Fairy Story: J. R. R. Tolkien and Robin McKinley's *Beauty.*" *Children's Literature in Education* (June 1991): 129–134.

Wright, Marjorie Evelyn. "The Cosmic Kingdom of Myth: A Study in the Myth-Philosophy of Charles Williams, C. S. Lewis, and J. R. R. Tokien." Ph.D. diss., University of Illinois, 1960.

Wynne, Patrick. "Sauron Gets Drafted." *Mythlore* 17 (Winter 1990): 4–12.

Wytenbroek, J. R. "Rites of Passage in *The Hobbit.*" *Mythlore* 50 (1987): 5–8+.

Yates, Jessica. "In Defense of Fantasy." *Mallorn* 21 (June 1984): 23–28.

———. "Tolkien's Influence on *The Chronicles of Narnia.*" *Mallorn* (June 18, 1982): 31–33.

Zimmerman, Manfred. "Rendering of Tolkien's Alliterative Verse." *Mythlore* 8 (1981): 21.

Zipes, Jack. *Breaking the Magic Spell: Radical Theories of Folk and Fairy Tales.* Univ. of Texas Press, 1979; New York: Methuen, 1984.

Tomalin, Ruth

Twentieth-Century Children's Writers. 3rd ed. Edited by Tracy Chevalier and D. L. Kirkpatrick. Chicago: St. James, 1989, pp. 968–969.

Torrey, Marjorie

More Junior Authors. Edited by Muriel Fuller. New York: Wilson, 1963, pp. 207–208.

Townsend, John Rowe

Barnes, Ron. "John Rowe Townsend's Novels of Adolescence." *Children's Literature in Education* 19 (Winter 1975): 178–190.

Crouch, Marcus. *The Nesbit Tradition.* London: Benn, 1972, pp. 206–208.

Fourth Book of Junior Authors and Illustrators. Edited by Doris De Montreville and Elizabeth D. Crawford. New York: Wilson, 1978, pp. 328–330.

Gilderdale, Betty. "John Rowe Townsend—A Sense of Place." *Children's Literature Association Yearbook.* New Zealand: Children's Literature Association, 1976, pp. 17–20.

Hansen, Carol A. "Recommended: John Rowe Townsend." *English Journal* 73 (Mar 1984): 89–90.

Moss, Elaine. "Coming of Age." *The Guardian* (Nov 13, 1974): 11.

The Oxford Companion to Children's Literature. Edited by Humphrey Carpenter and Mari Prichard. New York: Oxford Univ. Press, 1984, pp. 536–537.

Rees, David. "Children's Writers: John Rowe Townsend." *School Librarian* 31 (Mar 1983): 4–11.

———. "A Sense of Story—John Rowe Townsend." In *Painted Desert, Green Shade.* Boston: Horn Book, 1984, pp. 102–114.

Speaking for Ourselves: Autobiographical Sketches by Notable Authors of Books for Young Adults. Edited by Donald R. Gallo. Urbana, IL: National Council of Teachers of English, 1990, pp. 214–216.

Townsend, John Rowe. "Border Country." *Canadian Children's Literature* 48 (1987): 29–41.

———. "Didacticism in Modern Dress." *Horn Book* 43 (Apr 1967): 159–163.

———. "An Elusive Border." *Horn Book* 50 (Oct 1974): 33–42.

———. "Heights of Fantasy." In *Children's Literature Review,* vol. 5. Detroit: Gale, 1983, pp. 7–12. Guest essay.

———. "In Literary Terms." *Horn Book* 47 (Aug 1971): 347–353.

———. "The Life Journey." In *Innocence & Experience.* Edited by Barbara Harrison and Gregory Maguire. New York: Lothrop, 1987, pp. 138–147.

———. "The Now Child." *Horn Book* 49 (June 1973): 241–247.

———. *A Sense of Story: Essays on Contemporary Writers for Children.* Philadelphia: Lippincott, 1971.

———. *A Sounding of Storytellers: New and Revised Essays on Contemporary Writers for Children.* Philadelphia: Lippincott, 1979.

———. "Travellers in Time." *Times Educational Supplement* (Aug 4, 1989): 17.

———. "Under Two Hats." *Quarterly Journal of Library of Congress* 34 (Apr 1977): 116–128. Reprinted in Haviland. *The Openhearted Audience.* Washington, DC: Library of Congress, 1980, pp. 133–151.

———. "A Wholly Pragmatic Definition [of Children's Literature]." In Robert Bator. *Signposts to Criticism of Children's Literature.* Chicago: American Library Association, 1983, pp. 19–20. Excerpted from "Standards of Criticism for Children's Literature." In Zena Sutherland's *The Arbuthnot Lectures, 1970–1979.* Chicago: American Library Association, 1980, pp. 26–27.

———. *Written for Children: An Outline of English Language Children's Literature.* 4th ed. New York: Harper, 1992.

Twentieth-Century Children's Writers. 3rd ed. Edited by Tracy Chevalier and D. L. Kirkpatrick. Chicago: St. James, 1989, pp. 970–972.

Wintle, Justin, and Emma Fisher. "John Rowe Townsend." In *The Pied Pipers.* New York: Paddington Press, 1974, pp. 236–248.

"Writers and Critics: A Dialogue Between Jill Paton Walsh and John Rowe Townsend; Part I." *Horn Book* 58 (Oct 1982): 498–504; "Part II." *Horn Book* 58 (Dec 1982): 680–685.

Travers, P(amela) L(yndon)

"Authors and Editors." *Publishers Weekly* 188 (Dec 13, 1971): 7–9.

Bart, Peter, and Dorothy Bart. "As Told and Sold by Disney." *New York Times Book Review,* (May 9, 1965): 2, 32–34.

Bergsten, Staffan. *Mary Poppins and Myth.* Stockholm: Almqvist and Wiksell International, 1978.

Buckley, M. "Words of Power: Language and Reality in the Fantasy Novels of E. Nesbit and P. L. Travers." Ed.D. diss., East Texas State University, 1977.

Burness, E., and J. Griswold. "The Art of Fiction; P. L. Travers." *Paris Review* 24 (Winter 1982): 211–229. Interview.

Carpenter, Humphrey. "*Mary Poppins,* Force of Nature." *New York Times Book Review* (Aug 27, 1989): 29.

Cott, Jonathan. "The Wisdom of Mary Poppins: Afternoon Tea with P. L. Travers." In *Pipers at the Gate of Dawn.* New York: Random, 1983, pp. 195–240.

DeForest, Mary. "*Mary Poppins* and the Great Mother." *Classical and Modern Literature* 11 (Winter 1991): 139–154.

Demers, Patricia. *P. L. Travers.* Boston: Twayne, 1991.

Doyle, Brian. *The Who's Who of Children's Literature.* New York: Schocken, 1968, pp. 268–269.

"Elusive Author Expansive with Children." *Library Journal* 91 (Mar 15, 1966): 1640.

Field, M. "Reminiscing with P. L. Travers. *Publishers Weekly* 229 (Mar 21, 1986): 40–41.

Frankel, Haskel. "A Rose for *Mary Poppins.*" *Saturday Review* 47 (Nov 7, 1964): 24–25.

Gibson, Lois Rauch. "Beyond the Apron: Archetypes, Stereotypes, and Alternative Portrayals of Mothers in Children's Literature." *Children's Literature Association Quarterly* 13 (1988): 177–181.

Gilead, S. "Magic Abjured: Closure in Children's Fantasy Fiction." *Publications of the Modern Language Association* 106 (Mar 1991): 277–293.

Gillespie, John T., and Diana Lembo. *Introducing Books: A Guide for the Middle Grades.* New York: Bowker, 1970, pp. 256–258.

Hearn, Michael Patrick. "P. L. Travers in Fantasy Land." *Children's Literature,* vol. 6. Philadelphia: Temple Univ. Press, 1977, pp. 221–224.

Higgens, Regina. *Magic Kingdoms: Discovering the Joys of Childhood Classics with Your Child.* New York: Simon, 1992.

Hoffeld, Laura. "Where Magic Begins." *The Lion and the Unicorn* 3, no. 1 (Spring 1979): 4–13.

Hopkins, Lee Bennett. "P. L. Travers." In *More Books by More People.* New York: Citation Press, 1974, pp. 355–362.

The Junior Book of Authors. 2nd ed. rev. Edited by Stanley J. Kunitz and Howard Haycraft. New York: Wilson, 1951, pp. 287–288.

Lingeman, Richard R. "A Visit with Mary Poppins and P. L. Travers." *New York Times Magazine,* Dec 25, 1966, pp. 12–13.

Moore, Anne Carroll. *"Mary Poppins."* *Horn Book* 11 (Jan–Feb 1936): 6–7.

Moore, Robert B. *"Mary Poppins:* A Letter from a Critic." In *Children's Literature,* vol. 10. New Haven, CT: Yale Univ. Press, 1982, pp. 211–213.

The Oxford Companion to Children's Literature. Edited by Humphrey Carpenter and Mari Prichard. New York: Oxford Univ. Press, 1984, pp. 342, 540.

Pflieger, Pat, and Helen M. Hill. *A Reference Guide to Modern Fantasy for Children.* Westport, CT: Greenwood, 1984, pp. xiv, 351–357, 548–551.

Philip, Neil. "The Writer and the Nanny Who Never Explain." *Times Educational Supplement* (June 11, 1982): 42.

Roddy, Joseph. "A Visit with the Real Mary Poppins: Interview with P. L. Travers." *Look* (Dec 13, 1966): 84ff.

Schwartz, Albert V. "Mary Poppins Revised: An Interview with P. L. Travers." *Interracial Books for Children Bulletin* 5, no. 3 (1974): 1, 3–5. Reprinted in Donnarae MacCann and Gloria Woodard. *Cultural Conformity in Books for Children.* Metuchen, NJ: Scarecrow Press, 1977, pp. 134–140; and in White. *Children's Literature.* Columbus, OH: Merrill, 1976, pp. 75–77.

Searles, Baird, Beth Meacham, and Michael Franklin. *A Reader's Guide to Fantasy.* New York: Avon, 1982, pp. 147–148.

Smaridge, Norah. *Famous Modern Storytellers for Young People.* New York: Dodd, 1969, pp. 92–97.

Stone, Kay F. "Re-Awakening the Sleeping Beauty: P. L. Travers' Literary Folktale." *Proceedings of the Eighth Annual Conference of the Children's Literature Association.* Ypsilanti, MI: Children's Literature Association, 1982 pp. 84–90.

Travers, P. L. *About Sleeping Beauty.* New York: McGraw-Hill, 1975.

———. "The Black Sheep." *New York Times Book Review,* pt. II. (Nov 7, 1965): 1, 61.

———. "Grimm's Women." *New York Times Book Review,* (Nov 16, 1975): 59.

———. "The Heroes of Childhood, A Note on Nannies." *Horn Book* 11 (May–June 1935): 147–155.

———. "I Never Wrote for Children." *New York Times Magazine,* (July 2, 1978): 16–18, 30.

———. "Mary Poppins: A Letter from the Author." In *Children's Literature,* vol. 10. New Haven, CT: Yale Univ. Press, 1982, pp. 214–217.

———. "My Childhood Bends Beside Me." *New Statesman* 44 (Nov 29, 1952): 639.

———. "On Not Writing for Children." *Bookbird* 6, no. 4 (1967): 7–8. Reprinted in *Children's Literature,* vol. 4. Philadelphia: Temple University Press, 1975, pp. 15–22; *Reflections on Literature for Children.* Edited by Francelia Butler and Richard Rotert. Hamden, CT: Shoe String Press, 1984, pp. 58–65.

———. "Once I Saw a Fox Dancing Alone." *New York Herald Tribune Book Week* (May 9, 1965): 2.

———. "Only Connect." *Quarterly Journal of the Library of Congress* 24 (Oct 1967): 232–248. Reprinted in Sheila A. Egoff. *Only Connect.* New York: Oxford Univ. Press, 1980, pp. 182–206; and in *The Openhearted Audience.* Washington, DC: Library of Congress, 1980, pp. 2–23.

———. "Personal View." *Sunday* [London] *Times* (Dec 11, 1989): G4.

———. "A Radical Innocence." *New York Times Book Review,* pt. II, *Children's Book Section,* May 9, 1965, pp. 38–39.

———. "Threepenny Bit." *Parabola* [New York] 16 (Feb 1991): 70–75.

———. "Where Did She Come From, Why Did She Go?" *Saturday Evening Post* 237 (Nov 7, 1964): 76–77.

———. "Where Do Ideas Come From?" *Bookbird* 5, no. 4 (1967): 7–8.

———. "Who Is Mary Poppins?" *Junior Bookshelf* 18 (Mar 1964): 45–50.

———. "World Beyond World." *Chicago Sun Times Book Week,* Spring Children's Issue, May 7, 1965, pp. 4–5. Reprinted in Virginia Haviland. *Children and Literature.* Glenview, IL: Scott, Foresman, 1973, pp. 246–249.

Twentieth-Century Children's Writers. 3rd ed. Edited by Tracy Chevalier and D. L. Kirkpatrick. Chicago: St. James, 1989, pp. 973–974.

Ziner, Feenie. "Mary Poppins as a Zen Monk." *New York Times Book Review,* May 7, 1982, pp. 2, 22.

Tregarthen, Enys (pseud. of Nelie Sloggett)

Wright, Harriet S. "A Visit with Enys Tregarthen." *Horn Book* 26 (May 1950): 205–206.

Yates, Elizabeth. "Enys Tregarthen, 1851–1923." *Horn Book* 25 (May–June 1949): 231–238.

———. "How Enys Tregarthen's Cornish Legends Came to Light." *Horn Book* 16 (Sept 1940): 334–337.

Turkle, Brinton (Cassaday)

Hopkins, Lee Bennett. "Brinton Turkle." In *Books Are by People.* New York: Citation Press, 1969, pp. 289–291.

Roginski, Jim, ed. *Newbery and Caldecott Medalists and Honor Book Winners.* Littleton, CO: Libraries Unlimited, 1982, pp. 263–265.

Third Book of Junior Authors. Edited by Doris De Montreville and Donna Hill. New York: Wilson, 1972, pp. 288–289.

Turkle, Brinton. "Confessions of a Leprechaun: An Author and Illustrator of Children's Books." *Publishers Weekly* 186 (July 14, 1969): 33–35.

Twentieth-Century Children's Writers. 3rd ed. Edited by Tracy Chevalier and D. L. Kirkpatrick. New York: St. Martin, 1989, p. 986.

Twain, Mark (pseud. of Samuel Langhorne Clemens)

Bloom, Harold, ed. *Mark Twain.* Edgemont, PA: Chelsea House, 1986.

Branch, Edgar Marquess, et al., eds. *Mark Twain's Letters, Vol. I: 1853–1866.* Berkeley: Univ. of California Press, 1988.

Briden, E. F. "Advertising in *'A Connecticut Yankee.'*" *American Notes and Queries* 21 (Jan–Feb 1983): 74.

Budd, Louis J., ed. *Critical Essays on Mark Twain, 1867–1910.* Boston: G. K. Hall, 1982.

Cardwell, Guy. *The Man Who Was Mark Twain.* New Haven, CT: Yale Univ. Press, 1991.

Clareson, Thomas D. "Mark Twain." In *Supernatural Fiction Writers: Fantasy and Horror,* vol. 2. Edited by E. F. Bleiler. New York: Scribner, 1985, pp. 761–768.

Clemens, Susy. *Papa: An Intimate Biography of Mark Twain.* New York: Doubleday, 1985.

Collins, W. J. "Hank Morgan in the Garden of Forking Paths: *A Connecticut Yankee in King Arthur's Court* as Alternative History." *Modern Fiction Studies* 32 (Spring 1986): 109–114.

Cummings, Sherwood. *Mark Twain and Science: Adventures of a Mind.* Baton Rouge: Louisiana State Univ. Press, 1988.

Doyle, Brian. *The Who's Who of Children's Literature.* New York: Schocken, 1968, pp. 274–275.

Duram, James C. "Mark Twain and Middle Ages." *Wichita State University Studies* 47 (Aug 1971): 1–16.

Dusinberre, Juliet. *"Alice" to the Lighthouse: Children's Books and Radical Experimentalism in Art.* New York: St. Martin, 1987.

Fienberg, Lorne. "Twain's *Connecticut Yankee:* The Entrepreneur as a Daimonic Hero." *Modern Fiction Studies* 28 (Summer 1982): 155–167.

Gardiner, Jane. "'A More Splendid Necromancy': Mark Twain's *Connecticut Yankee* and the Electrical Revolution." *Studies in the Novel* 19 (Winter 1987): 448–458.

George, Roger. "'The Road Lieth Not Straight': Maps and Mental Models in *A Connecticut Yankee in King Arthur's Court.*" *ATQ: A Journal of New England Writing* 5 (Mar 1991): 66–67.

Gerber, John C. *Mark Twain* Boston: Twayne, 1988.

Hawkins, Hunt. "Mark Twain's Anti-Imperialism." *American Literary Realism* 25 (Winter 1993): 31–45.

Hearn, Michael Patrick. "Mark Twain." In *Writers for Children: Critical Studies of Major Authors Since the Seventeenth Century.* Edited by Jane M. Bingham. New York: Scribner, 1988, pp. 573–582.

Helbig, Alethea K., and Agnes Regan Perkins. *Dictionary of American Children's Fiction, 1859–1959.* Westport, CT: Greenwood, 1985, pp. 537–538.

Kaplan, Justin. "*A Connecticut Yankee* in Hell." *American Heritage* 40 (Nov 1989): 97–104.

———. *Mr. Clemens and Mark Twain: A Biography.* New York: Simon, 1983.

Ketterer, David. "Epoch-Eclipse and Apocalypse: Special Effects in *A Connecticut Yankee.*" *Publications of the Modern Language Association* 88 (Oct 1973): 1104–1114.

———. "*The Fortunate Island* by Max Adeler: Its Publication History and *A Connecticut Yankee.*" *Mark Twain Journal* 29 (Fall 1991): 28–34.

——— "Power Fantasy in the 'Science Fiction' of Mark Twain." In Slusser, Rabkin, and Scholes. *Bridges to Fantasy.* Carbondale: Southern Illinois Univ. Press, 1982, pp. 130–141.

———, ed. *The Science Fiction of Mark Twain.* Hamden, CT: Archon Books, 1984.

Kiskis, Michael J. *Mark Twain's Own Autobiography: The Chapters from "The North American Review."* Madison: University of Wisconsin Press, 1990.

Klass, Philip. "An Innocent in Time: Mark Twain in King Arthur's Court." *Extrapolation* 16 (1974): 17–32.

Kordecki, Lesley C. "Twain's Critique of Malory's Romance: *Forma Tractandi* and *A Connecticut Yankee.*" *Nineteenth-Century Literature* 41 (1986): 329–348.

Lawson, Lewis. "A Connecticut Agnostic in King Arthur's Court." In *American Literature in Belgium,* ed. by Gilbert Debusscher and Marc Maufort. Amsterdam: Rodopoi, 1988, pp. 67–76.

Michaels, Walter Benn. "An American Tragedy; or, the Promise of American Life: Classes and Individuals." *Representation* 25 (Winter 1989): 71–98.

Michelson, Bruce. "Realism, Romance and Dynamite: The Quarrel of *A Connecticut Yankee.*" *New England Quarterly* 64 (Dec 1991): 609–632.

Neider, Charles, ed. *The Selected Letters of Mark Twain.* New York: Harper, 1982.

The Oxford Companion to Children's Literature. Edited by Humphrey Carpenter and Mari Prichard. New York: Oxford Univ. Press, 1984, p. 546.

Rogers, R. O. "Twain, Taine, and Lecky: The Genesis of a Passage in *A Connecticut Yankee.*" *Modern Language Quarterly* 34 (Dec 1973): 436–447.

Scharnhorst, Gary. "Mark Twain and the Millerites: Notes on *A Connecticut Yankee in King Arthur's Court.*" *American Transcendental Quarterly* 3 (Sept 1989): 297–304.

Sewell, D. R. "Hank Morgan and the Colonization of Utopia." (Kingston: Univ. of Rhode Island) *ATQ* 3 (Mar 1989): 27–44.

Stableford, Brian. *"A Connecticut Yankee in King Arthur's Court."* In *Survey of Modern Fantasy Literature,* vol. 1. Edited by Frank N. Magill. Englewood Cliffs, NJ: Salem Press, 1983, pp. 319–323.

Stahl, J. D. "Satire and the Evolution of Perspective in Children's Literature: Mark Twain, E. B. White, and Louise Fitzhugh." *Children's Literature Association Quarterly* 15 (Fall 1990): 119–122.

Stanek, Lou Willet. "Twain's Farewell to His Art: A New Version of *The Mysterious Stranger.*" *Top of the News* 41, no. 2 (1985): 177–179.

Stott, Jon C. *Children's Literature from A to Z.* New York: McGraw-Hill, 1984, p. 275.

Tenney, Thomas Asa. *Mark Twain: A Reference Guide.* Boston: G. K. Hall, 1977.

———. "Mark Twain: A Reference Guide. 5th Annual Supplement." *American Literary Realism* 14 (1981): 157–194.

Twain, Mark. *Mark Twain's Autobiography.* 2 vols. New York: Harper, 1924.

Twentieth-Century Children's Writers. 3rd ed. Edited by Tracy Chevalier and D. L. Kirkpatrick. New York: St. Martin, 1989, pp. 986–988.

Twentieth-Century Science Fiction Writers. 3rd ed. Edited by Noelle Watson and Paul E. Schellinger. Chicago: St. James Press, 1991, pp. 812–817.

Winters, Donald E. "The Utopianism of Survival: Bellamy's *Looking Backward* and Twain's *A Connecticut Yankee.*" *American Studies* 21 (1980): 23–28.

Zall, Paul M., ed. *Mark Twain Laughing: Humorous Anecdotes by and about Samuel L. Clemens.* Knoxville: Univ. of Tennessee, 1985.

Zlatic, Thomas D. "Language Technologies in *A Connecticut Yankee.*" *Nineteenth Century Literature* 45 (Mar 1991): 453–477.

Unwin, Nora S(picer)

More Junior Authors. Edited by Muriel Fuller. New York: Wilson, 1963, p. 216.

Unwin, Nora S. "The Artist in England, 1929–1945." *Horn Book* 23 (Mar 1947): 121–124.

———. "With Small Victories a Lesson Is Crowned." *Horn Book* 36 (Oct 1960): 378–385.

Yates, Elizabeth. "Portrait of an Artist." *Horn Book* 26 (Mar 1950): 134–143.

Uttley, Alison (pseud. of Alice Jane Taylor Uttley)

Aers, Lesley. "The Treatment of Time in Four Children's Books." *Children's Literature in Education* 2 (July 1970): 69–81.

"Alison Uttley, Born 17th December, 1884." *Books for Your Children* (U.K.) 19 (Autumn/Winter 1984): 10–11.

Colwell, Eileen. "Dreams and Memories: A Tribute to Alison Uttley for Her 85th Birthday." *Junior Bookshelf* 34 (Feb 1970): 13–17.

Crouch, Marcus. "Memory and Alison Uttley." *Junior Bookshelf* 48 (Dec 1984): 239–242.

Doyle, Brian. *The Who's Who of Children's Literature.* New York: Schocken, 1968, pp. 277–278.

Graham, Eleanor. "Alison Uttley: An Appreciation." *Junior Bookshelf* 5 (Dec 1941): 115–120.

Gunn, Katherine. "The Children's Books of Alison Uttley." *Book and Magazine Collector* 25 (Apr 1986): 24–31.

Judd, Denis. *Alison Uttley: The Life of a Country Child.* London: Joseph, 1986.

———. "The Magic of Fairytale." *Radio Times* [London] (Dec 15–21, 1984): 76.

Kingsley, Madeleine. "A Child of Her Time." *Radio Times* [London] 217 (Dec 17–23, 1977): 15.

Lehnert-Rodiek, Gertrud. "Fantastic Children's Literature and Travel in Time." *Phaedrus* 13 (1988): 61–72.

MacIlroy, Barry. "'Those Magical Time-Slip Stories.'" *Souvenir* (U.K.) 21 (1992): 14–15. Discusses Violet Needham, David Severn, Mabel Esther Allan, and Alison Uttley.

"Obituary: Mrs. Alison Uttley: Author of Much-Loved Books for Children." [London] *Times* (May 8, 1976): 14.

The Oxford Companion to Children's Literature. Edited by Humphrey Carpenter and Mari Prichard. New York: Oxford Univ. Press, 1984, p. 555.

Pflieger, Pat, and Helen M. Hill. *A Reference Guide to Modern Fantasy for Children.* Westport, CT: Greenwood, 1984, pp. xiii, 546–548, 564–566.

Ray, Sheila. "Author Notes from Great Britain: Ted Hughes, John Masefield, and Alison Uttley." *Bookbird* 2 (1985): 29–30.

Saintsbury, Elizabeth. *The World of Alison Uttley: A Biography.* London: Baker, 1980.

Twentieth-Century Children's Writers. 3rd ed. Edited by Tracy Chevalier and D. L. Kirkpatrick. Chicago: St. James, 1989, pp. 995–997.

Uttley, Alison. *Country World: Memories of Childhood.* Selected by Lucy Meredith. London: Faber, 1984, 1986.

———. *Wild Honey.* Oxford: Issis, 1962, 1991.

Van Allsburg, Chris

Bernagozzi, T. "Curriculum Adventures with Chris Van Allsburg." *Learning '93* 21 (Apr–May 1993): 42–44.

Fifth Book of Junior Authors and Illustrators. Edited by Sally Holmes Holtze. New York: Wilson, 1983, pp. 316–317.

Ford, Elizabeth A. "Resurrection Twins: Visual Implications in *Two Bad Ants.*" *Children's Literature Association Quarterly* 15 (Spring 1990): 8–10.

Gardner, John. "Fun and Games and Dark Imaginings." *New York Times Book Review,* Apr 26, 1981, pp. 49, 64.

Heron, Kim. "Van Allsburg's *Express.*" *New York Times Magazine* (Dec 24, 1989): 12–28.

"Jumanji." In *Newbery and Caldecott Medal Books: 1976–1985.* Edited by Lee Kingman. Boston: Horn Book, 1986, pp. 229–237.

Kiefer, B. "Profile: Chris Van Allsburg in Three Dimensions." *Language Arts* 64 (Oct 1987): 664–673.

Macaulay, David. "Chris Van Allsburg." *Horn Book* 58 (Aug 1982): 385–387.

———. "Chris Van Allsburg." *Horn Book* 62 (July–Aug 1986): 425–429.

MacCann, Donnarae, and Olga Richard. "Picture Books for Children." *Wilson Library Bulletin* 56 (Nov 1981): 212–213.

McKee, Barbara. "Van Allsburg: From a Different Perspective." *Horn Book* 62 (Sept–Oct 1986): 566–571.

Neumeyer, Peter F. "How Picture Books Mean: The Case of Chris Van Allsburg." *Children's Literature Association Quarterly* 15 (Spring 1990): 2–7.

The Oxford Companion to Children's Literature. Edited by Humphrey Carpenter and Mari Prichard. New York: Oxford Univ. Press, 1984, pp. 204–207.

Rogers, S. "It's Only a Game . . . or Is It?" *School Library Journal* 38 (Mar 1992): 176–177.

Stan, Susan. "Chris Van Allsburg." *Five Owls* 2, no. 6 (1988): 86.

Thomas, Rebecca L. *Primaryplots 2: A Book Talk Guide for Use with Readers Ages 4–8.* New Providence, NJ: Bowker, 1993, pp. 218–220, 300–302.

Twentieth-Century Children's Writers. 3rd ed. Edited by Tracy Chevalier and D. L. Kirkpatrick. Chicago: St. James, 1989, pp. 997–998.

Van Allsburg, Chris. "1986 Caldecott Acceptance Speech." *Horn Book* 62 (July–Aug 1986): 420–424; also in *Top of the News* 42 (Summer 1986): 396–400.

Vance, Jack (pseud. of John Holbrook Vance)

Allen, Paul C. "Of Swords and Sorcery." *Fantasy Crossroads* 9 (1976): 25–27.

Chandler, A. Bertram. "An Appreciation of Jack Vance." *Science Fiction* 4 (June 1982): 53–54.

Close, Peter. "An Interview with Jack Vance." *Science Fiction Review* 6 (Nov 1977): 36–42.

Dean, John. "The Uses of Wilderness in American Science Fiction." *Science Fiction Studies* 9 (1982): 68–81.

Dirda, Michael. "Jack Vance." In *Supernatural Fiction Writers: Fantasy and Horror,* vol. 2. Edited by E. F. Bleiler. New York: Scribner, 1985, pp. 1105–1111.

Dowling, Terry. "A Xenographical Postscript." *Science Fiction* 2 (1980): 243–250.

Edwards, Malcolm. "Jack Vance." In *Science Fiction Writers.* Edited by E. F. Bleiler. New York: Scribner, 1982, pp. 543–550.

Letson, Russell. "Identity, Freedom and Will: Jack Vance." *Fantasy Review* 98 (1987): 12–14+.

———, ed. *Jack Vance: Light from a Lone Star.* Cambridge, MA: NESFA Press, 1985.

Levack, Daniel J. H. "Jack Vance: A Bibliography." *Science Fiction* 4 (June 1982): 82–84.

Levack, Daniel J. H., and Tim Underwood. *Fantasms: A Bibliography of the Literature of Jack Vance.* San Francisco: Underwood-Miller, 1978.

McFerran, Dave. "The Magic of *The Dying Earth.*" *Anduril* 6 (1976): 35–38.

Platt, Charles. *Dream Makers II.* New York: Berkley, 1983, pp. 159–166. Interview.

Rawline, Jack P. "Linear Man: Jack Vance and the Value of Plot in Science Fiction." *Extrapolation* 24 (1983): 356–369.

Schuyler, William M., Jr. "Recent Developments in Spell Construction." In *The Aesthetics of Fantasy Literature and Art.* Edited by Roger C. Schlobin. Notre Dame, IN: Univ. of Notre Dame, 1982, pp. 237–248.

Shreve, Gregory M. "Not with a Bang but with a Whimper: Anticatastrophic Elements in Vance's *Dying Earth.*" In *Phoenix from the Ashes: The Literature of the Remade World,* ed. by Carl B. Yoke. New York: Greenwood, 1987.

Silverberg, Robert. "Introduction." In Jack Vance. *Eyes of the Overworld.* Boston: Gregg, 1977.

Spinrad, Norman. "Introduction." In Jack Vance. *The Dragon Masters.* Boston: Gregg, 1976.

Twentieth-Century Science Fiction Writers. 3rd ed. Edited by Noelle Watson and Paul E. Schellinger. Chicago: St. James Press, 1991, pp. 820–822.

Underwood, Tim, and Chuck Miller, eds. *Jack Vance.* New York: Taplinger, 1980.

Watson, Christine. "*The Dying Earth* and *The Eyes of the Overworld.*" In *Survey of Modern Fantasy Literature,* vol. 1. Edited by Frank N. Magill. Englewood Cliffs, NJ: Salem Press, 1983, pp. 441–446.

Van Leeuwen, Jean

Fifth Book of Junior Authors and Illustrators. Edited by Sally Holmes Holtze. New York: Wilson, 1983, pp. 317–318.

Van Stockum (Marlin), Hilda (Gerarda)

Coblentz, Catherine Cate. "Birthdays in an Artist's Family." *Horn Book* 20 (Nov 1944): 461–468.

The Junior Book of Authors. 2nd ed. rev. Edited by Stanley J. Kunitz and Howard Haycraft. New York: Wilson, 1951, pp. 289–290.

Roginski, Jim, ed. *Newbery and Caldecott Medalists and Honor Book Winners.* Littleton, CO: Libraries Unlimited, 1982, pp. 268–269.

Twentieth-Century Children's Writers. 3rd ed. Edited by Tracy Chevalier and D. L. Kirkpatrick. New York: St. Martin, 1989, pp. 998–999.

Van Stockum, Hilda. "Holland During Invasion." *Horn Book* 22 (Jan 1946): 50–54.

———. "Storytelling in the Family." *Horn Book* 37 (June 1961): 246–252.

———. "Through an Illustrator's Eyes." *Horn Book* 20 (May 1944): 176–184.

Vaughan, Agnes Carr

Vaughan, Agnes Carr. "Lucian and His True Story." *Horn Book* 6 (May 1930): 127–130.

Vinge, Joan D(ennison)

Barr, Marleen S., et al. *Reader's Guide to Suzy McKee Charnas, Octavia Butler and Joan Vinge.* Mercer Island, WA: Starmont, 1985.

Frazier, Robert. "Interview: Joan Vinge." *Thrust* 16 (1980): 6–9.

Law, Richard. "Science Fiction Women: Victims, Rebels, Heroes." In *Patterns of the Fantastic.* Mercer Island, WA: Starmont, 1983, pp. 11–20.

Platt, Charles. *Dream Makers II: The Uncommon Men and Women Who Write Science Fiction.* New York: Berkley, 1983, pp. 211–218. Interview.

Schweitzer, Darrell. "An Interview with Joan D. Vinge." *Science Fiction Review* 8 (Mar–Apr 1979): 8–12.

Thompson, William B. "Interview: Joan D. Vinge." *Starship* 43 (1983): 15–18.

Twentieth-Century Science Fiction Writers. 3rd ed. Edited by Noelle Watson and Paul E. Schellinger. Chicago: St. James Press, 1989, pp. 829–831.

Yoke, Carl B. "From Alienation to Personal Triumph: The Science Fiction of Joan D. Vinge." *In the Feminine Eye.* Edited by Tom Staicar. New York. Ungar, 1982, pp. 103–130.

———. "Vinge and Vegetation." *Fantasy Newsletter* 53 (1982): 24–26.

Voigt, Cynthia

Fifth Book of Junior Authors and Illustrators. Edited by Sally Holmes Holtze. New York: Wilson, 1983, pp. 320–321.

Helbig, Alethea, and Agnes Regan Perkins. *Dictionary of American Children's Fiction, 1985–1989.* Westport, CT: Greenwood, 1993, pp. 36–37, 268.

———. *Dictionary of American Children's Fiction, 1960–1984.* Westport, CT: Greenwood, 1986, p. 700.

Henke, James T. "Dicey, Odysseus, and Hansel and Gretel: The Lost Children in Voigt's *Homecoming.*" *Children's Literature in Education* 16 (Spring 1985): 45–52.

Hoffman, Mary. "The Best Is Yet to Be: The Novels of Cynthia Voigt." *School Librarian* (U.K.) 41 (May 1993): 48–49.

Irving, Elsie K. "Cynthia Voigt." *Horn Book* 59 (Aug 1983): 410–412.

Kauffman, D. "Profile: Cynthia Voigt." *Language Arts* 62 (Dec 1985): 876–880.

Rochman, Hazel. "The *Booklist* Interview: Cynthia Voigt." *Booklist* 85 (Apr 15, 1989): 297–304.

Speaking for Ourselves: Autobiographical Sketches by Notable Authors of Books for Young Adults. Edited by Donald R. Gallo. Urbana, IL: National Council of Teachers of English, 1990, pp. 217–218.

Twentieth-Century Children's Writers. 3rd ed. Edited by Tracy Chevalier and D. L. Kirkpatrick. Chicago: St. James, 1989, pp. 1004–1005.

Voigt, Cynthia. "About Excellence." *Language Arts* 63, no. 1 (1986): 10–11.

———. "Newbery Medal Acceptance." *Horn Book* 59 (Aug 1983): 401–409.

Voigt, Jessica. "Cynthia Voigt." *Horn Book* 59 (Aug 1983): 413.

Waber, Bernard

Bader, Barbara. *American Picturebooks from Noah's Ark to the Beast Within.* New York: Macmillan, 1976, pp. 480–483.

Harmon, Mary K. "Bernard Waber." *Elementary English* 51 (Sept 1974): 773–776.

Third Book of Junior Authors. Edited by Doris De Montreville and Donna Hill. New York: Wilson, 1972, pp. 293–295.

Twentieth-Century Children's Writers. 3rd ed. Edited by Tracy Chevalier and D. L. Kirkpatrick. New York: St. Martin, 1989, pp. 1005–1006.

Waddell, Martin *see* Sefton, Catherine

Wagner, Lauren McGraw

Hanff, Peter E., and Douglas G. Greene. *Bibliographia Oziana.* Demorest, GA: International Wizard of Oz Club, 1976.

Wahl, Jan (Boyer)

Third Book of Junior Authors. Edited by Doris De Montreville and Donna Hill. New York: Wilson, 1972, pp. 295–296.

Twentieth-Century Children's Writers. 3rd ed. Edited by Tracy Chevalier and D. L. Kirkpatrick. New York: St. Martin, 1989, pp. 1009–1012.

Walsh, Jill Paton *see* Paton Walsh, Jill

Walton, Evangeline (pseud. of Evangeline Ensley)

Dowdy, David A. "The Figure of Taliesin." *Mythlore* 6, no. 23 (1979).

Evans, W. D. Emrys. "The Welsh Mabinogion: Tellings and Retellings." *Children's Literature in Education* 9 (Spring 1978): 17–33.

Herman, John. "Recommended: Evangeline Walton." *English Journal* 74 (Apr 1985): 75–76.

Spencer, Paul. "Evangeline Walton: An Interview." *Fantasy Review* 77 (1985): 7–10.
Spivack, Charlotte. *Merlin's Daughters: Contemporary Women Writers of Fantasy.* New York: Greenwood, 1987.
Sullivan, C. W., III. "Evangeline Walton and the Welsh Mythos." *Fantasy Review* 77 (1985): 35–36, 42.
———. "The Influence of Celtic Myth and Legend on Modern Imaginative Fiction." Ph.D. diss., University of Oregon, 1976.
———. "The Mabinogion Tetralogy." In *Survey of Modern Fantasy Literature,* vol. 2. Edited by Frank N. Magill. Englewood Cliffs, NJ: Salem Press, 1983, pp. 932–937.
———. *Welsh Celtic Myth in Modern Fantasy.* Westport, CT: Greenwood, 1989, pp. 13–23+.
Walton, Evangeline. "Celtic Myth in the 20th Century." *Mythlore* 3 (1976): 19–22.
Zahorski, Kenneth J., and Robert H. Boyer. *Lloyd Alexander, Evangeline Walton Ensley, Kenneth Morris: A Primary and Secondary Bibliography.* Boston: G. K. Hall, 1981.

Wangerin, Walter

Burger, Douglas A. *"The Book of the Dun Cow."* In *Survey of Modern Fantasy Literature,* vol. 1. Edited by Frank N. Magill. Englewood Cliffs, NJ: Salem Press, 1983, pp. 149–153.

Warburg, Sandol Stoddard (pseud. of Sandol Stoddard)

Hopkins, Lee Bennett. "Sandol Warburg." In *Books Are by People.* New York: Citation Press, 1969, pp. 299–302.

Warner, Sylvia Townsend

Crossley, Robert. "A Long Day's Dying: The Elves of J. R. R. Tolkien and Sylvia Townsend Warner." In *Death and the Serpent: Immortality in Science Fiction and Fantasy.* Edited by Carl B. Yoke and Donald M. Hassler. Westport, CT: Greenwood, 1985, pp. 57–70.
Morgan, Chris. *"Kingdoms of Elfin."* In *Survey of Modern Fantasy Literature,* vol. 2. Englewood Cliffs, NJ: Salem Press, 1984, pp. 855–858.
Paul, Lissa. "Escape Claws: Cover Stories on *Lolly Willowes* and *Crusoe's Daughter."* *Signal* 63 (Sept 1990): 206–220.

Weir, Rosemary (Green)

Twentieth-Century Children's Writers. 3rd ed. Edited by Tracy Chevalier and D. L. Kirkpatrick. Chicago: St. James, 1989, pp. 1022–1023.

Weis, Margaret

Fonstad, Karen Wynn. *The Atlas of the Dragonlance World.* Lake Geneva, WI: TSR, 1987.
Weis, Margaret, and Tracy Hickman, eds. *Leaves from the Inn of the Last Home: The Complete Krynn Source Book.* Lake Geneva, WI: TSR, 1987.

Welch, Ronald (pseud. of Ronald Oliver Felton)

Aers, Lesley. "The Treatment of Time in Four Children's Books." *Children's Literature in Education* 2 (July 1970): 69–81.
Crouch, Marcus. *The Nesbit Tradition.* London: Benn, 1972, pp. 72–74.

Doyle, Brian. *The Who's Who of Children's Literature.* New York: Schocken, 1968, pp. 287–288.

Twentieth-Century Children's Writers. 3rd ed. Edited by Tracy Chevalier and D. L. Kirkpatrick. New York: St. Martin, 1989, pp. 1023–1024.

Welch, Ronald. "Attention to Detail: The Workbooks of Ronald Welch." *Children's Literature in Education* 8 (Summer 1972): 30–38.

Wellman, Manly Wade

Benson, Gordon, Jr. *Manly Wade Wellman: The Gentleman from Chapel Hill.* Albuquerque: Benson, 1986.

Coulson, Robert. "The Recent Fantasies of Manly Wade Wellman." In *Discovering Modern Horror Fiction.* Edited by Darrell Schweitzer. Mercer Island, WA: Starmont, 1985.

Elliot, Jeffrey M. *Fantasy Voices: Interviews with American Fantasy Writers.* San Bernardino, CA: Borgo Press, 1982.

———. "Interview: Manly Wade Wellman—Better Things Waiting." *Fantasy Newsletter* 22 (1980): 16–25.

Meyers, Walter E. "Manly Wade Wellman." In *Supernatural Fiction Writers: Fantasy and Horror,* vol. 2. Edited by E. F. Bleiler. New York: Scribner, 1985, pp. 947–954.

———. "The Silver John Stories." In *Survey of Modern Fantasy Literature,* vol. 4. Edited by Frank N. Magill. Englewood Cliffs, NJ: Salem Press, 1983, pp. 1744–1748.

More Junior Authors. Edited by Muriel Fuller. New York: Wilson, 1963, pp. 222–223.

Schweitzer, Darrell. "*Amazing* Interview: An Interview with Manly Wade Wellman." *Amazing Stories,* Mar 1981, pp. 122–126.

Searles, Baird, Beth Meacham, and Michael Franklin. *A Reader's Guide to Fantasy.* New York: Avon, 1982, pp 149–150.

Twentieth-Century Science Fiction Writers. 3rd ed. Edited by Noelle Watson and Paul E. Schellinger. Chicago: St. James Press, 1991, pp. 850–852.

Waggoner, Diana. "Go Tell It on the Mountain: The Achievement of Manly Wade Wellman." *Fantasy Review* 90 (1986): 17–19, 50.

Wagner, Karl Edward. "Manly Wade Wellman: A Biography." *August Darleth Society Newsletter* 4 (1980): 4–9.

———. "The Old Captain Goes Home: Manly Wade Wellman, 1903–1986." *Fantasy Review* 90 (1986): 15–16, 34.

Wells, H(erbert) G(eorge)

Cook, Monte. "Tips for Time Travel." In *Philosophers Look at Science Fiction.* Edited by Nicholas D. Smith. Chicago: Nelson, 1982, pp. 47–55.

Costa, Richard Hauer. *H. G. Wells.* rev. ed. Boston: Twayne, 1985.

Crosley, Robert. *H. G. Wells.* Mercer Island, WA: Starmont, 1986.

Ferrell, Keith. *H. G. Wells: First Citizen of the Future.* New York: Evans, 1983.

Gardner, Martin. "H. G. Wells." In *Supernatural Fiction Writers: Fantasy and Horror,* vol. 1. Edited by E. F. Bleiler. New York: Scribner, 1985, pp. 397–402.

H. G. Wells. Maltoon, IL: Spectrum Educational Media, 1984. (Audiocassette)

H. G. Wells. Hawthorne, NJ: Peller, 1985. (Filmstrip-audiocassette)

H. G. Wells Society. *H. G. Wells: A Comprehensive Bibliography.* London: Polytechnic of North London, 1986.

Hammond, J. R. *Herbert George Wells: An Annotated Bibliography of His Works.* New York: Garland, 1977.

Hampson, R. G. "H. G. Wells and *The Arabian Nights.*" *The Wellsian* 6 (1983): 30–34.

Mullen, Michael, ed. *H. G. Wells: Reality and Beyond. A Collection of Critical Essays Prepared in Conjunction with the Exhibition and Symposium on H. G. Wells.* Champaign, IL: Champaign Public Library Information Center, 1986.

Neilson, Keith. "The Short Fiction of H. G. Wells." In *Survey of Modern Fantasy Literature,* vol. 4. Edited by Frank N. Magill. Englewood Cliffs, NJ: Salem Press, 1983, pp. 1729–1932.

Parrinder, Patrick, ed. *H. G. Wells: The Critical Heritage.* New York: Routledge, 1985.

Ponnau, Gwenhail. *La Folie Dans la Littérature Fantastique [Madness in Fantasy Literature].* Paris: Editions du Centre National de la Recherche Scientifique, 1987.

Reed, John R. *The Natural History of H. G. Wells.* Athens: Ohio Univ. Press, 1982.

Scheick, William J., and J. Randolph Cox. *H. G. Wells: A Reference Guide.* Boston: Hall, 1988.

Shiveley, James Ross. "Fantasy in the Fiction of H. G. Wells." Ph.D. diss., University of Nebraska, Lincoln, 1955.

Twentieth-Century Science Fiction Writers. 3rd ed. Edited by Noelle Watson and Paul E. Schellinger. Chicago: St. James Press, 1991, pp. 852–856.

West, Anthony. *H. G. Wells: Aspects of a Life.* New York: Random, 1984; NAL/Meridian, 1985.

Zanger, Jules. "Goblins, Morlocks and Weasels: Classic Fantasy and the Industrial Revolution." *Children's Literature in Education* 8 (Winter 1977): 154–162.

Wells, Rosemary

Fourth Book of Junior Authors and Illustrators. Edited by Doris De Montreville and Elizabeth D. Crawford. New York: Wilson, 1978, pp. 343–345.

Mercier, Jean F. "Rosemary Wells." *Publishers Weekly* 217 (Feb 29, 1980): 72–73.

Twentieth-Century Children's Writers. 3rd ed. Edited by Tracy Chevalier and D. L. Kirkpatrick. New York: St. Martin, 1989, pp. 1024–1025.

Wersba, Barbara

Cunningham, Julia. "Notes for Another's Music." *Horn Book* 47 (Dec 1971): 617. Discusses *Let Me Fall Before I Fly.*

Third Book of Junior Authors. Edited by Doris De Montreville and Donna Hill. New York: Wilson, 1972, pp. 298–299.

Twentieth-Century Children's Writers. 3rd ed. Edited by Tracy Chevalier and D. L. Kirkpatrick. Chicago: St. James, 1989, pp. 1025–1026.

Vandergrift, Kay E. "Barbara Wersba." In *American Authors for Children since 1960: Fiction. Dictionary of Literary Biography,* vol. 52. Detroit: Gale, 1986, pp. 374–379.

Westall, Robert (Atkinson)

Chambers, Aidan. "Letter from England: Children at War." *Horn Book* 52 (Aug 1976): 438–442.

Crouch, Marcus. "Robert Westall, 1929–1993." *Junior Bookshelf* (U.K.) 57 (1993): 85–87.

Davis, J. S. "An Examination of Robert Westall's Eleven Works of Young Adult Fiction Through the Use of Reviews and Wolfgang Iser's Reader Reception Theory." MSLS thesis, University of North Carolina at Chapel Hill, 1989.

Fifth Book of Junior Authors and Illustrators. Edited by Sally Holmes Holtze. New York: Wilson, 1983, pp. 322–324.

Gillespie, John T., and Corinne J. Naden. *Juniorplots 3: A Book Talk Guide for Use with Readers Ages 12–16.* New York: Bowker, 1987, pp. 231–234.

Hollindale, Peter. "A Freedom in Ghostliness." *British Book News Children's Books* (Dec 1986): 2–4.

Lehnert-Rodiek, Gertrud. "Fantastic Children's Literature and Travel in Time." *Phaedrus* 13 (1988): 61–72.

Lewis, Tom. "Know the Author: Robert Westall." *Magpies* (Australia) 6, no. 2 (May 1991): 15–17.

Nettell, Stephanie. "The Ruler of the Kingdom of the Imagination." *The Guardian* 28 (Mar 1991): 32.

The Oxford Companion to Children's Literature. Edited by Humphrey Carpenter and Mari Prichard. New York: Oxford Univ. Press, 1984, p. 565.

Pflieger, Pat, and Helen M. Hill. *A Reference Guide to Modern Fantasy for Children.* Westport, CT: Greenwood, 1984, pp. xiii, 150–152, 574–576, 587–589, 603–605.

Rees, David. "Macho Man, British Style—Robert Westall." In *Painted Desert, Green Shade.* Boston: Horn Book, 1984, pp. 115–125.

Robertson, Robbie. "Of Guns and Ghosts: An Introduction to the Novels of Robert Westall." *Bookmark* (Edinburgh) 2 (Sept 1978): 46–55.

Searles, Baird, Beth Meacham, and Michael Franklin. *A Reader's Guide to Fantasy.* New York: Avon, 1982, pp. 151–152.

Twentieth-Century Children's Writers. 3rd ed. Edited by Tracy Chevalier and D. L. Kirkpatrick. Chicago: St. James, 1989, pp. 1027–1028.

Westall, Robert. "The Hunt for Evil." *Signal* 34 (Jan 1981): 3–13.

Weston, John (Harrison)

Blakely, W. Paul. "Growing Pains in Arizona: Youth in the Fiction of John Weston." *Arizona English Bulletin* 14 (Apr 1972): 44–50.

White, Anne Hitchcock

Fourth Book of Junior Authors and Illustrators. Edited by Doris De Montreville and Elizabeth D. Crawford. New York: Wilson, 1978, pp. 347–348.

Gillespie, John T., and Diana Lembo. *Introducing Books: A Guide for the Middle Grades.* New York: Bowker, 1970, pp. 284–288.

Helbig, Alethea K., and Agnes Regan Perkins. *Dictionary of American Children's Fiction, 1859–1959.* Westport, CT: Greenwood, 1985, pp. 265–266, 496, 561.

More Junior Authors. Edited by Muriel Fuller. New York: Wilson, 1963, pp. 224–225.

White, Anne Hitchcock. "The Animals, One by One." *Horn Book* 34 (June 1958): 211–219.

White, E(lwin) B(rooks)

Alberghene, Janice M. "The Writing in *Charlotte's Web.*" *Children's Literature in Education* 16 (Spring 1985): 32–44.

Alitzer, Nell. "*Charlotte's Web* and the Wake of Language." In *Literature and Hawaii's Children,* ed. by Cristina Bacchilega and Steven Curry. Honolulu: Literature and Hawaii's Children, 1990, pp. 101–106.

Anderson, Arthur James. *E. B. White: A Bibliography.* Metuchen, NJ: Scarecrow Press, 1978.

"Anne Carroll Moore Urged Withdrawal of *Stuart Little.*" *Library Journal* 91 (Apr 15, 1966): 2187–2188; *School Library Journal* 13 (Apr 15, 1966): 71–72.

Apseloff, Marilyn. *"Charlotte's Web*: Flaws in the Weaving." In Douglas Street. *Children's Novels and the Movies.* New York: Ungar, 1983, pp. 171–181.

Arnold, A. "The Pig—Pet, Pork, or Sacrifice?" *Children's Literature in Education* 19 (Summer 1988): 80–85.

Benét, Laura. *Familiar English and American Essayists.* New York: Dodd, 1966.

Blount, Margaret. "The Tables Turned at the Zoo: Mowgli and Stuart Little." In *Animal Land: The Creatures of Children's Fiction.* New York: Morrow, 1975, pp. 226–244.

Breit, H. "Visit." *New York Herald Tribune Book Review,* Jan 17, 1954.

Cameron, Eleanor. "McLuhan, Youth and Literature." *Horn Book* 48 (Dec 1972): 572–579. Reprinted in Heins. *Crosscurrents of Criticism.* Boston: Horn Book, 1977, pp. 98–125.

"Charlotte's Web Tops 'Reading Is Fundamental's' Favorite Book List." *School Library Journal* 36 (Dec 1990): 15.

Curry, Steven. "Fate and Friendship: Lessons of Loss in *The Bridge to Terabithia* and *Charlotte's Web."* In *Literature and Hawaii's Children,* ed. by Cristina Bacchilega and Steven Curry. Honolulu: Literature and Hawaii's Children, 1990, pp. 96–100.

Doyle, Brian. *The Who's Who of Children's Literature.* New York: Schocken, 1968, pp. 289–290.

Elledge, Scott. *E. B. White: A Biography.* New York: Norton, 1984.

Frey, Charles, and John Griffiths. *The Literary Heritage of Childhood: An Appraisal of Children's Classics in the Western Tradition.* Westport, CT: Greenwood, 1987, pp. 219–226.

Gagnon, Laurence. "Webs of Concern: Heidegger, *The Little Prince,* and *Charlotte's Web."* In *Children's Literature,* vol. 2. Storrs, CT: Journal of the Modern Language Association, 1973, pp. 61–66. Reprinted in *Reflections on Literature for Children.* Edited by Francelia Butler and Richard Rotert. Hamden, CT: Shoe String Press, 1984, pp. 66–71.

Galda, Lee. "Readers, Texts, and Contexts: A Response-Based View of Literature in the Classroom." *The New Advocate* 1 (1988): 92–102.

Gillespie, John T., and Diana Lembo. *Introducing Books: A Guide for the Middle Grades.* New York: Bowker, 1970, pp. 259–262.

———. *Juniorplots: A Book Talk Manual for Teachers and Librarians.* New York: Bowker, 1967, pp. 199–201.

Glastonbury, Marion. "E. B. White's Unexpected Items of Enchantment." *Children's Literature in Education* 11 (May 1973): 3–12. Reprinted in Geoff Fox. *Writers, Critics and Children.* New York: Agathon Press, 1976, pp. 104–115.

Gose, Elliott. *Mere Creatures: A Study of Modern Fantasy Tales for Children.* Toronto: Univ. of Toronto Press, 1988, pp. 53–62.

Griffith, John. *"Charlotte's Web*: A Lonely Fantasy of Love." In *Children's Literature,* vol. 8. New Haven, CT: Yale Univ. Press, 1980, pp. 111–117.

Guth, Dorothy Lobrano, ed. *Letters of E. B. White.* New York: Harper, 1976.

Helbig, Alethea K., and Agnes Regan Perkins. *Dictionary of American Children's Fiction, 1859–1959.* Westport, CT: Greenwood, 1985, pp. 94, 500, 561–562.

———. *Dictionary of American Children's Fiction, 1960–1984.* Westport, CT: Greenwood, 1986, pp. 679, 716.

Hiller, Claire. "The World of Fantasy—the World Where Anything Can Happen." *English in Australia* 86 (Dec 1988): 54–59.

Hopkins, Lee Bennett. "E. B. White." In *More Books by More People.* New York: Citation Press, 1974, pp. 375–380.

———. "Profile in Memoriam: E. B. White." *Language Arts* 63 (Sept 1986): 491–494.

Inglis, Fred. *The Promise of Happiness.* New York: Cambridge Univ. Press, 1981, pp. 178–180.

Kinghorn, Norton D. "The Real Miracle of *Charlotte's Web." Children's Literature Association Quarterly* 11 (Spring 1986): 4–9.

Konigsburg, E. L. "Book Remembered." *The Calendar* (now *CBC Features*) 39 (Oct 1984–July 1985). Discusses *Charlotte's Web.*

Kurth, Ruth Justine. "Realism in Children's Books of Fantasy." *California Librarian* 39 (July 1978): 39–40.

Landes, Sonia. "E. B. White's *Charlotte's Web:* Caught in the Web." In *Touchstones.* Edited by Perry Nodelman. West Lafayette, IN: Children's Literature Association Publications, 1985, pp. 270–280.

Landes, Sonia, and Molly Flender. *"Charlotte's Web."* Norwood, MA: Christopher-Gordon, 1989.

Lukens, Rebecca J. *A Critical Handbook of Children's Literature.* 3rd ed. Glenview, IL: Scott, Foresman, 1986, pp. 95–97, 167–168.

McNulty, Faith. "Children's Books for Christmas" *The New Yorker* (Nov 25 1991): 137–148.

Mason, Bobbie Ann. "Profile: The Elements of E. B. White's Style." *Language Arts* 56 (Sept 1979): 692–696.

Milner, Joseph O'Beirne. "When Worlds Collide: The Humanist-Religious Ethos in Children's Literature." In *Webs and Wardrobes: Humanist and Religious World Views in Children's Literature,* ed. by Joseph O'Beirne Milner and Lucy Floyd Morcock Milner. Lanham, MD: University Press of America, 1987, pp. 1–5.

More Junior Authors. Edited by Muriel Fuller. New York: Wilson, 1963, pp. 225–226.

Neumeyer, Peter F. "The Creation of *Charlotte's Web:* From Drafts to Book." Pt. I. *Horn Book* 58 (Oct 1982): 489–497; Pt. II. *Horn Book* 58 (Dec 1982): 617–625.

———. "The Creation of E. B. White's *The Trumpet of the Swan:* The Manuscripts." *Horn Book* 61 (Jan–Feb 1985): 17–28. A shortened version of a paper presented at the conference of the Children's Literature Association, at the University of North Carolina, Charlotte, on May 25, 1984.

———. "E. B. White." In *American Writers for Children, 1900–1960.* Edited by John Cech. *Dictionary of Literary Biography,* vol. 22. Detroit: Gale, 1983, pp. 333–350.

———. "E. B. White: Aspects of Style." *Horn Book* 63 (Sept–Oct 1987): 568–591.

———. *"Stuart Little:* The Manuscripts." *Horn Book* 64 (Sept–Oct 1988): 593–600. Abstract in *The Child and the Family: Selected Papers from the 1988 International Conference of the Children's Literature Association,* ed. by Susan R. Gannon and Ruth A. Thompson. New York: Pace University, 1990, p. 81.

———. "What Makes a Good Children's Book? The Texture of *Charlotte's Web." South Atlantic Bulletin* 44 (1979): 66–75.

Nodelman, Perry. "Text as Teacher: The Beginning of *Charlotte's Web."* In *Children's Literature,* vol. 13. New Haven CT: Yale Univ. Press, 1985, pp. 109–127.

Nordstrom, Ursula. "Stuart, Wilbur, Charlotte: A Tale of Tales." *New York Times Book Review,* May 21, 1974, p. 8.

Nulton, Lucy. "Eight-Year-Olds in *Charlotte's Web." Elementary English* 31 (Jan 1954): 11–16.

The Oxford Companion to Children's Literature. Edited by Humphrey Carpenter and Mari Prichard. New York: Oxford Univ. Press, 1984, pp. 108, 568.

Paulus, P. C. "Claim to Fame and *Charlotte's Web." Teacher* 96 (May–June 1979): 48–49.

Pflieger, Pat, and Helen M. Hill. *A Reference Guide to Modern Fantasy for Children.* Westport, CT: Greenwood, 1984, pp. xii, xv, 107–108, 508–509, 552–553, 593–595.

Ragsdale, W. "Presentation of the Sixth Recognition of Merit to E. B. White for *Charlotte's Web." Claremont Reading Conference Yearbook* 34 (1970): 114–117.

Roginski, Jim, ed. *Newbery and Caldecott Medalists and Honor Book Winners.* Littleton, CO: Libraries Unlimited, 1982, pp. 279–280.

Rollin, Lucy. "The Reproduction of Mothering in *Charlotte's Web." Children's Literature* 18 (1990): 42–52.

Rushdy, Ashraf H. A. "'The Miracle of the Web': Community, Desire and Narrativity in *Charlotte's Web." The Lion and the Unicorn* 15 (Dec 1991): 35–60.

Rustin, Michael. "The Poetic Power of Ordinary Speech: E. B. White's Children's Stories." In Margaret Rustin and Michael Rustin, *Narratives of Love and Loss: Studies in Modern Children's Fiction.* London: Verso, 1987; New York: Routledge, 1988, pp. 146–162.

Sale, Roger. *Fairy Tales and After: From Snow White to E. B. White.* Cambridge, MA: Harvard Univ. Press, 1978, pp. 258–267.

Sampson, Edward C. *E. B. White.* Boston: Twayne, 1974.

Silvey, Anita. "In a Class By Himself." *Horn Book* 62 (Jan–Feb 1986): 17.

Singer, Dorothy G. *"Charlotte's Web:* Erickson's Life Cycle." *School Library Journal* 22 (Nov 1975): 17–19.

Smaridge, Norah. *Famous Modern Storytellers for Young People.* New York: Dodd, 1969, pp. 110–114.

Solheim, Helene. "Magic in the Web: Time, Pigs, and E. B. White." *South Atlantic Quarterly* 80 (Autumn 1981): 391–405.

Stahl, J. D. "Satire and the Evolution of Perspective in Children's Literature: Mark Twain, E. B. White, and Louise Fitzhugh." *Children's Literature Association Quarterly* 15 (Fall 1990): 119–122.

Stott, Jon C. *Children's Literature from A to Z.* New York: McGraw-Hill, 1984, p. 281.

Strunk, William, Jr. *The Elements of Style,* 3rd ed. With Revisions, an Introduction, and a New Chapter on Writing by E. B. White. New York: Macmillan, 1979.

Swinfen, Ann. *In Defense of Fantasy.* New York: Routledge, 1984, pp. 24–25. Discusses *Stuart Little.*

Twentieth-Century Children's Writers. 3rd ed. Edited by Tracy Chevalier and D. L. Kirkpatrick. Chicago: St. James, 1989, pp. 1032–1034.

"Typewriter Man." *Newsweek* 55 (Feb 22, 1960): 72.

Weales, Gerald. "The Designs of E. B. White." *New York Times,* sect. 7, pt. II, May 24, 1970, p. 2 ff. Reprinted in Miriam Hoffman and Eva Samuels. *Authors and Illustrators of Children's Books.* New York: Bowker, 1972, pp. 407–411.

White, E. B. *The Annotated Charlotte's Web,* ed. by Peter F. Neumeyer. New York: Harper, 1994.

———. "Children's Books." In *One Man's Meat.* rev. ed. New York: Harper, 1944, pp. 23–29.

———. "Death of a Pig." *Atlantic Monthly* 181 (Jan 1948): 30–33.

———. *The Essays of E. B. White.* New York: Harper, 1977.

———. "Laura Ingalls Wilder Acceptance." *Horn Book* 46 (Aug 1970): 349–351.

———. *The Letters of E. B. White.* Collected and edited by Dorothy Lobrano Guth. New York: Harper, 1976.

———. "Mr. Forbush's Friends." In *Essays of E. B. White.* New York: Harper, 1977.

———. "On Writing for Children." From "The Art of the Essay." *Paris Review,* no. 48 (Fall 1969). Reprinted in Virginia Haviland. *Children and Literature.* Glenview, IL: Scott, Foresman, 1973, p. 140.

———. *The Second Tree from the Corner.* New York: Harper, 1954; 1978.

Wintle, Justin, and Emma Fisher. "E. B. White." In *The Pied Pipers.* New York: Paddington Press, 1974, pp. 124–131.

White, Eliza Orne

"Eliza Orne White, Her Books for Children." *Horn Book* 1 (Jan 1925): 3–9.

The Junior Book of Authors. 2nd ed. rev. Edited by Stanley J. Kunitz and Howard Haycraft. New York: Wilson, 1951, pp. 295–296.

Miller, Bertha Mahony. "Eliza Orne White and Her Books for Children." *Horn Book* 31 (Apr 1955): 89–102. Reprinted in Andrews. *The Hewins Lectures, 1947–1962.* Boston: Horn Book, 1963, pp. 151–162.

Twentieth-Century Children's Writers. 3rd ed. Edited by Tracy Chevalier and D. L. Kirkpatrick. Chicago: St. James, 1989, pp. 1034–1036.

White, Eliza Orne. "Growing Old with the Radio." *Horn Book* 18 (Jan 1942): 47–82.

White, Stewart Edward

Alter, Judy. *Stewart Edward White.* Boise, ID: Boise State Univ., 1975.

White, T(erence) H(anbury)

Allen, Elizabeth M. "The Fellowship of Merlin: The Role of the Sorcerer in *The Once and Future King* and *The Lord of the Rings.*" Master's thesis, Baylor University, 1978.

Chapman, Ed. "Images of the Numinous in T. H. White and C. S. Lewis." *Mythlore* 4, 16 (June 1977): 3–10.

Chapman, Susan Elizabeth. "A Study of the Genre of T. H. White's Arthurian Books." Ph.D. diss., University of Wales (U.K.), 1988.

Clute, John. "T. H. White." In *Supernatural Fiction Writers: Fantasy and Horror,* vol. 2. Edited by E. F. Bleiler. New York: Scribner, 1985, pp. 651–660.

Crane, John K. *T. H. White.* Boston: Twayne, 1974.

———. "T. H. White: The Fantasy of the Here and Now." *Mosaic* 10, no. 2 (Winter 1976–1977): 33–46.

de Camp, L. Sprague. *Literary Swordsmen and Sorcerers: The Makers of Heroic Fantasy.* Sauk City, WI: Arkham House, 1976.

———, ed. *The Blade of Conan.* New York: Ace, 1979.

Doyle, Brian. *The Who's Who of Children's Literature.* New York: Schocken, 1968, pp. 290–291.

Floyd, Barbara. "A Critique of *The Once and Future King,* Part 1: Not Any Common Earth." *Riverside Quarterly* 1 (1965): 175–180.

Foust, R. E. "*Mistress Masham's Repose.*" In *Survey of Modern Fantasy Literature,* vol. 3. Edited by Frank N. Magill. Englewood Cliffs, NJ: Salem Press, 1983, pp. 1052–1056.

Fries, Maureen. "The Rationalization of the Arthurian Matter in T. H. White and Mary Stewart." *Philological Quarterly* 56 (1977): 258–265.

Gallix, Francois. "T. H. White et la Legende du Roi Arthur." *Mosaic* 10, no. 2 (Winter 1976–1977): 47–64.

Garnett, David, ed. *The White/Garnett Letters.* London: Cape, 1968.

Gillespie, John T., and Diana Lembo. *Juniorplots: A Book Talk Manual for Teachers and Librarians.* New York: Bowker, 1967, pp. 202–204.

Irwin, W. R. "Swift and the Novelists." *Philological Quarterly* 45, no. 1 (Jan 1966): 102–113.

Kellman, Martin Hirsch. "Arthur and Others: The Literary Career of T. H. White." Ph.D. diss., University of Pennsylvania, 1973.

Kellogg, Judith L. "The Dynamics of Dumbing: The Case of Merlin." *The Lion and the Unicorn* 17 (June 1993): 57–72. Discusses Heyer's *Excalibur,* White's *The Sword in the Stone,* Talbott's *King Arthur,* and Yolen's *Merlin's Booke.*

Kertzer, Adrienne. "T. H. White's *The Sword in the Stone:* Education and the Child Reader." In *Touchstones.* Edited by Perry Nodelman. West Lafayette, IN: Children's Literature Association Publications, 1985, pp. 281–290.

Langton, Jane. "A Second Look: *Mistress Masham's Repose.*" *Horn Book* 57 (Oct 1981): 565–570.

Lott, Herschel Woodley. "The Social and Political Ideals in the Major Writings of T. H. White." Ph.D. diss., University of Southern Mississippi, 1970.

MacLeod, Helen. "T. H. White, Author of *The Once and Future King.*" *Book and Magazine Collector* [London] 46 (Jan 1988): 30–39.

Manlove, C. N. "Fantasy and Loss: T. H. White." In C. N. Manlove. *The Impulse of Fantasy Literature.* Kent, OH: Kent State Univ. Press, 1983, pp. 93–114 (revised from an article in *Mosaic,* 1979)

———. "Flight to Aleppo: T. H. White's *The Once and Future King.*" *Mosaic* 10, no. 2 (Winter 1976–1977): 65–84.

Mitchell, Judith H. "The Boy Who Would Be King." *Journal of Popular Culture* 17 (Spring 1984): 134–137.

Nellis, Marilyn K. "Anachronistic Humor in Two Arthurian Romances of Education: *To the Chapel Perilous* and *The Sword and the Stone.*" *Studies in Medievalism* 2 (Fall 1983): 57–77.

Nelson, Marie. "Bird Language in T. H. White's *The Sword in the Stone.*" *Mythlore* 8, 28 (1981).

The Oxford Companion to Children's Literature. Edited by Humphrey Carpenter and Mari Prichard. New York: Oxford Univ. Press, 1984, pp. 353–354, 386, 511, 568.

Pflieger, Pat, and Helen M. Hill. *A Reference Guide to Modern Fantasy for Children.* Westport, CT: Greenwood, 1984, pp. xii, xiv, 372–373, 516–518, 595–597.

Searles, Baird, Beth Meacham, and Michael Franklin. *A Reader's Guide to Fantasy.* New York: Avon, 1982, p. 152.

Shippey, T. A. *"The Once and Future King."* In *Survey of Modern Fantasy Literature,* vol. 3. Englewood Cliffs, NJ: Salem Press, 1983, pp. 1149–1157.

Sprague, Kurth. "From a Troubled Heart: T. H. White and Women in *The Once and Future King.*" Ph.D. diss., University of Texas, Austin, 1978.

Stevenson, Lionel. "Purveyors of Myth and Magic." In *Yesterday and After: The History of the English Novel.* Totowa, NJ: Barnes and Noble, 1967, pp. 111–154.

Stott, Jon C. *Children's Literature from A to Z.* New York: McGraw-Hill, 1984, p. 284.

Swanson, Donald R. "The Uses of Tradition: King Arthur in the Modern World." *CEA Critic* 36, no. 3 (1974): 19–21.

Swinfen, Ann. *In Defense of Fantasy.* New York: Routledge, 1984, pp. 23–24, 26–30, 124, on *The Sword in the Stone;* pp. 125–126, 129–130, on *Mistress Masham's Repose.*

Twentieth-Century Children's Writers. 3rd ed. Edited by Tracy Chevalier and D. L. Kirkpatrick. Chicago: St. James, 1989, pp. 1036–1037.

Warner, Sylvia Ashton. *T. H. White: A Biography.* London: Cape, 1967.

Whitaker, Muriel. "Swords at Sunset and Bag-Puddings: Arthur in Modern Fiction." *Children's Literature in Education* 27, no. 8 (Winter 1977): 143–153.

Wood, Denis. "Growing Up Among the Stars." *Literary/Film Quarterly* 6 (1978): 327–341.

White, W(illiam) A(nthony) P(arker) *see* Boucher, Anthony

Whitney, Phyllis A(yame)

The Junior Book of Authors. 2nd ed. rev. Edited by Stanley J. Kunitz and Howard Haycraft. New York: Wilson, 1951, pp. 297–298.

Wibberley, Leonard (Patrick O'Connor)

Helbig, Alethea K., and Agnes Regan Perkins. *Dictionary of American Children's Fiction, 1859–1959.* Westport, CT: Greenwood, 1985, pp. 563–564.

———. *Dictionary of American Children's Fiction, 1960–1984.* Westport, CT: Greenwood, 1986, p. 722.

More Junior Authors. Edited by Muriel Fuller. New York: Wilson, 1963, pp. 226–227.

Morgan, Chris. *"The Quest of Excalibur."* In *Survey of Modern Fantasy Literature,* vol. 3. Edited by Frank N. Magill. Englewood Cliffs, NJ: Salem Press, 1983, pp. 1301–1303.

Searles, Baird, Beth Meacham, and Michael Franklin. *A Reader's Guide to Fantasy.* New York: Avon, 1982, p. 154.

Twentieth-Century Children's Writers. 3rd ed. Edited by Tracy Chevalier and D. L. Kirkpatrick. Chicago: St. James, 1989, pp. 1039–1041.

White, I. J. "The Historical Stories of Leonard Wibberley—An Appreciation." *Ontario Library Review* 47 (Aug 1963): 95–97.

Wibberley, Leonard. "I Go There Quite Often." *Horn Book* 54 (June 1978): 249–256.

Wiggin, Kate Douglas (Smith)

Benner, Helen Frances. *Kate Douglas Wiggin's Country of Childhood.* Orono: Univ. Press of Maine, 1956.

Boutwell, Edna. "Kate Douglas Wiggin—The Lady with the Golden Key." In Siri Andrews. *The Hewins Lectures, 1947–1962.* Boston: Horn Book, 1963, pp. 297–319.

Butler, Francelia. "Kate Douglas Wiggin." In *Writers for Children: Critical Studies of Major Authors Since the Seventeenth Century.* Edited by Jane M. Bingham. New York: Scribner, 1988, pp. 605–610.

Doyle, Brian. *The Who's Who of Children's Literature.* New York: Schocken, 1968, pp. 291–292.

Erisman, Fred. "Transcendentalism for American Youth: The Children's Books of Kate Douglas Wiggin." *New England Quarterly* 41, 2 (June 1968): 238–247.

Helbig, Alethea K., and Agnes Regan Perkins. *Dictionary of American Children's Fiction, 1859–1959.* Westport, CT: Greenwood, 1985, p. 564.

Kingston, Carolyn T. *The Tragic Mode in Children's Literature.* New York: Teachers College Press, 1974, pp. 127–130.

Moss, Anita. "Kate Douglas Wiggin." In *American Writers for Children before 1900. Dictionary of Literary Biography,* vol. 42. Detroit: Gale, 1985, pp. 380–392.

Stebbins, Lucy Ward. "Kate Douglas Wiggin as a Child Knew Her." *Horn Book* 26 (Nov–Dec 1950): 447–454.

Twentieth-Century Children's Writers. 3rd ed. Edited by Tracy Chevalier and D. L. Kirkpatrick. Chicago: St. James, 1989, pp. 1042–1044.

Wiggin, Kate Douglas. *My Garden of Memory: An Autobiography.* Boston: Houghton Mifflin, 1923.

———. "What Shall Children Read?" *Cosmopolitan* 7 (Aug 1889): 355–360.

Wilde, Oscar (pseud. of Fingal O'Flahertie Wills)

Bradley, Anna Y. "Oscar Wilde." In *Writers for Children: Critical Studies of Major Authors Since the Seventeenth Century.* Edited by Jane M. Bingham. New York: Scribner, 1988, pp. 611–616.

Cohen, Philip K. *The Moral Vision of Oscar Wilde.* Rutherford, NJ: Fairleigh Dickinson Univ. Press, 1978.

Cornwell, Charles Landrum. "From Self to the Shire: Studies in Victorian Fantasy." Ph.D. diss., University of Virginia, 1972.

Doyle, Brian. *The Who's Who of Children's Literature.* New York: Schocken, 1968, p. 292.

D'Yachenko, A. "Skazki Uaul'da [Wilde's Fairy Tales]." *Detskaya Literatura* (Moscow) 8 (Aug 1991): 64–69.

Edelson, Maria. "The Language of Allegory in Oscar Wilde's Tales." In *Anglo-Irish and*

Irish Literature: Aspects of Language and Culture, ed. by Birgit Bramsback and Martin Croghan. Uppsala: U. U., 1988, pp. 165–171.

Eisner, Greta. *"The Canterville Ghost."* In *Survey of Modern Fantasy Literature,* vol. 1. Edited by Frank N. Magill. Englewood Cliffs, NJ: Salem Press, 1983, pp. 190–192.

Elkins, Mary J. "Oscar Wilde." In *Supernatural Fiction Writers: Fantasy and Horror,* vol. 1. Edited by E. F. Bleiler. New York: Scribner, 1985, pp. 345–350.

Ellmann, Richard. *Oscar Wilde.* New York: Knopf, 1988.

Fido, Martin. *Oscar Wilde: An Illustrated Biography.* New York: Peter Bedrick, 1986.

Griswold, Jerome. "Sacrifice and Mercy in Wilde's *The Happy Prince.*" In *Children's Literature,* vol. 3. Storrs, CT: Journal of the Modern Language Association, 1974, pp. 103–106.

Hastings, Albert Waller. "Social Myth and Fictional Reality: The Decline of Fairy Tale Thinking in the Victorian Novel." Ph.D. diss., University of Wisconsin, Madison, 1988.

Jackson, Rosemary. *Fantasy: The Literature of Subversion.* New York: Methuen, 1980, pp. 45, 108, 112–114, 180.

Jacobs, Susan Tayor. "Oscar Wilde's Use of Fantasy." Ph.D. diss., State University of New Jersey at New Brunswick, 1987.

Kohl, Norbert. *Oscar Wilde: The Works of a Conformist Rebel.* Cambridge: Cambridge Univ. Press, 1989.

Kotzin, M. C. *"The Selfish Giant* as a Literary Fairy Tale." *Studies in Short Fiction* 16 (Fall 1979): 301–309.

Lawler, Donald L. *"The Picture of Dorian Gray."* In *Survey of Modern Fantasy Literature,* vol. 3. Edited by Frank N. Magill. Englewood Cliffs, NJ: Salem Press, 1983, pp. 1257–1261.

Martin, Robert K. "Oscar Wilde and the Fairy Tale: *The Happy Prince* as Self-Dramatization." *Studies in Short Fiction* 16 (Winter 1979): 74–77.

Monaghan, David M. "The Literary Fairy Tale: A Study of Oscar Wilde's *The Happy Prince* and *The Star Child.*" *Canadian Review of Comparative Literature* 1, no. 2 (Spring 1974): 156–166.

Morley, Sheridan. *Oscar Wilde.* New York: Holt, 1976.

Murray, Isobel, ed. *Oscar Wilde.* Oxford: Oxford Univ. Press, 1989.

Nassaar, Christopher S. *Into the Demon Universe: A Literary Exploration of Oscar Wilde.* New Haven, CT: Yale Univ. Press, 1974.

The Oxford Companion to Children's Literature. Edited by Humphrey Carpenter and Mari Prichard. New York: Oxford Univ. Press, 1984, p. 238.

Quintus, John Allen. "The Moral Prerogative in Oscar Wilde: A Look at the Fairy Tales." *Virginia Quarterly Review* 53 (Autumn 1977): 708–717.

Raby, Peter. *Oscar Wilde.* Cambridge: Cambridge Univ. Press, 1988.

Searles, Baird, Beth Meacham, and Michael Franklin. *A Reader's Guide to Fantasy.* New York: Avon, 1982, pp. 154–155.

Shewan, Rodney. *Oscar Wilde: Art and Egotism.* New York: Harper, 1977.

Spelman, Marilyn Kelly. "The Self-Realization Themes in *The Happy Prince* and *A House of Pomegranates.*" Ph.D. diss., University of Colorado at Boulder, 1978.

Stableford, Brian. *"The Happy Prince and Other Tales* and *A House of Pomegranates."* In *Survey of Modern Fantasy Literature,* vol. 2. Edited by Frank N. Magill. Englewood Cliffs, NJ: Salem Press, 1983, pp. 687–689.

Tremper, Ellen. "Commitment and Escape: The Fairy Tales of Thackeray, Dickens and Wilde." *The Lion and the Unicorn* 2 (Spring 1978): 38–47.

Wilburn, Lydia Reineck. "Oscar Wilde's 'The Canterville Ghost': The Power of an Audience." In *Papers on Language and Literature* 23 (Winter 1987): 41–55.

Wynne-Jones, T. *"The Selfish Giant*: The Adult Writing for Children." In *Lands of Pleasure.* Metuchen, NJ: Scarecrow Press, 1990, pp. 97–109.

Zhang, Longxi. "The Critical Legacy of Oscar Wilde." *Texas Studies in Literature and Language* 30 (Spring 1988): 87–103.

Zipes, Jack, ed. *Spells of Enchantment: The Wondrous Fairy Tales of Western Culture.* New York: Viking, 1991.

Wilder, Cherry (pseud. of Cherry Barbara Lockett Grimm)

"Awards, Awards." *Locus* 11 (Apr 1978): 3.

Brown, E. C. "Snapshot." *Vector* 117 (Dec 1983): 5–9, 38.

Twentieth-Century Science Fiction Writers. 3rd ed. Edited by Noelle Watson and Paul E. Schellinger. Chicago: St. James Press, 1991, pp. 862–863.

Wilhelm, Kate (Katie Gertrude)

Caldwell, Patrice. "Earth Mothers or Male Memories: Wilhelm, Lem, and Future Women." In *Women Worldwalkers: New Dimensions of Science Fiction and Fantasy,* ed. by Jane B. Weedman. Lubbock: Texas Tech Press, 1985.

Law, Richard. "Science Fiction Women: Victims, Rebels, Heroes." In *Patterns of the Fantastic.* Edited by Donald M. Hassler. Mercer Island, WA: Starmont, 1983, pp. 11–20.

Platt, Charles. *Dream Makers.* New York: Berkley, 1980, pp. 193–204.

Twentieth-Century Science Fiction Writers. 2nd ed. Edited by Curtis C. Smith. Chicago: St. James Press, 1986, pp. 792–794.

Villani, Jim. "The Women Science Fiction Writers and the Non-Heroic Male Protagonist." In *Patterns of the Fantastic.* Edited by Donald M. Hassler. Mercer Island, WA: Starmont, 1983, pp. 21–30.

Wilhelm, Kate. "The Book of Ylin: A Trilogy." *Fantasy Newsletter* 58 (1983): 8–9, 38.

———. "Something Happens." In *Teaching Science Fiction: Education for Tomorrow.* Edited by Jack Williamson. Philadelphia: Owlswick Press, 1980, pp. 184–189.

———. "The Uncertain Edge of Reality." *Locus* 237 (1980): 7–8, 17.

Wood, Susan. "Kate Wilhelm Is a Writer." *Starship* 40 (1980): 7–16.

Wilkins, Mary Huiskamp *see* Calhoun, Mary

Willard, Nancy (Margaret)

Fifth Book of Junior Authors and Illustrators. Edited by Sally Holmes Holtze. New York: Wilson, 1983, pp. 326–327.

Helbig, Alethea K., and Agnes Regan Perkins. *Dictionary of American Children's Fiction, 1960–1984.* Westport, CT: Greenwood, 1986, pp. 314–315, 570–571, 725.

Lucas, Barbara. "Nancy Willard." *Horn Book* 58 (Aug 1982): 374–379.

Perkins, Agnes Regan. "Nancy Willard: Scribe of Dreams." *Children's Literature Association Quarterly* 10 (Spring 1985): 38–40.

Twentieth-Century Children's Writers. 3rd ed. Edited by Tracy Chevalier and D. L. Kirkpatrick. Chicago: St. James, 1989, pp. 1048–1050.

Vousden, Charles E., and Laura Ingram. "Nancy Willard." In *American Writers for Children since 1960: Fiction. Dictionary of Literary Biography,* vol. 52. Detroit: Gale, 1986, pp. 386–391.

Willard, Nancy. "Angel in the Parlor: The Reading and Writing of Fantasy." *Antioch Review* 35 (Fall 1977): 426–437.

———. "A Child's Star." *Horn Book* 30 (Dec 1954): 447–454.

———. "A Drawing by Nancy Willard, Age Seventeen, Ann Arbor, Michigan." *Horn Book* 30 (June 1954): 191.

———. "Magic, Craft, and the Making of Children's Books." In *The Writer's Handbook.* Edited by Sylvia K. Burack. Boston: The Writer, 1985.

———. "Newbery Medal Acceptance Speech." *Horn Book* 58 (Aug 1982): 369–373.

———. "The Spinning Room: Symbols and Storytellers." *Horn Book* 56 (Oct 1980): 555–564.

———. *Telling Time: Angels, Ancestors, and Stories.* New York: Harcourt, 1993.

———. "The Watcher." In *Innocence & Experience.* Edited by Barbara Harrison and Gregory Maguire. New York: Lothrop, 1987, pp. 422–426.

———. "The Well-Tempered Falsehood: The Art of Storytelling." *Top of the News* 39 (Fall 1982): 104–113.

———. "When By Now and Tree By Leaf: Time and Timelessness in the Reading and Making of Children's Books." *Children's Literature Association Quarterly* 10 (Winter 1986): 166–172.

Williams, Garth (Montgomery)

Friedberg, Joan Brest. "Garth Williams." In Cech. *American Writers for Children, 1900–1960. Dictionary of Literary Biography,* vol. 22. Detroit: Gale, 1983, pp. 367–376.
More Junior Authors. Edited by Muriel Fuller. New York: Wilson, 1963, p. 227.
Stott, Jon C. *Children's Literature from A to Z.* New York: McGraw-Hill, 1984, p. 292.
Williams, Garth. *Self-Portrait, Garth Williams.* Reading, MA: Addison-Wesley, 1982.

Williams, Jay

Chambers, Aidan. "Letter from England: The Magic of the Mask." *Horn Book* 53 (Feb 1977): 92–96.
Fourth Book of Junior Authors and Illustrators. Edited by Doris De Montreville and Elizabeth D. Crawford. New York: Wilson, 1978, pp. 352–353.
Helbig, Alethea K., and Agnes Regan Perkins. *Dictionary of American Children's Fiction, 1859–1959.* Westport, CT: Greenwood, 1985, p. 566.
———. *Dictionary of American Children's Fiction, 1960–1984.* Westport, CT: Greenwood, 1986, pp. 275, 726.
Newman, Robert. "Jay Williams, 1914–1978." *Signal* 27 (Sept 1978): 112–118.
Twentieth-Century Children's Writers. 3rd ed. Edited by Tracy Chevalier and D. L. Kirkpatrick. Chicago: St. James, 1989, pp. 1050–1052.
Williams, Jay. "Looking for a Pattern." *Signal* 16 (Jan 1975): 3–4.
———. "A Sense of Wonder." *Pacific Northwest Library Association Quarterly* 26 (Jan 1962): 28–82; *Montana Libraries* 15 (Apr 1962): 16–21; and in *Top of the News* 18 (Mar 1962): 50–54.

Williams, Kit

"Kit Williams, Visual Photographer." *Locus* 17 (Sept 1984): 4.

Williams (John), Ursula Moray

Doyle, Brian. *The Who's Who of Children's Literature.* New York: Schocken, 1968, p. 294.
Fourth Book of Junior Authors and Illustrators. Edited by Doris De Montreville and Elizabeth D. Crawford. New York: Wilson, 1978, pp. 269–271.

Moss, Elaine. "Ursula Moray Williams and *Adventures of the Little Wooden Horse.*" *Signal* 5 (May 1971): 56–61. Reprinted in *Part of the Pattern.* New York: Greenwillow, 1986, pp. 53–57.

The Oxford Companion to Children's Literature. Edited by Humphrey Carpenter and Mari Prichard. New York: Oxford Univ. Press, 1984, p. 572.

Rahn, Suzanne. "Cat-Child: Rediscovering *Socks* and *Island MacKenzie.*" *The Lion and the Unicorn* 12 (1988): 111–120.

Twentieth-Century Children's Writers. 3rd ed. Edited by Tracy Chevalier and D. L. Kirkpatrick. Chicago: St. James, 1989, pp. 696–698.

Williams, Ursula Moray. "*Adventures of the Little Wooden Horse.*" *Books for Your Children* (U.K.) 12 (Winter 1976): 5.

———. "A Spontaneous Affair." *School Library Bulletin Supplement* (Australia) 10, no. 2 (1978): 67–68.

Wood, Anne. "A Taste for a Feeling Book?" *Books for Your Children* (U.K.) 21, no. 3 (1986): 2–3.

Wills, Fingal O'Flahertie *see* Wilde, Oscar

Wilson, Gahan

Schweitzer, Darrell, ed. *Science Fiction Voices.* Baltimore: T-K Graphics, 1976. Interview.

Wiater, Stanley. "Interview: Gahan Wilson." *Fantasy Newsletter* 6 (Oct–Nov 1983): 11–12, 46.

Wilson, Joyce Muriel Judson *see* Stranger, Joyce

Windsor, Patricia (Frances)

Fifth Book of Junior Authors and Illustrators. Edited by Sally Holmes Holtze. New York: Wilson, 1983, pp. 328–330.

Winterfeld, Henry

Third Book of Junior Authors. Edited by Doris De Montreville and Donna Hill. New York: Wilson, 1972, pp. 302–303.

Winthrop (Mahony), Elizabeth

Fifth Book of Junior Authors and Illustrators. Edited by Sally Holmes Holtze. New York: Wilson, 1983, pp. 330–331.

Wiseman, David

Fifth Book of Junior Authors and Illustrators. Edited by Sally Holmes Holtze. New York: Wilson, 1983, pp. 331–332.

Wisniewski, David

Thomas, Rebecca L. *Primaryplots 2: A Book Talk Guide for Use with Readers Ages 4–8.* New Providence, NJ: Bowker, 1993, pp. 304–306.

Wolfe, Gene (Rodman)

Barker, Chris. *"The Citadel of the Autarch,* and *The New Sun." Vector* 119 (1984): 35–37.

Clareson, Thomas D. "Variations and Design: The Fiction of Gene Wolfe." In *Voices for the Future: Volume Three.* Edited by Thomas D. Clareson and Thomas L. Wymer. Bowling Green, OH: Bowling Green Univ. Press, 1984, pp. 1–29.

Dickinson, Mike. "Why They're All Crying Wolfe." *Vector* 118 (1984): 13–20.

"A Few Minutes With Gene Wolfe." *American Fantasy* (Fall 1986): 20–21.

Frazier, Robert. "Interview: Gene Wolfe—'The Legerdemain of the Wolfe.'" *Thrust* 19 (1983): 5–9.

Gene Wolfe—Interview. Columbia, MO: American Audio Prose Library, 1984. (audio-cassette)

Gillespie, Bruce. "Gene Wolfe's Sleight of Hand." *Australian Science Fiction Review* (Mar 1986): 12–17.

Goldman, Stephen G. "In Search of New Worlds: The John N. Campbell Memorial Award." *Science Fiction Writers Association Bulletin* 85 (1988): 8–9.

Gordon, Joan. "Interview: Gene Wolfe." *Science Fiction Review* 39 (1983): 18–22.

———. "An Interview with Gene Wolfe." *Science Fiction Review* 38 (1981): 18–22.

Gordon, Ruth. *Gene Wolfe.* Mercer Island, WA: Starmont, 1986.

Greenland, Colin. "Riding a Bicycle Backwards: An Interview with Gene Wolfe." *Foundation* 31 (1984): 37–44.

Hanna, Judith, and Joseph Nicholas. "A Two-Foot Square of Gene Wolfe." *Vector* 118 (1984): 5–12.

Ingersoll, Earl G. "A Conversation with Gene Wolfe." *Australian Science Fiction Review* 5 (1986): 12–22.

Lane, Daryl, William Vernon, and David Carlson. *The Sound of Wonder: Interviews from "The Science Fiction Radio Show,"* vol. 2. Phoenix, AZ: Oryx Press, 1985, pp. 141–158.

Malekin, Peter. "Remembering the Future: Gene Wolfe's *The Book of the New Sun.*" In *The Fantastic in World Literature and the Arts.* New York: Greenwood, 1987.

Manlove, C. N. *"Terminus Non Est:* Gene Wolfe's *The Book of the New Sun." Kansas Quarterly* 16 (Summer 1984): 7–20.

Meyers, Walter E. *"The Book of the New Sun."* In *Survey of Modern Fantasy Literature,* vol. 1. Edited by Frank N. Magill. Englewood Cliffs, NJ: Salem Press, 1983, pp. 154–160.

Nelson, Chris. "Books by Gene Wolfe: A Checklist." *Science Fiction* 7 (1985): 15–17.

Schweitzer, Darrell. "Interview: Gene Wolfe." *Fantasy Newsletter* 49 (1982): 8–9, 37.

Swanson, Elliot. "Gene Wolfe." *Interzone* 17 (1986): 38–40.

Talbot, Norman. "The Audience and the Narrators in Gene Wolfe's *The Book of the New Sun."* In *Contrary Modes.* Edited by Jenny Blackford. Melbourne, Australia: Ebony Books, 1985.

Twentieth-Century Science Fiction Writers. 3rd ed. Edited by Noelle Watson and Paul E. Schellinger. Chicago: St. James Press, 1991, pp. 885–886.

Wolfe, Gene. "Aussiecon Two, Guest of Honor Speech." *Science Fiction Chronicle* 73 (1985): 1.

———. "The Ethos of Elfland." *Twilight Zone* 7 (1987): 32–35.

———. "The Profession of Science Fiction: XVIII." *Foundation* 18 (1980): 5–11.

———. "The Special Problems of Science Fiction." *The Writer* 89 (May 1976): 12–14.

———. "What Do They Mean, SF?" *The Writer* 93 (Aug 1980): 11–13, 45; *Science Fiction Writers Association Bulletin* 75 (1981): 20–25.

———. "Where I Get My Ideas." In *The Science Fiction Sourcebook.* Edited by David Wingrove. New York: Van Nostrand Reinhold, 1984, pp. 84–85.

Wood, James Playsted

Fourth Book of Junior Authors and Illustrators. Edited by Doris De Montreville and Elizabeth D. Crawford. New York: Wilson, 1978, pp. 353–355.

Wood, James Playsted. "The Honest Audience." *Horn Book* 43 (Oct 1967): 612–615.

———. "Writers Do Not Exist." *Horn Book* 42 (Dec 1966): 694–697.

Wright, Betty Ren

Helbig, Alethea K., and Agnes Regan Perkins. *Dictionary of American Children's Fiction, 1960–1984.* Westport, CT: Greenwood, 1986, p. 740.

Sixth Book of Junior Authors and Illustrators. Edited by Sally Holmes Holtze. New York: Wilson, 1989, pp. 323–325.

Wrightson, (Alice) Patricia (Furlonger)

Alberman, Belle. "The Dromkeen Medal Awarded to Patricia Wrightson." *Teacher and Librarian* (Australia) 77 (Mar 1985): 25–26.

Attebery, Brian. "Women's Coming of Age in Fantasy." *Extrapolation* 28 (Spring 1987): 10–22.

Barelli, Linnell. "Patricia Wrightson: Her Development in Style and Subject Matter." *Orana* 18 (Aug 1982): 75–83.

Bear, Elizabeth R. "'A Long Struggle with the Strangeness of Life': Patricia Wrightson's *A Little Fear.*" In *Literature and Hawaii's Children,* ed. by Stephen Canham. Honolulu: Univ. of Hawaii Manoa, 1992, pp. 45–53.

Boddington, Sandra. "A Discussion of Patricia Wrightson's Novels." *Orana* (Australia) 14 (Feb 1978): 22–25.

Cohen, John "Patricia Wrightson: The Making of Myth." *Reading Time* (Australia) 68 (July 1978): 11–14.

Cooper, Susan. "A Second Look: *The Nargun and the Stars.*" *Horn Book* 62 (Sept–Oct 1986): 572–574.

Crago, Hugh, and Maureen Crago. "Patricia Wrightson." *Signal* 19 (Jan 1976): 31–39.

Evans, Emrys. "Series as Epic: Patricia Wrightson's 'The Book of Wirrun.'" *Children's Literature Association Quarterly* 14 (Winter 1989): 165–170.

Fisher, Marjorie T. "Writers for Children: Patricia Wrightson." *School Librarian* 17 (Mar 1969): 22–26.

Fourth Book of Junior Authors and Illustrators. Edited by Doris De Montreville and Elizabeth D. Crawford. New York: Wilson, 1978, pp. 355–356.

Gilderdale, Betty. "The Novels of Patricia Wrightson." *Children's Literature in Education* 28, no. 1 (1978): 43–49.

Gough, John. "Ice, Dark Water and Wind in Patricia Wrightson's Wirrun Trilogy." *Idiom* (Australia) 19 (Summer 1984): 13–18.

———. "Patricia Wrightson's Wirrun: A Modern Aboriginal Mythic Hero." *Review Bulletin* (Australia) 2 (1987): 17–21; *Papers* (Australia) 1 (Dec 1990): 140–144.

Green, Carole. "Australian Fantasy." *Orana* (Australia) 15 (May 1979): 74–76.

———. "Waking Up to Our Dreaming: The New Australian Fantasy." *School Library Bulletin* (Australia) 10 (Aug 1978): 11–17, 28.

Grove, Trevor. "Top Books from Down Under." *Observer Magazine* [London] (Sept 2, 1984): 92–93.

Harranth, Wolf. "Der Andere Kosmos Patricia Wrightson—Versuch einer Anaheurung [The Other Cosmos of Patricia Wrightson—An Approach]." *1001 Buch* (Vienna) 3 (June 1991): 15–18.

Harrison, Cassandra. "*The Nargun*: A Closer Look." *Orana* (Australia) 14 (Nov 1978): 123–126.

Kleindienst, J. K. "From *Crooked Snake* to *Nargun*: The Growth of Patricia Wrightson's Art." *Children's Libraries Newsletter* (Australia) 11 (Jan 1975): 17–24.

Lenz, Millicent. "Humanity and Nature in Patricia Wrightson's *The Ice Is Coming*." In *Webs and Wardrobes: Humanist and Religious World Views in Children's Literature,* ed. by Joseph O'Beirne Milner and Lucy Floyd Morcock Milner. Lanham, MD: University Press of America, 1987, pp. 123–133.

McVitty, Walter. "Patricia Wrightson: At the Edge of Australian Vision." In *Innocence and Experience.* Melbourne, Australia: Nelson, 1981, pp. 99–132.

Manyweathers, Janet. "Patricia Wrightson: Mythologist of the Australian Hero." *Orana* (Australia) 25 (Nov 1989): 54–67.

Michaels, Wendy. "At the Dark Edge of Vision." *Orana* (Australia) 17 (Nov 1981): 145–148.

Middleton, Linda C. "Wirrun in Wonderland." In *Literature and Hawaii's Children,* ed. by Stephen Canham. Honolulu: Univ. of Hawaii Manoa, 1992, pp. 45–53.

Moon, Kenneth. "The Use of the Natural World in Patricia Wrightson's *The Ice Is Coming* and *The Dark Bright Water.*" *Orana* 22 (May 1986): 102–106.

Mower, Nancy Alpert. "Narguns, Turongs, Nyols and More: Earth Spirits in Three of Patricia Wrightson's Novels." In *Literature and Hawaii's Children,* ed. by Stephen Canham. Honolulu: Univ. of Hawaii Manoa, 1992, pp. 45–53.

Murray, John. "Hurtling into Freedom: Patricia Wrightson's *The Nargun and the Stars.*" *Papers* (Australia) 2 (Aug 1991): 75–86.

The Oxford Companion to Children's Literature. Edited by Humphrey Carpenter and Mari Prichard. New York: Oxford Univ. Press, 1984, p. 582.

Reeder, Stephanie Owen. "Australian Under the Magnifying Glass: The Work of Patricia Wrightson." *Reading Time* (Australia) 100 (July 1986): 22–24.

Rees, David. "Aboriginals and Happy Folk: Patricia Wrightson." In *"What Do Draculas Do?" Essays on Contemporary Writers of Fiction for Children and Young Adults,* ed. by David Rees. Metuchen, NJ: Scarecrow Press, 1990, pp. pp. 88–106.

Ryan, John S. *Australian Fantasy and Folklore.* Armidale, New South Wales: Univ. of New England, 1981.

———. "Australian Fantasy and Folklore: Pt. 3." *Orana* (Australia) 17 (Nov 1981): 145–148.

———. "The Developing Lore of the Nargun as Monster for Patricia Wrightson." *Orana* 22 (Aug 1986): 123–132.

Saxby, Maurice. "The Art of Patricia Wrightson." *Bookbird* 24 (Nov 2, 1986): 5–7.

———. "At Mrs. Tucker's House." *Horn Book* 64 (Mar–Apr 1988): 180–185.

Smith, Karen Patricia. "Preserving a Legacy: Traditional Australian Aboriginal Themes in Works for Children and Young People." *Wilson Library Bulletin* 66 (June 1992): 31–34, 147.

Townsend, John Rowe. "Guest Essay, Heights of Fantasy." *Children's Literature Review,* vol. 5. Detroit: Gale, 1983, p. 11.

———. "Patricia Wrightson." In *A Sense of Story.* Philadelphia: Lippincott, 1971, pp. 204–214.

———. "Patricia Wrightson." In *A Sounding of Storytellers.* Philadelphia: Lippincott, 1979, pp. 194–206.

Twentieth-Century Children's Writers. 3rd ed. Edited by Tracy Chevalier and D. L. Kirkpatrick. Chicago: St. James, 1989, pp. 1065–1066.

Williams, Stephen. "The Novels of Patricia Wrightson." *Review* (Australia) 6 (June 1978): 27–29.

Wrightson, Patricia. "Books Remembered." *C. B. C. Features* 43 (Jan–June 1990).

———. "Deeper Than You Think." *Horn Book* 67 (Mar–Apr 1991): 162–170.

———. "Ever Since My Accident: Aboriginal Folklore and Australian Fantasy." *Horn Book* 56 (Dec 1980): 609–617.

———. "The Fellowship of Man and Beast." *Horn Book* 61 (Jan–Feb 1985): 38–41.

———. "Folklore and Fantasy." *Orana* (Australia) 23 (May 1987): 77–82.

———. "The Geranium Leaf." *Horn Book* 62 (Mar–Apr 1986): 176–185. Anne Carroll Moore Spring Lecture, N.Y. Public Library.

———. "Hans Christian Andersen Award Acceptance Speech." *Bookbird* (Denmark) 3 & 4 (1986): 23–26; *Orana* (Australia) 23 (Feb 1987): 3–5.

———. "Hero and Everyman." *Magpies* (Australia) 8 (Mar 1993): 5–8.

———. "An Intimate Thing." *ALAN Review* 19 (Spring 1992): 20–29.

———. "Is Your Minority Group Really Necessary? [The Contribution of Aboriginal Culture to Australian Literature]." In *Pacific Rim Conference on Children's Literature.* Melbourne: Melbourne State College, 1979. Reprinted in *A Track to Unknown Water.* Metuchen, NJ: Scarecrow Press, 1977, pp. 129–148.

———. "Jag Skriver av Karlek [I Write for Love]." *Opsis Kalopsis* (Sweden) 2 (1986): 46–48.

———. "A Little Fear." *Reading Time* (Australia) 92 (July 1984): 14.

———. "The Nature of Fantasy." In *Readings in Children's Literature.* Edited by Moira Robinson. Frankston, Victoria, Australia: Frankston State College, 1975.

———. "The Slippery Stuff of Fantasy." *Educational Magazine* (Australia) 33, no. 6 (1976): 22–25.

———. "Some Comments on the Books of Wirrun." *Reading Time* (Australia) 84 (July 1982): 13.

———. "Stones into Pools." *Top of the News* 41 (Spring 1985): 283–292. May Hill Arbuthnot Honor Lecture. Reprinted in *The Arbuthnot Lectures, 1980–1989.* Chicago: American Library Association, 1990, pp. 67–77.

———. "The Square Professional: Patricia Wrightson Addresses her Critics." *Reading Time* (Australia) 70 (Jan 1979): 5–8.

Young, Donald A. "Patricia Wrightson." *Junior Bookshelf* 45 (Dec 1981): 234–237ff.

Wuorio, Eva-Lis

Third Book of Junior Authors. Edited by Doris De Montreville and Donna Hill. New York: Wilson, 1972, pp. 306–307.

Wyndham, Lee (pseud. of Jane Andrews Lee Hyndman)

More Junior Authors. Edited by Muriel Fuller. New York: Wilson, 1963, pp. 229–230.

Yep, Laurence M(ichael)

Burnson, Patrick. "In the Studio with Laurence Yep." *Publishers Weekly* 241 (May 16, 1994): 25–26.

Cai, Mingshui. "A Balanced View of Acculturation: Comments on Lawrence Yep's Three Novels." *Children's Literature in Education* 23 (June 1992): 107–118.

Dinchak, Maria. "Recommended: Laurence Yep." *English Journal* 71 (Mar 1982): 81–82.

Fifth Book of Junior Authors and Illustrators. Edited by Sally Holmes Holtze. New York: Wilson, 1983, pp. 339–340.

Helbig, Alethea K., and Agnes Regan Perkins. *Dictionary of American Children's Fiction, 1960–1984.* Westport, CT: Greenwood, 1986, p. 747.

Speaking for Ourselves: Autobiographical Sketches by Notable Authors of Books for Young

Adults. Edited by Donald R. Gallo. Urbana, IL: National Council of Teachers of English, 1990, pp. 222–224.

Stines, Joe. "Laurence Yep." In *American Writers for Children since 1960: Fiction. Dictionary of Literary Biography,* vol. 52. Detroit: Gale, 1986, pp. 392–397.

Twentieth-Century Children's Writers. 3rd ed. Edited by Tracy Chevalier and D. L. Kirkpatrick. Chicago: St. James, 1989, pp. 1074–1075.

Twentieth-Century Science Fiction Writers. 3rd ed. Edited by Noelle Watson and Paul E. Schellinger. Chicago: St. James Press, 1991, pp. 895–896.

Yep, Laurence. "Books Remembered." *CBC Features* 41 (Sept 1987–Apr 1988). Formerly *The Calendar.*

Yep, Laurence. "Books Remembered." *CBC Features* 41 (Sept 1987–Apr 1988). Formerly *The Calendar.*

———. "A Chinese Sense of Reality." In *Innocence & Experience.* Edited by Barbara Harrison and Gregory Maguire. New York: Lothrop, 1987, pp. 485–489.

———. "A Cord to the Past [A Chinese American's Identity]." *CMLEA Journal* (Burlingame, CA) 15 (Fall, 1991): 8–10.

———. "Fantasy and Reality." *Horn Book* 54 (Apr 1978): 137–143.

———. "A Garden of Dragons." *ALAN Review* 19 (Spring 1992): 6–8.

———. "The Green Cord [Thoughts on a Child's Version of History in Writing Historical Fiction]." *Horn Book* 65 (May–June 1989): 318–322.

———. "World Building." In *Innocence & Experience.* Edited by Barbara Harrison and Gregory Maguire. New York: Lothrop, 1987, pp. 182–183.

———. "Writing *Dragonwings.*" *Reading Teacher* 30 (Jan 1977): 359–363.

Yolen (Stemple), Jane H(yatt)

Abdullah, Cheryl. "Story for Story's Sake: The Gift of Jane Yolen." *Book Report* 7 (Sept–Oct 1988): 26–28.

Fourth Book of Junior Authors and Illustrators. Edited by Doris De Montreville and Elizabeth D. Crawford. New York: Wilson, 1978, pp. 356–358.

Frongia, Terri. "Merlin's Fathers: The Sacred and the Profane." *Children's Literature Association Quarterly* 18 (Fall 1993): 120–125. Discusses Peter Dickinson, Pamela Service, Rosemary Sutcliff, and Jane Yolen.

Gillespie, John T., and Corinne J. Naden. *Juniorplots 3: A Book Talk Guide for Use with Readers Ages 12–16.* New York: Bowker, 1987, pp. 205–209.

Greenlaw, M. Jean. "Books in the Classroom." *Horn Book* 64 (Nov–Dec 1988): 820–822.

Helbig, Alethea, and Agnes Regan Perkins. *Dictionary of American Children's Fiction, 1985–1989.* Westport, CT: Greenwood, 1993, pp. 99–100, 283.

"An Interview with Jane Yolen." *Mythlore* 47 (1986): 34–36, 48.

Kellogg, Judith L. "The Dynamics of Dumbing: The Case of Merlin." *The Lion and the Unicorn* 17 (June 1993): 57–72. Discusses Heyer's *Excalibur,* White's *The Sword in the Stone,* Talbott's *King Arthur,* and Yolen's *Merlin's Booke.*

Kreuger, William E. "Jane Yolen." In *American Writers for Children since 1960: Fiction. Dictionary of Literary Biography,* vol. 52. Detroit: Gale, 1986, pp. 398–404.

Raymond, A. "Jane Yolen: Creative Storyteller." *Early Years* 14 (Dec 1983): 22–24.

Roginski, Jim. *Behind the Covers: Interviews with Authors and Illustrators of Books for Children and Young Adults.* Littleton, CO: Libraries Unlimited, 1985, pp. 224–238.

Schweitzer, Darrell. "Jane Yolen: The Pornography of Innocence." *Fantasy Newsletter* 62 (1983): 12–13, 38. Interview.

Speaking for Ourselves: Autobiographical Sketches by Notable Authors of Books for Young Adults. Edited by Donald R. Gallo. Urbana, IL: National Council of Teachers of English, 1990, pp. 225–227.

Stott, Jon C. *Children's Literature from A to Z.* New York: McGraw-Hill, 1984, p. 295.

Twentieth-Century Children's Writers. 3rd ed. Edited by Tracy Chevalier and D. L. Kirk-patrick. Chicago: St. James, 1989, pp. 1075–1078.

Twentieth-Century Science Fiction Writers. 3rd ed. Edited by Noelle Watson and Paul E. Schellinger. Chicago: St. James, 1991, pp. 896–899.

White, David E. "Profile: Jane Yolen." *Language Arts* 60 (1983): 652–660.

Wiater, Stanley. "*Thrust* Profile: Jane Yolen." *Thrust* 23 (1985): 16–17.

Yolen, Jane. "The Author as Hero." *Foundation* (U.K.) 43 (Summer 1988): 47–49.

———. "Author's Bane." *The Lion and the Unicorn* 16 (June 1992): 75–76.

———. "The Creative Process: The Route to Story." *The New Advocate* 4 (Summer 1991): 143–150.

———. "Dealing With Dragons." *Horn Book* 60 (June 1984): 380–388.

———. "An Experiential Act [The Time Travel Story]." *Language Arts* 66 (Mar 1989): 246–251.

———. "[Children's Book Illustration:] The Eye and the Ear." *Children's Literature Association Quarterly* 6 (Winter 1981–82): 8–9. Excerpted from Jane Yolen. *Touch Magic.* New York: Philomel, 1981. Reprinted in Patricia Dooley. *The First Steps.* West Lafayette, IN: Children's Literature Association Publications, 1984, pp. 133–134.

———. "The Fault of the Nightingale." *California Medical and Library Educators Association Journal* 1 (Fall 1977): 8–12. Effects of fairy tales on children; speech given at Festival of Children's Books, May 1977.

———. "*The Girl*—From Where?—*Who Loved the Wind.*" *Wilson Library Bulletin* 46 (Oct 1973): 139–161.

———. "Here There Be Dragons." *Top of the News* 39 (Fall 1982): 54–56. Reprinted from Jane Yolen. *Touch Magic.* New York: Philomel, 1981.

———. "In the Spirit of Angels [Regina Medal Acceptance Speech]." *Catholic Library World* 63 (Oct–Dec 1991): 94–97.

———. "The Literary Underwater World." *Language Arts* 57 (1980): 403–412.

———. "Magic Mirrors: Social Reflections in the Glass of Fantasy." *Children's Literature Association Quarterly* 11 (Summer 1986): 88–90.

———. "Makers of Modern Myths." *Horn Book* 51 (Oct 1975): 496–497.

———. "The Modern Mythmakers." *Language Arts* 53 (May 1976): 491–495.

———. "Once Upon a Tale." *The New Advocate* 1 (Summer 1988): 137–142.

———. "The Profession of Science Fiction, 37: The Author as Hero." *Foundation* 43 (1988): 47–49.

———. "The Route to Story." *The New Advocate* 4 (Summer 1991): 143–150.

———. "The Story Between." *Language Arts* 62, no. 6 (1985): 590–592.

———. "Storytelling: The Oldest and Newest Art." In *The Writer's Handbook.* Edited by Sylvia K. Burack. Boston: The Writer, 1985.

———. "Strings That Touch the Sky." *The Writer* 97 (Jan 1984): 7–8. Reprinted in *The Writer's Handbook.* Edited by Sylvia K. Burack. Boston: The Writer, 1985.

———. *Touch Magic: Fantasy, Faerie and Folklore in the Literature of Childhood.* New York: Philomel, 1981, 1992.

———. "Touch Magic." *Parent's Choice* (Sept 1978). Reprinted in *Top of the News* 35 (Winter 1979): 183–187; and in Jane Yolen. *Touch Magic.* New York: Philomel, 1981, pp. 69–74.

———. "Traveling the Road to Ithaca." In *Innocence & Experience.* Edited by Barbara Harrison and Gregory Maguire. New York: Lothrop, 1987, p. 188.

———. "The Voice of Fantasy." *Advocate* 3 (Fall 1983): 50–56.

———. "The Wood Between the Worlds." *Mythlore* 41 (1985): 5–7. Fifteenth Mythopoetic Conference Guest of Honor Speech, on Fantasy.

———. *Writing Books for Children.* rev. ed. Boston: The Writer, 1983.

York, Carol Beach

Fifth Book of Junior Authors and Illustrators. Edited by Sally Holmes Holtze. New York: Wilson, 1983, pp. 340–341.

Young, Ella

Colum, Padraic. "Ella Young: A Druidess." *Horn Book* 15 (May 1939): 183–188.
———. *Ella Young: An Appreciation.* London: Longman, 1931.
Eaton, Anne. "Ella Young's Unicorns and Kyelins." *Horn Book* 9 (Aug 1933): 115–120.
Flanagan, Sylvia. "Ella Young at Home." *Horn Book* 15 (May 1939): 145–148.
Hadden, Anne. "Off the Beaten Path with Ella Young." *Horn Book* 15 (May 1939): 175–180.
Horn Book Magazine. Special Issue 15 (May 1939): 139–148, 175–188.
The Junior Book of Authors. 2nd ed. rev. Edited by Stanley J. Kunitz and Howard Haycraft. New York: Wilson, 1951, pp. 305–306.
Roginski, Jim, ed. *Newbery and Caldecott Medalists and Honor Book Winners.* Littleton, CO: Libraries Unlimited, 1982, pp. 295–296.
Sayers, Frances Clarke. "The Flowering Dusk of Ella Young." *Horn Book* 21 (May–June 1945): 214–220.
Terrill, Jane Verne. "Ella Young: How She Came to Know the Fairies." *Horn Book* 3 (May 1927): 3–5.
Whitney, Elinor. "A Draught from the Sacred Well." *Horn Book* 3 (May 1927): 6–9.
Young, Ella. "Faërie Music (Ceol Sidhe)." *Horn Book* 21 (May 1945): 211–213.
———. "The Poet's Fee." *Horn Book* 15 (May 1939): 139–144. Story.

Zelazny, Roger (Joseph Christopher)

Barbour, Douglas. "Roger Zelazny." In *Supernatural Fiction Writers: Fantasy and Horror,* vol. 2. Edited by E. F. Bleiler. New York: Scribner, 1985, pp. 1113–1120.
Braswell, Laurel. "The Visionary Voyage in Science Fiction and Medieval Allegory." *Mosaic* 14 (Winter 1981): 125–142.
Collings, Michael R. "Words and Worlds: The Creation of a Fantasy Universe in Zelazny, Lee, and Anthony." In *The Scope of the Fantastic—Theory, Technique, Major Authors.* Edited by Robert A. Collins and Howard D. Pearce. Westport, CT: Greenwood, 1985, pp. 173–182.
Francavilla, Joseph V. "Promethean Bound: Heroes and Gods in Roger Zelazny's Science Fiction." In *The Transcendent Adventure.* Edited by Robert Reilly. Westport, CT: Greenwood, 1985, pp. 207–224.
———. "These Immortals: An Alternative View of Immortality in Roger Zelazny's Science Fiction." *Extrapolation* 25 (1984): 20–33.
Krulik, Theodore. *Roger Zelazny.* New York: Ungar, 1986.
Levack, Daniel J. H. *"Amber" Dreams: A Roger Zelazny Bibliography.* Columbia, PA: Underwood-Miller, 1983.
Lindskold, Jane M. "All Roads Do Lead to Amber." *Extrapolation* 31 (Winter 1990): 326–332.
———. "The Pervasive Influence of Poetry in the Works of Roger Zelazny." *Extrapolation* 33 (Spring 1992): 41–58.
Lucy, N. J. *The Arthurian Encyclopedia.* New York: Garland, 1986, p. 648.
Mayo, Clark. "*Changeling* and *Madwand.*" In *Survey of Modern Fantasy Literature,* vol. 1. Englewood Cliffs, NJ: Salem Press, 1983, pp. 228–231.
———. "*Jack of Shadows.*" In *Survey of Modern Fantasy Literature,* vol. 2. Englewood Cliffs, NJ: Salem Press, 1983, pp. 794–797.

Monteleone, Thomas F. "Fire and Ice—On Roger Zelazny's Short Fiction." *Algol* 13 (1976): 9–14.

Morrissey, Thomas J. "Zelazny: Mythmaker of Nuclear War." *Science Fiction Studies* 13 (1986): 182–192.

Nichols, Peter. "Roger Zelazny." In *Science Fiction Writers.* Edited by E. F. Bleiler. New York: Scribner, 1982, pp. 563–570.

Sanders, Joseph L. "Dancing on the Tightrope: Immortality in Roger Zelazny." In *Death and the Serpent.* Edited by Carl B. Yoke and Donald M. Hassler. Westport, CT: Greenwood, 1985, pp. 135–144.

———. *Roger Zelazny: A Primary and Secondary Bibliography.* Boston: G. K. Hall, 1980.

———. "Zelazny: Unfinished Business." In *Voices for the Future: Essays on Major Science Fiction Writers,* vol. 2. Edited by Thomas D. Clareson. Bowling Green, OH: Bowling Green Univ. Press, 1979.

———. "Zelazny's 'Dilvish' Series: Enduring Concerns." *Fantasy Newsletter* 62 (1983): 31–32.

Schlobin, Roger C. "The Fool and the Fantastic." *Fantasy Newsletter* 43 (1981): 6–9, 29.

Schuyler, William M., Jr. "Recent Developments in Spell Construction." In *The Aesthetics of Fantasy Literature and Art.* Edited by Roger C. Schlobin. Notre Dame, IN: Univ. of Notre Dame, 1982, pp. 237–248.

Searles, Baird, Beth Meacham, and Michael Franklin. *A Reader's Guide to Fantasy.* New York: Avon, 1982, pp. 160–161.

Thomson, W. B. "Interview: Roger Zelazny." *Future Life* 25 (1981): 40–42.

Thurston, Robert. "Introduction." In Roger Zelazny. *Today We Choose Faces.* Boston: Gregg, 1978.

Twentieth-Century Science Fiction Writers. 3rd ed. Edited by Noelle Watson and Paul E. Schellinger. Chicago: St. James Press, 1991, pp. 906–909.

Vance, Michael, and Bill Eads. "An Interview with Roger Zelazny." *Fantasy Newsletter* 55 (1983): 8–10.

Walker, Paul. *Speaking of Science Fiction: The Paul Walker Interviews.* Oradell, NJ: Luna, 1978, pp. 78–84.

Wilgus, Neal. "Interview: Roger Zelazny." *Science Fiction Review* 36 (1980): 14–16.

Yoke, Carl B. *"The Amber Series."* In *Survey of Modern Fantasy Literature,* vol. 1. Englewood Cliffs, NJ: Salem Press, 1983, pp. 29–35.

———. *Roger Zelazny.* West Linn, OR: Starmont, 1979.

———. *Roger Zelazny and André Norton: Proponents of Individualism.* Columbus: State Library of Ohio, 1979.

———. "Roger Zelazny's Bold New Mythologies." In *Critical Encounters II: Writers and Themes in Science Fiction.* Edited by Tom Staicar. New York: Ungar, 1982.

———. "Roger Zelazny's Form and Chaos Philosophy." *Science Fiction* 2 (1979): 129–150.

Zelazny, Roger. "Constructing Science Fiction Novels." *The Writer* 97 (Oct 1984): 9–12, 46.

———. "Fantasy and Science Fiction: A Writer's View." In *Intersections: Science Fiction and Fantasy,* ed. by George E. Slusser and Eric S. Rabkin. Carbondale: Southern Illinois Univ. Press, 1987.

———. "The Process of Composing." In *The Science Fiction Sourcebook.* Edited by David Wingrove. New York: Van Nostrand Reinhold, 1984.

Zemach, Harve (pseud. of Harvey Fischtrom)

Stott, Jon C. *Children's Literature from A to Z.* New York: McGraw-Hill, 1984, p. 296.

Third Book of Junior Authors. Edited by Doris De Montreville and Donna Hill. New York: Wilson, 1972, pp. 310–312.

Zimnik, Reiner

Chambers, Aidan. *Booktalk: Occasional Writing on Literature and Children.* New York: Harper, 1986, pp. 19–24, 48, 69, 71, 148, 159.

Danischewsky, Nina. "Re-Viewing Reiner Zimnik." *Signal* 6 (Sept 1971): 115–125.

Third Book of Junior Authors. Edited by Doris De Montreville and Donna Hill. New York: Wilson, 1972, pp. 312–313.

Zindel, Paul

Angelotti, Michael. "Zindel on Writing and the Writing Process: An Interview." *The ALAN Review* 18 (Winter 1991): 37–42.

"Authorgraph no. 54: Paul Zindel." *Books for Keeps* (U.K.) 54 (1989): 14–16.

Eaglen, Audrey. "Of Life, Love, Death, Kids, and Inhalation Therapy: An Interview with Paul Zindel." *Top of the News* 34 (Winter 1978): 178–185.

Fifth Book of Junior Authors and Illustrators. Edited by Sally Holmes Holtze. New York: Wilson, 1983, pp. 343–344.

Hipple, Theodore W. "Paul Zindel." In *American Writers for Children since 1960: Fiction. Dictionary of Literary Biography,* vol. 52. Detroit: Gale, 1986, pp. 405–410.

Hoffman, Stanley. "Winning, Losing, But Above All Taking Risks: A Look at the Novels of Paul Zindel." *The Lion and the Unicorn* 2 (Fall 1978): 78–88.

Janeczko, P. "Interview: Paul Zindel." *English Journal* 66 (Oct 1977): 20–21.

The Oxford Companion to Children's Literature. Edited by Humphrey Carpenter and Mari Prichard. New York: Oxford Univ. Press, 1984, p. 587.

Twentieth-Century Children's Writers. 3rd ed. Edited by Tracy Chevalier and D. L. Kirkpatrick. Chicago: St. James, 1989, pp. 1078–1079.

Zindel, Paul. "Magic of Special People." *School Media Quarterly* 2 (Fall 1979): 29–32.

Zolotow, Charlotte S(hapiro)

Chapman, Karen Lenz. "Themes of Charlotte Zolotow's Books and Her Adult Development." Master's thesis, Claremont Graduate School, 1981.

Francis, Elizabeth. "Charlotte Zolotow." In *American Writers for Children since 1960: Fiction. Dictionary of Literary Biography,* vol. 52. Detroit: Gale, 1986, pp. 411–418.

More Junior Authors. Edited by Muriel Fuller. New York: Wilson, 1963, p. 235.

Twentieth-Century Children's Writers. 3rd ed. Edited by Tracy Chevalier and D. L. Kirkpatrick. Chicago: St. James, 1989, pp. 1080–1082.

Wintle, Justin, and Emma Fisher. *The Pied Pipers.* New York: Two Continents, 1975, pp. 87–100.

Zolotow, Charlotte. "Passion in Publishing." In *A Sea of Upturned Faces: Proceedings of the Third Pacific Rim Conference on Children's Literature,* ed. by Winifred Ragsdale. Metuchen, NJ: Scarecrow Press, 1989.

———. "Writing for the Very Young." *Horn Book* 61 (Sept 1985): 536–540.

———. "Writing for Young People: An Emotional Deja Vu." *Writer* (Apr 1986): 13–16.

Author and Illustrator Index

This Author and Illustrator Index provides references to the specific works of all authors and editors of books mentioned in Chapters 1 through 10, including out-of-print works. All numbers refer to entry numbers, not page numbers. Authors' and editors' last names are given in all capital letters, and a list of specific works follows. Illustrators are listed with reference to entry number only and do not list specific works.

AAMODT, Donald
  A Name to Conjure With, 1885
ABBEY, Lynn (pseud. of Marilyn Lorraine Abbey)
  The Black Flame, 1230
  Daughter of the Bright Moon, 1230
  Unicorn and Dragon, 1602
Abbey, Marilyn Lorraine. *See* ABBEY, Lynn
ABELL, Kathleen
  King Orville and the Bullfrogs, 1
ADAIR, Gilbert
  Alice Through the Needle's Eye: The Further Adventures of Lewis Carroll's "Alice," 1886
Adams, Adrienne, 17, 19, 207, 294, 296, 518, 2495, 2921, 2923, 2927, 2929
ADAMS, Hazard
  The Truth about Dragons: An Anti-Romance, 1231
ADAMS, Richard (George)
  The Plague Dogs, 378
  Shardik, 1232
  Watership Down, 379
ADAMS, Robert. *See* NORTON, André
ADKINS, Jan
  Solstice: A Mystery of the Season, 2678
  A Storm Without Rain, 2679
ADLER, C(arole) S(chwerdtfeger)
  Footsteps on the Stairs, 1004
  Eddie's Blue-Winged Dragon, 2337
ADLER, David A.
  Jeffrey's Ghost and the Leftover Baseball Team, 1005
Aggs, Patrice, 129
AHLBERG, Allan, 2089. *See also* AHLBERG, Janet

The Clothes Horse and Other Stories, 2088
Ten in a Bed, 2338
AHLBERG, Janet, 2088, 2882
  Jeremiah in the Dark Woods, 2089
AHLBERG, Janet, and AHLBERG, Allan
  The Bear Nobody Wanted, 2882
Aichinger, Helga, 371
AIKEN, Joan (Delano)
  Arabel and Mortimer, 2090
  Arabel's Raven, 2090
  Armitage, Armitage, Fly Away Home, 2091
  Black Hearts in Battersea, 1235
  The Cuckoo Tree, 1235
  Dido and Pa, 1235
  The Faithless Lollybird, 765
  The Far Forests: Tales of Romance, Fantasy and Suspense, 766
  A Foot in the Grave, 1006
  Give Yourself a Fright: Thirteen Stories of the Supernatural, 767
  The Green Flash and Other Tales of Horror, Suspense, and Fantasy, 768
  A Harp of Fishbones and Other Stories, 769
  The Haunting of Lamb House, 1007
  Is Underground, 1235
  The Kingdom and the Cave, 1233
  The Last Slice of Rainbow: And Other Stories, 770
  The Moon's Revenge, 2
  Mortimer Says Nothing, 2090
  Mortimer's Cross, 2090
  A Necklace of Raindrops and Other Stories, 771
  Nightbirds on Nantucket, 1235
  Not What You Expected: A Collection of Short Stories, 772

Past Eight O'Clock: Goodnight Stories, 773
Return to Harken House, 1008
The Shadow Guests, 1009
Smoke from Cromwell's Time and Other Stories, 774
The Stolen Lake, 1235
Street: A Play for Children, 3
A Touch of Chill: Tales for Sleepless Nights, 1010
Up the Chimney Down and Other Stories, 2092
A Whisper in the Night: Tales of Terror and Suspense, 1011
The Whispering Mountain, 1234
Winterthing: A Play for Children, 1603
The Wolves of Willoughby Chase, 1235
AINSWORTH (Gilbert), Ruth (Gallard)
    The Bear Who Liked Hugging People and Other Stories, 775
    The Phantom Carousel and Other Ghostly Tales, 1012
Akino, Fuku, 210, 1129, 2229
Alborough, Jez, 574
ALBRECHT, Lillie Vanderveer
    Deborah Remembers, 2883
ALCOCK, Vivien (Dolores)
    Ghostly Companions: A Feast of Chilling Tales, 1013
    The Haunting of Cassie Palmer, 1014
    The Monster Garden, 2339
    Singer to the Sea God, 1604
    The Stonewalkers, 1605
ALDEN, Raymond Macdonald
    Why the Chimes Rang and Other Stories, 777
ALDISS, Brian W(ilson)
    Helliconia Spring, 778
    Helliconia Summer, 778
    Helliconia Winter, 778
    Seasons in Flight, 778
Alexander, Gregory, 579
ALEXANDER, Lloyd (Chudley)
    The Beggar Queen, 1241
    The Black Cauldron, 1236
    The Book of Three, 1236
    The Castle of Llyr, 1236
    The Cat Who Wished to Be a Man, 380
    Coll and His White Pig, 1237
    The Drackenberg Adventure, 1888
    The El Dorado Adventure, 1888
    The First Two Lives of Lukas-Kasha, 1887
    The Foundling and Other Tales of Prydain, 1238
    The High King, 1236
    The Illyrian Adventure, 1888
    The Jedera Adventure, 1888
    The Kestrel, 1241
    The Marvelous Misadventures of Sebastian: Grand Extravaganza, Including a Performance by the Entire Cast of the Gallimaufry Theatricus, 1239
    The Philadelphia Adventure, 1888

The Remarkable Journey of Prince Jen, 4
Taran Wanderer, 1236
Time Cat: The Remarkable Journeys of Jason and Gareth, 2680
The Town Cats, and Other Tales, 381
The Truthful Harp, 1236, 1240
Westmark, 1241
The Wizard in the Tree, 2963
Aliki, 2902
ALLAN, Mabel E(sther)
    Romansgrove, 268
    Time to Go Back, 2682
ALLAN, Ted
    Willie the Squowse, 382
Allen, Jonathan, 641, 2243
ALLEN, Judy
    The Lord of the Dance, 1606
    The Spring on the Mountain, 5
Allen, Linda, 8
Alley, R. W., 1724
ALPHIN, Elaine Marie
    The Ghost Cadet, 1015
ALTON, Andrea I
    Demon of Undoing, 1243
AMADO, Jorge
    The Swallow and the Tom Cat: A Grown-Up Love Story, 383
Ambrus, Glenys, 140
Ambrus, Victor G., 140, 279, 580, 821, 962, 1233, 1829, 2069, 2905, 2985
AMOSS, Berthe
    Lost Magic, 2964
Amstutz, André, 2338
ANASTASIO, Dina
    A Question of Time, 1016
ANCKARSVÄRD, Karin (Inez Maria)
    Bonifacius the Green, 2340
ANDERSEN, Hans Christian
    Andersen's Fairy Tales, 779
    Ardizzone's Hans Andersen: Fourteen Classic Tales, 779
    The Complete Fairy Tales and Stories, 779
    Dulac's The Snow Queen and Other Stories from Hans Andersen, 779
    Eighty Fairy Tales, 779
    The Emperor's New Clothes, 6
    Fairy Tales, 779
    Fairy Tales from Hans Christian Andersen, 779
    Favorite Tales of Hans Andersen, 779
    The Fir Tree, 7
    Hans Andersen: His Classic Fairy Tales, 779
    Hans Andersen's Fairy Tales, 779
    Hans Andersen's Fairy Tales: A Selection, 779
    Hans Christian Andersen Fairy Tales, 779
    It's Perfectly True, and Other Stories, 779
    Little Ida's Flowers, 8
    The Little Match Girl, 9
    The Little Mermaid, 10

The Mermaid, and Other Fairy Tales, 779
Michael Hague's Favorite Hans Christian Andersen Fairy Tales, 779
The Nightingale, 11
The Old House, 12
The Red Shoes, 13
Seven Tales, 779
The Snow Queen, 14
The Steadfast Tin Soldier, 15
Stories from Hans Andersen, 779
The Stories of Hans Andersen, 779
The Swineherd, 16
Tales and Stories by Hans Christian Andersen, 779
Thumbelina, 17
The Tinderbox, 18
Twelve Tales, 779
The Ugly Duckling, 19
The Wild Swans, 20
ANDERSON, Joy
Juma and the Magic Jinn, 2341
ANDERSON, Karen, jt. auth. *See* ANDERSON, Poul
Anderson, Kathleen, 1068
ANDERSON, Margaret J(ean)
The Druid's Gift, 2683
The Ghost Inside the Monitor, 1017
In the Circle of Time, 2684
In the Keep of Time, 2684
The Mists of Time, 2684
To Nowhere and Back, 2685
ANDERSON, Mary
F*T*C* Superstar, 384
ANDERSON, Mildred Napier
A Gift for Merimond, 21
Sandra and the Right Prince, 22
ANDERSON, Poul (William)
Fantasy, 780
Guardians of Time, 2686
The Merman's Children, 1245
A Midsummer Tempest, 1246
Operation Chaos, 1246
The Shield of Time, 2686
Three Hearts and Three Lions, 1246
The Time Patrol, 2686
Time Patrolman, 2686
ANDERSON, Poul, and ANDERSON, Karen
Dahut, 1247
The Dog and the Wolf, 1247
Gallicenae, 1247
Roman Mater, 1247
ANDERSON, Wayne, 17
Dragon, 23
ANDREWS, Allen
Castle Crespin, 385
The Pig Plantagenet, 385
ANDREWS, Frank (Emerson)
The Upside-Down Town, 2093

ANDREWS, J(ames) S(ydney)
The Green Hill of Nendrum, 2687
Angel, Marie, 664
ANGELL, Judie
The Weird Disappearance of Jordan Hall, 2342
Angelo, Nicholas, 470
ANNETT (Pipitone Scott), Cora
How the Witch Got Alf, 386
When the Porcupine Moved In, 387
ANNIXTER, Paul (pseud. of Howard Allison Sturtzel)
The Cat That Clumped, 388
ANSA, Tina McElroy
Baby of the Family, 2343
Anstey, Caroline, 2611
Anstey, David, 3128
Anthony, Barbara. *See* BARBER, Antonia
ANTHONY, Piers (pseud. of Piers A. D. Jacob)
Alien Plot, 782
Bearing an Hourglass, 1249
Blue Adept, 1248
Castle Roogna, 1250
Centaur Aisle, 1250
Chaos Mode, 1889
The Color of Her Panties, 1250
Crewel Lye, 1250
Demons Don't Dream, 1250
Dragon on a Pedestal, 1250
Fractal Mode, 1889
Golem in the Gears, 1250
Harpy Thyme, 1250
Heaven Scent, 1250
Isle of View, 1250
Juxtaposition, 1248
Man from Mundania, 1250
Night Mare, 1250
Ogre, Ogre, 1250
On a Pale Horse, 1249
Out of Phaze, 1248
Phaze Doubt, 1248
Question Quest, 1250
Robot Adept, 1248
The Source of Magic, 1250
A Spell for Chameleon, 1250
Split Infinity, 1248
Unicorn Point, 1248
Vale of the Vole, 1250
Virtual Mode, 1889
Wielding a Red Sword, 1249
With a Tangled Skein, 1249
ANTHONY, Piers, and FARMER, Philip Jose
The Caterpillar's Question, 1890
ANTHONY, Piers, and KORNWISE, Robert Ian
Through the Ice, 1891
ANTHONY, Piers, and LACKEY, Mercedes
If I Pay Thee Not in Gold, 1251
Antonucci, Emil, 1686

APPEL, Allen
Till the End of Time, 2688
Time After Time, 2688
Twice Upon a Time, 2688
Apple, Margot, 575, 2533
ARCHAMBAULT, John, jt. auth. *See* MARTIN,
 Bill (William Ivan)
Ardizzone, Edward, 61, 495, 721, 750, 779, 860,
 861, 862, 863, 953, 2374, 2442, 3015
ARKIN, Alan (Wolf)
The Lemming Condition, 389
Armfield, Maxwell, 779
Armstrong, James, 2547
Arndt, Ursula, 2398
Arno, Enrico, 37, 800, 920
Arnold, Claire. *See* CROSS, Gillian
ARNOLD, Mark Alan. *See* WINDLING, Terri
ARNOLD, Tim
The Winter Mittens, 2344
Arnosky, Jim, 2550
ARTHUR, Ruth M(abel)
The Autumn People, 1019
Miss Ghost, 1020
On the Wasteland, 2689
Requiem for a Princess, 2690
The Whistling Boy, 1021
Artzybasheff, Boris, 1674
ARUNDEL, Honor
The Amazing Mr. Prothero, 390
ASCH, Frank
Pearl's Promise, 391
ASHLEY, Mike
*The Camelot Chronicles: Heroic Adventures
 from the Time of King Arthur*, 1632
*The Pendragon Chronicles: Heroic Fantasy from
 the Time of King Arthur*, 1801
ASIMOV, Isaac
Azazel, 2345
*Tomorrow's Children: 18 Tales of Fantasy and
 Science Fiction*, 974
ASIMOV, Isaac, CARR, Terry, and GREENBERG,
 Martin H.
100 Great Fantasy Short Stories, 937
ASIMOV, Isaac, GREENBERG, Charles G., and
 WAUGH, Martin H.
Atlantis, 784
Dragon Tales, 845
*Fantastic Creatures: An Anthology of Fantasy
 and Science Fiction*, 856
*Isaac Asimov Presents the Best Fantasy of the
 19th Century*, 903
*Isaac Asimov's Magical Worlds of Fantasy:
 Faeries*, 904
Witches, 3138
Young Ghosts, 1229
Young Witches and Warlocks, 3145
ASIRE, Nancy, jt. auth. *See* CHERRYH, C. J.
 (pseud. of Carolyn Janice Cherry)

ASKOUNIS, Christina
The Dream of the Stone, 1892
ASPRIN, Robert L(ynn)
Another Fine Myth, 2965
Hit or Myth, 2965
Little Myth Marker, 2965
M.Y.T.H. Inc. Link, 2965
Myth Conceptions, 2965
Myth Directions, 2965
Myth-ing Persons, 2965
Myth-Nomers and Im-Perfections, 2965
The Association for Childhood Education Literature
 Committee
*Told Under the Magic Umbrella: Modern
 Fanciful Stories for Young Children*, 973
Astrop, John, 2128
Atkinson, Allen, 1982, 2893
Atkinson, Leslie, 2815
ATTANASIO, A(lfred) A(ngelo)
Kingdom of the Grail, 1607
ATTWOOD, Frederic
Vavache, the Cow Who Painted Pictures, 392
ATWATER, Florence (Hasseltine Carroll), jt. auth.
 See ATWATER, Richard (Tupper)
ATWATER, Richard (Tupper), and ATWATER,
 Florence (Hasseltine Carroll)
Mr. Popper's Penguins, 2094
Atwood, Clara E., 2381
AULAIRE, Edgar Parin d', jt. auth. *See* AULAIRE,
 Ingri Mortenson d'
AULAIRE, Ingri Mortenson d', and d'AULAIRE,
 Edgar Parin d'
D'Aulaires' Trolls, 785
AULNOY, Marie Catherine Jumelle de Berneville,
 Comtesse d'
The Children's Fairy Land, 786
*The White Cat and Other Old French Fairy
 Tales*, 787
Austin, Alicia, 603
Austin, Erwin, 1115
AVERILL, Esther (Holden)
The Adventures of Jack Ninepins, 2884
*Captains of the City Streets: A Story of the Cat
 Club*, 393
The Cat Club, 393
The Hotel Cat, 393
How the Brothers Joined the Cat Club, 393
Jenny and the Cat Club, 393
Jenny's First Party, 393
Jenny's Moonlight Adventure, 393
The School for Cats, 393
AVI (pseud. of Avi Wortis)
Bright Shadow, 1252
*Emily Upham's Revenge: Or, How Deadwood
 Dick Saved the Banker's Niece: A
 Massachusetts Adventure*, 2095
Something Upstairs: A Tale of Ghosts, 2691
Ayer, Jacqueline, 231

AYMÉ, Marcel (André)
  The Magic Pictures: More about the Wonderful Farm, 394
  The Wonderful Farm, 394

B. B. (pseud. of D[enys] J[ames] Watkins-Pitchford)
  Down the Bright Stream, 1253
  The Little Grey Men, 1253
BABBITT, Lucy Cullyford
  Children of the Maker, 1254
  The Oval Amulet, 1254
  Where the Truth Lies, 1255
BABBITT, Natalie (Zane Moore)
  The Devil's Other Storybook, 2096
  The Devil's Storybook, 2096
  Goody Hall, 2097
  Knee-Knock Rise, 24
  The Search for Delicious, 25
  Tuck Everlasting, 1608
BABCOCK (Thompson), Betty (Elizabeth S.)
  The Expandable Pig, 2346
Baber, Frank, 2905
Bach, Peggie, 2812
BACH, Richard (David)
  Jonathan Livingston Seagull, 26
Bacharach, H(erman) I., 1915, 2916
BACON, Martha (Sherman)
  Moth Manor: A Gothic Tale, 2885
  The Third Road, 2692
Bacon, Peggy, 316, 515
  The Ghost of Opalina, or Nine Lives, 1022
  The Lion-Hearted Kitten and Other Stories, 395
  The Magic Touch, 2347
  Mercy and the Mouse and Other Stories, 396
BAILEY, Carolyn Sherwin
  Finnegan II: His Nine Lives, 397
  Miss Hickory, 2886
BAILEY, Margery
  The Little Man with One Shoe, 788
  Seven Peas in the Pod, 789
  Whistle for Good Fortune, in Which It Is Shown How Six from Six Makes Six and One to Carry, with Other Riddles Here and There Along the Way, 790
Bailey-Jones, Beryl, 488
Baker, Alan, 177, 1767, 3060
BAKER, Betty (Lou)
  Danby and George, 398
  Dupper, 399
  Save Sirrushany!, 27
  Seven Spells to Farewell, 28
BAKER, Elizabeth Whitemore
  Sonny-Boy Sim, 400
BAKER, Margaret
  The Black Cats and the Tinker's Wife, 29
  Cat's-Cradles for His Majesty, 30

Fifteen Tales for Lively Children, 791
  The Lost Merbaby, 31
  Noddy Goes A-Plowing, 32
  Patsy and the Leprechauns, 2348
  Pollie Who Did as She Was Told, 2349
  Tell Them Again Tales, 792
  Three for an Acorn, 401
  Victoria Josephine, 2887
  The Water Elf and the Miller's Child, 2350
BAKER, Margaret Joyce
  Bears Back in Business, 2888
  Hannibal and the Bears, 2888
  Hi Jinks Joins the Bears, 2888
  Homer Goes to Stratford, 402
  Homer Sees the Queen, 402
  Homer the Tortoise, 402
  The Magic Sea Shell, 2351
  Porterhouse Major, 2352
  The Shoe Shop Bears, 2888
Baker, Mary, 29, 30, 31, 32, 401, 791, 792, 2348, 2349, 2350, 2887
BAKER, Olaf
  Bengey and the Beast, 2353
BAKER, (Robert) Michael (Graham)
  The Mountain and the Summer Stars: An Old Tale Newly Ended, 1609
BAKKEN, Harald
  The Fields and the Hills, 1256
BALABAN, John
  The Hawk's Tale, 403
BALL, Brian
  The Quest for Queenie, 1893
BALL, Duncan
  Emily Eyefinger, 2354
BALL, Margaret
  Changeweaver, 1257
  Flameweaver, 1257
  The Shadow Gate, 1894
BANCROFT, Alberta
  The Goblins of Haubeck, 33
BANKS, Richard
  The Mysterious Leaf, 34
BARBER, Antonia (pseud. of Barbara Anthony)
  The Enchanter's Daughter, 35
  The Ghosts, 2693
BARKER, Clive
  The Thief of Always: A Fable, 1895
BARKER, M(uhammad) A(bd-Al-) R(ahman)
  The Man of Gold, 1258
BARKLEM, Jill
  Autumn Story, 404
  The Four Seasons of Brambly Hedge, 404
  The High Hills, 404
  Sea Story, 404
  The Secret Staircase, 404
  Spring Story, 404
  Summer Story, 404
  Winter Story, 404

Barlow, Wayne, 2645
Barrett, Angela, 14, 20, 152, 238, 1174
BARRETT, Nicholas
   Fledger, 405
Barrett, Ron, 2247
BARRIE, Sir J(ames) M(atthew)
   Peter Pan, 1896
   Peter Pan in Kensington Gardens, 1896
   When Wendy Grew Up: An Afterthought, 1896
BARRINGER, Marie
   Martin the Goose Boy, 2889
Barrish, Wendy, 1913
BARRON, T(homas) A
   The Ancient One, 2694
BARTHOLOMEW, Barbara
   Child of Tomorrow, 1897
   The Time Keeper, 1897
   When Dreamers Cease to Dream, 1897
Bartlett, Maurice, 567
Baskin, Leonard, 906
Batchelor, Joy, 642
Bates, Leo, 402
Batherman, Muriel, 2640
BATO, Joseph
   The Sorcerer, 2966
BATTLES, Edith
   The Witch in Room 6, 2967
BAUDINO, Gael
   Strands of Starlight, 1259
BAUER, Marion Dane
   Ghost Eye, 1023
   A Taste of Smoke, 1024
   Touch the Moon, 2355
BAUM, L(yman) Frank
   Dorothy and the Wizard in Oz, 1898
   The Emerald City of Oz, 1898
   Glinda of Oz, 1898
   The Land of Oz, 1898
   Little Wizard Stories of Oz, 1898
   The Lost Princess of Oz, 1898
   The Magic of Oz, 1898
   Ozma of Oz, 1898
   The Patchwork Girl of Oz, 1898
   Rinki-tink of Oz, 1898
   The Road to Oz, 1898
   The Scarecrow of Oz, 1898
   *The Surprising Adventures of the Magical
      Monarch of Mo and His People*, 794
   Tik-Tok of Oz, 1898
   The Tin Woodman of Oz, 1898
   The Visitors from Oz, 1898
   The Wizard of Oz, 1898
Baumgartner, Robert, 589
BAXTER, Caroline
   The Stolen Telesm, 2968
Baxter, Glen, 2214
BAXTER, Lorna
   The Eggchild, 2969

Bayley, Nicola, 234
Baynes, Pauline, 96, 124, 184, 332, 333, 2007, 2924
BEACHCROFT, Nina
   Well Met by Witchlight, 2970
   The Wishing People, 2356
BEAGLE, Peter S(oyer)
   The Fantasy Worlds of Peter S. Beagle, 795
   A Fine and Private Place, A Novel, 1025
   The Folk of the Air, 1610
   The Innkeeper's Song, 1260
   The Last Unicorn, 1261
BEAR, Greg(ory Dale)
   The Infinity Concerto, 1899
Beard, Daniel C., 2860
BEATON-JONES, Cynon
   The Adventures of So Hi, 1900
BECHDOLT, Jack (pseud. of John Ernest Bechdolt)
   Bandmaster's Holiday, 406
Bechdolt, John Ernest. *See* BECHDOLT, Jack
Becher, Arthur E., 2383
BECKER, Eve
   The Love Potion, 2357
   Thirteen Means Magic, 2357
Beckman, Kaj, 355
BEDARD, Michael
   A Darker Magic, 2971
   Painted Devil, 2971
   Redwork, 2972
Beddows, Eric, 89
Bedford, D., 219
Bedford, F(rancis) D., 224, 1896, 1923, 2549
BEEKS, Graydon
   *Hosea Globe and the Fantastical Peg-Legged
      Chu*, 2098
BEHN, Harry
   The Faraway Lurs, 36
   Roderick, 407
BELDEN, Wilianne Schneider
   Frankie!, 2358
BELL, Clare E.
   Clan Ground, 408
   The Jaguar Princess, 1262
   Ratha and Thistle–Chaser, 408
   Ratha's Creature, 408
   Tomorrow's Sphinx, 409
Bell, Corydon, 2359, 2451
BELL, Norman (Edward)
   The Weightless Mother, 2099
Bell, Owain, 503
BELL, Thelma Harrington
   Take It Easy, 2359
BELLAIRS, John
   The Dark Secret of Weatherend, 2360
   The Face in the Frost, 2973
   The Figure in the Shadows, 1026
   The Ghost in the Mirror, 1026
   The House with a Clock in Its Walls, 1026
   The Lamp from the Warlock's Tomb, 2360

The Letter, the Witch and the Ring, 1026
The Mansion in the Mist, 2360
The Treasure of Alpheus Winterborn, 2360
The Trolley to Yesterday, 2695
BELLAMY, Edward
Equality, 2696
Looking Backward: 2000–1887, 2696
BEMELMANS, Ludwig
The Happy Place, 2890
BEMMANN, Hans
The Stone and the Flute, 1263
BENARY-ISBERT, Margot
The Wicked Enchantment, 37
BENCHLEY, Nathaniel (Goddard)
Demo and the Dolphin, 1611
Feldman Fieldmouse: A Fable, 410
Kilroy and the Gull, 411
The Magic Sled, 2361
BENDICK, Jeanne
The Blonk from Beneath the Sea, 2100
The Goodknight Ghost, 1027
BENÉT, Stephen Vicent
The Devil and Daniel Webster, 1612
BENJAMIN, Alan
Appointment, 38
BENNETT, Anna Elizabeth
Little Witch, 2974
Bennett, Jill, 901, 1178, 2215, 2405, 2516, 2627
BENNETT, John
*The Pigtail of Ah Lee Ben Loo, with Seventeen
    Other Laughable Tales,* 2101
Bennett, Richard, 457, 779, 1148, 2235, 2331, 2455
BENNETT, Rodney
Eagle Boy, 2362
Bensell, E. B., 1915
BENSON, E(dward) F(rederic)
The Collected Ghost Stories of E. F. Benson,
    1028
David Blaize and the Blue Door, 1901
Benson, Patrick, 1930, 2255, 2566
Bentley, Nicolas, 2540
Berenzy, Alix, 770, 2292, 2355
BERESFORD, Elizabeth
Invisible Magic, 2697
The Invisible Womble, 412
MacWomble's Pipe Band, 412
The Snow Womble, 412
Travelling Magic, 2698
The Wandering Wombles, 412
The Wombles, 412
The Wombles at Work, 412
The Wombles Book, 412
The Wombles Go Round the World, 412
The Wombles in Danger, 412
The Wombles Make a Clean Sweep, 412
The Wombles of Wimbledon, 412
The Wombles to the Rescue, 412
Beresford, Marcus. *See* BRANDEL, Marc

Berg, Joan, 146
BERGENGREN, Ralph Wilhelm
David the Dreamer: His Book of Dreams, 1902
Susan and the Butterbees, 2363
BERGER, Barbara Helen
Gwinna, 39
BERGER, Thomas (Louis)
Arthur Rex: A Legendary Novel, 1613
Bernstein, Zena, 606, 639
Berry, Erick, 870, 2919
BERRY, James R.
The Magicians of Erianne, 1614
Berson, Harold, 1918, 2192, 2385, 2443, 2544
Bertelli, Luigi. *See* VAMBA
BERTON, Pierre
The Secret World of Og, 1903
Bertrand, Karen, 755
BEST, (Oswald) Herbert
Desmond and Dog Friday, 413
*Desmond and the Peppermint Ghost: The Dog
    Detective's Third Case,* 413
*Desmond the Dog Detective: The Case of the
    Lone Stranger,* 413
Desmond's First Case, 413
BESTERMAN, Catherine
*The Extraordinary Education of Johnny
    Longfoot in His Search for the Magic Hat,*
    414
*The Quaint and Curious Quest of Johnny
    Longfoot, the Shoe King's Son,* 414
BESTON, Henry B. (pseud. of Henry Beston
    Sheahan)
Henry Beston's Fairy Tales, 797
BETANCOURT, John Gregory
The Blind Archer, 1264
BETHANCOURT, T(homas) Ernesto (pseud. of
    Tom Paisley)
The Dog Days of Arthur Cane, 2364
The Tomorrow Connection, 2699
Tune in Yesterday, 2699
Bettina, 132, 2674
Bhend, Käthi, 555, 556, 625
Biamonte, Daniel, 165
BIANCO, Margery (Winifred) Williams
The Good Friends, 415
The House That Grew Smaller, 40
The Hurdy-Gurdy Man, 2365
The Little Wooden Doll, 2891
*Poor Cecco: The Wonderful Story of a Wonderful
    Wooden Dog Who Was the Jolliest Toy in the
    House Until He Went Out to Explore the
    World,* 2892
The Skin Horse, 2893
A Street of Little Shops, 798
*The Velveteen Rabbit; or, How Toys Became
    Real,* 2893
BIANCO, Pamela, 10, 2891, 2958
Little Houses Far Away, 2894

The Starlit Journey, a Story, 41
Toy Rose, 2895
BIEGEL, Paul
 The King of the Copper Mountains, 42
Bilbin, I., 273, 274
Bileck, Marvin, 91
Binder-Strassfurt, Eberhart, 2001
Binks, Robert, 153
BINNS, Archie (Fred)
 The Radio Imp, 2366
 Secret of the Sleeping River, 2366
Birch, Reginald B., 967, 1914
Bischoff, Ilse, 2918
BISSON, Terry
 Fire on the Mountain, 1265
 Talking Man, 1615
Bissot, Douglas, 497
Bjorklund, Lorence, 2176
BLACKWOOD, Algernon (Henry)
 The Adventures of Dudley and Gilderoy, 416
BLACKWOOD, Gary L.
 Beyond the Door, 1904
BLADOW, Suzanne Wilson
 *The Midnight Flight of Moose, Mops and
 Marvin*, 417
Blair, Eric Hugh. *See* ORWELL, George
Blair, Pauline (Clarke) Hunter. *See* CLARKE,
 Pauline
Blaisdell, Elinore, 1767
BLAISDELL, Mary Frances
 Bunny Rabbit's Diary, 418
Blake, Quentin, 144, 181, 348, 382, 471, 2090,
 2132, 2133, 2134, 2135, 2136, 2162, 2193, 2242,
 2244, 2417, 2999
BLATHWAYT, Benedict
 Stories from Firefly Island, 419
 Tangle and the Firesticks, 420
BLAYLOCK, James P(aul)
 The Disappearing Dwarf, 1266
 The Elfin Ship, 1266
 Land of Dreams, 1905
 The Paper Grail, 1616
 The Stone Giant, 1266
Blechman, R. O., 2124
Blegvad, Erik, 16, 84, 149, 421, 714, 779, 933,
 1402, 2078, 2143, 2526, 2586, 2946
BLISHEN, Edward, jt. auth. *See* GARFIELD, Leon
BLISS, Corinne Demas
 Matthew's Meadow, 43
BLOCH, Marie Halun
 The Dollhouse Story, 2896
Bloom, Lloyd, 1102
Blum, Zevi, 1688
BLUNT, Wilfrid (Jasper Walter)
 Omar; a Fantasy for Animal Lovers, 2102
Bock, Vera, 121, 122, 559
BODECKER, N(iels) M(ogens), 1946, 2433, 2434,
 2435, 2633

Carrot Holes and Frisbee Trees, 2103
The Lost String Quartet, 44
The Mushroom Center Disaster, 421
Quimble Wood, 1267
BODGER, Joan (Mercer)
 Clever-Lazy, the Girl Who Invented Herself, 45
Boix, Manuel, 61, 297
Bolam, Emily, 180
Bolognese, Don, 2447, 2712
BOMANS, Godfried (Jan Arnold)
 *The Wily Witch and All the Other Fairy Tales and
 Fables*, 801
BOND, Nancy (Barbara)
 Another Shore, 2700
 A String in the Harp, 2701
BOND, (Thomas) Michael
 A Bear Called Paddington, 422
 The Complete Adventures of Olga Da Polga, 424
 Here Comes Thursday, 423
 More about Paddington, 422
 Olga Carries On, 424
 Olga Counts Her Blessings, 424
 Olga Makes a Friend, 424
 Olga Makes a Wish, 424
 Olga Makes Her Mark, 424
 Olga Meets Her Match, 424
 Olga Takes a Bite, 424
 Olga's New Home, 424
 Olga's Second Home, 424
 Olga's Special Day, 424
 Paddington Abroad, 422
 Paddington at Large, 422
 Paddington at the Circus, 422
 Paddington at the Seaside, 422
 Paddington at the Tower, 422
 Paddington at Work, 422
 Paddington Goes to Town, 422
 Paddington Helps Out, 422
 Paddington Marches On, 422
 Paddington on Screen, 422
 Paddington on Stage, 422
 Paddington on Top, 422
 Paddington Takes the Air, 422
 Paddington Takes the Test, 422
 Paddington Takes to TV, 422
 Paddington's Garden, 422
 Paddington's Lucky Day, 422
 Paddington's Storybook, 422
 Tales of Olga Da Polga, 424
 Thursday Ahoy!, 423
 Thursday in Paris, 423
 Thursday Rides Again, 423
BONHAM, Frank
 The Friends of the Loony Lake Monster, 2367
BONTEMPS, Arna (Wendell), and CONROY, Jack
 The Fast Sooner Hound, 2104

BORGES, Jorge Luis, with GUERRERO, Margarita
   The Book of Imaginary Beings, 802
Born, Adolf, 924
BOSHINSKI, Blanche
   Aha and the Jewel of Mystery, 425
BOSSE, Malcolm J(oseph)
   Cave Beyond Time, 2702
BOSTON, L(ucy) M(aria Wood)
   The Castle of Yew, 2368
   The Children of Green Knowe, 1031
   An Enemy at Green Knowe, 1031, 2371
   The Fossil Snake, 2369
   The Guardians of the House, 1906
   Nothing Said, 2370
   The River at Green Knowe, 1031, 2371
   The Sea Egg, 2372
   The Stones of Green Knowe, 1031, 2703
   A Stranger at Green Knowe, 1031
   The Treasure of Green Knowe, 1031
Boston, Peter, 1031, 1906, 2369, 2370, 2371, 2372, 2703
BOUCHER, Anthony (pseud. of William Anthony Parker White)
   The Compleat Werewolf; and Other Stories of Fantasy and Science Fiction, 803
BOUMPHREY, Geoffrey, jt. auth. *See* WALKER, Kenneth Macfarlane
BOURLIAGUET, Léonce
   The Giant Who Drank from His Shoe and Other Stories, 804
   A Sword to Slice Through Mountains and Other Stories, 805
BOWEN, Vernon
   The Wonderful Adventures of Ting Ling, 46
BOWEN, William A(lvin)
   Merrimeg, 1907
   The Old Tobacco Shop: A True Account of What Befell a Little Boy in Search of Adventure, 2373
Bower, Barbara Euphan (Todd). *See* TODD, Barbara Euphan
Bowler, Jan Brett, 585
Bowman, Leslie W., 570, 1342
Boyd, Frank, 2591
BOYER, Elizabeth H.
   The Curse of Slagfid, 1908
   The Dragon's Carbuncle, 1908
   The Troll's Grindstone, 1908
BOYER, Robert H., and ZAHORSKI, Kenneth J.
   The Fantastic Imagination: An Anthology of High Fantasy, 1343
   The Phoenix Tree: An Anthology of Myth Fantasy, 1804
   Visions of Wonder: An Anthology of Christian Fantasy, 977
BOYLE, Kay
   The Youngest Camel, 47

Bozzo, Frank, 1234, 1655
BRADBURY, Ray (Douglas)
   Dinosaur Tales, 806
   The Halloween Tree, 2704
   The Illustrated Man, 807
   A Medicine for Melancholy, 808
   R Is for Rocket, 809
   Something Wicked This Way Comes, 2975
   The Stories of Ray Bradbury, 810
   The Toynbee Convector, 811
Bradfield, Margaret, 2390
BRADLEY, Marion Zimmer
   The Bloody Sun, 1270
   City of Sorcery, 1270
   Darkover Landfall, 1270
   Domains of Darkover, 1270
   The Firebrand, 1617
   The Forbidden Tower, 1270
   Four Moons of Darkover, 1270
   Free Amazons of Darkover, 1270
   Hawkmistress!, 1269, 1270
   The Heirs of Hammerfell, 1270
   The Heritage of Hastur, 1270
   The House Between the Worlds, 1909
   The Keeper's Price and Other Stories, 1270
   Leroni of Darkover, 1270
   Marion Zimmer Bradley's Darkover, 1270
   The Mists of Avalon, 1618
   Night's Daughter, 1619
   Oath of the Renunciates, 1270
   The Other Side of the Mirror: And Other Darkover Stories, 1270
   The Planet Savers, 1270
   Red Sun of Darkover, 1270
   Rediscovery: A Novel of Darkover, 1270
   Renunciates of Darkover, 1270
   Shaara's Exile, 1270
   The Shattered Chain: A Darkover Novel, 1270
   The Spell Sword, 1270
   Spells of Wonder, 1270, 1535
   Star of Danger, 1270
   Stormqueen, 1270
   Sword and Sorceress: An Anthology of Heroic Fantasy, 1547
   The Sword of Aldones, 1270
   Sword of Chaos and Other Stories, 1270
   Thendara House, 1270
   Towers of Darkness, 1270
   Two to Conquer, 1270
   Winds of Darkover, 1270
   The World Wreckers, 1270
BRADLEY, Marion Zimmer, and McINTYRE, Vonda
   Lythande, 2976
BRADLEY, Marion Zimmer, MAY, Julian, and NORTON, André
   Black Trillium, 1271

Blood Trillium, 1271
Golden Trillium, 1271
Bradley, Maureen, 2414
BRADSHAW, Gillian (Marucha)
  Beyond the North Wind, 1620
  The Dragon and the Thief, 1272
  Hawk of May, 1621
  In Winter's Shadow, 1621
  Kingdom of Summer, 1621
  The Land of Gold, 1272
BRAND, (Mary) Christianna (Milne Lewis)
  Nurse Matilda, 2374
  Nurse Matilda Goes to the Hospital, 2374
  Nurse Matilda Goes to Town, 2374
BRANDEL, Marc (pseud. of Marcus Beresford)
  The Mine of Lost Days, 2705
Brandenberg, Aliki. *See* Aliki
Bray, Phyllis, 2861
BRELIS, Nancy (Burns)
  The Mummy Market, 2105
BRENNAN, Herbie
  Emily and the Werewolf, 2977
BRENNAN, J. H.
  Shiva Accused, 1622
  Shiva: An Adventure of the Ice Age, 1622
  Shiva's Challenge, 1622
BRENNER, Anita
  *The Timid Ghost: Or What Would You Do with a
    Sackful of Gold?*, 1032
BRENNER, Barbara (Johnes)
  The Flying Patchwork Quilt, 2375
  Hemi: A Mule, 426
Brenner, Fred, 474, 2375
Brent, Isabelle, 580
BRENTANO, Clemens Maria
  Schoolmaster Whackwell's Wonderful Sons, 48
  The Tale of Gockel, Hinkel and Gackeliah, 49
Brett, Jan, 2935
Brewster, Anna Richards, 972
Brierly, Louise, 180
BRIGGS, K(atharine) M(ary)
  Hobberdy Dick, 1623
  Kate Crackernuts, 1624
Briggs, Raymond, 988
BRIGHT, Robert
  Richard Brown and the Dragon, 2106
BRIN, David
  The Practice Effect, 1910
BRINDEL, June Rachuy
  Ariadne, 1625
BRINK, Carol Ryrie
  Andy Buckram's Tin Men, 2107
  Baby Island, 2108
Brinkloe, Julie, 2779
Brisland, Janet Marjorie. *See* MARK, Jan
BRITTAIN, Bill (William)
  All the Money in the World, 2109
  The Devil's Donkey, 2978

Doctor Dredd's Wagon of Wonders, 2978
The Fantastic Freshman, 2376
The Ghost from Beneath the Sea, 1033
*Professor Popkin's Prodigious Polish: A Tale of
  Coven Tree*, 2978
Who Knew There'd Be Ghosts?, 1033
Wings, 2377
The Wish Giver: Three Tales of Coven Tree, 2978
BRO, Margueritte (Harmon)
  The Animal Friends of Peng-U, 427
BROCK, Betty
  No Flying in the House, 2378
  The Shades, 1034
Brock, Emma L., 477, 793, 1907, 2381, 2915
Brock, Margaret, 2915
BRÖGER, Achim
  Bruno, 2110
  Bruno Takes a Trip, 2110
  Little Harry, 2111
Broman, Polly, 376
BROOKE, William J.
  A Brush with Magic, 2379
  A Telling of the Tales: Five Stories, 812
  Untold Tales, 812
Brooks, Ron, 2865
BROOKS, Terry
  The Black Unicorn, 2112
  The Druids of Shannara, 1273
  The Elf Queen of Shannara, 1273
  The Elfstones of Shannara, 1273
  Magic Kingdom for Sale—Sold!, 2112
  The Scions of Shannara, 1273
  The Sword of Shannara, 1273
  The Talismans of Shannara, 1273
  The Tangle Box, 2112
  The Wishsong of Shannara, 1273
  Wizard at Large, 2112
BROOKS, Walter Rollin
  The Clockwork Twin, 428
  Collected Poems of Freddy the Pig, 428
  Freddy and Freginald, 428
  Freddy and Mr. Camphor, 428
  Freddy and Simon the Dictator, 428
  Freddy and the Baseball Team from Mars, 428
  Freddy and the Bean Home News, 428
  Freddy and the Dragon, 428
  Freddy and the Flying Saucer Plans, 428
  Freddy and the Ignormus, 428
  Freddy and the Men from Mars, 428
  Freddy and the Perilous Adventure, 428
  Freddy and the Popinjay, 428
  Freddy and the Space Ship, 428
  Freddy Goes Camping, 428
  Freddy Goes to Florida, 428
  Freddy Goes to the North Pole, 428
  Freddy Plays Football, 428
  Freddy Rides Again, 428
  Freddy the Cowboy, 428

Freddy the Detective, 428
Freddy the Magician, 428
Freddy the Pied Piper, 428
Freddy the Pilot, 428
Freddy the Politician, 428
Freddy's Cousin Weedly, 428
The Story of Freginald, 428
BROW, Thea J.
   The Secret Cross of Lorraine, 1035
BROWN, Abbie Farwell
   The Lonesomest Doll, 2897
BROWN, Jeff
   Flat Stanley, 2113
   A Lamp for the Lambchops, 2113
BROWN, Judith Gwyn, 505, 671, 830, 2129, 2397,
   2809, 3079
   The Mask of the Dancing Princess, 50
Brown, Judy, 2409
Brown, Marc, 96
Brown, Marcia, 15, 20
BROWN, Mary
   The Unlikely Ones, 2979
Brown, Neva Kanaga, 2485
BROWN, Palmer
   *Beyond the Pawpaw Trees: The Story of Anna
      Lavinia*, 2380
   Hickory, 429
   The Silver Nutmeg, 2380
BROWN, Rita Mae and BROWN, Sneaky Pie
   Wish You Were Here, 430
BROWN, Sneaky Pie, jt. auth. *See* BROWN, Rita
   Mae
Browne, Anthony, 1913
BROWNE, Frances
   *Granny's Wonderful Chair and Its Tales of Fairy
      Times*, 2381
Browne, Gordon, 194
BRUÈRE, Martha (Bensley)
   Sparky-for-Short, 2382
Bruner, Paul, 935
Brunsman, James, 602
BRUST, Steven K. (Zoltan)
   Brokedown Palace, 1626
   Five Hundred Years After, 1274
   Jhereg, 1275
   Phoenix, 1275
   The Phoenix Guards, 1274
   Taltos, 1275
   Tekla, 1275
   To Reign in Hell, 1627
   Yendi, 1275
Bryan, Ashley, 2403
BRYHER, Winifred (pseud. of Annie Winifred
   Ellerman)
   A Visa for Avalon, 1628
Bryson, Bernarda, 968, 2903
BUCHAN, John
   Lake of Gold, 2706

The Magic Walking-Stick, 2383
The Watcher by the Threshold and Other Tales,
   1629
Bucholtz-Ross, Linda, 636
BUCHWALD, Emilie
   Floramel and Esteban, 431
   *Gildaen: The Heroic Adventures of a Most
      Unusual Rabbit*, 432
BUCK, David
   The Small Adventures of Dog, 2898
Buel, Hubert, 2219
BUFFETT, Jimmy, and BUFFETT, Savannah Jane
   Trouble Dolls, 2899
BUFFETT, Savannah Jane, jt. auth. *See* BUFFETT,
   Jimmy
BUFFIE, Margaret
   The Haunting of Frances Rain, 2707
   The Warnings, 2384
Buffum, Katherine, 876
BUJOLD, Lois McMaster
   The Spirit Ring, 1276
BULL, Emma. *See also* SHETTERLY, Will
   War for the Oaks, 1630
BULLA, Clyde Robert
   The Moon Singer, 51
   My Friend the Monster, 52
   The Sword in the Tree, 53
BUNCH, Chris, jt. auth. *See* COLE, Allan
BUNTING, (Anne) Eve(lyn Bolton)
   Ghost Behind Me, 1036
   The Ghosts of Departure Point, 1037
BUNYAN, John
   The Pilgrim's Progress, 54
BURCH, Robert
   The Jolly Witch, 2980
Burchard, Peter, 646
Burd, Clara, 847
BURFORD, Lolah
   The Vision of Stephen: An Elegy, 2708
BURGESS, Barbara Hood
   Oren Bell, 1038
BURGESS, Thornton W(aldo)
   The Adventures of Bob White, 433
   The Adventures of Bobby Coon, 433
   The Adventures of Buster Bear, 433
   The Adventures of Chatterer the Red Squirrel,
      433
   The Adventures of Danny Meadowmouse, 433
   The Adventures of Grandfather Frog, 433
   The Adventures of Jerry Muskrat, 433
   The Adventures of Jimmy Skunk, 433
   The Adventures of Johnny Chuck, 433
   The Adventures of Lightfoot the Deer, 433
   The Adventures of Ol' Mistah Buzzard, 433
   The Adventures of Old Granny Fox, 433
   The Adventures of Old Man Coyote, 433
   The Adventures of Peter Cottontail, 433
   The Adventures of Poor Mrs. Quack, 433

The Adventures of Prickly Porky, 433
The Adventures of Reddy Fox, 433
The Adventures of Sammy Jay, 433
The Adventures of Unc' Billy Possum, 433
The Adventures of Whitefoot the Woodmouse, 433
Mother West Wind's Animal Friends, 433
Mother West Wind's Children, 433
Mother West Wind's "How" Stories, 433
Mother West Wind's Neighbors, 433
Mother West Wind's "When" Stories, 433
Mother West Wind's "Where" Stories, 433
Mother West Wind's "Why" Stories, 433
Old Mother West Wind, 433
Burgoyne, John, 2856
Burkert, Nancy Ekholm, 7, 11, 2418
BURMAN, Ben Lucien
Blow a Wild Bugle for Catfish Bend, 434
High Treason at Catfish Bend, 434
High Water at Catfish Bend, 434
The Owl Hoots Twice at Catfish Bend, 434
Seven Stars for Catfish Bend, 434
Three from Catfish Bend, 434
BURN, Doris
The Tale of Lazy Lizard Canyon, 2114
BURNETT (Townsend), Frances (Elizabeth) Hodgson
Queen Silverbell, 2385
Racketty-Packetty House, as Told by Queen Crosspatch, 2385
Spring Cleaning, as Told by Queen Crosspatch, 2385
BURNFORD, Sheila (Philip [née Every] Cochrane)
Mr. Noah and the Second Flood, 1631
Burningham, John, 523, 2174
Burns, Irene, 2072
Burroughs, Gail, 2885
BURTON, Philip
The Green Isle, 55
Burton, Virginia Lee, 6, 2104
Busoni, Rafaello, 215, 777, 2366
BUTLER, Beverly
Witch's Fire, 2981
Butler, E. F., 2950
BUTLER, Octavia E.
Kindred, 2709
BUTTERS, Dorothy G(ilman)
Papa Dolphin's Table, 435
BUTTERWORTH, Oliver
The Enormous Egg, 2115
The Narrow Passage, 2115
The Trouble with Jenny's Ear, 2116
Butterworth, Pam, 2236
BUZZATI, Dino
The Bears' Famous Invasion of Sicily, 436
Byard, Carole, 1773

BYARS, Betsy (Cromer)
Clementine, 2900
The Winged Colt of Casa Mia, 2386
BYFIELD, Barbara Ninde
Andrew and the Alchemist, 2982
The Haunted Churchbell, 1039
The Haunted Ghost, 1039
The Haunted Spy, 1039
The Haunted Tower, 1039
Byrd, Robert, 6

Cacciola, Concetta, 849
Caddy, Alice, 434
Caddy, Harrison, 2385, 433
CAIRE, Helen
Señor Castillo, Cock of the Island, 437
CALDECOTT, Moyra
Shadow on the Stones, 1277
The Tall Stones, 1277
The Temple of the Sun, 1277
CALHOUN, Mary (pseud. of Mary Huiskamp Wilkins)
Magic in the Alley, 2387
Ownself, 2388
CALIF, Ruth
The Over-the-Hill Ghost, 1040
CALLANDER, Don
Aquamancer, 2983
Geomancer, 2983
Pyromancer, 2983
CALLEN, Larry (Lawrence Willard, Jr.)
Pinch, 2117
CAMERON, Eleanor (Frances Butler)
The Beast with the Magical Horn, 56
Beyond Silence, 2710
The Court of the Stone Children, 1041
The Terrible Churnadryne, 2389
Time and Mr. Bass: A Mushroom Planet Book, 2711
CAMPBELL, Ann
Once Upon a Princess and a Pea, 57
CAMPBELL, Hope
Peter's Angel: A Story about Monsters, 438
CANFIELD, Dorothy (pseud. of Dorothea Frances [Canfield] Fisher)
Made-to-Order Stories, 813
CANNING, Victor
The Crimson Chalice, 1633
Canty, Thomas, 1882
Capek, Josef, 814
CAPEK, Karel
Nine Fairy Tales and One More Thrown In for Good Measure, 814
CARD, Orson Scott
Hart's Hope, 1278
Maps in a Mirror: The Short Fiction of Orson Scott Card, 815

Prentice Alvin, 1279
Red Prophet, 1279
Seventh Son, 1279
Songmaster, 1280
CAREW, Jan (Rynveld)
Children of the Sun, 58
CAREY, Valerie Soho
The Devil and Mother Crump, 2118
CARKEET, David
I Been There Before, 2119
Carloni, Giancarlo, 674
CARLSEN, Ruth Christoffer
Henrietta Goes West, 2120
Mr. Pudgins, 2390
Ride a Wild Horse, 1911
Sam Bottleby, 2391
CARLSON, Natalie Savage
Alphonse, That Bearded One, 2121
Evangeline, Pigeon of Paris, 439
The Ghost in the Lagoon, 1042
Hortense, the Cow for a Queen, 2122
Spooky Night, 1042
CARLYON, Richard
The Dark Lord of Pengersick, 1281
Carnabuci, Anthony, 2420
CARPENTER, Christopher
The Twilight Realm, 1912
CARR, Terry. *See also* ASIMOV, Isaac
Fantasy Annual V, 857
Into the Unknown: Eleven Tales of Imagination, 902
Worlds Near and Far: Nine Stories of Science Fiction, 991
Carrick, Donald, 151, 2993
CARRIS, Joan Davenport
A Ghost of a Chance, 1043
Witch-Cat, 2984
Carroll, John, 1642
CARROLL, Lewis (pseud. of Charles Ludwidge Dodgson)
Alice's Adventures in Wonderland, 1913
Through the Looking Glass and What Alice Found There, 1913
CARRYL, Charles Edward
The Admiral's Caravan, 1914
Davy and the Goblin, or What Followed Reading "Alice's Adventures in Wonderland," 1915
Carter, Abby, 2188
CARTER, Angela
The Donkey Prince, 59
Carter, Harry, 2255
CARTER, Lin
Callipygia, 1282
Dragonrouge, 1282
Kesrick, 1282
Kingdoms of Sorcery, 1408

Mandricardo: New Adventures of Terra Magica, 1282
The Year's Best Fantasy Stories, 6, 994
CARVER, Jeffrey A(llan)
Dragon Rigger, 1283
Dragons in the Stars, 1283
Star Rigger's Way, 1283
Casale, Paul, 2396, 2427
Casseau, Vera, 912
CASSEDY, Sylvia
Behind the Attic Wall, 1044
CASSERLEY, Anne Thomasine
Barney the Donkey, 440
Michael of Ireland, 816
Roseen, 441
The Whins on Knockattan, 817
Casson, Hugh, 2123
Catchpole, Diana, 2556
CATES, Emily
The Ghost Ferry, 1045
The Ghost in the Attic, 1045
The Mystery of Misty Island Inn, 1045
Cather, Carolyn, 1728
CATLING, Patrick Skene
The Chocolate Touch, 2392
John Midas in the Dreamtime, 2392
Catrow, David, 660
CAUFIELD, Don and CAUFIELD, Joan
The Incredible Detectives, 442
CAUFIELD, Joan, jt. auth. *See* CAUFIELD, Don
Cauley, Lorinda Bryan, 19, 176, 180
CAVANAGH, Helen
Panther Glade, 1634
CAYLUS, Anne Claude Phillipe, Comte de
Heart of Ice, 60
Cazet, Denys, 491
CECIL, Laura
Boo! Stories to Make You Jump, 1030
Listen to This, 919
Cellini, Joseph, 2498, 3046
CERVANTES, Saavedra Miguel de
The Adventures of Don Quixote de la Mancha, 61
Chaffin, Donald, 472
Chalk, Gary, 550
Challans, Mary. *See* RENAULT, Mary
Chalmers, Mary, 591
Chamberlain, Margaret, 2238, 2245
CHAMBERS, Aidan
Shades of Dark: Stories, 1180
CHANT, Joy (pseud. of Eileen Joyce Rutter)
The Grey Mane of Morning, 1284
The High Kings, 1635
Red Moon and Black Mountain: The End of the House of Kendreth, 1916
When Voiha Wakes, 1284, 1916
CHAPMAN, Vera
The Green Knight, 1636

Chappell, Warren, 61, 248, 1073, 2933
CHARLES, Prince of Wales
  The Old Man of Lochnagar, 2123
Charlot, Jean, 1032, 2497
CHARNAS, Suzy McKee
  The Bronze King, 2986
  The Golden Thread, 2986
  The Kingdom of Kevin Malone, 1917
  The Silver Glove, 2986
Chartier, Normand, 502
CHASE, Carol
  Hawk's Flight, 1285
CHASE, Mary (Coyle)
  Harvey, a Play, 2124
  Loretta Mason Potts, 1918
  Mrs. McThing: A Play, 2987
  The Wicked Pigeon Ladies in the Garden, 2712
Chee, Cheng-Khee, 369
CHEKHOV, Anton
  Kashtanka, 443
CHENOWETH, Russ
  Shadow Walkers, 444
Cherry, Carolyn Janice. *See* CHERRYH, C. J.
CHERRYH, C. J. (pseud. of Carolyn Janice Cherry)
  Angel with the Sword, 1286
  Chernevog, 2988
  Divine Right, 1286
  The Dreamstone, 1637
  Endgame, 1286
  Exile's Gate, 1287
  Festival Moon, 1346
  Fever Season, 1286
  The Fires of Azeroth, 1287
  Flood Tide, 1286
  Gate of Ivrel, 1287
  The Goblin Mirror, 1288
  Rusalka, 2988
  Smuggler's Gold, 1286
  The Tree of Swords and Jewels, 1637
  Troubled Waters, 1286
  Visible Light, 1287
  The Well of Shiuan, 1287
  Yvgenie, 2988
CHERRYH, C. J. (pseud. of Carolyn Janice Cherry)
  and ASIRE, Nancy
  A Dirge for Sabis, 1289
  Reap the Whirlwind, 1289
  Wizard Spawn, 1289
CHESNUTT, Charles Waddell
  Conjure Tales, 822
Chess, Victoria, 645, 3144
Chessare, Michele, 52, 1033, 1997, 2646
CHETWIN, Grace
  Child of the Air, 1290
  The Chimes of Alyafaleyn, 1291
  The Crystal Stair, 1292
  Friends in Time, 2713
  Gom on Windy Mountain: From Tales of Gom, 1292

  Out of the Dark World, 1919
  The Riddle and the Rune: From Tales of Gom in the Legends of Ulm, 1292
  The Starstone, 1292
CHEW, Ruth (Silver)
  Do-It-Yourself Magic, 1920
  Mostly Magic, 2393
  No Such Thing as a Witch, 2989
  The Would-Be Witch, 2990
Chodos-Irvine, Margaret, 600
Chorao, Kay, 252, 2933, 3012
CHRISMAN, Arthur Bowie
  Shen of the Sea: Chinese Stories for Children, 823
  The Wind That Wouldn't Blow: Stories of the Merry Middle Kingdom for Children and Myself, 824
Christelow, Eileen, 475, 627
CHRISTIAN, Catherine
  The Pendragon, 1638
CHRISTIAN, Mary Blount
  Sebastian [Super Sleuth] and the Baffling Bigfoot, 2125
  Sebastian [Super Sleuth] and the Bone to Pick Mystery, 2125
  Sebastian [Super Sleuth] and the Case of the Santa Claus Caper, 2125
  Sebastian [Super Sleuth] and the Clumsy Cowboy, 2125
  Sebastian [Super Sleuth] and the Copycat Crime, 2125
  Sebastian [Super Sleuth] and the Crummy Yummies Caper, 2125
  Sebastian [Super Sleuth] and the Egyptian Connection, 2125
  Sebastian [Super Sleuth] and the Hair of the Dog Mystery, 2125
  Sebastian [Super Sleuth] and the Impossible Crime, 2125
  Sebastian [Super Sleuth] and the Mystery Patient, 2125
  Sebastian [Super Sleuth] and the Purloined Sirloin, 2125
  Sebastian [Super Sleuth] and the Secret of the Skewered Skier, 2125
  Sebastian [Super Sleuth] and the Stars-in-His-Eyes Mystery, 2125
  Sebastian [Super Sleuth] and the Time Capsule Caper, 2125
CHRISTOPHER, John (pseud. of Christopher Samuel Youd)
  Beyond the Burning Lands, 1293
  Dragon Dance, 1921
  Fireball, 1921
  New Found Land, 1921
  The Prince in Waiting, 1293
  The Sword of the Spirits, 1293
CHRISTOPHER, Matt(hew F.)
  The Dog That Called the Signals, 2394

The Dog That Pitched a No-Hitter, 2394
The Dog That Stole Football Plays, 2394
Favor for a Ghost, 1048
The Kid Who Only Hit Homers, 2395
Return of the Home Run Kid, 2395
Skateboard Tough, 2396
CHURCH, Richard (Thomas)
    The French Lieutenant: A Ghost Story, 1049
Cingoli, Giulio, 674
Circolo, Priscilla Posey, 704
CLAPP, Patricia
    Jane-Emily, 1050
    King of the Doll House, 2397
Clark, Alan M., 1819
CLARK, Ann Nolan
    *Looking-for-Something: The Story of a Stray
        Burro of Ecuador*, 445
CLARK, Douglas W.
    Alchemy Unlimited, 2991
Clark, Emma Chichester, 320, 919, 1030
Clark, Matthew, 2432
CLARKE, J(udith)
    Teddy B. Zoot, 2901
CLARKE, Pauline (pseud. of Pauline [Clarke]
        Hunter Blair)
    Five Dolls and the Duke, 2902
    Five Dolls and the Monkey, 2902
    Five Dolls and Their Friends, 2902
    Five Dolls in a House, 2902
    Five Dolls in the Snow, 2902
    The Return of the Twelves, 2903
    The Two Faces of Silenus, 1639
Clarke, Peter, 1399
Claveloux, Nicole, 289
Claverie, Jean, 12, 355
CLAYTON, Jo
    A Bait of Dreams: A Five Summer Quest, 1294
    Changer's Moon, 1296
    The Magic Wars, 1295
    Moongather, 1296
    Moonscatter, 1296
    Shadowkill, 1297
    Shadowplay, 1297
    Shadowspeer, 1297
    Wild Magic, 1295
    Wildfire, 1295
CLEARY, Beverly (Bunn)
    The Mouse and the Motorcycle, 446
    Ralph S. Mouse, 446
    Runaway Ralph, 446
    Socks, 447
Clemens, Samuel. *See* TWAIN, Mark
CLEMENT, Aeron
    The Cold Moons, 448
CLÉMENT, Claude
    The Man Who Lit the Stars, 62
    The Voice of the Wood, 63
Clément, Frédéric, 63

CLEMENTS, Bruce
    Two Against the Tide, 1922
CLIFFORD, Eth
    Flatfoot Fox and the Case of the Missing Eye,
        449
    *Flatfoot Fox and the Case of the Missing
        Whoooo*, 449
    Flatfoot Fox and the Case of the Noisy Otter, 449
CLIFFORD, Sandy
    The Roquefort Gang, 450
CLIMO, Shirley
    T.J.'s Ghost, 1051
CLINE, Linda
    The Miracle Season, 451
Coalson, Glo, 2180
COATES, Anna
    Dog Magic, 452
COATSWORTH, Elizabeth (Jane)
    All-of-a-Sudden Susan, 2904
    The Cat and the Captain, 453
    The Cat Who Went to Heaven, 64
    Cricket and the Emperor's Son, 65
    The Enchanted: An Incredible Tale, 1640
    Knock at the Door, 1923
    Marra's World, 1641
    The Princess and the Lion, 66
    Pure Magic, 67
    Silky: An Incredible Tale, 1642
    The Snow Parlor and Other Bedtime Stories, 826
    Troll Weather, 2398
COBALT, Martin (pseud. of William Mayne)
    Pool of Swallows, 1052
Cober, Alan E., 95, 469, 1789
COBLENTZ, Catherine Cate
    The Blue Cat of Castle Town, 2399
COCHRAN, Molly, and MURPHY, Warren
    The Forever King, 1643
Cockerell, Olive, 839
COEHLO, Paulo
    *The Alchemist: A Fable About Following Your
        Dream*, 68
COHEN, Barbara
    Roses, 1644
    Unicorns in the Rain, 1645
COHEN, Daniel
    Great Ghosts, 1053
COLE, Adrian
    A Place among the Fallen, 1298
COLE, Allan, and BUNCH, Chris
    The Far Kingdoms, 1299
Cole, Babette, 2635
Cole, Brock, 2610
COLE, Joanna
    Bony-Legs, 2992
    Doctor Change, 2993
COLEMAN, Janet Wyman
    Fast Eddie, 454
Collard, Derek, 266
Collier, John, 1304

COLLINS, Meghan
  The Willow Maiden, 1646
COLLODI, Carlo (pseud. of Carlo Lorenzini)
  The Adventures of Pinocchio, 2905
COLOMA, Padre Luis
  Perez, the Mouse, 455
COLUM, Padraic
  The Big Tree of Bunlahy: Stories of My Own
    Countryside, 827
  The Boy Apprenticed to an Enchanter, 2994
  The Boy Who Knew What the Birds Said, 456
  The Fountain of Youth; Stories to Be Told, 828
  The Girl Who Sat by the Ashes, 69
  The King of Ireland's Son, 70
  The Peep-Show Man, 829
  The Stone of Victory and Other Tales, 830
  Where the Winds Never Blew and the Cocks
    Never Crew, 457
  The White Sparrow, 458
Conde, J. M., 647
CONEY, Michael Greatrex
  The Celestial Steam Locomotive, 1647
  Fang, the Gnome, 1647
  Gods of the Greatway, 1647
  King of the Scepter'd Isle, 1647
CONFORD, Ellen
  Genie with the Light Blue Hair, 2400
CONLY, Jane Leslie
  R–T, Margaret, and the Rats of NIMH, 459
  Racso and the Rats of NIMH (The Rats of NIMH
    series, book 2), 459
Conly, Robert Leslie. *See* O'BRIEN, Robert C.
Conner, Mac, 2810
Conor, Chris, 2733
Conover, Alida, 2501
Conover, Chris, 105, 3003
CONRAD, Pam
  Stonewords: A Ghost Story, 2714
CONROY, Jack, jt. auth. *See* BONTEMPS, Arna
  (Wendell)
COOK, Glen
  Ceremony, 460
  Doomstalker, 460
  Tower of Fear, 1300
  Warlock, 460
COOK, Hugh
  The Walrus and the Warwolf, 2995
  The Wizards and the Warriors, 2995
  The Women and the Warlords, 2995
  The Wordsmiths and the Warguild, 2995
COOK, Rick
  Wizard's Bane, 1924
  Wizardry Compiled, 1924
  Wizardry Cursed, 1924
COOKE, Catherine
  Mask of the Wizard, 1301
COOKE, Donald Edwin
  The Firebird, 71

Cooke, Edna, 928
COOKSON, Catherine (McMullen)
  Mrs. Flannagan's Trumpet, 1054
COOLIDGE, Olivia E(nsor)
  The King of Men, 1648
COOMBS, Patricia
  Dorrie and the Amazing Magic Elixir, 2996
  Dorrie and the Birthday Eggs, 2996
  Dorrie and the Blue Witch, 2996
  Dorrie and the Dreamyard Monsters, 2996
  Dorrie and the Fortune Teller, 2996
  Dorrie and the Goblin, 2996
  Dorrie and the Halloween Plot, 2996
  Dorrie and the Haunted House, 2996
  Dorrie and the Haunted Schoolhouse, 2996
  Dorrie and the Museum Case, 2996
  Dorrie and the Pin Witch, 2996
  Dorrie and the Screebit Ghost, 2996
  Dorrie and the Weather-Box, 2996
  Dorrie and the Witch Doctor, 2996
  Dorrie and the Witch's Imp, 2996
  Dorrie and the Witches' Camp, 2996
  Dorrie and the Witchville Fair, 2996
  Dorrie and the Wizard's Spell, 2996
  Dorrie's Magic, 2996
  Dorrie's Play, 2996
  The Lost Playground, 2906
  Molly Mullett, 72
Cooney, Barbara, 529, 604, 2929
COONTZ, Otto
  Hornswoggle Magic, 2401
  Isle of the Shape-Shifters, 1649
COOPER, Gale
  Unicorn Moon, 73
COOPER, Louise
  Avatar, 1303
  Infanta, 1303
  Inferno, 1303
  The Initiate, 1302
  The Master, 1302
  Nemesis, 1303
  Nocturne, 1303
  The Outcast, 1302
  Revenant, 1303
  The Sleep of Stone, 1304
  Troika, 1303
COOPER, Margaret
  The Ice Palace, 74
Cooper, Marion, 75
COOPER, Paul Fenimore
  Dindle, 75
  Tal: His Marvelous Adventures with Noom-Zor-
    Noom, 1925
COOPER (Grant), Susan (Mary)
  The Boggart, 2402
  The Dark Is Rising, 1650
  Greenwitch, 1650
  The Grey King, 1650

Jethro and the Jumbie, 2403
Over Sea, Under Stone, 1650
Seaward, 1926
The Selkie Girl, 1651
Silver on the Tree, 1650
Tam Lin, 1652
Copelman, Evelyn, 1898
CORBALIS, Judy
 The Ice Cream Heroes, 2126
 Porcellus, the Flying Pig, 461
CORBETT, Scott
 The Black Mask Trick, 2404
 Captain Butcher's Body, 1055
 The Disappearing Dog Trick, 2404
 The Discontented Ghost, 1056
 Dr. Merlin's Magic Shop, 2997
 Ever Ride a Dinosaur?, 2127
 The Foolish Dinosaur Fiasco, 2997
 The Great Custard Pie Panic, 2997
 The Hairy Horror Trick, 2404
 The Hateful Plateful Trick, 2404
 The Home Run Trick, 2404
 The Lemonade Trick, 2404
 The Limerick Trick, 2404
 The Mailbox Trick, 2404
 The Mysterious Zetabet, 1927
 The Turnabout Trick, 2404
CORBETT, W(illiam) J(esse)
 The Pentecost and the Chosen One, 462
 The Song of Pentecost, 462
COREN, Alan
 Arthur and the Bellybutton Diamond, 2128
 Arthur and the Great Detective, 2128
 Arthur and the Purple Panic, 2128
 Arthur the Kid, 2128
 Arthur versus the Rest, 2128
 Arthur's Last Stand, 2128
 Buffalo Arthur, 2128
 Klondike Arthur, 2128
 The Lone Arthur, 2128
 Railroad Arthur, 2128
CORRIN, Sara, and CORRIN, Stephen
 The Faber Book of Modern Fairy Tales, 853
 Imagine That! Fifteen Fantastic Tales, 901
 *Stories for Nine-Year-Olds and Other Young
  Readers*, 970
CORRIN, Stephen. *See* CORRIN, Sara
Corwin, June, 14
COSTIKYAN, Greg
 By the Sword: Magic of the Plains, 1305
Coudrille, Jonathon, 682
COUNSEL, June
 A Dragon in Class 4, 2405
COVILLE, Bruce
 The Dark Abyss, 1928
 Jennifer Murdley's Toad, 2406, 2407, 2408
 Jeremy Thatcher, Dragon Hatcher, 2406, 2407,
  2408

The Monster Ring, 2406, 2407, 2408
*The Unicorn Treasury: Stories, Poems and
 Unicorn Lore*, 975
Coville, Katherine, 2408, 2671
COWPER, Richard (pseud. of John Middleton-
 Murray)
 A Dream of Kinship, 1306
 The Road to Corlay, 1306
COX, Michael, and GILBERT, R. A.
 Victorian Ghost Stories: An Oxford Anthology,
  1201
COX, Palmer
 Another Brownie Book, 1307
 The Brownies Abroad, 1307
 The Brownies and Prince Florimel, 1307
 The Brownies around the World, 1307
 The Brownies at Home, 1307
 The Brownies in the Philippines, 1307
 The Brownies' Latest Adventure, 1307
 The Brownies Many More Nights, 1307
 The Brownies: Their Book, 1307
 The Brownies through the Union, 1307
Craft, Kinuko, 2009
Craig, Helen, 201, 258, 461, 3035
Craig, Mary Francis. *See* SHURA, Mary Francis
Craik, Dinah. *See* MULOCK, Diana
CRAMER, Kathryn, and HARTWELL, David G. *See
 also* HARTWELL, David G.
 Christmas Ghosts, 1046
Crane, Walter, 839, 2568
CREGAN, Maírín
 Old John, 463
CRESSWELL (Rowe), Helen
 Almost Goodbye, 2409
 The Beachcombers, 2410
 The Bongleweed, 2411
 A Game of Catch, 1057
 Moondial, 2715
 The Night Watchmen, 76
 The Piemakers, 2129
 The Secret World of Polly Flint, 2412
 Time Out, 2716
 Up the Pier, 2717
 The White Sea Horse, 2413
 The Winter of the Birds, 77
CRETAN, Gladys
 Joey's Head, 2130
CREW, Fleming, jt. auth. *See* GALL, Alice (Crew)
CREW, Gary
 Strange Objects, 1653
CROSS, Gilbert B.
 A Witch Across Time, 1058
CROSS, Gillian (pseud. of Claire Arnold)
 The Dark Behind the Curtain, 1059
 Twin and Super-Twin, 2414
CROSS, John Kier
 The Other Side of Green Hills, 1929
Cross, Peter, 473

CROTHERS, Samuel McChord
Miss Muffet's Christmas Party, 78
CROWLEY, Maude
Azor, 464
*Azor and the Blue-Eyed Cow: A Christmas
Story*, 464
Azor and the Haddock, 464
Tor and Azor, 464
Cruz, Ray, 3142
Cuffari, Richard, 632, 1018, 2045, 2386, 2904
CULLEN, Countee (Porter)
*The Lost Zoo (A Rhyme for the Young, but Not
Too Young) by Christopher Cat and Countee
Cullen*, 465
*My Lives and How I Lost Them, by Christopher
Cat and Countee Cullen*, 465
CULLEN, Lynn
The Backyard Ghost, 1060
CUMMINGS, e(dward) e(stlin)
Fairy Tales, 831
CUNNINGHAM, Julia (Woolfolk)
Candle Tales, 466
Come to the Edge, 79
Dorp Dead, 80
Macaroon, 467
Maybe, a Mole, 468
Oaf, 81
Tuppenny, 82
Viollet, 469
The Vision of Francois the Fox, 470
Wolf Roland, 83
CURLEY, Daniel
Ann's Spring, 1654
Billy Beg and the Bull, 1655
CURRY, Ann
The Book of Brendan, 1656
CURRY, Jane Louise
The Bassumtyte Treasure, 1061
Beneath the Hill, 1657
The Birdstones, 2718
The Change Child, 1657
The Daybreakers, 2718
Little Little Sister, 84
The Lost Farm, 2415
The Magical Cupboard, 2720
Mindy's Mysterious Miniature, 2415
Over the Sea's Edge, 2719
Parsley, Sage, Rosemary and Time, 2720
Poor Tom's Ghost, 1062
Shadow Dancers, 1308
The Sleepers, 1658
The Watchers, 2721
The Wolves of Aam, 1308
Curtis, Dora, 1985
CUTT, W(illiam) Towrie
Message from Arkmae, 2722
Seven for the Sea, 2722

CUYLER, Margery
Weird Wolf, 2131

D'Achille, Gino, 311
Dabcovich, Lydia, 859
DAHL, Roald
The BFG, 2132
Charlie and the Chocolate Factory, 2416
Charlie and the Great Glass Elevator, 2416
The Enormous Crocodile, 471
Esio Trot, 2133
Fantastic Mr. Fox, 472
George's Marvelous Medicine, 2417
James and the Giant Peach: A Children's Story,
2418
The Magic Finger, 2419
Matilda, 2134
The Minpins, 1930
*Roald Dahl's James and the Giant Peach: A
Play*, 2418
The Twits, 2135
Two Fables, 85
The Vicar of Nibbleswicke, 2136
The Witches, 2999
*The Wonderful Story of Henry Sugar and Six
More*, 832
DAHL, Tessa
Gwenda & the Animals, 2420
School Can Wait, 2137
DALBY, Richard
Ghosts for Christmas, 1088
The Mammoth Book of Ghost Stories 2, 1153
*Modern Ghost Stories by Eminent Women
Writers*, 1159
DALEY, Brian
A Tapestry of Magics, 1309
DALGLIESH, Alice
The Enchanted Book, 849
DALKEY, Kara
The Nightingale, 1659
DALLAS-SMITH, Peter
Trouble for Trumpets, 473
Trumpets in Grumpetland, 473
DALTON, Annie
Out of the Ordinary, 1931
DAMJAN, Mischa (pseud.)
December's Travels, 86
DANA, Barbara
Rutgers and the Watersnouts, 474
Zucchini, 475
Daniel, Alan, 547, 633
Daniels, Julia, 2437
Daniels, Stewart, 2358
DANK, Gloria Rand
The Forest of App, 87
DANN, Colin (Michael)
The Animals of Farthing Wood, 476

Escape from Danger, 476
In the Grip of Winter, 476
Siege of White Deer Park, 476
The Way to White Deer Park, 476
DANN, Jack
  Wandering Stars: An Anthology of Jewish
    Fantasy and Science Fiction, 979
DANN, Jack, and DOZOIS, Gardner
  Bestiary!, 796
  Magicats!, 617
  Unicorns!, 976
DARK, Larry
  The Literary Ghost: Great Contemporary Ghost
    Stories, 1134
Darke, Alison Claire, 11, 17
Darling, Louis, 446, 2115
Darwin, Beatrice, 447
DATLOW, Ellen, and WINDLING, Terri
  The Year's Best Fantasy: First Annual Collection,
    993
Daugherty, James, 543, 2205
DAVID, Peter
  Knight Life, 1660
Davidson, Andrew, 899
DAVIDSON, Lionel
  Under Plum Lake, 1932
DAVIDSON, Ronnie, jt. auth. *See* GOLDMAN,
  Kelly
DAVIES, Andrew (Wynford)
  Conrad's War, 2723
  Danger—Marmalade at Work, 2138
  Educating Marmalade, 2138
  Marmalade and Rufus, 2138
  Marmalade Atkins Hits the Big Time, 2138
  Marmalade Atkins in Space, 2138
DAVIES, Valentine
  It Happens Every Spring, 2139
  The Miracle on 34th Street, 88
Davine, 1954
Davis, Jack, 2313
Davis, Lambert, 581, 2899
DAVIS, Mary Gould
  A Baker's Dozen: Thirteen Stories to Tell and to
    Read Aloud, 793
  The Handsome Donkey, 477
  With Cap and Bells: Humorous Stories to Tell
    and to Read Aloud, 2331
DAVIS, Robert
  Padre Porko: The Gentlemanly Pig, 478
DAWSON, Carley
  Dragon's Run, 2724
  Mr. Wicker's Window, 2724
  The Sign of the Seven Seas, 2724
DAWSON, Mitchell
  The Magic Firecrackers, 2421
DAY, David
  The Emperor's Panda, 89
Day, Maurice, 102

Dean, Graham, 85
DEAN, Pamela
  Tam Lin, 1661
de Brissac, Malcolm. *See* DICKINSON, Peter
DE CAMP, Catherine Crook, jt. auth. *See* DE
  CAMP, L(yon) Sprague
DE CAMP, L(yon) Sprague
  The Clocks of Iraz, 1310
  The Golden Tower, 1310
  The Honorable Barbarian, 1310
  The Unbeheaded King, 1310
DE CAMP, L(yon) Sprague, and DE CAMP,
  Catherine Crook
  The Incorporated Knight, 1311
  The Pixilated Peeress, 1312
DE CHANCIE, John
  Castle Dreams, 3000
  Castle for Rent, 3000
  Castle Kidnapped, 3000
  Castle Murders, 3000
  Castle Perilous, 3000
  Castle War!, 3000
DE FELICE, Cynthia
  The Strange Night Writing of Jessamine Colter,
    90
DE FORD, Miriam Allen
  Elsewhere, Elsewhen, Elsehow, 848
Degen, Bruce, 185
de Groat, Diane, 2912
DE HAVEN, Tom
  The End-of-Everything Man, 1933
  The Last Human, 1933
  Walker of Worlds, 1933
DEITZ, Tom
  Darkthunder's Way, 1934
  Fireshaper's Doom, 1934
  The Gryphon King, 1662
  Sunshaker's War, 1934
  Windmaster's Bane, 1934
Delacorte, Carybé, 383
Delamare, David, 403
DE LA MARE, Walter (John)
  Animal Stories, 838
  Broomsticks and Other Tales, 833
  Crossings: A Fairy Play, 2422
  The Dutch Cheese, 834
  The Lord Fish, 835
  The Magic Jacket and Other Stories, 836
  Mr. Bumps and His Monkey, 479
  A Penny a Day, 837
  Tales Told Again, 838
  The Three Royal Monkeys, 480
  The Turnip, 838
Delaney, A., 2522
DELANEY, M. C.
  Henry's Special Delivery, 2140
DELANY, Samuel R.
  The Bridge of Lost Desire, 1313

Flight from Nevèryön, 1313
Nevèryöna, 1313
Tales of Nevèryön, 1313
de la Ramée, (Marie) Louise. *See* OUIDA
DE LARRABEITI, Michael
The Borribles, 1314
The Borribles Go for Broke, 1314
de Larrea, Victoria, 882, 883, 1034, 2196, 2488, 2676
DE LEEUW, Adele Louise
Nobody's Doll, 2907
Delessert, Etienne, 580
DE LINT, Charles
The Dreaming Place, 1935
Dreams Underfoot: The Newford Collection, 1315
Drink Down the Moon, 1663
Into the Green, 1316
Jack the Giant-Killer, 1663
The Little Country, 3001
Moonheart, 1664
Spiritwalk, 1664
Yarrow: An Autumn Tale, 1936
DELL, Joan
The Missing Boy, 1937
DEL REY, Lester, and KESSLER, Risa
Once Upon a Time: A Treasury of Modern Fairy Tales, 936
Demi, 11, 17
de Miskey, Julian, 2116
DE MORGAN, Mary (Augusta)
The Complete Fairy Tales of Mary De Morgan, 839
The Necklace of Princess Fiorimonde, 839
The Necklace of Princess Fiorimonde; and Other Stories, 840
On a Pincushion, 839
The Windfairies, 839
de Morgan, William, 839
Denison, Harold, 1612
Denslow, W. W., 1898
dePaola, Tomie, 88, 859, 2334, 2665
DE REGNIERS, Beatrice Schenk (Freedman)
The Boy, the Rat, and the Butterfly, 2423
Penny, 91
DERESKE, Jo
Glom Gloom, 1317
DERMAN, Martha
Tales from Academy Street, 2424
de Rosa, Dee, 2535
DE WEESE, (Thomas Eugene) Gene
The Adventures of a Two Minute Werewolf, 2141
DEXTER, Catherine
The Gilded Cat, 1063
Mazemaker, 2725
The Oracle Doll, 2908
Di Fiori, Lawrence, 494, 734
Di Grazia, Thomas, 15

Diamond, Donna, 171, 351, 375, 1654, 2811
DIAZ, Abby (Morton)
Polly Cologne, 2909
DICKENS, Charles (John Huffam)
A Christmas Carol, 93
The Magic Fishbone, 94
DICKINSON, Peter (pseud. of Malcolm de Brissac)
The Blue Hawk, 1318
A Box of Nothing, 1938
The Devil's Children, 1319
Giant Cold, 95
Heartsease, 1320
The Iron Lion, 96
Merlin Dreams, 1665
The Weathermonger, 1321
DICKS, Terrance
Nurse Sally Ann, 2910
Sally Ann and the Mystery Picnic, 2910
Sally Ann and the School Show, 2910
Sally Ann on Her Own, 2910
DICKSON, Gordon R(upert)
Dorsai!, 1322
The Dorsai Companion, 1322
The Dragon and the George, 1939
Dragon at War, 1939
The Dragon Knight, 1939
The Dragon on the Border, 1939
The Final Encyclopedia, 1322
The Genetic General, 1322
The Last Dream, 841
Lost Dorsai, 1322
Necromancer, 1322
No Room for Men, 1322
Soldier, Ask Not, 1322
The Spirit of Dorsai, 1322
Tactics of Mistake, 1322
Three to Dorsai!, 1322
DIGGS, Lucy
Selene Goes Home, 481
DILLON, Barbara
The Good-Guy Cake, 2425
A Mom by Magic, 2426
Mrs. Tooey and the Terrible Toxic Tar, 3002
My Stepfather Shrank!, 2427
The Teddy Bear Tree, 2911
What's Happened to Harry?, 3003
Who Needs a Bear?, 2912
Dillon, Diane, 58, 3137
Dillon, Leo, 58, 3137
DIXON, Larry, jt. auth. *See* LACKEY, Mercedes
DIXON, Marjorie (Mack)
The Forbidden Island, 1666
DOBBS, Rose
The Discontented Village, 97
No Room: An Old Story Retold, 98
Dobias, Frank, 2953
Dodge, Carlota, 2592

Dodgson, Charles Ludwidge. *See* CARROLL, Lewis
Dodson, Bert, 2138
DOLBIER, Maurice (Wyman)
    The Half-Pint Jinni, and Other Stories, 842
    A Lion in the Woods, 2142
    The Magic Shop, 2428
    Torten's Christmas Secret, 99
Domanska, Janina, 204
DONALDSON, Stephen R(upert)
    The Chronicles of Thomas Covenant, 1940
    Daughter of Regals and Other Tales, 1323
    The Illearth War, 1940
    Lord Foul's Bane, 1940
    A Man Rides Through, 1941
    The Mirror of Her Dreams, 1941
    The One Tree, 1940
    The Power That Preserves, 1940
    Strange Dreams: Unforgettable Fantasy, 971
    White Gold Wielder, 1940
    The Wounded Land, 1940
DONEHOWER, Bruce
    Miko, Little Hunter of the North, 100
DONOVAN, John
    Family: A Novel, 482
Dooling, Michael, 701
Doré, Gustave, 289, 2255
DOTY, Jean Slaughter
    Can I Get There by Candlelight?, 2726
DOUGLAS, Carole Nelson
    Cup of Clay, 1942
    Exiles of the Rynth, 3004
    Heir of Rengarth, 3004
    Keepers of Edanvant, 3004
    Seed upon the Wind, 1942
    Seven of Swords, 3004
    Six of Swords, 3004
Dowling, Victor J., 2353
DOWNER, Ann
    The Spellkey, 1324
Downing, Julie, 137, 203
DOYLE, Debra, and MacDONALD, James D.
    Knight's Wyrd, 1325
Doyle, Richard, 281
DOZOIS, Gardner. *See also* DANN, Jack
    Another World; Adventures in Otherness: A Science Fiction Anthology, 781
DRAGT, Tonke
    The Towers of February: A Diary By an Anonymous (for the Time Being) Author with Added Punctuation and Footnotes, 1943
DRAKE, David
    The Sea Hag, 1326
Drummond, V. H., 2636
DRUON, Maurice (Samuel Roger Charles)
    Tistou of the Green Thumbs, 101

DRURY, Roger W(olcott)
    The Champion of Merrimack County, 483
    The Finches Fabulous Furnace, 2143
DU BOIS, William (Sherman) Pène, 125, 222, 623, 2419, 3011, 3042
    The Alligator Case, 2144
    Call Me Bandicoot, 2145
    Elisabeth the Cow Ghost, 1065
    The Flying Locomotive, 2146
    The Forbidden Forest, 2147
    Gentleman Bear, 2913
    The Giant, 2148
    The Great Geppy, 2149
    The Horss in the Camel Suit, 2144
    Lazy Tommy Pumpkinhead, 2150
    Otto and the Magic Potatoes, 2151
    Otto at Sea, 2151
    Otto in Africa, 2151
    Otto in Texas, 2151
    Peter Graves, 2152
    The Squirrel Hotel, 2153
    The Three Policemen, or Young Bottsford of Farbe Island, 2154
    The Twenty-One Balloons, 2155
DUANE, Diane (Elizabeth)
    Deep Wizardry, 3006
    The Door into Fire, 3005
    The Door into Shadow, 3005
    The Door into Sunset, 3005
    High Wizardry, 3006
    So You Want to Be a Wizard, 3006
Duchesne, Janet, 2564
DUFFEY, Betsy
    A Boy in the Doghouse, 484
DUFFY, James
    The Christmas Gang, 485
    The Revolt of the Teddy Bears, 485
DUGGAN, Alice
    Violet's Finest Hour, 486
DUGGAN, Maurice (Noel)
    Falter Tom and the Water Boy, 1944
Duhème, Jacqueline, 101
Dulac, Edmund, 779
DUMAS, Gerald J.
    Rabbits Rafferty, 487
DUNBAR, Aldis
    Once There Was a Prince, 102
DUNCAN, Dave
    The Cutting Edge, 1327
    Faery Lands Forlorn, 1327
    Magic Casement, 1327
    The Stricken Field, 1327
    Upland Outlaws, 1327
DUNLOP, Eileen (Rhona)
    Clementina, 1667
    Elizabeth, Elizabeth, 2727
    Green Willow, 1066
    The House on Mayferry Street, 2430

The House on the Hill, 1067
The Maze Stone, 2728
The Valley of Deer, 2729
DUNSANY, Lord (pseud. of Edward John Morton
    Drax Plunkett)
    The Charwoman's Shadow, 3007
    The King of Elfland's Daughter, 1328
Duntze, Dorothée, 6, 16, 223
DURRELL, Gerald (Malcolm)
    The Fantastic Flying Journey, 2431
    The Talking Parcel, 1945
DUTTON, Sandra
    The Magic of Myrna C. Waxweather, 2432
Duvoisin, Roger, 392, 392, 1774
Dyer, Jane, 761

EAGAR, Frances
    Time Tangle, 2730
EAGER, Edward (McMaken)
    Half Magic, 2433
    Knight's Castle, 1946
    Magic by the Lake, 1946, 2433
    Magic or Not?, 2434
    Mouse Manor, 488
    Seven-Day Magic, 2435
    Time Garden, 1946, 2433
    The Well-Wishers, 2434
Eagle, Ellen, 1222
EASTON, M. Coleman
    The Fisherman's Curse, 1329
    Masters of Glass, 1329
    Spirits of Cavern and Hearth, 1330
Eaton, John, 831
Ebborn, Caroline, 182
Eckart, Chuck, 399
ECKERT, Allan W.
    The Dark Green Tunnel, 1947
    The Wand: The Return to Mesmeria, 1947
EDDINGS, David
    Aldur, 3008
    Castle of Wizardry, 3008
    Demon Lord of Karanda, 1333
    The Diamond Throne, 1331
    Domes of Fire, 1332
    Enchanter's End Game, 3008
    Guardians of the West, 1333
    The Hidden City, 1332
    King of the Murgos, 1333
    Magician's Gambit, 3008
    Pawn of Prophecy, 3008
    Queen of Sorcery, 3008
    The Ruby Knight, 1331
    The Sapphire Rose, 1331
    The Seeress of Kell, 1333
    The Shining Ones, 1331, 1332
    Sorceress of Darshiva, 1333

EDDISON, E(rik) R(ucker)
    A Fish Dinner in Memison, 1334
    The Menzian Gate, 1334
    Mistress of Mistresses, 1334
    The Worm Ouroboros, a Romance, 1334
EDGERTON, Teresa
    Child of Saturn, 3009
    The Gnome's Engine, 3010
    Goblin Moon, 3010
    The Moon in Hiding, 3009
    The Work of the Sun, 3009
EDGEWORTH, Maria
    Simple Susan and Other Tales, 847
EDMONDS, Walter D(umaux)
    Beaver Valley, 489
    Time to Go House, 490
    Uncle Ben's Whale, 2156
EDMONDSON, Madeline
    Anna Witch, 3011
    The Witch's Egg, 3012
EDWARDS, Dorothy (Brown)
    The Witches and the Grinnygog, 3013
Edwards, Gunvor, 2329, 2330
EGAN, Doris
    The Gate of Ivory, 1335
    Guilt-Edged Ivory, 1335
    Two-Bit Heroes, 1335
Egielski, Richard, 812, 2938
EGNER, Thorbjørn
    The Singing Town, 2157
EHRLICH, Amy
    Lucy's Winter Tale, 2436
Eichenberg, Fritz, 98, 478, 579, 897, 2179, 2428,
    2492, 2663
Eidrigevicius, Stasys, 277
EILERT, Bernd, jt. auth. *See* WAECHTER,
    Friedrich
Einzig, Susan, 2822
EISENBERG, Lawrence B(enjamin)
    The Villa of the Ferromonte, 2731
EISENSTEIN, Phyllis
    The Crystal Palace, 1337
    In the Red Lord's Reach, 1336
    Sorcerer's Son, 1337
Eldridge, Mildred, 480
ELDRIDGE, Roger
    The Shadow of the Gloom-World, 1338
ELGIN, (Patricia Anne) Suzette Haden
    And Then There'll Be Fireworks, 1339
    The Grand Jubilee, 1339
    Twelve Fair Kingdoms, 1339
ELIOT, Ethel (Augusta) Cook
    Buttercup Days, 2437
    The Wind Boy, 103
ELISH, Dan
    The Great Squirrel Uprising, 491
    Jason and the Baseball Bear, 492
    The Worldwide Dessert Contest, 2158

ELKIN, Benjamin
  Al and the Magic Lamp, 2438
Ellerman, Annie Winifred. *See* BRYHER, Winifred
Elson, Susan, 2351
EMBRY, Margaret (Jacob)
  The Blue-Nosed Witch, 3014
EMERSON, Ru, jt. auth. *See* LACKEY, Mercedes
  The Craft of Light, 1948
  Night Threads: The Calling of the Three, 1948
  One Land, One Duke, 1948
  The Two in Hiding, 1948
EMSHWILLER, Carol
  Carmen Dog, 493
ENDE, Michael
  Momo, 1341
  The Neverending Story, 1949
  *The Night of Wishes, or The Satanarcheolide-
    alcohellish Notion Potion*, 2159
ENGH, M(ary) J(ane)
  The House in the Snow, 1342
Enik, Ted, 667
ENRIGHT, Elizabeth (Wright)
  Tatsinda, 104
  Zeee, 2439
Ensley, Evangeline. *See* WALTON, Evangeline
Erhard, Walter, 2896
ERICKSON, Russell E(verett)
  A Toad for Tuesday, 494
  Warton and Morton, 494
  Warton and the Castaways, 494
  Warton and the Contest, 494
  Warton and the King of the Skies, 494
  Warton and the Traders, 494
  Warton's Christmas Eve Adventure, 494
ERSHOV, Petr Pavlovich
  The Little Hump-backed Horse: A Russian Tale,
    105
ERWIN, Betty K.
  Aggie, Maggie, and Tish, 2440
  Where's Aggie?, 2440
  Who Is Victoria?, 1068
ESSEX, Rosamund (Sibyl)
  Into the Forest, 106
Essley, Roger, 38
ESTERN, Anne Graham
  The Picolinis and the Haunted House, 2914
ESTES, Eleanor (Ruth Rosenfeld)
  The Curious Adventures of Jimmy McGee, 3015
  Miranda the Great, 495
  The Sleeping Giant and Other Stories, 851
  The Witch Family, 3015
ESTES, Rose
  Brother to the Lion, 1950
  The Name of the Game, 1950
  Spirit of the Hawk, 1950
ESTEY, Dale
  A Lost Tale, 1668

EUBANK, Judith
  Crossover, 2732
EUSTIS, Helen
  Mr. Death and the Redheaded Woman, 2160
EVANS, Sanford
  Naomi's Geese, 496
EVARTS, Hal G
  Jay-Jay and the Peking Monster, 2161
Everen, Jay Van, 2571
Ewell, Peter, 2716
Ewing, Carolyn, 2489
EWING, Juliana (Horatia Gatty)
  The Brownies, 2441
  The Brownies and Other Stories, 852
EZO (pseud.)
  Avril, 497
  My Son-in-Law, the Hippopotamus, 2162

FAIRSTAR, Mrs. (pseud. of Richard Henry Horne)
  Memoirs of a London Doll, Written by Herself,
    2915
FALKBERGET, Johan (Petter)
  Broomstick and Snowflake, 107
FANCIULLI, Guiseppe
  The Little Blue Man, 2916
FARALLA, Dana
  The Singing Cupboard, 2442
  The Wonderful Flying-Go-Round, 2443
FARBER, Norma (Holzman)
  Six Impossible Things Before Breakfast, 859
FARJEON, Eleanor
  The Glass Slipper, 1669
  Italian Peepshow and Other Tales, 860
  Jim at the Corner, 861
  *The Little Bookroom: Eleanor Farjeon's Short
    Stories for Children, Chosen by Herself*, 862
  Martin Pippin in the Apple Orchard, 108
  Martin Pippin in the Daisy Field, 108
  Mr. Garden, 2444
  The Old Nurse's Stocking Basket, 863
  One Foot in Fairyland: Sixteen Tales, 864
  The Silver Curlew, 1670
FARJEON, Eleanor, and MAYNE, William
  A Cavalcade of Queens, 821
Farley, Rick, 1834
FARMER (Mockridge), Penelope
  A Castle of Bone, 1671
  Charlotte Sometimes, 2733
  Emma in Winter, 2734
  Eve: Her Story, 1672
  The Magic Stone, 2445
  The Summer Birds, 2446
  Thicker Than Water, 1069
  William and Mary: A Story, 1951
  Year King, 1673
Farmer, Peter, 2727

FARMER, Philip Jose, jt. auth. *See* ANTHONY,
Piers
FARTHING, Alison
The Mystical Beast, 1952
FAST, Howard (Melvin)
*The General Zapped an Angel: New Stories of
Fantasy and Science Fiction*, 865
*A Touch of Infinity: Thirteen New Stories of
Fantasy and Science Fiction*, 866
Faulcon, Robert. *See* HOLDSTOCK, Robert (P.)
FAULKNER, William (Cuthbert)
The Wishing Tree, 2447
Fava, Rita, 134
FAWCETT, Bill. *See* STASHEFF, Christopher
Fax, Elton, 2468
FEAGLES, Anita MacRae
Casey, the Utterly Impossible Horse, 498
Feiffer, Jules, 1992
FEIL, Hila
Blue Moon, 1070
FEIST, Raymond E.
A Darkness at Sethanon, 1344
The King's Buccaneer, 1344
Magician, 1344
Prince of the Blood, 1344
Silverthorn, 1344
FEIST, Raymond E., and WURTS, Janny
Daughter of the Empire, 1345
Mistress of the Empire, 1345
Servant of the Empire, 1345
Felton, Ronald Oliver. *See* WELCH, Ronald
Felts, Shirley, 727, 2412
FENNER, Phyllis Reid
*Princesses and Peasant Boys: Tales of
Enchantment*, 948
FENTON, Edward
The Nine Questions, 109
FENWICK, Elizabeth
Cockleberry Castle, 110
Fetz, Ingrid, 67, 2554
FEYDY, Anne (Lindbergh Sapieyevski)
Osprey Island, 2448
FIELD, Rachel (Lyman), 40
Eliza and the Elves, 1953
Hitty, Her First Hundred Years, 2917
Little Dog Toby, 499
*The Magic Pawnshop; a New Year's Eve
Fantasy*, 2449
FIENBERG, Anna
The Magnificent Nose and Other Marvels, 2450
Wiggy and Boa, 2163
FINCH, Sheila
Infinity's Web, 1347
FINE, Anne
The Chicken Gave It to Me, 500
Finlay, Virgil, 2022
FINNEY, Charles G(randison)
The Circus of Dr. Lao, 1674

FINNEY, Jack (pseud. of Walter Branden Finney)
About Time: Twelve Stories, 2735
Marion's Wall: A Novel, 1071
Time and Again, 2736
Finney, Walter Branden. *See* FINNEY, Jack
Fiorentino, Al, 2223
FIRMIN, Peter, 255, 572, jt. auth. *See* POSTGATE,
Oliver
FISCHER, Marjorie
Red Feather, 1954
Fisher, Cynthia, 500
Fisher, Dorothea Frances (Canfield). *See*
CANFIELD, Dorothy
FISHER, Leonard Everett, 1724
*Noonan: A Novel about Baseball, ESP, and Time
Warps*, 2737
FISHER, Paul R.
The Ash Staff, 1348
The Hawks of Fellheath, 1348
Mont Cant Gold, 1349
The Princess and the Thorn, 1348
FISK, Pauline
Midnight Blue, 1955
Fitschen, Marilyn, 2973
Fitzhardinge, Margaret. *See* PHIPSON, Joan
Fix, Philippe, 886
FLACK, Marjorie
Walter the Lazy Mouse, 501
FLECKER, (Herman) James Elroy
The King of Alsander, 1956
FLEISCHMAN, Paul (Taylor)
The Birthday Tree, 111
Coming-and-Going Men: Four Tales, 112
Finzel the Farsighted, 2164
Graven Images: Three Stories, 1072
The Half-a-Moon Inn, 3016
FLEISCHMAN, (Albert) Sid(ney)
By the Great Horn Spoon, 2165
Chancy and the Grand Rascal, 2166
The Ghost in the Noonday Sun, 1073
The Ghost on Saturday Night, 2167
Here Comes McBroom! Three More Tall Tales,
2171
The Hey Hey Man, 113
Humbug Mountain, 2168
Jim Bridger's Alarm Clock, and Other Tall Tales,
2169
Jingo Django, 2170
McBroom and the Beanstalk, 2171
McBroom and the Big Wind, 2171
McBroom and the Great Race, 2171
McBroom Tells a Lie, 2171
McBroom Tells the Truth, 2171
McBroom the Rainmaker, 2171
McBroom's Almanac, 2171
McBroom's Ear, 2171
McBroom's Ghost, 2171
*McBroom's Wonderful One-Acre Farm: Three
Tall Tales*, 2171

McBroom's Zoo, 2171
Me and the Man on the Moon-Eyed Horse, 2172
The Midnight Horse, 1074
Mister Mysterious and Company, 2173
The Whipping Boy, 1350
FLEMING, Ian (Lancaster)
Chitty-Chitty Bang Bang: The Magical Car, 2174
FLETCHER, Susan
Dragon's Milk, 1351
Flight of the Dragon Kyn, 1352
FLINT, Kenneth C.
Challenge of the Clans, 1676
Champion of the Sidhe, 1677
Cromm, 1675
The Dark Druid, 1676
Master of the Sidhe, 1677
The Riders of the Sidhe, 1677
The Storm Shield, 1676
Floethe, Richard, 126, 969, 2466
FLORA, James (Royer), 683
Grandpa's Ghost Stories, 1075
Grandpa's Witched-Up Christmas, 1075
Wanda and the Bumbly Wizard, 3017
FLORY, Jane Trescott
The Lost and Found Princess, 114
Floyd, Gareth, 76, 1658, 1752, 2717
Flynn, Barbara, 432
FLYNN, Casey
Most Ancient Song, 1678
FOLLETT, Barbara Newhall
The House Without Windows and Eepersip's Life There, 115
FOOTE, Timothy (Gilson)
The Great Ringtail Garbage Caper, 502
Forberg, Ati, 1057, 1825
FORBUS, Ina B(ell)
The Magic Pin, 2451
Ford, H. J., 1901
FORD, John M.
The Dragon Waiting: A Masque of History, 1353
FORD, Richard
Quest for the Faradawn, 503
Foreman, Michael, 93, 163, 179, 357, 385, 580, 779, 1631, 2208, 2209, 2210
FORESTER, C(ecil) S(cott)
Poo Poo and the Dragons, 2175
FORREST, Elizabeth
Phoenix Fire, 1679
FORST, S.
Pipkin, 116
FORT, John
June the Tiger, 504
Fortnum, Peggy, 422, 984
FOSBURGH, Liza
Bella Arabella, 2452
FOSTER, Alan Dean, and GREENBERG, Martin H.
Smart Dragons, Foolish Elves, 2307

FOSTER, Elizabeth
Gigi in America: Further Adventures of a Merry-Go-Round Horse, 2918
Gigi: The Story of a Merry-Go-Round Horse, 2918
FOSTER, John T(homas)
Marco and the Tiger, 2176
FOSTER, Malcolm (Burton)
The Prince with a Hundred Dragons, 117
FOX, Denise P.
Through Tempest Trails, 505
FOX (Greenberg), Paula
Dear Prosper, 506
The Little Swineherd and Other Tales, 868
Fox-Davies, Sarah, 753
Frampton, David, 580, 1767
FRANCE, Anatole (pseud. of Jacques Anatole François Thibault)
Bee, the Princess of the Dwarfs, 1957
Frank, Mary, 1640
FRANKO, Ivan, and MELNYK, Bohdan
Fox Mykyta, 507
Frascino, Edward, 10, 745
Fraser, Betty, 2091
FRAZIER, Neta Lohnes
The Magic Ring, 2453
Freas, Frank Kelly, 1357
FREDDI, Cris
Pork, and Other Stories, 508
FREEMAN, Barbara C(onstance)
Broom-Adelaide, 118
A Haunting Air, 1076
The Other Face, 2738
A Pocket of Silence, 1077
Freeman, Don, 329
Freeman, Margaret, 914
Freeman, T. R., 2864
FREMLIN, Robert
Three Friends, 509
FRENCH, Fiona, 358
The Magic Vase, 119
Frenck, Hal, 2914
FRESCHET, Bernice (Louise Speck)
Bernard and the Catnip Caper, 510
Bernard of Scotland Yard, 510
Bernard Sees the World, 510
Freschet, Gina, 510
Freud, Tom, 1902
FRIEDMAN, C. S.
Black Sun Rising, 1354
When True Night Falls, 1354
Friedman, Marvin, 2117
FRIEDMAN, Mel. *See also* WEISS, Ellen
FRIEDMAN, Michael Jan
The Glove of Maiden's Hair, 1680
The Hammer and the Horn, 1680
The Seekers and the Sword, 1680
FRIESNER, Esther M., *See also* WATT-EVANS, Lawrence

Demon Blues, 2178
Druid's Blood, 1355
Elf Defense, 2177
Gnome Man's Land, 1958
Harpy High, 1958
Here be Demons, 2178
Hooray for Hellywood, 2178
Majyk by Accident, 3018
Mustapha and His Wise Dog, 1356
Spells of Mortal Weaving, 1356
Unicorn U, 1958
Wishing Season, 1357
Yesterday We Saw Mermaids, 1681
FRITZ, Jean (Guttery)
Magic to Burn, 2454
Fritz, Ronald, 2141
Frolich, Lorenz, 779
FROMAN, Elizabeth Hult
Eba, the Absent-Minded Witch, 3019
FROST, Frances
Then Came Timothy, 2455
Froud, Brian, 1935, 2041
FRY, Rosalie K(ingsmill), 175
The Mountain Door, 1959
Mungo, 2456
The Secret of the Ron Mor Skerry, 1682
The Wind Call, 511
FURLONG, Monica (Navis)
Juniper, 3020
Wise Child, 3020
Furukawa, Mel, 2361
FYLEMAN, Rose (Amy)
The Dolls' House, 2919
Forty Good-Morning Tales, 869
Forty Good-Night Tales, 869
Tea Time Tales, 870

GABALDON, Diana
A Dragonfly in Amber, 2739
Outlander: A Novel, 2739
Voyager, 2739
Gaber, Susan, 2439
GABHART, Ann
The Gifting, 3021
GACKENBACH, Dick
Beauty, Brave and Beautiful, 512
GAGE, Wilson (pseud. of Mary Q[uintard] Govan
    Steele)
The Ghost of Five Owl Farm, 1079
Miss Osborne-the-Mop, 2457
Gal, Laszlo, 260, 1646
Galdone, Paul, 15, 53, 659, 722, 723, 1079, 2289,
    2404, 2457
GALE, David
*Don't Give Up the Ghost: The Delacorte Book of
    Original Ghost Stories*, 1064

GALL, Alice (Crew), and CREW, Fleming
The Royal Mimkin, 1960
GALLICO, Paul (William)
The Abandoned, 513
The House That Wouldn't Go Away, 2458
The Snow Goose, 120
Gamble, Kim, 2450
Gammell, Stephen, 128, 212, 762, 900, 1389, 1611
GANGLOFF, Deborah
Albert and Victoria, 514
GANNETT (Kahn), Ruth Stiles
The Dragons of Blueland, 2459
Elmer and the Dragon, 2459
My Father's Dragon, 2459
The Wonderful House-Boat-Train, 2179
Gannett, Ruth Chrisman, 2459, 2886
GARD, Joyce (pseud. of Joyce Reeves)
The Mermaid's Daughter, 3022
Talargain, 1683
GARDAM, Jane (Pearson)
Through the Dolls' House Door, 2920
GARDEN, Nancy
The Door Between, 1684
Fours Crossing, 1684
Watersmeet, 1684
GARDINER, Judith, jt. auth. *See* WHITELAW,
    Stella
GARDNER, Craig Shaw
A Bad Day for Ali Baba, 1685
A Difficulty with Dwarves, 3023
A Disagreement with Death, 3023
An Excess of Enchantment, 3023
The Last Arabian Night, 1685
The Other Sinbad, 1685
GARDNER, John (Champlin) (Jr.)
Dragon, Dragon, and Other Timeless Tales, 871
Grendel, 1686
In the Suicide Mountains, 1358
GARFIELD, Leon
The Empty Sleeve, 1080
The Ghost Downstairs, 1081
Mister Corbett's Ghost, 1082
The Restless Ghost: Three Stories, 1083
The Wedding Ghost, 1687
GARFIELD, Leon, and BLISHEN, Edward
The God Beneath the Sea, 1688
*The Golden Shadows: A Recreation of Greek
    Legends*, 1689
Garland, Michael, 1724
Garland, Roger, 332, 333
GARNER, Alan
Alan Garner's Fairytales of Gold, 872
A Cavalcade of Goblins, 820
Elidor, 1961
The Moon of Gomrath, 1691
Once Upon a Time, 873
The Owl Service, 1690

The Red Shift, 2740
The Weirdstone of Brisingamen, 1691
GARNETT, David
Two by Two: A Story of Survival, 1692
GARRETT, Randall
Lord Darcy Investigates, 1359
Murder and Magic, 1359
Ten Little Wizards, 1359
Too Many Magicians, 1359
GASCOIGNE, Toss, GOODMAN, Jo, and
TYRELL, Margot
*Dream Time: New Stories by Sixteen
Award Winning Authors*, 846
GATE, Ethel May
The Fortunate Days, 874
Tales from the Enchanted Isles, 875
Tales from the Secret Kingdom, 876
GATES, Doris
The Cat and Mrs. Cary, 515
GATES, Susan P.
The Burnhope Wheel, 1084
GATHORNE-HARDY, Jonathan
The Airship Ladyship Adventure, 2180
Jane's Adventures In and Out of the Book, 2180
Operation Peeg, 2180
Gaul, Randy, 112
GAUNT, Michael (pseud. of [James] Dennis
Robertshaw)
Brim Sails Out, 516
Brim's Boat, 516
Brim's Valley, 516
GAUTIER, (Louise) Judith
The Memoirs of a White Elephant, 517
Gay, Zhenya, 679
Gayler, Winnie, 3106
Gaze, Gillian, 3126
GEAR, Kathleen O'Neal, jt. auth. *See* GEAR, W.
Michael
GEAR, W. Michael, and GEAR, Kathleen O'Neal
People of the Earth, 1693
People of the Fire, 1693
People of the River, 1693
People of the Wolf, 1693
GEE, Maurice (Gough)
The Halfmen of O, 1962
The World Around the Corner, 1963
Geer, Charles, 2593
Geisel, Theodor Seuss. *See* SEUSS, Dr.
Gekiere, Madeleine, 2987
Geldart, William, 159, 318, 2609
GEMMELL, David
Dark Prince, 1694
Lion of Macedon, 1694
GENTLE, Mary
The Architecture of Desire, 1360
A Hawk in Silver, 1964
Rats and Gargoyles, 1360

GERRARD, Roy
Sir Cedric, 2181
Sir Cedric Rides Again, 2181
GERROLD, David
The Man Who Folded Himself, 2741
GERSTEIN, Mordicai (adapt.)
The Seal Mother, 1695
Getz, Arthur, 673
GIBSON, Katharine
Cinders, 121
Jock's Castle, 122
Gider, Iskender, 680
GIFALDI, David
The Boy Who Spoke Colors, 123
Gregory, Maw and the Mean One, 2182
Gilbert, John, 324
GILBERT, R. A. *See* COX, Michael
Gili, Phillida, 2430
Gill, Margery, 283, 1019, 1021, 1650, 2368, 2689,
2690
Gillespie, Jessie, 354
GILLILAND, Alexis A(rnaldus)
Lord of the Troll-Bats, 3024
The Shadow Shaia, 3024
Wizenbeak, 3024
Gillman, Alec, 454
GILLULY, Sheila
Greenbriar Queen, 1361
GILMAN (Butters), Dorothy
The Maze in the Heart of the Castle, 1965
GILMORE, Kate
Enter Three Witches, 3025
Gilmour, J. L., 261
GINSBURG, Mirra
*The Air of Mars; and Other Stories of Time and
Space*, 776
Giventer, Abbi, 2481
Glanzman, Louis, 2230
Glass, Andrew, 698, 983, 1042, 1072, 2182, 2582,
2826, 2978, 3073
Glass, Marvin, 1190
Glasser, Judy, 2261, 2642
Glienke, Amelie, 2308
GLOSS, Molly
Outside the Gates, 1362
Gnoli, Domenico, 906
Gobbato, Imero, 69, 891, 1403, 1657
GODDEN (Dixon), (Margaret) Rumer
Candy Floss, 2921
The Dolls' House, 2922
The Dragon of Og, 124
The Fairy Doll, 2923
Four Dolls, 2924
Fu-Dog, 2925
Home Is the Sailor, 2926
Impunity Jane: The Story of a Pocket Doll, 2927
Little Plum, 2928
Miss Happiness and Miss Flower, 2928

Mouse House, 518
The Mousewife, 125
The Story of Holly and Ivy, 2929
Take Three Tenses; A Fugue in Time, 1089
GODWIN, Parke
Beloved Exile, 1696
Firelord, 1696
The Last Rainbow, 1696
Robin and the King, 1697
Sherwood, 1697
Goffe, Toni, 736
GOGOL, Nikolai
The Nose, 2183
GOLDIN, Stephen
Crystals of Air and Water, 1363
Shrine of the Desert Mage, 1363
The Storyteller and the Jann, 1363
GOLDMAN, Kelly and DAVIDSON, Ronnie
Sherlick Hound and the Valentine Mystery, 519
GOLDMAN, William W.
*The Princess Bride: S. Morgenstern's Classic
Tale of True Love and High Adventure*, 1364
GOLDS, Cassandra
Michael and the Secret War, 1966
GOLDSTEIN, Lisa
The Dream Years, 2742
The Red Magician, 3026
Strange Devices of the Sun and Moon, 1698
Goldstein, Nathan, 1320
Goodall, J. S., 2577, 2806
Goode, Diane, 139, 244, 1791, 1896, 2905
GOODMAN, Jo. *See also* GASCOIGNE, Toss
GOODWIN, Harold Leland, 74
Magic Number, 520
GOODWIN, Marie D.
Where the Towers Pierce the Sky, 2743
GOODWIN, Murray
Alonzo and the Army of Ants, 521
Googendijk, Wouter, 801
GORDON, John (William)
The Burning Baby and Other Ghosts, 1090
The Edge of the World, 1967
The Ghost on the Hill, 1091
The Giant under the Snow: A Story of Suspense,
1699
The House on the Brink: A Story of Suspense,
1700
Gordon, Margaret, 412
Gordon, Patricia. *See* HOWARD, Joan
Gorey, Edward, 1026, 2191
GORMLEY, Beatrice
Best Friend Insurance, 2460
Fifth Grade Magic, 2461
The Ghastly Glasses, 2462
Mail-Order Wings, 2462
More Fifth Grade Magic, 2461
Paul's Volcano, 2463

GOROG, Judith
*In a Messy, Messy Room, and Other Strange
Stories*, 877
No Swimming in Dark Pond, 878
*No Swimming in Dark Pond: And Other Chilling
Tales*, 1092
On Meeting Witches at Wells, 1093
Please Do Not Touch, 1094
A Taste for Quiet, 878
A Taste for Quiet, and Other Disquieting Tales,
1095
*Three Dreams and a Nightmare, and Other Tales
of the Dark*, 878
Winning Scheherazad, 1701
GOUDGE, Elizabeth (de Beauchamp)
Linnets and Valerians, 2464
The Little White Horse, 2465
Smoky-House, 2466
The Valley of Song, 126
Gough, Philip, 779, 945
GOULART, Ron(ald Joseph)
*The Chameleon Corps and Other Shape
Changers*, 1365
Flux, 1365
The Prisoner of Blackwood Castle, 1366
Spacehawk Inc., 1365
The Sword Swallower, 1365
A Whiff of Madness, 1365
GOULD, Joan
Otherborn, 1968
Gould, Robert, 1928, 2844
GRAHAME, Kenneth
Bertie's Escapade, 522
Dream Days, 879
The Golden Age, 879
Mole's Christmas, or, Home Sweet Home, 523
The Open Road, 523
The Reluctant Dragon, 127
The River Bank, 523
Toad of Toad Hall, 523
Wayfarers All, 523
The Wind in the Willows, 523
Grahame-Johnstone, Anne, 701
Grahame-Johnstone, Janet, 701
Grant, Leigh, 2980
GRAVES, Robert
The Big Green Book, 2467
GRAY, Genevieve S(tuck)
Ghost Story, 1096
The Seven Wishes of Joanna Peabody, 2468
GRAY, Nicholas Stuart
The Apple Stone, 2469
Grimbold's Other World, 1969
*Mainly in Moonlight: Ten Stories of Sorcery and
the Supernatural*, 880
A Wind from Nowhere, 881
Gray, Reg, 2697

GREAVES, Margaret
  Cat's Magic, 2744
  The Dagger and the Bird: A Story of Suspense,
    1970
  A Net to Catch the Wind, 128
GREELEY, Andrew M(oran)
  The Magic Cup: An Irish Legend, 1702
GREEN, Kathleen
  Leprechaun Tales, 882
  Philip and the Pooka and Other Irish Fairy Tales,
    883
GREEN, Phyllis
  Eating Ice Cream with a Werewolf, 2470
GREEN, Roger J(ames)
  The Devil Finds Work, 1703
  The Fear of Samuel Walton, 1703
  The Lengthening Shadow, 1703
  They Watched Him Die, 1703
GREEN, Roger (Gilbert) Lancelyn
  A Cavalcade of Dragons, 819
  A Cavalcade of Magicians, 2985
  Modern Fairy Stories, 927
Green, Sheila. *See* GREENWALD, Sheila
GREEN, Simon
  Blue Moon Rising, 1367
GREEN, Susan
  Self-Portrait with Wings, 2471
GREENBURG, Dan
  Young Santa, 2184
GREENBERG, Martin H. *See also* ASIMOV,
    Isaac; FOSTER, Alan Dean; GREENBERG,
    Rosalind M.; NORTON, André;
    SILVERBERG, Robert; WAUGH, Charles G.;
    YOLEN, Jane
  After the King: Stories in Honor of J. R. R.
    Tolkien, 764
GREENBERG, Rosalind M., and GREENBERG,
    Martin H.
  Dragon Fantastic, 844
GREENE, Jacqueline Dembar
  The Leveller, 1704
GREENO, Gayle
  Finders-Seekers, 1368
  Mind-Speaker's Call, 1368
GREENWALD, Sheila (pseud. of Sheila Green),
    1937, 3071
  The Secret Museum, 2930
Greer, Bill, 2708
GREER, Gerry, and RUDDICK, Bob
  Max and Me and the Time Machine, 2745
  Max and Me and the Wild West, 2745
Greger, Shana C., 123
GREGORIAN, Joyce Ballou
  The Broken Citadel, 1971
  Castledown, 1971
  The Great Wheeler, 1971

GREGORY, Philippa
  Florizella and the Wolves, 129
  The Wise Woman, 3027
GREGORY, Valiska
  Through the Mickle Woods, 130
Gretzer, John, 1484, 1715
Gribbon, William Lancaster. *See* MUNDY, Talbot
GRIFFIN, P. M., jt. auth. *See* NORTON, André
GRIFFIN, Peni R(ae)
  A Dig in Time, 2746
  Hobkin, 2472
  Otto from Otherwhere, 2473
  Switching Well, 2747
GRIFFITH, Helen V(irginia)
  Caitlin's Holiday, 2931
  Doll Trouble, 2931
  Emily and the Enchanted Frog, 2474
GRIMBLE, Rosemary
  Jonothon and Large, 2475
Grimm, Cherry Barbara Lockett. *See* WILDER,
    Cherry
GRIMSHAW, Nigel (Gilroy)
  Bluntstone and the Wildkeepers, 1369
  The Wildkeepers' Guest, 1369
GRIPARI, Pierre
  Tales of the Rue Broca, 884
Gripe, Harold, 1370, 1972, 3028
GRIPE, Maria (Kristina)
  Agnes Cecilia, 1097
  The Glassblower's Children, 3028
  In the Time of the Bells, 1370
  The Land Beyond, 1972
Gropper, William, 2156
GROSSER, Morton
  The Snake Horn, 2748
Grossman, Nancy, 3076
Grosvenor, Thelma Cudlipp, 869
Groth, John, 93
GUARD, David
  Deirdre: A Celtic Legend, 1705
GUILLOT, René
  Great Land of the Elephant, 131
  Master of the Elephants, 131
  Nicolette and the Mill, 2476
  The Three Hundred Ninety-seventh White
    Elephant, 131
Guitar, Jeremy, 526
GURNEY, James
  Dinotopia: A Land Apart from Time, 1973
Gurney, John Steven, 2158
Gustafson, Scott, 1896
GUY, Rosa (Cuthbert)
  My Love, My Love, or, the Peasant Girl, 1706
Gwyneth A. Jones. *See* HALAM, Ann

HAAS, Dorothy F. (Dee Francis)
  The Bears Up Stairs, 524

Haas, Irene, 34, 104, 2439
HACKETT, Walter Anthony
  The Swans of Ballycastle, 132
Hader, Berta, 2567
Hader, Elmer, 2567
Haeffele, Deborah, 700
Hague, Michael, 10, 127, 143, 233, 433, 523, 779, 984, 996, 1556, 1896, 1898, 1913, 2007, 2296, 2587, 2893
Hahn, Deborah, 16
HAHN, Harriet
  James, Fabulous Feline: Further Adventures of a Connoisseur Cat, 525
  James, the Connoisseur Cat, 525
HAHN, Mary Downing
  The Doll in the Garden: A Ghost Story, 2749
  The Time of the Witch, 3029
  Wait Till Helen Comes: A Ghost Story, 1098
HAINING, Peter
  The Ghost's Companion: A Haunting Anthology, 1087
HALAM, Ann (pseud. of Gwyneth A. Jones)
  The Daymaker, 1371
  Transformations, 1371
Halas, John, 642
HALDANE, J(ohn) B(urdon) S(anderson)
  My Friend Mr. Leakey, 3030
HALDEMAN, Linda (Wilson)
  Esbae: A Winter's Tale, 1707
  The Lastborn of Elvinwood, 1708
HALE, F. J.
  In the Sea Nymph's Lair, 3031
  Ogre Castle, 3031
HALE, Lucretia P(eabody)
  The Complete Peterkin Papers, 2185
  The Lady Who Put Salt in Her Coffee, 2185
HALEY, Gail E(inhart)
  Sea Tale, 133
HALL, Lynn
  Dagmar Schultz and the Angel Edna, 2186
  Dagmar Schultz and the Green-Eyed Monster, 2186
  Dagmar Schultz and the Powers of Darkness, 2186
  The Mystery of the Caramel Cat, 1099
Hall, Robin, 2783
Hallock, Robert, 103
HALLOWELL, Priscilla
  The Long-Nosed Princess: A Fairy Tale, 134
Halperin, Wendy Anderson, 1438
HAMBLY, Barbara
  The Armies of Daylight, 1975
  The Dark Hand of Magic, 1372
  Dog Wizard, 1974
  Dragonsbane, 3032
  The Ladies of Mandrigyn, 1372
  Search the Seven Hills, 1974
  The Silent Tower, 1974

The Silicon Mage, 1974
  Stranger at the Wedding, 1974
  The Time of the Dark, 1975
  The Unschooled Wizard, 1372
  The Walls of Air, 1975
  The Witches of Wenshar, 1372
HAMILTON (Adoff), Virginia (Esther)
  The All Jahdu Storybook, 2187
  Jahdu, 2187
  The Magical Adventures of Pretty Pearl, 1709
  Sweet Whispers, Brother Rush, 1100
  Time-Ago Lost: More Tales of Jahdu, 2187
  The Time-Ago Tales of Jahdu, 2187
HAMILTON, Carol
  The Dawn Seekers, 526
HAMLETT, Christina
  The Enchanter, 1710
HAMLEY, Dennis
  Blood Line, 2477
  Hare's Choice, 527
  Pageants of Despair, 2750
HANCOCK, Neil (Anderson)
  Dragon Winter, 528
  The Fires of Windameir, 528
HANLEY, Eve
  The Enchanted Toby Jug, 2478
HANLON, Emily
  Circle Home, 2751
HANSEN, Ron
  The Shadowmaker, 2479
Hanson, Peter E., 2545
HARDING, Lee
  Misplaced Persons, 1976
HARDY, Lyndon
  Master of the Five Magics, 3033
  Secret of the Sixth Magic, 3033
HARPER, Tara K.
  Shadow Leader, 1373
  Storm Runner, 1373
  Wolfwalker, 1373
HARPER, Wilhelmina
  The Lonely Little Pig and Other Animal Tales, 611
HARRIS, Christie (Lucy Irwin)
  Secret in the Stlalakum Wild, 1101
HARRIS, Deborah. *See also* KURTZ, Katherine
  The Burning Stone, 3034
  The Gauntlet of Malice, 3034
  Spiral of Fire, 3034
HARRIS, Dorothy Joan
  The House Mouse, 529
  The School Mouse, 529
HARRIS, Geraldine (Rachel)
  The Children of the Wind, 1374
  The Dead Kingdom, 1374
  Prince of the Godborn, 1374
  The Seventh Gate, 1374

HARRIS, Rosemary (Jeanne)
   The Bright and Morning Star, 1711
   The Moon in the Cloud, 1711
   Sea Magic and Other Stories of Enchantment,
    885
   The Seal-Singing, 1712
   The Shadow on the Sun, 1711
HARRISON, David Lee
   The Book of Giant Stories, 886
HARRISON, Harry
   The Hammer and the Cross, 1375
HARRISON, M(ichael) John
   The Floating Gods, 1376
   The Pastel City, 1376
   A Storm of Wings, 1376
   Virconium Nights, 1376
HARTWELL, David G. *See also* CRAMER,
   Kathryn
   Christmas Forever, 825
HARTWELL, David G., and CRAMER, Kathryn
   Masterpieces of Fantasy and Enchantment, 925
Harvard, Stephen, 564
HARVEY, Dean
   The Secret Elephant of Harlan Kooter, 2480
HARVEY, Jayne
   Great-Uncle Dracula, 2188
   Great-Uncle Dracula and the Dirty Rat, 2188
HASELEY, Dennis
   Doctor Gravity, 2189
   Ghost Catcher, 1102
HASS, E. A.
   Incognito Mosquito Flies Again, 530
   Incognito Mosquito, Private Insective, 530
   Incognito Mosquito Takes to the Air, 530
Hasselriis, Else, 823, 824
HASTINGS, Selina
   Sir Gawain and the Green Knight, 1713
   Sir Gawain and the Loathly Lady, 1713
HATCH, Richard Warren
   The Lobster Books, 531
HAUFF, Wilhelm
   The Adventures of Little Mouk, 135
   The Caravan, 887
   Dwarf Long-Nose, 136
   The Fairy Tales of Wilhelm Hauff, 888
   A Monkey's Uncle, 2190
HAUGAARD, Erik Christian
   Prince Boghole, 137
   Princess Horrid, 138
Hauman, Doris, 219
Hauman, George, 219
HAWDON, Robin
   A Rustle in the Grass, 532
HAWKINS, Laura
   Figment, Your Dog, Speaking, 533
HAWTHORNE, Julian
   Rumpty-Dudget's Tower: A Fairy Tale, 139

HAWTHORNE, Nathaniel
   The Snow Image, 889
HAYES, Geoffrey
   *The Alligator and His Uncle Tooth: A Novel of
    the Sea*, 534
   The Mystery of the Pirate Ghost, 534
   The Secret of Foghorn Island, 534
HAYES, Sarah
   Crumbling Castle, 3035
HAYNES, Betsy
   The Ghost of the Gravestone Hearth, 1105
HAYWOOD, Carolyn
   A Valentine Fantasy, 140
HAZEL, Paul
   Undersea, 1377
   The Wealdwife's Tale, 1377
   Winter King, 1377
   Yearwood, 1377
HEAL (Berrien), Edith
   What Happened to Jenny, 2481
Heale, Jonathan, 19, 751
Healy, Deborah, 345
Hearn, Dawson, 138
HEARNE, Betsy (Gould)
   Eli's Ghost, 1106
   Home, 1378
   South Star, 1378
HEATH, W(illiam) L.
   The Earthquake Man, 141
Hebley, Gary, 1963
HEIDE, Florence Parry
   The Shrinking of Treehorn, 2191
   Treehorn's Treasure, 2191
   Treehorn's Wish, 2191
Heinly, John, 3040
HELAKISA, Kaarina
   The Journey of Pietari and His Wolf, 142
Heller, Julek, 1767, 2945
HELPRIN, Mark
   Swan Lake, 1714
   Winter's Tale, 1379
Helweg, Hans, 424
Hemmant, Lynette, 568, 577
Henderson, Dave, 279
Henderson, Keith, 1334, 1983
HENDRICH, Paula (Griffith)
   Who Says So?, 2482
HENDRY, Diana
   A Camel Called April, 2483
HENDRY, Frances Mary
   Quest for a Maid, 3037
Henneberger, Robert, 99, 2142
HENRY, Jan
   Tiger's Chance, 2484
HENRY, Maeve
   A Gift for Gift: A Ghost Story, 1107
   The Witch King, 1380
Henstra, Friso, 364, 365, 542, 859

Henterly, Jamichael, 270, 1820
HESS, Fjeril
  The Magic Switch, 2485
HESSE, Hermann
  Pictor's Metamorphoses, and Other Fantasies,
    890
HEWETT, Anita
  The Bull Beneath the Walnut Tree and Other
    Stories, 891
Hewitt, Margaret, 2901
HICKMAN, Tracy, jt. auth. *See* WEIS, Margaret
HIEATT, Constance B(artlett)
  The Castle of the Ladies, 1715
  The Joy of the Court, 1715
  The Knight of the Cart, 1715
  The Knight of the Lion, 1715
  The Minstrel Knight, 1715
  Sir Gawain and the Green Knight, 1715
  The Sword and the Grail, 1715
Higginbottom, J(effrey) Winslow, 426
Hiken, Kathleen, 634
Hildebrandt, Brothers, 1273
Hildebrandt, Greg, 93, 1584
Hildebrandt, Tim, 975
Hilder, Rowland, 2560
HILDICK, E(dmund) W(allace)
  The Case of the Dragon in Distress: A McGurk
    Fantasy, 2752
  The Case of the Weeping Witch, 2752
  The Dragon That Lived Under Manhattan, 2192
  The Ghost Squad and the Ghoul of Grünberg,
    1108
  The Ghost Squad and the Halloween
    Conspiracy, 1108
  The Ghost Squad and the Menace of the Malves,
    1108
  The Ghost Squad and the Prowling Hermits,
    1108
  The Ghost Squad Breaks Through, 1108
  The Ghost Squad Flies Concorde, 1108
HILGARTNER, Beth
  Colors in the Dreamweaver's Loom, 1977
  The Feast of the Trickster, 1977
  A Necklace of Fallen Stars, 143
HILL, Douglas (Arthur)
  Blade of the Poisoner, 1381
  Master of Fiends, 1381
  Penelope's Pendant, 2486
HILL, Elizabeth Starr
  Ever-After Island, 2487
HILL, Susan
  The Random House Book of Ghost Stories, 1174
Hillenbrand, Will, 2670
HILLER, Catherine
  Abracatabby, 2488
HILTON, James
  Lost Horizon, 1978

HIMLER, Ann, jt. auth. *See* HIMLER, Ronald
  (Norbert)
Himler, Ronald, 168, 172, 535, 1106, 2110
HIMLER, Ronald (Norbert), and HIMLER, Ann
  Little Owl, Keeper of the Trees, 535
HISER, Constance
  The Missing Doll, 2932
  No Bean Sprouts, Please!, 2489
HITE, Sid
  Dither Farm, 2490
Hitz, Demi, 295
Hoban, Abrom, 539
HOBAN, Lillian, 145
  It's Really Christmas, 536
HOBAN, Russell C(onwell)
  Arthur's New Power, 538
  Dinner at Alberta's, 538
  How Tom Beat Captain Najork and His Hired
    Sportsmen, 2193
  Jim Hedgehog and the Lonesome Tower, 537
  Jim Hedgehog's Supernatural Christmas, 537
  The Marzipan Pig, 144
  The Mouse and His Child, 145
  A Near Thing for Captain Najork, 2193
  The Sea-Thing Child, 539
  The Twenty-Elephant Restaurant, 2194
HODGELL, P(atricia) C(hristine)
  Dark of the Moon, 1382
  God Stalk, 1382
HODGES, C(yril) Walter, 109, 2073, 2465, 2888
  Sky High: The Story of a House That Flew, 2195
HODGES, Elizabeth Jamison
  The Three Princes of Serendip, 146
Hoffman, Felix, 1857
HOFFMAN, Lee
  Change Song, 1383
HOFFMAN, Mary
  The Four-Legged Ghosts, 2491
HOFFMAN, Nina Kiriki, jt. auth. *See* WILLIAMS,
  Tad
HOFFMANN, E(rnst) T(heodor) A(madeus)
  The Nutcracker, 2933
  The Strange Child, 147
HOFFMANN, Eleanor
  The Four Friends, 540
  Mischief in Fez, 2492
Hogarth, Paul, 324
Hogrogian, Nonny, 299, 1826, 1840, 2921
HOKE, Helen
  Witches, Witches, Witches, 3139
Holden, Elizabeth Rhoda. *See* LAWRENCE,
  Louise
Holder, Heidi, 125
HOLDSTOCK, Robert (P.) (pseud. of Robert
  Faulcon)
  The Emerald Forest, 1979
  The Hollowing, 1717

Lavondyss, 1717
Mythago Wood, 1717
Holland, Janice, 2399
Hollander, Carl, 3064
HOLLANDER, John
   The Quest of the Gole, 148
Hollinger, Deanne, 2982
HOLMAN (Valen), Felice
   The Blackmail Machine, 2196
   The Cricket Winter, 541
   The Escape of the Giant Hogstalk, 2197
   The Future of Hooper Toote, 2198
   The Witch on the Corner, 3038
HOLT, Isabella
   The Adventures of Rinaldo, 149
HOLT, Tom
   Who's Afraid of Beowulf?, 1718
Holtan, Gene, 2638
Holub, Jean, 1040
Hood, George W., 139
HOOKS, William H(arris)
   The Ballad of Belle Dorcas, 150
   Mean Jake and the Devils, 2199
   Moss Gown, 151
HOOVER, H(elen) M(ary)
   The Dawn Palace: The Story of Medea, 1719
HOPE, Christopher, jt. auth. *See also* MENUHIN,
   Yehudi
   The Dragon Wore Pink, 152
HOPKINS, Lee Bennett
   Monsters, Ghoulies and Creepy Creatures:
     Fantastic Stories and Poems, 929
HOPP, Zinken
   The Magic Chalk, 2493
HOPPE, Joanne
   Dream Spinner, 2753
HOŘEJŠ, Vít
   Pig and Bear, 542
Hornby, Nicole, 2660
Horne, Daniel R., 1821, 1891
HORNE, Richard Henry. *See* FAIRSTAR, Mrs.
   The Good-Natured Bear: A Story for Children of
     All Ages, 2200
   King Penguin: A Legend of the South Sea Isles,
     543
HOROWITZ, Anthony
   The Devil's Door-Bell, 3039
   The Night of the Scorpion, 3039
   The Silver Citadel, 3039
Horvath, Ferdinand Huszti, 1778
HORWITZ, Elinor Lander
   The Strange Story of the Frog Who Became a
     Prince, 3040
HORWOOD, William
   Duncton Wood, 544
HOTZE, Sollace
   Acquainted with the Night, 1109

HOUGH, (Helen) Charlotte (Woodyatt)
   Red Biddy and Other Stories, 893
HOUGHTON, Eric
   Gates of Glass, 1980
   Steps Out of Time, 2754
Housman, Clemence, 894, 895
HOUSMAN, Laurence
   The Blue Moon, 894
   Cotton-Wooleena, 153
   A Doorway in Fairyland, 894
   A Farm in Fairyland, 894
   The Field of Clover, 894
   The House of Joy, 894
   Moonshine and Clover, 895
   The Rat-Catcher's Daughter: A Collection of
     Stories, 896
HOUSTON, James A(rchibald)
   Spirit Wrestler, 3041
Hovland, Gary, 2288
HOWARD, Alice (Woodbury)
   Ching-Li and the Dragons, 154
   Sokar and the Crocodile: A Fairy Story of Egypt,
     2494
HOWARD, Joan (pseud. of Patricia Gordon)
   The Oldest Secret, 1981
   The Summer Is Magic, 2495
   The Taming of Giants, 545
   The Thirteenth Is Magic, 2495
   Uncle Sylvester, 546
   The Witch of Scrapfaggot Green, 3042
HOWE, Deborah, and HOWE, James
   Bunnicula: A Rabbit Tale of Mystery, 547
   The Celery Stalks at Midnight, 547
   Harold and Chester in Hot Fudge, 547
   Harold and Chester in the Fright Before
     Christmas, 547
   Howliday Inn, 547
   Nighty-Nightmare, 547
   Rabbit–Cadabra!, 547
   Return to Howliday Inn, 547
   Scared Silly: A Halloween Treat, 547
   Teddy Bear's Scrapbook, 2934
HOWE, James. *See also* HOWE, Deborah
   Babes in Toyland, 1982
   Morgan's Zoo, 548
Howe, John, 62, 1725
Howell, Troy, 19, 562, 2436, 2905
HOYLAND, John
   The Ivy Garland, 1110
Hoys, James, 349
HUDDY, Delia
   Time Piper, 1720
HUDSON, W(illiam) H(enry)
   Green Mansions: A Romance of the Tropical
     Forest, 1983
   A Little Boy Lost: A Tale for Children, 155

HUFF, Tanya
Gate of Darkness, Circle of Light, 1721
The Last Wizard, 3043
HUGHART, Barry
*Bridge of Birds: A Novel of an Ancient China
That Never Was,* 1384
Eight Skilled Gentlemen, 1384
The Story of the Stone, 1384
Hughes, Arthur, 224, 922
HUGHES, Dean
Nutty's Ghost, 1111
Theo Zephyr, 2496
HUGHES, Frieda
Getting Rid of Aunt Edna, 3044
HUGHES, Monica
The Promise, 1385
Sandwriter, 1385
HUGHES, Richard (Arthur Warren)
Don't Blame Me!, 897
*The Wonder-Dog: The Collected Stories of
Richard Hughes,* 898
HUGHES, Robert Don
The Faithful Traitor, 3045
The Forging of the Dragon, 3045
Hughes, Shirley, 290, 779, 970, 1012, 2352, 2557,
2572, 2961, 3121
HUGHES, Ted (Edward James)
How the Whale Became, 549
The Iron Giant: A Story in Five Nights, 156
Tales of the Early World, 899
Hummel, Lisl, 2200
HUNT, Marigold
Hester and the Gnomes, 2497
HUNTER, Mollie (pseud. of Maureen Mollie
Hunter McVeigh McIlwraith)
Day of the Unicorn, 158
The Ferlie, 2498
A Furl of Fairy Wind: Four Stories, 900
The Haunted Mountain: A Story of Suspense,
1984
The Kelpie's Pearls, 157
The Knight of the Golden Plain, 158
The Mermaid Summer, 2499
The Smartest Man in Ireland, 2201
A Stranger Came Ashore, 1722
Thomas and the Warlock, 3046
The Three-Day Enchantment, 158
The Walking Stones: A Story of Suspense, 3047
The Wicked One, 2500
HUNTER, Norman (George Lorimer)
The Best of Branestawm, 2202
*The Incredible Adventures of Professor
Branestawm,* 2202
The Peculiar Triumph of Professor Branestawm,
2202
Professor Branestawm up the Pole, 2202
Professor Branestawm's Building Bust-Up, 2202
Professor Branestawm's Great Revolution, 2202

Professor Branestawm's Mouse War, 2202
Professor Branestawm's Treasure Hunt, 2202
Hurd, Clement, 308
HURLBUTT, Isabelle B.
Little Heiskell, 2501
HURMENCE, Belinda
A Girl Called Boy, 2755
HUTCHINS, Hazel (J.)
Anastasia Morningstar, 2502
The Three and Many Wishes of Jason Reid, 2503
Hutchins, Laurence, 2203, 2204
HUTCHINS, Pat (Goundry)
Follow That Bus!, 2203
The House That Sailed Away, 2204
The Mona Lisa Mystery, 2203
Hutchinson, William, 2084
Hutton, Warwick, 18, 1651, 1652
Hyman, Trina Schart, 51, 93, 227, 243, 307, 359,
360, 859, 997, 1023, 1191, 1378, 1716, 1896,
2032, 2033, 2085, 2482, 2506, 2508, 2721, 2860,
2955, 3047, 3062, 3085, 3110
Hyndman, Jane Andrews. *See* WYNDHAM, Lee

IBBOTSON, Eva
The Great Ghost Rescue, 1112
Ilsley, Velma, 916, 2456
ING, Dean, jt. auth. *See* REYNOLDS, Mack
INGELOW, Jean
Mopsa the Fairy, 1985
Ingraham, Erick, 27, 223, 618
INGRAM, Tom (Thomas Henry)
Garranane, 159
The Night Rider, 2756
Innocenti, Roberto, 93, 2905
IPCAR, Dahlov (Zorach)
A Dark Horn Blowing, 1986
The Queen of Spells, 1723
The Warlock of Night, 3048
IRESON, Barbara
The April Witch and Other Strange Tales, 1018
Haunting Tales, 1104
Tales out of Time, 2855
IRVING, Washington
Knickerbocker's History of New York, 2205
The Legend of Sleepy Hollow, 1724
Rip Van Winkle, 1725
Irwin, Patricia Kathleen Page. *See* PAGE, P(atricia)
K(athleen)
Isadora, Rachel, 9, 2933
ISH-KISHOR, Sulamith
*The Master of Miracle: A New Novel of the
Golem,* 1726
Iwasaki, Chihiro, 10, 13

Jacob, Piers A. D. *See* ANTHONY, Piers
Jacobi, Kathy, 3016, 3087

JACQUES, Brian
   Mariel of Redwall, 550
   Martin the Warrior, 550
   Mattimeo, 550
   Mossflower, 550
   Redwall, 550
   Salamandastron, 550
   Seven Strange and Ghostly Tales, 1113
Jacques, Robin, 116, 779, 1929, 2038, 2413, 2692, 2808
Jaffurs, Alexa, 2905
Jainschigg, Nicholas, 3119
James, Ann, 2163
JAMES, Betsy
   Dark Heart, 1387
   Long Night Dance, 1387
JAMES, J. Alison
   Runa, 1727
   Sing for a Gentle Rain, 2757
JAMES, M(ontague) R(hodes)
   The Five Jars, 2504
JAMES, Mary (pseud. of Marijane Meaker, a.k.a.
   M. E. Kerr)
   Shoebag, 551
   The Shuteyes, 1987
JANE, Pamela
   Noelle of the Nutcracker, 2935
JANEWAY, Elizabeth (Hall)
   Ivanov Seven, 2206
JANSSON, Tove (Marika), 1913
   A Comet in Moominland, 1388
   The Exploits of Moominpappa, 1388
   Finn Family Moomintroll, 1388
   Moomin, Mymble and Little My, 1388
   Moominland Midwinter, 1388
   Moominpappa at Sea, 1388
   Moominpappa's Memoirs, 1388
   Moominsummer Madness, 1388
   Moominvalley in November, 1388
   Tales from Moominvalley, 1388
JARRELL, Randall
   The Animal Family, 160
   The Bat-Poet, 552
   Fly by Night, 2505
Jauss, Anne, 418
Jeffers, Susan, 14, 17, 20
JEFFRIES, (John) Richard
   Bevis: The Story of a Boy, 553
   Wood Magic; a Fable, 553
JEKEL, Pamela
   The Jungle Book, 554
   The Second Jungle Book, 554
   The Third Jungle Book, 554
Jenkins, Jean, 1005
JENNINGS, Paul
   Unbelievable! More Surprising Stories, 905
   Uncanny! Even More Surprising Stories, 905

   Unmentionable! More Amazing Stories, 905
   Unreal! Eight Surprising Stories, 905
JENSEN, Dorothea
   The Riddle of Penncroft Farm, 1114
JETER, K. W.
   Infernal Devices: A Mad Victorian Fantasy, 2207
JOHANSEN, Hanna
   7 X 7 Tales of a Sevensleeper, 555
   A Tomcat's Tale, 556
JOHNSON, Annabel
   I Am Leaper, 557
JOHNSON, Charles
   Pieces of Eight, 2758
JOHNSON, Crockett (pseud. of David Leisk)
   Ellen's Lion: Twelve Stories, 2936
JOHNSON, Dorothy M(arie)
   Witch Princess, 1728
JOHNSON, Elizabeth
   Break a Magic Circle, 2506
   The Little Knight, 161
   No Magic, Thank You, 2507
   Stuck with Luck, 2508
   The Three-in-One Prince, 162
Johnson, Holly, 2385
Johnson, Pamela, 315, 715, 718, 1945
JOHNSON, Sally Patrick
   *The Princesses: Sixteen Stories about
      Princesses*, 947
Johnson, Steve, 2299
JOHNSTON, Johanna
   Great Gravity the Cat, 558
JOHNSTON, Norma
   Pride of Lions: The Story of the House of Atreus,
      1729
   Strangers Dark and Gold, 1730
Johnston, Pamela, 719
JONES, Adrienne
   The Hawks of Chelney, 1389
   The Mural Master, 1988
Jones, Carol, 2947
JONES, Courtway
   In the Shadow of the Oak King, 1731
   Witch of the North, 1731
JONES, David Lee
   Unicorn Highway, 2509
JONES, Diana Wynne
   Archer's Goon, 3049
   Aunt Maria, 3050
   Cart and Cwidder, 1390
   Castle in the Air, 1391
   Charmed Life, 2759
   Dogsbody, 1989
   Drowned Ammet, 1392
   Eight Days of Luke, 1732
   Fire and Hemlock, 3051
   *Hidden Turnings: A Collection of Stories
      Through Time and Space*, 892
   The Homeward Bounders, 1393

Howl's Moving Castle, 1391, 3052
The Lives of Christopher Chant, 1990
The Magicians of Caprona, 3053
The Ogre Downstairs, 2510
The Power of Three, 1733
The Spellcoats, 1394
Stopping for a Spell: Three Fantasies, 2511
A Sudden Wild Magic, 3054
A Tale of Time City, 1991
Warlock at the Wheel and Other Stories, 3055
Witch Week, 3056
Witch's Business, 3057
JONES, Elizabeth Orton, 973
Big Susan, 2937
Twig, 2512
Jones, Harold, 175, 609, 954, 2954
JONES, Louis C(lark)
Things That Go Bump in the Night, 1115
Jones, Margaret, 1849
Jones, Margot, 2325
JONES, McClure
Cast Down the Stars, 1395
Jones, Naimo, 2939
JONES, Terry
Fairy Tales, 2208
Fantastic Stories, 2209
Nicobobinus, 2210
The Saga of Erik the Viking, 163
JONSSON, Runer
Viki Viking, 2211
JORDAN, Anne Devereaux
*Fires of the Past: Thirteen Contemporary
   Fantasies about Hometowns*, 867
JORDAN, Robert
The Dragon Reborn, 1396
The Eye of the World, 1396
The Fires of Heaven, 1396
The Great Hunt, 1396
Lord of Chaos, 1396
The Shadow Rising, 1396
JORDAN, Sherryl
The Juniper Game, 2760
A Time of Darkness, 2761
Winter of Fire, 1397
Jorgensen, David, 15
Joyce, William, 2248
JUSTER, Norton
Alberic the Wise and Other Journeys, 906
The Phantom Tollbooth, 1992

Kaila, Kaarina, 17, 20
Kállay, Dušan, 86
Karasz, Ilonka, 2562
KARAZIN, Nikolaí Nikoleavich
Cranes Flying South, 559
Karlsson, Ewert, 2211

KARPIN, Florence
The Prince in the Golden Tower, 164
KARR, Kathleen
Gideon and the Mummy Professor, 2513
KARR, Phyllis Ann
The Idylls of the Queen, 1734
Kashiwagi, Isami, 2841
KÄSTNER, Erich
The Animal's Conference, 560
The Little Man, 2212
The Little Man and the Big Thief, 2212
The Little Man and the Little Miss, 2212
KATZ, Welwyn Wilton
Come Like Shadows, 3058
False Face, 1735
The Third Magic, 1993
Whalesinger, 561
Kauffer, E. McKnight, 1983
KAUFMAN, Charles
The Frog and the Beanpole, 562
Kaufmann, John, 2445, 2584
KAVANAUGH, James
A Fable, 165
Kay, Gertrude A., 219
KAY, Guy Gavriel
The Darkest Road, 1994
A Song for Arbonne, 1398
The Summer Tree, 1994
The Wandering Fire, 1994
KAYE, M(argaret) M(ary)
The Ordinary Princess, 166
KAYE, Marvin
The Amorous Umbrella, 1995
The Incredible Umbrella, 1995
KEANEY, Brian
No Need for Heroes, 1736
Keats, Ezra Jack, 413
KEELE, Luqman, and PINKWATER, D(aniel)
   Manus
Java Jack, 2213
Keeping, Charles, 176, 880, 1505, 1687, 1689,
   1802, 1848, 1969, 2201, 2469
KEHRET, Peg
Horror at the Haunted House, 1116
Keith, Eros, 59, 765, 2206
KELLEHER, Victor (pseud. of Michael Kitchener)
Baily's Bones, 1117
Brother Night, 1399
Master of the Grove, 3059
The Red King, 1400
KELLER, Beverly (Lou)
A Small, Elderly Dragon, 167
KELLER, Gottfried
The Fat of the Cat and Other Stories, 907
Kelley, Gary, 1724, 1725
Kelley, True Adelaide, 563
KELLEY, True Adelaide and LINDBLOM, Steven
   (Winther)

The Mouses' Terrible Christmas, 563
The Mouses' Terrible Halloween, 563
Kellogg, Steven, 386, 386, 730, 2252
KEMP, Gene
  Jason Bodger and the Priory Ghost, 1118
  Mr. Magus Is Waiting for You, 3060
KENDALL, Carol (Seeger)
  The Firelings, 1401
  The Gammage Cup, 1402
  The Whisper of Glocken, 1403
KENEALLY, Thomas (Michael)
  Ned Kelly and the City of the Bees, 1996
KENNEALY (Morrison), Patricia
  The Copper Crown, 1404, 1737
  The Hawk's Gray Feather: A Book of the Keltiad, 1737
  The Oak Above the Kings, 1737
  The Silver Branch, 1404, 1737
  The Throne of Scone, 1404, 1737
KENNEDY, Brendan, jt. auth. *See* KENNEDY, William
KENNEDY, (Jerome) Richard
  Amy's Eyes, 2938
  The Blue Stone, 168
  The Boxcar at the Center of the Universe, 169
  Come Again in the Spring, 170
  Crazy in Love, 2514
  The Dark Princess, 171
  Inside My Feet: The Story of a Giant, 172
  The Leprechaun's Story, 173
  The Lost Kingdom of Karnica, 174
  The Mouse God, 564
  Richard Kennedy: Collected Stories, 908
Kennedy, Joseph Charles. *See* KENNEDY, X. J.
Kennedy, Paul, 836, 837, 2440
Kennedy, Richard, 108, 1666
KENNEDY, William, and KENNEDY, Brendan
  Charlie Malarkey and the Belly-Button Machine, 2214
  Charlie Malarkey and the Singing Moose, 2214
KENNEDY, X. J. (pseud. of Joseph Charles Kennedy)
  The Owlstone Crown, 1997
KENNEMORE, Tim
  Changing Times, 2762
Kent, Pat, 586
Kerr, George, 433
KERR, Katharine
  The Bristling Wood, 3061
  Daggerspell, 3061
  Darkspell, 3061
  Days of Air and Darkness, 3061
  Days of Blood and Fire, 1405, 3061
  The Dragon Reverant, 3061
  A Time of Exile: A Novel of the Westlands, 1405
  A Time of Omens, 1405, 3061
Kerr, M. E. *See* JAMES, Mary

KESEY, Ken
  Little Tricker the Squirrel Meets Big Double the Bear, 565
  The Sea Lion: A Story of the Sea Cliff People, 1738
KESSLER, Risa. *See* DEL REY, Lester
KEY, Alexander (Hill)
  The Forgotten Door, 1998
  The Sword of Aradel, 2763
Khing, The Tjong, 267
Kidder, Harvey, 2395
KILWORTH, Garry
  The Foxes of Firstdark, 566
KIMMEL, Margaret Mary
  Magic in the Mist, 3062
KINDL, Patrice
  Owl in Love, 3063
King, Arthur, 2290
KING, Bernard
  Starkadder, 1739
  Vargr-Moon, 1739
KING, (David) Clive
  The Town That Went South, 567
KING, Stephen
  The Drawing of the Three, 1407
  The Eyes of the Dragon, 1406
  The Gunslinger, 1407
  The Wastelands, 1407
KING, Stephen, and STRAUB, Peter
  The Talisman, 1999
KING-SMITH, Dick
  Ace: The Very Important Pig, 568
  Babe: The Gallant Pig, 569
  The Cuckoo Child, 570
  The Fox-Busters, 571
  Harry's Mad, 2215
  The Jenius, 572
  Lady Daisy, 2939
  Magnus Powermouse, 573
  Martin's Mice, 574
  The Mouse Butcher, 575
  Paddy's Pot of Gold, 2515
  Pigs Might Fly, 576
  Pretty Polly, 2216
  The Queen's Nose, 2516
  The Toby Man, 577
KINGSLEY, Charles
  The Water Babies: A Fairy Tale for a Land Baby, 175
KINSELLA, W(illiam) P(atrick)
  Shoeless Joe, 1119
Kipling, John Lockwood, 579
KIPLING, (Joseph) Rudyard
  All the Mowgli Stories, 578
  The Beginning of the Armadilloes, 176
  The Butterfly That Stamped, 177
  The Cat That Walked by Himself, 178
  The Crab That Played with the Sea, 179

The Elephant's Child, 180
How the Camel Got His Hump, 181
How the Leopard Got His Spots, 182
How the Rhinoceros Got His Skin, 183
How the Whale Got His Throat, 184
The Jungle Book, 579
Just So Stories, 580
Kipling's Fantasy, 909
Phantoms and Fantasies: Twenty Tales, 1120
Puck of Pook's Hill, 2764
Rewards and Fairies, 2764
Rikki-Tikki-Tavi, 581
The Second Jungle Book, 579
KIRBY, Mansfield
    *The Secret of Thut-Mouse III; or Basil
        Beandesert's Revenge*, 582
Kirk, Maria L., 175, 219, 224, 779, 1725, 1767,
    2591
KIRWAN-VOGEL, Anna
    The Jewel of Life, 1409
KISLING, Lee
    The Fools' War, 1410
Kitchener, Michael. *See* KELLEHER, Victor
Kite, S. B., 517
KITTLEMAN, Laurence R
    Canyons Beyond the Sky, 2765
Kiuchi, Tatsuro, 2543
KLAVENESS, Jan O'Donnell
    The Griffin Legacy, 1121
KLEIN, Robin
    Thing, 2217
Knight, Hilary, 410, 859, 2484
KNIGHT, Marjorie
    Alexander's Birthday, 2940
    Alexander's Christmas Eve, 2940
    Alexander's Vacation, 2940
KNOWLES, Anne
    The Halcyon Island, 1122
Knowlton, Vianna, 874
Kocsis, J. C., 363, 2047
Koelsh, Michael, 2379
Koering, Ursula, 2319, 2553
KOFF, Richard M(yram)
    Christopher, 2517
KOLLER, Jackie French
    A Dragon in the Family, 1411
    The Dragonling, 1411
    If I Had One Wish. . ., 2518
Komoda, Kiyo, 442, 521
KONIGSBURG, E(laine) L(obl)
    Up from Jericho Tel, 2519
KOOIKER, Leonie (pseud. of Johanna Maria
        Kooyker-Romijn)
    Legacy of Magic, 3064
    The Magic Stone, 3064
KOONTZ, Dean R(ay)
    Oddkins: A Fable for All Ages, 2941

Kooyker-Romijn, Johanna Maria. *See* KOOIKER,
    Leonie
KORNWISE, Robert Ian, jt. auth. *See* ANTHONY,
    Piers
KORSCHUNOW, Irina
    Adam Draws Himself a Dragon, 2520
    Small Fur, 2521
    Small Fur is Getting Bigger, 2521
KORTUM, Jeanie
    Ghost Vision, 3065
KOTZWINKLE, William
    Doctor Rat, 583
    Hearts of Wood: And Other Timeless Tales, 910
    *Trouble in Bugland: A Collection of Inspector
        Mantis Mysteries*, 2218
KOVACS, Deborah
    Brewster's Courage, 584
Krahn, Fernando, 724
Kredel, Fritz., 779, 797, 2255, 2905
KRENSKY, Stephen (Alan)
    A Big Day for Scepters, 185
    Castles in the Air and Other Tales, 911
    The Dragon Circle, 2522
    A Ghostly Business, 2522
    The Perils of Putney, 186
    A Troll in Passing, 187
    The Witching Hour, 2522
    Woodland Crossings, 585
KROEBER, Theodora (Kracow)
    Carrousel, 2942
Kronen, Jeff, 169
KROPP, Lloyd
    The Drift, 2000
Krush, Beth, 56, 1911, 2389, 2454, 2587
Krush, Joe, 56, 1786, 1911, 2389, 2454, 2587
KRÜSS, James (Jacob Hinrich)
    Eagle and Dove, 586
    The Happy Islands Behind the Winds, 2001
    Return to the Happy Islands, 2001
Kubinyi, Coleman, 2494
Kubinyi, Laszlo, 381, 1970, 1984, 2963
KUMIN, Maxine (Winokur), and SEXTON, Anne
        (Harvey)
    The Wizard's Tears, 3066
Kurelek, William, 507
KURTZ, Katherine
    The Bastard Prince, 1414
    The Bishop's Heir, 1412
    Camber of Culdi, 1413
    Camber the Heretic, 1413
    The Deryni Archives, 1413
    Deryni Checkmate, 1413
    Deryni Magic, 1413
    Deryni Rising, 1413
    The Harrowing of Gwynedd, 1414
    High Deryni, 1413
    King Javin's Year, 1413, 1414
    The King's Justice, 1412

Lammas Night, 3067
The Quest for Saint Camber, 1412
Saint Camber, 1413
KURTZ, Katherine, and HARRIS, Deborah
The Adept, 3068
The Lodge of the Lynx, 3068
The Templar Treasure, 3068
KUSHNER, Donn
A Book Dragon, 2523
Uncle Jacob's Ghost Story, 188
The Violin-Maker's Gift, 189
KUSHNER, Ellen
Thomas the Rhymer, 1740
KUTTNER, Henry
The Startling Worlds of Henry Kuttner, 2002
KWITZ, Mary DeBall
The Bell Tolls at Mousehaven Manor, 587
Shadow Over Mousehaven Manor, 587

LACKEY, Mercedes. *See also* ANTHONY,
    Piers; NORTON, André
Arrow's Fall, 1415
Arrow's Flight, 1415
Arrows of the Queen, 1415
By the Sword, 1416
Magic's Pawn, 1417
Magic's Price, 1417
Magic's Promise, 1417
Storm Warning, 1415
Winds of Change, 1418
Winds of Fate, 1418
LACKEY, Mercedes, and DIXON, Larry
The Black Gryphon, 1415, 1417
Born to Run, 3069
LACKEY, Mercedes, and EMERSON, Ru
Castle of Deception, 3070
Fortress of Frost and Fire, 3070
Prison of Souls, 3070
LACKEY, Mercedes, and LISLE, Holly
When the Bough Breaks, 2003
LAGERLÖF, Selma (Ottilliana Lovisa)
The Changeling, 191
The Further Adventures of Nils, 2524
The Wonderful Adventures of Nils, 2524
LAHEY, Michael
Quest for Apollo, 2766
Laimgruber, Monika, 15, 19, 135
Lamb, Lynton, 2565
Lamb, Susan Condie, 2474, 2931
Lambert, J. K., 60, 2010
Lambert, Saul, 1083, 2614
LAMORISSE, Albert (Emmanuel)
The Red Balloon, 192
LA MOTTE FOUQUÉ, Baron Friedrich Heinrich
    Karl de
Undine, 190

LAMPLUGH, Lois
Falcon's Tor, 2767
LAMPMAN, Evelyn Sibley
Captain Apple's Ghost, 1123
The City Under the Back Steps, 2004
The Shy Stegosaurus of Cricket Creek, 2219
LANCASTER, Clay
Periwinkle Steamboat, 2525
LANCASTER, Osbert
The Saracen's Head; or, the Reluctant Crusader,
    193
LANDSMAN, Sandy
Castaways on Chimp Island, 588
LANG, Andrew
*Prince Prigio and Prince Ricardo: The
    Chronicles of Pantouflia*, 194
Tales of a Fairy Court, 194
LANGTON, Jane (Gillson)
The Astonishing Stereoscope, 2526, 2527
The Diamond in the Window, 2526, 2527
The Fledgling, 2527
The Swing in the Summerhouse, 2526, 2527
LANIER, Sterling E(dmund)
*The War for the Lot: A Tale of Fantasy and
    Terror*, 589
Larrecq, John, 640
Larsen, Suzanne, 3077
LARSON, Jean (Russell)
The Silkspinners, 195
Lasell, Fen, 2044
Lasker, Joe, 2677
LASKI, Marghanita
The Victorian Chaise Longue, 2768
LASKY (Knight), Kathryn
Home Free, 2769
LATHROP, Dorothy P(ulis), 10, 155, 222, 479, 813,
    834, 875, 889, 2422, 2917
An Angel in the Woods, 2943
The Colt from Moon Mountain, 2528
The Dog in the Tapestry Garden, 2529
The Fairy Circus, 196
The Little White Goat, 2530
The Lost Merry-Go-Round, 2531
The Snail Who Ran, 590
LATTIMORE, Deborah Nourse
The Dragon's Robe, 197
The Winged Cat: A Tale of Ancient Egypt, 1741
LAUBENTHAL, Sanders Anne
Excalibur, 1742
LAUBER, Patricia (Grace)
Home at Last! A Young Cat's Tale, 591
LAUGHLIN, Florence (Young)
The Little Leftover Witch, 3071
LAUMER, (John) Keith
The Shape Changer: A Science Fiction Novel,
    1419
LAURENCE, Margaret (Wemyss)
Jason's Quest, 592

LAWHEAD, Stephen R.
  In the Hall of the Dragon King, 1420
  The Paradise War, 1743
  Pendragon, 1744
  The Silver Hand, 1743
  The Sword and the Flame, 1420
  Taliesin, 1744
  The Warlords of Nin, 1420
LAWRENCE, Ann (Margaret)
  The Half Brothers, 1421
  Tom Ass: Or the Second Gift, 2532
Lawrence, John, 325, 2233
LAWRENCE, Louise (pseud. of Elizabeth Rhoda
    Holden)
  The Earth Witch, 1745
  Sing and Scatter Daisies, 1124
  Star Lord, 1746
  The Warriors of Taan, 1422
  The Wyndcliffe, 1124
Lawrie, Robin, 779
LAWSON, Amy
  Star Baby, 2533
LAWSON, John S(hults)
  The Spring Rider, 2770
  You Better Come Home with Me, 198
LAWSON, Julie
  The Dragon's Pearl, 199
LAWSON, Marie (Abrams)
  Dragon John, 200
LAWSON, Robert, 54, 194, 864, 2087, 2094, 2175,
    2365, 2561, 2647
  Ben and Me, 593
  Captain Kidd's Cat, 594
  Edward, Hoppy and Joe, 595
  The Fabulous Flight, 2534
  I Discover Columbus, 596
  McWhinney's Jaunt, 2220
  Mr. Revere and I, 597
  Mr. Twigg's Mistake, 598
  Rabbit Hill, 599
  Robbut: A Tale of Tails, 599
  Smeller Martin, 2221
  The Tough Winter, 599
Lazarevich, Mila, 2532
LAZARUS, Keo Felker
  The Shark in the Window, 2222
Leach, Alice Mary Doanne. *See* LEACH, Maria
LEACH, Christopher
  Rosalinda, 1125
LEACH, Maria (pseud. of Alice Mary Doanne
    Leach)
  *The Thing at the Foot of the Bed and Other Scary
    Tales*, 1126
LEAMY, Edmund
  *The Fairy Minstrel of Glenmalure, and Other
    Stories for Children*, 912
  The Golden Spears and Other Fairy Tales, 913
Leatham, Moyra, 131
Lebenson, Richard, 1782

LEBERMANN, Norbert
  New German Fairy Tales, 914
Lebiš, Ján, 950
Le Cain, Errol, 1, 14, 35, 280
Lee, Alan, 2, 1665
Lee, Doris, 326
LEE, John
  *The Unicorn Dilemma: A Saga of War and
    Magic*, 1423
  The Unicorn Quest, 1423
LEE, Josephine
  Joy Is Not Herself, 3072
LEE, Robert C.
  The Day It Rained Forever, 2223
  The Iron Arm of Michael Glenn, 2223
  Once upon Another Time, 2771
  Timequake, 2772
LEE, Tanith
  Anackire, 1424
  Animal Castle, 201
  Black Unicorn, 1425
  Companions on the Road: Two Novellas, 1426
  Cyrion, 1427
  Dark Castle, White Horse, 1428
  The Dragon Hoard, 1429
  *Dreams of Dark and Light: The Great Short
    Fiction of Tanith Lee*, 915
  East of Midnight, 1430
  A Heroine of the World, 1431
  Princess Hynchatti and Some Other Surprises,
    916
  Red as Blood; or Tales from the Sisters Grimmer,
    1747
  The Storm Lord, 1424
  Sung in Shadow, 1432
  Tamastara; or the Indian Nights, 1748
  The White Serpent, 1424
LEESON, Robert (Arthur)
  Genie on the Loose, 2224
  The Third Class Genie, 2224
Lefkowitz, Mark, 3095
Legett, Ann, 3074
LE GRAND (Henderson)
  How Baseball Began in Brooklyn, 2225
  How Space Rockets Began, 2226
  Matilda, 2227
LeGrand, Edy, 209
LE GUIN, Ursula K(roeber)
  The Beginning Place, 2005
  Buffalo Gals and Other Animal Presences, 600
  Catwings, 601
  Catwings Return, 601
  The Farthest Shore, 1433
  Fish Soup, 202
  Lesse Webster, 602
  A Ride on the Red Mare's Back, 203
  *Solomon Leviathan's Nine Hundred and Thirty-
    First Trip Around the World*, 603
  Tehanu: The Last Book of Earthsea, 1433

The Tombs of Atuan, 1433
The Wind's Twelve Quarters: Short Stories, 917
A Wizard of Earthsea, 1433
Wonderful Alexander and the Cat Wings, 601
Lehmann, E. A., 779
Leight, Edward, 2994
Leisk, David. *See* JOHNSON, Crockett
Lemieux, Michele, 1774
Lemoine, 11
L'ENGLE, Madeleine
    An Acceptable Time, 2773
    Many Waters, 2774
Lenski, Lois, 829, 2949
Lent, Blair, 9
LEONARD, Nellie Mabel
    Grandfather Whiskers, M. D., a Graymouse Story, 604
    The Graymouse Family, 604
Leone, Sergio, 321
LEROE, Ellen
    Ghost Dog, 1127
    Leap Frog Friday, 2535
LEROY, Gen
    Taxi Cat and Huey, 605
LESKOV, Nikolai
    The Steel Flea, a Story, 204
Leslie, Cecil, 2576
Leslie, Donna, 1913
Lester, Alison, 2217
Levenson, S., 2706
LE VERT, John
    The Flight of the Cassowary, 205
LEVIN, Betty (Lowenthal)
    A Binding Spell, 1128
    The Forespoken, 2776
    A Griffon's Nest, 2776
    The Ice Bear, 1434
    Landfall, 1749
    Mercy's Mill, 2775
    The Sword of Culann, 2776
LEVIN, Meyer
    The Spell of Time: A Tale of Love in Jerusalem, 206
Levine, Ed, 3044
Levit, Herschel, 1827
LEVITIN, Sonia (Wolff)
    Jason and the Money Tree, 2228
LEVOY, Myron
    The Magic Hat of Mortimer Wintergreen, 3073
Levrin, Nora, 2778
LEVY, Elizabeth
    Running Out of Magic with Houdini, 2777
    Running Out of Time, 2777
Levy, Jessica, 692
LEVY, Robert
    Escape from Exile, 2006
Lewin, Betsy, 91, 537, 2589
Lewin, Ted, 43, 1167, 2726, 3086

LEWIS, Beth (pseud. of Beth Lipkin)
    The Blue Mountain, 207
LEWIS, C(live) S(taples)
    The Horse and His Boy, 2007
    The Last Battle, 2007
    The Lion, the Witch, and the Wardrobe, 2007
    The Magician's Nephew, 2007
    Prince Caspian: The Return to Narnia, 2007
    The Silver Chair, 2007
    The Voyage of the Dawn Treader, 2007
LEWIS, Gogo. *See* MANLEY, Seon
LEWIS, Hilda (Winifred)
    The Ship That Flew, 2778
LEWIS, J. Patrick
    The Moonbow of Mr. B. Bones, 208
LEWIS, Naomi
    The Silent Playmate: A Collection of Doll Stories, 2954
LEY, Madeleine
    The Enchanted Eve, 209
LEZRA, Giggy (Grizzella Paull)
    The Cat, the Horse, and the Miracle, 606
Lieberman, Warren, 911
Lieblich, Irene, 300
Lies, Brian, 449, 2637
LIFTON, Betty Jean (Kirschner)
    The Cock and the Ghost Cat, 1129
    The Dwarf Pine Tree, 210
    Jaguar, My Twin, 3074
    The One-Legged Ghost, 2229
LILLINGTON, Kenneth (James)
    An Ash-Blond Witch, 3075
    Full Moon, 1130
    Jonah's Mirror, 2008
    Selkie, 1750
    What Beckoning Ghost?, 1131
Lindberg, Jeffrey, 2426
LINDBERGH, Anne Spencer
    Bailey's Window, 2009
    The Hunky-Dory Dairy, 2779
    The People in Pineapple Place, 1132
    The Prisoner of Pineapple Place, 1132
    The Shadow on the Dial, 2780
    Three Lives to Live, 2781
    Travel Far, Pay No Fare, 2536
LINDBLOM, Steven (Winther), jt. auth. *See* KELLEY, True Adelaide
LINDE, Gunnel (Geijerstam)
    The White Stone, 2537
LINDENBAUM, Pija
    Else-Marie and Her Seven Little Daddies, 2538
LINDGREN, Astrid
    The Brothers Lionheart, 2010
    Erik and Karlsson on the Roof, 2539
    The Ghost of Skinny Jack, 1133
    Karlsson Flies Again, 2539
    Karlsson-on-the-Roof, 2539
    Mio, My Son, 2011
    Pippi Goes on Board, 2230

Pippi in the South Seas, 2230
Pippi Longstocking, 2230
Pippi on the Run, 2230
Ronia, the Robber's Daughter, 1436
Sweden, 2539
The World's Best Karlsson, 2539
LINDHOLM, Megan
  Harpy's Flight, 1437
  The Limbreth Gate, 1437
  Luck of the Wheels, 1437
  The Windsingers, 1437
LINDOP, Audrey E.
  The Adventures of the Wuffle, 607
LINDSAY, Norman (Alfred William)
  *The Magic Pudding: Being the Adventures of
    Bunyip Bluegum and His Friends Bill
    Barnacle and Sam Sawnoff*, 2231
LINES, Kathleen
  *The Haunted and the Haunters: Tales of Ghosts
    and Other Apparitions*, 1103
  A Ring of Tales, 954
LINKLATER, Eric (Robert Russell)
  The Pirates in the Deep Green Sea, 2012
  The Wind on the Moon, 2540
Linn, David, 1053
Linton, Anne, 943
Lipkin, Beth. *See* LEWIS, Beth
Lippincott, Gary A., 2406, 2407
Lippman, Peter, 688
LISLE, Holly, jt. auth. *See* LACKEY, Mercedes
LISLE, Janet Taylor
  The Dancing Cats of Applesap, 2232
  Forest, 211
  The Great Dimpole Oak, 212
  The Lampfish of Twill, 1438
Lisowski, Gabriel, 288
LISSON, Deborah
  The Devil's Own, 2782
LITTLE, Jane
  The Philosopher's Stone, 2783
  Sneaker Hill, 3076
  Spook, 3077
Littlewood, Valerie, 2925
LIVELY, Penelope (Margaret Low)
  Astercote, 1751
  The Driftway, 1135
  The Ghost of Thomas Kempe, 1136
  The House in Norham Gardens, 2784
  A House Inside Out, 608
  The Revenge of Samuel Stokes, 1137
  A Stitch in Time, 1138
  Uninvited Ghosts and Other Stories, 2233
  The Voyage of Q V 66, 609
  The Whispering Knights, 1752
  The Wild Hunt of the Ghost Hounds, 1753
LLOYD, (Mary) Norris
  The Desperate Dragons, 213

LLYWELYN, Morgan
  Bard: The Odyssey of the Irish, 1754
  Druids, 1755
  The Elementals, 214
  The Horse Goddess, 3078
  The Isles of the Blest, 1756
  Lion of Ireland: The Legend of Brian Boru, 1757
  Red Branch, 1758
LOBE, Mira
  The Grandma in the Apple Tree, 2541
Lobel, Adrienne, 398
Lobel, Arnold, 1726, 2118, 3038
Loccisano, Karen, 2957
LOCKE, Angela
  Mr. Mullett Owns a Cloud, 2542
Locker, Thomas, 19, 1725
LOCKLEY, Ronald Mathias
  The Seal-Woman, 1759
Loestoeter, Lori, 182
Loewenstein, Bernice, 453, 504
LOFTING, Hugh
  Doctor Dolittle: A Treasury, 2234
  Doctor Dolittle and the Green Canary, 2234
  Doctor Dolittle and the Secret Lake, 2234
  Doctor Dolittle in the Moon, 2234
  Doctor Dolittle's Caravan, 2234
  Doctor Dolittle's Circus, 2234
  Doctor Dolittle's Garden, 2234
  Doctor Dolittle's Post Office, 2234
  Doctor Dolittle's Puddleby Adventures, 2234
  Doctor Dolittle's Return, 2234
  Doctor Dolittle's Zoo, 2234
  Gub-Gub's Book: An Encyclopedia of Food,
    2234
  The Story of Doctor Dolittle, 2234
  The Story of Mrs. Tubbs, 610
  The Twilight of Magic, 2543
  The Voyages of Doctor Dolittle, 2234
LOGAN, Carolyn F.
  The Power of the Rellard, 1760
LOGSTON, Anne
  Shadow, 1439
  Shadow Dance, 1439
  Shadow Hunt, 1439
Lohse, W. R., 3139
Long, Olive M., 78
LONGYEAR, Barry B(rookes)
  The God Box, 1440
LORD, Beman
  The Perfect Pitch, 2544
Lorenzini, Carlo. *See* COLLODI, Carlo
LORING, Selden M(elville)
  *Mighty Magic: An Almost-True Story of Pirates
    and Indians*, 2785
Lorraine, Walter, 278, 2171
LOVEJOY, Jack
  The Rebel Witch, 3079

LOVETT, Margaret (Rose)
  The Great and Terrible Quest, 1441
Low, Joseph, 458, 465, 644
Low, William, 229
LOWREY, Janette Sebring
  The Lavender Cat, 215
Lubin, Leonard, 459, 868
LUENN, Nancy
  Arctic Unicorn, 3080
  Goldclimbers, 1442
  The Ugly Princess, 216
  Unicorn Crossing, 2545
LUKEMAN, Tim
  Witchwood, 1443
LUNN, Janet (Louise Swoboda)
  The Root Cellar, 2786
  Shadow in Hawthorn Bay, 1139
  Twin Spell, 1140
LURIE, Alison
  The Oxford Book of Modern Fairy Tales,
    938
LYKKEN, Laurie
  Little Room of Terror, 1141
Lynch, P. J., 14, 15, 256, 984
LYNCH, Patricia (Nora)
  Brogeen and the Black Enchanter, 217
  Brogeen and the Bronze Lizard, 217
  Brogeen and the Little Wind, 217
  Brogeen and the Lost Castle, 217
  Brogeen and the Red Fez, 217
  Brogeen Follows the Magic Tune, 217
  Guests at the Beech Tree, 217
  *The Turf-Cutter's Donkey: An Irish Story of
    Mystery and Adventure*, 2546
  The Turf-Cutter's Donkey Kicks Up His Heels,
    2546
  The Turf-Cutters Donkey Goes Visiting, 2546
LYNN, Elizabeth A.
  The Dancers of Arun, 1444
  The Northern Girl, 1444
  Watchtower, 1444
  *The Woman Who Loved the Moon, and Other
    Stories*, 921

Maas, Dorothy, 2333, 3019
Mabel, Lucie Attwell, 1896
MacALPINE, Margaret H(esketh Murray)
  The Black Gull of Corie Lachan, 2547
MACAULAY, David, 2279
  BAAA, 218
MacAVOY, R(oberta) A(nn)
  The Belly of the Wolf, 1445
  The Book of Kells, 2787
  Damiano, 3081
  Damiano's Lute, 3081
  The Grey Horse, 3082
  King of the Dead, 1445
  Lens of the World, 1445

  Raphael, 3081
  Tea with the Black Dragon, 1761
  A Trio for Lute, 3081
  Twisting the Rope, 1761
McBRATNEY, Sam
  The Ghosts of Hungryhouse Lane, 1142
McCAFFREY, Anne (Inez)
  All the Weyrs of Pern, 1447
  The Chronicles of Pern: First Fall, 1447
  Crystal Line, 1446
  Crystal Singer, 1446
  The Dolphins of Pern, 1447
  Dragondrums, 1447
  Dragonflight, 1447
  Dragonquest, 1447
  Dragonsdawn, 1447
  Dragonsinger, 1447
  Dragonsong, 1448
  The Girl Who Heard Dragons, 1447
  The Harper Hall of Pern, 1448
  Killashandra, 1446
  Moreta: Dragon Lady of Pern, 1447
  Nerilka's Story: A Pern Adventure, 1447
  The Renegades of Pern, 1447
  The White Dragon, 1447
McCAUGHREAN, Geraldine (Jones)
  A Pack of Lies, 2548
McClintock, Barbara, 485
McCloskey, Robert, 741
McCord, Kathleen Garry, 626, 3131
McCormick, A. D., 155
McCOY, Neely
  Jupie and the Wise Old Owl, 612
  Jupie Follows His Tale, 612
  The Tale of the Good Cat Jupie, 612
McCue, Lisa, 735, 2125, 2140
McCully, Emily Arnold, 481, 760, 884, 1140, 2194,
  2460, 2461, 2462
MacDONALD, Betty (Campbell Bard)
  Hello, Mrs. Piggle-Wiggle, 2235
  Mrs. Piggle-Wiggle, 2235
  Mrs. Piggle-Wiggle's Farm, 2235
  Mrs. Piggle-Wiggle's Magic, 2235
MacDONALD, George
  At the Back of the North Wind, 219
  *The Complete Fairy Tales of George
    MacDonald*, 922
  The Fairy Fleet, 220
  The Golden Key, 221
  The Light Princess, 222
  Little Daylight, 223
  The Princess and Curdie, 224
  The Princess and the Goblin, 224
  The Wise Woman and Other Fantasy Stories, 225
MacDONALD, Greville
  *Billy Barnicoat: A Fairy Romance for Young and
    Old*, 2549
  Count Billy, 2549

McDONALD, Ian
  King of Morning, Queen of Day, 1762
MacDONALD, James D., jt. auth. *See* DOYLE,
  Debra
MacDONALD, Reby Edmond
  The Ghosts of Austwick Manor, 2788
McEwan, Chris, 2905
McGINLEY, Phyllis (Louise)
  The Plain Princess, 226
McGINNIS, Lila S(prague)
  The Ghost Upstairs, 1143
McGOWEN, Tom (Thomas E.)
  Dragon Stew, 227
  The Magical Fellowship, 3083
  The Magician's Apprentice, 3084
  The Magician's Challenge, 3084
  The Magician's Company, 3084
  Odyssey from River Bend, 613
  A Question of Magic, 3083
  The Shadow of Fomor, 2014
  Sir Machinery, 3085
  A Trial of Magic, 3083
McGRAW, Eloise Jarvis
  Joel and the Great Merlini, 2550
  A Really Weird Summer, 1144
  The Trouble with Jacob, 1145
McHARGUE, Georgess
  Beastie, 2551
  Elidor and the Golden Ball, 2015
  The Mermaid and the Whale, 228
  Stoneflight, 2552
McHUGH, Elizabet
  Beethoven's Cat, 614
  Wiggie Wins the West, 614
McIlwraith, Maureen Mollie Hunter McVeigh. *See*
  HUNTER, Mollie
McINERNEY, Judith Whitelock
  Judge Benjamin and the Purloined Sirloin, 615
  Judge Benjamin: Superdog, 615
  Judge Benjamin: The Superdog Gift, 615
  Judge Benjamin: The Superdog Rescue, 615
  Judge Benjamin: The Superdog Secret, 615
  Judge Benjamin: The Superdog Surprise, 615
McINERNY, Ralph M.
  Quick As a Dodo, 2236
McIntosh, John, 1927
McINTYRE, Vonda, jt. auth. *See* BRADLEY,
  Marion Zimmer
McKEAN, Thomas
  The Haunted Circus, 2789
  The Secret of the Seven Willows, 2789
MacKELLAR, William
  Alfie and Me and the Ghost of Peter Stuyvesant,
    1146
  A Ghost Around the House, 1147
  The Ghost in the Castle, 1148
  The Smallest Monster in the World, 2553
  The Witch of Glen Gowrie, 3086

McKENZIE, Ellen Kindt
  A Bowl of Mischief, 1449
  Drujienna's Harp, 2016
  Kashka, 1450
  The King, the Princess, and the Tinker, 229
  Taash and the Jesters, 1450
MacKenzie, Garry, 545, 546, 1981
MacKenzie, Thomas, 310
McKIERAN, Dennis L.
  The Brega Path, 1452
  Dragondoom, 1451
  Tales of Mithgar, 1452
  Trek to Kraggen-Cor, 1452
McKILLIP, Patricia A(nne)
  The Changeling Sea, 1453
  Cygnet and the Firebird, 1454
  The Forgotten Beasts of Eld, 1455
  Harpist in the Wind, 1457
  Heir of Sea and Fire, 1457
  The House on Parchment Street, 1149
  The Moon and the Face, 1456
  Moon-Flash, 1456
  Riddle of the Stars, 1457
  The Riddle-Master of Hed, 1457
  The Sorceress and the Cygnet, 1458
  The Throme of the Erril of Sherill, 1459
McKINLEY, (Jennifer Carolyn) Robin (Turrell)
  Beauty: A Retelling of the Story of Beauty and
    the Beast, 1763
  The Blue Sword, 1460
  Deerskin, 1460, 1764
  The Door in the Hedge, 923
  The Hero and the Crown, 1461
  Imaginary Lands, 1386
MacKinstry, Elizabeth, 224, 787, 1953, 2449
McKISSACK, Patricia C(arwell)
  The Dark-Thirty: Southern Tales of the
    Supernatural, 1150
MacKnight, Ninon, 1123
MacLACHLAN, Patricia
  Tomorrow's Wizard, 3087
McLachlin, Steve, 506
MacLEISH, Roderick
  Prince Ombra, 1765
MacLEOD, Charlotte (Matilda Hughes)
  The Curse of the Giant Hogweed, 2790
McLEOD, Emilie Warren
  Clancy's Witch, 3088
McMULLAN, Kate
  Under the Mummy's Spell, 1151
McNAUGHTON, Colin
  Jolly Roger and the Pirates of Abdul the
    Skinhead, 2237
McNEILL (Alexander), Janet
  A Monster Too Many, 2554
  Tom's Tower, 2017
McNutt, Mildred Coughlin, 2392

McPHAIL, (Michael) David, 2079
   Henry Bear's Park, 616
   Stanley, Henry Bear's Friend, 616
MACE, Elisabeth
   The Ghost Diviners, 2791
   Out There, 1462
   The Rushton Inheritance, 2792
   The Travelling Man, 1462
   Under Siege, 2018
MACOUREK, Miloš
   Curious Tales, 924
   Max and Sally and the Phenomenal Phone, 2555
Madden, Don, 519
Maestro, Giulio, 1112
MAETERLINCK, Maurice
   The Children's Blue Bird, 230
MAGUIRE, Gregory
   The Daughter of the Moon, 2019
   The Dream Stealer, 3089
   Lightning Time, 2793
   Lights on the Lake, 2793
MAHY, Margaret (May)
   *The Birthday Burglar & A Very Wicked
     Headmistress*, 2238
   *The Blood-and-Thunder Adventure on Hurricane
     Peak*, 2239
   Bubble Trouble and Other Poems and Stories,
     2240
   The Changeover: A Supernatural Romance,
     3090
   The Chewing-Gum Rescue and Other Stories,
     2241
   Dangerous Spaces, 2020
   The Door in the Air and Other Stories, 2556
   *The Downhill Crocodile Whizz and Other
     Stories*, 2557
   The First Margaret Mahy Storybook, 2557
   *The Girl with the Green Ear: Stories About
     Magic in Nature*, 2557
   *The Great Piratical Rumbustification, and The
     Librarian and the Robbers*, 2242
   *The Great White Man-Eating Shark: A
     Cautionary Tale*, 2243
   The Haunting, 3091
   Nonstop Nonsense, 2244
   *The Pirates' Mixed-Up Voyage: Dark Doings in
     the Thousand Islands*, 2245
   Raging Robots and Unruly Uncles, 2246
   The Second Margaret Mahy Storybook, 2557
   A Tall Story and Other Tales, 2558
   The Third Margaret Mahy Storybook, 2557
   The Tricksters, 1152
Maitland, Antony, 775, 898, 1081, 2599, 2601
MAJOR, Beverly
   Porcupine Stew, 618
MAJOR, Kevin (Gerald)
   Blood Red Ochre, 1766
Malick, Nancy, 554

Malone, Nola Langner, 167
MALORY, Sir Thomas
   *The Acts of Arthur and His Noble Knights from
     the Winchester Manuscripts of Thomas
     Malory and Other Sources*, 1767
   Arthur Pendragon of Britain, 1767
   The Book of King Arthur and His Noble Knights,
     1767
   The Boy's King Arthur, 1767
   King Arthur and His Knights, 1767
   King Arthur and the Legends of Camelot, 1767
   King Arthur: The Sword in the Stone, 1767
   La Morte D'Arthur, 1767
   The Legend of King Arthur, 1767
   *Of Swords and Sorcerers: The Adventures of
     King Arthur and His Knights*, 1767
   *The Romance of King Arthur and His Knights of
     the Round Table*, 1767
   Stories of King Arthur, 1767
   Stories of King Arthur and His Knights, 1767
   The Story of Idylls of the King, 1767
   The Story of King Arthur and His Knights, 1767
   *The Sword and Circle: King Arthur and Knights
     of the Round Table*, 1767
   Tales of King Arthur, 1767
MANES, Stephen
   *Chicken Trek: The Third Strange Thing That
     Happened to Oscar Noodleman*, 2247
   Monstra vs. Irving, 2559
   Some of the Adventures of Rhode Island Red,
     2248
MANGUELO, Alberto
   Black Water: The Book of Fantastic Literature,
     799
MANLEY, Seon
   The Ghost in the Far Garden and Other Stories,
     1154
MANLEY, Seon, and LEWIS, Gogo
   Christmas Ghosts: An Anthology, 1047
   Fun Phantoms: Tales of Ghostly Entertainment,
     1078
   *Masters of Shades and Shadows: An Anthology
     of Great Ghost Stories*, 1156
MANNING, Rosemary (Joy)
   Dragon in Danger, 2249
   Dragon in Summer, 2249
   The Dragon's Quest, 2249
   Green Smoke, 2249
Mansell, Dom, 357
Marcellino, Fred, 15, 684, 685
Marchesi, Stephen, 61
Marcks, Marie, 2328
MARK, Jan (pseud. of Janet Marjorie Brisland)
   Aquarius, 1464
   Divide and Rule, 1465
Marks, Alan, 19, 265, 1166
Marokvia, Artur, 286
Maroto, Esteban, 1485

Marriott, Pat, 1235, 2802, 3072
Mars, W. T., 2099, 2107, 2129
Marshall, Constance, 2249
MARSHALL, James (Edward), 538
   Rats on the Range and Other Stories, 619
   Rats on the Roof and Other Stories, 619
   A Summer in the South, 620
   Taking Care of Carruthers, 621
   What's the Matter with Carruthers?, 621
Marshall, Judith, 1411
Marshall, Laura, 1832
MARTIN, Ann M(atthews)
   Ma and Pa Dracula, 2250
MARTIN, Bill (William Ivan), and
      ARCHAMBAULT, John
   The Ghost-Eye Tree, 1155
MARTIN, Graham Dunstan
   Catchfire, 1466
   Giftwish, 1466
MARTINE-BARNES, Adrienne, jt. auth. *See*
      PAXON, Diana L.
MARZOLLO, Jean
   Halfway Down Paddy Lane, 2794
MASEFIELD, John (Edward)
   The Box of Delights: Or, When the Wolves Were
      Running, 2560
   The Midnight Folk: A Novel, 2560
Masline, Camille, 1960
MASON, Arthur
   From the Horn of the Moon, 2561
   The Wee Men of Ballywooden, 2561
MASON, Miriam E(vangeline)
   Hoppity, 622
MATHESON, Richard (Burton)
   Bid Time Return, 2795
Mathieu, Joseph, 417, 584, 2997
Mathis, Melissa Bay, 558
MATTHIESSEN, Peter
   The Seal Pool, 623
Mattotti, Lorenzo, 2905
Matus, Greta, 1096
MAUGHAM, W. Somerset
   Princess September, 231
MAXWELL, William (Keepers)
   The Heavenly Tenants, 2562
May, Darcy, 10, 2623
MAY, Julian, jt. auth. *See* BRADLEY, Marion
      Zimmer
MAYER, Marianna
   The Black Horse, 1768
   The Little Jewel Box, 232
   Noble-Hearted Kate: A Celtic Tale, 1769
   The Sorcerer's Apprentice: A Greek Fable, 1770
   The Unicorn and the Lake, 233
Mayer, Mercer, 349, 370
MAYHAR, Ardath
   Lords of the Triple Moons, 1467
   Makra Choria, 1468
   Runes of the Lyre, 1469, 1471

   The Saga of Grittel Sundotha, 1470
   Soul-Singer of Tyrnos, 1471
Mayne, William. *See* COBALT, Martin
MAYNE, William (James Carter) *See also*
      FARJEON, Eleanor
   All the King's Men, 2021
   Antar and the Eagles, 1472
   The Blue Boat, 2563
   The Blue Book of Hob Stories, 2566
   Earthfasts, 1771
   A Game of Dark, 2796
   Ghosts: An Anthology, 1086
   The Glass Ball, 2564
   A Grass Rope, 2565
   The Green Book of Hob Stories, 2566
   The Hill Road, 2797
   Hob and the Goblins, 2566
   It, 1157
   The Mouldy, 234
   The Red Book of Hob Stories, 2566
   William Mayne's Book of Giants, 988
   A Year and a Day, 235
   The Yellow Book of Hob Stories, 2566
MAZER, Anne
   The Oxboy, 236
MAZER, Norma Fox
   Saturday, the Twelfth of October, 2798
Meaker, Marijane, a.k.a. M. E. Kerr. *See* JAMES,
     Mary
MEANY, Dee Morrison
   Iseult: Dreams That Are Done, 1772
MEIER, Shirley, jt. auth. *See* STIRLING, S. M.
MEIGS, Cornelia (Lynde)
   The Kingdom of the Winding Road, 926
   The Wonderful Locomotive, 2567
Meise, Fred, 2711
MELENDEZ, Francisco
   The Mermaid and the Major: or, The True Story
     of the Invention of the Submarine, 2251
MELLECKER, Judith
   Randolph's Dream, 237
MELLING, O(rla) R
   The Singing Stone, 2799
MELNYK, Bohdan, jt. auth. *See* FRANKO, Ivan
Mendelson, S. T., 6
MENDEZ, Phil
   The Black Snowman, 1773
MENDOZA, George
   Gwot! Horribly Funny Hairticklers, 2252
MENOTTI, Gian Carlo
   Amahl and the Night Visitors, 1774
MENUHIN, Yehudi, and HOPE, Christopher
   The King, the Cat, and the Fiddle, 238
MERRILL, Jean (Fairbanks)
   The Black Sheep, 624
   The Pushcart War, 2253
   The Superlative Horse: A Tale of Ancient China,
     239
   The Toothpaste Millionaire, 2254

MERRITT, A(braham P.)
  The Ship of Ishtar, 2022
Merwin, Decie, 406, 648
Messenger, Norman, 873
MIAN, Mary (Lawrence Shipman)
  The Net to Catch War, 3092
  Take Three Witches, 3092
MICHAELS, Melisa C.
  Far Harbor, 1473
MICHELS, Tilde
  Rabbit Spring, 625
Michl, Reinhard, 2160
Micich, Paul, 321
Middleton-Murray, John. *See* COWPER, Richard
Mieke, Anne, 1952
MIESEL, Sandra
  Shaman, 2023
Mikolaycak, Charles, 305, 757, 859, 1883, 2341
MILES, (Mary) Patricia
  The Gods in Winter, 240
Milhous, Katherine, 2441
Millar, H. R., 2031, 2576, 2577, 2578, 2579, 2580,
  2805, 2806
Millard, C. E., 957
Miller, Jon, 571
MILLER, Judi
  Ghost in My Soup, 1158
MILLER (Mandelkorn), Eugenia
  The Sign of the Salamander, 2800
Miller, Marilyn, 1147, 3102, 3103
Miller, Mitchell, 343, 2190
MILLER, Phyllis, jt. auth. *See* NORTON, André
Miller, Warren, 2184
MILNE, A(lan) A(lexander)
  The Christopher Robin Story Book, 2944
  The House at Pooh Corner, 2944
  The Hums of Pooh, 2944
  Once on a Time, 241
  The Pooh Story Book, 2944
  Pooh's Bedtime Book, 2944
  *Prince Rabbit and the Princess Who Could Not
    Laugh*, 242
  Winnie-the-Pooh, 2944
  The World of Pooh, 2944
MINOT, Stephen
  Surviving the Flood, 1775
MIRRLEES, Hope
  Lud-in-the-Mist, 1474
Mitchell, Kurt, 2843
MOBLEY, Jane
  *Phantasmagoria: Tales of Fantasy and the
    Supernatural*, 940
MODESITT, L(eland) E(xton Jr.)
  The Magic Engineer, 1475
  The Magic of Recluce, 1475
  Towers of the Sunset, 1475
Moebius, 806

MOERI, Louise
  Star Mother's Youngest Child, 243
  The Unicorn and the Plow, 244
Mogensen, Jan, 180
Molan, Chris, 247
MOLESWORTH, Mary Louisa (Stewart)
  A Christmas Child, 2024
  The Cuckoo Clock, 2024
  Fairy Stories, 928
  The Tapestry Room: A Child's Romance, 2568
Molnar, George, 336
MONACO, Richard
  Ayesha, the Return of She, 2025
  Journey to the Flame, 2025
  She, 2025
  She and Allan, 2025
  Wisdom's Daughter, 2025
MONATH, Elizabeth
  Topper and the Giant, 2569
MONSELL, Mary Elise
  Crackle Creek, 626
  A Fish Named Yum, 627
  Mr. Pin: The Chocolate Files, 627
  The Mysterious Cases of Mr. Pin, 627
  The Spy Who Came North from the Pole, 627
  Toohy and Wood, 628
Monti, Sylvie, 840
Montresor, Beni, 11, 248, 713, 947
MONTROSE, Anne
  The Winter Flower, and Other Fairy Stories, 930
MOON, Carl, 2570. *See also* MOON, Grace
  Purdie
MOON, Elizabeth
  The Deed of Paksenarrion, 1476
  Divided Allegiance, 1476
  Oath of Gold, 1476
  Sheepfarmer's Daughter, 1476
  Surrender None: The Legacy of Gird, 1476
MOON, Grace Purdie, and MOON, Carl
  *Lost Indian Magic: A Mystery Story of the Red
    Man as He Lived Before the White Men
    Came*, 2570
MOON, Sheila (Elizabeth)
  Hunt Down the Prize, 2026
  Knee-Deep in Thunder, 2026
MOONEY, Bel
  The Stove Haunting, 2801
MOORCOCK, Michael (John)
  The Bane of the Black Pearl, 1478
  The City in the Autumn Stars, 245
  The Dragon in the Sword, 1477
  The Dreaming Jewels, 1478
  Elric at the End of Time, 1478
  Elric of Melnibone, 1478
  Elric, the Return to Melnibone, 1478
  The Eternal Champion: A Fantastic Romance,
    1477
  The Fortress of the Pearl, 1478
  The Ice Schooner: A Tale, 1479

Phoenix in Obsidian, 1477
The Revenge of the Rose, 1478
The Sailor on the Seas of Fate, 1478
The Silver Warrior, 1477
The Sleeping Sorceress, 1478
The Stealer of Souls and Other Stories, 1478
Stormbringer, 1478
The Vanishing Tower, 1478
The War Hound and the World's Pain: A Fable,
  245
The Weird of the White Wolf, 1478
MOORE, Annie Carroll
  Nicholas: A Manhattan Christmas Story, 2571
  Nicholas and the Golden Goose, 2571
Moore, Inga, 579
MOORE, John
  Slay and Rescue, 1776
MOORE, Katherine (Davis)
  The Little Stolen Sweep, 2802
MOORE, Lilian
  Adam Mouse's Book of Poems, 629
  Don't Be Afraid, Amanda, 629
  I'll Meet You at the Cucumbers, 629
MOORE, Margaret Eileen
  Willie Without, 630
Moore, Mary, 2596
Mordvinoff, Nicolas, 439, 2121, 2122, 2311, 2312
MORGAN, Alison (Mary Raikes)
  River Song, 631
MORGAN, Helen (Gertrude Louise Axford)
  Mother Farthing's Luck, 2572
  Satchkin Patchkin, 2572
Morgan, Judy, 2111
MORGAN, Robin
  *The Mer-Child: A Legend for Children and
    Other Adults*, 246
Morgan, Roy, 1767
Morin, Paul, 199
MORPURGO, Michael
  Jo-Jo the Melon Donkey, 247
  King of the Cloud Forests, 1777
MORRESSY, John
  Kedrigern and the Charming Couple, 3093
  Kedrigern in Wanderland, 3093
  The Questing of Kedrigern, 3093
  A Remembrance for Kedrigern, 3093
  A Voice for Princess, 3093
Morrill, Leslie, 484, 489, 548, 615, 687, 740, 1534
MORRIS, Kenneth
  The Book of the Three Dragons, 1778
  The Fates of the Princes of Dyfed, 1778
MORRIS, William
  The Well at the World's End, 1480
MORRISON, Dorothy Nafus
  Vanishing Act, 2573
Morrison, Seon, 1805
Moser, Barry, 18, 130, 443, 565, 669, 1724, 1725,
  1869, 1898, 1913, 2187

MOSKIN, Marietta D(unston)
  Dream Lake, 2803
Mostyn, David, 2282
Moy, Seong, 427
Moynihan, Roberta, 304
MOZART, Wolfgang Amadeus
  The Magic Flute, 248
Mozley, Charles, 984
Mugnaini, Joseph, 2704
Müller, Jörg, 309, 708
MULLER, Robin
  The Magic Paintbrush, 249
MULOCK, Diana (pseud. of Dinah Craik)
  *The Adventures of a Brownie as Told to My
    Child*, 2574
  *The Little Lame Prince and His Travelling
    Cloak*, 250
MÜNCHAUSEN, Karl
  The Adventures of Baron Münchausen, 2255
  The Baron All at Sea, 2255
  The Baron on the Island of Cheese, 2255
  The Baron Rides Out, 2255
MUNDY, Talbot (pseud. of William Lancaster
  Gribbon)
  C. I. D, 2027
  The Caves of Terror, 2027
  The Gunga Sahib, 2027
  Guns of the Gods, 2027
  Hira Singh's Tale, 2027
  The Hundred Days, 2027
  Jingrim, 2027
  Jingrim and Allah's Peace, 2027
  Jungle Jest, 2027
  The King in Check, 2027
  King—of the Khybers, 2027
  The Lion of Petra, 2027
  The Lost Trooper, 2027
  The Mystery of Khufu's Tomb, 2027
  The Nine Unknown, 2027
  Old Ugly Face, 2027
  OM, The Secret of Abhor Valley, 2027
  Ramsden, 2027
  The Red Flame of Erinpura, 2027
  The Seventeen Thieves of El-Kalil, 2027
  The Thunder Dragon Gate, 2027
  The Winds of the World, 2027
  The Woman Ayisha, 2027
Munsinger, Lynn, 729
Murdocca, Sal, 2813
Murphy, E(mmet) Jefferson. See MURPHY, Pat
MURPHY, Jill
  A Bad Spell for the Worst Witch, 3094
  Jeffrey Strangeways, 2256
  The Worst Witch, 3094
  The Worst Witch Strikes Again, 3094
MURPHY, Pat (pseud. of E[mmet] Jefferson
  Murphy)

The Falling Woman: A Fantasy, 1779
Points of Departure, 932
MURPHY, Shirley Rousseau
   The Castle of Hape, 1482
   The Catswold Portal, 2028
   Caves of Fire and Ice, 1482
   The Dragonbards, 1481
   Flight of the Fox, 632
   The Ivory Lyre, 1481
   The Joining of the Stone, 1482
   Nightpool, 1481
   The Pig Who Could Conjure the Wind, 3095
   The Ring of Fire, 1482
   Silver Woven in My Hair, 251
   Valentine for a Dragon, 252
MURPHY, Shirley Rousseau, and SUGGS, Welch
   Medallion of the Black Hound, 2029
MURPHY, Warren, jt. auth. *See* COCHRAN, Molly
Mussino, Atillo, 2905
MYERS, Bernice
   Sidney Rella and the Glass Sneaker, 2257
MYERS, John Myers
   The Moon's Fire-Eating Daughter, 2030
   Silverlock, 2030
MYERS, Walter Dean
   *The Black Pearl and the Ghost; or, One Mystery
     after Another*, 2258
   The Golden Serpent, 253
   The Legend of Tarik, 1780
MYRA, Harold
   Children in the Night, 1483
   The Shining Face, 1483

NABB, Magdalen
   The Enchanted Horse, 2945
Nadler, Robert, 156
Nantier, 984
NAPOLI, Donna Jo
   The Magic Circle, 3096
   *The Prince of the Pond: Otherwise Known as De
     Fawg Pin*, 2259
NASH, Mary (Hughes)
   Mrs. Coverlet's Detectives, 2260
   Mrs. Coverlet's Magicians, 2260
   While Mrs. Coverlet Was Away, 2260
NASTICK, Sharon
   Mr. Radagast Makes an Unexpected Journey,
     2261
NATHAN, Robert (Gruntal)
   The Elixir, 1781
   Mia, 1160
   Portrait of Jennie, 254
   The Snowflake and the Starfish, 3097
Natti, Susanna, 759, 2604
NAYLOR, Phyllis Reynolds
   Bernie and the Bessledorf Ghost, 1161
   Faces in the Water, 2804

Footprints at the Window, 2804
   The Grand Escape, 633
   Shadows on the Wall, 2804
Negri, Rocco, 1541, 1699, 1811
Neill, John Rea, 1767
Nelson, Jennie Ann, 2758
NESBIT (Bland), E(dith)
   The Complete Book of Dragons, 933
   The Deliverers of Their Country, 2575
   The Enchanted Castle, 2576
   Five Children and It, 2577
   *The Five Children; Containing Five Children
     and It; The Phoenix and the Carpet; The
     Story of the Amulet*, 2577
   Harding's Luck, 2805
   The House of Arden, 2805
   The Last of the Dragons, 255
   The Magic City, 2031
   The Magic World, 2578
   Melisande, 256
   The Phoenix and the Carpet, 2577, 2806
   The Story of the Amulet, 2806
   Wet Magic, 2579
   The Wonderful Garden; or the Three C's, 2580
Nesbitt, Jan, 2558
NESS, Evaline (Michelow), 66, 466, 467, 643,
   1237, 1240, 2829, 3066
   *The Girl and the Goatherd, or This and That and
     Thus and So*, 257
Neville, Vera, 611
NEWELL, Averil
   The Fly-By-Nights, 634
NEWMAN, Robert (Howard)
   Merlin's Mistake, 1782
   The Shattered Stone, 1484
   The Testing of Tertius, 1782
NEWMAN, Sharan
   The Chessboard Queen, 1783
   Guinevere, 1783
   Guinevere Evermore, 1783
Newsham, Ian, 1938, 2542
Newton, Rita, 2883
NICHOLS, (Joanna) Ruth
   The Left-Handed Spirit, 3098
   The Marrow of the World, 2032
   Song of the Pearl, 2807
   A Walk out of the World, 2033
Nicholson, William, 2893
Nicklaus, Carol, 2098, 2262
NICKLESS, Will
   Dotted Lines, 635
   Owlglass, 635
Nielsen, Kay, 779
NIMMO, Jenny
   The Chestnut Soldier, 2581
   Orchard of the Crescent Moon, 2581
   The Snow Spider, 2581
   Ultramarine, 1784

NIVEN, Larry
  The Magic Goes Away, 1485
  Magic May Return, 1485
  More Magic, 1485
NIXON, Joan Lowery
  The Gift, 2582
  Haunted Island, 1162
  Magnolia's Mixed-Up Magic, 636
Nolan, Dennis, 1865, 372
Noonan, Julia, 896, 1459, 1597
Norman, Marty, 2277
NORMAN, Roger
  Albion's Dream: A Novel of Terror, 1785
NORTH, Joan
  The Cloud Forest, 2583
  The Light Maze, 2034
North, Linda, 3135
Norton, Alice Mary. *See* NORTON, André
NORTON, André (pseud. of Alice Mary Norton).
    See also BRADLEY, Marion Zimmer
  The Crystal Gryphon, 1486
  Dragon Magic, 2808
  Fur Magic, 2584
  The Gate of the Cat, 2039
  Gryphon in Glory, 1486, 2039
  Gryphon's Eyrie, 1486, 2039
  Here Abide Monsters, 2035
  Horn Crown, 2039
  Huon of the Horn, 1786
  The Jargoon Pard, 1487
  Knave of Dreams, 2036
  Lavender Green Magic, 2809
  Lore of the Witch World, 2039
  The Mark of the Cat, 1488
  Moon Mirror, 934
  Octagon Magic, 2810
  Operation Time Search, 2037
  Quag Keep, 1787
  Red Hart Magic, 2811
  Small Shadows Creep, 1186
  Sorceress of the Witch World, 2039
  Spell of the Witch World, 2039
  Steel Magic, 2038
  Three Against the Witch World, 2039
  Trey of Swords, 2039
  'Ware Hawk, 2039
  Warlock of the Witch World, 2039
  Web of the Witch World, 2039
  Witch World, 2039
  Wizards' Worlds, 3099
  Wraiths of Time, 2040
  Year of the Unicorn, 2039
  Zarsthor's Bane, 2039
NORTON, André, and ADAMS, Robert
  Magic in Ithkar, 1463
NORTON, André, and GREENBERG, Martin H.
  Catfantastic: Nine Lives and Fifteen Tales, 818

NORTON, André, and GRIFFIN, P. M.
  Flight of Vengeance, 1489
  On Wings of Magic, 1489
  Storms of Victory, 1489
  Witch World, 1489
NORTON, André, and LACKEY, Mercedes
  *The Elvenbane: An Epic Fantasy of the
    Halfblood Chronicles*, 3100
NORTON, André, and MILLER, Phyllis
  House of Shadows, 1163
  Seven Spells to Sunday, 2585
NORTON, André, and SHWARTZ, Susan
  Imperial Lady: A Fantasy of Han China, 1788
NORTON, Mary (Pearson)
  Are All the Giants Dead?, 2041
  Bedknob and Broomstick, 2586
  The Borrowers, 2587
  The Borrowers Afield, 2587
  The Borrowers Afloat, 2587
  The Borrowers Aloft, 2587
  The Borrowers Avenged, 2587
  The Borrowers Omnibus, 2587
  Poor Stainless, 2587
NÖSTLINGER, Christine
  Konrad, 2262
NYE, Robert
  Beowulf; a New Telling, 1789
  The Mathematical Princess and Other Stories,
    935
  Wishing Gold, 258
NYGAARD, Jacob Bech
  Tobias the Magic Mouse, 637
NYGREN, Tord
  Fiddler and His Brothers, 259

OAKLEY, Graham, 1429, 2278
  The Church Cat Abroad, 638
  The Church Mice Adrift, 638
  The Church Mice and the Moon, 638
  The Church Mice and the Ring, 638
  The Church Mice at Bay, 638
  The Church Mice at Christmas, 638
  The Church Mice in Action, 638
  The Church Mice Spread Their Wings, 638
  The Church Mouse, 638
  Diary of a Churchmouse, 638
  Henry's Quest, 2263
Oberdieck, Bernhard, 225
Obligado, Lilian, 438
O'BRIEN, Robert C. (pseud. of Robert Leslie
    Conly)
  Mrs. Frisby and the Rats of NIMH, 639
  The Silver Crown, 2042
Obrist, Jürg, 186
O'CONNELL, Jean S.
  The Dollhouse Caper, 2946

ODGERS, Sally Farrell
  Drummond: The Search for Sarah, 2947
O'FAOLÁIN, Eileen (Gould)
  King of the Cats, 2588
  The Little Black Hen; An Irish Fairy Story, 2588
  Miss Pennyfeather and the Pooka, 2588
  Miss Pennyfeather in the Springtime, 2588
Ogden, Bill, 2394
OGIWARA, Noriko
  Dragon Sword and Wind Child, 1790
O'HANLON (Meek), Jacklyn
  The Door, 2043
Olcott, Harriet Mead, 786
Olsen, Ib Spang, 637
OLSON, Helen Kronberg
  *The Strange Thing That Happened to Oliver
    Wendell Iscovitch*, 2589
Omerod, Jan, 1896, 2241
OPPENHEIM, Shulamith (Levey)
  The Selchie's Seed, 1791
ORLOCK, Carol (Ellen)
  *The Goddess Letters: The Demeter-Persephone
    Myth Retold*, 1792
Ormai, Stella, 557, 587
Ormerod, Jan, 2612
ORMONDROYD, Edward
  All in Good Time, 2812
  Broderick, 640
  Castaways on Long Ago, 1164
  David and the Phoenix, 2590
  Time at the Top, 2812
O'ROURKE, Frank
  Burton and Stanley, 641
ORR, A.
  In the Ice King's Palace, 3101
  The World in Amber, 3101
ORWELL, George (pseud. of Eric Hugh Blair)
  Animal Farm, 642
OSBORNE, M(aurice) M(achado) (Jr.)
  Ondine: The Story of a Bird Who Was Different,
    643
  Rudi and the Mayor of Naples, 644
OSBORNE, Mary Pope
  Dinosaurs Before Dark, 2813
  Knight at Dawn, 2813
  Mummies in the Morning, 2813
  *Spider Kane and the Mystery at Jumbo
    Nightcrawlers*, 645
  *Spider Kane and the Mystery Under the May
    Apple*, 645
O'SHEA, Pat
  The Hounds of the Morrigan, 1793
Ottendorff, E. Pollak, 2077
OTTO, Margaret G(lover)
  The Tiny Man, 646
OUIDA (pseud. of [Marie] Louise de la Ramée)
  The Nürnberg Stove, 2591

Owens, Gail, 384, 2603, 2666, 2681

Pace, David, 2977
PAGE, P(atricia) K(athleen) (pseud. of Patricia
    Kathleen Page Irwin)
  A Flask of Sea Water, 260
PAGET, (Reverend) F(rancis) E(dward) (used the
    pseud. William Churne of Staffordshire)
  *The Hope of the Katzekopfs; or, the Sorrow of
    Selfishness: A Fairy Tale*, 261
Paget-Fredericks, J., 21, J., 22
Pagram, Edward, 855
PAINE, Albert Bigelow
  The Hollow Tree and Deep Woods Book, 647
  Hollow Tree Nights and Days, 647
  The Hollow Tree Snowed-In Book, 647
  How Mr. Dog Got Even, 647
  How Mr. Rabbit Lost His Tail, 647
  Making Up with Mr. Dog, 647
  Mr. Crow and the Whitewash, 647
  Mr. Possum's Great Balloon Trip, 647
  Mr. Rabbit's Big Dinner, 647
  Mr. Rabbit's Wedding, 647
  Mr. Turtle's Flying Adventure, 647
  When Jack Rabbit Was a Little Boy, 647
Paisley, Tom. See BETHANCOURT, T(homas)
    Ernesto
Palaček, Josef, 10, 11
Palazzo, Tony, 742
Palladini, David, 164, 998, 1000, 1001, 1406
PALMER, David R.
  Threshold, 2264
Palmer, Juliette, 65
PALMER, Mary
  The Dolmop of Dorkling, 2044
  The Magic Knight, 262
  The Teaspoon Tree, 2592
PALMER, Robin (Riggs)
  Wise House, 648
Pangrazio, Michael, 936
Panton, Doug, 189
PARDOE, M(argaret Mary)
  Argyle's Causeway, 2815
  Argyle's Oracle, 2815
  Curtain of Mist, 2815
PARK, (Rosina) Ruth (Lucia)
  Playing Beatie Bow, 2816
PARK, Ruth
  My Sister Sif, 1794
  Things in Corners, 1165
PARKER, (James) Edgar (Jr.)
  The Dream of the Dormouse, 649
  The Duke of Sycamore, 650
  The Enchantress, 263
  The Flower of the Realm, 651

The Question of a Dragon, 652
Rogue's Gallery, 2265
PARKER, Nancy Winslow
   *The Spotted Dog: The Strange Tale of a Witch's
      Revenge*, 2266
PARKER, Richard
   M for Mischief, 2593
   The Old Powder Line, 2817
   Spell Seven, 2594
   A Time to Choose: A Story of Suspense, 2818
Parker, Robert Andrew, 55, 228, 237, 1800, 2652
Parkins, David, 608, 1059, 1703, 2126
Parks, Phil, 2941
Parnall, Peter, 387, 387, 695, 2026
PARRISH, Anne
   Floating Island, 2948
   The Story of Appleby Capple, 2267
PARRISH, Anne, and PARRISH, Dillwyn
   The Dream Coach, 939
   Knee-High to a Grasshopper, 2595
PARRISH, Dillwyn, jt. auth. *See* PARRISH, Anne
Parrish, Maxfield, 879
Parry, Alan, 224
PASCAL, Francine
   Hangin' Out with Cici, 2819
PASSEY, Helen K.
   Speak to the Rain, 1795
Pastor, Rosita, 337
PATERSON, Katherine
   The King's Equal, 264
Paton, Jane, 390, 390, 2444, 2667
PATON WALSH, Jill (Gillian Bliss)
   Birdy and the Ghosties, 1166
   Matthew and the Sea Singer, 265
   Torch, 1490
   A Chance Child, 2820
PATTEN, Brian
   Mr. Moon's Last Case, 2596
PATTOU, Edith
   Hero's Song, 1796
Paul, Korky, 2137
Paull, Grace, 415, 798
Paus, Herbert, 230
PAXON, Diana L.
   Lady of Darkness, 1491
   Lady of Light, 1491
   The Serpent's Tooth, 1797
   Silverhair the Warrior, 1491
   The Wolf and the Raven, 1798
PAXON, Diana L., and MARTINE-BARNES,
   Adrienne
   Master of Earth and Water, 1799
   The Shield Between the Worlds, 1799
PAYNE, Bernal C., Jr.
   It's About Time, 2821
PAYNE, Joan Balfour (Dicks), 213
   Ambrose, 653
   The Leprechaun of Bayou Luce, 2597

Magnificent Milo, 2598
The Piebald Princess, 654
Payson, Dale, 1016, 2042
PEABODY, Paul
   Blackberry Hollow, 655
PEARCE, (Ann) Philippa
   A Dog So Small, 2599
   Lion at School: And Other Stories, 2600
   Mrs. Cockle's Cat, 2601
   *The Shadow-Cage and Other Tales of the
      Supernatural*, 1167
   The Squirrel Wife, 266
   Tom's Midnight Garden, 2822
   Who's Afraid? And Other Strange Stories, 1168
PEARSON, Kit
   A Handful of Time, 2823
PEASE, (Clarence) Howard
   *The Gypsy Caravan; Being the Merry Tale of the
      Travels of Betty and Joe With the Gypsies—
      Their Amazing Adventures with Robin
      Hood—with Richard-the-Lion-Hearted—with
      Roland—and Sundry Other Great and
      Famous Persons*, 2824
Peck, Beth, 120, 2984
Peck, Marshall, 2216
PECK, Richard (Wayne)
   Blossom Culp and the Sleep of Death, 1169
   The Dreadful Future of Blossom Culp, 1169
   The Ghost Belonged to Me: A Novel, 1169
   Ghosts I Have Been, 1169
   Voices After Midnight, 2825
PECK, Sylvia
   Seal Child, 1800
Pedersen, Vilhelm, 779
PEET, Bill (William Bartlett)
   Big Bad Bruce, 656
   The Whingdingdilly, 657
PELGROM, Els
   Little Sophie and Lanky Flop, 267
Pels, Winslow, 1769
PENDERGRAFT, Patricia
   The Legend of Daisy Flowerdew, 268
Percy, Graham, 2431
Perkins, David, 2515
Perl, Susan, 241
Petersham, Maud, 2296, 2889
Petersham, Miska, 2296, 2889
PETRIE, Stuart
   The Voyage of Barracks, 2268
PEYTON, K. M. (pseud. of Kathleen Wendy
   Peyton)
   A Pattern of Roses, 1170
Peyton, Kathleen Wendy. *See* PEYTON, K. M.
PFEFFER, Susan Beth
   Future Forward, 2826
   Rewind to Yesterday, 2826
PHILIP, Neil
   The Tale of Sir Gawain, 1802

PHILLIPS, Ann
  The Oak King and the Ash Queen, 1803
PHILLIPS, Ethel Calvert
  Little Rag Doll, 2949
  The Popover Family, 2950
PHIPSON, Joan (pseud. of Margaret Fitzhardinge)
  The Watcher in the Garden, 269
  The Way Home, 2827
PICARD, Barbara Leonie
  The Faun and the Woodcutter's Daughter, 942
  The Goldfinch Garden: Seven Tales, 943
  The Lady of the Linden Tree, 944
  The Mermaid and the Simpleton, 945
Pickard, Charles, 738
Pienkowski, Jan, 771, 773, 1006
PIERCE, Meredith Ann
  Birth of the Firebringer, 1492
  Dark Moon, 1492
  The Darkangel, 1493
  A Gathering of Gargoyles, 1493
  The Pearl of the Soul of the World, 1493
  Where the Wild Geese Go, 270
  The Woman Who Loved Reindeer, 1494
PIERCE, Tamora
  Alanna: The First Adventure, 1495
  In the Hand of the Goddess, 1495
  Lioness Rampant, 1495
  Wild Magic: The Immortals, 1496
  Wolf-Speaker, 1496
  The Woman Who Rides Like a Man, 1495
PIKE, Christopher
  Sati, 271
PINI, Richard, jt. auth. *See* PINI, Wendy
PINI, Wendy, and PINI, Richard
  Against the Wind, 1497
  The Blood of Ten Chiefs, 1497
  ElfQuest, Book 2, 1497
  ElfQuest, Book 3, 1497
  ElfQuest, Book 4, 1497
  ElfQuest: The Novel, Journey to Sorrow's End,
    1497
  Winds of Change, 1497
  Wolfsong, 1497
Pinkney, Brian, 150, 465, 1150
PINKWATER, D(aniel) Manus. *See also* KEELE,
  Luqman
  Blue Moose, 658
  The Frankenbagel Monster, 2269
  The Hoboken Chicken Emergency, 2270
  Jolly Roger: A Dog of Hoboken, 2271
  The Last Guru, 2272
  Lizard Music, 2273
  Magic Camera, 2602
  The Moospire, 658
  The Muffin Fiend, 2274
  Return of the Moose, 658
  Wingman, 2828
  The Worms of Kukumlima, 2275

Yobgorgle: Mystery Monster of Lake Ontario,
  2276
Pinto, Ralph, 217, 541
Pitz, Henry C., 948, 1767
PLACE, Marian T(empleton)
  The Resident Witch, 3102
  The Witch Who Saved Halloween, 3103
PLENN, Doris
  The Green Song, 659
Plume, Ilsa, 2893
Plunkett, Edward John Morton Drax. *See*
  DUNSANY, Lord
POCHOCKI, Ethel
  The Attic Mice, 660
Podwal, Mark, 1866
Pogány, Willy, 70, 2069
Pohrt, Tom, 100
POLESE, Carolyn
  Something About a Mermaid, 2603
Politi, Leo, 445
Pollack, Reginald, 148
POLLAND, Madeleine A(ngela Cahill)
  Deirdre, 1805
POLLOCK, Penny
  Stall Buddies, 661
POMERANTZ, Charlotte
  *Detective Poufy's First Case: Or the Missing
    Battery-Operated Pepper Grinder*, 2277
  The Downtown Fairy Godmother, 2604
POOLE, Josephine
  The Visitor: A Story of Suspense, 3104
POPE, Elizabeth Marie
  The Perilous Gard, 2045
  The Sherwood Ring, 2829
POPHAM, Hugh
  The Fabulous Voyage of the Pegasus, 2278
PORTE, Barbara Ann
  Jesse's Ghost and Other Stories, 946
PORTER, David Lord
  Help! Let Me Out!, 2279
Porter, Pat, 2228
Post, Mance, 582
POSTGATE, Oliver, and FIRMIN, Peter
  The Blackwash, 272
  The Flowers, 272
  The Game, 272
  The Ice Dragon, 272
  The Icebergs, 272
  King of the Nogs, 272
  The Monster, 272
  Nogbad and the Elephants, 272
  Nogbad Comes Back, 272
  Noggin and the Dragon, 272
  Noggin and the Money, 272
  Noggin and the Moon Mouse, 272
  Noggin and the Storks, 272
  Noggin and the Whale, 272
  Noggin the King, 272

Nogmania, 272
The Pie, 272
POSTMA, Lidia, 314
The Stolen Mirror, 2046
The Witch's Garden, 2605
POTTER, (Helen) Beatrix (Heelis)
The Fairy Caravan, 662
The Tale of Little Pig Robinson, 663
The Tale of the Faithful Dove, 664
POTTER, Miriam (S.) Clark
Sally Gabble and the Fairies, 2606
POWERS, Tim
The Stress of Her Regard, 1498
Prachatická, Markéta, 1913
PRANTERA, Amanda
The Cabalist, 3105
PRATCHETT, Terry
Diggers, 1499
Truckers, 1499
Wings, 1499
PRATT, (Murray) Fletcher
The Well of the Unicorn, 1500
PREISS, Byron (Cary), and REAVES, J. Michael
Dragonworld, 1501
Preston, Alice Bolan, 788, 789, 790
PREUSSLER, Otfried
The Final Adventures of the Robber Hotzenplotz, 2280
Further Adventures of the Robber Hotzenplotz, 2280
The Little Ghost, 1171
The Little Witch, 3106
The Robber Hotzenplotz, 2280
The Satanic Mill, 3107
The Wise Men of Schilda, 2281
Price, Christine, 437, 2049, 2861
Price, Garrett, 2260, 2507
PRICE, Susan
The Devil's Piper, 1806
The Ghost Drum: A Cat's Tale, 3108
Ghost Song, 3109
Primavera, Elise, 352, 353
Primrose, Jean, 2926, 2928
PROVENSEN, Alice, 253, 949
The Provensen Book of Fairy Tales, 949
Provensen, Martin, 253, 949
PROYSEN, Alf
Little Old Mrs. Pepperpot and Other Stories, 2607
Mrs. Pepperpot Again, 2607
Mrs. Pepperpot in the Magic Wood, 2607
Mrs. Pepperpot to the Rescue, 2607
Mrs. Pepperpot's Busy Day, 2607
Mrs. Pepperpot's Christmas, 2607
Mrs. Pepperpot's Outing, 2607
Mrs. Pepperpot's Year, 2607
Pryse, Spencer, 2578
Pulido, Shirley, 425

PULLMAN, Philip
Spring-Heeled Jack, 2282
PURTILL, Richard
Enchantment at Delphi, 1807
PUSHKIN, Alexander Sergeevich
The Golden Cockerel and Other Stories, 950
The Tale of Czar Saltan, or the Prince and the Swan Princess, 273
The Tale of the Golden Cockerel, 274
PYLE, Howard, 1767
The Garden Behind the Moon: A Real Story of the Moon Angel, 275
King Stork, 3110
Pepper and Salt; or, Seasoning for Young Folk, 951
The Story of King Arthur and His Knights, 1808
The Story of Sir Launcelot and His Companions, 1808
The Story of the Champions of the Round Table, 1808
The Story of the Grail and the Passing of Arthur, 1808
Twilight Land, 276
The Wonder Clock; or, Four and Twenty Marvelous Tales, Being One for Each Hour of the Day, 952
Pyle, Katherine, 2381

QUACKENBUSH, Robert M(ead), 1228, 2258
Bicycle to Treachery, 665
Danger in Tibet, 665
Dig to Disaster, 665
Dogsled to Dread, 665
Evil Under the Sea, 665
Express Train to Trouble: A Miss Mallard Mystery, 665
Gondola to Danger, 665
Lost in the Amazon, 665
Rickshaw to Horror, 665
Stage Door to Terror, 665
Stairway to Doom, 665
Taxi to Intrigue, 665
Quadflieg, Roswitha, 1949

RABINOWITZ, Ann
Knight on Horseback, 1172
Rackham, Arthur, 93, 190, 523, 779, 1724, 1725, 1767, 1913, 2069, 2764, 2892, 2897
Rader, Laura, 2675
RADFORD, Ken
The Cellar, 2830
Haunting at Mill Lane, 1173
Raglin, Tim, 183
Raible, Alton, 1187, 1188, 1532, 2639
RAMACHANDER, Akumal
Little Pig, 277
Ramos, Michael, 2310

Ramsey, Marcy, 2932
Rand, Ted, 1155
RASKIN, Ellen, 1648
   Figgs and Phantoms, 2283
   The Mysterious Disappearance of Leon (I Mean Noel), 2284
   The Tattooed Potato and Other Clues, 2285
RAWLINGS (Baskin), Marjorie Kinnan
   The Secret River, 2608
RAWN, Melanie
   Dragon Prince, 1502
   Dragon Token, 1503
   Skybowl, 1503
   The Star Scroll, 1502
   Stronghold, 1503
   Sunrunner's Fire, 1502
Ray, David, 1881
RAY, Mary (Eva Pedder)
   The Golden Bees, 1504
   Song of Thunder, 1504
Rayevsky, Robert, 301
RAYNER, Mary (Yoma, neé Grigson), 569, 573, 576
   Garth Pig and the Ice-Cream Lady, 666
   Garth Pig Steals the Show, 666
   Mr. and Mrs. Pig's Evening Out, 666
   Mrs. Pig Gets Cross; and Other Stories, 666
   Mrs. Pig's Bulk Buy, 666
RAYNER, William
   Stag Boy, 1809
Raysor, Joan, 2590
RAZZI, Jim (James), and RAZZI, Mary
   The Search for King Pup's Tomb, 667
RAZZI, Mary, jt. auth. *See* RAZZI, Jim (James)
REAVES, J. Michael, jt. auth. *See* PREISS, Byron (Cary)
REAVES, Michael
   The Shattered World, 3111
   Street Magic, 1810
REEVES, James (pseud. of John Morris Reeves)
   The Cold Flame, 1505
   Maildun the Voyager, 1811
   Sailor Rumbelow and Other Stories, 953
   The Strange Light, 2047
Reeves, John Morris. *See* REEVES, James
Reeves, Joyce. *See* GARD, Joyce
Reeves, Ruth, 1925
Reeves, William, 2012
REICHERT, Mickey Zucker
   Child of Thunder, 1506
   The Last of the Renshai, 1506
   The Western Wizard, 1506
REID, Alastair
   Allth, 278
   Fairwater, 278
REID BANKS, Lynne
   The Fairy Rebel, 2609
   The Farthest-Away Mountain, 279

   I Houdini: The Autobiography of a Self-Educated Hamster, 668
   The Indian in the Cupboard, 2610
   The Magic Hare, 669
   Melusine: A Mystery, 1812
   The Mystery of the Cupboard, 2610
   The Return of the Indian, 2610
   The Secret of the Indian, 2610
Reiner, Gertrude, 357
Reiner, Walter, 357
Reinertson, Barbara, 2517
REISS, Kathryn
   Dreadful Sorry, 2831
   Pale Phoenix, 2832
   Time Windows, 2832
REIT, Seymour
   Benvenuto, 2286
Remington, Barbara, 117, 739
RENAULT, Mary (pseud. of Mary Challans)
   The Bull from the Sea, 1813
   The King Must Die, 1813
RENDAL, Justine
   A Child of Their Own, 2951
REYNOLDS, Alfred
   Kiteman of Karanga, 1507
REYNOLDS, Mack, and ING, Dean
   The Other Time, 2833
REYNOLDS, Susan Lynn
   Strandia, 1508
RHYS, Mimpsey
   Mr. Hermit Crab: A Tale for Children by a Child, 2048
Ribbons, Ian, 2464
Ricci, Regolo, 11
RICE, Robert
   The Last Pendragon, 1814
Richards, George, 2314
Richardson, Frederick, 966
RICHARDSON, Jean
   Beware! Beware! Chilling Tales, 1029
Richardson, Mark, 2480
RICHEMONT, Enid
   The Glass Bird, 2611
   The Magic Skateboard, 2612
   The Time Tree, 2834
RICHLER, Mordecai
   Jacob Two-Two and the Dinosaur, 2287
RICHLER, Mordecai
   Jacob Two-Two Meets the Hooded Fang, 2287
RIDLEY, Philip
   Krindlekrax; or, How Ruskin Splinter Battled a Horrible Monster and Saved His Entire Neighborhood, 2288
Ridley, Trevor, 2594
Rieti, Fabio, 110
Riggio, Anita, 614
RILEY, Louise
   Train for Tiger Lily, 2049

Riley, Terry, 668
RINKOFF, Barbara (Jean)
  Elbert, the Mind Reader, 2289
RIORDAN, James
  The Three Magic Gifts, 280
RIOS, Tere (Teresa)
  The Fifteenth Pelican, 2290
RITCHIE, Alice
  The Treasure of Li-Po, 955
Ritchie, T., 955
Ritz, Karen, 605, 1221
Rivoli, Mario, 350
ROACH, Marilynne K(athleen)
  *Encounters with the InvisibleWorld; Being Ten
    Tales of Ghosts, Witches, and the Devil
    Himself in New England*, 956
  Presto: Or, the Adventures of a Turnspit Dog,
    670
Robb, Brian, 2255
ROBBINS, Ruth, 1164, 1433
  Taliesin and King Arthur, 1815
ROBERSON, Jennifer
  Daughters of Lion, 1509
  Flight of the Raven, 1509
  Lady of the Forest, 1816
  Legacy of the Sword, 1509
  A Pride of Princes, 1509
  Shapeshifters, 1509
  The Song of Homana, 1509
  Sword Dancer, 1510
  Sword-Breaker, 1510
  Sword-Maker, 1510
  Sword-Singer, 1510
  Track of the White Wolf, 1509
ROBERTS, Keith (John Kingston)
  Pavane, 1511
ROBERTS, Willo Davis
  The Magic Book, 2613
Robertshaw, (James) Dennis. *See* GAUNT, Michael
ROBERTSON, Mary Elsie
  Jemimalee, 671
Robinson, Charles, 241, 431, 779, 826, 984, 1149,
  1725, 1957, 2109, 2415, 2718, 2719, 2720
ROBINSON Joan (Mary) G(ale Thomas)
  When Marnie Was There, 1175
ROBINSON, Mabel L(ouise)
  Back-Seat Driver, 672
  Riley Goes to Obedience School, 672
  Skipper Riley, 672
ROBINSON, Marileta
  Mr. Goat's Bad Good Idea, 673
Robinson, Thomas H., 779
Robinson, W. Heath, 175, 779, 2202, 2255
ROCCA, Guido
  Gaetano the Pheasant: A Hunting Fable, 674
Rockwell, Anne, 6
ROCKWELL, Thomas
  Tin Cans, 2614

RODDA, Emily
  The Best-Kept Secret, 2835
  Finders Keepers, 2050
  The Pigs Are Flying!, 2615
  Something Special, 2616
  The Timekeeper, 2050
RODGERS (Guettel), Mary
  A Billion for Boris, 2291
  Freaky Friday, 2291
  Summer Switch, 2291
RODOWSKY, Colby F.
  The Gathering Room, 1176
  Keeping Time, 2836
Rogers, Jacqueline, 1217
ROGERS, Mark E.
  The Adventures of Samurai Cat, 675
  More Adventures of Samurai Cat, 675
  Samurai Cat Goes to the Movies, 675
  Samurai Cat in the Real World, 675
ROHAN, Michael Scott
  The Anvil of Ice, 3112
Rojankovsky, Feodor, 416, 580
Romano, Clare, 822
RONSON, Mark, jt. auth. *See* WHITELAW, Stella
Root, Kimberly Bulcken, 877
ROOT, Phyllis
  The Listening Silence, 1817
Rose, Carl, 3014
Rose, David S., 2911, 2934
Rose, Gerald, 804, 805
ROSENBERG, Joel
  D'Shai, 1512
  Heir Apparent, 2051
  Hour of the Octopus, 1512
  The Road to Ehvenor, 2051
  The Silver Crown, 2051
  The Sleeping Dragon, 2051
  The Sword and the Chain, 2051
  The Warrior Lives, 2051
Rosenberry, Vera, 929
Rosoman, L. H., 3030
ROSS, Eulalie Steinmetz
  The Blue Rose; a Collection of Stories for Girls,
    800
  The Lost Half-Hour: A Collection of Stories, 920
Ross, Gordon, 2255
Ross, John, 822
ROSS, Ramon Royal
  Prune, 676
ROSS, Tony, 1913
  A Fairy Tale, 2617
ROUNDS, David
  Cannonball River Tales, 2292
ROUNDS, Glen (Harold)
  The Day the Circus Came to Lone Tree, 2293
  Mr. Yowder and the Giant Bull Snake, 2293
  Mr. Yowder and the Lion Roar Capsules, 2293
  Mr. Yowder and the Steamboat, 2293

Mr. Yowder and the Train Robbers, 2293
Mr. Yowder and the Windwagon, 2293
Mr. Yowder, the Peripatetic Sign Painter: Three Tall Tales, 2294
Rowell, Kenneth, 1944
Rowen, Amy, 1143
Rowles, Daphne, 423
RUBIN, Amy Kateman
 Children of the Seventh Prophecy, 2052
RUCH, Sandi Barrett
 Junkyard Dog, 677
RUCKER, Rudy
 The Hollow Earth: The Narrative of Mason Algiers Reynolds of Virginia, 2053
RUDDICK, Bob, jt. auth. *See* GREER, Gerry
RUFF, Matt
 Fool on the Hill, 2618
RUFFELL, Ann
 Pyramid Power, 2054
RUSCH, Kristine Kathryn
 The White Mists of Power, 1513
RUSH, Alison
 The Last of Danu's Children, 1818
RUSHDIE, Salman
 Haroun and the Sea of Stories, 1514
RUSKIN, John
 The King of the Golden River, or the Black Brothers: A Legend of Stiria, 281
Russell, Craig P., 984
RUSSELL, Jean
 Supernatural Stories: 13 Tales of the Unexpected, 1195
RUSSELL, Sean
 The Initiate Brother, 1515
Russon, Mary, 2017
Rutherford, Jenny, 2777
Rutherford, Meg, 527, 580
Rutter, Eileen Joyce. *See* CHANT, Joy
Ryan, Stephen, 1996

SABERHAGEN, Fred
 After the Fact, 2055
 The Book of Swords, 1517
 The Complete Book of Swords, 1517
 Empire of the East, 1516
 The Fifth Book of Lost Swords: Coinspinner's Story, 1517
 The First Book of Lost Swords: Woundhealer's Story, 1517
 The First Book of Swords, 1518
 The Fourth Book of Lost Swords: Farslayer's Story, 1517
 The Last Book of Lost Swords: Shieldbreaker's Story, 1517, 1518
 Pyramids, 2055
 The Second Book of Lost Swords: Sightblinder's Story, 1517

The Second Book of Swords, 1518
The Seventh Book of Lost Swords: Wayfinder's Story, 1517
The Sixth Book of Lost Swords: Mindsword's Story, 1517
The Third Book of Lost Swords: Stonecutter's Story, 1517
The Third Book of Swords, 1518
SACHAR, Louis
 Sideways Arithmetic from Wayside School, 2295
 Sideways Stories from Wayside School, 2295
 Wayside School Is Falling Down, 2295
SAINT-EXUPÉRY, Antoine (Jean-Baptiste-Marie-Roger) de
 The Little Prince, 282
SAINTSBURY (Green), Dana
 The Squirrel That Remembered, 678
Sallak, Albert, 907
SALMONSON, Jessica Amanda
 Amazons!, 1244
 What Did Miss Darrington See? An Anthology of Feminist Supernatural Fiction, 1211
SALSITZ, R. A. V.
 Night of Dragons, 1520
 The Unicorn Dancer, 1519
 Where Dragons Lie, 1520
 Where Dragons Rule, 1520
SALSITZ, Rhodi Vilott
 The Twilight Gate, 1819
Salter, Safaya, 580
SALVATORE, R. A.
 The Dragon's Dagger, 2056
 The Woods Out Back, 2056
Sambourne, Linley, 175
SANCHEZ-SILVA, José
 The Boy and the Whale, 283
SANDBURG, Carl (August)
 More Rootabagas, 2296
 Potato Face, 2296
 Rootabaga Pigeons, 2296
 Rootabaga Stories, 2296
SANDERSON, Ruth, 1099
 The Enchanted Wood: An Original Fairy Tale, 284
Sandin, Joan, 389, 389
San Souci, Daniel, 346, 1724, 1725, 3113
SAN SOUCI, Robert D.
 Young Guinevere, 1820
 Young Merlin, 1821
 Feathertop: Based on the Tale by Nathaniel Hawthorne, 3113
Santore, Charles, 10, 1898
SARGENT, Sarah
 Jerry's Ghosts and the Mystery of the Blind Tower, 1177
SARGENT, Sarah
 Jonas McFee, A. T. P., 2619
 Lure of the Dark, 1822

Watermusic, 1823
Weird Henry Berg, 2620
Sauber, Rob, 2317
SAUER, Julia L(ina)
Fog Magic, 2837
SAWYER, Ruth
The Enchanted Schoolhouse, 2621
Say, Allen, 1035
SAYERS, Frances Clarke
Mr. Tidy Paws, 679
SCARBOROUGH, Elizabeth Ann
Bronwyn's Bane, 1521
The Christening Quest, 1521
The Drastic Dragon of Draco, Texas, 2297
The Harem of Aman Akbar; or The Djinn Decanted, 2298
The Healer's War: A Fantasy Novel of Vietnam, 1824
Phantom Banjo, 3114
Picking the Ballad's Bones, 3114
Song of Sorcery, 1521
Strum Again?, 3114
The Unicorn Creed, 1521
Schachner, Judith Byron, 2259
Schaeffer, Mead, 1767
SCHAEFFER, Susan Fromberg
The Dragons of North Chittendon, 2623
Scheel, Lita, 3134
SCHEFFLER, Ursel
The Return of Rinaldo, the Sly Fox, 680
Rinaldo, the Sly Fox, 680
SCHEIDL, Gerda Marie
Loretta and the Little Fairy, 2624
Schick, Joel, 2295, 2306
SCHILLER, Barbara
The Kitchen Knight, 1826
The Wandering Kinght, 1826
Schindelman, Joseph, 2416
Schindelman, Laurel, 2222
Schindler, S. D., 601
SCHLEIN, Miriam
The Raggle Taggle Fellow, 285
Schmidt, Eric Von, 3092
SCHMIDT, Werner (Felix)
The Forests of Adventure, 286
Schoengut, Emanuel, 974, 1154, 2015, 2851
Schoenherr, John, 411, 631
SCHOLES, Katherine
The Landing: A Night of Birds, 2625
Schramm, Ulrik, 888
SCHRANK, Joseph
The Plain Princess and the Lazy Prince, 287
Schreiter, Rick, 549, 989, 2212
Schroeder, Binette, 2255
Schwartz, Amy, 317
SCHWARZ, Eugene M
Two Brothers, 288

SCHWED, Antonia Holding
Noah and Me: A Novel, 681
SCIESZKA, Jon
The Frog Prince, Continued, 2299
The Good, the Bad and the Goofy, 2838
Knights of the Kitchen Table, 2838
The Not-So-Jolly Roger, 2838
The Stinky Cheese Man and Other Fairly Stupid Tales, 2300
The True Story of the 3 Little Pigs: By A. Wolf, 2301
Your Mother Was a Neanderthal, 2838
SCOTT, Dixon
A Fresh Wind in the Willows, 682
SCULLARD, Sue
Miss Fanshawe and the Great Dragon Adventure, 2302
SEABROOKE, Brenda
The Dragon That Ate Summer, 2626
Seaman, Mary, 2574
Seeley, Laura L., 2491
SEEMAN, Elizabeth (Brickel)
The Talking Dog and the Barking Man, 683
SEFTON, Catherine (pseud. of Martin Waddell)
The Emma Dilemma, 2627
The Ghost and Bertie Boggin, 1178
SÈGUR, Comtesse Sophie (Rostopchine) de
The Enchanted Forest, 289
SEIDLER, Tor
A Rat's Tale, 684
The Wainscott Weasel, 685
SELDEN (Thompson), George
Chester Cricket's New Home, 686
Chester Cricket's Pigeon Ride, 686
The Cricket in Times Square, 686
The Genie of Sutton Place, 2628
Harry Cat's Pet Puppy, 686
Harry Kitten and Tucker Mouse, 686
Irma and Jerry, 687
The Old Meadow, 686
Oscar Lobster's Fair Exchange, 688
Tucker's Countryside, 686
SELFRIDGE, Oliver
The Trouble with Dragons, 290
SELZNICK, Brian
The Houdini Box, 2629
SENDAK, Jack
The Second Witch, 3115
SENDAK, Maurice (Bernard), 48, 49, 136, 160, 221, 222, 291, 312, 313, 394, 552, 733, 779, 961, 2467, 2505, 2933
Higglety Pigglety Pop! Or, There Must Be More to Life, 689
Kenny's Window, 2630
SENDAK, Philip
In Grandpa's House, 291

SEREDY, Kate, 397
Lazy Tinka, 292
The White Stag, 1828
SERRAILLIER, Ian (Lucien)
The Challenge of the Green Knight, 1829
Servello, Joe, 910, 1358, 2218
SERVICE, Pamela F.
Being of Two Minds, 2631
The Reluctant God, 2839
Tomorrow's Magic, 1831
Vision Quest, 2840
Weirdos of the Universe, Unite!, 1830
When the Night Wind Howls, 3116
Winter of Magic's Return, 1831
Wizard of Wind and Rock, 1832
SEUSS, Dr. (pseud. of Theodor Seuss Geisel)
The 500 Hats of Bartholomew Cubbins, 293
Bartholomew and the Oobleck, 293
SEVERN, David (pseud. of David Unwin)
Dream Gold, 2841
The Girl in the Grove, 1179
Sewall, Marcia, 111, 170, 173, 347, 361, 908, 2164, 2514
Sewell, Helen, 107, 463, 464, 2048, 2108, 2606, 2987
SEXTON, Anne (Harvey), jt. auth. *See* KUMIN, Maxine (Winokur)
SEYMOUR, Miranda (pseud. of Miranda Sinclair)
Medea, 1833
SHACHTMAN, Tom
Beachmaster, 690
Driftwhistler: A Story of Daniel au Fond, 690
Wavebender, 690
SHANNON, Monica
California Fairy Tales, 957
More Tales from California, 957
SHAPIRO, Irwin
Twice upon a Time, 294
SHARMA, Partap
The Surangini Tales, 295
SHARMAT, Marjorie Weinman
The Trolls of Twelfth Street, 2303
SHARP (Castle), Margery
Bernard into Battle, 691
Bernard the Brave, 691
Miss Bianca, 691
Miss Bianca and the Bridesmaid, 691
Miss Bianca in the Antarctic, 691
Miss Bianca in the Arctic, 691
Miss Bianca in the Orient, 691
Miss Bianca in the Salt Mines, 691
The Rescuers, 691
The Turret, 691
Sharpe, Caroline, 2600
Sheahan, Henry Beston. *See* BESTON, Henry B.
SHECKLEY, Robert, jt. auth. *See* ZELAZNY, Roger

SHECTER, Ben, 2105, 2197, 2303
The Stocking Child, 2952
The Whistling Whirligig, 1181
SHEEDY, Alexandra E.
She Was Nice to Mice: The Other Side of Elizabeth I's Character Never Before Revealed by Previous Historians, 692
SHEEHAN, Carolyn, and SHEEHAN, Edmond
Magnifi-Cat, 693
SHEEHAN, Edmond, jt. auth. *See* SHEEHAN, Carolyn
Shefts, Joelle, 2232
Shekerjian, Haig, 2423
Shekerjian, Regina, 2423
SHELLEY, Rick
The Hero of Varay, 2057
Son of the Hero, 2057
Shepard, Ernest H., 127, 522, 523, 779, 852, 927, 1669, 1670, 2024, 2441, 2944
Shepard, Mary, 242, 2651
SHERBURNE, Zoa (Morin)
Why Have the Birds Stopped Singing?, 2842
SHERMAN, Josepha
Child of Faerie, Child of Earth, 1834
The Horse of Flame, 1522
The Shining Falcon, 1522
Strange and Ancient Name, 2058
Windleaf, 1523
SHETTERLY, Will
Elsewhere, 2059
Nevernever, 2059
SHETTERLY, Will, and BULL, Emma
Liavek, 1435
Shields, Charles, 871
Shore, Robert, 579
Shortall, Leonard, 672
SHOWELL, Ellen Harvey
Cecelia and the Blue Mountain Boy, 2632
Shpitalnik, Vladimir, 2653
SHULEVITZ, Uri, 174, 195, 1836, 3115
The Strange and Exciting Adventures of Jeremiah Hush, 694
SHURA, Mary Francis (pseud. of Mary Francis Craig)
Happles and Cinnamunger, 1182
The Nearsighted Knight, 296
A Shoe Full of Shamrock, 2633
Simple Spigott, 1183
A Tale of Middle Length, 695
SHUSTERMAN, Neal
The Eyes of Kid Midas, 2634
SHWARTZ, Susan M. *See also* NORTON, André
Arabesques 2, 783
Hecate's Cauldron, 3036
Moonsinger's Friends: In Honor of André Norton, 931
Silk Roads and Shadows, 1524

SHYER, Marlene Fanta
Ruby, the Red Hot Witch at Bloomingdale's, 3117
Sichel, Harold, 33
SIEBE, Josephine
Kasperle's Adventures, 2953
SIEGEL, Robert (Harold)
Alpha Centauri, 2843
SILVERBERG, Barbara
Phoenix Feathers: A Collection of Mythical Monsters, 941
SILVERBERG, Robert
Beyond the Gate of the Worlds, 1525
The Gate of Worlds, 1525
Gilgamesh the King, 1835
Kingdoms of the Wall, 1526
Letters from Atlantis, 2844
Lord Valentine's Castle, 1527
Lost Worlds, Unknown Horizons: Nine Stories of Science Fiction, 2013
The Majipoor Chronicles, 1527
Trips in Time: Nine Stories of Science Fiction, 2859
Valentine Pontifex, 1527
SILVERBERG, Robert, and GREENBERG, Martin H.
Fantasy Hall of Fame, 858
Silverman, Burt, 887, 1120
SILVERMAN, Maida
The Magic Well, 297
Silverman, Mel, 407
SILVERSTEIN, Herma
Mad, Mad Monday, 1184
SILVERSTEIN, Shel(by)
Uncle Shelby's Story of Lafcadio, the Lion Who Shot Back, 2304
SIMAK, Clifford D(onald)
Enchanted Pilgrimage, 1528
The Goblin Reservation, 2845
Where the Evil Dwells, 1529
Simms, Blanche, 2910
Simon, Howard, 2940
SIMONT, Marc, 158, 327, 328, 330
The Contest at Paca, 2305
Mimi, 696
Sims, Blanche, 2130, 2309, 2659, 2777
Sinclair, Miranda. *See* SEYMOUR, Miranda
SINCLAIR, Tom
Tales of a Wandering Warthog, 697
SINGER, Isaac Bashevis
Alone in the Wild Forest, 298
The Fearsome Inn, 299
The Golem, 1836
Naftali the Storyteller and His Horse, Sus, and Other Stories, 959
Stories for Children, 960
A Tale of Three Wishes, 300
Zlateh the Goat and Other Stories, 961

SINGER, Marilyn
California Demon, 3118
Charmed, 2060
The Fido Frame-Up, 698
Ghost Host, 1185
The Golden Heart of Winter, 301
Horsemaster, 2061
A Nose for Trouble, 698
Where There's a Will, There's a Wag, 698
Sis, Peter, 81, 1073, 1074, 1350
SISSON, Rosemary Anne
The Adventures of Ambrose, 699
SKURZYNSKI, Gloria (Joan)
What Happened in Hamelin, 1837
SLATER, Jim
Grasshopper and the Unwise Owl, 2635
SLEATOR, William (Warner III)
Among the Dolls, 2955
The Green Futures of Tycho, 2846
SLEIGH, Barbara (de Riemer)
Carbonel and Calidor, 2636
Carbonel: The King of the Cats, 2636
Jessamy, 2847
The Kingdom of Carbonel, 2636
Stirabout Stories, Brewed in Her Own Cauldron, 962
SLEPIAN, Jan
Back to Before, 2848
SLOAN, Carolyn
The Sea Child, 1838
SLOBODKIN, Louis, 94, 327, 2093
The Adventures of Arab, 2956
The Amiable Giant, 302
The Little Mermaid Who Could Not Sing, 303
Sloggett, Nellie. *See* TREGARTHEN, Enys
SLOTE, Alfred
My Robot Buddy, 2306
Small, David, 331, 2069
SMITH, Agnes
An Edge of the Forest, 304
SMITH, Alison
Come Away Home, 700
Smith, Cat Bowen, 2463
SMITH, Dodie (Dorothy Gladys)
The Hundred and One Dalmatians, 701
The Starlight Barking, 701
SMITH, Doris Buchanan
Voyages, 1839
SMITH, Emma
Emily: The Traveling Guinea Pig, 702
Emily's Voyage, 702
Smith, Jessie Willcox, 175, 219, 224
Smith, Joseph A., 1898, 2511
Smith, Kenneth, 806
Smith, L. H., 517
SMITH, L(isa) J.
Heart of Valor, 2062
Night of the Solstice, 2062

Smith, Lane, 2300, 2301, 2838
Smith, Maggie, 2448
Smith, Richard, 2915
SMITH, Sherwood
   Wren to the Rescue, 1530
   Wren's Quest, 1530
SMITH, Stephanie A.
   Snow-Eyes, 1531
Smith, Wendy, 2239
SNYDER, Dianne
   George and the Dragon Word, 2637
SNYDER, Zilpha Keatley
   And All Between, 1532
   Below the Root, 1532
   Black and Blue Magic, 2638
   The Changing Maze, 305
   Eyes in the Fishbowl, 1187
   A Season of Ponies, 2639
   Song of the Gargoyle, 1533
   Squeak Saves the Day and Other Tooley Tales,
      1534
   The Truth about Stone Hollow, 1188
   Until the Celebration, 1532
So, Meilo, 11
Sokol, Bill, 262, 2680
Solbert, Ronni, 47, 161, 162, 239, 624, 1875, 2253
SOMMER-BODENBURG, Angela
   If You Want to Scare Yourself, 1189
   My Friend the Vampire, 2308
   The Vampire in Love, 2308
   The Vampire Moves In, 2308
   The Vampire on the Farm, 2308
   The Vampire Takes a Trip, 2308
SOMTOW, S. P. (pseud. of Somtow Sucharitkul)
   The Wizard's Apprentice, 3119
SONNTAG, Linda
   The Ghost Story Treasury, 1085
Sours, Michael, 2559
SOYER, Abraham
   The Adventures of Yemima, 963
Soyer, Raphael, 963
Spanfeller, James J., 80, 2446, 2734
SPEARING, Judith (Mary Harlow)
   The Ghosts Who Went to School, 1190
   The Museum House Ghosts, 1190
Speiss, Helga, 1189
Spelman, Mary. *See* TOWNE, Mary
Spence, Geraldine, 2563
Spenceley, Annabel, 1085
Spiers, John, 1913
Spilka, Arnold, 198
SPIRIN, Gennady, 2069, 2183
   The Enchanter's Spell: Five Famous Tales, 850
SPRINGER, Nancy
   The Black Beast, 1538
   The Book of Vale, 1538
   Chains of Gold, 1536
   The Friendship Song, 2063

   Godbond, 1537
   The Golden Swan, 1538
   The Hex Witch of Seldom, 3120
   Madbond, 1537
   Mindbond, 1537
   Red Wizard, 2064
   The Sable Moon, 1538
   The Silver Sun, 1538
   The White Hart, 1538
   Wings of Flame, 1539
SPURR, Elizabeth
   Mrs. Minetta's Car Pool, 2309
ST. GEORGE, Judith
   The Mysterious Girl in the Garden, 2849
   Who's Scared? Not Me!, 2850
ST. JOHN, Wylly Folk
   The Ghost Next Door, 1191
Stadler, John, 492
Staffordshire, William Churne of. *See* PAGET,
      (Reverend) F(rancis) E(dward)
STAHL, Ben(jamin)
   Blackbeard's Ghost, 1192
   The Secret of Red Skull, 1192
Stanley, Diana, 1985
STANLEY, Diane, 2335
   Fortune, 306
STANTON, Mary
   The Heavenly Horse from the Outermost West,
      703
   Piper at the Gate, 703
Starr, Branka, 1267
STASHEFF, Christopher
   Her Majesty's Wizard, 2065
   The Oathbound Wizard, 2065
   The Witch Doctor, 2065
STASHEFF, Christopher, and FAWCETT, Bill
   The Crafters, 2998
STEARNS, Pamela (Fujimoto)
   The Fool and the Dancing Bear, 1540
   Into the Painted Bear Lair, 2066
   The Mechanical Doll, 307
STEARNS, Michael
   A Wizard's Dozen: Stories of the Fantastic, 990
STEELE, Mary Q(uintard Govan). *See* GAGE,
      Wilson
   Journey Outside, 1541
   The Owl's Kiss: Three Stories, 965
   The True Men, 1542
   Wish, Come True, 2640
STEELE, William O(wen)
   Andy Jackson's Water Well, 2310
   Daniel Boone's Echo, 2311
   Davy Crockett's Earthquake, 2312
   The No-Name Man of the Mountain, 2313
STEFANEC-OGREN, Cathy
   Sly, P. I.: The Case of the Missing Shoes, 704
STEIG, William
   Abel's Island, 705

Dominic, 706
The Real Thief, 707
STEIN, Gertrude
The World Is Round, 308
STEINER, Jörg
Rabbit Island, 708
The Sea People, 309
STEPHENS, James
The Crock of Gold, 310
Deirdre, 1840
Steranko, 806
STERMAN, Betsy, and STERMAN, Samuel
Backyard Dragon, 2641
Too Much Magic, 2642
STERMAN, Samuel, jt. auth. *See* STERMAN,
Betsy
Stermer, Dugald, 3065
Stern, Patti, 2470
STERN, Philip Van Doren
*The Other Side of the Clock: Stories Out of Time,
Out of Place*, 2814
STEUSSY, Marti
Forest of the Night, 1543
Stevens, Anthony, 709
STEVENS, Eden Vale
Abba, 709
Stevens, Janet, 6
Stevenson, Harvey, 486
STEVENSON, James
Here Comes Herb's Hurricane!, 710
Oliver, Clarence, and Violet, 711
The Supreme Souvenir Factory, 712
STEVENSON, Jocelyn
O'Diddy, 2643
STEVENSON, Laura C(aroline)
The Island and the Ring, 1544
Stevenson, Peter, 2246
STEVERMER, Caroline, jt. auth. *See* WREDE,
Patricia C(ollins)
Stewart, Arvis, 3, 1603, 2552
Stewart, Charles, 942, 944
STEWART, Mary (Florence Elinor)
The Crystal Cave, 1841
The Hollow Hills, 1841
The Last Enchantment, 1841
The Little Broomstick, 3121
Ludo and the Star Horse, 311
Thornyhold, 3122
A Walk in Wolf Wood, 2851
The Wicked Day, 1841
STIRLING, S. M., and MEIER, Shirley
The Cage, 1545
Stobbs, William, 178, 607, 1881
Stock, Catherine, 2452
STOCKTON, Frank (Francis) R(ichard)
The Bee-Man of Orn, 312
*The Casting Away of Mrs. Lecks and Mrs.
Aleshine*, 2314

The Griffin and the Minor Canon, 313
The Queen's Museum and Other Fanciful Tales,
966
*The Reformed Pirate: Stories from The Floating
Prince, Ting-a-Ling Tales and the Queen's
Museum*, 967
*The Storyteller's Pack, a Frank R. Stockton
Reader*, 968
Ting-a-Ling Tales, 969
Stoddard, Sandol. *See* WARBURG, Sandol
Stoddard
STOLP, Hans
The Golden Bird, 314
Stolpe, Daniel, 1569
STOLZ, Mary (Slattery)
Belling the Tiger, 713
Cat in the Mirror, 2852
Cat Walk, 714
The Cuckoo Clock, 315
Deputy Shep, 715
Frédou, 716
The Great Rebellion, 713
The Leftover Elf, 316
Maximilian's World, 713
Pigeon Flight, 717
Quentin Corn, 718
The Scarecrows and Their Child, 317
Siri the Conquistador, 713
Tales at the Mousehole, 719
Stone, David, 1146, 2748
Stone, Helen, 226, 2974
STONG, Phil(ip Duffield)
Prince and the Porker, 720
STORR, Catherine (Cole)
Clever Polly and the Stupid Wolf, 2315
Cold Marble and Other Ghost Stories, 1193
The Magic Drawing Pencil, 2644
Polly and the Wolf Again, 2315
Tales of Polly and the Hungry Wolf, 2315
Thursday, 1842
Stout, William, 806
STOVER, Marjorie Filley
Midnight in the Dollhouse, 2957
When the Dolls Woke, 2957
STRANGER, Joyce (pseud. of Joyce Muriel Judson
Wilson)
The Fox at Drummer's Darkness, 318
STRAUB, Peter (Francis). *See also* KING,
Stephen
Shadowland, 3123
STRAUSS, Victoria
Worldstone, 2067
STRICKLAND, Brad
*Dragon's Plunder, or, The Last Voyage of
Captain Deadmon: A Fantasy Adventure*,
2645

STRUGATSKII, Arkadii Natanovich, and
    STRUGATSKII, Boris Natanovich
    Monday Begins on Saturday, 3124
STRUGATSKII, Boris Natanovich, jt. auth. *See*
    STRUGATSKII, Arkadii Natanovich
Strugnell, Ann, 853, 1540, 2066
Sturtzel, Howard Allison. *See* ANNIXTER, Paul
Suba, Susanne, 400
Sucharitkul, Somtow. *See* SOMTOW, S. P.
SUCHARITKUL, Somtow
    Light on the Sound, 1546
    The Throne of Madness, 1546
    Utopia Hunters: Chronicles of the High Inquest,
        1546
SUDBERY, Rodie (Tutton)
    The Silk and the Skin, 1194
SUGGS, Welch, jt. auth. *See* MURPHY, Shirley
    Rousseau
Sumiko, 779
SUTCLIFF, Rosemary
    Chess-Dream in a Garden, 319
    *The Light Beyond the Forest: The Quest for the
        Holy Grail*, 1843
    The Minstrel and the Dragon Pup, 320
    The Road to Camlann, 1843
    *The Sword and the Circle: King Arthur and the
        Knights of the Round Table*, 1843
    Sword at Sunset, 1844
    Tristan and Iseult, 1845
SWAHN, Sven
    The Island Through the Gate, 2068
SWAYNE, Samuel, and SWAYNE, Zoa
    Great Grandfather in the Honey Tree, 2316
SWAYNE, Zoa, jt. auth. *See* SWAYNE, Samuel
Sweeney, Morgan J., 2909
SWIFT, Jonathan
    *Gulliver's Travels into Several Remote Nations
        of the World*, 2069
SYKES, Pamela
    Lucy Beware!, 2853
    Mirror of Danger, 2853
SYMONDS, John
    Away to the Moon, 2958
    Elfrida and the Pig, 721
SYMONS, (Dorothy) Geraldine
    Crocuses Were Over, Hitler Was Dead, 2854
SYNGE, (Phyllis) Ursula
    Land of Heroes: A Retelling of the Kalevala,
        1846
    Swan's Wing, 1847
    Weland, Smith of the Gods, 1848
Szekeres, Cyndy, 468, 501, 622

Tait, Douglas, 1101, 2942
Talbott, Hudson, 1767
TANNEN, Mary
    Huntley Nutley and the Missing Link, 2317

The Lost Legend of Finn, 2856
The Wizard Children of Finn, 2856
TAPP, Kathy Kennedy
    Flight of the Moth-Kin, 2646
    Moth-Kin Magic, 2646
    The Scorpio Ghosts and the Black Hole Gang,
        1196
TARN, (Sir) W(illiam) W(oodthorpe)
    *The Treasure of the Isle of Mist: A Tale of the Isle
        of Skye*, 2647
TARR, Judith
    Alamut, 1548
    Arrows of the Sun, 1550
    Ars Magica, 1549
    The Dagger and the Cross, 1548, 1551
    A Fall of Princes, 1550
    The Golden Horn, 1551
    The Hall of the Mountain King, 1550
    His Majesty's Elephant, 3125
    The Hounds of God, 1551
    The Isle of Glass, 1551
    The Lady of Han-Gilen, 1550
    Lord of the Two Lands, 1850
TASSIN, Algernon de Vivier
    The Rainbow String, 972
TAZEWELL, Charles
    The Littlest Angel, 321
TEMPEST, John
    Vision of the Hunter, 1851
Tenggren, Gustaf, 9
Tennent, Julie, 2502, 2503
Tenniel, John, 1913
TENNY, Dixie
    Call the Darkness Down, 1852
TENNYSON, Noel
    The Lady's Chair and the Ottoman, 322
TEPPER, Sheri S.
    Beauty: A Novel, 1853
    Dervish Daughter, 1552
    The Flight of Mavin Manyshaped, 1554
    Jinian Footseer, 1552
    Jinian Star-Eye, 1552
    Kings Blood Four, 1554
    Marianne, the Magus, and the Manticore, 2070
    Necromancer Nine, 1554
    Northshore, 1553
    The Search of Mavin Manyshaped, 1554
    The Song of Mavin Manyshaped, 1554
    Southshore, 1553
    Wizard's Eleven, 1554
TERLOUW, Jan (Cornelis)
    How to Become King, 323
THACKERAY, William Makepeace
    *The Rose and the Ring; or the History of Prince
        Giglio and Prince Bulbo: A Fireside
        Pantomime for Great and Small Children*, 324
Thamer, Katie, 1768

THEROUX, Paul
  A Christmas Card, 325
THESMAN, Jean
  Appointment with a Stranger, 1197
Thibault, Jacques Anatole François. *See* FRANCE,
  Anatole
Thiesing, Lisa, 1142, 1893
Thomas, Allan, 842
THOMAS, Jane Resh
  The Princess in the Pigpen, 2857
THOMPSON, Julian F(rancis)
  Gypsyworld, 2071
  Herb Seasoning, 2318
Thompson, Ralph, 319
Thorne, Jenny, 183, 1886
THURBER, James (Grover)
  The 13 Clocks, 328
  The Great Quillow, 326
  Many Moons, 327
  The White Deer, 329
  The Wonderful O, 330
Tiegreen, Alan, 251, 2425
Tikka, Saara, 142
TILLSTROM, Burr
  The Dragon Who Lived Downstairs, 331
Tinkelman, Murray, 717
Titherington, Jeanne, 194, 1095
TITUS, Eve
  Basil and the Lost Colony, 722
  Basil and the Pygmy Cats, 722
  Basil in Mexico, 722
  Basil in the Wild West, 722
  Basil of Baker Street, 722
Tobias, Beatrice, 97
TODD, Barbara Euphan (pseud. of Barbara Euphan
  [Todd] Bower)
  Earthy Mangold and Worzel Gummidge, 2319
  More about Worzel Gummidge, 2319
  Worzel Gummidge and Saucy Nancy, 2319
  Worzel Gummidge and the Railway Scarecrows,
    2319
  Worzel Gummidge and the Treasure Ship, 2319
  Worzel Gummidge at the Circus, 2319
  Worzel Gummidge Takes a Holiday, 2319
  *Worzel Gummidge, the Scarecrow of
    Scatterbrook Farm*, 2319
Todd, Justin, 1913
TODD, Ruthven
  Space Cat, 723
  Space Cat and the Kittens, 723
  Space Cat Meets Mars, 723
  Space Cat Visits Venus, 723
TOLKIEN, J(ohn) R(onald) R(euel)
  *The Adventures of Tom Bombadil and Other
    Verses from "The Red Book,"* 1555
  Bilbo's Last Song, 1556
  The Book of Lost Tales, 1555
  The Book of Lost Tales, Volume 2, 1555

  Farmer Giles of Ham, 332
  The Fellowship of the Ring, 1555
  The Hobbit; Or, There and Back Again, 1556
  The Lays of the Beleriad, 1555
  The Return of the King, 1555
  *The Shaping of Middle-Earth: The Quenta, the
    Ambrakanta, and the Annals*, 1555
  Smith of Wootton Major, 333
  The Treason of Isengard, 1555
  The Two Towers, 1555
  Unfinished Tales of Numenor and Middle-Earth,
    1555
TOLLE, Jean Bashor
  The Great Pete Penney, 2648
TOLSTOY, Nikolai
  *The Coming of the King: The First Book of
    Merlin*, 1854
TOMALIN, Ruth
  Gone Away, 1199
Tomes, Jacqueline, 1183
Tomes, Margot, 232, 2074, 2479, 2632, 2849
TOMLINSON, Jill
  Hilda the Hen Who Wouldn't Give Up, 724
Torell, Staffen, 592
Tormey, Bertram M., 1182
TORREY, Marjorie (Chanslor Hood)
  Artie and the Princess, 334
TOWNE, Mary (pseud. of Mary Spelman)
  Goldenrod, 2649
TOWNSEND, John Rowe
  The Fortunate Isles, 1557
  The Persuading Stick, 2650
  The Visitors, 2858
TRAVERS, P(amela) L(yndon)
  Mary Poppins, 2651
  Mary Poppins and the House Next Door, 2651
  Mary Poppins Comes Back, 2651
  Mary Poppins from A to Z, 2651
  Mary Poppins in Cherry Tree Lane, 2651
  Mary Poppins in the Park, 2651
  Mary Poppins Opens the Door, 2651
TREGARTHEN, Enys (pseud. of Nellie Sloggett)
  The Doll Who Came Alive, 2959
  The White Ring, 1855
Treherne, Katie Thamer, 10, 104, 222
Tresilian, Stuart, 516
TREVOR, Elleston
  Badger's Wood, 725
  Deep Wood, 725
  Heather Hill, 725
Trier, Walter, 560, 2255
Tripp, F. J., 2280, 2281
Tripp, Wallace, 487, 509, 2120, 2378, 2391
TROTT, Susan
  The Sea Serpent of Horse, 2072
Troughton, Joanna, 54
Troy, Hugh, 2621, 2622
Truesdell, Sue, 2643

Tryon, Leslie, 628
Tudor, Tasha, 2922
TURKLE, Brinton (Cassaday), 388, 388, 2785
   The Fiddler of High Lonesome, 335
   Mooncoin Castle; or Skulduggery Rewarded,
     1200
TURNBULL, Ann (Christine)
   The Frightened Forest, 3126
   The Wolf King, 1558
TURNER, Ann
   Rosemary's Witch, 3127
Turner, Corinne, 913
Turney, Elaine McGregor, 1118
Turska, Krystyna, 281, 819, 820, 1641
TWAIN, Mark (pseud. of Samuel Clemens)
   A Connecticut Yankee in King Arthur's Court,
     2860
   Legend of Sagenfeld, 336
TWOHILL, Maggie
   Jeeter, Mason and the Magic Headset, 2960
TYRELL, Margot. *See* GASCOIGNE, Toss

Ulrich, George, 2354
Ungerer, Tomi, 716, 2113
Unwin, David. *See* SEVERN, David
UNWIN, Nora S(picer), 224, 630, 1855, 1896,
     2478, 2959
   Two Too Many, 726
Unzer-Fischer, Christa, 2624
UPDIKE, David
   An Autumn Tale, 2652
Updike, John, 248
UPENSKY, Eduard
   Uncle Fedya, His Dog, and His Cat, 2653
URE, Jean
   The Wizard in the Woods, 3128
   Wizard in Wonderland, 3128
URQUHART, Elizabeth
   Horace, 337
Ursell, Martin, 462
Uttley, Alice Jane (Taylor). *See* UTTLEY, Alison
UTTLEY, Alison (pseud. of Alice Jane [Taylor]
     Uttley)
   Candlelight Tales, 727
   Foxglove Tales, 727
   Lavender Shoes, 727
   Moonshine and Magic, 727
   A Traveler in Time, 2861

Vaës, Alain, 15
Vagin, Vladimir, 264
VALENCAK, Hannelore
   When Half-Gods Go, 1856
Valintcourt, Honoré, 2004
Valpy, Judith, 2698
VAMBA (pseud. of Luigi Bertelli)
   The Prince and His Ants, 2654

VAN ALLSBURG, Chris, 1714
   Ben's Dream, 2655
   The Garden of Abdul Gasazi, 2656
   Jumanji, 2657
   The Stranger, 338
   The Sweetest Fig, 339
   Two Bad Ants, 728
   The Widow's Broom, 3129
   The Wreck of the Zephyr, 340
   The Wretched Stone, 341
VAN DE WETERING, Janwillem
   Hugh Pine, 729
   Hugh Pine and Something Else, 729
   Hugh Pine and the Good Place, 729
Van Everen, Jay, 828
VAN LEEUWEN, Jean
   The Great Cheese Conspiracy, 730
   The Great Christmas Kidnapping Caper, 730
   The Great Rescue Operation, 730
   The Great Summer Camp Catastrophe, 730
Van Nutt, Robert, 19
VAN SCYOC, Sydney J(oyce)
   Bluesong, 1562
   Darkchild, 1562
   Daughters of the Sunstone, 1562
   Drowntide, 1563
   Starsilk, 1562
VAN STOCKUM, Hilda (Gerarda)
   Kersti and Saint Nicholas, 2320
VAN THAL, Herbert Maurice
   Famous Tales of the Fantastic, 855
Van Veen, Stuyvesant, 220
Van Wely, Babs, 42
VANCE, Jack (pseud. of John Holbrook Vance)
   Cugel's Saga, 1559
   The Dying Earth, 1559
   The Eyes of the Overworld, 1559
   The Green Pearl, 1560
   Madouc, 1560
   A Quest for Simbils, 1559
   Rhialto the Marvellous, 1559
   Suldrun's Garden, 1560
Vance, John Holbrook. *See* VANCE, Jack
VANDE VELDE, Vivian
   Dragon's Bait, 1561
VASILIU, Mircea, 287, 930, 2127
   Hark, the Little Angel, 2321
VAUGHAN, Agnes Carr
   Lucian Goes A-Voyaging, 2322
Vaughan, Anne, 2363, 2907
Verling, John, 2705
Verney, John, 2102
Vicary, Richard, 1110
VICK, Helen Hughes
   Walker of Time, 2862
Victor, Joan, 490
VINGE, Joan D(ennison)
   Ladyhawke, 3130

VIVELO, Jackie
  A Trick of the Light: Stories to Read at Dusk, 978
VOEGELI, Max
  The Prince of Hindustan, 1857
  The Wonderful Lamp, 1857
VOIGT, Cynthia
  Building Blocks, 2863
  Jackaroo, 1564
  On Fortune's Wheel, 1565
  The Wings of a Falcon, 1566
VOLSKY, Paula
  The Luck of Relian Kru, 1567
  The Wolf of Winter, 1568
Von Schmidt, Eric, 2165, 2166, 2167, 2168, 2169,
  2170, 2172, 2173
Voorhis, Stephen, 725
Voute, Kathleen, 2453
Vyse, George Howard, 455

WABER, Bernard
  Dear Hildegarde, 73
  Mice on My Mind, 732
Waddell, Martin. *See* SEFTON, Catherine
WAECHTER, Friedrich, and EILERT, Bernd
  The Crown Snatchers, 342
WAHL, Jan (Boyer)
  How the Children Stopped the Wars, 343
  Pleasant Fieldmouse, 733
  The Pleasant Fieldmouse Storybook, 733
  Pleasant Fieldmouse's Halloween Party, 733
  Pleasant Fieldmouse's Valentine Trick, 733
  The Six Voyages of Pleasant Fieldmouse, 733
Wainwright, Francis, 2905
Wakeman, Marion Freeman, 531
Waldman, Neil, 1738
Walford, Astrid, 699
Walker, Dugald Stewart, 456
WALKER, Gwen
  The Golden Stile, 2073
WALKER, Kenneth Macfarlane, and
    BOUMPHREY, Geoffrey
  The Log of the Ark, 1858
WALKER, Mary Alexander
  The Scathach and Maeve's Daughters, 1859
WALLACE, Barbara Brooks
  The Barrel in the Basement, 2658
  *The Interesting Thing That Happened at Perfect
    Acres, Inc*, 2659
  Miss Switch to the Rescue, 3131
  Palmer Patch, 734
  The Trouble with Miss Switch, 3131
WALLACE, Bill
  Snot Stew, 735
WALLIN, Luke
  The Slavery Ghosts, 1202
Wallner, John C., 697

WALTON, Evangeline (pseud. of Evangeline
    Ensley)
  The Children of Llyr, 1860
  The Prince of Annwn, 1860
  The Song of Rhiannon, 1860
  The Virgin and the Swine, 1860
WANGERIN, Walter, Jr.
  The Book of Sorrows, 344
  The Book of the Dun Cow, 344
  Elisabeth and the Water-Troll, 345
  Potter, Come Fly to the First of the Earth, 346
  Thistle, 347
WARBURG, Sandol Stoddard (pseud. of Sandol
    Stoddard)
  On the Way Home, 1569
Ward, John, 1900
Ward, Lynd, 64, 154, 2724
WARD, Patricia A(nn)
  The Secret Pencil, 2660
Warhola, James, 18
WARNER, Sylvia Townsend
  Kingdoms of Elfin, 1570
  Lolly Willowes: or, the Loving Huntsman, 3132
WATKINS, Will
  Sid Seal, Houseman, 736
Watkins-Pitchford, D(enys) J(ames), 225, 2381. *See*
    B. B.
Watson, Aldren A., 2326, 2588
WATSON, Ian
  Queenmagic, Kingmagic, 1571
Watson, Richard Jesse, 2664
WATSON, Wendy, 2387
  Tales for a Winter's Eve, 737
WATT-EVANS, Lawrence (pseud. of Richard Watt
    Evans)
  Crosstime Traffic, 980
  Misenchanted Sword, 3133
  With a Single Spell, 3133
WATT-EVANS, Lawrence, and FRIESNER,
    Esther M.
  Split Heirs, 1572
Watts, Bernadette, 7, 14
Watts, Marjorie-Ann, 2315, 2644
WAUGH, Charles G. *See* ASIMOV, Isaac;
    YOLEN, Jane
WAUGH, Charles G., and GREENBERG,
    Martin H.
  *Alternative Histories: Eleven Stories of the World
    as It Might Have Been*, 1242
WEALES, Gerald (Clifford)
  Miss Grimsbee Is a Witch, 3134
  Miss Grimsbee Takes a Vacation, 3134
WEAVER, Jack
  Mr. O'Hara, 2323
WEBB, Clifford (Cyril)
  The North Pole Before Lunch, 2661
Weevers, Peter, 1913
Wegner, Fritz, 483, 2287

Weihs, Erika, 1609
Weil, Lisl, 3088
WEIN, Elizabeth E.
  The Winter Prince, 1861
WEIR, Rosemary (Green)
  Albert and the Dragonettes, 348
  Albert the Dragon, 348
  Albert the Dragon and the Centaur, 348
  Further Adventures of Albert the Dragon, 348
  Pyewacket, 738
WEIS, Margaret
  The Paladin of the Night, 1573
  The Prophet of Akhian, 1573
  The Will of the Wanderer, 1573
WEIS, Margaret, and HICKMAN, Tracy
  Doom of the Darksword, 1577
  Dragon Wing, 1574
  DragonLance Chronicles, 1575
  DragonLance Legends, 1576
  Dragons of Autumn Twilight, 1575
  Dragons of Spring Dawning, 1575
  Dragons of Winter Night, 1575
  Elvin Star, 1574
  Fire Sea, 1574
  Forging the Darksword, 1577
  The Hand of Chaos, 1574
  Into the Labyrinth, 1574
  Serpent Mage, 1574
  The Seventh Gate, 1574
  Test of the Twins, 1576
  Time of the Twins, 1576
  Triumph of the Darksword, 1577
  War of the Twins, 1576
Weisgard, Leonard, 180, 182, 183, 2608, 3097
WEISS, Ellen, and FRIEDMAN, Mel
  The Adventures of Ratman, 2324
Weiss, Harvey, 285
WELCH, Ronald (pseud. of Ronald Oliver Felton)
  The Gauntlet, 2864
WELDRICK, Valerie
  Time Sweep, 2865
WELLMAN, Manly Wade
  After Dark, 1863
  Cahena, 1862
  The Hanging Stones, 1863
  John the Balladeer, 1863
  The Lost and the Lurking, 1863
  The Old Gods Waken, 1863
  The Valley So Low, 1863
  The Voice of the Mountain, 1863
  Who Fears the Devil?, 1863
  Worse Things Waiting, 1863
WELLS, H(erbert) G(eorge)
  The Door in the Wall and Other Stories, 981
Wells, Rosemary, 250
WENNING, Elisabeth
  The Christmas Mouse, 739
Wenzel, David, 2641

WERSBA, Barbara
  The Brave Balloon of Benjamin Buckley, 2325
  The Land of Forgotten Beasts, 2074
  Let Me Fall Before I Fly, 349
  A Song for Clowns, 350
Werth, Kurt, 435, 1126, 2332
WESLEY, Mary
  Haphazard House, 2866
WESTALL, Robert (Atkinson)
  The Call and Other Stories, 1203
  The Cats of Seroster, 1578
  *Demons and Shadows: The Ghostly Best Stories
    of Robert Westall*, 1204
  The Devil on the Road, 2867
  Ghost Abbey, 1205
  The Haunting of Chas McGill and Other Stories,
    1206
  In Camera and Other Stories, 1207
  The Promise, 1208
  Rachel and the Angel and Other Stories, 982
  The Scarecrows, 1209
  *Shades of Darkness: More of the Ghostly Best
    Stories of Robert Westall*, 1204
  The Watch House, 1210
  The Wind Eye, 2868
Westcott, Nadine Bernard, 6, 113
WESTON, John (Harrison)
  The Boy Who Sang the Birds, 351
WETTERER, Margaret K.
  The Giant's Apprentice, 352
  The Mermaid's Cape, 353
WHAYNE, Susanne Santoro
  Watch the House, 740
WHEELER, Thomas
  Loose Chippings, 2075
  Lost Threshold: A Novel, 2076
Whelan, Michael, 1407
Whistler, Rex, 835
WHITCHER, Susan
  *Real Mummies Don't Bleed: Friendly Tales for
    October Nights*, 983
WHITE, Anne Hitchcock
  Junket, 741
  The Story of Serapina, 742
White, David, 1988
WHITE, E(lwyn) B(rooks)
  Charlotte's Web, 743
  Stuart Little, 744
  The Trumpet of the Swan, 745
WHITE, Eliza Orne
  The Enchanted Mountain, 2077
White, Frances, 926
White, Martin, 1284
WHITE, Stewart Edward
  The Magic Forest: A Modern Fairy Story, 2662
WHITE, T(erence) H(anbury)
  The Ill-Made Knight, 1864
  Mistress Masham's Repose, 2663

The Once and Future King, 1864
The Sword in the Stone, 1865
The Witch in the Wood, 1865
White, William Anthony Parker. *See* BOUCHER,
    Anthony
WHITEHEAD, Victoria
    Chimney Witch Chase, 3135
    The Chimney Witches, 3135
WHITELAW, Stella, GARDINER, Judith, and
    RONSON, Mark
    Grimalkin's Tales, 746
WHITNEY, Phyllis A(yame)
    The Island of Dark Woods, 1212
WIBBERLEY, Leonard (Patrick O'Connor)
    Beware of the Mouse, 2327
    The Crime of Martin Coverly, 2869
    McGillicuddy McGotham, 2326
    The Mouse on the Moon, 2327
    The Mouse on Wall Street, 2327
    The Mouse That Roared, 2327
    The Mouse That Saved the West, 2327
    The Quest of Excalibur, 1213
WICKENDEN, Dan
    The Amazing Vacation, 2078
Wickstrom, Thor, 2483
WIEMER, Rudolf Otto
    The Good Robber, Willibald, 2328
Wiese, Kurt, 46, 428, 540, 558, 578, 579, 720, 2421
WIESEL, Elie(zer)
    The Golem; the Story of a Legend, 1866
Wiesner, David, 216, 806, 1770, 1947
Wiesner, William, 2438
WIGGIN, Kate Douglas (Smith)
    The Bird's Christmas Carol, 354
Wigglesworth, Katherine, 702
WIGNELL, Edel
    Escape by Deluge, 1867
Wijngaard, Juan, 1713
Wikland, Ilon, 1133, 2011
WILDE, Nicholas
    Down Came a Blackbird, 2870
    Into the Dark, 1214
WILDE, Oscar (pseud. of Fingal O'Flahertie Wills)
    The Canterville Ghost, 1215
    Complete Fairy Tales of Oscar Wilde, 984
    The Fairy Tales of Oscar Wilde, 984
    The Happy Prince, 355
    The Happy Prince and Other Fairy Stories, 984
    The Happy Prince and Other Tales, 984
    The Picture of Dorian Gray, 356
    The Selfish Giant, 357
    The Star Child: A Fairy Tale, 358
    Stories for Children, 984
WILDER, Cherry (pseud. of Cherry Barbara
    Lockett Grimm)
    A Princess of the Chameln, 1579

The Summer's King, 1579
Yorath the Wolf, 1579
Wilgus, David, 999, 1409
WILHELM, Kate (Katie Gertrude)
    And the Angels Sing: Stories, 985
    Cambio Bay, 1868
    Children of the Wind: Five Novellas, 986
    *The Downstairs Room, and Other Speculative
        Fiction*, 987
WILKINS (Freeman), Mary E(leanor)
    Princess Rosetta and the Popcorn Man, 359
    The Pumpkin Giant, 360
WILLARD, Barbara
    Spell Me a Witch, 3136
WILLARD, Nancy (Margaret)
    Beauty and the Beast, 1869
    *The High Rise Glorious Skittle Skat Roarious Sky
        Pie Angel Food Cake*, 2664
    *The Island of the Grass King: The Further
        Adventures of Anatole*, 2079
    The Marzipan Moon, 361
    The Mountains of Quilt, 2665
    Sailing to Cythera, and Other Anatole Stories,
        2079
    The Sorcerer's Apprentice, 3137
    Things Invisible to See, 362
    Uncle Terrible: More Adventures of Anatole,
        2079
WILLETT, John (William Mills)
    The Singer in the Stone, 1580
WILLEY, Elizabeth
    *The Well-Favored Man: The Tale of the
        Sorcerer's Nephew*, 1581
WILLIAMS, A. Susan
    *The Lifted Veil: The Book of Fantastic Literature
        by Women, 1800–World War II*, 918
WILLIAMS, Anne
    Secret of the Round Tower, 363
WILLIAMS, Garth (Montgomery), 686, 691, 743,
    744
    The Adventures of Benjamin Pink, 747
WILLIAMS, Jay
    The Hero from Otherwhere, 2080
    The Magic Grandfather, 2666
    Petronella, 364
    The Practical Princess, 365
    *The Practical Princess and Other Liberating
        Fairy Tales*, 989
    The Time of the Kraken, 1582
WILLIAMS (John), Ursula Moray
    Bogwoppit, 749
    Castle Merlin, 1216
    The Cruise of the Happy-Go-Gay, 2329
    Malkin's Mountain, 2961
    The Moonball, 2667
    The Nine Lives of Island MacKenzie, 750
    The Three Toymakers, 2961

Tiger Nanny, 2330
The Toymaker's Daughter, 2961
WILLIAMS, Kit
Masquerade, 366
Williams, Marcia, 61
WILLIAMS, Ruth L.
The Silver Tree, 2871
WILLIAMS, Tad
The Dragonbone Chair, 1583
Stone of Farewell, 1583
Tailchaser's Song, 748
To Green Angel Tower, 1583
WILLIAMS, Tad, and HOFFMAN, Nina Kiriki
Child of an Ancient City, 1584
WILLIAMS, Thomas (Alonzo)
Tsuga's Children, 2081
WILLIS, Connie
Doomsday Book, 2872
Lincoln's Dreams, 2873
WILLIS, Paul J.
No Clock in the Forest, 2082
WILSON, A. N.
Hazel the Guinea Pig, 751
Stray, 752
Tabitha, 753
Wilson, Dagmar, 498
WILSON, David Henry
The Coachman Rat, 1870
WILSON, Gahan, 806, 2198
Harry and the Sea Serpent, 754
Harry the Fat Bear, 754
Wilson, Joyce Muriel Judson. *See* STRANGER,
Joyce
WILSON, Robert Charles
A Bridge of Years, 2874
Gypsies, 2083
WILSON, Willie
Up Mountain One Time, 755
Wilton, Charles, 2900
WINDLING, Terri. *See also* DATLOW, Ellen
Faery!, 854
WINDLING, Terri, and ARNOLD, Mark Alan
Borderland, No. 1, 1268
Elsewhere, vol. 1, 1340
WINDSOR, Patricia (Frances)
*How a Weirdo and a Ghost Can Change Your
Entire Life*, 1217
Wingham, Peter, 1725
Winslow, Will, 2286
Winter, Jeanette, 191
Winter, William, 1903
WINTERFELD, Henry
Castaways in Lilliput, 2084
Winters, Nina, 2103
WINTHROP (Mahony), Elizabeth
The Battle for the Castle, 2085
The Castle in the Attic, 2085

WISEMAN, David
Adam's Common, 2875
Blodwen and the Guardians, 2668
Jeremy Visick, 2876
Thimbles, 2877
A Tie to the Past, 2878
WISNIEWSKI, David
Elfwyn's Saga, 367
The Warrior and the Wise Man, 368
WOLF, Joan
The Road to Avalon, 1871
WOLF, Joyce
Between the Cracks, 3140
WOLFE, Gene (Rodman)
Castleview, 1872
The Citadel of the Autarch, 1585
The Claw of the Conciliator, 1585
Nightside the Long Sun, 1585
The Shadow of the Torturer, 1585
Soldier of Arete, 1586
Soldier of the Mist, 1586
The Sword of the Lictor, 1585
The Urth of the New Sun, 1585
WOLITZER, Meg
The Dream Book, 2669
Wong, David, 2625
WOOD, Douglas
Old Turtle, 369
Wood, Harrie, 2322, 2824
WOOD, James Playsted
The Elephant in the Barn, 2332
An Elephant in the Family, 2332
The Elephant on Ice, 2332
The Elephant Tells, 2332
WOOD, Marcia
The Secret Life of Hilary Thorne, 2086
Wooding, Sharon, 629, 2658
Woodman, Bill, 514
WOODRUFF, Elvira
Awfully Short for the Fourth Grade, 2670
Back in Action, 2670
The Disappearing Bike Shop, 2879
The Summer I Shrank My Grandmother, 2671
Woolf, Freda, 1104
WOOLLEY, Persia
Child of the Northern Spring, 1873
Guinevere: The Legend in Autumn, 1873
Queen of the Summer Stars, 1873
WORK, Rhoda O.
Mr. Dawson Had a Farm, 2333
Mr. Dawson Had a Lamb, 2333
Mr. Dawson Had an Elephant, 2333
Wortis, Avi. *See* AVI
Wray, Wendy, 430
WREDE, Patricia C(ollins)
Calling on Dragons, 1588
Caught in Crystal, 1587

Daughter of Witches, 1589
Dealing with Dragons, 1588
The Harp of Imach Thyssel, 1589
Mairelon the Magician, 1590
Searching for Dragons, 1588
The Seven Towers, 1591
Shadow Magic, 1589
Snow White and Rose Red, 1874
Sorcery and Cecilia, 1590
Talking to Dragons, 1588
WREDE, Patricia C(ollins), and STEVERMER,
    Caroline
Mairelon the Magician, 1592
Sorcery and Cecilia, 1592
Wriggins, Michelle, 1913
WRIGGINS, Sally
The White Monkey King: A Chinese Fable, 1875
WRIGHT, Betty Ren
Christina's Ghost, 1218
The Dollhouse Murders, 2962
A Ghost in the House, 1219
The Ghost of Ernie P, 1220
The Ghost of Popcorn Hill, 1221
The Ghost Witch, 1222
Ghosts Beneath Our Feet, 1223
The Ghosts of Mercy Manor, 1224
The Pike River Phantom, 1225
Wright, Freire, 357
WRIGHT, T. M.
Goodlow's Ghosts, 1226
WRIGHTSON, (Alice) Patricia (Furlonger)
Balyet, 1876
The Dark Bright Water, 1877
The Ice Is Coming, 1877
Journey Behind the Wind, 1877
A Little Fear, 2672
Moon–Dark, 756
The Nargun and the Stars, 1878
An Older Kind of Magic, 2673
Wunsch, Marjorie, 677
WUORIO, Eva-Lis
Tal and the Magic Barruget, 2674
WURTS, Janny. *See also* FEIST, Raymond E.
Keeper of the Keys, 3141
The Master of White Storm, 1593
Shadowfane, 3141
Sorcerer's Legacy, 1594
Stormwarden, 3141
Wyeth, Andrew, 1767
Wyeth, N. C., 1725, 1767
WYNDHAM, Lee (pseud. of Jane Andrews
    Hyndman)
Mourka, the Mighty Cat, 757
Wynne, Patrick, 202
WYSS, Thelma Hatch
A Stranger Here, 1227

Yeats, Jack B., 827, 2546
YEP, Laurence M(ichael)
The Curse of the Squirrel, 758
Dragon Cauldron, 1595
Dragon of the Lost Sea, 1595
Dragon Steel, 1595
Dragon War, 1595
YOLEN (Stemple), Jane H(yatt)
The Acorn Quest, 759
The Bird of Time, 370
The Boy Who Had Wings, 371
Briar Rose, 1879
The Devil's Arithmetic, 2880
Dove Isabeau, 372
Dragon's Blood, 1596
The Dragon's Boy, 1880
Dragonfield and Other Stories, 995
Dream Weaver, 996
*The Faery Flag: Stories and Poems of Fantasy
    and the Supernatural*, 997
The Giants' Farm, 2334
The Giants Go Camping, 2334
The Girl Who Cried Flowers and Other Tales,
    998
The Girl Who Loved the Wind, 373
*Greyling: A Picture Story from the Islands of
    Shetland*, 1881
Heart's Blood, 1596
Here There Be Dragons, 999
Hobo Toad and the Motorcycle Gang, 760
The Hundredth Dove and Other Tales, 1000
The Magic Three of Solatia, 1597
Merlin's Booke, 1882
The Mermaid's Three Wisdoms, 2675
The Moon Ribbon and Other Tales, 1001
Picnic with Piggins, 761
Piggins, 761
Piggins and the Royal Wedding, 761
A Sending of Dragons, 1596
The Seventh Mandarin, 374
*Shape Shifters: Fantasy and Science Fiction
    Tales about Humans Who Can Change Their
    Shapes*, 958
Sister Light, Sister Dark, 1598
Sleeping Ugly, 2335
Tam Lin: An Old Ballad, 1883
The Transfigured Hart, 375
White Jenna, 1598
The Wizard Islands, 1228
The Wizard of Washington Square, 3142
Wizard's Hall, 3143
Xanadu, 992
*Zoo 2000: Twelve Stories of Science Fiction and
    Fantasy Beasts*, 763
YOLEN, Jane, and GREENBERG, Martin H.
*Things That Go Bump in the Night: A Collection
    of Original Stories*, 1198

YOLEN, Jane, GREENBERG, Martin H., and
WAUGH, Charles G.
*Dragons & Dreams: A Collection of New
Fantasy and Science Fiction Stories*, 2429
*Spaceships and Spells: A Collection of New
Fantasy and Science-Fiction Stories*, 964
YORK, Carol Beach
The Christmas Dolls, 2676
Miss Know-It-All; A Butterfield Square Story,
2676
Miss Know-It-All Returns, 2676
Pudmuddles, 2336
Youd, Christopher Samuel. *See* CHRISTOPHER,
John
Young, Ed, 355, 373, 374
YOUNG, Ella
The Unicorn with Silver Shoes, 2087
Young, Kathy Osborn, 57
YOUNG, Miriam
The Witch Mobile, 3144
Young, Noela, 756, 2050, 2615, 2616, 2673, 2835
YOUNG, Robert F.
The Vizier's Second Daughter, 1884
ZAHORSKI, Kenneth J. *See* BOYER, Robert H.
ZAMBRENO, Mary Frances
Journeyman Wizard: A Magical Mystery, 3146
A Plague of Sorcerers, 3146
ZARING, Jane T(homas)
The Return of the Dragon, 376
ZELAZNY, Roger (Joseph Christopher)
Blood of Amber, 1599
Changeling, 3148
The Courts of Chaos, 1599
Frost and Fire, 1002
The Guns of Avalon, 1599
The Hand of Oberon, 1599
Jack of Shadows, 3147

Knight of Shadows, 1599
The Last Defender of Camelot, 1003
Madwand, 3148
Nine Princes in Amber, 1599
Prince of Chaos, 1599
Roger Zelazny's Visual Guide to Castle Amber,
1599
Sign of Chaos, 1599
The Sign of the Unicorn, 1599
Trumps of Doom, 1599
Wizard World, 3148
ZELAZNY, Roger, and SHECKLEY, Robert
Bring Me the Head of Prince Charming, 2881
If at Faust You Don't Succeed, 2881
Zeldich, Arieh, 14
Zelinsky, Paul O., 2095, 2576
ZEMACH, Harve(y Fischtrom)
The Tricks of Master Dabble, 377
Zemach, Margot, 298, 377, 959, 1238
Zerner, Jesse Spicer, 246
ZETTNER, Pat
The Shadow Warrior, 1600
Zimmer, Dirk, 208, 758, 2131, 2199, 2250, 2324,
2992
ZIMNIK, Reiner
The Bear and the People, 1601
ZINDEL, Paul
Let Me Hear You Whisper: A Play, 762
ZIPES, Jack
*Don't Bet on the Prince: Contemporary Feminist
Fairy Tales in North America and England*,
843
ZOLOTOW, Charlotte S(hapiro)
The Man with Purple Eyes, 2677
Zvorykin, Boris, 950
Zwerger, Lisbeth, 11, 16, 17, 93, 147, 357, 779,
1215, 2575, 293

Title Index

This index provides references to all titles mentioned in Chapters 1 through 10. The numbers that follow the titles refer to entry numbers, not page numbers. Author surnames appear in parentheses when titles by different authors are identical.

The Abandoned, 513
Abba, 709
Abel's Island, 705
About Time: Twelve Stories, 2735
Abracatabby, 2488
An Acceptable Time, 2773
Ace: The Very Important Pig, 568
The Acorn Quest, 759
Acquainted with the Night, 1109
The Acts of Arthur and His Noble Knights from the Winchester Manuscripts of Thomas Maloryand Other Sources, 1767
Adam Draws Himself a Dragon, 2520
Adam Mouse's Book of Poems, 629
Adam's Common, 2875
The Adept, 3068
The Admiral's Caravan, 1914
The Adventures of a Brownie as Told to My Child, 2574
The Adventures of a Two Minute Werewolf, 2141
The Adventures of Ambrose, 699
The Adventures of Arab, 2956
The Adventures of Baron Münchausen, 2255
The Adventures of Benjamin Pink, 747
The Adventures of Bob White, 433
The Adventures of Bobby Coon, 433
The Adventures of Buster Bear, 433
The Adventures of Chatterer the Red Squirrel, 433
The Adventures of Danny Meadowmouse, 433
The Adventures of Don Quixote de la Mancha, 61
The Adventures of Dudley and Gilderoy, 416
The Adventures of Grandfather Frog, 433
The Adventures of Jack Ninepins, 2884
The Adventures of Jerry Muskrat, 433
The Adventures of Jimmy Skunk, 433
The Adventures of Johnny Chuck, 433

The Adventures of Lightfoot the Deer, 433
The Adventures of Little Mouk, 135
The Adventures of Ol' Mistah Buzzard, 433
The Adventures of Old Granny Fox, 433
The Adventures of Old Man Coyote, 433
The Adventures of Peter Cottontail, 433
The Adventures of Pinocchio, 2905
The Adventures of Poor Mrs. Quack, 433
The Adventures of Prickly Porky, 433
The Adventures of Ratman, 2324
The Adventures of Reddy Fox, 433
The Adventures of Rinaldo, 149
The Adventures of Sammy Jay, 433
The Adventures of Samurai Cat, 675
The Adventures of So Hi, 1900
The Adventures of the Wuffle, 607
The Adventures of Tom Bombadil and Other Verses from "The Red Book," 1555
The Adventures of Unc' Billy Possum, 433
The Adventures of Whitefoot the Woodmouse, 433
The Adventures of Yemima, 963
After Dark, 1863
After the Fact, 2055
After the King: Stories in Honor of J. R. R. Tolkien, 764
Against the Wind, 1497
Aggie, Maggie, and Tish, 2440
Agnes Cecilia, 1097
Aha and the Jewel of Mystery, 425
The Air of Mars; and Other Stories of Time and Space, 776
The Airship Ladyship Adventure, 2180
Al and the Magic Lamp, 2438
Alamut, 1548
Alan Garner's Fairytales of Gold, 872
Alanna: The First Adventure, 1495

Alberic the Wise and Other Journeys, 906
Albert and the Dragonettes, 348
Albert and Victoria, 514
Albert the Dragon, 348
Albert the Dragon and the Centaur, 348
Albion's Dream: A Novel of Terror, 1785
The Alchemist: A Fable About Following Your Dream, 68
Alchemy Unlimited, 2991
Aldur, 3008
Alexander's Birthday, 2940
Alexander's Christmas Eve, 2940
Alexander's Vacation, 2940
Alfie and Me and the Ghost of Peter Stuyvesant, 1146
Alice Through the Needle's Eye: The Further Adventures of Lewis Carroll's "Alice," 1886
Alice's Adventures in Wonderland, 1913
Alien Plot, 782
All in Good Time, 2812
The All Jahdu Storybook, 2187
All the King's Men, 2021
All the Money in the World, 2109
All the Mowgli Stories, 578
All the Weyrs of Pern, 1447
All-of-a-Sudden Susan, 2904
The Alligator and His Uncle Tooth: A Novel of the Sea, 534
The Alligator Case, 2144
Allth, 278
Almost Goodbye, 2409
Alone in the Wild Forest, 298
Alonzo and the Army of Ants, 521
Alpha Centauri, 2843
Alphonse, That Bearded One, 2121
Alternative Histories: Eleven Stories of the World as It Might Have Been, 1242
Amahl and the Night Visitors, 1774
The Amazing Mr. Prothero, 390
The Amazing Vacation, 2078
Amazons!, 1244
Amazons II, 1244
Ambrose, 653
The Amiable Giant, 302
Among the Dolls, 2955
The Amorous Umbrella, 1995
Amy's Eyes, 2938
Anackire, 1424
Anastasia Morningstar, 2502
The Ancient One, 2694
And All Between, 1532
And the Angels Sing: Stories, 985
And Then There'll Be Fireworks, 1339
Andersen's Fairy Tales, 779
Andrew and the Alchemist, 2982
Andy Buckram's Tin Men, 2107
Andy Jackson's Water Well, 2310
An Angel in the Woods, 2943

Angel with the Sword, 1286
Animal Castle, 201
The Animal Family, 160
Animal Farm, 642
The Animal Friends of Peng-U, 427
Animal Stories, 838
The Animal's Conference, 560
The Animals of Farthing Wood, 476
Ann's Spring, 1654
Anna Witch, 3011
Another Brownie Book, 1307
Another Fine Myth, 2965
Another Shore, 2700
Another World; Adventures in Otherness: A Science Fiction Anthology, 781
Antar and the Eagles, 1472
The Anvil of Ice, 3112
The Apple Stone, 2469
Appointment, 38
Appointment with a Stranger, 1197
The April Witch and Other Strange Tales, 1018
Aquamancer, 2983
Aquarius, 1464
Arabel and Mortimer, 2090
Arabel's Raven, 2090
Arabesques 2, 783
Arabesques: More Tales of the Arabian Nights, 783
Archer's Goon, 3049
The Architecture of Desire, 1360
Arctic Unicorn, 3080
Ardizzone's Hans Andersen: Fourteen Classic Tales, 779
Are All the Giants Dead?, 2041
Argyle's Causeway, 2815
Argyle's Oracle, 2815
Ariadne, 1625
The Armies of Daylight, 1975
Armitage, Armitage, Fly Away Home, 2091
Arrow's Fall, 1415
Arrow's Flight, 1415
Arrows of the Queen, 1415
Arrows of the Sun, 1550
Ars Magica, 1549
Arthur and the Bellybutton Diamond, 2128
Arthur and the Great Detective, 2128
Arthur and the Purple Panic, 2128
Arthur Pendragon of Britain, 1767
Arthur Rex: A Legendary Novel, 1613
Arthur the Kid, 2128
Arthur versus the Rest, 2128
Arthur's Last Stand, 2128
Arthur's New Power, 538
Artie and the Princess, 334
The Ash Staff, 1348
An Ash-Blond Witch, 3075
Astercote, 1751
The Astonishing Stereoscope, 2526, 2527
At the Back of the North Wind, 219

Atlantis, 784
The Attic Mice, 660
Aunt Maria, 3050
The Autumn People, 1019
Autumn Story, 404
An Autumn Tale, 2652
Avatar, 1303
Avril, 497
Away to the Moon, 2958
Awfully Short for the Fourth Grade, 2670
Ayesha, the Return of She, 2025
Azazel, 2345
Azor, 464
Azor and the Blue-Eyed Cow: A Christmas Story, 464
Azor and the Haddock, 464

BAAA, 218
Babe: The Gallant Pig, 569
Babes in Toyland, 1982
Baby Island, 2108
Baby of the Family, 2343
Back in Action, 2670
Back to Before, 2848
Back-Seat Driver, 672
Backyard Dragon, 2641
The Backyard Ghost, 1060
A Bad Day for Ali Baba, 1685
A Bad Spell for the Worst Witch, 3094
Badger's Wood, 725
Bailey's Window, 2009
Baily's Bones, 1117
A Bait of Dreams: A Five Summer Quest, 1294
A Baker's Dozen: Thirteen Stories to Tell and to Read Aloud, 793
The Ballad of Belle Dorcas, 150
Balyet, 1876
Bandmaster's Holiday, 406
The Bane of the Black Pearl, 1478
Bard: The Odyssey of the Irish, 1754
Barney the Donkey, 440
The Baron All at Sea, 2255
The Baron on the Island of Cheese, 2255
The Baron Rides Out, 2255
The Barrel in the Basement, 2658
Bartholomew and the Oobleck, 293
Basil and the Lost Colony, 722
Basil and the Pygmy Cats, 722
Basil in Mexico, 722
Basil in the Wild West, 722
Basil of Baker Street, 722
The Bassumtyte Treasure, 1061
The Bastard Prince, 1414
The Bat-Poet, 552
The Battle for the Castle, 2085
The Beachcombers, 2410
Beachmaster, 690

The Bear and the People, 1601
A Bear Called Paddington, 422
The Bear Nobody Wanted, 2882
The Bear Who Liked Hugging People and Other Stories, 775
Bearing an Hourglass, 1249
Bears Back in Business, 2888
The Bears' Famous Invasion of Sicily, 436
The Bears Up Stairs, 524
The Beast with the Magical Horn, 56
Beastie, 2551
Beauty: A Novel, 1853
Beauty: A Retelling of the Story of Beauty and the Beast, 1763
Beauty and the Beast, 1869
Beauty, Brave and Beautiful, 512
Beaver Valley, 489
Bedknob and Broomstick, 2586
Bee, the Princess of the Dwarfs, 1957
The Bee-Man of Orn, 312
Beethoven's Cat, 614
The Beggar Queen, 1241
The Beginning of the Armadilloes, 176
The Beginning Place, 2005
Behind the Attic Wall, 1044
Being of Two Minds, 2631
The Bell Tolls at Mousehaven Manor, 587
Bella Arabella, 2452
Belling the Tiger, 713
The Belly of the Wolf, 1445
Beloved Exile, 1696
Below the Root, 1532
Ben and Me: A New and Astonishing Life of Benjamin Franklin as Written by His Good Mouse, Amos: Lately Discovered, 593
Ben's Dream, 2655
Beneath the Hill, 1657
Bengey and the Beast, 2353
Benvenuto, 2286
Beowulf; a New Telling, 1789
Bernard and the Catnip Caper, 510
Bernard into Battle, 691
Bernard of Scotland Yard, 510
Bernard Sees the World, 510
Bernard the Brave, 691
Bernie and the Bessledorf Ghost, 1161
Bertie's Escapade, 522
Best Friend Insurance, 2460
The Best of Branestawm, 2202
The Best-Kept Secret, 2835
Bestiary!, 796
Between the Cracks, 3140
Bevis: The Story of a Boy, 553
Beware! Beware! Chilling Tales, 1029
Beware of the Mouse, 2327
Beyond Silence, 2710
Beyond the Burning Lands, 1293
Beyond the Door, 1904

Beyond the Gate of the Worlds, 1525
Beyond the North Wind, 1620
Beyond the Pawpaw Trees: The Story of Anna Lavinia, 2380
The BFG, 2132
Bicycle to Treachery, 665
Bid Time Return, 2795
Big Bad Bruce, 656
A Big Day for Scepters, 185
The Big Green Book, 2467
Big Susan, 2937
The Big Tree of Bunlahy: Stories of My Own Countryside, 827
Bilbo's Last Song, 1556
A Billion for Boris, 2291
Billy Barnicoat: A Fairy Romance for Young and Old, 2549
Billy Beg and the Bull, 1655
A Binding Spell, 1128
The Bird of Time, 370
The Bird's Christmas Carol, 354
The Birdstones, 2718
Birdy and the Ghosties, 1166
Birth of the Firebringer, 1492
The Birthday Burglar & A Very Wicked Headmistress, 2238
The Birthday Tree, 111
The Bishop's Heir, 1412
Black and Blue Magic, 2638
The Black Beast, 1538
The Black Cats and the Tinker's Wife, 29
The Black Cauldron, 1236
The Black Flame, 1230
The Black Gryphon, 1415, 1417
The Black Gull of Corie Lachan, 2547
Black Hearts in Battersea, 1235
The Black Horse, 1768
The Black Mask Trick, 2404
The Black Pearl and the Ghost; or, One Mystery after Another, 2258
The Black Sheep, 624
The Black Snowman, 1773
Black Sun Rising, 1354
Black Trillium, 1271
Black Unicorn, 1425
The Black Unicorn, 2112
Black Water: The Book of Fantastic Literature, 799
Blackbeard's Ghost, 1192
Blackberry Hollow, 655
The Blackmail Machine, 2196
The Blackwash, 272
Blade of the Poisoner, 1381
The Blind Archer, 1264
Blodwen and the Guardians, 2668
The Blonk from Beneath the Sea, 2100
Blood Line, 2477
Blood of Amber, 1599
The Blood of Ten Chiefs, 1497

Blood Red Ochre, 1766
Blood Trillium, 1271
The Blood-and-Thunder Adventure on Hurricane Peak, 2239
The Bloody Sun, 1270
Blossom Culp and the Sleep of Death, 1169
Blow a Wild Bugle for Catfish Bend, 434
Blue Adept, 1248
The Blue Boat, 2563
The Blue Book of Hob Stories, 2566
The Blue Cat of Castle Town, 2399
The Blue Hawk, 1318
The Blue Moon, 894
Blue Moon, 1070
Blue Moon Rising, 1367
Blue Moose, 658
The Blue Mountain, 207
The Blue Rose; a Collection of Stories for Girls, 800
The Blue Stone, 168
The Blue Sword, 1460
The Blue-Nosed Witch, 3014
Bluesong, 1562
Bluntstone and the Wildkeepers, 1369
The Boggart, 2402
Bogwoppit, 749
The Bongleweed, 2411
Bonifacius the Green, 2340
Bony-Legs, 2992
Boo! Stories to Make You Jump, 1030
A Book Dragon, 2523
The Book of Brendan, 1656
The Book of Giant Stories, 886
The Book of Imaginary Beings, 802
The Book of Kells, 2787
The Book of King Arthur and His Noble Knights, 1767
The Book of Lost Tales, 1555
The Book of Lost Tales, Volume 2, 1555
The Book of Sorrows, 344
The Book of Swords, 1517
The Book of the Dun Cow, 344
The Book of the Three Dragons, 1778
The Book of Three, 1236
The Book of Vale, 1538
Borderland, No. 1, 1268
Bordertown, 1268
Born to Run, 3069
The Borribles, 1314
The Borribles Go for Broke, 1314
The Borrowers, 2587
The Borrowers Afield, 2587
The Borrowers Afloat, 2587
The Borrowers Aloft, 2587
The Borrowers Avenged, 2587
The Borrowers Omnibus, 2587
A Bowl of Mischief, 1449

The Box of Delights: Or, When the Wolves Were Running, 2560
A Box of Nothing, 1938
The Boxcar at the Center of the Universe, 169
The Boy and the Whale, 283
The Boy Apprenticed to an Enchanter, 2994
A Boy in the Doghouse, 484
The Boy, the Rat, and the Butterfly, 2423
The Boy Who Had Wings, 371
The Boy Who Knew What the Birds Said, 456
The Boy Who Sang the Birds, 351
The Boy Who Spoke Colors, 123
The Boy's King Arthur, 1767
The Brave Balloon of Benjamin Buckley, 2325
Break a Magic Circle, 2506
The Brega Path, 1452
Brewster's Courage, 584
Briar Rose, 1879
Bridge of Birds: A Novel of an Ancient China That Never Was, 1384
The Bridge of Lost Desire, 1313
A Bridge of Years, 2874
The Bright and Morning Star, 1711
Bright Shadow, 1252
Brim Sails Out, 516
Brim's Boat, 516
Brim's Valley, 516
Bring Me the Head of Prince Charming, 2881
The Bristling Wood, 3061
Broderick, 640
Brogeen and the Black Enchanter, 217
Brogeen and the Bronze Lizard, 217
Brogeen and the Little Wind, 217
Brogeen and the Lost Castle, 217
Brogeen and the Red Fez, 217
Brogeen Follows the Magic Tune, 217
Brokedown Palace, 1626
The Broken Citadel, 1971
Bronwyn's Bane, 1521
The Bronze King, 2986
Broom-Adelaide, 118
Broomstick and Snowflake, 107
Broomsticks and Other Tales, 833
Brother Night, 1399
Brother to the Lion, 1950
The Brothers Lionheart, 2010
The Brownies, 2441
The Brownies Abroad, 1307
The Brownies and Other Stories, 852
The Brownies and Prince Florimel, 1307
The Brownies around the World, 1307
The Brownies at Home, 1307
The Brownies in the Philippines, 1307
The Brownies' Latest Adventure, 1307
The Brownies Many More Nights, 1307
The Brownies: Their Book, 1307
The Brownies through the Union, 1307
Bruno, 2110

Bruno Takes a Trip, 2110
A Brush with Magic, 2379
Bubble Trouble and Other Poems and Stories, 2240
Buffalo Arthur, 2128
Buffalo Gals and Other Animal Presences, 600
Building Blocks, 2863
The Bull Beneath the Walnut Tree and Other Stories, 891
The Bull from the Sea, 1813
Bunnicula: A Rabbit Tale of Mystery, 547
Bunny Rabbit's Diary, 418
The Burnhope Wheel, 1084
The Burning Baby and Other Ghosts, 1090
The Burning Stone, 3034
Burton and Stanley, 641
Buttercup Days, 2437
The Butterfly That Stamped, 177
By the Great Horn Spoon, 2165
By the Sword, 1416
By the Sword: Magic of the Plains, 1305

C. I. D, 2027
The Cabalist, 3105
The Cage, 1545
Cahena, 1862
Caitlin's Holiday, 2931
California Demon, 3118
California Fairy Tales, 957
The Call and Other Stories, 1203
Call Me Bandicoot, 2145
Call the Darkness Down, 1852
Calling on Dragons, 1588
Callipygia, 1282
Camber of Culdi, 1413
Camber the Heretic, 1413
Cambio Bay, 1868
A Camel Called April, 2483
Camelot Chronicles, 1801
The Camelot Chronicles: Heroic Adventures from the Time of King Arthur, 1632
Can I Get There by Candlelight?, 2726
Candle Tales, 466
Candlelight Tales, 727
Candy Floss, 2921
Cannonball River Tales, 2292
The Canterville Ghost, 1215
Canyons Beyond the Sky, 2765
Captain Apple's Ghost, 1123
Captain Butcher's Body, 1055
Captain Kidd's Cat: Being the True and Dolorous Chronicle of Wm. Kidd, Gentleman and Merchant of New York; Late Captain of the Adventure Galley; Of the Vicissitudes Attending His Unfortunate Cruise in Eastern Waters, Of His Unjust Trial and Execution, as Narrated by His Faithful Cat, McDermot, Who Ought to Know, 594

Captains of the City Streets: A Story of the Cat Club, 393
The Caravan, 887
Carbonel and Calidor, 2636
Carbonel: The King of the Cats, 2636
Carmen Dog, 493
Carrot Holes and Frisbee Trees, 2103
Carrousel, 2942
Cart and Cwidder, 1390
The Case of the Dragon in Distress: A McGurk Fantasy, 2752
The Case of the Weeping Witch, 2752
Casey, the Utterly Impossible Horse, 498
Cast Down the Stars, 1395
Castaways in Lilliput, 2084
Castaways on Chimp Island, 588
Castaways on Long Ago, 1164
The Casting Away of Mrs. Lecks and Mrs. Aleshine, 2314
Castle Crespin, 385
Castle Dreams, 3000
Castle for Rent, 3000
Castle in the Air, 1391
The Castle in the Attic, 2085
Castle Kidnapped, 3000
Castle Merlin, 1216
Castle Murders, 3000
A Castle of Bone, 1671
Castle of Deception, 3070
The Castle of Hape, 1482
The Castle of Llyr, 1236
The Castle of the Ladies, 1715
Castle of Wizardry, 3008
The Castle of Yew, 2368
Castle Perilous, 3000
Castle Roogna, 1250
Castle War!, 3000
Castledown, 1971
Castles in the Air and Other Tales, 911
Castleview, 1872
The Cat and Mrs. Cary, 515
The Cat and the Captain, 453
The Cat Club, 393
Cat in the Mirror, 2852
The Cat That Clumped, 388
The Cat That Walked by Himself, 178
The Cat, the Horse, and the Miracle, 606
Cat Walk, 714
The Cat Who Went to Heaven, 64
The Cat Who Wished to Be a Man, 380
Cat's Magic, 2744
Cat's-Cradles for His Majesty, 30
Catchfire, 1466
The Caterpillar's Question, 1890
Catfantastic II, 818
Catfantastic III, 818
Catfantastic: Nine Lives and Fifteen Tales, 818
The Cats of Seroster, 1578

The Catswold Portal, 2028
Catwings, 601
Catwings Return, 601
Caught in Crystal, 1587
A Cavalcade of Dragons, 819
A Cavalcade of Goblins, 820
A Cavalcade of Kings, 821
A Cavalcade of Magicians, 2985
A Cavalcade of Queens, 821
Cave Beyond Time, 2702
Caves of Fire and Ice, 1482
The Caves of Terror, 2027
Cecelia and the Blue Mountain Boy, 2632
The Celery Stalks at Midnight, 547
The Celestial Steam Locomotive, 1647
The Cellar, 2830
Centaur Aisle, 1250
Ceremony, 460
Chains of Gold, 1536
Challenge of the Clans, 1676
The Challenge of the Green Knight, 1829
The Chameleon Corps and Other Shape Changers, 1365
The Champion of Merrimack County, 483
Champion of the Sidhe, 1677
A Chance Child, 2820
Chancy and the Grand Rascal, 2166
The Change Child, 1657
Change Song, 1383
The Changeling (Lagerlöf), 191
Changeling (Zelazny), 3148
The Changeling Sea, 1453
The Changeover: A Supernatural Romance, 3090
Changer's Moon, 1296
Changeweaver, 1257
The Changing Maze, 305
Changing Times, 2762
Chaos Mode, 1889
Charlie and the Chocolate Factory, 2416
Charlie and the Great Glass Elevator, 2416
Charlie Malarkey and the Belly-Button Machine, 2214
Charlie Malarkey and the Singing Moose, 2214
Charlotte Sometimes, 2733
Charlotte's Web, 743
Charmed, 2060
Charmed Life, 2759
The Charwoman's Shadow, 3007
Chernevog, 2988
Chess-Dream in a Garden, 319
The Chessboard Queen, 1783
Chester Cricket's New Home, 686
Chester Cricket's Pigeon Ride, 686
The Chestnut Soldier, 2581
The Chewing-Gum Rescue and Other Stories, 2241
The Chicken Gave It to Me, 500
Chicken Trek: The Third Strange Thing That Happened to Oscar Noodleman, 2247

Child of an Ancient City, 1584
Child of Faerie, Child of Earth, 1834
Child of Saturn, 3009
Child of the Air, 1290
Child of the Northern Spring, 1873
A Child of Their Own, 2951
Child of Thunder, 1506
Child of Tomorrow, 1897
Children in the Night, 1483
The Children of Green Knowe, 1031
The Children of Llyr, 1860
Children of the Maker, 1254
Children of the Seventh Prophecy, 2052
Children of the Sun, 58
The Children of the Wind, 1374
Children of the Wind: Five Novellas, 986
The Children's Blue Bird, 230
The Children's Fairy Land, 786
The Chimes of Alyafaleyn, 1291
Chimney Witch Chase, 3135
The Chimney Witches, 3135
Ching-Li and the Dragons, 154
Chitty-Chitty Bang Bang: The Magical Car, 2174
The Chocolate Touch, 2392
The Christening Quest, 1521
Christina's Ghost, 1218
A Christmas Card, 325
A Christmas Carol, 93
A Christmas Child, 2024
The Christmas Dolls, 2676
Christmas Forever, 825
The Christmas Gang, 485
Christmas Ghosts, 1046
Christmas Ghosts: An Anthology, 1047
The Christmas Mouse, 739
Christopher, 2517
The Christopher Robin Story Book, 2944
The Chronicles of Pern: First Fall, 1447
The Chronicles of Thomas Covenant, 1940
The Church Cat Abroad, 638
The Church Mice Adrift, 638
The Church Mice and the Moon, 638
The Church Mice and the Ring, 638
The Church Mice at Bay, 638
The Church Mice at Christmas, 638
The Church Mice in Action, 638
The Church Mice Spread Their Wings, 638
The Church Mouse, 638
Cinders, 121
Circle Home, 2751
The Circus of Dr. Lao, 1674
The Citadel of the Autarch, 1585
The City in the Autumn Stars, 245
City of Sorcery, 1270
The City Under the Back Steps, 2004
Clan Ground, 408
Clancy's Witch, 3088
The Claw of the Conciliator, 1585

Clementina, 1667
Clementine, 2900
Clever Polly and the Stupid Wolf, 2315
Clever-Lazy, the Girl Who Invented Herself, 45
The Clocks of Iraz, 1310
The Clockwork Twin, 428
The Clothes Horse and Other Stories, 2088
The Cloud Forest, 2583
The Coachman Rat, 1870
The Cock and the Ghost Cat, 1129
Cockleberry Castle, 110
The Cold Flame, 1505
Cold Marble and Other Ghost Stories, 1193
The Cold Moons, 448
Coll and His White Pig, 1237
The Collected Ghost Stories of E. F. Benson, 1028
Collected Poems of Freddy the Pig, 428
The Color of Her Panties, 1250
Colors in the Dreamweaver's Loom, 1977
The Colt from Moon Mountain, 2528
Come Again in the Spring, 170
Come Away Home, 700
Come Like Shadows, 3058
Come to the Edge, 79
A Comet in Moominland, 1388
The Coming of the King: The First Book of Merlin, 1854
Coming-and-Going Men: Four Tales, 112
Companions on the Road: Two Novellas, 1426
The Compleat Werewolf; and Other Stories of Fantasy and Science Fiction, 803
The Complete Adventures of Olga Da Polga, 424
The Complete Book of Dragons, 933
The Complete Book of Swords, 1517
The Complete Fairy Tales and Stories, 779
The Complete Fairy Tales of George MacDonald, 922
The Complete Fairy Tales of Mary De Morgan, 839
Complete Fairy Tales of Oscar Wilde, 984
The Complete Peterkin Papers, 2185
Conjure Tales, 822
A Connecticut Yankee in King Arthur's Court, 2860
Conrad's War, 2723
The Contest at Paca, 2305
The Copper Crown, 1404
Cotton-Wooleena, 153
Count Billy, 2549
The Court of the Stone Children, 1041
The Courts of Chaos, 1599
The Crab That Played with the Sea, 179
Crackle Creek, 626
The Craft of Light, 1948
The Crafters, 2998
The Crafters, vol. 2: Blessings and Curses, 2998
Cranes Flying South, 559
Crazy in Love, 2514
Crewel Lye, 1250
Cricket and the Emperor's Son, 65

The Cricket in Times Square, 686
The Cricket Winter, 541
The Crime of Martin Coverly, 2869
The Crimson Chalice, 1633
The Crock of Gold, 310
Crocuses Were Over, Hitler Was Dead, 2854
Cromm, 1675
Crossings: A Fairy Play, 2422
Crossover, 2732
Crosstime Traffic, 980
The Crown Snatchers, 342
The Cruise of the Happy-Go-Gay, 2329
Crumbling Castle, 3035
The Crystal Cave, 1841
The Crystal Gryphon, 1486
Crystal Line, 1446
The Crystal Palace, 1337
Crystal Singer, 1446
The Crystal Stair, 1292
Crystals of Air and Water, 1363
The Cuckoo Child, 570
The Cuckoo Clock (Stolz), 315
The Cuckoo Clock (Molesworth), 2024
The Cuckoo Tree, 1235
Cugel's Saga, 1559
Cup of Clay, 1942
The Curious Adventures of Jimmy McGee, 3015
Curious Tales, 924
The Curse of Slagfid, 1908
The Curse of the Giant Hogweed, 2790
The Curse of the Squirrel, 758
Curtain of Mist, 2815
The Cutting Edge, 1327
Cygnet and the Firebird, 1454
Cyrion, 1427

D'Aulaires' Trolls, 785
D'Shai, 1512
The Dagger and the Bird: A Story of Suspense, 1970
*The Dagger and the Cross: A Novel of the
    Crusades*, 1548, 1551
Daggerspell, 3061
Dagmar Schultz and the Angel Edna, 2186
Dagmar Schultz and the Green-Eyed Monster, 2186
Dagmar Schultz and the Powers of Darkness, 2186
Dahut, 1247
Damiano, 3081
Damiano's Lute, 3081
Danby and George, 398
The Dancers of Arun, 1444
The Dancing Cats of Applesap, 2232
Danger in Tibet, 665
Danger—Marmalade at Work, 2138
Dangerous Spaces, 2020
Daniel Boone's Echo, 2311
The Dark Abyss, 1928
The Dark Behind the Curtain, 1059

The Dark Bright Water, 1877
Dark Castle, White Horse, 1428
The Dark Druid, 1676
The Dark Green Tunnel, 1947
The Dark Hand of Magic, 1372
Dark Heart, 1387
A Dark Horn Blowing, 1986
The Dark Is Rising, 1650
The Dark Lord of Pengersick, 1281
Dark Moon, 1492
Dark of the Moon, 1382
Dark Prince, 1694
The Dark Princess, 171
The Dark Secret of Weatherend, 2360
*The Dark-Thirty: Southern Tales of the
    Supernatural*, 1150
The Darkangel, 1493
Darkchild, 1562
A Darker Magic, 2971
The Darkest Road, 1994
A Darkness at Sethanon, 1344
Darkover Landfall, 1270
Darkspell, 3061
Darkthunder's Way, 1934
Daughter of Regals and Other Tales, 1323
Daughter of the Bright Moon, 1230
Daughter of the Empire, 1345
The Daughter of the Moon, 2019
Daughter of Witches, 1589
Daughters of Lion, 1509
Daughters of the Sunstone, 1562
David and the Phoenix, 2590
David Blaize and the Blue Door, 1901
David the Dreamer: His Book of Dreams, 1902
*Davy and the Goblin, or What Followed Reading
    "Alice's Adventures in Wonderland,"* 1915
Davy Crockett's Earthquake, 2312
The Dawn Palace: The Story of Medea, 1719
The Dawn Seekers, 526
The Day It Rained Forever, 2223
Day of the Unicorn, 158
The Day the Circus Came to Lone Tree, 2293
The Daybreakers, 2718
The Daymaker, 1371
Days of Air and Darkness, 3061
Days of Blood and Fire, 1405, 3061
The Dead Kingdom, 1374
Dealing with Dragons, 1588
Dear Hildegarde, 731
Dear Prosper, 506
Deborah Remembers, 2883
December's Travels, 86
The Deed of Paksenarrion, 1476
Deep Wizardry, 3006
Deep Wood, 725
Deerskin, 1764
Deirdre (Polland), 1805
Deirdre (Stephens), 1840

Deirdre: A Celtic Legend, 1705
The Deliverers of Their Country, 2575
Demo and the Dolphin, 1611
Demon Blues, 2178
Demon Lord of Karanda, 1333
Demon of Undoing, 1243
Demons and Shadows: The Ghostly Best Stories of Robert Westall, 1204
Demons Don't Dream, 1250
Deputy Shep, 715
Dervish Daughter, 1552
The Deryni Archives, 1413
Deryni Checkmate, 1413
Deryni Magic, 1413
Deryni Rising, 1413
Desmond and Dog Friday, 413
Desmond and the Peppermint Ghost: The Dog Detective's Third Case, 413
Desmond the Dog Detective: The Case of the Lone Stranger, 413
Desmond's First Case, 413
The Desperate Dragons, 213
Detective Poufy's First Case: Or the Missing Battery-Operated Pepper Grinder, 2277
The Devil and Daniel Webster, 1612
The Devil and Mother Crump, 2118
The Devil Finds Work, 1703
The Devil on the Road, 2867
The Devil's Arithmetic, 2880
The Devil's Children, 1319
The Devil's Donkey, 2978
The Devil's Door-Bell, 3039
The Devil's Other Storybook, 2096
The Devil's Own, 2782
The Devil's Piper, 1806
The Devil's Storybook, 2096
The Diamond in the Window, 2526
The Diamond Throne, 1331
Diary of a Churchmouse, 638
Dido and Pa, 1235
A Difficulty with Dwarves, 3023
A Dig in Time, 2746
Dig to Disaster, 665
Diggers, 1499
Dindle, 75
Dinner at Alberta's, 538
Dinosaur Tales, 806
Dinosaurs Before Dark, 2813
Dinotopia: A Land Apart from Time, 1973
A Dirge for Sabis, 1289
A Disagreement with Death, 3023
The Disappearing Bike Shop, 2879
The Disappearing Dog Trick, 2404
The Disappearing Dwarf, 1266
The Discontented Ghost, 1056
The Discontented Village, 97
Dither Farm, 2490
Divide and Rule, 1465

Divided Allegiance, 1476
Divine Right, 1286, 1346
Do-It-Yourself Magic, 1920
Doctor Change, 2993
Doctor Dolittle: A Treasury, 2234
Doctor Dolittle and the Green Canary, 2234
Doctor Dolittle and the Secret Lake, 2234
Doctor Dolittle in the Moon, 2234
Doctor Dolittle's Caravan, 2234
Doctor Dolittle's Circus, 2234
Doctor Dolittle's Garden, 2234
Doctor Dolittle's Post Office, 2234
Doctor Dolittle's Puddleby Adventures, 2234
Doctor Dolittle's Return, 2234
Doctor Dolittle's Zoo, 2234
Doctor Dredd's Wagon of Wonders, 2978
Doctor Gravity, 2189
Doctor Rat, 583
The Dog and the Wolf, 1247
The Dog Days of Arthur Cane, 2364
The Dog in the Tapestry Garden, 2529
Dog Magic, 452
A Dog So Small, 2599
The Dog That Called the Signals, 2394
The Dog That Pitched a No-Hitter, 2394
The Dog That Stole Football Plays, 2394
Dog Wizard, 1974
Dogsbody, 1989
Dogsled to Dread, 665
The Doll in the Garden: A Ghost Story, 2749
Doll Trouble, 2931
The Doll Who Came Alive, 2959
The Dollhouse Caper, 2946
The Dollhouse Murders, 2962
The Dollhouse Story, 2896
The Dolls' House, 2919
The Dolls' House, 2922
The Dolmop of Dorkling, 2044
The Dolphins of Pern, 1447
Domains of Darkover, 1270
Domes of Fire, 1332
Dominic, 706
Don't Be Afraid, Amanda, 629
Don't Bet on the Prince: Contemporary Feminist Fairy Tales in North America and England, 843
Don't Blame Me!, 897
Don't Give Up the Ghost: The Delacorte Book of Original Ghost Stories, 1064
The Donkey Prince, 59
Doom of the Darksword, 1577
Doomsday Book, 2872
Doomstalker, 460
The Door, 2043
The Door Between, 1684
The Door in the Air and Other Stories, 2556
The Door in the Hedge, 923
The Door in the Wall and Other Stories, 981

The Door into Fire, 3005
The Door into Shadow, 3005
The Door into Sunset, 3005
A Doorway in Fairyland, 894
Dorothy and the Wizard in Oz, 1898
Dorp Dead, 80
Dorrie and the Amazing Magic Elixir, 2996
Dorrie and the Birthday Eggs, 2996
Dorrie and the Blue Witch, 2996
Dorrie and the Dreamyard Monsters, 2996
Dorrie and the Fortune Teller, 2996
Dorrie and the Goblin, 2996
Dorrie and the Halloween Plot, 2996
Dorrie and the Haunted House, 2996
Dorrie and the Haunted Schoolhouse, 2996
Dorrie and the Museum Case, 2996
Dorrie and the Pin Witch, 2996
Dorrie and the Screebit Ghost, 2996
Dorrie and the Weather-Box, 2996
Dorrie and the Witch Doctor, 2996
Dorrie and the Witch's Imp, 2996
Dorrie and the Witches' Camp, 2996
Dorrie and the Witchville Fair, 2996
Dorrie and the Wizard's Spell, 2996
Dorrie's Magic, 2996
Dorrie's Play, 2996
Dorsai!, 1322
The Dorsai Companion, 1322
Dotted Lines, 635
Dove Isabeau, 372
Down Came a Blackbird, 2870
Down the Bright Stream, 1253
The Downhill Crocodile Whizz and Other Stories,
  2557
*The Downstairs Room, and Other Speculative
  Fiction*, 987
The Downtown Fairy Godmother, 2604
Dr. Merlin's Magic Shop, 2997
The Drackenberg Adventure, 1888
Dragon, 23
The Dragon and the George, 1939
The Dragon and the Thief, 1272
Dragon at War, 1939
Dragon Cauldron, 1595
The Dragon Circle, 2522
Dragon Dance, 1921
Dragon, Dragon, and Other Timeless Tales, 871
Dragon Fantastic, 844
The Dragon Hoard, 1429
A Dragon in Class 4, 2405
Dragon in Danger, 2249
Dragon in Summer, 2249
A Dragon in the Family, 1411
The Dragon in the Sword, 1477
Dragon John, 200
The Dragon Knight, 1939
Dragon Magic, 2808
The Dragon of Og, 124

Dragon of the Lost Sea, 1595
Dragon on a Pedestal, 1250
The Dragon on the Border, 1939
Dragon Prince, 1502
The Dragon Reborn, 1396
The Dragon Reverant, 3061
Dragon Rigger, 1283
Dragon Steel, 1595
Dragon Stew, 227
Dragon Sword and Wind Child, 1790
Dragon Tales, 845
The Dragon That Ate Summer, 2626
The Dragon That Lived Under Manhattan, 2192
Dragon Token, 1503
The Dragon Waiting: A Masque of History, 1353
Dragon War, 1595
The Dragon Who Lived Downstairs, 331
Dragon Wing, 1574
Dragon Winter, 528
The Dragon Wore Pink, 152
The Dragonbards, 1481
The Dragonbone Chair, 1583
Dragondoom, 1451
Dragondrums, 1447
Dragonfield and Other Stories, 995
Dragonflight, 1447
A Dragonfly in Amber, 2739
DragonLance Chronicles, 1575
DragonLance Legends, 1576
The Dragonling, 1411
Dragonquest, 1447
Dragonrouge, 1282
*Dragons & Dreams: A Collection of New Fantasy
  and Science Fiction Stories*, 2429
Dragon's Bait, 1561
Dragon's Blood, 1596
The Dragon's Boy, 1880
The Dragon's Carbuncle, 1908
The Dragon's Dagger, 2056
Dragons in the Stars, 1283
Dragon's Milk, 1351
Dragons of Autumn Twilight, 1575
The Dragons of Blueland, 2459
The Dragons of North Chittendon, 2623
Dragons of Spring Dawning, 1575
Dragons of Winter Night, 1575
The Dragon's Pearl, 199
*Dragon's Plunder, or, The Last Voyage of Captain
  Deadmon: A Fantasy Adventure*, 2645
The Dragon's Quest, 2249
The Dragon's Robe, 197
Dragon's Run, 2724
Dragonsbane, 3032
Dragonsdawn, 1447
Dragonsinger, 1447
Dragonsong, 1448
Dragonworld, 1501
The Drastic Dragon of Draco, Texas, 2297

The Drawing of the Three, 1407
The Dreadful Future of Blossom Culp, 1169
Dreadful Sorry, 2831
The Dream Book, 2669
The Dream Coach, 939
Dream Days, 879
Dream Gold, 2841
Dream Lake, 2803
A Dream of Kinship, 1306
The Dream of the Dormouse, 649
The Dream of the Stone, 1892
Dream Spinner, 2753
The Dream Stealer, 3089
*Dream Time: New Stories by Sixteen Award
    Winning Authors*, 846
Dream Weaver, 996
The Dream Years, 2742
The Dreaming Jewels, 1478
The Dreaming Place, 1935
*Dreams of Dark and Light: The Great Short Fiction
    of Tanith Lee*, 915
Dreams Underfoot: The Newford Collection, 1315
The Dreamstone, 1637
The Drift, 2000
The Driftway, 1135
Driftwhistler: A Story of Daniel au Fond, 690
Drink Down the Moon, 1663
Drowned Ammet, 1392
Drowntide, 1563
Druid's Blood, 1355
The Druid's Gift, 2683
Druids, 1755
The Druids of Shannara, 1273
Drujienna's Harp, 2016
Drummond: The Search for Sarah, 2947
The Duke of Sycamore, 650
*Dulac's The Snow Queen and Other Stories from
    Hans Andersen*, 779
Duncton Wood, 544
Dupper, 399
The Dutch Cheese, 834
Dwarf Long-Nose, 136
The Dwarf Pine Tree, 210
The Dying Earth, 1559

Eagle and Dove, 586
Eagle Boy, 2362
The Earth Witch, 1745
Earthfasts, 1771
The Earthquake Man, 141
Earthy Mangold and Worzel Gummidge, 2319
East of Midnight, 1430
Eating Ice Cream with a Werewolf, 2470
Eba, the Absent-Minded Witch, 3019
Eddie's Blue-Winged Dragon, 2337
An Edge of the Forest, 304
The Edge of the World, 1967

Educating Marmalade, 2138
Edward, Hoppy and Joe, 595
The Eggchild, 2969
Eight Days of Luke, 1732
Eight Skilled Gentlemen, 1384
Eighty Fairy Tales, 779
The El Dorado Adventure, 1888
Elbert, the Mind Reader, 2289
The Elementals, 214
The Elephant in the Barn, 2332
An Elephant in the Family, 2332
The Elephant on Ice, 2332
The Elephant Tells, 2332
The Elephant's Child, 180
Elf Defense, 2177
The Elf Queen of Shannara, 1273
The Elfin Ship, 1266
ElfQuest, Book 2, 1497
ElfQuest, Book 3, 1497
ElfQuest, Book 4, 1497
ElfQuest: The Novel, Journey to Sorrow's End,
    1497
Elfrida and the Pig, 721
The Elfstones of Shannara, 1273
Elfwyn's Saga, 367
Eli's Ghost, 1106
Elidor, 1961
Elidor and the Golden Ball, 2015
Elisabeth and the Water-Troll, 345
Elisabeth the Cow Ghost, 1065
The Elixir, 1781
Eliza and the Elves, 1953
Elizabeth, Elizabeth, 2727
Ellen's Lion: Twelve Stories, 2936
Elmer and the Dragon, 2459
Elric at the End of Time, 1478
Elric of Melnibone, 1478
Elric, the Return to Melnibone, 1478
Else-Marie and Her Seven Little Daddies, 2538
Elsewhere, 2059
Elsewhere, Elsewhen, Elsehow, 848
Elsewhere, vol. 1, 1340
Elsewhere, vol. 2, 1340
Elsewhere, vol. 3, 1340
*The Elvenbane: An Epic Fantasy of the Halfblood
    Chronicles*, 3100
Elvin Star, 1574
The Emerald City of Oz, 1898
The Emerald Forest, 1979
Emily and the Enchanted Frog, 2474
Emily and the Werewolf, 2977
Emily Eyefinger, 2354
Emily: The Traveling Guinea Pig, 702
*Emily Upham's Revenge: Or, How Deadwood Dick
    Saved the Banker's Niece: A Massachusetts
    Adventure*, 2095
Emily's Voyage, 702
The Emma Dilemma, 2627

Emma in Winter, 2734
The Emperor's New Clothes, 6
The Emperor's Panda, 89
Empire of the East, 1516
The Empty Sleeve, 1080
The Enchanted: An Incredible Tale, 1640
The Enchanted Book, 849
The Enchanted Castle, 2576
The Enchanted Eve, 209
The Enchanted Forest, 289
The Enchanted Horse, 2945
The Enchanted Mountain, 2077
Enchanted Pilgrimage, 1528
The Enchanted Schoolhouse, 2621
The Enchanted Toby Jug, 2478
The Enchanted Wood: An Original Fairy Tale, 284
The Enchanter, 1710
The Enchanter's Daughter, 35
Enchanter's End Game, 3008
The Enchanter's Spell: Five Famous Tales, 850
Enchantment at Delphi, 1807
The Enchantress, 263
*Encounters with the Invisible World; Being Ten
    Tales of Ghosts, Witches, and the Devil
    Himself in New England*, 956
The End-of-Everything Man, 1933
Endgame, 1286, 1346
An Enemy at Green Knowe, 1031, 2371
The Enormous Crocodile, 471
The Enormous Egg, 2115
Enter Three Witches, 3025
Equality, 2696
Erec and Enid, 1825
Erik and Karlson on the Roof, 2539
Esbae: A Winter's Tale, 1707
Escape by Deluge, 1867
Escape from Danger, 476
Escape from Exile, 2006
The Escape of the Giant Hogstalk, 2197
Esio Trot, 2133
The Eternal Champion: A Fantastic Romance, 1477
Evangeline, Pigeon of Paris, 439
Eve: Her Story, 1672
Ever-After Island, 2487
Ever Ride a Dinosaur?, 2127
Evil Under the Sea, 665
Excalibur, 1742
An Excess of Enchantment, 3023
Exile's Gate, 1287
Exiles of the Rynth, 3004
The Expandable Pig, 2346
The Exploits of Moominpappa, 1388
Express Train to Trouble: A Miss Mallard Mystery,
    665
*The Extraordinary Education of Johnny Longfoot in
    His Search for the Magic Hat*, 414
The Eye of the World, 1396
Eyes in the Fishbowl, 1187

The Eyes of Kid Midas, 2634
The Eyes of the Dragon, 1406
The Eyes of the Overworld, 1559

F*T*C* Superstar, 384
The Faber Book of Modern Fairy Tales, 853
A Fable, 165
The Fabulous Flight, 2534
The Fabulous Voyage of the Pegasus, 2278
The Face in the Frost, 2973
Faces in the Water, 2804
Faery!, 854
*The Faery Flag: Stories and Poems of Fantasy and
    the Supernatural*, 997
Faery Lands Forlorn, 1327
Fairwater, 278
The Fairy Caravan, 662
The Fairy Circus, 196
The Fairy Doll, 2923
The Fairy Fleet, 220
*The Fairy Minstrel of Glenmalure, and Other
    Stories for Children*, 912
The Fairy Rebel, 2609
Fairy Stories, 928
A Fairy Tale, 2617
Fairy Tales (Andersen), 779
Fairy Tales (Cummings), 831
Fairy Tales (Jones), 2208
Fairy Tales from Hans Christian Andersen, 779
The Fairy Tales of Oscar Wilde, 984
The Fairy Tales of Wilhelm Hauff, 888
The Faithful Traitor, 3045
The Faithless Lollybird, 765
Falcon's Tor, 2767
A Fall of Princes, 1550
The Falling Woman: A Fantasy, 1779
False Face, 1735
Falter Tom and the Water Boy, 1944
Family: A Novel, 482
Famous Tales of the Fantastic, 855
Fang, the Gnome, 1647
*Fantastic Creatures: An Anthology of Fantasy and
    Science Fiction*, 856
The Fantastic Flying Journey, 2431
The Fantastic Freshman, 2376
*The Fantastic Imagination: An Anthology of High
    Fantasy*, 1343
The Fantastic Imagination, vol. 2, 1343
Fantastic Mr. Fox, 472
Fantastic Stories, 2209
Fantasy, 780
Fantasy Annual III, 857
Fantasy Annual IV, 857
Fantasy Annual V, 857
Fantasy Hall of Fame, 858
The Fantasy Worlds of Peter S. Beagle, 795

The Far Forests: Tales of Romance, Fantasy and Suspense, 766
Far Harbor, 1473
The Far Kingdoms, 1299
The Faraway Lurs, 36
A Farm in Fairyland, 894
Farmer Giles of Ham, 332
The Farthest Shore, 1433
The Farthest-Away Mountain, 279
Fast Eddie, 454
The Fast Sooner Hound, 2104
The Fat of the Cat and Other Stories, 907
The Fates of the Princes of Dyfed, 1778
The Faun and the Woodcutter's Daughter, 942
Favor for a Ghost, 1048
Favorite Tales of Hans Andersen, 779
The Fear of Samuel Walton, 1703
The Fearsome Inn, 299
The Feast of the Trickster, 1977
Feathertop: Based on the Tale by Nathaniel Hawthorne, 3113
Feldman Fieldmouse: A Fable, 410
The Fellowship of the Ring, 1555
The Ferlie, 2498
Festival Moon, 1346
Fever Season, 1286
Fiddler and His Brothers, 259
The Fiddler of High Lonesome, 335
The Fido Frame-Up, 698
The Field of Clover, 894
The Fields and the Hills, 1256
Fifteen Tales for Lively Children, 791
The Fifteenth Pelican, 2290
The Fifth Book of Lost Swords: Coinspinner's Story, 1517
Fifth Grade Magic, 2461
Figgs and Phantoms, 2283
Figment, Your Dog, Speaking, 533
The Figure in the Shadows, 1026
The Final Adventures of the Robber Hotzenplotz, 2280
The Final Encyclopedia, 1322
The Finches Fabulous Furnace, 2143
Finders Keepers, 2050
Finders-Seekers, 1368
A Fine and Private Place, A Novel, 1025
Finn Family Moomintroll, 1388
Finnegan II: His Nine Lives, 397
Finzel the Farsighted, 2164
The Fir Tree, 7
Fire and Hemlock, 3051
Fire on the Mountain, 1265
Fire Sea, 1574
Fireball, 1921
The Firebird, 71
The Firebrand, 1617
The Firelings, 1401
Firelord, 1696

The Fires of Azeroth, 1287
The Fires of Heaven, 1396
Fires of the Past: Thirteen Contemporary Fantasies about Hometowns, 867
The Fires of Windameir, 528
Fireshaper's Doom, 1934
The First Book of Lost Swords: Woundhealer's Story, 1517
The First Book of Swords, 1518
The First Margaret Mahy Storybook, 2557
The First Two Lives of Lukas-Kasha, 1887
A Fish Dinner in Memison, 1334
A Fish Named Yum, 627
Fish Soup, 202
The Fisherman's Curse, 1329
Five Children and It, 2577
The Five Children; Containing Five Children and It; The Phoenix and the Carpet; The Story of the Amulet, 2577
Five Dolls and the Duke, 2902
Five Dolls and the Monkey, 2902
Five Dolls and Their Friends, 2902
Five Dolls in a House, 2902
Five Dolls in the Snow, 2902
The 500 Hats of Bartholomew Cubbins, 293
Five Hundred Years After, 1274
The Five Jars, 2504
Flameweaver, 1257
A Flask of Sea Water, 260
Flat Stanley, 2113
Flatfoot Fox and the Case of the Missing Eye, 449
Flatfoot Fox and the Case of the Missing Whoooo, 449
Flatfoot Fox and the Case of the Noisy Otter, 449
Fledger, 405
The Fledgling, 2527
Flight from Nevèrÿon, 1313
The Flight of Mavin Manyshaped, 1554
The Flight of the Cassowary, 205
Flight of the Dragon Kyn, 1352
Flight of the Fox, 632
Flight of the Moth-Kin, 2646
Flight of the Raven, 1509
Flight of Vengeance, 1489
The Floating Gods, 1376
Floating Island, 2948
Flood Tide, 1286, 1346
Floramel and Esteban, 431
Florizella and the Wolves, 129
The Flower of the Realm, 651
The Flowers, 272
Flux, 1365
Fly by Night, 2505
The Fly-By-Nights, 634
The Flying Locomotive, 2146
The Flying Patchwork Quilt, 2375
Fog Magic, 2837
The Folk of the Air, 1610

Follow That Bus!, 2203
The Fool and the Dancing Bear, 1540
Fool on the Hill, 2618
The Foolish Dinosaur Fiasco, 2997
The Fools' War, 1410
A Foot in the Grave, 1006
Footprints at the Window, 2804
Footsteps on the Stairs, 1004
The Forbidden Forest, 2147
The Forbidden Island, 1666
The Forbidden Tower, 1270
The Forespoken, 2776
Forest, 211
The Forest of App, 87
Forest of the Night, 1543
The Forests of Adventure, 286
The Forever King, 1643
The Forging of the Dragon, 3045
Forging the Darksword, 1577
The Forgotten Beasts of Eld, 1455
The Forgotten Door, 1998
Fortress of Frost and Fire, 3070
The Fortress of the Pearl, 1478
The Fortunate Days, 874
The Fortunate Isles, 1557
Fortune, 306
Forty Good-Morning Tales, 869
Forty Good-Night Tales, 869
The Fossil Snake, 2369
The Foundling and Other Tales of Prydain, 1238
The Fountain of Youth; Stories to Be Told, 828
Four Dolls, 2924
The Four Friends, 540
Four Moons of Darkover, 1270
The Four Seasons of Brambly Hedge, 404
The Four-Legged Ghosts, 2491
Fours Crossing, 1684
The Fourth Book of Lost Swords: Farslayer's Story,
   1517
The Fox at Drummer's Darkness, 318
Fox Mykyta, 507
The Fox-Busters, 571
The Foxes of Firstdark, 566
Foxglove Tales, 727
Fractal Mode, 1889
The Frankenbagel Monster, 2269
Frankie!, 2358
Freaky Friday, 2291
Freddy and Freginald, 428
Freddy and Mr. Camphor, 428
Freddy and Simon the Dictator, 428
Freddy and the Baseball Team from Mars, 428
Freddy and the Bean Home News, 428
Freddy and the Dragon, 428
Freddy and the Flying Saucer Plans, 428
Freddy and the Ignormus, 428
Freddy and the Men from Mars, 428
Freddy and the Perilous Adventure, 428

Freddy and the Popinjay, 428
Freddy and the Space Ship, 428
Freddy Goes Camping, 428
Freddy Goes to Florida, 428
Freddy Goes to the North Pole, 428
Freddy Plays Football, 428
Freddy Rides Again, 428
Freddy the Cowboy, 428
Freddy the Detective, 428
Freddy the Magician, 428
Freddy the Pied Piper, 428
Freddy the Pilot, 428
Freddy the Politician, 428
Freddy's Cousin Weedly, 428
Frédou, 716
Free Amazons of Darkover, 1270
The French Lieutenant: A Ghost Story, 1049
A Fresh Wind in the Willows, 682
Friends in Time, 2713
The Friends of the Loony Lake Monster, 2367
The Friendship Song, 2063
The Frightened Forest, 3126
The Frog and the Beanpole, 562
The Frog Prince, Continued, 2299
From the Horn of the Moon, 2561
Frost and Fire, 1002
Fu-Dog, 2925
Full Moon, 1130
Fun Phantoms: Tales of Ghostly Entertainment,
   1078
Fur Magic, 2584
A Furl of Fairy Wind: Four Stories, 900
Further Adventures of Albert the Dragon, 348
The Further Adventures of Nils, 2524
Further Adventures of the Robber Hotzenplotz,
   2280
Future Forward, 2826
The Future of Hooper Toote, 2198

Gaetano the Pheasant: A Hunting Fable, 674
Gallicenae, 1247
The Game, 272
A Game of Catch, 1057
A Game of Dark, 2796
The Gammage Cup, 1402
*The Garden Behind the Moon: A Real Story of the
   Moon Angel*, 275
The Garden of Abdul Gasazi, 2656
Garranane, 159
Garth Pig and the Ice-Cream Lady, 666
Garth Pig Steals the Show, 666
Gate of Darkness, Circle of Light, 1721
The Gate of Ivory, 1335
Gate of Ivrel, 1287
The Gate of the Cat, 2039
The Gate of Worlds, 1525
Gates of Glass, 1980

A Gathering of Gargoyles, 1493
The Gathering Room, 1176
The Gauntlet, 2864
The Gauntlet of Malice, 3034
The General Zapped an Angel: New Stories of Fantasy and Science Fiction, 865
The Genetic General, 1322
The Genie of Sutton Place, 2628
Genie on the Loose, 2224
Genie with the Light Blue Hair, 2400
Gentleman Bear, 2913
Geomancer, 2983
George and the Dragon Word, 2637
George's Marvelous Medicine, 2417
Getting Rid of Aunt Edna, 3044
The Ghastly Glasses, 2462
Ghost Abbey, 1205
The Ghost and Bertie Boggin, 1178
A Ghost Around the House, 1147
Ghost Behind Me, 1036
The Ghost Belonged to Me: A Novel, 1169
The Ghost Cadet, 1015
Ghost Catcher, 1102
The Ghost Diviners, 2791
Ghost Dog, 1127
The Ghost Downstairs, 1081
The Ghost Drum: A Cat's Tale, 3108
Ghost Eye, 1023
The Ghost-Eye Tree, 1155
The Ghost Ferry, 1045
The Ghost from Beneath the Sea, 1033
Ghost Host, 1185
Ghost in My Soup, 1158
The Ghost in the Attic, 1045
The Ghost in the Castle, 1148
The Ghost in the Far Garden and Other Stories, 1154
A Ghost in the House, 1219
The Ghost in the Lagoon, 1042
The Ghost in the Mirror, 1026
The Ghost in the Noonday Sun, 1073
The Ghost Inside the Monitor, 1017
The Ghost Next Door, 1191
A Ghost of a Chance, 1043
The Ghost of Ernie P, 1220
The Ghost of Five Owl Farm, 1079
The Ghost of Opalina, or Nine Lives, 1022
The Ghost of Popcorn Hill, 1221
The Ghost of Skinny Jack, 1133
The Ghost of the Gravestone Hearth, 1105
The Ghost of Thomas Kempe, 1136
The Ghost on Saturday Night, 2167
The Ghost on the Hill, 1091
Ghost Song, 3109
The Ghost Squad and the Ghoul of Grünberg, 1108
The Ghost Squad and the Halloween Conspiracy, 1108

The Ghost Squad and the Menace of the Malves, 1108
The Ghost Squad and the Prowling Hermits, 1108
The Ghost Squad Breaks Through, 1108
The Ghost Squad Flies Concorde, 1108
Ghost Story, 1096
The Ghost Story Treasury, 1085
The Ghost Upstairs, 1143
Ghost Vision, 3065
The Ghost Witch, 1222
A Ghostly Business, 2522
Ghostly Companions: A Feast of Chilling Tales, 1013
The Ghosts, 2693
Ghosts: An Anthology, 1086
Ghosts Beneath Our Feet, 1223
The Ghost's Companion: A Haunting Anthology, 1087
Ghosts for Christmas, 1088
Ghosts I Have Been, 1169
The Ghosts of Austwick Manor, 2788
The Ghosts of Departure Point, 1037
The Ghosts of Hungryhouse Lane, 1142
The Ghosts of Mercy Manor, 1224
The Ghosts Who Went to School, 1190
The Giant, 2148
Giant Cold, 95
The Giant under the Snow: A Story of Suspense, 1699
The Giant Who Drank from His Shoe and Other Stories, 804
The Giant's Apprentice, 352
The Giants' Farm, 2334
The Giants Go Camping, 2334
Gideon and the Mummy Professor, 2513
The Gift, 2582
A Gift for Gift: A Ghost Story, 1107
A Gift for Merimond, 21
The Gifting, 3021
Giftwish, 1466
Gigi in America: Further Adventures of a Merry-Go-Round Horse, 2918
Gigi: The Story of a Merry-Go-Round Horse, 2918
Gildaen: The Heroic Adventures of a Most Unusual Rabbit, 432
The Gilded Cat, 1063
Gilgamesh the King, 1835
The Girl and the Goatherd, or This and That and Thus and So, 257
A Girl Called Boy, 2755
The Girl in the Grove, 1179
The Girl Who Cried Flowers and Other Tales, 998
The Girl Who Heard Dragons, 1447
The Girl Who Loved the Wind, 373
The Girl Who Sat by the Ashes, 69
The Girl with the Green Ear: Stories About Magic in Nature, 2557

Give Yourself a Fright: Thirteen Stories of the Supernatural, 767
The Glass Ball, 2564
The Glass Bird, 2611
The Glass Slipper, 1669
The Glassblower's Children, 3028
Glinda of Oz, 1898
Glom Gloom, 1317
The Glove of Maiden's Hair, 1680
Gnome Man's Land, 1958
The Gnome's Engine, 3010
The Goblin Mirror, 1288
Goblin Moon, 3010
The Goblin Reservation, 2845
The Goblins of Haubeck, 33
The God Beneath the Sea, 1688
The God Box, 1440
God Stalk, 1382
Godbond, 1537
The Goddess Letters: The Demeter-Persephone Myth Retold, 1792
The Gods in Winter, 240
Gods of the Greatway, 1647
Goldclimbers, 1442
The Golden Age, 879
The Golden Bees, 1504
The Golden Bird, 314
The Golden Cockerel and Other Stories, 950
The Golden Heart of Winter, 301
The Golden Horn, 1551
The Golden Key, 221
The Golden Serpent, 253
The Golden Shadows: A Recreation of Greek Legends, 1689
The Golden Spears and Other Fairy Tales, 913
The Golden Stile, 2073
The Golden Swan, 1538
The Golden Thread, 2986
The Golden Tower, 1310
Golden Trillium, 1271
Goldenrod, 2649
The Goldfinch Garden: Seven Tales, 943
The Golem, 1836
Golem in the Gears, 1250
The Golem; the Story of a Legend, 1866
Gom on Windy Mountain: From Tales of Gom, 1292
Gondola to Danger, 665
Gone Away, 1199
The Good Friends, 415
The Good Robber, Willibald, 2328
The Good, the Bad and the Goofy, 2838
The Good-Guy Cake, 2425
The Good-Natured Bear: A Story for Children of All Ages, 2200
The Goodknight Ghost, 1027
Goodlow's Ghosts, 1226
Goody Hall, 2097
The Grand Escape, 633

The Grand Jubilee, 1339
Grandfather Whiskers, M.D., a Graymouse Story, 604
The Grandma in the Apple Tree, 2541
Grandpa's Ghost Stories, 1075
Grandpa's Witched-Up Christmas, 1075
Granny's Wonderful Chair and Its Tales of Fairy Times, 2381
A Grass Rope, 2565
Grasshopper and the Unwise Owl, 2635
Graven Images: Three Stories, 1072
The Graymouse Family, 604
The Great and Terrible Quest, 1441
The Great Cheese Conspiracy, 730
The Great Christmas Kidnapping Caper, 730
The Great Custard Pie Panic, 2997
The Great Dimpole Oak, 212
The Great Geppy, 2149
The Great Ghost Rescue, 1112
Great Ghosts, 1053
Great Grandfather in the Honey Tree, 2316
Great Gravity the Cat, 558
The Great Hunt, 1396
Great Land of the Elephant, 131
The Great Pete Penney, 2648
The Great Piratical Rumbustification, and The Librarian and the Robbers, 2242
The Great Quillow, 326
The Great Rebellion, 713
The Great Rescue Operation, 730
The Great Ringtail Garbage Caper, 502
The Great Squirrel Uprising, 491
The Great Summer Camp Catastrophe, 730
The Great Wheeler, 1971
The Great White Man-Eating Shark: A Cautionary Tale, 2243
Great-Uncle Dracula, 2188
Great-Uncle Dracula and the Dirty Rat, 2188
The Green Book of Hob Stories, 2566
The Green Flash and Other Tales of Horror, Suspense, and Fantasy, 768
The Green Futures of Tycho, 2846
The Green Hill of Nendrum, 2687
The Green Isle, 55
The Green Knight, 1636
Green Mansions: A Romance of the Tropical Forest, 1983
The Green Pearl, 1560
Green Smoke, 2249
The Green Song, 659
Green Willow, 1066
Greenbriar Queen, 1361
Greenwitch, 1650
Gregory, Maw and the Mean One, 2182
Grendel, 1686
The Grey Horse, 3082
The Grey King, 1650
The Grey Mane of Morning, 1284

Greyling: A Picture Story from the Islands of Shetland, 1881
The Griffin and the Minor Canon, 313
The Griffin Legacy, 1121
A Griffon's Nest, 2776
Grimalkin's Tales, 746
Grimbold's Other World, 1969
Gryphon in Glory, 1486, 2039
The Gryphon King, 1662
Gryphon's Eyrie, 1486, 2039
The Guardians of the House, 1906
Guardians of the West, 1333
Guardians of Time, 2686
Gub-Gub's Book: An Encyclopedia of Food, 2234
Guests at the Beech Tree, 217
Guilt-Edged Ivory, 1335
Guinevere, 1783
Guinevere Evermore, 1783
Guinevere: The Legend in Autumn, 1873
Gulliver's Travels into Several Remote Nations of the World, 2069
The Gunga Sahib, 2027
The Guns of Avalon, 1599
Guns of the Gods, 2027
The Gunslinger, 1407
Gwenda & the Animals, 2420
Gwinna, 39
Gwot! Horribly Funny Hairticklers, 2252
Gypsies, 2083
The Gypsy Caravan; Being the Merry Tale of the Travels of Betty and Joe with the Gypsies— Their Amazing Adventures with Robin Hood—with Richard-the-Lion-Hearted—with Roland—and Sundry Other Great and Famous Persons, 2824
Gypsyworld, 2071

The Hairy Horror Trick, 2404
The Halcyon Island, 1122
The Half Brothers, 1421
Half Magic, 2433
The Half-a-Moon Inn, 3016
The Half-Pint Jinni, and Other Stories, 842
The Halfmen of O, 1962
Halfway Down Paddy Lane, 2794
The Hall of the Mountain King, 1550
The Halloween Tree, 2704
The Hammer and the Cross, 1375
The Hammer and the Horn, 1680
The Hand of Chaos, 1574
The Hand of Oberon, 1599
A Handful of Time, 2823
The Handsome Donkey, 477
Hangin' Out with Cici, 2819
The Hanging Stones, 1863
Hannibal and the Bears, 2888
Hans Andersen: His Classic Fairy Tales, 779

Hans Andersen's Fairy Tales, 779
Hans Andersen's Fairy Tales: A Selection, 779
Hans Christian Andersen Fairy Tales, 779
Haphazard House, 2866
Happles and Cinnamunger, 1182
The Happy Islands Behind the Winds, 2001
The Happy Place, 2890
The Happy Prince, 355
The Happy Prince and Other Fairy Stories, 984
The Happy Prince and Other Tales, 984
Harding's Luck, 2805
Hare's Choice, 527
The Harem of Aman Akbar; or The Djinn Decanted, 2298
Hark, the Little Angel, 2321
Harold and Chester in Hot Fudge, 547
Harold and Chester in the Fright Before Christmas, 547
Haroun and the Sea of Stories, 1514
A Harp of Fishbones and Other Stories, 769
The Harp of Imach Thyssel, 1589
The Harper Hall of Pern, 1448
Harpist in the Wind, 1457
Harpy High, 1958
Harpy Thyme, 1250
Harpy's Flight, 1437
The Harrowing of Gwynedd, 1414
Harry and the Sea Serpent, 754
Harry Cat's Pet Puppy, 686
Harry Kitten and Tucker Mouse, 686
Harry the Fat Bear, 754
Harry's Mad, 2215
Hart's Hope, 1278
Harvey, a Play, 2124
The Hateful Plateful Trick, 2404
The Haunted and the Haunters: Tales of Ghosts and Other Apparitions, 1103
The Haunted Churchbell, 1039
The Haunted Circus, 2789
The Haunted Ghost, 1039
Haunted Island, 1162
The Haunted Mountain: A Story of Suspense, 1984
The Haunted Spy, 1039
The Haunted Tower, 1039
The Haunting, 3091
A Haunting Air, 1076
Haunting at Mill Lane, 1173
The Haunting of Cassie Palmer, 1014
The Haunting of Chas McGill and Other Stories, 1206
The Haunting of Frances Rain, 2707
The Haunting of Lamb House, 1007
Haunting Tales, 1104
A Hawk in Silver, 1964
Hawk of May, 1621
Hawk's Flight, 1285
The Hawk's Gray Feather: A Book of the Keltiad, 1737

The Hawk's Tale, 403
Hawkmistress!, 1269
The Hawks of Chelney, 1389
The Hawks of Fellheath, 1348
Hazel the Guinea Pig, 751
The Healer's War: A Fantasy Novel of Vietnam,
    1824
Heart of Ice, 60
Heart of Valor, 2062
Heart's Blood, 1596
Hearts of Wood: And Other Timeless Tales, 910
Heartsease, 1320
Heather Hill, 725
Heaven Scent, 1250
The Heavenly Horse from the Outermost West, 703
The Heavenly Tenants, 2562
Hecate's Cauldron, 3036
Heir Apparent, 2051
Heir of Rengarth, 3004
Heir of Sea and Fire, 1457
The Heirs of Hammerfell, 1270
Helliconia Spring, 778
Helliconia Summer, 778
Helliconia Winter, 778
Hello, Mrs. Piggle-Wiggle, 2235
Help! Let Me Out!, 2279
Hemi: A Mule, 426
Henrietta Goes West, 2120
Henry Bear's Park, 616
Henry Beston's Fairy Tales, 797
Henry's Quest, 2263
Henry's Special Delivery, 2140
Her Majesty's Wizard, 2065
Herb Seasoning, 2318
Here Abide Monsters, 2035
Here be Demons, 2178
Here Comes Herb's Hurricane!, 710
Here Comes McBroom! Three More Tall Tales,
    2171
Here Comes Thursday, 423
Here There Be Dragons, 999
The Heritage of Hastur, 1270
The Hero and the Crown, 1461
The Hero from Otherwhere, 2080
The Hero of Varay, 2057
Hero's Song, 1796
A Heroine of the World, 1431
Hester and the Gnomes, 2497
The Hex Witch of Seldom, 3120
The Hey Hey Man, 113
Hi Jinks Joins the Bears, 2888
Hickory, 429
The Hidden City, 1332
*Hidden Turnings: A Collection of Stories Through
    Time and Space*, 892
*Higglety Pigglety Pop! Or, There Must Be More to
    Life*, 689
High Deryni, 1413

The High Hills, 404
The High King, 1236
The High Kings, 1635
*The High Rise Glorious Skittle Skat Roarious Sky
    Pie Angel Food Cake*, 2664
High Treason at Catfish Bend, 434
High Water at Catfish Bend, 434
High Wizardry, 3006
Hilda the Hen Who Wouldn't Give Up, 724
The Hill Road, 2797
Hira Singh's Tale, 2027
His Majesty's Elephant, 3125
Hit or Myth, 2965
Hitty, Her First Hundred Years, 2917
Hob and the Goblins, 2566
Hobberdy Dick, 1623
The Hobbit; Or, There and Back Again, 1556
Hobkin, 2472
Hobo Toad and the Motorcycle Gang, 760
The Hoboken Chicken Emergency, 2270
*The Hollow Earth: The Narrative of Mason Algiers
    Reynolds of Virginia*, 2053
The Hollow Hills, 1841
The Hollow Tree and Deep Woods Book, 647
Hollow Tree Nights and Days, 647
The Hollow Tree Snowed-In Book, 647
The Hollowing, 1717
Home, 1378
Home at Last! A Young Cat's Tale, 591
Home Free, 2769
Home Is the Sailor, 2926
The Home Run Trick, 2404
Homer Goes to Stratford, 402
Homer Sees the Queen, 402
Homer the Tortoise, 402
The Homeward Bounders, 1393
The Honorable Barbarian, 1310
Hooray for Hellywood, 2178
*The Hope of the Katzekopfs; or, the Sorrow of
    Selfishness: A Fairy Tale*, 261
Hoppity, 622
Horace, 337
Horn Crown, 2039
Hornswoggle Magic, 2401
Horror at the Haunted House, 1116
The Horse and His Boy, 2007
The Horse Goddess, 3078
The Horse of Flame, 1522
Horsemaster, 2061
The Horse in the Camel Suit, 2144
Hortense, the Cow for a Queen, 2122
Hosea Globe and the Fantastical Peg-Legged Chu,
    2098
The Hotel Cat, 393
The Houdini Box, 2629
The Hounds of God, 1551
The Hounds of the Morrigan, 1793
Hour of the Octopus, 1512

The House at Pooh Corner, 2944
The House Between the Worlds, 1909
The House in Norham Gardens, 2784
The House in the Snow, 1342
A House Inside Out, 608
The House Mouse, 529
The House of Arden, 2805
The House of Joy, 894
House of Shadows, 1163
The House of the Nightmare and Other Eerie Stories, 1103
The House on Mayferry Street, 2430
The House on Parchment Street, 1149
The House on the Brink: A Story of Suspense, 1700
The House on the Hill, 1067
The House That Grew Smaller, 40
The House That Sailed Away, 2204
The House That Wouldn't Go Away, 2458
The House with a Clock in Its Walls, 1026
The House Without Windows and Eepersip's Life There, 115
How a Weirdo and a Ghost Can Change Your Entire Life, 1217
How Baseball Began in Brooklyn, 2225
How Mr. Dog Got Even, 647
How Mr. Rabbit Lost His Tail, 647
How Space Rockets Began, 2226
How the Brothers Joined the Cat Club, 393
How the Camel Got His Hump, 181
How the Children Stopped the Wars, 343
How the Leopard Got His Spots, 182
How the Rhinoceros Got His Skin, 183
How the Whale Became, 549
How the Whale Got His Throat, 184
How the Witch Got Alf, 386
How to Become King, 323
How Tom Beat Captain Najork and His Hired Sportsmen, 2193
Howl's Moving Castle, 3052
Howliday Inn, 547
Hugh Pine, 729
Hugh Pine and Something Else, 729
Hugh Pine and the Good Place, 729
Humbug Mountain, 2168
The Hums of Pooh, 2944
The Hundred and One Dalmatians, 701
The Hundred Days, 2027
The Hundredth Dove and Other Tales, 1000
The Hunky-Dory Dairy, 2779
Hunt Down the Prize, 2026
Huntley Nutley and the Missing Link, 2317
Huon of the Horn, 1786
The Hurdy-Gurdy Man, 2365

I Am Leaper, 557
I Been There Before, 2119

I Discover Columbus: A True Chronicle of the Great Admiral and His Finding of the New World, Narrated by the Venerable Parrot Aurelio, Who Shared in the Glorious Venture, 596
I Houdini: The Autobiography of a Self-Educated Hamster, 668
I'll Meet You at the Cucumbers, 629
The Ice Bear, 1434
The Ice Cream Heroes, 2126
The Ice Dragon, 272
The Ice Is Coming, 1877
The Ice Palace, 74
The Ice Schooner: A Tale, 1479
The Icebergs, 272
The Idylls of the Queen, 1734
If at Faust You Don't Succeed, 2881
If I Had One Wish. . ., 2518
If I Pay Thee Not in Gold, 1251
If You Want to Scare Yourself, 1189
The Ill-Made Knight, 1864
The Illearth War, 1940
The Illustrated Man, 807
The Illyrian Adventure, 1888
Imaginary Lands, 1386
Imagine That! Fifteen Fantastic Tales, 901
Imperial Lady: A Fantasy of Han China, 1788
Impunity Jane: The Story of a Pocket Doll, 2927
In a Messy, Messy Room, and Other Strange Stories, 877
In Camera and Other Stories, 1207
In Grandpa's House, 291
In the Circle of Time, 2684
In the Grip of Winter, 476
In the Hall of the Dragon King, 1420
In the Hand of the Goddess, 1495
In the Ice King's Palace, 3101
In the Keep of Time, 2684
In the Red Lord's Reach, 1336
In the Sea Nymph's Lair, 3031
In the Shadow of the Oak King, 1731
In the Suicide Mountains, 1358
In the Time of the Bells, 1370
In Winter's Shadow, 1621
Incognito Mosquito Flies Again, 530
Incognito Mosquito, Private Insective, 530
Incognito Mosquito Takes to the Air, 530
The Incorporated Knight, 1311
The Incredible Adventures of Professor Branestawm, 2202
The Incredible Detectives, 442
The Incredible Umbrella, 1995
The Indian in the Cupboard, 2610
Infanta, 1303
Infernal Devices: A Mad Victorian Fantasy, 2207
Inferno, 1303
The Infinity Concerto, 1899
Infinity's Web, 1347
The Initiate, 1302

The Initiate Brother, 1515
The Innkeeper's Song, 1260
Inside My Feet: The Story of a Giant, 172
*The Interesting Thing That Happened at Perfect
    Acres, Inc*, 2659
Into the Dark, 1214
Into the Forest, 106
Into the Green, 1316
Into the Labyrinth, 1574
Into the Painted Bear Lair, 2066
Into the Unknown: Eleven Tales of Imagination, 902
Invisible Magic, 2697
The Invisible Womble, 412
Irma and Jerry, 687
The Iron Arm of Michael Glenn, 2223
The Iron Giant: A Story in Five Nights, 156
The Iron Lion, 96
Is Underground, 1235
*Isaac Asimov Presents the Best Fantasy of the 19th
    Century*, 903
Isaac Asimov's Magical Worlds of Fantasy: Faeries,
    904
Iseult: Dreams That Are Done, 1772
The Island and the Ring, 1544
The Island of Dark Woods, 1212
*The Island of the Grass King: The Further
    Adventures of Anatole*, 2079
The Island Through the Gate, 2068
The Isle of Glass, 1551
Isle of the Shape-Shifters, 1649
Isle of View, 1250
The Isles of the Blest, 1756
It, 1157
It Happens Every Spring, 2139
It's About Time, 2821
It's Perfectly True, and Other Stories, 779
It's Really Christmas, 536
Italian Peepshow and Other Tales, 860
Ivanov Seven, 2206
The Ivory Lyre, 1481
The Ivy Garland, 1110

Jack of Shadows, 3147
Jack the Giant-Killer, 1663
Jackaroo, 1564
Jacob Two-Two and the Dinosaur, 2287
Jacob Two-Two Meets the Hooded Fang, 2287
Jaguar, My Twin, 3074
The Jaguar Princess, 1262
Jahdu, 2187
James and the Giant Peach: A Children's Story,
    2418
*James, Fabulous Feline: Further Adventures of a
    Connoisseur Cat*, 525
James, the Connoisseur Cat, 525
Jane's Adventures In and Out of the Book, 2180
Jane-Emily, 1050

The Jargoon Pard, 1487
Jason and the Baseball Bear, 492
Jason and the Money Tree, 2228
Jason Bodger and the Priory Ghost, 1118
Jason's Quest, 592
Java Jack, 2213
Jay-Jay and the Peking Monster, 2161
The Jedera Adventure, 1888
Jeeter, Mason and the Magic Headset, 2960
Jeffrey Strangeways, 2256
Jeffrey's Ghost and the Leftover Baseball Team,
    1005
Jemimalee, 671
The Jenius, 572
Jennifer Murdley's Toad, 2406
Jenny and the Cat Club, 393
Jenny's First Party, 393
Jenny's Moonlight Adventure, 393
Jeremiah in the Dark Woods, 2089
Jeremy Thatcher, Dragon Hatcher, 2407
Jeremy Visick, 2876
Jerry's Ghosts and the Mystery of the Blind Tower,
    1177
Jessamy, 2847
Jesse's Ghost and Other Stories, 946
Jethro and the Jumbie, 2403
The Jewel of Life, 1409
Jheref, 1275
Jim at the Corner, 861
Jim Bridger's Alarm Clock, and Other Tall Tales,
    2169
Jim Hedgehog and the Lonesome Tower, 537
Jim Hedgehog's Supernatural Christmas, 537
Jingo Django, 2170
Jingrim, 2027
Jingrim and Allah's Peace, 2027
Jinian Footseer, 1552
Jinian Star-Eye, 1552
Jo-Jo the Melon Donkey, 247
Jock's Castle, 122
Joel and the Great Merlini, 2550
Joey's Head, 2130
John Midas in the Dreamtime, 2392
John the Balladeer, 1863
The Joining of the Stone, 1482
Jolly Roger: A Dog of Hoboken, 2271
Jolly Roger and the Pirates of Abdul the Skinhead,
    2237
The Jolly Witch, 2980
Jonah's Mirror, 2008
Jonas McFee, A. T. P, 2619
Jonathan Livingston Seagull, 26
Jonothon and Large, 2475
Journey Behind the Wind, 1877
The Journey of Pietari and His Wolf, 142
Journey Outside, 1541
Journey to the Flame, 2025
Journeyman Wizard: A Magical Mystery, 3146

Joy Is Not Herself, 3072
The Joy of the Court, 1715
Judge Benjamin and the Purloined Sirloin, 615
Judge Benjamin: Superdog, 615
Judge Benjamin: The Superdog Gift, 615
Judge Benjamin: The Superdog Rescue, 615
Judge Benjamin: The Superdog Secret, 615
Judge Benjamin: The Superdog Surprise, 615
Juma and the Magic Jinn, 2341
Jumanji, 2657
June the Tiger, 504
The Jungle Book, 554, 579
Jungle Jest, 2027
Juniper, 3020
The Juniper Game, 2760
Junket, 741
Junkyard Dog, 677
Jupie and the Wise Old Owl, 612
Jupie Follows His Tale, 612
Just So Stories, 580
Juxtaposition, 1248

Karlson Flies Again, 2539
Karlsson-on-the-Roof, 2539
Kashka, 1450
Kashtanka, 443
Kasperle's Adventures, 2953
Kate Crackernuts, 1624
Kedrigern and the Charming Couple, 3093
Kedrigern in Wanderland, 3093
Keeper of the Keys, 3141
The Keeper's Price and Other Stories, 1270
Keepers of Edanvant, 3004
Keeping Time, 2836
The Kelpie's Pearls, 157
Kenny's Window, 2630
Kersti and Saint Nicholas, 2320
Kesrick, 1282
The Kestrel, 1241
The Kid Who Only Hit Homers, 2395
Killashandra, 1446
Kilroy and the Gull, 411
Kindred, 2709
King Arthur and His Knights, 1767
King Arthur and the Legends of Camelot, 1767
King Arthur: The Sword in the Stone, 1767
The King in Check, 2027
King Javin's Year, 1413, 1414
The King Must Die, 1813
The King of Alsander, 1956
The King of Elfland's Daughter, 1328
The King of Ireland's Son, 70
The King of Men, 1648
King of Morning, Queen of Day, 1762
King of the Cats, 2588
King of the Cloud Forests, 1777
The King of the Copper Mountains, 42

King of the Dead, 1445
King of the Doll House, 2397
*The King of the Golden River, or the Black
    Brothers: A Legend of Stiria,* 281
King—of the Khybers, 2027
King of the Murgos, 1333
King of the Nogs, 272
King of the Scepter'd Isle, 1647
King Orville and the Bullfrogs, 1
King Penguin: A Legend of the South Sea Isles, 543
King Stork, 3110
The King, the Cat, and the Fiddle, 238
The King, the Princess, and the Tinker, 229
The Kingdom and the Cave, 1233
The Kingdom of Carbonel, 2636
The Kingdom of Kevin Malone, 1917
Kingdom of Summer, 1621
Kingdom of the Grail, 1607
The Kingdom of the Winding Road, 926
Kingdoms of Elfin, 1570
Kingdoms of Sorcery, 1408
Kingdoms of the Wall, 1526
Kings Blood Four, 1554
The King's Buccaneer, 1344
The King's Equal, 264
The King's Justice, 1412
Kipling's Fantasy, 909
The Kitchen Knight, 1826
The Kitchen Knight: A Tale of King Arthur, 1716
Kiteman of Karanga, 1507
Klondike Arthur, 2128
Knave of Dreams, 2036
Knee-Deep in Thunder, 2026
Knee-High to a Grasshopper, 2595
Knee-Knock Rise, 24
Knickerbocker's History of New York, 2205
Knight at Dawn, 2813
Knight Life, 1660
Knight of Shadows, 1599
The Knight of the Cart, 1715
The Knight of the Golden Plain, 158
The Knight of the Lion, 1715
Knight on Horseback, 1172
Knight's Castle, 1946
Knights of the Kitchen Table, 2838
Knight's Wyrd, 1325
Knock at the Door, 1923
Konrad, 2262
*Krindlekrax; or, How Ruskin Splinter Battled a
    Horrible Monster and Saved His Entire
    Neighborhood,* 2288

La Morte D'Arthur, 1767
The Ladies of Mandrigyn, 1372
Lady Daisy, 2939
Lady of Darkness, 1491
The Lady of Han-Gilen, 1550

Lady of Light, 1491
Lady of the Forest, 1816
The Lady of the Linden Tree, 944
The Lady Who Put Salt in Her Coffee, 2185
The Lady's Chair and the Ottoman, 322
Ladyhawke, 3130
Lake of Gold, 2706
Lammas Night, 3067
A Lamp for the Lambchops, 2113
The Lamp from the Warlock's Tomb, 2360
The Lampfish of Twill, 1438
The Land Beyond, 1972
Land of Dreams, 1905
The Land of Forgotten Beasts, 2074
The Land of Gold, 1272
Land of Heroes: A Retelling of the Kalevala, 1846
The Land of Oz, 1898
Landfall, 1749
The Landing: A Night of Birds, 2625
The Last Arabian Night, 1685
The Last Battle, 2007
*The Last Book of Lost Swords: Shieldbreaker's
     Story*, 1517, 1518
The Last Defender of Camelot, 1003
The Last Dream, 841
The Last Enchantment, 1841
The Last Guru, 2272
The Last Human, 1933
The Last of Danu's Children, 1818
The Last of the Dragons, 255
The Last of the Renshai, 1506
The Last Pendragon, 1814
The Last Rainbow, 1696
The Last Slice of Rainbow: And Other Stories, 770
The Last Unicorn, 1261
The Last Wizard, 3043
The Lastborn of Elvinwood, 1708
The Lavender Cat, 215
Lavender Green Magic, 2809
Lavender Shoes, 727
Lavondyss, 1717
The Lays of the Beleriad, 1555
Lazy Tinka, 292
Lazy Tommy Pumpkinhead, 2150
Leap Frog Friday, 2535
The Left-Handed Spirit, 3098
The Leftover Elf, 316
Legacy of Magic, 3064
Legacy of the Sword, 1509
The Legend of Daisy Flowerdew, 268
The Legend of King Arthur, 1767
Legend of Sagenfeld, 336
The Legend of Sleepy Hollow, 1724
The Legend of Tarik, 1780
The Lemming Condition, 389
The Lemonade Trick, 2404
The Lengthening Shadow, 1703
Lens of the World, 1445

The Leprechaun of Bayou Luce, 2597
Leprechaun Tales, 882
The Leprechaun's Story, 173
Leroni of Darkover, 1270
Lesse Webster, 602
Let Me Fall Before I Fly, 349
Let Me Hear You Whisper: A Play, 762
The Letter, the Witch and the Ring, 1026
Letters from Atlantis, 2844
The Leveller, 1704
Liavek, 1435
Liavek: Spells of Binding, 1435
Liavek: The Players of Luck, 1435
Liavek: Wizard's Row, 1435
*The Lifted Veil: The Book of Fantastic Literature by
     Women, 1800–World War II*, 918
*The Light Beyond the Forest: The Quest for the Holy
     Grail*, 1843
The Light Maze, 2034
Light on the Sound, 1546
The Light Princess, 222
Lightning Time, 2793
Lights on the Lake, 2793
The Limbreth Gate, 1437
The Limerick Trick, 2404
Lincoln's Dreams, 2873
Linnets and Valerians, 2464
Lion at School: And Other Stories, 2600
A Lion in the Woods, 2142
Lion of Ireland: The Legend of Brian Boru, 1757
Lion of Macedon, 1694
The Lion of Petra, 2027
The Lion, the Witch, and the Wardrobe, 2007
The Lion-Hearted Kitten and Other Stories, 395
Lioness Rampant, 1495
Listen to This, 919
The Listening Silence, 1817
*The Literary Ghost: Great Contemporary Ghost
     Stories*, 1134
The Little Black Hen; An Irish Fairy Story, 2588
The Little Blue Man, 2916
*The Little Bookroom: Eleanor Farjeon's Short
     Stories for Children, Chosen by Herself*, 862
A Little Boy Lost: A Tale for Children, 155
The Little Broomstick, 3121
The Little Country, 3001
Little Daylight, 223
Little Dog Toby, 499
A Little Fear, 2672
The Little Ghost, 1171
The Little Grey Men, 1253
Little Harry, 2111
Little Heiskell, 2501
Little Houses Far Away, 2894
The Little Hump-backed Horse: A Russian Tale, 105
Little Ida's Flowers, 8
The Little Jewel Box, 232
The Little Knight, 161

The Little Lame Prince and His Travelling Cloak, 250

The Little Leftover Witch, 3071

Little Little Sister, 84

The Little Man, 2212

The Little Man and the Big Thief, 2212

The Little Man and the Little Miss, 2212

The Little Man with One Shoe, 788

The Little Match Girl, 9

The Little Mermaid, 10

The Little Mermaid Who Could Not Sing, 303

Little Myth Marker, 2965

Little Old Mrs. Pepperpot and Other Stories, 2607

Little Owl, Keeper of the Trees, 535

Little Pig, 277

Little Plum, 2928

The Little Prince, 282

Little Rag Doll, 2949

Little Room of Terror, 1141

Little Sophie and Lanky Flop, 267

The Little Stolen Sweep, 2802

The Little Swineherd and Other Tales, 868

Little Tricker the Squirrel Meets Big Double the Bear, 565

The Little White Goat, 2530

The Little White Horse, 2465

Little Witch, 2974

The Little Witch, 3106

Little Wizard Stories of Oz, 1898

The Little Wooden Doll, 2891

The Littlest Angel, 321

The Lives of Christopher Chant, 1990

Lizard Music, 2273

The Lobster Books, 531

The Lodge of the Lynx, 3068

The Log of the Ark, 1858

Lolly Willowes: or, the Loving Huntsman, 3132

The Lone Arthur, 2128

The Lonely Little Pig and Other Animal Tales, 611

The Lonesomest Doll, 2897

Long Night Dance, 1387

The Long-Nosed Princess: A Fairy Tale, 134

Looking Backward: 2000–1887, 2696

Looking-for-Something: The Story of a Stray Burro of Ecuador, 445

Loose Chippings, 2075

Lord Darcy Investigates, 1359

The Lord Fish, 835

Lord Foul's Bane, 1940

Lord of Chaos, 1396

The Lord of the Dance, 1606

Lord of the Troll-Bats, 3024

Lord of the Two Lands, 1850

Lord Valentine's Castle, 1527

Lords of the Triple Moons, 1467

Lore of the Witch World, 2039

Loretta and the Little Fairy, 2624

Loretta Mason Potts, 1918

The Lost and Found Princess, 114

The Lost and the Lurking, 1863

Lost Dorsai, 1322

The Lost Farm, 2415

The Lost Half-Hour: A Collection of Stories, 920

Lost Horizon, 1978

Lost in the Amazon, 665

Lost Indian Magic: A Mystery Story of the Red Man as He Lived Before the White Men Came, 2570

The Lost Kingdom of Karnica, 174

The Lost Legend of Finn, 2856

Lost Magic, 2964

The Lost Merbaby, 31

The Lost Merry-Go-Round, 2531

The Lost Playground, 2906

The Lost Princess of Oz, 1898

The Lost String Quartet, 44

A Lost Tale, 1668

Lost Threshold: A Novel, 2076

The Lost Trooper, 2027

Lost Worlds, Unknown Horizons: Nine Stories of Science Fiction, 2013

The Lost Zoo (A Rhyme for the Young, but Not Too Young) by Christopher Cat and Countee Cullen, 465

The Love Potion, 2357

Lucian Goes A-Voyaging, 2322

The Luck of Relian Kru, 1567

Luck of the Wheels, 1437

Lucy Beware!, 2853

Lucy's Winter Tale, 2436

Lud-in-the-Mist, 1474

Ludo and the Star Horse, 311

Lure of the Dark, 1822

Lythande, 2976

M for Mischief, 2593

M.Y.T.H. Inc. Link, 2965

Ma and Pa Dracula, 2250

Macaroon, 467

MacWomble's Pipe Band, 412

Mad, Mad Monday, 1184

Madbond, 1531

Made-to-Order Stories, 813

Madouc, 1560

Madwand, 3148

The Magic Book, 2613

Magic by the Lake, 1946, 2433

Magic Camera, 2602

Magic Casement, 1327

The Magic Chalk, 2493

The Magic Circle, 3096

The Magic City, 2031

The Magic Cup: An Irish Legend, 1702

The Magic Drawing Pencil, 2644

The Magic Engineer, 1475

The Magic Finger, 2419

The Magic Firecrackers, 2421
The Magic Fishbone, 94
The Magic Flute, 248
The Magic Forest: A Modern Fairy Story, 2662
The Magic Goes Away, 1485
The Magic Grandfather, 2666
The Magus Hare, 669
The Magic Hat of Mortimer Wintergreen, 3073
Magic in Ithkar, 1463
Magic in Ithkar 2, 1463
Magic in Ithkar 3, 1463
Magic in Ithkar 4, 1463
Magic in the Alley, 2387
Magic in the Mist, 3062
The Magic Jacket and Other Stories, 836
Magic Kingdom for Sale—Sold!, 2112
The Magic Knight, 262
Magic May Return, 1485
Magic Number, 520
The Magic of Myrna C. Waxweather, 2432
The Magic of Oz, 1898
The Magic of Recluce, 1475
Magic or Not?, 2434
The Magic Paintbrush, 249
The Magic Pawnshop; a New Year's Eve Fantasy, 2449
The Magic Pin, 2451
The Magic Pudding: Being the Adventures of Bunyip Bluegum and His Friends Bill Barnacle and Sam Sawnoff, 2231
The Magic Ring, 2453
The Magic Sea Shell, 2351
The Magic Shop, 2428
The Magic Skateboard, 2612
The Magic Sled, 2361
The Magic Stone, 2445, 3064
The Magic Switch, 2485
The Magic Three of Solatia, 1597
Magic to Burn, 2454
The Magic Touch, 2347
The Magic Vase, 119
The Magic Walking-Stick, 2383
The Magic Wars, 1295
The Magic Well, 297
The Magic World, 2578
Magic's Pawn, 1417
Magic's Price, 1417
Magic's Promise, 1417
The Magical Adventures of Pretty Pearl, 1709
The Magical Cupboard, 2720
The Magical Fellowship, 3083
Magicats!, 617
Magician, 1344
The Magician's Apprentice, 3084
The Magician's Challenge, 3084
The Magician's Company, 3084
Magician's Gambit, 3008
The Magician's Nephew, 2007

The Magicians of Caprona, 3053
The Magicians of Erianne, 1614
Magnifi-Cat, 693
Magnificent Milo, 2598
The Magnificent Nose and Other Marvels, 2450
Magnolia's Mixed-Up Magic, 636
Magnus Powermouse, 573
Mail-Order Wings, 2462
The Mailbox Trick, 2404
Maildun the Voyager, 1811
Mainly in Moonlight: Ten Stories of Sorcery and the Supernatural, 880
Mairelon the Magician, 1590
The Majipoor Chronicles, 1527
Majyk by Accident, 3018
Making Up with Mr. Dog, 647
Makra Choria, 1468
Malkin's Mountain, 2961
The Mammoth Book of Ghost Stories, 1153
The Mammoth Book of Ghost Stories 2, 1153
Man from Mundania, 1250
The Man of Gold, 1258
A Man Rides Through, 1941
The Man Who Folded Himself, 2741
The Man Who Lit the Stars, 62
The Man with Purple Eyes, 2677
Mandricardo: New Adventures of Terra Magica, 1282
The Mansion in the Mist, 2360
Many Moons, 327
Many Waters, 2774
Maps in a Mirror: The Short Fiction of Orson Scott Card, 815
Marco and the Tiger, 2176
Marianne, the Magus, and the Manticore, 2070
Mariel of Redwall, 550
Marion Zimmer Bradley's Darkover, 1270
Marion's Wall: A Novel, 1071
The Mark of the Cat, 1488
Marmalade and Rufus, 2138
Marmalade Atkins Hits the Big Time, 2138
Marmalade Atkins in Space, 2138
Marra's World, 1641
The Marrow of the World, 2032
Martin Pippin in the Apple Orchard, 108
Martin Pippin in the Daisy Field, 108
Martin the Goose Boy, 2889
Martin the Warrior, 550
Martin's Mice, 574
The Marvelous Misadventures of Sebastian: Grand Extravaganza, Including a Performance by the Entire Cast of the Gallimaufry Theatricus, 1239
Mary Poppins, 2651
Mary Poppins and the House Next Door, 2651
Mary Poppins Comes Back, 2651
Mary Poppins from A to Z, 2651
Mary Poppins in Cherry Tree Lane, 2651

Mary Poppins in the Park, 2651
Mary Poppins Opens the Door, 2651
The Marzipan Moon, 361
The Marzipan Pig, 144
The Mask of the Dancing Princess, 50
Mask of the Wizard, 1301
Masquerade, 366
The Master, 1302
Master of Earth and Water, 1799
Master of Fiends, 1381
The Master of Miracle: A New Novel of the Golem, 1726
Master of the Elephants, 131
Master of the Five Magics, 3033
Master of the Grove, 3059
Master of the Sidhe, 1677
The Master of White Storm, 1593
Masterpieces of Fantasy and Enchantment, 925
Masters of Glass, 1329
Masters of Shades and Shadows: An Anthology of Great Ghost Stories, 1156
The Mathematical Princess and Other Stories, 935
Matilda (Dahl), 2134
Matilda (Le Grand), 2227
Matthew and the Sea Singer, 265
Matthew's Meadow, 43
Mattimeo, 550
Max and Me and the Time Machine, 2745
Max and Me and the Wild West, 2745
Max and Sally and the Phenomenal Phone, 2555
Maximilian's World, 713
Maybe, a Mole, 468
The Maze in the Heart of the Castle, 1965
The Maze Stone, 2728
Mazemaker, 2725
McBroom and the Beanstalk, 2171
McBroom and the Big Wind, 2171
McBroom and the Great Race, 2171
McBroom Tells a Lie, 2171
McBroom Tells the Truth, 2171
McBroom the Rainmaker, 2171
McBroom's Almanac, 2171
McBroom's Ear, 2171
McBroom's Ghost, 2171
McBroom's Wonderful One-Acre Farm: Three Tall Tales, 2171
McBroom's Zoo, 2171
McGillicuddy McGotham, 2326
McWhinney's Jaunt, 2220
Me and the Man on the Moon-Eyed Horse, 2172
Mean Jake and the Devils, 2199
The Mechanical Doll, 307
Medallion of the Black Hound, 2029
Medea, 1833
A Medicine for Melancholy, 808
Melisande, 256
Melusine: A Mystery, 1812

Memoirs of a London Doll, Written by Herself, 2915
The Memoirs of a White Elephant, 517
The Menzian Gate, 1334
The Mer-Child: A Legend for Children and Other Adults, 246
Mercy and the Mouse and Other Stories, 396
Mercy's Mill, 2775
Merlin Dreams, 1665
Merlin's Booke, 1882
Merlin's Mistake, 1782
The Mermaid, and Other Fairy Tales, 779
The Mermaid and the Major: or, The True Story of the Invention of the Submarine, 2251
The Mermaid and the Simpleton, 945
The Mermaid and the Whale, 228
The Mermaid Summer, 2499
The Mermaid's Cape, 353
The Mermaid's Daughter, 3022
The Mermaid's Three Wisdoms, 2675
The Merman's Children, 1245
Merrimeg, 1907
Message from Arkmae, 2722
Mia, 1160
Mice on My Mind, 732
Michael and the Secret War, 1966
Michael Hague's Favorite Hans Christian Andersen Fairy Tales, 779
Michael of Ireland, 816
Midnight Blue, 1955
The Midnight Flight of Moose, Mops and Marvin, 417
The Midnight Folk: A Novel, 2560
The Midnight Horse, 1074
Midnight in the Dollhouse, 2957
A Midsummer Tempest, 1246
Mighty Magic: An Almost-True Story of Pirates and Indians, 2785
Miko, Little Hunter of the North, 100
Mimi, 696
Mind-Speaker's Call, 1368
Mindbond, 1537
Mindy's Mysterious Miniature, 2415
The Mine of Lost Days, 2705
The Minpins, 1930
The Minstrel and the Dragon Pup, 320
The Minstrel Knight, 1715
Mio, My Son, 2011
The Miracle on 34th Street, 88
The Miracle Season, 451
Miranda the Great, 495
Mirror of Danger, 2853
The Mirror of Her Dreams, 1941
Mischief in Fez, 2492
Misenchanted Sword, 3133
Misplaced Persons, 1976
Miss Bianca, 691
Miss Bianca and the Bridesmaid, 691

Miss Bianca in the Antarctic, 691
Miss Bianca in the Arctic, 691
Miss Bianca in the Orient, 691
Miss Bianca in the Salt Mines, 691
Miss Fanshawe and the Great Dragon Adventure,
    2302
Miss Ghost, 1020
Miss Grimsbee Is a Witch, 3134
Miss Grimsbee Takes a Vacation, 3134
Miss Happiness and Miss Flower, 2928
Miss Hickory, 2886
Miss Know-It-All; A Butterfield Square Story, 2676
Miss Know-It-All Returns, 2676
Miss Muffet's Christmas Party, 78
Miss Osborne-the-Mop, 2457
Miss Pennyfeather and the Pooka, 2588
Miss Pennyfeather in the Springtime, 2588
Miss Switch to the Rescue, 3131
The Missing Boy, 1937
The Missing Doll, 2932
Mister Corbett's Ghost, 1082
Mister Mysterious and Company, 2173
Mistress Masham's Repose, 2663
Mistress of Mistresses, 1334
Mistress of the Empire, 1345
The Mists of Avalon, 1618
The Mists of Time, 2684
Modern Fairy Stories, 927
Modern Ghost Stories by Eminent Women Writers,
    1159
Mole's Christmas, or, Home Sweet Home, 523
Molly Mullett, 72
A Mom by Magic, 2426
Momo, 1341
The Mona Lisa Mystery, 2203
Monday Begins on Saturday, 3124
A Monkey's Uncle, 2190
The Monster, 272
The Monster Garden, 2339
The Monster Ring, 2406
A Monster Too Many, 2554
The Monster's Ring, 2408
Monsters, Ghoulies and Creepy Creatures:
    Fantastic Stories and Poems, 929
Monstra vs. Irving, 2559
Mont Cant Gold, 1349
Moomin, Mymble and Little My, 1388
Moominland Midwinter, 1388
Moominpappa at Sea, 1388
Moominpappa's Memoirs, 1388
Moominsummer Madness, 1388
Moominvalley in November, 1388
The Moon and the Face, 1456
Moon–Dark, 756
The Moon in Hiding, 3009
The Moon in the Cloud, 1711
Moon Mirror, 934
The Moon of Gomrath, 1691

The Moon Ribbon and Other Tales, 1001
The Moon Singer, 51
The Moon's Fire-Eating Daughter, 2030
The Moon's Revenge, 2
Moon-Flash, 1456
The Moonball, 2667
The Moonbow of Mr. B. Bones, 208
Mooncoin Castle; or Skulduggery Rewarded, 1200
Moondial, 2715
Moongather, 1296
Moonheart, 1664
Moonscatter, 1296
Moonshine and Clover, 895
Moonshine and Magic, 727
Moonsinger's Friends: In Honor of André Norton,
    931
The Moospire, 658
Mopsa the Fairy, 1985
More about Paddington, 422
More about Worzel Gummidge, 2319
More Adventures of Samurai Cat, 675
More Fifth Grade Magic, 2461
More Rootabagas, 2296
More Tales from California, 957
More Magic, 1485
Moreta: Dragon Lady of Pern, 1447
Morgan's Zoo, 548
Mortimer Says Nothing, 2090
Mortimer's Cross, 2090
Moss Gown, 151
Mossflower, 550
Most Ancient Song, 1678
Mostly Magic, 2393
Moth Manor: A Gothic Tale, 2885
Moth-Kin Magic, 2646
Mother Farthing's Luck, 2572
Mother West Wind's Animal Friends, 433
Mother West Wind's Children, 433
Mother West Wind's "How" Stories, 433
Mother West Wind's Neighbors, 433
Mother West Wind's "When" Stories, 433
Mother West Wind's "Where" Stories, 433
Mother West Wind's "Why" Stories, 433
The Mouldy, 234
The Mountain and the Summer Stars: An Old Tale
    Newly Ended, 1609
The Mountain Door, 1959
The Mountains of Quilt, 2665
Mourka, the Mighty Cat, 757
The Mouse and His Child, 145
The Mouse and the Motorcycle, 446
The Mouse Butcher, 575
The Mouse God, 564
Mouse House, 518
Mouse Manor, 488
The Mouse on the Moon, 2327
The Mouse on Wall Street, 2327
The Mouse That Roared, 2327

The Mouse That Saved the West, 2327
The Mouses' Terrible Christmas, 563
The Mouses' Terrible Halloween, 563
The Mousewife, 125
Mr. and Mrs. Pig's Evening Out, 666
Mr. Bumps and His Monkey, 479
Mr. Crow and the Whitewash, 647
Mr. Dawson Had a Farm, 2333
Mr. Dawson Had a Lamb, 2333
Mr. Dawson Had an Elephant, 2333
Mr. Death and the Redheaded Woman, 2160
Mr. Garden, 2444
Mr. Goat's Bad Good Idea, 673
Mr. Hermit Crab: A Tale for Children by a Child,
    2048
Mr. Magus Is Waiting for You, 3060
Mr. Moon's Last Case, 2596
Mr. Mullett Owns a Cloud, 2542
Mr. Noah and the Second Flood, 1631
Mr. O'Hara, 2323
Mr. Pin: The Chocolate Files, 627
Mr. Popper's Penguins, 2094
Mr. Possum's Great Balloon Trip, 647
Mr. Pudgins, 2390
Mr. Rabbit's Big Dinner, 647
Mr. Rabbit's Wedding, 647
Mr. Radagast Makes an Unexpected Journey, 2261
Mr. Revere and I: Being an Account of Certain
    Episodes in the Career of Paul Revere, Esq., as
    Recently Revealed by His Horse,
    Scheherazade, Late Pride of His Royal
    Majesty's 14th Regiment of Foot, 597
Mr. Tidy Paws, 679
Mr. Turtle's Flying Adventure, 647
Mr. Twigg's Mistake, 598
Mr. Wicker's Window, 2724
Mr. Yowder and the Giant Bull Snake, 2293
Mr. Yowder and the Lion Roar Capsules, 2293
Mr. Yowder and the Steamboat, 2293
Mr. Yowder and the Train Robbers, 2293
Mr. Yowder and the Windwagon, 2293
Mr. Yowder, the Peripatetic Sign Painter: Three Tall
    Tales, 2294
Mrs. Cockle's Cat, 2601
Mrs. Coverlet's Detectives, 2260
Mrs. Coverlet's Magicians, 2260
Mrs. Flannagan's Trumpet, 1054
Mrs. Frisby and the Rats of NIMH, 639
Mrs. McThing: A Play, 2987
Mrs. Minetta's Car Pool, 2309
Mrs. Pepperpot Again, 2607
Mrs. Pepperpot in the Magic Wood, 2607
Mrs. Pepperpot to the Rescue, 2607
Mrs. Pepperpot's Busy Day, 2607
Mrs. Pepperpot's Christmas, 2607
Mrs. Pepperpot's Outing, 2607
Mrs. Pepperpot's Year, 2607
Mrs. Pig Gets Cross; and Other Stories, 666

Mrs. Pig's Bulk Buy, 666
Mrs. Piggle-Wiggle, 2235
Mrs. Piggle-Wiggle's Farm, 2235
Mrs. Piggle-Wiggle's Magic, 2235
Mrs. Tooey and the Terrible Toxic Tar, 3002
The Muffin Fiend, 2274
Mummies in the Morning, 2813
The Mummy Market, 2105
Mungo, 2456
The Mural Master, 1988
Murder and Magic, 1359
The Museum House Ghosts, 1190
The Mushroom Center Disaster, 421
Mustapha and His Wise Dog, 1356
My Father's Dragon, 2459
My Friend Mr. Leakey, 3030
My Friend the Monster, 52
My Friend the Vampire, 2308
My Lives and How I Lost Them, by Christopher Cat
    and Countee Cullen, 465
My Love, My Love, or, the Peasant Girl, 1706
My Robot Buddy, 2306
My Sister Sif, 1794
My Son-in-Law, the Hippopotamus, 2162
My Stepfather Shrank!, 2427
The Mysterious Cases of Mr. Pin, 627
The Mysterious Disappearance of Leon (I Mean
    Noel), 2284
The Mysterious Girl in the Garden, 2849
The Mysterious Leaf, 34
The Mysterious Zetabet, 1927
The Mystery of Khufu's Tomb, 2027
The Mystery of Misty Island Inn, 1045
The Mystery of the Caramel Cat, 1099
The Mystery of the Cupboard, 2610
The Mystery of the Pirate Ghost, 534
The Mystical Beast, 1952
Myth Conceptions, 2965
Myth Directions, 2965
Myth-ing Persons, 2965
Myth-Nomers and Im-Perfections, 2965
Mythago Wood, 1717

Naftali the Storyteller and His Horse, Sus, and
    Other Stories, 959
The Name of the Game, 1950
A Name to Conjure With, 1885
Naomi's Geese, 496
The Nargun and the Stars, 1878
The Narrow Passage, 2115
A Near Thing for Captain Najork, 2193
The Nearsighted Knight, 296
A Necklace of Fallen Stars, 143
The Necklace of Princess Fiorimonde, 839
The Necklace of Princess Fiorimonde; and Other
    Stories, 840
A Necklace of Raindrops and Other Stories, 771

Necromancer, 1322
Necromancer Nine, 1554
Ned Kelly and the City of the Bees, 1996
Nemesis, 1303
Nerilka's Story: A Pern Adventure, 1447
A Net to Catch the Wind, 128
The Net to Catch War, 3092
The Neverending Story, 1949
Nevernever, 2059
Nevèryöna, 1313
New Found Land, 1921
New German Fairy Tales, 914
Nicholas: A Manhattan Christmas Story, 2571
Nicholas and the Golden Goose, 2571
Nicobobinus, 2210
Nicolette and the Mill, 2476
Night Mare, 1250
Night of Dragons, 1520
The Night of the Scorpion, 3039
Night of the Solstice, 2062
*The Night of Wishes, or The
    Satanarcheolidealcohellish Notion Potion*,
    2159
The Night Rider, 2756
Night Threads: The Calling of the Three, 1948
The Night Watchmen, 76
Night's Daughter, 1619
Nightbirds on Nantucket, 1235
The Nightingale (Andersen), 11
The Nightingale (Dalkey), 1659
Nightpool, 1481
Nightside the Long Sun, 1585
Nighty-Nightmare, 547
*Nine Fairy Tales and One More Thrown In for Good
    Measure*, 814
The Nine Lives of Island MacKenzie, 750
Nine Princes in Amber, 1599
The Nine Questions, 109
The Nine Unknown, 2027
No Bean Sprouts, Please!, 2489
No Clock in the Forest, 2082
No Flying in the House, 2378
No Magic, Thank You, 2507
No Need for Heroes, 1736
No Room: An Old Story Retold, 98
No Room for Men, 1322
No Such Thing as a Witch, 2989
No Swimming in Dark Pond, 878
*No Swimming in Dark Pond: And Other Chilling
    Tales*, 1092
The No-Name Man of the Mountain, 2313
Noah and Me: A Novel, 681
Noble-Hearted Kate: A Celtic Tale, 1769
Nobody's Doll, 2907
Nocturne, 1303
Noddy Goes A-Plowing, 32
Noelle of the Nutcracker, 2935
Nogbad and the Elephants, 272

Nogbad Comes Back, 272
Noggin and the Dragon, 272
Noggin and the Money, 272
Noggin and the Moon Mouse, 272
Noggin and the Storks, 272
Noggin and the Whale, 272
Noggin the King, 272
Nogmania, 272
Nonstop Nonsense, 2244
*Noonan: A Novel about Baseball, ESP, and Time
    Warps*, 2737
The North Pole Before Lunch, 2661
The Northern Girl, 1444
Northshore, 1553
The Nose, 2183
A Nose for Trouble, 698
*Not What You Expected: A Collection of Short
    Stories*, 772
The Not-So-Jolly Roger, 2838
Nothing Said, 2370
The Nürnberg Stove, 2591
Nurse Matilda, 2374
Nurse Matilda Goes to the Hospital, 2374
Nurse Matilda Goes to Town, 2374
Nurse Sally Ann, 2910
The Nutcracker, 2933
Nutty's Ghost, 1111

O'Diddy, 2643
Oaf, 81
The Oak Above the Kings, 1737
The Oak King and the Ash Queen, 1803
Oath of Gold, 1476
Oath of the Renunciates, 1270
The Oathbound Wizard, 2065
Octagon Magic, 2810
Oddkins: A Fable for All Ages, 2941
Odyssey from River Bend, 613
*Of Swords and Sorcerers: The Adventures of King
    Arthur and His Knights*, 1767
Ogre Castle, 3031
The Ogre Downstairs, 2510
Ogre, Ogre, 1250
The Old Gods Waken, 1863
The Old House, 12
Old John, 463
The Old Man of Lochnagar, 2123
The Old Meadow, 686
Old Mother West Wind, 433
The Old Nurse's Stocking Basket, 863
The Old Powder Line, 2817
*The Old Tobacco Shop: A True Account of What
    Befell a Little Boy in Search of Adventure*,
    2373
Old Turtle, 369
Old Ugly Face, 2027
An Older Kind of Magic, 2673

The Oldest Secret, 1981
Olga Carries On, 424
Olga Counts Her Blessings, 424
Olga Makes a Friend, 424
Olga Makes a Wish, 424
Olga Makes Her Mark, 424
Olga Meets Her Match, 424
Olga Takes a Bite, 424
Olga's New Home, 424
Olga's Second Home, 424
Olga's Special Day, 424
Oliver, Clarence, and Violet, 711
OM, The Secret of Abhor Valley, 2027
Omar; a Fantasy for Animal Lovers, 2102
On a Pale Horse, 1249
On a Pincushion, 839
On Fortune's Wheel, 1565
On Meeting Witches at Wells, 1093
On the Wasteland, 2689
On the Way Home, 1569
On Wings of Magic, 1489
The Once and Future King, 1864
Once on a Time, 241
Once There Was a Prince, 102
Once Upon a Princess and a Pea, 57
*Once Upon a Time: A Treasury of Modern Fairy
    Tales*, 936
*Once Upon a Time: Though It Wasn't in Your Time,
    and It Wasn't in My Time, and It Wasn't in
    Anybody Else's Time . . .* , 873
Once Upon Another Time, 2771
Ondine: The Story of a Bird Who Was Different, 643
One Foot in Fairyland: Sixteen Tales, 864
100 Great Fantasy Short Stories, 937
One Land, One Duke, 1948
The One Tree, 1940
The One-Legged Ghost, 2229
The Open Road, 523
Operation Chaos, 1246
Operation Peeg, 2180
Operation Time Search, 2037
The Oracle Doll, 2908
Orchard of the Crescent Moon, 2581
The Ordinary Princess, 166
Oren Bell, 1038
Oscar Lobster's Fair Exchange, 688
Osprey Island, 2448
The Other Face, 2738
The Other Side of Green Hills, 1929
*The Other Side of the Clock: Stories Out of Time,
    Out of Place*, 2814
*The Other Side of the Mirror: And Other Darkover
    Stories*, 1270
The Other Sinbad, 1685
The Other Time, 2833
Otherborn, 1968
Otto and the Magic Potatoes, 2151
Otto at Sea, 2151

Otto from Otherwhere, 2473
Otto in Africa, 2151
Otto in Texas, 2151
Out of Phaze, 1248
Out of the Dark World, 1919
Out of the Ordinary, 1931
Out There, 1462
The Outcast, 1302
Outlander: A Novel, 2739
Outside the Gates, 1362
The Oval Amulet, 1254
Over Sea, Under Stone, 1650
Over the Sea's Edge, 2719
The Over-the-Hill Ghost, 1040
The Owl Hoots Twice at Catfish Bend, 434
Owl in Love, 3063
The Owl Service, 1690
The Owl's Kiss: Three Stories, 965
Owlglass, 635
The Owlstone Crown, 1997
Ownself, 2388
The Oxboy, 236
The Oxford Book of Modern Fairy Tales, 938
Ozma of Oz, 1898

A Pack of Lies, 2548
Paddington Abroad, 422
Paddington at Large, 422
Paddington at the Circus, 422
Paddington at the Seaside, 422
Paddington at the Tower, 422
Paddington at Work, 422
Paddington Goes to Town, 422
Paddington Helps Out, 422
Paddington Marches On, 422
Paddington on Screen, 422
Paddington on Stage, 422
Paddington on Top, 422
Paddington Takes the Air, 422
Paddington Takes the Test, 422
Paddington Takes to TV, 422
Paddington's Garden, 422
Paddington's Lucky Day, 422
Paddington's Storybook, 422
Paddy's Pot of Gold, 2515
Padre Porko: The Gentlemanly Pig, 478
Pageants of Despair, 2750
Painted Devil, 2971
The Paladin of the Night, 1573
Pale Phoenix, 2832
Palmer Patch, 734
Panther Glade, 1634
Papa Dolphin's Table, 435
The Paper Grail, 1616
The Paradise War, 1743
Parsley, Sage, Rosemary and Time, 2720
Past Eight O'Clock: Goodnight Stories, 773

The Pastel City, 1376
The Patchwork Girl of Oz, 1898
Patsy and the Leprechauns, 2348
A Pattern of Roses, 1170
Paul's Volcano, 2463
Pavane, 1511
Pawn of Prophecy, 3008
The Pearl of the Soul of the World, 1493
Pearl's Promise, 391
The Peculiar Triumph of Professor Branestawm, 2202
The Peep-Show Man, 829
The Pendragon (Christian), 1638
Pendragon (Lawhead), 1744
The Pendragon Chronicles: Heroic Fantasy from the Time of King Arthur, 1801
Penelope's Pendant, 2486
Penny, 91
A Penny a Day, 837
The Pentecost and the Chosen One, 462
The People in Pineapple Place, 1132
People of the Earth, 1693
People of the Fire, 1693
People of the River, 1693
People of the Wolf, 1693
Pepper and Salt; or, Seasoning for Young Folk, 951
Perez, the Mouse, 455
The Perfect Pitch, 2544
The Perilous Gard, 2045
The Perils of Putney, 186
Periwinkle Steamboat, 2525
The Persuading Stick, 2650
Peter Graves, 2152
Peter Pan, 1896
Peter Pan in Kensington Gardens, 1896
Peter's Angel: A Story about Monsters, 438
Petronella, 364
Phantasmagoria: Tales of Fantasy and the Supernatural, 940
Phantom Banjo, 3114
The Phantom Carousel and Other Ghostly Tales, 1012
The Phantom Tollbooth, 1992
Phantoms and Fantasies: Twenty Tales, 1120
Phaze Doubt, 1248
The Philadelphia Adventure, 1888
Philip and the Pooka and Other Irish Fairy Tales, 883
The Philosopher's Stone, 2783
Phoenix, 1275
The Phoenix and the Carpet, 2577, 2806
Phoenix Feathers: A Collection of Mythical Monsters, 941
Phoenix Fire, 1679
The Phoenix Guards, 1274
Phoenix in Obsidian, 1477
The Phoenix Tree: An Anthology of Myth Fantasy, 1804

Picking the Ballad's Bones, 3114
Picnic with Piggins, 761
The Picolinis and the Haunted House, 2914
Pictor's Metamorphoses, and Other Fantasies, 890
The Picture of Dorian Gray, 356
The Pie, 272
The Piebald Princess, 654
Pieces of Eight, 2758
The Piemakers, 2129
Pig and Bear, 542
The Pig Plantagenet, 385
The Pig Who Could Conjure the Wind, 3095
Pigeon Flight, 717
Piggins, 761
Piggins and the Royal Wedding, 761
The Pigs Are Flying!, 2615
Pigs Might Fly, 576
The Pigtail of Ah Lee Ben Loo, with Seventeen Other Laughable Tales, 2101
The Pike River Phantom, 1225
The Pilgrim's Progress, 54
Pinch, 2117
Piper at the Gate, 703
Pipkin, 116
Pippi Goes on Board, 2230
Pippi in the South Seas, 2230
Pippi Longstocking, 2230
Pippi on the Run, 2230
The Pirates in the Deep Green Sea, 2012
The Pirates' Mixed-Up Voyage: Dark Doings in the Thousand Islands, 2245
The Pixilated Peeress, 1312
A Place among the Fallen, 1298
The Plague Dogs, 378
A Plague of Sorcerers, 3146
The Plain Princess, 226
The Plain Princess and the Lazy Prince, 287
The Planet Savers, 1270
Playing Beatie Bow, 2816
Pleasant Fieldmouse, 733
The Pleasant Fieldmouse Storybook, 733
Pleasant Fieldmouse's Halloween Party, 733
Pleasant Fieldmouse's Valentine Trick, 733
Please Do Not Touch, 1094
A Pocket of Silence, 1077
Points of Departure, 932
Pollie Who Did as She Was Told, 2349
Polly and the Wolf Again, 2315
Polly Cologne, 2909
Poo Poo and the Dragons, 2175
The Pooh Story Book, 2944
Pooh's Bedtime Book, 2944
Pool of Swallows, 1052
Poor Cecco: The Wonderful Story of a Wonderful Wooden Dog Who Was the Jolliest Toy in the House Until He Went Out to Explore the World, 2892
Poor Stainless, 2587

Poor Tom's Ghost, 1062
The Popover Family, 2950
Porcellus, the Flying Pig, 461
Porcupine Stew, 618
Pork, and Other Stories, 508
Porterhouse Major, 2352
Portrait of Jennie, 254
Potato Face, 2296
Potter, Come Fly to the First of the Earth, 346
The Power of the Rellard, 1760
The Power of Three, 1733
The Power That Preserves, 1940
The Practical Princess, 365
The Practical Princess and Other Liberating Fairy Tales, 989
The Practice Effect, 1910
Prentice Alvin, 1279
Presto: Or, the Adventures of a Turnspit Dog, 670
Pretty Polly, 2216
Pride of Lions: The Story of the House of Atreus, 1729
A Pride of Princes, 1509
The Prince and His Ants, 2654
Prince and the Porker, 720
Prince Boghole, 137
Prince Caspian: The Return to Narnia, 2007
The Prince in the Golden Tower, 164
The Prince in Waiting, 1293
The Prince of Annwn, 1860
Prince of Chaos, 1599
The Prince of Hindustan, 1857
Prince of the Blood, 1344
The Prince of the Godborn, 1374
The Prince of the Pond: Otherwise Known as De Fawg Pin, 2259
Prince Ombra, 1765
Prince Prigio and Prince Ricardo: The Chronicles of Pantouflia, 194
Prince Rabbit and the Princess Who Could Not Laugh, 242
The Prince with a Hundred Dragons, 117
The Princess and Curdie, 224
The Princess and the Goblin, 224
The Princess and the Lion, 66
The Princess and the Thorn, 1348
The Princess Bride: S. Morgenstern's Classic Tale of True Love and High Adventure, 1364
Princess Horrid, 138
Princess Hynchatti and Some Other Surprises, 916
The Princess in the Pigpen, 2857
A Princess of the Chameln, 1579
Princess Rosetta and the Popcorn Man, 359
Princess September, 231
Princesses and Peasant Boys: Tales of Enchantment, 948
The Princesses: Sixteen Stories about Princesses, 947
Prison of Souls, 3070

The Prisoner of Blackwood Castle, 1366
The Prisoner of Pineapple Place, 1132
Professor Branestawm up the Pole, 2202
Professor Branestawm's Building Bust-Up, 2202
Professor Branestawm's Great Revolution, 2202
Professor Branestawm's Mouse War, 2202
Professor Branestawm's Treasure Hunt, 2202
Professor Popkin's Prodigious Polish: A Tale of Coven Tree, 2978
The Promise (Westall), 1208
The Promise (Hughes), 1385
The Prophet of Akhian, 1573
The Provensen Book of Fairy Tales, 949
Prune, 676
Puck of Pook's Hill, 2764
Pudmuddles, 2336
The Pumpkin Giant, 360
Pure Magic, 67
The Pushcart War, 2253
Pyewacket, 738
Pyramid Power, 2054
Pyramids, 2055
Pyromancer, 2983

Quag Keep, 1787
The Quaint and Curious Quest of Johnny Longfoot, the Shoe King's Son, 414
Queen of Sorcery, 3008
The Queen of Spells, 1723
Queen of the Summer Stars, 1873
Queen Silverbell, 2385
The Queen's Museum and Other Fanciful Tales, 966
The Queen's Nose, 2516
Queenmagic, Kingmagic, 1571
Quentin Corn, 718
Quest for a Maid, 3037
Quest for Apollo, 2766
The Quest for Queenie, 1893
The Quest for Saint Camber, 1412
A Quest for Simbils, 1559
Quest for the Faradawn, 503
The Quest of Excalibur, 1213
The Quest of the Gole, 148
The Questing of Kedrigern, 3093
The Question of a Dragon, 652
A Question of Magic, 3083
A Question of Time, 1016
Question Quest, 1250
Quick As a Dodo, 2236
Quimble Wood, 1267

R Is for Rocket, 809
R–T, Margaret, and the Rats of NIMH, 459
Rabbit–Cadabra!, 547
Rabbit Hill, 599
Rabbit Island, 708
Rabbit Spring, 625

Rabbits Rafferty, 487
Rachel and the Angel and Other Stories, 982
Racketty-Packetty House, as Told by Queen Crosspatch, 2385
Racso and the Rats of NIMH (The Rats of NIMH series, book 2), 459
The Radio Imp, 2366
The Raggle Taggle Fellow, 285
Raging Robots and Unruly Uncles, 2246
Railroad Arthur, 2128
The Rainbow String, 972
Ralph S. Mouse, 446
Ramsden, 2027
Randolph's Dream, 237
The Random House Book of Ghost Stories, 1174
Raphael, 3081
The Rat-Catcher's Daughter: A Collection of Stories, 896
Ratha and Thistle–Chaser, 408
Ratha's Creature, 408
Rats and Gargoyles, 1360
Rats on the Range and Other Stories, 619
Rats on the Roof and Other Stories, 619
A Rat's Tale, 684
Real Mummies Don't Bleed: Friendly Tales for October Nights, 983
The Real Thief, 707
A Really Weird Summer, 1144
Reap the Whirlwind, 1289
The Rebel Witch, 3079
Red as Blood; or Tales from the Sisters Grimmer, 1747
The Red Balloon, 192
Red Biddy and Other Stories, 893
The Red Book of Hob Stories, 2566
Red Branch, 1758
Red Feather, 1954
The Red Flame of Erinpura, 2027
Red Hart Magic, 2811
The Red King, 1400
The Red Magician, 3026
Red Moon and Black Mountain: The End of the House of Kendreth, 1916
Red Prophet, 1279
The Red Shift, 2740
The Red Shoes, 13
Red Sun of Darkover, 1270
Red Wizard, 2064
Rediscovery: A Novel of Darkover, 1270
Redwall, 550
Redwork, 2972
The Reformed Pirate: Stories from The Floating Prince, Ting-a-Ling Tales and the Queen's Museum, 967
The Reluctant Dragon, 127
The Reluctant God, 2839
The Remarkable Journey of Prince Jen, 4
A Remembrance for Kedrigern, 3093

The Renegades of Pern, 1447
Renunciates of Darkover, 1270
Requiem for a Princess, 2690
The Rescuers, 691
The Resident Witch, 3102
The Restless Ghost: Three Stories, 1083
The Return of Rinaldo, the Sly Fox, 680
The Return of the Dragon, 376
Return of the Home Run Kid, 2395
The Return of the Indian, 2610
The Return of the King, 1555
Return of the Moose, 658
The Return of the Twelves, 2903
Return to Harken House, 1008
Return to Howliday Inn, 547
Return to the Happy Islands, 2001
Revenant, 1303
The Revenge of Samuel Stokes, 1137
The Revenge of the Rose, 1478
The Revolt of the Teddy Bears, 485
Rewards and Fairies, 2764
Rewind to Yesterday, 2826
Rhialto the Marvellous, 1559
Richard Brown and the Dragon, 2106
Richard Kennedy: Collected Stories, 908
Rickshaw to Horror, 665
The Riddle and the Rune: From Tales of Gom in the Legends of Ulm, 1292
The Riddle of Penncroft Farm, 1114
Riddle of the Stars, 1457
The Riddle-Master of Hed, 1457
Ride a Wild Horse, 1911
A Ride on the Red Mare's Back, 203
The Riders of the Sidhe, 1677
Rikki-Tikki-Tavi, 581
Riley Goes to Obedience School, 672
Rinaldo, the Sly Fox, 680
The Ring of Fire, 1482
A Ring of Tales, 954
Rinki-tink of Oz, 1898
Rip Van Winkle, 1725
The River at Green Knowe, 2371
The River Bank, 523
River Song, 631
The Road to Avalon, 1871
The Road to Camlann, 1843
The Road to Corlay, 1306
The Road to Ehvenor, 2051
The Road to Oz, 1898
Roald Dahl's James and the Giant Peach: A Play, 2418
The Robber Hotzenplotz, 2280
Robbut: A Tale of Tails, 599
Robin and the King, 1697
Robot Adept, 1248
Roderick, 407
Roger Zelazny's Visual Guide to Castle Amber, 1599

Rogue's Gallery, 2265

Roman Mater, 1247

The Romance of King Arthur and His Knights of the
    Round Table, 1767

Romansgrove, 2681

Ronia, the Robber's Daughter, 1436

The Root Cellar, 2786

Rootabaga Pigeons, 2296

Rootabaga Stories, 2296

The Roquefort Gang, 450

Rosalinda, 1125

The Rose and the Ring; or the History of Prince
    Giglio and Prince Bulbo: A Fireside
    Pantomime for Great and Small Children, 324

Roseen, 441

Rosemary's Witch, 3127

Roses, 1644

The Royal Mimkin, 1960

The Ruby Knight, 1331

Ruby, the Red Hot Witch at Bloomingdale's, 3117

Rudi and the Mayor of Naples, 644

Rumpty-Dudget's Tower: A Fairy Tale, 139

Runa, 1727

Runaway Ralph, 446

Runes of the Lyre, 1469

Running Out of Magic with Houdini, 2777

Running Out of Time, 2777

Rusalka, 2988

The Rushton Inheritance, 2792

A Rustle in the Grass, 532

Rutgers and the Watersnouts, 474

The Sable Moon, 1538

The Saga of Erik the Viking, 163

The Saga of Grittel Sundotha, 1470

Sailing to Cythera, and Other Anatole Stories, 2079

The Sailor on the Seas of Fate , 1478

Sailor Rumbelow and Other Stories, 953

Saint Camber, 1413

Salamandastron, 550

Sally Ann and the Mystery Picnic, 2910

Sally Ann and the School Show, 2910

Sally Ann on Her Own, 2910

Sally Gabble and the Fairies, 2606

Sam Bottleby, 2391

Samurai Cat Goes to the Movies, 675

Samurai Cat in the Real World, 675

Sandra and the Right Prince, 22

Sandwriter, 1385

The Sapphire Rose, 1331

The Saracen's Head; or, the Reluctant Crusader,
    193

The Satanic Mill, 3107

Satchkin Patchkin, 2572

Sati, 271

Saturday, the Twelfth of October, 2798

Save Sirrushany!, 27

The Scarecrow of Oz, 1898

The Scarecrows, 1209

The Scarecrows and Their Child, 317

Scared Silly: A Halloween Treat, 547

The Scathach and Maeve's Daughters, 1859

School Can Wait, 2137

The School for Cats, 393

The School Mouse, 529

Schoolmaster Whackwell's Wonderful Sons, 48

The Scions of Shannara, 1273

The Scorpio Ghosts and the Black Hole Gang, 1196

The Sea Child, 1838

The Sea Egg, 2372

The Sea Hag, 1326

The Sea Lion: A Story of the Sea Cliff People, 1738

Sea Magic and Other Stories of Enchantment, 885

The Sea People, 309

The Sea Serpent of Horse, 2072

Sea Story, 404

Sea Tale, 133

The Sea-Thing Child, 539

Seal Child, 1800

The Seal Mother, 1695

The Seal Pool, 623

The Seal-Singing, 1712

The Seal-Woman, 1759

The Search for Delicious, 25

The Search for King Pup's Tomb, 667

The Search of Mavin Manyshaped, 1554

Search the Seven Hills, 1974

Searching for Dragons, 1588

A Season of Ponies, 2639

Seasons in Flight, 778

Seaward, 1926

Sebastian [Super Sleuth] and the Baffling Bigfoot,
    2125

Sebastian [Super Sleuth] and the Bone to Pick
    Mystery, 2125

Sebastian [Super Sleuth] and the Case of the Santa
    Claus Caper, 2125

Sebastian [Super Sleuth] and the Clumsy Cowboy,
    2125

Sebastian [Super Sleuth] and the Copycat Crime,
    2125

Sebastian [Super Sleuth] and the Crummy Yummies
    Caper, 2125

Sebastian [Super Sleuth] and the Egyptian
    Connection, 2125

Sebastian [Super Sleuth] and the Hair of the Dog
    Mystery, 2125

Sebastian [Super Sleuth] and the Impossible Crime,
    2125

Sebastian [Super Sleuth] and the Mystery Patient,
    2125

Sebastian [Super Sleuth] and the Purloined Sirloin,
    2125

Sebastian [Super Sleuth] and the Secret of the
    Skewered Skier, 2125

Sebastian [Super Sleuth] and the Stars-in-His-Eyes Mystery, 2125

Sebastian [Super Sleuth] and the Time Capsule Caper, 2125

The Second Book of Lost Swords: Sightblinder's Story, 1517

The Second Book of Swords, 1518

The Second Jungle Book, 554, 579

The Second Margaret Mahy Storybook, 2557

The Second Witch, 3115

The Secret Cross of Lorraine, 1035

The Secret Elephant of Harlan Kooter, 2480

Secret in the Stlalakum Wild, 1101

The Secret Life of Hilary Thorne, 2086

The Secret Museum, 2930

The Secret of Foghorn Island, 534

The Secret of Red Skull, 1192

The Secret of the Indian, 2610

The Secret of the Ron Mor Skerry, 1682

Secret of the Round Tower, 363

The Secret of the Seven Willows, 2789

Secret of the Sixth Magic, 3033

Secret of the Sleeping River, 2366

The Secret of Thut-Mouse III; or Basil Beandesert's Revenge, 582

The Secret Pencil, 2660

The Secret River, 2608

The Secret Staircase, 404

The Secret World of Og, 1903

The Secret World of Polly Flint, 2412

Seed upon the Wind, 1942

The Seekers and the Sword, 1680

The Seeress of Kell, 1333

The Selchie's Seed, 1791

Selene Goes Home, 481

Self-Portrait with Wings, 2471

The Selfish Giant, 357

Selkie, 1750

The Selkie Girl, 1651

A Sending of Dragons, 1596

Señor Castillo, Cock of the Island, 437

Serpent Mage, 1574

The Serpent's Tooth, 1797

Servant of the Empire, 1345

7 X 7 Tales of a Sevensleeper, 555

Seven for the Sea, 2722

Seven of Swords, 3004

Seven Peas in the Pod, 789

Seven Spells to Farewell, 28

Seven Spells to Sunday, 2585

Seven Stars for Catfish Bend, 434

Seven Strange and Ghostly Tales, 1113

Seven Tales, 779

The Seven Towers, 1591

The Seven Wishes of Joanna Peabody, 2468

Seven-Day Magic, 2435

The Seventeen Thieves of El-Kalil, 2027

The Seventh Book of Lost Swords: Wayfinder's Story, 1517

The Seventh Gate (Harris), 1374

The Seventh Gate (Weis and Hickman), 1574

The Seventh Mandarin, 374

Seventh Son, 1279

Shaara's Exile, 1270

The Shades, 1034

Shades of Dark: Stories, 1180

Shades of Darkness: More of the Ghostly Best Stories of Robert Westall, 1204

Shadow, 1439

Shadow Dance, 1439

Shadow Dancers, 1308

The Shadow Gate, 1894

The Shadow Guests, 1009

Shadow Hunt, 1439

Shadow in Hawthorn Bay, 1139

Shadow Leader, 1373

Shadow Magic, 1589

The Shadow of Fomor, 2014

The Shadow of the Gloom-World, 1338

The Shadow of the Torturer, 1585

The Shadow on the Dial, 2780

Shadow on the Stones, 1277

The Shadow on the Sun, 1711

Shadow Over Mousehaven Manor, 587

The Shadow Rising, 1396

The Shadow Shaia, 3024

Shadow Walkers, 444

The Shadow Warrior, 1600

The Shadow-Cage and Other Tales of the Supernatural, 1167

Shadowfane, 3141

Shadowkill, 1297

Shadowland, 3123

The Shadowmaker, 2479

Shadowplay, 1297

Shadows on the Wall, 2804

Shadowspeer, 1297

Shaman, 2023

The Shape Changer: A Science Fiction Novel, 1419

Shape Shifters: Fantasy and Science Fiction Tales about Humans Who Can Change Their Shapes, 958

Shapeshifters, 1509

The Shaping of Middle-Earth: The Quenta, the Ambrakanta, and the Annals, 1555

Shardik, 1232

The Shark in the Window, 2222

The Shattered Chain: A Darkover Novel, 1270

The Shattered Stone, 1484

The Shattered World, 3111

She, 2025

She and Allan, 2025

She Was Nice to Mice: The Other Side of Elizabeth I's Character Never Before Revealed by Previous Historians, 692

Sheepfarmer's Daughter, 1476
Shen of the Sea: Chinese Stories for Children, 823
Sherlick Hound and the Valentine Mystery, 519
Sherwood, 1697
The Sherwood Ring, 2829
The Shield Between the Worlds, 1799
The Shield of Time, 2686
The Shining Face, 1483
The Shining Falcon, 1522
The Shining Ones, 1331, 1332
The Ship of Ishtar, 2022
The Ship That Flew, 2778
Shiva Accused, 1622
Shiva: An Adventure of the Ice Age, 1622
Shiva's Challenge, 1622
A Shoe Full of Shamrock, 2633
The Shoe Shop Bears, 2888
Shoebag, 551
Shoeless Joe, 1119
Shrine of the Desert Mage, 1363
The Shrinking of Treehorn, 2191
The Shuteyes, 1987
The Shy Stegosaurus of Cricket Creek, 2219
Sid Seal, Houseman, 736
Sideways Arithmetic from Wayside School, 2295
Sideways Stories from Wayside School, 2295
Sidney Rella and the Glass Sneaker, 2257
Siege of White Deer Park, 476
Sign of Chaos, 1599
The Sign of the Salamander, 2800
The Sign of the Seven Seas, 2724
The Sign of the Unicorn, 1599
The Silent Playmate: A Collection of Doll Stories, 2954
The Silent Tower, 1974
The Silicon Mage, 1974
The Silk and the Skin, 1194
Silk Roads and Shadows, 1524
The Silkspinners, 195
Silky: An Incredible Tale, 1642
The Silver Branch: A Novel of the Keltiad, 1404, 1737
The Silver Chair, 2007
The Silver Citadel, 3039
The Silver Crown (O'Brien), 2042
The Silver Crown (Rosenberg), 2051
The Silver Curlew, 1670
The Silver Glove, 2986
The Silver Hand, 1743
The Silver Nutmeg, 2380
Silver on the Tree, 1650
The Silver Sun, 1538
The Silver Tree, 2871
The Silver Warrior, 1477
Silver Woven in My Hair, 251
Silverhair the Warrior, 1491
Silverlock, 2030
Silverthorn, 1344

Simple Spigott, 1183
Simple Susan and Other Tales, 847
Sing and Scatter Daisies, 1124
Sing for a Gentle Rain, 2757
The Singer in the Stone, 1580
Singer to the Sea God, 1604
The Singing Cupboard, 2442
The Singing Stone, 2799
The Singing Town, 2157
Sir Cedric, 2181
Sir Cedric Rides Again, 2181
Sir Gawain and the Green Knight, 1713, 1715
Sir Gawain and the Loathly Lady, 1713
Sir Machinery, 3085
Siri the Conquistador, 713
Sister Light, Sister Dark, 1598
Six Impossible Things Before Breakfast, 859
Six of Swords, 3004
The Six Voyages of Pleasant Fieldmouse, 733
The Sixth Book of Lost Swords: Mindsword's Story, 1517
Skateboard Tough, 2396
The Skin Horse, 2893
Skipper Riley, 672
Sky High: The Story of a House That Flew, 2195
Skybowl, 1503
The Slavery Ghosts, 1202
Slay and Rescue, 1776
The Sleep of Stone, 1304
The Sleepers, 1658
The Sleeping Dragon, 2051
The Sleeping Giant and Other Stories, 851
The Sleeping Sorceress, 1478
Sleeping Ugly, 2335
Sly, P. I.: The Case of the Missing Shoes, 704
The Small Adventures of Dog, 2898
A Small, Elderly Dragon, 167
Small Fur, 2521
Small Fur is Getting Bigger, 2521
Small Shadows Creep, 1186
The Smallest Monster in the World, 2553
Smart Dragons, Foolish Elves, 2307
The Smartest Man in Ireland, 2201
Smeller Martin, 2221
Smith of Wootton Major, 333
Smoke from Cromwell's Time and Other Stories, 774
Smoky-House, 2466
Smuggler's Gold, 1286, 1346
The Snail Who Ran, 590
The Snake Horn, 2748
Sneaker Hill, 3076
Snot Stew, 735
The Snow Goose, 120
The Snow Image, 889
The Snow Parlor and Other Bedtime Stories, 826
The Snow Queen, 14
The Snow Spider, 2581

Snow White and Rose Red, 1874
The Snow Womble, 412
Snow-Eyes, 1531
The Snowflake and the Starfish, 3097
So You Want to Be a Wizard, 3006
Socks, 447
Sokar and the Crocodile: A Fairy Story of Egypt, 2494
Soldier, Ask Not, 1322
Soldier of Arete, 1586
Soldier of the Mist, 1586
Solomon Leviathan's Nine Hundred and Thirty First Trip Around the World, 603
Solstice: A Mystery of the Season, 2678
Some of the Adventures of Rhode Island Red, 2248
Something about a Mermaid, 2603
Something Special, 2616
Something Upstairs: A Tale of Ghosts, 2691
Something Wicked This Way Comes, 2975
Son of the Hero, 2057
A Song for Arbonne, 1398
A Song for Clowns, 350
The Song of Homana, 1509
The Song of Mavin Manyshaped, 1554
The Song of Pentecost, 462
The Song of Rhiannon, 1860
Song of Sorcery, 1521
Song of the Gargoyle, 1533
Song of the Pearl, 2807
Song of Thunder, 1504
Songmaster, 1280
Sonny-Boy Sim, 400
The Sorcerer, 2966
The Sorcerer's Apprentice, 3137
The Sorcerer's Apprentice: A Greek Fable, 1770
Sorcerer's Legacy, 1594
Sorcerer's Son, 1337
The Sorceress and the Cygnet, 1458
Sorceress of Darshiva, 1333
Sorceress of the Witch World, 2039
Sorcery and Cecilia, 1592
Soul-Singer of Tyrnos, 1471
The Source of Magic, 1250
South Star, 1378
Southshore, 1553
Space Cat, 723
Space Cat and the Kittens, 723
Space Cat Meets Mars, 723
Space Cat Visits Venus, 723
Spacehawk Inc., 1365
Spaceships and Spells: A Collection of New Fantasy and Science-Fiction Stories, 964
Sparky-for-Short, 2382
Speak to the Rain, 1795
A Spell for Chameleon, 1250
Spell Me a Witch, 3136
Spell of the Witch World, 2039
The Spell of Time: A Tale of Love in Jerusalem, 206

Spell Seven, 2594
The Spell Sword, 1270
The Spellcoats, 1394
The Spellkey, 1324
Spells of Mortal Weaving, 1356
Spells of Wonder, 1535
Spider Kane and the Mystery at Jumbo Nightcrawlers, 645
Spider Kane and the Mystery Under the May Apple, 645
Spiral of Fire, 3034
The Spirit of Dorsai, 1322
Spirit of the Hawk, 1950
The Spirit Ring, 1276
Spirit Wrestler, 3041
Spirits of Cavern and Hearth, 1330
Spiritwalk, 1664
Split Heirs, 1572
Split Infinity, 1248
Spook, 3077
Spooky Night, 1042
The Spotted Dog: The Strange Tale of a Witch's Revenge, 2266
Spring Cleaning, as Told by Queen Crosspatch, 2385
The Spring on the Mountain, 5
The Spring Rider, 2770
Spring Story, 404
Spring-Heeled Jack, 2282
The Spy Who Came North from the Pole, 627
Squeak Saves the Day and Other Tooley Tales, 1534
The Squirrel Hotel, 2153
The Squirrel That Remembered, 678
The Squirrel Wife, 266
Stag Boy, 1809
Stage Door to Terror, 665
Stairway to Doom, 665
Stall Buddies, 661
Stanley, Henry Bear's Friend, 616
Star Baby, 2533
The Star Child: A Fairy Tale, 358
Star Lord, 1746
Star Mother's Youngest Child, 243
Star of Danger, 1270
Star Rigger's Way, 1283
The Star Scroll, 1502
Starkadder, 1739
The Starlight Barking, 701
The Starlit Journey, a Story, 41
Starsilk, 1562
The Starstone, 1292
The Startling Worlds of Henry Kuttner, 2002
The Steadfast Tin Soldier, 15
The Stealer of Souls and Other Stories, 1478
The Steel Flea, a Story, 204
Steel Magic, 2038
Steps Out of Time, 2754

The Stinky Cheese Man and Other Fairly Stupid Tales, 2300

Stirabout Stories, Brewed in Her Own Cauldron, 962

A Stitch in Time, 1138

The Stocking Child, 2952

The Stolen Lake, 1235

The Stolen Mirror, 2046

The Stolen Telesm, 2968

The Stone and the Flute, 1263

The Stone Giant, 1266

Stone of Farewell, 1583

The Stone of Victory and Other Tales, 830

Stoneflight, 2552

The Stones of Green Knowe, 2703

The Stonewalkers, 1605

Stonewords: A Ghost Story, 2714

Stopping for a Spell: Three Fantasies, 2511

Stories for Children (Singer), 960

Stories for Children (Wilde), 984

Stories for Nine-Year-Olds and Other Young Readers, 970

Stories from Firefly Island, 419

Stories from Hans Andersen, 779

The Stories of Hans Andersen, 779

Stories of King Arthur, 1767

Stories of King Arthur and His Knights, 1767

The Stories of Ray Bradbury, 810

The Storm Lord, 1424

A Storm of Wings, 1376

Storm Runner, 1373

The Storm Shield, 1676

Storm Warning, 1415

A Storm Without Rain, 2679

Stormbringer, 1478

Stormqueen, 1270

Storms of Victory, 1489

Stormwarden, 3141

The Story of Appleby Capple, 2267

The Story of Doctor Dolittle, 2234

The Story of Freginald, 428

The Story of Holly and Ivy, 2929

The Story of Idylls of the King, 1767

The Story of King Arthur and His Knights (Malory), 1767

The Story of King Arthur and His Knights (Pyle), 1808

The Story of Mrs. Tubbs, 610

The Story of Serapina, 742

The Story of Sir Launcelot and His Companions, 1808

The Story of the Amulet, 2806

The Story of the Champions of the Round Table, 1808

The Story of the Grail and the Passing of Arthur, 1808

The Story of the Stone, 1384

The Storyteller and the Jann, 1363

The Storyteller's Pack, a Frank R. Stockton Reader, 968

The Stove Haunting, 2801

Strandia, 1508

Strands of Starlight, 1259

Strange and Ancient Name, 2058

The Strange and Exciting Adventures of Jeremiah Hush, 694

The Strange Child, 147

Strange Devices of the Sun and Moon, 1698

Strange Dreams: Unforgettable Fantasy, 971

The Strange Light, 2047

The Strange Night Writing of Jessamine Colter, 90

Strange Objects, 1653

The Strange Story of the Frog Who Became a Prince, 3040

The Strange Thing That Happened to Oliver Wendell Iscovitch, 2589

The Stranger, 338

A Stranger at Green Knowe, 1031

Stranger at the Wedding, 1974

A Stranger Came Ashore, 1722

A Stranger Here, 1227

Strangers Dark and Gold, 1730

Stray, 752

Street: A Play for Children, 3

Street Magic, 1810

A Street of Little Shops, 798

The Stress of Her Regard, 1498

The Stricken Field, 1327

A String in the Harp, 2701

Stronghold, 1503

Strum Again?, 3114

Stuart Little, 744

Stuck with Luck, 2508

A Sudden Wild Magic, 3054

Suldrun's Garden, 1560

The Summer Birds, 2446

The Summer I Shrank My Grandmother, 2671

A Summer in the South, 620

The Summer Is Magic, 2495

Summer Story, 404

Summer Switch, 2291

The Summer Tree, 1994

The Summer's King, 1579

Sung in Shadow, 1432

Sunrunner's Fire, 1502

Sunshaker's War, 1934

The Superlative Horse: A Tale of Ancient China, 239

Supernatural Stories: 13 Tales of the Unexpected, 1195

The Supreme Souvenir Factory, 712

The Surangini Tales, 295

The Surprising Adventures of the Magical Monarch of Mo and His People, 794

Surrender None: The Legacy of Gird, 1476

Surviving the Flood, 1775

Susan and the Butterbees, 2363

The Swallow and the Tom Cat: A Grown-Up Love Story, 383

Swan Lake (Diamond), 92

Swan Lake (Helprin), 1714

Swan's Wing, 1847

The Swans of Ballycastle, 132

Sweden, 2539

Sweet Whispers, Brother Rush, 1100

The Sweetest Fig, 339

The Swineherd, 16

The Swing in the Summerhouse, 2526, 2527

Switching Well, 2747

The Sword and Circle: King Arthur and Knights of the Round Table, 1767

Sword and Sorceress: An Anthology of Heroic Fantasy, 1547

Sword and Sorceress II, 1547

Sword and Sorceress III, 1547

Sword and Sorceress IV, 1547

Sword and Sorceress V, 1547

Sword and Sorceress VI, 1547

Sword and Sorceress VII, 1547

Sword and Sorceress VIII, 1547

Sword and Sorceress IX, 1547

Sword and Sorceress X, 1547

Sword and Sorceress XI, 1547

The Sword and the Chain, 2051

The Sword and the Circle: King Arthur and the Knights of the Round Table, 1843

The Sword and the Flame, 1420

The Sword and the Grail, 1715

Sword at Sunset, 1844

Sword-Breaker, 1510

Sword Dancer, 1510

The Sword in the Stone, 1865

The Sword in the Tree, 53

Sword-Maker, 1510

The Sword of Aldones, 1270

The Sword of Aradel, 2763

Sword of Chaos and Other Stories, 1270

The Sword of Culann, 2776

The Sword of Shannara, 1273

The Sword of the Lictor, 1585

The Sword of the Spirits, 1293

Sword-Singer, 1510

The Sword Swallower, 1365

A Sword to Slice Through Mountains and Other Stories, 805

T.J.'s Ghost, 1051

Taash and the Jesters, 1450

Tabitha, 753

Tactics of Mistake, 1322

Tailchaser's Song, 748

Take It Easy, 2359

Take Three Tenses; A Fugue in Time, 1089

Take Three Witches, 3092

Taking Care of Carruthers, 621

Tal and the Magic Barruget, 2674

Tal: His Marvelous Adventures with Noom-Zor-Noom, 1925

Talargain, 1683

The Tale of Czar Saltan, or the Prince and the Swan Princess, 273

The Tale of Gockel, Hinkel and Gackeliah, 49

The Tale of Lazy Lizard Canyon, 2114

The Tale of Little Pig Robinson, 663

A Tale of Middle Length, 695

The Tale of Sir Gawain, 1802

The Tale of the Faithful Dove, 664

The Tale of the Golden Cockerel, 274

The Tale of the Good Cat Jupie, 612

A Tale of Three Wishes, 300

A Tale of Time City, 1991

Tales and Stories by Hans Christian Andersen, 779

Tales at the Mousehole, 719

Tales for a Winter's Eve, 737

Tales from Academy Street, 2424

Tales from Moominvalley, 1388

Tales from the Enchanted Isles, 875

Tales from the Mabinogion, 1849

Tales from the Secret Kingdom, 876

Tales of a Fairy Court, 194

Tales of a Wandering Warthog, 697

Tales of King Arthur, 1767

Tales of Mithgar, 1452

Tales of Nevèrÿon, 1313

Tales of Olga Da Polga, 424

Tales of Polly and the Hungry Wolf, 2315

Tales of the Early World, 899

Tales of the Rue Broca, 884

Tales out of Time, 2855

Tales Told Again, 838

Taliesin, 1744

Taliesin and King Arthur, 1815

The Talisman, 1999

The Talismans of Shannara, 1273

The Talking Dog and the Barking Man, 683

Talking Man, 1615

The Talking Parcel, 1945

Talking to Dragons, 1588

The Tall Stones, 1277

A Tall Story and Other Tales, 2558

Taltos, 1275

Tam Lin (Cooper), 1652

Tam Lin (Dean), 1661

Tam Lin: An Old Ballad, 1883

Tamastara; or the Indian Nights, 1748

The Taming of Giants, 545

Tangle and the Firesticks, 420

The Tangle Box, 2112

A Tapestry of Magics, 1309

The Tapestry Room: A Child's Romance, 2568

Taran Wanderer, 1236

A Taste for Quiet, 878
A Taste for Quiet, and Other Disquieting Tales, 1095
A Taste of Smoke, 1024
Tatsinda, 104
The Tattooed Potato and Other Clues, 2285
Taxi Cat and Huey, 605
Taxi to Intrigue, 665
Tea Time Tales, 870
Tea with the Black Dragon, 1761
The Teaspoon Tree, 2592
Teddy B. Zoot, 2901
The Teddy Bear Tree, 2911
Teddy Bear's Scrapbook, 2934
Tehanu: The Last Book of Earthsea, 1433
Tekla, 1275
Tell Them Again Tales, 792
A Telling of the Tales: Five Stories, 812
The Templar Treasure, 3068
The Temple of the Sun, 1277
Ten in a Bed, 2338
Ten Little Wizards, 1359
The Terrible Churnadryne, 2389
Test of the Twins, 1576
The Testing of Tertius, 1782
The Magic Pictures: More about the Wonderful Farm, 394
Then Came Timothy, 2455
Thendara House, 1270
Theo Zephyr, 2496
They Watched Him Die, 1703
Thicker Than Water, 1069
The Thief of Always: A Fable, 1895
Thimbles, 2877
Thing, 2217
The Thing at the Foot of the Bed and Other Scary Tales, 1126
Things in Corners, 1165
Things Invisible to See, 362
Things That Go Bump in the Night, 1115
Things That Go Bump in the Night: A Collection of Original Stories, 1198
The Third Book of Lost Swords: Stonecutter's Story, 1517
The Third Book of Swords, 1518
The Third Class Genie, 2224
The Third Jungle Book, 554
The Third Magic, 1993
The Third Margaret Mahy Storybook, 2557
The Third Road, 2692
The 13 Clocks, 328
Thirteen Means Magic, 2357
The Thirteenth Is Magic, 2495
Thistle, 347
Thomas and the Warlock, 3046
Thomas the Rhymer, 1740
Thornyhold, 3122
Three Against the Witch World, 2039

The Three and Many Wishes of Jason Reid, 2503
Three Dreams and a Nightmare, and Other Tales of the Dark, 878
Three for an Acorn, 401
Three Friends, 509
Three from Catfish Bend, 434
Three Hearts and Three Lions, 1246
The Three Hundred Ninety-seventh White Elephant, 131
Three Lives to Live, 2781
The Three Magic Gifts, 280
The Three Policemen, or Young Bottsford of Farbe Island, 2154
The Three Princes of Serendip, 146
The Three Royal Monkeys, 480
Three to Dorsai!, 1322
The Three Toymakers, 2961
The Three-Day Enchantment, 158
The Three-in-One Prince, 162
Threshold, 2264
The Throme of the Erril of Sherill, 1459
The Throne of Madness, 1546
The Throne of Scone: A Novel of the Keltiad, 1404, 1737
Through Tempest Trails, 505
Through the Dolls' House Door, 2920
Through the Ice, 1891
Through the Looking Glass and What Alice Found There, 1913
Through the Mickle Woods, 130
Thumbelina, 17
The Thunder Dragon Gate, 2027
Thursday, 1842
Thursday Ahoy!, 423
Thursday in Paris, 423
Thursday Rides Again, 423
A Tie to the Past, 2878
Tiger Nanny, 2330
Tiger's Chance, 2484
Tik-Tok of Oz, 1898
Till the End of Time, 2688
Time After Time, 2688
Time and Again, 2736
Time and Mr. Bass: A Mushroom Planet Book, 2711
Time at the Top, 2812
Time Cat: The Remarkable Journeys of Jason and Gareth, 2680
Time Garden, 1946, 2433
The Time Keeper, 1897
A Time of Darkness, 2761
A Time of Exile: A Novel of the Westlands, 1405
A Time of Omens, 1405, 3061
The Time of the Dark, 1975
The Time of the Kraken, 1582
Time of the Twins, 1576
The Time of the Witch, 3029
Time Out, 2716
The Time Patrol, 2686

Time Patrolman, 2686

Time Piper, 1720

Time Sweep, 2865

Time Tangle, 2730

A Time to Choose: A Story of Suspense, 2818

Time to Go Back, 2682

Time to Go House, 490

The Time Tree, 2834

Time Windows, 2832

Time-Ago Lost: More Tales of Jahdu, 2187

The Time-Ago Tales of Jahdu, 2187

The Timekeeper, 2050

Timequake, 2772

The Timid Ghost: Or What Would You Do with a Sackful of Gold?, 1032

Tin Cans, 2614

The Tin Woodman of Oz, 1898

The Tinderbox, 18

Ting-a-Ling Tales, 969

The Tiny Man, 646

Tistou of the Green Thumbs, 101

To Green Angel Tower, 1583

To Nowhere and Back, 2685

To Reign in Hell, 1627

A Toad for Tuesday, 494

Toad of Toad Hall, 523

Tobias the Magic Mouse, 637

The Toby Man, 577

Told Under the Magic Umbrella: Modern Fanciful Stories for Young Children, 973

Tom Ass: Or the Second Gift, 2532

Tom's Midnight Garden, 2822

Tom's Tower, 2017

The Tombs of Atuan, 1433

A Tomcat's Tale, 556

The Tomorrow Connection, 2699

Tomorrow's Children: 18 Tales of Fantasy and Science Fiction, 974

Tomorrow's Magic, 1831

Tomorrow's Sphinx, 409

Tomorrow's Wizard, 3087

Too ManyMagicians, 1359

Too Much Magic, 2642

Toohy and Wood, 628

The Toothpaste Millionaire, 2254

Topper and the Giant, 2569

Tor and Azor, 464

Torch, 1490

Torten's Christmas Secret, 99

A Touch of Chill: Tales for Sleepless Nights, 1010

A Touch of Infinity: Thirteen New Stories of Fantasy and Science Fiction, 866

Touch the Moon, 2355

The Tough Winter, 599

Tower of Fear, 1300

Towers of Darkness, 1270

The Towers of February: A Diary By an Anonymous (for the Time Being) Author with Added Punctuation and Footnotes, 1943

Towers of the Sunset, 1475

The Town Cats, and Other Tales, 381

The Town That Went South, 567

Toy Rose, 2895

The Toymaker's Daughter, 2961

The Toynbee Convector, 811

Track of the White Wolf, 1509

Train for Tiger Lily, 2049

The Transfigured Hart, 375

Transformations, 1371

Travel Far, Pay No Fare, 2536

A Traveler in Time, 2861

Travelling Magic, 2698

The Travelling Man, 1462

The Treason of Isengard, 1555

The Treasure of Alpheus Winterborn, 2360

The Treasure of Green Knowe, 1031

The Treasure of Li-Po, 955

The Treasure of the Isle of Mist: A Tale of the Isle of Skye, 2647

The Tree of Swords and Jewels, 1637

Treehorn's Treasure, 2191

Treehorn's Wish, 2191

Trek to Kraggen-Cor, 1452

Trey of Swords, 2039

A Trial of Magic, 3083

A Trick of the Light: Stories to Read at Dusk, 978

The Tricks of Master Dabble, 377

The Tricksters, 1152

A Trio for Lute, 3081

Trips in Time: Nine Stories of Science Fiction, 2859

Tristan and Iseult, 1845

Triumph of the Darksword, 1577

Troika, 1303

A Troll in Passing, 187

Troll Weather, 2398

The Troll's Grindstone, 1908

The Trolley to Yesterday, 2695

The Trolls of Twelfth Street, 2303

Trouble Dolls, 2899

Trouble for Trumpets, 473

Trouble in Bugland: A Collection of Inspector Mantis Mysteries, 2218

The Trouble with Dragons, 290

The Trouble with Jacob, 1145

The Trouble with Jenny's Ear, 2116

The Trouble with Miss Switch, 3131

Troubled Waters, 1286

Truckers, 1499

The True Men, 1542

The True Story of the 3 Little Pigs: By A. Wolf, 2301

The Trumpet of the Swan, 745

Trumpets in Grumpetland, 473

Trumps of Doom, 1599

The Truth about Dragons: An Anti-Romance, 1231

The Truth about Stone Hollow, 1188
The Truthful Harp, 1240
Tsuga's Children, 2081
Tuck Everlasting, 1608
Tucker's Countryside, 686
Tune in Yesterday, 2699
Tuppenny, 82
The Turf-Cutter's Donkey: An Irish Story of Mystery
    and Adventure, 2546
The Turf-Cutter's Donkey Kicks Up His Heels, 2546
The Turf-Cutters Donkey Goes Visiting, 2546
The Turnabout Trick, 2404
The Turnip, 838
The Turret, 691
Twelve Fair Kingdoms, 1339
Twelve Tales, 779
The Twenty-Elephant Restaurant, 2194
The Twenty-One Balloons, 2155
Twice upon a Time (Shapiro), 294
Twice upon a Time (Appel), 2688
Twig, 2512
The Twilight Gate, 1819
Twilight Land, 276
The Twilight of Magic, 2543
The Twilight Realm, 1912
Twin and Super-Twin, 2414
Twin Spell, 1140
Twisting the Rope, 1761
The Twits, 2135
Two Against the Tide, 1922
Two Bad Ants, 728
Two Brothers, 288
Two by Two: A Story of Survival, 1692
Two Fables, 85
The Two Faces of Silenus, 1639
The Two in Hiding, 1948
Two to Conquer, 1270
Two Too Many, 726
The Two Towers, 1555
Two-Bit Heroes, 1335

The Ugly Duckling, 19
The Ugly Princess, 216
Ultramarine, 1784
The Unbeheaded King, 1310
Unbelievable! More Surprising Stories, 905
Uncanny! Even More Surprising Stories, 905
Uncle Ben's Whale, 2156
Uncle Fedya, His Dog, and His Cat, 2653
Uncle Jacob's Ghost Story, 188
Uncle Shelby's Story of Laficadio, the Lion Who
    Shot Back, 2304
Uncle Sylvester, 546
Uncle Terrible: More Adventures of Anatole, 2079
Under Plum Lake, 1932
Under Siege, 2018
Under the Mummy's Spell, 1151

Undersea, 1377
Undine, 190
Unfinished Tales of Numenor and Middle-Earth,
    1555
Unicorn and Dragon, 1602
The Unicorn and the Lake, 233
The Unicorn and the Plow, 244
The Unicorn Creed, 1521
Unicorn Crossing, 2545
The Unicorn Dancer, 1519
The Unicorn Dilemma: A Saga of War and Magic,
    1423
Unicorn Highway, 2509
Unicorn Moon, 73
Unicorn Point, 1248
The Unicorn Quest, 1423
The Unicorn Treasury: Stories, Poems and Unicorn
    Lore, 975
Unicorn U, 1958
The Unicorn with Silver Shoes, 2087
Unicorns!, 976
Unicorns in the Rain, 1645
Uninvited Ghosts and Other Stories, 2233
The Unlikely Ones, 2979
Unmentionable! More Amazing Stories, 905
Unreal! Eight Surprising Stories, 905
The Unschooled Wizard, 1372
Until the Celebration, 1532
Untold Tales, 812
Up from Jericho Tel, 2519
Up Mountain One Time, 755
Up the Chimney Down and Other Stories, 2092
Up the Pier, 2717
Upland Outlaws, 1327
The Upside-Down Town, 2093
The Urth of the New Sun, 1585
Utopia Hunters: Chronicles of the High Inquest,
    1546

Vale of the Vole, 1250
A Valentine Fantasy, 140
Valentine for a Dragon, 252
Valentine Pontifex, 1527
The Valley of Deer, 2729
The Valley of Song, 126
The Valley So Low, 1863
The Vampire in Love, 2308
The Vampire Moves In, 2308
The Vampire on the Farm, 2308
The Vampire Takes a Trip, 2308
Vanishing Act, 2573
The Vanishing Tower, 1478
Vargr-Moon, 1739
Vavache, the Cow Who Painted Pictures, 392
The Velveteen Rabbit; or, How Toys Became Real,
    2893
The Vicar of Nibbleswicke, 2136

Victoria Josephine, 2887
The Victorian Chaise Longue, 2768
Victorian Ghost Stories: An Oxford Anthology, 1201
Victorian Ghost Stories by Eminent Women Writers,
    1159
Viki Viking, 2211
The Villa of the Ferromonte, 2731
Violet's Finest Hour, 486
The Violin-Maker's Gift, 189
Viollet, 469
Virconium Nights, 1376
The Virgin and the Swine, 1860
Virtual Mode, 1889
A Visa for Avalon, 1628
Visible Light, 1287
The Vision of Francois the Fox, 470
The Vision of Stephen: An Elegy, 2708
Vision of the Hunter, 1851
Vision Quest, 2840
*Visions of Wonder: An Anthology of Christian
    Fantasy*, 977
The Visitor: A Story of Suspense, 3104
The Visitors, 2858
The Visitors from Oz, 1898
The Vizier's Second Daughter, 1884
A Voice for Princess, 3093
The Voice of the Mountain, 1863
The Voice of the Wood, 63
Voices After Midnight, 2825
The Voyage of Barracks, 2268
The Voyage of Q V 66, 609
The Voyage of the Dawn Treader, 2007
Voyager, 2739
Voyages, 1839
The Voyages of Doctor Dolittle, 2234

The Wainscott Weasel, 685
Wait Till Helen Comes: A Ghost Story, 1098
A Walk in Wolf Wood, 2851
A Walk out of the World, 2033
Walker of Time, 2862
Walker of Worlds, 1933
The Walking Stones: A Story of Suspense, 3047
The Walls of Air, 1975
The Walrus and the Warwolf, 2995
Walter the Lazy Mouse, 501
The Wand: The Return to Mesmeria, 1947
Wanda and the Bumbly Wizard, 3017
The Wandering Fire, 1994
The Wandering Kinght, 1826, 1827
*Wandering Stars: An Anthology of Jewish Fantasy
    and Science Fiction*, 979
The Wandering Wombles, 412
The War for the Lot: A Tale of Fantasy and Terror,
    589
War for the Oaks, 1630
The War Hound and the World's Pain: A Fable, 245

War of the Twins, 1576
'Ware Hawk, 2039
Warlock, 460
Warlock at the Wheel and Other Stories, 3055
The Warlock of Night, 3048
Warlock of the Witch World, 2039
The Warlords of Nin, 1420
The Warnings, 2384
The Warrior and the Wise Man, 368
The Warrior Lives, 2051
The Warriors of Taan, 1422
Warton and Morton, 494
Warton and the Castaways, 494
Warton and the Contest, 494
Warton and the King of the Skies, 494
Warton and the Traders, 494
Warton's Christmas Eve Adventure, 494
The Wastelands, 1407
The Watch House, 1210
Watch the House, 740
The Watcher by the Threshold and Other Tales,
    1629
The Watcher in the Garden, 269
The Watchers, 2721
Watchtower, 1444
The Water Babies: A Fairy Tale for a Land Baby,
    175
The Water Elf and the Miller's Child, 2350
Watermusic, 1823
Watership Down, 379
Watersmeet, 1684
Wavebender, 690
The Way Home, 2827
The Way to White Deer Park, 476
Wayfarers All, 523
Wayside School Is Falling Down, 2295
The Wealdwife's Tale, 1377
The Weathermonger, 1321
Web of the Witch World, 2039
The Wedding Ghost, 1687
The Wee Men of Ballywooden, 2561
The Weightless Mother, 2099
The Weird Disappearance of Jordan Hall, 2342
Weird Henry Berg, 2620
The Weird of the White Wolf, 1478
Weird Wolf, 2131
Weirdos of the Universe, Unite!, 1830
The Weirdstone of Brisingamen, 1691
Weland, Smith of the Gods, 1848
The Well at the World's End, 1480
Well Met by Witchlight, 2970
The Well of Shiuan, 1287
The Well of the Unicorn, 1500
*The Well-Favored Man: The Tale of the Sorcerer's
    Nephew*, 1581
The Well-Wishers, 2434
The Western Wizard, 1506
Westmark, 1241

Wet Magic, 2579
Whalesinger, 561
What Beckoning Ghost?, 1131
What Did Miss Darrington See? An Anthology of Feminist Supernatural Fiction, 1211
What Happened in Hamelin, 1837
What Happened to Jenny, 2481
What's Happened to Harry?, 3003
What's the Matter with Carruthers?, 621
When Dreamers Cease to Dream, 1897
When Half-Gods Go, 1856
When Jack Rabbit Was a Little Boy, 647
When Marnie Was There, 1175
When the Bough Breaks, 2003
When the Dolls Woke, 2957
When the Night Wind Howls, 3116
When the Porcupine Moved In, 387
When True Night Falls, 1354
When Voiha Wakes, 1284, 1916
When Wendy Grew Up: An Afterthought, 1896
Where Dragons Lie, 1520
Where Dragons Rule, 1520
Where the Evil Dwells, 1529
Where the Towers Pierce the Sky, 2743
Where the Truth Lies, 1255
Where the Wild Geese Go, 270
Where the Winds Never Blew and the Cocks Never Crew, 457
Where There's a Will, There's a Wag, 698
Where's Aggie?, 2440
A Whiff of Madness, 1365
While Mrs. Coverlet Was Away, 2260
The Whingdingdilly, 657
The Whins on Knockattan, 817
The Whipping Boy, 1350
A Whisper in the Night: Tales of Terror and Suspense, 1011
The Whisper of Glocken, 1403
The Whispering Knights, 1752
The Whispering Mountain, 1234
Whistle for Good Fortune, in Which It Is Shown How Six from Six Makes Six and One to Carry, with Other Riddles Here and There Along the Way, 790
The Whistling Boy, 1021
The Whistling Whirligig, 1181
The White Cat and Other Old French Fairy Tales, 787
The White Deer, 329
The White Dragon, 1447
White Gold Wielder, 1940
The White Hart, 1538
White Jenna, 1598
The White Mists of Power, 1513
The White Monkey King: A Chinese Fable, 1875
The White Ring, 1855
The White Sea Horse, 2413
The White Serpent, 1424

The White Sparrow, 458
The White Stag, 1828
The White Stone, 2537
Who Fears the Devil?, 1863
Who Is Victoria?, 1068
Who Knew There'd Be Ghosts?, 1033
Who Needs a Bear?, 2912
Who Says So?, 2482
Who's Afraid? And Other Strange Stories, 1168
Who's Afraid of Beowulf?, 1718
Who's Scared? Not Me!, 2850
Why Have the Birds Stopped Singing?, 2842
Why the Chimes Rang and Other Stories, 777
The Wicked Day, 1841
The Wicked Enchantment, 37
The Wicked One, 2500
The Wicked Pigeon Ladies in the Garden, 2712
The Widow's Broom, 3129
Wielding a Red Sword, 1249
Wiggie Wins the West, 614
Wiggy and Boa, 2163
The Wild Hunt of the Ghost Hounds, 1753
Wild Magic, 1295
Wild Magic: The Immortals, 1496
The Wild Swans, 20
Wildfire, 1295
The Wildkeepers' Guest, 1369
The Will of the Wanderer, 1573
William and Mary: A Story, 1951
William Mayne's Book of Giants, 988
Willie the Squowse, 382
Willie Without, 630
The Willow Maiden, 1646
The Wily Witch and All the Other Fairy Tales and Fables, 801
The Wind Boy, 103
The Wind Call, 511
The Wind Eye, 2868
A Wind from Nowhere, 881
The Wind in the Willows, 523
The Wind on the Moon, 2540
The Wind That Wouldn't Blow: Stories of the Merry Middle Kingdom for Children and Myself, 824
The Wind's Twelve Quarters: Short Stories, 917
The Windfairies, 839
Windleaf, 1523
Windmaster's Bane, 1934
Winds of Change, 1418
Winds of Change, 1497
Winds of Darkover, 1270
Winds of Fate, 1418
The Winds of the World, 2027
The Windsingers, 1437
The Winged Cat: A Tale of Ancient Egypt, 1741
The Winged Colt of Casa Mia, 2386
Wingman, 2828
Wings, 1499
Wings, 2377

The Wings of a Falcon, 1566
Wings of Flame, 1539
Winnie-the-Pooh, 2944
Winning Scheherazad, 1701
The Winter Flower, and Other Fairy Stories, 930
Winter King, 1377
The Winter Mittens, 2344
Winter of Fire, 1397
Winter of Magic's Return, 1831
The Winter of the Birds, 77
The Winter Prince, 1861
Winter Story, 404
Winter's Tale, 1379
Winterthing: A Play for Children, 1603
Wisdom's Daughter, 2025
Wise Child, 3020
Wise House, 648
The Wise Men of Schilda, 2281
The Wise Woman, 3027
The Wise Woman and Other Fantasy Stories, 225
Wish, Come True, 2640
The Wish Giver: Three Tales of Coven Tree, 2978
Wish You Were Here, 430
Wishing Gold, 258
The Wishing People, 2356
Wishing Season, 1357
The Wishing Tree, 2447
The Wishsong of Shannara, 1273
A Witch Across Time, 1058
Witch-Cat, 2984
The Witch Doctor, 2065
The Witch Family, 3015
The Witch in Room 6, 2967
The Witch in the Wood, 1865
The Witch King, 1380
The Witch Mobile, 3144
The Witch of Glen Gowrie, 3086
The Witch of Scrapfaggot Green, 3042
Witch of the North, 1731
The Witch on the Corner, 3038
Witch Princess, 1728
Witch Week, 3056
The Witch Who Saved Halloween, 3103
Witch World, 2039
The Witches, 2999
Witches, 3138
The Witches and the Grinnygog, 3013
The Witches of Wenshar, 1372
Witches, Witches, Witches, 3139
The Witching Hour, 2522
Witch's Business, 3057
The Witch's Egg, 3012
Witch's Fire, 2981
The Witch's Garden, 2605
Witchwood, 1443
With a Single Spell, 3133
With a Tangled Skein, 1249

With Cap and Bells: Humorous Stories to Tell and to Read Aloud, 2331
Wizard at Large, 2112
The Wizard Children of Finn, 2856
The Wizard in the Tree, 2963
The Wizard in the Woods, 3128
Wizard in Wonderland, 3128
The Wizard Islands, 1228
A Wizard of Earthsea, 1433
The Wizard of Oz, 1898
The Wizard of Washington Square, 3142
Wizard of Wind and Rock, 1832
Wizard Spawn, 1289
Wizard World, 3148
Wizardry Compiled, 1924
Wizardry Cursed, 1924
Wizards, 3138
The Wizards and the Warriors, 2995
The Wizard's Apprentice, 3119
Wizard's Bane, 1924
A Wizard's Dozen: Stories of the Fantastic, 990
Wizard's Eleven, 1554
Wizard's Hall, 3143
The Wizard's Tears, 3066
Wizards' Worlds, 3099
Wizenbeak, 3024
The Wolf and the Raven, 1798
The Wolf King, 1558
The Wolf of Winter, 1568
Wolf Roland, 83
Wolf-Speaker, 1496
Wolfsong, 1497
Wolfwalker, 1373
The Wolves of Aam, 1308
The Wolves of Willoughby Chase, 1235
The Woman Ayisha, 2027
The Woman Who Loved Reindeer, 1494
The Woman Who Loved the Moon, and Other Stories, 921
The Woman Who Rides Like a Man, 1495
The Wombles, 412
The Wombles at Work, 412
The Wombles Book, 412
The Wombles Go Round the World, 412
The Wombles in Danger, 412
The Wombles Make a Clean Sweep, 412
The Wombles of Wimbledon, 412
The Wombles to the Rescue, 412
The Women and the Warlords, 2995
The Wonder Clock; or, Four and Twenty Marvelous Tales, Being One for Each Hour of the Day, 952
The Wonder-Dog: The Collected Stories of Richard Hughes, 898
The Wonderful Adventures of Nils, 2524
The Wonderful Adventures of Ting Ling, 46
Wonderful Alexander and the Cat Wings, 601
The Wonderful Farm, 394

The Wonderful Flying-Go-Round, 2443
The Wonderful Garden; or the Three C's, 2580
The Wonderful House-Boat-Train, 2179
The Wonderful Lamp, 1857
The Wonderful Locomotive, 2567
The Wonderful O, 330
The Wonderful Story of Henry Sugar and Six More,
    832
Wood Magic; a Fable, 553
Woodland Crossings, 585
The Woods Out Back, 2056
The Wordsmiths and the Warguild, 2995
The Work of the Sun, 3009
The World Around the Corner, 1963
The World in Amber, 3101
The World Is Round, 308
The World of Pooh, 2944
The World Wreckers, 1270
The World's Best Karlson, 2539
*Worlds Near and Far: Nine Stories of Science
    Fiction*, 991
Worldstone, 2067
The Worldwide Dessert Contest, 2158
The Worm Ouroboros, a Romance, 1334
The Worms of Kukumlima, 2275
Worse Things Waiting, 1863
The Worst Witch, 3094
The Worst Witch Strikes Again, 3094
Worzel Gummidge and Saucy Nancy, 2319
Worzel Gummidge and the Railway Scarecrows,
    2319
Worzel Gummidge and the Treasure Ship, 2319
Worzel Gummidge at the Circus, 2319
Worzel Gummidge Takes a Holiday, 2319
*Worzel Gummidge, the Scarecrow of Scatterbrook
    Farm*, 2319
The Would-Be Witch, 2990
The Wounded Land, 1940
Wraiths of Time, 2040
The Wreck of the Zephyr, 340
Wren to the Rescue, 1530
Wren's Quest, 1530
The Wretched Stone, 341
The Wyndcliffe, 1124

Xanadu, 992
Xanadu 2, 992

Yarrow: An Autumn Tale, 1936
A Year and a Day, 235
Year King, 1673
Year of the Unicorn, 2039
*The Year's Best Fantasy and Horror: Fifth Annual
    Collection*, 993
*The Year's Best Fantasy and Horror: Fourth Annual
    Collection*, 993
*The Year's Best Fantasy and Horror: Sixth Annual
    Collection*, 993
*The Year's Best Fantasy and Horror: Third Annual
    Collection*, 993
The Year's Best Fantasy: First Annual Collection,
    993
The Year's Best Fantasy: Second Annual Collection,
    993
The Year's Best Fantasy Stories, 6, 994
The Year's Finest Fantasy, 1978, 857
The Year's Finest Fantasy, vol. 2, 857
Yearwood, 1377
The Yellow Book of Hob Stories, 2566
Yendi, 1275
Yesterday We Saw Mermaids, 1681
Yobgorgle: Mystery Monster of Lake Ontario, 2276
Yorath the Wolf, 1579
You Better Come Home with Me, 198
Young Ghosts, 1229
Young Guinevere, 1820
Young Merlin, 1821
Young Santa, 2184
Young Witches and Warlocks, 3145
The Youngest Camel, 47
Your Mother Was a Neanderthal, 2838
Yvgenie, 2988

Zarsthor's Bane, 2039
Zeee, 2439
Zlateh the Goat and Other Stories, 961
*Zoo 2000: Twelve Stories of Science Fiction and
    Fantasy Beasts*, 763
Zucchini, 475

Subject Index

This Subject Index provides topical headings for many areas of interest to children, young adults, and the librarians who serve them—historical periods, ethnic groups, folktales, imaginary beings and worlds, and mythical creatures. Also listed are series titles and subjects such as alcoholism, divorce, and other sensitive topics that are not usually tied to the realm of fantasy. Historical periods are listed under specific countries (for example, Revolutionary War can be found under United States—Revolutionary War). General headings such as mythology, folklore, legends, and fantasy are not listed here. All references are to entry numbers within chapters 1 to 10, not page numbers. Titles listed here are main entry titles. Other titles in a series and sequels are noted in the main entry annotation.

Aam
CURRY, Jane Louise. *The Wolves of Aam*, 1308
Abáloc trilogy
CURRY, Jane Louise. *The Daybreakers*, 2718;
Over the Sea's Edge, 2719
Abominable snowman
CORBALIS, Judy. *The Ice Cream Heroes*, 2126
MORPURGO, Michael. *King of the Cloud Forests*, 1777
Aboriginal mythology. *See* Australian Aboriginal mythology
Adept series
KURTZ, Katherine, and HARRIS, Deborah. *The Adept*, 3068
Aennorve
VOLSKY, Paula. *The Wolf of Winter*, 1568
Aesir
FRIEDMAN, Michael Jan. *The Seekers and the Sword*, 1680
Africa—1868
COVILLE, Bruce. *The Dark Abyss*, 1928
Africa, Northern
COEHLO, Paulo. *The Alchemist: A Fable About Following Your Dream*, 68
Africa, Northern—Alternate Middle Ages
MYERS, Walter Dean. *The Legend of Tarik*, 1780
Africa, Northern—Folklore
MYERS, Walter Dean. *The Legend of Tarik*, 1780

WELLMAN, Manly Wade. *Cahena*, 1862
Africa, Northern—World War II period
MELLECKER, Judith. *Randolph's Dream*, 237
Africa—Nubia—Alternate ancient history
BRADSHAW, Gillian (Marucha). *The Dragon and the Thief*, 1272
Africa—Sahara Desert
SAINT-EXUPÉRY, Antoine de. *The Little Prince*, 282
African Americans
ANSA, Tina McElroy. *Baby of the Family*, 2343
AVI. *Something Upstairs: A Tale of Ghosts*, 2691
BETHANCOURT, T(homas) Ernesto (pseud. of Tom Paisley). *Tune in Yesterday*, 2699
BISSON, Terry. *Fire on the Mountain*, 1265
BRITTAIN, Bill (William). *All the Money in the World*, 2109
BURGESS, Barbara Hood. *Oren Bell*, 1038
BUTLER, Octavia E. *Kindred*, 2709
CAREW, Jan (Rynveld). *Children of the Sun*, 58
CHESNUTT, Charles Waddell. *Conjure Tales*, 822
GRAY, Genevieve S(tuck). *The Seven Wishes of Joanna Peabody*, 2468
HALL, Lynn. *The Mystery of the Caramel Cat*, 1099
HAMILTON (Adoff), Virginia (Esther). *The Magical Adventures of Pretty Pearl*, 1709; *Sweet Whispers, Brother Rush*, 1100
HURMENCE, Belinda. *A Girl Called Boy*, 2755

MENDEZ, Phil. *The Black Snowman*, 1773

NORTON, André (pseud. of Alice Mary Norton). *Lavender Green Magic*, 2809; *Octagon Magic*, 2810

SHECTER, Ben. *The Whistling Whirligig*, 1181

WALLIN, Luke. *The Slavery Ghosts*, 1202

African-American folklore

HAMILTON (Adoff), Virginia (Esther). *The All Jahdu Storybook*, 2187

HOOKS, William H(arris). *The Ballad of Belle Dorcas*, 150

McKISSACK, Patricia C(arwell). *The Dark-Thirty: Southern Tales of the Supernatural*, 1150

After the Spell Wars trilogy

HALE, F. J. *Ogre Castle*, 3031

Agari

BAKKEN, Harald. *The Fields and the Hills*, 1256

The Age of Magic trilogy

McGOWEN, Tom (Thomas E.). *The Magical Fellowship*, 3083

Alcoholism

WILDE, Nicholas. *Down Came a Blackbird*, 2870

Alert

JAMES, Mary (pseud. of Maryjane Meaker; a.k.a. M. E. Kerr). *The Shuteyes*, 1987

Alex Balfour series

APPEL, Allen. *Time After Time*, 2688

Alexander Armsworth books

PECK, Richard (Wayne). *The Ghost Belonged to Me: A Novel*, 1169

Alfheim

FRIEDMAN, Michael Jan. *The Seekers and the Sword*, 1680

Alphenlicht

TEPPER, Sheri S. *Marianne, the Magus, and the Manticore*, 2070

Alyafaleyn

CHETWIN, Grace. *The Chimes of Alyafaleyn*, 1291

Amber series

ZELAZNY, Roger (Joseph Christopher). *Nine Princes in Amber*, 1599

Anasazi Indian tribe

JAMES, J. Alison. *Sing for a Gentle Rain*, 2757

Anatole trilogy

WILLARD, Nancy (Margaret). *Sailing to Cythera, and Other Anatole Stories*, 2079

Ancar

CHERRYH, C. J. (pseud. of Carolyn Janice Cherry) and ASIRE, Nancy. *Wizard Spawn*, 1289

Angels

ANDERSEN, Hans Christian. *The Red Shoes*, 13

CAMPBELL, Hope. *Peter's Angel: A Story about Monsters*, 438

FRIESNER, Esther M. *Hooray for Hellywood*, 2178

HALL, Lynn. *Dagmar Schultz and the Angel Edna*, 2186

KENNEDY, (Jerome) Richard. *The Blue Stone*, 168

LATHROP, Dorothy P(ulis). *An Angel in the Woods*, 2943

PYLE, Howard. *The Garden Behind the Moon*, 275

SCHAEFFER, Susan Fromberg. *The Dragons of North Chittendon*, 2623

TAZEWELL, Charles. *The Littlest Angel*, 321

VASILIU, Mircea. *Hark, the Little Angel*, 2321

WESTALL, Robert (Atkinson). *Rachel and the Angel and Other Stories*, 982

WILLARD, Nancy (Margaret). *The High Rise Glorious Skittle Skat Roarious Sky Pie Angel Food Cake*, 2664

Animal experimentation

ADAMS, Richard (George). *The Plague Dogs*, 378

CLIFFORD, Sandy. *The Roquefort Gang*, 450

DANN, Colin (Michael). *The Animals of Farthing Wood*, 476

LANDSMAN, Sandy. *Castaways on Chimp Island*, 588

O'BRIEN, Robert C. (pseud. of Robert Leslie Conly). *Mrs. Frisby and the Rats of NIMH*, 639

ZINDEL, Paul. *Let Me Hear You Whisper: A Play*, 762

Annabel Andrews trilogy

RODGERS (Guettel), Mary. *Freaky Friday*, 2291

Anthony Munday series

BELLAIRS, John. *The Dark Secret of Weatherend*, 2360

Appalachia—1940s

PENDERGRAFT, Patricia. *The Legend of Daisy Flowerdew*, 268

Apprentice Adept series

ANTHONY, Piers (pseud. of Piers A. D. Jacob). *Blue Adept*, 1248

Arabia

Arabesques 2, 783

FRIESNER, Esther M. *Wishing Season*, 1357

GARDNER, Craig Shaw. *The Other Sinbad*, 1685

GOROG, Judith. *Winning Scheherazad*, 1701

JONES, Diana Wynne. *Castle in the Air*, 1391

LONGYEAR, Barry B(rookes). *The God Box*, 1440

McKENZIE, Ellen Kindt. *A Bowl of Mischief*, 1449

RUSHDIE, Salman. *Haroun and the Sea of Stories*, 1514

Arabia—Alternate ancient history
WILLIAMS, Tad, and HOFFMAN, Nina Kiriki.
Child of an Ancient City, 1584
"Arabian Nights," adaptations of
DOLBIER, Maurice (Wyman). *The Half-Pint Jinni, and Other Stories*, 842
GOROG, Judith. *Winning Scheherazad*, 1701
HAUFF, Wilhelm. *The Fairy Tales of Wilhelm Hauff*, 888
SCARBOROUGH, Elizabeth Ann. *The Harem of Aman Akbar; or The Djinn Decanted*, 2298
VOEGELI, Max. *The Wonderful Lamp*, 1857
YOUNG, Robert F. *The Vizier's Second Daughter*, 1884
Arabian Nights trilogy
GARDNER, Craig Shaw. *The Other Sinbad*, 1685
Arafel's saga
CHERRYH, C. J. (pseud. of Carolyn Janice Cherry). *The Dreamstone*, 1637
Aragonia series
SCARBOROUGH, Elizabeth Ann. *Bronwyn's Bane*, 1521
Arbonne
KAY, Guy Gavriel. *A Song for Arbonne*, 1398
The Arctic
HOUSTON, James A(rchibald). *Spirit Wrestler*, 3041
LUENN, Nancy. *Arctic Unicorn*, 3080
PIERCE, Meredith Ann. *The Woman Who Loved Reindeer*, 1494
WEBB, Clifford (Cyril). *The North Pole Before Lunch*, 2661
Arden books
NESBIT (Bland), E(dith). *The House of Arden*, 2805
Arizona
VICK, Helen Hughes. *Walker of Time*, 2862
Arizona—1280
JAMES, J. Alison. *Sing for a Gentle Rain*, 2757
Arthur, King of Britain
ATTANASIO, A(lfred) A(ngelo). *Kingdom of the Grail*, 1607
BERGER, Thomas (Louis). *Arthur Rex: A Legendary Novel*, 1613
BERRY, James R. *The Magicians of Erianne*, 1614
BOND, Nancy (Barbara). *A String in the Harp*, 2701
BRADLEY, Marion Zimmer. *The Mists of Avalon*, 1618
BRADSHAW, Gillian (Marucha). *Hawk of May*, 1621
BRYHER, Winifred (pseud. of Annie Winifred Ellerman). *A Visa for Avalon*, 1628
The Camelot Chronicles: Heroic Adventures from the Time of King Arthur, 1632
CANNING, Victor. *The Crimson Chalice*, 1633

CHAPMAN, Vera. *The Green Knight*, 1636
CHRISTIAN, Catherine. *The Pendragon*, 1638
COCHRAN, Molly, and MURPHY, Warren. *The Forever King*, 1643
COLUM, Padraic. *The Boy Apprenticed to an Enchanter*, 2994
CONEY, Michael Greatrex. *The Celestial Steam Locomotive*, 1647
COOPER (Grant), Susan (Mary). *Over Sea, Under Stone*, 1650
CURRY, Ann. *The Book of Brendan*, 1656
CURRY, Jane Louise. *The Sleepers*, 1658
DAVID, Peter. *Knight Life*, 1660
DICKINSON, Peter (pseud. of Malcolm de Brissac). *Merlin Dreams*, 1665; *The Weathermonger*, 1321
GODWIN, Parke. *Beloved Exile*, 1696
HAMLETT, Christina. *The Enchanter*, 1710
HASTINGS, Selina. *Sir Gawain and the Green Knight*, 1713
HIEATT, Constance B(artlett). *The Knight of the Cart*, 1715
HODGES, Margaret, adapt. *The Kitchen Knight: A Tale of King Arthur*, 1716
JONES, Courtway. *In the Shadow of the Oak King*, 1731
JONES, Diana Wynne. *A Sudden Wild Magic*, 3054
KARR, Phyllis Ann. *The Idylls of the Queen*, 1734
KATZ, Welwyn Wilton. *The Third Magic*, 1993
KENNEALY (Morrison), Patricia. *The Hawk's Gray Feather: A Book of the Keltiad*, 1737
LAUBENTHAL, Sanders Anne. *Excalibur*, 1742
LAWHEAD, Stephen R. *Taliesin*, 1744
LIVELY, Penelope (Margaret Low). *The Whispering Knights*, 1752
MALORY, Sir Thomas. *La Morte D'Arthur*, 1767
MAYNE, William (James Carter). *Earthfasts*, 1771
MEANY, Dee Morrison. *Iseult: Dreams That Are Done*, 1772
NATHAN, Robert (Gruntal). *The Elixir*, 1781
NEWMAN, Robert (Howard). *Merlin's Mistake*, 1782
NEWMAN, Sharan. *Guinevere*, 1783
NORMAN, Roger. *Albion's Dream: A Novel of Terror*, 1785
NORTON, André (pseud. of Alice Mary Norton). *Steel Magic*, 2038
The Pendragon Chronicles: Heroic Fantasy from the Time of King Arthur, 1801
PHILIP, Neil. *The Tale of Sir Gawain*, 1802
PYLE, Howard. *The Story of King Arthur and His Knights*, 1808
RICE, Robert. *The Last Pendragon*, 1814
ROBBINS, Ruth. *Taliesin and King Arthur*, 1815

SAN SOUCI, Robert D. *Young Guinevere*, 1820; *Young Merlin*, 1821

SCHILLER, Barbara, adapt. *Erec and Enid*, 1825; *The Kitchen Knight*, 1826; *The Wandering Knight*, 1827

SCIESZKA, Jon. *Knights of the Kitchen Table*, 2838

SERRAILLIER, Ian (Lucien). *The Challenge of the Green Knight*, 1829

SERVICE, Pamela F. *Winter of Magic's Return*, 1831; *Wizard of Wind and Rock*, 1832

SMITH, L(isa) J. *Night of the Solstice*, 2062

STEWART, Mary (Florence Elinor). *The Crystal Cave*, 1841

SUTCLIFF, Rosemary. *The Sword and the Circle: King Arthur and the Knights of the Round Table*, 1843; *Sword at Sunset*, 1844; *Tristan and Iseult*, 1845

TOLSTOY, Nikolai. *The Coming of the King: The First Book of Merlin*, 1854

TWAIN, Mark (pseud. of Samuel Clemens). *A Connecticut Yankee in King Arthur's Court*, 2860

WEIN, Elizabeth E. *The Winter Prince*, 1861

WHITE, T(erence) H(anbury). *The Once and Future King*, 1864; *The Sword in the Stone*, 1865

WIBBERLEY, Leonard (Patrick O'Connor). *The Quest of Excalibur*, 1213

WOLF, Joan. *The Road to Avalon*, 1871

WOLFE, Gene. *Castleview*, 1872

WOOLLEY, Persia. *Child of the Northern Spring*, 1873

YOLEN (Stemple), Jane H(yatt). *The Dragon's Boy*, 1880; *Merlin's Booke*, 1882

Asgard

SMITH, Doris Buchanan. *Voyages*, 1839

Ash Staff series

FISHER, Paul R. *The Ash Staff*, 1348

Asia. *See* Arabia; Babylonia; Byzantium; China; India; Iran; Israel; Japan; Nepal; New Guinea; Persia; Sumeria; Tibet; Turkey; Vietnam

Astalon

AIKEN, Joan (Delano). *The Kingdom and the Cave*, 1233

Atlantis

Atlantis, 784

LAWHEAD, Stephen R. *Taliesin*, 1744

NORTON, André (pseud. of Alice Mary Norton). *Operation Time Search*, 2037

SILVERBERG, Robert. *Letters from Atlantis*, 2844

Aulnoy, Marie Catherine Jumelle de Berneville, Comtesse d'

SHERMAN, Josepha. *Child of Faerie, Child of Earth*, 1834

Austerneve

SNYDER, Zilpha Keatley. *Song of the Gargoyle*, 1533

Australia

Dream Time: New Stories by Sixteen Award Winning Authors, 846

GOLDS, Cassandra. *Michael and the Secret War*, 1966

HARDING, Lee. *Misplaced Persons*, 1976

KELLEHER, Victor (pseud. of Michael Kitchener). *Baily's Bones*, 1117

LINDSAY, Norman. *The Magic Pudding*, 2231

LOGAN, Carolyn F. *The Power of the Rellard*, 1760

PARK, Ruth. *My Sister Sif*, 1794; *Playing Beatie Bow*, 2816; *Things in Corners*, 1165

RODDA, Emily. *The Pigs Are Flying!*, 2615; *Something Special*, 2616

WELDRICK, Valerie. *Time Sweep*, 2865

WRIGHTSON, (Alice) Patricia (Furlonger). *The Ice Is Coming*, 1877; *A Little Fear*, 2672; *Moon–Dark*, 756; *The Nargun and the Stars*, 1878; *An Older Kind of Magic*, 2673

Australia—1629

LISSON, Deborah. *The Devil's Own*, 2782

Australia—1880s

PARK, (Rosina) Ruth (Lucia). *Playing Beatie Bow*, 2816

Australia, 1972

WIGNELL, Edel. *Escape by Deluge*, 1867

Australian Aboriginal mythology

Dream Time: New Stories by Sixteen Award Winning Authors, 846

WRIGHTSON, (Alice) Patricia (Furlonger). *Balyet*, 1876

Austria

LOBE, Mira. *The Grandma in the Apple Tree*, 2541

NÖSTLINGER, Christine. *Konrad*, 2262

Autism

LASKY (Knight), Kathryn. *Home Free*, 2769

Avalon

BRYHER, Winifred (pseud. of Annie Winifred Ellerman). *A Visa for Avalon*, 1628

NORTON, André (pseud. of Alice Mary Norton). *Here Abide Monsters*, 2035; *Steel Magic*, 2038

Avaryan Rising series

TARR, Judith. *The Hall of the Mountain King*, 1550

Awakeners series

NESBIT (Bland), E(dith). *The Story of the Amulet*, 2806

TEPPER, Sheri S. *Northshore*, 1553

Aztec Indian tribe

BELL, Clare E. *The Jaguar Princess*, 1262

REYNOLDS, Mack, and ING, Dean. *The Other Time*, 2833

Babylonia
MERRITT, A(braham P.). *The Ship of Ishtar*, 2022
Ballad of Wuntvor trilogy
GARDNER, Craig Shaw. *A Disagreement with Death*, 3023
Ballets
DIAMOND, Donna, adapt. *Swan Lake*, 92
HOFFMANN, E(rnst) T(heodor) A(madeus). *The Nutcracker*, 2933
Ballybran
McCAFFREY, Anne (Inez). *Crystal Singer*, 1446
Banshees
FRIESNER, Esther M. *Gnome Man's Land*, 1958
Bard's Tale series
LACKEY, Mercedes, and EMERSON, Ru. *Fortress of Frost and Fire*, 3070
"Beauty and the Beast," adaptations of
COHEN, Barbara. *Roses*, 1644
McKINLEY, (Jennifer Carolyn) Robin (Turrell). *Beauty: A Retelling of the Story of Beauty and the Beast*, 1763
WILLARD, Nancy (Margaret). *Beauty and the Beast*, 1869
Belgariad saga
EDDINGS, David. *Queen of Sorcery*, 3008
Bessledorf Mystery series
NAYLOR, Phyllis Reynolds. *Bernie and the Bessledorf Ghost*, 1161
Bible—New Testament, adaptations of
BUNYAN, John. *The Pilgrim's Progress*, 54
LEWIS, C(live) S(taples). *The Lion, the Witch, and the Wardrobe*, 2007
MENOTTI, Gian Carlo. *Amahl and the Night Visitors*, 1774
MOORCOCK, Michael (John). *The War Hound and the World's Pain: A Fable*, 245
SHEEHAN, Carolyn, and SHEEHAN, Edmond. *Magnifi-Cat*, 693
Visions of Wonder: An Anthology of Christian Fantasy, 977
WANGERIN, Walter, Jr. *The Book of the Dun Cow*, 344
Bible—Old Testament, adaptations of
BISSON, Terry. *Talking Man*, 1615
BRUST, Steven K. (Zoltan). *To Reign in Hell*, 1627
CARRYL, Charles Edward. *The Admiral's Caravan*, 1914
COHEN, Barbara. *Unicorns in the Rain*, 1645
CULLEN, Countee (Porter). *The Lost Zoo (A Rhyme for the Young, but Not Too Young) by Christopher Cat and Countee Cullen*, 465
FARMER (Mockridge), Penelope. *Eve: Her Story*, 1672
GARNETT, David. *Two by Two: A Story of Survival*, 1692

HARRIS, Rosemary (Jeanne). *The Moon in the Cloud*, 1711
HUGHES, Ted (Edward James). *Tales of the Early World*, 899
L'ENGLE, Madeleine. *Many Waters*, 2774
MINOT, Stephen. *Surviving the Flood*, 1775
WALKER, Kenneth Macfarlane, and BOUMPHREY, Geoffrey. *The Log of the Ark*, 1858
Blindness
WILDE, Nicholas. *Into the Dark*, 1214
WISNIEWSKI, David. *Elfwyn's Saga*, 367
Blood of Ten Chiefs series
PINI, Wendy, and PINI, Richard. *ElfQuest: The Novel, Journey to Sorrow's End*, 1497
Blossom Culp books
PECK, Richard (Wayne). *The Ghost Belonged to Me: A Novel*, 1169
Boggarts
COOPER (Grant), Susan (Mary). *The Boggart*, 2402
FRITZ, Jean (Guttery). *Magic to Burn*, 2454
Book of Swords trilogy
SABERHAGEN, Fred. *The Second Book of Swords*, 1518
Book of the New Sun series
WOLFE, Gene (Rodman). *The Shadow of the Torturer*, 1585
Books of Westria series
PAXON, Diana L. *Lady of Light*, 1491
Borderland
Borderland, No. 1, 1268
SHETTERLY, Will. *Elsewhere*, 2059
Borribles
DE LARRABEITI, Michael. *The Borribles*, 1314
Brambly Hedge series
BARKLEM, Jill. *Autumn Story*, 404
Brazil
AMADO, Jorge. *The Swallow and the Tomcat*, 383
HOLDSTOCK, Robert (P.) (pseud. of Robert Faulcon). *The Emerald Forest*, 1979
HUDSON, W(illiam) H(enry). *Green Mansions: A Romance of the Tropical Forest*, 1983
"Briar Rose," adaptation of
YOLEN (Stemple), Jane H(yatt). *Briar Rose*, 1879
Brightwater
ELGIN, (Patricia Anne) Suzette Haden. *Twelve Fair Kingdoms*, 1339
Brisingamen
GARNER, Alan. *The Weirdstone of Brisingamen*, 1691
British Isles. *See* England; Ireland, Scotland; Wales
Brobdingnag
SWIFT, Jonathan. *Gulliver's Travels into Several Remote Nations of the World*, 2069

Bromeliad trilogy
PRATCHETT, Terry. *Truckers*, 1499
Brownies
COX, Palmer. *The Brownies: Their Book*, 1307
EWING, Juliana (Horatia Gatty). *The Brownies*, 2441
GARDNER, Craig Shaw. *A Disagreement with Death*, 3023
GRIFFIN, Peni R(ae). *Hobkin*, 2472
HUNTER, Mollie (pseud. of Maureen Mollie Hunter McVeigh McIlwraith). *A Furl of Fairy Wind: Four Stories*, 900
McGOWEN, Tom (Thomas E.). *Sir Machinery*, 3085
MULOCK, Diana (pseud. of Dinah Craik). *The Adventures of a Brownie as Told to My Child*, 2574
Bunyips
LINDSAY, Norman (Alfred William). *The Magic Pudding: Being the Adventures of Bunyip Bluegum and His Friends Bill Barnacle and Sam Sawnoff*, 2231
WIGNELL, Edel. *Escape by Deluge*, 1867
Byzantium
SHWARTZ, Susan. *Silk Roads and Shadows*, 1524

Caer Cadwy
EDGERTON, Teresa. *Child of Saturn*, 3009
California
BLAYLOCK, James P(aul). *The Paper Grail*, 1616
EMERSON, Ru. *Night Threads: The Calling of the Three*, 1948
KATZ, Welwyn Wilton. *Whalesinger*, 561
SINGER, Marilyn. *California Demon*, 3118
SOMTOW, S. P. (pseud. of Somtow Sucharitkul). *The Wizard's Apprentice*, 3119
WILHELM, Kate (Katie Gertrude). *Cambio Bay*, 1868
California—1866
CLIMO, Shirley. *T.J.'s Ghost*, 1051
California—Los Angeles
FORREST, Elizabeth. *Phoenix Fire*, 1679
California—San Francisco
CAMERON, Eleanor. *The Court of the Stone Children*, 1041
REAVES, Michael. *Street Magic*, 1810
Camelot series
WHITE, T(erence) H(anbury). *The Sword in the Stone*, 1865
Camelot trilogy
GODWIN, Parke. *Beloved Exile*, 1696
Canada. *See also* Inuits; Nova Scotia; Ontario
BERTON, Pierre. *The Secret World of Og*, 1903
BUCHAN, John. *Lake of Gold*, 2706

BUFFIE, Margaret. *The Haunting of Frances Rain*, 2707
CARLSON, Natalie Savage. *Alphonse, That Bearded One*, 2121
DE LINT, Charles. *Jack the Giant-Killer*, 1663; *Yarrow: An Autumn Tale*, 1936
HARRIS, Christie (Lucy Irwin). *Secret in the Stlalakum Wild*, 1101
KUSHNER, Donn. *A Book Dragon*, 2523; *Uncle Jacob's Ghost Story*, 188; *The Violin-Maker's Gift*, 189
LUNN, Janet (Louise Swoboda). *The Root Cellar*, 2786; *Shadow in Hawthorn Bay*, 1139; *Twin Spell*, 1140
MAJOR, Kevin (Gerald). *Blood Red Ochre*, 1766
NICHOLS, (Joanna) Ruth. *Song of the Pearl*, 2807
PEARSON, Kit. *A Handful of Time*, 2823
RICHLER, Mordecai. *Jacob Two-Two Meets the Hooded Fang*, 2287
RILEY, Louise. *Train for Tiger Lily*, 2049
SAUER, Julia L(ina). *Fog Magic*, 2837
WHITE, Stewart Edward. *The Magic Forest: A Modern Fairy Story*, 2662
Canada—Prehistoric period
GEAR, W. Michael, and GEAR, Kathleen O'Neal. *People of the Fire*, 1693
Canada—17th century
WALKER, Mary Alexander. *The Scathach and Maeve's Daughters*, 1859
Canada—18th century
BUCHAN, John. *Lake of Gold*, 2706
Canada—1815
LUNN, Janet (Louise Swoboda). *Shadow in Hawthorn Bay*, 1139
Canada—1840s, Nova Scotia
SAUER, Julia L(ina). *Fog Magic*, 2837
Canada—1860 (U.S. Civil War)
LUNN, Janet (Louise Swoboda). *The Root Cellar*, 2786
Canada—1900, Toronto
NICHOLS, (Joanna) Ruth. *Song of the Pearl*, 2807
Caprona
JONES, Diana Wynne. *The Magicians of Caprona*, 3053
Car Do Prawn
NORTON, André (pseud. of Alice Mary Norton). *The Jargoon Pard*, 1487
Caribbean Islands. *See also* Virgin Islands—British
BUCHWALD, Emilie. *Floramel and Esteban*, 431
GUY, Rosa (Cuthbert). *My Love, My Love, or, the Peasant Girl*, 1706
RIOS, Tere (Teresa). *The Fifteenth Pelican*, 2290
Castle series
DE CHANCIE, John. *Castle Kidnapped*, 3000

Cat Club series
AVERILL, Esther (Holden). *Captains of the City Streets: A Story of the Cat Club*, 393
Catfish Bend
BURMAN, Ben Lucien. *High Water at Catfish Bend*, 434
Celtic folklore. *See* Ireland—Celtic folklore
Centaurs
Bestiary!, 796
LEWIS, C(live) S(taples). *The Lion, the Witch, and the Wardrobe*, 2007
PAYNE, Joan Balfour (Dicks). *Magnificent Milo*, 2598
SIEGEL, Robert (Harold). *Alpha Centauri*, 2843
Cerebral palsy
ADLER, C. S. *Eddie's Blue-Winged Dragon*, 2337
Chameleon Corps series
GOULART, Ron(ald Joseph). *The Chameleon Corps and Other Shape Changers*, 1365
Chameln
WILDER, Cherry (pseud. of Cherry Barbara Lockett Grimm). *A Princess of the Chameln*, 1579
Changeling saga
ZELAZNY, Roger (Joseph Christopher). *Madwand*, 3148
Changes trilogy
DICKINSON, Peter (pseud. of Malcolm de Brissac). *The Devil's Children*, 1319; *Heartsease*, 1320; *The Weathermonger*, 1321
Charlemagne, Emperor of France
TARR, Judith. *His Majesty's Elephant*, 3125
Charlotte and Emma trilogy
FARMER (Mockridge), Penelope. *Charlotte Sometimes*, 2733; *The Summer Birds*, 2446
Chelm. *See also* Jewish folklore
SINGER, Isaac Bashevis. *Naftali the Storyteller and His Horse, Sus, and Other Stories*, 959; *Zlateh the Goat and Other Stories*, 961
Chess
SUTCLIFF, Rosemary. *Chess-Dream in a Garden*, 319
WATSON, Ian. *Queenmagic, Kingmagic*, 1571
Chester Cricket books
SELDEN (Thompson), George. *The Cricket in Times Square*, 686
Cheysuli
ROBERSON, Jennifer. *A Pride of Princes*, 1509
Child abuse
GRIFFIN, Peni R(ae). *Hobkin*, 2472
McDONALD, Ian. *King of Morning, Queen of Day*, 1762
REID BANKS, Lynne. *Melusine: A Mystery*, 1812
REISS, Kathryn. *Time Windows*, 2832

Childe Cycle
DICKSON, Gordon R(upert). *The Dorsai Companion*, 1322
Children of Ynell series
MURPHY, Shirley Rousseau. *The Ring of Fire*, 1482
China—13th century
LATTIMORE, Deborah Nourse. *The Dragon's Robe*, 197
China—Alternate 18th century
HUGHART, Barry. *Bridge of Birds: A Novel of an Ancient China That Never Was*, 1384
China—Alternate 19th century
BALL, Margaret. *Changeweaver*, 1257
China—Alternate 20th century
CHRISTOPHER, John. *Dragon Dance*, 1921
China—Alternate history
DE CAMP, L(yon) Sprague. *The Honorable Barbarian*, 1310
SHWARTZ, Susan. *Silk Roads and Shadows*, 1524
China—Ancient
ALEXANDER, Lloyd (Chudley). *The Remarkable Journey of Prince Jen*, 4
BOWEN, Vernon. *The Wonderful Adventures of Ting Ling*, 46
BROOKE, William J. *A Brush with Magic*, 2379
DAY, David. *The Emperor's Panda*, 89
LAWSON, Julie. *The Dragon's Pearl*, 199
NICHOLS, (Joanna) Ruth. *The Left-Handed Spirit*, 3098
PINKWATER, D(aniel) Manus. *Wingman*, 2828
China—Ch'in Dynasty
FORREST, Elizabeth. *Phoenix Fire*, 1679
China—Folklore
BEATON-JONES, Cynon. *The Adventures of So Hi*, 1900
BENNETT, John. *The Pigtail of Ah Lee Ben Loo, with Seventeen Other Laughable Tales*, 2101
BODGER, Joan (Mercer). *Clever-Lazy, the Girl Who Invented Herself*, 45
BRO, Margueritte (Harmon). *The Animal Friends of Peng-U*, 427
BROOKE, William J. *A Brush with Magic*, 2379
CHRISMAN, Arthur Bowie. *Shen of the Sea: Chinese Stories for Children*, 823; *The Wind That Wouldn't Blow: Stories of the Merry Middle Kingdom for Children and Myself*, 824
DAY, David. *The Emperor's Panda*, 89
FORREST, Elizabeth. *Phoenix Fire*, 1679
HOWARD, Alice (Woodbury). *Ching-Li and the Dragons*, 154
LARSON, Jean (Russell). *The Silkspinners*, 195
MacAVOY, R(oberta) A(nn). *Tea with the Black Dragon*, 1761
MERRILL, Jean (Fairbanks). *The Superlative Horse: A Tale of Ancient China*, 239

NICHOLS, (Joanna) Ruth. *The Left-Handed Spirit*, 3098

NORTON, André, and SHWARTZ, Susan. *Imperial Lady: A Fantasy of Han China*, 1788

PINKWATER, D(aniel) Manus. *Wingman*, 2828

RITCHIE, Alice. *The Treasure of Li-Po*, 955

WRIGGINS, Sally. *The White Monkey King: A Chinese Fable*, 1875

YOLEN (Stemple), Jane H(yatt). *The Seventh Mandarin*, 374

China—Han period

NORTON, André, and SHWARTZ, Susan. *Imperial Lady: A Fantasy of Han China*, 1788

China—World War II era

MORPURGO, Michael. *King of the Cloud Forests*, 1777

Chinese culture—Anglo-Chinese

GODDEN (Dixon), (Margaret) Rumer. *Fu-Dog*, 2925

Chirudaks

EASTON, M. Coleman. *Spirits of Cavern and Hearth*, 1330

Chosen

JORDAN, Sherryl. *Winter of Fire*, 1397

Chrestomanci series

JONES, Diana Wynne. *Charmed Life*, 2759; *The Lives of Christopher Chant*, 1990; *The Magicians of Caprona*, 3053

Chretien de Troyes

SCHILLER, Barbara, adapt. *Erec and Enid*, 1825

Christian symbolism

GALLICO, Paul (William). *The Snow Goose*, 120

Christianity

L'ENGLE, Madeleine. *An Acceptable Time*, 2773

MYRA, Harold. *The Shining Face*, 1483

STOLP, Hans. *The Golden Bird*, 314

WANGERIN, Walter, Jr. *Potter, Come Fly to the First of the Earth*, 346

Christmas

ADKINS, Jan. *Solstice: A Mystery of the Season*, 2678

ANDERSEN, Hans Christian. *The Fir Tree*, 7; *The Little Match Girl*, 9

ARNOLD, Tim. *The Winter Mittens*, 2344

BLADOW, Suzanne Wilson. *The Midnight Flight of Moose, Mops and Marvin*, 417

Christmas Ghosts, 1046

Christmas Ghosts: An Anthology, 1047

Ghosts for Christmas, 1088

COATSWORTH, Elizabeth (Jane). *Silky: An Incredible Tale*, 1642

CROTHERS, Samuel McChord. *Miss Muffet's Christmas Party*, 78

CROWLEY, Maude. *Azor and the Blue-Eyed Cow: A Christmas Story*, 464

DAHL, Tessa. *School Can Wait*, 2137

DAMJAN, Mischa (pseud.). *December's Travels*, 86

DAVIES, Valentine. *The Miracle on 34th Street*, 88

DICKENS, Charles (John Huffam). *A Christmas Carol*, 93

DILLON, Barbara. *A Mom by Magic*, 2426

DOLBIER, Maurice (Wyman). *Torten's Christmas Secret*, 99

GODDEN (Dixon), (Margaret) Rumer. *The Story of Holly and Ivy*, 2929

GREENBURG, Dan. *Young Santa*, 2184

HOBAN, Lillian. *It's Really Christmas*, 536

HOFFMANN, E(rnst) T(heodor) A(madeus). *The Nutcracker*, 2933

HOFFMANN, Eleanor. *The Four Friends*, 540

HOWE, James. *Babes in Toyland*, 1982

HURLBUTT, Isabelle B. *Little Heiskell*, 2501

JONES, Elizabeth Orton. *Big Susan*, 2937

KELLEY, True Adelaide and LINDBLOM, Steven (Winther). *The Mouses' Terrible Christmas*, 563

KNIGHT, Marjorie. *Alexander's Christmas Eve*, 2940

KWITZ, Mary DeBall. *Shadow Over Mousehaven Manor*, 587

LATHROP, Dorothy P(ulis). *An Angel in the Woods*, 2943

MENDEZ, Phil. *The Black Snowman*, 1773

MENOTTI, Gian Carlo. *Amahl and the Night Visitors*, 1774

MOERI, Louise. *Star Mother's Youngest Child*, 243

NABB, Magdalen. *The Enchanted Horse*, 2945

SAWYER, Ruth. *The Year of the Christmas Dragon*, 2622

SHECTER, Ben. *The Whistling Whirligig*, 1181

TAZEWELL, Charles. *The Littlest Angel*, 321

THEROUX, Paul. *A Christmas Card*, 325

VAN LEEUWEN, Jean. *The Great Christmas Kidnapping Caper*, 730

VAN STOCKUM, Hilda (Gerarda). *Kersti and Saint Nicholas*, 2320

WENNING, Elisabeth. *The Christmas Mouse*, 739

WIGGIN, Kate Douglas (Smith). *The Bird's Christmas Carol*, 354

Chronicles of an Age of Darkness

COOK, Hugh. *The Wizards and the Warriors*, 2995

Chronicles of Deryni

KURTZ, Katherine. *The Deryni Archives*, 1413

Chronicles of Isle

SPRINGER, Nancy. *The Sable Moon*, 1538

Chronicles of Narnia

LEWIS, C(live) S(taples). *The Lion, the Witch, and the Wardrobe*, 2007

Chronicles of Pantouflia
LANG, Andrew. *Prince Prigio and Prince Ricardo: The Chronicles of Pantouflia*, 194
Chronicles of Prydain
ALEXANDER, Lloyd (Chudley). *The Book of Three*, 1236
Chronicles of the Cheysuli
ROBERSON, Jennifer. *A Pride of Princes*, 1509
Chronicles of the King's Tramp
DE HAVEN, Tom. *Walker of Worlds*, 1933
Chronicles of Thomas Covenant, the Unbeliever
DONALDSON, Stephen R(upert). *Lord Foul's Bane*, 1940
Chronicles of Tornor
LYNN, Elizabeth A. *Watchtower*, 1444
"Cinderella," adaptations of
COLUM, Padraic. *The Girl Who Sat by the Ashes*, 69
FARJEON, Eleanor. *The Glass Slipper*, 1669
GIBSON, Katharine. *Cinders*, 121
HOOKS, William H(arris). *Moss Gown*, 151
LEE, Tanith. *Red as Blood; or Tales from the Sisters Grimmer*, 1747
MOORE, John. *Slay and Rescue*, 1776
MURPHY, Shirley Rousseau. *Silver Woven in My Hair*, 251
MYERS, Bernice. *Sidney Rella and the Glass Sneaker*, 2257
WILSON, David Henry. *The Coachman Rat*, 1870
Claire Randall and Jamie Fraser series
GABALDON, Diana. *Outlander: A Novel*, 2739
Cockatrices
DURRELL, Gerald (Malcolm). *The Talking Parcel*, 1945
WANGERIN, Walter, Jr. *The Book of the Dun Cow*, 344
Cold Fire trilogy
FRIEDMAN, C. S. *Black Sun Rising*, 1354
Colorado—1280
JAMES, J. Alison. *Sing for a Gentle Rain*, 2757
The Commonwealth
MYERS, John Myers. *Silverlock*, 2030
Connecticut
L'ENGLE, Madeleine. *An Acceptable Time*, 2773
Coven Tree saga
BRITTAIN, Bill (William). *The Devil's Donkey*, 2978
Crafters series
The Crafters, 2998
Crete
KEANEY, Brian. *No Need for Heroes*, 1736
LLYWELYN, Morgan. *The Elementals*, 214
Cuchulain
LLYWELYN, Morgan. *Red Branch*, 1758
Cycle of Fire series
WURTS, Janny. *Stormwarden*, 3141

Cymdulock
GILLILAND, Alexis A(rnaldus). *Wizenbeak*, 3024
Czechoslovakia—16th century, Prague
ISH-KISHOR, Sulamith. *The Master of Miracle: A New Novel of the Golem*, 1726
SINGER, Isaac Bashevis. *The Golem*, 1836
WIESEL, Elie(zer). *The Golem; the Story of a Legend*, 1866
Czechoslovakia—Folklore
MACOUREK, Miloš. *Curious Tales*, 924

Dacaria
STEVENSON, Laura C(aroline). *The Island and the Ring*, 1544
Dagmar Schultz series
HALL, Lynn. *Dagmar Schultz and the Angel Edna*, 2186
Dalemark trilogy
JONES, Diana Wynne. *Cart and Cwidder*, 1390; *Drowned Ammet*, 1392; *The Spellcoats*, 1394
Damar series
McKINLEY, (Jennifer Carolyn) Robin (Turrell). *The Blue Sword*, 1460; *The Hero and the Crown*, 1461
Damiano series
MacAVOY, R(oberta) A(nn). *Damiano*, 3081
Daniel au Fond trilogy
SHACHTMAN, Tom. *Driftwhistler: A Story of Daniel au Fond*, 690
Dantari
ZETTNER, Pat. *The Shadow Warrior*, 1600
Dark Is Rising sequence
COOPER (Grant), Susan (Mary). *Over Sea, Under Stone*, 1650
Dark Tower trilogy
KING, Stephen. *The Gunslinger*, 1407
Darkangel trilogy
PIERCE, Meredith Ann. *The Darkangel*, 1493
Darkchild trilogy
VAN SCYOC, Sydney J(oyce). *Bluesong*, 1562
Darkover series
BRADLEY, Marion Zimmer. *Hawkmistress!*, 1269
BRADLEY, Marion Zimmer. *The Shattered Chain: A Darkover Novel*, 1270
Darksword trilogy
WEIS, Margaret, and HICKMAN, Tracy. *Forging the Darksword*, 1577
Darkwar trilogy
COOK, Glen. *Doomstalker*, 460
Dartars
COOK, Glen. *Tower of Fear*, 1300
Darwaeth trilogy
HAMBLY, Barbara. *The Time of the Dark*, 1975
Deafness
RICHEMONT, Enid. *The Time Tree*, 2834

Death

ANTHONY, Piers (pseud. of Piers A. D. Jacob). *On a Pale Horse*, 1249

BEAGLE, Peter S(oyer). *The Innkeeper's Song*, 1260

BENJAMIN, Alan. *Appointment*, 38

BUNTING, (Anne) Eve(lyn Bolton). *Ghost Behind Me*, 1036

BUTLER, Beverly. *Witch's Fire*, 2981

CROSS, Gilbert B. *A Witch Across Time*, 1058

DOYLE, Debra, and MacDONALD, James D. *Knight's Wyrd*, 1325

DUNLOP, Eileen (Rhona). *Green Willow*, 1066

EUSTIS, Helen. *Mr. Death and the Redheaded Woman*, 2160

GARDNER, Craig Shaw. *A Disagreement with Death*, 3023

HUFF, Tanya. *The Last Wizard*, 3043

KENNEDY, (Jerome) Richard. *Come Again in the Spring*, 170

MAHY, Margaret (May). *Dangerous Spaces*, 2020

MONSELL, Mary Elise. *Toohy and Wood*, 628

MOORCOCK, Michael (John). *The War Hound and the World's Pain: A Fable*, 245

PASSEY, Helen K. *Speak to the Rain*, 1795

SINGER, Marilyn. *The Golden Heart of Winter*, 301

SLEPIAN, Jan. *Back to Before*, 2848

STOLP, Hans. *The Golden Bird*, 314

WANGERIN, Walter, Jr. *Elisabeth and the Water-Troll*, 345; *Potter, Come Fly to the First of the Earth*, 346

WESTALL, Robert (Atkinson). *The Promise*, 1208; *Rachel and the Angel and Other Stories*, 982

WILLARD, Nancy (Margaret). *Things Invisible to See*, 362

Death Gate Cycle

WEIS, Margaret, and HICKMAN, Tracy. *Dragon Wing*, 1574

Decans

GENTLE, Mary. *Rats and Gargoyles*, 1360

Deed of Paksenarrion trilogy

MOON, Elizabeth. *Surrender None: The Legacy of Gird*, 1476

Demon trilogy

FRIESNER, Esther M. *Hooray for Hellywood*, 2178

Demons and devils

ALTON, Andrea I. *Demon of Undoing*, 1243

ANTHONY, Piers (pseud. of Piers A. D. Jacob). *On a Pale Horse*, 1249

ASIMOV, Isaac. *Azazel*, 2345

BABBITT, Natalie (Zane Moore). *The Devil's Storybook*, 2096

BALL, Margaret. *Changeweaver*, 1257

BENÉT, Stephen Vicent. *The Devil and Daniel Webster*, 1612

BOWEN, William A(lvin). *Merrimeg*, 1907

BRITTAIN, Bill (William). *The Devil's Donkey*, 2978

BROOKS, Terry. *Magic Kingdom for Sale— Sold!*, 2112

BRUST, Steven K. (Zoltan). *To Reign in Hell*, 1627

CAREY, Valerie Soho. *The Devil and Mother Crump*, 2118

COLE, Allan, and BUNCH, Chris. *The Far Kingdoms*, 1299

The Crafters, 2998

DAHL, Roald. *The Minpins*, 1930

EISENSTEIN, Phyllis. *Sorcerer's Son*, 1337

FLEISCHMAN, Paul (Taylor). *Coming-and-Going Men: Four Tales*, 112

FORREST, Elizabeth. *Phoenix Fire*, 1679

FRIESNER, Esther M. *Hooray for Hellywood*, 2178

GARDNER, Craig Shaw. *A Disagreement with Death*, 3023

GARFIELD, Leon. *The Ghost Downstairs*, 1081

GREEN, Simon. *Blue Moon Rising*, 1367

GREENE, Jacqueline Dembar. *The Leveller*, 1704

GRIPARI, Pierre. *Tales of the Rue Broca*, 884

HALDEMAN, Linda (Wilson). *Esbae: A Winter's Tale*, 1707

HAMLEY, Dennis. *Pageants of Despair*, 2750

HANSEN, Ron. *The Shadowmaker*, 2479

Hidden Turnings: A Collection of Stories Through Time and Space, 892

HOOKS, William H(arris). *Mean Jake and the Devils*, 2199

JACQUES, Brian. *Seven Strange and Ghostly Tales*, 1113

LEVIN, Meyer. *The Spell of Time: A Tale of Love in Jerusalem*, 206

McDONALD, Ian. *King of Morning, Queen of Day*, 1762

McGOWEN, Tom (Thomas E.). *Sir Machinery*, 3085

MAGUIRE, Gregory. *The Dream Stealer*, 3089

MOORCOCK, Michael (John). *The War Hound and the World's Pain: A Fable*, 245

MURPHY, Shirley Rousseau. *The Pig Who Could Conjure the Wind*, 3095

NORTON, André (pseud. of Alice Mary Norton). *Here Abide Monsters*, 2035

POOLE, Josephine. *The Visitor: A Story of Suspense*, 3104

POWERS, Tim. *The Stress of Her Regard*, 1498

PRICE, Susan. *The Devil's Piper*, 1806

ROACH, Marilynne K(athleen). *Encounters with the Invisible World; Being Ten Tales of Ghosts, Witches, and the Devil Himself in New England*, 956

SCARBOROUGH, Elizabeth Ann. *Phantom Banjo*, 3114

SERVICE, Pamela F. *When the Night Wind Howls*, 3116

SINGER, Isaac Bashevis. *Naftali the Storyteller and His Horse, Sus, and Other Stories*, 959; *Zlateh the Goat and Other Stories*, 961

SINGER, Marilyn. *California Demon*, 3118

TENNY, Dixie. *Call the Darkness Down*, 1852

WARNER, Sylvia Townsend. *Lolly Willowes: or, the Loving Huntsman*, 3132

WATT-EVANS, Lawrence. *Crosstime Traffic*, 980

WILDE, Oscar (pseud. of Fingal O'Flahertie Wills). *The Picture of Dorian Gray*, 356

Denmark

ANDERSON, Poul (William). *The Merman's Children*, 1245

BEHN, Harry. *The Faraway Lurs*, 36

Denmark—8th century

GARDNER, John (Champlin) (Jr.). *Grendel*, 1686

NYE, Robert. *Beowulf; a New Telling*, 1789

Denmark—13th century

ANDERSON, Poul (William). *The Merman's Children*, 1245

Denmark—Bronze Age

BEHN, Harry. *The Faraway Lurs*, 36

Denmark—Folklore

ANDERSEN, Hans Christian. *Fairy Tales*, 779

GARDNER, John (Champlin) (Jr.). *Grendel*, 1686

NYE, Robert. *Beowulf; a New Telling*, 1789

Deryni

KURTZ, Katherine. *The Deryni Archives*, 1413; *The Harrowing of Gwynedd*, 1414

Deverry series

KERR, Katharine. *Daggerspell*, 3061; *A Time of Exile: A Novel of the Westlands*, 1405

Didd

SEUSS, Dr. (pseud. of Theodor Seuss Geisel). *The 500 Hats of Bartholomew Cubbins*, 293

Dido Twite series

AIKEN, Joan (Delano). *The Wolves of Willoughby Chase*, 1235

Dinosaurs

BONHAM, Frank. *The Friends of the Loony Lake Monster*, 2367

BRADBURY, Ray (Douglas). *Dinosaur Tales*, 806

BRÖGER, Achim. *Bruno*, 2110

BUTTERWORTH, Oliver. *The Enormous Egg*, 2115

CORBETT, Scott. *Ever Ride a Dinosaur?*, 2127

KLEIN, Robin. *Thing*, 2217

LAMPMAN, Evelyn Sibley. *The Shy Stegosaurus of Cricket Creek*, 2219

PALMER, Mary. *The Teaspoon Tree*, 2592

PHIPSON, Joan (pseud. of Margaret Fitzhardinge). *The Way Home*, 2827

Divorce

McGRAW, Eloise Jarvis. *A Really Weird Summer*, 1144

PEARSON, Kit. *A Handful of Time*, 2823

SLEPIAN, Jan. *Back to Before*, 2848

Djinns. *See* Genies and djinns

"Donkeyskin," adaptations of

McKINLEY, (Jennifer Carolyn) Robin (Turrell). *Deerskin*, 1764

Doors into Time trilogy

McKEAN, Thomas. *The Secret of the Seven Willows*, 2789

Dorsai

DICKSON, Gordon R(upert). *The Dorsai Companion*, 1322

Dragaera

BRUST, Steven K. (Zoltan). *The Phoenix Guards*, 1274; *Taltos*, 1275

Dragon King trilogy

LAWHEAD, Stephen R. *In the Hall of the Dragon King*, 1420

Dragon Prince trilogy

RAWN, Melanie. *Dragon Prince*, 1502

Dragon quartet

YEP, Laurence M(ichael). *Dragon of the Lost Sea*, 1595

Dragon series

DICKSON, Gordon R(upert). *The Dragon and the George*, 1939

Dragon Star trilogy

RAWN, Melanie. *Stronghold*, 1503

Dragonbards trilogy

MURPHY, Shirley Rousseau. *Nightpool*, 1481

DragonLance Chronicles

WEIS, Margaret, and HICKMAN, Tracy. *DragonLance Chronicles*, 1575

DragonLance Legends

WEIS, Margaret, and HICKMAN, Tracy. *DragonLance Legends*, 1576

Dragonriders of Pern series

McCAFFREY, Anne (Inez). *Dragonflight*, 1447

Dragons

ADAMS, Hazard. *The Truth about Dragons: An Anti-Romance*, 1231

ADLER, C. S. *Eddie's Blue-Winged Dragon*, 2337

ANCKARSVÄRD, Karin (Inez Maria). *Bonifacius the Green*, 2340

ANDERSON, Wayne. *Dragon*, 23

ANTHONY, Piers (pseud. of Piers A. D. Jacob). *Blue Adept*, 1248

ASKOUNIS, Christina. *The Dream of the Stone*, 1892

BAKER, Betty (Lou). *Save Sirrushany!*, 27

BALL, Brian. *The Quest for Queenie*, 1893

BEATON-JONES, Cynon. *The Adventures of So Hi*, 1900

BENDICK, Jeanne. *The Goodknight Ghost*, 1027

BERRY, James R. *The Magicians of Erianne*, 1614

Bestiary!, 796

BOWEN, Vernon. *The Wonderful Adventures of Ting Ling*, 46

BRADSHAW, Gillian (Marucha). *The Dragon and the Thief*, 1272

BRIGHT, Robert. *Richard Brown and the Dragon*, 2106

CARVER, Jeffrey A(llan). *Dragon Rigger*, 1283

A Cavalcade of Dragons, 819

COOPER, Paul Fenimore. *Dindle*, 75

COSTIKYAN, Greg. *By the Sword: Magic of the Plains*, 1305

COUNSEL, June. *A Dragon in Class 4*, 2405

CURLEY, Daniel. *Billy Beg and the Bull*, 1655

DICKINSON, Peter (pseud. of Malcolm de Brissac). *Merlin Dreams*, 1665

DICKSON, Gordon R(upert). *The Dragon and the George*, 1939; *The Last Dream*, 841

DOYLE, Debra, and MacDONALD, James D. *Knight's Wyrd*, 1325

Dragon Fantastic, 844

Dragon Tales, 845

DRAKE, David. *The Sea Hag*, 1326

FLETCHER, Susan. *Dragon's Milk*, 1351; *Flight of the Dragon Kyn*, 1352

FLORY, Jane Trescott. *The Lost and Found Princess*, 114

FORESTER, C(ecil) S(cott). *Poo Poo and the Dragons*, 2175

FOSTER, Malcolm (Burton). *The Prince with a Hundred Dragons*, 117

GANNETT (Kahn), Ruth Stiles. *My Father's Dragon*, 2459

GARDNER, Craig Shaw. *A Disagreement with Death*, 3023

GARDNER, John (Champlin) (Jr.). *Dragon, Dragon, and Other Timeless Tales*, 871

GODDEN (Dixon), (Margaret) Rumer. *The Dragon of Og*, 124

GRAHAME, Kenneth. *The Reluctant Dragon*, 127

GREEN, Simon. *Blue Moon Rising*, 1367

HALDANE, J(ohn) B(urdon) S(anderson). *My Friend Mr. Leakey*, 3030

HAMBLY, Barbara. *Dragonsbane*, 3032

HAYES, Sarah. *Crumbling Castle*, 3035

HILDICK, E(dmund) W(allace). *The Dragon That Lived Under Manhattan*, 2192

HODGES, Elizabeth Jamison. *The Three Princes of Serendip*, 146

HOPE, Christopher. *The Dragon Wore Pink*, 152

HOUGH, (Helen) Charlotte (Woodyatt). *Red Biddy and Other Stories*, 893

HOWARD, Alice (Woodbury). *Ching-Li and the Dragons*, 154

HUGHES, Robert Don. *The Faithful Traitor*, 3045

HUGHES, Ted (Edward James). *The Iron Giant: A Story in Five Nights*, 156

JOHNSON, Elizabeth. *The Little Knight*, 161

JONES, Terry. *Nicobobinus*, 2210

KELLER, Beverly (Lou). *A Small, Elderly Dragon*, 167

KIMMEL, Margaret Mary. *Magic in the Mist*, 3062

KIRWAN-VOGEL, Anna. *The Jewel of Life*, 1409

KOLLER, Jackie French. *The Dragonling*, 1411

KRENSKY, Stephen (Alan). *The Dragon Circle*, 2522; *The Perils of Putney*, 186

KUSHNER, Donn. *A Book Dragon*, 2523

LACKEY, Mercedes, and EMERSON, Ru. *Fortress of Frost and Fire*, 3070

LATTIMORE, Deborah Nourse. *The Dragon's Robe*, 197

LAWSON, Julie. *The Dragon's Pearl*, 199

LAWSON, Marie (Abrams). *Dragon John*, 200

LEE, Tanith. *The Dragon Hoard*, 1429

LINDGREN, Astrid. *The Brothers Lionheart*, 2010

LIVELY, Penelope (Margaret Low). *Uninvited Ghosts and Other Stories*, 2233; *The Whispering Knights*, 1752

LLOYD, (Mary) Norris. *The Desperate Dragons*, 213

MacAVOY, R(oberta) A(nn). *Tea with the Black Dragon*, 1761

McCAFFREY, Anne (Inez). *Dragonflight*, 1447; *Dragonsong*, 1448

McGOWEN, Tom (Thomas E.). *Dragon Stew*, 227; *The Magical Fellowship*, 3083

McKIERAN, Dennis L. *Dragondoom*, 1451

MANNING, Rosemary (Joy). *Dragon in Danger*, 2249

MARTIN, Graham Dunstan. *Giftwish*, 1466

MAYNE, William (James Carter). *A Game of Dark*, 2796

Monsters, Ghoulies and Creepy Creatures: Fantastic Stories and Poems, 929

MONTROSE, Anne. *The Winter Flower, and Other Fairy Stories*, 930

MURPHY, Shirley Rousseau. *Nightpool*, 1481; *Valentine for a Dragon*, 252

NESBIT (Bland), E(dith). *The Complete Book of Dragons*, 933; *The Deliverers of Their Country*, 2575; *The Last of the Dragons*, 255

NORTON, André (pseud. of Alice Mary Norton). *Dragon Magic*, 2808

NORTON, André, and LACKEY, Mercedes. *The Elvenbane: An Epic Fantasy of the Halfblood Chronicles*, 3100

PALMER, Mary. *The Magic Knight*, 262

PARKER, (James) Edgar (Jr.). *The Question of a Dragon*, 652

Phoenix Feathers: A Collection of Mythical Monsters, 941

PIERCE, Tamora. *Wild Magic: The Immortals*, 1496

POMERANTZ, Charlotte. *Detective Poufy's First Case: Or the Missing Battery-Operated Pepper Grinder*, 2277

PREISS, Byron (Cary), and REAVES, J. Michael. *Dragonworld*, 1501

RAWN, Melanie. *Dragon Prince*, 1502; *Stronghold*, 1503

REID BANKS, Lynne. *The Magic Hare*, 669

REIT, Seymour. *Benvenuto*, 2286

REYNOLDS, Alfred. *Kiteman of Karanga*, 1507

RIDLEY, Philip. *Krindlekrax; or, How Ruskin Splinter Battled a Horrible Monster and Saved His Entire Neighborhood*, 2288

ROUNDS, David. *Cannonball River Tales*, 2292

RUFF, Matt. *Fool on the Hill*, 2618

SALSITZ, R. A. V. *The Unicorn Dancer*, 1519; *Where Dragons Lie*, 1520

SAN SOUCI, Robert D. *Young Guinevere*, 1820; *Young Merlin*, 1821

SARGENT, Sarah. *Weird Henry Berg*, 2620

SAWYER, Ruth. *The Year of the Christmas Dragon*, 2622

SCARBOROUGH, Elizabeth Ann. *The Drastic Dragon of Draco, Texas*, 2297

SCHRANK, Joseph. *The Plain Princess and the Lazy Prince*, 287

SCULLARD, Sue. *Miss Fanshawe and the Great Dragon Adventure*, 2302

SEABROOKE, Brenda. *The Dragon That Ate Summer*, 2626

SELFRIDGE, Oliver. *The Trouble with Dragons*, 290

SHELLEY, Rick. *Son of the Hero*, 2057

SHURA, Mary Francis (pseud. of Mary Francis Craig). *The Nearsighted Knight*, 296

SNYDER, Dianne. *George and the Dragon Word*, 2637

SOMTOW, S. P. (pseud. of Somtow Sucharitkul). *The Wizard's Apprentice*, 3119

STASHEFF, Christopher. *Her Majesty's Wizard*, 2065

STEARNS, Pamela (Fujimoto). *Into the Painted Bear Lair*, 2066

STERMAN, Betsy, and STERMAN, Samuel. *Backyard Dragon*, 2641

STRICKLAND, Brad. *Dragon's Plunder, or, The Last Voyage of Captain Deadmon: A Fantasy Adventure*, 2645

SUTCLIFF, Rosemary. *The Minstrel and the Dragon Pup*, 320

TERLOUW, Jan (Cornelis). *How to Become King*, 323

TILLSTROM, Burr. *The Dragon Who Lived Downstairs*, 331

TOLKIEN, J(ohn) R(onald) R(euel). *Farmer Giles of Ham*, 332; *The Hobbit; Or, There and Back Again*, 1556

TORREY, Marjorie (Chanslor Hood). *Artie and the Princess*, 334

URQUHART, Elizabeth. *Horace*, 337

VANDE VELDE, Vivian. *Dragon's Bait*, 1561

WATT-EVANS, Lawrence. *Crosstime Traffic*, 980; *With a Single Spell*, 3133

WEIR, Rosemary (Green). *Albert the Dragon*, 348

WERSBA, Barbara. *The Land of Forgotten Beasts*, 2074

WILLARD, Nancy (Margaret). *The Sorcerer's Apprentice*, 3137

WILLEY, Elizabeth. *The Well-Favored Man: The Tale of the Sorcerer's Nephew*, 1581

WILLIAMS, Jay. *The Practical Princess*, 365; *The Practical Princess and Other Liberating Fairy Tales*, 989

WILLIAMS, Tad. *The Dragonbone Chair*, 1583

WREDE, Patricia C(ollins). *Dealing with Dragons*, 1588

YEP, Laurence M(ichael). *Dragon of the Lost Sea*, 1595

YOLEN (Stemple), Jane H(yatt). *Dove Isabeau*, 372; *Dragon's Blood*, 1596; *The Dragon's Boy*, 1880

ZARING, Jane T(homas). *The Return of the Dragon*, 376

ZELAZNY, Roger (Joseph Christopher). *Madwand*, 3148

Dragons trilogy

SALSITZ, R. A. V. *Where Dragons Lie*, 1520

Druids

ANDERSON, Margaret J(ean). *The Druid's Gift*, 2683

Bestiary!, 796

FRIESNER, Esther M. *Druid's Blood*, 1355

HOROWITZ, Anthony. *The Devil's Door-Bell*, 3039

JONES, Courtway. *In the Shadow of the Oak King*, 1731

LLYWELYN, Morgan. *Druids*, 1755

Dryads

BOSTON, L(ucy) M(aria Wood). *Nothing Said*, 2370

FOLLETT, Barbara Newhall. *The House Without Windows and Eepersip's Life There*, 115

KEY, Alexander (Hill). *The Sword of Aradel*, 2763

D'Shai

ROSENBERG, Joel. *D'Shai*, 1512

Duel of Sorcery trilogy

CLAYTON, Jo. *Moongather*, 1296

Dungeon series
COVILLE, Bruce. *The Dark Abyss*, 1928
Dungeons and Dragons
WEIS, Margaret, and HICKMAN, Tracy. *DragonLance Chronicles*, 1575; *DragonLance Legends*, 1576
Dwarfs
BROOKS, Terry. *The Sword of Shannara*, 1273
COOPER, Paul Fenimore. *Dindle*, 75
EDGERTON, Teresa. *Goblin Moon*, 3010
FRANCE, Anatole (pseud. of Jacques Anatole François Thibault). *Bee, the Princess of the Dwarfs*, 1957
GARDNER, Craig Shaw. *A Disagreement with Death*, 3023
GARDNER, John (Champlin) (Jr.). *In the Suicide Mountains*, 1358
HAUFF, Wilhelm. *Dwarf Long-Nose*, 136
HAWTHORNE, Julian. *Rumpty-Dudget's Tower: A Fairy Tale*, 139
KING, Bernard. *Starkadder*, 1739
KRENSKY, Stephen (Alan). *The Perils of Putney*, 186
LACKEY, Mercedes, and EMERSON, Ru. *Fortress of Frost and Fire*, 3070
McKIERAN, Dennis L. *Dragondoom*, 1451; *Trek to Kraggen-Cor*, 1452
NICHOLS, (Joanna) Ruth. *A Walk out of the World*, 2033
SALSITZ, R. A. V. *Where Dragons Lie*, 1520
SALVATORE, R. A. *The Woods Out Back*, 2056
TOLKIEN, J(ohn) R(onald) R(euel). *The Hobbit; Or, There and Back Again*, 1556
WEIS, Margaret, and HICKMAN, Tracy. *Dragon Wing*, 1574; *DragonLance Chronicles*, 1575
Dwomor
WATT-EVANS, Lawrence (pseud. of Richard Watt Evans). *With a Single Spell*, 3133
Dyfed
MORRIS, Kenneth. *The Book of the Three Dragons*, 1778
WALTON, Evangeline (pseud. of Evangeline Ensley). *The Prince of Annwn*, 1860
Dying Earth Saga
VANCE, Jack (pseud. of John Holbrook Vance). *Cugel's Saga*, 1559
Dyslexia
DAHL, Roald. *The Vicar of Nibbleswicke*, 2136

Earthsea quartet
LE GUIN, Ursula K(roeber). *A Wizard of Earthsea*, 1433
Ecology. *See also* Endangered species
ADAMS, Hazard. *The Truth about Dragons: An Anti-Romance*, 1231
BARRON, T(homas) A. *The Ancient One*, 2694

BLISS, Corinne Demas. *Matthew's Meadow*, 43
BODECKER, N(iels) M(ogens). *The Mushroom Center Disaster*, 421
CLARK, Douglas W. *Alchemy Unlimited*, 2991
CLINE, Linda. *The Miracle Season*, 451
COLEMAN, Janet Wyman. *Fast Eddie*, 454
CORBETT, W(illiam) J(esse). *The Song of Pentecost*, 462
ELISH, Dan. *The Great Squirrel Uprising*, 491
ENDE, Michael. *The Night of Wishes, or The Satanarcheolidealcohellish Notion Potion*, 2159
EVANS, Sanford. *Naomi's Geese*, 496
LASKY (Knight), Kathryn. *Home Free*, 2769
LE GUIN, Ursula K(roeber). *Buffalo Gals and Other Animal Presences*, 600
LLYWELYN, Morgan. *The Elementals*, 214
MAHY, Margaret (May). *The Girl with the Green Ear: Stories About Magic in Nature*, 2557
McHARGUE, Georgess. *Beastie*, 2551
NIMMO, Jenny. *Ultramarine*, 1784
PARK, Ruth. *My Sister Sif*, 1794
ROUNDS, David. *Cannonball River Tales*, 2292
SHACHTMAN, Tom. *Driftwhistler: A Story of Daniel au Fond*, 690
STRANGER, Joyce (pseud. of Joyce Muriel Judson Wilson). *The Fox at Drummer's Darkness*, 318
THOMPSON, Julian F(rancis). *Gypsyworld*, 2071
WILLARD, Nancy (Margaret). *The Sorcerer's Apprentice*, 3137
WOOD, Douglas. *Old Turtle*, 369
WRIGHTSON, (Alice) Patricia (Furlonger). *Moon–Dark*, 756
Ecuador
CLARK, Ann Nolan. *Looking-for-Something: The Story of a Stray Burro of Ecuador*, 445
Edanvant
DOUGLAS, Carole Nelson. *Exiles of the Rynth*, 3004
Egypt
COEHLO, Paulo. *The Alchemist: A Fable About Following Your Dream*, 68
Egypt—2700 B.C.
ALEXANDER, Lloyd (Chudley). *Time Cat: The Remarkable Journeys of Jason and Gareth*, 2680
Egypt—Alternate ancient history
BRADSHAW, Gillian (Marucha). *The Dragon and the Thief*, 1272
LATTIMORE, Deborah Nourse. *The Winged Cat: A Tale of Ancient Egypt*, 1741
Egypt—Ancient
BELL, Clare E. *Tomorrow's Sphinx*, 409
BOSHINSKI, Blanche. *Aha and the Jewel of Mystery*, 425

DEXTER, Catherine. *The Gilded Cat*, 1063

DICKINSON, Peter (pseud. of Malcolm de Brissac). *The Blue Hawk*, 1318

GREAVES, Margaret. *Cat's Magic*, 2744

HARRIS, Rosemary (Jeanne). *The Moon in the Cloud*, 1711

HOWARD, Alice (Woodbury). *Sokar and the Crocodile: A Fairy Story of Egypt*, 2494

KARR, Kathleen. *Gideon and the Mummy Professor*, 2513

LEWIS, Hilda (Winifred). *The Ship That Flew*, 2778

McMULLAN, Kate. *Under the Mummy's Spell*, 1151

NESBIT (Bland), E(dith). *The Story of the Amulet*, 2806

SABERHAGEN, Fred. *Pyramids*, 2055

SERVICE, Pamela F. *The Reluctant God*, 2839

STOLZ, Mary (Slattery). *Cat in the Mirror*, 2852

TARR, Judith. *Lord of the Two Lands*, 1850

Eirren

PATTOU, Edith. *Hero's Song*, 1796

Elder Isles

VANCE, Jack (pseud. of John Holbrook Vance). *Suldrun's Garden*, 1560

Elenium Saga

EDDINGS, David. *The Diamond Throne*, 1331

Eleven Kingdoms

COOKE, Catherine. *Mask of the Wizard*, 1301

Elfin Sequence

BLAYLOCK, James P(aul). *The Stone Giant*, 1266

Elfland

BALL, Margaret. *The Shadow Gate*, 1894

SHELLEY, Rick. *Son of the Hero*, 2057

ElfQuest Saga

PINI, Wendy, and PINI, Richard. *ElfQuest: The Novel, Journey to Sorrow's End*, 1497

Elric Saga

MOORCOCK, Michael (John). *The Fortress of the Pearl*, 1478

Elves

AIKEN, Joan (Delano). *A Necklace of Raindrops and Other Stories*, 771

BALL, Margaret. *The Shadow Gate*, 1894

BAUDINO, Gael. *Strands of Starlight*, 1259

BOWEN, William A(lvin). *Merrimeg*, 1907

BOYER, Elizabeth H. *The Troll's Grindstone*, 1908

BROOKS, Terry. *The Sword of Shannara*, 1273

CALHOUN, Mary (pseud. of Mary Huiskamp Wilkins). *Magic in the Alley*, 2387

CALLANDER, Don. *Aquamancer*, 2983

DANK, Gloria Rand. *The Forest of App*, 87

DE LINT, Charles. *Yarrow: An Autumn Tale*, 1936

DOLBIER, Maurice (Wyman). *Torten's Christmas Secret*, 99

EDGERTON, Teresa. *Goblin Moon*, 3010

FIELD, Rachel (Lyman). *Eliza and the Elves*, 1953

FRIESNER, Esther M. *Elf Defense*, 2177

GRIFFITH, Helen V(irginia). *Emily and the Enchanted Frog*, 2474

Isaac Asimov's Magical Worlds of Fantasy: Faeries, 904

KERR, Katharine. *A Time of Exile: A Novel of the Westlands*, 1405

KORSCHUNOW, Irina. *Small Fur*, 2521

KUSHNER, Ellen. *Thomas the Rhymer*, 1740

LACKEY, Mercedes, and DIXON, Larry. *Born to Run*, 3069

LACKEY, Mercedes, and EMERSON, Ru. *Fortress of Frost and Fire*, 3070

LACKEY, Mercedes, and LISLE, Holly. *When the Bough Breaks*, 2003

LAGERLÖF, Selma (Ottilliana Lovisa). *The Wonderful Adventures of Nils*, 2524

LAWRENCE, Ann (Margaret). *Tom Ass: Or the Second Gift*, 2532

LOGSTON, Anne. *Shadow*, 1439

McDONALD, Ian. *King of Morning, Queen of Day*, 1762

McGOWEN, Tom (Thomas E.). *The Magical Fellowship*, 3083

NORTON, André, and LACKEY, Mercedes. *The Elvenbane: An Epic Fantasy of the Halfblood Chronicles*, 3100

PINI, Wendy, and PINI, Richard. *ElfQuest: The Novel, Journey to Sorrow's End*, 1497

POSTMA, Lidia. *The Witch's Garden*, 2605

SALVATORE, R. A. *The Woods Out Back*, 2056

SHELLEY, Rick. *Son of the Hero*, 2057

SHETTERLY, Will. *Elsewhere*, 2059

SLEIGH, Barbara (de Riemer). *Stirabout Stories, Brewed in Her Own Cauldron*, 962

STOLZ, Mary (Slattery). *The Leftover Elf*, 316

TARN, (Sir) W(illiam) W(oodthorpe). *The Treasure of the Isle of Mist*, 2647

TARR, Judith. *The Isle of Glass*, 1551

WALLACE, Barbara Brooks. *The Barrel in the Basement*, 2658

WARNER, Sylvia Townsend. *Kingdoms of Elfin*, 1570

WEIS, Margaret, and HICKMAN, Tracy. *Dragon Wing*, 1574; *DragonLance Chronicles*, 1575

WUORIO, Eva-Lis. *Tal and the Magic Barruget*, 2674

Elysia

CLEMENT, Aeron. *The Cold Moons*, 448

Elyssonne

STEVENSON, Laura C(aroline). *The Island and the Ring*, 1544

Elythia

FLETCHER, Susan. *Dragon's Milk*, 1351

Empire trilogy
FEIST, Raymond E., and WURTS, Janny.
Daughter of the Empire, 1345

Enchanted Forest Chronicles
WREDE, Patricia C(ollins). *Dealing with
Dragons*, 1588

Endangered species
LASKY (Knight), Kathryn. *Home Free*, 2769
McHARGUE, Georgess. *Beastie*, 2551

England. *See also* Arthur, King of Britain; Druids;
Ireland—Celtic folklore
FARMER (Mockridge), Penelope. *Thicker Than
Water*, 1069
GORDON, John (William). *The Burning Baby
and Other Ghosts*, 1090
ROSS, Tony. *A Fairy Tale*, 2617
WESLEY, Mary. *Haphazard House*, 2866

England—5th century B.C.
PAXON, Diana L. *The Serpent's Tooth*, 1797

England—5th century
GODWIN, Parke. *Beloved Exile*, 1696
JONES, Courtway. *In the Shadow of the Oak
King*, 1731

England—7th century
BURFORD, Lolah. *The Vision of Stephen: An
Elegy*, 2708
GARD, Joyce (pseud. of Joyce Reeves).
Talargain, 1683
WESTALL, Robert (Atkinson). *The Cats of
Seroster*, 1578

England—675
WESTALL, Robert. *The Wind Eye*, 2868

England—725
CURRY, Ann. *The Book of Brendan*, 1656

England—970
ANDREWS, J(ames) S(ydney). *The Green Hill
of Nendrum*, 2687

England—11th century
ABBEY, Lynn (pseud. of Marilyn Lorraine
Abbey). *Unicorn and Dragon*, 1602

England—1066
GODWIN, Parke. *Sherwood*, 1697

England—12th century
LITTLE, Jane. *The Philosopher's Stone*, 2783
PEASE, (Clarence) Howard. *The Gypsy
Caravan; Being the Merry Tale of the Travels
of Betty and Joe with the Gypsies—Their
Amazing Adventures with Robin Hood—with
Richard-the-Lion-Hearted—with Roland—and
Sundry Other Great and Famous Persons*,
2824
WALKER, Mary Alexander. *The Scathach and
Maeve's Daughters*, 1859

England—1120
BOSTON, L(ucy) M(aria Wood). *The Stones of
Green Knowe*, 2703

England—1175
HILDICK, E(dmund) W(allace). *The Case of the
Dragon in Distress: A McGurk Fantasy*, 2752

England—13th century
GREER, Gerry, and RUDDICK, Bob. *Max and
Me and the Time Machine*, 2745
ROBERSON, Jennifer. *Lady of the Forest*, 1816

England—14th century
NAYLOR, Phyllis Reynolds. *Shadows on the
Wall*, 2804

England—1326
WELCH, Ronald. *The Gauntlet*, 2864

England—1348
WILLIS, Connie. *Doomsday Book*, 2872

England—15th century
RABINOWITZ, Ann. *Knight on Horseback*,
1172

England—16th century
CURRY, Jane Louise. *The Bassumtyte Treasure*,
1061
EAGAR, Frances. *Time Tangle*, 2730
GIBSON, Katharine. *Jock's Castle*, 122
GREGORY, Philippa. *The Wise Woman*, 3027

England—16th-century Elizabethan period
RICHEMONT, Enid. *The Time Tree*, 2834

England—1558
POPE, Elizabeth Marie. *The Perilous Gard*, 2045

England—1588
ALEXANDER, Lloyd (Chudley). *Time Cat: The
Remarkable Journeys of Jason and Gareth*,
2680

England—1591
THOMAS, Jane Resh. *The Princess in the
Pigpen*, 2857

England—17th century
AIKEN, Joan (Delano). *Return to Harken House*,
1008
CURRY, Jane Louise. *Poor Tom's Ghost*, 1062
LIVELY, Penelope (Margaret Low). *The Ghost of
Thomas Kempe*, 1136
McKILLIP, Patricia A(nne). *The House on
Parchment Street*, 1149
WESTALL, Robert (Atkinson). *The Devil on the
Road*, 2867

England—1639
LIVELY, Penelope (Margaret Low). *The Ghost of
Thomas Kempe*, 1136

England—18th century
AIKEN, Joan (Delano). *The Haunting of Lamb
House*, 1007
DUNLOP, Eileen (Rhona). *Elizabeth, Elizabeth*,
2727
GARFIELD, Leon. *The Empty Sleeve*, 1080
KING-SMITH, Dick. *The Toby Man*, 577
LEACH, Christopher. *Rosalinda*, 1125
SEVERN, David (pseud. of David Unwin).
Dream Gold, 2841

WIBBERLEY, Leonard (Patrick O'Connor). *The Crime of Martin Coverly*, 2869

England—1760s

MAYNE, William (James Carter). *Earthfasts*, 1771

ROACH, Marilynne K(athleen). *Presto: Or, the Adventures of a Turnspit Dog*, 670

England—1770s

FREEMAN, Barbara C(onstance). *A Pocket of Silence*, 1077

England—19th century

AIKEN, Joan (Delano). *The Haunting of Lamb House*, 1007; *The Wolves of Willoughby Chase*, 1235

BARBER, Antonia (pseud. of Barbara Anthony). *The Ghosts*, 2693

MACE, Elisabeth. *The Rushton Inheritance*, 2792

MOORE, Katherine (Davis). *The Little Stolen Sweep*, 2802

England—1805

ST. GEORGE, Judith. *The Mysterious Girl in the Garden*, 2849

England—1819

WISEMAN, David. *Thimbles*, 2877

England—1820s

FREEMAN, Barbara C(onstance). *The Other Face*, 2738

England—1833

PATON WALSH, Jill (Gillian Bliss). *A Chance Child*, 2820

England—1835

MOONEY, Bel. *The Stove Haunting*, 2801

England—1849

WISEMAN, David. *Adam's Common*, 2875

England—1852

WISEMAN, David. *Jeremy Visick*, 2876

England—1862

WELDRICK, Valerie. *Time Sweep*, 2865

England—1864

LASKI, Marghanita. *The Victorian Chaise Longue*, 2768

England—1870s

ANDERSON, Margaret J(ean). *To Nowhere and Back*, 2685

England—1880s

PEARCE, (Ann) Philippa. *Tom's Midnight Garden*, 2822

England—1890s

NESBIT (Bland), E(dith). *The Deliverers of Their Country*, 2575

England—1900

MACE, Elisabeth. *The Ghost Diviners*, 2791

England—1902

ALLAN, Mabel E(sther). *Romansgrove*, 2681

England—1905

KING-SMITH, Dick. *Lady Daisy*, 2939

England—1914

SLEIGH, Barbara (de Riemer). *Jessamy*, 2847

England—1915

LAMPLUGH, Lois. *Falcon's Tor*, 2767

England—1918

FARMER (Mockridge), Penelope. *Charlotte Sometimes*, 2733

England—1920s

MASEFIELD, John (Edward). *The Midnight Folk: A Novel*, 2560

England—1930s

AIKEN, Joan (Delano). *Return to Harken House*, 1008

England—1933

TOMALIN, Ruth. *Gone Away*, 1199

England—1935

LILLINGTON, Kenneth (James). *Selkie*, 1750

England—1939

JONES, Diana Wynne. *A Tale of Time City*, 1991

England—1940s

KURTZ, Katherine. *Lammas Night*, 3067

MACE, Elisabeth. *The Ghost Diviners*, 2791

STEWART, Mary (Florence Elinor). *Thornyhold*, 3122

England—2084

WILLIS, Connie. *Doomsday Book*, 2872

England—Alternate 9th century

HARRISON, Harry. *The Hammer and the Cross*, 1375

England—Alternate 1478

FORD, John M. *The Dragon Waiting: A Masque of History*, 1353

England—Alternate 20th century

CHRISTOPHER, John. *Fireball*, 1921

England—Alternate Elizabethan period

WREDE, Patricia C(ollins). *Snow White and Rose Red*, 1874

England—Alternate history

GARRETT, Randall. *Lord Darcy Investigates*, 1359

England—Alternate Medieval period

MURPHY, Jill. *Jeffrey Strangeways*, 2256

England—Alternate Regency period

POWERS, Tim. *The Stress of Her Regard*, 1498

WREDE, Patricia C(ollins). *Mairelon the Magician*, 1590

WREDE, Patricia C(ollins), and STEVERMER, Caroline. *Sorcery and Cecilia*, 1592

England—Alternate Victorian era

FRIESNER, Esther M. *Druid's Blood*, 1355

PULLMAN, Philip. *Spring-Heeled Jack*, 2282

England—Bronze Age

CALDECOTT, Moyra. *The Tall Stones*, 1277

England—Celtic

CANNING, Victor. *The Crimson Chalice*, 1633

INGRAM, Tom (Thomas Henry). *The Night Rider*, 2756

KATZ, Welwyn Wilton. *The Third Magic*, 1993

LAWHEAD, Stephen R. *Taliesin*, 1744

PARDOE, M(argaret Mary). *Curtain of Mist*, 2815

England—Civil War

ANDERSON, Poul (William). *A Midsummer Tempest*, 1246

GARNER, Alan. *The Red Shift*, 2740

England—Cornwall

DE LINT, Charles. *The Little Country*, 3001

England—Elizabethan period

NICHOLS, (Joanna) Ruth. *Song of the Pearl*, 2807

RODOWSKY, Colby. F. *Keeping Time*, 2836

SHEEDY, Alexandra E. *She Was Nice to Mice: The Other Side of Elizabeth I's Character Never Before Revealed by Previous Historians*, 692

UTTLEY, Alison (pseud. of Alice Jane [Taylor] Uttley). *A Traveler in Time*, 2861

England—Folklore, Anglo-Saxon

GARDNER, John (Champlin) (Jr.). *Grendel*, 1686

NYE, Robert. *Beowulf; a New Telling*, 1789

SUTCLIFF, Rosemary. *Sword at Sunset*, 1844

England—Folklore, Cornish

TREGARTHEN, Enys (pseud. of Nellie Sloggett). *The White Ring*, 1855

England—Late Medieval period

AMOSS, Berthe. *Lost Magic*, 2964

England—London

GODDEN (Dixon), (Margaret) Rumer. *Fu-Dog*, 2925

England—London—1590

GOLDSTEIN, Lisa. *Strange Devices of the Sun and Moon*, 1698

England—London—1887

CRESSWELL (Rowe), Helen. *Time Out*, 2716

England—London—1909

WISEMAN, David. *A Tie to the Past*, 2878

England—Middle Ages

ARTHUR, Ruth M(abel). *On the Wasteland*, 2689

BULLA, Clyde Robert. *The Sword in the Tree*, 53

HAMLEY, Dennis. *Pageants of Despair*, 2750

KEY, Alexander (Hill). *The Sword of Aradel*, 2763

NYE, Robert. *Beowulf; a New Telling*, 1789

SUTCLIFF, Rosemary. *Sword at Sunset*, 1844

TARR, Judith. *The Isle of Glass*, 1551

TOMALIN, Ruth. *Gone Away*, 1199

WILLIAMS (John), Ursula Moray. *Castle Merlin*, 1216

England—Norman Britain

GODWIN, Parke. *Sherwood*, 1697

LEWIS, Hilda (Winifred). *The Ship That Flew*, 2778

England—Norman invasion, 1066

BURTON, Philip. *The Green Isle*, 55

England—Post-Roman

MAYNE, William (James Carter). *The Hill Road*, 2797

WOLF, Joan. *The Road to Avalon*, 1871

England—Pre-Druic

SIEGEL, Robert (Harold). *Alpha Centauri*, 2843

England—Roman Britain

ALEXANDER, Lloyd (Chudley). *Time Cat: The Remarkable Journeys of Jason and Gareth*, 2680

ANDERSON, Poul, and ANDERSON, Karen. *Gallicenae*, 1247

England—Rye, Sussex

AIKEN, Joan (Delano). *The Haunting of Lamb House*, 1007

England—Victorian period

BURFORD, Lolah. *The Vision of Stephen: An Elegy*, 2708

EUBANK, Judith. *Crossover*, 2732

GREAVES, Margaret. *Cat's Magic*, 2744

GREEN, Roger J(ames). *The Fear of Samuel Walton*, 1703

JETER, K. W. *Infernal Devices: A Mad Victorian Fantasy*, 2207

SCULLARD, Sue. *Miss Fanshawe and the Great Dragon Adventure*, 2302

SYKES, Pamela. *Mirror of Danger*, 2853

England—World War I

MONACO, Richard. *Journey to the Flame*, 2025

England—World War II era. *See also* World War II

GALLICO, Paul (William). *The Snow Goose*, 120

WESTALL, Robert (Atkinson). *The Promise*, 1208

Epic Tales of the Five series

DUANE, Diane (Elizabeth). *The Door into Fire*, 3005

Erd

SNYDER, Zilpha Keatley. *Below the Root*, 1532

Erianne

BERRY, James R. *The Magicians of Erianne*, 1614

Erna

FRIEDMAN, C. S. *Black Sun Rising*, 1354

Eskimos. *See* Inuits

Estcarp

NORTON, André (pseud. of Alice Mary Norton). *Witch World*, 2039

Esterness

PIERCE, Meredith Ann. *The Darkangel*, 1493

Eternal Champion Saga

MOORCOCK, Michael (John). *The Dragon in the Sword*, 1477

Europe. *See also* Austria; Czechoslovakia; Denmark; England; Finland; France; Germany; Greece; Hungary; Icelandic sagas; Ireland; Italy; Lapland; The Netherlands; Norway; Poland; Russia; Scotland; Spain; Sweden; Switzerland; Ukrania; Wales

Europe—1347
TEPPER, Sheri S. *Beauty: A Novel*, 1853

Europe—1648
MOORCOCK, Michael (John). *The War Hound and the World's Pain: A Fable*, 245

Europe—Alternate 14th century
BAUDINO, Gael. *Strands of Starlight*, 1259

Europe—Alternate 15th century
FORD, John M. *The Dragon Waiting: A Masque of History*, 1353

Europe—Alternate Medieval period
TARR, Judith. *Ars Magica*, 1549

Europe—Alternate Middle Ages
LOGSTON, Anne. *Shadow*, 1439
SNYDER, Zilpha Keatley. *Song of the Gargoyle*, 1533

Europe—Alternate Renaissance period
GENTLE, Mary. *Rats and Gargoyles*, 1360

Europe—The Crusades
LANCASTER, Osbert. *The Saracen's Head; or, the Reluctant Crusader*, 193

Europe—Middle Ages
CUNNINGHAM, Julia (Woolfolk). *Wolf Roland*, 83
GERRARD, Roy. *Sir Cedric*, 2181
JONES, Terry. *Nicobobinus*, 2210
LANCASTER, Osbert. *The Saracen's Head*, 193
LEVIN, Betty (Lowenthal). *The Ice Bear*, 1434
MURPHY, Shirley Rousseau. *Silver Woven in My Hair*, 251
PIERCE, Tamora. *Alanna: The First Adventure*, 1495
SHURA, Mary Francis (pseud. of Mary Francis Craig). *The Nearsighted Knight*, 296

Europe—Middle Ages—12th century
KEMP, Gene. *Jason Bodger and the Priory Ghost*, 1118

Europe, Northern—Prehistoric period
TEMPEST, John. *Vision of the Hunter*, 1851

Faerie
DEITZ, Tom. *Windmaster's Bane*, 1934
DE LINT, Charles. *Into the Green*, 1316
FRIESNER, Esther M. *Gnome Man's Land*, 1958
LACKEY, Mercedes, and LISLE, Holly. *When the Bough Breaks*, 2003
MURPHY, Shirley Rousseau. *The Catswold Portal*, 2028
REAVES, Michael. *Street Magic*, 1810

SHERMAN, Josepha. *Child of Faerie, Child of Earth*, 1834; *Strange and Ancient Name*, 2058; *Windleaf*, 1523
SHETTERLY, Will. *Elsewhere*, 2059
WREDE, Patricia C(ollins). *Snow White and Rose Red*, 1874

Fairies
AIKEN, Joan (Delano). *The Whispering Mountain*, 1234
ANDERSON, Mildred Napier. *A Gift for Merimond*, 21
ANDERSON, Poul (William). *A Midsummer Tempest*, 1246
BAILEY, Margery. *The Little Man with One Shoe*, 788
BAKER, (Robert) Michael (Graham). *The Mountain and the Summer Stars: An Old Tale Newly Ended*, 1609
BARRIE, Sir J(ames) M(atthew). *Peter Pan*, 1896
BERGENGREN, Ralph Wilhelm. *Susan and the Butterbees*, 2363
BIANCO, Margery (Winifred) Williams. *The Velveteen Rabbit; or, How Toys Became Real*, 2893
BOWEN, William A(lvin). *Merrimeg*, 1907
BROCK, Betty. *No Flying in the House*, 2378
BULL, Emma. *War for the Oaks*, 1630
BURNETT (Townsend), Frances (Elizabeth) Hodgson. *Racketty-Packetty House, as Told by Queen Crosspatch*, 2385
CALHOUN, Mary (pseud. of Mary Huiskamp Wilkins). *Ownself*, 2388
CASSERLEY, Anne Thomasine. *Michael of Ireland*, 816
CHERRYH, C. J. (pseud. of Carolyn Janice Cherry). *The Dreamstone*, 1637
COATSWORTH, Elizabeth (Jane). *Knock at the Door*, 1923
COLUM, Padraic. *The Stone of Victory and Other Tales*, 830
CREGAN, Maírín. *Old John*, 463
CURRY, Jane Louise. *Over the Sea's Edge*, 2719
DEAN, Pamela. *Tam Lin*, 1661
DE LA MARE, Walter (John). *Crossings: A Fairy Play*, 2422
DE LINT, Charles. *Into the Green*, 1316
DU BOIS, William (Sherman) Pène. *The Flying Locomotive*, 2146
DUNLOP, Eileen (Rhona). *The Maze Stone*, 2728
EDGERTON, Teresa. *Goblin Moon*, 3010
ELIOT, Ethel (Augusta) Cook. *Buttercup Days*, 2437; *The Wind Boy*, 103
ENRIGHT, Elizabeth (Wright). *Zeee*, 2439 *Faery!*, 854
FISCHER, Marjorie. *Red Feather*, 1954

FOLLETT, Barbara Newhall. *The House Without Windows and Eepersip's Life There*, 115

FRY, Rosalie K(ingsmill). *The Mountain Door*, 1959; *The Wind Call*, 511

GODWIN, Parke. *Beloved Exile*, 1696

GOLDSTEIN, Lisa. *Strange Devices of the Sun and Moon*, 1698

GRAY, Genevieve S(tuck). *The Seven Wishes of Joanna Peabody*, 2468

GREAVES, Margaret. *The Dagger and the Bird: A Story of Suspense*, 1970

GREEN, Kathleen. *Philip and the Pooka and Other Irish Fairy Tales*, 883

GUILLOT, René. *Nicolette and the Mill*, 2476

HALDEMAN, Linda (Wilson). *The Lastborn of Elvinwood*, 1708

HAUFF, Wilhelm. *Dwarf Long-Nose*, 136

HOFFMANN, E(rnst) T(heodor) A(madeus). *The Strange Child*, 147

HOUGH, (Helen) Charlotte (Woodyatt). *Red Biddy and Other Stories*, 893

HOUSMAN, Laurence. *Cotton-Wooleena*, 153

HOWARD, Joan (pseud. of Patricia Gordon). *The Oldest Secret*, 1981

HUNTER, Mollie (pseud. of Maureen Mollie Hunter McVeigh McIlwraith). *The Ferlie*, 2498; *A Furl of Fairy Wind: Four Stories*, 900; *The Haunted Mountain: A Story of Suspense*, 1984; *The Smartest Man in Ireland*, 2201

INGELOW, Jean. *Mopsa the Fairy*, 1985

IPCAR, Dahlov (Zorach). *The Queen of Spells*, 1723

Isaac Asimov's Magical Worlds of Fantasy: Faeries, 904

JAMES, M(ontague) R(hodes). *The Five Jars*, 2504

JOHNSON, Elizabeth. *Break a Magic Circle*, 2506

JONES, Elizabeth Orton. *Twig*, 2512

KINGSLEY, Charles. *The Water Babies: A Fairy Tale for a Land Baby*, 175

KIPLING, (Joseph) Rudyard. *Puck of Pook's Hill*, 2764

KOTZWINKLE, William. *Hearts of Wood: And Other Timeless Tales*, 910

KURTZ, Katherine, and HARRIS, Deborah. *The Adept*, 3068

LATHROP, Dorothy P(ulis). *The Fairy Circus*, 196; *The Snail Who Ran*, 590

LLYWELYN, Morgan. *The Isles of the Blest*, 1756

LYNCH, Patricia (Nora). *Brogeen Follows the Magic Tune*, 217

MacALPINE, Margaret H(esketh Murray). *The Black Gull of Corie Lachan*, 2547

MacAVOY, R(oberta) A(nn). *The Grey Horse*, 3082

MacDONALD, George. *The Fairy Fleet*, 220

McHARGUE, Georgess. *Elidor and the Golden Ball*, 2015

MASON, Arthur. *The Wee Men of Ballywooden*, 2561

MAYER, Marianna. *Noble-Hearted Kate: A Celtic Tale*, 1769

MAYNE, William (James Carter). *All the King's Men*, 2021; *A Grass Rope*, 2565

MIRRLEES, Hope. *Lud-in-the-Mist*, 1474

MOLESWORTH, Mary Louisa (Stewart). *Fairy Stories*, 928

NESBIT (Bland), E(dith). *Five Children and It*, 2577

NESBIT (Bland), E(dith). *Melisande*, 256

O'FAOLÁIN, Eileen (Gould). *The Little Black Hen; An Irish Fairy Story*, 2588

PAGET, (Reverend) F(rancis) E(dward) (used the pseud. William Churne of Staffordshire). *The Hope of the Katzekopfs; or, the Sorrow of Selfishness: A Fairy Tale*, 261

PATTOU, Edith. *Hero's Song*, 1796

PEARCE, (Ann) Philippa. *The Squirrel Wife*, 266

PHILLIPS, Ethel Calvert. *Little Rag Doll*, 2949

POPE, Elizabeth Marie. *The Perilous Gard*, 2045

POTTER, Miriam (S.) Clark. *Sally Gabble and the Fairies*, 2606

REAVES, Michael. *Street Magic*, 1810

REID BANKS, Lynne. *The Fairy Rebel*, 2609

ROSS, Tony. *A Fairy Tale*, 2617

SÈGUR, Comtesse Sophie (Rostopchine) de. *The Enchanted Forest*, 289

SALVATORE, R. A. *The Woods Out Back*, 2056

SCHEIDL, Gerda Marie. *Loretta and the Little Fairy*, 2624

SHERMAN, Josepha. *Child of Faerie, Child of Earth*, 1834; *Strange and Ancient Name*, 2058; *Windleaf*, 1523

SHURA, Mary Francis (pseud. of Mary Francis Craig). *Happles and Cinnamunger*, 1182

SILVERMAN, Maida. *The Magic Well*, 297

SLEIGH, Barbara (de Riemer). *Stirabout Stories, Brewed in Her Own Cauldron*, 962

STORR, Catherine (Cole). *Thursday*, 1842

TARR, Judith. *Alamut*, 1548

TEPPER, Sheri S. *Beauty: A Novel*, 1853

THACKERAY, William Makepeace. *The Rose and the Ring; or the History of Prince Giglio and Prince Bulbo: A Fireside Pantomime for Great and Small Children*, 324

TOLKIEN, J(ohn) R(onald) R(euel). *Smith of Wootton Major*, 333

TREGARTHEN, Enys (pseud. of Nellie Sloggett). *The Doll Who Came Alive*, 2959; *The White Ring*, 1855

TURNBULL, Ann (Christine). *The Wolf King*, 1558

WARNER, Sylvia Townsend. *Kingdoms of Elfin*, 1570

WILLIAMS, Jay. *The Practical Princess*, 365;
*The Practical Princess and Other Liberating
Fairy Tales*, 989
WISEMAN, David. *Blodwen and the Guardians*,
2668
WREDE, Patricia C(ollins). *Snow White and
Rose Red*, 1874
YOLEN (Stemple), Jane H(yatt). *Tam Lin: An
Old Ballad*, 1883
Fantasy role-playing games
CARPENTER, Christopher. *The Twilight Realm*,
1912
MACE, Elisabeth. *Under Siege*, 2018
WEIS, Margaret, and HICKMAN, Tracy.
DragonLance Chronicles, 1575
Fauns
LEWIS, C(live) S(taples). *The Lion, the Witch,
and the Wardrobe*, 2007
PICARD, Barbara Leonie. *The Faun and the
Woodcutter's Daughter*, 942
"Faust" legend, adaptations of
BENÉT, Stephen Vicent. *The Devil and Daniel
Webster*, 1612
GARFIELD, Leon. *The Ghost Downstairs*, 1081
GREENE, Jacqueline Dembar. *The Leveller*,
1704
HALDEMAN, Linda (Wilson). *Esbae: A
Winter's Tale*, 1707
LEVIN, Meyer. *The Spell of Time: A Tale of Love
in Jerusalem*, 206
SERVICE, Pamela F. *When the Night Wind
Howls*, 3116
WARNER, Sylvia Townsend. *Lolly Willowes: or,
the Loving Huntsman*, 3132
WILDE, Oscar (pseud. of Fingal O'Flahertie
Wills). *The Picture of Dorian Gray*, 356
ZELAZNY, Roger, and SHECKLEY, Robert. *If
at Faust You Don't Succeed*, 2881
Fayre Farre
CHARNAS, Suzy McKee. *The Kingdom of
Kevin Malone*, 1917
Fellheath
FISHER, Paul R. *The Ash Staff*, 1348
Felmargue
ABBEY, Lynn (pseud. of Marilyn Lorraine
Abbey). *The Black Flame*, 1230
Feydom
MARTIN, Graham Dunstan. *Giftwish*, 1466
Finland—Folklore
SYNGE, (Phyllis) Ursula. *Land of Heroes: A
Retelling of the Kalevala*, 1846
Finn MacCool trilogy
PAXSON, Diana L., and MARTINE-BARNES,
Adrienne. *Master of Earth and Water*, 1799
Finnbranch trilogy
HAZEL, Paul. *Yearwood*, 1377
Fionavar Tapestry trilogy
KAY, Guy Gavriel. *The Summer Tree*, 1994

Fireball trilogy
CHRISTOPHER, John (pseud. of Christopher
Samuel Youd). *Fireball*, 1921
Firefly Island
BLATHWAYT, Benedict. *Stories from Firefly
Island*, 419
Five Children trilogy
NESBIT (Bland), E(dith). *Five Children and It*,
2577
Flameweaver series
BALL, Margaret. *Changeweaver*, 1257
Flatfoot Fox Mystery series
CLIFFORD, Eth. *Flatfoot Fox and the Case of
the Missing Eye*, 449
Florida
HARVEY, Dean. *The Secret Elephant of Harlan
Kooter*, 2480
Florida Everglades
BUFFETT, Jimmy, and BUFFETT, Savannah
Jane. *Trouble Dolls*, 2899
CAVANAGH, Helen. *Panther Glade*, 1634
ECKERT, Allan W. *The Dark Green Tunnel*,
1947
The Flux
CARVER, Jeffrey A(llan). *Dragon Rigger*, 1283
Fomor
FLYNN, Casey. *Most Ancient Song*, 1678
Forest Land
GREEN, Simon. *Blue Moon Rising*, 1367
Foster children
ROBINSON, Joan G. *When Marnie Was There*,
1175
WRIGHT, Betty Ren. *The Ghosts of Mercy
Manor*, 1224
Fraglund
BEMMANN, Hans. *The Stone and the Flute*,
1263
France. *See also* Roman Gaul
ANDREWS, Allen. *The Pig Plantagenet*, 385
ATTWOOD, Frederic. *Vavache, the Cow Who
Painted Pictures*, 392
AYMÉ, Marcel (André). *The Wonderful Farm*,
394
BATO, Joseph. *The Sorcerer*, 2966
BROW, Thea J. *The Secret Cross of Lorraine*,
1035
CAMERON, Eleanor (Frances Butler). *The
Court of the Stone Children*, 1041
CARLSON, Natalie Savage. *Evangeline, Pigeon
of Paris*, 439
DRUON, Maurice (Samuel Roger Charles).
Tistou of the Green Thumbs, 101
EZO (pseud.). *Avril*, 49; *My Son-in-Law, the
Hippopotamus*, 2162
GRIPARI, Pierre. *Tales of the Rue Broca*, 884
GUILLOT, René. *Nicolette and the Mill*, 2476
LAMORISSE, Albert (Emmanuel). *The Red
Balloon*, 192

LEY, Madeleine. *The Enchanted Eve*, 209

MAETERLINCK, Maurice. *The Children's Blue Bird*, 230

MILLER (Mandelkorn), Eugenia. *The Sign of the Salamander*, 2800

MOLESWORTH, Mary Louisa (Stewart). *The Tapestry Room: A Child's Romance*, 2568

REID BANKS, Lynne. *Melusine: A Mystery*, 1812

SAINT-EXUPÉRY, Antoine de. *The Little Prince*, 282

SHERMAN, Josepha. *Child of Faerie, Child of Earth*, 1834

STOLZ, Mary (Slattery). *Frédou*, 716

VINGE, Joan D(ennison). *Ladyhawke*, 3130

WESTALL, Robert (Atkinson). *The Cats of Seroster*, 1578

France—802 A.D.

TARR, Judith. *His Majesty's Elephant*, 3125

France—12th century

KAY, Guy Gavriel. *A Song for Arbonne*, 1398

France—13th century

ANDREWS, Allen. *The Pig Plantagenet*, 385

France—1429

GOODWIN, Marie D. *Where the Towers Pierce the Sky*, 2743

France—16th century

MILLER (Mandelkorn), Eugenia. *The Sign of the Salamander*, 2800

SHERMAN, Josepha. *Windleaf*, 1523

France—1790

CAMERON, Eleanor (Frances Butler). *The Court of the Stone Children*, 1041

France—1920s

GOLDSTEIN, Lisa. *The Dream Years*, 2742

France—1940

GALLICO, Paul (William). *The Snow Goose*, 120

France—Alternate 15th century

CLARK, Douglas W. *Alchemy Unlimited*, 2991

France—Folklore

AULNOY, Marie Catherine Jumelle de Berneville, Comtesse d'. *The White Cat and Other Old French Fairy Tales*, 787

BOURLIAGUET, Léonce. *The Giant Who Drank from His Shoe and Other Stories*, 804

CAYLUS, Anne Claude Phillipe, Comte de. *Heart of Ice*, 60

FRANCE, Anatole (pseud. of Jacques Anatole François Thibault). *Bee, the Princess of the Dwarfs*, 1957

LA MOTTE FOUQUÉ, Baron Friedrich Heinrich Karl de. *Undine*, 190

SÈGUR, Comtesse Sophie (Rostopchine) de. *The Enchanted Forest*, 289

WILLARD, Nancy (Margaret). *Beauty and the Beast*, 1869

France—Middle Ages

NORTON, André (pseud. of Alice Mary Norton). *Huon of the Horn*, 1786

VINGE, Joan D(ennison). *Ladyhawke*, 3130

France—Paris

DUFFY, James. *The Revolt of the Teddy Bears*, 485

GOLDSTEIN, Lisa. *The Dream Years*, 2742

VAN ALLSBURG, Chris. *The Sweetest Fig*, 339

France—Stone Age

BATO, Joseph. *The Sorcerer*, 2966

WESTALL, Robert. *The Cats of Seroster*, 1578

France—World War II

BROW, Thea J. *The Secret Cross of Lorraine*, 1035

"The Frog Prince," adaptations of

NAPOLI, Donna Jo. *The Prince of the Pond: Otherwise Known as De Fawg Pin*, 2259

Futuristic tales

ANDERSON, Margaret J(ean). *In the Circle of Time*, 2684

BELLAMY, Edward. *Looking Backward: 2000–1887*, 2696

COWPER, Richard (pseud. of John Middleton-Murray). *The Road to Corlay*, 1306

LEE, Robert C. *Timequake*, 2772

LIVELY, Penelope (Margaret Low). *The Voyage of Q V 66*, 609

MOORCOCK, Michael (John). *The Ice Schooner: A Tale*, 1479

OAKLEY, Graham. *Henry's Quest*, 2263

SERVICE, Pamela F. *Winter of Magic's Return*, 1831

SILVERBERG, Robert. *Lord Valentine's Castle*, 1527

WILLIS, Connie. *Doomsday Book*, 2872

WOLFE, Gene (Rodman). *The Shadow of the Torturer*, 1585

Gaelic legend. *See* Ireland—Folklore

Gale'tin

BLACKWOOD, Gary L. *Beyond the Door*, 1904

Game

TEPPER, Sheri S. *Jinian Footseer*, 1552; *The Song of Mavin Manyshaped*, 1554

Gargoyles

GENTLE, Mary. *Rats and Gargoyles*, 1360

SNYDER, Zilpha Keatley. *Song of the Gargoyle*, 1533

Garillon

HARRIS, Deborah Turner. *The Burning Stone*, 3034

Genies and djinns

BELL, Thelma Harrington. *Take It Easy*, 2359

CONFORD, Ellen. *Genie with the Light Blue Hair*, 2400

CRESSWELL (Rowe), Helen. *Almost Goodbye*, 2409

DOLBIER, Maurice (Wyman). *The Half-Pint Jinni, and Other Stories*, 842

ELKIN, Benjamin. *Al and the Magic Lamp*, 2438

FRIESNER, Esther M. *Wishing Season*, 1357; *Yesterday We Saw Mermaids*, 1681

GOROG, Judith. *Winning Scheherazad*, 1701

HOFFMANN, Eleanor. *Mischief in Fez*, 2492

JONES, Diana Wynne. *Castle in the Air*, 1391

KIPLING, (Joseph) Rudyard. *How the Camel Got His Hump*, 181

LEESON, Robert (Arthur). *Genie on the Loose*, 2224

SCARBOROUGH, Elizabeth Ann. *The Harem of Aman Akbar; or The Djinn Decanted*, 2298

SELDEN (Thompson), George. *The Genie of Sutton Place*, 2628

WHITCHER, Susan. *Real Mummies Don't Bleed: Friendly Tales for October Nights*, 983

Georgia

ANSA, Tina McElroy. *Baby of the Family*, 2343

DEITZ, Tom. *The Gryphon King*, 1662

Germany. *See also* World War II

BENARY-ISBERT, Margot. *The Wicked Enchantment*, 37

BRÖGER, Achim. *Bruno*, 2110

DAVIES, Andrew (Wynford). *Conrad's War*, 2723

ENDE, Michael. *Momo*, 1341

HOFFMANN, E(rnst) T(heodor) A(madeus). *The Nutcracker*, 2933

KORSCHUNOW, Irina. *Adam Draws Himself a Dragon*, 2520

MONACO, Richard. *Journey to the Flame*, 2025

PREUSSLER, Otfried. *The Robber Hotzenplotz*, 2280; *The Satanic Mill*, 3107

SIEBE, Josephine. *Kasperle's Adventures*, 2953

SOMMER-BODENBURG, Angela. *My Friend the Vampire*, 2308

SYMONS, (Dorothy) Geraldine. *Crocuses Were Over, Hitler Was Dead*, 2854

WIEMER, Rudolf Otto. *The Good Robber, Willibald*, 2328

WINTERFELD, Henry. *Castaways in Lilliput*, 2084

ZIMNIK, Reiner. *The Bear and the People*, 1601

Germany—5th century

PAXON, Diana L. *The Wolf and the Raven*, 1798

Germany—1284

SKURZYNSKI, Gloria (Joan). *What Happened in Hamelin*, 1837

Germany—1600

ALEXANDER, Lloyd (Chudley). *Time Cat: The Remarkable Journeys of Jason and Gareth*, 2680

Germany—17th century

PREUSSLER, Otfried. *The Satanic Mill*, 3107

Germany—Folklore

BRENTANO, Clemens Maria. *Schoolmaster Whackwell's Wonderful Sons*, 48; *The Tale of Gockel, Hinkel and Gackeliah*, 49

HAUFF, Wilhelm. *The Adventures of Little Mouk*, 135; *Dwarf Long-Nose*, 136

HOFFMANN, E(rnst) T(heodor) A(madeus). *The Strange Child*, 147

LEBERMANN, Norbert. *New German Fairy Tales*, 914

MÜNCHAUSEN, Karl. *The Adventures of Baron Münchausen*, 2255

NAPOLI, Donna Jo. *The Magic Circle*, 3096

PAXON, Diana L. *The Wolf and the Raven*, 1798

PREUSSLER, Otfried. *The Wise Men of Schilda*, 2281

SKURZYNSKI, Gloria (Joan). *What Happened in Hamelin*, 1837

Germany—Hamelin

HUDDY, Delia. *Time Piper*, 1720

Germany—Nazi era

MOORCOCK, Michael (John). *The Dragon in the Sword*, 1477

Germany—World War I

MONACO, Richard. *Journey to the Flame*, 2025

Ghatti's Tale series

GREENO, Gayle. *Finders-Seekers*, 1368

Ghosts

BRADBURY, Ray (Douglas). *The Toynbee Convector*, 811

Giants

ALDEN, Raymond Macdonald. *Why the Chimes Rang and Other Stories*, 777

Bestiary!, 796

BOSTON, L(ucy) M(aria Wood). *The River at Green Knowe*, 2371

BOURLIAGUET, Léonce. *The Giant Who Drank from His Shoe and Other Stories*, 804

BRENTANO, Clemens Maria. *Schoolmaster Whackwell's Wonderful Sons*, 48

CURLEY, Daniel. *Billy Beg and the Bull*, 1655

DAHL, Roald. *The BFG*, 2132

DAVIDSON, Lionel. *Under Plum Lake*, 1932

DICKINSON, Peter (pseud. of Malcolm de Brissac). *Giant Cold*, 95

DU BOIS, William (Sherman) Pène. *The Giant*, 2148

ENRIGHT, Elizabeth (Wright). *Tatsinda*, 104

ESTES, Eleanor (Ruth Rosenfeld). *The Sleeping Giant and Other Stories*, 851

FALKBERGET, Johan (Petter). *Broomstick and Snowflake*, 107

FLORA, James (Royer). *Wanda and the Bumbly Wizard*, 3017

GARDNER, Craig Shaw. *A Disagreement with Death*, 3023

GARDNER, John (Champlin) (Jr.). *Dragon, Dragon, and Other Timeless Tales*, 871

GORDON, John (William). *The Giant under the Snow: A Story of Suspense*, 1699

GOUDGE, Elizabeth (de Beauchamp). *Linnets and Valerians*, 2464

HARRISON, David Lee. *The Book of Giant Stories*, 886

HEARNE, Betsy (Gould). *South Star*, 1378

HOUGH, (Helen) Charlotte (Woodyatt). *Red Biddy and Other Stories*, 893

HUGHES, Ted (Edward James). *The Iron Giant: A Story in Five Nights*, 156

JOHNSON, Elizabeth. *The Little Knight*, 161

JONES, Diana Wynne. *The Power of Three*, 1733

KENNEDY, (Jerome) Richard. *Inside My Feet: The Story of a Giant*, 172

KRENSKY, Stephen (Alan). *The Perils of Putney*, 186

MANNING, Rosemary (Joy). *Dragon in Danger*, 2249

MAYHAR, Ardath. *The Saga of Grittel Sundotha*, 1470

MAYNE, William (James Carter). *The Blue Boat*, 2563

MONATH, Elizabeth. *Topper and the Giant*, 2569

NORTON, Mary (Pearson). *Are All the Giants Dead?*, 2041

REID BANKS, Lynne. *The Magic Hare*, 669

SALVATORE, R. A. *The Woods Out Back*, 2056

SENDAK, Philip. *In Grandpa's House*, 291

SLOBODKIN, Louis. *The Amiable Giant*, 302

SWIFT, Jonathan. *Gulliver's Travels into Several Remote Nations of the World*, 2069

THURBER, James (Grover). *The Great Quillow*, 326

WANGERIN, Walter, Jr. *The Book of the Dun Cow*, 344

WEIS, Margaret, and HICKMAN, Tracy. *Dragon Wing*, 1574

WETTERER, Margaret K. *The Giant's Apprentice*, 352

WILDE, Oscar (pseud. of Fingal O'Flahertie Wills). *The Selfish Giant*, 357

WILKINS (Freeman), Mary E(leanor). *The Pumpkin Giant*, 360

William Mayne's Book of Giants, 988

WILLIAMS, Tad. *The Dragonbone Chair*, 1583

YOLEN (Stemple), Jane H(yatt). *The Bird of Time*, 370

YOLEN (Stemple), Jane H(yatt). *The Giants' Farm*, 2334

ZETTNER, Pat. *The Shadow Warrior*, 1600

Glass Mistress series

EASTON, M. Coleman. *The Fisherman's Curse*, 1329

Gnomes

AULAIRE, Ingri Mortenson d', and AULAIRE, Edgar Parin d'. *D'Aulaires' Trolls*, 785

B. B. (pseud. of D(enys) J(ames) Watkins-Pitchford). *The Little Grey Men*, 1253

BOWEN, William A(lvin). *Merrimeg*, 1907

BROOKS, Terry. *The Sword of Shannara*, 1273

DE LINT, Charles. *Yarrow: An Autumn Tale*, 1936

FALKBERGET, Johan (Petter). *Broomstick and Snowflake*, 107

FORST, S. *Pipkin*, 116

HOFFMANN, E(rnst) T(heodor) A(madeus). *The Strange Child*, 147

HOUSMAN, Laurence. *The Rat-Catcher's Daughter: A Collection of Stories*, 896

HUNT, Marigold. *Hester and the Gnomes*, 2497

JANSSON, Tove (Marika). *Finn Family Moomintroll*, 1388

Goblins

BANCROFT, Alberta. *The Goblins of Haubeck*, 33

BRIGGS, K(atharine) M(ary). *Hobberdy Dick*, 1623

CARRYL, Charles Edward. *Davy and the Goblin, or What Followed Reading "Alice's Adventures in Wonderland,"* 1915

A Cavalcade of Goblins, 820

CHERRYH, C. J. (pseud. of Carolyn Janice Cherry). *The Goblin Mirror*, 1288

DE LINT, Charles. *Dreams Underfoot: The Newford Collection*, 1315

EDGERTON, Teresa. *Goblin Moon*, 3010

Ghosts: An Anthology, 1086

KRENSKY, Stephen (Alan). *A Big Day for Scepters*, 185

LINDGREN, Astrid. *Ronia, the Robber's Daughter*, 1436

MacDONALD, George. *The Princess and the Goblin*, 224

MAYNE, William (James Carter). *The Blue Boat*, 2563

SALVATORE, R. A. *The Woods Out Back*, 2056

ZETTNER, Pat. *The Shadow Warrior*, 1600

Gods of Ireland series

FLYNN, Casey. *Most Ancient Song*, 1678

Godsland

BABBITT, Lucy Cullyford. *Where the Truth Lies*, 1255

The Golem

HARRISON, M(ichael) John. *The Pastel City*, 1376

ISH-KISHOR, Sulamith. *The Master of Miracle: A New Novel of the Golem*, 1726

SINGER, Isaac Bashevis. *The Golem*, 1836

WIESEL, Elie(zer). *The Golem; the Story of a Legend*, 1866

Gorhaut

KAY, Guy Gavriel. *A Song for Arbonne*, 1398

Grand Fenwick series
WIBBERLEY, Leonard (Patrick O'Connor). *The Mouse That Roared*, 2327
The Great Land
MOON, Sheila (Elizabeth). *Knee-Deep in Thunder*, 2026
Greece
PATON WALSH, Jill. *Torch*, 1490
PURTILL, Richard. *Enchantment at Delphi*, 1807
WOLFE, Gene (Rodman). *Soldier of the Mist*, 1586
Greece—Alexandrian period
TARR, Judith. *Lord of the Two Lands*, 1850
Greece—Alternate ancient history
TOWNSEND, John Rowe. *The Fortunate Isles*, 1557
Greece—Ancient. *See also* Olympic Games
ALCOCK, Vivien (Dolores). *Singer to the Sea God*, 1604
RAY, Mary (Eva Pedder). *The Golden Bees*, 1504
WOLFE, Gene (Rodman). *Soldier of the Mist*, 1586
Greece—Mythology
ALCOCK, Vivien (Dolores). *Singer to the Sea God*, 1604
BENCHLEY, Nathaniel (Goddard). *Demo and the Dolphin*, 1611
BRADLEY, Marion Zimmer. *The Firebrand*, 1617
BRADSHAW, Gillian (Marucha). *Beyond the North Wind*, 1620
BRINDEL, June Rachuy. *Ariadne*, 1625
COOLIDGE, Olivia E(nsor). *The King of Men*, 1648
DEXTER, Catherine. *The Oracle Doll*, 2908
GARFIELD, Leon, and BLISHEN, Edward. *The God Beneath the Sea*, 1688; *The Golden Shadows: A Recreation of Greek Legends*, 1689
HOOVER, H(elen) M(ary). *The Dawn Palace: The Story of Medea*, 1719
JOHNSON, Dorothy M(arie). *Witch Princess*, 1728
JOHNSTON, Norma. *Pride of Lions: The Story of the House of Atreus*, 1729; *Strangers Dark and Gold*, 1730
KEANEY, Brian. *No Need for Heroes*, 1736
ORLOCK, Carol (Ellen). *The Goddess Letters: The Demeter-Persephone Myth Retold*, 1792
PURTILL, Richard. *Enchantment at Delphi*, 1807
RENAULT, Mary (pseud. of Mary Challans). *The King Must Die*, 1813
SEYMOUR, Miranda (pseud. of Miranda Sinclair). *Medea*, 1833
SPRINGER, Nancy. *The Friendship Song*, 2063

VALENCAK, Hannelore. *When Half-Gods Go*, 1856
VAUGHAN, Agnes Carr. *Lucian Goes A-Voyaging*, 2322
Greece—Pre-Alexandrian
GEMMELL, David. *Lion of Macedon*, 1694
Greece—World War II
PURTILL, Richard. *Enchantment at Delphi*, 1807
Greek folklore
MAYER, Marianna. *The Sorcerer's Apprentice: A Greek Fable*, 1770
Green Knowe books
BOSTON, L(ucy) M(aria Wood). *The Children of Green Knowe*, 1031
Green Lion trilogy
EDGERTON, Teresa. *Child of Saturn*, 3009
Green-Sky trilogy
SNYDER, Zilpha Keatley. *Below the Root*, 1532
Griffins (gryphons)
BELDEN, Wilianne Schneider. *Frankie!*, 2358
Bestiary!, 796
BRADSHAW, Gillian (Marucha). *Beyond the North Wind*, 1620
KROEBER, Theodora (Kracow). *Carrousel*, 2942
McHARGUE, Georgess. *Stoneflight*, 2552
ORMONDROYD, Edward. *David and the Phoenix*, 2590
Phoenix Feathers: A Collection of Mythical Monsters, 941
PIERCE, Meredith Ann. *Birth of the Firebringer*, 1492
PIERCE, Tamora. *Wild Magic: The Immortals*, 1496
STOCKTON, Frank (Francis) R(ichard). *The Griffin and the Minor Canon*, 313
WERSBA, Barbara. *The Land of Forgotten Beasts*, 2074
WILLARD, Nancy (Margaret). *The Sorcerer's Apprentice*, 3137
Grollicans
HUNTER, Mollie (pseud. of Maureen Mollie Hunter McVeigh McIlwraith). *The Wicked One*, 2500
Guardians of the Flame series
ROSENBERG, Joel. *The Sleeping Dragon*, 2051
Guatemalan Trouble Dolls
BUFFETT, Jimmy, and BUFFETT, Savannah Jane. *Trouble Dolls*, 2899
Guinevere trilogy
NEWMAN, Sharan. *Guinevere*, 1783
WOOLLEY, Persia. *Child of the Northern Spring*, 1873
Gwyn Griffiths trilogy
NIMMO, Jenny. *The Snow Spider*, 2581

Gwynedd
KURTZ, Katherine. *The Bishop's Heir*, 1412; *The Harrowing of Gwynedd*, 1414
Gypsyworld
THOMPSON, Julian F(rancis). *Gypsyworld*, 2071

Hakhans
EASTON, M. Coleman. *Spirits of Cavern and Hearth*, 1330
Halfblood Chronicles
NORTON, André, and LACKEY, Mercedes. *The Elvenbane: An Epic Fantasy of the Halfblood Chronicles*, 3100
Halloween
KEHRET, Peg. *Horror at the Haunted House*, 1116
UPDIKE, David. *An Autumn Tale*, 2652
Handful of Men tetralogy
DUNCAN, Dave. *The Cutting Edge*, 1327
Hansel and Gretel
NAPOLI, Donna Jo. *The Magic Circle*, 3096
Harper-Hall trilogy
McCAFFREY, Anne (Inez). *Dragonsong*, 1448
Harry Cat books
SELDEN (Thompson), George. *The Cricket in Times Square*, 686
Haunting with Louisa trilogy
CATES, Emily. *The Ghost in the Attic*, 1045
Hawthorne, Nathaniel
SAN SOUCI, Robert D., reteller. *Feathertop: Based on the Tale by Nathaniel Hawthorne*, 3113
Hed
McKILLIP, Patricia A(nne). *The Riddle-Master of Hed*, 1457
Heirs of Saint Camber trilogy
KURTZ, Katherine. *The Harrowing of Gwynedd*, 1414
Heralds of Valdemar trilogy
LACKEY, Mercedes. *Arrows of the Queen*, 1415
Hidden folk
WISNIEWSKI, David. *Elfwyn's Saga*, 367
Histories of King Kelson
KURTZ, Katherine. *The Bishop's Heir*, 1412
History of Middle-Earth
TOLKIEN, J(ohn) R(onald) R(euel). *The Fellowship of the Ring*, 1555
Hlanter
ANTHONY, Piers (pseud. of Piers A. D. Jacob). *Virtual Mode*, 1889
Hobbits
TOLKIEN, J(ohn) R(onald) R(euel). *The Hobbit; Or, There and Back Again*, 1556
Holocaust
YOLEN (Stemple), Jane H(yatt). *Briar Rose*, 1879; *The Devil's Arithmetic*, 2880

Holy Grail. *See also* Arthur, King of Britain
ATTANASIO, A(lfred) A(ngelo). *Kingdom of the Grail*, 1607
Homana
ROBERSON, Jennifer. *A Pride of Princes*, 1509
Homosexuality
LACKEY, Mercedes. *Magic's Pawn*, 1417
MacAVOY, R(oberta) A(nn). *Lens of the World*, 1445
Hookywalker
MAHY, Margaret (May). *The Pirates' Mixed-Up Voyage: Dark Doings in the Thousand Islands*, 2245
Hound and the Falcon trilogy
TARR, Judith. *The Isle of Glass*, 1551
Hounds of God series
TARR, Judith. *Alamut*, 1548
Hungary—1930s
GOLDSTEIN, Lisa. *The Red Magician*, 3026
Hungary—Folklore
BRUST, Steven K. (Zoltan). *Brokedown Palace*, 1626
GOLDSTEIN, Lisa. *The Red Magician*, 3026
SEREDY, Kate. *The White Stag*, 1828
Hydrangea
WATT-EVANS, Lawrence, and FRIESNER, Esther M. *Split Heirs*, 1572
Hylor
WILDER, Cherry (pseud. of Cherry Barbara Lockett Grimm). *A Princess of the Chameln*, 1579

Ianon
TARR, Judith. *The Hall of the Mountain King*, 1550
Ice Age
BRENNAN, J. H. *Shiva: An Adventure of the Ice Age*, 1622
Icelandic sagas. *See also* Norse mythology
WISNIEWSKI, David. *Elfwyn's Saga*, 367
Idaho—1960
WYSS, Thelma Hatch. *A Stranger Here*, 1227
Illinois
WOLFE, Gene. *Castleview*, 1872
Illyria
MOORE, John. *Slay and Rescue*, 1776
Imkaira
ALTON, Andrea I. *Demon of Undoing*, 1243
The Immortals series
PIERCE, Tamora. *Wild Magic: The Immortals*, 1496
Impire
DUNCAN, Dave. *The Cutting Edge*, 1327
Imps
BINNS, Archie (Fred). *The Radio Imp*, 2366

Incarnations of Immortality series
ANTHONY, Piers (pseud. of Piers A. D. Jacob). *On a Pale Horse*, 1249

Incest
LACKEY, Mercedes, and LISLE, Holly. *When the Bough Breaks*, 2003
McKINLEY, (Jennifer Carolyn) Robin (Turrell). *Deerskin*, 1764
WEIN, Elizabeth E. *The Winter Prince*, 1861

India
GAUTIER, (Louise) Judith. *The Memoirs of a White Elephant*, 517
HODGES, Elizabeth Jamison. *The Three Princes of Serendip*, 146
KARPIN, Florence. *The Prince in the Golden Tower*, 164
KIPLING, (Joseph) Rudyard. *The Jungle Book*, 579; *Phantoms and Fantasies: Twenty Tales*, 1120; *Rikki-Tikki-Tavi*, 581
MORPURGO, Michael. *King of the Cloud Forests*, 1777
MUNDY, Talbot (pseud. of William Lancaster Gribbon). *OM, The Secret of Abhor Valley*, 2027
SHARMA, Partap. *The Surangini Tales*, 295

India—1920s
MUNDY, Talbot (pseud. of William Lancaster Gribbon). *OM, The Secret of Abhor Valley*, 2027

India—Folklore
HODGES, Elizabeth Jamison. *The Three Princes of Serendip*, 146
KIPLING, (Joseph) Rudyard. *Kipling's Fantasy*, 909
LEE, Tanith. *Tamastara; or the Indian Nights*, 1748

Indiana—South Bend
GOODWIN, Marie D. *Where the Towers Pierce the Sky*, 2743

Indigo series
COOPER, Louise. *Nemesis*, 1303

Inquestor trilogy
SUCHARITKUL, Somtow. *Utopia Hunters: Chronicles of the High Inquest*, 1546

Inuits
HOUSTON, James A(rchibald). *Spirit Wrestler*, 3041
KORTUM, Jeanie. *Ghost Vision*, 3065
LUENN, Nancy. *Arctic Unicorn*, 3080
PIERCE, Meredith Ann. *The Woman Who Loved Reindeer*, 1494

Iowa
GREENBURG, Dan. *Young Santa*, 2184
SERVICE, Pamela F. *Weirdos of the Universe, Unite!*, 1830
THOMAS, Jane Resh. *The Princess in the Pigpen*, 2857

Iran. *See also* Persia
HODGES, Elizabeth Jamison. *The Three Princes of Serendip*, 146

Iraq
BENJAMIN, Alan. *Appointment*, 38

Ireland. *See also* Ireland—Celtic folklore
BRANDEL, Marc (pseud. of Marcus Beresford). *The Mine of Lost Days*, 2705
CASSERLEY, Anne Thomasine. *Barney the Donkey*, 440; *Michael of Ireland*, 816; *Roseen*, 441
COLUM, Padraic. *The Big Tree of Bunlahy: Stories of My Own Countryside*, 827; *The King of Ireland's Son*, 70; *The Peep-Show Man*, 829; *The Stone of Victory and Other Tales*, 830
CREGAN, Maírín. *Old John*, 463
DIXON, Marjorie (Mack). *The Forbidden Island*, 1666
FLINT, Kenneth C. *The Dark Druid*, 1676
GATE, Ethel May. *Tales from the Enchanted Isles*, 875
GREEN, Kathleen. *Leprechaun Tales*, 882; *Philip and the Pooka and Other Irish Fairy Tales*, 883
HAUGAARD, Erik Christian. *Prince Boghole*, 137
HEATH, W(illiam) L. *The Earthquake Man*, 141
HUNTER, Mollie (pseud. of Maureen Mollie Hunter McVeigh McIlwraith). *The Smartest Man in Ireland*, 2201
KING-SMITH, Dick. *Paddy's Pot of Gold*, 2515
LEAMY, Edmund. *The Fairy Minstrel of Glenmalure, and Other Stories for Children*, 912; *The Golden Spears and Other Fairy Tales*, 913
LEVIN, Betty (Lowenthal). *The Sword of Culann*, 2776
LLYWELYN, Morgan. *Bard: The Odyssey of the Irish*, 1754; *The Elementals*, 214
LOCKLEY, Ronald Mathias. *The Seal-Woman*, 1759
LYNCH, Patricia (Nora). *Brogeen Follows the Magic Tune*, 217; *The Turf-Cutter's Donkey: An Irish Story of Mystery and Adventure*, 2546
MacAVOY, R(oberta) A(nn). *The Book of Kells*, 2787; *The Grey Horse*, 3082
McDONALD, Ian. *King of Morning, Queen of Day*, 1762
McGOWEN, Tom (Thomas E.). *The Shadow of Fomor*, 2014
MASON, Arthur. *The Wee Men of Ballywooden*, 2561
MELLING, O(rla) R. *The Singing Stone*, 2799
O'FAOLÁIN, Eileen (Gould). *The Little Black Hen; An Irish Fairy Story*, 2588
PAXON, Diana L., and MARTINE-BARNES, Adrienne. *Master of Earth and Water*, 1799

SHURA, Mary Francis (pseud. of Mary Francis Craig). *A Shoe Full of Shamrock*, 2633

STEPHENS, James. *The Crock of Gold*, 310

TANNEN, Mary. *The Wizard Children of Finn*, 2856

Ireland—4th century

FLINT, Kenneth C. *Cromm*, 1675

Ireland—411 A.D.

ALEXANDER, Lloyd (Chudley). *Time Cat: The Remarkable Journeys of Jason and Gareth*, 2680

Ireland—10th century

LLYWELYN, Morgan. *Lion of Ireland: The Legend of Brian Boru*, 1757

MacAVOY, R(oberta) A(nn). *The Book of Kells*, 2787

Ireland—19th century

The Crafters, 2998

Ireland—1870s

BRANDEL, Marc (pseud. of Marcus Beresford). *The Mine of Lost Days*, 2705

Ireland—Celtic era

COLUM, Padraic. *The King of Ireland's Son*, 70

GREELEY, Andrew M(oran). *The Magic Cup: An Irish Legend*, 1702

LEVIN, Betty (Lowenthal). *The Sword of Culann*, 2776

LLYWELYN, Morgan. *Bard: The Odyssey of the Irish*, 1754

MELLING, O(rla) R. *The Singing Stone*, 2799

REEVES, James (pseud. of John Morris Reeves). *Maildun the Voyager*, 1811

TANNEN, Mary. *The Wizard Children of Finn*, 2856

Ireland—Celtic folklore

AMOSS, Berthe. *Lost Magic*, 2964

BEAR, Greg(ory Dale). *The Infinity Concerto*, 1899

BUCHAN, John. *The Watcher by the Threshold and Other Tales*, 1629

CHANT, Joy (pseud. of Eileen Joyce Rutter). *The High Kings*, 1635

COLLINS, Meghan. *The Willow Maiden*, 1646

COOPER (Grant), Susan (Mary). *Tam Lin*, 1652

CURRY, Ann. *The Book of Brendan*, 1656

DEITZ, Tom. *Windmaster's Bane*, 1934

FLINT, Kenneth C. *Cromm*, 1675; *The Riders of the Sidhe*, 1677

FLYNN, Casey. *Most Ancient Song*, 1678

FRIESNER, Esther M. *Druid's Blood*, 1355

GARDEN, Nancy. *Fours Crossing*, 1684

GODWIN, Parke. *Beloved Exile*, 1696

GUARD, David. *Deirdre: A Celtic Legend*, 1705

HAZEL, Paul. *Yearwood*, 1377

KENNEALY (Morrison), Patricia. *The Hawk's Gray Feather: A Book of the Keltiad*, 1737

KERR, Katharine. *Daggerspell*, 3061; *A Time of Exile: A Novel of the Westlands*, 1405

LAWHEAD, Stephen R. *The Silver Hand*, 1743

LEVIN, Betty (Lowenthal). *The Sword of Culann*, 2776

LIVELY, Penelope (Margaret Low). *The Wild Hunt of the Ghost Hounds*, 1753

LLYWELYN, Morgan. *Bard: The Odyssey of the Irish*, 1754; *Druids*, 1755; *The Horse Goddess*, 3078; *The Isles of the Blest*, 1756; *Red Branch*, 1758

MacAVOY, R(oberta) A(nn). *The Book of Kells*, 2787

MAYER, Marianna. *The Black Horse*, 1768; *Noble-Hearted Kate: A Celtic Tale*, 1769

NORMAN, Roger. *Albion's Dream: A Novel of Terror*, 1785

PATTOU, Edith. *Hero's Song*, 1796

PAXON, Diana L. *The Serpent's Tooth*, 1797

PAXON, Diana L., and MARTINE-BARNES, Adrienne. *Master of Earth and Water*, 1799

PECK, Sylvia. *Seal Child*, 1800

POLLAND, Madeleine A(ngela Cahill). *Deirdre*, 1805

RAYNER, William. *Stag Boy*, 1809

SPRINGER, Nancy. *Chains of Gold*, 1536

STEPHENS, James. *Deirdre*, 1840

TOLSTOY, Nikolai. *The Coming of the King: The First Book of Merlin*, 1854

WALKER, Mary Alexander. *The Scathach and Maeve's Daughters*, 1859

WELLMAN, Manly Wade. *The Old Gods Waken*, 1863

Ireland—Folklore

COLUM, Padraic. *The Big Tree of Bunlahy: Stories of My Own Countryside*, 827; *The King of Ireland's Son*, 70; *The Stone of Victory and Other Tales*, 830

CURLEY, Daniel. *Billy Beg and the Bull*, 1655

FLINT, Kenneth C. *Cromm*, 1675; *The Dark Druid*, 1676

FLYNN, Casey. *Most Ancient Song*, 1678

GATE, Ethel May. *Tales from the Enchanted Isles*, 875

GREELEY, Andrew M(oran). *The Magic Cup: An Irish Legend*, 1702

LEAMY, Edmund. *The Fairy Minstrel of Glenmalure, and Other Stories for Children*, 912; *The Golden Spears and Other Fairy Tales*, 913

LLYWELYN, Morgan. *The Isles of Blest*, 1756; *Lion of Ireland: The Legend of Brian Boru*, 1757; *Red Branch*, 1758

LOCKLEY, Ronald Mathias. *The Seal-Woman*, 1759

McGOWEN, Tom (Thomas E.). *The Shadow of Fomor*, 2014

REEVES, James (pseud. of John Morris Reeves). *Maildun the Voyager*, 1811

STEPHENS, James. *The Crock of Gold*, 310

Ireland—Middle Ages
HAUGAARD, Erik Christian. *Prince Boghole*,
137
Irissa and Kendric trilogy
DOUGLAS, Carole Nelson. *Exiles of the Rynth*,
3004
Iron Tower trilogy
McKIERAN, Dennis L. *Dragondoom*, 1451
Isle
SPRINGER, Nancy. *The Sable Moon*, 1538
Israel
LEVIN, Meyer. *The Spell of Time: A Tale of Love
in Jerusalem*, 206
Italy. *See also* Roman Empire
BUZZATI, Dino. *The Bears' Famous Invasion of
Sicily*, 436
CLARKE, Pauline (pseud. of Pauline [Clarke]
Hunter Blair). *The Two Faces of Silenus*, 1639
COLLODI, Carlo (pseud. of Carlo Lorenzini).
The Adventures of Pinocchio, 2905
ESTES, Eleanor (Ruth Rosenfeld). *Miranda the
Great*, 495
FANCIULLI, Guiseppe. *The Little Blue Man*,
2916
FARJEON, Eleanor. *Italian Peepshow and Other
Tales*, 860
MENOTTI, Gian Carlo. *Amahl and the Night
Visitors*, 1774
NICHOLS, (Joanna) Ruth. *The Left-Handed
Spirit*, 3098
OSBORNE, M(aurice) M(achado) (Jr.). *Rudi and
the Mayor of Naples*, 644
ROCCA, Guido. *Gaetano the Pheasant: A
Hunting Fable*, 674
VAMBA (pseud. of Luigi Bertelli). *The Prince
and His Ants*, 2654
Italy—14th century
MacAVOY, R(oberta) A(nn). *Damiano*, 3081
Italy—1468
ALEXANDER, Lloyd (Chudley). *Time Cat: The
Remarkable Journeys of Jason and Gareth*,
2680
Italy—Alternate Renaissance period
BUJOLD, Lois McMaster. *The Spirit Ring*, 1276
Italy—Renaissance period
LEE, Tanith. *Sung in Shadow*, 1432
WOODRUFF, Elvira. *The Disappearing Bike
Shop*, 2879
Italy—Venice—16th century
MORPURGO, Michael. *Jo-Jo the Melon
Donkey*, 247
Italy—Venice—Renaissance period
CLÉMENT, Claude. *The Voice of the Wood*, 63
Ithkar
Magic in Ithkar, 1463
Ivory series
EGAN, Doris. *The Gate of Ivory*, 1335

"Jack and the Beanstalk," adaptations of
DE LINT, Charles. *Jack the Giant-Killer*, 1663
Japan
WISNIEWSKI, David. *The Warrior and the Wise
Man*, 368
Japan—998 A.D.
ALEXANDER, Lloyd (Chudley). *Time Cat: The
Remarkable Journeys of Jason and Gareth*,
2680
Japan—Alternate 10th-century Heian period
DALKEY, Kara. *The Nightingale*, 1659
Japan—Alternate ancient history
RUSSELL, Sean. *The Initiate Brother*, 1515
Japan—Folklore
COATSWORTH, Elizabeth (Jane). *The Cat Who
Went to Heaven*, 64
LIFTON, Betty Jean (Kirschner). *The Cock and
the Ghost Cat*, 1129; *The Dwarf Pine Tree*,
210; *The One-Legged Ghost*, 2229
OGIWARA, Noriko. *Dragon Sword and Wind
Child*, 1790
Japan—Hokusai period
BLAYLOCK, James P(aul). *The Paper Grail*,
1616
Jerusalem
LEVIN, Meyer. *The Spell of Time: A Tale of Love
in Jerusalem*, 206
Jerusalem—12th century
ATTANASIO, A(lfred) A(ngelo). *Kingdom of the
Grail*, 1607
Jerusalem—Alternate Medieval period
TARR, Judith. *Alamut*, 1548
Jewish folklore
ISH-KISHOR, Sulamith. *The Master of Miracle:
A New Novel of the Golem*, 1726
SINGER, Isaac Bashevis. *Alone in the Wild
Forest*, 298; *The Fearsome Inn*, 299; *The
Golem*, 1836; *Naftali the Storyteller and His
Horse, Sus, and Other Stories*, 959; *A Tale of
Three Wishes*, 300; *Zlateh the Goat and Other
Stories*, 961
SOYER, Abraham. *The Adventures of Yemima*,
963
WIESEL, Elie(zer). *The Golem; the Story of a
Legend*, 1866
Jewish life, prewar Eastern Europe
SENDAK, Philip. *In Grandpa's House*, 291
Jews. *See also* Holocaust; Israel
ATTANASIO, A(lfred) A(ngelo). *Kingdom of the
Grail*, 1607
FRIESNER, Esther M. *Yesterday We Saw
Mermaids*, 1681
GOLDSTEIN, Lisa. *The Red Magician*, 3026
KUSHNER, Donn. *Uncle Jacob's Ghost Story*,
188
LEVIN, Meyer. *The Spell of Time: A Tale of Love
in Jerusalem*, 206
PRANTERA, Amanda. *The Cabalist*, 3105

Wandering Stars: An Anthology of Jewish Fantasy and Science Fiction, 979
YOLEN (Stemple), Jane H(yatt). *Briar Rose*, 1879
YOLEN (Stemple), Jane H(yatt). *The Devil's Arithmetic*, 2880
Jingrim/Ramsden series
MUNDY, Talbot (pseud. of William Lancaster Gribbon). *OM, The Secret of Abhor Valley*, 2027
Jinian trilogy
TEPPER, Sheri S. *Jinian Footseer*, 1552
Johnny Dixon series
BELLAIRS, John. *The Trolley to Yesterday*, 2695
Journey Once Begun series
BAKKEN, Harald. *The Fields and the Hills*, 1256

Kansas—1940s
JONES, David Lee. *Unicorn Highway*, 2509
Karintepe
CLAYTON, Jo. *Shadowspeer*, 1297
Karmiss
LEE, Tanith. *Anackire*, 1424
"Kate Crackernuts," adaptations of
MAYER, Marianna. *Noble-Hearted Kate: A Celtic Tale*, 1769
Kay Harker books
MASEFIELD, John (Edward). *The Midnight Folk*, 2560
Kedrigern series
MORRESSY, John. *A Voice for Princess*, 3093
Keltia
KENNEALY (Morrison), Patricia. *The Copper Crown*, 1404; *The Hawk's Gray Feather: A Book of the Keltiad*, 1737
Kemi
HARRIS, Rosemary (Jeanne). *The Moon in the Cloud*, 1711
Kencyrs
HODGELL, P(atricia) C(hristine). *God Stalk*, 1382
Kendark
MARTIN, Graham Dunstan. *Giftwish*, 1466
Kender
WEIS, Margaret, and HICKMAN, Tracy. *DragonLance Legends*, 1576
Kentucky
LEWIS, J. Patrick. *The Moonbow of Mr. B. Bones*, 208
Kerovan and Joisan books
NORTON, André (pseud. of Alice Mary Norton). *The Crystal Gryphon*, 1486
Khentor series
CHANT, Joy (pseud. of Eileen Joyce Rutter). *Red Moon and Black Mountain: The End of the House of Kendreth*, 1916

Ki series
LINDHOLM, Megan. *Luck of the Wheels*, 1437
King Arthur quartet
PYLE, Howard. *The Story of King Arthur and His Knights*, 1808
King Arthur trilogy
BRADSHAW, Gillian (Marucha). *Hawk of May*, 1621
SUTCLIFF, Rosemary. *The Sword and the Circle: King Arthur and the Knights of the Round Table*, 1843
King Lear
PAXON, Diana L. *The Serpent's Tooth*, 1797
King of Ys series
ANDERSON, Poul, and ANDERSON, Karen. *Gallicenae*, 1247
Kingdom of Faery
Faery!, 854
Kubal
MURPHY, Shirley Rousseau. *The Ring of Fire*, 1482

The Land
DONALDSON, Stephen R(upert). *Lord Foul's Bane*, 1940
The Land Between the Mountains
KENDALL, Carol. *The Gammage Cup*, 1402
Landover
BROOKS, Terry. *Magic Kingdom for Sale—Sold!*, 2112
Lapland
DONEHOWER, Bruce. *Miko, Little Hunter of the North*, 100
Last Herald Mage trilogy
LACKEY, Mercedes. *Magic's Pawn*, 1417
Leprechauns
BAKER, Margaret. *Patsy and the Leprechauns*, 2348
BRITTAIN, Bill (William). *All the Money in the World*, 2109
GREEN, Kathleen. *Leprechaun Tales*, 882
HUTCHINS, Hazel (J.). *The Three and Many Wishes of Jason Reid*, 2503
JOHNSON, Elizabeth. *Stuck with Luck*, 2508
KENNEDY, (Jerome) Richard. *The Leprechaun's Story*, 173
KING-SMITH, Dick. *Paddy's Pot of Gold*, 2515
LYNCH, Patricia (Nora). *Brogeen Follows the Magic Tune*, 217; *The Turf-Cutter's Donkey: An Irish Story of Mystery and Adventure*, 2546
NIXON, Joan Lowery. *The Gift*, 2582
ORMONDROYD, Edward. *David and the Phoenix*, 2590
PATTEN, Brian. *Mr. Moon's Last Case*, 2596
PAYNE, Joan Balfour (Dicks). *The Leprechaun of Bayou Luce*, 2597
SALVATORE, R. A. *The Woods Out Back*, 2056

SAWYER, Ruth. *The Enchanted Schoolhouse*, 2621

SHURA, Mary Francis (pseud. of Mary Francis Craig). *A Shoe Full of Shamrock*, 2633

STEPHENS, James. *The Crock of Gold*, 310

TOLLE, Jean Bashor. *The Great Pete Penney*, 2648

WIBBERLEY, Leonard (Patrick O'Connor). *McGillicuddy McGotham*, 2326

Lewis Barnavelt series
BELLAIRS, John. *The House with a Clock in Its Walls*, 1026

Liavek
Liavek, 1435

Lilliputians
SWIFT, Jonathan. *Gulliver's Travels into Several Remote Nations of the World*, 2069

WHITE, T(erence) H(anbury). *Mistress Masham's Repose*, 2663

WINTERFELD, Henry. *Castaways in Lilliput*, 2084

Lithia
LEVY, Robert. *Escape from Exile*, 2006

"The Little Mermaid," adaptations of
GUY, Rosa (Cuthbert). *My Love, My Love, or, the Peasant Girl*, 1706

"Little Red Riding Hood," adaptations of
STORR, Catherine (Cole). *Clever Polly and the Stupid Wolf*, 2315

The Living God
DUNCAN, Dave. *The Cutting Edge*, 1327

Lord Darcy series
GARRETT, Randall. *Lord Darcy Investigates*, 1359

Lord of the Rings trilogy
TOLKIEN, J(ohn) R(onald) R(euel). *The Fellowship of the Ring*, 1555

The Lost Sea
YEP, Laurence M(ichael). *Dragon of the Lost Sea*, 1595

Lost Swords series
SABERHAGEN, Fred. *The First Book of Lost Swords: Woundhealer's Story*, 1517

Louisiana
KOVACS, Deborah. *Brewster's Courage*, 584

Louisiana—1855
KARR, Kathleen. *Gideon and the Mummy Professor*, 2513

Lower Forest
LISLE, Janet Taylor. *Forest*, 211

Lyonesse series
VANCE, Jack (pseud. of John Holbrook Vance). *Suldrun's Garden*, 1560

Lyra series
WREDE, Patricia C(ollins). *The Harp of Imach Thyssel*, 1589

Mabinogion, retellings of
MORRIS, Kenneth. *The Book of the Three Dragons*, 1778

Tales from the Mabinogion, 1849

WALTON, Evangeline (pseud. of Evangeline Ensley). *The Prince of Annwn*, 1860

McGurk Fantasy series
HILDICK, E(dmund) W(allace). *The Case of the Dragon in Distress: A McGurk Fantasy*, 2752

Mage Winds trilogy
LACKEY, Mercedes. *Winds of Fate*, 1418

Mages of Garillon series
HARRIS, Deborah Turner. *The Burning Stone*, 3034

Maggiar
CHERRYH, C. J. (pseud. of Carolyn Janice Cherry). *The Goblin Mirror*, 1288

"The Magic Flute," adaptations of
BRADLEY, Marion Zimmer. *Night's Daughter*, 1619

MOZART, Wolfgang Amadeus. *The Magic Flute*, 248

Magic of the Plains series
COSTIKYAN, Greg. *By the Sword: Magic of the Plains*, 1305

Magic of Xanth series
ANTHONY, Piers (pseud. of Piers A. D. Jacob). *A Spell for Chameleon*, 1250

Magic Shop books
COVILLE, Bruce. *Jennifer Murdley's Toad*, 2406; *Jeremy Thatcher, Dragon Hatcher*, 2407

Magic Tree House series
OSBORNE, Mary Pope. *Dinosaurs Before Dark*, 2813

Magic trilogy
NIVEN, Larry. *The Magic Goes Away*, 1485

Magician trilogy
McGOWEN, Tom (Thomas E.). *The Magician's Apprentice*, 3084

Maine
ADKINS, Jan. *Solstice: A Mystery of the Season*, 2678

PECK, Sylvia. *Seal Child*, 1800

ZELAZNY, Roger, and SHECKLEY, Robert. *If at Faust You Don't Succeed*, 2881

Maine—1824
HOTZE, Sollace. *Acquainted with the Night*, 1109

Maine—1912
REISS, Kathryn. *Dreadful Sorry*, 2831

Maine—1970
HOTZE, Sollace. *Acquainted with the Night*, 1109

Majipoor trilogy
SILVERBERG, Robert. *Lord Valentine's Castle*, 1527

Malloreon series
EDDINGS, David. *Guardians of the West*, 1333

Mandragora
BALL, Brian. *The Quest for Queenie*, 1893
Mandrigyn
HAMBLY, Barbara. *The Ladies of Mandrigyn*, 1372
Manitou
DE LINT, Charles. *The Dreaming Place*, 1935
Manticore
TEPPER, Sheri S. *Marianne, the Magus, and the Manticore*, 2070
Maris books
MOON, Sheila (Elizabeth). *Knee-Deep in Thunder*, 2026
Martin Hopkins trilogy
HOROWITZ, Anthony. *The Devil's Door-Bell*, 3039
Massachusetts
CHENOWETH, Russ. *Shadow Walkers*, 444
CLAPP, Patricia. *Jane-Emily*, 1050
CROSS, Gilbert B. *A Witch Across Time*, 1058
DEXTER, Catherine. *The Oracle Doll*, 2908
FEIL, Hila. *Blue Moon*, 1070
LANGTON, Jane (Gillson). *The Diamond in the Window*, 2526; *The Fledgling*, 2527
LASKY (Knight), Kathryn. *Home Free*, 2769
WATKINS, Will. *Sid Seal, Houseman*, 736
Massachusetts—17th century
The Crafters, 2998
Massachusetts—1600s
LEVIN, Betty (Lowenthal). *Mercy's Mill*, 2775
Massachusetts—1775
ALEXANDER, Lloyd (Chudley). *Time Cat: The Remarkable Journeys of Jason and Gareth*, 2680
Massachusetts—1850s
LEVIN, Betty (Lowenthal). *Mercy's Mill*, 2775
Massachusetts—1862
GURNEY, James. *Dinotopia: A Land Apart from Time*, 1973
Master Li series
HUGHART, Barry. *Bridge of Birds: A Novel of an Ancient China That Never Was*, 1384
Mavin Manyshaped trilogy
TEPPER, Sheri S. *The Song of Mavin Manyshaped*, 1554
May Gray Mystery series
DUFFY, James. *The Revolt of the Teddy Bears*, 485
Mazonia
ANTHONY, Piers, and LACKEY, Mercedes. *If I Pay Thee Not in Gold*, 1251
Meged
LUENN, Nancy. *Goldclimbers*, 1442
Meldrith
SMITH, Sherwood. *Wren to the Rescue*, 1530
Melnibone
MOORCOCK, Michael (John). *The Fortress of the Pearl*, 1478

Memory, Sorrow and Thorn trilogy
WILLIAMS, Tad. *The Dragonbone Chair*, 1583
Mensandor
LAWHEAD, Stephen R. *In the Hall of the Dragon King*, 1420
Mental illness. *See also* Autism
CREW, Gary. *Strange Objects*, 1653
Merilon
WEIS, Margaret, and HICKMAN, Tracy. *Forging the Darksword*, 1577
Merlin trilogy
STEWART, Mary (Florence Elinor). *The Crystal Cave*, 1841
TOLSTOY, Nikolai. *The Coming of the King: The First Book of Merlin*, 1854
Mermaids. *See* Merpeople
Merovin
Festival Moon, 1346
Merovingen Nights series
CHERRYH, C. J. (pseud. of Carolyn Janice Cherry). *Angel with the Sword*, 1286
Festival Moon, 1346
Merpeople
AIKEN, Joan (Delano). *The Faithless Lollybird*, 765
AINSWORTH (Gilbert), Ruth (Gallard). *The Bear Who Liked Hugging People and Other Stories*, 775
ANDERSEN, Hans Christian. *The Little Mermaid*, 10
BABBITT, Natalie (Zane Moore). *The Search for Delicious*, 25
BAKER, Margaret. *The Lost Merbaby*, 31; *The Water Elf and the Miller's Child*, 2350
BAKER, Margaret Joyce. *The Magic Sea Shell*, 2351
BOSTON, L(ucy) M(aria Wood). *The Sea Egg*, 2372
CALHOUN, Mary (pseud. of Mary Huiskamp Wilkins). *Magic in the Alley*, 2387
DE LINT, Charles. *Dreams Underfoot: The Newford Collection*, 1315
DUGGAN, Maurice (Noel). *Falter Tom and the Water Boy*, 1944
HALEY, Gail E(inhart). *Sea Tale*, 133
HILL, Elizabeth Starr. *Ever-After Island*, 2487
HUNTER, Mollie (pseud. of Maureen Mollie Hunter McVeigh McIlwraith). *The Kelpie's Pearls*, 157; *The Mermaid Summer*, 2499
JARRELL, Randall. *The Animal Family*, 160
LA MOTTE FOUQUÉ, Baron Friedrich Heinrich Karl de. *Undine*, 190
MacDONALD, Greville. *Billy Barnicoat: A Fairy Romance for Young and Old*, 2549
McHARGUE, Georgess. *The Mermaid and the Whale*, 228
MacKELLAR, William. *The Smallest Monster in the World*, 2553

MELENDEZ, Francisco. *The Mermaid and the Major: or, The True Story of the Invention of the Submarine*, 2251

MORGAN, Robin. *The Mer-Child: A Legend for Children and Other Adults*, 246

NATHAN, Robert (Gruntal). *The Snowflake and the Starfish*, 3097

NESBIT (Bland), E(dith). *Wet Magic*, 2579

NIMMO, Jenny. *Ultramarine*, 1784

PICARD, Barbara Leonie. *The Mermaid and the Simpleton*, 945

POLESE, Carolyn. *Something about a Mermaid*, 2603

POPHAM, Hugh. *The Fabulous Voyage of the Pegasus*, 2278

SLOAN, Carolyn. *The Sea Child*, 1838

SLOBODKIN, Louis. *The Little Mermaid Who Could Not Sing*, 303

VAN SCYOC, Sydney J(oyce). *Drowntide*, 1563

WETTERER, Margaret K. *The Mermaid's Cape*, 353

YOLEN (Stemple), Jane H(yatt). *The Mermaid's Three Wisdoms*, 2675

YOUNG, Ella. *The Unicorn with Silver Shoes*, 2087

Meryn

MURPHY, Shirley Rousseau, and SUGGS, Welch. *Medallion of the Black Hound*, 2029

Mesmeria

ECKERT, Allan W. *The Dark Green Tunnel*, 1947

Mesmerian Annals

ECKERT, Allan W. *The Dark Green Tunnel*, 1947

Methuen

GREENO, Gayle. *Finders-Seekers*, 1368

Mexico. See also Aztec Indian tribe

LIFTON, Betty Jean (Kirschner). *Jaguar, My Twin*, 3074

Mexico—16th century

REYNOLDS, Mack, and ING, Dean. *The Other Time*, 2833

Michigan—Detroit

BURGESS, Barbara Hood. *Oren Bell*, 1038

Michigan—Upper Peninsula

WRIGHT, Betty Ren. *Ghosts Beneath Our Feet*, 1223

Middle-Earth

TOLKIEN, J(ohn) R(onald) R(euel). *The Fellowship of the Ring*, 1555; *The Hobbit; Or, There and Back Again*, 1556

Miniature people

ANDERSEN, Hans Christian. *Thumbelina*, 17

BERTON, Pierre. *The Secret World of Og*, 1903

BLATHWAYT, Benedict. *Tangle and the Firesticks*, 420

BODECKER, N(iels) M(ogens). *Quimble Wood*, 1267

BOSTON, L(ucy) M(aria Wood). *The Castle of Yew*, 2368

BUFFETT, Jimmy, and BUFFETT, Savannah Jane. *Trouble Dolls*, 2899

CAYLUS, Anne Claude Phillipe, Comte de. *Heart of Ice*, 60

CHASE, Mary (Coyle). *Loretta Mason Potts*, 1918

CHEW, Ruth (Silver). *Do-It-Yourself Magic*, 1920; *The Would-Be Witch*, 2990

CLAPP, Patricia. *King of the Doll House*, 2397

CURRY, Jane Louise. *Little Little Sister*, 84; *Mindy's Mysterious Miniature*, 2415; *The Wolves of Aam*, 1308

DAHL, Roald. *The Magic Finger*, 2419; *The Minpins*, 1930

DE LINT, Charles. *The Little Country*, 3001

DE REGNIERS, Beatrice Schenk (Freedman). *Penny*, 91

DICKINSON, Peter (pseud. of Malcolm de Brissac). *Giant Cold*, 95

DILLON, Barbara. *My Stepfather Shrank!*, 2427

ESTERN, Anne Graham. *The Picolinis and the Haunted House*, 2914

FARJEON, Eleanor. *Mr. Garden*, 2444

GRIMSHAW, Nigel (Gilroy). *Bluntstone and the Wildkeepers*, 1369

HALDEMAN, Linda (Wilson). *The Lastborn of Elvinwood*, 1708

HOUGH, (Helen) Charlotte (Woodyatt). *Red Biddy and Other Stories*, 893

IRVING, Washington. *Rip Van Winkle*, 1725

KÄSTNER, Erich. *The Little Man*, 2212

KENDALL, Carol (Seeger). *The Firelings*, 1401; *The Gammage Cup*, 1402; *The Whisper of Glocken*, 1403

KENEALLY, Thomas (Michael). *Ned Kelly and the City of the Bees*, 1996

LAGERLÖF, Selma (Ottilliana Lovisa). *The Wonderful Adventures of Nils*, 2524

LAWSON, Robert. *The Fabulous Flight*, 2534

LINDENBAUM, Pija. *Else-Marie and Her Seven Little Daddies*, 2538

MACE, Elisabeth. *Under Siege*, 2018

MANES, Stephen. *Some of the Adventures of Rhode Island Red*, 2248

MAYNE, William (James Carter). *The Green Book of Hob Stories*, 2566

MOORE, Annie Carroll. *Nicholas: a Manhattan Christmas Story*, 2571

MORGAN, Helen (Gertrude Louise Axford). *Satchkin Patchkin*, 2572

NORTON, Mary (Pearson). *The Borrowers*, 2587

OSBORNE, Mary Pope. *Spider Kane and the Mystery Under the May Apple*, 645

OTTO, Margaret G(lover). *The Tiny Man*, 646

PARRISH, Anne, and PARRISH, Dillwyn. *Knee-High to a Grasshopper*, 2595

PRATCHETT, Terry. *Truckers*, 1499

PROYSEN, Alf. *Little Old Mrs. Pepperpot and Other Stories*, 2607

REID BANKS, Lynne. *The Indian in the Cupboard*, 2610

RENDAL, Justine. *A Child of Their Own*, 2951

SNYDER, Zilpha Keatley. *Squeak Saves the Day and Other Tooley Tales*, 1534

STEELE, Mary Q(uintard Govan). *Wish, Come True*, 2640

SWIFT, Jonathan. *Gulliver's Travels into Several Remote Nations of the World*, 2069

TAPP, Kathy Kennedy. *Moth-Kin Magic*, 2646

TOLKIEN, J(ohn) R(onald) R(euel). *The Hobbit; Or, There and Back Again*, 1556

WALLACE, Barbara Brooks. *The Barrel in the Basement*, 2658

WERSBA, Barbara. *Let Me Fall Before I Fly*, 349

WHITE, T(erence) H(anbury). *Mistress Masham's Repose*, 2663

WINTERFELD, Henry. *Castaways in Lilliput*, 2084

WINTHROP (Mahony), Elizabeth. *The Castle in the Attic*, 2085

WOODRUFF, Elvira. *Awfully Short for the Fourth Grade*, 2670

WRIGHT, Betty Ren. *The Dollhouse Murders*, 2962

YOLEN (Stemple), Jane H(yatt). *The Wizard of Washington Square*, 3142

Minnesota

BAUER, Marion Dane. *A Taste of Smoke*, 1024

BELLAIRS, John. *The Dark Secret of Weatherend*, 2360

DEAN, Pamela. *Tam Lin*, 1661

DOUGLAS, Carole Nelson. *Cup of Clay*, 1942

Minnipins books

KENDALL, Carol (Seeger). *The Gammage Cup*, 1402; *The Whisper of Glocken*, 1403

Minotaur

KEANEY, Brian. *No Need for Heroes*, 1736

Minpins

DAHL, Roald. *The Minpins*, 1930

Miss Bianca series

SHARP (Castle), Margery. *The Rescuers*, 691

Miss Mallard mysteries

QUACKENBUSH, Robert M(ead). *Express Train to Trouble: A Miss Mallard Mystery*, 665

Mississippi

JAMES, Mary (pseud. of Maryjane Meaker; a.k.a. M. E. Kerr). *The Shuteyes*, 1987

Mississippi River

KARR, Kathleen. *Gideon and the Mummy Professor*, 2513

Mithgar

McKIERAN, Dennis L. *Trek to Kraggen-Cor*, 1452

Mode series

ANTHONY, Piers (pseud. of Piers A. D. Jacob). *Virtual Mode*, 1889

Mole and Arien trilogy

FISHER, Paul R. *The Ash Staff*, 1348

Monsters

ALCOCK, Vivien (Dolores). *The Monster Garden*, 2339

BABBITT, Natalie (Zane Moore). *Knee-Knock Rise*, 24

BARRON, T(homas) A. *The Ancient One*, 2694

Bestiary!, 796

BRADSHAW, Gillian (Marucha). *Beyond the North Wind*, 1620

BULLA, Clyde Robert. *My Friend the Monster*, 52

CAMERON, Eleanor (Frances Butler). *The Terrible Churnadryne*, 2389

CAMPBELL, Hope. *Peter's Angel: A Story about Monsters*, 438

CHARNAS, Suzy McKee. *The Bronze King*, 2986

COVILLE, Bruce. *The Monster's Ring*, 2408

DAHL, Roald. *The Minpins*, 1930

EASTON, M. Coleman. *The Fisherman's Curse*, 1329

FRY, Rosalie K(ingsmill). *Mungo*, 2456

GRIMBLE, Rosemary. *Jonothon and Large*, 2475

HARRIS, Rosemary (Jeanne). *Sea Magic and Other Stories of Enchantment*, 885

HAYES, Geoffrey. *The Alligator and His Uncle Tooth: A Novel of the Sea*, 534

LARSON, Jean (Russell). *The Silkspinners*, 195

LITTLE, Jane. *Sneaker Hill*, 3076

McHARGUE, Georgess. *Beastie*, 2551

MacKELLAR, William. *The Smallest Monster in the World*, 2553

McNEILL (Alexander), Janet. *A Monster Too Many*, 2554

MAHY, Margaret (May). *A Tall Story and Other Tales*, 2558

MANES, Stephen. *Monstra vs. Irving*, 2559

MAYNE, William (James Carter). *A Game of Dark*, 2796

MENDOZA, George. *Gwot! Horribly Funny Hairticklers*, 2252

Monsters, Ghoulies and Creepy Creatures: Fantastic Stories and Poems, 929

NESBIT (Bland), E(dith). *The Enchanted Castle*, 2576

NYE, Robert. *Beowulf; a New Telling*, 1789

ORMONDROYD, Edward. *David and the Phoenix*, 2590

PALMER, Mary. *The Magic Knight*, 262; *The Teaspoon Tree*, 2592
PHIPSON, Joan (pseud. of Margaret Fitzhardinge). *The Way Home*, 2827
PINKWATER, D(aniel) Manus. *The Frankenbagel Monster*, 2269; *Yobgorgle: Mystery Monster of Lake Ontario*, 2276
SENDAK, Philip. *In Grandpa's House*, 291
SLEIGH, Barbara (de Riemer). *Stirabout Stories, Brewed in Her Own Cauldron*, 962
SMITH, Alison. *Come Away Home*, 700
TROTT, Susan. *The Sea Serpent of Horse*, 2072
WARBURG, Sandol Stoddard (pseud. of Sandol Stoddard). *On the Way Home*, 1569
WILLEY, Elizabeth. *The Well-Favored Man: The Tale of the Sorcerer's Nephew*, 1581

Moomins series
JANSSON, Tove (Marika). *Finn Family Moomintroll*, 1388

Mordant's Need series
DONALDSON, Stephen R(upert). *The Mirror of Her Dreams*, 1941

Morgaine series
CHERRYH, C. J. (pseud. of Carolyn Janice Cherry). *Exile's Gate*, 1287

Moth-Kins
TAPP, Kathy Kennedy. *Moth-Kin Magic*, 2646

The Mouldiwarp
NESBIT (Bland), E(dith). *The House of Arden*, 2805

Mr. Pin Mystery series
MONSELL, Mary Elise. *The Mysterious Cases of Mr. Pin*, 627

Mr. Yowder series
ROUNDS, Glen (Harold). *The Day the Circus Came to Lone Tree*, 2293

Mulberia
KISLING, Lee. *The Fools' War*, 1410

Mundania
ANTHONY, Piers (pseud. of Piers A. D. Jacob). *A Spell for Chameleon*, 1250

Murry Family series
L'ENGLE, Madeleine. *Many Waters*, 2774

Mushroom Planet books
CAMERON, Eleanor (Frances Butler). *Time and Mr. Bass: A Mushroom Planet Book*, 2711

Mycetia
CAMERON, Eleanor (Frances Butler). *Time and Mr. Bass: A Mushroom Planet Book*, 2711

Myth Adventure series
ASPRIN, Robert L(ynn). *Hit or Myth*, 2965

Narguns
WRIGHTSON, (Alice) Patricia (Furlonger). *The Ice Is Coming*, 1877; *The Nargun and the Stars*, 1878

Narnia
LEWIS, C(live) S(taples). *The Lion, the Witch, and the Wardrobe*, 2007

Native American folklore
CAVANAGH, Helen. *Panther Glade*, 1634
DE LINT, Charles. *The Dreaming Place*, 1935
DOUGLAS, Carole Nelson. *Cup of Clay*, 1942
GEAR, W. Michael, and GEAR, Kathleen O'Neal. *People of the Fire*, 1693
MOON, Sheila. *Knee-Deep in Thunder*, 2026
ROOT, Phyllis. *The Listening Silence*, 1817
WILHELM, Kate (Katie Gertrude). *Cambio Bay*, 1868

Native Americans. *See also* Inuits; Aztec Indian tribe
APPEL, Allen. *Time After Time*, 2688
BARRON, T(homas) A. *The Ancient One*, 2694
BELL, Claire E. *The Jaguar Princess*, 1262
BOSSE, Malcolm J(oseph). *Cave Beyond Time*, 2702
COATSWORTH, Elizabeth (Jane). *The Enchanted: An Incredible Tale*, 1640
COONTZ, Otto. *Isle of the Shape-Shifters*, 1649
CURRY, Jane Louise. *The Daybreakers*, 2718; *Over the Sea's Edge*, 2719; *The Watchers*, 2721
FRENCH, Fiona. *The Magic Vase*, 119
HARRIS, Christie (Lucy Irwin). *Secret in the Stlalakum Wild*, 1101
JAMES, J. Alison. *Sing for a Gentle Rain*, 2757
KITTLEMAN, Laurence R. *Canyons Beyond the Sky*, 2765
LE GRAND (Henderson). *How Baseball Began in Brooklyn*, 2225
LIFTON, Betty Jean (Kirschner). *Jaguar, My Twin*, 3074
LORING, Selden M(elville). *Mighty Magic: An Almost-True Story of Pirates and Indians*, 2785
MAJOR, Kevin (Gerald). *Blood Red Ochre*, 1766
MOON, Grace Purdie, and MOON, Carl. *Lost Indian Magic: A Mystery Story of the Red Man as He Lived Before the White Men Came*, 2570
NICHOLS, (Joanna) Ruth. *Song of the Pearl*, 2807
NORTON, André (pseud. of Alice Mary Norton). *Fur Magic*, 2584
REID BANKS, Lynne. *The Indian in the Cupboard*, 2610
REYNOLDS, Mack, and ING, Dean. *The Other Time*, 2833
SERVICE, Pamela F. *Vision Quest*, 2840
SNYDER, Zilpha Keatley. *The Truth about Stone Hollow*, 1188
VICK, Helen Hughes. *Walker of Time*, 2862
WELLMAN, Manly Wade. *The Old Gods Waken*, 1863

WHITE, Stewart Edward. *The Magic Forest: A Modern Fairy Story*, 2662

Native Americans—Calusa tribe
CAVANAGH, Helen. *Panther Glade*, 1634

Native Americans—Canada
HARRIS, Christie (Lucy Irwin). *Secret in the Stlalakum Wild*, 1101

Native Americans—Halami tribe
BARRON, T(homas) A. *The Ancient One*, 2694

Native Americans—Historical
BOSSE, Malcolm J(oseph). *Cave Beyond Time*, 2702
CURRY, Jane Louise. *Over the Sea's Edge*, 2719; *The Watchers*, 2721
KITTLEMAN, Laurence R. *Canyons Beyond the Sky*, 2765
LORING, Selden M(elville). *Mighty Magic: An Almost-True Story of Pirates and Indians*, 2785
MOON, Grace Purdie, and MOON, Carl. *Lost Indian Magic: A Mystery Story of the Red Man as He Lived Before the White Men Came*, 2570

Native Americans—Historical, Canada
NICHOLS, (Joanna) Ruth. *Song of the Pearl*, 2807
WHITE, Stewart Edward. *The Magic Forest: A Modern Fairy Story*, 2662

Native Americans—Hopi tribe
VICK, Helen Hughes. *Walker of Time*, 2862

Native Americans—Iroquois tribe
KATZ, Welwyn Wilton. *False Face*, 1735

Native Americans—Pacific Northwest Coast
KESEY, Ken. *The Sea Lion: A Story of the Sea Cliff People*, 1738
PASSEY, Helen K. *Speak to the Rain*, 1795

Native Americans—Zinacantec tribe
LIFTON, Betty Jean (Kirschner). *Jaguar, My Twin*, 3074

Nazhuret Saga
MacAVOY, R(oberta) A(nn). *Lens of the World*, 1445

Nazor
McKENZIE, Ellen Kindt. *Taash and the Jesters*, 1450

Nemedians
FLYNN, Casey. *Most Ancient Song*, 1678

Nepal
MORPURGO, Michael. *King of the Cloud Forests*, 1777

The Netherlands
BIEGEL, Paul. *The King of the Copper Mountains*, 42
BOMANS, Godfried. *The Wily Witch and All the Other Fairy Tales and Fables*, 801
DRAGT, Tonke. *The Towers of February*, 1943
KIRBY, Mansfield. *The Secret of Thut-Mouse III*, 582

KOOIKER, Leonie (pseud. of Johanna Maria Kooyker-Romijn). *The Magic Stone*, 3064
POSTMA, Lidia. *The Stolen Mirror*, 2046; *The Witch's Garden*, 2605

Netherworld
MURPHY, Shirley Rousseau. *The Catswold Portal*, 2028

Nevada
SERVICE, Pamela F. *Vision Quest*, 2840

Nevèryön trilogy
DELANY, Samuel R. *Tales of Nevèryön*, 1313

New Guinea—Stone Age
LIVELY, Penelope (Margaret Low). *The House in Norham Gardens*, 2784

New Hampshire
LLYWELYN, Morgan. *The Elementals*, 214

New Jersey
STERMAN, Betsy, and STERMAN, Samuel. *Backyard Dragon*, 2641

New Mexico—1280
JAMES, J. Alison. *Sing for a Gentle Rain*, 2757

New York—Brooklyn
FRIESNER, Esther M. *Gnome Man's Land*, 1958
SLEPIAN, Jan. *Back to Before*, 2848

New York—Ithaca
RUFF, Matt. *Fool on the Hill*, 2618

New York—Manhattan
CHARNAS, Suzy McKee. *The Kingdom of Kevin Malone*, 1917
GILMORE, Kate. *Enter Three Witches*, 3025

New York City
DAVID, Peter. *Knight Life*, 1660
ELISH, Dan. *The Great Squirrel Uprising*, 491
GANGLOFF, Deborah. *Albert and Victoria*, 514
SHYER, Marlene Fanta. *Ruby, the Red Hot Witch at Bloomingdale's*, 3117
ST. GEORGE, Judith. *Who's Scared? Not Me!*, 2850

New York City—1882
FINNEY, Jack. *Time and Again*, 2736

New York City—1888
PECK, Richard. *Voices After Midnight*, 2825

New York City—1900
WILLARD, Nancy (Margaret). *Beauty and the Beast*, 1869

New York City—1962
WILSON, Robert Charles. *A Bridge of Years*, 2874

New York City—2000
HELPRIN, Mark. *Winter's Tale*, 1379
WALKER, Mary Alexander. *The Scathach and Maeve's Daughters*, 1859

New York State—1780
NORTON, André, and MILLER, Phyllis. *House of Shadows*, 1163

New Zealand
  GEE, Maurice. *The Halfmen of O*, 1962; *The World Around the Corner*, 1963
  MAHY, Margaret (May). *The Changeover: A Supernatural Romance*, 3090; *Dangerous Spaces*, 2020; *The Haunting*, 3091; *The Tricksters*, 1152
New Zealand—15th century
  JORDAN, Sherryl. *The Juniper Game*, 2760
Night Threads series
  EMERSON, Ru. *Night Threads: The Calling of the Three*, 1948
Nightpool
  MURPHY, Shirley Rousseau. *Nightpool*, 1481
Nile trilogy
  HARRIS, Rosemary (Jeanne). *The Moon in the Cloud*, 1711
Nineteenth century—Alternate history
  ALEXANDER, Lloyd (Chudley). *The Illyrian Adventure*, 1888
  GOULART, Ron(ald Joseph). *The Prisoner of Blackwood Castle*, 1366
Ninya
  WRIGHTSON, (Alice) Patricia (Furlonger). *The Ice Is Coming*, 1877
Njimbin
  WRIGHTSON, (Alice) Patricia (Furlonger). *A Little Fear*, 2672
Nogs
  POSTGATE, Oliver, and FIRMIN, Peter. *King of the Nogs*, 272
Nomes
  PRATCHETT, Terry. *Truckers*, 1499
Norse mythology. *See also* Icelandic sagas; Vikings
  FRIEDMAN, Michael Jan. *The Seekers and the Sword*, 1680
  HOLT, Tom. *Who's Afraid of Beowulf?*, 1718
  JAMES, J. Alison. *Runa*, 1727
  JONES, Diana Wynne. *Eight Days of Luke*, 1732
  JONES, Terry. *The Saga of Erik the Viking*, 163
  JONSSON, Runer. *Viki Viking*, 2211
  KING, Bernard. *Starkadder*, 1739
  SARGENT, Sarah. *Lure of the Dark*, 1822
  SMITH, Doris Buchanan. *Voyages*, 1839
  SYNGE, (Phyllis) Ursula. *Weland, Smith of the Gods*, 1848
North Carolina
  CARRIS, Joan Davenport. *A Ghost of a Chance*, 1043
North Dakota
  ROUNDS, David. *Cannonball River Tales*, 2292
Northland
  REICHERT, Mickey Zucker. *The Last of the Renshai*, 1506
Norway
  EGNER, Thorbjørn. *The Singing Town*, 2157
  FALKBERGET, Johan. *Broomstick and Snowflake*, 107

  HOPP, Zinken. *The Magic Chalk*, 2493
Norway—13th century
  HENDRY, Frances Mary. *Quest for a Maid*, 3037
Nova Scotia, Canada—1744
  BOND, Nancy (Barbara). *Another Shore*, 2700
Nwm
  KATZ, Welwyn Wilton. *The Third Magic*, 1993

Ogres
  CHERRYH, C. J. (pseud. of Carolyn Janice Cherry). *The Goblin Mirror*, 1288
  COOMBS, Patricia. *Molly Mullett*, 72
  DOYLE, Debra, and MacDONALD, James D. *Knight's Wyrd*, 1325
  MURPHY, Jill. *Jeffrey Strangeways*, 2256
Ohio
  HASELEY, Dennis. *Doctor Gravity*, 2189
Olympic Games
  PATON WALSH, Jill. *Torch*, 1490
Ontario, Canada
  KATZ, Welwyn Wilton. *Come Like Shadows*, 3058; *False Face*, 1735
Ontario, Canada—Toronto
  COOPER (Grant), Susan (Mary). *The Boggart*, 2402
Operas
  BRADLEY, Marion Zimmer. *Night's Daughter*, 1619
  MENOTTI, Gian Carlo. *Amahl and the Night Visitors*, 1774
  MOZART, Wolfgang Amadeus. *The Magic Flute*, 248
Operettas
  EGNER, Thorbjørn. *The Singing Town*, 2157
  HOWE, James. *Babes in Toyland*, 1982
Orathi
  HILGARTNER, Beth. *Colors in the Dreamweaver's Loom*, 1977
Oregon
  BARRON, T(homas) A. *The Ancient One*, 2694
Oregon—Early 1900s
  ANDERSON, Margaret J(ean). *The Ghost Inside the Monitor*, 1017
  BAUER, Marion Dane. *A Taste of Smoke*, 1024
Orissa
  COLE, Allan, and BUNCH, Chris. *The Far Kingdoms*, 1299
Orphans
  AIKEN, Joan. *The Whispering Mountain*, 1234; *The Wolves of Willoughby Chase*, 1235
  ALEXANDER, Lloyd. *Westmark*, 1241
  BAKKEN, Harald. *The Fields and the Hills*, 1256
  BAUER, Marion Dane. *A Taste of Smoke*, 1024
  BUNTING, Eve. *Ghost Behind Me*, 1036

BUTLER, Beverly. *Witch's Fire*, 2981

CASSEDY, Sylvia. *Behind the Attic Wall*, 1044

CHETWIN, Grace. *Child of the Air*, 1290; *Gom on Windy Mountain*, 1292

CROSS, Gilbert B. *A Witch Across Time*, 1058

CURRY, Jane Louise. *The Wolves of Aam*, 1308

DICKINSON, Peter. *The Devil's Children*, 1319

DOWNER, Ann. *The Spellkey*, 1324

FISHER, Paul R. *The Ash Staff*, 1348

FLEISCHMAN, Sid. *The Midnight Horse*, 1074

GRIPE, Maria (Kristina). *Agnes Cecilia*, 1097

HEARNE, Betsy (Gould). *South Star*, 1378

JONES, Adrienne. *The Hawks of Chelney*, 1389

JONES, Diana Wynne. *The Spellcoats*, 1394

KING, Stephen. *The Eyes of the Dragon*, 1406

MacAVOY, R. A. *Lens of the World*, 1445

McKENZIE, Ellen Kindt. *Taash and the Jesters*, 1450

McKILLIP, Patricia A(nne). *The Changeling Sea*, 1453; *The Forgotten Beasts of Eld*, 1455

MAHY, Margaret. *Dangerous Spaces*, 2020

PASSEY, Helen K. *Speak to the Rain*, 1795

SABERHAGEN, Fred. *Empire of the East*, 1516

SLEPIAN, Jan. *Back to Before*, 2848

SMITH, Sherwood. *Wren to the Rescue*, 1530

SPRINGER, Nancy. *Wings of Flame*, 1539

STOPP, Hans. *The Golden Bird*, 314

VANDE VELDE, Vivian. *Dragon's Bait*, 1561

WANGERIN, Walter, Jr. *Elisabeth and the Water-Troll*, 345

WILDER, Cherry. *A Princess of the Chameln*, 1579

WRIGHT, Betty Ren. *The Ghosts of Mercy Manor*, 1224

YOLEN (Stemple), Jane H(yatt). *Sister Light, Sister Dark*, 1598

"Orpheus and Eurydice," retellings of

SPRINGER, Nancy. *The Friendship Song*, 2063

Oscar Noodleman trilogy

MANES, Stephen. *Chicken Trek: The Third Strange Thing That Happened to Oscar Noodleman*, 2247

Osten Ard

WILLIAMS, Tad. *The Dragonbone Chair*, 1583

Oz series

BAUM, L(yman) Frank. *The Wizard of Oz*, 1898

Ozark trilogy

ELGIN, (Patricia Anne) Suzette Haden. *Twelve Fair Kingdoms*, 1339

Pacifica

SHACHTMAN, Tom. *Driftwhistler: A Story of Daniel au Fond*, 690

Pandemia

DUNCAN, Dave. *The Cutting Edge*, 1327

Pantouflia

LANG, Andrew. *Prince Prigio and Prince Ricardo: The Chronicles of Pantouflia*, 194

Parsina Saga

GOLDIN, Stephen. *Crystals of Air and Water*, 1363

Pendaire

WURTS, Janny. *Sorcerer's Legacy*, 1594

Pendragon Cycle

LAWHEAD, Stephen R. *Taliesin*, 1744

Pennsylvania

JENSEN, Dorothea. *The Riddle of Penncroft Farm*, 1114

SPRINGER, Nancy. *The Hex Witch of Seldom*, 3120

Pennsylvania—1876

APPEL, Allen. *Time After Time*, 2688

Pern

McCAFFREY, Anne (Inez). *Dragonflight*, 1447

Perrenland

ESTES, Rose. *The Name of the Game*, 1950

Perryth

HAMBLY, Barbara. *The Silent Tower*, 1974

Persia. *See also* Iran

STANLEY, Diane. *Fortune*, 306

Peru—1555

ALEXANDER, Lloyd (Chudley). *Time Cat: The Remarkable Journeys of Jason and Gareth*, 2680

Phar-Tracil

ORR, A. *The World in Amber*, 3101

Phaze

ANTHONY, Piers (pseud. of Piers A. D. Jacob). *Blue Adept*, 1248

The Phoenix

FORREST, Elizabeth. *Phoenix Fire*, 1679

NESBIT (Bland), E(dith). *Five Children and It*, 2577

ORMONDROYD, Edward. *David and the Phoenix*, 2590

Phoenix Feathers: A Collection of Mythical Monsters, 941

Physical disabilities. *See also* Blindness; Cerebral palsy; Deafness

BENNETT, Rodney. *Eagle Boy*, 2362

BUTLER, Beverly. *Witch's Fire*, 2981

"The Pied Piper of Hamelin," adaptations of

HUDDY, Delia. *Time Piper*, 1720

LEE, Tanith. *Red as Blood; or Tales from the Sisters Grimmer*, 1747

PRICE, Susan. *The Devil's Piper*, 1806

SKURZYNSKI, Gloria (Joan). *What Happened in Hamelin*, 1837

Pit Dragons trilogy

YOLEN (Stemple), Jane H(yatt). *Dragon's Blood*, 1596

Plays

AIKEN, Joan (Delano). *Street: A Play for Children*, 3; *Winterthing: A Play for Children*, 1603

BARRIE, Sir J(ames) M(atthew). *Peter Pan*, 1896

CHASE, Mary (Coyle). *Harvey, a Play*, 2124; *Mrs. McThing: A Play*, 2987

DAHL, Roald. *James and the Giant Peach: A Children's Story*, 2418

DE LA MARE, Walter (John). *Crossings: A Fairy Play*, 2422

EGNER, Thorbjørn. *The Singing Town*, 2157

MAETERLINCK, Maurice. *The Children's Blue Bird*, 230

ZINDEL, Paul. *Let Me Hear You Whisper: A Play*, 762

Poland—1942

YOLEN (Stemple), Jane H(yatt). *The Devil's Arithmetic*, 2880

Prehistoric period

BRENNAN, J. H. *Shiva: An Adventure of the Ice Age*, 1622

HANLON, Emily. *Circle Home*, 2751

JORDAN, Sherryl. *A Time of Darkness*, 2761

KITTLEMAN, Laurence R. *Canyons Beyond the Sky*, 2766

L'ENGLE, Madeleine. *An Acceptable Time*, 2773

MAZER, Norma Fox. *Saturday, the Twelfth of October*, 2798

OSBORNE, Mary Pope. *Dinosaurs Before Dark*, 2813

PHIPSON, Joan (pseud. of Margaret Fitzhardinge). *The Way Home*, 2827

Prejudice

BABBITT, Lucy Cullyford. *Where the Truth Lies*, 1255

BETHANCOURT, T(homas) Ernesto. *Tune in Yesterday*, 2699

HOPE, Christopher. *The Dragon Wore Pink*, 152

JORDAN, Sherryl. *Winter of Fire*, 1397

MAZER, Anne. *The Oxboy*, 236

The Principles of Magic books

HARDY, Lyndon. *Secret of the Sixth Magic*, 3033

Professor Kurtz books

CURRY, Jane Louise. *Mindy's Mysterious Miniature*, 2415

Proton

ANTHONY, Piers (pseud. of Piers A. D. Jacob). *Blue Adept*, 1248

Pryan

WEIS, Margaret, and HICKMAN, Tracy. *Dragon Wing*, 1574

Prydain

ALEXANDER, Lloyd (Chudley). *The Book of Three*, 1236

Prydein

TOLSTOY, Nikolai. *The Coming of the King: The First Book of Merlin*, 1854

The Psammead

NESBIT (Bland), E(dith). *Five Children and It*, 2577

Pyra

CHETWIN, Grace. *Child of the Air*, 1290

Pyromancer series

CALLANDER, Don. *Aquamancer*, 2983

Quelled

JORDAN, Sherryl. *Winter of Fire*, 1397

Quest of Morgaine series

CHERRYH, C. J. (pseud. of Carolyn Janice Cherry). *Exile's Gate*, 1287

Qushmarrah

COOK, Glen. *Tower of Fear*, 1300

Raeth

REYNOLDS, Susan Lynn. *Strandia*, 1508

Ralph S. Mouse trilogy

CLEARY, Beverly (Bunn). *The Mouse and the Motorcycle*, 446

Ratlords

GENTLE, Mary. *Rats and Gargoyles*, 1360

Rats of NIMH series

CONLY, Jane Leslie. *Racso and the Rats of NIMH (The Rats of NIMH series, book 2)*, 459

O'BRIEN, Robert C. (pseud. of Robert Leslie Conly). *Mrs. Frisby and the Rats of NIMH*, 639

Ravan

GOLDIN, Stephen. *Crystals of Air and Water*, 1363

The Realm

CARVER, Jeffrey A(llan). *Dragon Rigger*, 1283

Recluce

MODESITT, L(eland) E(xton Jr.). *The Magic of Recluce*, 1475

Red Hand people

GEAR, W. Michael, and GEAR, Kathleen O'Neal. *People of the Fire*, 1693

Redwall Saga

JACQUES, Brian. *Redwall*, 550

Reluctant King trilogy

DE CAMP, L(yon) Sprague. *The Honorable Barbarian*, 1310

Renshai trilogy

REICHERT, Mickey Zucker. *The Last of the Renshai*, 1506

Reuben trilogy

HARRIS, Rosemary (Jeanne). *The Moon in the Cloud*, 1711

Rhaetia

DE CAMP, L(yon) Sprague, and DE CAMP, Catherine Crook. *The Pixilated Peeress*, 1312

Rhazaulle
VOLSKY, Paula. *The Wolf of Winter*, 1568
Rhiyana
TARR, Judith. *Alamut*, 1548
Rhode Island
MANES, Stephen. *Some of the Adventures of Rhode Island Red*, 2248
Rhode Island—1800
AVI. *Something Upstairs: A Tale of Ghosts*, 2691
Rifkind books
ABBEY, Lynn. *The Black Flame*, 1230
Riftwar saga
FEIST, Raymond E. *Silverthorn*, 1344
Rising folk
CHETWIN, Grace. *Child of the Air*, 1290
Rivan
EDDINGS, David. *Guardians of the West*, 1333
Riverworld
McKILLIP, Patricia A(nne). *Moon-Flash*, 1456
"Robin Hood," adaptations of
ROBERSON, Jennifer. *Lady of the Forest*, 1816
Robin Hood duology
GODWIN, Parke. *Sherwood*, 1697
Roman Empire
ESTES, Eleanor (Ruth Rosenfeld). *Miranda the Great*, 495
LAHEY, Michael. *Quest for Apollo*, 2766
NESBIT (Bland), E(dith). *The Story of the Amulet*, 2806
NICHOLS, (Joanna) Ruth. *The Left-Handed Spirit*, 3098
Roman Empire—Alternate 20th century
CHRISTOPHER, John (pseud. of Christopher Samuel Youd). *Fireball*, 1921
Roman Empire—Alternate Middle Ages
SIMAK, Clifford D(onald). *Where the Evil Dwells*, 1529
Roman Empire—England
ALEXANDER, Lloyd (Chudley). *Time Cat: The Remarkable Journeys of Jason and Gareth*, 2680
ANDERSON, Poul, and ANDERSON, Karen. *Gallicenae*, 1247
GARD, Joyce (pseud. of Joyce Reeves). *The Mermaid's Daughter*, 3022
GARNER, Alan. *The Red Shift*, 2740
LAURENCE, Margaret (Wemyss). *Jason's Quest*, 592
NAYLOR, Phyllis Reynolds. *Shadows on the Wall*, 2804
Roman Gaul
LLYWELYN, Morgan. *Druids*, 1755
Roman mythology
LAHEY, Michael. *Quest for Apollo*, 2766
"Romeo and Juliet," adaptations of
LEE, Tanith. *Sung in Shadow*, 1432
Rose of the Prophet trilogy
WEIS, Margaret. *The Prophet of Akhian*, 1573

Roshan
HUGHES, Monica. *Sandwriter*, 1385
Rulers of Hylor trilogy
WILDER, Cherry (pseud. of Cherry Barbara Lockett Grimm). *A Princess of the Chameln*, 1579
"Rumplestiltskin," adaptations of
FARJEON, Eleanor. *The Silver Curlew*, 1670
Runaways
LACKEY, Mercedes. *Arrows of the Queen*, 1415
LACKEY, Mercedes, and DIXON, Larry. *Born to Run*, 3069
MICHAELS, Melisa C. *Far Harbor*, 1473
PARK, Ruth. *My Sister Sif*, 1794
REAVES, Michael. *Street Magic*, 1810
SHETTERLY, Will. *Elsewhere*, 2059
TOWNSEND, John Rowe. *The Fortunate Isles*, 1557
WILLIS, Paul J. *No Clock in the Forest*, 2082
Russia
GOGOL, Nikolai. *The Nose*, 2183
JANEWAY, Elizabeth (Hall). *Ivanov Seven*, 2206
PATERSON, Katherine. *The King's Equal*, 264
PRICE, Susan. *Ghost Song*, 3109
SCHWARZ, Eugene M. *Two Brothers*, 288
STRUGATSKII, Arkadii Natanovich, and STRUGATSKII, Boris Natanovich. *Monday Begins on Saturday*, 3124
Russia—1917
APPEL, Allen. *Time After Time*, 2688
Russia—Folklore
CHERRYH, C. J. (pseud. of Carolyn Janice Cherry). *Rusalka*, 2988
COLE, Joanna. *Bony-Legs*, 2992
COOKE, Donald Edwin. *The Firebird*, 71
ERSHOV, Petr Pavlovich. *The Little Humpbacked Horse: A Russian Tale*, 105
KARAZIN, Nikolaí Nikoleavich. *Cranes Flying South*, 559
LESKOV, Nikolai. *The Steel Flea, a Story*, 204
MAGUIRE, Gregory. *The Dream Stealer*, 3089
PRICE, Susan. *The Ghost Drum: A Cat's Tale*, 3108
PUSHKIN, Alexander Sergeevich. *The Golden Cockerel and Other Stories*, 950; *The Tale of Czar Saltan, or the Prince and the Swan Princess*, 273; *The Tale of the Golden Cockerel*, 274
RIORDAN, James. *The Three Magic Gifts*, 280
Russia—Pre-Christian era
CHERRYH, C. J. (pseud. of Carolyn Janice Cherry). *Rusalka*, 2988
Ruwenda
BRADLEY, Marion Zimmer, MAY, Julian, and NORTON, André. *Black Trillium*, 1271
Rynth
DOUGLAS, Carole Nelson. *Exiles of the Rynth*, 3004

Sabis trilogy
CHERRYH, C. J. (pseud. of Carolyn Janice Cherry) and ASIRE, Nancy. *Wizard Spawn*, 1289
Sacred Stones series
CALDECOTT, Moyra. *The Tall Stones*, 1277
Saga of the Lost Lands trilogy
ESTES, Rose. *The Name of the Game*, 1950
Sally Ann series
DICKS, Terrance. *Sally Ann on Her Own*, 2910
Sam Spayed series
SINGER, Marilyn. *The Fido Frame-Up*, 698
Samurai Cat trilogy
ROGERS, Mark E. *The Adventures of Samurai Cat*, 675
Saphier
McKILLIP, Patricia A(nne). *Cygnet and the Firebird*, 1454
Satyrs
ANTHONY, Piers, and KORNWISE, Robert Ian. *Through the Ice*, 1891
Scatterlings
REAVES, Michael. *Street Magic*, 1810
Scotland
ANDERSON, Margaret J(ean). *The Druid's Gift*, 2683
ARTHUR, Ruth M(abel). *The Autumn People*, 1019
CHARLES, Prince of Wales. *The Old Man of Lochnagar*, 2123
DUNLOP, Eileen (Rhona). *Clementina*, 1667; *Green Willow*, 1066; *The Maze Stone*, 2728
HARRIS, Rosemary. *The Seal-Singing*, 1712
HOLT, Tom. *Who's Afraid of Beowulf?*, 1718
KURTZ, Katherine, and HARRIS, Deborah. *The Adept*, 3068
McHARGUE, Georgess. *Beastie*, 2551
MacKELLAR, William. *The Ghost in the Castle*, 1148
SMITH, Alison. *Come Away Home*, 700
TARN, (Sir) W(illiam) W(oodthorpe). *The Treasure of the Isle of Mist: A Tale of the Isle of Skye*, 2647
Scotland—7th century
BRIGGS, K(atharine) M(ary). *Kate Crackernuts*, 1624
Scotland—13th century
HENDRY, Frances Mary. *Quest for a Maid*, 3037
KUSHNER, Ellen. *Thomas the Rhymer*, 1740
Scotland—17th century
MacKELLAR, William. *The Ghost in the Castle*, 1148
Scotland—1700s
DUNLOP, Eileen (Rhona). *The Valley of Deer*, 2729
Scotland—1743
GABALDON, Diana. *Outlander: A Novel*, 2739

Scotland—1746
DUNLOP, Eileen (Rhona). *Clementina*, 1667
Scotland—19th century
HUNTER, Mollie (pseud. of Maureen Mollie Hunter McVeigh McIlwraith). *The Mermaid Summer*, 2499
Scotland—1901
ARTHUR, Ruth M(abel). *The Autumn People*, 1019
Scotland—1941
DUNLOP, Eileen (Rhona). *The Maze Stone*, 2728
Scotland—1945
GABALDON, Diana. *Outlander: A Novel*, 2739
Scotland—Folklore
BRIGGS, K(atharine) M(ary). *Kate Crackernuts*, 1624
COOPER (Grant), Susan (Mary). *The Selkie Girl*, 1651; *Tam Lin*, 1652
DEAN, Pamela. *Tam Lin*, 1661
DE LINT, Charles. *Jack the Giant-Killer*, 1663
FRY, Rosalie K(ingsmill). *The Secret of the Ron Mor Skerry*, 1682
GERSTEIN, Mordicai (adapt.). *The Seal Mother*, 1695
HARRIS, Rosemary (Jeanne). *The Seal-Singing*, 1712
HUNTER, Mollie (pseud. of Maureen Mollie Hunter McVeigh McIlwraith). *A Furl of Fairy Wind: Four Stories*, 900; *The Haunted Mountain: A Story of Suspense*, 1984; *A Stranger Came Ashore*, 1722
JONES, Diana Wynne. *Fire and Hemlock*, 3051
LEVIN, Betty (Lowenthal). *Landfall*, 1749
LILLINGTON, Kenneth (James). *Selkie*, 1750
LOCKLEY, Ronald Mathias. *The Seal-Woman*, 1759
MAYER, Marianna. *Noble-Hearted Kate: A Celtic Tale*, 1769
YOLEN (Stemple), Jane H(yatt). *Tam Lin: An Old Ballad*, 1883
Scotland—Western Highlands
COOPER (Grant), Susan (Mary). *The Boggart*, 2402
Sea King trilogy
SPRINGER, Nancy. *Madbond*, 1537
Selkies (selchies)
ANDERSON, Poul (William). *The Merman's Children*, 1245
COATSWORTH, Elizabeth (Jane). *Marra's World*, 1641
COOPER (Grant), Susan (Mary). *The Selkie Girl*, 1651
CUTT, W(illiam) Towrie. *Seven for the Sea*, 2722
FRY, Rosalie K(ingsmill). *The Secret of the Ron Mor Skerry*, 1682
GARD, Joyce (pseud. of Joyce Reeves). *Talargain*, 1683

GERSTEIN, Mordicai (adapt.). *The Seal Mother*, 1695

HUNTER, Mollie (pseud. of Maureen Mollie Hunter McVeigh McIlwraith). *A Stranger Came Ashore*, 1722

LEVIN, Betty (Lowenthal). *Landfall*, 1749

LILLINGTON, Kenneth (James). *Selkie*, 1750

LOCKLEY, Ronald Mathias. *The Seal-Woman*, 1759

MURPHY, Pat. *Points of Departure*, 932

OPPENHEIM, Shulamith (Levey). *The Selchie's Seed*, 1791

PARK, Ruth. *My Sister Sif*, 1794

PECK, Sylvia. *Seal Child*, 1800

YOLEN (Stemple), Jane H(yatt). *Greyling: A Picture Story from the Islands of Shetland*, 1881

Serendip

HODGES, Elizabeth Jamison. *The Three Princes of Serendip*, 146

Serrated Edge series

LACKEY, Mercedes, and DIXON, Larry. *Born to Run*, 3069

Seven Citadels quartet

HARRIS, Geraldine (Rachel). *Prince of the Godborn*, 1374

Shadow series

CLAYTON, Jo. *Shadowspeer*, 1297

LOGSTON, Anne. *Shadow*, 1439

Shannara series

BROOKS, Terry. *The Sword of Shannara*, 1273

She series

MONACO, Richard. *Journey to the Flame*, 2025

Sherluck Bones Mystery–Detective books

RAZZI, Jim (James), and RAZZI, Mary. *The Search for King Pup's Tomb*, 667

Shimmer and Thorn books

YEP, Laurence M(ichael). *Dragon of the Lost Sea*, 1595

Shiva trilogy

BRENNAN, J. H. *Shiva: An Adventure of the Ice Age*, 1622

Sidhe

DEITZ, Tom. *Windmaster's Bane*, 1934

Sidhe trilogy

FLINT, Kenneth C. *The Riders of the Sidhe*, 1677

Sigfrid and Brunahild trilogy

PAXON, Diana L. *The Wolf and the Raven*, 1798

Silver Call duology

McKIERAN, Dennis L. *Trek to Kraggen-Cor*, 1452

Silver John series

WELLMAN, Manly Wade. *The Old Gods Waken*, 1863

Simon Tregarth sequence

NORTON, André (pseud. of Alice Mary Norton). *Witch World*, 2039

Sinagua Indians

VICK, Helen Hughes. *Walker of Time*, 2862

Sinbad the Sailor

GARDNER, Craig Shaw. *The Other Sinbad*, 1685

Slavery

ALCOCK, Vivien (Dolores). *Singer to the Sea God*, 1604

AVI. *Something Upstairs: A Tale of Ghosts*, 2691

BISSON, Terry. *Fire on the Mountain*, 1265

BUTLER, Octavia E. *Kindred*, 2709

CHESNUTT, Charles Waddell. *Conjure Tales*, 822

HALL, Lynn. *The Mystery of the Caramel Cat*, 1099

HAMILTON, Virginia. *The Magical Adventures of Pretty Pearl*, 1709

HURMENCE, Belinda. *A Girl Called Boy*, 2755

JORDAN, Sherryl. *Winter of Fire*, 1397

NORTON, André. *Octagon Magic*, 2810

SHECTER, Ben. *The Whistling Whirligig*, 1181

VOIGT, Cynthia. *The Wings of a Falcon*, 1566

WALLIN, Luke. *The Slavery Ghosts*, 1202

Slavic folklore

SHERMAN, Josepha. *The Shining Falcon*, 1522

"Sleeping Beauty," adaptations of

GARFIELD, Leon. *The Wedding Ghost*, 1687

MOORE, John. *Slay and Rescue*, 1776

TEPPER, Sheri S. *Beauty: A Novel*, 1853

YOLEN (Stemple), Jane H(yatt). *Briar Rose*, 1879

"Snow White," adaptations of

LEE, Tanith. *Red as Blood; or Tales from the Sisters Grimmer*, 1747

MOORE, John. *Slay and Rescue*, 1776

"Snow White and Rose Red," adaptations of

WREDE, Patricia C(ollins). *Snow White and Rose Red*, 1874

Song of Albion series

LAWHEAD, Stephen R. *The Silver Hand*, 1743

Song of the Earth series

CONEY, Michael Greatrex. *The Celestial Steam Locomotive*, 1647

Song of the Lioness series

PIERCE, Tamora. *Alanna: The First Adventure*, 1495; *Wild Magic: The Immortals*, 1496

Songkiller saga

SCARBOROUGH, Elizabeth Ann. *Phantom Banjo*, 3114

Sorcery Hall trilogy

CHARNAS, Suzy McKee. *The Bronze King*, 2986

South America. *See also* Brazil; Ecuador; Peru

HUDSON, W(illiam) H(enry). *A Little Boy Lost: A Tale for Children*, 155

MURPHY, Pat (pseud. of E[mmet] Jefferson Murphy). *The Falling Woman: A Fantasy*, 1779

Spain
ARTHUR, Ruth M(abel). *Requiem for a Princess*, 2690
BACON, Martha (Sherman). *The Third Road*, 2692
CAIRE, Helen. *Señor Castillo, Cock of the Island*, 437
CERVANTES, Saavedra Miguel de. *The Adventures of Don Quixote de la Mancha*, 61
COEHLO, Paulo. *The Alchemist: A Fable About Following Your Dream*, 68
COLOMA, Padre Luis. *Perez, the Mouse*, 456
DUNSANY, Lord (pseud. of Edward John Morton Drax Plunkett). *The Charwoman's Shadow*, 3007
LAWSON, Robert. *I Discover Columbus*, 596
MELENDEZ, Francisco. *The Mermaid and the Major: or, The True Story of the Invention of the Submarine*, 2251
SANCHEZ-SILVA, José. *The Boy and the Whale*, 283

Spain—1492
FRIESNER, Esther M. *Yesterday We Saw Mermaids*, 1681
LAWSON, Robert. *I Discover Columbus*, 596

Spain—16th century
ARTHUR, Ruth M(abel). *Requiem for a Princess*, 2690

Spain—17th century
BACON, Martha (Sherman). *The Third Road*, 2692

Spain—Middle Ages
DUNSANY, Lord (pseud. of Edward John Morton Drax Plunkett). *The Charwoman's Shadow*, 3007

Spearwielder's Tale series
SALVATORE, R. A. *The Woods Out Back*, 2056

Star-Bearer trilogy
McKILLIP, Patricia A(nne). *The Riddle-Master of Hed*, 1457

Star-Rigger series
CARVER, Jeffrey A(llan). *Dragon Rigger*, 1283

Starlit Land
CHANT, Joy (pseud. of Eileen Joyce Rutter). *Red Moon and Black Mountain: The End of the House of Kendreth*, 1916

Stone Cycle
GREEN, Roger J(ames). *The Fear of Samuel Walton*, 1703

Story of the Dragon's Heirs trilogy
JONES, Courtway. *In the Shadow of the Oak King*, 1731

Strandia
REYNOLDS, Susan Lynn. *Strandia*, 1508

Stronghold
RAWN, Melanie. *Dragon Prince*, 1502

Suicide
ANTHONY, Piers (pseud. of Piers A. D. Jacob). *On a Pale Horse*, 1249; *Virtual Mode*, 1889
LUNN, Janet. *Shadow in Hawthorn Bay*, 1139

Sumeria
NICHOLS, (Joanna) Ruth. *Song of the Pearl*, 2807

Sumeria—Folklore
SILVERBERG, Robert. *Gilgamesh the King*, 1835

Sunrunners
RAWN, Melanie. *Stronghold*, 1503

Sweden
ANCKARSVÄRD, Karin. *Bonifacius the Green*, 2340
GRIPE, Maria (Kristina). *Agnes Cecilia*, 1097; *The Glassblower's Children*, 3028; *In the Time of the Bells*, 1370; *The Land Beyond*, 1972
JAMES, J. Alison. *Runa*, 1727
JONSSON, Runer. *Viki Viking*, 2211
LAGERLÖF, Selma. *The Changeling*, 191; *The Wonderful Adventures of Nils*, 2524
LE GUIN, Ursula K(roeber). *A Ride on the Red Mare's Back*, 203
LINDE, Gunnel (Geijerstam). *The White Stone*, 2537
LINDENBAUM, Pija. *Else-Marie and Her Seven Little Daddies*, 2538
LINDGREN, Astrid. *The Ghost of Skinny Jack*, 1133; *Karlsson-on-the-Roof*, 2539; *Pippi Longstocking*, 2230; *Ronia, the Robber's Daughter*, 1436
PROYSEN, Alf. *Little Old Mrs. Pepperpot and Other Stories*, 2607
SWAHN, Sven. *The Island Through the Gate*, 2068

Switzerland
DU BOIS, William (Sherman) Pène. *The Flying Locomotive*, 2146
KÄSTNER, Erich. *The Little Man*, 2212
KELLER, Gottfried. *The Fat of the Cat and Other Stories*, 907

Sword and Circlet trilogy
DOUGLAS, Carole Nelson. *Exiles of the Rynth*, 3004

Sword and Sorceress series
Spells of Wonder, 1535
Sword and Sorceress: An Anthology of Heroic Fantasy, 1547

Sybil Barron trilogy
GREGORIAN, Joyce Ballou. *The Broken Citadel*, 1971

Taitastigon
HODGELL, P(atricia) C(hristine). *God Stalk*, 1382

Tales of Aeron trilogy
KENNEALY (Morrison), Patricia. *The Copper Crown*, 1404
Tales of Alvin Maker
CARD, Orson Scott. *Seventh Son*, 1279
Tales of Arthur series
KENNEALY (Morrison), Patricia. *The Hawk's Gray Feather: A Book of the Keltiad*, 1737
Tales of Gom series
CHETWIN, Grace. *Gom on Windy Mountain: From Tales of Gom*, 1292
Taliswoman trilogy
DOUGLAS, Carole Nelson. *Cup of Clay*, 1942
Tam
BAKKEN, Harald. *The Fields and the Hills*, 1256
"Tam Lin, The Ballad of," adaptations of
COOPER (Grant), Susan (Mary). *Tam Lin*, 1652
DEAN, Pamela. *Tam Lin*, 1661
IPCAR, Dahlov (Zorach). *The Queen of Spells*, 1723
JONES, Diana Wynne. *Fire and Hemlock*, 3051
MAYER, Marianna. *Noble-Hearted Kate: A Celtic Tale*, 1769
SILVERMAN, Maida. *The Magic Well*, 297
YOLEN (Stemple), Jane H(yatt). *Tam Lin: An Old Ballad*, 1883
Tamul
EDDINGS, David. *Domes of Fire*, 1332
The Tamuli trilogy
EDDINGS, David. *The Diamond Throne*, 1331
EDDINGS, David. *Domes of Fire*, 1332
Tasavalta
SABERHAGEN, Fred. *The First Book of Lost Swords: Woundhealer's Story*, 1517
Tebriel trilogy
MURPHY, Shirley Rousseau. *Nightpool*, 1481
Tekumel
BARKER, M(uhammad) A(bd-Al-) R(ahman). *The Man of Gold*, 1258
Tembreabrezi
LE GUIN, Ursula K. *The Beginning Place*, 2005
Terra Magica trilogy
CARTER, Lin. *Mandricardo: New Adventures of Terra Magica*, 1282
Terran
MICHAELS, Melisa C. *Far Harbor*, 1473
Tertius books
NEWMAN, Robert (Howard). *Merlin's Mistake*, 1782
Texas—San Antonio
GRIFFIN, Peni R(ae). *A Dig in Time*, 2746
Texas—San Antonio, 1891
GRIFFIN, Peni R(ae). *Switching Well*, 2747
Texas, West
GRIFFIN, Peni R(ae). *Hobkin*, 2472
"Thomas the Rhymer," adaptations of
KUSHNER, Ellen. *Thomas the Rhymer*, 1740

"Thousand and One Nights," adaptations of
GOROG, Judith. *Winning Scheherazad*, 1701
Three Damsels trilogy
CHAPMAN, Vera. *The Green Knight*, 1636
Thulgaria
SERVICE, Pamela F. *Being of Two Minds*, 2631
Tibet
HILTON, James. *Lost Horizon*, 1978
MORPURGO, Michael. *King of the Cloud Forests*, 1777
Tiger and Del series
ROBERSON, Jennifer. *Sword-Breaker*, 1510
Tim Desmond trilogy
FRIESNER, Esther M. *Gnome Man's Land*, 1958
Time Master trilogy
COOPER, Louise. *The Master*, 1302
Time Patrol series
ANDERSON, Poul (William). *The Time Patrol*, 2686
Time trilogy
ANDERSON, Margaret J(ean). *In the Circle of Time*, 2684
Time Warp Trio series
SCIESZKA, Jon. *Knights of the Kitchen Table*, 2838
Timeways trilogy
BARTHOLOMEW, Barbara. *The Time Keeper*, 1897
Torloc
DOUGLAS, Carole Nelson. *Exiles of the Rynth*, 3004
Tornor
LYNN, Elizabeth A. *Watchtower*, 1444
Trecler
GREGORIAN, Joyce Ballou. *The Broken Citadel*, 1971
Tredana
GREGORIAN, Joyce Ballou. *The Broken Citadel*, 1971
Treehorn trilogy
HEIDE, Florence Parry. *The Shrinking of Treehorn*, 2191
The Tribes
BABBITT, Lucy Cullyford. *Where the Truth Lies*, 1255
Trillium Saga
BRADLEY, Marion Zimmer, MAY, Julian, and NORTON, André. *Black Trillium*, 1271
Trolls
AULAIRE, Ingri Mortenson d', and AULAIRE, Edgar Parin d'. *D'Aulaires' Trolls*, 785
Bestiary!, 796
BROOKS, Terry. *The Sword of Shannara*, 1273
COATSWORTH, Elizabeth (Jane). *Troll Weather*, 2398
DOYLE, Debra, and MacDONALD, James D. *Knight's Wyrd*, 1325

EDDINGS, David. *Domes of Fire*, 1332
EDGERTON, Teresa. *Goblin Moon*, 3010
FALKBERGET, Johan (Petter). *Broomstick and Snowflake*, 107
HEATH, W(illiam) L. *The Earthquake Man*, 141
JANSSON, Tove (Marika). *Finn Family Moomintroll*, 1388
KRENSKY, Stephen (Alan). *A Troll in Passing*, 187
LAGERLÖF, Selma. *The Changeling*, 191
LE GUIN, Ursula K(roeber). *A Ride on the Red Mare's Back*, 203
McGOWEN, Tom (Thomas E.). *The Magical Fellowship*, 3083
PIERCE, Meredith Ann. *The Woman Who Loved Reindeer*, 1494
PINI, Wendy, and PINI, Richard. *ElfQuest: The Novel, Journey to Sorrow's End*, 1497
REID BANKS, Lynne. *The Farthest-Away Mountain*, 279
RUBIN, Amy Kateman. *Children of the Seventh Prophecy*, 2052
SHARMAT, Marjorie Weinman. *The Trolls of Twelfth Street*, 2303
SIMAK, Clifford D(onald). *Enchanted Pilgrimage*, 1528
WANGERIN, Walter, Jr. *Elisabeth and the Water-Troll*, 345
WILLIAMS, Tad. *The Dragonbone Chair*, 1583

True Game trilogy
TEPPER, Sheri S. *The Song of Mavin Manyshaped*, 1554

Trumpets
DALLAS-SMITH, Peter. *Trouble for Trumpets*, 473

Tucker Mouse books
SELDEN (Thompson), George. *The Cricket in Times Square*, 686

Turkey—Constantinople
BELLAIRS, John. *The Trolley to Yesterday*, 2695
GATE, Ethel May. *The Fortunate Days*, 874

Twelve Kingdoms series
FRIESNER, Esther M. *Spells of Mortal Weaving*, 1356

Twill
LISLE, Janet Taylor. *The Lampfish of Twill*, 1438

Tyrnos books
MAYHAR, Ardath. *Soul-Singer of Tyrnos*, 1471

Ukrania—Folklore
FRANKO, Ivan, and MELNYK, Bohdan. *Fox Mykyta*, 507

Ulm
CHETWIN, Grace. *Gom on Windy Mountain: From Tales of Gom*, 1292
NORTON, André (pseud. of Alice Mary Norton). *The Crystal Gryphon*, 1486

Ulster
LLYWELYN, Morgan. *Red Branch*, 1758

Unicorns
ANTHONY, Piers (pseud. of Piers A. D. Jacob). *Blue Adept*, 1248
BARTHOLOMEW, Barbara. *The Time Keeper*, 1897
BEAGLE, Peter S(oyer). *The Last Unicorn*, 1261 *Bestiary!*, 796
BROWN, Mary. *The Unlikely Ones*, 2979
CAMERON, Eleanor (Frances Butler). *The Beast with the Magical Horn*, 56
CHANT, Joy (pseud. of Eileen Joyce Rutter). *The Grey Mane of Morning*, 1284
COHEN, Barbara. *Unicorns in the Rain*, 1645
COOPER, Gale. *Unicorn Moon*, 73
DICKINSON, Peter (pseud. of Malcolm de Brissac). *Merlin Dreams*, 1665
ESTEY, Dale. *A Lost Tale*, 1668
FARBER, Norma (Holzman). *Six Impossible Things Before Breakfast*, 859
GARDNER, Craig Shaw. *A Disagreement with Death*, 3023
GENTLE, Mary. *A Hawk in Silver*, 1964
GREAVES, Margaret. *A Net to Catch the Wind*, 128
GREEN, Simon. *Blue Moon Rising*, 1367
JONES, David Lee. *Unicorn Highway*, 2509
LATHROP, Dorothy P(ulis). *The Colt from Moon Mountain*, 2528
LEE, John. *The Unicorn Quest*, 1423
LITTLE, Jane. *Sneaker Hill*, 3076
LUENN, Nancy. *Arctic Unicorn*, 3080; *Unicorn Crossing*, 2545
MAYER, Marianna. *The Unicorn and the Lake*, 233
MAYNE, William (James Carter). *A Grass Rope*, 2565
MOERI, Louise. *The Unicorn and the Plow*, 244
NEWMAN, Sharan. *Guinevere*, 1783
Phoenix Feathers: A Collection of Mythical Monsters, 941
PIERCE, Meredith Ann. *Birth of the Firebringer*, 1492
RODDA, Emily. *The Pigs Are Flying!*, 2615
SALSITZ, Rhondi Vilott. *The Twilight Gate*, 1819
The Unicorn Treasury: Stories, Poems and Unicorn Lore, 975
Unicorns!, 976
WILLIAMS, Anne. *Secret of the Round Tower*, 363
YOUNG, Ella. *The Unicorn with Silver Shoes*, 2087

United States. *See also* Appalachia; Arizona; California; Colorado; Connecticut; Florida; Georgia; Idaho; Illinois; Indiana; Iowa; Kansas; Kentucky; Louisiana; Maine; Massachusetts; Michigan; Minnesota; Mississippi; Nevada; New

Hampshire; New Jersey; New Mexico; New York; North Carolina; North Dakota; Ohio; Oregon; Pennsylvania; Rhode Island; Texas; Vermont; Virginia; Washington, D.C.

United States—17th century
CURRY, Jane Louise. *Parsley, Sage, Rosemary and Time*, 2720
LE GRAND (Henderson). *How Baseball Began in Brooklyn*, 2225
MacKELLAR, William. *Alfie and Me and the Ghost of Peter Stuyvesant*, 1146
ROACH, Marilynne K(athleen). *Encounters with the InvisibleWorld; Being Ten Tales of Ghosts, Witches, and the Devil Himself in New England*, 956

United States—18th century
GREENE, Jacqueline Dembar. *The Leveller*, 1704
LAWSON, Robert. *Ben and Me: A New and Astonishing Life of Benjamin Franklin as Written by His Good Mouse, Amos: Lately Discovered*, 593; *Captain Kidd's Cat*, 594
MOSKIN, Marietta D(unston). *Dream Lake*, 2803
ROACH, Marilynne K(athleen). *Encounters with the InvisibleWorld; Being Ten Tales of Ghosts, Witches, and the Devil Himself in New England*, 956

United States—1712
HAYNES, Betsy. *The Ghost of the Gravestone Hearth*, 1105

United States—1771
McKEAN, Thomas. *The Secret of the Seven Willows*, 2789

United States—1779
POPE, Elizabeth Marie. *The Sherwood Ring*, 2829

United States—19th century
DOTY, Jean Slaughter. *Can I Get There by Candlelight?*, 2726
FLEISCHMAN, (Albert) Sid(ney). *The Midnight Horse*, 1074
LINDBERGH, Anne Spencer. *The Hunky-Dory Dairy*, 2779
SCARBOROUGH, Elizabeth Ann. *The Drastic Dragon of Draco, Texas*, 2297

United States—1800s
FLEISCHMAN, Paul (Taylor). *Coming-and-Going Men: Four Tales*, 112
IRVING, Washington. *The Legend of Sleepy Hollow*, 1724; *Rip Van Winkle*, 1725

United States—1819
BUTLER, Octavia E. *Kindred*, 2709

United States—1846
CHETWIN, Grace. *Friends in Time*, 2713

United States—1850s
MARZOLLO, Jean. *Halfway Down Paddy Lane*, 2794

SHERBURNE, Zoa (Morin). *Why Have the Birds Stopped Singing?*, 2842
WALLIN, Luke. *The Slavery Ghosts*, 1202

United States—1853
HURMENCE, Belinda. *A Girl Called Boy*, 2755

United States—1862
GURNEY, James. *Dinotopia: A Land Apart from Time*, 1973

United States—1876
IPCAR, Dahlov (Zorach). *The Queen of Spells*, 1723

United States—1881
ORMONDROYD, Edward. *Time at the Top*, 2812

United States—1882
FINNEY, Jack (pseud. of Walter Branden Finney). *Time and Again*, 2736

United States—1887
BELLAMY, Edward. *Looking Backward: 2000–1887*, 2696

United States—1890s
SHURA, Mary Francis (pseud. of Mary Francis Craig). *A Shoe Full of Shamrock*, 2633

United States—1896
FISHER, Leonard Everett. *Noonan: A Novel about Baseball, ESP, and Time Warps*, 2737
MATHESON, Richard (Burton). *Bid Time Return*, 2795

United States—1897
CATES, Emily. *The Ghost in the Attic*, 1045

United States—1900
CALHOUN, Mary (pseud. of Mary Huiskamp Wilkins). *Ownself*, 2388
FRAZIER, Neta Lohnes. *The Magic Ring*, 2453
HOPPE, Joanne. *Dream Spinner*, 2753
KUSHNER, Donn. *Uncle Jacob's Ghost Story*, 188

United States—1904
ADKINS, Jan. *A Storm Without Rain*, 2679
REISS, Kathryn. *Time Windows*, 2832

United States—1906
GIFALDI, David. *Gregory, Maw and the Mean One*, 2182

United States—1912
LEVY, Elizabeth. *Running Out of Magic with Houdini*, 2777

United States—1918
PECK, Richard (Wayne). *The Ghost Belonged to Me: A Novel*, 1169

United States—1920s
EISENBERG, Lawrence B(enjamin). *The Villa of the Ferromonte*, 2731

United States—1933
ERWIN, Betty K. *Who Is Victoria?*, 1068

United States—1935
O'ROURKE, Frank. *Burton and Stanley*, 641

United States—1937
VOIGT, Cynthia. *Building Blocks*, 2863

United States—1938
NATHAN, Robert (Gruntal). *Portrait of Jennie*, 254
SNYDER, Zilpha Keatley. *The Truth about Stone Hollow*, 1188
United States—1940s
REISS, Kathryn. *Time Windows*, 2832
United States—1942
BETHANCOURT, T(homas) Ernesto (pseud. of Tom Paisley). *Tune in Yesterday*, 2699
LEE, Robert C. *Once upon Another Time*, 2771
United States—1944
PASCAL, Francine. *Hangin' Out with Cici*, 2819
United States—1946
KLAVENESS, Jan O'Donnell. *The Griffin Legacy*, 1121
United States—1950s
SILVERSTEIN, Herma. *Mad, Mad Monday*, 1184
United States—1955
PAYNE, Bernal C., Jr. *It's About Time*, 2821
United States—1957
MURPHY, Shirley Rousseau. *The Catswold Portal*, 2028
United States—Alternate 19th century
CARD, Orson Scott. *Seventh Son*, 1279
United States—Alternate 20th century
CHRISTOPHER, John. *New Found Land*, 1921
SILVERBERG, Robert. *The Gate of Worlds*, 1525
United States—Alternate Civil War era
Alternative Histories: Eleven Stories of the World as It Might Have Been, 1242
BISSON, Terry. *Fire on the Mountain*, 1265
United States—Alternate Revolutionary War era
Alternative Histories: Eleven Stories of the World as It Might Have Been, 1242
United States—Atlantic Coast, 1716
JOHNSON, Charles. *Pieces of Eight*, 2758
United States—California Gold Rush
FLEISCHMAN, (Albert) Sid(ney). *By the Great Horn Spoon*, 2165
United States—Civil War
ALPHIN, Elaine Marie. *The Ghost Cadet*, 1015
CULLEN, Lynn. *The Backyard Ghost*, 1060
HALL, Lynn. *The Mystery of the Caramel Cat*, 1099
LAWSON, John S(hults). *The Spring Rider*, 2770
NORTON, André (pseud. of Alice Mary Norton). *Octagon Magic*, 2810
SHECTER, Ben. *The Whistling Whirligig*, 1181
WILLIS, Connie. *Lincoln's Dreams*, 2873
United States—Folklore
BENÉT, Stephen Vincent. *The Devil and Daniel Webster*, 1612
BONTEMPS, Arna (Wendell), and CONROY, Jack. *The Fast Sooner Hound*, 2104

CHESNUTT, Charles Waddell. *Conjure Tales*, 822
HAMILTON (Adoff), Virginia (Esther). *The Magical Adventures of Pretty Pearl*, 1709
HOOKS, William H(arris). *Moss Gown*, 151
IPCAR, Dahlov (Zorach). *The Queen of Spells*, 1723
IRVING, Washington. *Knickerbocker's History of New York*, 2205; *Rip Van Winkle*, 1725
ROACH, Marilynne K(athleen). *Encounters with the InvisibleWorld; Being Ten Tales of Ghosts, Witches, and the Devil Himself in New England*, 956
SHANNON, Monica. *California Fairy Tales*, 957
STEELE, William O(wen). *Andy Jackson's Water Well*, 2310; *Daniel Boone's Echo*, 2311; *Davy Crockett's Earthquake*, 2312; *The No-Name Man of the Mountain*, 2313
WELLMAN, Manly Wade. *The Old Gods Waken*, 1863
United States—French and Indian Wars
REID BANKS, Lynne. *The Indian in the Cupboard*, 2610
United States—Pacific Northwest Coast
KESEY, Ken. *The Sea Lion: A Story of the Sea Cliff People*, 1738
PASSEY, Helen K. *Speak to the Rain*, 1795
United States—Pre-Civil War
CHESNUTT, Charles Waddell. *Conjure Tales*, 822
HAMILTON (Adoff), Virginia (Esther). *The Magical Adventures of Pretty Pearl*, 1709
United States—Revolutionary War
DAWSON, Carley. *Mr. Wicker's Window*, 2724
JENSEN, Dorothea. *The Riddle of Penncroft Farm*, 1114
KLAVENESS, Jan O'Donnell. *The Griffin Legacy*, 1121
LAWSON, Robert. *Mr. Revere and I*, 597
United States—Southern states
BISSON, Terry. *Fire on the Mountain*, 1265
United States—Southwest—1280
JAMES, J. Alison. *Sing for a Gentle Rain*, 2757
United States—Stone Age
HANLON, Emily. *Circle Home*, 2751
KITTLEMAN, Laurence R. *Canyons Beyond the Sky*, 2765
MAZER, Norma Fox. *Saturday, the Twelfth of October*, 2798
United States—Western states—Alternate history
KING, Stephen. *The Gunslinger*, 1407
Upper Forest
LISLE, Janet Taylor. *Forest*, 211
Upslope
JAMES, Betsy. *Long Night Dance*, 1387

Valdemar
    LACKEY, Mercedes. *Arrows of the Queen*, 1415; *By the Sword*, 1416; *Magic's Pawn*, 1417; *Winds of Fate*, 1418

Valleria
    BROWN, Judith Gwyn. *The Mask of the Dancing Princess*, 50

Vampire series
    SOMMER-BODENBURG, Angela. *My Friend the Vampire*, 2308

Vampires
    DE LINT, Charles. *Yarrow: An Autumn Tale*, 1936
    FORD, John M. *The Dragon Waiting: A Masque of History*, 1353
    GOULART, Ron(ald Joseph). *The Prisoner of Blackwood Castle*, 1366
    HARVEY, Jayne. *Great-Uncle Dracula*, 2188
    JACQUES, Brian. *Seven Strange and Ghostly Tales*, 1113
    MARTIN, Ann M(atthews). *Ma and Pa Dracula*, 2250
    PIERCE, Meredith Ann. *The Darkangel*, 1493
    POWERS, Tim. *The Stress of Her Regard*, 1498
    SOMMER-BODENBURG, Angela. *If You Want to Scare Yourself*, 1189; *My Friend the Vampire*, 2308
    WILLIAMS, Tad, and HOFFMAN, Nina Kiriki. *Child of an Ancient City*, 1584
    ZELAZNY, Roger (Joseph Christopher). *Frost and Fire*, 1002

Vanalaria
    McKIERAN, Dennis L. *Dragondoom*, 1451; *Trek to Kraggen-Cor*, 1452

Vandarei series
    CHANT, Joy (pseud. of Eileen Joyce Rutter). *The Grey Mane of Morning*, 1284; *Red Moon and Black Mountain: The End of the House of Kendreth*, 1916

Vanima
    LYNN, Elizabeth A. *Watchtower*, 1444

Varay
    SHELLEY, Rick. *Son of the Hero*, 2057

Varayan Memoir series
    SHELLEY, Rick. *Son of the Hero*, 2057

Veil
    DOUGLAS, Carole Nelson. *Cup of Clay*, 1942

Vermont
    LINDBERGH, Anne Spencer. *Travel Far, Pay No Fare*, 2536
    SCHAEFFER, Susan Fromberg. *The Dragons of North Chittendon*, 2623
    SLEPIAN, Jan. *Back to Before*, 2848

Vesper Holly Adventure series
    ALEXANDER, Lloyd (Chudley). *The Illyrian Adventure*, 1888

Vietnam War
    SCARBOROUGH, Elizabeth Ann. *The Healer's War: A Fantasy Novel of Vietnam*, 1824

Vikings. *See also* Norse mythology
    JONSSON, Runer. *Viki Viking*, 2211
    WISNIEWSKI, David. *Elfwyn's Saga*, 367

Virconium series
    HARRISON, M(ichael) John. *The Pastel City*, 1376

Virgin Islands—British
    BOND, Nancy (Barbara). *A String in the Harp*, 2701
    COOPER (Grant), Susan (Mary). *Jethro and the Jumbie*, 2403
    CRESSWELL (Rowe), Helen. *Up the Pier*, 2717
    MacLEOD, Charlotte (Matilda Hughes). *The Curse of the Giant Hogweed*, 2790

Virginia
    HITE, Sid. *Dither Farm*, 2490

Virginia—Alternate 1836
    RUCKER, Rudy. *The Hollow Earth: The Narrative of Mason Algiers Reynolds of Virginia*, 2053

Viridian
    MAHY, Margaret (May). *Dangerous Spaces*, 2020

Vlad Taltos series
    BRUST, Steven K. (Zoltan). *Taltos*, 1275

Wales
    AIKEN, Joan (Delano). *The Whispering Mountain*, 1234
    BAKER, (Robert) Michael (Graham). *The Mountain and the Summer Stars: An Old Tale Newly Ended*, 1609
    GARNER, Alan. *The Owl Service*, 1690
    MORRIS, Kenneth. *The Book of the Three Dragons*, 1778
    RADFORD, Ken. *The Cellar*, 2830
    SERVICE, Pamela F. *Wizard of Wind and Rock*, 1832
    STERMAN, Betsy, and STERMAN, Samuel. *Backyard Dragon*, 2641
    WEIN, Elizabeth E. *The Winter Prince*, 1861
    ZARING, Jane T(homas). *The Return of the Dragon*, 376

Wales—6th century
    BOND, Nancy (Barbara). *A String in the Harp*, 2701

Wales—11th century
    BURTON, Philip. *The Green Isle*, 55

Wales—12th century
    ATTANASIO, A(lfred) A(ngelo). *Kingdom of the Grail*, 1607
    CURRY, Jane Louise. *Over the Sea's Edge*, 2719

Wales—14th century
WELCH, Ronald (pseud. of Ronald Oliver Felton). *The Gauntlet*, 2864

Wales—19th century
AIKEN, Joan (Delano). *The Whispering Mountain*, 1234

Wales—1900
RADFORD, Ken. *Haunting at Mill Lane*, 1173

Wales—1921
CRESSWELL (Rowe), Helen. *Up the Pier*, 2717

Wales—Folklore
ALEXANDER, Lloyd (Chudley). *The Book of Three*, 1236

BAKER, (Robert) Michael (Graham). *The Mountain and the Summer Stars: An Old Tale Newly Ended*, 1609

BOND, Nancy (Barbara). *A String in the Harp*, 2701

CARRIS, Joan Davenport. *Witch-Cat*, 2984

CURRY, Jane Louise. *Over the Sea's Edge*, 2719

DE LINT, Charles. *Moonheart*, 1664

FARMER (Mockridge), Penelope. *Year King*, 1673

GARNER, Alan. *The Owl Service*, 1690

LAWRENCE, Louise. *The Earth Witch*, 1745

MORRIS, Kenneth. *The Book of the Three Dragons*, 1778

MURPHY, Shirley Rousseau, and SUGGS, Welch. *Medallion of the Black Hound*, 2029

Tales from the Mabinogion, 1849

TENNY, Dixie. *Call the Darkness Down*, 1852

WALTON, Evangeline (pseud. of Evangeline Ensley). *The Prince of Annwn*, 1860

WELCH, Ronald (pseud. of Ronald Oliver Felton). *The Gauntlet*, 2864

Wales—Middle Ages
MacLEOD, Charlotte (Matilda Hughes). *The Curse of the Giant Hogweed*, 2790

War
LISLE, Janet Taylor. *Forest*, 211

Warrow
McKIERAN, Dennis L. *Trek to Kraggen-Cor*, 1452

Wars of Vis trilogy
LEE, Tanith. *Anackire*, 1424

Warton the Toad series
ERICKSON, Russell E(verett). *A Toad for Tuesday*, 494

Washington, D.C.
HAMLETT, Christina. *The Enchanter*, 1710

Wayfolk
McKILLIP, Patricia A(nne). *The Sorceress and the Cygnet*, 1458

Werewolves
BRENNAN, Herbie. *Emily and the Werewolf*, 2977

CUYLER, Margery. *Weird Wolf*, 2131

DE WEESE, (Thomas Eugene) Gene. *The Adventures of a Two Minute Werewolf*, 2141

EDGERTON, Teresa. *Child of Saturn*, 3009

GREEN, Phyllis. *Eating Ice Cream with a Werewolf*, 2470

HARVEY, Jayne. *Great-Uncle Dracula*, 2188

SOMMER-BODENBURG, Angela. *If You Want to Scare Yourself*, 1189

Western Kingdom
GARDNER, Craig Shaw. *A Disagreement with Death*, 3023

Westlands series
KERR, Katharine. *A Time of Exile: A Novel of the Westlands*, 1405

Westmark trilogy
ALEXANDER, Lloyd (Chudley). *Westmark*, 1241

Westria trilogy
PAXON, Diana L. *Lady of Light*, 1491

Wheel of Time Saga
JORDAN, Robert. *The Eye of the World*, 1396

The White Isle
COOPER, Louise. *The Master*, 1302

Wild Magic trilogy
CLAYTON, Jo. *The Magic Wars*, 1295

"The Wild Swans," adaptations of
SYNGE, (Phyllis) Ursula. *Swan's Wing*, 1847

Wildkeepers
GRIMSHAW, Nigel (Gilroy). *Bluntstone and the Wildkeepers*, 1369

Winchester trilogy
CHRISTOPHER, John (pseud. of Christopher Samuel Youd). *The Prince in Waiting*, 1293

Windrose Chronicles
HAMBLY, Barbara. *The Silent Tower*, 1974

Winged horses
BAUER, Marion Dane. *Touch the Moon*, 2355

Bestiary!, 796

BOSTON, L(ucy) M(aria Wood). *The River at Green Knowe*, 2371

BULL, Emma. *War for the Oaks*, 1630

BYARS, Betsy (Cromer). *The Winged Colt of Casa Mia*, 2386

CRESSWELL (Rowe), Helen. *The White Sea Horse*, 2413

ERSHOV, Petr Pavlovich. *The Little Hump-backed Horse: A Russian Tale*, 105

GOUDGE, Elizabeth (de Beauchamp). *The Little White Horse*, 2465

GREEN, Kathleen. *Philip and the Pooka and Other Irish Fairy Tales*, 883

KROEBER, Theodora (Kracow). *Carrousel*, 2942

LATHROP, Dorothy P(ulis). *The Colt from Moon Mountain*, 2528

MAYER, Marianna. *The Black Horse*, 1768

MURPHY, Shirley Rousseau. *The Ring of Fire*, 1482

NIXON, Joan Lowery. *The Gift*, 2582
SINGER, Marilyn. *Horsemaster*, 2061
SNYDER, Zilpha Keatley. *A Season of Ponies*, 2639
WERSBA, Barbara. *The Land of Forgotten Beasts*, 2074
Winter of the World trilogy
ROHAN, Michael Scott. *The Anvil of Ice*, 3112
Winter Solstice
ADKINS, Jan. *Solstice: A Mystery of the Season*, 2678
Wirrun trilogy
WRIGHTSON, (Alice) Patricia (Furlonger). *The Ice Is Coming*, 1877
Witch World series
NORTON, André (pseud. of Alice Mary Norton). *Witch World*, 2039
Witch World: The Turning series
NORTON, André (pseud. of Alice Mary Norton). *Witch World*, 2039
Wizard and Dragon series
HUGHES, Robert Don. *The Faithful Traitor*, 3045
Wizard Sequence
DUANE, Diane (Elizabeth). *So You Want to Be a Wizard*, 3006
Wizard series
STASHEFF, Christopher. *Her Majesty's Wizard*, 2065
Wizard's War trilogy
BOYER, Elizabeth H. *The Troll's Grindstone*, 1908
Wizardry trilogy
COOK, Rick. *Wizardry Compiled*, 1924
Wolfriders
PINI, Wendy, and PINI, Richard. *ElfQuest: The Novel, Journey to Sorrow's End*, 1497
Wombles
BERESFORD, Elizabeth. *The Wombles*, 412
Women's suffrage
WISEMAN, David. *A Tie to the Past*, 2878
Wood spirits
FLEISCHMAN, (Albert) Sid(ney). *The Hey Hey Man*, 113
World of Crystal Walls series
DRAKE, David. *The Sea Hag*, 1326
World War I—England
MONACO, Richard. *Journey to the Flame*, 2025
World War I—Germany
MONACO, Richard. *Journey to the Flame*, 2025
World War II. *See also* Holocaust
MELLECKER, Judith. *Randolph's Dream*, 237
WYSS, Thelma Hatch. *A Stranger Here*, 1227
YOLEN (Stemple), Jane H(yatt). *The Devil's Arithmetic*, 2880

World War II—England
ESTEY, Dale. *A Lost Tale*, 1668
GALLICO, Paul (William). *The Snow Goose*, 120
SYMONS, (Dorothy) Geraldine. *Crocuses Were Over, Hitler Was Dead*, 2854
WESTALL, Robert (Atkinson). *The Haunting of Chas McGill and Other Stories*, 1206; *The Promise*, 1208
World War II—France
BROW, Thea J. *The Secret Cross of Lorraine*, 1035
GALLICO, Paul (William). *The Snow Goose*, 120
World War II—Germany
DAVIES, Andrew (Wynford). *Conrad's War*, 2723
MOORCOCK, Michael (John). *The Dragon in the Sword*, 1477
SYMONS, (Dorothy) Geraldine. *Crocuses Were Over, Hitler Was Dead*, 2854
World War II—Greece
PURTILL, Richard. *Enchantment at Delphi*, 1807
Worst Witch trilogy
MURPHY, Jill. *The Worst Witch*, 3094

Xanth series
ANTHONY, Piers (pseud. of Piers A. D. Jacob). *A Spell for Chameleon*, 1250

The Year's Best Fantasy and Horror series
The Year's Best Fantasy: First Annual Collection, 993
Yeti
MORPURGO, Michael. *King of the Cloud Forests*, 1777
Ynell
MURPHY, Shirley Rousseau. *The Ring of Fire*, 1482
York trilogy
NAYLOR, Phyllis Reynolds. *Shadows on the Wall*, 2804
Ys
ANDERSON, Poul, and ANDERSON, Karen. *Gallicenae*, 1247

Zarathandra
AAMODT, Donald. *A Name to Conjure With*, 1885
Zimiamvian trilogy
EDDISON, E(rik) R(ucker). *The Worm Ouroboros, a Romance*, 1334
Zindar
HARRIS, Geraldine (Rachel). *Prince of the Godborn*, 1374